Study and prepare
for your pilot and
aircraft dispatcher
FAA Knowledge Exam

Airline Transport Pilot

2024 Test Prep

AVIATION SUPPLIES & ACADEMICS, INC.
NEWCASTLE, WASHINGTON

The FAA Knowledge Exam questions can change throughout the year. Stay current with test changes; sign up for ASA's free email update service at **asa2fly.com/testupdate**

Airline Transport Pilot Test Prep
2024 Edition

Aviation Supplies & Academics, Inc.
7005 132nd Place SE
Newcastle, Washington 98059
asa@asa2fly.com | 425.235.1500 | asa2fly.com

Visit **asa2fly.com/TPATP** for additional information and resources related to this book.

Sample Federal Aviation Administration (FAA) questions herein contain information as of: September 2023. Stay informed of changes since the book was printed: **asa2fly.com/testupdate**

None of the material in this publication supersedes any documents, procedures or regulations issued by the Federal Aviation Administration.

Cover photo by Daniel Eledut on Unsplash

ASA-TPP-ATP-FE-24
Softcover book plus software download
ISBN 978-1-64425-337-3

Additional format available:
eBook PDF ISBN 978-1-64425-323-6

Printed in the United States of America

2024 2023 5 4 3 2 1

About the Contributors

Jackie Spanitz
General Manager
Aviation Supplies & Academics, Inc.

As ASA General Manager, Jackie Spanitz oversees maintenance and development of more than 1,000 titles and pilot supplies in the ASA product line. Ms. Spanitz has worked with airman training and testing for more than 25 years, including participation in the Airman Certification Standards (ACS) development committees. Jackie holds a Bachelor of Science in Aviation Technology from Western Michigan University, a Master of Science from Embry-Riddle Aeronautical University, and Instructor and Commercial Pilot certificates. She is the author of *Guide to the Flight Review*, and the technical editor for ASA's Test Prep and FAR/AIM series.

Andrea Georgio
Associate Professor
Middle Tennessee State University (MTSU)

Andrea Georgiou is an associate professor and the flight dispatch coordinator in the MTSU Aerospace department. She earned a B.S. in Aerospace and Master of Aerospace Education from MTSU and a PhD in General Psychology from Capella University. Dr. Georgiou holds an FAA Aircraft Dispatch Certificate and a Private Pilot Certificate. She serves as an honors faculty member and teaches a wide range of undergraduate and graduate courses including flight dispatch, aviation laws and regulations, advanced aviation weather, professional pilot, introduction to aerospace, human factors, and aviation industries.

Aviation Supplies & Academics, Inc. (ASA) is an industry leader in the development and sale of aviation supplies and publications for pilots, flight instructors, aviation maintenance technicians, aircraft dispatchers, air traffic controllers, flight attendants, and drone operators. We manufacture and publish more than 1,000 products and have been providing trusted and reliable training materials to the aviation industry for over 80 years. Visit **asa2fly.com** to learn more.

Contents

Instructions

Chapter 1 **Regulations**

Chapter 2 **Equipment, Navigation, and Facilities**

Chapter 3 **Aerodynamics**

Chapter 4 **Performance**

Chapter 5 **Weight and Balance**

Chapter 6 **Flight Operations**

Chapter 7 **Emergencies, Hazards, and Flight Physiology**

Chapter 8 **Meteorology and Weather Services**

Cross References

FAA Figures

Airman Knowledge Testing Supplement for Airline Transport Pilot and Aircraft Dispatcher (FAA-CT-8080-7D)

Updates and Practice Tests

Free Test Updates for the One-Year Life Cycle of Test Prep Books

The FAA modifies tests as needed throughout the year. ASA keeps abreast of changes to the tests and posts free Test Updates on the ASA website. Before taking your test, be certain you have the most current information by visiting the ASA Test Updates webpage: **asa2fly.com/testupdate**. Additionally, sign up for free email notifications, which are sent when new Test Updates are available.

We Invite Your Feedback

After you take your FAA exam, let us know how you did. Were you prepared? Did ASA's products meet your needs and exceed your expectations? We want to continue to improve these products to ensure applicants are prepared and become safe aviators. Send your feedback to: **cfi@asa2fly.com**.

Introduction

Welcome to the Aviation Supplies & Academics, Inc., (ASA) Test Prep Series. This series has been helping pilots prepare for the FAA Knowledge Tests for more than 60 years with great success. We are confident that with proper use of this book you will score very well on any of the Airline Transport Pilot tests.

Begin your studies with a classroom or home-study ground school course, which will involve reading a comprehensive textbook. Visit the Reader Resources for this Test Prep (**asa2fly.com/TPATP**) and become familiar with the FAA guidance materials available for the certification exam. Then use this Test Prep to prepare for your exam: read the question, select your choice for the correct answer, and then read the explanation. Use the references that conclude each explanation to identify additional resources for further study of a subject. Upon completion of your studies, take practice tests at **prepware.com** (see inside the front cover for your activation code).

The questions in this book have been arranged into chapters based on subject matter to promote better understanding, aid recall, and provide a more efficient study guide. Place emphasis on questions most likely to be included in your test (identified by the aircraft category above each question). For example, a pilot preparing for the ATP Multi-engine test would focus on the questions marked "ALL" and "ATM"; a pilot preparing for the ATP Single-engine test would focus on the questions marked "ALL" and "ATS"; a pilot preparing for the ATP Helicopter (135) test would focus on the questions marked "ALL" and "RTC"; and candidates for the Dispatcher certificate would focus on the questions marked "ALL" and "ADX."

Prior to taking an FAA Airman Knowledge Test, all applicants must establish an FAA Tracking Number (FTN) by creating a profile in the Integrated Airman Certification and Rating Application (IACRA) system at **iacra.faa.gov**. Then visit **faa.psiexams.com** to register for your exam and take FAA-created practice tests to become familiar with the computer testing platform.

It is important to answer every question assigned on your FAA Knowledge Test. If in their ongoing review, the FAA decides a question has no correct answer, is no longer applicable, or is otherwise defective, your answer will be marked correct no matter which one you chose. However, you will not be given the automatic credit if you have not marked an answer. Unlike some other exams you may have taken, there is no penalty for guessing in this instance.

The FAA exams are "closed tests" which means the exact database of questions is not available to the public. The question and answer choices in this book are based on our extensive history and experience with the FAA testing and airman certification process. You might see similarly worded questions on your official FAA exam, or answer stems might be rearranged from the order you see in this book. Therefore, be sure to fully understand the intent of each question and corresponding answer while studying, rather than memorizing the letter associated with the correct response. You may be asked a question that has unfamiliar wording; studying and understanding the information in this book and the associated references will give you the tools to answer question variations with confidence.

If your study leads you to question an answer choice, we recommend you seek the assistance of a local instructor. We welcome your questions, recommendations, and concerns—send them to:

Aviation Supplies & Academics, Inc.
7005 132nd Place SE
Newcastle, WA 98059-3153
Phone: 425.235.1500
Email: cfi@asa2fly.com
Website: asa2fly.com

The FAA appreciates testing experience feedback. You can contact them at:

Federal Aviation Administration
AFS-630, Airman Testing Standards Branch
PO Box 25082
Oklahoma City, OK 73125
Email: afs630comments@faa.gov

Description of the Tests

The FAA Knowledge Exam is an objective, multiple choice test. Each question can be answered by one of the three choices. Each test question is independent of the others—a correct response to one question does not depend on the correct response to another. You must score at least 70 percent to pass the test.

The FAA Knowledge Exams are designed to test your knowledge in many subject areas. If you are pursuing an airline transport pilot certificate or added rating, you should review the appropriate sections of 14 CFR Part 61 for the specific knowledge areas on each test. Those taking the ATM or "ATP–Airline Transport Pilot Multi-engine" exam will be tested on Part 121 as one of the knowledge areas. Those taking the ATS or "ATP–Airline Transport Pilot Single-engine" exam will be tested on Part 135 as one of the knowledge areas.

An applicant for an Aircraft Dispatcher Certificate should review the appropriate sections of 14 CFR Part 65 for the specific knowledge areas on the test. The applicant will be tested on Part 121 as one of the knowledge areas. If Part 135 commuter operators (as defined in DOT Part 298) are required to have aircraft dispatchers in the future, Part 135 questions will be added to the test. The aircraft dispatcher applicant is not required to have the flying skills of an airline transport pilot but is expected to have the same knowledge.

If it's been more than 24 months since you took the initial ATP FAA Knowledge Exam, we recommend that you prepare for the Add-On test using the "ATP Single-engine" or "ATP–Helictoper (Part 135)" test. This will better prepare you for all questions that may be included on your add-on test.

The table below lists the number of questions and the allotted time for each test. Each question in this book is preceded by a category. Use these categories to study the content that may appear on your test. Study all the questions first, then refer to the following table, placing emphasis on those questions most likely to be included on your test (identified by the test prep category above each question number).

Test Code	Test Name	Test Prep Study	Number of Questions	Min. Age	Allotted Time (hrs)
ADX	Aircraft Dispatcher	ALL, ADX	80	21	3.5
ATM	ATP Multi-engine Airplane	ALL, ATM	125	18	3.5
ATS	ATP Single-engine Airplane (Part 135)	ALL, ATS	90	21	2.5
ATH	ATP–Helicopter (Part 135)	ALL, RTC	80	21	3.0
ARH	ATP–Helicopter–Added Rating (Part 135)*	ALL, RTC	50	21	2.5
ACM	ATP Canadian Conversion ME**	ALL, ATM	60	23	2.5
ASC	ATP Canadian Conversion SE**	ALL, ATS	40	23	2.0
ACH	ATP Canadian Conversion–Helicopter**	ALL, RTC	40	23	2.0

* This test focuses on U.S. regulations, procedures, and operations.

Note: All applicants transitioning from ATP airplane and/or helicopter need to take the additional knowledge test. For example, an applicant adding a helicopter rating to an existing ATP airplane certificate will need to take the 50-question add-on test.

Knowledge Test Registration

The FAA testing provider authorizes hundreds of test center locations that offer a full range of airman knowledge tests. For information on authorized testing centers and to register for the knowledge test, visit **faa.psiexams.com**.

When you contact a knowledge testing center, be prepared to select a test date and make payment. You may register for test(s) several weeks in advance online or by phone, and you may cancel in accordance with the testing center's cancellation policy.

Regardless of your registration method, you will need an FAA Tracking Number (FTN) prior to registering for the FAA Airman Knowledge Test. This FTN will follow you throughout your aviation career. You will obtain your FTN as part of the test registration process, by creating a profile in the Integrated Airman Certificate and Rating Application (IACRA) system at **iacra.faa.gov/IACRA**. This FTN will be printed on your Airman Knowledge Test Report (AKTR).

The test registration process includes collection of this information: name, FTN, physical address, date of birth, email address, photo identification, phone number, test authorization (credentials for an individual, such as a graduation certificate for an authorized ATP certification training program [CTP]), and previous number of test attempts.

Step 1: Create a profile using the IACRA system and login to obtain your FTN.
Step 2: Register for your knowledge test with PSI by phone or online.

For more information, contact:
PSI Services LLC
844-704-1487 or examschedule@psionline.com
faa.psiexams.com

Knowledge Test Eligibility

When you take your FAA Knowledge Test, you will be required to show proper identification. The ATP and dispatcher tests do not require instructor endorsements or other form of written authorization, except in the case of retesting (see Retesting Procedures).

An applicant taking the ATM test must present a graduation certificate that shows completion of an ATP Certification Training Program (CTP) described in 14 CFR §61.156. A graduation certificate must contain the following information in order to be considered valid:

1. The full name, address, and FAA certificate number of the training provider authorized to conduct the course.
2. The full name, FAA pilot certificate number, and address of the graduate.
3. The following statement: "The applicant named above has successfully completed the airline transport pilot Certification Training Program as required by §61.156, and therefore has met the prerequisite required by §61.35(a)(2) for the airline transport pilot airplane knowledge test."
4. The date of issuance.
5. The signature of the authorized instructor who completed the academic portion of the course.
6. A sequential number on the certificate starting with the first four identifiers of the training provider's certificate number.

Acceptable Materials

The applicant may use test aids and materials within the guidelines listed below during the test, if actual test questions or answers are not revealed.

Acceptable Materials	Unacceptable Materials	Notes
Supplement book provided by proctor.	Written materials that are handwritten, printed, or electronic.	Testing centers may provide calculators and/or deny the use of personal calculators.
All models of aviation-oriented calculators or small electronic calculators that perform only arithmetic functions.	Electronic calculators incorporating permanent or continuous type memory circuits without erasure capability.	Test proctor may prohibit the use of your calculator if he or she is unable to determine the calculator's erasure capability.
Calculators with simple programmable memories, which allow addition to, subtraction from, or retrieval of one number from the memory; or simple functions, such as square root and percentages.	Magnetic cards, magnetic tapes, modules, computer chips, or any other device upon which pre-written programs or information related to the test can be stored and retrieved.	Printouts of data must be surrendered at the completion of the test if the calculator incorporates this design feature.
Scales, straight-edges, protractors, plotters, navigation computers, blank log sheets, holding pattern entry aids, and electronic or mechanical calculators that are directly related to the test.	Dictionaries.	Before, and upon completion of the test, while in the presence of the test proctor, actuate the ON/OFF switch or RESET button, and perform any other function that ensures erasure of any data stored in memory circuits.
Manufacturer's permanently inscribed instructions on the front and back of such aids, such as formulas, conversions, regulations, signals, weather data, holding pattern diagrams, frequencies, weight and balance formulas, and ATC procedures.	Any booklet or manual containing instructions related to use of test aids.	Test proctor makes the final determination regarding aids, reference materials, and test materials.

Testing Procedures for Applicants Requesting Special Accommodations

If you are an applicant with a learning or reading disability, you may request approval from the local FAA office to take an airman knowledge test, using the special accommodations procedures outlined in the most current version of FAA Order 8080.6 Conduct of Airman Knowledge Tests.

Prior to approval of any option, the FAA Aviation Safety Inspector must advise you of the regulatory certification requirement of being able to read, write, speak, and understand the English language.

Test Reports

Your test will be graded immediately upon completion and your score will display on the computer screen. You will receive your Airman Knowledge Test Report (AKTR), which will state your score. See sample AKTR on next page.

Visit **faa.psiexams.com** to request a duplicate or replacement AKTR due to loss or destruction.

Airman Knowledge Test Reports are valid for 24 calendar months. If the AKTR expires before completion of the practical test, you must retake the knowledge test.

The AKTR lists the Airman Certification Standard (ACS) code (if an Airman Certification Standard is available for the certificate and rating specific to the test) or Learning Statement Code (LSCs) (if a Practical Test Standard is in effect for the certificate and rating specific to the test) for questions answered incorrectly. The total number of ACSs/LSCs shown on the AKTR is not necessarily an indication of the total number of questions answered incorrectly. Study these knowledge areas to improve your understanding of the subject matter. See Cross-Reference B in the back of this book for a listing of ACSs/LSCs and their associated questions.

Your instructor is required to provide instruction on each of the knowledge areas listed on your AKTR and to complete an endorsement of this instruction. You must present this to the examiner prior to taking the practical test. During the oral portion of the practical test, the examiner is required to evaluate the noted areas of deficiency.

Retesting Procedures

Applicants retesting ***after failure*** are required to submit the applicable AKTR indicating failure, along with an endorsement (on the test report) from an authorized instructor, who gave the applicant the additional training, certifying the applicant is competent to pass the test. The original failed AKTR and retest endorsement presented as authorization shall be retained by the proctor and attached to the applicable sign-in/out log. The latest test taken will reflect the official score.

Applicants retesting ***in an attempt to achieve a higher passing score*** may retake the same test for a better grade after 30 days. The latest test taken will reflect the official score. Applicants are required to submit the original applicable AKTR indicating previous passing score to the testing center prior to testing. Testing center personnel must collect and destroy this report prior to issuing the new test report.

Dispatcher (ADX) retests do not require a 30-day waiting period if the applicant presents a signed statement from an airman holding a certificate and rating sought by the applicant. This statement must certify that the airman has given the applicant additional instruction in each of the subjects failed, and that the airman considers the applicant ready for retesting. However, this test requires a 30-day waiting period for retesting if the applicant presents a failed test report without a signed statement.

Cheating or Other Unauthorized Conduct

Computer testing centers must follow strict security procedures to avoid test compromise. These procedures are established by the FAA and are covered in FAA Order 8080.6 Conduct of Airman Knowledge Tests. The FAA has directed testing centers to terminate a test at any time a test proctor suspects a cheating incident has occurred. An FAA investigation will then be conducted. If the investigation determines that cheating or unauthorized conduct has occurred, then any airman certificate or rating that you hold may be revoked, and you will be prohibited for one year from applying for or taking any test for a certificate or rating under Part 61.

U.S. DEPARTMENT OF TRANSPORTATION
Federal Aviation Administration
Airman Knowledge Test Report

NAME: TAYLOR SMITH

FAA TRACKING NUMBER (FTN): C1234567 **EXAM ID:** 98765432109876543

EXAM: ATP Single-engine Airplane (Part 135) (ATS)

EXAM DATE: 09/15/2023 **EXAM SITE:** ABC12345

SCORE: 88% **GRADE:** Pass **TAKE:** 1

The Airman Certification Standards (ACS) codes listed below represent incorrectly answered questions. These ACS codes and their associated Areas of Operation/Tasks/Elements may be found in the appropriate ACS document at http://www.faa.gov/training_testing/testing/acs.

A single code may represent more than one incorrect response.

AA.I.B.K3e AA.I.G.K5 AA.I.D.K9 AA.II.A.K7 AA.III.B.R1 AA.IV.A.K2d AA.VI.E.K1

EXPIRATION DATE: 09/30/2025

DO NOT LOSE THIS REPORT

- -

AUTHORIZED INSTRUCTOR'S STATEMENT: (if applicable)
On __________ (date) I gave the above named applicant _____ hours of additional instruction, covering each subject area shown to be deficient, and consider the applicant competent to pass the knowledge test.

Name ____

Cert. No. ____ *(print clearly)*

Type of instructor certificate ____

Signature ____

FRAUDULENT ALTERATION OF THIS FORM BY ANY PERSON IS A BASIS FOR SUSPENSION OR REVOCATION OF ANY CERTIFICATES OR RATINGS HELD BY THAT PERSON.
ISSUED BY: PSI Services LLC
FEDERAL AVIATION ADMINISTRATION

THIS INFORMATION IS PROTECTED BY THE PRIVACY ACT. FOR OFFICIAL USE ONLY.

Sample Airman Knowledge Test Report

Test-Taking Tips

Prior to launching the actual test, the test proctor's testing software will provide you with an opportunity to practice navigating through the test. This practice (or tutorial) session may include a "sample" question(s). These sample questions have no relation to the content of the test, but are meant to familiarize you with the look and feel of the system screens, including selecting an answer, marking a question for later review, time remaining for the test, and other features of the testing software.

Follow these time-proven tips, which will help you develop a skillful, smooth approach to test-taking:

- Visit **faa.psiexams.com** to take a small sample test to become familiar with the latest PSI exam interface you will see on your actual FAA knowledge test.
- Be careful to fully understand the intent of each question and corresponding answer while studying, rather than memorize the A, B, C answer choice—answer stems may appear in a different order than you studied and have some wording differences.
- Remember to bring an ATP-CTP graduation certificate (as applicable), photo I.D., the testing fee, calculator, flight computer (ASA's E6-B or CX-3 Flight Computer), plotter, magnifying glass, and a sharp pointer, such as a safety pin.
- Your first action when you sit down should be to write any formulas and information you can remember from your study on the scratch paper they will provide. Remember, some of the formulas may be on your E6-B.
- Read each question carefully before looking at the possible answers. You should clearly understand the problem before attempting to solve it.
- After formulating an answer, determine which answer choice corresponds the closest with your answer. The answer chosen should completely resolve the problem.
- From the answer choices given, it may appear that there is more than one possible answer. However, there is only one answer that is correct and complete. The other answers are either incomplete, erroneous, or represent popular misconceptions.
- Answer each question in accordance with the latest regulations and guidance publications.
- If a certain question is difficult for you, tag it for REVIEW and proceed to the other questions. After you answer the less difficult questions, return to those which you tagged and answer them. Be sure to untag these questions once you have answered them. The review marking procedure will be explained to you prior to starting the test. Although the computer should alert you to unanswered questions, make sure every question has an answer recorded. This will allow you to use the available time to your maximum advantage.
- Perform each math calculation twice to confirm your answer. If adding or subtracting a column of numbers, reverse your direction the second time to reduce the possibility of error.
- When solving a calculation problem, select the answer nearest to your solution.
- Remember that information is provided in the Legends and Figures contained within the Airman Knowledge Testing Supplement (FAA-CT-8080 document) you'll be using during the test.
- Remember to answer every question, even the ones with no completely correct answer, to ensure the FAA gives you credit for a bad question.
- Take your time and be thorough but relaxed. Take a minute off every half-hour or so to relax your brain and body. Stay hydrated.

ATP Certificate Eligibility Requirements

If you are pursuing an airline transport or aircraft dispatcher certificate, you should review 14 CFR §61.23 "Medical Certificates: Requirement and Duration," §61.35 "Knowledge Test: Prerequisites and Passing Grades," and Part 61 (ATP or Part 65 (ADX) for certificate requirements.

To be eligible for an Airline Transport Pilot Certificate, a person must:

1. Be at least 23 years old (or 21 if meeting §61.160 requirements).
2. Be of good moral character.
3. Read, write, and understand English, and speak it without impediment that would interfere with radio conversation.
4. Have a current third-class medical certificate.
5. Pass a knowledge examination on the appropriate subjects with a score of at least 70 percent.
6. Pass an oral and flight check on the subjects and maneuvers in the Airline Transport Pilot and Type Rating Airman Certification Standards (ASA-ACS-11).
7. Have a Commercial Pilot Certificate or foreign or military equivalent.
8. For an ATP–Airplane Multi-Engine or an ATP obtained concurrently with an airplane type rating, receive a graduation certificate from an authorized training provider certifying completion of an ATP certification training program specified in §61.156 before applying for the knowledge test.
9. For an ATP certificate with an airplane category and class rating, have at least 1,500 hours of total time as a pilot that includes at least:
    a. 500 hours of cross-country flight time.
    b. 100 hours of night flight time.
    c. 50 hours of flight time in the class of airplane for the rating sought.
    d. 75 hours of instrument flight time, in actual or simulated instrument conditions.
    e. 250 hours of PIC time.
10. For a rotorcraft category and helicopter class rating, have 1,200 hours pilot time including:
    a. 500 hours cross-country flight time.
    b. 100 hours night time, at least 15 hours in helicopters.
    c. 200 hours in helicopters including 75 hours PIC time.
    d. 75 hours of actual or simulated instrument time with at least 50 hours in flight and 25 hours PIC time in helicopters.

Knowledge Exam References

The FAA references the following documents to write the FAA Knowledge Exam questions. You should be familiar with all of these as part of your ground school studies, which you should complete before starting test preparation.

Aerodynamics for Naval Aviators
Aeronautical Chart User's Guide

FAA-H-8083-1 *Aircraft Weight and Balance Handbook*
FAA-H-8083-2 *Risk Management Handbook*
FAA-H-8083-3 *Airplane Flying Handbook*
FAA-H-8083-15 *Instrument Flying Handbook*
FAA-H-8083-16 *Instrument Procedures Handbook*
FAA-H-8083-21 *Helicopter Flying Handbook*
FAA-H-8083-25 *Pilot's Handbook of Aeronautical Knowledge*
FAA-H-8083-28 *Aviation Weather Handbook*

FAA-S-ACS-11 *Airline Transport Pilot and Type Rating for Airplane Airman Certification Standards*

AC 00-24 *Thunderstorms*
AC 00-30 *Atmospheric Turbulence Avoidance*
AC 00-54 *Pilot Wind Shear Guide*
AC 20-117 *Hazards Following Ground Deicing & Ground Operations in Conditions Conducive to Aircraft Icing*
AC 91-6 *Water, Slush and Snow on the Runway*
AC 91-43 *Unreliable Airspeed Indication*
AC 91-51 *Effect of Icing on Aircraft Control and Airplane Deice and Anti-Ice Systems*
AC 91-74 *Pilot Guide: Flight in Icing Conditions*
AC 135-17 *Pilot Guide-Small Aircraft Ground Deicing*
AC 120-51 *Crew Resource Management Training*
AC 120-100 *Basics of Aviation Fatigue*
AC 120-58 *Pilot Guide for Large Aircraft Ground Deicing*

Chart Supplements U.S.
IFR Enroute High Altitude Chart
IFR Enroute Low Altitude Chart
U.S. Terminal Procedures

Aeronautical Information Manual (AIM)
14 CFR Parts 1, 23, 25, 61, 63, 71, 91, 97, 110, 111, 117, 119, 121, 135
49 CFR Parts 172, 175, 830, 1544

Visit **asa2fly.com** for these and many more titles and pilot supplies for your aviation endeavors.
Visit **asa2fly.com/TPATP** for reader resources useful to airline transport pilots and aircraft dispatchers.

Acronyms

For reference, acronyms appearing in this book are defined below.

AC	Advisory Circular
AC	Convective Outlook
ADC	air data computer
ADF	automatic direction finder
ADIZ	Air Defense Identification Zone
ADM	aeronautical decision making
ADS-B	Automatic Dependent Surveillance–Broadcast
AFM	aircraft flight manual
AGL	above ground level
AIRMET	airmen's meteorological information
ALD	available landing distance
ANU	airplane nose up
ARFF	aircraft rescue and firefighting
ARTCC	Air Route Traffic Control Center
ASDE-X	Airport Surface Detection Equipment–Model X
ASOS	Automated Surface Observing System
ASR	airport surveillance radar
ASSC	airport surface surveillance capability
ATC	air traffic control
ATD	along-track distance (RNAV/GPS)
ATP	airline transport pilot
BHP	brake horsepower
BMEP	brake mean effective pressure
BOW	basic operating weight
CAS	calibrated airspeed
CAT	clear air turbulence
CDI	course deviation indicator
CFIT	controlled flight into terrain
CG	center of gravity
CONUS	continental/contiguous United States
CRM	crew resource management
CVR	cockpit voice recorder
CWA	center weather advisory
DA	decision altitude
DC	dry chemical (firefighting)
DH	decision height
DME	distance measuring equipment
DP	departure procedure
EDCT	estimated departure clearance time
EFC	expect further clearance
EFD	electronic flight display
EGT	exhaust gas temperature
ELT	emergency locator transmitter
EPR	engine pressure ratio
ESHP	equivalent shaft horsepower
ETA	estimated time of arrival
ETOPS	extended range twin-engine operations
FAF	final approach fix
FAR	Federal Aviation Regulation
FAROS	final approach occupancy signal
FB	winds and temperatures aloft forecast
FDP	flight duty period
FIS-B	Flight Information Services–Broadcast
FL	flight level
FPD	freezing point depressant
FSDO	Flight Standards District Office
FSS	Flight Service Station
GBAS	ground-based augmentation system
GNSS	Global Navigation Satellite System
GPS	Global Positioning System
GPWS	ground proximity warning system
GS	ground speed
GTG-2	Graphical Turbulence Guidance
HAT	height above touchdown
HEMES	hospital emergency medical evacuation service
HIRL	high intensity runway lights
HS	hot spot (runway)
HSI	horizontal situation indicator
IAP	instrument approach procedure
IAS	indicated airspeed
ICAO	International Civil Aviation Organization
IFR	instrument flight rules
ILS	instrument landing system

IMC	instrument meteorological conditions
INS	internal navigation system
IR	Instrument Route (MTR)
IRU	inertial reference unit (DME)
ISA	international standard atmosphere
KIAS	knots indicated airspeed
LAHSO	land and hold short operations
LDA	localizer directional aid
LEMAC	leading edge of mean aerodynamic chord
LLWAS	Low-Level Wind Shear Alert System
LNAV	lateral navigation
LOC	localizer (ILS)
LPV	localizer performance with vertical guidance
LTE	loss of tail rotor effectiveness
MAC	mean aerodynamic chord
MAP	manifold pressure
MAWP	missed approach waypoint
MDA	minimum descent altitude
MEA	minimum enroute altitude
MEL	Minimum Equipment List
METAR	aviation routine weather report
MFD	multi-function display
MGT	measured gas temperature
MHA	minimum holding altitude
MLS	microwave landing system
MOA	Military Operating Area
MOCA	minimum obstacle clearance altitude
MON	Minimum Operational Network (VOR)
MSA	minimum safe/sector altitude
MSL	mean sea level
MTOW	maximum takeoff weight
MTR	Military Training Route
MVA	minimum vectoring altitude
NAS	National Airspace System
NAVAID	navigational aid
NDB	non-directional beacon
NM	nautical mile
NMAC	near midair collision
NOTAM	Notice to Air Missions
NTSB	National Transportation Safety Board
NTW	net total weight
OAT	outside air temperature
OBS	omni bearing selector
OCS	obstacle clearance surface
OIS	obstacle identification surface
OROCA	off-route obstruction clearance altitude
PAPI	precision approach path indicator
PAR	precision approach radar
PDSC	pre-departure service check
PFD	primary flight display
PIC	pilot-in-command
PIREP	pilot report
POH	pilot's operating handbook
PPH	pounds per hour
PRM	precision runway monitor
psi	pounds per square inch
RA	resolution advisory
RAFC	Regional Aera Forecast Center
RAIM	receiver autonomous integrity monitoring
RCAM	runway condition assessment matrix
RCLS	runway centerline lighting system
REIL	runway end identifier lights
REL	runway entrance lights
RFFS	rescue and firefighting services
RFM	rotorcraft flight manual
RIL	runway intersection lights
RNAV	area navigation
RNP	required navigation performance
RVR	runway visual range
RVSM	reduced vertical separate minimum
RwyCC	runway condition code
SDF	simplified directional facility
SIAP	standard instrument approach procedure
SIC	second-in-command
SID	standard instrument departure
SIGMET	significant meteorological information
SL	sea level
SM	statute mile
STAR	standard terminal arrival route
TA	traffic advisory

TAF	terminal aerodrome forecast
TAS	true airspeed
TAT	total air temperature
TAWS	terrain awareness system
TDZE	touchdown zone elevation
TDZL	touchdown zone lights
THL	takeoff hold lights
TIBS	Telephone Information Briefing Service
TIS-B	Traffic Information Service–Broadcast
TIT	turbine inlet temperature
UAT	Universal Access Transceiver
VASI	visual approach slope indicator
VDP	visual descent point
VFR	visual flight rules
VHF	very high frequency
VOR	VHF Omnidirectional Range
VORTAC	VOR-TACAN navigation system
VOT	VOR Test Facility
VR	Visual Route (MTR)
WAAS	Wide Area Augmentation System
WW	severe weather watch bulletin
ZFW	zero fuel weight

ASA Test Prep Layout

Sample FAA questions have been sorted into chapters according to subject matter. Within each chapter, similar questions are grouped together following introductory chapter text. Figures referenced in the chapter text are numbered with the appropriate chapter number, e.g., "Figure 1-1" is Chapter 1's first chapter text figure.

Some sample FAA questions refer to Figures or Legends immediately following the question number, e.g., "8201. (Refer to Figure 14.)." These are FAA Figures and Legends from the Airman Knowledge Testing Supplement (FAA-CT-8080-7D) that can be found at the back of this book. This supplement will be provided to you as a separate booklet when you take your FAA test.

Following each sample FAA test question is ASA's explanation in italics. The last line of the explanation contains a Learning Statement Code (LSC), for those tests referencing an FAA Practical Test Standard (PTS), or Airman Certification Standards (ACS) code, for those tests with an ACS, as well as a reference for further study. Some questions include an explanation for the incorrect answers for added clarity. When you encounter a difficult question, find the LSC or ACS code in Cross-Reference B, and then look for material relating to the subject description within the given reference(s). Refer to Cross-Reference B for more information on how to use LSCs or ACS codes for effective studying.

Answers to each question are found at the bottom of each page.

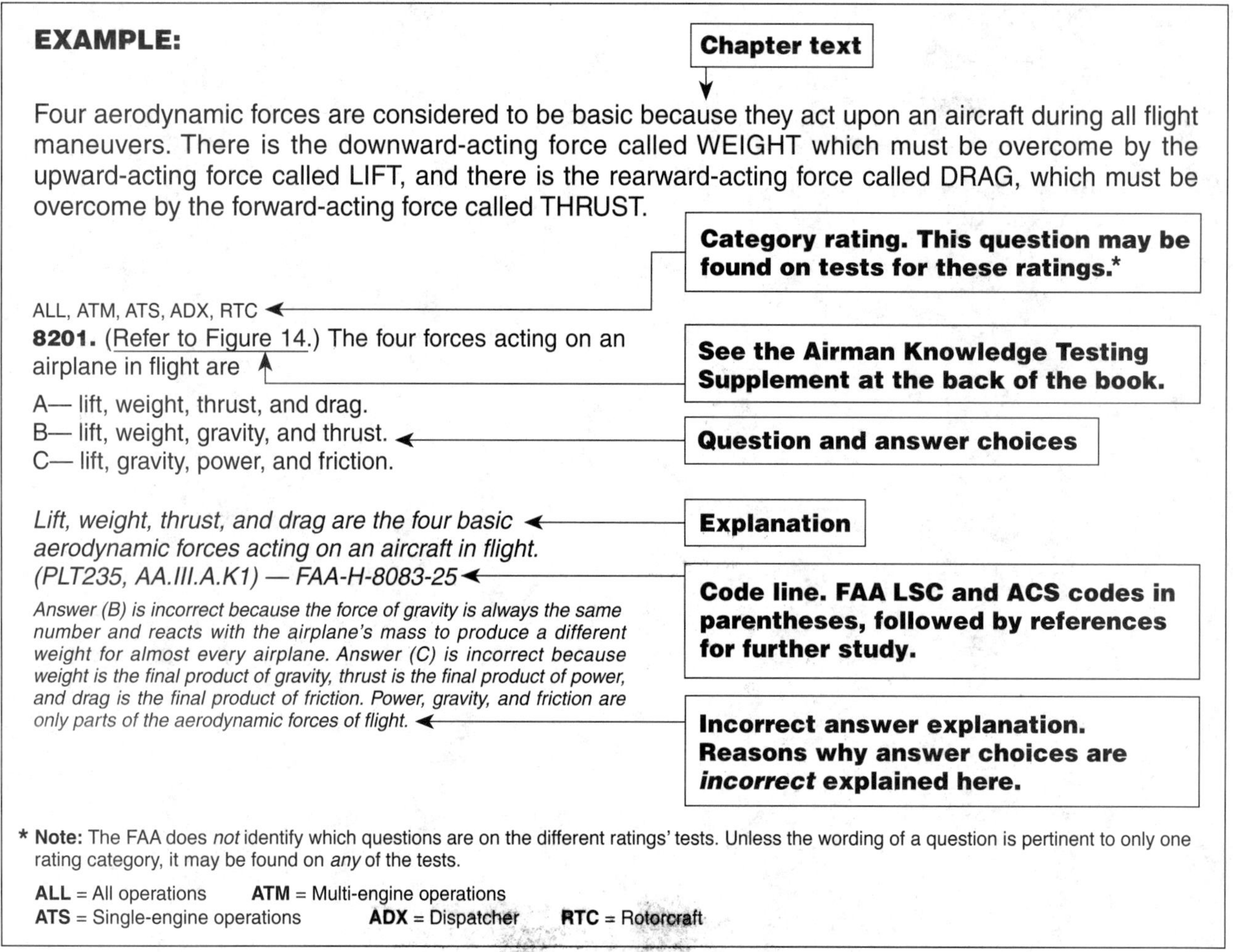

EXAMPLE:

Chapter text

Four aerodynamic forces are considered to be basic because they act upon an aircraft during all flight maneuvers. There is the downward-acting force called WEIGHT which must be overcome by the upward-acting force called LIFT, and there is the rearward-acting force called DRAG, which must be overcome by the forward-acting force called THRUST.

Category rating. This question may be found on tests for these ratings.*

ALL, ATM, ATS, ADX, RTC

8201. (Refer to Figure 14.) The four forces acting on an airplane in flight are

See the Airman Knowledge Testing Supplement at the back of the book.

A— lift, weight, thrust, and drag.
B— lift, weight, gravity, and thrust.
C— lift, gravity, power, and friction.

Question and answer choices

Lift, weight, thrust, and drag are the four basic aerodynamic forces acting on an aircraft in flight.

Explanation

(PLT235, AA.III.A.K1) — FAA-H-8083-25

Code line. FAA LSC and ACS codes in parentheses, followed by references for further study.

Answer (B) is incorrect because the force of gravity is always the same number and reacts with the airplane's mass to produce a different weight for almost every airplane. Answer (C) is incorrect because weight is the final product of gravity, thrust is the final product of power, and drag is the final product of friction. Power, gravity, and friction are only parts of the aerodynamic forces of flight.

Incorrect answer explanation. Reasons why answer choices are *incorrect* explained here.

* **Note:** The FAA does *not* identify which questions are on the different ratings' tests. Unless the wording of a question is pertinent to only one rating category, it may be found on *any* of the tests.

ALL = All operations **ATM** = Multi-engine operations
ATS = Single-engine operations **ADX** = Dispatcher **RTC** = Rotorcraft

Chapter 1
Regulations

Applicable Regulations

Although "FAR" is used as the acronym for "Federal Aviation Regulations," and found throughout the regulations themselves and hundreds of other publications, the FAA is now actively discouraging its use. "FAR" also means "Federal Acquisition Regulations." To eliminate any possible confusion, the FAA is now citing the federal aviation regulations with reference to Title 14 of the Code of Federal Regulations. For example, "FAR Part 91.3" is now referenced as "14 CFR Part 91 Section 3." The regulations change frequently; answer all questions in compliance with the most current regulations.

Three different Federal Aviation Regulation Parts can apply to operations of aircraft covered by this chapter: Parts 91, 121, and 135. Part 91 encompasses the general operation and flight rules for all aircraft operating within the United States. Often the rules of Part 121 or 135 supplement or even supersede Part 91. When an airplane is not operated for compensation, only the Part 91 rules apply. For the test, assume Part 121 or 135 rules apply unless the question specifically states otherwise.

Part 121 applies to air carriers (airlines) engaged in interstate or overseas air transportation. Carriers which operate under Part 121 engage in **common carriage**. This means that they offer their services to the public and receive compensation for those services.

Part 121 operators are subdivided into five categories: commuter, on-demand, domestic, flag, and supplemental. **Commuter operation** means any scheduled operation that makes at least five round trips per week on at least one route between two or more points according to the published flight schedules and that is conducted with a rotorcraft or with an airplane or powered-lift aircraft that is not turbojet-powered, has 9 seats or fewer excluding crewmember seats, and has a maximum payload capacity of 7,500 pounds or less. **On-demand operation** means any operation for compensation or hire that carries passengers with a negotiated schedule or that uses a turbojet-powered airplane or powered-lift aircraft with 30 or fewer seats. Carriers authorized to conduct scheduled operations within the 48 contiguous states are **domestic air carriers**. **Flag air carriers** conduct scheduled operations inside and outside the 48 contiguous states. A **supplemental carrier** conducts its operations anywhere that its operations specifications permit but only on a nonscheduled basis. There is a sixth category, **commercial operators of large aircraft**, but they must comply with the rules covering supplemental carriers and the distinction is unimportant to this discussion.

Part 135 applies to air taxi operators. These operators are subdivided into two categories, commuter and on-demand operations.

Other parts of the regulations apply as well. Part 61 governs certification of pilots and flight instructors. Part 67 covers the issuing and standards for medical certificates. Part 1 contains definitions and abbreviations.

The ATP Certificate

All required flight crew of an air carrier flight must hold Airline Transport Pilot (ATP) certificates with the appropriate type rating.

The pilot-in-command of a large aircraft (gross weight over 12,500 pounds) or of a turbojet powered airplane must have a type rating from that aircraft issued under 14 CFR Part 61.

Any type rating(s) on the pilot certificate of an applicant who successfully completes an ATP checkride will be included on the ATP Certificate with the privileges and limitations of the ATP Certificate, provided the applicant passes the checkride in the same category and class of aircraft for which the applicant holds the type rating(s). However, if a type rating for that category and class of aircraft on the superseded pilot certificate is limited to VFR, that limitation will be carried forward to the person's ATP Certificate level.

An ATP certificate holder may give instruction in "air transportation service" in aircraft for which he/she holds category, class and type ratings as an ATP. An ATP may not instruct more than 8 hours a day and not more than 36 hours in any 7-day period.

If a person's pilot or medical certificate is lost or destroyed he/she can request the FAA to send a FAX confirming that they were issued. This FAX can be used as a temporary replacement for the certificates for up to 60 days.

If a pilot certificate holder is convicted of driving under the influence of alcohol or drugs, the pilot must report that conviction to the FAA, Civil Aviation Security Division within 60 days. Failure to do so is grounds for suspending or revoking any pilot or flight instructor certificates held by that person.

A **crewmember** is a person assigned to duty in the aircraft during flight. This includes pilots, flight engineers, navigators, flight attendants or anyone else assigned to duty in the airplane. A **flight crewmember** is a pilot, flight engineer or flight navigator assigned to duty in the aircraft during flight.

No one may serve as a pilot on an air carrier after that person has reached his/her 65th birthday. Note that this rule applies to any pilot position in the aircraft, but it does not apply to other flight crew positions such as flight engineer or navigator. This is known as the "Age 65 Rule."

To exercise **ATP privileges** (such as pilot-in-command of an air carrier flight), a pilot must hold a first-class medical certificate issued within the preceding (6 or 12) calendar months—depending on whether the applicant is over or under 40 years of age. To exercise commercial pilot privileges (e.g. flying a parachute jump operation) a pilot must hold either a first- or second-class medical certificate within the preceding (6 or 12) calendar months. For example, a first-class certificate issued in February to a pilot over 40 years of age would be good anytime in February for ATP privileges through August 31 and then good through the last day of February the next year for commercial pilot privileges.

A prerequisite for taking a practical test requires the applicant hold at least a current third-class medical certificate, if a medical certificate is required. If the practical test is scheduled in an aircraft, the applicant is required to have the third-class medical certificate. The applicant is not required to hold a medical certificate when taking a test or check for a certificate, rating, or authorization conducted in a flight simulator or flight training device.

ALL

9350. Unless otherwise authorized, when is the pilot-in-command required to hold a type rating?

A—When operating an aircraft that is certificated for more than one pilot.
B—When operating an aircraft having a gross weight of more than 12,500 pounds.
C—When operating a multiengine aircraft having a gross weight of more than 6,000 pounds.

A person must hold a type rating to act as pilot-in-command of a large aircraft (over 12,500 pounds gross takeoff weight), or of a turbojet-powered airplane. (PLT443, AA.I.G.K1) — 14 CFR §61.31

Answer (A) is incorrect because an aircraft requiring more than one pilot does not constitute the need for a type rating. Answer (C) is incorrect because it does not matter if the aircraft is single-engine or multi-engine, and the aircraft must weigh over 12,500 lbs., not 6,000.

ALL

9350-1. According to 14 CFR Part 121, what requirements must the second-in-command possess?

A—ATP certificate with appropriate type rating.
B—ATP certificate with appropriate second-in-command type rating.
C—ATP certificate and Third Class Medical Certificate.

No certificate holder may use nor may any pilot act as second-in-command (SIC) unless the pilot holds an airline transport pilot certificate and an appropriate aircraft type rating for the aircraft being flown. A second-in-command type rating obtained under 61.55 does not satisfy these requirements. (PLT450, AA.I.G.K4) — 14 CFR §121.436

Answers

9350 [B]   9350-1 [A]

ALL
9328. A commercial pilot has a type rating in a B-727 and B-737. A flight test is completed in a B-747 for the Airline Transport Pilot Certificate. What pilot privileges may be exercised regarding these airplanes?

A—Commercial – B-737; ATP – B-727 and B-747.
B—ATP – B-747; Commercial – B-727 and B-737.
C—ATP – B-747, B-727, and B-737.

Any type rating(s) on the pilot certificate of an applicant who successfully completes an ATP checkride will be included on the ATP Certificate with the privileges and limitations of the ATP Certificate, provided the applicant passes the checkride in the same category and class of aircraft for which the applicant holds the type rating(s). However, if a type rating for that category and class of aircraft on the superseded pilot certificate is limited to VFR, that limitation shall be carried forward to the person's ATP Certificate level. (PLT443, AA.I.G.K1)—14 CFR §61.157

ALL
9329. A commercial pilot has DC-3 and DC-9 type ratings. A flight test is completed for an Airline Transport Pilot Certificate in a B-727. What pilot privileges may be exercised?

A—ATP – B-727 and DC-3; Commercial – DC-9.
B—ATP – B-727 only; Commercial – DC-9 and DC 3.
C—ATP – B-727, DC-3, and DC-9.

Any type rating(s) on the pilot certificate of an applicant who successfully completes an ATP checkride will be included on the ATP Certificate with the privileges and limitations of the ATP Certificate, provided the applicant passes the checkride in the same category and class of aircraft for which the applicant holds the type rating(s). However, if a type rating for that category and class of aircraft on the superseded pilot certificate is limited to VFR, that limitation shall be carried forward to the person's ATP Certificate level. (PLT442, AA.I.G.K1) — 14 CFR §61.157

ALL
9329-1. The lowest CAT II minimums are

A—DH 100 and RVR 1200.
B—DH 150 and RVR 1600.
C—DH 50 and RVR 1200.

A Category II or Category III pilot authorization is issued by a letter of authorization as part of an applicant's instrument rating or ATP certificate. Upon original issue, the authorization contains the following limitations: for Category II operations, the limitation is 1,600 feet RVR and a 150-foot decision height. (PLT442, AA.I.G.K1) — 14 CFR §61.13

ALL
9329-2. The lowest authorized ILS minimums associated with CAT II approaches are

A—Decision Height (DH) 200 feet and Runway Visual Range (RVR) 2,400 feet (with touchdown zone and centerline lighting, RVR 1,800 feet).
B—DH 100 feet and RVR 1,200 feet.
C—No DH or DH below 50 feet and RVR less than 700 feet but not less than 150 feet.

Category I (CAT I) operation is a precision instrument approach and landing with a decision altitude that is not lower than 200 feet (60 meters) above the threshold and with either a visibility of not less than 1/2 statute mile (800 meters), or a runway visual range of not less than 1,800 feet (550 meters). Category II (CAT II) operation is a precision instrument approach and landing with a decision height lower than 200 feet (60 meters), but not lower than 100 feet (30 meters), and with a runway visual range of not less than 1,200 feet (350 meters). Category III (CAT III) operation is a precision instrument approach and landing with a decision height lower than 100 feet (30 meters) or no DH, and with a runway visual range less than 1200 feet (350 meters). (PLT442, AA.I.C.K5) — FAA-H-8083-16

ALL
9330. In a 24-hour consecutive period, what is the maximum time, excluding briefing and debriefing, that an airline transport pilot may instruct other pilots in air transportation service?

A—6 hours.
B—8 hours.
C—10 hours.

An airline transport pilot may instruct other pilots in air transportation service in aircraft of the category, class and type for which he/she is rated. However, the ATP may not instruct for more than 8 hours in one day nor more than 36 hours in any 7-day period. (PLT460, AA.I.G.K1) — 14 CFR §61.167

Answers

9328 [C] 9329 [C] 9329-1 [B] 9329-2 [B] 9330 [B]

ALL
9331. The flight instruction of other pilots in air transportation service by an airline transport pilot is restricted to

A—30 hours in any 7-consecutive-day period.
B—7 hours in any 24-consecutive-hour period.
C—36 hours in any 7-consecutive-day period.

The ATP may not instruct for more than 8 hours in one day nor more than 36 hours in any 7-day period. (PLT460, AA.I.G.K1) — 14 CFR §61.167

ALL
9351. When a replacement is received for an airman's medical certificate, for what maximum time is this document valid?

A—30 days.
B—60 days.
C—90 days.

A person who has lost an Airman's Certificate or a Medical Certificate, or both, may obtain a document from the FAA confirming that it was issued. The document may be carried as temporary certificate(s) for a period not to exceed 60 days. (PLT447, AA.I.G.K1) — 14 CFR §61.29

ALL
9332. How soon after the conviction for driving while intoxicated by alcohol or drugs shall it be reported to the FAA, Civil Aviation Security Division?

A—No later than 30 working days after the motor vehicle action.
B—No later than 60 days after the motor vehicle action.
C—Required to be reported upon renewal of medical certificate.

Each person holding a certificate issued under this part shall provide a written report of each motor vehicle action to the FAA, Civil Aviation Security Division, no later than 60 days after the motor vehicle action. (PLT463, AA.I.G.K1) — 14 CFR §61.15

ALL
9325. Which is a definition of the term "crewmember"?

A—Only a pilot, flight engineer, or flight navigator assigned to duty in an aircraft during flight time.
B—A person assigned to perform duty in an aircraft during flight time.
C—Any person assigned to duty in an aircraft during flight except a pilot or flight engineer.

"Crewmember" means a person assigned to perform duty in an aircraft during flight time. (PLT395, AA.I.G.K4) — 14 CFR §1.1

Answer (A) is incorrect because "crewmember" pertains to anyone assigned duty in the aircraft during flight. Answer (C) is also incorrect because "crewmember" also includes the pilot and flight engineer.

ATM, ATS, RTC
9349. When a type rating is to be added to an airline transport pilot certificate, and the practical test is scheduled in an approved flight simulator and an aircraft, the applicant is

A—required to have a least a current third-class medical certificate.
B—required to have a current first-class medical certificate.
C—not required to hold a medical certificate.

A prerequisite for taking a practical test requires that the applicant hold at least a current third-class medical certificate, if a medical certificate is required. In this case, since part of the practical test is scheduled in an aircraft, the applicant is required to have at least a current third-class medical certificate. (PLT427, AA.I.G.K1) — 14 CFR §61.39

ATM, ATS, RTC
9335. An applicant who is taking a practical test for a type rating to be added to a commercial pilot certificate, in an approved simulator, is

A—required to have a first-class medical certificate.
B—required to have a second-class medical certificate.
C—not required to have a medical certificate.

A prerequisite for taking a practical test requires that the applicant hold at least a current third-class medical certificate, if a medical certificate is required. The applicant is not required to hold a medical certificate when taking a test or check for a certificate, rating, or authorization conducted in a flight simulator or flight training device. In this case, since the practical test is scheduled in an approved flight simulator, the applicant is not required to have a medical certificate. (PLT427, AA.I.G.K1) — 14 CFR §§61.39, 61.23

Answers

9331 [C]	9351 [B]	9332 [B]	9325 [B]	9349 [A]	9335 [C]

ATM, ATS, RTC
9333. An applicant who is scheduled for a practical test for an airline transport pilot certificate, in an approved flight simulator, is

A—required to have at least a current third-class medical certificate.
B—not required to have a medical certificate.
C—required to have a first-class medical certificate.

A prerequisite for taking a practical test requires that the applicant hold at least a current third-class medical certificate, if a medical certificate is required. The applicant is not required to hold a medical certificate when taking a test or check for a certificate, rating, or authorization conducted in a flight simulator or flight training device. In this case, since the practical test is scheduled in an approved flight simulator, the applicant is not required to have a medical certificate. (PLT427, AA.I.G.K1) — 14 CFR §61.39 and §61.23

ATM, ATS, RTC
9343. When a type rating is to be added to an airline transport pilot certificate, and the practical test is scheduled in an approved flight training device and/or approved flight simulator, the applicant is

A—required to have at least a third-class medical certificate.
B—is not required to have a medical certificate.
C—required to have a first-class medical certificate.

A prerequisite for taking a practical test requires that the applicant hold at least a current third-class medical certificate, if a medical certificate is required. The applicant is not required to hold a medical certificate when taking a test or check for a certificate, rating, or authorization conducted in a flight simulator or flight training device. In this case, since the practical test is scheduled in an approved flight training device and/or approved flight simulator, the applicant is not required to have a medical certificate. (PLT427, AA.I.G.K1) — 14 CFR §§61.39, 61.23

ATM, ATS, RTC
9340. An applicant who is scheduled for a practical test for an airline transport pilot certificate, in an aircraft, needs

A—a first-class medical certificate.
B—at least a current third-class medical certificate.
C—a second-class medical certificate.

A prerequisite for taking a practical test requires that the applicant hold at least a current third-class medical certificate, if a medical certificate is required. In this case, since the practical test is scheduled in an aircraft, the applicant is required to have at least a current third-class medical certificate. (PLT427, AA.I.G.K1) — 14 CFR §61.39

ATM, ADX
8191. The "age 65 rule" of 14 CFR Part 121 applies to

A—any required pilot crewmember.
B—any flight crewmember.
C—the pilot-in-command only.

No person may serve as a pilot on an airplane engaged in operations under 14 CFR Part 121 if that person has reached his/her 65th birthday. (PLT443, AA.I.G.K4) — 14 CFR §121.383

Answer (B) is incorrect because the "age 65" rule excludes flight engineers and navigators. Answer (C) is incorrect because the "age 65" rule applies to every pilot crewmember.

Answers

9333 [B]	9343 [B]	9340 [B]	8191 [A]

Flight Engineer Requirements

Many air carrier aircraft have a **flight engineer** as a required flight crewmember. All older airplanes that have a maximum takeoff weight of more than 80,000 pounds must have a flight engineer. On aircraft types certified after 1963, the aircraft's "type certificate" states whether or not a flight engineer is required.

On each flight that requires a flight engineer, at least one other member of the flight crew must be qualified to provide emergency performance of the flight engineer's duties if he/she becomes ill or incapacitated. Either pilot can fulfill the function and they need not hold a Flight Engineer Certificate to be "qualified."

ATM, ADX
8189. Under which condition is a flight engineer required as a flight crewmember in 14 CFR Part 121 operations?

A—If the airplane is being flown on proving flights, with revenue cargo aboard.
B—If the airplane is powered by more than two turbine engines.
C—If required by the airplane's type certificate.

No certificate holder may operate an airplane for which a type certificate was issued before January 2, 1964, having a maximum certificated takeoff weight of more than 80,000 pounds without a flight crewmember holding a current Flight Engineer Certificate. For each airplane type certificated after January 1, 1964, the requirement for a flight engineer is determined under the type certification requirements of 14 CFR §25.1523. (PLT409, AA.I.G.K4) — 14 CFR §121.387

Answer (A) is incorrect because the type certificate is the determining factor for a flight engineer. Answer (B) is incorrect because the type certificate is the determining factor for a flight engineer.

ATM, ADX
8190. When the need for a flight engineer is determined by aircraft weight, what is the takeoff weight that requires a flight engineer?

A—80,000 pounds.
B—More than 80,000 pounds.
C—300,000 pounds.

No certificate holder may operate an airplane for which a type certificate was issued before January 2, 1964, having a maximum certificated takeoff weight of more than 80,000 pounds without a flight crewmember holding a current Flight Engineer Certificate. (PLT440, AA.I.G.K4) — 14 CFR §121.387

ATM, ADX
8212. An air carrier uses an airplane that is certified for operation with a flightcrew of two pilots and one flight engineer. In case the flight engineer becomes incapacitated,

A—at least one other flight crewmember must be qualified to perform the flight engineer duties.
B—one crewmember must be qualified to perform the duties of the flight engineer.
C—one pilot must be qualified and have a flight engineer certificate to perform the flight engineer duties.

On each flight requiring a flight engineer at least one flight crewmember, other than the flight engineer, must be qualified to provide emergency performance of the flight engineer's functions for the safe completion of the flight if the flight engineer becomes ill or is otherwise incapacitated. A pilot need not hold a Flight Engineer's Certificate to perform the flight engineer's functions in such a situation. (PLT440, AA.I.G.K4) — 14 CFR §121.385

ATM, ADX
8213. When a flight engineer is a required crewmember on a flight, it is necessary for

A—one pilot to hold a flight engineer certificate and be qualified to perform the flight engineer duties in an emergency.
B—the flight engineer to be properly certificated and qualified, but also at least one other flight crewmember must be qualified and certified to perform flight engineer duties.
C—at least one other flight crewmember to be qualified to perform flight engineer duties, but a certificate is not required.

On each flight requiring a flight engineer at least one flight crewmember, other than the flight engineer, must be qualified to provide emergency performance of the flight engineer's functions for the safe completion of the flight if the flight engineer becomes ill or is otherwise incapacitated. A pilot need not hold a Flight Engineer's Certificate to perform the flight engineer's functions in such a situation. (PLT440, AA.I.G.K4) — 14 CFR §121.385

Answers

8189 [C] 8190 [B] 8212 [A] 8213 [C]

ATM, ADX
8188. If a flight engineer becomes incapacitated during flight, who may perform the flight engineer's duties?

A—The second in command only.
B—Any flight crewmember, if qualified.
C—Either pilot, if they have a flight engineer certificate.

On each flight requiring a flight engineer at least one flight crewmember, other than the flight engineer, must be qualified to provide emergency performance of the flight engineer's functions for the safe completion of the flight if the flight engineer becomes ill or is otherwise incapacitated. A pilot need not hold a Flight Engineer's Certificate to perform the flight engineer's functions in such a situation. (PLT440, AA.I.G.K4) — 14 CFR §121.385

Flight Attendants

One or more **flight attendants** are required on each passenger carrying airplane operating under Part 121 that has more than nine passenger seats. The number of flight attendants is determined by the number of installed passenger seats—not by the actual number of passengers on board.

One flight attendant is required on airplanes that can seat from 10 through 50 passengers. Two flight attendants are required on airplanes having a seating capacity from 51 through 100 seats. After that, an additional flight attendant is required for each unit (or partial unit) of 50 seats above 100. For example, three flight attendants are required on airplanes having from 101 through 150 seats, and four flight attendants must be on aircraft with 151 through 200 seats.

ATM, ADX
8192. An airplane has seats for 149 passengers and eight crewmembers. What is the minimum number of flight attendants required with 97 passengers aboard?

A—Four.
B—Three.
C—Two.

For airplanes having a seating capacity of more than 100 passengers, each certificate holder shall provide at least two flight attendants plus one additional flight attendant for a unit (or partial unit) of 50 passenger seats above a seating capacity of 100 passengers. The number of flight attendants is determined by the number of installed passenger seats (not by the actual number of passengers on board). For an airplane with a seating capacity of 149 passengers, three flight attendants are required. (PLT389, AA.II.A.K7) — 14 CFR §121.391

ATM, ADX
8193. When an air carrier airplane with a seating capacity of 187 has 137 passengers on board, what is the minimum number of flight attendants required?

A—Five.
B—Four.
C—Three.

For airplanes having a seating capacity of more than 100 passengers, each certificate holder shall provide at least two flight attendants plus one additional flight attendant for a unit (or partial unit) of 50 passenger seats above a seating capacity of 100 passengers. The number of flight attendants is determined by the number of installed passenger seats (not by the actual number of passengers on board). For an airplane with a seating capacity of 187 passengers, four flight attendants are required. (PLT389, AA.II.A.K7) — 14 CFR §121.391

ATM, ADX
8201. What is the minimum number of flight attendants required on an airplane having a passenger seating capacity of 188 with only 117 passengers aboard?

A—Five.
B—Four.
C—Three.

For airplanes having a seating capacity of more than 100 passengers, each certificate holder shall provide at least two flight attendants plus one additional flight attendant for a unit (or partial unit) of 50 passenger seats above a seating capacity of 100 passengers. The number of flight attendants is determined by the number of installed passenger seats (not by the actual number of passengers on board). For an airplane with a seating capacity of 188 passengers, four flight attendants are required. (PLT389, AA.II.A.K7) — 14 CFR §121.391

Answers

8188 [B] 8192 [B] 8193 [B] 8201 [B]

ATM, ADX

8202. What is the minimum number of flight attendants required on an airplane with a passenger seating capacity of 333 when 296 passengers are aboard?

A—Seven.
B—Six.
C—Five.

For airplanes having a seating capacity of more than 100 passengers, each certificate holder shall provide at least two flight attendants plus one additional flight attendant for a unit (or partial unit) of 50 passenger seats above a seating capacity of 100 passengers. The number of flight attendants is determined by the number of installed passenger seats (not by the actual number of passengers on board). For an airplane with a seating capacity of 333 passengers, seven flight attendants are required. (PLT389, AA.II.A.K7) — 14 CFR §121.391

Experience and Training Requirements

For these definitions of training, aircraft are divided into two "groups." **Group I** aircraft are propeller driven. Turbojet aircraft are **Group II**. **Initial training** is the training required for crewmembers and dispatchers who have not qualified and served in the same capacity (i.e., flight engineer, co-pilot, pilot-in-command) on another aircraft of the same group. **Transition training** is the training required for crewmembers or dispatchers who have qualified and served in the same capacity on another aircraft of the same group. **Upgrade training** is the training required for crewmembers who have qualified and served as second-in-command or flight engineer on a particular airplane type (e.g., Boeing 727) before they can serve as pilot-in-command or second-in-command, respectively, on that airplane. **Differences training** is the training required for crewmembers or dispatchers who have qualified and served on a particular type of airplane before they can serve in the same capacity on a variation of that airplane. For example, a crewmember who is qualified on a Boeing 727-100 would need differences training to serve on a Boeing 727-200.

The pilot-in-command (PIC) of an air carrier flight must have had a proficiency check within the preceding 12 calendar months. In addition, within the preceding 6 calendar months the pilot-in-command must have either passed a proficiency check or completed an approved simulator training course. Pilots other than the PIC must have either passed a proficiency check or completed "line oriented" simulator training within the last 24 calendar months. In addition, the co-pilot must have had a **proficiency check** or any other kind of simulator training within the last 12 calendar months.

The pilot-in-command of an air carrier flight must have completed a **line check** in one of the aircraft types he/she is qualified to fly within the preceding 12 calendar months. If the PIC is qualified in more than one type aircraft, a line check in any of them satisfies this requirement.

Recurrent training and **checkrides** are always due during a calendar month rather than by a certain date. In addition, if recurrent training or a check is taken during, before, or after the month, it is considered to have been taken during the month it was due. For example, if a crewmember had a check due in December, he/she could take it November, December or January and it would be considered as having been done in December. Also, January would be considered a "grace month" in that the crewmember could fly, even though he/she had technically gone beyond the due date of the check.

Every pilot on an air carrier flight must have made at least 3 takeoffs and landings in the type of airplane flown within the preceding 90 days. If a pilot doesn't meet these requirements, he/she must re-establish the recency of experience by making 3 takeoffs and 3 landings under the supervision of a check airman. These takeoffs and landings must meet the following:

Answers

8202 [A]

- At least 1 takeoff must be made with a simulated failure of the most critical engine.
- At least 1 landing must be made from an ILS approach to the lowest ILS minimums authorized for the certificate holder.
- At least 1 landing must be made to a full stop.

Air Carriers' Operations Specifications are usually written so that the instrument experience requirements of 14 CFR Part 61 do not apply to their pilots. This test asks four questions on the Part 61 requirements: 9333, 9339, 9342, 9344.

The pilot-in-command of an airplane who has less than one hundred hours in the aircraft type has higher than published landing minimums at the destination airport. Such a pilot-in-command must add 100 feet to the published DH or MDA and add 1/2-mile (or 2,400 feet RVR) to the required visibility. If a flight diverts to an alternate airport, the pilot-in-command may use the published minimums for the approach there, but in no event may the landing minimums be less than 300 and 1. If a pilot has at least 100 hours PIC in another aircraft under Part 121 operations, he/she may reduce the current restriction by 1 hour for each landing, up to 50 hours maximum.

A Category II Instrument Approach is an ILS approach with a published minimum visibility of less than 1,800 RVR but equal to or greater than 1,200 RVR. Most CAT II approaches have published decision heights of 150 and 100 feet HAT. To fly a published CAT II approach, the aircraft must meet certain equipment and maintenance requirements and the pilots must be trained and qualified. Part 61 sets forth requirements for pilot qualification and an Air Carrier's Operations Specifications may modify or replace those requirements. The test limits its questions to Part 61 rules. To qualify for CAT II approach authorization, a pilot must take a CAT II checkride. To be eligible for the checkride he/she must meet all recent experience requirements of Part 61 and have certain recent experience with regard to ILS approaches. Within the previous 6 months the pilot must have made at least 6 ILS approaches down to minimums (CAT I minimums are OK). At least 3 of the approaches must have been hand flown. The other 3 may have been flown using an approach coupler. When issued an original CAT II certification, a pilot is restricted to a DH of 150 feet and a minimum RVR of 1,600. This restriction is lifted when the pilot logs 3 CAT II approaches to the 150-foot DH within the previous 6 months.

An aircraft dispatcher must have spent at least five hours observing flight deck operations within the preceding 12 calendar months. The dispatcher must have done this for at least one of the types for each group he/she is to dispatch.

ATM, ATS, RTC

9339. A pilot, acting as second-in-command, successfully completes the instrument competency check specified in 14 CFR Part 61. How long does this pilot remain current if no further IFR flights are made?

A—12 months.
B—90 days.
C—6 months.

No pilot may act as pilot-in-command under IFR unless he/she has, within the preceding 6 calendar months in the aircraft category for the instrument privileges sought, logged at least 6 instrument approaches, performed holding procedures, and intercepted and tracked courses through the use of navigation systems, or passed an instrument competency check in the category of aircraft involved. (PLT442, AA.I.G.K1) — 14 CFR §61.57

Answer (A) is incorrect because, upon completion of an instrument competency check, a pilot will remain current for 6 months. Answer (B) is incorrect because ninety days defines the 3 takeoffs and landings experience required to carry passengers.

Answers

9339 [C]

ATM, ATS, RTC

9344. To satisfy the minimum required instrument experience for IFR operations, a pilot must accomplish during the past 6 months at least

A—six instrument approaches, holding, intercepting and tracking courses through the use of navigation systems in an approved flight training device/simulator or in the category of aircraft to be flown.
B—six instrument approaches, three of which must be in the same category and class of aircraft to be flown, plus holding, intercepting and tracking courses in any aircraft.
C—six instrument approaches and 6 hours of instrument time, three of which may be in a glider.

No pilot may act as pilot-in-command under IFR unless he/she has, within the preceding 6 calendar months in the aircraft category for the instrument approaches, performed holding procedures, and intercepted and tracked courses through the use of navigation systems. (PLT442, AA.I.G.K1) — 14 CFR §61.57

ALL

9342. What instrument flight time may be logged by a second-in-command of an aircraft requiring two pilots?

A—All of the time the second-in-command is controlling the airplane solely by reference to flight instruments.
B—One-half the time the flight is on an IFR flight plan.
C—One-half the time the airplane is in actual IFR conditions.

A pilot may log as instrument flight time only that time during which he/she operates the aircraft solely by reference to the instruments, under actual or simulated instrument flight conditions. (PLT409, AA.I.G.K1) — 14 CFR §61.51

Answers (B) and (C) are incorrect because only when the pilot is flying in actual or simulated instrument flying conditions and is the sole manipulator of the controls may he/she log instrument flight time.

ALL

9342-1. An example of air carrier experience a pilot may use towards the 1,000 hours required to serve as PIC in Part 121 is flight time as an SIC

A—in Part 121 operations.
B—in Part 91, subpart K operations.
C—in Part 135 operations.

ATP certificate holders may use the 1,000 hours required to serve as PIC in Part 121 operations, as SIC in Part 121 operations, or PIC in Part 91 and 135 operations. (PLT450, AA.I.G.K4) — 14 CFR §121.436

ALL

9342-2. The holder of an ATP certificate with restricted privileges or an ATP certificate who also holds an aircraft type rating for the aircraft to be flown may act as

A—a PIC for a Part 121 supplemental air carrier.
B—a PIC for a Part 121 air carrier with 500 hours as a Part 121 SIC.
C—an SIC for a Part 121 air carrier.

The holder of an ATP-Restricted certificate may serve as second-in-command (SIC) for Part 121 operations requiring less than three pilots. (PLT450, AA.I.G.K4) — 14 CFR §61.167

ATM, ATS, RTC

9334. What recent experience is required to be eligible for the practical test for the original issue of a Category II authorization?

A—Within the previous 6 months, six ILS approaches flown manually to the Category I DH.
B—Within the previous 12 calendar months, six ILS approaches flown by use of an approach coupler to the Category I or Category II DH.
C—Within the previous 6 months, six ILS approaches, three of which may be flown to the Category I DH by use of an approach coupler.

To be eligible for Category II authorization, a pilot must have made at least 6 ILS approaches since the beginning of the 6th month before the test. These approaches must be under actual or simulated instrument flight conditions down to the minimum landing altitude for the ILS approach in the type aircraft in which the flight test is to be conducted. However, the approaches need not be conducted down to the decision heights authorized for Category II operations. At least 3 of these approaches must have been conducted manually, without the use of an approach coupler. (PLT442, AA.I.G.K1) — 14 CFR §61.67

Answer (A) is incorrect because only 3 of the approaches must be flown manually to Category I DH. Answer (B) is incorrect because the 6 ILS approaches must be flown within the preceding 6 calendar months and 3 of the approaches must be flown without an approach coupler.

Answers

9344 [A]	9342 [A]	9342-1 [A]	9342-2 [C]	9334 [C]

ATM, ATS, RTC

9345. To be eligible for the practical test for the renewal of a Category II authorization, what recent instrument approach experience is required?

A—Within the previous 6 months, six ILS approaches, three of which may be flown to the Category I DH by use of an approach coupler.
B—Within the previous 6 months, six ILS approaches flown by use of an approach coupler to the Category I DH.
C—Within the previous 12 calendar months, three ILS approaches flown by use of an approach coupler to the Category II DH.

To be eligible for Category II authorization, a pilot must have made at least 6 ILS approaches since the beginning of the 6th month before the test. These approaches must be under actual or simulated instrument flight conditions down to the minimum landing altitude for the ILS approach in the type aircraft in which the flight test is to be conducted. However, the approaches need not be conducted down to the decision heights authorized for Category II operations. At least 3 of these approaches must have been conducted manually, without the use of an approach coupler. (PLT442, AA.VI.E.K1) — 14 CFR §61.67

Answer (B) is incorrect because only 3 of the 6 approaches may be flown using an approach coupler. Answer (C) is incorrect because the requirement is for a total of 6 approaches, only 3 of which may be flown by the use of an approach coupler. The approaches are not required to be flown down to Category II DH. Also, they must have been flown within the preceding 6 calendar months.

ATM, ATS, RTC

9346. When may a Category II ILS limitation be removed?

A—When three Cat II ILS approaches have been completed to a 150-foot decision height and landing.
B—When six ILS approaches to Category II minimums and landing have been completed in the past 6 months.
C—120 days after issue or renewal.

Upon original issue, a Category II authorization contains a limitation for Category II operations of 1,600 feet RVR and a 150-foot decision height. This limitation is removed when the holder shows that since the beginning of the 6th preceding month he/she has made 3 Category II ILS approaches to a landing under actual or simulated instrument conditions with a 150-foot decision height. (PLT407, AA.VI.E.K1) — 14 CFR §61.13

ALL

9347. A Category II ILS pilot authorization, when originally issued, is normally limited to

A—Category II operations not less than 1600 RVR and a 150-foot DH.
B—pilots who have completed an FAA-approved Category II training program.
C—Category II operations not less than 1200 RVR and a 100-foot DH.

Upon original issue, a Category II authorization contains a limitation for Category II operations of 1,600 feet RVR and a 150-foot decision height. This limitation is removed when the holder shows that since the beginning of the 6th preceding month he/she has made 3 Category II ILS approaches to a landing under actual or simulated instrument conditions with a 150-foot decision height. (PLT407, AA.VI.E.K1) — 14 CFR §61.13

Answer (B) is incorrect because all pilots must undergo FAA-approved training for a Category II authorization. The initial limitation is to RVR and DH for 6 months. Answer (C) is incorrect because a 1,200 RVR and a 100-foot DH are the Category II minimums after the initial limitation is removed by the pilot completing 3 ILS approaches to a 150-foot DH in the preceding 6 months.

ALL

9348. What is the lowest decision height for which a Category II applicant can be certified during the original issuance of the authorization?

A—100 feet AGL.
B—150 feet AGL.
C—200 feet AGL.

Upon original issue, a Category II authorization contains a limitation for Category II operations of 1,600 feet RVR and a 150-foot decision height. (PLT420, AA.VI.E.K1) — 14 CFR §61.13

Answer (A) is incorrect because a 100-foot DH is allowed only after completion of 3 Category II ILS approaches to a 150-foot DH. Answer (C) is incorrect because 200 feet is the standard Category I ILS DH.

Answers

9345 [A]	9346 [A]	9347 [A]	9348 [B]

ATM, ADX

8215. The training required by flight crewmembers who have not qualified and served in the same capacity on another airplane of the same group (e.g., turbojet powered) is

A—upgrade training.
B—transition training.
C—initial training.

Initial training is the training required for crewmembers and dispatchers who have not qualified and served in the same capacity on another airplane of the same group. (PLT407, AA.I.G.K4) — 14 CFR §121.400

Answer (A) is incorrect because upgrade training is required of a flight engineer or second-in-command when he/she trains for the next higher position in a particular airplane type. Answer (B) is incorrect because transition training is the training required for crewmembers and dispatchers who have qualified and served in the same capacity on another airplane of the same group.

ATM, ADX

8216. A crewmember who has served as second-in-command on a particular type airplane (e.g., B-727-100), may serve as pilot-in-command upon completing which training program?

A—Upgrade training.
B—Recurrent training.
C—Initial training.

Upgrade training is the training required for crewmembers who have qualified and served as second-in-command or flight engineer on a particular airplane type, before they serve as pilot-in-command or second-in-command respectively, on that airplane. (PLT407, AA.I.G.K4) — 14 CFR §121.400

Answer (B) is incorrect because recurrent training is a periodic requirement of crewmembers who are qualified in their positions. Answer (C) is incorrect because initial training is the first training received for crewmembers who have not previously qualified and served in the same airplane group (e.g., turboprop or turbojet).

ATM, ADX

8217. The training required for crewmembers or dispatchers who have been qualified and served in the same capacity on other airplanes of the same group is

A—difference training.
B—transition training.
C—upgrade training.

Transition training is the training required for crewmembers and dispatchers who have qualified and served in the same capacity on another airplane of the same group. (PLT407, AA.I.G.K4) — 14 CFR §121.400

Answer (A) is incorrect because difference training is required of a crewmember who is qualified on a particular type of airplane prior to becoming qualified in a variation of that same type. Answer (C) is incorrect because upgrade training is required of a crewmember who is qualified in a particular type of airplane and then desires to advance to the next higher position in that airplane, e.g., from copilot to pilot.

ATM, ADX

8205. A pilot-in-command must complete a proficiency check or simulator training within the preceding

A—6 calendar months.
B—12 calendar months.
C—24 calendar months.

For a person to serve as pilot-in-command he/she must have completed a proficiency check within the preceding 12 calendar months and, in addition, within the preceding 6 calendar months, either a proficiency check or an approved simulator training course. (PLT407, AA.I.G.K4) — 14 CFR §121.441

Answer (B) is incorrect because a proficiency check is mandatory within the preceding 12 months. Additionally, a proficiency check or simulator training is required within the preceding 6 months. Answer (C) is incorrect because a 24-month time frame applies to pilots other than the pilot-in-command.

ATM

8207. A pilot flight crewmember, other than pilot-in-command, must have received a proficiency check or line-oriented simulator training within the preceding

A—6 calendar months.
B—12 calendar months.
C—24 calendar months.

Pilots other than the pilot-in-command must have completed either a proficiency check or a line-oriented simulator training course within the preceding 24 calendar months. (PLT407, AA.I.G.K4) — 14 CFR §121.441

Answer (A) is incorrect because 6 months is the requirement for pilot-in-command to complete a proficiency check or simulator training. Answer (B) is incorrect because 12 months is the requirement for pilots other than pilot-in-command to receive a proficiency check or "any other kind of simulation training" (not necessarily line-oriented simulator training).

Answers

8215 [C] 8216 [A] 8217 [B] 8205 [A] 8207 [C]

ATM, ADX

8210. What are the line check requirements for the pilot-in-command for a domestic air carrier?

A—The line check is required every 12 calendar months in one of the types of airplanes to be flown.
B—The line check is required only when the pilot is scheduled to fly into special areas and airports.
C—The line check is required every 12 months in each type aircraft in which the pilot may fly.

No certificate holder may use any person nor may any person serve as pilot-in-command of an airplane unless, within the preceding 12 calendar months that person has passed a line check in which he/she satisfactorily performs the duties and responsibilities of a pilot-in-command in one of the types of airplanes to be flown. (PLT442, AA.I.G.K4) — 14 CFR §121.440

ATM, ADX

8214. If a flight crewmember completes a required annual flight check in December 2010 and the required annual recurrent flight check in January 2012, the latter check is considered to have been taken in

A—November 2010.
B—December 2011.
C—January 2011.

Whenever a crewmember or aircraft dispatcher who is required to take recurrent training, a flight check, or a competency check, takes the check or completes the training in the calendar month before or after the month in which that training or check is required, he/she is considered to have taken or completed it in the calendar month in which it was required. (PLT449, AA.I.G.K4) — 14 CFR §121.401

ATM

8208. Which is one of the requirements that must be met by a required pilot flight crewmember in re-establishing recency of experience?

A—At least one landing must be made with a simulated failure of the most critical engine.
B—At least one ILS approach to the lowest ILS minimums authorized for the certificate holder and a landing from that approach.
C—At least three landings must be made to a complete stop.

When a pilot has not made 3 takeoffs and landings within the preceding 90 days, the pilot must make at least 3 takeoffs and landings in the type of airplane in which that person is to serve or in an advanced simulator. These takeoffs and landings must include:

1. *At least 1 takeoff with a simulated failure of the most critical powerplant;*
2. *At least 1 landing from an ILS approach to the lowest ILS minimum authorized for the certificate holder; and*
3. *At least 1 landing to a full stop.*

(PLT442, AA.I.G.K4) — 14 CFR §121.439

Answer (A) is incorrect because at least 1 takeoff is required with a simulated failure of the most critical powerplant. Answer (C) is incorrect because only 1 landing to a complete stop is required.

ATM

8209. What is one of the requirements that must be met by an airline pilot to re-establish recency of experience?

A—At least one landing must be made from a circling approach.
B—At least one full stop landing must be made.
C—At least one precision approach must be made to the lowest minimums authorized for the certificate holder.

When a pilot has not made 3 takeoffs and landings within the preceding 90 days, the pilot must make at least 3 takeoffs and landings in the type of airplane in which that pilot is to serve, or in an advanced simulator. These takeoffs and landings must include:

1. *At least 1 takeoff with a simulated failure of the most critical powerplant;*
2. *At least 1 landing from an ILS approach to the lowest ILS minimum authorized for the certificate holder; and*
3. *At least 1 landing to a full stop.*

(PLT442, AA.I.G.K4) — 14 CFR §121.439

Answers (A) and (C) are incorrect because the only instrument approach required is an ILS approach to the lowest minimums authorized for the certificate holder.

Answers

8210 [A] 8214 [B] 8208 [B] 8209 [B]

ATM, ADX

8289. When a pilot's flight time consists of 80 hours' pilot-in-command in a particular type airplane, how does this affect the minimums for the destination airport?

A—Has no effect on destination but alternate minimums are no less than 300 and 1.
B—Minimums are decreased by 100 feet and 1/2 mile.
C—Minimums are increased by 100 feet and 1/2 mile.

If the pilot-in-command has not served 100 hours as pilot-in-command in operations under Part 121 in the type of airplane he/she is operating, the MDA or DH and visibility landing minimums in the certificate holder's operations specifications for regular, provisional, or refueling airports are increased by 100 feet and 1/2 mile (or the RVR equivalent). (PLT443, AA.I.G.K4) — 14 CFR §121.652

ATM

8285. Category II ILS operations below 1600 RVR and a 150-foot DH may be approved after the pilot-in-command has

A—logged 90 hours' flight time, 10 takeoffs and landings in make and model airplane and three Category II ILS approaches in actual or simulated IFR conditions with 150-foot DH since the beginning of the sixth preceding month, in operations under 14 CFR parts 91 and 121.
B—made at least six Category II approaches in actual IFR conditions with 100-foot DH within the preceding 12 calendar months.
C—logged 100 hours' flight time in make and model airplane under 14 CFR part 121 and three Category II ILS approaches in actual or simulated IFR conditions with 150-foot DH since the beginning of the sixth preceding month.

If the pilot-in-command of an airplane has not served 100 hours as pilot-in-command in operations under 14 CFR Part 121 in the type of airplane he/she is operating, the MDA or DH and visibility landing minimums in the certificate holder's operations specifications for regular, provisional, or refueling airports are increased by 100 feet and 1/2 mile (or the RVR equivalent). In addition, CAT II minimums and the sliding scale do not apply. Upon original issue, a Category II authorization contains a limitation for Category II operations of 1,600 feet RVR and a 150-foot decision height. This limitation is removed when the holder shows that since the beginning of the 6th preceding month he/she has made 3 Category II ILS approaches to a landing under actual or simulated instrument conditions with a 150-foot decision height. (PLT444, AA.VI.E.K1) — 14 CFR §121.652 and §61.13

ADX

8230. To remain current as an aircraft dispatcher, a person must, in addition to other requirements,

A—within the preceding 12 calendar months, spend 2.5 hours observing flight deck operations, plus two additional takeoff and landings, in one of the types of airplanes in each group he/she is to dispatch.
B—within the preceding 12 calendar months, spend at least 5 hours observing flight deck operations in one of the types of airplanes in each group he/she is to dispatch.
C—within the preceding 12 calendar months, spend at least 5 hours observing flight deck operations in each type of airplane, in each group that he/she is to dispatch.

No domestic or flag air carrier may use any person as an aircraft dispatcher unless, within the preceding 12 calendar months, he/she has satisfactorily completed operating familiarization consisting of at least 5 hours observing operations from the flight deck under 14 CFR Part 121 in one of the types of airplanes in each group he/she is to dispatch. (PLT450) — 14 CFR §121.463

Answers

8289 [C]   8285 [C]   8230 [B]

Part 135 Flight Crew Requirements

ATS
8082. What are the minimum certificate and rating requirements for the pilot-in-command of a multiengine airplane being operated by a commuter air carrier?

A—Airline transport pilot; airplane category; multiengine class.
B—Commercial pilot; airplane category; multiengine class; instrument rating; airplane type rating, if required.
C—Airline transport pilot; airplane category; multiengine class; airplane type rating, if required.

No certificate holder may use a person, nor may any person serve, as pilot-in-command in passenger-carrying operations of a turbojet airplane, or an airplane having a passenger seating configuration, excluding any crewmember seat, of 10 seats or more, or a multi-engine airplane being operated by "commuter operations," unless that person holds an Airline Transport Pilot Certificate with appropriate category and class ratings and, if required, an appropriate type rating for that aircraft. (PLT443, AA.I.G.K5) — 14 CFR §135.243

ATS
8083. What are the minimum certificate and rating requirements for the pilot-in-command of a multiengine airplane in commuter air carrier service under IFR?

A—Airline transport pilot of any category; multiengine class rating.
B—Airline transport pilot; airplane category; multiengine class rating; airplane type rating, if required.
C—Commercial pilot; airplane category; multiengine class and instrument rating.

No certificate holder may use a person, nor may any person serve, as pilot-in-command in passenger-carrying operations of a turbojet airplane, or an airplane having a passenger seating configuration, excluding any crewmember seat, of 10 seats or more, or a multi-engine airplane being operated by "commuter operations," unless that person holds an Airline Transport Pilot Certificate with appropriate category and class ratings and, if required, an appropriate type rating for that aircraft. (PLT443, AA.I.G.K5) — 14 CFR §135.243

ATS
8094. Which takeoff computation must not exceed the length of the runway plus the length of the stopway for a turbine-engine-powered small transport category airplane?

A—Takeoff distance.
B—Acceleration-stop distance.
C—Acceleration-climb distance.

The accelerate-stop distance, as defined in 14 CFR §25.109, must not exceed the length of the runway plus the length of any stopway. (PLT456, AA.I.G.K5) — 14 CFR §135.379 and §135.397

ATS
8100. A person is assigned as pilot-in-command to fly both single-engine and multiengine airplanes and has passed the initial instrument proficiency check in a multiengine airplane. Which requirement applies regarding each succeeding instrument check?

A—The instrument check must be taken every 6 calendar months in both a single-engine and a multiengine airplane.
B—The instrument check must be taken alternately in single-engine and multiengine airplanes every 6 calendar months.
C—The instrument check may be taken in either a single-engine or multiengine airplane if taken at intervals of 6 calendar months.

No certificate holder may use a pilot, nor may any person serve as a pilot-in-command of an aircraft under IFR unless, since the beginning of the 6th calendar month before that service, that pilot has passed an instrument proficiency check given by the FAA or authorized check pilot. If the pilot-in-command is assigned to both single-engine aircraft and multi-engine aircraft, that pilot must initially take the instrument proficiency check in a multi-engine aircraft and each succeeding check alternately in single-engine and multi-engine aircraft. (PLT442, AA.I.G.K5) — 14 CFR §135.297

Answers

8082 [C] 8083 [B] 8094 [B] 8100 [B]

ATS

8103. A person is acting as pilot-in-command of a multiengine, turboprop-powered airplane operated in passenger-carrying service by a commuter air carrier. If eight takeoffs and landings are accomplished in that make and basic model, which additional pilot-in-command experience meets the requirement for designation as pilot-in-command?

A—7 hours, and two takeoffs and landing.
B—10 hours, and three takeoffs and landings.
C—10 hours, and two takeoffs and one landings.

No certificate holder may use any person, nor may any person serve, as a pilot-in-command of an aircraft operated by "commuter operations" in passenger-carrying operations, unless that person has completed, on that make and basic model aircraft and in that crewmember position the following operating experience:

1. *Aircraft, single-engine—10 hours;*
2. *Aircraft, multi-engine, reciprocating engine-powered—15 hours;*
3. *Aircraft, multi-engine, turbine engine-powered—20 hours; or*
4. *Airplane, turbojet-powered—25 hours.*

The hours of operating experience may be reduced to not less than 50% of the hours required above by the substitution of one additional takeoff and landing for each hour of flight. (PLT407, AA.I.G.K5) — 14 CFR §135.244

ATS

8107. What are the minimum certificate and rating requirements for the pilot-in-command of a turbojet airplane with two engines being operated by a Commuter Air Carrier?

A—Airline transport pilot; airplane category; multiengine class rating; airplane type rating, if required.
B—Airline transport pilot of any category; multiengine class rating; airplane type rating.
C—Commercial pilot; airplane category; multiengine class rating; instrument rating; airplane type rating.

No certificate holder may use a person, nor may any person serve, as pilot-in-command in passenger-carrying operations of a turbojet airplane, or an airplane having a passenger seating configuration, excluding any crewmember seat, of 10 seats or more, or a multiengine airplane being operated by "commuter operations" unless that person holds an Airline Transport Pilot Certificate with appropriate category and class ratings and, if required, an appropriate type rating for that aircraft. (PLT443, AA.I.G.K5) — 14 CFR §135.243

ATS

8108. A person is acting as pilot-in-command of a multiengine, reciprocating engine powered airplane operated in passenger-carrying service by a commuter air carrier. If five takeoffs and landings have been accomplished in that make and basic model, which additional pilot-in-command experience meets the requirement for designation as the pilot-in-command?

A—Two takeoffs and landings, and 8 hours.
B—Five takeoffs and landings, and 5 hours.
C—Three takeoffs and landings, and 7 hours.

No certificate holder may use any person, nor may any person serve, as a pilot-in-command of an aircraft operated by "commuter operations" in passenger-carrying operations, unless that person has completed, on that make and basic model aircraft and in that crewmember position the following operating experience:

1. *Aircraft, single-engine—10 hours;*
2. *Aircraft, multi-engine, reciprocating engine-powered—15 hours;*
3. *Aircraft, multi-engine, turbine engine-powered—20 hours; or*
4. *Airplane, turbojet-powered — 25 hours.*

The hours of operating experience may be reduced to not less than 50% of the hours required above by the substitution of one additional takeoff and landing for each hour of flight. (PLT407, AA.I.G.K5) — 14 CFR §135.244

ATS

8109. A person is acting as pilot-in-command of a turbojet powered airplane operated in passenger-carrying service by a commuter air carrier. If 10 takeoffs and landings have been accomplished in that make and basic model, which additional pilot-in-command experience meets the requirement for designation as pilot-in-command?

A—10 hours.
B—15 hours.
C—10 hours, and five takeoffs and landings.

No certificate holder may use any person, nor may any person serve, as a pilot-in-command of an aircraft operated by "commuter operations" in passenger-carrying operations, unless that person has completed, on that make and basic model aircraft and in that crewmember position the following operating experience:

1. *Aircraft, single-engine—10 hours;*
2. *Aircraft, multi-engine, reciprocating engine-powered—15 hours;*

Answers

8103 [B] 8107 [A] 8108 [A] 8109 [B]

3. Aircraft, multi-engine, turbine engine-powered—20 hours; or

4. Airplane, turbojet-powered—25 hours.

The hours of operating experience may be reduced to not less than 50% of the hours required above by the substitution of one additional takeoff and landing for each hour of flight. (PLT407, AA.I.G.K5) — 14 CFR §135.244

ATS

8110. A pilot's experience includes 8 hours in a particular make and basic model multiengine, turboprop airplane while acting as pilot-in-command. Which additional pilot-in-command experience meets the requirements for designation as pilot-in-command of that airplane when operated by a commuter air carrier in passenger-carrying service?

A—Twelve takeoffs and landings.
B—Five takeoffs and landings, and 2 hours.
C—Ten takeoffs and landings, and 2 hours.

No certificate holder may use any person, nor may any person serve, as a pilot-in-command of an aircraft operated by "commuter operations" in passenger-carrying operations, unless that person has completed, on that make and basic model aircraft and in that crewmember position the following operating experience:

1. Aircraft, single-engine—10 hours;

2. Aircraft, multi-engine, reciprocating engine-powered—15 hours;

3. Aircraft, multi-engine, turbine engine-powered—20 hours; or

4. Airplane, turbojet-powered—25 hours.

The hours of operating experience may be reduced to not less than 50% of the hours required above by the substitution of one additional takeoff and landing for each hour of flight. (PLT407, AA.I.G.K5) — 14 CFR §135.244

ATS

8111. A person is acting as pilot-in-command of a single-engine airplane operated in passenger-carrying service by a commuter air carrier. If six takeoffs and landings have been accomplished in that make and basic model, which additional pilot-in-command experience meets the requirement for designation as pilot-in-command?

A—4 hours
B—5 hours
C—6 hours

No certificate holder may use any person, nor may any person serve, as a pilot-in-command of an aircraft operated by "commuter operations" in passenger-carrying operations, unless that person has completed, on that make and basic model aircraft and in that crewmember position the following operating experience:

1. Aircraft, single-engine—10 hours;

2. Aircraft, multi-engine, reciprocating engine-powered—15 hours;

3. Aircraft, multi-engine, turbine engine-powered—20 hours; or

4. Airplane, turbojet-powered—25 hours.

The hours of operating experience may be reduced to not less than 50% of the hours required above by the substitution of one additional takeoff and landing for each hour of flight. (PLT407, AA.I.G.K5) — 14 CFR §135.244

ATS

9618. (Refer to Figure 301.) The PIC (single pilot 135 with A/P) of PTZ 70 has less than 100 hours of PIC time in the BE 1900. Due to BUF weather being 100 feet, 1/4 mile in blowing snow, which is below landing minimums, the PIC requested and received clearance to SYR, the filed alternate. Under Part 135, what are the PIC's minimums at SYR for the ILS RWY 10?

A—800/2.
B—719/42.
C—619/50.

The MDA or DA/DH and visibility landing minimums prescribed in 14 CFR Part 97 or in the operator's operations specifications are increased by 100 feet and 1/2 mile respectively, but not to exceed the ceiling and visibility minimums for that airport when used as an alternate airport, for each pilot-in-command of a turbine-powered airplane who has not served at least 100 hours as pilot-in-command in that type of airplane. Since the pilot is operating with an autopilot, as noted in the question with "(single pilot 135 with A/P)," the chart notes indicate that an RVR of 1800 is authorized. Adding a 1/2 mile (or 2400 RVR) to that would make the visibility requirement 4200 RVR. (PLT407, AA.I.G.K5) — 14 CFR §135.225

Answers

8110 [C] 8111 [B] 9618 [B]

ATS, RTC

8018. Which person, other than the second in command, may the pilot-in-command permit to manipulate the flight controls?

A—A member of the National Transportation Safety Board who holds a pilot certificate appropriate for the aircraft.
B—An authorized FAA safety representative who is qualified in the aircraft, and is checking flight operations.
C—A pilot employed by an engineering firm who is authorized by the certificate holder to conduct flight tests.

No pilot-in-command may allow any person to manipulate the controls of an aircraft during flight unless that person is:

1. *A pilot employed by the certificate holder and qualified in the aircraft; or*
2. *An authorized safety representative of the Administrator who has permission of the pilot-in-command, is qualified in the aircraft, and is checking flight operations.*

(PLT444, AA.I.G.K5) — 14 CFR §135.115

ATS, RTC

8026. A flight attendant crewmember is required on aircraft having a passenger seating configuration, excluding any pilot seat, of

A—15 or more.
B—19 or more.
C—20 or more

No certificate holder may operate an aircraft that has a passenger seating configuration, excluding any pilot seat, of more than 19 unless there is a flight attendant crewmember on board the aircraft. (PLT440, AA.I.G.K5) — 14 CFR §135.107

ATS, RTC

8027. Before each takeoff, the pilot-in-command of an aircraft carrying passengers shall ensure that all passengers have been orally briefed on the

A—location of normal and emergency exits, oxygen masks, and life preservers.
B—use of safety belts, location and operation of fire extinguishers, and smoking.
C—use of seatbelts, smoking, and location and use of survival equipment.

Before each takeoff the pilot-in-command shall ensure that all passengers have been orally briefed on:

1. *Smoking;*
2. *Use of seatbelts;*
3. *The placement of seat backs in an upright position before takeoff and landing;*
4. *Location and means of opening the passenger entry door and emergency exits;*
5. *Location of survival equipment;*
6. *If the flight involves extended overwater operation, ditching procedures and the use of required flotation equipment;*
7. *If the flight involves operations above 12,000 feet MSL, the normal and emergency use of oxygen; and*
8. *Location and operation of fire extinguishers.*

(PLT384, AA.I.G.K5) — 14 CFR §135.117

ATS, RTC

8028. Before takeoff, the pilot-in-command of an aircraft carrying passengers shall ensure that all passengers have been orally briefed on the normal and emergency use of oxygen

A—if the flight involves operations above 12,000 feet MSL.
B—regardless of the altitude at which the flight will operate.
C—if the flight involves operations at or above 12,000 feet MSL for more than 30 minutes.

Before each takeoff the pilot-in-command shall ensure that all passengers have been orally briefed on the normal and emergency use of oxygen if the flight involves operations above 12,000 feet MSL. (PLT438, AA.I.G.K5) — 14 CFR §135.117

Answers

8018 [B]	8026 [C]	8027 [B]	8028 [A]

ATS, RTC

8029. The oral before flight briefing required on passenger-carrying aircraft shall be

A—supplemented by an actual demonstration of emergency exit door operation by a crewmember.
B—presented by the pilot-in-command or another flight crewmember, as a crewmember demonstrates the operation of the emergency equipment.
C—conducted by a crewmember or the pilot-in-command and supplemented by printed cards for the use of each passenger.

The required oral briefing must be given by the pilot-in-command or other crewmember. It must be supplemented by printed cards which must be carried in the aircraft in locations convenient for the use of each passenger. (PLT384, AA.I.G.K5) — 14 CFR §135.117

ATS, RTC

8034. A commuter air carrier certificate holder plans to assign a pilot as pilot-in-command of an aircraft having eight passenger seats to be used in passenger-carrying operations. Which experience requirement must that pilot meet if the aircraft is to be flown with an operative approved autopilot and no second in command?

A—100 hours as pilot-in-command in the category, class, and type.
B—50 hours and 10 landings as pilot-in-command in the make and model.
C—100 hours as pilot-in-command in the make and model.

When using an autopilot in lieu of a second-in-command in commuter airline passenger-carrying operations, the pilot-in-command must have at least 100 hours of PIC time in the make and model of aircraft to be flown. (PLT407, AA.I.G.K5) — 14 CFR §135.105

ATS, RTC

8035. Which is a condition that must be met by a commuter air carrier certificate holder to have an aircraft approved for operation with an autopilot system and no second in command?

A—The passenger seating configuration is 10 or more, including any pilot seat.
B—The autopilot system is capable of operating the controls to maintain flight and to maneuver the aircraft about the three axes.
C—The operation is restricted to VFR or VFR over-the-top.

The autopilot used in lieu of a second-in-command must be capable of operating the aircraft controls to maintain flight and maneuver it about the three axes. (PLT443, AA.I.G.K5) — 14 CFR §135.105

ATS, RTC

8036. An autopilot may not be used in place of a second in command in any aircraft

A—being operated in commuter air carrier service.
B—having a passenger seating configuration, excluding any pilot's seat, of 10 seats or more.
C—having a total seating capacity of 10 or more seats and being operated in commuter air service.

Unless two pilots are required by 14 CFR for operations under VFR, a person may operate an aircraft without a second-in-command, if it is equipped with an operative approved autopilot system and the use of that system is authorized by appropriate operations specifications. No certificate holder may operate an aircraft without a second-in-command if that aircraft has a passenger seating configuration, excluding any pilot seat, of 10 seats or more. (PLT443, AA.I.G.K5) — 14 CFR §135.99 and §135.105

ATS, RTC

8044. What is the minimum passenger seating configuration that requires a second in command?

A—15 seats.
B—12 seats.
C—10 seats.

No certificate holder may operate an aircraft without a second-in-command if that aircraft has a passenger seating configuration, excluding any pilot seat, of 10 seats or more. (PLT443, AA.I.G.K5) — 14 CFR §135.99

Answers

8029 [C] 8034 [C] 8035 [B] 8036 [B] 8044 [C]

ATS, RTC

8076. When is a pilot not required to keep the shoulder harness fastened during takeoff and landing while at a pilot station?

A—When operating an aircraft having a passenger seating configuration, excluding any pilot seat, of 10 seats or less.
B—When the pilot cannot perform the required duties with the shoulder harness fastened.
C—When serving as pilot-in-command or second in command of an aircraft having a total seating capacity of eight seats or less.

Each flight crewmember occupying a station equipped with a shoulder harness must fasten the shoulder harness during takeoff and landing, except that the shoulder harness may be unfastened if the crewmember is unable to perform required duties with the shoulder harness fastened. (PLT464, AA.I.G.K5) — 14 CFR §135.171

ATS, RTC

8095. To serve as pilot-in-command in an IFR operation, a person must have passed a line check

A—consisting of a flight over the route to be flown, with at least three instrument approaches at representative airports, within the past 12 calendar months, in one type of aircraft which that pilot is to fly.
B—within the past 12 months, which include a portion of a civil airway and one instrument approach at one representative airport, in one of the types of aircraft which that pilot is to fly.
C—since the beginning of the 12th month before that service, which included at least one flight over a civil airway, or approved off-airway route, or any portion of either, in one type of aircraft which that pilot is to fly.

No certificate holder may use a pilot, nor may any person serve, as a pilot-in-command of a flight unless, since the beginning of the 12th calendar month before that service, that pilot has passed a flight check (line check) in one of the types of aircraft that pilot is to fly. The flight check shall:

1. *Be given by an approved check pilot or by the FAA;*
2. *Consist of at least one flight over one route segment; and*
3. *Include takeoffs and landings at one or more representative airports;*
4. *For a pilot authorized for IFR operations, at least one flight shall be flown over a civil airway, an approved off-airway route, or a portion of either of them.*

(PLT442, AA.I.G.K5) — 14 CFR §135.299

ATS, RTC

8096. What are the minimum requirements for the line check required of each pilot-in-command authorized for IFR air taxi operations? The line check shall be given over

A—one route segment in each type of airplane the pilot is to fly and includes takeoffs and landings at one or more representative airports.
B—a civil airway or an approved off-airway route, or a portion of either of them, in one type of airplane the pilot is to fly and includes takeoffs and landings at one or more representative airports.
C—a civil airway or an approved off-airway route in each make and model airplane the pilot is to fly and includes takeoffs and landings at one or more representative airports.

No certificate holder may use a pilot, nor may any person serve, as a pilot-in-command of a flight unless, since the beginning of the 12th calendar month before that service, that pilot has passed a flight check (line check) in one of the types of aircraft that pilot is to fly. The flight check shall:

1. *Be given by an approved check pilot or by the FAA;*
2. *Consist of at least one flight over one route segment; and*
3. *Include takeoffs and landings at one or more representative airports;*
4. *For a pilot authorized for IFR operations, at least one flight shall be flown over a civil airway, an approved off-airway route, or a portion of either of them.*

(PLT442, AA.I.G.K5) — 14 CFR §135.299

ATS, RTC

8097. No certificate holder may use a person as pilot-in-command unless that person has passed a line check

A—since the beginning of the 12th month before serving as pilot-in-command.
B—since the beginning of the 6th month before serving as pilot-in-command.
C—within the past 6 months.

No certificate holder may use a pilot, nor may any person serve, as a pilot-in-command of a flight unless, since the beginning of the 12th calendar month before that service, that pilot has passed a flight check (line check) in one of the types of aircraft that pilot is to fly. (PLT442, AA.I.G.K5) — 14 CFR §135.299

Answers

8076 [B] 8095 [C] 8096 [B] 8097 [A]

ATS, RTC

8098. A person may act as pilot-in-command of both type A and type B aircraft under IFR, if an instrument proficiency check has been passed in

A—either type A or B since the beginning of the 12th month before time to serve.
B—type A since the beginning of the 12th month, and in type B since the beginning of the 6th month before time to serve.
C—type A since the beginning of the 12th month, and in type B since the beginning of the 24th month before time to serve.

No certificate holder may use a pilot, nor may any person serve, as a pilot-in-command of an aircraft under IFR unless, since the beginning of the 6th calendar month before that service, that pilot has passed an instrument proficiency check given by the FAA or authorized check pilot. If the pilot-in-command is assigned to pilot more than one type of aircraft, that pilot must take the instrument proficiency check for each type of aircraft to which that pilot is assigned in rotation, but not more than one flight check in each period. (PLT442, AA.I.G.K5) — 14 CFR §135.297

ATS, RTC

8099. A pilot-in-command is authorized to use an autopilot system in place of a second in command. During the instrument proficiency check, that person is required to demonstrate (without a second in command) the ability to

A—comply with complex ATC instructions with, but not without, the autopilot.
B—properly conduct air-ground communications with, but not without, the autopilot.
C—properly conduct instrument operations competently both with, and without, the autopilot.

If the pilot-in-command is authorized to use an autopilot system in place of a second-in-command, that pilot must show during the required instrument proficiency check, that the pilot is able both with and without using the autopilot to:

1. *Conduct instrument operations competently; and*
2. *Properly conduct air-ground communications and comply with complex air traffic control instructions.*

(PLT442, AA.I.G.K5) — 14 CFR §135.297

ATS, RTC

8101. A person may not serve as pilot-in-command in an IFR operation unless that person has passed an

A—aircraft competency, an instrument proficiency, and autopilot check within the previous 6 calendar months prior to the date to serve.
B—instrument proficiency check in the airplane in which to serve, or in an approved aircraft simulator, within the previous 12 calendar months.
C—instrument proficiency check under actual or simulated IFR conditions, since the beginning of the 6th calendar month prior to the date to serve.

No certificate holder may use a pilot, nor may any person serve as a pilot-in-command of an aircraft under IFR unless, since the beginning of the 6th calendar month before that service, that pilot has passed an instrument proficiency check given by the FAA or authorized check pilot. If the pilot-in-command is assigned to both single-engine aircraft and multi-engine aircraft, that pilot must initially take the instrument proficiency check in a multi-engine aircraft and each succeeding check alternately in single-engine and multi-engine aircraft. (PLT442, AA.I.G.K5) — 14 CFR §135.297

ATS, RTC

8102. A pilot-in-command who is authorized to use an autopilot system, in place of a second in command, may take the autopilot check

A—concurrently with the instrument proficiency check, but at 12 month intervals.
B—in any aircraft appropriately equipped, providing the check is taken at 6 month intervals.
C—concurrently with the competency check, providing the check is taken at 12 month intervals.

If the pilot-in-command is authorized to use an autopilot system in place of a second-in-command, that pilot must show during the required instrument proficiency check, that the pilot is able both with and without using the autopilot to:

1. *Conduct instrument operations competently; and*
2. *Properly conduct air-ground communications and comply with complex air traffic control instructions.*

(PLT424, AA.I.G.K5) — 14 CFR §135.297

Answers

8098 [B] 8099 [C] 8101 [C] 8102 [A]

ATS, RTC

8104. Pilot flight time limitations under 14 CFR Part 135 are based

A—on the flight time accumulated in any commercial flying.
B—solely on flight time accumulated in air taxi operations.
C—solely on flight time accumulated during commercial flying, in the last 30 day and/or 12 month period.

Pilot flight time limitations are based on the flight time accumulated under 14 CFR Part 135 and any other commercial flying time. (PLT409, AA.I.G.K5) — 14 CFR §135.265

ATS, RTC

8105. No person may serve, as second in command of an aircraft (under part 135), unless they hold a commercial pilot certificate with the appropriate category, class rating and an instrument rating. For flight under IFR, that person must have accomplished within the last 6 months, the recent instrument requirements of

A—using the navigation systems for interception and tracking of courses, 6 instrument low approaches and holding.
B—using the navigation systems to intercept and track 3 inbound/3 outbound courses, 6 holding patterns and 6 instrument approaches.
C—holding procedures, using the navigation systems for intercepting and tracking courses, and 6 instrument approaches.

To act as second-in-command under IFR, a person must meet the recent instrument experience requirements of 14 CFR Part 61. These requirements are: in the last 6 months, the pilot must have logged 6 instrument approaches, performed holding procedures, and intercepted and tracked courses through the use of navigation systems. (PLT442, AA.I.G.K5) — 14 CFR §135.245

ATS, RTC

8106. With regard to flight crewmember duties, which operations are considered to be in the "critical phase of flight"?

A—All ground operations involving taxi, takeoff, landing, and all other operations conducted below 10,000 feet MSL, including cruise flight.
B—Descent, approach, landing, and taxi operations, irrespective of altitudes MSL.
C—All ground operations involving taxi, takeoff, landing, and all other operations conducted below 10,000 feet, excluding cruise flight.

For the purpose of this section, critical phases of flight include all ground operations involving taxi, takeoff and landing, and all other flight operations conducted below 10,000 feet, except cruise flight. (PLT029, AA.I.G.K5) — 14 CFR §135.100

ATS, RTC

8113. Other than in cruise flight, below what altitude are non-safety related cockpit activities by flight crewmembers prohibited?

A—12,000 feet.
B—10,000 feet.
C—8,000 feet.

No certificate holder shall require, nor may any flight crewmember perform, any duties during a critical phase of flight except those duties required for the safe operation of the aircraft. For purposes of this section, critical phases of flight include all ground operations involving taxi, takeoff and landing, and all other flight operations conducted below 10,000 feet, except cruise flight. (PLT440, AA.I.G.K5) — 14 CFR §135.100

Answers

8104 [A] 8105 [C] 8106 [C] 8113 [B]

Flight Crew Duty Time Limits

Familiarize yourself with 14 CFR Part 117 to understand flight crew duty time limits. The limitations of Part 117 apply to all flying by flightcrew members on behalf of any certificate holder or 91K program manager during the applicable periods. Each flightcrew member must report for any flight duty period rested and prepared to perform his or her assigned duties. Each certificate holder must develop and implement an education and awareness training program that is approved by the Administrator. This program must provide the training to all employees of the certificate holder who are responsible for administering the provisions of Part 117, including flightcrew members, dispatchers, individuals directly involved in the scheduling of flightcrew members or in operational control, and any employee providing direct management oversight of these areas.

A person cannot be assigned to any ground or flight duties during required rest periods. The term "**deadhead**" is used to describe the transportation of crewmembers by the air carrier to or from their flight assignments when that transportation is not local in character. Time spent in deadhead air transportation cannot be considered as part of a required rest period.

Other new terms and definitions associated with Part 117 to be aware of are as follows:

Airport/standby reserve means a defined duty period during which a flightcrew member is required by a certificate holder to be at an airport for a possible assignment. For airport/standby reserve, all time spent in a reserve status is part of the flightcrew member's flight duty period.

Augmented, or unaugmented operations. An unaugmented flight contains the minimum number of flightcrew members necessary to safely pilot an aircraft. An augmented flight contains additional flightcrew members and at least one onboard rest facility, which allows flightcrew members to work in shifts and sleep during the flight.

Calendar day means a 24-hour period from 0000 through 2359 using Coordinated Universal Time or local time.

Fatigue means a physiological state of reduced mental or physical performance capability resulting from lack of sleep or increased physical activity, which can reduce a flightcrew member's alertness and ability to safely operate an aircraft or perform safety-related duties.

Physiological night's rest means 10 hours of rest that encompasses the hours of 0100 and 0700 at the flightcrew member's home base, unless the individual has acclimated to a different theater. If the flightcrew member has acclimated to a different theater, the rest must encompass the hours of 0100 and 0700 at the acclimated location.

Rest period means a continuous period determined prospectively during which the flightcrew member is free from all restraint by the certificate holder, including freedom from present responsibility for work should the occasion arise.

Short-call reserve means a period of time in which a flightcrew member is assigned to a reserve availability period. For short-call reserve, the reserve availability period may not exceed 14 hours.

Theater means a geographical area in which the distance between the flightcrew member's flight duty period departure point and arrival point differs by no more than 60 degrees longitude. The applicable flight duty period is based on the local time at the theater in which the flightcrew member was last acclimated.

Unforeseen operational circumstance means an unplanned event of insufficient duration to allow for adjustments to schedules, including unforecast weather, equipment malfunction, or air traffic delay that is not reasonably expected. For augmented and unaugmented operations, if unforeseen operational circumstances arise **prior** to takeoff, the pilot-in-command and the certificate holder may extend the maximum flight duty period permitted up to 2 hours. For augmented and unaugmented operations, if unforeseen operational circumstances arise **after** takeoff, the pilot-in-command and the certificate holder may extend maximum flight duty periods to the extent necessary to safely land the aircraft at the next destination airport or alternate airport, as appropriate.

Window of circadian low means a period of maximum sleepiness that occurs between 0200 and 0559 during a physiological night's rest. No certificate holder may schedule and no flightcrew member may accept more than three consecutive flight duty periods that infringe upon the window of circadian low.

Flight Duty Periods

No certificate holder may schedule, and no flightcrew member may accept an assignment if the flightcrew member's total flight duty period (FDP) will exceed 60 flight duty hours in any 168 consecutive hours. Before beginning any reserve or flight duty period, a flightcrew member must be given at least 30 consecutive hours free from all duty within the past 168 consecutive-hour period.

No certificate holder may schedule, and no flightcrew member may accept an assignment if the flightcrew member's total flight duty period will exceed 190 FDP hours in any 672 consecutive hours.

No certificate holder may schedule, and no flightcrew member may accept an assignment for any reserve or flight duty period unless the flightcrew member is given a rest period of at least 10 consecutive hours immediately before beginning the reserve or flight duty period measured from the time the flightcrew member is released from duty. The 10-hour rest period must provide the flightcrew member with a minimum of 8 uninterrupted hours of sleep opportunity. If a flightcrew member determines that this rest period will not provide eight uninterrupted hours of sleep opportunity, he or she must notify the certificate holder. The flightcrew member cannot report for the assigned flight duty period until he or she receives this specified rest period.

For an unaugmented operation only, if a flightcrew member is provided with a rest opportunity (an opportunity to sleep) in a suitable accommodation during his or her flight duty period, the time that the flightcrew member spends there is not part of his/her flight duty period if the time spent in that accommodation is at least 3 hours, measured from the time that the flightcrew member arrives there.

A Part 117 excerpt will be available for your reference during the FAA test. You will not be required to memorize the tables; however, you will need to know which table to use—that is, which one is applicable to the question being asked.

The maximum flight time for unaugmented operations is as follows (14 CFR §117.11 Table A):

Time of report (acclimated)	Maximum flight time (hours)
0000-0459	8
0500-1959	9
2000-2359	8

The maximum flight duty period (hours) for lineholders is based on the number of flight segments and the scheduled time of start (14 CFR §117.13 Table B):

Scheduled time of start (acclimated time)	Maximum flight duty period (hours) for lineholders based on number of flight segments						
	1	2	3	4	5	6	7+
0000-0359	9	9	9	9	9	9	9
0400-0459	10	10	10	10	9	9	9
0500-0559	12	12	12	12	11.5	11	10.5
0600-0659	13	13	12	12	11.5	11	10.5
0700-1159	14	14	13	13	12.5	12	11.5
1200-1259	13	13	13	13	12.5	12	11.5
1300-1659	12	12	12	12	11.5	11	10.5
1700-2159	12	12	11	11	10	9	9
2200-2259	11	11	10	10	9	9	9
2300-2359	10	10	10	9	9	9	9

If the flightcrew member is not acclimated, the maximum flight duty period in Table C of Part 117 is reduced by 30 minutes (14 CFR Part 117 Table C):

Scheduled time of start (acclimated time)	Maximum flight duty period (hours) based on rest facility and number of pilots					
	Class 1 rest facility		Class 2 rest facility		Class 3 rest facility	
	3 pilots	4 pilots	3 pilots	4 pilots	3 pilots	4 pilots
0000-0559	15	17	14	15.5	13	13.5
0600-0659	16	18.5	15	16.5	14	14.5
0700-1259	17	19	16.5	18	15	15.5
1300-1659	16	18.5	15	16.5	14	14.5
1700-2359	15	17	14	15.5	13	13.5

ALL

8706. Fatigue can be evident in others if they

A—talk more than usual.
B—yawn excessively.
C—are overly helpful.

Physical signs of fatigue include yawning repeatedly, heavy eyelids or microsleeps, eye-rubbing, nodding off or head dropping, headaches, nausea, upset stomach, slowed reaction time, lack of energy, weakness, and light headedness. (PLT409, AA.I.F.K1h) — FAA-H-8083-2

ALL

8706-1. Which of the following is an effect of acute fatigue on performance?

A—Loss of accuracy and smoothness in control movements.
B—Heightened acuity in peripheral vision.
C—Mild euphoria, impaired judgment, and increased reaction time.

Acute fatigue is characterized by inattention, distractibility, errors in timing, neglect of secondary tasks, loss of accuracy and control, lack of awareness of error accumulation, and irritability. (PLT409, AA.I.F.K1h) — AIM ¶8-1-1

Answers

8706 [B] 8706-1 [A]

ALL
8707. You did not get a good night's rest and have been on duty for several hours. A sign you may be fatigued is

A—improved dexterity.
B—decreased short term memory.
C—mental acuteness.

Short term memory loss is a sign of mental fatigue. Additional signs of mental fatigue include: difficulty concentrating on tasks, lapse in attention, failure to communicate important information, failure to anticipate events or actions, making mistakes even on well-practiced tasks, forgetfulness, difficulty thinking clearly, and poor decision making. (PLT409, AA.I.F.K1h) — FAA-H-8083-2

ATM, ADX
8708. Under 14 CFR 121, a required flightcrew member of an unaugmented two-pilot flag operation may not exceed how many hours duty in a seven consecutive day period?

A—48.
B—52.
C—32.

No pilot may fly more than 32 hours during any seven consecutive days, and each pilot must be relieved from all duty for at least 24 consecutive hours at least once during any seven consecutive days. (PLT409, AA.I.G.K3) — 14 CFR §121.481

ATM, ADX
8709. Under 14 CFR 121, a required flightcrew member of an unaugmented two-pilot flag operation may not exceed how many hours duty in a one calendar month period?

A—120.
B—100.
C—80.

No pilot may fly as a member of a crew more than 100 hours during any one calendar month. (PLT409, AA.I.G.K3) — 14 CFR §121.481

ATM, ADX
8227. How does deadhead transportation, going to or from a duty assignment, affect the computation of flight time limits for air carrier flight crewmembers? It is

A—considered part of the rest period if the flightcrew includes more than two pilots.
B—considered part of the rest period for flight engineers and navigators.
C—not considered to be part of a rest period.

Time spent in deadhead transportation to or from duty assignment is not considered part of a rest period. (PLT409, AA.I.G.K3) — 14 CFR §§121.471, 121.491, and 121.519

Answer (A) is incorrect because deadhead transportation does not count for part of the required rest period. Answer (B) is incorrect because flight engineers and navigators are defined as flight crewmembers. The same rest period requirements apply to them as to pilot and copilot.

ATM, ADX
8228. Flight duty period hours for flightcrew members are limited to

A—190 hours in any 672 consecutive hours.
B—180 hours in any 672 consecutive hours.
C—170 hours in any 672 consecutive hours.

No certificate holder may schedule and no flightcrew member may accept an assignment if the flightcrew member's total Flight Duty Period will exceed 190 flight duty period hours in any 672 consecutive hours. (PLT409, AA.I.G.K3) — 14 CFR §117.23

ATM, ADX
8220. Flight duty period hours for flightcrew members are limited to

A—180 hours in any 28 consecutive days.
B—190 hours in any 672 consecutive hours.
C—170 hours in any 672 consecutive hours.

No certificate holder may schedule and no flightcrew member may accept an assignment if the flightcrew member's total Flight Duty Period will exceed 190 flight duty period hours in any 672 consecutive hours. (PLT409, AA.I.G.K3) — 14 CFR §117.23

Answers

8707 [B] 8708 [C] 8709 [B] 8227 [C] 8228 [A] 8220 [B]

ATM, ADX
8221. "Window of circadian low" means a period of maximum sleepiness that occurs between

A—0100 – 0500.
B—1200 – 0459.
C—0200 – 0559.

Window of circadian low means a period of maximum sleepiness that occurs between 0200 and 0559 during a physiological night's rest. (PLT409, AA.I.G.K3) — 14 CFR §117.3

ATM, ADX
8219. For a short-call reserve, the reserve availability period may not exceed

A—12 hours.
B—14 hours.
C—16 hours.

Short-call reserve means a period of time in which a flightcrew member is assigned to a reserve availability period. For short-call reserve, the reserve availability period may not exceed 14 hours. (PLT409, AA.I.G.K3) — 14 CFR §117.21

ATM, ADX
8222. If the crew van breaks down en route to the rest facility and delays arrival for nearly 2 hours, does the flightcrew member need to notify the certificate holder?

A—No, as long as the crew member has the opportunity for 9 hours of uninterrupted rest.
B—No, as long as the crew member has the opportunity for 8 hours rest.
C—Yes, if the flightcrew member does not have the opportunity for 10 hours of uninterrupted hours free from duty.

No certificate holder may schedule and no flightcrew member may accept an assignment for any reserve or flight duty period unless the flightcrew member is given a rest period of at least 10 consecutive hours immediately before beginning the reserve or flight duty period measured from the time the flightcrew member is released from duty. The 10 hour rest period must provide the flightcrew member with a minimum of 8 uninterrupted hours of sleep opportunity. If a flightcrew member determines that this rest period will not provide eight uninterrupted hours of sleep opportunity, the flightcrew member must notify the certificate holder. The flightcrew member cannot report for the assigned flight duty period until he or she receives this specified rest period. (PLT409, AA.I.G.K3) — 14 CFR §117.25

ATM, ADX
8223. "Airport standby reserve" means

A—a specified 15-hour period of reserve in close proximity of assignment being available for flight duty assignments in less than 2 hours.
B—being within 90 minutes of the airport and available for immediate flight duty assignments of 8 hours duration.
C—a defined duty period during which a flight crewmember is required by the certificate holder to be available for possible assignment.

Airport/standby reserve means a defined duty period during which a flightcrew member is required by a certificate holder to be at an airport for a possible assignment. (PLT409, AA.I.G.K3) — 14 CFR §117.3

ATM, ADX
9714. Each flightcrew member must report

A—in uniform and properly prepared to accomplish all assignments.
B—to the airport on time and fully prepared to accomplish assigned duty.
C—for any flight duty period rested and prepared to perform his duty.

Each flightcrew member must report for any flight duty period rested and prepared to perform his or her assigned duties. (PLT409, AA.I.G.K3) — 14 CFR §117.5

ATM, ADX
8211. You are on the last day of a four day trip and haven't slept well. What is a warning sign that you are fatigued?

A—Improved dexterity.
B—Head bobbing.
C—Mental acuteness.

Common physical signs of fatigue include yawning repeatedly, heavy eyelids, microsleeps, eye rubbing, nodding off or head dropping, headaches, nausea, or upset stomach, slowed reaction time, lack of energy, weakness, or light headedness. (PLT409, AA.I.G.K3) — FAA-H-8083-2, 14 CFR §117.3

Answers

8221 [C]	8219 [B]	8222 [B]	8223 [C]	9714 [C]	8211 [B]

ATM, ADX

8224. No flightcrew member may accept an assignment for any reserve or flight duty period unless the flight crew member is given

A—10 consecutive hours of rest immediately before beginning a flight duty period or a reserve period.
B—12 consecutive hours of rest immediately before beginning a flight duty period or a reserve period.
C—8 consecutive hours of rest immediately before beginning a flight duty period or a reserve period.

No certificate holder may schedule and no flightcrew member may accept an assignment for any reserve or flight duty period unless the flightcrew member is given a rest period of at least 10 consecutive hours immediately before beginning the reserve or flight duty period measured from the time the flightcrew member is released from duty. The 10-hour rest period must provide the flightcrew member with a minimum of 8 uninterrupted hours of sleep opportunity. (PLT409, AA.I.G.K3) — 14 CFR §117. 25

ATM, ADX

8229. You are a pilot operating under 14 CFR Part 121 and are in a required rest period. When can you be contacted about your next day duty assignment?

A—At any time during your required rest period.
B—At the end of your required rest period.
C—No earlier than 1 hour before the end of your required rest period.

No certificate holder may assign and no flightcrew member may accept assignment to any reserve or duty with the certificate holder during any required rest period. (PLT409, AA.I.G.K3) — 14 CFR §117.25

ATM, ADX

8231. "Rest period" means

A—an 8-hour continuous period determined prospectively during which the flightcrew member is free from all restraint by the certificate holder.
B—a continuous period determined prospectively during which the flightcrew member is free from all restraint by the certificate holder.
C—a 12-hour continuous period determined prospectively during which the flightcrew member is free from all restraint by the certificate holder.

Rest period means a continuous period determined prospectively during which the flightcrew member is free from all restraint by the certificate holder, including freedom from present responsibility for work should the occasion arise. (PLT409, AA.I.G.K3) — 14 CFR §117.3

ATM, ADX

8231-1. For passenger-carrying operations under 14 CFR Part 121, which situation would be considered part of the required rest period?

A—Deadheading to home base after the last scheduled flight.
B—Electing to fly as a passenger from home base after the flight duty period ends.
C—Training conducted in a flight simulator.

Duty means any task that a flight crewmember performs as required by the certificate holder, including but not limited to flight duty period, flight duty, pre- and post-flight duties, administrative work, training, deadhead transportation, aircraft positioning on the ground, aircraft loading, and aircraft servicing. Rest period means a continuous period determined prospectively during which the flightcrew member is free from all restraint by the certificate holder, including freedom from present responsibility for work should the occasion arise. (PLT409, AA.I.G.K3) — 14 CFR §117.3

Answer (A) is incorrect because deadhead transportation is considered duty time and does not count for part of the required rest period. Answer (C) is incorrect because no training counts for part of the required rest period.

ATM, ADX

8238. "Theater" means

A—a geographical area in which the distance between the flightcrew member flight duty period departure point and arrival point differs by no more than 90 degrees longitude.
B—a geographical area in which the distance between the flightcrew member flight duty period departure point and arrival point differs by no more than 75 degrees longitude.
C—a geographical area in which the distance between the flightcrew member flight duty period departure point and arrival point differs by no more than 60 degrees longitude.

Answers

8224 [A] 8229 [B] 8231 [B] 8231-1 [B] 8238 [C]

Theater means a geographical area in which the distance between the flightcrew member's flight duty period departure point and arrival point differs by no more than 60 degrees longitude. The applicable flight duty period is based on the local time at the theater in which the flightcrew member was last acclimated. (PLT409, AA.I.G.K3) — 14 CFR §117.3 and §117.13

ATM, ADX
9837. "Physiological night's rest" means

A—9 hours of rest that encompasses the hours of 0100 and 0700 at the crewmember's home base.
B—10 hours of rest that encompasses the hours of 0100 and 0700 at the crewmember's home base.
C—12 hours of rest that encompasses any continuous 8 hour period for uninterrupted or disturbed rest.

Physiological night's rest means 10 hours of rest that encompasses the hours of 0100 and 0700 at the flightcrew member's home base, unless the individual has acclimated to a different theater. If the flightcrew member has acclimated to a different theater, the rest must encompass the hours of 0100 and 0700 at the acclimated location. (PLT395), AA.I.G.K3 — 14 CFR §117.3

ATM, ADX
9838. In order to be assigned for duty, each flightcrew member must report

A—on time, in uniform, and properly prepared to accomplish all assigned duties.
B—to the airport on time, after the designated rest period and fully prepared to accomplish assigned duties.
C—for any flight duty period rested and prepared to perform his/her assigned duties.

Each flightcrew member must report for any flight duty period rested and prepared to perform his or her assigned duties. (PLT409, AA.I.G.K3) — 14 CFR §117.5

ATM, ADX
9839. Flightcrew members must receive fatigue education and awareness training

A—with all required air carrier dispatcher and every flightcrew member training activity.
B—annually for flightcrew members and every 24 months for dispatchers, flightcrew member schedulers, and operational control individuals.
C—annually for flightcrew member schedulers, operational control individuals and flightcrew members and dispatchers.

Each certificate holder must develop and implement an education and awareness training program that is approved by the Administrator. This program must provide the training to all employees of the certificate holder responsible for administering the provisions of Part 117, including flightcrew members, dispatchers, individuals directly involved in the scheduling of flightcrew members or in operational control, and any employee providing direct management oversight of these areas. (PLT409, AA.I.G.K3) — 14 CFR §117.9

ATM, ADX
9840. In an airplane assigned with a minimum flight crew of two, your flight time may not exceed

A—9 hours if assigned to report at 0330.
B—9 hours if assigned to report at 0500.
C—9 hours if assigned to report at 2030.

The maximum flight time for unaugmented operations is as follows:

Time of report (acclimated)	***Maximum flight time (hours)***
0000-0459	*8*
0500-1959	*9*
2000-2359	*8*

A Part 117 excerpt will be available for your reference during the FAA test. You will not be required to memorize the tables; however, you will need to know which table to use as applicable to the question being asked. (PLT409, AA.I.G.K3) — 14 CFR §117.11 and Table A

Answers

9837 [B] 9838 [C] 9839 [C] 9840 [B]

ATM, ADX
9841. For unaugmented flightcrew operations, your maximum flight duty period limit is

A—13 hours if assigned to report at 0700 for 4 flight segments.
B—13 hours if assigned to report at 2030 for 3 flight segments.
C—10.5 hours if assigned to report at 1730 for 6 flight segments.

The maximum flight duty period (hours) for lineholders is based on the number of flight segments and the scheduled time of start.

Scheduled time of start (acclimated time)	Maximum flight duty period (hours) for lineholders base on number of flight segments						
	1	2	3	4	5	6	7+
0000-0359	9	9	9	9	9	9	9
0400-0459	10	10	10	10	9	9	9
0500-0559	12	12	12	12	11.5	11	10.5
0600-0659	13	13	12	12	11.5	11	10.5
0700-1159	14	14	13	13	12.5	12	11.5
1200-1259	13	13	13	13	12.5	12	11.5
1300-1659	12	12	12	12	11.5	11	10.5
1700-2159	12	12	11	11	10	9	9
2200-2259	11	11	10	10	9	9	9
2300-2359	10	10	10	9	9	9	9

A Part 117 excerpt will be available for your reference during the FAA test. You will not be required to memorize the tables; however, you will need to know which table to use as applicable to the question being asked. (PLT409, AA.I.G.K3) — 14 CFR §117.13 and Table B

ATM, ADX
9842. In an airplane with an augmented crew of three flightcrew members assigned, the maximum flight duty period is

A—17 hours if assigned to report at 1200 with a Class 3 rest facility available.
B—16 hours if assigned to report at 0630 with a Class 1 rest facility available
C—15 hours if assigned to report at 1730 with a Class 2 rest facility available.

Scheduled time of start (acclimated time)	Maximum flight duty period (hours) for lineholders base on number of flight segments					
	Class 1 rest facility		Class 2 rest facility		Class 3 rest facility	
	3 pilots	4 pilots	3 pilots	4 pilots	3 pilots	4 pilots
0000-0559	15	17	14	15.5	13	13.5
0600-0659	16	18.5	15	16.5	14	14.5
0700-1259	17	19	16.5	18	15	15.5
1300-1659	16	18.5	15	16.5	14	14.5
1700-2359	15	17	14	15.5	13	13.5

A Part 117 excerpt will be available for your reference during the FAA test. You will not be required to memorize the tables; however, you will need to know which table to use as applicable to the question being asked. (PLT409, AA.I.G.K3) — 14 CFR §117.17 and Table C

ATM, ADX
9843. The time spent resting during unaugmented operations will not be counted towards the flight duty period limitation if the rest period is at least

A—3 hours long after reaching suitable accommodations.
B—4 hours long after reaching suitable accommodations.
C—4 hours long which can include transportation to suitable accommodations.

For an unaugmented operation only, if a flightcrew member is provided with a rest opportunity (an opportunity to sleep) in a suitable accommodation during his or her flight duty period, the time that the flightcrew member spends in the suitable accommodation is not part of that flightcrew member's flight duty period if the time spent in that accommodation is at least 3 hours, measured from the time that the flightcrew member reaches the accommodation. (PLT409, AA.I.G.K3) — 14 CFR §117.15

Answers
9841 [A] 9842 [B] 9843 [A]

ATM, ADX

9844. Notification of the rest opportunity period during unaugmented operations, must be

A—given before the next to last flight segment.
B—given before the beginning of the flight duty period.
C—provided no later than after the first flight segment offered after the first flight segment is completed.

For an unaugmented operation only, if a flightcrew member is provided with a rest opportunity (an opportunity to sleep) in a suitable accommodation during his or her flight duty period, the time that the flightcrew member spends in that accommodation is not part of that flightcrew member's flight duty period if the rest opportunity is scheduled before the beginning of the flight duty period in which that rest is taken. (PLT409, AA.I.G.K3) — 14 CFR §117.15

ATM, ADX

9845. If the augmented flightcrew member is not acclimated, the

A—maximum flight duty period given in 14 CFR part 117, Table C (not included herein) is reduced by 30 minutes.
B—flight duty period assignment must be reduced 15 minutes by each 15 degrees of longitude difference from the previous rest location.
C—minimum rest period must be extended by 3 hours.

If the flightcrew member is not acclimated the maximum flight duty period in Table C of Part 117 is reduced by 30 minutes. (PLT409, AA.I.G.K3) — 14 CFR §117.17

ATM, ADX

9846. The flight duty period may be extended due to unforeseen circumstances before takeoff by as much as

A—2 hours.
B—1 hour.
C—30 minutes.

For augmented and unaugmented operations, if unforeseen operational circumstances arise prior to takeoff, the pilot-in-command and the certificate holder may extend the maximum flight duty period permitted up to 2 hours. (PLT409, AA.I.G.K3) — 14 CFR §117.19

ATM, ADX

9847. After takeoff, unforeseen circumstances arise. In this case, the flight duty period may be extended by as much as

A—2 hours.
B—necessary to reach the closest suitable alternate crew base airport.
C—necessary to land at the next destination airport or alternate airport.

For augmented and unaugmented operations, if unforeseen operational circumstances arise after takeoff, the pilot-in-command and the certificate holder may extend maximum flight duty periods to the extent necessary to safely land the aircraft at the next destination airport or alternate airport, as appropriate. (PLT409, AA.I.G.K3) — 14 CFR §117.19

ATM, ADX

9847-1. "Unforeseen operational circumstance" means an

A—unplanned event of insufficient duration to allow for adjustments to schedules.
B—unforecast weather and expected ATC delays.
C—event of sufficient duration to create increased flight times for the certificate holder's operation.

Unforeseen operational circumstance means an unplanned event of insufficient duration to allow for adjustments to schedules, including unforecast weather, equipment malfunction, or air traffic delay that is not reasonably expected. (PLT407, AA.I.G.K3) — 14 CFR §117.3

ATM, ADX

9847-2. For passenger operations under Part 121, a flightcrew member may exceed maximum flight time limitations if

A—immediately followed by 11 hours of rest.
B—unforeseen operational circumstances arise after takeoff.
C—known ATC delays do not exceed 30 minutes.

For augmented and unaugmented operations, if unforeseen operational circumstances arise after takeoff, the PIC and the certificate holder may extend maximum flight duty periods to the extent necessary to safely land the aircraft at the next destination airport or alternate airport, as appropriate. (PLT409, AA.I.G.K3) — 14 CFR §117.3

Answers

9844 [B]	9845 [A]	9846 [A]	9847 [C]	9847-1 [A]	9847-2 [B]

ATM, ADX

9848. For airport/standby reserve, all time spent in airport/standby reserve time is

A—not part of the flightcrew member's flight duty period.
B—part of the flightcrew member's flight duty period.
C—part of the flightcrew member's flight duty period after being alerted for flight assignment.

For airport/standby reserve, all time spent in a reserve status is part of the flightcrew member's flight duty period (PLT409, AA.I.G.K3) — 14 CFR §117.21

ATM, ADX

9849. Limiting flight time for all flightcrew members will include

A—instruction flight hours, commercial flying, and flying for any certificate holder.
B—any flying by flightcrew members for any certificate holder or 91K program manager.
C—flying by flightcrew members for any certificate holder or 91K program manager and any other commercial flight time.

The limitations of Part 117 include all flying by flightcrew members on behalf of any certificate holder or 91K program manager during the applicable periods. (PLT409, AA.I.G.K3) — 14 CFR §117.23

ATM, ADX

9850. Flightcrew member's flight duty periods are limited to

A—60 hours in any 168 consecutive hours.
B—70 hours in any 168 consecutive hours.
C—60 hours in any 7 days.

No certificate holder may schedule and no flightcrew member may accept an assignment if the flightcrew member's total flight duty period will exceed 60 flight duty hours in any 168 consecutive hours. (PLT409, AA.I.G.K3) — 14 CFR §117.23

ATM, ADX

9851. A flightcrew member must be given a rest period before beginning any reserve or flight duty period of

A—24 consecutive hours free from any duty in the past 7 consecutive calendar days.
B—36 consecutive hours in the past 168 consecutive hours.
C—30 consecutive hours in the past 168 consecutive hours.

Before beginning any reserve or flight duty period, a flightcrew member must be given at least 30 consecutive hours free from all duty within the past 168 consecutive-hour period. (PLT409, AA.I.G.K3) — 14 CFR §117.25

ATM, ADX

9852. No flightcrew member may accept an assignment without scheduled rest opportunities for

A—more than 3 consecutive nighttime flights that infringe on the window of circadian low.
B—more than 4 consecutive nighttime flights that infringe on the window of circadian low in a 168 hour period.
C—consecutive nighttime flights beginning after 0001 hours local home base time.

No certificate holder may schedule and no flightcrew member may accept more than three consecutive flight duty periods that infringe on the window of circadian low. (PLT409, AA.I.G.K3) — 14 CFR §117.27

ADX

8194. Normally, a dispatcher for domestic or flag operations should be scheduled for no more than

A—10 hours of duty in any 24 consecutive hours.
B—8 hours of service in any 24 consecutive hours.
C—10 consecutive hours of duty.

Except in cases where circumstances or emergency conditions beyond the control of the certificate holder, no certificate holder conducting domestic or flag operations may schedule a dispatcher for more than 10 consecutive hours of duty. (PLT450, AA.I.G.K3) — 14 CFR §121.465

ATM, ADX

8724. What is the minimum rest period required before a flight or reserve duty period?

A—8 consecutive hours rest.
B—10 consecutive hours rest.
C—12 consecutive hours rest.

No certificate holder may schedule and no flightcrew member may accept an assignment for any reserve or flight duty period unless the flightcrew member is given a rest period of at least 10 consecutive hours immediately before beginning the reserve or flight duty period measured from the time the flightcrew member is released from duty. The 10 hour rest period must provide the flightcrew member with a minimum of 8 uninterrupted hours of sleep opportunity. (PLT409, AA.I.G.K3) — 14 CFR §117.25

Answers

9848 [B]	9849 [B]	9850 [A]	9851 [C]	9852 [A]	8194 [C]
8724 [B]					

Dispatching and Flight Release

Operational control with respect to a flight, means the exercise of authority over initiating, conducting or terminating a flight.

The air carrier or commercial operator is responsible for operational control. The pilot-in-command and the director of operations are jointly responsible for the initiation, continuation, diversion, and termination of flight in compliance with regulations and the company's operations specifications. The pilot-in-command is responsible for the preflight planning and the operation of the flight.

Each flag and domestic flight must have a **dispatch release** on board. The dispatch release can be in any form but must contain the following information.

- The identification number of the aircraft
- The trip number
- The departure, destination, intermediate and alternate airports
- The type of operation (IFR or VFR)
- The minimum fuel supply
- The latest weather reports and forecasts for the complete flight (may be attached to the release rather than be part of it)

The aircraft dispatcher must provide the pilot-in-command with all available current reports or information on airport conditions and irregularities of navigation facilities that may affect the safety of flight. The aircraft dispatcher must provide the pilot-in-command with all available weather reports and forecasts of weather phenomena that may affect the safety of flight including adverse weather. The aircraft dispatcher must update this information during a flight.

When a domestic flight lands at an intermediate airport named in its original dispatch release and departs again within 1 hour, it does not need a new dispatch release. If it remains on the ground for more than 1 hour, a redispatch release must be issued.

When a flag flight lands at an intermediate airport named in its original dispatch release and departs again within 6 hours, it does not need a new dispatch release. If it remains on the ground for more than 6 hours, a redispatch is required.

The pilot-in-command of a flight shall carry in the airplane to its destination:

- A copy of the completed load manifest
- A copy of the dispatch release
- A copy of the flight plan.

The air carrier must keep copies of these documents for at least 3 months.

Each supplemental carrier or commercial operator flight must have a **flight release** on board. The flight release can be in any form but must contain the following information:

- The company or organization name
- Make, model and registration number of the aircraft used
- The flight or trip number and the date of the flight
- The name of each flight crewmember, flight attendant and the pilot designated as pilot-in-command
- The departure, destination, intermediate and alternate airports and route
- The type of operation (e.g., IFR or VFR)
- The minimum fuel supply
- The latest weather reports and forecasts for the complete flight (may be attached to the release rather than be part of it)

Before beginning a flight, the pilot-in-command must obtain all available current reports or information on airport conditions and irregularities of navigation facilities that may affect the safety of the flight. During a flight, the pilot-in-command must obtain any additional available information of meteorological conditions and irregularities of facilities and services that may affect the safety of the flight.

A provisional airport is defined as an airport approved by the Administrator for use by a certificate holder for the purpose of providing service to a community when the regular airport used by the certificate holder is not available. A person who is not authorized to conduct direct air carrier operations, but who is authorized by the Administrator to conduct operations as a U.S. commercial operator, will be issued an Operating Certificate. Each certificate holder conducting domestic, flag, or commuter operations must obtain operations specifications containing, among many other provisions, the kinds of operations authorized.

Extended-range twin-engine operational performance standards (ETOPS) is a rating accompanied by a time limit (such as 180-minute ETOPS) that allows twin-engine civil transport aircraft to fly over oceans and deserts provided that the aircraft is never more than 180 minutes away from a suitable airfield. An ETOPS "entry point" is the first point on an ETOPS route at which the airplane is farther than a distance of 60 minutes flying time, with one engine inoperative, from an emergency or diversion airport that is adequate for an airplane with two engines.

When filing an alternate using the 180-minute ETOPS rule, the alternate airport must have rescue and fire fighting services (RFFS) that meet ICAO Category 4 standard or higher. If filing an alternate using the beyond-180-minute ETOPS rule, the alternate must have RFFS that meet the ICAO Category 4 standard or higher, and the aircraft must remain within the ETOPS authorized diversion time from an adequate airport that has RFFS equal to ICAO Category 7 or higher.

ALL

9326. "Operational control" of a flight refers to

A—the specific duties of any required crewmember.
B—exercising authority over initiating, conducting, or terminating a flight.
C—exercising the privileges of pilot-in-command of an aircraft.

"Operational Control," with respect to flight, means the exercise of authority over initiating, conducting or terminating a flight. (PLT432, AA.I.G.K4) — 14 CFR §1.1

Answer (A) is incorrect because "crewmember" refers to any person assigned to perform duty in an aircraft during flight time, which includes cabin crew as well as cockpit crew. Answer (C) is incorrect because "pilot-in-command" refers to the pilot responsible for the operation and safety of an aircraft during flight time, which does not include the initiation of a flight.

ALL

8003. Which document specifically authorizes a person to operate an aircraft in a particular geographic area?

A—Operations Specifications.
B—Operating Certificate.
C—Dispatch Release.

Each certificate holder conducting domestic, flag, or commuter operations must obtain operations specifications containing authorization and limitations for routes and areas of operations. (PLT389, AA.II.A.K7) — 14 CFR §119.49

Answers

9326 [B]   8003 [A]

ALL

9745. No person may operate a U.S. registered civil aircraft

A—for which an AFM or RFM is required by part 21 section 21.5 unless there is a current, approved operator's manual available.
B—for which an AFM or RFM is required by part 21 section 21.5 unless there is a current, approved AFM or RFM available.
C—for which an AFM or RFM is required by part 21 section 21.5 unless there is a current, approved AFM or RFM available or the manual specified in part 135 section 135.19(b).

No person may operate a U.S.-registered civil aircraft for which an Airplane or Rotorcraft Flight Manual is required by §21.5 unless there is available in the aircraft a current, approved Airplane or Rotorcraft Flight Manual or the manual provided for in §121.141(b). (PLT373, AA.II.A.K7) — 14 CFR §91.9

ALL

8429. An airport approved by the Administrator for use by an air carrier certificate holder for the purpose of providing service to a community when the regular airport is not available is a/an:

A—destination airport.
B—provisional airport.
C—alternate airport.

A provisional airport is defined as an airport approved by the Administrator for use by a certificate holder for the purpose of providing service to a community when the regular airport used by the certificate holder is not available. (PLT395, AA.II.A.K7) — 14 CFR §110.2

Answer (A) is incorrect because the destination airport is the term used to describe the primary airport of intended landing. Answer (C) is incorrect because the alternate airport is generally defined as an airport at which an aircraft may land if a landing at the intended airport becomes inadvisable.

ALL

8430. A provisional airport is an airport approved by the Administrator for use by an air carrier certificate holder for the purpose of

A—obtaining provisions and fuel when unable, due to winds, to proceed direct to the regular airport.
B—having the aircraft catered (foods, beverages, or supplies).
C—providing service to a community when the regular airport is unavailable.

A provisional airport is defined as an airport approved by the Administrator for use by a certificate holder for the purpose of providing service to a community when the regular airport used by the certificate holder is not available. (PLT389, AA.II.A.K7) — 14 CFR §110.2

ALL

8767. A person who is not authorized to conduct direct air carrier operations, but who is authorized by the Administrator to conduct operations as a U.S. commercial operator, will be issued

A—an Air Carrier Certificate.
B—a Supplemental Air Carrier Certificate.
C—an Operating Certificate.

A person who is not authorized to conduct direct air carrier operations, but who is authorized by the Administrator to conduct operations as a U.S. commercial operator, will be issued an Operating Certificate. (PLT389, AA.II.A.K7) — 14 CFR §119.5

Answer (A) is incorrect because a person authorized by the Administrator to conduct operations as a direct air carrier is issued an Air Carrier Certificate. Answer (B) is incorrect because wherever in the Federal Aviation Regulations the term "supplemental air carrier operating certificate" appears, it shall be deemed to mean an "Air Carrier Operating Certificate."

ALL

8768. The kinds of operation that a certificate holder is authorized to conduct are specified in the

A—certificate holder's operations specifications.
B—application submitted for an Air Carrier or Operating Certificate, by the applicant.
C—Air Carrier Certificate or Operating Certificate.

Each certificate holder conducting domestic, flag, or commuter operations must obtain operations specifications containing, among many other provisions, the kinds of operations authorized. (PLT389, AA.II.A.K7) — 14 CFR §119.49

Answers (B) and (C) are incorrect because the operations specifications are continually updated and amended relative to the operator's needs and not contained in the original application or on the certificate itself.

Answers

9745 [B]	8429 [B]	8430 [C]	8767 [C]	8768 [A]

ALL

9782. All 14 CFR Part 139 airports must report

A—accident and incident data annually.
B—noise complaint statistics for each departure procedure or runway.
C—declared distances for each runway.

All 14 CFR Part 139 airports report declared runway distance for each runway. (PLT078, AA.II.A.K2b) — AIM ¶4-3-6

Answers (A) and (B) are incorrect because this information is only furnished upon request by the administrator per 14 CFR §139.301.

ATM, ADX

8243. The persons jointly responsible for the initiation, continuation, diversion, and termination of a supplemental air carrier or commercial operator flight are the

A—pilot-in-command and chief pilot.
B—pilot-in-command and director of operations.
C—pilot-in-command and the flight follower.

For operations of supplemental air carriers or commercial operators, the pilot-in-command and the director of operations are jointly responsible for the initiation, continuation, diversion, and termination of a flight. (PLT444, AA.II.A.K2e) — 14 CFR §121.537

ATM, ADX

8243-1. You are the pilot-in-command of a 14 CFR Part 121 domestic operation flight. In addition to yourself, who is jointly responsible for preflight planning, delay, and dispatch release of the flight?

A—The director of operations.
B—The chief pilot or designed.
C—The aircraft dispatcher.

The PIC and the aircraft dispatcher are jointly responsible for the preflight planning, delay, and dispatch release of a flight in compliance with this chapter and operations specifications. (PLT444, AA.I.E.K9) — 14 CFR §121.533

ATM, ADX

8290. Which information must be contained in, or attached to, the dispatch release for a flag air carrier flight?

A—Type of operation (e.g., IFR, VFR), trip number.
B—Total fuel supply and minimum fuel required on board the airplane.
C—Passenger manifest, company or organization name, and cargo weight.

The dispatch release of a flag or domestic air carrier may be in any form but must contain at least the following information concerning the flight:

1. *Identification number of the aircraft;*
2. *Trip number;*
3. *Departure airport, intermediate stops, destination airports, and alternate airports;*
4. *A statement of the type of operation (IFR, VFR);*
5. *Minimum fuel supply.*

(PLT455, AA.II.A.K2e) — 14 CFR §121.687

Answers (B) and (C) are incorrect because fuel on board, a passenger list, and cargo weights are found in the load manifest. Although separate items, both the dispatch release and the load manifest are required to be carried on the flight.

ATM, ADX

8292. What information must be contained in, or attached to, the dispatch release for a domestic air carrier flight?

A—Departure airport, intermediate stops, destinations, alternate airports, and trip number.
B—Names of all passengers on board and minimum fuel supply.
C—Cargo load, weight and balance data, and identification number of the aircraft.

The dispatch release of a flag or domestic air carrier may be in any form but must contain at least the following information concerning the flight:

1. *Identification number of the aircraft;*
2. *Trip number;*
3. *Departure airport, intermediate stops, destination airports, and alternate airports;*
4. *A statement of the type of operation (IFR, VFR);*
5. *Minimum fuel supply.*

(PLT400, AA.II.A.K2e) — 14 CFR §121.687

Answers (B) and (C) are incorrect because the passenger names, cargo load, and weight and balance data are part of the required load manifest. A copy of the load manifest must also be carried on the flight. The load manifest is not part of the dispatch release.

Answers

9782 [C] 8243 [B] 8243-1 [C] 8290 [A] 8292 [A]

ATM, ADX

8293. What information must be included on a domestic air carrier dispatch release?

A—Evidence that the airplane is loaded according to schedule, and a statement of the type of operation.
B—Minimum fuel supply and trip number.
C—Company or organization name and identification number of the aircraft.

The dispatch release of a flag or domestic air carrier may be in any form but must contain at least the following information concerning the flight:

1. *Identification number of the aircraft;*
2. *Trip number;*
3. *Departure airport, intermediate stops, destination airports, and alternate airports;*
4. *A statement of the type of operation (IFR, VFR);*
5. *Minimum fuel supply.*

(PLT412, AA.II.A.K2e) — 14 CFR §121.687

Answer (A) is incorrect because the proper loading of the airplane is documented in the load manifest. Answer (C) is incorrect because the company or organization name is not required on the dispatch release.

ATM, ADX

8294. A dispatch release for a flag or domestic air carrier must contain or have attached to it

A—minimum fuel supply and weather information for the complete flight.
B—trip number and weight and balance data.
C—weather information for the complete flight and a crew list.

The dispatch release must contain, or have attached to it, weather reports, available weather forecasts, or a combination thereof, for the destination airport, intermediate stops, and alternate airports, that are the latest available at the time the release is signed by the pilot-in-command and dispatcher. It may include any additional available weather reports or forecasts that the pilot-in-command or the aircraft dispatcher considers necessary or desirable. (PLT412, AA.II.A.K2e) — 14 CFR §121.687

ATM, ADX

8280. By regulation, who shall provide the pilot-in-command of a domestic or flag air carrier airplane information concerning weather, and irregularities of facilities and services?

A—The aircraft dispatcher.
B—Air route traffic control center.
C—Director of operations.

The aircraft dispatcher for a flag or domestic flight shall provide the pilot-in-command all available reports or information on airport conditions and irregularities of navigation facilities that may affect safety of the flight. (PLT398, AA.II.A.K2e) — 14 CFR §121.601

Answer (B) is incorrect because air route traffic control center may have information concerning irregularities of facilities and service, but it is not the proper source of that information. That information should be provided by the aircraft dispatcher. Answer (C) is incorrect because the director of operations (who may also be the general manager) is an administrative person, responsible for the day-to-day operations and not usually involved in specific flight operations.

ATM, ADX

8283. Where can the pilot of a flag air carrier airplane find the latest FDC NOTAMs?

A—Any company dispatch facility.
B—Notices to Air Missions publication.
C—Chart Supplements U.S.

The aircraft dispatcher for a flag or domestic flight shall provide the pilot-in-command all available reports or information on airport conditions and irregularities of navigation facilities that may affect safety of the flight. Since FDC NOTAMs are regulatory in nature and apply to instrument approach procedures and enroute charts, they would have to be available. (PLT323, AA.I.E.K14) — 14 CFR §121.601

ATM, ADX

8284. Who is responsible, by regulation, for briefing a domestic or flag air carrier pilot-in-command on all available weather information?

A—Company meteorologist.
B—Aircraft dispatcher.
C—Director of operations.

Before the beginning of a flag or domestic flight, the aircraft dispatcher shall provide the pilot-in-command with all available weather reports and forecasts of weather phenomena that may affect the safety of flight. (PLT398, AA.I.G.K4) — 14 CFR §121.601

Answers

8293 [B]	8294 [A]	8280 [A]	8283 [A]	8284 [B]

ATM, ADX

8232. A domestic air carrier flight has a delay while on the ground, at an intermediate airport. How long before a redispatch release is required?

A—Not more than 1 hour.
B—Not more than 2 hours.
C—More than 6 hours.

Except when a domestic air carrier airplane lands at an intermediate airport specified in the original dispatch release and remains there for not more than 1 hour, no person may start a flight unless an aircraft dispatcher specifically authorizes that flight. (PLT452, AA.II.A.K2e) — 14 CFR §121.593

Answer (B) is incorrect because domestic air carriers may remain at an intermediate stop for 1 hour before a redispatch release is required. Answer (C) is incorrect because flag, supplemental, and commercial operators may remain at an intermediate stop up to 6 hours before a redispatch release is required.

ATM, ADX

8260. A domestic air carrier airplane lands at an intermediate airport at 1815Z. The latest time it may depart without a specific authorization from an aircraft dispatcher is

A—1945Z.
B—1915Z.
C—1845Z.

Except when a domestic air carrier airplane lands at an intermediate airport specified in the original dispatch release and remains there for not more than 1 hour, no person may start a flight unless an aircraft dispatcher specifically authorizes that flight. (PLT398, AA.II.A.K2e) — 14 CFR §121.593

ATM, ADX

8259. A flag air carrier flight lands at an intermediate airport at 1805Z. The latest time that it may depart without being redispatched is

A—2005Z.
B—1905Z.
C—0005Z.

No person may continue a flag air carrier flight from an intermediate airport without redispatch if the airplane has been on the ground more than 6 hours. (PLT398, AA.II.A.K2e) — 14 CFR §121.595

ATM, ADX

8266. When a flag air carrier airplane lands at an intermediate airport at 1822Z, what is the latest time it may continue a flight without receiving a redispatch authorization?

A—1922Z.
B—1952Z.
C—0022Z.

No person may continue a flag air carrier flight from an intermediate airport without redispatch if the airplane has been on the ground more than 6 hours. (PLT398, AA.II.A.K2e) — 14 CFR §121.595

ATM, ADX

8267. If a flag air carrier flight lands at an intermediate airport at 1845Z, and experiences a delay, what is the latest time it may depart for the next airport without a redispatch release?

A—1945Z.
B—2015Z.
C—0045Z.

No person may continue a flag air carrier flight from an intermediate airport without redispatch if the airplane has been on the ground more than 6 hours. (PLT398, AA.II.A.K2e) — 14 CFR §121.595

ATM, ADX

8226. What information must the pilot-in-command of a supplemental air carrier flight or commercial operator carry to the destination airport?

A—Cargo and passenger distribution information.
B—Copy of the flight plan.
C—Names of all crewmembers and designated pilot-in-command.

The pilot-in-command shall carry in the airplane to its destination: load manifest, flight release, airworthiness release, pilot route certification, and flight plan. (PLT400, AA.II.A.K2e) — 14 CFR §121.687

Answer (A) is incorrect because this information is only part of the load manifest. Answer (C) is incorrect because this is only one element of the flight release which is required on board.

Answers

8232 [A] 8260 [B] 8259 [C] 8266 [C] 8267 [C] 8226 [B]

ATM, ADX
8286. Which documents are required to be carried aboard each domestic air carrier flight?

A—Load manifest (or information from it) and flight release.
B—Dispatch release and weight and balance release.
C—Dispatch release, load manifest (or information from it), and flight plan.

The pilot-in-command of a domestic or flag air carrier flight shall carry in the airplane to its destination:

1. *A copy of the completed load manifest;*
2. *A copy of the dispatch release; and*
3. *A copy of the flight plan.*

(PLT400, AA.II.A.K2e) — 14 CFR §121.695

ATM, ADX
8288. A domestic or flag air carrier shall keep copies of the flight plans, dispatch releases, and load manifests for at least

A—3 months.
B—6 months.
C—30 days.

The air carrier shall keep copies of the flight plans, dispatch releases, and load manifests for at least 3 months. (PLT453, AA.II.A.K2e) — 14 CFR §121.695

ATM, ADX
8296. Which documents are required to be carried aboard each flag air carrier flight?

A—Dispatch release, flight plan, and weight and balance release.
B—Load manifest, flight plan, and flight release.
C—Dispatch release, load manifest, and flight plan.

The pilot-in-command of a domestic or flag air carrier flight shall carry in the airplane to its destination:

1. *A copy of the completed load manifest;*
2. *A copy of the dispatch release; and*
3. *A copy of the flight plan.*

(PLT400, AA.II.A.K2e) — 14 CFR §121.695

Answer (A) is incorrect because a dispatch release is required but there is no required document called a weight and balance release. Answer (B) is incorrect because a flight release is used by supplemental air carriers and commercial operators.

ATM, ADX
8287. How long shall a supplemental air carrier or commercial operator retain a record of the load manifest, airworthiness release, pilot route certification, flight release, and flight plan?

A—1 month.
B—3 months.
C—12 months.

A supplemental air carrier must retain a copy of each load manifest, flight release and flight plan at its principal operations base for at least 3 months. (PLT453, AA.II.A.K2e) — 14 CFR §121.697

ATM, ADX
8291. The certificated air carrier and operators who must attach to, or include on, the flight release form the name of each flight crewmember, flight attendant, and designated pilot-in-command are

A—supplemental and commercial.
B—supplemental and domestic.
C—flag and commercial.

Supplemental air carrier and commercial operators must attach to, or include on, the flight release form, containing at least the following information concerning each flight:

1. *Company or organization name;*
2. *Make, model and registration number of the aircraft being used;*
3. *Flight or trip number and the date of the flight;*
4. *Name of each flight crewmember, flight attendant, and pilot designated as pilot-in-command;*
5. *Departure airport, destination airports, alternate airports, and route;*
6. *Minimum fuel supply; and*
7. *A statement of the type of operation (IFR, VFR).*

(PLT455, AA.II.A.K2e) — 14 CFR §121.689

Answers (B) and (C) are incorrect because domestic and flag carriers, unlike supplemental and commercial operators, utilize a dispatch release. Commercial operators and supplemental carriers utilize a flight release. A flight release contains the crew names, but a dispatch release does not.

Answers

8286 [C] 8288 [A] 8296 [C] 8287 [B] 8291 [A]

ATM, ADX

8295. The information required in the flight release for supplemental air carriers and commercial operators that is not required in the dispatch release for flag and domestic air carriers is the

A—weather reports and forecasts.
B—names of all crewmembers.
C—minimum fuel supply.

The flight release of a supplemental air carrier or commercial operator may be in any form but must contain at least the following information concerning each flight:

1. *Company or organization name;*
2. *Make, model and registration number of the aircraft being used;*
3. *Flight or trip number and the date of the flight;*
4. *Name of each flight crewmember, flight attendant, and pilot designated as pilot-in-command;*
5. *Departure airport, destination airports, alternate airports, and route;*
6. *Minimum fuel supply; and*
7. *A statement of the type of operation (IFR, VFR).*

The dispatch release of a flag or domestic air carrier may be in any form but must contain at least the following information concerning the flight:

1. *Identification number of the aircraft;*
2. *Trip number;*
3. *Departure airport, intermediate stops, destination airports, and alternate airports;*
4. *A statement of the type of operation (IFR, VFR);*
5. *Minimum fuel supply.*

(PLT412, AA.II.A.K2e) — 14 CFR §121.689

Answers (A) and (C) are incorrect because weather reports and forecasts and minimum fuel supply information are required in the flight release for supplemental and commercial operators and in the dispatch release for flag and domestic air carriers.

ATM

9746. Before an ETOPS flight may commence, an ETOPS

A—preflight check must be conducted by a certified A&P and signed off in the logbook.
B—pre-departure service check must be certified by a PDSC Signatory Person.
C—pre-departure check must be signed off by an A&P or the PIC for the flight.

An appropriately-trained, ETOPS-qualified maintenance person must accomplish and certify by signature ETOPS specific tasks. Before an ETOPS flight may commence, an ETOPS pre-departure service check (PDSC) Signatory Person, who has been authorized by the certificate holder, must certify by signature, that the ETOPS PDSC has been completed. (PLT425, AA.II.A.K2e) — 14 CFR §121.374

ATM

9746-1. An ETOPS entry point means

A—the first entry point on the route of flight of an ETOPS flight using one-engine-inoperative cruise speed that is more than 60 minutes from an adequate airport for airplanes having two engines.
B—the first entry point on the route of flight of an ETOPS flight using one-engine-inoperative cruise speed that is more than 200 minutes from an adequate airport for airplanes having more than two engines.
C—the first entry point on the route of flight of an ETOPS flight using one-engine-inoperative cruise speed that is more than 90 minutes from an adequate airport for airplanes having two engines.

"ETOPS entry point" means the first point on the route of an ETOPS flight that is (1) more than 60 minutes from an adequate airport for airplanes with two engines, and (2) more than 180 minutes from an adequate airport for passenger-carrying airplanes with more than two engines. This is determined using a one-engine-inoperative cruise speed under standard conditions in still air. (PLT425, AA.I.G.K4) — 14 CFR §121.7

Answers

8295 [B] 9746 [B] 9746-1 [A]

ATM

9746-2. For flight planning, a Designated ETOPS Alternate Airport

A—for ETOPS up to 180 minutes, must have RFFS equivalent to that specified by ICAO category 4, unless the airport's RFFS can be augmented by local fire fighting assets within 30 minutes.
B—for ETOPS up to 180 minutes, must have RFFS equivalent to that specified by ICAO category 3, unless the airport's RFFS can be augmented by local fire fighting assets within 45 minutes.
C—for ETOPS up to 180 minutes, must have RFFS equivalent to that specified by ICAO category 4, unless the airport's RFFS can be augmented by local fire fighting assets within 45 minutes.

For ETOPS up to 180 minutes, each designated ETOPS alternate airport must have RFFS equivalent to that specified by ICAO as Category 4 or higher. If the equipment and personnel required are not immediately available at an airport, the certificate holder may still list the airport on the dispatch or flight release if the airport's RFFS can be augmented from local fire fighting assets. A 30-minute response time for augmentation is adequate if the local assets can be notified while the diverting airplane is en route. (PLT398, AA.I.G.K4) — 14 CFR §121.106

ALL

9761. What is considered "north polar"?

A—north of 60° N latitude.
B—north of 68° N latitude.
C—north of 78° N latitude.

As an example, operations in the "North Polar Area" and "South Polar Area" require a specific passenger recovery plan for each diversion airport. North Polar Area means the entire area north of 78° N latitude. (PLT425, AA.I.G.K4) — 14 CFR §121.7

ALL

9762. What is considered "south polar"?

A—south of 60° S latitude.
B—south of 68° S latitude.
C—south of 78° S latitude.

As an example, operations in the "North Polar Area" and "South Polar Area" require a specific passenger recovery plan for each diversion airport. South Polar Area means the entire area south of 60° S latitude. (PLT425, AA.I.G.K4) — 14 CFR §121.7

ATM, ADX

8281. Who is responsible for obtaining information on all current airport conditions, weather, and irregularities of navigation facilities for a supplemental air carrier flight?

A—Aircraft dispatcher.
B—Director of operations or flight follower.
C—Pilot-in-command.

Before beginning a flight, each pilot-in-command of a supplemental air carrier or commercial operator flight shall obtain all available current reports or information on airport conditions and irregularities or navigation facilities that may affect the safety of the flight. (PLT444, AA.II.A.K5) — 14 CFR §121.603

Answer (A) is incorrect because an aircraft dispatcher is responsible for briefing a flag or domestic (not supplemental) air carrier pilot. Answer (B) is incorrect because the director of operations (who may also be the general manager) is an administrative person, responsible for the day-to-day operations and not usually involved in specific flight operations.

ATM, ADX

8282. During a supplemental air carrier flight, who is responsible for obtaining information on meteorological conditions?

A—Aircraft dispatcher.
B—Pilot-in-command.
C—Director of operations or flight follower.

During a flight, the pilot-in-command of a supplemental air carrier or commercial operator flight shall obtain any additional available information of meteorological conditions and irregularities of facilities and services that may affect the safety of the flight. (PLT444, AA.II.A.K5) — 14 CFR §121.603

Answer (A) is incorrect because an aircraft dispatcher is responsible for obtaining weather information for a flag or domestic air carrier flight. Answer (C) is incorrect because the director of operations (who may also be the general manager) or flight follower is an administrative person, responsible for day-to-day operations and not usually involved in specific flight operations.

Answers

9746-2 [A]	9761 [C]	9762 [A]	8281 [C]	8282 [B]

Fuel Requirements

All **domestic flights** must have enough fuel to:

1. Fly to the airport to which the flight was dispatched;
2. Thereafter, fly to and land at the most distant alternate airport (if an alternate is required) and
3. Thereafter, fly for 45 minutes at normal cruising fuel consumption.

(The fuel required for a **flag flight** landing in the 48 contiguous states or the District of Columbia is the same as for domestic flights.)

(The fuel requirements for **reciprocating-powered supplemental or commercial operations** landing in the contiguous 48 states is the same as for domestic operations.)

If an **alternate is not required** or the flight is being made to a remote airport where **no alternate is available**, the fuel requirements are:

1. Enough fuel to fly to the destination, and then;
2. Fly for two hours at normal cruising fuel consumption.

A **turbojet supplemental flight** (with an alternate available) landing outside the 48 contiguous states must have fuel to:

1. Fly to the destination, then
2. Fly 10% of the total time required to fly to the destination, then
3. Fly to the alternate, then
4. Fly for 30 minutes at holding speed at 1,500 feet above the alternate.

Propeller driven flag flights must have enough fuel to:

1. Fly to the airport to which the flight was dispatched;
2. Thereafter, fly to and land at the most distant alternate; and
3. Thereafter, fly for 30 minutes plus 15% of the total flying time to the destination and the alternate at normal cruising fuel consumption; or fly for 90 minutes, whichever is less.

If an **alternate is not required** or the flight is being made to a remote airport where **no alternate is available**, the fuel requirements for **reciprocating engine powered flights** are:

1. Enough fuel to fly to the destination, and then;
2. Fly for 3 hours at normal cruising fuel consumption.

ATM, ADX

8268. The reserve fuel supply for a domestic air carrier flight is

A—30 minutes plus 15 percent at normal fuel consumption in addition to the fuel required to the alternate airport.

B—45 minutes at normal fuel consumption in addition to the fuel required to fly to and land at the most distant alternate airport.

C—45 minutes at normal fuel consumption in addition to the fuel required to the alternate airport.

For domestic operations, no person may dispatch or takeoff an airplane unless it has enough fuel to:

1. *Fly to the airport to which it was dispatched;*
2. *Thereafter, to fly to and land at the most distant alternate airport (if an alternate is required); and*
3. *Thereafter, to fly for 45 minutes at normal cruising fuel consumption.*

(PLT413, AA.I.G.K4) — 14 CFR §121.639

Answers

8268 [B]

ATM, ADX

8269. The minimum amount (planned) of fuel to be aboard a flag air carrier turbojet airplane on a flight within the 48 contiguous United States, after reaching the most distant alternate airport, should be

A—45 minutes at normal cruising fuel consumption.
B—2 hours at normal cruising fuel consumption.
C—enough fuel to return to the destination airport or to fly for 90 minutes at normal cruising fuel consumption, whichever is less.

A turbine-engined flag air carrier operation within the 48 contiguous United States and the District of Columbia may use the fuel requirements of a domestic air carrier. For domestic operations, no person may dispatch or takeoff in an airplane unless it has enough fuel to:

1. *Fly to the airport to which it was dispatched;*
2. *Thereafter, to fly to and land at the most distant alternate airport (if an alternate is required); and*
3. *Thereafter, to fly for 45 minutes at normal cruising fuel consumption.*

(PLT413, AA.I.G.K4) — 14 CFR §121.639

Answer (B) is incorrect because 2 hours normal cruising fuel is required at the destination airport when an alternate is not specified and the flight is conducted outside the 48 contiguous United States. Answer (C) is incorrect because there is no provision for return to the destination airport in calculating fuel requirements.

ATM, ADX

8271. For a flag air carrier flight to be released to an island airport for which an alternate airport is not available, a turbojet-powered airplane must have enough fuel to fly to that airport and thereafter to fly

A—at least 2 hours at normal cruising fuel consumption.
B—for 3 hours at normal cruising fuel consumption.
C—back to the departure airport.

No person may dispatch a turbojet-powered airplane to an airport for which no alternate is available unless it has enough fuel, considering wind and other weather conditions, to fly to that airport and thereafter to fly for at least 2 hours at normal cruising fuel consumption. (PLT413, AA.I.G.K4) — 14 CFR §121.645

ATM, ADX

8272. An alternate airport is not required for a supplemental or commercial air carrier, turbojet-powered airplane on an IFR flight outside the 48 contiguous United States, if enough fuel

A—is aboard to fly to the destination at normal cruise speed and thereafter at least 2 hours at normal holding speed.
B—is aboard the airplane to fly to the destination and then to fly for at least 2 more hours at normal cruising fuel consumption.
C—to fly over the destination for 30 minutes at holding airspeed at 1,500 feet AGL is carried aboard the airplane.

No person may dispatch a turbojet-powered airplane to an airport for which no alternate is available unless it has enough fuel, considering wind and other weather conditions, to fly to that airport and thereafter to fly for at least 2 hours at normal cruising fuel consumption. (PLT413, AA.I.G.K4) — 14 CFR §121.645

ATM, ADX

8276. A turbine-engine-powered flag air carrier airplane is released to an airport which has no available alternate. What is the required fuel reserve?

A—2 hours at normal cruise speed in a no wind condition fuel consumption.
B—2 hours at normal cruise fuel consumption.
C—30 minutes, plus 10 percent of the total flight time.

No person may dispatch a turbojet-powered airplane to an airport for which no alternate is available unless it has enough fuel, considering wind and other weather conditions, to fly to that airport and thereafter to fly for at least 2 hours at normal cruising fuel consumption. (PLT413, AA.I.G.K4) — 14 CFR §121.645

Answers

8269 [A] 8271 [A] 8272 [B] 8276 [B]

ATM, ADX

8273. The fuel reserve required for a turbine-engine-powered (other than turbopropeller) supplemental air carrier airplane upon arrival over the most distant alternate airport outside the 48 contiguous United States is

A—30 minutes at holding speed, at 1,500 feet over the airport.
B—30 minutes, over the airport, at 1,500 feet, at cruising speed.
C—2 hours at the normal cruising fuel consumption rate.

For any flag air carrier, supplemental air carrier, or commercial operator operation outside the 48 contiguous United States or District of Columbia, no person may release for flight or takeoff a turbine engine-powered airplane (other than a turbopropeller-powered airplane) unless, considering wind and other weather conditions expected, it has enough fuel:

1. *To fly to and land at the airport to which it was released;*
2. *After that, to fly for a period of 10% of the total time required to fly from the airport of departure to and land at, the airport to which it was released;*
3. *After that, to fly to and land at the most distant alternate airport specified in the flight release, if an alternate is required; and*
4. *After that, to fly for 30 minutes at holding speed at 1,500 feet above the alternate airport (or destination airport if no alternate is required) under standard temperature conditions.*

(PLT413, AA.I.G.K4) — 14 CFR §121.645

ATM, ADX

8270. What is the fuel reserve requirement for a commercially operated reciprocating-engine-powered airplane flying within the 48 contiguous United States upon arrival at the most distant alternate airport specified in the flight release? Enough fuel to fly

A—30 minutes plus 15 percent of total time required to fly at normal cruising consumption to the alternate.
B—to fly for 90 minutes at normal cruising fuel consumption.
C—45 minutes at normal cruising fuel consumption.

No person may release for flight or takeoff a nonturbine or turbopropeller-powered airplane unless, considering the wind and other weather conditions expected, it has enough fuel to:

1. *Fly to the airport to which it was released;*
2. *Thereafter, to fly to and land at the most distant alternate airport specified in the flight release; and*
3. *Thereafter, to fly for 45 minutes at normal cruising fuel consumption.*

(PLT413, AA.I.G.K4) — 14 CFR §121.643

ATM, ADX

8277. The fuel reserve required for a reciprocating-engine-powered supplemental air carrier airplane upon arrival at the most distant alternate airport during a flight in the 48 contiguous United States is

A—45 minutes at normal cruising fuel consumption.
B—the fuel required to fly to the alternate, plus 10 percent.
C—3 hours at normal cruising fuel consumption.

No person may release for flight or takeoff a nonturbine or turbopropeller-powered airplane unless, considering the wind and other weather conditions expected, it has enough fuel to:

1. *Fly to the airport to which it was released;*
2. *Thereafter, to fly to and land at the most distant alternate airport specified in the flight release; and*
3. *Thereafter, to fly for 45 minutes at normal cruising fuel consumption.*

(PLT413, AA.I.G.K4) — 14 CFR §121.643

ATM, ADX

8274. Upon arriving at the most distant airport, what is the fuel reserve requirement for a turbopropeller flag air carrier airplane?

A—90 minutes at holding altitude and speed fuel consumption or 30 minutes plus 15 percent of cruise fuel consumption, whichever is less.
B—45 minutes at holding altitude.
C—30 minutes plus 15 percent of the total time required, or 90 minutes at normal cruise, whichever is less.

Answers

8273 [A] 8270 [C] 8277 [A] 8274 [C]

No person may dispatch or takeoff in a flag air carrier nonturbine or turbopropeller-powered airplane unless, considering the wind and other weather conditions expected, it has enough fuel:

1. *To fly to and land at the airport to which it is dispatched;*
2. *Thereafter, to fly to and land at the most distant alternate airport specified in the dispatch release; and*
3. *Thereafter to fly for 30 minutes plus 15% of numbers 1 and 2 above, or to fly for 90 minutes at normal cruising fuel consumption, whichever is less.*

(PLT413, AA.I.G.K4) — 14 CFR §121.641

ATM, ADX

8275. The fuel reserve required, for a turbopropeller supplemental air carrier airplane upon the arrival at a destination airport for which an alternate airport is not specified, is

A—3 hours at normal consumption, no wind condition.
B—3 hours at normal cruising fuel consumption.
C—2 hours at normal cruising fuel consumption.

No supplemental air carrier or commercial operator may release a nonturbine or turbopropeller-powered airplane to an airport for which no alternate is specified unless it has enough fuel, considering wind and weather conditions expected, to fly to that airport and thereafter to fly for 3 hours at normal cruising fuel consumption. (PLT413, AA.I.G.K4) — 14 CFR §121.643

Carriage of Passengers and Cargo

Before takeoff all the passengers must be briefed on:

- Smoking,
- the location of emergency exits,
- the use of seatbelts,
- the location and use of any required means of emergency flotation.

After the seatbelt sign has been turned off in flight, the passengers must be briefed to keep their seatbelts fastened while seated. In addition to the required briefings, passengers must be provided with printed cards that contain diagrams of and methods of operating the emergency exits and the use of other emergency equipment. Before flight is conducted above FL250, a crewmember must instruct the passengers on the necessity of using oxygen in the event of cabin depressurization, and must point out to them the location and demonstrate the use of the oxygen dispensing equipment.

Each passenger two years old and older must have their own seat or berth and approved seatbelt. During takeoff and landing, all passengers must be in their seat with their seatbelts fastened. A child under two may be held by an adult. During the enroute portion of a flight, two passengers may share a seatbelt while seated in a multiple lounge or divan seat.

There are certain persons who have to be admitted to the flight deck in flight (such as crewmembers, FAA inspectors, etc.) and certain others who may be admitted (e.g., deadheading crew), but the pilot-in-command has emergency authority to exclude any person from the flight deck in the interest of safety. In what is commonly known as the "sterile cockpit rule," crewmembers are required to refrain from nonessential activities during critical phases of flight. As defined in the regulation, critical phases of flight are all ground operations involving taxi, takeoff, and landing, and all other flight operations below 10,000 feet except cruise flight. Nonessential activities include such activities as eating, reading a newspaper, or chatting.

Law enforcement officers may carry firearms on board an air carrier flight if their duties so require. Except in an emergency, the carrier should be given at least one hour prior notice that a person carrying a deadly weapon is going to be on the flight. If a passenger is carrying a firearm in their checked

Answers

8275 [B]

baggage, the weapon must be unloaded and the bag locked. The passenger must retain the key to the bag. The bag must be stowed in a portion of the aircraft that is inaccessible to both the passenger and to crewmembers in flight.

Prisoners are sometimes carried on air carrier flights. The prisoners are always escorted and no more than one prisoner who is classified as "maximum risk" can be allowed on the aircraft. Certain rules apply to the carriage of prisoners. These include:

- The prisoner and escort must be boarded before all other passengers and must stay on board until all other passengers have deplaned.
- The prisoner and escort must sit in the most rearward passenger seats and the escort must sit between the prisoner and the aisle.
- The carrier may serve the prisoner and the escort food and beverages, but neither of them may be served alcohol.

If a person who appears to be intoxicated creates a disturbance on a flight, a report of the incident must be made to the Administrator (the FAA) within 5 days.

Certain passengers may be carried on an all-cargo flight without the carrier having to comply with all the passenger-carrying rules. Passengers carried on an all-cargo flight must have a seat with an approved seatbelt in the cargo compartment. They must have access to the pilot compartment or to an exit. The pilot-in-command must be able to notify them when they must have their seatbelt fastened and when smoking is prohibited. They must receive an emergency briefing from a crewmember prior to takeoff. The pilot-in-command may authorize the passenger to be admitted to the flight crew compartment.

Cargo (including carry-on baggage) may be carried in the passenger compartment of an aircraft if certain conditions are met. If the cargo is carried in an approved cargo bin, it can be located anywhere in the passenger compartment. The bin:

- Must withstand the load factor required of passenger seats multiplied by 1.15.
- May not be installed in a position that restricts access to or use of any required emergency exit, or of the aisle in the passenger cabin.
- Must be completely enclosed and made of material that is at least flame resistant.

If the cargo is not placed in an approved cargo bin it must be located aft of a bulkhead or divider (i.e., not aft of a passenger) and it must meet certain other requirements. These include:

- It must be properly secured by a safety belt or other tie down.
- It must be packaged or covered in a manner so as to avoid injury to occupants of the passenger cabin.
- It must not impose an excessive load on the floor or seat structures of the aircraft.
- Its location must not restrict access to or use of the aisle, any regular exit or any required emergency exit.
- Its location must not obscure any passenger's view of the "seatbelt," "no smoking," or required "exit" signs unless an auxiliary sign is installed.

Each person who has duties concerning the handling or carriage of dangerous articles or magnetized materials must have completed a training course within the preceding 12 calendar months.

ALL
8131. A certificate holder is notified that a person specifically authorized to carry a deadly weapon is to be aboard an aircraft. Except in an emergency, how long before loading that flight should the air carrier be notified?

A—Notification is not required, if the certificate holder has a security coordinator.
B—A minimum of 1 hour.
C—A minimum of 2 hours.

The certificate holder, except in an emergency, must be given at least 1 hour notice when an authorized person intends to have a weapon accessible in flight. (PLT498, AA.I.G.S1) — 49 CFR §1544.219

ALL
8137. When a passenger notifies the certificate holder prior to checking baggage that an unloaded weapon is in the baggage, what action is required by regulation regarding this baggage?

A—The baggage may be carried in the flightcrew compartment, provided the baggage remains locked, and the key is given to the pilot-in-command.
B—The baggage must remain locked and carried in an area that is inaccessible to the passenger, and only the passenger retains the key.
C—The baggage must remain locked and stored where it would be inaccessible, and custody of the key shall remain with a designated crewmember.

No certificate holder may knowingly permit any person to transport any unloaded firearm in checked baggage unless the baggage in which it is carried is locked and only the passenger checking the baggage retains the key or combination. The baggage containing the firearm must be carried in an area, other than the flight crew compartment, that is inaccessible to passengers. (PLT498, AA.I.G.S1) — 49 CFR §1544.203(f)

Answers (A) and (C) are incorrect because the baggage containing the unloaded firearm will be carried in the baggage area, and only the passenger checking the baggage retains the key.

ALL
9763. What is meant by "sterile cockpit"?

A—All preflight checks are complete and the aircraft is ready for engine starting.
B—Crewmembers refrain from nonessential activities during critical phases of flight.
C—Crewmembers are seated and buckled at their required stations.

Commonly known as the "sterile cockpit rule," 14 CFR §121.542 requires flight crewmembers to refrain from nonessential activities during critical phases of flight. As defined in the regulation, critical phases of flight are all ground operations involving taxi, takeoff, and landing, and all other flight operations below 10,000 feet except cruise flight. Nonessential activities include such activities as eating, reading a newspaper, or chatting. (PLT498, AA.I.E.K8) — 14 CFR §121.542

ALL
9763-1. Under 14 CFR Part 121, when may nonessential communications take place below 10,000 feet?

A—In VMC conditions.
B—Before the final approach fix.
C—During cruise flight.

Commonly known as the sterile cockpit rule, 14 CFR §121.542 requires flight crewmembers to refrain from nonessential activities during critical phases of flight. As defined in the regulation, critical phases of flight are all ground operations involving taxi, takeoff, and landing, and all other flight operations below 10,000 feet except cruise flight. Nonessential activities include such activities as eating, reading a newspaper, or chatting. (PLT498, AA.I.G.K4) — 14 CFR §121.542

ALL
8132. When a person in the custody of law enforcement personnel is scheduled on a flight, what procedures are required regarding boarding of this person and the escort?

A—They shall be boarded before all other passengers board, and deplaned after all the other passengers have left the aircraft.
B—They shall be boarded after all other passengers board, and deplaned before all the other passengers leave the aircraft.
C—They shall board and depart before the other passengers.

When a person in custody of law enforcement is to be carried on a flight, the prisoner and escort must be boarded before any other passengers and deplaned after all other passengers have deplaned. (PLT325, AA.I.G.S1) — 49 CFR §1544.221(f)(1)

Answers

8131 [B]	8137 [B]	9763 [B]	9763-1 [C]	8132 [A]

ALL

8136. Which applies to the carriage of a person in the custody of law enforcement personnel?

A—The air carrier is not allowed to serve beverages to the person in custody or the law enforcement escort.
B—No more than one person considered to be in the maximum risk category may be carried on a flight, and that person must have at least two armed law enforcement escorts.
C—The person in custody must be seated between the escort and the aisle.

No more than one passenger, of whom the certificate holder has been notified as being in a maximum risk category, can be carried on an airplane. (PLT325, AA.I.G.S1) — 49 CFR §1544.221(c)(2), (d)(3)

ATM, ADX

8225. Which announcement must be made if the seat belt sign will be turned off during flight?

A—Clearly explain the location of the fire extinguishers and emergency exits.
B—Passenger should keep their seat belts fastened while seated.
C—Passengers are free to leave their seats once the seat belt sign is turned off.

After each takeoff, immediately before or immediately after turning the seat belt sign off, an announcement shall be made that passengers should keep their seat belts fastened, while seated, even when the seat belt sign is off. (PLT384, AA.I.G.K4) — 14 CFR §121.571

ATM, ADX

8181. A passenger briefing by a crewmember shall be given, instructing passengers on the necessity of using oxygen in the event of cabin depressurization, prior to flights conducted above

A—FL200.
B—FL240.
C—FL250.

Before flight is conducted above FL250, a crewmember shall instruct the passengers on the necessity of using oxygen in the event of cabin depressurization, and shall point out to them the location and demonstrate the use of the oxygen dispensing equipment. (PLT438, AA.I.A.K11) — 14 CFR §121.333

ATM, ADX

8153. When may two persons share one approved safety belt in a lounge seat?

A—When one is an adult and one is a child under 3 years of age.
B—Only during the en route flight.
C—During all operations except the takeoff and landing portion of a flight.

No person may operate an airplane unless there are available during the takeoff, enroute flight, and landing an approved seatbelt for separate use by each person on board the airplane who has reached his/her second birthday, except that two persons occupying a berth may share one approved seatbelt and two persons occupying a multiple lounge or divan seat may share one approved seatbelt during en route flight only. (PLT465, AA.I.G.K4) — 14 CFR §121.311

Answer (A) is incorrect because the regulations do not specify an age of persons sharing a seatbelt on a lounge seat. Sharing a seatbelt in a lounge seat can only be done during the enroute portion of the flight. Answer (C) is incorrect because two persons may share one seatbelt in a lounge seat only during the enroute portion of the flight, which excludes taxi and takeoff as well as landing.

ATM, ADX

8244. The pilot-in-command has emergency authority to exclude any and all persons from admittance to the flight deck

A—except a FAA inspector doing enroute checks.
B—in the interest of safety.
C—except persons who have authorization from the certificate holder and the FAA or NTSB.

The pilot-in-command has the emergency authority to exclude anyone from the flight deck in the interest of safety. (PLT444, AA.I.G.K4) — 14 CFR §121.547

Answers (A) and (C) are incorrect because persons who have specific authorization of the certificate holder and FAA inspectors may be admitted to the flight deck except when excluded in an emergency.

Answers

8136 [B] 8225 [B] 8181 [C] 8153 [B] 8244 [B]

ATM, ADX

8233. If an intoxicated person creates a disturbance aboard an air carrier aircraft, the certificate holder must submit a report, concerning the incident, to the Administrator within

A—7 days.
B—5 days.
C—48 hours.

If an intoxicated person causes an incident on the aircraft the certificate holder shall, within 5 days, report that incident to the Administrator. (PLT366, AA.I.G.K4) — 14 CFR §121.575

ATM, ADX

8234. When carrying a passenger aboard an all-cargo aircraft, which of the following applies?

A—The passenger must have access to a seat in the pilot compartment.
B—The pilot-in-command may authorize the passenger to be admitted to the crew compartment.
C—Crew-type oxygen must be provided for the passenger.

When a passenger is allowed on an all-cargo flight, the pilot-in-command may authorize admittance to the flight deck. (PLT444, AA.I.G.K4) — 14 CFR §121.583

Answer (A) is incorrect because the seat does not have to be on the flight deck, but there must be an approved seat with an approved seatbelt for each person. Answer (C) is incorrect because crew-type oxygen is not required for passengers. It is only required that the person be briefed on the use of oxygen and emergency oxygen equipment.

ATM, ADX

8139. What requirement must be met regarding cargo that is carried anywhere in the passenger compartment of an air carrier airplane?

A—The bin in which the cargo is carried may not be installed in a position that restricts access to, or use of, any exit.
B—The bin in which the cargo is carried may not be installed in a position that restricts access to, or use of, any aisle in the passenger compartment.
C—The container or bin in which the cargo is carried must be made of material which is at least flash resistant.

Cargo may be carried anywhere in the passenger compartment if it is carried in an approved cargo bin. The bin must meet the following requirements:

1. *The bin must be able to withstand the load factors and emergency landing conditions applicable to the passenger seats of the airplane in which it is installed, multiplied by a factor of 1.15;*
2. *The cargo bin may not be installed in a position that restricts access to or use of any required emergency exit, or of the aisle in the passenger compartment;*
3. *The bin must be fully enclosed and made of material that is at least flame resistant.*

(PLT385, AA.I.G.K4) — 14 CFR §121.285

Answer (A) is incorrect because the bin may not be installed in a position that restricts access to or use of any required emergency exit. Answer (C) is incorrect because the bin must be fully enclosed and made of material that is at least flame resistant.

ATM, ADX

8175. Which restriction applies to a cargo bin in a passenger compartment? The bin

A—may have an open top if it is placed in front of the passengers and the cargo is secured by a cargo net.
B—must withstand the load factor required of passenger seats, multiplied by 1.15, using the combined weight of the bin and the maximum weight of the cargo that may be carried in the bin.
C—must be constructed of flame retardant material and fully enclosed.

Cargo may be carried anywhere in the passenger compartment if it is carried in an approved cargo bin. The bin must meet the following requirements:

1. *The bin must be able to withstand the load factors and emergency landing conditions applicable to the passenger seats of the airplane in which it is installed, multiplied by a factor of 1.15;*
2. *The cargo bin may not be installed in a position that restricts access to or use of any required emergency exit, or of the aisle in the passenger compartment;*
3. *The bin must be fully enclosed and made of material that is at least flame resistant.*

(PLT385, AA.I.G.K4) — 14 CFR §121.285

Answers (A) and (C) are incorrect because the cargo bin must be fully enclosed, and be constructed of materials that are at least flame resistant.

Answers

8233 [B]   8234 [B]   8139 [B]   8175 [B]

ATM, ADX

8138. What restrictions must be observed regarding the carrying of cargo in the passenger compartment of an airplane operated under 14 CFR Part 121?

A—All cargo must be separated from the passengers by a partition capable of withstanding certain load stresses.
B—All cargo must be carried in a suitable flame resistant bin and the bin must be secured to the floor structure of the airplane.
C—Cargo may be carried aft of a divider if properly secured by a safety belt or other tiedown having enough strength to eliminate the possibility of shifting.

Cargo may be carried aft of a bulkhead or divider in any passenger compartment provided the cargo is restrained to required load factors, and it is properly secured by a safety belt or other tiedown having enough strength to eliminate the possibility of shifting under all normally anticipated flight and ground conditions. (PLT385, AA.I.G.K4) — 14 CFR §121.285

Answers (A) and (B) are incorrect because cargo may be carried in the passenger compartment if it is properly covered and secured so as not to be a hazard.

Part 135 Carriage of Passengers and Cargo Requirements

ATS, RTC

8007. Where must a certificate holder keep copies of completed load manifests and for what period of time?

A—1 month at its principal operations base, or at a location approved by the Administrator.
B—30 days at its principal operations base, or another location used by it and approved by the Administrator.
C—30 days, at the flight's destination.

The certificate holder shall keep copies of completed load manifests for at least 30 days at its principal operations base, or at another location used by it and approved by the Administrator. (PLT400, AA.I.G.K5) — 14 CFR §135.63

ATS, RTC

8008. Which is NOT a required item on the load manifest?

A—List of passenger names and the weight of each.
B—Aircraft registration number or flight number.
C—Identification of crewmembers and their crew position.

The load manifest must be prepared before each takeoff and must include:

1. *The number of passengers;*
2. *The total weight of the loaded aircraft;*
3. *The maximum allowable takeoff weight for that flight;*
4. *The center of gravity limits;*
5. *The center of gravity of the loaded aircraft;*
6. *The registration number of the aircraft or flight number;*
7. *The origin and destination; and*
8. *Identification of crewmembers and their crew position assignments.*

(PLT440, AA.I.G.K5) — 14 CFR §135.63

ATS, RTC

8009. Who is responsible for the preparation of a required load manifest?

A—PIC or the Dispatcher.
B—Company official designated by the Administrator.
C—The certificate holder.

For multi-engine aircraft, each certificate holder is responsible for the preparation and accuracy of a load manifest. (PLT440, AA.I.G.K5) — 14 CFR §135.63

ATS, RTC

8032. Which restriction must be observed regarding the carrying of cargo in the passenger compartment?

A—It is packaged or covered to avoid possible injury to occupants.
B—All cargo must be carried in a suitable bin and secured to a passenger seat or the floor structure of the aircraft.
C—Cargo carried in passenger seats must be forward of all passengers.

Answers

8138 [C] 8007 [B] 8008 [A] 8009 [C] 8032 [A]

No person may carry cargo, including carry-on baggage, in or on any aircraft unless one of the three following criteria is met:

1. *It is carried in an approved cargo rack, bin or compartment;*
2. *It is secured by approved means; or*
3. *If number 1 or 2 is not met, then all of the following are met:*
   a. *For cargo, it is properly secured by a safety belt or other tie-down having enough strength to eliminate the possibility of shifting under all normally anticipated flight and ground conditions, or for carry-on baggage, it is restrained so as to prevent its movement during air turbulence;*
   b. *It is packaged or covered to avoid possible injury to occupants;*
   c. *It does not impose any load on seats or on the floor structure that exceeds the load limitation for those components;*
   d. *It is not located in a position that obstructs the access to, or use of, any required emergency or regular exit, or the use of the aisle between the crew and passenger compartment, or located in a position that obscures any passenger's view of the "seatbelt" sign, "no smoking" sign or any required exit sign;*
   e. *It is not carried directly above seated occupants.*

(PLT385, AA.I.G.K5) — 14 CFR §135.87

ATS, RTC

9720. A person whose duties include the handling or carriage of dangerous articles and/or magnetized materials must have satisfactorily completed an approved training program established by the certificate holder within the previous

A—6 calendar months.
B—12 calendar months.
C—24 calendar months.

No certificate holder may use any person or perform, and no person may perform, any assigned duties and responsibilities for the handling or carriage of hazardous materials unless within the preceding 12 calendar months that person has satisfactorily completed initial or recurrent training in an appropriate training program established by the certificate holder. (PLT407, AA.I.G.K5) — 14 CFR, SFAR 99

ATS, RTC

8039. In a cargo-only operation, cargo must be loaded

A—so that it does not obstruct the aisle between the crew and cargo compartments.
B—in such a manner that at least one emergency or regular exit is available to all occupants.
C—in such a manner that at least one emergency or regular exit is available to all crewmembers, if an emergency occurs.

For cargo-only operations, the cargo must be loaded so at least one emergency or regular exit is available to provide all occupants of the aircraft a means of unobstructed exit from the aircraft if an emergency occurs. (PLT385, AA.I.G.K5) — 14 CFR §135.87

ATS, RTC

8040. Which is a requirement governing the carriage of cargo, on a scheduled passenger flight?

A—Cargo must be carried in an approved rack, bin, or compartment.
B—Cargo not stowed in an approved bin must be secured by a safety belt or approved tiedown device.
C—All cargo carried in the passenger compartment must be packaged and stowed ahead of the foremost seated passenger.

No person may carry cargo, including carry-on baggage, in or on any aircraft unless one of the three following criteria is met:

1. *It is carried in an approved cargo rack, bin or compartment;*
2. *It is secured by approved means; or*
3. *If number 1 or 2 is not met, then all of the following are met:*
   a. *For cargo, it is properly secured by a safety belt or other tie-down having enough strength to eliminate the possibility of shifting under all normally anticipated flight and ground conditions, or for carry-on baggage, it is restrained so as to prevent its movement during air turbulence;*
   b. *It is packaged or covered to avoid possible injury to occupants;*
   c. *It does not impose any load on seats or on the floor structure that exceeds the load limitation for those components;*
   d. *It is not located in a position that obstructs the access to, or use of, any required emergency or*

Answers

9720 [B] 8039 [B] 8040 [B]

regular exit, or the use of the aisle between the crew and passenger compartment, or located in a position that obscures any passenger's view of the "seatbelt" sign, "no smoking" sign or any required exit sign;

e. It is not carried directly above seated occupants.

(PLT385, AA.I.G.K5) — 14 CFR §135.87

ATS, RTC

8041. Which is a requirement governing the carriage of carry-on baggage?

A—All carry-on baggage must be restrained so that its movement is prevented during air turbulence.
B—Carry-on baggage must be stowed under the seat in front of the owner.
C—Pieces of carry-on baggage weighing more than 10 pounds must be carried in an approved rack or bin.

No person may carry cargo, including carry-on baggage, in or on any aircraft unless one of the three following criteria is met:

1. *It is carried in an approved cargo rack, bin or compartment;*
2. *It is secured by approved means; or*
3. *If number 1 or 2 is not met, then all of the following are met:*
   a. *For cargo, it is properly secured by a safety belt or other tie-down having enough strength to eliminate the possibility of shifting under all normally anticipated flight and ground conditions, or for carry-on baggage, it is restrained so as to prevent its movement during air turbulence;*
   b. *It is packaged or covered to avoid possible injury to occupants;*
   c. *It does not impose any load on seats or on the floor structure that exceeds the load limitation for those components;*
   d. *It is not located in a position that obstructs the access to, or use of, any required emergency or regular exit, or the use of the aisle between the crew and passenger compartment, or located in a position that obscures any passenger's view of the "seatbelt" sign, "no smoking" sign or any required exit sign;*
   e. *It is not carried directly above seated occupants.*

(PLT385, AA.I.G.K5) — 14 CFR §135.87

ATS, RTC

8042. If carry-on baggage or cargo is carried in the passenger compartment, it must be

A—stowed ahead of the foremost seated passengers and secured by approved means.
B—placed in an approved rack, bin, or compartment installed in the aircraft.
C—so located that it does not obstruct the access to, or the use of, any required emergency or regular exit.

No person may carry cargo, including carry-on baggage, in or on any aircraft unless one of the three following criteria is met:

1. *It is carried in an approved cargo rack, bin or compartment;*
2. *It is secured by approved means; or*
3. *If number 1 or 2 is not met, then all of the following are met:*
   a. *For cargo, it is properly secured by a safety belt or other tie-down having enough strength to eliminate the possibility of shifting under all normally anticipated flight and ground conditions, or for carry-on baggage, it is restrained so as to prevent its movement during air turbulence;*
   b. *It is packaged or covered to avoid possible injury to occupants;*
   c. *It does not impose any load on seats or on the floor structure that exceeds the load limitation for those components;*
   d. *It is not located in a position that obstructs the access to, or use of, any required emergency or regular exit, or the use of the aisle between the crew and passenger compartment, or located in a position that obscures any passenger's view of the "seatbelt" sign, "no smoking" sign or any required exit sign;*
   e. *It is not carried directly above seated occupants.*

(PLT385, AA.I.G.K5) — 14 CFR §135.87

ATS, RTC

8043. The load manifest must be prepared prior to each takeoff for

A—any aircraft with a passenger seating capacity of 10 seats or more.
B—any aircraft with more than one engine.
C—all helicopters and large aircraft operated by a commuter air carrier.

For multi-engine aircraft, each certificate holder is responsible for the preparation and accuracy of a load manifest. (PLT440, AA.I.G.K5) — 14 CFR §135.63

Answers

8041 [A] 8042 [C] 8043 [B]

Emergency Equipment and Operations

Certain emergency equipment must be carried on every air carrier airplane. This equipment includes fire extinguishers, megaphones, first aid kits, and a crash ax. All this equipment must:

- Be inspected regularly.
- Be readily accessible to the crew and, for items carried in the passenger cabin, to the passengers.
- Be clearly identified and marked with its method of operation (this applies to any containers in which the equipment is carried).

Only one crash ax is required on the airplane and must be carried on the flight deck. At least one hand fire extinguisher must be carried on the flight deck. The number of extinguishers carried in the cabin is determined by the number of installed passenger seats. The following table applies.

Minimum Number of Hand Fire Extinguishers in the Passenger Cabin:

Passenger Seating Capacity	Extinguishers Required
6 through 30	1
31 through 60	2
61 through 200	3
201 through 300	4
301 through 400	5
401 through 500	6
501 through 600	7
601 or more	8

The number of megaphones carried on the airplane is determined by the number of installed passenger seats. On airplanes with a seating capacity of 60 through 99 passengers, one megaphone must be carried in the most rearward location in the passenger cabin that is readily accessible to a normal flight attendant seat. On airplanes with a seating capacity of 100 or more seats, one megaphone must be carried at the rear of the cabin and another megaphone must be carried at the front of the cabin.

Passenger carrying airplanes must have an emergency exit light system. This system must be operable manually from both the flight crew station and from a point in the passenger compartment readily accessible to a flight attendant. When the system is armed it must come on automatically with the interruption of the airplane's normal electrical power. The exit lights must be armed or turned on during taxiing, takeoff and landing. Every emergency exit (other than an over wing exit) that is more than 6 feet from the ground must have a means of assisting occupants to the ground in the event of an emergency evacuation. The most common means of complying with this requirement is an inflatable slide that deploys automatically when the door is opened. If such an automatic escape slide is installed, it must be armed during taxi, takeoff and landing. If any required emergency exit for passengers is located in other than the passenger compartment (such as the flight deck), the door separating the compartments must be latched open during takeoff and landing.

A public address system and a separate crewmember interphone system must be installed on all airplanes with a seating capacity of more than 19 seats.

Each crewmember on a flight must have a flashlight in good working order readily available.

When operating at flight altitudes above 10,000 feet there must be enough oxygen for all crewmembers for the entire flight at those altitudes, and in no event less than a 2-hour supply.

When operating at flight altitudes above FL410 each flight crewmember on flight deck duty must have an oxygen mask, within immediate reach, so designed that it can be rapidly placed on his/her face. This is commonly referred to as a "quick-donning" oxygen mask. To meet the requirements, regulations require that the mask be designed so that it can be put on the user's face within 5 seconds. If, while operating above FL410, one pilot leaves his/her station, the other pilot must put on his/her oxygen mask.

Above FL410 one pilot must wear his/her mask at all times. Notice that the rule applies only to the pilots. Above FL250 the flight engineer need only have a quick-donning mask readily available. *Note:* For Part 135 operations one pilot must wear the oxygen mask above FL350.

The oxygen requirements for passengers vary with the type of aircraft, but oxygen must be provided to all passengers for the entire time the cabin altitude is above 15,000 feet.

Passengers on turbine powered airplanes must be supplied oxygen according to the following schedule.

- For flights at cabin pressure altitudes above 10,000 feet, up to and including 14,000 feet, there must be enough oxygen to supply 10% of the passengers for any time at those altitudes in excess of 30 minutes.
- For flights at cabin pressure altitudes above 14,000 feet, up to and including 15,000 feet, there must be enough oxygen for 30% of the passengers for the entire time at those altitudes.
- For flights at cabin pressure altitudes above 15,000 feet there must be enough oxygen for all the passengers for the entire time of flight at those altitudes.

The amount of oxygen carried for passengers in the event of loss of pressurization varies depending on the ability of the airplane to make an emergency descent. If the aircraft can make a descent to 14,000 feet within 4 minutes it may carry less oxygen than would otherwise be required.

A certain amount of **first aid oxygen** must be carried for passengers on flights that operate above FL250. The amount of oxygen is determined by the actual number of passengers but in no case may there be less than 2 oxygen dispensing units.

On extended over-water flights (more than 50 nautical miles from the shoreline) the airplane must have a life preserver for each occupant of the aircraft, and enough life rafts to accommodate all the occupants. This equipment must be easily accessible in the event of a ditching.

- Each life raft and each life vest must be equipped with a survivor locator light.
- A survival kit, appropriate for the route flown, must be attached to each life raft.
- There must be at least one portable emergency radio transmitter carried on the airplane.

When flag or supplemental carriers or commercial operators fly over uninhabited terrain, the following survival equipment must be carried on the airplane:

- Suitable pyrotechnic signaling devices.
- A survival-type emergency locator transmitter.
- Enough survival kits, appropriate for the route flown, for all the occupants of the airplane.

In an emergency situation that requires immediate decision and action, the pilot-in-command may take any action that he/she considers necessary under the circumstances. In such a case the PIC may deviate from prescribed procedures and methods, weather minimums and regulations to the extent required in the interest of safety. In an emergency situation arising during flight that requires immediate decision and action by an aircraft dispatcher, the dispatcher must advise the pilot-in-command of the emergency, shall ascertain the decision of the pilot-in-command and shall have that decision recorded.

If the dispatcher cannot communicate with the pilot, he/she shall declare an emergency and take any action he/she considers necessary under the circumstances.

Each certificate holder (airline) must, for each type and model of airplane, assign to each category of crewmember, as appropriate, the necessary functions to be performed in an emergency or in a situation requiring emergency evacuation. The certificate holder must describe those duties in its manual.

Crewmembers must receive emergency training annually on several subjects. Besides the training they must perform emergency drills in:

- The operation of emergency exits;
- Hand fire extinguishers;
- The emergency oxygen system and protective breathing equipment;
- Donning, inflation and use of individual flotation equipment; and
- Ditching.

Crewmembers who serve above 25,000 feet must receive instruction in hypoxia, respiration and decompression. Crewmembers must actually operate certain emergency equipment in their recurrent training at least once every 24 months.

The pilot-in-command must make a report to the appropriate ground radio station of the stoppage of an engine's rotation in flight (due either to failure or intentional shutdown) as soon as practicable and must keep that station informed of the progress of the flight. As a general rule, when an engine fails or is shutdown, the pilot-in-command must land the aircraft at the nearest suitable airport, time-wise, at which a safe landing can be made. There is an exception to the rule for airplanes with 3 or more engines. If only 1 engine has failed, the pilot-in-command may elect to continue to a more distant airport (possibly the original destination) if this is considered as safe as landing at the nearest suitable airport.

The certificate holder must provide a **cockpit check procedure** (checklist) for each type of aircraft it operates. The procedures must include each item necessary for flight crewmembers to check for safety before starting engines, taking-off or landing, and in engine and systems emergencies. The procedures must be designed so that a flight crewmember will not need to rely on memory for items to be checked. The flight crew must use the approved check procedure.

Whenever a pilot-in-command or dispatcher exercises emergency authority, he/she shall keep the appropriate ATC facility and dispatch centers fully informed of the progress of the flight. The person declaring the emergency shall send a written report of any deviation through the air carrier's operations manager to the Administrator (FAA). A dispatcher must send this report within 10 days after the date of the emergency. A pilot-in-command must send the report within 10 days after returning to his/her home base.

When ATC gives priority to an aircraft in an emergency, the chief of the ATC facility involved may ask the pilot-in-command to submit a report. If asked, the pilot-in-command must submit a detailed written report to the ATC facility manager within 48 hours. This is required whether or not there was a deviation from regulations.

ALL

9636. (Refer to Legend 12.) Newport News/Williamsburg Intl is a 14 CFR Part 139 airport. The Chart Supplements U.S. (previously A/FD) contains the following entry: ARFF Index A. What is the minimum number of aircraft rescue and fire fighting vehicles, and the type and amount of fire fighting agents that the airport should have?

A—Two vehicles and 600 pounds dry chemical (DC) or Halon 1211 or 500 pounds of DC plus 100 gallons of water.
B—One vehicle and 500 pounds of dry chemical (DC) or Halon 1211 or 450 pounds DC plus 100 gallons of water.
C—One vehicle and 500 pounds of dry chemical (DC) or Halon 1211 or 350 pounds DC and 1,000 gallons of water.

FAA Legend 15 indicates that an index A airport must have at least one vehicle with either 500 pounds of dry chemical or Halon 1211, or 450 pounds of dry chemical plus 100 gallons of water. (PLT143, AA.II.A.K5) — Chart Supplements U.S.

ALL

9668. (Refer to Legend 12 and Figure 185A.) McCarran Intl (LAS) is a 14 CFR Part 139 airport. What is the minimum number of aircraft rescue and fire fighting vehicles and the type and amount of fire fighting agents that the airport should have?

A—Three vehicles and 500 pounds of dry chemical (DC) or HALON 1211, or 450 pounds of DC and 100 gallons of water plus 6,000 gallons of water.
B—Two vehicles and 600 pounds dry chemical (DC) or Halon 1211 or 500 pounds of DC plus 4,000 gallons of water.
C—Three vehicles and 500 pounds of dry chemical (DC) or Halon 1211 or 450 pounds DC plus 3,000 gallons of water.

Using FAA Figure 185A, the second line of the McCarran entry indicates it is an ARFF (Aircraft Rescue and Fire Fighting) index E airport. FAA Legend 12 indicates that an index E airport must have the requirements for Index A plus 6,000 gallons of water. An index E airport must have at least three vehicles and 500 pounds of dry chemical (DC) or HALON 1211, or 450 pounds of DC and 100 gallons of water plus 6,000 gallons of water. (PLT143, AA.II.A.K5) — Chart Supplements U.S.

ATM, ATS, RTC

9379. During an emergency, a pilot-in-command does not deviate from a 14 CFR rule but is given priority by ATC. To whom or under what condition is the pilot required to submit a written report?

A—To the manager of the General Aviation District Office within 10 days.
B—To the manager of the facility in control within 10 days.
C—Upon request by ATC, submit a written report within 48 hours to the ATC manager.

Each pilot-in-command who (though not deviating from a rule) is given priority by ATC in an emergency, shall, if requested by ATC, submit a detailed report of that emergency within 48 hours to the chief of that ATC facility. (PLT383, AA.I.G.K2) — 14 CFR §91.123

ATM, ATS, RTC

9388. When may ATC request a detailed report on an emergency even though a rule has not been violated?

A—When priority has been given.
B—Anytime an emergency occurs.
C—When the emergency occurs in controlled airspace.

Each pilot-in-command who (though not deviating from a rule) is given priority by ATC in an emergency, shall, if requested by ATC, submit a detailed report of that emergency within 48 hours to the chief of that ATC facility. (PLT044, AA.I.G.K2) — 14 CFR §91.123

Answer (B) is incorrect because a pilot may deviate from a regulation in order to meet an emergency, as long as ATC is notified immediately. A detailed report is usually not required if ATC priority was not given. Answer (C) is incorrect because, regardless of the type of airspace in which it occurs, only when priority has been given may a detailed report be requested by ATC.

ATM, ATS, RTC

9388-1. If available, what action could a pilot of an air carrier take if they violate a federal regulation because of an air traffic control direction?

A—File a report through the Voluntary Disclosure Reporting Program (VDRP).
B—File a report through the Aviation Safety Action Program (ASAP).
C—File a report through the Flight Operational Quality Assurance Program (FOQA).

Answers

9636 [B] 9668 [A] 9379 [C] 9388 [A] 9388-1 [A]

The VDRP is used to collect information on 14 CFR regulation violations to improve the overall safety of the NAS. (PLT044, AA.I.E.K13) — AC 00-58

Answer (B) is incorrect because ASAP is used is to encourage employees of air carriers or repair stations to voluntarily report safety information that may be critical to identifying potential precursors to accidents. Answer (C) is incorrect because an FOQA program is used to reveal operational situations in which risk is increased in order to enable early corrective action before that risk results in an incident or accident.

ALL

9388-2. What is the purpose of a Flight Operational Quality Assurance (FOQA) program?

A—To identify pilots who are having problems operationally.
B—To identify aggregate information for error trends.
C—To provide accountability within the air carrier system.

FOQA is a voluntary safety program that is designed to make commercial aviation safer by allowing commercial airlines and pilots to share de-identified aggregate information with the FAA, so that the FAA can monitor national trends in aircraft operations and target its resources to address operational risk issues (e.g., flight operations, ATC, airports). (PLT044, AA.I.E.K13) — AC 120-82

ALL

9388-3. Your airline recently initiated a new safety partnership with the FAA utilizing the Aviation Safety Action Program (ASAP) for all pilots, flight attendants, dispatchers, and mechanics. What does ASAP encourage?

A—Encourages an employee to utilize an ASAP report after receiving a criminal substance abuse conviction so they do not face additional FAA enforcement.
B—Encourages operational situations in which risk is increased in order to enable early corrective action before that risk results in an incident or accident.
C—Encourages airline management to utilize ASAP reports and voluntarily report safety information to derive synergies and cost savings for the airline.

ASAP is used is to encourage employees of air carriers or repair stations to voluntarily report safety information that may be critical to identifying potential precursors to accidents. (PLT044, AA.I.E.K13) — AC 120-66

ATM, ADX

8177. Which requirement applies to emergency equipment (fire extinguishers, megaphones, first-aid kits, and crash ax) installed in an air carrier airplane?

A—All emergency equipment, must be readily accessible to the passengers.
B—Emergency equipment cannot be located in a compartment or area where it is not immediately visible to a flight attendant in the passenger compartment.
C—Emergency equipment must be clearly identified and clearly marked to indicate its method of operation.

Each item of required emergency equipment must be clearly identified and clearly marked to indicate its method of operation. (PLT404, AA.I.G.K4) — 14 CFR §121.309

Answers (A) and (B) are incorrect because the requirement is that the emergency equipment be "readily accessible" to the crew.

ATM, ADX

8176. Which factor determines the minimum number of hand fire extinguishers required for flight under 14 CFR Part 121?

A—Number of passengers and crewmembers aboard.
B—Number of passenger cabin occupants.
C—Airplane passenger seating accommodations.

The minimum number of hand fire extinguishers carried on an air carrier flight is determined by the seating capacity of the airplane. (PLT408, AA.I.A.K14) — 14 CFR §121.309

Answers (A) and (B) are incorrect because passenger capacity, not actual passenger count, determines the number of extinguishers required.

ATM, ADX

8160. Where should the portable battery-powered megaphone be located if only one is required on a passenger-carrying airplane?

A—The most forward location in the passenger cabin.
B—In the cabin near the over-the-wing emergency exit.
C—The most rearward location in the passenger cabin.

One megaphone must be installed on each airplane with a seating capacity of more than 60 and less than 100 passengers, at the most rearward location in the passenger cabin where it would be readily accessible to a normal flight attendant seat. (PLT462, AA.I.A.K14) — 14 CFR §121.309

Answers

9388-2 [B]	9388-3 [C]	8177 [C]	8176 [C]	8160 [C]

ATM, ADX

8161. How many portable battery-powered megaphones are required on an air carrier airplane with a seating capacity of 100 passengers on a trip segment when 45 passengers are carried?

A—Two; one at the forward end, and the other at the most rearward location in the passenger cabin.
B—Two; one at the most rearward and one in the center of the passenger cabin.
C—Two; one located near or accessible to the flightcrew, and one located near the center of the passenger cabin.

Two megaphones are required in the passenger cabin of each airplane with a seating capacity of more than 99 passengers, one installed at the forward end and the other at the rearward location where it would be readily accessible to a normal flight attendant seat. (PLT462, AA.I.A.K14) — 14 CFR §121.309

ATM, ADX

8162. How many portable battery-powered megaphones are required on an air carrier airplane with a seating capacity of 150 passengers on a trip segment when 75 passengers are carried?

A—Two; one located near or accessible to the flightcrew, and one located near the center of the passenger cabin.
B—Two; one at the most rearward and one in the center of the passenger cabin.
C—Two; one at the forward end, and the other at the most rearward location of the passenger cabin.

Two megaphones are required in the passenger cabin of each airplane with a seating capacity of more than 99 passengers, one installed at the forward end and the other at the rearward location where it would be readily accessible to a normal flight attendant seat. (PLT462, AA.I.A.K14) — 14 CFR §121.309

ATM, ADX

8144. The emergency lights on a passenger-carrying airplane must be armed or turned on during

A—taxiing, takeoff, cruise, and landing.
B—taxiing, takeoff, and landing.
C—takeoff, cruise, and landing.

Each emergency exit light must be armed or turned on during taxiing, takeoff, and landing. (PLT404, AA.I.G.K4) — 14 CFR §121.310

Answers (A) and (C) are incorrect because the emergency lights are not required to be armed or turned on during cruise.

ATM, ADX

8159. Federal Aviation Regulations require that interior emergency lights must

A—operate automatically when subjected to a negative G load.
B—be operable manually from the flightcrew station and a point in the passenger compartment.
C—be armed or turned on during taxiing and all flight operations.

The emergency exit light system must be operable from both the flight crew station and from a point in the passenger compartment that is readily accessible to a normal flight attendant seat. Each emergency exit light must be armed or turned on during taxiing, takeoff, and landing. (PLT404, AA.I.G.K4) — 14 CFR §121.310

Answer (A) is incorrect because interior emergency lights must operate automatically with the interruption of the airplane's normal electrical power. Answer (C) is incorrect because the interior emergency light system must only be armed during taxi, takeoff, and landing portions of the flight.

ATM, ADX

8157. If a passenger-carrying landplane is required to have an automatic deploying escape slide system, when must this system be armed?

A—For taxi, takeoff, and landing.
B—Only for takeoff and landing.
C—During taxi, takeoff, landing, and after ditching.

Each passenger-carrying landplane with an emergency exit (other than over-the-wing) that is more than 6 feet from the ground must have an approved means to assist the occupants in descending to the ground. An assisting means that deploys automatically must be armed during taxi, takeoffs, and landings. (PLT404, AA.I.G.K4) — 14 CFR §121.310

Answers

8161 [A] 8162 [C] 8144 [B] 8159 [B] 8157 [A]

ATM, ADX
8158. If there is a required emergency exit located in the flightcrew compartment, the door which separates the compartment from the passenger cabin must be

A—unlocked during takeoff and landing.
B—locked at all times, except during any emergency declared by the pilot-in-command.
C—latched open during takeoff and landing.

If it is necessary to pass through a doorway separating the passenger cabin from other areas to reach a required emergency exit from any passenger seat, the door must have means to latch it open, and the door must be latched open during each takeoff and landing. (PLT459, AA.I.G.K4) — 14 CFR §121.310

Answers (A) and (B) are incorrect because the door must always be latched open during takeoff and landing.

ATM, ADX
8178. A crewmember interphone system is required on which airplane?

A—A large airplane.
B—A turbojet airplane.
C—An airplane with more than 19 passenger seats.

No person may operate an airplane with a seating capacity of more than 19 passengers unless the airplane is equipped with a crewmember interphone system. (PLT462, AA.I.G.K4) — 14 CFR §121.319

Answers (A) and (B) are incorrect because the crewmember interphone system requirement is based upon the number of seats.

ATM, ADX
8179. An air carrier airplane must have an operating public address system if it

A—has a seating capacity of 19 passengers.
B—has a seating capacity for more than 19 passengers.
C—weighs more than 12,500 pounds.

No person may operate an airplane with a seating capacity of more than 19 passengers unless the airplane is equipped with an operating public address system. (PLT462, AA.I.G.K4) — 14 CFR §121.318

ATM, ADX
8235. Each crewmember shall have readily available for individual use on each flight a

A—key to the flight deck door.
B—certificate holder's manual.
C—flashlight in good working order.

Each crewmember shall, on each flight, have readily available for use a flashlight that is in good working order. (PLT405, AA.I.G.K4) — 14 CFR §121.549

ATM, ADX
8173. How much supplemental oxygen for emergency descent must a pressurized turbine-powered air transport airplane carry for each flight crewmember on flight deck duty when operating at flight altitudes above 10,000 feet?

A—A minimum of 2-hours' supply.
B—Sufficient for the duration of the flight above 8,000 feet cabin pressure altitude.
C—Sufficient for the duration of the flight at 10,000 feet flight altitude, not to exceed 1 hour and 50 minutes.

When operating at flight altitudes above 10,000 feet, the certificate holder shall supply enough oxygen for each crewmember for the entire flight at those altitudes and not less than a 2-hour supply for each flight crewmember on flight deck duty. (PLT438, AA.I.G.K4) — 14 CFR §121.331 and §121.333

ATM, ADX
8183. Each air carrier flight deck crewmember on flight deck duty must be provided with an oxygen mask that can be rapidly placed on his face when operating at flight altitudes

A—of FL260.
B—of FL250.
C—above FL250.

When operating at flight altitudes above flight level 250, each flight crewmember on flight deck duty must be provided with an oxygen mask so designed that it can be rapidly placed on his/her face from its ready position, properly secured, sealed, and supplying oxygen within 5 seconds; and so designed that after being placed on the face it does not prevent immediate communication between the flight crewmember and other crewmembers over the airplane intercom system. When not being used at flight altitudes above flight level 250, the mask must be kept ready for use and within immediate reach. (PLT438, AA.I.G.K4) — 14 CFR §121.333

Answers

8158 [C] 8178 [C] 8179 [B] 8235 [C] 8173 [A] 8183 [C]

ATM, ADX
8184. A flight crewmember must be able to don and use a quick-donning oxygen mask within

A—5 seconds.
B—10 seconds.
C—15 seconds.

When operating at flight altitudes above flight level 250, each flight crewmember on flight deck duty must be provided with an oxygen mask so designed that it can be rapidly placed on his/her face from its ready position, properly secured, sealed, and supplying oxygen within 5 seconds; and so designed that after being placed on the face it does not prevent immediate communication between the flight crewmember and other crewmembers over the airplane intercom system. When not being used at flight altitudes above flight level 250, the mask must be kept ready for use and within immediate reach. (PLT438, AA.I.G.K4) — 14 CFR §121.333

ATM, ADX
8155. If either pilot of an air carrier airplane leaves the duty station while flying at FL410, the other pilot

A—and the flight engineer shall put on their oxygen masks and breathe oxygen.
B—shall put on the oxygen mask and breathe oxygen.
C—must have a quick-donning type oxygen mask available.

When operating at flight altitudes above FL410 each flight crewmember on flight deck duty must have an oxygen mask, within immediate reach, so designed that it can be rapidly placed on his/her face. This is commonly referred to as a "quick-donning" oxygen mask. To meet the requirements, regulations require that the mask be designed so that it can be put on the user's face within 5 seconds. If, while operating above FL410, one pilot leaves his/her station, the other pilot must put on his/her oxygen mask. (PLT440, AA.I.G.K4) — 14 CFR §121.333

ATM, ADX
8156. If a turbine-engine-powered, pressurized airplane is not equipped with quick-donning oxygen masks, what is the maximum flight altitude authorized without one pilot wearing and using an oxygen mask?

A—FL200.
B—FL300.
C—FL250.

When operating at flight altitudes above flight level 250, one pilot at the controls of the airplane shall at all times wear and use an oxygen mask secured, sealed, and supplying oxygen, except that the one pilot need not wear and use an oxygen mask while at or below flight level 410 if each flight crewmember on flight deck duty has a quick-donning type oxygen mask. (PLT438, AA.I.G.K4) — 14 CFR §121.333

ATM, ADX
8187. What is the highest flight level that operations may be conducted without the pilot at the controls wearing and using an oxygen mask, while the other pilot is away from the duty station?

A—FL410.
B—FL250.
C—Above FL410.

If for any reason, at any time it is necessary for one pilot to leave the controls of the airplane when operating at flight altitudes above FL410, the remaining pilot at the controls shall put on and use his or her oxygen mask until the other pilot has returned to their duty station. (PLT438, AA.I.G.K4) — 14 CFR §121.333

ATM, ADX
8174. What is the passenger oxygen supply requirement for a flight, in a turbine-powered aircraft, with a cabin pressure altitude in excess of 15,000 feet? Enough oxygen for

A—each passengers for the entire flight above 15,000 feet cabin altitude.
B—30 percent of the passengers.
C—10 percent of the passengers for 30 minutes.

For flights at cabin pressure altitudes above 15,000 feet, the certificate holder must provide enough oxygen for each passenger carried during the entire flight at those altitudes. (PLT438, AA.I.G.K4) — 14 CFR §§121.327, 121.329

ATM, ADX
8186. For flights above which cabin altitude must oxygen be provided for all passengers during the entire flight at those altitudes?

A—15,000 feet.
B—16,000 feet.
C—14,000 feet.

For flights at cabin pressure altitudes above 15,000 feet, the certificate holder must provide enough oxygen for each passenger carried during the entire flight at those altitudes. (PLT438, AA.I.G.K4) — 14 CFR §§121.327, 121.329

Answers

8184 [A] 8155 [C] 8156 [C] 8187 [A] 8174 [A] 8186 [A]

ATM, ADX

8185. For a 2-hour flight in a reciprocating engine-powered airplane at a cabin pressure altitude of 12,000 feet, how much supplemental oxygen for sustenance must be provided? Enough oxygen for

A—30 minutes for 10 percent of the passengers.
B—10 percent of the passengers for 1.5 hours.
C—each passenger for 30 minutes.

For flight in reciprocating-engine-powered airplanes, at cabin pressure altitudes above 8,000 feet, up to and including 14,000 feet, each certificate holder shall provide enough oxygen for 30 minutes for 10% of the passengers. (PLT438, AA.I.G.K4) — 14 CFR §121.327

ATM, ADX

8182. The supplemental oxygen requirements for passengers when a flight is operated at FL250 is dependent upon the airplane's ability to make an emergency descent to a flight altitude of

A—10,000 feet within 4 minutes.
B—14,000 feet within 4 minutes.
C—12,000 feet within 4 minutes or at a minimum rate of 2,500 ft/min, whichever is quicker.

The supplemental oxygen requirements for passengers on pressurized aircraft is dependent upon the ability of the aircraft to descend to 14,000 feet within 4 minutes in the event of a loss of pressurization. (PLT438, AA.I.G.K4) — 14 CFR §121.333

ATM, ADX

8180. What is the minimum number of acceptable oxygen-dispensing units for first-aid treatment of occupants who might require undiluted oxygen for physiological reasons?

A—Two.
B—Four.
C—Three.

There must be an appropriate number of oxygen dispensing units for first aid treatment of passengers, but in no case less than 2. (PLT438, AA.I.G.K4) — 14 CFR §121.333

ATM, ADX

8164. Which emergency equipment is required for a flag air carrier flight between John F. Kennedy International Airport and London, England?

A—A life preserver equipped with an approved survivor locator light or other flotation device for the full seating capacity of the airplane.
B—An appropriately equipped survival kit attached to each required liferaft.
C—A self-buoyant, water resistant, portable survival-type emergency locator transmitter for each required liferaft.

No person may operate an airplane in extended overwater operations without having on the airplane the following equipment:

1. *A life preserver equipped with an approved survivor locator light for each occupant of the airplane;*
2. *Enough life rafts (each equipped with an approved survivor locator light) to accommodate the occupants of the airplane;*
3. *At least one pyrotechnic signaling device for each life raft;*
4. *One survival-type emergency locator transmitter;*
5. *A survival kit, appropriately equipped for the route to be flown, must be attached to each life raft.*

(PLT404, AA.I.G.K4) — 14 CFR §121.339

Answer (A) is incorrect because a life preserver or other flotation device for each occupant is required. The requirement is not based upon seating capacity. Answer (C) is incorrect because only one survival type emergency locator transmitter is required to be carried in the aircraft, not one for each life raft.

ATM, ADX

8166. Each large aircraft operating over water must have a life preserver for each

A—aircraft occupant.
B—seat on the aircraft.
C—passenger seat, plus 10 percent.

No person may operate an airplane in extended overwater operations without having on the airplane the following equipment:

1. *A life preserver equipped with an approved survivor locator light for each occupant of the airplane;*
2. *Enough life rafts (each equipped with an approved survivor locator light) to accommodate the occupants of the airplane;*
3. *At least one pyrotechnic signaling device for each life raft;*

Answers

8185 [A] 8182 [B] 8180 [A] 8164 [B] 8166 [A]

4. One survival-type emergency locator transmitter;

5. A survival kit, appropriately equipped for the route to be flown, must be attached to each life raft.

(PLT417, AA.I.G.K4) — 14 CFR §121.339

Answers (B) and (C) are incorrect because unlike some regulations that are based upon the number of seats in the aircraft, the number of life preservers required is based on the number of occupants for a particular flight.

ATM, ADX

8169. Life preservers required for overwater operations are stored

A—within easy reach of each passenger.
B—under each occupant seat.
C—within easy reach of each seated occupant.

The required life rafts, life preservers, and survival-type emergency locator transmitter must be easily accessible in the event of a ditching without appreciable time for preparatory procedures. (PLT417, AA.I.G.K4) — 14 CFR §121.339

ATM, ADX

8167. For a flight over uninhabited terrain, an airplane operated by a flag or supplemental air carrier must carry enough appropriately equipped survival kits for

A—all of the passengers, plus 10 percent.
B—all aircraft occupants.
C—all passenger seats.

Unless it has the following equipment, no flag or supplemental carrier or commercial operator may conduct an operation over an uninhabited area:

1. Suitable pyrotechnic signaling devices;

2. A survival-type emergency locator transmitter; and

3. Enough survival kits, appropriately equipped for the route to be flown, for the number of occupants of the airplane.

(PLT404, AA.I.G.K4) — 14 CFR §121.353

ATM, ADX

8168. When a supplemental air carrier is operating over an uninhabited area, how many appropriately equipped survival kits are required aboard the aircraft?

A—One for each passenger seat.
B—One for each passenger, plus 10 percent.
C—One for each occupant of the aircraft.

Unless it has the following equipment, no flag or supplemental carrier or commercial operator may conduct an operation over an uninhabited area:

1. Suitable pyrotechnic signaling devices;

2. A survival-type emergency locator transmitter; and

3. Enough survival kits, appropriately equipped for the route to be flown, for the number of occupants of the airplane.

(PLT404, AA.I.G.K4) — 14 CFR §121.353

ATM, ADX

8170. An airplane operated by a supplemental air carrier flying over uninhabited terrain must carry which emergency equipment?

A—Survival kit for each passenger.
B—Suitable pyrotechnic signaling devices.
C—Colored smoke flares and a signal mirror.

Unless it has the following equipment, no flag or supplemental carrier or commercial operator may conduct an operation over an uninhabited area:

1. Suitable pyrotechnic signaling devices;

2. A survival-type emergency locator transmitter; and

3. Enough survival kits, appropriately equipped for the route to be flown, for the number of occupants of the airplane.

(PLT404, AA.I.G.K4) — 14 CFR §121.353

ATM, ADX

8171. An airplane operated by a commercial operator flying over uninhabited terrain must carry which emergency equipment?

A—A signal mirror and colored smoke flares.
B—Survival kit for each passenger.
C—An approved survival-type emergency locator transmitter.

Unless it has the following equipment, no flag or supplemental carrier or commercial operator may conduct an operation over an uninhabited area:

1. Suitable pyrotechnic signaling devices;

2. A survival-type emergency locator transmitter; and

3. Enough survival kits, appropriately equipped for the route to be flown, for the number of occupants of the airplane.

(PLT402, AA.I.G.K4) — 14 CFR §121.353

Answers

8169 [C] 8167 [B] 8168 [C] 8170 [B] 8171 [C]

ATM, ADX

8172. An airplane operated by a flag air carrier operator flying over uninhabited terrain must carry which emergency equipment?

A—Suitable pyrotechnic signaling devices.
B—Colored smoke flares and a signal mirror.
C—Survival kit for each passenger.

Unless it has the following equipment, no flag or supplemental carrier or commercial operator may conduct an operation over an uninhabited area:

1. *Suitable pyrotechnic signaling devices;*
2. *A survival-type emergency locator transmitter; and*
3. *Enough survival kits, appropriately equipped for the route to be flown, for the number of occupants of the airplane.*

(PLT404, AA.I.G.K4) — 14 CFR §121.353

ATM, ADX

8245. If an aircraft dispatcher cannot communicate with the pilot of an air carrier flight during an emergency, the aircraft dispatcher should

A—take any action considered necessary under the circumstances.
B—comply with the company's lost aircraft plan.
C—phone the ARTCC where the flight is located and ask for a phone patch with the flight.

If the aircraft dispatcher cannot communicate with the pilot, he/she shall declare an emergency and take any action considered necessary under the circumstances. (PLT403, AA.I.G.K4) — 14 CFR §121.557

ATM, ADX

8198. Which 14 CFR Part 121 required document includes descriptions of the required crewmember functions to be performed in the event of an emergency?

A—Airplane Flight Manual.
B—Certificate holder's manual.
C—Pilot's Emergency Procedures Handbook.

Each certificate holder shall, for each type and model of airplane, assign to each category of required crewmember, as appropriate, the necessary functions to be performed in an emergency or a situation requiring emergency evacuation. The certificate holder shall describe in its manual the functions of each category of required crewmember. (PLT436, AA.I.G.K4) — 14 CFR §121.397

Answer (A) is incorrect because the Airplane Flight Manual may contain emergency procedures as a convenience, but they are not required by 14 CFR §121.141. Answer (C) is incorrect because an "Emergency Procedures Handbook" does not exist.

ATM, ADX

8200. The required crewmember functions that are to be performed in the event of an emergency shall be assigned by the

A—pilot-in-command.
B—air carrier's chief pilot.
C—certificate holder.

Each certificate holder shall, for each type and model of airplane, assign to each category of required crewmember, as appropriate, the necessary functions to be performed in an emergency or a situation requiring emergency evacuation. The certificate holder shall describe in its manual the functions of each category of required crewmember. (PLT374, AA.I.G.K4) — 14 CFR §121.397

Answer (A) is incorrect because, although the pilot-in-command may assign duties as necessary during an emergency, the required crewmember functions shall be assigned and described in the certificate holder's manual. Answer (B) is incorrect because the chief pilot does not have the authority to assign crewmember functions that are to be performed in the event of an emergency. Those functions shall be described in the certificate holder's manual.

ATM, ADX

8204. The air carrier must give instruction on such subjects as respiration, hypoxia, and decompression to crewmembers serving on pressurized airplanes operated above

A—FL180.
B—FL200.
C—FL250.

Crewmembers who serve in operations above 25,000 feet must receive instruction in respiration, hypoxia, and decompression. (PLT460, AA.I.G.K4) — 14 CFR §121.417

ATM, ADX

8218. How often must a crewmember actually operate the airplane emergency equipment, after initial training? Once every

A—6 calendar months.
B—12 calendar months.
C—24 calendar months.

Emergency drill requirements must be accomplished during initial training and once each 24 calendar months during recurrent training. (PLT407, AA.I.G.K4) — 14 CFR §121.417

Answers

8172 [A] 8245 [A] 8198 [B] 8200 [C] 8204 [C] 8218 [C]

ATM, ADX
8236. If an engine's rotation is stopped in flight, the pilot-in-command must report it, as soon as practicable, to the

A—appropriate ground radio station.
B—nearest FAA district office.
C—operations manager (or director of operations).

The pilot-in-command shall report each stoppage of engine rotation in flight to the appropriate ground radio station as soon as practicable and shall keep that station fully informed of the progress of the flight. (PLT366, AA.I.G.K4) — 14 CFR §121.565

ATM, ADX
8237. If it becomes necessary to shut down one engine on a domestic air carrier three-engine turbojet airplane, the pilot-in-command

A—must land at the nearest suitable airport, in point of time, at which a safe landing can be made.
B—may continue to the planned destination if approved by the company aircraft dispatcher.
C—may continue to the planned destination if this is considered as safe as landing at the nearest suitable airport.

If not more than one engine of an airplane that has three or more engines fails or its rotation is stopped, the pilot-in-command may proceed to an airport that he/she selects if, after considering the following, he/she decides that proceeding to that airport is as safe as landing at the nearest suitable airport. (PLT406, AA.I.G.K4) — 14 CFR §121.565

ATM, ADX
8241. What action shall the pilot-in-command take if it becomes necessary to shut down one of the two engines on an air carrier airplane?

A—Land at the airport which the pilot considers to be as safe as the nearest suitable airport in point of time.
B—Land at the nearest suitable airport in point of time at which a safe landing can be made.
C—Land at the nearest airport, including military, that has a crash and rescue unit.

Whenever an engine of an airplane fails or whenever the rotation of an engine is stopped to prevent possible damage, the pilot-in-command shall land the airplane at the nearest suitable airport, time-wise, at which a safe landing can be made. Note: There are no exceptions to this rule for two-engine airplanes. (PLT223, AA.I.G.K4) — 14 CFR §121.565

ATM, ADX
8163. In the event of an engine emergency, the use of a cockpit check procedure by the flightcrew is

A—encouraged; it helps to ensure that all items on the procedure are accomplished.
B—required by regulations to prevent reliance upon memorized procedures.
C—required by the FAA as a doublecheck after the memorized procedure has been accomplished.

Each certificate holder shall provide an approved cockpit check procedure for each type of aircraft. The approved procedures must include each item necessary for flight crewmembers to check for safety before starting engines, taking off, or landing, and in engine and systems emergencies. The procedures must be designed so that a flight crewmember will not need to rely upon memory for items to be checked. (PLT404, AA.I.G.K4) — 14 CFR §121.315

ATM, ADX
8240. When the pilot-in-command is responsible for a deviation during an emergency, the pilot should submit a written report within

A—10 days after the deviation.
B—10 days after returning home.
C—10 days after returning to home base.

A pilot-in-command declaring an emergency shall send a written report of any deviation, through the air carrier's director of operations, to the Administrator within 10 days after returning to the home base. (PLT403, AA.I.G.K4) — 14 CFR §121.557

ATM, ADX
8246. Who is required to submit a written report on a deviation that occurs during an emergency?

A—Pilot-in-command.
B—Dispatcher.
C—Person who declares the emergency.

The person declaring the emergency shall send a written report of any deviation, through the air carrier's director of operations, to the Administrator within 10 days. (PLT366, AA.I.G.K4) — 14 CFR §121.557

Answers

8236 [A]	8237 [C]	8241 [B]	8163 [B]	8240 [C]	8246 [C]

ADX
8239. An aircraft dispatcher declares an emergency for a flight and a deviation results. A written report shall be sent through the air carrier's operations manager by the

A—dispatcher to the FAA Administrator within 10 days of the event.
B—certificate holder to the FAA Administrator within 10 days of the event.
C—pilot-in-command to the FAA Administrator within 10 days of the event.

An aircraft dispatcher declaring an emergency shall send a written report of any deviation, through the air carrier's director of operations, to the Administrator within 10 days after the date of the emergency. (PLT394) — 14 CFR §121.557

ATM, ATS
8725. Bird strikes in flight will be reported to the

A—nearest state or federal wildlife office on company letterhead.
B—FAA on an FAA form 5200-7.
C—nearest FSS via telephone.

Pilots are urged to report any bird or other wildlife strike using FAA Form 5200–7, Bird/Other Wildlife Strike Report (Appendix 1). (PLT366, AA.I.G.K4) — AIM ¶7-4-3

Part 135 Oxygen Requirements

ATS
8020. Which is a requirement for flightcrew use of oxygen masks in a pressurized cabin airplane?

A—Both pilots at the controls shall use oxygen masks above FL350.
B—At altitudes above 25,000 feet MSL, if one pilot leaves the pilot duty station, the remaining pilot at the controls shall use an oxygen mask.
C—At altitudes above FL250, one of the two pilots at the controls shall use an oxygen mask continuously.

One pilot of a pressurized aircraft must wear an oxygen mask any time the aircraft is flown above 35,000 feet MSL. In addition, one pilot must wear an oxygen mask above a flight altitude of 25,000 feet MSL if the other pilot leaves the duty station. (PLT438, AA.I.G.K5) — 14 CFR §135.89

ATS
8022. Which is a requirement for pilot use of oxygen in a pressurized airplane?

A—The pilot at the controls shall use oxygen continuously any time the cabin pressure altitude is more than 12,000 feet MSL.
B—At FL250 and above, each pilot shall have an approved quick-donning oxygen mask.
C—At FL250 and above, the pilot at the controls must have an approved oxygen mask any time the other pilot is away from the duty station.

Each pilot of an unpressurized aircraft shall use oxygen continuously when flying:

1. *At altitudes above 10,000 feet through 12,000 feet MSL for that part of the flight at those altitudes that is more than 30 minutes duration; and*
2. *Above 12,000 feet MSL.*

Whenever a pressurized aircraft is operated with the cabin pressure altitude more than 10,000 feet MSL, each pilot shall comply with the rules for unpressurized aircraft.

Whenever a pressurized airplane is operated above 25,000 feet MSL flight altitude both pilots must have a "quick-donning"-type oxygen mask.

One pilot of a pressurized aircraft must wear an oxygen mask any time the aircraft is flown above 35,000 feet MSL. In addition, one pilot must wear an oxygen mask above a flight altitude of 25,000 feet MSL if the other pilot leaves the duty station. (PLT438, AA.I.G.K5) — 14 CFR §135.89

Answer (B) is incorrect because the regulation states "above 25,000 feet MSL." Answer (C) is incorrect because above 25,000 feet MSL, the pilot at the controls must wear an approved oxygen mask any time the other pilot is away from the duty station.

Answers

8239 [A] 8725 [B] 8020 [B] 8022 [A]

ATS

8055. The two pilot stations of a pressurized aircraft are equipped with approved quick-donning oxygen masks. What is the maximum altitude authorized if one pilot is not wearing an oxygen mask and breathing oxygen?

A—41,000 feet MSL.
B—35,000 feet MSL.
C—25,000 feet MSL.

One pilot of a pressurized aircraft must wear an oxygen mask any time the aircraft is flown above 35,000 feet MSL. (PLT438, AA.I.G.K5) — 14 CFR §135.89

ATS

8056. At altitudes above 10,000 feet through 12,000 feet MSL, each pilot of an unpressurized airplane must use supplemental oxygen for that part of the flight that is of a duration of more than

A—20 minutes.
B—30 minutes.
C—45 minutes.

Each pilot of an unpressurized aircraft shall use oxygen continuously when flying:

1. *At altitudes above 10,000 feet through 12,000 feet MSL for the part of the flight, at those altitudes, that is more than 30 minutes duration; and*
2. *Above 12,000 feet MSL.*

(PLT438, AA.I.G.K5) — 14 CFR §135.89

ATS

8072. A pressurized airplane being operated at FL330 can descend safely to 15,000 feet MSL in 3.5 minutes. What oxygen supply must be carried for all occupants other than the pilots?

A—60 minutes.
B—45 minutes.
C—30 minutes.

No person may operate a pressurized aircraft above 15,000 feet MSL unless it is equipped to supply oxygen to each occupant, other than the pilots, for 1 hour. This is reduced to a 30-minute supply if the aircraft, at all times during flight above 15,000 feet MSL, can safely descend to 15,000 feet within 4 minutes. (PLT438, AA.I.G.K5) — 14 CFR §135.157

ATS

8073. At what altitude, in an unpressurized airplane, must all passengers be supplied oxygen?

A—Above 12,000 feet MSL.
B—Above 14,000 feet MSL.
C—Above 15,000 feet MSL.

In unpressurized aircraft, at altitudes above 10,000 feet MSL through 15,000 feet MSL, oxygen must be available for 10% of the occupants, other than the pilots, for the part of the flight, at those altitudes, in excess of 30-minute duration. Above 15,000 feet MSL, oxygen must be available to all occupants, other than the pilots. (PLT438, AA.I.G.K5) — 14 CFR §135.157

ATS

8074. Between what altitudes must oxygen be available to at least 10 percent of the occupants, in an unpressurized airplane, other than the pilots?

A—Above 12,000 feet through 16,000 feet MSL, for any time period.
B—Above 10,000 feet through 15,000 feet MSL, if flight at those altitudes is of more than a 30-minute duration.
C—10,000 feet to 15,000 feet MSL, if flight at those altitudes is of more than a 30-minute duration.

In unpressurized aircraft, at altitudes above 10,000 feet MSL through 15,000 feet MSL, oxygen must be available for 10% of the occupants, other than the pilots, for that part of the flight at those altitudes in excess of 30-minute duration. Above 15,000 feet MSL, oxygen must be available to all occupants. (PLT438, AA.I.G.K5) — 14 CFR §135.157

ATS

8080. The oxygen requirements for occupants of a pressurized airplane operated at altitudes above FL250 is dependent upon the airplane's ability to descend safely to an altitude of

A—10,000 feet MSL in 4 minutes.
B—12,000 feet MSL at a minimum rate of 2,500 ft/min.
C—15,000 feet MSL in 4 minutes.

No person may operate a pressurized aircraft above 15,000 feet MSL unless it is equipped to supply oxygen to each occupant, other than the pilots, for 1 hour. This is reduced to a 30-minute supply if the aircraft, at all times during flight above 15,000 feet MSL, can safely descend to 15,000 feet within 4 minutes. (PLT438, AA.I.G.K5) — 14 CFR §135.157

Answers

8055 [B]	8056 [B]	8072 [C]	8073 [C]	8074 [B]	8080 [C]

ATS, RTC

8021. Above which altitude/flight level must at least one of the two pilots, at the controls of a pressurized aircraft (with quick-donning masks) wear a secured and sealed oxygen mask?

A—FL300.
B—FL350.
C—FL250.

One pilot of a pressurized aircraft must wear an oxygen mask any time the aircraft is flown above 35,000 feet MSL. (PLT438, AA.I.G.K5) — 14 CFR §135.89

ATS, RTC

8023. Which is a pilot requirement for oxygen?

A—Each pilot of a pressurized aircraft operating at FL180 and above shall have an approved quick-donning type oxygen mask.
B—On pressurized aircraft requiring a flightcrew of two pilots, both shall continuously wear oxygen masks whenever the cabin pressure altitude exceeds 12,000 feet MSL.
C—On unpressurized aircraft, flying above 12,000 feet MSL, pilots shall use oxygen continuously.

Each pilot of an unpressurized aircraft shall use oxygen continuously when flying:

1. *At altitudes above 10,000 feet through 12,000 feet MSL for that part of the flight at those altitudes that is more than 30 minutes duration; and*
2. *Above 12,000 feet MSL.*

(PLT438, AA.I.G.K5) — 14 CFR §135.89

Answer (A) is incorrect because quick-donning type oxygen masks are required above 25,000 feet MSL. Answer (B) is incorrect because both pilots should continuously use oxygen masks when the cabin pressure altitude is more than 10,000 feet MSL.

ATS, RTC

8024. Which requirement applies when oxygen is stored in liquid form?

A—Smoking is not permitted within 50 feet of stored liquid oxygen.
B—Liquefied oxygen is a hazardous material and must be kept in an isolated storage facility.
C—The equipment used to store liquid oxygen must be covered in the certificate holder's approved maintenance program.

When the oxygen is stored in the form of a liquid, the equipment must have been under the certificate holder's approved maintenance program since its purchase new, or since the storage container was last purged. (PLT438, AA.I.G.K5) — 14 CFR §135.91

ATS, RTC

8025. Which is a condition that must be met when a person is administered medical oxygen in flight?

A—The distance between a person using medical oxygen and any electrical unit must not be less than 5 feet.
B—A person using oxygen equipment must be seated to avoid restricting access to, or use of, any required exit.
C—A person being administered oxygen must be monitored by equipment that displays and records pulse and respiration.

Oxygen equipment must be stowed, and each person using the equipment must be seated, so as not to restrict access to or use of any required emergency or regular exit, or of the aisle in the passenger compartment. (PLT438, AA.I.G.K5) — 14 CFR §135.91

ATS, RTC

8030. Which is a requirement regarding the carriage and operation of oxygen equipment for medical use by passengers?

A—No person may smoke within 10 feet of oxygen storage and dispensing equipment.
B—When oxygen equipment is used for the medical treatment of a patient, the rules pertaining to emergency exit access are waived.
C—No person may connect oxygen bottles or any other ancillary equipment until all passengers are aboard the aircraft and seated.

No person may smoke within 10 feet of oxygen-dispensing equipment. (PLT438, AA.I.G.K5) — 14 CFR §135.91

Answers

8021 [B]	8023 [C]	8024 [C]	8025 [B]	8030 [A]

ATS, RTC

8031. If a certificate holder deviates from the provisions of regulations which pertain to medical use of oxygen by passengers, a complete report of the incident shall be sent to the FAA within

A—7 working days.
B—10 working days.
C—10 days of the deviation.

Each certificate holder who deviates from the provisions of the regulations pertaining to use of medical oxygen by passengers, must send a report of the deviation to the FAA Flight Standards District Office within 10 days excluding Saturdays, Sundays, and federal holidays. (PLT438, AA.I.G.K5) — 14 CFR §135.91

ATS, RTC

8081. An unpressurized aircraft with 20 occupants other than the pilots will be cruising at 14,000 feet MSL for 25 minutes. For how many, if any, of these occupants must there be an oxygen supply?

A—Five.
B—Two.
C—None.

In unpressurized aircraft, at altitudes above 10,000 feet MSL through 15,000 feet MSL, oxygen must be available for 10% of the occupants, other than the pilots, for the part of the flight, at those altitudes, in excess of 30-minutes duration. Above 15,000 feet MSL, oxygen must be available to all occupants, other than the pilots. (PLT438, AA.I.G.K5) — 14 CFR §135.157

ATS, RTC

9819. What are the oxygen requirements for passengers if operating at 14,000 feet?

A—30 minutes for each passenger.
B—available for 10% of the occupants.
C—available for 10% of the occupants other than the pilots.

In unpressurized aircraft at altitudes above 10,000 feet MSL through 15,000 feet MSL, oxygen must be available for 10% of the occupants, other than the pilots, for the part of the flight at those altitudes in excess of 30-minutes duration. Above 15,000 feet MSL, oxygen must be available to all occupants, other than the pilots. (PLT438, AA.I.G.K5) — 14 CFR §135.157

RTC

9638. (Refer to Figures 186, 187, 188, and 188A.) What are the passenger oxygen requirements on this 14 CFR Part 135 flight from Las Vegas to Provo?

A—When above 10,000 feet through 15,000 feet, oxygen must be supplied to at least 10 percent of the aircraft occupants, including the pilots.
B—Starting 30 minutes after climbing through 10,000 feet, 10 percent of the aircraft occupants until reaching cruise at 15,000 feet then all occupants must be supplied oxygen until descending below 15,000 feet, then 10 percent down to 10,000 feet.
C—Starting 30 minutes after climbing through 10,000 feet, 10 percent of the aircraft occupants, except pilots, must be supplied oxygen until descending below 10,000 feet.

No person may operate an unpressurized aircraft at altitudes prescribed in this section unless it is equipped with enough oxygen dispensers and oxygen to supply the pilots under §135.89(a) and to supply when flying—

1. *At altitudes above 10,000 feet through 15,000 MSL, oxygen to at least 10% of the occupants of the aircraft, other than pilots, for the part of the flight at those altitudes that is more than 30 minutes duration; and*
2. *Above 15,000 feet MSL, oxygen to each occupant of the aircraft other than the pilots.*

(PLT438) — 14 CFR §135.157

Answers

8031 [B] 8081 [C] 9819 [C] 9638 [C]

National Transportation Safety Board (NTSB)

Aircraft accident means an occurrence associated with the operation of an aircraft that takes place between the time any person boards the aircraft with the intention of flight, and the time all such persons have disembarked, and in which any person suffers death or serious injury, or in which the aircraft receives substantial damage.

Serious injury means any injury that:

- Requires hospitalization for more than 48 hours commencing within 7 days from the date the injury was received.
- Results in fracture of any bone (except simple fractures of fingers, toes or nose).
- Causes severe hemorrhages, nerve, muscle or tendon damage.
- Involves any internal organ.
- Involves second or third degree burns or any burns affecting more than 5% of the body surface.

Substantial damage means damage or failure that adversely affects the structural strength, performance or flight characteristics of the aircraft and that would normally require major repair or replacement of the affected component. Damage not considered substantial for accident reporting purposes are as follows: engine failure or damage limited to an engine if only one engine fails or is damaged, bent fairings or cowling, dented skin, small punctured holes in the skin or fabric, ground damage to rotor or propeller blades, and damage to the landing gear, wheels, tires, flaps, engine accessories, brakes or wing tips.

The operator of an aircraft must immediately notify the nearest National Transportation Safety Board field office if any of the following occur:

- Flight control system malfunction.
- An aircraft accident.
- Inability of any required flight crewmember to perform his normal flight duties as the result of injury or illness.
- Failure of structural components of a turbine engine excluding compressor and turbine blades and vanes.
- Inflight fire.
- Aircraft collide in flight.
- Damage to property, other than the aircraft, estimate to exceed $25,000 for repair or fair market value in the event of total loss whichever is less.
- Certain incidents on large, multi-engine airplanes.
- An aircraft is overdue and is believed to have been involved in an accident.

The operator of an aircraft must submit a written report of an aircraft accident within 10 days of the accident. The operator of an overdue aircraft must submit a written report within 7 days if the aircraft is still missing. The operator of an aircraft that was involved in an incident requiring immediate notification of the NTSB must submit a written report of the incident only if requested to do so by the NTSB.

ALL
8317. What period of time must a person be hospitalized before an injury may be defined by the NTSB as a "serious injury"?

A—72 hours; commencing within 10 days after date of injury.
B—48 hours; commencing within 7 days after date of the injury.
C—10 days, with no other extenuating circumstances.

"Serious injury" means any injury which requires hospitalization for more than 48 hours, commencing within 7 days from the date the injury was received. (PLT366, AA.I.G.K6) — NTSB §830.2

ALL
8319. Which of the following constitutes "substantial damage" according to NTSB Part 830?

A—Ground damage to landing gear, wheels, or tires.
B—Damage to wingtips (or rotor blades, in the case of a helicopter).
C—Failure of a component which would adversely affect the performance, and which would require replacement.

"Substantial damage" is defined as damage or failure which would adversely affect the structural strength, performance, or flight characteristics of the aircraft which would normally require major repair or replacement of the damaged component. (PLT395, AA.I.G.K6) — NTSB §830.2

Answer (A) is incorrect because ground damage to landing gear, wheels, or tires is not considered "substantial damage" for the purpose of NTSB Part 830. Answer (B) is incorrect because damage to wing tips (or rotorblades, in the case of a helicopter) is not considered "substantial damage" for the purpose of NTSB Part 830.

ALL
8320. Which of the following meets the requirements of a "serious injury" as defined by the NTSB?

A—A simple fracture of the nose or other extremity.
B—An injury which caused severe tendon damage.
C—First-degree burns over 5 percent of the body.

"Serious injury" includes severe tendon damage and second or third degree burns covering more than five percent of the body. (PLT395, AA.I.G.K6) — NTSB §830.2

Answer (A) is incorrect because simple fractures, such as of the finger, toe, or nose, are not considered a serious injury. Answer (C) is incorrect because only second and third degree burns or first degree burns over more than 5% of the body are defined as a serious injury. (First degree burns are less serious than second and third degree burns.)

ALL
8318. Within what time period should the nearest NTSB field office be notified when an aircraft is involved in an accident which results in substantial damage?

A—Immediately.
B—7 calendar days.
C—10 days.

The operator of an aircraft shall immediately, and by the most expeditious means available, notify the nearest NTSB field office when an aircraft accident occurs. (PLT366, AA.I.G.K6) — NTSB §830.5

ALL
8321. Which incident requires an immediate notification to NTSB?

A—Aircraft colliding on the ground.
B—Flight control system malfunction.
C—Damage to property, other than the aircraft, estimated to exceed $10,000.

The NTSB lists a flight control malfunction or failure as an incident requiring immediate notification to the field office. (PLT416, AA.I.G.K6) — NTSB §830.5

ALL
8322. Within how many days must the operator of an aircraft involved in an accident file a report to the NTSB?

A—3 days.
B—7 days.
C—10 days.

The NTSB requires a report to be filed within 10 days of the accident. (PLT366, AA.I.G.K6) — NTSB §830.15

ALL
8323. When is an operator of an aircraft, which has been involved in an incident, required to submit a report to the nearest field office of the NTSB?

A—Within 7 days.
B—Within 10 days.
C—Only if requested to do so by the NTSB.

An aircraft involved in an incident is required to file a report only on request from the NTSB. (PLT366, AA.I.G.K6) — NTSB §830.15

Answers

8317 [B]	8319 [C]	8320 [B]	8318 [A]	8321 [B]	8322 [C]
8323 [C]					

ALL
9836. Pilots and/or flightcrew members involved in near midair collision (NMAC) occurrences are urged to report each incident immediately

A—by cell phone to the nearest Flight Standards District Office, as this is an emergency.
B—to local law enforcement.
C—by radio or telephone to the nearest FAA ATC facility or FSS.

The primary purpose of the Near Midair Collision (NMAC) Reporting Program is to provide information for use in enhancing the safety and efficiency of the National Airspace System. Pilots and/or flightcrew members involved in NMAC occurrences are urged to report each incident immediately by radio or telephone to the nearest FAA ATC facility or FSS. (PLT526, AA.I.G.K6) — AIM ¶7-7-3

ALL
9836-1. What information is de-identified when a report is submitted through the Aviation Safety Reporting System (ASRS)?

A—Crew identity information when criminal offenses have occurred.
B—Crew identity information involving time-sensitive data.
C—Crew identity information when prompt NTSB reporting is required.

The ASRS is a voluntary, confidential, and non-punitive incident reporting system. All identifying information is removed from the report before the data is entered into the ASRS database. The FAA will not use reports submitted to this program (or information derived therefrom) in any enforcement action except information concerning accidents or criminal offenses which are wholly excluded from the program. (PLT526, AA.I.E.K13) — AC 00-46

Part 135 Regulations

ATS
8053. What aircraft operating under 14 CFR Part 135 are required to have a third gyroscopic bank-and-pitch indicator installed?

A—All airplanes that are turbojet powered.
B—All multiengine airplanes that require a two pilot flightcrew.
C—All turbine powered aircraft having a passenger seating capacity of 30 seats or more.

A third gyroscopic pitch-and-bank indicator is required on all turbojet-powered airplanes. (PLT405, AA.I.G.K5) — 14 CFR §135.149

ATS
8054. In airplanes where a third gyroscopic bank-and-pitch indicator is required, that instrument must

A—continue reliable operation for at least 30 minutes after the output of the airplane's electrical generating system falls below an optimum level.
B—be operable by a selector switch which may be actuated from either pilot station.
C—continue reliable operation for a minimum of 30 minutes after total failure of the electrical generating system.

A third gyroscopic pitch-and-bank indicator is required on all turbojet-powered airplanes. This indicator must be able to continue reliable operation for at least 30 minutes after the failure of the aircraft's electrical generating system. (PLT405, AA.I.G.K5) — 14 CFR §135.149

ATS
8069. In which airplanes is a Class A TAWS required?

A—All airplanes having a passenger seating configuration, excluding any pilot seat, of 10 seats or more.
B—Turbine-powered airplanes having a passenger seating configuration, excluding any pilot seat, of 10 seats or more.
C—Turbine-powered aircraft having a passenger seating configuration, including any pilot seat, of 10 seats or more.

No person may operate a turbine-powered airplane having a passenger seating configuration, excluding any pilot seat, of 10 seats or more unless it is equipped with a terrain awareness system (TAWS). (PLT139, AA.I.G.K5) — 14 CFR §135.154

Answers

9836 [C]	9836-1 [B]	8053 [A]	8054 [C]	8069 [B]

ATS

8075. Which airplanes must have a shoulder harness installed at each flight crewmember station?

A—All airplanes used in commuter air service, having a passenger seating configuration of 9, excluding any pilot seat.
B—All airplanes operating under 14 CFR Part 135, having a seating configuration for 10 persons.
C—All turbojet-powered airplanes.

No person may operate a turbojet aircraft or an aircraft having a passenger seating configuration, excluding any pilot seat, of 10 seats or more unless it is equipped with an approved shoulder harness installed for each flight crewmember station. (PLT464, AA.I.G.K5) — 14 CFR §135.171

ATS, ADX

8165. What emergency equipment is required for extended overwater operations?

A—A portable survival emergency locator transmitter for each liferaft.
B—A pyrotechnic signaling device for each life preserver.
C—A life preserver equipped with a survivor locator light, for each person on the airplane.

No person may operate an aircraft in extended overwater operations unless it carries an approved life preserver (easily accessible to each seated occupant) equipped with an approved survivor locator light for each occupant of the aircraft, and enough approved life rafts of a rated capacity and buoyancy to accommodate the occupants of the aircraft. An approved survival-type emergency locator transmitter must be attached to one of the life rafts. (PLT404, AA.I.G.K5) — 14 CFR §135.167

Answer (A) is incorrect because only one survival emergency locator transmitter is required to be carried on the airplane. Answer (B) is incorrect because one pyrotechnic signaling device is required for each life raft.

ATS

8088. If the weather forecasts do not require the listing of an alternate airport on an IFR flight, the airplane must carry sufficient fuel to fly to the destination airport and

A—make one missed approach and thereafter have a 45-minute reserve at normal cruising speed.
B—fly thereafter for 45 minutes at normal cruising speed.
C—fly for 45 minutes thereafter at normal cruise climb speed.

No person may operate an aircraft in IFR conditions unless it carries enough fuel (considering weather reports and forecasts) to:

1. *Complete the flight to the first airport of intended landing;*
2. *Fly from that airport to the alternate airport (if one is required); and*
3. *Fly after that for 45 minutes at normal cruising speed.*

(PLT413, AA.I.G.K5) — 14 CFR §135.223

ATS

8089. If the weather forecasts require the listing of an alternate airport on an IFR flight, the airplane must carry enough fuel to fly to the first airport of intended landing, then to the alternate, and fly thereafter for a minimum of

A—45 minutes at normal holding speed.
B—45 minutes at normal cruise speed and then complete an approach and landing.
C—45 minutes at normal cruise speed.

No person may operate an aircraft in IFR conditions unless it carries enough fuel (considering weather reports and forecasts) to:

1. *Complete the flight to the first airport of intended landing;*
2. *Fly from that airport to the alternate airport (if one is required); and*
3. *Fly after that for 45 minutes at normal cruising speed.*

(PLT413, AA.I.G.K5) — 14 CFR §135.223

ATS

8115. When computing the takeoff data for reciprocating powered airplanes, what is the percentage of the reported headwind component that may be applied to the "still air" data?

A—Not more than 150 percent.
B—Not more than 100 percent.
C—Not more than 50 percent.

When computing takeoff data not more than 50% of the reported headwind component may be taken into account. (PLT011, AA.I.B.K2b) — 14 CFR §135.389

Answers

8075 [C] 8165 [C] 8088 [B] 8089 [C] 8115 [C]

ATS
8116. When computing takeoff data, what is the percentage of the effective tailwind component which may be applied to the "still air" data?

A—Not less than 150 percent.
B—Not less than 100 percent.
C—Not more than 50 percent.

When computing takeoff data not less than 150% of the reported tailwind component may be taken into account. (PLT011, AA.I.B.K2b) — 14 CFR §135.389

ATS
8050. Which performance requirement applies to passenger-carrying land airplanes being operated over water?

A—Multiengine airplanes must be able to climb, with the critical engine inoperative, at least 50 ft/min at 1,500 feet above the surface.
B—Single-engine airplanes must be operated at an altitude that will allow them to reach land in case of engine failure.
C—Multiengine airplanes must be able to climb, with the critical engine inoperative, at least 100 ft/min at 1,000 feet above the surface.

No person may operate a land aircraft carrying passengers over water unless it is operated at an altitude that allows it to reach land in the case of engine failure. (PLT437, AA.I.G.K5) — 14 CFR §135.183

ATS
8051. What performance is required of a multiengine airplane with the critical engine inoperative, while carrying passengers for hire in IFR weather conditions?

A—Climb at least 100 ft/min at the highest MEA of the route to be flown or 5,000 feet MSL, whichever is higher.
B—Climb at least 50 ft/min at the MEA's of the route to be flown or 5,000 feet AGL, whichever is higher.
C—Climb at least 50 ft/min at the MEA's of the route to be flown or 5,000 feet MSL, whichever is higher.

No person may operate a multi-engine airplane carrying passengers Over-The-Top or in IFR conditions at a weight that will not allow it to climb, with the critical engine inoperative, at least 50 feet a minute when operating at the MEAs of the route to be flown or 5,000 feet MSL, whichever is higher. (PLT223, AA.I.G.K5) — 14 CFR §135.181

ATS
8792. The crewmember interphone system on a large turbojet-powered airplane provides a means of two-way communications between ground personnel and at least one of two flight crewmembers in the pilot compartment, when the aircraft is on the ground. The interphone station for use by ground personnel must be located so that those using the system from that station

A—are always visible, from within the airplane.
B—are able to avoid the intake areas of the engines.
C—may avoid visible detection from within the airplane.

The interphone system station for use by ground personnel must be so located that personnel using the system may avoid visible detection from within the airplane. (PLT462, AA.I.G.K5) — 14 CFR §135.150

ATS
8831. For which of these aircraft may part of the "clearway" distance, for a particular runway, be considered in computing the takeoff distance?

A—Passenger-carrying transport aircraft.
B—Turbine-engine-powered transport airplanes, certificated after September 30, 1958.
C—U.S. certified transport airplane, certificated before August 26, 1957.

"Clearway" may be used in computing the takeoff distance of turbine-engine-powered airplanes certificated after September 30, 1958. (PLT456, AA.I.G.K5) — 14 CFR §1.1

ATS
8832. What requirement must be met regarding cargo that is carried anywhere in the passenger compartment of a commuter air carrier airplane?

A—Cargo may not be carried anywhere in the rear of the passenger compartment.
B—The bin in which the cargo is carried may not be installed in a position that restricts access to, or use of the aisle between the crew and the passenger compartment.
C—The container or bin in which the cargo is carried must be made of material which is at least flash resistant.

No person may carry cargo, including carry-on baggage in an aircraft unless it is in an approved cargo rack, bin, or compartment, and it does not obstruct access to, or use of, the aisle between the passenger and crew compartment. (PLT385, AA.I.G.K5) — 14 CFR §135.87

Answers

8116 [A] 8050 [B] 8051 [C] 8792 [C] 8831 [B] 8832 [B]

ATS
8833. Information recorded during normal operation of a cockpit voice recorder in a multiengine turbine powered airplane

A—may all be erased or otherwise obliterated except for the last 30 minutes.
B—may all be erased or otherwise obliterated except for the last 30 minutes prior to landing.
C—may all be erased, prior to each flight, unless the NTSB has requested that it be kept for 60 days.

Information recorded more than 30 minutes earlier may be erased or obliterated. (PLT388, AA.I.G.K5) — 14 CFR §135.151

ATS
8842. An airplane, operated by a commuter air carrier, flying in extended overwater operations must carry enough approved liferafts of a rated capacity and buoyancy to accommodate the occupants of the aircraft. Each liferaft must be equipped with

A—one approved pyrotechnic signaling device.
B—colored smoke flares and a signal mirror.
C—one fishing kit for each person the raft is rated to carry.

Every aircraft flown in extended overwater operations must carry enough appropriately equipped life rafts to accommodate the occupants of the aircraft. Each raft must have an approved pyrotechnic signaling device (either smoke or flare type flare). (PLT082, AA.I.G.K5) — 14 CFR §135.167

Answer (B) is incorrect because the survival kit is not required to have colored smoke flares. Answer (C) is incorrect because the survival kit is only required to have one fishing kit per liferaft, not one per person.

ATS, RTC
8001. A certificate holder must have "exclusive use" of

A—at least one aircraft that meets the requirements of each kind of operation authorized in the Operations Specifications.
B—at least one aircraft that meets the requirements of at least one kind of operation authorized in the certificate holder's Operations Specifications.
C—at least one aircraft that meets the requirements of the specific operations authorized in the certificate holder's Operations Specifications.

Each certificate holder must have the exclusive use of at least one aircraft that meets the requirements for at least one kind of operation authorized in the certificate holder's operations specifications. (PLT454, AA.I.G.K5) — 14 CFR §135.25

ATS, RTC
8005. Where is the certificate holder required to list the name and title of each person authorized to exercise operational control for a particular flight?

A—Operations Specifications.
B—Attached to the load manifest.
C—Certificate holder's manual.

Each certificate holder is responsible for operational control and shall list in the manual the name and title of each person authorized to exercise operational control. (PLT282, AA.I.G.K5) — 14 CFR §135.77

ATS, RTC
8010. An aircraft being operated outside of the United States, over a foreign country, by a 14 CFR part 135 operator must comply with

A—the International Civil Aviation Organization (ICAO), Annex 3, Rules of the Air.
B—regulations of the foreign country.
C—rules of the U.S. State Department and the foreign country.

Each person operating an aircraft under Part 135 while operating outside the United States, shall comply with Annex 2, Rules of the Air, to the Convention of International Civil Aviation or the regulations of any foreign country, whichever applies. (PLT392, AA.I.G.K5) — 14 CFR §135.3

ATS, RTC
8011. Who is responsible for keeping copies of the certificate holder's manual up to date with approved changes or additions?

A—Each of the certificate holder's employees who are furnished a manual.
B—An employee designated by the certificate holder.
C—A representative of the certificate holder approved by the Administrator.

Each employee of the certificate holder to whom a manual (or appropriate portions of it) is furnished shall keep it up to date with changes and additions furnished to them. (PLT282, AA.I.G.K5) — 14 CFR §135.21

Answers

8833 [A]	8842 [A]	8001 [B]	8005 [C]	8010 [B]	8011 [A]

ATS, RTC

9807. No person may operate a U.S. registered civil aircraft

A—for which an AFM or RFM is required by part 21 section 21.5 unless there is a current, approved operator's manual available.
B—for which an AFM or RFM is required by part 21 section 21.5 unless there is a current, approved AFM or RFM available.
C—for which an AFM or RFM is required by part 21 section 21.5 unless there is a current, approved AFM or RFM available or the manual specified in part 135 section 135.19(b).

Per 14 CFR §21.5, with each airplane or rotorcraft not type certificated with an Airplane or Rotorcraft Flight Manual and having no flight time before March 1, 1979, the holder of a type certificate (including amended or supplemental type certificates) or the licensee of a type certificate must make available to the owner at the time of delivery of the aircraft a current approved Airplane or Rotorcraft Flight Manual. (PLT373, AA.I.G.S1) — 14 CFR §21.5

ATS, RTC

8013. What is the lowest altitude above the terrain that an autopilot may be used during en route operations, if the Airplane Flight Manual specifies a malfunction under cruise conditions?

A—1,000 feet.
B—500 feet.
C—100 feet.

Except for approaches, no person may use an autopilot at an altitude above the terrain which is less than 500 feet or less than twice the maximum altitude loss specified in the approved Aircraft Flight Manual or equivalent for a malfunction of the autopilot, whichever is higher. (PLT424, AA.I.G.K5) — 14 CFR §135.93

ATS, RTC

8033. Who may be allowed to carry a deadly weapon on board an aircraft operated under 14 CFR Part 135?

A—Official bodyguards attached to foreign legations.
B—Crewmembers and/or others authorized by the certificate holder.
C—Employees of a municipality or a state, or of the United States.

No person may carry a deadly weapon on a Part 135 flight except for:

1. *Officials or employees of a municipality or a state or of the United States, who are authorized to carry arms; or*
2. *Crewmembers and other persons authorized by the certificate holder to carry arms.*

(PLT440, AA.I.G.K5) — 14 CFR §135.119

ATS, RTC

8038. Which person may be carried aboard an aircraft without complying with the passenger-carrying requirements of 14 CFR Part 135?

A—An individual who is necessary for the safe handling of hazardous material on the aircraft.
B—A representative of the Administrator, traveling to attend a meeting.
C—A member of the United States diplomatic corps on an official courier mission.

The following persons may be carried on an aircraft without complying with the passenger-carrying rules of Part 135:

1. *A crewmember or other employee of the certificate holder;*
2. *A person necessary for the safe handling of animals on the aircraft;*
3. *A person necessary for the safe handling of hazardous materials;*
4. *A person performing duty as a security or honor guard accompanying a shipment made by or under the authority of the U.S. Government;*
5. *A military courier or a military route supervisor carried by a military cargo contract air carrier or commercial operator;*
6. *An authorized representative of the Administrator conducting an enroute inspection; or*
7. *A person, authorized by the Administrator, who is performing a duty connected with a cargo operation of the certificate holder.*

(PLT385, AA.I.G.K5) — 14 CFR §135.85

Answers

9807 [B] 8013 [B] 8033 [B] 8038 [A]

ATS, RTC

8004. If previous arrangements have not been made by the operator, where can the procedures for servicing the aircraft be found?

A—Certificate holder's maintenance manual.
B—Certificate holder's manual.
C—Pilot's Handbook.

The certificate holder's manual must contain procedures to be followed by the pilot-in-command to obtain maintenance, preventative maintenance, and servicing of the aircraft at a place where previous arrangements have not been made by the operator, when the pilot is authorized to so act for the operator. (PLT282, AA.I.G.K5) — 14 CFR §135.23

ATS, RTC

8006. Who is directly responsible for determining the status of each mechanical irregularity previously entered in the aircraft maintenance log?

A—Aircraft dispatcher.
B—Line maintenance supervisor.
C—The next pilot-in-command.

Before each flight, the pilot-in-command shall determine, if the pilot does not already know, the status of each irregularity entered in the maintenance log at the end of the preceding flight. (PLT374, AA.I.G.K5) — 14 CFR §135.65

ATS, RTC

8012. What document contains procedures that explain how the required return-to-service conditions have been met?

A—Maintenance manual.
B—Pilot's Handbook.
C—Certificate holder's manual.

The certificate holder's manual must include procedures for ensuring that the pilot-in-command knows that required airworthiness inspections have been made and that the aircraft has been returned to service in compliance with applicable maintenance requirements. (PLT375, AA.I.G.K5) — 14 CFR §135.23

ATS, RTC

8019. Procedures for keeping copies of the aircraft maintenance log in the aircraft and available to appropriate personnel shall be set forth in

A—the certificate holder's manual.
B—the maintenance procedures handbook.
C—the Operations Specifications.

Each certificate holder shall establish a procedure for keeping copies of the aircraft maintenance log in the aircraft for access by appropriate personnel and shall include that procedure in the manual. (PLT282, AA.I.G.K5) — 14 CFR §135.65

ATS, RTC

8093. If a certificate holder makes arrangements for another person to perform aircraft maintenance, that maintenance shall be performed in accordance with the

A—certificate holder's manual and 14 CFR Parts 43, 91, and 135.
B—provisions of a contract prepared by a certificate holder and approved by the supervising FAA district office.
C—provisions and standards as outlined in the certificate holder's manual.

The certificate holder shall ensure that any maintenance, preventative maintenance, or alteration that is performed by another person is performed under the certificate holder's manual and regulations. (PLT282, AA.I.G.K5) — 14 CFR §135.413

ATS, RTC

8112. Who is responsible for submitting a Mechanical Reliability Report?

A—Each certificate holder.
B—Director of maintenance at the facility that discovers the reportable condition.
C—Chief inspector at the facility where the condition is found.

The certificate holder is responsible for submitting required mechanical reliability reports. (PLT443, AA.I.G.K5) — 14 CFR §135.415

Answers

8004 [B]	8006 [C]	8012 [C]	8019 [A]	8093 [A]	8112 [A]

ATS, RTC

8014. The maximum altitude loss specified for malfunction of a certain autopilot under cruise conditions is 50 feet. What is the lowest altitude this autopilot may be used en route?

A—500 feet AGL.
B—550 feet AGL.
C—600 feet AGL.

Except for approaches, no person may use an autopilot at an altitude above the terrain which is less than 500 feet or less than twice the maximum altitude loss specified in the approved Aircraft Flight Manual or equivalent for a malfunction of the autopilot, whichever is higher. (PLT424, AA.I.G.K5) — 14 CFR §135.93

ATS, RTC

8015. The maximum altitude loss for a particular malfunctioning autopilot under approach conditions is 55 feet. If the TDZE is 571 feet and the MDA is 1,100 feet, to which minimum altitude may you use this autopilot?

A—626 feet MSL.
B—990 feet MSL.
C—1,050 feet MSL.

When using an instrument approach facility other than ILS, no person may use an autopilot at an altitude above the terrain that is less than 50 feet below the approved minimum descent altitude for that procedure, or less than twice the maximum loss specified in the approved Airplane Flight Manual or equivalent for malfunction of the autopilot under approach conditions, whichever is higher. (PLT424, AA.I.G.K5) — 14 CFR §135.93

ATS, RTC

8016. The maximum altitude loss for a malfunctioning autopilot with an approach coupler is 40 feet. To which minimum altitude may the autopilot be used during an ILS approach in less than basic VFR conditions?

A—40 feet AGL.
B—50 feet AGL.
C—80 feet AGL.

For ILS approaches, when reported weather is less than VFR, no person may use an autopilot with an approach coupler at an altitude that is less than 50 feet above the terrain, or the maximum altitude loss specified in the approved Airplane Flight Manual or equivalent, for the malfunction of the autopilot with an approach coupler, whichever is higher. (PLT424, AA.I.G.K5) — 14 CFR §135.93

ATS, RTC

8017. The maximum altitude loss for a malfunctioning autopilot without an approach coupler is 45 feet. If the MDA is 1,620 feet MSL and the TDZE is 1,294 feet, to which minimum altitude may you use the autopilot?

A—1,510 feet MSL.
B—1,339 feet MSL.
C—1,570 feet MSL.

When using an instrument approach facility other than ILS, no person may use an autopilot at an altitude above the terrain that is less than 50 feet below the approved minimum descent altitude for that procedure, or less than twice the maximum loss specified in the approved Airplane Flight Manual or equivalent for malfunction of the autopilot under approach conditions, whichever is higher. (PLT424, AA.I.G.K5) — 14 CFR §135.93

ATS, RTC

8037. The altitude loss for a particular malfunctioning autopilot with an approach coupler is 60 feet. If the reported weather is below basic VFR minimums and an ILS approach using the approach coupler is to be used, what minimum altitude may be used?

A—50 feet AGL.
B—55 feet AGL.
C—60 feet AGL.

For ILS approaches, when reported weather is less than VFR, no person may use an autopilot with an approach coupler at an altitude that is less than 50 feet above the terrain, or the maximum altitude loss specified in the approved Airplane Flight Manual or equivalent, for the malfunction of the autopilot with an approach coupler, whichever is higher. (PLT424, AA.I.G.K5) — 14 CFR §135.93

ATS, RTC

8045. During which time period must a required voice recorder of a passenger-carrying airplane be continuously operated?

A—From the beginning of taxi to the end of the landing roll.
B—From engine start at departure airport to engine shutdown at landing airport.
C—From the use of the checklist before the flight to completion of the final check at the end of the flight.

Answers

8014 [A]	8015 [C]	8016 [B]	8017 [C]	8037 [C]	8045 [C]

No person may operate a multi-engine, turbine-powered airplane or rotorcraft having a passenger seating configuration of 20 or more seats unless it is equipped with an approved cockpit voice recorder that:

1. *Is installed in compliance with Part 23, 25, 27 or 29 as applicable to Part 135; and*
2. *Is operated continuously from the use of the checklist before the flight to completion of the final check at the end of the flight.*

(PLT405, AA.I.G.K5) — 14 CFR §135.151

ATS, RTC

8046. An approved cockpit voice recorder is required equipment in

A—large turbine-powered airplanes having a maximum passenger capacity of 20 or more seats.
B—multiengine, turbine-powered airplanes having a passenger seating configuration of 20 or more seats.
C—all aircraft operated in commuter air carrier service having a passenger seating configuration of 20 seats or more.

No person may operate a multi-engine, turbine-powered airplane or rotorcraft having a passenger seating configuration of 20 or more seats unless it is equipped with an approved cockpit voice recorder. (PLT405, AA.I.G.K5) — 14 CFR §135.151

ATS, RTC

8047. Ilnformation recorded during normal operation of a cockpit voice recorder in a large turbine powered airplane

A—may be erased or otherwise obliterated except for the last 30 minutes prior to landing.
B—may all be erased or otherwise obliterated except for the last 30 minutes.
C—may all be erased, as the voice recorder is not required on an aircraft with reciprocating engines.

No person may operate a multi-engine, turbine-powered airplane or rotorcraft having a passenger seating configuration of 20 or more seats unless it is equipped with an approved cockpit voice recorder that:

1. *Is installed in compliance with Part 23, 25, 27 or 29 as applicable to Part 135; and*
2. *Is operated continuously from the use of the checklist before the flight to completion of the final check at the end of the flight.*

In complying with this section, information recorded more than 30 minutes earlier may be erased or otherwise obliterated. (PLT388, AA.I.G.K5) — 14 CFR §135.151

ATS, RTC

8048. Which aircraft must be equipped with an approved public address and crewmember interphone system?

A—All turbine-engine-powered aircraft having a seating configuration of more than 19 seats.
B—Aircraft having a passenger seating configuration, excluding any pilot seat, of more than 19 seats.
C—Multiengine aircraft having a passenger seating configuration of 10 seats or more.

No person may operate an aircraft having a passenger seating configuration, excluding any pilot seat, of more than 19 unless an approved public address and crew interphone system is installed. (PLT462, AA.I.G.K5) — 14 CFR §135.150

ATS, RTC

8052. To operate an aircraft with certain equipment inoperative under the provisions of a minimum equipment list, what document authorizing it must be issued to the certificate holder?

A—Letter of Authorization from the Regional Airworthiness Office authorizing such an operation.
B—Operations specifications issued by the FAA district office having certification responsibility.
C—Letter of Authorization issued by the FAA district office having certification responsibility.

No person may takeoff with inoperable instruments or equipment installed unless the following conditions are met:

1. *An approved Minimum Equipment List exists for that aircraft.*
2. *The certificate-holding district office has issued the certificate holder operations specifications authorizing operations in accordance with an approved Minimum Equipment List. The flight crew shall have direct access at all times prior to flight to all of the information contained in the approved Minimum Equipment List through printed or other means approved by the Administrator in the certificate holders operations specifications. An approved Minimum Equipment List, as authorized by the operations specifications, constitutes an approved change to the type design without requiring recertification*

(PLT428, AA.I.G.K5) — 14 CFR §135.179

Answers

8046 [B] 8047 [A] 8048 [B] 8052 [B]

ATS, RTC
8058. When a crash ax is required equipment on an aircraft, where should it be located?

A—In the flight crew compartment.
B—At a location inaccessible to the passengers during normal operations.
C—At a location accessible to both the crew and passengers during normal operations.

No person may operate an aircraft having a passenger seating configuration, excluding any pilot seat, of more than 19 seats unless it is equipped with a crash ax carried that is accessible to the crew but inaccessible to passengers during normal operations. (PLT404, AA.I.G.K5) — 14 CFR §135.177

ATS, RTC
8059. How many, if any, approved first aid kits are required on an aircraft having a passenger seating configuration of 20 seats and a passenger load of 14?

A—None.
B—One.
C—Two.

No person may operate an aircraft having a passenger seating configuration, excluding any pilot seat, of more than 19 seats unless it is equipped with one approved first aid kit for the treatment of injuries likely to occur in flight or in a minor accident. (PLT404, AA.I.G.K5) — 14 CFR §135.177

ATS, RTC
8060. An aircraft has a passenger seating configuration of 19 seats, excluding any pilot seats. How many, if any, approved first aid kits are required?

A—One.
B—Two.
C—None.

No person may operate an aircraft having a passenger seating configuration, excluding any pilot seat, of more than 19 seats unless it is equipped with one approved first aid kit for the treatment of injuries likely to occur in flight or in a minor accident. (PLT404, AA.I.G.K5) — 14 CFR §135.177

ATS, RTC
8061. Airborne weather radar equipment must be installed in large transport category aircraft, in the conterminous 48 United States,

A—that are engaged in passenger-carrying operations.
B—that are engaged in either cargo or passenger-carrying operations.
C—and be fully operational, although weather forecasts indicate no hazardous conditions.

No person may operate a large, transport category aircraft in passenger-carrying operations unless approved airborne weather radar equipment is installed in the aircraft. (PLT367, AA.I.G.K5) — 14 CFR §135.175

ATS, RTC
8062. In which aircraft, or under what conditions, is airborne thunderstorm detection equipment required?

A—Large multiengine turbine-powered aircraft having a passenger seating configuration of 19 seats or more being operated by a commuter air carrier.
B—Any aircraft having a passenger seating configuration of 19 seats or more that is engaged in passenger-carrying operations under IFR or at night.
C—Small aircraft having a passenger seating configuration of 10 seats or more, excluding any pilot seat, that are engaged in passenger-carrying operations.

No person may operate an aircraft that has a passenger seating configuration, excluding any pilot seat, of 10 seats or more in passenger-carrying operations unless the aircraft is equipped with either approved thunderstorm detection equipment or approved airborne weather radar equipment. (PLT367, AA.I.G.K5) — 14 CFR §135.173

Answers

8058 [B] 8059 [B] 8060 [C] 8061 [A] 8062 [C]

ATS, RTC
8070. When a ground proximity warning system is required under 14 CFR Part 135, it must

A—convey warnings of any deviation below glide slope and of excessive closure rate with the terrain.
B—convey warnings for excessive closure rates with the terrain but not for deviation from an ILS glide slope.
C—alert the pilot by an audible and visual warning signals when deviation above or below glide slope occurs.

An approved ground proximity warning system must convey warnings of excessive closure rates with the terrain and any deviations below glide slope by visual and audible means. (PLT139, AA.I.G.K5) — 14 CFR §135.154

ATS, RTC
8071. When a ground proximity warning system is required, it must

A—apply corrective control pressure when deviation below glide slope occurs.
B—incorporate a means of alerting the pilot when a system malfunction occurs.
C—incorporate a backup feature that activates automatically upon total failure of the aircraft's electrical generating system.

An approved ground proximity warning system must convey warnings of excessive closure rates with the terrain and any deviations below glide slope by visual and audible means. It must also incorporate a means of alerting the pilot when a malfunction occurs. (PLT139, AA.I.G.K5) — 14 CFR §135.154

ATS, RTC
8077. Which group of aircraft must have a shoulder harness installed at each flight crewmember station?

A—Aircraft having a passenger seating configuration, excluding any pilot seat, of 10 seats or more.
B—All passenger-carrying aircraft operating under 14 CFR Part 135, having a seating configuration for 10 persons.
C—Large aircraft being operated in commuter air service, having a passenger seating configuration of 9, excluding any pilot seat.

No person may operate a turbojet aircraft or an aircraft having a passenger seating configuration, excluding any pilot seat, of 10 seats or more unless it is equipped with an approved shoulder harness installed for each flight crewmember station. (PLT464, AA.I.G.K5) — 14 CFR §135.171

ATS, RTC
8078. Which is a requirement for life preservers during extended overwater operations? Each life preserver must be equipped with

A—a dye marker.
B—an approved survivor locator light.
C—one flashlight having at least two size "D" cells or equivalent.

No person may operate an aircraft in extended overwater operations unless it carries an approved life preserver equipped with an approved survivor locator light for each occupant of the aircraft. (PLT437, AA.I.G.K5) — 14 CFR §135.167

ATS, RTC
8079. In addition to fully-equipped liferafts and life preservers, what emergency equipment must be provided during extended overwater operations?

A—One water resistant, self-buoyant, portable survival-type emergency radio transmitter for each liferaft.
B—Each aircraft must have at least one liferaft, equipped with a survival-type emergency locator transmitter.
C—One pyrotechnic signaling device for each aircraft.

No person may operate an aircraft in extended overwater operations unless there is attached to one of the required life rafts, a survival-type emergency locator transmitter. (PLT437, AA.I.G.K5) — 14 CFR §135.167

Answers
8070 [A] 8071 [B] 8077 [A] 8078 [B] 8079 [B]

ATS, RTC

8057. A pilot may make an IFR departure from an airport that does not have an approved standard instrument approach procedure if

A—there is a departure alternate within 60 minutes and the weather there is above landing minimums.
B—the Administrator has issued Operations Specifications to the certificate holder approving the procedure.
C—the departure airport is within 30 minutes flying time of another airport that has an approved standard instrument approach procedure.

The Administrator may issue operations specifications to the certificate holder to allow it to depart at an airport that does not have an approved standard instrument approach procedure when the Administrator determines that it is necessary to make an IFR departure from that airport and that the proposed operations can be conducted safely. (PLT459, AA.I.G.K5) — 14 CFR §135.215

ATS, RTC

8063. Assuming the required ceiling exists, an alternate for the destination airport is not required under 14 CFR 135 if, for at least 1 hour before and after the ETA, the forecast visibility is at least

A—5 miles, or 3 miles more than the lowest applicable visibility minimums for the instrument approach procedure to be used, whichever is greater.
B—3 miles, or 2 miles more than the lowest applicable visibility minimums for the instrument approach procedure to be used, whichever is greater.
C—3 nautical miles, or 2 nautical miles more than the lowest applicable visibility minimums for the approach procedure to be used, which ever is greater.

An alternate airport need not be designated if the ceiling criteria is met and the visibility is forecast to be at least 3 miles or 2 miles more than the lowest applicable visibility minimums, whichever is the greater, for the instrument approach procedure to be used at the destination airport. (PLT379, AA.I.G.K5) — 14 CFR §135.223

ATS, RTC

8064. A pilot may not designate an airport as an alternate unless the weather reports, or forecasts, or any combination of them indicate that it will be at or above alternate airport landing minimum at the

A—time of departure.
B—estimated time of arrival, plus or minus 1 hour.
C—estimated time of arrival.

No person may designate an alternate airport unless the weather reports or forecasts, or any combination of them, indicate that the weather conditions will be at or above authorized alternate airport landing minimums for that airport at the estimated time of arrival. (PLT379, AA.I.G.K5) — 14 CFR §135.221

ATS, RTC

8065. A takeoff may not be made from an airport that is below the authorized IFR landing minimums unless

A—there is an alternate airport with the required IFR landing minimums within 60 minutes flying time, at normal cruising speed in still air.
B—the departure airport is forecast to have the required IFR landing minimums within 1 hour.
C—there is an alternate airport with the required IFR landing minimums within 60 minutes flying time, at normal cruising speed in still air with one engine inoperative.

No person may takeoff an aircraft under IFR from an airport where weather conditions are at or above takeoff minimums, but are below landing minimums, unless there is an alternate airport within one hour's flying time (at normal cruising speed in still air) of the airport of departure. (PLT459, AA.I.G.K5) — 14 CFR §135.217

ATS, RTC

8066. A pilot may not begin an IFR operation unless the next airport of intended landing is forecast to be at or above authorized IFR landing minimums at

A—the estimated time of arrival, ±1 hour.
B—the estimated time of arrival.
C—the estimated time of arrival, ±30 minutes.

No person may takeoff an aircraft under IFR or begin an IFR or over-the-top operation unless the latest weather reports or forecasts, or any combination of them, indicate that weather conditions at the estimated time of arrival at the next airport of intended landing will be at or above authorized IFR landing minimums. (PLT459, AA.I.G.K5) — 14 CFR §135.219

Answers

8057 [B] 8063 [B] 8064 [C] 8065 [A] 8066 [B]

ATS, RTC

8068. Which condition must be met to conduct IFR operations from an airport that is not at the location where weather observations are made?

A—An "Authorization Letter" permitting the procedure must be issued by the FAA district office charged with the overall inspection of the certificate holder.

B—A "Letter of Waiver" authorizing the procedure must be issued by the Administrator, after an investigation by the U.S. National Weather Service and the FSDO which find the standard of safety to be satisfactory.

C—The Administrator must issue Operations Specifications that permit the procedure.

The Administrator may issue operations specifications to the certificate holder to allow it to depart at an airport that does not have an approved standard instrument approach procedure when the Administrator determines that it is necessary to make an IFR departure from that airport and that the proposed operations can be conducted safely. (PLT282, AA.I.G.K5) — 14 CFR §135.215

ATS, RTC

8084. Which is an operational requirement concerning ice, snow, or frost on structural surfaces?

A—A takeoff may be made with ice, snow, or frost adhering to the wings or stabilizing or control surfaces, but polished smooth, if the anti-icing and deicing equipment is operating.

B—If snow, ice, or frost is adhering to the airplane's lift or control surfaces, but polished smooth, a takeoff may be made.

C—A takeoff may not be made if ice or snow is adhering to the wings or stabilizing or control surfaces.

No pilot may takeoff in an aircraft that has snow or ice adhering to the wings, stabilizing, or control surfaces. (PLT493, AA.I.G.K5) — 14 CFR §135.227

ATS, RTC

8085. Which is one required condition for a pilot to take off under IFR with less-than-standard takeoff minimums at an airport where a straight-in instrument approach procedure is authorized and there is an approved weather reporting source?

A—The pilot must have at least 100 hours as pilot-in-command in the type airplane to be flown.

B—The certificate holder has been approved for such operation and the visibility at the time of takeoff must be at least RVR 16.

C—Wind direction and velocity must be such that a straight-in approach can be made to the runway served by the procedure.

At airports where straight-in instrument approach procedures are authorized, a pilot may takeoff in an aircraft under IFR when the weather conditions are equal to or better than the lowest straight-in landing minimums if:

1. *The wind direction and velocity at the time of takeoff are such that a straight-in instrument approach can be made to the runway served by instrument approach;*
2. *The associated ground facilities upon which the landing minimums are predicated and the related airborne equipment are in normal operation; and*
3. *The certificate holder has been approved for such operations.*

(PLT459, AA.I.G.K5) — 14 CFR §135.225

ATS, RTC

8086. After passing the final approach fix on a VOR approach, a weather report is received indicating the visibility is below prescribed minimums. In this situation, the pilot

A—may continue the approach and land, if at the MDA, the actual weather conditions are at least equal to the minimums prescribed for the procedure.

B—may continue the approach and land regardless of the visibility observed at the MDA, if prior to beginning the approach, the visibility was reported at or above minimums.

C—should leveloff and continue to fly the approach to the MAP, and execute the missed approach.

Answers

8068 [C] 8084 [C] 8085 [C] 8086 [A]

If a pilot has begun the final approach segment of a VOR, NDB or comparable approach procedure and has passed the final approach fix when he/she receives a weather report indicating below minimum conditions, he/she may continue the approach and, if upon reaching the MDA finds the weather at least equal to the prescribed minimums, may land. (PLT379, AA.I.G.K5) — 14 CFR §135.225

ATS, RTC

8087. An alternate for a destination airport (circling not authorized) is not required if, for at least 1 hour before and after the ETA, the required visibility exists, and the forecast ceiling is at least

A—1,500 feet above the lowest published minimum, or 2,000 feet above the airport elevation, whichever is higher.
B—1,500 feet above the lowest MDA or 2,000 feet above the runway touchdown zone elevation, whichever is higher.
C—1,000 feet above the lowest published minimum, or 1,500 feet above the airport elevation, whichever is higher.

An alternate airport need not be designated if the required visibility criteria exists and the ceiling is forecast to be at least 1,500 feet above the lowest circling approach MDA. If no circling approach is authorized the ceiling must be forecast to be 1,500 feet above the lowest published minimum, or 2,000 feet above the airport elevation, whichever is higher. (PLT380, AA.I.G.K5) — 14 CFR §135.223

ATS, RTC

8090. At a military airport, a pilot may not take off under IFR unless the reported weather conditions indicate that the

A—visibility is at least 1 mile.
B—ceiling is at least 500 feet and the visibility is 1 mile or more.
C—airport has landing minimums.

Each pilot making an IFR takeoff or approach and landing at a military or foreign airport shall comply with applicable instrument approach procedures and weather minimums prescribed by the authority having jurisdiction over that airport. In addition, no pilot may takeoff at that airport when the visibility is less than one mile. (PLT459, AA.I.G.K5) — 14 CFR §135.225

ATS, RTC

8091. A pilot may not take off under IFR at a foreign airport unless the visibility is

A—1/2 mile or more above landing minimums.
B—1 mile or more and the ceiling is 500 feet or more.
C—at least 1 mile.

Each pilot making an IFR takeoff or approach and landing at a military or foreign airport shall comply with applicable instrument approach procedures and weather minimums prescribed by the authority having jurisdiction over that airport. In addition, no pilot may takeoff at that airport when the visibility is less than one mile. (PLT459, AA.I.G.K5) — 14 CFR §135.225

ATS, RTC

8092. An instrument approach procedure to an airport may not be initiated unless the latest weather report issued by an authorized weather reporting facility indicates that weather conditions

A—are at or above the circling minimums for the runway the pilot intends to use.
B—are at or above the authorized IFR landing minimums for that procedure.
C—exceed the straight-in minimums for all nonprecision approaches.

No pilot may begin an instrument approach procedure to an airport unless the latest weather report issued by that weather reporting facility indicates that weather conditions are at or above the authorized IFR landing minimums for that airport. (PLT420, AA.I.G.K5) — 14 CFR §135.225

ATS, RTC

8114. What is the minimum ceiling and visibility for an airplane to operate under VFR in Class G airspace?

A—2,000-foot ceiling; 1-mile visibility.
B—2,000-foot ceiling; 1-mile flight visibility.
C—1,000-foot ceiling; 2-miles flight visibility.

No person may operate an airplane under VFR in uncontrolled airspace when the ceiling is less than 1,000 feet unless flight visibility is at least 2 miles. (PLT163, AA.I.G.K5) — 14 CFR §135.205

Answers

8087 [A] 8090 [A] 8091 [C] 8092 [B] 8114 [C]

ATS, RTC

8807. Which document would constitute an approved change to the type design without requiring a recertification?

A—An approved Minimum Equipment List.
B—The Operations Specifications as approved by the Administrator.
C—A special flight permit.

An approved Minimum Equipment List, as authorized by the operations specifications, constitutes an approved change to the type design without requiring recertification. (PLT428, AA.I.G.K5) — 14 CFR §135.179

ATS, RTC

8808. No person may operate an aircraft under 14 CFR Part 135, carrying passengers under VFR at night, unless

A—each flight crewmember has a flashlight having at least two size "D" batteries or the equivalent.
B—it is equipped with a flashlight having at least two size "D" cell or the equivalent.
C—each crewmember has a flashlight having at least two size "D" cells and a spare bulb.

No person may operate an aircraft carrying passengers under VFR at night unless it is equipped with a flashlight having at least two size "D" cells or equivalent. (PLT405, AA.I.G.K5) — 14 CFR §135.159

ATS, RTC

8809. For operations during the period beginning 1 hour after sunset and ending 1 hour before sunrise (as published in the Air Almanac), no certificate holder may use any person, nor may any person serve, as pilot-in-command of an aircraft carrying passengers unless that person has made three takeoffs and three landings, within the preceding 90 days,

A—as the sole manipulator of the flight controls in an aircraft of the same category and class and, if a type rating is required, of the same type in which that person is to serve.
B—as pilot-in-command of an aircraft of the same category and class and, if a type rating is required, of the same type in which that person is to serve.
C—as the sole manipulator of the flight controls in an aircraft of the same type in which that person is to serve.

No person may serve as pilot-in-command of an aircraft carrying passengers unless, within the preceding 90 days, that person has, for operation during the period beginning 1 hour after sunset and ending 1 hour before sunrise (as published in the air almanac), made 3 takeoffs and 3 landings as the sole manipulator of the flight controls in an aircraft of the same category and class and, if a type rating is required, of the same type in which the person is to serve. (PLT442, AA.I.G.K5) — 14 CFR §135.247

ATS, RTC

8813. An employee who performs safety-sensitive functions, for a certificate holder, who has actual knowledge of an accident involving an aircraft for which he or she performed a safety-sensitive function at or near the time of the accident shall not use alcohol

A—until 4 hours after the accident.
B—within 8 hours of the accident.
C—until given a release by the NTSB or FAA.

No covered employee who has actual knowledge of an accident involving an aircraft for which he or she has performed a safety-sensitive function at or near the time of the accident shall use alcohol for 8 hours following the accident. (PLT463, AA.I.G.K5) — 14 CFR §120.215

ATS, RTC

8814. What is the maximum number of hours that a pilot may fly in 7 consecutive days as a pilot in commercial flying and as a pilot for a commuter air carrier?

A—32 hours.
B—34 hours.
C—35 hours.

No certificate holder may schedule any flight crewmember for flight in scheduled operations if that crewmember's total time in commercial flying will exceed:

1. 1,200 hours in any calendar year.

2. 120 hours in any calendar month.

3. 34 hours in any seven consecutive days.

(PLT409, AA.I.G.K5) — 14 CFR §135.265

Answers

8807 [A]   8808 [B]   8809 [A]   8813 [B]   8814 [B]

ATS, RTC

8815. What is the maximum number of hours that a commuter air carrier may schedule a flight crewmember to fly in scheduled operations and other commercial flying in any calendar month?

A—100.
B—110.
C—120.

No certificate holder may schedule any flight crewmember for flight in scheduled operations if that crewmember's total time in commercial flying will exceed:

1. *1,200 hours in any calendar year.*
2. *120 hours in any calendar month.*
3. *34 hours in any seven consecutive days.*

(PLT409, AA.I.G.K5) — 14 CFR §135.265

ATS, RTC

8819. The pilot-in-command may deviate from 14 CFR Part 135 during an emergency involving the safety of persons or property only

A—after ATC is notified of the emergency and the extent of deviation required.
B—to the extent required to meet that emergency.
C—if required to, by the emergency cockpit checklist.

In an emergency involving the safety of persons or property, the pilot-in-command may deviate from the rules of 14 CFR Part 135 to the extent required to meet that emergency. (PLT444, AA.I.G.K5) — 14 CFR §135.19

ATS, RTC

8820. The training required for flight crewmembers who have not qualified and served in the same capacity on an aircraft is

A—upgrade training.
B—transition training.
C—initial training.

Initial training is the term used for the training required for crewmembers who have not qualified and served in the same capacity on an aircraft. (PLT407, AA.I.G.K5) — 14 CFR §135.321

ATS, RTC

8821. A crewmember who has served as second in command on a particular aircraft type (e.g., BE-1900), may serve as pilot-in-command upon completing which training program?

A—Upgrade training.
B—Transition training.
C—Initial training.

Upgrade training is the training required of crewmembers who have qualified and served as second-in-command on a particular aircraft before they serve as pilot-in-command of that aircraft. (PLT407, AA.I.G.K5) — 14 CFR §135.321

ATS, RTC

8827. The training required for crewmembers who have been qualified and served in the same capacity on another aircraft is

A—difference training.
B—transition training.
C—upgrade training.

Transition training is the training required of crewmembers who have qualified and served in the same capacity on another aircraft. (PLT407, AA.I.G.K5) — 14 CFR §135.321

ATS, RTC

8828. The certificate holder must give instruction on such subjects as respiration, hypoxia, gas expansion, and decompression to crewmembers who serve in operations above

A—FL180.
B—FL200.
C—FL250.

Crewmembers who serve in operations above 25,000 feet must receive instruction in respiration, hypoxia, duration of consciousness without supplemental oxygen at altitude, gas expansion, gas bubble formation and physical phenomena and incidents of decompression. (PLT460, AA.I.G.K5) — 14 CFR §135.331

Answers

8815 [C]	8819 [B]	8820 [C]	8821 [A]	8827 [B]	8828 [C]

ATS, RTC

8829. The air carrier must give instruction on such subjects as gas bubble formation, hypoxia, decompression, and length of consciousness without supplemental oxygen at altitude to crewmembers serving on aircraft operated above

A—FL250.
B—FL200.
C—FL180.

Crewmembers who serve in operations above 25,000 feet must receive instruction in respiration, hypoxia, duration of consciousness without supplemental oxygen at altitude, gas expansion, gas bubble formation and physical phenomena and incidents of decompression. (PLT407, AA.I.G.K5) — 14 CFR §135.331

ATS, RTC

8830. What is one of the requirements that must be met by a pilot-in-command to re-establish recency of experience?

A—At least one full stop landing must be made from a circling approach.
B—Three takeoffs and landings must be made as the sole manipulator of the controls, in the type, if a type rating is required, if not in the same category and class aircraft that the person is to serve.
C—At least one nonprecision approach must be made to the lowest minimums authorized for the certificate holder.

No person may serve as pilot-in-command of an aircraft carrying passengers unless, within the preceding 90 days, that person has made 3 takeoffs and 3 landings as the sole manipulator of the flight controls in an aircraft of the same category and class and, if a type rating is required, of the same type in which the person is to serve. (PLT442, AA.I.G.K5) — 14 CFR §135.247

ATS, RTC

8834. Federal Aviation Regulations require that interior emergency lights, on aircraft having a passenger seating configuration of 20 to

A—operate automatically when subjected to a negative G load.
B—be operable manually from the flight crew station and a point in the passenger compartment.
C—be armed or turned on during taxiing and all flight operations.

Emergency exit lights must be operable manually from the flight crew station and from a station in the passenger compartment that is readily accessible to a normal flight attendant seat. (PLT404, AA.I.G.K5) — 14 CFR §135.178

Answer (A) is incorrect because the lights must operate automatically either with loss of normal electrical power or when an emergency assist means is activated, depending on the aircraft certification. Answer (C) is incorrect because the lights must be armed or turned on during taxi, takeoff and landing but not necessarily during all other flight operations.

ATS, RTC

8838. What emergency equipment is required for extended overwater operations?

A—A portable survival emergency locator transmitter for each life raft.
B—A pyrotechnic signaling device for each life preserver.
C—A life preserver equipped with a survivor locator light, for each person on the airplane.

Every aircraft flown in extended overwater operations must carry an approved life preserver for every occupant of the aircraft. This life preserver must be equipped with an approved survivor locator light. A life preserver must be readily accessible to each seated occupant. In addition, there must be enough appropriately equipped life rafts to accommodate all the occupants of the aircraft. One of the life rafts must have a survival type emergency locator transmitter. (PLT437, AA.I.G.K5) — 14 CFR §135.167

ATS, RTC

8840. Each aircraft being operated in extended overwater operations, must have a life preserver for each

A—aircraft occupant.
B—seat on the aircraft.
C—passenger seat, plus 10 percent.

Every aircraft flown in extended overwater operations must carry an approved life preserver for every occupant of the aircraft. (PLT437, AA.I.G.K5) — 14 CFR §135.167

Answers

8829 [A]　8830 [B]　8834 [B]　8838 [C]　8840 [A]

ATS, RTC

8841. Life preservers required for extended overwater operations are stored

A—within easy reach of each passenger.
B—under each occupant seat.
C—within easy access of each seated occupant.

Every aircraft flown in extended overwater operations must carry an approved life preserver for every occupant of the aircraft. A life preserver must be readily accessible to each seated occupant. (PLT437, AA.I.G.K5) — 14 CFR §135.167

ATS, RTC

8843. No person may takeoff an aircraft under IFR from an airport that has takeoff weather minimums but that is below landing minimums unless there is an alternate airport within

A—1 hour at normal indicated airspeed of the departure airport.
B—1 hour at normal cruise speed in still air of the departure airport.
C—1 hour at normal cruise speed in still air with one engine operating.

No person may takeoff an aircraft under IFR from an airport where weather conditions are at or above take-off minimums, but are below authorized IFR landing minimums unless there is an alternate airport within 1 hour's flying time (in still air) of the airport of departure. (PLT459, AA.I.G.K5) — 14 CFR §135.217

Helicopter Regulations

RTC

8002. What minimum rest period must be provided for a pilot assigned to Helicopter Hospital Emergency Medical Evacuation Service (HEMES) who has been on duty for a 47 hour period?

A—16 consecutive hours.
B—14 consecutive hours.
C—12 consecutive hours.

Each pilot must be given a rest period upon completion of the HEMES assignment and prior to being assigned any further duty with the certificate holder of at least 12 consecutive hours for an assignment of less than 48 hours, and at least 16 consecutive hours for an assignment of more than 48 hours. (PLT409) — 14 CFR §135.271

RTC

9043. What is a helicopter pilot's responsibility when cleared to "air taxi" on the airport?

A—Taxi direct to destination as quickly as possible.
B—Taxi at hover altitude using taxiways.
C—Taxi below 100 feet AGL avoiding other aircraft and personnel.

Air taxi is the preferred method for helicopter ground movements on airports. Unless otherwise requested or instructed, pilots are expected to remain below 100 feet AGL. Helicopters should avoid overflight of other aircraft, vehicles, and personnel during air taxi operations. (PLT112) — AIM ¶4-3-17

RTC

9336. What minimum instrument experience in the past 6 calendar months meets the second-in-command requirement to maintain IFR currency in a helicopter?

A—6 hours in actual IFR conditions or 3 hours actual and 3 hours simulated IFR in a helicopter plus six instrument approaches.
B—Holding procedures, intercepting and tracking courses using the navigation equipment, six instrument approaches logged in actual or simulated IFR in a helicopter, simulator or a flight training device.
C—6 hours of actual or simulated time in a helicopter of the same type, plus six instrument approaches.

For flight under IFR, the second-in-command must meet the recent instrument requirements of Part 61: No pilot may act as pilot-in-command under IFR unless the pilot has performed and logged, within the past 6 calendar months, at least 6 instrument approaches, holding procedures, and intercepting and tracking courses through the use of navigation systems in the appropriate category of aircraft for the instrument privileges sought. (PLT442) — 14 CFR §135.245 and §61.57

Answers

8841 [C]	8843 [B]	8002 [C]	9043 [C]	9336 [B]

RTC
9337. What minimum conditions are necessary for the instrument approaches required for second-in-command IFR currency in a helicopter?

A—Six must be performed and logged under actual or simulated instrument conditions in a rotorcraft.
B—Six must be performed and logged under actual or simulated instrument conditions; three must be in a rotorcraft, three may be in an airplane or an approved flight simulator.
C—All must be made in a rotorcraft category of aircraft, or approved simulator, or flight training device and logged while under actual or simulated IFR conditions.

For flight under IFR, the second-in-command must meet the recent instrument requirements of Part 61: No pilot may act as pilot-in-command under IFR unless the pilot has performed and logged, within the past 6 calendar months, at least 6 instrument approaches, holding procedures, and intercepting and tracking courses through the use of navigation systems in the appropriate category of aircraft for the instrument privileges sought. (PLT442) — 14 CFR §135.245 and §61.57

RTC
9338. Within the past 6 months, a pilot has accomplished:

Two approaches in a helicopter.
Two approaches in an airplane.
Two approaches in a glider.

What additional instrument experience must the pilot obtain prior to acting as second in command (under 14 CFR part 135) on an IFR flight?

A—Four approaches in an aircraft, approved training device, flight simulator (that is representative of the aircraft category), holding, intercepting and tracking courses using the navigation systems.
B—Passes an instrument proficiency check in any category aircraft, approved simulator or training device.
C—Holding, intercepting and tracking courses (using the navigation systems) in an aircraft, approved simulator or approved flight training device.

For flight under IFR, the second-in-command must meet the recent instrument requirements of Part 61: No pilot may act as pilot-in-command under IFR unless the pilot has performed and logged, within the past 6 calendar months, at least 6 instrument approaches, holding procedures, and intercepting and tracking courses through the use of navigation systems in the appropriate category of aircraft for the instrument privileges sought. (PLT442) — 14 CFR §135.245 and §61.57

RTC
9341. Within the past 6 months, a pilot has accomplished:

Two approaches and intercepting, tracking courses using the navigation systems in a helicopter.
Two approaches, missed approaches and holding in an approved airplane flight simulator.
Two approaches and holding in an approved rotorcraft flight training device.

What additional instrument experience, if any, must the pilot perform to act as second in command (under 14 CFR part 135) on an IFR helicopter flight?

A—None.
B—Two approaches in a rotorcraft category aircraft.
C—Two approaches in either a helicopter or an airplane.

For flight under IFR, the second-in-command must meet the recent instrument requirements of Part 61: No pilot may act as pilot-in-command under IFR unless the pilot has performed and logged, within the past 6 calendar months, at least 6 instrument approaches, holding procedures, and intercepting and tracking courses through the use of navigation systems in the appropriate category of aircraft for the instrument privileges sought. (PLT442) — 14 CFR §135.245, §61.57

RTC
9366. Unless otherwise prescribed, what is the rule regarding altitude and course to be maintained by a helicopter during an off-airways IFR flight over non-mountainous terrain?

A—1,000 feet above the highest obstacle within 4 nautical miles of course.
B—2,000 feet above the highest obstacle within 5 statute miles of course.
C—1,500 feet above the highest obstacle within a horizontal distance of 3 statute miles of course.

Answers

9337 [C] 9338 [A] 9341 [B] 9366 [A]

In the case of operations over areas that are not designated as mountainous areas; no person may operate an aircraft under IFR below an altitude of 1,000 feet above the highest obstacle within a horizontal distance of 4 nautical miles from the course to be flown. (PLT430) — 14 CFR §91.177

RTC

9367. Unless otherwise prescribed, what is the rule regarding altitude and course to be maintained by a helicopter during an IFR off-airways flight over mountainous terrain?

A—1,000 feet above the highest obstacle within a horizontal distance of 4 nautical miles.
B—2,500 feet above the highest obstacle within a horizontal distance of 3 nautical miles of course.
C—2,000 feet above the highest obstacle within a horizontal distance of 4 nautical miles.

In the case of operations over areas designated as mountainous, no person may operate an aircraft under IFR below an altitude of 2,000 feet above the highest obstacle within a horizontal distance of 4 nautical miles from the course to be flown. (PLT430) — 14 CFR §91.177

RTC

9371. According to 14 CFR Part 91, when takeoff minimums are not prescribed for a civil airport, what are the takeoff minimums under IFR for a multiengine helicopter?

A—1 SM visibility.
B—1/2 SM visibility.
C—1200 RVR.

If takeoff minimums are not prescribed under Part 97, the takeoff minimums under IFR for helicopters are 1/2 statute mile visibility. (PLT459) — 14 CFR §91.175

RTC

9372. According to 14 CFR Part 91, when takeoff minimums are not prescribed for a civil airport, what are the takeoff minimums under IFR for a single-engine helicopter?

A—1/2 SM visibility.
B—1 SM visibility.
C—1200 RVR.

If takeoff minimums are not prescribed under Part 97, the takeoff minimums under IFR for helicopters are 1/2 statute mile visibility. (PLT459) — 14 CFR §91.175

RTC

9373. What minimum altitude should a helicopter maintain while en route?

A—Over congested areas such as towns, no lower than 1,000 feet over the highest obstacle within a horizontal radius of 2,000 feet of the helicopter.
B—That specifically prescribed by the air carrier for the operation.
C—That prescribed by the Administrator.

Each person operating a helicopter shall comply with routes or altitudes specifically prescribed for helicopters by the Administrator. (PLT430) — 14 CFR §91.119

RTC

9414. In addition to a two-way radio capable of communicating with ATC on appropriate frequencies, which equipment is the helicopter required to have to operate within Class B airspace? (Letter of agreement not applicable.)

A—A VOR or TACAN receiver.
B—DME, a VOR or TACAN receiver, and an appropriate transponder beacon.
C—An appropriate ATC transponder.

An operable ATC transponder is required to operate all aircraft in Class B airspace except for helicopters operated at or below 1,000 feet AGL under the terms of a letter of agreement. (PLT405) — 14 CFR §91.131 and §91.215

RTC

9415. Which of the following is a transponder requirement for helicopter operations?

A—Helicopters with a certified gross weight of more than 12,500 pounds that are engaged in commercial operations are required to be equipped with operable ATC transponders.
B—Helicopters may not be operated at or below 1,000 feet AGL within Class B airspace without an operable ATC transponder.
C—Operable ATC transponders are required when operating helicopters within Class D airspace at night under special VFR.

An operable ATC transponder is required to operate all aircraft in Class B airspace except as authorized by ATC. (PLT405) — 14 CFR §91.215

Answers

9367 [C]	9371 [B]	9372 [A]	9373 [C]	9414 [C]	9415 [B]

RTC

8975. Which of the following are required for a helicopter ILS approach with a decision height lower than 200 feet HAT?

A—Special aircrew training and aircraft certification.
B—Both a marker beacon and a radio altimeter.
C—ATP helicopter certificate and CAT II certification.

Approaches with a HAT below 200 feet are annotated with the note: "Special Aircraft & Aircraft Certification Required" since the FAA must approve the helicopter and its avionics, and the flight crew must have the required experience, training, and checking. (PLT356) — FAA-H-8083-16

Answers

8975 [A]

Chapter 2
Equipment, Navigation, and Facilities

Inoperative Equipment

A certificate holder's manual must contain enroute flight, navigation and communication procedures, including procedures for the dispatch, release or continuance of a flight if a required piece of equipment becomes inoperative.

When any required instrument or equipment in an aircraft is inoperative, the airplane cannot be flown unless that aircraft's **Minimum Equipment List (MEL)** allows such a flight.

The pilot-in-command of an aircraft operating IFR in controlled airspace shall report to ATC immediately any malfunction of navigational, approach or communications equipment that occurs in flight. The report must include:

- Aircraft identification;
- Equipment affected;
- Degree to which the capability of the aircraft to operate IFR in the ATC system is impaired; and
- Nature and extent of assistance desired from ATC.

ALL

9407. An approved minimum equipment list or FAA Letter of Authorization allows certain instruments or equipment

A—to be inoperative prior to beginning a flight in an aircraft if prescribed procedures are followed.
B—to be inoperative anytime with no other documentation required or procedures to be followed.
C—to be inoperative for a one-time ferry flight of a large airplane to a maintenance base without further documentation from the operator or FAA with passengers on board.

The Minimum Equipment List and the letter of authorization constitute a supplemental type certificate for the aircraft. The approved Minimum Equipment List must provide for the operation of the aircraft with the instruments and equipment in an inoperable condition (PLT405, AA.II.A.K2c) — 14 CFR §91.213

ATM, ATS, RTC

9380. What action is necessary when a partial loss of ILS receiver capability occurs while operating in controlled airspace under IFR?

A—Continue as cleared and file a written report to the Administrator if requested.
B—If the aircraft is equipped with other radios suitable for executing an instrument approach, no further action is necessary.
C—Report the malfunction immediately to ATC.

The pilot-in-command of an aircraft operating IFR in controlled airspace shall report to ATC as soon as practical any malfunction of navigational, approach or communication equipment that occurs in flight. (PLT356, AA.VI.E.K1) — 14 CFR §91.187

Answer (A) is incorrect because any malfunction of approach equipment must be reported in flight, not by a written report. Answer (B) is incorrect because, although another type of instrument approach may be executed if permission is granted by ATC, any malfunction of approach equipment should be reported.

ATM, ATS, RTC

9381. What action should be taken if one of the two VHF radios fail while IFR in controlled airspace?

A—Notify ATC immediately.
B—Squawk 7600.
C—Monitor the VOR receiver.

The pilot-in-command of an aircraft operating IFR in controlled airspace shall report to ATC as soon as practical any malfunction of navigational, approach or communication equipment that occurs in flight. (PLT162, AA.VI.D.K3) — 14 CFR §91.187

Answer (B) is incorrect because, although you have experienced a communications failure, it is only a partial one. You still have one operational VHF radio and all other radios are working normally, so a squawk of 7600 is not needed. Answer (C) is incorrect because you still have an operable VHF radio for communication, so monitoring of a NAVAID is not needed. The only pilot action required is notification to ATC of the problem.

Answers

9407 [A] 9380 [C] 9381 [A]

ATM, ATS, RTC

9386. While flying IFR in controlled airspace, if one of the two VOR receivers fails, which course of action should the pilot-in-command follow?

A—No call is required if one of the two VOR receivers is operating properly.
B—Advise ATC immediately.
C—Notify the dispatcher via company frequency.

The pilot-in-command of an aircraft operating IFR in controlled airspace shall report to ATC as soon as practical any malfunction of navigational, approach or communication equipment that occurs in flight. (PLT406, AA.VI.D.K3) — 14 CFR §91.187

Answer (A) is incorrect because any malfunction of a navigational radio should be reported, no matter how slightly it may affect the conduct of the flight. Answer (C) is incorrect because, although this may be a common practice among the air carriers, the regulations require notification to ATC of the malfunction.

ATM, ATS, RTC

9387. While flying in controlled airspace under IFR, the ADF fails. What action is required?

A—Descend below Class A airspace.
B—Advise dispatch via company frequency.
C—Notify ATC immediately.

The pilot-in-command of an aircraft operating IFR in controlled airspace shall report to ATC as soon as practical any malfunction of navigational, approach or communication equipment that occurs in flight. (PLT406, AA.VI.D.K3) — 14 CFR §91.187

Answer (A) is incorrect because controlled airspace exists far below positive control airspace (base of 18,000 feet MSL), and any loss of a navigational aid should be reported to ATC. Answer (B) is incorrect because, although this may be a common practice among the air carriers, the regulations require notification to ATC of the malfunction.

ATM, ADX

8278. If a required instrument on a multi-engine airplane becomes inoperative, which document required under 14 CFR Part 121 dictates whether the flight may continue en route?

A—A Master Minimum Equipment List for the airplane.
B—Original dispatch release.
C—Certificate holder's manual.

Each certificate holder's manual must contain enroute flight, navigation, and communication procedures for the dispatch, release or continuance of flight if any item of equipment required for the particular type of operation becomes inoperative or unserviceable en route. (PLT436, AA.I.G.K4) — 14 CFR §121.135

Pitot-Static Instruments

Modern jet transports usually have three pitot-static systems. There are separate systems for the captain's and co-pilot's instruments plus an auxiliary system that provides a backup for either of the two primary systems. The instruments that require static pressure input are **airspeed, Mach, altitude** and **vertical speed indicators**. In addition, the airspeed and Mach indicators need a source of pitot pressure. Besides the flight instruments, static pressure input is required for the Mach warning, autopilot, flight director, flight recorder and cabin differential pressure. Pitot input is required for all those systems except for cabin differential pressure. The usual source for these non-flight instruments is the auxiliary pitot-static system. See Figure 2-1.

Altimeters compare the sea level pressure setting in their window with the outside air pressure sensed through the static system. The difference is displayed as the altitude above sea level. Part of the preflight check is to verify the accuracy of the altimeters. An altimeter should be considered questionable if the indicated altitude varies by more the 75 feet from a known field elevation.

The altimeter setting used by pilots is always the station pressure of the reporting station corrected to sea level. **Station pressure** is the actual pressure at field elevation.

True altitude is the actual height of the aircraft above sea level. This is the same as indicated altitude when standard temperatures exist. When the temperature is warmer than standard, true altitude is higher than indicated altitude. When the temperature is colder than standard day conditions, just the opposite is true. Corrected altitude (approximately true altitude) can be calculated but it is neither practical

Answers

9386 [B] 9387 [C] 8278 [C]

nor useful to do so in most situations. When setting an altimeter, a pilot should just use the appropriate altimeter setting and disregard the effects of nonstandard atmospheric pressures and temperatures.

Pressure altitude is the altitude indicated when the altimeter is set to standard sea level pressure of 29.92" Hg. Density altitude is used in aircraft performance computations. It is pressure altitude corrected for nonstandard temperatures. If the temperature is warmer than standard, density altitude will be higher than pressure altitude.

The local altimeter setting is used when flying below FL180 and the altimeter is 31.00" Hg or less. Special procedures apply when the local pressure is more than 31.00" Hg because most altimeters cannot be set higher than that. In the United States, all altimeters are set to 29.92" Hg when climbing through FL180. Caution: outside the United States the transition altitude is often something other than FL180.

A common reason for altimeter errors is incorrect setting of the altimeter. If the setting in the altimeter is higher than the actual sea level pressure, the altimeter will read higher than the actual altitude. If the setting is too low, the altimeter will read lower than it really is. As a rough rule of thumb, the magnitude of the error is about 1,000 feet for each 1" Hg that the altimeter is off. For example, if the altimeter is set to 29.92" Hg, but the real sea level pressure is 30.57" Hg, the altimeter will read about 650 feet lower than the actual airplane's altitude (30.57 – 29.92 = .65" Hg = 650 feet). In this example, the airplane would be 650 feet higher than the indicated altitude.

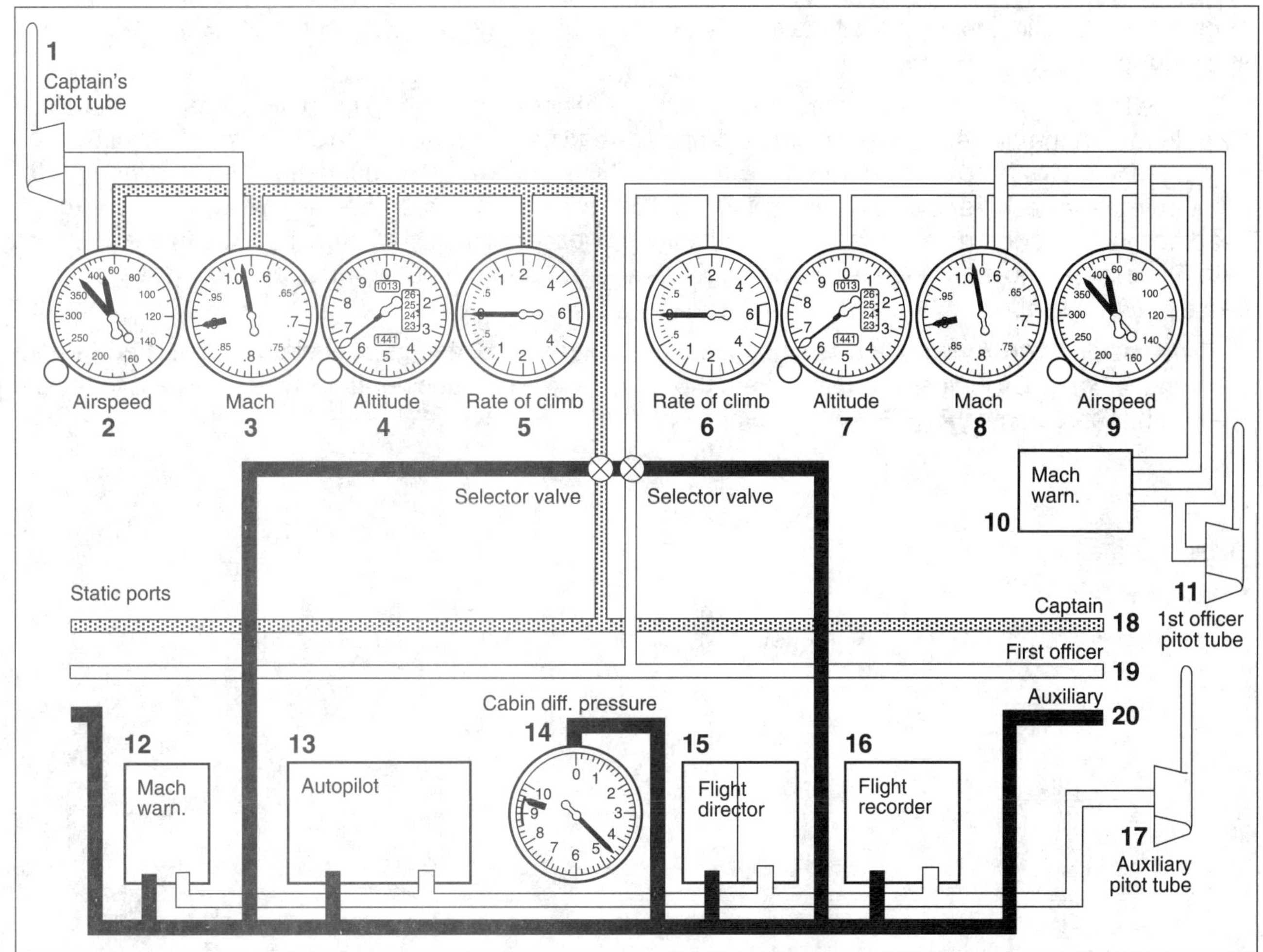

Figure 2-1. Typical pitot-static system

The airspeed indicators compare pitot pressure with static pressure and display the difference as **indicated airspeed**. This indicated airspeed equals the aircraft's actual speed through the air (True Airspeed) only under standard day conditions at sea level. Under almost all flight conditions, true airspeed will be higher than indicated airspeed because of the lower ambient pressures at altitude.

The Machmeter displays aircraft speed as a percentage of the speed of sound. For example, an aircraft cruising at a Mach number of .82 is flying at 82% of the speed of sound. The Machmeter works in a manner similar to the airspeed indicator in that it compares pitot and static pressure, but these inputs are corrected by an altimeter mechanism.

If a pitot tube becomes blocked, the airspeed and Mach indicators will read inaccurately. If pressure is trapped in the pitot line, the airspeed will read inaccurately high as the aircraft climbs, low as it descends, and will be unresponsive to changes in airspeed. The airspeed indicator acts as an altimeter because only the static pressure changes. This situation occurs in icing conditions if both the ram air inlet and the drain hole of the pitot tube become completely blocked by ice.

If the pitot tube is blocked but the static port and the pitot drain hole remain open, the indicated airspeed will drop to zero. The drain pitot tube drain hole allows the pressure in the pitot line to drop to atmospheric and therefore there is no differential between the static and pitot pressures.

Pitot tubes and static ports are electrically heated to prevent ice formations that could interfere with proper operation of the systems. They are required to have "power on" indicator lights to show proper operation. In addition, many aircraft have an ammeter that shows the actual current flow to the pitot and static ports.

Since the magnetic compass is the only direction-seeking instrument in most airplanes, the pilot must be able to turn the airplane to a magnetic compass heading and maintain this heading. It is influenced by magnetic dip which causes northerly turning error and acceleration/deceleration error. When northerly turning error occurs, the compass will lag behind the actual aircraft heading while turning through headings in the northern half of the compass rose, and lead the aircraft's actual heading in the southern half. The error is most pronounced when turning through north or south, and is approximately equal in degrees to the latitude.

The acceleration/deceleration error is most pronounced on headings of east and west. When accelerating, the compass indicates a turn toward the north, and when decelerating it indicates a turn toward the south. The acronym **ANDS** is a good memory aid:

A accelerate

N north

D decelerate

S south

No errors are apparent while on east or west headings, when turning either north or south.

ALL

9174. Which pressure is defined as station pressure?

A—Altimeter setting.
B—Actual pressure at field elevation.
C—Station barometric pressure reduced to sea level.

The pressure measured at a station or airport is "station pressure" or the actual pressure at field elevation. (PLT166, AA.I.A.K13) — FAA-H-8083-28

Answer (A) is incorrect because altimeter setting is the value to which the scale of a pressure altimeter is adjusted to read field elevation. Answer (C) is incorrect because station barometric pressure reduced to sea level is a method to readily compare station pressures between stations at different altitudes.

ALL

9164. What is corrected altitude (approximate true altitude)?

A—Pressure altitude corrected for instrument error.
B—Indicated altitude corrected for temperature variation from standard.
C—Density altitude corrected for temperature variation from standard.

True altitude is indicated altitude corrected for the fact that nonstandard temperatures will result in nonstandard pressure lapse rates. (PLT023, AA.I.A.K13) — FAA-H-8083-28

Answer (A) is incorrect because pressure altitude corrected for instrument error is a nonexistent concept. Answer (C) is incorrect because density altitude is pressure altitude corrected for temperature variation from standard. Density altitude is a final figure and not subject to additional adjustments.

ATM, ATS, RTC

9099. When setting the altimeter, pilots should disregard

A—effects of nonstandard atmospheric temperatures and pressures.
B—corrections for static pressure systems.
C—corrections for instrument error.

Pilots should disregard the effect of nonstandard atmospheric temperatures and pressures except that low temperatures and pressures need to be considered for terrain clearance purposes. (PLT166, AA.I.A.K13) — AIM ¶7-2-2

Answers (B) and (C) are incorrect because altimeters are subject to instrument errors and to errors in the static pressure system. A pilot should set the current reported altimeter setting on the altimeter setting scale. The altimeter should read within 75 feet of field elevation. If not, it is questionable and should be evaluated by a repair station.

ALL

9173. If the ambient temperature is colder than standard at FL310, what is the relationship between true altitude and pressure altitude?

A—They are both the same, 31,000 feet.
B—True altitude is lower than 31,000 feet.
C—Pressure altitude is lower than true altitude.

True altitude is indicated altitude corrected for the fact that nonstandard temperatures will result in nonstandard pressure lapse rates. In warm air, you fly at a true altitude higher than indicated. In cold air, you fly at a true altitude lower than indicated. Pressure altitude is the altitude indicated when the altimeter is set to the standard sea level pressure (29.92" Hg). In the United States, altimeters are always set to 29.92" Hg at and above 18,000 feet. This question assumes the difference between the pressure altitude and the indicated altitude (local altimeter setting) is not significant enough to reverse the effects of the temperature. (PLT023, AA.I.D.K3) — FAA-H-8083-28

Answer (A) is incorrect because both true and pressure altitude would be the same at FL310 if the ambient air temperature was standard. Answer (C) is incorrect because pressure altitude would be lower than true altitude in warmer than standard air temperature.

ALL

9173-1. When the temperature is -20°C at 15,000 feet indicated, you know that

A—altimeters automatically compensate for temperature variations.
B—the altimeter is indicating higher than true altitude.
C—the altimeter is indicating lower than true altitude.

The ISA for 15,000 feet is -15°C. When the temperature is colder than standard, the altimeter will indicate higher than true altitude. (PLT023, AA.I.D.K3) — FAA-H-8083-28

Answers

9174 [B] 9164 [B] 9099 [A] 9173 [B] 9173-1 [B]

ALL

9172. If the ambient temperature is warmer than standard at FL350, what is the density altitude compared to pressure altitude?

A—Lower than pressure altitude.
B—Higher than pressure altitude.
C—Impossible to determine without information on possible inversion layers at lower altitudes.

Pressure altitude is the altitude indicated when the altimeter is set to the standard sea level pressure (29.92" Hg). Density altitude is pressure altitude corrected for nonstandard temperature. A warmer than standard temperature will result in a density altitude higher than the pressure altitude. (PLT023, AA.I.D.K3) — FAA-H-8083-28

Answer (A) is incorrect because density altitude is higher when air temperature is warmer than standard. Answer (C) is incorrect because density altitude is pressure altitude corrected for non-standard temperatures. Pressure altitude is based on a standard pressure atmosphere at a particular altitude, and inversion layers at lower levels have no effect on pressure altitude.

ALL

9813. Given

Pressure altitude.. 1,000 ft
True air temperature .... 10°C

From the conditions given, the approximate density altitude is

A—1,000 feet MSL
B—650 feet MSL
C—450 feet MSL

1. *Using an E6B flight computer, refer to the right-hand "Density Altitude" window. Note that the scale above the window is labeled air temperature (°C). The scale inside the window itself is labeled pressure altitude (in thousands of feet). Rotate the disc and place the pressure altitude of 1,000 feet opposite an air temperature of 10°C.*
2. *The density altitude shown in the window is 650 feet.*

You can also answer this using an electronic flight computer, such as the CX-3. Select Altitude from the CX-3 FLT menu. (PLT005, AA.I.D.K3) — FAA-H-8083-28

ALL

9163. En route at FL270, the altimeter is set correctly. On descent, a pilot fails to set the local altimeter setting of 30.57. If the field elevation is 650 feet, and the altimeter is functioning properly, what will it indicate upon landing?

A—585 feet.
B—1,300 feet.
C—Sea level.

One inch of Hg pressure is equal to about 1,000 feet of altitude. In the United States, altimeters are always set to 29.92" Hg at and above 18,000 feet. If the altimeter is not reset when descending into an area with a local altimeter setting of 30.57" Hg, an error of 650 feet will result (30.57 – 29.92 = .65 = 650 feet). If the altimeter is set lower than the actual setting, it will read lower than the actual altitude. (PLT166, AA.I.D.K3) — FAA-H-8083-28

Answer (A) is incorrect because 585 feet is the result of subtracting 65 feet rather than subtracting 650 feet. Answer (B) is incorrect because 1,300 feet is the result of adding 650 feet rather than subtracting 650 feet.

ATM, ATS, RTC

9080. During an en route descent in a fixed-thrust and fixed-pitch attitude configuration, both the ram air input and drain hole of the pitot system become completely blocked by ice. What airspeed indication can be expected?

A—Increase in indicated airspeed.
B—Decrease in indicated airspeed.
C—Indicated airspeed remains at the value prior to icing.

If both the ram air input and the drain hole are blocked, the pressure trapped in the pitot line cannot change and the airspeed indicator may react as an altimeter. The airspeed will not change in level flight even when actual airspeed is varied by large power changes. During a climb the airspeed indication will increase. During a descent the airspeed indication will decrease. (PLT128, AA.I.D.K3) — AC 91-43

Answer (A) is incorrect because indicated airspeed will decrease in a descent. Answer (C) is incorrect because indicated airspeed will remain at the same value during level flight.

Answers

9172 [B]	9813 [B]	9163 [C]	9080 [B]

ATM, ATS, RTC

9081. What can a pilot expect if the pitot system ram air input and drain hole are blocked by ice?

A—The airspeed indicator may act as an altimeter.
B—The airspeed indicator will show a decrease with an increase in altitude.
C—No airspeed indicator change will occur during climbs or descents.

If both the ram air input and the drain hole are blocked, the pressure trapped in the pitot line cannot change and the airspeed indicator may react as an altimeter. The airspeed will not change in level flight even when actual airspeed is varied by large power changes. During a climb the airspeed indication will increase. During a descent the airspeed indication will decrease. (PLT337, AA.VII.A.K6) — AC 91-43

Answer (B) is incorrect because the airspeed indicator will show an increase (not decrease) with an increase in altitude. Answer (C) is incorrect because differential pressure between the pitot tube and static air source changes, and so does indicated airspeed.

ATM, ATS, RTC

9082. If both the ram air input and drain hole of the pitot system are blocked by ice, what airspeed indication can be expected?

A—No variation of indicated airspeed in level flight if large power changes are made.
B—Decrease of indicated airspeed during a climb.
C—Constant indicated airspeed during a descent.

If both the ram air input and the drain hole are blocked, the pressure trapped in the pitot line cannot change and the airspeed indicator may react as an altimeter. The airspeed will not change in level flight even when actual airspeed is varied by large power changes. During a climb the airspeed indication will increase. During a descent the airspeed indication will decrease. (PLT337, AA.VII.A.K6) — AC 91-43

Answer (B) is incorrect because, during a climb, it will indicate an increase due to the stronger differential pressure in the blocked pitot tube relative to the static vents. Answer (C) is incorrect because indicated airspeed would change with changes in altitude.

ATM, ATS, RTC

9222. How will the airspeed indicator react if the ram air input to the pitot head is blocked by ice, but the drain hole and static port are not?

A—Indication will drop to zero.
B—Indication will rise to the top of the scale.
C—Indication will remain constant but will increase in a climb.

If the pitot tube becomes blocked but pressure is not trapped in the pitot lines, the indicated airspeed will drop to zero since the pitot pressure will be approximately equal to the static pressure. (PLT337, AA.VII.A.K6) — FAA-H-8083-28

Answer (B) is incorrect because the airspeed indication will drop if only the ram air input is blocked. Answer (C) is incorrect because the pressure in the airspeed line will vent out through the hole and the indication will drop to zero.

ATM, ATS, RTC

9934. During a constant-rate climb in IMC above the freezing level, you notice that both the airspeed and altitude are increasing. This indicates the

A—aircraft is in an unusual attitude.
B—gyroscopic instruments have failed.
C—pitot-static system has malfunctioned.

If the pitot tube ram pressure hole and drain hole become obstructed, the airspeed indicator operates like an altimeter as the aircraft climbs and descends. In this situation as the aircraft climbs and the altimeter increases, so will the airspeed indicator. (PLT337, AA.VII.A.K6) — FAA-H-8083-15

Answer (A) is incorrect because an aircraft in an unusual attitude with an increasing airspeed will result in a decreasing altitude. Answer (B) is incorrect because the airspeed indicator and altimeter operate off the pitot-static system.

Answers

9081 [A]	9082 [A]	9222 [A]	9934 [C]

Electronic Flight Instruments

Electronic flight instrument systems integrate many individual instruments into a single presentation called a primary flight display (PFD). Flight instrument presentations on a PFD differ from conventional instrumentation not only in format, but sometimes in location as well. For example, the attitude indicator on the PFD is often larger than conventional round-dial presentations of an artificial horizon. Airspeed and altitude indications are presented on vertical tape displays that appear on the left and right sides of the primary flight display. The vertical speed indicator is depicted using conventional analog presentation. Turn coordination is shown using a segmented triangle near the top of the attitude indicator. The rate-of-turn indicator appears as a curved line display at the top of the heading/navigation instrument in the lower half of the PFD.

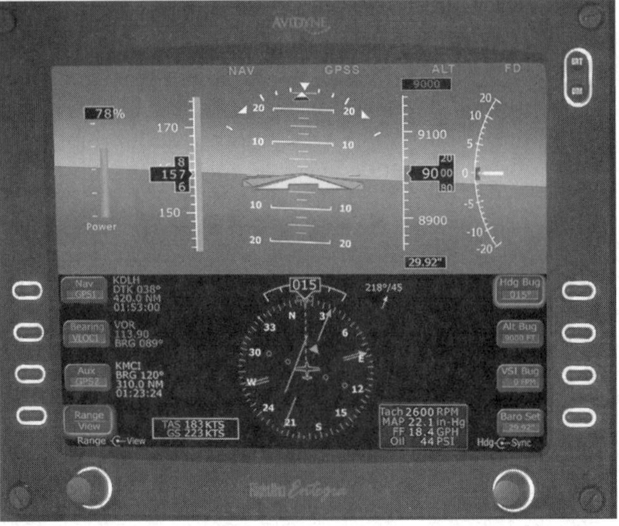

Figure 2-2. A typical primary flight display (PFD)

ATM, ATS, RTC

8206. (See Figure shown below.) You see the indication in the figure on your PFD, but your standby indicator reads 120 knots and the power is set for 120-knot cruise in level flight. You decide the

A—pitot tube may be plugged with ice or a bug.
B—standby indicator is defective because there is no red 'X' on the speed tape display.
C—airspeed means attitude is incorrect.

The airspeed indicator on the PFD is indicating a TAS of 64 knots. If this instrument had failed, the numbers would be replaced with a large red X. The stand-by airspeed indicator reading 120 knots suggests this instrument is working fine. The line coming out of the pitot tube splits to feed multiple instruments. The most likely culprit is a bug or ice blockage occurring past the split, in the line that feeds the Air Data Computer (ADC) for the PFD. This would allow the stand-by gauge to work properly, but cause the ASI on the PFD to give a false indication. True Airspeed is calculated in the ADC by correcting CAS with OAT probe data, so this explains why the TAS is correspondingly low. The pitot lines need to be cleared; applying pitot heat may or may not help at this point. (PLT524, AA.I.A.K9) — FAA-H-8083-6

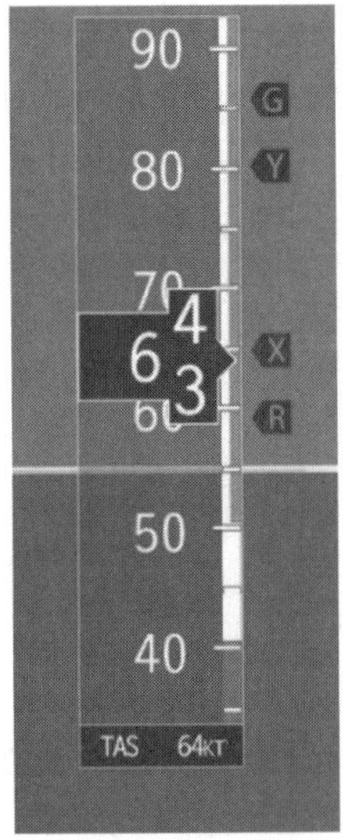

Question 8206

Answer (B) is incorrect because you cannot assume the standby is failed if you have cruise power and level attitude; the red Xs appear on the speed tape when the ADC fails or when one of the pressure transducers fail. Answer (C) is incorrect because an attitude instrument savvy pilot would discern attitude correctness by cross referencing other instruments and hearing the pitch of the engine would decide that power and a level attitude must be an indicator problem and have nothing to do with attitude correctness.

ALL

9769. Automated flight decks or cockpits

A—enhance basic pilot flight skills.
B—decrease the workload in terminal areas.
C—often create much larger pilot errors than traditional cockpits.

Advanced avionics were designed to increase safety as well as the utility of the aircraft, particularly during increased workload phases, such as in the terminal areas. (PLT524, AA.I.E.K2) — FAA-H-8083-6

Answer (A) is incorrect because automation has been shown to erode some flying skills when they are not kept proficient. Answer (C) is incorrect because while automation can make some errors more evident and hide others, it does not result in larger pilot errors than traditional cockpits.

Answers

8206 [A]
9769 [B]

ALL

9769-1. Automated flight decks or cockpits

A—improve basic flight skills.
B—decrease the workload in terminal areas.
C—sometimes hide errors.

Automation can make some errors more evident and hide others. (PLT524, AA.I.E.K2) — FAA-H-8083-6

ALL

9769-2. When flying an aircraft with electronic flight displays (EFDs), risk increases

A—if the pilot expects the electronics to enhance flight safety and remove pilot error.
B—when the pilot expects the equipment to malfunction on occasion.
C—if the pilot believes the EFD will compensate for lack of skill and knowledge.

Automation has been shown to erode some flying skills when they are not kept proficient. (PLT524, AA.I.E.K2) — FAA-H-8083-6

ALL

9830. Automation has been found to

A—create higher workloads in terminal areas.
B—improve crew situational awareness skills.
C—substitute for a lack of aviation experience.

Advanced avionics were designed to increase safety as well as the utility of the aircraft. Safety is enhanced by enabling better situational awareness. (PLT104, AA.I.A.R3) — FAA-H-8083-6

ALL

9853. When a pilot believes advanced avionics enable operations closer to personal or environmental limits,

A—greater utilization of the aircraft is achieved.
B—risk is increased.
C—risk is decreased.

Advanced avionics can sometimes have a negative effect on pilot risk-taking behavior, where more information results in pilots taking more risk than they might be willing to accept without the information. Advanced avionics should be used to increase safety, not risk. (PLT104, AA.I.A.R3) — FAA-H-8083-6

ALL

9853-1. In advanced avionics aircraft, proper automation management requires

A—relying on flight management systems to navigate in order for the pilot to perform other tasks.
B—a thorough understanding of how the autopilot interacts with other systems.
C—the pilot to refrain from monitoring the automation after initial programming.

Advanced avionics offer multiple levels of automation, from strictly manual flight to highly automated flight. No one level of automation is appropriate for all flight situations, but in order to avoid potentially dangerous distractions when flying with advanced avionics, the pilot must know how to manage the CDI, the navigation source, and the autopilot. It is important for a pilot to know the peculiarities of the particular automated system being used. (PLT104, AA.I.F.K3) — FAA-H-8083-25

ALL

9854. Automation in aircraft has proven

A—to present new hazards in its limitations.
B—that automation is basically flawless.
C—effective in preventing accidents.

Advanced avionics were designed to increase safety as well as the utility of the aircraft. However, the systems are not infallible. While automation does help prevent many existing types of errors, it has also created new kinds of errors. (PLT104, AA.I.A.R3) — FAA-H-8083-6

ALL

9855. The lighter workloads associated with glass (digital) flight instrumentation

A—are useful in decreasing flightcrew fatigue.
B—have proven to increase safety in operations.
C—may lead to complacency by the flightcrew.

Risk management is the last of the three flight management skills needed for mastery of the advanced avionics aircraft. The enhanced situational awareness and automation capabilities offered by a glass flight deck vastly expand its safety and utility, especially for personal transportation use. At the same time, there is some risk that lighter workloads could lead to complacency. (PLT104, AA.I.A.R3) — FAA-H-8083-2

Answers

9769-1 [C]	9769-2 [C]	9830 [B]	9853 [B]	9853-1 [B]	9854 [A]
9855 [C]					

ALL
9857. Humans are characteristically

A—disposed to appreciate the workload imposed by automation.
B—disposed to expect automation to fail often.
C—poor monitors of automated systems.

Humans are characteristically poor monitors of automated systems. When passively monitoring an automated system for faults, abnormalities, or other infrequent events, humans perform poorly. The more reliable the system is, the worse the human performance becomes. For example, the pilot monitors only a backup alert system, rather than the situation that the alert system is designed to safeguard. It is a paradox of automation that technically advanced avionics can both increase and decrease pilot awareness. (PLT104, AA.I.A.R3) — FAA-H-8083-2

ALL
8711. Reliance on automation can translate to

A—decreased cockpit workload.
B—increased error awareness.
C—lack of manual handling skills.

A reliance on automation translates into a lack of basic flying skills that may affect the pilot's ability to cope with an in-flight emergency, such as a sudden mechanical failure. (PLT104, AA.I.A.R3) — FAA-8083-25

ALL
9941. Risk is increased when flightcrew members

A—fail to monitor automated navigation systems.
B—allocate time to verify expected performance of automated systems.
C—question the performance of each other's duties.

Flightcrew members must stay vigilant and actively involved throughout the flight, and avoid being complacent and overly dependent on the automated navigation systems. (PLT047, AA.I.A.R3) — FAA-H-8083-2

Safety of Flight Equipment

Airborne weather radar is used to detect and avoid areas of heavy precipitation such as thunderstorms. With few exceptions, all air carrier aircraft must be equipped with an approved airborne weather radar unit. The radar must be in satisfactory operating condition prior to dispatch on an IFR or night VFR flight if thunderstorms (or other hazardous weather) that could be detected by the radar are forecast along the intended route of flight. An aircraft may be dispatched with an inoperative radar unit if one of two conditions is met:

- The flight will be able to remain in day VFR flight conditions, or
- Hazardous weather is not forecast.

An air carrier's operations manual must contain procedures for the flight crew to follow if the weather radar fails in flight.

A ground proximity warning system (GPWS) must be installed on all large turbine powered airplanes. The GPWS gives aural and visual warnings when an aircraft too close to the terrain is in an improper configuration for landing, or when it deviates below glide slope on an ILS approach.

TCAS I (Traffic Alert and Collision Avoidance System) provides proximity warning only, to assist the pilot in the visual acquisition of intruder aircraft. No recommended avoidance maneuvers are provided nor authorized as a result of a TCAS I warning. TCAS II provides traffic advisories (TAs) and resolution advisories (RAs). Resolution advisories provide recommended maneuvers in a vertical direction to avoid conflicting traffic. TCAS does not alter or diminish the pilot's basic authority and responsibility to ensure safe flight. After the conflict, return to the ATC clearance in effect. If a deviation occurs, contact ATC as soon as practical.

Answers

9857	[C]	8711	[C]	9941	[A]

Cockpit voice recorders are required on large turbine engine powered airplanes and large four engine reciprocating powered airplanes. The recorder must operate from before the start of the before starting checklist to the completion of the secure cockpit checklist. Although the recorder runs for the entire flight, only the most recent 30 minutes of information need be retained on the recorder tape.

An approved flight recorder must be installed on all airplanes certified for operations above 25,000 feet and on all turbine powered airplanes. What the flight recorder must record varies from airplane to airplane, but at a minimum it must record:

- Time.
- Altitude.
- Airspeed.
- Vertical acceleration.
- Heading.
- Time of each radio transmission to or from ATC.

An air carrier must keep the flight recorder data until an aircraft has been operated at least 25 hours after the data was removed. However, 1 hour of the oldest recorded data may be erased to test the flight recorder.

The cockpit voice and flight recorder data can be used to identify malfunctions and irregularities with the aircraft and in carrying out investigations under NTSB Part 830. It cannot be used by the FAA for enforcement purposes. If an incident occurs which would require the immediate notification of the NTSB, the data must be kept by the operator for at least 60 days.

ALL

9410. Information obtained from flight data and cockpit voice recorders shall be used only for determining

A—who was responsible for any accident or incident.
B—evidence for use in civil penalty or certificate action.
C—possible causes of accidents or incidents.

Information obtained from flight data and cockpit voice recorders is used to assist in determining the cause of accidents or occurrences in connection with investigation under NTSB Part 830. The Administrator does not use the cockpit voice recorder record in any civil penalty or certificate action. (PLT388, AA.I.G.K2) — 14 CFR §91.609

Answer (A) is incorrect because flight data or cockpit voice recorders are only used to determine possible causes of accidents or incidents. Answer (B) is incorrect because flight data or cockpit voice recorders may not be used for any civil penalty or certificate action.

ALL

9356. For what purpose may cockpit voice recorders and flight data recorders NOT be used?

A—Determining causes of accidents and occurrences under investigation by the NTSB.
B—Determining any certificate action, or civil penalty, arising out of an accident or occurrence.
C—Identifying procedures that may have been conducive to any accident, or occurrence resulting in investigation under NTSB Part 830.

Information obtained from flight data and cockpit voice recorders is used to assist in determining the cause of accidents or occurrences in connection with investigation under NTSB Part 830. The Administrator does not use the cockpit voice recorder record in any civil penalty or certificate action. (PLT388, AA.I.G.K2) — 14 CFR §91.609

Answer (A) is incorrect because cockpit voice recorders and flight data recorders are used to determine causes of accidents or occurrences. Answer (C) is incorrect because flight data recorders and cockpit voice recorders are used to identify any procedures, malfunction, or failure that may have contributed to an accident or occurrence.

Answers

9410 [C] 9356 [B]

ALL

9357. How long is cockpit voice recorder and flight recorder data kept, in the event of an accident or occurrence resulting in terminating the flight?

A—60 days.
B—90 days.
C—30 days.

In the event of an accident or occurrence requiring immediate notification to NTSB Part 830, and that results in the termination of a flight, any operator who has installed approved flight recorders and approved cockpit voice recorders shall keep the recorded information for at least 60 days. (PLT388, AA.I.G.K2) — 14 CFR §91.609

ATM, ATS

9428. Each pilot who deviates from an ATC clearance in response to a TCAS II, resolution advisory (RA) is expected to

A—maintain the course and altitude resulting from the deviation, as ATC has radar contact.
B—request ATC clearance for the deviation.
C—notify ATC of the deviation as soon as practicable.

Each pilot who deviates from an ATC clearance in response to a TCAS II RA shall notify ATC of that deviation as soon as practicable and expeditiously return to the current ATC clearance when the traffic conflict is resolved. (PLT195, AA.I.E.K4) — AIM ¶4-4-16

ATM, ATS, RTC

9425. TCAS I provides

A—traffic and resolution advisories.
B—proximity warning.
C—recommended maneuvers to avoid conflicting traffic.

TCAS I provides proximity warning only, to assist the pilot in the visual acquisition of intruder aircraft. No recommended avoidance maneuvers are provided nor authorized as a result of a TCAS I warning. (PLT195, AA.I.E.K4) — AIM ¶4-4-16

Answer (A) is incorrect because traffic and resolution advisories are provided by TCAS II. Answer (C) is incorrect because no recommended avoidance maneuvers are provided nor authorized as a result of a TCAS I warning.

ATM, ATS, RTC

9426. TCAS II provides

A—traffic and resolution advisories.
B—proximity warning.
C—maneuvers in all directions to avoid the conflicting traffic.

TCAS II provides traffic advisories (TAs) and resolution advisories (RAs). (PLT195, AA.I.E.K4) — AIM ¶4-4-16

Answer (B) is incorrect because TCAS I provides proximity warning only. Answer (C) is incorrect because resolution advisories provide recommended maneuvers in a vertical direction only to avoid conflicting traffic.

ATM, ATS, RTC

9427. Each pilot who deviates from an ATC clearance in response to a TCAS advisory is expected to notify ATC and

A—maintain the course and altitude resulting from the deviation, as ATC has radar contact.
B—request a new ATC clearance.
C—expeditiously return to the ATC clearance in effect prior to the advisory, after the conflict is resolved.

Each pilot who deviates from an ATC clearance in response to a TCAS II RA shall notify ATC of that deviation as soon as practicable and expeditiously return to the current ATC clearance when the traffic conflict is resolved. (PLT195, AA.I.E.K4) — AIM ¶4-4-16

ALL

9427-1. With no traffic identified by TCAS when in 10 miles of visibility, you

A—can rest assured that no other aircraft is near.
B—must continually scan for other traffic.
C—must scan only for hot air balloons and gliders.

TCAS does not alter or diminish the pilot's basic authority and responsibility to ensure safe flight. Since TCAS does not respond to aircraft that are not transponder-equipped or aircraft with a transponder failure, TCAS alone does not ensure safe separation in every case. (PLT195), AA.I.E.K4 — AIM ¶4-4-16

Answers

9357 [A]	9428 [C]	9425 [B]	9426 [A]	9427 [C]	9427-1 [B]

ATM, ADX

8150. If an air carrier airplane's airborne radar is inoperative and thunderstorms are forecast along the proposed route of flight, an airplane may be dispatched only

A—when able to climb and descend VFR and maintain VFR/OT en route.
B—in VFR conditions.
C—in day VFR conditions.

No person may dispatch an airplane under IFR or night VFR conditions when current weather reports indicate that thunderstorms, or other potentially hazardous weather conditions that can be detected with airborne weather radar, may reasonably be expected along the route to be flown, unless the weather radar is in satisfactory operating condition. (PLT469, AA.I.E.K3) — 14 CFR §121.357

ATM, ADX

8151. An air carrier airplane's airborne radar must be in satisfactory operating condition prior to dispatch, if the flight will be

A—conducted under VFR conditions at night with scattered thunderstorms reported en route.
B—carrying passengers, but not if it is "all cargo."
C—conducted IFR, and ATC is able to radar vector the flight around areas of weather.

No person may dispatch an airplane under IFR or night VFR conditions when current weather reports indicate that thunderstorms, or other potentially hazardous weather conditions that can be detected with airborne weather radar, may reasonably be expected along the route to be flown, unless the weather radar is in satisfactory operating condition. (PLT469, AA.I.E.K3) — 14 CFR §121.357

Answer (B) is incorrect because there is no difference between "all cargo" and "passenger" air carrier operations. The airborne radar must be operational prior to dispatch into an area of expected thunderstorms. Answer (C) is incorrect because airborne radar needs to be in operating condition for IFR or night VFR conditions, regardless of ATC's ability to vector the flight around the areas of weather.

ATM, ADX

8148. What action should be taken by the pilot-in-command of a transport category airplane if the airborne weather radar becomes inoperative en route on an IFR flight for which weather reports indicate possible thunderstorms?

A—Request radar vectors from ATC to the nearest suitable airport and land.
B—Proceed in accordance with the approved instructions and procedures specified in the operations manual for such an event.
C—Return to the departure airport if the thunderstorms have not been encountered, and there is enough fuel remaining.

No person may dispatch an airplane under IFR or night VFR conditions when current weather reports indicate that thunderstorms, or other potentially hazardous weather conditions that can be detected with airborne weather radar, may reasonably be expected along the route to be flown, unless the weather radar is in satisfactory operating condition. If the airborne radar becomes inoperative en route, the airplane must be operated in accordance with the approved instructions and procedures specified in the operations manual for such an event. (PLT469, AA.I.E.K3) — 14 CFR §121.357

Answer (A) is incorrect because radar vectors to land at the nearest suitable airport are not required when airborne weather detection radar malfunctions. Radar vectors to avoid weather would be a wise request. Answer (C) is incorrect because return to the departure airport upon malfunction of airborne weather detection radar would be the correct action if it were the procedure specified in the air carrier's operations manual. However, it is not required by regulation.

ATM, ADX

8154. Which airplanes are required to be equipped with a ground proximity warning glide slope deviation alerting system?

A—All turbine powered airplanes.
B—Passenger-carrying turbine-powered airplanes only.
C—Large turbine-powered airplanes only.

No person may operate a turbine-powered airplane unless it is equipped with a ground proximity warning/glide slope deviation alerting system. (PLT139, AA.I.E.K4) — 14 CFR §121.356

Answers

8150 [C] 8151 [A] 8148 [B] 8154 [A]

ATM, ADX

8140. Information recorded during normal operation of a cockpit voice recorder in a large pressurized airplane with four reciprocating engines

A—may all be erased or otherwise obliterated except for the last 30 minutes.
B—may be erased or otherwise obliterated except for the last 30 minutes prior to landing.
C—may all be erased, as the voice recorder is not required on an aircraft with reciprocating engines.

When a cockpit voice recorder is required on an airplane, it must be operated continuously from the start of the use of the checklist (before starting engines for the purpose of flight), to completion of the final checklist at the termination of flight. Information recorded more than 30 minutes earlier may be erased or otherwise obliterated. (PLT405, AA.I.G.K2) — 14 CFR §121.359

Answer (B) is incorrect because there is no requirement for information to be retained for 30 minutes after landing. However, under some circumstances involving an accident or occurrence, the certificate holder may be required to retain the information up to 60 days. Answer (C) is incorrect because a cockpit voice recorder is required in large pressurized airplanes with four reciprocating engines.

ATM, ADX

8141. Which rule applies to the use of the cockpit voice recorder erasure feature?

A—All recorded information may be erased, except for the last 30 minutes prior to landing.
B—Any information more than 30 minutes old may be erased.
C—All recorded information may be erased, unless the NTSB needs to be notified of an occurrence.

When a cockpit voice recorder is required on an airplane, it must be operated continuously from the start of the use of the checklist (before starting engines for the purpose of flight), to completion of the final checklist at the termination of flight. Information recorded more than 30 minutes earlier may be erased or otherwise obliterated. (PLT388, AA.I.G.K2) — 14 CFR §121.359

Answer (A) is incorrect because the requirement is that any information more than 30 minutes old may be erased. Answer (C) is incorrect because the requirement is to retain any information that was recorded within the last 30 minutes.

ATM, ADX

8143. A cockpit voice recorder must be operated

A—from the start of the before starting engine checklist to completion of final checklist upon termination of flight.
B—from the start of the before starting engine checklist to completion of checklist prior to engine shutdown.
C—when starting to taxi for takeoff to the engine shutdown checklist after termination of the flight.

When a cockpit voice recorder is required on an airplane, it must be operated continuously from the start of the use of the checklist (before starting engines for the purpose of flight), to completion of the final checklist at the termination of flight. Information recorded more than 30 minutes earlier may be erased or otherwise obliterated. (PLT388, AA.I.G.K2) — 14 CFR §121.359

ATM, ADX

8142. For the purpose of testing the flight recorder system,

A—a minimum of 1 hour of the oldest recorded data must be erased to get a valid test.
B—a total of 1 hour of the oldest recorded data accumulated at the time of testing may be erased.
C—a total of no more than 1 hour of recorded data may be erased.

A total of 1 hour of recorded data may be erased for the purpose of testing a flight recorder or flight recorder system. Any erasure must be of the oldest recorded data accumulated at the time of testing. (PLT388, AA.I.G.K2) — 14 CFR §121.343

Answer (A) is incorrect because a maximum of 1 hour of data may be erased for testing. Answer (C) is incorrect because a total of no more than 1 hour of flight recorder data may be erased, but it must be 1 hour of the oldest recorded data.

Answers

8140 [A] 8141 [B] 8143 [A] 8142 [B]

Communications

Each flag and domestic operator must have a two-way radio system that, under normal conditions, allows reliable and rapid communications between its aircraft and the appropriate dispatch office. For operations within the 48 contiguous states, this system must be independent of any operated by the U.S. government.

ATM, ATS, RTC

9258. ATC asks you to follow the B737 3 NM ahead of you on the approach path. ATC is responsible to ensure

A—wake turbulence avoidance.
B—traffic separation only.
C—wind shear avoidance.

A pilot's acceptance of instructions to follow another aircraft or provide visual separation from it is an acknowledgment that the pilot will maneuver the aircraft as necessary to avoid the other aircraft or to maintain in-trail separation. In operations conducted behind heavy jet aircraft, it is also an acknowledgment that the pilot accepts the responsibility for wake turbulence separation. (PLT149, AA.II.C.K6) — AIM ¶4-4-14

ATM

8135. Who must the crew of a domestic or flag air carrier airplane be able to communicate with, under normal conditions, along the entire route (in either direction) of flight?

A—ARINC.
B—Any FSS.
C—Appropriate dispatch office.

Each domestic and flag air carrier must show that a two-way air/ground radio communications system is available at points that will ensure reliable and rapid communications, under normal operating conditions over the entire route (either direct or via approved point to point circuits) between each airplane and the appropriate dispatch office, and between each airplane and the appropriate air traffic control unit. (PLT390, AA.I.G.K4) — 14 CFR §121.99

Answer (A) is incorrect because the aircraft must be able to communicate directly with the air carrier dispatch office, not just ARINC. ARINC is a commercial message company which subscribers may use to relay messages, telephone calls, etc. Answer (B) is incorrect because regulations require that the company communications system be independent of any system operated by the FAA or any other third party.

ATM, ATS, RTC

9783. When should transponders be operated on the ground while taxiing?

A—Only when ATC specifically requests that the transponder to be activated.
B—Any time the airport is operating under IFR.
C—All the time when at an airport with ASDE-X.

If operating at an airport with Airport Surface Detection Equipment - Model X (ASDE-X), transponders should be transmitting "on" with altitude reporting continuously while moving on the airport surface if so equipped. (PLT149, AA.II.C.K6) — AIM ¶4-1-20

ATM, ATS, RTC

9783-1. If you notice ATC is unusually quiet and one of your VHF transmit lights is illuminated, then you should suspect

A—your VHF receiver is inoperative.
B—your VHF transmitter is keyed and you probably have a stuck microphone.
C—the radio is performing a self-test function.

If radio communications are unusually quiet, suspect radio problems or a stuck microphone, and then contact ATC and look for light gun signals. (PLT542, AA.I.A.K9) — AIM

ATM, ATS, RTC

9784. When taxiing on an airport with ASDE-X, you should

A—operate the transponder only when the airport is under IFR or at night during your taxi.
B—operate the transponder with altitude reporting all of the time during taxiing.
C—be ready to activate the transponder upon ATC request while taxing.

If operating at an airport with Airport Surface Detection Equipment – Model X (ASDE-X), transponders should be transmitting "on" with altitude reporting continuously while moving on the airport surface if so equipped. (PLT149, AA.II.C.K6) — AIM ¶4-1-20

Answers

9258 [B] 8135 [C] 9783 [C] 9783-1 [B] 9784 [B]

Navigation Equipment

When an aircraft is flown IFR or VFR Over-the-Top it must have a dual installation of the navigation radios required to fly that route. This means that an aircraft flying Victor airways or jet routes must have two operable VOR systems. Only one ILS system and one marker beacon system is required under Part 121.

When an aircraft is navigating over routes using low frequency, ADF or Radio Range, it only needs one receiver for those NAVAIDs, if it is also equipped with two VOR receivers. If that is the case, the VOR stations must be located such that the aircraft could complete the flight to a suitable airport and make an instrument approach if the low frequency system fails. The airplane must also be fueled to allow for such a failure.

Whenever a different VOR station is tuned, the pilot must listen to the Morse code identification. This will ensure that the correct frequency has been tuned and that a usable signal is available. Occasionally, when a VOR station is undergoing routine maintenance, it will broadcast a signal that is not reliable enough to use for navigation. This condition is indicated in one of two ways. Either the coded ident will be turned off or the ident will be changed to the letters T - E - S - T. Other than the identifier, the station may appear to be broadcasting a normal signal.

To be flown IFR, an aircraft must have had its VORs checked within the past 30 days. The pilots may check the accuracy of the VORs in one of several ways.

The VORs may be checked using a VOT facility on an airport. The VOT broadcasts the 360° radial and so the CDI needle should center either on a setting of 360° with a FROM indication or on 180° with a TO indication. A deviation of ±4° is acceptable for a VOT check.

If a VOT is not available, a VOR checkpoint may be used instead. The aircraft must be moved to the checkpoint and the designated radial set in the CDI course. The acceptable variation for a ground check is ±4°. For an airborne check the allowable variation is ±6°.

If no VOT or VOR check point is available, the VORs may be checked against each other. This is called a "dual VOR check." Tune the VORs to the same station and check the difference in indicated bearing. If they are within 4° of each other, the check is satisfactory. This check can be performed on the ground or in the air.

The person making a VOR check must make an entry in the aircraft log or other record. A proper entry includes the date, place and bearing error. The checker must sign the entry. Besides the VOR check, the altimeter system and the transponder must have been checked within the last 24 calendar months (14 CFR §91.411 and §91.413).

Whenever VOR receivers are required on board an aircraft operating within the United States, it must also have at least one DME receiver on board as well. *Note:* 14 CFR §91.205 requires a DME only if the aircraft is operated above FL240. 14 CFR §121.349 makes the DME required equipment for all air carrier aircraft operating in the U.S. If the DME fails in flight, the pilot must inform ATC as soon as possible.

DME indicates the actual distance from the station to the receiving aircraft in nautical miles. That is different from the horizontal distance because the aircraft is always higher than the DME ground station and altitude is included in the slant range. As a practical matter, the difference between the horizontal distance and the "slant range" is insignificant at distances of more than 10 miles from the station. There is a considerable error close to the station when the aircraft is at high altitudes. In such a situation, almost all of the slant range distance is vertical. When an aircraft passes over a DME station, the distance indicated at station passage is the altitude of the aircraft above the station in nautical miles. For example, if an airplane flew over a VORTAC site 12,000 feet above the station, the DME would indicate 2.0 NM.

A multi-function display (MFD) presents information drawn from a variety of aircraft information systems. The moving map function uses the MFD to provide a pictorial view of the present position of the aircraft, the route programmed into the flight management system, the surrounding airspace, and geographical features. The MFD and moving map can help you maintain the "big picture" and awareness of potential landing sites.

ALL

9019. What would be the identification when a VORTAC is undergoing routine maintenance and is considered unreliable?

A—A test signal, "TESTING," is sent every 30 seconds.
B—Identifier is preceded by "M" and an intermittent "OFF" flag would appear.
C—The identifier would be removed.

During periods of routine or emergency maintenance, coded identification (or code and voice, where applicable) is removed from certain FAA NAVAIDs. During periods of maintenance, VHF ranges may radiate a T-E-S-T code. (PLT300, AA.I.A.K9) — AIM ¶1-1-3

Answer (A) is incorrect because a facility may send a T-E-S-T code (not "TESTING") during periods of maintenance. Answer (B) is incorrect because an identifier preceded by "M" designates an identification group for the Microwave Landing System (MLS), a system no longer in operation.

ALL

9020. Which indication may be received when a VOR is undergoing maintenance and is considered unreliable?

A—Coded identification T-E-S-T.
B—Identifier is preceded by "M" and an intermittent "OFF" flag might appear.
C—An automatic voice recording stating the VOR is out-of-service for maintenance.

During periods of routine or emergency maintenance, coded identification (or code and voice, where applicable) is removed from certain FAA NAVAIDs. During periods of maintenance, VHF ranges may radiate a T-E-S-T code. (PLT300, AA.I.A.K9) — AIM ¶1-1-3

Answer (B) is incorrect because an identifier preceded by "M" designates an identification group for the Microwave Landing System (MLS), a system no longer in operation. Answer (C) is incorrect because this is used to identify a station and it is removed when the VOR is undergoing maintenance and is considered unreliable.

ALL

9020-1. Why does the FAA maintain a VOR Minimum Operational Network (MON)?

A—To provide VOR navigation service in the western mountainous United States below GPS signal coverage.
B—To maintain the enroute Victor airway structure on overwater routes in the Gulf of Mexico.
C—To support navigation of non-DME/DME equipped RNAV aircraft in the event of GPS outage.

For those aircraft that do not carry DME, the FAA is retaining a limited network of VORs, called the VOR MON, to provide a basic conventional navigation service for operators to use if GNSS becomes unavailable. (PLT300, AA.II.A.K6) — AIM ¶1-1-3

ALL

9375. What is the maximum permissible variation between the two bearing indicators on a dual VOR system when checking one VOR against the other?

A—4° on the ground and in flight.
B—6° on the ground and in flight.
C—6° in flight and 4° on the ground.

If a dual system VOR (units independent of each other except for the antenna) is installed in the aircraft, the person checking the equipment may check one system against the other. The maximum permissible variation between the two indicated bearings is 4°. (PLT508, AA.I.A.K9) — 14 CFR §91.171

Answer (B) is incorrect because 6° is the maximum permissible bearing error when checking a single VOR system against a published radial while in the air, not when checking a dual VOR system. Answer (C) is incorrect because 6° is the maximum permissible bearing error when checking a single VOR system while in the air. Regardless of whether you are on the ground or airborne, the maximum permissible bearing error is only 4° when using a cross-check between dual VORs.

Answers

9019 [C] 9020 [A] 9020-1 [C] 9375 [A]

ALL

9405. During a VOT check of the VOR equipment, the course deviation indicator centers on 356° with the TO/FROM reading FROM. This VOR equipment may

A—be used if 4° is entered on a correction card and subtracted from all VOR courses.
B—be used during IFR flights, since the error is within limits.
C—not be used during IFR flights, since the TO/FROM should read TO.

With the course deviation indicator (CDI) centered, the omni-bearing selector should read 0° (±4°) with the TO/FROM indicator showing FROM or 180° (±4°) with the TO/FROM indicator showing TO. (PLT508, AA.I.A.K9) — 14 CFR §91.171

Answer (A) is incorrect because 4° is the maximum permissible bearing error for a VOT check, and no correction card exists for VORs. VORs are either within or not within acceptable limits. Answer (C) is incorrect because a "TO" reading would be indicated if the omni-bearing selector were selected to 180°, not 0°.

ALL

9406. If an airborne checkpoint is used to check the VOR system for IFR operations, the maximum bearing error permissible is

A—plus or minus 6°.
B—plus 6° or minus 4°.
C—plus or minus 4°.

If neither a VOT nor a designated ground checkpoint is available, a pilot may use a designated airborne checkpoint for the VOR check. The maximum permissible bearing error is ±6°. (PLT508, AA.I.A.K9) — 14 CFR §91.171

Answer (B) is incorrect because the maximum bearing error is ±6. Answer (C) is incorrect because ±4° is the maximum permissible bearing error when using a VOT check or a radio repair facility.

ALL

9376. Which entry shall be recorded by the person performing a VOR operational check?

A—Frequency, radial and facility used, and bearing error.
B—Flight hours and number of days since last check, and bearing error.
C—Date, place, bearing error, and signature.

Each person making the VOR operational check required by regulations shall enter the date, place, bearing error and sign the aircraft log or other record. (PLT508, AA.I.A.K9) — 14 CFR §91.171

Answer (A) is incorrect because the frequency and radial used are not required entry items. Answer (B) is incorrect because flight hours and number of days since last check are not required entry items.

ALL

9404. What record shall be made by the pilot performing a VOR operational check?

A—The date, frequency of VOR or VOT, number of hours flown since last check, and signature in the aircraft log.
B—The date, place, bearing error, and signature in the aircraft log or other record.
C—The date, approval or disapproval, tach reading, and signature in the aircraft log or other permanent record.

Each person making the VOR operational check required by regulations shall enter the date, place, bearing error and sign the aircraft log or other record. (PLT508, AA.I.A.K9) — 14 CFR §91.171

Answer (A) is incorrect because neither the frequency nor number of hours flown since the last check need to be entered in the log or record. Answer (C) is incorrect because neither the tach reading nor approval or disapproval need to be entered in the record of a VOR operational check.

ALL

9377. Which checks and inspections of flight instruments or instrument systems must be accomplished before an aircraft can be flown under IFR?

A—VOR within 30 days and altimeter systems and transponder within 24 calendar months.
B—ELT test within 30 days, altimeter systems within 12 calendar months, and transponder within 24 calendar months.
C—Airspeed indicator within 24 calendar months, altimeter system within 24 calendar months, and transponder within 12 calendar months.

No person may operate an aircraft under IFR using the VOR system of radio navigation unless the VOR equipment of that aircraft has been operationally checked within the preceding 30 days. No person may operate an airplane in controlled airspace under IFR unless, within the preceding 24 calendar months, each static pressure system, each altimeter instrument, and each automatic pressure altitude reporting system has been tested and inspected. No person may use an ATC transponder required by regulations unless, within the preceding 24 calendar months, it has been tested and inspected. (PLT508, AA.I.A.K9) — 14 CFR §§91.171, 91.411, 91.413

Answer (B) is incorrect because ELTs do not have to be tested every 30 days, and the altimeter must be checked along with transponder every 24 calendar months (not 12 months). Answer (C) is incorrect because the airspeed indicator is part of the pitot-static system which must be inspected every 24 calendar months and the transponder which must be inspected every 24 calendar months.

Answers

9405 [B]	9406 [A]	9376 [C]	9404 [B]	9377 [A]

ALL

9408. When is DME or suitable RNAV required for an instrument flight?

A—At or above 24,000 feet MSL if VOR navigational equipment is required.
B—In terminal radar service areas.
C—Above 12,500 feet MSL.

If VOR navigational equipment is required, no person may operate a U.S.-registered civil aircraft within the 50 states and District of Columbia, at or above 24,000 feet MSL, unless that aircraft is equipped with approved distance measuring equipment (DME) or a suitable RNAV system. (PLT429, AA.I.A.K9) — 14 CFR §91.205

ALL

9023. What DME indications should a pilot observe when directly over a VORTAC site at 12,000 feet?

A—0 DME miles.
B—2 DME miles.
C—2.3 DME miles.

Distance information displayed on DME equipment is slant range from the station in nautical miles. 12,000 feet directly over a VORTAC is almost exactly 2 NM. (PLT202, AA.I.A.K9) — FAA-H-8083-15

Answer (A) is incorrect because the DME would indicate 0 DME miles if the DME were sitting on top of the VORTAC site. Answer (C) is incorrect because 2.3 DME miles would be indicated if the airplane were at 13,800 feet (6,000 × 2.3) above the VORTAC site.

ALL

9024. Where does the DME indicator have the greatest error between the ground distance and displayed distance to the VORTAC?

A—High altitudes close to the VORTAC.
B—Low altitudes close to the VORTAC.
C—Low altitudes far from the VORTAC.

Distance information displayed on DME equipment is slant range from the station in nautical miles. The greatest difference between displayed distance and ground distance will occur at high altitudes close to the VORTAC. (PLT202, AA.I.A.K9) — FAA-H-8083-15

Answer (B) is incorrect because at low altitudes close to the VORTAC, the slant-range error is less than at high altitudes close to the VORTAC. Answer (C) is incorrect because the slant-range error is at its smallest at low altitudes far from the VORTAC.

ATM, ADX

8145. When an air carrier flight is operated under IFR or over-the-top on "victor airways," which navigation equipment is required to be installed in duplicate?

A—VOR.
B—ADF.
C—VOR and DME.

No person may operate IFR or Over-the-Top unless the airplane is equipped with the radio equipment necessary for the route, and is able to satisfactorily receive radio navigational signals from all primary en route and approach navigational facilities intended for use, by either of two independent systems. (PLT322, AA.I.A.K9) — 14 CFR §121.349

ATM, ADX

8195. An air carrier operates a flight in VFR over-the-top conditions. What radio navigation equipment is required to be a dual installation?

A—VOR.
B—VOR and ILS.
C—VOR and DME.

No person may operate IFR or Over-the-Top unless the airplane is equipped with the radio equipment necessary for the route and is able to satisfactorily receive radio navigational signals from all primary en route and approach navigational facilities intended for use, by either of two independent systems. (PLT429, AA.I.A.K9) — 14 CFR §121.349

ATM, ADX

8195-1. An air carrier operates a flight in VFR over-the-top conditions where pilotage is not used. What radio navigation equipment is required?

A—single VOR and DME installed.
B—dual approved independent navigation systems.
C—dual VOR, ILS's, and DME.

No person may operate IFR or over-the-top unless the airplane is equipped with the radio equipment necessary for the route and is able to satisfactorily receive radio navigational signals from all primary en route and approach navigational facilities intended for use, by either of two independent systems. (PLT429, AA.I.A.K9) — 14 CFR §121.349

Answers

9408 [A]	9023 [B]	9024 [A]	8145 [A]	8195 [A]	8195-1 [B]

ATM, ADX

8149. If an air carrier airplane is flying IFR using a single ADF navigation receiver and the ADF equipment fails, the flight must be able to

A—proceed safely to a suitable airport using VOR aids and complete an instrument approach by use of the remaining airplane radio system.
B—continue to the destination airport by means of dead reckoning navigation.
C—proceed to a suitable airport using VOR aids, complete an instrument approach and land.

In the case of IFR operation over routes in which navigation is based on low-frequency radio range or automatic direction finding, only one low-frequency radio range or ADF receiver need be installed if the airplane is equipped with two VOR receivers, and VOR navigational aids are so located and the airplane is fueled so that, in the case of failure of the low-frequency radio range or ADF receiver, the flight may proceed safely to a suitable airport by means of VOR aids and complete an instrument approach by use of the remaining airplane radio system. (PLT429, AA.I.A.K9) — 14 CFR §121.349

ATM, ADX

8147. When a pilot plans a flight using NDB NAVAIDs, which rule applies?

A—The airplane must have sufficient fuel to proceed, by means of one other independent navigation system, to a suitable airport and complete an instrument approach by use of the remaining airplane radio system.
B—The pilot must be able to return to the departure airport using other navigation radios anywhere along the route with 150% of the forecast headwinds.
C—The airplane must have sufficient fuel to proceed, by means of VOR NAVAIDS, to a suitable airport and land anywhere along the route with 150% of the forecast headwinds.

In the case of IFR operation over routes in which navigation is based on low-frequency radio range or automatic direction finding, only one low-frequency radio range or ADF receiver need be installed if the airplane is equipped with two VOR receivers, and VOR navigational aids are so located and the airplane is fueled so that, in the case of failure of the low-frequency radio range or ADF receiver, the flight may proceed safely to a suitable airport by means of VOR aids and complete an instrument approach by use of the remaining airplane radio system. (PLT322, AA.I.A.K9) — 14 CFR §121.349

ATM, ADX

8146. When must an air carrier airplane be DME/suitable RNAV system equipped?

A—In Class E airspace for all IFR or VFR on Top operations.
B—Whenever VOR navigation equipment is required.
C—For flights at or above FL180.

Whenever VOR navigational receivers are required by regulation, at least one approved distance measuring equipment (DME) unit or suitable RNAV system capable of receiving and indicating distance information from VORTAC facilities must be installed on each airplane when operated in the 50 states and the District of Columbia. (PLT405, AA.I.A.K9) — 14 CFR §121.349

Answer (A) is incorrect because DME is only required if VOR equipment is required and not only in Class E airspace. Answer (C) is incorrect because DME is only required if VOR receivers are required.

ATM, ADX

8152. While on an IFR flight in controlled airspace, the failure of which unit will precipitate an immediate report to ATC?

A—One engine, on a multiengine aircraft.
B—Airborne radar.
C—DME.

If the distance measuring equipment (DME) becomes inoperative enroute, the pilot shall notify ATC of that failure as soon as it occurs. (PLT429, AA.I.A.K9) — 14 CFR §121.349

Answers

8149 [A] 8147 [A] 8146 [B] 8152 [C]

ALL

9751. (See Figure shown at right.) The moving map below reflects a loss of

A—position information.
B—the AHRS.
C—the ADC.

Failure indications on the moving map can be quite subtle. The MFD in Figure 242 reflects a loss of position information, indicated by the removal of the aircraft symbol, compass labels, and other subtle differences. (PLT524, AA.I.A.K9) — FAA-H-8083-6

Answers (B) and (C) are incorrect because an AHRS or ADC failure would be depicted by red X's on the PFD.

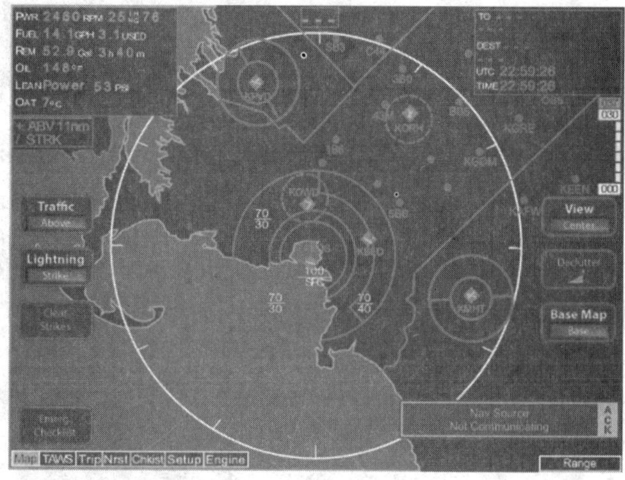

Question 9751

Horizontal Situation Indicator (HSI)

The **Horizontal Situation Indicator (HSI)** is a combination of two instruments: the heading indicator and the VOR. See Figure 2-3.

The aircraft heading displayed on the rotating azimuth card under the upper lubber line in Figure 2-2 is 330°. The course-indicating arrowhead that is shown is set to 300°. The tail of the course-indicating arrow indicates the reciprocal, or 120°.

The course deviation bar operates with a VOR/LOC navigation receiver to indicate either left or right deviations from the course that is selected with the course-indicating arrow. It moves left or right to indicate deviation from the centerline in the same manner that the angular movement of a conventional VOR/LOC needle indicates deviation from course.

The desired course is selected by rotating the course-indicating arrow in relation to the azimuth card by means of the course set knob. This gives the pilot a pictorial presentation. The fixed aircraft symbol and the course deviation bar display the aircraft relative to the selected course as though the pilot was above the aircraft looking down.

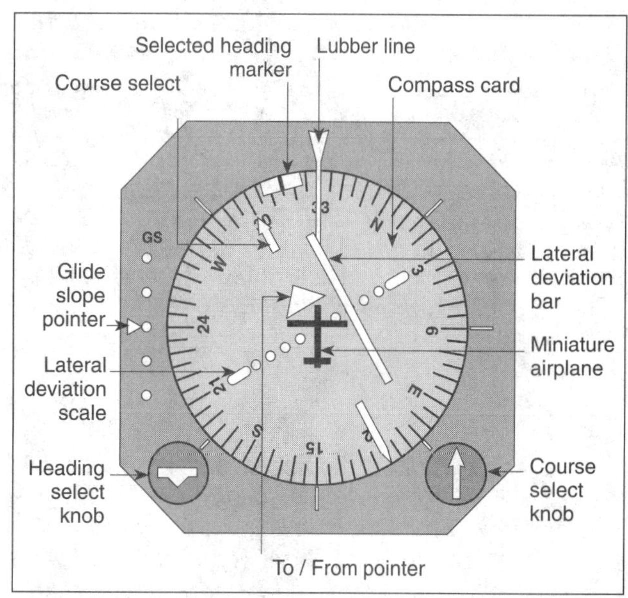

Figure 2-3. Horizontal Situation Indicator (HSI)

The TO/FROM indicator is a triangular-shaped pointer. When this indicator points to the head of the course arrow, it indicates that the course selected, and if properly intercepted and flown, will take the aircraft TO the selected facility, and vice versa.

The glide slope deviation pointer indicates the relationship of the aircraft to the glide slope. When the pointer is below the center position, the aircraft is above the glide slope and an increased rate of descent is required.

Answers

9751 [A]

To orient where the aircraft is in relation to the facility, first determine which radial is selected (look at the arrowhead). Next, determine whether the aircraft is flying to or away from the station (look at the TO/FROM indicator) to find which hemisphere the aircraft is in. Next, determine how far from the selected course the aircraft is (look at the deviation bar) to find which quadrant the aircraft is in. Last, consider the aircraft heading (under the lubber line) to determine the aircraft's position within the quadrant.

Aircraft displacement from course is approximately 200 feet per dot per nautical mile. For example, at 30 NM from the station, 1-dot deflection indicates approximately 1 NM displacement of the aircraft from the course centerline. Therefore, a 2.5-dot deflection at 60 NM would mean the aircraft is approximately 5 NM from the course centerline.

ATM, ATS, RTC

8999. (Refer to Figures 142 and 143.) To which aircraft position does HSI presentation "D" correspond?

A—4.
B—15.
C—17.

HSI Indicator "D" has a course selection of 180°, and the TO/FROM indicator is pointing to the tail of the course arrow. So the aircraft is flying away FROM the station, and is south of R-270 and R-090. The CDI bar is deflected left, which means the aircraft is west of R-180. The aircraft heading is 180°, which describes position 17. (PLT355, AA.VI.D.K3) — FAA-H-8083-15

Answer (A) is incorrect because position 4 is to the north of the 270/090 radials, which would require a TO indication. Answer (B) is incorrect because the course deflection bar on position 15 would have a centered deflection bar and a heading of 360°.

ATM, ATS, RTC

9000. (Refer to Figures 142 and 143.) To which aircraft position does HSI presentation "E" correspond?

A—5.
B—6.
C—15.

HSI Indicator "E" has a course selection of 360°, and the TO/FROM indicator is pointing to the tail of the course arrow. So the aircraft is flying away FROM the station, and is north of R-270 and R-090. The CDI bar is deflected left, which means the aircraft is east of R-180. The aircraft heading is 360°, which describes position 6. (PLT355, AA.VI.D.K3) — FAA-H-8083-15

Answer (A) is incorrect because position 5 would have a centered deflection bar and a heading of 180°. Answer (C) is incorrect because position 15 is to the south of the R-270 and R-090, which would require a TO indication, and the deflection bar would be centered.

ATM, ATS, RTC

9001. (Refer to Figures 142 and 143.) To which aircraft position does HSI presentation "F" correspond?

A—10.
B—14.
C—16.

HSI Indicator "F" has a course selection of 180°, and the TO/FROM indicator is pointing to the tail of the course arrow. So the aircraft is flying away FROM the station, and is south of R-270 and R-090. The CDI bar is centered, which means the aircraft is on R-180. The aircraft heading is 045°, which describes position 16. (PLT355, AA.VI.D.K3) — FAA-H-8083-15

Answer (A) is incorrect because position 10 is north of R-270 and R-090 and east of R-360 and R-180, which would require a TO indication and a right course deflection. Answer (B) is incorrect because position 14 is to the east of R-180, which would require a right course deflection.

ATM, ATS, RTC

9002. (Refer to Figures 142 and 143.) To which aircraft position does HSI presentation "A" correspond?

A—1.
B—8.
C—11.

HSI Indicator "A" has a course selection of 090°, and the TO/FROM indicator is pointing to the head of the course arrow. So the aircraft is flying TO the station, and is west of R-180 and R-000. The CDI bar is deflected right, which means the aircraft is north of R-270. The aircraft heading is 205°, which describes position 1. (PLT355, AA.VI.D.K3) — FAA-H-8083-15

Answer (B) is incorrect because position 8 is to the right of R-360 and R-180, which would require a FROM indication. Answer (C) is incorrect because airplane 11 is to the right of R-360 and R-180 and is south of R-270 and R-090, which would require a FROM indication and a left deviation indication.

Answers

8999 [C] 9000 [B] 9001 [C] 9002 [A]

ATM, ATS, RTC

9003. (Refer to Figures 142 and 143.) To which aircraft position does HSI presentation "B" correspond?

A—9.
B—13.
C—19.

HSI Indicator "B" has a course selection of 270°, and the TO/FROM indicator is pointing to the tail of the course arrow. So the aircraft is flying away FROM the station, and is west of R-180 and R-000. The CDI bar is deflected right, which means the aircraft is south of R-270. The aircraft heading is 135°, which describes position 19. (PLT355, AA.VI.D.K3) — FAA-H-8083-15

Answer (A) is incorrect because position 9 would require a left course deflection bar indication and a TO indication. Answer (B) is incorrect because position 13 is to the right of R-360 and R-180 and would require a TO indication.

ATM, ATS, RTC

9004. (Refer to Figures 142 and 143.) To which aircraft position does HSI presentation "C" correspond?

A—6.
B—7.
C—12.

HSI Indicator "C" has a course selection of 360°, and the TO/FROM indicator is pointing to the head of the course arrow. So the aircraft is flying TO the station, and is south of R-270 and R-090. The CDI bar is deflected left, which means the aircraft is east of R-180. The aircraft heading is 310°, which describes position 12. (PLT355, AA.VI.D.K3) — FAA-H-8083-15

Answer (A) is incorrect because position 6 has a heading of 360° and is north of R-270 and R-090, which would require a FROM indication. Answer (B) is incorrect because position 7 is north of R-270 and R-090 radials, which would require a FROM indication.

ATM, ATS, RTC

8984. (Refer to Figure 139.) What is the lateral displacement of the aircraft in nautical miles from the radial selected on the No. 1 NAV?

A—5.0 NM.
B—7.5 NM.
C—10.0 NM.

Aircraft displacement from course is approximately 200 feet per dot per nautical mile. For example, at 30 NM from the station, 1-dot deflection indicates approximately 1 NM displacement of the aircraft from the course centerline. Therefore, a 2.5-dot deflection at 60 NM would mean the aircraft is approximately 5 NM from the course centerline. (PLT276, AA.VI.D.K3) — FAA-H-8083-15

Answer (B) is incorrect because 7.5 NM would be indicated by a displacement of almost 4 dots. Answer (C) is incorrect because 10.0 NM would be indicated by a full deflection.

ATM, ATS, RTC

8985. (Refer to Figure 139.) On which radial is the aircraft as indicated by the No. 1 NAV?

A—R-175.
B—R-165.
C—R-345.

The No. 1 Nav has a course selection of 350°, and the TO/FROM indicator is pointing to the tail of the course arrow. So the aircraft is flying away FROM the station, and is in the north hemisphere. The CDI bar is deflected right, which means the aircraft is in the northwestern quadrant. The aircraft heading is 140°. The only answer choice in the northwest is R-345. (PLT276, AA.VI.D.K3) — FAA-H-8083-15

Answer (A) is incorrect because R-175 would require a TO indicator. Answer (B) is incorrect because R-165 would require a TO indicator and a left deflection.

ATM, ATS, RTC

8986. (Refer to Figure 139.) Which OBS selection on the No. 1 NAV would center the CDI and change the ambiguity indication to a TO?

A—175.
B—165.
C—345.

The No. 1 Nav has a course selection of 350°, and the TO/FROM indicator is pointing to the tail of the course arrow. So the aircraft is flying away FROM the station, and is in the north hemisphere. The CDI bar is deflected 2.5° right and the aircraft heading is 140°, which would put the aircraft on R-345. To center the CDI and change the ambiguity indication to a TO, rotate the OBS to 165° (the reciprocal of R-345). (PLT276, AA.VI.D.K3) — FAA-H-8083-15

Answers (A) and (C) are incorrect because the aircraft is currently on R-345.

Answers

9003 [C]	9004 [C]	8984 [A]	8985 [C]	8986 [B]

ATM, ATS, RTC

8987. (Refer to Figure 139.) What is the lateral displacement in degrees from the desired radial on the No. 2 NAV?

A—1°.
B—2°.
C—4°.

Full scale deflection is 10°, so each dot represents 2°. The CDI is displaced two dots. Therefore, the lateral displacement is: 2 dots × 2°/dot = 4°. (PLT276, AA.VI.D.K3) — FAA-H-8083-15

Answer (A) is incorrect because a 1° lateral displacement would be indicated by a 1/2-dot displacement of the CDI. Answer (B) is incorrect because a 2° lateral displacement would be indicated by a 1-dot displacement of the CDI.

ATM, ATS, RTC

8988. (Refer to Figure 139.) Which OBS selection on the No. 2 NAV would center the CDI?

A—174.
B—166.
C—335.

Full scale deflection is 10°, so each dot represents 2°. The CDI is displaced two dots (4°). The OBS is set at 170° with a FROM indication, and the aircraft is 4° to the right of course (or on R-174). Simply rotating the OBS to 174° would center the CDI. (PLT276, AA.VI.D.K3) — FAA-H-8083-15

Answer (B) is incorrect because a right deflection would indicate R-166. Answer (C) is incorrect because the TO-FROM indicator is on FROM, not TO.

ATM, ATS, RTC

8989. (Refer to Figure 139.) Which OBS selection on the No. 2 NAV would center the CDI and change the ambiguity indication to a TO?

A—166.
B—346.
C—354.

Rotating the OBS to the reciprocal of 170° (350°) under the course arrow will cause the ambiguity indication to change to a TO. The CDI indicates that the aircraft is 4° to the left of course. Rotating the OBS to 354° will center the CDI. (PLT276, AA.VI.D.K3) — FAA-H-8083-15

Answer (A) is incorrect because a right deflection would currently mean the airplane is on R-166. To change the ambiguity indicator to a TO, 180° must be added to the current radial. Answer (B) is incorrect because a right deflection would mean the airplane is currently on R-166.

ATM, ATS, RTC

8990. (Refer to Figures 140 and 141.) To which aircraft position(s) does HSI presentation "A" correspond?

A—9 and 6.
B—9 only.
C—6 only.

HSI Indicator "A" is set up with the head of the arrow pointing to 270° (normal sensing). The Course Deviation Indicator is centered; therefore, the aircraft is on the extended centerline of runway #9 and #27. With a heading of 360, Indicator "A" represents an aircraft at position #6 or #9. (PLT355, AA.VI.D.K3) — FAA-H-8083-15

Answers (B) and (C) are incorrect because the indication will be the same on both the front course and the back course.

ATM, ATS, RTC

8991. (Refer to Figures 140 and 141.) To which aircraft position(s) does HSI presentation "B" correspond?

A—11.
B—5 and 13.
C—7 and 11.

HSI Indicator "B" is set up with the head of the arrow pointing to 090° (reverse sensing). The CDI indication is deflected right, which means the aircraft is actually to the south of the extended centerline. Indicator "B" then, with the aircraft flying on a heading of 090°, could be at position #13 and #5. Remember that the local receiver does not know where you are in relationship to the antenna site. (PLT355, AA.VI.D.K3) — FAA-H-8083-15

Answer (A) is incorrect because position 11 has a 270° heading. Answer (C) is incorrect because positions 7 and 11 have 270° headings.

ATM, ATS, RTC

8992. (Refer to Figures 140 and 141.) To which aircraft position does HSI presentation "C" correspond?

A—9.
B—4.
C—12.

HSI Indicator "C" is set up with the head of the arrow pointing to 090° (reverse sensing). With the CDI centered, the aircraft is on the extended centerline. With a heading of 090°, position #12 is the only one which would have that indication. (PLT355, AA.VI.D.K3) — FAA-H-8083-15

Answer (A) is incorrect because position 9 has a 360° heading. Answer (B) is incorrect because position 4 has a 270° heading.

Answers

8987 [C]	8988 [A]	8989 [C]	8990 [A]	8991 [B]	8992 [C]

ATM, ATS, RTC

8993. (Refer to Figures 140 and 141.) To which aircraft position does HSI presentation "D" correspond?

A—1.
B—10.
C—2.

HSI Indicator "D" is set up with the head of the arrow pointing to 090° (reverse sensing). The CDI is deflected right, which means the aircraft is to the south of course. On a heading of 310°, position #2 is the only choice. (PLT355, AA.VI.D.K3) — FAA-H-8083-15

Answer (A) is incorrect because position 1 is on a 225° heading and is north of the localizer. Answer (B) is incorrect because position 10 has a 135° heading, and is north of the localizer.

ATM, ATS, RTC

8994. (Refer to Figures 140 and 141.) To which aircraft position(s) does HSI presentation "E" correspond?

A—8 only.
B—8 and 3.
C—3 only.

HSI Indicator "E" is set up with the head of the arrow pointing to 090° (reverse sensing). With the CDI deflected right, the aircraft is to the south of the extended centerline. On a heading of 045°, position #8 or #3 are the only answers. (PLT355, AA.VI.D.K3) — FAA-H-8083-15

Answers (A) and (C) are incorrect because both positions 8 and 3 have a 045° heading and are south of the localizer.

ATM, ATS, RTC

8995. (Refer to Figures 140 and 141.) To which aircraft position does HSI presentation "F" correspond?

A—4.
B—11.
C—5.

HSI Indicator "F" is set up with the head of the arrow pointing to 270° (normal sensing). The CDI is centered; therefore, the aircraft is on the extended centerline of runway #9 and #27. With a heading of 270°, Indicator "F" represents an aircraft at position #4. (PLT355, AA.VI.D.K3) — FAA-H-8083-15

Answer (B) is incorrect because position 11 has a left CDI deflection. Answer (C) is incorrect because position 5 has a 090° heading. It also should have a right deflection because it is south of the localizer.

ATM, ATS, RTC

8996. (Refer to Figures 140 and 141.) To which aircraft position(s) does HSI presentation "G" correspond?

A—4 only.
B—11 only.
C—12 only.

HSI indicator "G" is set up with the head of the arrow pointing to 270° (normal sensing). The CDI is centered. Therefore, the aircraft is on the extended centerline of Runway 9 and 27. With a heading of 270°, indicator "G" represents an aircraft at position 4. (PLT355, AA.VI.D.K3) — FAA-H-8083-15

Answer (B) is incorrect because position 11 has a left CDI deflection. Answer (C) is incorrect because position 12 has a 090° heading.

ATM, ATS, RTC

8998. (Refer to Figures 140 and 141.) To which aircraft position does HSI presentation "I" correspond?

A—12 only.
B—9 only.
C—4 only.

HSI Indicator "I" is set up with the head of the arrow pointing to 090° (reverse sensing). The CDI is centered. Therefore, the aircraft is on the extended centerline of Runway 9 and 27. With a heading of 270°, indicator "I" represents an aircraft at position 4. (PLT355, AA.VI.D.K3) — FAA-H-8083-15

Answer (A) is incorrect because position 12 is on a heading of 090°. Answer (B) is incorrect because position 9 is on a heading of 360°.

ATM, ATS, RTC

9932. (Refer to Figures 140 and 141.) To which HSI presentation does aircraft 8 correspond, if on a back course to the Runway 9 approach?

A—Figure H.
B—Figure I.
C—Figure E.

Position 8 shows the aircraft just south of the extended centerline for Runway 9 on a northeast heading. HSI "E" is the only one that corresponds to aircraft position 8, and shows the aircraft on a heading of 045° with the head of the arrowing pointing to 090°. (PLT355, AA.VI.D.K3) — FAA-H-8083-15

Answer (A) is incorrect because it depicts the aircraft on the extended centerline of Runway 9 and 27 with a heading of 215°. Answer (B) is incorrect because it also depicts the aircraft on the extended centerline of Runway 9 and 27 with a heading of 270°.

Answers

8993 [C]	8994 [B]	8995 [A]	8996 [A]	8998 [C]	9932 [C]

Global Navigation

When an air carrier operates on routes outside of the 48 contiguous states where the aircraft's position cannot be reliably fixed for more than one hour, special rules apply. The aircraft must either be equipped with a "specialized means of navigation" (INS or Doppler Radar), or one of the flight crewmembers must have a current flight navigator certificate. The FAA may also require either a navigator or the specialized navigation on routes which meet the one hour rule if they feel it's necessary. All routes that require either the navigator or specialized means of navigation must be listed in the air carrier's operations specifications.

Certain routes over the North Atlantic Ocean between North America and Europe require better than normal standards of navigation. Appendix C of 14 CFR Part 91 defines these routes and the required navigation standards. The Administrator (the FAA) has the authority to grant a deviation from the navigation standards of Appendix C if an operator requests one.

ATM, ADX
8196. Routes that require a flight navigator are listed in the

A—Airplane Flight Manual.
B—International Flight Information Manual.
C—Air Carrier's Operations Specifications.

Operations where a flight navigator, special navigation equipment, or both are required, are specified in the operations specifications of the air carrier or commercial operator. (PLT389, AA.II.A.K7) — 14 CFR §121.389

ATM, ADX
8197. Where is a list maintained for routes that require special navigation equipment?

A—Air Carrier's Operations Specifications.
B—International Flight Information Manual.
C—Airplane Flight Manual.

Operations where a flight navigator, special navigation equipment, or both are required, are specified in the operations specifications of the air carrier or commercial operator. (PLT389, AA.II.A.K7) — 14 CFR §121.389

Answers (B) and (C) are incorrect because while the International Flight Information Manual and Airplane Flight Manual may contain information on the location and operation for the flight, the air carrier's operations specifications determine the routes in which special navigation equipment or a flight navigator is required.

ATM, ATS, ADX
8197-1. What would authorize an air carrier to conduct a special instrument approach procedure?

A—Operations specifications.
B—Compliance statement.
C—Training specifications.

No person may make an instrument approach at an airport except in accordance with IFR weather minimums and instrument approach procedures set forth in the certificate holder's operations specifications. (PLT389, AA.II.A.K7) — 14 CFR §§121.389 and 135.78

ADX
9811. What document(s) must be in a person's possession for that person to act as a flight navigator?

A—Third-Class Medical Certificate and current Flight Navigator Certificate.
B—Current Flight Navigator Certificate and a current Second-Class (or higher) Medical Certificate.
C—Current Flight Navigator Certificate and a valid passport.

No person may act as a flight navigator of a civil aircraft of U.S. registry unless he has in his personal possession a current flight navigator certificate issued to him under this part and a second-class (or higher) medical certificate issued to him under Part 67 within the preceding 12 months. (PLT427) — 14 CFR §63.3

Answers

8196 [C]	8197 [A]	8197-1 [A]	9811 [B]

ATM, ADX

8199. A flight navigator or a specialized means of navigation is required aboard an air carrier airplane operated outside the 48 contiguous United States and District of Columbia when

A—operations are conducted IFR or VFR on Top.

B—operations are conducted over water more than 50 miles from shore.

C—the airplane's position cannot be reliably fixed for a period of more than 1 hour.

No certificate holder may operate an airplane outside the 48 contiguous states and the District of Columbia, when its position cannot be reliably fixed for a period of more than one hour, without a flight crewmember who holds a current flight navigator certificate, or unless the aircraft is equipped with an approved specialized means of navigation. (PLT374, AA.I.G.K4) — 14 CFR §121.389

Answer (A) is incorrect because whether IFR or VFR-On-Top, the requirement applies if the airplane's position cannot be reliably fixed for more than 1 hour. Answer (B) is incorrect because the requirement applies over water or land if the airplane's position cannot be reliably fixed for more than 1 hour.

Approach Systems

The primary instrument approach system in the United States is the **Instrument Landing System (ILS)**. The system can be divided operationally into three parts: guidance, range and visual information. If any of the elements is unusable, the approach minimums may be raised or the approach may not be authorized at all.

The guidance information consists of the localizer for horizontal guidance and the glide slope for vertical guidance. The localizer operates on one of 40 frequencies from 108.10 MHz to 111.95 MHz. The glide slope operates on one of 40 paired UHF frequencies. The Morse code identifier of the localizer is the letter "I" (• •) followed by three other letters unique to that facility. The portion of the localizer used for the ILS approach is called the front course. The portion of the localizer extending from the far end of the runway is called the back course. The back course may be used for missed approach procedures or for a back course approach if one is published.

Range information is usually provided by 75 MHz marker beacons or, occasionally, by DME. There are four types of marker beacons associated with ILS approaches—the outer marker, the middle marker, the inner marker and the back course marker. Flying over any marker beacon will result in both visual and aural indications. The outer marker is identified by a blue light and continuous dashes in Morse code at a rate of 2 per second. The middle marker is indicated by a flashing amber light and alternating dots and dashes at a rate of 2 per second. The inner marker flashes the white light and sounds continuous dots at 6 per second. The back course marker will also flash the white light and sound a series of 2-dot combinations. See Figure 2-4.

Often, an ADF facility (called a compass locator) is associated with an ILS approach. Usually it is located at the outer marker, but occasionally it is co-located with the middle marker. An outer compass locator is identified with the first 2 letters of the localizer identification group. A middle compass locator is identified by the last 2 letters of the localizer.

If a middle marker is out of service, the middle compass locator or PAR radar can be substituted. The middle marker being inoperative does not affect minimums during a Category I ILS approach.

The visual information portion of the ILS consists of approach lights, touchdown and centerline lights and runway lights.

The localizer is very narrow. In fact a full scale deflection (CDI moving from the center to full scale left or right) is only about 700 feet at the runway threshold.

Different aircraft will require different rates of descent to stay on glide slope. A good rule of thumb is that the vertical speed in feet per minute will be equal to about five times the ground speed in knots.

Answers

8199 [C]

For example, an aircraft with an approach speed of 140 knots will require a descent rate of about 700 feet per minute (140 × 5 = 700).

The lowest approach minimums that can be used for a normal (Category I) ILS approach are a DH of 200 feet and 1,800 feet RVR. A Category II ILS approach will have minimums as low as a DH of 100 feet and a visibility requirement of 1,200 feet RVR. The approach has to be approved for Category II minimums. In addition to suitable localizer, glide slope and marker beacons, the approach must have certain additional equipment working on the landing runway. This equipment includes an approach light

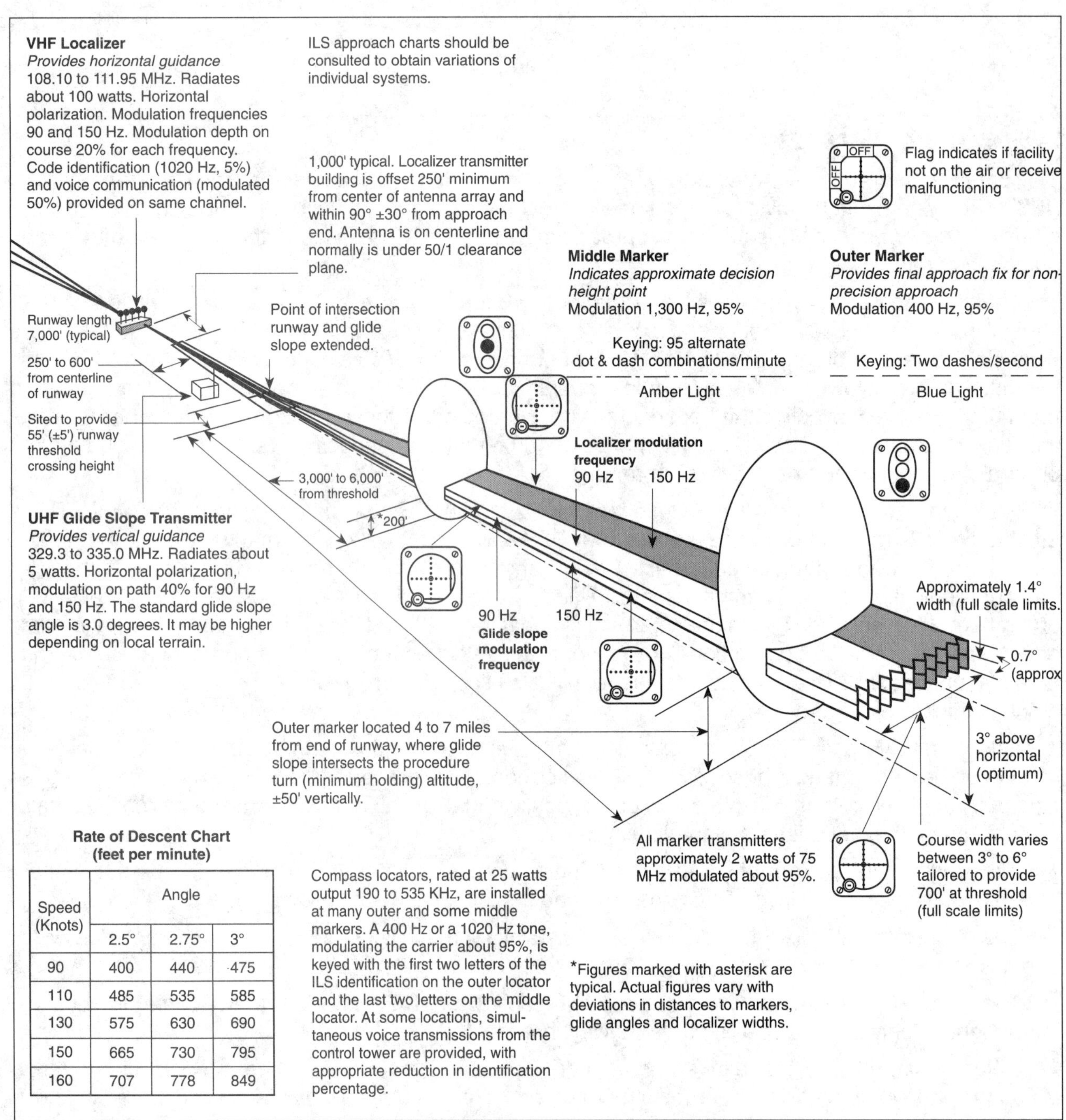

Speed (Knots)	Angle		
	2.5°	2.75°	3°
90	400	440	475
110	485	535	585
130	575	630	690
150	665	730	795
160	707	778	849

Figure 2-4. Instrument Landing System (ILS)

system, High Intensity Runway Lights (HIRL), Touchdown Zone Lights (TDZL), Runway Centerline Lights (CL) and Runway Visual Range (RVR). Radar, VASI and Runway End Identifier Lights (REIL) are not required components of a Category II approach system. To descend below the DH from a Category II approach the pilot must be able to see one of the following:

- The runway threshold;
- The threshold markings;
- The threshold lights;
- The touchdown zone or the touchdown zone markings;
- The touchdown zone lights; or
- The approach light system, except that a pilot may not descend below 100 feet above the touchdown zone unless the red terminating bars or the red side row bars are distinctly visible and identifiable.

The Simplified Directional Facility (SDF) and the Localizer-type Directional Air (LDA) are approach systems that give a localizer-type indication to the pilot, but with some significant differences. The LDA is essentially a localizer, but it is not aligned within 3° of the runway as a localizer must be. The localizer can be any width from 3° to 6° wide. If the LDA is within 30°, straight-in minimums will be published for it; if not, only circling minimums will be published. The SDF may or may not be aligned with the runway. The main difference between it and a localizer is that its width is fixed at either 6° or 12°.

ALL
8961. Within what frequency range does the localizer transmitter of the ILS operate?

A—108.10 to 118.10 MHz.
B—108.10 to 111.95 MHz.
C—108.10 to 117.95 MHz.

The localizer transmitter operates on one of 40 ILS channels within the frequency range of 108.10 to 111.95 MHz. (PLT358, AA.VI.E.K1) — AIM ¶1-1-9

Answer (A) is incorrect because communications frequencies are above 117.95 MHz. Answer (C) is incorrect because 108.10 to 117.95 MHz is the frequency band in which VORs operate.

ALL
8966. What functions are provided by ILS?

A—Azimuth, distance, and vertical angle.
B—Azimuth, range, and vertical angle.
C—Guidance, range, and visual information.

The ILS system may be divided into three functional parts:

1. *Guidance information—localizer, glide slope;*
2. *Range information—marker beacon, DME; and*
3. *Visual information—approach lights, touchdown and centerline lights, runway lights.*

(PLT356, AA.VI.E.K3) — AIM ¶1-1-9

Answer (A) is incorrect because azimuth and distance information are provided by a TACAN. Answer (B) is incorrect because a localizer/DME approach provides azimuth and range information.

ALL
8958. What aural and visual indications should be observed over an ILS inner marker?

A—Continuous dots at the rate of six per second.
B—Continuous dashes at the rate of two per second.
C—Alternate dots and dashes at the rate of two per second.

The code and light identifications of marker beacons are as follows:

Marker	***Code***	***Light***
OM	— — —	*BLUE*
MM	• — • —	*AMBER*
IM	• • • •	*WHITE*
BC	• • • •	*WHITE*

(PLT356, AA.VI.E.K3) — AIM ¶1-1-9

Answer (B) is incorrect because continuous dashes at the rate of two per second indicate the ILS outer marker. Answer (C) is incorrect because alternate dots and dashes at the rate of two per second indicate the ILS middle marker.

Answers
8961 [B]   8966 [C]   8958 [A]

ALL

8959. What aural and visual indications should be observed over an ILS middle marker?

A—Continuous dots at the rate of six per second, identified as a high pitch tone.
B—Continuous dashes at the rate of two per second, identified as a low-pitched tone.
C—Alternate dots and dashes identified as a low-pitched tone.

The code and light identifications of marker beacons are as follows:

Marker	*Code*	*Light*
OM	— — —	*BLUE*
MM	• — • —	*AMBER*
IM	• • • •	*WHITE*
BC	• • • •	*WHITE*

(PLT277, AA.VI.E.K3) — AIM ¶1-1-9

Answer (A) is incorrect because continuous dots at the rate of six per second indicate an ILS inner marker. Answer (B) is incorrect because continuous dashes at the rate of two per second indicate an ILS outer marker.

ALL

8960. What aural and visual indications should be observed over an ILS outer marker?

A—Continuous dots at the rate of six per second.
B—Continuous dashes at the rate of two per second.
C—Alternate dots and dashes at the rate of two per second.

The code and light identifications of marker beacons are as follows:

Marker	*Code*	*Light*
OM	— — —	*BLUE*
MM	• — • —	*AMBER*
IM	• • • •	*WHITE*
BC	• • • •	*WHITE*

(PLT277, AA.VI.E.K3) — AIM ¶1-1-9

Answer (A) is incorrect because continuous dots at the rate of six per second indicate an ILS inner marker. Answer (C) is incorrect because alternating dots and dashes at the rate of two per second indicate an ILS middle marker.

ALL

8962. If installed, what aural and visual indications should be observed over the ILS back course marker?

A—A series of two dot combinations, and a white marker beacon light.
B—Continuous dashes at the rate of one per second, and a white marker beacon light.
C—A series of two dash combinations, and a white marker beacon light.

The code and light identifications of marker beacons are as follows:

Marker	*Code*	*Light*
OM	— — —	*BLUE*
MM	• — • —	*AMBER*
IM	• • • •	*WHITE*
BC	• • • •	*WHITE*

(PLT277, AA.VI.E.K3) — AIM ¶1-1-9

Answer (B) is incorrect because this is not a marker indication of any kind, but it most closely resembles an ILS outer marker. Answer (C) is incorrect because this is not marker indication of any kind, but it most closely resembles an ILS middle marker.

ALL

8956. Which component associated with the ILS is identified by the last two letters of the localizer group?

A—Inner marker.
B—Middle compass locator.
C—Outer compass locator.

Compass locators transmit two-letter identification groups. The outer locator transmits the first two letters of the localizer identification group, and the middle locator transmits the last two letters of the localizer identification group. (PLT356, AA.VI.E.K1) — AIM ¶1-1-9

Answer (A) is incorrect because a simple marker beacon is not identified by letters; only compass locators are so identified. Answer (C) is incorrect because an outer compass locator is identified by the first two letters of the localizer identification group.

Answers

8959 [C] 8960 [B] 8962 [A] 8956 [B]

ALL

8957. Which component associated with the ILS is identified by the first two letters of the localizer identification group?

A—Inner marker.
B—Middle compass locator.
C—Outer compass locator.

Compass locators transmit two-letter identification groups. The outer locator transmits the first two letters of the localizer identification group, and the middle locator transmits the last two letters of the localizer identification group. (PLT356, AA.VI.E.K1) — AIM ¶1-1-9

Answer (A) is incorrect because marker beacons are not identified by letters; only compass locators. Answer (B) is incorrect because a middle compass locator is identified by the last two letters of the localizer identification group.

ALL

9403. Which facility may be substituted for the middle marker during a Category I ILS approach?

A—VOR/DME FIX.
B—Surveillance radar.
C—Compass locator.

A compass locator or precision radar may be substituted for the outer or middle marker. (PLT356, AA.VI.E.K1)—14 CFR §91.175

Answer (A) is incorrect because VOR/DME may be substituted for the outer marker only. Answer (B) is incorrect because surveillance radar may be substituted for the outer marker only.

ALL

8970. If the middle marker for a Category I ILS approach is inoperative,

A—the RVR required to begin the approach in increased by 20%.
B—the DA/DH is increased by 50 feet.
C—the inoperative middle marker has no effect on straight-in minimums.

The middle marker being inoperative does not affect minimums. (PLT277, AA.VI.E.K3) — 14 CFR §91.175

ALL

8968. When is the course deviation indicator (CDI) considered to have a full-scale deflection?

A—When the CDI deflects from full-scale left to full-scale right, or vice versa.
B—When the CDI deflects from the center of the scale to full-scale left or right.
C—When the CDI deflects from half-scale left to half-scale right, or vice versa.

Full-scale deflection is 5 dots to either side of center. (PLT276, AA.VI.E.K2) — FAA-H-8083-15

Answers (A) and (C) are incorrect because when the CDI deflects full-scale left to full-scale right (or vice versa), this represents 2 full-scale deflections.

ALL

8969. Which "rule-of-thumb" may be used to approximate the rate of descent required for a 3° glidepath?

A—5 times groundspeed in knots.
B—8 times groundspeed in knots.
C—10 times groundspeed in knots.

The descent rate in feet per minute required to maintain a 3° glide slope is roughly five times your ground speed in knots. (PLT170, AA.VI.E.K4) — FAA-P-8740-48

Answer (B) is incorrect because 8 times the ground speed in knots would result in a 5% glide slope. Answer (C) is incorrect because 10 times the ground speed in knots would result in a 6% glide slope.

ALL

9749. The rate of descent for a 3.5° angle of descent glidescope is

A—740 ft/min at 105 knots groundspeed.
B—740 ft/min at 120 knots airspeed.
C—740 ft/min at 120 knots groundspeed.

Refer to Legend 72. Follow 3.5° to right to 740 ft/min and go up to find the ground speed of 120. (PLT045, AA.VI.E.K1) — AIM ¶1-1-20

Answers

8957 [C]	9403 [C]	8970 [C]	8968 [B]	8969 [A]	9749 [C]

ALL

8963. The lowest ILS Category II minimums are

A—DH 50 feet and RVR 1,200 feet.
B—DH 100 feet and RVR 1,000 feet.
C—DH 150 feet and RVR 1,500 feet.

The lowest authorized ILS minimums with all required ground and airborne systems components operative, are:

Category I—Decision Height (DH) 200 feet and Runway Visual Range (RVR) 2,400 feet (with touchdown zone and runway centerline lighting, RVR 1,800 Category A, B, C; RVR 2,000 Category D),

Category II—DH 100 feet and RVR 1,000 feet, and

Category IIIA—RVR 700 feet.

(PLT356, AA.VI.E.K3) — AIM ¶1-1-9

Answer (A) is incorrect because a DH of 50 feet is for Category III operations. Answer (C) is incorrect because a DH of 150 feet is for a pilot's initial Category II authorization (for the initial 6-month period) only and is not the lowest DH for Category II operations.

ALL

9411. Which ground components are required to be operative for a Category II approach in addition to LOC, glide slope, marker beacons, and approach lights?

A—Radar, VOR, ADF, taxiway lead-off lights and RVR.
B—RCLS and REIL.
C—All of the required ground components.

No person may operate a civil aircraft in a Category II or Category III operation unless each ground component required for that operation and the related airborne equipment is installed and operating. (PLT420, AA.VI.E.K3) — 14 CFR §91.189

Answer (A) is incorrect because radar is not a required Category II ILS ground component. Answer (B) is incorrect because runway end identifier lights (REIL) are used to provide rapid identification of the approach component for Category II ILS.

ALL

9412. When may a pilot descend below 100 feet above the touchdown zone elevation during a Category II ILS instrument approach when only the approach lights are visible?

A—After passing the visual descent point (VDP).
B—When the RVR is 1,600 feet or more.
C—When the red terminal bar of the approach light systems are in sight.

A pilot may descend below the DH on a Category II approach using the approach light system as the sole visual reference. However, the pilot may not descend below 100 feet above touchdown zone elevation (TDZE) using the approach lights as a reference unless the red terminating bars or the red side row bars are also distinctly visible and identifiable. (PLT356, AA.VI.E.K3) — 14 CFR §91.189

Answer (A) is incorrect because a VDP is not used in conjunction with Category II ILS instrument approaches. Answer (B) is incorrect because, although 1,600 feet may be the required inflight visibility, in order to descend below 100 feet above the touchdown zone elevation based on the approach lights also requires sighting of the red terminating bars.

ALL

9413. In addition to the localizer, glide slope, marker beacons, approach lighting, and HIRL, which ground components are required to be operative for a Category II instrument approach to a DH below 150 feet AGL?

A—RCLS and REIL.
B—Radar, VOR, ADF, runway exit lights, and RVR.
C—Each required ground component.

In addition to localizer, glide slope, marker beacons, and approach light system a Category II ILS must have high-intensity runway lights (HIRL), runway centerline lights (RCLS), touchdown zone lights (TDZL), and runway visual range (RVR). (PLT420, AA.VI.E.K3) — 14 CFR §91.189

Answer (A) is incorrect because runway end identifier lights (REIL) are used to provide rapid identification of the approach end of a runway. Answer (B) is incorrect because radar is not a required ground component for Category II ILS operations.

Answers

8963 [B] 9411 [C] 9412 [C] 9413 [C]

ATM, ATS, RTC

8967. How does the LDA differ from an ILS LOC?

A—LDA. 6° or 12° wide, ILS – 3° to 6°.
B—LDA. offset from runway plus 3°, ILS – aligned with runway.
C—LDA. 15° usable off course indications, ILS – 35°.

The LDA is not aligned with the runway. (PLT356, AA.VI.E.K3) — AIM ¶1-1-9

Answer (A) is incorrect because an SDF (not LDA) is fixed at either 6° or 12° wide. Answer (C) is incorrect because the usable off-course indications are limited to 35° for both types of approaches within 10 NM.

ATM, ATS, RTC

8965. How does the SDF differ from an ILS LOC?

A—SDF – 6° or 12° wide, ILS – 3° to 6°.
B—SDF – offset from runway plus 4°, ILS – aligned with runway.
C—SDF – 15° usable off course indications, ILS – 35°.

The SDF signal is fixed at either 6° or 12° as necessary to provide maximum flyability and optimum course quality. (PLT356, AA.VI.E.K3) — AIM ¶1-1-10

Answer (B) is incorrect because an SDF may or may not be aligned with the centerline of the runway. Answer (C) is incorrect because the usable off course indications are limited to 35° for both types of approaches.

ALL

9794. (Refer to Figure 251). You are cleared to HNL and plan to use the RNAV (RNP) RWY 26L approach. Assuming you have received the training, you

A—should be prepared to program the FMS/GPS with the radio frequency to fly this approach.
B—can use the GPS and radio frequency communications to fly this approach to minimums.
C—must know ahead of time whether or not your FMS/GPS has GPS and radius-to-fix capability.

Some RNP approaches have a curved path, also called a radius-to-fix (RF) leg. Since not all aircraft have the capability to fly these arcs, pilots are responsible for knowing ahead of time whether or not they can conduct an RNP approach with an arc. (PLT354, AA.VI.E.K2) — AIM ¶5-4-18

RTC

9795. (Refer to Figure 253.) You are cleared to LXV in your helicopter and expect to be given the GPS RWY 16 approach. Your helicopter is equipped with an IFR certified WAAS GPS. Your approach minimums will be

A—11,360' MDA and 3/4 mi.
B—11,360' MDA and 1-1/4 mi.
C—11,360' MDA and 6,600 RVR, or 1-1/2 mi.

Helicopters flying conventional (non-copter) SIAP's may reduce the visibility minima to not less than one half the published Category A landing visibility minima, or 1/4 statute mile visibility/1200 RVR, whichever is greater unless the procedure is annotated with "Visibility Reduction by Helicopters NA." (PLT354) — AIM ¶10-1-2

ALL

9796. (Refer to Figure 250.) You arrive at DUMBB for the RNAV (GPS) at CHA. The preflight briefer issued an unreliable advisory before takeoff. Your avionics are good and you have full GPS service. You

A—can descend to the LNAV MDA of 1,200 feet and 2,400 RVR due to the FSS advisory.
B—descend to the LPV minima of 882 feet and 2,400 RVR in your CAT B aircraft.
C—can descend to the LNAV MDA of 518 feet due to the FSS advisory.

Upon commencing an approach at locations with a "WAAS UNRELIABLE" NOTAM, if the WAAS avionics indicate LNAV/VNAV or LPV service is available, then vertical guidance may be used to complete the approach using the displayed level of service. (PLT354, AA.VI.E.K2) — AIM ¶1-1-20

Answers

8967 [B] 8965 [A] 9794 [C] 9795 [A] 9796 [B]

ALL

9796-1. (Refer to Figure 249.) You arrive at PILOC. The preflight briefer issued you an "unreliable" advisory on the approach before you took off. Your avionics indicates good signal. You

A—know you can only fly the approach down to LNAV DA minimum of 459 ft. because of the FSS advisory.
B—can use the LPV minimum of 368'DA and 2400 RVR in your CAT B airplane.
C—can only fly the approach down to the LNAV MDA of 560'.

Upon commencing an approach at locations with a "WAAS UNRELIABLE" NOTAM, if the WAAS avionics indicate LNAV/VNAV or LPV service is available, then vertical guidance may be used to complete the approach using the displayed level of service. (PLT354, AA.VI.E.K2) — AIM ¶1-1-20

ALL

8703. (Refer to Figure 251.) In the RNAV (RNP) RWL 26L at HNL profile, what does the shaded triangle below the DA indicate?

A—The visual segment below the DA is not clear of obstacles.
B—The approach does not have a visual glide slope landing aid.
C—The visual segment is clear.

The shaded fan (or triangle) indicates visual segment below DA is clear of obstacles on a 34:1 slope. (PLT354, AA.VI.E.K2) — Instrument Approach Procedures

GPS

The Global Positioning System (GPS) is a satellite-based radio navigational, positioning, and time transfer system. The GPS receiver verifies the integrity (usability) of the signals received from the GPS satellites through receiver autonomous integrity monitoring (RAIM) to determine if a satellite is providing corrupted information. Without RAIM capability, the pilot has no assurance of the accuracy of the GPS position. If RAIM is not available, another type of navigation and approach system must be used, another destination selected, or the trip delayed until RAIM is predicted to be available on arrival. The authorization to use GPS to fly instrument approaches is limited to U.S. airspace. The use of GPS in any other airspace must be expressly authorized by the appropriate sovereign authority.

If a visual descent point (VDP) is published, it will not be included in the sequence of waypoints. Pilots are expected to use normal piloting techniques for beginning the visual descent. The database may not contain all of the transitions or departures from all runways and some GPS receivers do not contain DPs in the database. The GPS receiver must be set to terminal (±1 NM) course deviation indicator (CDI) sensitivity and the navigation routes contained in the database in order to fly published IFR charted departures and DPs. Terminal RAIM should be automatically provided by the receiver. Terminal RAIM for departure may not be available unless the waypoints are part of the active flight plan rather than proceeding direct to the first destination. Overriding an automatically selected sensitivity during an approach will cancel the approach mode annunciation. The RAIM and CDI sensitivity will not ramp down, and the pilot should not descend to MDA, but fly to the MAWP and execute a missed approach.

It is necessary that helicopter procedures be flown at 70 knots or less since helicopter departure procedures and missed approaches use a 20:1 obstacle clearance surface (OCS), which is double the fixed-wing OCS, and turning areas are based on this speed as well.

The pilot must be thoroughly familiar with the activation procedure for the particular GPS receiver installed in the aircraft and must initiate appropriate action after the missed approach waypoint (MAWP). Activating the missed approach prior to the MAWP will cause CDI sensitivity to immediately change to terminal (±1 NM) sensitivity and the receiver will continue to navigate to the MAWP. The receiver will not

Answers

9796-1 [B]   8703 [C]

sequence past the MAWP. Turns should not begin prior to the MAWP. A GPS missed approach requires pilot action to sequence the receiver past the MAWP to the missed approach portion of the procedure. If the missed approach is not activated, the GPS receiver will display an extension of the inbound final approach course and the ATD will increase from the MAWP until it is manually sequenced after crossing the MAWP.

Any required alternate airport must have an approved instrument approach procedure other than GPS, which is anticipated to be operational and available at the estimated time of arrival and which the aircraft is equipped to fly. Missed approach routings in which the first track is via a course rather than direct to the next waypoint require additional action by the pilot to set the course. Being familiar with all of the inputs required is especially critical during this phase of flight.

ALL

9429. If Receiver Autonomous Integrity Monitoring (RAIM) is not available when setting up for GPS approach, the pilot should

A—continue to the MAP and hold until the satellites are recaptured.
B—proceed as cleared to the IAF and hold until satellite reception is satisfactory.
C—select another type of approach using another type of navigation aid.

If RAIM is not available, another type of navigation and approach system must be used, another destination selected, or the trip delayed until RAIM is predicted to be available on arrival. (PLT354, AA.VI.D.K2) — AIM ¶1-1-19

ALL

9430. Without Receiver Autonomous Integrity Monitoring (RAIM) capability, the accuracy of the GPS derived

A—altitude information should not be relied upon to determine aircraft altitude.
B—position is not affected.
C—velocity information should be relied upon to determine aircraft groundspeed.

The GPS receiver verifies the integrity (usability) of the signals received from the GPS constellation through RAIM, to determine if a satellite is providing corrupted information. Without RAIM capability, the pilot has no assurance of the accuracy of the GPS position. (PLT354, AA.VI.D.K2) — AIM ¶1-1-19

ALL

9431. Overriding an automatically selected sensitivity during a GPS approach will

A—cancel the approach mode annunciation.
B—require flying point-to-point on the approach to comply with the published approach procedure.
C—have no affect if the approach is flown manually.

Overriding an automatically selected sensitivity during an approach will cancel the approach mode annunciation. The RAIM and CDI sensitivity will not ramp down, and the pilot should not descend to MDA, but fly to the MAWP and execute a missed approach. (PLT354, AA.VI.D.K2) — AIM ¶1-1-19

ALL

9432. If a visual descent point (VDP) is published on a GPS approach, it

A—will be coded in the waypoint sequence and identified using ATD.
B—will not be included in the sequence of waypoints.
C—must be included in the normal waypoints.

If a visual descent point (VDP) is published, it will not be included in the sequence of waypoints. Pilots are expected to use normal piloting techniques for beginning the visual descent. (PLT354, AA.VI.D.K2) — AIM ¶1-1-19

ALL

9722. GPS instrument approach operations, outside the United States, must be authorized by

A—the FAA-approved aircraft flight manual (AFM) or flight manual supplement.
B—a sovereign country or governmental unit.
C—the FAA Administrator only.

The authorization to use GPS to fly instrument approaches is provided by a sovereign country or governmental unit. (PLT354, AA.VI.D.K2) — AIM ¶1-1-19

Answers

9429 [C] 9430 [A] 9431 [A] 9432 [B] 9722 [B]

ALL

9723. Authorization to conduct any GPS operation under IFR requires that

A—the equipment be approved in accordance with TSO C-115a.
B—the pilot review appropriate weather, aircraft flight manual (AFM), and operation of the particular GPS receiver.
C—air carrier and commercial operators must meet the appropriate provisions of their approved operations specifications.

The GPS operation must be conducted in accordance with the FAA-approved aircraft flight manual (AFM) or flight manual supplement. Flight crewmembers must be thoroughly familiar with the particular GPS equipment installed in the aircraft, the receiver operation manual, and the AFM or flight manual supplement. Air carrier and commercial operators must meet the appropriate provisions of their approved operations specifications. (PLT354, AA.VI.D.K2) — AIM ¶1-1-19

Answer (A) is incorrect because the equipment must be approved in accordance with TSO C-129, not TSO C-115a. Answer (B) is incorrect because while the pilot is responsible for reviewing the weather before any flight, this requirement is not specific to GPS operations.

ALL

9812. What does the absence of the shaded arrowhead after the VDP on a GPS approach indicate?

A—Obstacle obstructions between the VDP and the runway.
B—A 20:1 glideslope.
C—A 60:1 glideslope.

Absence of the shaded area indicates that the 34:1 visual surface area is not clear of obstructions. (PLT354, AA.VI.D.K2) — AIM ¶5-4-5

ALL

9812-1. (Refer to Figure 252.) In reviewing the RNAV/GPS procedure RWY 4 LEW, the lack of shaded fan from the 1.6 NM point to the runway indicates

A—the visual segment below the MDA/DA is not clear of obstacles on a 34-to-1 slope.
B—it does not have VASI.
C—you can descend on a 20-to-1 slope and remain clear of all obstacles.

This question is referring to the area near the black triangle symbol in the IAP profile view that is pointing to the 1.6 NM to RW04 location. For RNAV approaches only, the presence of a gray-shaded line (or "fan," or arrowhead-shaped symbol) from the MDA to the runway symbol in the profile view, is an indication that the visual segment below the MDA is clear of obstructions on the 34:1 slope. Absence of this gray-shaded area indicates that the 34:1 visual surface area is not free of obstructions. (PLT354, AA.VI.D.K2) — AIM ¶5-4-5, FAA-H-8083-16

ALL

9742. A pilot employed by an air carrier and/or commercial operator may conduct GPS/WAAS instrument approaches

A—if they are not prohibited by the FAA-approved aircraft flight manual and the flight manual supplement.
B—only if approved in their air carrier/commercial operator operations specifications.
C—only if the pilot was evaluated on GPS/WAAS approach procedures during their most recent proficiency check.

Air carrier and commercial operators must meet the appropriate provisions of their approved operations specifications. (PLT420, AA.VI.E.K3) — AIM ¶1-1-20

ALL

9724. Authorization to conduct any GPS operation under IFR requires that

A—the pilot review appropriate weather, aircraft flight manual (AFM), and operation of the particular GPS receiver.
B—air carrier and commercial operators must meet the appropriate provisions of their approved operations specifications.
C—the equipment be approved in accordance with TSO C-115a.

Properly certified GPS equipment may be used as a supplemental means of IFR navigation for domestic enroute, terminal operations, and certain instrument approach procedures (IAPs). This approval permits the use of GPS in a manner that is consistent with current navigation requirements as well as approved air carrier operations specifications. (PLT389, AA.II.A.K7) — AIM ¶1-1-19

Answer (A) is incorrect because while the pilot is responsible for reviewing the weather before any flight, this requirement is not specific to GPS operation. Answer (C) is incorrect because the equipment must be approved in accordance with TSO C-129, not TSO C-115a.

Answers

9723 [C]	9812 [A]	9812-1 [A]	9742 [B]	9724 [B]

ALL

9725. When using GPS for navigation and instrument approaches, a required alternate airport must have

A—an approved instrument approach procedure, besides GPS, that is expected to be operational and available at the ETA.
B—a GPS approach that is expected to be operational and available at the ETA.
C—authorization to fly approaches under IFR using GPS avionics.

Use of a GPS for IFR requires that the avionics necessary to receive all of the ground based facilities appropriate for the route to the destination airport and any required alternate airport must be installed and operational. (PLT354, AA.VI.D.K3) — AIM ¶1-1-19

Answer (B) is incorrect because the operational nature of GPS is not facility dependent. Answer (C) is incorrect because the GPS equipment, not the pilot-in-command, is authorized for use under IFR.

ALL

9727. A GPS missed approach requires that the pilot take action to sequence the receiver

A—over the MAWP.
B—after the MAWP.
C—just prior to the MAWP.

The pilot must be thoroughly familiar with the activation procedure for the particular GPS receiver installed in the aircraft and must initiate appropriate action after the MAWP. Activating the missed approach prior to the MAWP will cause CDI sensitivity to immediately change to terminal (±1 NM) sensitivity and the receiver will continue to navigate to the MAWP. The receiver will not sequence past the MAWP. Turns should not begin prior to the MAWP. (PLT354, AA.VI.E.K2) — AIM ¶1-1-19

ALL

9728. If the missed approach is not activated, the GPS receiver will display

A—an extension of the outbound final approach course, and the ATD will increase from the MAWP.
B—an extension of the outbound final approach course.
C—an extension of the inbound final approach course.

A GPS missed approach requires pilot action to sequence the receiver past the MAWP to the missed approach portion of the procedure. If the missed approach is not activated, the GPS receiver will display an extension of the inbound final approach course and the ATD will increase from the MAWP until it is manually sequenced after crossing the MAWP. (PLT354, AA.VI.E.K2) — AIM ¶1-1-19

ALL

9739. "Unreliable," as indicated in the following GPS NOTAMs: SFO 12/051 SFO WAAS LNAV/VNAV AND LPV MNM UNRELBL WEF0512182025-0512182049 means

A—within the time parameters of the NOTAM, the predicted level of service will not support LPV approaches.
B—satellite signals are currently unavailable to support LPV and LNAV/VNAV approaches.
C—within the time parameters of the NOTAM, the predicted level of service will not support RNAV and MLS approaches.

The term "unreliable" is used in conjunction with GPS NOTAMs; the term is an advisory to pilots indicating the expected level of service may not be available. GPS operation may be NOTAMed UNRELIABLE due to testing or anomalies. (PLT354, AA.VI.E.K2) — AIM ¶1-1-19

ALL

9743. What does "UNREL" indicate in the following GPS and WAAS NOTAM: BOS WAAS LPV AND LNAV/VNAV MNM UNREL WEF 0305231700 -0305231815?

A—Satellite signals are currently unavailable to support LPV and LNAV/VNAV approaches to the Boston airport.
B—The predicted level of service, within the time parameters of the NOTAM, may not support LPV approaches.
C—The predicted level of service, within the time parameters of the NOTAM, will not support LNAV/VNAV and MLS approaches.

The term UNRELIABLE is used in conjunction with GPS and WAAS NOTAMs for flight planning purposes. The term UNRELIABLE is an advisory to pilots indicating the expected level of WAAS service (LNAV/VNAV, LPV) may not be available. (PLT354, AA.VI.E.K2) — AIM ¶1-1-20

Answer (A) is incorrect because UNREL indicates the expected level of WAAS service merely might not be available, and this states that it is definitely unavailable. Answer (C) is incorrect because MLS approaches are not included in the UNREL advisory.

Answers

9725 [A] 9727 [B] 9728 [C] 9739 [A] 9743 [B]

ALL

9917. It is important for a pilot to ask for site-specific WAAS UNRELIABLE NOTAMs for your destination airport before a flight because

A—Air Traffic Control will not advise pilots of site-specific WAAS UNRELIABLE NOTAMs.
B—Air Traffic Control will confirm that you have site-specific information from a pre-flight briefing.
C—this provides for a second level of safety in the National Airspace System.

Site-specific WAAS MAY NOT BE AVBL NOTAMs indicate an expected level of service; for example, LNAV/VNAV, LP, or LPV may not be available. Pilots must request site-specific WAAS NOTAMs during flight planning. In flight, Air Traffic Control will not advise pilots of WAAS MAY NOT BE AVBL NOTAMs. (PLT354, AA.VI.E.K2) — AIM ¶1-1-18

ALL

9729. If flying a published GPS departure,

A—the data base will contain all of the transition or departures from all runways.
B—and if RAIM is available, manual intervention by the pilot should not be required.
C—the GPS receiver must be set to terminal course deviation indicator sensitivity.

The GPS receiver must be set to terminal (±1 NM) course deviation indicator (CDI) sensitivity and the navigation routes contained in the data base in order to fly published IFR charted departures and SIDs. Terminal RAIM should be automatically provided by the receiver. Terminal RAIM for departure may not be available unless the waypoints are part of the active flight plan rather than proceeding direct to the first destination. (PLT354, AA.VI.E.K2) — AIM ¶1-1-19

Answer (A) is incorrect because the data base may ***not*** *contain all of the transitions or departures from all runways and some GPS receivers do not contain SIDs in the data base. Answer (B) is incorrect because certain segments of a SID may require some manual intervention by the pilot, especially when radar vectored to a course or required to intercept a specific course to a waypoint.*

ALL

9729-1. To use a substitute means of guidance on departure procedures, pilots of aircraft with RNAV systems using DME/DME/IRU without GPS input must

A—ensure their aircraft navigation system position is confirmed within 1,000 feet at the start point of takeoff roll.
B—ensure their aircraft navigation system position is confirmed within 2,000 feet of the initialization point.
C—ensure their aircraft navigation system position is confirmed within 1,000 feet of pushback.

For RNAV 1 DPs and STARs, pilots of aircraft without GPS using DME/DME/IRU, must ensure the aircraft navigation system position is confirmed within 1,000 feet at the start point of take-off roll. (PLT354, AA.VI.E.K2) — AIM ¶5-5-16

ALL

9730. Missed approach routing in which the first track is via a course rather than direct to the next waypoint requires

A—that the GPS receiver be sequenced to the missed approach portion of the procedure.
B—manual intervention by the pilot, but will not be required, if RAIM is available.
C—additional action by the operator to set the course.

Missed approach routings in which the first track is via a course rather than direct to the next waypoint require additional action by the pilot to set the course. Being familiar with all of the inputs required is especially critical during this phase of flight. (PLT354, AA.VI.E.K2) — AIM ¶1-1-19

Answer (A) is incorrect because a GPS missed approach requires pilot action to sequence the receiver, and routing in which the first track is via a course requires additional action by the operator. Answer (B) is incorrect because manual intervention for GPS missed approach routing is not dependent upon RAIM availability.

Answers

9917 [A] 9729 [C] 9729-1 [A] 9730 [C]

ALL

9310. An aircraft not equipped with DME/DME experiences a Global Navigation Satellite System (GNSS) disruption while en route. The flight crew will need to navigate using

A—RNAV.
B—VOR MON.
C—GPS.

VOR Minimum Operational Network (MON) provides a basic conventional navigation service for operators to use if GNSS becomes unavailable. During a GNSS disruption, the MON will enable aircraft to navigate through the affected area or to a safe landing at a MON airport without reliance on GNSS. (PLT354, AA.I.E.K3) — AIM ¶1-1-3

Answer (A) is incorrect because in the event of a GNSS disruption only an aircraft that carries DME/DME equipment can use RNAV which provides a backup to continue flying Performance Based Navigation (PBN). Answer (C) is incorrect because a GNSS disruption will not allow for GPS navigation.

ALL

8837. Outside the Western U.S. Mountainous Area, the VOR MON will provide nearly continuous navigation signal coverage across the national airspace system an altitude of

A—5,000 feet AGL.
B—5,000 feet MSL.
C—10,000 feet MSL.

Use of the MON will provide nearly continuous VOR signal coverage at 5,000 feet AGL across the NAS, outside of the Western U.S. Mountainous Area (WUSMA). There is no plan to change the NAVAID and route structure in the WUSMA. (PLT354, AA.I.E.K3) — AIM ¶1-1-3

ALL

8839. Over the contiguous U.S., the VOR MON assures that a MON airport will be available within how many miles of the aircrafts position?

A—80 NM.
B—100 NM.
C—120 NM.

The VOR MON will ensure that regardless of an aircraft's position in the contiguous U.S. (CONUS), a MON airport (equipped with legacy ILS or VOR approaches) will be within 100 NM. (PLT354, AA.I.E.K3) — AIM ¶1-1-3

RTC

9721. Obstacles in most areas where "Copter GPS" instrument approaches are needed, require the approach speed must be limited to

A—80 knots on initial and final segments.
B—60 knots on all segments except the missed approach.
C—70 knots on final and missed approach segments.

As long as the obstacle environment permits, helicopter approaches can be flown at a speed of 70 knots from the initial approach waypoint until reaching the missed approach holding waypoint. It is necessary that helicopter procedures be flown at 70 knots or less since helicopter departure procedures and missed approaches use a 20:1 obstacle clearance surface. (PLT382) — AIM ¶1-1-19

RTC

9726. The maximum speed and obstacle clearance surface (OCS) that a "Copter GPS" standard instrument departure (SID) or departure procedure (DP) is based upon is

A—70 knots and 20:1 OCS.
B—70 knots and 10:1 OCS.
C—60 knots and 20:1 OCS.

As long as the obstacle environment permits, helicopter approaches can be flown at a speed of 70 knots from the initial approach waypoint until reaching the missed approach holding waypoint. It is necessary that helicopter procedures be flown at 70 knots or less since helicopter departure procedures and missed approaches use a 20:1 obstacle clearance surface. (PLT354) — AIM ¶1-1-19

Answers

9310 [B] 8837 [A] 8839 [B] 9721 [C] 9726 [A]

Automatic Dependent Surveillance–Broadcast (ADS-B)

Aircraft operating in airspace previously requiring the use of a transponder are required to have an Automatic Dependent Surveillance–Broadcast (ADS-B) system that includes a certified position source capable of meeting requirements defined in 14 CFR §91.227. For altitudes below FL180 this system can be either a 1090-ES or Universal Access Transceiver (UAT). Operations in Class A airspace require the use of extended squitter ADS-B and Traffic Information Services–Broadcast (TIS-B) equipment operating on the radio frequency of 1090 MHz. This equipment is simply referred to as 1090-ES.

ADS-B Out is a function of an aircraft's avionics that periodically broadcasts the aircraft's three-dimnesional position and velocity along with additional identifying information prescribed by §91.227. If the aircraft is equipped with ADS-B Out, it must be operated in transmit mode at all times. At any time, the pilot of an aircraft with inoperable ADS-B equipment may request a deviation from the ATC facility that has jurisdiction over the airspace for flight to the ultimate destination airport, including any intermediate stops, or to proceed to a place where suitable repairs can be made.

ALL

9944. Flight operations conducted in Class A airspace require the aircraft be equipped with a

A—Extended Squitter ADS-B operating on radio frequency 1090 MHz.
B—Universal Access Transceiver ADS-B operating on the frequency of 978 MHz.
C—Extended Squitter ADS-B operating on radio frequency 978 MHz.

Extended squitter ADS-B operates on radio frequency 1090 MHz. (PLT354, AA.I.A.K9) 14 CFR §91.225

Answer (B) is incorrect because this equipment is only allowed for operations below FL180. Answer (C) is incorrect because, for operations in Class A airspace, the ADS-B must operate on radio frequency 1090 MHz.

ALL

9945. Operations at and above FL180 require the use of what onboard avionics equipment?

A—Flight Information Services – Broadcast and Automatic Dependent Surveillance – Broadcast.
B—Traffic Information Services – Broadcast and Automatic Dependent Surveillance – Broadcast.
C—Traffic Information Services – Broadcast and Flight Information Services – Broadcast.

Operation at and above FL180 in Class A airspace require the use of Automatic Dependent Surveillance–Broadcast (ADS-B) and Traffic Information Services–Broadcast (TIS-B) equipment. (PLT354, AA.I.A.K9) — 14 CFR §91.227

ALL

9946. Requests for deviations for inoperable ADS-B equipment may be made to

A—the ATC facility having jurisdiction over the airspace at any time.
B—the ATC facility having jurisdiction over the airspace at least 1-hour prior.
C—the Federal Aviation Administration 24 hours before the scheduled operation.

Requests for deviations for inoperable ADS-B equipment may be made at any time to the ATC facility having jurisdiction over the airspace. (PLT354, AA.I.A.K9) — 14 CFR §91.225

ALL

9946-1. Each person operating an aircraft equipped with ADS-B Out must operate it in the transmit mode

A—at all times unless otherwise authorized by the FAA or directed by ATC.
B—when operating in Class B and C airspace, excluding operations conducted under day VFR.
C—all classes of airspace when the flight is operated for compensation or hire but not otherwise.

Regardless of airspace or whether the aircraft was originally certificated with an electrical system, it must operate any installed ADS-B Out equipment in transmit mode. (PLT354, AA.I.G.K2) — 14 CFR §91.225

Answers

9944 [A] 9945 [B] 9946 [A] 9946-1 [A]

Airport Lighting and Marking

A rotating beacon not only aids in locating an airport at night or in low visibility, it can also help to identify which airport is seen. Civilian airports have a beacon that alternately flashes green and white. A military airport has the same green and white beacon but the white beam is split to give a dual flash of white. A lighted heliport has a green, yellow and white beacon.

FAA Figure 129 shows the basic marking and lighting for a runway with a nonprecision approach. The threshold is marked with 4 stripes on either side of the centerline. 1,000 feet from the threshold, a broad "fixed distance" marker is painted on either side of the centerline (A). The runway lights are white for the entire length of the runway (as are the centerline lights if installed). The threshold is lit with red lights.

FAA Figure 130 shows the somewhat more elaborate ICAO markings for a nonprecision runway. In addition to the fixed distance marker, there are stripes painted on the runway every 500 feet to a distance of 3,000 feet from the threshold. This runway has either High Intensity Runway Lights (HIRL) or Medium Intensity Runway Lights (MIRL) installed. These lights are amber rather than white in the areas within 2,000 feet of the threshold. This gives the pilot a "caution zone" on landing rollout.

FAA Figure 131 shows the lighting and marking for a precision instrument runway. The runway striping has been modified to make it easier to tell exactly how much runway remains. The stripes are still at 500 foot intervals for the 3,000 feet from the threshold. The HIRL or MIRL turns amber for the 2,000 feet closest to the threshold. The centerline lighting has alternating red and white lights from 3,000 feet to 1,000 feet to go, and has all red lights in the 1,000 feet closest to the threshold.

In addition to the markings discussed above, some runways have distance remaining markers. These are simply signs showing the remaining runway in thousands of feet.

Taxi leadoff lights associated with runway centerline lights are green and yellow alternating lights, curving from the centerline of the runway to a point on the exit.

Some runways have Runway End Identifier Lights (REIL) installed at the threshold. These are synchronized flashing lights (usually strobes) placed laterally at either side of the runway threshold. Their purpose is to facilitate identification of a runway surrounded by numerous other lighting systems.

LAHSO is an acronym for "Land And Hold Short Operations." These operations include landing and holding short of an intersecting runway, an intersecting taxiway, or some other designated point on a runway other than an intersecting runway or taxiway. At controlled airports, ATC may clear a pilot to land and hold short. The pilot-in-command has the final authority to accept or decline any land and hold short clearance. The safety and operation of the aircraft remain the responsibility of the pilot. To conduct LAHSO, pilots should become familiar with all available information concerning LAHSO at their destination airport. Pilots should have, readily available, the published Available Landing Distance (ALD) and runway slope information for all LAHSO runway combinations at each airport of intended landing. Additionally, knowledge about landing performance data permits the pilot to readily determine that the ALD for the assigned runway is sufficient for safe LAHSO. If, for any reason, such as difficulty in discerning the location of a LAHSO intersection, wind conditions, aircraft condition, etc., the pilot elects to request to land on the full length of the runway, to land on another runway, or to decline LAHSO, a pilot is expected to promptly inform ATC, ideally even before the clearance is issued. A LAHSO clearance, once accepted, must be adhered to, just as any other ATC clearance, unless an amended clearance is obtained or an emergency occurs. However, a LAHSO clearance does not preclude a rejected landing. The airport markings, signage, and lighting associated with LAHSO consist of a three-part system of yellow hold-short markings, red and white signage and, in certain cases, in-pavement lighting.

A hot spot is a location on an airport movement area with a history or potential risk of collision or runway incursion, and where heightened attention by pilots and drivers is necessary. The FAA depicts hot spots in Chart Supplements with symbols using three shapes with two distinct meanings: a circle or ellipse for ground movement hot spots and a cylinder for wrong-surface hot spots. To address wrong-surface events where an aircraft lines up to or lands on the incorrect runway, taxiway, or airport, the FAA is releasing Arrival Alert Notices (AANs) at several airports with a history of misalignment risk. AANs include graphics that visually depict the approach to a particular airport with a history of misalignment risk and language that describes the misalignment risk. AANs incorporate the standardized hot spot symbology.

ATM, ATS, RTC
8905. How can a pilot identify a military airport at night?

A—Green, yellow, and white beacon light.
B—White and red beacon light with dual flash of the white.
C—Green and white beacon light with dual flash of the white.

Military airport beacons flash alternately white and green, but are differentiated from civil beacons by a dual peaked (two quick) white flashes between the green flashes. (PLT141, AA.II.C.K3) — AIM ¶2-1-9

Answer (A) is incorrect because a sequential green, yellow, and white beacon light identifies a lighted civilian heliport. Answer (B) is incorrect because no type of airfield is marked by a beacon with a red and white light with dual flash of the white.

ATM, ATS, RTC
8906. How can a pilot identify a lighted heliport at night?

A—Green, yellow, and white beacon light.
B—White and red beacon light with dual flash of the white.
C—Green and white beacon light with dual flash of the white.

A rotating beacon flashing green, yellow and white identifies a lighted heliport. (PLT141, AA.II.C.K3) — AIM ¶2-1-9

Answer (B) is incorrect because no type of airfield is marked by a white and red beacon with a dual flash of white. Answer (C) is incorrect because a green and white beacon light with a dual flash of the white identifies a military airfield.

ATM, ATS, RTC
9421. Holding position signs have

A—white inscriptions on a red background.
B—red inscriptions on a white background.
C—yellow inscriptions on a red background.

Holding position signs are mandatory instruction signs, and mandatory instruction signs have a red background with a white inscription. (PLT141, AA.II.C.K3) — AIM ¶2-3-8

ATM, ATS, RTC
9421-1. The most important markings on an airport are

A—ILS critical area.
B—hold markings.
C—taxiway identification markings.

The hold markings depict where the aircraft is supposed to stop and are a critical component to safe airport operations. (PLT141, AA.II.C.K3) — AIM ¶2-3-5

ALL
9421-2. In the United States, there is an average of

A—2 runway incursions every week.
B—3 runway incursions every day.
C—4 runway incursions every month.

Runway safety is a significant challenge and a top priority for everyone in aviation. In the United States, an average of three runway incursions occur daily. (PLT141, AA.I.E.K10) — FAA-H-8083-25

ALL
9421-3. Detailed investigations of runway incursions have identified

A—2 major areas of contributing factors.
B—3 major areas of contributing factors.
C—4 major areas of contributing factors.

Detailed investigations of runway incursions have identified 3 major areas contributing to these events: (1) failure to comply with ATC instructions; (2) lack of airport familiarity; (3) nonconformance with standard operating procedures. (PLT149, AA.II.C.K6) — FAA-H-8083-25

Answers

8905 [C]	8906 [A]	9421 [A]	9421-1 [B]	9421-2 [B]	9421-3 [B]

ATM, ATS, RTC

9422. Airport information signs, used to provide destination or information, have

A—yellow inscriptions on a black background.
B—white inscriptions on a black background.
C—black inscriptions on a yellow background.

Information signs have a yellow background with a black inscription. They are used to provide the pilot with information on such things as areas that cannot be seen from the control tower, applicable radio frequencies, and noise abatement procedures. (PLT141, AA.II.C.K3) — AIM ¶2-3-12

ATM, ATS, RTC

9735. (Refer to Figure 223.) The "runway hold position" sign denotes

A—an area protected for an aircraft approaching a runway.
B—an entrance to runway from a taxiway.
C—intersecting runways.

Runway holding position signs are located at the holding position on taxiways that intersect a runway or on runways that intersect other runways. (PLT141, AA.II.C.K3) — AIM ¶2-3-8

ATM, ATS, RTC

9735-1. (Refer to Figure 228.) What is the purpose of the runway/runway hold position sign?

A—Denotes entrance to runway from a taxiway.
B—Denotes area protected for an aircraft approaching or departing a runway.
C—Denotes intersecting runways.

Mandatory instruction signs are used to denote an entrance to a runway or critical area and areas where an aircraft is prohibited from entering. The runway holding position sign is located at the holding position on taxiways that intersect a runway or on runways that intersect other runways. (PLT141, AA.II.C.K3) — AIM ¶2-3-8

ATM, ATS, RTC

9735-2. (Refer to Figure 225.) What is the purpose of No Entry sign?

A—Identifies paved area where aircraft are prohibited from entering.
B—Identifies area that does not continue beyond intersection.
C—Identifies the exit boundary for the runway protected area.

The no entry sign prohibits an aircraft from entering an area. Typically, this sign would be located on a taxiway intended to be used in only one direction or at the intersection of vehicle roadways with runways, taxiways or aprons where the roadway may be mistaken as a taxiway or other aircraft movement surface. (PLT141, AA.II.C.K3) — AIM ¶2-3-8

Answer (B) is incorrect because this is the purpose of a hold position sign. Answer (C) is incorrect because this is the purpose of the runway boundary sign.

ATM, ATS, RTC

9735-3. (Refer to Figure 226.) What does the outbound destination sign identify?

A—Identifies entrance to the runway from a taxiway.
B—Identifies runway on which an aircraft is located.
C—Identifies direction to take-off runways.

Outbound destination signs define directions to takeoff runways. (PLT141, AA.II.C.K3) — AIM ¶2-3-11

Answer (A) is incorrect because this is a runway marking. Answer (B) is incorrect because this is a runway location sign.

ALL

8901. What is the advantage of HIRL or MIRL on an IFR runway as compared to a VFR runway?

A—Lights are closer together and easily distinguished from surrounding lights.
B—Amber lights replace white on the last 2,000 feet of runway for a caution zone.
C—Alternate red and white lights replace the white on the last 3,000 feet of runway for a caution zone.

Runway edge lights (HIRL or MIRL) are white on VFR runways. On IFR runways, HIRL or MIRL lights are amber on the last 2,000 feet or half the runway length (whichever is less), to indicate a caution zone for landing. (PLT148, AA.III.A.K4) — AIM ¶2-1-4

Answer (A) is incorrect because MIRL and HIRL are runway edge light systems, and are not spaced closer together on instrument runways. Answer (C) is incorrect because alternate red and white runway centerline lights are on the last 3,000 feet of a runway to the last 1,000 feet of runway (the last 1,000 feet of runway centerline lights are marked by red lights).

Answers

9422 [C]	9735 [C]	9735-1 [C]	9735-2 [A]	9735-3 [C]	8901 [B]

ALL

8901-1. What is the advantage of HIRL or MIRL on a VFR runway as compared to an IFR Runway?

A—Yellow lights replace white on the last 2,000 feet or half of the runway length.
B—Lights are spaced closer together.
C—Runway edge lights are white.

Runway edge lights (HIRL or MIRL) are white on VFR runways. On IFR runways, HIRL or MIRL lights are amber on the last 2,000 feet or half the runway length (whichever is less), to indicate a caution zone for landing. (PLT148, AA.II.C.K3) — AIM ¶ 2-1-4

ATM, ATS, RTC

8902. Identify touchdown zone lighting (TDZL).

A—Two rows of transverse light bars disposed symmetrically about the runway centerline.
B—Flush centerline lights spaced at 50-foot intervals extending through the touchdown zone.
C—Alternate white and green centerline lights extending from 75 feet from the threshold through the touchdown zone.

Touchdown Zone Lighting (TDZL) consists of two rows of transverse light bars disposed symmetrically about the runway centerline in the runway touchdown zone. (PLT148, AA.III.A.K4) — AIM ¶2-1-5

Answer (B) is incorrect because flush centerline lights spaced at 50-foot intervals extending the length of the runway, including the touchdown zone, are runway centerline lighting. Answer (C) is incorrect because runway centerline lights extend from 75 feet from the threshold through the touchdown zone and are white, not alternating white and green.

ATM, ATS, RTC

8722. When approaching a holding position sign for a runway approach area you must

A—obtain ATC clearance prior to crossing.
B—hold only when specifically instructed by ATC.
C—hold only when the weather is below 800 feet and 2 miles visibility.

At some airports, it is necessary to hold an aircraft on a taxiway located in the approach or departure area for a runway so that the aircraft does not interfere with operations on that runway. In these situations, a sign with the designation of the approach end of the runway followed by a "dash" (-) and letters "APCH" will be located at the holding position on the taxiway. (PLT141, AA.II.C.K2) — AIM ¶2-3-8

ATM, ATS, RTC

8903. Identify runway remaining lighting on centerline lighting systems.

A—Amber lights from 3,000 feet to 1,000 feet, then alternate red and white lights to the end.
B—Alternate red and white lights from 3,000 feet to 1,000 feet, then red lights to the end.
C—Alternate red and white lights from 3,000 feet to the end of the runway.

Centerline lighting systems consist of alternating red and white lights from 3,000 feet remaining to the 1,000-foot point, and all red lights for the last 1,000 feet of the runway. (PLT141, AA.III.A.K4) — AIM ¶2-1-5

Answer (A) is incorrect because alternate red and white lights are from 3,000 feet to 1,000 feet, then red lights to the end. Answer (C) is incorrect because runway remaining lighting alternates red and white lights from 3,000 feet to 1,000 feet, and red lights from 1,000 feet to the end of the runway.

ATM, ATS, RTC

8904. Identify taxi leadoff lights associated with the centerline lighting system.

A—Alternate green and yellow lights curving from the centerline of the runway to the centerline of the taxiway.
B—Alternate green and yellow lights curving from the centerline of the runway to the edge of the taxiway.
C—Alternate green and yellow lights curving from the centerline of the runway to a point on the exit.

Taxiway leadoff lights extend from the runway centerline to a point on an exit taxiway to expedite movement of aircraft from the runway. These lights alternate green and yellow from the runway centerline to the runway holding position or the ILS critical area, as appropriate. (PLT141, AA.III.A.K4) — AIM ¶2-1-5

ATM, ATS, RTC

8907. Identify the runway distance remaining markers.

A—Signs with increments of 1,000 feet distance remaining.
B—Red markers laterally placed across the runway at 3,000 feet from the end.
C—Yellow marker laterally placed across the runway with signs on the side denoting distance to end.

Runway distance remaining markers are signs located along the sides of a runway to indicate the remaining runway distance in increments of 1,000 feet. (PLT141, AA.II.C.K3) — AIM ¶2-3-3

Answers (B) and (C) are incorrect because distance remaining markers are along the side of the runway and are black and white.

Answers

8901-1 [C]	8902 [A]	8722 [A]	8903 [B]	8904 [C]	8907 [A]

ALL

8907-1. Runway centerline lights as seen from the flight deck begin to alternate white and red in the last

A—1,000 feet of runway distance remaining.
B—2,000 feet of runway distance remaining.
C—3,000 feet of runway distance remaining.

Runway centerline lights as seen from the approach end of the runway are white until the last 3,000 feet of the runway. The white lights begin to alternate red for the next 2,000 feet, and for the last 1,000 feet of the runway, all centerline lights are red. (PLT141, AA.VI.F.K2) — AIM ¶2-1-5

ATM, ATS, RTC

8922. (Refer to Figure 129.) What is the runway distance remaining at "A" for a daytime takeoff on runway 9?

A—1,000 feet.
B—1,500 feet.
C—2,000 feet.

The fixed distance marker is located 1,000 feet from the threshold (in this case the end of the runway). (PLT141, AA.II.C.K3) — AIM ¶2-3-3

Answer (B) is incorrect because the 1,500 feet distance of runway remaining is not marked on an FAA nonprecision runway. Answer (C) is incorrect because 2,000 feet is the distance remaining on an ICAO (not FAA) nonprecision instrument runway where the runway edge lights are amber.

ATM, ATS, RTC

8923. (Refer to Figure 130.) What is the runway distance remaining at "A" for a nighttime takeoff on runway 9?

A—1,000 feet.
B—2,000 feet.
C—2,500 feet.

According to the key, a half-shaded circle indicates yellow lights. Each fixed-distance marker marks off 500 feet. Four markers from the departure end to the first yellow light measures 2,000 feet remaining. (PLT141, AA.III.A.K4) — AIM ¶2-3-3

Answers (A) and (C) are incorrect because the beginning of yellow runway edge lights on an ICAO nonprecision instrument runway indicates 2,000 feet of runway remaining.

ATM, ATS, RTC

8924. (Refer to Figure 130.) What is the runway distance remaining at "B" for a daytime takeoff on runway 9?

A—2,000 feet.
B—2,500 feet.
C—3,000 feet.

Each fixed-distance marker measures 500 feet. From the departure end, it is 3,000 feet. (PLT141, AA.III.A.K4) — AIM ¶2-3-3

Answer (A) is incorrect because 2,000 feet would be the third distance marker encountered. At night, 2,000 feet is identified by the beginning of amber runway edge lights. Answer (B) is incorrect because 2,500 feet would be the second distance marker encountered.

ATM, ATS, RTC

8925. (Refer to Figure 130.) What is the runway distance remaining at "C" for a daytime takeoff on runway 9?

A—2,500 feet.
B—2,000 feet.
C—1,500 feet.

Since each fixed-distance marker in this problem represents 500 feet, the distance to "C" from the departure end is 2,000 feet. (PLT141, AA.III.A.K4) — AIM ¶2-3-3

Answer (A) is incorrect because 2,500 feet would be the second distance marker encountered. Answer (C) is incorrect because 1,500 feet would be the fourth distance marker encountered.

ATM, ATS, RTC

8926. (Refer to Figure 130.) What is the runway distance remaining at "D" for a daytime takeoff on runway 9?

A—500 feet.
B—1,000 feet.
C—1,500 feet.

The fixed-distance marker at "D" corresponds to 1,000 feet remaining. (PLT141, AA.III.A.K4) — AIM ¶2-3-3

Answer (A) is incorrect because 500 feet would be the sixth distance marker encountered. Answer (C) is incorrect because 1,500 feet would be the fourth distance marker encountered.

ATM, ATS, RTC

8927. (Refer to Figure 131.) What is the runway distance remaining at "E" for a daytime takeoff on runway 9?

A—1,500 feet.
B—2,000 feet.
C—2,500 feet.

Each fixed-distance marker marks off 500 feet. "E" is 2,000 feet from the departure end. (PLT141, AA.III.A.K4) — AIM ¶2-3-3

Answer (A) is incorrect because 1,500 feet would be the second pair of double markers encountered on either side of the centerline. Answer (C) is incorrect because 2,500 feet would be the second pair of single markers encountered on either side of the centerline.

Answers

8907-1 [C]	8922 [A]	8923 [B]	8924 [C]	8925 [B]	8926 [B]
8927 [B]					

ATM, ATS, RTC
8928. (Refer to Figure 131.) What is the runway distance remaining at "A" for a nighttime takeoff on runway 9?

A—2,000 feet.
B—3,000 feet.
C—3,500 feet.

This question and figure reference remaining runway lighting/centerline lighting systems in the final 2,000 feet as viewed from the takeoff or approach position. Alternate red and white lights are seen from the 3,000-foot points to the 1,000-foot points, and all red lights are seen for the last 1,000 feet of the runway. (PLT141, AA.III.A.K4) — AIM ¶2-1-5

Answer (A) is incorrect because 2,000 feet is marked by the beginning of amber runway edge lights. Answer (C) is incorrect because the runway remaining lights begin alternating between red and white at 3,000 feet of remaining runway.

ATM, ATS, RTC
8929. (Refer to Figure 131.) What is the runway distance remaining at "D" for a daytime takeoff on runway 9?

A—3,000 feet.
B—2,500 feet.
C—1,500 feet.

Each fixed-distance marker marks off 500 feet. "D" corresponds to 3,000 feet. (PLT141, AA.III.A.K4) — AIM ¶2-3-3

Answer (B) is incorrect because 2,500 feet would be the second pair of single markers encountered on either side of the centerline. Answer (C) is incorrect because 1,500 feet would be the second pair of double markers encountered on either side of the centerline.

ATM, ATS, RTC
8930. (Refer to Figure 131.) What is the runway distance remaining at "B" for a nighttime takeoff on runway 9?

A—1,000 feet.
B—2,000 feet.
C—2,500 feet.

The runway edge lights are white, except on instrument runways. There, amber replaces white on the last 2,000 feet or half the runway length, whichever is less, to form a caution zone for landings. (PLT141, AA.III.A.K4) — AIM ¶2-1-4

Answer (A) is incorrect because 1,000 feet would be indicated by the start of red centerline lighting. Answer (C) is incorrect because the beginning of yellow runway edge lights on an instrument runway indicates 2,000 feet of remaining runway.

ATM, ATS, RTC
8931. (Refer to Figure 131.) What is the runway distance remaining at "F" for a daytime takeoff on runway 9?

A—2,000 feet.
B—1,500 feet.
C—1,000 feet.

Each fixed-distance marker marks off 500 feet. "F" corresponds to the 1,000-foot fixed-distance marker. (PLT141, AA.III.A.K4) — AIM ¶2-3-3

Answer (A) is incorrect because 2,000 feet would be the first pair of double markers encountered on either side of the centerline. At night it is marked by the beginning of amber runway edge lights. Answer (B) is incorrect because 1,500 feet would be the second pair of double markers encountered on either side of the centerline.

ATM, ATS, RTC
8932. (Refer to Figure 131.) What is the runway distance remaining at "C" for a takeoff on runway 9?

A—1,000 feet.
B—1,500 feet.
C—1,800 feet.

All red lights along the runway centerline correspond to the last 1,000 feet of runway. (PLT141, AA.III.A.K4) — AIM ¶2-1-5

Answer (B) is incorrect because the start of red lights on centerline lighting indicates 1,000 feet of remaining runway. Answer (C) is incorrect because the start of red lights on centerline lighting indicates 1,000 feet of remaining runway.

ATM, ATS, RTC
8914. What is the purpose of REIL?

A—Identification of a runway surrounded by a preponderance of other lighting.
B—Identification of the touchdown zone to prevent landing short.
C—Establish visual descent guidance information during an approach.

Runway End Identifier Lights (REIL) are effective for:

1. *Identification of a runway surrounded by numerous other lighting systems,*
2. *Identification of a runway which lacks contrast with surrounding terrain, or*
3. *Identification of a runway during reduced visibility.*

(PLT145, AA.III.A.K4) — AIM ¶2-1-3

Answer (B) is incorrect because the touchdown zone is identified by in-runway lighting of two rows of transverse light bars on either side of the runway centerline from 100 feet to 3,000 feet from the landing threshold. Answer (C) is incorrect because a VASI (not REIL) assists in providing visual descent guidance information during an approach.

Answers

8928 [B]	8929 [A]	8930 [B]	8931 [C]	8932 [A]	8914 [A]

ATM, ATS, RTC

8915. Identify REIL.

A—Amber lights for the first 2,000 feet of runway.
B—Green lights at the threshold and red lights at far end of runway.
C—Synchronized flashing lights laterally at each side of the runway threshold.

The REIL system consists of a pair of synchronized flashing lights located laterally on each side of the runway threshold. (PLT145, AA.III.A.K4) — AIM ¶2-1-3

Answer (A) is incorrect because amber lights are used on the last 2,000 feet of runway edge lights to form a caution zone on instrument runways. Answer (B) is incorrect because green lights at the threshold mark the runway edge for landing aircraft and red lights at the far end mark the runway edge to a departing or landing aircraft.

ATM, ATS, RTC

9731. Land and Hold Short Operations (LAHSO) include landing and holding short:

A—of an intersecting taxiway only.
B—of some designated point on the runway.
C—only of an intersecting runway or taxiway.

Land And Hold Short Operations (LAHSO) include landing and holding short of an intersecting runway, an intersecting taxiway, or some other designated point on a runway other than an intersecting runway or taxiway. (PLT140, AA.VI.F.R3b) — AIM ¶4-3-11

ATM, ATS, RTC

9732. A Land and Hold Short Operations (LAHSO) clearance, that the pilot accepts:

A—must result in a landing.
B—does not preclude a rejected landing.
C—precludes a rejected landing.

A LAHSO clearance, once accepted, must be adhered to unless an amended clearance is obtained or an emergency occurs. However, a LAHSO clearance does not preclude a rejected landing. (PLT140, AA.VI.F.R3b) — AIM ¶4-3-11

ATM, ATS, RTC

9733. In conducting Land and Hold Short Operations (LAHSO), the pilot should have readily available:

A—the published Available Landing Distance (ALD), landing performance of the aircraft, and slope of all LAHSO combinations at the destination airport.
B—the published runway length and slope for all LAHSO combinations at the airport of intended landing.
C—the landing performance of the aircraft, published Available Landing Distance (ALD) for all LAHSO combinations at the airport of intended landing, plus the forecast winds.

To conduct LAHSO, pilots should become familiar with all available information concerning LAHSO at their destination airport. Pilots should have, readily available, the published Available Landing Distance (ALD) and runway slope information for all LAHSO runway combinations at each airport of intended landing. Additionally, knowledge about landing performance data permits the pilot to readily determine that the ALD for the assigned runway is sufficient for safe LAHSO. (PLT140, AA.VI.F.R3b) — AIM ¶4-3-11

ATM, ATS, RTC

9734. The airport markings, signage and lighting associated with Land and Hold Short (LAHSO) consists of:

A—yellow hold-short markings, red and white signage, and in-pavement lights.
B—red and white signage, yellow hold-short markings, and at some airports, in-pavement lights.
C—red and black signage, in-pavement lights, and yellow hold-short markings.

The airport markings, signage, and lighting associated with LAHSO consist of a three-part system of yellow hold-short markings, red and white signage and, in certain cases, in-pavement lighting. (PLT140, AA.VI.F.R3b) — AIM ¶4-3-11

Answers

8915 [C]	9731 [B]	9732 [B]	9733 [A]	9734 [B]

ATM, ATS, RTC

9416-1. (Refer to Figure 224.) The ILS critical area markings denote

A—where you are clear of the runway.
B—where you must be to start your ILS procedure.
C—where you are clear of the ILS critical area.

The ILS critical area sign is located adjacent to the ILS holding position marking on the pavement and can be seen by pilots leaving the critical area. The sign is intended to provide pilots with another visual cue which they can use as a guide in deciding when they are clear of the ILS critical area. (PLT141, AA.II.C.S3) — AIM ¶2-3-9

ATM, ATS, RTC

9416-2. The ILS critical area sign indicates

A—where aircraft are prohibited.
B—the edge of the ILS critical area.
C—the exit boundary.

The ILS critical area sign is located adjacent to the ILS holding position marking on the pavement and can be seen by pilots leaving the critical area. The sign is intended to provide pilots with another visual cue to use as a guide in deciding when they are clear of the ILS critical area. (PLT141, AA.II.C.S3) — AIM ¶2-3-9

ATM, ATS, RTC

9423-1. (Refer to Figure 227.) The "taxiway ending" marker

A—identifies area where aircraft are prohibited.
B—indicates taxiway does not continue.
C—provides general taxiing direction to named taxiway.

Taxiway ending marker is an airport sign indicating the taxiway does not continue. (PLT141, AA.II.C.K3) — AIM ¶2-3-11

Answer (A) is incorrect because this is the purpose of a no entry sign. Answer (C) is incorrect because this is the purpose of direction signs.

ATM, ATS, RTC

9423. Hold line markings at the intersection of taxiways and runways consist of four lines (two solid and two dashed) that extend across the width of the taxiway. These lines are

A—white in color and the dashed lines are nearest the runway.
B—yellow in color and the dashed lines are nearest the runway.
C—yellow in color and the solid lines are nearest the runway.

Holding position markings for taxiway/runway intersections consist of four yellow lines—two solid and two dashed. The solid lines are always on the same side where the aircraft is to hold. (PLT141, AA.II.C.K3) — AIM ¶2-3-5

ATM, ATS, RTC

8203. All runway hold markings consist of

A—2 dashed and 1 solid yellow line.
B—2 dashed and 2 solid yellow lines.
C—1 dashed and 1 solid yellow line.

Holding position markings for taxiway/runway intersections consist of four yellow lines—two solid and two dashed. The solid lines are always on the same side where the aircraft is to hold. (PLT149, AA.II.C.K3) — AIM ¶2-3-5

ATM, ATS, RTC

9436. (Refer to Figure 156.) This sign, which is visible to the pilot on the runway, indicates

A—a point at which the pilot should contact ground control without being instructed by the tower.
B—a point at which the aircraft will be clear of the runway.
C—the point at which the emergency arresting gear is stretched across the runway.

The runway boundary sign has a yellow background with a black inscription with a graphic depicting the pavement holding position. This sign, which faces the runway and is visible to the pilot exiting the runway, is located adjacent to the holding position marking on the pavement. The sign is intended to provide pilots with another visual cue which they can use as a guide in deciding when they are "clear of the runway." (PLT141, AA.I.E.K4) — AIM ¶2-3-9

Answers

9416-1 [C]	9416-2 [B]	9423-1 [B]	9423 [B]	8203 [B]	9436 [B]

ATM, ATS, RTC

9417. You have just landed at JFK and the tower tells you to call ground control when clear of the runway. You are considered clear of the runway when

A—the aft end of the aircraft is even with the taxiway location sign.
B—the flight deck area of the aircraft is even with the hold line.
C—all parts of the aircraft have crossed the hold line.

An aircraft is not "clear of the runway" until all parts have crossed the applicable holding position marking. (PLT141, AA.II.C.K3) — AIM ¶2-3-5

ATM, ATS, RTC

9764. Taxiway Centerline Lead-Off Lights are color coded to warn pilots that

A—they are within the runway environment or run-up danger critical area.
B—they are within the runway environment or ILS critical area.
C—they are within the taxiway end environment or ILS critical area.

Taxiway centerline lead-off lights provide visual guidance to persons exiting the runway. They are color-coded to warn pilots and vehicle drivers that they are within the runway environment or ILS critical area, whichever is more restrictive. Alternate green and yellow lights are installed, beginning with green, from the runway centerline to one centerline light position beyond the runway holding position or ILS critical area holding position. (PLT141, AA.III.A.K4) — AIM ¶2-1-5

ATM, ATS, RTC

9785. THL is the acronym for

A—Takeoff hold lights.
B—Taxi holding lights.
C—Terminal holding lights.

The Takeoff Hold Lights (THL) system is composed of in-pavement, unidirectional fixtures in a double longitudinal row aligned either side of the runway centerline lighting. Fixtures are focused toward the arrival end of the runway at the "position and hold" point, and they extend for 1,500 feet in front of the holding aircraft. Illuminated red lights provide a signal, to an aircraft in position for takeoff or rolling, indicating that it is unsafe to takeoff because the runway is occupied or about to be occupied by another aircraft or ground vehicle. Two aircraft, or a surface vehicle and an aircraft, are required for the lights to illuminate. The departing aircraft must be in position for takeoff or beginning takeoff roll. Another aircraft or a surface vehicle must be on or about to cross the runway. (PLT141, AA.III.A.K4) — AIM ¶2-1-6

ATM, ATS, RTC

9785-1. Takeoff hold lights (THL) are a part of the

A—automatic runway status light system.
B—tower operated runway stop light system.
C—ground controller operated ramp status holding light system.

Runway Status Light (RWSL) System is a fully automated system that provides runway status information to pilots and surface vehicle operators to clearly indicate when it is unsafe to enter, cross, takeoff from, or land on a runway. The RWSL system processes information from surveillance systems and activates Runway Entrance Lights (REL), Takeoff Hold Lights (THL), Runway Intersection Lights (RIL), and Final Approach Runway Occupancy Signal (FAROS) in accordance with the position and velocity of the detected surface traffic and approach traffic. REL, THL, and RIL are in-pavement light fixtures that are directly visible to pilots and surface vehicle operators. (PLT141, AA.III.A.K4) — AIM ¶2-1-6

ATM, ATS, RTC

9786. REL is the acronym for

A—Runway exit lights.
B—Runway entrance lights.
C—Ramp entry lights.

The Runway Entrance Lights (REL) system is composed of flush mounted, in-pavement, unidirectional fixtures that are parallel to and focused along the taxiway centerline and directed toward the pilot at the hold line. A specific array of REL lights include the first light at the hold line followed by a series of evenly spaced lights to the runway edge; and one additional light at the runway centerline in line with the last two lights before the runway edge. When activated, these red lights indicate that there is high-speed traffic on the runway or there is an aircraft on final approach within the activation area. (PLT141, AA.III.A.K4) — AIM ¶2-1-6

Answers

9417 [C]	9764 [B]	9785 [A]	9785-1 [A]	9786 [B]

ATM, ATS, RTC

9786-1. Runway Status Lights (REL) are

A—an independent light system.
B—automatically activated.
C—ATC tower controlled.

The runway status light (RWSL) system, which includes runway entrance lights (REL), is a fully automated system that provides runway status information to pilots and surface vehicle operators to clearly indicate when it is unsafe to enter, cross, takeoff from, or land on a runway. RWSL is an independent safety enhancement that does not substitute for or convey an ATC clearance. (PLT141, AA.III.A.K4) — AIM ¶2-1-6

ATM, ATS, RTC

9786-2. A runway status light (RWSL) system at an airport

A—relies on ASDE-X/airport surface surveillance capability (ASSC).
B—allows ATC to override any RWSL false indications.
C—does not require pilots to tell ATC when executing a go-around.

RWSL is an independent safety enhancement that does not substitute for or convey an ATC clearance. ATC maintains all authority over airport operations. (PLT141, AA.III.A.K4) — AIM ¶2-1-6

ATM, ATS, RTC

9787. (Refer to Figure 241). Hot Spots are depicted on airport diagrams as

A—circle, ellipse, or cylinder.
B—circle, ellipse, or square.
C—ellipse, square, or cylinder.

A circle or ellipse depicts ground movement hot spots such as:

- *hold short line infractions*
- *approach hold issues*
- *complex taxiway configurations*
- *movement/nonmovement boundary area issues*
- *tower line of sight problems*
- *marking and signage issues.*

A cylinder depicts wrong-surface hot spots, locations where an aircraft has inadvertently attempted to or actually departed or landed on the wrong surface. (PLT149, AA.II.C.K6) — FAA-H-8083-16

ATM, ATS, RTC

9437. (Refer to Figure 157.) This is an example of

A—an ILS Critical Area Holding Position Sign.
B—a Runway Boundary Sign.
C—an ILS Critical Area Boundary Sign.

This sign has a yellow background with a black inscription with a graphic depicting the ILS pavement holding position marking. This is located adjacent to the ILS holding position marking on the pavement and can be seen by the pilots leaving the critical area. (PLT141, AA.II.C.K3) — AIM ¶2-3-9

ATM, ATS, RTC

9416. When instructed by ATC to "Hold short of a runway (ILS critical area, etc.)," the pilot should stop

A—with the nose gear on the hold line.
B—so that no part of the aircraft extends beyond the hold line.
C—so the flight deck area of the aircraft is even with the hold line.

When the ILS critical area is being protected the pilot should stop so no part of the aircraft extends beyond the holding position marking. (PLT141, AA.II.C.K2) — AIM ¶2-3-5

ATM, ATS, RTC

9798. When you see this pavement marking from the cockpit, you

A—can taxi past this point at your own risk.
B—must hold short until "cleared" to taxi onto or past the runway.
C—may not cross the line until ATC allows you to "enter" or "cross" by instruction.

This question will likely include an onscreen image depicting runway hold position markings. These markings indicate where an aircraft is supposed to stop when approaching a runway. ATC will not use the word "cleared" in conjunction with authorization for aircraft to taxi. (PLT141, AA.II.C.K3) — AIM ¶2-3-5, 4-3-18

Answers

9786-1 [A]	9786-2 [B]	9787 [A]	9437 [C]	9416 [B]	9798 [C]

ATM, ATS, RTC
9799. The sign shown is an example of

A—a mandatory instruction sign.
B—runway heading notification signage.
C—an airport directional sign.

This question will likely include an onscreen image depicting a runway hold position sign. This is a mandatory instruction sign, used to hold an aircraft on a taxiway located in the approach or departure area for a runway so the aircraft does not interfere with operations on that runway. (PLT141, AA.II.C.K3) — AIM ¶2-3-8

ATM, ATS, RTC
8701. Airport "hot spots" are

A—reserved for contaminated aircraft.
B—parking spots for military aircraft.
C—known hazardous runway intersections.

A hot spot is defined as a location on an airport movement area with a history of potential risk of collision or runway incursion, and where heightened attention by pilots and drivers is necessary. (PLT149, AA.II.C.K6) — FAA-H-8083-16

Approach Lighting

An airplane approaching to land on a runway served by a **Visual Approach Slope Indicator (VASI)** must remain on or above the glide slope (except for normal bracketing) until a lower altitude is necessary for a safe landing.

A VASI gives the pilot a visual glide slope to follow when landing on certain runways. A VASI glide slope is normally about 3° (the same as an ILS) and the aim point is about 1,000 feet down the runway from the threshold. The angle and aim point of the VASI can be adjusted as necessary to accommodate the runway conditions. If a pilot of a high performance airplane is flying a VASI with a glide slope steeper than 3.5°, he/she should be aware that a longer than normal roll-out may result from the flare maneuver required by the steep angle.

Many runways used by air carrier aircraft have a three-bar VASI system to accommodate aircraft with a high cockpit such as Boeing 747 or DC-10. These aircraft need a glide slope that has an aim point further down the runway to ensure adequate clearance for the landing gear at the runway threshold. The pilot of such an airplane must use the two upwind lights (middle and far bars) for glide slope information.

The **Precision Approach Path Indicator (PAPI)** approach light system consists of a row of four lights perpendicular to the runway. Each light can be either red or white depending on the aircraft's position relative to the glide slope. The glide slope indications of a PAPI are as follows:

- High—4 white lights
- Slightly high—1 red, 3 white lights
- On glidepath—2 red, 2 white lights
- Slightly low—1 white, 3 red lights
- Low—4 red lights

Pulsating visual approach slope indicators normally consist of a single light unit projecting a two-color visual approach path. The below glidepath indication is normally pulsating red and the above glidepath indication is normally pulsating white. The "on glide slope" indication for one type of system is a steady white light, while for another type it is an alternating red and white.

Answers

9799 [A] 8701 [C]

ATM, ATS, RTC

9378. A pilot approaching to land a turbine-powered aircraft on a runway served by a VASI shall

A—not use the VASI unless a clearance for a VASI approach is received.
B—use the VASI only when weather conditions are below basic VFR.
C—maintain an altitude at or above the glide slope until a lower altitude is necessary for a safe landing.

An airplane approaching to land on a runway served by a visual approach slope indicator (VASI), shall maintain an altitude at or above the glide slope until a lower altitude is necessary for a safe landing. (PLT147, AA.III.B.K4) — 14 CFR §91.129

Answer (A) is incorrect because a VASI should be used at all times when available, and is not considered an instrument approach. Answer (B) is incorrect because a VASI should be used at all times in both VFR and when transitioning out of IFR weather.

ATM, ATS, RTC

8912. A pilot of a high-performance airplane should be aware that flying a steeper-than-normal VASI glide slope angle may result in

A—a hard landing.
B—increased landing rollout.
C—landing short of the runway threshold.

Although normal VASI glidepath angles are 3°, angles at some locations may be as high as 4.5° to give proper obstacle clearance. Pilots of high performance aircraft are cautioned that use of VASI angles in excess of 3.5° may cause an increase in runway length required for landing and rollout. (PLT147, AA.III.B.K4) — AIM ¶2-1-2

Answer (A) is incorrect because flying a steeper-than-normal VASI may result in an increased landing rollout in a high-performance airplane. Answer (C) is incorrect because a landing short of the runway threshold would be a result of flying a lower-than-normal VASI glide slope angle.

ATM, ATS, RTC

8911. What is the advantage of a three-bar VASI?

A—Pilots have a choice of glide angles.
B—A normal glide angle is afforded both high and low cockpit aircraft.
C—The three-bar VASI is much more visible and can be used at a greater height.

Three-bar VASI installations provide two visual glidepaths. The lower glidepath is provided by the near and middle bars and is normally set at 3° while the upper glidepath, provided by the middle and far bars is normally 1/4° higher. This higher glidepath is intended for use only by high cockpit aircraft to provide a sufficient threshold crossing height. (PLT147, AA.III.B.K4) — AIM ¶2-1-2

Answer (A) is incorrect because the three-bar VASI provides a glide slope for high cockpit aircraft, not a choice of glide angles for pilots. Answer (C) is incorrect because both the two- and three-bar VASI are visible from 3-5 miles during the day and up to 20 miles or more at night, and the three-bar VASI does not provide use at a greater height.

ATM, ATS, RTC

8913. The higher glide slope of the three-bar VASI is intended for use by

A—high performance aircraft.
B—helicopters.
C—high cockpit aircraft.

Three-bar VASI installations provide two visual glidepaths. The lower glidepath is provided by the near and middle bars and is normally set at 3° while the upper glidepath, provided by the middle and far bars is normally 1/4° higher. This higher glidepath is intended for use only by high cockpit aircraft to provide a sufficient threshold crossing height. (PLT147, AA.III.B.K4) — AIM ¶2-1-2

Answer (A) is incorrect because the higher glide slope of a three-bar VASI is for use only by high cockpit aircraft, which may or may not be high performance aircraft. Answer (B) is incorrect because the higher glide slope of a three-bar VASI is for use only by high cockpit aircraft, not specifically for use by helicopters.

ATM, ATS, RTC

8921. What does the Precision Approach Path Indicator (PAPI) consist of?

A—Row of four lights parallel to the runway; red, white, and green.
B—Row of four lights perpendicular to the runway; red and white.
C—One light projector with two colors; red and white.

The Precision Approach Path Indicator (PAPI) uses light units similar to the VASI but are installed in a single row of either two- or four-light units. (PLT147, AA.III.B.K4) — AIM ¶2-1-2

Answer (A) is incorrect because PAPI has a row of four lights perpendicular to the runway, and projects red and white light. Answer (C) is incorrect because PAPI consists of a row of four light projectors emitting red or white light.

Answers

9378 [C]	8912 [B]	8911 [B]	8913 [C]	8921 [B]

ATM, ATS, RTC

8908. What are the indications of Precision Approach Path Indicator (PAPI)?

A—High – white, on glidepath – red and white; low – red.
B—High – white, on glidepath – green; low – red.
C—High – white and green, on glidepath – green; low – red.

The Precision Approach Path Indicator (PAPI) uses light units similar to the VASI but are installed in a single row of either two or four light units:

High .... 4 white lights

Slightly high .... 1 red, 3 white lights

On glide path .... 2 red, 2 white lights

Slightly low .... 1 white, 3 red lights

Low .... 4 red lights

(PLT147, AA.III.B.K4) — AIM ¶2-1-2

Answer (B) is incorrect because the on glidepath indication of PAPI is both red and white lights. Answer (C) is incorrect because above the glidepath indication of PAPI is all white, on glidepath is two red and two white, and below glidepath is all red.

ATM, ATS, RTC

8909. What does the pulsating VASI consist of?

A—Three-light system, two pulsing and one steady.
B—Two-light projectors, one pulsing and one steady.
C—One-light projector, pulsing white when above glide slope or red when more than slightly below glide slope, steady white when on glide slope, steady red for slightly below glide path.

Pulsating visual approach slope indicators normally consist of a single light unit projecting a two-color visual approach path into the final approach area of the runway upon which the indicator is installed. The below glidepath indication is normally pulsating red, and the above glidepath indication is normally pulsating white. The on glidepath indication for one type of system is a steady white light, while for another type system, the on glidepath indication consists of an alternating red and white. (PLT147, AA.III.B.K4) — AIM ¶2-1-2

Answer (A) is incorrect because the pulsating VASI is a two-light system, in which below glidepath is pulsating red, above glidepath is pulsating white, and on glidepath is a steady white light. Answer (B) is incorrect because the pulsating VASI is a single light projecting unit emitting a two-color visual approach path into the final approach area of the runway.

ATM, ATS, RTC

8910. What are the indications of the pulsating VASI?

A—High – pulsing white, on glidepath – green, low – pulsing red.
B—High – pulsing white, on glidepath – steady white, slightly below glide slope steady red, low – pulsing red.
C—High – pulsing white, on course and on glidepath – steady white, off course but on glidepath – pulsing white and red; low – pulsing red.

Pulsating visual approach slope indicators normally consist of a single light unit projecting a two-color visual approach path into the final approach area of the runway upon which the indicator is installed. The below glidepath indication is normally pulsating red, and the above glidepath indication is normally pulsating white. The on glidepath indication for one type of system is a steady white light, while for another type system the on glidepath indication consists of an alternating red and white. (PLT147, AA.III.B.K4) — AIM ¶2-1-2

Answer (A) is incorrect because the on glidepath indication of a pulsating VASI is either a pulsing red and white or steady white, not green. Answer (C) is incorrect because the pulsating VASI only provides glidepath indications, not lateral, or course, indications. Above glidepath is pulsing white, on glidepath is pulsing red and white or steady white, and below glidepath is pulsing red.

ATM, ATS, RTC

8705. Lights which indicate the runway is occupied are

A—strobe lights located next to the PAPIs.
B—flashing PAPIs.
C—yellow flashing lights located below the PAPIs.

The standalone final approach runway occupancy signal (FAROS) is a fully automated system that provides runway occupancy status to pilots on final approach to indicate whether it may be unsafe to land. When an aircraft or vehicle is detected on the runway, the precision approach path indicator (PAPI) light fixtures flash as a signal to indicate the runway is occupied and that it may be unsafe to land. (PLT147, AA.III.B.K4) — AIM ¶2-1-7

Answers

8908 [A] 8909 [C] 8910 [B] 8705 [B]

Chapter 3
Aerodynamics

Lift and Drag

The four forces acting on an aircraft in flight are **lift, weight, thrust** and **drag**. Weight always acts vertically toward the center of the earth. Lift acts perpendicular to the relative wind (not always vertically). Thrust and drag act opposite each other and parallel to the relative wind.

Lift is produced by air flowing over the curved wing surfaces. The air flowing over the upper surface of the wing is deflected further than that flowing across the lower surface and therefore is accelerated. **Bernoulli's Principle** states that when a gas is accelerated, its pressure decreases. Thus the pressure on the upper wing surface is lower than that on the lower surface and lift is produced.

Angle of attack is the angle between the relative wind and chord line of wing. At zero angle of attack, the pressure on the upper surface of the wing is still less than atmospheric, but the wing is producing minimum lift. As the angle of attack is increased, the lift developed by the wing increases proportionately. This is true until the angle of attack exceeds a critical value, when the air flowing over the top of the wing breaks up into a turbulent flow and the wing stalls.

Angle of attack and indicated airspeed determine the total lift. An increase in either indicated airspeed or angle of attack increases total lift (up to the stalling angle of attack) and a decrease in either decreases total lift. To maintain the same total lift (i.e., maintain level flight), a pilot has to change the angle of attack anytime indicated airspeed is changed. For example, as indicated airspeed is decreased, the angle of attack must be increased to compensate for the loss of lift. The relationship between indicated airspeed and lift for a given angle of attack involves the law of squares. If the angle of attack does not change, total lift varies with the square of the indicated airspeed. For example, if the airspeed doubles, the lift will increase by four times.

Indicated airspeed can be thought of as having two elements—the actual speed of the airplane through the air (true airspeed) and the density of the air. As altitude increases, air density decreases. To maintain the same indicated airspeed at altitude an aircraft must fly at a higher true airspeed. To produce the same amount of lift at altitude, a higher true airspeed is required for a given angle of attack.

A wing will always stall at the same angle of attack. The load factor, weight and density altitude will cause the stalling true airspeed to vary, but the stall angle of attack will always be the same.

A curve comparing total drag to parasite and induced drag reveals an airspeed at which drag is at a minimum value. At higher airspeeds, total drag increases because of increasing parasite drag. At lower airspeeds, induced drag increases which increases the total drag. Since the lift stays constant (equal to weight), the low point on the curve is the airspeed that produces the best lift to drag (L/D) ratio. This point is referred to as **L/D_{MAX}**. See Figure 3-1.

A change in weight changes the L/D curve. The amount of parasite drag is mainly a function of indicated airspeed. The amount of induced drag is a function of angle of attack. When an aircraft's weight is increased, any indicated airspeed will require a higher angle of attack to produce the required lift. This means that induced drag will increase with increases in weight while there will be little change in parasite drag.

When an airplane is within about one wingspan of the ground, the flow of air around the wingtips is inhibited by the close proximity of the ground. This **ground effect** reduces induced drag (and therefore total drag) and increases lift. As an airplane flies out of ground effect on takeoff, the increased induced drag will require a higher angle of attack.

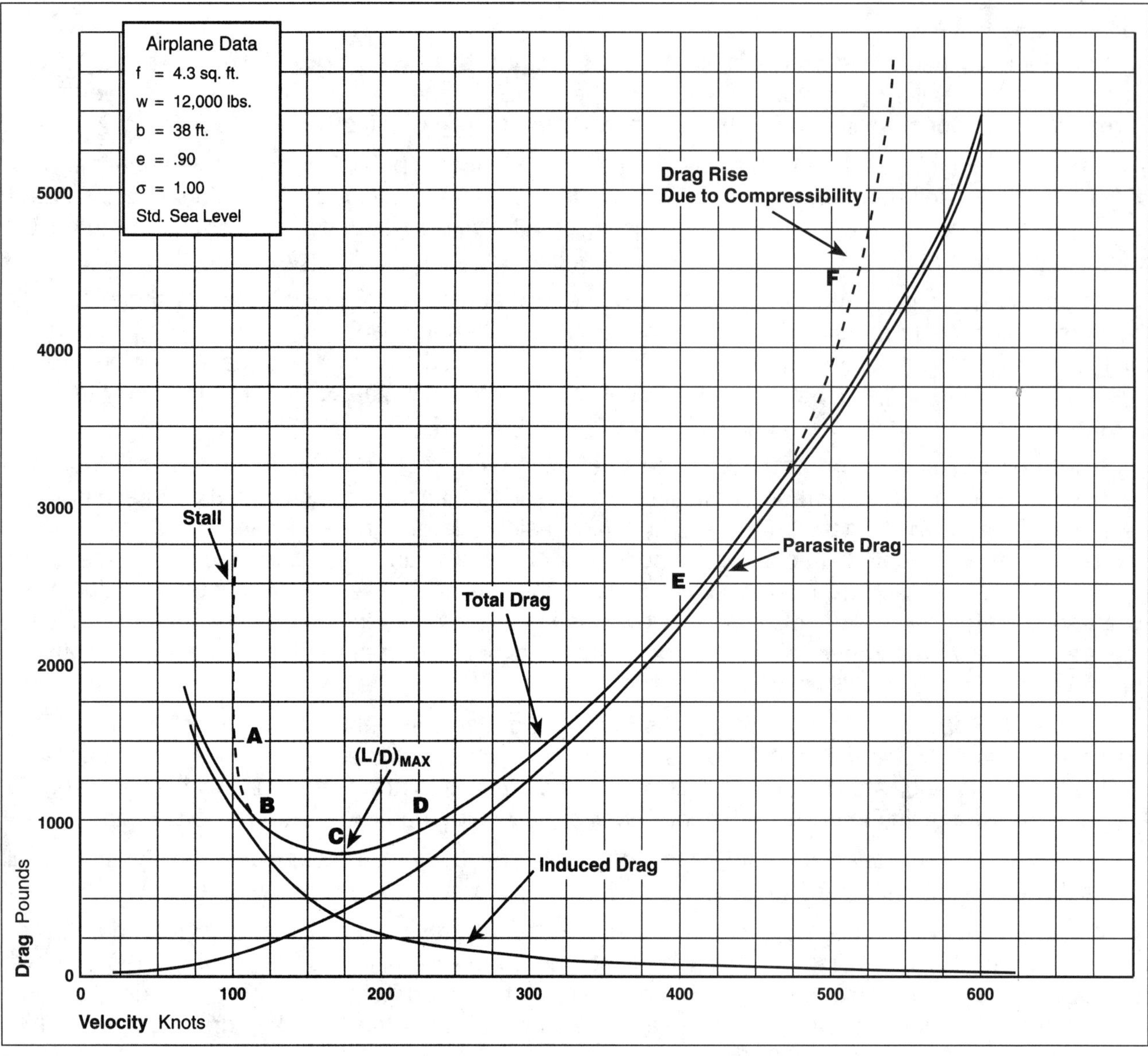

Figure 3-1. Typical drag curves

ALL

8377. What will be the ratio between airspeed and lift if the angle of attack and other factors remain constant and airspeed is doubled? Lift will be

A—the same.
B—two times greater.
C—four times greater.

Lift is proportional to the square of the airplane's velocity. For example, an airplane traveling at 200 knots has four times the lift as the same airplane traveling at 100 knots if the angle of attack and other factors remain constant. (PLT242, AA.I.B.K4) — FAA-H-8083-25

Answer (A) is incorrect because lift is proportional to the square of the airplane's velocity, it is not constant. Answer (B) is incorrect because, as airspeed is doubled, the lift will be four times greater.

Answers

8377 [C]

ALL

8378. What true airspeed and angle of attack should be used to generate the same amount of lift as altitude is increased?

A—The same true airspeed and angle of attack.
B—A higher true airspeed for any given angle of attack.
C—A lower true airspeed and higher angle of attack.

If the density factor is decreased and the total lift must equal the total weight to remain in flight, it follows that one of the other factors must be increased. The factors usually increased are the airspeed or the angle of attack, because these can be controlled by the pilot. (PLT168, AA.I.B.K4) — FAA-H-8083-25

Answer (A) is incorrect because true airspeed must be increased (not remain the same) as altitude increases. Answer (C) is incorrect because true airspeed must increase (not decrease) for any given angle of attack.

ALL

8348. What affects indicated stall speed?

A—Weight, load factor, and power.
B—Load factor, angle of attack, and power.
C—Angle of attack, weight, and air density.

An airplane will always stall at the same angle of attack. The indicated airspeed at which the stalling angle of attack is reached will vary with weight, load factor, and (to an extent) power setting. (PLT477, AA.I.B.K4) — FAA-H-8083-25

Answers (B) and (C) are incorrect because indicated stall speed is not affected by the angle of attack or air density.

ALL

9808. The stall speed of an airplane

A—is constant regardless of weight or airfoil configuration.
B—is affected by weight, and bank angle.
C—is not affected by dynamic pressures and lift coefficient.

Airplanes stall at the same angle of attack regardless of weight, dynamic pressure, bank angle, etc. The stall speed of the aircraft will be affected by weight, bank angle, and other factors since the product of dynamic pressure, wing area, and lift coefficient must produce the required lift. (PLT477, AA.I.B.K4) — ANA

ALL

8346. What is the effect on total drag of an aircraft if the airspeed decreases in level flight below that speed for maximum L/D?

A—Drag increases because of increased induced drag.
B—Drag increases because of increased parasite drag.
C—Drag decreases because of lower induced drag.

Note in the following figure that the airspeed at which minimum drag occurs is the same airspeed at which the maximum lift/drag ratio (L/D) takes place. At speeds below maximum L/D, any decrease in airspeed will result in an increase in total drag due to the increase in induced drag. (PLT303, AA.I.B.K4) — FAA-H-8083-25

Answer (B) is incorrect because parasite drag varies directly (not inversely) with airspeed. Answer (C) is incorrect because drag increases (not decreases) from any speed other than that for maximum L/D.

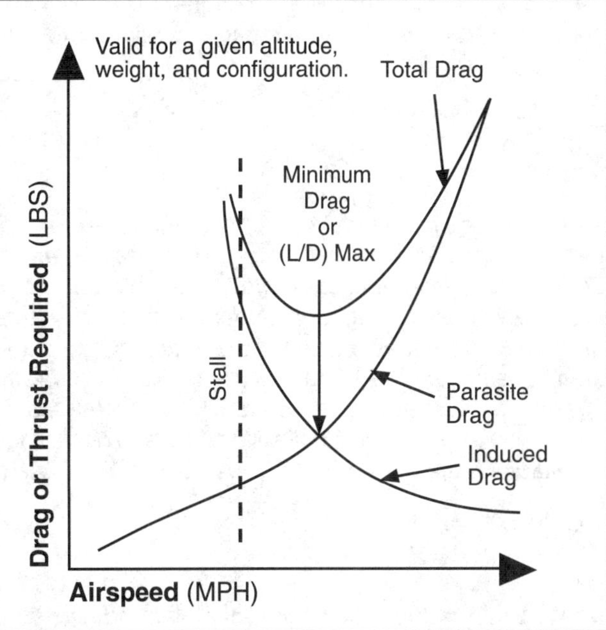

Question 8346

Answers

8378 [B] 8348 [A] 9808 [B] 8346 [A]

ALL

9942. How does the stall speed (KCAS) vary as you climb from sea level to 33,000 feet?

A—It varies directly with a change in altitude.
B—It remains relatively unchanged throughout the climb.
C—It varies indirectly with a change in altitude.

The indicated airspeed (or calibrated airspeed) at which an aircraft stalls can be considered constant, but the true airspeed at which it stalls increases with altitude because of the lower air density. (PLT124, AA.I.B.K4) — FAA-H-8083-25

Answers (A) and (C) are incorrect because the question is specifically asking about the knots calibrated airspeed (KCAS) and not true airspeed (TAS) or Mach.

ALL

9942-1. As an airplane climbs to higher altitudes, what happens to the calibrated airspeed in relation to true airspeed?

A—It remains equal.
B—It decreases.
C—It increases.

True airspeed is calibrated airspeed corrected for altitude and nonstandard temperature. Because air density decreases with an increase in altitude, an aircraft has to be flown faster at higher altitudes to cause the same pressure difference between pitot impact pressure and static pressure. Therefore, for a given calibrated airspeed, true airspeed increases as altitude increases; or for a given true airspeed, calibrated airspeed decreases as altitude increases. (PLT124, AA.I.B.K3a) — FAA-H-8083-25

ALL

8397. What is the relationship between induced and parasite drag when the gross weight is increased?

A—Parasite drag increases more than induced drag.
B—Induced drag increases more than parasite drag.
C—Both parasite and induced drag are equally increased.

Lift is required to counteract the aircraft's weight. If weight is increased, lift must be also. To increase lift, angle of attack must be increased, so induced drag also increases. Parasite drag is due to form and friction drag, so there would be little or no change in parasite drag. (PLT015, AA.I.B.K4) — ANA

Answer (A) is incorrect because parasite drag increases less (not more) than induced drag as airplane weight increases. Answer (C) is incorrect because induced drag increases more than parasite drag with increases in airplane gross weight.

ALL

8397-1. How does an increase in an aircraft's weight affect its climb performance?

A—The aircraft will climb at a lower angle of attack, which allows for a higher TAS and higher rate of climb.
B—Both parasite and induced drag are increased, which will lower the reserve thrust available to climb.
C—A higher aircraft weight requires that the aircraft is configured for climb earlier in the departure which allows a greater climb gradient.

Climb performance is most critical at high weight, high altitude, or during a malfunction of a powerplant. A change in aircraft weight affects both climb angle and climb rate and will alter the drag and power required. Generally, an increase in weight will reduce the maximum rate of climb, but the airplane must be operated at an increased speed to achieve the reduced maximum rate of climb. (PLT015, AA.I.B.K2c) — ANA

ALL

9767. How does V_S (KTAS) speed vary with altitude?

A—Remains the same at all altitudes.
B—Varies directly with altitude.
C—Varies inversely with altitude.

True airspeed (KTAS) is based on the density of the air, which is affected by pressure, temperature, and humidity—together, these determine air density. While flying at a constant indicated airspeed, an increase in density altitude will indicate that the air has become less dense, and the true airspeed as well as ground speed will increase. (PLT124, AA.V.B.K1) — FAA-H-8083-25

Answers

9942 [B]	9942-1 [B]	8397 [B]	8397-1 [A]	9767 [B]

ALL

8368. What is the reason for variations in geometric pitch along a propeller or rotor blade?

A—It permits a relatively constant angle of attack along its length when in cruising flight.
B—It prevents the portion of the blade near the hub or root from stalling during cruising flight.
C—It permits a relatively constant angle of incidence along its length when in cruising flight.

"Twisting," or variations in the geometric pitch of the blades permits the propeller to operate with a relatively constant angle of attack along its length when in cruising flight. (PLT214, AA.I.B.K4) — FAA-H-8083-25

ALL

8375. What flight condition should be expected when an aircraft leaves ground effect?

A—An increase in induced drag requiring a higher angle of attack.
B—A decrease in parasite drag permitting a lower angle of attack.
C—An increase in dynamic stability.

An airplane leaving ground effect will require an increase in angle of attack to maintain the same lift coefficient, experience an increase in induced drag and thrust required, experience a decrease in stability with a nose-up change in pitch, and produce a reduction in static source pressure and increase in indicated airspeed. (PLT131, AA.I.B.K4) — FAA-H-8083-25

Answer (B) is incorrect because, at slow airspeeds when taking off, induced (not parasite) drag predominates. Answer (C) is incorrect because, when leaving ground effect, expect a decrease in stability and a nose-up change in moment.

ATM, ATS, ADX

8382. By changing the angle of attack of a wing, the pilot can control the airplane's

A—lift, gross weight, and drag.
B—lift, airspeed, and drag.
C—lift and airspeed, but not drag.

By changing the angle of attack, the pilot can control lift, airspeed, and drag. Even the total load supported in flight by the wing may be modified by variations in angle of attack. (PLT004, AA.I.B.K1) — FAA-H-8083-3

Answer (A) is incorrect because angle of attack cannot control the airplane's gross weight. Answer (C) is incorrect because the pilot can control the amount of induced drag by changing the angle of attack.

ATM, ATS, ADX

8399. At which speed will increasing the pitch attitude cause an airplane to climb?

A—Low speed.
B—High speed.
C—Any speed.

When operating at speeds below L/D_{MAX}, an increase in pitch or decrease in speed causes total drag to increase, thus causing a descent with a fixed power setting. When operating at speeds above L/D_{MAX} and pitch is increased (or airspeed is decreased), total drag will decrease, thus causing a climb with a fixed power setting. (PLT303, AA.I.B.K4) — ANA

Answers (A) and (C) are incorrect because below L/D_{MAX}, performance decreases with increases in pitch.

ATM, ATS, ADX

8379. How can an airplane produce the same lift in ground effect as when out of ground effect?

A—The same angle of attack.
B—A lower angle of attack.
C—A higher angle of attack.

The reduction of the wing-tip vortices due to ground effect alters the spanwise lift distribution and reduces the induced angle of attack and induced drag. Therefore, the wing will require a lower angle of attack in ground effect to produce the same lift coefficient. (PLT131, AA.I.B.K4) — FAA-H-8083-3

Answer (A) is incorrect because, if the same angle of attack is maintained, an increase in lift coefficient will result. Answer (C) is incorrect because a lower angle of attack is required to produce the same lift in ground effect.

ATM, ATS, ADX

8379-1. What is the absolute ceiling of an airplane?

A—The point where the minimum rate of climb becomes lower than the optimum L/D_{MAX} speed.
B—The altitude at which the aircraft is unable to climb at more than 100 feet per minute.
C—When the maximum rate of climb and the maximum angle of climb speeds converge.

At the absolute ceiling, there is no excess of power and only one speed will allow steady level flight. Consequently, the absolute ceiling of the airplane produces zero rate of climb. This occurs when the maximum rate of climb and the maximum angle of climb speeds converge. (PLT131, AA.I.B.K2c) — FAA-H-8083-25

Answers

8368 [A] 8375 [A] 8382 [B] 8399 [B] 8379 [B] 8379-1 [C]

Critical Engine and V_{MC}

Because of "P-Factor" on most propeller-driven airplanes, the loss of one particular engine at high angles of attack would be more detrimental to performance than the loss of the other. One of the engines has its thrust line closer to the aircraft centerline (see Figure 3-2). The loss of this engine would more adversely affect the performance and handling of the aircraft; therefore this is the "critical engine."

For unsupercharged engines, V_{MC} decreases as altitude is increased. Stalls should never be practiced with one engine inoperative because of the potential for loss of control. Engine out approaches and landings should be made the same as normal approaches and landings.

Banking at least 5° into the good engine ensures the airplane will be controllable at any speed above the certificated V_{MC}, that the airplane will be in a minimum drag configuration for best climb performance, and that the stall characteristics will not be degraded. Engine out flight with the ball centered is never correct.

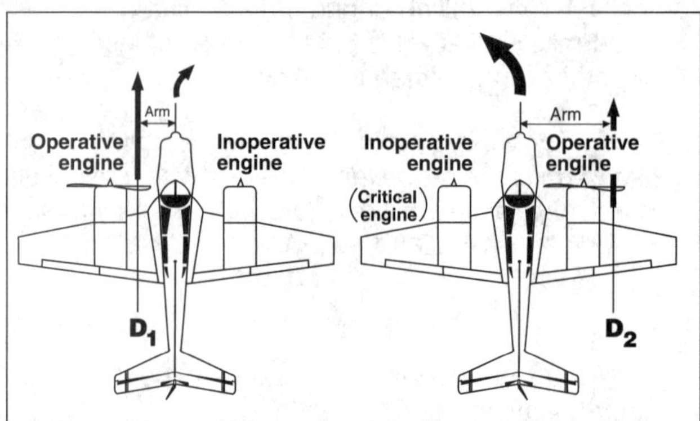

Figure 3-2

ATM
8357. In a light, twin-engine airplane with one engine inoperative, when is it acceptable to allow the ball of a slip-skid indicator to be deflected outside the reference lines?

A—While maneuvering at minimum controllable airspeed or less to avoid overbanking.
B—When operating at any airspeed of V_{MC} or greater with only enough deflection to zero the side slip.
C—When practicing imminent stalls in a banked attitude of over 60°.

Banking at least 5° into the good engine ensures that the airplane will be controllable at any speed above the certificated V_{MC}, that the airplane will be in a minimum drag configuration for best climb performance, and that the stall characteristics will not be degraded. Engine out flight with the ball centered is never correct. (PLT223, AA.VII.B.K1) — FAA-H-8083-3

ATM
8358. What is the safest and most efficient takeoff and initial climb procedure in a light, twin-engine airplane? Accelerate to

A—best engine-out, rate-of-climb airspeed while on the ground, then lift off and climb at that speed.
B—V_{MC}, then lift off at that speed and climb at maximum angle-of-climb airspeed.
C—an airspeed slightly above V_{MC}, then lift off and climb at the best rate-of-climb airspeed.

Lift-off should be made at no less than V_{MC} + 5. After lift-off, the airplane should be allowed to accelerate to the all-engine best-rate-of-climb speed V_Y, and then the climb maintained at this speed with takeoff power until a safe maneuvering altitude is attained. (PLT459, AA.VII.B.K1) — FAA-H-8083-3

ATM
8360. What performance should a pilot of a light, twin-engine airplane be able to maintain at V_{MC}?

A—Heading.
B—Heading and altitude.
C—Heading, altitude, and ability to climb 50 ft/min.

V_{MC} can be defined as the minimum airspeed at which the airplane is controllable when the critical engine is suddenly made inoperative, and the remaining engine is producing takeoff power. This does not mean that the airplane must be able to climb or even hold altitude. It only means that a heading can be maintained. (PLT208, AA.VII.B.K1) — FAA-H-8083-3

Answers

8357 [B] 8358 [C] 8360 [A]

ATM

8364. What does the blue radial line on the airspeed indicator of a light, twin-engine airplane represent?

A—Maximum single-engine rate of climb.
B—Maximum single-engine angle of climb.
C—Minimum controllable airspeed for single-engine operation.

The airspeed indicator in a twin-engine airplane is marked with a red radial line at the minimum controllable airspeed with the critical engine inoperative (V_{MC}), and a blue radial line at the best rate of climb airspeed with one engine inoperative (V_{YSE}). (PLT132, AA.VII.B.K1) — FAA-H-8083-3

ATM, ADX

8359. What procedure is recommended for an engine-out approach and landing?

A—The flightpath and procedures should be almost identical to a normal approach and landing.
B—The altitude and airspeed should be considerably higher than normal throughout the approach.
C—A normal approach, except do not extend the landing gear or flaps until over the runway threshold.

Essentially, an engine-out approach and landing is the same as a normal approach and landing. (PLT223, AA.VII.C.K2) — FAA-H-8083-3

ATM, ADX

8361. Which engine is the "critical" engine of a twin-engine airplane?

A—The one with the center of thrust closest to the centerline of the fuselage.
B—The one designated by the manufacturer which develops most usable thrust.
C—The one with the center of thrust farthest from the centerline of the fuselage.

The critical engine is defined as the engine whose failure would most adversely affect performance or handling. Because of "P-factor," most propeller-driven airplanes do not develop symmetrical thrust at high angles of attack. If the engine with the thrust line closest to the airplane centerline fails, the resulting yawing moment will be greater than if the other engine had failed. (PLT347, AA.VII.B.K2) — FAA-H-8083-3

ATM, ADX

8362. What effect, if any, does altitude have on V_{MC} for an airplane with unsupercharged engines?

A—None.
B—Increases with altitude.
C—Decreases with altitude.

For an airplane without supercharged engines, V_{MC} decreases as altitude is increased. Consequently, directional control can be maintained at a lower airspeed than at sea level. (PLT314, AA.VII.B.K1) — FAA-H-8083-3

ATM, ATS

9813-1. High density altitude can reduce turbojet aircraft performance in which of the following ways?

A—It reduces the likelihood of maintaining laminar flow over the airfoils as airspeed and altitude increase.
B—It reduces thrust because there is a reduced mass of gases to force out of the exhaust.
C—It reduces thrust because there is an increased mass of gases that inhibits the outflow of exhaust.

The engine's compressor section has to work harder when air density is decreased. Power capability is reduced at high density altitudes, and power use may have to be modulated to keep engine temperature within limits. (PLT005, AA.I.B.K3a) — FAA-H-8083-3

ATM, ADX

8363. Under what condition should stalls never be practiced in a twin-engine airplane?

A—With one engine inoperative.
B—With climb power on.
C—With full flaps and gear extended.

With full power applied to the operative engine, as the airspeed drops below V_{MC}, the airplane tends to roll as well as yaw into the inoperative engine. This tendency becomes greater as the airspeed is further reduced. Since this tendency must be counteracted by aileron control, the yaw condition is aggravated by aileron roll (the "down" aileron creates more drag than the "up" aileron). If a stall occurs in this condition, a violent roll into the dead engine may be experienced. (PLT459, AA.VII.B.K1) — FAA-H-8083-3

Answers

8364 [A] 8359 [A] 8361 [A] 8362 [C] 9813-1 [B] 8363 [A]

Maneuvering Flight

In a **turn**, centrifugal force is counterbalanced by a portion of the lift of the wing. The horizontal component of lift turns the airplane and the vertical component of lift opposes gravity. When the pilot rolls the airplane into a turn he must increase the total lift of the wing so that the vertical component is equal to the airplane's weight. This is done by increasing the angle of attack. If no compensation is made for the loss of vertical component of lift in a turn, the aircraft will develop a sink rate.

Load factor is the ratio of the weight supported by the wings to the actual weight of the aircraft. For example, if an aircraft with a gross weight of 2,000 pounds were subjected to a total load of 6,000 pounds in flight, the load factor would be 3 Gs. On the ground or in unaccelerated flight the load factor is one. Conditions which can increase the load factor are vertical gusts (turbulence) and level turns. In a **level turn**, the load factor is dependent only on the angle of bank. Airspeed, turn rate or aircraft weight have no effect on load factor.

Rate of turn is the number of degrees per second at which the aircraft turns. The rate of turn is dependent on both the aircraft's airspeed and its angle of bank. To increase the rate of turn, the pilot must increase the angle of bank or decrease the airspeed or both. The rate of turn will decrease if the bank angle is decreased or if the airspeed is increased. The **radius of turn** is also dependent on both the bank angle and the airspeed. If angle of bank is increased or airspeed is decreased, the radius of turn will decrease. If bank angle is shallowed or if airspeed is increased, the radius of turn will increase.

ALL

8349. If no corrective action is taken by the pilot as angle of bank is increased, how is the vertical component of lift and sink rate affected?

A—Lift increases and the sink rate increases.
B—Lift decreases and the sink rate decreases.
C—Lift decreases and the sink rate increases.

When an airplane is banked, its lift can be broken into two vectors, a vertical component of lift and a horizontal component. If the airplane is to maintain altitude in the turn, the vertical component of lift must be equal to the aircraft's weight. This means that total lift must be increased. Lift can be increased either by increasing airspeed or by increasing angle of attack. If the vertical component of lift is less than the aircraft's weight, the airplane will descend. (PLT348, AA.IV.A.K2e) — FAA-H-8083-3

Answer (A) is incorrect because lift will decrease, not increase. Answer (B) is incorrect because the sink rate increases as the lift decreases.

ALL

8350. Why must the angle of attack be increased during a turn to maintain altitude?

A—Compensate for loss of vertical component of lift.
B—Increase the horizontal component of lift equal to the vertical component.
C—Compensate for increase in drag.

When an airplane is banked, its lift can be broken into two vectors, a vertical component of lift and a horizontal component. If the airplane is to maintain altitude in the turn, the vertical component of lift must be equal to the aircraft's weight. This means that total lift must be increased. Lift can be increased either by increasing airspeed or by increasing angle of attack. If the vertical component of lift is less than the aircraft's weight, the airplane will descend. (PLT348, AA.IV.A.K2e) — FAA-H-8083-3

Answer (B) is incorrect because angle of attack is increased in order to increase the vertical component of lift to equal weight. Answer (C) is incorrect because additional thrust (power) is used to compensate for increase in drag.

Answers

8349 [C] 8350 [A]

ALL

8347. What is load factor?

A—Lift multiplied by the total weight.
B—Lift subtracted from the total weight.
C—Lift divided by the total weight.

Load factor is the ratio of the total load supported by the airplane's wings to the actual weight of the airplane and its contents, or the actual load supported by the wings' lift divided by the total weight of the airplane. (PLT310, AA.IV.A.K2d) — FAA-H-8083-25

ALL

9823. During a turn with constant power

A—the aircraft nose will pitch down.
B—the aircraft will decelerate.
C—the rate of descent will increase.

While in a turn, part of the vertical component of lift has been diverted to horizontal lift. If total lift is not increased (increase in angle of attack) the aircraft nose will pitch down. (PLT348, AA.IV.A.K2e) — FAA-H-8083-3

ALL

9740. During a skidding turn to the right, what is the relationship between the component of lift and centrifugal force?

A—Centrifugal force is less than the horizontal lift component and the load factor is increased.
B—Centrifugal force is greater than the horizontal lift component.
C—Centrifugal force and the horizontal lift component are equal, and the load factor is decreased.

A skidding turn results from excess centrifugal force over the horizontal lift component, pulling the aircraft toward the outside of the turn. As centrifugal force increases, the load factor also increases. (PLT234, AA.IV.A.K2e) — FAA-H-8083-15

Answer (A) is incorrect because a slipping turn will occur if centrifugal force is less than horizontal lift. Answer (C) is incorrect because centrifugal force and horizontal lift are equal in a coordinated turn and load factor will increase.

ALL

8354. If an aircraft with a gross weight of 2,000 pounds were subjected to a total load of 6,000 pounds in flight, the load factor would be

A—2 Gs.
B—3 Gs.
C—9 Gs.

Load factor is the ratio of the total load supported by the airplane's wings to the actual weight of the airplane and its contents, or the actual load supported by the wings divided by the total weight of the airplane:

6,000 pounds ÷ 2,000 pounds = 3 Gs

(PLT018, AA.IV.A.K2d) — FAA-H-8083-25

ALL

8353. Upon which factor does wing loading during a level coordinated turn in smooth air depend?

A—Rate of turn.
B—Angle of bank.
C—True airspeed.

Load factor is independent of airspeed and dependent on angle of bank; therefore, with a constant bank angle, load factor is not affected. There is no change in centrifugal force for any given bank — the load factor remains the same. (PLT248, AA.IV.A.K2d) — FAA-H-8083-25

Answer (A) is incorrect because in a coordinated turn, the rate of turn does not have any impact on the load factor — it is determined wholly by the angle of bank. Answer (C) is incorrect because true airspeed has no impact on the load factor.

ALL

8396. For a given angle of bank, the load factor imposed on both the aircraft and pilot in a coordinated constant-altitude turn

A—increases with an increase in airspeed.
B—remains constant regardless of airspeed changes.
C—decreases with an increase in airspeed.

For any given angle of bank, the load factor remains constant. (PLT309, AA.IV.A.K2d) — FAA-H-8083-25

Answers

8347 [C]	9823 [A]	9740 [B]	8354 [B]	8353 [B]	8396 [B]

ALL

8351. How can the pilot increase the rate of turn and decrease the radius at the same time?

A—Steepen the bank and increase airspeed.
B—Steepen the bank and decrease airspeed.
C—Shallow the bank and increase airspeed.

Any increase in the angle of bank will increase the rate of turn and decrease the radius of turn. Turn radius will decrease with decreasing airspeed. (PLT348, AA.IV.A.K2e) — FAA-H-8083-3

ALL

8352. What is the relationship of the rate of turn with the radius of turn with a constant angle of bank but increasing airspeed?

A—Rate will decrease and radius will increase.
B—Rate will increase and radius will decrease.
C—Rate and radius will increase.

For any given angle of bank, the rate of turn varies with the airspeed. If the angle of bank is held constant and the airspeed is increased, the rate of turn will decrease. The radius of turn will vary with airspeed. As airspeed is increased the radius will also increase. (PLT248, AA.IV.A.K2d) — FAA-H-8083-3

Answer (B) is incorrect because to maintain a constant angle of bank while increasing airspeed, the radius of turn will increase. Answer (C) is incorrect because to maintain a constant angle of bank while increasing airspeed, the rate of turn will decrease.

ALL

8345. What effect does an increase in airspeed have on a coordinated turn while maintaining a constant angle of bank and altitude?

A—The rate of turn will decrease resulting in a decreased load factor.
B—The rate of turn will increase resulting in an increased load factor.
C—The rate of turn will decrease resulting in no changes in load factor.

For any given angle of bank, the rate of turn varies with the airspeed. A constant bank angle does not change the load factor. If the angle of bank is held constant and the airspeed is increased, the rate of turn will decrease. The radius of turn will vary with airspeed. As airspeed is increased the radius will also increase. (PLT248, AA.IV.A.K2d) — FAA-H-8083-25

Answer (A) is incorrect because, at a constant bank angle, the higher airspeed will decrease the rate of turn to compensate for added centrifugal force, allowing the load factor to remain the same. Answer (B) is incorrect because, for any bank angle, the rate of turn varies with the airspeed; the higher the speed, the slower the rate of turn.

ATM, ATS, ADX

8345-1. Generally, the turning performance of an airplane is defined by

A—structural and power limits at high altitude.
B—aerodynamic and structural limits at low altitude.
C—control and structural limits at high altitude.

Each of the three limiting factors (aerodynamic, structural, and power) may combine to define the turning performance of an airplane. Generally, aerodynamic and structural limits predominate at low altitude while aerodynamic and power limits predominate at high altitude. The knowledge of this turning performance is particularly necessary for effective operation of fighter and interceptor types of airplanes. (PLT237, AA.IV.A.K2d) — ANA

ATM, ATS, ADX

8345-2. A bank angle of 15° will increase induced drag by about

A—3%.
B—7%.
C—15%.

Due to the increased load factor in a coordinated turn, there will be an increase in stall speed and—of greater importance to engine-out performance—an increase in induced drag. A bank angle of 15 degrees will increase induced drag by about 7%. (PLT237, AA.IV.A.K2d) — ANA

Answers

8351 [B]	8352 [A]	8345 [C]	8345-1 [B]	8345-2 [B]

Stability

Static stability describes the initial reaction of an aircraft after it has been disturbed from equilibrium in one or more of its axes of rotation. If the aircraft has an initial tendency to return to its original attitude of equilibrium, it has **positive static stability**. When it continues to diverge, it exhibits **negative static** stability. If an aircraft tends to remain in its new, disturbed state, it has **neutral static stability**. Most airplanes have positive static stability in pitch and yaw, and are close to neutrally stable in roll.

When an aircraft exhibits positive static stability in one of its axes, the term "dynamic stability" describes the long term tendency of the aircraft. When an aircraft is disturbed from equilibrium and then tries to return, it will invariably overshoot the original attitude and then pitch back. This results in a series of oscillations. If the oscillations become smaller with time, the aircraft has positive dynamic stability. If the aircraft diverges further away from its original attitude with each oscillation, it has negative dynamic stability.

The entire design of an aircraft contributes to its **stability** (or lack of it) in each of its axes of rotation. However, the vertical tail is the primary source of direction stability (yaw), and the horizontal tail is the primary source of pitch stability. The **center of gravity (CG)** location also affects stability. If the CG is toward its rearward limit, the aircraft will be less stable in both roll and pitch. As the CG is moved forward, the stability improves. Even though an airplane will be less stable with a rearward CG, it will have some desirable aerodynamic characteristics due to reduced aerodynamic loading of horizontal tail surface. This type of an airplane will have a slightly lower stall speed and will cruise faster for a given power setting.

ALL

8365. Identify the type stability if the aircraft attitude remains in the new position after the controls have been neutralized.

A—Negative longitudinal static stability.
B—Neutral longitudinal dynamic stability.
C—Neutral longitudinal static stability.

Neutral static stability is the initial tendency of an airplane to remain in a new position after its equilibrium has been disturbed. (PLT236, AA.I.B.K3e) — FAA-H-8083-25

Answer (A) is incorrect because a negative longitudinal static stability means the airplane would tend to move even further from the original position. Answer (B) is incorrect because, with neutral longitudinal dynamic stability, the airplane would continue to oscillate without a tendency to increase or decrease.

ALL

8372. Identify the type stability if the aircraft attitude tends to move farther from its original position after the controls have been neutralized.

A—Negative static stability.
B—Positive static stability.
C—Negative dynamic stability.

Negative static stability is the initial tendency of the airplane to continue away from the original state of equilibrium after being disturbed. (PLT213, AA.I.B.K3e) — FAA-H-8083-25

ALL

8373. Identify the type stability if the aircraft attitude tends to return to its original position after the controls have been neutralized.

A—Positive dynamic stability.
B—Positive static stability.
C—Neutral dynamic stability.

Positive static stability is the initial tendency of the airplane to return to the original state of equilibrium after being disturbed. (PLT236, AA.I.B.K3e) — FAA-H-8083-25

Answer (A) is incorrect because positive dynamic stability refers to oscillations being dampened or decreasing. Answer (C) is incorrect because neutral dynamic stability refers to oscillations continuing without a tendency to increase or decrease.

ALL

8366. What is a characteristic of longitudinal instability?

A—Pitch oscillations becoming progressively greater.
B—Bank oscillations becoming progressively greater.
C—Aircraft constantly tries to pitch down.

A longitudinally unstable airplane has a tendency to dive or climb progressively into a very steep dive or climb, or even a stall. (PLT213, AA.I.B.K3e) — FAA-H-8083-25

Answer (B) is incorrect because longitudinal stability refers to pitch (not bank) oscillations. Answer (C) is incorrect because this is not considered a stability problem. Stability is the reaction of the airplane when its equilibrium is disturbed.

Answers

8365 [C] | 8372 [A] | 8373 [B] | 8366 [A]

ALL

8367. Describe dynamic longitudinal stability.

A—Motion about the longitudinal axis.
B—Motion about the lateral axis.
C—Motion about the vertical axis.

Longitudinal stability is the quality which makes an airplane stable about its lateral axis. (PLT236, AA.I.B.K3e) — FAA-H-8083-25

Answer (A) is incorrect because motion about the airplane's longitudinal axis is lateral (not longitudinal) stability. Answer (C) is incorrect because motion about the vertical axis is directional stability.

ALL

8367-1. When does a typical aircraft exhibit reduced longitudinal stability?

A—With the center of gravity (CG) near the aft limit.
B—With the center of gravity (CG) near the forward limit.
C—With the center of gravity (CG) at a mid-range location.

A tail-heavy condition has a serious effect on longitudinal stability and reduces the capability to recover from stalls and spins. (PLT236, AA.I.B.K5) — FAA-H-8083-25

ALL

8376. What characteristic should exist if an airplane is loaded to the rear of its CG range?

A—Sluggish in aileron control.
B—Sluggish in rudder control.
C—Unstable about the lateral axis.

If an airplane is loaded too far rearward it may not dampen out a vertical displacement of the nose. Instead, when the nose is momentarily pulled up, it may alternately climb and dive becoming steeper with each oscillation. (PLT236, AA.I.B.K3e) — FAA-H-8083-25

Answer (A) is incorrect because an aft location of the CG has a greater effect on the longitudinal stability, not the lateral (aileron) controllability. Answer (B) is incorrect because an aft CG has a greater effect on the longitudinal stability, not vertical (rudder) controllability.

ATM, ATS, ADX

8380. What are some characteristics of an airplane loaded with the CG at the aft limit?

A—Lowest stall speed, highest cruise speed, and least stability.
B—Highest stall speed, highest cruise speed, and least stability.
C—Lowest stall speed, lowest cruise speed, and highest stability.

An airplane loaded with the CG at its aft limit will have a lower stall speed, higher cruise speed, but be less stable. (PLT240, AA.I.B.K5) — FAA-H-8083-3

Answer (B) is incorrect because an aft CG would cause the airplane to have the lowest stall speed. Answer (C) is incorrect because an aft CG would cause an airplane to have the highest cruise speed and the least stability.

ADX

8380-1. An airplane loaded with the CG at the aft limit will

A—fly more efficiently.
B—be very unbalanced in lateral control forces.
C—feel heavy in the longitudinal axis.

The stick force gradient is low at low airspeeds; when the airplane is at low speeds, high power, and with a CG positioned near the aft limit, the "feel" for airspeed will be weak. (PLT240) — ANA

ATM, ATS, ADX

9921. An airplane loaded with the CG aft of the rear-CG limit could

A—make it easier to recover from stalls and spins.
B—make it more difficult to flare for landing.
C—increase the likelihood of inadvertent overstress.

If an airplane is loaded too far rearward, it may not dampen out a vertical displacement of the nose. Instead, when the nose is momentarily pulled up, such as when flaring for landing, it may alternately climb and dive becoming steeper with each oscillation. (PLT240, AA.I.B.K5) — FAA-H-8083-25

Answers

8367 [B]	8367-1 [A]	8376 [C]	8380 [A]	8380-1 [C]	9921 [B]

High Speed Flight

Mach number is the ratio of the true airspeed to the speed of sound (TAS ÷ Speed of Sound). For example, an aircraft cruising at Mach .80 is flying at 80% of the speed of sound. The speed of sound is Mach 1.0.

A large increase in drag occurs when the air flow around the aircraft exceeds the speed of sound (Mach 1.0). Because lift is generated by accelerating air across the upper surface of the wing, local air flow velocities will reach sonic speeds while the aircraft Mach number is still considerably below the speed of sound. With respect to **Mach cruise control**, flight speeds can be divided into three regimes—subsonic, transonic and supersonic. The **subsonic regime** can be considered to occur at aircraft Mach numbers where all the local air flow is less than the speed of sound. The **transonic range** is where some but not all the local air flow velocities are Mach 1.0 or above. In **supersonic** flight, all the air flow around the aircraft exceeds Mach 1.0. The exact Mach numbers will vary with each aircraft type but as a very rough rule of thumb the subsonic regime occurs below Mach .75, the transonic regime between Mach .75 and Mach 1.20, and the supersonic regime over Mach 1.20.

A limiting speed for a subsonic transport aircraft is its critical Mach number (M_{CRIT}). That is the speed at which airflow over the wing first reaches, but does not exceed, the speed of sound. At M_{CRIT} there may be sonic but no supersonic flow.

When an airplane exceeds its critical Mach number, a shock wave forms on the wing surface that can cause a phenomenon known as shock stall. If this shock stall occurs symmetrically at the wing roots, the loss of lift and loss of downwash on the tail will cause the aircraft to pitch down or "tuck under." This tendency is further aggravated in sweptwing aircraft because the center of pressure moves aft as the wing roots shock stall. If the wing tips of a sweptwing airplane shock stall first, the wing's center of pressure would move inward and forward causing a pitch up motion. See Figure 3-3.

The less airflow is accelerated across the wing, the higher the critical Mach number (i.e., the maximum flow velocity is closer to the aircraft's Mach number). Two ways of increasing M_{CRIT} in jet transport designs are to give the wing a lower camber and increase wing sweep. A thin airfoil section (lower camber) causes less airflow acceleration. The sweptwing design has the effect of creating a thin airfoil section by inducing a spanwise flow, thus increasing the effective chord length. See Figure 3-4.

Although a sweptwing design gives an airplane a higher critical Mach number (and therefore a higher maximum cruise speed), it results in some undesirable flight characteristics. One of these is a reduced maximum coefficient of lift. This requires that sweptwing airplanes extensively employ high lift devices, such as slats and slotted flaps, to get acceptably low takeoff and landing speeds. The purpose of high lift devices such as flaps, slats and slots is to increase lift at low airspeeds and to delay stall to a higher angle of attack.

Another disadvantage of the sweptwing design is the tendency, at low airspeeds, for the wing tips to stall first. This results in loss of aileron control early in the stall, and in very little aerodynamic buffet on the tail surfaces.

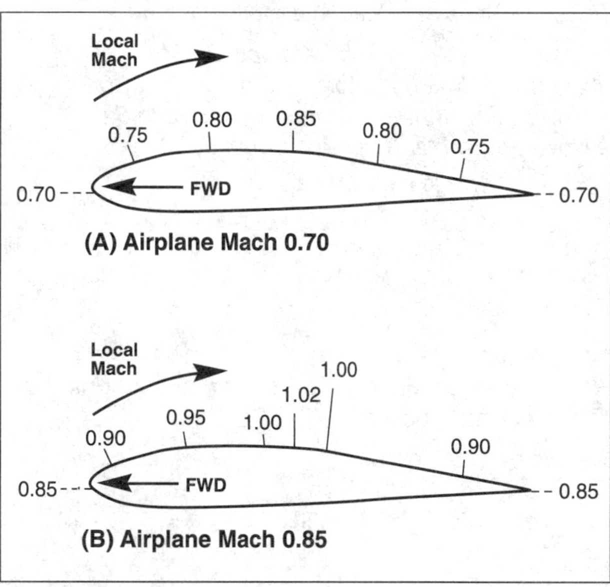

Figure 3-3. Local airstream Mach numbers

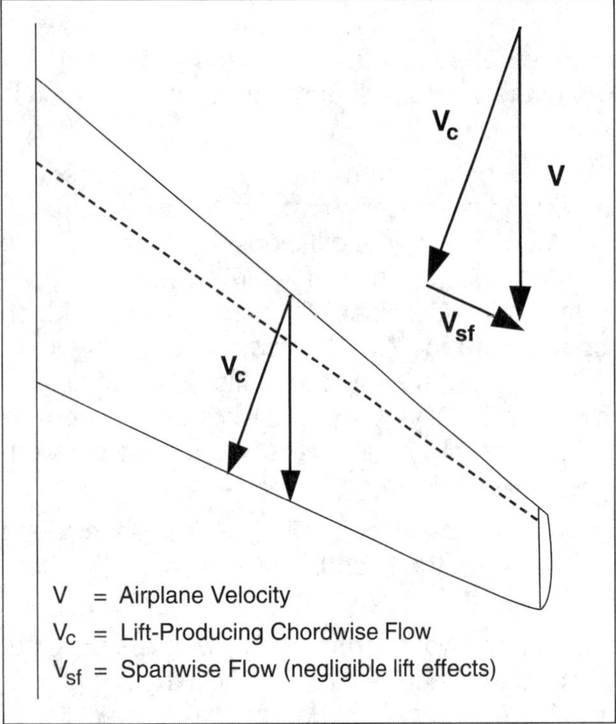

Figure 3-4. Effect of wing sweep on M_{CRIT}

ATM, ATS, ADX

8387. Within what Mach range does transonic flight regimes usually occur?

A—.50 to .75 Mach.
B—.75 to 1.20 Mach.
C—1.20 to 2.50 Mach.

Flight regimes are defined as follows:

Subsonic – Mach numbers below 0.75
Transonic – Mach numbers from 0.75 to 1.20
Supersonic – Mach numbers from 1.20 to 5.00
Hypersonic – Mach numbers above 5.00.

(PLT032, AA.I.D.K1) — ANA

Answer (A) is incorrect because .50 to .75 Mach would be subsonic flight. Answer (C) is incorrect because 1.20 to 2.50 Mach would be supersonic flight.

ATM, ATS, ADX

8390. At what Mach range does the subsonic flight range normally occur?

A—Below .75 Mach.
B—From .75 to 1.20 Mach.
C—From 1.20 to 2.50 Mach.

Flight regimes are defined as follows:

Subsonic – Mach numbers below 0.75
Transonic – Mach numbers from 0.75 to 1.20
Supersonic – Mach numbers from 1.20 to 5.00
Hypersonic – Mach numbers above 5.00.

(PLT214, AA.I.D.K1) — ANA

Answer (B) is incorrect because .75 to 1.20 Mach would be transonic flight. Answer (C) is incorrect because 1.20 to 2.50 Mach would be supersonic flight.

ATM, ATS, ADX

8388. What is the highest speed possible without supersonic flow over the wing?

A—Initial buffet speed.
B—Critical Mach number.
C—Transonic index.

The highest speed possible without supersonic flow is called the Critical Mach Number. (PLT214, AA.I.D.K1) — ANA

ATM, ATS, ADX

8389. What is the free stream Mach number which produces first evidence of local sonic flow?

A—Supersonic Mach number.
B—Transonic Mach number.
C—Critical Mach number.

The highest speed possible without supersonic flow is called the Critical Mach Number. (PLT214, AA.I.D.K1) — ANA

ATM, ATS, ADX

8389-1. When piloting a turbojet transport airplane, what is a possible result when operating at speeds 5 to 10 percent above the critical Mach number?

A—Increased aerodynamic efficiency.
B—Decreased control surface effectiveness.
C—Occasional low speed Mach buffet warnings.

Critical Mach number is the boundary between subsonic and transonic flight. When shock waves form on the aircraft, airflow separation followed by buffet and aircraft control difficulties can occur. Shock waves, buffet, and airflow separation take place above critical Mach number. (PLT214, AA.I.B.K4) — FAA-H-8083-25

Answers

8387 [B] 8390 [A] 8388 [B] 8389 [C] 8389-1 [B]

ATM, ATS, ADX
8392. What is the result of a shock-induced separation of airflow occurring symmetrically near the wing root of a sweptwing aircraft?

A—A high-speed stall and sudden pitchup.
B—A severe moment or "Mach tuck."
C—Severe porpoising.

If the shock-induced separation occurs symmetrically near the wing root, there is an accompanying loss of lift. A decrease in downwash on the horizontal tail will create a diving moment and the aircraft will "tuck under." (PLT214, AA.I.D.K1) — ANA

Answer (A) is incorrect because there is a sudden pitch down when a shock-induced separation of airflow occurs symmetrically near the wing root of a sweptwing aircraft. Answer (C) is incorrect because there is a diving moment when a shock-induced separation of airflow occurs symmetrically near the wing root of a sweptwing aircraft.

ATM, ATS, ADX
8395. What is the movement of the center of pressure when the wingtips of a sweptwing airplane are shock-stalled first?

A—Inward and aft.
B—Inward and forward.
C—Outward and forward.

Shock formation at the wing tip first moves the center of pressure forward and inboard and the resulting climbing moment and tail downwash can contribute to "pitch up." (PLT214, AA.I.D.K1) — ANA

Answer (A) is incorrect because when the wing tips are shock-stalled first, the center of pressure moves forward. Answer (C) is incorrect because when the wing tips are shock-stalled first, the center of pressure moves inward.

ATM, ATS, ADX
8391. What is the principal advantage of a sweepback design wing over a straightwing design?

A—The critical Mach number will increase significantly.
B—Sweepback will increase changes in the magnitude of force coefficients due to compressibility.
C—Sweepback will accelerate the onset of compressibility effect.

One of the most important advantages of sweep is an increase in critical Mach number, force divergence Mach number, and the Mach number at which the drag rise will peak. In other words, the sweep will delay the onset of compressibility effects. (PLT214, AA.I.D.K1) — ANA

ATM, ATS, ADX
8391-1. Swept wings

A—improve specific fuel consumption.
B—increase the critical Mach number.
C—increase the speed of sound quotient.

One of the advantages of sweep in wing design is the increase in the critical Mach number it creates. The increase in critical Mach number, force divergence Mach number, and the Mach number at which the drag-rise peaks will delay the onset of compressibility effects. (PLT094, AA.I.D.K1) — ANA

ATM, ATS, ADX
8391-2. For significant benefit, wing sweep must be at least

A—30 to 35°.
B—45 to 50°.
C—55°or more to substantially delay compressibility effects.

If sweepback is to be used at all, at least 30 to 35 degrees must be used to produce any significant benefit. (PLT094, AA.I.D.K1) — ANA

ATM, ATS, ADX
8391-3. What is an advantage of a sweptback wing?

A—It allows shock wave induced flow separation.
B—The design delays the onset of compressibility.
C—The wings tend to stall at the wing root first.

The sweptback wing design delays the onset of compressibility. (PLT094, AA.I.B.K4) — ANA

Answer (A) is incorrect because sweptback wings are designed to avoid the formation of shock waves. Answer (C) is incorrect because sweptback wings stall at the tip first.

ATM, ATS, ADX
8393. What is one disadvantage of a sweptwing design?

A—The wing root stalls prior to the wingtip section.
B—The wingtip section stalls prior to the wing root.
C—Severe pitchdown moment when the center of pressure shifts forward.

When sweepback is combined with taper there is an extremely powerful tendency for the wing tip to stall first. (PLT214, AA.I.D.K1) — ANA

Answers

8392 [B]	8395 [B]	8391 [A]	8391-1 [B]	8391-2 [A]	8391-3 [B]
8393 [B]					

ATM, ATS, ADX
9803. Swept wings causes a significant

A—increase in effectiveness of flaps.
B—reduction in effectiveness of flaps.
C—flap actuation reliability issue.

Thin airfoil sections with sweepback impose distinct limitations on the effectiveness of flaps. (PLT266, AA.I.D.K1) — ANA

ATM, ATS, ADX
8394-2. A turbojet airplane has an increase in specific range with altitude, which can be attributed to three factors. One of those factors is

A—an increase in altitude in the troposphere results in higher energy air flow.
B—an increase in proportion of velocity versus thrust required.
C—decreased engine turbine speeds.

One of the three factors that leads to the increase in specific range with altitude in a turbojet airplane is that higher altitude increases the proportion of V/Tr (velocity versus required thrust), which in turn provides a greater true airspeed for the same amount of thrust.

The other two factors involved are that, (1) an increase in tropospheric altitude produces a lower inlet air temperature, which then reduces the specific fuel consumption, and (2) an increase in altitude requires increased engine RPM for cruise thrust, and then the specific fuel consumption is reduced as the engine approaches the normal-rated RPM. (PLT094, AA.I.D.K1) — ANA

ATM, ATS, ADX.
8394-3. While operating a turbojet transport airplane at high altitude, which of the following is most likely to cause a low speed Mach buffet?

A—Reducing the angle of attack after a high speed Mach buffet.
B—The airplane is flown too fast for its weight and altitude.
C—The airplane is flown too slow for its weight and altitude.

Mach buffet is a function of the speed of the airflow over the wing—not necessarily the speed of the aircraft. An aircraft flown at a speed too slow for its weight and altitude necessitating a high angle of attack is the most likely situation to cause a low speed Mach buffet. (PLT094, AA.I.D.K9) — FAA-H-8083-25

Primary Flight Controls

Because of the high air loads, it is very difficult to move the flight control surfaces of jet aircraft with just mechanical and aerodynamic forces. So flight controls are usually moved by hydraulic actuators. Flight controls are divided into **primary flight controls** and **secondary** or **auxiliary flight controls**. The primary flight controls are those that maneuver the aircraft in roll, pitch and yaw. These include the ailerons, elevator and rudder. Secondary (or auxiliary) flight controls include tabs, trailing-edge flaps, leading-edge flaps, spoilers and slats. See Figure 3-5.

Roll control of most jet aircraft is accomplished by ailerons and flight spoilers. The exact mix of controls is determined by the aircraft's flight regime. In low speed flight all control surfaces operate to provide the desired roll control. As the aircraft moves into higher speed operations, control surface movement is reduced to provide approximately the same roll response to a given input through a wide range of speeds.

Many aircraft have two sets of ailerons—inboard and outboard. The inboard ailerons operate in all flight regimes. The outboard ailerons work only when the wing flaps are extended and are automatically

Answers
9803 [B] 8394-2 [B] 8394-3 [C]

locked out when flaps are retracted. This allows good roll response in low speed flight with the flaps extended and prevents excessive roll and wing bending at high speeds when the flaps are retracted.

Spoilers increase drag and reduce lift on the wing. If raised on only one wing, they aid roll control by causing that wing to drop. If the spoilers raise symmetrically in flight, the aircraft can either be slowed in level flight or can descend rapidly without an increase in airspeed. When the spoilers rise on the ground at high speeds, they destroy the wing's lift which puts more of the aircraft's weight on its wheels which in turn makes the brakes more effective.

Often aircraft have both flight and ground spoilers. The flight spoilers are available both in flight and on the ground. However, the ground spoilers can only be raised when the weight of the aircraft is on the landing gear. When the spoilers deploy on the ground, they decrease lift and make the brakes more effective. In flight, a ground-sensing switch on the landing gear prevents deployment of the ground spoilers.

Vortex generators are small (an inch or so high) aerodynamic surfaces located in different places on different airplanes. They prevent undesirable airflow separation from the surface by mixing the boundary airflow with the high energy airflow just above the surface. When located on the upper surface of a wing, the vortex generators prevent shock-induced separation from the wing as the aircraft approaches its critical Mach number. This increases aileron effectiveness at high speeds.

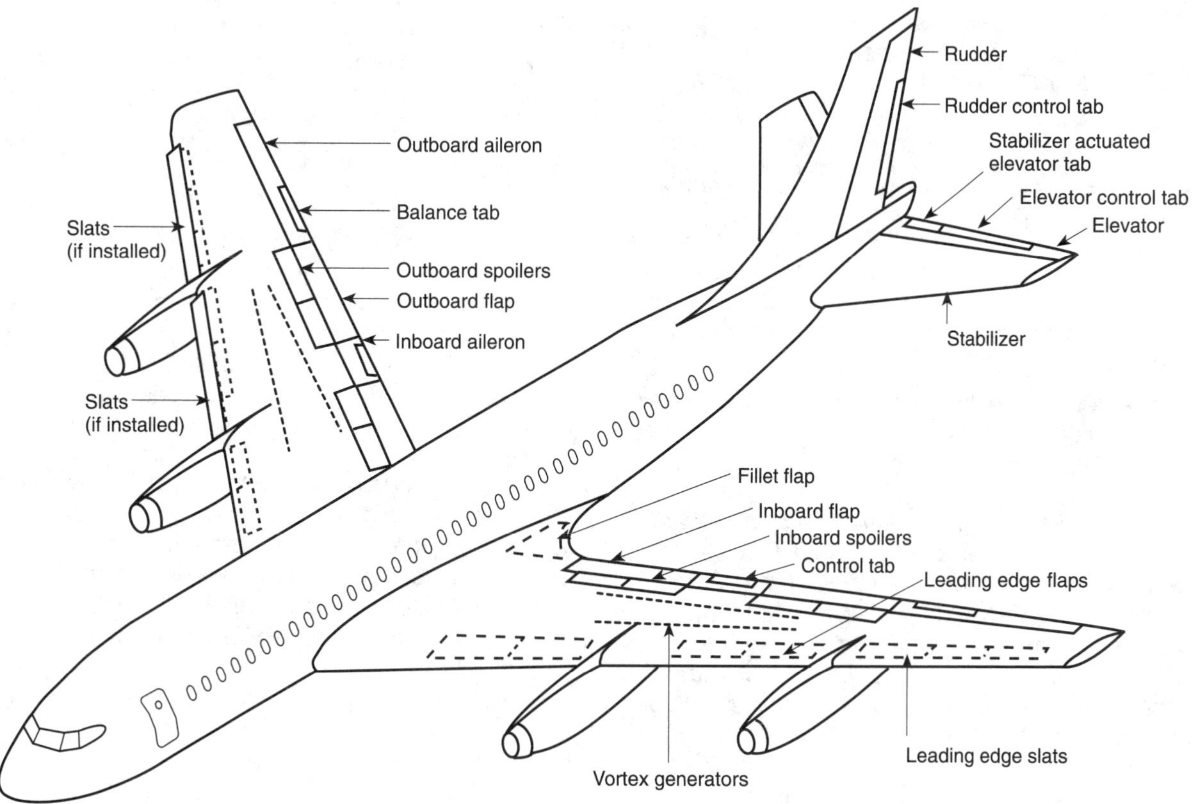

Figure 3-5. Typical transport aircraft flight controls

ATM, ATS, ADX

8326. Which of the following is considered a primary flight control?

A—Slats.
B—Elevator.
C—Dorsal fin.

The primary group of flight control surfaces consists of ailerons, elevators, and rudders. (PLT346, AA.I.A.K12) — FAA-H-8083-25

Answer (A) is incorrect because slats are high-lift devices, not a flight control device. Answer (C) is incorrect because a dorsal fin is not a primary flight control, but is used to provide directional stability.

ATM, ATS, ADX

8327. Which of the following is considered an auxiliary flight control?

A—Ruddervator.
B—Upper rudder.
C—Leading-edge flaps.

Auxiliary wing flight surfaces include trailing edge flaps, leading edge flaps, speed brakes, spoilers, and leading edge slats. (PLT473, AA.I.A.K12) — FAA-H-8083-25

Answer (A) is incorrect because a ruddervator is a primary flight control surface that incorporates both a rudder and elevator into one surface. Answer (B) is incorrect because upper rudders (found on the B-727) are stand-by rudders, which are used in the event of a hydraulic system failure.

ATM, ATS, ADX

8343. Precise roll control using a rudder on a transport category airplane

A—can be effective when turbulence is encountered.
B—is difficult and therefore not recommended.
C—should be considered to assist the yaw damper.

The lateral control of an airplane is accomplished by producing differential lift on the wings. The differential lift for control in roll is usually obtained by some type of ailerons or spoilers. Rudders are not recommended as the primary method to achieve precise roll control as they can contribute to dihedral effect. Excessive dihedral effect can lead to many problems including Dutch rolls. (PLT346, AA.I.A.K12) — ANA

ATM, ATS, ADX

8324. When are inboard ailerons normally used?

A—Low-speed flight only.
B—High-speed flight only.
C—Low-speed and high-speed flight.

During low-speed flight, all lateral control surfaces operate to provide maximum stability. This includes all four ailerons, flaps, and spoilers. (PLT346, AA.I.A.K12) — FAA-H-8083-25

Answers (A) and (B) are incorrect because the inboard ailerons are used during both high- and low-speed flight.

ATM, ATS, ADX

8325. When are outboard ailerons normally used?

A—Low-speed flight only.
B—High-speed flight only.
C—Low-speed and high-speed flight.

At high speeds, flaps are retracted and the outboard ailerons are locked out of the aileron control system. (PLT346, AA.I.A.K12) — FAA-H-8083-25

Answers (B) and (C) are incorrect because the outboard ailerons are locked when airspeed is increased and flaps are raised.

ATM, ATS, ADX

8342. Why do some airplanes equipped with inboard/outboard ailerons use the outboards for slow flight only?

A—Increased surface area provides greater controllability with flap extension.
B—Aerodynamic loads on the outboard ailerons tend to twist the wingtips at high speeds.
C—Locking out the outboard ailerons in high-speed flight provides variable flight control feel.

Aerodynamic loads on the outboard ailerons tend to twist the wing tips at high speeds. This results in deformation great enough to nullify the effect of aileron deflection and create rolling moments opposite to the direction commanded. Because of this, outboard ailerons are used for slow flight only. (PLT346, AA.I.A.K12) — FAA-H-8083-25

Answers

8326 [B]	8327 [C]	8343 [B]	8324 [C]	8325 [A]	8342 [B]

ATM, ATS, ADX
8332. What is a purpose of flight spoilers?

A—Increase the camber of the wing.
B—Reduce lift without decreasing airspeed.
C—Direct airflow over the top of the wing at high angles of attack.

The purpose of the spoilers is to disturb the smooth airflow across the top of the wing thereby creating an increased amount of drag and a reduced amount of lift. (PLT473, AA.I.A.K12) — FAA-H-8083-25

Answer (A) is incorrect because flaps (not spoilers) increase the camber of the wing. Answer (C) is incorrect because slots and slats direct airflow over the top of the wing at high angles of attack.

ATM, ATS, ADX
8333. For which purpose may flight spoilers be used?

A—Reduce the wings' lift upon landing.
B—Increase the rate of descent without increasing aerodynamic drag.
C—Aid in longitudinal balance when rolling an airplane into a turn.

An additional purpose or use for flight spoilers is to reduce lift when the aircraft lands. (PLT473, AA.I.A.K12) — FAA-H-8083-25

Answer (B) is incorrect because spoilers will increase the aerodynamic drag. Answer (C) is incorrect because trim devices (not spoilers) aid in balancing forces on an aircraft about the three axes.

ATM, ATS, ADX
8336. Which is a purpose of ground spoilers?

A—Reduce the wings' lift upon landing.
B—Aid in rolling an airplane into a turn.
C—Increase the rate of descent without gaining airspeed.

Ground spoilers are speed brakes extended on the ground or landing roll to kill lift and keep the aircraft from flying again after touchdown. (PLT473, AA.I.A.K12) — FAA-H-8083-25

Answer (B) is incorrect because an aid in rolling an airplane into a turn is a flight spoiler. Answer (C) is incorrect because increasing the rate of descent without gaining airspeed is the purpose of a flight spoiler.

ATM, ATS, ADX
9793. Upon landing, spoilers

A—decrease directional stability on the landing rollout.
B—function by increasing tire to ground friction.
C—should be extended after the thrust reversers have been deployed.

Spoilers should be deployed immediately after touchdown because they are most effective at high speed. The spoilers increase wheel loading by as much as 200% in the landing flap configuration. This increases the tire ground friction force making the maximum tire braking and cornering forces available. (PLT170, AA.I.A.K12) — FAA-H-8083-3A

ATM, ATS, ADX
9793-1. Aerodynamic braking is only effective up to approximately

A—30% of touchdown speed.
B—40 to 50% of touchdown speed.
C—60 to 70% of touchdown speed.

The aerodynamic drag of the airplane must be considered during the landing roll. Because of the reduced induced drag when in ground effect, aerodynamic braking will be of greatest significance only when partial stalling of the wing can be accomplished. The reduced drag when in ground effect accounts for the fact that the brakes are the most effective source of deceleration for the majority of airplane configurations. At speeds less than 60 to 70% of the touchdown speed, aerodynamic drag is so slight as to be of little use, and therefore aerodynamic braking must be utilized to produce continued deceleration of the airplane. (PLT247, AA.I.A.K12) — ANA

ATM, ATS, ADX
9793-2. Ground spoilers used after landing are

A—more effective at low speed.
B—equally effective at any speed.
C—more effective at high speed.

Spoilers should be deployed immediately after touchdown because they are most effective at high speed. (PLT473, AA.I.A.K12) — FAA-H-8083-3

Answers

8332 [B]	8333 [A]	8336 [A]	9793 [B]	9793-1 [C]	9793-2 [C]

ATM, ATS, ADX

8341. Which is a purpose of wing-mounted vortex generators?

A—Delays the onset of drag divergence at high speeds and aids in maintaining aileron effectiveness at high speeds.
B—Increase the onset of drag divergence and aid in aileron effectiveness at low speeds.
C—Breaks the airflow over the wing so the stall will progress from the root out to the tip of the wing.

"Vortex generators" are used to delay or prevent shock wave-induced boundary layer separation encountered in transonic flight. Vortex generators create a vortex which mixes the boundary airflow with the high energy airflow just above the surface. This produces higher surface velocities and increases the energy of the boundary layer. Thus, a stronger shock wave will be necessary to produce airflow separation. (PLT266, AA.I.A.K12) — FAA-H-8083-25

Answer (B) is incorrect because vortex generators are most effective at high speeds and the increased drag that they produce is not their primary function. Answer (C) is incorrect because a stall strip breaks the airflow over the wing so the stall will progress from the root out to the tip of the wing.

ATM, ATS, ADX

8356. Airflow separation over the wing can be delayed by using vortex generators

A—directing high pressure air over the top of the wing or flap through slots and making the wing surface smooth.
B—directing a suction over the top of the wing or flap through slots and making the wing surface smooth.
C—making the wing surface rough and/or directing high pressure air over the top of the wing or flap through slots.

Vortex generators prevent undesirable airflow separation from the surface by mixing the boundary airflow with the high energy airflow just above the surface. The vortex generators mix the turbulent outer layers of the boundary layers with the slow moving laminar lower layers thus reenergizing them. (PLT266, AA.I.A.K12) — FAA-H-8083-25

ALL

9759. If the boundary layer separates

A—drag is decreased.
B—the wing is about to stall and stop producing lift.
C—ice will sublimate and not freeze.

The boundary layer gives any object an "effective" shape that is usually slightly different from the physical shape. The boundary layer may also separate from the body, thus creating an effective shape much different from the physical shape of the object. This change in the physical shape of the boundary layer causes a dramatic decrease in lift and an increase in drag. When this happens, the airfoil has stalled. (PLT266, AA.V.A.K1) — FAA-H-8083-25

Answers

8341 [A] 8356 [C] 9759 [B]

Tabs

Flight control surfaces are sometimes equipped with **servo tabs**. These tabs are on the trailing edge of the control surface and are mechanically linked to move opposite the direction of the surface. If the tab moves up, the surface moves down. This "servo" movement moves the control surface. See Figure 3-6.

One method of modifying the downward tail load through changes in airspeed and configuration is by using **trim tabs**. Trim tabs are moved by a separate trim control from the cockpit. Movement of the trim tab (like the servo tab) is opposite that of the primary control surface.

Anti-servo tabs move in the same direction as the primary control surface. This means that as the control surface deflects, the aerodynamic load is increased by movement of the anti-servo tab. This helps to prevent the control surface from moving to a full deflection. It also makes a hydraulically-boosted flight control more aerodynamically effective than it would otherwise be.

Some jet aircraft have **control tabs** for use in the event of loss of all hydraulic pressure. Movement of the control wheel moves the control tab which causes the aerodynamic movement of the control surface. The control tab is used only during manual reversion; that is, with the loss of hydraulic pressure. They work the same as a servo tab but only in the manual mode.

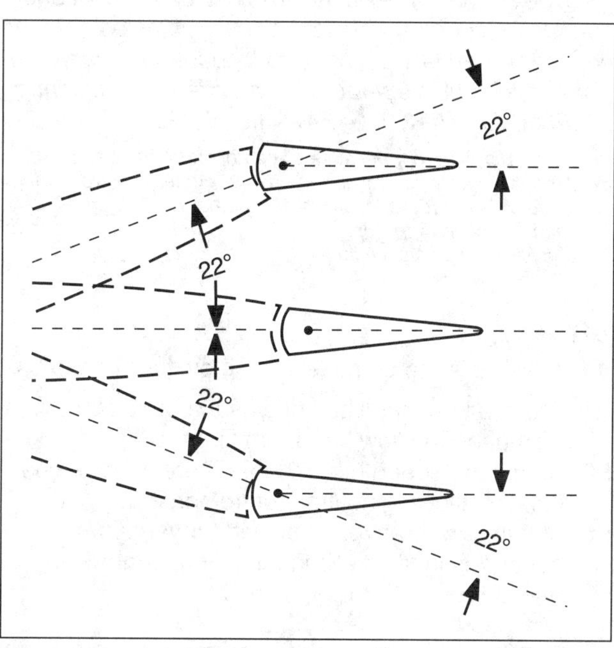

Figure 3-6

ATM, ATS, ADX

8330. What is the purpose of a servo tab?

A—Move the flight controls in the event of manual reversion.

B—Reduce control forces by deflecting in the proper direction to move a primary flight control.

C—Prevent a control surface from moving to a full-deflection position due to aerodynamic forces.

The servo tab moves in response to the cockpit control. The force of the airflow on the servo tab then moves the primary control surface. (PLT473, AA.I.A.K12) — FAA-H-8083-25

Answer (A) is incorrect because, in the event of "manual reversion" on some transport category aircraft, the control tabs would move the flight controls. Answer (C) is incorrect because the purpose of the anti-servo tab is to preclude full deflection of control surfaces.

ATM, ATS, ADX

8338. Which direction from the primary control surface does a servo tab move?

A—Same direction.

B—Opposite direction.

C—Remains fixed for all positions.

The servo tab attached to the flight control moves in the opposite direction, to assist in moving and holding the flight control by way of the airflow against it. (PLT473, AA.I.A.K12) — FAA-H-8083-25

Answer (A) is incorrect because an anti-servo tab, as found on the trailing edge of stabilators, moves in the same direction as the stabilator to provide a feel to the pilot control pressures. Answer (C) is incorrect because servo tabs move in response to the pilot's control movements.

Answers

8330 [B]   8338 [B]

ATM, ATS, ADX

8339. Which direction from the primary control surface does an elevator adjustable trim tab move when the control surface is moved?

A—Same direction.
B—Opposite direction.
C—Remains fixed for all positions.

Trim tabs remain fixed for all positions of primary control surface movement until mechanically adjusted from the cockpit. A trim tab is hinged to its parent primary control surface but is operated by an independent control. (PLT473, AA.I.A.K12) — FAA-H-8083-25

Answer (A) is incorrect because once adjusted, trim tabs remain fixed to the primary control surface as the primary control surface is moved. Answer (B) is incorrect because a tab having a linkage designed to move in the opposite direction from the main control surface is called a balance tab.

ATM, ATS, ADX

8340. What is the purpose of an elevator trim tab?

A—Provide horizontal balance as airspeed is increased to allow hands-off flight.
B—Adjust the speed tail load for different airspeeds in flight allowing neutral control forces.
C—Modify the downward tail load for various airspeeds in flight eliminating flight-control pressures.

The air flowing downward behind the trailing edge of the wing strikes the upper surface of the horizontal stabilizer, creating a downward tail force. The use of the trim tab will allow the pilot to reduce the hinge moment to zero and trim the control forces to zero for a given flight condition. (PLT473, AA.I.A.K12) — FAA-H-8083-25

Answer (A) is incorrect because the elevator trim tab permits "hands-off" flight at any airspeed, not only when the airspeed is increasing, and provides longitudinal balance. Answer (B) is incorrect because the elevator trim tab adjusts the downward tail load for various airspeeds in flight allowing neutral control forces.

ATM, ATS, ADX

8329. What is the purpose of an anti-servo tab?

A—Move the flight controls in the event of manual reversion.
B—Reduce control forces by deflecting in the proper direction to move a primary flight control.
C—Prevent a control surface from moving to a full-deflection position due to aerodynamic forces.

Anti-servo tabs add resistance and increase control forces required as the surface moves toward its limit to avoid overcontrolling and offset deflection caused by aerodynamic forces rather than control input. (PLT473, AA.I.A.K12) — FAA-H-8083-25

Answer (A) is incorrect because in the event of "manual reversion" the control tabs (not servo or anti-servo tabs) would move the flight controls. Answer (B) is incorrect because the anti-servo usually will increase the pressure required to deflect the control surfaces (the anti-servo tab moves in the same direction as the control surface).

ATM, ATS, ADX

8337. Which direction from the primary control surface does an anti-servo tab move?

A—Same direction.
B—Opposite direction.
C—Remains fixed for all positions.

Anti-servo tabs move in the same direction as the primary control surface. (PLT346, AA.I.A.K12) — FAA-H-8083-25

Answer (B) is incorrect because a servo tab moves in the opposite direction from the primary control surface. Answer (C) is incorrect because trim tabs remain fixed during control inputs.

ATM, ATS, ADX

8328. What is the purpose of a control tab?

A—Move the flight controls in the event of manual reversion.
B—Reduce control forces by deflecting in the proper direction to move a primary flight control.
C—Prevent a control surface from moving to a full-deflection position due to aerodynamic forces.

The flight controls of large jet airplanes are usually hydraulically powered. They are equipped with control tabs in the event of a total hydraulic failure. When this happens, the control tab can still be moved with control wheel input and the tab displacement creates an aerodynamic force which moves the control surface. (PLT473, AA.I.A.K12) — FAA-H-8083-25

Answer (B) is incorrect because servo tabs reduce control forces by deflecting primary flight controls in the proper direction. Answer (C) is incorrect because this is the purpose and function of an anti-servo tab.

Answers

8339 [C]	8340 [C]	8329 [C]	8337 [A]	8328 [A]

High-Lift Devices

Sweptwing jet aircraft are equipped with a number of high-lift devices. These include leading edge flaps, slots or slats, and trailing edge flaps. The primary purpose of high-lift devices (flaps, slots, slats, etc.) is to increase the **maximum coefficient of lift** (CL_{MAX}) of the airplane and reduce the stall speed. The takeoff and landing speeds are consequently reduced.

The two most common types of **leading-edge devices** are **slats** and **Krueger flaps**. The Krueger flap extends from the leading edge of the wing, increasing its camber. The slat also extends from the wing's leading edge but it creates a gap or slot. This slot allows high energy from under the wing to flow over the top of the wing that delays stall to a higher angle of attack than would otherwise occur. It is common to find Krueger flaps and slats on the same wing.

ATM, ATS, ADX

8384. The primary purpose of high-lift devices is to increase the

A—L/D_{MAX}.
B—lift at low speeds.
C—drag and reduce airspeed.

The primary purpose of high-lift devices (flaps, slots, slats, etc.) is to increase the CL_{MAX} of the airplane and to reduce the stall speed. The takeoff and landing speeds are consequently reduced. (PLT266, AA.I.A.K12) — ANA

Answer (A) is incorrect because increasing the lift component is an objective of high-lift devices which increase the ratio of L/D. The primary purpose of high-lift devices is to increase lift at low speeds. Answer (C) is incorrect because increasing the drag to reduce airspeed is the function of spoilers, not high-lift devices.

ATM, ATS, ADX

8331. Which is a purpose of leading-edge flaps?

A—Increase the camber of the wing.
B—Reduce lift without increasing airspeed.
C—Direct airflow over the top of the wing at high angles of attack.

The leading-edge flap extends in a downward direction to increase the camber or total curve of the wing's shape. (PLT473, AA.I.A.K12) — ANA

Answer (B) is incorrect because leading-edge flaps increase the maximum lift coefficient at higher angles of attack. Answer (C) is incorrect because a slot will direct airflow over the top of the wing at high angles of attack.

ATM, ATS, ADX

8385. What is the primary function of the leading edge flaps in landing configuration during the flare before touchdown?

A—Prevent flow separation.
B—Decrease rate of sink.
C—Increase profile drag.

The primary purpose of high-lift devices (flaps, slots, slats, etc.) is to increase the CL_{MAX} of the airplane and to reduce the stall speed. The takeoff and landing speeds are consequently reduced. (PLT305, AA.I.A.K12) — ANA

Answer (B) is incorrect because, to decrease the rate of sink, the coefficient of lift (CL) must increase. This is done by using leading-edge lift devices, slats, flaps, and other devices with the correct power setting. Answer (C) is incorrect because spoilers increase profile drag and are usually deployed after touchdown to reduce lift.

ATM, ATS, ADX

8334. What effect does extending leading edge slats have on an airplane's wing?

A—Increases the pitch up moment of an airfoil.
B—Increases the camber and CL_{MAX}.
C—Allows for earlier airflow separation.

The primary purpose of high-lift devices (flaps, slots, slats, etc.) is to increase the CL_{MAX} of the airplane and reduce the stall speed. The takeoff and landing speeds are consequently reduced. (PLT473, AA.I.A.K12) — ANA

Answers

8384 [B]	8331 [A]	8385 [A]	8334 [B]

ATM, ATS, ADX

8386. What effect does the leading edge slot in the wing have on performance?

A—Decreases profile drag.
B—Changes the stalling angle of attack to a higher angle.
C—Decelerates the upper surface boundary layer air.

The slot delays stall to a higher angle of attack. (PLT305, AA.I.A.K12) — ANA

Answer (A) is incorrect because, at low angles of attack, there is little or no profile drag increase. At high angles of attack, the slot delays the stall characteristics of the wing. Answer (C) is incorrect because the leading-edge slot actually increases airflow on the upper wing surface to allow higher angles of attack.

ATM, ATS, ADX

9765. What is a difference between the fowler flap system and split flap system?

A—Fowler flaps produce the greatest change in pitching moment.
B—Fowler flaps produce more drag.
C—Split flaps cause the greatest change in twisting loads.

Fowler flaps slide out and downward from the trailing edge of the wing. When lowered, they increase the wing area as well as the wing camber. The Fowler flap is characterized by the largest increase in CL_{MAX} with the least changes in drag. The Fowler flap also creates the greatest change in pitching moment. Split flaps consist of a hinged plate that deflects downward from the lower surface of the wing and produce the least change in the pitching moments of a wing when it is lowered. The deflection of a flap causes large nose-down moments which create significant twisting loads on the structure and pitching moments that must be controlled with the horizontal tail. Unfortunately, the flap types producing the greatest increases in CL_{MAX} usually cause the greatest twisting moments. The Fowler flap causes the greatest change in twisting moment while the split flap causes the least. (PLT266, AA.I.A.K12) — ANA

ATM, ATS, ADX

9766. On which type of wing are flaps most effective?

A—Thin wing.
B—Thick wing.
C—Sweptback wing.

The effectiveness of flaps on a wing configuration depends on many different factors, of which an important one is the amount of the wing area affected by the flaps. Since a certain amount of the span is reserved for ailerons, the actual wing maximum lift properties will be less than that resulting from the flapped two-dimensional section. If the basic wing has a low thickness, any type of flap will be less effective than on a wing of greater thickness. Sweepback of the wing can also cause a significant reduction in the effectiveness of flaps. (PLT266, AA.I.A.K12) — ANA

ATM, ATS, ADX

9771. When compared to plain flaps, split flaps

A—produce more lift with less drag.
B—produce only slightly more lift, but much more drag.
C—enhance takeoff performance in high density conditions.

The split flap produces a slightly greater change in CL_{MAX} than the plain flap. However, a much larger change in drag results from the substantial and turbulent wake produced by this type of flap; although greater drag may be advantageous, for example, when steeper landing approaches over obstacles are required. (PLT266, AA.I.A.K12) — ANA

Answers

8386 [B]	9765 [A]	9766 [B]	9771 [B]

Helicopter Aerodynamics

RTC
8355. What is the ratio between the total load supported by the rotor disc and the gross weight of a helicopter in flight?

A—Power loading.
B—Load factor.
C—Aspect ratio.

The load factor is the actual load on the rotor blades at any time, divided by the gross weight (or apparent gross weight; i.e., when the helicopter is in a bank, the apparent gross weight increases). (PLT310) — FAA-H-8083-21

RTC
8402. How should the pilot execute a pinnacle-type approach to a rooftop heliport in conditions of high wind and turbulence?

A—Steeper-than-normal approach, maintaining the desired angle of descent with collective.
B—Normal approach, maintaining a slower-than-normal rate of descent with cyclic.
C—Shallow approach, maintaining a constant line of descent with cyclic.

High winds can cause severe turbulence and downdrafts on the leeward side of rooftop helipads. Under these conditions, a steeper-than-normal approach to avoid downdrafts is desired. Angle of descent is maintained with collective and rate of closure (airspeed) is controlled with cyclic. (PLT170) — FAA-H-8083-21

RTC
8403. How should a quick stop be initiated?

A—Raise collective pitch.
B—Apply aft cyclic.
C—Decrease RPM while raising collective pitch.

The deceleration (or slowing) is initiated by applying aft cyclic to reduce forward speed and simultaneously lowering the collective to counteract any ballooning or climbing tendency. (PLT170) — FAA-H-8083-21

RTC
8404. How does V_{NE} speed vary with altitude?

A—Remains the same at all altitudes.
B—Increases with an increase in altitude.
C—Decreases with altitude an increase in altitude.

V_{NE} will decrease with an increase in altitude. Several factors contribute to V_{NE} including temperature, weight, altitude, and design limitations. (PLT124) — FAA-H-8083-21

RTC
8405. What limits the high airspeed potential of a helicopter?

A—Harmonic resonance.
B—Retreating blade stall.
C—Rotor RPM limitations.

The airflow over the retreating blade decreases and the airflow over the advancing blade increases in forward flight. To correct for the resulting dissymmetry of lift, the retreating blade must operate at increasingly higher angles of attack as the forward speed increases, until the retreating blade will stall at some high forward airspeed. (PLT124) — FAA-H-8083-21

RTC
8406. What corrective action can a pilot take to recover from vortex ring state?

A—Increase forward speed and raise collective pitch.
B—Decrease forward speed and partially raise collective pitch.
C—Increase forward speed and partially lower collective pitch.

By increasing forward speed and/or (if possible) partially lowering collective pitch, the conditions necessary for vortex ring state are reduced or eliminated. (PLT208) — FAA-H-8083-21

Answers

8355 [B]	8402 [A]	8403 [B]	8404 [C]	8405 [B]	8406 [C]

RTC
8406-1. A traditional recovery from a vortex ring state condition is accomplished by

A—increasing collective pitch.
B—increasing airspeed and/or partially lowering collective pitch.
C—lateral cyclic thrust combined with an increase in power and lateral antitorque thrust.

The traditional recovery is accomplished by increasing airspeed and/or partially lowering collective pitch to exit the vortex. (PLT208) — FAA-H-8083-21

Answer (A) is incorrect because increasing collective pitch only results in increasing the stalled area of the rotor, thereby increasing the rate of descent. Answer (C) is incorrect because this is the Vuichard recovery technique.

RTC
8406-2. A loss of tail rotor effectiveness (LTE) is a condition that occurs when

A—the flow of air through a tail rotor is altered in some way
B—the flow of air through the main rotor is altered in some way.
C—power to the tail rotor is substantially reduced or lost.

LTE is a condition that occurs when the flow of air through a tail rotor is altered in some way, by changing the angle or speed at which the air passes through the rotating blades of the tail rotor disk. (PLT262) — FAA-H-8083-21

RTC
8408. The lift differential that exists between the advancing main rotor blade and the retreating main rotor blade is known as

A—Coriolis effect.
B—dissymmetry of lift.
C—translating tendency.

Dissymmetry of lift is created by horizontal flight or by wind during hovering flight, and is the difference in lift that exists between the advancing blade of the rotor disc and the retreating blade of the rotor disc. (PLT470) — FAA-H-8083-21

RTC
8409. During a hover, a helicopter tends to drift in the direction of tail rotor thrust. What is this movement called?

A—Translating tendency.
B—Transverse flow effect.
C—Gyroscopic precession.

The entire helicopter has a tendency to move in the direction of tail rotor thrust when hovering, which is often referred to as "drift or translating tendency." (PLT268) — FAA-H-8083-21

RTC
8410. What is the purpose of the lead-lag (drag) hinge in a three-bladed, fully articulated helicopter rotor system?

A—Offset lateral instability during autorotation.
B—Compensate for Coriolis effect.
C—Provide geometric balance.

When a rotor blade of a three-bladed rotor system flaps upward, the center mass of that blade moves closer to the axis of rotation and blade acceleration takes place. When the blade flaps downward, its center of mass moves further from the axis of rotation and blade deceleration (or slowing) occurs. This increase and decrease of blade velocity in the plane of rotation due to mass movement is known as Coriolis effect. The acceleration and deceleration actions (leading and lagging) are absorbed by dampers or the blade structure itself (hinges) in a three-bladed system. (PLT470) — FAA-H-8083-21

RTC
8411. During an autorotation (collective pitch full down), what is an increase in rotor RPM associated with?

A—An increase in airflow through the rotor system.
B—A decrease in airflow through the rotor system.
C—A decrease in airspeed.

During an autorotation, the flow of air is upward through the rotor. The portion of the blade that produces the forces causing the rotor to turn in autorotation (approximately 25 to 70% of the radius outward from the center) is the driving region. An increase in the aerodynamic forces along the driving region (increase in the airflow through the rotor) tends to speed up the blade rotation. (PLT470) — FAA-H-8083-21

Answers

8406-1 [B] 8406-2 [A] 8408 [B] 8409 [A] 8410 [B] 8411 [A]

RTC

8412. What corrective action can a pilot take to prevent a retreating blade stall at its onset?

A—Reduce collective pitch and increase rotor RPM.
B—Increase collective pitch and increase rotor RPM.
C—Reduce collective pitch and decrease rotor RPM.

At the onset of blade stall vibration, the pilot should reduce collective pitch, increase rotor RPM, reduce forward airspeed and minimize maneuvering. (PLT470) — FAA-H-8083-21

RTC

8413. Which is a major warning of approaching retreating blade stall?

A—High frequency vibration.
B—Tendency to roll opposite the stalled side of the rotor.
C—Pitchup of the nose.

The major warnings of approaching retreating blade stall are: low-frequency vibration equal to the number of blades per revolution of the main rotor system, pitchup of the nose and tendency for the helicopter to roll towards the stalled (retreating blade) side of the rotor system. (PLT470) — FAA-H-8083-21

RTC

8417. How does high density altitude affect helicopter performance?

A—Engine and rotor efficiency are increased.
B—Engine and rotor efficiency are reduced.
C—Engine efficiency is reduced, but rotor efficiency is increased.

High elevations, high temperatures, and high moisture content (relative humidity) all contribute to high density altitude, which lessens helicopter performance. The thinner air at high density altitudes reduces the amount of lift of the rotor blades, and unsupercharged engines produce less power. (PLT124) — FAA-H-8083-21

RTC

8418. How is helicopter climb performance most adversely affected?

A—Higher-than-standard temperature and high relative humidity.
B—Lower-than-standard temperature and high relative humidity.
C—Higher-than-standard temperature and low relative humidity.

High elevations, high temperatures, and high moisture content (relative humidity) all contribute to high density altitude, which lessens helicopter performance. The thinner air at high density altitudes reduces the amount of lift of the rotor blades, and unsupercharged engines produce less power. (PLT124) — FAA-H-8083-21

RTC

8420. What causes Coriolis effect?

A—Differential thrust of rotor blades.
B—Changing angle of attack of blades during rotation.
C—Shift in center of mass of flapping blade.

When a rotor blade of a three-bladed rotor system flaps upward, the center mass of that blade moves closer to the axis of rotation and blade acceleration takes place. When the blade flaps downward, its center of mass moves further from the axis of rotation and blade deceleration (or slowing) occurs. This increase and decrease of blade velocity in the plane of rotation due to mass movement is known as Coriolis effect. (PLT197) — FAA-H-8083-21

RTC

8421. Why are the rotor blades more efficient when operating in ground effect?

A—Induced drag is reduced.
B—Induced angle of attack is increased.
C—Downwash velocity is accelerated.

When a helicopter is operated near the surface, the downwash velocity of the rotor blades cannot be fully developed. The reduction in downwash velocity causes the induced angle of attack of each rotor blade to be reduced, which causes the induced drag to be less. (PLT237) — FAA-H-8083-21

Answers

8412 [A]	8413 [C]	8417 [B]	8418 [A]	8420 [C]	8421 [A]

RTC

8422. What result does a level turn have on the total lift required and load factor with a constant airspeed?

A—Lift required remains constant and the load factor increases.
B—Lift required increases and the load factor decreases.
C—Both total lift force and load factor increase.

When a helicopter is placed in a bank, the resultant lifting force acts more horizontally and less vertically. To maintain a level turn, the resultant lifting force (total lift force) must be increased. When a helicopter assumes a curved flight path, centrifugal force causes additional stresses (load factor) to be imposed. (PLT248) — FAA-H-8083-21

RTC

8423. What causes a helicopter to turn?

A—Centrifugal force.
B—Horizontal component of lift.
C—Greater angle of attack of rotor blades on upward side of the rotor disc.

When a helicopter is placed in a bank, the rotor disc is tilted sideward causing the horizontal component of lift to be increased. The increased horizontal lift component pulls the helicopter from its straight course. (PLT248) — FAA-H-8083-21

RTC

8424. What is the primary purpose of the tail rotor system?

A—Maintain heading during forward flight.
B—Act as a rudder to assist in coordinated turns.
C—Counteract the torque effect of the main rotor.

As the main rotor of a helicopter turns in one direction, the fuselage tends to rotate in the opposite direction (Newton's Third Law of Motion: For every action there is an equal and opposite reaction). This tendency to rotate is called torque. The tail rotor is used to produce thrust to counteract the torque effect of the main rotor. (PLT470) — FAA-H-8083-21

RTC

8425. Under what condition would it be necessary to cause the tail rotor to direct thrust to the left on an American-made helicopter?

A—To maintain heading with a left crosswind.
B—To counteract the drag of the transmission during autorotation.
C—To execute hovering turns to the right.

The capability for tail rotors to produce thrust to the left (negative pitch angle) is necessary because during autorotation, the drag of the transmission (with no torque effect present) tends to yaw the nose to the left, in the same direction that the main rotor is turning. (PLT470) — FAA-H-8083-21

RTC

9318. Which statement describes the term "V_{TOSS}"?

A—The takeoff safety speed in a turbine-engine powered transport category airplane.
B—The takeoff safety speed in a Category A helicopter.
C—The takeoff stall speed in the takeoff configuration in a turbopropeller powered airplane.

V_{TOSS} means takeoff safety speed for Category A helicopters. (PLT466) — 14 CFR §1.2

RTC

9831. A level attitude in flight in a helicopter indicates

A—acceleration.
B—descent.
C—stable flight.

In straight-and-level, unaccelerated forward flight, lift equals weight and thrust equals drag (straight-and-level flight is flight with a constant heading and at a constant altitude). If lift exceeds weight, the helicopter climbs; if lift is less than weight, the helicopter descends. If thrust exceeds drag, the helicopter speeds up; if thrust is less than drag, it slows down. (PLT219) — FAA-H-8083-21

Answers

8422 [C]	8423 [B]	8424 [C]	8425 [B]	9318 [B]	9381 [C]

Chapter 4
Performance

Note applicable to Chapters 4 and 5: The ATP Single-engine exam (ATS) focuses on performance comparable to the Cessna 208 and the ATP Multi-engine exam (ATM) focuses on performance comparable to the Bombardier CRJ200 and Q400.

Engine Performance

There are four types of engines in use on modern airplanes: **reciprocating engine, turboprop engine, turbofan engine,** and **turbojet engine**. The type of engine selected for a particular airplane design depends primarily on the speed range of the aircraft. The reciprocating engine is most efficient for aircraft with cruising speeds below 250 MPH, the turboprop works best in the 250 MPH to 450 MPH range and the turbofan and turbojet engines are most efficient above 450 MPH.

Manifold pressure (MAP) is a measurement of the power output of a reciprocating engine. It is basically the pressure in the engine's air inlet system. In a normally-aspirated (unsupercharged) engine, the MAP will drop as the aircraft climbs to altitude. This severely limits a piston-powered airplane's altitude capability.

Most piston-powered airplanes flown by air carriers are turbocharged. On this type of engine, exhaust gas from the engine is used as a power source for a compressor that in turn raises the MAP at any given altitude. The flow of exhaust gas to the turbocharger is controlled by a device called a **waste gate**.

Turbocharging allows an aircraft to fly at much higher altitudes than it would be able to with normally-aspirated engines. The term **critical altitude** is used to describe the effect of turbocharging on the aircraft's performance. The critical altitude of a turbocharged reciprocating engine is the highest altitude at which a desired manifold pressure can be maintained.

The pilots of reciprocating-engine-powered aircraft must be very careful to observe the published limits on manifold pressure and engine RPM. In particular, high RPM and low MAP can produce severe wear, fatigue and damage.

Turboprops, turbofans and turbojet engines are types of **gas turbine engines**. Turbine engines are classified by the type of compressors they use—centrifugal flow, axial flow, and centrifugal-axial flow. All gas turbine engines consist of an air inlet section, a compressor section, the combustion section, the turbine section and the exhaust. Air enters the inlet at roughly ambient temperature and pressure. As it passes through the compressor the pressure increases and so does the temperature due to the heat of compression. **Bleed air** is tapped off the compressor for such accessories as air conditioning and thermal anti-icing.

The section connecting the compressor and the combustion sections is called the diffuser. In the diffuser, the cross sectional area of the engine increases. This allows the air stream from the compressor to slow and its pressure to increase. In fact, the highest pressure in the engine is attained at this point.

Next, the air enters the combustion section where it is mixed with fuel and the mixture is ignited. Note that after the initial start of the engine there is no need for an ignition system that operates continuously (such as the spark plugs in a piston engine) because the uninterrupted flow of fuel and air will sustain combustion after the initial "light off." The combustion of the fuel-air mixture causes a great increase in volume and because there is higher pressure at the diffuser, the gas exits through the turbine section. The temperature of the gas rises rapidly as it passes from the front to the rear of the combustion section. It reaches its highest point in the engine at the turbine inlet. The maximum turbine inlet temperature is a major limitation on turbojet performance, and without cooling, it could easily reach up to 4,000°F, far beyond the limits of the materials used in the turbine section. To keep the temperature down to an acceptable 1,100° to 1,500°F, surplus cooling air from the compressor is mixed aft of the burners.

The purpose of the turbine(s) is to drive the compressor(s) and they are connected by a drive shaft. Since the turbines take energy from the gas, both the temperature and pressure drop.

The gases exit the turbine section at very high velocity into the tailpipe. The tailpipe is shaped so that the gas is accelerated even more, reaching maximum velocity as it exits into the atmosphere. See Figure 4-1.

Combinations of slow airspeed and high engine RPM can cause a phenomenon in turbine engines called **compressor stall**. This occurs when the angle of attack of the engine's compressor blades becomes excessive and they stall. If a transient stall condition exists, the pilot will hear an intermittent "bang" as backfires and flow reversals in the compressor take place. If the transient condition develops into a steady state stall, the pilot will hear a loud roar and experience severe engine vibrations. The steady state compressor stall has the most potential for severe engine damage, which can occur literally within seconds of the onset of the stall.

If a compressor stall occurs in flight, the pilot should reduce fuel flow, reduce the aircraft's angle of attack and increase airspeed.

The turboprop is a turbine engine that drives a conventional propeller. It can develop much more power per pound than can a piston engine and is more fuel efficient than the turbojet engine. Compared to a turbojet engine, it is limited to slower speeds and lower altitudes (25,000 feet to the tropopause). The term **equivalent shaft horsepower (ESHP)** is used to describe the total engine output. This term combines its output in shaft horsepower (used to drive the propeller) and the jet thrust it develops.

As the density altitude is increased, engine performance will decrease. When the air becomes less dense, there is not as much oxygen available for combustion and the potential thrust output is decreased accordingly. Density altitude is increased by increasing the pressure altitude or by increasing the ambient temperature. Relative humidity will also affect engine performance. Reciprocating engines in particular will experience a significant loss of BHP (Brake Horsepower). Turbine engines are not affected as much by high humidity and will experience very little loss of thrust.

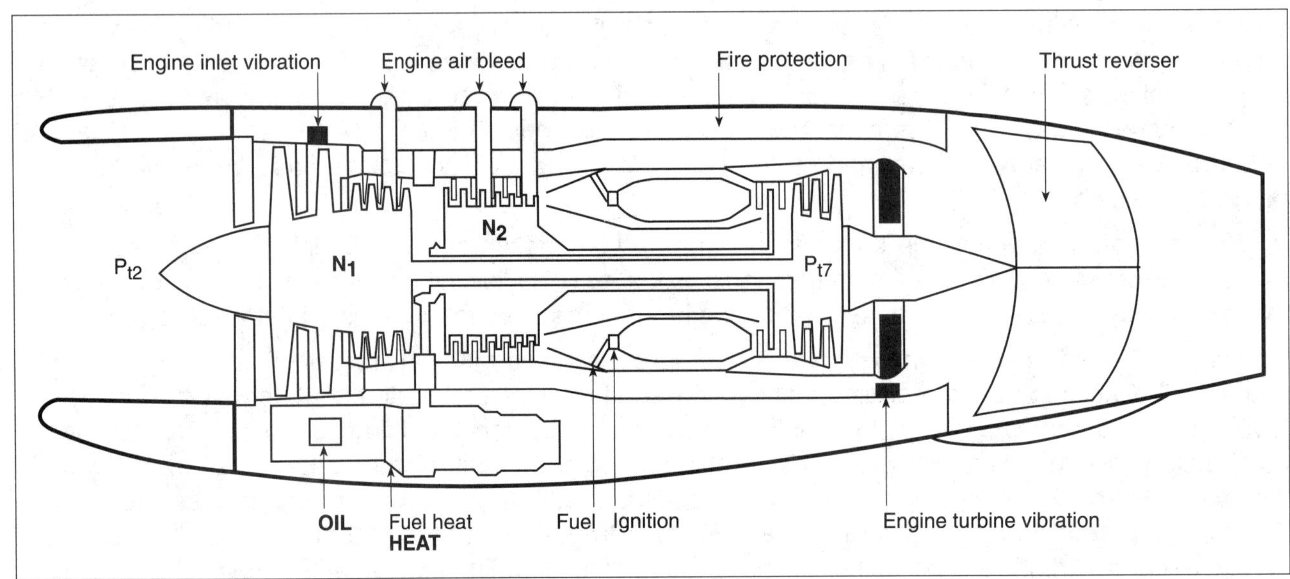

Figure 4-1. Turbojet engine

ALL

9072. Where is the critical altitude of a supercharged-reciprocating engine?

A—The highest altitude at which a desired manifold pressure can be obtained.
B—Highest altitude where the mixture can be leaned to best power ratio.
C—The altitude at which maximum allowable BMEP can be obtained.

The critical altitude of a supercharged reciprocating engine is the highest altitude at which a desired MAP can be maintained. (PLT343, AA.I.A.K2) — FAA-H-8083-25

Answer (B) is incorrect because critical altitude is the highest altitude at which a manifold pressure can be obtained. Answer (C) is incorrect because BMEP is pressure representing the mean gas load on the piston during the power stroke.

ALL

9073. What is controlled by the waste gate of a turbocharged-reciprocating engine?

A—Supercharger gear ratio.
B—Exhaust gas discharge.
C—Throttle opening.

A turbocharger drives exhaust gas from the engine. The waste gate controls the flow of the exhaust gas through the turbocharger's turbine. (PLT343, AA.I.A.K2) — FAA-H-8083-25

Answer (A) is incorrect because supercharger gear ratio is not controlled by the waste gate. Answer (C) is incorrect because the throttle opening sets the desired manifold pressure.

ALL

9068. Under normal operating conditions, which combination of MAP and RPM produce the most severe wear, fatigue, and damage to high performance reciprocating engines?

A—High RPM and low MAP.
B—Low RPM and high MAP.
C—High RPM and high MAP.

The most severe rate of wear and fatigue damage occurs at high RPM and low MAP. (PLT365, AA.I.A.K2) — FAA-H-8083-25

Answer (B) is incorrect because while low RPM and high MAP produce severe wear to high performance reciprocating engines, the most damage is done by high RPM and low manifold pressure. Answer (C) is incorrect because a high RPM and a low MAP produce the most severe wear to high performance reciprocating engines.

ALL

9068-1. How are turbine engines classified?

A—The type of compressor or combination of compressors they use.
B—The method in which the air/fuel mixture is ignited.
C—The flow of air through the engine and how power is produced.

Turbine engines are classified by the type of compressors they use—centrifugal flow, axial flow, and centrifugal-axial flow. (PLT365, AA.I.A.K2) — FAA-H-8083-25

ALL

9058. Which place in the turbojet engine is subjected to the highest temperature?

A—Compressor discharge.
B—Fuel spray nozzles.
C—Turbine inlet.

The highest temperatures in any turbine engine will occur at the turbine inlet. This TIT (Turbine Inlet Temperature) is usually the limiting factor in the engine operation. (PLT499, AA.I.A.K2) — FAA-H-8083-25

ALL

8394. A hot start in a turbine engine is caused by

A—failed ignition.
B—the engine's failure to accelerate.
C—too much fuel in the combustion chamber.

A hot start occurs when the exhaust gas temperature exceeds the safe limit of an aircraft. Caused by either too much fuel entering the combustion chamber or insufficient turbine RPM, this condition is also known as a hung start. (PLT499, AA.I.A.K2) — FAA-H-8083-25

ALL

8394-1. What could cause a turbine engine hot start?

A—Lack of airflow due to insufficient turbine RPM.
B—Inlet and compressor airflow imbalance.
C—Insufficient fuel in the combustion chamber.

A hot start occurs when the exhaust gas temperature exceeds the safe limit of an aircraft. Caused by either too much fuel entering the combustion chamber or insufficient turbine RPM, this condition is also known as a hung start. (PLT499, AA.I.A.K2) — FAA-H-8083-25

Answers

9072 [A]	9073 [B]	9068 [A]	9068-1 [A]	9058 [C]	8394 [C]
8394-1 [A]					

ALL

9060. The most important restriction to the operation of turbojet or turboprop engines is

A—limiting compressor speed.
B—limiting exhaust gas temperature.
C—limiting torque.

The highest temperatures in any turbine engine will occur at the turbine inlet. This TIT (Turbine Inlet Temperature) is usually the limiting factor in the engine operation. In many engines, TIT is measured indirectly as EGT (Exhaust Gas Temperature). (PLT499, AA.I.A.K2) — FAA-H-8083-25

Answer (A) is incorrect because the turbine section is the most critical element of the turbojet engine. Temperature control is more restrictive than compressor speed, which may operate above 10,000 RPM continuously. Answer (C) is incorrect because torque is a performance measure used on turbopropeller airplanes, but not generally applicable to turbojet engines. The most important restriction is temperature, even though in cooler weather a torque limitation may be reached before the temperature limitation in a turbopropeller airplane.

ALL

9064. What characterizes a transient compressor stall?

A—Loud, steady roar accompanied by heavy shuddering.
B—Sudden loss of thrust accompanied by a loud whine.
C—Intermittent "bang," as backfires and flow reversals take place.

If a compressor stall is transient and intermittent, the indication will be an intermittent "bang" as backfire and flow reversal take place. If the stall develops and becomes steady, strong vibration and a loud roar develop from the continuous flow reversal. The possibility of damage is immediate from a steady stall. Recovery must be accomplished quickly by reducing throttle setting, lowering the airplane angle of attack, and increasing airspeed. (PLT343, AA.I.A.K2) — FAA-H-8083-25

Answer (A) is incorrect because this describes a developed and steady stall. Answer (B) is incorrect because a transient stall is characterized by an intermittent "bang."

ALL

9768. What prevents turbine engines from developing compressor stalls?

A—Deice valves-fuel heat.
B—TKS system.
C—Compressor bleed valves.

At a low RPM, sudden full power application will tend to overfuel the engine resulting in possible compressor surge, excessive turbine temperatures, compressor stall, and/or flameout. To prevent this, various limiters such as compressor bleed valves are contained in the system and serve to restrict the engine until it is at an RPM at which it can respond to a rapid acceleration demand without distress. (PLT499, AA.I.A.K2) — FAA-H-8083-3

ALL

9065. What indicates that a compressor stall has developed and become steady?

A—Strong vibrations and loud roar.
B—Occasional loud "bang" and flow reversal.
C—Complete loss of power with severe reduction in airspeed.

If a compressor stall is transient and intermittent, the indication will be an intermittent "bang" as backfire and flow reversal take place. If the stall develops and becomes steady, strong vibration and a loud roar develop from the continuous flow reversal. The possibility of damage is immediate from a steady stall. Recovery must be accomplished quickly by reducing throttle setting, lowering the airplane angle of attack, and increasing airspeed. (PLT343, AA.I.A.K2) — FAA-H-8083-25

Answer (B) is incorrect because this describes an indication of a transient stall. Answer (C) is incorrect because a compressor stall will not cause a complete loss of power.

ALL

9066. Which type of compressor stall has the greatest potential for severe engine damage?

A—Intermittent "backfire" stall.
B—Transient "backfire" stall.
C—Steady, continuous flow reversal stall.

If a compressor stall is transient and intermittent, the indication will be an intermittent "bang" as backfire and flow reversal take place. If the stall develops and becomes steady, strong vibration and a loud roar develop from the continuous flow reversal. The possibility of damage is immediate from a steady stall. Recovery must be accomplished quickly by reducing throttle setting, lowering the airplane angle of attack, and increasing airspeed. (PLT343, AA.I.A.K2) — FAA-H-8083-25

Answers

9060 [B]	9064 [C]	9768 [C]	9065 [A]	9066 [C]

ALL

8974. Which part(s) in the turbojet engine is subjected to the high temperatures and severe centrifugal forces?

A—Turbine wheel(s).
B—Turbine vanes.
C—Compressor rotor(s) or impeller(s).

The turbine wheels are found at the back of the turbine section, in the area of very high temperatures and high centrifugal forces. Very hot, high pressure gases enter the turbine section from the combustor. The function of the gas generator's turbine wheels is to transfer the energy from the hot, high pressure gases to drive the shaft which is connected to the compressor wheel at the front of the engine. This in turn compresses air into the combustor where fuel is added and ignited. During normal operations, the turbine wheel rotates at many thousands of RPM. (PLT499, AA.I.A.K2) — FAA-H-8083-25

Answer (B) is incorrect because although turbine vanes (inlet guide vanes) are exposed to higher temperatures, they are stationary and thus are not subject to centrifugal forces. Answer (C) is incorrect because turbine wheels, or disks, with their attached blades, are the most highly stressed components on a turbojet engine.

ALL

9067. What recovery would be appropriate in the event of compressor stall?

A—Reduce the throttle and then rapidly advance the throttle to decrease the angle of attack on the compressor blades, creating more airflow.
B—Reduce the throttle and then slowly advance the throttle again and decrease the aircraft's angle of attack.
C—Advance the throttle slowly to increase airflow and decrease the angle of attack on one or more compressor blades.

If a compressor stall is transient and intermittent, the indication will be an intermittent "bang" as backfire and flow reversal take place. If the stall develops and becomes steady, strong vibration and a loud roar develop from the continuous flow reversal. The possibility of damage is immediate from a steady stall. Recovery must be accomplished quickly by reducing throttle setting, lowering the airplane angle of attack, and increasing airspeed. (PLT343, AA.I.A.K2) — FAA-H-8083-25

ALL

9067-1. While on an ILS approach, what is the proper way to recover from an impending stall?

A—Engaging the autopilot.
B—Changing flap settings.
C—Reducing the angle of attack.

The most important action to take to recover from an impending stall or a full stall is to reduce the angle of attack. (PLT343, AA.V.C.K5) — FAA-H-8083-3

ALL

9070. Equivalent shaft horsepower (ESHP) of a turboprop engine is a measure of

A—turbine inlet temperature.
B—shaft horsepower and jet thrust.
C—propeller thrust only.

Turboprop engines get 15 to 25% of their total thrust output from jet exhaust. ESHP (Equivalent Shaft Horsepower) is the term used to describe the shaft horsepower applied to the propeller plus this jet thrust. (PLT500, AA.I.A.K2) — FAA-H-8083-25

ALL

9071. Minimum specific fuel consumption of the turboprop engine is normally available in which altitude range?

A—10,000 feet to 25,000 feet.
B—25,000 feet to the tropopause.
C—The tropopause to 45,000 feet.

Minimum specific fuel consumption of a turboprop engine will be obtained in an altitude range of 25,000 to 35,000 feet. The tropopause will be in the neighborhood of 35,000 feet depending on the season and latitude. (PLT130, AA.I.A.K4) — FAA-H-8083-25

ALL

9059. What effect would a change in ambient temperature or air density have on gas-turbine-engine performance?

A—As air density decreases, thrust increases.
B—As temperature increases, thrust increases.
C—As temperature increases, thrust decreases.

Turbine engine thrust varies directly with air density. As air density decreases, so does thrust. An increase in temperature will decrease air density. (PLT127, AA.I.B.K3a) — FAA-H-8083-25

Answers

8974 [A]	9067 [B]	9067-1 [C]	9070 [B]	9071 [B]	9059 [C]

ALL

9061. As outside air pressure decreases, thrust output will

A—increase due to greater efficiency of jet aircraft in thin air.
B—remain the same since compression of inlet air will compensate for any decrease in air pressure.
C—decrease due to higher density altitude.

Thrust output decreases with increasing density altitude. Decreasing air pressure increases density altitude. (PLT127, AA.I.B.K3a) — FAA-H-8083-25

ALL

9061-1. Low pressure air decreases aircraft performance because

A—the air is denser than higher pressure air.
B—the air is less dense than high pressure air.
C—air expands in the engine during the combustion process.

Thrust output decreases with increasing density altitude. Decreasing air pressure increases density altitude. (PLT127, AA.I.B.K3a) — FAA-H-8083-25

ALL

9062. What effect will an increase in altitude have upon the available equivalent shaft horsepower (ESHP) of a turboprop engine?

A—Lower air density and engine mass flow will cause a decrease in power.
B—Higher propeller efficiency will cause an increase in usable power (ESHP) and thrust.
C—Power will remain the same but propeller efficiency will decrease.

As altitude is increased, the ESHP of a turboprop engine will decrease due to lower engine mass flow and decreased propeller efficiency. (PLT127, AA.I.B.K2) — FAA-H-8083-25

ALL

9063. What effect, if any, does high ambient temperature have upon the thrust output of a turbine engine?

A—Thrust will be reduced due to the decrease in air density.
B—Thrust will remain the same, but turbine temperature will be higher.
C—Thrust will be higher because more heat energy is extracted from the hotter air.

Turbine engine thrust varies directly with air density. As air density decreases, so does thrust. An increase in temperature will decrease air density. (PLT127, AA.I.B.K3a) — FAA-H-8083-25

ALL

9069. What effect does high relative humidity have upon the maximum power output of modern aircraft engines?

A—Neither turbojet nor reciprocating engines are affected.
B—Reciprocating engines will experience a significant loss of BHP.
C—Turbojet engines will experience a significant loss of thrust.

While turbojet engines are almost unaffected by high relative humidity, reciprocating engines will experience a significant loss of BHP (Brake Horsepower). (PLT365, AA.I.B.K3a) — FAA-H-8083-25

Answer (A) is incorrect because both reciprocating and turbojet engines are affected by high relative humidity to some degree. Answer (C) is incorrect because turbojet engines will have a negligible loss of thrust.

Answers

9061 [C] 9061-1 [B] 9062 [A] 9063 [A] 9069 [B]

Helicopter Systems

RTC
8407. Which type rotor system is more susceptible to ground resonance?

A—Fully articulated rotor system.
B—Semi-rigid rotor system.
C—Rigid rotor system.

Due to the lead/lag of the blades in a fully articulated rotor system, a shock from a landing gear striking the surface can be transmitted through the fuselage to the rotor, forcing the blades straddling the contact point closer together and unbalancing the rotor system. This can cause a pendulum-like oscillation which will increase rapidly unless immediate corrective action is taken. (PLT470) — FAA-H-8083-21

RTC
9781. Ground resonance occurs when

A—a fully articulated rotor system is unbalanced.
B—a semi-rigid rotor system is out of balance.
C—a pilot lands with over inflated tires.

Ground resonance is an aerodynamic phenomenon associated with fully articulated rotor systems. It develops when the rotor blades move out of phase with each other and cause the rotor disc to become unbalanced. (PLT470) — FAA-H-8083-21

RTC
8414. What type frequency vibration is associated with a defective transmission?

A—Low frequency only.
B—Medium or low frequency.
C—High or medium frequency.

High-frequency vibrations (2,000 cycles per minute or higher) are associated with the engine in most helicopters. Any bearings in the transmission that go bad will result in vibrations with frequencies directly related to the speed of the engine. (PLT472) — FAA-H-8083-21

RTC
8415. What type frequency vibration is associated with the main rotor system?

A—Low frequency.
B—Medium frequency.
C—High frequency.

Abnormal vibrations in the low-frequency range (100 to 400 cycles per minute) are always associated with the main rotor system, and will be somewhat related to the rotor RPM and the number of blades of the main rotor. (PLT472) — FAA-H-8083-21

RTC
9800. A medium or higher frequency vibration mainly present in the anti-torque pedals is

A—usually traceable to engine cooling fan assembly.
B—probably caused by the tail rotor.
C—to be expected and accepted as normal.

Medium-frequency vibrations are a result of trouble with the tail rotor in most helicopters. Improper rigging, imbalance, defective blades, or bad bearings in the tail rotor are all sources of these vibrations. If the vibration occurs only during turns, the trouble may be caused by insufficient tail rotor flapping action. (PLT472) — FAA-H-8083-21

RTC
8416. What type frequency vibration is indicative of a defective tail rotor system?

A—Low and medium frequency.
B—Medium and high frequency.
C—Low and high frequency.

Medium frequency vibrations (1,000–2,000 cycles per minute) and high frequency vibrations (2,000 cycles per minute or higher) are normally associated with out-of-balance components that rotate at a high RPM, such as the tail rotor, engine, cooling fans, and components of the drive train, including transmissions, drive shafts, bearings, pulleys, and belts. (PLT472) — FAA-H-8083-21

Answers

8407 [A]	9781 [A]	8414 [C]	8415 [A]	9800 [B]	8416 [B]

RTC

8426. What is the primary purpose of the free-wheeling unit?

A—To provide speed reduction between the engine, main rotor system, and tail rotor system.
B—To provide disengagement of the engine from the rotor system for autorotation purposes.
C—To transmit engine power to the main rotor, tail rotor, generator/alternator, and other accessories.

The freewheeling coupling provides for autorotative capabilities by disconnecting the rotor system from the engine when the engine stops or slows below the RPM of the rotor system. This allows the transmission to be driven by the main rotor. The tail rotor will continue to be turned by the transmission. (PLT470) — FAA-H-8083-21

RTC

8427. The main rotor blades of a fully articulated rotor system can

A—flap, drag, and feather collectively.
B—flap, drag, and feather independently of each other.
C—flap and drag individually, but can only feather collectively.

Fully articulated rotor systems usually have three or more rotor blades, each of which is attached to the rotor hub by a horizontal hinge (flapping), a vertical hinge (drag), and can be feathered (rotated about their spanwise axis) independently of the other blades. (PLT470) — FAA-H-8083-21

RTC

8428. The main rotor blades of a semi-rigid system can

A—flap and feather as a unit.
B—flap, drag, and feather independently.
C—flap and drag individually, but can only feather collectively.

In a semirigid (two-bladed) rotor system, the blades are rigidly interconnected to the hub and flap as a unit (when one blade flaps up, the other blade flaps down an equal amount). The swash plate changes the pitch angle in each blade (feathers) an equal amount. (PLT470) — FAA-H-8083-21

Takeoff Performance Terminology

Clearway—a plane beyond the end of a runway which does not contain obstructions and can be considered when calculating takeoff performance of turbine-powered transport category airplanes. The first segment of the takeoff of a turbine-powered airplane is considered complete when it reaches a height of 35 feet above the runway and has achieved V_2 speed. Clearway may be used for the climb to 35 feet.

Stopway—an area designated for use in decelerating an aborted takeoff. It cannot be used as a part of the takeoff distance but can be considered as part of the accelerate-stop distance. See Figure 4-2.

Regulation requires that a transport category airplane's takeoff weight be such that, if at any time during the takeoff run the critical engine fails, the airplane can either be stopped on the runway and stopway remaining, or that it can safely continue the takeoff. This means that a **maximum takeoff weight** must be computed for each takeoff. Factors which determine the maximum takeoff weight for an airplane include runway length, wind, flap position, runway braking action, pressure altitude and temperature.

In addition to the runway-limited takeoff weight, each takeoff requires a computation of a climb-limited takeoff weight that will guarantee acceptable climb performance after takeoff with an engine inoperative. The climb-limited takeoff weight is determined by flap position, pressure altitude and temperature.

When the runway-limited and climb-limited takeoff weights are determined, they are compared to the maximum structural takeoff weight. The lowest of the three weights is the limit that must be observed for that takeoff. If the airplane's actual weight is at or below the lowest of the three limits, adequate takeoff performance is ensured. If the actual weight is above any of the limits a takeoff cannot be made until the weight is reduced or one or more limiting factors (runway, flap setting, etc.) is changed to raise the limiting weight.

Answers

8426 [B] 8427 [B] 8428 [A]

After the maximum takeoff weight is computed and it is determined that the airplane's actual weight is within limits, then V_1, V_R and V_2 are computed. These takeoff speed limits are contained in performance charts and tables of the airplane flight manual, and are observed on the captain's airspeed indicator. By definition they are indicated airspeeds. See Figure 4-3.

V_1 (takeoff decision speed) is the speed during the takeoff at which the airplane can experience a failure of the critical engine and the pilot can abort the takeoff and come to a full safe stop on the runway and stopway remaining, or the pilot can continue the takeoff safely. If an engine fails at a speed less than V_1, the pilot must abort; if the failure occurs at a speed above V_1 he/she must continue the takeoff.

V_R (rotation speed) is the IAS at which the aircraft is rotated to its takeoff attitude with or without an engine failure. V_R is at or just above V_1.

V_2 (takeoff safety speed) ensures that the airplane can maintain an acceptable climb gradient with the critical engine inoperative.

V_{MU} (minimum unstick speed) is the minimum speed at which the airplane may be flown off the runway without a tail strike. This speed is determined by manufacturer's tests and establishes minimum V_1 and V_R speeds. The flight crew does not normally compute the V_{MU} speed separately.

V_1 is computed using the actual airplane gross weight, flap setting, pressure altitude and temperature. Raising the pressure altitude, temperature or gross weight will all increase the computed V_1 speed. Lowering any of those variables will lower the V_1 speed.

A wind will change the takeoff distance. A headwind will decrease it and a tailwind will increase it. While a headwind or tailwind component does affect the runway limited takeoff weight, it usually has no direct effect on the computed V_1 speed. The performance tables for a few airplanes include a small correction to V_1 for very strong winds. For those airplanes, a headwind will increase V_1 and a tailwind will decrease it.

A runway slope has the same effect on takeoff performance as a wind. A runway which slopes uphill will increase the takeoff distance for an airplane and a downslope will decrease it. A significant slope may require an adjustment in the V_1 speed. An upslope will require an increase in V_1 and a downslope will require a decrease.

If there is slush on the runway or if the antiskid system is inoperative, the stopping performance of the airplane is degraded. This requires that any aborted takeoff be started at a lower speed and with more runway and stopway remaining. This means that both the runway-limited takeoff weight and the V_1 used for takeoff be lower than normal.

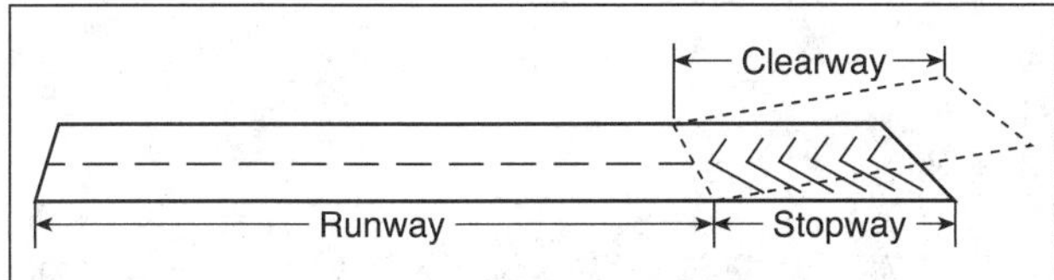

Figure 4-2. Takeoff runway definitions

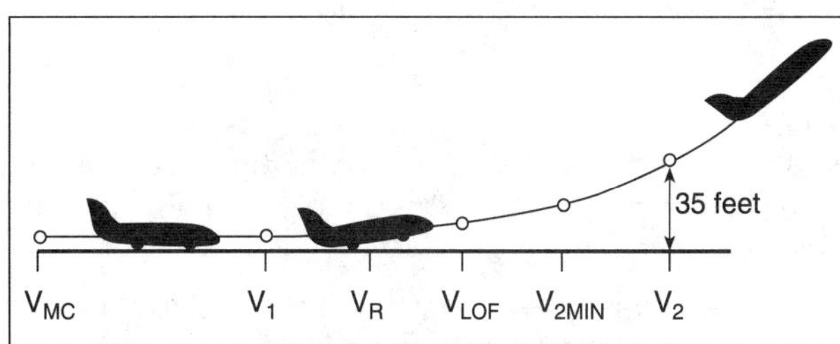

Figure 4-3. Takeoff speeds

ATM, ATS, ADX

9324. What is the name of an area beyond the end of a runway which does not contain obstructions and can be considered when calculating takeoff performance of turbine-powered aircraft?

A—Clearway.
B—Stopway.
C—Obstruction clearance plane.

"Clearway" means, for turbine-powered airplanes, an area beyond the end of the runway, centrally located about the extended centerline and under the control of the airport authorities. Clearway distance may be used in the calculation of takeoff distance. (PLT395, AA.I.B.K2b) — 14 CFR §1.1

Answer (B) is incorrect because a stopway is an area beyond the takeoff runway, not any less wide than the runway, centered upon the extended centerline of the runway, and able to support the airplane during an aborted takeoff. Answer (C) is incorrect because an obstruction clearance plane is not defined in 14 CFR Part 1.

ATM, ATS, ADX

9327. What is an area identified by the term "stopway"?

A—An area, at least the same width as the runway, capable of supporting an airplane during a normal takeoff.
B—An area designated for use in decelerating an aborted takeoff.
C—An area, not as wide as the runway, capable of supporting an airplane during a normal takeoff.

"Stopway" means an area beyond the takeoff runway, able to support the airplane, for use in decelerating the airplane during an aborted takeoff. (PLT395, AA.I.B.K2b) — 14 CFR §1.1

Answer (A) is incorrect because it describes the nonlanding portion of a runway behind a displaced threshold, which may be suitable for taxiing, landing rollout, and takeoff of aircraft. Answer (C) is incorrect because it would describe an area that exists before a displaced threshold.

ATM, ATS, ADX

8134. For which of these aircraft is the "clearway" for a particular runway considered in computing takeoff weight limitations?

A—Those passenger-carrying transport aircraft certificated between August 26, 1957 and August 30, 1959.
B—Turbine-engine-powered transport airplanes certificated after September 30, 1958.
C—U.S. certified air carrier airplanes certificated after August 29, 1959.

"Clearway" may be considered when determining the takeoff distance of turbine-engine-powered transport category airplane certificated after August 29, 1959. (PLT034, AA.I.B.K2b) — 14 CFR §121.189 and §1.1

Answers (A) and (C) are incorrect because the passenger-carrying transport aircraft and air carrier airplane would have to be turbine-engine-powered in order to include the clearway in determining runway length for takeoff purposes.

ATM, ATS, ADX

9317. Which is a definition of V_2 speed?

A—Takeoff decision speed.
B—Takeoff safety speed.
C—Minimum takeoff speed.

V_2 means takeoff safety speed. (PLT466, AA.I.B.K2b) — 14 CFR §1.2

Answer (A) is incorrect because V_1 is takeoff decision speed. Answer (C) is incorrect because minimum takeoff speed doesn't describe a defined speed.

ATM, ATS, ADX

9319. What is the correct symbol for minimum unstick speed?

A—V_{MU}.
B—V_{MD}.
C—V_{FC}.

V_{MU} means minimum unstick speed. (PLT466, AA.I.B.K2b) — 14 CFR §1.2

Answer (B) is incorrect because V_{MD} is not a concept that is defined in 14 CFR §1.2. Answer (C) is incorrect because V_{FC}/M_{FC} is maximum speed for stability characteristics.

ATM, ATS, ADX

8774. The maximum speed during takeoff that the pilot may abort the takeoff and stop the airplane within the accelerate-stop distance is

A—V_2.
B—V_{REF}.
C—V_1.

The takeoff decision speed, V_1, is the calibrated airspeed on the ground at which, as a result of engine failure or other reasons, the pilot is assumed to have made a decision to continue or discontinue the takeoff. (PLT506, AA.I.B.K2a) — 14 CFR §1.2

Answer (A) is incorrect because V_2 is the takeoff safety speed. Answer (B) is incorrect because V_{REF} is the reference landing speed, an airspeed used for final approach, which adjusts the normal approach speed for winds and gusty conditions.

Answers

9324 [A] 9327 [B] 8134 [B] 9317 [B] 9319 [A] 8774 [C]

ATM, ATS, ADX

8775. The minimum speed during takeoff, following a failure of the critical engine at V_{EF}, at which the pilot may continue the takeoff and achieve the required height above the takeoff surface within the takeoff distance is indicated by symbol

A—V_{2min}.
B—V_1.
C—V_{LOF}.

The takeoff decision speed, V_1, is the calibrated airspeed on the ground at which, as a result of engine failure or other reasons, the pilot is assumed to have made a decision to continue or discontinue the takeoff. V_1 is also the speed at which the airplane can be rotated for takeoff and shown to be adequate to safely continue the takeoff, using normal piloting skill, when the critical engine is suddenly made inoperative. (PLT466, AA.I.B.K2a) — 14 CFR §1.2

Answer (A) is incorrect because V_{2min} is the minimum takeoff safety speed. Answer (C) is incorrect because V_{LOF} is the liftoff speed.

ATM, ATS, ADX

8780. The symbol for the speed at which the critical engine is assumed to fail during takeoff is

A—V_2.
B—V_1.
C—V_{EF}.

V_{EF} is the calibrated airspeed at which the critical engine is assumed to fail. V_{EF} must be selected by the applicant but must not be less than 1.05 V_{MC} or, at the option of the applicant, not less than V_{MCG}. (PLT466, AA.I.B.K2b) — 14 CFR Part 25

Answer (A) is incorrect because V_2 is the takeoff safety speed. Answer (B) is incorrect because V_1 is takeoff decision speed.

ATM, ATS, ADX

9076. Which performance factor decreases as airplane gross weight increases, for a given runway?

A—Critical engine failure speed.
B—Rotation speed.
C—Accelerate-stop distance.

Critical Engine Failure Speed (also called V_1) increases with an increase in weight, resulting in a decrease in performance. (PLT011, AA.I.B.K2a) — ANA

ATM, ATS, ADX

9085. Which condition has the effect of reducing critical engine failure speed?

A—Slush on the runway or inoperative antiskid.
B—Low gross weight.
C—High density altitude.

Critical Engine Failure Speed is an obsolete term for V_1 which is now called Takeoff Decision Speed. Lowering the airplane's weight will always have the effect of decreasing V_1, while increasing the density altitude will have the effect of increasing V_1. However, inoperative antiskid or slush on the runway will cause a reduction in the maximum allowable takeoff weight which has the effect of lowering V_1. (PLT347, AA.I.B.K2b) — ANA

ATM, ATS, ADX

9083. What effect does an uphill runway slope have upon takeoff performance?

A—Increases takeoff distance.
B—Decreases takeoff speed.
C—Decreases takeoff distance.

An uphill runway will have the effect of decreasing an airplane's rate of acceleration during the takeoff roll thus causing it to reach its takeoff speeds (V_1 and V_R) further down the runway than would otherwise be the case. An uphill runway will also necessitate an increased V_1 speed in some airplanes. (PLT129, AA.I.B.K2b) — ANA

ATM, ATS, ADX

9075. Which condition reduces the required runway for takeoff?

A—Higher-than-recommended airspeed before rotation.
B—Lower-than-standard air density.
C—Increased headwind component.

A headwind, in effect, gives an airplane part of its airspeed prior to starting the takeoff roll. This allows the airplane to reach its takeoff speed after a shorter takeoff roll than in no wind conditions. High rotation speeds and lower air density (high density altitude) both have the effect of increasing takeoff distance. (PLT134, AA.I.B.K2b) — ANA

Answers (A) and (B) are incorrect because higher-than-recommended airspeed before rotation and lower-than-standard air density would increase the required runway for takeoff.

Answers

8775 [B]	8780 [C]	9076 [A]	9085 [A]	9083 [A]	9075 [C]

ATM, ATS, ADX

9797. You are rolling out after touchdown and decide you really need to abort your landing, and takeoff. Your airplane is at 116 knots and your engines have spooled down to 71% idle. You need a V_2 of 142 to safely lift off and climb. The airplane will require 6 seconds to accelerate after the engines spool up to takeoff thrust, which requires 4 seconds. How much runway will you require for a safe landing abort from your decision point? (Use an average of 129 knots ground speed.)

A—1,738 feet.
B—2,178 feet.
C—3,601 feet.

At a ground speed of 129 knots, the question assumes it takes 10 seconds to takeoff. The distance required to fly to the decision point would be calculated using 129 knots ground speed. 1 knot = 1.69 feet per second = 218 ft/seconds. 218 × 10 sec = 2,180 feet. (PLT011, AA.I.B.K2a) — FAA-H-8083-25

ATM, ATS, ADX

9797-1. You touchdown long with a speed of 145 knots on a 9,001 foot runway and the braking is not working, so you decide to takeoff and climb out. The engines require 5 seconds to spool up and then the airplane requires 10 seconds of acceleration time to lift off again. The 5,000 foot marker flashes by. Do you have enough runway to lift off? (Use 132 knots for the average groundspeed.)

A—Yes, there will be a margin of 850 feet and almost 3 seconds of decision time.
B—Yes, there will be a margin of 2,001 feet and almost 5 seconds of decision time.
C—No, the runway is 1,340 feet too short and my decision is about 6 seconds too late.

1. *Calculate distance traveled per second (1 knot = 1.69 feet per second) at 132 knots × 1.69 feet per second for 223.08 feet per second.*
2. *Calculate Liftoff Distance—Total of 15 seconds (5 for spool up and 10 for liftoff) multiplied by distance traveled per second 223.08 = 3,346.2 feet of liftoff distance needed.*
3. *Calculate Distance remaining (at 5000 marker) 5,000 - 3,346.2 (liftoff distance) = 1,653.8 feet remaining.*
4. *Calculate time for decision by dividing 1,653.8 by 223.08 (distance traveled per second) = 7.41 seconds available to make a decision.*

(PLT011, AA.I.B.K2a) — FAA-H-8083-25

ATM, ATS, ADX

9797-2. You touchdown long with a speed of 145 knots on a 8,501 foot runway and the braking is not working, so you decide to takeoff and climbout. The engines require 5 seconds to spool up and then the airplane requires 10 seconds of acceleration to lift off again. The 4,000 foot marker flashed by 2 seconds ago. Do you have enough runway to lift off? (Use 143 knots for average ground speed due to the tailwind.)

A—Yes, there will be a margin of about 850 feet which is almost 3 seconds of decision time.
B—Yes, there will be a margin of almost 101 feet which is about 1.5 seconds of decision time.
C—No, the runway is 99 feet too short and my decision was about 0.4 seconds too late.

1. *Calculate distance traveled per second (1 knot = 1.69 feet per second) at 143 knots × 1.69 feet per second for 241.67 feet per second.*
2. *Calculate distance past 4,000 marker by 241.67 (distance traveled per second) × 2 (time past marker) = 483.34 feet.*
3. *Subtract distance past marker from the marker passed (4,000 - 483.34 = 3,516.66) to find remaining runway.*
4. *Calculate Liftoff Distance—Total of 15 seconds (5 for spool up and 10 for liftoff) multiplied by distance traveled per second 241.67 = 3,625.05 feet of liftoff distance needed.*
5. *Calculate if any excess runway is present—3,516.66 feet remaining - 3,625.05 required for liftoff = -108.39 feet available*

This calculation indicates an extra 108.39 feet would be needed to make this takeoff.

6. *Calculate time needed to make a decision 108.39 feet required / 241.67 feet per second =.448 seconds*

This calculation indicates the decision would have needed to be made .448 seconds ago. (PLT011, AA.I.B.K2a) — FAA-H-8083-25

Answers

9797 [B]   9797-1 [B]   9797-2 [C]

ATM, ATS, ADX

9801. One typical takeoff error is

A—delayed rotation, which may extend the climb distance.
B—premature rotation, which may increase takeoff distance.
C—extended rotation, which may degrade acceleration.

In training it is common for the pilot to overshoot V_R and then overshoot V_2 because the pilot not flying will call for rotation at, or just past V_R. The reaction of the pilot flying is to visually verify V_R and then rotate. The airplane then leaves the ground at or above V_2. The excess airspeed may be of little concern on a normal takeoff, but a delayed rotation can be critical when runway length or obstacle clearance is limited. (PLT134, AA.I.B.K2b) — FAA-H-8083-3

ATM, ATS, ADX

9802. Excessive takeoff speeds may result in approximately a

A—4% takeoff distance increase for each 1% of additional takeoff speed.
B—1% takeoff distance increase for each 2% of additional takeoff speed.
C—2% takeoff distance increase for each 1% of additional takeoff speed.

An excessive airspeed at takeoff may improve the initial rate of climb and "feel" of the airplane but will produce an undesirable increase in takeoff distance. Assuming that the acceleration is essentially unaffected, the takeoff distance varies as the square of the takeoff velocity. Thus, a 10% increase excess airspeed would increase the takeoff distance 21%. (PLT134, AA.I.B.K2b) — ANA

Calculating V-Speeds

CRJ200 V-Speeds

V_1, V_R, and V_2 are calculated by using the charts in FAA Figures 450, 452, and 454. In order to use these charts, you must first find a "Reference A" speed in FAA Figure 451. Once you have the Reference A speed, enter the chart in either Figure 452 or 454 at that speed and then move across directly right to determine the minimum V_{1MCA}.

From there, continuing to the right, intersect the aircraft weight line and proceed directly down, correcting for runway slope (if present), to note the V_R speed. If V_R is greater than 1.05 × V_{1MCA}, proceed to the right until entering the Chart B region; otherwise, use Chart A. Once intersecting the aircraft weight line in Chart A or B, move directly down and read the V_2 speed.

Q400 V-Speeds

V_1, V_R and V_2 for the Q400 are calculated from the charts contained in FAA Figure 470. Using operating conditions given either through airport diagrams or as part of the question, you must be able to calculate these important speeds.

Figure 470 is the chart used to determine V_1 and V_R. Start on this chart at the lower left with the OAT and move up to the field elevation. Move across to the right until intersecting the reference line. Then proceed diagonally until intersecting the aircraft weight line. From there, move across to the right and note the V_R speed. Continue to the right and intersect the reference line, then move down and to the left in parallel with the diagonal lines until intersecting the correct V_1/V_R ratio. Move directly right and find your V_1 speed. Note that V_1 cannot be less than V_R.

Transport Aircraft 2 V-Speeds

Using Operating Conditions R-1 (FAA Figure 53), follow the steps for determining the V-speeds (See FAA Figure 55). Enter the table at the top left in the row appropriate for the pressure altitude and go across until in a column containing a temperature range which includes the given value. In this case, enter in the

Answers

9801 [A] 9802 [C]

row labeled -1 to 1 (pressure altitude = 500 feet, refer to FAA Figure 54) and go to the first column which contains the temperature of +50°F (be sure to use the Fahrenheit or Celsius ranges as appropriate). Go down the first column until in the row appropriate for a flap setting of 15° and a gross weight of 90,000 pounds. The V_1 speed is 120 knots, the V_R speed is 121 knots and the V_2 speed is 128 knots. There are two possible adjustments to make to the V_1 speed only. They are noted at the bottom of the table.

Transport Aircraft 1 V-Speeds

The first step for calculating V_1 and V_R is to find the basic speeds in the table at the top of FAA Figure 47. Using the conditions from Operating Conditions A-1 from FAA Figure 45, the V-speeds for a weight of 75,000 pounds are: V_1 = 120.5, and V_R = 123.5 knots. Next, a series of corrections must be applied for pressure altitude, ambient temperature, runway slope, wind component, and engine and wing ice protection. There are table values for all these corrections at the bottom of FAA Figure 47 except for pressure altitude and ambient temperature.

The first step in the altitude correction is to use the table in FAA Figure 46 to determine the pressure altitude. Using the altimeter setting from Operating Conditions A-1 (29.40" Hg), the table shows a correction of +500 feet. The pressure altitude then is 3,000 feet (2,500 + 500).

Next, enter the graphs as shown in FAA Figure 47. Draw two vertical lines representing the pressure altitude of 3,000 feet. Next, draw a horizontal line through the ambient temperature (+10°F) to intersect each of the vertical lines. In this case, the lines meet in the "zero" correction area for both V_1 and V_R. Notice that the correction is marked by bands. For example, if the lines crossed anywhere in the highest shaded band, the correction would be +1 knot.

Next, set up a table similar to the one below to apply any necessary corrections:

	V_1	V_R
Table Value	120.5	123.5
Pressure Alt & Temp	0	0
Slope (+1%)	+ 1.5	+ .9
10 HW	+ .3	0
Ice Protection	+ .8	+ .8
Corrected Speeds	123.1	125.2

ATM, ADX

8717. (Refer to Figures 340, 451, and 452.) With a reported temperature of 20°C, flaps set at 8, engine bleeds closed, and a takeoff weight of 79,500 pounds, the takeoff safety speed is

A—154 knots.
B—160 knots.
C—162 knots.

1. *On Figure 340, find an airport elevation of 23 feet.*
2. *Use Figure 451 to find Reference A. Locate the portion of the chart marked Engine Bleeds Closed. Enter the chart at 20°C and work your way up to a Pressure Altitude of 23 feet. Move right to find a Reference A of 15.*
3. *On Figure 452, enter the chart from the left at Reference A of 15. Move right to the chart B area—the notes indicate this is the correct area because V_{MCA} is 114 knots and V_R is 146 knots (V_R is greater than 1.05 × V_{MCA} of 114). Intersect your takeoff weight of 79,500 pounds, then read the takeoff speed below of 154 knots.*

(PLT011, AA.I.B.K2b) — FAA-H-8083-25

ATM, ADX

8718. (Refer to Figures 336, 451, and 452). With a reported temperature of 5°C, flaps set at 8, engine bleeds closed, and a takeoff weight off 82,000 pounds, the V_R is

A—150 knots.
B—147 knots.
C—158 knots.

1. *On Figure 336, find a field elevation of 9 feet.*
2. *Use Figure 451 to find a Reference A. Locate the portion of the graph with column marked Engine Bleeds Closed. Enter the chart at 5°C moving up to intersect an altitude of 9 feet. Move straight across to the right to find a Reference A of 15.4.*
3. *On Figure 452, enter the chart from the left at Reference A of 15.4. Move right to intersect your takeoff weight of 82,000 pounds. Moving straight down, locate the V_R of 147 knots.*

(PLT011, AA.I.B.K2b) — FAA-H-8083-25

ATM, ADX

8719. (Refer to Figures 340 and 450.) With a reported temperature of 35°C, flaps set at 8, and 5 knots of headwind at a takeoff weight of 82,300 pounds, the V_{1MBE} is

A—174 knots.
B—169 knots.
C—154 knots.

1. *On Figure 340, the field elevation is 23 feet. Note that there is no runway slope indicated for runway 10.*
2. *On Figure 450, start with the ambient temperature of 35°C, and move right to intersect an airport pressure altitude of 23 feet. Then move straight down all the way to the REF. LINE in the wind section. From this reference line, move up and right in parallel with the diagonal lines until you reach the 5 knot wind mark. From here, proceed straight down to the REF. LINE in the runway slope section. Because there is no slope, move straight down and determine the V_{1MBE} speed of 171 knots.*
3. *Reference Note 2 in the upper right side of chart and see that for each 2,200 pounds under 84,500 pounds, add 3 knots. Since 84,500 – 82,300 = 2,200, add 3 knots, with the result of an V_{1MBE} speed of 174 knots.*

(PLT089, AA.I.B.K2b) — FAA-H-8083-25

ATM, ADX

8720. (Refer to Figures 342 and 450.) With a reported temperature of 40°C, flaps set at 20, and a 3 knot tailwind at a takeoff weight of 84,500, the V_{1MBE} is

A—160 knots.
B—143 knots.
C—166 knots.

In Figure 450, enter the chart on the left at 40°C. Move right to locate an airport altitude of 10 feet. Move straight down to intersect the tailwind portion of the chart following the line parallel and to the right to -3 knots. Read a V_{1MBE} of 165 on the bottom portion of the chart. Note 1 states with flaps set at 20 degrees increase V_{1MBE} value by 1 knot.

165 + 1 = 166 knots

(PLT012, AA.I.B.K2b) — FAA-H-8083-25

Answers

8717 [A] 8718 [B] 8719 [A] 8720 [C]

ATM, ADX
8721. (Refer to Figures 342, 451, and 452.) With a reported temperature of -10°C, flaps set at 8, cowl anti-ice on, and at a takeoff weight off 77,000 lbs, the V_R and V_2 speeds are

A—143 and 153 knots.
B—153 and 143 knots.
C—123 and 133 knots.

1. *Start with Figure 342 to determine an airport elevation of 10 feet.*
2. *Enter Figure 451 at -10°C in the first column labeled Cowl and Anti-Ice On, and proceed up to a pressure altitude of approximately 10 feet. Move straight across to the right to determine a Reference A of 13.9.*
3. *On Figure 452, enter the chart at your Reference A of 13.9. Move across to intersect the take-off weight of 77,000 lbs. Proceed straight down to note a V_R speed of 143.*
4. *To find V_2 speed, once again enter the chart at 13.9 moving straight across to intersect the weight of 77,000 lbs on Chart B. Proceed straight down to note a V_2 speed of 153 knots.*

(PLT012, AA.I.B.K2b) — FAA-H-8083-25

ATM, ADX
8584. (Refer to Figure 465.) At a weight of 60,000 pounds with 35 flaps, the Reference Stall Speed is

A—96 knots.
B—93 knots.
C—89 knots.

Start at the bottom of Figure 465 at the weight of 60,000 pounds. Move straight up until you intersect the 35° flap angle reference line. Move straight left and note a stall speed of 96 knots. (PLT123, AA.I.B.K5) — FAA-H-8083-25

ATM, ADX
8585. (Refer to Figure 465.) What is the reference stall speed if you will be landing the aircraft at 55,000 pounds with 35° of flaps?

A—92 knots.
B—97 knots.
C—102 knots.

Start at the bottom of Figure 465 at the weight of 55,000 pounds. Move straight up until you intersect the 35° flap angle reference line. Move straight to the left and note a reference stall speed (V_{REF}) of 92 knots. (PLT123, AA.I.B.K5) — FAA-H-8083-25

ATM, ADX
8586. (Refer to Figure 470.) What are the V_1 and V_R speeds at 25°C at sea level for an aircraft weighing 54,500 lbs. and a maximum V_1/V_R ratio of .93?

A—110 and 114 knots.
B—112 and 121 knots.
C—97 and 102 knots.

1. *Start at the bottom left on Figure 470 and find 25°C. Move straight up until intersecting the sea level line. Move straight to the right until intersecting the reference line. Move diagonally up and to the right staying parallel with the lines until you intersect the 54,500 lbs line. Move directly to the right and note a V_R speed of 121 knots.*
2. *Continue to the right until intersecting the reference line. Move diagonally down and to the left in parallel with the lines until intersecting the 0.93 V_1/V_R ratio line. Move directly to the right and note a V_1 of 112 knots.*

(PLT123, AA.I.B.K2b) — FAA-H-8083-25

ATM, ADX
8587. (Refer to Figure 470.) What are the V_1 and V_R speeds at ISA+30°C and a field elevation of 4,500 feet for an aircraft weighing 64,000 lbs. and a maximum V_1/V_R ratio of .98?

A—100 and 104 knots.
B—112 and 115 knots.
C—135 and 137 knots.

1. *Start at the ISA+30°C point in the middle left portion of Figure 470. Move down and to the right until intersecting the 4,500 foot line. Move straight to the right until intersecting the reference line. Move diagonally up and to the right staying parallel with the lines until you intersect the 64,000 lbs line. Move directly to the right and note a V_R speed of 137 knots.*
2. *Continue to the right until intersecting the reference line. Move diagonally down and to the left in parallel with the lines until intersecting the 0.98 V_1/V_R ratio line. Move directly to the right and note a V_1 of 135 knots.*

(PLT123, AA.I.B.K2b) — FAA-H-8083-25

Answers

8721 [A]	8584 [A]	8585 [A]	8586 [B]	8587 [C]

ADX

8618. (Refer to Figures 46, 53, and 55.) What is the takeoff safety speed for Operating Conditions R-1?

A—128 knots.
B—121 knots.
C—133 knots.

Pressure altitude = 500 feet
$V_1 = 120 + 1$ *(slope)* $= 121$
$V_R = 121$
$V_2 = 128$

Note: V_2 *is defined as Takeoff Safety Speed.*

(PLT011) — FAA-H-8083-25

Answer (B) is incorrect because 121 knots is the rotation (V_R) *speed. Answer (C) is incorrect because 133 knots is the* V_2 *speed using 5 flaps.*

ADX

8619. (Refer to Figures 46, 53, and 55.) What is the rotation speed for Operating Conditions R-2?

A—147 knots.
B—152 knots.
C—146 knots.

Pressure altitude = 3,500 feet
$V_1 = 144 - 1$ *(Wind)* $- 1$ *(Slope)* $= 142$
$V_R = 146$
$V_2 = 150$

Note: V_R *is defined as Rotation Speed.*

(PLT011) — FAA-H-8083-25

ADX

8620. (Refer to Figures 46, 53, and 55.) What are V_1, V_R, and V_2 speeds for Operating Conditions R-3?

A—143, 143, and 147 knots.
B—138, 138, and 142 knots.
C—136, 138, and 143 knots.

Pressure altitude = 1,450 feet
$V_1 = 136 + 1$ *(Wind)* $+ 1$ *(Slope)* $= 138$
$V_R = 138$
$V_2 = 142$

(PLT011) — FAA-H-8083-25

ADX

8621. (Refer to Figures 46, 53, and 55.) What are critical engine failure and takeoff safety speeds for Operating Conditions R-4?

A—131 and 133 knots.
B—123 and 134 knots.
C—122 and 130 knots.

Pressure altitude = 1,900 feet
$V_1 = 127 - 2$ *(Wind)* $- 2$ *(Slope)* $= 123$
$V_R = 129$
$V_2 = 134$

Note: Critical Engine Failure Speed is an obsolete term for V_1. V_2 *is Takeoff Safety Speed.*

(PLT012) — FAA-H-8083-25

ADX

8622. (Refer to Figures 46, 53, and 55.) What are rotation and V_2 bug speeds for Operating Conditions R-5?

A—138 and 143 knots.
B—136 and 138 knots.
C—134 and 141 knots.

Pressure altitude = -150 feet
$V_R = 138$
$V_2 = 143$

(PLT012) — FAA-H-8083-25

Answers

8618 [A] 8619 [C] 8620 [B] 8621 [B] 8622 [A]

ADX

8642-4. (Refer to Figures 237 and 238.) Given the following conditions, what are the takeoff V speeds?

Weight ....170,000 lb
Flaps ....10°
Temperature (OAT) ....25°C
Field pressure altitude ....427 ft.
Runway slope 0%
Wind (kts) headwind ....8 kts
Runway condition ....wet runway

For V_R more than or equal to .1 V_R, round up V_R to the next value (example: 140 + .1 = 141)

A—V_1 133 kts, V_R 140 kts, V_2 145 kts.
B—V_1 140 kts, V_R 140 kts, V_2 145 kts.
C—V_1 138 kts, V_R 141 kts, V_2 145 kts.

1. *Start on FAA Figure 238 since a wet runway is specified.*
2. *Enter the Takeoff speeds chart at 170 (1,000 pounds) and proceed to the Flaps 10 column for V_1 – 133, V_R – 139, V_2 – 145.*
3. *Enter the adjustments table at 27°C and interpolate in each column for pressure altitude of 500 feet.*
4. *Enter the V_1 Slope and Wind adjustments table at the given weight of 170 (1,000 lbs). Since there is no runway slope, continue right to the wind column of 10 knots (rounding up from the given 8-knot headwind). Note a minimal -1 knot decrease adjustment for V_1.*
5. *For V_1, round down to 133 knots, for V_R round up to 140 knots, for V_2 the adjustment is 0 so it remains 145.*

(PLT011) — FAA-H-8083-25

Calculating Takeoff Power

CRJ200 Takeoff Thrust Settings

Calculating the appropriate thrust settings for the CRJ200 is accomplished by using FAA Figures 428 through 431. Pay special attention to the "Notes" at the bottom of each of these figures, as this tells how to determine the correct chart to use. For example, Figure 428 depicts thrust settings based on all engines operating with the bleed valves closed, which is a typical takeoff for the CRJ200. Enter the chart at the left at the correct temperature and move to the right until intersecting the correct pressure altitude. This will yield the correct N_1 power thrust setting to be used during takeoff.

Q400 Takeoff Power

The Q400 takeoff power settings are determined by the charts in FAA Figures 467 and 468. Figure 467 depicts the appropriate power settings while on the ground and Figure 468 is used in flight (during the climb). To determine the correct takeoff torque setting, use Figure 467. Start at the bottom of the chart at the OAT, then move directly up until intersecting the airport elevation. Move directly to the right to find the torque setting.

Transport Aircraft 2 Takeoff EPR

In the table of FAA Figure 55, two EPR values are found: one for temperature and one for altitude (be sure to use the table in FAA Figure 54 to determine the pressure altitude). The lower of the two is the takeoff EPR. For example if the temperature is 50°F at a pressure altitude of 500 feet, the temperature-limited EPR is 2.04 and the altitude-limited EPR is 2.035. (The altitude-limited EPR is 2.01 from sea level up to 1,000 feet.) The only possible correction would be for if the air conditioning bleeds are off.

Answers

8642-4 [A]

ATM, ADX

8712. (Refer to Figures 363 and 429.) At a reported temperature of 10°C with cowl anti-ice on and packs on, the takeoff thrust setting is

A—90.0%.
B—89.1%.
C—87.4%.

Using Figure 363, determine an airport elevation of 3,877 feet. On Figure 429, find the row marked 10°C and column marked 4,000. Determine an approximate takeoff thrust setting of 90.0%. (PLT011, AA.I.B.K2b) — FAA-H-8083-25

ATM, ADX

8713. (Refer to Figures 330 and 428.) At a reported temperature of 30°C with engine bleeds closed, the takeoff thrust setting is

A—91.9%.
B—87.4%.
C—90.9%.

Using Figure 330, determine an airport elevation of 13 feet. On Figure 428, find the row marked 30°C and column marked zero. Determine an approximate takeoff thrust setting of 91.9%. (PLT011, AA.I.B.K2b) — FAA-H-8083-25

ATM, ADX

8714. (Refer to Figures 329 and 428.) At a reported temperature of 20°C with engine bleeds closed, the takeoff thrust setting is

A—92.1%.
B—92.3%.
C—88.4%.

Using Figure 329, determine an airport elevation of 4,473 feet. On Figure 428, find the row marked 30°C and column marked 4,000. Interpolate to find an approximate takeoff thrust setting of 92.3%. (PLT011, AA.I.B.K2b) — FAA-H-8083-25

ATM, ADX

8715. (Refer to Figures 329 and 429.) At a reported temperature of -10°C with cowl anti-ice on and packs on, the takeoff thrust setting is

A—87.0%.
B—87.2%.
C—87.7%.

Using Figure 329, determine an airport elevation of 4,473 feet. On Figure 429 find the row marked -10°C and column marked 4,000. Interpolate to find an approximate takeoff thrust setting of 87.2%. (PLT011, AA.I.B.K2b) — FAA-H-8083-25

ATM, ADX

8716. (Refer to Figures 332 and 428.) At a reported temperature of 5°C with engine bleeds off, the takeoff thrust setting is

A—87.0%.
B—87.2%.
C—88.2%.

Using Figure 332, determine an airport elevation of 13 feet. On Figure 428, find the row marked 5°C and column marked zero. Interpolate to find an approximate takeoff thrust setting of 88.2%. (PLT011, AA.I.B.K2b) — FAA-H-8083-25

ATM, ATS, ADX

8613. (Refer to Figure 393.) (Note: Applicants may request a printed copy of the chart(s) or graph(s) for use while computing the answer. All printed pages must be returned to test proctor.) With an OAT of 10°C, inertial separator in bypass and cabin heater, you calculate maximum torque for climb to be

A—1,795 ft-lbs.
B—1,695 ft-lbs.
C—1,615 ft-lbs.

On Figure 393, find the OAT of 10°C at the bottom of the chart and move straight up. No pressure altitude is given, therefore you can move to the maximum torque limit of 1,865 foot-pounds. Because the inertial separator is on, the torque is reduced by 100. Furthermore, assuming the question is asking for cabin heat on, the torque is reduced by another 80 pounds. This yields a torque of 1,685 foot-pounds. (PLT011, AA.I.B.K2b) — FAA-H-8083-25

Answers

8712 [A]	8713 [A]	8714 [B]	8715 [B]	8716 [C]	8613 [B]

ADX
9874. (Refer to Figures 46, 53, and 55.) What is the takeoff EPR for Operating Conditions R-1?

A—2.04.
B—2.01.
C—2.035.

Pressure altitude = 500 feet
Altitude-limited EPR = 2.035
Temperature-limited EPR = 2.04

(PLT007) — FAA-H-8083-25

ADX
8614. (Refer to Figures 46, 53, and 55.) What is the takeoff EPR for Operating Conditions R-2?

A—2.19.
B—2.18.
C—2.16.

Pressure altitude = 3,500 feet
Altitude-limited EPR = 2.19
Temperature-limited EPR = 2.19

(PLT011) — FAA-H-8083-25

ADX
8615. (Refer to Figures 46, 53, and 55.) What is the takeoff EPR for Operating Conditions R-3?

A—2.01.
B—2.083.
C—2.04.

Pressure altitude = 1,450 feet
Altitude-limited EPR = 2.083
Temperature-limited EPR = 2.01

Add .03 for air conditioning off.

(PLT007) — FAA-H-8083-25

ADX
8616. (Refer to Figures 46, 53, and 55.) What is the takeoff EPR for Operating Conditions R-4?

A—2.06.
B—2.105.
C—2.11.

Pressure altitude = 1,900 feet
Altitude-limited EPR = 2.105
Temperature-limited EPR = 2.11

(PLT007) — FAA-H-8083-25

ADX
8617. (Refer to Figures 46, 53, and 55.) What is the takeoff EPR for Operating Conditions R-5?

A—1.98.
B—1.95.
C—1.96.

Pressure altitude = -150 feet
Altitude-limited EPR = 2.003
Temperature-limited EPR = 1.95

Add .03 for air conditioning off.

(PLT007) — FAA-H-8083-25

Climb Performance

The **best rate-of-climb speed** for any airplane is the speed at which there is the greatest difference between the power required for level flight and the power available from the engines. The L/D_{MAX} speed for any airplane is the one that requires the least power for level flight since it is the lowest drag speed. Because the power output of prop-driven airplanes is relatively constant at all speeds, L/D_{MAX} is the best rate-of-climb speed for them.

Turbojet engines produce more power as the aircraft speed increases. Even though drag increases at speeds above L/D_{MAX}, the engine's power output increases even more so that the maximum difference between power required and power available is achieved at a higher airspeed. For a turbojet, the best rate-of-climb speed is faster than L/D_{MAX}.

CRJ200 Performance Tables

FAA Figures 432 through 454 contain the information needed to correctly calculate takeoff performance data, including V-speeds, takeoff weights, and climb performance. It is very important to note that these

Answers

9874 [C] 8614 [A] 8615 [C] 8616 [B] 8617 [A]

tables are divided into two categories based upon flap setting used on takeoff. Note the boxed "Flaps 8" or "Flaps 20" usually found in the lower right-hand side of the figure in order to choose the correct chart.

Q400 Performance Tables

FAA Figures 475 and 476 contain the data needed to calculate first- and second-segment climb performance. This is done with one engine operating and is part of the performance pre-planning conducted prior to each flight. Note that you will start with the OAT on the bottom of the chart and move up. Most of the time you do not need to worry about the ISA lines—simply intersect the appropriate pressure altitude. Move right to the "Reference Line," follow the diagonal lines to the aircraft weight, and then move across to the right to find your climb gradient.

Q400 Climb and Cruise Power Tables

The Q400 figures include FAA Figures 481 (radius of turn), and Figure 482 (maximum-climb ceiling chart). The radius of turn depicts the radius in feet that will be flown given a 15-degree steady-state turn. This can be helpful when calculating distance needed to maneuver during single-engine operations. The enroute climb ceiling chart (Figure 482) uses two parameters—aircraft weight and temperature—to determine the maximum ceiling during single-engine operations.

Transport Aircraft 2 Climb Performance Tables

The tables in FAA Figures 57 and 58 allow you to determine the time and fuel required for a climb to cruising altitude after takeoff. The table in FAA Figure 57 is for ISA temperatures, and the table in FAA Figure 58 is for ISA +10°C. Each intersection of Brake Release Weight and Cruise Altitude has a box with four numbers. These are the time, the fuel, the distance and the TAS required to climb from a sea level airport to cruise altitude in calm wind conditions. For example, with a brake release weight of 110,000 pounds, a climb to 33,000 feet in ISA +10°C conditions will require 26 minutes, 4,100 pounds of fuel and cover a distance of 154 NM.

A headwind or tailwind component in the climb will change the distance flown. Assume that there is an average 20-knot headwind in the climb described above. The first step is to compute the average "no wind" GS. A distance of 154 NM flown in 26 minutes works out to a GS of 355.4 knots. A headwind component of 20 knots will reduce this GS to 335.4 knots. The distance flown in 26 minutes at 335.4 knots is 145.3 NM.

Note: Using a CX-3 computer, select "Ground Speed" from the FLT menu and enter Duration and GS. Do not use the TAS from the table as that will result in an inaccurate answer.

Departure from an airport that is significantly above sea level will reduce the fuel required for the climb. Notice that departure from a 2,000-foot airport will reduce the climb fuel by 100 pounds, however the effect on time and distance flown is negligible.

Transport Aircraft 2 Climb and Cruise Power Tables

The Max Climb & Max Continuous EPR Table at the top of FAA Figure 60 is similar to the one discussed in Takeoff EPR. In this table two EPR values are found—one for temperature and one for altitude. The lower of the two is the maximum climb/continuous EPR. For example, if the temperature is +10°C at a pressure altitude of 10,000 feet, the temperature-limited EPR is 2.04 and the altitude-limited EPR is 2.30. (The altitude-limited EPR is 2.30 from 5,660 feet and up.) The max EPR is 2.04.

The Max Cruise EPR Table supplies one EPR value for a given TAT (Total Air Temperature) in one of two altitude ranges. The correction tables are similar to ones used previously and apply to both tables.

ATM, ATS, ADX

8400. At what speed, with reference to L/D_{MAX}, does maximum rate-of-climb for a jet airplane occur?

A—A speed greater than that for L/D_{MAX}.
B—A speed equal to that for L/D_{MAX}.
C—A speed less than that for L/D_{MAX}.

An airplane's best rate-of-climb is achieved at the airspeed where there is the maximum difference between the power available from the engines and the power required for level flight. The L/D_{MAX} airspeed will require the minimum power for level flight since drag is at its minimum. However, turbojet engines produce more power at high speed than at lower speeds and so the speed with the greatest difference between power required and power available is higher than L/D_{MAX}. (PLT303, AA.I.B.K2c) — ANA

Answer (B) is incorrect because a speed equal to that of L/D_{MAX} is the maximum rate-of-climb for a propeller airplane. Answer (C) is incorrect because the maximum rate-of-climb is at a speed greater than L/D_{MAX}.

ATM, ATS, ADX

8400-1. (Refer to Figure 271.) For a takeoff from Runway 25L at LAX, what is the minimum climb gradient that ATC expects the aircraft to maintain?

A—500 feet per minute climb.
B—200 feet per minute climb.
C—400 feet per minute climb.

At the top of Figure 271, the departure indicates Runway 25L has a standard climb gradient. The standard climb gradient rate is 200 feet per minute. (PLT052, AA.I.B.K2c) — FAA-H-8083-25

ATM, ADX

8593. (Refer to Figures 273 and 475.) With a reported temperature of 32°C, and a weight of 58,000 pounds, the second segment takeoff gross climb gradient is

A—0.057%.
B—0.062%.
C—0.034%.

1. *From Figure 273, find the field elevation of 1,135 feet.*
2. *On Figure 475, start at the bottom left and find 32°C. Move straight up until you intersect the 1,135 foot line. Move straight to the right until you intersect the reference line. Move down and to the right following the diagonal lines in parallel until you intersect the 58,000 pound line. Move directly to the right and note a second segment climb gradient of .057%.*

(PLT004, AA.I.B.K2c) — FAA-H-8083-25

ATM, ADX

8594. (Refer to Figures 273 and 474.) With a reported temperature of 45°C, and a weight of 52,000 pounds, the first segment takeoff gross climb gradient is

A—0.048%.
B—0.044%.
C—0.0419%.

1. *From Figure 273, find the field elevation of 1,135 feet.*
2. *On Figure 474, start at the bottom left side of chart and note the temperature of 45°C. Move straight up until you intersect the 1,135 foot line. Move straight to the right until intersecting the reference line. Move down and to the right following the diagonal lines in parallel until you intersect the 52,000 pound line. Move directly to the right and note a first segment climb gradient of .045%.*

(PLT004, AA.I.B.K2c) — FAA-H-8083-25

ATM, ATS, ADX

9935. (Refer to Figure 474.) What is the gross climb gradient with the following conditions?

Outside air temperature.. 0°C
Airfield altitude.. 4,000 feet
Weight .... 55,000 pounds

A—0.052%
B—0.020%
C—0.074%

On Figure 474, start at the bottom left side of the chart and note the temperature of 0°C. Move straight up until you intersect the 4,000 foot line. Move straight to the right until intersecting the reference line. Following the diagonal line, move down until you intersect the 55,000 pound line. Move directly to the right and note a gross climb gradient of .052%. (PLT004, AA.I.B.K2c) — FAA-H-8083-25

ATM, ADX

8628. (Refer to Figures 56, 57, and 58.) What is the ground distance covered during en route climb for Operating Conditions V-1?

A—145 NM.
B—137 NM.
C—134 NM.

Answers

8400 [A]	8400-1 [B]	8593 [A]	8594 [B]	9935 [A]	8628 [A]

No wind time = 26 minutes
No wind distance = 154 NM
No wind GS = 355.4 knots
Wind adjusted GS = 335.4 knots
Wind adjusted distance = 145.3 NM

(PLT004, AA.I.B.K2c) — FAA-H-8083-25

ATM, ADX
8629. (Refer to Figures 56, 57, and 58.) What is the ground distance covered during en route climb for Operating Conditions V-2?

A—84 NM.
B—65 NM.
C—69 NM.

No wind time = 13 minutes
No wind distance = 65 NM
No wind GS = 300 knots
Wind adjusted GS = 320 knots
Wind adjusted distance = 69.3 NM

(PLT004, AA.I.B.K2c) — FAA-H-8083-25

ATM, ADX
8630. (Refer to Figures 56, 57, and 58.) What is the ground distance covered during en route climb for Operating Conditions V-3?

A—95 NM.
B—79 NM.
C—57 NM.

No wind time = 16 minutes
No wind distance = 87 NM
No wind GS = 326.3 knots
Wind adjusted GS = 296.3 knots
Wind adjusted distance = 79 NM

(PLT004, AA.I.B.K2c) — FAA-H-8083-25

ATM, ADX
8631. (Refer to Figures 56, 57, and 58.) What is the ground distance covered during en route climb for Operating Conditions V-4?

A—63 NM.
B—53 NM.
C—65 NM.

No wind time = 13 minutes
No wind distance = 61 NM
No wind GS = 281.5 knots
Wind adjusted GS = 291.5 knots
Wind adjusted distance = 63.2 NM

(PLT004, AA.I.B.K2c) — FAA-H-8083-25

ATM, ADX
8632. (Refer to Figures 56, 57, and 58.) What is the ground distance covered during en route climb for Operating Conditions V-5?

A—70 NM.
B—52 NM.
C—61 NM.

No wind time = 13 minutes
No wind distance = 70 NM
No wind GS = 323.1 knots
Wind adjusted GS = 283.1 knots
Wind adjusted distance = 61.3 NM

(PLT004, AA.I.B.K2c) — FAA-H-8083-25

ATM, ADX
8633. (Refer to Figures 56, 57, and 58.) How much fuel is burned during en route climb for Operating Conditions V-1?

A—4,100 pounds.
B—3,600 pounds.
C—4,000 pounds.

Fuel to climb from sea level = 4,100 lbs
Correction factor = -100 lbs

(PLT012, AA.I.B.K2c) — FAA-H-8083-25

ATM, ADX
8634. (Refer to Figures 56, 57, and 58.) How much fuel is burned during en route climb for Operating Conditions V-2?

A—2,250 pounds.
B—2,600 pounds.
C—2,400 pounds.

Fuel to climb from sea level = 2,400 lbs
Correction factor = -150 lbs

(PLT012, AA.I.B.K2c) — FAA-H-8083-25

Answers

8629 [C]	8630 [B]	8631 [A]	8632 [C]	8633 [C]	8634 [A]

ATM, ADX

8635. (Refer to Figures 56, 57, and 58.) What is the aircraft weight at the top of climb for Operating Conditions V-3?

A—82,100 pounds.
B—82,500 pounds.
C—82,200 pounds.

Fuel to climb from sea level = 2,600 lbs
Correction factor = -100 lbs
Final weight = 85,000 – 2,500 = 82,500 lbs

(PLT004, AA.I.B.K1) — FAA-H-8083-25

ATM, ADX

8636. (Refer to Figures 56, 57, and 58.) What is the aircraft weight at the top of climb for Operating Conditions V-4?

A—102,900 pounds.
B—102,600 pounds.
C—103,100 pounds.

Fuel to climb from sea level = 2,400 lbs
Correction factor = -300 lbs
Final weight = 105,000 – 2,100 = 102,900 lbs

(PLT004, AA.I.B.K1) — FAA-H-8083-25

ATM, ADX

8637. (Refer to Figures 56, 57, and 58.) What is the aircraft weight at the top of climb for Operating Conditions V-5?

A—73,000 pounds.
B—72,900 pounds.
C—72,800 pounds.

Fuel to climb from sea level = 2,100 lbs
Correction factor = -100 lbs
Final weight = 75,000 – 2,000 = 73,000 lbs

(PLT004, AA.I.B.K1) — FAA-H-8083-25

ATM, ADX

8638. (Refer to Figures 59 and 60.) What is the max climb EPR for Operating Conditions T-1?

A—1.82.
B—1.96.
C—2.04.

Altitude-limited EPR = 2.30
TAT-limited EPR = 1.90
Correction for engine anti-ice = -.08
Max climb EPR setting = 1.82

(PLT007, AA.I.B.K2c) — FAA-H-8083-25

Answer (B) is incorrect because 1.96 is the max continuous EPR. Answer (C) is incorrect because 2.04 is the max continuous EPR without the bleed air correction for the engine anti-ice ON.

ATM, ADX

8639. (Refer to Figures 59 and 60.) What is the max continuous EPR for Operating Conditions T-2?

A—2.10.
B—1.99.
C—2.02.

Altitude-limited EPR = 2.20
TAT-limited EPR = 2.10
Engine and wing anti-ice correction = -.12
Air conditioning off correction = +.04
Max continuous EPR setting = 2.02

(PLT007, AA.I.B.K2c) — FAA-H-8083-25

ATM, ADX

8640. (Refer to Figures 59 and 60.) What is the max cruise EPR for Operating Conditions T-3?

A—2.11.
B—2.02.
C—1.90.

Max cruise EPR = 2.02
Engine and wing anti-ice correction = -.12
Max cruise EPR setting = 1.90

(PLT007, AA.I.B.K2c) — FAA-H-8083-25

ATM, ADX

8641. (Refer to Figures 59 and 60.) What is the max climb EPR for Operating Conditions T-4?

A—2.20.
B—2.07.
C—2.06.

Altitude-limited EPR = 2.30
TAT-limited EPR = 2.20
Engine and wing anti-ice correction = -.14
Max climb EPR setting = 2.06

(PLT007, AA.I.B.K2c) — FAA-H-8083-25

Answers

8635 [B] 8636 [A] 8637 [A] 8638 [A] 8639 [C] 8640 [C]
8641 [C]

ATM, ADX

8642-1. (Refer to Figures 59 and 60.) What is the max continuous EPR for Operating Conditions T-5?

A—2.00.
B—2.04.
C—1.96.

Altitude-limited EPR = 2.30
TAT-limited EPR = 2.00
Air conditioning off correction = +.04
Max continuous EPR setting = 2.04

(PLT007, AA.I.B.K2c) — FAA-H-8083-25

ATM, ADX

8642-2. (Refer to Figure 231.) Given the following conditions, what is the takeoff climb limit?

Airport OAT..38°C
Airport Pressure Altitude .... 14 ft.
Flaps.. 15°
Engine Bleed for packs .... On
Anti-ice .... Off

A— 136,000 lb.
B— 137,500 lb.
C— 139,000 lb.

1. *Enter FAA Figure 231 at 38° OAT and proceed up to the 0 ft pressure altitude (this is closest to 14 feet).*
2. *From the point of intersection on the pressure altitude line, draw a line horizontally to the Climb Limit Brake Release Weight of 136,000 pounds.*

(PLT085, AA.I.B.K2c) — FAA-H-8083-25

ADX

9875. (Refer to Figures 48, 49, and 50.) What is the ground distance covered during en route climb for Operating Conditions W-1?

A—104.0 NM.
B—99.2 NM.
C—109.7 NM.

Long range climb:

No wind time = 17.1 minutes
No wind distance = 109.7 NM
No wind GS = 384.9 knots
Wind adjusted GS = 364.9 knots
Wind adjusted distance = 104 NM

(PLT004) — FAA-H-8083-25

ADX

9876. (Refer to Figures 48, 49, and 50.) What is the ground distance covered during en route climb for Operating Conditions W-2?

A—85.8 NM.
B—87.8 NM.
C—79.4 NM.

High speed climb:

No wind time = 12.8 minutes
No wind distance = 85.8 NM
No wind GS = 402.2 knots
Wind adjusted GS = 372.2 knots
Wind adjusted distance = 79.4 NM

(PLT004) — FAA-H-8083-25

ADX

9877. (Refer to Figures 48, 49, and 50.) What is the ground distance covered during en route climb for Operating Conditions W-3?

A—86.4 NM.
B—84.2 NM.
C—85.1 NM.

Long range climb:

No wind time = 13.3 minutes
No wind distance = 84.2 NM
No wind GS = 379.8 knots
Wind adjusted GS = 389.8 knots
Wind adjusted distance = 86.4 NM

(PLT004) — FAA-H-8083-25

ADX

8596. (Refer to Figures 48, 49, and 50.) What is the ground distance covered during en route climb for Operating Conditions W-4?

A—58.4 NM.
B—61.4 NM.
C—60.3 NM.

High speed climb:

No wind time = 9.1 minutes
No wind distance = 58.4 NM
No wind GS = 385.1 knots
Wind adjusted GS = 405.1 knots
Wind adjusted distance = 61.4 NM

(PLT004) — FAA-H-8083-25

Answers

8642-1 [B] 8642-2 [A] 9875 [A] 9876 [C] 9877 [A] 8596 [B]

ADX
8597. (Refer to Figures 48, 49, and 50.) What is the ground distance covered during en route climb for Operating Conditions W-5?

A—68.0 NM.
B—73.9 NM.
C—66.4 NM.

High speed climb:

No wind time = 11.3 minutes
No wind distance = 73.9 NM
No wind GS = 392.4 knots
Wind adjusted GS = 352.4 knots
Wind adjusted distance = 66.4 NM

(PLT004) — FAA-H-8083-25

ADX
8598. (Refer to Figures 48, 49, and 50.) What is the aircraft weight at the top of climb for Operating Conditions W-1?

A—81,600 pounds.
B—81,400 pounds.
C—81,550 pounds.

Long range climb:

Initial weight	*84,000*
Burn	*– 2,570*
TOC weight	*81,430*

(PLT004) — FAA-H-8083-25

ADX
8599. (Refer to Figures 48, 49, and 50.) What is the aircraft weight at the top of climb for Operating Conditions W-2?

A—82,775 pounds.
B—83,650 pounds.
C—83,775 pounds.

High speed climb:

Initial weight	*86,000*
Burn	*– 2,225*
TOC weight	*83,775*

(PLT004) — FAA-H-8083-25

ADX
8600. (Refer to Figures 48, 49, and 50.) What is the aircraft weight at the top of climb for Operating Conditions W-3?

A—75,750 pounds.
B—75,900 pounds.
C—76,100 pounds.

Long range climb:

Initial weight	*78,000*
Burn	*– 2,102*
TOC weight	*75,898*

(PLT004) — FAA-H-8083-25

ADX
8601. (Refer to Figures 48, 49, and 50.) What is the aircraft weight at the top of climb for Operating Conditions W-4?

A—86,150 pounds.
B—86,260 pounds.
C—86,450 pounds.

High speed climb:

Initial weight	*88,000*
Burn	*– 1,738*
TOC weight	*86,262*

(PLT004) — FAA-H-8083-25

ADX
8602. (Refer to Figures 48, 49, and 50.) What is the aircraft weight at the top of climb for Operating Conditions W-5?

A—89,900 pounds.
B—90,000 pounds.
C—90,100 pounds.

Long-range climb:

Initial weight	*92,000*
Burn	*– 2,079*
TOC weight	*89,921*

(PLT004) — FAA-H-8083-25

Answers

8597 [C]	8598 [B]	8599 [C]	8600 [B]	8601 [B]	8602 [A]

Cruise Performance

The maximum range speed for an aircraft is determined by its L/D curve. Propeller-driven airplanes will achieve best range performance if they are flown at the speed that yields L/D_{MAX}. In turbojet aircraft, a somewhat more complex relationship between lift and drag determines best range. Turbojets always have a best range speed higher than L/D_{MAX}.

A headwind or tailwind will affect the miles per unit of fuel burned. If an airplane is operating at its best-range airspeed and encounters a headwind, it should speed up to minimize the time in the adverse wind. By the same token, an airplane with a tailwind can slow down and let the wind maintain its ground speed with a lower fuel flow. The exact amount of airspeed change that is useful varies with airplane type.

Turbojet engines have a strong preference for operations at high altitudes and airspeeds. Both lower temperatures and higher altitudes increase engine efficiency by requiring a lower fuel flow for a given thrust. Besides increased engine efficiency, lift and drag both decrease at higher altitudes, so less thrust is required.

Turbine engines are much more efficient when operated at the upper end of their RPM range. Generally, the optimum cruise altitude for a turbojet airplane is the highest at which it is possible to maintain the optimum aerodynamic conditions (best angle of attack) at maximum continuous power. The optimum altitude is determined mainly by the aircraft's gross weight at the beginning of cruise.

As an aircraft burns fuel and becomes lighter, the optimum cruise altitude slowly increases and the speed that yields the optimum cruise performance slowly decreases. Since it is seldom practical to change speed and altitude constantly, it is common procedure to maintain a constant Mach cruise at a flight level close to optimum. As fuel is burned, thrust is reduced to maintain the constant Mach number.

ATM, ATS, ADX

8383. What performance is characteristic of flight at maximum L/D in a propeller-driven airplane?

A—Maximum range and distance glide.
B—Best angle of climb.
C—Maximum endurance.

Maximum range and glide distance is achieved at L/D_{MAX}. (PLT242, AA.I.B.K2d) — FAA-H-8083-3

Answer (B) is incorrect because best angle of climb is at a high angle of attack with both high lift and high drag coefficients, which would not result in a maximum L/D ratio. Answer (C) is incorrect because maximum endurance would be obtained at the point of minimum power required, since this would require the lowest fuel flow to keep the airplane in steady, level flight. This is not at maximum L/D.

ATM, ATS, ADX

8401. At what speed, with reference to L/D_{MAX}, does maximum range for a jet airplane occur?

A—A speed less than that for L/D_{MAX}.
B—A speed equal to that for L/D_{MAX}.
C—A speed greater than that for L/D_{MAX}.

Maximum range is obtained at the aerodynamic condition which produces a maximum proportion between the square root of the lift coefficient and the drag coefficient. It occurs where the proportion between velocity and thrust required is greatest. This point is located by a straight line from the origin tangent to the curve, and is consequently at a higher airspeed than L/D_{MAX}. (PLT303, AA.I.B.K2d) — ANA

Answer (A) is incorrect because a speed greater than L/D_{MAX} will obtain maximum range for a jet airplane. Answer (B) is incorrect because a speed equal to that of L/D_{MAX} is a jet airplane's maximum endurance, not range.

Answers

8383 [A] 8401 [C]

ATM, ATS, ADX
8398. What should a pilot do to maintain "best range" airplane performance when a tailwind is encountered?

A—Increase speed.
B—Maintain speed.
C—Decrease speed.

While it is only necessary to consider wind velocity effect on cruise speed at wind velocities that exceed 25% of the zero wind cruise speed, generally you should increase cruise speed with a headwind and decrease cruise speed with a tailwind. (PLT303, AA.I.B.K2d) — FAA-H-8083-25

ATM, ATS, ADX
9078. Which procedure produces the minimum fuel consumption for a given leg of the cruise flight?

A—Increase speed for a headwind.
B—Increase speed for a tailwind.
C—Increase altitude for a headwind, decrease altitude for a tailwind.

When flying into a headwind the airspeed should be increased above that used for maximum range in calm winds. Airspeed should be decreased for a tailwind. (PLT015, AA.I.B.K2d) — ANA

ATM, ATS, ADX
8381. Which maximum range factor decreases as weight decreases?

A—Angle of attack.
B—Altitude.
C—Airspeed.

As fuel is consumed and the airplane's weight decreases, the optimum airspeed and power setting may decrease, or the optimum altitude may increase. The optimum angle of attack does not change with changes in weight. (PLT006, AA.I.B.K2d) — FAA-H-8083-3

Answer (A) is incorrect because the factors of maximum range are weight, altitude, and aerodynamic configuration of the airplane, not angle of attack. Answer (B) is incorrect because maximum range altitude may increase with a decrease in weight.

ATM, ATS, ADX
9077. Maximum range performance of a turbojet aircraft is obtained by which procedure as aircraft weight reduces?

A—Increasing speed or altitude.
B—Increasing altitude or decreasing speed.
C—Increasing speed or decreasing altitude.

As a turbojet-powered airplane burns fuel, its maximum range of profile can be maintained by increasing the cruise altitude to improve the specific fuel consumption of the engines and by decreasing airspeed to maintain the optimum L/D ratio. (PLT015, AA.I.B.K2d) — ANA

Answer (A) is incorrect because, as weight decreases, the optimum speed decreases, or altitude increases. Answer (C) is incorrect because, as weight decreases, speed decreases, or altitude increases.

Landing Considerations

V_S—stalling speed or the minimum steady flight speed at which the airplane is controllable.

V_{S0}—stalling speed or the minimum steady flight speed in the landing configuration.

V_{REF}—reference speed. It is normally $1.3 \times V_{S0}$.

Even with all the aircraft's high lift devices extended, a typical air carrier airplane has a high approach speed and a long landing roll. An airplane is normally flown at 1.3 times the V_{S0} speed for the aircraft's weight. Of course, 1.3 times V_{S0} is an indicated airspeed and the ground speed will vary depending on wind, altitude and temperature. A high temperature or high altitude approach will increase an aircraft's ground speed for any given approach speed.

Once an airplane has touched down on a runway there are 3 ways of slowing it to a stop: aerodynamic braking, use of the wheel brakes, and reverse thrust.

Answers

8398 [C]   9078 [A]   8381 [C]   9077 [B]

The typical technique for stopping an aircraft on a normal landing is to apply reverse thrust (or prop reverse) once the nosewheel is on the ground. This takes maximum advantage of reverse thrust when it is most effective and it saves wear on the wheel brakes, which heat up very rapidly at high ground speeds. Shortly after touchdown, the spoilers are deployed. This reduces lift and increases drag. As the aircraft slows, the main wheel brakes are applied to bring it down to taxiing speed. The brakes are most effective when lift has been reduced (by spoilers and low airspeed) and more of the aircraft's weight is carried by the landing gear.

Water on a runway will increase the landing rollout because the reduced coefficient of friction makes the wheel brakes less effective. This is particularly true at high ground speeds.

A very dangerous possibility when landing on a wet runway is **hydroplaning**. When hydroplaning occurs, the wheel brakes are almost totally ineffective. This not only greatly increases the landing rollout, but also introduces the possibility of losing directional control on sliding off the side of the runway. There are three types of hydroplaning.

Dynamic hydroplaning occurs when a tire rolls through standing water, forms a bow wave, and then rolls up on top of the wave, losing all contact with the runway. The minimum speed at which dynamic hydroplaning can start is related to tire pressure. As a rule of thumb, dynamic hydroplaning will start at speeds of greater than nine times the square root of the tire pressure in pounds per square inch. The practical application is that your nose wheel can hydroplane at a lower speed than the mains because of its lower pressure. Once dynamic hydroplaning has started, it can continue to much lower speeds.

Viscous hydroplaning occurs when there is a thin film of water covering a smooth surface such as a painted or rubber-coated portion of the runway. Viscous hydroplaning can occur at much lower speeds than dynamic hydroplaning.

Reverted rubber hydroplaning occurs during a locked wheel skid. Water trapped between the tire and the runway is heated by friction, and the tire rides along a pocket of steam.

When landing on a water-covered runway, fly the approach as close to "on speed" as possible. Landing at a higher than recommended speed will greatly increase the potential for hydroplaning. After touchdown, use aerodynamic braking and reverse thrust to maximum possible extent, saving the use of wheel brakes until the speed is low enough to minimize the possibility of hydroplaning.

Regulations (14 CFR §121.195) require that when a turbojet aircraft is dispatched to an airport where the runways are forecast to be wet or slippery, the effective length of the landing runway must be 115% of what is required under dry conditions. Since runways cannot be lengthened, the effect of this rule is to lower the maximum allowable landing weight of aircraft on wet runways for dispatch purposes.

ATM, ATS, ADX

9323. Which is the correct symbol for the stalling speed or the minimum steady flight speed at which the airplane is controllable?

A—V_{S0}.
B—V_S.
C—V_{S1}.

V_S means the stalling speed or the minimum steady flight speed at which the airplane is controllable. (PLT466, AA.I.B.K2d) — 14 CFR §1.2

Answer (A) is incorrect because V_{S0} is the stalling speed or the minimum steady flight speed in the landing configuration. Answer (C) is incorrect because V_{S1} is the stalling speed or the minimum steady flight speed in a specific configuration.

ATM, ATS, ADX

9322. Which is the correct symbol for the minimum steady-flight speed or stalling speed in the landing configuration?

A—V_S.
B—V_{S1}.
C—V_{S0}.

V_{S0} means the stalling speed or the minimum steady flight speed in the landing configuration. (PLT466, AA.I.B.K2d) — 14 CFR §1.2

Answer (A) is incorrect because V_S is the stalling speed or the minimum steady flight speed at which the airplane is controllable. Answer (B) is incorrect because V_{S1} is the stalling speed or the minimum steady flight speed in a specific configuration.

Answers

9323 [B] 9322 [C]

ATM, ATS, ADX
8374. What effect does landing at high elevation airports have on groundspeed with comparable conditions relative to temperature, wind, and airplane weight?

A—Higher than at low elevation.
B—Lower than at low elevation.
C—The same as at low elevation.

An airplane at altitude will land at the same indicated airspeed as at sea level but, because of the reduced air density, the true airspeed will be greater. Given the same wind conditions, this will also make the ground speed higher than at sea level. (PLT124, AA.V.B.K1) — FAA-H-8083-25

Answer (B) is incorrect because at high elevation there is reduced air density, and thus TAS will increase. As TAS increases, ground speed will increase. Answer (C) is incorrect because, under comparable conditions, TAS will increase and cause the ground speed to be higher, at higher elevation.

ATM, ATS, ADX
9074. How should thrust reversers be applied to reduce landing distance for turbojet aircraft?

A—Immediately after ground contact.
B—Immediately prior to touchdown.
C—After applying maximum wheel braking.

Thrust reversers are most effective at high speeds and should be deployed immediately after touchdown. (PLT170, AA.I.E.K1) — FAA-H-8083-3

ATM, ATS, ADX
9074-1. Upon landing, thrust reversers

A—are required to obtain the calculated stopping distances.
B—should be deployed as soon as the nose wheel is in firm contact with the runway.
C—should be deployed immediately upon landing when airspeeds are highest.

If operating an aircraft such as the MD-80, thrust reversers should be deployed as soon as the nose wheel is in firm contact with the runway. (PLT170, AA.I.E.K1) — FAA-H-8083-3

ATM, ATS, ADX
9079. How should reverse thrust propellers be used during landing for maximum effectiveness in stopping?

A—Gradually increase reverse power to maximum as rollout speed decreases.
B—Use maximum reverse power as soon as possible after touchdown.
C—Select reverse-pitch after landing and use idle power setting of the engines.

Reverse thrust is most effective at high airspeeds. It should be used as soon as possible after touchdown. (PLT244, AA.VI.E.K4) — FAA-H-8083-25

ATM, ATS, ADX
9084. Under which condition during the landing roll are the main wheel brakes at maximum effectiveness?

A—When wing lift has been reduced.
B—At high groundspeeds.
C—When the wheels are locked and skidding.

Wheel brakes are at maximum effectiveness when the weight of the airplane is used to hold the tires in contact with the runway and the rate of wheel deceleration (or slowing) is just below that which would induce a skid. To place the maximum weight on the tires it is necessary to reduce lift as soon as possible after touchdown by lowering the nose wheel to the runway and deploying wing spoilers. Wheel brakes become more effective as an airplane decelerates (or slows down) because of loss of residual lift as the airspeed decreases. (PLT170, AA.VI.E.K4) — FAA-H-8083-25

Answer (B) is incorrect because, at high ground speeds, the lift is greater and the normal force on the wheels is small, thus the braking friction force is small. Answer (C) is incorrect because, when the wheels are locked and skidding, the braking friction force is small.

ATM, ATS
9084-1. When is braking performance optimized during landing?

A—Before the nose wheel touches down.
B—Wheel spin-up at touchdown.
C—Maximum weight on main wheels.

Braking effectiveness is greatest when the aircraft weight is transferred to the wheels. (PLT170, AA.I.A.K1) — FAA-H-8083-25

Answers

8374 [A]	9074 [A]	9074-1 [B]	9079 [B]	9084 [A]	9084-1 [C]

ATM, ATS, ADX

8935. At what minimum speed (rounded off) could dynamic hydroplaning occur on main tires having a pressure of 121 PSI?

A—90 knots.
B—99 knots.
C—110 knots.

Dynamic hydroplaning occurs when there is standing water on the runway surface. Water about 1/10th of an inch deep acts to lift the tire off the runway. The minimum speed at which dynamic hydroplaning occurs has been determined to be about 9 times the square root of the tire pressure in pounds per square inch:

Square root of 121 = 11
11 × 9 = 99

(PLT144, AA.III.B.R1) — FAA-H-8083-3

ATM, ATS, ADX

8936. At what minimum speed will dynamic hydroplaning begin if a tire has an air pressure of 70 PSI?

A—85 knots.
B—80 knots.
C—75 knots.

Dynamic hydroplaning occurs when there is standing water on the runway surface. Water about 1/10th of an inch deep acts to lift the tire off the runway. The minimum speed at which dynamic hydroplaning occurs has been determined to be about 9 times the square root of the tire pressure in pounds per square inch:

Square root of 70 = 8.37
8.37 × 9 = 75.3

(PLT144, AA.III.B.R1) — FAA-H-8083-3

Answer (A) is incorrect because hydroplaning would occur at 85 knots with a tire pressure of 95 PSI. Answer (B) is incorrect because hydroplaning would occur at 80 knots with a tire pressure of 84 PSI.

ATM, ATS, ADX

8933. A definition of the term "viscous hydroplaning" is where

A—the airplane rides on standing water.
B—a film of moisture covers the painted or rubber-coated portion of the runway.
C—the tires of the airplane are actually riding on a mixture of steam and melted rubber.

Either the moisture or the originally slick surface could cause problems, and the combination is especially dangerous. (PLT144, AA.III.B.R1) — FAA-H-8083-3

Answer (A) is incorrect because dynamic hydroplaning occurs when the airplane tires ride on standing water. Answer (C) is incorrect because reverted rubber hydroplaning occurs when the tires of the airplane are actually riding on a mixture of steam and melted rubber.

ATM, ATS, ADX

8938. Compared to dynamic hydroplaning, at what speed does viscous hydroplaning occur when landing on a smooth, wet runway?

A—At approximately 2.0 times the speed that dynamic hydroplaning occurs.
B—At a lower speed than dynamic hydroplaning.
C—At the same speed as dynamic hydroplaning.

Viscous hydroplaning occurs due to the viscous properties of water. In this type, a thin film of fluid (not more than 1/1,000 of an inch in depth) cannot be penetrated by the tire and the tire rolls on top of the film. This can occur at a much lower speed than dynamic hydroplaning but requires a smooth acting surface. (PLT144, AA.III.B.R1) — FAA-H-8083-3

ATM, ATS, ADX

8934. Which term describes the hydroplaning which occurs when an airplane's tire is effectively held off a smooth runway surface by steam generated by friction?

A—Reverted rubber hydroplaning.
B—Dynamic hydroplaning.
C—Viscous hydroplaning.

This would typically occur if excessive braking kept a wheel from rotating. (PLT144, AA.III.B.R1) — FAA-H-8083-3

Answer (B) is incorrect because dynamic hydroplaning occurs when there is standing water or slush on the runway which forms a wedge that lifts the tire away from contact with the runway surface. Answer (C) is incorrect because viscous hydroplaning occurs on a thin film of water on a smooth (e.g., painted or rubber-coated) runway surface.

Answers

8935 [B] 8936 [C] 8933 [B] 8938 [B] 8934 [A]

ATM, ATS, ADX

8937. What is the best method of speed reduction if hydroplaning is experienced on landing?

A—Apply full main wheel braking only.
B—Apply nosewheel and main wheel braking alternately and abruptly.
C—Apply aerodynamic braking to the fullest advantage.

Since occurrence of dynamic hydroplaning is related to speed, it is prudent to slow the aircraft with spoilers, reverse thrust, etc., as much as possible prior to applying the brakes. (PLT144, AA.III.B.R1) — FAA-H-8083-3

Answer (A) is incorrect because applying full main wheel braking may increase or compound the problems associated with hydroplaning. If any brakes are used, a pumping or modulating motion like an antiskid system can be used. Aerodynamic braking is recommended. Answer (B) is incorrect because abrupt use of either the nose wheel or main wheel brakes will lock the wheels and compound the problem.

ATM, ATS, ADX

8937-1. Under what conditions might a pilot expect the possibility of hydroplaning?

A—When landing on a wet runway that is covered in rubber from previous landings.
B—When departing a grooved runway with less than a thousandth of an inch of water.
C—When the adiabatic lapse rate is high, and steam is rising from the landing surface.

Viscous hydroplaning requires a smooth, or smooth-acting surface such as asphalt or accumulated rubber from a past landing coating the touchdown area. To cause this hydroplaning, all that is needed is a thin film of fluid no more than 1/1,000th of an inch in depth. (PLT144, AA.III.B.R1) — FAA-H-8083-3

ATM, ATS, ADX

8939. What effect, if any, will landing at a higher-than-recommended touchdown speed have on hydroplaning?

A—No effect on hydroplaning, but increases landing roll.
B—Reduces hydroplaning potential if heavy braking is applied.
C—Increases hydroplaning potential regardless of braking.

Hydroplaning is most likely to occur during conditions of standing water or slush on a runway with a smooth textured surface. The higher the aircraft speed, the more likely it is to hydroplane. (PLT144, AA.III.B.R1) — FAA-H-8083-3

ATM, ADX

8133. What effective runway length is required for a turbojet-powered airplane at the destination airport if the runways are forecast to be wet or slippery at the ETA?

A—70 percent of the actual runway available, from a height of 50 feet over the threshold.
B—115 percent of the runway length required for a dry runway.
C—115 percent of the runway length required for a wet runway.

No person may takeoff in a turbojet-powered airplane when the appropriate weather reports and forecasts, or combination thereof, indicate that the runways at the destination airport may be wet or slippery at the estimated time of arrival unless the effective runway length at the destination airport is at least 115% of the runway length required for a landing on a dry runway. (PLT144, AA.III.B.R1) — 14 CFR §121.195

Answer (A) is incorrect because 70% is the requirement for the turbopropeller aircraft. Answer (C) is incorrect because the effective runway length is based on a dry runway.

Landing Performance Tables and Graphs

FAA Figures 457 and 458 are examples of landing performance charts. These are used to calculate both the appropriate landing reference speeds and landing distances. As in most performance charts, OAT, pressure altitude, wind and runway slope are the determining factors for calculating speeds and distances used. As a general rule, always move to the next reference line on the chart, before making any adjustments.

Answers

8937 [C] 8937-1 [A] 8939 [C] 8133 [B]

ALL

9791. Approaching the runway 1° below glidepath can add how many feet to the landing distance?

A—250 feet.
B—500 feet.
C—1,000 feet.

On final approach, at a constant airspeed, the glidepath angle and rate of descent is controlled with pitch attitude and elevator. The optimum glidepath angle is 2.5° to 3° whether or not an electronic glidepath reference is being used. On visual approaches, pilots may have a tendency to make flat approaches. A flat approach, however, will increase landing distance and should be avoided. For example, an approach angle of 2° instead of a recommended 3° will add 500 feet to landing distance. (PLT170, AA.I.B.K2e) — FAA-H-8083-3

ALL

9792. Arriving over the runway 10 knots over V_{REF} would add approximately how many feet to the dry landing distance?

A—800 feet.
B—1,700 feet.
C—2,800 feet.

Excess approach speed carried through the threshold window and onto the runway will increase the minimum stopping distance required by 20–30 feet per knot of excess speed for a dry runway. Worse yet, the excess speed will increase the chances of an extended flare, which will increase the distance to touchdown by approximately 250 feet for each excess knot in speed. (PLT170, AA.I.B.K2e) — FAA-H-8083-3

ATM

8742. (Refer to Figures 327 and 457.) With a weight of 69,000 pounds, flaps 45, calm winds, the V_{REF} is

A—136 knots.
B—133 knots.
C—129 knots.

1. *On Figure 327, note the field elevation of 7,680 feet.*
2. *On Figure 457, start at 69,000 pounds on lower left of chart. Move straight up until you intersect the 10,000 foot line. Move directly to the right and note a V_{REF} speed of 136 knots.*

(PLT008, AA.I.B.K2f) — FAA-H-8083-25

ATM

8743. (Refer to Figure 460.) At a weight of 77,500 pounds, and a landing elevation below 5,000 feet, the V_{REF} is

A—139 knots.
B—141 knots.
C—143 knots.

On Figure 460, start on the right side of chart and locate 77,500 pounds. Move left until intersecting the reference line for 5,000 feet and below. Move straight down and note the V_{REF} speed of 143 knots. (PLT008, AA.I.B.K1) — FAA-H-8083-25

ATM, ADX

8744. (Refer to Figures 331 and 461.) At a weight of 73,500 pounds, the expected landing field length is

A—6,700 feet.
B—5,650 feet.
C—6,450 feet.

1. *On Figure 331, note the field elevation of 13 feet.*
2. *On Figure 461, start on the right side of the page at 73,500 pounds. Move directly to the left until you intersect the S.L. line. Move straight down and note the 5,650 feet landing field length.*

(PLT008, AA.I.B.K1) — FAA-H-8083-25

ATM, ADX

8745. (Refer to Figures 331 and 461.) What is the maximum landing weight which will permit stopping 2,000 feet short of the end of a 7,500-foot dry runway?

A—32,200 pounds.
B—71,000 pounds.
C—72,500 pounds.

A landing weight of about 71,000 pounds will require a distance of about 5,500 feet. (PLT008, AA.I.B.K1) — FAA-H-8083-25

Answer (A) is incorrect because 32,000 is shown on the chart in kg. Answer (C) is incorrect because a landing weight of 72,500 pounds would require a landing distance greater than 5,500 feet.

Answers

9791 [B]	9792 [C]	8742 [A]	8743 [C]	8744 [B]	8745 [B]

ATM, ADX

8746. (Refer to Figures 321 and 458.) With a reported temperature of 15°C, a 0.8% upslope, and calm winds, the maximum permissible quick turn-around landing weight is

A—81,000 pounds.
B—81,600 pounds.
C—82,000 pounds.

1. *On Figure 321, note the field elevation of 6,535 feet.*
2. *On Figure 458, start at the temperature of 15°C and move directly right. Intersect the airport pressure altitude of 6,535 feet. Move down until intersecting the wind reference line. Winds are calm, so you can move down to the runway slope reference line. Move diagonally up and to the right in parallel with the diagonal lines until intersecting the .8% upslope line. Move directly down and note the 81,000 pound maximum permissible landing weight.*

(PLT121, AA.I.B.K3e) — FAA-H-8083-25

ATM, ADX

8750. (Refer to Figure 461.) What is the maximum landing weight which will permit stopping 700 feet short of the end of a 5,600 foot runway at sea level?

A—61,000 pounds.
B—59,000 pounds.
C—63,000 pounds.

A landing weight of 61,000 pounds will cause the aircraft to stop approximately 700 feet short of the end of the runway. (PLT008, AA.I.B.K2f) — FAA-8083-25

Answer (B) is incorrect because the aircraft will stop 950 feet short. Answer (C) is incorrect because the aircraft will stop more than 700 feet short of the end of the runway.

ATM, ADX

8753. (Refer to Figures 273 and 457). What is the landing field length on a wet runway with a headwind of 7 knots and an aircraft weight of 83,000 pounds?

A—6,600 feet.
B—7,200 feet.
C—5,900 feet.

1. *On Figure 273, note the field elevation of 1,135 feet.*
2. *On Figure 457, start in the left section at the bottom of the graph, at 83,000 pounds. Move up until you intersect the 1,135 foot pressure altitude line. Move directly to the right until you intersect the reference line. Move diagonally down and to the right in parallel with the diagonal lines until you intersect the 7 knot line. Move right until you intersect the REF line. Move up and to the right in parallel with the diagonal line until intersecting the WET reference line. Move directly to the right and note a landing field length of 6,600 feet.*

(PLT008, AA.I.B.K1) — FAA-H-8083-25

ATM, ADX

8756. (Refer to Figures 331 and 457.) What approach speed and landing distance will be needed when landing at a weight of 75,000 pounds on a dry runway with calm winds?

A—131 knots and 5,600 feet.
B—141 knots and 4,600 feet.
C—141 knots and 5,600 feet.

Figure 331 shows an approximate airport elevation of 13 feet. At 75,000 pounds, the vertical line indicates a V_{REF} *speed of 141 knots and a landing distance of 5,600 feet in calm dry conditions. (PLT008, AA.I.B.K1) — FAA-H-8083-25*

Answers

8746 [A]	8750 [A]	8753 [A]	8756 [C]

Miscellaneous Performance

V_C—design cruising speed.

V_{MO}/M_{MO}—maximum operating limit speed.

An encounter with strong turbulence can result in structural damage to an aircraft, or inadvertent stall. The sudden changes in wind direction and speed can result in very rapid changes in an aircraft's angle of attack. A sudden increase in angle of attack will cause the airplane to accelerate upward, increasing both the load factor and the stalling speed.

For any combination of weight and altitude there will be a recommended "rough air" speed that provides the best protection from stalls and from the possibility of overstressing the aircraft. When clear air turbulence has been reported in the area, a pilot should slow to the rough air speed upon encountering the first ripple of turbulence.

In severe turbulence, it may be impossible to maintain a constant airspeed or altitude. If this happens, the pilot should set the power to that which would maintain the desired airspeed and maintain a level flight attitude, accepting large variations in airspeed and altitude.

ALL

9321. Which is the correct symbol for design cruising speed?

A—V_C.
B—V_S.
C—V_A.

V_C—design cruising speed.

(PLT132, AA.I.B.K2d) — 14 CFR §1.2

Answer (B) is incorrect because V_S is the stalling speed or minimum steady flight speed at which the airplane is controllable. Answer (C) is incorrect because V_A is maneuvering speed.

ALL

8344. How can turbulent air cause an increase in stalling speed of an airfoil?

A—An abrupt change in relative wind.
B—A decrease in angle of attack.
C—Sudden decrease in load factor.

When an airplane flying at a high speed with a low angle of attack suddenly encounters a vertical current of air moving upward, the relative wind changes in an upward direction as it meets the airfoil. This increases the angle of attack. A downward gust would have the effect of decreasing the angle of attack. (PLT245, AA.I.B.K4) — FAA-H-8083-25

Answer (B) is incorrect because a decrease in angle of attack would decrease the possibility of a stall. Answer (C) is incorrect because a sudden decrease in load factor would decrease the stalling speed.

ALL

9129. If severe turbulence is encountered, which procedure is recommended?

A—Maintain a constant altitude.
B—Maintain a constant attitude.
C—Maintain constant airspeed and altitude.

In severe turbulence, the airspeed indicator is inaccurate; therefore the pilot should set power for the recommended rough air speed and then maintain a level flight attitude, accepting variations in indicated airspeed and altitude. (PLT501, AA.I.B.K4) — AC 00-30

Answers (A) and (C) are incorrect because severe turbulence causes large variations in both indicated airspeed and altitude. Any attempt to maintain constant airspeed and altitude may overstress the aircraft.

ATM, ATS, ADX

9320. Which speed symbol indicates the maximum operating limit speed for an airplane?

A—V_{LE}.
B—V_{MO}/M_{MO}.
C—V_{LO}/M_{LO}.

V_{MO}/M_{MO}—maximum operating limit speed.

(PLT466, AA.I.B.K2d) — 14 CFR §1.2

Answer (A) is incorrect because V_{LE} is maximum landing gear extended speed. Answer (C) is incorrect because V_{LO}/M_{LO} is the maximum speed for operating the landing gear.

Answers

9321 [A]	8344 [A]	9129 [B]	9320 [B]

ATM, ADX

8668. (Refer to Figures 68 and 69.) What are the recommended IAS and EPR settings for holding under Operating Conditions O-1?

A—219 knots and 1.83 EPR.
B—223 knots and 2.01 EPR.
C—217 knots and 1.81 EPR.

Interpolation is required for FL310 and 102,000 pounds. At FL350, the EPR value for 102,000 is 1.97. At FL300, the EPR value for 102,000 is 1.77. Interpolation for FL310 results in an EPR value of 1.81. At FL350 the IAS for 102,000 is 219 knots. At FL300 the IAS for 102,000 is 217 knots. Interpolating for FL310 results in an IAS value of 217 knots. (PLT007, AA.I.B.K1) — FAA-H-8083-25

ATM, ADX

8669. (Refer to Figures 68 and 69.) What are the recommended IAS and EPR settings for holding under Operating Conditions O-2?

A—210 knots and 1.57 EPR.
B—210 knots and 1.51 EPR.
C—210 knots and 1.45 EPR.

Interpolation is required for FL230 and 93,000 pounds. At FL250, the EPR value for 93,000 is 1.56. At FL200, the EPR value for 93,000 is 1.44. Interpolation for FL230 results in an EPR value of 1.51. At FL250, the IAS for 93,000 is 210 knots. At FL200, the IAS for 93,000 is 210 knots. Interpolating for FL230 results in an IAS value of 210 knots. (PLT007, AA.I.B.K1) — FAA-H-8083-25

ATM, ADX

8670. (Refer to Figures 68 and 69.) What are the recommended IAS and EPR settings for holding under Operating Conditions O-3?

A—217 knots and 1.50 EPR.
B—215 knots and 1.44 EPR.
C—216 knots and 1.40 EPR.

Interpolation is required for FL170 and 104,000 pounds. At FL200, the EPR value for 104,000 is 1.50. At FL150, the EPR value for 104,000 is 1.40. Interpolation for FL170 results in an EPR value of 1.44. At FL200, the IAS for 104,000 is 216 knots. At FL150, the IAS for 104,000 is 215 knots. Interpolating for FL170 results in an IAS value of 215 knots. (PLT007, AA.I.B.K1) — FAA-H-8083-25

ATM, ADX

8671. (Refer to Figures 68 and 69.) What are the recommended IAS and EPR settings for holding under Operating Conditions O-4?

A—223 knots and 1.33 EPR.
B—225 knots and 1.33 EPR.
C—220 knots and 1.28 EPR.

Interpolation is required for FL080 and 113,000 pounds. At FL100, the EPR value for 113,000 is 1.35. At FL050, the EPR value for 113,000 is 1.29. Interpolation for FL080 results in an EPR value of 1.33. At FL100, the IAS for 113,000 is 223 knots. At FL050, the IAS for 113,000 is 222 knots. Interpolating for FL080 results in an IAS value of 223 knots. (PLT007, AA.I.B.K1) — FAA-H-8083-25

ATM, ADX

8672. (Refer to Figures 68 and 69.) What are the recommended IAS and EPR settings for holding under Operating Conditions O-5?

A—219 knots and 1.28 EPR.
B—214 knots and 1.26 EPR.
C—218 knots and 1.27 EPR.

Interpolation is required for FL040 and 109,000 pounds. At FL050, the EPR value for 109,000 is 1.28. At FL015, the EPR value for 109,000 is 1.24. Interpolation for FL040 results in an EPR value of 1.27. At FL050, the IAS for 109,000 is 218 knots. At FL015, the IAS for 109,000 is 218 knots. Interpolating for FL040 results in an IAS value of 218 knots. (PLT007, AA.I.B.K1) — FAA-H-8083-25

ATM, ADX

8673. (Refer to Figures 68 and 69.) What is the approximate fuel consumed when holding under Operating Conditions O-1?

A—1,625 pounds.
B—1,950 pounds.
C—2,440 pounds.

Compute the fuel flow for the holding time as follows:

Fuel flow per engine = 2,434 × 2 = 4,868 ÷ 60 × 20 = 1,623

(PLT012, AA.VI.J.K2) — FAA-H-8083-25

Answers

8668 [C]	8669 [B]	8670 [B]	8671 [A]	8672 [C]	8673 [A]

ATM, ADX

8674. (Refer to Figures 68 and 69.) What is the approximate fuel consumed when holding under Operating Conditions O-2?

A—2,250 pounds.
B—2,500 pounds.
C—3,000 pounds.

Compute the fuel used for the holding time as follows:

Fuel flow per engine = 2,248 × 2 = 4,496 ÷ 60 × 40 = 2,997

(PLT012, AA.VI.J.K2) — FAA-H-8083-25

ATM, ADX

8675. (Refer to Figures 68 and 69.) What is the approximate fuel consumed when holding under Operating Conditions O-3?

A—2,940 pounds.
B—2,520 pounds.
C—3,250 pounds.

Compute the fuel used for the holding time as follows:

Fuel flow per engine = 2,518 × 2 = 5,036 ÷ 60 × 35 = 2,938

(PLT012, AA.VI.J.K2) — FAA-H-8083-25

ATM, ADX

8676. (Refer to Figures 68 and 69.) What is the approximate fuel consumed when holding under Operating Conditions O-4?

A—2,870 pounds.
B—2,230 pounds.
C—1,440 pounds.

Compute the fuel used for the holding time as follows:

Fuel flow per engine = 2,866 × 2 = 5,732 ÷ 60 × 15 = 1,433

(PLT012, AA.VI.J.K2) — FAA-H-8083-25

ATM, ADX

8677. (Refer to Figures 68 and 69.) What is the approximate fuel consumed when holding under Operating Conditions O-5?

A—2,950 pounds.
B—2,870 pounds.
C—2,400 pounds.

Compute the fuel used for the holding time as follows:

Fuel flow per engine = 2,873 × 2 = 5,746 ÷ 60 × 25 = 2,394

(PLT012, AA.VI.J.K2) — FAA-H-8083-25

ATM, ADX

9943. (Refer to Figure 69.) Before departure, you learn that your destination airport's arrivals are holding for 30 minutes on the arrival. In a two-engine aircraft, how many pounds of fuel would be required to hold at 10,000 feet with an EPR of 1.26 and an airplane weight of 85,000 pounds?

A—1,155 pounds.
B—2,310 pounds.
C—4,620 pounds.

Compute the fuel used for the holding time as follows:

Fuel flow per engine = 2,310 × 2 = 4,620 ÷ 60 × 30 = 2,310 pounds.

(PLT012, AA.VI.J.K2) — FAA-H-8083-25

ATM, ATS, ADX

8727-1. (Refer to Figure 21.) You are taking off from a runway with a 330° magnetic course. Tower reported winds are 290° at 25 knots. The computed headwind component for takeoff is

A—19 knots.
B—25 knots.
C—16 knots.

First, subtract the wind direction from takeoff heading: 330 – 290 = 40 degrees. Then, find the intersection of 40 degrees (angle between wind and runway) and 25 knots (wind velocity). Going to the left, find a headwind component of 19 knots. (PLT013, AA.III.A.K1) — FAA-H-8083-25

Answers

8674 [C]	8675 [A]	8676 [C]	8677 [C]	9943 [B]	8727-1 [A]

ATM, ADX

8727. (Refer to Figures 287 and 421.) The winds are reported as 220/15. You compute tailwind component, hoping for a Runway 33 takeoff. You compute the tailwind to be

A—14 knots.
B—10 knots.
C—5 knots.

The angle between the winds and the runway is 110°. On Figure 421, starting on the left side of the chart at zero, move down and to the right along the 110 line until intersecting the 15 knots point. Then move directly to the left and note a tailwind (indicated by the minus sign) of 5 knots. (PLT013, AA.III.A.K1) — FAA-H-8083-25

ATM, ADX

8728. (Refer to Figure 422.) At a weight of 68,500 pounds with gear and flaps up, you find the reference stall speed to be

A—148 knots.
B—145 knots.
C—142 knots.

On Figure 422, use the upper chart that indicates FLAP 0/GEAR UP. Find the gross weight of 68,500 pounds at the bottom of the chart and move up until intersecting the reference line. Then move directly to the left and note a reference stall speed of 142 knots. (PLT 018, AA.V.B.K1) — FAA-H-8083-25

ATM, ADX

8729. (Refer to Figure 459.) With a payload of 20,000 pounds, the still-air range is

A—1,350 NM.
B—1,410 NM.
C—1,590 NM.

On Figure 459, find the payload of 20,000 pounds on the bottom of the chart. Move directly up until you intersect the MTOW 82500 LB line. Then move directly to the right and note the still-air range of 1,410 NM. (PLT121, AA.I.B.K3f) — FAA-H-8083-25

ATM, ADX

8730. (Refer to Figure 459.) For a supplemental charter, a still-air range of 2,250 NM is required. The payload for this nonstop trip is

A—5,100 pounds.
B—5,900 pounds.
C—6,100 pounds.

On Figure 459, and maintaining the portrait perspective, start at the right side of the chart and find the still-air range of 2,250 NM. Move directly to the left until you intersect the MAX FUEL 19450 LB reference line. Then move straight down and note the payload of 5,900 pounds. (PLT121, AA.I.B.K3f) — FAA-H-8083-25

ATM, ADX

8731. (Refer to Figure 417.) You find one air data computer listed on the MEL as inoperative, leaving one ADC operative during your preflight logbook inspection. This means the flight

A—must fly non-RVSM flight levels above FL330.
B—can only fly between FL290.
C—must remain below FL290 unless dispatch obtains a deviation from ATC.

Figure 417 indicates that two air data computers (ADCs) are required for RVSM operations. Because RVSM airspace starts at FL290, you will not be able to climb above FL290 unless you receive special permission or a deviation from ATC. (PLT428, AA.I.A.K17) — FAA-H-8083-25

ATM, ADX

8732. (Refer to Figure 438.) With an actual runway length of 6,400 feet with 8 flaps, a 1% downslope, a 200 foot clearway, and 4 knots of tailwind, the Reference A is

A—2.12.
B—2.02.
C—1.94.

On Figure 438, start on the left side and find 6,400 feet. Move right until you intersect the REF LINE. Move up and right in parallel with the diagonal lines until you intersect the 200-foot clearway line. Move directly to the right until you intersect the next REF LINE. Move up and left in parallel with the diagonal lines until you intersect the -1 runway slope line. Move directly right until intersecting the Reported Wind REF LINE. Move down and left in parallel with the diagonal lines until you intersect the -4 wind line. Move directly to the right and note the 1.94 Reference A. (PLT428, AA.I.B.K2f) — FAA-H-8083-25

Answers

8727 [C]	8728 [C]	8729 [B]	8730 [B]	8731 [C]	8732 [C]

ATM, ADX
8733. (Refer to Figures 318 and 439.) With a reported temperature of 30°C with packs on and anti-ice off, the Reference B is

A—28.2.
B—29.8.
C—30.7.

1. *On Figure 318 note the field elevation of 4,227 feet.*
2. *On Figure 439, find the section of the chart that indicates ANTI-ICE OFF PACKS ON and start at the bottom of that section at 30°C. Move straight up until you intersect the 4,227 feet line. Move directly to the right and note the Reference B of 29.8.*

(PLT328, AA.I.B.K6) — FAA-H-8083-25

ATM, ADX
8734. (Refer to Figure 440, All Engines.) With a Reference A of 3.00 and Reference B of 28.5, the takeoff weight is limited to

A—78,500 pounds.
B—76,500 pounds.
C—75,000 pounds.

On Figure 440, start at the right side of the chart and find the Reference B of 28.5. Move directly right until you intersect the REF LINE. Move up and to the right diagonally until you intersect the Reference A line of 3.00. Move directly to the right and note the aircraft weight of 76,500 pounds. (PLT328, AA.I.B.K2b) — FAA-H-8083-25

ATM, ADX
9128. What action is appropriate when encountering the first ripple of reported clear air turbulence (CAT)?

A—Extend flaps to decrease wing loading.
B—Extend gear to provide more drag and increase stability.
C—Adjust airspeed to that recommended for rough air.

In an area where significant clear air turbulence has been reported or is forecast, the pilot should adjust the speed to fly at the recommended rough air speed on encountering the first ripple, since the intensity of such turbulence may build up rapidly. (PLT501, AA.I.D.R4) — AC 00-30

Answer (A) is incorrect because use of flaps increases the camber of the wing and angle of attack, but does not decrease the amount of wing loading. Answer (B) is incorrect because extending the gear would increase the drag, but would not change the stability of the airplane.

ATM, ADX
9937. (Refer to Figure 473.) What is the maximum permissible takeoff weight with an airfield altitude of 7,300 feet and an outside air temperature of 24°C?

A—65,000 pounds.
B—62,400 pounds.
C—63,800 pounds.

On Figure 473, start at the bottom and find 24°C. Move straight up until you intersect the 7,300 foot airfield altitude line. Move straight to the right and note a maximum permissible takeoff weight of 63,800 pounds. (PLT011, AA.I.B.K2b) — FAA-H-8083-25

Engine-Out Procedures

V_{MC}—minimum control speed with the critical engine inoperative.

V_{XSE}—best single engine angle-of-climb speed.

V_{YSE}—best single engine rate-of-climb speed.

When an engine fails in flight, the effect on aircraft performance is drastic. For example, the loss of one engine on a two-engine aircraft will result in a loss of climb performance in excess of 50%. Climb performance is determined by the amount of power available in excess of that required for level flight. The one remaining engine must provide all of the power required for level flight. It may be able to develop little or no excess power that would allow for a climb.

When an engine fails in cruise flight, the pilot should slow the aircraft to its best single-engine rate-of-climb speed (V_{YSE}) and apply maximum continuous power on the remaining engine. The airplane may or may not be able to climb. If it cannot climb at the present altitude, at least it will descend at the

Answers

8733 [B] 8734 [B] 9128 [C] 9937 [C]

minimum possible rate of sink and level off at its maximum engine-out altitude. It may be necessary to dump fuel to improve the altitude capability of the aircraft.

A multi-engine airplane should never be flown below its minimum control speed (V_{MC}). If it is below V_{MC} and an engine failure occurs, it may be impossible to maintain directional control with the other engine operating at full power. V_{MC} will vary with the aircraft's center of gravity location. V_{MC} will be highest with the CG at its most rearward-allowed position.

A three- or four-engine turbine-powered airplane, used by an air carrier, may be ferried to a maintenance base with one engine inoperative if certain requirements are met. These requirements include:

- The airplane model must have been test flown to show that such an operation is safe.
- The operator's approved flight manual must contain performance data for such an operation.
- The operating weight of the aircraft must be limited to the minimum required for flight plus any required reserve fuel.
- Takeoffs are usually limited to dry runways.
- The computed takeoff performance must be within acceptable limits (this will vary depending on the type of aircraft).
- The initial climb cannot be over thickly-populated areas.
- Only required flight crewmembers may be on the aircraft.
- Weather conditions at the takeoff and destination airports must be VFR.

ATM, ATS, ADX

8369. If an engine failure occurs at an altitude above single-engine ceiling, what airspeed should be maintained?

A—V_{MC}.
B—V_{YSE}.
C—V_{XSE}.

If an airplane is not capable of maintaining altitude with an engine inoperative under existing circumstances, the airspeed should be maintained within ±5 knots of the engine-out best rate-of-climb speed (V_{YSE}), in order to conserve altitude as long as possible to reach a suitable landing area. (PLT208, AA.I.B.K2g) — FAA-H-8083-3

ATM, ATS, ADX

8370. What is the resulting performance loss when one engine on a twin-engine airplane fails?

A—Reduction of cruise airspeed by 50 percent.
B—Reduction of climb by 80 to 90 percent.
C—Reduction of all performance by 50 percent.

When one engine fails on a light twin, performance is not really halved, but is actually reduced by 80% or more. The performance loss is greater than 50% because an airplane's climb performance is a function of the thrust horsepower, which is in excess of that required for level flight. (PLT223, AA.I.B.K2g) — FAA-H-8083-3

Answer (A) is incorrect because the power loss affects climb capability much more than it does cruise speed. Answer (C) is incorrect because climb capability is significantly (more than 50%) reduced.

ATM, ATS, ADX

8371. Under what condition is V_{MC} the highest?

A—Gross weight is at the maximum allowable value.
B—CG is at the most rearward allowable position.
C—CG is at the most forward allowable position.

V_{MC} is greater when the center of gravity is at the most rearward-allowed position. (PLT466, AA.I.B.K3e) — FAA-H-8083-3

Answer (A) is incorrect because the location of the weight (i.e., CG) is more critical than the amount of weight. Answer (C) is incorrect because a forward CG increases rudder effectiveness and reduces V_{MC}.

Answers

8369 [B] 8370 [B] 8371 [B]

ATM, ATS, ADX

9355. Which operational requirement must be observed by a commercial operator when ferrying a large, three-engine, turbojet-powered airplane from one facility to another to repair an inoperative engine?

A—The computed takeoff distance to reach V_1 must not exceed 70 percent of the effective runway length.
B—The existing and forecast weather for departure, en route, and approach must be VFR.
C—No passengers may be carried.

A commercial operator of large aircraft may conduct a ferry flight of a four-engine airplane or a turbine-engine-powered, three-engine airplane with one engine inoperative, to a base for the purpose of repairing the engine. Several restrictions apply to such flights. These include:

1. *The Airplane Flight Manual must include procedures and performance data which allow for the safe operation of such a flight.*
2. *The initial climb cannot be over thickly-populated areas.*
3. *Weather conditions at the takeoff and destination airports must be VFR.*
4. *Only required flight crewmembers may be on board the aircraft.*

(PLT367, AA.I.G.K2) — 14 CFR §91.611

Answer (A) is incorrect because runway length allowing V_1 in less than 70% of the runway is not required for ferry flights with one engine inoperative. Answer (B) is incorrect because the weather conditions must be VFR only for takeoff and landing.

ATM, ATS, ADX

9355-1. You are assigned to ferry a large, three-engine, turbojet-powered airplane from one facility to another to repair an inoperative engine. You know you are restricted to

A—VFR weather for takeoff, en route, and landing.
B—flight crewmembers only aboard.
C—a computed takeoff distance to reach V_1 that cannot exceed 70 percent of the effective runway length.

A commercial operator of large aircraft may conduct a ferry flight of a four-engine airplane or a turbine-engine-powered, three-engine airplane with one engine inoperative, to a base for the purpose of repairing the engine. Several restrictions apply to such flights. These include:

1. *The Airplane Flight Manual must include procedures and performance data which allow for the safe operation of such a flight.*
2. *The initial climb cannot be over thickly-populated areas.*
3. *Weather conditions at the takeoff and destination airports must be VFR.*
4. *Only required flight crewmembers may be on board the aircraft.*

(PLT367, AA.I.G.K2) — 14 CFR §91.611

ATM, ATS, ADX

9358. A commercial operator plans to ferry a large, four-engine, reciprocating-engine-powered airplane from one facility to another to repair an inoperative engine. Which is an operational requirement for the three-engine flight?

A—The gross weight at takeoff may not exceed 75 percent of the maximum certificated gross weight.
B—Weather conditions at the takeoff and destination airports must be VFR.
C—The computed takeoff distance to reach V_1 must not exceed 70 percent of the effective runway length.

A commercial operator of large aircraft may conduct a ferry flight of a four-engine airplane or a turbine-engine-powered, three-engine airplane with one engine inoperative, to a base for the purpose of repairing the engine. Several restrictions apply to such flights. These include:

1. *The Airplane Flight Manual must include procedures and performance data which allow for the safe operation of such a flight.*
2. *The initial climb cannot be over thickly-populated areas.*
3. *Weather conditions at the takeoff and destination airports must be VFR.*
4. *Only required flight crewmembers may be on board the aircraft.*

(PLT367, AA.I.G.K2) — 14 CFR §91.611

Answers

9355 [C] 9355-1 [B] 9358 [B]

ATM, ATS, ADX

9359. Which operational requirement must be observed when ferrying an air carrier airplane when one of its three turbine engines is inoperative?

A—The weather conditions at takeoff and destination must be VFR.
B—The flight cannot be conducted between official sunset and official sunrise.
C—Weather conditions must exceed the basic VFR minimums for the entire route, including takeoff and landing.

A commercial operator of large aircraft may conduct a ferry flight of a four-engine airplane or a turbine-engine-powered, three-engine airplane with one engine inoperative, to a base for the purpose of repairing the engine. Several restrictions apply to such flights. These include:

1. *The Airplane Flight Manual must include procedures and performance data which allow for the safe operation of such a flight.*
2. *The initial climb cannot be over thickly-populated areas.*
3. *Weather conditions at the takeoff and destination airports must be VFR.*
4. *Only required flight crewmembers may be on board the aircraft.*

(PLT367, AA.I.G.K2) — 14 CFR §91.611

Answer (B) is incorrect because a ferry flight may be conducted after sunset and before sunrise as long as the takeoff and destination airports are VFR. Answer (C) is incorrect because the weather conditions must be VFR only for takeoff and landing.

ATM, ATS, ADX

9360. Which operational requirement must be observed when ferrying a large, turbine-engine-powered airplane when one of its engines is inoperative?

A—The weather conditions at takeoff and destination must be VFR.
B—Weather conditions must exceed the basic VFR minimums for the entire route, including takeoff and landing.
C—The flight cannot be conducted between official sunset and sunrise.

A commercial operator of large aircraft may conduct a ferry flight of a four-engine airplane or a turbine-engine-powered, three-engine airplane with one engine inoperative, to a base for the purpose of repairing the engine. Several restrictions apply to such flights. These include:

1. *The Airplane Flight Manual must include procedures and performance data which allow for the safe operation of such a flight.*
2. *The initial climb cannot be over thickly-populated areas.*
3. *Weather conditions at the takeoff and destination airports must be VFR.*
4. *Only required flight crewmembers may be on board the aircraft.*

(PLT367, AA.I.G.K2) — 14 CFR §91.611

Answer (B) is incorrect because the weather conditions must be VFR only for takeoff and landing. Answer (C) is incorrect because a ferry flight may be conducted after sunset and before sunrise as long as the takeoff and destination airports are VFR.

ATM, ATS, ADX

9361. When a turbine-engine-powered airplane is to be ferried to another base for repair of an inoperative engine, which operational requirement must be observed?

A—Only the required flight crewmembers may be on board the airplane.
B—The existing and forecast weather for departure, en route, and approach must be VFR.
C—No passengers except authorized maintenance personnel may be carried.

A commercial operator of large aircraft may conduct a ferry flight of a four-engine airplane or a turbine-engine-powered, three-engine airplane with one engine inoperative, to a base for the purpose of repairing the engine. Several restrictions apply to such flights. These include:

1. *The Airplane Flight Manual must include procedures and performance data which allow for the safe operation of such a flight.*
2. *The initial climb cannot be over thickly-populated areas.*
3. *Weather conditions at the takeoff and destination airports must be VFR.*
4. *Only required flight crewmembers may be on board the aircraft.*

(PLT367, AA.I.G.K2) — 14 CFR §91.611

Answer (B) is incorrect because the weather conditions must be VFR only for takeoff and landing. Answer (C) is incorrect because only the required flight crewmembers may be aboard.

Answers

9359 [A] 9360 [A] 9361 [A]

ATM, ADX

8678. (Refer to Figure 70.) How many minutes of dump time is required to reach a weight of 144,500 pounds?

Initial weight... 180,500 lb
Zero fuel weight... 125,500 lb

A—13 minutes.
B—15 minutes.
C—16 minutes.

1. Initial weight 180,500
Zero fuel wt. – 125,500
Initial fuel wt. 55,000
2. Ending weight 144,500
Zero fuel wt. – 125,500
Ending fuel wt. 19,000
3. Dump time = 15.25 minutes

(PLT016, AA.I.B.K1) — FAA-H-8083-25

ATM, ADX

8679. (Refer to Figure 70.) How many minutes of dump time is required to reduce fuel load to 25,000 pounds?

Initial weight...179,500 lb
Zero fuel weight... 136,500 lb

A—10 minutes.
B—9 minutes.
C—8 minutes.

1. Initial weight 179,500
Zero fuel wt. – 136,500
Initial fuel wt. 43,000
2. Ending fuel wt. 25,000
3. Dump time = 7.6 minutes

(PLT016, AA.I.B.K1) — FAA-H-8083-25

ATM, ADX

8680. (Refer to Figure 70.) How many minutes of dump time is required to reach a weight of 151,500 pounds?

Initial weight...181,500 lb
Zero fuel weight... 126,000 lb

A—15 minutes.
B—14 minutes.
C—13 minutes.

1. Initial weight 181,500
Zero fuel wt. – 126,000
Initial fuel wt. 55,500
2. Ending weight 151,500
Zero fuel wt. – 126,000
Ending fuel wt. 25,500
3. Dump time = 12.875 minutes

(PLT016, AA.I.B.K1) — FAA-H-8083-25

ATM, ADX

8681. (Refer to Figure 70.) How many minutes of dump time is required to reduce fuel load to 16,000 pounds (at 2,350 lbs/min)?

Initial weight...175,500 lb
Zero fuel weight... 138,000 lb

A—9 minutes.
B—10 minutes.
C—8 minutes.

1. Initial weight 175,500
Zero fuel wt. – 138,000
Initial fuel wt. 37,500
2. Ending fuel wt. 16,000
3. Dump time = 8.8125 minutes

(PLT016, AA.I.B.K1) — FAA-H-8083-25

ATM, ADX

8682. (Refer to Figures 71 and 72.) What is the approximate level-off pressure altitude after drift-down under Operating Conditions D-1?

A—19,400 feet.
B—18,000 feet.
C—20,200 feet.

Assume the aircraft weighs 100,000 pounds at the time of its engine failure and the engine anti-ice is on. If the temperature is ISA, the level-off altitude is 19,400 feet. (PLT004, AA.I.B.K2c) — FAA-H-8083-25

Answers

8678 [B] 8679 [C] 8680 [C] 8681 [A] 8682 [A]

ATM, ADX

8683. (Refer to Figures 71 and 72.) What is the approximate level-off pressure altitude after drift-down under Operating Conditions D-2?

A—14,700 feet.
B—17,500 feet.
C—18,300 feet.

Assume the aircraft weighs 110,000 pounds at the time of its engine failure. If the temperature is ISA +10°C, the level-off altitude is 17,500 feet. (PLT004, AA.I.B.K2c) — FAA-H-8083-25

ATM, ADX

8684. (Refer to Figures 71 and 72.) What is the approximate level-off pressure altitude after drift-down under Operating Conditions D-3?

A—22,200 feet.
B—19,800 feet.
C—21,600 feet.

Assume the aircraft weighs 90,000 pounds at the time of its engine failure. If the temperature is ISA -10°C, the level-off altitude is 21,600 feet. (PLT004, AA.I.B.K2c) — FAA-H-8083-25

ATM, ADX

8685. (Refer to Figures 71 and 72.) What is the approximate level-off pressure altitude after drift-down under Operating Conditions D-4?

A—27,900 feet.
B—22,200 feet.
C—24,400 feet.

Assume the aircraft weighs 80,000 pounds at the time of its engine failure. If the temperature is ISA -10°C, the level-off altitude is 24,400 feet. (PLT004, AA.I.B.K2c) — FAA-H-8083-25

ATM, ADX

8686. (Refer to Figures 71 and 72.) What is the approximate level-off pressure altitude after drift-down under Operating Conditions D-5?

A—8,800 feet.
B—9,600 feet.
C—13,000 feet.

Assume the aircraft weighs 120,000 pounds at the time of its engine failure. If the temperature is ISA +20°C, the level-off altitude is 8,800 feet. When engine bleed-air for air conditioning is off below 17,000 feet, increase level-off altitude by 800 feet. Therefore, the level-off altitude is 9,600 feet (8,800 + 800). (PLT004, AA.I.B.K2c) — FAA-H-8083-25

C208 Aircraft Performance

ATS, ADX

8459. (Refer to Figure 392.) Given the following conditions, what is the maximum torque for takeoff?

Pressure altitude..9,000 ft
Temperature (OAT)..+3°C
Cabin Heat..OFF

A—1,800 foot-pounds.
B—1,840 foot-pounds.
C—1,775 foot-pounds.

Enter the graph at +3°C and proceed up to 9,000 feet, then over to the left to read 1,840 foot-pounds of torque. Note that the pressure altitude levels are given in thousand feet increments, therefore 8 is equal to 8,000, 10 is equal to 10,000, etc. (PLT169, AA.I.B.K2b) — FAA-H-8083-25

ATS, ADX

8460. (Refer to Figure 392.) Given the following conditions, what is the maximum torque for takeoff?

Pressure altitude..4,500 ft
Temperature (OAT)..+35°C
Cabin Heat..OFF

A—1,760 foot-pounds.
B—1,840 foot-pounds.
C—1,675 foot-pounds.

Enter the graph at +35°C and proceed up to 4,500 feet, then over to the left to read 1,760 foot-pounds of torque. Note that the pressure altitude levels are given in thousand feet increments, therefore 8 is equal to 8,000, 10 is equal to 10,000, etc. (PLT169, AA.I.B.K2b) — FAA-H-8083-25

Answers

8683 [B]	8684 [C]	8685 [C]	8686 [B]	8459 [B]	8460 [A]

ATS, ADX

8461. (Refer to Figure 392.) Given the following conditions, what is the maximum torque for takeoff?

Pressure altitude..1,000 ft
Temperature (OAT)..+40°C
Cabin Heat..OFF

A—1,800 foot-pounds.
B—1,725 foot-pounds.
C—1,865 foot-pounds.

Enter the graph at +40°C and proceed up to 1,000 feet, then over to the left to read 1,865 foot-pounds of torque. Note that the pressure altitude levels are given in thousand feet increments, therefore 8 is equal to 8,000, 10 is equal to 10,000, etc. (PLT169, AA.I.B.K2b) — FAA-H-8083-25

ATS, ADX

8462. (Refer to Figure 392.) Given the following conditions, what is the maximum torque for takeoff?

Pressure altitude..6,000 ft
Temperature (OAT)..+25°C
Cabin Heat...ON

A—1,800 foot-pounds.
B—1,735 foot-pounds.
C—1,865 foot-pounds.

Enter the graph at +25°C and proceed up to 6,000 feet, then over to the left to read 1,800 foot-pounds of torque. Note 4 states that with cabin heat on, decrease torque setting by 65 foot-pounds: 1,800 – 65 = 1,735 foot-pounds. Note that the pressure altitude levels are given in thousand feet increments, therefore 8 is equal to 8,000, 10 is equal to 10,000, etc. (PLT169, AA.I.B.K2b) — FAA-H-8083-25

ATS, ADX

8463. (Refer to Figure 392.) Given the following conditions, what is the maximum torque for takeoff?

Pressure altitude..9,000 ft
Temperature (OAT)...+15°C
Cabin Heat...ON

A—1,645 foot-pounds.
B—1,710 foot-pounds.
C—1,675 foot-pounds.

Enter the graph at +15°C and proceed up to 9,000 feet, then over to the left to read 1,710 foot-pounds of torque. Note 4 states that with cabin heat on, decrease torque setting by 65 foot-pounds: 1,710 – 65 = 1,645 foot-pounds. Note that the pressure altitude levels are given in thousand feet increments, therefore 8 is equal to 8,000, 10 is equal to 10,000, etc. (PLT169, AA.I.B.K2b) — FAA-H-8083-25

ATS, ADX

8464. (Refer to Figures 394 and 395.) Given the following conditions, what is the takeoff distance over a 50-foot obstacle?

Pressure Altitude.......................................Sea Level
Temperature (OAT)..+20°C
Wind ....11 knots headwind

A—2,570 feet.
B—2,313 feet.
C—2,160 feet.

Find the column marked 20°C and "Total Distance to Clear 50 foot obstacle." Move down to intersect a pressure altitude of sea level, and find 2,570. Note 2 on Figure 394 requires you to reduce the distance by 10% for each 11 knots of headwind.

2,570 × .10 = 257

2,570 – 257 = 2,313 feet

(PLT169, AA.I.B.K2b) — FAA-H-8083-25

ATS, ADX

8465. (Refer to Figures 394 and 395.) Given the following conditions, what is the takeoff ground roll?

Pressure Altitude...4,000 ft
Temperature (OAT)...0°C
Wind ....4 knots tailwind

A—1,655 feet.
B—1,820 feet.
C—1,986 feet.

Find the column marked 0°C and "Ground Roll Feet." Move down to intersect a pressure altitude of 4,000 feet and find 1,655 feet. Note 2 requires you to increase ground roll by 10% for each two knots of tailwind, therefore 4 knots total would equal a 20% increase.

1655 × .20 = 331

1655 + 331 = 1,986 feet

(PLT169, AA.I.B.K2b) — FAA-H-8083-25

Answers

8461 [C] 8462 [B] 8463 [A] 8464 [B] 8465 [C]

ATS, ADX

8466. (Refer to Figures 394 and 395.) Given the following conditions, what is the takeoff distance over a 50-foot obstacle?

Pressure altitude .... 2,000 ft
Temperature (OAT) .... +15°C
Weight .... 8750 lbs
Wind .... Calm

A—2,823 feet.
B—1,595 feet.
C—2,905 feet.

At 2,000 feet and 10°C, find 2,740 feet to clear a 50-foot obstacle. At 2,000 and 20°C, find 2,905 feet to clear a 50-foot obstacle. To find the distance to clear a 50-foot obstacle at 15°C, interpolate to find the difference: 2740 + 2905 = 5675 / 2 = 2,823 feet. (PLT011, AA.I.B.K2b) — FAA-H-8083-25

ATS, ADX

8467. (Refer to Figures 394 and 395.) Given the following conditions, what is the takeoff ground roll?

Pressure altitude .... 4,000 ft
Temperature (OAT) .... +10°C
Weight .... 8750 lbs
Wind .... HW 11 knots

A—1,760 feet.
B—1,584 feet.
C—1,936 feet.

At 4,000 feet and 10°C, find a ground roll of 1,760 feet. On Figure 394, Note 2 requires you to decrease distance 10% for each 11 knots of headwind.

1760 × .10 = 176

1760 – 176 = 1,584 feet

(PLT011, AA.I.B.K2b) — FAA-H-8083-25

ATS, ADX

8468. (Refer to Figures 394 and 395.) Given the following conditions, what is the takeoff distance over a 50-foot obstacle?

Pressure altitude .... 5,000 ft
Temperature (OAT) .... +20°C
Weight .... 8,750 lbs
Wind .... Calm

A—3,530 feet.
B—3,765 feet.
C—2,010 feet.

At 4,000 feet and 20°C, find 3,295 feet to clear a 50-foot obstacle. At 6,000 and 20°C, find 3,765 feet to clear a 50-foot obstacle. To find the distance to clear a 50-foot obstacle at 5,000 feet, interpolate between 4,000 feet and 6,000 feet to find 3,530 feet. (PLT011, AA.I.B.K2b) — FAA-H-8083-25

ATS, ADX

9918. (Refer to Figures 394 and 395.) With an airport pressure altitude of 6,000 feet and an OAT of 10°C, INERTIAL SEPARATOR NORMAL, and a 2 knot tailwind, the short field takeoff ground roll distance is computed as

A—3,540 feet.
B—2,015 feet.
C—2,217 feet.

At 6,000 feet and 20°C, find 2,015 feet for the ground roll. This needs to be increased 10% for the 2-knot tailwind: 2,015 + 201.5 = 2,216.5 feet. (PLT011, AA.I.B.K2b) — FAA-H-8083-25

ATS, ADX

8479. (Refer to Figures 298, 394, and 395.) With an OAT of 30°C, inertial separator set to normal, and a 12-knot headwind, you calculate the short field takeoff distance to clear a 50-foot obstacle to be

A—3,510 feet.
B—3,833 feet.
C—4,370 feet.

1. *On Figure 298, find the field elevation of 5,837 feet.*
2. *On Figure 395, find the OAT of 30°C and note the distances over a 50-foot obstacle to be 3,510 feet at a 4,000-foot pressure altitude and 4,370 feet at a 6,000-foot pressure altitude. Interpolating for 5,837 feet yields a distance of 4,300 feet.*
3. *Because of the 12-knot headwind, you must reduce the distance by approximately 10.9% (10% for each 11 knots): 4,300 – 469 = 3,831 feet.*

(PLT011, AA.I.B.K2b) — FAA-H-8083-25

Answers

8466 [A]	8467 [B]	8468 [A]	9918 [C]	8479 [B]

ATS, ADX

8480. (Refer Figure 398.) With an OAT of 20°C, inertial separator normal, and gross weight of 8,750 pounds, you calculate the climb gradient at 8,000 feet to be

A—495 ft/NM.
B—410 ft/NM.
C—330 ft/NM.

On Figure 398, locate the gross weight figure of 8,750 in the upper left side of the chart. Proceed to the right at the 8,000 feet pressure altitude level until you intersect the 20°C and note the climb gradient of 330 feet per NM. (PLT004, AA.I.B.K2b) — FAA-H-8083-25

ATS, ADX

9919. (Refer to Figure 398.) With an OAT of 0°C, INERTIAL SEPARATOR in BYPASS, CABIN HEAT ON, and a gross weight of 8,750 pounds, calculation of the climb gradient at 6,000 feet is

A—495 feet per nautical mile.
B—535 feet per nautical mile.
C—545 feet per nautical mile.

On Figure 398, locate the gross weight of 8,750 pounds in the upper left side of the chart. Proceed to the right at the 6,000 feet pressure altitude level until you intersect the 0°C and note the climb gradient of 545 ft/NM. The notes at the bottom of the figure indicate that the climb needs to be decreased 10 ft/NM for inertial separator in bypass and 40 ft/NM for cabin heat on: 545–50 = 495 feet per nautical mile. (PLT004, AA.I.B.K2b) — FAA-H-8083-25

ATS, ADX

8481. (Refer to Figure 399.) With an OAT of 15°C, inertial separator set in bypass, and a gross weight of 8,750 pounds, you calculate the climb fuel to 12,000 feet to be

A—105 lbs.
B—112 lbs.
C—147 lbs.

On Figure 399, start at the gross weight of 8,750 pounds and move to the right across the 12,000 feet pressure altitude level until you intersect the "Standard Temperature/Fuel LBS" column. Note the 105 lbs of fuel used in the climb. Note 3 states that for each 2,000 feet of climb, add 1% to this figure. Because of the climb to 12,000 feet, increase the 105 figure by 6% (1% for each 2,000 feet to 12,000). 6% of 105 is 6.3 feet. 105 + 6.3 = 111.3 feet. Note that 15°C is the standard temperature at sea level where the climb begins. (PLT004, AA.I.B.K2b) — FAA-H-8083-25

ATS

8117. (Refer to Figure 1.) What is the maximum landing distance that may be used by a turbopropeller-powered, small transport category airplane to land on Rwy 24 (dry) at the alternate airport?

A—5,490 feet.
B—6,210 feet.
C—6,405 feet.

The maximum landing percentages for turboprop small transport category airplanes are 60% at destination and 70% at alternate of effective runway length (actual runway minus shaded obstruction clearance portion). Compute for runway 24 as follows:

10,350
– 1,200
9,150 × .7 = 6,405

(PLT008, AA.I.B.K2f) — 14 CFR §§135.385, 135.387, 135.397

ATS

8118. (Refer to Figure 1.) What is the maximum landing distance that may be used by a reciprocating-engine-powered, small transport category airplane to land on Rwy 24 (dry) at the destination airport?

A—5,490 feet.
B—6,210 feet.
C—6,405 feet.

The maximum landing percentages for reciprocating transport category airplanes are 60% at destination and 70% at alternate of effective runway length (actual runway minus shaded obstruction clearance portion). Compute for runway 24 as follows:

10,350
– 1,200
9,150 × .6 = 5,490

(PLT008, AA.I.B.K2f) — 14 CFR §§135.375, 135.377, 135.397

Answers

8480 [C] 9919 [A] 8481 [B] 8117 [C] 8118 [A]

ATS

8119. (Refer to Figure 1.) What is the maximum landing distance that may be used by a turbopropeller-powered, small transport category airplane to land on Rwy 6 (dry) at the alternate airport?

A—5,460 feet.
B—6,210 feet.
C—6,370 feet.

The maximum landing percentages for turboprop small transport category airplanes are 60% at destination and 70% at alternate of effective runway length (actual runway minus shaded obstruction clearance portion). Compute for runway 6 as follows:

10,350
– 1,250
9,100 × .7 = 6,370

(PLT008, AA.I.B.K2f) — 14 CFR §§135.385, 135.387, 135.395

ATS

8120. (Refer to Figure 1.) What is the maximum landing distance that may be used by a reciprocating-engine-powered, small transport category airplane to land on Rwy 6 (dry) at the destination airport?

A—5,460 feet.
B—6,210 feet.
C—6,370 feet.

The maximum landing percentages for reciprocating transport category airplanes are 60% at destination and 70% at alternate of effective runway length (actual runway minus shaded obstruction clearance portion). Compute for runway 6 as follows:

10,350
– 1,250
9,100 × .6 = 5,460

(PLT008, AA.I.B.K2f) — 14 CFR §§135.375, 135.377, 135.397

ATS

8121. (Refer to Figure 1.) What is the maximum landing distance that may be used by a turbine-engine-powered, small transport category airplane to land on Rwy 24 (dry) at the destination airport?

A—5,460 feet.
B—5,490 feet.
C—6,210 feet.

The maximum landing percentages for turbine-engine-powered small transport category airplanes are 60% at destination and 70% at alternate of effective runway length (actual runway minus shaded obstruction clearance portion). Compute for runway 24 as follows:

10,350
– 1,200
9,150 × .6 = 5,490

(PLT008, AA.I.B.K2f) — 14 CFR §§135.385, 135.387, 135.395

ATS

8122. (Refer to Figure 1.) What is the maximum landing distance that may be used by a turbine-engine-powered, small transport category airplane to land on Rwy 6 (wet) at the destination airport?

A—5,460 feet.
B—9,100 feet.
C—6,279 feet.

The maximum landing percentages for turbine-engine-powered small transport category airplanes are 60% at destination and 70% at alternate of effective runway length (actual runway minus shaded obstruction clearance portion). Compute for runway 6 as follows:

10,350
– 1,250
9,100 × .6 = 5,460

14 CFR §135.385 is misleading here because you must increase actual landing distance by 115% to find the effective runway length wet, but the question asks for maximum landing distance, not effective landing distance. (PLT008, AA.I.B.K2f) — 14 CFR §§135.385, 135.387, 135.395

Answers

8119 [C] 8120 [A] 8121 [B] 8122 [A]

ATS

8123. (Refer to Figure 2.) What is the maximum landing distance that may be used by a turbopropeller-powered, small transport category airplane to land on Rwy 19 (dry) at the destination airport?

A—6,020 feet.
B—5,820 feet.
C—5,160 feet.

The maximum landing percentages for turboprop small transport category airplanes are 60% at destination and 70% at alternate of effective runway length (actual runway minus shaded obstruction clearance portion). Compute for runway 19 as follows:

9,700
– 1,100
8,600 × .6 = 5,160

(PLT008, AA.I.B.K2f) — 14 CFR §§135.377, 135.385, 135.387, 135.397

ATS

8124. (Refer to Figure 2.) What is the maximum landing distance that may be used by a reciprocating-engine-powered, small transport category airplane to land on Rwy 1 (dry) at the destination airport?

A—5,010 feet.
B—5,820 feet.
C—5,845 feet.

The maximum landing percentages for reciprocating transport category airplanes are 60% at destination and 70% at alternate of effective runway length (actual runway minus shaded obstruction clearance portion). Compute for runway 1 as follows:

9,700
– 1,350
8,350 × .6 = 5,010

(PLT008, AA.I.B.K2f) — 14 CFR §§135.375, 135.377, 135.395

ATS

8125. (Refer to Figure 2.) What is the maximum landing distance that may be used by a turbine-engine-powered, small transport category airplane to land on Rwy 1 (dry) at the destination airport?

A—5,010 feet.
B—5,820 feet.
C—5,845 feet.

The maximum landing percentages for turbine-engine-powered small transport category airplanes are 60% at destination and 70% at alternate of effective runway length (actual runway minus shaded obstruction clearance portion). Compute for runway 1 as follows:

9,700
– 1,350
8,350 × .6 = 5,010

(PLT008, AA.I.B.K2f) — 14 CFR §§135.385, 135.387, 135.395

ATS

8126. (Refer to Figure 2.) What is the maximum landing distance that may be used by a turbine-engine-powered, small transport category airplane to land on Rwy 19 (dry) at the destination airport?

A—5,160 feet.
B—5,820 feet.
C—6,020 feet.

The maximum landing percentages for turbine-engine-powered small transport category airplanes are 60% at destination and 70% at alternate of effective runway length (actual runway minus shaded obstruction clearance portion). Compute for runway 19 as follows:

9,700
– 1,100
8,600 × .6 = 5,160

(PLT008, AA.I.B.K2f) — 14 CFR §§135.385, 135.387, 135.395

Answers

8123 [C] 8124 [A] 8125 [A] 8126 [A]

ATS

8127. (Refer to Figure 2.) May a small transport category, turbine-engine-powered airplane that has a computed landing distance of 5,500 feet use one or both of the runways depicted in the illustration at the destination airport?

A—Neither Rwy 1 nor Rwy 19 may be used if dry conditions exist.
B—Only Rwy 19 may be used provided dry conditions exist.
C—Rwy 1 or Rwy 19 may be used whether conditions are wet or dry.

The maximum landing percentages for turbine-engine-powered small transport category airplanes are 60% at destination and 70% at alternate of effective runway length (actual runway minus shaded obstruction clearance portion). Compute as follows:

1. *Runway 1*

$$\begin{array}{r} 9{,}700 \\ -\ 1{,}350 \\ \hline 8{,}350 \end{array} \times .6 = 5{,}010$$

2. *Runway 19*

$$\begin{array}{r} 9{,}700 \\ -\ 1{,}100 \\ \hline 8{,}600 \end{array} \times .6 = 5{,}160$$

3. *Computed landing distance is given as 5,500. Since computed landing distance exceeds both runway landing distances even in dry conditions, neither runway 1 nor 19 may be used if dry conditions exist.*

(PLT456, AA.I.B.K2f) — 14 CFR §135.385

ATS

8128. (Refer to Figure 2.) May a small transport category, turboprop airplane that has a computed landing distance of 6,000 feet use either or both runways depicted in the illustration at the destination airport?

A—Only Rwy 19 may be used if dry conditions exist.
B—Neither Rwy 1 nor Rwy 19 may be used under any conditions.
C—Either Rwy 1 or Rwy 19 may be used whether conditions are wet or dry.

The maximum landing percentages for turboprop small transport category airplanes are 60% at destination and 70% at alternate of effective runway length (actual runway minus shaded obstruction clearance portion). Compute as follows:

1. *Runway 1*

$$\begin{array}{r} 9{,}700 \\ -\ 1{,}350 \\ \hline 8{,}350 \end{array} \times .6 = 5{,}010$$

2. *Runway 19*

$$\begin{array}{r} 9{,}700 \\ -\ 1{,}100 \\ \hline 8{,}600 \end{array} \times .6 = 5{,}160$$

3. *Computed landing distance is given as 6,000; therefore neither runway may be used.*

(PLT456, AA.I.B.K2f) — 14 CFR §§135.385, 135.387, 135.395

ATS

8129. (Refer to Figure 2.) What is the maximum landing distance that may be used for a non-transport category, turbopropeller-driven airplane to land on Rwy 1 (dry) at the alternate airport?

A—5,010 feet.
B—5,845 feet.
C—6,020 feet.

The maximum landing percentages for turboprop small transport category airplanes are 60% at destination and 70% at alternate of effective runway length (actual runway minus shaded obstruction clearance portion). Compute as follows:

$$\begin{array}{r} 9{,}700 \\ -\ 1{,}350 \\ \hline 8{,}350 \end{array} \times .7 = 5{,}845$$

(PLT008, AA.I.B.K2f) — 14 CFR §§135.385, 135.387, 135.395

Answers

8127 [A] 8128 [B] 8129 [B]

ATS

8130. (Refer to Figure 2.) Which condition meets 14 CFR Part 135 operational requirements for a small, transport category, turboprop airplane to land at the destination airport that has the runway environment given in the illustration?

A—The airport may be listed as the destination airport if the landing distance does not exceed 5,160 feet for Rwy 19.

B—The airport may NOT be listed as the destination airport if the landing distance exceeds 5,100 feet for Rwy 19.

C—The airport may be listed as the destination airport if the landing distance does not exceed 5,350 feet for either runway, wet or dry conditions.

The maximum landing percentages for turboprop small transport category airplanes are 60% at destination and 70% at alternate of effective runway length (actual runway minus shaded obstruction clearance portion). Compute as follows:

1. *Runway 1*

   9,700
   – 1,350
   8,350 × .6 = 5,010

2. *Runway 19*

   9,700
   – 1,100
   8,600 × .6 = 5,160

3. *The best answer is to not exceed 5,160 feet.*

(PLT456, AA.I.B.K2f) — 14 CFR §135.385

Cessna 208 Performance Tables

The Cessna 208 performance tables start with FAA Figure 392 and continue through Figure 403. With Cessna charts, be sure to always read closely the "Notes" associated with a particular chart. A good example of why it's important to read the Notes is shown in the "Engine torque on takeoff" charts in Figures 392 and 393. The inertial separator is set to "Normal" for the chart readings, but when it is placed in bypass, adjustments need to be made. For example, in Figure 392, if you calculate a maximum torque setting of 1,750, you will have to decrease the torque setting by 15 (see Note 3).

The takeoff and landing distance charts (FAA Figures 395 and 402) are tabular charts that often require interpolation to obtain accurate results. For example, a landing ground-roll distance is needed (Figure 402) for a sea level airport at 20°C. Examining the chart, this distance is 930 feet. But it gets more complicated if the pressure altitude is 1,000 feet. In this case, the value would be halfway between the sea level value of 930 and the 2,000-foot value of 1,000—or, 965 feet (930 + 1,000 = 1,930 ÷ 2 = 965).

Sometimes the interpolation requires a calculation beyond the simple "halfway-in-between" two published values. There are a few techniques available for solving these problems but the basic idea is to set up a ratio. Let's say the pressure altitude in the above example is a field elevation of 683 feet. We know from the chart that between sea level and 2,000 feet (a difference of 2,000), the ground roll increased 70 feet. That makes a ratio of 70/2000, or, for every 2,000 feet, the ground roll increases by 70 feet. (Note that this relationship only works at *this* altitude, and will change at the higher altitudes.)

In the example, calculate how many feet the ground roll increases when the pressure altitude increases 683 feet. To do this, we cross-multiply: just multiply 683 by 70, and divide by 2,000. This yields 24 feet. Therefore, add 24 to the 930 sea level value, and calculate a ground roll of 954 feet at a pressure altitude of 683 feet. Interpolation can also work between temperature settings.

Again—don't forget to read the Notes in these chart figures; sometimes they can be found on a further page as in FAA Figure 401.

Answers

8130 [A]

ATS, ADX

8505. (Refer to Figures 298, 401, and 402.) With an OAT of 30°C, inertial separator set to Normal, 10 knots of headwind, and a gross weight of 8,500 pounds, you calculate the landing roll to be about

A—1,080 feet.
B—1,200 feet.
C—2,140 feet.

1. *On Figure 298, note the field elevation of 5,837 feet.*
2. *On Figure 402, find the pressure altitude of 4,000 and 6,000 feet at 30°C and note 1,115 feet (at 4,000 feet pressure altitude) and 1,200 feet (at 6,000 feet pressure altitude). Interpolating for 5,837 feet, calculate a ground roll of 1,193 feet.*
3. *Due to the 10-knot headwind, reduce this distance by 9.1% (reduce 10% for each 11 knots of headwind—see Figure 401 for the corresponding note): 1,193 – 109 = 1,084 feet.*

(PLT008, AA.I.B.K2f) — FAA-H-8083-25

ATS, ADX

8506. (Refer to Figures 299 and 409.) What is your landing distance over a 50-foot obstacle at 10°C and 8,500 pounds?

A—1,715 feet.
B—965 feet.
C—1,747 feet.

1. *On Figure 299, note the field elevation of 647 feet.*
2. *On Figure 409, find the sea level and 2,000-foot pressure altitudes and move across to the right until you find the distances to clear a 50-foot obstacle. Note the 1,715 feet at sea level and the 1,815 feet at 2,000 feet pressure altitude. Interpolating for the field elevation of 647 feet, calculate a distance of 1,747 feet.*

(PLT008, AA.I.B.K2f) — FAA-H-8083-25

ATS, ADX

8507. (Refer to Figures 295 and 409.) Calculate your landing distance with an OAT of 20°C.

A—1,000 feet.
B—1,016 feet.
C—1,884 feet.

1. *On Figure 295, note the field elevation of 2,417 feet.*
2. *On Figure 409, find the 2,000-foot pressure altitude and the 4,000-foot pressure altitude. Move across to the right until you find the ground roll distances at 20°C. Note the 1,000 feet at 2,000-foot pressure altitude and the 1,075 feet at 4,000-foot pressure altitude. Interpolating for the field elevation of 2,417 feet, calculate a distance of 1,016 feet.*

(PLT008, AA.I.B.K2f) — FAA-H-8083-25

ATS, ADX

8508. (Refer to Figure 409.) Given the following conditions, what would your distance to clear a 50-foot obstacle be?

Pressure Altitude .... 2,000 feet
OAT .... 40°C
Wind .... calm
Weight .... 8,500 pounds
Runway condition .... Paved, level and dry

A—1,960 feet.
B—1,070 feet.
C—1,742 feet.

On Figure 409, find the 2,000-foot pressure altitude and move across until you intersect the 40°C column. Note the 1,960 feet needed to clear the 50-foot obstacle. (PLT008, AA.I.B.K2f) — FAA-H-8083-25

ATS, ADX

8509. (Refer to Figure 409.) Given the following conditions, what would your ground roll distance be?

Pressure Altitude .... 4,000 feet
OAT .... 15°C
Wind .... calm
Weight .... 8,500 pounds
Runway condition .... Paved, level and dry

A—1,040 feet.
B—1,058 feet.
C—1,075 feet.

On Figure 409, find the 4,000-foot pressure altitude and move across until you intersect the 10°C and 20°C columns. Note the ground roll distances of 1,040 feet for 10°C and 1,075 feet for 20°C feet. Interpolating for 15°C, find a value of 1,058 feet. (PLT008, AA.I.B.K2f) — FAA-H-8083-25

Answers

8505 [A] 8506 [C] 8507 [B] 8508 [A] 8509 [B]

ATS, ADX

8510. (Refer to Figure 409.) Given the following conditions, what would your ground roll distance be?

Pressure Altitude .... 1,000 feet
OAT.. -10°C
Wind ....calm
Weight .... 8,500 pounds
Runway condition ....Paved, level and dry

A—868 feet.
B—835 feet.
C—900 feet.

On Figure 409, find the sea level and 2,000-foot pressure altitudes and move across until you intersect the -10°C. Note the ground roll distances of 835 feet at sea level and 900 feet at the 2,000-foot pressure altitude. Interpolating for 1,000 feet pressure altitude, find a value of 868 feet. (PLT008, AA.I.B.K2f) — FAA-H-8083-25

ATS, ADX

8511. (Refer to Figures 342 and 409.) Calculate your landing distance with an OAT of 5°C.

A—865 feet.
B—883 feet.
C—900 feet.

1. *On Figure 342, note the field elevation of 10 feet.*
2. *On Figure 409, find the sea level pressure altitude. Move across to the right until you find the ground roll distances at 0°C and at 10°C. Note the 0°C distance of 865 feet, and the 10°C distance of 900 feet. Interpolating for the temperature of 5°C, calculate a distance of 883 feet.*

(PLT008, AA.I.B.K2f) — FAA-H-8083-25

ATS, ADX

8512. (Refer to Figures 327 and 409.) Calculate your landing distance over a 50-foot obstacle with an OAT of 10°C.

A—2,135 feet.
B—2,030 feet.
C—2,155 feet.

1. *On Figure 327, note the field elevation of 7,680 feet.*
2. *On Figure 409, find the pressure altitudes of 6,000 and 8,000 feet. Move across to the right until you find the 10°C distances over a 50-foot obstacle at both pressure altitudes. Note the distance of 2,030 feet at the pressure altitude of 6,000 feet, and the distance of 2,155 at the pressure altitude of 8,000 feet. Interpolating for the field elevation of 7,680 feet, calculate a distance of 883 feet.*

(PLT008, AA.I.B.K2f) — FAA-H-8083-25

Answers

8510 [A] 8511 [B] 8512 [A]

Commuter Aircraft Performance

ADX

9899. (Refer to Figure 13.) Given the following conditions, what is the takeoff distance over a 50-foot obstacle?

Pressure altitude.. Sea Level
Temperature (OAT).. +12°C
Weight.. 16,000 lb
Wind component.. 16 kts HW
Ice vanes.. Retracted

A—1,750 feet.
B—2,800 feet.
C—2,550 feet.

1. *Enter FAA Figure 13 at the bottom left-hand side at +12°C OAT and proceed upward to the line representing sea level (SL) pressure altitude.*
2. *From the point of intersection on the "pressure altitude" lines, draw a horizontal line to the reference line, then parallel the line which represents an aircraft weight of 16,000 pounds.*
3. *From the point of intersection in the "weight" portion of the graph, draw a horizontal line to the next reference line (wind component), then parallel the line until intersecting with the 16-knot headwind.*
4. *From the point of intersection on the "wind" portion of the graph draw a horizontal line to the next reference line (0-foot obstacle height), then parallel the line required to clear a 50-foot obstacle.*
5. *The distance required is 2,550 feet.*

(PLT011) — FAA-H-8083-25

ADX

9900. (Refer to Figure 13.) Given the following conditions, what is the takeoff ground roll and V_1 speed?

Pressure altitude.. 4,000 ft
Temperature (OAT).. 0°C
Weight.. 15,500 lb
Wind component.. 10 kts TW
Ice vanes.. Extended

A—2,900 feet, 106 knots.
B—4,250 feet, 102 knots.
C—2,700 feet, 107 knots.

1. *Enter FAA Figure 13 at the bottom left-hand side at +5°C OAT (adding 5°C to the actual OAT since the ice vanes are extended) and proceed upward to the line representing 4,000 feet pressure altitude.*
2. *From the point of intersection on the "pressure altitude" lines, draw a horizontal line to the reference line, then parallel the line which represents an aircraft weight of 15,500 pounds.*
3. *From the point of intersection in the "weight" portion of the graph, draw a horizontal line to the next reference line (wind component), then parallel the line until intersecting with the 10-knot tailwind.*
4. *From the point of intersection on the "wind" portion of the graph continue to the edge of the graph to find the ground roll required: 2,900 feet.*
5. *The V_1 speed is found using the table in the upper right corner of FAA Figure 13. Interpolate between 16,000 and 14,000 to find 106 knots for 15,500 pounds.*

(PLT011) — FAA-H-8083-25

ADX

9901. (Refer to Figure 13.) Given the following conditions, what is the takeoff distance over a 50-foot obstacle?

Pressure altitude.. 2,000 ft
Temperature (OAT).. +15°C
Weight.. 16,600 lb
Wind component.. Calm
Ice vanes.. Retracted

A—3,400 feet.
B—3,700 feet.
C—4,200 feet.

1. *Enter FAA Figure 13 at the bottom left-hand side at +15°C OAT and proceed upward to the line representing 2,000 feet pressure altitude.*
2. *From the point of intersection on the "pressure altitudes" lines, draw a horizontal line to the reference line, then parallel the line which represents an aircraft weight of 16,600 pounds.*
3. *Continue past the second reference line to the third reference line (since the wind is calm).*
4. *From the third reference line (0-foot obstacle height), parallel the line required to clear a 50-foot obstacle.*
5. *The distance required is 3,700 feet.*

(PLT011) — FAA-H-8083-25

Answers

9899 [C] 9900 [A] 9901 [B]

ADX
9902. (Refer to Figure 13.) Given the following conditions, what is the takeoff ground roll and V_1 speed?

Pressure altitude..3,000 ft
Temperature (OAT)... -10°C
Weight .... 15,000 lb
Wind component ....8 kts TW
Ice vanes ....Extended

A—2,200 feet, 105 knots.
B—2,000 feet, 113 knots.
C—1,900 feet, 103 knots.

1. *Enter FAA Figure 13 at the bottom left-hand side at -5°C OAT (adding 5°C to the actual OAT since the ice vanes are extended) and proceed upward to the line representing 3,000 feet pressure altitude.*
2. *From the point of intersection on the "pressure altitude" lines, draw a horizontal line to the reference line, then parallel the line which represents an aircraft weight of 15,000 pounds.*
3. *From the point of intersection in the "weight" portion of the graph, draw a horizontal line to the next reference line (wind component), then parallel the line until intersecting with the 8-knot tailwind.*
4. *From the point of intersection on the "wind" portion of the graph continue to the edge of the graph to find the ground roll required: 2,200 feet.*
5. *The V_1 speed is found using the table in the upper right corner of FAA Figure 13. Interpolate between 16,000 and 14,000 to find 105 knots for 15,000 pounds.*

(PLT011) — FAA-H-8083-25

ADX
9903. (Refer to Figure 13.) Given the following conditions, what is the takeoff distance over a 50 foot obstacle?

Pressure altitude..6,000 ft
Temperature (OAT)..+35°C
Weight .... 14,500 lb
Wind component ....10 kts HW
Ice vanes ....Retracted

A—4,150 feet.
B—4,550 feet.
C—2,600 feet.

1. *Enter FAA Figure 13 at the bottom left-hand side at +35°C OAT and proceed upward to the line representing 6,000 feet pressure altitude.*
2. *From the point of intersection on the "pressure altitude" lines, draw a horizontal line to the reference line, then parallel the line which represents an aircraft weight of 14,500 pounds.*
3. *From the point of intersection in the "weight" portion of the graph, draw a horizontal line to the next reference line (wind component), then parallel the line until intersecting with the 10-knot headwind.*
4. *From the point of intersection on the "wind" portion of the graph draw a horizontal line to the next reference line (0-foot obstacle height), then parallel the line required to clear a 50-foot obstacle.*
5. *The distance required is 4,150 feet.*

(PLT011) — FAA-H-8083-25

ADX
8469. (Refer to Figure 14.) Given the following conditions, what is the accelerate-stop field length?

Pressure altitude..5,000 ft
Temperature (OAT)..+20°C
Weight .... 15,000 lb
Wind component ....10 kts HW
Ice vanes ....Retracted

A—6,300 feet.
B—4,700 feet.
C—4,300 feet.

1. *Enter FAA Figure 14 at the bottom left-hand side at +20°C OAT and proceed upward to the line representing 5,000 feet pressure altitude.*
2. *From the point of intersection on the "pressure altitude" lines, draw a horizontal line to the reference line, then parallel the line which represents an aircraft weight of 15,000 pounds.*
3. *From the point of intersection in the "weight" portion of the graph, draw a horizontal line to the next reference line (wind component), then parallel the line until intersecting with the 10-knot headwind.*
4. *Proceed from the wind line to the edge of the chart to read the accelerate/stop distance of 4,300 feet.*

(PLT011) — FAA-H-8083-25

Answers

9902 [A] 9903 [A] 8469 [C]

ADX

8470. (Refer to Figure 14.) Given the following conditions, what is the accelerate-stop field length?

Pressure altitude..2,000 ft
Temperature (OAT).. -15°C
Weight .... 16,000 lb
Wind component ....5 kts TW
Ice vanes ....Extended

A—3,750 feet.
B—4,600 feet.
C—4,250 feet.

1. *Enter FAA Figure 14 at the bottom left-hand side at -12°C OAT (adding 3°C to the actual OAT for extended ice vanes) and proceed upward to the line representing 2,000 feet pressure altitude.*
2. *From the point of intersection on the "pressure altitude" lines, draw a horizontal line to the reference line, then parallel the line which represents an aircraft weight of 16,000 pounds.*
3. *From the point of intersection in the "weight" portion of the graph, draw a horizontal line to the next reference line (wind component), then parallel the line until intersecting with the 5-knot tailwind.*
4. *Proceed from the wind line to the edge of the chart to read the accelerate/stop distance of 4,250 feet.*

(PLT011) — FAA-H-8083-25

ADX

8471. (Refer to Figure 14.) Given the following conditions, what is the accelerate-stop field length?

Pressure altitude..6,000 ft
Temperature (OAT).. +10°C
Weight .... 16,600 lb
Wind component ....15 kts HW
Ice vanes ....Retracted

A—4,950 feet.
B—4,800 feet.
C—5,300 feet.

1. *Enter FAA Figure 14 at the bottom left-hand side at +10°C OAT and proceed upward to the line representing 6,000 feet pressure altitude.*
2. *From the point of intersection on the "pressure altitude" lines, draw a horizontal line to the reference line, then parallel the line which represents an aircraft weight of 16,600 pounds.*
3. *From the point of intersection in the "weight" portion of the graph, draw a horizontal line to the next reference line (wind component), then parallel the line until intersecting with the 15-knot headwind.*
4. *Proceed from the wind line to the edge of the chart to read the accelerate/stop distance of 4,950 feet.*

(PLT011) — FAA-H-8083-25

ADX

8472. (Refer to Figure 14.) Given the following conditions, what is the accelerate-stop field length?

Pressure altitude..8,000 ft
Temperature (OAT)... -5°C
Weight .... 14,000 lb
Wind component ....4 kts TW
Ice vanes ....Extended

A—4,500 feet.
B—4,800 feet.
C—5,300 feet.

1. *Enter FAA Figure 14 at the bottom left-hand side at -2°C OAT (adding 3°C to the actual OAT for extended ice vanes) and proceed upward to the line representing 8,000 feet pressure altitude.*
2. *From the point of intersection on the "pressure altitude" lines, draw a horizontal line to the reference line, then parallel the line which represents an aircraft weight of 14,000 pounds.*
3. *From the point of intersection in the "weight" portion of the graph, draw a horizontal line to the next reference line (wind component), then parallel the line until intersecting with the 4-knot tailwind.*
4. *Proceed from the wind line to the edge of the chart to read the accelerate/stop distance of 4,800 feet.*

(PLT011) — FAA-H-8083-25

Answers

8470 [C] 8471 [A] 8472 [B]

ADX
8473. (Refer to Figure 14.) Given the following conditions, what is the accelerate-stop field length?

Pressure altitude.. Sea Level
Temperature (OAT).. +30°C
Weight .... 13,500 lb
Wind component .... 14 kts HW
Ice vanes ....Retracted

A—2,500 feet.
B—2,850 feet.
C—3,050 feet.

1. *Enter FAA Figure 14 at the bottom left-hand side at +30°C OAT and proceed upward to the line representing sea level (SL) pressure altitude.*
2. *From the point of intersection on the "pressure altitude" lines, draw a horizontal line to the reference line, then parallel the line which represents an aircraft weight of 13,500 pounds.*
3. *From the point of intersection in the "weight" portion of the graph, draw a horizontal line to the next reference line (wind component), then parallel the line until intersecting with the 14-knot headwind.*
4. *Proceed from the wind line to the edge of the chart to read the accelerate/stop distance of 3,050 feet.*

(PLT011) — FAA-H-8083-25

ATM, ATS, ADX
9936. (Refer to Figure 478.) With a reported temperature of 5°C, and a weight of 57,000 pounds, an altitude of 5,355 feet, and V_1/V_R ratio of 1.0, the accelerate-stop distance is

A—4,100 feet.
B—4,900 feet.
C—5,700 feet.

On Figure 478, start at the bottom of the chart and find the intersecting point of 5°C and an altitude of 5,355 feet. Move straight up until you hit the first reference line and then follow the arching line until you intersect a weight of 57,000 pounds. Move straight up to the second reference line. Note that the reference line also intersects a V_1/V_R of 1.0, so from here you can move straight up to determine an accelerate-stop distance of approximately 5,700 feet. (PLT011, AA.I.B.K2b) — FAA-H-8083-25

ADX
8474. (Refer to Figures 15, 16, and 17.) What is the two-engine rate of climb after takeoff in climb configuration for Operating Conditions BE-21?

A—1,350 ft/min.
B—2,450 ft/min.
C—2,300 ft/min.

1. *Enter FAA Figure 16 at the bottom left-hand side at +10°C OAT and proceed upward to the line representing 2,000 feet pressure altitude.*
2. *From the point of intersection on the "pressure altitude" lines, draw a horizontal line to the reference line, then parallel the line which represents an aircraft weight of 16,600 pounds.*
3. *From the point of intersection in the "weight" portion of the graph, draw a horizontal line to the edge of the chart to read 2,300 fpm.*

(PLT004) — FAA-H-8083-25

ADX
8475. (Refer to Figures 15, 16, and 17.) What is the single-engine climb gradient after takeoff in climb configuration for Operating Conditions BE-22?

A—6.8 percent gradient.
B—7.5 percent gradient.
C—5.6 percent gradient.

1. *Enter FAA Figure 17 at the bottom left-hand side at 0°C OAT and proceed upward to the line representing 1,000 feet pressure altitude.*
2. *From the point of intersection on the "pressure altitude" lines, draw a horizontal line to the reference line, then parallel the line which represents an aircraft weight of 14,000 pounds.*
3. *From the point of intersection in the "weight" portion of the graph, draw a horizontal line to the edge of the chart to read 870 fpm.*
4. *Adjust the rate of climb for the extended ice vanes, as indicated at the top of the graph. The single-engine rate of climb with ice vanes extended is 755 fpm (870 – 115).*
5. *Find 755 fpm at the right edge of the chart and proceed right to the reference line and determine a climb gradient of 5.6%.*

(PLT004) — FAA-H-8083-25

Answers

8473 [C] 9936 [C] 8474 [C] 8475 [C]

ADX

8476. (Refer to Figures 15, 16, and 17.) What is the two-engine rate of climb after takeoff in climb configuration for Operating Conditions BE-23?

A—1,500 ft/min.
B—2,600 ft/min.
C—2,490 ft/min.

1. *Enter FAA Figure 16 at the bottom left-hand side at +20°C OAT and proceed upward to the line representing 3,000 feet pressure altitude.*
2. *From the point of intersection on the "pressure altitude" lines, draw a horizontal line to the reference line, then parallel the line which represents an aircraft weight of 15,000 pounds.*
3. *From the point of intersection in the "weight" portion of the graph, draw a horizontal line to the edge of the chart to read 2,600 fpm.*

(PLT004) — FAA-H-8083-25

ADX

8477. (Refer to Figures 15, 16, and 17.) What is the two-engine rate of climb after takeoff in climb configuration for Operating Conditions BE-24?

A—2,100 ft/min.
B—2,400 ft/min.
C—1,500 ft/min.

1. *Enter FAA Figure 16 at the bottom left-hand side at +25°C OAT and proceed upward to the line representing 4,000 feet pressure altitude.*
2. *From the point of intersection on the "pressure altitude" lines, draw a horizontal line to the reference line, then parallel the line which represents an aircraft weight of 16,000 pounds.*
3. *From the point of intersection in the "weight" portion of the graph, draw a horizontal line to the edge of the chart to read 2,100 fpm.*

(PLT004) — FAA-H-8083-25

ADX

8478. (Refer to Figures 15, 16, and 17.) What is the single-engine rate of climb after takeoff in climb configuration for Operating Conditions BE-25?

A—385 ft/min.
B—780 ft/min.
C—665 ft/min.

1. *Enter FAA Figure 17 at the bottom left-hand side at -10°C OAT and proceed upward to the line representing 5,000 feet pressure altitude.*
2. *From the point of intersection on the "pressure altitude" lines, draw a horizontal line to the reference line, then parallel the line which represents an aircraft weight of 14,000 pounds.*
3. *From the point of intersection in the "weight" portion of the graph, draw a horizontal line to the edge of the chart to read 780 fpm.*
4. *Adjust the rate of climb for the extended ice vanes, as indicated at the top of the graph. The single-engine rate-of-climb with ice vanes extended is 665 fpm (780 – 115).*

(PLT004) — FAA-H-8083-25

ADX

9904. (Refer to Figures 15 and 18.) What are the time, fuel, and distance from the start of climb to cruise altitude for Operating Conditions BE-21?

A—10.0 minutes; 290 pounds; 35 NM.
B—10.0 minutes; 165 pounds; 30 NM.
C—11.5 minutes; 165 pounds; 30 NM.

1. *Enter FAA Figure 18 at the bottom left-hand side at -20°C OAT and proceed upward to the line representing 16,000-foot cruise altitude.*
2. *From the point of intersection on the "pressure altitude" lines, draw a horizontal line to the line which represents an aircraft weight of 16,600 pounds.*
3. *From the point of intersection in the "weight" portion of the graph, draw a line down to the bottom of the chart to read the time to climb of 11.5 minutes.*
4. *Continue down to the fuel to climb line to read 190 pounds fuel burned.*
5. *Continue down to the distance-to-climb line to read 32 NM.*
6. *Repeat steps 1 through 5 using an OAT of +10°C OAT and 2,000 feet pressure altitude, and find the time to climb 1.5 minutes, fuel burn 25 pounds, and distance 2 NM.*
7. *Subtract the results of the airport altitudes from the cruise altitude results. Therefore, from 2,000 feet to 16,000 feet, it will take 10 minutes (11.5 – 1.5), 165 pounds of fuel (190 – 25), and 30 NM (32 – 2).*

(PLT012) — FAA-H-8083-25

Answers

8476 [B]	8477 [A]	8478 [C]	9904 [B]

ADX

9905. (Refer to Figures 15 and 18.) What are the time, fuel, and distance from the start of climb to cruise altitude for Operating Conditions BE-22?

A—12.0 minutes; 220 pounds; 40 NM.
B—11.0 minutes; 185 pounds; 37 NM.
C—10.5 minutes; 175 pounds; 32 NM.

1. *Enter FAA Figure 18 at the bottom left-hand side at -15°C OAT (accounting for the extended ice vanes) and proceed upward to the line representing 18,000-foot cruise altitude.*
2. *From the point of intersection on the "pressure altitude" lines, draw a horizontal line to the line which represents an aircraft weight of 14,000 pounds.*
3. *From the point of intersection in the "weight" portion of the graph, draw a line down to the bottom of the chart to read the time to climb of 12 minutes.*
4. *Continue down to the fuel-to-climb line to read 200 pounds fuel burned.*
5. *Continue down to the distance-to-climb line to read 37.5 NM.*
6. *Repeat steps 1 through 5 using an OAT of +10°C OAT and 1,000 feet pressure altitude, and find the time to climb 1 minute, fuel burn 15 pounds, and distance 0.5 NM.*
7. *Subtract the results of the airport altitudes from the cruise altitude results. Therefore, from 1,000 feet to 18,000 feet, it will take 11 minutes (12 – 1), 185 pounds of fuel (200 – 15), and 37 NM (37.5 – 0.5).*

(PLT012) — FAA-H-8083-25

ADX

9906. (Refer to Figures 15 and 18.) What are the time, fuel, and distance from the start of climb to cruise altitude for Operating Conditions BE-23?

A—13.0 minutes; 180 pounds; 35 NM.
B—14.0 minutes; 210 pounds; 40 NM.
C—15.0 minutes; 240 pounds; 46 NM.

1. *Enter FAA Figure 18 at the bottom left-hand side at ISA and proceed upward to the line representing 20,000-foot cruise altitude.*
2. *From the point of intersection on the "pressure altitude" lines, draw a horizontal line to the line which represents an aircraft weight of 15,000 pounds.*
3. *From the point of intersection in the "weight" portion of the graph, draw a line down to the bottom of the chart to read the time to climb of 15 minutes.*
4. *Continue down to the fuel-to-climb line to read 235 pounds fuel burned.*
5. *Continue down to the distance-to-climb line to read 44 NM.*
6. *Repeat steps 1 through 5 using an OAT of +20°C OAT and 3,000 feet pressure altitude, and find the time to climb 1 minutes, fuel burn 25 pounds, and distance 4 NM.*
7. *Subtract the results of the airport altitudes from the cruise altitude results. Therefore, from 3,000 feet to 20,000 feet, it will take 14 minutes (15–1), 210 pounds of fuel (235–25), and 40 NM (44–4).*

(PLT012) — FAA-H-8083-25

ADX

8482. (Refer to Figures 15 and 18.) What are the time, fuel, and distance from the start of climb to cruise altitude for Operating Conditions BE-24?

A—12.0 minutes; 220 pounds; 45 NM.
B—9.0 minutes; 185 pounds; 38 NM.
C—10.0 minutes; 170 pounds; 30 NM.

1. *Enter FAA Figure 18 at the bottom left-hand side at 0°C OAT and proceed upward to the line representing 14,000-foot cruise altitude.*
2. *From the point of intersection on the "pressure altitude" lines, draw a horizontal line to the line which represents an aircraft weight of 16,000 pounds.*
3. *From the point of intersection in the "weight" portion of the graph, draw a line down to the bottom of the chart to read the time to climb of 13 minutes.*
4. *Continue down to the fuel-to-climb line to read 210 pounds fuel burned.*
5. *Continue down to the distance-to-climb line to read 38 NM.*
6. *Repeat steps 1 through 5 using an OAT of +25°C OAT and 4,000 feet pressure altitude, and find the time to climb 3 minutes, fuel burn 60 pounds, and distance 8 NM.*
7. *Subtract the results of the airport altitudes from the cruise altitude results. Therefore, from 4,000 feet to 14,000 feet, it will take 10 minutes (13–3), 150 pounds of fuel (210–60), and 30 NM (38–8).*

(PLT004) — FAA-H-8083-25

Answers

9905 [B] 9906 [B] 8482 [C]

ADX

8483. (Refer to Figures 15 and 18.) What are the time, fuel, and distance from the start of climb to cruise altitude for Operating Conditions BE-25?

A—11.5 minutes; 170 pounds; 31 NM.
B—8.0 minutes; 270 pounds; 28 NM.
C—12.5 minutes; 195 pounds; 38 NM.

1. *Enter FAA Figure 18 at the bottom left-hand side at -30°C OAT (accounting for the extended ice vanes) and proceed upward to the line representing 22,000-foot cruise altitude.*
2. *From the point of intersection on the "pressure altitude" lines, draw a horizontal line to the line which represents an aircraft weight of 14,000 pounds.*
3. *From the point of intersection in the "weight" portion of the graph, draw a line down to the bottom of the chart to read the time to climb of 14.5 minutes.*
4. *Continue down to the fuel-to-climb line to read 235 pounds fuel burned.*
5. *Continue down to the distance-to-climb line to read 44 NM.*
6. *Repeat steps 1 through 5 using an OAT of 0°C OAT and 5,000 feet pressure altitude, and find the time to climb 2 minutes, fuel burn 40 pounds, and distance 6 NM.*
7. *Subtract the results of the airport altitudes from the cruise altitude results. Therefore, from 5,000 feet to 22,000 feet, it will take 12.5 minutes (14.5 – 2), 195 pounds of fuel (235 – 40), and 38 NM (44 – 6).*

(PLT012) — FAA-H-8083-25

ADX

8484. (Refer to Figures 19 and 20.) At what altitude is the service ceiling with one engine inoperative for Operating Conditions BE-26?

A—13,000 feet.
B—14,200 feet.
C—13,600 feet.

1. *Enter FAA Figure 20 at the bottom left-hand side (for bleed air on) at -8°C OAT and proceed upward to the line representing 15,500 pounds.*
2. *From the point of intersection in the "weight" portion of the graph, draw a line to the edge of the chart to determine a pressure altitude service ceiling of 13,000 feet with one engine inoperative.*

(PLT065) — FAA-H-8083-25

ADX

8485. (Refer to Figures 19 and 20.) Which statement is true regarding performance with one engine inoperative for Operating Conditions BE-27?

A—Climb rate at the MEA is more than 50 ft/min.
B—Service ceiling is below the MEA.
C—Bleed air OFF improves service ceiling by 3,000 feet.

1. *Enter FAA Figure 20 at the bottom left-hand side (for bleed air on) at +30°C OAT and proceed upward to the line representing 16,600 pounds.*
2. *From the point of intersection in the "weight" portion of the graph, draw a line to the edge of the chart to determine a pressure altitude service ceiling of 5,000 feet with one engine inoperative.*
3. *Therefore, the 5,000-foot service ceiling is below the MEA of 5,500 feet.*

(PLT065) — FAA-H-8083-25

ADX

8486. (Refer to Figures 19 and 20.) At what altitude is the service ceiling with one engine inoperative for Operating Conditions BE-28?

A—1,500 feet above the MEA.
B—10,400 feet.
C—11,800 feet.

1. *Enter FAA Figure 20 at the bottom right-hand side (for bleed air off) at +5°C OAT and proceed upward to the line representing 16,000 pounds.*
2. *From the point of intersection in the "weight" portion of the graph, draw a line to the edge of the chart to determine a pressure altitude service ceiling of 11,800 feet with one engine inoperative.*
3. *11,800 feet is 2,800 feet above the 9,000-foot MEA.*

(PLT065) — FAA-H-8083-25

Answers

8483 [C] 8484 [A] 8485 [B] 8486 [C]

ADX

8487. (Refer to Figures 19 and 20.) Which statement is true regarding performance with one engine inoperative for Operating Conditions BE-29?

A—Service ceiling is more than 100 feet above the MEA.
B—Bleed air must be OFF to obtain a rate of climb of 50 ft/min at the MEA.
C—Climb is not possible at the MEA.

1. *Enter FAA Figure 20 at the bottom left-hand side (for bleed air on) at +18°C OAT and proceed upward to the line representing 16,300 pounds.*
2. *From the point of intersection in the "weight" portion of the graph, draw a line to the edge of the chart to determine a pressure altitude service ceiling of 7,700 feet with one engine inoperative.*
3. *Therefore, the 7,700-foot service ceiling is above the MEA of 7,000 feet by more than 100 feet.*

(PLT065) — FAA-H-8083-25

ADX

8488. (Refer to Figures 19 and 20.) At what altitude is the service ceiling with one engine inoperative for Operating Conditions BE-30?

A—9,600 feet.
B—13,200 feet.
C—2,100 feet above the MEA.

1. *Enter FAA Figure 20 at the bottom right-hand side (for bleed air off) at +22°C OAT and proceed upward to the line representing 14,500 pounds.*
2. *From the point of intersection in the "weight" portion of the graph, draw a line to the edge of the chart to determine a pressure altitude service ceiling of 11,600 feet with one engine inoperative.*
3. *Therefore, the 11,600-foot service ceiling is above the MEA of 9,500 feet.*

(PLT065) — FAA-H-8083-25

ADX

8489. (Refer to Figures 21, 22, 23, 24, and 25.) What is the en route time of the cruise leg for Operating Conditions BE-31?

A—1 hour 11 minutes.
B—1 hour 17 minutes.
C—1 hour 19 minutes.

Temperature = ISA +10°C
TAS = 228 knots
GS = 216.0 knots
Time = 1 hour 17 minutes 47 seconds

(PLT012) — FAA-H-8083-25

ADX

8490. (Refer to Figures 21, 22, 23, 24, and 25.) What is the en route time of the cruise leg for Operating Conditions BE-32?

A—1 hour 13 minutes.
B—1 hour 15 minutes.
C—1 hour 20 minutes.

Temperature = -19°C
TAS = 252 knots
GS = 261.8 knots
Time = 1 hour 13 minutes 20 seconds

(PLT012) — FAA-H-8083-25

ADX

8491. (Refer to Figures 21, 22, 23, 24, and 25.) What is the en route time of the cruise leg for Operating Conditions BE-33?

A—1 hour 50 minutes.
B—1 hour 36 minutes.
C—1 hour 46 minutes.

Temperature = ISA -10°C
TAS = 256.5 knots
GS = 225.2 knots
Time = 1 hour 46 minutes 33 seconds

(PLT012) — FAA-H-8083-25

ADX

8492. (Refer to Figures 21, 22, 23, 24, and 25.) What is the en route time of the cruise leg for Operating Conditions BE-34?

A—1 hour 7 minutes.
B—1 hour 2 minutes.
C—1 hour 12 minutes.

Temperature = ISA
TAS = 228 knots
GS = 208 knots
Time = 1 hour 06 minutes 15 seconds

(PLT012) — FAA-H-8083-25

Answers

8487 [A] 8488 [C] 8489 [B] 8490 [A] 8491 [C] 8492 [A]

ADX
8493. (Refer to Figures 21, 22, 23, 24, and 25.) What is the en route time of the cruise leg for Operating Conditions BE-35?

A—1 hour 6 minutes.
B—1 hour 8 minutes.
C—1 hour 10 minutes.

Temperature = ISA +10°C
TAS = 253 knots
GS = 252.4 knots
Time = 1 hour 11 minutes 19 seconds

(PLT012) — FAA-H-8083-25

ADX
8494. (Refer to Figures 21, 22, 23, 24, and 25.) What is the fuel consumption during the cruise leg for Operating Conditions BE-31?

A—812 pounds.
B—749 pounds.
C—870 pounds.

Temperature = ISA +10°C
Time = 1 hour 17 minutes (see Question 8489)
Fuel flow = 633
Fuel burn = 812.3 pounds

(PLT012) — FAA-H-8083-25

ADX
8495. (Refer to Figures 21, 22, 23, 24, and 25.) What is the fuel consumption during the cruise leg for Operating Conditions BE-32?

A—1,028 pounds.
B—896 pounds.
C—977 pounds.

Temperature = ISA
Time = 1 hour 13 minutes (see Question 8490)
Fuel flow = 803
Fuel burn = 977.0 pounds

(PLT012) — FAA-H-8083-25

ADX
8496. (Refer to Figures 21, 22, 23, 24, and 25.) What is the fuel consumption during the cruise leg for Operating Conditions BE-33?

A—1,165 pounds.
B—1,373 pounds.
C—976 pounds.

Temperature = ISA -10°C
Time = 1 hour 46 minutes (see Question 8491)
Fuel flow = 777
Fuel burn = 1,372.7 pounds

(PLT012) — FAA-H-8083-25

ADX
8497. (Refer to Figures 21, 22, 23, 24, and 25.) What is the fuel consumption during the cruise leg for Operating Conditions BE-34?

A—668 pounds.
B—718 pounds.
C—737 pounds.

Temperature = ISA
Time = 1 hour 06 minutes (see Question 8492)
Fuel flow = 653
Fuel burn = 718.3 pounds

(PLT012) — FAA-H-8083-25

ADX
8498. (Refer to Figures 21, 23, 24, and 25.) What is the fuel consumption during the cruise leg for Operating Conditions BE-35?

A—900 pounds.
B—1,030 pounds.
C—954 pounds.

Temperature = ISA +10°C
Time = 1 hour 10 minutes (see Question 8493)
Fuel flow = 818
Fuel burn = 954.3 pounds

(PLT012) — FAA-H-8083-25

Answers

8493 [C]	8494 [A]	8495 [C]	8496 [B]	8497 [B]	8498 [C]

ADX

8499. (Refer to Figure 26.) What are the time and distance to descend from 18,000 feet to 2,500 feet?

A—10.3 minutes, 39 NM.
B—9.8 minutes, 33 NM.
C—10.0 minutes, 36 NM.

Enter FAA Figure 26 from initial pressure altitude on the left side of the graph. Proceed to heavy reference line, then drop to minutes, pounds and/or distance scales as needed. Repeat this process with the final altitude.

	Time	***NM***
Descent to SL	*12.0*	*45*
Field alt.	*– 1.5*	*– 5*
Descent	*10.5*	*40*

(PLT012) — FAA-H-8083-25

ADX

8500. (Refer to Figure 26.) What are the distance and fuel consumption to descend from 22,000 feet to 4,500 feet?

A—44 NAM, 117 pounds.
B—48 NAM, 112 pounds.
C—56 NAM, 125 pounds.

Enter FAA Figure 26 from initial pressure altitude on the left side of the graph. Proceed to heavy reference line, then drop to minutes, pounds and/or distance scales as needed. Repeat this process with the final altitude.

	NM	***Fuel***
Descent to SL	*58*	*142*
Field alt.	*– 10*	*– 30*
Descent	*48*	*112*

(PLT012) — FAA-H-8083-25

ADX

8501. (Refer to Figure 26.) What are the time and distance to descend from 16,500 feet to 3,500 feet?

A—9.3 minutes, 37 NAM.
B—9.1 minutes, 35 NAM.
C—8.7 minutes, 33 NAM.

Enter FAA Figure 26 from initial pressure altitude on the left side of the graph. Proceed to heavy reference line, then drop to minutes, pounds and/or distance scales as needed. Repeat this process with the final altitude.

	Time	***NM***
Descent to SL	*11.1*	*41*
Field alt.	*– 2.4*	*– 8*
Descent	*8.7*	*33*

(PLT045) — FAA-H-8083-25

ADX

8502. (Refer to Figure 26.) What are the distance and fuel consumption to descend from 13,500 feet to 1,500 feet?

A—30 NAM, 87 pounds.
B—29 NAM, 80 pounds.
C—38 NAM, 100 pounds.

Enter FAA Figure 26 from initial pressure altitude on the left side of the graph. Proceed to heavy reference line, then drop to minutes, pounds and/or distance scales as needed. Repeat this process with the final altitude.

	NM	***Fuel***
Descent to SL	*32.5*	*90*
Field alt.	*– 3.5*	*– 10*
Descent	*29*	*80*

(PLT045) — FAA-H-8083-25

ADX

8503. (Refer to Figure 26.) What are the time and distance to descend from 23,000 feet to 600 feet with an average 15-knot headwind?

A—14.2 minutes, 50 NAM.
B—14.6 minutes, 56 NAM.
C—14.9 minutes, 59 NAM.

Enter FAA Figure 26 from initial pressure altitude on the left side of the graph. Proceed to heavy reference line, then drop to minutes, pounds and/or distance scales as needed. Repeat this process with the final altitude.

	Time	***NM***
Descent to SL	*15.4*	*62*
Field alt.	*– .5*	*– 2*
Descent	*14.9*	*60*

Note: The answers are in NM so no wind correction is necessary.

(PLT045) — FAA-H-8083-25

Answers

8499 [A] 8500 [B] 8501 [C] 8502 [B] 8503 [C]

ADX
8504. (Refer to Figures 27 and 28.) What is the landing distance over a 50-foot obstacle for Operating Conditions B-36?

A—1,900 feet.
B—1,625 feet.
C—950 feet.

1. *Enter FAA Figure 28 at the bottom left-hand side at +30°C OAT and proceed upward to the line representing sea level (SL) pressure altitude.*
2. *From the point of intersection on the "pressure altitude" lines, draw a horizontal line to the reference line, then parallel the line which represents an aircraft weight of 16,000 pounds.*
3. *From the point of intersection in the "weight" portion of the graph, draw a horizontal line to the next reference line (wind component), then parallel the line until intersecting with the 20-knot headwind.*
4. *From the point of intersection on the "wind" portion of the graph draw a horizontal line to the next reference line (0-foot obstacle height), then parallel the line required to clear a 50-foot obstacle.*
5. *The distance required is 1,900 feet.*

(PLT008) — FAA-H-8083-25

ADX
9907. (Refer to Figures 27 and 28.) What are the approach speed and ground roll when landing under Operating Conditions B-36?

A—113 knots and 950 feet.
B—113 knots and 1,950 feet.
C—112 knots and 900 feet.

1. *Enter FAA Figure 28 at the bottom left-hand side at +30°C OAT and proceed upward to the line representing sea level (SL) pressure altitude.*
2. *From the point of intersection on the "pressure altitude" lines, draw a horizontal line to the reference line, then parallel the line which represents an aircraft weight of 16,000 pounds.*
3. *From the point of intersection in the "weight" portion of the graph, draw a horizontal line to the next reference line (wind component), then parallel the line until intersecting with the 20-knot headwind.*
4. *From the point of intersection on the "wind" portion of the graph draw a horizontal line to the edge of the chart to find a ground roll of 950 feet.*
5. *The approach speed is found using the table at the top of figure. Interpolate between 16,100 and 14,000 to find the approach speed for 16,000 pounds at 113 knots.*

(PLT008) — FAA-H-8083-25

ADX
9908. (Refer to Figures 27 and 28.) What is the remaining runway length when stopped after landing over a 50-foot obstacle for Operating Conditions B-37?

A—2,500 feet.
B—2,000 feet.
C—2,600 feet.

1. *Enter FAA Figure 28 at the bottom left-hand side at +16°C OAT and proceed upward to the line representing 1,000 feet pressure altitude.*
2. *From the point of intersection on the "pressure altitude" lines, draw a horizontal line to the reference line, then parallel the line which represents an aircraft weight of 14,500 pounds.*
3. *From the point of intersection in the "weight" portion of the graph, draw a horizontal line to the next reference line (wind component), then parallel the line until intersecting with the 10-knot tailwind.*
4. *From the point of intersection on the "wind" portion of the graph draw a horizontal line to the next reference line (0-foot obstacle height), then parallel the line required to clear a 50-foot obstacle.*
5. *The distance required is 2,500 feet.*
6. *The remaining runway length when stopped is the runway distance minus the distance required, which is 2,000 feet (4,500 – 2,500).*

(PLT008) — FAA-H-8083-25

Answers

8504 [A]   9907 [A]   9908 [B]

ADX

9909. (Refer to Figures 27 and 28.) What are the approach speed and ground roll when landing under Operating Conditions B-37?

A—108 knots and 1,400 feet.
B—109 knots and 900 feet.
C—107 knots and 1,350 feet.

1. *Enter FAA Figure 28 at the bottom left-hand side at +16°C OAT and proceed upward to the line representing 1,000 feet pressure altitude.*
2. *From the point of intersection on the "pressure altitude" lines, draw a horizontal line to the reference line, then parallel the line which represents an aircraft weight of 14,500 pounds.*
3. *From the point of intersection in the "weight" portion of the graph, draw a horizontal line to the next reference line (wind component), then parallel the line until intersecting with the 10-knot tailwind.*
4. *From the point of intersection on the "wind" portion of the graph draw a horizontal line to the edge of the chart to find a ground roll of 1,400 feet.*
5. *The approach speed is found using the table at the top of figure. Interpolate between 16,100 and 14,000 to find the approach speed for 14,500 pounds at 108 knots.*

(PLT008) — FAA-H-8083-25

ADX

9910. (Refer to Figures 27 and 28.) What is the landing distance over a 50-foot obstacle for Operating Conditions B-38?

A—1,850 feet.
B—1,700 feet.
C—1,800 feet.

1. *Enter FAA Figure 28 at the bottom left-hand side at 0°C OAT and proceed upward to the line representing 2,000 feet pressure altitude.*
2. *From the point of intersection on the "pressure altitude" lines, draw a horizontal line to the reference line, then parallel the line which represents an aircraft weight of 13,500 pounds.*
3. *From the point of intersection in the "weight" portion of the graph, draw a horizontal line to the next reference line (wind component), then parallel the line until intersecting with the 15-knot headwind.*
4. *From the point of intersection on the "wind" portion of the graph draw a horizontal line to the next reference line (0-foot obstacle height), then parallel the line required to clear a 50-foot obstacle.*
5. *The distance required is 1,700 feet.*

(PLT008) — FAA-H-8083-25

ADX

9911. (Refer to Figures 27 and 28.) What is the total runway used when touchdown is at the 1,000 foot marker for Operating Conditions B-38?

A—2,000 feet.
B—1,700 feet.
C—1,800 feet.

1. *Enter FAA Figure 28 at the bottom left-hand side at 0°C OAT and proceed upward to the line representing 2,000 feet pressure altitude.*
2. *From the point of intersection on the "pressure altitude" lines, draw a horizontal line to the reference line, then parallel the line which represents an aircraft weight of 13,500 pounds.*
3. *From the point of intersection in the "weight" portion of the graph, draw a horizontal line to the next reference line (wind component), then parallel the line until intersecting with the 15-knot headwind.*
4. *From the point of intersection on the "wind" portion of the graph draw a horizontal line to the edge of the chart to find the ground roll distance is 800 feet.*
5. *The total runway used is the distance from the threshold of the runway to the touchdown point, plus the ground roll distance, which is 1,800 feet (1,000 + 800).*

(PLT008) — FAA-H-8083-25

Answers

9909 [A] 9910 [B] 9911 [C]

ADX

9912. (Refer to Figures 27 and 28.) What is the remaining runway length when stopped after landing over a 50-foot obstacle for Operating Conditions B-39?

A—2,300 feet.
B—2,400 feet.
C—2,500 feet.

1. *Enter FAA Figure 28 at the bottom left-hand side at +20°C OAT and proceed upward to the line representing 4,000 feet pressure altitude.*
2. *From the point of intersection on the "pressure altitude" lines, draw a horizontal line to the reference line, then parallel the line which represents an aircraft weight of 15,000 pounds.*
3. *From the point of intersection in the "weight" portion of the graph, draw a horizontal line to the next reference line (wind component), then parallel the line until intersecting with the 5-knot tailwind.*
4. *From the point of intersection on the "wind" portion of the graph draw a horizontal line to the next reference line (0-foot obstacle height), then parallel the line required to clear a 50-foot obstacle, which is 2,500 feet.*
5. *The remaining runway length when stopped is the runway length minus the landing distance, which is 2,500 feet (5,000 – 2,500).*

(PLT008) — FAA-H-8083-25

ADX

9913. (Refer to Figures 27 and 28.) What are the approach speed and ground roll when landing under Operating Conditions B-39?

A—111 knots and 1,550 feet.
B—110 knots and 1,400 feet.
C—109 knots and 1,300 feet.

1. *Enter FAA Figure 28 at the bottom left-hand side at +20°C OAT and proceed upward to the line representing 4,000 feet pressure altitude.*
2. *From the point of intersection on the "pressure altitude" lines, draw a horizontal line to the reference line, then parallel the line which represents an aircraft weight of 15,000 pounds.*
3. *From the point of intersection in the "weight" portion of the graph, draw a horizontal line to the next reference line (wind component), then parallel the line until intersecting with the 5-knot tailwind.*
4. *From the point of intersection on the "wind" portion of the graph draw a horizontal line to the edge of the chart to find a ground roll of 1,400 feet.*
5. *The approach speed is found using the table at the top of figure. Interpolate between 16,100 and 14,000 to find the approach speed for 15,000 pounds at 110 knots.*

(PLT008) — FAA-H-8083-25

ADX

9914. (Refer to Figures 27 and 28.) What is the landing distance over a 50-foot obstacle for Operating Conditions B-40?

A—1,500 feet.
B—1,750 feet.
C—1,650 feet.

1. *Enter FAA Figure 28 at the ISA line and proceed to the line representing 5,000 feet pressure altitude.*
2. *From the point of intersection on the "pressure altitude" lines, draw a horizontal line to the reference line, then parallel the line which represents an aircraft weight of 12,500 pounds.*
3. *From the point of intersection in the "weight" portion of the graph, draw a horizontal line to the next reference line (wind component), then parallel the line until intersecting with the 25-knot headwind.*
4. *From the point of intersection on the "wind" portion of the graph draw a horizontal line to the next reference line (0-foot obstacle height), then parallel the line required to clear a 50-foot obstacle, which is 1,650 feet.*

(PLT008) — FAA-H-8083-25

Answers

9912 [C] 9913 [B] 9914 [C]

Helicopter Performance

RTC

8533. (Refer to Figure 36.) Given the following conditions, what is the maximum allowable measured gas temperature (MGT) during the power assurance check?

Engine torque .... 57 percent
Pressure altitude.. 2,500 ft
Temperature (OAT) .... +5°C

A—810°C.
B—815°C.
C—828°C.

Follow the example in the inset, upper left corner of FAA Figure 36. Begin at 57% torque, draw a line with a straight-edge parallel to the bold line through pressure altitude. From the point where your line intersects with 2,500 feet, draw a second line through the OAT lines. From the intersection of that line and +5°C OAT, draw a perpendicular line to maximum allowable MGT. Read the correct answer of 828°C. (PLT009) — FAA-H-8083-21

RTC

8534. (Refer to Figure 36.) Given the following conditions, what is the maximum allowable measured gas temperature (MGT) during the power assurance check?

Engine torque .... 49 percent
Pressure altitude.. 5,500 ft
Temperature (OAT) .... +25°C

A—870°C.
B—855°C.
C—880°C.

Follow the example in the inset, upper left corner FAA Figure 36. Begin at 49% torque, draw a line with a straight-edge parallel to the bold line through pressure altitude. From the point where your line intersects with 5,500 feet, draw a second line through the OAT lines. From the intersection of that line and +25°C OAT, draw a perpendicular line to maximum allowable MGT. Read the correct answer of 870°C. (PLT009) — FAA-H-8083-21

RTC

8535. (Refer to Figure 36.) Given the following conditions, what is the maximum allowable measured gas temperature (MGT) during the power assurance check?

Engine torque .... 54 percent
Pressure altitude... 500 ft
Temperature (OAT) .... +25°C

A—840°C.
B—830°C.
C—820°C.

Follow the example in the inset, upper left corner FAA Figure 36. Begin at 54% torque, draw a line with a straight-edge parallel to the bold line through pressure altitude. From the point where your line intersects with 500 feet, draw a second line through the OAT lines. From the intersection of that line and +25°C OAT, draw a perpendicular line to maximum allowable MGT. Read the correct answer of 840°C. (PLT009) — FAA-H-8083-21

RTC

8536. (Refer to Figure 36.) Given the following conditions, what is the maximum allowable measured gas temperature (MGT) during the power assurance check?

Engine torque .... 43 percent
Pressure altitude.. 9,000 ft
Temperature (OAT) .... -15°C

A—782°C.
B—768°C.
C—750°C.

Follow the example in the inset, upper left corner FAA Figure 36. Begin at 43% torque, draw a line with a straight-edge parallel to the bold line through pressure altitude. From the point where your line intersects with 9,000 feet, draw a second line through the OAT lines. From the intersection of that line and -15°C OAT, draw a perpendicular line to maximum allowable MGT. Read the correct answer of 768°C. (PLT009) — FAA-H-8083-21

Answers

8533 [C] 8534 [A] 8535 [A] 8536 [B]

RTC

8537. (Refer to Figure 36.) Given the following conditions, what is the maximum allowable measured gas temperature (MGT) during the power assurance check?

Engine torque .... 52 percent
Pressure altitude.. 1,500 ft
Temperature (OAT)... +35°C

A—880°C.
B—865°C.
C—872°C.

Follow the example in the inset, upper left corner FAA Figure 36. Begin at 52% torque, draw a line with a straight-edge parallel to the bold line through pressure altitude. From the point where your line intersects with 1,500 feet, draw a second line through the OAT lines. From the intersection of that line and +35°C OAT, draw a perpendicular line to maximum allowable MGT. Read the correct answer of 865°C. (PLT009) — FAA-H-8083-21

RTC

8538. (Refer to Figure 37.) What is the maximum gross weight for hovering in ground effect at 3,000 feet pressure altitude and +25°C?

A—17,300 pounds.
B—14,700 pounds.
C—16,600 pounds.

To determine the maximum gross weight, begin in the lower left corner of FAA Figure 37 at +25°C OAT. With a straight-edge, draw a line vertically to intersect 3,000 feet pressure altitude. Draw a second perpendicular line from that point to the right to intersect +25°C OAT. Draw a third line from this intersection vertically to gross weight. Read the correct answer of 17,300 pounds. (PLT048) — FAA-H-8083-21

RTC

8539. (Refer to Figure 37.) What is the maximum gross weight for hovering in ground effect at 6,000 feet pressure altitude and +15°C?

A—17,200 pounds.
B—16,600 pounds.
C—14,200 pounds.

To determine the maximum gross weight, begin in the lower left corner of FAA Figure 37 at +15°C OAT. With a straight-edge, draw a line vertically to intersect 6,000 feet pressure altitude. Draw a second perpendicular line from that point to the right to intersect +15°C OAT. Draw a third line from this intersection vertically to gross weight. Read the correct answer of 16,600 pounds. (PLT048) — FAA-H-8083-21

RTC

8540. (Refer to Figure 37.) What is the maximum gross weight for hovering in ground effect at 7,000 feet pressure altitude and +35°C?

A—13,500 pounds.
B—14,700 pounds.
C—12,100 pounds.

To determine the maximum gross weight, begin in the lower left corner of FAA Figure 37 at +35°C OAT. With a straight-edge, draw a line vertically to intersect 7,000 feet pressure altitude. Draw a second perpendicular line from that point to the right to intersect +35°C OAT. Draw a third line from this intersection vertically to gross weight. Read the correct answer of 13,500 pounds. (PLT048) — FAA-H-8083-21

RTC

8541. (Refer to Figure 37.) What is the maximum gross weight for hovering in ground effect at 4,500 feet pressure altitude and +20°C?

A—14,500 pounds.
B—16,500 pounds.
C—17,000 pounds.

To determine the maximum gross weight, begin in the lower left corner of FAA Figure 37 at +20°C OAT. With a straight-edge, draw a line vertically to intersect 4,500 feet pressure altitude. Draw a second perpendicular line from that point to the right to intersect +20°C OAT. Draw a third line from this intersection vertically to gross weight. Read the correct answer of 17,000 pounds. (PLT048) — FAA-H-8083-21

Answers

8537 [B]   8538 [A]   8539 [B]   8540 [A]   8541 [C]

RTC

8542. (Refer to Figure 37.) What is the maximum gross weight for hovering in ground effect at 2,500 feet pressure altitude and +35°C?

A—16,200 pounds.
B—16,600 pounds.
C—14,600 pounds.

To determine the maximum gross weight, begin in the lower left corner of FAA Figure 37 at +35°C OAT. With a straight-edge, draw a line vertically to intersect 2,500 feet pressure altitude. Draw a second perpendicular line from that point to the right to intersect +35°C OAT. Draw a third line from this intersection vertically to gross weight. Read the correct answer of 16,200 pounds. (PLT048) — FAA-H-8083-21

RTC

8543. (Refer to Figure 38.) What is the maximum gross weight for hovering out of ground effect at 3,000 feet pressure altitude and +30°C?

A—17,500 pounds.
B—14,300 pounds.
C—13,400 pounds.

To determine the maximum gross weight, begin in the lower left corner of FAA Figure 38 at +30°C OAT. With a straight-edge, draw a line vertically to intersect 3,000 feet pressure altitude. Draw a second perpendicular line from that point to the right to intersect +30°C OAT. Draw a third line from this intersection vertically to gross weight. Read the correct answer of 14,300 pounds. (PLT048) — FAA-H-8083-21

RTC

8544. (Refer to Figure 38.) What is the maximum gross weight for hovering out of ground effect at 6,000 feet pressure altitude and +15°C?

A—16,800 pounds.
B—13,500 pounds.
C—14,400 pounds.

To determine the maximum gross weight, begin in the lower left corner of FAA Figure 38 at +15°C OAT. With a straight-edge, draw a line vertically to intersect 6,000 feet pressure altitude. Draw a second perpendicular line from that point to the right to intersect +15°C OAT. Draw a third line from this intersection vertically to gross weight. Read the correct answer of 14,400 pounds. (PLT048) — FAA-H-8083-21

RTC

8545. (Refer to Figure 38.) What is the maximum gross weight for hovering out of ground effect at 7,000 feet pressure altitude and +35°C?

A—14,000 pounds.
B—11,600 pounds.
C—12,500 pounds.

To determine the maximum gross weight, begin in the lower left corner of FAA Figure 38 at +35°C OAT. With a straight-edge, draw a line vertically to intersect 7,000 feet pressure altitude. Draw a second perpendicular line from that point to the right to intersect +35°C OAT. Draw a third line from this intersection vertically to gross weight. Read the correct answer of 11,600 pounds. (PLT048) — FAA-H-8083-21

RTC

8546. (Refer to Figure 38.) What is the maximum gross weight for hovering out of ground effect at 4,500 feet pressure altitude and +20°C?

A—14,500 pounds.
B—14,000 pounds.
C—17,000 pounds.

To determine the maximum gross weight, begin in the lower left corner of FAA Figure 38 at +20°C OAT. With a straight-edge, draw a line vertically to intersect 4,500 feet pressure altitude. Draw a second perpendicular line from that point to the right to intersect +20°C OAT. Draw a third line from this intersection vertically to gross weight. Read the correct answer of 14,500 pounds. (PLT048) — FAA-H-8083-21

RTC

8547. (Refer to Figure 38.) What is the maximum gross weight for hovering out of ground effect at 2,500 feet pressure altitude and +30°C?

A—17,400 pounds.
B—15,000 pounds.
C—14,500 pounds.

To determine the maximum gross weight, begin in the lower left corner of FAA Figure 38 at +30°C OAT. With a straight-edge, draw a line vertically to intersect 2,500 feet pressure altitude. Draw a second perpendicular line from that point to the right to intersect +30°C OAT. Draw a third line from this intersection vertically to gross weight. Read the correct answer of 14,500 pounds. (PLT048) — FAA-H-8083-21

Answers

8542 [A]	8543 [B]	8544 [C]	8545 [B]	8546 [A]	8547 [C]

RTC
8548. (Refer to Figure 39.) What is the takeoff distance over a 50-foot obstacle?

Pressure altitude..3,500 ft
Temperature (OAT)..+20°C
Gross weight ....15,000 lb

A—1,070 feet.
B—1,020 feet.
C—1,100 feet.

To determine the takeoff distance, begin at +20°C OAT in the lower left corner of FAA Figure 39. Draw a vertical line upward to intersect 3,500 feet pressure altitude. From that point, draw a perpendicular line to 15,000 pounds gross weight. From this point, draw a vertical line downward to takeoff distance. Read the distance of 1,070 feet. (PLT011) — FAA-H-8083-21

RTC
8549. (Refer to Figure 39.) What is the takeoff distance over a 50-foot obstacle?

Pressure altitude..5,000 ft
Temperature (OAT)..-10°C
Gross weight ....11,000 lb

A—1,000 feet.
B—920 feet.
C—870 feet.

To determine the takeoff distance, begin at -10°C OAT in the lower left corner of FAA Figure 39. Draw a vertical line upward to intersect 5,000 feet pressure altitude. From that point, draw a perpendicular line to 11,000 pounds gross weight. From this point, draw a vertical line downward to takeoff distance. Read the distance of 870 feet. (PLT011) — FAA-H-8083-21

RTC
8550. (Refer to Figure 39.) What is the takeoff distance over a 50-foot obstacle?

Pressure altitude..6,500 ft
Temperature (OAT)..0°C
Gross weight ....13,500 lb

A—1,500 feet.
B—1,050 feet.
C—1,100 feet.

To determine the takeoff distance, begin at +0°C OAT in the lower left corner of FAA Figure 39. Draw a vertical line upward to intersect 6,500 feet pressure altitude. From that point, draw a perpendicular line to 13,500 pounds gross weight. From this point, draw a vertical line downward to takeoff distance. Read the distance of 1,050 feet. (PLT011) — FAA-H-8083-21

RTC
8551. (Refer to Figure 39.) What is the takeoff distance over a 50-foot obstacle?

Pressure altitude..9,000 ft
Temperature (OAT)..+20°C
Gross weight ....15,000 lb

A—1,300 feet.
B—1,350 feet.
C—1,250 feet.

To determine the takeoff distance, begin at +20°C OAT in the lower left corner of FAA Figure 39. Draw a vertical line upward to intersect 9,000 feet pressure altitude. From that point, draw a perpendicular line to 15,000 pounds gross weight. From this point, draw a vertical line downward to takeoff distance. Read the distance of 1,350 feet. (PLT011) — FAA-H-8083-21

RTC
8552. (Refer to Figure 39.) What is the takeoff distance over a 50-foot obstacle?

Pressure altitude..-1,000 ft
Temperature (OAT)..+25°C
Gross weight ....14,000 lb

A—1,000 feet.
B—900 feet.
C—950 feet.

To determine the takeoff distance, begin at +25°C OAT in the lower left corner of FAA Figure 39. Draw a vertical line upward to intersect -1,000 feet pressure altitude. From that point, draw a perpendicular line to 14,000 pounds gross weight. From this point, draw a vertical line downward to takeoff distance. Read the distance of 900 feet. (PLT011) — FAA-H-8083-21

Answers

8548 [A] 8549 [C] 8550 [B] 8551 [B] 8552 [B]

RTC

8553. (Refer to Figure 40.) What is the climb performance with both engines operating?

Pressure altitude..9,500 ft
Temperature (OAT)...-5°C
Heater...ON

A—925 ft/min.
B—600 ft/min.
C—335 ft/min.

1. *Enter FAA Figure 40 at the left side with 9,500 pressure altitude and draw a horizontal line to the curved line representing -5°C temperature (interpolate between temperatures as necessary).*
2. *From that point of intersection, draw a vertical line to the bottom of the graph and read the rate of climb of 915 fpm.*
3. *With the heater on above 1,800 feet, the rate of climb is 315 fpm less, therefore our rate of climb is 600 fpm.*

(PLT004) — FAA-H-8083-21

RTC

8554. (Refer to Figure 40.) What is the climb performance with both engines operating?

Pressure altitude.. 7,500 ft
Temperature (OAT)... +5°C
Heater...ON

A—905 ft/min.
B—765 ft/min.
C—1,080 ft/min.

1. *Enter FAA Figure 40 at the left side with 7,500 pressure altitude and draw a horizontal line to the curved line representing +5°C temperature (interpolate between temperatures as necessary).*
2. *From that point of intersection, draw a vertical line to the bottom of the graph and read the rate of climb of 1,080 fpm.*
3. *With the heater on above 1,800 feet, the rate of climb is 315 fpm less; therefore, our rate of climb is 765 fpm.*

(PLT004) — FAA-H-8083-21

RTC

8555. (Refer to Figure 40.) What is the climb performance with both engines operating?

Pressure altitude..6,500 ft
Temperature (OAT)... +25°C
Heater...OFF

A—285 ft/min.
B—600 ft/min.
C—400 ft/min.

1. *Enter FAA Figure 40 at the left side with 6,500 pressure altitude and draw a horizontal line to the curved line representing +25°C temperature (interpolate between temperatures as necessary).*
2. *From that point of intersection, draw a vertical line to the bottom of the graph and read the rate of climb of 600 fpm.*

(PLT004) — FAA-H-8083-21

RTC

8556. (Refer to Figure 40.) What is the climb performance with both engines operating?

Pressure altitude...11,500 ft
Temperature (OAT)... -15°C
Heater...ON

A—645 ft/min.
B—375 ft/min.
C—330 ft/min.

1. *Enter FAA Figure 40 at the left side with 11,500 pressure altitude and draw a horizontal line to the curved line representing -15°C temperature (interpolate between temperatures as necessary).*
2. *From that point of intersection, draw a vertical line to the bottom of the graph and read the rate of climb of 645 fpm.*
3. *With the heater on above 1,800 feet, the rate of climb is 315 fpm less; therefore, the rate of climb is 330 fpm.*

(PLT004) — FAA-H-8083-21

Answers

8553 [B] 8554 [B] 8555 [B] 8556 [C]

RTC
8557. (Refer to Figure 40.) What is the climb performance with both engines operating?

Pressure altitude..3,500 ft
Temperature (OAT)..-10°C
Heater..ON

A—985 ft/min.
B—1,300 ft/min.
C—1,360 ft/min.

1. *Enter FAA Figure 40 at the left side with 3,500 pressure altitude and draw a horizontal line to the curved line representing -10°C temperature (interpolate between temperatures as necessary).*
2. *From that point of intersection, draw a vertical line to the bottom of the graph and read the rate of climb of 1,300 fpm.*
3. *With the heater on above 1,800 feet, the rate of climb is 315 fpm less; therefore, our rate of climb is 985 fpm.*

(PLT004) — FAA-H-8083-21

RTC
8558. (Refer to Figure 41.) What is the single-engine climb or descent performance?

Pressure altitude..7,500 ft
Temperature (OAT)..0°C

A—80 ft/min descent.
B—10 ft/min climb.
C—50 ft/min climb.

1. *Enter FAA Figure 41 at the left side with 7,500 pressure altitude and draw a horizontal line to the curved line representing 0°C temperature (interpolate between temperatures as necessary).*
2. *From that point of intersection, draw a vertical line to the bottom of the graph and read the rate of descent of 80 fpm.*

(PLT004) — FAA-H-8083-21

RTC
8559. (Refer to Figure 41.) Given the following, what is the single-engine climb or descent performance?

Pressure altitude..3,000 ft
Temperature (OAT)..+35°C

A—150 ft/min descent.
B—350 ft/min climb.
C—100 ft/min descent.

1. *Enter FAA Figure 41 at the left side with 3,000 pressure altitude and draw a horizontal line to the curved line representing +35°C temperature (interpolate between temperatures as necessary).*
2. *From that point of intersection, draw a vertical line to the bottom of the graph and read the rate of descent of 100 fpm.*

(PLT004) — FAA-H-8083-21

RTC
8560. (Refer to Figure 41.) Given the following, what is the single-engine climb or descent performance?

Pressure altitude..4,700 ft
Temperature (OAT)..+20°C

A—420 ft/min climb.
B—60 ft/min climb.
C—60 ft/min descent.

1. *Enter FAA Figure 41 at the left side with 4,700 pressure altitude and draw a horizontal line to the curved line representing +20°C temperature (interpolate between temperatures as necessary).*
2. *From that point of intersection, draw a vertical line to the bottom of the graph and read the rate of climb of 60 fpm.*

(PLT004) — FAA-H-8083-21

Answers

8557 [A] 8558 [A] 8559 [C] 8560 [B]

RTC

8561. (Refer to Figure 41.) Given the following, what is the single-engine climb or descent performance?

Pressure altitude..9,500 ft
Temperature (OAT)..-10°C

A—600 ft/min descent.
B—840 ft/min descent.
C—280 ft/min descent.

1. *Enter FAA Figure 41 at the left side with 9,500 pressure altitude and draw a horizontal line to the curved line representing -10°C temperature (interpolate between temperatures as necessary).*
2. *From that point of intersection, draw a vertical line to the bottom of the graph and read the rate of descent of 280 fpm.*

(PLT004) — FAA-H-8083-21

RTC

8562. (Refer to Figure 41.) Given the following, what is the single-engine climb or descent performance?

Pressure altitude..1,500 ft
Temperature (OAT)..+45°C

A—100 ft/min descent.
B—360 ft/min climb.
C—200 ft/min descent.

1. *Enter FAA Figure 41 at the left side with 1,500 pressure altitude and draw a horizontal line to the curved line representing +45°C temperature (interpolate between temperatures as necessary).*
2. *From that point of intersection, draw a vertical line to the bottom of the graph and read the rate of descent of 100 fpm.*

(PLT004) — FAA-H-8083-21

RTC

8563. (Refer to Figure 42.) Given the following, what is the airspeed limit (V_{NE})?

Gross weight..16,500 lb
Pressure altitude..5,000 ft
Temperature (OAT)..-15°C

A—128 KIAS.
B—133 KIAS.
C—126 KIAS.

1. *Use the right-middle table for an aircraft weighing 16,500 pounds.*
2. *Start at an OAT of -15°C and interpolate between 6,000 (126) and 4,000 (131) feet to find V_{NE} for 5,000.*
3. *V_{NE} for 5,000 feet at -15°C is 128.5 knots.*

(PLT002) — FAA-H-8083-21

RTC

8564. (Refer to Figure 42.) What is the airspeed limit (V_{NE})?

Gross weight..17,500 lb
Pressure altitude..4,000 ft
Temperature (OAT)..+10°C

A—114 KIAS.
B—120 KIAS.
C—130 KIAS.

1. *Use the right-bottom table for an aircraft weighing 17,500 pounds.*
2. *Interpolate between 0°C and 20°C for 4,000 feet to find V_{NE} for +10°C.*
3. *V_{NE} for 5,000 feet at +10°C is 120 knots.*

(PLT002) — FAA-H-8083-21

RTC

8565. (Refer to Figure 42.) What is the airspeed limit (V_{NE})?

Gross weight..15,000 lb
Pressure altitude..6,000 ft
Temperature (OAT)..0°C

A—135 KIAS.
B—127 KIAS.
C—143 KIAS.

1. *Use the table for 14,500 pounds and 16,500 to interpolate for an aircraft weighing 15,000 pounds.*
2. *Start at an OAT of 0°C and find 6,000 for both 14,500 pounds (138) and 16,500 pounds (122) feet to find V_{NE} for 15,000 pounds.*
3. *V_{NE} for 15,000 feet at 0°C is 135 knots.*

(PLT002) — FAA-H-8083-21

Answers

8561 [C] 8562 [A] 8563 [A] 8564 [B] 8565 [A]

RTC

8566. (Refer to Figure 42.) What is the airspeed limit (V_{NE})?

Gross weight .... 14,000 lb
Pressure altitude.. 8,000 ft
Temperature (OAT)... -15°C

A—121 KIAS.
B—123 KIAS.
C—113 KIAS.

1. *Use the table for 13,500 pounds and 14,500 to interpolate for an aircraft weighing 14,000 pounds.*
2. *Start at an OAT of -15°C and find 8,000 for both 13,500 pounds (121) and 14,500 pounds (121) feet to find V_{NE} for 14,000 pounds.*
3. *V_{NE} for 14,000 feet at -15°C is 121 knots.*

(PLT002) — FAA-H-8083-21

RTC

8567. (Refer to Figure 42.) What is the airspeed limit (V_{NE})?

Gross weight .... 12,500 lb
Pressure altitude... 14,000 ft
Temperature (OAT)... -20°C

A—99 KIAS.
B—108 KIAS.
C—103 KIAS.

1. *Use the table for an aircraft weighing 12,500 pounds.*
2. *Interpolate between -15°C and -25°C for 14,000 feet to find V_{NE} for -20°C.*
3. *V_{NE} for 14,000 feet at -20°C is 103 knots.*

(PLT002) — FAA-H-8083-21

RTC

8568. (Refer to Figure 43.) What is the single-engine landing distance over a 50-foot obstacle?

Gross weight .... 12,000 lb
Pressure altitude.. 3,500 ft
Temperature (OAT)... +30°C

A—850 feet.
B—900 feet.
C—1,000 feet.

1. *Enter FAA Figure 43 on the left side at the bottom and draw a vertical line from +30°C OAT to the 3,500 feet pressure altitude (interpolate as necessary).*
2. *From that point of intersection, draw a horizontal line to the diagonal representing 12,000 pounds, and then a vertical line from there down to the landing distance of 1,000 feet.*

(PLT011) — FAA-H-8083-21

RTC

8569. (Refer to Figure 43.) What is the single-engine landing distance over a 50-foot obstacle?

Gross weight .... 16,500 lb
Pressure altitude.. 5,500 ft
Temperature (OAT)... -10°C

A—1,700 feet.
B—1,550 feet.
C—1,600 feet.

1. *Enter FAA Figure 43 on the left side at the bottom and draw a vertical line from -10°C OAT to the 5,500 feet pressure altitude (interpolate as necessary).*
2. *From that point of intersection, draw a horizontal line to the diagonal representing 16,500 pounds, and then a vertical line from there down to the landing distance of 1,550 feet.*

(PLT011) — FAA-H-8083-21

RTC

8570. (Refer to Figure 43.) What is the single-engine landing distance over a 50-foot obstacle?

Gross weight .... 15,000 lb
Pressure altitude.. 8,000 ft
Temperature (OAT)... +20°C

A—1,900 feet.
B—1,800 feet.
C—2,000 feet.

1. *Enter FAA Figure 43 on the left side at the bottom and draw a vertical line from +20°C OAT to the 8,000 feet pressure altitude (interpolate as necessary).*
2. *From that point of intersection, draw a horizontal line to the diagonal representing 15,000 pounds, and then a vertical line from there down to the landing distance of 1,900 feet.*

(PLT011) — FAA-H-8083-21

Answers

8566 [A] 8567 [C] 8568 [C] 8569 [B] 8570 [A]

RTC
8571. (Refer to Figure 43.) What is the single-engine landing distance over a 50-foot obstacle?

Gross weight .... 14,000 lb
Pressure altitude.. 1,000 ft
Temperature (OAT).. +10°C

A—650 feet.
B—920 feet.
C—800 feet.

1. *Enter FAA Figure 43 on the left side at the bottom and draw a vertical line from +10°C OAT to the 1,000 feet pressure altitude (interpolate as necessary).*
2. *From that point of intersection, draw a horizontal line to the diagonal representing 14,000 pounds, and then a vertical line from there down to the landing distance of 920 feet.*

(PLT011) — FAA-H-8083-21

RTC
8572. (Refer to Figure 43.) What is the single-engine landing distance over a 50-foot obstacle?

Gross weight .... 17,000 lb
Pressure altitude.. 4,000 ft
Temperature (OAT).. +40°C

A—1,850 feet.
B—2,200 feet.
C—2,000 feet.

1. *Enter FAA Figure 43 on the left side at the bottom and draw a vertical line from +40°C OAT to the 4,000 feet pressure altitude (interpolate as necessary).*
2. *From that point of intersection, draw a horizontal line to the diagonal representing 17,000 pounds, and then a vertical line from there down to the landing distance of 2,000 feet.*

(PLT011) — FAA-H-8083-21

Flight Planning Graphs and Tables

Aircraft manufacturers publish flight planning graphs or tables that enable flight crews to quickly estimate the time and fuel required to fly certain trips. These tables or graphs allow adjustments for aircraft weight, wind, altitude, cruise speed, and other variables.

FAA Figure 399 represents a performance chart that is often used for performance questions on the Cessna 208: the "time, fuel and distance to climb" chart. This chart is fairly easy to use in that you simply find your weight, and the altitude you are climbing to. Just make sure to subtract your departure elevation altitude. For example, if you were departing from a field elevation of 4,000 feet and climbing to a cruise altitude of 16,000 feet, you would first calculate everything at the 16,000-foot level and then subtract the 4,000-foot field elevation.

In this example, at 8,750 pounds and standard temperature, you would expect to spend 23 minutes in the climb; however, subtract the 4,000-foot time of 5 minutes, which yields a time-to-climb of 18 minutes.

ATM, ADX
8643. (Refer to Figures 61 and 62.) What is the trip time for Operating Conditions X-1?

A—4 hours 5 minutes.
B—4 hours 15 minutes.
C—4 hours.

1. *Enter the bottom of FAA Figure 62 at 2,000 and move up to the reference line.*
2. *From the reference line, follow the diagonal line representing a 50-knot tailwind.*
3. *Move up to the line representing a pressure altitude of 27,000 feet and move left to the reference line.*
4. *From the reference line, follow the diagonal line representing ISA +10°C and continue to the edge of the chart.*
5. *Determine a trip time of 4 hours.*

(PLT012, AA.I.B.K1) — FAA-H-8083-25

Answers
8571 [B] 8572 [C] 8643 [C]

ATM, ADX

8644. (Refer to Figures 61 and 62.) What is the trip time for Operating Conditions X-2?

A—5 hours 5 minutes.
B—6 hours 15 minutes.
C—5 hours 55 minutes.

1. *Enter the bottom of FAA Figure 62 at 2,400 and move up to the reference line.*
2. *From the reference line, follow the diagonal line representing a 50-knot headwind.*
3. *Move up to the line representing a pressure altitude of 35,000 feet and move left to edge of the chart.*
4. *Determine a trip time of 6 hours 15 minutes.*

(PLT012, AA.I.B.K1) — FAA-H-8083-25

ATM, ADX

8645. (Refer to Figures 61 and 62.) What is the trip time for Operating Conditions X-3?

A—4 hours 15 minutes.
B—3 hours 40 minutes.
C—4 hours.

1. *Enter the bottom of FAA Figure 62 at 1,800 and move up to the reference line.*
2. *From the reference line, follow the diagonal line representing a 20-knot headwind.*
3. *Move up to the line representing a pressure altitude of 20,000 feet and move left to the reference line.*
4. *From the reference line, follow the diagonal line representing ISA +20°C and continue to the edge of the chart.*
5. *Determine a trip time of 4 hours.*

(PLT012, AA.I.B.K1) — FAA-H-8083-25

ATM, ADX

8646. (Refer to Figures 61 and 62.) What is the trip time for Operating Conditions X-4?

A—6 hours 50 minutes.
B—5 hours 45 minutes.
C—5 hours 30 minutes.

1. *Enter the bottom of FAA Figure 62 at 2,800 and move up to the reference line.*
2. *From the reference line, follow the diagonal line representing a 50-knot tailwind.*
3. *Move up to the line representing a pressure altitude of 29,000 feet and move left to the reference line.*
4. *From the reference line, follow the diagonal line representing ISA -10°C and continue to the edge of the chart.*
5. *Determine a trip time of 5 hours 45 minutes.*

(PLT012, AA.I.B.K1) — FAA-H-8083-25

ATM, ADX

8647. (Refer to Figures 61 and 62.) What is the trip time for Operating Conditions X-5?

A—2 hours 55 minutes.
B—3 hours 10 minutes.
C—2 hours 59 minutes.

1. *Enter the bottom of FAA Figure 62 at 1,200 and move up to the reference line.*
2. *From the reference line, follow the diagonal line representing a 30-knot headwind.*
3. *Move up to the line representing a pressure altitude of 37,000 feet and move left to the reference line.*
4. *From the reference line, follow the diagonal line representing ISA +10°C and continue to the edge of the chart.*
5. *Determine a trip time of 2 hours 55 minutes.*

(PLT012, AA.I.B.K1) — FAA-H-8083-25

ATM, ADX

8648. (Refer to Figures 61 and 62.) What is the trip fuel for Operating Conditions X-1?

A—25,000 pounds.
B—26,000 pounds.
C—24,000 pounds.

1. *Enter the bottom of FAA Figure 62 at 2,000 and move up to the reference line.*
2. *From the reference line, follow the diagonal line representing a 50-knot tailwind.*
3. *Move up to the line representing a pressure altitude of 27,000 feet and move right to the reference line.*
4. *From the reference line, follow the diagonal line representing 70,000 pounds and continue to the edge of the chart.*
5. *Determine a trip fuel of 26,000 pounds.*

(PLT012, AA.I.B.K1) — FAA-H-8083-25

Answers

8644 [B]	8645 [C]	8646 [B]	8647 [A]	8648 [B]

ATM, ADX

8649. (Refer to Figures 61 and 62.) What is the trip fuel for Operating Conditions X-2?

A—33,000 pounds.
B—28,000 pounds.
C—35,000 pounds.

1. *Enter the bottom of FAA Figure 62 at 2,400 and move up to the reference line.*
2. *From the reference line, follow the diagonal line representing a 50-knot headwind.*
3. *Move up to the line representing a pressure altitude of 35,000 feet and move right to the reference line.*
4. *From the reference line, follow the diagonal line representing 75,000 pounds and continue to the edge of the chart.*
5. *Determine a trip fuel of 35,000 pounds.*

(PLT012, AA.I.B.K1) — FAA-H-8083-25

ATM, ADX

8650. (Refer to Figures 61 and 62.) What is the trip fuel for Operating Conditions X-3?

A—36,000 pounds.
B—34,500 pounds.
C—33,000 pounds.

1. *Enter the bottom of FAA Figure 62 at 1,800 and move up to the reference line.*
2. *From the reference line, follow the diagonal line representing a 20-knot headwind.*
3. *Move up to the line representing a pressure altitude of 20,000 feet and move right to the reference line.*
4. *From the reference line, follow the diagonal line representing 75,000 pounds and continue to the edge of the chart.*
5. *Determine a trip fuel of 34,500 pounds.*

(PLT012, AA.I.B.K1) — FAA-H-8083-25

ATM, ADX

8651. (Refer to Figures 61 and 62.) What is the trip fuel for Operating Conditions X-4?

A—33,000 pounds.
B—31,500 pounds.
C—34,000 pounds.

1. *Enter the bottom of FAA Figure 62 at 2,800 and move up to the reference line.*
2. *From the reference line, follow the diagonal line representing a 50-knot tailwind.*
3. *Move up to the line representing a pressure altitude of 29,000 feet and move right to the reference line.*
4. *From the reference line, follow the diagonal line representing 65,000 pounds and continue to the edge of the chart.*
5. *Determine a trip fuel of 33,000 pounds.*

(PLT012, AA.I.B.K1) — FAA-H-8083-25

ATM, ADX

8652. (Refer to Figures 61 and 62.) What is the trip fuel for Operating Conditions X-5?

A—15,000 pounds.
B—20,000 pounds.
C—19,000 pounds.

1. *Enter the bottom of FAA Figure 62 at 1,200 and move up to the reference line.*
2. *From the reference line, follow the diagonal line representing a 30-knot headwind.*
3. *Move up to the line representing a pressure altitude of 37,000 feet and move right to the reference line.*
4. *From the reference line, follow the diagonal line representing 90,000 pounds and continue to the edge of the chart.*
5. *Determine a trip fuel of 19,000 pounds.*

(PLT012, AA.I.B.K1) — FAA-H-8083-25

ATM, ATS, ADX

8658. (Refer to Figures 66 and 67.) What is the trip time corrected for wind under Operating Conditions Z-1?

A—58.1 minutes.
B—51.9 minutes.
C—54.7 minutes.

Change in time = Time × Wind Component ÷ TAS
55 × (-25) ÷ 438 = -3.1 minutes

Therefore, the trip time corrected for wind is 51.9 minutes (55 – 3.1).

(PLT012, AA.I.B.K1) — FAA-H-8083-25

Answers

8649 [C]	8650 [B]	8651 [A]	8652 [C]	8658 [B]

ATM, ATS, ADX

8659. (Refer to Figures 66 and 67.) What is the trip time corrected for wind under Operating Conditions Z-2?

A—1 hour 35 minutes.
B—1 hour 52 minutes.
C—1 hour 46 minutes.

Table time = 96 minutes
Change in time = 96 minutes × 45 ÷ 433 = +10 minutes
Trip time = 96 min + 10 min = 106 minutes = 1 hour 46 minutes

(PLT012, AA.I.B.K1) — FAA-H-8083-25

ATM, ATS, ADX

8660. (Refer to Figures 66 and 67.) What is the trip time corrected for wind under Operating Conditions Z-3?

A—2 hours 9 minutes.
B—1 hour 59 minutes.
C—1 hour 52 minutes.

Table time = 129 minutes
Change in time = 129 min × (-35) ÷ 433 = -10.4 minutes
Trip time = 129 min – 10.4 min = 118.6 minutes = 1 hour 59 minutes

(PLT012, AA.I.B.K1) — FAA-H-8083-25

ATM, ATS, ADX

8661. (Refer to Figures 66 and 67.) What is the trip time corrected for wind under Operating Conditions Z-4?

A—48.3 minutes.
B—50.7 minutes.
C—51.3 minutes.

Table time = 48 minutes
Change in time = 48 min × 25 ÷ 443 = 2.7 minutes
Trip time = 48 min + 2.7 min = 50.7 minutes

(PLT012, AA.I.B.K1) — FAA-H-8083-25

ATM, ATS, ADX

8662. (Refer to Figures 66 and 67.) What is the trip time corrected for wind under Operating Conditions Z-5?

A—1 hour 11 minutes.
B—56 minutes.
C—62 minutes.

Table time = 62 minutes
Change in time = 62 min × 60 ÷ 433 = 8.6 minutes
Trip time = 62 min + 8.6 min = 70.6 minute = 1 hour 11 minutes

(PLT012, AA.I.B.K1) — FAA-H-8083-25

ATM, ATS, ADX

8663. (Refer to Figures 66 and 67.) What is the estimated fuel consumption for Operating Conditions Z-1?

A—5,230 pounds.
B—5,970 pounds.
C—5,550 pounds.

Table fuel = 5,550 lbs
Change in fuel = 5,500 × (-25) ÷ 438 = -316.8 lbs
Trip fuel = 5,500 lbs – 316.8 lbs = 5,233.2 lbs

(PLT012, AA.I.B.K1) — FAA-H-8083-25

ATM, ATS, ADX

8664. (Refer to Figures 66 and 67.) What is the estimated fuel consumption for Operating Conditions Z-2?

A—10,270 pounds.
B—9,660 pounds.
C—10,165 pounds.

Table fuel = 9,300 lbs
Change in fuel = 9,300 × 45 ÷ 433 = 967 lbs
Trip fuel = 9,300 lbs + 967 lbs = 10,267 lbs

(PLT012, AA.I.B.K1) — FAA-H-8083-25

ATM, ATS, ADX

8665. (Refer to Figures 66 and 67.) What is the estimated fuel consumption for Operating Conditions Z-3?

A—12,300 pounds.
B—11,300 pounds.
C—13,990 pounds.

Table fuel = 12,300 lbs
Change in fuel = 12,300 × (-35) ÷ 433 = -994 lbs
Trip fuel = 12,300 lbs – 994 lbs = 11,306 lbs

(PLT012, AA.I.B.K1) — FAA-H-8083-25

ATM, ATS, ADX

8666. (Refer to Figures 66 and 67.) What is the estimated fuel consumption for Operating Conditions Z-4?

A—4,950 pounds.
B—5,380 pounds.
C—5,230 pounds.

Table fuel = 4,950 lbs
Change in fuel = 4,950 × 25 ÷ 443 = 279 lbs
Trip fuel = 4,950 lbs + 279 lbs = 5,229 lbs

(PLT012, AA.I.B.K1) — FAA-H-8083-25

Answers

8659 [C]	8660 [B]	8661 [B]	8662 [A]	8663 [A]	8664 [A]
8665 [B]					

ATM, ATS, ADX

8667. (Refer to Figures 66 and 67.) What is the estimated fuel consumption for Operating Conditions Z-5?

A—6,250 pounds.
B—5,380 pounds.
C—7,120 pounds.

Table fuel = 6,250 lbs
Change in fuel = 6,250 × 60 ÷ 433 = 866 lbs
Trip fuel = 6,250 lbs + 866 lbs = 7,116 lbs

(PLT012, AA.I.B.K1) — FAA-H-8083-25

ATM, ATS, ADX

8603. (Refer to Figures 297 and 481.) With a reported temperature of 0°C, at 500 feet AGL after takeoff, and airspeed of 145 knots IAS, the radius of turn is

A—7,850 feet.
B—8,150 feet.
C—8,450 feet.

1. *On Figure 297, note the field elevation of 5,355 feet.*
2. *On Figure 481, start on the lower left side of the chart at 0°C and move straight up until you intersect the altitude of 5,855 feet (field elevation of 5,355 + 500 feet AGL). Move directly to the right until intersecting the REF LINE. Move up and to the right in parallel with the diagonal lines until intersecting the airspeed of 145 knots. Move directly to the right and note the radius of turn of 8,150 feet.*

(PLT011, AA.I.B.K1) — FAA-H-8083-25

ATM, ADX

8604. (Refer to Figure 469.) With an OAT of -20°C at 20,000 feet and an IAS of 150, the Maximum Continuous Power Torque Setting is

A—64%.
B—66%.
C—68%.

On Figure 469, start at the bottom of the chart and locate -20°C. Move straight up until intersecting the 20,000 feet line. Move directly to the right and stop at the REF LINE. Because 150 knots intersects with the REF LINE, you continue to the right and note the maximum continuous power torque setting is 66%. (PLT009, AA.I.B.K1) — FAA-H-8083-25

Typical Flight Logs

Flight logs are used to accurately plan the time and fuel required for a flight. In the following paragraphs we describe all the steps required to complete a flight log.

1. Determine the magnetic courses for each leg and determine the leg distances.
2. Apply variations to the winds aloft.
3. Determine the temperature in relation to ISA.
4. Determine Mach number and convert to TAS.
5. Compute ground speed.
6. Calculate and record the time for each leg.
7. Compute fuel flow.
8. Compute total fuel.
9. Determine the reserve fuel.
10. Compute fuel burn to alternate.
11. Add the en route, reserve, and alternate fuel to find the total fuel required for the flight.

Answers

8666 [C] 8667 [C] 8603 [B] 8604 [B]

Computation of Temperature at Cruise Altitude

Temperature is often expressed as a deviation from ISA which is the standard day temperature (i.e., ISA -2°). This temperature can be computed by the following procedure:

1. Compute ISA by multiplying the altitude in thousands of feet times -2° and then adding 15°. For example: ISA at 27,000 feet = 27 × (-2°) +15 = -39°
2. Apply the deviation from ISA: ISA -2° at 27,000 feet = (-39°) + (-2°) = -41°

Computation of True Airspeed Using Mach Number

True Airspeed (TAS) can be computed from Mach number and Outside Air Temperature (OAT).

Using the CX-3 Flight Computer, select "Airspeed" from the FLT menu, then enter the OAT and the Mach number at the appropriate prompts to get TAS.

Using an E6-B computer, follow these steps:

1. In the small window labeled "Airspeed Correction" or "True Airspeed," align the arrow labeled "Mach Number" with the OAT on the scale adjacent the window.
2. Find the Mach number on the inner of the two main scales and then read the TAS opposite it on the outer scale.

Note: Some "CR"-type mechanical computers have a window in which a Mach Index is aligned with a Mach number inside the window. Don't use this scale. It is designed to use Indicated Temperature and will give an inaccurate TAS when OAT is used.

See the instruction manual of your individual computer for more detailed instructions.

Specific Range

Specific range is the term used to describe the rate of fuel burn per nautical air mile flown. It is calculated by using TAS and fuel flow only. Wind has no effect on specific range. To calculate specific range in nautical air miles per 1,000 pounds, use the formula:

NM/1,000 = TAS × 1,000 ÷ PPH.

TAS should be calculated from the Mach number as in the paragraph above. PPH can be taken directly from the flight log.

ATM, ATS, ADX
8702. A jet airplane is flying at .72 Mach with an OAT of -40°C. What is the true airspeed?

A—430 knots.
B—452 knots.
C—464 knots.

Using your CX-3 Flight Computer select Airspeed from the FLT menu. Enter a MACH of .72 and OAT of -40°C to get a TAS of 428.41 KTS. The closest available answer is 430 knots. (PLT012, AA.I.D.K3) — FAA-H-8083-15

Answers
8702 [A]

Chapter 5
Weight and Balance

Note applicable to Chapters 4 and 5: The ATP Single-engine exam (ATS) focuses on performance comparable to the Cessna 208 and the ATP Multi-engine exam (ATM) focuses on performance comparable to the Bombardier CRJ200 and Q400.

Center of Gravity Computation

The start of the solution to any weight and balance problem is the calculation of the total weight of the aircraft (gross weight) and the total moment. All weight and balance problems on the ATP test use a moment index rather than the actual moment. The moment index is the actual moment divided by 1,000.

Basic Operating Weight (BOW) is defined as the empty weight of the aircraft plus the weight of the required crew, their baggage and other standard items such as meals and potable water. The BOW and the Basic Operating Index (Moment/1,000) are the same for all questions.

The Moment Index (MOM/1,000) is calculated by using the formula:

Weight × Arm/1,000 = MOM/1,000

The Center of Gravity (CG) in inches aft of the Datum line can be determined by using the formula:

CG = Total Moment / Total Weight

Since some FAA questions use a Moment Index instead of Moment, for these it is necessary to modify this formula by multiplying the (Total Moment/Total Weight) by the reduction factor (1,000). The formula then becomes:

CG = (Total Moment Index / Total Weight) × 1,000

ATM, ADX

8697. (Refer to Figures 405 through 416.) (Note: Applicants may request a printed copy of the chart(s) or graph(s) for use while computing the answer. All printed pages must be returned to test proctor.) With the load weights shown in Figure 414, you fill the fuel tanks to the maximum fuel to remain under maximum gross weight and compute the center of gravity. Your computations indicate

A—at a CG of 200.1, your loading is satisfactory for flight operations.
B—at a CG of 180.19, you need to redistribute your loads.
C—at a CG of 190.27, you only need to change the cargo pod loading.

1. *On Figure 405, note the maximum gross weight of 8,785 lbs.*
2. *On Figure 410, note the 200-pound pilot yields a 27.1 moment.*
3. *Using Figure 411, using maximum fuel at a weight of 2,224 lbs, the moment is 451.7.*
4. *On Figure 414, using the pilot weight of 200 lbs and 27.1 moment, and the fuel of 2,224 and moment of 451.7, the calculated ramp weight is 7,429 lbs. Adding all the moments together yields 1408.2.*
5. *The CG is calculated by taking the total moment (1,408.2 × 1,000) and dividing by aircraft weight. 14,082,000 ÷ 7,429 lbs = 189.6.*
6. *On Figure 415, note the aircraft is out of CG, but can be brought into CG by changing the cargo pad loading.*

(PLT003, AA.I.B.K3e) — FAA-H-8083-25

Answers

8697 [C]

ALL

8697-1. Given the following, what would be the maximum payload?

Basic operating weight (BOW): 100,500 lbs.
Maximum zero fuel weight: 138,000 lbs.
Maximum landing weight: 142,000 lbs.
Maximum takeoff weight: 184,200 lbs.
Fuel load: 40,000 lbs.
Fuel tank capacity: 54,000 lbs.

A—43,700 lbs.
B—37,500 lbs.
C—29,700 lbs.

The payload is the maximum combination of passengers, baggage, and cargo that the airplane is capable of carrying. A zero fuel weight, if published, is the limiting weight: 138,000 – 100,500 = 37,500. (PLT003, AA.I.B.K3e) — FAA-H-8083-3

ALL

8697-2. What is the purpose of a zero fuel weight limitation?

A—To limit load forces on the wing spars with heavy fuselage loads.
B—To limit load forces on the fuselage with a heavy wing fuel load.
C—To prevent overstressing the landing gear during a hard landing.

The zero fuel weight of an aircraft includes all useful load except fuel. The purpose of a zero fuel weight is to limit load forces on the wing spars with heavy fuselage loads. (PLT003, AA.I.B.K3e) — FAA-H-8083-3

ALL

8697-3. What adverse flight characteristics could result from operating an aircraft with the center of gravity (CG) beyond the published forward limitations?

A—The flight control forces may become very light.
B—It could be difficult or impossible to flare for landing.
C—It could be difficult or impossible to recover from a stall.

In extreme cases, a CG location that is beyond the forward limit may result in nose heaviness, making it difficult or impossible to flare for landing. (PLT003, AA.I.B.K5) — FAA-H-8083-25

ALL

8697-4. What adverse flight characteristics could result from operating an aircraft with the center of gravity (CG) beyond the published aft limitations?

A—The flight control forces may become very heavy.
B—It could be difficult to flare for landing.
C—It could be impossible to recover from a stall.

As the CG moves aft, a less stable condition occurs, which decreases the ability of the aircraft to right itself after maneuvering or turbulence, including recovery from a stall or spin. (PLT003, AA.I.B.K5) — FAA-H-8083-25

ATM, ATS, ADX

8698. (Refer to Figures 405 through 416.) What is the CG in inches from datum under the following loading conditions?

	Weight (lbs.)
Basic empty weight	5,005
Pilot	185
Cargo	
Zone 1	200
Zone 2	240
Zone 3	500
Zone 4	400
Zone 5	200
Zone 6	50
Cargo Pod	
Zone A	0
Zone B	0
Zone C	0
Zone D	0
Fuel	275 gallons

A—Station 202.6.
B—Station 198.5.
C—Station 205.6.

1. *Use Figure 410 to calculate the weight and moment for the pilot. The arm is 135.5 inches, so multiply 185 × 135.5 to get a moment of 25,067.5. Record these numbers under "Your Airplane" in the Figure 414 worksheet.*
2. *Use Figure 412 to calculate the cargo weights at each zone by multiplying the weight by the arm, to get the following results:*

Answers

8697-1 [B] 8697-2 [A] 8697-3 [B] 8697-4 [C] 8698 [A]

	Weight	× Arm	= Moment
Zone 1	200	172.1	34,420
Zone 2	240	217.8	52,272
Zone 3	500	264.4	132,200
Zone 4	400	294.5	117,800
Zone 5	200	319.5	63,900
Zone 6	50	344	17,200

Record these in the Figure 414 worksheet.

3. *Using Figure 411, calculate the weight and moment of 275 gallons of fuel and find 1,843 pounds, and a moment of 374,500. Record in Figure 414 worksheet.*
4. *Add all the items from the Figure 414 worksheet, including the basic empty weight and moment:*

	Weight	Moment
Basic empty weight	5,005	929,400
Pilot	185	25,067.5
Zone 1	200	34,420
Zone 2	240	52,272
Zone 3	500	132,200
Zone 4	400	117,800
Zone 5	200	63,900
Zone 6	50	17,200
Zone A	0	
Zone B	0	
Zone C	0	
Zone D	0	
Fuel	1,843	374,500
Total	8,623 lbs	1,746,760 in-lbs

5. *Divide the total moment by the total weight to get a CG of 202.6 inches.*

(PLT121, AA.I.B.K3e) — FAA-H-8083-1

ATM, ATS, ADX

8699. (Refer to Figures 405 through 416.) What is the CG in inches from datum under the following loading conditions?

Weight (lbs.)

Basic empty weight 5,005
Pilot 190
Front seat passenger 200
Cargo
Zone 1 180
Zone 2 505
Zone 3 198
Zone 4 600
Zone 5 0
Zone 6 60
Cargo Pod
Zone A 100
Zone B 80
Zone C 200
Zone D 180
Fuel .... 180 gallons

A—196.4 inches aft of datum.
B—200.4 inches aft of datum.
C—204.1 inches aft of datum.

1. *Use Figure 410 to calculate the weight and moment for the pilot and passenger. The arm is 135.5 inches, so multiply 390 × 135.5 to get a moment of 52,845. Record these numbers under "Your Airplane" in the Figure 414 worksheet.*
2. *Use Figure 412 to calculate the cargo weights at each zone by multiplying the weight by the arm, to get the following results:*

	Weight	× Arm	= Moment
Zone 1	180	172.1	30,978
Zone 2	505	217.8	109,989
Zone 3	198	264.4	52,351.2
Zone 4	600	294.5	176,700
Zone 5	0	319.5	0
Zone 6	60	344	20,640
Zone A	100	132.4	13,240
Zone B	80	182.1	14,568
Zone C	200	233.4	46,680
Zone D	180	287.6	51,768

Record these in the Figure 414 worksheet.

Answers

8699 [B]

3. *Using Figure 411, calculate the weight and moment of 180 gallons of fuel and find 1,206 pounds, and a moment of 245,200. Record in Figure 414 worksheet.*
4. *Add all the items from the Figure 414 worksheet, including the basic empty weight and moment:*

	Weight	***Moment***
Basic empty weight	*5,005*	*929,400*
Pilot	*190*	*25,745*
Front Passenger	*200*	*27,100*
Zone 1	*180*	*30,978*
Zone 2	*505*	*109,989*
Zone 3	*198*	*52,351.2*
Zone 4	*600*	*176,700*
Zone 5	*0*	*0*
Zone 6	*60*	*20,640*
Zone A	*100*	*13,240*
Zone B	*80*	*14,568*
Zone C	*200*	*46,680*
Zone D	*180*	*51,768*
Fuel	*1206*	*245,200*
Total	*8,704 lbs*	*1,744,359 in-lbs*

5. *Divide the total weight to arrive at a CG of 200.4 inches.*

(PLT121, AA.I.B.K3e) — FAA-H-8083-1

ATM, ATS, ADX

8699-1. (Refer to Figure 419.) With the following conditions, would the airplane be in the approved weight and CG envelope for landing?

CG location: 25% MAC
Aircraft Weight: 74,000 lbs.

A—No, the airplane is over the maximum approved landing weight.
B—Yes, the airplane is within the approved weight and CG envelope.
C—No, the airplane is below the maximum landing weight, but the CG is aft of limits.

The airplane is over the maximum approved landing weight of 73,500 lbs. (PLT121, AA.I.B.K3e) — FAA-H-8083-25

ATM, ATS, ADX

8699-2. (Refer to Figure 419.) You are preparing for a flight, with the following planned loading at takeoff. Would the aircraft be within the approved weight limitations?

Basic operating weight (including crew): 49,500 lbs.
Passengers, baggage, and cargo: 20,850 lbs.
Fuel weight: 9,500 lbs.

A—Yes, the weight would be within limits.
B—No, max zero fuel weight would be exceeded.
C—No, the max takeoff weight would be exceeded.

The total weight for this flight is 49,500 + 20,850 + 9,500 = 79,850 lbs. This is below the maximum takeoff weight but above the zero fuel weight limit of 70,000 at 70,350 lbs. (PLT121, AA.I.B.K3e) — FAA-H-8083-25

Answers

8699-1 [A] 8699-2 [B]

Stabilizer Trim Setting

The correct horizontal stabilizer trim setting is very critical for proper takeoff performance of jet aircraft. The main determinants are the CG location and possibly the flap setting. Some aircraft, such as the DC-9, have their stabilizer trim indicators calibrated in percent of MAC, so it is necessary to calculate the CG to know the trim setting. Other aircraft (such as the B-737) have their trim indicators marked off in units of nose up trim. In such cases it is necessary to refer to the trim table to determine the proper setting for a given CG. See FAA Figure 55.

The **Stab Trim Setting** Table at the bottom left side of FAA Figure 55 is used to determine the takeoff trim setting for a B-737. CG location in percent of MAC is used to determine the setting. For example, if the CG is at 8.0% of MAC, the stab trim setting is 7-3/4 units ANU (Airplane Nose Up).

ATM
8623. (Refer to Figures 53 and 55.) What is the STAB TRIM setting for Operating Conditions R-1?

A—8 ANU.
B—7-5/8 ANU.
C—7-3/4 ANU.

CG (inches aft of LEMAC) = 635.7" – 625.0" = 10.7"
CG (% of MAC) = 10.7"/134.0" = 8.0%
Stab Trim = 7-3/4 ANU

(PLT010, AA.III.A.K3) — FAA-H-8083-25

ATM
8624. (Refer to Figures 53 and 55.) What is the STAB TRIM setting for Operating Conditions R-2?

A—5-3/4 ANU.
B—7 ANU.
C—6-3/4 ANU.

CG (inches aft of LEMAC) = 643.8" – 625.0" = 18.8"
CG (% of MAC) = 18.8"/134.0" = 14.0%
Stab Trim = 6-3/4 ANU

(PLT010, AA.III.A.K3) — FAA-H-8083-25

ATM,
8625. (Refer to Figures 53 and 55.) What is the STAB TRIM setting for Operating Conditions R-3?

A—3 ANU.
B—4-1/2 ANU.
C—5 ANU.

CG (inches aft of LEMAC) = 665.2" – 625.0" = 40.2"
CG (% of MAC) = 40.2"/134.0" = 30.0%
Stab Trim = 3 ANU

(PLT010, AA.III.A.K3) — FAA-H-8083-25

ATM
8626. (Refer to Figures 53 and 55.) What is the STAB TRIM setting for Operating Conditions R-4?

A—4-1/4 ANU.
B—4-1/2 ANU.
C—5 ANU.

CG (inches aft of LEMAC) = 657.2" – 625.0" = 32.2"
CG (% of MAC) = 32.2"/134.0" = 24.0%
Stab Trim = 4-1/2 ANU

(PLT010, AA.III.A.K3) — FAA-H-8083-25

ATM
8627. (Refer to Figures 53 and 55.) What is the STAB TRIM setting for Operating Conditions R-5?

A—6-3/4 ANU.
B—8 ANU.
C—7-1/2 ANU.

CG (inches aft of LEMAC) = 638.4" – 625.0" = 13.4"
CG (% of MAC) = 13.4"/134.0" = 10.0%
Stab Trim = 7-1/2 ANU

(PLT010, AA.III.A.K3) — FAA-H-8083-25

Answers

8623 [C] 8624 [C] 8625 [A] 8626 [B] 8627 [C]

Changing Loading Conditions

Whenever weight is either added to or subtracted from a loaded airplane, both the gross weight and the center of gravity location will change. The solution to such a calculation is really a simplified loading problem. Instead of calculating a weight and moment for every section of the aircraft, it is only necessary to compute the original weight and moment—then, the *effect* of the change in weight. Often in these problems, the original CG is expressed in percent of MAC and it is necessary to convert this to an arm for the entire aircraft.

For example, if an aircraft's total weight was 8,600 pounds, and you shifted 100 pounds from station (or, arm) 100 to arm 150, a simple weight shift formula can be applied:

$$\frac{\text{Weight to be Shifted (100 pounds)}}{\text{Total Weight (8,600 pounds)}} = \frac{\text{Change in CG}}{\text{Distance CG Shifted (50 inches)}}$$

This is solved easily by cross-multiplying: 50 × 100 ÷ 8,600 = .06 inches. Therefore, the CG shifts .06 inches aft.

ATM, ATS, ADX

8700. (Refer to Figures 405 through 416.) What is the old and new CG if 300 pounds of cargo is moved from Zone 2 to Zone 3 given the following conditions?

	Weight (lbs.)
Basic empty weight	5,005
Pilot	190
Front seat passenger	200
Cargo	
Zone 1	180
Zone 2	505
Zone 3	198
Zone 4	600
Zone 5	0
Zone 6	60
Cargo Pod	
Zone A	100
Zone B	80
Zone C	200
Zone D	180
Fuel	180 gallons

A—200.2 and 198.6.
B—196.4 and 199.2.
C—200.4 and 202.

First, calculate the old CG by using the following procedure:

1. *Use Figure 410 to calculate the weight and moment for the pilot and passenger. The arm is 135.5 inches, so multiply 390 × 135.5 to get a moment of 52,845. Record these numbers under "Your Airplane" in the Figure 414 worksheet.*
2. *Use Figure 412 to calculate the cargo weights at each zone by multiplying the weight by the arm, to get the following results:*

	Weight	***× Arm***	***= Moment***
Zone 1	*180*	*172.1*	*30,978*
Zone 2	*505*	*217.8*	*109,989*
Zone 3	*198*	*264.4*	*52,351.2*
Zone 4	*600*	*294.5*	*176,700*
Zone 5	*0*	*319.5*	*0*
Zone 6	*60*	*344*	*20,640*
Zone A	*100*	*132.4*	*13,240*
Zone B	*80*	*182.1*	*14,568*
Zone C	*200*	*233.4*	*46,680*
Zone D	*180*	*287.6*	*51,768*

Record these in the Figure 414 worksheet.

3. *Using Figure 411, calculate the weight and moment of 180 gallons of fuel and find 1,206 pounds, and a moment of 245,200. Record in Figure 414 worksheet.*

Answers

8700 [C]

4. *Add all the items from the Figure 414 worksheet, including the basic empty weight and moment:*

	Weight	***Moment***
Basic empty weight	*5,005*	*929,400*
Pilot	*190*	*25,745*
Front Passenger	*200*	*27,100*
Zone 1	*180*	*30,978*
Zone 2	*505*	*109,989*
Zone 3	*198*	*52,351.2*
Zone 4	*600*	*176,700*
Zone 5	*0*	*0*
Zone 6	*60*	*20,640*
Zone A	*100*	*13,240*
Zone B	*80*	*14,568*
Zone C	*200*	*46,680*
Zone D	*180*	*51,768*
Fuel	*1206*	*245,200*
Total	*8,704 lbs*	*1,744,359 in-lbs*

5. *Divide the total moment by the total weight to arrive at a CG of 200.4 inches. This is the old CG.*
6. *You are moving 300 pounds from Zone 2 (arm 217.8) to Zone 3 (arm 264.4). This is a distance of (264.4 – 217.8) 46.6 inches. The formula for weight shift is given as:*

$$\frac{\text{Weight to be shifted}}{\text{Total weight}} = \frac{\text{Change in CG}}{\text{Distance CG is shifted}}$$

$$\frac{300}{8{,}704} = \frac{\text{Change in CG}}{46.6}$$

Using cross-multiplication, 46.6 × 300 ÷ 8,704 equals 1.6 inches. Since Zone 3 is aft of Zone 2, the CG also shifts aft and the new CG is 200.4 + 1.6 = 202 inches. (PLT121, AA.I.B.K3e) — FAA-H-8083-1

ATM, ATS

8578. (Refer to Figure 44.) What is the new CG if the weight is removed from the forward compartment under Loading Conditions WS 1?

A—27.1 percent MAC.
B—26.8 percent MAC.
C—30.0 percent MAC.

1. *Calculate original CG in inches aft of datum:*

   CG (inches aft of LEMAC) = (22.5% / 100%) × 141.5" = 31.84"

   CG (inches aft of Datum) = 549.13" + 31.84" = 580.97"
2. *Use the original weight and the CG to calculate the original Moment/1,000. Next use the weight change and station to determine the Moment/1,000 change:*

	Weight	***Moment/1,000***
Original Weight	*90,000*	*52,287.08*
Weight Change	*– 2,500*	*– 880.25*
New Weight	*87,500*	*51,406.83*

3. *Determine the new CG:*

   CG = (51,406.83/87,500) × 1,000 = 587.51"
4. *Convert CG to percent of MAC:*

   CG (inches aft of LEMAC) = 587.51" – 549.13" = 38.38"

   CG (% of MAC) = (38.38/141.5) = 27.1%

(PLT021, AA.I.B.K3e) — FAA-H-8083-1

ATM, ATS

8579. (Refer to Figure 44.) Where is the new CG if the weight is added to the aft compartment under Loading Conditions WS 2?

A—+17.06 index arm.
B—+14.82 index arm.
C—+12.13 index arm.

1. *Calculate original CG in inches aft of datum:*

   CG (inches aft of LEMAC) = (28.4% / 100%) × 141.5" = 40.19"

   CG (inches aft of Datum) = 549.13" + 40.19" = 589.32"
2. *Use the original weight and the CG to calculate the original Moment/1,000. Next use the weight change and station to determine the Moment/1,000 change:*

	Weight	***Moment/1,000***
Original Weight	*85,000*	*50,091.87*
Weight Change	*+ 1,800*	*+ 1,304.82*
New Weight	*86,800*	*51,396.69*

3. *Determine the new CG:*

   CG = (51,396.69/86,800) × 1,000 = 592.13"
4. *Convert to Index Arm (0 Index Arm = 580.0"):*

   CG (Index Arm) = 592.13" – 580" = +12.13"

(PLT021, AA.I.B.K3e) — FAA-H-8083-1

Answers

8578 [A] 8579 [C]

ATM, ATS

8580. (Refer to Figure 44.) What is the new CG if the weight is added to the forward compartment under Loading Conditions WS 3?

A—11.4 percent MAC.
B—14.3 percent MAC.
C—14.5 percent MAC.

1. *Calculate original CG in inches aft of datum:*

   CG (inches aft of LEMAC) = (19.8% / 100%) × 141.5" = 28.02"
   CG (inches aft of Datum) = 549.13" + 28.02" = 577.15"

2. *Use the original weight and the CG to calculate the original Moment/1,000. Next use the weight change and station to determine the Moment/1,000 change:*

	Weight	***Moment/1,000***
Original Weight	*84,500*	*48,768.92*
Weight Change	*+ 3,000*	*+ 1,056.30*
New Weight	*87,500*	*49,825.22*

3. *Determine the new CG:*

   CG = (49,825.22/87,500) × 1,000 = 569.43

4. *Convert CG to percent of MAC:*

   CG (inches aft of LEMAC) = 569.43" – 549.13" = 20.3"
   CG (% of MAC) = (20.3"/141.5") × 100% = 14.3%

(PLT021, AA.I.B.K3e) — FAA-H-8083-1

ATM, ATS

8581. (Refer to Figure 44.) Where is the new CG if the weight is removed from the aft compartment under Loading Conditions WS 4?

A—+15.53 index arm.
B—+8.50 index arm.
C—-93.51 index arm.

1. *Calculate original CG in inches aft of datum:*

   CG (inches aft of LEMAC) = (30.3% / 100%) × 141.5" = 42.87"
   CG (inches aft of Datum) = 549.13" + 42.87" = 592.00"

2. *Use the original weight and the CG to calculate the original Moment/1,000. Next use the weight change and station to determine the Moment/1,000 change:*

	Weight	***Moment/1,000***
Original Weight	*81,700*	*48,366.40*
Weight Change	*– 2,100*	*– 1,522.29*
New Weight	*79,600*	*46,844.11*

3. *Determine the new CG:*

   CG = (46,844.11/79,600) × 1,000 = 588.49"

4. *Convert to Index Arm:*

   CG (Index Arm) = 588.49" – 580" = +8.50"

(PLT021, AA.I.B.K3e) — FAA-H-8083-1

ATM, ATS

8582. (Refer to Figure 44.) What is the new CG if the weight is removed from the forward compartment under Loading Conditions WS 5?

A—31.9 percent MAC.
B—19.1 percent MAC.
C—35.2 percent MAC.

1. *Calculate original CG in inches aft of datum:*

   CG (inches aft of LEMAC) = (25.5% / 100%) × 141.5" = 36.08"
   CG (inches aft of Datum) = 549.13" + 36.08" = 585.21"

2. *Use the original weight and the CG to calculate the original Moment/1,000. Next use the weight change and station to determine the Moment/1,000 change:*

	Weight	***Moment/1,000***
Original Weight	*88,300*	*51,674.04*
Weight Change	*– 3,300*	*– 1,161.93*
New Weight	*85,000*	*50,512.11*

3. *Determine the new CG:*

   CG = (50,512.11 ÷ 85,000) × 1,000 = 594.26"

4. *Convert CG to percent of MAC:*

   CG (inches aft of LEMAC) = 594.26" – 549.13" = 45.13"
   CG(% of MAC) = (45.13"/141.5") × 100% = 31.9%

(PLT021, AA.I.B.K3e) — FAA-H-8083-1

Answers

8580 [B] 8581 [B] 8582 [A]

ADX

8573. (Refer to Figure 44.) What is the new CG if the weight is shifted from the forward to the aft compartment under Loading Conditions WS 1?

A—15.2 percent MAC.
B—29.8 percent MAC.
C—30.0 percent MAC.

Change in CG = (2,500 lbs × 372.8)/90,000 lbs = +10.4"
Change in CG (% of MAC) = (10.4"/141.5") × 100% = 7.35%
New CG = 22.5% + 7.35% = 29.85%

(PLT021) — FAA-H-8083-1

ATM, ATS

8574. (Refer to Figure 44.) What is the new CG if the weight is shifted from the aft to the forward compartment under Loading Conditions WS 2?

A—26.1 percent MAC.
B—20.5 percent MAC.
C—22.8 percent MAC.

Change in CG = (1,800 lbs × (-372.8))/85,000 lbs = -7.89"
Change in CG (% of MAC) = (-7.89"/141.5") × 100% = -5.6%
New CG = 28.4% – 5.6% = 22.8%

(PLT021, AA.I.B.K3e) — FAA-H-8083-1

ATM, ATS

8575. (Refer to Figure 44.) What is the new CG if the weight is shifted from the forward to the aft compartment under Loading Conditions WS 3?

A—29.2 percent MAC.
B—33.0 percent MAC.
C—28.6 percent MAC.

Change in CG = (3,000 lbs × 372.8")/84,500 lbs = 13.24"
Change in CG (% of MAC) = (13.24"/141.5") × 100% = 9.4%
New CG = 19.8% + 9.4% = 29.2%

(PLT021, AA.I.B.K3e) — FAA-H-8083-1

ATM, ATS

8576. (Refer to Figure 44.) What is the new CG if the weight is shifted from the aft to the forward compartment under Loading Conditions WS 4?

A—37.0 percent MAC.
B—23.5 percent MAC.
C—24.1 percent MAC.

Change in CG = (2,100 lbs × (-372.8")/81,700 lbs = -9.58"
Change in CG (% of MAC) = (-9.58"/141.5") × 100% = -6.8%
New CG = 30.3% – 6.8% = 23.5%.

(PLT021, AA.I.B.K3e) — FAA-H-8083-1

ATM, ATS

8577. (Refer to Figure 44.) Where is the new CG if the listed weight is shifted from the forward to the aft compartment under Loading Conditions WS 5?

A—+19.15 index arm.
B—+13.93 index arm.
C—-97.92 index arm.

CG (inches aft of LEMAC) = (25.5%/100%) × 141.5 = 36.08"
CG (inches aft of Datum) = 549.13" + 36.08" = 585.21"
CG (Index Arm) = 585.21" – 580" = +5.21"
Change in CG = (3,300 lbs × 372.8")/88,300 lbs = 13.93"
New CG (Index Arm) = +5.21" + 13.93" = 19.14"

(PLT021, AA.I.B.K3e) — FAA-H-8083-1

Answers

8573 [B]	8574 [C]	8575 [A]	8576 [B]	8577 [A]

C208 Weight and Balance

Note: By definition, "basic empty weight" does not include crew weight, so you must include crew in the calculation. By definition, "basic operating weight" includes crew weight so you do not include crew in the calculation.

The other key to C208 weight and balance is to use the actual arms listed (FAA Figure 405) for each position. You can use the charts and pre-calculated moments as depicted in FAA Figure 412, but the actual calculation is more accurate and probably quicker. The only exception to this is fuel, as the arm changes based upon fuel weight, therefore the chart in FAA Figure 411 should be used.

ATS, ADX

8049. The weight and CG of an aircraft used in 135 operations must have been calculated from those values established by actual weighing of the aircraft within what period of time?

A—Multiengine aircraft, preceding 36 calendar months.
B—Multiengine and single-engine aircraft, preceding 36 calendar months.
C—Multiengine aircraft, last 36 calendar months; single-engine, last 24 calendar months.

No person may operate a multi-engine aircraft unless the current empty weight and center of gravity are calculated from values established by actual weighing of the aircraft within the preceding 36 calendar months. (PLT454, AA.I.G.K5) — 14 CFR §135.185

ATS, ADX

8067. What are the empty weight and balance currency requirements for aircraft used in 135 operations?

A—The empty weight and CG of multiengine and single-engine aircraft must have been calculated from an actual weighing within the previous 36 calendar months.
B—The empty weight and CG must have been calculated from an actual weighing within the previous 24 calendar months unless the original Airworthiness Certificate was issued within the previous 36 calendar months.
C—The empty weight and CG of multiengine aircraft must have been calculated from an actual weighing within the previous 36 calendar months.

No person may operate a multi-engine aircraft unless the current empty weight and center of gravity are calculated from values established by actual weighing of the aircraft within the preceding 36 calendar months. (PLT454, AA.I.G.K5) — 14 CFR §135.185

Answers

8049 [A] 8067 [C]

Commuter Aircraft Weight and Balance

Note: By definition, "basic empty weight" does not include crew weight, so you must include crew in the calculation. By definition, "basic operating weight" includes crew weight so you do not include crew in the calculation.

ATS

8439. (Refer to Figures 3, 6, 8, 9, 10, and 11.) What is the CG shift if the passengers in row 1 are moved to seats in row 9 under Loading Conditions AC-1?

A—1.5 inches aft.
B—5.6 inches aft.
C—6.2 inches aft.

	Weight	***Moment/100***
Basic Empty Wt.	*9,226*	*25,823*
Crew	*360*	*464*
Row 1	*350*	*700*
Row 2	*260*	*598*
Row 3	*200*	*520*
Row 4	*340*	*986*
Row 5	*120*	*384*
Row 6	*400*	*1,400*
Row 7	*120*	*456*
Row 8	*250*	*1,025*
Row 9	—	—
Baggage		
Nose	*60*	*39*
FWD Cabin	*250*	*409*
Aft (FWD Sec)	*500*	*2,418*
Aft (Aft Sec)	—	—
Fuel (Jet B @ 6.6)	*+ 2,442*	*+ 7,299*
Total	*14,878*	*42,521*

Change in CG = 350 lbs × 240" ÷ 14,878 lbs = 5.6 aft

(PLT021, AA.I.B.K3e) — FAA-H-8083-1

ATS

8440. (Refer to Figures 3, 6, 8, 9, 10, and 11.) What is the CG shift if the passengers in row 1 are moved to row 8, and the passengers in row 2 are moved to row 9 under Loading Conditions AC-2?

A—9.2 inches aft.
B—5.7 inches aft.
C—7.8 inches aft.

	Weight	***Moment/100***
Basic Empty Wt.	*9,226*	*25,823*
Crew	*340*	*439*
Row 1	*300*	*600*
Row 2	*250*	*575*
Row 3	*190*	*494*
Row 4	*170*	*493*
Row 5	*190*	*608*
Row 6	*340*	*1,190*
Row 7	*190*	*722*
Row 8	—	—
Row 9	—	—
Baggage		
Nose	—	—
FWD Cabin	*100*	*164*
Aft (FWD Sec)	*200*	*967*
Aft (Aft Sec)	*600*	*3,198*
Fuel (Jet A @ 6.6)	*+ 2,652*	*+ 7,924*
Total	*14,748*	*43,197*

Change in CG = 550 lbs × 210" ÷ 14,748 lbs = 7.8" aft

(PLT021, AA.I.B.K3e) — FAA-H-8083-1

Answers

8439 [B] 8440 [C]

ATS

8441. (Refer to Figures 3, 6, 8, 9, 10, and 11.) What is the CG shift if four passengers weighing 170 pounds each are added; two to seats in row 6 and two to seats in row 7 under Loading Conditions AC-3?

A—3.5 inches aft.
B—2.2 inches forward.
C—1.8 inches aft.

Use the following steps:

1. Compute the CG position prior to changes:

	Weight	***Moment/100***
Basic Empty Wt.	*9,226*	*25,823*
Crew	*350*	*452*
Row 1	*120*	*240*
Row 2	*340*	*782*
Row 3	*350*	*910*
Row 4	*300*	*870*
Row 5	*170*	*544*
Row 6	—	—
Row 7	—	—
Row 8	—	—
Row 9	—	—
Baggage		
Nose	*80*	*52*
FWD Cabin	*120*	*197*
Aft (FWD Sec)	*250*	*1,209*
Aft (Aft Sec)	*500*	*2,665*
Fuel (Jet B @ 6.7)	*+ 2,680*	*+ 8,007*
Total	*14,486*	*41,751*

CG = (41,751 ÷ 14,486) × 100 = 288.2"

2. Calculate the weight additions:

	Weight	***Moment/100***
Original Wt.	*14,486*	*41,751*
2 pax in row 6	*+ 340*	*+ 1,190*
2 pax in row 7	*+ 340*	*+ 1,292*
New Total	*15,166*	*44,233*

3. CG = (44,233 ÷ 15,166) × 100 = 291.7"

4. The CG moved from station 288.2 to station 291.7, a movement of 3.5 inches aft.

(PLT021, AA.I.B.K3e) — FAA-H-8083-1

ATS

8442. (Refer to Figures 3, 6, 8, 9, 10, and 11.) What is the CG shift if all passengers in rows 2 and 4 are deplaned under Loading Conditions AC-4?

A—2.5 inches aft.
B—2.5 inches forward.
C—2.0 inches aft.

Use the following steps:

1. Compute the CG position prior to changes:

	Weight	***Moment/100***
Basic Empty Wt.	*9,226*	*25,823*
Crew	*340*	*439*
Row 1	—	—
Row 2	*370*	*851*
Row 3	*400*	*1,040*
Row 4	*290*	*841*
Row 5	*200*	*640*
Row 6	*170*	*595*
Row 7	*210*	*798*
Row 8	*190*	*779*
Row 9	*420*	*1,848*
Baggage		
Nose	—	—
FWD Cabin	—	—
Aft (FWD Sec)	*800*	*3,868*
Aft (Aft Sec)	—	—
Fuel (Jet A @ 6.8)	*+1,972*	*+ 5,912*
Total	*14,588*	*43,434*

CG = (43,434 ÷ 14,588) × 100 = 297.7"

2. Calculate the weight reductions:

	Weight	***Moment/100***
Original Wt.	*14,588*	*43,434*
2 pax in row 2	*– 370*	*– 851*
2 pax in row 4	*– 290*	*– 841*
New Total	*13,928*	*41,742*

3. Calculate the new CG:

CG = (41,742 ÷ 13,928) × 100 = 299.7"

4. The CG moved from station 297.7 to station 299.7, a movement of 2.0 inches aft.

(PLT021, AA.I.B.K3e) — FAA-H-8083-1

Answers

8441 [A] 8442 [C]

ATS

8443. (Refer to Figures 3, 6, 8, 9, 10, and 11.) What is the CG shift if the passengers in row 8 are moved to row 2, and the passengers in row 7 are moved to row 1 under Loading Conditions AC-5?

A—1.0 inches forward.
B—8.9 inches forward.
C—6.5 inches forward.

	Weight	***Moment/100***
Basic Empty Wt.	*9,226*	*25,823*
Crew	*360*	*464*
Row 1	—	—
Row 2	—	—
Row 3	*170*	*442*
Row 4	*200*	*580*
Row 5	*290*	*928*
Row 6	*400*	*1,400*
Row 7	*370*	*1,406*
Row 8	*340*	*1,394*
Row 9	*430*	*1,892*
Baggage		
Nose	*100*	*66*
FWD Cabin	*200*	*327*
Aft (FWD Sec)	—	—
Aft (Aft Sec)	—	—
Fuel (Jet B @ 6.5)	*+ 2,210*	*+ 6,610*
Total	*14,296*	*41,332*

Change in CG = 710 lbs × 180" ÷ 14,296 lbs = 8.9" forward

(PLT021, AA.I.B.K3e) — FAA-H-8083-1

ADX

8444. (Refer to Figures 4, 7, 9, 10, and 11.) What is the CG in inches from datum under Loading Conditions AC-6?

A—Station 300.5.
B—Station 296.5.
C—Station 300.8.

	Weight	***Moment/100***
Basic Operating Wt.	*9,005*	*25,934*
Sec A	*500*	*1,125*
Sec B	*500*	*1,275*
Sec C	*550*	*1,567.5*
Sec D	*550*	*1,732.5*
Sec E	*600*	*2,070*
Sec F	*600*	*2,250*
Sec G	*450*	*1,822.5*
Sec H	—	—
Sec J	*350*	*1,627.5*
Sec K	—	—
Sec L	—	—
Fuel (Jet B @ 6.5)	*+2,210*	*+ 6,610*
Total	*15,315*	*46,014*

CG = (46,014 ÷ 15,315) × 100 = 300.5"

(PLT021) — FAA-H-8083-1

ADX

8445. (Refer to Figures 4, 7, 9, 10, and 11.) What is the CG in inches from datum under Loading Conditions AC-7?

A—Station 296.0.
B—Station 297.8.
C—Station 299.9.

	Weight	***Moment/100***
Basic Operating Wt.	*9,005*	*25,934*
Sec A	—	—
Sec B	*400*	*1,020*
Sec C	*450*	*1,282.5*
Sec D	*600*	*1,890*
Sec E	*600*	*2,070*
Sec F	*600*	*2,250*
Sec G	*500*	*2,025*
Sec H	—	—
Sec J	—	—
Sec K	—	—
Sec L	—	—
Fuel	*+ 2,442*	*+ 7,299*
Total	*14,597*	*43,770.5*

CG = (43,770.5 ÷ 14,597) × 100 = 299.9"

(PLT021) — FAA-H-8083-1

Answers

8443 [B] 8444 [A] 8445 [C]

ADX

8446. (Refer to Figures 4, 7, 9, 10, and 11.) What is the CG in inches from datum under Loading Conditions AC-8?

A—Station 297.4.
B—Station 298.1.
C—Station 302.0.

	Weight	*Moment/100*
Basic Operating Wt.	*9,005*	*25,934*
Sec A	*600*	*1,350*
Sec B	*200*	*510*
Sec C	*400*	*1,140*
Sec D	*400*	*1,260*
Sec E	*200*	*690*
Sec F	*200*	*750*
Sec G	*200*	*810*
Sec H	*200*	*870*
Sec J	*300*	*1,395*
Sec K	*250*	*1,248.75*
Sec L	*100*	*533*
Fuel	*+ 2,652*	*+ 7,924*
Total	*14,707*	*44,414.75*

CG = (44,414.75 ÷ 14,707) × 100 = 302.0"

(PLT021) — FAA-H-8083-1

ADX

8447. (Refer to Figures 4, 7, 9, 10, and 11.) What is the CG in inches from datum under Loading Conditions AC-9?

A—Station 296.7.
B—Station 297.1.
C—Station 301.2.

	Weight	*Moment/100*
Basic Operating Wt.	*9,005*	*25,934*
Sec A	*600*	*1,350*
Sec B	*600*	*1,530*
Sec C	*600*	*1,710*
Sec D	*600*	*1,890*
Sec E	*550*	*1,897.5*
Sec F	*350*	*1,312.5*
Sec G	*250*	*1,012.5*
Sec H	*250*	*1,087.5*
Sec J	*150*	*697.5*
Sec K	*200*	*999*
Sec L	*100*	*533*
Fuel (Jet A @ 6.8)	*+ 1,972*	*+ 5,912*
Total	*15,227*	*45,865.5*

CG = (45,865.5 ÷ 15,227) × 100 = 301.2"

(PLT021) — FAA-H-8083-1

ATS

8449. (Refer to Figures 4, 7, 9, 10, and 11.) What is the CG shift if 300 pounds of cargo in section A is moved to section H under Loading Conditions AC-6?

A—4.1 inches aft.
B—3.5 inches aft.
C—4.0 inches aft.

	Weight	*Moment/100*
Basic Operating Wt.	*9,005*	*25,934*
Sec A	*500*	*1,125*
Sec B	*500*	*1,275*
Sec C	*550*	*1,567.5*
Sec D	*550*	*1,732.5*
Sec E	*600*	*2,070*
Sec F	*600*	*2,250*
Sec G	*450*	*1,822.5*
Sec H	—	—
Sec J	*350*	*1,627.5*
Sec K	—	—
Sec L	—	—
Fuel (Jet B @ 6.5)	*+ 2,210*	*+ 6,610*
Total	*15,315*	*46,014*

Change in CG = 300 lbs × 210" ÷ 15,315 lbs = 4.1" aft

(PLT021, AA.I.B.K3e) — FAA-H-8083-1

ATS

8450. (Refer to Figures 4, 7, 9, 10, and 11.) What is the CG shift if the cargo in section F is moved to section A, and 200 pounds of the cargo in section G is added to the cargo in section B, under Loading Conditions AC-7?

A—7.5 inches forward.
B—8.0 inches forward.
C—8.2 inches forward.

	Weight	*Moment/100*
Basic Operating Wt.	*9,005*	*25,934*
Sec A	—	—
Sec B	*400*	*1,020*
Sec C	*450*	*1,282.5*
Sec D	*600*	*1,890*
Sec E	*600*	*2,070*
Sec F	*600*	*2,250*
Sec G	*500*	*2,025*
Sec H	—	—
Sec J	—	—
Sec K	—	—
Sec L	—	—
Fuel	*+ 2,442*	*+ 7,299*
Total	*14,597*	*43,770.5*

Answers

8446 [C] 8447 [C] 8449 [A] 8450 [C]

CG change moving weight from F to A is:
600 × 150 ÷ 14,597 = 6.2 inches forward
CG change moving weight from G to B is:
200 × 150 ÷ 14,597 = 2.1 inches forward
Total change:
6.2 inches + 2.1 inches = 8.3 inches forward

(PLT021, AA.I.B.K3e) — FAA-H-8083-1

ATS

8451. (Refer to Figures 4, 7, 9, 10, and 11.) What is the CG if all cargo in sections A, B, J, K, and L are off-loaded under Loading Conditions AC-8?

A—Station 292.7.
B—Station 297.0.
C—Station 294.6.

Calculate the weight and CG accounting for the off-loaded items:

	Weight	**Moment/100**
Basic Operating Wt.	*9,005*	*25,934*
Sec A	—	—
Sec B	—	—
Sec C	*400*	*1,140*
Sec D	*400*	*1,260*
Sec E	*200*	*690*
Sec F	*200*	*750*
Sec G	*200*	*810*
Sec H	*200*	*870*
Sec J	—	—
Sec K	—	—
Sec L	—	—
Fuel	*+ 2,652*	*+ 7,924*
Total	*13,257*	*39,378*

CG = (39,378 ÷ 13,257) × 100 = 297.0"

(PLT021, AA.I.B.K3e) — FAA-H-8083-1

ATS

8452. (Refer to Figures 4, 7, 9, 10, and 11.) What is the CG if cargo is loaded to bring sections F, G, and H to maximum capacity under Loading Conditions AC-9?

A—Station 307.5.
B—Station 305.4.
C—Station 303.5.

Use the following steps:

1. *Calculate the weight and CG prior to weight changes:*

	Weight	**Moment/100**
Basic Operating Wt.	*9,005*	*25,934*
Sec A	*600*	*1,350*
Sec B	*600*	*1,530*
Sec C	*600*	*1,710*
Sec D	*600*	*1,890*
Sec E	*550*	*1,897.5*
Sec F	*350*	*1,312.5*
Sec G	*250*	*1,012.5*
Sec H	*250*	*1,087.5*
Sec J	*150*	*697.5*
Sec K	*200*	*999*
Sec L	*100*	*533*
Fuel (Jet A @ 6.8)	*+ 1,972*	*+ 5,912*
Total	*15,227*	*45,865.5*

CG = (45,865.5 ÷ 15,227) × 100 = 301.2"

2. *250 pounds can be added to Section F, 350 pounds to Section G and 350 pounds to Section H. Apply these weight additions to the previously calculated weight and Moment/100, then calculate the new CG:*

	Weight	**Moment/100**
Original Wt.	*15,227*	*45,865.5*
Sec F	*250*	*937.5*
Sec G	*350*	*1,417.5*
Sec H	*+ 350*	*+1,522.5*
New Wt.	*16,177*	*49,743*

CG = (49,743 ÷ 16,177) × 100 = 307.5"

(PLT021, AA.I.B.K3e) — FAA-H-8083-1

Answers

8451 [B] 8452 [A]

ATS

8453. (Refer to Figures 4, 7, 9, 10, and 11.) What is the CG shift if the cargo in section G is moved to section J under Loading Conditions AC-10?

A—2.7 inches aft.
B—2.4 inches aft.
C—3.2 inches aft.

	Weight	***Moment/100***
Basic Operating Wt.	*9,005*	*25,934*
Sec A	*350*	*787.5*
Sec B	*450*	*1,147.5*
Sec C	*450*	*1,282.5*
Sec D	*550*	*1,732.5*
Sec E	*550*	*1,897.5*
Sec F	*600*	*2,250*
Sec G	*600*	*2,430*
Sec H	—	—
Sec J	—	—
Sec K	—	—
Sec L	—	—
Fuel (Jet B @ 6.7)	*+ 2,680*	*+ 8,007*
Total	*15,235*	*45,468.5*

Change in CG = 600 lbs × 60" ÷ 15,235 lbs = 2.4" aft

(PLT021, AA.I.B.K3e) — FAA-H-8083-1

ADX

8454. (Refer to Figures 5, 7, 9, and 11.) What limit is exceeded under Operating Conditions AC-11?

A—ZFW limit is exceeded.
B—Aft CG limit is exceeded at takeoff weight.
C—Aft CG limit is exceeded at landing weight.

Use the following steps:

1. *Calculate the Zero Fuel Weight (ZWF) using Operating Conditions BE-11:*

	Weight	***Moment/100***
Basic Empty Wt.	*9,225*	*25,820*
Crew	*340*	*439*
Pax & Bags	*+ 4,200*	*+ 15,025*
Zero Fuel Wt.	*13,765*	*41,284*

2. *Determine the Takeoff Weight:*

	Weight	***Moment/100***
Zero Fuel Wt.	*13,765*	*41,284*
T/O Fuel (340 gal)	*+ 2,312*	*+ 6,915*
Takeoff Wt.	*16,077*	*48,199*

3. *Calculate the Takeoff CG:*

   CG = (48,199 ÷ 16,077) × 100 = 299.8

4. *Determine the Landing Weight:*

	Weight	***Moment/100***
Zero Fuel Wt.	*13,765*	*41,284*
Land Fuel (100 gal)	*+ 680*	*+ 2,068*
Land Wt.	*14,445*	*43,352*

5. *Calculate the Landing Weight CG. Refer to CG = (43,352 ÷ 14,445) × 100 = 300.1*

This exceeds the aft CG limit (300.0) at landing.

(PLT021) — FAA-H-8083-1

ADX

8455. (Refer to Figures 5, 7, 9, and 11.) What limit(s) is(are) exceeded under Operating Conditions AC-12?

A—ZFW limit is exceeded.
B—Landing aft CG limit is exceeded.
C—ZFW and maximum takeoff weight limits are exceeded.

Use the following steps:

1. *Calculate the Zero Fuel Weight using Operating Conditions BE-12:*

	Weight	***Moment/100***
Basic Empty Wt.	*9,100*	*24,990*
Crew	*380*	*490*
Pax & Bags	*+ 4,530*	*+ 16,480*
Zero Fuel Wt.	*14,010*	*41,960*

2. *Determine the Takeoff Weight:*

	Weight	***Moment/100***
Zero Fuel Wt.	*14,010*	*41,960*
T/O Fuel (300 gal)	*+ 2,040*	*+ 6,112*
Takeoff Wt.	*16,050*	*48,072*

3. *Calculate the Takeoff CG:*

   CG = (48,172 ÷ 16,050) × 100 = 299.5

4. *Determine the Landing Weight:*

	Weight	***Moment/100***
Zero Fuel Wt.	*14,010*	*41,960*
Land Fuel (160 gal)	*+ 1,088*	*+ 3,303*
Land Wt.	*15,098*	*45,263*

5. *Calculate the Landing Weight CG. Refer to CG = (45,263 ÷ 15,098) × 100 = 299.8*

This exceeds the maximum Zero Fuel Weight.

(PLT021) — FAA-H-8083-1

Answers

8453 [B] 8454 [C] 8455 [A]

ADX
8456. (Refer to Figures 5, 7, 9, and 11.) What limit, if any, is exceeded under Operating Conditions AC-13?

A—Takeoff forward CG limit is exceeded.
B—No limit is exceeded.
C—Landing aft CG limit is exceeded.

Use the following steps:

1. *Calculate the Zero Fuel Weight using Operating Conditions BE-13:*

	Weight	***Moment/100***
Basic Empty Wt.	*9,000*	*24,710*
Crew	*360*	*464*
Pax & Bags	*+ 4,630*	*+ 16,743*
Zero Fuel Wt.	*13,990*	*41,917*

2. *Determine the Takeoff Weight:*

	Weight	***Moment/100***
Zero Fuel Wt.	*13,990*	*41,917*
T/O Fuel (330 gal)	*+ 2,244*	*+ 6,713*
Takeoff Wt.	*16,234*	*48,630*

3. *Calculate the Takeoff CG:*

   CG = (48,630 ÷ 16,234) × 100 = 299.6

4. *Determine the Landing Weight:*

	Weight	***Moment/100***
Zero Fuel Wt.	*13,990*	*41,917*
Land Fuel (140 gal)	*+ 952*	*+ 2,893*
Land Wt.	*14,942*	*44,810*

5. *Calculate the Landing Weight CG. Refer to CG = (44,810 ÷ 14,942) × 100 = 299.9*

No limits are exceeded.

(PLT021) — FAA-H-8083-1

ADX
8457. (Refer to Figures 5, 7, 9, and 11.) What limit(s) is(are) exceeded under Operating Conditions AC-14?

A—Maximum ZFW limit is exceeded.
B—Takeoff forward CG limit is exceeded.
C—Maximum landing weight and landing forward CG limits are exceeded.

Use the following steps:

1. *Calculate the Zero Fuel Weight using Operating Conditions BE-14:*

	Weight	***Moment/100***
Basic Empty Wt.	*8,910*	*24,570*
Crew	*400*	*516*
Pax & Bags	*+ 4,690*	*+ 13,724*
Zero Fuel Wt.	*14,000*	*38,810*

2. *Determine the Takeoff Weight:*

	Weight	***Moment/100***
Zero Fuel Wt.	*14,000*	*38,810*
T/O Fuel (290 gal)	*+ 1,972*	*+ 5,912*
Takeoff Wt.	*15,972*	*44,722*

3. *Calculate the Takeoff CG:*

   CG = (44,722 ÷ 15,972) × 100 = 280.0

The forward takeoff CG limit is exceeded.

(PLT021) — FAA-H-8083-1

ADX
8458. (Refer to Figures 5, 7, 9, and 11.) What limit(s) is(are) exceeded under Operating Conditions AC-15?

A—Maximum takeoff weight limit is exceeded.
B—Maximum ZFW and takeoff forward CG limits are exceeded.
C—Maximum takeoff weight and takeoff forward CG limits are exceeded.

Use the following steps:

1. *Calculate the Zero Fuel Weight using Operating Conditions BE-15:*

	Weight	***Moment/100***
Basic Empty Wt.	*9,150*	*25,240*
Crew	*370*	*477*
Pax & Bags	*+ 4,500*	*+ 13,561*
Zero Fuel Wt.	*14,020*	*39,278*

2. *Determine the Takeoff Weight:*

	Weight	***Moment/100***
Zero Fuel Wt.	*14,020*	*39,278*
T/O Fuel (380 gal)	*+ 2,584*	*+ 7,722*
Takeoff Wt.	*16,604*	*47,000*

3. *Calculate the Takeoff CG:*

   CG = (47,000 ÷ 16.604) × 100 = 283.1

This exceeds the maximum takeoff gross weight of 16,600.

(PLT021) — FAA-H-8083-1

Answers

8456 [B] 8457 [B] 8458 [A]

Helicopter Weight and Balance

RTC

8419. What is the result of loading a helicopter so that the CG is aft of the rearward limit?

A—Insufficient aft cyclic control to decelerate properly during an approach.
B—Inability of the pilot to recognize this dangerous condition when hovering in a strong headwind.
C—Insufficient forward cyclic control to fly in the upper allowable airspeed range.

If the center of gravity is too far aft of the mast, the helicopter hangs with the nose tilted up. If flight is attempted in this condition, the pilot may find it impossible to fly in the upper allowable airspeed range due to insufficient forward cyclic displacement to maintain a nose low attitude. (PLT240) — FAA-H-8083-21

RTC

8513. (Refer to Figures 29, 31, 32, and 33.) Where is the longitudinal CG located under Operating Conditions BL-1?

A—Station 214.3.
B—Station 235.6.
C—Station 237.8.

Condition	*BL-1*	*Weight*	*Moment*
Empty		*9,387.5*	*2,327,105*
Crew		*340.0*	*39,780*
Pax Row	*1*	*700.0*	*109,830*
	2	*830.0*	*154,546*
	3	*800.0*	*172,320*
	4	*—*	*—*
Baggage	*Center*	*500.0*	*148,500*
	L & R	*200.0*	*59,040*
Fuel		*+ 2,040.0*	*+ 475,400*
Total		*14,797.5*	*3,486,521*

Total Moment ÷ Total Weight = Longitudinal CG

$$\frac{3,486,521}{14,797.5} = 235.6$$

(PLT021) — FAA-H-8083-1

RTC

8514. (Refer to Figures 29, 31, 32, and 33.) Where is the longitudinal CG located under Operating Conditions BL-2?

A—Station 237.6.
B—Station 238.5.
C—Station 262.3.

Condition	*BL-2*	*Weight*	*Moment*
Empty		*9387.5*	*2,327,105*
Crew		*400.0*	*46,800*
Pax Row	*1*	*620.0*	*97,278*
	2	*700.0*	*130,340*
	3	*680.0*	*146,472*
	4	*400.0*	*97,840*
Baggage	*Center*	*550.0*	*163,350*
	L & R	*250.0*	*73,800*
Fuel		*+ 1,625.0*	*+ 389,400*
Total		*14,612.5*	*3,472,385*

Total Moment ÷ Total Weight = Longitudinal CG

$$\frac{3,472,385}{14,612.5} = 237.6$$

(PLT021) — FAA-H-8083-1

RTC

8515. (Refer to Figures 29, 31, 32, and 33.) Where is the longitudinal CG located under Operating Conditions BL-3?

A—Station 223.4.
B—Station 239.0.
C—Station 240.3.

Condition	*BL-3*	*Weight*	*Moment*
Empty		*9,387.5*	*2,327,105*
Crew		*360.0*	*42,120*
Pax Row	*1*	*—*	*—*
	2	*750.0*	*139,650*
	3	*810.0*	*174,474*
	4	*650.0*	*158,990*
Baggage	*Center*	*300.0*	*89,100*
	L & R	*—*	*—*
Fuel		*+ 2,448.0*	*+ 583,900*
Total		*14,705.5*	*3,515,339*

Total Moment ÷ Total Weight = Longitudinal CG

$$\frac{3,515,339}{14,705.5} = 239.05$$

(PLT021) — FAA-H-8083-1

Answers

8419 [C] 8513 [B] 8514 [A] 8515 [B]

RTC

8516. (Refer to Figures 29, 31, 32, and 33.) Where is the longitudinal CG located under Operating Conditions BL-4?

A—Station 238.1.
B—Station 220.4.
C—Station 236.5.

Condition	*BL-4*	*Weight*	*Moment*
Empty		*9,387.5*	*2,327,105*
Crew		*380.0*	*44,460*
Pax Row	*1*	*180.0*	*28,242*
	2	*800.0*	*148,960*
	3	*720.0*	*155,088*
	4	*200.0*	*48,920*
Baggage	*Center*	*200.0*	*59,400*
	L & R	*100.0*	*29,520*
Fuel		*+ 2,600.0*	*+ 627,400*
Total		*14,567.5*	*3,469,095*

Total Moment ÷ Total Weight = Longitudinal CG

$$\frac{3,469,095}{14,567.5} = 238.14$$

(PLT021) — FAA-H-8083-1

RTC

8517. (Refer to Figures 29, 31, 32, and 33.) Where is the longitudinal CG located under Operating Conditions BL-5?

A—Station 232.0.
B—Station 235.4.
C—Station 234.9.

Condition	*BL-5*	*Weight*	*Moment*
Empty		*9,387.5*	*2,327,105*
Crew		*370.0*	*43,290*
Pax Row	*1*	*680.0*	*106,692*
	2	*950.0*	*176,890*
	3	*850.0*	*183,090*
	4	*500.0*	*122,300*
Baggage	*Center*	*450.0*	*133,650*
	L & R	—	—
Fuel		*+ 1,768.0*	*+ 420,000*
Total		*14,955.5*	*3,513,017*

Total Moment ÷ Total Weight = Longitudinal CG

$$\frac{3,513,017}{14,955.5} = 234.9$$

(PLT021) — FAA-H-8083-1

Helicopter Weight and Balance: CG Shifts

These questions require a re-computation of CG based on a shift of weight only, i.e., CG will change but total weight does not change. AC 91-23A, Chapter 5 gives us a formula for working this type of problem.

$$\frac{\text{Weight Shifted}}{\text{Total Weight}} = \frac{\text{Change of CG}}{\text{Distance of Shift}}$$

These problems may also be worked with a flight computer as shown in AC 91-23A, Chapter 5 in the following manner:

1. Set Weight Shifted (mile scale) over Total Weight (minute scale).
2. Find the Change in CG on the mile scale over the distance shifted on the minute scale.

Question 8518 is solved using both methods.

Answers

8516 [A] 8517 [C]

RTC

8518. (Refer to Figures 29, 31, 32, and 33.) What is the CG shift if all passengers in row 1 are moved to row 4 under Operating Conditions BL-1?

A—5.0 inches aft.
B—4.1 inches aft.
C—0.19 inch aft.

Using FAA Figure 29:
Weight shifted = 700 lbs, Total weight = 14,797.5
The distance shifted is the difference between Row 4 (Station 244.6) and Row 1 (Station 156.9):

244.6 – 156.9 = 87.7

To find the CG shift:

$$\frac{700}{14{,}797.5} = \frac{\text{CG Shift}}{87.7}$$

The shift from Row 1 to Row 4 is 4.15 aft.

or:

On the E6-B, set 700 (miles scale) over 14,797.5 (round it out: 14,800) on the minutes scale. Find 87.7 on the minutes scale and read 4.15 above it.

(PLT021) — FAA-H-8083-1

RTC

8519. (Refer to Figures 29, 31, 32, and 33.) What is the CG shift if one passenger weighing 150 pounds in row 2 is moved to row 4 under Operating Conditions BL-2?

A—0.1 inch aft.
B—0.6 inch aft.
C—1.1 inches aft.

$$\frac{\text{Weight Shifted (150)}}{\text{Total Weight (14,612.5)}} = \frac{\text{CG Shift}}{\text{Distance of Shift (58.4)}}$$

= .60 aft

(PLT021) — FAA-H-8083-1

RTC

8520. (Refer to Figures 29, 31, 32, and 33.) What is the CG shift if all passengers in row 4 are moved to row 1 under Operating Conditions BL-3?

A—3.7 inches forward.
B—0.4 inch forward.
C—3.9 inches forward.

$$\frac{\text{Weight Shifted (650)}}{\text{Total Weight (14,705.5)}} = \frac{\text{CG Shift}}{\text{Distance of Shift (87.7)}}$$

= -3.88 FWD

(PLT021) — FAA-H-8083-1

RTC

8521. (Refer to Figures 29, 31, 32, and 33.) What is the CG shift if the passengers in row 1 are moved to row 4 under Operating Conditions BL-4?

A—1.1 inches aft.
B—1.6 inches aft.
C—0.2 inch aft.

$$\frac{\text{Weight Shifted (180)}}{\text{Total Weight (14,567.5)}} = \frac{\text{CG Shift}}{\text{Distance of Shift (87.7)}}$$

= 1.08 aft

(PLT021) — FAA-H-8083-1

RTC

8522. (Refer to Figures 29, 31, 32, and 33.) What is the CG shift if one passenger, weighing 100 pounds, seated in row 1 is moved to row 3 under Operating Conditions BL-5?

A—1.0 inch aft.
B—0.4 inch aft.
C—1.3 inches aft.

$$\frac{\text{Weight Shifted (100)}}{\text{Total Weight (14,955.5)}} = \frac{\text{CG Shift}}{\text{Distance of Shift (58.5)}}$$

= .39 aft

(PLT021) — FAA-H-8083-1

Answers

8518 [B]	8519 [B]	8520 [C]	8521 [A]	8522 [B]

Helicopter Weight and Balance: Load Limits

In these questions, it will be necessary to compute both a takeoff and a landing weight and balance. Since the stations (CG) for fuel vary with weight, the most simple method of solving these problems is to compute the zero fuel weight for the given conditions, then perform a separate weight and balance for takeoff and landing. Some moments are given; others are not and therefore must be computed. Also, the fuel is stated in gallons, not pounds, which can be converted using the Jet A Table (FAA Figure 33).

RTC

8523. (Refer to Figures 30, 32, 33, and 35.) What limits are exceeded under Loading Conditions BL-6?

A—Aft CG limits are exceeded at takeoff and landing.
B—Takeoff aft CG and landing forward CG limits are exceeded.
C—Maximum takeoff weight and takeoff aft CG limits are exceeded.

Condition BL-6	***Weight***	***Moment***
Empty/basic	*10,225*	*2,556,250*
Crew	*340*	*39,780*
Passengers	*3,280*	*672,250*
Baggage Center	*+ 700*	*+ 207,900*
Zero Fuel wt.	*14,545*	*3,476,180*

Takeoff	***Weight***	***Moment***
Zero fuel wt.	*14,545*	*3,476,180*
Fuel 435 gal.	*+ 2,958*	*+ 719,900*
Total	*17,503*	*4,196,080*

Landing	***Weight***	***Moment***
Zero fuel wt.	*14,545*	*3,476,180*
Fuel 80 gal.	*+ 544*	*+ 125,600*
Total	*15,089*	*3,601,780*

CG = 4,196,080 ÷ 17,503 = 239.73
CG = 3,601,780 ÷ 15,089 = 238.7

Checking the longitudinal CG envelope (FAA Figure 35), we find that at takeoff, the aircraft is both over maximum gross weight and out of aft CG. (PLT021) — FAA-H-8083-1

RTC

8524. (Refer to Figures 30, 32, 33, and 35.) What limit, if any, is exceeded under Loading Conditions BL-7?

A—No limit is exceeded.
B—Forward CG limit is exceeded at landing only.
C—Forward CG limit is exceeded at takeoff and landing.

Condition BL-7	***Weight***	***Moment***
Empty/basic	*9,450*	*2,323,600*
Crew	*380*	*44,460*
Passengers	*2,880*	*541,860*
Baggage (center)	*+ 600*	*+ 178,200*
Zero Fuel	*13,310*	*3,088,120*

Takeoff	***Weight***	***Moment***
Zero fuel wt.	*13,310*	*3,088,120*
Fuel 290 gal.	*+ 1,972*	*+ 457,900*
Total	*15,282*	*3,546,020*

Takeoff CG = 3,546,020 ÷ 15,282 = 232.04

Original fuel load (Fig 30) is 290 gal. Trip fuel burn is indicated at 190 gal. Fuel upon landing is 100 gal. 100 gal × 6.8 lbs/gal = 680 lbs. Figure 33 shows the CG for 680 lbs is 228.2. 680 × 228.2 = 155,176.

Landing	***Weight***	***Moment***
Zero fuel wt.	*13,310*	*3,088,120*
Fuel 100 gal.	*+ 680*	*+ 155,176*
Total	*13,990*	*3,243,296*

CG = 3,243,296 ÷ 13,990 = 231.82

Checking the longitudinal CG envelope (FAA Figure 35), we find that at landing only, the forward CG limit is exceeded. (PLT021) — FAA-H-8083-1

Answers

8523 [C] 8524 [B]

RTC
8525. (Refer to Figures 30, 32, 33, and 35.) What limit, if any, is exceeded under Loading Conditions BL-8?

A—No limit is exceeded.
B—Forward CG limit is exceeded at landing only.
C—Forward CG limit is exceeded at takeoff and landing.

Condition BL-8	*Weight*	*Moment*
Empty/basic	*9,000*	*2,202,050*
Crew	*410*	*47,970*
Passengers	*3,150*	*642,580*
Bags center	*+ 300*	*+ 89,100*
Zero Fuel	*12,860*	*2,981,700*

Takeoff	*Weight*	*Moment*
Zero fuel wt.	*12,860*	*2,981,700*
Fuel 220 gal.	*+ 1,496*	*+ 369,400*
Total	*14,356*	*3,351,100*

Takeoff CG = 3,351,100 ÷ 14,356 = 233.43

Original fuel load (Fig 30) is 220 gal. Trip fuel burn is indicated at 190 gal. Fuel upon landing is 30 gal. 30 gal × 6.8 lbs/gal = 204 lbs. Figure 33 shows the CG for 204 lbs is 244.4. 204 × 244.4 = 49,857.6.

Landing	*Weight*	*Moment*
Zero fuel wt.	*12,860*	*2,981,700*
Fuel 30 gal.	*+ 204*	*+ 49,857.6*
Total	*13,064*	*3,031,557*

Landing CG = 3,031,557 ÷ 13,064 = 232.05

Checking the longitudinal CG envelope (FAA Figure 35), we find that no limits are exceeded. (PLT021) — FAA-H-8083-1

RTC
8526. (Refer to Figures 30, 32, 33, and 35.) What limit, if any, is exceeded under Loading Conditions BL-9?

A—No limit is exceeded.
B—Aft CG limit is exceeded at takeoff only.
C—Aft CG limit is exceeded at takeoff and landing.

Condition BL-9	*Weight*	*Moment*
Empty/basic	*9,510*	*2,349,990*
Crew	*360*	*42,120*
Passengers	*2,040*	*473,220*
Bags center	*+ 550*	*+ 163,350*
Zero Fuel	*12,460*	*3,028,680*

Takeoff	*Weight*	*Moment*
Zero fuel wt.	*12,460*	*3,028,680*
Fuel 435 gal.	*+ 2,958*	*+ 719,900*
Total	*15,418*	*3,748,580*

Landing	*Weight*	*Moment*
Zero fuel wt.	*12,460*	*3,028,680*
Fuel 110 gal.	*+ 748*	*+ 170,900*
Total	*13,208*	*3,199,580*

CG = 3,748,580 ÷ 15,418 = 243.13
CG = 3,199,580 ÷ 13,208 = 242.24

Checking the longitudinal CG envelope (FAA Figure 35), we find that aft CG is exceeded at takeoff only. (PLT021) — FAA-H-8083-1

RTC
8527. (Refer to Figures 30, 32, 33, and 35.) What limit, if any, is exceeded under Loading Conditions BL-10?

A—No limit is exceeded.
B—Aft CG limit is exceeded at takeoff.
C—Forward CG limit is exceeded at landing.

Condition BL-10	*Weight*	*Moment*
Empty/basic	*9,375*	*2,329,680*
Crew	*400*	*46,800*
Passengers	*2,400*	*456,070*
Baggage (center)	*+ 650*	*+ 193,050*
Zero Fuel	*12,825*	*3,025,600*

Note: For this problem, it is easier to compute the landing data by subtracting the weight and moment of the fuel used from the takeoff data.

Takeoff	*Weight*	*Moment*
Zero fuel wt.	*12,825*	*3,025,600*
Fuel 380 gal.	*+ 2,584*	*+ 620,200*
Total	*15,409*	*3,645,800*

Landing	*Weight*	*Moment*
Takeoff	*15,409*	*3,645,800*
Fuel 330 gal.	*– 2,244*	*– 529,600*
Total	*13,165*	*3,116,200*

CG = 3,645,800 ÷ 15,409 = 236.6
CG = 3,116,200 ÷ 13,165 = 236.7

Checking the longitudinal CG envelope (FAA Figure 35), we find that no limits are exceeded. (PLT021) — FAA-H-8083-1

Answers

8525 [A] 8526 [B] 8527 [A]

Helicopter Weight and Balance: Lateral CG

These questions are answered by using the formula given in AC 91-23A.

1. For shifted weight:

$$\frac{\text{Weight Shifted (WS)}}{\text{Total Weight (TW)}} = \frac{\text{CG Shift (CS)}}{\text{Distance Shifted (DS)}}$$

2. For added/removed weight (WA or WR):

$$\frac{\text{(WA or WR)}}{\text{New Total Weight (NTW)}} = \frac{\text{CG Shift (CS)}}{\text{Distance shifted (DS)}}$$

Refer to answers to Questions 8523 through 8527 for total weights.

RTC

8528. (Refer to Figures 30, 31, 32, 33, and 34.) Given Loading Conditions BL-6, what is the effect on lateral CG if the outside passengers from each row on the left side are deplaned? Deplaned passenger weights are 170 pounds each.

A—CG shifts 1.5 inches right, out of limits.
B—CG shifts 1.4 inches right, within limits.
C—CG shifts 1.6 inches left, out of limits.

1. *Total weight for BL-6 = 17,503 (from Question 8523)*
2. *Weight removed = 170 × 4 = 680*
3. *New total weight = 17,503 – 680 = 16,823*
4. *Distance shifted = the average arm of the four outboard seats (34 + 35.4 + 35.4 + 39.4) ÷ 4 = 36.05.*

$$\frac{WR}{NTW} = \frac{CS}{DS}$$

(Very close to 1.5 inches.)

Since the deplaned passengers were all on the left, CG shift is to the right. Referring to FAA Figure 34, at our new weight of 16,823, the lateral CG is out of limits to the right. (PLT021) — FAA-H-8083-1

RTC

8529. (Refer to Figures 30, 31, 32, 33, and 34.) Given Loading Conditions BL-7, what is the effect on lateral CG if additional passengers, each weighing 200 pounds, are seated, one in each outside right seat of rows 1, 2, 3, and 4?

A—CG shifts 1.5 inches left, out of limits.
B—CG shifts 0.2 inch right, within limits.
C—CG shifts 1.8 inches right, out of limits.

1. *Total weight for BL-7 = 15,282 (from Question 8524)*
2. *Weight added = 800*
3. *New total weight = 15,282 + 800 = 16,082*
4. *Distance shifted = the average arm of the four outboard seats (34 + 35.4 + 35.4 + 39.4) ÷ 4 = 36.05.*

$$\frac{WA}{NTW} = \frac{CS}{DS}$$

CG shifts right 1.79 inches, out of limits.

(PLT021) — FAA-H-8083-1

Answers

8528 [A] 8529 [C]

RTC

8530. (Refer to Figures 30, 31, 32, 33, and 34.) Given Loading Conditions BL-8, what is the effect on lateral CG if a passenger weighing 200 pounds is added to the outer left seat of row 1, and a passenger weighing 220 pounds is added to the outer left seat of row 4?

A—CG shifts 1.5 inches left, out of limits.
B—CG shifts 1.2 inches left, within limits.
C—CG shifts 1.0 inch left, within limits.

1. *Total weight for BL-8 = 14,356 (from Question 8525)*
2. *Weight added = 420*
3. *New total weight = 14,356 + 420 = 14,776*
4. *Distance shifted = the average arm of Row 1 and Row 4 (34 + 39.4) ÷ 2 = 36.7*

$$\frac{WA}{NTW} = \frac{CS}{DS}$$

CG shifts left 1.04 inches, within limits.

(PLT021) — FAA-H-8083-1

RTC

8531. (Refer to Figures 30, 31, 32, 33, and 34.) Given Loading Conditions BL-9, what is the effect on lateral CG if passengers, each weighing 160 pounds, are added to the outer left seats of rows 1 and 2; and passengers, each weighing 180 pounds, are added to the outer right seats of rows 3 and 4?

A—CG shifts 0.14 inch left.
B—CG shifts 0.15 inch right.
C—CG does not shift.

It is obvious without doing the math, considering the weights and arms involved, that answer B is the only possible answer. However:

1. *Total weight for BL-9 = 15,418 (from Question 8526)*
2. *Weight added = 680*
3. *New total weight = 15,418 + 680 = 16,098*
4. *Distance shifted = the difference between the average left and right arms. If we consider the left side as negative, then distance shifted = [-(34 + 35.4) ÷ 2] + (35.4 + 39.4) ÷ 2 = -34.7 + 37.4 = + 2.7 inches.*

$$\frac{WA}{NTW} = \frac{CS}{DS}$$

CG shifts .11 inches right.

(PLT021) — FAA-H-8083-1

RTC

8532. (Refer to Figures 30, 31, 32, 33, and 34.) Given Loading Conditions BL-10, what is the effect on lateral CG if a passenger, weighing 240 pounds, is shifted from the outer right seat of row 4 to the outer left seat of row 1?

A—CG shifts 1.1 inches left, within limits.
B—CG shifts 1.5 inches left, out of limits.
C—CG shifts 1.7 inches left, out of limits.

1. *Total weight for BL-10 = 15,409 (from Question 8527)*
2. *Weight Shifted = 240*
3. *Distance shifted = the distance between Row 1 and Row 4 (34 + 39.4) = 73.4*

$$\frac{WS}{NTW} = \frac{CS}{DS}$$

CG shifts left 1.14 inches, within limits.

(PLT021) — FAA-H-8083-1

Answers

8530 [C] 8531 [B] 8532 [A]

Floor Loading Limits

In addition to ensuring that an aircraft is loaded within its weight and balance limits, it is important to make sure that the floor of a cargo compartment is not overloaded. The load limit of a floor is stated in pounds per square foot. The questions on the test require you to determine the maximum load that can be placed on a pallet of certain dimensions.

For example: what is the maximum weight that may be carried on a pallet which has the dimensions of 37 × 39 inches, when the floor load limit is 115 pounds per square foot, the pallet weight is 37 pounds, and the weight of the tiedown devices is 21 pounds?

The first step is to determine the area of the floor (in square feet) covered by the pallet. This is done by multiplying the given dimensions (which calculates the area in square inches) and dividing by 144 (which converts the area to square feet):

37 inches × 39 inches ÷ 144 square inches = 10.02 square feet.

The next step is to determine the total weight that the floor under the pallet can support, by multiplying the area times the floor load limit given in the question:

10.02 square feet × 115 pounds per square foot = 1,152.39 pounds.

The final step is to determine the maximum weight which can be placed on the pallet by subtracting the weight of the pallet and the tiedown devices from the total load limit:

1,152.39 pounds – 58 pounds = 1,094.39 pounds.

The weight on the pallet must be equal to or less than this number (1,094.39, in this example). If it is more than this number, the combination of cargo, pallet, and tiedown weight would exceed the floor load limit. A review of the test questions reveals that the closest answer choice is always equal to or slightly less than the floor limit. All the calculations in this section were performed with a calculator carrying all digits to the right of the decimal point forward for the next step of the problem. The explanations show only two places to the right of the decimal.

A variation of the pallet loading problem is to determine the minimum floor load limit (in pounds per square foot) required to carry a particular loaded pallet. For example: what is the minimum floor load limit to carry a pallet of cargo with a pallet dimension of 78.9 inches × 98.7 inches, and a combination weight of pallet, cargo, and tiedown devices of 9,896.5 pounds?

The first step is to determine the floor area, multiplying the dimensions and dividing by 144 (78.9 × 98.7 ÷ 144 = 54.08 square feet). The second step is to determine the minimum required floor limit by dividing the total weight of the pallet, cargo, and tiedowns by the pallet area (9,896.5 ÷ 54.08 = 183.00 pounds). The correct answer must be at or *above* this weight (183.00 pounds, in this example).

ATM, ATS, RTC

8769. What is the maximum allowable weight that may be carried on a pallet which has the dimensions of 33.5 × 48.5 inches?

Floor load limit ....76 lb/sq ft
Pallet weight .... 44 lb
Tiedown devices.. 27 lb

A—857.4 pounds.
B—830.4 pounds.
C—786.5 pounds.

1. *Determine the area.*

   33.5 × 48.5 ÷ 144 = 11.28 square feet.
2. *Determine the floor load limit.*

   11.28 × 76 = 857.51 pounds.
3. *Subtract the weight of the pallet and tiedown devices.*

   857.51 – 71 = 786.51 pounds.

(PLT121, AA.I.B.K3e) — FAA-H-8083-1

Answers

8769 [C]

ATM, ATS, RTC

8770. What is the maximum allowable weight that may be carried on a pallet which has the dimensions of 36.5 × 48.5 inches?

Floor load limit .... 112 lb/sq ft
Pallet weight .... 45 lb
Tiedown devices .... 29 lb

A—1,331.8 pounds.
B—1,302.8 pounds.
C—1,347.8 pounds.

1. *Determine the area.*

   36.5 × 48.5 ÷ 144 = 12.29 square feet.

2. *Determine the floor load limit.*

   12.29 × 112 = 1,376.86 pounds.

3. *Subtract the weight of the pallet and tiedown devices.*

   1,376.86 – 74 = 1,302.86 pounds.

(PLT121, AA.I.B.K3e — FAA-H-8083-1

ATM, ATS, RTC

8771. What is the maximum allowable weight that may be carried on a pallet which has the dimensions of 42.6 × 48.7 inches?

Floor load limit .... 121 lb/sq ft
Pallet weigh .... 47 lb
Tiedown devices .... 33 lb

A—1,710.2 pounds.
B—1,663.2 pounds.
C—1,696.2 pounds.

1. *Determine the area.*

   42.6 × 48.7 ÷ 144 = 14.41 square feet.

2. *Determine the floor load limit.*

   14.41 × 121 = 1,743.25 pounds.

3. *Subtract the weight of the pallet and tiedown devices.*

   1,743.25 – 80 = 1,663.25 pounds.

(PLT121, AA.I.B.K3e) — FAA-H-8083-1

ATM, ATS, RTC

8772. What is the maximum allowable weight that may be carried on a pallet which has the dimensions of 24.6 × 68.7 inches?

Floor load limit .... 85 lb/sq ft
Pallet weight .... 44 lb
Tiedown devices .... 29 lb

A—924.5 pounds.
B—968.6 pounds.
C—953.6 pounds.

1. *Determine the area.*

   24.6 × 68.7 ÷ 144 = 11.74 square feet.

2. *Determine the floor load limit.*

   11.74 × 85 = 997.58 pounds.

3. *Subtract the weight of the pallet and tiedown devices.*

   997.58 – 73 = 924.58 pounds.

(PLT121, AA.I.B.K3e) — FAA-H-8083-1

ATM, ATS, RTC

8773. What is the maximum allowable weight that may be carried on a pallet which has the dimensions of 34.6 × 46.4 inches?

Floor load limit .... 88 lb/sq ft
Pallet weight .... 41 lb
Tiedown devices .... 26 lb

A—914.1 pounds.
B—940.1 pounds.
C—981.1 pounds.

1. *Determine the area.*

   34.6 × 46.4 ÷ 144 = 11.15 square feet.

2. *Determine the floor load limit.*

   11.15 × 88 = 981.10 pounds.

3. *Subtract the weight of the pallet and tiedown devices.*

   981.10 – 67 = 914.10 pounds.

(PLT121, AA.I.B.K3e) — FAA-H-8083-1

Answers

8770 [B] 8771 [B] 8772 [A] 8773 [A]

ATM, ATS, RTC

8776. What is the maximum allowable weight that may be carried on a pallet which has the dimensions of 33.5 × 48.5 inches?

Floor load limit .... 66 lb/sq ft
Pallet weight .... 34 lb
Tiedown devices.. 29 lb

A—744.6 pounds.
B—681.6 pounds.
C—663.0 pounds.

1. *Determine the area.*

   33.5 × 48.5 ÷ 144 = 11.28 square feet.

2. *Determine the floor load limit.*

   11.28 × 66 = 744.68 pounds.

3. *Subtract the weight of the pallet and tiedown devices.*

   744.68 – 63 = 681.68 pounds.

(PLT121, AA.I.B.K3e) — FAA-H-8083-1

ATM, ATS, RTC

8777. What is the maximum allowable weight that may be carried on a pallet which has the dimensions of 36.5 × 48.5 inches?

Floor load limit ....107 lb/sq ft
Pallet weight .... 37 lb
Tiedown devices.. 33 lb

A—1,295.3 pounds.
B—1,212.3 pounds.
C—1,245.3 pounds.

1. *Determine the area.*

   36.5 × 48.5 ÷ 144 = 12.29 square feet.

2. *Determine the floor load limit.*

   12.29 × 107 = 1,315.39 pounds.

3. *Subtract the weight of the pallet and tiedown devices.*

   1,315.39 – 70 = 1,245.39 pounds.

(PLT121, AA.I.B.K3e) — FAA-H-8083-1

ATM, ATS, RTC

8778. What is the maximum allowable weight that may be carried on a pallet which has the dimensions of 42.6 × 48.7 inches?

Floor load limit .... 117 lb/sq ft
Pallet weight .... 43 lb
Tiedown devices.. 31 lb

A—1,611.6 pounds.
B—1,654.6 pounds.
C—1,601.6 pounds.

1. *Determine the area.*

   42.6 × 48.7 ÷ 144 = 14.41 square feet.

2. *Determine the floor load limit.*

   14.41 × 117 = 1,685.63 pounds.

3. *Subtract the weight of the pallet and tiedown devices.*

   1,685.63 – 74 = 1,611.63 pounds.

(PLT121, AA.I.B.K3e) — FAA-H-8083-1

ATM, ATS, RTC

8779. What is the maximum allowable weight that may be carried on a pallet which has the dimensions of 24.6 × 68.7 inches?

Floor load limit ....79 lb/sq ft
Pallet weight .... 43 lb
Tiedown devices.. 27 lb

A—884.1 pounds.
B—857.1 pounds.
C—841.1 pounds.

1. *Determine the area.*

   24.6 × 68.7 ÷ 144 = 11.74 square feet.

2. *Determine the floor load limit.*

   11.74 × 79 = 927.16 pounds.

3. *Subtract the weight of the pallet and tiedown devices.*

   927.16 – 70 = 857.16 pounds.

(PLT121, AA.I.B.K3e) — FAA-H-8083-1

Answers

8776 [B]	8777 [C]	8778 [A]	8779 [B]

ATM, ATS, ADX

9920. What is the maximum pallet weight for a floor with a limit of 140 pounds per square foot and the following information?

Pallet dimensions .... 32.4 inches × 34.9 inches
Pallet weight .... 45 pounds
Tiedown devices....................................... 20 pounds

A—1,099 pounds.
B—1,129 pounds.
C—1,034 pounds.

1. *Determine the area. 32.4 × 34.9 ÷ 144 = 7.85 square feet.*
2. *Determine the floor load limit. 7.85 × 140 = 1,099.35 pounds.*
3. *Subtract the weight of the pallet and tiedown devices. 1,099.35 – 65 = 1,034.35 pounds.*

(PLT121, AA.I.B.K3e) — FAA-H-8083-1

ATM, ATS, ADX

9938. What is the maximum load that can be placed on a pallet without exceeding the floor weight limit of 260 pounds per square inch?

Pallet dimensions ....95.2 inches × 140.1 inches
Pallet weight .... 350 pounds
Tiedown devices...................................... 120 pounds

A—23,606 pounds.
B—24,076 pounds.
C—24,546 pounds.

1. *Determine the area. 95.2 × 140.1 ÷ 144 = 92.62 square feet.*
2. *Determine the floor load limit. 92.62 × 260 = 24,081.20 pounds.*
3. *Subtract the weight of the pallet and tiedown devices. 24,081.20 – 470 = 23,611.20 pounds.*

(PLT121, AA.I.B.K3e) — FAA-H-8083-1

ATM, ATS, RTC

8781. What is the maximum allowable weight that may be carried on a pallet which has the dimensions of 143 × 125.2 inches?

Floor load limit .... 209 lb/sq ft
Pallet weight ....197 lb
Tiedown devices... 66 lb

A—25,984.9 pounds.
B—25,787.9 pounds.
C—25,721.9 pounds.

1. *Determine the area.*

   143 × 125.2 ÷ 144 = 124.33 square feet.
2. *Determine the floor load limit.*

   124.33 × 209 = 25,985.09 pounds.
3. *Subtract the weight of the pallet and tiedown devices.*

   25,985.09 – 263 = 25,722.09 pounds.

(PLT121, AA.I.B.K3e) — FAA-H-8083-1

ATM, ATS, RTC

8787. What is the maximum allowable weight that may be carried on a pallet which has the dimensions of 138.5 × 97.6 inches?

Floor load limit .... 235 lb/sq ft
Pallet weight ....219 lb
Tiedown devices.. 71 lb

A—21,840.9 pounds.
B—21,769.9 pounds.
C—22,059.9 pounds.

1. *Determine the area.*

   138.5 × 97.6 ÷ 144 = 93.87 square feet.
2. *Determine the floor load limit.*

   93.87 × 235 = 22,059.97 pounds.
3. *Subtract the weight of the pallet and tiedown devices.*

   22,059.97 – 290 = 21,769.97 pounds.

(PLT121, AA.I.B.K3e) — FAA-H-8083-1

Answers

9920 [C] 9938 [A] 8781 [C] 8787 [B]

ATM, ATS, RTC

8788. What is the maximum allowable weight that may be carried on a pallet which has the dimensions of 96.1 × 133.3 inches?

Floor load limit .... 249 lb/sq ft
Pallet weight .... 347 lb
Tiedown devices .... 134 lb

A—21,669.8 pounds.
B—21,803.8 pounds.
C—22,120.8 pounds.

1. *Determine the area.*

   96.1 × 133.3 ÷ 144 = 88.96 square feet.

2. *Determine the floor load limit.*

   88.96 × 249 = 22,150.85 pounds.

3. *Subtract the weight of the pallet and tiedown devices.*

   22,150.85 – 481 = 21,669.85 pounds.

(PLT121, AA.I.B.K3e) — FAA-H-8083-1

ATM, ATS, RTC

8789. What is the maximum allowable weight that may be carried on a pallet which has the dimensions of 87.7 × 116.8 inches?

Floor load limit .... 175 lb/sq ft
Pallet weight .... 137 lb
Tiedown devices .... 49 lb

A—12,262.4 pounds.
B—12,448.4 pounds.
C—12,311.4 pounds.

1. *Determine the area.*

   87.7 × 116.8 ÷ 144 = 71.13 square feet.

2. *Determine the floor load limit.*

   71.13 × 175 = 12,448.52 pounds.

3. *Subtract the weight of the pallet and tiedown devices.*

   12,448.52 – 186 = 12,262.52 pounds.

(PLT121, AA.I.B.K3e) — FAA-H-8083-1

ATM, ATS, RTC

8790. What is the maximum allowable weight that may be carried on a pallet which has the dimensions of 98.7 × 78.9 inches?

Floor load limit .... 183 lb/sq ft
Pallet weight .... 161 lb
Tiedown devices .... 54 lb

A—9,896.5 pounds.
B—9,735.5 pounds.
C—9,681.5 pounds.

1. *Determine the area.*

   98.7 × 78.9 ÷ 144 = 54.08 square feet.

2. *Determine the floor load limit.*

   54.08 × 183 = 9,896.53 pounds.

3. *Subtract the weight of the pallet and tiedown devices.*

   9,896.53 – 215 = 9,681.53 pounds.

(PLT121, AA.I.B.K3e) — FAA-H-8083-1

ATM, ATS, RTC

8791. What minimum floor load limit must an aircraft have to carry the following pallet of cargo?

Pallet dimensions .... 78.9 wide × 98.7 inches
Pallet weight .... 161 lb
Tiedown devices .... 54 lb
Cargo weight .... 9,681.5 lb

A—182 lb/sq ft.
B—180 lb/sq ft.
C—183 lb/sq ft.

1. *Determine the area.*

   78.9 × 98.7 ÷ 144 = 54.08 square feet.

2. *Determine the total weight.*

   9,681.5 + 54 + 161 = 9,896.5

3. *Determine the minimum floor load limit.*

   9,896.5 ÷ 54.08 = 183.00 lbs/sq ft.

(PLT121, AA.I.B.K3e) — FAA-H-8083-1

Answers

8788 [A] 8789 [A] 8790 [C] 8791 [C]

ATM, ATS, RTC

8844. What is the minimum floor load limit that an aircraft must have to carry the following pallet of cargo?

Pallet dimensions ....39 × 37 inches.
Pallet weight ....37 lbs.
Tiedown devices...21 lbs
Cargo weight ....1,094.3 lbs.

A—115 lbs/sq ft.
B—112 lbs/sq ft.
C—109 lbs/sq ft.

1. *Determine the area.*

   39 × 37 ÷ 144 = 10.02 sq ft.

2. *Determine the total weight.*

   1,094.3 + 21 + 37 = 1,152.3

3. *Determine the minimum floor load limit.*

   1,152.3 ÷ 10.02 = 114.99 lbs/sq ft.

(PLT121, AA.I.B.K3e) — FAA-H-8083-1

ATM, ATS, RTC

8845. What is the minimum floor load limit that an aircraft must have to carry the following pallet of cargo?

Pallet dimensions ....37.5 × 35 inches.
Pallet weight .... 34 lbs.
Tiedown devices..23 lbs.
Cargo weight ....1,255.4 lbs.

A—152 lbs/sq ft.
B—148 lbs/sq ft.
C—144 lbs/sq ft.

1. *Determine the area.*

   37.5 × 35 ÷ 144 = 9.12 sq ft.

2. *Determine the total weight.*

   1,255.4 + 23 + 34 = 1,312.4

3. *Determine the minimum floor load limit.*

   1,312.4 ÷ 9.12 = 143.99 lbs/sq ft.

(PLT121, AA.I.B.K3e) — FAA-H-8083-1

ATM, ATS, RTC

8846. What is the minimum floor load limit that an aircraft must have to carry the following pallet of cargo?

Pallet dimensions .... 48.5 × 33.5 inches.
Pallet weight .... 44 lbs.
Tiedown devices..27 lbs.
Cargo weight ....786.5 lbs.

A—79 lbs/sq ft.
B—76 lbs/sq ft.
C—73 lbs/sq ft.

1. *Determine the area.*

   48.5 × 33.5 ÷ 144 = 11.28 sq ft.

2. *Determine the total weight.*

   786.5 + 27 + 44 = 857.5

3. *Determine the minimum floor load limit.*

   857.5 ÷ 11.28 = 76.00 lbs/sq ft.

(PLT121, AA.I.B.K3e) — FAA-H-8083-1

ATM, ATS, RTC

8847. What is the minimum floor load limit that an aircraft must have to carry the following pallet of cargo?

Pallet dimensions ....116.8 × 87.7 inches.
Pallet weight ....137 lbs.
Tiedown devices..49 lbs.
Cargo weight ....12,262.4 lbs.

A—172 lbs/sq ft.
B—176 lbs/sq ft.
C—179 lbs/sq ft.

1. *Determine the area.*

   116.8 × 87.7 ÷ 144 = 71.13 sq ft.

2. *Determine the total weight.*

   12,262.4 + 49 + 137 = 12,448.4

3. *Determine the minimum floor load limit.*

   12,448.4 ÷ 71.13 = 175.00 lbs/sq ft.

(PLT121, AA.I.B.K3e) — FAA-H-8083-1

Answers

8844 [A] 8845 [C] 8846 [B] 8847 [B]

ATM, ATS, RTC

8848. What is the minimum floor load limit that an aircraft must have to carry the following pallet of cargo?

Pallet dimensions .... 78.9 × 98.7 inches.
Pallet weight .... 161 lbs.
Tiedown devices.. 54 lbs.
Cargo weight .... 9,681.5 lbs.

A—180 lbs/sq ft.
B—186 lbs/sq ft.
C—183 lbs/sq ft.

1. *Determine the area.*

   78.9 × 98.7 ÷ 144 = 54.08 sq ft.

2. *Determine the total weight.*

   9,681.5 + 54 + 161 = 9,896.5

3. *Determine the minimum floor load limit.*

   9,896.5 ÷ 54.08 = 183.00 lbs/sq ft.

(PLT121, AA.I.B.K3e) — FAA-H-8083-1

ATM, ATS

8431. What is the maximum allowable weight that may be carried on a pallet which has the dimensions of 36 × 48 inches?

Floor load limit .... 169 lbs/sq ft
Pallet weight .... 47 lbs
Tiedown devices.. 33 lbs

A—1,948.0 pounds.
B—1,995.0 pounds.
C—1,981.0 pounds.

Pallet area = (36 × 48) ÷ 144 = 12 sq ft
Floor load limit = 12 sq ft × 169 lbs/sq ft = 2,028 lbs
Allowable weight = 2,028 lbs – 80 lbs = 1,948 lbs

(PLT121, AA.I.B.K3e) — FAA-H-8083-1

ATM, ATS

8432. What is the maximum allowable weight that may be carried on a pallet which has the dimensions of 76 × 74 inches?

Floor load limit .... 176 lbs/sq ft
Pallet weight .... 77 lbs
Tiedown devices.. 29 lbs

A—6,767.8 pounds.
B—6,873.7 pounds.
C—6,796.8 pounds.

Floor load limit – 176 lbs/sq ft
Pallet weight – 77 lbs
Tiedown devices – 29 lbs
Pallet area = (76 × 74) ÷ 144 = 39.1 sq ft
Floor load limit = 39.1 sq ft × 176 lbs/sq ft = 6,873.8 lbs
Allowable weight = 6,873.8 lbs – 106 lbs = 6,767.8 lbs

(PLT121, AA.I.B.K3e) — FAA-H-8083-1

ATM, ATS

8433. What is the maximum allowable weight that may be carried on a pallet which has the dimensions of 81 × 83 inches?

Floor load limit .... 180 lbs/sq ft
Pallet weight .... 82 lbs
Tiedown devices.. 31 lbs

A—8,403.7 pounds.
B—8,321.8 pounds.
C—8,290.8 pounds.

Floor load limit – 180 lbs/sq ft
Pallet weight – 82 lbs
Tiedown devices – 31 lbs
Pallet area = (81 × 83) ÷ 144 = 46.7 sq ft
Floor load limit = 46.7 sq ft × 180 lbs/sq ft = 8,403.8 lbs
Allowable weight = 8,403.8 lbs – 113 lbs = 8,290.8 lbs

(PLT121, AA.I.B.K3e) — FAA-H-8083-1

Answers

8848 [C] 8431 [A] 8432 [A] 8433 [C]

Chapter 6
Flight Operations

Airspace

A turbine-powered airplane or a large airplane must enter **Class D airspace** at an altitude of at least 1,500 feet AGL and maintain that altitude in the traffic pattern until a lower altitude is necessary for a safe landing. When taking off, the pilot of a turbine-powered airplane or a large airplane must climb as rapidly as practicable to an altitude of 1,500 feet AGL.

No person may operate an aircraft within **Class B airspace** unless a proper authorization from ATC has been received prior to entry. An IFR clearance is not necessarily required. Unless otherwise authorized by ATC, every person flying a large turbine-engine-powered airplane to or from the primary airport in Class B airspace must operate at or above the floor of Class B airspace.

All **Class C airspace** has the same dimensions with minor site variations. They are composed of two circles both centered on the primary airport. The surface area has a radius of 5 nautical miles and extends from the surface up to 4,000 feet above the airport. The shelf area has a radius of 10 nautical miles and extends vertically from 1,200 feet AGL up to 4,000 feet above the primary airport. In addition to the Class C airspace proper, there is an outer area with a radius of 20 nautical miles and vertical coverage from the lower limits of the radio/radar coverage up to the top of the approach control facility's delegated airspace.

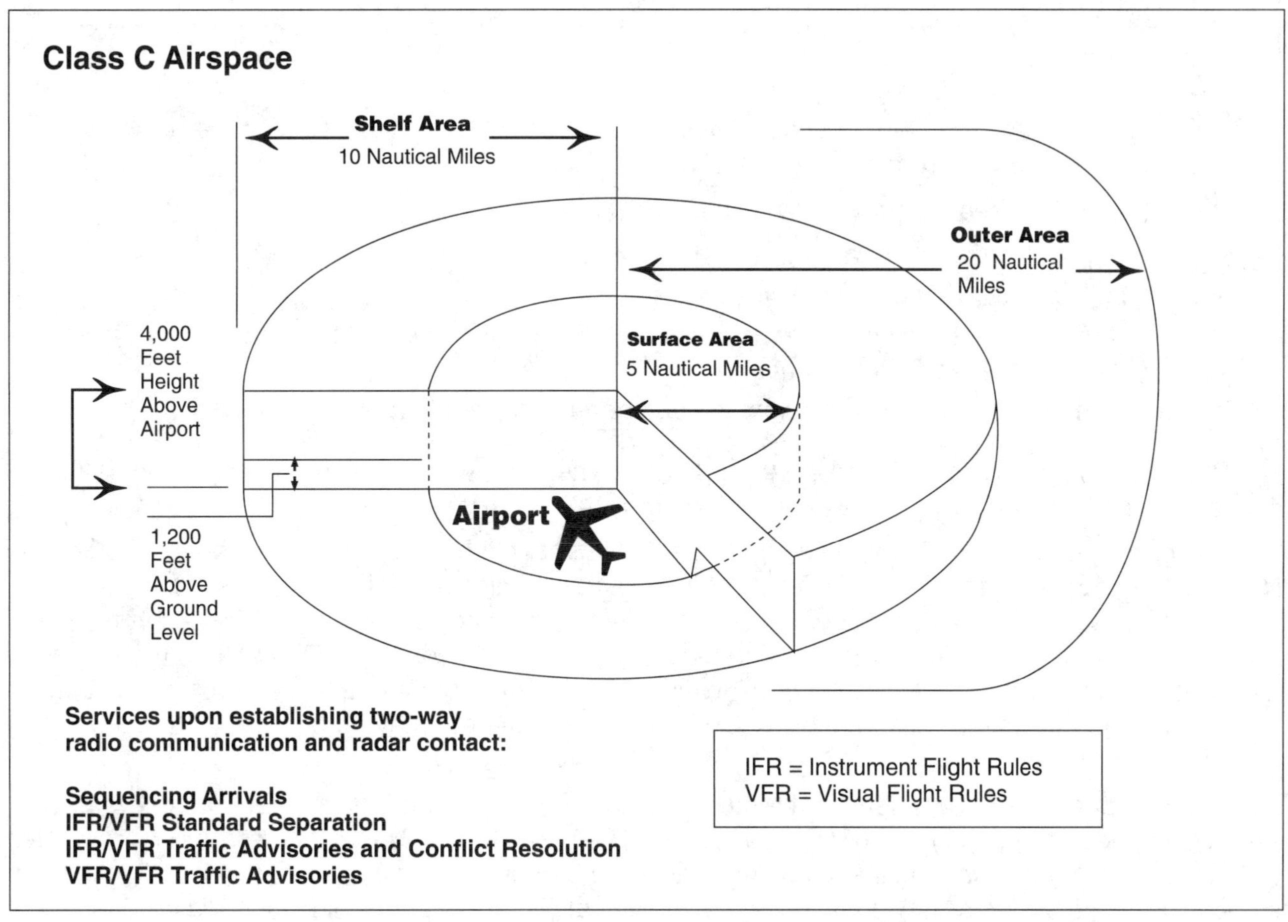

Figure 6-1. Class C airspace

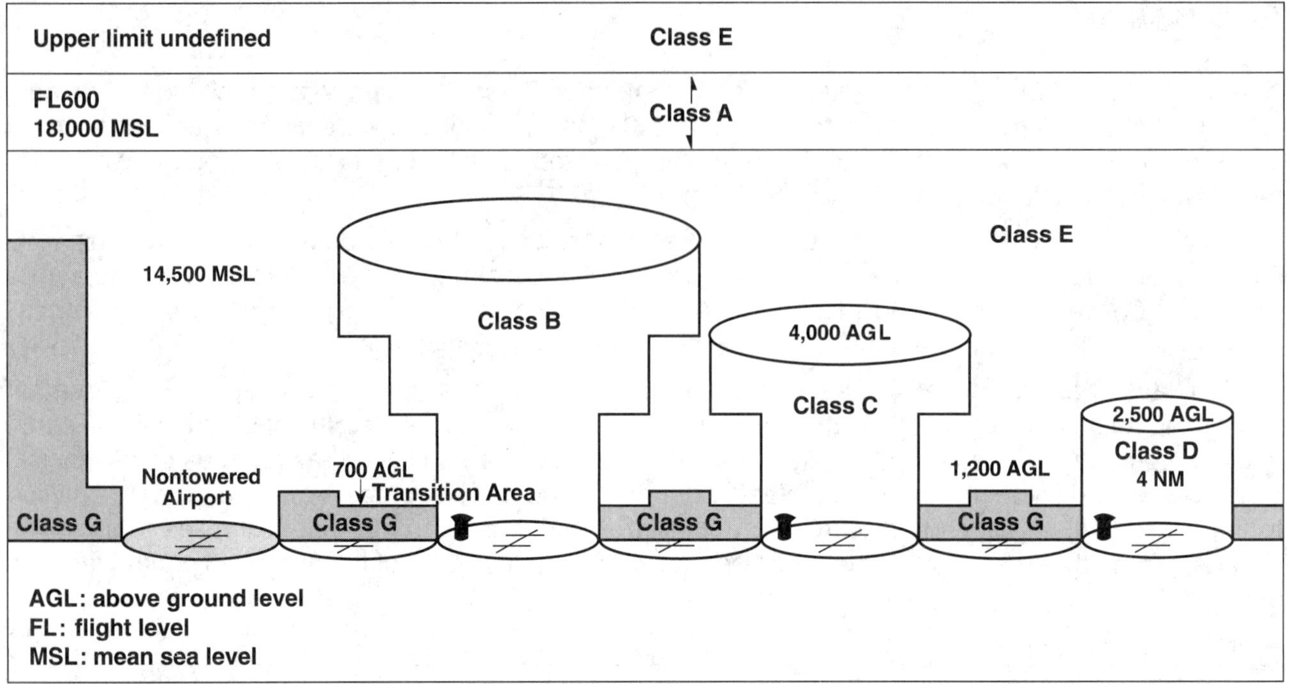

Figure 6-2. Airspace

The only equipment requirements for an aircraft to operate within Class C airspace are a two-way radio and a transponder. No specific pilot certification is required.

The following services are provided within Class C airspace:

- Sequencing of all arriving aircraft to the primary airport.
- Standard IFR separation between IFR aircraft.
- Between IFR and VFR aircraft — traffic advisories and conflict resolution so that radar targets do not touch, or 500 feet vertical separation.
- Between VFR aircraft, traffic advisories and as appropriate, safety alerts.

The same services are provided in the outer area when two-way radio and radar contact is established. There is no requirement for VFR participation in the outer area.

No one may operate an aircraft below 10,000 feet MSL at an indicated speed greater than 250 knots. No one may operate an aircraft within Class D airspace at an indicated airspeed of more than 200 knots. There is no special speed limit for operations within Class B airspace other than the 250-knot limit when below 10,000 feet MSL. When operating beneath the lateral limits of Class B airspace, the indicated airspeed cannot exceed 200 knots. If the minimum safe airspeed for any particular operation is greater than the maximum speed prescribed by 14 CFR §91.117, the aircraft may be operated at that minimum speed.

Warning Areas are so designated because they are located in international (and therefore uncontrolled) airspace and have invisible hazards to flight. The purpose of a **Military Operating Area (MOA)** is to separate IFR traffic from military training activities. Normally, ATC will not clear an IFR flight into an MOA if it is in use by the military. In an MOA, the individual pilots are responsible for collision avoidance. **VR** Military Training Routes which extend above 1,500 feet AGL, and **IR** Training Routes are depicted on IFR Enroute Low Altitude Charts.

When a flight is to penetrate an **Air Defense Identification Zone (ADIZ)**, it must be on either an IFR or a DVFR flight plan. The flight must penetrate the ADIZ within ±5 minutes of the flight plan estimate and within 10 miles when over land or within 20 miles when over water. These were formerly referred to as domestic and coastal ADIZs in the AIM.

A **VFR-On-Top** clearance is an IFR authorization to fly the cleared route at the VFR altitude of the pilot's choice. To request VFR-On-Top, the flight must be able to maintain the minimum VFR visibility and cloud clearances appropriate for the airspace and altitude. This may be done above, below or between the clouds, if any. While the pilot is expected to comply with all IFR rules, ATC will provide traffic advisories only. VFR-On-Top will not be authorized in Class A airspace. VFR weather minimums must be observed when operating under a VFR-On-Top clearance.

An air carrier flight may conduct day Over-the-Top operations below the minimum IFR altitude if the following are observed:

- The flight must be at least 1,000 feet above the top of a broken or overcast layer.
- The top of the clouds are generally uniform and level.
- The flight visibility is at least five miles.
- The base of any higher ceiling is at least 1,000 feet above the minimum IFR altitude.

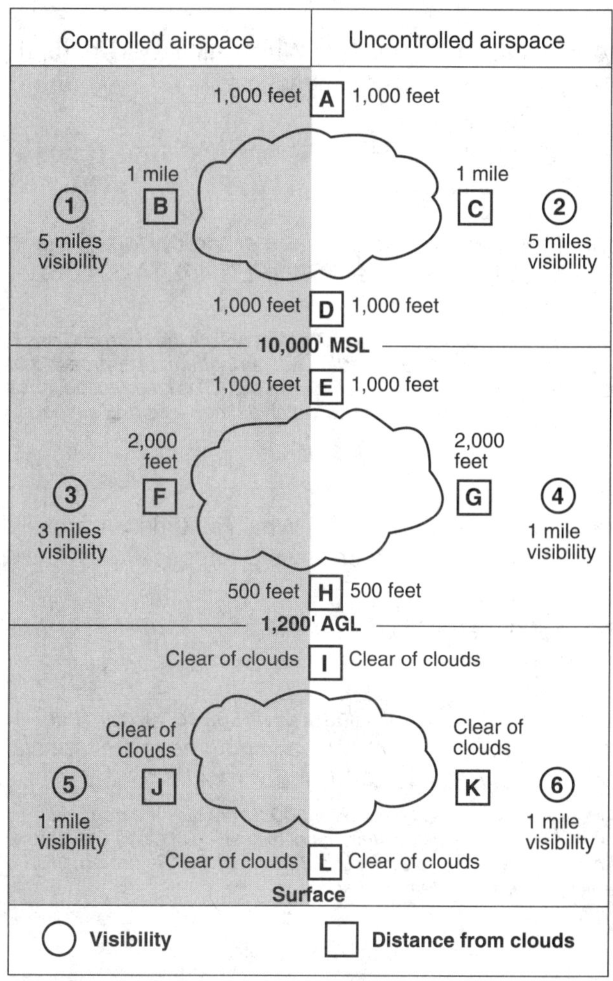

Figure 6-3. Minimum in-flight visibility and distance from clouds

OROCA is an off-route altitude which provides obstruction clearance with a 1,000-foot buffer in nonmountainous terrain areas, and a 2,000-foot buffer in designated mountainous areas within the U.S. **Minimum Vectoring Altitudes (MVAs)** are established for use by ATC when radar is exercised; MVA charts are prepared by air traffic facilities at locations where there are many different minimum IFR altitudes. **Minimum Safe/Sector Altitudes (MSA)** are published for emergency use on IAP charts; they are expressed in MSL and normally have a 25 NM radius; however, this radius may be expanded to 30 NM if necessary to encompass the airport landing surfaces.

ALL
8881. (Refer to Figure 127.) Which altitude is appropriate for the top of Class G airspace?

A—700 feet AGL.
B—1,200 feet AGL.
C—1,500 feet AGL.

The floor of controlled airspace or the ceiling of Class G airspace is 1,200 feet AGL. (PLT040, AA.II.A.S6) — AIM ¶3-2-1

Answer (A) is incorrect because 700 feet AGL is the base of Class E airspace when used in conjunction with an instrument approach that has been prescribed, as in circle 6. Answer (C) is incorrect because 1,500 feet AGL is not an altitude which defines a certain airspace.

ALL
8882. (Refer to Figure 127.) Which altitude is normally appropriate for the top of Class D airspace?

A—1,000 feet AGL.
B—2,500 feet AGL.
C—3,000 feet AGL.

The top or ceiling of Class D airspace is normally at 2,500 feet AGL. There will be variations to suit special conditions. (PLT040, AA.II.A.S6) — AIM ¶3-2-5

Answer (A) is incorrect because 1,000 feet AGL is the normal traffic pattern altitude for piston aircraft, not the ceiling of Class D airspace. Answer (C) is incorrect because 3,000 feet AGL is not an altitude which defines a certain airspace.

ALL
8883. (Refer to Figure 127.) Which altitude is appropriate for the top of Class G airspace?

A—700 or 2,500 feet AGL.
B—500 or 2,000 feet AGL.
C—700 or 1,200 feet AGL.

The ceiling of Class G airspace could be 700 or 1,200 feet AGL. (PLT040, AA.II.A.S6) — AIM ¶3-2-1

ALL
8884. (Refer to Figure 127.) Which altitude is appropriate for the top of Class E airspace?

A—14,000 feet MSL.
B—14,500 feet MSL.
C—18,000 feet MSL.

The top or ceiling of Class E airspace is at 18,000 feet MSL. (PLT040, AA.II.A.S6) — AIM ¶3-2-1

Answer (A) is incorrect because 14,000 feet MSL is not an altitude which defines a certain airspace. Answer (B) is incorrect because 14,500 MSL is the base of Class E airspace when it is not set lower.

ALL
8885. (Refer to Figure 127.) Which altitude is appropriate for the top of Class C airspace?

A—3,000 feet AGL.
B—4,000 feet AGL.
C—3,500 feet MSL.

The top or ceiling of Class C airspace is generally at 4,000 feet AGL. (PLT040, AA.II.A.S6) — AIM ¶3-2-4

Answers (A) and (C) are incorrect because neither 3,000 feet AGL nor 3,500 feet MSL are altitudes which define a certain airspace.

ALL
8886. (Refer to Figure 127.) Which altitude is appropriate for the top of Class A airspace??

A—FL600.
B—FL450.
C—FL500.

The top or upper limits of Class A airspace is at FL600. (PLT040, AA.II.A.S6) — AIM ¶3-2-1

Answers (B) and (C) are incorrect because neither FL450 nor FL500 are altitudes which define a certain airspace.

ALL
8888. (Refer to Figure 127.) What is the base of the Class A airspace?

A—12,000 feet AGL.
B—14,500 feet MSL.
C—FL180.

The base of Class A airspace is 18,000 feet MSL. (PLT040, AA.II.A.S6) — AIM ¶3-2-1

Answer (A) is incorrect because 12,000 feet AGL is not an altitude which defines a certain airspace. Answer (B) is incorrect because 14,500 MSL is the base of Class E airspace when it is not set lower.

ALL
9409. In what altitude structure is a transponder required when operating in controlled airspace?

A—Above 12,500 feet MSL, excluding the airspace at and below 2,500 feet AGL.
B—Above 10,000 feet MSL, excluding the airspace at and below 2,500 feet AGL.
C—Above 14,500 feet MSL, excluding the airspace at and below 2,500 feet AGL.

Answers

8881 [B]	8882 [B]	8883 [C]	8884 [C]	8885 [B]	8886 [A]
8888 [C]	9409 [B]				

A transponder is required at and above 10,000 feet MSL and below the floor of Class A airspace, excluding the airspace at and below 2,500 feet AGL. (PLT429, AA.I.A.K9) — 14 CFR §91.215

Answer (A) is incorrect because 12,500 feet MSL was the old altitude above which a transponder was needed; it is now 10,000 feet MSL. Answer (C) is incorrect because 14,500 feet MSL is the base of Class E airspace when it is not set lower.

ALL

9424. Pilots should state their position on the airport when calling the tower for takeoff

A—from a runway intersection.
B—from a runway intersection, only at night.
C—from a runway intersection, only during instrument conditions.

Pilots should state their position on the airport when calling the tower for takeoff from a runway intersection. (PLT434, AA.II.C.K7) — AIM ¶4-3-10

Answers (B) and (C) are incorrect because this rule applies to all operations.

ALL

9780. When flying in the airspace underlying Class B airspace, the maximum speed authorized is

A—200 knots.
B—230 knots.
C—250 knots.

No person may operate an aircraft in the airspace underlying Class B airspace at a speed of more than 200 knots. (PLT161, AA.I.G.K2) — 14 CFR §91.117

ALL

8889. What restriction applies to a large, turbine-powered airplane operating to or from a primary airport in Class B airspace?

A—Must not exceed 200 knots within Class B airspace.
B—Must operate above the floor when within lateral limits of Class B airspace.
C—Must operate in accordance with IFR procedures regardless of weather conditions.

Unless otherwise authorized by ATC, each person operating a large turbine-engine-powered airplane to or from a primary airport in Class B airspace shall operate at or above the designated floors while within the lateral limits of the Class B airspace. (PLT161, AA.I.G.K2) — AIM ¶3-2-3

Answer (A) is incorrect because the speed limit within a Class B airspace is 250 knots for all aircraft. Answer (C) is incorrect because VFR is permitted in Class B airspace; i.e., an IFR clearance is not required as it is at FL180 and above.

ALL

8872. (Refer to Figure 126.) What is the normal radius from the airport of the outer area, B?

A—10 miles.
B—20 miles.
C—25 miles.

The normal radius of the outer area of Class C airspace is 20 NM. (PLT040, AA.II.A.S6) — AIM ¶3-2-4

Answer (A) is incorrect because 10 NM is the radius of the outer circle of Class C airspace. Answer (C) is incorrect because 25 NM does not pertain to any set radius of Class C airspace.

ALL

8873. (Refer to Figure 126.) What is the usual radius from the airport of the inner circle, C?

A—5 miles.
B—7 miles.
C—10 miles.

The usual radius from the airport of the inner circle is 5 NM in Class C airspace. (PLT040, AA.II.A.S6) — AIM ¶3-2-4

Answer (B) is incorrect because 7 NM is not established as the radius for any portion of Class C airspace. Answer (C) is incorrect because 10 NM is the radius of the outer circle of Class C airspace.

ALL

8874. (Refer to Figure 126.) What is the radius from the airport of the outer circle, A?

A—5 miles.
B—10 miles.
C—15 miles.

The radius of the outer circle is 10 NM in Class C airspace. (PLT040, AA.II.A.S6) — AIM ¶3-2-4

Answer (A) is incorrect because 5 NM is the radius of the surface area of Class C airspace. Answer (C) is incorrect because 15 NM is not established as the radius for any area of Class C airspace.

Answers

9424 [A]	9780 [A]	8889 [B]	8872 [B]	8873 [A]	8874 [B]

ALL

8875. (Refer to Figure 126.) Which altitude (box 2) is applicable to the base of the outer circle?

A—700 feet AGL.
B—1,000 feet AGL.
C—1,200 feet AGL.

The base of the outer circle is 1,200 feet AGL. (PLT040, AA.II.A.S6) — AIM ¶3-2-4

Answer (A) is incorrect because 700 feet AGL is not applicable to Class C airspace (it is the base of some Class E airspace). Answer (B) is incorrect because 1,000 feet AGL is not applicable to Class C airspace (it is the normal traffic pattern altitude for propeller airplanes).

ALL

8876. (Refer to Figure 126.) Which altitude (box 1) is applicable to the vertical extent of the inner and outer circles?

A—3,000 feet AGL.
B—3,000 feet above airport.
C—4,000 feet above airport.

The vertical extent of the inner and outer circles is 4,000 feet above the airport. (PLT040, AA.II.A.S6) — AIM ¶3-2-4

Answers (A) and (B) are incorrect because 3,000 feet AGL does not define an airspace.

ALL

8877. What minimum aircraft equipment is required for operation within Class C airspace?

A—Two-way communications.
B—Two-way communications and transponder.
C—Transponder and DME.

An encoding transponder and two-way radio is required in order to operate within Class C airspace. (PLT040, AA.II.A.S6) — AIM ¶3-2-4

Answer (A) is incorrect because a Mode C transponder is also required. Answer (C) is incorrect because two-way communications are also required and DME is not required.

ALL

8878. What service is provided for aircraft operating within the outer area of Class C airspace?

A—The same as within Class C airspace when communications and radar contact is established.
B—Radar vectors to and from secondary airports within the outer area.
C—Basic radar service only when communications and radar contact is established.

The same services are provided for aircraft operating within the outer area, as within the Class C airspace, when two-way communication and radar contact are established. (PLT161, AA.II.A.S6) — AIM ¶3-2-4

Answer (B) is incorrect because providing radar vectors to and from secondary airports within the outer circle is not a mandated service of ATC. Answer (C) is incorrect because the same services are provided in the outer area as within Class C airspace, once two-way communications and radar contact are established.

ALL

8879. What services are provided for aircraft operating within Class C airspace?

A—Sequencing of arriving aircraft, separation of aircraft (except between VFR aircraft), and traffic advisories.
B—Sequencing of arriving aircraft (except VFR aircraft), separation between all aircraft, and traffic advisories.
C—Sequencing of all arriving aircraft, separation between all aircraft, and traffic advisories.

ATC services within an Class C airspace include:

1. *Sequencing of all arriving aircraft to the primary Class C airport,*
2. *Standard IFR separation between IFR aircraft,*
3. *Between IFR and VFR aircraft — traffic advisories and conflict resolution so that radar targets do not touch, or 500 feet vertical separation, and*
4. *Between VFR aircraft — traffic advisories and as appropriate, safety alerts.*

(PLT161, AA.II.A.S6) — AIM ¶3-2-4

Answer (B) is incorrect because the services in the Class C airspace provide sequencing of all aircraft to the primary/Class C airspace airport. Answer (C) is incorrect because the services in the Class C airspace do not provide separation between VFR aircraft, only traffic advisories and safety alerts.

Answers

8875 [C]	8876 [C]	8877 [B]	8878 [A]	8879 [A]

ALL
8880. What pilot certification and aircraft equipment are required for operating in Class C airspace?

A—No specific certification but a two-way radio.
B—At least a Private Pilot Certificate and two-way radio.
C—At least a Private Pilot Certificate, two-way radio, and a TSO-C74b transponder.

No specific pilot certification is required for operation within Class C airspace. The aircraft must be equipped with a two-way radio for operations within Class C airspace. (PLT161, AA.II.A.S6) — AIM ¶3-2-4

Answers (B) and (C) are incorrect because there is no specific pilot certificate required, although two-way radio and transponder are required.

ALL
9399. What is the maximum indicated airspeed a turbine-powered aircraft may be operated below 10,000 feet MSL?

A—288 knots.
B—250 knots.
C—230 knots.

Unless otherwise authorized by the Administrator, no person may operate an aircraft below 10,000 feet MSL at an indicated airspeed of more than 250 knots (288 MPH). (PLT161, AA.I.G.K2) — 14 CFR §91.117

ALL
8890. Why are certain areas that start 3 nautical miles from the coastline of the U.S. and extend outward, classified as Warning Areas?

A—To inform pilots of participating aircraft to maintain extreme vigilance while conducting flight within the area.
B—To warn all aircraft pilots that flying within the area may be extremely hazardous to aircraft and occupants.
C—To warn pilots of nonparticipating aircraft of a potential danger within the area.

A Warning Area is airspace of defined dimensions, extending from three nautical miles outward from the coast of the United States, that contains activity that may be hazardous to nonparticipating aircraft. The purpose of such warning areas is to warn nonparticipating pilots of the potential danger. A warning area may be located over domestic or international waters or both. (PLT161, AA.II.A.S6) — AIM ¶3-4-4

ALL
8891. What is the purpose of MOAs?

A—To protect military aircraft operations from civil aircraft.
B—To separate military training activities from IFR traffic.
C—To separate military training activities from both IFR and VFR traffic.

Military Operations Areas (MOAs) consist of airspace of defined vertical and lateral limits established for the purpose of separating certain military training activities from IFR traffic. (PLT161, AA.II.A.S6) — AIM ¶3-4-5

Answer (A) is incorrect because MOAs are to separate (not protect) military training activities from IFR traffic. Answer (C) is incorrect because MOAs are established for the purpose of separating IFR traffic from military training activities.

ATM, ATS, RTC
8892. Who is responsible for collision avoidance in an MOA?

A—Military controllers.
B—ATC controllers.
C—Each pilot.

Pilots operating under VFR should exercise extreme caution while flying within an MOA when military activity is being conducted. (PLT162, AA.II.A.S6) — AIM ¶3-4-5

ALL
9049. Which aeronautical chart depicts Military Training Routes (MTR) above 1,500 feet?

A—IFR Low Altitude En Route Chart.
B—IFR High Altitude En Route Chart.
C—IFR Planning Chart.

The IFR Enroute Low Altitude Chart depicts all Military Training Routes (MTR) that accommodate operations above 1,500 feet AGL. (PLT100, AA.II.A.S6) — AIM ¶3-5-2

Answer (B) is incorrect because IFR High Altitude Enroute Charts do not depict MTRs. Answer (C) is incorrect because VFR Planning Charts depict MTRs.

Answers

8880 [A] 9399 [B] 8890 [C] 8891 [B] 8892 [C] 9049 [A]

ALL

9100. What is the maximum acceptable position tolerance for penetrating a domestic ADIZ over land?

A—Plus or minus 10 miles; plus or minus 10 minutes.
B—Plus or minus 20 miles; plus or minus 5 minutes.
C—Plus or minus 10 miles; plus or minus 5 minutes.

The aircraft position tolerances over land in a domestic ADIZ is within ±5 minutes from the estimated time over a reporting point or point of penetration and within 10 NM from the centerline of an intended track over an estimated reporting point or penetration point. (PLT161, AA.II.A.S6) — AIM ¶5-6-1

Answer (A) is incorrect because penetration of an ADIZ within 10 minutes is not an acceptable tolerance for either over water or land. Answer (B) is incorrect because the maximum acceptable tolerance for penetrating over water (a coastal ADIZ) is within 20 NM of the intended track and within 5 minutes of the estimated penetration time.

ALL

9741. What is the maximum acceptable position tolerance for penetrating a domestic ADIZ over water?

A—Plus or minus 10 miles; plus or minus 10 minutes.
B—Plus or minus 10 miles; plus or minus 5 minutes.
C—Plus or minus 20 miles; plus or minus 5 minutes.

The aircraft position tolerances over water in a domestic ADIZ is plus or minus five minutes from the estimated time over a reporting point or point of penetration and within 20 NM from the centerline of the intended track over an estimated reporting point or point of penetration. (PLT161, AA.II.A.S6) — AIM ¶5-6-1

ALL

9046. Under what conditions may a pilot on an IFR flight plan comply with authorization to maintain "VFR on Top"?

A—Maintain IFR flight plan but comply with visual flight rules while in VFR conditions.
B—Maintain VFR altitudes, cloud clearances, and comply with applicable instrument flight rules.
C—Maintain IFR altitudes, VFR cloud clearances, and comply with applicable instrument flight rules.

When operating in VFR conditions with an ATC authorization to "maintain VFR-On-Top" pilots on IFR flight plans must:

1. *Fly an appropriate VFR altitude,*
2. *Comply with VFR visibility and distance from cloud criteria, and*
3. *Comply with instrument flight rules that are applicable to the flight.*

(PLT370, AA.II.A.S6) — AIM ¶5-5-13

Answer (A) is incorrect because not only will a pilot remain on the IFR flight plan and comply with VFR altitudes, visibility, and cloud clearances, he/she must also comply with applicable IFR rules, e.g., position reporting, minimum IFR altitudes. Answer (C) is incorrect because, while operating on a "VFR-On-Top" clearance, a pilot must maintain VFR altitudes.

ALL

9047. What cloud clearance must be complied with when authorized to maintain "VFR on Top"?

A—May maintain VFR clearance above, below, or between layers.
B—Must maintain VFR clearance above or below.
C—May maintain VFR clearance above or below, but not between layers.

ATC authorization to "maintain VFR-On-Top" is not intended to restrict pilots so that they must operate only above an obscuring meteorological formation. Instead, it permits operations above, below, between or in areas where there is no meteorological obstruction. (PLT370, AA.II.A.S6) — AIM ¶5-5-13

ALL

9048. In what airspace will ATC not authorize "VFR on Top"?

A—Class C airspace.
B—Class B airspace.
C—Class A airspace.

ATC will not authorize VFR or VFR-On-Top operations in Class A airspace. (PLT161, AA.II.A.S6) — AIM ¶5-5-13

ALL

9093. What separation or service by ATC is afforded pilots authorized "VFR on Top"?

A—The same afforded all IFR flights.
B—3 miles horizontally instead of 5.
C—Traffic advisories only.

Pilots operating VFR-On-Top may receive traffic information from ATC on other pertinent IFR or VFR aircraft. (PLT172, AA.II.A.S6) — AIM ¶5-5-13

Answer (A) is incorrect because separation will be provided for all IFR flights except those operating with a VFR-On-Top clearance. In that case, only traffic advisories may be provided. Answer (B) is incorrect because, when radar is employed for separation of aircraft at the same altitude, a minimum of 3 miles separation is provided between airplanes operating within 40 miles of the radar antenna site, and 5 miles between aircraft operating beyond 40 miles from the antenna site.

Answers

9100 [C]	9741 [C]	9046 [B]	9047 [A]	9048 [C]	9093 [C]

ALL

9018. A minimum instrument altitude for enroute operations off of published airways which provides obstruction clearance of 1,000 feet in nonmountainous terrain areas and 2,000 feet in designated mountainous areas within the United States is called

A—Minimum Obstruction Clearance Altitude (MOCA).
B—Off-Route Obstruction Clearance Altitude (OROCA).
C—Minimum Safe/Sector Altitude (MSA).

OROCA is an off-route altitude which provides obstruction clearance with a 1,000-foot buffer in nonmountainous terrain areas, and a 2,000-foot buffer in designated mountainous areas within the U.S. (PLT162, AA.II.A.S6) — AIM ¶4-4-9

Answer (A) is incorrect because MOCAs provide the lowest published altitude in effect between radio fixes on VOR airways, off-airway routes, or route segments which meets obstacle clearance requirements for the entire route segment and which ensures acceptable navigational signal coverage only within 25 SM (22 NM) of a VOR. Answer (C) is incorrect because MSAs are published for emergency use on IAP charts; they are expressed in feet above mean sea level and normally have a 25 NM radius; however, this radius may be expanded to 30 NM if necessary to encompass the airport landing surfaces.

ALL

8893. What is the required flight visibility and distance from clouds if you are operating in Class E airspace at 9,500 feet with a VFR-on-Top clearance during daylight hours?

A—3 statute miles, 1,000 feet above, 500 feet below, and 2,000 feet horizontal.
B—5 statute miles, 500 feet above, 1,000 feet below, and 2,000 feet horizontal.
C—3 statute miles, 500 feet above, 1,000 feet below, and 2,000 feet horizontal.

A pilot receiving authorization for VFR-On-Top must comply with VFR visibility, distance from cloud criteria, and minimum IFR altitudes. When operating at more than 1,200 feet AGL but less than 10,000 feet MSL, pilots are required to maintain flight visibility of 3 statute miles and a distance from clouds of 1,000 feet above, 500 feet below, and 2,000 feet horizontal. (PLT163, AA.I.G.K2) — 14 CFR §91.155

Answer (B) is incorrect because the visibility requirement is 3 miles (not 5 miles) and the distances from clouds above and below are reversed. They should be 1,000 feet above and 500 feet below. Answer (C) is incorrect because the distances from clouds above and below are reversed. They should be 1,000 feet above and 500 feet below.

ALL

8900. What is the minimum flight visibility and distance from clouds for flight at 10,500 feet, in Class E airspace, with a VFR-on-Top clearance during daylight hours?

A—3 statute miles, 1,000 feet above, 500 feet below, and 2,000 feet horizontal.
B—5 statute miles, 1,000 feet above, 1,000 feet below, and 1 mile horizontal.
C—5 statute miles, 1,000 feet above, 500 feet below, and 1 mile horizontal.

A pilot on an IFR flight plan requesting and receiving authorization to operate VFR-On-Top must comply with instrument flight rules as well as VFR visibilities and distances from clouds. When operating at more than 1,200 feet AGL and at or above 10,000 feet MSL pilots are required to maintain flight visibility of 5 statute miles and distances of 1,000 feet above, 1,000 feet below, and 1 mile horizontally from clouds. (PLT163, AA.I.G.K2) — 14 CFR §91.155

Answer (A) is incorrect because it presents the VFR weather minimums for below 10,000 feet MSL. Answer (C) is incorrect because the vertical separation from clouds is 1,000 feet both above and below.

ATM, ADX

8253. Which in-flight conditions are required by a supplemental air carrier to conduct a day, over-the-top flight below the specified IFR minimum en route altitude?

A—The flight must remain clear of clouds by at least 1,000 feet vertically and 1,000 feet horizontally and have at least 3 miles flight visibility.
B—The flight must be conducted at least 1,000 feet above an overcast or broken cloud layer, any higher broken/overcast cloud cover is a minimum of 1,000 feet above the IFR MEA, and have at least 5 miles flight visibility.
C—The height of any higher overcast or broken layer must be at least 500 feet above the IFR MEA.

A person may conduct day Over-the-Top operations in an airplane at flight altitudes lower than the minimum enroute IFR altitudes if—

1. *The operation is conducted at least 1,000 feet above the top of lower broken or overcast cloud cover;*
2. *The top of the lower cloud cover is generally uniform and level;*
3. *Flight visibility is at least 5 miles; and*
4. *The base of any higher broken or overcast cloud cover is generally uniform and level, and is at least 1,000 feet above the minimum enroute IFR altitude for that route segment.*

(continued)

Answers

9018 [B] 8893 [A] 8900 [B] 8253 [B]

(PLT468, AA.I.G.K4) — 14 CFR §121.657

Answer (A) is incorrect because the flight must remain at least 1,000 feet above the cloud layer with a flight visibility of at least 5 miles. Answer (C) is incorrect because the height of any higher ceiling must be at least 1,000 feet above the IFR MEA.

ATM, ATS

9395. At what minimum altitude is a turbine-engine-powered, or large airplane, required to enter Class D airspace?

A—1,500 feet AGL.
B—2,000 feet AGL.
C—2,500 feet AGL.

When operating to an airport with an operating control tower, each pilot of a turbine-powered airplane or a large airplane shall, unless otherwise required by the applicable distance from cloud criteria, enter Class D airspace at an altitude of at least 1,500 feet above the surface of the airport. (PLT161, AA.I.G.K2) — 14 CFR §91.129

ATM, ATS

9401. A pilot of a turbine-powered airplane should climb as rapidly as practicable after taking off to what altitude?

A—1,000 feet AGL.
B—1,500 feet AGL.
C—5,000 feet AGL.

When taking off from an airport with an operating control tower, each pilot of a turbine-powered airplane shall climb to an altitude of 1,500 feet above the surface as rapidly as practicable. (PLT459, AA.I.G.K2) — 14 CFR §91.129

ATM, ATS, ADX

9396. What is the maximum indicated airspeed a reciprocating-engine-powered airplane may be operated within Class B airspace?

A—180 knots.
B—230 knots.
C—250 knots.

Unless otherwise authorized by the Administrator, no person may operate an aircraft below 10,000 feet MSL at an indicated airspeed of more than 250 knots (288 MPH). There is no specific speed restriction which applies to operation within Class B airspace. (PLT161, AA.I.G.K2) — 14 CFR §91.117

Answer (A) is incorrect because 180 knots is the old maximum airspeed for turbine-powered aircraft while operating within Class D airspace (it is now 200 knots). Answer (B) is incorrect because 230 knots is the maximum authorized holding speed for all civil turbojet aircraft while operating from the minimum holding altitude to 14,000 feet. It is not an airspeed limitation in Class B airspace.

ATM, ATS, ADX

8887. The maximum indicated airspeed that an aircraft may be flown in Class B airspace, after departing the primary airport, while at 1,700 feet AGL and 3.5 nautical miles from the airport is

A—200 knots.
B—230 knots.
C—250 knots.

Unless otherwise authorized by the Administrator, no person may operate an aircraft below 10,000 feet MSL at an indicated airspeed of more than 250 knots (288 MPH). (PLT161, AA.I.G.K2) — 14 CFR §91.117

ATM, ATS, ADX

9397. At what maximum indicated airspeed can a B-727 operate within Class B airspace without special ATC authorization?

A—230 knots.
B—250 knots.
C—275 knots.

Unless otherwise authorized by the Administrator, no person may operate an aircraft below 10,000 feet MSL at an indicated airspeed of more than 250 knots (288 MPH). There is no specific speed restriction which applies to operation within Class B airspace. (PLT161, AA.I.G.K2) — 14 CFR §91.117

Answer (A) is incorrect because 230 knots is not an airspeed limitation in Class B airspace. Answer (C) is incorrect because 275 knots is not an established maximum speed for any type of operation.

ATM, ATS, ADX

9398. At what maximum indicated airspeed may a reciprocating-engine-powered airplane be operated within Class D airspace?

A—156 knots.
B—180 knots.
C—200 knots.

Unless otherwise authorized or required by ATC, no person may operate an aircraft within Class D airspace at an indicated airspeed of more than 200 knots. (PLT161, AA.I.G.K2) — 14 CFR §91.117

Answer (A) is incorrect because 156 knots was the old maximum authorized airspeed for reciprocating aircraft in Class D airspace (it is now 200 knots). Answer (B) is incorrect because 180 knots was the old maximum authorized airspeed for turbine-powered aircraft in Class D airspace (it is now 200 knots).

Answers

9395 [A] 9401 [B] 9396 [C] 8887 [C] 9397 [B] 9398 [C]

ATM, ATS, ADX

9400. At what maximum indicated airspeed can a reciprocating-engine airplane operate in the airspace underlying Class B airspace?

A—180 knots.
B—200 knots.
C—230 knots.

No person may operate an aircraft in the airspace underlying Class B airspace at an indicated airspeed of more than 200 knots (230 MPH). (PLT161, AA.I.G.K2) — 14 CFR §91.117

Answer (A) is incorrect because 180 knots was the old published maximum airspeed for turbine-powered aircraft in Class D airspace (it is now 200 knots). Answer (C) is incorrect because the limitation is 200 knots or 230 MPH, not 230 knots.

NOTAMs (Notices to Air Missions)

Notices to Air Missions (NOTAMs) provide the most current information available. They provide time-critical information on airports and changes that affect the national airspace system and are of concern to instrument flight rule (IFR) operations. NOTAM information is classified into five categories: NOTAM (D) or distant, Flight Data Center (FDC) NOTAMs, pointer NOTAMs, Special Activity Airspace (SAA) NOTAMs, and military NOTAMs.

NOTAM (D)s are attached to hourly weather reports and are available at flight service stations (AFSS/FSS). FDC NOTAMs are issued by the National Flight Data Center and contain regulatory information, such as temporary flight restrictions or an amendment to instrument approach procedures.

Pointer NOTAMs highlight or point out another NOTAM, such as an FDC or NOTAM (D). This type of NOTAM will assist pilots in cross-referencing important information that may not be found under an airport or NAVAID identifier. Military NOTAMs pertain to U.S. Air Force, Army, Marine, and Navy NAVAIDs/airports that are part of the NAS.

SAA NOTAMs are issued when Special Activity Airspace will be active outside the published schedule times and when required by the published schedule. Pilots and other users are still responsible to check published schedule times for Special Activity Airspace as well as any NOTAMs for that airspace.

NOTAM (D)s and FDC NOTAMs are contained in the Notices to Air Missions publication, which is issued every 28 days. Prior to any flight, pilots should check for any NOTAMs that could affect their intended flight.

ALL

9086. What are FDC NOTAMs?

A—Conditions of facilities en route that may cause delays.
B—Time critical aeronautical information of a temporary nature from distant centers.
C—Regulatory amendments to published IAPs and charts not yet available in normally published charts.

FDC NOTAMs contain such things as amendments to published IAPs and other current aeronautical charts and other information which is considered regulatory in nature. (PLT323, AA.II.C.K1) — AIM ¶5-1-3

Answer (A) is incorrect because NOTAM (D) contains information on navigational facilities en route that may cause delays. Answer (B) is incorrect because time critical aeronautical information of a temporary nature from distant centers will be included in a NOTAM (D) ("distant").

ALL

9087. What type information is disseminated by NOTAM (D)s?

A—Status of navigation aids, ILSs, radar service available, and other information essential to planning.
B—Airport or primary runway closings, runway and taxiway conditions, and airport lighting aids outages.
C—Temporary flight restrictions, changes in status in navigational aids, and updates on equipment such as VASI.

NOTAM (D) information is disseminated for all navigational facilities that are part of the national airspace system, all IFR airports with approved instrument approaches, and those VFR airports annotated with the NOTAM service symbol (§) in the Chart Supplements U.S. (previously A/FD). NOTAM (D) information could affect a pilot's decision to make a flight. It includes

Answers

9400 [B] 9086 [C] 9087 [A]

such information as airport or primary runway closures, changes in the status of navigational aids, ILS's, radar service availability, and other information essential to planned en route, terminal or landing operations. (PLT323, AA.II.C.K1) — AIM ¶5-1-3

ALL

9089. How often are NOTAMs broadcast to pilots on a scheduled basis?

A—15 minutes before and 15 minutes after the hour.
B—Between weather broadcasts on the hour.
C—Hourly, appended to the weather broadcast.

NOTAM (D) information is appended to the hourly weather reports via the Service A (ATC/FSS) telecommunications system. (PLT323, AA.II.C.K1) — AIM ¶5-1-3

Answer (A) is incorrect because SIGMETs and AIRMETs are broadcast by FSSs to pilots 15 minutes before and 15 minutes after the hour during the valid period. Answer (B) is incorrect because NOTAM (D)s are appended to the hourly weather broadcast, not a separate broadcast between weather reports.

ATS, RTC

9931. Which of the following would meet the requirements for 14 CFR Part 135 flight locating when an FAA flight plan is not filed?

A—Receiving VFR flight following services from air traffic control.
B—Operating an aircraft equipped with an approved satellite phone and ELT.
C—Relaying flight plan information to a company flight locator before departure.

Each certificate holder must have procedures established for locating each flight for which an FAA flight plan is not filed, providing the certificate holder with the location, date, and estimated time for reestablishing communications, if the flight will operate in an area where communications cannot be maintained. Flight locating information shall be retained at the certificate holder's principal place of business, or at other places designated by the certificate holder in the flight locating procedures, until the completion of the flight. (PLT433, AA.I.G.K5) — 14 CFR §135.79

Flight Plans

An IFR flight plan should be filed at least 30 minutes prior to the departure time, and pilots should request their IFR clearance no more than 10 minutes prior to taxi.

If the flight is to be flown on established airways, the route should be defined using the airways or jet routes with transitions. Intermediate VORs and fixes on an airway need not be listed. If filing for an off-airway direct route, list all the radio fixes over which the flight will pass. Pilots of appropriately equipped aircraft may file for random RNAV routes. The following rules must be observed:

- Radar monitoring by ATC must be available along the entire proposed route.
- Plan the random route portion to begin and end over appropriate departure and arrival transition fixes or navigation aids appropriate for the altitude structure used for the flight. Use of DPs and STARs, where available, is recommended.
- Define the random route by waypoints. Use degree-distance fixes based on navigational aids appropriate for the altitude structure used. Above FL390 latitude/longitude fixes may be used to define the route.
- List at least one waypoint for each Air Route Traffic Control Center through which the flight will pass. The waypoint must be within 200 NM of the preceding Center's boundary.

A pilot may file a flight plan to an airport containing a special or privately-owned instrument approach procedure only upon approval of the owner.

Air ambulance flights and air carrier flights responding to medical emergencies will receive expedited handling by ATC when necessary. When appropriate, the word "Lifeguard" should be entered in the remarks section of the flight plan. It should also be used in the flight's radio call sign as in, "Lifeguard Delta Thirty-Seven."

Answers

9089 [C] 9931 [C]

ALL

9031. What is the suggested time interval for filing and requesting an IFR flight plan?

A—File at least 30 minutes prior to departure and request the clearance not more than 10 minutes prior to taxi.
B—File at least 30 minutes prior to departure and request the clearance at least 10 minutes prior to taxi.
C—File at least 1 hour prior to departure and request the clearance at least 10 minutes prior to taxi.

Pilots should file IFR flight plans at least 30 minutes prior to the estimated time of departure to preclude possible delay in receiving a departure clearance from ATC. Pilots should call clearance delivery or ground control for their IFR clearance not more than 10 minutes before the proposed taxi time. (PLT224, AA.I.E.K14) — AIM ¶5-1-8, 5-2-1

ALL

9032. How should the route of flight be defined on an IFR flight plan?

A—A simplified route via airways or jet routes with transitions.
B—A route via airways or jet routes with VORs and fixes used.
C—A route via airways or jet routes with only the compulsory reporting points.

Pilots are requested to file via airways or jet routes established for use at the altitude or flight level planned. If the flight is to be conducted via designated airways or jet routes, describe the route by indicating the type and number designators of the airway(s) or jet route(s) requested. If more than one airway or jet route is to be used, clearly indicate points of transition. (PLT224, AA.I.G.K2) — AIM ¶5-1-8

Answer (B) is incorrect because, to simplify the route, all VORs and fixes are not used to define a route on an IFR flight plan. Answer (C) is incorrect because compulsory reporting points might not define the transitions between airways or jet routes.

ALL

9033. How should an off-airway direct flight be defined on an IFR flight plan?

A—The initial fix, the true course, and the final fix.
B—All radio fixes over which the flight will pass.
C—The initial fix, all radio fixes which the pilot wishes to be compulsory reporting points, and the final fix.

Any portions of the route which will not be flown on the radials or courses of established airways or routes, such as direct route flights, must be clearly defined by indicating the radio fixes over which the flight will pass. (PLT225, AA.I.G.K2) — AIM ¶5-1-8

Answer (A) is incorrect because true course is not an item that is reported on an IFR flight plan. The initial fix and the final fix are listed as radio fixes that define the start and finish points of a flight. Answer (C) is incorrect because initial and final fixes are required to define random RNAV (not direct flight) routes. All radio fixes that define the route of a direct flight automatically become compulsory reporting points, not just those the pilot chooses.

ALL

9026. How are random RNAV routes below FL390 defined on the IFR flight plan?

A—Define route waypoints using degree-distance fixes based on appropriate navigational aids for the route and altitude.
B—List the initial and final fix with at least one waypoint each 200 NM.
C—Begin and end over appropriate arrival and departure transition fixes or navigation aids for the altitude being flown, define the random route waypoints by using degree-distance fixes based on navigation aids appropriate for the altitude being flown.

Pilots of aircraft equipped with operational area navigation equipment may file for random RNAV routes throughout the national airspace system, where radar monitoring by ATC is available, in accordance with the following:

1. *File airport-to-airport flight plans prior to departure.*
2. *File the appropriate RNAV capability suffix in the flight plan.*
3. *Plan the random route portion of the flight plan to begin and end over appropriate arrival and departure fixes.*
4. *Define the random route by waypoints. File route description waypoints by using degree/distance fixes based on navigation aids which are appropriate to the altitude.*
5. *File a minimum of one route description waypoint for each ARTCC through whose area the random route will be flown. These waypoints must be located within 200 NM of the preceding center's boundary.*

(PLT224, AA.I.G.K2) — AIM ¶5-1-8

Answer (A) is incorrect because RNAV routes defined on an IFR flight plan must also begin and end over an established radio fix. Answer (B) is incorrect because RNAV waypoints have no established distance requirement. A minimum of one waypoint must be filed for each ARTCC through which the route is planned, and this must be located within 200 NM of the preceding center's boundary.

Answers

9031 [A] 9032 [A] 9033 [B] 9026 [C]

ALL

9027. What is one limitation when filing a random RNAV route on an IFR flight plan?

A—The waypoints must be located within 200 NM of each other.
B—The entire route must be within radar environment.
C—The waypoints may only be defined by degree-distance fixes based on appropriate navigational aids.

Random RNAV routes can only be approved in a radar environment. Aircraft operating at or above FL390 may file waypoints based on latitude/longitude fixes, under some circumstances. (PLT225, AA.I.G.K2) — AIM ¶5-1-8

Answer (A) is incorrect because VOR/VORTAC facilities must be within 200 NM of each other when operating above FL450 to define a direct route. Answer (C) is incorrect because random RNAV waypoints may be defined by degree-distance fixes based on appropriate navigational aids, of latitude/longitude coordinate navigation, independent of VOR/TACAN references, operating at and above FL390 in the conterminous U.S.

ALL

9040. Under what condition may a pilot file an IFR flight plan containing a special or privately owned IAP?

A—Upon approval of ATC.
B—Upon approval of the owner.
C—Upon signing a waiver of responsibility.

Pilots planning flights to locations served by special IAPs should obtain advance approval from the owner of the procedure. Approval by the owner is necessary because special procedures are for the exclusive use of the single interest unless otherwise authorized by the owner. Controllers assume a pilot has obtained approval and is aware of any details of the procedure if he/she files an IFR flight plan to that airport. (PLT083, AA.VI.D.K1) — AIM ¶5-4-7

Answer (A) is incorrect because ATC is not required to question pilots to determine whether they have the owner's permission to use the procedure. Answer (C) is incorrect because a pilot is responsible for the safe operation of the airplane. To sign a waiver of responsibility is contrary to a pilot's duty.

ALL

9053. To assure expeditious handling of a civilian air ambulance flight, the word "LIFEGUARD" should be entered in which section of the flight plan?

A—Aircraft type/special equipment block.
B—Pilot's name and address block.
C—Remarks block.

When expeditious handling is necessary because of a medical emergency, add the word "LIFEGUARD" in the remarks section of the flight plan. (PLT225, AA.I.G.K2) — AIM ¶4-2-4

Answer (A) is incorrect because only the airplane's designator or manufacturer's name and the transponder DME and/or RNAV equipment code is entered in the aircraft type/special equipment block. Answer (B) is incorrect because the complete name, address, and telephone number of the pilot-in-command are entered in the pilot's name and address block. Sufficient information is listed here to identify home base, airport, or operator. This information would be essential in the event of a search and rescue operation.

ALL

9809. Before requesting RVSM clearance, each person

A—shall correctly annotate the flight plan.
B—must file an ICAO RVSM flight plan.
C—should file for odd altitudes only.

Each person requesting a clearance to operate within reduced vertical separate minimum (RVSM) airspace shall correctly annotate the flight plan filed with air traffic control with regard to RVSM approval. (PLT367, AA.I.G.K2) — AIM ¶4-6-4

Answers

9027 [B] 9040 [B] 9053 [C] 9809 [A]

Alternate Airport Planning

An airport may not be available for alternate use if the airport NAVAID is unmonitored, is GPS-based, or if it does not have weather-reporting capabilities.

For an airport to be used as an alternate, the forecast weather at that airport must meet certain qualifications at the estimated time of arrival. Standard alternate minimums for a precision approach are a 600-foot ceiling and 2 SM visibility. For a nonprecision approach, the minimums are an 800-foot ceiling and 2 SM visibility. Standard alternate minimums apply unless higher alternate minimums are listed for an airport.

Alternate Airport for Destination—Domestic Air Carriers: Unless the weather at the destination meets certain criteria, an alternate must be listed in the dispatch release (and flight plan) for each destination airport. If the weather at the first listed alternate is marginal (as defined by the operations specifications) at least one additional alternate must be listed.

Alternate Airport for Destination—Flag Carriers: An alternate airport must be listed in the dispatch release (and flight plan) for all flag air carrier flights longer than 6 hours. An alternate is not required for a flag air carrier flight if it is scheduled for less than 6 hours and the weather forecast for the destination meets certain criteria. For the period from 1 hour before to 1 hour after the estimated time of arrival:

- The ceiling must be forecast to be at least 1,500 feet above the lowest minimums or 2,000 feet, whichever is higher; and
- The visibility must be forecast to be 3 miles, or 2 miles greater than the lowest applicable visibility minimum, whichever is greater.

Alternate Airport for Destination—Supplemental Air Carriers and Commercial Operators: Except for certain operations, a supplemental air carrier or commercial operator must always list an alternate airport regardless of existing or forecast weather conditions.

An airport cannot be listed as an alternate in the dispatch or flight release unless the appropriate weather reports and forecasts indicate that the weather conditions will be at or above the alternate weather minimums specified in the certificate holder's operations specifications for that airport, when the flight arrives. Alternate weather minimums are for planning purposes only and do not apply to actual operations. If an air carrier flight actually diverts to an alternate airport, the crew may use the actual weather minimums shown on the IAP (Instrument Approach Procedure) Chart for that airport.

If the weather conditions at the departure airport are below landing minimums in the airline's operations specifications, a departure alternate must be listed in the dispatch or the flight release. Weather at alternate airports must meet the conditions for alternates in the operations specifications. The maximum distance to the departure alternate for a two-engine airplane cannot be more than 1 hour from the departure airport in still air with one engine operating. The distance to the departure alternate for an airplane with three or more engines cannot be more than 2 hours from the departure airport in still air with one engine inoperative.

ALL

9394-1. When proceeding to the alternate airport, which minimums apply?

A—The IFR alternate minimums section in front of the NOAA IAP book.
B—2000-3 for at least 1 hour before until 1 hour after the ETA.
C—The actual minimums shown on the IAP chart for the airport.

When the approach procedure being used provides for and requires the use of a DH or MDA, the authorized decision height or authorized minimum descent altitude is the DH or MDA prescribed by the approach procedure, the DH or MDA prescribed for the pilot-in-command, or the DH or MDA for which the aircraft is equipped, whichever is highest.

Note: The alternate airport minimums are used only during preflight planning to determine the suitability of an airport as an IFR alternate. They impose no additional restrictions should a flight actually divert to the filed alternate. (PLT421, AA.I.G.K2) — 14 CFR §91.175

Answer (A) is incorrect because the alternate minimums listed in the NOAA IAP (National Oceanic and Atmospheric Administration Instrument Approach Procedure) book refer to the ceiling and visibility requirements for that airport in order to file it as an alternate, not the ceiling and visibility required to execute an instrument approach. Answer (B) is incorrect because 2000-3 minimums apply to the destination airport. If your destination airport has a forecast ceiling of at least 2,000 feet and a visibility of at least 3 miles, an alternate airport need not be filed in the flight plan.

ALL

9394-2. An airport may not be qualified for alternate use if

A—the airport has AWOS-3 weather reporting.
B—the airport is located next to a restricted or prohibited area.
C—the NAVAIDs used for the final approach are unmonitored.

Not all airports can be used as an alternate. An airport may not be qualified for alternate use if the airport NAVAID is unmonitored, is GPS-based, or if it does not have weather reporting capability. (PLT379, AA.I.G.K4) — FAA-H-8083-16

Answer (A) is incorrect because an airport can qualify for alternate use if it has any weather reporting capability. Answer (B) is incorrect because an airport can qualify for alternate use even if it is located in a restricted or prohibited area.

ALL

9770. When planning to use RNAV equipment with GPS input for an instrument approach at a destination airport, any required alternate airport must have an available instrument approach procedure that does not

A—require the use of GPS except when the RNAV system has a WAAS input.
B—require the use of GPS except when the RNAV system has an IRU input.
C—require the use of GPS except when dual, independent GPS receivers are installed.

Aircraft using GPS navigation equipment under IFR for domestic en route, terminal operations, and certain IAPs must be equipped with an approved and operational alternate means of navigation appropriate to the flight. However, a required alternate airport may be selected if it uses an RNAV system with WAAS equipment. (PLT420, AA.I.G.K4) — FAA-H-8083-15

ATM, ADX

8247. When the forecast weather conditions for a destination and alternate airport are considered marginal for a domestic air carrier's operation, what specific action should the dispatcher or pilot-in-command take?

A—List an airport where the forecast weather is not marginal as the alternate.
B—Add 1 additional hour of fuel based on cruise power settings for the airplane in use.
C—List at least one additional alternate airport.

When weather conditions forecast for the destination and first alternate airport are marginal, at least one additional alternate must be designated. (PLT379, AA.I.G.K4) — 14 CFR §121.619

ATM, ADX

8256. Which dispatch requirement applies to a flag air carrier that is scheduled for a 7-hour IFR flight?

A—No alternate airport is required if the forecast weather at the ETA at the destination airport is at least 1,500 feet and 3 miles.
B—An alternate airport is not required if the ceiling will be at least 1,500 feet above the lowest circling MDA.
C—An alternate airport is required.

All flag air carrier flights over 6 hours require an alternate airport. (PLT379, AA.I.G.K4) — 14 CFR §121.621

Answers (A) and (B) are incorrect because whenever the scheduled flight exceeds 6 hours, a flag air carrier must list an alternate regardless of the weather.

Answers

9394-1 [C]	9394-2 [C]	9770 [A]	8247 [C]	8256 [C]

ATM, ADX
8262. An alternate airport is not required to dispatch a flag air carrier airplane for a flight of less than 6 hours when the visibility for at least 1 hour before and 1 hour after the ETA at the destination airport is forecast to be

A—2 miles or greater.
B—at least 3 miles, or 2 miles more than the lowest applicable minimum.
C—3 miles.

An alternate airport need not be listed if the destination weather, from an hour before to an hour after the ETA, is forecast to have the required ceiling criteria and the visibility is forecast to be at least 3 miles, or 2 miles more than the lowest visibility minimums, whichever is greater, for the instrument approach procedures to be used at the destination airport. (PLT379, AA.I.G.K4) — 14 CFR §121.621

ATM, ADX
8251. When is a supplemental air carrier, operating under IFR, required to list an alternate airport for each destination airport within the 48 contiguous United States?

A—When the forecast weather indicates the ceiling will be less than 1,000 feet and visibility less than 2 miles at the estimated time of arrival.
B—On all flights, an alternate is required regardless of existing or forecast weather conditions at the destination.
C—When the flight is scheduled for more than 6 hours en route.

A supplemental air carrier must declare an alternate airport for all IFR operations. (PLT379, AA.I.G.K4) — 14 CFR §121.623

ATM, ADX
8254. Prior to listing an airport as an alternate airport in the dispatch or flight release, weather reports and forecasts must indicate that weather conditions will be at or above authorized minimums at that airport

A—for a period 1 hour before or after the ETA.
B—during the entire flight.
C—when the flight arrives.

No person may list an airport as an alternate airport in the dispatch release or flight release unless the appropriate weather reports or forecasts, or any combination thereof, indicate that the weather conditions will be at or above the alternate weather minimums specified in the certificate holder's operations specifications for that airport when the flight arrives. (PLT380, AA.I.G.K4) — 14 CFR §121.625

ATM, ADX
8255. As required by Part 121, an airport may be listed as an alternate in the flight release only if the weather forecast indicates that conditions will be at or above the

A—alternate weather minima specified in the operation specifications at the time of arrival.
B—lowest available IAP minima at the time of arrival.
C—lowest available IAP minima for 1 hour before to 1 hour after the time of arrival.

No person may list an airport as an alternate airport in the dispatch release or flight release unless the appropriate weather reports or forecasts, or any combination thereof, indicate that the weather conditions will be at or above the alternate weather minimums specified in the certificate holder's operations specifications for that airport when the flight arrives. (PLT380, AA.I.G.K4) — 14 CFR §121.625

ATM, ADX
8248. An alternate airport for departure is required

A—if weather conditions are below authorized landing minimums at the departure airport.
B—when the weather forecast at the ETD is for landing minimums only at the departure airport.
C—when destination weather is marginal VFR (ceiling less than 3,000 feet and visibility less than 5 SM).

If the weather conditions at the airport of takeoff are below the landing minimums in the certificate holder's operations specifications for that airport, no person may dispatch or release an aircraft from that airport unless the dispatch or flight release specifies an alternate airport located within the following distances from the airport of takeoff.

1. *Aircraft having two engines: Not more than 1 hour from the departure airport at normal cruising speed in still air with one engine inoperative.*
2. *Aircraft having three or more engines: Not more than 2 hours from the departure airport at normal cruising speed in still air with one engine inoperative.*

(PLT379, AA.I.G.K4) — 14 CFR §121.617

Answers

8262 [B] 8251 [B] 8254 [C] 8255 [A] 8248 [A]

ATM, ADX

8249. What is the maximum distance that a departure alternate airport may be from the departure airport for a two-engine airplane?

A—1 hour at normal cruise speed in still air with both engines operating.
B—1 hour at normal cruise speed in still air with one engine operating.
C—2 hours at normal cruise speed in still air with one engine operating.

If the weather conditions at the airport of takeoff are below the landing minimums in the certificate holder's operations specifications for that airport, no person may dispatch or release an aircraft from that airport unless the dispatch or flight release specifies an alternate airport located within the following distances from the airport of takeoff.

1. *Aircraft having two engines: Not more than 1 hour from the departure airport at normal cruising speed in still air with one engine inoperative.*
2. *Aircraft having three or more engines: Not more than 2 hours from the departure airport at normal cruising speed in still air with one engine inoperative.*

(PLT379, AA.I.G.K4) — 14 CFR §121.617

Answer (A) is incorrect because the maximum distance is determined with one engine operating. Answer (C) is incorrect because 2 hours is the limit for airplanes with three or more engines with one engine inoperative.

ATM, ADX

8250. If a four-engine air carrier airplane is dispatched from an airport that is below landing minimums, what is the maximum distance that a departure alternate airport may be located from the departure airport?

A—Not more than 2 hours at cruise speed with one engine inoperative.
B—Not more than 2 hours at normal cruise speed in still air with one engine inoperative.
C—Not more than 1 hour at normal cruise speed in still air with one engine inoperative.

If the weather conditions at the airport of takeoff are below the landing minimums in the certificate holder's operations specifications for that airport, no person may dispatch or release an aircraft from that airport unless the dispatch or flight release specifies an alternate airport located within the following distances from the airport of takeoff.

1. *Aircraft having two engines: Not more than 1 hour from the departure airport at normal cruising speed in still air with one engine inoperative.*
2. *Aircraft having three or more engines: Not more than 2 hours from the departure airport at normal cruising speed in still air with one engine inoperative.*

(PLT396, AA.I.G.K4) — 14 CFR §121.617

ATM, ADX

8252. When a departure alternate is required for a three-engine air carrier flight, it must be located at a distance not greater than

A—2 hours from the departure airport at normal cruising speed in still air with one engine not functioning.
B—1 hour from the departure airport at normal cruising speed in still air with one engine inoperative.
C—2 hours from the departure airport at normal cruising speed in still air.

If the weather conditions at the airport of takeoff are below the landing minimums in the certificate holder's operations specifications for that airport, no person may dispatch or release an aircraft from that airport unless the dispatch or flight release specifies an alternate airport located within the following distances from the airport of takeoff.

1. *Aircraft having two engines: Not more than 1 hour from the departure airport at normal cruising speed in still air with one engine inoperative.*
2. *Aircraft having three or more engines: Not more than 2 hours from the departure airport at normal cruising speed in still air with one engine inoperative.*

(PLT379, AA.I.G.K4) — 14 CFR §121.617

Answer (B) is incorrect because 1 hour is correct for a two-engine airplane. Answer (C) is incorrect because it does not contain the words "with one engine inoperative."

Answers

8249 [B] 8250 [B] 8252 [A]

ATC Clearances

No one may operate an aircraft in Class A, B, C, D or E airspace under Instrument Flight Rules (IFR) unless he/she has filed an IFR flight plan and received an appropriate ATC clearance. No flight plan or clearance is required for IFR operations in Class G airspace.

IFR clearances always contain:

- A clearance limit (usually the destination);
- Route of flight;
- Altitude assignment; and
- Departure instructions (could be a DP).

The words "cleared as filed" replace only the route of flight portion of a normal clearance. The controller will still state the destination airport, the enroute altitude (or initial altitude and expected final altitude) and DP if appropriate. If a STAR is filed on the flight plan, it is considered part of the enroute portion of the flight plan and is included in the term "cleared as filed."

When an ATC clearance has been received, you may not deviate from it (except in an emergency) unless an amended clearance is received. If you are uncertain of the meaning of an ATC clearance or the clearance appears to be contrary to a regulation, you should immediately request a clarification. When you receive a clearance you should always read back altitude assignments, altitude restrictions, and vectors. A Departure Procedure (DP) may contain these elements but they need not be included in the readback unless the ATC controller specifically states them.

At airports with pretaxi clearance delivery, a pilot should call for the clearance 10 minutes prior to the desired taxi time. After receiving clearance on the clearance delivery frequency, the pilot should call ground control for taxi when ready.

Occasionally, an aircraft with an IFR release will be held on the ground for traffic management reasons. The traffic may be too heavy or weather may be causing ATC delays. If this happens to an aircraft waiting for takeoff, it will be given a hold for release instruction.

When ATC can anticipate long delays for IFR aircraft, they will establish gate hold procedures. The idea is to hold aircraft at the gate rather than cause congestion and unnecessary fuel burn on the taxiways while waiting for an IFR release. Ground control will instruct aircraft when to start engines. ATC expects that turbine-powered aircraft will be ready for takeoff as soon as they reach the runway after having been released from gate hold.

When departing uncontrolled airports, IFR flights will often receive a void time with their clearance. The void time is a usually a 30-minute window of time during which the aircraft must takeoff for its IFR clearance to be valid. If unable to comply with the void time, a pilot must receive another clearance with an amended void time.

The flight plan of an airborne IFR aircraft may only be canceled when the aircraft is in VFR weather conditions and outside of Class A airspace.

ALL

9374. A pilot is operating in Class G airspace. If existing weather conditions are below those for VFR flight, an IFR flight plan must be filed and an ATC clearance received prior to

A—takeoff if weather conditions are below IFR minimums.
B—entering controlled airspace.
C—entering IFR weather conditions.

No person may operate an aircraft in Class A, B, C, D or E airspace under IFR unless an IFR flight plan has been filed and an appropriate ATC clearance has been received. (PLT162, AA.I.G.K2) — 14 CFR §91.173

Answers (A) and (C) are incorrect because an IFR flight plan and an ATC clearance are not required to fly in IMC (instrument meteorological conditions) in Class G airspace.

ALL

9006. What minimum information does an abbreviated departure clearance "cleared as filed" include?

A—Clearance limit and en route altitude.
B—Clearance limit, transponder code, and DP, if appropriate.
C—Destination airport, en route altitude, transponder code, and DP, if appropriate.

The following apply to "cleared as filed" clearances:

1. *The clearance as issued will include the destination airport filed in the flight plan. "Cleared to (destination) as filed."*
2. *The controller will state the DP name and number.*
3. *STARs, when filed in a flight plan, are considered a part of the filed route of flight and will not normally be stated in an initial clearance.*
4. *An enroute altitude will be stated in the clearance or the pilot will be advised to expect an assigned or filed altitude within a given time frame or at a certain point after departure. This may be done verbally in the departure clearance or stated in the DP.*

(PLT370, AA.I.G.K2) — AIM ¶5-2-5

Answer (A) is incorrect because a clearance limit may be a fix, point, or location. An abbreviated clearance will be a clearance to the destination airport. In some cases, a clearance is issued to a fix (limit) from which another clearance limit will be issued. DPs are stated in all IFR departure clearances when appropriate. Answer (B) is incorrect because a clearance will state the destination airport's name, not a clearance limit.

ALL

9439. An ATC "instruction"

A—is the same as an ATC "clearance."
B—is a directive issued by ATC for the purpose of requiring a pilot to take a specific action.
C—must be "read back" in full to the controller and confirmed before becoming effective.

Instructions are directives issued by air traffic control for the purpose of requiring a pilot to take specific actions; e.g., "Turn left heading two five zero," "Go around," "Clear the runway." (PLT370, AA.I.G.K2) — Pilot/Controller Glossary

Answer (A) is incorrect because an ATC clearance is not the same as an ATC instruction. Answer (C) is incorrect because an ATC instruction does not have to be read back in full to the controller and confirmed before becoming effective.

ALL

9402. What action should a pilot take when a clearance is received from ATC that appears to be contrary to a regulation?

A—Read the clearance back in its entirety.
B—Request a clarification from ATC.
C—Do not accept the clearance.

If a pilot is uncertain of the meaning of an ATC clearance, he/she shall immediately request clarification from ATC. (PLT444, AA.I.G.K2) — 14 CFR §91.123

Answer (A) is incorrect because reading the clearance back in its entirety does not inform ATC of the possible conflict to a regulation. A pilot should actively seek clarification if there is any doubt. Answer (C) is incorrect because not accepting a clearance is not the proper procedure to use when, in a pilot's opinion, it would conflict with a regulation. First, a pilot should receive a clarification from ATC, then ask for an amended clearance, if necessary.

ALL

9402-1. While airborne and below the MEA, the pilot accepts an IFR clearance. Sole responsibility for terrain and obstruction clearance remains with the pilot unless

A—the flight continues in clouds or above a ceiling and ATC transmits "RADAR CONTACT."
B—an appropriate minimum IFR altitude providing obstruction clearance is attained.
C—the pilot advises ATC that he or she is unable to maintain terrain/obstruction clearance.

Answers

9374 [B] 9006 [C] 9439 [B] 9402 [B] 9402-1 [C]

It is the pilot's responsibility to maintain terrain/obstruction clearance when flying below the minimum IFR altitude, unless the pilot advises ATC that they are unable to do so. (PLT444, AA.VI.B.K3) — FAA-H-8083-15

Answer (A) is incorrect because simply hearing "radar contact" does not relieve the pilot of responsibility. Answer (B) is incorrect because a controller cannot issue an IFR clearance until an aircraft is above the minimum IFR altitude, unless it is able to climb in VFR conditions.

ALL

9045. What is the pilot's responsibility for clearance or instruction readback?

A—Except for SIDs, acknowledge altitude assignments, altitude restrictions, and vectors.

B—If the clearance or instruction is understood, an acknowledgment is sufficient.

C—Read back the entire clearance or instruction to confirm the message is understood.

Pilots of airborne aircraft should read back those parts of ATC clearances and instructions containing altitude assignments or vectors. Altitudes contained in charted procedures such as DPs, instrument approaches, etc., should not be read back unless they are specifically stated by the controller. (PLT370, AA.I.G.K2) — AIM ¶4-4-7

Answer (B) is incorrect because the best way to know that the clearance or instruction is understood is to read back the "numbers" as a double-check between the pilot and ATC. This reduces the kinds of communication errors that occur when a number is either misheard or is incorrect. Answer (C) is incorrect because the pilot's responsibility is to read back the clearances and instructions containing altitude assignments, altitude restrictions, and vectors, not the entire clearance or instruction.

ALL

9008. What is the normal procedure for IFR departures at locations with pretaxi clearance programs?

A—Pilots request IFR clearance when ready to taxi. The pilot will receive taxi instruction with clearance.

B—Pilots request IFR clearance when ready to taxi. Pilots will receive taxi clearance, then receive IFR clearance while taxiing or on runup.

C—Pilots request IFR clearance 10 minutes or less prior to taxi, then request taxi clearance from ground control.

When operating at airports with pretaxi clearance delivery, participating pilots should call clearance delivery or ground control not more than 10 minutes before taxi. When the IFR clearance is received on clearance delivery frequency, pilots should call ground control when ready to taxi. (PLT370, AA.I.G.K2) — AIM ¶5-2-1

Answers (A) and (B) are incorrect because the pilot will first be given the IFR clearance, then the taxi instruction or clearance.

ALL

9009. What is the purpose of the term "hold for release" when included in an IFR clearance?

A—A procedure for delaying departure for traffic volume, weather, or need to issue further instructions.

B—When an IFR clearance is received by telephone, the pilot will have time to prepare for takeoff prior to being released.

C—Gate hold procedures are in effect and the pilot receives an estimate of the time the flight will be released.

ATC may issue "hold for release" instructions in a clearance to delay an aircraft's departure for traffic management reasons (i.e., weather, traffic volume, etc.). (PLT370, AA.II.C.K2) — AIM ¶5-2-6

Answer (B) is incorrect because, when a pilot receives an IFR clearance via telephone, it is normally because he/she is departing from an uncontrolled airport. In this case, ATC would issue a clearance void time, not a hold for release. Answer (C) is incorrect because gate hold procedures are in effect whenever departure delays exceed (or are expected to exceed) 15 minutes. This procedure is not a way for ATC to delay an airplane's departure.

ALL

9056. What action should the pilot take when "gate hold" procedures are in effect?

A—Contact ground control prior to starting engines for sequencing.

B—Taxi into position and hold prior to requesting clearance.

C—Start engines, perform pretakeoff check, and request clearance prior to leaving the parking area.

When gate hold procedures are in effect, pilots should contact ground control or clearance delivery prior to starting engines, because departure delays are expected to exceed 15 minutes. (PLT434, AA.II.C.K2) — AIM ¶4-3-15

Answer (B) is incorrect because taxi into position means that the pilot is on the active runway and ready for takeoff. This is not a position where ATC would issue an IFR clearance. Answer (C) is incorrect because pilots should contact ground control for sequencing before starting engines.

Answers

9045 [A] 9008 [C] 9009 [A] 9056 [A]

ALL

9057. What special consideration is given for turbine-powered aircraft when "gate hold" procedures are in effect?

A—They are given preference for departure over other aircraft.
B—They are expected to be ready for takeoff when they reach the runway or warmup block.
C—They are expected to be ready for takeoff prior to taxi and will receive takeoff clearance prior to taxi.

Even with gate holds in effect, the tower controller will consider that pilots of turbine-powered aircraft are ready for takeoff when they reach the runway or warm up block unless advised otherwise. (PLT149, AA.II.C.K2) — AIM ¶4-3-15

Answer (A) is incorrect because, when gate hold procedures are in effect, sequencing of all airplanes is based on the initial call-up to ground control or clearance delivery. Answer (C) is incorrect because a pilot of any airplane should be ready to taxi prior to requesting taxi, and takeoff clearance is received prior to takeoff.

ALL

9007. Under what condition does a pilot receive a "void time" specified in the clearance?

A—On an uncontrolled airport.
B—When "gate hold" procedures are in effect.
C—If the clearance is received prior to starting engines.

If operating from an airport not served by a control tower, the pilot may receive a clearance containing a provision that if the flight has not departed by a specific time, the clearance is void. (PLT370, AA.II.C.K2) — AIM ¶5-2-6

Answer (B) is incorrect because gate hold procedures are in effect whenever departure delays exceed or are anticipated to exceed 15 minutes. Answer (C) is incorrect because clearances can be issued before starting the airplane's engine(s).

ALL

9005. Under what condition may a pilot cancel an IFR flight plan prior to completing the flight?

A—Anytime it appears the clearance will cause a deviation from FARs.
B—Anytime within controlled airspace by contacting ARTCC.
C—Only if in VFR conditions in other than Class A airspace.

An IFR flight plan may be canceled anytime the flight is operating in VFR conditions outside Class A airspace. (PLT224, AA.II.C.S5) — AIM ¶5-1-14

Answer (A) is incorrect because anytime a clearance appears to deviate from a regulation, the pilot should request clarification from ATC and an amended clearance. Answer (B) is incorrect because all aircraft in Class A airspace (above FL180) or when operating in IMC in Class B, C, D or E must be operating under an IFR flight plan.

ATM, ATS, RTC

9737. (Refer to Runway Incursion Figure.) You have requested taxi instructions for takeoff using Runway 16. The controller issues the following taxi instructions: "N123, Taxi to runway 16." Where are you required to stop in order to be in compliance with the controller's instructions?

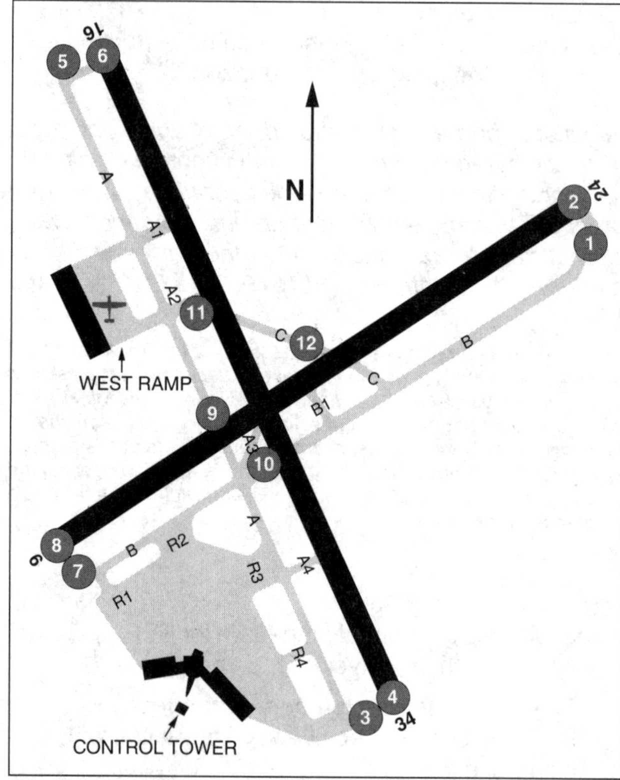

Runway Incursion

A—5 (Five).
B—6 (Six).
C—9 (Nine).

Answers

9057 [B]   9007 [A]   9005 [C]   9737 [A]

When ATC clears an aircraft to "taxi to" an assigned takeoff runway, the absence of holding instructions does not authorize the aircraft to "cross" all runways which the taxi route intersects except the assigned takeoff runway. A clearance must be obtained prior to crossing any runway. It does not include authorization to "taxi onto" or "cross" the assigned takeoff runway at any point. You should taxi and hold short of runway 16, which is position 5. (PLT141, AA.II.C.K2) — AIM 4-3-18

Answer (B) is incorrect because "taxi to" does not authorize the aircraft to "taxi onto" the assigned takeoff runway. Answer (C) is incorrect because the airplane should taxi the most direct route to the assigned runway unless instructed otherwise; position 9 would not be encountered for the airplane at the west ramp to taxi to runway 16.

ATM, ATS, RTC

9788. As you call for taxi instructions, the key words to understand are

A—cleared to runway.
B—hold short of or "cross."
C—taxi to and "expedite."

When issuing taxi instructions to any point other than an assigned takeoff runway, ATC will specify the point to taxi to, issue taxi instructions, and state any hold short instructions or runway crossing clearances if the taxi route will cross a runway. (PLT149, AA.II.C.K2) — AIM ¶4-3-18

Answer (A) is incorrect because ATC will not use the word "cleared" in conjunction with authorization for aircraft to taxi. Answer (C) is incorrect because "expedite" is not as critical as being told to hold short or cross.

ATM, ATS, RTC

9789. You received these ATC taxi instructions: "Taxi to Runway 30 via Lima and hold short of Runway 25L". Your airplane is on the ramp by the terminal and NWS on the east side of the airport. Your taxi route

A—requires crossing of Runway 25L at Lima.
B—involves transiting HS 4.
C—requires crossing Runway 34R en route to the assigned runway.

When assigned a takeoff runway, ATC will first specify the runway, issue taxi instructions, and state any hold short instructions or runway crossing clearances if the taxi route will cross a runway. (PLT149, AA.II.C.K8) — AIM ¶4-3-18

ATM, ATS, RTC

9790. (Refer to Figure 241 and 242.) As you rolled out long on Runway 30 after landing at Long Beach (LGB), you slowed and turned left on very wide pavement and now see Taxiway D signs on both sides of your pavement. You notice your heading is about 250°. Tower is urging you to turn left on D, cross 16R/34L, then taxi to G and hold short of Runway 30. You now know you

A—exited onto Runway 25R and transited HS 2.
B—exited onto Taxiway G.
C—exited at Taxiway J and transited HS 4.

The very wide pavement and taxiway D signs on both sides of the pavement indicate you are now on runway 25R in the HS1 and HS2 region. (PLT149, AA.II.C.K3) — AIM ¶4-3-18

ATM, ATS, RTC

9790-1. (Refer to Figures 241 and 242.) You land on Runway 12 at LGB and plan to exit the runway to the right on Taxiway J. What potential risk should you be aware of on the airport diagram?

A—Convergence of Taxiways D and J.
B—Convergence of Taxiways C and J.
C—Convergence of Runways 16R-34L and 07R-25L

LGB has a hot spot when departing Runway 12 at Taxiway J with the convergence of Taxiway D. This is noted as HS 4 on the airport diagram. Refer to Figure 241 to note the description of hot spot 4. (PLT149, AA.II.C.K6) — AIM ¶4-3-18

ALL

9818. When should an aircraft depart if issued an EDCT?

A—No earlier than 5 minutes before and no later than 5 minutes after the EDCT.
B—No later than 5 minutes before and no earlier than 5 minutes after the EDCT.
C—No earlier than 15 minutes before and no later than 15 minutes after the EDCT.

The EDCT is the runway release time assigned to an aircraft included in traffic management programs. Aircraft are expected to depart no earlier than 5 minutes before, and no later than 5 minutes after the EDCT. (PLT080, AA.II.C.S3) — AIM ¶5-2-6

Answers

9788 [B]	9789 [A]	9790 [A]	9790-1 [B]	9818 [A]

Takeoff Procedures

Unless otherwise authorized by the FAA, an air carrier flight may not takeoff unless the weather meets the prescribed takeoff minimums for that airport. If takeoff minimums are not published for the airport, the following visibility is required for takeoff:

- For aircraft having two engines or less: 1 statute mile visibility.
- For aircraft having three or more engines: 1/2 statute mile visibility.

If an air carrier flight is going to takeoff from an airport that is not listed in its operations specifications, the pilot must observe the takeoff weather minimums published for that airport. If no takeoff weather minimums are published for that airport, then the pilot must be sure that the ceiling and visibility meet a sliding scale requirement of 800-2 or 900-1-1/2 or 1,000-1.

V_1 is the critical engine failure speed or decision speed. Engine failure below this speed shall result in an aborted takeoff; above this speed the takeoff run should be continued.

V_R is defined as the speed at which the rotation of the aircraft should be initiated to takeoff attitude. Rotation speed (V_R) cannot be less than V_1. If it is greater than V_1 and it is found that, at V_R, rotation cannot be achieved, a subsequent rejected take off may not be possible within the remaining runway length and is likely to result in a Runway Excursion.

ATM, ATS, ADX

9370. When takeoff minimums are not prescribed for a civil airport, what are the takeoff minimums under IFR for a three-engine airplane?

A—1 SM.
B—1/2 SM.
C—300 feet and 1/2 SM.

If takeoff minimums are not prescribed under 14 CFR Part 97, the takeoff minimums under IFR for aircraft having more than two engines are 1/2 statute mile visibility. (PLT421, AA.VI.B.K1) — 14 CFR §91.175

Answer (A) is incorrect because 1 SM visibility is for aircraft, other than helicopters, having two engines or less. Answer (C) is incorrect because minimum ceilings are not specified for takeoff minimums.

ATM, ADX

8257. An airport is not listed in a domestic Air Carrier's Operations Specifications and does not have the prescribed takeoff weather minimums. What are the minimum weather conditions required for takeoff?

A—800-2.
B—900-1.
C—1000-1/2.

When departing from an alternate airport within the United States which is not listed in the operations specifications, an air carrier must use the 14 CFR Part 97 takeoff minimums. When no takeoff minimums are specified, the air carrier must use a ceiling and visibility of 800-2, 900-1-1/2, or 1,000-1. (PLT398, AA.VI.B.K1) — 14 CFR §121.637

Answer (B) is incorrect because a 900-foot ceiling requires 1.5 miles visibility. Answer (C) is incorrect because a 1,000-foot ceiling requires 1 mile visibility.

ATM, ADX

8261. The weather conditions that meet the minimum requirements for a flag air carrier to take off from an alternate airport that is not listed in the Operations Specifications are

A—800-2, 900-1-1/2, or 1000-1.
B—800-1/2, 900-1, or 1000-2.
C—800-1, 900-2, or 1000-3.

When departing from an alternate airport within the United States which is not listed in the operations specifications, an air carrier must use the 14 CFR Part 97 takeoff minimums. When no takeoff minimums are specified, the air carrier must use a ceiling and visibility of 800-2, 900-1-1/2, or 1,000-1. (PLT380, AA.VI.B.K1) — 14 CFR §121.637

Answers

9370 [B]   8257 [A]   8261 [A]

ATM, ADX

8263. The minimum weather conditions that must exist for a domestic air carrier flight to take off from an airport that is not listed in the Air Carrier's Operations Specifications (takeoff minimums are not prescribed for that airport) is

A—800-2, 1,100-1, or 900-1-1/2.
B—1,000-1, 900-1-1/4, or 800-2.
C—1,000-1, 900-1-1/2, or 800-2.

When departing from an alternate airport within the United States which is not listed in the operations specifications, an air carrier must use the 14 CFR Part 97 takeoff minimums. When no takeoff minimums are specified, the air carrier must use a ceiling and visibility of 800-2, 900-1-1/2, or 1,000-1. (PLT459, AA.VI.B.K1) — 14 CFR §121.637

ATM, ADX

8264. When an alternate airport outside the United States has no prescribed takeoff minimums and is not listed in a Flag Air Carrier's Operations Specifications, the minimum weather conditions that will meet the requirements for takeoff is

A—800-1-1/2.
B—600-2.
C—900-1-1/2.

When departing from an alternate airport outside the United States which is not listed in the operations specifications, an air carrier must use the takeoff minimums approved by the government of the country in which the airport is located. When no takeoff minimums are specified, the air carrier must use a ceiling and visibility of 800-2, 900-1-1/2, or 1,000-1. (PLT380, AA.VI.B.K1) — 14 CFR §121.637

ATM, ADX

9826. An air carrier flight is preparing to depart from a domestic airport which is not listed in the carrier's operation specifications. There are no takeoff minimums prescribed for the airport, and the weather is currently reporting a 900-foot overcast ceiling and 1-mile visibility in mist. The flight may

A—not depart until the weather improves.
B—depart if an alternate departure airport is filed.
C—depart without an alternate departure airport.

When departing from an alternate airport within the United States which is not listed in the operations specifications, an air carrier must use the 14 CFR Part 97 takeoff minimums. When no takeoff minimums are specified, the air carrier must use a ceiling and visibility of 800-2, 900-1½, or 1,000-1. (PLT459, AA.VI.B.K1) — 14 CFR §121.637

ATM, ADX

9827-1. You are rolling on takeoff in a 14 CFR Part 25 certified jet and you see an engine oil pressure caution light as you approach V_1. You should

A—continue the takeoff as briefed and handle the illumination as an inflight emergency.
B—promptly abort the takeoff and plan on only having asymmetrical reverse thrust.
C—abort the takeoff and plan for a maximum reverse thrust for deceleration.

V_1 is the critical engine failure speed or decision speed. Engine failure below this speed shall result in an aborted takeoff; above this speed the takeoff run should be continued. (PLT208, AA.VII.B.K1) — FAA-H-8083-25

ATM, ADX

9827-2. You are rolling on takeoff in a 14 CFR Part 25 certified jet and you see an engine oil pressure caution light as you pass V_1. You should

A—continue the takeoff as briefed and handle the illumination as an inflight emergency.
B—promptly abort the takeoff and plan on only having asymmetrical reverse thrust.
C—abort the takeoff and plan for a maximum reverse thrust for deceleration.

V_1 is the critical engine failure speed or decision speed. Engine failure below this speed shall result in an aborted takeoff; above this speed the takeoff run should be continued. (PLT208, AA.VII.B.K1) — FAA-H-8083-25

Answers

8263 [C] 8264 [C] 9826 [A] 9827-1 [B] 9827-2 [A]

ATM, ADX

9827-3. During takeoff roll with runway remaining, you receive a master caution light after V_R. What action should you take?

A—Reject the takeoff.
B—Hold the nose down to takeoff speed.
C—Continue the takeoff.

V_R is defined as the speed at which the rotation of the aircraft should be initiated to takeoff attitude. V_R or rotation speed cannot be less than V_1. If it is greater than V_1 and it is found that, at V_R, rotation cannot be achieved, a subsequent rejected takeoff may not be possible within the remaining runway length and is likely to result in a runway excursion. In these circumstances (after V_R, runway remaining), you should continue the takeoff. (PLT208, AA.VII.B.K1) — FAA-H-8083-3

Instrument Approaches

This section is limited to rules and procedures common to most, or all approaches, or procedures that may be used in connection with published instrument approaches.

Contact and visual approaches are both IFR authorizations to proceed to an airport visually. A **visual approach** may be authorized by ATC to reduce pilot or controller workload and to expedite traffic by shortening flight paths to the airport. The weather must be VFR and the pilot must report either the airport or the preceding aircraft in sight. Either the pilot or ATC may initiate a visual approach. A **contact approach** may be initiated only by the pilot. The weather need not be VFR but the aircraft must be clear of the clouds, have at least 1 mile visibility and be able to proceed to the landing airport visually.

When an airport has ILS or MLS approaches to parallel runways at least 4,300 feet apart, ATC may conduct approaches to both runways simultaneously. The pilots will be informed if simultaneous approaches are in progress. To ensure safe separation between aircraft, radar monitoring is provided on the tower frequency. A pilot must report any malfunctioning aircraft receivers if he/she has been informed that simultaneous approaches are in progress.

Occasionally, a pilot will be asked to fly an instrument approach to a runway and then fly a visual "sidestep" maneuver to land on a parallel runway. This sidestep maneuver should be executed as soon as possible after the runway environment is in sight.

If a pilot is being radar vectored when an approach clearance is received, he/she must maintain the last assigned altitude until the aircraft is established on a segment of a published route or approach procedure unless a different altitude is assigned by ATC. If a flight is being radar vectored to the final approach course and intercepts a published portion of the course, the pilot may not descend to the published altitudes until cleared for the approach. If a flight has not been cleared for approach while on a radar vector and it becomes apparent that the current vector will take it across the final approach course, the pilot should advise ATC of the situation. Do not turn to intercept the approach course unless cleared to do so.

Unless ATC issues a clearance otherwise, no pilot may make a procedure turn on an instrument approach if any of the following apply:

- The flight is radar vectored to the final approach course or fix.
- The flight makes a timed approach from a holding fix.
- The approach procedure specifies "No PT."

Answers

9827-3 [C]

When the approach procedure involves a procedure turn, a maximum speed of not greater than 200 KIAS should be observed from first overheading the course reversal IAF through the procedure turn maneuver, to ensure containment with the obstruction clearance area.

Except for Category II and III approaches, if RVR minimums for takeoff or landing are prescribed in an instrument approach procedure, but the RVR is not reported for the runway intended, the ground visibilities may be substituted. These may be found in FAA Legend 7.

A pilot may not continue an approach past the final approach fix or on to the final approach segment unless the latest weather report for the airport indicates that the visibility is equal to, or greater than, the visibility required for the approach procedure. If a pilot has begun the final approach segment and then receives a report of below minimum conditions, he/she may continue the approach to the DH or MDA.

To descend below the published DH or MDA on an instrument approach, one of the following must be distinctly visible and identifiable to the pilot:

- Approach light system, except that the pilot may not descend below 100 feet above the touchdown zone elevation using the approach lights as a reference unless the red terminating bars or red side row bars are also distinctly visible and identifiable.
- Threshold.
- Threshold markings.
- Threshold lights.
- Runway end identifier lights.
- Visual approach slope indicator.
- Touchdown zone or touchdown zone markings.
- Touchdown zone lights.
- Runway or runway markings.
- Runway lights.

A pilot must initiate a missed approach from an ILS upon arrival at the DH on the glide slope if none of the required visual references is distinctly visible. If visual contact is lost anytime after descending below the DH but before touchdown, the pilot must start a missed approach.

If a pilot loses visual reference while circling to land from an instrument approach, he/she should follow the missed approach procedure published for the approach used. The pilot should make an initial climbing turn toward the landing runway to establish the aircraft on the missed approach course.

An **Airport Surveillance Radar (ASR)** approach is one in which an ATC radar controller provides directional guidance and distance to the runway information to the pilot. The only airborne equipment required is an operating radio receiver. The controller will tell the pilot when the aircraft is at the missed approach point and give missed approach instructions as required. If the pilot desires to execute a missed approach prior to the missed approach point, he/she should inform the controller, who will then issue missed approach instructions.

Precision Runway Monitor (PRM) is a high update-rate radar surveillance system, certified to provide simultaneous independent approaches to closely-spaced parallel runways.

If there is penetration of the obstacle identification surfaces (OIS), the published approach visibility can be no lower than 3/4 SM.

ALL

9091. What is the difference between a visual and a contact approach?

A—A visual approach is an IFR authorization while a contact approach is a VFR authorization.
B—A visual approach is initiated by ATC while a contact approach is initiated by the pilot.
C—Both are the same but classified according to the party initiating the approach.

Visual approaches are initiated by ATC to reduce pilot/controller workload and expedite traffic. Pilots operating on IFR flight plans may request a contact approach if the appropriate weather conditions exist. (PLT170, AA.VI.E.K4) — AIM ¶5-4-22, 5-4-24

Answer (A) is incorrect because both a visual and contact approach are initiated from an IFR flight plan. Answer (C) is incorrect because a visual approach is one in which the pilot has a preceding aircraft or the airport in sight and can maintain basic VFR weather minimums. A contact approach is used by a pilot in lieu of conducting a standard or special instrument approach to an airport.

ALL

8953. When simultaneous approaches are in progress, how does each pilot receive radar advisories?

A—On tower frequency.
B—On approach control frequency.
C—One pilot on tower frequency and the other on approach control frequency.

Whenever simultaneous approaches are in progress, radar advisories will be provided on the tower frequency. (PLT420, AA.VI.C.K3) — AIM ¶5-4-15

Answer (B) is incorrect because pilots will be advised to monitor the tower (not approach control) frequency to receive radar advisories and instructions. Answer (C) is incorrect because both pilots would receive radar advisories on the tower frequency.

ALL

8955. When simultaneous ILS approaches are in progress, which of the following should approach control be advised of immediately?

A—Any inoperative or malfunctioning aircraft receivers.
B—If a simultaneous ILS approach is desired.
C—If radar monitoring is desired to confirm lateral separation.

When advised that simultaneous ILS approaches are in progress, pilots shall advise approach control immediately of malfunctioning or inoperative receivers or if simultaneous approach is not desired. (PLT170, AA.VI.E.K1) — AIM ¶5-4-15

Answer (B) is incorrect because simultaneous approaches are issued at any time according to ATC needs, and it is not the responsibility of the pilot to request such an approach. Answer (C) is incorrect because radar monitoring is always provided during simultaneous approaches.

ALL

8954. When cleared to execute a published side-step maneuver, at what point is the pilot expected to commence this maneuver?

A—At the published DH.
B—At the MDA published or a circling approach.
C—As soon as possible after the runway environment is in sight.

Pilots are expected to execute the side-step maneuver as soon as possible after the runway or runway environment is in sight. (PLT083, AA.VI.D.K1) — AIM ¶5-4-19

Answers (A) and (B) are incorrect because the side-step maneuver can only be performed and should be performed as soon as possible after the runway or runway environment is in sight.

ATM, ATS, RTC

9438. When cleared to execute a published side-step maneuver for a specific approach and landing on the parallel runway, at what point is the pilot expected to commence this maneuver?

A—At the published minimum altitude for a circling approach.
B—As soon as possible after the runway or runway environment is in sight.
C—At the localizer MDA minimums and when the runway is in sight.

Pilots are expected to execute the side-step maneuver as soon as possible after the runway or runway environment is in sight. (PLT170, AA.VI.E.K4) — AIM ¶5-4-19

Answers (A) and (C) are incorrect because the maneuver should be started as soon as the runway environment is in sight not at a DH or MDA of an approach.

ALL

9037. While being vectored to the final approach course of an IFR approach, when may the pilot descend to published altitudes?

A—Anytime the flight is on a published leg of an approach chart.
B—When the flight is within the 10-mile ring of a published approach.
C—Only when approach control clears the flight for the approach.

Answers

9091 [B]	8953 [A]	8955 [A]	8954 [C]	9438 [B]	9037 [C]

When operating on an unpublished route or while being radar vectored, the pilot, when approach clearance is received, in addition to complying with the minimum altitudes for IFR operations, shall maintain the last assigned altitude unless a different altitude is assigned by ATC, or until the aircraft is established on a segment of published route or IAP. This implies that even if a radar vector should happen to put a flight on a published route, the pilot may not descend until cleared for the approach. (PLT420, AA.VI.D.K1) — AIM ¶5-4-7

Answer (A) is incorrect because you may only descend if cleared. Answer (B) is incorrect because the 10-mile ring has nothing to do with descent clearance.

ALL

9383. What action should be taken when a pilot is "cleared for approach" while being radar vectored on an unpublished route?

A—Descend to minimum vector altitude.
B—Remain at last assigned altitude until established on a published route segment.
C—Descend to initial approach fix altitude.

When operating on an unpublished route or while being radar vectored, the pilot, when an approach clearance is received, shall maintain the last altitude assigned until the aircraft is established on a segment of a published route or instrument approach procedure, unless a different altitude is assigned by ATC. (PLT421, AA.VI.D.K1) — 14 CFR §91.175

Answer (A) is incorrect because a pilot should maintain the last altitude assigned by ATC and should use the minimum vector altitude only during lost communication procedures. Answer (C) is incorrect because a pilot should maintain the last altitude assigned by ATC.

ALL

9385. What altitude is a pilot authorized to fly when cleared for an ILS approach? The pilot

A—may begin a descent to the procedure turn altitude.
B—must maintain the last assigned altitude until established on a published route or segment of the approach with published altitudes.
C—may descend from the assigned altitude only when established on the final approach course.

When operating on an unpublished route or while being radar vectored, the pilot, when an approach clearance is received, shall maintain the last altitude assigned until the aircraft is established on a segment of a published route or instrument approach procedure, unless a different altitude is assigned by ATC. (PLT421, AA.VI.E.K1) — 14 CFR §91.175

Answer (A) is incorrect because descent to the procedure turn altitude can be commenced only when you are established on that route segment or instrument approach. Answer (C) is incorrect because the pilot does not have to be established on the final approach course to descend from the last assigned altitude, if established on a published route segment with a specified lower minimum altitude than the last assigned altitude.

ALL

9036. What action(s) should a pilot take if vectored across the final approach course during an IFR approach?

A—Continue on the last heading issued until otherwise instructed.
B—Contact approach control, and advise that the flight is crossing the final approach course.
C—Turn onto final, and broadcast in the blind that the flight has proceeded on final.

Aircraft will normally be informed when it is necessary to vector across the final approach course for spacing or other reasons. If approach course crossing is imminent and the pilot has not been informed that he will be vectored across the final approach course, he should query the controller. (PLT420, AA.VI.D.K1) — AIM ¶5-4-3

Answer (A) is incorrect because the pilot should maintain last heading issued, but should also advise approach control that the flight is crossing the final approach course. Answer (C) is incorrect because a pilot should broadcast in the blind that the flight has turned onto final when operating VFR at an uncontrolled airport.

ALL

9369. If being radar vectored to the final approach course of a published instrument approach that specifies "NO PT," the pilot should

A—advise ATC that a procedure turn will not be executed.
B—not execute the procedure turn unless specifically cleared to do so by ATC.
C—execute a holding-pattern type procedure turn.

In the case of a radar vector to a final approach course or fix, a timed approach from a holding fix, or an approach for which the approach procedure specifies "NoPT," no pilot may make a procedure turn unless cleared to do so by ATC. (PLT420, AA.VI.D.K2) — 14 CFR §91.175

Answer (A) is incorrect because a procedure turn is not authorized or expected to be executed for this instrument approach; therefore, advising ATC of your intention to omit a procedure turn is not necessary. Answer (C) is incorrect because if the published instrument approach specifies "NoPT," you should follow the published procedure rather than automatically reverting to a holding-pattern-type procedure turn.

Answers

9383 [B]	9385 [B]	9036 [B]	9369 [B]

ALL

9021. When the approach procedure involves a procedure turn the maximum speed that should be observed from first overheading the course reversal IAF through the procedure turn is

A—180 knots IAS.
B—200 knots TAS.
C—200 knots IAS.

When the approach procedure involves a procedure turn, a maximum speed of not greater than 200 knots (IAS) should be observed from first overheading the course reversal IAF through the procedure turn maneuver, to ensure containment within the obstruction clearance area. (PLT420, AA.VI.D.K1) — AIM ¶5-4-9

ALL

9391. What minimum ground visibility may be used instead of a prescribed visibility criteria of RVR 16 when that RVR value is not reported?

A—1/4 SM.
B—3/4 SM.
C—1/2 SM.

RVR minimum may be converted to ground visibility using FAA Legend 27. (PLT420, AA.VI.D.K1) — 14 CFR §91.175

ALL

9392. The prescribed visibility criteria of RVR 32 for the runway of intended operation is not reported. What minimum ground visibility may be used instead of the RVR value?

A—3/8 SM.
B—5/8 SM.
C—3/4 SM.

RVR minimum may be converted to ground visibility using FAA Legend 27. (PLT420, AA.VI.D.K1) — 14 CFR §91.175

ALL

9393. The visibility criteria for a particular instrument approach procedure is RVR 40. What minimum ground visibility may be substituted for the RVR value?

A—5/8 SM.
B—3/4 SM.
C—7/8 SM.

RVR minimum may be converted to ground visibility using FAA Legend 27. (PLT420, AA.VI.D.K1) — 14 CFR §91.175

ALL

9384. Under which condition, if any, may a pilot descend below DH or MDA when using the ALSF-1 approach light system as the primary visual reference for the intended runway?

A—Under no condition can the approach light system serve as a necessary visual reference for descent below DH or MDA.
B—Descent to the intended runway is authorized as long as any portion of the approach light system can be seen.
C—The approach light system can be used as a visual reference, except that descent below 100 feet above TDZE requires that the red light bars be visible and identifiable.

A pilot may descend below the MDA or DH using the approach light system as the sole visual reference. However, the pilot may not descend below 100 feet above touchdown zone elevation (TDZE) using the approach lights as a reference unless the red terminating bars or the red side row bars are also distinctly visible and identifiable. (PLT420, AA.VI.D.K1) — 14 CFR §91.175

Answer (A) is incorrect because approach lighting systems can be used as a reference below the DH or MDA up to 100 feet above the TDZE, at which point the red terminating bars must be in sight. Answer (B) is incorrect because the approach lighting system can only be used to within 100 feet of the TDZE, at which point the red side row bars must be in sight.

ALL

8726. (Refer to Figure 310.) What is the required minimum reported weather to initiate the ILS Rwy 9L approach at PHL in your CAT C turbine-powered airplane with no MEL items?

A—Ceiling at least 200 feet and RVR 2400.
B—Ceiling 300 feet minimum.
C—Visibility 1800 RVR.

The approach plates notes a minimum RVR of 1800 in the top left portion of the approach plate. (PLT420, AA.VI.E.K1) — Instrument Approach Procedures

Answers

9021 [C] 9391 [A] 9392 [B] 9393 [B] 9384 [C] 8726 [C]

ALL

9368. When must the pilot initiate a missed approach procedure from an ILS approach?

A—At the DA/DH when the runway is not clearly visible.
B—When the time has expired after reaching the DA/DH and the runway environment is not clearly visible.
C—At the DA/DH, if the visual references for the intended runway are not distinctly visible or anytime thereafter that visual reference is lost.

A pilot must initiate a missed approach procedure from an ILS approach at the DA/DH, if the required visual references for intended runway are not distinctly visible or anytime thereafter if visual reference is lost. (PLT420, AA.VI.I.K1) — 14 CFR §91.175

Answer (A) is incorrect because the runway itself does not have to be visible at the DA/DH to continue with the approach; a pilot may use the required visual references. Answer (B) is incorrect because as soon as the DA/DH is reached on an ILS approach, regardless of the elapsed time, a missed approach procedure should be executed if visual references are not obtained, or any time thereafter that visual reference is lost.

ALL

9382. Assuming that all ILS components are operating and the required visual references are not acquired, the missed approach should be initiated upon

A—arrival at the DH on the glide slope.
B—arrival at the visual descent point.
C—expiration of the time listed on the approach chart for missed approach.

A pilot must initiate a missed approach procedure from an ILS approach at the DH, if the required visual references for intended runway are not distinctly visible or any time thereafter if visual reference is lost. (PLT356, AA.VI.I.K1) — 14 CFR §91.175

Answer (B) is incorrect because a visual descent point is a point in which an aircraft operating visually can descend from a specified altitude to the runway and land. If on an ILS approach and no visual flight is encountered, a missed approach should be executed at the DH. Answer (C) is incorrect because time listed on the approach chart is used only if the glide slope were to fail. If the aircraft reaches the DH prior to the time listed on the chart, the pilot should execute a missed approach.

ALL

9041. When may a pilot execute a missed approach during an ASR approach?

A—Anytime at the pilot's discretion.
B—Only at the MAP.
C—Only when advised by the controller.

Controllers will terminate guidance on an ASR approach and instruct the pilot to execute a missed approach unless at the MAP, the pilot has the runway or airport in sight. Also, if at any time during an ASR approach the controller considers that safe guidance for the remainder of the approach cannot be provided, he will terminate the approach and instruct the pilot to execute a missed approach. A missed approach will also be effected upon pilot request. (PLT420, AA.VI.I.K1) — AIM ¶5-4-10

Answer (B) is incorrect because the controller will instruct the pilot to execute a missed approach at the MAP or anytime during the approach that the controller considers that safe guidance cannot be provided. Answer (C) is incorrect because a missed approach will be effected upon pilot request.

ALL

9090-1. If visual reference is lost while circling to land from an instrument approach, what action(s) should the pilot take?

A—Make a climbing turn toward the landing runway until established on the missed approach course.
B—Turn toward the landing runway maintaining MDA, and if visual reference is not regained, perform missed approach.
C—Make a climbing turn toward the VOR/NDB, and request further instructions.

If visual reference is lost while circling to land from an instrument approach, the missed approach specified for that particular procedure must be followed. To become established on the prescribed missed approach course, the pilot should make an initial climbing turn toward the landing runway and continue the turn until he is established on the missed approach course. (PLT170, AA.VI.D.R6) — AIM ¶5-4-21

Answer (B) is incorrect because while turning toward the runway, a climbing turn should be established. Answer (C) is incorrect because a pilot should make a climbing turn toward the runway to ensure obstacle clearance while becoming established on the missed approach course.

Answers

9368 [C]	9382 [A]	9041 [A]	9090-1 [A]

ALL

9090-2. Precision Runway Monitoring (PRM) is

A—an airborne RADAR system for monitoring approaches to two runways.
B—a RADAR system for monitoring approaches to closely spaced parallel runways.
C—a high update rate RADAR system for monitoring multiple aircraft ILS approaches to a single runway.

Precision Runway Monitoring (PRM) is a high update-rate radar surveillance system, certified to provide simultaneous independent approaches to closely spaced parallel runways. (PLT172, AA.VI.E.K2) — FAA-H-8083-16

Answer (A) is incorrect because PRM is not an airborne radar system; it is ground based. Answer (C) is incorrect because PRM monitors simultaneous approaches to two closely spaced parallel runways.

ALL

9760. Precision runway monitoring requires

A—pilot responsibility to monitor 2 simultaneous radios.
B—pilot responsibility to monitor 2 ILS receivers.
C—detailed performance during the "decision region": 1/3 dot localizer and 1/2 dot glideslope.

The aircraft flying the ILS/PRM or LDA/PRM approach must have the capability of enabling the pilots to listen to two communications frequencies simultaneously. (PLT172, AA.VI.E.K2) — AIM ¶5-4-16

ALL

9090-3. How can the pilot determine, for an ILS runway equipped with MALSR, that there may be penetration of the obstacle identification surfaces (OIS), and care should be taken in the visual segment to avoid any obstacles?

A—The runway has a visual approach slope indicator (VASI).
B—The published visibility for the ILS is no lower than 3/4 SM.
C—The approach chart has a visual descent point (VDP) published.

The visibility published on an approach chart is dependent on many variables, including the height above touchdown for straight-in approaches, or height above airport elevation for circling approaches. Other factors include the approach light system coverage, and type of approach procedure, such as precision, nonprecision, circling or straight-in. Another factor determining the minimum visibility is the penetration of the 34:1 and 20:1 surfaces. These surfaces are inclined planes that begin 200 feet out from the runway and extend outward to 10,000 feet. If there is a penetration of the 34:1 surface, the published visibility can be no lower than 3/4 SM. If there is penetration of the 20:1 surface, the published visibility can be no lower than 1 SM with a note prohibiting approaches to the affected runway at night (both straight-in and circling). Pilots should be aware of these penetrating obstacles when entering the visual and/or circling segments of an approach and take adequate precautions to avoid them. (PLT170, AA.VI.E.K3) — FAA-H-8083-16

Answers (A) and (C) are incorrect because a VASI or VDP are not indicators to a possible penetration of the OIS.

ALL

9738. To conduct an RNAV (GPS) approach to LPV minimums, the aircraft must be furnished with

A—a GPS/WAAS receiver approved for an LPV approach by the AFM supplement.
B—a GPS (TSO-129) receiver certified for IFR operations.
C—an IFR approach-certified system with required navigation performance (RNP) of 0.5.

"LPV" is the acronym for localizer performance with vertical guidance. LPV identifies the APV minimums with electronic lateral and vertical guidance. The lateral guidance is equivalent to localizer, and the protected area is considerably smaller than the protected area for the present LNAV and LNAV/VNAV lateral protection. Aircraft can fly this minima line with a statement in the Aircraft Flight Manual that the installed equipment supports LPV approaches. This includes Class 3 and 4 TSO-C146 WAAS equipment, and future LAAS equipment. (PLT354, AA.VI.D.K2) — AIM ¶5-4-5

Answers

9090-2 [B]	9760 [A]	9090-3 [B]	9738 [A]

ALL

9744. Pilots are not authorized to fly a published RNAV or RNP procedure unless it is retrievable by the procedure name from

A—the aircraft navigation database, or manually loaded with each individual waypoint in the correct sequence.
B—the aircraft navigation database, or manually loaded with each individual waypoint and verified by the pilot(s).
C—the aircraft navigation database.

Pilots are not authorized to fly a published RNAV or RNP procedure (instrument approach, departure, or arrival procedure) unless it is retrievable by the procedure name from the aircraft navigation database and conforms to the charted procedure. (PLT354, AA.VI.D.K2) — AIM ¶5-5-16

ALL

9744-1. GBAS approaches are

A—flown using the same techniques as an ILS once selected and identified.
B—flown the same as an LDA with glide slope tuning and identification.
C—automatically tuned and displayed after selection of the three character procedure identifier.

GBAS is a ground-based augmentation to GPS that focuses its service on the airport area (approximately a 20-30 mile radius) for precision approach, departure procedures, and terminal area operations. GBAS is the ICAO term for Local Area Augmentation System (LAAS). LAAS was developed as an "ILS look-alike" system from the pilot perspective. (PLT354, AA.VI.E.K2) — AIM ¶1-1-19

ALL

9773. Pilots are responsible for knowing

A—if they can conduct an RNP approach with an arc at a designated airspeed.
B—if the RNP missed approach is normal or reduced.
C—if the RNP registration is complete.

Some RNP approaches have a curved path, also called a radius-to-a-fix (RF) leg. Since not all aircraft have the capability to fly these arcs, pilots are responsible for knowing whether or not they can conduct an RNP approach with an arc. (PLT300, AA.VI.D.K2) — AIM ¶5-4-18

ATM, ADX

8279. Under what conditions may an air carrier pilot continue an instrument approach to the DH, after receiving a weather report indicating that less than minimum published landing conditions exist at the airport?

A—If the instrument approach is conducted in a radar environment.
B—When the weather report is received as the pilot passes the FAF.
C—When the weather report is received after the pilot has begun the final approach segment of the instrument approach.

If a pilot has begun the final approach segment of an instrument approach procedure with the reported weather at or above landing minimums and later receives a report indicating below minimum conditions, he may continue the approach to DH or MDA. The pilot may land from that approach if he discovers that the visibility is at least that required by the approach, he/she has the required visual references in sight and a normal descent and landing can be made. (PLT420, AA.VI.E.R7) — 14 CFR §121.651

ALL

9817. When executing a stabilized approach, you should use

A—no more than 1000 FPM rate of descent for a non-precision or precision approach from 1,000 feet above the airport or TDZE.
B—no more than 1000 FPM for a precision approach or 1200 FPM for a non-precision approach.
C—no more than 800 FPM for a non-precision approach or 1000 FPM for a precision approach.

For all straight-in-instrument approaches in IFR weather conditions, the approach must be stabilized (descent rate of less than 1,000 fpm) before descending below 1,000 feet above the airport or TDZE. (PLT420, AA.VI.E.S12) — FAA-H-8083-16

Answers

9744 [C] 9744-1 [A] 9773 [A] 8279 [C] 9817 [A]

ATM, ATS

9817-1. You are in IMC and descending below 1,000 feet above the TDZE on a straight-in instrument approach in a turbojet. The approach is considered stabilized when the airplane is

A—fully configured and on the correct speed with a descent rate of less than 1,000 FPM.
B—fully configured with the engines spooled up and a descent rate of no more than 500 FPM.
C—at least partially configured and on the correct speed with a descent rate of no more than 1,200 FPM.

For all straight-in-instrument approaches in IFR weather conditions, the approach must be stabilized (descent rate of less than 1,000 FPM) before descending below 1,000 feet above the airport or TDZE (PLT170, AA.VI.E.K4) — FAA-H-8083-16

ALL

8736. (Refer to Figure 1.) What does the 20:1 ratio represent?

A—Displaced threshold.
B—Final approach fix.
C—Obstacle clearance surface (OCS).

The obstacle clearance surface (OCS). The OCS used to evaluate the missed approach is a 20:1 inclined plane. This surface is twice as steep for the helicopter as the OCS used to evaluate the airplane missed approach segment. (PLT170, AA.VI.E.K1) — FAA-H-8083-16

Landing

Except for emergencies, the landing priority of aircraft arriving at a tower controlled airport is on "first-come, first-served" basis. When landing at a tower controlled airport, an aircraft should exit the runway at the first suitable taxiway and remain on the tower frequency until instructed to do otherwise. The aircraft should not turn onto any other taxiway unless a clearance to do so has been received.

If a flight is making an IFR approach at an uncontrolled airport, radar service will be terminated when the aircraft lands or when the controller tells the pilot to change to advisory frequency. After changing to the advisory frequency, the pilot should broadcast his/her intentions and continually update position reports. The advisory frequency will be an FSS frequency, or if there is no FSS on the field, a UNICOM frequency.

ATC furnishes pilot braking action reports using the terms good, good to medium, medium, medium to poor, poor, or nil. If you give a braking action report to ATC, you should use the same terminology. See Figure 6-4.

ALL

9092. Except during an emergency, when can a pilot expect landing priority?

A—When cleared for an IFR approach.
B—When piloting a large, heavy aircraft.
C—In turn, on a first-come, first-serve basis.

Air Traffic Control towers handle all aircraft, regardless of the type of flight plan, on a "first-come, first-served" basis. (PLT170, AA.VI.E.K1) — AIM ¶5-4-25

Answer (A) is incorrect because a clearance for an IFR approach does not mean landing priority will be given over other traffic. Answer (B) is incorrect because a large, heavy aircraft will be sequenced for landing on a first-come, first-served basis, with no special priority over other traffic.

ALL

9044. What action is expected of an aircraft upon landing at a controlled airport?

A—Continue taxiing in the landing direction until advised by the tower to switch to ground control frequency.
B—Exit the runway at the nearest suitable taxiway and remain on tower frequency until instructed otherwise.
C—Exit the runway at the nearest suitable taxiway and switch to ground control upon crossing the taxiway holding lines.

Answers

9817-1 [A]	8736 [C]	9092 [C]	9044 [B]

Assessment Criteria		Control/Braking Assessment Criteria	
Runway Condition Description	**RwyCC**	**Deceleration or Directional Control Observation**	**Pilot Reported Braking Action**
• Dry	6	—	—
• Frost • Wet (Includes damp and 1/8 inch depth or less of water) ***1/8 inch (3 mm) depth or less of:*** • Slush • Dry Snow • Wet Snow	5	Braking deceleration is normal for the wheel braking effort applied AND directional control is normal.	Good
-15°C and Colder outside air temperature: • Compacted Snow	4	Braking deceleration OR directional control is between Good and Medium.	Good to Medium
• Slippery When Wet (wet runway) • Dry Snow or Wet Snow (any depth) over Compacted Snow ***Greater than 1/8 inch (3 mm) depth of:*** • Dry Snow • Wet Snow ***Warmer than -15°C outside air temperature:*** • Compacted Snow	3	Braking deceleration is noticeably reduced for the wheel braking effort applied OR directional control is noticeably reduced.	Medium
Greater than 1/8 inch (3 mm) depth of: • Water • Slush	2	Braking deceleration OR directional control is between Medium and Poor.	Medium to Poor
• Ice	1	Braking deceleration is significantly reduced for the wheel braking effort applied OR directional control is significantly reduced.	Poor
• Wet Ice • Slush over Ice • Water over Compacted Snow • Dry Snow or Wet Snow over Ice	0	Braking deceleration is minimal to non-existent for the wheel braking effort applied OR directional control is uncertain.	Nil

Figure 6-4. Runway Condition Assessment Matrix (RCAM)

After landing, unless otherwise instructed by the control tower, continue to taxi in the landing direction, proceed to the nearest suitable taxiway and exit the runway without delay. Do not turn on another runway or make a 180° turn to taxi back on an active runway or change to ground control frequency while on the active runway without authorization from the tower. A pilot who has just landed should not change from the tower frequency to the ground control frequency until he is directed to do so by the controller. (PLT434, AA.VI.C.K3) — AIM ¶4-3-20

Answer (A) is incorrect because upon landing, the pilot should exit the runway at the nearest suitable taxiway to clear the runway for other traffic. Answer (C) is incorrect because while the crossing of the taxiway hold lines indicates clearing of the active runway, a pilot should not switch to ground control until directed to do so by the controller. Switching without permission may be confusing to ATC.

ALL

9038. When is radar service terminated while vectored for an IFR approach at an uncontrolled airport?

A—Only upon landing or advised to change to advisory frequency.
B—When aligned on the final approach course.
C—When cleared for the approach.

Whether aircraft are vectored to the appropriate final approach course or provide their own navigation on published routes to it, radar service is automatically terminated when the landing is completed or when instructed to change to advisory frequency at uncontrolled airports, whichever occurs first. (PLT420, AA.VI.E.K3) — AIM ¶5-4-3

Answer (B) is incorrect because when established on the final approach course, radar separation will be maintained and the pilot is expected to complete the approach utilizing the approach aid designated in the clearance (ILS, VOR, etc.). Answer (C) is incorrect because when cleared for the approach, approach control will continue to maintain radar separation and the pilot is expected to complete the approach utilizing the approach aid designated in the clearance (ILS, VOR, etc.).

Answers

9038 [A]

ALL

9039. When cleared for an IFR approach to an uncontrolled airport with no FSS, what precaution should the pilot take after being advised to change to advisory frequency?

A—Monitor ATC for traffic advisories as well as UNICOM.
B—Broadcast position and intentions on the Common Traffic Advisory Frequency and monitor the frequency.
C—Wait until visual contact is made with the airport and then broadcast position and intentions to land on UNICOM.

When making an IFR approach to an airport not served by a tower or FSS, after the ATC controller advises, "CHANGE TO ADVISORY FREQUENCY APPROVED" you should broadcast your intentions, including the type of approach being executed, your position, and when you are over the outer marker or final approach fix. Continue to monitor the appropriate frequency (UNICOM, etc.) for reports from other pilots. (PLT170, AA.VI.E.K3) — AIM ¶5-4-4

Answer (A) is incorrect because after ATC advises the pilot to change to advisory frequency, ATC will no longer be able to provide traffic advisories. Answer (C) is incorrect because a pilot should always broadcast intentions and continually update position reports on UNICOM, not wait until visual contact is made with airport.

ALL

9055. What terms or values should be used when providing a quality of braking action report to ATC?

A—Good, Medium, Poor, and Nil.
B—Good, Good to Medium, Medium, Medium to Poor, Poor, and Nil.
C—0, 1, 2, 3, 4, 5, 6.

Pilots should use these terms when providing a braking action report: good, good to medium, medium, medium to poor, poor, and nil. (PLT144, AA.I.B.K9) — AIM ¶4-3-9

Answer (A) is incorrect because it is missing some of the descriptive terms. Answer (C) is incorrect because numbers 0 through 6 are used in runway condition reports.

ALL

9055-1. A runway condition code (RwyCC) will not be issued by ATC if all three segments of a runway are reporting values of

A—0.
B—5.
C—6.

When a value of 6 is reported for all three segments of a runway, ATC will not issue a RwyCC and the pilot can expect the runway to be dry with no contaminants. (PLT144, AA.I.B.K9) — AIM ¶4-3-9

ALL

9055-2. What information does a FICON NOTAM provide for a paved runway?

A—Contaminant measurements.
B—Braking action.
C—Contaminant measurements and braking action.

FICON NOTAMs will provide contaminant measurements for paved runways, but a FICON NOTAM for braking action will only be used for non-paved runway surfaces, taxiways, and aprons. (PLT144, AA.I.B.K9) — AIM ¶4-3-8

ALL

9055-3. A Runway Condition Code (RwyCC) of 0 is used to delineate a braking action report of

A—Good.
B—Nil.
C—Poor.

Nil indicates a RwyCC of 0. (PLT144, AA.I.B.K9) — AIM ¶4-3-9

Answer (A) is incorrect because the RwyCC for Good is 5. Answer (C) is incorrect because the RwyCC for Poor is 1.

ATM, ATS, ADX

9005-1. A landing weight increase of 10% will result in a landing distance increase of approximately

A—7%.
B—10%.
C—15%.

The minimum landing distance will vary directly as the gross weight varies. For example, a 10% increase in gross weight at landing would cause a 5% increase in landing velocity and a 10% increase in landing distance. (PLT247, AA.I.B.K3f) — ANA

Answers

9039 [B] 9055 [B] 9055-1 [C] 9055-2 [A] 9055-3 [B] 9005-1 [B]

ATM, ATS, ADX
9005-2. A landing weight increase of 10% will result in

A—7% increase in kinetic energy.
B—21% increase in kinetic energy.
C—33% increase in kinetic energy.

As an example of measuring the effectiveness of aircraft brakes, a 30,000-pound aircraft landing at 175 knots has a kinetic energy of 41,000,000 ft-lbs at the instant of touchdown. While a 10% increase in landing weight causes a 5% higher landing speed and a 10% greater landing distance, it also produces a 21% increase in the kinetic energy of the airplane to be dissipated during the landing roll. (PLT247, AA.I.B.K3f) — ANA

Communications

The "Sterile Cockpit" Rule: Regulations say only those duties required for the safe operation of the aircraft are allowed during critical phases of flight. Critical phases of flight are defined as climb and descent when below 10,000 feet, taxi, takeoff, and landing. Excluded from the definition of critical phase of flight are any operations at or above 10,000 feet and cruise flight below 10,000 feet. Activities which are prohibited during critical phases of flight include filling out logs, ordering galley supplies, making passenger announcements or pointing out sights of interest. Activities such as eating meals or engaging in nonessential conversations are also prohibited.

The following should be reported without ATC request:

- Vacating a previously assigned altitude for a newly assigned one.
- An altitude change when operating under a VFR-On-Top clearance.
- When unable to climb or descend at a rate of at least 500 feet per minute.
- When an approach has been missed.
- A change in cruising true airspeed of 10 knots or 5%, whichever is greater.
- The time and altitude (or Flight Level) upon reaching a holding fix or clearance limit.
- When leaving an assigned holding fix or point.
- The malfunction of navigation, approach or communication equipment.
- Any information pertaining to the safety of flight.

In addition to the reports listed above, when not in radar contact a pilot must report:

- When over designated compulsory reporting points.
- When leaving the final approach fix inbound on an instrument approach.
- When it becomes apparent that an estimate of arrival time over a fix is in error by more than 3 minutes.

Occasionally an ATC controller will query a pilot about the aircraft's altitude or course. For example, a controller says "Verify 9000," meaning he/she wants confirmation that the aircraft is at 9,000 feet altitude. If the aircraft is not at that altitude, the pilot should reply, "Negative, maintaining 8,000 as assigned." No climb or descent should be started unless specifically assigned by the controller.

Pilots should notify controllers on initial contact that they have received the ATIS broadcast by repeating the alphabetical code used appended to the broadcast. For example, "Information Sierra received."

Answers

9005-2 [B]

ALL

8854. What report should the pilot make at a clearance limit?

A—Time and altitude/flight level arriving or leaving.
B—Time, altitude/flight level, and expected holding speed.
C—Time, altitude/flight level, expected holding speed, and inbound leg length.

Pilots should report to ATC the time and altitude/flight level at which the aircraft reaches the clearance limit, and report when leaving the clearance limit. (PLT171, AA.II.D.K2) — AIM ¶5-3-2

Answer (B) is incorrect because ATC does not need the expected holding speed reported since it will be below the maximum holding airspeed. For all aircraft between MHA and 6,000 feet MSL, holding speed is 200 KIAS; for all aircraft between 6,001 and 14,000 feet MSL, holding speed is 230 KIAS; for all aircraft 14,001 feet MSL and above, holding speed is 265 KIAS. For turbojet airplanes, the maximum holding airspeed is 230 knots IAS from minimum holding altitude to 14,000 feet. Answer (C) is incorrect because inbound leg lengths are set by time or DME distance. At or below 14,000 feet MSL there is a 1-minute inbound leg. Above 14,000 feet MSL the inbound leg is 1-1/2 minutes.

ALL

9014. Where are position reports required on an IFR flight on airways or routes?

A—Over all designated compulsory reporting points.
B—Only where specifically requested by ARTCC.
C—When requested to change altitude or advise of weather conditions.

A position report is required by all flights regardless of altitude over each designated compulsory reporting point along the route being flown.

Note: When the controller states "radar contact," this requirement is removed. However, the question states nothing about being in "radar contact." (PLT421, AA.II.D.K2) — AIM ¶5-3-2

Answer (B) is incorrect because the "on request" reporting point is indicated on enroute charts by an open triangle. Reports passing an "on request" reporting point are only necessary when requested by ARTCC. Answer (C) is incorrect because pilots in IFR are expected to report weather conditions which have not been forecast, or hazardous conditions which have been forecast.

ALL

9015. Which reports are required when operating IFR in radar environment?

A—Position reports, vacating an altitude, unable to climb 500 ft/min, and time and altitude reaching a holding fix or point to which cleared.
B—Position reports, vacating an altitude, unable to climb 500 ft/min, time and altitude reaching a holding fix or point to which cleared, and a change in average true airspeed exceeding 5 percent or 10 knots.
C—Vacating an altitude, unable to climb 500 ft/min, time and altitude reaching a holding fix or point to which cleared, a change in average true airspeed exceeding 5 percent or 10 knots, and leaving any assigned holding fix or point.

The following reports should be made to ATC or FSS facilities without specific ATC request:

1. *Vacating any previously assigned altitude.*
2. *Making an altitude change when VFR-On-Top.*
3. *Unable to climb or descend at least 500 feet per minute.*
4. *Making a missed approach.*
5. *Changing true airspeed from flight plan by 5% or 10 knots (whichever is greater).*
6. *Time and altitude of reaching a clearance holding fix or point.*
7. *Leaving any holding fix.*

(PLT171, AA.VI.C.K3) — AIM ¶5-3-3

Answers (A) and (B) are incorrect because position reports are not required in a radar environment.

ALL

9016. Which reports are always required when on an IFR approach not in radar contact?

A—Leaving FAF inbound or outer marker inbound and missed approach.
B—Leaving FAF inbound, leaving outer marker inbound or outbound, and missed approach.
C—Leaving FAF inbound, leaving outer marker inbound or outbound, procedure turn outbound and inbound, and visual contact with the runway.

The following reports should be made when not in radar contact:

1. *When over designated compulsory reporting points*
2. *When leaving the final approach fix inbound*

Answers

8854 [A] 9014 [A] 9015 [C] 9016 [A]

3. When it becomes apparent that an ETA is in error by more than 3 minutes.

(PLT171, AA.VI.C.K3) — AIM ¶5-3-3

Answer (B) is incorrect because a pilot is required to report leaving the outer marker inbound on final approach. Answer (C) is incorrect because a pilot is not required to report leaving the outer marker outbound, the execution of a procedure turn, and/or visual contact with the runway.

ALL

9013. What action should a pilot take if asked by ARTCC to "VERIFY 9,000" and the flight is actually maintaining 8,000?

A—Immediately climb to 9,000.
B—Report climbing to 9,000.
C—Report maintaining 8,000.

At times controllers will ask pilots to verify that they are at a particular altitude. Pilots should confirm that they are at the altitude stated. If this is not the case, they should inform the controller of the actual altitude being maintained. Pilots should not take action to change their actual altitude to the altitude stated in the controller's verification request unless the controller specifically authorizes a change. (PLT171, AA.II.D.K2) — AIM ¶5-3-1

Answers (A) and (B) are incorrect because pilots should not take action to change their actual altitude to the altitude stated in the controller's verification request unless the controller specifically authorizes a change.

ALL

9022. Pilots should notify controllers on initial contact that they have received the ATIS broadcast by

A—stating "Have Numbers".
B—stating "Have Weather".
C—repeating the alphabetical code word appended to the broadcast.

Pilots should notify controllers on initial contact that they have received the ATIS broadcast by repeating the alphabetical code word appended to the broadcast. For example, "Information Sierra received." (PLT196, AA.VI.C.K3) — AIM ¶4-1-13

ALL

9022-1. While holding short for an intersection takeoff runway 36 at taxiway C, tower clears you to "line up and wait runway 36." You should

A—line up and wait for takeoff on taxiway C.
B—line up and wait on runway 36 at intersection C for departure.
C—hold short and advise tower that you are at intersection C short of runway 36.

"Line up and wait" is an ATC phrase used to instruct pilots to taxi onto the departure runway, line up, and wait for imminent departure. (PLT171, AA.II.C.K2) — AIM Chapter 5

ATM, ADX

8297. Except when in cruise flight, below what altitude are non-safety related cockpit activities by flight crewmembers prohibited?

A—10,000 feet.
B—14,500 feet.
C—FL180.

No certificate holder shall require, nor may any flight crewmember perform, any duties during a critical phase of flight except those duties required for the safe operation of the aircraft. For purposes of this section, critical phases of flight include all ground operations involving taxi, takeoff and landing, and all other flight operations conducted below 10,000 feet, except cruise flight. (PLT430, AA.I.E.K8) — 14 CFR §121.542

Answers

9013 [C] 9022 [C] 9022-1 [B] 8297 [A]

ATM, ADX

8298. With regard to flight crewmember duties, which of the following operations are considered to be in the "critical phase of flight"?

A—Taxi, takeoff, landing, and all other operations conducted below 10,000 feet MSL, including cruise flight.
B—Descent, approach, landing, and taxi operations, irrespective of altitudes MSL.
C—Taxi, takeoff, landing, and all other operations conducted below 10,000 feet, excluding cruise flight.

No certificate holder shall require, nor may any flight crewmember perform, any duties during a critical phase of flight except those duties required for the safe operation of the aircraft. For purposes of this section, critical phases of flight include all ground operations involving taxi, takeoff and landing, and all other flight operations conducted below 10,000 feet, except cruise flight. (PLT029, AA.I.E.K8) — 14 CFR §121.542

Answer (A) is incorrect because critical phase of flight includes all operations (except cruise flight) below 10,000 feet. Answer (B) is incorrect because 14,500 feet is the base of Class E airspace (if not set lower).

ALL

8298-1. When is the pilot responsible to see and avoid other traffic, terrain, or obstacles?

A—ATC maintains responsibility if the pilot is operating under IFR.
B—When meteorological conditions permit, regardless of flight rules.
C—When they have accepted an instruction to "maintain visual separation."

When weather conditions permit, regardless of whether an operation is conducted under IFR or VFR, vigilance shall be maintained by each person operating an aircraft so as to see and avoid other aircraft. (PLT029, AA.VI.C.K3) — 14 CFR §91.113

Speed Adjustments

ATC controllers often issue speed adjustments to radar controlled aircraft to achieve or maintain the desired separation. The following minimum speeds are usually observed:

- Turbine-powered aircraft below 10,000 feet: 210 knots.
- Turbine-powered aircraft departing an airport: 230 knots.

If an ATC controller assigns a speed which is too fast or too slow for the operating limitations of the aircraft under the existing circumstances, the pilot should advise ATC of the speed that will be used. The controller will then issue instructions based on that speed.

Because of the great differences in speed and operating characteristics of helicopters and airplanes, they are usually assigned different routing. Occasionally, larger/faster helicopters are integrated with fixed-wing aircraft. These situations could occur on IFR flights, routes that avoid noise-sensitive areas, or when the helicopter is assigned runways or taxiways to avoid downwash in congested areas.

Answers

8298 [C]   8298-1 [B]

ALL

9094. When a speed adjustment is necessary to maintain separation, what minimum speed may ATC request of a turbine-powered aircraft operating below 10,000 feet?

A—200 knots.
B—210 knots.
C—250 knots.

When a speed adjustment is necessary to maintain separation, the minimum airspeed for a turbine-powered aircraft operated below 10,000 feet is 210 knots. (PLT161, AA.I.E.K10) — AIM ¶4-4-12

Answer (A) is incorrect because 200 knots is the maximum airspeed of any airplane operating within Class C or D airspace, a VFR-designated corridor through Class B airspace, or in airspace underlying Class B airspace. Answer (C) is incorrect because 250 knots is the maximum airspeed of any airplane operating below 10,000 feet MSL.

ALL

9094-1. When ATC assigns a speed adjustment to an aircraft operating at FL270, it will be at a speed not less than

A—250 knots.
B—210 knots.
C—200 knots.

When ATC assigns speed adjustments to aircraft operating between FL280 and 10,000 feet, it will be to a speed not less than 250 knots or the equivalent Mach number. (PLT161, AA.VI.C.K3) — AIM ¶4-4-12

ALL

9095. When a speed adjustment is necessary to maintain separation, what minimum speed may ATC request of a turbine-powered aircraft departing an airport?

A—188 knots.
B—210 knots.
C—230 knots.

When a speed adjustment is necessary to maintain separation, the minimum airspeed for a turbine-powered aircraft on departure is 230 knots. (PLT161, AA.I.E.K10) — AIM ¶4-4-12

Answer (A) is incorrect because 188 knots is not an applicable airspeed for any ATC operation. All airspeeds used by ATC/regulations are expressed in 10-knot increments. Answer (B) is incorrect because it is the minimum airspeed that ATC can request of a turbine-powered airplane operating below 10,000 feet, excluding departing airplanes.

ALL

9096. If ATC requests a speed adjustment that is not within the operating limits of the aircraft, what action must the pilot take?

A—Maintain an airspeed within the operating limitations as close to the requested speed as possible.
B—Attempt to use the requested speed as long as possible, then request a reasonable airspeed from ATC.
C—Advise ATC of the airspeed that will be used.

The pilots retain the prerogative of rejecting the application of speed adjustment by ATC if the minimum safe airspeed for any particular operation is greater than the speed adjustment. In such cases, the pilots are expected to advise ATC of the speed that will be used. (PLT172, AA.I.E.K10) — AIM ¶4-4-12

Answer (A) is incorrect because while a pilot should maintain at least the minimum safe airspeed for any particular operation, a pilot is expected to advise ATC of the airspeed being used when it differs from ATC's requested speed adjustment. Answer (B) is incorrect because a pilot who uses an airspeed that is not within the operating limits of the airplane is not only in violation of regulations, but is also risking the safety of all on board the airplane. A pilot must operate the airplane in a safe manner and advise ATC of the airspeed that will be used.

RTC

9042. Under what situations are faster/larger helicopters integrated with fixed-wing aircraft?

A—IFR flights, noise avoidance routes, and use of runways or taxiways.
B—Use of taxiways, sequencing for takeoff and landing, and use of the same traffic patterns.
C—Use of taxiways, sequencing for takeoff and landing, and use of the same loading ramps.

There will be situations where faster/larger helicopters may be integrated with fixed-wing aircraft. These include IFR flights, avoidance of noise-sensitive areas, or use of runway/taxiways to minimize the hazardous effects of rotor downwash in congested areas. (PLT434) — AIM ¶4-3-17

Answers

9094 [B] 9094-1 [A] 9095 [C] 9096 [C] 9042 [A]

Holding

Holding may be necessary when ATC is unable to clear a flight to its destination. VORs, nondirectional beacons, airway intersections, and DME fixes may all be used as holding points. Flying a holding pattern involves two turns and two straight-and-level legs as shown in Figure 6-5.

At and below 14,000 feet MSL (no wind), the aircraft flies the specified course inbound to the fix, turns to the right 180°, flies a parallel course outbound for 1 minute, again turns 180° to the right, and flies 1 minute inbound to the fix. Above 14,000 feet MSL, the inbound leg length is 1-1/2 minutes. If a nonstandard pattern is to be flown, ATC will specify left turns.

When 3 minutes or less from the holding fix, the pilot is expected to start a speed reduction so as to cross the fix at or below the maximum holding airspeed. For all aircraft between MHA (minimum holding altitude) and 6,000 feet MSL, holding speed is 200 KIAS. For all aircraft between 6,001 and 14,000 feet MSL, holding speed is 230 KIAS. For all aircraft 14,001 feet MSL and above, holding speed is 265 KIAS. Exceptions to these speeds will be indicated by an icon.

The aircraft is in a holding pattern as of the initial time of arrival over the fix, and that time should be reported to ATC. The initial outbound leg is flown for 1 minute at or below 14,000 feet MSL. Subsequently, timing of the outbound leg should be adjusted as necessary to arrive at the proper inbound leg length. Timing of the outbound leg begins over or abeam the fix, whichever occurs later. If the abeam position cannot be determined, start timing when the turn to outbound is completed. The same entry and holding procedures apply to DME holding, except distance in nautical miles are used to establish leg length.

The FAA has three recommended methods for entering a holding pattern, as shown in Figure 6-6. An aircraft approaching from within sector (A) would fly a parallel entry by turning left to parallel the outbound course, making another left turn to remain in protected airspace, and returning to the holding fix. Aircraft approaching from sector (B) would fly a teardrop entry, by flying outbound on a track of 30° or less to the holding course, and then making a right turn to intercept the holding course inbound to the fix. Those approaching from within sector (C) would fly a direct entry by turning right to fly the pattern.

If the holding pattern is charted, the controller may omit all holding instructions, except the holding direction and the statement "as published." Pilots are expected to hold in the pattern depicted even if it means crossing the clearance limit. If the holding pattern to be used is not depicted on charts, ATC will issue general holding instructions. The holding clearance will include the following information: direction of holding from the fix in terms of the eight cardinal compass points; holding fix; radial, course, bearing, airway, or route on which the aircraft is to hold; leg length in miles if DME or RNAV is to be used; direction of turn if left turns are to be made; time to expect further clearance and any pertinent additional delay information.

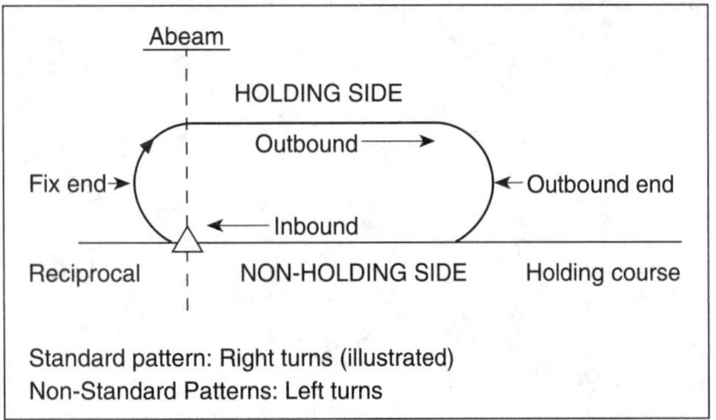

Figure 6-5

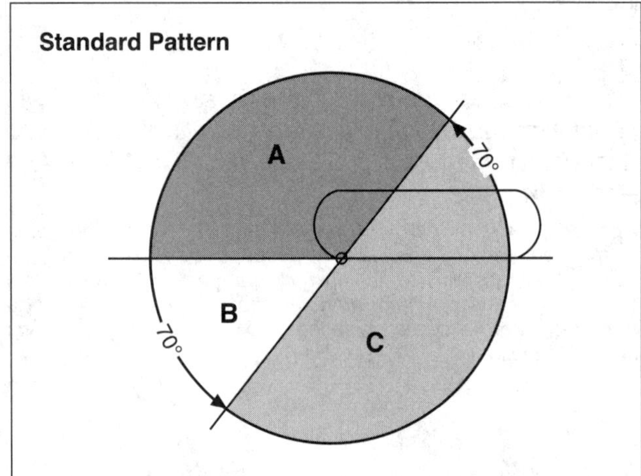

Figure 6-6

ALL

8853. What action should a pilot take if within 3 minutes of a clearance limit and further clearance has not been received?

A—Assume lost communications and continue as planned.
B—Plan to hold at cruising speed until further clearance is received.
C—Start a speed reduction to holding speed in preparation for holding.

When an aircraft is 3 minutes or less from a clearance limit and a clearance beyond the fix has not been received, the pilot is expected to start a speed reduction so that he will cross the fix, initially, at or below the maximum holding airspeed. (PLT296, AA.VI.J.K1) — AIM ¶5-3-7

Answer (A) is incorrect because if two-way communications are lost, the pilot is required to hold at the clearance limit in a standard pattern on the course that was used to approach the fix. If an expected further clearance time was received, plan on leaving the fix at that time. If none was given and the fix is an IAF, plan your arrival as close as possible to the estimated time of arrival. Answer (B) is incorrect because cruising speed may be greater than maximum holding speed.

ALL

8855. The maximum speed a propeller-driven airplane may hold at is

A—265 knots.
B—230 knots.
C—156 knots.

For all aircraft between MHA and 6,000 feet MSL, holding speed is 200 KIAS. For all aircraft between 6,001 and 14,000 feet MSL, holding speed is 230 KIAS. For all aircraft 14,000 feet MSL and above, holding speed is 265 KIAS. Exceptions to these speeds will be indicated by an icon. Since this question does not specify what altitude the airplane is holding at, both answers (A) and (B) are correct. Choosing either of these will result in a correct response. (PLT296, AA.VI.J.K1) — AIM ¶5-3-7

ALL

8856. Maximum holding speed for a turbojet airplane above 14,000 feet is

A—210 knots.
B—230 knots.
C—265 knots.

For all aircraft between MHA (minimum holding altitude) and 6,000 feet MSL, holding speed is 200 KIAS. For all aircraft between 6,001 and 14,000 feet MSL, holding speed is 230 KIAS. For all aircraft 14,000 feet MSL and above, holding speed is 265 KIAS. Exceptions to these speeds will be indicated by an icon. (PLT296, AA.VI.J.K1) — AIM ¶5-3-7

ALL

8857. Maximum holding speed for a civil turbojet aircraft at a joint use airport (civil/Navy) between 7,000 and 14,000 feet is

A—265 knots.
B—230 knots.
C—200 knots.

The following are exceptions to the maximum holding airspeeds: Holding patterns at Navy fields only 230 KIAS maximum, unless otherwise depicted. (PLT296, AA.VI.J.K1) — AIM ¶5-3-7

ALL

9418. What is the maximum holding speed for a civil turbojet holding at a civil airport at 15,000 feet MSL, unless a higher speed is required due to turbulence or icing and ATC is notified?

A—265 knots.
B—230 knots.
C—250 knots.

For all aircraft between MHA (minimum holding altitude) and 6,000 feet MSL, holding speed is 200 KIAS. For all aircraft between 6,001 and 14,000 feet MSL, holding speed is 230 KIAS. For all aircraft 14,000 feet MSL and above, holding speed is 265 KIAS. Exceptions to these speeds will be indicated by an icon. (PLT296, AA.VI.J.K1) — AIM ¶5-3-7

ALL

9419. Civil aircraft holding at an altitude of 14,000 feet at a military or joint civil/military use airports should expect to operate at which holding pattern airspeed?

A—250 knots.
B—260 knots.
C—230 knots.

Aircraft holding at military or joint civil/military use airports should expect to operate at a maximum holding pattern airspeed of 230 knots up to and including 14,000 feet. (PLT296, AA.VI.J.K1) — AIM ¶5-3-7

Answers

8853 [C]	8855 [A] or [B]	8856 [C]	8857 [B]	9418 [A]	9419 [C]

ALL

8858. When using a flight director system, what rate of turn or bank angle should a pilot observe during turns in a holding pattern?

A—3° per second or 25° bank, whichever is less.
B—3° per second or 30° bank, whichever is less.
C—1-1/2° per second or 25° bank, whichever is less.

When making turns in the holding pattern, use whichever of the following requires the least angle of bank:

1. *3° per second;*
2. *30° bank angle; or*
3. *25° bank provided a flight director system is used.*

(PLT047, AA.VI.J.K1) — AIM ¶5-3-7

ALL

8859. When holding at an NDB, at what point should the timing begin for the second leg outbound?

A—Abeam the holding fix or when the wings are level after completing the turn to the outbound heading, whichever occurs first.
B—At the end of a 1-minute standard rate turn after station passage.
C—When abeam the holding fix.

Outbound leg timing begins over or abeam the holding fix, whichever occurs later. If the abeam position cannot be determined, start timing when the turn to outbound is complete. (PLT296, AA.VI.J.K1) — AIM ¶5-3-7

Answer (A) is incorrect because the pilot should start the timing when the turn is complete, only when a position abeam the fix cannot be determined. Answer (B) is incorrect because abeam the fix is preferable and should be used rather than at the completion of a standard rate turn, especially if turn completion occurs before coming abeam the fix.

ALL

8860. When entering a holding pattern above 14,000 feet, the initial outbound leg should not exceed

A—1 minute.
B—1-1/2 minutes.
C—1-1/2 minutes or 10 NM, whichever is less.

Inbound leg time should not exceed 1 minute when holding at or below 14,000 feet, or 1-1/2 minutes when holding above 14,000 feet. The outbound leg should be flown for 1 minute or 1-1/2 minutes as appropriate on the first leg and then adjusted on subsequent legs to get the correct time on the inbound leg. (PLT296, AA.VI.J.K1) — AIM ¶5-3-7

Answer (A) is incorrect because an initial outbound leg of 1 minute should be used only when below 14,000 feet. Answer (C) is incorrect because a DME distance is issued only by the specified controller for aircraft equipped with DME capability. A DME distance is not required unless specified by the controller.

ATM, ATS, RTC

8861. (Refer to Figure 123.) You receive this ATC clearance:

"...HOLD EAST OF THE ABC VORTAC ON THE ZERO NINER ZERO RADIAL, LEFT TURNS..."

What is the recommended procedure to enter the holding pattern?

A—Parallel only.
B—Direct only.
C—Teardrop only.

Determine the holding pattern by placing your pencil on the holding fix and dragging it on the holding radial given by ATC, then returning back to the fix. Then draw the pattern from the fix with turns in the direction specified. Holding east on the 090° radial with left turns means you will be south of R-090.

The entry procedure is based on the aircraft's heading. To determine which entry procedure to use, draw a line at a 70° angle from the holding fix, and cutting the outbound leg at about one-third its length. With a heading of 055°, we are in the middle-size piece of pie, so a parallel entry would be used. (PLT296, AA.VI.J.K1) — AIM ¶5-3-7

Answer (B) is incorrect because a direct entry would be appropriate if you were coming in on R-340 to R-160. Answer (C) is incorrect because a teardrop entry would be appropriate if you were coming in from R-270 to R-340.

ATM, ATS, RTC

8862. (Refer to Figure 123.) You receive this ATC clearance:

"...CLEARED TO THE ABC VORTAC. HOLD SOUTH ON THE ONE EIGHT ZERO RADIAL..."

What is the recommended procedure to enter the holding pattern?

A—Teardrop only.
B—Direct only.
C—Parallel only.

Determine the holding pattern by placing your pencil on the holding fix and dragging it on the holding radial given by ATC, then returning back to the fix. Then draw the pattern from the fix with turns in the direction specified.

Answers

8858 [A]	8859 [C]	8860 [B]	8861 [A]	8862 [B]

Holding south on the 180° radial with right turns means you will be east of R-180.

The entry procedure is based on the aircraft's heading. To determine which entry procedure to use, draw a line at a 70° angle from the holding fix, and cutting the outbound leg at about one-third its length. With a heading of 055°, we are in the largest piece of pie, so a direct entry would be used. (PLT087, AA.VI.J.K1) — AIM ¶5-3-7

Answer (A) is incorrect because a teardrop entry would be appropriate only from R-290 to R-360. Answer (C) is incorrect because a parallel entry would only be appropriate from R-360 to R-110.

ATM, ATS, RTC

8863. (Refer to Figure 123.) You receive this ATC clearance:

"...CLEARED TO THE XYZ VORTAC. HOLD NORTH ON THE THREE SIX ZERO RADIAL, LEFT TURNS..."

What is the recommended procedure to enter the holding pattern?

A—Parallel only.
B—Direct only.
C—Teardrop only.

Determine the holding pattern by placing your pencil on the holding fix and dragging it on the holding radial given by ATC, then returning back to the fix. Then draw the pattern from the fix with turns in the direction specified. Holding north on the 360° radial with left turns means you will be east of R-090.

The entry procedure is based on the aircraft's heading. To determine which entry procedure to use, draw a line at a 70° angle from the holding fix, and cutting the outbound leg at about one-third its length. With a heading of 055°, we are in the smallest piece of pie, so a teardrop entry would be used. (PLT296, AA.VI.J.K1) — AIM ¶5-3-7

Answer (A) is incorrect because a parallel entry would be appropriate only from R-070 to R-180. Answer (B) is incorrect because a direct entry would only be appropriate from R-250 to R-070.

ATM, ATS, RTC

8864. (Refer to Figure 123.) You receive this ATC clearance:

"...CLEARED TO THE ABC VORTAC. HOLD WEST ON THE TWO SEVEN ZERO RADIAL..."

What is the recommended procedure to enter the holding pattern?

A—Parallel only.
B—Direct only.
C—Teardrop only.

Determine the holding pattern by placing your pencil on the holding fix and dragging it on the holding radial given by ATC, then returning back to the fix. Then draw the pattern from the fix with turns in the direction specified. Holding west on the 270° radial with right turns means you will be south of R-090.

The entry procedure is based on the aircraft's heading. To determine which entry procedure to use, draw a line at a 70° angle from the holding fix, and cutting the outbound leg at about one-third its length. With a heading of 055°, we are in the largest piece of pie, so a direct entry would be used. (PLT296, AA.VI.J.K1) — AIM ¶5-3-7

Answer (A) is incorrect because a parallel entry would be appropriate only from R-090 to R-200. Answer (C) is incorrect because a teardrop entry would only be appropriate from R-020 to R-090.

ATM, ATS, RTC

8865. (Refer to Figure 124.) A pilot receives this ATC clearance:

"...CLEARED TO THE ABC VORTAC. HOLD WEST ON THE TWO SEVEN ZERO RADIAL..."

What is the recommended procedure to enter the holding pattern?

A—Parallel or teardrop.
B—Parallel only.
C—Direct only.

Determine the holding pattern by placing your pencil on the holding fix and dragging it on the holding radial given by ATC, then returning back to the fix. Then draw the pattern from the fix with turns in the direction specified. Holding west on the 270° radial with right turns means you will be south of R-090.

The entry procedure is based on the aircraft's heading. To determine which entry procedure to use, draw a line at a 70° angle from the holding fix, and cutting the outbound leg at about one-third its length. With a heading of 155°, we are in the largest piece of pie, so a direct entry would be used. (PLT296, AA.VI.J.K1) — AIM ¶5-3-7

Answer (A) is incorrect because the parallel or teardrop entries are alternatives only when approaching on R-090. Answer (B) is incorrect because a parallel entry would only be appropriate when approaching from R-090 to R-200.

Answers

8863 [C] 8864 [B] 8865 [C]

ATM, ATS, RTC

8866. (Refer to Figure 124.) A pilot receives this ATC clearance:

"...CLEARED TO THE XYZ VORTAC. HOLD NORTH ON THE THREE SIX ZERO RADIAL, LEFT TURNS..."

What is the recommended procedure to enter the holding pattern?

A—Teardrop only.
B—Parallel only.
C—Direct.

Determine the holding pattern by placing your pencil on the holding fix and dragging it on the holding radial given by ATC, then returning back to the fix. Then draw the pattern from the fix with turns in the direction specified. Holding north on the 360° radial with left turns means you will be east of R-360.

The entry procedure is based on the aircraft's heading. To determine which entry procedure to use, draw a line at a 70° angle from the holding fix, and cutting the outbound leg at about one-third its length. With a heading of 155°, we are in the largest piece of pie, so a direct entry would be used. (PLT296, AA.VI.J.K1) — AIM ¶5-3-7

Answer (A) is incorrect because a teardrop entry would be appropriate only from R-180 to R-250. Answer (B) is incorrect because, if you were approaching on R-070 to R-180, you would make a parallel entry.

ATM, ATS, RTC

8867. (Refer to Figure 124.) A pilot receives this ATC clearance:

"...CLEARED TO THE ABC VORTAC. HOLD SOUTH ON THE ONE EIGHT ZERO RADIAL..."

What is the recommended procedure to enter the holding pattern?

A—Teardrop only.
B—Parallel only.
C—Direct only.

Determine the holding pattern by placing your pencil on the holding fix and dragging it on the holding radial given by ATC, then returning back to the fix. Then draw the pattern from the fix with turns in the direction specified. Holding south on the 180° radial with right turns means you will be east of R-360.

The entry procedure is based on the aircraft's heading. To determine which entry procedure to use, draw a line at a 70° angle from the holding fix, and cutting the outbound leg at about one-third its length. With a heading of 155°, we are in the smallest piece of pie, so a teardrop entry would be used. (PLT296, AA.VI.J.K1) — AIM ¶5-3-7

Answer (B) is incorrect because a parallel entry would be appropriate only from R-360 to R-110. Answer (C) is incorrect because a direct entry would only be appropriate from R-110 to R-290.

Charts

The pilot-in-command must ensure that the appropriate aeronautical charts are on board the aircraft for each flight.

There are a number of questions that require reference to a segment of the *Chart Supplements U.S.* (previously A/FD). The legend for this publication is available in Appendix 1 of the Airman Knowledge Testing Supplement (FAA Legends) for ATP.

Most of the questions concerning interpretation of Approach Charts, DPs and STARs can be answered by referring to the appropriate legend. These legends are available during the test in CT-8080 you will be issued at the testing center.

There are a few questions that require you to interpret the symbology on Enroute Charts. Unlike the other charts, no legend is available in the test book.

Departure Procedures (DPs) are depicted in one of two basic forms. Pilot Navigation (Pilot NAV) DPs are established where the pilot is primarily responsible for navigation on the DP route. Vector DPs are established where ATC will provide radar navigational guidance to an assigned route or fix. A vector DP will often include procedures to be followed in the event of a two-way communication radio failure.

Standard Terminal Arrival Routes (STARs) are ATC-coded IFR arrival routes established for certain airports. STARs purpose is to simplify clearance delivery procedures. ATC will assign a STAR to a civil aircraft whenever they deem it appropriate.

Answers

8866 [C] 8867 [A]

The Jet Route system consists of jet routes established from 18,000 feet MSL to FL450 inclusive.

The GPS Approach Overlay Program permits pilots to use GPS avionics under IFR for flying existing instrument approach procedures, except localizer (LOC), localizer directional aid (LDA), and simplified directional facility (SDF) procedures. Aircraft navigating by GPS are considered to be RNAV aircraft. Therefore, the appropriate equipment suffix must be included in the ATC flight plan. The word "or" in the approach title indicates that approach is in Phase III of the GPS Overlay Program. This allows the approach to be flown without reference of any kind to the ground-based NAVAIDs associated with the approach. When using GPS for the approach at the destination airport, the alternate must be an approach other than a GPS.

ALL

9012. In what way are SIDs depicted in plan view?

A—"Vectors" provided for navigational guidance or "Pilot NAV" with courses the pilot is responsible to follow.
B—"Vectors" and "Pilot NAV" for pilots to use at their discretion.
C—Combined textual and graphic form which are mandatory routes and instructions.

Pilot navigation (Pilot NAV) DPs (previously called SIDs) are established where the pilot is primarily responsible for navigation on the DP route. Vector DPs are established where ATC will provide radar navigational guidance to a filed/assigned route or to a fix depicted on the DP. (PLT201, AA.VI.C.K1) — AIM ¶5-2-8

Answer (B) is incorrect because DPs are departure procedures and must be followed as depicted (not at the pilot's discretion). If a pilot does not wish to use a DP, then he/she must notify ATC. Answer (C) is incorrect because a NOS DP does not list the textual description in the plan view. The plan view depicts a DP as either a "pilot nav" or "vector" to signify if navigation is provided by the pilot or by radar vectors.

ALL

9034. What is the primary purpose of a STAR?

A—Provide separation between IFR and VFR traffic.
B—Simplify clearance delivery procedures.
C—Decrease traffic congestion at certain airports.

A STAR is an ATC-coded IFR arrival route established for application to arriving IFR aircraft destined for certain airports. Its purpose is to simplify clearance delivery procedures. (PLT170, AA.VI.C.K1) — AIM ¶5-4-1

Answer (A) is incorrect because separation between IFR and VFR traffic is provided by Stage III radar service, not a STAR. Answer (C) is incorrect because controlled airspace, e.g., Class B, Class C, can be used to decrease traffic congestion at some airports by allowing ATC to regulate traffic flow and volume.

ALL

9035. When does ATC issue a STAR?

A—Only when ATC deems it appropriate.
B—Only to high priority flights.
C—Only upon request of the pilot.

Pilots of IFR civil aircraft destined to locations for which STARs have been published may be issued a clearance containing a STAR whenever ATC deems it appropriate. (PLT170, AA.VI.C.K1) — AIM ¶5-4-1

Answer (B) is incorrect because any type of IFR flight can be issued a STAR. High priority flights will normally be handled in an expeditious manner by ATC. Answer (C) is incorrect because a STAR is a clearance delivery procedure that is issued by ATC. A pilot has the responsibility to accept or refuse that clearance. A pilot can list a STAR in the flight plan, but ATC will issue one only if appropriate.

ATM, ATS, RTC

9554. (Refer to Figure 259.) When performing the LOC RWY 33R approach and sidestep, at what point would you initiate the missed approach?

A—anytime after the FAF.
B—4.5 NM after JOLTE.
C—IAH DME 1.0.

The FAF to MAP for the LOC approach is listed in the bottom left corner of the approach plate. FAF to MAP is 4.5 NM. (PLT083, AA.VI.C.K1) — Instrument Approach Procedures

Answers

9012 [A]   9034 [B]   9035 [A]   9554 [B]

ALL

9555. (Refer to Figures 360 and 388.) N60JB desired to list ROC as an alternate for BUF. The active RWY at ROC was expected to be RWY 28. What weather forecast was required at Greater Rochester Intl, for N60JB to list it as an alternate?

A—Nonprecision approach 800-2, precision approach 800-2.
B—Nonprecision approach 800-2, precision approach 600-2.
C—Nonprecision approach 800-2 1/4, precision approach 600-2.

The A in the triangle in the top left-hand corner of the approach chart indicates Rochester has nonstandard alternate minimums. FAA Figure 388 lists all the approaches at Rochester which have nonstandard alternate minimums. Find the Rochester minimums in the top left of FAA Figure 388. Assuming N60JB is in approach category A, B, or C, the minimums for the ILS 28 approach are 800-2. Since alternate minimums are not stated for a nonprecision approach to Runway 28, we can assume that standard alternate minimums apply. (PLT083, AA.VI.C.K1) — Instrument Approach Procedures

Answers (B) and (C) are incorrect because the lowest minimums for a precision approach in any category aircraft is 800-2.

ALL

9571. (Refer to Figure 259.) Which approach lighting is available for RWY 33R?

A—MALSR and RAIL.
B—MIRL.
C—TDZ and CL.

The A_5 inside the circle with the dot indicates that runway 33R has MALSR approach lights with RAIL. See FAA Legend 38. (PLT083, AA.VI.C.K1) — Instrument Approach Procedures

Answer (B) is incorrect because MIRL indicates Medium Intensity Runway Lights. Answer (C) is incorrect because TDZ and CL lighting is not available for RWY 33R and it is in-runway, not approach lighting.

ALL

9588. (Refer to Figure 273.) The touchdown zone elevation of the ILS RWY 25L approach at Phoenix Sky Harbor International Airport is

A—1,126 feet.
B—1,135 feet.
C—1,458 feet.

The notation "TDZE 1126" indicates the touchdown zone elevation on runway 25L is 1,126 feet MSL. See FAA Legend 4. (PLT049, AA.VI.C.K1) — Instrument Approach Procedures

ALL

9599. (Refer to Figure 293.) The distance from the FAF to the MAP for the VOR or GPS RWY 13L/13R approach is

A—6.2 NM.
B—3.2 NM.
C—2.6 NM.

The airport diagram indicates the FAF to the MAP is 2.6 NM. (PLT083, AA.VI.C.K1) — FAA-H-8083-15

ALL

9600. (Refer to Figure 293.) The La Guardia weather goes below minimums and New York Approach Control issues a clearance to N711JB, via radar vectors, to ASALT Intersection. As N711JB is approaching ASALT, Approach Control clears the aircraft to fly the VOR RWY 13L/13R approach. What is the distance from ASALT Intersection to RWY 13L?

A—11.2 NM
B—12.2 NM.
C—8.6 NM.

The profile view indicates that the distance from ASALT INT to CRI VOR is 6.0 NM, CRI VOR to MAP is 2.6 NM. On the plan view it is noted that from MAP to Rwy 13L is 3.6NM. 6 + 2.6 + 3.6 = 12.2 (PLT083, AA.VI.C.K1) — Instrument Approach Procedures

ALL

9601. (Refer to Figure 293.) The La Guardia weather goes below minimums and New York Approach Control issues a clearance to N711JB, via radar vectors, to ASALT Intersection. What is the lowest altitude that Approach Control may clear N711JB to cross ASALT Intersection?

A—3,000 feet.
B—2,500 feet.
C—2,000 feet.

The profile view shows a mandatory altitude of 3,000 feet at ASALT unless advised by ATC, then 2,000 feet is the minimum. (PLT049, AA.VI.C.K1) — Instrument Approach Procedures

Answers

9555 [A] 9571 [A] 9588 [A] 9599 [C] 9600 [B] 9601 [C]

ALL

9602. (Refer to Figure 293.) For landing on RWY 13R at JFK, how much RWY is available?

A—12,468 feet.
B—14,511 feet.
C—9,095.

The runway landing distance for 13R is listed in the upper center left portion of the approach plate and is 12,468. (PLT083, AA.VI.C.K1) — Instrument Approach Procedures

Answer (B) is incorrect because 14,511 is the overall length of runway 13R/31L. Answer (C) is incorrect because 9,905 is the runway landing distance for 13L.

ALL

9603. (Refer to Figure 293.) What must be operational for N711JB to execute the VOR RWY 13L/13R approach to JFK?

A—DME or radar.
B—LDIN and VOR.
C—VOR, LDIN, and DME or radar.

VOR is required, as indicated by the approach title. The plan view indicates that DME or radar is required. The notes section at the top of the chart shows that the lead-in light system must be operational to execute the procedure. (PLT083, AA.VI.C.K1) — Instrument Approach Procedures

ALL

9604. (Refer to Figure 293.) The distance from Canarsie (CRI) to RWY 13R at JFK is

A—5.2 NM.
B—6.2 NM.
C—8.6 NM.

The profile view indicates that the distance from CRI VOR to MAP is 2.6 NM and the distance from the MAP to Rwy 13R is 2.6 NM. (PLT083, AA.VI.C.K1) — Instrument Approach Procedures

ALL

9614. (Refer to Figure 269.) The flight is filed Senic One Departure, Daggett transition. Before reaching MOXIE intersection, ATC clears you to turn left heading 030 and proceed direct LAHAB intersection. After the turn, you realize you cannot cross LAHAB at 15,000 feet. What. should you do if you are in IMC?

A—Enter holding at LAHAB on the 185 degree radial until reaching 15,000 feet.
B—Advise departure control you cannot make the clearance and request radar vectors.
C—Turn toward the Long Beach Airport temporarily and continue the climb until you can cross LAHAB at 15,000 feet.

Advise departure control whenever you cannot make the clearance and request radar vectors to ensure you maintain obstacle and traffic avoidance. (PLT052, AA.VI.C.K1) — Instrument Approach Procedures

ALL

9615. (Refer to Figure 293.) What is the distance from ASALT intersection to the MAP?

A—8.6 NM.
B—2.6 NM.
C—6 NM.

The profile view shows the distance between ASALT and the final approach fix is 6 miles. The distance between the FAF and MAP is 2.6 NM. Therefore, the distance between ASALT and the MAP is 8.6 NM. (PLT090, AA.VI.C.K1) — Instrument Approach Procedure

ATM, ATS, RTC

9617. (Refer to Figure 258.) As you approach DEPEW on the RNAV (GPS) RWY 32 approach, your GPS changes from "armed" to "active," and the CDI needle begins to show increasing deviation to the left with no increase in cross track. In this situation, you

A—should immediately execute the missed approach.
B—know that the sensitivity of the CDI has increased.
C—would turn to the right to center the CDI needle.

When within 2 NM of the final approach waypoint (FAWP) of DEPEW on the RNAV (GPS) Runway 32 approach, with the approach mode "armed," the approach mode will switch to "active" which results in a change in CDI sensitivity. (PLT354, AA.VI.C.K1) — AIM ¶1-1-17

Answers

9602 [A]	9603 [C]	9604 [A]	9614 [B]	9615 [A]	9617 [B]

ALL

9619. (Refer to Figure 301.) During the approach (ILS RWY 10 at SYR) while maintaining an on glide slope indication with a groundspeed of 110 knots, what was the approximate rate of descent for PTZ 70?

A—475 feet per minute.
B—585 feet per minute.
C—690 feet per minute.

The profile view indicates that the final approach angle is 3.0°. The table in FAA Legend 72 shows that a 555 fpm descent rate is required for 105 knots, and 635 fpm is required for 120 knots. 585 is the only answer choice to fall within these limits. (PLT049, AA.VI.C.K1) — FAA-H-8083-15, Chapter 7

ALL

9644. (Refer to Figure 192.) On the airway J10 between OBH and LBF, the MAA is 41,000 feet. What is the MAA on J197 between FSD and OBH?

A—43,000 feet.
B—45,000 feet.
C—60,000 feet.

The Maximum Authorized Altitude is the maximum usable altitude or flight level on an airway or jet route which has a published MEA. FL450 is the upper limit of all jet routes. (PLT100, AA.VI.C.K1) — Pilot/Controller Glossary

Answer (A) is incorrect because the upper limit of the jet route system includes FL450 unless marked otherwise. Answer (C) is incorrect because this is the upper limit of Class A airspace, but the jet route system stops above 45,000 feet.

ALL

9645. (Refer to Figure 373.) Inbound to DEN from Dallas/Fort Worth (DFW), Center gives you a vector and a frequency for Denver Approach Control, but you miss-copy the frequency. You determine you probably were assigned

A—119.3 and should expect a tower frequency of 124.3.
B—120.35 and should expect a tower frequency of 132.35.
C—120.35 and should expect a tower frequency of 124.3.

Approaching Denver from Dallas, you will use the Denver Approach Center designed for "South" which is 120.35, and 132.35 for Denver tower. (PLT049, AA.VI.C.K1) — Instrument Approach Procedures

ALL

9645-1. (Refer to Figure 374.) Inbound to DEN from Dallas/Fort Worth (DFW), Center gives you a vector and a frequency for Denver Approach Control, but you miss-copy the frequency. You determine you probably were assigned

A—119.3 and should expect a tower frequency of 124.3.
B—120.35 and should expect a tower frequency of 124.3.
C—120.35 and should expect a tower frequency of 132.35.

Approaching Denver from Dallas, you will use the Denver Approach Center designed for "South" which is 120.35, and 124.3 for Denver tower. (PLT049, AA.VI.C.K1) — Instrument Approach Procedures

ALL

9655. (Refer to Figures 201 and 201A.) What type of weather information would normally be expected to be available from the Weather Data Source at Ogden-Hinckley?

A—Cloud height, weather, obstructions to vision, temperature, dewpoint, altimeter, surface winds, and any pertinent remarks.
B—Cloud bases/tops, obstructions to vision, altimeter, winds, precipitation, and the intensity of the precipitation.
C—Cloud height, obstructions to vision, temperature, dewpoint, altimeter, wind data, and density altitude.

The Chart Supplements U.S. (previously A/FD) indicates the weather source for Ogden-Hinckley is ASOS. Observations report cloud height, weather, obstructions to vision, temperature and dew point (in most cases), surface wind, altimeter, and pertinent remarks. See FAA Legends 19 and 20. (PLT078, AA.VI.C.K1) — Chart Supplements U.S.

Answer (B) is incorrect because it does not report cloud bases or tops, nor precipitation and intensity. Answer (C) is incorrect because it does not report wind data and density altitude.

Answers

9619 [B]	9644 [B]	9645 [B]	9645-1 [B]	9655 [A]

ALL

9658. (Refer to Figures 185 and 185A.) The maximum gross weight that an L1011 can be operated on RWY 01L/19R at McCarran Intl is

A—496,000 pounds.
B—833,000 pounds.
C—620,000 pounds.

The runway weight limit for a dual tandem gear airplane on Runway 01L/19R is listed as 2D/2D2-833, which is 833,000 pounds. However, the remarks section states the maximum weight for an L1011 is 496,000 pounds. (PLT078, AA.VI.C.K1) — Chart Supplements U.S.

ALL

9659. (Refer to Figure 185A.) The threshold of RWY 07L at McCarran Intl is displaced

A—878 feet, due to a pole.
B—2,138 feet, due to a hangar.
C—1,659 feet, due to a pole.

The Chart Supplement U.S. (previously A/FD) listing for Runway 07L states the threshold is displaced 2,138 feet for a hangar. (PLT078, AA.VI.C.K1) — Chart Supplements U.S.

ALL

9666. (Refer to Figure 335.) At San Francisco Intl (SFO), the runway hold position signs are

A—all on the left-hand side of the taxiways.
B—all on the right-hand side of the taxiways.
C—on either side of the taxiways.

The note on the airport diagram states that several runway hold position signs are on the right rather than the left side of the taxiways. (PLT083, AA.VI.C.K1) — Instrument Approach Procedures

ALL

9670. (Refer to Figure 210.) The route between FIS (near Key West) and MTH, which is labeled B646, is an example of a

A—LF/MF Airway.
B—LF/MF Oceanic Route.
C—Military Training Route.

The brown color and airway designation (Blue 646) indicate it is a LF/MF airway. A solid narrow line indicates that it is an Oceanic route. A domestic LF/MF airway would be represented by a broader, shaded line. (PLT058, AA.VI.C.K1) — Enroute Low Altitude Chart Legend

ALL

9686. (Refer to Figure 343.) The airport diagram of Bradley Intl Airport has a symbol (appears to be a triangle balanced on top of another triangle) located close to the approach end of RWY 19. What does this symbol indicate?

A—Runway Radar Reflectors.
B—Practice hover area for the Army National Guard helicopters.
C—Two course lights, back to back, which flash beams of light along the course of an airway.

The double triangle symbol in the airport diagram stands for runway radar reflectors. (PLT083, AA.VI.C.K1) — Instrument Approach Procedures

ALL

9692. Aircraft navigating by GPS are considered, on the flight plan, to be

A—RNAV equipped.
B—in compliance with ICAO Annex 10.
C—FMS/EFIS equipped.

Aircraft navigating by GPS are considered to be RNAV aircraft. Therefore, the appropriate equipment suffix must be included in the ATC flight plan. (PLT354, AA.VI.C.K1) — Pilot/Controller Glossary

ALL

9694. The weather forecast requires an alternate for LUKACHUKAI (GPS RWY 25) ARIZONA. The alternate airport must have an approved instrument approach procedure, which is anticipated to be operational and available at the estimated time of arrival, other than

A—GPS or VOR.
B—ILS or GPS.
C—GPS.

When using GPS for the approach at the destination airport, the alternate must be an approach other than a GPS. (PLT354, AA.VI.C.K1) — AIM ¶1-1-19

ALL

8793. (Refer to Figures 348 and 361.) Determine the DEP CON frequency for the TUS7.GBN transition after takeoff from Rwy 11R at Tucson Intl.

A—125.1 MHz.
B—118.5 MHz.
C—128.5 MHz.

Answers

9658 [A]	9659 [B]	9666 [C]	9670 [B]	9686 [A]	9692 [A]
9694 [C]	8793 [A]				

The Chart Supplements U.S. (previously A/FD) indicates that the Departure Control Frequency for runway 11, departures on bearings 090° through 285° from the airport, is 125.1 Mhz. (PLT078, AA.VI.C.K1) — Chart Supplements U.S.

Answer (B) is incorrect because 118.5 MHz is for departures from RWY 11 with a departure heading between 286° to 089°. Answer (C) is incorrect because 128.5 is the general approach/departure control frequency.

ALL
8796. (Refer to Figure 348.) How can the pilot receive the latest NOTAMs for the TUS LAX flight?

A—Monitor ATIS on 123.8 MHz.
B—Contact the RCO on 122.2 MHz.
C—Request ADCUS on any FSS or Tower frequency.

NOTAMs can be received through the FSS located on the airport. The standard RCO frequency is 122.2 MHz. (PLT078, AA.VI.C.K1) — Chart Supplements U.S.

ALL
8797. (Refer to Figure 348.) What distance is available for takeoff on RWY 11R at Tucson Intl?

A—6,998 feet.
B—8,408 feet.
C—10,996 feet.

Runway 11R-29L is 8,408 feet long. The displaced threshold does not reduce takeoff distance. (PLT078, AA.VI.C.K1) — Chart Supplements U.S.

Answer (A) is incorrect because 6,998 feet is the length of the runway without the displaced threshold. Answer (C) is incorrect because 10,996 feet is the length of RWY 11L-29R.

ALL
8798. (Refer to Figure 348.) What effect on the takeoff run can be expected on RWY 11R at Tucson Intl?

A—Takeoff length shortened to 6,986 feet by displaced threshold.
B—Takeoff run shortened by 0.7 percent runway slope to the SE.
C—Takeoff run will be lengthened by the 0.7 percent upslope of the runway.

There is a 0.7% upslope to the southeast on runway 11R-29L. (PLT078, AA.VI.C.K1) — Chart Supplements U.S.

Answer (A) is incorrect because a displaced threshold will shorten the usable runway but has no effect on an airplane's required takeoff distance. Answer (B) is incorrect because the takeoff run is lengthened due to the 0.7% upslope to the southeast.

ALL
8782. (Refer to Figures 99, 101, and 101A.) Which frequency should be selected to check airport conditions and weather prior to departure at DFW Intl?

A—123.775 MHz.
B—122.95 MHz.
C—135.95 MHz.

The departure ATIS for DFW airport is listed as 135.95. (PLT078, AA.VI.C.K1) — Chart Supplements U.S.

Answer (A) is incorrect because 123.775 is the listed ATIS frequency for arriving airplanes. Answer (B) is incorrect because 122.95 is the UNICOM frequency.

ALL
8784. (Refer to Figure 100, Area 8.) Where is the VOR changeover point on V571 between Navasota (TNV) and Humble (IAH)?

A—24 miles from IAH.
B—18 miles from IAH.
C—Halfway between TNV and IAH

The changeover should be made at the changeover symbol if depicted, where there is a change in the direction of the airway, or in the absence of these at the halfway point between the VORs. In this case, the changeover point (COP) is indicated with a symbol, and the changeover should be made 24 miles from IAH and 18 miles from TNV. (PLT058, AA.VI.C.K1) — Enroute Low Altitude Chart Legend

ALL
8824. (Refer to Figure 114.) The changeover point on V8 southwest bound between HEC VORTAC and PDZ VORTAC is

A—halfway.
B—27 DME miles from HEC VORTAC.
C—31 DME miles from the HEC VORTAC.

There is a changeover point marked on the enroute chart at 31 NM from HEC VORTAC and 44 NM from PDZ VORTAC. Next to number 9 in the lower right corner of the figure note "PDZ TO HEC." (PLT058, AA.VI.C.K1) — Enroute Low Altitude Chart

Answer (A) is incorrect because when the changeover point is not located at the midway point, aeronautical charts will depict the location and give mileage to the radio aids. Answer (B) is incorrect because 27 DME miles from HEC VORTAC is the LUCER intersection, the flag represents a minimum crossing altitude not a changeover point.

Answers

8796 [B]	8797 [B]	8798 [C]	8782 [C]	8784 [A]	8824 [C]

ALL

8825. (Refer to Figure 114.) The minimum crossing altitude at APLES INT southwest bound on V394 is

A—7,500 feet.
B—9,100 feet.
C—11,500 feet.

There is a Minimum Crossing Altitude (MCA) of 9,100 feet at APLES INT when southwest bound on V394. (PLT058, AA.VI.C.K1) — Enroute Low Altitude Chart Legend

Answer (A) is incorrect because 7,500 feet is the minimum enroute altitude (MEA) from DAG VORTAC to APLES INT on V394, not the MCA at APLES INT. Answer (C) is incorrect because 11,500 feet is the minimum enroute altitude after APLES INT, not the MCA at APLES INT.

ALL

8826. (Refer to Figure 114, Area 9.) What is the minimum altitude southwest bound on V8 at LUCER intersection?

A—9,300 feet.
B—9,000 feet.
C—10,500 feet.

The flag at LUCER intersection signifies a minimum crossing altitude of 9,300 feet for aircraft flying southwest along V8-21-282-587. The MEA on V8 SW at this intersection changes from 9,000 to 10,500 feet; aircraft must be at a minimum altitude of 9,300 feet when crossing. (PLT058, AA.VI.C.K1) — Enroute Low Altitude Chart Legend

Answer (A) is incorrect because 9,000 feet is the MEA on V8 SW prior to reaching LUCER. Answer (B) is incorrect because 10,500 feet is the MEA on V8 SW after passing LUCER.

ALL

8852. (Refer to Figure 279 and Legend 72.) What is the approximate rate of descent required (for planning purposes) to maintain the electronic glide slope at 120 KIAS with a reported headwind component of 15 knots?

A—637 ft/min.
B—478 ft/min.
C—558 ft/min.

The ILS RWY 32R approach into Chicago-O'Hare has a 3° glide slope as indicated within the profile section of the approach chart. Using FAA Legend 72 along with a ground speed of 105 (120 KIAS — 15 knot headwind component), the rate of descent is 557.5 FPM. (PLT083, AA.VI.C.K1) — IFR Approach Procedures

Answer (A) is incorrect because a rate of descent of 637 FPM is appropriate for the indicated airspeed of 120 knots. Answer (B) is incorrect because a rate of descent of 478 FPM is appropriate for a 3.0° glide slope angle at 90 knots.

ALL

8852-1. (Refer to Legend 72 and Figure 361.) With a speed of 140 knots, what is the minimum rate of climb after taking off from Rwy 3 at TUS to reach 9,900 feet? Interpolation required.

A—963 FPM.
B—1,065 FPM.
C—930 FPM.

Using Figure 361, standard takeoff minimums for Runway 3 is 400 ft/NM. Using Legend 72 and the 140 knots provided in the question, interpolate the rate of climb by finding 400 ft/NM on the left-hand column and 140 knots on the top of the chart for the groundspeed. The minimum rate of climb is 963 FPM. (PLT058, AA.I.B.K2c) — FAA-H-8083-3

Answer (B) is incorrect because a minimum rate of climb of 1,065 FPM is for 425ft/NM at 150 knots. Answer (C) is incorrect because a minimum rate of climb of 930 FPM is for 370 ft/NM at 150 knots.

ALL

9933. (Refer to Figure 279.) Where does the final approach segment begin on the ILS RWY 32R at ORD?

A—Glide slope intercept, 2,700 feet MSL.
B—INDDY OM, 2,663 feet MSL.
C—MUNDAY ORD, 4,000 feet MSL.

The "lightning bolt" symbol depicts the beginning of the final approach segment, in this case at 2,700 feet MSL. (PLT049, AA.VI.C.K1) — IFR Approach Procedures

ALL

8799. (Refer to Figures 255A and 255B). Which approach control frequency is indicated for the TNP. DOWNE4 Arrival with LAX as the destination?

A—128.5 MHz
B—124.9 MHz
C—124.05 MHz

Figure 255A lists the approach frequency as 124.05 on the top left under SOCAL APP CON for the TNP. DOWNE4 Arrival. (PLT080, AA.VI.C.K1) — Chart Supplements U.S.

Answers (A) and (B) are incorrect because the Chart Supplements U.S. frequencies do not apply when using the TNP.DOWNE3 arrival.

Answers

8825 [B]	8826 [C]	8852 [C]	8852-1 [A]	9933 [A]	8799 [C]

ALL
8800. (Refer to Figure 257A.) At what point does the flight enter the final approach phase of the ILS RWY 25L at LAX?

A—FUELR INT.
B—HUNDA INT.
C—Intercept of glide slope.

The lightning bolt symbol indicates that 1,900 feet is the glide slope interception altitude. An aircraft is considered to be on the final approach segment past this point when on an ILS approach. (PLT083, AA.VI.C.K1) — Instrument Approach Procedure

Answer (A) is incorrect because FUELR INT is an initial approach fix (IAF) and does not mark the point at which the flight enters the final approach phase. Answer (B) is incorrect because HUNDA INT is a fix at which the pilot should intercept the glide slope, but the intersection itself does not mark the point at which the airplane enters the final approach phase.

ALL
8802. (Refer to Figure 257B.) The radio altimeter indication for the DH at the inner marker on the ILS RWY 24R approach at LAX is

A—120.
B—115.
C—126.

The RA height at the IM is also the DH for the 100-foot minimums. At this point, the radio altimeter will indicate 111 feet. (PLT083, AA.VI.C.K1) — Instrument Approach Procedure

Answer (A) is incorrect because 120 feet is the touchdown zone elevation (TDZE). Answer (C) is incorrect because 126 feet is the airport elevation.

ALL
8803. (Refer to Figure 257A.) If the glide slope indication is lost upon passing LIMMA INT on the ILS RWY 25L approach at LAX, what action should the pilot take?

A—Continue to the MAP, and execute the missed approach as indicated.
B—Continue the approach as an LOC, and add 100 feet to the DH.
C—Immediately start the missed approach left turn to CATLY INT.

Obstacle clearance on a missed approach is predicated on the assumption that the abort is initiated at the MAP and not lower than the DH or MDA. When an early missed approach is executed, pilots should, unless otherwise authorized by ATC, fly the instrument approach procedure to the MAP at or above the DH or MDA before executing any turning maneuver. (PLT083, AA.VI.C.K1) — AIM ¶5-5-5

Answer (B) is incorrect because the LOC minimums for this approach are 540 feet MDA and 24 RVR. Answer (C) is incorrect because protected obstacle clearance areas for missed approaches are made on the assumption that the abort is made at the MAP. No consideration is made for an abnormally early turn, unless otherwise directed by ATC.

ALL
8804. (Refer to Figure 257A and Legend 38.) What approach lights are available for the ILS RWY 25L approach at LAX?

A—ALSF-2 with sequenced flashing lights.
B—MALSR with a displayed threshold.
C—HIRL and TDZ/CL.

The airport diagram in Figure 257A has an "A" with a dot and in a circle next to Runway 25L. Legend 38 states the dot and "A" indicates sequenced flashing lights are installed with the approach lighting system (ALSF-2). A dot in a circle represents an approach lighting system. (PLT078, AA.VI.C.K1) — Chart Supplements U.S.

Answer (B) is incorrect because RWY 25R has an out of service (see Remarks) MALSR and a displaced threshold. Answer (C) is incorrect because high intensity runway lights (HIRL), touchdown zone lights (TDZ), and centerline lights (CL) are runway lighting systems.

ALL
8806. (Refer to Figures 256 and 257A.) How should the IFR flight plan be closed upon landing at LAX?

A—Contact UNICOM on 122.95.
B—Phone ASOS on 310-568-2486.
C—LAX tower will close it automatically.

If operating IFR to an airport with a functioning control tower, the flight plan is automatically closed upon landing. (PLT224, AA.VI.C.K1) — AIM ¶5-1-14

Answer (A) is incorrect because an IFR flight plan would not be closed by contacting UNICOM. Answer (B) is incorrect because an IFR flight plan would not be closed with ASOS by phone.

Answers

8800 [C] 8802 [B] 8803 [A] 8804 [A] 8806 [C]

ATM, ADX

8950. (Refer to Figure 145.) The minimums for the nonprecision approach at KAMA are 3/4-mile visibility and 400 feet. When operating under Part 121, can the pilot legally execute the approach with the given METAR data?

A—Yes, they meet the minimum visibility requirements.
B—No, they do not meet the minimum visibility requirements.
C—No, they do not meet the minimum ceiling requirements.

The pilot cannot legally execute the approach because the ceiling will be too low. Figure 145 indicates visibilities will be 3/4 SM with an overcast ceiling of 300 feet. (PLT059, AA.VI.C.K1) — FAA-H-8083-15

ALL

8836. (Refer to Figure 273.) Straight-in minimums for a Category B aircraft on the LOC RWL 25L approach are

A—1326-½.
B—1520-½.
C—1740-1.

The straight-in approach minimums for the LOC 25L approach are an MDA of 1,520 feet and visibility of 1/2 mile at the 0.2 DME from I-RJG. (PLT083, AA.VI.C.K1) — Instrument Approach Procedure

ATM, ATS

8704. (Refer to Figures 262 and 263.) In a turbojet airplane, when assigned the RIICE THREE ARRIVAL, at what speed would ATC expect you to cross RIICE intersection when landing EAST at IAH?

A—200 knots.
B—220 knots.
C—250 knots.

The chart notes "Turbojets: Landing east at IAH cross RIICE at 250 KIAS, expect clearance to cross RIICE at 10000." (PLT083, AA.VI.C.K1) — Instrument Approach Procedures

ATM, ATS

8704-1. (Refer to Figure 163A) Arriving at Ryan Field at 1600Z under visual meteorological conditions (VMC) in a turbine-powered airplane, at what altitude should you enter the traffic pattern and remain at that altitude until further descent is required for a safe landing?

A—1,000 feet AGL.
B—2,500 feet AGL.
C—1,500 feet AGL.

The chart supplement does not specify any changes from regular procedures. Large and turbine-powered aircraft enter the traffic pattern at an altitude of not less than 1,500 feet AGL or 500 feet above the established pattern altitude. (PLT083, AA.I.G.K2) — AIM ¶4-3-3

ATM, ADX

8242. Assuring that appropriate aeronautical charts are aboard an aircraft is the responsibility of the

A—aircraft dispatcher.
B—first officer.
C—pilot-in-command.

The pilot-in-command shall ensure that appropriate aeronautical charts containing adequate information concerning navigation aids and instrument approach procedures are aboard the aircraft for each flight. (PLT444, AA.VI.C.K1) — 14 CFR §121.549

Answer (A) is incorrect because the dispatcher may be hundreds of miles from the origination of the flight, e.g., in a central dispatch office. Answer (B) is incorrect because although a first officer may be assigned the task of carrying aeronautical charts, the pilot-in-command is responsible for ensuring that adequate charts are aboard the aircraft.

Answers

8950 [C]	8836 [B]	8704 [C]	8704-1 [C]	8242 [C]

Chapter 7
Emergencies, Hazards, and Flight Physiology

Flight Emergencies and Hazards

The Pilot/Controller Glossary divides emergencies into two categories: **distress** and **urgency**. Distress is a condition of being threatened by serious and/or imminent danger and of requiring immediate assistance. Distress conditions include fire, mechanical failure or structural damage. An urgency condition is one of being concerned about safety and of requiring timely but not immediate assistance. At least an urgency condition exists the moment a pilot becomes doubtful about position, fuel endurance, weather or any other condition that could adversely affect the safety of flight. A pilot should declare an emergency when either an urgency or a distress condition exists.

When a distress or urgency condition exists, the pilot should set the radar beacon transponder to code 7700. If an aircraft is being hijacked or illegally interfered with, the pilot can alert ATC to that fact by setting the transponder to code 7500. If an aircraft has experienced a two-way communications radio failure, the pilot should set the transponder to code 7600. The pilot should also conform to the radio failure procedures of 14 CFR §91.185 (IFR operations: Two-way radio communications failure). In order to avoid false alarms, pilots should take care not to inadvertently switch through codes 7500, 7600 and 7700 when changing the transponder.

If a two-way radio failure occurs in VFR conditions, or if VFR conditions are encountered after the failure, the pilot must continue the flight under VFR and land as soon as practicable. If IFR conditions prevail, the pilot must follow the rules listed below for route, altitude and time to leave a clearance limit:

Route to be Flown

- The route assigned in the last ATC clearance received.
- If being radar vectored, fly by the direct route from the point of the radio failure to the fix, route or airway specified in the vector clearance.
- In the absence of an assigned route, fly by the route that ATC has advised may be expected in a further clearance.
- In the absence of an assigned route or expected further routing, fly by the route filed in the flight plan.

Altitude

Fly the highest of the following altitudes or flight levels for the route segment being flown:

- The altitude or flight level assigned in the last ATC clearance received.
- The minimum IFR altitude for the route segment being flown (MEA).
- The altitude or flight level that ATC has advised may be expected in a further clearance.

When to Leave a Clearance Limit

- When the clearance limit is a fix from which an approach begins, commence descent or descent and approach as close as possible to the expect further clearance (EFC) time if one has been received; or if one has not been received, as close as possible to the estimated time of arrival (ETA) as calculated from the filed or amended estimated time en route.
- If the clearance limit is not a fix from which an approach begins, leave the clearance limit at the expect further clearance (EFC) time if one has been received; or if none has been received, upon arrival over the clearance limit, and proceed to a fix from which an approach begins and commence descent or descent and approach as close as possible to the estimated time of arrival (ETA) as calculated from the filed or amended time en route.

A near midair collision is defined as an occurrence in which the possibility of a collision existed as the result of two aircraft coming within 500 feet or less of each other.

A minimum fuel advisory is used by a pilot to inform ATC that the fuel supply has reached a state where the pilot cannot accept any undue delay upon arrival at the destination. The minimum fuel advisory is not a declaration of an emergency, nor is it a request for priority. It does indicate that an emergency situation may develop if any undue delay occurs during the rest of the flight.

Some airports have a number of wind indicators located around the perimeter of the field as well as a center field windsock. When there is a significant difference in speed or direction between the center field windsock and one or more of the boundary wind indicators, the tower can report that a wind shear condition exists.

A safety alert will be issued to pilots being controlled by ATC in either of two circumstances. A controller will issue a safety alert when, in the controller's opinion, the aircraft's altitude will put it in unsafe proximity to the surface or an obstacle. A controller will also issue an alert if he/she becomes aware of another aircraft, not controlled by him/her, that will put both aircraft in an unsafe proximity to each other.

The **wake turbulence** developed by large aircraft can present a significant flight hazard to other aircraft that encounter them. The main component of wake turbulence is **wing-tip vortices**. These are twin vortices of air trailing behind an aircraft in flight. The **vortex** is a by-product of lift. The pressure under each wing is greater than the pressure above it and this induces a flow of air outward, upward and around the wing tip. This leaves two counter-rotating spirals of air trailing behind the aircraft. See Figure 7-1.

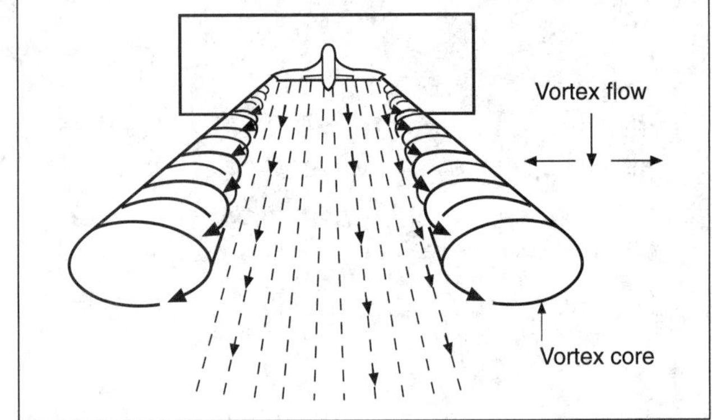

Figure 7-1

The characteristics of a vortex can be altered by changing the aircraft's configuration. The most intense vortices will be produced by an airplane that is heavy, flying slowly, and with the landing gear and flaps retracted.

The vortices generated by a large aircraft will slowly sink below its flight path and dissipate by the time they have descended about 1,000 feet. They will also tend to drift away from each other at a speed of about five knots. In a light crosswind, the upwind vortex will tend to stay over the same position on the ground while the downwind vortex will move away at about twice its normal rate. It is good wake turbulence avoidance technique to stay above and on the upwind side of the flight path of a preceding large airplane.

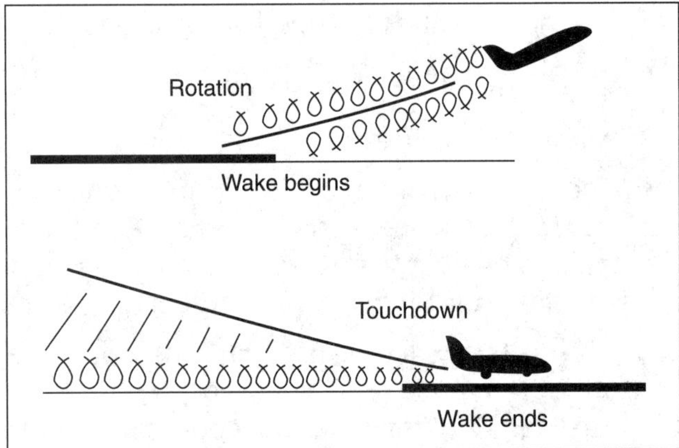

Figure 7-2

If the vortices reach the ground before dissipating, they will move away from each other as noted above. In a light crosswind, the upwind vortex can remain on the runway long after a large airplane has taken off or landed. The most hazardous situation is a light quartering tailwind, which not only keeps a vortex on the runway but also inhibits its dissipation.

If you plan to take off behind a large airplane, try to rotate prior to that airplane's point of rotation and climb out above and on the upwind side of the other airplane's flight path. If you plan to takeoff from a runway on which a large airplane has just landed, try to plan your lift-off point to be beyond the point where that aircraft touched down. See Figure 7-2.

ALL

9097. What minimum condition is suggested for declaring an emergency?

A—Anytime the pilot is doubtful of a condition that could adversely affect flight safety.
B—When fuel endurance or weather will require an en route or landing priority.
C—When distress conditions such as fire, mechanical failure, or structural damage occurs.

An aircraft is in an emergency condition the moment the pilot becomes doubtful about position, fuel endurance, weather or any other condition that could adversely affect flight safety. (PLT394, AA.VII.A.K2) — AIM ¶6-1-2

Answer (B) is incorrect because, if fuel endurance or weather will require an en route or landing priority, this is beyond an urgency situation and is now a distress condition. Answer (C) is incorrect because this is the step after an urgency condition, one that has the potential to become a distress condition.

ALL

9051. What is the hijack code?

A—7200.
B—7500.
C—7777.

Only nondiscrete transponder code 7500 will be decoded as the hijack code. (PLT497, AA.I.A.K9) — AIM ¶4-1-20

Answer (A) is incorrect because 7200 is a code that is used for normal operating procedures. Answer (C) is incorrect because code 7777 is reserved for military interceptor operations.

ALL

9052. Which range of codes should a pilot avoid switching through when changing transponder codes?

A—0000 through 1000.
B—7200 and 7500 series.
C—7500, 7600, and 7700 series.

When making routine transponder code changes, pilot should avoid inadvertent selection of codes 7500, 7600 or 7700 thereby causing momentary false alarms at automated ground facilities. (PLT497, AA.I.A.K9) — AIM ¶4-1-20

Answer (A) is incorrect because codes 0000 through 1000 are acceptable codes that may be used during normal operations. Answer (B) is incorrect because the 7200 series can be used during normal operations, while 7500 should be avoided except in the case of a hijack.

ALL

9362. After experiencing two-way radio communications failure en route, when should a pilot begin the descent for the instrument approach?

A—Upon arrival at any initial approach fix for the instrument approach procedure but not before the flight plan ETA as amended by ATC.
B—Upon arrival at the holding fix depicted on the instrument approach procedure at the corrected ETA, plus or minus 3 minutes.
C—At the primary initial approach fix for the instrument approach procedure at the ETA shown on the flight plan or the EFC time, whichever is later.

During a two-way radio communications failure, if the clearance limit is a fix from which an approach begins, commence descent or descent and approach as close as possible to the expect further clearance (EFC) time, if one has been received. If no EFC time has been received, commence descent and approach as close as possible to the estimated time of arrival as calculated from the filed or amended (with ATC) estimated time en route. (PLT391, AA.VI.C.K4) — 14 CFR §91.185

Answer (B) is incorrect because an approach should begin at the initial approach fix, not at a holding fix, as close as possible to the ETA. Answer (C) is incorrect because an EFC time supersedes a flight plan ETA and should be used if one has been received (no matter if the EFC is sooner or later than the flight plan ETA).

ALL

9363. If a pilot is being radar vectored in IFR conditions and loses radio communications with ATC, what action should be taken?

A—Fly directly to the next point shown on the IFR flight plan and continue the flight.
B—Squawk 7700 and climb to VFR on Top.
C—Fly direct to a fix, route, or airway specified in the vector clearance.

If a two-way radio communication failure occurs while in IFR conditions the pilot should continue the flight by the following route:

1. *By the route assigned in the last ATC clearance;*
2. *If being radar vectored, by the direct route from the point of the radio failure to the fix, route or airway specified in the vector clearance;*
3. *In the absence of an assigned route, by the route that ATC has advised may be expected in a further clearance; or*

Answers

9097 [A]	9051 [B]	9052 [C]	9362 [A]	9363 [C]

4. *In the absence of an assigned route or a route that ATC has advised may be expected in a further clearance, by the route filed in the flight plan.*

(PLT406, AA.VI.C.K4) — 14 CFR §91.185

Answer (A) is incorrect because the route shown on the flight plan should be the last route to be used and only if an assigned route, vector, or expected route has not been received. Answer (B) is incorrect because a climb should only be initiated in order to establish the highest of either the assigned, MEA, or expected altitude. The squawk of 7700 is no longer correct.

ALL

9364. A pilot is flying in IFR weather conditions and has two-way radio communications failure. What altitude should be used?

A—Last assigned altitude, altitude ATC has advised to expect, or the MEA, whichever is highest.
B—An altitude that is at least 1,000 feet above the highest obstacle along the route.
C—A VFR altitude that is above the MEA for each leg.

A pilot should maintain the highest altitude or flight level of the following for each route segment:

1. *The altitude or flight level assigned in the last ATC clearance received;*
2. *The minimum altitude or flight level for IFR operations (MEA); or*
3. *The altitude that ATC has advised may be expected in a further clearance.*

(PLT391, AA.VI.C.K4) — 14 CFR §91.185

Answer (B) is incorrect because 1,000 feet above the highest obstacle along the route is what a MOCA, (minimum obstruction clearance altitude) provides. Answer (C) is incorrect because VFR altitudes or regulations should never be used while flying in IFR weather conditions.

ALL

9365. A pilot is holding at an initial approach fix after having experienced two-way radio communications failure. When should that pilot begin descent for the instrument approach?

A—At the EFC time, if this is within plus or minus 3 minutes of the flight plan ETA as amended by ATC.
B—At flight plan ETA as amended by ATC.
C—At the EFC time as amended by ATC.

During a two-way radio communications failure, if the clearance limit is a fix from which an approach begins, commence descent or descent and approach as close as possible to the expect further clearance (EFC) time, if one has been received. If no EFC time has been received, commence descent and approach as close as possible to the estimated time of arrival as calculated from the filed or amended (with ATC) estimated time enroute. (PLT391, AA.VI.C.K4) — 14 CFR §91.185

Answer (A) is incorrect because the approach should begin at the EFC time, regardless of whether it is close to the planned ETA or not; ETA is only used if an EFC has not been received. Answer (B) is incorrect because a pilot who is holding at an initial approach fix after having experienced a two-way radio communication failure without an EFC time should begin descent for the instrument approach so that the arrival will coincide as closely as possible with the ETA.

ALL

9389. What altitude and route should be used if the pilot is flying in IFR weather conditions and has two-way radio communications failure?

A—Continue on the route specified in the clearance and fly the highest of the following: the last assigned altitude, altitude ATC has informed the pilot to expect, or to the MEA.
B—Descend to MEA and, if clear of clouds, proceed to the nearest appropriate airport. If not clear of clouds, maintain the highest of the MEAs along the clearance route.
C—Fly the most direct route to the destination, maintaining the last assigned altitude or MEA, whichever is higher.

If a two-way radio communication failure occurs while in IFR conditions the pilot should continue the flight by the following route:

1. *By the route assigned in the last ATC clearance;*
2. *If being radar vectored, by the direct route from the point of the radio failure to the fix, route or airway specified in the vector clearance;*
3. *In the absence of an assigned route, by the route that ATC has advised may be expected in a further clearance; or*
4. *In the absence of an assigned route or a route that ATC has advised may be expected in a further clearance, by the route filed in the flight plan.*

A pilot should maintain the highest altitude or flight level of the following for each route segment:

1. *The altitude or flight level assigned in the last ATC clearance received;*

Answers

9364 [A]	9365 [C]	9389 [A]

2. *The minimum altitude or flight level for IFR operations (MEA); or*
3. *The altitude that ATC has advised may be expected in a further clearance.*

(PLT391, AA.VI.C.K4) — 14 CFR §91.185

Answer (B) is incorrect because the highest of either the MEA, expected altitude, or assigned altitude should be used. Answer (C) is incorrect because, if ATC advises you may expect an altitude after reaching a clearance limit, and it is higher than the published MEA or assigned altitude, the expected altitude should be used. The route to be used should be the one assigned by ATC, as specified in a vector clearance, by the route ATC has advised may be expected, or in the absence of all of these, the route as filed in the flight plan, not the most direct route.

ALL

9390. While in IFR conditions, a pilot experiences two-way radio communications failure. Which route should be flown in the absence of an ATC assigned route or a route ATC has advised to expect in a further clearance?

A—The most direct route to the filed alternate airport.
B—An off-airway route to the point of departure.
C—The route filed in the flight plan.

If a two-way radio communication failure occurs while in IFR conditions the pilot should continue the flight by the following route:

1. *By the route assigned in the last ATC clearance;*
2. *If being radar vectored, by the direct route from the point of the radio failure to the fix, route or airway specified in the vector clearance;*
3. *In the absence of an assigned route, by the route that ATC has advised may be expected in a further clearance; or*
4. *In the absence of an assigned route or a route that ATC has advised may be expected in a further clearance, by the route filed in the flight plan.*

(PLT391, AA.VI.C.K4) — 14 CFR §91.185

ALL

9098. It is the responsibility of the pilot and crew to report a near midair collision as a result of proximity of at least

A—50 feet or less to another aircraft.
B—500 feet or less to another aircraft.
C—1,000 feet or less to another aircraft.

A near midair collision is defined as an incident associated with the operation on an aircraft in which a possibility of collision occurs as a result of proximity of less than 500 feet to another aircraft, or a report is received from a pilot or flight crewmember stating that a collision hazard existed between two or more aircraft. (PLT366, AA.I.E.K4) — AIM ¶7-7-3

ALL

9010. Under what condition should a pilot on IFR advise ATC of minimum fuel status?

A—When the fuel supply becomes less than that required for IFR.
B—If the remaining fuel suggests a need for traffic or landing priority.
C—If the remaining fuel precludes any undue delay.

A pilot should advise ATC of his/her minimum fuel status when the fuel supply has reached a state where, upon reaching destination, he/she cannot accept any undue delay. It indicates a possible future emergency, but does not declare one and does not get priority handling. (PLT318, AA.VI.J.K2) — AIM ¶5-5-15

Answer (A) is incorrect because a pilot must ensure the minimum amount of fuel is on board the airplane for the planned IFR flight and alternatives, if needed, during the flight planning phase. Answer (B) is incorrect because, if the remaining fuel suggests a need for traffic or landing priority, the pilot should declare an emergency (not minimum fuel status), and report fuel remaining in minutes.

ALL

9011. What does the term "minimum fuel" imply to ATC?

A—Traffic priority is needed to the destination airport.
B—Emergency handling is required to the nearest suitable airport.
C—Advisory that indicates an emergency situation is possible should an undue delay occur.

A pilot should advise ATC of his/her minimum fuel status when the fuel supply has reached a state where, upon reaching destination, he/she cannot accept any undue delay. It indicates a possible future emergency, but does not declare one and does not get priority handling. (PLT318, AA.VI.J.K2) — AIM ¶5-5-15

Answer (A) is incorrect because a pilot should declare an emergency and report fuel remaining in minutes if traffic priority is needed to the destination airport. Answer (B) is incorrect because emergency handling to the nearest suitable airport would be required in a distress or urgent type of emergency.

Answers

9390 [C] 9098 [B] 9010 [C] 9011 [C]

ALL

9420. You should advise ATC of minimum fuel status when your fuel supply has reached a state where, upon reaching your destination, you cannot accept any undue delay.

A—This will ensure your priority handling by ATC.
B—ATC will consider this action as if you had declared an emergency.
C—If your remaining usable fuel supply suggests the need for traffic priority to ensure a safe landing, declare an emergency due to low fuel and report fuel remaining in minutes.

If the remaining usable fuel supply suggests the need for traffic priority to ensure a safe landing, you should declare an emergency due to low fuel and report fuel remaining in minutes. (PLT318, AA.VI.J.K2) —AIM ¶5-5-15

Answer (A) is incorrect because minimum fuel advisory does not imply a need for a traffic priority. Answer (B) is incorrect because minimum fuel advisory is not an emergency situation, but merely an advisory that indicates an emergency situation is possible should any undue delay occur.

ALL

9054. What airport condition is reported by the tower when more than one wind condition at different positions on the airport is reported?

A—Light and variable.
B—Wind shear.
C—Frontal passage.

The Low-Level Wind Shear Alert System (LLWAS) is a computerized system which detects low level wind shear by continuously comparing the winds measured by sensors installed around the periphery of an airport with the wind measured at the center field location. When a significant difference exists, the tower controller will provide aircraft with an advisory of the situation which includes the center field wind plus the remote site location and wind. (PLT518, AA.I.C.K3b) — AIM ¶4-3-7

Answer (A) is incorrect because "light and variable" is used to report the wind conditions when wind speed is less than 5 knots. Answer (C) is incorrect because a frontal passage is normally indicated by a change in wind direction, but it is usually not reported by the tower.

ALL

9050. What conditions would cause an air traffic controller to issue you a safety alert?

A—When your approach has become unstable, and you are required to execute a go-around.
B—When the aircraft altitude places it in unsafe proximity to terrain, obstructions, or other aircraft.
C—When they have implemented a temporary reduction in approach control separation minimums.

A safety alert will be issued to pilots of aircraft being controlled by ATC if the controller is aware the aircraft is at an altitude which, in the controller's judgment, places the aircraft in unsafe proximity to terrain, obstructions or other aircraft. (PLT172, AA.VI.J.K2) — AIM ¶4-1-16

Answer (A) is incorrect because a safety alert is issued to a pilot if ATC believes that his/her airplane is at an altitude which would place it in unsafe proximity to another airplane. Answer (C) is incorrect because, when weather conditions are extreme and wind shear or large hail is in the vicinity, a Convective SIGMET would be broadcast.

ALL

9119. Which flight conditions of a large jet airplane create the most severe flight hazard by generating wingtip vortices of the greatest strength?

A—Heavy, slow, gear and flaps up.
B—Heavy, slow, gear and flaps down.
C—Heavy, fast, gear and flaps down.

The greatest vortex strength occurs when the generating aircraft is heavy, clean (gear and flaps up) and slow. (PLT509, AA.VI.A.K1) — AIM ¶7-4-3

Answers

9420 [C]	9054 [B]	9050 [B]	9119 [A]

ALL

9120. Hazardous vortex turbulence that might be encountered behind large aircraft is created only when that aircraft is

A—developing lift.
B—operating at high airspeeds.
C—using high power settings.

Lift is generated by the creation of a pressure differential over the wing surface. The lowest pressure occurs over the upper wing surface and the highest pressure under the wing. This pressure differential triggers the roll up of the airflow aft of the wing resulting in swirling air masses trailing downstream of the wing tips. (PLT509, AA.VI.A.K1) — AIM ¶7-4-2

Answer (B) is incorrect because hazardous vortex turbulence is created only when the aircraft is developing lift, which can be while operating at low or high airspeeds. A slow, heavy, and clean airplane will generate the most hazardous vortex turbulence. Answer (C) is incorrect because most takeoff rolls are at high power settings, but the generation of vortices does not occur until lift is produced. Landing approaches are also conducted at lower power settings; vortex turbulence is produced whenever an airplane is producing lift.

ALL

9121. Wingtip vortices created by large aircraft tend to

A—sink below the aircraft generating the turbulence.
B—rise from the surface to traffic pattern altitude.
C—accumulate and remain for a period of time at the point where the takeoff roll began.

Flight tests have shown that the vortices from large aircraft sink at a rate of several hundred feet per minute. They tend to level off at a distance about 900 feet below the flight path of the generating aircraft. (PLT509, AA.VI.A.K1) — AIM ¶7-4-4

Answer (B) is incorrect because vortices created by large aircraft tend to sink from (not rise into) the traffic pattern altitude. Answer (C) is incorrect because wing-tip vortices are not generated until the aircraft's wings develop lift, so no wing-tip vortices are generated at the point where the takeoff roll begins.

ALL

9122. How does the wake turbulence vortex circulate around each wingtip?

A—Inward, upward, and around the wingtip.
B—Counterclockwise when viewed from behind the aircraft.
C—Outward, upward, and around the wingtip.

The vortex circulation is outward, upward and around the wing tips when viewed from either ahead or behind the aircraft. (PLT509, AA.VI.A.K1) — AIM ¶7-4-4

ALL

9123. Which statement is true concerning the wake turbulence produced by a large transport aircraft?

A—Vortices can be avoided by flying 300 feet below and behind the flightpath of the generating aircraft.
B—The vortex characteristics of any given aircraft may be altered by extending the flaps or changing the speed.
C—Wake turbulence behind a propeller-driven aircraft is negligible because jet engine thrust is a necessary factor in the formation of vortices.

The strength of the vortex is governed by the weight, speed and shape of the wing of the generating aircraft. The vortex characteristics of a given aircraft can be changed by extension of flaps or other wing configuring devices as well as by a change in speed. (PLT509, AA.VI.A.K1) — AIM ¶7-4-3

Answer (A) is incorrect because the vortices generated by large transport aircraft tend to sink below and behind, thus vortices can be expected by flying 300 feet below and behind the flight path of the generating aircraft. Answer (C) is incorrect because wake turbulence vortices are generated by lift produced by any airplane. It does not matter whether the airplane is powered by propeller or jet engines.

ALL

9124. What effect would a light crosswind have on the wingtip vortices generated by a large airplane that has just taken off?

A—The upwind vortex will tend to remain on the runway longer than the downwind vortex.
B—A crosswind will rapidly dissipate the strength of both vortices.
C—The downwind vortex will tend to remain on the runway longer than the upwind vortex.

A crosswind will decrease the lateral movement of the upwind vortex and increase the movement of the downwind vortex. Thus, a light wind of 3 to 7 knots could result in the upwind vortex remaining in the touchdown zone for a period of time and hasten the drift of the downwind vortex toward another runway. (PLT509, AA.VI.A.K1) — AIM ¶7-4-4

Answer (B) is incorrect because a crosswind will hold the upwind vortex in the vicinity of the runway. Answer (C) is incorrect because the downwind vortex moves away at a faster rate than the upwind vortex.

Answers

9120 [A] 9121 [A] 9122 [C] 9123 [B] 9124 [A]

ALL

9125. To avoid the wingtip vortices of a departing jet airplane during takeoff, the pilot should

A—lift off at a point well past the jet airplane's flightpath.
B—climb above and stay upwind of the jet airplane's flightpath.
C—remain below the flightpath of the jet airplane.

When departing behind a large aircraft, note its rotation point and rotate prior to that point. During the climb, stay above and upwind of the large aircraft's climb path until turning clear of its wake. (PLT509, AA.VI.A.R2) — AIM ¶7-4-4

Answer (A) is incorrect because, if you rotate beyond the jet's rotation point, you will have to fly up into the jet's vortices. Answer (C) is incorrect because the jet's vortices will sink. If you stay below the jet's flight path, you will fly in the area of the vortices.

ALL

9126. What wind condition prolongs the hazards of wake turbulence on a landing runway for the longest period of time?

A—Direct tailwind.
B—Light quartering tailwind.
C—Light quartering headwind.

A crosswind will decrease the lateral movement of the upwind vortex and increase the movement of the downwind vortex. Thus a light wind of 3 to 7 knots could result in the upwind vortex remaining in the touchdown zone for a period of time and hasten the drift of the downwind vortex toward another runway. Similarly, a tailwind condition can move the vortices of the preceding aircraft forward into the touchdown zone. The light, quartering tailwind requires maximum caution. (PLT509, AA.VI.A.R2) — AIM ¶7-4-4

Answer (A) is incorrect because, even though a direct tailwind can move the vortices of a preceding aircraft forward into the touchdown zone, it is not as hazardous because both vortices would move to the sides (and not remain on the runway). Answer (C) is incorrect because a light quartering headwind would move the vortices toward the runway threshold, away from (not into) the touchdown zone on a landing runway.

ALL

9127. If you take off behind a heavy jet that has just landed, you should plan to lift off

A—prior to the point where the jet touched down.
B—beyond the point where the jet touched down.
C—at the point where the jet touched down and on the upwind edge of the runway.

When departing behind a large aircraft which has just landed, note the aircraft's touchdown point and rotate past that point on the runway. (PLT509, AA.VI.A.R2) — AIM ¶7-4-6

Answer (A) is incorrect because a lift-off prior to the point where the jet touched down would force you to climb through the jet's vortices. Answer (C) is incorrect because lift-off should be planned beyond the point of touchdown to ensure that you avoid the vortices, and you should remain on the center of the runway during takeoff.

ALL

9715. To allow pilots of in-trail lighter aircraft to make flight path adjustments to avoid wake turbulence, pilots of heavy and large jet aircraft should fly

A—below the established glidepath and slightly to either side of the on-course centerline.
B—on the established glidepath and on the approach course centerline or runway centerline extended.
C—above the established glidepath and slightly downwind of the on-course centerline.

Pilots of aircraft that produce strong wake vortices should make every attempt to fly on the established glidepath, and as closely as possible to the approach course centerline or to the extended centerline of the runway of intended landing. (PLT509, AA.VI.A.R2) — AIM ¶7-4-8

ALL

9858. Which phase of flight has the greatest occurrence of fatal accidents?

A—Takeoff.
B—Landing.
C—Approach.

The pilot's work requirements vary depending on the mode of flight. The tasks increase significantly during the landing phase, creating greater risk to the pilot and warranting actions that require greater precision and attention, but the greatest percentage of fatal accidents occurs during the approach phase of flight. (PLT509, AA.VI.F.R9) — FAA-H-8083-2

Answers

9125 [B]	9126 [B]	9127 [B]	9715 [B]	9858 [C]

Flight Physiology

Even small amounts of alcohol have an adverse effect on reaction and judgment. This effect is magnified as altitude increases. No one may serve as a crewmember on a civil aircraft:

- Within 8 hours of the consumption of any alcoholic beverage.
- While having a blood alcohol level of .04% or higher.

Runway width illusion—A runway that is narrower than usual can create the illusion that the aircraft is higher than it really is. This can cause an unwary pilot to descend too low on approach. A wide runway creates an illusion of being too low on glide slope.

Featureless terrain illusion—An absence of ground feature, as when landing over water, darkened areas and terrain made featureless by snow can create the illusion that the aircraft is higher than it really is.

Autokinesis—In the dark, a static light will appear to move about when stared at for a period of time.

An effective scan pattern is necessary to ensure that a pilot will see other aircraft in time to avoid potential midair collisions. This means that 2/3 to 3/4 of a pilot's time should be spent scanning outside the aircraft. The best method would be to look outside for about 15 seconds and then inside for about 5 seconds. It is much easier to see an aircraft which is moving relative to the observer. Unfortunately, aircraft which present a collision hazard are usually on the horizon with little or no apparent horizontal or vertical movement. The image only grows larger as the threat aircraft gets closer. Special vigilance must be exercised for this type of situation. A pilot's most acute night vision is off-center in his/her peripheral vision. When looking for other aircraft at night, scan slowly to allow sufficient time for this off-center viewing.

All pilots who fly in instrument conditions or at night are subject to spatial disorientation. This occurs when body sensations are used to interpret flight attitudes, and there is no visual reference to the horizon. The only reliable way to overcome this disorientation is to rely entirely on the indications of the flight instruments. Some types of vertigo include:

The leans—An abrupt correction of a banked angle can create the illusion of banking in the opposite direction.

Coriolis illusion—An abrupt head movement during a constant rate turn can create the illusion of rotation in an entirely different axis. This illusion can be overwhelming and so rapid head movements in turns should be avoided.

Inversion illusion—An abrupt change from a climb to straight and level flight can create the illusion of tumbling backwards.

Somatogravic illusion—A rapid acceleration during takeoff can create the illusion of being in a nose up attitude.

Hypoxia is caused by insufficient oxygen reaching the brain. The most usual reason is the low partial pressure of oxygen encountered at altitude. Carbon monoxide poisoning is similar to hypoxia in that it causes too little oxygen to reach the brain. Carbon monoxide (usually from an exhaust leak) binds with the hemoglobin in the blood, preventing its usual oxygen-carrying function. The symptoms of both are similar and include dizziness, tingling of the hands, feet and legs, loss of higher thought processes, and unconsciousness. The sufferer may not notice or react to any of the symptoms due to his degraded mental faculties. Hyperventilation is caused by a reduction of carbon dioxide in the blood, usually due to rapid breathing in a stressful situation. The symptoms of hyperventilation are similar to hypoxia, but recovery is rapid once the rate of breathing is brought under control.

ALL

9354. Under 14 CFR Part 91, what are the minimum number of hours that must pass after a person consumes alcohol before they may act as a crewmember?

A—8.
B—10.
C—12.

No person may act or attempt to act as a crewmember of a civil aircraft within 8 hours after the consumption of any alcoholic beverage. (PLT463, AA.I.F.K2) — 14 CFR §91.17

ALL

9354-1. A pilot should be aware the alcohol in one beer can be detected for as long as

A—minimum of 60 minutes.
B—2 hours.
C—3 hours.

As little as one ounce of liquor, one bottle of beer or four ounces of wine can impair flying skills, with the alcohol consumed in these drinks being detectable in the breath and blood for at least 3 hours. (PLT104, AA.I.F.K2) — AIM ¶8-1-1

ALL

9111. What is the effect of alcohol consumption on functions of the body?

A—Alcohol has an adverse effect, especially as altitude increases.
B—Small amounts of alcohol in the human system increase judgment and decision-making abilities.
C—Alcohol has little effect if followed by an ounce of black coffee for every ounce of alcohol.

The adverse effect of alcohol is greatly multiplied when a person is exposed to altitude. Two drinks on the ground are equivalent to three or four at altitude. (PLT205, AA.I.F.K2) — AIM ¶8-1-1

Answer (B) is incorrect because even small amounts of alcohol impair judgment and decision-making abilities. Answer (C) is incorrect because there is no way to increase the body's metabolism of alcohol or to alleviate a hangover (including drinking black coffee).

ALL

9111-1. Pilot performance can be seriously degraded by

A—prescribed and over-the-counter medications.
B—prescription medications only.
C—over-the-counter medications only.

Pilot performance can be seriously degraded by both prescribed and over-the-counter medications, as well as by the medical conditions for which they are taken. Many medications have primary effects that may impair judgment, memory, alertness, coordination, vision, and the ability to make calculations. Others have side effects that may impair the same critical functions. Any medication that depresses the nervous system, such as a sedative, tranquilizer or antihistamine, can make a pilot much more susceptible to hypoxia. Pilots are prohibited from performing crewmember duties while using any medication that affects the faculties in any way contrary to safety. (PLT354, AA.I.F.K2) — AIM ¶8-1-1

ALL

9111-2. While experiencing a hangover, a pilot

A—will have impaired motor and mental responses.
B—is no longer under the influence of alcohol.
C—may experience discomfort, but no impairment.

While experiencing a hangover, a pilot is still under the influence of alcohol. Although a pilot may think he or she is functioning normally, motor and mental response impairment is still present. Alcohol can remain in the body for over 16 hours, so pilots should be cautious about flying too soon after drinking. (PLT205, AA.I.F.K2) — AIM ¶8-1-1

ALL

9111-3. Consumption of alcohol

A—can severely impair a person for more than 8 hours.
B—is of no concern in aviation after 8 hours regardless of amount consumed.
C—in small amounts has no effect on judgment and decision-making.

The CFRs prohibit pilots from performing crewmember duties within 8 hours after drinking any alcoholic beverages or while under the influence of alcohol. However, due to the slow metabolism of alcohol, a pilot may still be under the influence 8 hours after a moderate amount of alcohol. Therefore, allow at least 12 to 24 hours between "bottle and throttle" depending on the amount of alcoholic beverage consumed. (PLT205, AA.I.F.K2) — AIM ¶8-1-1

Answers

9354 [A] 9354-1 [C] 9111 [A] 9111-1 [A] 9111-2 [A] 9111-3 [A]

ALL

9107. When making an approach to a narrower-than-usual runway, without VASI assistance, the pilot should be aware that the approach

A—altitude may be higher than it appears.
B—altitude may be lower than it appears.
C—may result in leveling off too high and landing hard.

An approach to a narrower-than-usual runway can create the illusion that the aircraft is higher than it actually is. (PLT280, AA.I.F.K1k) — AIM ¶8-1-5

Answer (A) is incorrect because wider-than-usual runways may result in higher than desired approaches. Answer (C) is incorrect because leveling off too high is not affected by the runway width, but rather by the pilot's landing proficiency.

ALL

9107-1. You have just touched down hard in the rain on a narrower-than-usual runway at night. You realize you have just experienced

A—runway length illusion.
B—an atmospheric height illusion.
C—ground lighting illusion.

An approach to a narrower-than-usual runway can create the illusion that the aircraft is higher than it actually is. (PLT280, AA.I.F.K1k) — AIM ¶8-1-5

ALL

9107-2. The illusion associated with landing on a narrower than usual runway may result in the pilot flying a

A—lower approach with the risk of striking objects along the approach path or landing short.
B—slower approach with the risk of reducing airspeed below V_{SO} or landing hard.
C—higher approach with the risk of leveling out high and landing hard or overshooting the runway.

An approach to a narrower-than-usual runway can create the illusion that the aircraft is higher than it actually is. (PLT280, AA.I.F.K1k) — AIM ¶8-1-5

ALL

9109. In the dark, a stationary light will appear to move when stared at for a period of time. This illusion is known as

A—somatogravic illusion.
B—ground lighting illusion.
C—autokinesis.

In the dark, a stationary light will appear to move about when stared at for many seconds. This illusion is known as Autokinesis. (PLT280, AA.I.F.K1k) — AIM ¶8-1-5

Answer (A) is incorrect because somatogravic illusion occurs with a rapid acceleration during takeoff, creating the illusion of being in a nose-up attitude. Answer (B) is incorrect because a ground lighting illusion refers to lights on a straight path such as a road being mistaken by a pilot for runway or approach lights.

ALL

9110. When making a landing over darkened or featureless terrain such as water or snow, a pilot should be aware of the possibility of illusion. The approach may appear to be too

A—high.
B—low.
C—shallow.

An absence of ground features, when landing over water, darkened areas and terrain made featureless by snow, can create the illusion that the aircraft is at a higher altitude than it actually is. (PLT280, AA.I.F.K1k) — AIM ¶8-1-5

ALL

9110-1. You have just touched down on the runway faster than planned in the haze at night. You realize that you have just experienced

A—an atmospheric distance illusion.
B—a gravotopic height illusion.
C—the elevator illusion.

An absence of ground features, when landing over water, darkened areas and terrain made featureless by snow, can create the illusion that the aircraft is at a higher altitude than it actually is. (PLT280, AA.I.F.K1k) — AIM ¶8-1-5

ALL

9108. The illusion of being in a noseup attitude which may occur during a rapid acceleration takeoff is known as

A—inversion illusion.
B—autokinesis.
C—somatogravic illusion.

A rapid acceleration during takeoff can create the illusion of being in a nose-up attitude. This is known as a Somatogravic Illusion. (PLT280, AA.I.F.K1k) — AIM ¶8-1-5

Answer (A) is incorrect because the inversion illusion results from an abrupt change from climb to straight-and-level flight which can create an illusion of tumbling backwards. Answer (B) is incorrect because autokinesis refers to a stationary light appearing to move about when stared at for many seconds in the dark.

Answers

9107 [B] 9107-1 [B] 9107-2 [A] 9109 [C] 9110 [A] 9110-1 [A]
9108 [C]

ALL
9114. What is the most effective way to use the eyes during night flight?

A—Look only at far away, dim lights.
B—Scan slowly to permit offcenter viewing.
C—Concentrate directly on each object for a few seconds.

One should scan slowly at night to permit off-center viewing of dim objects. (PLT099, AA.I.F.K1k) — FAA-H-8083-3

Answer (A) is incorrect because pilots must look at their gauges and instruments, which are about 2 feet in front of them. Answer (C) is incorrect because peripheral (off-center) vision is more effective at night.

ALL
9114-1. When is ear blockage most likely to occur?

A—Upon descent and is aggravated by upper respiratory infection.
B—During initial climb-out as expanding air in the middle ear pushes the eustachian tube open.
C—During cruise flight as the pressure between the middle ear and aircraft cabin equalizes.

As the aircraft cabin pressure decreases during ascent, the expanding air in the middle ear pushes the eustachian tube open, and by escaping down into the nasal passages, equalizes in pressure with the cabin pressure. But during descent, a pilot must periodically open the eustachian tube to equalize pressure. This can be accomplished by swallowing, yawning, or tensing muscles in the throat. Either an upper respiratory infection or a nasal allergic condition can produce enough congestion around the eustachian tube to make equalization difficult. Consequently, the difference in pressure between the middle ear and aircraft cabin can build up to a level that will hold the eustachian tube closed, making equalization difficult if not impossible to open. The problem is commonly referred to as ear block. (PLT099, AA.I.F.K1c) — AIM ¶8-1-2

ALL
9116. Which observed target aircraft would be of most concern with respect to collision avoidance?

A—One which appears to be ahead and moving from left to right at high speed.
B—One which appears to be ahead and moving from right to left at slow speed.
C—One which appears to be ahead with no lateral or vertical movement and is increasing in size.

Any aircraft that appears to have no relative motion and stays in one scan quadrant is likely to be on a collision course. If a target shows no lateral or vertical motion, but increases in size, take evasive action. (PLT099, AA.I.F.K1k) — AIM ¶8-1-8

Answers (A) and (B) are incorrect because an airplane which is ahead of you and moving from left to right, or from right to left, should pass in front of you.

ALL
9117. Scanning procedures for effective collision avoidance should constitute

A—looking outside for 15 seconds, then inside for 5 seconds, then repeat.
B—1 minute inside scanning, then 1 minute outside scanning, then repeat.
C—looking outside every 30 seconds except in radar contact when outside scanning is unnecessary.

Studies show that the time a pilot spends on visual tasks inside the cabin should represent no more than 1/4 to 1/3 of the scan time outside, or no more than 4 to 5 seconds on the instrument panel for every 16 seconds outside. (PLT099, AA.I.F.K1k) — AIM ¶8-1-6

Answer (B) is incorrect because pilots should spend the majority of scan time outside the airplane when in VFR conditions. Answer (C) is incorrect because pilots should spend the majority of scan time outside the airplane, and outside scanning is necessary when in radar contact in VFR conditions.

ALL
9118. When using the Earth's horizon as a reference point to determine the relative position of other aircraft, most concern would be for aircraft

A—above the horizon and increasing in size.
B—on the horizon with little relative movement.
C—on the horizon and increasing in size.

Any aircraft that appears to have no relative motion and stays in one scan quadrant is likely to be on a collision course. If a target shows no lateral or vertical motion, but increases in size, take evasive action. (PLT099, AA.I.F.K1k) — AIM ¶8-1-8

Answer (A) is incorrect because an airplane above the horizon is probably at a higher altitude. Answer (B) is incorrect because an airplane on the horizon without movement may be traveling in the same direction as you.

Answers

9114 [B]	9114-1 [A]	9116 [C]	9117 [A]	9118 [C]

ALL

9112. A pilot is more subject to spatial disorientation when

A—ignoring or overcoming the sensations of muscles and inner ear.
B—eyes are moved often in the process of cross-checking the flight instruments.
C—body sensations are used to interpret flight attitudes.

When seated on an unstable moving platform at altitude with your vision cut off from the earth, horizon or other fixed reference, you are susceptible to misinterpreting certain body sensations caused by angular accelerations. (PLT334, AA.I.F.K1d) — AIM ¶8-1-5

Answer (A) is incorrect because ignoring or overcoming the sensations of muscles and inner ear is a means of avoiding (not becoming subject to) spatial disorientation. Answer (B) is incorrect because rapid eye movements have little or no impact on spatial disorientation and vision reference to reliable flight instruments helps avoid spatial disorientation.

ALL

9113. Which procedure is recommended to prevent or overcome spatial disorientation?

A—Reduce head and eye movement to the greatest possible extent.
B—Rely on the kinesthetic sense.
C—Rely entirely on the indications of the flight instruments.

The best method to prevent or overcome spatial disorientation is to rely entirely on the indications of the flight instruments. (PLT334, AA.I.F.K1d) — AIM ¶8-1-5

Answer (A) is incorrect because head and eye movement have little effect on spatial disorientation. Answer (B) is incorrect because relying on the kinesthetic sense encourages (not prevents) spatial disorientation.

ALL

9115. While making prolonged constant rate turns under IFR conditions, an abrupt head movement can create the illusion of rotation on an entirely different axis. This is known as

A—autokinesis.
B—Coriolis illusion.
C—the leans.

An abrupt head movement while making a prolonged constant rate turn, can produce a strong sensation of rotation or movement in an entirely different axis. The phenomenon is known as Coriolis Illusion. (PLT280, AA.I.F.K1k) — AIM ¶8-1-5

Answer (A) is incorrect because Autokinesis refers to a stationary light appearing to move about when stared at for many seconds in the dark. Answer (C) is incorrect because the "leans" refer to an abrupt correction of a banked attitude which can create the illusion of bank in the opposite direction.

ALL

9433. Haze can give the illusion that the aircraft is

A—closer to the runway than it actually is.
B—farther from the runway than it actually is.
C—the same distance from the runway as when there is no restriction to visibility.

Atmospheric haze can create an illusion of being at a greater distance from the runway than you actually are. (PLT280, AA.I.F.K1k) — AIM ¶8-1-5

ALL

9434. Sudden penetration of fog can create the illusion of

A—pitching up.
B—pitching down.
C—leveling off.

Penetration of fog can create an illusion of pitching up. (PLT280, AA.I.F.K1k) — AIM ¶8-1-5

ALL

9434-1. Penetrating fog while flying an approach at night, you might experience the illusion of

A—pitching up.
B—flying at a lower altitude.
C—constant turning.

Penetration of fog can create an illusion of pitching up. (PLT280, AA.I.F.K1k) — AIM ¶8-1-5

Answers

9112 [C]	9113 [C]	9115 [B]	9433 [B]	9434 [A]	9434-1 [A]

ALL
9435. What illusion, if any, can rain on the windscreen create?

A—Does not cause illusions.
B—Lower than actual.
C—Higher than actual.

Rain on the windscreen can create an illusion of being at a higher altitude than you are. (PLT280, AA.I.F.K1k) — AIM ¶8-1-5

ALL
9101. What is a symptom of carbon monoxide poisoning?

A—Rapid, shallow breathing.
B—Pain and cramping of the hands and feet.
C—Dizziness.

Carbon monoxide poisoning produces the same symptoms as hypoxia, which include dizziness. (PLT097, AA.I.F.K1f) — AIM ¶8-1-4

Answer (A) is incorrect because rapid breathing can result in hyperventilation, but it is not a symptom of carbon monoxide poisoning. Answer (B) is incorrect because tingling in the extremities (not pain and cramping) is one symptom of hyperventilation (not carbon monoxide poisoning).

ALL
9102. Which would most likely result in hyperventilation?

A—A stressful situation causing anxiety.
B—The excessive consumption of alcohol.
C—An extremely slow rate of breathing and insufficient oxygen.

You are most likely to hyperventilate when under stress or at high altitudes. (PLT332, AA.I.F.K1b) — AIM ¶8-1-3

Answer (B) is incorrect because excessive consumption of alcohol results in intoxication, not hyperventilation. Answer (C) is incorrect because a slow rate of breathing is the cure for hyperventilation, and insufficient oxygen is the cause of hypoxia, not hyperventilation.

ALL
9103. Altitude-induced hypoxia is caused by what atmospheric condition?

A—Significantly less oxygen molecules at high altitude.
B—Insufficient partial pressure of the inhaled oxygen.
C—Incorrect balance of oxygen and carbon dioxide.

Low partial pressure of oxygen causes hypoxia. (PLT330, AA.I.F.K1a) — AIM ¶8-1-2

ALL
9104. Which is a common symptom of hyperventilation?

A—Tingling sensations.
B—Visual acuity.
C—Decreased breathing rate.

Symptoms of hyperventilation include dizziness, tingling of the extremities, sensation of body heat, rapid heart rate, blurring of vision, muscle spasm and, finally, unconsciousness. (PLT332, AA.I.F.K1b) — AIM ¶8-1-3

Answer (B) is incorrect because hyperventilation distorts one's abilities. Answer (C) is incorrect because decreasing the breathing rate overcomes hyperventilation and is not a symptom of it.

ALL
9105. Loss of cabin pressure may result in hypoxia because as cabin altitude increases

A—the percentage of nitrogen in the air is increased.
B—the percentage of oxygen in the air is decreased.
C—oxygen partial pressure is decreased.

Low partial pressure of oxygen causes hypoxia. (PLT330, AA.I.F.K1a) — AIM ¶8-1-2

Answers (A) and (B) are incorrect because the percentage of nitrogen, carbon dioxide and oxygen in the atmosphere remains constant with changes in altitude, but there is less pressure as you increase in altitude.

ALL
9106. Hypoxia is the result of which of these conditions?

A—Insufficient oxygen reaching the brain.
B—Excessive carbon dioxide in the bloodstream.
C—Limited oxygen reaching the heart muscles.

Hypoxia is a result of too little oxygen reaching the brain. (PLT330, AA.I.F.K1a) — AIM ¶8-1-2

Answer (B) is incorrect because excessive carbon dioxide in the blood stream causes hyperventilation. Answer (C) is incorrect because it is the result of insufficient oxygen to the brain.

ALL
9856. Human behavior

A—rarely results in accidents unless deliberate actions are performed.
B—is responsible for three out of four accidents.
C—is well understood, so behavioral induced accidents are exceedingly rare occurrences.

Three out of four accidents result from improper human performance. The human element is the most flexible, adaptable, and valuable part of the aviation system,

Answers

9435 [C]	9101 [C]	9102 [A]	9103 [B]	9104 [A]	9105 [C]
9106 [A]	9856 [B]				

but it is also the most vulnerable to influences that can adversely affect its performance. (PLT104, AA.I.F.K3) — FAA-H-8083-2

ALL

9778. An experienced pilot trying to meet a schedule

A—can expect the flight crew to alert them to problems or areas of concern.
B—will always err on the side of caution.
C—can fail to perceive operational pitfalls.

Although more experienced pilots are likely to make more automatic decisions, there are tendencies or operational pitfalls that come with the development of pilot experience. These are classic behavioral traps into which pilots have been known to fall. More experienced pilots (as a rule) try to complete a flight as planned, please passengers, and meet schedules. The desire to meet these goals can have an adverse effect on safety and contribute to an unrealistic assessment of piloting skills. (PLT104, AA.I.F.K3) — FAA-H-8083-25

ALL

9778-1. Automatic Decision-Making is

A—a reflexive type of decision-making.
B—an impulsive type of decision-making.
C—an internalized type of decision-making.

Automatic decision-making is a reflexive type of decision-making anchored in training and experience and is most often used in times of emergency when there is no time to practice analytical decision-making. (PLT104, AA.I.F.K3) — FAA-H-8083-2

ALL

9804. The crew monitoring function is essential,

A—particularly during high altitude cruise flight modes to prevent CAT issues.
B—particularly during approach and landing to prevent CFIT.
C—during RNAV departures in class B airspace.

Effective monitoring and cross-checking can be the last line of defense that prevents an accident because detecting an error or unsafe situation may break the chain of events leading to an accident. This monitoring function is always essential, and particularly so during approach and landing when controlled flight into terrain (CFIT) accidents are most common. (PLT104, AA.I.F.K3) — AC 120-71A

ALL

9804-1. In order to achieve the highest level of safety,

A—each flight crewmember must carefully monitor the aircraft's flight path.
B—the crewmembers must continually monitor their seat dependent tasks.
C—the captain's judgment must not be questioned.

The FAA expects the flight crew to monitor the aircraft's flight path. (PLT354, AA.I.F.K3) — AC 120-71A

ALL

9805-8. In a multicrew environment, who is responsible for the tone, pace, and outcome of decisions made, and will be held accountable for all outcomes in air carrier flights?

A—First officer.
B—Air carrier.
C—Captain.

The captain is responsible for the tone, pace, and outcome of decisions, and will be held accountable for all outcomes of the flight. (PLT104, AA.I.E.K11) — AC 120-51

ALL

9805. CRM training refers to

A—the two components of flight safety and resource management, combined with mentor feedback.
B—the three components of initial indoctrination awareness, recurrent practice and feedback, and continual reinforcement.
C—the five components of initial indoctrination awareness, communication principles, recurrent practice and feedback, coordination drills, and continual reinforcement.

The critical components of effective crew resource management (CRM) training include initial indoctrination awareness, recurrent practice and feedback, and continual reinforcement. (PLT104, AA.I.F.K3) — AC120-51

Answers

9778 [C]	9778-1 [A]	9804 [B]	9804-1 [A]	9805-8 [C]	9805 [B]

ALL

9805-1. CRM error management includes

A—effective use of all available resources: human resources, hardware, and information.
B—error callout and error guidance training.
C—error prevention, error detection, and recovery from the error.

It is now understood that pilot errors cannot be entirely eliminated. It is important, therefore, that pilots develop appropriate error management skills and procedures. It is certainly desirable to prevent as many errors as possible, but since they cannot all be prevented, detection and recovery from errors should be addressed in training. Evaluation of pilots should also consider error management (error prevention, detection, and recovery). (PLT104, AA.I.F.K3) — AC 120-51

ALL

9805-2. CRM is defined as

A—application of team management in the flight deck environment.
B—the use of human factors principles in the aviation environment.
C—a human error avoidance approach to aviation management in the flight deck.

Crew resource management (CRM) is the application of team management concepts in the flight deck environment. It was initially known as cockpit resource management, but as CRM programs evolved to include cabin crews, maintenance personnel, and others, the phrase "crew resource management" was adopted. (PLT104, AA.I.F.K3) — FAA-H-8083-2

ALL

9805-3. Cultural issues in CRM

A—are not appropriate subjects for effective CRM training in any population.
B—must be addressed for each training population.
C—can be discussed if the training syllabus allows training time for those topics.

While individuals and even teams of individuals may perform well under many conditions, they are subject to the influence of at least three cultures: the professional cultures of the individuals themselves, the cultures of their organizations, and the national cultures surrounding the individuals and their organizations. If not recognized and addressed, factors related to culture may degrade crew performance. Hence, effective CRM training must address culture issues, as appropriate in each training population. (PLT104, AA.I.F.K3) — AC 120-51

ALL

9805-4. Crew resource management (CRM) is

A—a dilution of the captain's authority.
B—the only method of accident avoidance and error prevention.
C—one way to make good decisions.

CRM refers to the effective use of all available resources: human resources, hardware, and information. CRM training is one way of addressing the challenge of optimizing the human/machine interface and accompanying interpersonal activities, including decisionmaking. (PLT104, AA.I.F.K3) — AC 120-51

ALL

9805-5. Risk management, as part of the aeronautical decision making (ADM) process, relies on which features to reduce the risks associated with each flight?

A—Application of stress management and risk element procedures.
B—Situational awareness, problem recognition, and good judgment.
C—The mental process of analyzing all information in a particular situation and making a timely decision on what action to take.

Risk management is the part of the decision making process which relies on situational awareness, problem recognition, and good judgment to reduce risks associated with each flight. (PLT104, AA.I.F.K3) — FAA-H-8083-2

ALL

9805-6. In order to assess risk in aeronautical decision making, what two basic considerations are recommended?

A—Convenience and effort required.
B—Likelihood and severity.
C—Time and cost efficiency.

The degree of risk posed by a given hazard can be measured in terms of exposure (number of people or resources affected), severity (extent of possible loss), and probability (the likelihood that a hazard will cause a loss). (PLT104, AA.I.F.K3) — FAA-H-8083-25

Answers

9805-1 [C]	9805-2 [A]	9805-3 [B]	9805-4 [C]	9805-5 [B]	9805-6 [B]

ALL

9805-7. To improve the effectiveness and safety of the entire operations team as a working system, CRM training should include

A—usage of seat-dependent checklists.
B—employee groups beyond the flight crew.
C—failures the flight crew must work through as a team.

CRM is the application of team management concepts in the flight deck environment. CRM is one way of addressing the challenge of optimizing the human/machine interface and accompanying interpersonal activities. (PLT104, AA.I.E.K12) — FAA-H-8083-25

ALL

9940. One purpose of crew resource management (CRM) is to give crews the tools to

A—recognize and mitigate hazards.
B—maintain currency with regulations.
C—reduce the need for outside resources.

CRM training is one way of addressing the challenge of optimizing the human/machine interface and accompanying interpersonal activities, including recognizing and mitigating hazards. (PLT104, AA.I.F.K3) — AC 120-51

ALL

9806. Error management evaluation

A—should recognize not all errors can be prevented.
B—may include error evaluation that should have been prevented.
C—must mark errors as disqualifying.

It is certainly desirable to prevent as many errors as possible, but since they cannot all be prevented, detection and recovery from errors should be addressed in training. Error management (error prevention, detection, and recovery) should be considered in the evaluation of pilots, as well as the fact that since not all errors can be prevented, it is important that errors be managed properly. (PLT104, AA.I.F.K3) — AC120-51

ALL

9806-1. The most important key to risk management is

A—understanding pilot predisposition.
B—management of external pressures.
C—the sense of security provided by experience.

Management of external pressure is the single most important key to risk management because it is the one risk factor category that can cause a pilot to ignore all the other risk factors. External pressures put time-related pressure on the pilot and figure into a majority of accidents. (PLT271, AA.I.F.K3) — FAA-H-8083-25

ALL

9816. An experienced pilot mistakes the runway heading for the instructed heading for departure. What kind of error is this?

A—Experience error.
B—Detection error.
C—Insight detection.

Problem detection is the first step in the decision-making process. It begins with recognizing that a change occurred or that an expected change did not occur. A problem is perceived first by the senses and then it is determined through insight and experience. These same abilities, as well as an objective analysis of all available information, are used to determine the nature and severity of the problem. Therefore, incorrectly detecting the problem to begin with is an error that is critical during a decision-making process. (PLT104, AA.I.F.K3) — FAA-H-8083-25A

ALL

9816-1. An experienced, current, and proficient pilot fails to notice the landing gear is not extended for landing. This is an example of

A—systems training.
B—problem detection.
C—procedures knowledge.

Problem detection is the first step in the decision-making process. It begins with recognizing that a change occurred or that an expected change did not occur. A problem is perceived first by the senses and then it is determined through insight and experience. These same abilities, as well as an objective analysis of all available information, are used to determine the nature and severity of the problem. Therefore, incorrectly detecting a problem to begin with is an error that is critical during a decision-making process. (PLT104, AA.I.F.K3) — FAA-H-8083-25

Answers

9805-7 [C]	9940 [A]	9806 [A]	9806-1 [B]	9816 [B]	9816-1 [B]

ALL

9832. Accident-prone pilots tend to

A—have disdain toward rules.
B—follow methodical information gathering techniques.
C—excessively utilize outside resources.

One of the primary characteristics exhibited by accident-prone pilots was their disdain toward rules. (PLT103, AA.I.F.K3) — FAA-H-8083-2

ALL

9815. When a recently certificated pilot decides to not wait any longer for the fog and low ceilings to burn off, this pilot may be exhibiting the hazardous

A—resigned attitude.
B—macho attitude.
C—impulsive attitude.

ADM addresses the following five hazardous attitudes: Antiauthority (don't tell me!), Impulsivity (do something quickly!), Invulnerability (it won't happen to me), Macho (I can do it), Resignation (what's the use?). This pilot is exhibiting an impulsive attitude by departing before conditions warrant. (PLT103, AA.I.F.R2) — FAA-H-8083-2

ALL

9815-1. When an aircraft pilot takes off as ordered in the afternoon when embedded thunderstorms are indicated on radar and NOAA is broadcasting weather watches, it might be described as an example of

A—the resigned effect.
B—an anti-authority attitude.
C—an impulsive attitude.

ADM addresses the following five hazardous attitudes: Antiauthority (don't tell me!), Impulsivity (do something quickly!), Invulnerability (it won't happen to me), Macho (I can do it), and Resignation (what's the use?). This pilot is exhibiting a resigned attitude by leaving the departure decision up to others. Pilots who think, "What's the use?" will leave the action to others and may even go along with unreasonable requests. (PLT103, AA.I.F.R2) — FAA-H-8083-25

Answer (B) is incorrect because the question involves an example of the pilot following the authority to a fault. Answer (C) is incorrect because the question involves an example of a pilot following orders; the impulsive attitude is demonstrated when the pilot does not select the best alternative and they do the first thing that comes to mind.

ALL

9833. An air carrier crew fixated on completing the last flight of a four day trip often may exhibit

A—get-there-itis.
B—staged decision-making.
C—naturalistic decision-making.

There are a number of classic behavioral traps into which pilots have been known to fall. These dangerous tendencies or behavior patterns, which must be identified and eliminated, include: peer pressure, mind set, get-there-itis, duck-under syndrome, scud running, continuing visual flight rules into instrument conditions, getting behind the aircraft, loss of positional or situation awareness, operating without adequate fuel reserves, descent below the minimum enroute altitude, flying outside the envelope, neglect of flight planning, preflight inspections, checklists, etc. (PLT104, AA.I.F.R2) — FAA-H-8083-2

ALL

9834. An air carrier aircraft flown into the ground while troubleshooting a landing gear fault is an example of

A—neglect and reliance on memory.
B—loss of situational awareness.
C—lack of aviation experience.

Instances of human factor accidents include operational errors that relate to loss of situational awareness and flying outside the envelope. These can be termed as operational pitfalls. (PLT104, AA.I.F.K3) — FAA-H-8083-2

ALL

9927. A pilot making a blood donation in order to help a sick associate should be aware that for several weeks

A—sufficient oxygen may not reach the cells in the body.
B—fewer oxygen molecules will be available to the respiratory membranes.
C—the ability of the body tissues to effectively use oxygen is decreased.

Hypemic hypoxia occurs when the blood is not able to take up and transport a sufficient amount of oxygen to the cells in the body. Hypemic hypoxia can be caused by the loss of blood due to blood donation. Blood volume can require several weeks to return to normal following a donation. Although the effects of the blood loss are slight at ground level, there are risks when flying during this time. (PLT330, AA.I.F.K1a) — FAA-H-8083-25

Answers

9832 [A]	9815 [C]	9815-1 [A]	9833 [A]	9834 [B]	9927 [A]

ALL

9928. Stress distraction can interfere with judgment to the extent that

A—unwarranted risks are taken.
B—physical response rates to stimuli are impaired.
C—perceptions are clouded.

Stress causes concentration and performance problems. (PLT098, AA.I.F.K1g) — FAA-H-8083-25

ALL

9928-1. What type of stressor can lead to poor decision making?

A—Lack of sleep.
B—Lack of high workload.
C—Lack of motivation.

Fatigue is frequently associated with pilot error. Some of the effects of fatigue include degradation of attention and concentration, impaired coordination, and decreased ability to communicate. These factors seriously influence the ability to make effective decisions. (PLT098, AA.I.F.K3) — FAA-H-8083-25

ALL

9929. Sleep inertia refers to a period of

A—heightened alertness and visual acuity following a rest period.
B—alignment between a person`s internal biological clock and local external time cues.
C—impaired performance following awakening from a regular sleep cycle or nap.

Sleep inertia (also termed sleep drunkenness) refers to a period of impaired performance and reduced vigilance following awakening from the regular sleep episode or nap. This impairment may be severe, last from minutes to hours, and be accompanied by micro-sleep episodes. (PLT104, AA.I.F.K1h) — AC 120-100

ALL

9929-1. The maximum tailwind component of the airplane is 10 knots. The actual tailwind calculated is 11 knots. Other aircraft are continuing to land, so you decide to ignore the limitation and land as well. Which hazardous attitude are you displaying?

A—Impulsivity.
B—Resignation.
C—Anti-authority.

The anti-authority attitude is demonstrated by someone ignoring the rules. (PLT104, AA.I.F.R2) — FAA-H-8083-2

Answer (A) is incorrect because impulsivity is the attitude of people who frequently feel the need to do something, anything, immediately. Answer (B) is incorrect because resignation attitude is demonstrated by someone thinking "what's the use."

ALL

9929-2. Which of the following is one of the five traits discovered to be common in pilots who have had accidents in their past?

A—A low correlation between traffic safety violations and flying safety mishaps.
B—A tendency to be impulsive rather than disciplined, especially in decision making.
C—A sense of respect for rules and procedures.

The five traits discovered in pilots prone to having accidents are: (1) disdain toward rules; (2) very high correlation between accidents on their flying records and safety violations on their driving records; (3) frequently fall into the "thrill and adventure seeking" personality category; (4) impulsive rather than methodical and disciplined, both in their information gathering and in the speed and selection of actions to be taken; (5) a disregard for or tend to underutilize outside sources of information, including copilots, flight attendants, flight service personnel, flight instructors, and ATC. (PLT104, AA.I.F.K3) — FAA-H-8083-25

Answers

9928 [A]	9928-1 [A]	9929 [C]	9929-1 [C]	9929-2 [B]

Chapter 8
Meteorology and Weather Services

The Atmosphere

The primary cause of all the Earth's weather is the variation in solar radiation received at the surface. When the surface is warmed by the sun, the air next to it is, in turn, heated and it expands. This creates a low pressure area where the air rises and, at altitude, expands outward. Air from regions of relatively high pressure descends and then moves away from the center of the high toward the lower pressure areas. On both a global and local scale, this movement of air sets off an immensely complex process that generates all the Earth's weather. See Figure 8-1.

Another major influence in the pattern of the weather is a phenomenon known as **Coriolis effect**. This is an apparent force, caused by the Earth's rotation, acting on any movement of air. If the Earth did not rotate, air would move directly from areas of high pressure to areas of low pressure. Coriolis force bends the track of the air over the ground to right in the northern hemisphere and to the left in the southern hemisphere. Viewed from above (as on a weather map) this makes air rotate clockwise around high pressure areas in the northern hemisphere and counterclockwise around lows. In the southern hemisphere, the rotation around highs and lows is just the opposite. In the northern hemisphere, the rotation of air around a low pressure area is called a cyclone and that around a high is called an anticyclone.

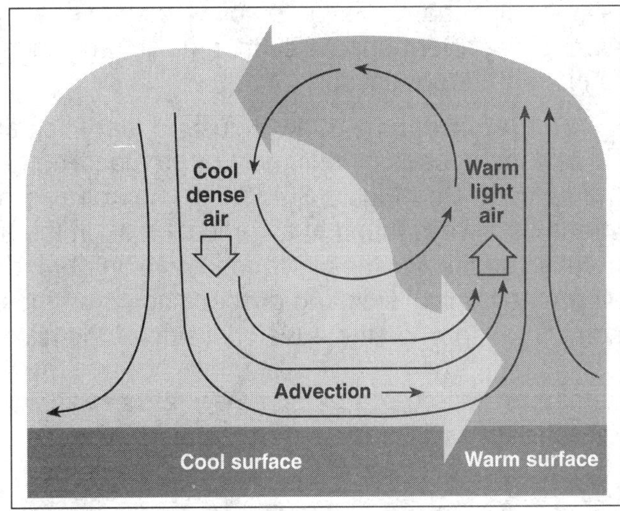

Figure 8-1. Circulation of air due to uneven surface heating

The strength of the Coriolis force is determined by wind speed and the latitude. Coriolis has the least effect at the equator and the most at the poles. It is also reduced in effect when wind speed decreases. Air moving near the Earth's surface is slowed by friction. This reduces the Coriolis force. However, the gradient pressure causing the air to move remains the same. The reduced Coriolis allows air to spiral out away from the center of a high and in toward the center of a low, and at an angle to winds aloft which are out of the friction level.

If the Earth did not rotate, air would move from the poles to the equator at the surface and from the equator to the poles at altitude. Because the Earth does rotate, Coriolis force and the pressure gradients tend to form three bands of prevailing winds in each hemisphere. Weather systems tend to move from east to west in the subtropical regions on the "trade winds." In the mid latitudes, the prevailing westerlies move weather systems from west to east. See Figure 8-2.

North Pole
60° latitude
Low-level Polar Easterlies
High-level Subtropical Westerlies
30° latitude
Equator

Figure 8-2. Global wind systems

All air carrier flights take place in the two lowest levels of the atmosphere. These are the **troposphere** and the **stratosphere**. The troposphere starts at the surface and extends vertically to roughly 35,000 feet. The thickness of the troposphere varies with latitude, being thicker over the equator than over the poles and with the season of the year (thicker in the summer than in the winter). The stratosphere extends from the top of the troposphere to about 26 to 29 miles altitude. See Figure 8-3. The main characteristic that distinguishes the troposphere from the stratosphere is the temperature lapse rate. In the troposphere, the temperature decreases with increasing altitude at an average rate of two degrees Celsius per one thousand feet of altitude. In the stratosphere, there is little or no change in temperature with altitude. In fact, in some regions the temperature increases with increasing altitude causing temperature inversions.

The thin boundary layer between the troposphere and the stratosphere is called the **tropopause**. The height of the tropopause is of great interest to the pilots of jet aircraft for two reasons. First, there is an abrupt change in the temperature lapse rate at the tropopause and that has a significant effect on jet engine performance. Second, maximum winds (the jet stream) and narrow zones of wind shear are found at the tropopause.

The **jet stream** is a few thousand feet thick and a few hundred miles wide. By arbitrary definition, it has wind speeds of fifty knots or greater. The highest wind speeds can be found on the polar side of the jet core. See Figure 8-4. There may be two or more jet streams in existence at one time. The jet stream is always found at a vertical break in the tropopause where the tropical and polar tropopauses meet. In addition to the high speed horizontal winds, the jet stream contains a circular rotation with rising air on the tropical side and descending air on the polar side. Because of the rising air, cirrus clouds will sometimes form on the equatorial side of the jet.

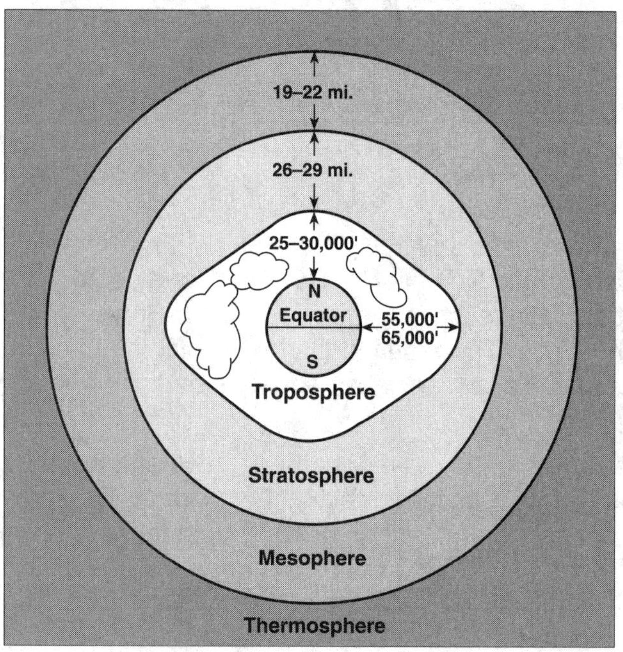

Figure 8-3. Levels of atmosphere

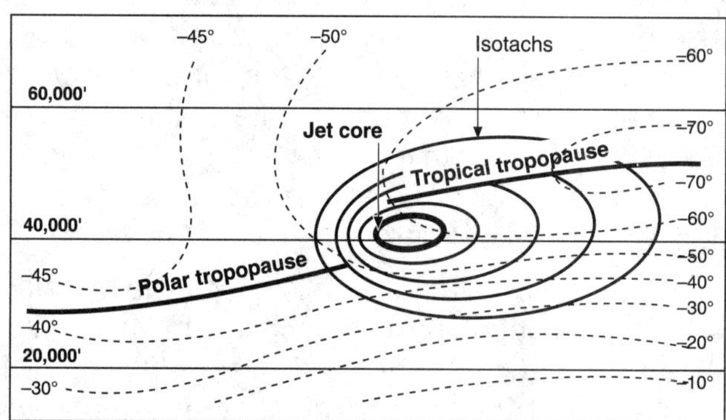

Figure 8-4. Cross-section of the jet stream

ALL

9152. What is the primary cause of all changes in the Earth's weather?

A—Variations of solar energy at the Earth's surface.
B—Changes in air pressure over the Earth's surface.
C—Movement of air masses from moist areas to dry areas.

Every physical process of weather is accompanied by or is the result of a heat exchange. Differences in solar energy create temperature variations. These temperature variations create forces that drive the atmosphere in its endless motion. (PLT510, AA.I.C.K3c) — FAA-H-8083-28

Answer (B) is incorrect because changes in air pressure are due to temperature variations. Answer (C) is incorrect because movement of air masses is a result of varying temperatures and pressures.

Answers

9152 [A]

ALL

9160. Where is the usual location of a thermal low?

A—Over the arctic region.
B—Over the eye of a hurricane.
C—Over the surface of a dry, sunny region.

A dry, sunny region can become quite warm from intense surface heating, thus generating a surface low-pressure area. This is called a thermal low. (PLT511, AA.I.C.K3e) — FAA-H-8083-28

Answer (A) is incorrect because thermal lows develop over dry, sunny regions, not in the arctic. Answer (B) is incorrect because the eye of a hurricane marks the center of a well-developed tropical cyclone.

ALL

9159. What is a feature of air movement in a high pressure area?

A—Ascending from the surface high to lower pressure at higher altitudes.
B—Descending to the surface and then outward.
C—Moving outward from the high at high altitudes and into the high at the surface.

Air in a high pressure system (in the northern hemisphere) tends to descend to the surface and then spiral out from the center of the high. (PLT173, AA.I.C.K3e) — FAA-H-8083-28

ALL

9157. At lower levels of the atmosphere, friction causes the wind to flow across isobars into a low because the friction

A—decreases windspeed and Coriolis force.
B—decreases pressure gradient force.
C—creates air turbulence and raises atmospheric pressure.

Frictional force slows wind speed near the surface and Coriolis force is decreased. The stronger pressure gradient force turns the wind at an angle across the isobars toward lower pressure until the three forces (Coriolis, pressure gradient, and friction) are in balance. (PLT173, AA.I.C.K3e) — FAA-H-8083-28

Answer (B) is incorrect because friction does not affect the pressure gradient force. Answer (C) is incorrect because of surface obstructions.

ALL

9176. At which location does Coriolis force have the least effect on wind direction?

A—At the poles.
B—Middle latitudes (30° to 60°).
C—At the Equator.

Coriolis force varies with latitude from zero at the Equator to a maximum at the poles. (PLT510, AA.I.C.K3e) — FAA-H-8083-28

ALL

9177. How does Coriolis force affect wind direction in the Southern Hemisphere?

A—Causes clockwise rotation around a low.
B—Causes wind to flow out of a low toward a high.
C—Has exactly the same effect as in the Northern Hemisphere.

Coriolis force deflects air flow to the right causing winds above the friction level to flow parallel to the isobars. In the northern hemisphere, winds flow clockwise around high-pressure areas and counterclockwise around low-pressure areas. In the southern hemisphere, Coriolis force causes a counterclockwise flow around highs and a clockwise flow around lows. (PLT516, AA.I.C.K3e) — FAA-H-8083-28

Answer (B) is incorrect because the wind flows from a high to a low (not a low to a high) in both the northern and southern hemispheres. Answer (C) is incorrect because the Coriolis force deflects air to the left in the southern hemisphere, which is the opposite effect from the northern hemisphere.

ALL

9178. Which weather condition is defined as an anticyclone?

A—Calm.
B—High pressure area.
C—Col.

The clockwise flow of air around a high-pressure area in the northern hemisphere is called an anticyclone. (PLT173, AA.I.C.K3e) — FAA-H-8083-28

Answer (A) is incorrect because calm is defined as the absence of wind or of apparent motion of the air. Answer (C) is incorrect because Col is the neutral area between two highs or two lows. It is also the intersection of a trough and a ridge.

Answers

9160 [C] 9159 [B] 9157 [A] 9176 [C] 9177 [A] 9178 [B]

ALL
9178-1. A cyclone is

A—a hurricane force storm in the Indian Ocean.
B—a tropical depression with sustained winds of 63 knots.
C—a tropical depression with a barometric pressure in the center of the feature that is 35 mb lower than pressure outside the weather feature.

The low pressure and its wind system is a cyclone. Strong tropical cyclones are known by different names in different regions of the world. A tropical cyclone in the Atlantic and eastern Pacific is a "hurricane"; in the western Pacific, "typhoon"; near Australia, "willy-willy"; and in the Indian Ocean, simply "cyclone." (PLT517, AA.I.C.K3e) — FAA-H-8083-28

ALL
9156. Which area or areas of the Northern Hemisphere experience a generally east to west movement of weather systems?

A—Arctic only.
B—Arctic and subtropical.
C—Subtropical only.

Polar easterlies carry storms from east to west. The northeasterly trade winds carry tropical storms from east to west. The prevailing westerlies drive mid-latitude storms generally from west to east. (PLT510, AA.I.C.K3e) — FAA-H-8083-28

ALL
9233. Summer thunderstorms in the arctic region will generally move

A—northeast to southwest in polar easterlies.
B—southwest to northeast with the jetstream flow.
C—directly north to south with the low-level polar airflow.

Arctic thundershowers, usually circumnavigable, move generally from northeast to southwest in the polar easterlies which is opposite from the general movement in mid-latitudes. (PLT495, AA.I.C.K3e) — FAA-H-8083-28

ALL
9151. What is a characteristic of the troposphere?

A—It contains all the moisture of the atmosphere.
B—There is an overall decrease of temperature with an increase of altitude.
C—The average altitude of the top of the troposphere is about 6 miles.

The troposphere is the layer of atmosphere from the surface to an average altitude of 7 miles. It is characterized by an overall decrease of temperature with increasing altitude. (PLT203, AA.I.C.K3a) — FAA-H-8083-28

Answer (A) is incorrect because moisture can be found in the stratosphere, as evidenced by some of the largest thunderstorms. Answer (C) is incorrect because the average altitude of the top of the troposphere is about 7 miles.

ALL
9240. What weather feature occurs at altitude levels near the tropopause?

A—Maximum winds and narrow wind shear zones.
B—Abrupt temperature increase above the tropopause.
C—Thin layers of cirrus (ice crystal) clouds at the tropopause level.

Maximum winds generally occur at levels near the tropopause. These strong winds create narrow zones of wind shear which often generate hazardous turbulence. (PLT203, AA.I.C.K3a) — FAA-H-8083-28

Answer (B) is incorrect because temperature is fairly constant above the tropopause. Answer (C) is incorrect because thin layers of cirrus (ice crystal) clouds can develop at altitudes below the tropopause level and extend into the lower stratosphere.

ALL
9209. Which feature is associated with the tropopause?

A—Absence of wind and turbulence.
B—Absolute upper limit of cloud formation.
C—Abrupt change of temperature lapse rate.

An abrupt change in the temperature lapse rate characterizes the tropopause. (PLT203, AA.I.C.K3a)—FAA-H-8083-28

Answer (A) is incorrect because the jet stream (wind) and clear air turbulence are found extensively in the tropopause. Answer (B) is incorrect because clouds can be present into the stratosphere, as in very large thunderstorms and cirrus clouds made up of ice crystals.

ALL
9168. Where is a common location for an inversion?

A—At the tropopause.
B—In the stratosphere.
C—At the base of cumulus clouds.

Inversions are common in the stratosphere. (PLT203, AA.I.C.K3a) — FAA-H-8083-28

Answer (A) is incorrect because a common location for an inversion is in the stratosphere, not at the tropopause. Answer (C) is incorrect because the base of cumulus clouds is where the dew point lapse rate and the dry adiabatic lapse rate converge. It is not a common location for an inversion.

Answers

9178-1 [A] 9156 [B] 9233 [A] 9151 [B] 9240 [A] 9209 [C]
9168 [B]

ALL
9241. Where are jetstreams normally located?

A—In areas of strong low pressure systems in the stratosphere.
B—In a break in the tropopause where intensified temperature gradients are located.
C—In a single continuous band, encircling the Earth, where there is a break between the equatorial and polar tropopause.

The jet stream is usually associated with a break in the tropopause where intensified temperature gradients are located. (PLT302, AA.I.C.K3a) — FAA-H-8083-28

Answer (A) is incorrect because a jet stream is located in a break in the tropopause, not in the stratosphere. Answer (C) is incorrect because there may be more than one jet stream at any time; up to three at one time are not uncommon.

ALL
9779. The tropopause is generally found when the free air temperatures are

A—between -55°C and -65°C.
B—between -40°C and -55°C.
C—colder than -60°C.

In the absence of other information, the tropopause will generally have a temperature of between -55°C and -65°C. (PLT302, AA.I.C.K3a) — AC 00-30

ALL
9229. Which type clouds may be associated with the jetstream?

A—Cumulonimbus cloud line where the jetstream crosses the cold front.
B—Cirrus clouds on the equatorial side of the jetstream.
C—Cirrostratus cloud band on the polar side and under the jetstream.

When high-level moisture is present, cirriform clouds form on the equatorial side of the jet stream. (PLT302, AA.I.C.K3f) — FAA-H-8083-28

Answer (A) is incorrect because cirriform, not cumulonimbus, clouds are associated with the jet stream. Answer (C) is incorrect because cirriform clouds form on the equatorial side of the jet stream.

ALL
9229-1. When high level moisture is available, cirrus clouds form on the

A—polar side of the jet stream.
B—equatorial side of the jet stream.
C—acute angle side of the jet stream.

When high-level moisture is present, cirriform clouds form on the equatorial side of the jet stream. (PLT226, AA.I.C.K3f) — FAA-H-8083-28

ALL
9238. Where do the maximum winds associated with the jetstream usually occur?

A—In the vicinity of breaks in the tropopause on the polar side of the jet core.
B—Below the jet core where a long straight stretch of the jetstream is located.
C—On the equatorial side of the jetstream where moisture has formed cirriform clouds.

Maximum winds in a jet stream occur near a break in the tropopause and on the polar side. (PLT302, AA.I.C.K3b) — FAA-H-8083-28

Answer (B) is incorrect because in the jet stream, the maximum winds are found in, not below, the core. Answer (C) is incorrect because when moisture is available, cirriform clouds will form on the upward motion of air of the jet stream on the equatorial side. This will occur in the slower winds of the jet stream.

ALL
9238-1. The rate of decrease in wind speed from the jet stream core is considerably greater on the

A—equatorial side.
B—polar side.
C—acute angle side.

The rate of decrease of wind speed is considerably greater on the polar side than on the equatorial side; hence, the magnitude of wind shear is greater on the polar side than on the equatorial side. (PLT226, AA.I.C.K3b) — FAA-H-8083-28

ALL
9810. Large areas of land

A—tend to increase temperature variations.
B—do not influence the troposhere.
C—minimize temperature variations.

Land and water surfaces underlying the atmosphere greatly affect cloud and precipitation development. (PLT512, AA.I.C.K3e) — FAA-H-8083-28

Answers

9241 [B]	9779 [A]	9229 [B]	9229-1 [B]	9238 [A]	9238-1 [B]
9810 [A]					

ALL

8710. For a flight to an airport in the vicinity of the coast, land surface cooling means you can expect to encounter

A—sea breezes.
B—land breezes.
C—a chinook wind.

During the day, the sun heats up both the ocean surface and the land. However, water heats up much more slowly than land and so the air above the land will be warmer compared to the air over the ocean. The warm air over the land will rise throughout the day, causing low pressure at the surface. Over the water, high surface pressure will form because of the colder air. To compensate, the air will sink over the ocean. The wind will blow from the higher pressure over the water to lower pressure over the land causing the sea breeze. The opposite occurs at night, with land surface cooling causing a land breeze. (PLT512, AA.I.C.K3e) — FAA-H-8083-28

Answer (A) is incorrect because a sea breeze is cause by land surface warming. Answer (C) is incorrect because a chinook wind is associated with mountainous terrain.

Weather Systems

When air masses of different temperature or moisture content collide, they force air aloft along the area where they meet. An elongated line of low pressure is referred to as a trough.

A **front** is defined as the boundary between two different air masses. The formation of a front is called frontogenesis. When a front dissipates, the area experiences frontolysis. All fronts lie in troughs. This means that winds flow around a front more or less parallel to the front, and in a counterclockwise direction. As an aircraft flies toward a front in the northern hemisphere, the pilot will notice a decreasing pressure and a wind from the left of the aircraft. After passing through the front, the pilot will note a wind shift to the right and increasing air pressure.

A front is usually the boundary between air masses of different temperatures. If cold air is displacing warm air, it is called a cold front. When warm air displaces cold air, it is a warm front. The speed of movement of the front is determined by the winds aloft. A cold front will move at about the speed of the wind component perpendicular to the front just above the friction level. It is harder for warm air to displace cold air and so warm fronts move at about half the speed of cold fronts under the same wind conditions.

A stationary front is one with little or no movement. Stationary fronts or slow moving cold fronts can form frontal waves and low pressure areas. A small disturbance can cause a bend in the frontal line that induces a counterclockwise flow of air around a deepening low pressure area. The wave forms into a warm front followed by a cold front. The cold front can then overtake the warm front and force the warm air between the two aloft. This is called an occluded front or an occlusion.

Most fronts mark the line between two air masses of different temperature. However, this is not always the case. Sometimes, air masses with virtually the same temperatures will form a front. The only difference between the two is the moisture content. The front formed in such conditions is called a dew point front or a dry line.

The surface position of a front often marks the line where an arctic and a tropical air mass meet at the surface. The jet stream is located in the area where these air masses meet at the altitude of the tropopause. There is often a rough correlation between the surface position of a front and the location of the jet stream. Generally speaking, the jet stream will lie to the north of the surface position of a front. As a frontal wave forms, the jet will move toward the center of the deepening low pressure area. If an occluded front forms, the jet stream will often cross the front near the point of the occlusion.

Answers

8710 [B]

ALL

9165. What term describes an elongated area of low pressure?

A—Trough.
B—Ridge.
C—Hurricane or typhoon.

A trough is an elongated area of low pressure with the lowest pressure along a line marking maximum anticyclonic curvature. (PLT173, AA.I.C.K3e) — FAA-H-8083-28

Answer (B) is incorrect because a ridge is an elongated area of high pressure. Answer (C) is incorrect because a hurricane or typhoon is a tropical cyclone (low) with highest sustained winds of 65 knots or greater.

ALL

9165-1. Low pressure areas are areas of

A—stagnant air.
B—descending air.
C—ascending air.

At the surface when air converges into a low, it cannot go outward against the pressure gradient, nor can it go downward into the ground; it must go upward. Therefore, a low or trough is an area of rising air. (PLT173, AA.I.C.K3e) — FAA-H-8083-28

ALL

9191. What is a feature of a stationary front?

A—The warm front surface moves about half the speed of the cold front surface.
B—Weather conditions are a combination of strong cold front and strong warm front weather.
C—Surface winds tend to flow parallel to the frontal zone.

The opposing forces exerted by adjacent air masses in a stationary front are such that the frontal surface between them shows little or no movement. In such cases, the surface winds tend to blow parallel to the frontal zone. (PLT511, AA.I.C.K3e) — FAA-H-8083-28

Answer (A) is incorrect because the movement of a warm front surface in comparison to a cold front surface has nothing to do with a stationary front. Answer (B) is incorrect because weather conditions that are a combination of strong cold front and strong warm front weather are a feature of an occluded front.

ALL

9192. Which event usually occurs after an aircraft passes through a front into the colder air?

A—Temperature/dewpoint spread decreases.
B—Wind direction shifts to the left.
C—Atmospheric pressure increases.

A front lies in a pressure trough, and pressure generally is higher in the cold air. Thus, when crossing a front directly into colder air, the pressure will usually rise abruptly. (PLT511, AA.I.C.K3e) — FAA-H-8083-28

Answer (A) is incorrect because the temperature/dew point spread usually differs across a front. But it might not decrease if you fly in to a cold, dry air mass. Answer (B) is incorrect because in the northern hemisphere the wind always shifts to the right due to the Coriolis force.

ALL

9213. If the winds aloft are blowing parallel to the front,

A—the front can be expected to move with the upper winds.
B—the winds aloft can be expected to turn at the frontal boundary.
C—the front moves slowly if at all.

The upper winds will dictate to a great extent the movement of the front, along with the amount of cloudiness and rain accompanying the frontal system. If winds aloft parallel a front, the front moves slowly if at all. If winds aloft blow across a front it tends to move with the wind. (PLT511, AA.I.C.K3e) — FAA-H-8083-28

ALL

9215. Which atmospheric factor causes rapid movement of surface fronts?

A—Upper winds blowing across the front.
B—Upper low located directly over the surface low.
C—The cold front overtaking and lifting the warm front.

Cold fronts move at about the speed of the wind component perpendicular to the front just above the frictional layer. (PLT511, AA.I.C.K3e) — FAA-H-8083-28

Answer (B) is incorrect because an upper low located directly over a surface low would be a factor in how extensive the weather would be, not in how fast it would move. Answer (C) is incorrect because a cold front overtaking and lifting the warm front is a characteristic of an advancing cold front.

Answers

9165 [A]	9165-1 [C]	9191 [C]	9192 [C]	9213 [C]	9215 [A]

ALL

9215-1. Dew point fronts result from

A—air density differences due to the humidity levels.
B—air density due to temperature.
C—temperatures aloft.

During a considerable part of the year, dew point fronts are common in Western Texas and New Mexico northward over the Plains States. Moist air flowing north from the Gulf of Mexico abuts the drier and therefore slightly denser air flowing from the southwest. Except for moisture differences, there is seldom any significant air mass contrast across this "front": therefore, it is commonly called a "dry line." Nighttime and early morning fog and low level clouds often prevail on the moist side of the line while generally clear skies mark the dry side. (PLT511, AA.I.C.K3e) — FAA-H-8083-28

ALL

9216. In which meteorological conditions can frontal waves and low pressure areas form?

A—Warm fronts or occluded fronts.
B—Slow-moving cold fronts or stationary fronts.
C—Cold front occlusions.

Frontal waves and cyclones (areas of low pressure) usually form on slow moving cold fronts or on stationary fronts. (PLT511, AA.I.C.K3e) — FAA-H-8083-28

Answer (A) is incorrect because occluded fronts are formed by frontal waves and areas of low pressure which cause a cold front to close together with a warm front. Frontal waves and low pressure areas normally form on slow-moving cold fronts. Answer (C) is incorrect because a cold front occlusion occurs when the air behind the cold front is colder than the air in advance of the warm front, lifting the warm front aloft.

ALL

9217. What weather difference is found on each side of a "dry line"?

A—Extreme temperature difference.
B—Dewpoint difference.
C—Stratus versus cumulus clouds.

A dew point front or "dry line" is formed when two air masses of similar density and temperature meet. Except for the moisture differences, there is little contrast across the front. (PLT511, AA.I.C.K3e) — FAA-H-8083-28

Answer (A) is incorrect because except for moisture (not extreme temperature) difference, there is seldom any significant air mass contrast across the "dry line." Answer (C) is incorrect because the side with moisture may have clouds, while generally clear skies mark the dry side.

ALL

9227. Where is the normal location of the jetstream relative to surface lows and fronts?

A—The jetstream is located north of the surface systems.
B—The jetstream is located south of the low and warm front.
C—The jetstream is located over the low and crosses both the warm front and the cold front.

Development of a surface low is usually south of the jet stream. As the low deepens, it moves nearer the jet center. When a low occludes, the jet stream usually crosses the frontal system at the point of the occlusion. (PLT302, AA.I.C.K3e) — FAA-H-8083-28

Answer (B) is incorrect because the jet stream is located to the north of the low and warm front. Answer (C) is incorrect because the jet stream crosses the occlusion of the warm and cold front at the point of occlusion.

ALL

9228. Which type frontal system is normally crossed by the jetstream?

A—Cold front and warm front.
B—Warm front.
C—Occluded front.

Development of a surface low is usually south of the jet stream. As the low deepens, it moves nearer the jet center. When a low occludes, the jet stream usually crosses the frontal system at the point of the occlusion. (PLT302, AA.I.C.K3e) — FAA-H-8083-28

ALL

9228-1. Steep frontal surfaces are usually associated with

A—fast moving warm front.
B—fast moving cold front.
C—dry lines.

The leading edge of an advancing cold air mass is a cold front. Warm fronts on the surface are seldom as well marked as cold fronts, and they usually move about half as fast when the general wind flow is the same in each case. (PLT511, AA.I.C.K3e) — FAA-H-8083-28

Answers

9215-1 [A]	9216 [B]	9217 [B]	9227 [A]	9228 [C]	9228-1 [B]

ALL

9228-2. If a sample of air is forced upward and it is colder than the surrounding air, it

A—sinks until it reaches denser air.
B—gets energy from surrounding air and remains in place.
C—warms from the surrounding air and rises to expansion.

If the upward moving air becomes colder than surrounding air, it sinks; but if it remains warmer it is accelerated upward as a convective current. Whether it sinks or rises depends on the ambient or existing temperature lapse rate. (PLT511, AA.I.C.K3e) — FAA-H-8083-28

ALL

9776. A jet stream is a narrow, shallow, meandering river of maximum winds extending around the globe in a wavelike pattern with speeds of

A—50 knots or greater.
B—71 knots or greater.
C—100 knots or greater.

The concentrated winds, by arbitrary definition, must be 50 knots or greater to be classified as a jet stream. (PLT302, AA.I.C.K3b) — FAA-H-8083-28

ALL

9776-1. Jet streams are strongest during which season in the Northern Hemisphere?

A—Spring.
B—Summer.
C—Winter.

Jet streams follow the boundaries between hot and cold air. Since these hot and cold air boundaries are most pronounced in winter, jet streams are strongest during Northern and Southern Hemisphere winters. (PLT302, AA.I.C.K3e) — FAA-H-8083-28

Stability and Instability of Air

When a parcel of air is forced to rise it expands because its pressure decreases. Air that is forced to descend is compressed. When the pressure and volume change, so does the temperature. When air expands, it cools and when it is compressed, it warms. This cooling or heating is referred to as being **adiabatic**, meaning that no heat was removed from or added to the air.

When unsaturated air is forced to rise or descend it cools or heats at a rate of about 3°C per 1,000 feet of altitude change. This called the dry adiabatic rate. The saturated adiabatic rate is normally much lower.

When moist air is forced upward, the temperature and the dew point converge on each other at a rate of about 2.5°C per 1,000 feet. At the altitude where the dew point lapse rate and the dry adiabatic rate meet, cloud bases will form. Once the condensation starts taking place the adiabatic rate slows considerably because the process of condensation releases latent heat into the air and partially offsets the expansional cooling.

Saturated air flowing downward will also warm at less than the dry adiabatic rate because vaporization of water droplets uses heat. Once the air is no longer saturated it will heat at the normal dry rate. An example of this is the "katabatic wind" which becomes warmer and dryer as it flows downslope.

The adiabatic rate should not be confused with the actual (ambient) lapse rate. The actual lapse rate is the rate at which the air temperature varies with altitude when air is not being forced to rise or descend. The actual lapse averages about 2°C per 1,000 feet, but that is highly variable. When a parcel of air is forced to rise, the adiabatic rate may be different than the ambient rate.

When a parcel of air becomes colder (and more dense) than the air around it, it will tend to sink back toward its original altitude. If the parcel becomes warmer than the surrounding air, it will tend to rise

Answers

9228-2 [A] 9776 [A] 9776-1 [C]

convectively even though the original lifting force may have disappeared. If this happens, the air is said to be unstable. When a parcel of air resists convective movement through it, it is said to be stable.

The best indication of the stability or instability of an air mass is the ambient temperature lapse rate. If the temperature drops rapidly as the altitude increases, the air is unstable. If the temperature remains unchanged or decreases only slightly as altitude is increased, the air mass is stable. If the temperature actually increases as altitude increases, a temperature inversion exists. This is the most stable of weather conditions.

ALL

9170. Which term applies when the temperature of the air changes by compression or expansion with no heat added or removed?

A—Katabatic.
B—Advection.
C—Adiabatic.

When air expands, it cools; and when compressed, it warms. These changes are adiabatic, meaning that no heat is removed from or added to the air. (PLT024, AA.I.C.K3a) — FAA-H-8083-28

Answer (A) is incorrect because katabatic is a wind blowing down an incline caused by cold, heavier air spilling down the incline displacing warmer, less dense air. Answer (B) is incorrect because advection is the horizontal flow in a convective current, i.e., wind.

ALL

9186. Which process causes adiabatic cooling?

A—Expansion of air as it rises.
B—Movement of air over a colder surface.
C—Release of latent heat during the vaporization process.

When air expands, it cools; and when compressed, it warms. These changes are adiabatic, meaning that no heat is removed from or added to the air. (PLT024, AA.I.C.K3a) — FAA-H-8083-28

Answer (B) is incorrect because adiabatic cooling means that no heat is removed from the air, as would be the case if the air was moved over a colder surface. Answer (C) is incorrect because adiabatic cooling is the process in which no heat is removed from or added to the air.

ALL

9158. Which type wind flows downslope becoming warmer and dryer?

A—Land breeze.
B—Valley wind.
C—Katabatic wind.

A katabatic wind is any wind blowing down an incline when the incline is influential in causing the wind. Any katabatic wind originates because cold, heavy air spills down sloping terrain displacing warmer, less dense air ahead of it. Air is heated and dried as it flows downslope. (PLT516, AA.I.C.K3a) — FAA-H-8083-28

Answer (A) is incorrect because a land breeze is a wind that flows from the cooler land toward warmer water. Answer (B) is incorrect because a valley wind is wind flowing up out of a valley because colder, denser air settles downward and forces the warmer air near the ground up a mountain slope.

ALL

9171. What is the approximate rate unsaturated air will cool flowing upslope?

A—3°C per 1,000 feet.
B—2°C per 1,000 feet.
C—4°C per 1,000 feet.

Unsaturated air moving upward and downward cools and warms at about 3.0°C (5.4°F) per 1,000 feet. (PLT024, AA.I.C.K3a) — FAA-H-8083-28

Answers (B) and (C) are incorrect because unsaturated air will cool flowing upslope at 3°C per 1,000 feet.

ALL

9182. What is the result when water vapor changes to the liquid state while being lifted in a thunderstorm?

A—Latent heat is released to the atmosphere.
B—Latent heat is transformed into pure energy.
C—Latent heat is absorbed from the surrounding air by the water droplet.

When water vapor condenses to liquid water or sublimates directly to ice, energy originally used in the evaporation reappears as heat and is released to the atmosphere. This energy is "latent heat." (PLT512, AA.I.C.K3h) — FAA-H-8083-28

Answer (B) is incorrect because latent heat cannot create pure energy. Latent heat is returned to the surrounding atmosphere. Answer (C) is incorrect because this is the process of latent heat in vaporization, which is changing liquid water to vapor.

Answers

9170 [C] 9186 [A] 9158 [C] 9171 [A] 9182 [A]

ALL
9185. What weather condition occurs at the altitude where the dewpoint lapse rate and the dry adiabatic lapse rate converge?

A—Cloud bases form.
B—Precipitation starts.
C—Stable air changes to unstable air.

Unsaturated air in a convective current cools at about 5.4°F (3°C) per 1,000 feet. The dew point decreases at about 1°F (5/9°C) per 1,000 feet. When the temperature and dew point converge, cloud bases will form. (PLT512, AA.I.C.K3a) — FAA-H-8083-28

Answer (B) is incorrect because precipitation starts when precipitation particles have grown to a size and weight that the atmosphere can no longer suspend, and the particles fall as precipitation. Answer (C) is incorrect because air stability depends on the ambient or existing temperature lapse rate, not the convergence of the dew point lapse rate and the dry adiabatic lapse rate.

ALL
9185-1. Adiabatic warming is also described as

A—chronographic warming.
B—expansional heating.
C—compressional heating.

The adiabatic process is the change of the temperature of air without transferring heat. In an adiabatic process, compression results in warming, and expansion results in cooling. (PLT512, AA.I.C.K3a) — FAA-H-8083-28

ALL
9185-2. Temperature and radiation variations over land with a clear sky typically lead to

A—minimum temperature occurring after sunrise.
B—incoming terrestrial radiation peaking at noon.
C—temperature reaching a maximum closer to noon than to sunset.

The warming and cooling of the Earth depends on an imbalance between solar and terrestrial radiation. Shortly after sunrise, incoming solar radiation received at the Earth's surface (insolation) becomes greater than outgoing terrestrial radiation and the Earth's surface warms. Peak insolation occurs around noon, but maximum surface air temperature usually occurs during the midafternoon. (PLT510, AA.I.C.K3c) — FAA-H-8083-28

ALL
9187. When saturated air moves downhill, its temperature increases

A—at a faster rate than dry air because of the release of latent heat.
B—at a slower rate than dry air because vaporization uses heat.
C—at a slower rate than dry air because condensation releases heat.

The saturated adiabatic rate of heating is slower than the dry rate because vaporization uses heat. (PLT024, AA.I.C.K3a) — FAA-H-8083-28

Answer (A) is incorrect because when saturated air moves downhill, its temperature increases at a slower rate than dry air because of the absorption of latent heat. Answer (C) is incorrect because as air moves downhill, its temperature increases at a slower rate than dry air because vaporization uses heat, not because of the release of heat through condensation.

ALL
9154. What feature is associated with a temperature inversion?

A—A stable layer of air.
B—An unstable layer of air.
C—Air mass thunderstorms.

A temperature inversion is defined as an increase in temperature with increasing altitude, or a negative temperature lapse rate. Stable air masses have a low or negative lapse rate. (PLT301, AA.I.C.K3c) — FAA-H-8083-28

Answer (B) is incorrect because instability occurs when the temperature decreases (not increases as in a temperature inversion) with an increase in altitude, and the rising air continues to rise. Answer (C) is incorrect because air mass thunderstorms result from instability. They do not occur when there is a temperature inversion.

ALL
9923. The stability of an air mass can usually be determined by

A—the height of the tropopause.
B—measuring the dry adiabatic lapse rate.
C—cloud types and the type of precipitation.

Characteristics of an unstable air mass include cumuliform clouds, showery precipitation, rough air (turbulence), and good visibility. Characteristics of a stable air mass include stratiform clouds and fog, continuous precipitation, smooth air, and fair to poor visibility in haze and smoke. (PLT511, AA.I.C.K3a) — FAA-H-8083-28

Answers

9185 [A]	9185-1 [C]	9185-2 [B]	9187 [B]	9154 [A]	9923 [C]

ALL

9924. Clouds with extensive vertical development over mountainous terrain are a sign of

A—a dry adiabatic lapse rate.
B—a stable air mass.
C—an unstable air mass.

When operating in the vicinity of towering cumulus (i.e., moderate/strong development), pilots can expect very strong turbulence and some clear icing above the freezing level. (PLT511, AA.I.C.K3f) — FAA-H-8083-28

ALL

9925. Cumulus clouds often indicate

A—possible turbulence.
B—a temperature inversion.
C—a dry adiabatic lapse rate.

Fair weather cumulus clouds often indicate bumpy turbulence beneath and in the clouds but good visibility. The cloud tops indicate the approximate upper limit of convection; flight above them is usually smooth. (PLT192, AA.I.C.K3f) — FAA-H-8083-28

ALL

9184. What is indicated about an air mass if the temperature remains unchanged or decreases slightly as altitude is increased?

A—The air is unstable.
B—A temperature inversion exists.
C—The air is stable.

A mass of air in which the temperature decreases rapidly with height favors instability. Air tends to be stable if the temperature changes little or not at all with altitude. (PLT512, AA.I.C.K3e) — FAA-H-8083-28

Answer (A) is incorrect because unstable air would have a uniform decrease (approaching 3°C/1,000 feet) in temperature with an increase in altitude. Answer (B) is incorrect because in a temperature inversion, the temperature increases with increases in altitude.

ALL

9188. Which condition is present when a local parcel of air is stable?

A—The parcel of air resists convection.
B—The parcel of air cannot be forced uphill.
C—As the parcel of air moves upward, its temperature becomes warmer than the surrounding air.

A parcel of air which resists convection when forced upward is called stable. (PLT173, AA.I.C.K3a) — FAA-H-8083-28

Answer (B) is incorrect because stable air can be forced uphill to form a mountain wave. Answer (C) is incorrect because rising air, warmer than the surrounding air, describes unstable air.

ALL

9195. How can the stability of the atmosphere be determined?

A—Ambient temperature lapse rate.
B—Atmospheric pressure at various levels.
C—Surface temperature/dewpoint spread.

A mass of air in which the temperature decreases rapidly with height favors instability. Air tends to be stable if the temperature changes little or not at all with altitude. The rate of temperature decrease with altitude is referred to as the temperature lapse rate. (PLT173, AA.I.C.K3a) — FAA-H-8083-28

Answer (B) is incorrect because the difference between ambient temperature and adiabatic lapse rate, not atmospheric pressure at various levels, determines stability. Answer (C) is incorrect because the surface temperature/dew point spread is used to indicate probability of fog, not atmospheric stability.

Answers

9924 [C] 9925 [A] 9184 [C] 9188 [A] 9195 [A]

Fog and Rain

Fog is a surface-based cloud that always forms in stable air conditions. The three main types are radiation fog, advection fog and upslope fog.

Radiation fog occurs when there is a surface-based temperature inversion. On a clear, relatively calm night the surface rapidly cools by radiating heat into space. This in turn cools the air within a few hundred feet of the surface and leaves warmer air aloft. If the temperature drops to the dew point, fog will form. Since the minimum temperature during the day occurs just after sunrise, this type of fog often forms then. This fog will dissipate when the air warms up enough to raise the temperature above the dew point again. However, if the inversion persists, visibility can remain limited due to lingering fog and haze. Wind or any significant movement of air will disperse both radiation fog and haze.

Advection fog and **upslope fog** both require wind to form. Advection fog forms when warm moist air flows over a colder surface. The temperature of the air drops to the dew point and fog forms. This commonly occurs over bodies of water such as lakes or oceans. The fog can drift over land on the leeward (downwind) side of the body of water lowering visibility at nearby airports. If the wind increases to over about 15 knots, the fog will tend to lift into low stratus clouds.

Upslope fog forms when moist, stable air is gradually moved over higher ground by the wind. As the air rises, it cools adiabatically and fog forms. This type of fog is common in mountainous areas.

All clouds are composed of tiny droplets of water (or ice crystals). As these drops of water collide with each other, they form larger drops until they precipitate out as rain. As a general rule, clouds need to be at least 4,000 feet thick to produce precipitation reported as light or greater intensity.

ALL

9153. What characterizes a ground-based inversion?

A—Convection currents at the surface.
B—Cold temperatures.
C—Poor visibility.

Inversions can occur in warm and cold temperatures in stable air, and usually trap particles in the air causing poor visibility. (PLT301, AA.I.C.K3c) — FAA-H-8083-28

Answer (A) is incorrect because convective currents at the surface do not occur when there is a ground-based inversion. Answer (B) is incorrect because when the temperature is cold, it is difficult for the earth to radiate enough heat to become colder than the overlying air.

ALL

9155. When does minimum temperature normally occur during a 24-hour period?

A—After sunrise.
B—About 1 hour before sunrise.
C—At midnight.

At night, solar radiation ceases, but terrestrial radiation continues and cools the surface. Cooling continues after sunrise until solar radiation again exceeds terrestrial radiation. Minimum temperature usually occurs after sunrise, sometimes as much as 1 hour after. (PLT512, AA.I.C.K3c) — FAA-H-8083-28

Answer (B) is incorrect because the minimum temperature normally occurs after sunrise. Answer (C) is incorrect because the minimum temperature normally occurs after sunrise, not at midnight.

Answers

9153 [C]
9155 [A]

ALL

9169. What condition produces the most frequent type of ground- or surface-based temperature inversion?

A—The movement of colder air under warm air or the movement of warm air over cold air.
B—Widespread sinking of air within a thick layer aloft resulting in heating by compression.
C—Terrestrial radiation on a clear, relatively calm night.

An inversion often develops near the ground on clear, cool nights when the wind is light. The ground radiates and cools much faster than the overlying air. Air in contact with the ground becomes cold while the temperature a few hundred feet above changes very little. Thus, temperature increases with height. (PLT301, AA.I.C.K3c) — FAA-H-8083-28

Answer (A) is incorrect because the movement of colder air under warm air is what happens when a cold front is advancing, and the movement of warm air over cold air is the process of an advancing warm front. Answer (B) is incorrect because widespread sinking of air describes compressional or adiabatic heating.

ALL

9208. How are haze layers cleared or dispersed?

A—By convective mixing in cool night air.
B—By wind or the movement of air.
C—By evaporation similar to the clearing of fog.

Haze or smoke must be dispersed by movement of air. (PLT510, AA.I.C.K3l) — FAA-H-8083-28

Answer (A) is incorrect because convective mixing would be caused by heating during the day, not by the cool night air. Answer (C) is incorrect because haze must be dispersed by movement of air, it cannot evaporate in a similar manner to the clearing of fog.

ALL

9206. You are planning a flight to the West Coast of the United States, which is currently below the published weather minimums for an ILS approach to that airport. Winds are forecast to increase to above 20 knots from the west at your scheduled arrival time. What weather conditions should you expect?

A—Visual meteorological conditions.
B—Advection fog will deepen with winds above 20 knots.
C—A layer of low stratus or stratocumulus is expected.

Advection fog is most common along coastal areas and will develop into a layer of stratus of stratocumulus clouds with wind speeds in excess of 15 knots. (PLT226, AA.I.C.K3j) — FAA-H-8083-28

ALL

9207. Which conditions are necessary for the formation of upslope fog?

A—Moist, stable air being moved over gradually rising ground by a wind.
B—A clear sky, little or no wind, and 100 percent relative humidity.
C—Rain falling through stratus clouds and a 10- to 25-knot wind moving the precipitation up the slope.

Upslope fog forms as a result of moist, stable air being cooled adiabatically as it moves up sloping terrain. (PLT226, AA.I.C.K3j) — FAA-H-8083-28

Answer (B) is incorrect because these are conditions necessary for the formation of radiation fog which usually occurs at night. Answer (C) is incorrect because upslope fog is formed by moist air being moved gradually over rising ground, not by rain falling through stratus clouds and not by a wind blowing the precipitation up the slope.

ALL

9207-1. Precipitation induced fog

A—results from relatively warm rain or drizzle falling through cooler air.
B—results from relatively cooler rain or drizzle falling through warmer air.
C—is usually of short duration.

When relatively warm rain or drizzle falls through cool air, evaporation from the precipitation saturates the cool air and forms fog. (PLT226, AA.I.C.K3j) — FAA-H-8083-28

ALL

9207-2. You are approaching an airport to land in 20 minutes. The METAR reports temperature 10°C, dew point 10°C, winds 310/04, scattered clouds and rain. You expect

A—radiation fog.
B—deepening fog.
C—clearing conditions.

Conditions favorable for radiation fog are clear sky, little or no wind, and small temperature-dew point spread. (PLT226, AA.I.C.K3j) — FAA-H-8083-28

Answers

9169 [C]	9208 [B]	9206 [C]	9207 [A]	9207-1 [A]	9207-2 [A]

ALL

9194. Which condition produces weather on the lee side of a large lake?

A—Warm air flowing over a colder lake may produce fog.
B—Cold air flowing over a warmer lake may produce advection fog.
C—Warm air flowing over a cool lake may produce rain showers.

When warm air flows over a colder lake, the air may become saturated by evaporation from the water while also becoming cooler in the low levels by contact with the cool water. Fog often becomes extensive and dense to the lee (downwind) side of the lake. (PLT226, AA.I.C.K3j) — FAA-H-8083-28

Answer (B) is incorrect because cold air flowing over a warmer lake may produce rain showers, not advection fog, on the lee side of the lake. Answer (C) is incorrect because warm air flowing over a cool lake may produce fog, not rain showers, on the lee side of the lake.

ALL

9193. What minimum thickness of cloud layer is indicated if precipitation is reported as light or greater intensity?

A—4,000 feet thick.
B—2,000 feet thick.
C—A thickness which allows the cloud tops to be higher than the freezing level.

When arriving at or departing from a terminal reporting precipitation of light or greater intensity, expect clouds to be more than 4,000 feet thick. (PLT192, AA.I.C.K3f) — FAA-H-8083-28

Answer (B) is incorrect because to produce significant precipitation (light or greater intensity), clouds are normally at least 4,000 feet thick. Answer (C) is incorrect because a cloud thickness resulting in cloud tops above the freezing level means ice droplets and super-cooled water will develop.

ALL

8723. A flight is scheduled at daybreak. The current weather is rainy but is expected to clear, with temperature/dew point spread forecast to be 10°C/10°C and winds 330° at 5 knots. What weather conditions should you expect?

A—Visual meteorological conditions until later in the day.
B—These conditions could produce radiation fog.
C—Dense fog that deepens later in the day.

Conditions favorable for radiation fog are clear sky, little or no wind, and small temperature/dew point spread (high relative humidity). Radiation fog is restricted to land because water surfaces cool little from nighttime radiation. (PLT226, AA.I.C.K3j) — FAA-H-8083-28

Answers

9194 [A] 9193 [A] 8723 [B]

Thunderstorms

Thunderstorms are always generated in very unstable conditions. Warm, moist air is forced upward either by heating from below or by frontal lifting, and becomes unstable. When the rising air cools to its dew point, a cumulus cloud forms. This "cumulus stage" is the first of three in a thunderstorm's life. It is characterized by a continuous updraft as the cloud builds. As the raindrops and ice pellets in the cloud grow larger, their weight begins to overpower the lifting force of the updrafts. As the drops fall through the cloud, they cool the air making it more dense than in the surrounding updrafts. This process causes downdrafts to form within the cloud.

When the **downdrafts** become strong enough to allow the first precipitation to reach the surface, the mature stage of the thunderstorm has begun. Eventually, the downdrafts cut off the updrafts and the storm loses the source of warm air that is its driving force. When the storm is characterized predominantly by downdrafts, it is in the dissipating stage.

Air mass thunderstorms are associated with local surface heating. On a clear, sunny day, local hot spots form that are capable of making the air over them unstable enough to generate a thunderstorm. Because the downdrafts in an air mass thunderstorm shut off the updrafts fairly quickly, this type of storm is relatively short-lived.

Steady-state thunderstorms are usually associated with weather systems. Fronts, converging winds and troughs aloft force upward motion. In a steady-state storm the precipitation falls outside the updraft allowing the storm to continue without abating for several hours.

The most violent type of steady-state thunderstorms are those generated by cold fronts or by squall lines. A **squall line** is a non-frontal instability line that often forms ahead of a fast moving cold front. Thunderstorms generated under these conditions are the most likely to develop cumulonimbus mamma clouds, funnel clouds and tornadoes. A severe thunderstorm is one which has surface winds of 50 knots or more, and/or has hail 3/4-inch or more in diameter.

Pressure usually falls rapidly with the approach of a thunderstorm, then rises sharply with onset of the first gust and arrival of the cold downdraft and heavy rain showers. As the storm passes on, the pressure returns to normal.

Even though thunderstorms are cumulus clouds formed in unstable air they can sometimes penetrate overlying bands of stratiform clouds. These are known as "**embedded thunderstorms**." Because these thunderstorms are obscured by other clouds and it is impossible for a pilot to visually detour around them, they present a particular hazard to IFR flight.

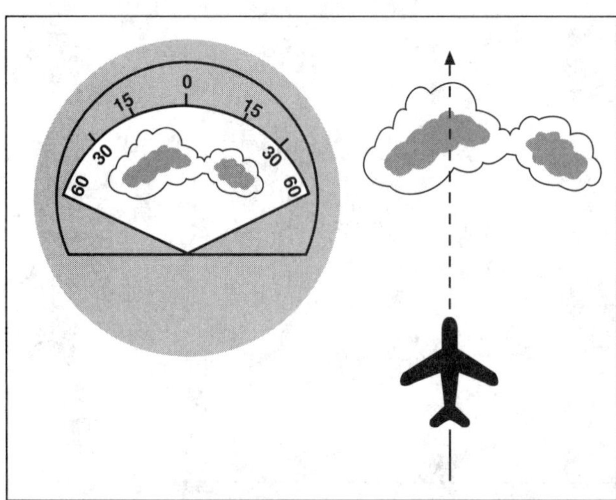

Figure 8-5. Radar display of a thunderstorm

When they can, most pilots prefer to visually avoid thunderstorms by flying around them or, if they can maintain a high enough altitude, by flying over the storm. If you are going to fly over the top of a thunderstorm, a good rule of thumb to follow is that the cloud should be overflown by at least 1,000 feet for each 10 knots of wind speed. Radar is a very useful tool in thunderstorm avoidance, especially at night or in IFR weather. The radar displays an area of precipitation size rain drops as a bright spot on the screen. Since thunderstorms often contain large water drops, they usually show up on the radar screen. A dark area on the screen is one in which no precipitation drops are detected. Areas of clouds may or may not be displayed depending on the size of the drops that make up the clouds. See Figure 8-5.

ALL

9196. Which weather phenomenon signals the beginning of the mature stage of a thunderstorm?

A—The appearance of an anvil top.
B—The start of rain at the surface.
C—Growth rate of the cloud is at its maximum.

Precipitation beginning to fall from the cloud base is the indication that a downdraft has developed and a thunderstorm cell has entered the mature stage. (PLT495, AA.I.C.K3h) — FAA-H-8083-28

Answer (A) is incorrect because the appearance of an anvil top occurs during the dissipating stage. Answer (C) is incorrect because the growth rate of a thunderstorm is at its greatest during the cumulus stage.

ALL

9197. During the life cycle of a thunderstorm, which stage is characterized predominately by downdrafts?

A—Cumulus.
B—Dissipating.
C—Mature.

Downdrafts characterize the dissipating stage of the thunderstorm. (PLT495, AA.I.C.K3h) — FAA-H-8083-28

Answer (A) is incorrect because the cumulus stage is the building stage characterized by updrafts. Answer (C) is incorrect because the mature stage has both updrafts and downdrafts, which create strong wind shears.

ALL

9198. What feature is normally associated with the cumulus stage of a thunderstorm?

A—Beginning of rain at the surface.
B—Frequent lightning.
C—Continuous updraft.

The key feature of the cumulus stage is a continuous updraft. (PLT495, AA.I.C.K3h) — FAA-H-8083-28

Answer (A) is incorrect because the beginning of rain at a surface marks the beginning of the mature stage. Answer (B) is incorrect because frequent lightning occurs after the downdrafts have developed and produce the static electricity which causes lightning.

ALL

9203. Why are downdrafts in a mature thunderstorm hazardous?

A—Downdrafts are kept cool by cold rain which tends to accelerate the downward velocity.
B—Downdrafts converge toward a central location under the storm after striking the surface.
C—Downdrafts become warmer than the surrounding air and reverse into an updraft before reaching the surface.

Precipitation beginning to fall from the cloud base is the indication that a downdraft has developed and a thunderstorm cell has entered the mature stage. Cold rain in the downdraft retards compressional heating, and the downdraft remains cooler than surrounding air. Therefore, its downward speed is accelerated and may exceed 2,500 feet per minute. (PLT495, AA.I.C.K3h) — FAA-H-8083-28

Answer (B) is incorrect because after striking the ground the downdrafts will move away from the storm's center. Answer (C) is incorrect because downdrafts remain colder than the surrounding air and accelerate downward into an updraft.

ALL

9200. Where do squall lines most often develop?

A—In an occluded front.
B—Ahead of a cold front.
C—Behind a stationary front.

A squall line is a non-frontal, narrow band of active thunderstorms. Often it develops ahead of a cold front in moist, unstable air. (PLT475, AA.I.C.K3h) — FAA-H-8083-28

Answer (A) is incorrect because squall lines most often develop ahead of a cold front, not in an occluded front. Answer (C) is incorrect because squall lines most often develop ahead of a cold front, not behind a stationary front.

ALL

9204. What is a difference between an air mass thunderstorm and a steady-state thunderstorm?

A—Air mass thunderstorms produce precipitation which falls outside of the updraft.
B—Air mass thunderstorm downdrafts and precipitation retard and reverse the updrafts.
C—Steady-state thunderstorms are associated with local surface heating.

Air mass thunderstorms most often result from surface heating. When the storm reaches the mature stage, rain falls through or immediately beside the updraft. Falling precipitation induces frictional drag, retards the updraft and reverses it to a downdraft. Such a self-destructive cell usually has a life cycle of 20 minutes to 1-1/2 hours. In a steady-state thunderstorm, the precipitation falls outside the downdraft and so the cell can last several hours. (PLT495, AA.I.C.K3h) — FAA-H-8083-28

Answer (A) is incorrect because steady-state, not air mass, thunderstorms produce precipitation which falls outside the updraft. Answer (C) is incorrect because air mass, not steady-state, thunderstorms are associated with local surface heating.

Answers

9196 [B]	9197 [B]	9198 [C]	9203 [A]	9200 [B]	9204 [B]

ALL

9205. Which type storms are most likely to produce funnel clouds or tornadoes?

A—Air mass thunderstorms.
B—Cold front or squall line thunderstorms.
C—Storms associated with icing and supercooled water.

Tornadoes occur with isolated thunderstorms at times, but much more frequently, they form with steady-state thunderstorms associated with cold fronts or squall lines. (PLT495, AA.I.C.K3h) — FAA-H-8083-28

Answer (A) is incorrect because even though air mass thunderstorms may produce funnel clouds or tornadoes, they are most likely to occur with steady-state thunderstorms. Answer (C) is incorrect because all thunderstorms that have updrafts and carry water above the freezing level can produce icing and supercooled water. But thunderstorms associated with cold fronts and squall lines are most likely to produce funnel clouds or tornadoes.

ALL

9210. Which type cloud is associated with violent turbulence and a tendency toward the production of funnel clouds?

A—Cumulonimbus mammatus.
B—Standing lenticular.
C—Stratocumulus.

Frequently, cumulonimbus mammatus clouds occur in connection with violent thunderstorms and tornadoes. (PLT501, AA.I.C.K3f) — FAA-H-8083-28

Answer (B) is incorrect because standing lenticular clouds mark mountain waves that are the product of stable air flowing over an obstruction. Answer (C) is incorrect because stratocumulus sometimes form from the breaking up of stratus or the spreading out of cumulus, and they are associated with some turbulence and possible icing at subfreezing levels.

ALL

9214. Which weather condition is an example of a nonfrontal instability band?

A—Squall line.
B—Advective fog.
C—Frontogenesis.

An instability line is a narrow, nonfrontal line or band of convective activity. If the activity is fully developed thunderstorms, the line is a squall line. (PLT511, AA.I.C.K3h) — FAA-H-8083-28

Answer (B) is incorrect because advective fog occurs when warm moist air moves over a cool surface. It forms in stable air. Answer (C) is incorrect because frontogenesis is the generation of a frontal zone.

ALL

9706. A severe thunderstorm is one in which the surface wind is

A—58 MPH or greater and/or surface hail is 3/4 inch or more in diameter.
B—50 knots or greater and/or surface hail is 1/2 inch or more in diameter.
C—45 knots or greater and/or surface hail is 1 inch or more in diameter.

A severe thunderstorm is one which has surface winds of 50 knots (58 MPH) or more, and/or has hail 3/4 inch or more in diameter. (PLT495, AA.I.C.K3h) — FAA-H-8083-28

ALL

9708. A squall is a sudden increase of at least 15 knots in average wind speed to a sustained speed of

A—24 knots or more for at least 1 minute.
B—22 knots or more for at least 1 minute.
C—20 knots or more for at least 1 minute.

A squall (SQ) means there has been a sudden increase in wind speed of at least 15 knots to a speed of 20 knots or more, and it lasted at least one minute. (PLT475, AA.I.C.K3h) — FAA-H-8083-28

ALL

9708-1. Shear turbulence from a thunderstorm has been encountered

A—10 miles from the severe thunderstorm.
B—15 miles from the severe thunderstorm.
C—20 miles from the severe thurnderstorm.

Hazardous turbulence is present in all thunderstorms; and in a severe thunderstorm, it can damage an airframe. Strongest turbulence within the cloud occurs with shear between updrafts and downdrafts. Outside the cloud, shear turbulence has been encountered several thousand feet above and 20 miles laterally from a severe storm. (PLT475, AA.I.C.K3g) — FAA-H-8083-28

ALL

9202. Atmospheric pressure changes due to a thunderstorm will be at the lowest value

A—during the downdraft and heavy rain showers.
B—when the thunderstorm is approaching.
C—immediately after the rain showers have stopped.

Answers

9205 [B]	9210 [A]	9214 [A]	9706 [A]	9708 [C]	9708-1 [C]
9202 [B]					

Pressure usually falls rapidly with the approach of a thunderstorm, then rises sharply with the onset of the first gust and the arrival of the cold downdraft and heavy rain showers, falling back to normal as the storm moves on. (PLT495, AA.I.C.K3h) — FAA-H-8083-28

Answer (A) is incorrect because during the downdraft and heavy rain showers the pressure rises sharply. Answer (C) is incorrect because immediately after the rain showers have stopped the pressure will return to normal.

ALL

9189. Convective clouds which penetrate a stratus layer can produce which threat to instrument flight?

A—Freezing rain.
B—Clear air turbulence.
C—Embedded thunderstorms.

A layer of stratiform clouds may sometimes form in a mildly stable layer while a few convective clouds penetrate the layer thus merging stratiform with cumuliform. Under the right conditions, the cumuliform clouds can become thunderstorms which are completely obscured by the surrounding stratus clouds. (PLT192, AA.I.C.K3f) — FAA-H-8083-28

Answer (A) is incorrect because the formation of freezing rain is dependent on rain falling through colder air. Convective clouds that penetrate a stratus layer may or may not produce precipitation. Answer (B) is incorrect because clear air turbulence is turbulence encountered in air where no clouds are present.

ALL

9189-1. Embedded thunderstorms, which can be hazardous during instrument flight, are most likely to occur

A—behind a fast-moving cold front.
B—in a warm front occlusion.
C—in a cold front occlusion.

A warm front occlusion occurs when the air ahead of the warm front is colder than the air of the cold front. When this occurs, the cold front rides up and over the warm front. If the air forced aloft by the warm front occlusion is unstable, the weather will be more severe than the weather found in a cold front occlusion. Embedded thunderstorms, rain, and fog are likely to occur. (PLT192, AA.I.C.K3h) — FAA-H-8083-25

ALL

9199. What is indicated by the term "embedded thunderstorms"?

A—Severe thunderstorms are embedded in a squall line.
B—Thunderstorms are predicted to develop in a stable air mass.
C—Thunderstorms are obscured by other types of clouds.

A layer of stratiform clouds may sometimes form in a mildly stable layer while a few convective clouds penetrate the layer, thus merging stratiform with cumuliform. Under the right conditions, the cumuliform clouds can become thunderstorms which are completely obscured by the surrounding stratus clouds. (PLT495, AA.I.C.K3h) — FAA-H-8083-28

Answer (A) is incorrect because a squall line consists of severe thunderstorms which can always be seen. Answer (B) is incorrect because thunderstorms do not occur in stable air masses.

ALL

9211. A clear area in a line of thunderstorm echoes on a radar scope indicates

A—the absence of clouds in the area.
B—an area of no convective turbulence.
C—an area where precipitation drops are not detected.

Airborne weather radar detects only precipitation size raindrops and hail. Absence of a radar return does indicate an area free of clouds or turbulence. (PLT495, AA.I.C.K3h) — FAA-H-8083-28

Answer (A) is incorrect because weather radar detects only precipitation drops, not clouds. Answer (B) is incorrect because convective turbulence, which would not be detected by radar, could be found under cumulus clouds. Radar does not detect turbulence.

ALL

9212. When flying over the top of a severe thunderstorm, the cloud should be overflown by at least

A—1,000 feet for each 10 knots windspeed.
B—2,500 feet.
C—500 feet above any moderate to severe turbulence layer.

When flying over the top of a severe thunderstorm, clear the top by 1,000 feet for each 10 knots of wind at the cloud top. (PLT495, AA.I.C.K3h) — FAA-H-8083-28

Answer (B) is incorrect because the cloud should be overflown by at least 1,000 feet for each 10 knots wind speed, which would normally be greater than 2,500 feet with a severe thunderstorm. Answer (C) is incorrect because the exact location of a turbulence layer will not usually be known.

Answers

9189 [C]	9189-1 [B]	9199 [C]	9211 [C]	9212 [A]

ALL

9835. A steady state thunderstorm is associated with

A—surface heating.
B—weather systems.
C—mature stage.

Steady state thunderstorms usually are associated with weather systems. Fronts, converging winds, and troughs aloft force upward motion spawning these storms which often form into squall lines. Afternoon heating intensifies them. (PLT495, AA.I.C.K3h) — FAA-H-8083-28

Wind Shear

Normally we think of changes in wind speed or direction as having an effect only on an aircraft's ground speed and track. However, when there is a very rapid shift in wind speed or direction there is a noticeable change in the aircraft's indicated airspeed as well.

In a situation where there is a sudden increase in headwind (or decrease in tailwind) the aircraft's momentum keeps it moving through space at the same ground speed as before. This means that the aircraft will be moving through the air faster than before and there will be an increase in its indicated airspeed. The aircraft will react to this increase by pitching up and by tending to climb (or descend more slowly). When there is a sudden increase in a tailwind (or decrease in the headwind), just the opposite occurs. There will be a loss of indicated airspeed accompanied by a tendency to pitch down and descend.

Wind shear is defined as any rapid change in wind direction or velocity. Often, there is little or no turbulence associated with wind shear. Severe wind shear is defined as a rapid change in wind direction or velocity causing airspeed changes greater than 15 knots or vertical speed changes greater than 500 feet per minute.

Wind shear may be associated with either a wind shift or a wind speed gradient at any level in the atmosphere. Three common generators of wind shear conditions are thunderstorms, temperature inversions and jet stream winds. Thunderstorms generate a very significant wind shear hazard for two reasons. The shear from thunderstorms is usually encountered close to the ground where there is little time or altitude to recover. The magnitude of the shear is often very severe, especially in situations involving microbursts, which we will discuss shortly. Wind shear can be encountered on all sides and directly under the thunderstorm cell. Often, in a low altitude temperature inversion the winds are very light but just above the inversion layer the wind is much stronger. When an aircraft either climbs or descends through the top of the inversion it can encounter significant wind shear because of the change in wind speed. A jet stream is a narrow "river" of wind where the speed can change a great deal over a very short distance. This is the very definition of wind shear.

Microbursts are a very localized, but very dangerous, wind shear condition. They can occur anywhere that convective weather conditions exist. This includes rain showers, virga and thunderstorms. It is believed that about 5 percent of thunderstorms produce a microburst.

A microburst is a very narrow downdraft of very high speed wind. The downdraft is typically a few hundred to 3,000 feet across with vertical speeds up to 6,000 feet per minute. When the downdraft approaches the surface, the wind flows outward from the core in all directions. Not only are these outflow winds very strong (up to 45 knots) but their effect is doubled when an aircraft flies through the shear. For example, a 45 knot headwind approaching the microburst will be a 45 knot tailwind flying out the other side—a change of 90 knots. This is usually a short-lived phenomena, seldom lasting more than 15 minutes from the time the burst strikes the ground until it dissipates.

An aircraft approaching a microburst will first experience an increasing headwind as it encounters the outflow. The increasing headwind shear causes the indicated airspeed to increase and gives the aircraft a tendency to pitch up and climb. This increase in performance without an increase in power might induce

Answers

9835 [B]

an unwary pilot into reducing power to maintain airspeed and flight path. As the aircraft flies into the core of the microburst the headwind shifts to a downdraft. The sudden loss of headwind will cause indicated airspeed to drop and cause the aircraft to pitch down and descend. The strong downdraft increases the tendency to descend and the aircraft can quickly get into the situation of having low airspeed and a very high rate of descent. As the aircraft flies out the backside of the microburst, it encounters an increasing tailwind shear that further reduces indicated airspeed and performance.

There are some wind shear conditions that exceed the performance capability of typical air carrier aircraft. For this reason it is imperative that pilots avoid situations where severe wind shear is either reported or is likely to exist. At this time only a couple of airports in the United States have experimental Doppler radar units capable of detecting wind shear. Many airports have the less sophisticated Low-Level Wind Shear Alert System (LLWAS), which is used to alert pilots to the possibility of wind shear on or near the airport. This system consists of wind sensors located around the perimeter of the airport as well as a center field wind sensor. When there is a significant difference in speed or direction between any of these sensors and the center field sensor, the tower will broadcast the difference. A typical tower transmission would be:

> "SOUTH BOUNDARY WIND ONE SIX ZERO AT TWO FIVE, WEST BOUNDARY WIND TWO FOUR ZERO AT THREE FIVE."

The greatest danger from a wind shear encounter at low altitude is that the aircraft will pick up such a high rate of descent that the pilots will be unable to stop it before hitting the ground. The technique to be used during a wind shear encounter essentially involves trading airspeed for altitude. The exact procedures vary from one aircraft to another but if an aircraft encounters severe wind shear, the pilot should maintain or increase the pitch attitude, increase power to the maximum available and accept lower than normal airspeed indications. If this does not arrest the descent, the pilot should continue to pitch up until the descent does stop or until "stick shaker" is encountered.

ALL

9139. Which is a definition of "severe wind shear"?

A—Any rapid change of horizontal wind shear in excess of 25 knots; vertical shear excepted.
B—Any rapid change in wind direction or velocity which causes airspeed changes greater than 15 knots or vertical speed changes greater than 500 ft/min.
C—Any change of airspeed greater than 20 knots which is sustained for more than 20 seconds or vertical speed changes in excess of 100 ft/min.

Severe wind shear is defined as any rapid change in wind direction or velocity which causes airspeed changes greater than 15 knots or vertical speed changes greater than 500 feet per minute. (PLT518, AA.I.C.K3b) — AC 00-54

Answer (A) is incorrect because a severe wind shear can be caused to both horizontal and vertical shears. Answer (C) is incorrect because a severe wind shear causes airspeed changes greater than 15 knots or vertical speed changes greater than 500 fpm.

ALL

9220. In comparison to an approach in a moderate headwind, which is an indication of a possible wind shear due to a decreasing headwind when descending on the glide slope?

A—Less power is required.
B—Higher pitch attitude is required.
C—Lower descent rate is required.

When a headwind shears to calm or a tailwind, the aircraft tends to lose airspeed, get low, and pitch nose down. The aircraft will require more power and a higher pitch attitude to stay on glide slope. (PLT518, AA.I.C.K3b) — AC 00-54

Answer (A) is incorrect because as airspeed decreases, more power is required. Answer (C) is incorrect because as the headwind decreases, ground speed will increase, requiring a higher descent rate.

Answers

9139 [B] 9220 [B]

ALL

9133. Which INITIAL cockpit indications should a pilot be aware of when a headwind shears to a calm wind?

A—Indicated airspeed decreases, aircraft pitches up, and altitude decreases.
B—Indicated airspeed increases, aircraft pitches down, and altitude increases.
C—Indicated airspeed decreases, aircraft pitches down, and altitude decreases.

With a headwind shearing to a calm wind there is a loss of lift as airspeed decreases, the aircraft pitches down, and the aircraft drops below glide slope (altitude decreases). Responding promptly by adding power and pitching up, a pilot may overshoot the glide slope and airspeed target but then recover. (PLT518, AA.I.C.K3b) — AC 00-54

Answer (A) is incorrect because the aircraft will pitch down due to the relatively small angle of attack used during the headwind and the sudden decrease in the airflow over the wing when the wind shears to calm. Answer (B) is incorrect because less power is required to maintain an indicated airspeed in a headwind than in calm air because of ram air; thus, a shear from a headwind to calm would be indicated by a decrease in airspeed and a decrease in altitude.

ALL

9134. Which condition would INITIALLY cause the indicated airspeed and pitch to increase and the sink rate to decrease?

A—Sudden decrease in a headwind component.
B—Tailwind which suddenly increases in velocity.
C—Sudden increase in a headwind component.

An increase in headwind component (which could also be caused by a tailwind shearing to calm) causes airspeed and pitch to increase, sink rate to decrease. (PLT518, AA.I.C.K3b) — AC 00-54

Answer (A) is incorrect because a sudden decrease in a headwind component would decrease aircraft performance and would be indicated by a decrease in airspeed, pitch, and altitude. Answer (B) is incorrect because an increase in tailwind velocity would decrease performance and be indicated by a decrease in airspeed, pitch, and altitude.

ALL

9135. Which INITIAL cockpit indications should a pilot be aware of when a constant tailwind shears to a calm wind?

A—Altitude increases; pitch and indicated airspeed decrease.
B—Altitude, pitch, and indicated airspeed decrease.
C—Altitude, pitch, and indicated airspeed increase.

When a tailwind on final shears to calm (or headwind), descent rate decreases. The closest answer suggests altitude decreases, which is still true when one considers the ground speed decreases in this situation. Indicated airspeed and pitch increase. An overshoot can result from insufficient power reduction. (PLT518, AA.I.C.K3b) — AC 00-54

Answer (A) is incorrect because pitch and indicated airspeed also increase. Answer (B) is incorrect because altitude, pitch, and indicated airspeed decrease when a headwind (not tailwind) shears to a calm wind.

ALL

9135-1. Which initial cockpit indications should a pilot be aware of when a constant headwind shears to a calm wind?

A—Altitude increases; pitch and indicated airspeed decrease.
B—Altitude, pitch, and indicated airspeed decrease.
C—Altitude, pitch, and indicated airspeed increase.

An increasing tailwind (or decreasing headwind) shear will decrease indicated airspeed and performance capability. Due to airspeed loss, the airplane may tend to pitch down to regain trim speed. (PLT518, AA.I.C.K3b) — AC 00-54

ALL

9137. Which wind-shear condition results in a loss of airspeed?

A—Decreasing headwind or tailwind.
B—Decreasing headwind and increasing tailwind.
C—Increasing headwind and decreasing tailwind.

Decreasing headwind by itself or with a shear to a tailwind will result in loss of indicated airspeed. (PLT518, AA.I.C.K3b) — AC 00-54

Answer (A) is incorrect because in a decreasing tailwind condition, airspeed initially increases. Answer (C) is incorrect because an increasing headwind and a decreasing tailwind both initially increase airspeed.

Answers

9133 [C]	9134 [C]	9135 [C]	9135-1 [B]	9137 [B]

ALL

9138. Which wind-shear condition results in an increase in airspeed?

A—Increasing tailwind and decreasing headwind.
B—Increasing tailwind and headwind.
C—Decreasing tailwind and increasing headwind.

A headwind increasing against the pitot and airframe will result in an airspeed increase. (PLT518, AA.I.C.K3b) — AC 00-54

Answers (A) and (B) are incorrect because when a headwind shears to a tailwind, increasing tailwind component and decreasing headwind component, the reduction of the ram air pressure on the pitot tube causes an initial reduction of indicated airspeed. The reduced headwind component will also cause a pitch down moment and a decrease in altitude.

ALL

9141. Which airplane performance characteristics should be recognized during takeoff when encountering a tailwind shear that increases in intensity?

A—Loss of, or diminished, airspeed performance.
B—Decreased takeoff distance.
C—Increased climb performance immediately after takeoff.

When a tailwind is encountered at liftoff, airspeed will decrease. The pilot must overcome the instinct to lower pitch attitude to recover airspeed or the aircraft may sink beyond recovery limits. Use all available performance by commanding a higher-than-normal pitch attitude and accepting the lower airspeed. (PLT518, AA.I.C.K3b) — AC 00-54

Answer (B) is incorrect because as a tailwind shear increases, takeoff distance is increased because more power or distance is required to attain lift-off speed. Answer (C) is incorrect because as a tailwind shear increases during climb-out, the climb performance will decrease.

ALL

9142. Thrust is being managed to maintain desired indicated airspeed and the glide slope is being flown. Which characteristics should be observed when a tailwind shears to a constant headwind?

A—PITCH ATTITUDE: Increases. VERTICAL SPEED: Increases. INDICATED AIRSPEED: Decreases, then increases to approach speed.
B—PITCH ATTITUDE: Increases. VERTICAL SPEED: Decreases. INDICATED AIRSPEED: Increases, then decreases.
C—PITCH ATTITUDE: Decreases. VERTICAL SPEED: Decreases. INDICATED AIRSPEED: Decreases, then increases to approach speed.

Shearing to a headwind will create an increased airspeed condition, causing a pitch up with a vertical speed decrease. (PLT518, AA.I.C.K3b) — AC 00-54

Answer (A) is incorrect because indicated airspeed will initially increase. Answer (C) is incorrect because pitch and indicated airspeed will both initially increase.

ALL

9166. What is an important characteristic of wind shear?

A—It is primarily associated with the lateral vortices generated by thunderstorms.
B—It usually exists only in the vicinity of thunderstorms, but may be found near a strong temperature inversion.
C—It may be associated with either a wind shift or a windspeed gradient at any level in the atmosphere.

Wind shear may be associated with either a wind shift or a wind speed gradient at any level in the atmosphere. (PLT518, AA.I.C.K3b) — FAA-H-8083-28

Answer (A) is incorrect because wind shear can be vertical (as well as lateral) in thunderstorm clouds between the updrafts and downdrafts, as well as in other areas such as frontal zones and low-level temperature inversions. Answer (B) is incorrect because wind shear can be encountered in areas other than thunderstorms; e.g., within a frontal zone, in and near the jet stream, low level inversions.

ALL

9201. Where can the maximum hazard zone caused by wind shear associated with a thunderstorm be found?

A—In front of the thunderstorm cell (anvil side) and on the southwest side of the cell.
B—Ahead of the roll cloud or gust front and directly under the anvil cloud.
C—On all sides and directly under the thunderstorm cell.

Wind shear can be found on all sides of a thunderstorm cell and in the downdraft directly under the cell. (PLT495, AA.I.C.K3h) — AC 00-54

Answer (A) is incorrect because the wind shear associated with a thunderstorm is on all sides and directly under the cell, not just in the front and on the southwest side. Answer (B) is incorrect because the wind shear associated with a thunderstorm is on all sides and directly under the cell. A roll cloud is not present on all thunderstorms, and when present it marks the eddies of the shear zone between the downdraft and surrounding air.

Answers

9138 [C]	9141 [A]	9142 [B]	9166 [C]	9201 [C]

ALL
9225. Which is a necessary condition for the occurrence of a low-level temperature inversion wind shear?

A—The temperature differential between the cold and warm layers must be at least 10°C.
B—A calm or light wind near the surface and a relatively strong wind just above the inversion.
C—A wind direction difference of at least 30° between the wind near the surface and the wind just above the inversion.

When taking off or landing in calm wind under clear skies within a few hours before or after sunrise, a pilot should be prepared for a temperature inversion near the ground. A shear zone in the inversion is relatively certain if the wind at 2,000 to 4,000 is 25 knots or more. (PLT501, AA.I.C.K3c) — FAA-H-8083-28

Answer (A) is incorrect because magnitude of temperature differential in the inversion is not important; the wind shear is caused by the variation in wind speed. Answer (C) is incorrect because surface wind and a relatively strong wind just above the inversion, not a wind direction difference of at least 30°, are needed to form a low-level temperature inversion wind shear. The wind shear is caused by wind speed variation, not variation in wind direction.

ALL
9701. The horizontal wind shear, critical for turbulence (moderate or greater) per 150 miles is

A—18 knots or less.
B—greater than 18 knots.
C—not a factor, only vertical shear is a factor.

Horizontal wind shear can be determined from the spacing of isotachs. The horizontal wind shear critical for turbulence (moderate or greater) is greater than 18 knots per 150 miles. 150 nautical miles is equal to 2-1/2 degrees latitude. (PLT263, AA.I.C.K3b) — FAA-H-8083-28

ALL
9130. What is the expected duration of an individual microburst?

A—Two minutes with maximum winds lasting approximately 1 minute.
B—One microburst may continue for as long as 2 to 4 hours.
C—Seldom longer than 15 minutes from the time the burst strikes the ground until dissipation.

Wind speeds intensify for about 5 minutes after a microburst initially contacts the ground. An encounter during the initial stage of microburst development may not be considered significant, but an airplane following may experience an airspeed change two to three times greater. Microbursts typically dissipate within 10 to 20 minutes after ground contact. (PLT317, AA.I.C.K3h) — AIM ¶7-1-25

ALL
9131. Maximum downdrafts in a microburst encounter may be as strong as

A—8,000 ft/min.
B—7,000 ft/min.
C—6,000 ft/min.

The downdrafts can be as strong as 6,000 feet per minute. Horizontal winds near the surface can be as strong as 45 knots resulting in a 90-knot shear across the microburst. (PLT317, AA.I.C.K3h) — AIM ¶7-1-25

ALL
9814. Maximum downdrafts in a microburst encounter are strong and may include horizontal winds near the surface as strong as

A—34 knots.
B—20 knots.
C—45 knots.

Microburst downdrafts can be as strong as 6,000 feet per minute. Horizontal winds near the surface can be as strong as 45 knots resulting in a 90-knot shear across the microburst. (PLT317, AA.I.C.K3h) — AIM ¶7-1-25

ALL
9132. An aircraft that encounters a headwind of 40 knots, within a microburst, may expect a total shear across the microburst of

A—40 knots.
B—80 knots.
C—90 knots.

With a headwind of 40 knots, the pilot may expect a total shear of 80 knots across the microburst. (PLT317, AA.I.C.K3h) — AIM ¶7-1-25

Answers (A) and (C) are incorrect because the total shear is the total headwind to tailwind change of a traversing airplane, thus a 40-knot headwind would shear 80 knots to a 40-knot tailwind.

Answers

9225 [B]	9701 [B]	9130 [C]	9131 [C]	9814 [C]	9132 [B]

ALL

9140. Doppler wind measurements indicate that the windspeed change a pilot may expect when flying through the peak intensity of a microburst is approximately

A—15 knots.
B—25 knots.
C—45 knots.

The downdrafts can be as strong as 6,000 feet per minute. Horizontal winds near the surface can be as strong as 45 knots resulting in a 90-knot shear across the microburst. (PLT317, AA.I.C.K3h) — AIM ¶7-1-25

ALL

9143. Maximum downdrafts in a microburst encounter may be as strong as

A—8,000 ft/min.
B—7,000 ft/min.
C—6,000 ft/min.

The downdrafts can be as strong as 6,000 feet per minute. Horizontal winds near the surface can be as strong as 45 knots resulting in a 90-knot shear across the microburst. (PLT317, AA.I.C.K3h) — AIM ¶7-1-25

ALL

9144. An aircraft that encounters a headwind of 45 knots, within a microburst, may expect a total shear across the microburst of

A—40 knots.
B—80 knots.
C—90 knots.

With a headwind of 45 knots, the pilot may expect a total shear of 90 knots across the microburst. (PLT317, AA.I.C.K3h) — AIM ¶7-1-25

Answer (A) is incorrect because the total shear is the total headwind to tailwind change of a traversing airplane, thus a 45-knot headwind would shear 90 knots, not 40 knots, to a 45-knot tailwind. Answer (B) is incorrect because the total shear is the total headwind to tailwind change of a traversing airplane, thus a 45-knot headwind would shear 90 knots, not 80 knots, to a 45-knot tailwind.

ALL

9145. (Refer to Figure 144.) If involved in a microburst encounter, in which aircraft positions will the most severe downdraft occur?

A—4 and 5.
B—2 and 3.
C—3 and 4.

An airplane flying through the microburst as depicted in FAA Figure 144 would encounter increasing performance in position 1, followed by a decreasing headwind in position 2. At position 3 the aircraft would encounter the strong downdraft followed by a strong tailwind at position 4. Position 5 represents the situation just before ground contact. (PLT317, AA.I.C.K3h) — AIM ¶7-1-25

Answer (A) is incorrect because position 5 has significantly less downdraft even though it has considerably more tailwind. Answer (B) is incorrect because position 2 has not as significant a downdraft as 3 and 4, but it contains a significant headwind even though it is decreasing.

ALL

9146. (Refer to Figure 144.) When penetrating a microburst, which aircraft will experience an increase in performance without a change in pitch or power?

A—3.
B—2.
C—1.

An airplane flying through the microburst as depicted in FAA Figure 144 would encounter increasing performance in position 1, followed by a decreasing headwind in position 2. At position 3 the aircraft would encounter the strong downdraft followed by a strong tailwind at position 4. Position 5 represents the situation just before ground contact. (PLT317, AA.I.C.K3h) — AIM ¶7-1-25

Answer (A) is incorrect because position 3 indicates where the most severe downdraft occurs, which results in a decrease in performance. Answer (B) is incorrect because position 2 does not have as significant a headwind component as position 1, and thus performance is less than at position 1.

ALL

9147. (Refer to Figure 144.) What effect will a microburst encounter have upon the aircraft in position 3?

A—Decreasing headwind.
B—Increasing tailwind.
C—Strong downdraft.

An airplane flying through the microburst as depicted in FAA Figure 144 would encounter increasing performance in position 1, followed by a decreasing headwind in position 2. At position 3 the aircraft would encounter the strong downdraft followed by a strong tailwind at position 4. Position 5 represents the situation just before ground contact. (PLT317, AA.I.C.K3h) — AIM ¶7-1-25

Answer (A) is incorrect because at position 2, not 3, the airplane encounters decreasing headwind. Answer (B) is incorrect because at position 5 the airplane encounters an increasing tailwind and it may result in an extreme situation as pictured, i.e., just before impact.

Answers

9140 [C]	9143 [C]	9144 [C]	9145 [C]	9146 [C]	9147 [C]

ALL

9148. (Refer to Figure 144.) What effect will a microburst encounter have upon the aircraft in position 4?

A—Strong tailwind.
B—Strong updraft.
C—Significant performance increase.

An airplane flying through the microburst as depicted in FAA Figure 144 would encounter increasing performance in position 1, followed by a decreasing headwind in position 2. At position 3 the aircraft would encounter the strong downdraft followed by a strong tailwind at position 4. Position 5 represents the situation just before ground contact. (PLT317, AA.I.C.K3h) — AIM ¶7-1-25

Answer (B) is incorrect because updrafts will occur in thunderstorms, not in microbursts from thunderstorms. Answer (C) is incorrect because the significant increase in performance occurs at position 1 where the headwind component is the greatest.

ALL

9149. (Refer to Figure 144.) How will the aircraft in position 4 be affected by a microburst encounter?

A—Performance increasing with a tailwind and updraft.
B—Performance decreasing with a tailwind and downdraft.
C—Performance decreasing with a headwind and downdraft.

An airplane flying through the microburst as depicted in FAA Figure 144 would encounter increasing performance in position 1, followed by a decreasing headwind in position 2. At position 3 the aircraft would encounter the strong downdraft followed by a strong tailwind at position 4. Position 5 represents the situation just before ground contact. (PLT317, AA.I.C.K3h) — AIM ¶7-1-25

Answer (A) is incorrect because performance will decrease with a tailwind, and thunderstorms (not microbursts) will have updrafts. Answer (C) is incorrect because the airplane at position 2 indicates where performance will decrease due to a headwind and downdraft.

ALL

9926. (Refer to Figure 144.) On final approach to the airport, airplane in position #5 would experience

A—decreased ground speed.
B—downdraft.
C—poor performance.

During a microburst encounter, the airplane first comes upon a headwind (which is performance increasing), followed by a downdraft and tailwind (both are performance decreasing). Position 5 represents an extreme situation just prior to impact. (PLT317, AA.I.C.K3h) — AIM ¶7-1-25

ALL

9150. What is the expected duration of an individual microburst?

A—Two minutes with maximum winds lasting approximately 1 minute.
B—One microburst may continue for as long as 2 to 4 hours.
C—Seldom longer than 15 minutes from the time the burst strikes the ground until dissipation.

An individual microburst will seldom last longer than 15 minutes from the time it strikes the ground until dissipation. The horizontal winds continue to increase during the first 5 minutes with the maximum intensity winds lasting approximately 2 to 4 minutes. (PLT317, AA.I.C.K3h) — AIM ¶7-1-25

Answer (A) is incorrect because microbursts last 15, not 2 minutes, and maximum winds last 2 to 4 minutes, not 1 minute. Answer (B) is incorrect because the maximum winds last 2 to 4 minutes, not 2 to 4 hours, and the microburst is usually limited to about 15 minutes.

ALL

9167. What information from the control tower is indicated by the following transmission?

"SOUTH BOUNDARY WIND ONE SIX ZERO AT TWO FIVE, WEST BOUNDARY WIND TWO FOUR ZERO AT THREE FIVE."

A—A downburst is located at the center of the airport.
B—Wake turbulence exists on the west side of the active runway.
C—There is a possibility of wind shear over or near the airport.

The Low-Level Wind Shear Alert System (LLWAS) is a computerized system which detects the presence of a possible hazardous low-level wind shear by continuously comparing the winds measured by sensors installed around the periphery on an airport with the wind measured at the center field location. If the difference between the center field wind sensor and peripheral sensor becomes excessive, a thunderstorm or thunderstorm gust front wind shear is probable. When this condition exists, the tower controller will provide arrival and departure aircraft with an advisory of the situation which includes the center field wind plus the remote location and wind. The broadcast quoted in the question is an example of this type of advisory. (PLT044, AA.I.C.K2) — AIM ¶4-3-7

Answer (A) is incorrect because a downburst is a vertical movement of air which is not measured by the LLWAS until it has horizontal movement. Also the wind direction is toward the center of the airport, not away from it. Answer (B) is incorrect because wake turbulence does not produce wind. It is generated by an aircraft that is producing lift, which could be on either side of the active runway.

Answers

9148 [A]	9149 [B]	9926 [C]	9150 [C]	9167 [C]

ALL

9136. What is the recommended technique to counter the loss of airspeed and resultant lift from wind shear?

A—Lower the pitch attitude and regain lost airspeed.
B—Avoid overstressing the aircraft, "pitch to airspeed," and apply maximum power.
C—Maintain, or increase, pitch attitude and accept the lower-than-normal airspeed indications.

Pitch attitude must be maintained or increased even when lower-than-normal airspeed indications are required. (PLT518, AA.I.C.K3b) — AC 00-54

Answer (A) is incorrect because lowering the pitch attitude to regain lost airspeed is a result of past training emphasis on airspeed control, not recovering from a wind shear. Answer (B) is incorrect because the recommended technique to recover from a wind shear is to maintain or increase pitch attitude and not "pitch to airspeed," which may decrease pitch to regain lost airspeed.

Frost and Ice

No person may dispatch or release an aircraft, continue to operate en route, or land when in the opinion of the pilot-in-command or aircraft dispatcher, icing conditions are expected or met that might adversely affect the safety of the flight. No person may takeoff when frost, snow or ice is adhering to the wings, control surfaces or propellers of the aircraft.

Deicing is a procedure in which frost, ice, or snow is removed from the aircraft in order to provide clean surfaces. Anti-icing is a process that provides some protection against the formation of frost or ice for a limited period of time.

The equipment most commonly used for **deicing** and **anti-icing** airplanes on the ground is the truck-mounted mobile deicer/anti-icer. The two basic types of fluids used are Type 1 (unthickened) fluids and Type 2 (thickened) fluids. Type 1 fluids have a minimum 80% glycol content and a relatively low viscosity, except at very low temperatures. The viscosity of Type 1 fluids depends only on temperature. The holdover time is relatively short for Type 1 fluids. Type 2 fluids have a significantly higher holdover time. Type 2 fluids have a minimum glycol content of 50% with 45% to 50% water plus thickeners and inhibitors. Water decreases the freeze point. The freeze point should be no greater than 20°F below ambient or surface temperature, whichever is less.

There is a one-step process and a two-step process for deicing and anti-icing. The one-step process uses heated fluid to remove snow, ice and frost. The primary advantage of this process is that it is quick and uncomplicated. However, where large deposits of snow or ice must be flushed off, fluid usage will be greater than with the two-step process. The two-step process consists of separate deicing and anti-icing steps. A diluted fluid, usually heated, is used to deice and a more concentrated fluid (either 100% or diluted, depending on the weather), usually cold, is used to anti-ice. Type 1 or 2 fluids can be used for both steps, or Type 1 for step 1 and Type 2 for step 2.

Two precautions to observe when using this equipment are:

1. Do not spray deice/anti-ice fluid at or into pitot inlets, TAT probes, or static ports; and
2. Apply deice/anti-ice fluid on pressure relief doors, lower door sills, and bottom edges of doors prior to closing for flight.

Icing

For ice to form, there must be moisture present in the air and the air must be cooled to a temperature of 0°C (32°F) or less. Aerodynamic cooling can lower the temperature of an airfoil to 0°C even though the ambient temperature is a few degrees warmer.

Ice is identified as clear, rime, or mixed. *Rime ice* forms if the droplets are small and freeze immediately when contacting the aircraft surface. This type of ice usually forms on areas such as the leading

Answers

9136 [C]

edges of wings or struts. It has a somewhat rough looking appearance and is a milky white color. *Clear ice* is usually formed from larger water droplets or freezing rain that can spread over a surface. This is the most dangerous type of ice since it is clear, hard to see, and can change the shape of the airfoil. *Mixed ice* is a mixture of clear ice and rime ice. It has the bad characteristics of both types and can form rapidly.

There are two kinds of icing that are significant to aviation: structural icing and induction icing. *Structural icing* refers to the accumulation of ice on the exterior of the aircraft; *induction icing* affects the powerplant operation. Structural icing occurs on an aircraft whenever supercooled droplets of water make contact with any part of the aircraft that is also at a temperature below freezing.

One inflight condition necessary for structural icing is visible moisture (clouds or raindrops). *Freezing rain* always occurs in a temperature inversion. As the rain falls through air that is below freezing, its temperature begins to fall below freezing yet it does not freeze solid—i.e., freezing rain. The process requires the temperature of the rain to be above freezing before it becomes supercooled. Eventually, the water drops will freeze into ice pellets. Any encounter with ice pellets in flight indicates that there is freezing rain at a higher altitude.

Aircraft structural ice will most likely have the highest accumulation in freezing rain; therefore, an operational consideration if you fly into rain which freezes on impact is that temperatures are above freezing at some higher altitude.

Hazards of Structural Icing

The most hazardous aspect of structural icing is its aerodynamic effects. Ice can alter the shape of an airfoil. This can cause control problems, change the angle of attack at which the aircraft stalls, and cause the aircraft to stall at a significantly higher airspeed. Ice can reduce the amount of lift that an airfoil will produce and increase the amount of drag by several times. It can partially block or limit control surfaces, which will limit or make control movements ineffective. If the extra weight caused by ice accumulation is too great, the aircraft might not be able to become airborne, and if in flight, might not be able to maintain altitude.

For this reason, regulations prohibit takeoff when snow, ice, or frost is adhering to wings, propellers, or control surfaces of an aircraft. Yet another hazard of structural icing is the possible uncommanded and uncontrolled roll phenomenon referred to as “roll upset,” which is associated with severe inflight icing. Therefore, pilots flying airplanes certificated for flight in known icing conditions should be aware that severe icing is a condition that is outside of the airplane’s certificated icing envelope.

Structural icing can also cause tailplane (empennage) stall. The tail can collect ice faster than the wing and because it is not visible to the pilot inflight, the situation could go undetected. A tailplane stall occurs when, same as with the wing, the critical angle of attack is exceeded. Since the horizontal stabilizer counters the natural nose-down tendency caused by the center of lift of the main wing, the airplane will react by pitching down, sometimes uncontrollably, when the tailplane is stalled. Application of flaps can aggravate or initiate the stall.

Because of this, the pilot should use caution when applying flaps during an approach if there is the possibility of icing on the tailplane. Ice buildup will cause the airplane to require more power to maintain cruise airspeed. Ice on the tailplane can cause diminished nose-up pitch control and heavy elevator forces, and the aircraft may buffet if flaps are applied. Ice on the rudder or ailerons can cause control oscillations or vibrations.

For an airplane to be approved for flight into icing conditions, the airplane must be equipped with systems that will adequately protect various components. Not all airplanes with these components are approved for flight into known icing; check your POH to know if your airplane has been certificated to operate in known icing conditions.

Frost Formation

Frost is described as ice deposits formed by sublimation on a surface when the temperature of the collecting surface is at or below the dew point of the adjacent air and the dew point is below freezing. Frost causes early airflow separation on an airfoil resulting in a loss of lift. Therefore, all frost should be removed from the lifting surfaces of an airplane before flight or it may prevent the airplane from becoming airborne.

Snow always forms in colder than freezing temperatures by the process of sublimation. This is when water goes straight from its vapor state into ice without ever being a liquid. Wet snow occurs when it falls to altitudes with above freezing temperatures and begins to melt.

Test data indicate that ice, snow, or frost formations having a thickness and surface roughness similar to medium or course sandpaper on the leading edge and upper surface of a wing can reduce wing lift by as much as 30% and increase drag by 40%.

ALL

9440. Which is an effect of ice, snow, or frost formation on an airplane?

A—Increased stall speed.
B—Increased pitchdown tendencies.
C—Increased angle of attack for stalls.

Aircraft with ice, snow, or frost on the wings may experience increased stall speed, decreased angle of attack for stalls, and increased pitchup tendencies. (PLT493, AA.I.B.K6) — AC 20-117

ALL

9440-1. Frozen dew is

A—white and opaque.
B—hard and opaque.
C—hard and transparent.

Frost forms in much the same way as dew. The difference is that the dew point of surrounding air must be colder than freezing. Water vapor then sublimates directly as ice crystals or frost rather than condensing as dew. Sometimes dew forms and later freezes; however, frozen dew is easily distinguished from frost. Frozen dew is hard and transparent while frost is white and opaque. (PLT493, AA.I.C.K3k) — FAA-H-8083-28

ALL

9449. Clear ice generally forms in outside temperature ranges of

A—-15 to -25°C.
B—0 to -10°C.
C—colder than -25°C.

Temperatures close to the freezing point, large amounts of liquid water, high aircraft velocities, and large droplets are conducive to the formation of clear ice. (PLT493, AA.I.C.K3i) — AC 91-51

ALL

9451. Test data indicate that ice, snow, or frost having a thickness and roughness similar to medium or coarse sandpaper on the leading edge and upper surface of a wing can

A—reduce lift by as much as 40 percent and increase drag by 30 percent.
B—increase drag and reduce lift by as much as 40 percent.
C—reduce lift by as much as 30 percent and increase drag by 40 percent.

Test data indicate that ice, snow, or frost formations having a thickness and surface roughness similar to medium or coarse sandpaper on the leading edge and upper surface of a wing can reduce wing lift by as much as 30% and increase drag by 40%. (PLT128, AA.I.B.K6) — AC 120-58

Answers

9440 [A] 9440-1 [C] 9449 [B] 9451 [C]

ALL
9695. The adverse effects of ice, snow, or frost on aircraft performance and flight characteristics include decreased lift and

A—increased thrust.
B—a decreased stall speed.
C—an increased stall speed.

Ice, frost, or snow on an aircraft can cause decreased lift, increased stall speed, and loss of thrust. (PLT493, AA.I.B.K6) — AC 120-58

ALL
9302. Even a small amount of frost, ice, or snow may

A—increase takeoff performance.
B—hinder lift production to a point where takeoff will be impossible.
C—decrease takeoff ground run.

Aircraft that have ice, snow, or frost on their surfaces must be carefully cleaned prior to beginning a flight because of the possible airflow disruption and loss of lift. (PLT128, AA.I.B.K6) — FAA-H-8083-25

ALL
9441. Which is a disadvantage of the one-step over the two-step process when deicing/anti-icing an airplane?

A—It is more complicated.
B—The holding time is increased.
C—More fluid is used with the one-step method when large deposits of ice and snow must be flushed off airplane surfaces.

Use the two-stage process to remove ice deposits with hot water or a mix of FPD (Freezing Point Depressant) and water. This reduces the amount of fluid required. (PLT108, AA.I.B.K7) — AC 120-58

Answer (A) is incorrect because the one-step process is less complicated. Answer (B) is incorrect because one of the advantages of the one-step process is increased holding time.

ALL
9442. The purpose of diluting ethylene glycol deicing fluid with water in non-precipitation conditions is to

A—raise the eutectic point.
B—decrease the freeze point.
C—increase the minimum freezing point (onset of crystallization).

Pure ethylene glycol will freeze at warmer temperatures than aqueous solutions of ethylene glycol. (PLT108, AA.I.B.K7) — AC 20-117

Answer (A) is incorrect because diluting ethylene glycol lowers the eutectic point. Answer (C) is incorrect because diluting ethylene glycol decreases the minimum freezing point (onset of crystallization).

ALL
9443. Which procedure increases holding time when deicing/anti-icing an airplane using a two-step process?

A—Heated Type 1 fluid followed by cold Type 2 fluid.
B—Cold Type 2 fluid followed by hot Type 2 fluid.
C—Heated Type 1 or 2 fluid followed by cold Type 1 fluid.

Type 2 fluid is applied cold to increase its thickness and increase holding time. (PLT108, AA.I.B.K7) — AC 120-58

Answer (B) is incorrect because cold Type 2 would not be an effective deicer. Answer (C) is incorrect because step 2 should be Type 2.

ALL
9444. Which of the following will decrease the holding time during anti-icing using a two-step process?

A—Apply heated Type 2 fluid.
B—Decrease the water content.
C—Increase the viscosity of Type 1 fluid.

Heating fluids increases their deicing effectiveness; however, in the anti-icing process, unheated fluids are more effective. (PLT108, AA.I.B.K7) — AC 120-58

Answer (B) is incorrect because decreasing the water content will increase the holding time. Answer (C) is incorrect because increasing the viscosity of Type 1 fluid will increase the holding time.

Answers

9695 [C]	9302 [B]	9441 [C]	9442 [B]	9443 [A]	9444 [A]

ALL

9753. When icing is detected, particularly while operating an aircraft without deicing equipment, the pilot should

A—fly to an area with liquid precipitation.
B—fly to a lower altitude.
C—leave the area of precipitation or go to an altitude where the temperature is above freezing.

When icing is detected, a pilot should do one of two things, particularly if the aircraft is not equipped with deicing equipment: leave the area of precipitation or go to an altitude where the temperature is above freezing. This "warmer" altitude may not always be a lower altitude. Proper preflight action includes obtaining information on the freezing level and the above-freezing levels in precipitation areas. (PLT493, AA.VII.A.K6) — FAA-H-8083-15

Answer (A) is incorrect because pilots should leave the area of any precipitation; even liquid precip can result in an icing scenario. Answer (B) is incorrect because a "warmer" altitude may not always be a lower altitude.

ALL

9756. If icing is suspected on an airplane equipped with deicing equipment, the pilot should

A—first confirm ice with the ice light prior to deploying the pneumatic boots.
B—operate the pneumatic deicing system several times to clear the ice.
C—operate the pneumatic deicing system once to allow time for the ice removal.

Pneumatic boots are one method capable of removing ice from an aircraft surface. This system is commonly used on smaller aircraft and usually provides ice removal for the wing and tail section by inflating a rubber boot. (PLT493, AA.VII.A.K6) — FAA-H-8083-15

Answer (A) is incorrect because the deicing system should be used as soon as icing is suspected. Answer (C) is incorrect because the pneumatic boots should be inflated/deflated several times to try to remove the ice.

ALL

9445. What should the deice/anti-ice fluid temperature be during the last step of a two-phase process?

A—Hot.
B—Warm.
C—Cold.

The two-step procedure involves both deicing and anti-icing. Deicing is accomplished with hot water or a hot mixture of FPD and water. The ambient weather conditions and the type of accumulation to be removed from the aircraft must be considered when determining which type of deicing fluid to use. The second (anti-icing) step involves applying a mixture of SAE or ISO Type 2 and water to the critical surfaces of the aircraft. (PLT108, AA.I.B.K7) — AC 120-58

Answers (A) and (B) are incorrect because heated fluids are used during the first step of a two-phase process.

ALL

9446. What is the minimum glycol content of Type 1 deicing/anti-icing fluid?

A—30 percent.
B—50 percent.
C—80 percent.

SAE and ISO Type 1 fluids in the concentrated form contain a minimum of 80% glycols and are considered "unthickened" because of their relatively low viscosity. (PLT108, AA.I.B.K7) — AC 120-58

ALL

9447. What is the minimum glycol content of Type 2 deicing/anti-icing fluid?

A—30 percent.
B—50 percent.
C—80 percent.

SAE and ISO Type 2 fluids contain a minimum of 50% glycols and are considered "thickened" because of added thickening agents that enable the fluid to be deposited in a thicker film and to remain on the aircraft surfaces until the time for takeoff. (PLT108, AA.I.B.K7) — AC 120-58

Answers

9753 [C] 9756 [B] 9445 [C] 9446 [C] 9447 [B]

ALL

9448. Anti-icing fluid should provide freezing point protection to

A—-20°F ambient temperature.
B—+32°F outside temperature or below.
C—a freezing point no greater than 20°F below the ambient or airplane surface temperature.

In any case the freezing point of residual fluids (water, FPD fluids or mixtures) should not be greater than 20°F below ambient or surface temperature, whichever is less. (PLT108, AA.I.B.K7) — AC 20-117

Answers (A) and (B) are incorrect because anti-icing fluid should protect from icing to a freezing point no greater than 20°F below the ambient or aircraft surface temperature.

ALL

9450. Freezing Point Depressant (FPD) fluids used for deicing

A—provide ice protection during flight.
B—are intended to provide ice protection on the ground only.
C—on the ground, cause no performance degradation during takeoff.

FPD fluids are used to aid the ground deicing process and provide a protective film to delay formations of frost, snow, or other ice. (PLT108, AA.I.B.K7) — AC 120-58

Answer (A) is incorrect because FPD does not provide inflight protection. Answer (C) is incorrect because some large aircraft experience performance degradation and may require weight or other compensation.

ALL

9452. Snow on top of deicing or anti-icing fluids

A—need not be considered as adhering to the aircraft.
B—must be considered as adhering to the aircraft.
C—must be considered as adhering to the aircraft, but a safe takeoff can be made as it will blow off.

FPD fluids are highly soluble in water; however, ice is slow to absorb FPD or to melt when in contact with it. If frost, ice, or snow is adhering to an aircraft surface, the formation may be melted by repeated application of proper quantities of FPD fluid. This process can be significantly accelerated by thermal energy from heated fluids. As the ice melts, the FPD mixes with the water thereby diluting the FPD. As dilution occurs, the resulting mixture may begin to run off. If all the ice is not melted, additional applications of FPD become necessary until the fluid penetrates to the aircraft surface. When all the ice has melted, the remaining liquid residue is a mixture of water and FPD. The resulting film could freeze (begin to crystallize) with only a slight temperature decrease. (PLT108, AA.I.B.K7) — AC 120-58

Answer (A) is incorrect because snow (ice) needs to be considered as adhering to the aircraft (see explanation). Answer (C) is incorrect because snow may not necessarily blow off during takeoff.

ALL

9453. Freezing Point Depressant (FPD) fluids are highly soluble in water; however,

A—ice is slow to absorb it but fast to melt when in contact with FPD.
B—ice absorbs it very fast but is slow to melt when in contact with it.
C—ice is slow to absorb it, and to melt when in contact with it.

FPD fluids are highly soluble in water; however, ice is slow to absorb FPD or to melt when in contact with it. (PLT108, AA.I.B.K7) — AC 120-58

Answer (A) is incorrect because FPD fluids are slow to melt. Answer (B) is incorrect because FPD fluids are slow to absorb.

ALL

9454. Freezing Point Depressant (FPD) fluid residue on engine fan or compressor blades

A—can increase performance and cause stalls or surges.
B—could cause FPD vapors to enter the aircraft but would have no affect on engine thrust or power.
C—can reduce engine performance and cause surging and/or compressor stalls.

Fluid residue on engine fan or compressor blades can reduce engine performance or cause stall or surge. (PLT108, AA.I.B.K7) — AC 120-58

Answer (A) is incorrect because fluid residue would cause a decrease in performance. Answer (B) is incorrect because fluid residue would have an affect on engine thrust or power.

Answers

9448 [C]	9450 [B]	9452 [B]	9453 [C]	9454 [C]

ALL

9698. The practice developed and accepted by the North American air carrier industry using traditional North American fluids is to ensure that the freeze point of the remaining film is below ambient temperature by at least

A—10°F.
B—20°F.
C—20°C.

As it is applied, deicing fluid is often diluted by melted snow and ice. It is standard practice to ensure that the remaining film of diluted fluid has a freeze point at least 20°F below the ambient temperature. (PLT108, AA.I.B.K7) — AC 120-58

ALL

9700. What is the effect of Freezing Point Depressant (FPD) fluid residue on engine fan or compressor blades?

A—could cause FPD vapors to enter the aircraft but would have no affect on engine thrust or power.
B—It can increase performance and cause stalls or surges.
C—It can reduce engine performance and cause surging and/or compressor stalls.

Fluid residue on engine fan or compressor blades can reduce engine performance or cause stall or surge. In addition, this could increase the possibility of, or the quantity of, glycol vapors entering the aircraft through the engine bleed air system. (PLT108, AA.I.B.K7) — AC 120-58

ALL

9183. What is a feature of supercooled water?

A—The water drop sublimates to an ice particle upon impact.
B—The unstable water drop freezes upon striking an exposed object.
C—The temperature of the water drop remains at 0°C until it impacts a part of the airframe, then clear ice accumulates.

Rain or drizzle is always formed in temperatures which are above freezing. Rain falling through colder air may become supercooled, freezing on impact as freezing rain. (PLT512, AA.I.C.K3i) — FAA-H-8083-28

Answer (A) is incorrect because sublimation is the process of changing water vapor to ice crystals (not liquid water to ice). Answer (C) is incorrect because supercooled water temperature is below 0°C.

ALL

9221. What condition is necessary for the formation of structural icing in flight?

A—Supercooled water drops.
B—Water vapor.
C—Visible water.

For structural icing to form, the aircraft must be flying through visible moisture and the temperature where the moisture strikes the aircraft must 0°C or colder. Note that the moisture does not need to be supercooled. (PLT274, AA.I.C.K3i) — FAA-H-8083-28

Answer (A) is incorrect because supercooled water drops increase the rate of icing, but are not a condition necessary for the formation of structural icing. Answer (B) is incorrect because water must be visible, not in a gaseous (vapor) state.

ALL

9224. Which type of icing is associated with the smallest size of water droplet similar to that found in low-level stratus clouds?

A—Clear ice.
B—Frost ice.
C—Rime ice.

Rime ice forms when drops are small, such as those in stratified clouds or light drizzle. (PLT274, AA.I.C.K3i) — FAA-H-8083-28

Answer (A) is incorrect because clear ice forms when drops are large, not small, as found in rain or cumuliform clouds. Answer (B) is incorrect because frost is not a structural icing condition found in flight; it happens to airplanes parked on the ground as well.

ALL

9161. Freezing rain encountered during climb is normally evidence that

A—a climb can be made to a higher altitude without encountering more than light icing.
B—a layer of warmer air exists above.
C—ice pellets at higher altitudes have changed to rain in the warmer air below.

Rain or drizzle is always formed in temperatures which are above freezing. Rain falling through colder air may become supercooled, freezing on impact as freezing rain. (PLT512, AA.I.C.K3d) — FAA-H-8083-28

Answer (A) is incorrect because freezing rain only means that a layer of warmer air exists above; it does not indicate the amount of icing that may be encountered during a climb. Answer (C) is incorrect because freezing rain is formed by rain falling through colder air, not from ice pellets melting through warmer air.

Answers

9698 [B] 9700 [C] 9183 [B] 9221 [C] 9224 [C] 9161 [B]

ALL

9161-1. What course of action should the pilot take if encountering freezing rain?

A—Climb because the temperature is warmer at a higher altitude.
B—Descend because the temperature is warmer at a lower altitude.
C—No change is necessary if all anti-ice/deice equipment is working.

Freezing rain occurs when there is a deep layer aloft with above freezing temperatures and with a shallow layer of below freezing air at the surface. Pilots should climb to warmer temperatures if encountering freezing rain. (PLT512, AA.I.C.K3d) — FAA-H-8083-28

ALL

9223. Which type precipitation is an indication that supercooled water is present?

A—Wet snow.
B—Freezing rain.
C—Ice pellets.

Rain or drizzle is always formed in temperatures which are above freezing. Rain falling through colder air may become supercooled, freezing on impact as freezing rain. (PLT344, AA.I.C.K3d) — FAA-H-8083-28

Answer (A) is incorrect because wet snow is an indication that temperature is above freezing at the present level. Answer (C) is incorrect because ice pellets indicate that water has frozen, not that is has become supercooled.

ALL

9180. What condition is indicated when ice pellets are encountered during flight?

A—Thunderstorms at higher levels.
B—Freezing rain at higher levels.
C—Snow at higher levels.

Rain or drizzle is always formed in temperatures which are above freezing. Rain falling through colder air may become supercooled, freezing on impact as freezing rain. As it continues to fall in the freezing temperature, it will form into ice pellets. (PLT493, AA.I.C.K3d) — FAA-H-8083-28

Answer (A) is incorrect because ice pellets always indicate freezing rain, not thunderstorms, at higher altitudes. Answer (C) is incorrect because freezing rain, not snow, is indicated at higher altitude when ice pellets are encountered.

ALL

9774. The most likely condition in which to experience severe inflight icing with the ambient temperature below 0°C is

A—rain.
B—visible moisture.
C—fog.

For structural icing to occur two conditions must be present: The aircraft must be flying through visible water such as rain or cloud droplets and temperature at the point where the moisture strikes the aircraft must be 0° or colder. (PLT274, AA.I.C.K3i) — FAA-H-8083-28

ALL

9775. Which of the following weather conditions are conducive to inflight icing?

A—Visible rain with temperatures below 0°C.
B—Visible rain with temperatures below 10°C.
C—Visible moisture with temperatures below 5°C.

The following weather conditions may be conducive to severe in-flight icing: visible rain at temperatures below 0°C ambient air temperature; droplets that splash or splatter on impact at temperatures below 0°C ambient air temperature. (PLT274, AA.I.C.K3i) — AC 91-51

ALL

9162. What temperature condition is indicated if precipitation in the form of wet snow occurs during flight?

A—The temperature is above freezing at flight altitude.
B—The temperature is above freezing at higher altitudes.
C—There is an inversion with colder air below.

Snowflakes are formed by sublimation in below-freezing temperatures. If the snow falls into an area of above-freezing temperatures it will start to melt, become wet snow and eventually turn into rain. (PLT493, AA.I.C.K3d) — FAA-H-8083-28

Answer (B) is incorrect because wet snow indicates above-freezing temperature at flight level, not at higher altitudes. The temperature was below freezing at the altitudes where the snow formed. Answer (C) is incorrect because wet snow indicates falling snow that has begun to melt due to above-freezing temperature at flight level. An inversion may or may not be the cause of the warmer air.

Answers

9161-1 [A]	9223 [B]	9180 [B]	9774 [A]	9775 [A]	9162 [A]

ALL

9179. Which conditions result in the formation of frost?

A—The temperature of the collecting surface is at or below freezing and small droplets of moisture are falling.
B—Dew collects on the surface and then freezes because the surface temperature is lower than the air temperature.
C—Temperature of the collecting surface is below the dewpoint and the dewpoint is also below freezing.

Frost forms when both the temperature and the dew point of the collecting surface are below freezing. When this occurs, water vapor sublimates directly into frost. This condition most often occurs on clear nights with little or no wind. (PLT493, AA.I.C.K3k) — FAA-H-8083-28

Answer (A) is incorrect because moisture that falls on a collecting surface that is at or below freezing will form ice. Answer (B) is incorrect because frozen dew is hard and transparent, while frost is the sublimation of vapor into ice, and is white and opaque.

ALL

9748. When flying in the rain and an air temperature of 1°C, a pilot should

A—not expect icing until the air temperature is 0°C or less.
B—Use autopilot in icing to lower the work load.
C—be aware of the possibility of airframe icing.

Pilots should be vigilant and aware of icing possibilities, particularly when flying in conditions between -5 and +2°C. (PLT274, AA.I.C.K3k) — AC 91-74

ALL

9181. When will frost most likely form on aircraft surfaces?

A—On clear nights with stable air and light winds.
B—On overcast nights with freezing drizzle precipitation.
C—On clear nights with convective action and a small temperature/dewpoint spread.

Frost forms when both the temperature and the dew point of the collecting surface are below freezing. When this occurs, water vapor sublimates directly into frost. This condition most often occurs on clear nights with little or no wind. (PLT493, AA.I.C.K3k) — FAA-H-8083-28

Answer (B) is incorrect because freezing drizzle would produce ice on the aircraft surfaces, not frost. Answer (C) is incorrect because stable air is required. Convective action requires unstable conditions.

ALL

9736. During an IFR cross-country flight you picked up rime icing which you estimate is 1/2" thick on the leading edge of the wings. You are now below the clouds at 2000 feet AGL and are approaching your destination airport under VFR. Visibility under the clouds is more than 10 miles, winds at the destination airport are 8 knots right down the runway, and the surface temperature is 3 degrees Celsius. You decide to:

A—use a faster than normal approach and landing speed.
B—approach and land at your normal speed since the ice is not thick enough to have any noticeable effect.
C—fly your approach slower than normal to lessen the "wind chill" effect and break up the ice.

Ice will accumulate unevenly on the airplane. It will add weight and drag, and decrease thrust and lift. With ice accumulations, landing approaches should be made with a minimum wing flap setting and with an added margin of airspeed. Sudden and large configuration and airspeed changes should be avoided. (PLT274, AA.I.C.K3k) — FAA-H-8083-3

Answer (B) is incorrect because ice having a thickness similar to sandpaper on the leading edge and upper surface of a wing can reduce wing lift by as much as 30% and increase drag by 40%. Answer (C) is incorrect because ice will increase drag, requiring additional lift (airspeed); "wind chill" effect cannot be relied upon to melt/remove the ice that has already accumulated; flying slower than normal increases the possibility of a stall due to the decreased lift.

ATM, ADX

8258. The pilot-in-command of an airplane en route determines that icing conditions can be expected that might adversely affect safety of the flight. Which action is appropriate?

A—The pilot-in-command may continue to the original destination airport, after climbing to a higher altitude.
B—The pilot-in-command shall not continue flight into the icing conditions.
C—The flight may continue to the original destination airport, provided all anti-icing and deicing equipment is operational and is used.

No person may dispatch or release an aircraft, continue to operate an aircraft en route, or land an aircraft when, in the opinion of the pilot-in-command or aircraft dispatcher, icing conditions are expected or met that might adversely affect the safety of flight. (PLT379, AA.I.C.K3k) — 14 CFR §121.629

Answers

9179 [C]	9748 [C]	9181 [A]	9736 [A]	8258 [B]

ATM, ADX
8265. What action is required prior to takeoff if snow is adhering to the wings of an air carrier airplane?

A—Sweep off as much snow as possible and the residue must be polished smooth.
B—Assure that the snow is removed from the airplane.
C—Add 15 knots to the normal V_R speed as the snow will blow off.

No person may take off in an aircraft when frost, snow, or ice is adhering to the wings, control surfaces, or propellers of the aircraft. (PLT493, AA.I.C.K3k) — 14 CFR §121.629

Answer (A) is incorrect because all of the snow must be removed prior to takeoff. Answer (C) is incorrect because there is no V-speed adjustment authorized to compensate for snow on the wings; it must be removed prior to takeoff.

ATS
9696. A pretakeoff contamination check for snow, ice or frost is required by 14 CFR Part 135. This check is required to

A—be made within 2 minutes of starting the takeoff roll.
B—be completed within 5 minutes prior to beginning the taxi to the runway.
C—see that the aircraft is clean, therefore, a safe takeoff can be made during the next 5 minutes.

A pre-takeoff inspection for ice, snow, or frost must be completed no more than 5 minutes prior to takeoff anytime conditions require it. (PLT108, AA.I.C.K3k) — 14 CFR §135.227

ATS
9697. Deicing procedures and equipment developed for large transport airplanes

A—will not be appropriate for the smaller aircraft, used under 14 CFR Part 135.
B—will be appropriate for all of the smaller aircraft, used under 14 CFR Part 135.
C—may not be appropriate for some of the smaller aircraft, used under 14 CFR Part 135.

Deicing procedures developed for large transport aircraft may not be appropriate for smaller, slower aircraft. (PLT108, AA.I.B.K7) — AC 120-58

Turbulence

Light chop causes slight, rapid and somewhat erratic bumpiness without appreciable changes in altitude or attitude. Light turbulence causes momentary slight erratic changes in altitude and/or attitude. Light chop causes rapid bumps or jolts without appreciable changes in aircraft altitude or attitude. Moderate turbulence is similar to light turbulence, but of greater intensity. Changes in altitude or attitude occur but the aircraft remains in positive control at all times. It usually causes variations in indicated airspeed. Severe turbulence causes large, abrupt changes in altitude or attitude. It usually causes large variations in indicated airspeed. The aircraft may be momentarily out of control. In extreme turbulence the aircraft is violently tossed about and is practically impossible to control. Extreme turbulence may cause structural damage.

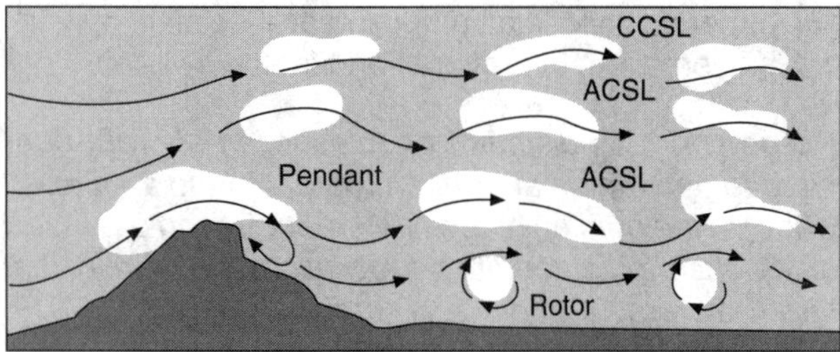

Figure 8-6. Mountain wave and associated clouds

Turbulence that occurs less than 1/3 of the time should be reported as occasional. Turbulence that occurs 1/3 to 2/3 of the time is intermittent. Turbulence that occurs more than 2/3 of the time is continuous. High altitude turbulence (normally above 15,000 feet MSL) not associated with cumuliform cloudiness should be reported as **CAT (Clear Air Turbulence)**.

Answers

8265 [B] 9696 [C] 9697 [C]

Strong winds across mountain crests can cause turbulence for 100 or more miles downwind of the mountains and to altitudes as high as 5,000 feet above the tropopause. If there is enough moisture in the air, a mountain wave can be marked by standing lenticular clouds. These clouds mark the crest of each wave. Under the right conditions, several lenticulars can form one above another. A rotor current forms below the crest of a mountain wave. This is sometimes marked by a rotor cloud which will be the lowest of a group of stationary clouds. See Figure 8-6.

The jet stream is a common source of CAT. The strong winds and steep wind gradients will almost always produce some turbulence. The most likely place to find turbulence is on the polar side of the stream in an upper trough. The strongest turbulence will be found in a curving jet stream associated with such a trough. If you encounter turbulence in the jet stream and you have a direct headwind or tailwind you should change course or altitude. With the wind parallel to your heading, you are likely to remain in the jet and the turbulence for a considerable distance. If you approach a jet stream from the polar side the temperature will drop. When you approach it from the tropical side, the temperature rises. Recall that there is a downdraft on the polar side and an updraft on the tropical side. Therefore, to avoid jet stream turbulence descend if the temperature is falling and climb if the temperature is rising as you approach the stream.

Fronts often have turbulence due to the wind shift associated with a sharp pressure trough. Try to cross the front at right angles to minimize the time you are exposed to this turbulence.

ALL

9262. What type turbulence should be reported when it causes slight, rapid, and somewhat rhythmic bumpiness without appreciable changes in attitude or altitude, less than one-third of the time?

A—Occasional light chop.
B—Moderate turbulence.
C—Moderate chop.

This description meets the criteria for occasional light chop. (PLT501, AA.I.C.K3g) — FAA-H-8083-28

Answer (B) is incorrect because moderate turbulence causes a change in the aircraft's attitude and/or altitude. Answer (C) is incorrect because moderate chop causes rapid, not rhythmic, bumps or jolts, which are not "slight."

ALL

9263. What type turbulence should be reported when it causes changes in altitude and/or attitude more than two-thirds of the time, with the aircraft remaining in positive control at all times?

A—Continuous severe chop.
B—Continuous moderate turbulence.
C—Intermittent moderate turbulence.

This description meets the criteria for continuous moderate turbulence. (PLT501, AA.I.C.K3g) — FAA-H-8083-28

Answer (A) is incorrect because severe chop is not a turbulence reporting term. Answer (C) is incorrect because intermittent means that turbulence is occurring from one-third to two-thirds of the time.

ALL

9264. What type turbulence should be reported when it momentarily causes slight, erratic changes in altitude and/or attitude, one-third to two-thirds of the time?

A—Occasional light chop.
B—Moderate chop.
C—Intermittent light turbulence.

This description meets the criteria for intermittent light turbulence. (PLT501, AA.I.C.K3g) — FAA-H-8083-28

Answer (A) is incorrect because light chop does not cause any appreciable changes in altitude and/or attitude, and occasional is less than one-third of the time. Answer (B) is incorrect because moderate chop does not cause any appreciable changes in altitude and/or attitude.

ALL

9235. Turbulence encountered above 15,000 feet AGL, not associated with cloud formations, should be reported as

A—convective turbulence.
B—high altitude turbulence.
C—clear air turbulence.

High-level turbulence (normally above 15,000 feet AGL) not associated with cumuliform cloudiness, including thunderstorms, should be reported as CAT (Clear Air Turbulence). (PLT501, AA.I.C.K3g) — FAA-H-8083-28

Answer (A) is incorrect because convective turbulence is normally associated with cumuliform clouds and is reported as turbulence. Answer (B) is incorrect because turbulence above 15,000 feet AGL, not associated with clouds, is termed clear air turbulence, not high altitude turbulence.

Answers

9262 [A]	9263 [B]	9264 [C]	9235 [C]

ALL

9190. Which type clouds are indicative of very strong turbulence?

A—Nimbostratus.
B—Standing lenticular.
C—Cirrocumulus.

Standing lenticular clouds form at the crests of waves created by barriers to the wind flow. Though the clouds do not move, they are indicative of strong winds and possible turbulence. (PLT192, AA.I.C.K3g) — FAA-H-8083-28

Answer (A) is incorrect because nimbostratus is a gray or dark massive cloud layer, diffused by continuous rain, snow, or ice pellets. The stratus feature indicates very little turbulence. Answer (C) is incorrect because cirrocumulus are thin clouds appearing as small white flakes or patches of cotton. Their presence indicates some turbulence and possible icing.

ALL

9226. What is the lowest cloud in the stationary group associated with a mountain wave?

A—Rotor cloud.
B—Standing lenticular.
C—Low stratus.

Mountain waves can generate standing lenticular clouds and rotor clouds. Of these, the rotor cloud is likely to be the lowest. (PLT501, AA.I.C.K3f) — FAA-H-8083-28

Answer (B) is incorrect because the standing lenticular clouds mark the crest, or the top, of each standing wave. Answer (C) is incorrect because low stratus clouds are not associated with a mountain wave.

ALL

9232. Clear air turbulence (CAT) associated with a mountain wave may extend as far as

A—1,000 miles or more downstream of the mountain.
B—5,000 feet above the tropopause.
C—100 miles or more upwind of the mountain.

Mountain wave CAT may extend from the mountain crests to as high as 5,000 feet above the tropopause, and can range 100 miles or more downwind from the mountains. (PLT501, AA.I.C.K3g) — FAA-H-8083-28

Answer (A) is incorrect because mountain wave CAT can range 100, not 1,000, miles or more downstream of the mountain. Answer (C) is incorrect because mountain wave CAT is downwind of the mountain.

ALL

9777. Clear air turbulence associated with a jet stream is

A—most commonly found in temperatures between -40 and -50 degrees C.
B—most commonly found in the vicinity of the tropopause.
C—similar to that associated with a tropical maritime front.

Maximum winds generally occur at levels near the tropopause. These strong winds create narrow zones of wind shear which often generate hazardous turbulence. (PLT501, AA.I.C.K3g) — FAA-H-8083-28

Answer (A) is incorrect because temperatures are not a primary factor for CAT. Answer (C) is incorrect because CAT is associated with the tropopause, not a tropical maritime front.

ALL

9777-1. The threshold wind speed in the jet stream for clear air turbulence is generally considered to be

A—100 kts.
B—110 kts.
C—120 kts.

The threshold wind speed in the jet stream for CAT is generally considered to be 110 knots. Wind speed in jet streams can be much stronger than 110 knots and the probability of encountering CAT increases proportionally with the wind speed and the wind shear it generates. It is not the wind speed itself that causes CAT; it is the wind shear or difference in wind speed from one level or point to another that causes the wave motion or overturning in the atmosphere that is turbulence to an aircraft. (PLT501, AA.I.C.K3g) — AC 00-30B

ALL

9237. What is a likely location of clear air turbulences?

A—In an upper trough on the polar side of a jetstream.
B—Near a ridge aloft on the equatorial side of a high pressure flow.
C—Downstream of the equatorial side of a jetstream.

A likely location of CAT is in an upper trough on the cold (polar) side of the jet stream. (PLT302, AA.I.C.K3g) — FAA-H-8083-28

Answer (B) is incorrect because CAT is likely to occur on the polar side of the jet stream in an upper trough. Answer (C) is incorrect because CAT is likely on the polar, not equatorial, side of a jet stream.

Answers

9190 [B]	9226 [A]	9232 [B]	9777 [B]	9777-1 [B]	9237 [A]

ALL
9239. Which type jetstream can be expected to cause the greater turbulence?

A—A straight jetstream associated with a high pressure ridge.
B—A jetstream associated with a wide isotherm spacing.
C—A curving jetstream associated with a deep low pressure trough.

A frequent CAT location is along the jet stream where it curves north and northeast of a rapidly deepening surface low. (PLT302, AA.I.C.K3g) — FAA-H-8083-28

Answer (A) is incorrect because greater turbulence is expected in a curved, not a straight jet stream. Answer (B) is incorrect because greater turbulence is more pronounced when isotherm spacing is narrow.

ALL
9230. Which action is recommended if jetstream turbulence is encountered with a direct headwind or tailwind?

A—Increase airspeed to get out of the area quickly.
B—Change course to fly on the polar side of the jetstream.
C—Change altitude or course to avoid a possible elongated turbulent area.

If jet stream turbulence is encountered with direct tailwinds or headwinds, a change of flight level or course should be initiated since these turbulent areas are elongated with the wind, and are shallow and narrow. (PLT263, AA.I.C.K3g) — AC 00-30, Appendix 1

Answer (A) is incorrect because an increase in airspeed may overstress the airplane in turbulent conditions. Normally, a reduction in airspeed is required for turbulent air penetration. Answer (B) is incorrect because CAT is normally on the polar side of the jet stream, so you would be flying into more turbulent weather.

ALL
9231. Which action is recommended regarding an altitude change to get out of jetstream turbulence?

A—Descend if ambient temperature is falling.
B—Descend if ambient temperature is rising.
C—Maintain altitude if ambient temperature is not changing.

If you want to traverse an area of CAT more quickly, watch the temperature gauge for a minute or two. If the temperature is rising—climb; if the temperature is falling—descend. Application of these rules will prevent you from following the sloping tropopause and staying in the turbulent area. If the temperature remains constant, the flight is probably close to the level of the core, so either climb or descend as is convenient. (PLT263, AA.I.C.K3g) — AC 00-30, Appendix 1

Answer (B) is incorrect because to get out of jet stream turbulence with a rising ambient temperature you would climb, not descend. Answer (C) is incorrect because you would need to make an altitude change due to jet stream turbulence, and there should be a temperature change due to a sloping tropopause.

ALL
9219. What action is recommended when encountering turbulence due to a wind shift associated with a sharp pressure trough?

A—Establish a straight course across the storm area.
B—Climb or descend to a smoother level.
C—Increase speed to get out of the trough as soon as possible.

If turbulence is encountered in an abrupt wind shift associated with a sharp pressure storm area, establish a straight course across the storm area rather than parallel to it. A change in flight level is not likely to alleviate the bumpiness. (PLT501, AA.I.C.K3g) — AC 00-30, Appendix 1

Answer (B) is incorrect because there is no indication to identify in which direction the turbulence is stronger. A change in altitude will normally remove the aircraft from the turbulent zone. Answer (C) is incorrect because speed should be decreased to the recommended airspeed for rough air. This will avoid overstressing the airplane.

Answers

9239 [C]   9230 [C]   9231 [A]   9219 [A]

Arctic and Tropical Weather Hazards

"Whiteout" is a visibility restricting phenomenon that occurs in the Arctic when a layer of cloudiness of uniform thickness overlies a snow or ice covered surface. Parallel rays of the sun are broken up and diffused when passing through the cloud layer so that they strike the snow surface from many angles. The diffused light then reflects back and forth between the clouds and the snow eliminating all shadows. The result is a loss of depth perception that makes takeoff or landing on snow-covered surfaces very dangerous.

"Tropical Cyclone" is the term for any low that originates over tropical oceans. Tropical cyclones are classified according to their intensity based on average one minute wind speeds. These classifications are:

Tropical Depression—highest sustained winds up to 34 knots.

Tropical Storm—highest sustained winds of 35 knots through 64 knots.

Hurricane or Typhoon—highest sustained winds of 65 knots or more.

The movement of hurricanes is erratic and very difficult to predict with any degree of precision. As a general rule, hurricanes in the northern hemisphere tend to move to the northwest while they are in the lower latitudes and under the influence of the trade winds. Once they move far enough north to come under the influence of the prevailing westerlies of the mid-latitudes their track tends to curve back to the northeast.

ALL

9234. Which arctic flying hazard is caused when a cloud layer of uniform thickness overlies a snow or ice covered surface?

A—Ice fog.
B—Whiteout.
C—Blowing snow.

"Whiteout" is a visibility restricting phenomenon that occurs in the Arctic when a layer of cloudiness of uniform thickness overlies a snow or ice covered surface. The result is a loss of depth perception. (PLT512, AA.I.C.K3l) — FAA-H-8083-28

Answer (A) is incorrect because ice fog forms in moist air during extremely cold conditions. It is not formed by a cloud layer overlying a snow-covered surface. Answer (C) is incorrect because blowing snow is snow that is blown by light or greater winds, causing decreased visibility. It is not formed by a cloud layer overlying a snow-covered surface.

ALL

9259. Which weather condition is present when the tropical storm is upgraded to a hurricane?

A—Highest windspeed, 100 knots or more.
B—A clear area or hurricane eye has formed.
C—Sustained winds of 65 knots or more.

Tropical cyclone international classifications are:

1. *Tropical depression — highest sustained winds up to 34 knots;*
2. *Tropical storm — highest sustained winds of 35 through 64 knots;*
3. *Hurricane or typhoon — highest sustained winds of 65 knots or more.*

(PLT511, AA.I.C.K3e) — FAA-H-8083-28

Answer (A) is incorrect because tropical cyclones are classified based on the sustained winds, not the highest wind speed. Answer (B) is incorrect because a clear area, or eye, usually forms in the tropical storm stage and continues through the hurricane stage.

ALL

9260. What is the general direction of movement of a hurricane located in the Caribbean or Gulf of Mexico region?

A—Northwesterly curving to northeasterly.
B—Westerly, until encountering land, then easterly.
C—Counterclockwise over open water, then dissipating outward over land.

Hurricanes located in the Caribbean or Gulf of Mexico move northwesterly in the lower latitudes curving to northeasterly in the higher latitudes. (PLT068, AA.I.C.K3e) — FAA-H-8083-28

Answer (B) is incorrect because a hurricane will curve easterly because of prevailing winds, not because of land. Answer (C) is incorrect because the windflow in the hurricane is counterclockwise, not the general movement of the hurricane itself.

Answers

9234 [B] 9259 [C] 9260 [A]

Aviation Routine Weather Report (METAR)

Weather reports (METAR) and forecasts (TAF) follow the format shown in Figure 8-7.

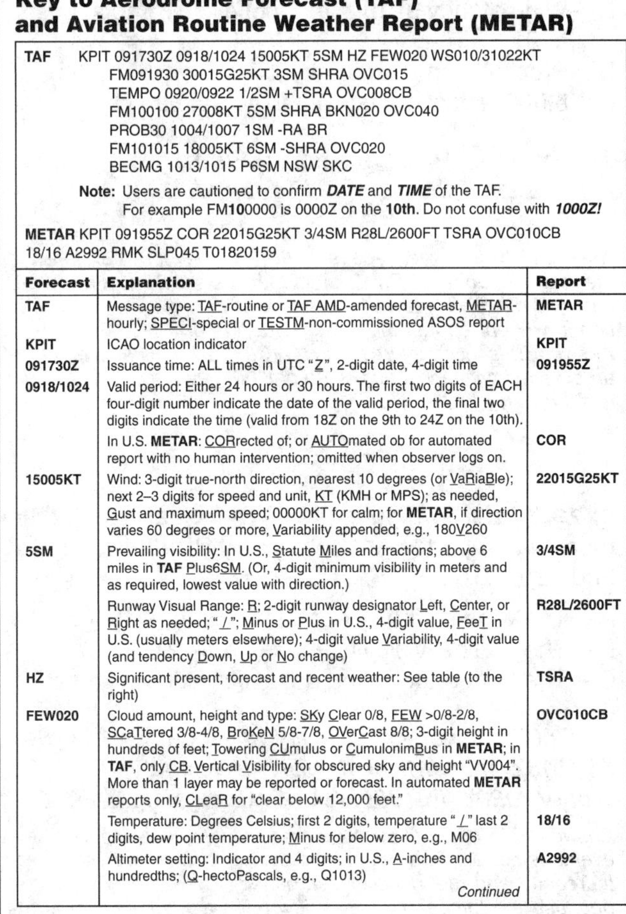

Key to Aerodrome Forecast (TAF) and Aviation Routine Weather Report (METAR)

TAF KPIT 091730Z 0918/1024 15005KT 5SM HZ FEW020 WS010/31022KT
FM091930 30015G25KT 3SM SHRA OVC015
TEMPO 0920/0922 1/2SM +TSRA OVC008CB
FM100100 27008KT 5SM SHRA BKN020 OVC040
PROB30 1004/1007 1SM -RA BR
FM101015 18005KT 6SM -SHRA OVC020
BECMG 1013/1015 P6SM NSW SKC

Note: Users are cautioned to confirm ***DATE*** and ***TIME*** of the TAF. For example FM**100000** is 0000Z on the **10th**. Do not confuse with ***1000Z!***

METAR KPIT 091955Z COR 22015G25KT 3/4SM R28L/2600FT TSRA OVC010CB 18/16 A2992 RMK SLP045 T01820159

Forecast	Explanation	Report
TAF	Message type: TAF-routine or TAF AMD-amended forecast, METAR-hourly; SPECI-special or TESTM-non-commissioned ASOS report	**METAR**
KPIT	ICAO location indicator	**KPIT**
091730Z	Issuance time: ALL times in UTC "Z", 2-digit date, 4-digit time	**091955Z**
0918/1024	Valid period: Either 24 hours or 30 hours. The first two digits of EACH four-digit number indicate the date of the valid period, the final two digits indicate the time (valid from 18Z on the 9th to 24Z on the 10th).	
	In U.S. **METAR**: CORrected of; or AUTOmated ob for automated report with no human intervention; omitted when observer logs on.	**COR**
15005KT	Wind: 3-digit true-north direction, nearest 10 degrees (or VaRiaBle); next 2–3 digits for speed and unit, KT (KMH or MPS); as needed, Gust and maximum speed; 00000KT for calm; for **METAR**, if direction varies 60 degrees or more, Variability appended, e.g., 180V260	**22015G25KT**
5SM	Prevailing visibility: In U.S., Statute Miles and fractions; above 6 miles in **TAF** Plus6SM. (Or, 4-digit minimum visibility in meters and as required, lowest value with direction.)	**3/4SM**
	Runway Visual Range: R; 2-digit runway designator Left, Center, or Right as needed; "/"; Minus or Plus in U.S., 4-digit value, FeeT in U.S. (usually meters elsewhere); 4-digit value Variability, 4-digit value (and tendency Down, Up or No change)	**R28L/2600FT**
HZ	Significant present, forecast and recent weather: See table (to the right)	**TSRA**
FEW020	Cloud amount, height and type: SKy Clear 0/8, FEW >0/8-2/8, SCaTtered 3/8-4/8, BroKeN 5/8-7/8, OVerCast 8/8; 3-digit height in hundreds of feet; Towering CUmulus or CumulonimBus in **METAR**; in **TAF**, only CB. Vertical Visibility for obscured sky and height "VV004". More than 1 layer may be reported or forecast. In automated **METAR** reports only, CLeaR for "clear below 12,000 feet."	**OVC010CB**
	Temperature: Degrees Celsius; first 2 digits, temperature "/" last 2 digits, dew point temperature; Minus for below zero, e.g., M06	**18/16**
	Altimeter setting: Indicator and 4 digits; in U.S., A-inches and hundredths; (Q-hectoPascals, e.g., Q1013)	**A2992**

Continued

Key to Aerodrome Forecast (TAF) and Aviation Routine Weather Report (METAR)

Forecast	Explanation	Report
WS010/ 31022KT	In U.S. **TAF**, non-convective low-level (≤2,000 feet) Wind Shear; 3-digit height (hundreds of feet); "/"; 3-digit wind direction and 2–3 digit wind speed above the indicated height, and unit, KT	
	In **METAR**, ReMarK indicator and remarks. For example: Sea-Level Pressure in hectoPascals and tenths, as shown: 1004.5 hPa; Temp/dew point in tenths °C, as shown: temp. 18.2°C, dew point 15.9°C	**RMK SLP045 T01820159**
FM091930	FroM: Changes are expected at: 2-digit date, 2-digit hour, and 2-digit minute **beginning** time: indicates significant change. Each FM starts on a new line, indented 5 spaces	
TEMPO 0920/0922	TEMPOrary: Changes expected for <1 hour and in total, < half of the period between the 2-digit date and 2-digit hour **beginning**, and 2-digit date and 2-digit hour **ending** time	
PROB30 1004/1007	PROBability and 2-digit percent (30 or 40): Probable condition in the period between the 2-digit date and 2-digit hour **beginning** time, and the 2-digit date and 2-digit hour **ending** time	
BECMG 1013/1015	BECoMinG: Change expected in the period between the 2-digit date and 2-digit hour **beginning** time, and the 2-digit date and 2-digit hour **ending** time	

Table of Significant Present, Forecast and Recent Weather–Grouped in categories and used in the order listed below; or as needed in TAF, No Significant Weather

QUALIFIERS
Intensity or Proximity
"–" = Light **No sign** = Moderate "+" = Heavy
"VC" = Vicinity, but not at aerodrome. In the U.S. **METAR**, 5 to 10 SM from the point of observation. In the U.S. **TAF**, 5 to 10 SM from the center of the runway complex. Elsewhere, within 8000m.

Descriptor
BC Patches **BL** Blowing **DR** Drifting **FZ** Freezing
MI Shallow **PR** Partial **SH** Showers **TS** Thunderstorm

WEATHER PHENOMENA
Precipitation
DZ Drizzle **GR** Hail **GS** Small hail or snow pellets
IC Ice crystals **PL** Ice pellets **RA** Rain **SG** Snow grains
SN Snow **UP** Unknown precipitation in automated observations

Obscuration
BR Mist (≥5/8SM) **DU** Widespread dust **FG** Fog (<5/8SM) **FU** Smoke
HZ Haze **PY** Spray **SA** Sand **VA** Volcanic ash

Other
DS Dust storm **FC** Funnel cloud **+FC** Tornado or waterspout
PO Well-developed dust or sand whirls **SQ** Squall **SS** Sandstorm

- Explanations in parentheses "( )" indicate different worldwide practices.
- Ceiling is not specified; defined as the lowest broken or overcast layer, or the vertical visibility.
- NWS **TAFs** exclude BECMG groups and temperature forecasts, NWS **TAFs** do not use PROB in the first 9 hours of a TAF; NWS **METARs** exclude trend forecasts. U.S. Military **TAFs** include Turbulence and Icing groups.

Figure 8-7. TAF/METAR weather card

ALL

9266. (Refer to Figure 145.) What was the local Central Standard Time of the Aviation Routine Weather Report at Austin (KAUS)?

A—11:53 a.m.
B—5:53 p.m.
C—10:53 p.m.

"131753Z" indicates that this METAR report is for the thirteenth day of the month, at 1753 Coordinated Universal Time (UTC). Central Standard Time is UTC minus 6 hours (1753 – 6 = 1153). (PLT059, AA.I.C.K2) — FAA-H-8083-28

ALL

9267. (Refer to Figure 145.) What type of report is listed for Lubbock (KLBB) at 1818Z?

A—An Aviation selected special weather report.
B—A special report concerning very low station pressure.
C—A Special METAR weather observation, concerning significant weather changes.

The designation "SPECI" means that this is a special weather observation. (PLT059, AA.I.C.K2) — FAA-H-8083-28

Answers

9266 [A] 9267 [A]

ALL

9268. (Refer to Figure 146.) What method was used to obtain the METAR at Tyler (KTYR) at 1753Z?

A—Automated Surface Observing System (ASOS), having a precipitation discriminator.
B—Automatic Meteorological Observing Station (AMOS), with a precipitation discriminator.
C—Automated Weather Observing System (AWOS), without a precipitation discriminator.

The word "AUTO" after the date-time group indicates that this is an automated weather report. The "A02" in the remarks section indicate that it was made by an unattended Automated Surface Observing System (ASOS). The ASOS will automatically report precipitation amounts. (PLT059, AA.I.C.K2) — FAA-H-8083-28

ALL

9269. (Refer to Figure 145.) What condition is reported at Childress (KCDS)?

A—Light rain showers.
B—Heavy rain showers began 42 minutes after the hour.
C—The ceiling is solid overcast at an estimated 1,800 feet above sea level.

"-SHRA" indicates an observation of light rain showers. (PLT059, AA.I.C.K2) — FAA-H-8083-28

Answer (B) is incorrect because the remark "RERAB42" means an observed recent weather event was that rain began at 42 minutes past the previous hour. Answer (C) is incorrect because the abbreviation "OVC180" indicated the base of an overcast layer is at 18,000 feet above the station.

ALL

9270. (Refer to Figure 145.) What condition is reported at Dallas (KDAL)?

A—The tops of the overcast is 10,000 feet.
B—Temperature/dewpoint spread is 8°F.
C—Altimeter setting is 30.07.

"A3007" indicates an altimeter setting of 30.07" Hg. (PLT059, AA.I.C.K2) — FAA-H-8083-28

Answer (A) is incorrect because "OVC100" indicates the base of the overcast layer is 10,000 feet above the station. Answer (B) is incorrect because the reported temperature/dew point are given in degrees Celsius, not Fahrenheit.

ALL

9272. SPECI KGLS 131802Z 10012G21KT 060V140 2SM +SHRA SCT005 BKN035 OVC050CB 24/23 A2980 RMK RAB1757 WS TKO RW09L WSHFT 58 FROPA.

This SPECI report at Galveston (KGLS) indicates which condition?

A—Wind steady at 100° magnetic at 12 knots, gusts to 21.
B—Precipitation started at 1757.
C—5,000 feet overcast with towering cumulus.

The remark "RAB1757" indicates rain began at 57 minutes past the hour. (PLT059, AA.I.C.K2) — FAA-H-8083-28

Answer (A) is incorrect because "10012G21KT 060V140" indicates the wind was from 100° at 12 knots with gusts to 21 knots; however, the wind direction was variable between 60-140°, and wind direction in written reports and forecasts are referenced to true north. Answer (C) is incorrect because "OVC050CB" indicates there was an overcast cumulonimbus cloud at 5,000 feet. Towering cumulus is abbreviated "TCU."

ALL

9273. (Refer to Figure 145.) What weather improvement was reported at Lubbock (KLBB) between 1750 and 1818 UTC?

A—The wind shift and frontal passage at 1812Z.
B—The vertical visibility improved by 2,000 feet.
C—The temperature and dew point spread improved.

At 1750Z, the vertical visibility was 1,000 feet (VV010). At 1818Z, the vertical visibility had improved to 3,000 feet (VV030). (PLT059, AA.I.C.K2) — FAA-H-8083-28

Answer (A) is incorrect because even though the description of the events is correct, it is not an improvement since the wind speed increased and the visibility decreased. Answer (C) is incorrect because the temperature and dew point actually converged. At 1750Z, the spread was 4°C (03/M01), but by 1818Z, there was a 0° spread (M01/M01).

ALL

8735. What hazard should you expect for a morning departure from KPDX, based on this METAR?

KPDX 271154Z 00000KT 9SM CLR -10/-10 A2979.

A—Wind shear.
B—Frost on the aircraft.
C—Sea breeze.

On calm clear nights with little-to-no wind, and a temperature at or below the dew point, you should expect dew or frost. Because the temperature and dew point are both -10 there is a high likelihood of the presence

Answers

9268 [A] 9269 [A] 9270 [C] 9272 [B] 9273 [B] 8735 [B]

of frost on the aircraft surfaces. (PLT059, AA.I.C.K2) — FAA-H-8083-28

Answers (A) and (C) are incorrect because the wind is calm.

ALL

9274. METAR KMAF 131756Z 02020KT 12SM BKN025 OVC250 27/18 A3009 RMK RAE44.

Which weather condition is indicated by this METAR report at Midland (KMAF)?

A—Rain of unknown intensity ended 16 minutes before the hour.
B—The ceiling was at 25,000 feet MSL.
C—Wind was 020° magnetic at 20 knots.

"RAE44" indicates the rain ended 44 minutes past the hour, which is the same thing as 16 minutes before the hour. (PLT059, AA.I.C.K2) — FAA-H-8083-28

Answer (B) is incorrect because a ceiling is the lowest broken or overcast layer. "BKN025" indicates a broken layer (not a ceiling) at 2,500 feet. The base of the higher overcast layer is at 25,000 feet above the station (not sea level). Answer (C) is incorrect because the winds are 020° true at 20 knots.

ALL

9275. METAR KSPS 131757Z 09014KT 6SM -RA SCT025 OVC090 24/22 A3005.
SPECI KSPS 131820Z 01025KT 3SM +RA FC OVC015 22/21 A3000.

Which change took place at Wichita Falls (KSPS) between 1757 and 1820 UTC?

A—The rain became lighter.
B—Atmospheric pressure increased.
C—A funnel cloud was observed.

"FC" in the 1820Z report indicates that a funnel cloud/tornado/waterspout was observed. (PLT059, AA.I.C.K2) — FAA-H-8083-28

Answer (A) is incorrect because the rain increased in intensity. At 1757Z, the abbreviation "-RA" indicated light rain; at 1820Z, "+RA" indicates heavy rain. Answer (B) is incorrect because the atmospheric pressure is decreased. The altimeter went from 30.05" Hg (A3005) at 1757Z, to 30.00" Hg (A3000) at 1820Z.

ALL

9276. (Refer to Figure 146.) What was the ceiling at Walnut Ridge (KARG)?

A—1,000 feet AGL.
B—2,400 feet AGL.
C—1,000 feet MSL.

"OVC010" indicates an overcast layer with bases at 1,000 feet AGL. (PLT059, AA.I.C.K2) — FAA-H-8083-28

Answer (B) is incorrect because 2,400 feet is the RVR for runway 28 at Walnut Ridge airport. Answer (C) is incorrect because the sky condition is reported in feet above the ground.

ALL

9277. METAR KHRO 131753Z 09007KT 7SM FEW020 BKN040 30/27 A3001.
SPECI KHRO 131815Z 13017G26KT 3SM +TSRA SCT020 BKN045TCU 29/24 A2983 RMK
RAB12 WS TKO LDG RW14R FRQ LTGICCG VC.

What change has taken place between 1753 and 1815 UTC at Harrison (KHRO)?

A—The ceiling lowered and cumulonimbus clouds developed.
B—Thundershowers began at 12 minutes past the hour.
C—Visibility reduced to IFR conditions.

At 1815Z, the station was reporting heavy thunderstorms and rain (+TSRA). "RAB12" indicates that the rain began at 12 minutes past the hour. (PLT059, AA.I.C.K2) — FAA-H-8083-28

ALL

9824. In this METAR excerpt, "SLP993 SNINCR 1/10" means

A—0.1" of snow on the runway land zone during the last hour.
B—1" of snow in the last 10 hours.
C—1" and a total of 10" of snow is on the ground with 1" in the last hour.

At designated stations, the "snow increasing rapidly" remark is reported in the next METAR whenever the snow depth increases by 1 inch or more in the past hour. The remark is coded in the following format: the remark indicator SNINCR, the depth increase in the past hour, and the total depth on the ground, separated from each other by a "/". (PLT059, AA.I.C.K2) — FAA-H-8083-28

Answers

9274 [A]   9275 [C]   9276 [A]   9277 [B]   9824 [C]

ALL

9704. Data that may be added (manual weather augmentation) to the Automated Weather Observing System (AWOS) report is limited to

A—the precipitation accumulation report, an automated variable visibility, and wind direction remark.
B—thunderstorms (intensity and direction), precipitation (type and intensity), and obstructions to visibility (dependent on the visibility being 3 miles or less).
C—density Altitude, NOTAMs, and reported slant range visibility.

In addition to the information automatically included in an AWOS report, information can be manually added. The remarks are limited to thunderstorms (type and intensity), and obstructions to vision when the visibility is 3 SM or less. Augmentation is identified in the observation as "observer weather." (PLT515, AA.I.C.K2) — AIM ¶7-1-11

ALL

9716. The prevailing visibility in the following METAR is

METAR KFSM 131756Z AUTO 00000KT M1/4SM R25/0600V1000FT -RA FG VV004 06/05
A2989 RMK AO2 $

A—less than 1/4 statute mile.
B—measured 1/4 statute mile.
C—a mean (average) of 1/4 statute mile.

The prevailing visibility is less than 1/4 statute miles, indicated by the "M1/4SM." (PLT059, AA.I.C.K2) — AIM ¶7-1-11

ALL

9717. The symbol ($) at the end of the following METAR indicates that

METAR KFSM 131756Z AUTO 00000KT M1/4SM R25/0600V1000FT -RA FG VV004 06/05
A2989 RMK AO2 $

A—the latest information is transmitted over a discrete VHF frequency at KFSM.
B—the latest information is broadcast on the voice portion of a local navaid at KFSM.
C—maintenance is needed on the system.

The dollar symbol ($) indicates the system may need maintenance. (PLT059, AA.I.C.K2) — AIM ¶7-1-11

ALL

9718. The VV001 in the following METAR indicates

METAR KFSM 131756Z AUTO 00000KT M1/4SM R25/0600V1000FT -RA FG VV001
A2989 RMK AO2 VIS 3/4 RWY19 CHINO RWY19 $

A—an observer reported the vertical visibility as 100 feet.
B—a 100 foot indefinite ceiling.
C—the variability value is 100 feet.

The height into an indefinite ceiling is preceded by "VV" and followed by three digits indicating the vertical visibility in hundreds of feet. This layer indicates total obscuration. The indefinite ceiling is 100 feet. (PLT059, AA.I.C.K2) — AIM ¶7-1-11

ALL

9242. METAR KFSO 030900Z VRB02KT 7SM MIFG SKC 15/14 A3012 RMK SLP993 6//// T01500139 56012

In the above METAR, the "SLP993 6////" indicates

A—sea-level pressure 993.6 hectopascals that has dropped .4 hectopascals in the last 6 hours.
B—sea-level pressure 993.6 hectopascals and that an indeterminable amount of precipitation has occurred over the last 3 hours.
C—sea-level pressure 993.6 hectopascals and that four-tenths of an inch of precipitation has fallen in the last 6 hours.

The "SLP993 6////" in the Remarks section of the METAR indicates sea-level pressure 993.6 hectopascals and that an indeterminable amount of precipitation has occurred over the last 3 hours. (PLT059, AA.I.C.K2) — FAA-H-8083-28

Answers

9704 [B] 9716 [A] 9717 [C] 9718 [B] 9242 [B]

The Terminal Aerodrome Forecast (TAF)

TAFs use the same code used in the METAR weather reports. (See Figure 8-7 in the previous section.)

ALL

9244. Which primary source contains information regarding the expected weather at the destination airport, at the ETA?

A—Low-Level Prog Chart.
B—Weather Depiction Charts.
C—Terminal Aerodrome Forecast.

A Terminal Aerodrome Forecast (TAF) is a concise statement of the expected meteorological conditions at an airport during a specified period (usually 24 hours). (PLT288, AA.I.C.K2) — FAA-H-8083-28

Answer (A) is incorrect because a Low-Level Prog Chart is a forecast of significant weather for the United States, not a forecast for a specific destination. Answer (B) is incorrect because Weather Depiction Charts are national weather maps of observed weather at a specific time; they do not provide specific information about a particular destination.

ALL

9245. Weather conditions expected to occur in the vicinity of the airport, but not at the airport, are denoted by the letters "VC." When VC appears in a Terminal Aerodrome Forecast, it covers a geographical area of

A—a 5 to 10 statute mile radius from the airport.
B—a 5-mile radius of the center of a runway complex.
C—10 miles of the station originating the forecast.

Proximity applies to weather conditions expected to occur in the vicinity of the airport (between a 5 to 10 mile radius of the airport), but not at the airport itself. It is denoted by the letters "VC." (PLT288, AA.I.C.K2) — FAA-H-8083-28

ALL

9248. What weather is predicted by the term VCTS in a Terminal Aerodrome Forecast?

A—Thunderstorms are expected in the vicinity.
B—Thunderstorms may occur over the station and within 50 miles of the station.
C—Thunderstorms are expected between 5 and 25 miles of the runway complex.

"VC" applies to weather conditions expected to occur in the vicinity of the airport (between a 5 to 10 statute mile radius of the airport), but not at the airport itself. "TS" denotes thunderstorms. Therefore, "VCTS" in a Terminal Aerodrome Forecast indicates thunderstorms are expected between a 5 to 10 mile radius of the airport, but not at the airport itself. (PLT288, AA.I.C.K2) — FAA-H-8083-28

ALL

9246. Which are the only cloud types forecast in the Terminal Aerodrome Forecast?

A—Altocumulus
B—Cumulonimbus
C—Stratocumulus

If cumulonimbus clouds are expected at the airport, the contraction "CB" is appended to the cloud layer which represents the base of the cumulonimbus cloud(s). Cumulonimbus clouds are the only cloud type forecast in TAFs. (PLT288, AA.I.C.K2) — FAA-H-8083-28

ALL

9278. A PROB40 (PROBability) HHhh group in an International Terminal Aerodrome Forecast (TAF) indicates the probability of

A—thunderstorms or other precipitation.
B—precipitation or low visibility.
C—thunderstorms or high wind.

A PROB40 (PROBability) HHhh group in a TAF indicates the probability of occurrence of thunderstorms or other precipitation events. (PLT072, AA.I.C.K2) — FAA-H-8083-28

ALL

9709. A calm wind that is forecast, in the International Terminal Aerodrome Forecast (TAF) is encoded as

A—VRB00KT.
B—00000KT.
C—00003KT.

A forecast of "00000KT" (calm) on a TAF means winds are expected at 3 knots or less. (PLT072, AA.I.C.K2) — FAA-H-8083-28

Answers

9244 [C]	9245 [A]	9248 [A]	9246 [B]	9278 [A]	9709 [B]

ALL

9710. In the International Terminal Aerodrome Forecast (TAF), a variable wind direction is noted by "VRB" where the three digit direction usually appears. A calm wind appears in the TAF as

A—00003KT.
B—VRB00KT.
C—00000KT.

Calm wind forecasts in a TAF are entered as "00000KT." (PLT072, AA.I.C.K2) — FAA-H-8083-28

ALL

9711. You are planning to arrive at the KHOU airport at 0900Z, what conditions can be expected as indicated by this TAF:

KHOU 151720Z 1518/1618 22009KT P6SM SCT030 SCT250
FM160000 18005KT P6SM BKN050 BKN120 FM160600 21007KT P6SM VCSH SCT025 BKN200
FM160900 34010KT P6SM VCTS BKN035CB BKN250
TEMPO 1611/1613 TSRA BKN012 OVC025CB
FM161600 35007KT P6SM BKN020

A—Winds from the south blowing to the north at 10 knots.
B—Thunderstorm activity 5 to 10 miles from the airport's runway complex.
C—Rain showers, scattered clouds at 2,500 feet, and overcast at 20,000 feet.

At 0900Z (FM160900), the TAF indicates the wind will be from 340° at 10 knots, with visibilities greater than 6 miles, thunderstorms in the vicinity of the airport, skies broken at 3,500 feet. (PLT283, AA.I.C.K2) — FAA-H-8083-28

Enroute Forecasts

Winds and temperatures aloft are forecast for various stations around the country. Wind directions are always relative to true north and the speed is in knots. Temperatures, in degrees Celsius, are forecast for all altitudes except for 3,000 feet. At altitudes where the wind or temperature is not forecast, a blank space is used to signify the omission. At 30,000 feet and above the minus sign is deleted from the temperature to save space.

When winds are light and variable the notation 9900 is used. When wind speeds exceed 99 knots, fifty is added to the wind direction and only the last two digits of the wind speed is printed. For example, an FB (previously FD) forecast of "731960" at FL390 is 230° true (73 – 50 = 23) at 119 knots with a temperature of -60°C. When winds exceed 199 knots they are indicated as a forecast speed of 199 knots. For example, winds from 280° at 205 knots are coded as 7899.

The temperature in the tropopause (36,000 feet and above) is approximately -56°C. ISA at sea level is 15°C and decreases at a rate of 2°/1,000 feet up to 36,000 feet MSL.

Forecast winds and temperatures aloft for international flights may be obtained by consulting wind and temperature aloft charts prepared by a Regional Area Forecast Center (RAFC).

ALL

9281. Constant Pressure Analysis Charts contain contours, isotherms and some contain isotachs. The contours depict

A—ridges, lows, troughs and highs aloft.
B—highs, lows, troughs, and ridges on the surface.
C—highs, lows, troughs, and ridges corrected to MSL.

Heights of the specified pressure for each station are analyzed through the use of solid lines called contours. This contour analysis gives the charts a height pattern. The contours depict highs, lows, troughs, and ridges, and all heights are given as pressure altitude. (PLT283, AA.I.C.K2) — FAA-H-8083-28

Answers

9710 [C] 9711 [B] 9281 [A]

ALL

9283. Vertical wind shear can be determined by comparing winds on vertically adjacent constant pressure charts. The vertical wind shear that is critical for probability of turbulence is

A—4 knots or greater per 1,000 feet.
B—6 knots or more per 1,000 feet.
C—greater than 8 knots per 1,000 feet.

Vertical wind shear can be identified by comparing winds on vertically adjacent constant pressure charts. The vertical shear critical for probable turbulence is 6 knots per 1,000 feet. (PLT518, AA.I.C.K3b) — FAA-H-8083-28

ALL

9287. (Refer to Figure 149.) What approximate wind direction, speed, and temperature (relative to ISA) are expected for a flight over OKC at FL370?

A—265° true; 27 knots; ISA +1°C.
B—260° true; 27 knots; ISA +6°C.
C—260° magnetic; 27 knots; ISA +10°C.

The Winds Aloft forecast (FB) for OKC at 34,000 feet shows a wind of 250° at 27 knots and a temperature of -43°C. At 39,000 feet the winds are 270° at 27 knots with a temperature of -54°C. Interpolation of these forecasts yields a forecast for 37,000 feet of winds from 260° at 27 knots with a temperature of -50°C. The ISA temperature at 37,000 feet is -56°C. All wind directions on a FD are relative to true north. (PLT076, AA.I.C.K2) — FAA-H-8083-28

Answer (A) is incorrect because the direction is rounded to the nearest 10° and temperature is ISA +6°C. Answer (C) is incorrect because winds are in degrees true, not magnetic.

ALL

9288. (Refer to Figure 149.) What approximate wind direction, speed, and temperature (relative to ISA) are expected for a flight over TUS at FL270?

A—347° magnetic; 5 knots; ISA -10°C.
B—350° true; 5 knots; ISA +5°C.
C—010° true; 5 knots; ISA +13°C.

The FB forecast of TUS at 24,000 feet is 050° at 5 knots with a temperature of -17°C. At 30,000 feet, the winds are 330° at 5 knots with a temperature of -33°C. Interpolation of these forecasts yields a forecast for 27,000 feet of winds from 010° at 5 knots with a temperature of -25°C. ISA temperature at 27,000 feet is -39°C. All wind directions on an FB are referenced to true north. (PLT076, AA.I.C.K2) — FAA-H-8083-28

Answer (A) is incorrect because wind direction is degrees true (not magnetic). Answer (B) is incorrect because wind direction is 010° true, not 350° true.

ALL

9289. (Refer to Figure 149.) What will be the wind and temperature trend for an SAT ELP TUS flight at 16,000 feet?

A—Temperature decrease slightly.
B—Windspeed decrease.
C—Wind direction shift from southwest to east.

SAT — Winds 196° at 8 knots, temperature -2°C.
ELP — Winds 026° at 14 knots, temperature -1°C.
TUS — Winds 080° at 11 knots, temperature 0°C.

(PLT076, AA.I.C.K2) — FAA-H-8083-28

Answer (A) is incorrect because temperatures increase slightly. Answer (B) is incorrect because wind speed increases between SAT and ELP, but decreases from ILP to TUS.

ALL

9290. (Refer to Figure 149.) What will be the wind and temperature trend for an STL MEM MSY flight at FL330?

A—Windspeed decrease.
B—Wind shift from west to north.
C—Temperature increase 5°C.

Interpolation of the FB forecasts for 30,000 and 34,000 feet yield a forecast at 33,000 feet of:

STL — Wind 260° at 56 knots, temperature -42°C.
MEM — Wind 260° at 20 knots, temperature -41°C.
MSY — Wind light and variable (9900), temperature -41°C.

(PLT076, AA.I.C.K2) — FAA-H-8083-28

Answer (B) is incorrect because the wind direction remains westerly and becomes light and variable (not shifting to the north). Answer (C) is incorrect because temperature increases 1°C.

ALL

9291. (Refer to Figure 149.) What will be the wind and temperature trend for a DEN ICT OKC flight at 11,000 feet?

A—Temperature decrease.
B—Windspeed increase slightly.
C—Wind shift from calm to a westerly direction.

Interpolation of the FB forecasts for 9,000 and 12,000 feet yield a forecast at 11,000 feet of:

DEN — Wind light and variable (9900), temperature +6°C.
ICT — Wind 060° at 2 knots, temperature +5°C.
OKC — Wind 110° at 2 knots, temperature +6°C.

(PLT076, AA.I.C.K2) — FAA-H-8083-28

Answer (A) is incorrect because the temperature increases at OKC to a temperature higher than DEN. Answer (C) is incorrect because the wind shifts from calm to an easterly direction.

Answers

9283 [B]	9287 [B]	9288 [C]	9289 [C]	9290 [A]	9291 [B]

ALL

9292. (Refer to Figure 149.) What will be the wind and temperature trend for a DSM LIT SHV flight at 12,000 feet?

A—Windspeed decrease.
B—Temperature decrease.
C—Wind direction shift from northwest to southeast.

The FB forecasts for 12,000 feet are:

DSM — Wind 300° at 22 knots, temperature 0°C.
LIT — Wind 280° at 8 knots, temperature +6°C.
SHV — Wind 210° at 6 knots, temperature +6°C.

(PLT076, AA.I.C.K2) — FAA-H-8083-28

Answer (B) is incorrect because the temperature increases en route. Answer (C) is incorrect because the wind direction shifts from northwest to southwest.

ALL

9293. (Refer to Figure 149.) What is the forecast temperature at ATL for the 3,000-foot level?

A—+6°C.
B—+6°F.
C—Not reported.

Temperatures are not forecast on the FB at the 3,000 feet level when within 2,500 of the surface. (PLT076, AA.I.C.K2) — FAA-H-8083-28

Answer (A) is incorrect because no temperature is reported at the 3,000-foot level or for a level within 2,500 feet of station elevation. Answer (B) is incorrect because no temperature is reported at the 3,000-foot level, and temperatures are depicted in degrees Celsius, not Fahrenheit. The 06 indicates wind velocity of 6 knots.

ALL

9294. (Refer to Figure 149.) What approximate wind direction, speed, and temperature (relative to ISA) are expected for a flight over MKC at FL260?

A—260° true; 43 knots; ISA +10°C.
B—260° true; 45 knots; ISA -10°C.
C—260° magnetic; 42 knots; ISA +9°C.

The FB forecast for MKC at 24,000 feet is winds of 260° at 38 knots with a temperature of -21°C. At 30,000 feet, the winds are forecast to be 260° at 50 knots with a temperature of -36°C. Interpolation for 26,000 feet yields a forecast of 260° at 42 knots with a temperature of -26°C. ISA temperature for 26,000 feet is -36°C. All wind directions on an FB are referenced to true north. (PLT076, AA.I.C.K2) — FAA-H-8083-28

Answer (B) is incorrect because forecast temperature is warmer than ISA. Answer (C) is incorrect because wind direction is degrees true, not magnetic.

ALL

9295. What wind direction and speed aloft are forecast by this WINDS AND TEMPERATURE ALOFT FORECAST (FD) for FL390 — "750649"?

A—350° at 64 knots.
B—250° at 106 knots.
C—150° at 6 knots.

For FB forecasts of wind speeds from 100 knots through 199 knots, subtract 50 from the wind direction code and add 100 to the speed code. The forecast of 750649 decodes as a wind of 250° (75 – 50 = 25) at 106 knots (100 + 06 = 106) with a temperature of –49°C (temperatures above FL240 are always negative). (PLT076, AA.I.C.K2) — FAA-H-8083-28

Answer (A) is incorrect because direction is the first two, not three, digits, and 50 must be subtracted from the first two digits. Speed is the second group of digits, not the fourth and fifth digits. Answer (C) is incorrect because 50 must be subtracted from the first two digits and 100 added to the second two digits, because the wind speed is forecast to be greater than 100 knots.

ALL

9296. What wind direction and speed aloft are forecast by this WINDS AND TEMPERATURE ALOFT FORECAST (FD) for FL390 — "731960"?

A—230° at 119 knots.
B—131° at 96 knots.
C—073° at 196 knots.

FB forecasts of wind speeds from 100 knots through 199 knots have 50 added to the wind direction code and 100 subtracted from the speed. The forecast of 731960 decodes as a wind of 230° at 119 knot with a temperature of -60°C. (PLT076, AA.I.C.K2) — FAA-H-8083-28

Answer (B) is incorrect because coded directions with wind speed over 100 knots range from 51 through 86. The direction is 230° (not 131°) at 119 knots (not 96 knots). Answer (C) is incorrect because 50 must be subtracted from the first two digits and 100 added to the second two digits. The last two digits are the temperature.

ALL

9251. Forecast winds and temperatures aloft for an international flight may be obtained by consulting

A—Area Forecasts published by the departure location host country.
B—The current International Weather Depiction Chart appropriate to the route.
C—Wind and Temperature Aloft Charts prepared by the U.S. National Centers of Environmental Prediction (NCEP).

Answers

9292	[A]	9293	[C]	9294	[A]	9295	[B]	9296	[A]	9251	[C]

Computer-generated forecast charts of winds and temperatures aloft are available for international flights at specified levels. The U.S. National Centers for Environmental Prediction (NCEP), near Washington D.C., prepares and supplies to users charts of forecast winds, temperatures, and significant weather. (PLT284, AA.I.C.K1) — FAA-H-8083-28

Answer (A) is incorrect because Area Forecasts are forecasts of general weather conditions over an area of several states and do not contain forecasts of the winds and temperatures aloft. Answer (B) is incorrect because the International Weather Depiction Chart indicates current weather and does not forecast winds and temperatures aloft.

ALL

9255. A station is forecasting wind and temperature aloft to be 280° at 205 knots; temperature –51°C at FL390. How would this data be encoded in the FB?

A—780051.
B—789951.
C—280051.

FB forecasts of wind speeds from 100 knots through 199 knots have 50 added to the wind direction code and 100 subtracted from the speed code. Winds over 200 knots are coded as 199 knots. A wind of 280° at 205 knots with a temperature of –51°C is coded as "789951." (PLT076, AA.I.C.K2) — FAA-H-8083-28

Answer (A) is incorrect because it indicates a wind at 280° at 100 knots. The minus sign is to be omitted above 24,000 feet MSL. Answer (C) is incorrect because if the wind is 0 knots, the direction and wind group is coded "9900."

ALL

9939. (Refer to Figure 149A, Area 10.) What is the forecasted wind direction, speed, and temperature over ELY at 30,000 feet?

A—330°, 35 knots, 33 °C.
B—040°, 35 knots, -33 °C.
C—220°, 35 knots, -33 °C.

The FB forecast for ELY at 30,000 feet is winds of 220 degrees at 35 knots with a temperature of –33°C. All wind directions on an FB are referenced to true north. (PLT076, AA.I.C.K2) — FAA-H-8083-28

Surface Analysis and Constant Pressure Charts

The Surface Analysis Chart shows pressure patterns, fronts and information on individual reporting stations. The pressure patterns are shown by lines called **isobars**. The isobars on a surface weather map represent lines of equal pressure reduced to sea level.

Constant pressure charts are similar in many ways to the surface analysis chart in that they show the pressure patterns and some weather conditions for reporting stations. These charts show conditions at one of five pressure levels from 850 millibars to 200 millibars. These pressure levels correspond roughly with altitudes from 5,000 feet MSL to 39,000 feet MSL. The chart is for a pressure level rather than an altitude. The altitude (in meters) of the pressure level is shown by height contours. In addition to the height contour lines, constant pressure charts can contain lines of equal temperature (isotherms) and lines of equal wind speed (isotachs). Since these are both dotted lines, be careful not to get them confused when looking at a chart. Six items of information are shown on the charts for reporting stations. These are the wind, temperature, temperature/dew point spread, height of the pressure level and the change of the height level over the previous 12 hours.

These charts can be used to locate the jet stream and its associated turbulence and wind shear. When there is a large change in wind speed over a short distance, as indicated by closely spaced isotachs, the probability of turbulence is greatly increased. Since the jet stream is associated with discontinuities in the temperature lapse rate at breaks in the tropopause, closely spaced isotherms indicate the possibility of turbulence or wind shear.

Charts can be used together to get a three dimensional view of the weather. For example, lows usually slope to the west with increasing height. If a low stops moving, it will extend almost vertically. This type of low is typical of a slow moving storm that may cause extensive and persistent cloudiness, precipitation, and generally adverse flying weather.

Answers

9255 [B]   9939 [C]

ALL

9175. Isobars on a surface weather chart represent lines of equal pressure

A—at the surface.
B—reduced to sea level.
C—at a given atmospheric pressure altitude.

Sea level pressures are plotted on a surface weather chart and lines are drawn connecting lines of equal pressure. These lines of equal pressure are called isobars. (PLT287, AA.I.C.K2) — FAA-H-8083-28

Answer (A) is incorrect because the isobars are depicted at the sea level pressure pattern at 4 MB intervals, not just at the surface. Answer (C) is incorrect because the isobars are reduced to sea level pressure, not any given atmospheric pressure altitude.

ALL

9218. Under what conditions would clear air turbulence (CAT) most likely be encountered?

A—When constant pressure charts show 20-knot isotachs less than 150 NM apart.
B—When constant pressure charts show 60-knot isotachs less than 20 NM apart.
C—When a sharp trough is moving at a speed less than 20 knots.

Clear Air Turbulence (CAT) is likely in areas where the vertical wind shear exceeds 6 knots per 1,000 feet or horizontal shear exceeds 40 knots per 150 miles. (PLT501, AA.I.C.K3g) — FAA-H-8083-28

Answer (B) is incorrect because when constant pressure charts show 20-knot isotachs less than 60 NM, CAT is most likely to be encountered, and "60-knot isotachs" do not exist. Answer (C) is incorrect because CAT can be expected upwind of the base of a deep upper trough, not because a sharp trough is moving.

ALL

9236. A strong wind shear can be expected

A—on the low pressure side of a 100-knot jetstream core.
B—where the horizontal wind shear is 15 knots, in a distance equal to 2.5° longitude.
C—if the 5°C isotherms are spaced 100 NM or closer together.

Jet streams stronger than 110 knots are apt to have significant turbulence in them in the sloping tropopause above the core, in the jet stream front below the core and on the low-pressure side of the core. (PLT518, AA.I.C.K3b) — AC 00-30, Appendix 1

Answers

9175 [B] 9218 [A] 9236 [A]

Reports and Forecasts of Hazardous Weather

A **Convective Outlook (AC)** describes the prospects for general thunderstorm activity during the following 24 hours. Areas in which there is a high, moderate or slight risk of severe thunderstorms are included as well as areas where thunderstorms may approach severe limits.

The **Severe Weather Outlook Chart** is a preliminary 24-hour outlook for thunderstorms presented in two panels. A line with an arrowhead delineates an area of probable general thunderstorm activity. An area labeled APCHG indicates probable general thunderstorm activity may approach severe intensity. "Approaching" means winds of 35 to 50 knots or hail 1/2 to 3/4 of an inch in diameter.

AIRMETs and **SIGMETs** are issued to alert pilots to potentially hazardous weather. They are broadcast by the FSS upon issue and at H+15 and H+45 while they are in effect. ARTCC facilities will announce that a SIGMET is in effect and the pilot can then contact the nearest FSS for the details.

AIRMET forecast:

- Moderate icing
- Moderate turbulence
- Sustained winds of 30 knots or more at the surface
- Widespread areas of ceilings less than 1,000 feet or visibilities of less than 3 miles
- Extensive mountain obscurement

SIGMET forecast:

- Severe and extreme turbulence
- Severe icing
- Widespread dust storms, sandstorms or volcanic ash lowering visibility to below three miles

Convective SIGMETs cover the following:

- Tornadoes
- Lines of thunderstorms
- Embedded thunderstorms
- Thunderstorm areas greater than or equal to intensity level 4
- Hail greater than 3/4 of an inch in diameter

Convective SIGMETs are each valid for one hour and are removed at H+40. They are reissued as necessary. On an hourly basis, an outlook is made up for each of the WST regions. This outlook covers the prospects for 2 to 6 hours.

Telephone Information Briefing Service (TIBS) is provided by automated flight service stations (AFSS). It is a continuous recording of meteorological and aeronautical information, available by telephone by calling 1-800-WX-BRIEF. Each AFSS provides at least four route and/or area briefings. In addition, airspace procedures and special announcements (if applicable) concerning aviation interests may also be available. Depending on user demand, other items may be provided, such as METAR observations, terminal aerodrome forecasts, wind/temperatures aloft forecasts, etc. TIBS is not intended to substitute for specialist-provided preflight briefings. It is, however, recommended for use as a preliminary briefing, and often will be valuable in helping you to make a "go or no go" decision.

ALL

9305. What information is provided by a Convective Outlook (AC)?

A—It describes areas of probable severe icing and severe or extreme turbulence during the next 24 hours.
B—It provides prospects of both general and severe thunderstorm activity during the following 24 hours.
C—It indicates areas of probable convective turbulence and the extent of instability in the upper atmosphere (above 500 mb).

A Convective Outlook (AC) describes the prospects for general and severe thunderstorm activity during the following 24 hours. Use the outlook primarily for planning (or canceling) flights later in the day. (PLT066, AA.I.C.K2) — FAA-H-8083-28

Answer (A) is incorrect because severe icing and severe or extreme turbulence are the subjects of SIGMETs. Answer (C) is incorrect because it describes a 500-mb Constant Pressure Analysis Chart.

ALL

9758. When does the National Weather Service release an Aviation Notification Watch Message (SAW)?

A—At 0000 (UTC).
B—At 0000 and 1200 (UTC).
C—Unscheduled and issued as required.

A SAW provides threat alerts on an unscheduled and as-needed basis to forecast organized severe thunderstorms that may produce tornadoes, large hail, and/or convective damaging winds. (PLT316, AA.I.C.K2) — FAA-H-8083-28

ALL

9257. If a SIGMET alert is announced, how can information contained in the SIGMET be obtained?

A—ATC will announce the hazard and advise when information will be provided in the FSS broadcast.
B—By contacting a weather watch station.
C—By contacting the nearest flight service.

SIGMETs, CWAs, and AIRMETs are broadcast by FSS's upon receipt and at 30-minute intervals at H+15 and H+45 for the first hour after issuance. Thereafter, a summarized alert notice will be broadcast at H+15 and H+45 during the valid period of the advisories. If a pilot has not previously received the SIGMET, etc., he/she should call the nearest FSS. (PLT290, AA.I.C.K2) — FAA-H-8083-28

Answer (A) is incorrect because ATC does not advise when to listen to an FSS broadcast, rather they tell you to contact FSS. Answer (B) is incorrect because the pilot may monitor an FSS broadcast or contact any FSS. "Weather watch station" is a nonexistent term.

ALL

9249. If squalls are reported at the destination airport, what wind conditions exist?

A—Sudden increases in windspeed of at least 15 knots, to a sustained wind speed of 20 knots, lasting for at least 1 minute.
B—A sudden increase in wind speed of at least 16 knots, the speed rising to 22 knots or more for 1 minute or longer.
C—Rapid variation in wind direction of at least 20° and changes in speed of at least 10 knots between peaks and lulls.

A squall (SQ) is a sudden increase in wind speed of at least 16 knots, the speed rising to 22 knots or more, and lasting at least 1 minute. (PLT475, AA.I.C.K3b) — FAA-H-8083-28

ALL

9284. (Refer to Figure 148.) Which system in the Convective SIGMET listing has the potential of producing the most severe storm?

A—The storms in Texas and Oklahoma.
B—The storms in Colorado, Kansas, and Oklahoma.
C—The isolated storm 50 miles northeast of Memphis (MEM).

Convective SIGMET 44C forecasts level 5 thunderstorms 50 miles northeast of MEM. (PLT067, AA.I.C.K2) — FAA-H-8083-28

ALL

9285. When you hear a SIGMET on an ATC frequency forecasting severe icing conditions on the route to your destination, you plan for

A—the installed transport category aircraft ice protection system protecting against all types and levels of icing as designed.
B—very little airframe icing because of an OAT of –10°C or colder, the moisture is already frozen and cannot adhere to aircraft surfaces.
C—the possibility of freezing rain and freezing drizzle that can accumulate on and beyond the limits of any deicing/anti-icing equipment.

Severe icing means the rate of accumulation is such that deicing/anti-icing equipment fails to reduce or control the hazard. Immediate diversion is necessary. (PLT274, AA.I.C.K2) — FAA-H-8083-28

Answers

9305 [B]	9758 [C]	9257 [C]	9249 [B]	9284 [C]	9285 [C]

ALL

9286. Which type weather conditions are covered in the Convective SIGMET?

A—Embedded thunderstorms, lines of thunderstorms, and thunderstorms with 3/4-inch hail or tornadoes.
B—Cumulonimbus clouds with tops above the tropopause and thunderstorms with 1/2-inch hail or funnel clouds.
C—Any thunderstorm with a severity level of VIP 2 or more.

Convective SIGMET forecast:

1. *Severe thunderstorms which have either surface winds greater than 50 knots, hail equal to or greater than 3/4 inches in diameter, or tornadoes;*
2. *Embedded thunderstorms;*
3. *Lines of thunderstorms; or*
4. *Thunderstorms equal to or greater than VIP level 4 affecting 40% or more of an area at least 3,000 square miles.*

(PLT290, AA.I.C.K2) — FAA-H-8083-28

Answer (B) is incorrect because cumulonimbus clouds with tops above the tropopause is not a weather condition covered in a Convective SIGMET. Answer (C) is incorrect because thunderstorms must be at least VIP level 4.

ALL

9747. Volcanic Ash Advisory charts are updated every

A—4 hours.
B—6 hours.
C—12 hours.

Volcanic Ash Advisories (VAAs) are issued as necessary, but at least every 6 hours until such time as the volcanic ash cloud is no longer identifiable from satellite data, no further reports of volcanic ash are received from the area, and no further eruptions of the volcano are reported. (PLT514, AA.I.C.K2) — FAA-H-8083-28

ALL

9747-1. All ATC facilities using radar weather processors with the ability to determine precipitation intensities will describe the intensity as

A—light, moderate, heavy, intense, extreme, or severe.
B—light, moderate, heavy, extreme, severe.
C—light, moderate, heavy, extreme.

All ATC facilities using radar weather processors with the ability to determine precipitation intensity describes the intensity to pilots as: "LIGHT" (< 30 dBZ), "MODERATE" (30 to 40 dBZ), "HEAVY" (>40 to 50 dBZ), or "EXTREME" (>50 dBZ). (PLT515, AA.I.C.K2) — FAA-H-8083-15

ALL

9747-2. Maximum turbulence potential charts (GTG-2) are issued

A—every morning at 0400.
B—two times a day.
C—hourly.

The Graphical Turbulence Guidance (GTG-2) graphics are computer-generated four-dimensional forecasts of information related to the likelihood of encountering Clear Air Turbulence (CAT) associated with upper-level fronts and jet streams. The GTG-2 product consists of a 00, 01, 02, and 03 hour forecast, which are updated every hour, and a 06, 09, and 12 hour forecast, which are updated every three hours starting at 00Z. GTG-2 graphics are "snapshot" graphics, intended to depict forecasted clear air turbulence conditions at the valid time (for example, at 1200Z), not for a valid time range (for example, from 1200Z to 1300Z). (PLT515, AA.I.C.K2) — FAA-H-8083-28

ALL

9747-3. Airborne weather radar is installed to help the crew

A—penetrate weather between storm cells.
B—avoid severe weather.
C—avoid storm turbulence and hail.

Airborne weather radar is used primarily for the detection of hazardous windshear conditions, precipitation, and winds aloft on and near major airports situated in climates with great exposure to thunderstorms. (PLT105, AA.I.C.K2) — FAA-H-8083-28

Answers

9286 [A] 9747 [B] 9747-1 [C] 9747-2 [C] 9747-3 [B]

PIREPs

A pilot weather report (PIREP) is often the most timely source of information about such weather conditions as icing and multiple cloud layers. While area forecasts and freezing level charts can give the pilot a good idea of the potential for icing, only a PIREP can let the pilot know what is happening currently. A typical PIREP appended to an SA is:

FTW UA /OV DFW 18005/TM1803/FL095/TP PA 30/SK 036 OVC 060/070 OVC 075/OVC ABV

The translation is:

FTW / UA — PIREP from reporting station FTW.

OV DFW 18005 — location is the DFW 180° radial at 5 miles.

TM 1803 — time of the report is 1803.

FL095 — altitude is 9,500 feet.

TP PA 30 — Type of aircraft is a PA 30.

SK 036 OVC 060/070 OVC 075/OVC ABV — Sky condition. The base of an overcast layer is at 3,600 feet with top at 6,000 feet. A second overcast layer has its base at 7,000 feet and its top is 7,500 feet. There is another overcast layer above the aircraft's altitude of 9,500 feet.

ALL

9247. What sources reflect the most accurate information on current and forecast icing conditions?

A—Low-Level Sig Weather Prog Chart, RADATs, and the Area Forecast.
B—PIREPs, Area Forecast, and the Freezing Level Chart.
C—AIRMET Zulus.

AIRMET Zulu describes moderate icing and provides freezing level heights. (PLT294, AA.I.C.K2) — FAA-H-8083-28

Answer (A) is incorrect because Low-Level Sig Weather Prog Charts do not forecast icing conditions but do forecast freezing levels. Answer (B) is incorrect because although the Freezing Level Panel of the Composite Moisture Stability Chart gives you the lowest observed freezing level, it does not indicate the presence of clouds or precipitation, which must be present for icing to occur.

ALL

9250. Which type of weather can only be directly observed during flight and then reported in a PIREP?

A—Turbulence and structural icing.
B—Jetstream-type winds and icing.
C—Level of the tropopause and turbulence.

Aircraft in flight are the only means of directly observing cloud tops, icing and turbulence. (PLT061, AA.I.C.K2) — FAA-H-8083-28

Answer (B) is incorrect because a pilot would not be able to determine from observation if jet stream type winds or other CAT were encountered. Answer (C) is incorrect because the level of the tropopause is determined by radiosondes released by ground weather observing stations. It is not a type of weather that can be directly observed by a pilot during flight.

Answers

9247 [C] 9250 [A]

ALL

9271. (Refer to Figure 145.) The peak wind at KAMA was reported to be from 320° true at 39 knots,

A—which occurred at 1743Z.
B—with gusts to 43 knots.
C—with .43 of an inch liquid precipitation since the last report.

"PK WND 32039/43" indicates that the peak wind was reported to be from 320° true at 39 knots, which occurred at 43 minutes past the hour. (PLT059, AA.I.C.K2) — FAA-H-8083-28

ALL

9713. KFTW UA/OV DFW/TM 1645/FL100/TP PA30/ SK SCT031-TOP043/BKN060-TOP085/OVC097-TOPUNKN/WX FV00SM RA/TA 07.

This pilot report to Fort Worth (KFTW) indicates

A—the aircraft is in light rain.
B—that the top of the ceiling is 4,300 feet.
C—the ceiling at KDFW is 6,000 feet.

"BKN060-TOP085" indicates the ceiling (defined as the lowest broken or overcast layer aloft) is broken at 6,000 feet with tops at 8,500 feet. (PLT061, AA.I.C.K2) — FAA-H-8083-28

Answer (A) is incorrect because "WX FV00SM RA" indicates the flight visibility is 0 statute miles due to moderate rain. Answer (B) is incorrect because the scattered layer has tops at 4,300 feet, but this does not constitute a ceiling.

ALL

9922. What is indicated by the following report?

TYR UUA/OV TYR180015/TM 1757/FL310/TP B737/ TB MOD-SEV CAT 350-390

A—An urgent pilot report for moderate to severe clear air turbulence.
B—A routine pilot report for overcast conditions from flight levels 350-390.
C—A special METAR issued on the 18th day of the month at 1757Z.

UUA at the start indicates this is an urgent pilot report. MOD-SEV CAT 350-390 indicates moderate to severe clear air turbulence between FL350 and FL390. (PLT061, AA.I.C.K2) — FAA-H-8083-28

Answers

9271 [A] 9713 [C] 9922 [A]

Cross-Reference A
Question Number and Page Number

This cross-reference lists all of the questions in this book in sequential order. Use this list in combination with Cross-Reference B to find specific questions to aid your studies. For more information about the questions included in ASA Test Preps, please see pages vi–vii and xviii.

Cross-Reference A Question Number and Page Number

Question Number	Page Number
8177	1–59
8178	1–61
8179	1–61
8180	1–63
8181	1–50
8182	1–63
8183	1–61
8184	1–62
8185	1–63
8186	1–62
8187	1–62
8188	1–9
8189	1–8
8190	1–8
8191	1–7
8192	1–9
8193	1–9
8194	1–34
8195	2–21
8195-1	2–21
8196	2–28
8197	2–28
8198	1–65
8199	2–29
8200	1–65
8201	1–9
8202	1–10
8203	2–50
8204	1–65
8205	1–14
8206	2–10
8207	1–14
8208	1–15
8209	1–15
8210	1–15
8211	1–29
8212	1–8
8213	1–8
8214	1–15
8215	1–14
8216	1–14
8217	1–14
8218	1–65
8219	1–29
8220	1–28
8221	1–29
8222	1–29
8223	1–29
8224	1–30
8225	1–50
8226	1–40
8227	1–28
8228	1–28
8229	1–30
8230	1–16
8231	1–30
8231-1	1–30
8232	1–40
8233	1–51
8234	1–51
8235	1–61
8236	1–66
8237	1–66
8238	1–30
8239	1–67
8240	1–66
8241	1–66
8242	6–57
8243	1–38
8243-1	1–38
8244	1–50
8245	1–65
8246	1–66
8247	6–18
8248	6–19
8249	6–20
8250	6–20
8251	6–19
8252	6–20
8253	6–11
8254	6–19
8255	6–19
8256	6–18
8257	6–26
8258	8–37
8259	1–40
8260	1–40
8261	6–26
8262	6–19
8263	6–27
8264	6–27
8265	8–38
8266	1–40
8267	1–40
8268	1–44
8269	1–45
8270	1–46
8271	1–45
8272	1–45
8273	1–46
8274	1–46
8275	1–47
8276	1–45
8277	1–46
8278	2–4
8279	6–35
8280	1–39
8281	1–43
8282	1–43
8283	1–39
8284	1–39
8285	1–16
8286	1–41
8287	1–41
8288	1–41
8289	1–16
8290	1–38
8291	1–41
8292	1–38
8293	1–39
8294	1–39
8295	1–42
8296	1–41
8297	6–41
8298	6–42
8298-1	6–42
8317	1–72
8318	1–72
8319	1–72
8320	1–72
8321	1–72
8322	1–72
8323	1–72
8324	3–20
8325	3–20
8326	3–20
8327	3–20
8328	3–24
8329	3–24
8330	3–23
8331	3–25
8332	3–21
8333	3–21
8334	3–25
8336	3–21
8337	3–24
8338	3–23
8339	3–24
8340	3–24
8341	3–22
8342	3–20
8343	3–20
8344	4–37
8345	3–12
8345-1	3–12
8345-2	3–12
8346	3–5
8347	3–11
8348	3–5
8349	3–10
8350	3–10
8351	3–12
8352	3–12
8353	3–11
8354	3–11
8355	3–27
8356	3–22
8357	3–8
8358	3–8
8359	3–9
8360	3–8
8361	3–9
8362	3–9
8363	3–9
8364	3–9
8365	3–13
8366	3–13
8367	3–14
8367-1	3–14
8368	3–7
8369	4–42
8370	4–42
8371	4–42
8372	3–13
8373	3–13
8374	4–32
8375	3–7
8376	3–14
8377	3–4
8378	3–5
8379	3–7
8379-1	3–7
8380	3–14
8380-1	3–14
8381	4–30
8382	3–7
8383	4–29
8384	3–25
8385	3–25
8386	3–26
8387	3–16
8388	3–16
8389	3–16
8389-1	3–16
8390	3–16
8391	3–17
8391-1	3–17
8391-2	3–17
8391-3	3–17
8392	3–17
8393	3–17
8394	4–5
8394-1	4–5
8394-2	3–18
8394-3	3–18
8395	3–17

Question Number	Page Number
8396	3–11
8397	3–6
8397-1	3–6
8398	4–30
8399	3–7
8400	4–24
8400-1	4–24
8401	4–29
8402	3–27
8403	3–27
8404	3–27
8405	3–27
8406	3–27
8406-1	3–28
8406-2	3–28
8407	4–9
8408	3–28
8409	3–28
8410	3–28
8411	3–28
8412	3–29
8413	3–29
8414	4–9
8415	4–9
8416	4–9
8417	3–29
8418	3–29
8419	5–20
8420	3–29
8421	3–29
8422	3–30
8423	3–30
8424	3–30
8425	3–30
8426	4–10
8427	4–10
8428	4–10
8429	1–37
8430	1–37
8431	5–33
8432	5–33
8433	5–33
8439	5–13
8440	5–13
8441	5–14
8442	5–14
8443	5–15
8444	5–15
8445	5–15
8446	5–16
8447	5–16
8449	5–16
8450	5–16
8451	5–17
8452	5–17
8453	5–18
8454	5–18
8455	5–18
8456	5–19
8457	5–19
8458	5–19
8459	4–46
8460	4–46
8461	4–47
8462	4–47
8463	4–47
8464	4–47
8465	4–47
8466	4–48
8467	4–48
8468	4–48
8469	4–57
8470	4–58
8471	4–58
8472	4–58
8473	4–59
8474	4–59
8475	4–59
8476	4–60
8477	4–60
8478	4–60
8479	4–48
8480	4–49
8481	4–49
8482	4–61
8483	4–62
8484	4–62
8485	4–62
8486	4–62
8487	4–63
8488	4–63
8489	4–63
8490	4–63
8491	4–63
8492	4–63
8493	4–64
8494	4–64
8495	4–64
8496	4–64
8497	4–64
8498	4–64
8499	4–65
8500	4–65
8501	4–65
8502	4–65
8503	4–65
8504	4–66
8505	4–54
8506	4–54
8507	4–54
8508	4–54
8509	4–54
8510	4–55
8511	4–55
8512	4–55
8513	5–20
8514	5–20
8515	5–20
8516	5–21
8517	5–21
8518	5–22
8519	5–22
8520	5–22
8521	5–22
8522	5–22
8523	5–23
8524	5–23
8525	5–24
8526	5–24
8527	5–24
8528	5–25
8529	5–25
8530	5–26
8531	5–26
8532	5–26
8533	4–69
8534	4–69
8535	4–69
8536	4–69
8537	4–70
8538	4–70
8539	4–70
8540	4–70
8541	4–70
8542	4–71
8543	4–71
8544	4–71
8545	4–71
8546	4–71
8547	4–71
8548	4–72
8549	4–72
8550	4–72
8551	4–72
8552	4–72
8553	4–73
8554	4–73
8555	4–73
8556	4–73
8557	4–74
8558	4–74
8559	4–74
8560	4–74
8561	4–75
8562	4–75
8563	4–75
8564	4–75
8565	4–75
8566	4–76
8567	4–76
8568	4–76
8569	4–76
8570	4–76
8571	4–77
8572	4–77
8573	5–11
8574	5–11
8575	5–11
8576	5–11
8577	5–11
8578	5–9
8579	5–9
8580	5–10
8581	5–10
8582	5–10
8584	4–18
8585	4–18
8586	4–18
8587	4–18
8593	4–24
8594	4–24
8596	4–27
8597	4–28
8598	4–28
8599	4–28
8600	4–28
8601	4–28
8602	4–28
8603	4–81
8604	4–81
8613	4–21
8614	4–22
8615	4–22
8616	4–22
8617	4–22
8618	4–19
8619	4–19
8620	4–19
8621	4–19
8622	4–19
8623	5–7
8624	5–7
8625	5–7
8626	5–7
8627	5–7
8628	4–24

Question Number	Page Number
8908	2–55
8909	2–55
8910	2–55
8911	2–54
8912	2–54
8913	2–54
8914	2–48
8915	2–49
8921	2–54
8922	2–47
8923	2–47
8924	2–47
8925	2–47
8926	2–47
8927	2–47
8928	2–48
8929	2–48
8930	2–48
8931	2–48
8932	2–48
8933	4–33
8934	4–33
8935	4–33
8936	4–33
8937	4–34
8937-1	4–34
8938	4–33
8939	4–34
8950	6–57
8953	6–30
8954	6–30
8955	6–30
8956	2–32
8957	2–33
8958	2–31
8959	2–32
8960	2–32
8961	2–31
8962	2–32
8963	2–34
8965	2–35
8966	2–31
8967	2–35
8968	2–33
8969	2–33
8970	2–33
8974	4–7
8975	1–92
8984	2–25
8985	2–25
8986	2–25
8987	2–26
8988	2–26
8989	2–26
8990	2–26
8991	2–26
8992	2–26
8993	2–27
8994	2–27
8995	2–27
8996	2–27
8998	2–27
8999	2–24
9000	2–24
9001	2–24
9002	2–24
9003	2–25
9004	2–25
9005	6–24
9005-1	6–38
9005-2	6–39
9006	6–22
9007	6–24
9008	6–23
9009	6–23
9010	7–7
9011	7–7
9012	6–49
9013	6–41
9014	6–40
9015	6–40
9016	6–40
9018	6–11
9019	2–19
9020	2–19
9020-1	2–19
9021	6–32
9022	6–41
9022-1	6–41
9023	2–21
9024	2–21
9026	6–15
9027	6–16
9031	6–15
9032	6–15
9033	6–15
9034	6–49
9035	6–49
9036	6–31
9037	6–30
9038	6–37
9039	6–38
9040	6–16
9041	6–33
9042	6–43
9043	1–89
9044	6–36
9045	6–23
9046	6–10
9047	6–10
9048	6–10
9049	6–9
9050	7–8
9051	7–5
9052	7–5
9053	6–16
9054	7–8
9055	6–38
9055-1	6–38
9055-2	6–38
9055-3	6–38
9056	6–23
9057	6–24
9058	4–5
9059	4–7
9060	4–6
9061	4–8
9061-1	4–8
9062	4–8
9063	4–8
9064	4–6
9065	4–6
9066	4–6
9067	4–7
9067-1	4–7
9068	4–5
9068-1	4–5
9069	4–8
9070	4–7
9071	4–7
9072	4–5
9073	4–5
9074	4–32
9074-1	4–32
9075	4–13
9076	4–13
9077	4–30
9078	4–30
9079	4–32
9080	2–8
9081	2–9
9082	2–9
9083	4–13
9084	4–32
9084-1	4–32
9085	4–13
9086	6–13
9087	6–13
9089	6–14
9090-1	6–33
9090-2	6–34
9090-3	6–34
9091	6–30
9092	6–36
9093	6–10
9094	6–43
9094-1	6–43
9095	6–43
9096	6–43
9097	7–5
9098	7–7
9099	2–7
9100	6–10
9101	7–16
9102	7–16
9103	7–16
9104	7–16
9105	7–16
9106	7–16
9107	7–13
9107-1	7–13
9107-2	7–13
9108	7–13
9109	7–13
9110	7–13
9110-1	7–13
9111	7–12
9111-1	7–12
9111-2	7–12
9111-3	7–12
9112	7–15
9113	7–15
9114	7–14
9114-1	7–14
9115	7–15
9116	7–14
9117	7–14
9118	7–14
9119	7–8
9120	7–9
9121	7–9
9122	7–9
9123	7–9
9124	7–9
9125	7–10
9126	7–10
9127	7–10
9128	4–41
9129	4–37
9130	8–26
9131	8–26
9132	8–26
9133	8–24
9134	8–24
9135	8–24
9135-1	8–24

Cross-Reference B

Airman Knowledge Test Report Codes and Question Numbers

When you take the applicable FAA Knowledge Exam required for an airman certificate or rating, you will receive an Airman Knowledge Test Report (AKTR). This test report will list the Learning Statement Codes (LSC) or Airman Certification Codes (ACS) for questions you have answered incorrectly. Match the codes given on your AKTR to the ones listed in this cross-reference. Use Cross-Reference A in this book to find the page number for the question numbers listed below.

Your AKTR will list the codes accordingly:

- If an ACS exists for the certificate or rating you're seeking, the report will list an ACS code. Reference the ACS specific to the certificate or rating to determine the subject you missed on the test: **faa.gov/training_testing/testing/acs/**
- If an ACS does not yet exist for the certificate or rating you're seeking, the report will list an LSC. Reference the Learning Statement Reference Guide to determine the subject you missed on the test: **faa.gov/training_testing/testing/media/LearningStatementReferenceGuide.pdf**

Your instructor is required to provide instruction on each of the areas of deficiency listed on your AKTR and give you an endorsement for this instruction. The AKTR must be presented to the examiner conducting your practical test. During the oral portion of the practical test, the examiner is required to evaluate the noted areas of deficiency.

If you received a code on your AKTR that is not listed in this cross-reference, email ASA at **cfi@asa2fly.com**. We will provide the definition so you can review that subject area.

Learning Statement Codes and Question Numbers

Learning Statement Code	***FAA Reference***	***Subject Description*** *(or* ***Topic*** 〉 ***Content*** 〉 ***Specific*** *classification)* ***Question Numbers***
PLT002	FAA-H-8083-25	Aircraft Performance 〉 Computations 〉 Airspeeds *8563, 8564, 8565, 8566, 8567*
PLT003	FAA-H-8083-25	Aircraft Performance 〉 Computations 〉 Center of Gravity *8697, 8697-1, 8697-2, 8697-3, 8697-4*
PLT004	FAA-H-8083-25	Aircraft Performance 〉 Charts 〉 Climb; Engine Out Performance *8382, 8474, 8475, 8476, 8477, 8478, 8480, 8481, 8482, 8553, 8554, 8555, 8556, 8557, 8558, 8559, 8560, 8561, 8562, 8593, 8594, 8596, 8597, 8598, 8599, 8600, 8601, 8602, 8628, 8629, 8630, 8631, 8632, 8635, 8636, 8637, 8682, 8683, 8684, 8685, 8686, 9875, 9876, 9877, 9919, 9935*
PLT005	FAA-H-8083-25 FAA-H-8083-28	Aircraft Performance 〉 Computations 〉 Density Altitude *9813, 9813-1*
PLT006	FAA- H-8083-3	Calculate aircraft performance—glide *8381*
PLT007	FAA-H-8083-25	Aircraft Performance 〉 Charts 〉 Holding; Landing; Takeoff *8615, 8616, 8617, 8638, 8639, 8640, 8641, 8642-1, 8668, 8669, 8670, 8671, 8672, 8763, 9874*
PLT008	FAA-H-8083-25	Aircraft Performance 〉 Charts 〉 Landing *8117, 8118, 8119, 8120, 8121, 8122, 8123, 8124, 8125, 8126, 8129, 8504, 8505, 8506, 8507, 8508, 8509, 8510, 8511, 8512, 8742, 8743, 8744, 8745, 8750, 8753, 8756, 9907, 9908, 9909, 9910, 9911, 9912, 9913, 9914*

Learning Statement Code	*FAA Reference*	***Subject Description** (or **Topic** 〉 **Content** 〉 **Specific** classification)* ***Question Numbers***
PLT009	FAA-H-8083-21	Aircraft Performance 〉 Charts 〉 Power Check; Turbine Engine *8533, 8534, 8535, 8536, 8537, 8604*
PLT010	FAA-H-8083-25	Aircraft Performance 〉 Charts 〉 Takeoff *8623, 8624, 8625, 8626, 8627*
PLT011	FAA-H-8083-25	Aircraft Performance 〉 Charts 〉 Takeoff *8115, 8116, 8466, 8467, 8468, 8469, 8470, 8471, 8472, 8743, 8479, 8548, 8549, 8550, 8551, 8552, 8568, 8569, 8570, 8571, 8572, 8603, 8613, 8614, 8618, 8619, 8620, 8642-4, 8712, 8713, 8714, 8715, 8716, 8717, 8718, 9076, 9797, 9797-1, 9797-2, 9899, 9900, 9901, 9902, 9903, 9918, 9937*
PLT012	FAA-H-8083-15 FAA-H-8083-25	Aircraft Performance 〉 Computations 〉 ETE; Fuel; Mach; Preflight Planning Aircraft Performance 〉 Charts 〉 Alternate; Cruise Navigation 〉 Radio 〉 VOR *8483, 8489, 8490, 8491, 8492, 8493, 8494, 8495, 8496, 8497, 8498, 8499, 8500, 8621, 8622, 8633, 8634, 8643, 8644, 8645, 8646, 8647, 8648, 8649, 8650, 8651, 8652, 8658, 8659, 8660, 8661, 8662, 8663, 8664, 8665, 8666, 8667, 8673, 8674, 8675, 8676, 8677, 8702, 8720, 8721, 9557, 9904, 9905, 9906*
PLT013	FAA-H-8083-25	Aircraft Performance 〉 Charts 〉 Takeoff *8727, 8727-1*
PLT015	ANA FAA-H-8083-25	Aerodynamics 〉 Performance 〉 Normal Flight Aircraft Performance 〉 Computations 〉 Specific Range: NAM/1000# Fuel Aircraft Performance 〉 Limitations 〉 Best Range *8397, 8397-1, 9077, 9078*
PLT016	FAA-H-8083-1	Aircraft Performance 〉 Computations 〉 Fuel Dump *8678, 8679, 8680, 8681*
PLT018	FAA-H-8083-25	Aerodynamics 〉 Load Factor 〉 Angle of Bank *8354, 8728*
PLT021	FAA-H-8083-1 FAA-H-8083-25	Aircraft Performance 〉 Charts 〉 Climb; Landing Weight and Balance 〉 Aircraft Loading 〉 Weight/Moment Indexes Weight and Balance 〉 Center of Gravity 〉 Computations; Shifting Weight *8439, 8440, 8441, 8442, 8443, 8444, 8445, 8446, 8447, 8449, 8450, 8451, 8452, 8453, 8454, 8455, 8456, 8457, 8458, 8513, 8514, 8515, 8516, 8517, 8518, 8519, 8520, 8521, 8522, 8523, 8524, 8525, 8526, 8527, 8528, 8529, 8530, 8531, 8532, 8573, 8574, 8575, 8576, 8577, 8578, 8579, 8580, 8581, 8582*
PLT023	FAA-H-8083-28	Navigation 〉 Instrument 〉 Altimeter *9164, 9172, 9173, 9173-1*
PLT024	FAA-H-8083-28	Meteorology 〉 Atmosphere 〉 Stability *9170, 9171, 9186, 9187*
PLT029	14 CFR 121 FAA-H-8083-16	Regulations 〉 14 CFR Part 121 〉 Flight Crewmember Duties *8106, 8298, 8298-1*
PLT032	FAA-H-8083-25	Aerodynamics 〉 Airspeed 〉 Mach *8387*
PLT034	14 CFR 121	Regulations 〉 14 CFR Part 121 〉 Takeoff Minimums *8134*
PLT040	14 CFR 71 AIM	Navigation 〉 Airspace 〉 Class B Regulations 〉 14 CFR Part 91 〉 Airspace *8872, 8873, 8874, 8875, 8876, 8877, 8881, 8882, 8883, 8884, 8885, 8886, 8888*

Learning Statement Code	*FAA Reference*	***Subject Description** (or **Topic** 〉 **Content** 〉 **Specific** classification)* ***Question Numbers***
PLT044	AIM	Air Traffic Control Procedures 〉 Arrival 〉 After Landing Air Traffic Control Procedures 〉 Departure 〉 Speed Adjustments; Takeoff Air Traffic Control Procedures 〉 En Route 〉 Speed Adjustments Air Traffic Control Procedures 〉 Ground 〉 Ground Hold Delays *9167, 9388, 9388-1, 9388-2, 9388-3*
PLT045	FAA-H-8083-25	Aircraft Performance 〉 Charts 〉 Descent *8501, 8502, 8503, 9749*
PLT047	AIM	Navigation 〉 Avionics 〉 Airborne Equipment *8858, 9941*
PLT048	FAA-H-8083-21	Aircraft Performance 〉 Charts 〉 Hovering *8538, 8539, 8540, 8541, 8542, 8543, 8544, 8545, 8546, 8547*
PLT049	14 CFR 61 14 CFR 91 FAA-H-8083-28 AIM U.S. Terminal Procedures	Navigation 〉 Avionics 〉 Airborne Equipment Navigation 〉 Flight Operations 〉 Approach Chart Navigation 〉 Radio 〉 ILS; Instrument Approach; Non-precision approach *9588, 9601, 9619, 9645, 9645-1, 9933*
PLT052	14 CFR 21 AIM U.S. Terminal Procedures	Instrument Procedures 〉 Instrument Departures 〉 SID Regulations 〉 14 CFR Part 121/135 〉 Performance Requirements *8400-1, 9614*
PLT055	AIM IFR Enroute High Altitude Chart	Air Traffic Control Procedures 〉 En Route 〉 Airways and Route Systems Navigation 〉 Flight Operations 〉 IFR En Route Charts *9596*
PLT058	FAA-H-8083-15 FAA-H-8083-16 IFR Enroute Low Altitude Chart	Instrument Procedures 〉 En Route 〉 Chart Interpretation Publications 〉 Aeronautical Charts 〉 IFR En Route *8784, 8824, 8825, 8826, 8852-1, 9670*
PLT059	FAA-H-8083-28	Weather 〉 Aeronautical Weather Reports 〉 Aviation Routine Weather Reports (METAR); Aviation Selected Special Report (SPECI); Aviation Weather Reports *8735, 8950, 9242, 9266, 9267, 9268, 9269, 9270, 9271, 9272, 9273, 9274, 9275, 9276, 9277, 9716, 9717, 9718, 9824, 9939*
PLT061	FAA-H-8083-28	Weather 〉 Aeronautical Weather Reports 〉 PIREPS *9250, 9713*
PLT065	FAA-H-8083-25	Aircraft Performance 〉 Charts 〉 Engine Out Performance *8484, 8485, 8486, 8487, 8488*
PLT066	FAA-H-8083-28	Weather 〉 Charts/Maps 〉 Severe Weather Outlook Charts *9305*
PLT067	FAA-H-8083-28	Weather 〉 Aeronautical Weather Forecasts 〉 Inflight Aviation Weather Advisories; SIGMETS *9284*
PLT068	FAA-H-8083-28	Weather 〉 Aeronautical Weather Reports 〉 Significant Weather Prognostic Charts *9260*
PLT072	FAA-H-8083-28	Weather 〉 Aeronautical Weather Forecasts 〉 Terminal Aerodrome Forecasts (TAF) *9278, 9709, 9710*

Learning Statement Code	*FAA Reference*	***Subject Description** (or **Topic** 〉 **Content** 〉 **Specific** classification)* ***Question Numbers***
PLT076	FAA-H-8083-28	National Weather Service (NWS) 〉 Functions 〉 Aeronautical Weather Forecasts Weather 〉 Aeronautical Weather Forecasts 〉 Winds/Temperatures Aloft Forecasts *9255, 9287, 9288, 9289, 9290, 9291, 9292, 9293, 9294, 9295, 9296*
PLT078	Chart Supplements U.S. U.S. Terminal Procedures	Air Traffic Control Procedures 〉 Communications 〉 Pilot Procedures Air Traffic Control Procedures 〉 Ground 〉 Taxi National Weather Service 〉 Functions 〉 Aeronautical Weather Reports; Weather Outlets Navigation 〉 Flight Operations 〉 Airport; Communications; Runway *8782, 8793, 8796, 8797, 8798, 8804, 9587, 9655, 9658, 9659, 9782*
PLT080	AIM U.S. Terminal Procedures	Air Traffic Control Procedures 〉 Arrival 〉 Approach Control Air Traffic Control Procedures 〉 Communications 〉 ATC Communications; Clearances Navigation 〉 Flight Operations 〉 Arrivals Navigation 〉 Radio 〉 STAR *8799, 9818*
PLT082	U.S. Terminal Procedures	Regulations 〉 14 CFR Parts 121/135 〉 Flight Planning *8842, 9618*
PLT083	AIM FAA-H-8083-15 U.S. Terminal Procedures	Air Traffic Control Procedures 〉 Arrival 〉 Instrument Approach Procedures; Missed Approach Navigation 〉 Flight Operations 〉 Approach Chart Navigation 〉 Radio 〉 DME; ILS *8704, 8704-1, 8800, 8803, 8805, 8836, 8852, 8954, 9040, 9554, 9555, 9571, 9589, 9590, 9599, 9600, 9602, 9603, 9604, 9666, 9686*
PLT085	FAA-H-8083-25	Aircraft Performance 〉 Charts 〉 Takeoff *8642-2*
PLT087	FAA-H-8083-15	Navigation 〉 Radio 〉 DME; Holding *8862*
PLT089	FAA-H-8083-25	Aircraft Performance 〉 Charts 〉 Takeoff *8719*
PLT090	Instrument Approach Procedures	Recall VOR interpretation—charts/indications/CDI/NAV *9615*
PLT094	ANA	Aerodynamics 〉 Stalls/Spins 〉 Angle of Attack *8391-1, 8391-2, 8391-3, 8394-2, 8394-3*
PLT097	AIM	Human Factors 〉 Aeromedical Factors 〉 Physiological *9101*
PLT098	FAA-H-8083-25	Recall aeromedical factors—fitness for flight *9928, 9928-1*
PLT099	AIM	Human Factors 〉 Aeromedical Factors 〉 Flight Illusions; Physiological *9114, 9114-1, 9116, 9117, 9118*
PLT100	AIM IFR Enroute Low Altitude Chart	Recall aeronautical charts—IFR En Route Low Altitude *9049, 9644*
PLT103	FAA-H-8083-25	Aeronautical Decision Making 〉 Judgment 〉 Hazardous; Training *9832, 9815, 9815-1*

Learning Statement Code	***FAA Reference***	***Subject Description** (or **Topic** 〉 **Content** 〉 **Specific** classification)* ***Question Numbers***
PLT104	FAA-H-8083-25	Aeronautical Decision Making (ADM), CRM 〉 Judgment 〉 Automatic Decisions Aeronautical Decision Making (ADM), CRM 〉 Risk Management 〉 Phase of Flight Human Factors 〉 Aeronautical Decision Making (ADM), CRM 〉 Problem Detection *8711, 9354-1, 9778, 9778-1, 9804, 9805, 9805-1, 9805-2, 9805-3, 9805-4, 9805-5, 9805-6, 9805-7, 9805-8, 9806, 9816, 9816-1, 9830, 9833, 9834, 9853, 9853-1, 9854, 9855, 9856, 9857, 9929, 9929-1, 9929-2, 9940*
PLT105	FAA-H-8083-28	Recall airborne radar/thunderstorm detection equipment—use/limitations *9747-3*
PLT108	AC 120-58 AC 135-17	Aerodynamics 〉 Powerplant 〉 Turbine Meteorology 〉 Hazardous 〉 Icing *9441, 9442, 9443, 9444, 9445, 9446, 9447, 9448, 9450, 9452, 9453, 9454, 9696, 9697, 9698, 9700*
PLT112	AIM	Recall aircraft controls—proper use/techniques *9043*
PLT121	FAA-H-8083-1	Weight and Balance 〉 Aircraft Loading 〉 Limitations *8431, 8432, 8433, 8698, 8699, 8699-1, 8699-2, 8700, 8729, 8730, 8746, 8769, 8770, 8771, 8772, 8773, 8776, 8777, 8778, 8779, 8781, 8787, 8788, 8789, 8790, 8791, 8844, 8845, 8846, 8847, 8848, 9920, 9938*
PLT123	FAA-H-8083-25	Aircraft Performance 〉 Charts 〉 Takeoff *8584, 8585, 8586, 8587*
PLT124	FAA-H-8083-25	Aircraft Performance 〉 Atmospheric Effects 〉 Instrumentation Error *8374, 8404, 8405, 8417, 8418, 9767, 9942, 9942-1*
PLT127	FAA-8083-3	Aerodynamics 〉 Powerplant 〉 Turbine; Turboprop Aircraft Performance 〉 Atmospheric Effects 〉 Density Altitue *9059, 9061, 9061-1, 9062, 9063*
PLT128	AC 91-74 AC 120-58 AC 135-17	Aerodynamics 〉 Flight Characteristics 〉 Flight Hazards Meteorology 〉 Hazards 〉 Icing *9080, 9302, 9451*
PLT129	FAA-H-8083-25	Aircraft Performance 〉 Charts 〉 Runway *9083*
PLT130	FAA-H-8083-25	Recall aircraft performance—fuel *9071*
PLT131	FAA-H-8083-25	Aerodynamics 〉 Principles of Flight 〉 Ground Effect *8375, 8379, 8379-1*
PLT132	FAA-H-8083-25	Navigation 〉 Instrumentation 〉 Airspeed Indicator *8364, 9321*
PLT134	ANA	Recall aircraft performance—takeoff *9075, 9801, 9802*
PLT139	14 CFR 121 ANA	Aerodynamics 〉 Stall/Spins 〉 Stall Warning Devices Regulations 〉 14 CFR Part 121 Subpart K 〉 Navigation Equipment *8069, 8070, 8071, 8154*
PLT140	AIM	Recall airport operations—LAHSO *9731, 9732, 9733, 9734*

Learning Statement Code	*FAA Reference*	*Subject Description (or Topic 〉 Content 〉 Specific classification) Question Numbers*
PLT141	AIM	Air Traffic Control Procedures 〉 Ground 〉 Landing Roll Out Navigation 〉 Flight Operations 〉 Airport; Heliport; Runway Navigation 〉 Pilotage 〉 Runway Markings; Runway Signs; Taxiway Markings; Taxiway Signs *8722, 8903, 8904, 8905, 8906, 8907, 8907-1, 8922, 8923, 8924, 8925, 8926, 8927, 8928, 8929, 8930, 8931, 8932, 9416, 9416-1, 9416-2, 9417, 9421, 9421-1, 9421-2, 9422, 9423, 9423-1, 9436, 9437, 9735, 9735-1, 9735-2, 9735-3, 9737, 9764, 9785, 9785-1, 9786, 9786-1, 9786-2, 9798, 9799*
PLT143	Chart Supplements U.S.	Navigation 〉 Flight Operations 〉 Airport *9636, 9668*
PLT144	AIM FAA-H-8083-3	Air Traffic Control Procedures 〉 Ground 〉 Braking Action Aircraft Performance 〉 Atmospheric Effects 〉 Braking Action Aircraft Performance 〉 Limitations 〉 Braking Action *8133, 8933, 8934, 8935, 8936, 8937, 8937-1, 8938, 8939, 9055, 9055-1, 9055-2, 9055-3*
PLT145	AIM	Navigation 〉 Flight Operations 〉 Runway *8914, 8915*
PLT147	AIM U.S. Terminal Procedures	Navigation 〉 Flight Operations 〉 Airport; Runway *8705, 8908, 8909, 8910, 8911, 8912, 8913, 8921, 9378*
PLT148	AIM Chart Supplements U.S.	Navigation 〉 Flight Operations 〉 Runway Navigation 〉 Pilotage 〉 Approach Lights *8901, 8901-1, 8902*
PLT149	AIM	Air Traffic Control Procedures 〉 Communications 〉 Gate Hold Procedures; Pilot Procedures *8203, 8701, 9057, 9258, 9421-3, 9783, 9784, 9787, 9788, 9789, 9790, 9790-1*
PLT161	14 CFR 91 AIM	Air Traffic Control Procedures 〉 Communications 〉 Airspace Requirements Air Traffic Control Procedures 〉 En Route 〉 ADIZ Navigation 〉 14 CFR Part 91 〉 Airspace; Equipment/Instrument/Certificate Requirement; Flight Rules *8878, 8879, 8880, 8887, 8889, 8890, 8891, 9048, 9094, 9094-1, 9095, 9100, 9395, 9396, 9397, 9398, 9399, 9400, 9741, 9780*
PLT162	14 CFR 91 AIM	Air Traffic Control Procedures 〉 Communications 〉 Traffic Alert/Collision Avoidance Air Traffic Control Procedures 〉 En Route 〉 MOA Air Traffic Control Procedures 〉 Services 〉 Outer Class C Regulations 〉 14 CFR Part 91 〉 Flight Rules *8892, 9018, 9374, 9381*
PLT163	14 CFR 91 14 CFR 121	Regulations 〉 14 CFR Part 91 〉 Enroute Regulations 〉 14 CFR Part 121 〉 Flight Rules *8114, 8893, 8900*
PLT166	FAA-H-8083-28	Navigation 〉 Instrumentation 〉 Altimeter *9099, 9163, 9174*
PLT168	FAA-H-8083-25	Recall angle of attack—characteristics/forces/principles *8378*
PLT169	FAA-H-8083-25	Recall antitorque system—components/functions *8459, 8460, 8461, 8462, 8463, 8464, 8465*

Learning Statement Code	*FAA Reference*	***Subject Description** (or **Topic** 〉 **Content** 〉 **Specific** classification)* ***Question Numbers***
PLT170	FAA-H-8083-3 FAA-H-8083-16	Aerodynamics 〉 Performance 〉 Brakes Navigation 〉 Flight Operations 〉 Approach *8402, 8403, 8736, 8955, 8969, 9034, 9035, 9039, 9074, 9074-1, 9084, 9084-1, 9090-1, 9090-3, 9091, 9092, 9438, 9791, 9792, 9793, 9817-1, 9943*
PLT171	AIM	Air Traffic Control Procedures 〉 En Route 〉 Reporting Air Traffic Control Procedures 〉 Communications 〉 Pilot Procedures; Radio Procedures *8854, 9013, 9015, 9016, 9022-1*
PLT172	AIM	Air Traffic Control Procedures 〉 Approach 〉 Priority Air Traffic Control Procedures 〉 Arrival 〉 Approach Control; Uncontrolled Field Air Traffic Control Procedures 〉 Communications 〉 ATC Altitude Alerts Air Traffic Control Procedures 〉 Services 〉 Class C; IFR Flight Plans; Weather Radar *9050, 9090-2, 9093, 9096, 9760*
PLT173	FAA-H-8083-28	Meteorology 〉 Atmosphere 〉 Pressure; Stability; Temperature *9157, 9159, 9165, 9165-1, 9178, 9188, 9195*
PLT192	FAA-H-8083-28	Meteorology 〉 Clouds 〉 Turbulence *9189, 9189-1, 9190, 9193, 9925*
PLT195	AIM	Air Traffic Control Procedures 〉 Communications 〉 Traffic Alert/Collision Avoidance System *9425, 9426, 9427, 9427-1, 9428*
PLT196	AIM	Recall communications—ATIS broadcasts *9022*
PLT197	FAA-H-8083-21	Aerodynamics 〉 Principles of Flight 〉 Forces Acting on Rotary Wing *8420*
PLT201	FAA-H-8083-16	Navigation 〉 Radio 〉 Departure Obstruction Clearance *9012*
PLT202	FAA-H-8083-15	Navigation 〉 Radio 〉 DME *9023, 9024*
PLT203	FAA-H-8083-28	Meteorology 〉 Atmosphere 〉 Temperature; Troposphere *9151, 9168, 9209, 9240*
PLT205	AIM	Human Factors 〉 Aeromedical Factors 〉 Alcohol *9111, 9111-2, 9111-3*
PLT208	14 CFR 91 14 CFR 121	Navigation 〉 Flight Operations 〉 Communications Regulations 〉 14 CFR Part 121 〉 Crew Equipment/Publications/Checklists *8360, 8369, 8406, 8406-1, 9827-1, 9827-2, 9827-3*
PLT213	FAA-H-8083-25	Aerodynamics 〉 Stability/Control 〉 Static *8366, 8372*
PLT214	FAA-H-8083-3 FAA-H-8083-25	Aerodynamics 〉 Flight Controls 〉 Normal Flight Aerodynamics 〉 Principles of Flight 〉 Forces Acting on Aircraft; Lift *8368, 8388, 8389, 8389-1, 8390, 8391, 8392, 8393, 8395*
PLT219	FAA-H-8083-3 FAA-H-8083-21	Flight Operations 〉 Maneuvers 〉 Basics *9831*
PLT223	FAA-H-8083-3	Aerodynamics 〉 Airspeed 〉 V_Y Aerodynamics 〉 Principles of Flight 〉 Drag *8051, 8241, 8357, 8359, 8370*

Learning Statement Code	***FAA Reference***	***Subject Description** (or **Topic** 〉 **Content** 〉 **Specific** classification)* ***Question Numbers***
PLT224	AIM	Air Traffic Control Procedures 〉 Preflight 〉 Flight Plan *8806, 9005, 9026, 9031, 9032*
PLT225	AIM	Air Traffic Control Procedures 〉 Preflight 〉 Flight Plan *9027, 9033, 9053*
PLT226	FAA-H-8083-28	Meteorology 〉 Clouds 〉 Fog *8723, 9194, 9206, 9207, 9207-1, 9207-2, 9229-1, 9238-1*
PLT234	FAA-H-8083-15	Recall forces acting on aircraft—3 axis intersect *9740*
PLT236	FAA-H-8083-25	Recall forces acting on aircraft—airfoil/center of pressure/mean camber line *8365, 8367, 8367-1, 8373, 8376*
PLT237	ANA	Aerodynamics 〉 Load Factor 〉 Lift *8345-1, 8345-2, 8421*
PLT240	FAA-H-8083-25	Weight and Balance 〉 Center of Gravity 〉 Effect of Load Distribution *8380, 8380-1, 8419, 9921*
PLT242	FAA-H-8083-3 FAA-H-8083-25	Aerodynamics 〉 Airspeed 〉 General Aerodynamics 〉 Principles of Flight 〉 Forces Acting on Wing; Lift *8377, 8383*
PLT244	FAA-H-8083-25	Recall forces acting on aircraft—stability/controllability *9079*
PLT245	FAA-H-8083-25	Aerodynamics 〉 Load Factor 〉 Lift *8344*
PLT247	ANA	Aerodynamics 〉 Normal Flight 〉 Landing *9005-1, 9005-2, 9793-1*
PLT248	FAA-H-8083-3 FAA-H-8083-25	Aerodynamics 〉 Principles of Flight 〉 Forces Acting on Aircraft; Load Factor *8345, 8352, 8353, 8422, 8423*
PLT262	FAA-H-8083-21	Recall helicopter hazards—dynamic rollover / Low G / LT *8406-2*
PLT263	FAA-H-8083-28	Weather 〉 Meteorology 〉 Icing; Moisture Windshear/Turbulence 〉 Clear Air Turbulence 〉 Jet Stream; Windshear *9230, 9231, 9701*
PLT266	ANA FAA-H-8083-25	Aerodynamics 〉 Performance 〉 Normal Flight Aerodynamics 〉 Principles of Flight 〉 Lift *8341, 8356, 8384, 9759, 9766, 9771, 9803*
PLT268	FAA-H-8083-25	Aerodynamics 〉 Principles of Flight 〉 Forces Acting on Aircraft *8409*
PLT271	FAA-H-8083-25	Recall human factors (ADM)—judgment *9806-1*
PLT274	AC 91-74 FAA-H-8083-28	Meteorology 〉 Hazardous 〉 Icing Meteorology 〉 Icing 〉 Freezing Rain *9221, 9224, 9285, 9736, 9748, 9774, 9775*
PLT276	FAA-H-8083-15	Navigation 〉 Radio 〉 VOR *8968, 8984, 8985, 8986, 8987, 8988, 8989*
PLT277	FAA-H-8083-15	Navigation 〉 Radio 〉 ILS *8959, 8960, 8962, 8970*

Learning Statement Code	*FAA Reference*	***Subject Description*** *(or* ***Topic*** *〉* ***Content*** *〉* ***Specific*** *classification)* ***Question Numbers***
PLT280	AIM	Human Factors 〉 Aeromedical Factors 〉 Flight Illusions; Spatial Disorientation *9107, 9107-1, 9107-2, 9108, 9109, 9110, 9110-1, 9115, 9433, 9434, 9434-1, 9435*
PLT282	14 CFR 121	Regulations 〉 14 CFR Part 121 〉 Dispatch/Redispatch *8004, 8005, 8011, 8019, 8068, 8093*
PLT283	FAA-H-8083-28	Weather 〉 Aeronautical Weather Reports 〉 Constant Pressure Analysis Charts *9281, 9711*
PLT284	FAA-H-8083-28	Recall information on a Forecast Winds and Temperatures Aloft (FD) *9251*
PLT287	FAA-H-8083-28	Meteorology 〉 Air Masses and Fronts 〉 Pressure *9175*
PLT288	FAA-H-8083-28	Weather 〉 Aeronautical Weather Forecasts 〉 Aviation Weather Forecasts; TAF *9244, 9245, 9246, 9248, 9709, 9710*
PLT290	FAA-H-8083-28	National Weather Service (NWS) 〉 Functions 〉 Aeronautical Weather Forecasts; Aeronautical Weather Reports Weather 〉 Aeronautical Weather Forecasts 〉 SIGMETS *9257, 9286*
PLT294	AIM FAA-H-8083-28	National Weather Service (NWS) 〉 Functions 〉 Aeronautical Weather Forecasts; En Route Flight Advisory Service *9247*
PLT296	AIM FAA-H-8083-15	Navigation 〉 Radio 〉 ADF/NDB; Holding; Instrument Approach *8853, 8855, 8856, 8857, 8859, 8860, 8861, 8863, 8864, 8865, 8866, 8867, 9418, 9419*
PLT300	AIM	Recall instrument/navigation system checks/inspections—limits/tuning/identifying/logging *9019, 9020, 9020-1, 9773*
PLT301	FAA-H-8083-28	Meteorology 〉 Atmosphere 〉 Temperature *9153, 9154, 9169*
PLT302	FAA-H-8083-28	Meteorology 〉 High Altitude 〉 Jet Stream Windshear/Turbulence 〉 Clear Air Turbulence 〉 High Altitude *9227, 9228, 9229, 9237, 9238, 9239, 9241, 9776, 9776-1, 9779*
PLT303	ANA FAA-H-8083-3 FAA-H-8083-25	Recall L/D ratio *8346, 8398, 8399, 8400, 8401*
PLT305	ANA	Recall leading edge devices -types / effect / purpose / operation *8385, 8386*
PLT309	FAA-H-8083-25	Aerodynamics 〉 Load Factor 〉 Angle of Bank *8396*
PLT310	FAA-H-8083-25	Aerodynamics 〉 Load Factor 〉 Lift *8347, 8355*
PLT314	FAA-H-8083-3	Recall longitudinal axis—aerodynamics/center of gravity/direction of motion *8362*
PLT316	FAA-H-8083-28	Weather 〉 Hazardous 〉 Thunderstorms *9758*

Learning Statement Code	*FAA Reference*	*Subject Description (or Topic 〉 Content 〉 Specific classification) Question Numbers*
PLT317	AC 00-54 AIM	Weather/Turbulence 〉 Microbursts 〉 Performance; Windshear *9130, 9131, 9132, 9140, 9143, 9144, 9145, 9146, 9147, 9148, 9149, 9150, 9814, 9926*
PLT318	AIM	Air Traffic Control Procedures 〉 Arrival 〉 Low Fuel Air Traffic Control Procedures 〉 Communications 〉 Pilot Procedures *9010, 9011, 9420*
PLT322	14 CFR 121	Regulations 〉 14 CFR Part 121 Subpart K 〉 Navigation Equipment *8145, 8147*
PLT323	14 CFR 121 AIM	Air Traffic Control Procedures 〉 Preflight 〉 NOTAMs Regulations 〉 14 CFR Part 121 〉 Crew Equipment/Publications/Checklists *8283, 9086, 9087, 9089*
PLT325	49 CFR 830	Recall operations manual—transportation of prisoner *8132, 8136*
PLT328	FAA-H-8083-25	Recall performance planning, aircraft loading *8733, 8734*
PLT330	AIM FAA-H-8083-25	Human Factors 〉 Aeromedical Factors 〉 Physiological *9103, 9105, 9106, 9927*
PLT332	AIM	Human Factors 〉 Aeromedical Factors 〉 Fitness for Flight; Physiological *9102, 9104*
PLT334	AIM	Human Factors 〉 Aeromedical Factors 〉 Flight Illusions *9112, 9113*
PLT337	AC 91-43	Navigation 〉 Instrumentation 〉 Airspeed Indicator *9081, 9082, 9222, 9934*
PLT343	14 CFR 1 FAA-H-8083-25	Aerodynamics 〉 Powerplant 〉 Reciprocating *9064, 9065, 9066, 9067, 9067-1, 9072, 9073*
PLT344	FAA-H-8083-28	Meteorology 〉 Hazardous 〉 Icing *9223*
PLT346	AC 65-15	Aerodynamics 〉 Flight Characteristics 〉 Normal Flight Aerodynamics 〉 Flight Controls 〉 Primary; Secondary *8324, 8325, 8326, 8337, 8342, 8343*
PLT347	ANA FAA-H-8083-3	Recall principles of flight—critical engine *8361, 9085*
PLT348	FAA-H-8083-3	Aerodynamics 〉 Principles of Flight 〉 Forces Acting on Wing *8349, 8350, 8351, 9823*
PLT354	AIM Instrument Approach Procedure Charts U.S. Terminal Procedures	Air Traffic Control Procedures 〉 Preflight 〉 Flight Plan Navigation 〉 Avionics 〉 Airborne Equipment; GPS Navigation 〉 Flight Operations 〉 Approach Chart; Preflight Planning/Calculations Navigation 〉 Radio 〉 GPS; Non-precision Approach *8703, 8837, 8839, 9111-1, 9310, 9429, 9430, 9431, 9432, 9617, 9692, 9694, 9722, 9723, 9725, 9726, 9727, 9728, 9729, 9729-1, 9730, 9738, 9739, 9743, 9744, 9744-1, 9794, 9795, 9796, 9796-1, 9804-1, 9812, 9812-1, 9917, 9944, 9945, 9946, 9946-1*
PLT355	FAA-H-8083-15	Navigation 〉 Radio 〉 HSI; ILS *8990, 8991, 8992, 8993, 8994, 8995, 8996, 8998, 8999, 9000, 9001, 9002, 9003, 9004, 9932*

Learning Statement Code	*FAA Reference*	***Subject Description** (or **Topic** 〉 **Content** 〉 **Specific** classification)* ***Question Numbers***
PLT356	AIM	Navigation 〉 Radio 〉 ILS *8956, 8957, 8958, 8963, 8966, 8967, 8975, 9380, 9382, 9403, 9412*
PLT358	AIM	Navigation 〉 Radio 〉 ILS *8961*
PLT365	FAA-H-8083-25	Recall reciprocating engine—components/operating principles/characteristics *9068, 9068-1, 9069*
PLT366	49 CFR 830	Regulations 〉 NTSB Part 830 〉 Definitions; Reports/Reporting *8233, 8236, 8246, 8317, 8318, 8322, 8323, 8725, 9098*
PLT367	14 CFR 91 14 CFR 121 14 CFR 135	Regulations 〉 14 CFR Part 91 〉 Limitations Regulations 〉 14 CFR Part 121 〉 Aircraft Equipment Regulations 〉 14 CFR Part 135 〉 Aircraft Equipment *8061, 8062, 9355, 9355-1, 9358, 9359, 9360, 9361, 9809*
PLT370	14 CFR 91 AIM	Air Traffic Control Procedures 〉 Communications 〉 ATC Communications; Clearances Air Traffic Control Procedures 〉 Departure 〉 Clearances Air Traffic Control Procedures 〉 En Route 〉 Speed Adjustments Regulations 〉 14 CFR Part 91 〉 Flight Rules *9006, 9007, 9008, 9009, 9045, 9046, 9047, 9439*
PLT373	14 CFR 121	Regulations 〉 14 CFR Part 121 〉 Flight Crewmember Duties *9745, 9807*
PLT374	14 CFR 121 14 CFR 135	Recall regulations—aircraft owner/operator responsibilities *8006, 8199, 8200*
PLT375	14 CFR 135	Regulations 〉 14 CFR Part 135 Subpart B 〉 Records Keeping *8012*
PLT379	14 CFR 121	Regulations 〉 14 CFR Part 121 〉 Flight Release *8063, 8064, 8086, 8247, 8248, 8249, 8251, 8252, 8256, 8258, 8262, 9394-2*
PLT380	14 CFR 121	Regulations 〉 14 CFR Part 121 〉 Alternate/Weather/Fuel/Requirements *8087, 8254, 8255, 8261, 8264*
PLT382	14 CFR 121 U.S. Terminal Procedures	Navigation 〉 Radio 〉 VOR Regulations 〉 14 CFR Part 121 〉 Landing Minimums *9721*
PLT383	14 CFR 121	Regulations 〉 14 CFR Part 121 〉 Icing Conditions *9379*
PLT384	14 CFR 121	Regulations 〉 14 CFR Part 121 〉 Seat Belts/Cabin Announcements *8027, 8029, 8225*
PLT385	14 CFR 121	Regulations 〉 14 CFR Part 121 〉 Cargo *8032, 8038, 8039, 8040, 8041, 8042, 8138, 8139, 8175, 8832*
PLT388	14 CFR 91 14 CFR 121	Regulations 〉 14 CFR Part 91 〉 Equipment/Instrument/Certificate Rating; Limitations Regulations 〉 14 CFR Part 121 Subpart K 〉 FDR *8047, 8141, 8142, 8143, 8833, 9356, 9357, 9410*
PLT389	14 CFR 119 AIM	Navigation 〉 Radio 〉 GPS Regulations 〉 14 CFR Part 119 〉 Definitions *8003, 8192, 8193, 8196, 8197, 8201, 8202, 8430, 8767, 8768, 9724*
PLT390	14 CFR 121 AIM	Air Traffic Control Procedures 〉 En Route 〉 Reporting Regulations 〉 14 CFR Part 121 〉 Communications *8135*

Learning Statement Code	*FAA Reference*	***Subject Description** (or **Topic** 〉 **Content** 〉 **Specific** classification)* ***Question Numbers***
PLT391	14 CFR 91	Regulations 〉 14 CFR Part 91 〉 Instrument Flight Rules *9362, 9364, 9365, 9389, 9390, 9616*
PLT392	14 CFR 135	Regulations 〉 14 CFR Part 135 〉 Operator/Control/Manual(s) *8010*
PLT394	14 CFR 121 AIM	Recall regulations—declaration of an emergency *8239, 9097*
PLT395	14 CFR 1 14 CFR 119	Regulations 〉 14 CFR Part 1 〉 General Definitions Regulations 〉 14 CFR Part 119 〉 Definitions *8319, 8320, 8429, 9324, 9325, 9327, 9837*
PLT396	14 CFR 121	Regulations 〉 14 CFR Part 121 〉 Takeoff Minimums *8250*
PLT398	14 CFR 121	Navigation 〉 Flight Operations 〉 Preflight Planning/Calculations Regulations 〉 14 CFR Part 121 〉 Dispatch/Redispatch Regulations 〉 14 CFR Part 121 Subpart E 〉 ETOPS *8257, 8259, 8260, 8266, 8267, 8280, 8284, 9746-2*
PLT400	14 CFR 121	Regulations 〉 14 CFR Part 121 〉 Dispatch/Redispatch *8007, 8226, 8286, 8292, 8296*
PLT402	14 CFR 121	Regulations 〉 14 CFR Part 121 〉 Emergency Equipment/Survival *8171*
PLT403	14 CFR 121	Regulations 〉 14 CFR Part 121 〉 Emergency Authority/Actions/Reports *8240, 8245*
PLT404	14 CFR 121	Regulations 〉 14 CFR Part 121 〉 Emergency Equipment/Survival Regulations 〉 14 CFR Part 121 Subpart K 〉 Emergency Equipment *8058, 8059, 8060, 8144, 8157, 8159, 8163, 8164, 8165, 8167, 8168, 8170, 8172, 8177, 8834*
PLT405	14 CFR 91 14 CFR 121	Regulations 〉 14 CFR Part 91 〉 Equipment/Instrument/Certificate Requirement Regulations 〉 14 CFR Part 121 〉 Crew Equipment/Publications/Checklists; Dispatch/ Redispatch *8045, 8046, 8053, 8054, 8140, 8146, 8235, 8808, 9407, 9414, 9415*
PLT406	14 CFR 91	Regulations 〉 14 CFR Part 91 〉 Equipment/Instrument/Certificate Requirement; Flight Rules *8237, 9363, 9386, 9387*
PLT407	14 CFR 61 14 CFR 121	Regulations 〉 14 CFR Part 61 〉 Limitations Regulations 〉 14 CFR Part 121 〉 Landing Minimums; Line-Oriented Simulator Training Course; Training/Currency *8034, 8103, 8108, 8109, 8110, 8111, 8205, 8207, 8215, 8216, 8217, 8218, 8820, 8821, 8827, 8829, 9346, 9347, 9618, 9720, 9847-1*
PLT408	14 CFR 121	Regulations 〉 14 CFR Part 121 〉 Emergency Equipment/Survival *8176*
PLT409	14 CFR 61 14 CFR 121	Regulations 〉 14 CFR Part 61 〉 Limitations Regulations 〉 14 CFR Part 121 〉 Flight Time/Duty/Rest/Requirements *8002, 8104, 8189, 8211, 8219, 8220, 8221, 8222, 8223, 8224, 8227, 8228, 8229, 8231, 8231-1, 8238, 8706, 8706-1, 8707, 8708, 8709, 8724, 8814, 8815, 9342, 9714, 9838, 9839, 9840, 9841, 9842, 9843, 9844, 9845, 9846, 9847, 9847-2, 9848, 9849, 9850, 9851, 9852*
PLT412	14 CFR 121	Regulations 〉 14 CFR Part 121 〉 Flight Release *8293, 8294, 8295*

Learning Statement Code	***FAA Reference***	***Subject Description*** *(or* ***Topic*** *〉* ***Content*** *〉* ***Specific*** *classification)* ***Question Numbers***
PLT413	14 CFR 121	Regulations 〉 14 CFR Part 121 〉 Alternate/Weather/Fuel/Requirements *8088, 8089, 8268, 8269, 8270, 8271, 8272, 8273, 8274, 8275, 8276, 8277*
PLT416	49 CFR 830	Regulations 〉 NTSB Part 830 〉 Reports/Reporting *8321*
PLT417	14 CFR 121	Regulations 〉 14 CFR Part 121 Subpart K 〉 Emergency Equipment *8166, 8169*
PLT420	14 CFR 91	Regulations 〉 14 CFR Part 91 〉 Instrument Flight Rules *8092, 8279, 8726, 8953, 9021, 9036, 9037, 9038, 9041, 9348, 9368, 9369, 9384, 9391, 9392, 9393, 9411, 9413, 9742, 9770, 9817*
PLT421	14 CFR 91 AIM	Recall regulations—instrument flight rules *9014, 9370, 9383, 9385, 9394-1*
PLT424	14 CFR 135	Regulations 〉 14 CFR Part 135 〉 Aircraft Equipment; Flight Operations Regulations 〉 14 CFR Part 135 Subpart B 〉 Flight/Crewmember Duties *8013, 8014, 8015, 8016, 8017, 8037, 8102*
PLT425	14 CFR 135	Regulations 〉 14 CFR Part 135 Subpart B 〉 Records Keeping *9746, 9746-1, 9761, 9762*
PLT427	14 CFR 61	Regulations 〉 14 CFR Part 61 〉 Limitations *9333, 9335, 9340, 9343, 9349, 9811*
PLT428	14 CFR 135	Regulations 〉 14 CFR Part 135 〉 MEL/CDL; Operator/Control/Manual(s)/Operation Specs *8052, 8731, 8732, 8807*
PLT429	14 CFR 121	Regulations 〉 14 CFR Part 121 Subpart K 〉 Navigation Equipment *8149, 8152, 8195, 8195-1, 9408, 9409*
PLT430	14 CFR 91	Regulations 〉 14 CFR Part 91 〉 Instrument Flight Rules *8297, 9366, 9367, 9373*
PLT432	14 CFR 1	Regulations 〉 14 CFR Part 1 〉 General Definitions *9326*
PLT433	14 CFR 135	Recall regulations—operational flight plan requirements *9931*
PLT434	AIM	Airport Operations 〉 Taxiing 〉 Airport Taxi Modes; Taxiing After Landing Airport Operations 〉 Tower Controlled 〉 ATC Procedures *9042, 9044, 9056, 9424*
PLT436	14 CFR 121	Regulations 〉 14 CFR Part 121 〉 Crew Equipment/Publications/Checklists; Enroute *8198, 8278*
PLT437	14 CFR 135	Regulations 〉 14 CFR Part 135 〉 Aircraft Equipment; Performance Requirements *8050, 8078, 8079, 8838, 8840, 8841*
PLT438	14 CFR 121	Regulations 〉 14 CFR Part 121 〉 Supplemental; Oxygen for Sustenance: Turbine Engine Regulations 〉 14 CFR Part 121 Subpart K 〉 Emergency Equipment *8020, 8021, 8022, 8023, 8024, 8025, 8028, 8030, 8031, 8055, 8056, 8072, 8073, 8074, 8080, 8081, 8156, 8173, 8174, 8180, 8181, 8182, 8183, 8184, 8185, 8186, 8187, 9638, 9819*
PLT440	14 CFR 121	Regulations 〉 14 CFR Part 121 Subpart M 〉 Flight Engineer Requirements *8008, 8009, 8026, 8033, 8043, 8113, 8155, 8188, 8190, 8212, 8213*

Learning Statement Code	*FAA Reference*	***Subject Description** (or **Topic** 〉 **Content** 〉 **Specific** classification)* ***Question Numbers***
PLT442	14 CFR 61 14 CFR 121 14 CFR 135	Regulations 〉 14 CFR Part 61 〉 Instrument Currency Regulations 〉 14 CFR Part 121 〉 Recent Experience; Training Currency Regulations 〉 14 CFR Part 135 〉 Crew Requirements *8095, 8096, 8097, 8098, 8099, 8100, 8101, 8105, 8208, 8209, 8210, 8809, 8830, 9329, 9329-2, 9334, 9336, 9337, 9338, 9339, 9341, 9344, 9345*
PLT443	14 CFR 61 14 CFR 121	Regulations 〉 14 CFR Part 61 〉 Type Rating Regulations 〉 14 CFR Part 121 〉 Flight Time/Duty/Rest/Requirements Regulations 〉 14 CFR Part 121 Subpart M 〉 Flight Engineer Requirements *8035, 8036, 8044, 8082, 8083, 8107, 8112, 8191, 8289, 9328, 9329-1, 9350*
PLT444	14 CFR 121	Regulations 〉 14 CFR Part 121 〉 Crew Equipment/Publications/Checklists; Emergency Authority/Actions/ Reports; Operational Control/ Flight Release *8018, 8234, 8242, 8243, 8243-1, 8244, 8281, 8282, 8285, 8819, 9402, 9402-1*
PLT447	14 CFR 61	Regulations 〉 14 CFR Part 61 〉 Limitations *9351*
PLT449	14 CFR 121	Regulations 〉 14 CFR Part 121 〉 Training/Currency *8214*
PLT450	14 CFR 63 14 CFR 121	Regulations 〉 14 CFR Part 63 〉 Experience Requirements Regulations 〉 14 CFR Part 121 〉 Flight Time/Duty/Rest Requirements Regulations 〉 14 CFR Part 121 Subpart P 〉 Dispatcher Duty Limitations *8194, 8230, 9342-1, 9342-2, 9350-1*
PLT452	14 CFR 121	Recall regulations—re-dispatch *8232*
PLT453	14 CFR 121	Regulations 〉 14 CFR Part 121 〉 Records Keeping *8287, 8288*
PLT454	14 CFR 135	Regulations 〉 14 CFR Part 135 〉 Aircraft Equipment *8001, 8049, 8067*
PLT455	14 CFR 121	Regulations 〉 14 CFR Part 121 〉 Dispatch/Redispatch *8290, 8291*
PLT456	14 CFR 121	Regulations 〉 14 CFR Part 121 〉 Landing Minimums *8094, 8127, 8128, 8130, 8831*
PLT459	14 CFR 91 14 CFR 121	Regulations 〉 14 CFR Part 91 〉 Instrument Flight Rules Regulations 〉 14 CFR Part 121 〉 Takeoff Minimums *8057, 8065, 8066, 8085, 8090, 8091, 8158, 8263, 8358, 8363, 8843, 9371, 9372, 9401, 9826*
PLT460	14 CFR 121 14 CFR 135	Regulations 〉 14 CFR Part 121 〉 Training/Currency Regulations 〉 14 CFR Part 121/135 〉 Training *8204, 8828, 9330, 9331*
PLT462	14 CFR 121 14 CFR 135	Regulations 〉 14 CFR Part 121 Subpart K 〉 Emergency Equipment Regulations 〉 14 CFR Part 121/135 〉 Aircraft Equipment *8048, 8160, 8161, 8162, 8178, 8179, 8792*
PLT463	14 CFR 61 14 CFR 121	Regulations 〉 14 CFR Part 61 〉 Limitations Regulations 〉 14 CFR Part 121 〉 Passenger/Flight Events/Disturbances *8813, 9332, 9354,*
PLT464	14 CFR 135	Regulations 〉 14 CFR 135 〉 Aircraft Equipment Regulations 〉 14 CFR Part 135 Subpart B 〉 Flight/Crewmember Duties *8075, 8076, 8077*

Learning Statement Code	*FAA Reference*	***Subject Description** (or **Topic** 〉 **Content** 〉 **Specific** classification)* ***Question Numbers***
PLT465	14 CFR 121	Regulations 〉 14 CFR Part 121 〉 Seat Belts/Cabin Announcements *8153*
PLT466	FAA-H-8083-3	Weight and Balance 〉 Center of Gravity 〉 Limitations *8371, 8775, 8780, 9317, 9318, 9319, 9320, 9322, 9323*
PLT468	14 CFR 121	Recall regulations—Visual Meteorological Conditions (VMC) *8253*
PLT469	14 CFR 121	Regulations 〉 14 CFR Part 121 Subpart K 〉 Navigation Equipment *8148, 8150, 8151*
PLT470	ANA	Aerodynamics 〉 Flight Characteristics 〉 Flight Limitations; Rotocraft Hazards Aerodynamics 〉 Principles of Flight 〉 Forces Acting on Aircraft; Forces Acting on Rotor Wings; Hazards; Lift *8407, 8408, 8410, 8411, 8412, 8413, 8424, 8425, 8426, 8427, 8428, 9781*
PLT472	FAA-H-8083-21	Aerodynamics 〉 Flight Characteristics 〉 Abnormal Flight *8414, 8415, 8416, 9800*
PLT473	AC 65-15	Aerodynamics 〉 Flight Controls 〉 Secondary Flight Controls; Servos *8327, 8328, 8329, 8330, 8331, 8332, 8333, 8334, 8336, 8338, 8339, 8340, 9793-2*
PLT474	FAA-H-8083-25	Recall soaring—normal procedures *9936*
PLT475	FAA-H-8083-28	Meteorology 〉 Hazards 〉 Definitions; Thunder Storms *9200, 9249, 9708, 9708-1*
PLT477	ANA FAA-H-8083-25	Aerodynamics 〉 Load Factor 〉 Stall Speed Aerodynamics 〉 Stall/Spins 〉 Angle of Attack; Stall Warning Devices *8348, 9808*
PLT493	14 CFR 121 AC 20-117 AC 135-17 FAA-H-8083-28	Aerodynamics 〉 Principles of Flight 〉 Hazards Regulations 〉 14 CFR Part 121 〉 Icing Conditions Meteorology 〉 Icing 〉 Frost *8084, 8265, 9162, 9179, 9180, 9181, 9440, 9440-1, 9449, 9695, 9753, 9756*
PLT495	AC 00-24 FAA-H-8083-28	Meteorology 〉 Hazardous 〉 Arctic Flying; Thunderstorms Windshear/Turbulence 〉 Clear Air Turbulence 〉 Windshear *9196, 9197, 9198, 9199, 9201, 9202, 9203, 9204, 9205, 9211, 9212, 9233, 9706, 9835*
PLT497	AIM	Navigation 〉 Avionics 〉 Transponder Equipment *9051, 9052*
PLT498	49 CFR 830	Recall Transportation Security Regulations *8131, 8137, 9763, 9763-1*
PLT499	FAA-H-8083-25	Aerodynamics 〉 Performance 〉 Normal Flight Aerodynamics 〉 Powerplant 〉 Turbine *8394, 8394-1, 8974, 9058, 9060, 9768*
PLT500	FAA-H-8083-3	Aerodynamics 〉 Powerplant 〉 Turboprop *9070*
PLT501	AC 00-30 AIM FAA-H-8083-28	Meteorology 〉 High Altitude 〉 Jet Stream Windshear/Turbulence 〉 Clear Air Turbulence 〉 Encountering; Reports; Windshear *9128, 9129, 9210, 9218, 9219, 9225, 9226, 9232, 9235, 9262, 9263, 9264, 9777, 9777-1*
PLT506	14 CFR 1	Regulations 〉 14 CFR Part 1 〉 General Definitions *8774*

Learning Statement Code	*FAA Reference*	***Subject Description** (or **Topic** 〉 **Content** 〉 **Specific** classification)* ***Question Numbers***
PLT508	14 CFR 91	Regulations 〉 14 CFR Part 91 〉 Equipment/Instrument/Certificate Requirement *9375, 9376, 9377, 9404, 9405, 9406*
PLT509	AIM FAA-H-8083-28	Aerodynamics 〉 Principles of Flight 〉 Forces Acting on Wing Windshear/Turbulence 〉 Wake Turbulence 〉 Turbulence Factors *9119, 9120, 9121, 9122, 9123, 9124, 9125, 9126, 9127, 9715, 9858*
PLT510	FAA-H-8083-28	Meteorology 〉 Air Masses and Fronts 〉 Winds Meteorology 〉 Airflow 〉 Temp Meteorology 〉 Atmosphere 〉 Haze *9152, 9156, 9176, 9185-2, 9208*
PLT511	FAA-H-8083-28	Meteorology 〉 Air Masses and Fronts 〉 Dry Line; Fronts Meteorology 〉 Atmosphere 〉 Pressure Meteorology 〉 Hazardous 〉 Thunderstorms *9160, 9191, 9192, 9213, 9214, 9215, 9215-1, 9216, 9217, 9228-1, 9228-2, 9259, 9923, 9924*
PLT512	FAA-H-8083-28	Meteorology 〉 Atmosphere 〉 Temperature Meteorology 〉 Moisture 〉 Change of State *8710, 9155, 9161, 9161-1, 9182, 9183, 9184, 9185, 9185-1, 9234, 9810*
PLT514	FAA-H-8083-28	Meteorology 〉 Atmosphere 〉 Pressure *9747*
PLT515	AIM	National Weather Service (NWS) 〉 Functions 〉 Aeronautical Weather Forecasts; Aeronautical Weather Reports *9704, 9747-1, 9747-2*
PLT516	FAA-H-8083-28	Meteorology 〉 Air Masses and Fronts 〉 Winds *9158, 9177*
PLT517	FAA-H-8083-28	Meteorology 〉 Hazardous 〉 Tropic Storms *9178-1*
PLT518	AC 00-54 AIM FAA-H-8083-28	Windshear/Turbulence 〉 Clear Air Turbulence 〉 Windshear Windshear/Turbulence 〉 Microbursts 〉 Loss of Airspeed Recovery; Windshear Windshear/Turbulence 〉 Windshear 〉 Characteristics; LLWAS *9054, 9133, 9134, 9135, 9135-1, 9136, 9137, 9138, 9139, 9141, 9142, 9166, 9220, 9236, 9283*
PLT524	FAA-H-8083-6	Navigation 〉 Avionics 〉 Primary Flight Displays (PFD) Navigation 〉 Radio 〉 Electronic Displays *8206, 9750, 9751, 9769, 9769-1, 9769-2*
PLT526	AIM	Recall near midair collision report *9836, 9836-1*
PLT542	AIM	Recall airport operations—radio failure *9783-1*

Airman Certification Codes and Question Numbers

ACS Code	***Question Numbers***
AA.I.A.K1	*9084-1*
AA.I.A.K2	*8394, 8394-1, 8974, 9058, 9060, 9062, 9064, 9065, 9066, 9067, 9068, 9068-1, 9070, 9072, 9073, 9768*
AA.I.A.K4	*9071*
AA.I.A.K9	*8145, 8146, 8147, 8149, 8152, 8195, 8195-1, 8206, 9019, 9020, 9023, 9024, 9051, 9052, 9375, 9376, 9377, 9404, 9405, 9406, 9408, 9409, 9751, 9783-1, 9944, 9945, 9946*
AA.I.A.K11	*8181*
AA.I.A.K12	*8324, 8325, 8326, 8327, 8328, 8329, 8330, 8331, 8332, 8333, 8334, 8336, 8337, 8338, 8339, 8340, 8341, 8342, 8343, 8356, 8384, 8385, 8386, 9765, 9766, 9771, 9793, 9793-1, 9793-2*
AA.I.A.K13	*9099, 9164, 9174*
AA.I.A.K14	*8160, 8161, 8162, 8176*
AA.I.A.K17	*8731*
AA.I.A.R3	*8711, 9830, 9853, 9854, 9855, 9857, 9941*
AA.I.B.K1	*8382, 8603, 8604, 8635, 8636, 8637, 8643, 8644, 8645, 8646, 8647, 8648, 8649, 8650, 8651, 8652, 8658, 8659, 8660, 8661, 8662, 8663, 8664, 8665, 8666, 8667, 8668, 8669, 8670, 8671, 8672, 8678, 8679, 8680, 8681, 8743, 8744, 8745, 8753, 8756*
AA.I.B.K2a	*8774, 8775, 9076, 9797, 9797-1, 9797-2*
AA.I.B.K2b	*8115, 8116, 8134, 8459, 8460, 8461, 8462, 8463, 8464, 8465, 8466, 8467, 8468, 8479, 8480, 8481, 8586, 8587, 8613, 8712, 8713, 8714, 8715, 8716, 8717, 8718, 8719, 8720, 8721, 8734, 8780, 9075, 9083, 9085, 9317, 9319, 9324, 9327, 9801, 9802, 9918, 9919, 9936, 9937*
AA.I.B.K2c	*8379-1, 8397-1, 8400, 8400-1, 8593, 8594, 8628, 8629, 8630, 8631, 8632, 8633, 8634, 8638, 8639, 8640, 8641, 8642-1, 8642-2, 8682, 8683, 8684, 8685, 8686, 8852-1, 9935*
AA.I.B.K2d	*8381, 8383, 8398, 8401, 9077, 9078, 9320, 9321, 9322, 9323*
AA.I.B.K2e	*9791, 9792*
AA.I.B.K2f	*8117, 8118, 8119, 8120, 8121, 8122, 8123, 8124, 8125, 8126, 8127, 8128, 8129, 8130, 8505, 8506, 8507, 8508, 8509, 8510, 8511, 8512, 8732, 8742, 8750*
AA.I.B.K2g	*8369, 8370*
AA.I.B.K3a	*9059, 9061, 9061-1, 9063, 9069, 9813-1, 9942-1*
AA.I.B.K3e	*8365, 8366, 8367, 8371, 8372, 8373, 8376, 8431, 8432, 8433, 8439, 8440, 8441, 8442, 8443, 8449, 8450, 8451, 8452, 8453, 8574, 8575, 8576, 8577, 8578, 8579, 8580, 8581, 8582, 8697, 8697-1, 8697-2, 8698, 8699, 8699-1, 8699-2, 8700, 8746, 8769, 8770, 8771, 8772, 8773, 8776, 8777, 8778, 8779, 8781, 8787, 8788, 8789, 8790, 8791, 8844, 8845, 8846, 8847, 8848, 9920, 9938*
AA.I.B.K3f	*8729, 8730, 9005-1, 9005-2*
AA.I.B.K4	*8344, 8346, 8348, 8368, 8375, 8377, 8378, 8379, 8389-1, 8391-3, 8397, 8399, 9129, 9808, 9942*
AA.I.B.K5	*8367-1, 8380, 8584, 8585, 8697-3, 8697-4, 9921*
AA.I.B.K6	*8733, 9302, 9440, 9451, 9695*
AA.I.B.K7	*9441, 9442, 9443, 9444, 9445, 9446, 9447, 9448, 9450, 9452, 9453, 9454, 9697, 9698, 9700*
AA.I.B.K9	*9055, 9055-1, 9055-2, 9055-3*
AA.I.C.K1	*9251*

ACS Code	***Question Numbers***
AA.I.C.K2	*8735, 9167, 9175, 9242, 9244, 9245, 9246, 9247, 9248, 9250, 9255, 9257, 9266, 9267, 9268, 9269, 9270, 9271, 9272, 9273, 9274, 9275, 9276, 9277, 9278, 9281, 9284, 9285, 9286, 9287, 9288, 9289, 9290, 9291, 9292, 9293, 9294, 9295, 9296, 9305, 9704, 9709, 9710, 9711, 9713, 9716, 9717, 9718, 9747, 9747-1, 9747-2, 9747-3, 9758, 9824, 9922, 9939*
AA.I.C.K3a	*9151, 9158, 9168, 9170, 9171, 9185, 9185-1, 9186, 9187, 9188, 9195, 9209, 9240, 9241, 9779, 9923*
AA.I.C.K3b	*9054, 9133, 9134, 9135, 9135-1, 9136, 9137, 9138, 9139, 9141, 9142, 9166, 9220, 9236, 9238, 9238-1, 9249, 9283, 9701, 9776*
AA.I.C.K3c	*9152, 9153, 9154, 9155, 9169, 9185-2, 9225*
AA.I.C.K3d	*9161, 9161-1, 9162, 9180, 9223*
AA.I.C.K3e	*8710, 9156, 9157, 9159, 9160, 9165, 9165-1, 9176, 9177, 9178, 9178-1, 9184, 9191, 9192, 9213, 9215, 9215-1, 9216, 9217, 9227, 9228, 9228-1, 9228-2, 9233, 9259, 9260, 9776-1, 9810*
AA.I.C.K3f	*9189, 9193, 9210, 9226, 9229, 9229-1, 9924, 9925*
AA.I.C.K3g	*9190, 9218, 9219, 9230, 9231, 9232, 9235, 9237, 9239, 9262, 9263, 9264, 9708-1, 9777, 9777-1*
AA.I.C.K3h	*9130, 9131, 9132, 9140, 9143, 9144, 9145, 9146, 9147, 9148, 9149, 9150, 9182, 9189-1, 9196, 9197, 9198, 9199, 9200, 9201, 9202, 9203, 9204, 9205, 9211, 9212, 9214, 9706, 9708, 9814, 9835, 9926*
AA.I.C.K3i	*9183, 9221, 9224, 9449, 9774, 9775*
AA.I.C.K3j	*8723, 9194, 9206, 9207, 9207-1, 9207-2*
AA.I.C.K3k	*8258, 8265, 9179, 9181, 9440-1, 9696, 9736, 9748*
AA.I.C.K3l	*9208, 9234*
AA.I.C.K5	*9329-2*
AA.I.D.K1	*8387, 8388, 8389, 8390, 8391, 8391-1, 8391-2, 8392, 8393, 8394-2, 8395, 9803*
AA.I.D.K3	*8702, 9080, 9163, 9172, 9173, 9173-1, 9813*
AA.I.D.K9	*8394-3*
AA.I.D.R4	*9128*
AA.I.E.K1	*9074, 9074-1*
AA.I.E.K10	*9094, 9095, 9096, 9421-2*
AA.I.E.K13	*9388-1, 9388-2, 9388-3, 9836-1*
AA.I.E.K14	*8283, 9031*
AA.I.E.K2	*9769, 9769-1, 9769-2*
AA.I.E.K3	*8148, 8150, 8151, 8837, 8839, 9310*
AA.I.E.K4	*8154, 9098, 9425, 9426, 9427, 9427-1, 9428, 9436*
AA.I.E.K8	*8297, 8298, 9763*
AA.I.E.K9	*8243-1*
AA.I.E.K11	*9805-8*
AA.I.E.K12	*9805-7*
AA.I.F.K1a	*9103, 9105, 9106, 9927*
AA.I.F.K1b	*9102, 9104*
AA.I.F.K1c	*9114-1*
AA.I.F.K1d	*9112, 9113*

ACS Code	*Question Numbers*
AA.I.F.K1f	*9101*
AA.I.F.K1g	*9928*
AA.I.F.K1h	*8706-1, 9929*
AA.I.F.K1k	*9107, 9107-1, 9107-2, 9108, 9109, 9110, 9110-1, 9114, 9115, 9116, 9117, 9118, 9433, 9434, 9434-1, 9435*
AA.I.F.K2	*9111, 9111-1, 9111-2, 9111-3, 9354, 9354-1*
AA.I.F.K3	*9778, 9778-1, 9804, 9804-1, 9805, 9805-1, 9805-2, 9805-3, 9805-4, 9805-5, 9805-6, 9806, 9806-1, 9816, 9816-1, 9832, 9834, 9853-1, 9856, 9928-1, 9929-2, 9940*
AA.I.F.R2	*9815, 9815-1, 9833, 9929-1*
AA.I.G.K1	*9328, 9329, 9329-1, 9330, 9331, 9332, 9333, 9334, 9335, 9339, 9340, 9342, 9343, 9344, 9349, 9350, 9351*
AA.I.G.K2	*8140, 8141, 8142, 8143, 8704-1, 8887, 8889, 8893, 8900, 9006, 9008, 9026, 9027, 9032, 9033, 9045, 9053, 9355, 9355-1, 9356, 9357, 9358, 9359, 9360, 9361, 9374, 9379, 9388, 9394-1, 9395, 9396, 9397, 9398, 9399, 9400, 9401, 9402, 9410, 9439, 9780, 9809, 9946-1*
AA.I.G.K3	*8194, 8211, 8219, 8220, 8221, 8222, 8223, 8224, 8227, 8228, 8229, 8231, 8231-1, 8238, 8706, 8707, 8708, 8709, 8724, 9714, 9837, 9838, 9839, 9840, 9841, 9842, 9843, 9844, 9845, 9846, 9847, 9847-1, 9847-2, 9848, 9849, 9850, 9851, 9852*
AA.I.G.K4	*8135, 8138, 8139, 8144, 8153, 8155, 8156, 8157, 8158, 8159, 8163, 8164, 8166, 8167, 8168, 8169, 8170, 8171, 8172, 8173, 8174, 8175, 8177, 8178, 8179, 8180, 8182, 8183, 8184, 8185, 8186, 8187, 8188, 8189, 8190, 8191, 8198, 8199, 8200, 8204, 8205, 8207, 8208, 8209, 8210, 8212, 8213, 8214, 8215, 8216, 8217, 8218, 8225, 8233, 8234, 8235, 8236, 8237, 8240, 8241, 8244, 8245, 8246, 8247, 8248, 8249, 8250, 8251, 8252, 8253, 8254, 8255, 8256, 8262, 8268, 8269, 8270, 8271, 8272, 8273, 8274, 8275, 8276, 8277, 8278, 8284, 8289, 8725, 9325, 9326, 9342-1, 9342-2, 9350-1, 9394-2, 9746-1, 9746-2, 9761, 9762, 9763-1, 9770*
AA.I.G.K5	*8001, 8004, 8005, 8006, 8007, 8008, 8009, 8010, 8011, 8012, 8013, 8014, 8015, 8016, 8017, 8018, 8019, 8020, 8021, 8022, 8023, 8024, 8025, 8026, 8027, 8028, 8029, 8030, 8031, 8032, 8033, 8034, 8035, 8036, 8037, 8038, 8039, 8040, 8041, 8042, 8043, 8044, 8045, 8046, 8047, 8048, 8049, 8050, 8051, 8052, 8053, 8054, 8055, 8056, 8057, 8058, 8059, 8060, 8061, 8062, 8063, 8064, 8065, 8066, 8067, 8068, 8069, 8070, 8071, 8072, 8073, 8074, 8075, 8076, 8077, 8078, 8079, 8080, 8081, 8082, 8083, 8084, 8085, 8086, 8087, 8088, 8089, 8090, 8091, 8092, 8093, 8094, 8095, 8096, 8097, 8098, 8099, 8100, 8101, 8102, 8103, 8104, 8105, 8105, 8107, 8108, 8109, 8110, 8111, 8112, 8113, 8165, 8792, 8807, 8808, 8809, 8813, 8814, 8815, 8819, 8820, 8821, 8827, 8828, 8829, 8830, 8831, 8832, 8833, 8834, 8838, 8840, 8841, 8842, 8843, 9618, 9720, 9819, 9931*
AA.I.G.K6	*8317, 8318, 8319, 8320, 8321, 8322, 8323, 9836*
AA.I.G.S1	*8131, 8132, 8136, 8137, 9807*
AA.II.A.K2b	*9782*
AA.II.A.K2c	*9407*
AA.II.A.K2e	*8226, 8232, 8243, 8259, 8260, 8266, 8267, 8280, 8286, 8287, 8288, 8290, 8291, 8292, 8293, 8294, 8295, 8296, 9746*
AA.II.A.K5	*8281, 8282, 9636, 9668*
AA.II.A.K6	*9020-1*
AA.II.A.K7	*8003, 8192, 8193, 8196, 8197, 8197-1, 8201, 8202, 8429, 8430, 8767, 8768, 9724, 9745*
AA.II.A.S6	*8872, 8873, 8874, 8875, 8876, 8877, 8878, 8879, 8880, 8881, 8882, 8883, 8884, 8885, 8886, 8888, 8890, 8891, 8892, 9018, 9046, 9047, 9048, 9049, 9093, 9100, 9741*
AA.II.C.K1	*9086, 9087, 9089*

ACS Code	Question Numbers
AA.II.C.K2	8722, 9007, 9009, 9022-1, 9056, 9057, 9416, 9737, 9788
AA.II.C.K3	8203, 8901-1, 8905, 8906, 8907, 8922, 9417, 9421, 9421-1, 9422, 9423, 9423-1, 9437, 9735, 9735-1, 9735-2, 9735-3, 9790, 9798, 9799
AA.II.C.K6	8701, 9258, 9421-3, 9783, 9784, 9787, 9790-1
AA.II.C.K7	9424
AA.II.C.K8	9789
AA.II.C.S3	9416-1, 9416-2, 9818
AA.II.C.S5	9005
AA.II.D.K2	8854, 9013, 9014
AA.III.A.K1	8727, 8727-1
AA.III.A.K3	8623, 8624, 8625, 8626, 8627
AA.III.A.K4	8901, 8902, 8903, 8904, 8914, 8915, 8923, 8924, 8925, 8926, 8927, 8928, 8929, 8930, 8931, 8932, 9764, 9785, 9785-1, 9786, 9786-1, 9786-2
AA.III.B.K4	8705, 8908, 8909, 8910, 8911, 8912, 8913, 8921, 9378
AA.III.B.R1	8133, 8933, 8934, 8935, 8936, 8937, 8937-1, 8938, 8939
AA.IV.A.K2d	8345, 8345-1, 8345-2, 8347, 8352, 8353, 8354, 8396
AA.IV.A.K2e	8349, 8350, 8351, 9740, 9823
AA.V.A.K1	9759
AA.V.B.K1	8374, 8728, 9767
AA.V.C.K5	9067-1
AA.VI.A.K1	9119, 9120, 9121, 9122, 9123, 9124
AA.VI.A.R2	9125, 9126, 9127, 9715
AA.VI.B.K1	8257, 8261, 8263, 8264, 9370, 9826
AA.VI.B.K3	9402-1
AA.VI.C.K1	8242, 8704, 8782, 8784, 8793, 8796, 8797, 8798, 8799, 8800, 8802, 8803, 8804, 8806, 8824, 8825, 8826, 8836, 8852, 8950, 9012, 9034, 9035, 9554, 9555, 9571, 9588, 9599, 9600, 9601, 9602, 9603, 9604, 9614, 9615, 9617, 9619, 9644, 9645, 9645-1, 9655, 9658, 9659, 9666, 9670, 9686, 9692, 9694, 9933
AA.VI.C.K3	8298-1, 8953, 9015, 9016, 9022, 9044, 9094-1
AA.VI.C.K4	9362, 9363, 9364, 9365, 9389, 9390
AA.VI.D.K1	8954, 9021, 9036, 9037, 9040, 9383, 9384, 9391, 9392, 9393
AA.VI.D.K2	9369, 9429, 9430, 9431, 9432, 9722, 9723, 9738, 9744, 9773, 9812, 9812-1
AA.VI.D.K3	8984, 8985, 8986, 8987, 8988, 8989, 8990, 8991, 8992, 8993, 8994, 8995, 8996, 8998, 8999, 9000, 9001, 9002, 9003, 9004, 9381, 9386, 9387, 9725, 9932
AA.VI.D.R6	9090-1
AA.VI.E.K1	8285, 8726, 8736, 8955, 8956, 8957, 8961, 9092, 9345, 9346, 9347, 9348, 9380, 9385, 9403, 9749
AA.VI.E.K2	8703, 8968, 9090-2, 9727, 9728, 9729, 9729-1, 9730, 9739, 9743, 9744-1, 9760, 9794, 9796, 9796-1, 9917
AA.VI.E.K3	8958, 8959, 8960, 8962, 8963, 8965, 8966, 8967, 8970, 9038, 9039, 9090-3, 9411, 9412, 9413, 9742

ACS Code	***Question Numbers***
AA.VI.E.K4	*8969, 9079, 9084, 9091, 9438, 9817-1*
AA.VI.E.R7	*8279*
AA.VI.E.S12	*9817*
AA.VI.F.K2	*8907-1*
AA.VI.F.R3b	*9731, 9732, 9733, 9734*
AA.VI.F.R9	*9858*
AA.VI.I.K1	*9041, 9368, 9382*
AA.VI.J.K1	*8853, 8855, 8856, 8857, 8858, 8859, 8860, 8861, 8862, 8863, 8864, 8865, 8866, 8867, 9418, 9419*
AA.VI.J.K2	*8673, 8674, 8675, 8676, 8677, 9010, 9011, 9050, 9420, 9943*
AA.VII.A.K2	*9097*
AA.VII.A.K6	*9081, 9082, 9222, 9753, 9756, 9934*
AA.VII.B.K1	*8357, 8358, 8360, 8362, 8363, 8364, 9827-1, 9827-2, 9827-3*
AA.VII.B.K2	*8361*
AA.VII.C.K2	*8359*

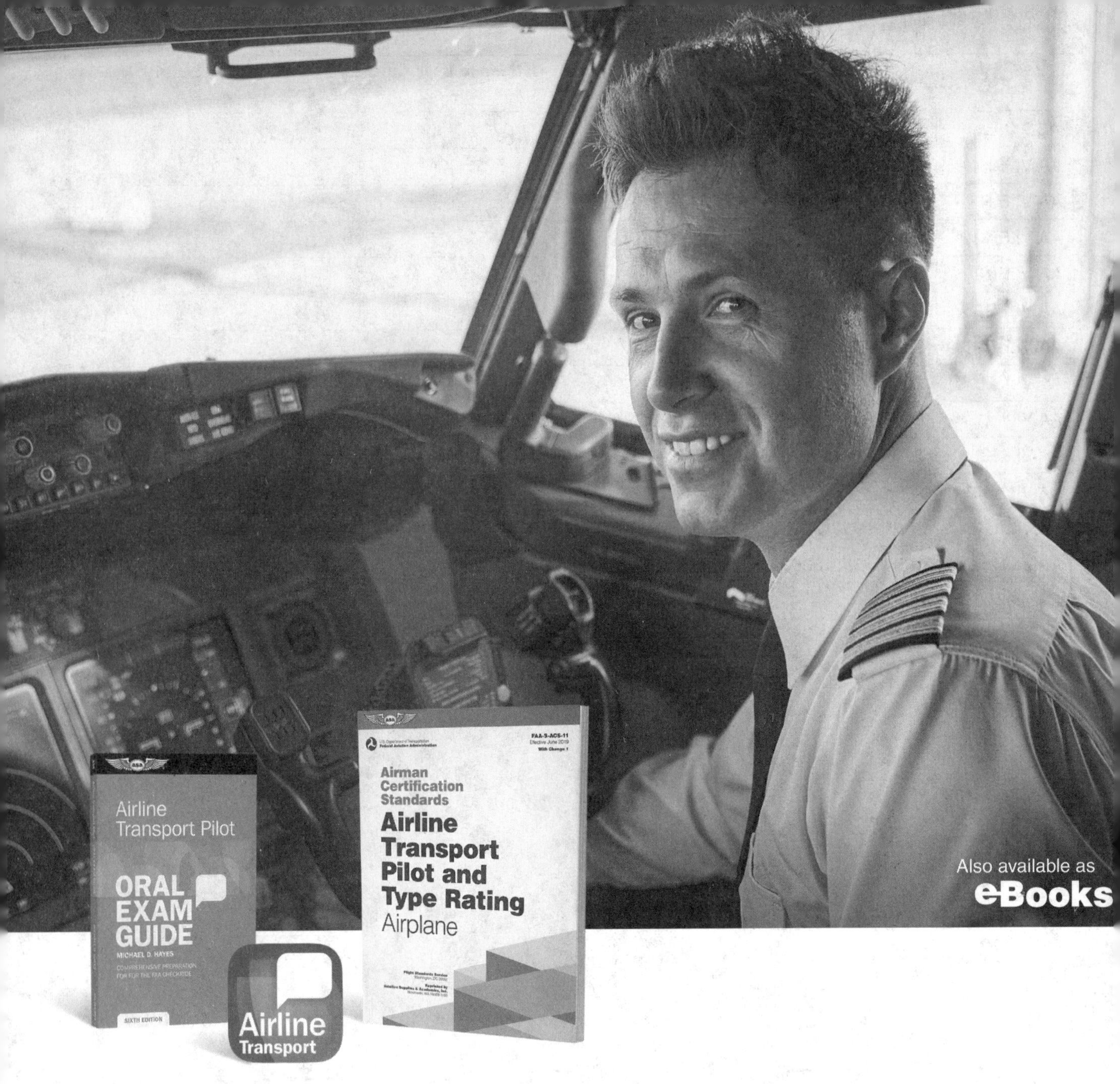

FAA-CT-8080-7D

Airman Knowledge Testing Supplement for Airline Transport Pilot and Aircraft Dispatcher

2019

This publication was formerly known as "Computer Testing Supplement for Airline Transport Pilot and Aircraft Dispatcher"

U.S. Department of Transportation
FEDERAL AVIATION ADMINISTRATION
Flight Standards Service

Preface

This Airman Knowledge Testing Supplement is designed by the Federal Aviation Administration (FAA) Flight Standards Service. It is intended for use by Airman Knowledge Testing (AKT) Organization Designation Authorization (ODA) Holders and other entities approved and/or authorized to administer airman knowledge tests on behalf of the FAA in the following knowledge areas:

Airline Transport Pilot (FAR 121) Multiengine Airplane (ATM)
Airline Transport Pilot (FAR 135) Single-Engine Airplane (ATS)
Airline Transport Pilot (FAR 135) Added Rating—Airplane (ARA)
Airline Transport Pilot (FAR 135) Helicopter (ATH)
Airline Transport Pilot (FAR 135) Added Rating—Helicopter (ARH)
Airline Transport Pilot Multiengine Airplane **Canadian Conversion** (ACM)
Airline Transport Pilot Single-Engine Airplane **Canadian Conversion** (ASC)
Airline Transport Pilot Helicopter **Canadian Conversion** (ACH)
Aircraft Dispatcher (ADX)
Flight Navigator (FNX)

FAA-CT-8080-7D supersedes FAA-CT-8080-7C dated 2005.

All figures in this supplement are for testing purposes only and are not to be used for flight or flight planning.

Comments regarding this supplement, or any Airman Testing publication, should be emailed to AFS630comments@faa.gov.

Contents

Appendix 2

Appendix 1

GENERAL INFORMATION

ABBREVIATIONS

The following abbreviations/acronyms are those commonly used within this Directory. Other abbreviations/acronyms may be found in the Legend and are not duplicated below. The abbreviations presented are intended to represent grammatical variations of the basic form. (Example–"req" may mean "request", "requesting", "requested", or "requests").

Abbreviation	Description
A/G	air/ground
AAF	Army Air Field
AAS	Airport Advisory Service
AB	Airbase
abm	abeam
ABn	Aerodrome Beacon
abv	above
ACC	Air Combat Command Area Control Center
acft	aircraft
ACLS	Automatic Carrier Landing System
act	activity
ACWS	Aircraft Control and Warning Squadron
ADA	Advisory Area
ADCC	Air Defense Control Center
ADCUS	Advise Customs
addn	addition
ADF	Automatic Direction Finder
adj	adjacent
admin	administration
ADR	Advisory Route
advs	advise
advsy	advisory
AEIS	Aeronautical Enroute Information Service
AER	approach end rwy
AFA	Army Flight Activity
AFB	Air Force Base
afct	affect
AFFF	Aqueous Film Forming Foam
AFHP	Air Force Heliport
AFIS	Aerodrome Flight Information Service
afld	airfield
AFOD	Army Flight Operations Detachment
AFR	Air Force Regulation
AFRC	Armed Forces Reserve Center/Air Force Reserve Command
AFRS	American Forces Radio Stations
AFS	Air Force Station
AFSS	Automated Flight Service Station
AFTN	Aeronautical Fixed Telecommunication Network
AG	Agriculture
A–G, A–GEAR	Arresting Gear
agcy	Agency
AGL	above ground level
AHP	Army heliport
AID	Airport Information Desk
AIS	Aeronautical Information Services
AL	Approach and Landing Chart
ALF	Auxiliary Landing Field
ALS	Approach Light System
ALSF–1	High Intensity ALS Category I configuration with sequenced Flashers (code)
ALSF–2	High Intensity ALS Category II configuration with sequenced Flashers (code)
alt	altitude
altn	alternate

Abbreviation	Description
AM	Amplitude Modulation, midnight til noon
AMC	Air Mobility Command
amdt	amendment
AMSL	Above Mean Sea Level
ANGS	Air National Guard Station
ant	antenna
AOE	Airport/Aerodrome of Entry
AP	Area Planning
APAPI	Abbreviated Precision Approach Path Indicator
apch	approach
apn	apron
APP	Approach Control
Apr	April
aprx	approximate
APU	Auxiliary Power Unit
apv, apvl	approve, approval
ARB	Air Reserve Base
ARCAL (CANADA)	Aircraft Radio Control of Aerodrome Lighting
ARFF	Aircraft Rescue and Fire Fighting
ARINC	Aeronautical Radio Inc
arng	arrange
arpt	airport
arr	arrive
ARS	Air Reserve Station
ARSA	Airport Radar Service Area
ARSR	Air Route Surveillance Radar
ARTCC	Air Route Traffic Control Center
AS	Air Station
ASAP	as soon as possible
ASDA	Accelerate–Stop Distance Available
ASDE	Airport Surface Detection
ASDE–X	Airport Surface Detection Equipment–Model X
asgn	assign
ASL	Above Sea Level
ASOS	Automated Surface Observing System
ASR	Airport Surveillance Radar
ASSC	Airport Surface Surveillance Capability
ASU	Aircraft Starting Unit
ATA	Actual Time of Arrival
ATC	Air Traffic Control
ATCC	Air Traffic Control Center
ATCT	Airport Traffic Control Tower
ATD	Actual Time of Departure Along Track Distance
ATIS	Automatic Terminal Information Service
ATS	Air Traffic Service
attn	attention
Aug	August
auth	authority
auto	automatic
AUW	All Up Weight (gross weight)
aux	auxiliary
AVASI	abbreviated VASI
avbl	available
AvGas	Aviation gasoline
avn	aviation
AvOil	aviation oil

Legend 1. Chart Supplement Abbreviations.

GENERAL INFORMATION 5

Abbreviation	Description
AWOS	Automatic Weather Observing System
AWSS	Automated Weather Sensor System
awt	await
awy	airway
az	azimuth
BA	braking action
BASH	Bird Aircraft Strike Hazard
BC	back course
bcn	beacon
bcst	broadcast
bdry	boundary
bldg	building
blkd	blocked
blo, blw	below
BOQ	Bachelor Officers Quarters
brg	bearing
btn	between
bus	business
byd	beyond
C	Commercial Circuit (Telephone)
CAC	Centralized Approach Control
cap	capacity
cat	category
CAT	Clear Air Turbulence
CCW or cntclkws	counterclockwise
ceil	ceiling
CERAP	Center Radar Approach Control
CG	Coast Guard
CGAF	Coast Guard Air Facility
CGAS	Coast Guard Air Station
CH, chan	channel
CHAPI	Chase Helicopter Approach Path Indicator
chg	change
cht	chart
cir	circle, circling
CIV, civ	Civil, civil, civilian
ck	check
CL	Centerline Lighting System
cl	class
clnc	clearance
clsd	closed
CNATRA	Chief of Naval Air Training
cnl	cancel
cntr	center
cntrln	centerline
Co	Company, County
CO	Commanding Officer
com	communication
comd	command
Comdr	Commander
coml	commercial
compul	compulsory
comsn	commission
conc	concrete
cond	condition
const	construction
cont	continue
CONUS	Continental United States
convl	conventional
coord	coordinate
copter	helicopter
corr	correct
CPDLC	Controller Pilot Data Link Communication
crdr	corridor
cros	cross
CRP	Compulsory Reporting Point
crs	course
CS	call sign
CSTMS	Customs
CTA	Control Area
CTAF	Common Traffic Advisory Frequency
ctc	contact
ctl	control
CTLZ	Control Zone
CVFR	Controlled Visual Flight Rules Areas
CW	Clockwise, Continuous Wave, Carrier Wave
dalgt	daylight
D–ATIS	Digital Automatic Terminal Information Service
daylt	daylight
db	decibel
DCL	Departure Clearance
Dec	December
decom	decommission
deg	degree
del	delivery
dep	depart
DEP	Departure Control
destn	destination
det	detachment
DF	Direction Finder
DH	Decision Height
DIAP	DoD Instrument Approach Procedure
direc	directional
disem	disseminate
displ	displace
dist	district, distance
div	division
DL	Direct Line to FSS
dlt	delete
dly	daily
DME	Distance Measuring Equipment (UHF standard, TACAN compatible)
DNVT	Digital Non–Secure Voice Telephone
DoD	Department of Defense
drct	direct
DSN	Defense Switching Network (Telephone)
DSN	Defense Switching Network
dsplcd	displaced
DT	Daylight Savings Time
dur	during
durn	duration
DV	Distinguished Visitor
E	East
ea	each
EAT	Expected Approach Time
ECN	Enroute Change Notice
EFAS	Enroute Flight Advisory Service
eff	effective, effect
E–HA	Enroute High Altitude
E–LA	Enroute Low Altitude
elev	elevation
ELT	Emergency Locator Transmitter
EMAS	Engineered Material Arresting System
emerg	emergency
eng	engine

Legend 2. Chart Supplement Abbreviations.

6 **GENERAL INFORMATION**

Abbreviation	Description
EOR	End of Runway
eqpt	equipment
ERDA	Energy Research and Development Administration
E–S	Enroute Supplement
est	estimate
estab	establish
ETA	Estimated Time of Arrival
ETD	Estimated Time of Departure
ETE	Estimated Time Enroute
ETS	European Telephone System
EUR	European (ICAO Region)
ev	every
evac	evacuate
exc	except
excld	exclude
exer	exercise
exm	exempt
exp	expect
extd	extend
extn	extension
extv	extensive
F/W	Fixed Wing
FAA	Federal Aviation Administration
fac	facility
FAWS	Flight Advisory Weather Service
fax	facsimile
FBO	Fixed Base Operator
FCC	Flight Control Center
FCG	Foreign Clearance Guide
FCLP	field carrier landing practice
fcst	forecast
Feb	February
FIC	Flight Information Center
FIH	Flight Information Handbook
FIR	Flight Information Region
FIS	Flight Information Service
FL	flight level
fld	field
flg	flashing
FLIP	Flight Information Publication
flt	flight
flw	follow
FM	Fan Marker, Frequency Modulation
FOC	Flight Operations Center
FOD	Foreign Object Damage
fone	telephone
FPL	Flight Plan
fpm	feet per minute
fr	from
freq	frequency, frequent
Fri	Friday
frng	firing
FSC	Flight Service Center
FSS	Flight Service Station
ft	foot
ftr	fighter
GA	Glide Angle
gal	gallon
GAT	General Air Traffic (Europe–Asia)
GCA	Ground Control Approach
GCO	Ground Communication Outlet
gldr	glider
GND	Ground Control
gnd	ground

Abbreviation	Description
govt	government
GP	Glide Path
Gp	Group
GPI	Ground Point of Intercept
grad	gradient
grd	guard
GS	glide slope
GWT	gross weight
H	Enroute High Altitude Chart (followed by identification)
H+	Hours or hours plus...minutes past the hour
H24	continuous operation
HAA	Height Above Airport/Aerodrome
HAL	Height Above Landing Area
HAR	Height Above Runway
HAT	Height Above Touchdown
haz	hazard
hdg	heading
HDTA	High Density Traffic Airport/Aerodrome
HF	High Frequency (3000 to 30,000 KHz)
hgr	hangar
hgt	height
hi	high
HIRL	High Intensity Runway Lights
HIWAS	Hazardous Inflight Weather Advisory Service
HO	Service available to meet operational requirements
hol	holiday
HOLF	Helicopter Outlying Field
hosp	hospital
HQ	Headquarters
hr	hour
HS	Service available during hours of scheduled operations
hsg	housing
hvy	heavy
HW	Heavy Weight
hwy	highway
HX	station having no specific working hours
Hz	Hertz (cycles per second)
I	Island
IAP	Instrument Approach Procedure
IAS	Indicated Air Speed
IAW	in accordance with
ICAO	International Civil Aviation Organization
ident	identification
IFF	Identification, Friend or Foe
IFR	Instrument Flight Rules
IFR–S	FLIP IFR Supplement
IFSS	International Flight Service Station
ILS	Instrument Landing System
IM	Inner Marker
IMC	Instrument Meteorological Conditions
IMG	Immigration
immed	immediate
inbd	inbound
Inc	Incorporated
incl	include
incr	increase
indef	indefinite
info	information
inop	inoperative
inst	instrument

Legend 3. Chart Supplement Abbreviations.

GENERAL INFORMATION

Abbreviation	Description
instl	install
instr	instruction
int	intersection
intcntl	intercontinental
intcp	intercept
intl	international
intmt	intermittent
ints	intense, intensity
invof	in the vicinity of
irreg	Irregularly
Jan	January
JASU	Jet Aircraft Starting Unit
JATO	Jet Assisted Take–Off
JOAP	Joint Oil Analysis Program
JOSAC	Joint Operational Support Airlift Center
JRB	Joint Reserve Base
Jul	July
Jun	June
K or Kt	Knots
kHz	kilohertz
KIAS	Knots Indicated Airspeed
KLIZ	Korea Limited Identification Zone
km	Kilometer
kw	kilowatt
L	Compass locator (Component of ILS system) under 25 Watts, 15 NM, Enroute Low Altitude Chart (followed by identification)
L	Local Time
LAA	Local Airport Advisory
LAHSO	Land and Hold–Short Operations
L–AOE	Limited Airport of Entry
LAWRS	Limited Aviation Weather Reporting Station
lb, lbs	pound (weight)
LC	local call
lcl	local
LCP	French Peripheral Classification Line
lctd	located
lctn	location
lctr	locator
LCVASI	Low Cost Visual Approach Slope Indicator
lczr	localizer
LD	long distance
LDA	Landing Distance Available
ldg	landing
LDIN	Lead–in Lights
LDOCF	Long Distance Operations Control Facility
len	length
lgt, lgtd, lgts	light, lighted, lights
LIRL	Low Intensity Runway Lights
LLWAS	Low–Level Wind Shear Alert System
LLZ	Localizer (Instrument Approach Procedures Identification only)
LMM	Compass locator at Middle Marker ILS
lo	low
LoALT or LA	Low Altitude
LOC	Localizer
LOM	Compass locator at Outer Marker ILS
LR	Long Range, Lead Radial
LRA	Landing Rights Airport
LRRS	Long Range RADAR Station

Abbreviation	Description
LSB	lower side band
ltd	limited
M	meters, magnetic (after a bearing), Military Circuit (Telephone)
MACC	Military Area Control Center
mag	magnetic
maint	maintain, maintenance
maj	major
MALS	Medium Intensity Approach Lighting System
MALSF	MALS with Sequenced Flashers
MALSR	MALS with Runway Alignment Indicator Lights
Mar	March
MARA	Military Activity Restricted Area
MATO	Military Air Traffic Operations
MATZ	Military Aerodrome Traffic Zone
max	maximum
mb	millibars
MCAC	Military Common Area Control
MCAF	Marine Corps Air Facility
MCALF	Marine Corps Auxiliary Landing Field
MCAS	Marine Corps Air Station
MCB	Marine Corps Base
MCC	Military Climb Corridor
MCOLF	Marine Corps Outlying Field
MDA	Minimum Descent Altitude
MEA	Minimum Enroute Altitude
med	medium
MEHT	Minimum Eye Height over Threshold
mem	memorial
MET	Meteorological, Meteorology
METAR	Aviation Routine Weather Report (in international MET figure code)
METRO	Pilot–to–Metro voice cell
MF	Medium Frequency (300 to 3000 KHz), Mandatory Frequency (Canada)
MFA	Minimum Flight Altitude
mgmt	Management
mgr	manager
MHz	Megahertz
mi	mile
MID/ASIA	Middle East/Asia (ICAO Region)
MIJI	Meaconing, Intrusion, Jamming, and Interference
Mil, mil	military
min	minimum, minute
MIRL	Medium Intensity Runway Lights
misl	missile
mkr	marker (beacon)
MM	Middle Marker of ILS
mnt	monitor
MOA	Military Operations Area
MOCA	Minimum Obstruction Clearance Altitude
mod	modify
MOG	Maximum (aircraft) on the Ground
Mon	Monday
MP	Maintenance Period
MR	Medium Range
MRA	Minimum Reception Altitude
mrk	mark, marker
MSAW	minimum safe altitude warning
msg	message
MSL	Mean Sea Level
msn	Mission

Legend 4. Chart Supplement Abbreviations

GENERAL INFORMATION

Abbreviation	Description
mt	mount, mountain
MTAF	Mandatory Traffic Advisory Frequency
MTCA	Military Terminal Control Area
mthly	monthly
MUAC	Military Upper Area Control
muni	municipal
MWARA	Major World Air Route Area
N	North
N/A	not applicable
NA	not authorized (For Instrument Approach Procedure take–off and alternate MINIMA only)
NAAS	Naval Auxiliary Air Station
NADC	Naval Air Development Center
NADEP	Naval Air Depot
NAEC	Naval Air Engineering Center
NAES	Naval Air Engineering Station
NAF	Naval Air Facility
NALCO	Naval Air Logistics Control Office
NALF	Naval Auxiliary Landing Field
NALO	Navy Air Logistics Office
NAS	Naval Air Station
NAT	North Atlantic (ICAO Region)
natl	national
nav	navigation
navaid	navigation aid
NAVMTO	Navy Material Transportation Office
NAWC	Naval Air Warfare Center
NAWS	Naval Air Weapons Station
NCRP	Non–Compulsory Reporting Point
NDB	Non–Directional Radio Beacon
NE	Northeast
nec	necessary
NEW	Net Explosives Weight
ngt	night
NM	nautical miles
nml	normal
NMR	nautical mile radius
No or Nr	number
NOLF	Naval Outlying Field
NORDO	Lost communications or no radio installed/available in aircraft
NOTAM	Notice to Airmen
Nov	November
npi	non precision instrument
Nr or No	number
NS	Naval Station
NS ABTMT	Noise Abatement
NSA	Naval Support Activity
NSF	Naval Support Facility
NSTD, nstd	nonstandard
ntc	notice
NVD	Night Vision Devices
NVG	Night Vision Goggles
NW	Northwest
NWC	Naval Weapons Center
O/A	On or about
O/S	out of service
O/R	On Request
OAT	Operational Air Traffic
obsn	observation
obst	obstruction
OCA	Oceanic Control Area
ocnl	occasional
Oct	October

Abbreviation	Description
ODALS	Omnidirectional Approach Lighting System
ODO	Operations Duty Officer
offl	official
OIC	Officer In Charge
OLF	Outlying Field
OLS	Optical Landing System
OM	Outer Marker, ILS
opr	operate, operator, operational
OPS, ops	operations
orig	original
OROCA	Off Route Obstruction Clearance Altitude
ORTCA	Off Route Terrain Clearance Altitude
OT	other times
OTS	out of service
outbd	outbound
ovft	overflight
ovrn	overrun
OX	oxygen
P/L	plain language
PAC	Pacific (ICAO Region)
PAEW	personnel and equipment working
PALS	Precision Approach and Landing System (NAVY)
PAPI	Precision Approach Path Indicator
PAR	Precision Approach Radar
para	paragraph
parl	parallel
pat	pattern
PAX	Passenger
PCL	pilot controlled lighting
pent	penetrate
perm	permanent
perms	permission
pers	personnel
PFC	Porous Friction Courses
PJE	Parachuting Activities/Exercises
p–line	power line
PM	Post meridian, noon til midnight
PMRF	Pacific Missile Range Facility
PMSV	Pilot–to–Metro Service
PN	prior notice
POB	persons on board
POL	Petrol, Oils and Lubricants
posn	position
PPR	prior permission required
prcht	parachute
pref	prefer
prev	previous
prim	primary
prk	park
PRM	Precision Runway Monitor
pro	procedure
proh	prohibited
pt	point
PTD	Pilot to Dispatcher
pub	publication
publ	publish
PVASI	Pulsating Visual Approach Slope Indicator
pvt	private
pwr	power
QFE	Altimeter Setting above station

Legend 5. Chart Supplement Abbreviations.

GENERAL INFORMATION

Abbreviation	Description
QNE	Altimeter Setting of 29.92 inches which provides height above standard datum plane
QNH	Altimeter Setting which provides height above mean sea level
qtrs	quarters
quad	quadrant
R/T	Radiotelephony
R/W	Rotary/Wing
RACON	Radar Beacon
rad	radius, radial
RAIL	Runway Alignment Indicator Lights
RAMCC	Regional Air Movement Control Center
R–AOE	Regular Airport of Entry
RAPCON	Radar Approach Control (USAF)
RATCF	Radar Air Traffic Control Facility (Navy)
RCAG	Remote Center Air to Ground Facility
RCAGL	Remote Center Air to Ground Facility Long Range
RCL	runway centerline
RCLS	Runway Centerline Light System
RCO	Remote Communications Outlet
rcpt	reception
RCR	Runway Condition Reading
rcv	receive
rcvr	receiver
rdo	radio
reconst	reconstruct
reful	refueling
reg	regulation, regular
REIL	Runway End Identifier Lights
rel	reliable
relctd	relocated
REP	Reporting Point
req	request
RETIL	Rapid Exit Taxiway Indicator Light
Rgn	Region
Rgnl	Regional
rgt	right
rgt tfc	right traffic
rlgd	realigned
RLLS	Runway Lead-in Light System
rmk	remark
rng	range, radio range
RNP	Required Navigation Performance
RON	Remain Overnight
Rot Lt or Bcn	Rotating Light or Beacon
RPI	Runway Point of Intercept
rpt	report
rqr	require
RR	Railroad
RRP	Runway Reference Point
RSC	Runway Surface Condition
RSDU	Radar Storm Detection Unit
RSE	Runway Starter Extension/Starter Strip
RSRS	Reduced Same Runway Separation
rstd	restricted
rte	route
ruf	rough
RVR	Runway Visual Range
RVSM	Reduced Vertical Separation Minima
rwy	runway
S	South
S/D	Seadrome
SALS	Short Approach Lighting System

Abbreviation	Description
SAR	Search and Rescue
Sat	Saturday
SAVASI	Simplified Abbreviated Visual Approach Slope Indicator
SAWRS	Supplement Aviation Weather Reporting Station
sby	standby
Sched	scheduled services
sctr	sector
SDF	Simplified Directional Facility
SE	Southeast
sec	second, section
secd	secondary
SELCAL	Selective Calling System
SELF	Strategic Expeditionary Landing Field
SEng	Single Engine
Sep	September
SFA	Single Frequency Approach
sfc	surface
SFL	Sequence Flashing Lights
SFRA	Special Flight Rules Area
SID	Standard Instrument Departure
SIDA	Secure Identification Display Area
SIF	Selective Identification Feature
sked	schedule
SM	statute miles
SOAP	Spectrometric Oil Analysis Program
SOF	Supervisor of Flying
SPB	Seaplane Base
SR	sunrise
SRE	Surveillance Radar Element of GCA (Instrument Approach Procedures Identification only)
SS	sunset
SSALS/R	Simplified Short Approach Lighting System/with RAIL
SSB	Single Sideband
SSR	Secondary Surveillance Radar
STA	Straight-in Approach
std	standard
stn	station
stor	storage
str–in	Straight–in
stu	student
subj	subject
sum	summer
Sun	Sunday
sur	surround
survl	survival, surveillance
suspd	suspended
svc	service
svcg	servicing
SW	Southwest
sys	system
TA	Transition Altitude
TAC	Tactical Air Command
TAF	Aerodrome (terminal or alternate) forecast in abbreviated form
TALCE	Tanker Aircraft Control Element
TCA	Terminal Control Area
TCH	Threshold Crossing Height
TCTA	Transcontinental Control Area
TD	Touchdown
TDWR	Terminal Doppler Weather Radar
TDZ	Touchdown Zone
TDZL	Touchdown Zone Lights

Legend 6. Chart Supplement Abbreviations.

GENERAL INFORMATION

Abbreviation	Description
tfc	traffic
thld	threshold
thou	thousand
thru	through
Thu	Thursday
til	until
tkf, tkof	take–off
TLv	Transition Level
tmpry	temporary
TODA	Take–Off Distance Available
TORA	Take–Off Run Available
TP	Tire Pressure
TPA	Traffic Pattern Altitude
TRACON	Terminal Radar Approach Control (FAA)
tran	transient
trans	transmit
trml	terminal
trng	training
trns	transition
TRSA	Terminal Radar Service Area
Tue	Tuesday
TV	Television
TWEB	Transcribed Weather Broadcast
twr	tower
twy	taxiway
UACC	Upper Area Control Center (used outside US)
UAS	Unmanned Aerial Systems
UC	Under Construction
UCN	Urgent Change Notice
UDA	Upper Advisory Area
UDF	Ultra High Frequency Direction Finder
UFN	until further notice
UHF	Ultra High Frequency (300 to 3000 MHz)
UIR	Upper Flight Information Region
unauthd	unauthorized
unavbl	unavailable
unctl	uncontrolled
unk	unknown
unlgtd	unlighted
unltd	unlimited
unmrk	unmarked
unmto	unmonitored
unrel	unreliable
unrstd	unrestricted
unsatfy	unsatisfactory
unsked	unscheduled
unsvc	unserviceable
unuse, unusbl	unusable
USA	United States Army
USAF	United States Air Force
USB	Upper Side Band
USCG	United States Coast Guard
USMC	United States Marine Corps
USN	United States Navy
UTA	Upper Control Area
UTC	Coordinated Universal Time
V	Defense Switching Network (telephone, formerly AUTOVON)
V/STOL	Vertical and Short Take–off and Landing aircraft
VAL	Visiting Aircraft Line
var	variation (magnetic variation)
VASI	Visual Approach Slope Indicator
vcnty	vicinity
VDF	Very High Frequency Direction Finder
veh	vehicle
vert	vertical
VFR	Visual Flight Rules
VFR–S	FLIP VFR Supplement
VHF	Very High Frequency (30 to 300 MHz)
VIP	Very Important Person
vis	visibility
VMC	Visual Meteorological Conditions
VOIP	Voice Over Internet Protocol
VOLMET	Meteorological Information for Aircraft in Flight
VOT	VOR Receiver Testing Facility
W	Warning Area (followed by identification), Watts, West, White
WCH	Wheel Crossing Height
Wed	Wednesday
Wg	Wing
WIE	with immediate effect
win	winter
WIP	work in progress
WSO	Weather Service Office
WSFO	Weather Service Forecast Office
wk	week
wkd	weekday
wkly	weekly
wng	warning
wo	without
WSP	Weather System Processor
wt	weight
wx	weather
yd	yard
yr	year
Z	Greenwich Mean Time (time groups only)

Legend 7. Chart Supplement Abbreviations.

AIRPORT/FACILITY DIRECTORY LEGEND

SAMPLE

(1) **CITY NAME**

AIRPORT NAME (ALTERNATE NAME) (LTS)(KLTS) CIV/MIL 3 N UTC–6(–5DT) N34°41.93′ W99°20.20′ **JACKSONVILLE**
200 B TPA—1000(800) AOE LRA Class IV, ARFF Index A NOTAM FILE ORL Not insp. **COPTER**
H–4G, L–19C
IAP, DIAP, AD

(2) (3) (4) (5) (6) (7) (8) (9) (11) (12) (13) (14) (15) (16) (17)

(18)→ **RWY 18–36:** H12004X200 (ASPH–CONC–GRVD)
S–90, D–160, 2D–300 PCN 80 R/B/W/T HIRL CL
RWY 18: RLLS. MALSF. TDZL. REIL. PAPI(P2R)—GA 3.0° TCH 36′. RVR–TMR. Thld dsplcd 300′. Trees. Rgt tfc. 0.3% up.
RWY 36: ALSF1. 0.4% down.
RWY 09–27: H6000X150 (ASPH) MIRL
RWY 173–353: H3515X150 (ASPH–PFC) AUW PCN 59 F/A/W/T

(19)→ **LAND AND HOLD–SHORT OPERATIONS**

LDG RWY	HOLD–SHORT POINT	AVBL LDG DIST
RWY 18	09–27	6500
RWY 36	09–27	5400

(20)→ **RUNWAY DECLARED DISTANCE INFORMATION**
RWY 18: TORA–12004 TODA–12004 ASDA–11704 LDA–11504
RWY 36: TORA–12004 TODA–12004 ASDA–12004 LDA–11704

(21)→ **ARRESTING GEAR/SYSTEM**
RWY 18 HOOK E5 (65′ OVRN) BAK–14 BAK–12B (1650′)
BAK–14 BAK–12B (1087′) HOOK E5 (74′ OVRN) **RWY 36**

(22)→ **SERVICE:** S4 **FUEL** 100LL, JET A **OX** 1, 3 **LGT** ACTIVATE MALSR Rwy 29, REIL Rwy 11, VASI Rwy 11, HIRL Rwy 11–29, PAPI Rwy 17 and Rwy 35, MIRL Rwy 17–35—CTAF. **MILITARY— A–GEAR** E–5 connected on dep end, disconnected on apch end.
JASU 3(AM32A–60) 2(A/M32A–86) **FUEL** J8(Mil)(NC–100, A)
FLUID W SP PRESAIR LOX **OIL** O–128 **MAINT** S1 Mon–Fri 1000–2200Z‡
TRAN ALERT Avbl 1300–0200Z‡ svc limited weekends.

(23)→ **AIRPORT REMARKS:** Special Air Traffic Rules—Part 93, see Regulatory Notices. Attended 1200–0300Z‡. Parachute Jumping. Deer invof arpt. Heavy jumbo jet training surface to 9000′. Twy A clsd indef. Flight Notification Service (ADCUS) avbl.

(24)→ **MILITARY REMARKS: ANG** PPR/Official Business Only. Base OPS DSN 638–4390, C503–335–4222. Ctc Base OPS 15 minutes prior to ldg and after dep. Limited tran parking.

(25)→ **AIRPORT MANAGER:** (580) 481–5739

(26)→ **WEATHER DATA SOURCES: AWOS–1** 120.3 (202) 426–8000. LAWRS.

(27)→ **COMMUNICATIONS: SFA CTAF** 122.8 **UNICOM** 122.95 **ATIS** 127.25 273.5 (202) 426–8003 **PTD** 372.2
NAME FSS (ORL) on arpt. 123.65 122.65 122.2
NAME RCO 112.2T 112.1R (NAME RADIO)
Ⓡ **NAME APP/DEP CON** 128.35 257.725 (1200–0400Z‡)
TOWER 119.65 255.6 (1200–0400Z‡) **GND CON** 121.7 **GCO** 135.075 (ORLANDO CLNC) **CLNC DEL** 125.55
CPDLC D–HZWXR, D–TAXI, DCL (LOGON KMEM)
NAME COMD POST (GERONIMO) 311.0 321.4 6761 **PMSV METRO** 239.8 **NAME OPS** 257.5

(28)→ **AIRSPACE: CLASS B** See VFR Terminal Area Chart.

(29)→ **VOR TEST FACILITY (VOT):** 116.7

(30)→ **RADIO AIDS TO NAVIGATION:** NOTAM FILE ORL. VHF/DF ctc FSS.
(H) VORTAC 112.2 MCO Chan 59 N28°32.55′ W81°20.12′ at fld. 1110/8E.
(H) TACAN Chan 29 CBU (109.2) N28°32.65′ W81°21.12′ at fld. 1115/8E.
HERNY NDB (LOM) 221 OR N28°37.40′ W81°21.05′ 177° 5.4 NM to fld.
ILS/DME 108.5 I–ORL Chan 22 Rwy 18. Class IIE. LOM HERNY NDB.
ASR/PAR (1200–0400Z‡)

(31)→ **COMM/NAV/WEATHER REMARKS:** Emerg frequency 121.5 not avbl at twr.

• • • • • • • • • • • • • • • • • •

HELIPAD H1: H100X75 (ASPH)
HELIPAD H2: H60X60 (ASPH)
HELIPORT REMARKS: Helipad H1 lctd on general aviation side and H2 lctd on air carrier side of arpt. (1)

• • • • • • • • • • • • • • • • • •

187 TPA 1000(813)
WATERWAY 15–33: 5000X425 (WATER)
SEAPLANE REMARKS: Birds roosting and feeding areas along river banks. Seaplanes operating adjacent to SW side of arpt not visible from twr and are required to ctc twr.

All bearings and radials are magnetic unless otherwise specified. All mileages are nautical unless otherwise noted.
All times are Coordinated Universal Time (UTC) except as noted. All elevations are in feet above/below Mean Sea Level (MSL) unless otherwise noted.
The horizontal reference datum of this publication is North American Datum of 1983 (NAD83), which for charting purposes is considered equivalent to World Geodetic System 1984 (WGS 84).

Legend 8. Airport/Facility Directory Legend from Chart Supplement.

(10)

SKETCH LEGEND

RUNWAYS/LANDING AREAS

Hard Surfaced . . . .

Metal Surface . . . .

Sod, Gravel, etc. . . . .

Light Plane, ...
Ski Landing Area or Water

Under Construction . . . . .

Closed Rwy . . . .

Closed Pavement . . . .

Helicopter Landings Area . . . . (H)

Displaced Threshold . . . .

Taxiway, Apron and Stopways . .

MISCELLANEOUS BASE AND CULTURAL FEATURES

Buildings . . . .

Power Lines . . . . –T——T–

Fence . . . .

Towers . . . .

Wind Turbine. . . . .

Tanks . . . .

Oil Well . . . .

Smoke Stack . . . .

Obstruction 5812

Controlling Obstruction . . . . +5812

Trees . . . .

Populated Places . . . .

Cuts and Fills . . . . . . Cut Fill

Cliffs and Depressions . .

Ditch . . . .

Hill . . . .

RADIO AIDS TO NAVIGATION

VORTAC . . . VOR . . . .

VOR/DME . . NDB . . . .

TACAN . . . . NDB/DME . . . .

DME . . . .

MISCELLANEOUS AERONAUTICAL FEATURES

Airport Beacon . . . .

Wind Cone . . . .

Landing Tee . . . .

Tetrahedron . . . .

Control Tower . . . . or TWR

When control tower and rotating beacon are co-located beacon symbol will be used and further identified as TWR.

APPROACH LIGHTING SYSTEMS

A dot "•" portrayed with approach lighting letter identifier indicates sequenced flashing lights (F) installed with the approach lighting system e.g. (A1) Negative symbology, e.g., (A1) (V) indicates Pilot Controlled Lighting (PCL).

Runway Centerline Lighting . . . . .

(A) Approach Lighting System ALSF-2 . .

(A1) Approach Lighting System ALSF-1 . .

(A2) Short Approach Lighting System SALS/SALSF . . . .

(A3) Simplified Short Approach Lighting System (SSALR) with RAIL . . . . .

(A4) Medium Intensity Approach Lighting System (MALS and MALSF)/(SSALS and SSALF) . . . .

(A5) Medium Intensity Approach Lighting System (MALSR) and RAIL . . . . .

Omnidirectional Approach Lighting System (ODALS) . . . .

(D) Navy Parallel Row and Cross Bar . . .

(‡) Air Force Overrun . . . .

(V) Visual Approach Slope Indicator with Standard Threshold Clearance provided

(V2) Pulsating Visual Approach Slope Indicator (PVASI)

(V3) Visual Approach Slope Indicator with a threshold crossing height to accomodate long bodied or jumbo aircraft

(V4) Tri-color Visual Approach Slope Indicator (TRCV)

(V5) Approach Path Alignment Panel (APAP)

(P) Precision Approach Path Indicator (PAPI)

Legend 9. Airport/Facility Directory Legend from Chart Supplement.

AIRPORT/FACILITY DIRECTORY LEGEND

LEGEND

This directory is a listing of data on record with the FAA on public–use airports, military airports and selected private–use airports specifically requested by the Department of Defense (DoD) for which a DoD Instrument Approach Procedure has been published in the U.S. Terminal Procedures Publication. Additionally this listing contains data for associated terminal control facilities, air route traffic control centers, and radio aids to navigation within the conterminous United States, Puerto Rico and the Virgin Islands. Civil airports and joint Civil/Military airports which are open to the public are listed alphabetically by state, associated city and airport name and cross–referenced by airport name. Military airports and private–use (limited civil access) joint Military/Civil airports are listed alphabetically by state and official airport name and cross–referenced by associated city name. Navaids, flight service stations and remote communication outlets that are associated with an airport, but with a different name, are listed alphabetically under their own name, as well as under the airport with which they are associated.

The listing of an airport as open to the public in this directory merely indicates the airport operator's willingness to accommodate transient aircraft, and does not represent that the airport conforms with any Federal or local standards, or that it has been approved for use on the part of the general public. Military airports, private–use airports, and private–use (limited civil access) joint Military/Civil airports are open to civil pilots only in an emergency or with prior permission. See Special Notice Section, Civil Use of Military Fields.

The information on obstructions is taken from reports submitted to the FAA. Obstruction data has not been verified in all cases. Pilots are cautioned that objects not indicated in this tabulation (or on the airports sketches and/or charts) may exist which can create a hazard to flight operation. Detailed specifics concerning services and facilities tabulated within this directory are contained in the Aeronautical Information Manual, Basic Flight Information and ATC Procedures.

The legend items that follow explain in detail the contents of this Directory and are keyed to the circled numbers on the sample on the preceding pages.

① CITY/AIRPORT NAME

Civil and joint Civil/Military airports which are open to the public are listed alphabetically by state and associated city. Where the city name is different from the airport name the city name will appear on the line above the airport name. Airports with the same associated city name will be listed alphabetically by airport name and will be separated by a dashed rule line. A solid rule line will separate all others. FAA approved helipads and seaplane landing areas associated with a land airport will be separated by a dotted line. Military airports and private–use (limited civil access) joint Military/Civil airports are listed alphabetically by state and official airport name.

② ALTERNATE NAME

Alternate names, if any, will be shown in parentheses.

③ LOCATION IDENTIFIER

The location identifier is a three or four character FAA code followed by a four–character ICAO code, when assigned, to airports. If two different military codes are assigned, both codes will be shown with the primary operating agency's code listed first. These identifiers are used by ATC in lieu of the airport name in flight plans, flight strips and other written records and computer operations. Zeros will appear with a slash to differentiate them from the letter "O".

④ OPERATING AGENCY

Airports within this directory are classified into two categories, Military/Federal Government and Civil airports open to the general public, plus selected private–use airports. The operating agency is shown for military, private–use and joint use airports. The operating agency is shown by an abbreviation as listed below. When an organization is a tenant, the abbreviation is enclosed in parenthesis. No classification indicates the airport is open to the general public with no military tenant.

A	US Army	MC	Marine Corps
AFRC	Air Force Reserve Command	MIL/CIV	Joint Use Military/Civil Limited Civil Access
AF	US Air Force	N	Navy
ANG	Air National Guard	NAF	Naval Air Facility
AR	US Army Reserve	NAS	Naval Air Station
ARNG	US Army National Guard	NASA	National Air and Space Administration
CG	US Coast Guard	P	US Civil Airport Wherein Permit Covers Use by Transient Military Aircraft
CIV/MIL	Joint Use Civil/Military Open to the Public		
DND	Department of National Defense Canada	PVT	Private Use Only (Closed to the Public)

⑤ AIRPORT LOCATION

Airport location is expressed as distance and direction from the center of the associated city in nautical miles and cardinal points, e.g., 4 NE.

⑥ TIME CONVERSION

Hours of operation of all facilities are expressed in Coordinated Universal Time (UTC) and shown as "Z" time. The directory indicates the number of hours to be subtracted from UTC to obtain local standard time and local daylight saving time UTC–5(–4DT). The symbol ‡ indicates that during periods of Daylight Saving Time (DST) effective hours will be one hour earlier than shown. In those areas where daylight saving time is not observed the (–4DT) and ‡ will not be shown. Daylight saving time is in effect from 0200 local time the second Sunday in March to 0200 local time the first Sunday in November. Canada and all U.S. Conterminous States observe daylight saving time except Arizona and Puerto Rico, and the Virgin Islands. If the state observes daylight saving time and the operating times are other than daylight saving times, the operating hours will include the dates, times and no ‡ symbol will be shown, i.e., April 15–Aug 31 0630–1700Z, Sep 1–Apr 14 0600–1700Z.

Legend 10. Airport/Facility Directory Legend from Chart Supplement.

AIRPORT/FACILITY DIRECTORY LEGEND

⑦ GEOGRAPHIC POSITION OF AIRPORT—AIRPORT REFERENCE POINT (ARP)

Positions are shown as hemisphere, degrees, minutes and hundredths of a minute and represent the approximate geometric center of all usable runway surfaces.

⑧ CHARTS

Charts refer to the Sectional Chart and Low and High Altitude Enroute Chart and panel on which the airport or facility is depicted. Helicopter Chart depictions will be indicated as COPTER. IFR Gulf of Mexico West and IFR Gulf of Mexico Central will be referenced as GOMW and GOMC.

⑨ INSTRUMENT APPROACH PROCEDURES, AIRPORT DIAGRAMS

IAP indicates an airport for which a prescribed (Public Use) FAA Instrument Approach Procedure has been published. DIAP indicates an airport for which a prescribed DoD Instrument Approach Procedure has been published in the U.S. Terminal Procedures. See the Special Notice Section of this directory, Civil Use of Military Fields and the Aeronautical Information Manual 5–4–5 Instrument Approach Procedure Charts for additional information. AD indicates an airport for which an airport diagram has been published. Airport diagrams are located in the back of each Chart Supplement volume alphabetically by associated city and airport name.

⑩ AIRPORT SKETCH

The airport sketch, when provided, depicts the airport and related topographical information as seen from the air and should be used in conjunction with the text. It is intended as a guide for pilots in VFR conditions. Symbology that is not self–explanatory will be reflected in the sketch legend. The airport sketch will be oriented with True North at the top. Airport sketches will be added incrementally.

⑪ ELEVATION

The highest point of an airport's usable runways measured in feet from mean sea level. When elevation is sea level it will be indicated as "00". When elevation is below sea level a minus "–" sign will precede the figure.

⑫ ROTATING LIGHT BEACON

B indicates rotating beacon is available. Rotating beacons operate sunset to sunrise unless otherwise indicated in the AIRPORT REMARKS or MILITARY REMARKS segment of the airport entry.

⑬ TRAFFIC PATTERN ALTITUDE

Traffic Pattern Altitude (TPA)—The first figure shown is TPA above mean sea level. The second figure in parentheses is TPA above airport elevation. Multiple TPA shall be shown as "TPA—See Remarks" and detailed information shall be shown in the Airport or Military Remarks Section. Traffic pattern data for USAF bases, USN facilities, and U.S. Army airports (including those on which ACC or U.S. Army is a tenant) that deviate from standard pattern altitudes shall be shown in Military Remarks.

⑭ AIRPORT OF ENTRY, LANDING RIGHTS, AND CUSTOMS USER FEE AIRPORTS

U.S. CUSTOMS USER FEE AIRPORT—Private Aircraft operators are frequently required to pay the costs associated with customs processing.

AOE—Airport of Entry. A customs Airport of Entry where permission from U.S. Customs is not required to land. However, at least one hour advance notice of arrival is required.

LRA—Landing Rights Airport. Application for permission to land must be submitted in advance to U.S. Customs. At least one hour advance notice of arrival is required.

NOTE: Advance notice of arrival at both an AOE and LRA airport may be included in the flight plan when filed in Canada or Mexico. Where Flight Notification Service (ADCUS) is available the airport remark will indicate this service. This notice will also be treated as an application for permission to land in the case of an LRA. Although advance notice of arrival may be relayed to Customs through Mexico, Canada, and U.S. Communications facilities by flight plan, the aircraft operator is solely responsible for ensuring that Customs receives the notification. (See Customs, Immigration and Naturalization, Public Health and Agriculture Department requirements in the International Flight Information Manual for further details.)

U.S. CUSTOMS AIR AND SEA PORTS, INSPECTORS AND AGENTS

Northeast Sector (New England and Atlantic States—ME to MD)	407–975–1740
Southeast Sector (Atlantic States—DC, WV, VA to FL)	407–975–1780
Central Sector (Interior of the US, including Gulf states—MS, AL, LA)	407–975–1760
Southwest East Sector (OK and eastern TX)	407–975–1840
Southwest West Sector (Western TX, NM and AZ)	407–975–1820
Pacific Sector (WA, OR, CA, HI and AK)	407–975–1800

⑮ CERTIFICATED AIRPORT (14 CFR PART 139)

Airports serving Department of Transportation certified carriers and certified under 14 CFR part 139 are indicated by the Class and the ARFF Index; e.g. Class I, ARFF Index A, which relates to the availability of crash, fire, rescue equipment. Class I airports can have an ARFF Index A through E, depending on the aircraft length and scheduled departures. Class II, III, and IV will always carry an Index A.

AIRPORT CLASSIFICATIONS

Type of Air Carrier Operation	Class I	Class II	Class III	Class IV
Scheduled Air Carrier Aircraft with 31 or more passenger seats	X			
Unscheduled Air Carrier Aircraft with 31 or more passengers seats	X	X		X
Scheduled Air Carrier Aircraft with 10 to 30 passenger seats	X	X	X	

Legend 11. Airport/Facility Directory Legend from Chart Supplement.

AIRPORT/FACILITY DIRECTORY LEGEND

INDICES AND AIRCRAFT RESCUE AND FIRE FIGHTING EQUIPMENT REQUIREMENTS

Airport Index	Required No. Vehicles	Aircraft Length	Scheduled Departures	Agent + Water for Foam
A	1	<90′	≥1	500#DC or HALON 1211 or 450#DC + 100 gal H_2O
B	1 or 2	≥90′, <126′	≥5	Index A + 1500 gal H_2O
		≥126′, <159′	<5	
C	2 or 3	≥126′, <159′	≥5	Index A + 3000 gal H_2O
		≥159′, <200′	<5	
D	3	≥159′, <200′		Index A + 4000 gal H_2O
		>200′	<5	
E	3	≥200′	≥5	Index A + 6000 gal H_2O

> Greater Than; < Less Than; ≥ Equal or Greater Than; ≤ Equal or Less Than; H_2O–Water; DC–Dry Chemical.

NOTE: The listing of ARFF index does not necessarily assure coverage for non–air carrier operations or at other than prescribed times for air carrier. ARFF Index Ltd.—indicates ARFF coverage may or may not be available, for information contact airport manager prior to flight.

⑯ NOTAM SERVICE

All public use landing areas are provided NOTAM service. A NOTAM FILE identifier is shown for individual landing areas, e.g., "NOTAM FILE BNA". See the AIM, Basic Flight Information and ATC Procedures for a detailed description of NOTAMs. Current NOTAMs are available from flight service stations at 1–800–WX–BRIEF (992–7433) or online through the FAA PilotWeb at https://pilotweb.nas.faa.gov. Military NOTAMs are available using the Defense Internet NOTAM Service (DINS) at https://www.notams.faa.gov. Pilots flying to or from airports not available through the FAA PilotWeb or DINS can obtain assistance from Flight Service.

⑰ FAA INSPECTION

All airports not inspected by FAA will be identified by the note: Not insp. This indicates that the airport information has been provided by the owner or operator of the field.

⑱ RUNWAY DATA

Runway information is shown on two lines. That information common to the entire runway is shown on the first line while information concerning the runway ends is shown on the second or following line. Runway direction, surface, length, width, weight bearing capacity, lighting, and slope, when available are shown for each runway. Multiple runways are shown with the longest runway first. Direction, length, width, and lighting are shown for sea–lanes. The full dimensions of helipads are shown, e.g., 50X150. Runway data that requires clarification will be placed in the remarks section.

RUNWAY DESIGNATION

Runways are normally numbered in relation to their magnetic orientation rounded off to the nearest 10 degrees. Parallel runways can be designated L (left)/R (right)/C (center). Runways may be designated as Ultralight or assault strips. Assault strips are shown by magnetic bearing.

RUNWAY DIMENSIONS

Runway length and width are shown in feet. Length shown is runway end to end including displaced thresholds, but excluding those areas designed as overruns.

RUNWAY SURFACE AND SURFACE TREATMENT

Runway lengths prefixed by the letter "H" indicate that the runways are hard surfaced (concrete, asphalt, or part asphalt–concrete). If the runway length is not prefixed, the surface is sod, clay, etc. The runway surface composition is indicated in parentheses after runway length as follows:

(AFSC)—Aggregate friction seal coat
(AM2)—Temporary metal planks coated with nonskid material
(ASPH)—Asphalt
(CONC)—Concrete
(DIRT)—Dirt
(GRVD)—Grooved
(GRVL)—Gravel, or cinders
(MATS)—Pierced steel planking, landing mats, membranes
(PEM)—Part concrete, part asphalt
(PFC)—Porous friction courses
(PSP)—Pierced steel plank
(RFSC)—Rubberized friction seal coat
(SAND)—Sand
(TURF)—Turf
(TRTD)—Treated
(WC)—Wire combed

Legend 12. Airport/Facility Directory Legend from Chart Supplement.

AIRPORT/FACILITY DIRECTORY LEGEND

RUNWAY WEIGHT BEARING CAPACITY

Runway strength data shown in this publication is derived from available information and is a realistic estimate of capability at an average level of activity. It is not intended as a maximum allowable weight or as an operating limitation. Many airport pavements are capable of supporting limited operations with gross weights in excess of the published figures. Permissible operating weights, insofar as runway strengths are concerned, are a matter of agreement between the owner and user. When desiring to operate into any airport at weights in excess of those published in the publication, users should contact the airport management for permission. Runway strength figures are shown in thousand of pounds, with the last three figures being omitted. Add 000 to figure following S, D, 2S, 2T, AUW, SWL, etc., for gross weight capacity. A blank space following the letter designator is used to indicate the runway can sustain aircraft with this type landing gear, although definite runway weight bearing capacity figures are not available, e.g., S, D. Applicable codes for typical gear configurations with S=Single, D=Dual, T=Triple and Q=Quadruple:

CURRENT	NEW	NEW DESCRIPTION
S	S	Single wheel type landing gear (DC3), (C47), (F15), etc.
D	D	Dual wheel type landing gear (BE1900), (B737), (A319), etc.
T	D	Dual wheel type landing gear (P3, C9).
ST	2S	Two single wheels in tandem type landing gear (C130).
TRT	2T	Two triple wheels in tandem type landing gear (C17), etc.
DT	2D	Two dual wheels in tandem type landing gear (B707), etc.
TT	2D	Two dual wheels in tandem type landing gear (B757, KC135).
SBTT	2D/D1	Two dual wheels in tandem/dual wheel body gear type landing gear (KC10).
None	2D/2D1	Two dual wheels in tandem/two dual wheels in tandem body gear type landing gear (A340–600).
DDT	2D/2D2	Two dual wheels in tandem/two dual wheels in double tandem body gear type landing gear (B747, E4).
TTT	3D	Three dual wheels in tandem type landing gear (B777), etc.
TT	D2	Dual wheel gear two struts per side main gear type landing gear (B52).
TDT	C5	Complex dual wheel and quadruple wheel combination landing gear (C5).

AUW—All up weight. Maximum weight bearing capacity for any aircraft irrespective of landing gear configuration.

SWL—Single Wheel Loading. (This includes information submitted in terms of Equivalent Single Wheel Loading (ESWL) and Single Isolated Wheel Loading).

PSI—Pounds per square inch. PSI is the actual figure expressing maximum pounds per square inch runway will support, e.g., (SWL 000/PSI 535).

Omission of weight bearing capacity indicates information unknown.

The ACN/PCN System is the ICAO standard method of reporting pavement strength for pavements with bearing strengths greater than 12,500 pounds. The Pavement Classification Number (PCN) is established by an engineering assessment of the runway. The PCN is for use in conjunction with an Aircraft Classification Number (ACN). Consult the Aircraft Flight Manual, Flight Information Handbook, or other appropriate source for ACN tables or charts. Currently, ACN data may not be available for all aircraft. If an ACN table or chart is available, the ACN can be calculated by taking into account the aircraft weight, the pavement type, and the subgrade category. For runways that have been evaluated under the ACN/PCN system, the PCN will be shown as a five–part code (e.g. PCN 80 R/B/W/T). Details of the coded format are as follows:

NOTE: Prior permission from the airport controlling authority is required when the ACN of the aircraft exceeds the published PCN or aircraft tire pressure exceeds the published limits.

(1) The PCN NUMBER—The reported PCN indicates that an aircraft with an ACN equal or less than the reported PCN can operate on the pavement subject to any limitation on the tire pressure.

(2) The type of pavement:
R — Rigid
F — Flexible

(3) The pavement subgrade category:
A — High
B — Medium
C — Low
D — Ultra–low

(4) The maximum tire pressure authorized for the pavement:
W — Unlimited, no pressure limit
X — High, limited to 254 psi (1.75 MPa)
Y — Medium, limited to 181 psi (1.25MPa)
Z — Low, limited to 73 psi (0.50 MPa)

(5) Pavement evaluation method:
T — Technical evaluation
U — By experience of aircraft using the pavement

RUNWAY LIGHTING

Lights are in operation sunset to sunrise. Lighting available by prior arrangement only or operating part of the night and/or pilot controlled lighting with specific operating hours are indicated under airport or military remarks. At USN/USMC facilities lights are available only during airport hours of operation. Since obstructions are usually lighted, obstruction lighting is not included in this code. Unlighted obstructions on or surrounding an airport will be noted in airport or military remarks. Runway lights nonstandard (NSTD) are systems for which the light fixtures are not FAA approved L–800 series: color, intensity, or spacing does not meet FAA standards. Nonstandard runway lights, VASI, or any other system not listed below will be shown in airport remarks or military

Legend 13. Airport/Facility Directory Legend from Chart Supplement.

AIRPORT/FACILITY DIRECTORY LEGEND

service. Temporary, emergency or limited runway edge lighting such as flares, smudge pots, lanterns or portable runway lights will also be shown in airport remarks or military service. Types of lighting are shown with the runway or runway end they serve.

NSTD—Light system fails to meet FAA standards.
LIRL—Low Intensity Runway Lights.
MIRL—Medium Intensity Runway Lights.
HIRL—High Intensity Runway Lights.
RAIL—Runway Alignment Indicator Lights.
REIL—Runway End Identifier Lights.
CL—Centerline Lights.
TDZL—Touchdown Zone Lights.
ODALS—Omni Directional Approach Lighting System.
AF OVRN—Air Force Overrun 1000′ Standard Approach Lighting System.
MALS—Medium Intensity Approach Lighting System.
MALSF—Medium Intensity Approach Lighting System with Sequenced Flashing Lights.
MALSR—Medium Intensity Approach Lighting System with Runway Alignment Indicator Lights.
RLLS—Runway Lead–in Light System
SALS—Short Approach Lighting System.
SALSF—Short Approach Lighting System with Sequenced Flashing Lights.
SSALS—Simplified Short Approach Lighting System.
SSALF—Simplified Short Approach Lighting System with Sequenced Flashing Lights.
SSALR—Simplified Short Approach Lighting System with Runway Alignment Indicator Lights.
ALSAF—High Intensity Approach Lighting System with Sequenced Flashing Lights.
ALSF1—High Intensity Approach Lighting System with Sequenced Flashing Lights, Category I, Configuration.
ALSF2—High Intensity Approach Lighting System with Sequenced Flashing Lights, Category II, Configuration.
SF—Sequenced Flashing Lights.
OLS—Optical Landing System.
WAVE–OFF.

NOTE: Civil ALSF2 may be operated as SSALR during favorable weather conditions. When runway edge lights are positioned more than 10 feet from the edge of the usable runway surface a remark will be added in the "Remarks" portion of the airport entry. This is applicable to Air Force, Air National Guard and Air Force Reserve Bases, and those joint use airfields on which they are tenants.

VISUAL GLIDESLOPE INDICATORS

APAP—A system of panels, which may or may not be lighted, used for alignment of approach path.

PNIL	APAP on left side of runway	PNIR	APAP on right side of runway

PAPI—Precision Approach Path Indicator

P2L	2–identical light units placed on left side of runway	P4L	4–identical light units placed on left side of runway
P2R	2–identical light units placed on right side of runway	P4R	4–identical light units placed on right side of runway

PVASI—Pulsating/steady burning visual approach slope indicator, normally a single light unit projecting two colors.

PSIL	PVASI on left side of runway	PSIR	PVASI on right side of runway

SAVASI—Simplified Abbreviated Visual Approach Slope Indicator

S2L	2–box SAVASI on left side of runway	S2R	2–box SAVASI on right side of runway

TRCV—Tri–color visual approach slope indicator, normally a single light unit projecting three colors.

TRIL	TRCV on left side of runway	TRIR	TRCV on right side of runway

VASI—Visual Approach Slope Indicator

V2L	2–box VASI on left side of runway	V6L	6–box VASI on left side of runway
V2R	2–box VASI on right side of runway	V6R	6–box VASI on right side of runway
V4L	4–box VASI on left side of runway	V12	12–box VASI on both sides of runway
V4R	4–box VASI on right side of runway	V16	16–box VASI on both sides of runway

NOTE: Approach slope angle and threshold crossing height will be shown when available; i.e., –GA 3.5° TCH 37′.

PILOT CONTROL OF AIRPORT LIGHTING

Key Mike	Function
7 times within 5 seconds	Highest intensity available
5 times within 5 seconds	Medium or lower intensity (Lower REIL or REIL–Off)
3 times within 5 seconds	Lowest intensity available (Lower REIL or REIL–Off)

Available systems will be indicated in the Service section, e.g., **LGT** ACTIVATE HIRL Rwy 07–25, MALSR Rwy 07, and VASI Rwy 07—122.8.

Where the airport is not served by an instrument approach procedure and/or has an independent type system of different specification installed by the airport sponsor, descriptions of the type lights, method of control, and operating frequency will be explained in clear text. See AIM, "Basic Flight Information and ATC Procedures," for detailed description of pilot control of airport lighting.

RUNWAY SLOPE

When available, runway slope data will be provided. Runway slope will be shown only when it is 0.3 percent or greater. On runways less than 8000 feet, the direction of the slope up will be indicated, e.g., 0.3% up NW. On runways 8000 feet or greater, the slope will be shown (up or down) on the runway end line, e.g., RWY 13: 0.3% up., RWY 31: Pole. Rgt tfc. 0.4% down.

Legend 14. Airport/Facility Directory Legend from Chart Supplement.

RUNWAY END DATA

Information pertaining to the runway approach end such as approach lights, touchdown zone lights, runway end identification lights, visual glideslope indicators, displaced thresholds, controlling obstruction, and right hand traffic pattern, will be shown on the specific runway end. "Rgt tfc"—Right traffic indicates right turns should be made on landing and takeoff for specified runway end. Runway Visual Range shall be shown as "RVR" appended with "T" for touchdown, "M" for midpoint, and "R" for rollout; e.g., RVR-TMR.

⑲ LAND AND HOLD–SHORT OPERATIONS (LAHSO)

LAHSO is an acronym for "Land and Hold–Short Operations" These operations include landing and holding short of an intersection runway, an intersecting taxiway, or other predetermined points on the runway other than a runway or taxiway. Measured distance represents the available landing distance on the landing runway, in feet.

Specific questions regarding these distances should be referred to the air traffic manager of the facility concerned. The Aeronautical Information Manual contains specific details on hold–short operations and markings.

⑳ RUNWAY DECLARED DISTANCE INFORMATION

TORA—Take–off Run Available. The length of runway declared available and suitable for the ground run of an aeroplane take–off.
TODA—Take–off Distance Available. The length of the take–off run available plus the length of the clearway, if provided.
ASDA—Accelerate–Stop Distance Available. The length of the take–off run available plus the length of the stopway, if provided.
LDA—Landing Distance Available. The length of runway which is declared available and suitable for the ground run of an aeroplane landing.

㉑ ARRESTING GEAR/SYSTEMS

Arresting gear is shown as it is located on the runway. The a–gear distance from the end of the appropriate runway (or into the overrun) is indicated in parentheses. A–Gear which has a bi–direction capability and can be utilized for emergency approach end engagement is indicated by a (B). Up to 15 minutes advance notice may be required for rigging A–Gear for approach and engagement. Airport listing may show availability of other than US Systems. This information is provided for emergency requirements only. Refer to current aircraft operating manuals for specific engagement weight and speed criteria based on aircraft structural restrictions and arresting system limitations.

Following is a list of current systems referenced in this publication identified by both Air Force and Navy terminology:

BI–DIRECTIONAL CABLE (B)

TYPE	DESCRIPTION
BAK–9	Rotary friction brake.
BAK–12A	Standard BAK–12 with 950 foot run out, 1–inch cable and 40,000 pound weight setting. Rotary friction brake.
BAK–12B	Extended BAK–12 with 1200 foot run, 1¼ inch Cable and 50,000 pounds weight setting. Rotary friction brake.
E28	Rotary Hydraulic (Water Brake).
M21	Rotary Hydraulic (Water Brake) Mobile.

The following device is used in conjunction with some aircraft arresting systems:

BAK–14	A device that raises a hook cable out of a slot in the runway surface and is remotely positioned for engagement by the tower on request. (In addition to personnel reaction time, the system requires up to five seconds to fully raise the cable.)
H	A device that raises a hook cable out of a slot in the runway surface and is remotely positioned for engagement by the tower on request. (In addition to personnel reaction time, the system requires up to one and one–half seconds to fully raise the cable.)

UNI–DIRECTIONAL CABLE

TYPE	DESCRIPTION
MB60	Textile brake—an emergency one–time use, modular braking system employing the tearing of specially woven textile straps to absorb the kinetic energy.
E5/E5–1/E5–3	Chain Type. At USN/USMC stations E–5 A–GEAR systems are rated, e.g., E–5 RATING–13R–1100 HW (DRY), 31L/R–1200 STD (WET). This rating is a function of the A–GEAR chain weight and length and is used to determine the maximum aircraft engaging speed. A dry rating applies to a stabilized surface (dry or wet) while a wet rating takes into account the amount (if any) of wet overrun that is not capable of withstanding the aircraft weight. These ratings are published under Service/Military/A-Gear in the entry.

FOREIGN CABLE

TYPE	DESCRIPTION	US EQUIVALENT
44B–3H	Rotary Hydraulic (Water Brake)	
CHAG	Chain	E–5

UNI–DIRECTIONAL BARRIER

TYPE	DESCRIPTION
MA–1A	Web barrier between stanchions attached to a chain energy absorber.
BAK–15	Web barrier between stanchions attached to an energy absorber (water squeezer, rotary friction, chain). Designed for wing engagement.

NOTE: Landing short of the runway threshold on a runway with a BAK–15 in the underrun is a significant hazard. The barrier in the down position still protrudes several inches above the underrun. Aircraft contact with the barrier short of the runway threshold can cause damage to the barrier and substantial damage to the aircraft.

OTHER

TYPE	DESCRIPTION
EMAS	Engineered Material Arresting System, located beyond the departure end of the runway, consisting of high energy absorbing materials which will crush under the weight of an aircraft.

Legend 15. Airport/Facility Directory Legend from Chart Supplement.

㉒ SERVICE

SERVICING—CIVIL

S1: Minor airframe repairs.
S2: Minor airframe and minor powerplant repairs.
S3: Major airframe and minor powerplant repairs.
S4: Major airframe and major powerplant repairs.
S5: Major airframe repairs.
S6: Minor airframe and major powerplant repairs.
S7: Major powerplant repairs.
S8: Minor powerplant repairs.

FUEL

CODE	FUEL
80	Grade 80 gasoline (Red)
100	Grade 100 gasoline (Green)
100LL	100LL gasoline (low lead) (Blue)
115	Grade 115 gasoline (115/145 military specification) (Purple)
A	Jet A, Kerosene, without FS–II*, FP** minus 40° C.
A+	Jet A, Kerosene, with FS–II*, FP** minus 40°C.
A++	Jet A, Kerosene, with FS–II*, CI/LI#, SDA##, FP** minus 40°C.
A++100	Jet A, Kerosene, with FS–II*, CI/LI#, SDA##, FP** minus 40°C, with +100 fuel additive that improves thermal stability characteristics of kerosene jet fuels.
A1	Jet A–1, Kerosene, without FS–II*, FP** minus 47°C.
A1+	Jet A–1, Kerosene with FS–II*, FP** minus 47° C.
B	Jet B, Wide–cut, turbine fuel without FS–II*, FP** minus 50° C.
B+	Jet B, Wide–cut, turbine fuel with FS–II*, FP** minus 50° C
J4 (JP4)	(JP–4 military specification) FP** minus 58° C.
J5 (JP5)	(JP–5 military specification) Kerosene with FS–II, FP** minus 46°C.
J8 (JP8)	(JP–8 military specification) Jet A–1, Kerosene with FS–II*, CI/LI#, SDA##, FP** minus 47°C.
J8+100	(JP–8 military specification) Jet A–1, Kerosene with FS–II*, CI/LI#, SDA##,FP** minus 47°C, with +100 fuel additive that improves thermal stability characteristics of kerosene jet fuels.
J	(Jet Fuel Type Unknown)
MOGAS	Automobile gasoline which is to be used as aircraft fuel.
UL91	Unleaded Grade 91 gasoline
UL94	Unleaded Grade 94 gasoline

*(Fuel System Icing Inhibitor) **(Freeze Point) # (Corrosion Inhibitors/Lubricity Improvers) ## (Static Dissipator Additive)

NOTE: Certain automobile gasoline may be used in specific aircraft engines if a FAA supplemental type certificate has been obtained. Automobile gasoline, which is to be used in aircraft engines, will be identified as "MOGAS", however, the grade/type and other octane rating will not be published.

Data shown on fuel availability represents the most recent information the publisher has been able to acquire. Because of a variety of factors, the fuel listed may not always be obtainable by transient civil pilots. Confirmation of availability of fuel should be made directly with fuel suppliers at locations where refueling is planned.

OXYGEN—CIVIL

OX 1 High Pressure
OX 2 Low Pressure
OX 3 High Pressure—Replacement Bottles
OX 4 Low Pressure—Replacement Bottles

SERVICE—MILITARY

Specific military services available at the airport are listed under this general heading. Remarks applicable to any military service are shown in the individual service listing.

JET AIRCRAFT STARTING UNITS (JASU)—MILITARY

The numeral preceding the type of unit indicates the number of units available. The absence of the numeral indicates ten or more units available. If the number of units is unknown, the number one will be shown. Absence of JASU designation indicates non–availability.

The following is a list of current JASU systems referenced in this publication:

USAF JASU (For variations in technical data, refer to T.O. 35–1–7.)

ELECTRICAL STARTING UNITS:

A/M32A–86	AC: 115/200v, 3 phase, 90 kva, 0.8 pf, 4 wire DC: 28v, 1500 amp, 72 kw (with TR pack)
MC–1A	AC: 115/208v, 400 cycle, 3 phase, 37.5 kva, 0.8 pf, 108 amp, 4 wire DC: 28v, 500 amp, 14 kw
MD–3	AC: 115/208v, 400 cycle, 3 phase, 60 kva, 0.75 pf, 4 wire DC: 28v, 1500 amp, 45 kw, split bus
MD–3A	AC: 115/208v, 400 cycle, 3 phase, 60 kva, 0.75 pf, 4 wire DC: 28v, 1500 amp, 45 kw, split bus
MD–3M	AC: 115/208v, 400 cycle, 3 phase, 60 kva, 0.75 pf, 4 wire DC: 28v, 500 amp, 15 kw
MD–4	AC: 120/208v, 400 cycle, 3 phase, 62.5 kva, 0.8 pf, 175 amp, "WYE" neutral ground, 4 wire, 120v, 400 cycle, 3 phase, 62.5 kva, 0.8 pf, 303 amp, "DELTA" 3 wire, 120v, 400 cycle, 1 phase, 62.5 kva, 0.8 pf, 520 amp, 2 wire

Legend 16. Airport/Facility Directory Legend from Chart Supplement.

AIRPORT/FACILITY DIRECTORY LEGEND

AIR STARTING UNITS

AM32–95	150 +/– 5 lb/min (2055 +/– 68 cfm) at 51 +/– 2 psia
AM32A–95	150 +/– 5 lb/min @ 49 +/– 2 psia (35 +/– 2 psig)
LASS	150 +/– 5 lb/min @ 49 +/– 2 psia
MA–1A	82 lb/min (1123 cfm) at 130° air inlet temp, 45 psia (min) air outlet press
MC–1	15 cfm, 3500 psia
MC–1A	15 cfm, 3500 psia
MC–2A	15 cfm, 200 psia
MC–11	8,000 cu in cap, 4000 psig, 15 cfm

COMBINED AIR AND ELECTRICAL STARTING UNITS:

AGPU	AC: 115/200v, 400 cycle, 3 phase, 30 kw gen DC: 28v, 700 amp AIR: 60 lb/min @ 40 psig @ sea level
AM32A–60*	AIR: 120 +/– 4 lb/min (1644 +/– 55 cfm) at 49 +/– 2 psia AC: 120/208v, 400 cycle, 3 phase, 75 kva, 0.75 pf, 4 wire, 120v, 1 phase, 25 kva DC: 28v, 500 amp, 15 kw
AM32A–60A	AIR: 150 +/– 5 lb/min (2055 +/– 68 cfm at 51 +/– psia AC: 120/208v, 400 cycle, 3 phase, 75 kva, 0.75 pf, 4 wire DC: 28v, 200 amp, 5.6 kw
AM32A–60B*	AIR: 130 lb/min, 50 psia AC: 120/208v, 400 cycle, 3 phase, 75 kva, 0.75 pf, 4 wire DC: 28v, 200 amp, 5.6 kw

*NOTE: During combined air and electrical loads, the pneumatic circuitry takes preference and will limit the amount of electrical power available.

USN JASU

ELECTRICAL STARTING UNITS:

NC–8A/A1	DC: 500 amp constant, 750 amp intermittent, 28v; AC: 60 kva @ .8 pf, 115/200v, 3 phase, 400 Hz.
NC–10A/A1/B/C	DC: 750 amp constant, 1000 amp intermittent, 28v; AC: 90 kva, 115/200v, 3 phase, 400 Hz.

AIR STARTING UNITS:

GTC–85/GTE–85	120 lbs/min @ 45 psi.
MSU–200NAV/A/U47A–5	204 lbs/min @ 56 psia.
WELLS AIR START SYSTEM	180 lbs/min @ 75 psi or 120 lbs/min @ 45 psi. Simultaneous multiple start capability.

COMBINED AIR AND ELECTRICAL STARTING UNITS:

NCPP–105/RCPT	180 lbs/min @ 75 psi or 120 lbs/min @ 45 psi. 700 amp, 28v DC. 120/208v, 400 Hz AC, 30 kva.

ARMY JASU

59B2–1B	28v, 7.5 kw, 280 amp.

OTHER JASU

ELECTRICAL STARTING UNITS (DND):

CE12	AC 115/200v, 140 kva, 400 Hz, 3 phase
CE13	AC 115/200v, 60 kva, 400 Hz, 3 phase
CE14	AC/DC 115/200v, 140 kva, 400 Hz, 3 phase, 28vDC, 1500 amp
CE15	DC 22–35v, 500 amp continuous 1100 amp intermittent
CE16	DC 22–35v, 500 amp continuous 1100 amp intermittent soft start

AIR STARTING UNITS (DND):

CA2	ASA 45.5 psig, 116.4 lb/min

COMBINED AIR AND ELECTRICAL STARTING UNITS (DND)

CEA1	AC 120/208v, 60 kva, 400 Hz, 3 phase DC 28v, 75 amp AIR 112.5 lb/min, 47 psig

ELECTRICAL STARTING UNITS (OTHER)

C–26	28v 45kw 115–200v 15kw 380–800 Hz 1 phase 2 wire
C–26–B, C–26–C	28v 45kw: Split Bus: 115–200v 15kw 380–800 Hz 1 phase 2 wire
E3	DC 28v/10kw

AIR STARTING UNITS (OTHER):

A4	40 psi/2 lb/sec (LPAS Mk12, Mk12L, Mk12A, Mk1, Mk2B)
MA–1	150 Air HP, 115 lb/min 50 psia
MA–2	250 Air HP, 150 lb/min 75 psia

CARTRIDGE:

MXU–4A	USAF

Legend 17. Airport/Facility Directory Legend from Chart Supplement.

AIRPORT/FACILITY DIRECTORY LEGEND

FUEL—MILITARY

Fuel available through US Military Base supply, DESC Into–Plane Contracts and/or reciprocal agreement is listed first and is followed by (Mil). At commercial airports where Into–Plane contracts are in place, the name of the refueling agent is shown. Military fuel should be used first if it is available. When military fuel cannot be obtained but Into–Plane contract fuel is available, Government aircraft must refuel with the contract fuel and applicable refueling agent to avoid any breach in contract terms and conditions. Fuel not available through the above is shown preceded by NC (no contract). When fuel is obtained from NC sources, local purchase procedures must be followed. The US Military Aircraft Identaplates DD Form 1896 (Jet Fuel), DD Form 1897 (Avgas) and AF Form 1245 (Avgas) are used at military installations only. The US Government Aviation Into–Plane Reimbursement (AIR) Card (currently issued by AVCARD) is the instrument to be used to obtain fuel under a DESC Into–Plane Contract and for NC purchases if the refueling agent at the commercial airport accepts the AVCARD. A current list of contract fuel locations is available online at https://cis.energy.dla.mil/ip_cis/. See legend item 14 for fuel code and description.

SUPPORTING FLUIDS AND SYSTEMS—MILITARY

CODE	
ADI	Anti–Detonation Injection Fluid—Reciprocating Engine Aircraft.
W	Water Thrust Augmentation—Jet Aircraft.
WAI	Water–Alcohol Injection Type, Thrust Augmentation—Jet Aircraft.
SP	Single Point Refueling.
PRESAIR	Air Compressors rated 3,000 PSI or more.
De–Ice	Anti–icing/De–icing/Defrosting Fluid (MIL–A–8243).

OXYGEN:

LPOX	Low pressure oxygen servicing.
HPOX	High pressure oxygen servicing.
LHOX	Low and high pressure oxygen servicing.
LOX	Liquid oxygen servicing.
OXRB	Oxygen replacement bottles. (Maintained primarily at Naval stations for use in acft where oxygen can be replenished only by replacement of cylinders.)
OX	Indicates oxygen servicing when type of servicing is unknown.

NOTE: Combinations of above items is used to indicate complete oxygen servicing available;

LHOXRB	Low and high pressure oxygen servicing and replacement bottles;
LPOXRB	Low pressure oxygen replacement bottles only, etc.

NOTE: Aircraft will be serviced with oxygen procured under military specifications only. Aircraft will not be serviced with medical oxygen.

NITROGEN:

LPNIT — Low pressure nitrogen servicing.

HPNIT — High pressure nitrogen servicing.

LHNIT — Low and high pressure nitrogen servicing.

OIL—MILITARY

US AVIATION OILS (MIL SPECS):

CODE	GRADE, TYPE
O–113	1065, Reciprocating Engine Oil (MIL–L–6082)
O–117	1100, Reciprocating Engine Oil (MIL–L–6082)
O–117+	1100, O–117 plus cyclohexanone (MIL–L–6082)
O–123	1065, (Dispersant), Reciprocating Engine Oil (MIL–L–22851 Type III)
O–128	1100, (Dispersant), Reciprocating Engine Oil (MIL–L–22851 Type II)
O–132	1005, Jet Engine Oil (MIL–L–6081)
O–133	1010, Jet Engine Oil (MIL–L–6081)
O–147	None, MIL–L–6085A Lubricating Oil, Instrument, Synthetic
O–148	None, MIL–L–7808 (Synthetic Base) Turbine Engine Oil
O–149	None, Aircraft Turbine Engine Synthetic, 7.5c St
O–155	None, MIL–L–6086C, Aircraft, Medium Grade
O–156	None, MIL–L–23699 (Synthetic Base), Turboprop and Turboshaft Engines
JOAP/SOAP	Joint Oil Analysis Program. JOAP support is furnished during normal duty hours, other times on request. (JOAP and SOAP programs provide essentially the same service, JOAP is now the standard joint service supported program.)

TRANSIENT ALERT (TRAN ALERT)—MILITARY

Tran Alert service is considered to include all services required for normal aircraft turn–around, e.g., servicing (fuel, oil, oxygen, etc.), debriefing to determine requirements for maintenance, minor maintenance, inspection and parking assistance of transient aircraft. Drag chute repack, specialized maintenance, or extensive repairs will be provided within the capabilities and priorities of the base. Delays can be anticipated after normal duty hours/holidays/weekends regardless of the hours of transient maintenance operation. Pilots should not expect aircraft to be serviced for TURN–AROUNDS during time periods when servicing or maintenance manpower is not available. In the case of airports not operated exclusively by US military, the servicing indicated by the remarks will not always be available for US military aircraft. When transient alert services are not shown, facilities are unknown. NO PRIORITY BASIS—means that transient alert services will be provided only after all the requirements for mission/tactical assigned aircraft have been accomplished.

Legend 18. Airport/Facility Directory Legend from Chart Supplement.

AIRPORT/FACILITY DIRECTORY LEGEND

㉓ AIRPORT REMARKS

The Attendance Schedule is the months, days and hours the airport is actually attended. Airport attendance does not mean watchman duties or telephone accessibility, but rather an attendant or operator on duty to provide at least minimum services (e.g., repairs, fuel, transportation).

Airport Remarks have been grouped in order of applicability. Airport remarks are limited to those items of information that are determined essential for operational use, i.e., conditions of a permanent or indefinite nature and conditions that will remain in effect for more than 30 days concerning aeronautical facilities, services, maintenance available, procedures or hazards, knowledge of which is essential for safe and efficient operation of aircraft. Information concerning permanent closing of a runway or taxiway will not be shown. A note "See Special Notices" shall be applied within this remarks section when a special notice applicable to the entry is contained in the Special Notices section of this publication.

Parachute Jumping indicates parachute jumping areas associated with the airport. See Parachute Jumping Area section of this publication for additional Information.

Landing Fee indicates landing charges for private or non–revenue producing aircraft. In addition, fees may be charged for planes that remain over a couple of hours and buy no services, or at major airline terminals for all aircraft.

Note: Unless otherwise stated, remarks including runway ends refer to the runway's approach end.

㉔ MILITARY REMARKS

Joint Civil/Military airports contain both Airport Remarks and Military Remarks. Military Remarks published for these airports are applicable only to the military. Military and joint Military/Civil airports contain only Military Remarks. Remarks contained in this section may not be applicable to civil users. When both sets of remarks exist, the first set is applicable to the primary operator of the airport. Remarks applicable to a tenant on the airport are shown preceded by the tenant organization, i.e., (A) (AF) (N) (ANG), etc. Military airports operate 24 hours unless otherwise specified. Airport operating hours are listed first (airport operating hours will only be listed if they are different than the airport attended hours or if the attended hours are unavailable) followed by pertinent remarks in order of applicability. Remarks will include information on restrictions, hazards, traffic pattern, noise abatement, customs/agriculture/immigration, and miscellaneous information applicable to the Military.

Type of restrictions:

CLOSED: When designated closed, the airport is restricted from use by all aircraft unless stated otherwise. Any closure applying to specific type of aircraft or operation will be so stated. USN/USMC/USAF airports are considered closed during non–operating hours. Closed airports may be utilized during an emergency provided there is a safe landing area.

OFFICIAL BUSINESS ONLY: The airfield is closed to all transient military aircraft for obtaining routine services such as fueling, passenger drop off or pickup, practice approaches, parking, etc. The airfield may be used by aircrews and aircraft if official government business (including civilian) must be conducted on or near the airfield and prior permission is received from the airfield manager.

AF OFFICIAL BUSINESS ONLY OR NAVY OFFICIAL BUSINESS ONLY: Indicates that the restriction applies only to service indicated.

PRIOR PERMISSION REQUIRED (PPR): Airport is closed to transient aircraft unless approval for operation is obtained from the appropriate commander through Chief, Airfield Management or Airfield Operations Officer. Official Business or PPR does not preclude the use of US Military airports as an alternate for IFR flights. If a non–US military airport is used as a weather alternate and requires a PPR, the PPR must be requested and confirmed before the flight departs. The purpose of PPR is to control volume and flow of traffic rather than to prohibit it. Prior permission is required for all aircraft requiring transient alert service outside the published transient alert duty hours. All aircraft carrying hazardous materials must obtain prior permission as outlined in AFJI 11–204, AR 95–27, OPNAVINST 3710.7.

Note: OFFICIAL BUSINESS ONLY AND PPR restrictions are not applicable to Special Air Mission (SAM) or Special Air Resource (SPAR) aircraft providing person or persons on aboard are designated Code 6 or higher as explained in AFJMAN 11–213, AR 95–11, OPNAVINST 3722–8J. Official Business Only or PPR do not preclude the use of the airport as an alternate for IFR flights.

㉕ AIRPORT MANAGER

The phone number of the airport manager.

㉖ WEATHER DATA SOURCES

Weather data sources will be listed alphabetically followed by their assigned frequencies and/or telephone number and hours of operation.

ASOS—Automated Surface Observing System. Reports the same as an AWOS–3 plus precipitation identification and intensity, and freezing rain occurrence;

AWOS—Automated Weather Observing System

AWOS–A—reports altimeter setting (all other information is advisory only).

AWOS–AV—reports altimeter and visibility.

AWOS–1—reports altimeter setting, wind data and usually temperature, dew point and density altitude.

AWOS–2—reports the same as AWOS–1 plus visibility.

AWOS–3—reports the same as AWOS–1 plus visibility and cloud/ceiling data.

AWOS–3P reports the same as the AWOS–3 system, plus a precipitation identification sensor.

AWOS–3PT reports the same as the AWOS–3 system, plus precipitation identification sensor and a thunderstorm/lightning reporting capability.

Legend 19. Airport/Facility Directory Legend from Chart Supplement.

AWOS–3T reports the same as AWOS–3 system and includes a thunderstorm/lightning reporting capability.
See AIM, Basic Flight Information and ATC Procedures for detailed description of Weather Data Sources.

AWOS–4—reports same as AWOS–3 system, plus precipitation occurrence, type and accumulation, freezing rain, thunderstorm and runway surface sensors.

HIWAS—See RADIO AIDS TO NAVIGATION

LAWRS—Limited Aviation Weather Reporting Station where observers report cloud height, weather, obstructions to vision, temperature and dewpoint (in most cases), surface wind, altimeter and pertinent remarks.

LLWAS—indicates a Low Level Wind Shear Alert System consisting of a center field and several field perimeter anemometers.

SAWRS—identifies airports that have a Supplemental Aviation Weather Reporting Station available to pilots for current weather information.

SWSL—Supplemental Weather Service Location providing current local weather information via radio and telephone.

TDWR—indicates airports that have Terminal Doppler Weather Radar.

WSP—indicates airports that have Weather System Processor.

When the automated weather source is broadcast over an associated airport NAVAID frequency (see NAVAID line), it shall be indicated by a bold ASOS, AWOS, or HIWAS followed by the frequency, identifier and phone number, if available.

㉗ COMMUNICATIONS

Airport terminal control facilities and radio communications associated with the airport shall be shown. When the call sign is not the same as the airport name the call sign will be shown. Frequencies shall normally be shown in descending order with the primary frequency listed first. Frequencies will be listed, together with sectorization indicated by outbound radials, and hours of operation. Communications will be listed in sequence as follows:

Single Frequency Approach (SFA), Common Traffic Advisory Frequency (CTAF), Aeronautical Advisory Stations (UNICOM) or (AUNICOM), and Automatic Terminal Information Service (ATIS) along with their frequency is shown, where available, on the line following the heading "COMMUNICATIONS." When the CTAF and UNICOM frequencies are the same, the frequency will be shown as CTAF/UNICOM 122.8.

The FSS telephone nationwide is toll free 1–800–WX–BRIEF (1–800–992–7433). When the FSS is located on the field it will be indicated as "on arpt". Frequencies available at the FSS will follow in descending order. Remote Communications Outlet (RCO) providing service to the airport followed by the frequency and FSS RADIO name will be shown when available. FSS's provide information on airport conditions, radio aids and other facilities, and process flight plans. Airport Advisory Service (AAS) is provided on the CTAF by FSS's for select non–tower airports or airports where the tower is not in operation.

(See AIM, Para 4–1–9 Traffic Advisory Practices at Airports Without Operating Control Towers or AC 90–42C.)

Aviation weather briefing service is provided by FSS specialists. Flight and weather briefing services are also available by calling the telephone numbers listed.

Remote Communications Outlet (RCO)—An unmanned air/ground communications facility that is remotely controlled and provides UHF or VHF communications capability to extend the service range of an FSS.

Civil Communications Frequencies–Civil communications frequencies used in the FSS air/ground system are operated on 122.0, 122.2, 123.6; emergency 121.5; plus receive–only on 122.1.

a. 122.0 is assigned as the Enroute Flight Advisory Service frequency at selected FSS RADIO outlets.

b. 122.2 is assigned as a common enroute frequency.

c. 123.6 is assigned as the airport advisory frequency at select non–tower locations. At airports with a tower, FSS may provide airport advisories on the tower frequency when tower is closed.

d. 122.1 is the primary receive–only frequency at VOR's.

e. Some FSS's are assigned 50 kHz frequencies in the 122–126 MHz band (eg. 122.45). Pilots using the FSS A/G system should refer to this directory or appropriate charts to determine frequencies available at the FSS or remoted facility through which they wish to communicate.

Emergency frequency 121.5 and 243.0 are available at all Flight Service Stations, most Towers, Approach Control and RADAR facilities.

Frequencies published followed by the letter "T" or "R", indicate that the facility will only transmit or receive respectively on that frequency. All radio aids to navigation (NAVAID) frequencies are transmit only. In cases where communications frequencies are annotated with (R) or (E), (R) indicates Radar Capability and (E) indicates Emergency Frequency.

TERMINAL SERVICES

SFA—Single Frequency Approach.

CTAF—A program designed to get all vehicles and aircraft at airports without an operating control tower on a common frequency.

ATIS—A continuous broadcast of recorded non–control information in selected terminal areas.

D–ATIS—Digital ATIS provides ATIS information in text form outside the standard reception range of conventional ATIS via landline & data link communications and voice message within range of existing transmitters.

AUNICOM—Automated UNICOM is a computerized, command response system that provides automated weather, radio check capability and airport advisory information selected from an automated menu by microphone clicks.

UNICOM—A non–government air/ground radio communications facility which may provide airport information.

PTD—Pilot to Dispatcher.

APP CON—Approach Control. The symbol Ⓡ indicates radar approach control.

TOWER—Control tower.

GCA—Ground Control Approach System.

GND CON—Ground Control.

Legend 20. Airport/Facility Directory Legend from Chart Supplement.

AIRPORT/FACILITY DIRECTORY LEGEND

GCO—Ground Communication Outlet—An unstaffed, remotely controlled, ground/ground communications facility. Pilots at uncontrolled airports may contact ATC and FSS via VHF to a telephone connection to obtain an instrument clearance or close a VFR or IFR flight plan. They may also get an updated weather briefing prior to takeoff. Pilots will use four "key clicks" on the VHF radio to contact the appropriate ATC facility or six "key clicks" to contact the FSS. The GCO system is intended to be used only on the ground.

DEP CON—Departure Control. The symbol ® indicates radar departure control.

CLNC DEL—Clearance Delivery.

CPDLC—Controller Pilot Data Link Communication. FANS ATC data communication capability from the aircraft to the ATC Data Link system.

PRE TAXI CLNC—Pre taxi clearance.

VFR ADVSY SVC—VFR Advisory Service. Service provided by Non–Radar Approach Control.
Advisory Service for VFR aircraft (upon a workload basis) ctc APP CON.

COMD POST—Command Post followed by the operator call sign in parenthesis.

PMSV—Pilot–to–Metro Service call sign, frequency and hours of operation, when full service is other than continuous. PMSV installations at which weather observation service is available shall be indicated, following the frequency and/or hours of operation as "Wx obsn svc 1900–0000Z‡" or "other times" may be used when no specific time is given. PMSV facilities manned by forecasters are considered "Full Service". PMSV facilities manned by weather observers are listed as "Limited Service".

OPS—Operations followed by the operator call sign in parenthesis.

CON

RANGE

FLT FLW—Flight Following

MEDIVAC

NOTE: Communication frequencies followed by the letter "X" indicate frequency available on request.

㉘ AIRSPACE

Information concerning Class B, C, and part–time D and E surface area airspace shall be published with effective times, if available.

CLASS B—Radar Sequencing and Separation Service for all aircraft in CLASS B airspace.

CLASS C—Separation between IFR and VFR aircraft and sequencing of VFR arrivals to the primary airport.

TRSA—Radar Sequencing and Separation Service for participating VFR Aircraft within a Terminal Radar Service Area.

Class C, D, and E airspace described in this publication is that airspace usually consisting of a 5 NM radius core surface area that begins at the surface and extends upward to an altitude above the airport elevation (charted in MSL for Class C and Class D). Class E surface airspace normally extends from the surface up to but not including the overlying controlled airspace.

When part–time Class C or Class D airspace defaults to Class E, the core surface area becomes Class E. This will be formatted as:
AIRSPACE: CLASS C svc "times" ctc **APP CON** other times CLASS E:
or
AIRSPACE: CLASS D svc "times" other times CLASS E.

When a part–time Class C, Class D or Class E surface area defaults to Class G, the core surface area becomes Class G up to, but not including, the overlying controlled airspace. Normally, the overlying controlled airspace is Class E airspace beginning at either 700´ or 1200´ AGL and may be determined by consulting the relevant VFR Sectional or Terminal Area Charts. This will be formatted as:
AIRSPACE: CLASS C svc "times" ctc **APP CON** other times CLASS G, with CLASS E 700´ (or 1200´) AGL & abv:
or
AIRSPACE: CLASS D svc "times" other times CLASS G with CLASS E 700´ (or 1200´) AGL & abv:
or
AIRSPACE: CLASS E svc "times" other times CLASS G with CLASS E 700´ (or 1200´) AGL & abv.

NOTE: AIRSPACE SVC "TIMES" INCLUDE ALL ASSOCIATED ARRIVAL EXTENSIONS. Surface area arrival extensions for instrument approach procedures become part of the primary core surface area. These extensions may be either Class D or Class E airspace and are effective concurrent with the times of the primary core surface area. For example, when a part–time Class C, Class D or Class E surface area defaults to Class G, the associated arrival extensions will default to Class G at the same time. When a part–time Class C or Class D surface area defaults to Class E, the arrival extensions will remain in effect as Class E airspace.

NOTE: CLASS E AIRSPACE EXTENDING UPWARD FROM 700 FEET OR MORE ABOVE THE SURFACE, DESIGNATED IN CONJUNCTION WITH AN AIRPORT WITH AN APPROVED INSTRUMENT PROCEDURE.
Class E 700´ AGL (shown as magenta vignette on sectional charts) and 1200´ AGL (blue vignette) areas are designated when necessary to provide controlled airspace for transitioning to/from the terminal and enroute environments. Unless otherwise specified, these 700´/1200´ AGL Class E airspace areas remain in effect continuously, regardless of airport operating hours or surface area status. These transition areas should not be confused with surface areas or arrival extensions.

(See Chapter 3, AIRSPACE, in the Aeronautical Information Manual for further details)

Legend 21. Airport/Facility Directory Legend from Chart Supplement.

AIRPORT/FACILITY DIRECTORY LEGEND

㉙ VOR TEST FACILITY (VOT)

The VOT transmits a signal which provided users a convenient means to determine the operational status and accuracy of an aircraft VOR receiver while on the ground. Ground based VOTs and the associated frequency shall be shown when available. VOTs are also shown with identifier, frequency and referenced remarks in the VOR Receiver Check section in the back of this publication.

㉚ RADIO AIDS TO NAVIGATION

The Airport/Facility Directory section of the Chart Supplement lists, by facility name, all Radio Aids to Navigation that appear on FAA, Aeronautical Information Services Visual or IFR Aeronautical Charts and those upon which the FAA has approved an Instrument Approach Procedure, with exception of selected TACANs. All VOR, VORTAC, TACAN and ILS equipment in the National Airspace System has an automatic monitoring and shutdown feature in the event of malfunction. Unmonitored, as used in this publication, for any navigational aid, means that monitoring personnel cannot observe the malfunction or shutdown signal. The NAVAID NOTAM file identifier will be shown as "NOTAM FILE IAD" and will be listed on the Radio Aids to Navigation line. When two or more NAVAIDS are listed and the NOTAM file identifier is different from that shown on the Radio Aids to Navigation line, it will be shown with the NAVAID listing. NOTAM file identifiers for ILSs and its components (e.g., NDB (LOM) are the same as the associated airports and are not repeated. Automated Surface Observing System (ASOS), Automated Weather Observing System (AWOS), and Hazardous Inflight Weather Advisory Service (HIWAS) will be shown when this service is broadcast over selected NAVAIDs.

NAVAID information is tabulated as indicated in the following sample:

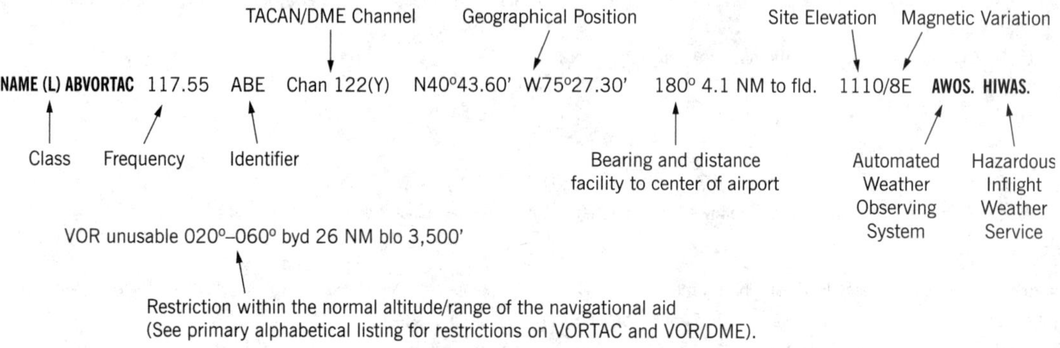

Note: Those DME channel numbers with a (Y) suffix require TACAN to be placed in the "Y" mode to receive distance information.

HIWAS—Hazardous Inflight Weather Advisory Service is a continuous broadcast of inflight weather advisories including summarized SIGMETs, convective SIGMETs, AIRMETs and urgent PIREPs. HIWAS is presently broadcast over selected VOR's throughout the U.S.

ASR/PAR—Indicates that Surveillance (ASR) or Precision (PAR) radar instrument approach minimums are published in the U.S. Terminal Procedures. Only part–time hours of operation will be shown.

Legend 22. Airport/Facility Directory Legend from Chart Supplement.

AIRPORT/FACILITY DIRECTORY LEGEND

RADIO CLASS DESIGNATIONS

VOR/DME/TACAN Standard Service Volume (SSV) Classifications

SSV Class	Altitudes	Distance (NM)
(T) Terminal	1000´ to 12,000´	25
(L) Low Altitude	1000´ to 18,000´	40
(H) High Altitude	1000´ to 14,500´	40
	14,500´ to 18,000´	100
	18,000´ to 45,000´	130
	45,000´ to 60,000´	100

NOTE: Additionally, (H) facilities provide (L) and (T) service volume and (L) facilities provide (T) service. Altitudes are with respect to the station's site elevation. Coverage is not available in a cone of airspace directly above the facility.

The term VOR is, operationally, a general term covering the VHF omnidirectional bearing type of facility without regard to the fact that the power, the frequency protected service volume, the equipment configuration, and operational requirements may vary between facilities at different locations.

AB	Automatic Weather Broadcast.
DF	Direction Finding Service.
DME	UHF standard (TACAN compatible) distance measuring equipment.
DME(Y)	UHF standard (TACAN compatible) distance measuring equipment that require TACAN to be placed in the "Y" mode to receive DME.
GS	Glide slope.
H	Non–directional radio beacon (homing), power 50 watts to less than 2,000 watts (50 NM at all altitudes).
HH	Non–directional radio beacon (homing), power 2,000 watts or more (75 NM at all altitudes).
H–SAB	Non–directional radio beacons providing automatic transcribed weather service.
ILS	Instrument Landing System (voice, where available, on localizer channel).
IM	Inner marker.
LDA	Localizer Directional Aid.
LMM	Compass locator station when installed at middle marker site (15 NM at all altitudes).
LOM	Compass locator station when installed at outer marker site (15 NM at all altitudes).
MH	Non–directional radio beacon (homing) power less than 50 watts (25 NM at all altitudes).
MM	Middle marker.
OM	Outer marker.
S	Simultaneous range homing signal and/or voice.
SABH	Non–directional radio beacon not authorized for IFR or ATC. Provides automatic weather broadcasts.
SDF	Simplified Direction Facility.
TACAN	UHF navigational facility–omnidirectional course and distance information.
VOR	VHF navigational facility–omnidirectional course only.
VOR/DME	Collocated VOR navigational facility and UHF standard distance measuring equipment.
VORTAC	Collocated VOR and TACAN navigational facilities.
W	Without voice on radio facility frequency.
Z	VHF station location marker at a LF radio facility.

Legend 23. Airport/Facility Directory Legend from Chart Supplement.

AIRPORT/FACILITY DIRECTORY LEGEND

ILS FACILITY PEFORMANCE CLASSIFICATION CODES

Codes define the ability of an ILS to support autoland operations. The two portions of the code represent Official Category and farthest point along a Category I, II, or III approach that the Localizer meets Category III structure tolerances.

Official Category: I, II, or III; the lowest minima on published or unpublished procedures supported by the ILS.

Farthest point of satisfactory Category III Localizer performance for Category I, II, or III approaches: A – 4 NM prior to runway threshold, B – 3500 ft prior to runway threshold, C – glide angle dependent but generally 750–1000 ft prior to threshold, T – runway threshold, D – 3000 ft after runway threshold, and E – 2000 ft prior to stop end of runway.

ILS information is tabulated as indicated in the following sample:

ILS/DME 108.5 I–ORL Chan 22 Rwy 18. Class IIE. LOM HERNY NDB.

ILS Facility Performance Classification Code

FREQUENCY PAIRING TABLE

VHF FREQUENCY	TACAN CHANNEL	VHF FREQUENCY	TACAN CHANNEL	VHF FREQUENCY	TACAN CHANNEL	VHF FREQUENCY	TACAN CHANNEL
108.10	18X	108.55	22Y	111.05	47Y	114.85	95Y
108.30	20X	108.65	23Y	111.15	48Y	114.95	96Y
108.50	22X	108.75	24Y	111.25	49Y	115.05	97Y
108.70	24X	108.85	25Y	111.35	50Y	115.15	98Y
108.90	26X	108.95	26Y	111.45	51Y	115.25	99Y
109.10	28X	109.05	27Y	111.55	52Y	115.35	100Y
109.30	30X	109.15	28Y	111.65	53Y	115.45	101Y
109.50	32X	109.25	29Y	111.75	54Y	115.55	102Y
109.70	34X	109.35	30Y	111.85	55Y	115.65	103Y
109.90	36X	109.45	31Y	111.95	56Y	115.75	104Y
110.10	38X	109.55	32Y	113.35	80Y	115.85	105Y
110.30	40X	109.65	33Y	113.45	81Y	115.95	106Y
110.50	42X	109.75	34Y	113.55	82Y	116.05	107Y
110.70	44X	109.85	35Y	113.65	83Y	116.15	108Y
110.90	46X	109.95	36Y	113.75	84Y	116.25	109Y
111.10	48X	110.05	37Y	113.85	85Y	116.35	110Y
111.30	50X	110.15	38Y	113.95	86Y	116.45	111Y
111.50	52X	110.25	39Y	114.05	87Y	116.55	112Y
111.70	54X	110.35	40Y	114.15	88Y	116.65	113Y
111.90	56X	110.45	41Y	114.25	89Y	116.75	114Y
108.05	17Y	110.55	42Y	114.35	90Y	116.85	115Y
108.15	18Y	110.65	43Y	114.45	91Y	116.95	116Y
108.25	19Y	110.75	44Y	114.55	92Y	117.05	117Y
108.35	20Y	110.85	45Y	114.65	93Y	117.15	118Y
108.45	21Y	110.95	46Y	114.75	94Y	117.25	119Y

FREQUENCY PAIRING TABLE

The following is a list of paired VOR/ILS VHF frequencies with TACAN channels.

TACAN CHANNEL	VHF FREQUENCY	TACAN CHANNEL	VHF FREQUENCY	TACAN CHANNEL	VHF FREQUENCY	TACAN CHANNEL	VHF FREQUENCY
2X	134.5	25X	108.80	36X	109.90	47X	111.00
2Y	134.55	25Y	108.85	36Y	109.95	47Y	111.05
11X	135.4	26X	108.90	37X	110.00	48X	111.10
11Y	135.45	26Y	108.95	37Y	110.05	48Y	111.15
12X	135.5	27X	109.00	38X	110.10	49X	111.20
12Y	135.55	27Y	109.05	38Y	110.15	49Y	111.25
17X	108.00	28X	109.10	39X	110.20	50X	111.30
17Y	108.05	28Y	109.15	39Y	110.25	50Y	111.35
18X	108.10	29X	109.20	40X	110.30	51X	111.40
18Y	108.15	29Y	109.25	40Y	110.35	51Y	111.45
19X	108.20	30X	109.30	41X	110.40	52X	111.50
19Y	108.25	30Y	109.35	41Y	110.45	52Y	111.55
20X	108.30	31X	109.40	42X	110.50	53X	111.60
20Y	108.35	31Y	109.45	42Y	110.55	53Y	111.65
21X	108.40	32X	109.50	43X	110.60	54X	111.70
21Y	108.45	32Y	109.55	43Y	110.65	54Y	111.75
22X	108.50	33X	109.60	44X	110.70	55X	111.80
22Y	108.55	33Y	109.65	44Y	110.75	55Y	111.85
23X	108.60	34X	109.70	45X	110.80	56X	111.90
23Y	108.65	34Y	109.75	45Y	110.85	56Y	111.95
24X	108.70	35X	109.80	46X	110.90	57X	112.00
24Y	108.75	35Y	109.85	46Y	110.95	57Y	112.05

Legend 24. Airport/Facility Directory Legend from Chart Supplement.

AIRPORT/FACILITY DIRECTORY LEGEND

TACAN CHANNEL	VHF FREQUENCY	TACAN CHANNEL	VHF FREQUENCY	TACAN CHANNEL	VHF FREQUENCY	TACAN CHANNEL	VHF FREQUENCY
58X	112.10	77X	113.00	96X	114.90	115X	116.80
58Y	112.15	77Y	113.05	96Y	114.95	115Y	116.85
59X	112.20	78X	113.10	97X	115.00	116X	116.90
59Y	112.25	78Y	113.15	97Y	115.05	116Y	116.95
60X	133.30	79X	113.20	98X	115.10	117X	117.00
60Y	133.35	79Y	113.25	98Y	115.15	117Y	117.05
61X	133.40	80X	113.30	99X	115.20	118X	117.10
61Y	133.45	80Y	113.35	99Y	115.25	118Y	117.15
62X	133.50	81X	113.40	100X	115.30	119X	117.20
62Y	133.55	81Y	113.45	100Y	115.35	119Y	117.25
63X	133.60	82X	113.50	101X	115.40	120X	117.30
63Y	133.65	82Y	113.55	101Y	115.45	120Y	117.35
64X	133.70	83X	113.60	102X	115.50	121X	117.40
64Y	133.75	83Y	113.65	102Y	115.55	121Y	117.45
65X	133.80	84X	113.70	103X	115.60	122X	117.50
65Y	133.85	84Y	113.75	103Y	115.65	122Y	117.55
66X	133.90	85X	113.80	104X	115.70	123X	117.60
66Y	133.95	85Y	113.85	104Y	115.75	123Y	117.65
67X	134.00	86X	113.90	105X	115.80	124X	117.70
67Y	134.05	86Y	113.95	105Y	115.85	124Y	117.75
68X	134.10	87X	114.00	106X	115.90	125X	117.80
68Y	134.15	87Y	114.05	106Y	115.95	125Y	117.85
69X	134.20	88X	114.10	107X	116.00	126X	117.90
69Y	134.25	88Y	114.15	107Y	116.05	126Y	117.95
70X	112.30	89X	114.20	108X	116.10		
70Y	112.35	89Y	114.25	108Y	116.15		
71X	112.40	90X	114.30	109X	116.20		
71Y	112.45	90Y	114.35	109Y	116.25		
72X	112.50	91X	114.40	110X	116.30		
72Y	112.55	91Y	114.45	110Y	116.35		
73X	112.60	92X	114.50	111X	116.40		
73Y	112.65	92Y	114.55	111Y	116.45		
74X	112.70	93X	114.60	112X	116.50		
74Y	112.75	93Y	114.65	112Y	116.55		
75X	112.80	94X	114.70	113X	116.60		
75Y	112.85	94Y	114.75	113Y	116.65		
76X	112.90	95X	114.80	114X	116.70		
76Y	112.95	95Y	114.85	114Y	116.75		

(31) **COMM/NAV/WEATHER REMARKS:** These remarks consist of pertinent information affecting the current status of communications, NAVAIDs, weather, and in the absence of air-ground radio outlets identified in the Communications section some approach control facilities will have a clearance delivery phone number listed here.

Legend 25. Airport/Facility Directory Legend from Chart Supplement.

INOP COMPONENTS 18088

INOPERATIVE COMPONENTS OR VISUAL AIDS TABLE
(For Civil Use Only)

Straight-in and Sidestep landing minimums published on instrument approach procedure charts are based on full operation of all components and visual aids associated with the particular approach chart being used. Higher minimums are required with inoperative components or visual aids as indicated below. If more than one component is inoperative, each minimum is raised to the highest minimum required by any single component that is inoperative. ILS glideslope inoperative minimums are published on the instrument approach charts as localizer minimums. This table applies to approach categories A thru D and is to be used unless amended by notes on the approach chart. Such notes apply only to the particular approach category(ies) as stated. Category E inoperative notes will be specified when published on civil charts. The inoperative table does not apply to Circling minimums. See legend page for description of components indicated below.

(1) ILS, PAR, LPV, GLS minima

Inoperative Component or Visual Aid	Increase Visibility
All ALS types (except ODALS)	¼ mile

(2) ILS, LPV, GLS with visibility minima of RVR 1800†/2000*/2200*

Inoperative Component or Visual Aid	Increase Visibility
ALSF 1 & 2, MALSR, SSALR	To RVR 4000† To RVR 4500*
TDZL or RCLS	To RVR 2400#
RVR	To ½ mile

#For ILS, LPV, GLS procedures with a 200 foot HAT, RVR 1800 authorized with use of FD or AP or HUD to DA.

(3) All Approach Types and all lines of minima other than (1) & (2) above

Inoperative Component or Visual Aid	Increase Visibility
ALSF 1 & 2, MALSR, SSALR	½ mile
MALSF, MALS, SSALF, SSALS, SALSF, SALS	¼ mile

(4) Sidestep minima (CAT C-D)

Inoperative Component or Visual Aid to Sidestep Runway	Increase Visibility
ALSF 1 & 2, MALSR, SSALR	½ mile

(5) All Approach Types, All lines of minima

Inoperative Component or Visual Aid	Increase Visibility
ODALS (CAT A-B)	¼ mile
ODALS (CAT C-D)	⅛ mile

INOP COMPONENTS 18088

Legend 26. U.S. Terminal Procedures Inoperative Components or Visual Aids Table.

TERMS/LANDING MINIMA DATA 17117

IFR LANDING MINIMA

The United States Standard for Terminal Instrument Procedures (TERPS) is the approved criteria for formulating instrument approach procedures. Landing minima are established for six aircraft approach categories (ABCDE and COPTER). In the absence of COPTER MINIMA, helicopters may use the CAT A minimums of other procedures.

LANDING MINIMA FORMAT

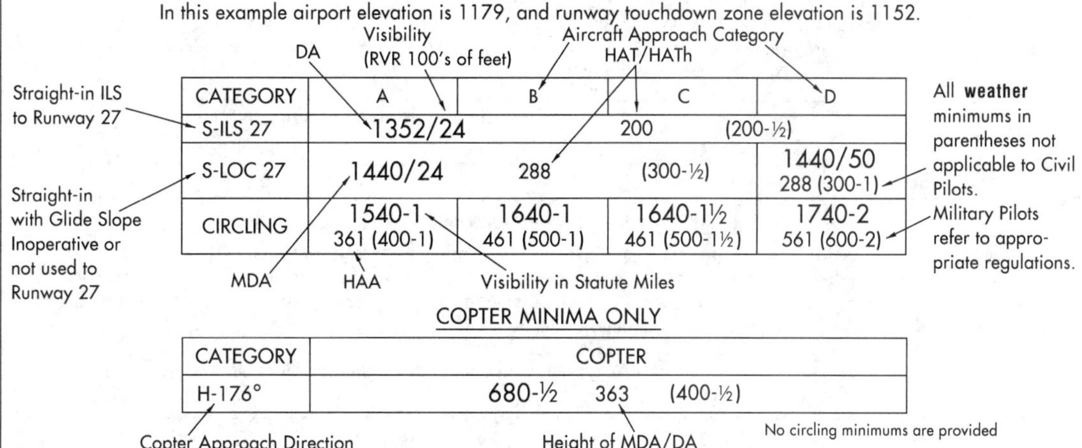

In this example airport elevation is 1179, and runway touchdown zone elevation is 1152.
DA
Visibility (RVR 100's of feet)
Aircraft Approach Category
HAT/HATh
Straight-in ILS to Runway 27
Straight-in with Glide Slope Inoperative or not used to Runway 27
CATEGORY
A
B
C
D
S-ILS 27
1352/24
200
(200-½)
S-LOC 27
1440/24
288
(300-½)
1440/50
288 (300-1)
CIRCLING
1540-1
361 (400-1)
1640-1
461 (500-1)
1640-1½
461 (500-1½)
1740-2
561 (600-2)
All weather minimums in parentheses not applicable to Civil Pilots.
Military Pilots refer to appropriate regulations.
MDA
HAA
Visibility in Statute Miles
COPTER MINIMA ONLY
CATEGORY
COPTER
H-176°
680-½
363
(400-½)
Copter Approach Direction
Height of MDA/DA Above Landing Area (HAL)
No circling minimums are provided

NOTE: The W symbol indicates outages of the WAAS vertical guidance may occur daily at this location due to initial system limitations. WAAS NOTAMS for vertical outages are not provided for this approach. Use LNAV minima for flight planning at these locations, whether as a destination or alternate. For flight operations at these locations, when the WAAS avionics indicate that LNAV/VNAV or LPV service is available, then vertical guidance may be used to complete the approach using the displayed level of service. Should an outage occur during the procedure, reversion to LNAV minima may be required. As the WAAS coverage is expanded, the W will be removed.

RNAV minimums are dependent on navigation equipment capability, as stated in the applicable AFM, AFMS, or other FAA approved document. See AIM paragraph 5-4-5, AC 90-105 and AC 90-107 for detailed requirements for each line of minima.

COLD TEMPERATURE RESTRICTED AIRPORTS

NOTE: A ❄-12°C symbol indicates a cold temperature altitude correction is required at this airport when reported temperature is at or below the published restricted temperature. Pilots familiar with cold temperature procedure in the Notice to Airman Publication (NTAP) and correcting all altitudes from the IAF to the MA final holding altitude do not have to reference the NTAP. Pilots wishing to correct on individual segments must reference the NTAP airport list for affected segments. See Notice to Airman Publication (NTAP) Graphic Notices General for complete list of published airports, temperature, segments, and procedure information. www.faa.gov/air_traffic/publications/notices. Pilots will advise ATC with the required altitude correction when making a correction to any segment other than the final segment. See following Cold Temperature Error Table to make manual corrections.

COLD TEMPERATURE ERROR TABLE

HEIGHT ABOVE AIRPORT IN FEET

REPORTED TEMP °C	200	300	400	500	600	700	800	900	1000	1500	2000	3000	4000	5000
+10	10	10	10	10	20	20	20	20	20	30	40	60	80	90
0	20	20	30	30	40	40	50	50	60	90	120	170	230	280
-10	20	30	40	50	60	70	80	90	100	150	200	290	390	490
-20	30	50	60	70	90	100	120	130	140	210	280	420	570	710
-30	40	60	80	100	120	140	150	170	190	280	380	570	760	950
-40	50	80	100	120	150	170	190	220	240	360	480	720	970	1210
-50	60	90	120	150	180	210	240	270	300	450	590	890	1190	1500

AIRCRAFT APPROACH CATEGORIES

Aircraft approach category indicates a grouping of aircraft based on a speed of VREF, if specified, or if VREF not specified, 1.3 VSO at the maximum certificated landing weight. VREF, VSO, and the maximum certificated landing weight are those values as established for the aircraft by the certification authority of the country of registry. Helicopters are Category A aircraft. An aircraft shall fit in only one category. However, if it is necessary to operate at a speed in excess of the upper limit of the speed range for an aircraft's category, the minimums for the category for that speed shall be used. For example, an airplane which fits into Category B, but is circling to land at a speed of 145 knots, shall use the approach Category D minimums. As an additional example, a Category A airplane (or helicopter) which is operating at 130 knots on a straight-in approach shall use the approach Category C minimums. See following category limits:

MANEUVERING TABLE

Approach Category	A	B	C	D	E
Speed (Knots)	0-90	91-120	121-140	141-165	Abv 165

TERMS/LANDING MINIMA DATA 17117

Legend 27. U.S. Terminal Procedures Terms/Landing Minima Data.

TERMS/LANDING MINIMA DATA 17229

CIRCLING APPROACH OBSTACLE PROTECTED AIRSPACE

The circling MDA provides vertical obstacle clearance during a circle-to-land maneuver. The circling MDA protected area extends from the threshold of each runway authorized for landing following a circle-to-land maneuver for a distance as shown in the tables below. The resultant arcs are then connected tangentially to define the protected area.

STANDARD CIRCLING APPROACH MANEUVERING RADIUS

Circling approach protected areas developed prior to late 2012 used the radius distances shown in the following table, expressed in nautical miles (NM), dependent on aircraft approach category. The approaches using standard circling approach areas can be identified by the absence of the C symbol on the circling line of minima.

Circling MDA in feet MSL	Approach Category and Circling Radius (NM)				
	CAT A	CAT B	CAT C	CAT D	CAT E
All Altitudes	1.3	1.5	1.7	2.3	4.5

C EXPANDED CIRCLING APPROACH MANEUVERING AIRSPACE RADIUS

Circling approach protected areas developed after late 2012 use the radius distance shown in the following table, expressed in nautical miles (NM), dependent on aircraft approach category, and the altitude of the circling MDA, which accounts for true airspeed increase with altitude. The approaches using expanded circling approach areas can be identified by the presence of the C symbol on the circling line of minima.

Circling MDA in feet MSL	Approach Category and Circling Radius (NM)				
	CAT A	CAT B	CAT C	CAT D	CAT E
1000 or less	1.3	1.7	2.7	3.6	4.5
1001-3000	1.3	1.8	2.8	3.7	4.6
3001-5000	1.3	1.8	2.9	3.8	4.8
5001-7000	1.3	1.9	3.0	4.0	5.0
7001-9000	1.4	2.0	3.2	4.2	5.3
9001 and above	1.4	2.1	3.3	4.4	5.5

Comparable Values of RVR and Visibility

The following table shall be used for converting RVR to ground or flight visibility. For converting RVR values that fall between listed values, use the next higher RVR value; do not interpolate. For example, when converting 1800 RVR, use 2400 RVR with the resultant visibility of ½ mile.

RVR (feet)	Visibility (statute miles)	RVR (feet)	Visibility (statute miles)
1600	¼	4500	⅞
2400	½	5000	1
3200	⅝	6000	1¼
4000	¾		

RADAR MINIMA

	RWY	GP/TCH/RPI	CAT	DA/ MDA-VIS	HAT/ HATh/ HAA	CEIL-VIS	CAT	DA/ MDA-VIS	HAT/ HATh/ HAA	CEIL-VIS
PAR	10	2.5°/42/1000	ABCDE	**195**/16	100	(100-¼)				
	28	2.5°/48/1068	ABCDE	**187**/16	100	(100-¼)				
ASR	10		ABC	**560**/40	463	(500-¾)	DE	**560**/50	463	(500-1)
	28		AB	**600**/50	513	(600-1)	CDE	**600**/60	513	(600-1¼)
CIR	10		AB	**560**-1¼	463	(500-1¼)	CDE	**560**-1½	463	(500-1½)
	28		AB	**600**-1¼	503	(600-1¼)	CDE	**600**-1½	503	(600-1½)

Visibility (RVR 100's of feet)

Visibility in Statute Miles

All minimums in parentheses not applicable to Civil Pilots. Military Pilots refer to appropriate regulations.

Radar Minima:

1. Minima shown are the lowest permitted by established criteria. Pilots should consult applicable directives for their category of aircraft.
2. The circling MDA and weather minima to be used are those for the runway to which the final approach is flown- not the landing runway. In the above RADAR MINIMA example, a category C aircraft flying a radar approach to runway 10, circling to land on runway 28, must use an MDA of 560 feet with weather minima of 500-1½.

NOTE: Military RADAR MINIMA may be shown with communications symbology that indicates emergency frequency monitoring capability by the radar facility as follows: (E) VHF and UHF emergency frequencies monitored
(V) VHF emergency frequency (121.5) monitored
(U) UHF emergency frequency (243.0) monitored

Additionally, unmonitored frequencies which are available on request from the controlling agency may be annotated with an "x".

A Alternate Minimums not standard. Civil users refer to tabulation. USA/USN/USAF pilots refer to appropriate regulations.

A NA Alternate minimums are Not Authorized due to unmonitored facility or absence of weather reporting service.

T Airport is published in the Takeoff Minimums, (Obstacle) Departure Procedures, and Diverse Vector Area (Radar Vectors) tabulation.

TERMS/LANDING MINIMA DATA 17229

Legend 28. U.S. Terminal Procedures Terms/Landing Minima Data.

GENERAL INFO 18088

GENERAL INFORMATION

This publication is issued every 56 days and includes Standard Instrument Approach Procedures (SIAPS), Standard Instrument Departures (SIDs), Standard Terminal Arrivals (STARs), IFR Takeoff Minimums and (Obstacle) Departure Procedures (ODPs), IFR Alternate Minimums, and Radar Instrument Approach Minimums for use by civil and military aviation. The organization responsible for SIAPs, Radar Minimums, SIDs, STARs and graphic ODPs is identified in parentheses in the top margin of the procedure; e.g., (FAA), (FAA-O), (USA), (USAF), (USN). SIAPS with the (FAA) and (FAA-O) designation are regulated under 14 CFR, Part 97. SIAPs with the (FAA-O) designation have been developed under Other Transaction Agreement (OTA) by private providers and have been certified by the FAA. See 14 CFR, Part 91.175 (a) and the AIM for further details. 14 CFR, Part 91.175 (g) and the Special Notices section of the Chart Supplement contains information on civil operations at military airports.

The FAA uses an internal numbering system on all charts in the TPP. This Approach and Landing (AL) number is located on the top center margin of the chart followed by the organization responsible for the procedure in parentheses, e.g., AL-18 (FAA), AL-227 (USAF).

CHART CURRENCY INFORMATION

Date of Latest Revision 09365

The Date of Latest Revision identifies the Julian date the chart was added or last revised for any reason. The first two digits indicate the year, the last three digits indicate the day of the year (001 to 365/6) in which the latest revision of any kind has been made to the chart.

FAA Procedure Amendment Number → Orig 31DEC09 ← Procedure Amendment Effective Date
Amdt 2B 12MAR09

The FAA Procedure Amendment Number represents the most current amendment of a given procedure. The Procedure Amendment Effective Date represents the AIRAC cycle date on which the procedure amendment was incorporated into the chart. Updates to the amendment number & effective date represent procedural/criteria revisions to the charted procedure, e.g., course, fix, altitude, minima, etc.

NOTE: Inclusion of the "Procedure Amendment Effective Date" will be phased in as procedures are amended. As this occurs, the Julian date will be relocated to the upper right corner of the chart.

MISCELLANEOUS

★ Indicates a non-continuously operating facility, see Chart Supplement.
For Civil (FAA) instrument procedures, "RADAR REQUIRED" in the planview of the chart indicates that ATC radar must be available to assist the pilot when transitioning from the en route environment. "Radar required" in the pilot briefing portion of the chart indicates that ATC radar is required on portions of the procedure outside the final approach segment, including the missed approach. Some military procedures also have equipment requirements such as "Radar Required", but do not conform to the same charting application standards used by the FAA.
Distances in nautical miles (except visibility in statute miles and Runway Visual Range in hundreds of feet). Runway Dimensions in feet. Elevations in feet. Mean Sea Level (MSL). Ceilings in feet above airport elevation. Radials/bearings/headings/courses are magnetic. Horizontal Datum: Unless otherwise noted on the chart, all coordinates are referenced to North American Datum 1983 (NAD 83), which for charting purposes is considered equivalent to World Geodetic System 1984 (WGS 84).

Terrain is scaled within the neat lines (planview boundaries) and does not accurately underlie not-to-scale distance depictions or symbols.

GENERAL INFO 18088

Legend 29. U.S. Terminal Procedures General Information.

GENERAL INFO 18088

STANDARD TERMINAL ARRIVALS AND DEPARTURE PROCEDURES

The use of the associated codified STAR/DP and transition identifiers are requested of users when filing flight plans via teletype and are required for users filing flight plans via computer interface. It must be noted that when filing a STAR/DP with a transition, the first three coded characters of the STAR and the last three coded characters of the DP are replaced by the transition code. Examples: ACTON SIX ARRIVAL, file (AQN.AQN6); ACTON SIX ARRIVAL, EDNAS TRANSITION, file (EDNAS.AQN6). FREEHOLD THREE DEPARTURE, file (FREH3.RBV), FREEHOLD THREE DEPARTURE, ELWOOD CITY TRANSITION, file (FREH3.EWC).

RNAV DP and STAR. Effective March 15,2007, these procedures, formerly identified as Type-A and Type-B, will be designated as RNAV 1 in accordance with amended Advisory Circular (AC) and ICAO terminology.

Refer to AC 90-100A U.S. TERMINAL AND EN ROUTE AREA NAVIGATION (RNAV) OPERATIONS and the Aeronautical Information Manual for additional guidance regarding these procedures.

Standard RNAV 1 Procedure Chart Notes

NOTE: RNAV 1
NOTE: DME/DME/IRU or GPS required

Some procedures may require use of GPS and will be identified by a "GPS required" note.

RNAV 1 Procedure Characteristics and Operations

1. Require use of an RNAV system with DME/DME/IRU, and/or GPS inputs.
2. Require use of a CDI, flight director, and/or autopilot, in lateral navigation mode, for flight guidance while operating on RNAV paths (track, course, or direct leg). Other methods providing an equivalent level of performance may be acceptable.
3. RNAV paths may start as low as 500 feet above airport elevation.

PROCEDURE EQUIPMENT REQUIREMENTS

Users will begin to see Performance-Based Navigation (PBN) Requirements and ground-based Equipment Requirements prominently displayed in separate, standardized notes boxes. For procedures with PBN elements, the PBN box will contain the procedure's navigation specification(s); and, if required: specific sensors or infrastructure needed for the navigation solution; any additional or advanced functional requirements; the minimum Required Navigation Performance (RNP) value and any amplifying remarks. Items listed in this PBN box are REQUIRED for the procedure's PBN elements. The separate Equipment Requirements Box will list ground-based equipment requirements. On procedures with both PBN elements and equipment requirements, the PBN requirements box will be listed first. The publication of these notes will continue incrementally until all charts have been amended to comply with the new standard.

Ground-Based Procedure with PBN Elements

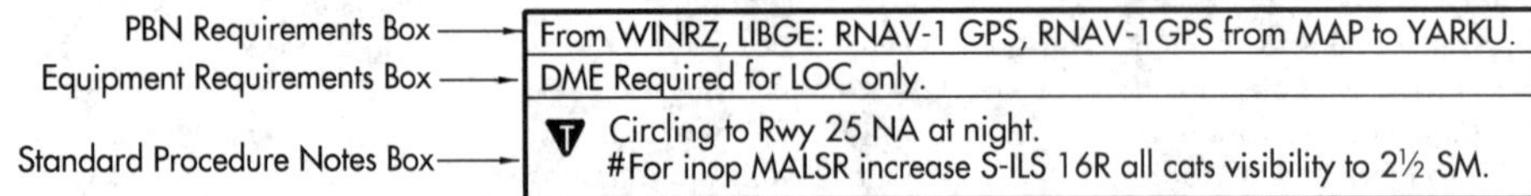

PBN Requirements Box
From WINRZ, LIBGE: RNAV-1 GPS, RNAV-1GPS from MAP to YARKU.
Equipment Requirements Box
DME Required for LOC only.
Standard Procedure Notes Box
Circling to Rwy 25 NA at night.
#For inop MALSR increase S-ILS 16R all cats visibility to 2½ SM.

PILOT CONTROLLED AIRPORT LIGHTING SYSTEMS

Available pilot controlled lighting (PCL) systems are indicated as follows:
1. Approach lighting systems that bear a system identification are symbolized using negative symbology, e.g., A1, V,
2. Approach lighting systems that do not bear a system identification are indicated with a negative "L" beside the name.
A star (★) indicates non-standard PCL, consult Chart Supplement, e.g., L★
To activate lights, use frequency indicated in the communication section of the chart with a L or the appropriate lighting system identification e.g., UNICOM 122.8 L, A1, V

KEY MIKE	FUNCTION
7 times within 5 seconds	Highest intensity available
5 times within 5 seconds	Medium or lower intensity (Lower REIL or REIL-off)
3 times within 5 seconds	Lowest intensity available (Lower REIL or REIL-off)

GENERAL INFO 18088

Legend 30. U.S. Terminal Procedures General Information.

GENERAL INFO 17117

ABBREVIATIONS

AAUP	Attention All Users Page
ADF	Automatic Direction Finder
ADIZ	Air Defense Identification Zone
AFIS	Automatic Flight Information Service
ALS	Approach Light System
ALSF	Approach Light System with Sequenced Flashing Lights
AP	Autopilot System
APCH	Approach
APP CON	Approach Control
ARR	Arrival
ASOS	Automated Surface Observing System
ASR/PAR	Published Radar Minimums at this Airport
ASSC	Airport Surface Surveillance Systems
ATIS	Automatic Terminal Information Service
AUNICOM	Automated UNICOM
AWOS	Automated Weather Observing System
AZ	Azimuth
BC	Back Course
BND	Bound
C	Circling
CAT	Category
CCW	Counter Clockwise
CDI	Course Deviation Indicator
Chan	Channel
CIFP	Coded Instrument Flight Procedures
CIR	Circling
CLNC DEL	Clearance Delivery
CNF	Computer Navigation Fix
CTAF	Common Traffic Advisory Frequency
CW	Clockwise
D-ATIS	Digital-Automatic Terminal Information Service
DA	Decision Altitude
DER	Departure End of Runway
DH	Decision Height
DME	Distance Measuring Equipment
DTHR	Displaced Threshold
DVA	Diverse Vector Area
ELEV	Elevation
EMAS	Engineered Material Arresting System
FAF	Final Approach Fix
FD	Flight Director System
FM	Fan Marker
FMS	Flight Management System
GBAS	Ground Based Augmentation System
GCO	Ground Communications Outlet
GLS	Ground Based Augmentation System Landing System
GP	Glidepath
GPI	Ground Point of Interception
GPS	Global Positioning System
GS	Glide Slope
HAA	Height above Airport
HAL	Height above Landing
HAT	Height above Touchdown
HATh	Height Above Threshold
HGS	Head-up Guidance System
HIRL	High Intensity Runway Lights
HUD	Head-up Display
IAF	Initial Approach Fix
ICAO	International Civil Aviation Organization
IF	Intermediate Fix
IM	Inner Marker
INOP	Inoperative
INT	Intersection
K	Knots
KIAS	Knots Indicated Airspeed
LAAS	Local Area Augmentation System
LDA	Localizer Type Directional Aid
Ldg	Landing
LIRL	Low Intensity Runway Lights
LNAV	Lateral Navigation
LOC	Localizer
LP	Localizer Performance
LPV	Localizer Performance with Vertical Guidance
LR	Lead Radial. Provides at least 2 NM (Copter 1 NM) of lead to assist in turning onto the intermediate/final course.
MAA	Maximum Authorized Altitude
MALS	Medium Intensity Approach Light System
MALSF	Medium Approach Lighting System with Sequenced Flashers
MALSR	Medium Intensity Approach Light System with RAIL
MAP	Missed Approach Point
MDA	Minimum Descent Altitude
MIRL	Medium Intensity Runway Lights
MM	Middle Marker
MRA	Minimum Reception Altitude
N/A	Not Applicable
NA	Not Authorized
NDB	Non-directional Radio Beacon
NFD	National Flight Database
NM	Nautical Mile
NoPT	No Procedure Turn Required (Procedure Turn shall not be executed without ATC clearance)
ODALS	Omnidirectional Approach Light System
ODP	Obstacle Departure Procedure
OM	Outer Marker
PAR	Precision Approach Radar
PRM	Precision Runway Monitor

GENERAL INFO 17117

Legend 31. U.S. Terminal Procedures Abbreviations.

GENERAL INFO 17117 ABBREVIATIONS

R.. Radial
RA...................................... Radio Altimeter setting height
RAIL.................................... Runway Alignment Indicator Lights
RCLS.................................... Runway Centerline Light System
REIL..................................... Runway End Identifier Lights
RF....................................... Radius-to-Fix
RLLS.................................... Runway Lead-in Light System
RNAV................................... Area Navigation
RNP..................................... Required Navigation Performance
RPI...................................... Runway Point of Intercept(ion)
RRL..................................... Runway Remaining Lights
Rwy..................................... Runway
RVR..................................... Runway Visual Range
S... Straight-in
SALS.................................... Short Approach Light System
SALSF.................................. Short Approach Lighting System with Sequenced Flashing Lights
SSALF.................................. Simplified Short Approach Lighting System with Sequenced Flashers
SSALR.................................. Simplified Short Approach Light System with RAIL
SSALS.................................. Simplified Short Approach Lighting System
SDF..................................... Simplified Directional Facility
SM...................................... Statute Mile
SOIA.................................... Simultaneous Offset Instrument Approach
TAA..................................... Terminal Arrival Area
TAC..................................... TACAN
TCH..................................... Threshold Crossing Height (height in feet Above Ground level)
TDZ..................................... Touchdown Zone
TDZE................................... Touchdown Zone Elevation
TDZ/CL................................ Touchdown Zone and Runway Centerline Lighting
TDZL................................... Touchdown Zone Lights
THR.................................... Threshold
THRE.................................. Threshold Elevation
TODA.................................. Takeoff Distance Available
TORA.................................. Takeoff Run Available
TR...................................... Track
VASI.................................... Visual Approach Slope Indicator
VCOA.................................. Visual Climb Over Airport
VDP.................................... Visual Descent Point
VGSI................................... Visual Glide Slope Indicator
VNAV.................................. Vertical Navigation
WAAS................................. Wide Area Augmentation System
WP/WPT.............................. Waypoint (RNAV)

GENERAL INFO 17117

Legend 32. U.S. Terminal Procedures Abbreviations.

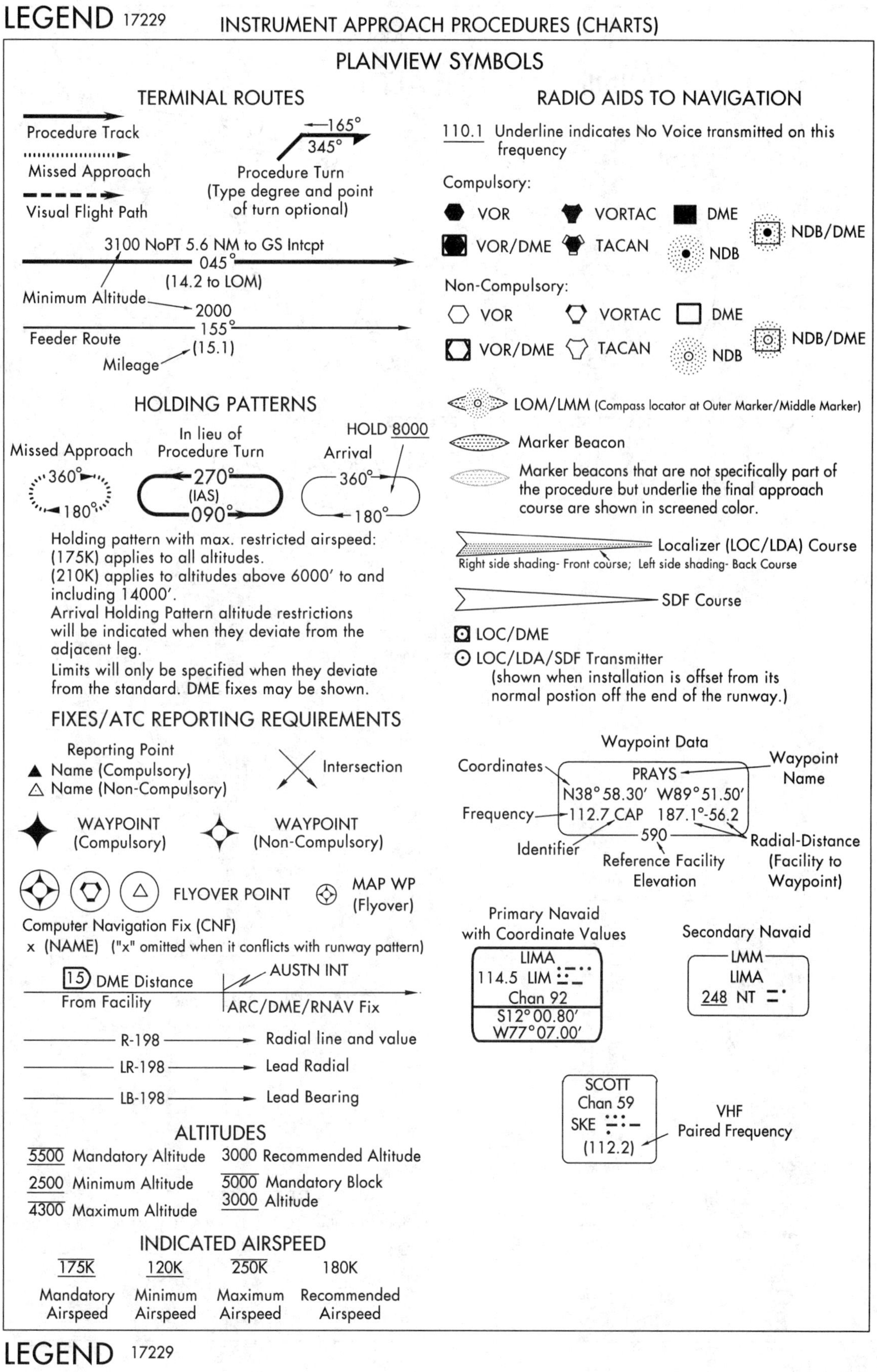

LEGEND 17229 INSTRUMENT APPROACH PROCEDURES (CHARTS)

PLANVIEW SYMBOLS

TERMINAL ROUTES

Procedure Track

Missed Approach

Visual Flight Path

165°
345°
Procedure Turn
(Type degree and point of turn optional)

3100 NoPT 5.6 NM to GS Intcpt
045°
(14.2 to LOM)
Minimum Altitude
2000
155°
Feeder Route
(15.1)
Mileage

HOLDING PATTERNS

Missed Approach — 360° 180°

In lieu of Procedure Turn — 270° (IAS) 090°

Arrival — HOLD 8000 — 360° 180°

Holding pattern with max. restricted airspeed:
(175K) applies to all altitudes.
(210K) applies to altitudes above 6000′ to and including 14000′.
Arrival Holding Pattern altitude restrictions will be indicated when they deviate from the adjacent leg.
Limits will only be specified when they deviate from the standard. DME fixes may be shown.

FIXES/ATC REPORTING REQUIREMENTS

Reporting Point
▲ Name (Compulsory)
△ Name (Non-Compulsory)

Intersection

WAYPOINT (Compulsory)

WAYPOINT (Non-Compulsory)

FLYOVER POINT

MAP WP (Flyover)

Computer Navigation Fix (CNF)
x (NAME) ("x" omitted when it conflicts with runway pattern)

15 DME Distance From Facility

AUSTN INT
ARC/DME/RNAV Fix

R-198 — Radial line and value

LR-198 — Lead Radial

LB-198 — Lead Bearing

ALTITUDES

5500 Mandatory Altitude

3000 Recommended Altitude

2500 Minimum Altitude

5000 / 3000 Mandatory Block Altitude

4300 Maximum Altitude

INDICATED AIRSPEED

175K	120K	250K	180K
Mandatory Airspeed	Minimum Airspeed	Maximum Airspeed	Recommended Airspeed

RADIO AIDS TO NAVIGATION

110.1 Underline indicates No Voice transmitted on this frequency

Compulsory:
VOR, VORTAC, DME, NDB/DME
VOR/DME, TACAN, NDB

Non-Compulsory:
VOR, VORTAC, DME, NDB/DME
VOR/DME, TACAN, NDB

LOM/LMM (Compass locator at Outer Marker/Middle Marker)

Marker Beacon

Marker beacons that are not specifically part of the procedure but underlie the final approach course are shown in screened color.

Localizer (LOC/LDA) Course
Right side shading- Front course; Left side shading- Back Course

SDF Course

LOC/DME

LOC/LDA/SDF Transmitter (shown when installation is offset from its normal postion off the end of the runway.)

Waypoint Data

Coordinates
PRAYS
N38°58.30′ W89°51.50′
Frequency — 112.7 CAP 187.1°-56.2
590
Identifier
Reference Facility Elevation
Waypoint Name
Radial-Distance (Facility to Waypoint)

Primary Navaid with Coordinate Values

LIMA
114.5 LIM
Chan 92
S12°00.80′
W77°07.00′

Secondary Navaid

LMM
LIMA
248 NT

SCOTT
Chan 59
SKE
(112.2)
VHF Paired Frequency

LEGEND 17229

Legend 33. U.S. Terminal Procedures Planview Symbols.

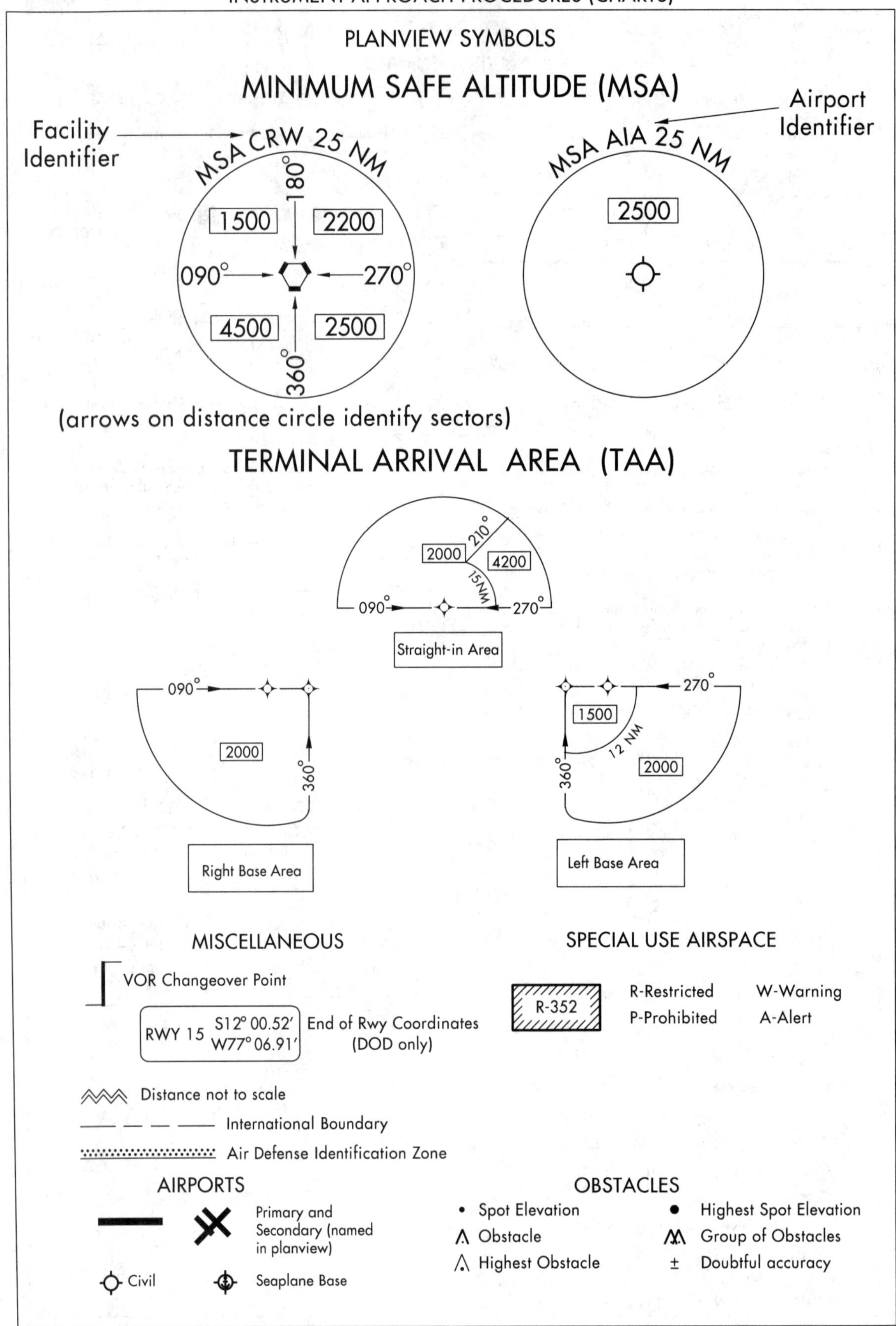
LEGEND 15232
INSTRUMENT APPROACH PROCEDURES (CHARTS)
PLANVIEW SYMBOLS
MINIMUM SAFE ALTITUDE (MSA)
Facility Identifier
MSA CRW 25 NM
180°
1500
2200
090°
270°
4500
2500
360°
Airport Identifier
MSA AIA 25 NM
2500
(arrows on distance circle identify sectors)
TERMINAL ARRIVAL AREA (TAA)
210°
2000
4200
15NM
090°
270°
Straight-in Area
090°
2000
360°
Right Base Area
270°
1500
12 NM
2000
360°
Left Base Area
MISCELLANEOUS
VOR Changeover Point
RWY 15 S12° 00.52′ W77° 06.91′
End of Rwy Coordinates (DOD only)
Distance not to scale
International Boundary
Air Defense Identification Zone
SPECIAL USE AIRSPACE
R-352
R-Restricted
P-Prohibited
W-Warning
A-Alert
AIRPORTS
Primary and Secondary (named in planview)
Civil
Seaplane Base
OBSTACLES
Spot Elevation
Obstacle
Highest Obstacle
Highest Spot Elevation
Group of Obstacles
± Doubtful accuracy
LEGEND 15232

Legend 34. U.S. Terminal Procedures Planview Symbols.

LEGEND 17229 INSTRUMENT APPROACH PROCEDURES (CHARTS)

PROFILE VIEW

Three different methods are used to depict either electronic or vertical guidance: "GS", "GP", or "VDA".

1. "GS" indicates that an Instrument Landing System (ILS) electronic glide slope (a ground antenna) provides vertical guidance. The profile section of ILS procedures depict a GS angle and TCH in the following format: GS 3.00°/TCH 55.

2. "GP" on GLS and RNAV procedures indicates that either electronic vertical guidance (via Wide Area Augmentation System - WAAS or Ground Based Augmentation System - GBAS) or barometric vertical guidance is provided. GLS and RNAV procedures with a published decision altitude (DA/H) depict a GP angle and TCH in the following format: GP 3.00°/TCH 50.

3. An advisory vertical descent angle (VDA) is provided on non-vertically guided conventional procedures and RNAV procedures with only a minimum descent altitude (MDA) to assist in preventing controlled flight into terrain. On Civil (FAA) procedures, this information is placed above or below the procedure track following the fix it is based on. Absence of a VDA or a note that the VDA is not authorized indicates that the prescribed obstacle clearance surface is not clear and the VDA must not be used below MDA. VDA is depicted in the following format: ∠3.00°/TCH 55.

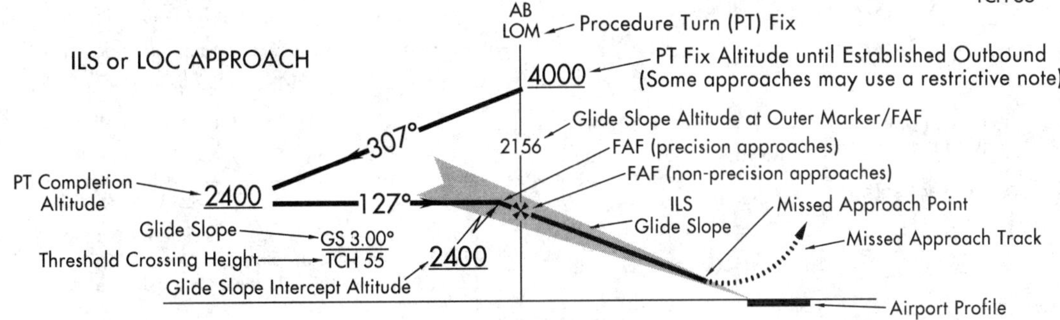

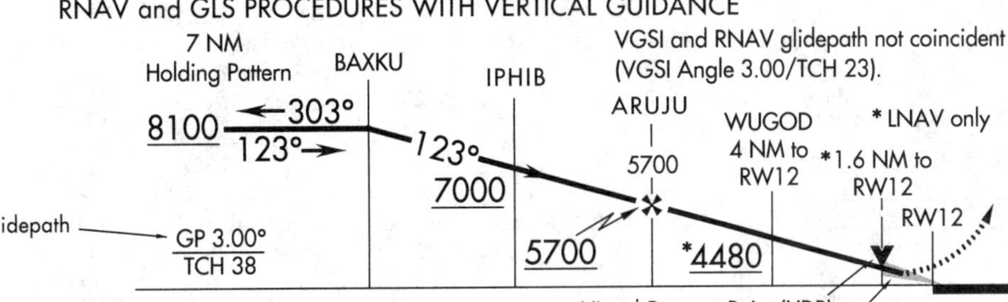

NON-VERTICALLY GUIDED CONVENTIONAL PROCEDURES AND RNAV PROCEDURES WITH MDA ONLY

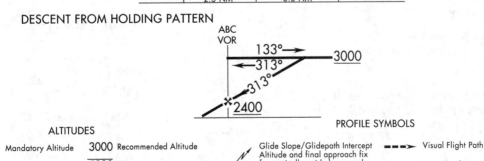

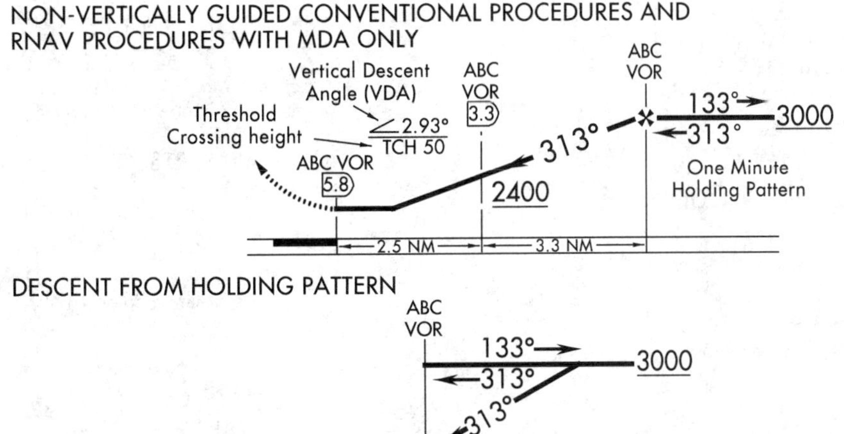

ALTITUDES

5500	Mandatory Altitude	3000	Recommended Altitude
2500	Minimum Altitude	5000 / 3000	Mandatory Block Altitude
4300	Maximum Altitude		

PROFILE SYMBOLS

2400 — Glide Slope/Glidepath Intercept Altitude and final approach fix for vertically guided approach procedures.

▼ — Visual Descent Point (VDP)

— — —➤ Visual Flight Path

Note: Facilities and waypoints are depicted as a solid vertical line while fixes and intersections are depicted as a dashed vertical line.

LEGEND 17229

Legend 35. U.S. Terminal Procedures Profile View.

LEGEND 17229

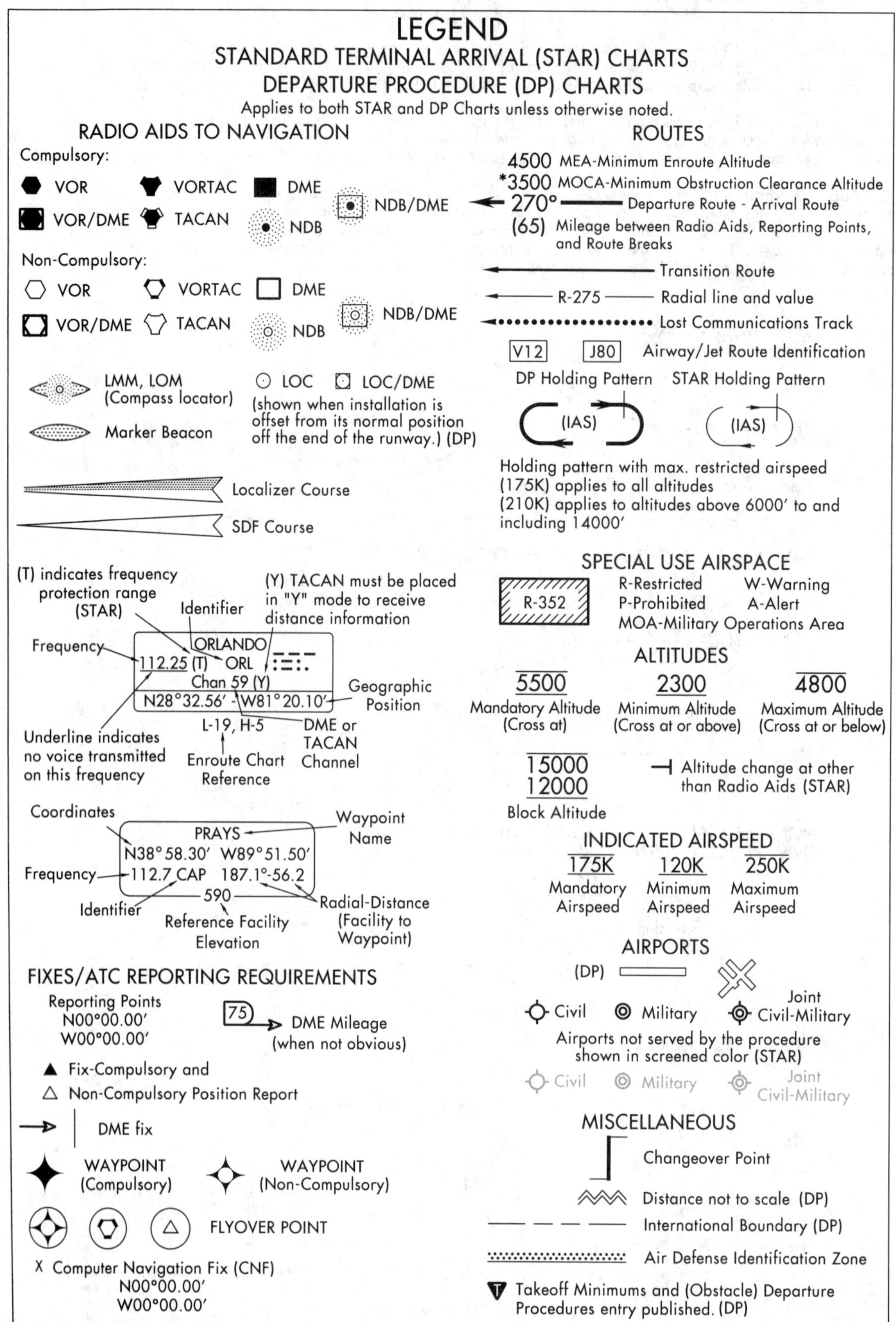

LEGEND 17229

Legend 36. U.S. Terminal Procedures STAR and DP Charts.

LEGEND

INSTRUMENT APPROACH PROCEDURES (CHARTS)

AIRPORT DIAGRAM/AIRPORT SKETCH

Runways

Hard Surface — Other Than Hard Surface — Stopways, Taxiways, Parking Areas, Water Runways — Displaced Threshold

Closed Runway — Closed Pavement — Under Construction — Metal Surface

ARRESTING GEAR: Specific arresting gear systems; e.g., BAK12, MA-1A etc., shown on airport diagrams, not applicable to Civil Pilots. Military Pilots refer to appropriate DOD publications.

uni-directional — bi-directional — Jet Barrier

ARRESTING SYSTEM (EMAS)

REFERENCE FEATURES

Hot Spot ....

Runway Holding Position Markings......................

Buildings..

24-Hour Self-Serve Fuel ##.................................

Tanks..

Obstructions..

Airport Beacon #...

Runway Radar Reflectors..................................

Control Tower #..TWR

When Control Tower and Rotating Beacon are co-located, Beacon symbol will be used and further identified as TWR.

A fuel symbol is shown to indicate 24-hour self-serve fuel available, see appropriate Chart Supplement for information.

Runway length depicted is the physical length of the runway (end-to-end, including displaced thresholds if any) but excluding areas designated as stopways.

A D symbol is shown to indicate runway declared distance information available, see appropriate Chart Supplement for distance information.

Helicopter Alighting Areas

Negative Symbols used to identify Copter Procedures landing point....................

Runway Threshold elevation...........THRE 123

Runway TDZ elevation...................TDZE 123

Runway Slope...............................0.8% UP (0.3% DOWN)

(shown when runway slope is greater than or equal to 0.3%)

NOTE:
Runway Slope measured to midpoint on runways 8000 feet or longer.

U.S. Navy Optical Landing System (OLS) "OLS" location is shown because of its height of approximately 7 feet and proximity to edge of runway may create an obstruction for some types of aircraft.

Approach light symbols are shown in the Flight Information Handbook.

Airport diagram scales are variable.

True/magnetic North orientation may vary from diagram to diagram

Coordinate values are shown in 1 or ½ minute increments. They are further broken down into 6 second ticks, within each 1 minute increments.

Positional accuracy within ±600 feet unless otherwise noted on the chart.

NOTE:
All new and revised airport diagrams are shown referenced to the World Geodetic System (WGS) (noted on appropriate diagram), and may not be compatible with local coordinates published in FLIP. (Foreign Only)

Runway Weight Bearing Capacity/or PCN Pavement Classification Number is shown as a codified expression.
Refer to the appropriate Supplement/Directory for applicable codes e.g., RWY 14-32 PCN 80 F/D/X/U S-75, D-185, 2S-175, 2D-325

SCOPE

Airport diagrams are specifically designed to assist in the movement of ground traffic at locations with complex runway/taxiway configurations. Airport diagrams are not intended to be used for approach and landing or departure operations. For revisions to Airport Diagrams: Consult FAA Order 7910.4.

LEGEND

Legend 37. U.S. Terminal Procedures Airport Diagram/Airport Sketch.

LEGEND 15344

INSTRUMENT APPROACH PROCEDURES (CHARTS)

APPROACH LIGHTING SYSTEM - UNITED STATES

Approach lighting and visual glide slope systems are indicated on the airport sketch by an identifier, e.g., (A2), (V), etc.

A dot " • " portrayed with approach lighting letter identifier indicates sequenced flashing lights (F) installed with the approach lighting system e.g., (A1). Negative symbology, e.g., (A1), (V) indicates Pilot Controlled Lighting (PCL).

RUNWAY TOUCHDOWN ZONE AND CENTERLINE LIGHTING SYSTEMS

TDZ/CL

RUNWAY CENTERLINE LIGHTS

CL

TDZL

TDZL

AVAILABILITY of TDZ/CL will be shown by NOTE in SKETCH e.g. "TDZ/CL Rwy 15"

APPROACH LIGHTING SYSTEM

(A)

ALSF-2

GREEN

500'

1000'

WHITE

RED

RED

2400'/3000'

WHITE

SEQUENCED FLASHING LIGHTS

NOTE: CIVIL ALSF-2 MAY BE OPERATED AS SSALR DURING FAVORABLE WEATHER CONDITIONS

(High Intensity)
LENGTH 2400/3000 FEET

APPROACH LIGHTING SYSTEM

(A1)

ALSF-1

RED

GREEN

1000'

2400'/3000'

WHITE

SEQUENCED FLASHING LIGHTS

(High Intensity)
LENGTH 2400/3000 FEET

SHORT APPROACH LIGHTING SYSTEM

(A2)

SALS/SALSF

(High Intensity)

SAME AS INNER 1500' OF ALSF-1

SIMPLIFIED SHORT APPROACH LIGHTING SYSTEM with Runway Alignment Indicator Lights

(A3)

SSALR

1000'

2400'/3000'

GREEN

WHITE

SEQUENCED FLASHING LIGHTS

(High Intensity)
LENGTH 2400/3000 FEET

MEDIUM INTENSITY (**MALS** and **MALSF**) OR SIMPLIFIED SHORT (**SSALS** and **SSALF**) APPROACH LIGHTING SYSTEMS

(A4)

GREEN

1000'

1400'

400'

WHITE

SEQUENCED FLASHING LIGHTS FOR MALSF/SSALF ONLY

LENGTH 1400 FEET

MEDIUM INTENSITY APPROACH LIGHTING SYSTEM with Runway Alignment Indicator Lights

(A5)

MALSR

SAME LIGHT CONFIGURATION AS SSALR.

OMNIDIRECTIONAL APPROACH LIGHTING SYSTEM

ODALS

36

THRESHOLD

1500'

SEQUENCED FLASHING LIGHTS

LENGTH 1500 FEET

VISUAL APPROACH SLOPE INDICATOR

(V)

VASI

VISUAL APPROACH SLOPE INDICATOR WITH STANDARD THRESHOLD CLEARANCE PROVIDED.

ALL LIGHTS WHITE — TOO HIGH

FAR LIGHTS RED / NEAR LIGHTS WHITE — ON GLIDE SLOPE

ALL LIGHTS RED — TOO LOW

VASI 2

36

THRESHOLD

700'

800'

VASI 4

36

THRESHOLD

VASI 12

36

THRESHOLD

VISUAL APPROACH SLOPE INDICATOR

(V3)

VASI

3-BAR, 6 OR 16 BOX, VISUAL APPROACH SLOPE INDICATOR THAT PROVIDES 2 GLIDE ANGLES AND 2 THRESHOLD CROSSING HEIGHTS.

VASI 6

36

THRESHOLD

VASI 16

36

THRESHOLD

LEGEND 15344

Legend 38. U.S. Terminal Procedures Approach Lighting System.

LEGEND 04330

INSTRUMENT APPROACH PROCEDURES (CHARTS)

APPROACH LIGHTING SYSTEM - UNITED STATES

Approach lighting and visual glide slope systems are indicated on the airport sketch by an identifier, (A2), (V) etc.

A dot " • " portrayed with approach lighting letter identifier indicates sequenced flashing lights (F) installed with the approach lighting system e.g., (A1). Negative symbology, e.g., (A1), (V) indicates Pilot Controlled Lighting (PCL).

(P) PRECISION APPROACH PATH INDICATOR

PAPI

Too low

Slightly low

On correct approach path

Slightly high

Too high

Legend: □ White ■ Red

(V1) "T"-VISUAL APPROACH SLOPE INDICATOR

"T"-VASI

"T" ON BOTH SIDES OF RWY
ALL LIGHTS VARIABLE WHITE.
CORRECT APPROACH SLOPE-ONLY CROSS BAR VISIBLE.
UPRIGHT "T"- FLY UP.
INVERTED "T"- FLY DOWN.
RED "T"- GROSS UNDERSHOOT.

(V2) PULSATING VISUAL APPROACH SLOPE INDICATOR

PVASI

CAUTION: When viewing the pulsating visual approach slope indicators in the pulsating white or pulsating red sectors, it is possible to mistake this lighting aid for another aircraft or a ground vehicle. Pilots should exercise caution when using this type of system.

(V4) TRI-COLOR VISUAL APPROACH SLOPE INDICATOR

TRCV

CAUTION: When the aircraft descends from green to red, the pilot may see a dark amber color during the transition from green to red.

(V5) ALIGNMENT OF ELEMENTS SYSTEMS

APAP

Painted panels which may be lighted at night.
To use the system the pilot positions the aircraft so the elements are in alignment.

LEGEND 04330

Legend 39. U.S. Terminal Procedures Approach Lighting System.

FREQ PAIRING 15008

FREQUENCY PAIRING TABLE

TACAN CHANNEL	VHF FREQUENCY	TACAN CHANNEL	VHF FREQUENCY	TACAN CHANNEL	VHF FREQUENCY
17Y	108.05	40X	110.30	88Y	114.15
18X	108.10	40Y	110.35	89Y	114.25
18Y	108.15	41Y	110.45	90Y	114.35
19Y	108.25	42X	110.50	91Y	114.45
20X	108.30	42Y	110.55	92Y	114.55
20Y	108.35	43Y	110.65	93Y	114.65
21Y	108.45	44X	110.70	94Y	114.75
22X	108.50	44Y	110.75	95Y	114.85
22Y	108.55	45Y	110.85	96Y	114.95
23Y	108.65	46X	110.90	97Y	115.05
24X	108.70	46Y	110.95	98Y	115.15
24Y	108.75	47Y	111.05	99Y	115.25
25Y	108.85	48X	111.10	100Y	115.35
26X	108.90	48Y	111.15	101Y	115.45
26Y	108.95	49Y	111.25	102Y	115.55
27Y	109.05	50X	111.30	103Y	115.65
28X	109.10	50Y	111.35	104Y	115.75
28Y	109.15	51Y	111.45	105Y	115.85
29Y	109.25	52X	111.50	106Y	115.95
30X	109.30	52Y	111.55	107Y	116.05
30Y	109.35	53Y	111.65	108Y	116.15
31Y	109.45	54X	111.70	109Y	116.25
32X	109.50	54Y	111.75	110Y	116.35
32Y	109.55	55Y	111.85	111Y	116.45
33Y	109.65	56X	111.90	112Y	116.55
34X	109.70	56Y	111.95	113Y	116.65
34Y	109.75	80Y	113.35	114Y	116.75
35Y	109.85	81Y	113.45	115Y	116.85
36X	109.90	82Y	113.55	116Y	116.95
36Y	109.95	83Y	113.65	117Y	117.05
37Y	110.05	84Y	113.75	118Y	117.15
38X	110.10	85Y	113.85	119Y	117.25
38Y	110.15	86Y	113.95		
39Y	110.25	87Y	114.05		

FREQ PAIRING 15008

Legend 40. U.S. Terminal Procedures Frequency Pairing.

EXPLANATION OF IFR ENROUTE TERMS

FAA charts are prepared in accordance with specifications of the Interagency Air Committee (IAC), and are approved by representatives of the Federal Aviation Administration and the Department of Defense (DoD). Some information on these charts may only apply to military pilots.

The explanations of symbols used on Instrument Flight Rule (IFR) Enroute Charts and examples in this section are based primarily on the IFR Enroute Low Altitude Charts. Other IFR products use similar symbols in various colors. The chart legends portray aeronautical symbols with a brief description of what each symbol depicts. This section provides more details of the symbols and how they are used on IFR Enroute charts.

AIRPORTS

Active airports are shown on IFR Enroute Charts.

Low Charts:

- All IAP Airports are shown on the Low Altitude Charts (US and Alaska).
- Non-IAP Airports are shown on the U.S. Low Altitude Charts (Contiguous US) have a minimum hard surface runway of 3,000'.
- Non-IAP airports are shown on the U.S. Low Altitude Alaska Charts are show if the runway is 3000' or longer, hard or soft surface.
- Public heliports with an Instrument Approach Procedure (IAP) or requested by the FAA or DoD are depicted on the IFR Enroute Low Altitude Charts.
- Seaplane bases requested by the FAA or DoD are depicted on the IFR Enroute Low Altitude Charts.

On IFR Enroute Low Altitude Charts, airport tabulation is provided which identifies airport names, IDs and the panels they are located on.

High Charts:

- Airports shown on the U.S. High Enroute Charts (Contiguous US) have a minimum hard surface runway of 5000'.
- Airports shown on the U.S. High Enroute Alaska Charts have a minimum hard surface runway of 4000'.

Charted airports are classified according to the following criteria:

Blue - Airports with an Instrument Approach Procedure and/or RADAR MINIMA published in the high altitude DoD Flight Information Publications (FLIPs)

Green - Airports which have an approved Instrument Approach Procedure and/or RADAR MINIMA published in either the U.S. Terminal Procedures Publications (TPPs) or the DoD FLIPs

Brown - Airports without a published Instrument Approach Procedure or RADAR MINIMA

Airports are plotted at their true geographic position.

Airports are identified by the airport name. In the case of military airports, Air Force Base (AFB), Naval Air Station (NAS), Naval Air Facility (NAF), Marine Corps Air Station (MCAS), Army Air Field (AAF), etc., the abbreviated letters appear as part of the airport name.

Legend 41. Explanation of IFR Enroute Terms.

Airports marked "Pvt" immediately following the airport name are not for public use, but otherwise meet the criteria for charting as specified above.

Runway length is the length of the longest active runway (including displaced thresholds but excluding overruns) and is shown to the nearest 100 feet using 70 feet as the division point; e.g., a runway of 8,070' is labeled 81. The following runway compositions (materials) constitute a hard-surfaced runway: asphalt, bitumen, chip seal, concrete, and tar macadam. Runways that are not hard-surfaced have a small letter "s" following the runway length, indicating a soft surface.

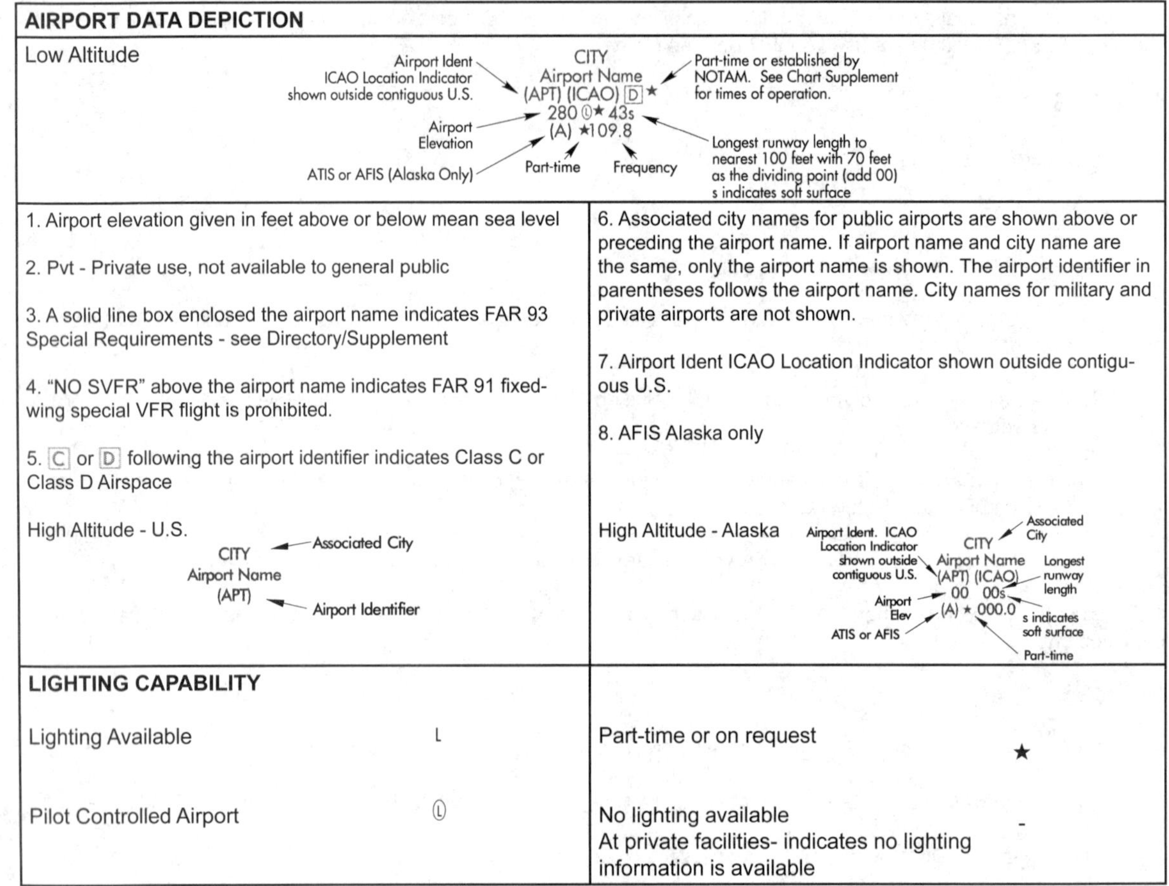

AIRPORT DATA DEPICTION

Low Altitude

1. Airport elevation given in feet above or below mean sea level 2. Pvt - Private use, not available to general public 3. A solid line box enclosed the airport name indicates FAR 93 Special Requirements - see Directory/Supplement 4. "NO SVFR" above the airport name indicates FAR 91 fixed-wing special VFR flight is prohibited. 5. C or D following the airport identifier indicates Class C or Class D Airspace	6. Associated city names for public airports are shown above or preceding the airport name. If airport name and city name are the same, only the airport name is shown. The airport identifier in parentheses follows the airport name. City names for military and private airports are not shown. 7. Airport Ident ICAO Location Indicator shown outside contiguous U.S. 8. AFIS Alaska only
High Altitude - U.S.	High Altitude - Alaska

LIGHTING CAPABILITY			
Lighting Available	L	Part-time or on request	★
Pilot Controlled Airport	Ⓛ	No lighting available At private facilities- indicates no lighting information is available	-

A L symbol between the airport elevation and runway length means that runway lights are in operation sunset to sunrise. A Ⓛ symbol indicates there is Pilot Controlled Lighting. A L★ symbol means the lighting is part-time or on request, the pilot should consult the Chart Supplement for light operating procedures. The Aeronautical Information Manual (AIM) thoroughly explains the types and uses of airport lighting aids.

RADIO AIDS TO NAVIGATION

All IFR radio NAVAIDs that have been flight checked and are operational are shown on all IFR Enroute Charts. Very High Frequency/Ultrahigh Frequency (VHF/UHF) NAVAIDs, Very high frequency Omnidirectional Radio range (VORs), Tactical Air Navigation (TACANs) are shown in black, and Low Frequency/Medium Frequency (LF/MF) NAVAIDs, (Compass Locators and Aeronautical or Marine NDBs) are shown in brown.

On IFR Enroute Charts, information about NAVAIDs is boxed as illustrated below. To avoid duplication of data, when two or more NAVAIDs in a general area have the same name, the name is usually printed only once inside an identification box with the frequencies, TACAN channel numbers, identification letters, or Morse Code Identifications of the different NAVAIDs are shown in appropriate colors.

Legend 42. Explanation of IFR Enroute Terms.

NAVAIDs in a shutdown status have the frequency and channel number crosshatched. Use of the NAVAID status "shutdown" is only used when a facility has been decommissioned but cannot be published as such because of pending airspace actions.

NAVIGATION AND COMMUNICATION BOXES - COMMON ELEMENTS	
LOW ENROUTE CHARTS *RCO Frequencies* *NAVAID Name* *FREQ, Ident, CH, Morse Code* *Latitude, Longitude* *Controlling FSS Name* 000.0 NAME 000.0 IDT 000 N00°00.00' W000°00.00' NAME	**HIGH ENROUTE CHARTS** *RCO Frequencies* *NAVAID Name* *Frequency, Ident, Channel,* *Latitude, Longitude* *Controlling FSS Name* 000.0 NAME 000.0 IDT 000 N00°00.00' W000°00.00' NAME
COMMON ELEMENTS (HIGH AND LOW CHARTS)	
RCO FREQUENCY *Single Frequency* *Multiple Frequencies* *Frequencies transmit and receive except those followed by R and T:* *R - Receive Only* *T - Transmit Only*	122.6 255.4 243.0 123.6 122.65 122.2 122.1R 121.5
NAVAID BOX *Thin line NAVAID boxes without frequency(s) and FSS radio name indicates no FSS frequencies available.* *Shadow NAVAID box indicates NAVAID and Flight Service Station (FSS) have same name.*	VHF/UHF LF/MF
FREQUENCY PROTECTION *Frequency Protection usable range at 18,000' AGL - 40 NM* *Frequency Protection usable range at 12,000' AGL - 25 NM*	(L) (T)
DISTANCE MEASURING EQUIPMENT *Facilities that operate in the "Y" mode for DME reception*	(Y)
VOICE COMMUNICATIONS VIA NAVAID *Voice Transmitted* *No Voice Transmitted*	112.6 111.0
NAVAID SHUTDOWN STATUS	**VHF/UHF** **LF/MF**
PART TIME OR ON-REQUEST	**VHF/UHF** ★ **LF/MF** ★
AUTOMATED WEATHER BROADCAST SERVICES **ASOS/AWOS** - *Automated Surface Observing Station/Automated Weather Observing Station* **HIWAS** - *Hazardous Inflight Weather Advisory Service* **TWEB** - *Transcribed Weather Broadcast*	VHF/UHF LF/MF Ⓐ Ⓐ Ⓗ Ⓗ Ⓣ Ⓣ *Automated weather, when available, is broadcast on the associated NAVAID frequency.*
LATITUDE AND LONGTITUDE *Latitude and Longitude coordinates are provided for those NAVAIDs that make up part of a route/airway or a holding pattern.*	**LOW ENROUTE** N00°00.00' W000°00.00' **HIGH ENROUTE** N00°00.00' W000°00.00'

Legend 43. Explanation of IFR Enroute Terms.

AIRSPACE INFORMATION

CONTROLLED AIRSPACE

Controlled airspace consists of those areas where some or all aircraft are subjected to air traffic control within the following airspace classifications of A, B, C, D, & E.

Air Route Traffic Control Centers (ARTCC) are established to provide Air Traffic Control to aircraft operating on IFR flight plans within controlled airspace, particularly during the enroute phase of flight. Boundaries of the ARTCCs are shown in their entirety using the symbol below.

NEW YORK / WASHINGTON — Air Route Traffic Control Center (ARTCC)

The responsible ARTCC Center names are shown adjacent and parallel to the boundary line. ARTCC sector frequencies are shown in boxes outlined by the same symbol.

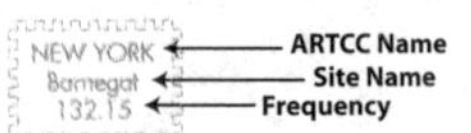

ARTCC Remoted Sites with discrete VHF and UHF frequencies

Class A Airspace is depicted as open area (white) on the IFR Enroute High Altitude Charts. It consists of airspace from 18,000 Mean Sea Level (MSL) to 60,000 MSL. In aviation terms those altitudes are written as FL 180 to FL 600, (18,000 MSL, is Flight Level (FL)180, 60,000 MSL, is FL 600).

Class B Airspace is depicted as screened blue area with a solid line encompassing the area.

Class C Airspace is depicted as screened blue area with a dashed line encompassing the area with a following the airport name.

Class B and Class C Airspace consist of controlled airspace extending upward from the surface or a designated floor to specified altitudes, within which all aircraft and pilots are subject to the operating rules and requirements specified in the Federal Aviation Regulations (UHF) 71. Class B and C Airspace are shown in abbreviated forms on IFR Enroute Low Altitude Charts. A general note adjacent to Class B airspace refers the user to the appropriate VFR Terminal Area Chart.

Class D Airspace (airports with an operating control tower) are depicted as open area (white) with a following the airport name.

Class E Airspace is depicted as open area (white) on the IFR Enroute Low Altitude Charts. It consists of airspace below FL180.

UNCONTROLLED AIRSPACE

Class G Airspace within the United States extends to 14,500' MSL. This uncontrolled airspace is shown as screened brown.

On Area Charts any uncontrolled airspace boundaries are depicted with a .012" brown line and a .060" screen brown band on the uncontrolled side, so as to be seen over the terrain.

Legend 44. Explanation of IFR Enroute Terms – Airspace Information.

SPECIAL USE AIRSPACE

Special Use Airspace (SUA) confines certain flight activities, restricts entry, or cautions other aircraft operating within specific boundaries. SUA areas are shown in their entirety, even when they overlap, adjoin, or when an area is designated within another area. SUA with altitudes from the surface and above are shown on the IFR Enroute Low Altitude Charts. Similarly, SUA that extends above 18,000' MSL are shown on IFR Enroute High Altitude Charts. On IFR Enroute Altitude Charts tabulations, identify the type of SUA, ID, effective altitudes, times of use, controlling agency and the panel it is located on.

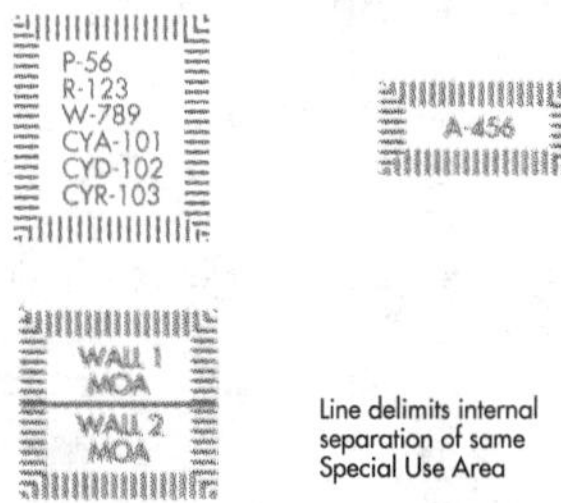

High and Low	Low Altitude Only	Canada Only	Caribbean Only
P - Prohibited Area	MOA - Military Operations Area	CYA - Advisory	D - Danger
R - Restricted Area	A - Alert Area	CYD - Danger Area	
W - Warning Area		CYR - Restricted Area	
See Airspace Tabulation on chart for complete information.			

OTHER AIRSPACE

FAR 91 Special Air Traffic Rules are shown with the type NO SVFR above the airport name.

FAR 93 Special Airspace Traffic Rules are shown with a solid line box around the airport name, indicating FAR 93 Special Requirements see Chart Supplement.

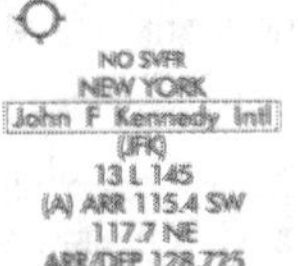

Mode C Required Airspace (from the surface to 10,000' MSL) within 30 NM radius of the primary airport(s) for which a Class B airspace is designated, is depicted on IFR Enroute Low Altitude Charts as a blue circle labeled MODE C 30 NM.

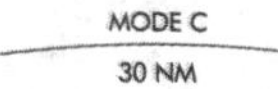

Mode C is also required for operations within and above all Class C airspace up to 10,000' MSL, but not depicted. See FAR 91.215 and the AIM.

Legend 45. Explanation of IFR Enroute Terms – Special Use Airspace.

INSTRUMENT AIRWAYS

The FAA has established two fixed route systems for air navigation. The VOR and LF/MF system-designated from 1,200' Above Ground Level (AGL) to but not including FL 180 is shown on IFR Enroute Low Altitude Charts, and the Jet Route system designated from FL 180 to FL 450 inclusive is shown on IFR Enroute High Altitude Charts.

VOR LF/MF AIRWAY SYSTEM (IFR LOW ALTITUDE ENROUTE CHARTS)

In this system VOR airways - airways based on VOR or VORTAC NAVAIDs - are depicted in black and identified by a "V" (Victor) followed by the route number (e.g., "V12").

LF/MF airways - airways based on LF/MF NAVAIDs - are sometimes called "colored airways" because they are identified by color name and number (e.g., "Amber One", charted as "A1"). In Alaska Green and Red airways are plotted east and west, and Amber and Blue airways are plotted north and south. Regardless of their color identifier, LF/MF airways are shown in brown.

AIRWAY/ROUTE DATA

On both series of IFR Enroute Charts, airway/route data such as the airway identifications, magnetic courses bearings or radials, mileages, and altitudes (e.g., Minimum Enroute Altitudes (MEAs), Minimum Reception Altitudes (MRAs), Maximum Authorized Altitudes (MAAs), Minimum Obstacle Clearance Altitudes (MOCAs), Minimum Turning Altitudes (MTAs) and Minimum Crossing Altitudes (MCAs)) are shown aligned with the airway.

As a rule the airway/route data is charted and in the same color as the airway, with one exception. Charted in blue, Global Navigation Satellite System (GNSS) MEAs, identified with a "G" suffix, have been added to "V" and "colored airways" for aircraft flying those airways using Global Positioning System (GPS) navigation.

Airways/Routes predicated on VOR or VORTAC NAVAIDs are defined by the outbound radial from the NAVAID. Airways/Routes predicated on LF/MF NAVAIDs are defined by the inbound bearing.

- **Minimum Enroute Altitude (MEA)** - The MEA is the lowest published altitude between radio fixes that assures acceptable navigational signal coverage and meets obstacle clearance requirements between those fixes. The MEA prescribed for a Federal airway or segment, RNAV low or high route, or other direct route applies to the entire width of the airway, segment, or route between the radio fixes defining the airway, segment, or route. MEAs for routes wholly contained within controlled airspace normally provide a buffer above the floor of controlled airspace consisting of at least 300 feet within transition areas and 500 feet within control areas. MEAs are established based upon obstacle clearance over terrain and manmade objects, adequacy of navigation facility performance, and communications requirements.

- **Minimum Reception Altitude (MRA)** - MRAs are determined by FAA flight inspection traversing an entire route of flight to establish the minimum altitude the navigation signal can be received for the route and for off-course NAVAID facilities that determine a fix. When the MRA at the fix is higher than the MEA, an MRA is established for the fix and is the lowest altitude at which an intersection can be determined.

- **Maximum Authorized Altitude (MAA)** - An MAA is a published altitude representing the maximum usable altitude or flight level for an airspace structure or route segment. It is the highest altitude on a Federal airway, jet route, RNAV low or high route, or other direct route for which an MEA is designated at which adequate reception of navigation signals is assured.

- **Minimum Obstruction Clearance Altitude (MOCA)** - The MOCA is the lowest published altitude in effect between fixes on VOR airways, off-airway routes, or route segments that meets obstacle clearance requirements for a VOR. The MOCA seen on the enroute chart may have been computed by adding the required obstacle clearance (ROC) to the controlling obstacle in the primary area or computed by using a TERPS chart if the controlling obstacle is located in the secondary area. This figure is then rounded to the nearest 100 foot increment (i.e., 2,049 feet becomes 2,000, and 2,050 feet becomes 2,100 feet). An extra 1,000 feet is added in mountainous areas, in most cases.

- **Minimum Turning Altitude (MTA)** - Minimum turning altitude (MTA) is a charted altitude providing vertical and lateral obstruction clearance based on turn criteria over certain fixes, NAVAIDs, waypoints, and on charted route segments. When a VHF airway or route terminates at a NAVAID or fix, the primary area extends beyond that

Legend 46. Explanation of IFR Enroute Terms – Instrument Airways.

termination point. When a change of course on VHF airways and routes is necessary, the enroute obstacle clearance turning area extends the primary and secondary obstacle clearance areas to accommodate the turn radius of the aircraft. Since turns at or after fix passage may exceed airway and route boundaries, pilots are expected to adhere to airway and route protected airspace by leading turns early before a fix. The turn area provides obstacle clearance for both turn anticipation (turning prior to the fix) and flyover protection (turning after crossing the fix). Turning fixes requiring a higher MTA are charted with a flag along with accompanying text describing the MTA restriction.

- **Minimum Crossing Altitude (MCA)** - An MCA is the lowest altitude at certain fixes at which the aircraft must cross when proceeding in the direction of a higher minimum enroute IFR altitude. MCAs are established in all cases where obstacles intervene to prevent pilots from maintaining obstacle clearance during a normal climb to a higher MEA after passing a point beyond which the higher MEA applies. The same protected enroute area vertical obstacle clearance requirements for the primary and secondary areas are considered in the determination of the MCA.

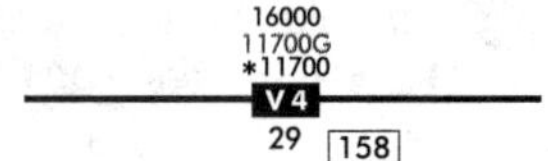

Victor Route (with RNAV/GPS MEA shown in blue)

AREA NAVIGATION (RNAV) "T" ROUTE SYSTEM

The FAA has created new low altitude area navigation (RNAV) "T" routes for the enroute and terminal environments. The RNAV routes will provide more direct routing for IFR aircraft and enhance the safety and efficiency of the National Airspace System. To utilize these routes aircraft are required to be equipped with IFR approved GNSS. In Alaska, TSO-145a and 146a equipment is required.

Low altitude RNAV only routes are identified by the prefix "T", and the prefix "TK" for RNAV helicopter routes followed by a three digit number (T-200 to T-500). Routes are depicted in blue on the IFR Enroute Low Altitude Charts. RNAV route data (route line, identification boxes, mileages, waypoints, waypoint names, magnetic reference courses and MEAs) will also be printed in blue. Magnetic reference courses will be shown originating from a waypoint, fix/reporting point or NAVAID. GNSS MEA for each segment is established to ensure obstacle clearance and communications reception. GNSS MEAs are identified with a "G" suffix.

REVUD
4000G
*3200
257
T616
077
16
077
13
258
VITOV
AGDUT

1800G
*1500
057
TK504
237
14
CIDOB
RUSEY

Joint Victor/RNAV routes are charted as outlined above except as noted. The joint Victor route and the RNAV route identification boxes are shown adjacent to each other. Magnetic reference courses are not shown. MEAs are charted above the appropriate identification box or stacked in pairs, GNSS and Victor. On joint routes, RNAV specific information will be printed in blue.

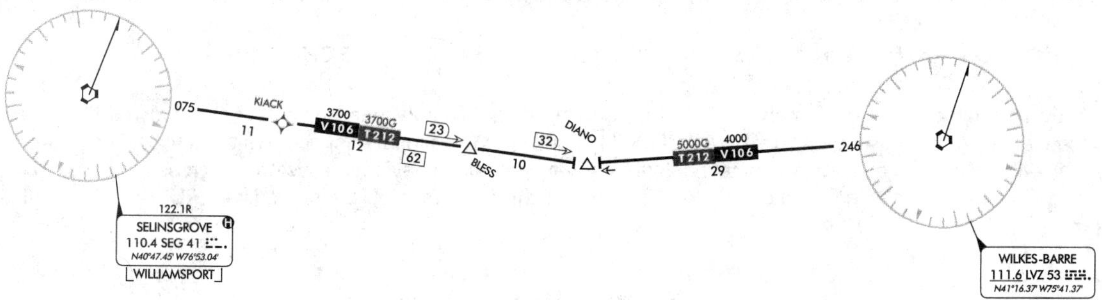

Legend 47. Explanation of IFR Enroute Terms – Instrument Airways.

OFF ROUTE OBSTRUCTION CLEARANCE ALTITUDE (OROCA)

The Off Route Obstruction Clearance Altitude (OROCA) is depicted on IFR Enroute Low Altitude and Pacific charts and is represented in thousands and hundreds of feet above MSL. OROCAs are shown in every 30 x 30 minute quadrant on Area Charts, every one degree by one degree quadrant for IFR Enroute Low Altitude Charts - U.S. and every two degree by two degree quadrant on IFR Enroute Low Altitude Charts - Alaska. The OROCA represents the highest possible obstruction elevation including both terrain and other vertical obstruction data (towers, trees, etc.) bounded by the ticked lines of latitude/longitude including data 4 NM outside the quadrant. In this example the OROCA represents 12,500 feet.

OROCA is computed just as the Maximum Elevation Figure (MEF) found on Visual Flight Rule (VFR) Charts except that it provides an additional vertical buffer of 1,000 feet in designated non-mountainous areas and a 2,000 foot vertical buffer in designated mountainous areas within the United States. For areas in Mexico and the Caribbean, located outside the U.S. Air Defense Identification Zone (ADIZ), the OROCA provides obstruction clearance with a 3,000 foot vertical buffer. Evaluating the area around the quadrant provides the chart user the same lateral clearance an airway provides should the line of intended flight follow a ticked line of latitude or longitude. OROCA does not provide for NAVAID signal coverage, communication coverage and would not be consistent with altitudes assigned by Air Traffic Control. OROCAs can be found over all land masses and open water areas containing man-made obstructions (such as oil rigs).

12 5

MILITARY TRAINING ROUTES (MTRs)

Military Training Routes (MTRs) are routes established for the conduct of low-altitude, high-speed military flight training (generally below 10,000 feet MSL at airspeeds in excess of 250 knots Indicated Air Speed). These routes are depicted in brown on IFR Enroute Low Altitude Charts, and are not shown on inset charts or on IFR Enroute High Altitude Charts. IFR Enroute Low Altitude Charts depict all IFR Military Training Routes (IRs) and VFR Military Training Routes (VRs), except those VRs that are entirely at or below 1,500 feet AGL.

MTRs are identified by designators (IR-107, VR-134) which are shown in brown on the route centerline. Arrows are shown to indicate the direction of flight along the route. The width of the route determines the width of the line that is plotted on the chart:

Route segments with a width of 5 NM or less, both sides of the centerline, are shown by a .02" line.

IR-000

Route segments with a width greater than 5 NM, either or both sides of the centerline, are shown by a .035" line.

VR-000

MTRs for particular chart pairs (ex. L1/2, etc.) are alphabetically, then numerically tabulated. The tabulation includes MTR type and unique identification and altitude range.

JET ROUTE SYSTEM (HIGH ALTITUDE ENROUTE CHARTS)

Jet routes are based on VOR or VORTAC NAVAIDs, and are depicted in black with a "J" identifier followed by the route number (e.g., "J12"). In Alaska, Russia and Canada some segments of jet routes are based on LF/MF NAVAIDs.

AREA NAVIGATION (RNAV) "Q" ROUTE SYSTEM (IFR Enroute HIGH ALTITUDE CHARTS)

The FAA has adopted certain amendments to Title 14, Code of Federal Regulations which paved the way for the development of new area high altitude navigation (RNAV) "Q" routes in the U.S. National Airspace System (NAS). These amendments enable the FAA to take advantage of technological advancements in navigation systems such as the GPS. RNAV "Q" Route MEAs are shown when other than FL 180 MEAs for DME/DME/Inertial Reference Unit (IRU) RNAV aircraft have a "D" suffix.

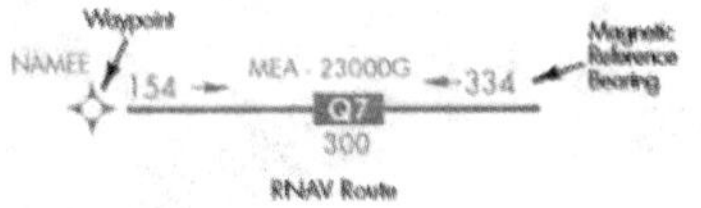

Waypoint
NAMEE
154
MEA - 23000G
334
Magnetic Reference Bearing
Q7
300
RNAV Route

RNAV routes and associated data are charted in blue.

Legend 48. Explanation of IFR Enroute Terms – Instrument Airways.

"Q" Routes on the IFR Gulf of Mexico charts are shown in black. Magnetic reference courses are shown originating from a waypoint, fix/reporting point, or NAVAID.

Joint Jet/RNAV route identification boxes will be located adjacent to each other with the route charted in black. With the exception of Q-Routes in the Gulf of Mexico, GNSS or DME/DME/IRU RNAV are required, unless otherwise indicated. DME/DME/IRU RNAV aircraft should refer to the Chart Supplement for DME information. Q-Routes in Alaska are GNSS Only. Altitude values are stacked highest to lowest.

TERRAIN CONTOURS ON AREA CHARTS

Based on a recommendation of the National Transportation Safety Board, terrain contours have been added to the Enroute Area Charts and are intended to increase pilots' situational awareness for safe flight over changes in terrain. The following Area Charts portray terrain: Anchorage, Denver, Fairbanks, Juneau, Los Angeles, Nome, Phoenix, San Francisco, Vancouver and Washington.

When terrain rises at least a 1,000 feet above the primary airports' elevation, terrain is charted using shades of brown with brown contour lines and values. The initial contour will be 1,000 or 2,000 feet above the airports' elevation. Subsequent intervals will be 2,000 or 3,000 foot increments.

Contours are supplemented with a representative number of spots elevations and are shown in solid black. The highest elevation on an Area Chart is shown with a larger spot and text.

The following boxed note is added to the affected Area Charts.

NOTE: TERRAIN CONTOURS HAVE BEEN ADDED TO THOSE AREA CHARTS WHERE THE TERRAIN ON THE CHART IS 1000 FOOT OR GREATER THAN THE ELEVATION OF THE PRIMARY AIRPORT

Legend 49. Explanation of IFR Enroute Terms – Instrument Airways.

IFR ENROUTE LOW / HIGH ALTITUDE SYMBOLS (U.S., PACIFIC AND ALASKA CHARTS)

AIRPORTS

Airport Data - Low/High Altitude

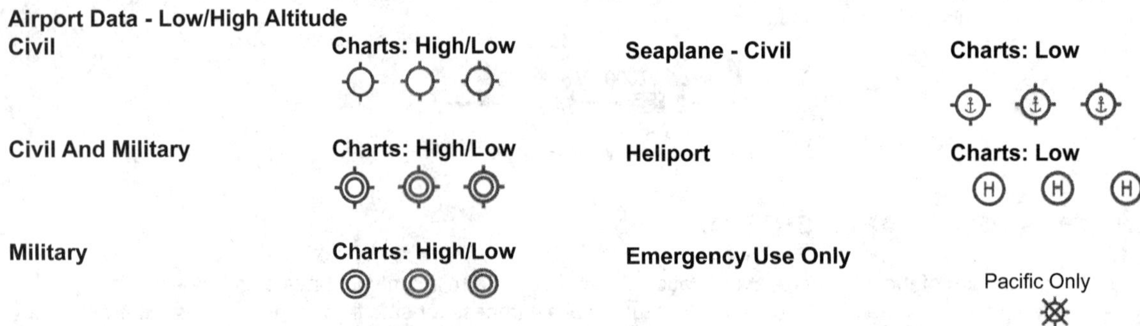

Facilities in BLUE or GREEN have an approved Instrument Approach Procedure and/or RADAR MINIMA published in either the FAA Terminal Procedures Publication or the DoD FLIPs. Those in BLUE have an Instrument Approach Procedure and/or RADAR MINIMA published at least in the High Altitude DoD FLIPs. Facilities in BROWN do not have a published Instrument Procedure or RADAR MINIMA.

All IAP Airports are shown on the Low Altitude Charts.

Non-IAP Airports shown on the U.S. Low Altitude Charts have a minimum hard surface runway of 3000'.

Airports shown on the U.S. High Altitude Charts have a minimum hard surface runway of 5000'.

Airports shown on the Alask High Altitude Charts have a minimum hard or soft surface runway of 4000'.

Associated city names for public airports are shown above or preceding the airport name and city name are the same only the airport name is shown. City names for military and private airports are not shown.

The airport identifier in parentheses follows the airport name or Pvt.

Pvt - Private Use

AIRPORT DATA DEPICTION

Low Altitude

Airport Ident ICAO Location Indicator shown outside contiguous U.S.
CITY
Airport Name
(APT) (ICAO) D ★
280 Ⓛ★ 43s
(A) ★109.8
Part-time or established by NOTAM. See Chart Supplement for times of operation.
Airport Elevation
ATIS or AFIS (Alaska Only)
Part-time
Frequency
Longest runway length to nearest 100 feet with 70 feet as the dividing point (add 00) s indicates soft surface

1. Airport elevation given in feet above or below mean sea level

2. Pvt - Private use, not available to general public

3. A solid line box enclosed the airport name indicates FAR 93 Special Requirements - see Directory/Supplement

4. "NO SVFR" above the airport name indicates FAR 91 fixed-wing special VFR flight is prohibited.

5. C or D following the airport identifier indicates Class C or Class D Airspace

High Altitude - U.S.

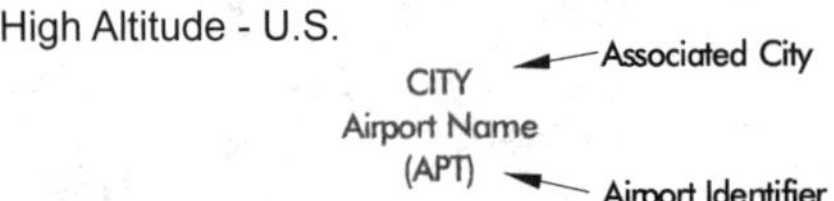

6. Associated city names for public airports are shown above or preceding the airport name. If airport name and city name are the same, only the airport name is shown. The airport identifier in parentheses follows the airport name. City names for military and private airports are not shown.

7. Airport Ident ICAO Location Indicator shown outside contiguous U.S.

8. AFIS Alaska only

High Altitude - Alaska

Associated City
Airport Ident. ICAO Location Indicator shown outside contiguous U.S.
CITY
Airport Name
(APT) (ICAO)
00 00s
(A) ★ 000.0
Longest runway length
Airport Elev
ATIS or AFIS
s indicates soft surface
Part-time

Legend 50. IFR Enroute Low/High Altitude Symbols.

Airports (Continued)

LIGHTING CAPABILITY

Lighting Available	L	Part-time or on request	★
Pilot Controlled Airport	Ⓛ	No lighting available At private facilities- indicates no lighting information is available	-

RADIO AIDS TO NAVIGATION

NAVAIDS

VOR	VOR/DME	TACAN	DME	NDB	NDB/DME	Reporting Function
						Non Compulsory Reporting or Off Airway
						Compulsory Reporting

Note: VHF/UHF is depicted in Black. LF/MF is depicted in Brown. RNAV is depicted in Blue

Compass Roses

VHF/UHF

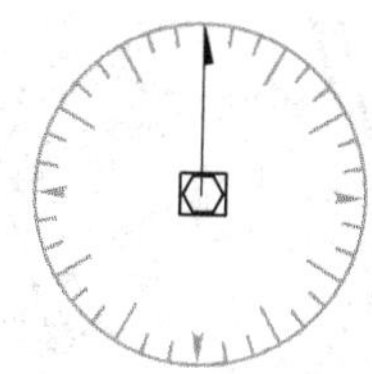

LF/MF

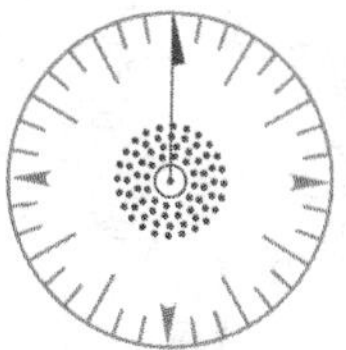

Compass Roses are orientated to Magnetic North of the NAVAID which may not be adjusted to the charted isogonic values.

Compass Locator Beacon

LOW ALTITUDE

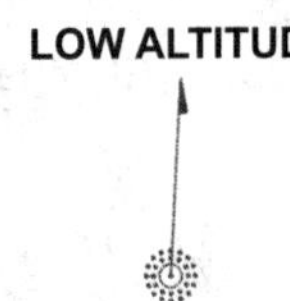

Chart Example : Enroute Low L-16 US

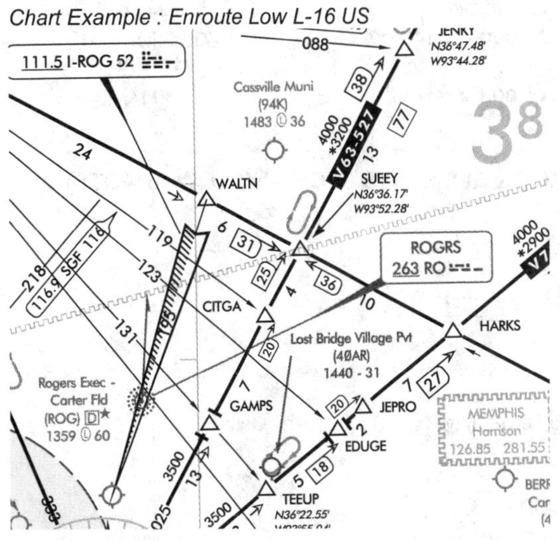

Legend 51. IFR Enroute Low/High Altitude Symbols.

RADIO AIDS TO NAVIGATION (Continued)

ILS LOCALIZER

LOW ALTITUDE

ILS Localizer Course with additional navigation function

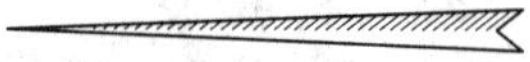

ILS Localizer Back Course with additional navigation function

BACK COURSE

ILS Localizer Example with Back Course (Chart: Enroute Low L-1 US)

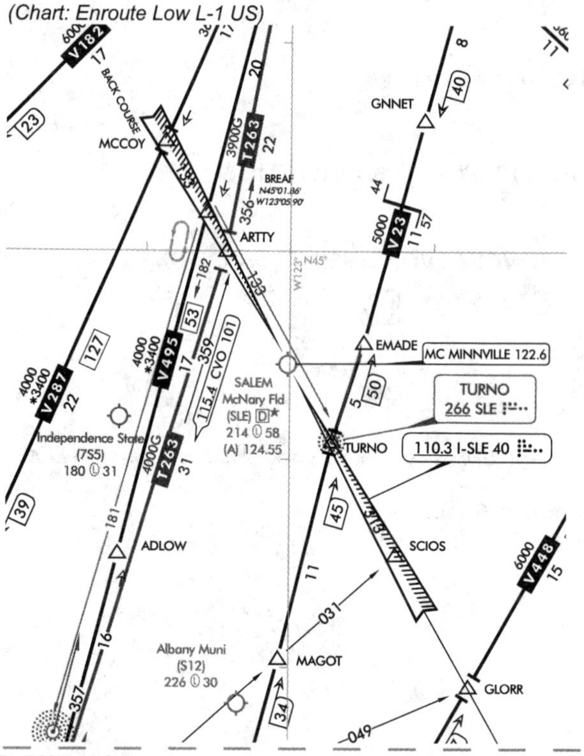

VOR/DME RNAV WAYPOINT DATA

HIGH ALTITUDE - ALASKA

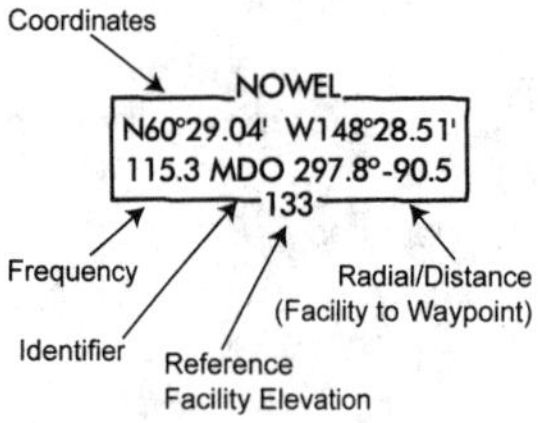

Coordinates

NOWEL
N60°29.04' W148°28.51'
115.3 MDO 297.8°-90.5
133

Frequency
Identifier
Reference Facility Elevation
Radial/Distance (Facility to Waypoint)

NAVIGATION AND COMMUNICATION BOXES - COMMON ELEMENTS

LOW ENROUTE CHARTS

RCO Frequencies
NAVAID Name
FREQ, Ident, CH, Morse Code
Latitude, Longitude
Controlling FSS Name

000.0
NAME
000.0 IDT 000
N00°00.00' W000°00.00'
NAME

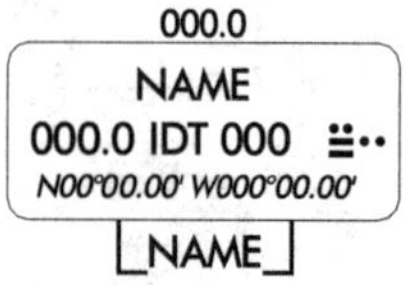

HIGH ENROUTE CHARTS

RCO Frequencies
NAVAID Name
Frequency, Ident, Channel,
Latitude, Longitude

Controlling FSS Name

000.0
NAME
000.0 IDT 000
N00°00.00'
W000°00.00'
NAME

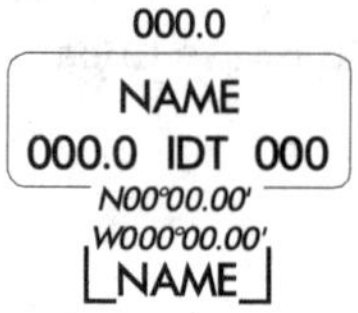

COMMON ELEMENTS (HIGH AND LOW CHARTS)

RCO Frequency

Single Frequency

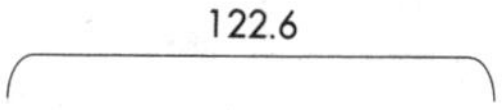

122.6

Multiple Frequencies
Frequencies transmit and receive except those followed by R and T:
R - Receive Only T - Transmit Only

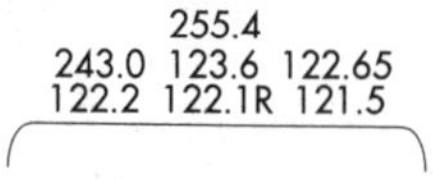

255.4
243.0 123.6 122.65
122.2 122.1R 121.5

NAVAID Box

VHF/UHF LF/MF

Thin line NAVAID boxes without frequency(s) and FSS radio name indicates no FSS frequencies available.

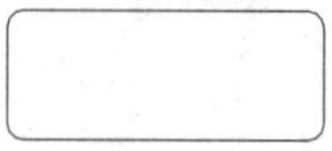

Shadow NAVAID box indicates NAVAID and Flight Service Station (FSS) have same name.

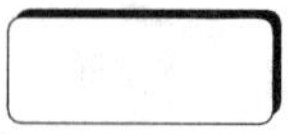

Legend 52. IFR Enroute Low/High Altitude Symbols.

RADIO AIDS TO NAVIGATION (Continued)

Navigation and Communication Boxes - Common Elements

Frequency Protection

Frequency Protection usable range at 18,000' AGL - 40 NM	(L)
Frequency Protection usable range at 12,000' AGL - 25 NM	(T)

DISTANCE MEASURING EQUIPMENT

Facilities that operate in the "Y" mode for DME reception	(Y)

VOICE COMMUNICATIONS VIA NAVAID

Voice Transmitted	112.6
No Voice Transmitted	111.0 (underlined)

NAVAID SHUTDOWN STATUS

VHF/UHF LF/MF

PART TIME OR ON-REQUEST

VHF/UHF ★ LF/MF ★

AUTOMATED WEATHER BROADCAST SERVICES

	VHF/UHF	LF/MF
ASOS/AWOS - Automated Surface Observing Station/Automated Weather Observing Station	Ⓐ	Ⓐ
HIWAS - Hazardous Inflight Weather Advisory Service	Ⓗ	Ⓗ
TWEB - Transcribed Weather Broadcast	Ⓣ	Ⓣ

LATITUDE AND LONGTITUDE

Latitude and Longtitude coordinates are provided for those NAVAIDs that make up part of a route/airway or a holding pattern.

LOW ENROUTE
N00°00.00' W000°00.00'

HIGH ENROUTE
N00°00.00'
W000°00.00'

Navigation and Communication Boxes - Examples

LOW ENROUTE CHARTS

VOR

R - Receive only 122.1R

Controlling FSS Name - ANDERSON

122.1R
ALLENDALE
116.7 ALD
N33°00.75' W81°17.53'
ANDERSON

(T) - Service Volume

POLK (T)
108.4 FXU

Receive & Transmit on 122.35
(T) - Service Volume
Latitude and Longitude
Controlling FSS Name - MACON

122.35
TIFT MYERS (T)
112.5 IFM
N31°25.72' W83°29.33'
MACON

HIGH ENROUTE CHARTS

VOR

CECIL
117.9 VQQ
N30°12.78'
W81°53.45'

Legend 53. IFR Enroute Low/High Altitude Symbols.

RADIO AIDS TO NAVIGATION (Continued)

Navigation And Communication Boxes - Examples (Continued)

LOW ENROUTE CHARTS

VOR/DME

No Voice Communications
(Y) Mode DME

SAWMILL
113.75 SWB 84(Y)

R - Receive only 122.1R
Controlling FSS Name - BUFFALO

122.1R
ROCKDALE
112.6 RKA 73
N42°27.98' W75°14.36'
BUFFALO

Shadow NAVAID Box
FSS Associated with NAVAID

119.1
MIRABEL
116.7 YMX 114
N45°53.30' W74°22.54'

TACAN

TACAN Channels are without voice but not underlined

SANTA ROSA
63 NGS (133.6)
N30°36.91' W86°56.24'

Part Time NAVAID

PENSACOLA
★119 NPA (117.2)
N30°21.48' W87°18.99'

VORTAC

H - HIWAS Available

255.4 243.0 122.55 121.5
ALEXANDRIA
116.1 AEX 108
N31°15.40' W92°30.06'
DE RIDDER

Shutdown status

BRUNSWICK
NHZ
N43°52.41' W69°55.31'

DME

DME Channel, Ident, Morse Code, VHF Frequency

MOULTRIE
25 MGR (108.8)
N31°04.94' W83°48.25'

NDB

A - ASOS/AWOS Available

SILVER BAY
350 BFW

Shutdown status

SHEMYA
SYA
N52°43.32' E174°03.62'

NDB/DME

No Voice Communications
(Y) Mode DME

122.3
CAPE LISBURNE
385 LUR 20(Y) (108.35)
N68°52.28' W166°04.58'
KOTZEBUE

T- TWEB Available
Shadow NAVAID Box
FSS Associated with NAVAID

123.6
ILIAMNA
411 ILI 91 (114.4)
N59°44.88' W154°54.58'

Notes:

HIGH ENROUTE CHARTS

VOR/DME

Off Route (Greyed NAVAID Box and NAVAID)

ITHACA
111.8 ITH (L) 55

Service Volume - L
DME in Y Mode

ELMIRA
109.65 ULW (L) 33(Y)
N42°05.65'
W77°01.49'

Shadow NAVAID Box
FSS Associated with NAVAID

119.1
MIRABEL
116.7 YMX 114
N45°53.30'
W74°22.54'

TACAN

Off Route

TYNDALL
64 PAM (133.7)
N30°04.44'
W85°34.34'

Off Route - Part Time NAVAID
(Greyed NAVAID Box and NAVAID)
Service Volume - L

PENSACOLA
119 NPA (L) (117.2)
N30°21.48'
W87°18.99'

VORTAC

H - HIWAS Available

122.55
ALEXANDRIA
116.1 AEX 108
N31°15.40'
W92°30.06'
DE RIDDER

Off Route (Greyed NAVAID Box and NAVAID)
Service Volume - L

HANDLE
114.3 HLL (L) 90

DME

NDB

T - TWEB Available

FORT DAVIS
529 FDV
N64°29.68'
W165°18.91'

NDB/DME

No Voice Communications
(Y) Mode DME

CAPE NEWENHAM
385 EHM 18(Y) (108.15)
N58°39.36'
W162°04.42'

T-TWEB Available
Shadow NAVAID Box
FSS Associated with NAVAID

ILIAMNA
411 ILI 91 (114.4)

Notes: *Morse Code is not shown on High NAVAID Boxes.*

Legend 54. IFR Enroute Low/High Altitude Symbols.

RADIO AIDS TO NAVIGATION (Continued)

Stand Alone Flight Services and Communication Outlets

LOW CHARTS | **HIGH CHARTS**

Flight Service Station (FSS)

Shadow NAVAID boxes indicate Flight Service Station (FSS) locations. Frequencies 122.2, 255.4 and emergency 121.5 and 243.0 are available at many FSSs and are not shown. All other frequencies are show above the box.

Certain FSSs provide Local Airport Advisory (LAA) on 123.6.

Frequencies transmit and receive except those followed by R and T:
R - Receive Only
T - Transmit Only

Stand Alone FSS

122.55
DAYTON DAY

Stand Alone FSS

HARBOR HBR

Stand Alone FSS Associated with an Airport

Stand Alone FSS Associated with an Airport

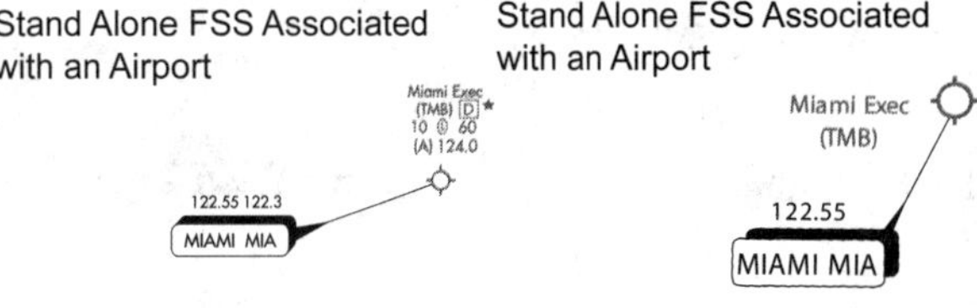

Part-time FSS

123.6 122.4
PALMER PAQ
FSS VOICE AVAILABLE
1700-0300Z‡ MON-FRI
1500-0630Z‡ SAT
1800-0400Z‡ SUN
OTHER TIMES CONTACT
KENAI FSS

Stand Alone FSS within Canadian Airspace

Stand Alone FSS within Canadian Airspace

In Canada, shadow boxes indicate FSSs with standard group frequencies of 121.5, 126.7 and 243.0.

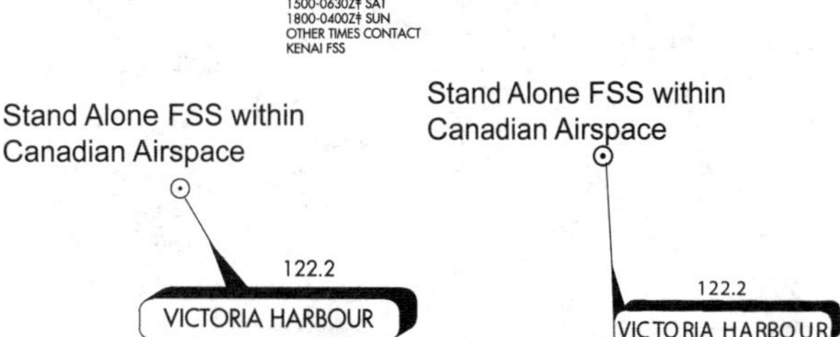

Remote Communications Outlet (RCO)

Thin line NAVAID boxes without frequencies and controlling FSS name indicate no FSS frequencies available. Frequencies positioned above the thin line boxes are remoted to the NAVAID sites. Other frequencies at the controlling FSS named are available, however altitude and terrain may determine their reception.

In Canada, a "D" after the frequency indicates a dial-up remote communications outlet.

Stand Alone RCO

Stand Alone RCO

RCO Associated/Co-located with an Airport

RCO Associated/Co-located with an Airport

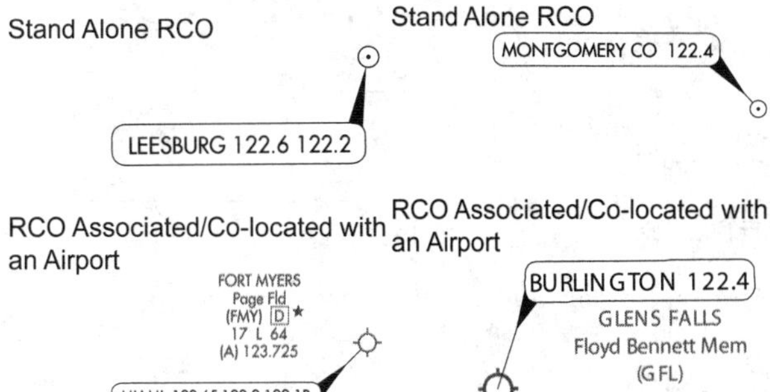

Stand Alone AWOS & ASOS

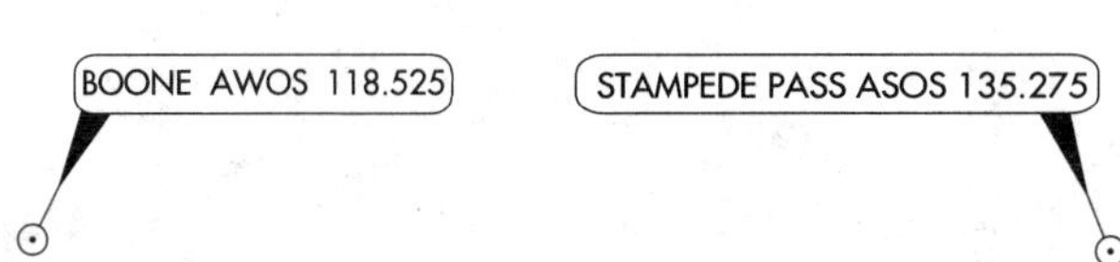

Legend 55. IFR Enroute Low/High Altitude Symbols.

AIRSPACE INFORMATION

Airway/Route Types
Low and High Enroute Airway Data:

VHF/UHF Data is depicted in Black.
LF/MF Data is depicted in Brown.
RNAV Route data is depicted in Blue

Low Enroute Charts

Victor Airways — V0

LF/MF Airway — A0

Uncontrolled LF/MF Airway — A0

RNAV T Route — T000

GNSS Required

RNAV TK Helicopter Route — TK000

GNSS Required

Preferred Single Direction Victor Route — V0

Unusable Route Segment

Direction of Flight Indicator Canadian Routes Only — EVEN

Military Training Routes (Mtr)

MTRs 5NM or less both sides of centerline — IR-000, VR-000

MTRs greater than 5NM either or both sides of centerline — IR-000, VR-000

Arrow indicates direction of route

See MTR tabulation for altitude range information

All IR and VR MTRs are shown except those VRs at or bleow 1500' AGL

CAUTION: Inset charts do not depict MTRs

High Enroute Charts

Jet Routes — J000

Atlantic Routes — ARO ARO

Bahama Routes — BROL BROL

RNAV Q Routes — Q00

Alaska Q Routes require GNSS and radar surveillance. Within the CONUS, GNSS or DME/DME/IRU RNAV required, unless otherwise indicated. DME/DME/IRU aircraft require radar surveillance. Refer to Chart Supplement for DME information.

Preferred Single Direction Jet Routes — J0

Preferred Single Direction RNAV Q Routes — Q0

Single Direction ATS Route — R000

Unusable Route Segment

By-Pass Route

Jet Route Centerline by-passing a facility which is not part of that specific route.

Low and High Enroute Charts

ATS Route — A0 A0

Oceanic Route — A00 A00

Substitute Route

All relative and supporting data shown in brown.

See NOTAMs or appropriate publication for specific information.

Legend 56. IFR Enroute Low/High Altitude Symbols.

Airspace Information (Continued)

FIXES VHF/UHF	FIXES LF/MF	REPORTING FUNCTION	WAYPOINTS RNAV
▲	▲	**Compulsory Position Reporting**	✦
△	△	**Non-Compulsory Position Reporting**	✧
N25°46.47' W76°16.28'	N29°36.00' W88°01.00'	**Fix or Waypoint Coordinates** *Fix Coordinates are shown for compulsory, offshore and holding fixes.* *Waypoints Coordinates are shown when waypoint is not part of a RNAV route and when located on or beyond the boundary of the U.S. Continental Control (12 mile limit).*	*N44°25.36' W64°11.00'*
		Off-set arrows indicate facility forming a fix *- Arrow points away from the VHF/UHF NAVAID* *- Arrow points towards the LF/MF NAVAID*	N/A
		Distance Measuring Equipment (DME) Fix *Denotes DME fix (distance same as airway / route mileage)*	N/A
VHF/UHF 15		**Distance Measuring Equipment (DME) Fix** *Denotes DME fix (encircled mileage shown when not otherwise obvious)*	RNAV N/A
5 10 15		**Example:** *First segment, 5NM; second segment 10NM; total milage provided in encircled DME arrow.*	N/A
VHF/UHF 229	LF/MF 149	**Total Mileages between Compulsory Reporting Points or NAVAIDs** *Note: All mileages are in Nautical Miles*	RNAV N/A
54	125	**MILEAGE BETWEEN OTHER FIXES, NAVAIDs AND/OR MILEAGE BREAKDOWN**	125
X (AFWOX)	X (MSABI)	**Mileage Breakdown or Computer Navigation Fix (CNF)** *Five letter identifier in parentheses indicates CNF with no ATC function*	N/A
000.0 IDT 000 000.0 IDT 000	000 ID 000 ID	**FACILITY LOCATOR BOATS** *Crosshatch indicates Shutdown status of NAVAID*	N/A
000	N/A	**RADIAL OUTBOUND FROM A VHF/UHF NAVAID** *All Radials are magnetic.*	N/A
N/A	000	**BEARING INBOUND TO AN LF/MF NAVAID** *All Bearings are magnetic.*	N/A
N/A	N/A	**MAGNETIC REFERENCE BEARING**, outbound from a NAVAID or Fix *Note: Not shown on joint Victor/RNAV or Jet/RNAV Routes.*	000

Legend 57. IFR Enroute Low/High Altitude Symbols.

Airspace Information (Continued)

VHF/UHF	LF/MF		RNAV
LOW CHARTS 0000	*LOW CHARTS* 0000	**MINIMUM ENROUTE ALTITUDE (MEA)** All Altitudes Are MSL Unless Otherwise Noted.	*LOW CHARTS* 0000G
13000 → ← 10000 ∗8100 18		Directional MEAs	
HIGH CHARTS MEA-29000	*HIGH CHARTS* MEA-FL240	MEAs are shown on IFR High Altitude Charts when MEA is other than 18,000'.	*HIGH CHARTS* MEA for GNSS RNAV aircraft MEA-24000G MEA for DME/DME/IRU RNAV aircraft MEA-24000D
LOW CHARTS 15000 13300G ∗13300 V465 MEA GAP 51 35 114 63 *HIGH CHARTS* MEA GAP TWISP MEA-24000 J505 65 108 91 279		**MINIMUM ENROUTE ALTITUDE (MEA) GAP** MEA is established when there is a gap in navigation signal coverage.	N/A
LOW / HIGH CHARTS MAA-00000	*LOW / HIGH CHARTS* MAA-00000	**Maximum Authorized Altitude (MAA)** All Altitudes Are MSL Unless Otherwise Noted. MAAs are shown on IFR High Altitude Charts when MAA is other than 45,000'.	*LOW / HIGH CHARTS* MAA-00000
LOW CHARTS ∗0000	*LOW CHARTS* ∗0000	**Minimum Obstruction Clearance Altitude (MOCA)** All Altitudes Are MSL Unless Otherwise Noted.	*LOW CHARTS* ∗0000
LOW CHARTS X	*LOW CHARTS* X	**Minimum Turning Altitude (MTA) and Minimum Crossing Altitude (MCA)** See Low Enroute Chart Example below for examples of both MTAs and MCAs.	*LOW CHARTS* X
R	R	**MINIMUM RECEPTION ALTITUDE (MRA)**	N/A
⊣ ⊢	⊣ ⊢	**ALTITUDE CHANGE** MEA, MOCA and/or MAA change at other than NAVAIDs	⊣ ⊢
LOW / HIGH CHARTS 00 00	*LOW / HIGH CHARTS* 00 00	**CHANGEOVER POINT** Changeover Point giving mileage to NAVAIDs (Not shown at midpoint locations.)	N/A
RADDY N47°04.47' W121°30.97' 210K	LARGE N39°17.12' W89°18.07'	**HOLDING PATTERNS** RNAV Holding Pattern Magnetic Reference Bearing is determined by the isogonic value at the waypoint or fix. Holding Pattern with maximum restriction airspeed 210K applies to altitudes 6000' to and including 14000'. 175K applied to all altitudes. Airspeed depicted is Indicated Airspeed (IAS)	290 CULTI

Legend 58. IFR Enroute Low/High Altitude Symbols.

AIRSPACE INFORMATION (Continued)

Enroute Chart Examples

Low Enroute Chart

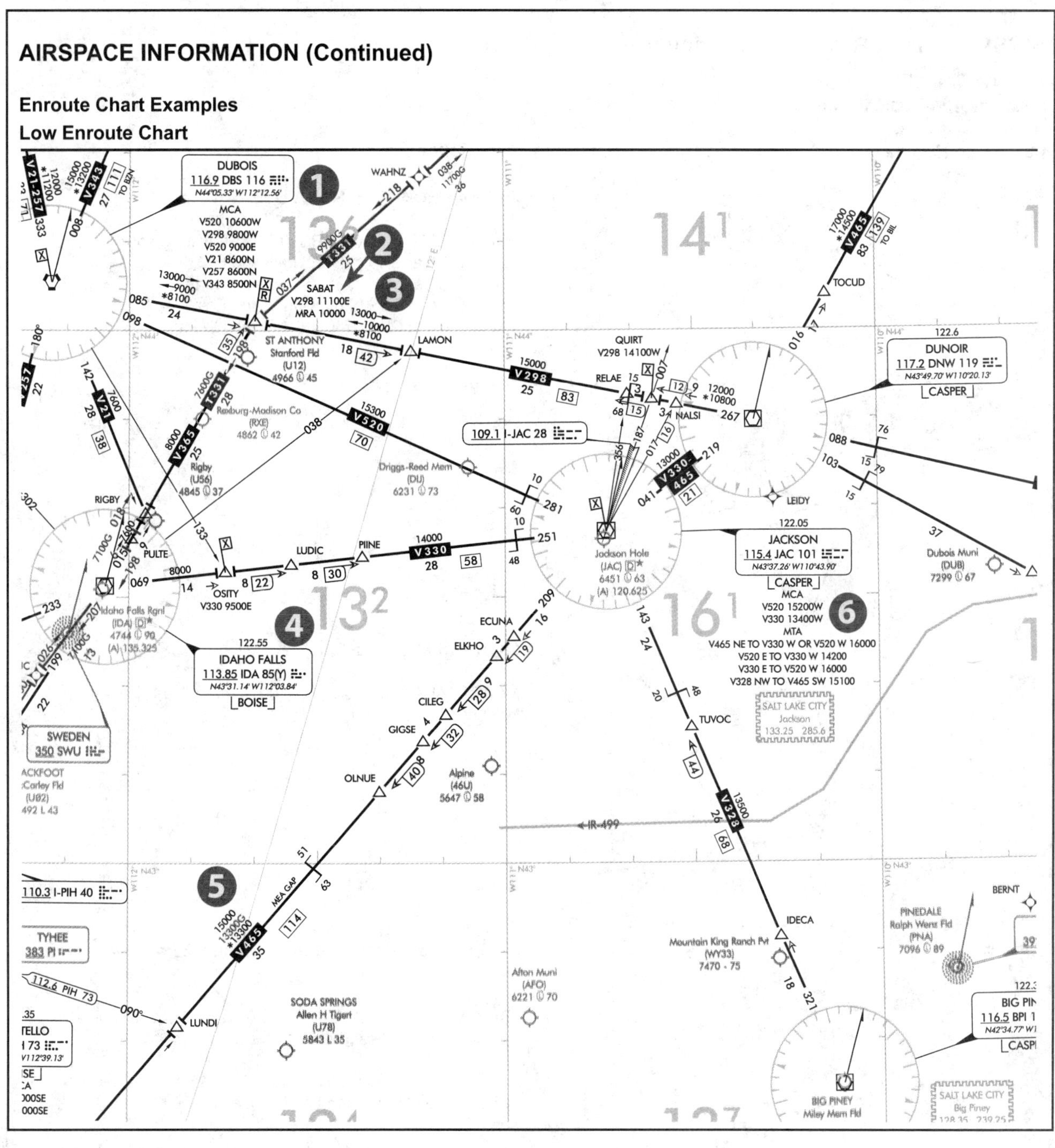

Legend 59. IFR Enroute Low/High Altitude Symbols.

AIRSPACE INFORMATION (Continued)

Enroute Chart Examples
Low Enroute Chart (Continued)

Reference Number | **Description**

1

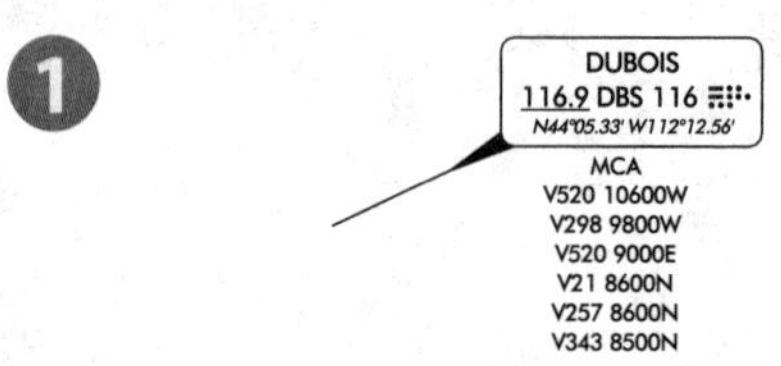

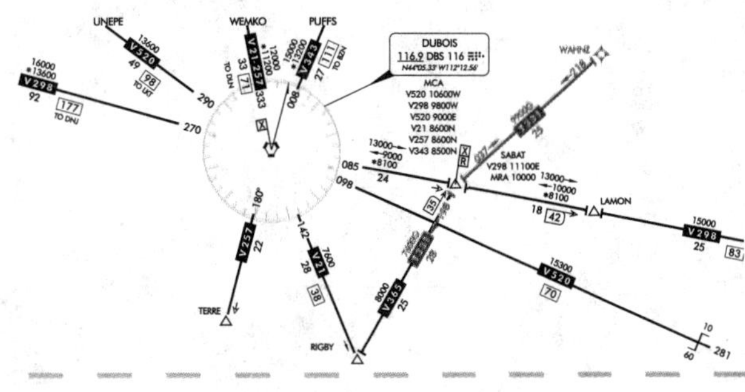

Multiple MCAs at a NAVAID

V21 and V257 - MCA at DBS of 8600' traveling North
V298 - MCA at DBS of 9800' traveling West
V343 - MCA at DBS of 8500' traveling North
V520 - MCA at DBS of 9000' traveling East
V520 - MCA at DBS of 10600' traveling West

2

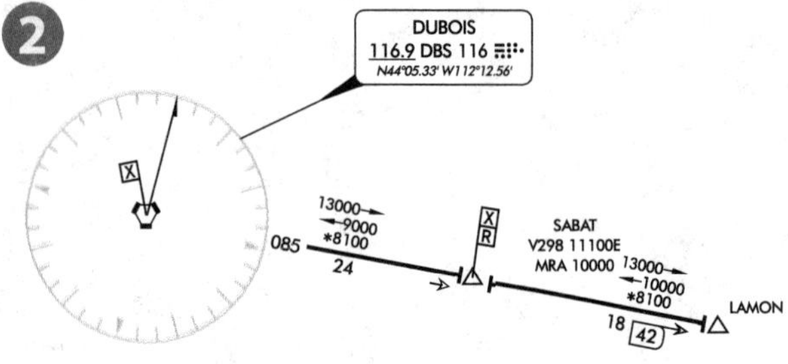

MCA and MRA at a Fix

MCA at SABAT on V298 of 11,100 traveling East.
MRA at SABAT of 10000.

3

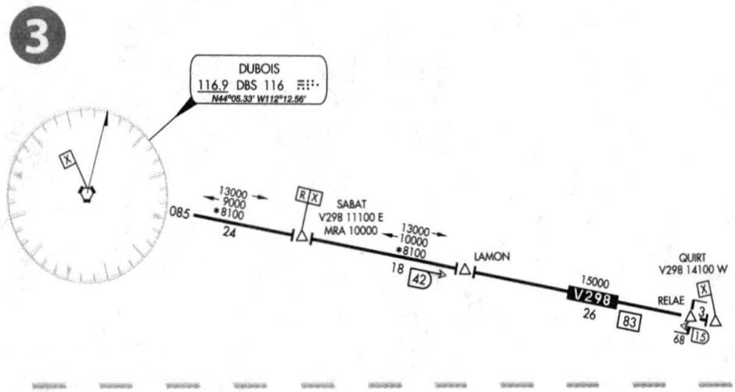

Example of MOCA and directional MEAs along a Victor Route

Traveling East from DBS, MEA 13,000' the first two segments, 15,000 along third segment.

Traveling West from QUIRT, MEA of 15,000' the first segment, MEA of 10,000 the second segment and MEA of 9,000 the third segment.

MOCA for DBS to SABAT and SABAT to LAMON segments of 8100

4

MCA Example

MCA at OSITY on V330. MCA of 9500' traveling East on V330 from Idaho Falls (IDA) VOR-DME.

Legend 60. IFR Enroute Low/High Altitude Symbols.

AIRSPACE INFORMATION (Continued)

Enroute Chart Examples

Low Enroute Chart (Continued)

Reference Number | **Description**

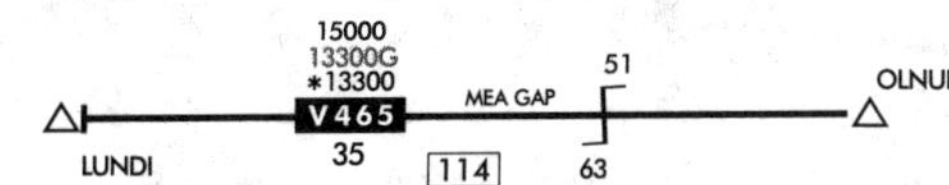

MEA VHF and RNAV Example

MEA for aircraft utilizing VHF NAVAID of 15000’
MEA for aircraft utilizing RNAV of 13300’

MOCA of 13300’

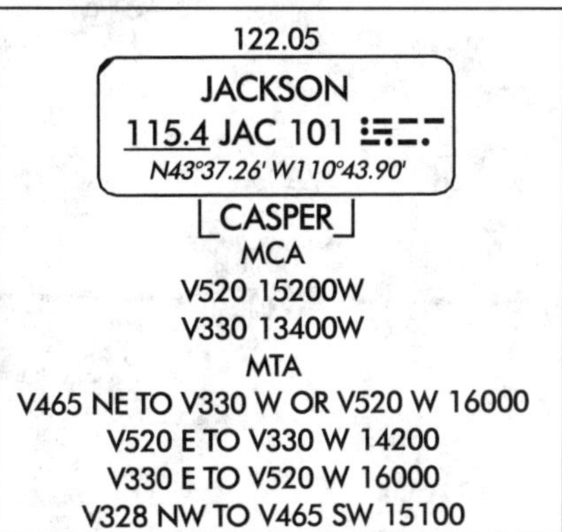

MCA and MTA Example at a NAVAID

MCA for aircraft traveling West along V520 to cross JAC at 15200’
MCA for aircraft traveling West along V330 to cross JAC at 13400’

MTA for aircraft crossing over and turning at JAC:

Aircraft traveling NE on V465 and turning to V330 on a W heading or turning to V520 on a W heading must turn at altitude of 16000’ or higher

Aircraft traveling E on V520 and turning to V330 on a W heading must turn at altitude of 14200’

Aircraft traveling E on V330 and turning to V520 on a W heading must turn at altitude of 16000’ or higher

Aircraft traveling NW on V328 and turning to V465 on a SW heading must turn at altitude of 15100’ or higher.

Legend 61. IFR Enroute Low/High Altitude Symbols.

Airspace Information (Continued)

Enroute Chart Examples

High Enroute Chart

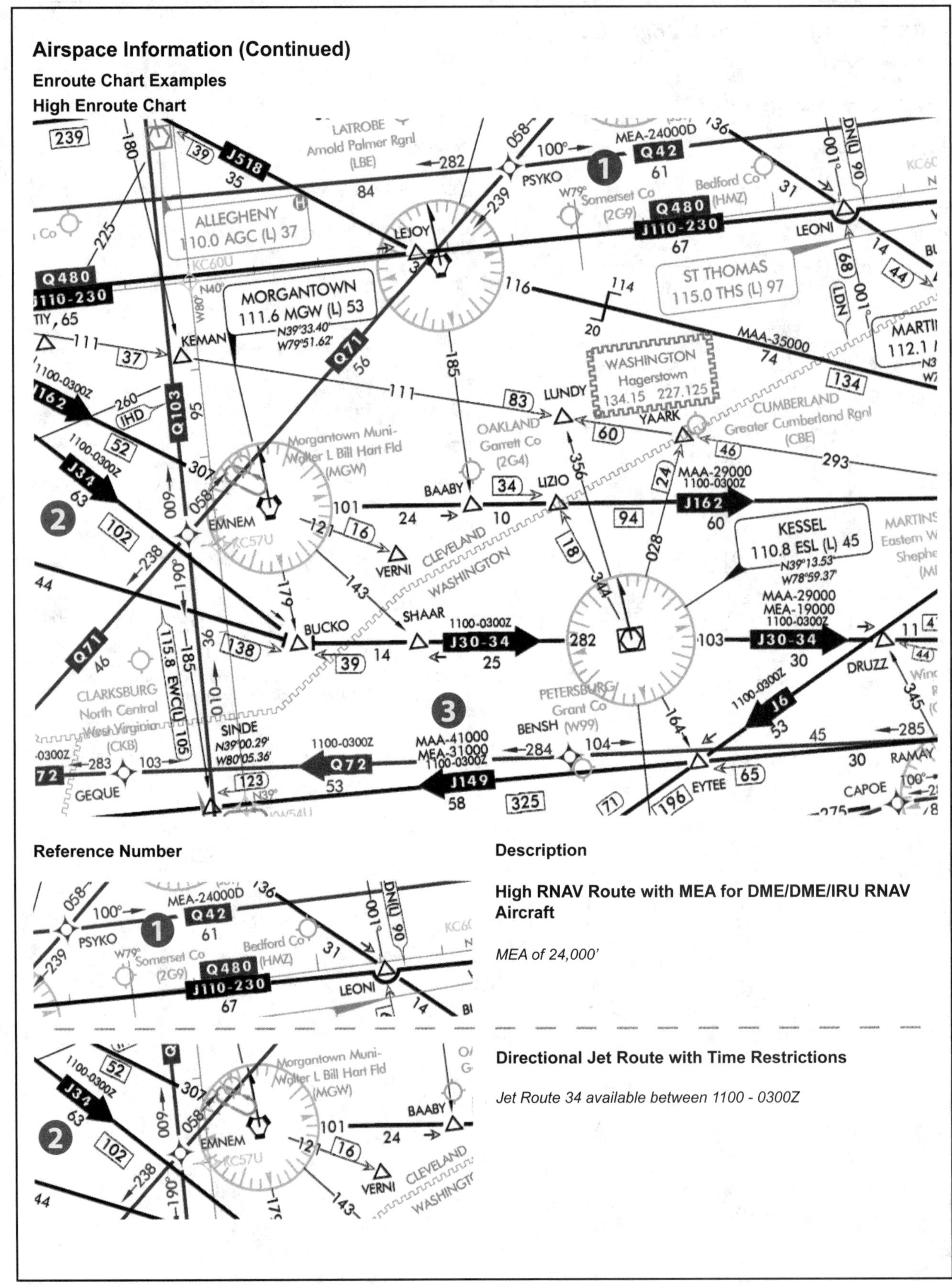

Reference Number | **Description**

High RNAV Route with MEA for DME/DME/IRU RNAV Aircraft

MEA of 24,000'

Directional Jet Route with Time Restrictions

Jet Route 34 available between 1100 - 0300Z

Legend 62. IFR Enroute Low/High Altitude Symbols.

AIRSPACE INFORMATION (Continued)

Enroute Chart Examples
High Enroute Chart (Continued)

Reference Number	Description
 3	**Directional Jet Route with Time Restrictions, MAA and MEA** Jet Route 149 available between 1100 - 0300Z MAA - 41,000' MEA - 31,000'

AIRSPACE BOUNDARIES

Air Defense Identification Zone (ADIZ)

LOW / HIGH CHARTS

Adjoining ADIZ

Air Traffic Service Identification Data

LOW / HIGH CHARTS

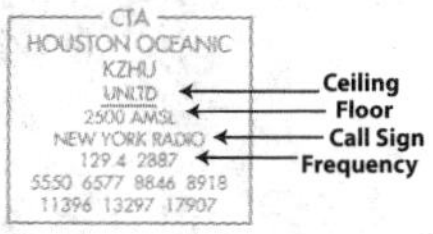

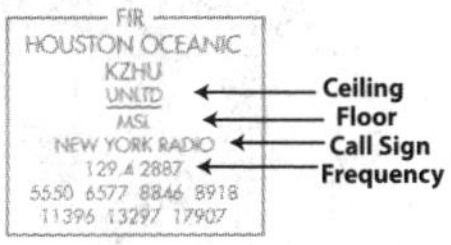

Flight Information Regions (FIR)

LOW / HIGH CHARTS

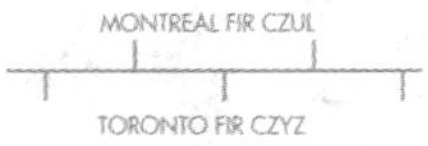

Upper Information Regions (UIR)

Upper Control Areas (UTA)

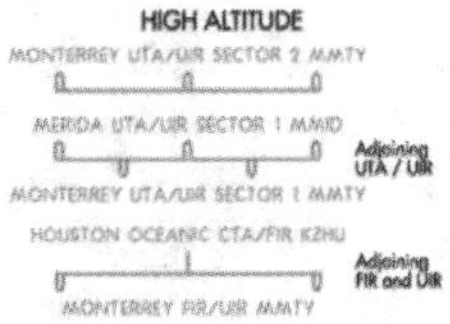

Air Route Traffic Control Center (ARTCC)

LOW / HIGH CHARTS

ARTCC Remoted Sites with discrete VHF and UHF frequencies

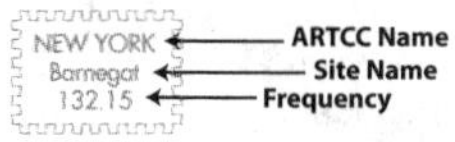

Altimeter Setting Change

Control Areas (CTA)

LOW / HIGH CHARTS

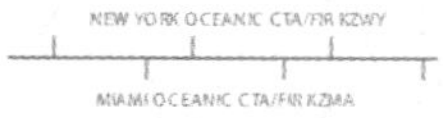

Adjoining CTA

Additional Control Areas

LOW ALTITUDE

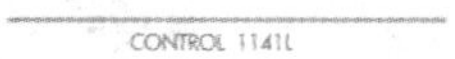

HIGH ALTITUDE

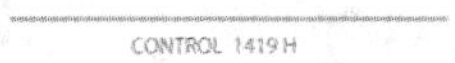

Legend 63. IFR Enroute Low/High Altitude Symbols.

AIRSPACE INFORMATION (Continued)

Airspace - U.S.

Class A — Open Area (White)

High Chart Only

Controlled Airspace

That airspace from 18,000' MSL to and including FL 600, including the airspace overflying the waters within 12 NM of the coast of the contiguous United States and Alaska and designated offshore areas, excluding Santa Barbara Island, Farallon Island, the airspace south of latitude 25° 04'00" N, the Alaska peninsula west of longitude 160°00'00" W, and the airspace less than 1,500' AGL.

That airspace from 18,000' MSL to and including FL 450, including Santa Barbara Island, Farallon Island, the Alaska peninsula west of longitude 160°00'00" W, and designated offshore areas.

Class B

Low Chart Only

Controlled Airspace

Screened Blue with a Solid Blue Outline

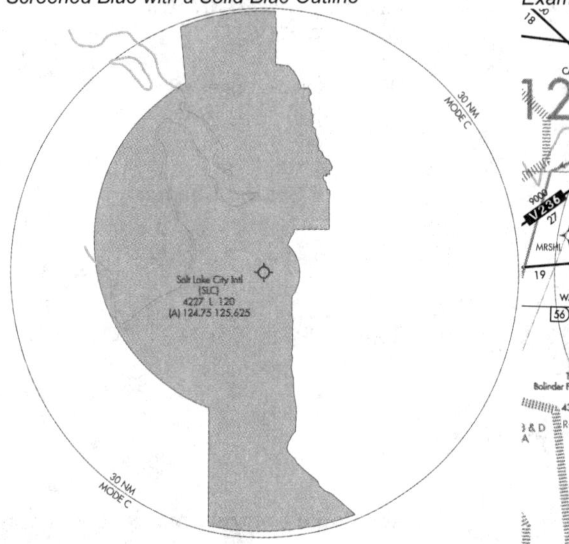

That airspace from the surface to 10,000' MSL (unless otherwise designated) surrounding the nation's busiest airports. Each Class B airspace area is individually tailored and consists of a surface area and two or more layers.

Example:

Mode C Area

Low Chart Only

Controlled Airspace

A Solid Blue Outline

That airspace within 30 NM of the primary airports of Class B airspace and within 10 NM of designated airports. Mode-C transponder equipment is required. (See FAR 91.215)

Example:

See Chart example above.

Legend 64. IFR Enroute Low/High Altitude Symbols.

AIRSPACE INFORMATION (Continued)

Airspace - U.S. (Continued)

CLASS C

Low Chart Only

Controlled Airspace

Screened Blue with a Solid Blue Dashed Outline

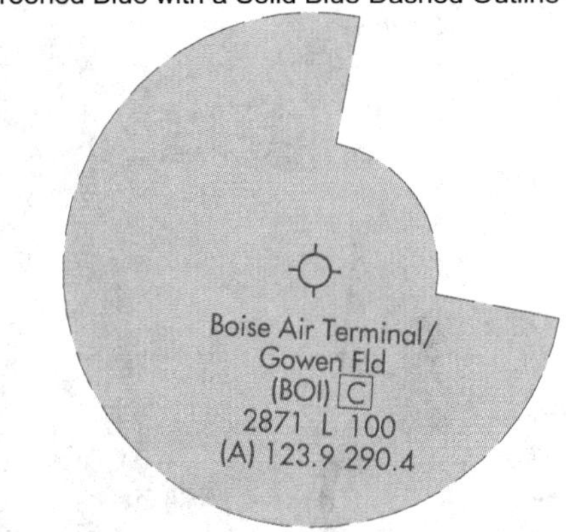

Example:

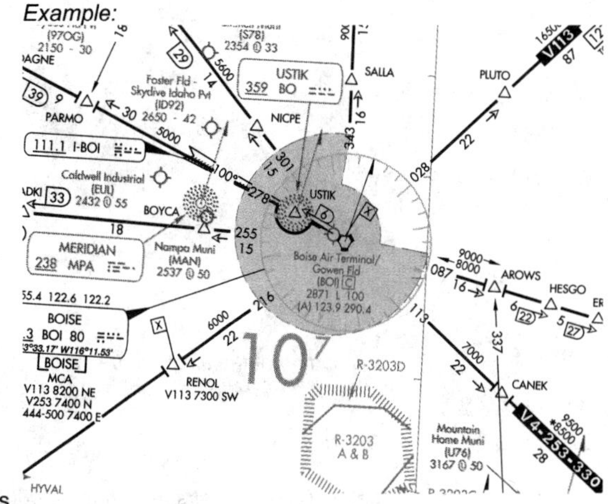

That airspace from the surface to 4,000' (unless otherwise designated) above the elevation of selected airports (charted in MSL). The normal radius of the outer limits of Class C airspace is 10NM. Class C airspace is also indicated by the letter C in a box following the airport name.

CLASS D

Low Chart Only

Controlled Airspace

Open Area (White)

Groton-New London
(GON) D ★
9 Ⓛ 50
(A) 127.0

Example:

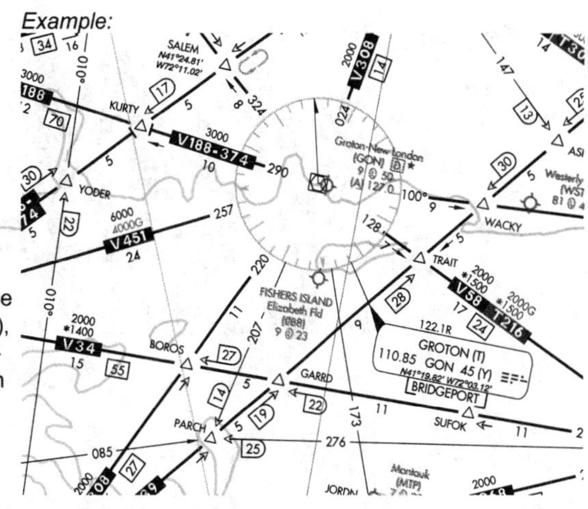

That airspace from the surface to 2,500' unless otherwise designated) above the airport elevation (charted in MSL), surrounding those airports that have an operational control tower. Class D airspace is indicated by the letter D in a box following the airport name.

CLASS E

Low Chart Only

Controlled Airspace

Open Area (White)

That controlled airpsace below 14,500' MSL which is not Class B, C or D.

Federal Airways from 1,200' AGL to but not including 18,000' MSL (unless otherwise specified).

Other designated control areas below 14,500' MSL.

Not Charted

That airspace from 14,500' MSL to but not including 18,000' MSL, including the airspace overflying the waters within 12 NM of the coast of the contiguous United States and Alaska and designated offshore areas, excluding the Alaska peninsula west of longitude 160°00'00" W, and the airspace less than 1,500' AGL.

Legend 65. IFR Enroute Low/High Altitude Symbols.

Airspace Information (Continued)

AIRSPACE - U.S.

CLASS G *Screened Brown Area*

High and Low Chart

Uncontrolled Airspace

Low Altitude

That portion of the airspace below 14,500' MSL that has not been designated as Class B, C, D or E Airspace.

High Altitude

That portion of the airspace from 18,000' MSL and above that has not been designated as Class A airspace.

Example:

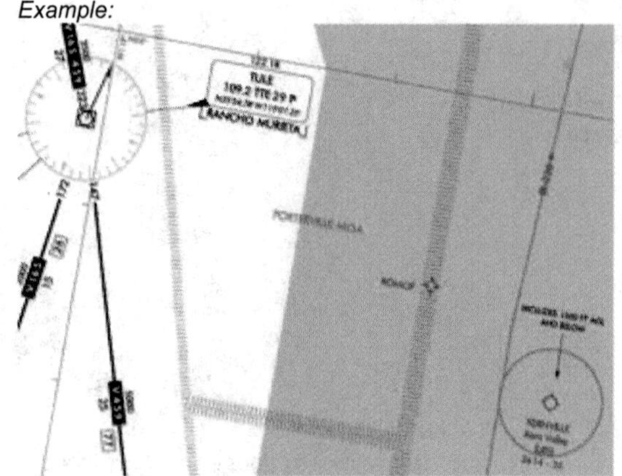

AIRSPACE - CANADIAN

CLASS B *Screened Brown Checkered Area*

Low Charts Only

Controlled Airspace

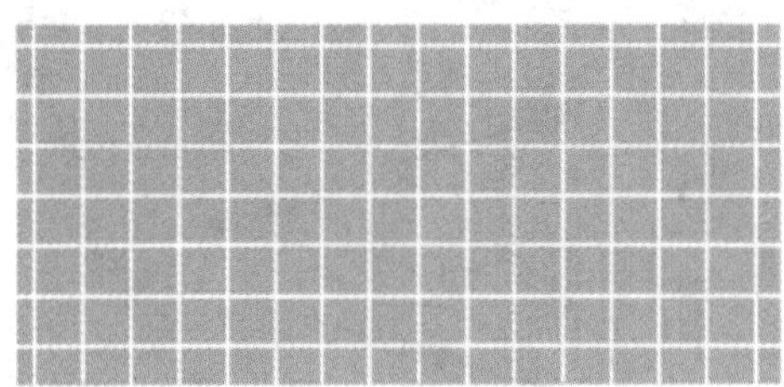

Controlled airspace above 12,500' MSL

Example:

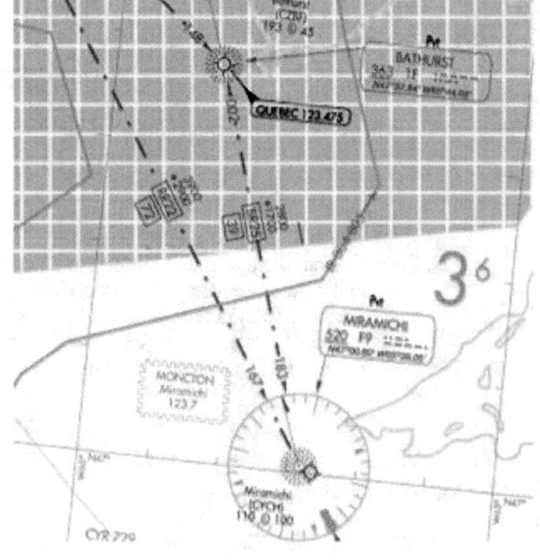

Legend 66. IFR Enroute Low/High Altitude Symbols.

AIRSPACE INFORMATION (Continued)

Special Use Airspace - U.S.

Low and High Charts

P - Prohibited Area

Example: P-56 -
Washington DC, Area A-1 Chart

P-56

Example: P-40 and R-4009 -
Washington DC, Area A-1 Chart

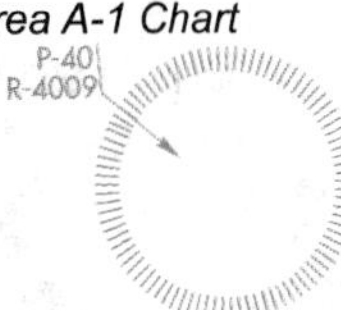

R - Restricted Area

Example: R3601A -

W - Warning Area

See Airspace Tabulation on each chart for complete documentation information on:

Area Identification
Effective Altitude
Operating Times
Controlling Agency Voice Call

Example: W-50

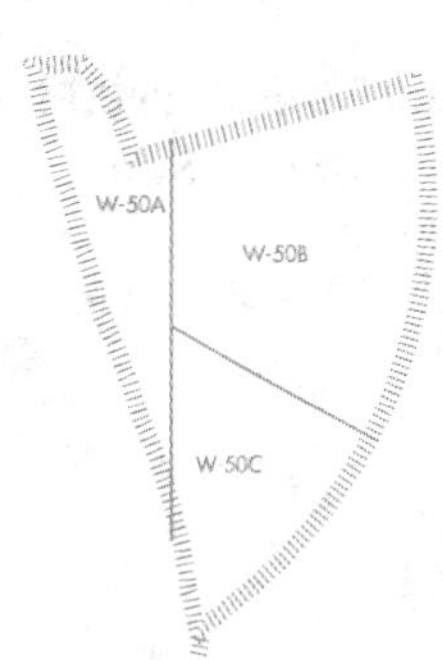

W-122
EXCLUDES THE AIRSPACE
ABOVE FL 240
W-122

Low Charts Only

A - Alert Area

A-562B

MOA - Military Operations Area

See Airspace Tabulation on each chart for complete documentation information on:
Area Identification
Effective Altitude
Operating Times
Controlling Agency Voice Call

SUNDANCE MOA
EXCLUDES AIRSPACE AT AND BELOW 1500 AGL

Legend 67. IFR Enroute Low/High Altitude Symbols.

AIRSPACE INFORMATION (Continued)

Off Route Obstruction Clearance Altitude (OROCA)

Low Charts Only

OROCA is computed similarly to the Maximum Elevation Figure (MEF) found on Visual charts except that it provides an additional vertical buffer of 1,000 feet in designated non-mountainous areas and a 2,000 foot vertical buffer in designated mountainous areas within the United States.

Example: 12,500 feet

12⁵

Example: Low L-13 Chart

Special Flight Rules Area (SFRA)

Low and High Charts

SFRA Symbology

Example: Low Chart (Washington Area Chart)

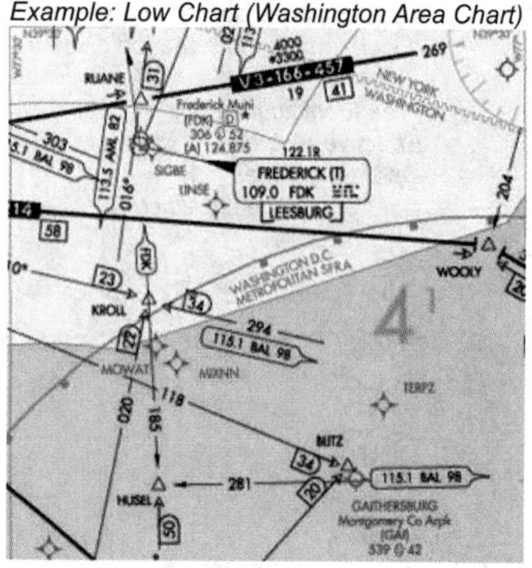

Example: High Chart (H-12)

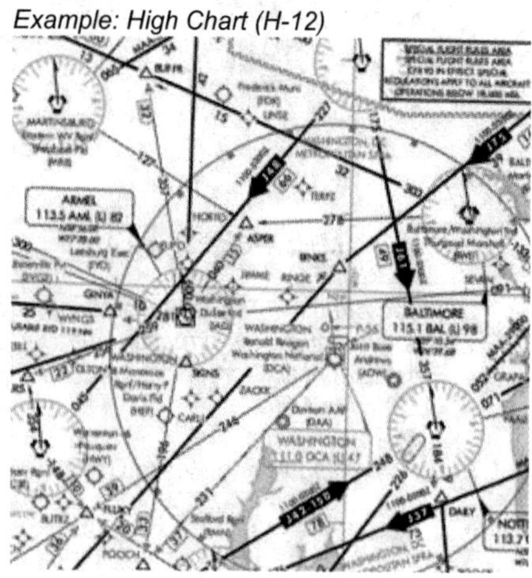

Legend 68. IFR Enroute Low/High Altitude Symbols.

AIRSPACE INFORMATION (Continued)

Special Use Airspace - Canada & Caribbean

Low and High Charts

Canada Only

CYA - Advisory Area

CYD - Danger Area

CYR - Restricted Area

Caribbean Only
D - Danger Area

In the Caribbean, the first two letters represent the country code, i.e. (MY) Bahamas, (MU) Cuba

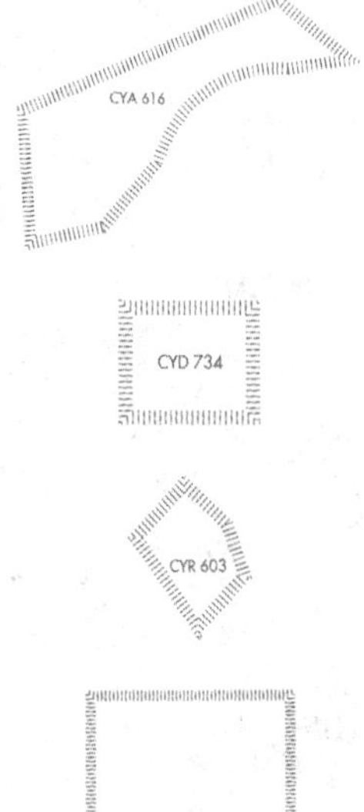

NAVIGATIONAL AND PROCEDURAL INFORMATION

Cruising Altitudes - Low Charts - U.S. Only

IFR outside controlled airspace.

IFR within controlled airspace as assigned by ATC.

ALL courses are magnetic.

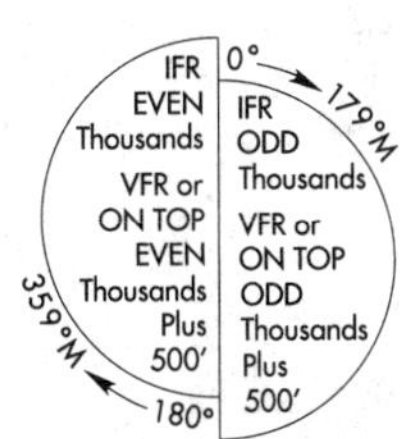

VFR above 3000' AGL unless otherwise authorized by ATC.

Cruising Altitudes - High Charts - U.S. Only

IFR within controlled airspace as assigned by ATC

All courses are magnetic.

18,000' MSL to FL280

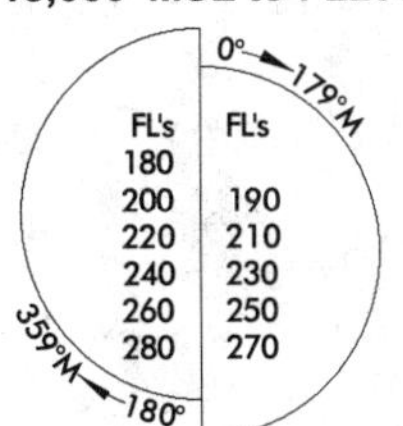

VFR or VFR On Top add 500'

No VFR flights within Class A Airspace above 3000' AGL unless otherwise authorized

RVSM Levels FL290 to FL410

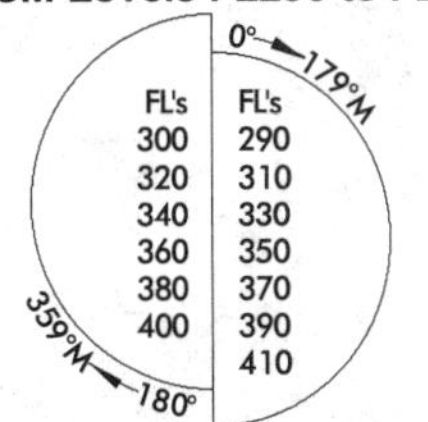

No VFR or VFR On Top authorized above FL285 in RVSM airspace.

FL430 and above

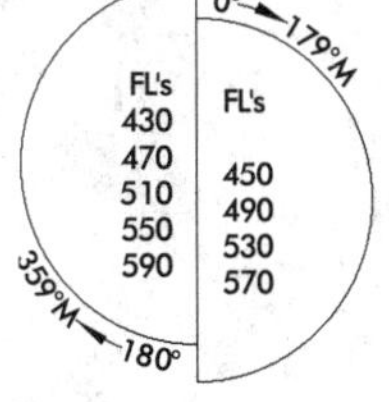

Legend 69. IFR Enroute Low/High Altitude Symbols.

Navigational and Procedural Information (Continued)

ISOGONIC LINE AND VALUE — LOW/HIGH CHARTS

10°W

ENLARGEMENT AREA

SEE WASHINGTON AREA CHART A-1 FOR DETAIL

TIME ZONE

All time is Coordinated Universal Time (UTC)

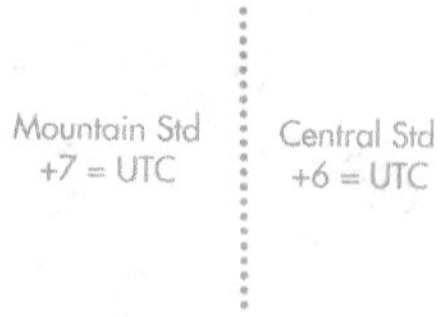

Mountain Std +7 = UTC | Central Std +6 = UTC

During periods of Daylights Savings Time (DT), effective hours will be one hour earlier than shown. All states observe DT except Arizona and Hawaii

MATCH MARK — LOW/HIGH CHARTS

MORSE CODE

A .–	F ..–.	K –.–	P .––.	U ..–	1 .––––	6 –....
B –...	G ––.	L .–..	Q ––.–	V ...–	2 ..–––	7 ––...
C –.–.	H	M ––	R .–.	W .––	3 ...––	8 –––..
D –..	I ..	N –.	S ...	X –..–	4 ....–	9 ––––.
E .	J .–––	O –––	T –	Y –.––	5	0 –––––
				Z ––..		

CULTURE

Boundaries

International — LOW/ HIGH ALTITUDE

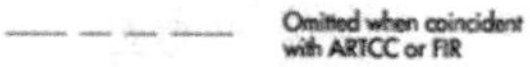

Omitted when coincident with ARTCC or FIR

U.S./Russia Maritime Line — LOW/ HIGH ALTITUDE

RUSSIA

UNITED STATES

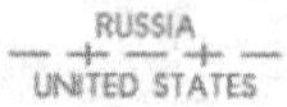

Date Line — LOW/ HIGH ALTITUDE

INTERNATIONAL DATE LINE — MONDAY SUNDAY

HYDROGRAPHY

SHORELINES

TOPOGRAPHY

TERRAIN
Area Charts

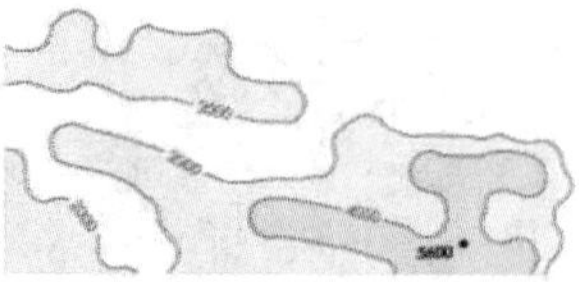

2000 3000 4000 5600

Legend 70. IFR Enroute Low/High Altitude Symbols.

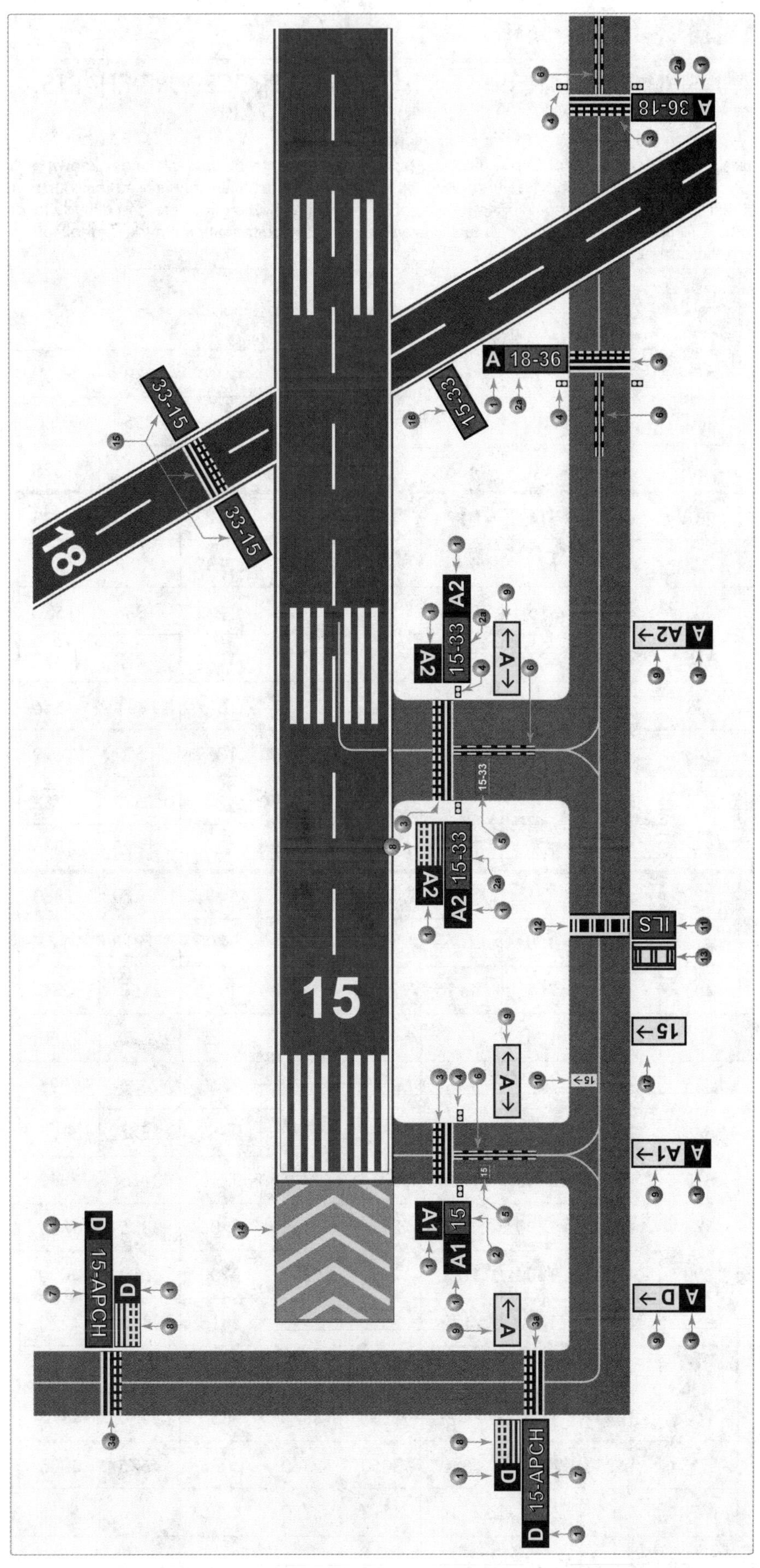

Legend 71. Examples of Airport Signs and Markings.

CLIMB/DESCENT TABLE 10042

INSTRUMENT TAKEOFF OR APPROACH PROCEDURE CHARTS
RATE OF CLIMB/DESCENT TABLE

(ft. per min)

A rate of climb/descent table is provided for use in planning and executing climbs or descents under known or approximate ground speed conditions. It will be especially useful for approaches when the localizer only is used for course guidance. A best speed, power, altitude combination can be programmed which will result in a stable glide rate and altitude favorable for executing a landing if minimums exist upon breakout. Care should always be exercised so that minimum descent altitude and missed approach point are not exceeded.

CLIMB/ DESCENT ANGLE (degrees and tenths)	ft/NM	GROUND SPEED (knots)										
		60	90	120	150	180	210	240	270	300	330	360
2.0	210	210	320	425	530	635	743	850	955	1060	1165	1275
2.5	265	265	400	530	665	795	930	1060	1195	1325	1460	1590
VERTICAL PATH ANGLE 2.7	287	287	430	574	717	860	1003	1147	1290	1433	1576	1720
2.8	297	297	446	595	743	892	1041	1189	1338	1486	1635	1783
2.9	308	308	462	616	770	924	1078	1232	1386	1539	1693	1847
3.0	318	318	478	637	797	956	1115	1274	1433	1593	1752	1911
3.1	329	329	494	659	823	988	1152	1317	1481	1646	1810	1975
3.2	340	340	510	680	850	1020	1189	1359	1529	1699	1869	2039
3.3	350	350	526	701	876	1052	1227	1402	1577	1752	1927	2103
3.4	361	361	542	722	903	1083	1264	1444	1625	1805	1986	2166
3.5	370	370	555	745	930	1115	1300	1485	1670	1860	2045	2230
4.0	425	425	640	850	1065	1275	1490	1700	1915	2125	2340	2550
4.5	480	480	715	955	1195	1435	1675	1915	2150	2390	2630	2870
5.0	530	530	795	1065	1330	1595	1860	2125	2390	2660	2925	3190
5.5	585	585	880	1170	1465	1755	2050	2340	2635	2925	3220	3510
6.0	640	640	960	1275	1595	1915	2235	2555	2875	3195	3510	3830
6.5	690	690	1040	1385	1730	2075	2425	2770	3115	3460	3805	4155
7.0	745	745	1120	1490	1865	2240	2610	2985	3355	3730	4105	4475
7.5	800	800	1200	1600	2000	2400	2800	3200	3600	4000	4400	4800
8.0	855	855	1280	1710	2135	2560	2990	3415	3845	4270	4695	5125
8.5	910	910	1360	1815	2270	2725	3180	3630	4085	4540	4995	5450
9.0	960	960	1445	1925	2405	2885	3370	3850	4330	4810	5295	5775
9.5	1015	1015	1525	2035	2540	3050	3560	4065	4575	5085	5590	6100
10.0	1070	1070	1605	2145	2680	3215	3750	4285	4820	5355	5890	6430

CLIMB/DESCENT TABLE 10042

Legend 72. Rate of Climb/Descent Table.

Appendix 2

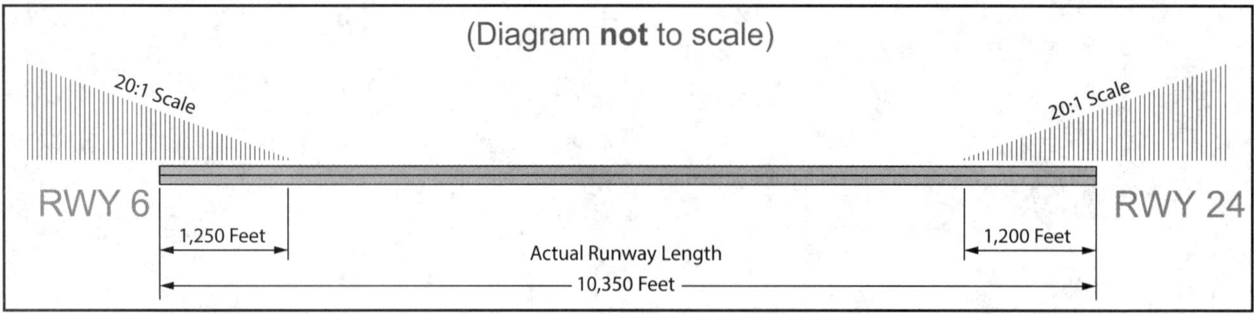

Figure 1. Runway Diagram.

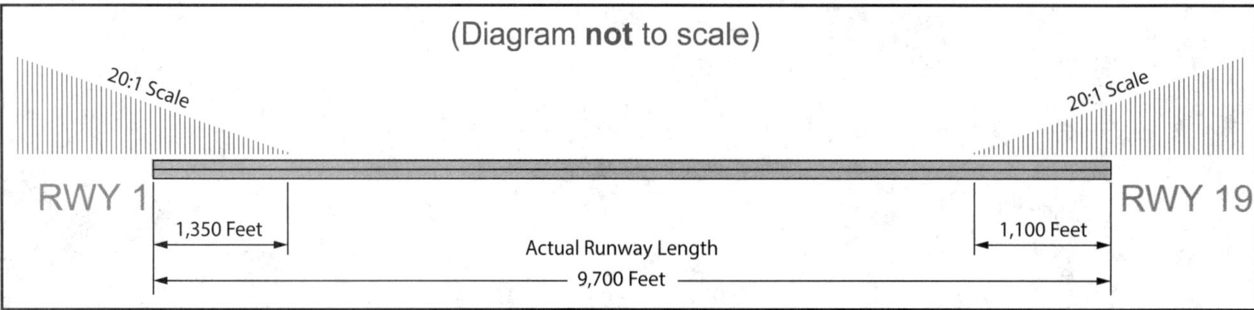

Figure 2. Runway Diagram.

LOADING CONDITIONS		AC-1	AC-2	AC-3	AC-4	AC-5
CREW		360	340	350	340	360
PASSENGERS	ROW 1	350	300	120	-	-
	ROW 2	260	250	340	370	-
	ROW 3	200	190	350	400	170
	ROW 4	340	170	300	290	200
	ROW 5	120	190	170	200	290
	ROW 6	400	340	-	170	400
	ROW 7	120	190	-	210	370
	ROW 8	250	-	-	190	340
	ROW 9	-	-	-	420	430
BAGGAGE	NOSE	60	-	80	-	100
	FWD CABIN	250	100	120	-	200
	AFT (FWD SEC)	500	200	250	800	-
	AFT (AFT SEC)	-	600	500	-	-
FUEL	GAL	370	390	400	290	340
	TYPE	JET B	JET A	JET B	JET A	JET B
	TEMP	+5 °C	+15 °C	−15 °C	+10 °C	+25 °C

Figure 3. Commuter Aircraft—Loading Passenger Configuration.

LOADING CONDITIONS		AC-6	AC-7	AC-8	AC-9	AC-10
CREW		360	340	350	370	420
CARGO SECTION	A	500	-	600	600	350
	B	500	400	200	600	450
	C	550	450	400	600	450
	D	550	600	400	600	550
	E	600	600	200	550	550
	F	600	600	200	350	600
	G	450	500	200	250	600
	H	-	-	200	250	-
	J	350	-	300	150	-
	K	-	-	250	200	-
	L	-	-	100	100	-
FUEL	GAL	340	370	390	290	400
	TYPE	JET B	JET B	JET A	JET A	JET B
	TEMP	+25 °C	+5 °C	+15 °C	+10 °C	−15 °C
BASIC OPERATING WEIGHT – 9,005 POUNDS, 25,934 MOM/100						

Figure 4. Commuter Aircraft—Loading Cargo Configuration.

OPERATING CONDITIONS	AC-11	AC-12	AC-13	AC-14	AC-15
BASIC EMPTY WT					
WEIGHT	9,225	9,100	9,000	8,910	9,150
MOM/100	25,820	24,990	24,710	24,570	25,240
CREW WEIGHT	340	380	360	400	370
PASS AND BAG					
WEIGHT	4,200	4,530	4,630	4,690	4,500
MOM/100	15,025	16,480	16,743	13,724	13,561
FUEL (6.8 LB/GAL)					
RAMP LOAD-GAL	360	320	340	310	410
USED START AND TAXI	20	20	10	20	30
REMAIN AT LDG	100	160	140	100	120

Figure 5. Commuter Aircraft—Loading Limitations.

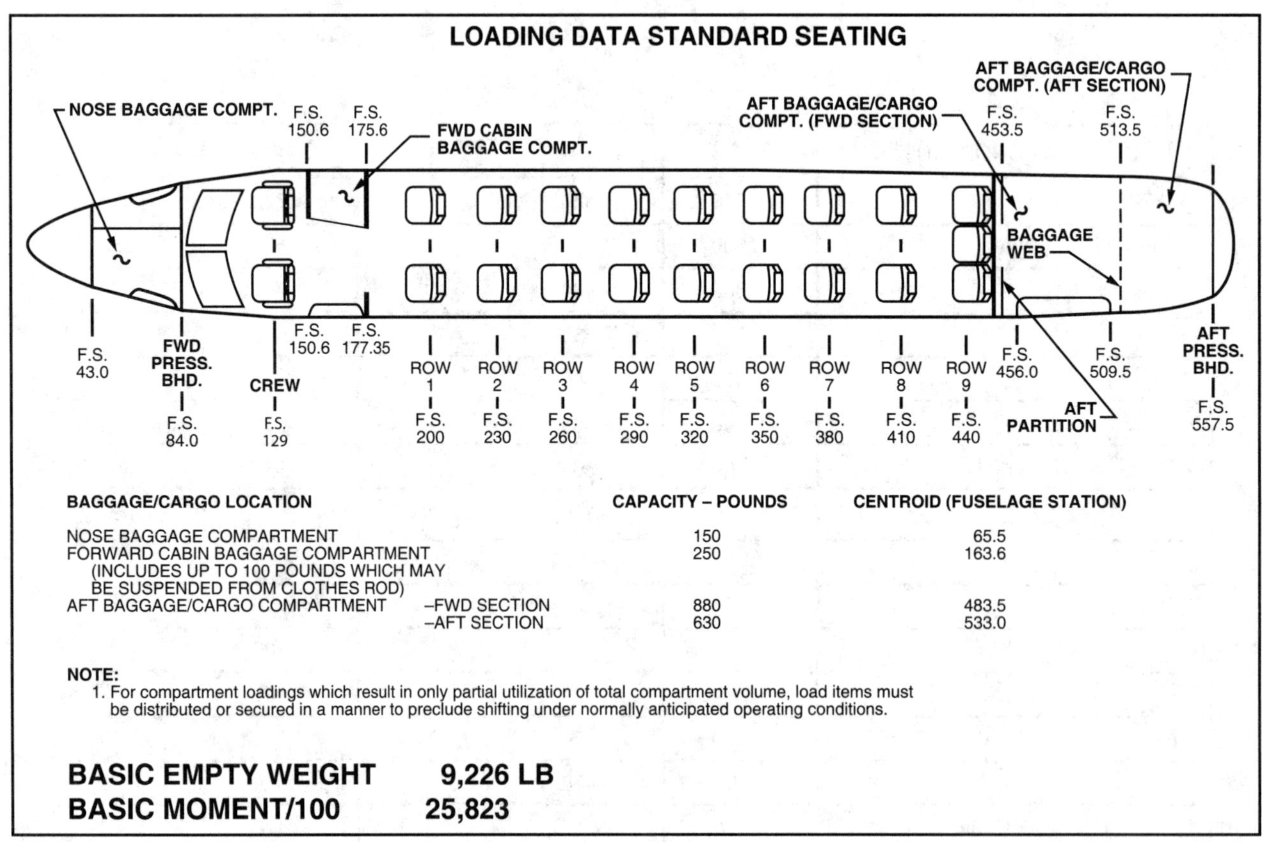

BAGGAGE/CARGO LOCATION		CAPACITY – POUNDS	CENTROID (FUSELAGE STATION)
NOSE BAGGAGE COMPARTMENT		150	65.5
FORWARD CABIN BAGGAGE COMPARTMENT (INCLUDES UP TO 100 POUNDS WHICH MAY BE SUSPENDED FROM CLOTHES ROD)		250	163.6
AFT BAGGAGE/CARGO COMPARTMENT	–FWD SECTION	880	483.5
	–AFT SECTION	630	533.0

NOTE:
1. For compartment loadings which result in only partial utilization of total compartment volume, load items must be distributed or secured in a manner to preclude shifting under normally anticipated operating conditions.

BASIC EMPTY WEIGHT 9,226 LB
BASIC MOMENT/100 25,823

Figure 6. Airplane—Loading Data.

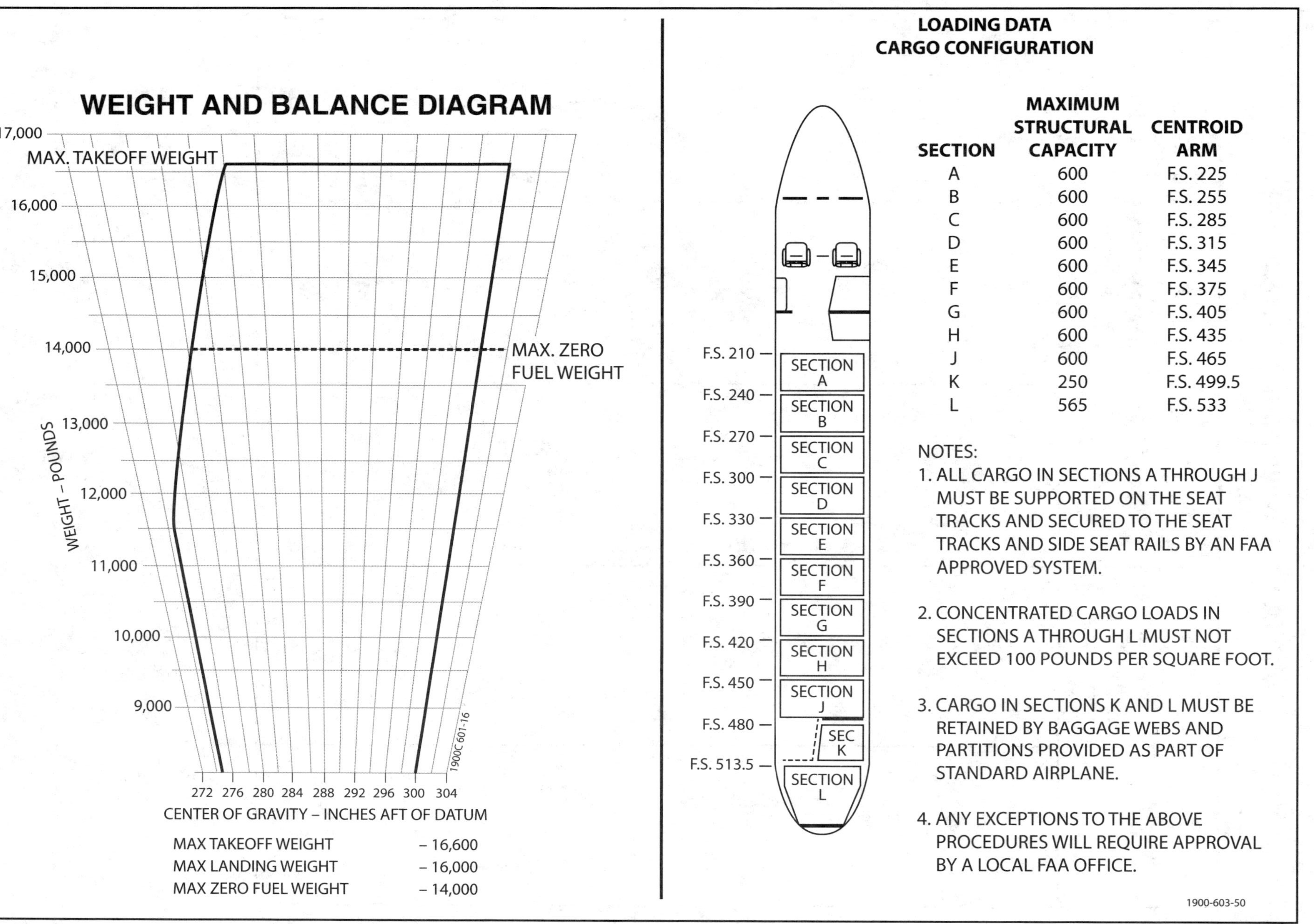

Figure 7. Commuter Aircraft—CG Envelope and Cargo Loading Data.

USEFUL LOAD WEIGHTS AND MOMENTS
BAGGAGE

WEIGHT	NOSE BAGGAGE COMPARTMENT F.S. 65.5	FORWARD CABIN BAGGAGE COMPARTMENT F.S. 163.6	AFT BAGGAGE/CARGO COMPARTMENT (FORWARD SECTION) F.S. 483.5	AFT BAGGAGE/CARGO COMPARTMENT (AFT SECTION) F.S. 533.0
	MOMENT/100			
10	7	16	48	53
20	13	33	97	107
30	20	49	145	160
40	26	65	193	213
50	33	82	242	266
60	39	98	290	320
70	46	115	338	373
80	52	131	387	426
90	59	147	435	480
100	66	164	484	533
150	98	245	725	800
200		327	967	1,066
250		409	1,209	1,332
300			1,450	1,599
350			1,692	1,866
400			1,934	2,132
450			2,176	2,398
500			2,418	2,665
550			2,659	2,932
600			2,901	3,198
630			3,046	3,358
650			3,143	
700			3,384	
750			3,626	
800			3,868	
850			4,110	
880			4,255	

Figure 8. Commuter Aircraft—Weights and Moments—Baggage.

USEFUL LOAD WEIGHTS AND MOMENTS
OCCUPANTS

WEIGHT	CREW	CABIN SEATS								
	F.S. 129	F.S. 200	F.S. 230	F.S. 260	F.S. 290	F.S. 320	F.S. 350	F.S. 380	F.S. 410	F.S. 440
	MOMENT/100									
80	103	160	184	208	232	256	280	304	328	352
90	116	180	207	234	261	288	315	342	369	396
100	129	200	230	260	290	320	350	380	410	440
110	142	220	253	286	319	352	385	418	451	484
120	155	240	276	312	348	384	420	456	492	528
130	168	260	299	338	377	416	455	494	533	572
140	181	280	322	364	406	448	490	532	574	616
150	194	300	345	390	435	480	525	570	615	660
160	206	320	368	416	464	512	560	608	656	704
170	219	340	391	442	493	544	595	646	697	748
180	232	360	414	468	522	576	630	684	738	792
190	245	380	437	494	551	608	665	722	779	836
200	258	400	460	520	580	640	700	760	820	880
210	271	420	483	546	609	672	735	798	861	924
220	284	440	506	572	638	704	770	836	902	968
230	297	460	529	598	667	736	805	874	943	1,012
240	310	480	552	624	696	768	840	912	984	1,056
250	323	500	575	650	725	800	875	950	1,025	1,100

NOTE: Weights reflected in above table represent weight per seat.

Figure 9. Commuter Aircraft—Weights and Moments—Occupants.

DENSITY VARIATION OF AVIATION FUEL

BASED ON AVERAGE SPECIFIC GRAVITY

FUEL	AVERAGE SPECIFIC GRAVITY AT 15 ˚C (59 ˚F)
AVIATION KEROSENE JET A AND JET A1	.812
JET B (JP-4)	.785
AV GAS GRADE 100/130	.703

NOTE: THE FUEL QUANTITY INDICATOR IS CALIBRATED FOR CORRECT INDICATION WHEN USING AVIATION KEROSENE JET A AND JET A1. WHEN USING OTHER FUELS, MULTIPLY THE INDICATED FUEL QUANTITY IN POUNDS BY .99 FOR JET B (JP-4) OR BY .98 FOR AVIATION GASOLINE (100/130) TO OBTAIN ACTUAL FUEL QUANTITY IN POUNDS.

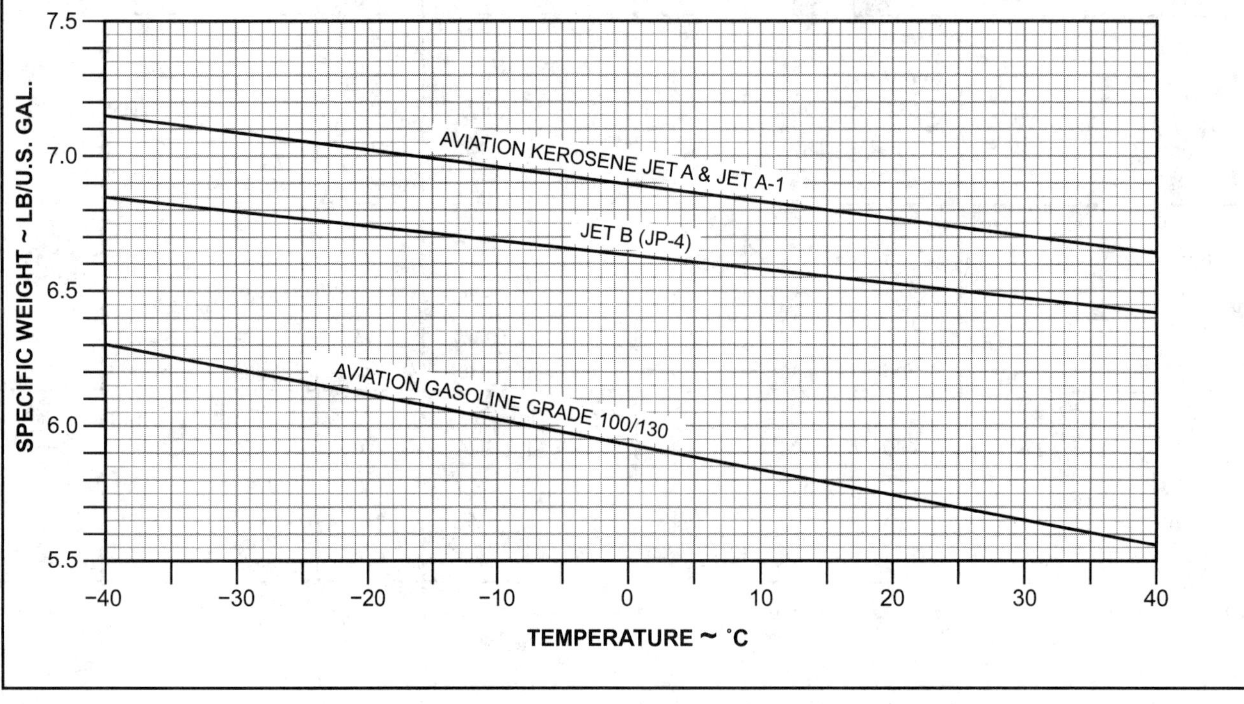

Figure 10. Density Variation of Aviation Fuel.

USEFUL LOAD WEIGHTS AND MOMENTS
USABLE FUEL

GALLONS	6.5 LB/GAL		6.6 LB/GAL		6.7 LB/GAL		6.8 LB/GAL	
	WEIGHT	MOMENT 100	WEIGHT	MOMENT 100	WEIGHT	MOMENT 100	WEIGHT	MOMENT 100
10	65	197	66	200	67	203	68	206
20	130	394	132	401	134	407	136	413
30	195	592	198	601	201	610	204	619
40	260	789	264	802	268	814	272	826
50	325	987	330	1,002	335	1,018	340	1,033
60	390	1,185	396	1,203	402	1,222	408	1,240
70	455	1,383	462	1,404	469	1,426	476	1,447
80	520	1,581	528	1,605	536	1,630	544	1,654
90	585	1,779	594	1,806	603	1,834	612	1,861
100	650	1,977	660	2,007	670	2,038	680	2,068
110	715	2,175	726	2,208	737	2,242	748	2,275
120	780	2,372	792	2,409	804	2,445	816	2,482
130	845	2,569	858	2,608	871	2,648	884	2,687
140	910	2,765	924	2,808	938	2,850	952	2,893
150	975	2,962	990	3,007	1,005	3,053	1,020	3,099
160	1,040	3,157	1,056	3,205	1,072	3,254	1,088	3,303
170	1,105	3,351	1,122	3,403	1,139	3,454	1,156	3,506
180	1,170	3,545	1,188	3,600	1,206	3,654	1,224	3,709
190	1,235	3,739	1,254	3,797	1,273	3,854	1,292	3,912
200	1,300	3,932	1,320	3,992	1,340	4,053	1,360	4,113
210	1,365	4,124	1,386	4,187	1,407	4,250	1,428	4,314
220	1,430	4,315	1,452	4,382	1,474	4,448	1,496	4,514
230	1,495	4,507	1,518	4,576	1,541	4,646	1,564	4,715
240	1,560	4,698	1,584	4,770	1,608	4,843	1,632	4,915
250	1,625	4,889	1,650	4,964	1,675	5,040	1,700	5,115
260	1,690	5,080	1,716	5,158	1,742	5,236	1,768	5,315
270	1,755	5,271	1,782	5,352	1,809	5,433	1,836	5,514
280	1,820	5,462	1,848	5,546	1,876	5,630	1,904	5,714
290	1,885	5,651	1,914	5,738	1,943	5,825	1,972	5,912
300	1,950	5,842	1,980	5,932	2,010	6,022	2,040	6,112
310	2,015	6,032	2,046	6,125	2,077	6,218	2,108	6,311
320	2,080	6,225	2,112	6,321	2,144	6,416	2,176	6,512
330	2,145	6,417	2,178	6,516	2,211	6,615	2,244	6,713
340	2,210	6,610	2,244	6,711	2,278	6,813	2,312	6,915
350	2,275	6,802	2,310	6,907	2,345	7,011	2,380	7,116
360	2,340	6,995	2,376	7,103	2,412	7,210	2,448	7,318
370	2,405	7,188	2,442	7,299	2,479	7,409	2,516	7,520
380	2,470	7,381	2,508	7,495	2,546	7,609	2,584	7,722
390	2,535	7,575	2,574	7,691	2,613	7,808	2,652	7,924
400	2,600	7,768	2,640	7,888	2,680	8,007	2,720	8,127
410	2,665	7,962	2,706	8,085	2,747	8,207	2,788	8,330
420	2,730	8,156	2,772	8,282	2,814	8,407	2,856	8,532
425	2,763	8,259	2,805	8,386	2,848	8,513	2,890	8,640

Figure 11. Commuter Aircraft—Weights and Moments—Usable Fuel.

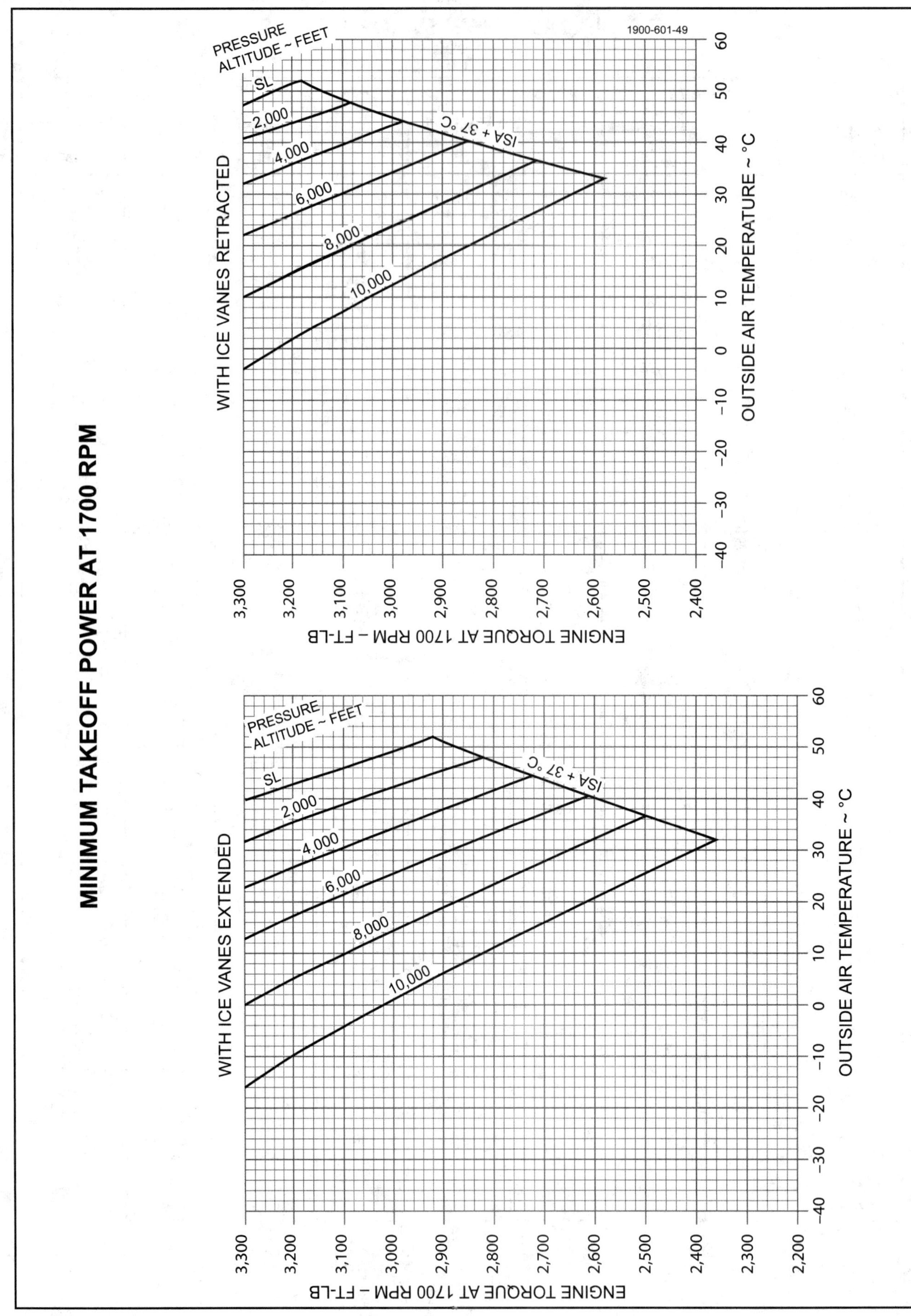

Figure 12. Minimum Takeoff Power at 1700 RPM.

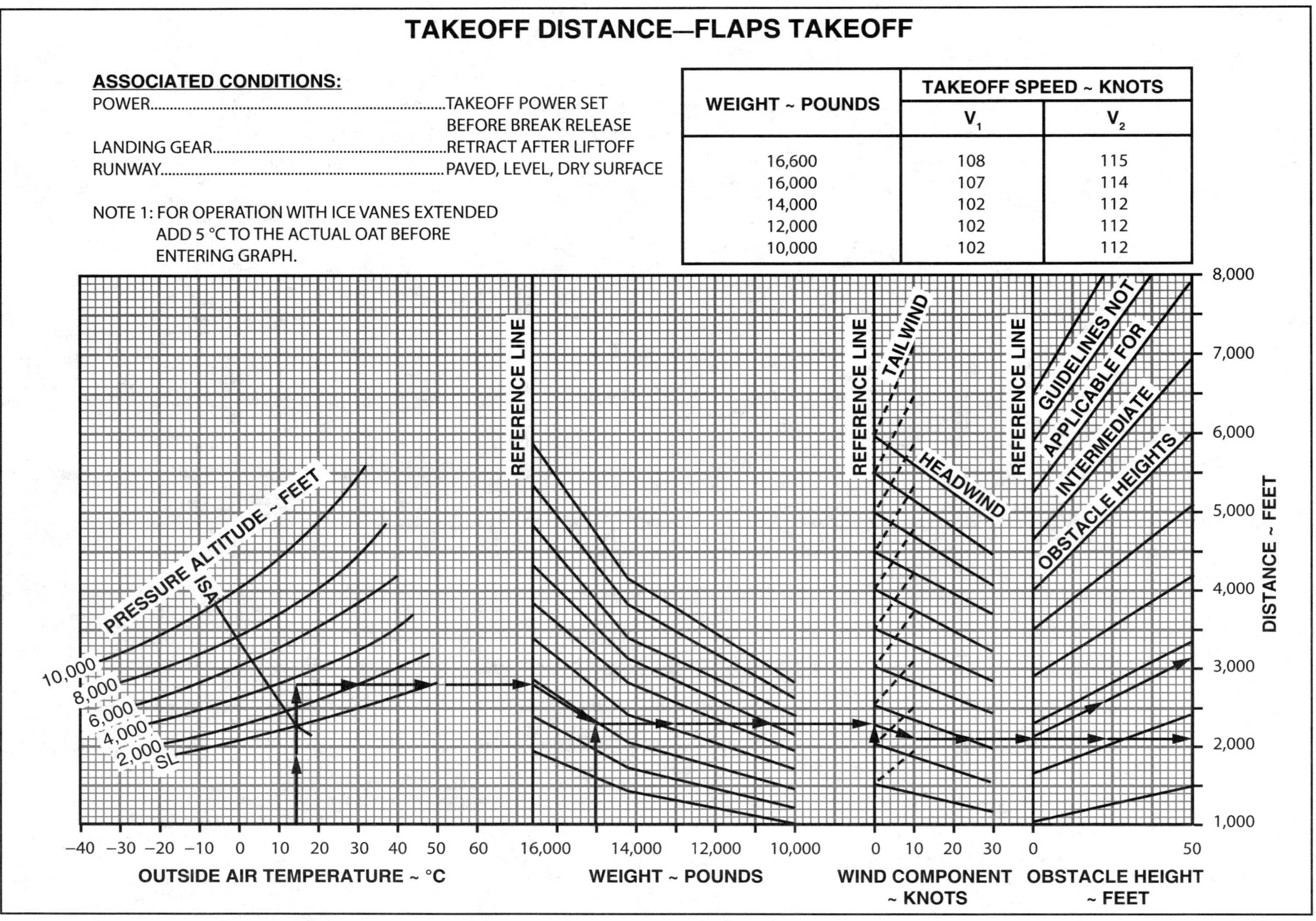

Figure 13. Takeoff Distance—Flaps Takeoff.

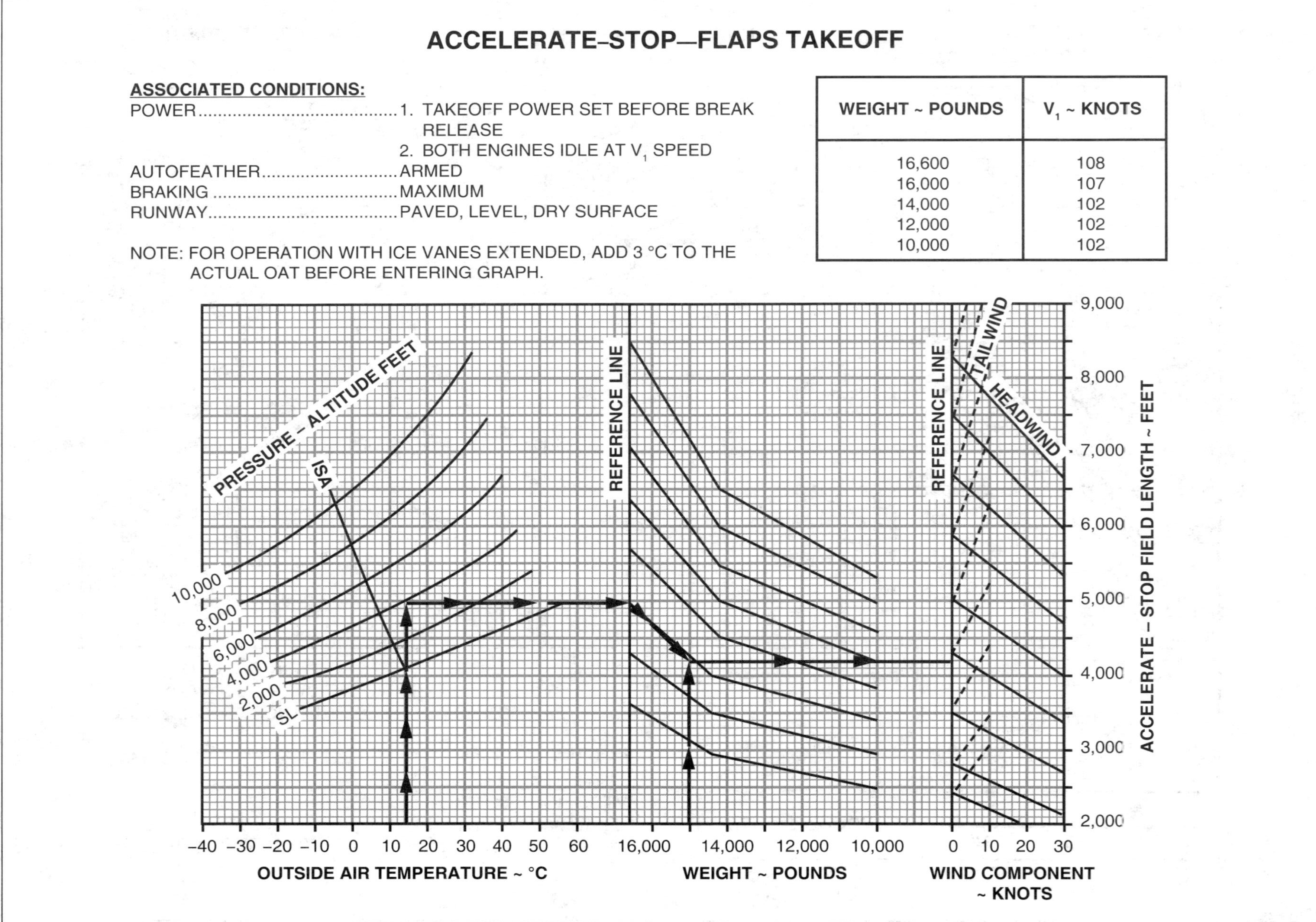

Figure 14. Accelerate-Stop–Flaps Takeoff.

OPERATING CONDITIONS	AC-21	AC-22	AC-23	AC-24	AC-25
OAT AT TAKEOFF	+10 °C	0 °C	+20 °C	+25 °C	−10 °C
OAT AT CRUISE	−20 °C	−25 °C	ISA	0 °C	−40 °C
AIRPORT PRESS ALTITUDE	2,000	1,000	3,000	4,000	5,000
CRUISE ALTITUDE	16,000	18,000	20,000	14,000	22,000
INITIAL CLIMB WEIGHT	16,600	14,000	15,000	16,000	14,000
ICE VANES	RETRACT	EXTEND	RETRACT	RETRACT	EXTEND

Figure 15. Commuter Aircraft—Climb.

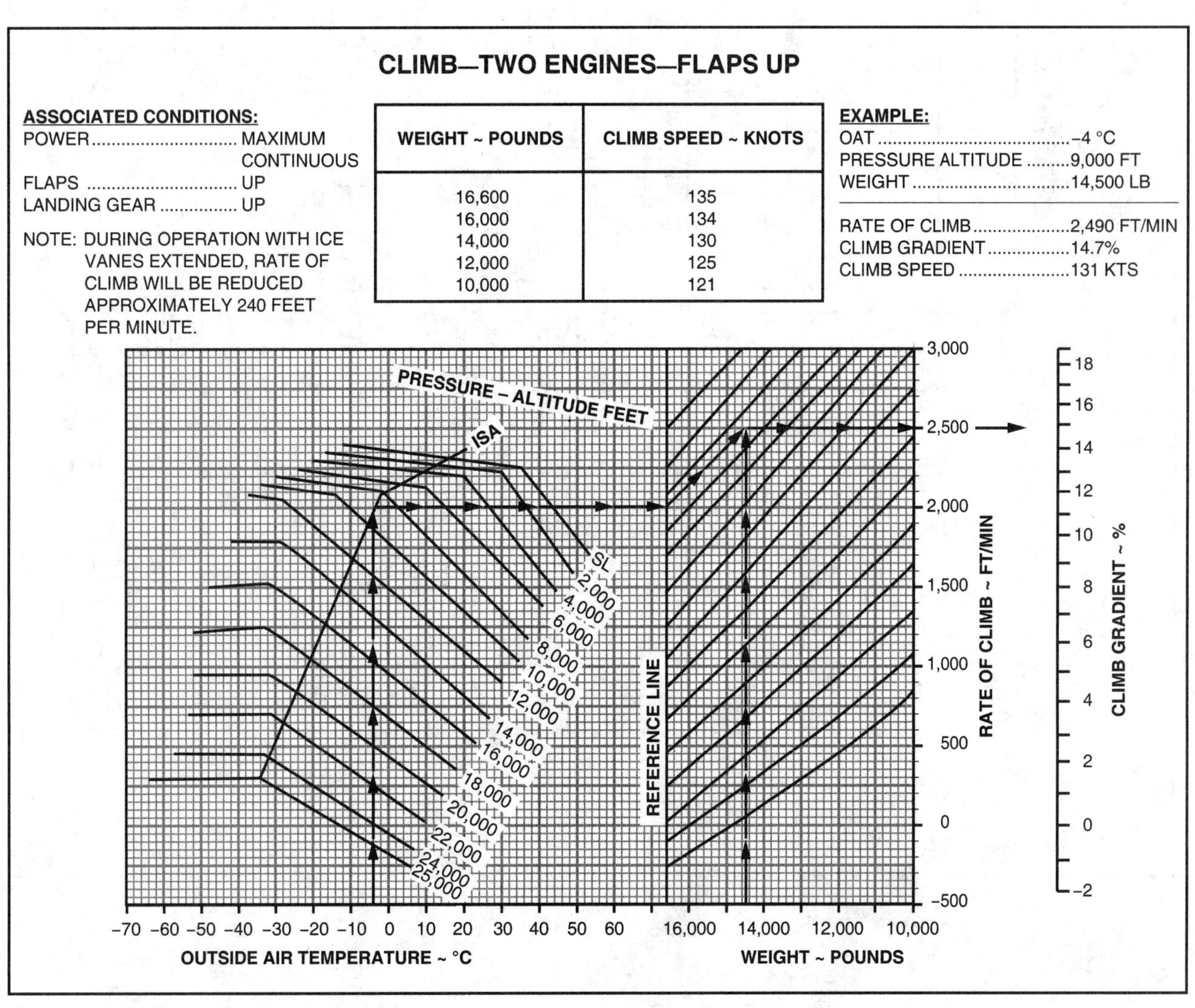

Figure 16. Climb—Two Engines—Flaps Up.

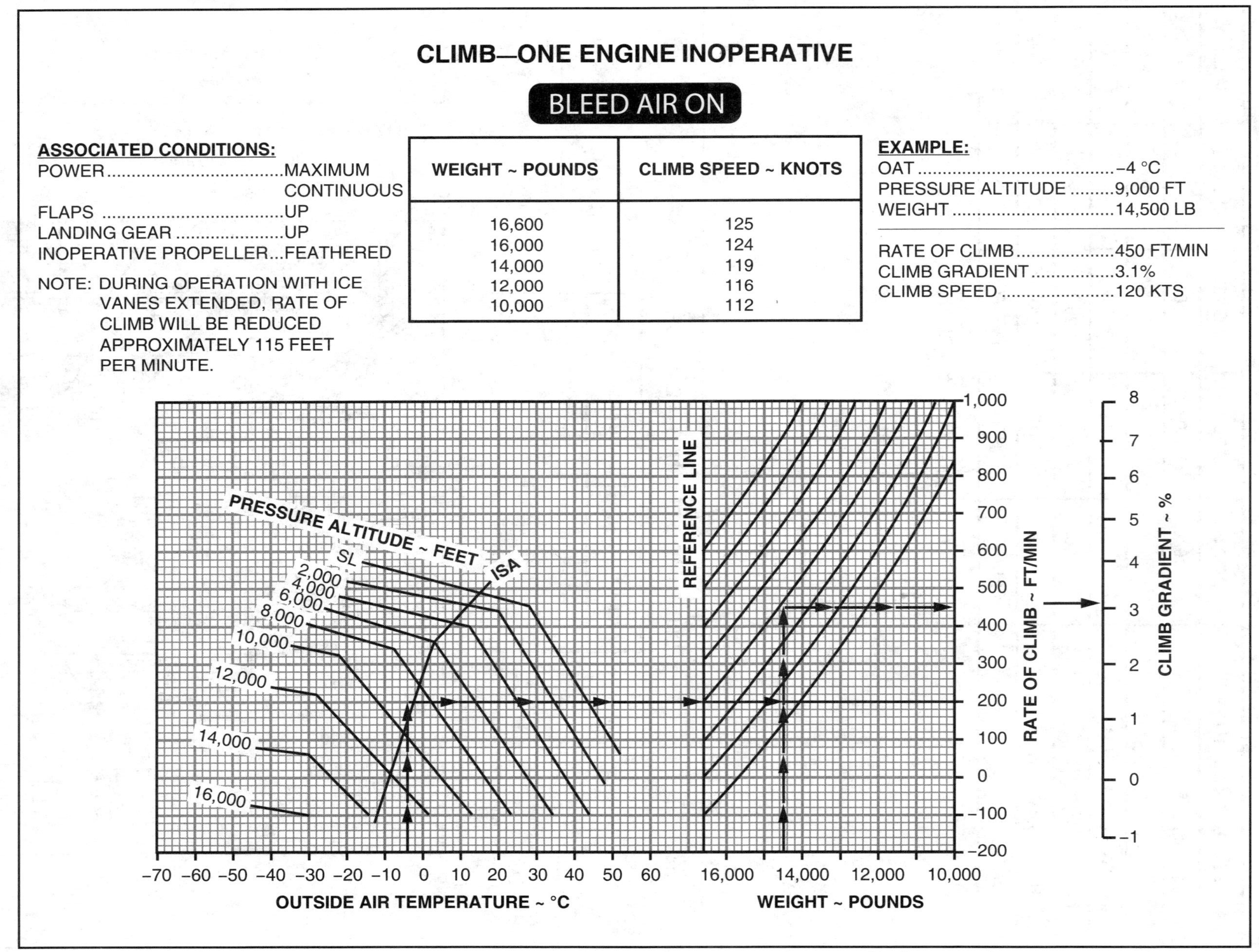

Figure 17. Climb—One Engine Inoperative.

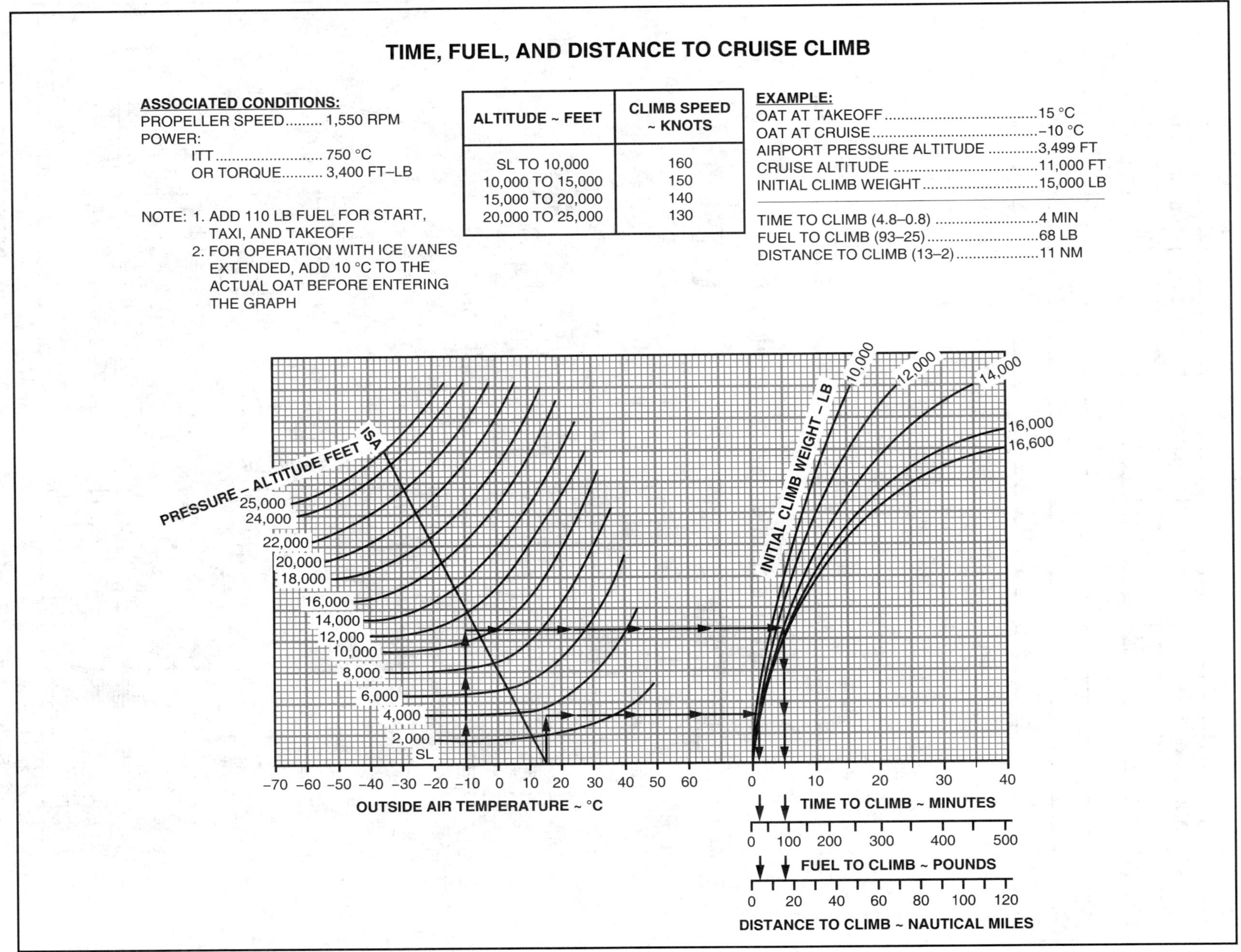

Figure 18. Time, Fuel and Distance to Cruise Climb.

OPERATING CONDITIONS	AC-26	AC-27	AC-28	AC-29	AC-30
OAT AT MEA	−8 °C	+30 °C	+5 °C	+18 °C	+22 °C
WEIGHT	15,500	16,600	16,000	16,300	14,500
ROUTE SEGMENT MEA	6,000	5,500	9,000	7,000	9,500
BLEED AIR	ON	ON	OFF	ON	OFF

Figure 19. Commuter Aircraft—Service Ceiling.

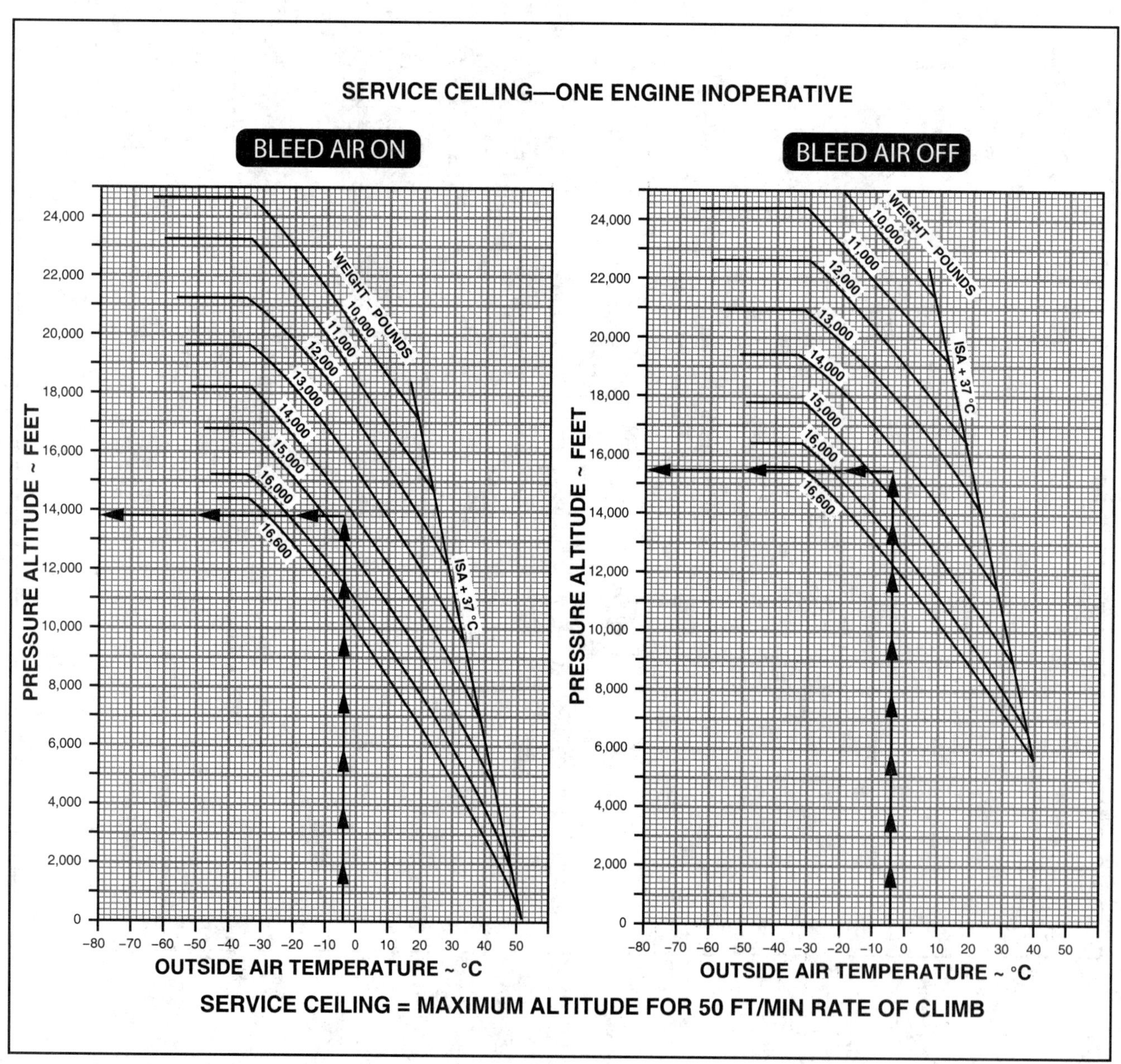

Figure 20. Service Ceiling—One Engine Inoperative.

OPERATING CONDITIONS	BE-31	BE-32	BE-33	BE-34	BE-35
WEIGHT	15,000	14,000	13,000	16,000	11,000
PRESSURE ALTITUDE	22,000	17,000	20,000	23,000	14,000
TEMPERATURE (OAT)	−19 °C	−19 °C	−35 °C	−31 °C	−3 °C
TRUE COURSE	110	270	185	020	305
WIND	180/30	020/35	135/45	340/25	040/50
CRUISE DISTANCE	280	320	400	230	300

Figure 21. Commuter Aircraft—Cruise.

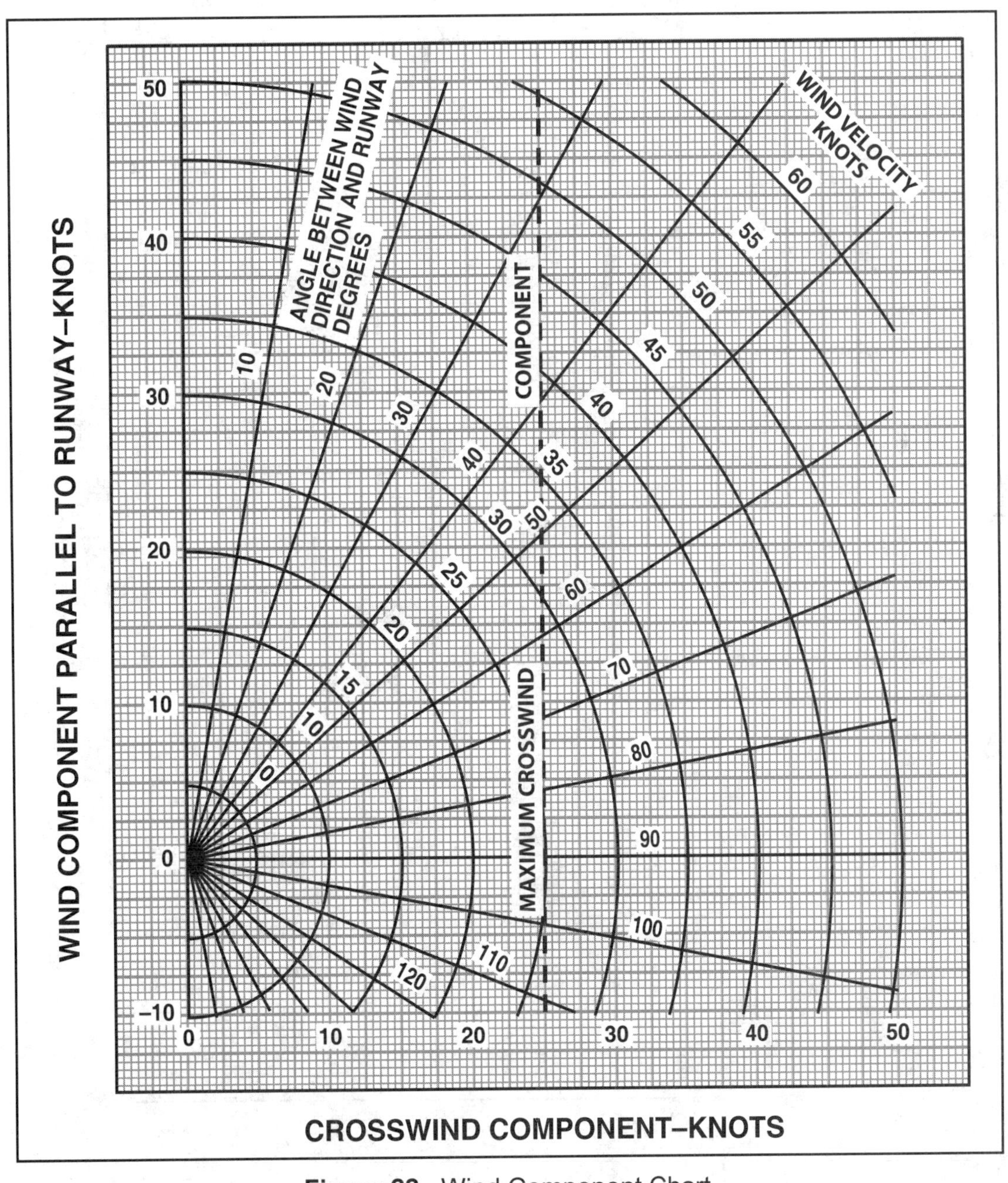

Figure 22. Wind Component Chart.

RECOMMENDED CRUISE POWER
1550 RPM

ISA + 10 °C

WEIGHT			16,000 POUNDS					14,000 POUNDS					12,000 POUNDS					10,000 POUNDS				
PRESSURE ALTITUDE	IOAT	OAT	TORQUE PER ENG	FUEL FLOW PER ENG	TOTAL FUEL FLOW	IAS	TAS	TORQUE PER ENG	FUEL FLOW PER ENG	TOTAL FUEL FLOW	IAS	TAS	TORQUE PER ENG	FUEL FLOW PER ENG	TOTAL FUEL FLOW	IAS	TAS	TORQUE PER ENG	FUEL FLOW PER ENG	TOTAL FUEL FLOW	IAS	TAS
FEET	°C	°C	FT-LB	LB/HR	LB/HR	KTS	KTS	FT-LB	LB/HR	LB/HR	KTS	KTS	FT-LB	LB/HR	LB/HR	KTS	KTS	FT-LB	LB/HR	LB/HR	KTS	KTS
SL	30	25	3,294	577	1,154	232	239	3,301	577	1,154	235	241	3,307	577	1,154	237	243	3,312	577	1,154	238	245
2,000	26	21	3,191	551	1,102	227	240	3,198	551	1,102	230	243	3,204	552	1,104	232	245	3,209	552	1,104	233	247
4,000	22	17	3,092	527	1,054	222	242	3,100	528	1,056	224	244	3,106	528	1,056	227	247	3,111	528	1,056	228	249
6,000	19	13	2,992	504	1,008	216	243	3,000	505	1,010	219	246	3,006	505	1,010	222	249	3,012	505	1,010	224	251
8,000	15	9	2,886	481	962	211	244	2,896	482	964	214	247	2,903	482	964	216	250	2,909	482	964	219	253
10,000	11	5	2,778	458	916	205	244	2,789	458	916	208	248	2,797	459	918	211	252	2,804	459	918	213	254
12,000	7	1	2,636	432	864	198	243	2,648	433	866	202	248	2,657	433	866	205	252	2,664	434	868	207	255
14,000	3	−3	2,495	408	816	190	241	2,508	409	818	195	247	2,518	409	818	198	251	2,525	409	818	201	255
16,000	−1	−7	2,352	384	768	182	239	2,367	385	770	188	246	2,378	385	770	192	251	2,386	386	772	195	255
18,000	−6	−11	2,208	361	722	174	235	2,226	362	724	180	243	2,239	363	726	185	250	2,248	363	726	188	254
20,000	−10	−15	2,063	338	676	164	229	2,085	340	680	172	240	2,100	341	682	177	248	2,111	341	682	181	253
22,000	−14	−19	1,911	316	632	153	221	1,939	317	634	163	235	1,957	319	638	169	245	1,969	319	638	174	252
24,000	−19	−23	1,749	292	584	137	206	1,790	295	590	152	229	1,812	297	594	161	241	1,827	298	596	167	249
25,000	−21	−25	1,649	279	558	122	187	1,714	284	568	147	224	1,739	286	572	156	238	1,756	287	574	163	248

Figure 23. Recommended Cruise Power—ISA +10 °C.

RECOMMENDED CRUISE POWER
1550 RPM

ISA

WEIGHT			16,000 POUNDS					14,000 POUNDS					12,000 POUNDS					10,000 POUNDS				
PRESSURE ALTITUDE	IOAT	OAT	TORQUE PER ENG	FUEL FLOW PER ENG	TOTAL FUEL FLOW	IAS	TAS	TORQUE PER ENG	FUEL FLOW PER ENG	TOTAL FUEL FLOW	IAS	TAS	TORQUE PER ENG	FUEL FLOW PER ENG	TOTAL FUEL FLOW	IAS	TAS	TORQUE PER ENG	FUEL FLOW PER ENG	TOTAL FUEL FLOW	IAS	TAS
FEET	°C	°C	FT-LB	LB/HR	LB/HR	KTS	KTS	FT-LB	LB/HR	LB/HR	KTS	KTS	FT-LB	LB/HR	LB/HR	KTS	KTS	FT-LB	LB/HR	LB/HR	KTS	KTS
SL	20	15	3,400	586	1,172	237	239	3,400	585	1,170	239	241	3,400	585	1,170	241	243	3,400	585	1,170	242	244
2,000	17	11	3,400	573	1,146	234	244	3,400	573	1,146	236	246	3,400	572	1,144	238	248	3,400	572	1,144	240	249
4,000	13	7	3,400	560	1,120	232	248	3,400	559	1,118	234	250	3,400	559	1,118	236	252	3,400	559	1,118	237	254
6,000	9	3	3,397	548	1,096	229	252	3,400	548	1,096	231	255	3,400	547	1,094	233	257	3,400	547	1,094	235	259
8,000	5	−1	3,253	521	1,042	223	253	3,260	522	1,044	225	256	3,265	522	1,044	228	258	3,270	522	1,044	229	260
10,000	1	−5	3,092	494	988	216	252	3,100	494	988	219	256	3,107	495	990	221	258	3,112	495	990	223	261
12,000	−3	−9	2,929	466	932	208	251	2,937	467	934	212	255	2,945	467	934	214	258	2,950	467	934	217	261
14,000	−7	−13	2,772	440	880	201	250	2,781	441	882	205	255	2,789	441	882	208	258	2,795	442	884	210	261
16,000	−11	−17	2,606	414	828	193	248	2,618	414	828	197	253	2,626	415	830	201	258	2,633	415	830	203	261
18,000	−15	−21	2,435	288	776	184	244	2,449	389	778	189	251	2,459	389	778	193	256	2,467	390	780	196	260
20,000	−19	−25	2,263	363	726	175	239	2,282	364	728	181	248	2,294	365	730	186	254	2,302	365	730	189	259
22,000	−24	−29	2,094	338	676	164	233	2,118	340	680	172	244	2,133	341	682	178	251	2,144	342	684	182	257
24,000	−28	−33	1,931	315	630	152	223	1,960	317	634	163	238	1,979	318	636	169	248	1,991	319	638	174	255
25,000	−30	−35	1,846	303	606	145	216	1,880	305	610	157	235	1,901	307	614	165	246	1,915	308	616	170	253

Figure 24. Recommended Cruise Power—ISA.

RECOMMENDED CRUISE POWER
1550 RPM

ISA –10 °C

WEIGHT			16,000 POUNDS					14,000 POUNDS					12,000 POUNDS					10,000 POUNDS				
PRESSURE ALTITUDE	IOAT	OAT	TORQUE PER ENG	FUEL FLOW PER ENG	TOTAL FUEL FLOW	IAS	TAS	TORQUE PER ENG	FUEL FLOW PER ENG	TOTAL FUEL FLOW	IAS	TAS	TORQUE PER ENG	FUEL FLOW PER ENG	TOTAL FUEL FLOW	IAS	TAS	TORQUE PER ENG	FUEL FLOW PER ENG	TOTAL FUEL FLOW	IAS	TAS
FEET	°C	°C	FT-LB	LB/HR	LB/HR	KTS	KTS	FT-LB	LB/HR	LB/HR	KTS	KTS	FT-LB	LB/HR	LB/HR	KTS	KTS	FT-LB	LB/HR	LB/HR	KTS	KTS
SL	10	5	3,400	582	1,164	238	237	3,400	582	1,164	240	239	3,400	581	1,162	242	240	3,400	581	1,162	243	242
2,000	6	1	3,400	569	1,138	236	241	3,400	569	1,138	238	243	3,400	568	1,136	240	245	3,400	568	1,136	241	246
4,000	3	–3	3,400	558	1,116	233	245	3,400	557	1,114	236	248	3,400	557	1,114	237	249	3,400	557	1,114	239	251
6,000	–1	–7	3,400	548	1,096	231	250	3,400	547	1,094	233	252	3,400	547	1,094	235	254	3,400	546	1,092	236	256
8,000	–5	–11	3,400	538	1,076	228	254	3,400	538	1,076	231	257	3,400	538	1,076	232	259	3,400	537	1,074	234	261
10,000	–9	–15	3,400	530	1,060	226	259	3,400	530	1,060	228	262	3,400	530	1,060	230	264	3,400	529	1,058	232	266
12,000	–13	–19	3,200	499	998	218	258	3,208	500	1,000	221	261	3,215	500	1,000	223	264	3,220	501	1,002	225	266
14,000	–17	–23	3,010	470	940	210	256	3,019	471	942	213	260	3,026	471	942	216	263	3,032	472	944	218	266
16,000	–21	–27	2,823	442	884	202	254	2,833	442	884	205	258	2,841	443	886	209	262	2,848	443	886	211	265
18,000	–25	–31	2,641	414	828	193	251	2,652	415	830	198	256	2,661	416	832	201	261	2,668	416	832	204	264
20,000	–29	–35	2,456	387	774	184	247	2,471	388	776	189	254	2,481	389	778	193	259	2,489	390	780	196	263
22,000	–33	–39	2,277	361	722	174	242	2,296	363	726	181	250	2,308	363	726	185	256	2,318	364	728	189	261
24,000	–37	–43	2,105	336	672	163	234	2,128	338	676	172	246	2,144	339	678	177	254	2,155	340	680	181	260
25,000	–40	–45	2,017	324	648	157	230	2,044	326	652	167	243	2,061	327	654	173	252	2,073	328	656	177	258

Figure 25. Recommended Cruise Power—ISA –10 °C.

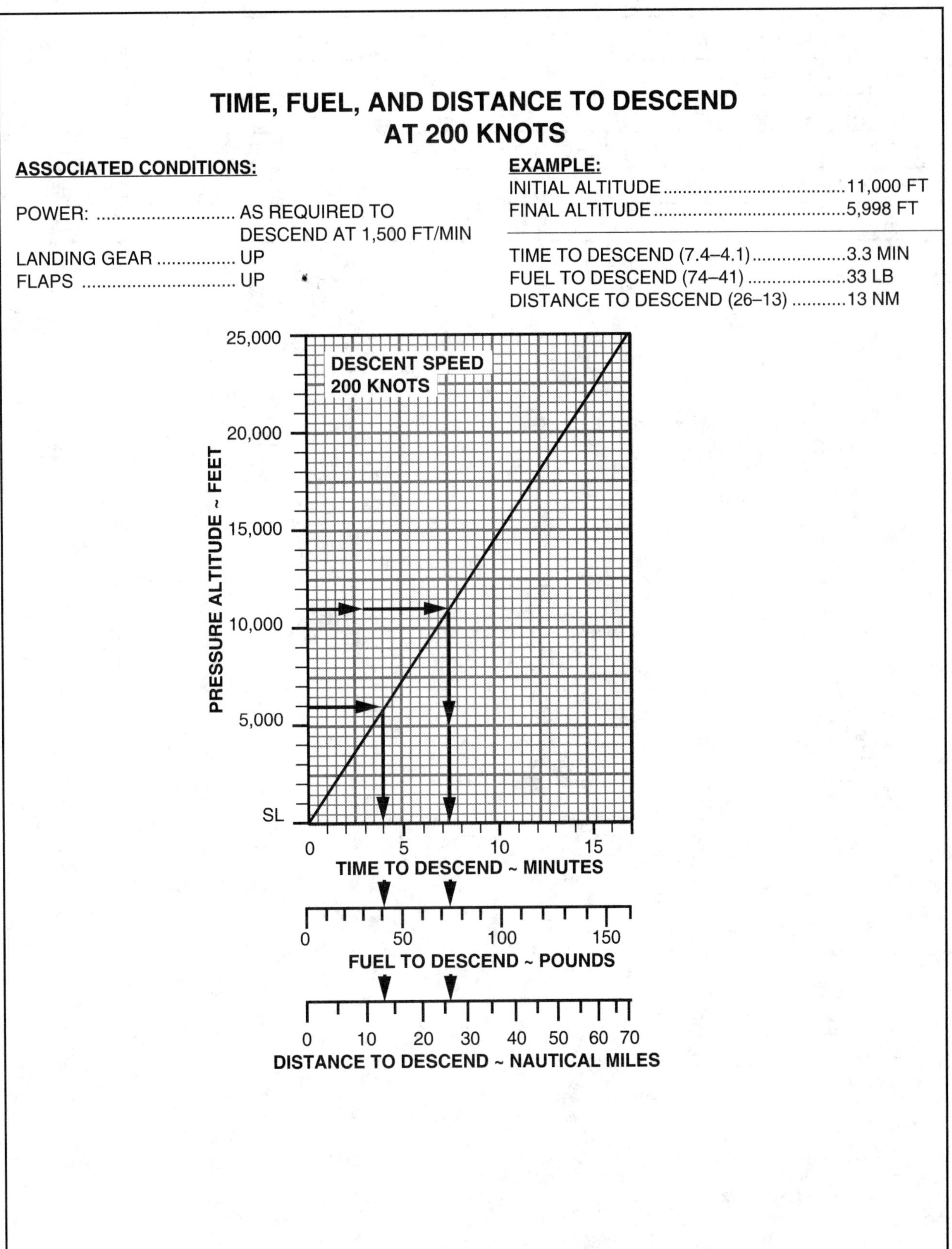

Figure 26. Time, Fuel, and Distance to Descend.

OPERATING CONDITIONS	AC-36	AC-37	AC-38	AC-39	AC-40
PRESSURE ALTITUDE	SL	1,000	2,000	4,000	5,000
TEMPERATURE (OAT)	+30 °C	+16 °C	0 °C	+20 °C	ISA
WEIGHT	16,000	14,500	13,500	15,000	12,500
WIND COMPONENT (KTS)	20 HW	10 TW	15 HW	5 TW	25 HW
RUNWAY LENGTH (FT)	4,000	4,500	3,800	5,000	4,000

Figure 27. Commuter Aircraft—Landing.

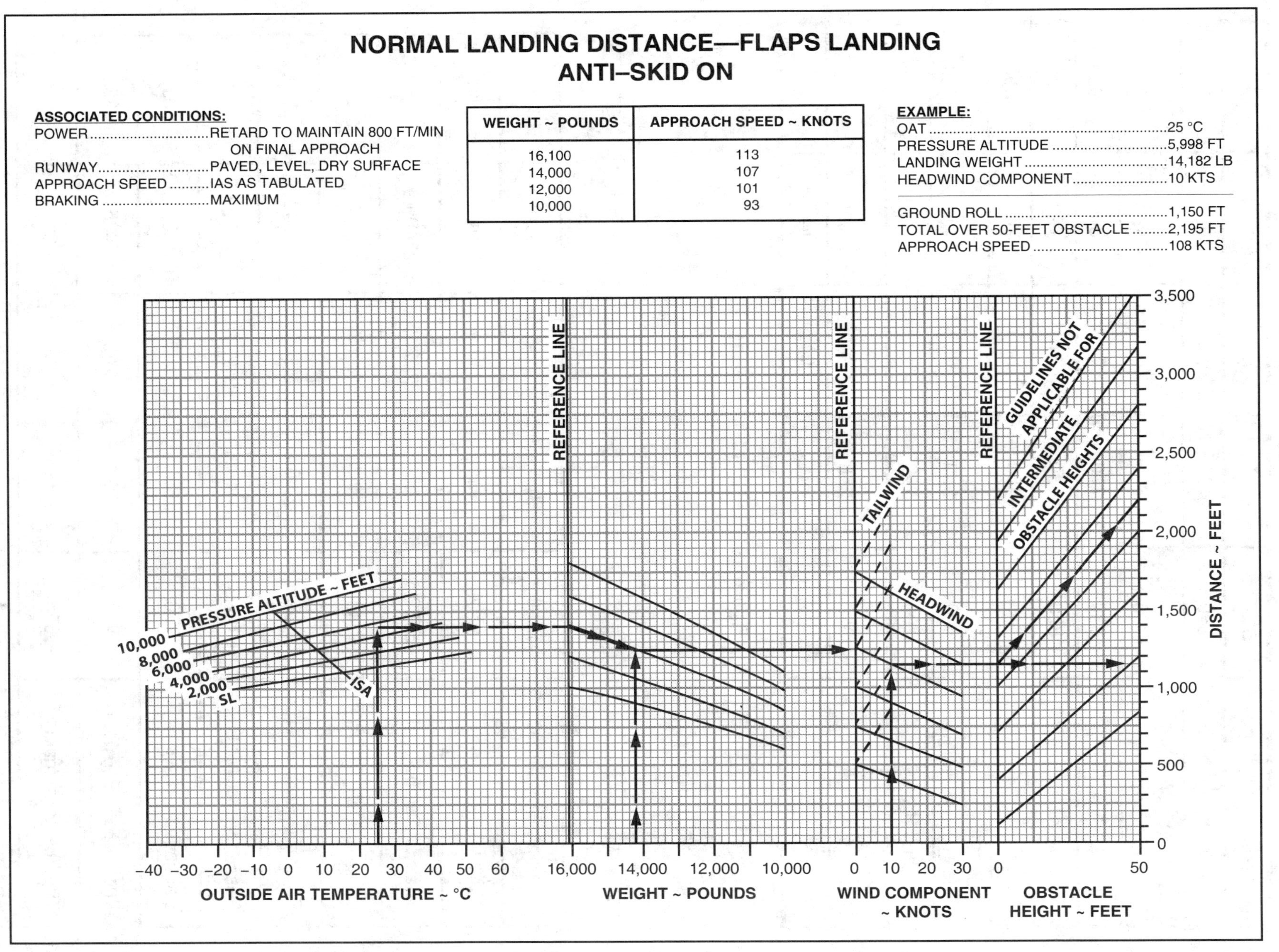

Figure 28. Normal Landing Distance—Flaps Landing.

Operating Conditions	BL-1	BL-2	BL-3	BL-4	BL-5
Crew Weight	340	400	360	380	370
Passenger Weight Row 1	700	620	-	180	680
Row 2	830	700	750	800	950
Row 3	800	680	810	720	850
Row 4	-	400	650	200	500
Baggage Center	500	550	300	200	450
Left and Right	200	250	-	100	-
Fuel Gallons	300	250	360	400	260
Type	Jet A	Jet B	Jet A	Jet B	Jet A

Figure 29. Bell 214 ST - Loading.

Loading Conditions	BL-6	BL-7	BL-8	BL-9	BL-10
Basic Weight	10,225	9,450	9,000	9,510	9,375
Basic MOM/100	25562.5	23236.0	22020.5	23499.9	23296.8
Crew Weight	340	380	410	360	400
Passenger Weight	3,280	2,880	3,150	2,040	2,400
Passenger MOM/100	6722.5	5418.6	6425.8	4732.2	4560.7
Baggage (center)	700	600	300	550	650
Fuel Load (6.8 lb/gal.)	435	290	220	435	380
Trip Fuel Burn (gal.)	355	190	190	325	330
Lateral CG is on longitudinal axis.					

Figure 30. Bell 214 ST - Weight Shift and Limits.

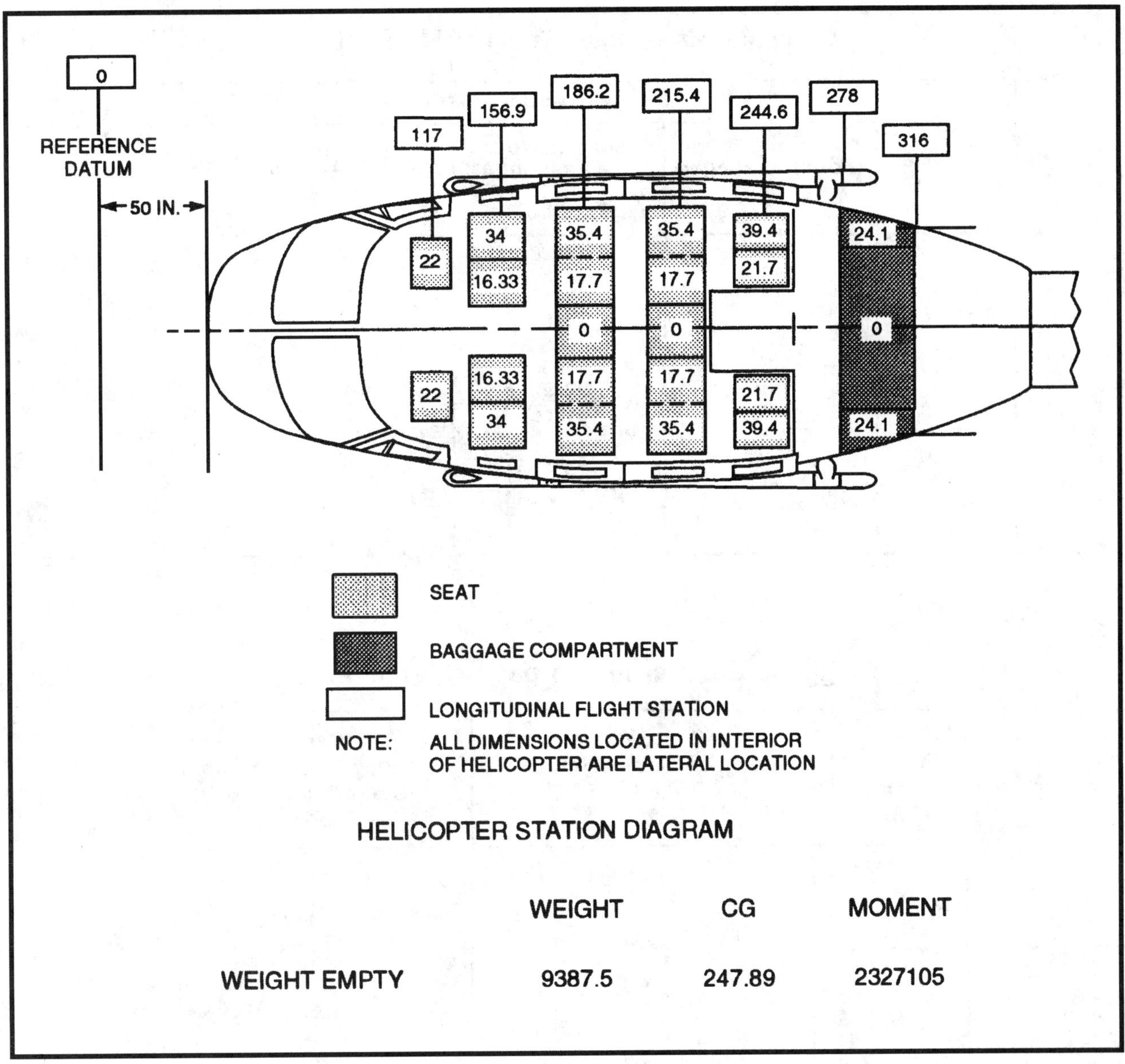

	WEIGHT	CG	MOMENT
WEIGHT EMPTY	9387.5	247.89	2327105

Figure 31. Helicopter - Loading Data.

Crew and Passenger Table of Moments (in-lb)

Weight lbs	Crew Seats F.S. 117	Airline Passenger Seats			
		First Row (Four Passenger) Seats F.S. 156.9	Second Row (Five Passenger) Seats F.S. 186.2	Third Row (Five Passenger) Seats F.S. 215.4	Fourth Row (Four Passenger) Seats F.S. 244.6
100	11700	15690	18620	21540	24460
110	12870	17259	20482	23694	26906
120	14040	18828	22344	25848	29352
130	15210	20397	24206	28002	31798
140	16380	21966	26068	30156	34244
150	17550	23535	27930	32310	36690
160	18720	25104	29792	34464	39136
170	19890	26673	31654	36618	41582
180	21060	28242	33516	38772	44028
190	22230	29811	35378	40926	46474
200	23400	31380	37240	43080	48920
210	24570	32949	39102	45234	51366
220	25740	34518	40964	47388	53812

Baggage Compartment Loading Table (in-lb ÷ 100)

Baggage Weight lbs	Left and Right Baggage Compartment Sta. 278.0 to 316.0 F.S. 295.2	Center Baggage Compartment Sta. 278.0 to 316.0 F.S. 297.0
50	147.6	148.5
100	295.2	297.0
150	442.8	445.5
200	590.4	594.0
250	738.0	742.5
300	885.6	891.0
350	1033.2	1039.5
400	1180.8	1188.0
450	1328.4	1336.5
500	1476.0	1485.0
530	1564.6	1574.1
550		1633.5
600		1782.0
650		1930.5
700		2079.0
740		2197.8

Figure 32. Helicopter - Weights and Moments - Crew, Passengers, and Baggage.

Usable Fuel Loading Table (English)

Jet A, Jet A-1, JP-5 (6.8 lbs/gal)							
U.S. gal	Weight lbs	C.G.	Moment in. lb. ÷ 100	U.S. gal	Weight lbs	C.G.	Moment in. lb. ÷ 100
10	68	244.3	166	220	1496	246.9	3694
20	136	244.3	332	230	1564	244.3	3820
30	204	244.4	499	240	1632	241.8	3947
**37.1	252	244.4	616	250	1700	239.6	4073
40	272	242.8	660	260	1768	237.6	4200
50	340	237.8	808	270	1836	235.6	4326
60	408	234.5	957	280	1904	233.9	4453
70	476	232.1	1105	290	1972	232.2	4579
80	544	230.9	1256	**291.4	1982	232.0	4597
90	612	229.2	1403	300	2040	233.1	4754
*99.7	678	228.2	1546	310	2108	234.0	4934
*109.2	743	228.2	1695	320	2176	235.1	5115
110	748	228.5	1709	330	2244	236.0	5296
120	816	231.7	1890	340	2312	236.9	5477
130	884	234.4	2072	350	2380	237.7	5658
140	952	236.7	2253	360	2448	238.5	5839
150	1020	238.6	2434	370	2516	239.3	6021
160	1088	240.4	2615	380	2584	240.0	6202
170	1156	242.0	2798	390	2652	240.7	6383
180	1224	243.3	2978	400	2720	241.3	6564
190	1292	244.5	3159	410	2788	241.9	6745
00	1360	245.6	3340	420	2856	242.5	6927
210	1428	246.6	3521	430	2924	243.1	7108
*218.4	1484	247.3	3673	435.0	2958	243.4	7199

Jet B, JP-4 (6.5 lbs/gal)							
U.S. gal	Weight lbs	C.G.	Moment in. lb. ÷ 100	U.S. gal	Weight lbs	C.G.	Moment in. lb. ÷ 100
10	65	244.3	159	220	1430	246.9	3531
20	130	244.3	318	230	1495	244.3	3652
30	195	244.5	477	240	1560	241.8	3772
**37.1	241	244.4	589	250	1625	239.6	3894
40	260	242.8	631	260	1690	237.6	4015
50	325	237.8	773	270	1755	235.6	4135
60	390	234.5	915	280	1820	233.9	4257
70	455	232.1	1056	290	1885	232.2	4377
80	520	230.9	1201	**291.4	1894	232.0	4394
90	585	229.2	1341	300	1950	233.1	4545
*99.7	648	228.2	1479	310	2015	234.0	4715
*109.2	710	228.2	1620	320	2080	235.1	4890
110	715	228.5	1634	330	2145	236.0	5062
120	780	231.7	1807	340	2210	236.9	5235
130	845	234.4	1981	350	2275	237.7	5408
140	910	236.7	2154	360	2340	238.5	5581
150	975	238.6	2326	370	2405	239.3	5755
160	1040	240.4	2500	380	2470	240.5	5928
170	1105	242.0	2674	390	2535	240.7	6102
180	1170	243.3	2847	400	2600	241.3	6274
190	1235	244.5	3020	410	2665	241.9	6447
200	1300	245.6	3193	420	2730	242.5	6620
210	1365	246.6	3366	430	2795	243.1	6795
*218.4	1420	247.3	3512	435	2827.5	243.4	6882

* Extreme limits of fuel C.G.
** Point of C.G. direction change.

Weights given are nominal weights at 15 °C.

Figure 33. Helicopter - Weights and Moments - Usable Fuel.

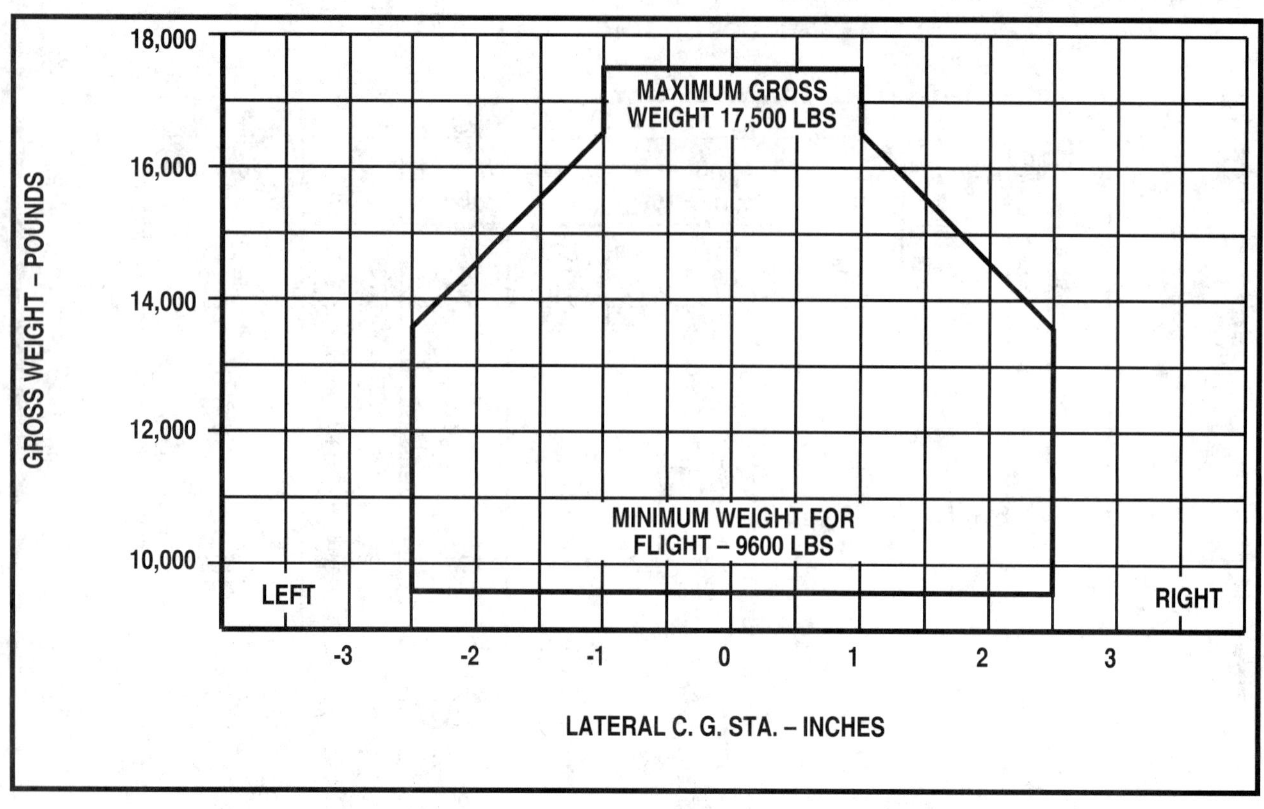

Figure 34. Helicopter - Lateral CG Envelope.

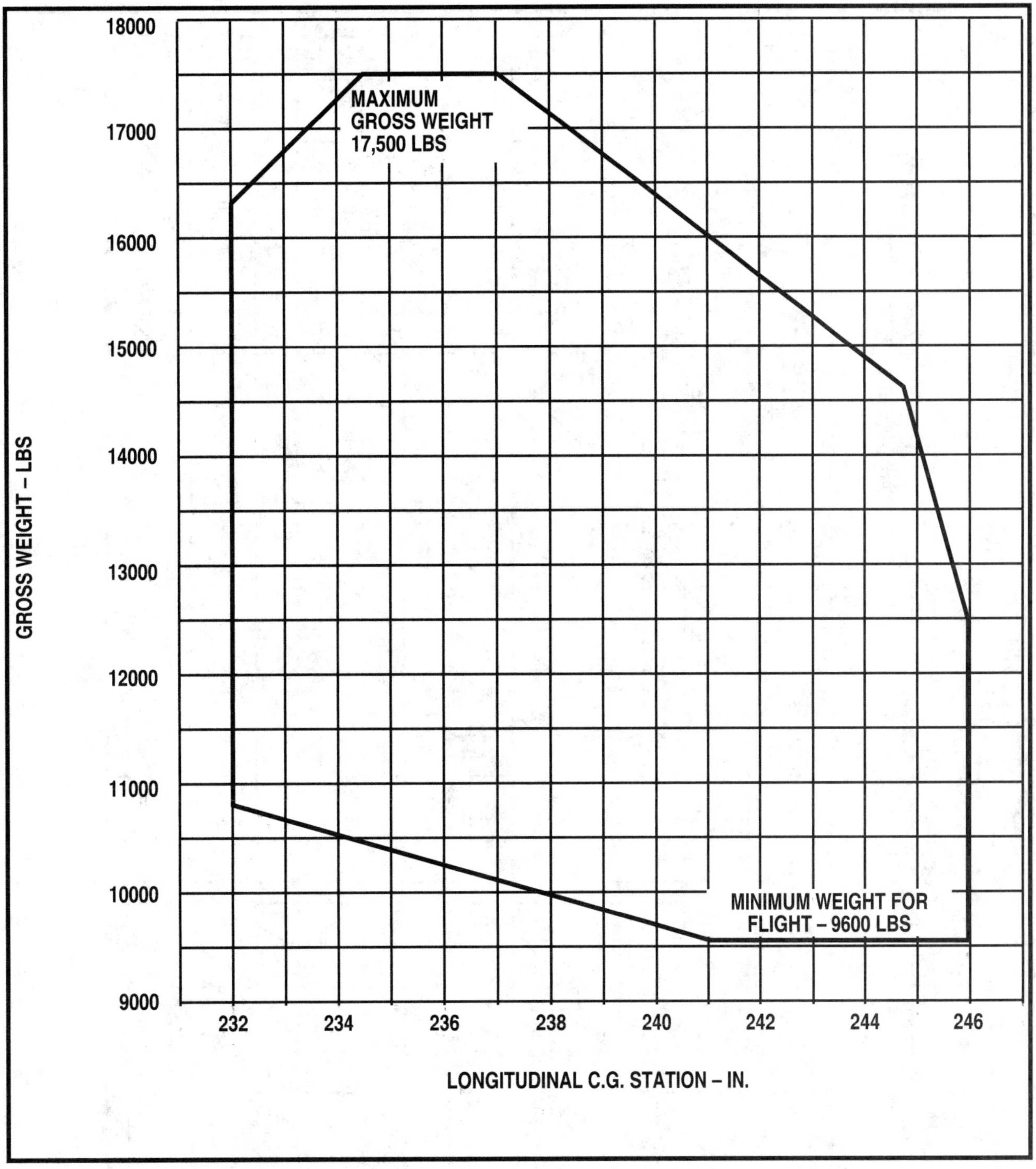

Figure 35. Helicopter - Longitudinal CG Envelope.

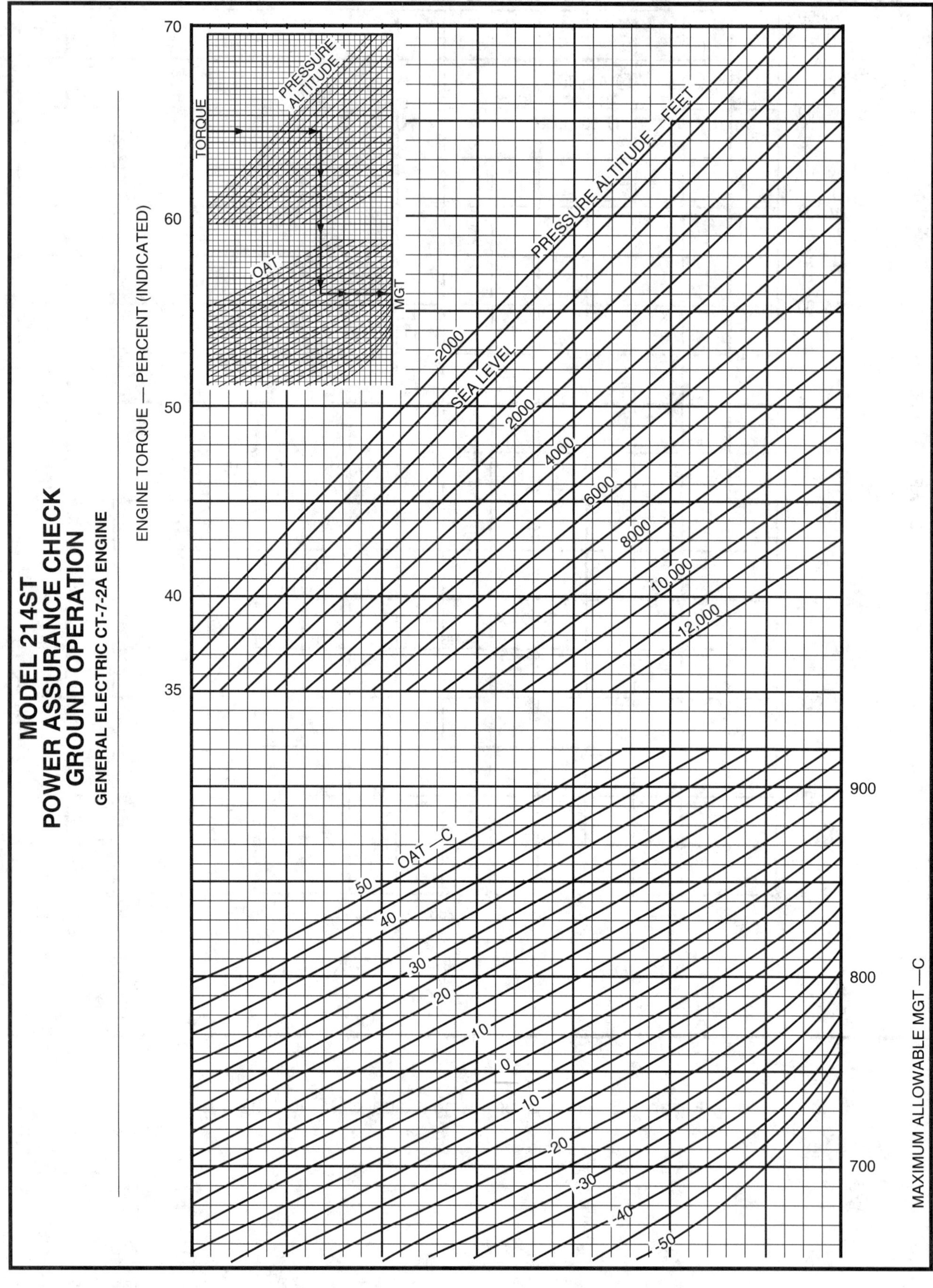

Figure 36. Bell 214 - Power Assurance Check.

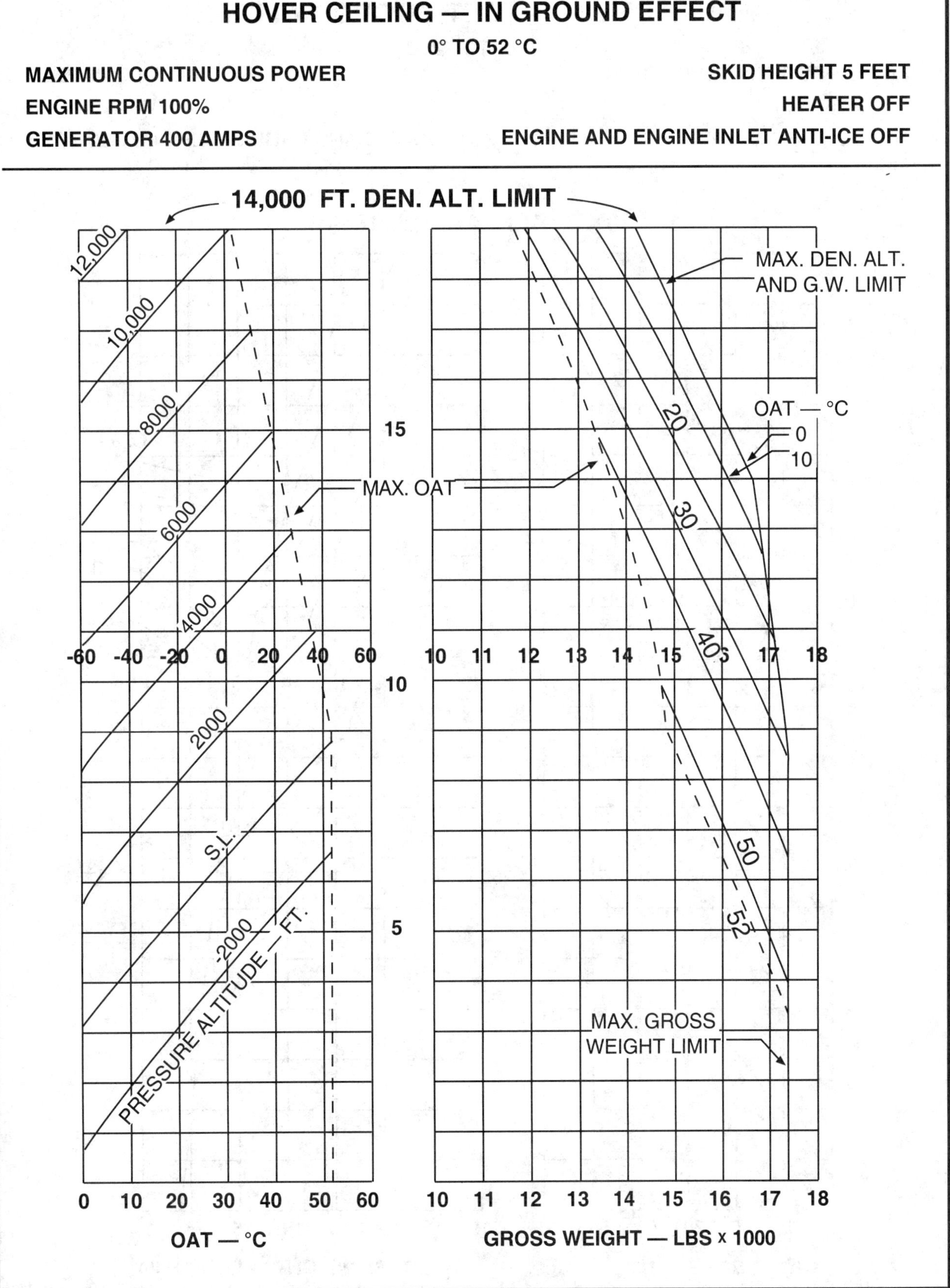

Figure 37. Hovering Ceiling - In Ground Effect.

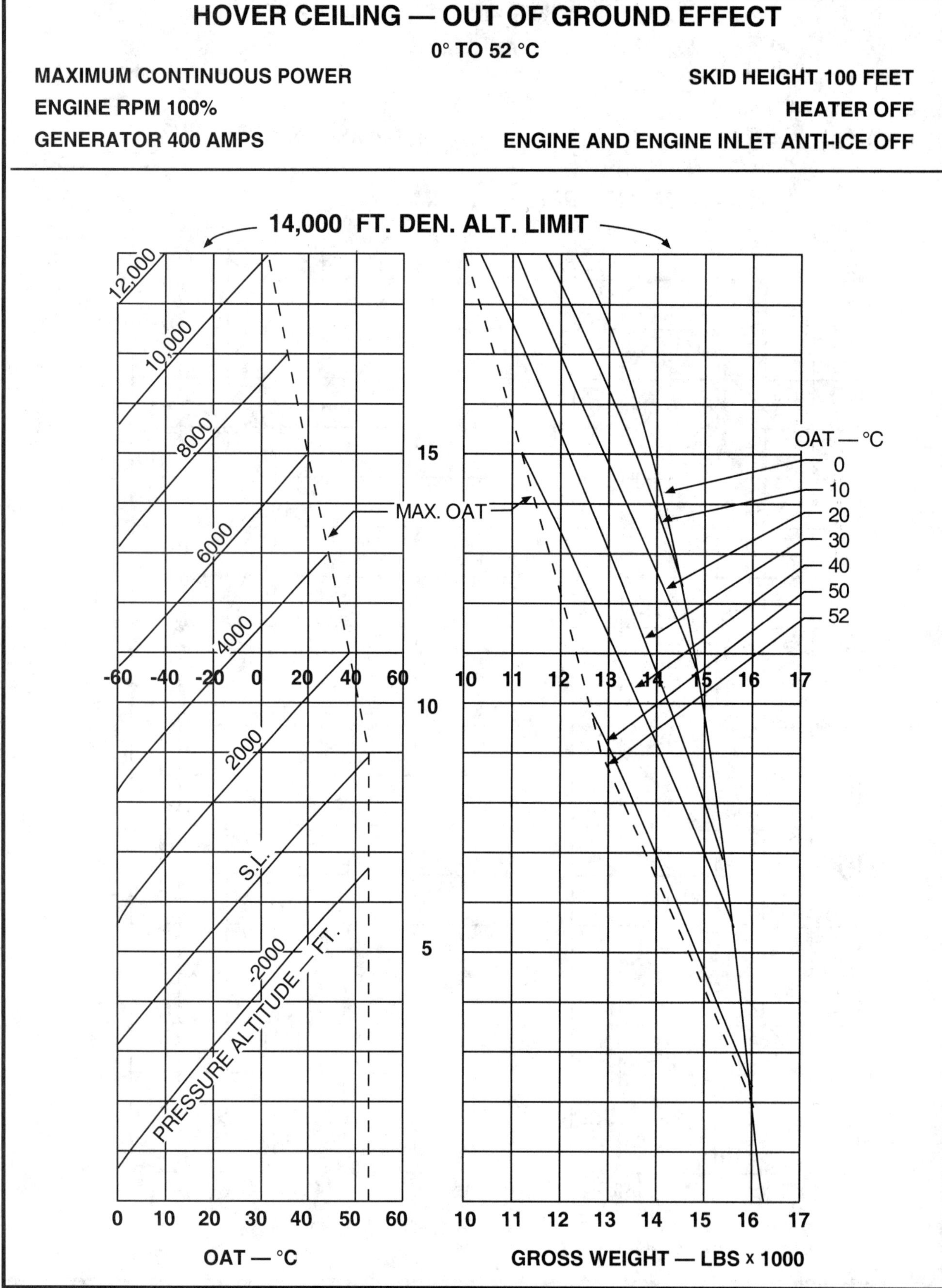

Figure 38. Hovering Ceiling - Out of Ground Effect.

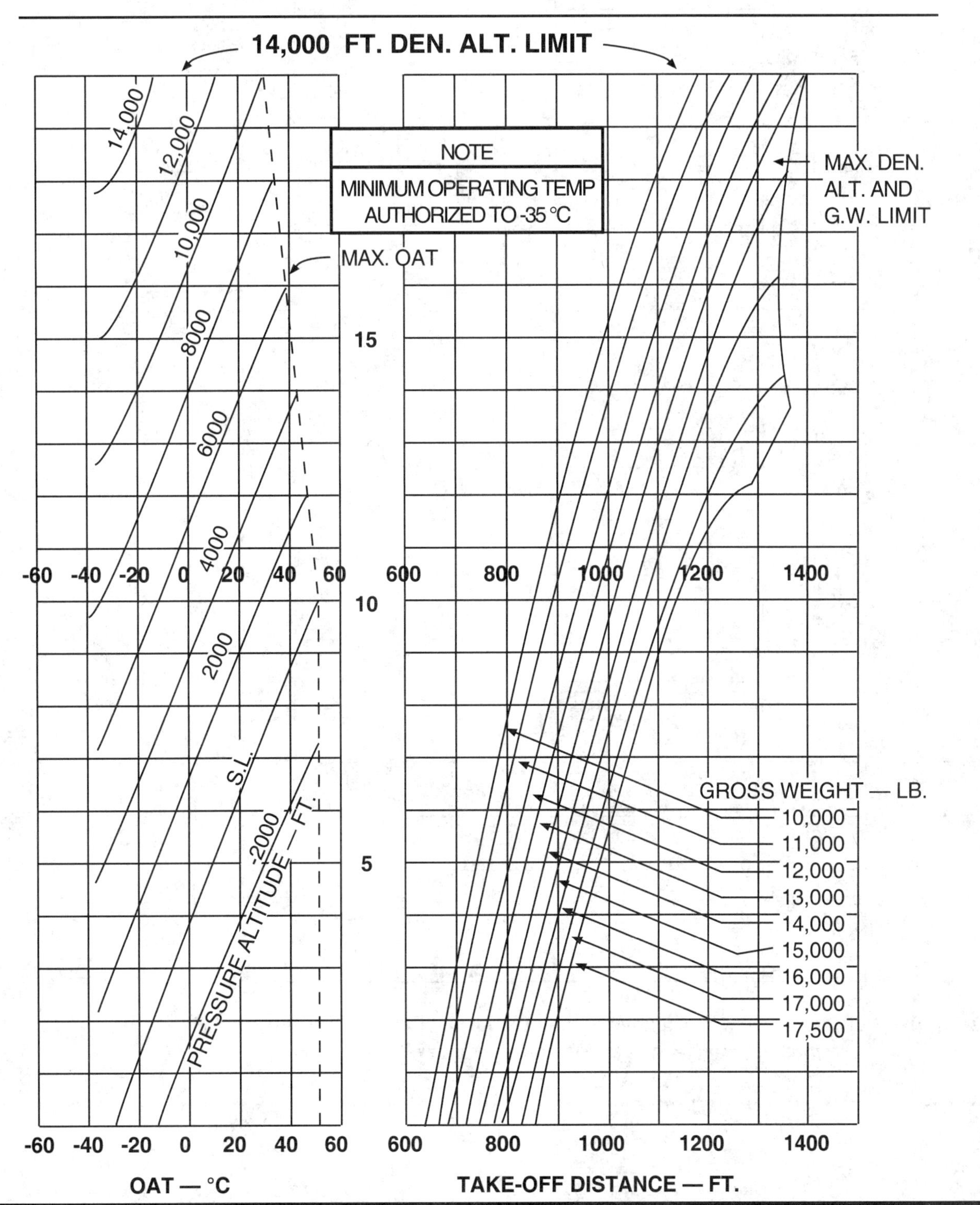

Figure 39. Takeoff Distance Over 50-foot Obstacle.

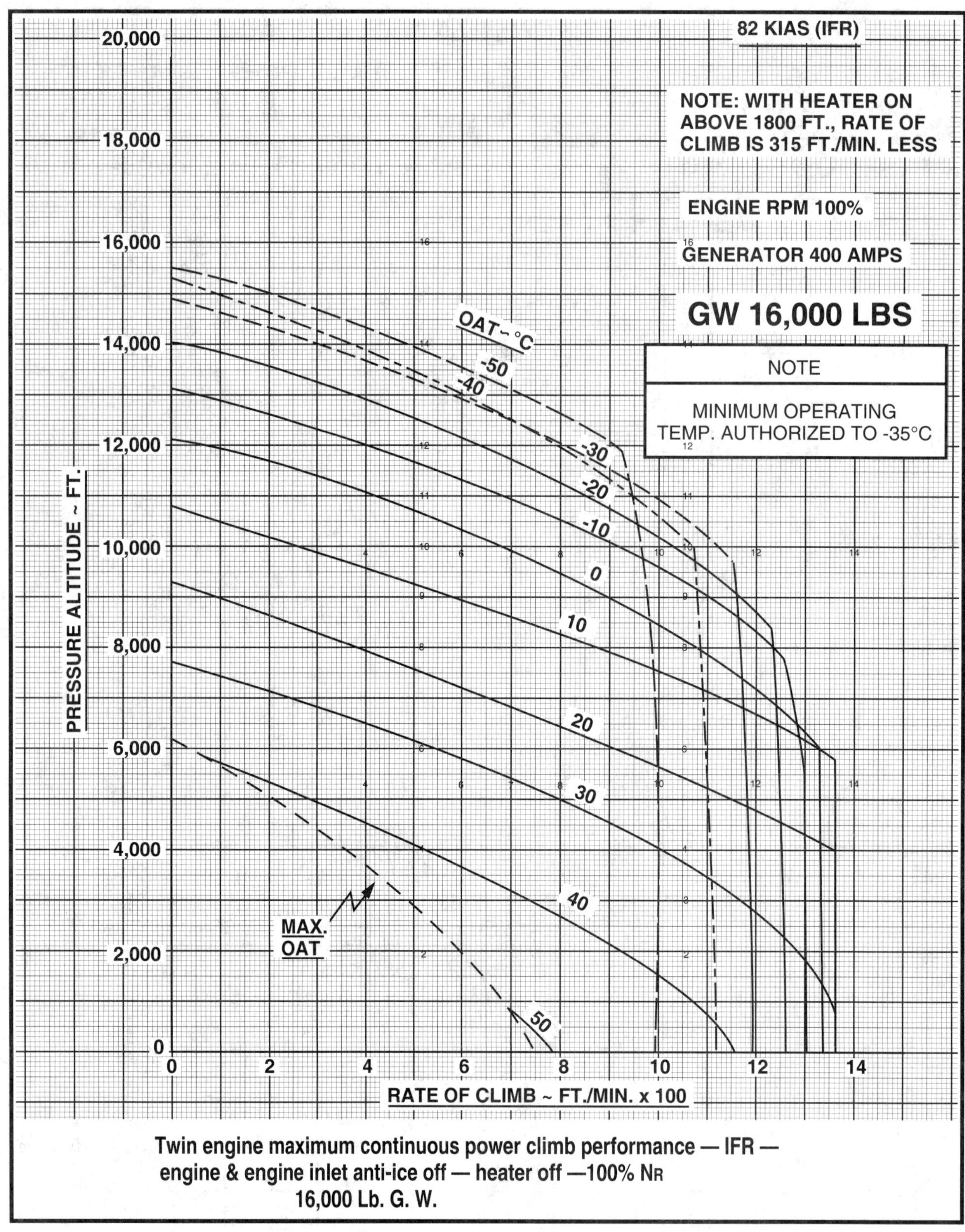

Figure 40. Twin-Engine Climb Performance.

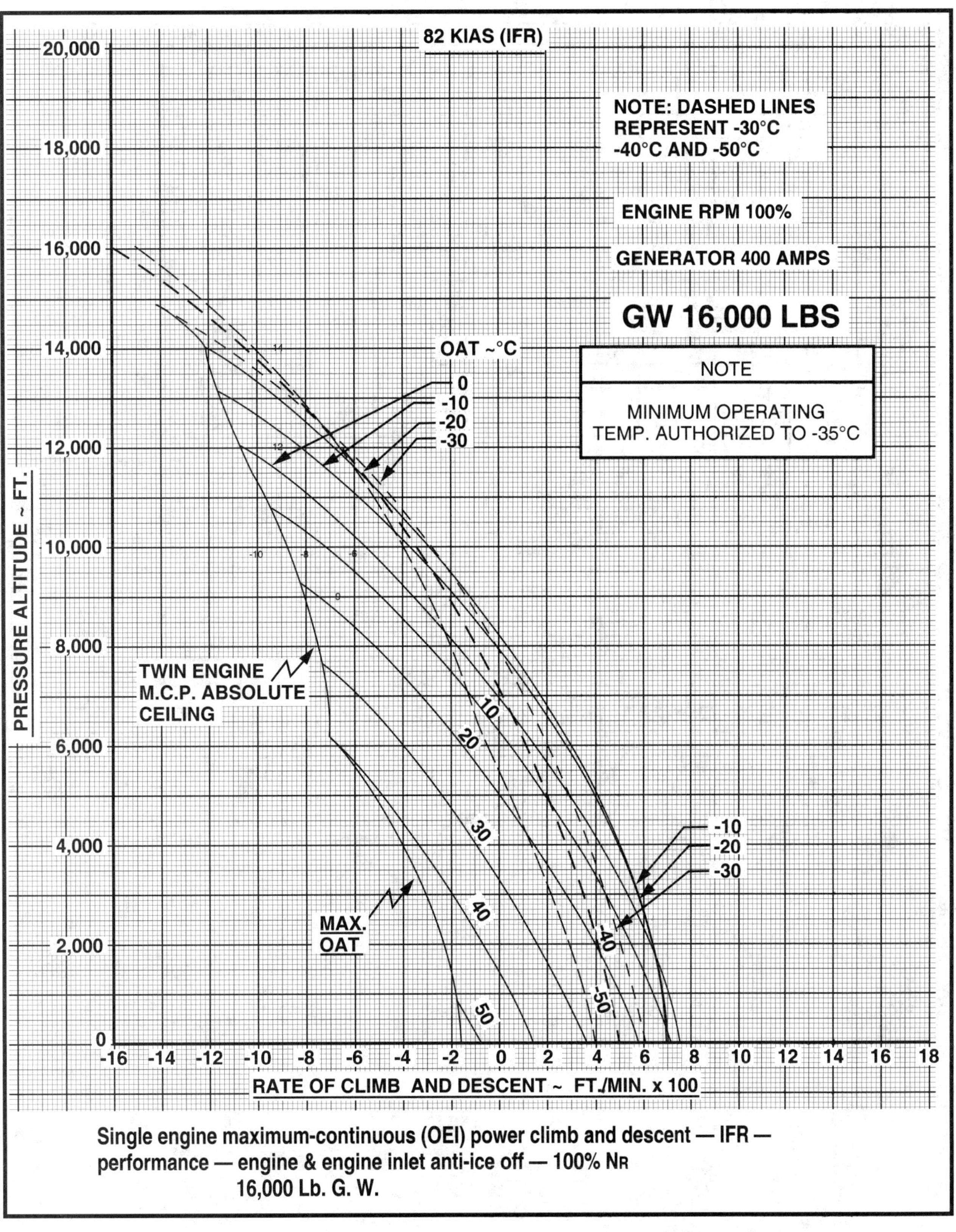

Single engine maximum-continuous (OEI) power climb and descent — IFR — performance — engine & engine inlet anti-ice off — 100% NR
16,000 Lb. G. W.

Figure 41. Single-Engine Climb Performance.

12500 LB	Airspeed Limit (V_{NE}) - KIAS										
OAT °C	Press Alt - FT x1,000										
	0	2	4	6	8	10	12	14	16	18	20
51.7	155	-	-	-	-	-	-	-	-	-	-
40	159	150	140	-	-	-	-	-	-	-	-
20	159	159	149	139	128	118	109	99	-	-	-
0	155	150	144	139	134	128	118	108	98	-	-
-15	142	136	131	126	121	116	112	106	103	95	-
-25	132	127	122	117	113	108	104	100	96	92	88
-35	122	117	113	108	104	100	96	92	88	84	81

15500 LB	Airspeed Limit (V_{NE}) - KIAS										
OAT °C	Press Alt - FT x1,000										
	0	2	4	6	8	10	12	14	16	18	20
51.7	139	-	-	-	-	-	-	-	-	-	-
40	144	134	122	-	-	-	-	-	-	-	-
20	144	143	133	121	110	99	89	78	-	-	-
0	144	144	143	132	120	109	98	88	77	-	-
-15	142	136	131	126	121	116	105	94	83	72	-
-25	132	127	122	117	113	108	104	100	89	77	-
-35	122	117	113	108	104	100	96	92	88	83	-

13500 LB	Airspeed Limit (V_{NE}) - KIAS										
OAT °C	Press Alt - FT x1,000										
	0	2	4	6	8	10	12	14	16	18	20
51.7	150	-	-	-	-	-	-	-	-	-	-
40	154	154	135	-	-	-	-	-	-	-	-
20	154	154	144	134	123	113	104	94	-	-	-
0	154	150	144	139	133	123	113	103	93	-	-
-15	142	136	131	126	121	116	112	105	99	89	-
-25	132	127	122	117	113	108	104	100	96	92	86
-35	122	117	113	108	104	100	96	92	88	84	81

16500 LB	Airspeed Limit (V_{NE}) - KIAS										
OAT °C	Press Alt - FT x1,000										
	0	2	4	6	8	10	12	14	16	18	20
51.7	133	-	-	-	-	-	-	-	-	-	-
40	139	124	110	-	-	-	-	-	-	-	-
20	139	138	123	108	93	79	-	-	-	-	-
0	139	139	138	122	107	92	78	-	-	-	-
-15	139	136	131	126	118	103	87	72	-	-	-
-25	132	127	122	117	113	108	93	78	-	-	-
-35	122	117	113	108	104	100	96	87	75	-	-

14500 LB	Airspeed Limit (V_{NE}) - KIAS										
OAT °C	Press Alt - FT x1,000										
	0	2	4	6	8	10	12	14	16	18	20
51.7	145	-	-	-	-	-	-	-	-	-	-
40	149	140	129	-	-	-	-	-	-	-	-
20	149	149	139	128	118	108	99	89	-	-	-
0	149	149	144	138	127	118	108	98	88	-	-
-15	142	136	131	126	121	116	112	104	94	84	-
-25	132	127	122	117	113	108	104	100	96	88	79
-35	122	117	113	108	104	100	96	92	88	84	81

17500 LB	Airspeed Limit (V_{NE}) - KIAS										
OAT °C	Press Alt - FT x1,000										
	0	2	4	6	8	10	12	14	16	18	20
51.7	122	-	-	-	-	-	-	-	-	-	-
40	128	115	102	-	-	-	-	-	-	-	-
20	128	127	114	101	-	-	-	-	-	-	-
0	128	128	127	113	100	-	-	-	-	-	-
-15	128	128	128	123	110	94	-	-	-	-	-
-25	128	127	122	117	113	101	87	-	-	-	-
-35	122	117	113	108	104	100	93	-	-	-	-

Figure 42. Airspeed Limit.

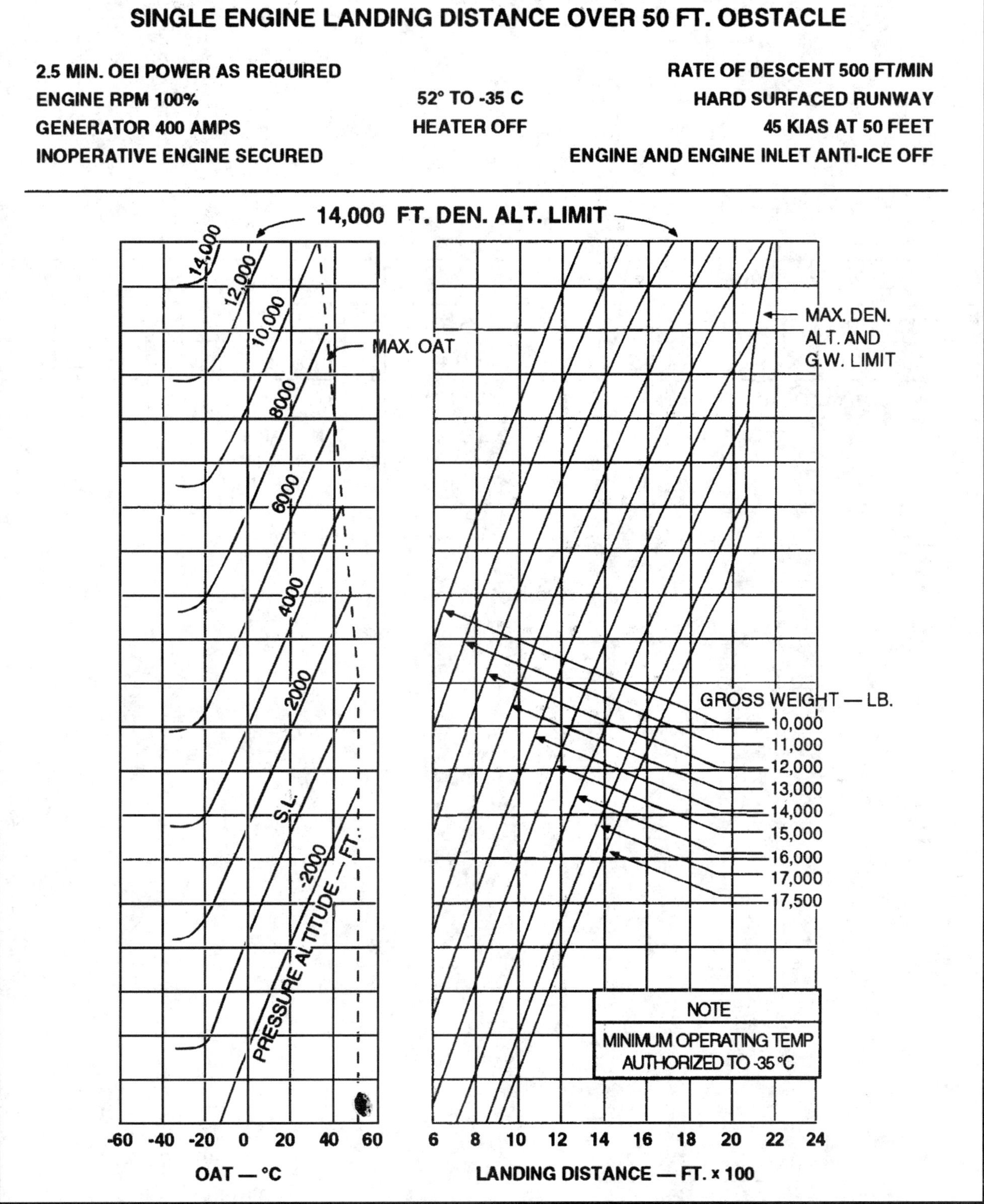

Figure 43. Single-engine Landing Distance Over 50-foot Obstacle.

LOADING CONDITIONS	WS-1	WS-2	WS-3	WS-4	WS-5
LOADED WEIGHT	90,000	85,000	84,500	81,700	88,300
LOADED CG (% MAC)	22.5%	28.4%	19.8%	30.3%	25.5%
WEIGHT CHANGE (POUNDS)	2,500	1,800	3,000	2,100	3,300
FWD COMPT CENTROID – STA 352.1 AND −227.9 INDEX ARM AFT COMPT CENTROID – STA 724.9 AND +144.9 INDEX ARM MAC – 141.5 INCHES, LEMAC – STA 549.13 AND −30.87 INDEX ARM					

Figure 44. Transport Aircraft 1—Weight Shift.

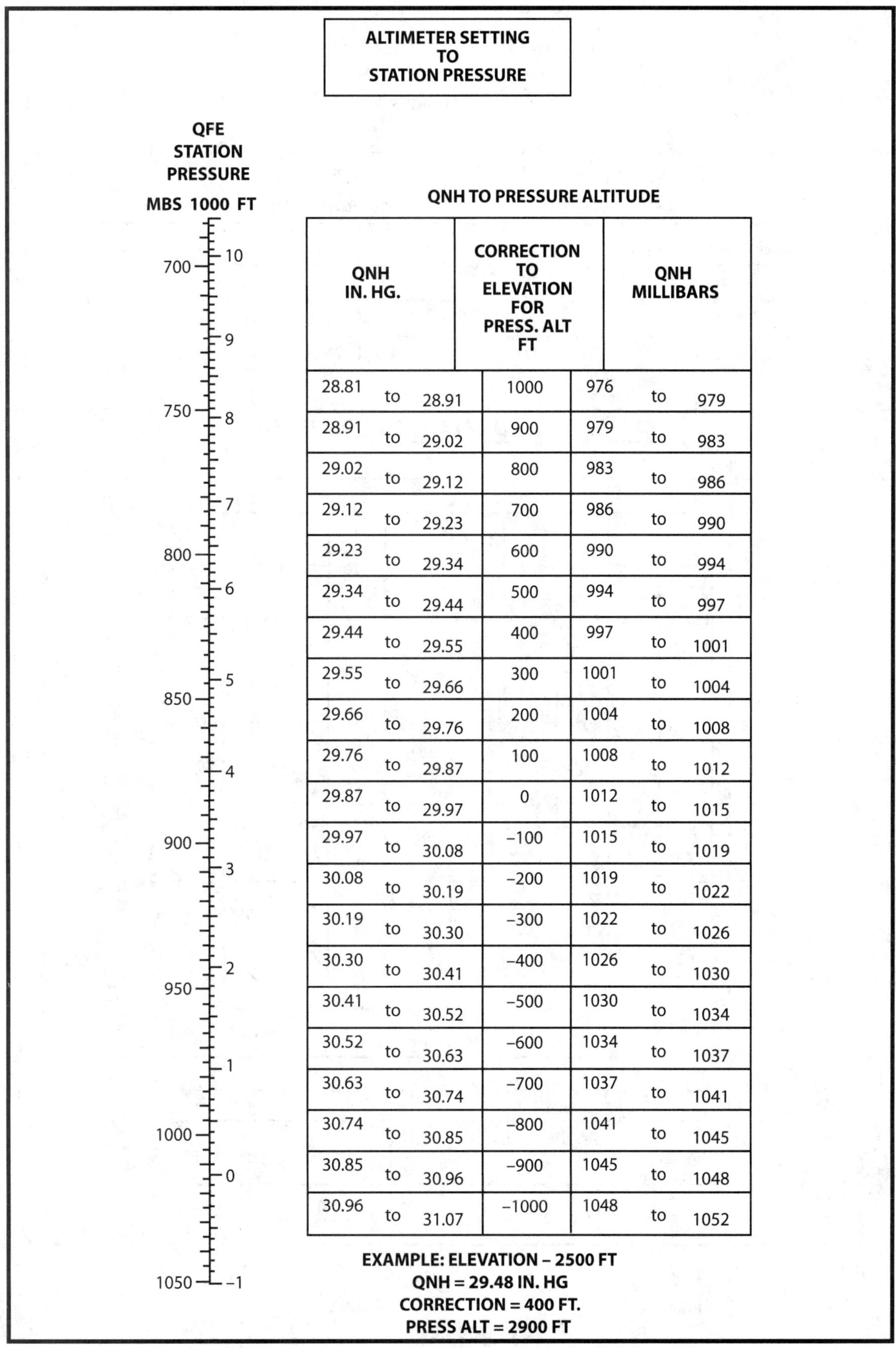

QNH IN. HG.	CORRECTION TO ELEVATION FOR PRESS. ALT FT	QNH MILLIBARS
28.81 to 28.91	1000	976 to 979
28.91 to 29.02	900	979 to 983
29.02 to 29.12	800	983 to 986
29.12 to 29.23	700	986 to 990
29.23 to 29.34	600	990 to 994
29.34 to 29.44	500	994 to 997
29.44 to 29.55	400	997 to 1001
29.55 to 29.66	300	1001 to 1004
29.66 to 29.76	200	1004 to 1008
29.76 to 29.87	100	1008 to 1012
29.87 to 29.97	0	1012 to 1015
29.97 to 30.08	–100	1015 to 1019
30.08 to 30.19	–200	1019 to 1022
30.19 to 30.30	–300	1022 to 1026
30.30 to 30.41	–400	1026 to 1030
30.41 to 30.52	–500	1030 to 1034
30.52 to 30.63	–600	1034 to 1037
30.63 to 30.74	–700	1037 to 1041
30.74 to 30.85	–800	1041 to 1045
30.85 to 30.96	–900	1045 to 1048
30.96 to 31.07	–1000	1048 to 1052

Figure 46. Altimeter Setting to Pressure Altitude.

TRANSPORT AIRCRAFT TAKEOFF SPEEDS

JT8D-1 ENGINES

TAKEOFF SPEED –20 ° FLAPS EITHER NO ICE PROTECTION OR ENGINE ICE PROTECTION ONLY								
TAKEOFF WEIGHT (1000 LB)	60	65	70	75	80	85	90	95
V_1 (KNOTS, IAS)	104.0	110.0	115.0	120.5	125.0	129.5	133.5	136.0
V_R (KNOTS, IAS)	106.5	112.5	118.0	123.5	129.0	134.0	139.0	143.5
V_2 (KNOTS, IAS)	117.0	121.5	126.5	130.5	135.0	139.0	143.0	147.0

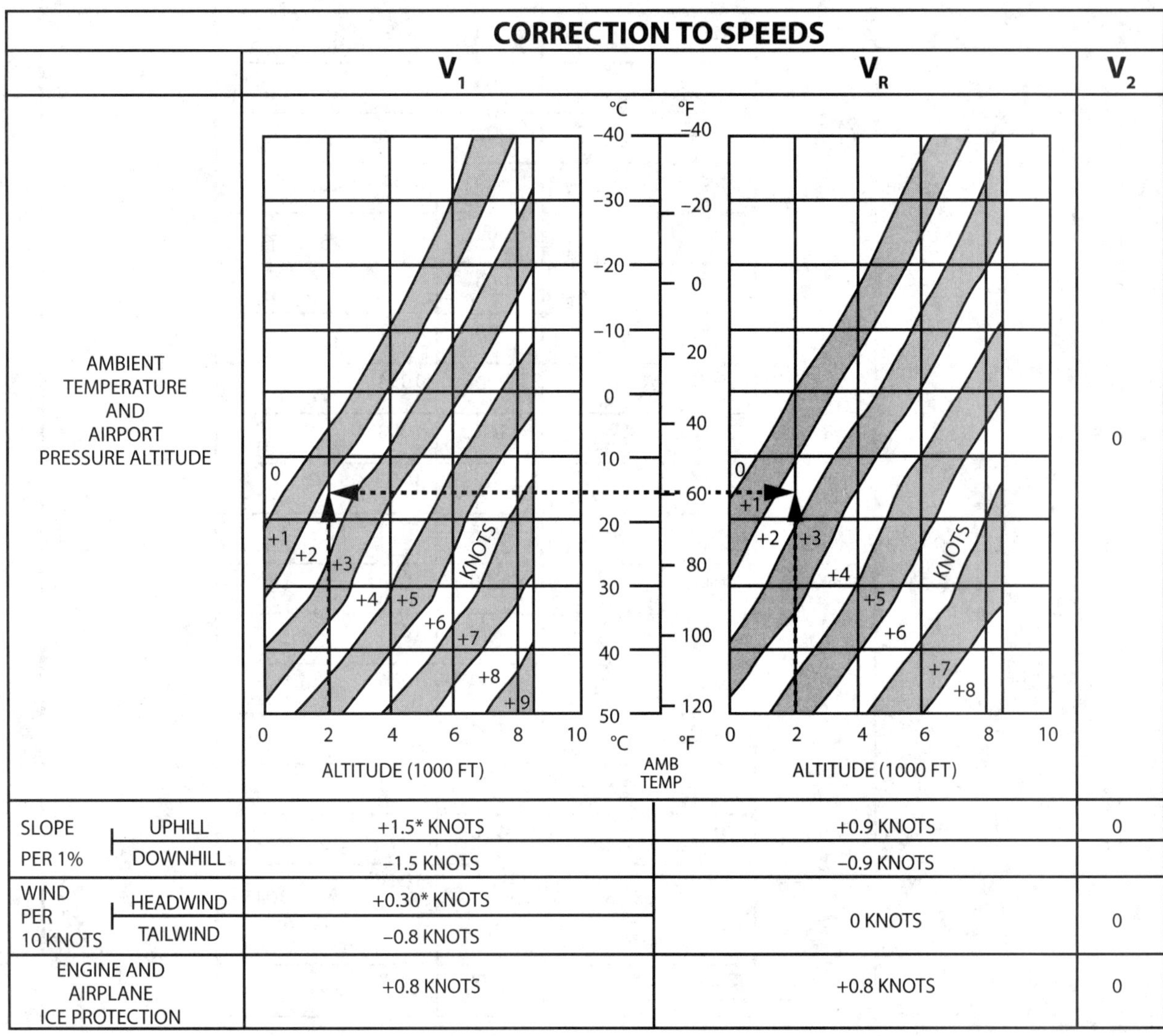

CORRECTION TO SPEEDS			
	V_1	V_R	V_2
AMBIENT TEMPERATURE AND AIRPORT PRESSURE ALTITUDE	(chart)	(chart)	0
SLOPE PER 1% — UPHILL	+1.5* KNOTS	+0.9 KNOTS	0
SLOPE PER 1% — DOWNHILL	–1.5 KNOTS	–0.9 KNOTS	
WIND PER 10 KNOTS — HEADWIND	+0.30* KNOTS	0 KNOTS	0
WIND PER 10 KNOTS — TAILWIND	–0.8 KNOTS		
ENGINE AND AIRPLANE ICE PROTECTION	+0.8 KNOTS	+0.8 KNOTS	0

* IF V_1 EXCEEDS V_R, SET V_1 EQUAL TO V_R

Figure 47. Transport Aircraft 1—Takeoff Speeds.

OPERATING CONDITIONS	W-1	W-2	W-3	W-4	W-5
CLIMB SCHEDULE	LR	HS	LR	HS	HS
INITIAL WEIGHT (X1000)	84	86	78	88	92
CRUISE PRESS ALTITUDE	34,000	28,000	32,000	22,000	24,000
ISA TEMPERATURE	ISA	ISA	ISA	ISA	ISA
AVG WIND COMP (KTS)	20 HW	30 HW	10 TW	20 TW	40 HW

Figure 48. Transport Aircraft 1—En Route Climb.

TIME, FUEL, AND DISTANCE TO CLIMB
JT8D-1 ENGINES - NORMAL BLEED
DC-9 SERIES 10 - HIGH SPEED CLIMB SCHEDULE
CLIMB AT 320 KNOTS IAS TO 23500 FT ALTITUDE THEN CLIMB AT M .74

INITIAL WEIGHT = 86000. POUNDS				INITIAL WEIGHT = 90000. POUNDS			
PRES. ALT. FEET	TIME MIN.	FUEL BURNED LB.	DIST. N. MI.	PRES. ALT. FEET	TIME MIN.	FUEL BURNED LB.	DIST. N. MI.
0.	0.	0.	0.	0.	0.	0.	0.
2000.	0.5	133.	2.8	2000.	0.6	140.	3.0
4000.	1.1	267.	5.9	4000.	1.1	282.	6.3
6000.	1.7	403.	9.3	6000.	1.8	426.	9.8
8000.	2.3	541.	13.0	8000.	2.5	573.	13.8
10000.	3.0	684.	17.2	10000.	3.2	724.	18.2
12000.	3.8	830.	21.3	12000.	4.0	879.	23.1
14000.	4.6	982.	27.0	14000.	4.8	1041.	28.6
16000.	5.5	1141.	32.9	16000.	5.8	1211.	34.9
18000.	6.4	1309.	39.6	18000.	6.9	1390.	42.1
20000.	7.6	1489.	47.4	20000.	8.0	1583.	50.4
22000.	8.8	1684.	56.6	22000.	9.4	1793.	60.3
23500.	9.9	1845.	64.7	23500.	10.6	1968.	69.1
23500.	9.9	1845.	64.7	23500.	10.6	1968.	69.1
24000.	10.2	1886.	66.8	24000.	10.9	2013.	71.5
26000.	11.4	2052.	75.9	26000.	12.3	2196.	81.5
28000.	12.8	2225.	85.8	28000.	13.8	2389.	92.6
30000.	14.3	2410.	97.1	30000.	15.5	2598.	105.4
32000.	16.2	2613.	110.3	32000.	17.6	2833.	120.6
34000.	18.4	2844.	126.3	34000.	20.3	3110.	139.8
36000.	21.4	3136.	147.8	36000.	24.3	3494.	168.0
INITIAL WEIGHT = 88000. POUNDS				INITIAL WEIGHT = 92000. POUNDS			
0.	0.	0.	0.	0.	0.	0.	0.
2000.	0.5	136.	2.9	2000.	0.6	144.	3.1
4000.	1.1	274.	6.1	4000.	1.2	290.	6.4
6000.	1.7	414.	9.6	6000.	1.8	438.	10.1
8000.	2.4	557.	13.4	8000.	2.5	589.	14.2
10000.	3.1	703.	17.7	10000.	3.3	744.	18.7
12000.	3.9	855.	22.5	12000.	4.1	905.	23.8
14000.	4.7	1012.	27.8	14000.	5.0	1072.	29.5
16000.	5.6	1176.	33.9	16000.	6.0	1247.	36.0
18000.	6.6	1349.	40.8	18000.	7.1	1432.	43.4
20000.	7.8	1535.	48.9	20000.	8.3	1631.	52.0
22000.	9.1	1738.	58.4	22000.	9.7	1850.	62.3
23500.	10.3	1906.	66.9	23500.	11.0	2032.	71.5
23500.	10.3	1906.	66.9	23500.	11.0	2032.	71.5
24000.	10.6	1949.	69.1	24000.	11.3	2079.	73.9
26000.	11.9	2123.	78.6	26000.	12.7	2272.	84.4
28000.	13.3	2306.	89.1	28000.	14.3	2476.	96.2
30000.	14.9	2502.	101.2	30000.	16.2	2693.	109.8
32000.	16.9	2720.	115.3	32000.	18.4	2951.	126.2
34000.	19.3	2973.	132.8	34000.	21.4	3258.	147.4
36000.	22.7	3304.	157.2	36000.	26.1	3713.	181.0

Figure 49. High-Speed Climb Schedule.

TIME, FUEL, AND DISTANCE TO CLIMB
ENGINES - NORMAL BLEED
LONG RANGE CLIMB SCHEDULE
CLIMB AT 290 KNOTS IAS TO 26860 FT ALTITUDE THEN CLIMB AT M .72

INITIAL WEIGHT = 78000. POUNDS				INITIAL WEIGHT = 82000. POUNDS			
PRES. ALT. FEET	TIME MIN.	FUEL BURNED LB.	DIST. N. MI.	PRES. ALT. FEET	TIME MIN.	FUEL BURNED LB.	DIST. N. MI.
0.	0.	0.	0.	0.	0.	0.	0.
2000.	0.5	113.	2.2	2000.	0.5	120.	2.4
4000.	0.9	227.	4.6	4000.	1.0	241.	4.9
6000.	1.5	342.	7.3	6000.	1.5	363.	7.7
8000.	2.0	457.	10.2	8000.	2.1	486.	10.8
10000.	2.6	574.	13.3	10000.	2.7	610.	14.2
12000.	3.2	693.	16.8	12000.	3.4	737.	17.9
14000.	3.9	815.	20.7	14000.	4.1	868.	22.1
16000.	4.6	941.	25.0	16000.	4.9	1002.	26.7
18000.	5.4	1070.	29.9	18000.	5.7	1141.	31.9
20000.	6.3	1205.	35.4	20000.	6.7	1286.	37.9
22000.	7.2	1347.	41.7	22000.	7.7	1439.	44.6
24000.	8.3	1498.	49.0	24000.	8.9	1602.	52.5
26000.	9.5	1661.	57.6	26000.	10.2	1780.	61.9
26860.	10.1	1736.	61.8	26860.	10.9	1863.	66.5
26860.	10.1	1736.	61.8	26860.	10.9	1863.	66.5
28000.	10.7	1813.	66.2	28000.	11.6	1948.	71.4
30000.	11.9	1953.	74.6	30000.	12.9	2104.	80.8
32000.	13.3	2102.	84.2	32000.	14.4	2274.	91.7
34000.	14.9	2267.	95.4	34000.	16.3	2464.	104.6
36000.	16.9	2456.	109.2	36000.	18.7	2693.	121.3
INITIAL WEIGHT = 80000. POUNDS				INITIAL WEIGHT = 84000. POUNDS			
0.	0.	0.	0.	0.	0.	0.	0.
2000.	0.5	117.	2.3	2000.	0.5	124.	2.4
4000.	1.0	234.	4.8	4000.	1.0	248.	5.1
6000.	1.5	352.	7.5	6000.	1.6	374.	8.0
8000.	2.1	471.	10.5	8000.	2.2	500.	11.1
10000.	2.7	592.	13.7	10000.	2.8	629.	14.6
12000.	3.3	715.	17.4	12000.	3.5	760.	18.5
14000.	4.0	841.	21.4	14000.	4.2	894.	22.8
16000.	4.7	971.	25.9	16000.	5.1	1033.	27.6
18000.	5.6	1105.	30.9	18000.	5.9	1177.	33.0
20000.	6.5	1245.	36.6	20000.	6.9	1327.	39.1
22000.	7.5	1392.	43.2	22000.	8.0	1486.	46.2
24000.	8.6	1549.	50.7	24000.	9.2	1656.	54.4
26000.	9.9	1719.	59.7	26000.	10.6	1841.	64.1
26860.	10.5	1798.	64.1	26860.	11.3	1928.	69.0
26860.	10.5	1798.	64.1	26860.	11.3	1928.	69.0
28000.	11.1	1879.	68.7	28000.	12.0	2018.	74.1
30000.	12.4	2027.	77.7	30000.	13.4	2183.	84.1
32000.	13.8	2186.	87.8	32000.	15.0	2364.	95.7
34000.	15.6	2362.	99.8	34000.	17.1	2570.	109.7
36000.	17.7	2570.	114.9	36000.	19.7	2826.	128.3

Figure 50. Long-Range Climb Schedule.

OPERATING CONDITIONS	L-1	L-2	L-3	L-4	L-5
WEIGHT (START TO ALT)	85,000	70,000	86,000	76,000	82,000
DISTANCE (NAM)	110	190	330	50	240
WIND COMPONENT (KTS)	15 HW	40 TW	50 HW	20 TW	45 HW
HOLDING TIME AT ALT (MIN)	15	15	15	15	15

Figure 51. Transport Aircraft 1—Alternate Planning.

OPERATING CONDITIONS	R-1	R-2	R-3	R-4	R-5
FIELD ELEVATION	100	4,000	950	2,000	50
ALTIMETER SETTING	29.50"	1032 mb	29.40"	1017 mb	30.15"
TEMPERATURE (OAT)	+50 °F	−15 °C	+59 °F	0 °C	+95 °C
WEIGHT (X1000)	90	110	100	85	95
FLAP POSITION	15°	5°	5°	1°	1°
WIND COMPONENT (KTS)	5 HW	5 TW	20 HW	10 TW	7 HW
RUNWAY SLOPE %	1% UP	1% DN	1% UP	2% DN	1.5% UP
AIR CONDITIONING	ON	ON	OFF	ON	OFF
ENGINE ANTI-ICE	OFF	ON	OFF	ON	OFF
CG STATION	635.7	643.8	665.2	657.2	638.4
LEMAC – STA 625.0, MAC 134.0					

Figure 53. Transport Aircraft 2—Takeoff.

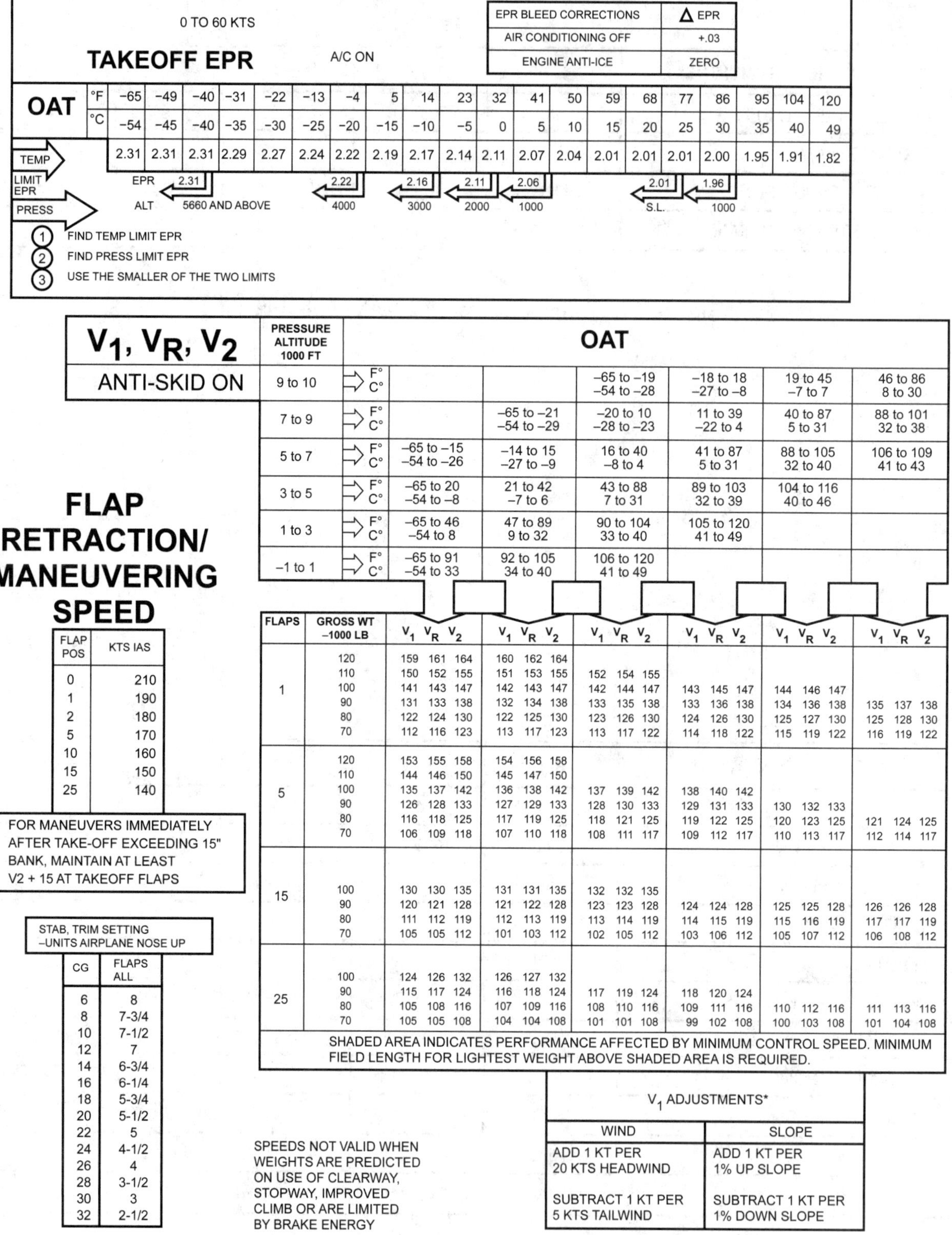

TAKEOFF EPR

0 TO 60 KTS — A/C ON

EPR BLEED CORRECTIONS	Δ EPR
AIR CONDITIONING OFF	+.03
ENGINE ANTI-ICE	ZERO

OAT °F	-65	-49	-40	-31	-22	-13	-4	5	14	23	32	41	50	59	68	77	86	95	104	120
OAT °C	-54	-45	-40	-35	-30	-25	-20	-15	-10	-5	0	5	10	15	20	25	30	35	40	49
TEMP LIMIT EPR	2.31	2.31	2.31	2.29	2.27	2.24	2.22	2.19	2.17	2.14	2.11	2.07	2.04	2.01	2.01	2.01	2.00	1.95	1.91	1.82

PRESS LIMIT EPR	2.31	2.22	2.16	2.11	2.06	2.01	1.96
ALT	5660 AND ABOVE	4000	3000	2000	1000	S.L.	1000

1. FIND TEMP LIMIT EPR
2. FIND PRESS LIMIT EPR
3. USE THE SMALLER OF THE TWO LIMITS

V1, VR, V2 — ANTI-SKID ON

PRESSURE ALTITUDE 1000 FT		OAT					
9 to 10	F° / C°			-65 to -19 / -54 to -28	-18 to 18 / -27 to -8	19 to 45 / -7 to 7	46 to 86 / 8 to 30
7 to 9	F° / C°		-65 to -21 / -54 to -29	-20 to 10 / -28 to -23	11 to 39 / -22 to 4	40 to 87 / 5 to 31	88 to 101 / 32 to 38
5 to 7	F° / C°	-65 to -15 / -54 to -26	-14 to 15 / -27 to -9	16 to 40 / -8 to 4	41 to 87 / 5 to 31	88 to 105 / 32 to 40	106 to 109 / 41 to 43
3 to 5	F° / C°	-65 to 20 / -54 to -8	21 to 42 / -7 to 6	43 to 88 / 7 to 31	89 to 103 / 32 to 39	104 to 116 / 40 to 46	
1 to 3	F° / C°	-65 to 46 / -54 to 8	47 to 89 / 9 to 32	90 to 104 / 33 to 40	105 to 120 / 41 to 49		
-1 to 1	F° / C°	-65 to 91 / -54 to 33	92 to 105 / 34 to 40	106 to 120 / 41 to 49			

FLAPS	GROSS WT -1000 LB	V_1 V_R V_2	V_1 V_R V_2	V_1 V_R V_2	V_1 V_R V_2	V_1 V_R V_2	V_1 V_R V_2
1	120	159 161 164	160 162 164				
	110	150 152 155	151 153 155	152 154 155			
	100	141 143 147	142 143 147	142 144 147	143 145 147	144 146 147	
	90	131 133 138	132 134 138	133 135 138	133 136 138	134 136 138	135 137 138
	80	122 124 130	122 125 130	123 126 130	124 126 130	125 127 130	125 128 130
	70	112 116 123	113 117 123	113 117 122	114 118 122	115 119 122	116 119 122
5	120	153 155 158	154 156 158				
	110	144 146 150	145 147 150				
	100	135 137 142	136 138 142	137 139 142	138 140 142		
	90	126 128 133	127 129 133	128 130 133	129 131 133	130 132 133	
	80	116 118 125	117 119 125	118 121 125	119 122 125	120 123 125	121 124 125
	70	106 109 118	107 110 118	108 111 117	109 112 117	110 113 117	112 114 117
15	100	130 130 135	131 131 135	132 132 135			
	90	120 121 128	121 122 128	123 123 128	124 124 128	125 125 128	126 126 128
	80	111 112 119	112 113 119	113 114 119	114 115 119	115 116 119	117 117 119
	70	105 105 112	101 103 112	102 105 112	103 106 112	105 107 112	106 108 112
25	100	124 126 132	126 127 132				
	90	115 117 124	116 118 124	117 119 124	118 120 124		
	80	105 108 116	107 109 116	108 110 116	109 111 116	110 112 116	111 113 116
	70	105 105 108	104 104 108	101 101 108	99 102 108	100 103 108	101 104 108

SHADED AREA INDICATES PERFORMANCE AFFECTED BY MINIMUM CONTROL SPEED. MINIMUM FIELD LENGTH FOR LIGHTEST WEIGHT ABOVE SHADED AREA IS REQUIRED.

FLAP RETRACTION/ MANEUVERING SPEED

FLAP POS	KTS IAS
0	210
1	190
2	180
5	170
10	160
15	150
25	140

FOR MANEUVERS IMMEDIATELY AFTER TAKE-OFF EXCEEDING 15" BANK, MAINTAIN AT LEAST V2 + 15 AT TAKEOFF FLAPS

STAB, TRIM SETTING –UNITS AIRPLANE NOSE UP

CG	FLAPS ALL
6	8
8	7-3/4
10	7-1/2
12	7
14	6-3/4
16	6-1/4
18	5-3/4
20	5-1/2
22	5
24	4-1/2
26	4
28	3-1/2
30	3
32	2-1/2

SPEEDS NOT VALID WHEN WEIGHTS ARE PREDICTED ON USE OF CLEARWAY, STOPWAY, IMPROVED CLIMB OR ARE LIMITED BY BRAKE ENERGY

V_1 ADJUSTMENTS*

WIND	SLOPE
ADD 1 KT PER 20 KTS HEADWIND	ADD 1 KT PER 1% UP SLOPE
SUBTRACT 1 KT PER 5 KTS TAILWIND	SUBTRACT 1 KT PER 1% DOWN SLOPE

*V_1 MUST NOT EXCEED V_R

Figure 55. Transport Aircraft 2—Takeoff Performance.

OPERATING CONDITIONS	V-1	V-2	V-3	V-4	V-5
BRK REL WEIGHT (X1000)	110	95	85	105	75
CRUISE PRESS ALT	33,000	27,000	35,000	22,000	31,000
AIRPORT ELEVATION	2,000	3,000	2,000	4,000	2,000
ISA TEMPERATURE	+10°	ISA	ISA	+10°	+10°
AVG WIND COMP (KTS)	20 HW	20 TW	30 HW	10 TW	40 HW

Figure 56. Transport Aircraft 2—En Route Climb.

EN ROUTE CLIMB 280/.70 ISA

PRESSURE ALTITUDE - FT	UNITS MIN/LB NM/KNOTS	BRAKE RELEASE WEIGHT - LB										
		120000	115000	110000	105000	100000	95000	90000	85000	80000	75000	65000
37000	TIME/FUEL DIST./TAS		41/5700 251/387	32/4700 192/384	27/4100 162/382	24/3700 140/380	21/3400 124/379	19/3100 111/378	17/2800 100/377	16/2500 90/376	14/2300 82/375	12/1900 67/374
36000	TIME/FUEL DIST./TAS	41/5900 246/386	33/4900 194/383	28/4300 164/381	25/3900 143/379	22/3500 127/378	20/3200 114/377	18/2900 103/376	16/2700 93/375	15/2500 84/374	14/2300 77/374	11/1900 63/373
35000	TIME/FUEL DIST./TAS	33/5100 197/382	29/4500 168/380	25/4100 147/378	23/3700 131/377	21/3400 117/376	19/3100 106/375	17/2800 96/374	16/2600 87/373	14/2400 80/373	13/2200 73/372	11/1800 60/371
34000	TIME/FUEL DIST./TAS	29/4700 171/379	26/4300 150/377	23/3900 134/376	21/3500 120/375	19/3200 109/374	18/3000 99/373	16/2700 90/372	15/2500 82/372	14/2300 75/371	12/2100 69/371	10/1800 57/370
33000	TIME/FUEL DIST./TAS	27/4400 153/376	24/4000 137/375	22/3700 123/374	20/3400 112/373	18/3100 102/372	17/2900 93/371	15/2700 85/370	14/2500 78/370	13/2300 71/369	12/2100 65/369	10/1700 54/368
32000	TIME/FUEL DIST./TAS	25/4200 139/374	23/3900 126/372	21/3600 114/371	19/3300 104/370	17/3000 95/370	16/2800 87/369	15/2600 80/368	14/2400 74/368	12/2200 67/367	11/2000 62/367	10/1700 51/366
31000	TIME/FUEL DIST./TAS	23/4000 128/371	21/3700 117/370	19/3400 107/369	18/3200 98/368	16/2900 90/367	15/2700 82/367	14/2500 76/366	13/2300 70/366	12/2100 64/365	11/2000 59/365	9/1700 49/364
30000	TIME/FUEL DIST./TAS	22/3900 119/368	20/3600 109/367	18/3300 100/366	17/3100 92/365	16/2800 84/365	15/2600 78/364	13/2400 72/364	12/2300 66/363	11/2100 61/363	11/1900 56/363	9/1600 47/362
29000	TIME/FUEL DIST./TAS	21/3700 111/365	19/3400 102/364	18/3200 93/363	16/3000 86/363	15/2700 79/362	14/2500 73/362	13/2400 68/361	12/2200 62/361	11/2000 57/361	10/1900 53/360	9/1600 44/360
28000	TIME/FUEL DIST./TAS	19/3600 103/362	18/3300 95/361	17/3100 88/360	15/2900 81/360	14/2700 75/359	13/2500 69/359	12/2300 64/359	11/2100 59/358	11/2000 54/358	10/1800 50/358	8/1500 42/357
27000	TIME/FUEL DIST./TAS	19/3400 96/358	17/3200 89/358	16/3000 82/357	15/2800 76/357	14/2600 71/356	13/2400 65/356	12/2200 60/356	11/2100 56/356	10/1900 52/355	9/1800 47/355	8/1500 40/355
26000	TIME/FUEL DIST./TAS	17/3300 88/354	16/3000 82/354	15/2800 76/353	14/2600 70/353	13/2500 65/352	12/2300 60/352	11/2100 56/352	10/2000 52/352	10/1800 48/351	9/1700 44/351	7/1400 37/351
25000	TIME/FUEL DIST./TAS	16/3100 81/350	15/2900 75/350	14/2700 70/349	13/2500 65/349	12/2400 60/349	11/2200 56/348	11/2000 52/348	10/1900 48/348	9/1800 45/348	8/1600 41/348	7/1400 35/347
24000	TIME/FUEL DIST./TAS	15/3000 75/346	14/2800 69/346	13/2600 65/345	12/2400 60/345	12/2300 56/345	11/2100 52/345	10/2000 48/345	9/1800 45/344	9/1700 41/344	8/1600 38/344	7/1300 32/344
23000	TIME/FUEL DIST./TAS	14/2800 69/342	13/2700 64/342	13/2500 60/342	12/2300 56/342	11/2200 52/342	10/2000 48/341	9/1900 45/341	9/1800 41/341	8/1600 38/341	8/1500 35/341	6/1300 30/341
22000	TIME/FUEL DIST./TAS	14/2700 63/339	13/2500 59/339	12/2400 55/338	11/2200 51/338	10/2100 48/338	10/1900 45/338	9/1800 41/338	8/1700 38/338	8/1600 36/338	7/1400 33/338	6/1200 28/337
6000	TIME/FUEL DIST./TAS	4/1000 9/295	4/1000 9/295	4/900 8/295	4/800 8/295	3/800 7/295	3/700 7/295	3/700 6/295	3/700 6/295	3/600 5/295	2/600 5/295	2/500 4/295
1500	TIME/FUEL	2/600	2/600	2/500	2/500	2/500	2/400	2/400	2/400	1/400	1/300	1/300

FUEL ADJUSTMENT FOR HIGH ELEVATION AIRPORTS	AIRPORT ELEVATION	2000	4000	6000	8000	10000	12000
EFFECT ON TIME AND DISTANCE IS NEGLIGIBLE	FUEL ADJUSTMENT	−100	−200	−400	−500	−600	−700

Figure 57. En Route Climb 280/.70 ISA.

EN ROUTE CLIMB 280/.70 ISA +10 °C

PRESSURE ALTITUDE - FT	UNITS MIN/LB NM/KNOTS	BRAKE RELEASE WEIGHT - LB										
		120000	115000	110000	105000	100000	95000	90000	85000	80000	75000	65000
37000	TIME/FUEL DIST./TAS			42/5700 263/395	34/4700 206/391	29/4100 174/389	25/3700 151/388	23/3300 133/386	20/3000 119/385	18/2700 107/384	16/2500 96/384	13/2100 78/382
36000	TIME/FUEL DIST./TAS		43/5900 266/394	35/5000 211/391	30/4400 179/389	26/3900 156/387	23/3500 138/385	21/3200 123/384	19/2900 111/383	17/2700 100/383	16/2400 90/382	13/2000 74/381
35000	TIME/FUEL DIST./TAS	45/6200 275/394	36/5300 219/390	31/4600 186/388	27/4100 162/386	24/3700 143/385	22/3400 128/384	20/3100 115/383	10/2800 104/382	16/2600 94/381	15/2400 85/380	12/2000 70/379
34000	TIME/FUEL DIST./TAS	38/5600 228/390	32/4900 193/387	28/4400 168/386	25/3900 149/384	23/3600 133/383	21/3300 120/382	19/3000 108/381	17/2700 98/380	16/2500 89/379	14/2300 81/379	12/1900 67/378
33000	TIME/FUEL DIST./TAS	34/5100 200/387	30/4600 174/385	26/4100 154/383	24/3800 138/382	22/3400 124/381	20/3100 113/380	18/2900 102/379	16/2600 93/378	15/2400 85/378	14/2200 77/377	11/1900 64/376
32000	TIME/FUEL DIST./TAS	31/4800 180/384	28/4400 160/382	25/4000 143/381	23/3600 129/379	21/3300 116/378	19/3000 106/378	17/2800 96/377	16/2600 88/376	14/2400 80/376	13/2200 73/375	11/1800 61/374
31000	TIME/FUEL DIST./TAS	29/4600 165/381	26/4200 147/379	23/3800 133/378	21/3500 120/377	20/3200 109/376	18/2900 100/375	16/2700 91/375	15/2500 83/374	14/2300 76/374	13/2100 70/373	11/1800 58/372
30000	TIME/FUEL DIST./TAS	27/4400 152/378	24/4000 137/376	22/3700 124/375	20/3400 113/374	19/3100 103/374	17/2900 94/373	16/2600 86/372	14/2400 79/372	13/2200 72/371	12/2100 66/371	10/1700 55/370
29000	TIME/FUEL DIST./TAS	25/4200 141/375	23/3800 128/374	21/3500 116/373	19/3200 106/372	18/3000 97/371	16/2800 89/370	15/2600 82/370	14/2400 75/369	13/2200 69/369	12/2000 63/369	10/1700 52/368
28000	TIME/FUEL DIST./TAS	24/4000 131/371	22/3700 119/370	20/3400 109/369	18/3100 100/369	17/2900 91/368	16/2700 84/368	14/2500 77/367	13/2300 71/367	12/2100 65/366	11/1900 60/366	9/1600 50/365
27000	TIME/FUEL DIST./TAS	22/3800 121/368	21/3500 111/367	19/3300 102/366	18/3000 93/366	16/2800 86/365	15/2600 79/364	14/2400 73/364	13/2200 67/364	12/2000 61/363	11/1900 56/363	9/1600 47/363
26000	TIME/FUEL DIST./TAS	21/3600 110/363	19/3400 101/362	18/3100 93/362	16/2900 86/361	15/2700 79/361	14/2500 73/360	13/2300 67/360	12/2100 62/360	11/2000 57/359	10/1800 52/359	9/1500 44/359
25000	TIME/FUEL DIST./TAS	19/3400 101/358	18/3200 93/358	17/3000 85/357	15/2800 79/357	14/2600 73/357	13/2400 67/356	12/2200 62/356	11/2000 57/356	10/1900 53/356	10/1700 48/355	8/1500 41/355
24000	TIME/FUEL DIST./TAS	18/3300 92/354	17/3000 85/354	16/2800 78/353	15/2600 72/353	13/2400 67/353	12/2300 62/352	12/2100 57/352	11/1900 53/352	10/1800 49/352	9/1700 45/352	8/1400 38/351
23000	TIME/FUEL DIST./TAS	17/3100 84/350	16/2900 78/350	15/2900 72/350	14/2500 67/349	13/2300 62/349	12/2200 57/349	11/2000 53/349	10/1900 49/348	9/1700 45/348	9/1600 42/348	7/1300 35/348
22000	TIME/FUEL DIST./TAS	16/3000 77/346	15/2800 71/346	14/2600 66/346	13/2400 61/346	12/2200 57/345	11/2100 53/345	10/1900 49/345	10/1800 45/345	9/1700 42/345	8/1500 38/345	7/1300 32/344
6000	TIME/FUEL DIST./TAS	5/1100 10/301	4/1000 10/301	4/900 9/301	4/900 9/301	4/800 8/301	3/800 8/301	3/700 7/301	3/700 7/301	3/600 6/301	3/600 6/301	2/500 5/301
1500	TIME/FUEL	3/600	2/600	2/500	2/500	2/500	2/500	2/400	2/400	2/400	1/300	1/300

FUEL ADJUSTMENT FOR HIGH ELEVATION AIRPORTS	AIRPORT ELEVATION	2000	4000	6000	8000	10000	12000
EFFECT ON TIME AND DISTANCE IS NEGLIGIBLE	FUEL ADJUSTMENT	−100	−300	−400	−500	−600	−800

Figure 58. En Route Climb 280/.70 ISA +10 °C.

OPERATING CONDITIONS	T-1	T-2	T-3	T-4	T-5
TOTAL AIR TEMP (TAT)	+10 °C	0 °C	−15 °C	−30 °C	+15 °C
ALTITUDE	10,000	5,000	25,000	35,000	18,000
ENGINE ANTI-ICE	ON	ON	ON	ON	OFF
WING ANTI-ICE	OFF	2 ON	2 ON	1 ON	OFF
AIR CONDITIONING	ON	OFF	ON	ON	OFF

Figure 59. Transport Aircraft 2—Climb and Cruise Power.

EN ROUTE

MAX CLIMB & MAX CONTINUOUS EPR

A/C AIRBLEED ON

MAX. CLIMB	MAX. CONT.	TAT °C																		
		−40	−35	−30	−25	−20	−15	−10	−5	0	5	10	15	20	25	30	35	40	45	50
S.L. TO 30000	S.L. TO 1500 20000 TO 30000	2.25	2.23	2.21	2.18	2.15	2.12	2.09	2.04	1.99	1.94	1.90	1.86	1.82	1.79	1.76	1.73	1.70	1.67	1.64
	1500 TO 20000	2.30	2.28	2.26	2.24	2.21	2.19	2.16	2.13	2.10	2.07	2.04	2.00	1.95	1.91	1.86	1.81	1.75	1.71	1.66
	35000 & 37000	2.24	2.22	2.20	2.17	2.14	2.11	2.07	2.02	1.97	1.92									

2.30	2.20	2.14	2.09	2.04	1.98
5660 AND ABOVE	4000	3000	2000	1000	S.L.

TEMP

PRESS

LIMIT EPR

1. FIND TEMP LIMIT EPR
2. FIND PRESS LIMIT EPR
3. USE THE SMALLER OF THE TWO LIMITS

MAX CRUISE EPR

TAT °C		−50	−45	−40	−35	−30	−25	−20	−15	−10	−5	0	5	10	15	20	25	30	35	40
PRESS ALT 1000 FT	6 TO 30	2.18	2.16	2.14	2.12	2.10	2.07	2.05	2.02	1.99	1.95	1.91	1.85	1.79	1.73	1.68	1.64	1.61	1.57	1.54
	35 & 37	2.28	2.26	2.24	2.22	2.20	2.17	2. 14	2.11	2.07	2.02	1.97	1.92	1.87	1.84	1.80				

ANTI-ICE BLEED CORRECTIONS	Δ EPR
ENGINE ANTI-ICE	−.08
WING ANTI-ICE	2 ENG −.04
	1 ENG −.06

AIR COND-BLEED CORRECTIONS Δ EPR	A/C OFF
S.L. TO 37000	+.04

BLEED CORRECTIONS APPLY TO MAX CLIMB, MAX CONTINUOUS, AND MAX CRUISE EPR SETTINGS

Figure 60. Transport Aircraft 2—Climb and Cruise Power.

OPERATING CONDITIONS	X-1	X-2	X-3	X-4	X-5
DISTANCE (NM)	2,000	2,400	1,800	2,800	1,200
WIND COMPONENT (KTS)	50 TW	50 HW	20 HW	50 TW	30 HW
CRUISE PRESS ALTITUDE	27,000	35,000	20,000	29,000	37,000
ISA TEMPERATURE	+10°	ISA	+20°	−10°	+10°
LANDING WEIGHT (X1000)	70	75	75	65	90

Figure 61. Flight Planning at .78 Mach Cruise.

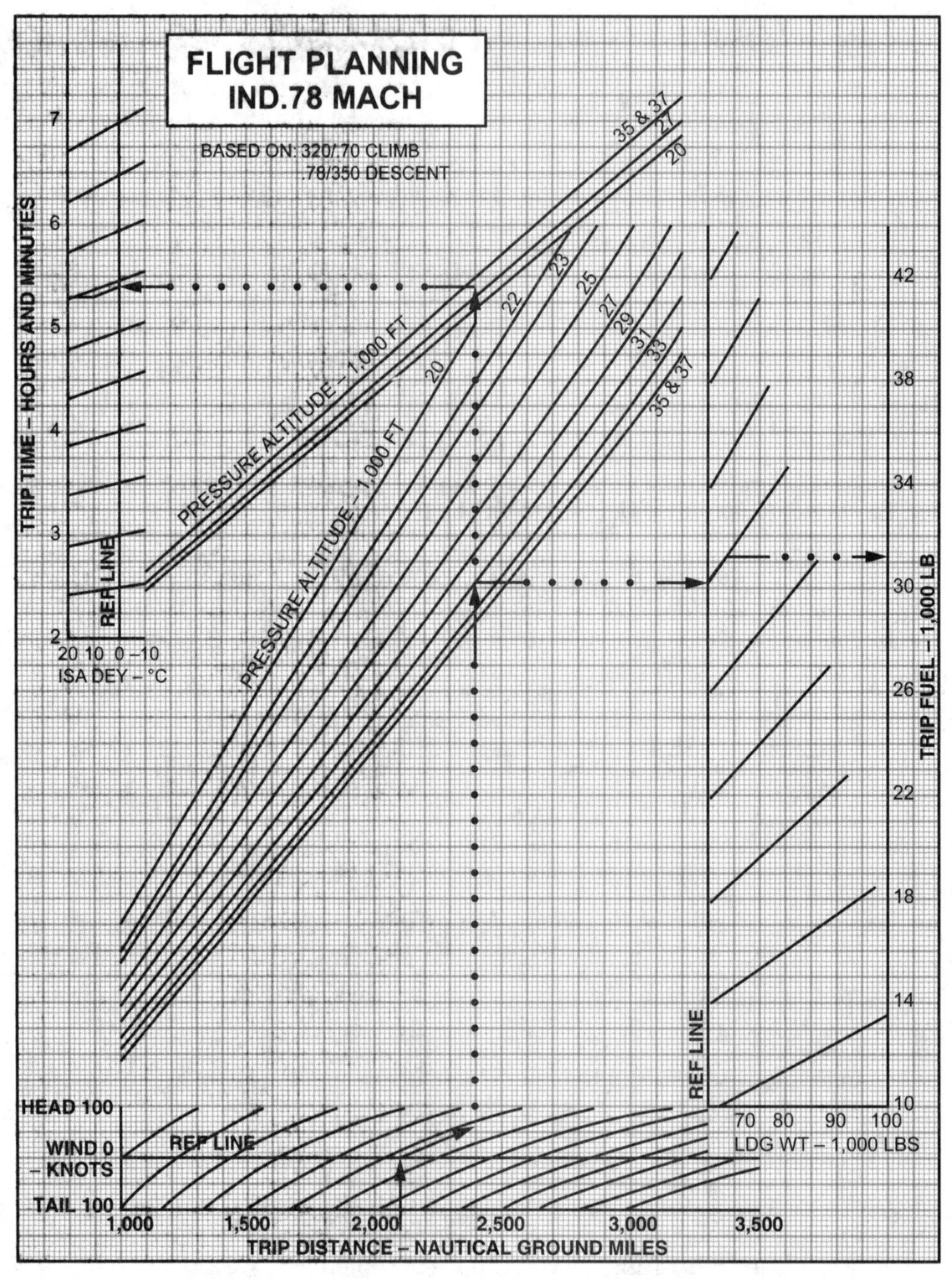

Figure 62. Transport Aircraft 2—Flight Planning at .78 Mach Indicated.

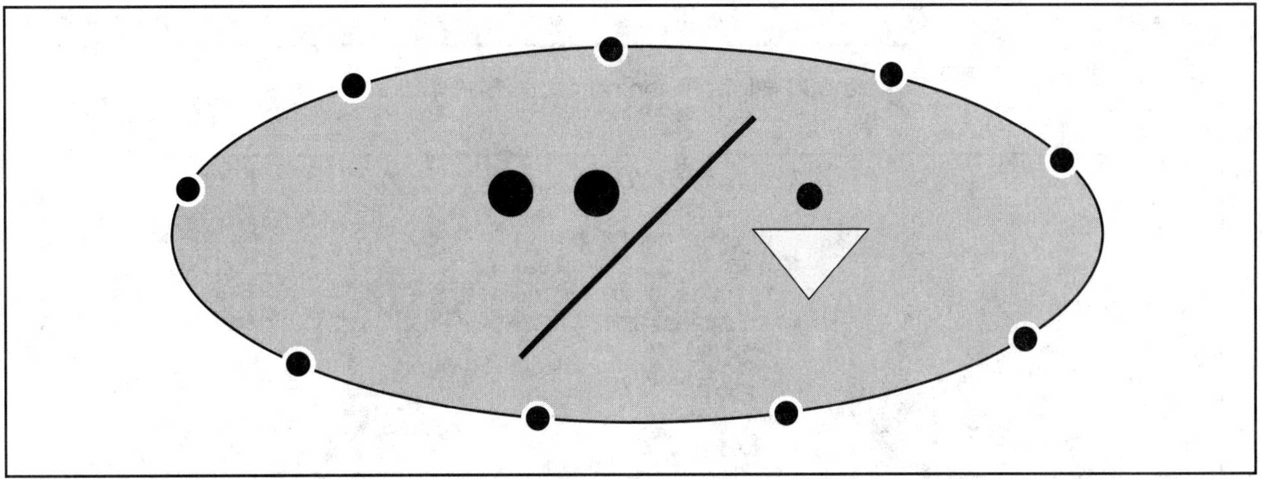

Figure 65. Symbol Used on U.S. Low Level Significant Weather Prog Chart.

OPERATING CONDITIONS	Z-1	Z-2	Z-3	Z-4	Z-5
DISTANCE (NM)	340	650	900	290	400
AVG WIND COMP (KTS)	25 TW	45 HW	35 TW	25 HW	60 HW

Figure 66. Flight Planning at .74 Mach Cruise.

ABBREVIATED FLIGHT PLANNING
.280/.70 CLIMB
.74/320/340 DESCENT
250 KTS CRUISE BELOW 10000 FT.
320 KTS CRUISE 10000 THRU 23000 FT.
.74 MACH CRUISE 24000 FT. AND ABOVE

DIST. N. MI.	REC. ALT.	TAS KTS	AIR TIME MINS.	FUEL LBS.
50	6000-7000	279	16	1800
60	6000-7000	279	18	1950
260	26000-27000	447	44	4600
270	26000-27000	447	45	4750
280	27000-28000	445	47	4850
290	28000-29000	443	48	4950
300	28000-29000	443	49	5100
310	28000-29000	443	51	5200
320	29000-31000	441	52	5300
330	29000-31000	441	53	5400
340	31000-33000	438	55	5550
350	31000-33000	438	56	5650
400	33000-35000	433	62	6250
450	33000-35000	433	69	6850
500	33000-35000	433	76	7500
550	33000-35000	433	82	8100
600	33000-35000	433	89	8700
650	33000-35000	433	96	9300
700	33000-35000	433	102	9900
750	33000-35000	433	109	10500
800	33000-35000	433	115	11100
850	33000-35000	433	122	11700
900	33000-35000	433	129	12300
950	33000-35000	433	135	12900
1000	33000-35000	433	142	13500

TIME AND FUEL CORRECTION FOR WIND

Δ TIME = TIME X WIND COMPONENT ÷ TAS

Δ FUEL = FUEL X WIND COMPONENT ÷ TAS

EXAMPLE: DIST. = 250
STILL AIR TIME = 43 MIN.
STILL AIR FUEL = 4500 LBS
WIND COMPONENT = 20 KTS.

Δ TIME = 43 X 20 ÷ 449 = MIN.

Δ FUEL = 4500 X 20 ÷ 449 = 200 LBS.

ADD Δ TIME AND Δ FUEL FOR THE HEADWIND; SUBTRACT FOR TAILWIND

Figure 67. Abbreviated Flight Planning.

OPERATING CONDITIONS	O-1	O-2	O-3	O-4	O-5
ALTITUDE	31,000	23,000	17,000	8,000	4,000
WEIGHT (X1000)	102	93	104	113	109
ENGINES OPERATING	2	2	2	2	2
HOLDING TIME (MIN)	20	40	35	15	25

Figure 68. Transport Aircraft 2—Holding.

HOLDING

EPR
ISA KNOTS
FF PER ENGINE LB/HR

FLIGHT LEVEL	GROSS WEIGHT 1000 LB										
	115	110	105	100	95	90	85	80	75	70	65
350	2.13 234 2830	2.07 228 2810	2.01 223 2630	1.95 217 2460	1.90 211 2290	1.85 210 2180	1.80 210 2070	1.76 210 1960	1.71 210 1870	1.67 210 1780	1.64 210 1700
300	1.86 231 2740	1.82 226 2600	1.79 220 2470	1.75 215 2370	1.71 210 2250	1.67 210 2140	1.64 210 2050	1.60 210 1960	1.57 210 1880	1.54 210 1790	1.51 210 1720
250	1.69 229 2710	1.66 224 2610	1.63 218 2490	1.60 213 2370	1.57 210 2260	1.54 210 2180	1.51 210 2080	1.48 210 1980	1.45 210 1920	1.43 210 1840	1.41 210 1780
200	1.56 227 2716	1.53 222 2590	1.50 217 2490	1.48 211 2390	1.45 210 2310	1.43 210 2230	1.40 210 2130	1.38 210 2060	1.36 210 2000	1.34 210 1920	1.32 210 1860
150	1.45 226 2790	1.43 221 2668	1.40 216 2570	1.38 210 2470	1.36 210 2380	1.34 210 2290	1.32 210 2220	1.31 210 2140	1.29 210 2070	1.27 210 2000	1.26 210 1990
100	1.36 225 2860	1.34 220 2780	1.33 215 2670	1.31 210 2560	1.29 210 2470	1.28 210 2390	1.26 210 2310	1.25 210 2240	1.24 210 2170	1.22 210 2100	1.21 210 2030
050	1.29 224 2960	1.28 219 2870	1.27 214 2770	1.25 210 2670	1.24 210 2580	1.23 210 2500	1.21 210 2420	1.20 210 2350	1.19 210 2290	1.18 210 2230	1.17 210 2150
015	1.25 224 3050	1.24 219 2950	1.23 214 2850	1.22 210 2790	1.21 210 2670	1.20 210 2590	1.19 210 2510	1.18 210 2430	1.17 210 2370	1.16 210 2300	1.15 210 2240

Figure 69. Transport Aircraft 2—Holding Performance Chart.

INITIAL FUEL WEIGHT 1000 LB	ENDING FUEL WEIGHT - 1000 LB															
	10	14	18	22	26	30	34	38	42	46	50	54	58	62	64	70
70	28	27	25	23	22	20	18	17	15	13	12	10	8	5	3	0
66	26	25	23	21	20	18	16	15	13	12	10	8	5	3	0	
62	23	23	20	18	17	15	13	11	10	8	7	5	3	0		
58	21	20	18	16	15	13	11	10	8	6	5	3	0			
54	18	16	15	13	12	10	8	7	5	3	2	0				
50	16	15	13	12	10	8	7	5	3	2	0					
46	15	13	12	10	8	7	5	3	2	0						
42	13	12	10	8	7	5	3	2	0			**FUEL DUMP TIME**				
38	12	10	8	7	5	3	2	0								
34	10	8	7	5	3	2	0									
30	8	7	5	3	2	0										
26	7	5	3	2	0											
22	5	3	2	0												
18	3	2	0							**FUEL JETTISON TIME-MINUTES**						
14	2	0														
10	0															

Figure 70. Fuel Dump Time.

OPERATING CONDITIONS	D-1	D-2	D-3	D-4	D-5
WT AT ENG FAIL (X1000)	100	110	90	80	120
ENGINE ANTI-ICE	ON	OFF	ON	ON	ON
WING ANTI-ICE	OFF	OFF	ON	ON	OFF
ISA TEMPERATURE	ISA	+10°	−10°	−10°	+20°
AIR CONDITIONING	OFF	OFF	OFF	OFF	OFF

Figure 71. Transport Aircraft 2—Drift-Down.

1 ENGINE INOP

ENGINE A/I OFF

GROSS WEIGHT 1000 LB		OPTIMUM DRIFTDOWN SPEED KIAS	ISA DEV °C			
AT ENGINE FAILURE	AT LEVEL OFF (APPROX)		−10	0	10	20
			APPROX GROSS LEVEL OFF PRESS ALT FT			
80	77	184	27900	26800	25400	22800
90	86	195	25000	23800	21700	20000
100	96	206	22000	20500	20000	18500
110	105	216	20000	19100	17500	15400
120	114	224	18200	16600	14700	12200

ENGINE A/I ON

GROSS WEIGHT 1000 LB		OPTIMUM DRIFTDOWN SPEED KIAS	ISA DEV °C			
AT ENGINE FAILURE	AT LEVEL OFF (APPROX)		−10	0	10	20
			APPROX GROSS LEVEL OFF PRESS ALT FT			
80	77	184	25500	24600	22800	20000
90	86	195	23000	21400	20000	19400
100	96	206	20000	19400	18700	15600
110	105	216	18100	16600	14700	12200
120	114	224	15500	13800	11800	8800

ENGINE AND WING A/I ON

GROSS WEIGHT 1000 LB		OPTIMUM DRIFTDOWN SPEED KIAS	ISA DEV °C			
AT ENGINE FAILURE	AT LEVEL OFF (APPROX)		−10	0	10	20
			APPROX GROSS LEVEL OFF PRESS ALT FT			
80	77	184	24400	23400	21400	20000
90	86	195	21600	20100	19800	18000
100	96	206	19600	18000	16400	14200
110	105	216	16800	15100	13300	10700
120	114	224	14000	12200	10300	7200

NOTE:
WHEN ENGINE BLEED FOR AIR CONDITIONING IS OFF BELOW 17,000 FT., INCREASE LEVEL OFF ALTITUDE BY 800 FT.

Figure 72. Drift-Down Performance Chart.

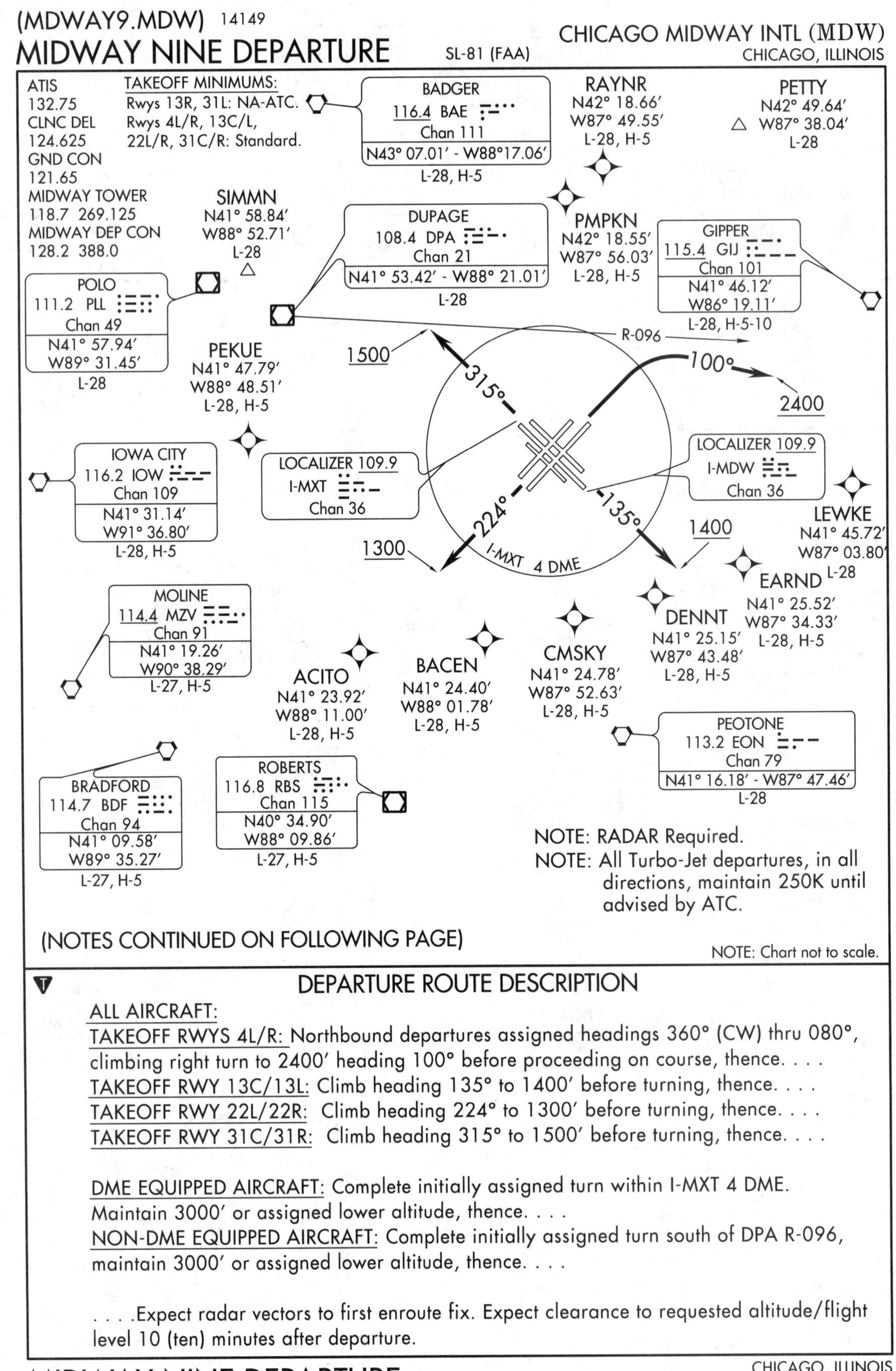

Figure 95. MIDWAY NINE Departure (MDWAY9.MDW).

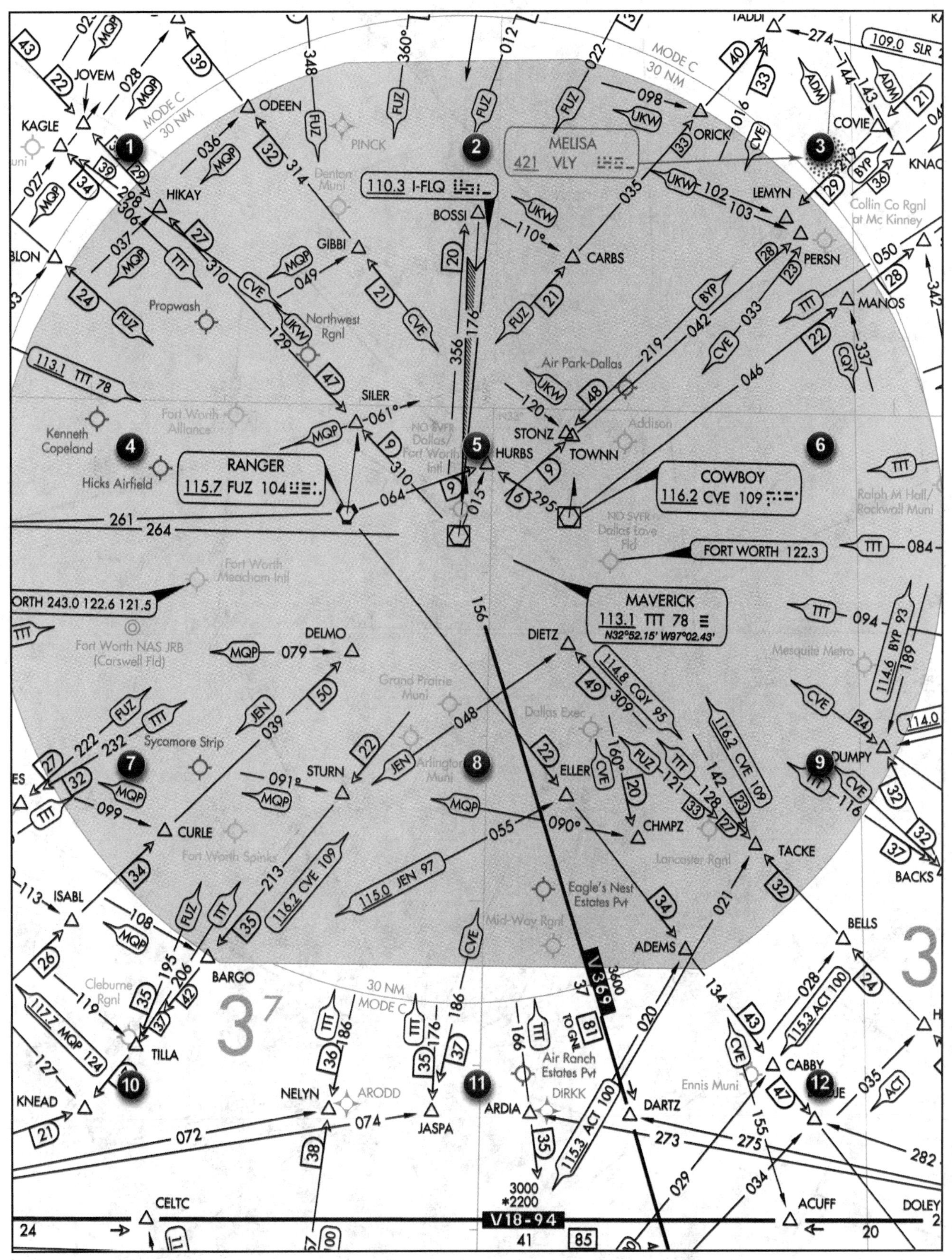

Figure 99. IFR Area Chart Segment.

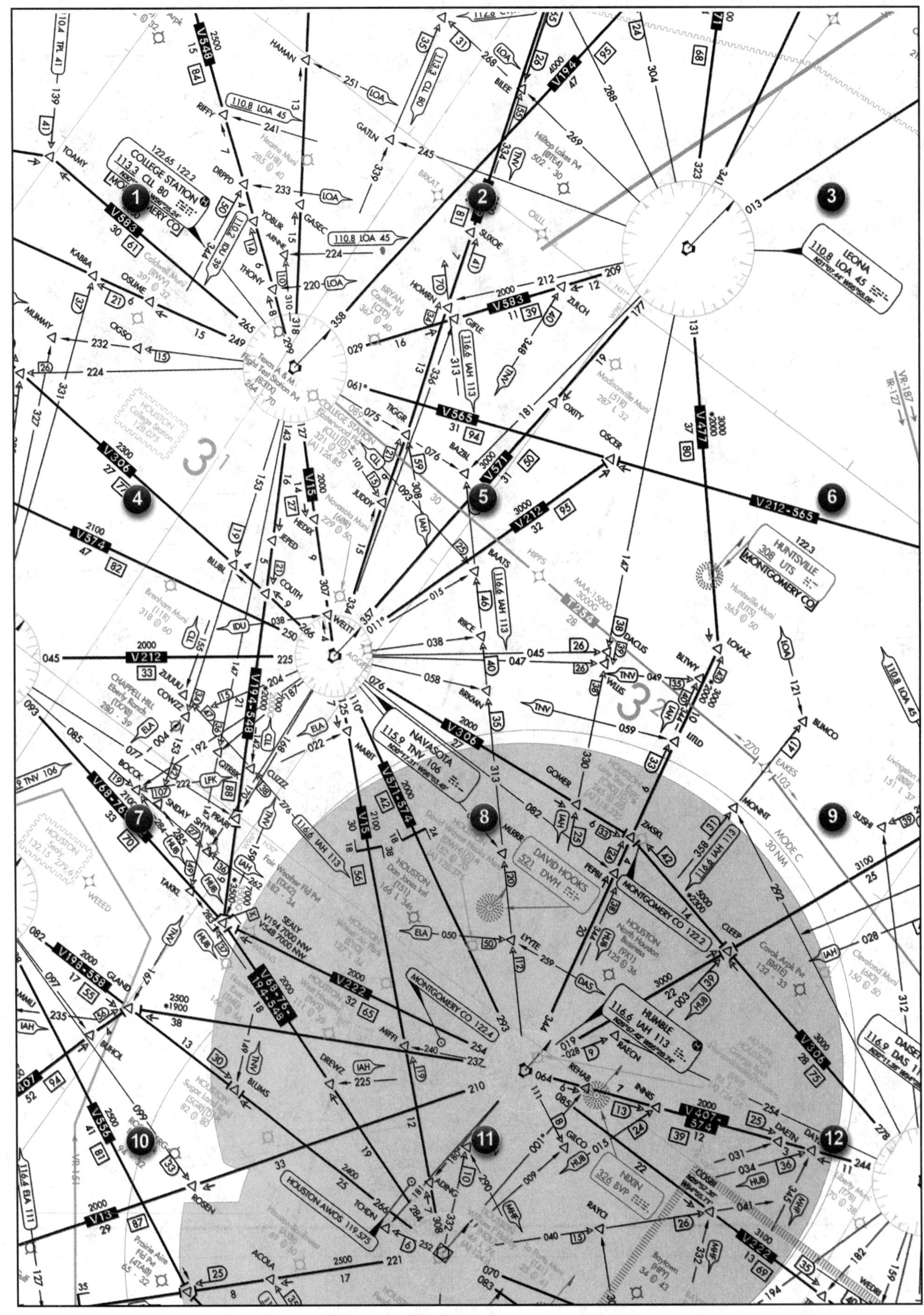

Figure 100. IFR En Route Low Altitude Chart Segment.

This page intentionally left blank.

DALLAS–FORT WORTH INTL (DFW)(KDFW) 12 NW UTC–6(–5DT) N32°53.83′ W97°02.26′ **DALLAS–FT WORTH**
607 B AOE Class I, ARFF Index E NOTAM FILE DFW **COPTER**
RWY 17C–35C: H13401X150 (CONC–GRVD) S–120, D–200, 2S–175, 2D–600, 2D/2D2–850 **H–6H, L–17C, A**
PCN 82 R/B/W/T HIRL CL **IAP, AD**
RWY 17C: ALSF2. TDZL. PAPI(P4L)—GA 3.0° TCH 74′. RVR–TMR
RWY 35C: ALSF2. TDZL. PAPI(P4L)—GA 3.0° TCH 76′. RVR–TMR
RWY 17R–35L: H13401X200 (CONC–GRVD) S–120, D–200, 2S–175, 2D–600, 2D/2D2–850 PCN 78 R/B/W/T HIRL CL
RWY 17R: MALSR. TDZL. PAPI(P4L)—GA 3.0° TCH 68′. RVR–TMR
RWY 35L: MALSR. TDZL. PAPI(P4L)—GA 3.0° TCH 63′. RVR–TMR
RWY 18L–36R: H13400X200 (CONC–GRVD) S–120, D–200, 2S–175, 2D–600, 2D/2D2–850 PCN 83 R/B/W/T HIRL CL
RWY 18L: MALSR. TDZL. PAPI(P4L)—GA 3.0° TCH 70′. RVR–TMR
RWY 36R: MALSR. TDZL. PAPI(P4L)—GA 3.0° TCH 66′. RVR–TMR
RWY 18R–36L: H13400X150 (CONC–GRVD) S–120, D–200, 2S–175, 2D–600, 2D/2D2–850 PCN 82 R/B/W/T HIRL CL
RWY 18R: ALSF2. TDZL. PAPI(P4L)—GA 3.0° TCH 74′. RVR–TMR
RWY 36L: MALSR. TDZL. PAPI(P4L)—GA 3.0° TCH 72′. RVR–TMR
RWY 13R–31L: H9301X150 (CONC–GRVD) S–120, D–200, 2S–175, 2D–600, 2D/2D2–850 PCN 83 R/B/W/T HIRL CL
RWY 13R: MALSR. TDZL. PAPI(P4L)—GA 3.0° TCH 71′. RVR–TR
RWY 31L: REIL. PAPI(P4L)—GA 3.13° TCH 72′. RVR–TR
RWY 13L–31R: H9000X200 (CONC–GRVD) S–120, D–200, 2S–175, 2D–600, 2D/2D2–850 PCN 97 R/B/W/T HIRL CL
RWY 13L: REIL. PAPI(P4L)—GA 3.0° TCH 82′. RVR–TMR Thld dsplcd 625′. 0.5% down.
RWY 31R: MALSR. TDZL. PAPI(P4L)—GA 3.0° TCH 69′. RVR–TMR 0.5% up.
RWY 17L–35R: H8500X150 (CONC–GRVD) S–120, D–200, 2S–175, 2D–600, 2D/2D2–850 PCN 97 R/B/W/T HIRL CL
RWY 17L: ALSF2. TDZL. PAPI(P4L)—GA 3.0° TCH 77′. RVR–TMR Antenna. 0.6% up.
RWY 35R: ALSF2. TDZL. PAPI(P4R)—GA 3.0° TCH 73′. RVR–TMR 0.6% down.

LAND AND HOLD–SHORT OPERATIONS

LDG RWY	HOLD–SHORT POINT	AVBL LDG DIST
RWY 17C	TWY B	10460
RWY 18R	TWY B	10100
RWY 35C	TWY EJ	9050
RWY 36L	TWY Z	10650

RUNWAY DECLARED DISTANCE INFORMATION

RWY	TORA	TODA	ASDA	LDA
RWY 13L:	TORA–9000	TODA–9000	ASDA–9000	LDA–8375
RWY 13R:	TORA–9301	TODA–9301	ASDA–9301	LDA–9301
RWY 17C:	TORA–13401	TODA–13401	ASDA–13401	LDA–13401
RWY 17L:	TORA–8500	TODA–8500	ASDA–8500	LDA–8500
RWY 17R:	TORA–13401	TODA–13401	ASDA–13401	LDA–13401
RWY 18L:	TORA–13400	TODA–13400	ASDA–13400	LDA–13400
RWY 18R:	TORA–13400	TODA–13400	ASDA–13400	LDA–13400
RWY 31L:	TORA–9301	TODA–9301	ASDA–9301	LDA–9301
RWY 31R:	TORA–8375	TODA–8375	ASDA–8375	LDA–8375
RWY 35C:	TORA–13401	TODA–13401	ASDA–13401	LDA–13401
RWY 35L:	TORA–13401	TODA–13401	ASDA–13401	LDA–13401
RWY 35R:	TORA–8500	TODA–8500	ASDA–8500	LDA–8500
RWY 36L:	TORA–13400	TODA–13400	ASDA–13400	LDA–13400
RWY 36R:	TORA–13400	TODA–13400	ASDA–13400	LDA–13400

SERVICE: **FUEL** 100LL, JET A **OX** 1, 3 **LGT** PAPI unusable byd 7° right of centerline.

CONTINUED ON NEXT PAGE

Figure 101. Chart Supplement.

TEXAS

CONTINUED FROM PRECEDING PAGE

AIRPORT REMARKS: Attended continuously. Rwy 17L–35R CLOSED 0400–1200Z‡ exc PPR. Rwy 13R–31L CLOSED 0400–1200Z‡ except PPR. Rwy 13L–31R CLOSED 0400–1200Z‡ exc PPR. Visual screen 20´ AGL 1180´ south AER 35C. Visual screen 22´ AGL 1179´ south AER 35L. ASDE–X in use. Opr transponders with altitude reporting mode and ADS–B (if equipped) enabled on all airport surfaces. Runway Status Lights in operation. Acft at East Air Freight must contact DFW Twr at 127.5 prior to taxi out. PPR for acft with wingspan 215´ or greater (GROUP VI), call arpt ops 972–973–3112 for flw–me svcs while taxiing to and from ramp and rwys. Arpt under const, PAEW in movement areas. Birds on and invof arpt. B747–8 and A380 ops only authorized on Rwys 18R–36L and Rwy 18L–36R, contact arpt ops for additional info. Tkf distance for Rwy 17L from Twy Q2 is 8196´. Tkf distance for Rwy 35R from Twy Q9 is 8196´. Tkf distance for Rwy 17R from Twy EG is 13082´ and from Twy EH is 12816´. Tkf distance for Rwy 35L from Twy EQ is 13084´ and from Twy EP is 12811´. Tkf distance for Rwy 36R from Twy WP is 12815´, from Twy WQ is 13082´. Tkf distance for Rwy 18L from Twy WG is 13082´, from Twy WH is 12815´. Tkf distance for Rwy 17C from Twy EG is 13,082´. Tkf distance for Rwy 18R from Twy WG is 13,082´. Land And Hold Short signs on Rwy 17C at Twy B 10,460´ south of Rwy 17C thld, Rwy 18R at Twy B 10,100´ south of Rwy 18R thld, Rwy 35C at Twy EJ 9050´ north of Rwy 35C thld, Rwy 36L at Twy Z 10,650´ north of Rwy 36L thld, lgtd and marked with in–pavement pulsating white lgts. Acft using Terminal D gates D6–17 must obtain approval from DFW ramp tower 129.95 prior to entering ramp and prior to pushback 0600L–2200L(1200–0400Z‡). Use extreme care at other times. Acft using terminal E gates must obtain approval from DFW ramp 131.0 prior to entering ramp and prior to pushback 1030–0730Z‡ during time change only. Apron entrance/exit points 1 and 2 clsd to acft with wingspan greater than 89´ except PPR. Apron entrance/exit points 3 and 4 clsd to acft with wingspan greater than 118´ except PPR. Apron entrance/exit points 5, 7, 42, 44, 49, 51, 52, and 122 clsd to acft with wingspan greater than 118´. Apron entrance/exit points 22, 24, 105, and 107 clsd to acft with wingspan 125´ and greater. Apron entrance/exit points 31 and 39 clsd to acft with wingspan greater than 167´. Apron entrance/exit points 9, 32, 33, 34, 35, 36, 37, 38, and 53 clsd to acft with wingspan greater than 135´. Apron entrance/exit point 48 clsd to acft with wingspan greater than 195´. Apron entrance/exit point 124 clsd to acft with wingspan greater than 213´. Unless otherwise specified, all apron entrance/exit points clsd to acft with wingspan greater than 214´ except PPR. Terminal B apron taxilane btn apron entrance/exit point taxilanes 107 and 115 clsd to acft with wingspan 118´ and greater. Twy A5 clsd to acft with wingspan 171´ and greater. Twys may rqr judgemental oversteering for large acft. PPR general aviation ops 0600–1100Z‡, call arpt ops 972–973–3112. PPR from arpt ops for general aviation acft to proceed to airline terminal gate exc to general aviation fac. PPR from the primary tenant airlines to opr within the central terminal area. Proper minimum object free area distances may not be maintained for ramp/apron taxi lanes. Twy edge reflectors along all twys. Ldg fee. Flight Notification Service (ADCUS) available. NOTE: See Land and Hold Short Operations, Intersection Departures During Periods of Darkness, Noise Abatement Procedures and Continuous Power Facilities.

AIRPORT MANAGER: 972-973-3112

WEATHER DATA SOURCES: ASOS (972) 615–2608 LLWAS.

COMMUNICATIONS: D–ATIS ARR 123.775 (972) 615–2701 **D–ATIS DEP** 135.925 (972) 615–2701 **UNICOM** 122.95

Ⓡ **RGNL APP CON** 118.1 135.975 124.3(North) 125.2 135.975(South) 119.875(West) 125.025(East)

DFW TOWER 126.55 127.5 (E) 124.15 134.9 (W) **GND CON** 121.65 121.8 (E) 121.85 (W)

CLNC DEL 128.25

Ⓡ **RGNL DEP CON** 118.1 135.975 124.825(North) 125.125 135.975(South) 126.475(West) 118.55(East)

CPDLC (LOGON KUSA)

AIRSPACE: CLASS B See VFR Terminal Area Chart

RADIO AIDS TO NAVIGATION: NOTAM FILE FTW.

MAVERICK (H) VORW/DME 113.1 TTT Chan 78 N32°52.15´ W97°02.43´ 359° 1.7 NM to fld. 540/6E.

All acft arriving DFW are requested to turn DME off until departure due to traffic overload of Maverick DME

DME unusable:

180°–190°

ILS/DME 109.5 I–LWN Chan 32 Rwy 13R. Class IIE. DME unusable wi 2.5 NM (4.2 DME).

ILS/DME 110.3 I–FLQ Chan 40 Rwy 17C. Class IIIE. DME also serves Rwy 35C.

ILS/DME 111.75 I–PPZ Chan 54(Y) Rwy 17L. Class IIIE. DME also serves Rwy 35R.

ILS/DME 111.35 I–JHZ Chan 50(Y) Rwy 17R. Class IE. DME also serves Rwy 35L.

ILS/DME 110.55 I–CIX Chan 42(Y) Rwy 18L. Class IE. DME also serves Rwy 36R.

ILS/DME 111.9 I–VYN Chan 56 Rwy 18R. Class IIIE. DME also serves Rwy 36L.

ILS/DME 110.9 I–RRA Chan 46 Rwy 31R. Class IE.

ILS/DME 110.3 I–PKQ Chan 40 Rwy 35C. Class IIIE. DME also serves Rwy 17C.

ILS/DME 111.35 I–UWX Chan 50(Y) Rwy 35L. Class IE. LOC unusable byd 14 NM blo 3,400´. DME also serves Rwy 17R.

ILS/DME 111.75 I–AJQ Chan 54(Y) Rwy 35R. Class IIIE. DME also serves Rwy 17L. LOC unusable byd 16 NM 5° right of course.

ILS/DME 111.9 I–BXN Chan 56 Rwy 36L. Class ID. DME also serves Rwy 18R. LOC unusable byd 15 NM 5° right of course.

ILS/DME 110.55 I–FJN Chan 42(Y) Rwy 36R. Class IE. DME also serves Rwy 18L.

DAN E RICHARDS MUNI (See PADUCAH on page 358)

Figure 101A. Chart Supplement.

GEORGE BUSH INTERCONTINENTAL/HOUSTON (IAH)(KIAH) 15 N UTC–6(–5DT) **HOUSTON**
N29°59.07′ W95°20.49′ **COPTER**
96 B LRA Class I, ARFF Index E NOTAM FILE IAH **H–7C, L–19E, 21A, GOMW**
RWY 15L–33R: H12001X150 (CONC–GRVD) S–100, D–200, 2S–175, 2D–400, 2D/2D2–800 PCN 72 R/A/W/T HIRL CL **IAP, AD**
RWY 15L: PAPI(P4R)—GA 3.0° TCH 58′. RVR–TMR
RWY 33R: MALSR. RVR–TMR
RWY 09–27: H10000X150 (CONC–GRVD) D–210, 2S–175, 2D–560 PCN 67 R/A/W/T HIRL CL
RWY 09: MALSR. PAPI(P4R)—GA 3.0° TCH 71′. RVR–TMR
RWY 27: ALSF2. TDZL. PAPI(P4L)—GA 3.0° TCH 70′. RVR–TMR
RWY 15R–33L: H10000X150 (CONC–GRVD) S–75, D–200, 2S–175, 2D–400, 2D/2D2–873 PCN 94 R/B/W/T HIRL CL
RWY 15R: MALSR. TDZL. PAPI(P4L)—GA 3.0° TCH 71′. RVR–TMR
RWY 33L: TDZL. PAPI(P4R)—GA 3.0° TCH 59′. RVR–TMR
RWY 08R–26L: H9402X150 (CONC–GRVD) S–75, D–210, 2S–175, 2D–498, 2D/2D2–873 PCN 72 R/A/W/T HIRL CL
RWY 08R: MALSR. TDZL. PAPI(P4L)—GA 3.0° TCH 72′. RVR–TMR
RWY 26L: ALSF2. TDZL. PAPI(P4R)—GA 3.0° TCH 71′. RVR–TMR
RWY 08L–26R: H9000X150 (CONC–GRVD) S–75, D–210, 2S–175, 2D–409, 2D/2D2–873 PCN 72 R/A/W/T HIRL CL
RWY 08L: ALSF2. TDZL. RVR–TMR
RWY 26R: ALSF2. TDZL. RVR–TMR

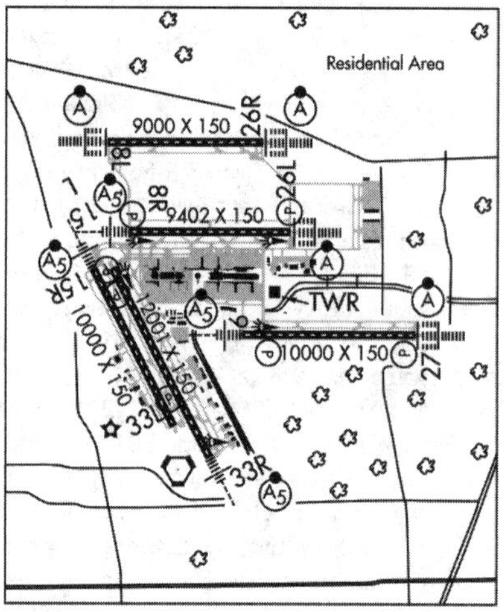

Residential Area
9000 X 150
9402 X 150
12001 X 150
10000 X 150
10000 X 150
TWR

LAND AND HOLD–SHORT OPERATIONS

LDG RWY	HOLD–SHORT POINT	AVBL LDG DIST
RWY 08R	TWY NP	9019
RWY 26L	TWY NE	9010

RUNWAY DECLARED DISTANCE INFORMATION

RWY	TORA	TODA	ASDA	LDA
RWY 08L:	TORA–9000	TODA–9000	ASDA–9000	LDA–9000
RWY 08R:	TORA–9402	TODA–9402	ASDA–9402	LDA–9402
RWY 09:	TORA–10000	TODA–10000	ASDA–10000	LDA–10000
RWY 15L:	TORA–12001	TODA–12001	ASDA–12001	LDA–12001
RWY 15R:	TORA–9999	TODA–9999	ASDA–9999	LDA–9999
RWY 26L:	TORA–9402	TODA–9402	ASDA–9402	LDA–9402
RWY 26R:	TORA–9000	TODA–9000	ASDA–9000	LDA–9000
RWY 27:	TORA–10000	TODA–10000	ASDA–10000	LDA–10000
RWY 33L:	TORA–9999	TODA–9999	ASDA–9999	LDA–9999
RWY 33R:	TORA–12001	TODA–12001	ASDA–12001	LDA–12001

SERVICE: S4 **FUEL** 100LL, JET A **OX** 2

AIRPORT REMARKS: Attended continuously. Rwy 09–27 CLOSED to acft with wingspan 215′ and abv. Birds on and invof arpt. ASDE–X in use. Opr transponders with altitude reporting mode and ADS–B (if equipped) enabled on all airport surfaces. Acft equipped with dual antennas should use top antenna. Rwy status lgts are in opr. Pilots/crews should be aware of dep turns on crs in excess of 180°. Pilot read–back of direction of turns is highly encouraged. Rwy 15L–33R magnetic anomalies may affect compass hdg for tkf. Noise sensitive area north, east and west of arpt. North ramp north and south taxilanes clsd to acft with wing spans greater than 125′. Taxilane RC clsd to acft with wingspan greater than 135′. Twy NR clsd to acft with wing spans greater than 125′ between Twy WD and Twy WB. Twy NR btn Twy NC and Twy WW clsd to acft wingspan more than 214′. Apron taxilane RA btn Twy SC and taxilane R2 irregular sfc steel plate over centerline lgt. Twy SC btn taxilane RA and taxilane RB steel plate over centerline lgt fixture. Twy SF between Rwy 09–27 up to and including the east bridge clsd to acft with wingspan 215′ and over. Twy WA clsd indef btn Twy WG and Twy WL barricaded and lgtd. Twy WA clsd indef btn Twy WL and Twy WN barricaded and lgtd. Twy WG clsd indef btn Rwy 15L–33R and Twy WA. Twy WH clsd indef btn Rwy 15L–33R and Twy WB; barricaded and lgtd. Twy WJ clsd indef btn Rwy 15L–33R and Twy WA barricaded and lgtd. Twy WK clsd indef btn Rwy 15L–33R and Twy WB barricaded and lgtd. Twy WL lgts btn Rwy 15L–33R and Twy WB OTS indef. Twy WM clsd indef btn Rwy 15L–33R and Twy WB barricaded and lgtd. Twy WW run–up pad for Rwy 15L clsd acft with wingspan 135′ and over. Twy WW btn Twy NR and Twy WB clsd to acft wingspan more than 214′. Twy WZ clsd indef btn Rwy 15L–33R and Twy WB barricaded and lgtd. The following movement areas are not visible from the twr: portions of Twys WA and WB from Twy WH to the AER 33R, Twys WA and WB from Twy WD north for 400′, Twy WD from Twy WA to Twy NR, Twy NR, Twy WL from Rwy 15L to Twy WB and Twy WM. Taxilane RA, RB, RC, R2, and Twy SC north of Twy SB are designated non–movement areas operated by UAL ramp ctl. Twy SF btn Twy NB and Taxilane RA is designated non–movement area. Dual twy ops Twy NK btn Twy NB and North Ramp, west cntrln rstd to acft max wing spans 125′ and east cntrln max wing spans 214′. Twy NR btn Twy WW and WB is designated non–movement area. Twy NK btn Twy NB and terminal D ramp simultaneous acft ops prohibited when middle taxilane in use. Twy WC west of Rwy 15R–33L rstd to acft with 118′ wingspan and blo. Twy WA and Twy WB magnetic anomalies may affect compass hdg. North Ramp taxilane btn Twys NF and NR rstd to acft with wing span 125′ and blo. 9′ AGL unmarked security fence adjacent to FBO and corporate base operator ramps and non–movement area taxilanes. Helicopter hover/taxi rstd to hard sfc movement areas only. Ldg fee. Flight Notification Service (ADCUS) available. NOTE: See Special Notices—Continuous Power Facilities.

Figure 102. Chart Supplement.

CONTINUED FROM PRECEDING PAGE

AIRPORT MANAGER: 281-230-3100
WEATHER DATA SOURCES: ASOS (281) 443–6397 **HIWAS** 116.6 IAH. TDWR.
COMMUNICATIONS: D–ATIS 124.05 (281–209–8665) **UNICOM** 122.95
RCO 122.4 (MONTGOMERY COUNTY RADIO)
® **HOUSTON APP CON** 124.35 (West) 120.05 (East)
® **HOUSTON DEP CON** 123.8 (West) 119.7 (North) 133.6 (East) 127.125
TOWER 135.15 (Rwy 09 and Rwy 27) 127.3 (Rwy 15R–33L and Rwy 15L–33R) 125.35 (Rwy 08R and Rwy 26L) 120.725 (Rwy 08L and Rwy 26R) **GND CON** 121.7 (Rwy 15L–33R, and Rwy 15R–33L) 118.575 (Rwy 08L–26R, Rwy 08R–26L and Rwy 09–27)
GND METERING 119.95 **CLNC DEL** 128.1
CPDLC (LOGON KUSA)
AIRSPACE: CLASS B See VFR Terminal Area Chart
RADIO AIDS TO NAVIGATION: NOTAM FILE IAH.
HUMBLE (H) VORTACW 116.6 IAH Chan 113 N29°57.42´ W95°20.74´ 003° 1.7 NM to fld. 81/5E. **HIWAS.**
VORTAC Monitored by ATCT
VOR portion unusable:
060°–070° byd 35 NM
175°–185° byd 20 NM blo 3,000´
Byd 30 NM blo 2,000´
DME unusable:
015°–090° byd 30 NM blo 2,000´
130°–320° byd 30 NM blo 2,000´
175°–185° byd 20 NM blo 3,000´
230°–250°
Byd 25° left of course
TACAN AZIMUTH unusable:
040°–055° blo 5,000´
150°–320° blo 4,500´
150°–320° byd 10 NM
NIXIN NDB (MHW) 326 BVP N29°59.60´ W95°12.90´ 260° 6.6 NM to fld. 72/5E. NOTAM FILE CXO.
ILS/DME 111.55 I–BZU Chan 52(Y) Rwy 08L. Class IIIE.
ILS/DME 109.7 I–IAH Chan 34 Rwy 08R. Class IE. DME also serves Rwy 26.
ILS/DME 110.9 I–UYO Chan 46 Rwy 09. DME also serves Rwy 27.
ILS 111.15 I–LKM Rwy 15R. Class IE. LOC unusable byd 30° right of course. DME unusable byd 25° left of course.
ILS/DME 109.7 I–JYV Chan 34 Rwy 26L. Class IIIE. DME also serves Rwy 08.
ILS/DME 111.55 I–OND Chan 52(Y) Rwy 26R. Class IIIE.
ILS/DME 110.9 I–GHI Chan 46 Rwy 27. Class IIIE. DME also serves Rwy 09.
ILS 111.9 I–CDG Rwy 33R. Class IE.
COMM/NAV/WEATHER REMARKS: Ground Based Augmentation System (GBAS) approach service volume 20 NM from threshold for all GLS approaches.

HOUSTON EXECUTIVE (TME)(KTME) 28 W UTC–6(–5DT) N29°48.30´ W95°53.87´ **HOUSTON**
166 B NOTAM FILE CXO **H–7C, L–19D, 21A, GOMW**
IAP, AD
RWY 18–36: H6610X100 (ASPH) D–101 MIRL
RWY 18: REIL. PAPI(P4L)—GA 3.0° TCH 40´. P–line.
RWY 36: REIL. PAPI(P4L)—GA 3.0° TCH 40´. Rgt tfc.
SERVICE: S4 **FUEL** 100LL, JET A **OX** 3, 4 **LGT** ACTIVATE MIRL Rwy 18–36, REIL Rwy 18 and REIL Rwy 36—CTAF.
AIRPORT REMARKS: Attended continuously. Birds on and invof arpt. Noise sensitive area east of arpt in effect, avoid housing area. Touch and go ldgs prohibited.
AIRPORT MANAGER: 281-945-5000
WEATHER DATA SOURCES: AWOS–3 119.525 (281) 945–5451. or 713–932–8437. TDWR.
COMMUNICATIONS: CTAF 126.975 **UNICOM** 122.975 **ATIS** 119.525 (24 hr 281–945–5451)
® **HOUSTON APP/DEP CON** 123.8
TOWER 126.975 (1200–0400Z‡)
GND CON 132.075 **CLNC DEL** 132.075
AIRSPACE: CLASS D svc 1200–0400Z‡ other times CLASS E.
RADIO AIDS TO NAVIGATION: NOTAM FILE ELA.
EAGLE LAKE (H) VORW/DME 116.4 ELA Chan 111 N29°39.75´ W96°19.03´ 061° 23.5 NM to fld. 193/8E.
COMM/NAV/WEATHER REMARKS: For Clnc Del when ATCT is clsd ctc Houston Apch at 281–443–5844, to cancel IFR call 281–443–5888.

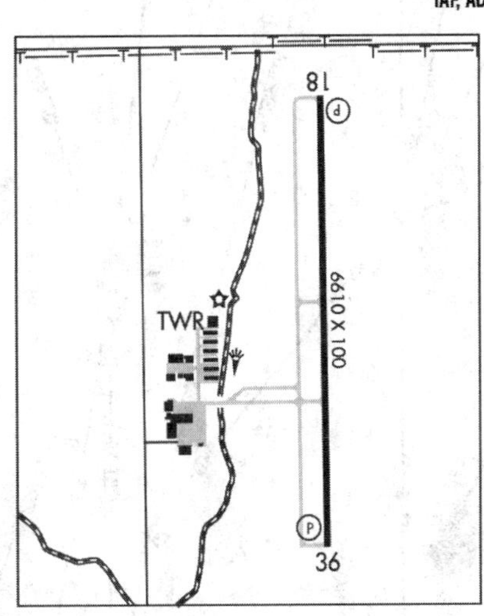

Figure 102A. Chart Supplement.

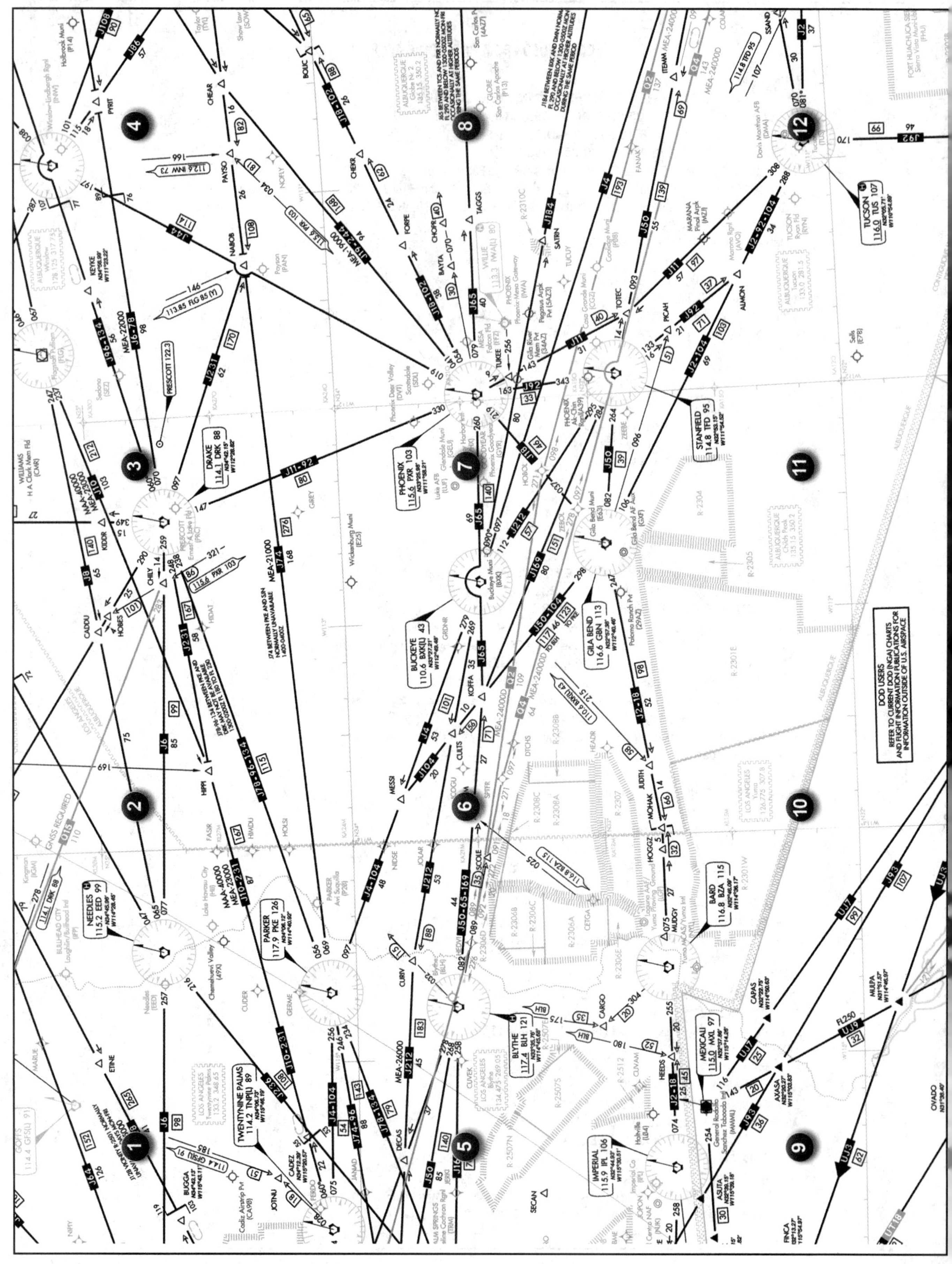

Figure 105. IFR En Route High Altitude Chart Segment.

BAKERSFIELD

BAKERSFIELD MUNI (L45) 3 S UTC–8(–7DT) N35°19.49′ W118°59.76′ **LOS ANGELES**
378 B S4 **FUEL** 100LL TPA—1178(800) NOTAM FILE RIU **L–3D, 7B**
RWY 16–34: H4000X75 (ASPH) S–20 MIRL **IAP**
RWY 16: Road. Rgt tfc.
RWY 34: REIL. PAPI(P2L)—GA 4.1° TCH 53′. P–line.
AIRPORT REMARKS: Attended 1500–0100Z‡. 100′ pole line 1/2 mile south of arpt. Rwy lgts are pilot controlled frequency 122.8, three clicks for on. Lgts go out after 15 minutes.
AIRPORT MANAGER: 661-326-3781
COMMUNICATIONS: CTAF/UNICOM 122.8
RCO 122.45 (RANCHO MURIETA RADIO)
Ⓡ **BAKERSFIELD APP/DEP CON** 126.45 (1400–0700Z‡)
Ⓡ **L.A. CENTER APP/DEP CON** 127.1 (0700–1400Z‡)
RADIO AIDS TO NAVIGATION: NOTAM FILE BFL.
SHAFTER (H) VORTACW 115.4 EHF Chan 101 N35°29.07′ W119°05.84′ 139° 10.8 NM to fld. 548/14E. **HIWAS.**

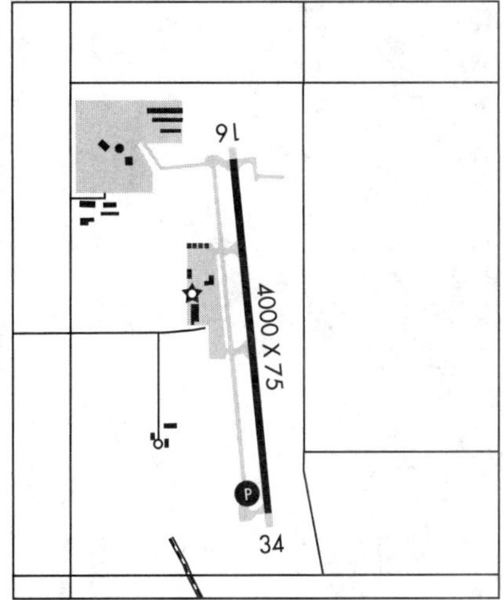

MEADOWS FLD (BFL)(KBFL) 3 NW UTC–8(–7DT) N35°26.03′ W119°03.46′ **LOS ANGELES**
510 B S4 **FUEL** 100, 100LL, JET A OX 4 ARFF Index—See Remarks NOTAM FILE BFL **H–4H, L–3D, 7B**
IAP, AD
RWY 12L–30R: H10855X150 (ASPH-GRVD) S–110, D–200, 2S–175, 2D–500, 2D/2D2–850 HIRL CL
RWY 12L: VASI(V4L)—GA 3.0° TCH 52′. 0.4% down.
RWY 30R: MALSR. TDZL. PAPI(P4L)—GA 3.0° TCH 64′. Thld dsplcd 3426′. Rgt tfc. 0.3% up.
RWY 12R–30L: H7703X100 (ASPH) S–18 MIRL 0.3% up NW
RWY 12R: PAPI(P4L)—GA 3.0° TCH 25′. Rgt tfc.
RWY 30L: PAPI(P4L)—GA 3.0° TCH 25′. Thld dsplcd 3382′. Tree.
AIRPORT REMARKS: Attended continuously. Rwy 12R–30L CLOSED when twr clsd. Right base ops for Rwy 30R establish wings level on final apch no lower than 300′ AGL. Arpt ops not authorized below 1200 RVR without Surface Movement Guidance & Control System (SMGCS). Arpt oprs not authorized below 600 RVR. Noise sensitive areas S and E of arpt recommended turbojet training hrs weekdays 1600–0600Z‡, weekends 2000–0600Z‡ no more than ten practice approaches per hour. Rwy 12R–30L NSTD holding position markings/sign locations. Rwy 30R 50:1 to dspld thld. Class I, ARFF Index B. Index C ARFF avbl. Centerline lgts Rwy 30R only. Rwy pilot control lighting avbl. When twr clsd ACTIVATE HIRL Rwy 12L–30R, PAPI and MALSR Rwy 30R—CTAF. PAPI Rwy 12R and PAPI Rwy 30L not opr when twr clsd.
AIRPORT MANAGER: 661-391-1870
WEATHER DATA SOURCES: ASOS (661) 393–3766
COMMUNICATIONS: CTAF 118.1 **ATIS** 118.6 661–399–9425 **UNICOM** 122.95
BAKERSFIELD RCO 122.45 (RANCHO MURIETA RADIO)
Ⓡ **BAKERSFIELD APP CON** 118.9 (N) 118.8 (S) (1400–0700Z‡)
Ⓡ **BAKERSFIELD DEP CON** 126.45 (N,S) (1400–0700Z‡)
Ⓡ **L.A. CENTER APP/DEP CON** 127.1 (0700–1400Z‡)
BAKERSFIELD TOWER 118.1 (1400–0700Z‡) **GND CON** 121.7
AIRSPACE: CLASS D svc 1400–2300Z‡, other times CLASS E.
VOR TEST FACILITY (VOT) 111.2
RADIO AIDS TO NAVIGATION: NOTAM FILE BFL.
SHAFTER (H) VORTACW 115.4 EHF Chan 101 N35°29.07′ W119°05.84′ 133° 3.6 NM to fld. 548/14E. **HIWAS.**
ILS/DME 111.9 I-BFL Chan 56 Rwy 30R. Unmonitored when ATCT clsd.

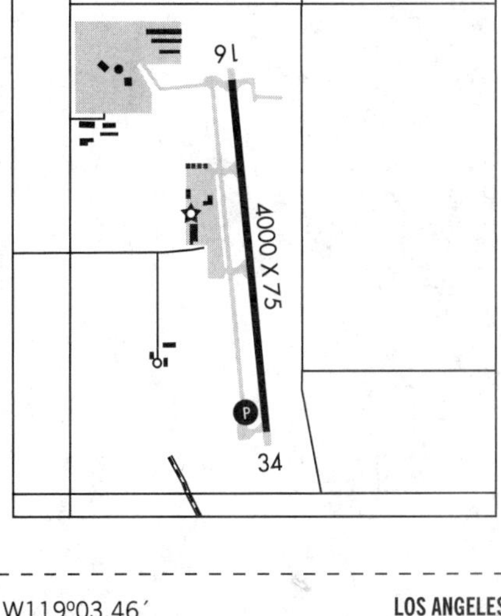

Figure 113B. Data from Southwest U.S. Chart Supplement.

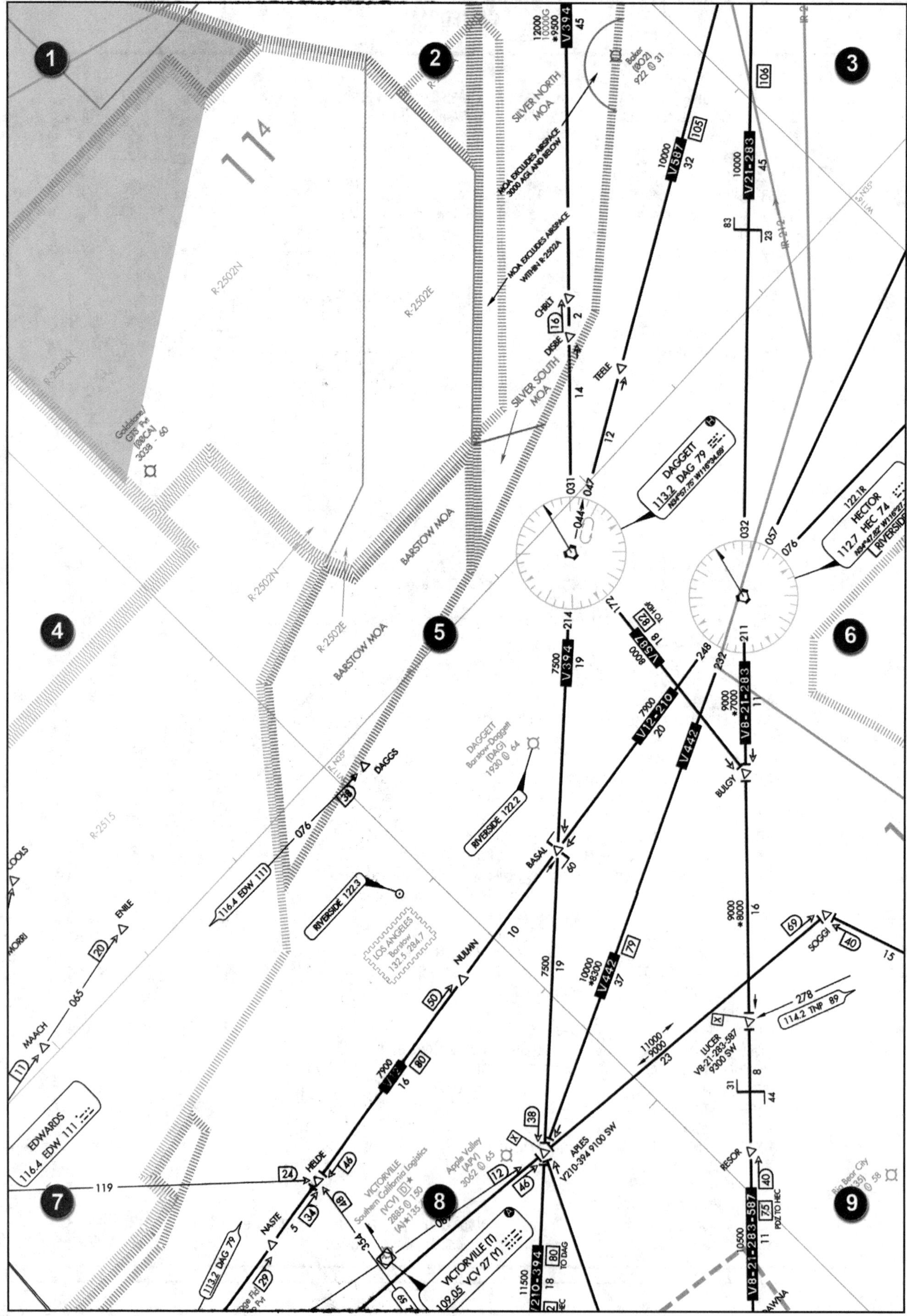

Figure 114. En Route Low Altitude Chart Segment.

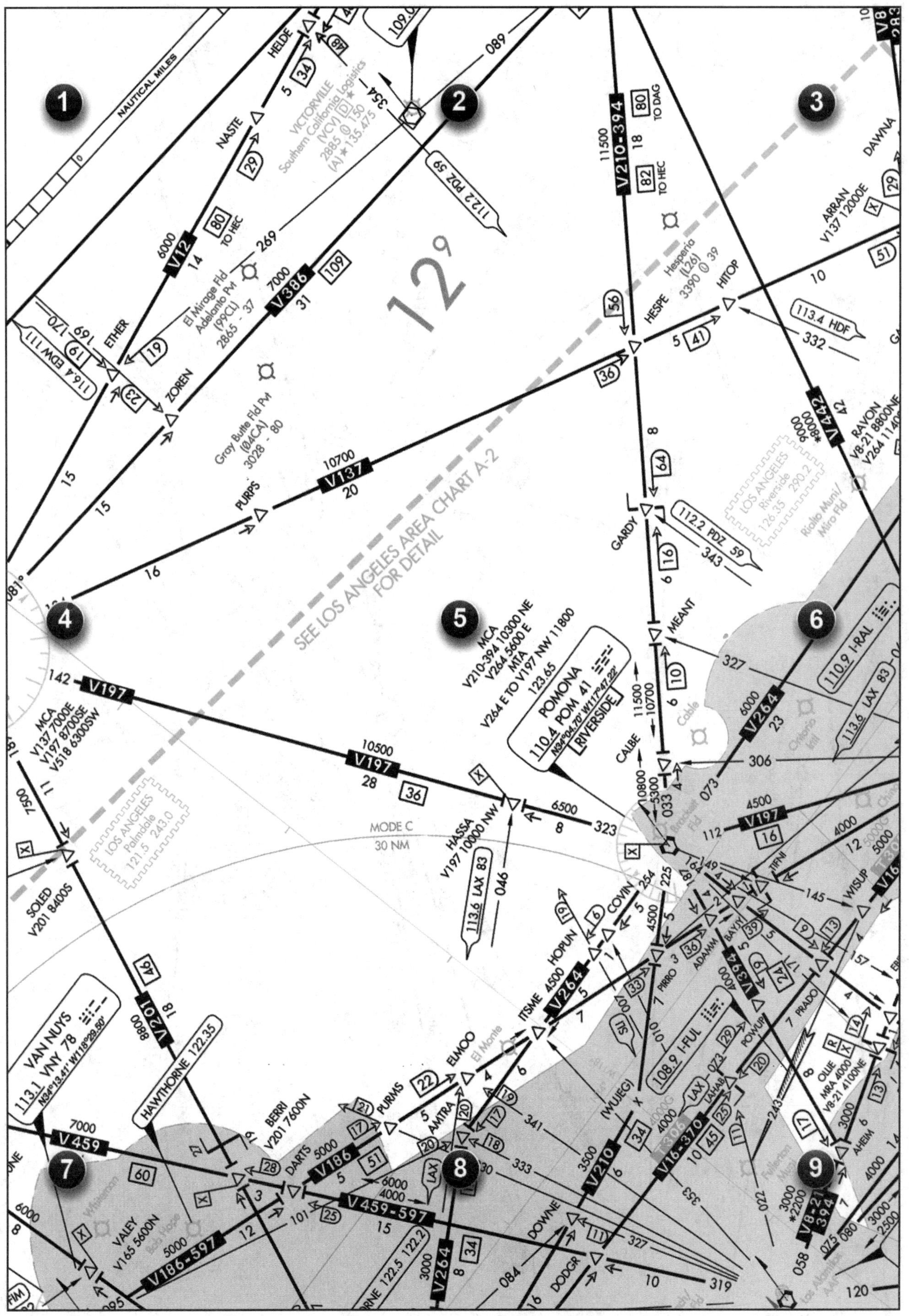

Figure 114A. En Route Low Altitude Chart Segment.

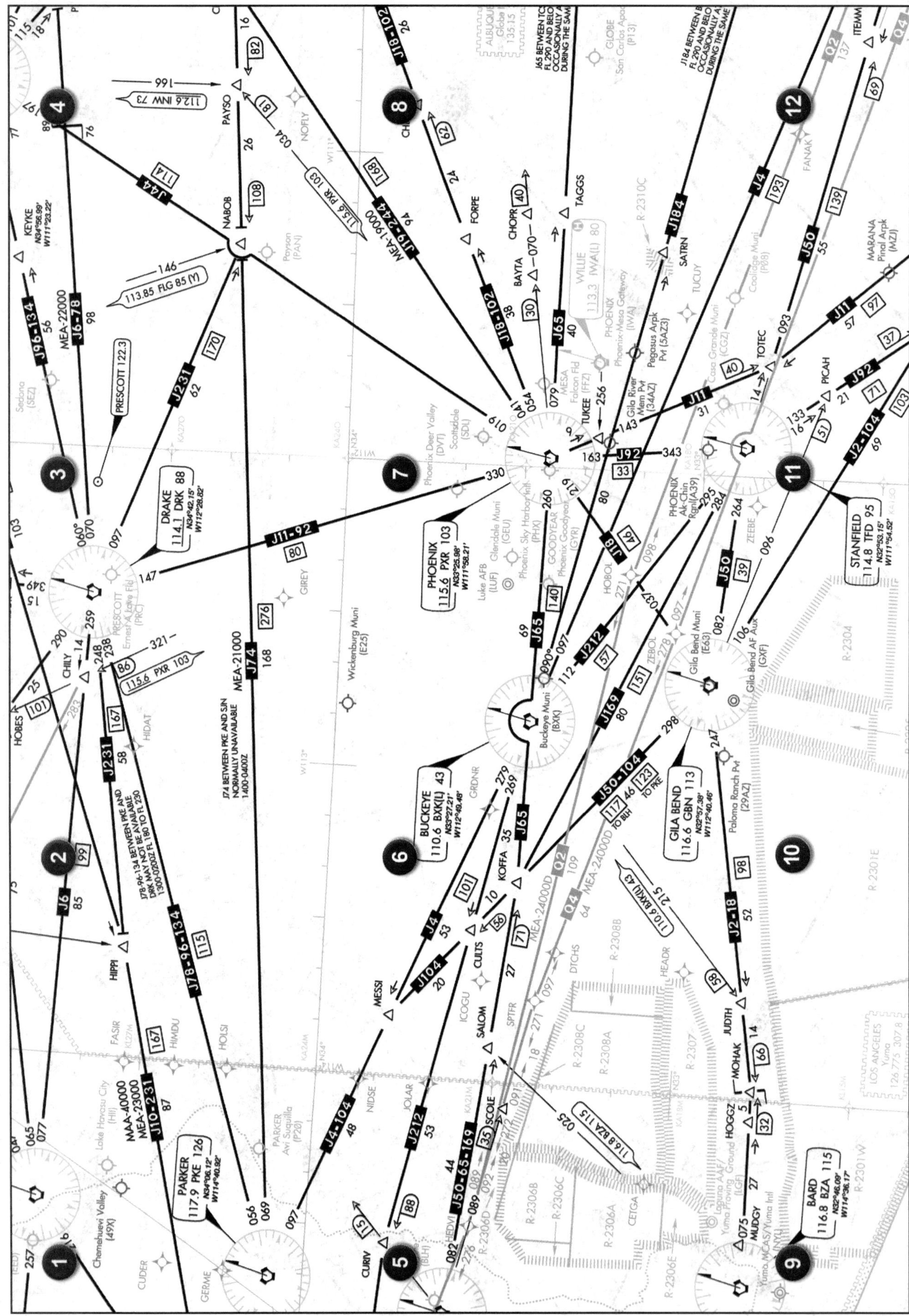

Figure 117. IFR En Route High Altitude Chart Segment.

This page intentionally left blank.

PHOENIX SKY HARBOR INTL (PHX)(KPHX) P (ANG) 3 E UTC–7 N33°26.06´ W112°00.70´ **PHOENIX**
1135 B S4 **FUEL** 100LL, JET A OX 1, 2, 3, 4 TPA—See Remarks LRA Class I, ARFF Index D **H–4J, L–5B, A**
NOTAM FILE PHX **IAP, AD**

RWY 08–26: H11489X150 (CONC–GRVD) S–30, D–200, 2S–175, 2D–400, 2D/2D2–620 PCN 74 R/B/W/T HIRL
RWY 08: MALSF. PAPI(P4L)—GA 3.0° TCH 69´. Thld dsplcd 898´. Bldg.
RWY 26: REIL. PAPI(P4L)—GA 3.0° TCH 60´. Road. Rgt tfc.
RWY 07L–25R: H10300X150 (CONC–GRVD) S–30, D–200, 2S–175, 2D–400, 2D/2D2–620 PCN 70 R/B/W/T HIRL
RWY 07L: MALSR. PAPI(P4L)—GA 3.0° TCH 73´. Pole. Rgt tfc.
RWY 25R: PAPI(P4L)—GA 3.0° TCH 70´. Antenna.
RWY 07R–25L: H7800X150 (CONC–GRVD) S–30, D–200, 2S–175, 2D–400, 2D/2D2–620 PCN 79 R/B/W/T HIRL
RWY 07R: MALSR. PAPI(P4L)—GA 3.0° TCH 70´. Pole.
RWY 25L: MALSR. PAPI(P4L)—GA 3.0° TCH 66´. Antenna.

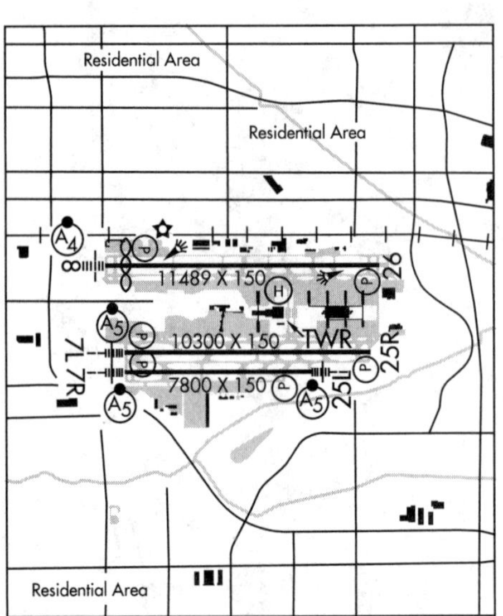

RUNWAY DECLARED DISTANCE INFORMATION
RWY 08: TORA–11489 TODA–11489 ASDA–11489 LDA–10591
RWY 26: TORA–11489 TODA–11489 ASDA–11489 LDA–11489

MILITARY SERVICE: JASU 1(MD–3M) 1(MA–1A) **FUEL** J4–Ltd supply (MIL), A+ (C602–273–3770.) (NC–100LL, A) **FLUID** LPOX LOX **OIL** O–148 (Mil)

AIRPORT REMARKS: Attended continuously. Bird activity within 10 miles of arpt up to 10,000´ MSL. ASDE–X Surveillance System in use. Opr transponders with Mode C on all twys and rwys. TPA—2135(1000) lgt acft and non–turbo jets; 2635(1500) heavy acft and turbojets. Noise abatement procedures are in effect at all times ctc 602–273–4300 for more information. Rwy 07L touchdown and Rwy 25R rollout rwy visual range avbl. Twy R and portions of Twy S and Twy T directly blo the twr are non–visible areas from the twr. Phoenix Twr unable to provide ATC services to acft while on Twr R, and portions of Twy S and Twy T. Twy D between intersections Twy D8 and Twy D9 rstd to acft with wingspan 135´ or less. Twy R overhead train bridge at midpoint provides 82´ –4" clnc. Tran acft use FBO for svc 602–273–3770, 132.0. FAA navigational antennas located 114´ north and south of Twy F centerline, 525´ west of Twy G3 intersection. FAA navigation equipment shacks located 117´ north and 117´ south of Twy F centerline between Twys G2 and G3 intersections. No experimental flt of ground demonstration on arpt without prior written consent from the arpt. This arpt has been surveyed by the National Geodetic Survey. National guard has ltd tran maintenance and parking RON by prior permission. Acft design group VI opr with PPR. No touch and go or stop and go ops allowed between 1300 and 0600Z without prior written consent from arpt. No engine runs on arpt without prior coordination with arpt ops 48 hrs prior to arrival. International ldg rights rqr US CSTMS and Border Protection notification 48 hrs prior to ldg. GA should review arpt safety video http://skyharbor.com/about/forpilots.html. General aviation should ctc arpt manager 602–273–3300 as to how to view/review arpt video. Rwy status lgts are in opr. Landing fee. Overnight parking fee. Fee for all charters, travel clubs and certain revenue producing aircraft. Flight Notification Service (ADCUS) available. NOTE: See Special Notices—Continuous Power Facilities.

AIRPORT MANAGER: 602-273-3300

WEATHER DATA SOURCES: ASOS (602) 231–8557 TDWR.

COMMUNICATIONS: D–ATIS 127.575
RCO 122.6 122.2 (PRESCOTT RADIO)
Ⓡ **APP/DEP CON** 124.1 (119°–138° 7500´–14,500´) (192°–263° 7500´–12,500´) 119.2 (319°–057° 7500´ and abv) 120.7 (319°–057° blo 7500´) 123.7 (119°–138° blo 7500´) (139°–191° blo 8500´) 124.9 (058°–118° blo 10,500´) 126.8 (058°–118° 10,500´ and abv) (119°–138° abv 14,500´) (139°–191° 8500´ and above) (192°–263° abv 12,500´) 126.375
TOWER 118.7 (Rwy 08–26) 120.9 (Rwy 07R–25L and Rwy 07L–25R) **GND CON** 119.75 (North) 132.55 (South)
CLNC DEL 118.1

AIRSPACE: CLASS B See VFR Terminal Area Chart

VOR TEST FACILITY (VOT) 109.0

Figure 118. Excerpt from Chart Supplement.

CONTINUED FROM PRECEDING PAGE

RADIO AIDS TO NAVIGATION: NOTAM FILE PRC.
(H) VORTACW 115.6 PXR Chan 103 N33°25.98′ W111°58.21′ 260° 2.1 NM to fld. 1182/12E.
VOR unusable:
345°–360° byd 33 NM blo 10,000′
DME unusable:
215°–315°
345°–360° byd 33 NM blo 11,000′
VORTAC unusable:
015°–034° byd 33 NM blo 10,000′
090°–100° byd 15 NM blo 8,000′
185°–190° byd 30 NM blo 8,000′
185°–190° byd 38 NM blo 9,000′
190°–230° byd 20 NM blo 10,000′
345°–034° byd 10 NM blo 6,000′
345°–034° byd 20 NM blo 8,000′
360°–015° byd 33 NM blo 11,000′
ILS/DME 111.5 I–PHX Chan 52 Rwy 07L. Class IA. LOC front course unusable byd 15° left and right of CL. LOC unusable within 0.3 NM of rwy thld.
ILS/DME 110.75 I–AHA Chan 44(Y) Rwy 07R. Class ID. DME also serves RJG ILS Rwy 25L.
ILS/DME 111.75 I–SYQ Chan 54(Y) Rwy 08. Class IT. LOC unusable 25° left of course.
ILS/DME 110.75 I–RJG Chan 44(Y) Rwy 25L. Class IT. DME also serves AHA ILS Rwy 07R.
ILS/DME 111.75 I–CWJ Chan 54(Y) Rwy 26. Class IB.

• • • • • • • • • • • • • • • • • •

HELIPAD H1: H60X60 (CONC)
HELIPORT REMARKS: Helipad H1 weight bearing capacity 12,000 lbs gross weight.

PHOENIX–MESA GATEWAY (IWA)(KIWA) 20 SE UTC–7 N33°18.47′ W111°39.33′ **PHOENIX**
1384 B S1 **FUEL** 100LL, JET A OX 3, 4 TPA—See Remarks Class I, ARFF Index C **H–4J, L–5B, A**
NOTAM FILE IWA **IAP, AD**

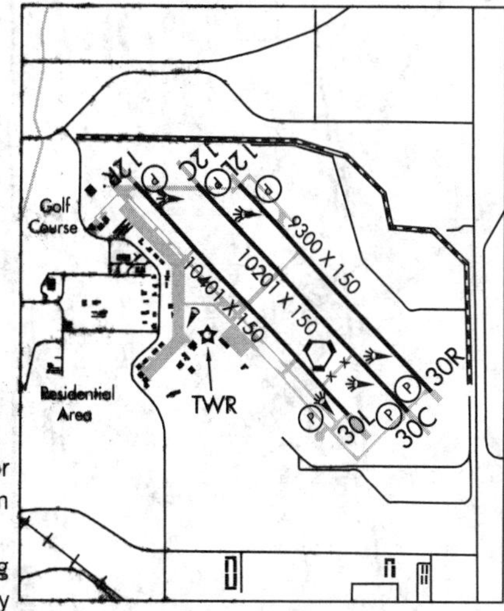

RWY 12R–30L: H10401X150 (CONC) S–55, D–95, 2S–120, 2D–185, 2D/2D2–550 MIRL
RWY 12R: PAPI(P4L)—GA 3.0° TCH 60′. Rgt tfc. 0.3% up.
RWY 30L: PAPI(P4L)—GA 3.0° TCH 60′. 0.3% down.
RWY 12C–30C: H10201X150 (ASPH–CONC) S–55, D–95, 2S–120, 2D–185, 2D/2D2–550 HIRL
RWY 12C: PAPI(P4L)—GA 3.0° TCH 50′. 0.3% up.
RWY 30C: PAPI(P4L)—GA 3.0° TCH 49′. 0.3% down.
RWY 12L–30R: H9300X150 (CONC) S–75, D–210, 2S–175, 2D–590, 2D/2D2–850 HIRL
RWY 12L: REIL. PAPI(P4L)—GA 3.0° TCH 74′. 0.3% up.
RWY 30R: REIL. PAPI(P4L)—GA 3.0° TCH 75′. Rgt tfc. 0.3% down.
AIRPORT REMARKS: Attended continuously. Fuel avbl continuously ctc 480–988–7700 or 129.875. Be alert for crop dusting activity at or below 2000′ MSL 3 miles west of the apch end of Rwy 12R. Be alert for crop dusting activity at or below 2000′ MSL between 2 and 3 miles on apch for Rwy 30R, Rwy 30L and Rwy 30C. Occasional wildlife invof arpt. Rwy 12C first 1000′ conc, Rwy 30C first 3500′ conc, remaining center portion asph. Large/heavy acft taxi with inboard engines only. Twy T rstd to acft with wingspan less than 79′. Twy W between Twy H and Twy V rstd to acft with wingspan less than 135′. Twy W between Twy T and Twy V rstd to acft with wingspan less than 118′. Twy Y rstd to acft with wing span less than 79′. 7′ chain link fence on southern portion of middle ramp. Voluntary noise abatement procedures in effect. Avoid low overflight of noise sensitive areas surrounding arpt. For noise abatement information ctc arpt 480–988–7637 between 1300–0500Z or 480–988–7700 between 0500–1300Z. TPA—Fixed Wing 2602(1218), Jet 3102(1718), Rotorcraft 2102(718). No ldg fee for U.S. Government owned, non–revenue and flight training acft up to 35,000 lbs. For REIL Rwy 12L and Rwy 30R ctc twr. After twr clsd, arpt lgts remain on.
AIRPORT MANAGER: 480-988-7700
WEATHER DATA SOURCES: AWOS–3 133.5 (480) 988–9428. **HIWAS** 113.3 IWA.
COMMUNICATIONS: CTAF 120.6 **ATIS** 133.5
® **PHOENIX APP/DEP CON** 124.9
GATEWAY TOWER 120.6 1200–0700Z **GND CON** 128.25
CLNC DEL 135.05
AIRSPACE: CLASS D svc 1200–0700Z other times CLASS G.

Figure 118A. Excerpt from Chart Supplement.

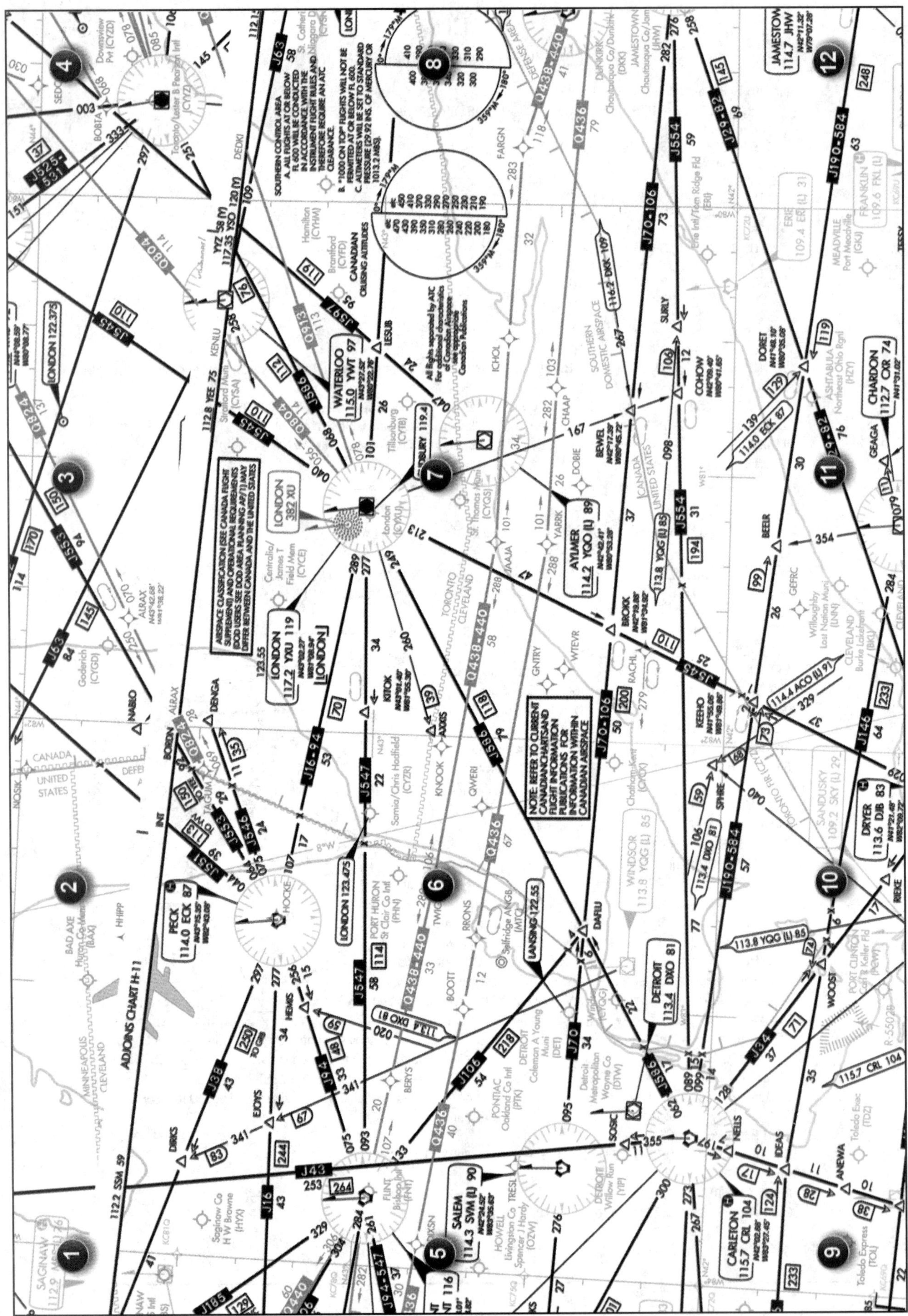

Figure 121. IFR En Route High Altitude Chart Segment.

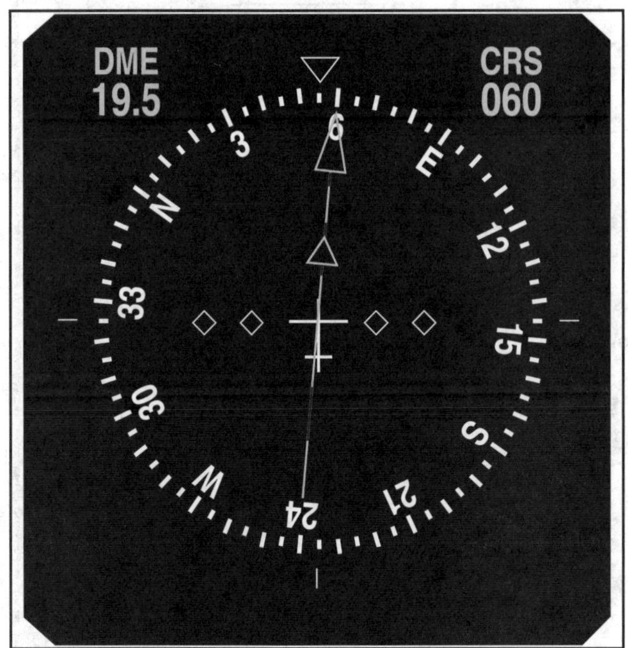

Figure 123. Aircraft Course and DME Indicator.

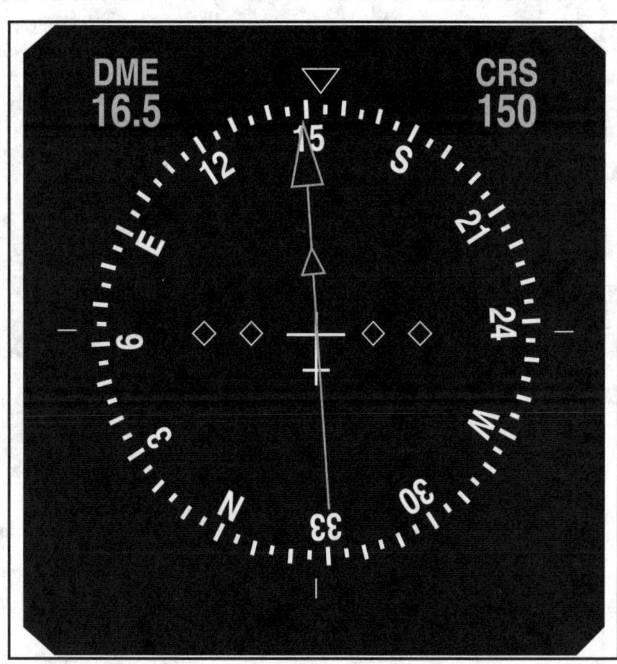

Figure 124. Aircraft Course and DME Indicator.

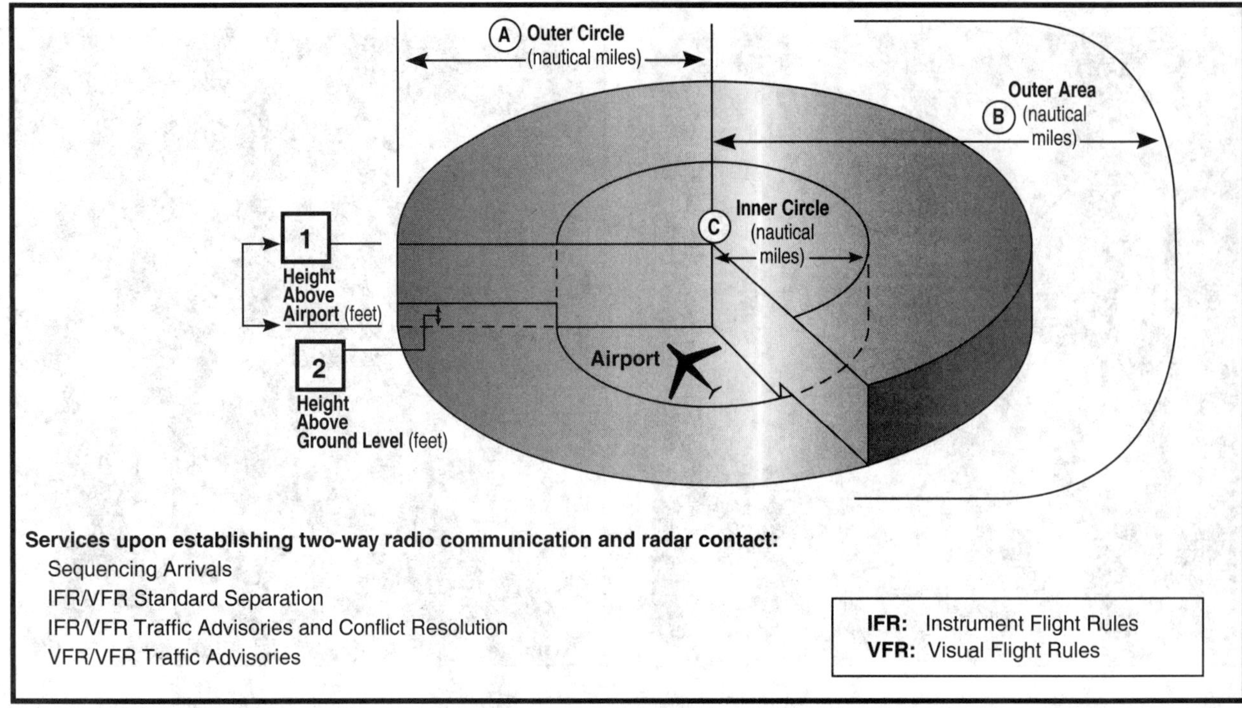

Figure 126. Class C Airspace.

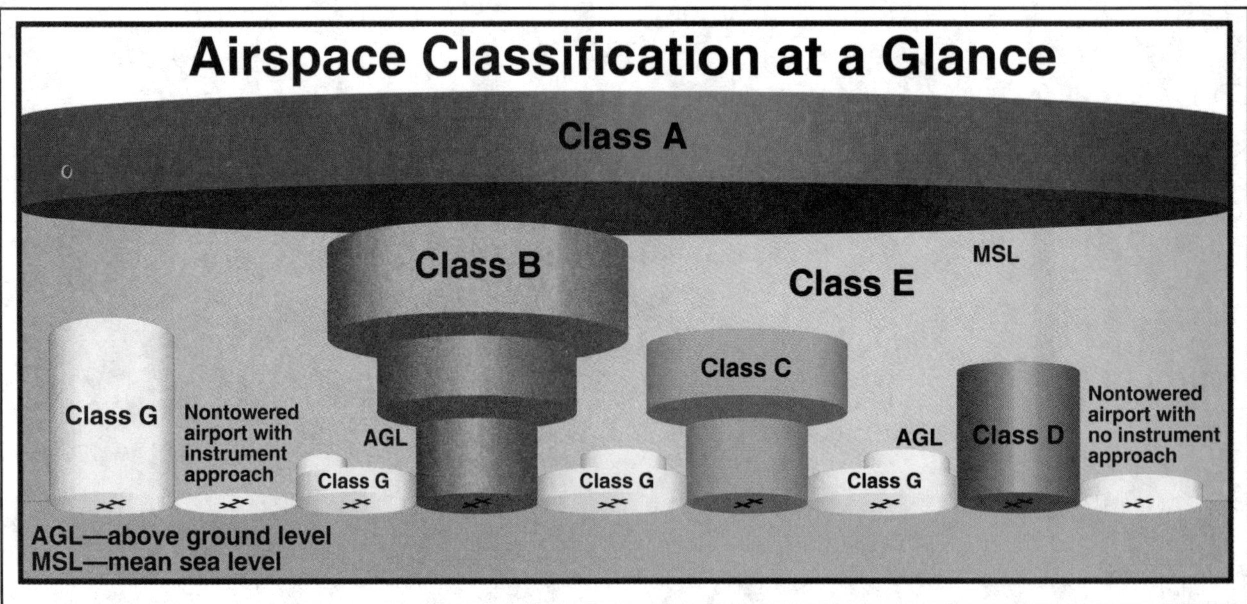

Figure 127. Airspace Classification.

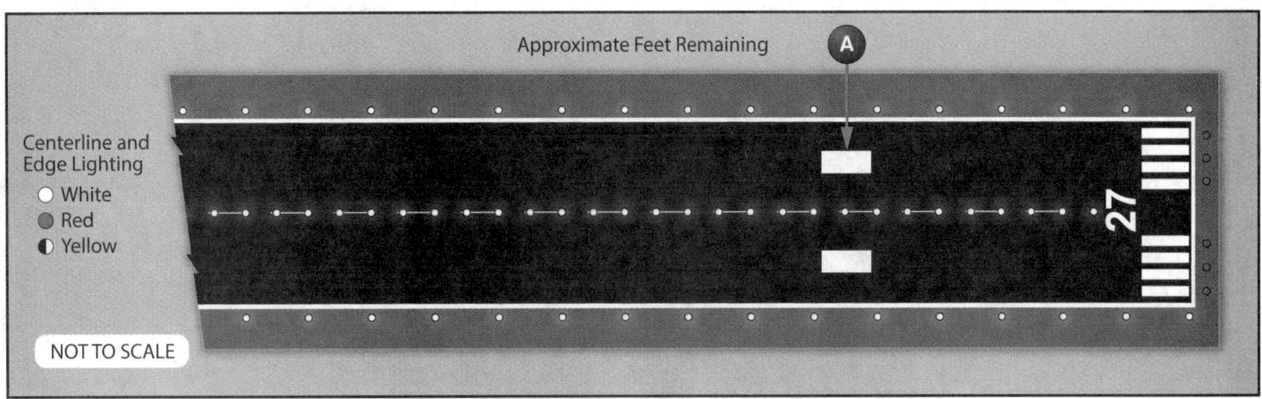

Figure 129. FAA Nonprecision Approach Runway Markings and Lighting.

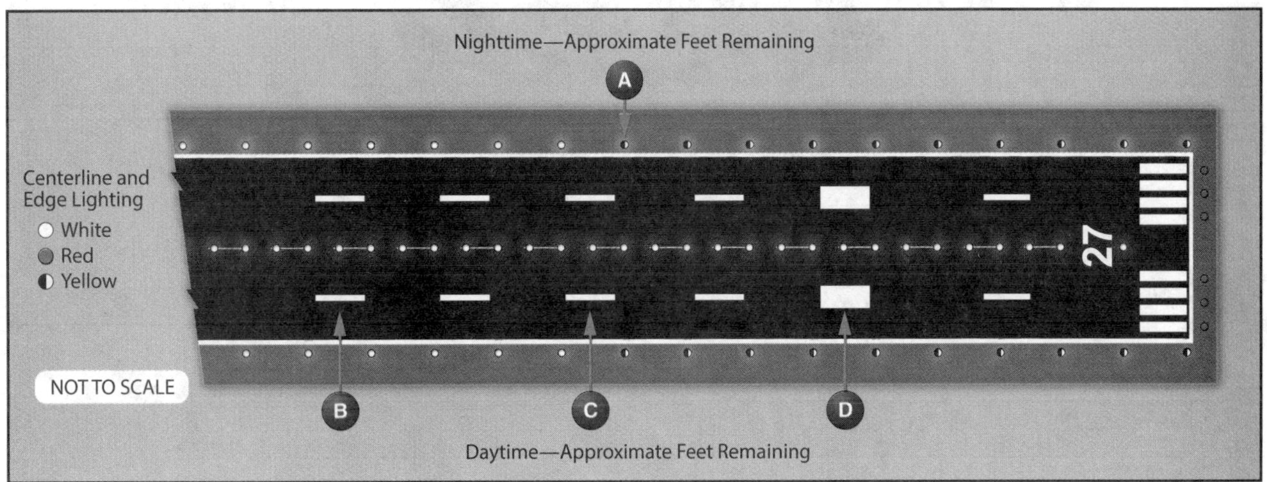

Figure 130. ICAO Nonprecision Approach Runway Markings and Lighting.

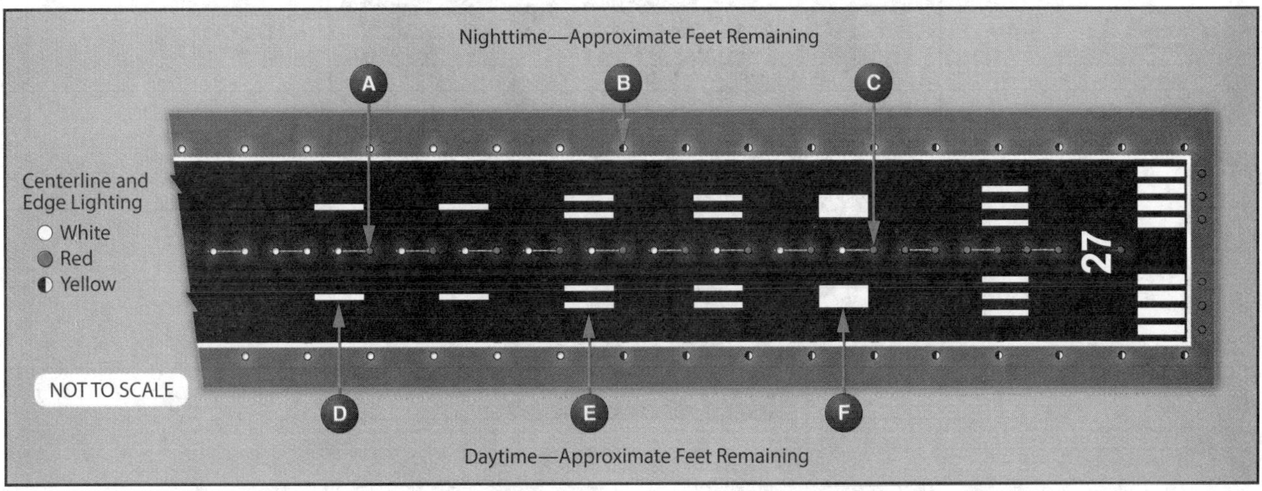

Figure 131. FAA ICAO Precision Approach Runway Markings and Lighting.

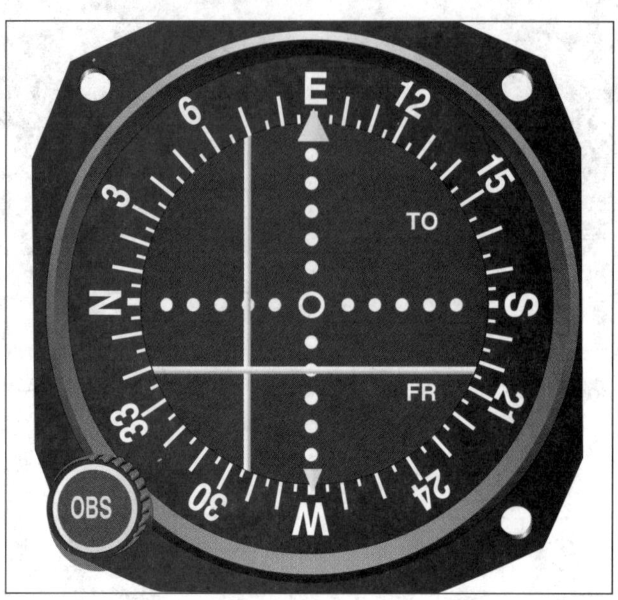

Figure 135. OBS, ILS, and GS Displacement.

Figure 136. OBS, ILS, and GS Displacement.

Figure 137. OBS, ILS, and GS Displacement.

FREQ	N.M.	KNOTS	MIN
115.0	60.0	180	20.0

Figure 139. No. 1 and No. 2 NAV Presentation.

Figure 140. HSI Presentation.

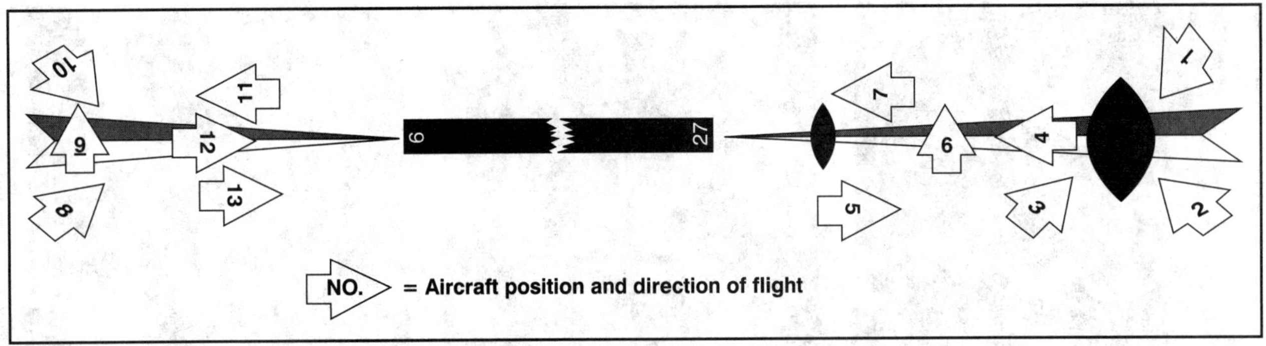

Figure 141. Aircraft Position and Direction of Flight.

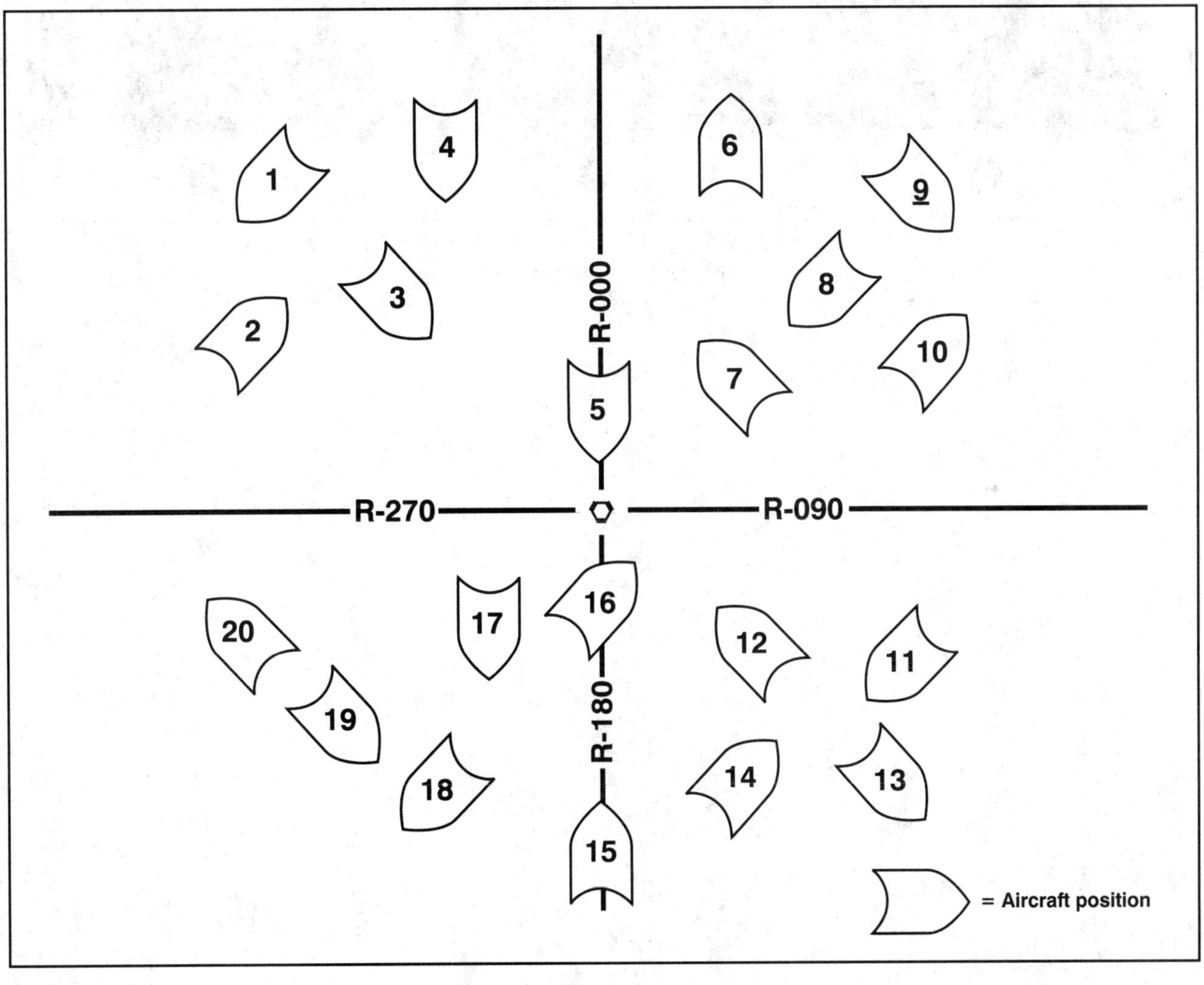

R-000
4
6
1
9
3
8
2
10
7
5
R-270
R-090
16
17
20
12
11
19
R-180
14
13
18
15
= Aircraft position

Figure 142. Aircraft Position.

Figure 143. HSI Presentation.

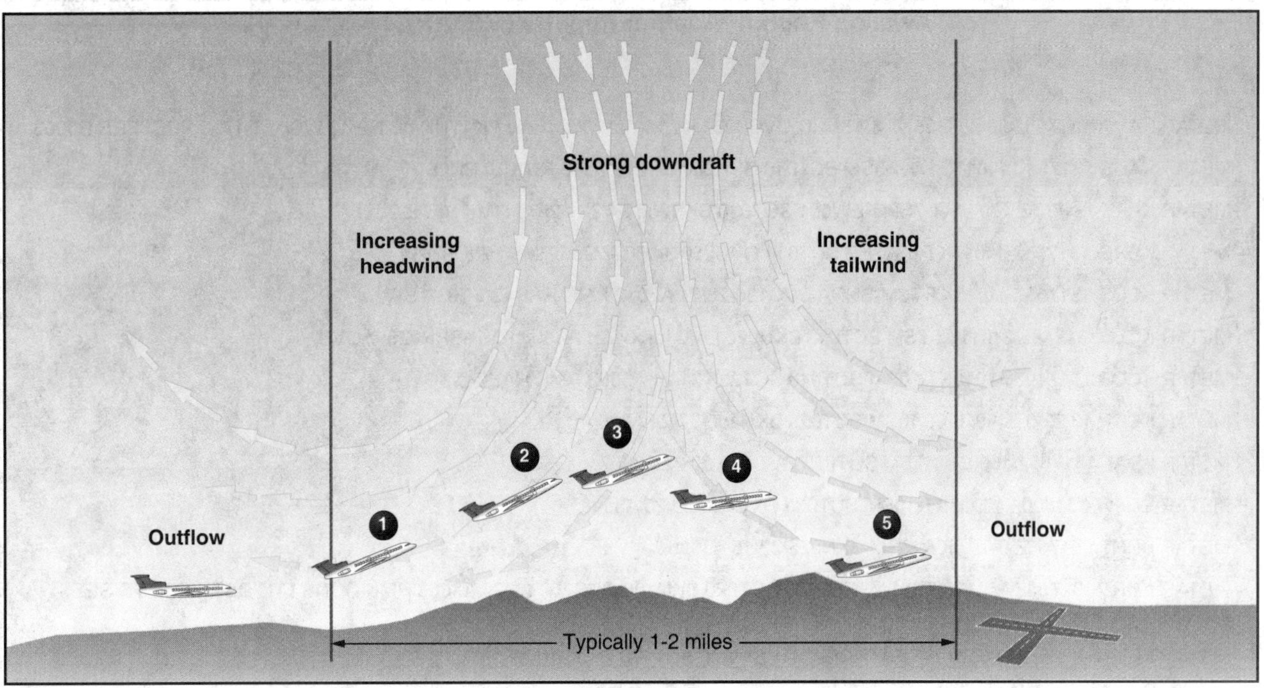

Figure 144. Microburst Section Chart.

Aviation Routine Weather Reports (METAR)

TX

METAR KAMA 131755Z 33025G35KT 3/4SM IC OVC003 M02/M01 A2952 RMK PK WND 32039/43 WSHFT 1735 PRESFER P0003.

METAR KAUS 131753Z 19011G17KT 8SM SCT040 BKN250 31/21 A3006 RMK SLPNO.

METAR KBPT 131755Z 17004KT 7SM FEW001 SCT030 BKN250 34/23 A2979 RMK VIS E 2.

METAR KBRO 131755Z 14015KT 6SM HZ SCT034 OVC250 34/30 A2985 RMK PRESRR.

METAR KCDS 131758Z 11013KT 7SM-SHRA OVC180 23/21 A3012 RMK RAB42 VIRGA SW.

METAR KCLL 131749Z 21011KT 7SM SCT003 BKN025 OVC100 34/21 A3008 RMK BKN025 V OVC.

METAR KCOT 131749Z 13010KT 10SM SCT040 SCT200 31/21 A3002 RMK RAE24.

METAR KCRP 131753Z 16016KT 10SM SCT028 BKN250 32/24 A3003.

METAR KDAL 131755Z 16005KT 7SM SCT023 OVC100 30/22 A3007.

METAR KDFW 131800Z 17007KT 10SM SCT035 OVC120 29/20 A3008.

METAR KDHT 131756Z 04014KT 15SM BKN025 22/15 A3026.

METAR KDRT 131756Z 12012KT 10SM FEW006 SCT020 BKN100 OVC250 29/22 A3000 RMK CONS LTG DSTN ESE TS SE MOVG NW VIRGA W.

METAR KELP 131755Z 09007KT 60SM VCBLDU FEW070 SCT170 BKN210 29/13 A3015.

METAR KFTW 131750Z 18007KT 7SM SCT025 OVC100 29/20 A3008.

FTW 131815Z UA/OV DFW/TM 1803/FL095/TP PA30/SK 036 OVC 060/075 OVC/RM TOPS UNKN.

METAR KGGG 131745Z 15008KT 15SM SKC 32/21 A3011.

METAR KGLS 131750Z VRB04KT 6SM VCSH SCT041 BKN093 26/22 A2995.

SPECI KGLS 13180ZZ 10012G21KT 060V140 2SM +SHRA SCT005 BKN035 OVC050CB 24/23 A2980 RMK RAB57 WSHFT 58 FROPA

METAR KHOU 131752Z 15008KT 7SM SCT030 OVC250 31/27 A3008.

METAR KHRL 131753Z 14015KT 8SM SKC 30/25 A3010.

METAR KIAH 131755Z VRB03KT 1/4SM R33L/1200FT BCFG VV007 27/26 A3005.

METAR KINK 131755Z 04027G36KT 2SM BLSA PO OVC015TCU 24/13 A2985.

METAR KLBB 131750Z 06029G43KT 1SM BLSNDU SQ VV010 03/M01 A2949.

LBB 131808Z UUA/OV LBB /TM 1800/FL UNKN /TP B737 /TB MDT /RM LLWS -17 KT SFC-010 DURC RWY 36LBB.

SPECI KLBB 131818Z 35031G40KT 1/2SM FZDZ VV030 M01/M01 A2946 RMK WSHFT 12 FROPA.

LBB 131821Z UUA/OV LBB/TM1817/FL011/TPB727/SK UNKN OVC/TA -06/TB MOD/IC MDT CLR.

METAR KLFK 131756Z 24007KT 7SM BKN100 33/19 A3008.

METAR KMAF 131756Z 02020KT 12SM BKN025 OVC250 27/18 A3009 RMK RAE44.

METAR KMFF 131756Z 13015KT 7SM BKN125 33/19 A2998.

METAR KMRF 131752Z 09012G20KT 60SM SKC 28/14 A3000.

MRF 131801Z UUA/OV MRF/TM1758/FL450/TP B767/TB MDT CAT.

Figure 145. Aviation Routine Weather Reports (METAR).

METARs & PIREPs

TX

METAR KABI 131755Z AUTO 21016G24KT 180V240 1SM R11/P6000FT -RA BR BKN015 OVC025 19/15 A2900 RMK AO2 PK WND 20035/25 WSHFT 1715 VIS 3/4V1 1/2 VIS 3/4 RWY11 RAB07 CIG 013V 017 CIG 014 RWY11 PRESFR SLP125 P0003 60009 T01940154 10196 20172 58033 TSNO $.

METAR KMWL 131756Z 13011KT 10SM BKN011 OVC050 25/23 A3006.

METAR KPSX 131755Z 20010KT 7SM SCT018 OVC200 31/24 A3007.

METAR KPVW 131750Z 05006KT 10SM SCT012 OVC030 30/20 A3011 RMK RAE47.

METAR KSAT 131756Z 15016KT 7SM SCT028 OVC250 30/20 A3005.

SAT 131756Z UA /OV SAT/TM 1739Z/FL UNKN/TP UNKN/SK OVC 040.

METAR KSIT 131755Z 22012KT 7SM BKN018 OVC070 25/23 A3002.

METAR KSPS 131757Z 09014KT 6SM -RA SCT025 OVC090 24/22 A3005.

SPECI KSPS 131820Z 01025KT 2SM +RA OVC015TCU 22/21 A3000 RMK DSNT TORNADO B15 N MOV E.

SPS 131820Z UA/OV SPS/TM 1818/FL090/TP C402/SK OVC 075.

METAR KTPL 131751Z 17015KT 15SM SCT015 SCT100 OVC250 31/20 A3007.

METAR KTYR 131753Z AUTO 26029G41KT 2SM +TSRA BKN008 OVC020 31/24 A3001 RMK A02 TSB44 RAB46.

METAR KVCT 131755Z 17013KT 7SM SCT030 OVC250 30/24 A3005.

AR

METAR KARG 131753Z AUTO 22015G25KT 3/4SM R28/2400FT +RA OVC010 29/28 A2985 RMK AO2.

METAR KELD 131755Z 06005G10KT 3SM FU BKN050 OVC100 30/21 A3010.

METAR KFSM 131756Z 00000KT 5SM SKC 30/20 A2982.

FSM 131830Z UA/OV HRO-FSM/TM 1825/FL290/TP B737/SK SCT 290.

METAR KFYV 131755Z 170018G32KT 2SM +TSRA SQ SCT030 BKN060OVC100CB 28/21 A2978 RMK RAB47.

FYV 131801Z UA/OV 1 E DAK/TM 1755Z/FL 001/TP CV 440/RM WS LND RWY16FYV.

METAR KHOT 131751Z 34006KT 18SM SCT040 OVC150 32/18 A3010.

METAR KHRO 131753Z 09007KT 7SM FEW020 BKN040CB 30/27 A3001.

SPECI KHRO 131815Z 13017G26KT 2SM +TSRA SCT020 BKN045TCU 29/24A2983 RMK RAB12 FRQ LTGICCG VC PRESFR.

HRO 131830Z UUA/OV 6 S HRO/TM 1825Z/FL 001/TP DC6/RM WS TKO RWY 18.

METAR KLIT 131754Z 07004KT 10SM SCT030 BKN250 34/29 A3007.

METAR KPBF 131753Z 29007KT 5SM SCT040 BKN100 35/19 A3008.

METAR KTXK 131753Z 25003KT 7SM SCT100 BKN200 33/19 A3010.

Figure 146. METARs & PIREPs.

Terminal Aerodrome Forecasts (TAF)

TX

TAF
KAMA 091120Z 0912/1012 15010KT P6SM SKC
TEMPO 0912/0914 09010KT
FM091900 16015KT P6SM SKC

TAF
KAUS 091322Z 0913/1018 20007KT P6SM SCT005 BKN015
TEMPO 0913/0915 BKN005
FM091600 18012G22KT P6SM FEW250
FM100100 16011KT P6SM SCT250
FM100900 18007KT P6SM BKN015

TAF
KCRP 091120Z 0912/1012 15004KT P6SM FEW015 BKN250
FM091500 16014KT P6SM SCT035
FM091900 14017G24KT P6SM FEW040
FM100200 15010KT P6SM FEW250

TAF
KDFW 091125Z 0912/1018 18016KT P6SM SCT150 BKN300

TAF
KELP 091130Z 0912/1012 25009KT P6SM SKC
FM100400 25006KT P6SM FEW250

TAF
KIAH 091120Z 0912/1018 00000KT P6SM SCT250
FM091300 19006KT P6SM SCT250
FM092000 17010KT P6SM FEW070 SCT200
FM100400 17005KT P6SM SKC
FM101000 18002KT 6SM MIFG FEW250
FM101300 18007KT P6SM FEW015 SCT250

TAF
KLBB 091120Z 0912/1012 16010KT P6SM FEW250
FM091700 18015KT P6SM FEW250

TAF
KSAT 091434Z 0915/1018 17008KT P6SM BKN020 BKN250
FM091600 16012G22KT P6SM FEW250
FM100100 15011KT P6SM SCT250
FM100900 18006KT P6SM BKN015

TAF
KSPS 091121Z 0912/1012 VRB10G15KT P6SM VCSH BKN150 WS015/23035KT
FM091400 18014G20KT P6SM SCT150
FM100100 17012KT P6SM BKN250

Figure 147. Terminal Aerodrome Forecasts (TAF).

Convective SIGMET

MKCC WST Ø31755
CONVECTIVE SIGMET 42C
VALID UNTIL 1955Z
TX OK
FROM 5W MLC–PEQ–SJT–5W MLC
AREA SCT EMBDD TSTMS MOVG LTL. TOPS 3ØØ.

CONVECTIVE SIGMET 43C
VALID UNTIL 1955Z
CO KS OK
FROM AKO–OSW–3ØWNW OKC–AKO
AREA SCT TSTMS OCNLY EMBDD MOVG FROM 322Ø. TOPS 38Ø.

CONVECTIVE SIGMET 44C
VALID UNTIL 1955Z
5ØNE MEM
ISOLD INSTD LVL5 TSTM DIAM 1Ø MOVG FROM 2625. TOP ABV 45Ø.

OUTLOOK VALID UNTIL 2355Z
TSTMS OVR TX AND SE OK WL MOV SEWD 15 KTS.
TSTMS OVER CO, KS, AND N OK WL CONT MOVG SEWD 2Ø KTS.
TSTM OVR TN WL CONT MOVG EWD 25 KTS.

Figure 148. Convective SIGMET.

Winds and Temperatures Aloft Forecasts

DATA BASED ON 031200Z
VALID 040000Z FOR USE 1800-0300Z. TEMPS NEG ABV 24000

FT	3000	6000	9000	12000	18000	24000	30000	34000	39000
ABI		1306+16	1607+11	1807+06	2108-07	2208-18	240833	250942	300753
ABO			0810+14	0511+08	3415-06	3220-18	312333	312543	302554
AMA		0614	0814+10	0709+05	3210-07	2914-19	281934	282243	292554
ATL	0906	9900+17	9900+12	0205+07	3507-07	3305-19	290534	280543	990054
BNA	9900	9900+17	3205+12	3109+07	3018-07	2918-19	272134	262444	262855
BRO	1510	1614+20	1611+14	1708+08	9900-07	9900-19	990034	990043	990055
DAL	0910	1706+17	2009+11	2011+06	2015-08	2214-19	231333	241342	271153
DEN			9900+09	9900+04	3020-10	3029-21	303636	304145	294756
DSM	3615	3315+07	3118+04	3022+00	2835-12	2748-24	276438	277348	277957
ELP		0610	0614+13	0615+08	0113-05	3614-17	361433	361442	251354
GCK		0611+11	0809+08	9900+03	2817-09	2823-20	273135	273644	284155
HLC		0409+09	0405+07	3106+02	2822-10	2730-21	273936	274545	275256
HOU	0909	1607+19	1606+13	1606+07	1605-08	9900-20	990034	990043	990054
ICT	0516	0613+12	0607+08	9900+04	2718-09	2626-20	263635	264144	274655
IND	3611	3207+12	2912+08	2818+03	2733-09	2643-21	265635	265944	256255
INK		0609+16	0709+12	0608+07	0107-06	3607-18	350833	340842	350855
JAN	3612	3613+18	3611+13	3609+07	0105-08	9900-19	990034	990043	230854
LIT	0310	3608+16	3206+11	2808+06	2517-08	2518-19	252034	252243	262454
LOU	0105	9900+15	2908+10	2913+05	2825-08	2731-20	263834	264143	254454
MEM	0109	0108+17	3408+12	3110+06	2916-07	2717-19	261934	262144	262555
MKC	0316	0211+11	3409+07	3013+03	2728-10	2638-21	265036	265645	276356
MSY	0315	0216+19	0315+13	0414+07	0510-08	0605-20	990034	990043	210854
OKC	0715	0810+14	1106+10	9900+05	2414-08	2419-19	252534	252743	272754
SAT	1107	1713+18	1813+13	1911+07	2006-07	1906-19	180734	170743	990054
SGF	0414	0410+14	3605+09	2908+04	2624-09	2632-20	254135	264444	264655
SHV	0509	9900+18	9900+12	2106+06	2012-08	2109-19	220734	240743	260754
STL	0314	0110+12	3210+08	2915+03	2730-09	2741-21	265435	265744	266055
TUS		0807+23	0814+16	0814+10	0810-05	0505-17	330533	310842	290954

Figure 149. Winds and Temperatures Aloft Forecasts.

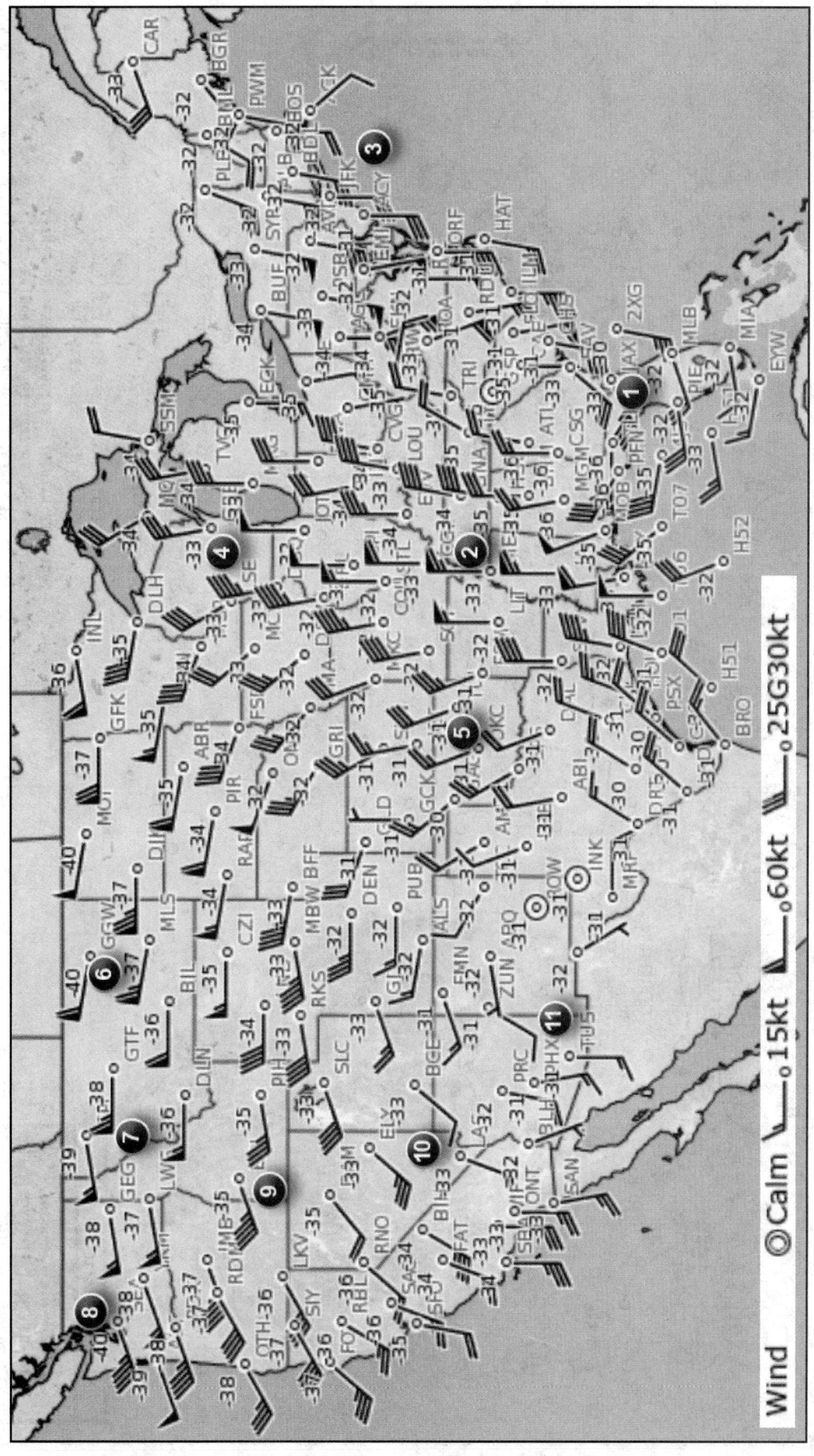

Figure 149A. Winds and Temperatures Aloft Forecast.

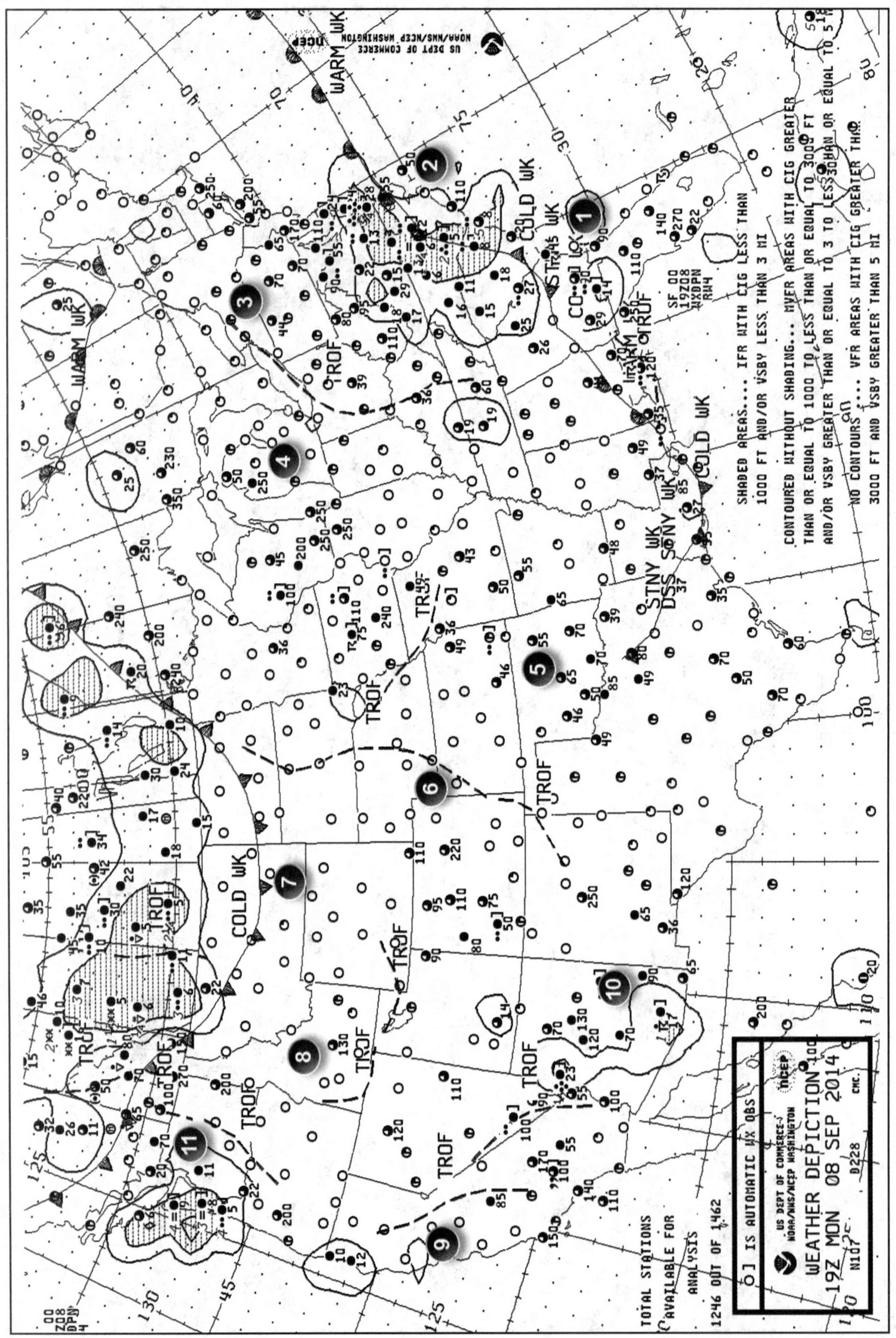

Figure 150. Weather Depiction Chart.

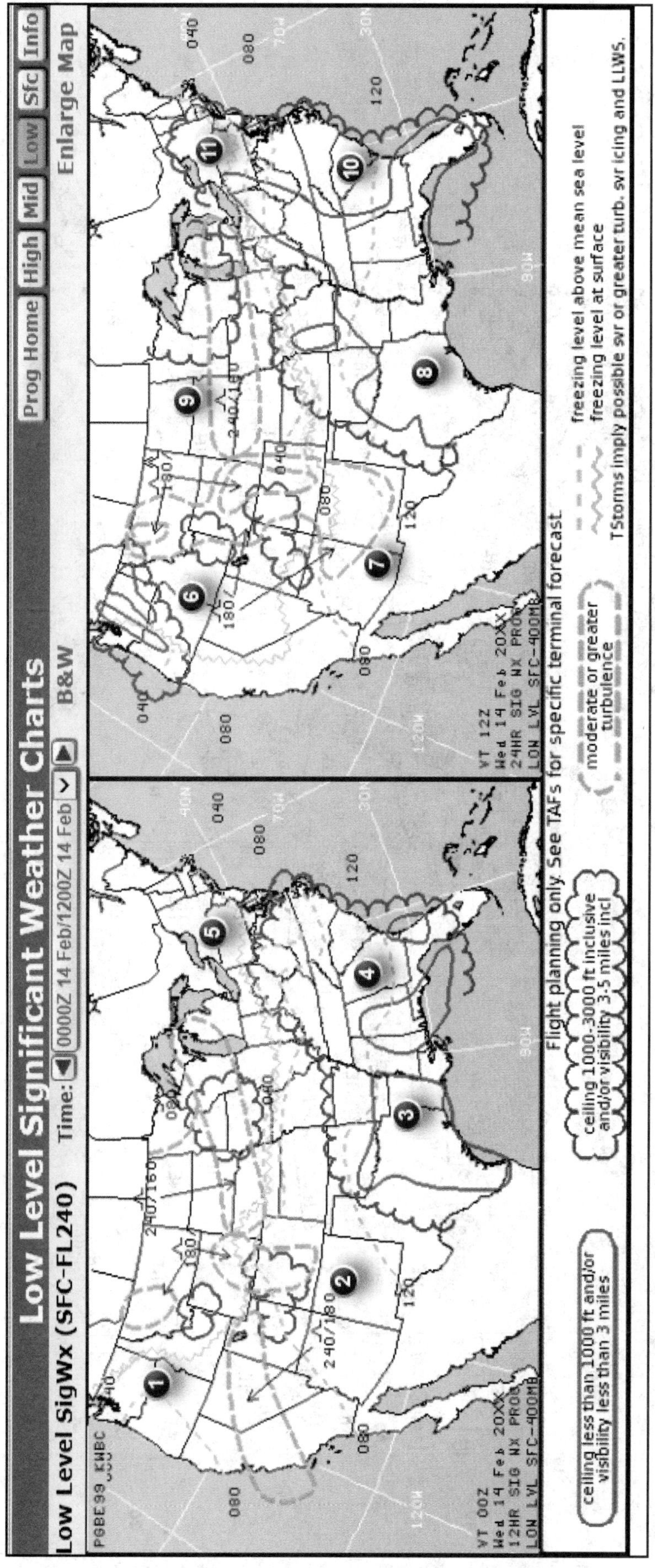

Figure 151. Low-Level Significant Weather Chart.

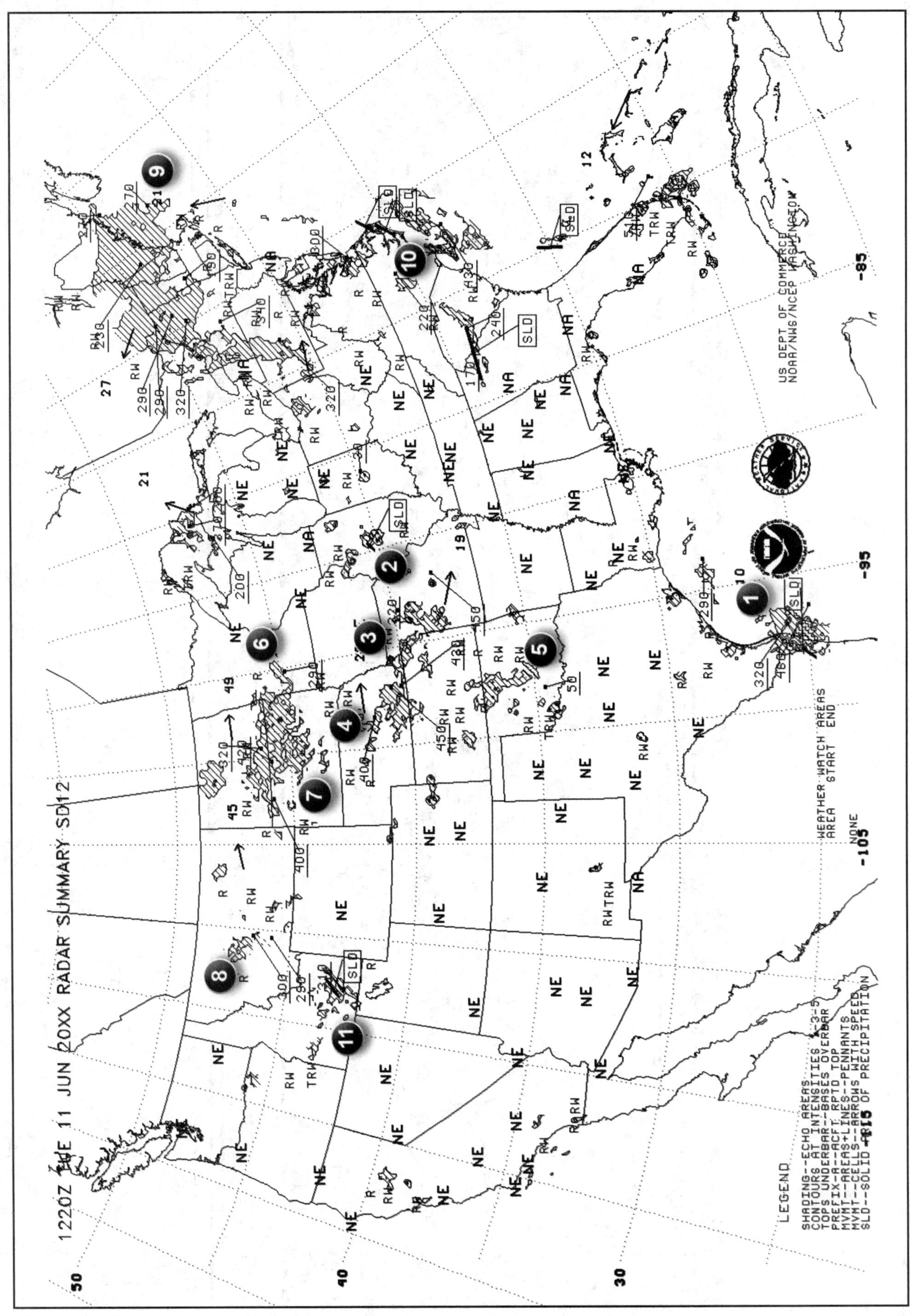

Figure 152. Radar Summary Chart.

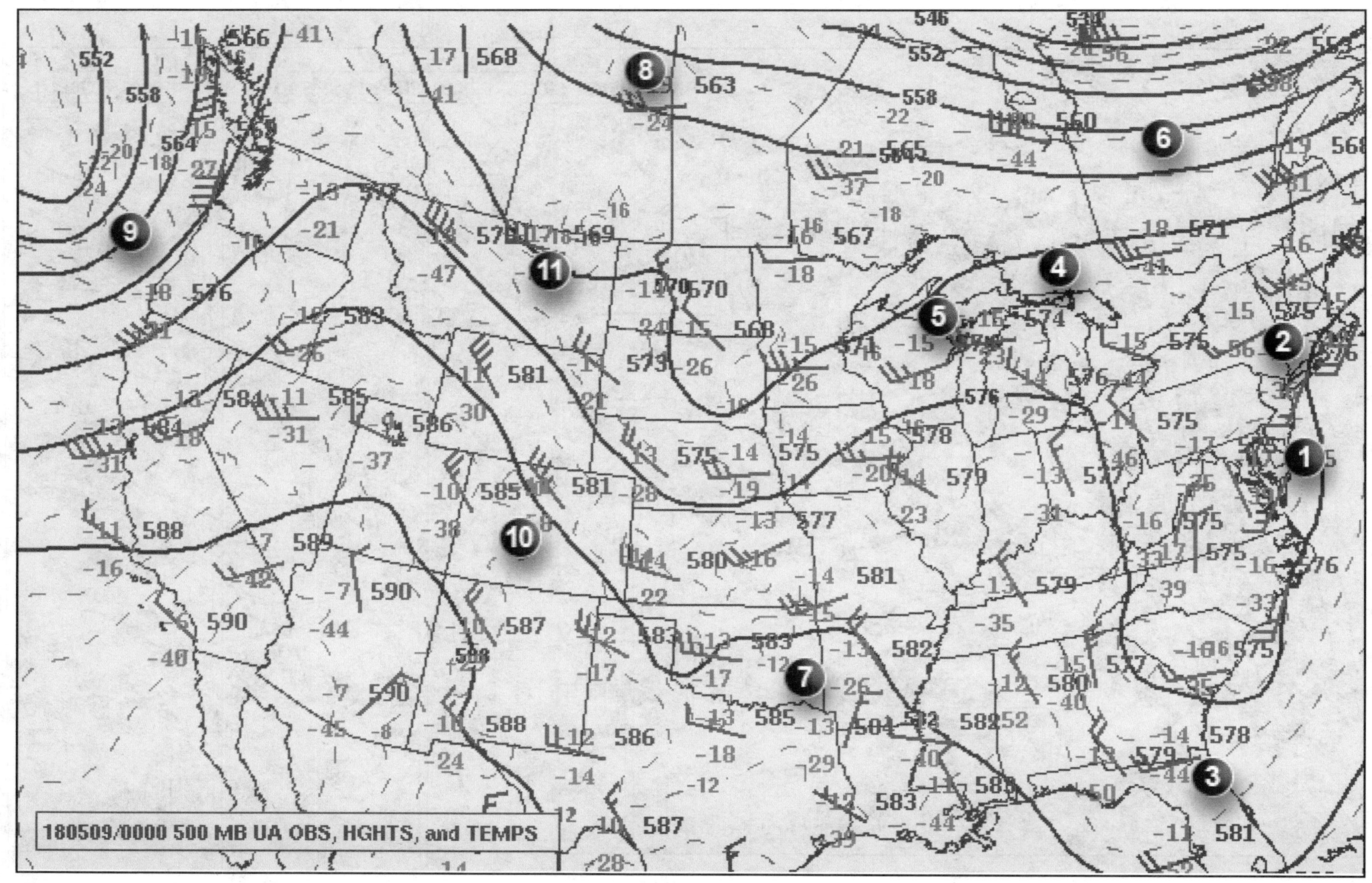

Figure 153. 500 MB Analysis Heights/Temperature Chart.

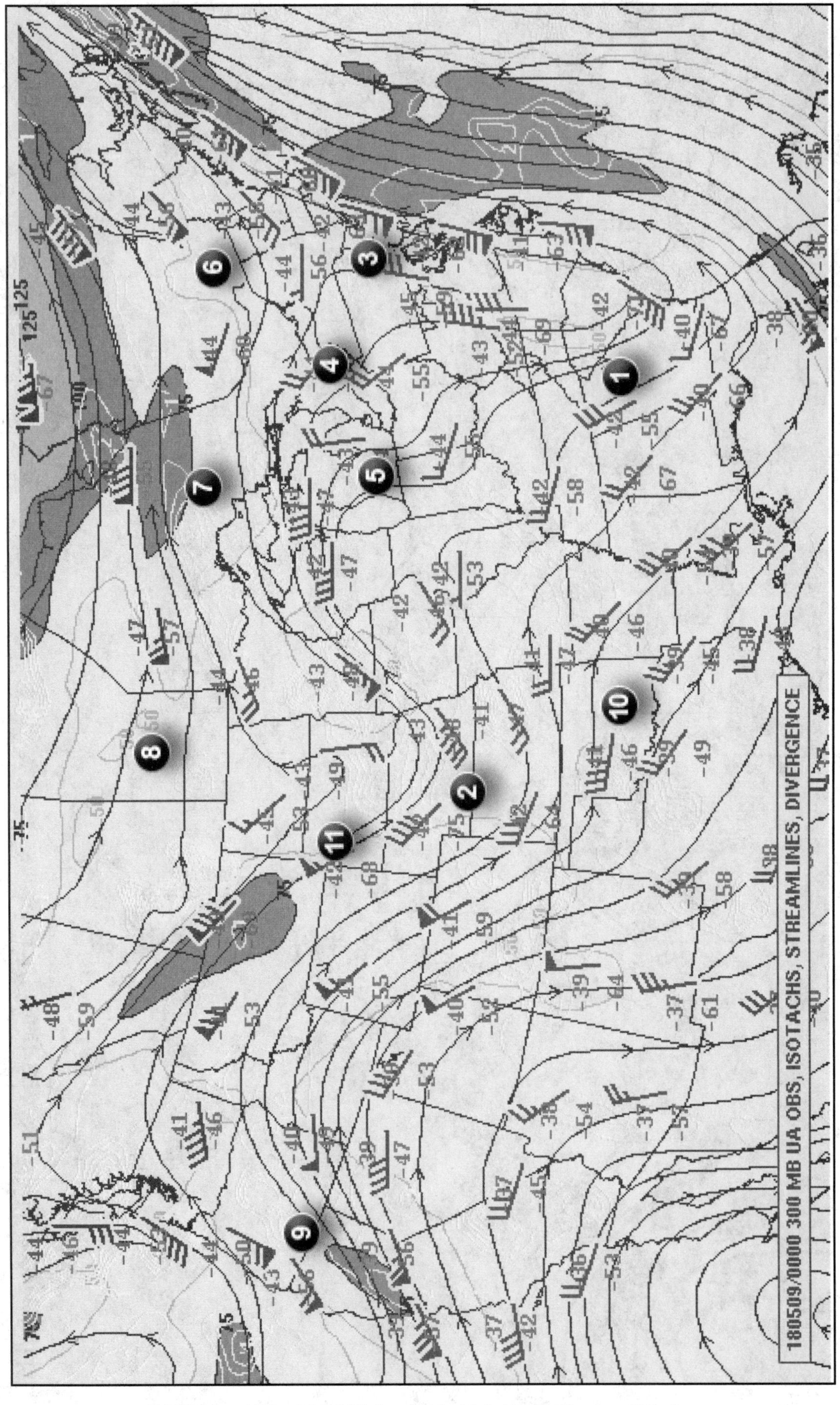

Figure 154. 300 MB Analysis Heights/Isotachs Chart.

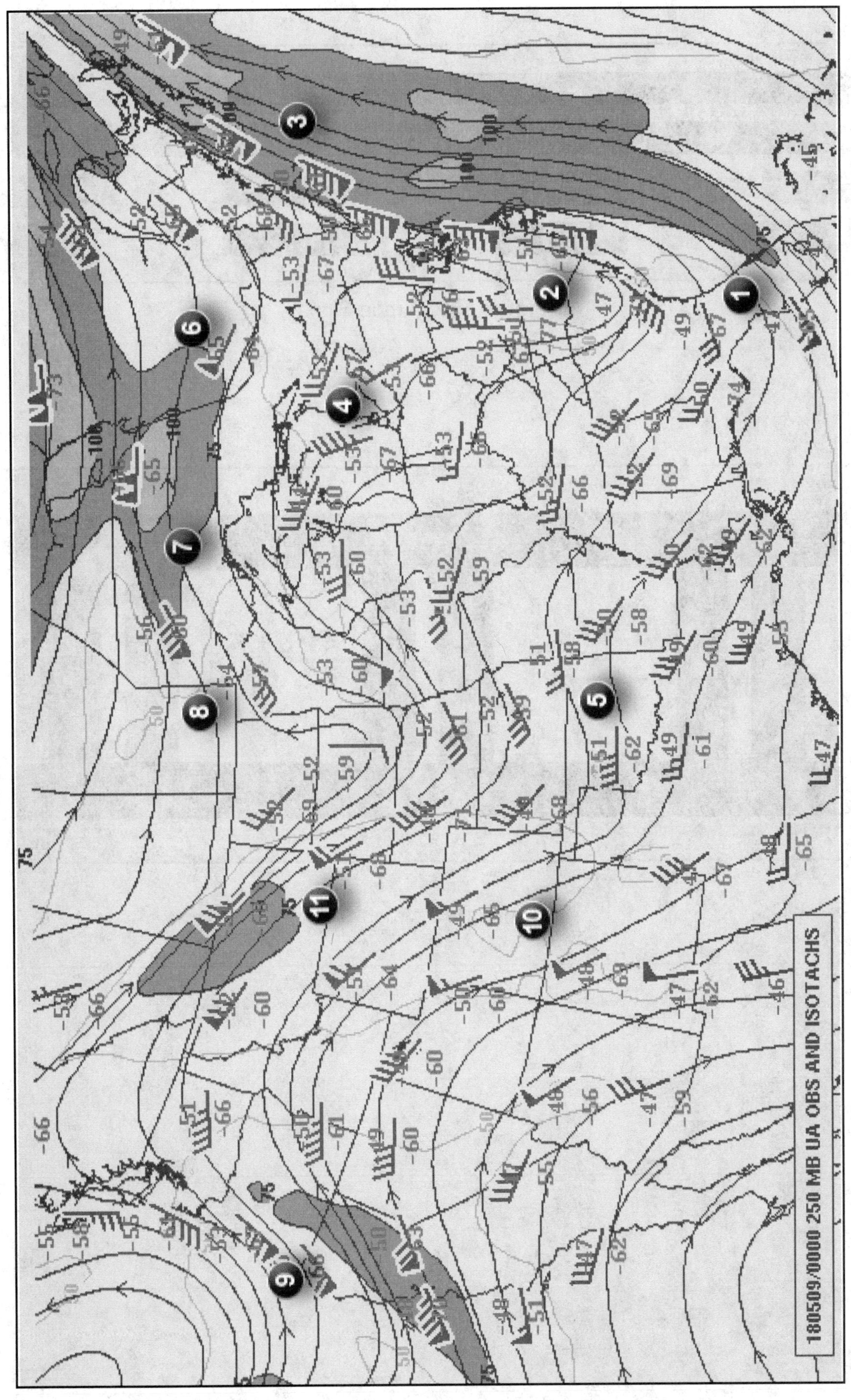

Figure 155. 200 MB Analysis Heights/Isotachs Chart.

Figure 156. Airport Sign.

Figure 157. Airport Sign.

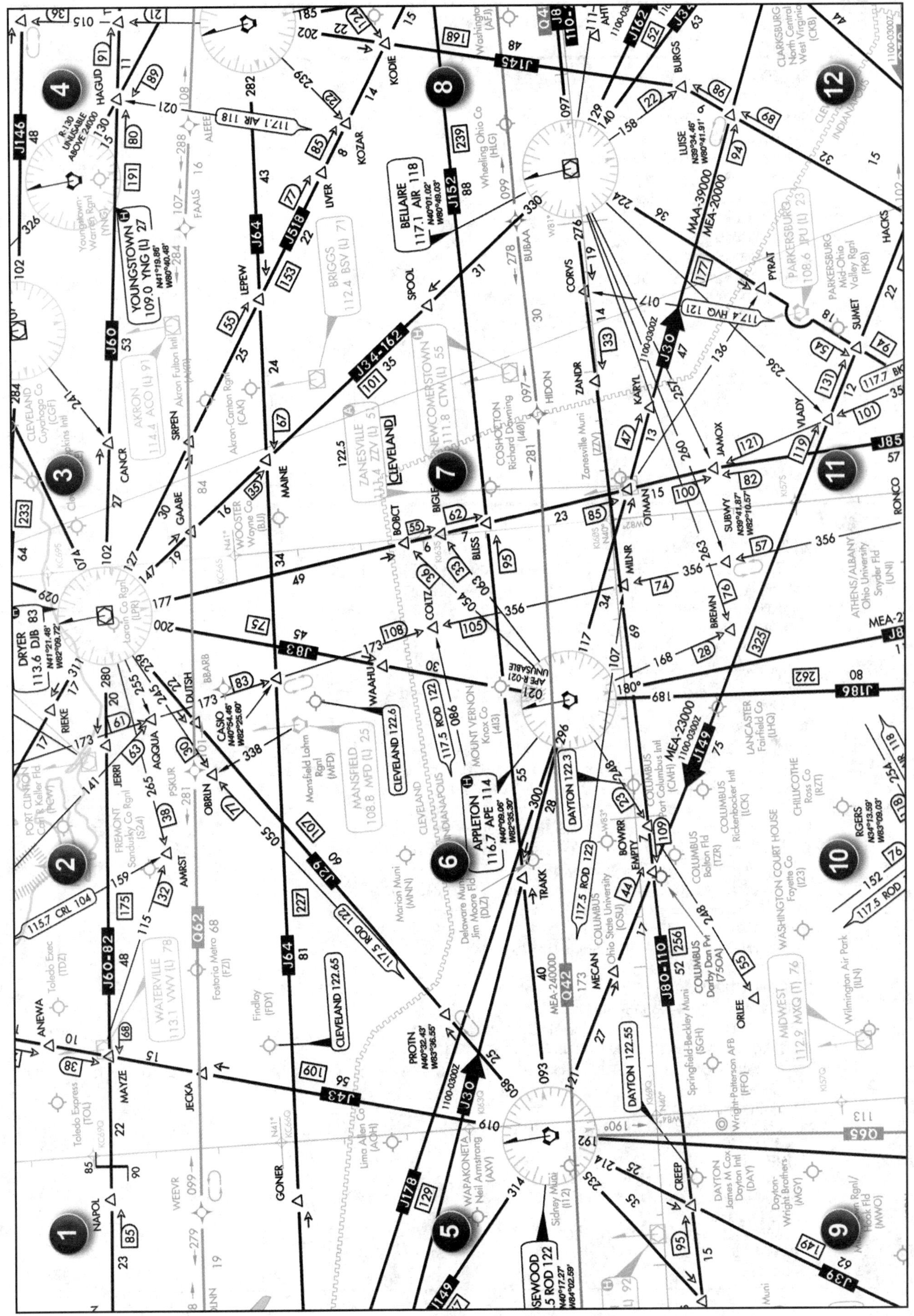

Figure 159. High Altitude Airways.

68 **ARIZONA**

TUBA CITY (TØ3) 5 W UTC–7 N36°05.56′ W111°22.99′
4513 B NOTAM FILE PRC

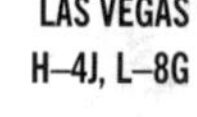

LAS VEGAS
H–4J, L–8G

RWY 15–33: H6230X75 (ASPH) S–12.5 MIRL
RWY 15: VASI(V2L)—GA 3.0° TCH 40′. Thld dsplcd 1520′. Hill.
RWY 33: VASI(V2L)—GA 3.0° TCH 40′.
AIRPORT REMARKS: Unattended. Rwy 15–33 uneven and rough 1500–2400′ from thld of Rwy 15 and cracked. Livestock on airport. ACTIVATE MIRL Rwy 15–33, VASI Rwy 15 and Rwy 33—CTAF.
AIRPORT MANAGER: 505-371-8327
COMMUNICATIONS: CTAF 122.9
RADIO AIDS TO NAVIGATION: NOTAM FILE PRC.
(H) VORTAC 113.5 TBC Chan 82 N36°07.28′ W111°16.18′ 238° 5.8 NM to fld. 5045/15E.

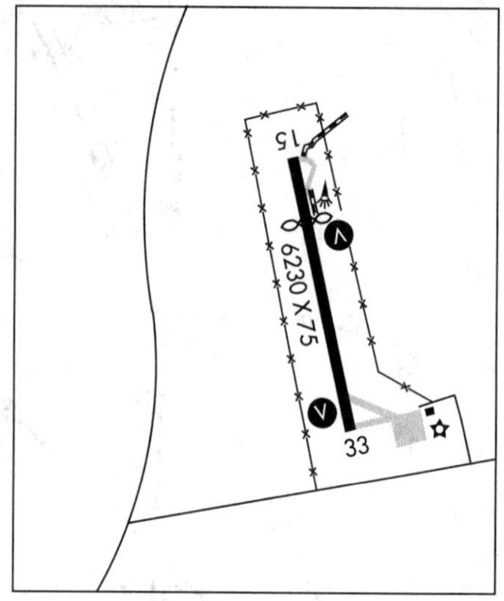

TUCSON

RYAN FLD (RYN)(KRYN) 10 SW UTC–7 N32°08.53′ W111°10.48′
2419 B S4 **FUEL** 100LL, JET A TPA—3219(800) NOTAM FILE PRC

PHOENIX
H–4J, L–5C
IAP, AD

RWY 06R–24L: H5503X75 (ASPH) S–12.5, D–30 MIRL
RWY 06R: REIL. Brush.
RWY 24L: VASI(V4L)—GA 3.0° TCH 26′. Brush.
RWY 06L–24R: H4900X75 (ASPH) S–12.5, D–30
RWY 06L: Tree.
RWY 15–33: H4000X75 (ASPH) 0.8% up S
RWY 33: Brush.
AIRPORT REMARKS: Attended Mon–Fri 1500–0000Z, Sat 1500–2200Z. After hrs, Jet A avbl as an on–call svc, and a $100 fee applies. Prior arrangements can be made by calling 520–744–7474, self serve 100LL avbl 24 hrs with major credit card. Rwy 15–33 CLOSED between SS–SR. Frequent practice of ILS approaches to Rwy 06R. Rwy 06R and Rwy 06L preferential rwy up to 10 knot tailwind. Afternoon winds usually favor Rwy 24L and Rwy 24R. Use landing lights in pattern. When twr clsd ACTIVATE MIRL Rwy 06R–24L—CTAF. VASI Rwy 24L opr continuously. REIL Rwy 06R opr dalgt hrs only. Note: See Special Notices—Glider Operations Northwest of Tucson, Arizona.
AIRPORT MANAGER: 520-573-8182
WEATHER DATA SOURCES: AWOS–3 133.35 (520) 578–0269.
COMMUNICATIONS: CTAF 125.8
Ⓡ **TUCSON APP/DEP CON** 128.5
TOWER 125.8 (1300–0300Z) **GND CON** 118.2
AIRSPACE: CLASS D svc 1300–0300Z other times CLASS E.
RADIO AIDS TO NAVIGATION: NOTAM FILE TUS.
TUCSON (H) VORTACW 116.0 TUS Chan 107 N32°05.71′ W110°54.89′ 270° 13.5 NM to fld. 2671/12E. **HIWAS.**
VORTAC unusable:
050°–080° byd 30 NM blo 11,500′
350°–020° byd 30 NM blo 13,000′
DME unusable:
155°–165° byd 35 NM blo 13,000′
NDB (HW) 338 RYN N32°08.33′ W111°09.69′ at fld. NOTAM FILE PRC. NDB unmonitored.
NDB unusable:
025°–050° byd 25 NM blo 14,500′
ILS/DME 111.1 I–IVI Chan 48 Rwy 06R. Unmonitored when ATCT clsd.

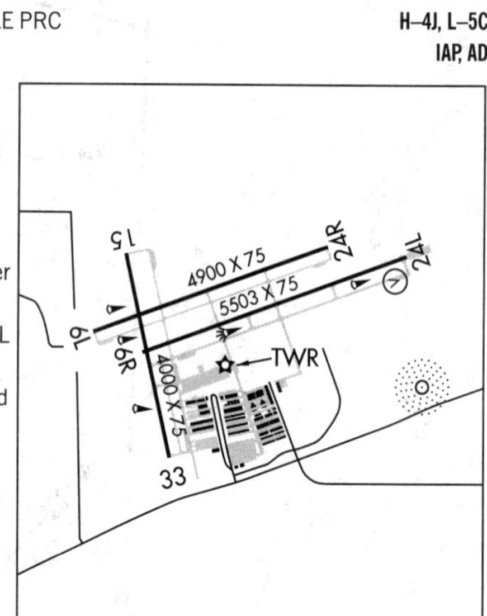

Figure 163A. Excerpt from Chart Supplement.

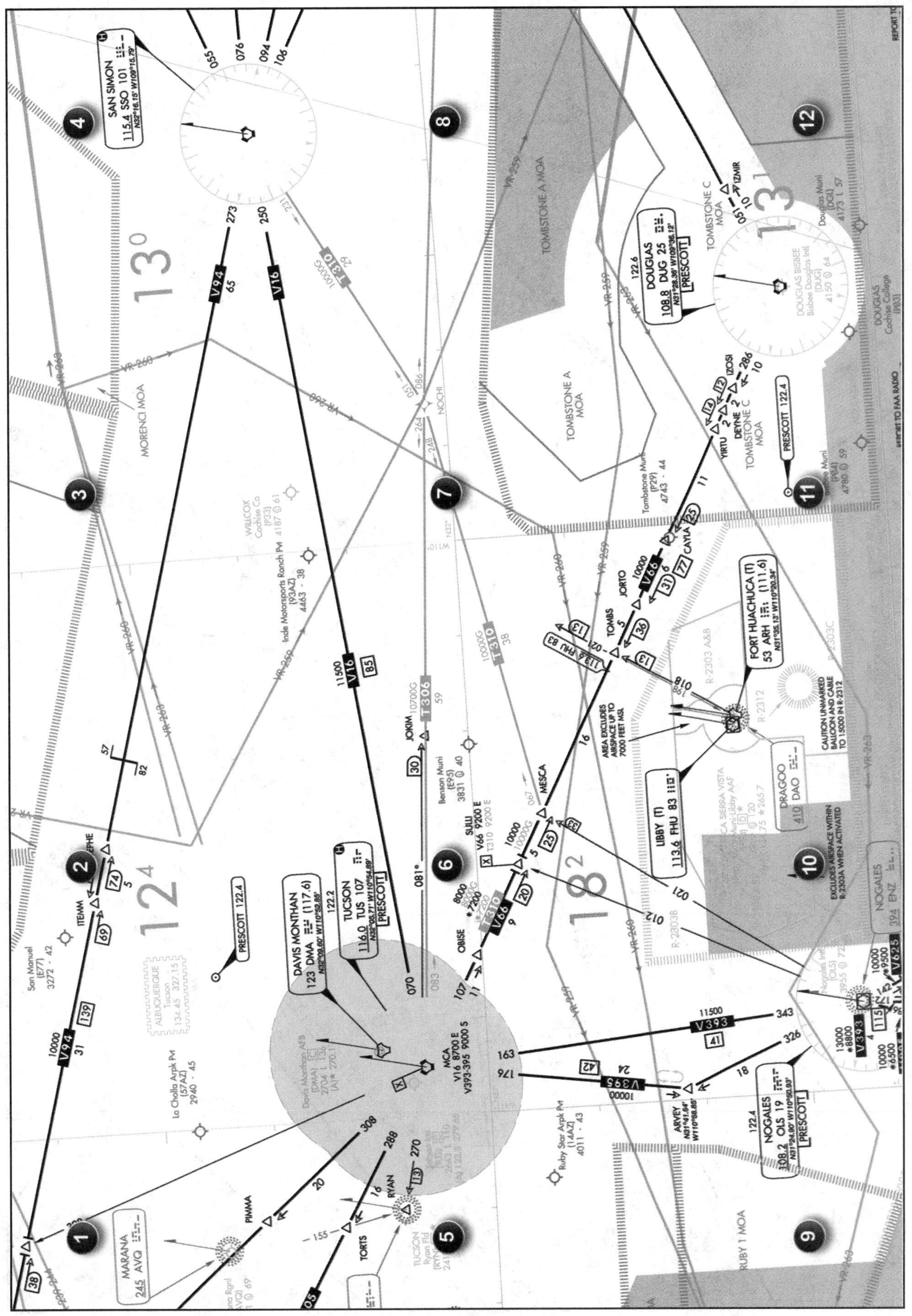

Figure 164. Low Altitude Airways.

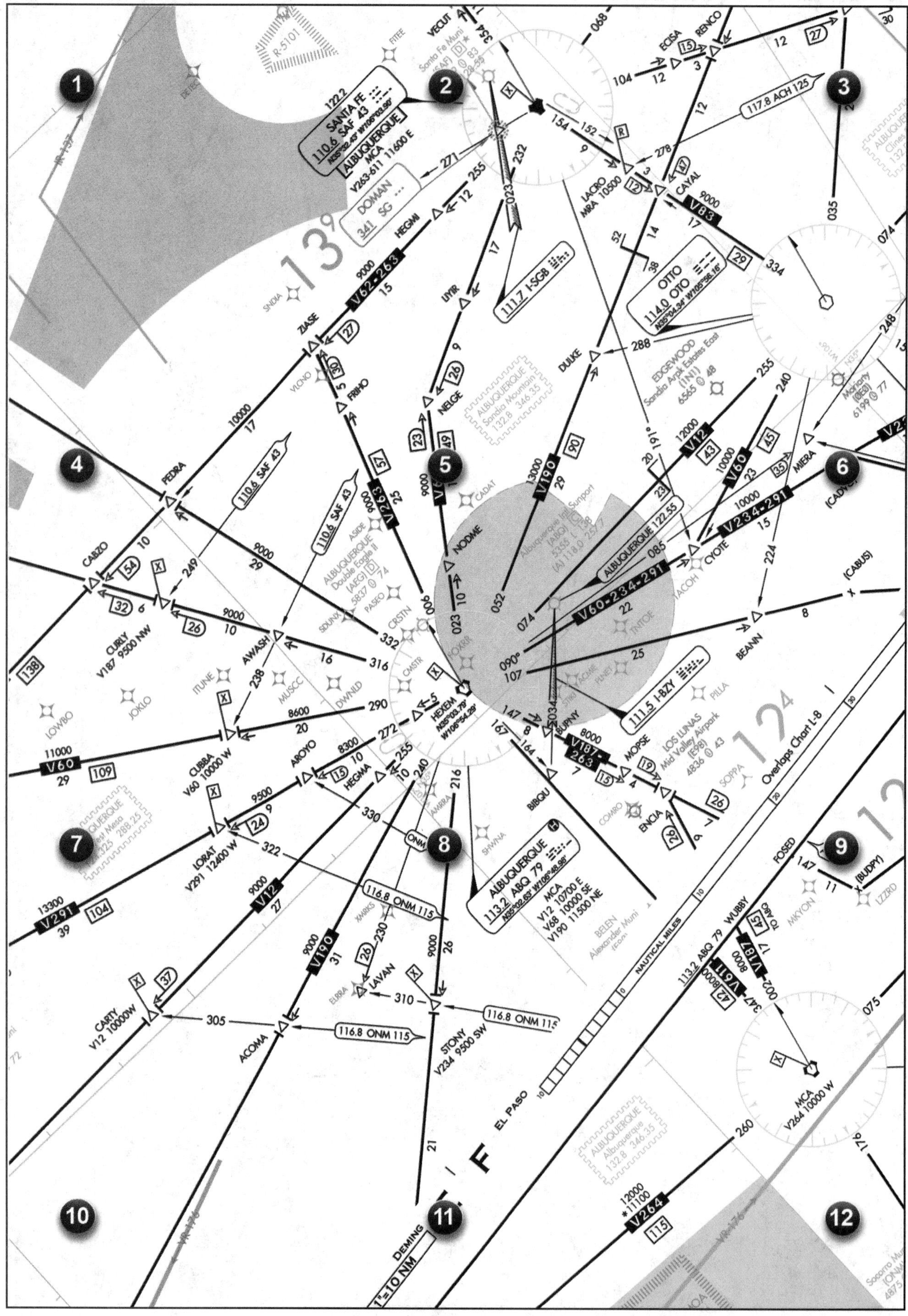

Figure 165. Low Altitude Airways.

ALBUQUERQUE

ALBUQUERQUE INTL SUNPORT (ABQ)(KABQ) 3 SE UTC–7(–6DT) N35°02.34′ W106°36.50′ **ALBUQUERQUE**
5355 B S4 **FUEL** 100LL, JET A, A1, A1+ OX 1, 2, 3, 4 LRA ARFF Index—See Remarks **H–4L, L–8I**
NOTAM FILE ABQ **IAP, AD**

RWY 08–26: H13793X150 (CONC–GRVD) S–100, D–210, 2S–175, 2D–360, 2D/2D2–720 HIRL CL
RWY 08: MALSR. TDZL. VASI(V6L)—GA 2.95° TCH 54′. Thld dsplcd 1000′. Rgt tfc.
RWY 26: REIL. PAPI(P4L)—GA 3.0° TCH 83′. 0.5% down.
RWY 03–21: H10000X150 (CONC–GRVD) S–100, D–210, 2S–175, 2D–360, 2D/2D2–720 HIRL CL
RWY 03: MALSR. TDZL. REIL. PAPI(P4L)—GA 3.0° TCH 62′. Rgt tfc.
RWY 21: REIL. PAPI(P4L).
RWY 12–30: H6000X150 (CONC–GRVD) S–65, D–120, 2S–155, 2D–155 MIRL
RWY 12: Rgt tfc.
RWY 30: REIL. PAPI(P4L)—GA 3.0° TCH 40′.

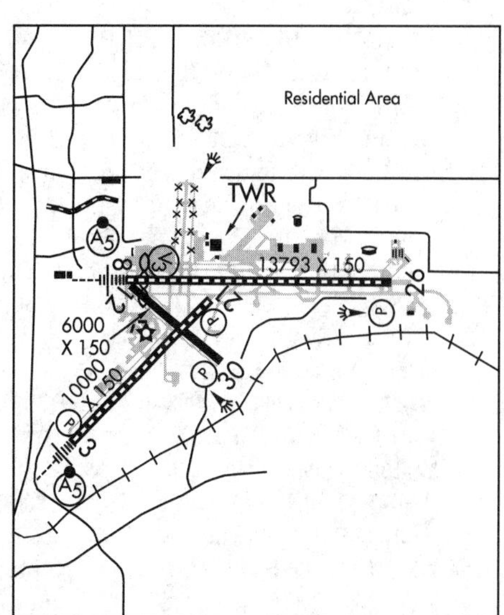

RUNWAY DECLARED DISTANCE INFORMATION
RWY 03: TORA–10000 TODA–10000 ASDA–10000 LDA–10000
RWY 08: TORA–13793 TODA–13793 ASDA–13793 LDA–12793
RWY 12: TORA–6000 TODA–6000 ASDA–6000 LDA–6000
RWY 21: TORA–10000 TODA–10000 ASDA–10000 LDA–10000
RWY 26: TORA–13793 TODA–13793 ASDA–13793 LDA–13793
RWY 30: TORA–6000 TODA–6000 ASDA–6000 LDA–6000

AIRPORT REMARKS: Attended continuously. Bird hazard Oct–Dec, and Mar–May. Heavy student copter tfc, ctl firing area south of arpt. Departures on Rwy 03 are rstd and rqr prior coordination. Rwy 03 and Rwy 08 touchdown rwy visual range avbl. Rwy 08–26, Rwy 03–21 and Rwy 12–30 grooved 130′ wide. Use extreme care taxiing north on Twy E–1 to Rwy 08, holding position for Rwy 08–26 collocated with Rwy 12–30 holding position prior to Rwy 12 thld. Ramp north of Rwy 08–26 clsd to helicopters and general aviation acft. Class I, ARFF Index C. ARFF protection provided by USAF. Fighter acft depart south only. Air carrier ground handling not avbl btn the hrs of 0800–1130Z‡. Twy D north of Twy B clsd indef. Twy H military use only. Flight Notification Service (ADCUS) available. NOTE: See Special Notices—Continuous Power Facilities.

AIRPORT MANAGER: 505-244-7778

WEATHER DATA SOURCES: ASOS (505) 242–4044 **HIWAS** 113.2 ABQ. LLWAS. WSP.

COMMUNICATIONS: D–ATIS 118.0 505–856–4928 UNICOM 122.95
RCO 122.55 (ALBUQUERQUE RADIO)
® **APP CON** 123.9 (S of V12) 127.4 (on or N of V12) 126.3
® **DEP CON** 127.4 (on or N of V12) 123.9 (S of V12)
TOWER 120.3 123.775 **GND CON** 121.9 **CLNC DEL** 119.2

AIRSPACE: CLASS C svc ctc **APP CON**

VOR TEST FACILITY (VOT) 111.0

RADIO AIDS TO NAVIGATION: NOTAM FILE ABQ.
(H) VORTACW 113.2 ABQ Chan 79 N35°02.63′ W106°48.98′ 079° 10.3 NM to fld. 5749/13E. **HIWAS.**
TACAN AZIMUTH unusable:
040°–055° byd 30 NM blo 15,000′
ILS 111.5 I–BZY Rwy 03. Class IE.
ILS/DME 111.9 I–SPT Chan 56 Rwy 08. Class IE.
ASR

Figure 166A. Excerpt from Chart Supplement.

DOUBLE EAGLE II (AEG)(KAEG) 7 NW UTC–7(–6DT) N35°08.71´ W106°47.71´ **ALBUQUERQUE**
5837 B S4 **FUEL** 100LL, JET A, A1 OX 3 NOTAM FILE AEG **H–4K, L–8I**
RWY 04–22: H7398X100 (ASPH–PFC) S–30 MIRL 0.4% up SW **IAP, AD**
RWY 04: PAPI(P4L)—GA 3.0° TCH 44´.
RWY 22: MALSR. Rgt tfc.
RWY 17–35: H5993X100 (ASPH–PFC) S–30 MIRL
RWY 17: REIL. PAPI(P4L)—GA 3.0° TCH 44´.
RWY 35: REIL. Rgt tfc.

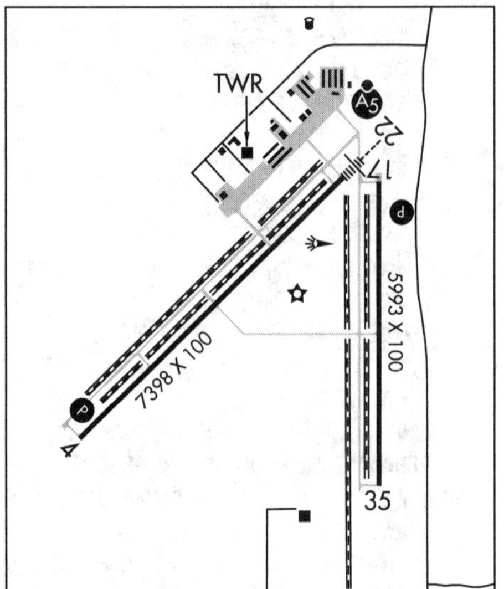

AIRPORT REMARKS: Attended 1300–0100Z‡. 100LL avbl 24 hrs self svc with major credit card. For attendant after hrs call 505–884–4530. Wildlife on and invof arpt. Twy A clsd between Twy A1 and Twy B 0500–1300Z‡. Twy B1 and Twy B between main ramp and Twy B2 clsd 0500–1300Z‡. When twr clsd ACTIVATE MIRL Rwy 04–22 and Rwy 17–35, REIL Rwy 17 and Rwy 35, MALSR Rwy 22, PAPI Rwy 04 and Rwy 17—CTAF.
AIRPORT MANAGER: 505-244-7888
WEATHER DATA SOURCES: AWOS–3PT 119.025 (505) 842–2009.
COMMUNICATIONS: CTAF 120.15
Ⓡ **ALBUQUERQUE APP/DEP CON** 127.4
TOWER 120.15 (1300–0500Z‡) **GND CON** 121.625
CLNC DEL 124.8 (when twr clsd)
AIRSPACE: CLASS D svc airport 1300–0500Z‡ other times CLASS G.
RADIO AIDS TO NAVIGATION: NOTAM FILE ABQ.
ALBUQUERQUE (H) VORTACW 113.2 ABQ Chan 79 N35°02.63´ W106°48.98´ 357° 6.2 NM to fld. 5749/13E. **HIWAS.**
TACAN AZIMUTH unusable:
040°–055° byd 30 NM blo 15,000´
DUDLE NDB (LOM) 351 AE N35°13.04´ W106°42.77´ 212° 5.9 NM to fld. LOM unmonitored.
ILS 110.1 I–AEG Rwy 22. LOM DUDLE NDB. Unmonitored when ATCT clsd. LOM unmonitored.

ALEXANDER MUNI (See BELEN on page 297)

ANGEL FIRE (AXX)(KAXX) 1 N UTC–7(–6DT) N36°25.32´ W105°17.39´ **DENVER**
8380 B **FUEL** 100LL, JET A NOTAM FILE ABQ **H–4L, 6F, L–8J**
RWY 17–35: H8900X100 (ASPH) S–30, D–45 MIRL **IAP**
RWY 17: PVASI(PSIL). Ground. 0.6% up.
RWY 35: Road.
AIRPORT REMARKS: Attended 1500–0000Z‡. Arpt located in mountain valley, rising terrain in all directions. Strong gusty crosswinds possible. High density altitude probable. Deer and elk invof arpt. 6–8 inch drop offs east side of rwy. Avoid overflight of Taos Pueblo World Heritage site west of arpt. ACTIVATE rotating bcn, MIRL Rwy 17–35—CTAF.
AIRPORT MANAGER: 575-643-8066
WEATHER DATA SOURCES: AWOS–3 118.025 (575) 377–0526.
COMMUNICATIONS: CTAF/UNICOM 122.8
ALBUQUERQUE CENTER APP/DEP CON 132.8
RADIO AIDS TO NAVIGATION: NOTAM FILE SKX.
TAOS (L) VORTAC 117.6 TAS Chan 123 N36°36.53´ W105°54.38´ 097° 31.8 NM to fld. 7860/13E.
DME portion unusable:
020°–100° byd 30 NM blo 18,000´
260°–330° byd 30 NM blo 17,000´

ANTON CHICO N35°06.70´ W105°02.40´ NOTAM FILE ABQ. **ALBUQUERQUE**
(H) VORTAC 117.8 ACH Chan 125 106° 22.2 NM to Santa Rosa Route 66. 5450/12E. **H–4L, 6F, L–8J**
TACAN AZM unusable:
Wi 20 NM blo 20,000´
RCO 122.1R 117.8T (ALBUQUERQUE RADIO)

Figure 167A. Excerpt from Chart Supplement.

TAKEOFF MINIMUMS AND (OBSTACLE) DEPARTURE PROCEDURES

14205

CENTRALIA, IL

CENTRALIA MUNI (ENL)
AMDT 2 12152 (FAA)

NOTE: **Rwy 9,** trees beginning 208' from DER, 494' right of centerline, up to 100' AGL/624' MSL. Trees beginning 528' from DER, 653 ' left of centerline, up to 100' AGL/624' MSL. **Rwy 18,** trees beginning 60' from DER, 265' left of centerline, up to 100' AGL/562' MSL. Trees beginning 77' from DER, 207' right of centerline, up to 100' AGL/603' MSL. Silo 1115' from DER, 755' right of centerline, 73' AGL/608' MSL. **Rwy 27,** trees beginning 1169' from DER, 493' left of centerline, up to 100' AGL/624' MSL. Trees beginning 1793' from DER, 377' right of centerline, up to 100' AGL/619' MSL. **Rwy 36,** trees and poles beginning 37' from DER, 5' right of centerline, up to 100' AGL/604' MSL. Trees, poles, and buildings beginning 203' from DER, 363' left of centerline, up to 100' AGL/610' MSL.

CHAMPAIGN/URBANA, IL

UNIVERSITY OF ILLINOIS-WILLARD (CMI)
ORIG 09015 (FAA)

DEPARTURE PROCEDURE: **Rwy 4,** climb heading 041° to 1300 before turning left.

NOTE: **Rwy 4,** trees beginning 56' from DER, 23' left of centerline, up to 63' AGL/808' MSL. Trees beginning 56' from DER, 89' right of centerline, up to 98' AGL/843' MSL. **Rwy 14R,** rod on obstruction light 520' from DER, 383' left of centerline, 17' AGL/760' MSL. Glide slope 541' from DER, 439' left of centerline, 36' AGL/779' MSL. Rod on obstruction light 543' from DER, 439' left of centerline, 37' AGL/780' MSL. **Rwy 18,** Terrain beginning 2' from DER, from left to right of centerline, up to 0' AGL/749' MSL. **Rwy 32L,** terrain 20' from DER, 152' right of centerline, 0' AGL/752' MSL. Antenna on ASR 1920' from DER, 331' left of centerline, 82' AGL/831' MSL.

CHETEK, WI

CHETEK MUNI-SOUTHWORTH (Y23)
ORIG-A 14065 (FAA)

NOTE: **Rwy 17,** trees beginning 44' from DER, 13' left of centerline, up to 100' AGL/1120' MSL. Vehicle on road 355' from DER, across centerline, 15' AGL/1070' MSL. Multiple poles beginning 338' from DER, 278' left of centerline, up to 29' AGL/1079' MSL. AG equipment beginning 27' from DER, 451' right of centerline, 19' AGL/1073' MSL. Pole 294' from DER, 299' right of centerline, 16' AGL/1070' MSL. Trees beginning 343' from DER, 7' right of centerline, up to 100' AGL/1137' MSL. **Rwy 35,** beacon 79' from DER, 448' left of centerline, 48' AGL/1103' MSL. Multiple buildings beginning 154' from DER, 339' left of centerline, up to 28' AGL/1082' MSL. Multiple poles beginning 881' from DER, 135' left of centerline, up to 34' AGL/1088' MSL. Multiple antennas beginning 1141' from DER, 40' left of centerline, up to 58' AGL/1107' MSL. Trees beginning 324' from DER, 4' left of centerline, up to 100' AGL/1146' MSL. Fence 80' from DER, 145' right of centerline, 6' AGL/1061' MSL. Multiple buildings beginning 144' from DER, 102' right of centerline, up to 22' AGL/1081' MSL. Multiple poles beginning 452' from DER, 14' right of centerline, up to 75' AGL/1088' MSL. Trees beginning 64' from DER, 1' right of centerline, up to 100' AGL/1141' MSL.

CHICAGO, IL

CHICAGO MIDWAY INTL (MDW)
AMDT 11 14205 (FAA)

DEPARTURE PROCEDURE: **Rwys 4L,4R,** Climbing right turn to 2400 heading 100° before proceeding on course. **Rwys 13C, 13L, 13R,** Climb heading 138° to 1400 before turning. **Rwys 22L, 22R,** Climb heading 227° to 1400 before turning. **Rwys 31C, 31L, 31R,** Climb heading 318° to 1400 before turning.

NOTE: **Rwy 4L,** fence 18' from DER, 257' left of centerline, 12' AGL/616' MSL. Vehicle on road 143' from DER, 163' left of centerline, 16' AGL/620' MSL. Poles and building beginning 167' from DER, 64' left of centerline, 25' AGL/630' MSL. Rising terrain 10' from DER, 492' right of centerline, 606' MSL. Signs beginning 1596' from DER, left and right of centerline, up to 88' AGL/692' MSL. Light poles, trees, towers and pole beginning 281' from DER, left and right of centerline, up to 75' AGL/679' MSL. **Rwy 4R,** navaid 300' from DER, on centerline, 9' AGL/614' MSL. Blast fence 278' from DER, 44' left of centerline, 9' AGL/613' MSL. Tower 3984' from DER, 1142' left of centerline, 109' AGL/708' MSL. Tramway 1491' from DER, 571' right of centerline, 48' AGL/654' MSL. Fence and wall beginning 249' from DER, left and right of centerline, up to 13' AGL/616' MSL. Light poles, transmission line towers and poles beginning 40' from DER, left and right of centerline, up to 39' AGL/644' MSL. Trees and sign beginning 905' from DER, 416' left of centerline, up to 75' AGL/679' MSL. Trees and flagpole beginning 921' from DER, 67' right of centerline, up to 53' AGL/657' MSL. Tower 1823' from DER, 110' right of centerline, 61' AGL/672' MSL. **Rwy 13C,** navaid 249' from DER, on centerline, 9' AGL/619' MSL. Building and trees beginning 37' from DER, 470' right of centerline, up to 27' AGL/641' MSL. Building and blast fence beginning 102' from DER, 51' left of centerline, up to 15' AGL/625' MSL. Light poles, sign and transmission line towers beginning 179' from DER, left and right of centerline, up to 39' AGL/650' MSL. Buildings and trees beginning 271' from DER, 569' left of centerline, up to 70' AGL/680' MSL. Buildings beginning 565' from DER, left and right of centerline, up to 42' AGL/654' MSL. Trees beginning 823' from DER, left and right of centerline, up to 81' AGL/700' MSL. **Rwy 13L,** buildings beginning 665' from DER, left and right of centerline, up to 33' AGL/641' MSL. Fence and wall beginning 178' from DER, 462' left of centerline, up to 15' AGL/622' MSL. Light poles, trees and transmission line towers beginning 362' from DER, left and right of centerline, up to 75' AGL/684' MSL. **Rwy 13R,** wind sock 263' from DER, 256' left of centerline, 11' AGL/621' MSL. Building 80' from DER, 334' right of centerline, 23' AGL/636' MSL. Buildings beginning 459' from DER, 291' right of centerline, up to 50' AGL/663' MSL. Light poles, trees and transmission line towers beginning 978' from DER, 52' right of centerline, up to 53' AGL/692' MSL. **Rwy 22L,** building and light poles beginning 73' from DER, 489' left of centerline, up to 31' AGL/648' MSL. Buildings, light poles, trees and transmission line towers beginning 211' from DER, left and right of centerline, up to 60' AGL/689' MSL. Tank 4100' from DER, 161' right of centerline, 113' AGL/728' MSL. Poles beginning 3991' from DER, 571' left of centerline, up to 107' AGL/743' MSL. **Rwy 22R,** tank 4332' from DER, 763' left of centerline, 113' AGL/728' MSL. Fence and wall beginning 8' from DER, left and right of centerline, up to 13' AGL/630' MSL. Building 946' from DER, 568' left of centerline, 62' AGL/677' MSL. Building, light poles, trees and transmission line towers beginning 84' from DER, left and right of centerline, up to 43' AGL/659' MSL. Trees beginning 1' from DER, 306' right of centerline, up to 52' AGL/669' MSL. Trees beginning 493' from DER, 30' right of centerline, up to 75' AGL/689' MSL.

14205

TAKEOFF MINIMUMS AND (OBSTACLE) DEPARTURE PROCEDURES

Figure 170. Takeoff Minimums and (Obstacle) Departure Procedures.

TAKEOFF MINIMUMS AND (OBSTACLE) DEPARTURE PROCEDURES

14205

CHICAGO, IL (CON'T)

CHICAGO MIDWAY INTL (MDW)
AMDT 11 14205 (FAA)

NOTE: **Rwy 31C,** navaid 238' from DER, on centerline, 12' AGL/617' MSL. Navaid 182' from DER, 309' right of centerline, 19' AGL/624' MSL. Tank and water tower beginning 5575' from DER, 1418' right of centerline, 162' AGL/757' MSL. Spire 2213' from DER, 711' left of centerline, 77' AGL/682' MSL. Trees beginning 82' from DER, 107' left of centerline, up to 45' AGL/658' MSL. Trees, poles and building beginning 450' from DER, 37' left of centerline, up to 75' AGL/670' MSL. Trees and transmission line towers beginning 83' from DER, 449' left of centerline, up to 66' AGL/670' MSL. Poles, trees and buildings beginning 141' from DER, 20' right of centerline, up to 39' AGL/647' MSL. Poles and trees beginning 1116' from DER, 12' right of centerline, up to 75' AGL/673' MSL. **Rwy 31L,** rising terrain 15' from DER, 502' right of centerline, 608' MSL. Signs beginning 68' from DER, left and right of centerline, up to 5' AGL/611' MSL. Buildings beginning 338' from DER, 451' left of centerline, up to 53' AGL/661' MSL. Trees and light poles beginning 958' from DER, 36' left of centerline, up to 65' AGL/674' MSL. Trees beginning 1411' from DER, 7' right of centerline, up to 63' AGL/667' MSL. **Rwy 31R,** navaid 614' from DER, 474' left of centerline, 19' AGL/624' MSL. Sign 494' from DER, 190' left of centerline, 23' AGL/638' MSL. Trees, poles and building beginning 16' from DER, 90' right of centerline, up to 34' AGL/638' MSL. Trees, poles and buildings beginning 208' from DER, 18' right of centerline, up to 63' AGL/667' MSL. Trees, poles and buildings beginning 256' from DER, 6' left of centerline, up to 33' AGL/650' MSL. Trees, poles and buildings beginning 574' from DER, 3' left of centerline, up to 60' AGL/664' MSL.

CHICAGO-O'HARE INTL (ORD)
AMDT 19 13290 (FAA)

TAKEOFF MINIMUMS: **Rwy 27L,** std. w/ min. climb of 220' per NM to 1700. **Rwy 27R,** std. w/ min. climb of 228' per NM to 1800. **Rwy 28C,** std. w/ min. climb of 236' per NM to 1700. **Rwy 28R,** std. w/ min. climb of 222' per NM to 1700. **Rwy 32L**, std. w/ min. climb of 240' per NM to 1800.

NOTE: **Rwy 4L,** building 3302' from DER, 1249' right of centerline, 109' AGL/750' MSL. **Rwy 4R,** tree 810' from DER, 611' right of centerline, 36' AGL/675' MSL. Trees beginning 2149' from DER, 834' left of centerline, up to 100' AGL/749' MSL. Parked aircraft on ramp 153' from DER, 329' left of centerline, 80' AGL/735' MSL. **Rwy 9L,** building 2771' from DER, 1234' right of centerline, 94' AGL/745' MSL. **Rwy 9R,** street light 877' from DER, 689' right of centerline, 40' AGL/673' MSL. Tree 3492' from DER, 1054' left of centerline, 100' AGL/744' MSL. **Rwy 10L**, parked aircraft on ramp 33' from DER, 440' left of centerline, 80' AGL/735' MSL. Parked aircraft on ramp 940' from DER, 541' left of centerline, 80' AGL/735' MSL. Towers beginning 2522' from DER, 983' right of centerline, up to 127' AGL/771' MSL. **Rwy 10C,** rod on RTR tower 790' from DER, 38' left of centerline, up to 65' AGL/715' MSL. Antenna beginning 656' from DER, 1' left of centerline, up to 48' AGL/697' MSL. Obstruction light on GS 1170' from DER, 777' left of centerline, up to 45' AGL/694' MSL. **Rwy 14L,** light poles beginning 981' from DER, 745' left of centerline, up to 40' AGL/684' MSL. Parked aircraft on ramp 100' from DER, 363' right of centerline, 80' AGL/729' MSL. Sign 1292' from DER, 724' right of centerline, 37' AGL/682' MSL. **Rwy 14R,** parked aircraft on ramp 1104' from DER, 766' right of centerline, 80' AGL/736' MSL. **Rwy 22R,** parked aircraft on ramp 34' from DER, 430' left of centerline, 80' AGL/736' MSL. **Rwy 27L,** parked aircraft on ramp 70' from DER, 405' left of centerline, 80' AGL/740' MSL. Pole 5584' from DER, 1824' left of centerline, 147' AGL/812' MSL. Parked aircraft on ramp 3627' from DER, 1225' right of centerline, 80' AGL/754' MSL. **Rwy 27R,** obstruction light on tank 1489' from DER, 886' left of centerline, 53' AGL/726' MSL. Elevator 2778' from DER, 1020' left of centerline, 111' AGL/776' MSL. **Rwy 28C,** railroad beginning 90' from DER, 81' left of centerline, 23' AGL/689' MSL. Trees beginning 3525' from DER, 697' left of centerline, up to 100' AGL/771' MSL. Trees beginning 2689' from DER, 126' left of centerline, up to 100' AGL/746' MSL. Trees beginning 2408' from DER, 197' right of centerline, up to 100' AGL/739' MSL. Trees beginning 2372' from DER, 1100' left of centerline, up to 100' AGL/737' MSL. **Rwy 28R,** trees beginning 1717' from DER, 752' left of centerline, up to 100' AGL/789' MSL. **Rwy 32L,** pole 1993' from DER, 791' left of centerline, 49' AGL/716' MSL.

14205

TAKEOFF MINIMUMS AND (OBSTACLE) DEPARTURE PROCEDURES

Figure 170A. Takeoff Minimums and (Obstacle) Departure Procedures.

TAKEOFF MINIMUMS AND (OBSTACLE) DEPARTURE PROCEDURES

14205

CHICAGO, IL (CON'T)

LANSING MUNI (IGQ)
AMDT 5 09183 (FAA)

TAKEOFF MINIMUMS: **Rwy 36,** 300-1¼ or std. w/ min. climb of 322' per NM to 900.

DEPARTURE PROCEDURE: **Rwy 36,** climb heading 002° to 1200 before proceeding on course.

NOTE: **Rwy 9,** poles beginning 1203' from DER, from left to right of centerline, up to 32' AGL/647' MSL. Building 1882' from DER, 964' left of centerline, 50' AGL/668' MSL. Tower 4314' from DER, 664' left of centerline, 149' AGL/764' MSL. **Rwy 18,** trees beginning 381' from DER, 440' right of centerline, up to 42' AGL/661' MSL. **Rwy 27,** hangar and building beginning 254' from DER, 69' right of centerline, up to 26' AGL/641' MSL. Trees, antennas, antennas on buildings, signs, light poles, and road with vehicles beginning 326' from DER, from left to right of centerline, up to 68' AGL/683' MSL. Tank 575' from DER, 65' left of centerline, 16' AGL/630' MSL. **Rwy 36,** pole 5546' from DER, 1932' right of centerline, 164' AGL/777' MSL.

CHICAGO/AURORA, IL

AURORA MUNI (ARR)
AMDT 1 07298 (FAA)

NOTE: **Rwy 9,** vehicle on road 794' from DER, right and left of centerline, 15' AGL/734' MSL. Multiple trees beginning 4126' from DER, on centerline, 100' AGL/819' MSL. **Rwy 15,** multiple trees, power poles and road beginning 900' from DER, 47' right of centerline, up to 100' AGL/809' MSL. Power pole 1313' from DER, 47' left of centerline, 34' AGL/733' MSL. **Rwy 18,** multiple power poles beginning 1218' from DER, 190' right of centerline, up to 35' AGL/734' MSL. Multiple trees beginning 3646' from DER, on centerline up to 100' AGL/809' MSL. **Rwy 27,** vehicle on road 1020' from DER, right and left of centerline, 15' AGL/734' MSL. **Rwy 33,** multiple trees and road beginning 788' from DER, 238' right of centerline, up to 79' AGL/788' MSL. Road and power pole beginning 577' from DER, 137' left of centerline, up to 38' AGL/747' MSL. **Rwy 36,** tree, pole and fence beginning 31' from DER, 169' left of centerline, up to 35' AGL/734' MSL. Vehicle on road beginning 1099' from DER, right and left of centerline, 15' AGL/734' MSL.

CHICAGO/LAKE IN THE HILLS, IL

LAKE IN THE HILLS (3CK)
ORIG-A 12096 (FAA)

NOTE: **Rwy 8,** road beginning 118' from DER, left/right and on centerline, 15' AGL/901' MSL. Multiple trees beginning 2174' from DER, 294' left of centerline, up to 100' AGL/986' MSL. Multiple trees beginning 3312' from DER, 1023' right of centerline, up to 100' AGL/994' MSL. **Rwy 26,** multiple trees beginning 55' from DER, 288' right of centerline, up to 100' AGL/999' MSL. Multiple trees beginning 299' from DER, 101' left of centerline, up to 100' AGL/959' MSL. Power lines beginning 1714' from DER, 12' right of centerline, up to 36' AGL/937' MSL. Power lines beginning 1879' from DER, 87' left of centerline, up to 52' AGL/952' MSL.

CHICAGO/PROSPECT HEIGHTS/ WHEELING, IL

CHICAGO EXECUTIVE (PWK)
AMDT 3 11125 (FAA)

TAKEOFF MINIMUMS: **Rwy 12,** 300-1½ or std. w/min. climb of 230' per NM to 900. Or alternatively, with standard takeoff minimums and a normal 200' per NM climb gradient, takeoff must occur no later than 1700' prior to DER. **Rwy 30,** 300-1 or std. w/min. climb of 250' per NM to 900, or alternatively, with standard takeoff minimums and a normal 200' per NM climb gradient, takeoff must occur no later than 2000' prior to DER.

NOTE: **Rwy 6,** trees beginning 10' from DER, left and right of centerline, up to 100' AGL/764' MSL. Vehicles on road beginning 102' from DER, left and right of centerline, up to 17' AGL/661' MSL. **Rwy 12,** vehicles on roads beginning 6' from DER, left and right of centerline, up to 17' AGL/661' MSL. Trees beginning 34' from DER, left and right of centerline, up to 100' AGL/764' MSL. Multiple antennas, buildings and poles beginning 164' from DER, right and left of centerline, up to 174' AGL/834' MSL. **Rwy 16,** multiple antennas, buildings, and poles beginning 91' from DER, left and right of centerline, up to 30' AGL/675' MSL. Vehicles on road beginning 288' from DER, left and right of centerline, up to 17' AGL/658' MSL. Trees beginning 442' from DER, left and right of centerline, up to 68' AGL/712' MSL. **Rwy 24,** vehicles on roads beginning 1' from DER, left and right of centerline, up to 17' AGL/666' MSL. Multiple buildings, poles and tower beginning 63' from DER, left and right of centerline, up to 130' AGL/783' MSL. Trees beginning 842' from DER, left and right of centerline, up to 48' AGL/693' MSL. **Rwy 30,** vehicles on road beginning 4' from DER, left and right of centerline, up to 17' AGL/666' MSL. Fence 63' from DER, 24' right of centerline, 12' AGL/652' MSL. Multiple buildings, poles and transmission towers beginning 70' from DER, left and right of centerline, up to 128' AGL/778' MSL. Trees beginning 77' from DER, left and right of centerline, up to 100' AGL/759' MSL. Antenna 5087' from DER, 759' right of centerline, 152' AGL/802' MSL. **Rwy 34,** trees beginning 116' from DER, left and right of centerline, up to 85' AGL/725' MSL. Building 718' from DER, 541' right of centerline, 53' AGL/693' MSL.

14205

TAKEOFF MINIMUMS AND (OBSTACLE) DEPARTURE PROCEDURES

Figure 170B. Takeoff Minimums and (Obstacle) Departure Procedures.

Figure 171. High Altitude Airways.

M1

ALTERNATE MINS

14205

INSTRUMENT APPROACH PROCEDURE CHARTS

IFR ALTERNATE AIRPORT MINIMUMS

Standard alternate minimums for non-precision approaches and approaches with vertical guidance [NDB, VOR, LOC, TACAN, LDA, SDF, VOR/DME, ASR, RNAV (GPS) or RNAV (RNP)] are 800-2. Standard alternate minimums for precision approaches (ILS, PAR, or GLS) are 600-2. Airports within this geographical area that require alternate minimums other than standard or alternate minimums with restrictions are listed below. NA - means alternate minimums are not authorized due to unmonitored facility, absence of weather reporting service, or lack of adequate navigation coverage. Civil pilots see FAR 91. IFR Alternate Minimums: Ceiling and Visibility Minimums not applicable to USA/USN/USAF. Pilots must review the IFR Alternate Minimums Notes for alternate airfield suitability.

NAME — ALTERNATE MINIMUMS

ALLENTOWN, PA

LEHIGH VALLEY
INTL (ABE)........................... **ILS or LOC Rwy 13**[1]

[1]Categories A, B, 900-2; Category C, 900-2½; Category D, 900-2¾.

ALLENTOWN QUEEN
CITY MUNI (XLL)................. **RNAV (GPS) Rwy 7**
VOR-B[1]

NA when local weather not available
Categories A, B, 900-2; Category C, 900-2½.

.TOONA, PA

-TOONA-BLAIR
OUNTY (AOO)................. **ILS or LOC Rwy 21**[12]
RNAV (GPS) Rwy 3[5]
RNAV (GPS) Rwy 21[13]
RNAV (GPS) Y Rwy 3[13]
RNAV (GPS) Z Rwy 3[1]
VOR-A1[14]

NA when local weather not available.
ILS, Categories A, B, 800-2; Category C, 1300-3; Category D, 1400-3; LOC, Category C, 1300-3; Category D, 1400-3.
[3]Category D, 1200-3.
[4]Categories A, B, 1000-2; Category C, 1000-2¾; Category D, 1200-3.
[5]Categories A, B, 900-2; Category C, 900-2½, Category D, 1200-3.

NAME — ALTERNATE MINIMUMS

BECKLEY, WV

RALEIGH COUNTY
MEMORIAL (BKW)............ **ILS or LOC Rwy 19**[12]
RNAV (GPS) Rwy 1[13]
RNAV (GPS) Rwy 10[13]
RNAV (GPS) Rwy 19[13]
RNAV (GPS) Rwy 28[14]
VOR Rwy 10[13]
VOR Rwy 19[13]

[1]NA when local weather not available.
[2]ILS, Categories A, B, C, 700-2; Category D, 700-2¼. LOC, Category D, 800-2¼.
[3]Category D, 800-2¼.
[4]Categories A, B, 900-2; Category C, 900-2½; Category D, 900-2¾.

BLUEFIELD, WV

MERCER
COUNTY (BLF)....................**ILS or LOC Rwy 23**[1]
RNAV (GPS) Rwy 5[2]
RNAV (GPS) Rwy 23[3]
VOR/DME Rwy 23[2]
VOR Rwy 23[4]

NA when local weather not available.
[1]ILS, Categories A, B, 700-2; Category C, 800-2; Category D, 800-2¼. LOC, Category D, 800-2¼.
[2]Category D, 800-2¼.
[3]Category C, 800-2¼; Category D, 800-2½.
[4]Categories A, B, 1000-2; Category C, 1000-2¾; Category D, 1000-3.

BRADFORD, PA

BRADFORD
RGNL (BFD)......................... **ILS or LOC Rwy 32**
RNAV (GPS) Rwy 14
RNAV (GPS) Rwy 32
VOR Rwy 14[1]
VOR/DME Rwy 14

NA when local weather not available.
[1]Category C, 800-2½; Category D, 800-2¾.

ALTERNATE MINS

NE-4

Figure 173. IFR Alternate Airport Minimums.

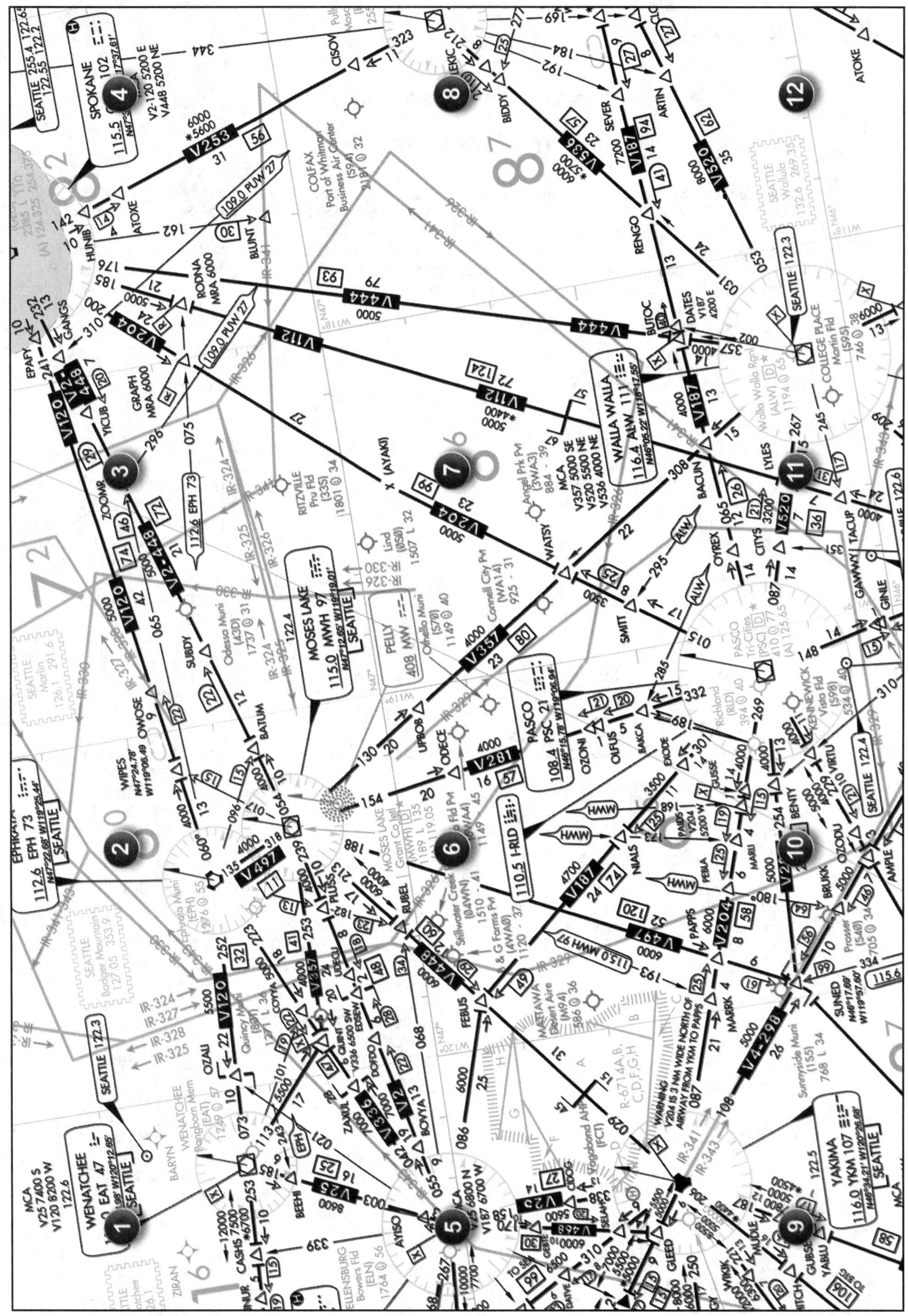

Figure 175. Low Altitude Airways.

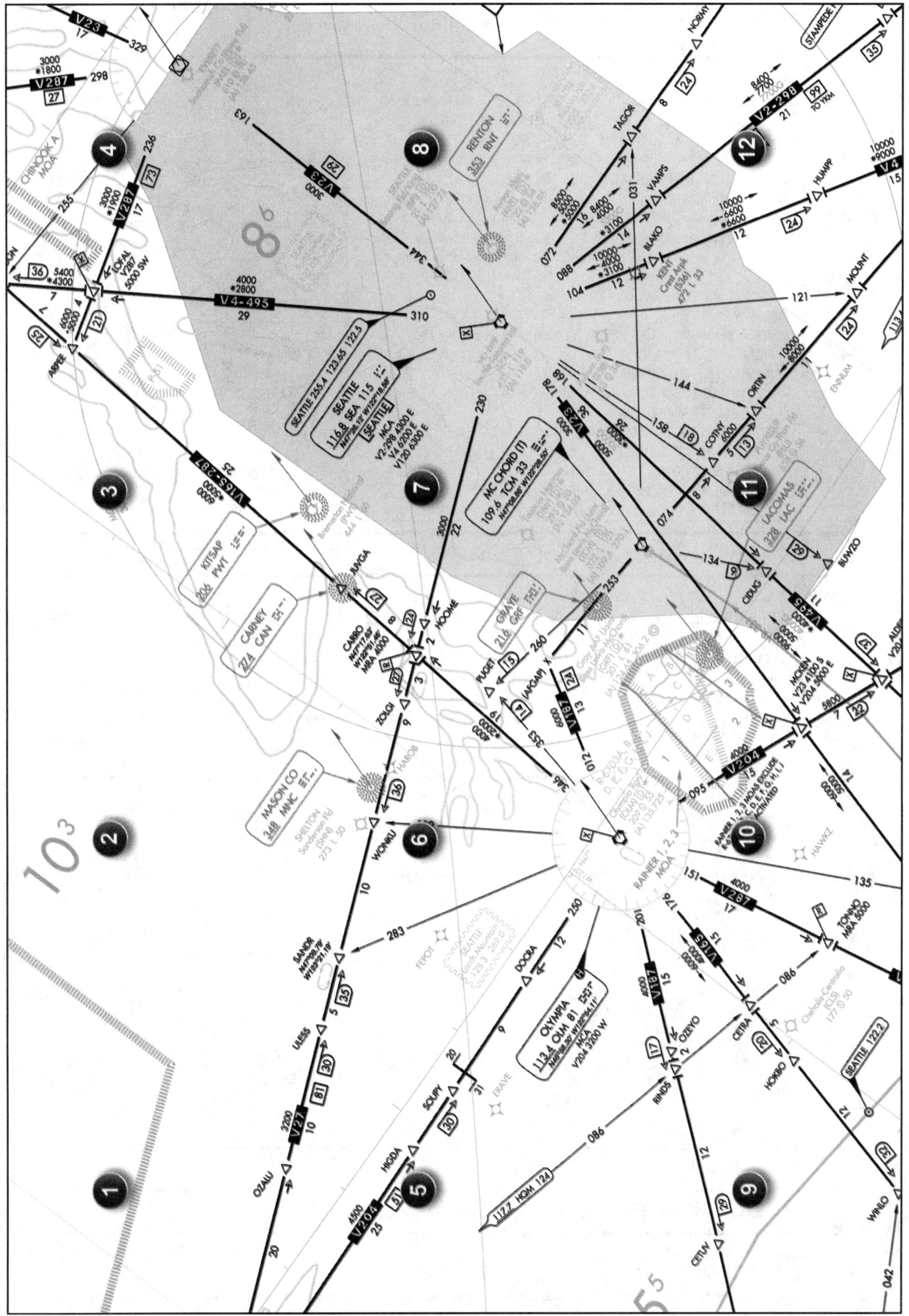

Figure 176. Low Altitude Airways.

HOQUIAM

BOWERMAN (HQM)(KHQM) 2 W UTC–8(–7DT) N46°58.27′ W123°56.19′ **SEATTLE**
18 B **FUEL** 100LL, JET A LRA NOTAM FILE HQM **H–1B, L–1D**
RWY 06–24: H5000X150 (ASPH) S–30, D–40, 2D–80 HIRL **IAP**
RWY 06: REIL. PAPI(P4R)—GA 3.0° TCH 40′. Rgt tfc.
RWY 24: MALSR. PAPI(P4L)—GA 3.5° TCH 55′.
AIRPORT REMARKS: Unattended. 100LL avbl 24 hrs a day with a major credit card. For Jet A call 360–593–0949 24 hrs a day. Flocks of waterfowl on and invof arpt. 103′ crane 0.2 NM southwest of AER 24. Svc road south of rwy in primary sfc. Ultralights prohibited without written permission from arpt mgr. ACTIVATE HIRL Rwy 06–24, MALSR Rwy 24 and REIL Rwy 06—CTAF.
AIRPORT MANAGER: 360-533-9544
WEATHER DATA SOURCES: ASOS 135.775 (360) 538–7021. **HIWAS** 117.7 HQM.
COMMUNICATIONS: CTAF/UNICOM 122.7
HOQUIAM RCO 122.2 (SEATTLE RADIO)
SEATTLE CENTER APP/DEP CON 128.3
AIRSPACE: CLASS E svc 1400–0600Z‡ other times CLASS G.
RADIO AIDS TO NAVIGATION: NOTAM FILE HQM.
HOQUIAM (H) VORTACW 117.7 HQM Chan 124 N46°56.82′ W124°08.96′ 062° 8.9 NM to fld. 10/19E. **HIWAS.**
ILS/DME 108.7 I–HQM Chan 24 Rwy 24. Class IT.

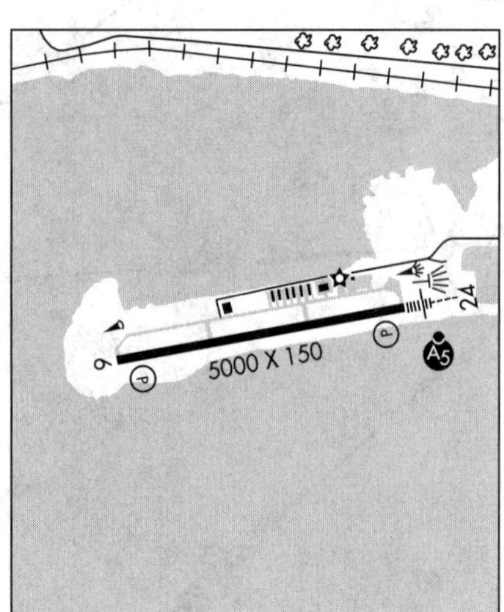

HOSKINS FLD (See OLYMPIA on page 188)

ILWACO

PORT OF ILWACO (7W1) 2 E UTC–8(–7DT) N46°18.89′ W124°00.23′ **SEATTLE**
13 B NOTAM FILE SEA
RWY 10–28: H2080X50 (ASPH) S–5 MIRL
RWY 10: Trees.
RWY 28: PAPI(P2L)—GA 4.0°. Thld dsplcd 300′. Trees.
AIRPORT REMARKS: Unattended. Rwy 10–28 markings faded. ACTIVATE MIRL Rwy 10–28—CTAF.
AIRPORT MANAGER: 360-642-3143
COMMUNICATIONS: CTAF 122.9

IONE MUNI (S23) 2 S UTC–8(–7DT) N48°42.48′ W117°24.78′ **SEATTLE**
2108 B NOTAM FILE SEA **L–13B**
RWY 15–33: H4059X45 (ASPH) MIRL
RWY 15: Fence.
AIRPORT REMARKS: Unattended. Wildlife invof rwy.
AIRPORT MANAGER: 509-442-3416
COMMUNICATIONS: CTAF 122.9
RADIO AIDS TO NAVIGATION: NOTAM FILE GEG.
SPOKANE (H) VORTACW 115.5 GEG Chan 102 N47°33.90′ W117°37.61′ 346° 69.2 NM to fld. 2756/21E. **HIWAS.**
VOR portion unusable:
300°–330° byd 30 NM blo 9,000′
335°–360° byd 18 NM blo 7,000′
335°–360° byd 25 NM
360°–015° byd 26 NM blo 7,000′
NDB (MHW) 379 ION N48°42.61′ W117°24.81′ at fld. NOTAM FILE SEA. VFR only.

• • • • • • • • • • • • • • • • • •

HELIPAD H1: H60X60 (CONC) MIRL

JEFFERSON CO INTL (See PORT TOWNSEND on page 192)

JOINT BASE LEWIS–MCCHORD (See MCCHORD FLD (JOINT BASE LEWIS–MCCHORD) on page 183)

JUMP–OFF–JOE N46°06.24′ W119°07.92′ **SEATTLE**
RCO 122.4 (SEATTLE RADIO) **L–13A**

Figure 177. Excerpt from Chart Supplement.

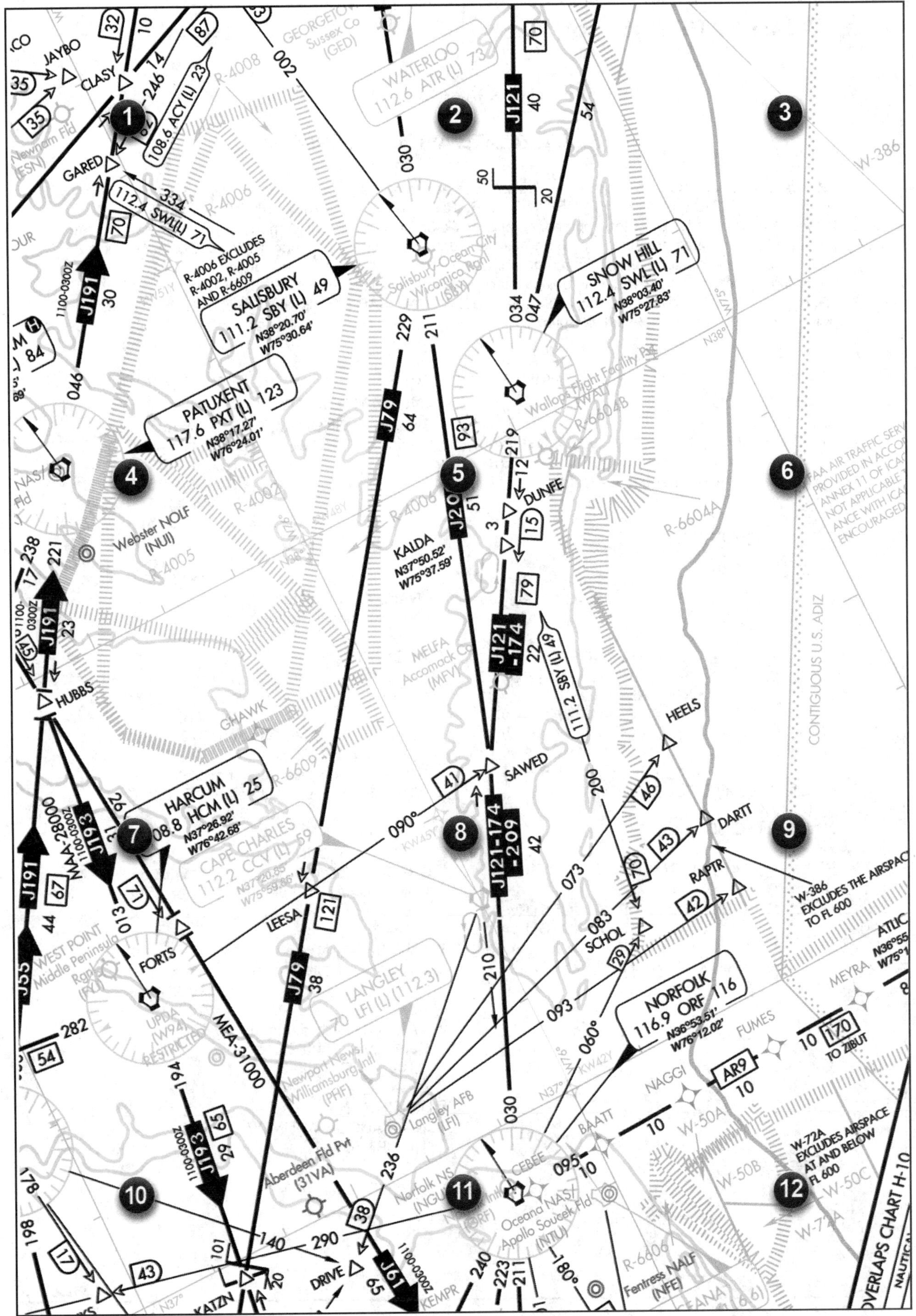

Figure 181. High Altitude Airways.

ALTERNATE MINS M1 

14205

INSTRUMENT APPROACH PROCEDURE CHARTS

IFR ALTERNATE AIRPORT MINIMUMS

Standard alternate minimums for non-precision approaches and approaches with vertical guidance [NDB, VOR, LOC, TACAN, LDA, SDF, VOR/DME, ASR, RNAV (GPS) or RNAV (RNP)] are 800-2. Standard alternate minimums for precision approaches (ILS, PAR, or GLS) are 600-2. Airports within this geographical area that require alternate minimums other than standard or alternate minimums with restrictions are listed below. NA - means alternate minimums are not authorized due to unmonitored facility, absence of weather reporting service, or lack of adequate navigation coverage. Civil pilots see FAR 91. IFR Alternate Minimums: Ceiling and Visibility Minimums not applicable to USA/USN/USAF. Pilots must review the IFR Alternate Minimums Notes for alternate airfield suitability.

NAME ALTERNATE MINIMUMS

ANDOVER, NJ

AEROFLEX-
ANDOVER (12N).................. **RNAV (GPS) Rwy 3**
VOR-A

NA when local weather not available.
Category A, 1000-2.

ATLANTIC CITY, NJ

ATLANTIC CITY
INTL (ACY).......................... **ILS or LOC Rwy 13**[1]
ILS or LOC/DME Rwy 31[1]
RADAR-1[2]
RNAV (GPS) Rwy 4[2]
RNAV (GPS) Y Rwy 13[2]
RNAV (GPS) Rwy 22[2]
RNAV (GPS) Y Rwy 31[2]
VOR/DME Rwy 22[2]
VOR Rwy 4[2]
VOR Rwy 13[2]
VOR Rwy 31[2]

[1]ILS, Category E, 700-2½. LOC, Category E, 800-2½.
[2]Category E, 800-2½.

BELMAR/FARMINGDALE, NJ

MONMOUTH
EXECUTIVE (BLM) .... **RNAV (GPS) Rwy 14**
RNAV (GPS) Rwy 32
VOR-A

NA when local weather not available.

NAME ALTERNATE MINIMUMS

BINGHAMTON, NY

GREATER BINGHAMTON/EDWIN A.
LINK FIELD (BGM) ....**ILS or LOC Rwy 16**[1]
ILS or LOC Rwy 34[12]
RNAV (GPS) Rwy 10[2]
RNAV (GPS) Rwy 16[2]
RNAV (GPS) Rwy 28[2]
RNAV (GPS) Rwy 34[2]
VOR Rwy 10[2]
VOR/DME Rwy 28[2]

[1]NA when control tower closed.
[2]NA when local weather not available.

CALDWELL, NJ

ESSEX COUNTY (CDW)... **RNAV (GPS) Rwy 4**[12]
RNAV (GPS) Rwy 10[12]
RNAV (GPS) Rwy 22[23]

[1]Category B, 900-2; Category C, 900-2½; Category D, 1000-3.
[2]NA when local weather not available.
[3]Category B, 900-2; Category C, 900-2½.

CORTLAND, NY

CORTLAND COUNTY-
CHASE FIELD (N03)................... **VOR or GPS-A**

Categories A, B, 1100-2, Categories C, D, 1100-3.

DANSVILLE, NY

DANSVILLE MUNI (DSV)............. **RNAV (GPS)-A**
RNAV (GPS) Rwy 14
RNAV (GPS) Rwy 18

NA when local weather not available.
Category A, 1300-2; Category B, 1500-2; Category C, 1500-3.

DUNKIRK, NY

CHAUTAUQUA COUNTY/
DUNKIRK (DKK) ....**VOR Rwy 6**
VOR Rwy 24

Category D, 900-2¾.

 **ALTERNATE MINS** NE-2

Figure 183. IFR Alternate Airport Minimums.

This page intentionally left blank.

NEVADA

CONTINUED FROM PRECEDING PAGE

AIRPORT REMARKS: Attended continuously. Large numbers of birds and bats invof arpt btn SS–SR. Lgtd golf range 1400′ south of Rwy 01R–19L and Rwy 01L–19R. Extensive glider/soaring ops weekends and hol, SR–SS, LAS 187/020, alts up to but not including FL 180. Gliders remain clear of the terminal ctl area but otherwise opr within the entire southwest quadrant of the terminal ctl area Veil. Acft may experience reflection of sun from glass hotels lctd northwest of arpt. Reflection may occur at various alts, headings and distances from arpt. Numerous helicopter ops on west side of arpt. Rwy 01L–19R 496,000 lbs GWT for L–1011, 555,000 lbs GWT for DC–10, 602,500 lbs GWT for MD–11. Acft using full length departure on Rwy 07L use minimal power until passing the power–up point on rwy. Power–up point is 348′ east of blast pad and marked with sign and std markings for beginning of rwy. Turbojet dep not permitted Rwy 01R–19L or Rwy 01L–19R 0400–1600Z‡. Exception for wx or operational necessity. All NSTD rwy ops PPR from Department of Aviation. ASDE–X surveillance system in use. Opr transponders with Mode C on all twys and rwys. Acft taxiing westbound on Twy B near Twy E use caution not to enter the rwy on Twy Y, acft taxiing westbound on Twy W near Twy E use caution not to enter the rwy on Twy U. Twy C no centerline lgts west of Twy B6, has edge lgts on south side of twy in this area. Directional twy signs will be incomplete due to construction. Acft larger than B757 PPR from Department of Aviation to use Twy H. Ops at all terminal gates and cargo ramp controlled by Department of Aviation 1330–0900Z‡. All acft ctc ramp ctl on freq 124.4 for ops at A, B, and C gates, ctc ramp ctl on freq 127.9 for ops at D and E gates and cargo ramp prior to entering ramp or pushing back from gate or parking spot. From 0900–1330Z‡ ctc Gnd Con on freq 121.1 for ops at all gates and cargo ramp. Acft opr near the intersection of Twys S, D, G and the north end of Twy Z should be alert as there are closely aligned twy centerlines and radius turns. Acft that departure full length of Rwy 01L and Rwy 07L must hold at the same hold line, as there is no room to hold between the rwy ends, and such acft should verify that they are on the correct rwy. Acft dep Rwy 19R use minimal power passing the rwy thld. Rwy 19R thld has std rwy markings and is 780′ south of the blast pad. Ldg Rights Arpt: Customs avbl to general aviation acft 1600–0600Z‡, all other times PPR call 702–2615539. General aviation acft rqrg immigration/customs svcs must ctc Department of Aviation for parking arrangements minimum 2 hrs prior to arr 702–261–4411. General aviation acft using the west side customs facility must ctc ramp ctl 124.4. General aviation parking very ltd. For parking availability ctc either FBO 702–736–1830 or 702–739–1100. Rotating bcn not visible 115°–240° southeast to southwest from twr. Rwy status lgts are in ops. Tiedown fee. General aviation customs and immigration lctd west side of afld between FBO′s. Flight Notification Service (ADUCS) avbl. NOTE: See Special Notices—Intersection Departures During Period of Darkness, Grand Canyon Special Flight Rules Area.

AIRPORT MANAGER: 702-261-5211

WEATHER DATA SOURCES: ASOS (702) 736–1416

COMMUNICATIONS: D–ATIS 132.4 702–736–0950 **UNICOM** 122.95

Ⓡ **LAS VEGAS APP CON** 125.025 125.6 (Rwy 25L and Rwy 25R)

Ⓡ **LAS VEGAS DEP CON** 125.02 (North)125.9 (South)

LAS VEGAS TOWER 119.9 (Rwy 07L–25R and Rwy 07R–25L) 118.75 (Rwy 01L–19R and Rwy 01R–19L)

GND CON 121.9 (West of Rwy 01R–19L) 121.1 (East of Rwy 01R–19L) **RAMP CON** 124.4 (Terminal A, B, C) 127.9 (D, Gates and Cargo Ramp) 129.175 (A, B, C Gates) **CLNC DEL** 118.0

AIRSPACE: CLASS B See VFR Terminal Area Chart

RADIO AIDS TO NAVIGATION: NOTAM FILE LAS.

LAS VEGAS (H) VORTACW 116.9 LAS Chan 116 N36°04.78′ W115°09.59′ at fld. 2136/15E.

No NOTAM MP: 1600–1800Z‡ Sat

VORTAC unusable:

025°–160° byd 20 NM blo 6,000′
160°–200° byd 20 NM blo 9,000′
200°–025° byd 25 NM blo 11,000′
200°–220° byd 15 NM blo 9,000′
220°–245° byd 35 NM blo 15,000′
245°–260° byd 35 NM blo 14,000′
260°–275° byd 35 NM blo 14,000′
275°–310° byd 35 NM blo 16,500′

ILS/DME 110.1 I–CUA Chan 38 Rwy 01L. Class IB. LOC unusable byd 30° left of course. LOC unusable within .2 NM from threshold.

ILS/DME 111.75 I–RLE Chan 54(Y) Rwy 25L. Class IE. LOC unusable byd 19° south of course.

ILS/DME 110.3 I–LAS Chan 40 Rwy 25R.

Figure 185. Excerpt from Chart Supplement.

LAS VEGAS

HENDERSON EXECUTIVE (HND)(KHND) 11 S UTC–8(–7DT) N35°58.37′ W115°08.07′ **LAS VEGAS**
2492 B **FUEL** 100LL, JET A OX 1, 2 TPA—3492(1000) NOTAM FILE HND **H–4I, L–7E**
RWY 17R–35L: H6501X100 (ASPH) S–30, D–60 MIRL 1.4% up S **IAP, AD**
RWY 17R: REIL. PAPI(P4L)—GA 3.0° TCH 40′.
RWY 35L: REIL. PAPI(P4L)—GA 4.3° TCH 52′. Road.
RWY 17L–35R: H5001X75 (ASPH) S–30, D–30 MIRL 1.4% up S
RWY 17L: REIL. PAPI(P4L)—GA 3.0° TCH 40′.
RWY 35R: REIL. PAPI(P4L)—GA 4.3° TCH 52′.
AIRPORT REMARKS: Attended 1300–0600Z‡. Self–svc fuel 100LL 24 hrs. Rwy 17L–35R is CLOSED 0400–1500Z‡. Extensive commercial air tour tfc arriving from southeast at different times during dalgt hrs. Acft departure Rwy 17R or Rwy 35L should verify that they are taking off from the rwy and not the parallel twy. MIRl Rwy 17L–35R OTS unless Rwy 17R–35L is clsd. ACTIVATE MIRL Rwy 17R–35L and Rwy 17L–35R, PAPI Rwy 17R and Rwy 35L, PAPI Rwy 17L and Rwy 35R REIL Rwy 17R and 35L REIL Rwy 17L and 35R and twy—CTAF. REIL Rwy 17L and 35R avbl only when Rwy 17R and 35L clsd.
AIRPORT MANAGER: 702-261-4802
WEATHER DATA SOURCES: ASOS 120.775 (702) 614–4537.
COMMUNICATIONS: CTAF 125.1 **ATIS** 120.775 **UNICOM** 122.95
MOUNT POTOSI RCO 122.35 (RENO RADIO)
®**LAS VEGAS APP/DEP CON** 118.4
TOWER 125.1 (1400–0400Z‡) **GND CON** 127.8
AIRSPACE: CLASS D svc 1400–0400Z‡ other times CLASS G.
RADIO AIDS TO NAVIGATION: NOTAM FILE RNO.
BOULDER CITY (H) VORTACW 116.7 BLD Chan 114 N35°59.75′ W114°51.81′ 249° 13.3 NM to fld. 3642/15E.
HIWAS.
Unusable:
155°–180° byd 30 NM blo 9,000′

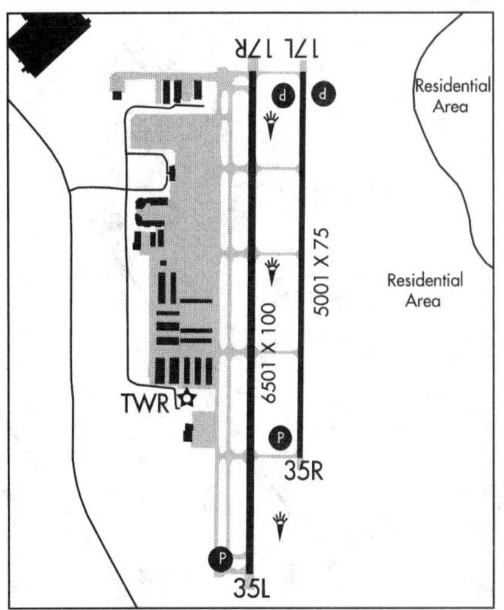

MC CARRAN INTL (LAS)(KLAS) 5 S UTC–8(–7DT) N36°04.80′ W115°09.14′ **LAS VEGAS**
2181 B S4 **FUEL** 100, 100LL, JET A1+ OX 1, 2, 3 LRA Class I, ARFF Index E NOTAM FILE LAS **H–4I, L–7E**
RWY 07L–25R: H14512X150 (ASPH–PFC) S–23, D–220, 2S–175, 2D–633, 2D/2D2–877 HIRL **IAP, AD**
RWY 07L: PAPI(P4L)—GA 3.0° TCH 76′. Thld dsplcd 2138′. Hangar. 1.1% down.
RWY 25R: MALSR. PAPI(P4L)—GA 3.0° TCH 84′. Thld dsplcd 1397′. 0.9% up.
RWY 07R–25L: H10525X150 (CONC–GRVD) S–23, D–220, 2S–175, 2D–633, 2D/2D2–914 HIRL
RWY 07R: REIL. PAPI(P4L)—GA 3.0° TCH 61′. Pole. 1.1% down.
RWY 25L: MALSF. PAPI(P4L)—GA 3.0° TCH 84′. 0.9% up.
RWY 01R–19L: H9771X150 (CONC–GRVD) S–23, D–220, 2S–175, 2D–633, 2D/2D2–877 MIRL
RWY 01R: REIL. PAPI(P4L)—GA 3.0° TCH 76′. Thld dsplcd 491′. Railroad. Rgt tfc. 1.1% down.
RWY 19L: REIL. PAPI(P4L)—GA 3.0° TCH 75′. Thld dsplcd 878′. Pole. 0.9% up.
RWY 01L–19R: H8988X150 (CONC–GRVD) S–30, D–145, 2S–175, 2D–460, 2D/2D2–833 HIRL
RWY 01L: MALSF. PAPI(P4L)—GA 3.4° TCH 57′. Thld dsplcd 587′. Railroad. 1.1% down.
RWY 19R: REIL. PAPI(P4L)—GA 3.0° TCH 80′. Fence. Rgt tfc. 1.0% up.
RUNWAY DECLARED DISTANCE INFORMATION
RWY 01L:TORA–8985 TODA–8985 ASDA–8985 LDA–8401
RWY 01R:TORA–9775 TODA–10172 ASDA–9441 LDA–8681
RWY 07L:TORA–14510 TODA–15099 ASDA–14099 LDA–11966
RWY 19L:TORA–9775 TODA–10175 ASDA–9685 LDA–8745
RWY 19R:TORA–8985 TODA–9397 ASDA–8397 LDA–8397
RWY 25R:TORA–14510 TODA–15155 ASDA–14155 LDA–12755

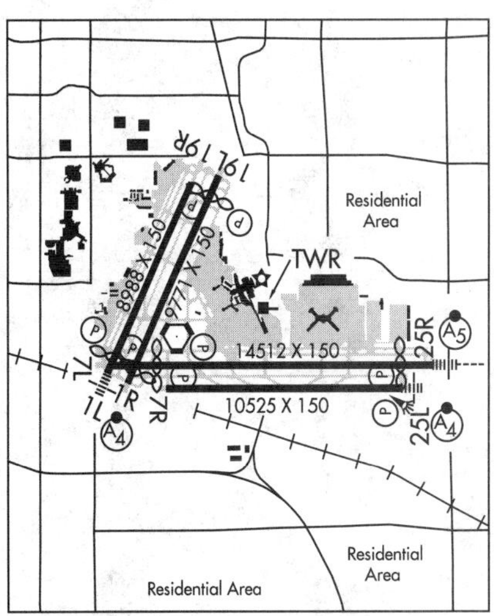

Figure 185A. Excerpt from Chart Supplement.

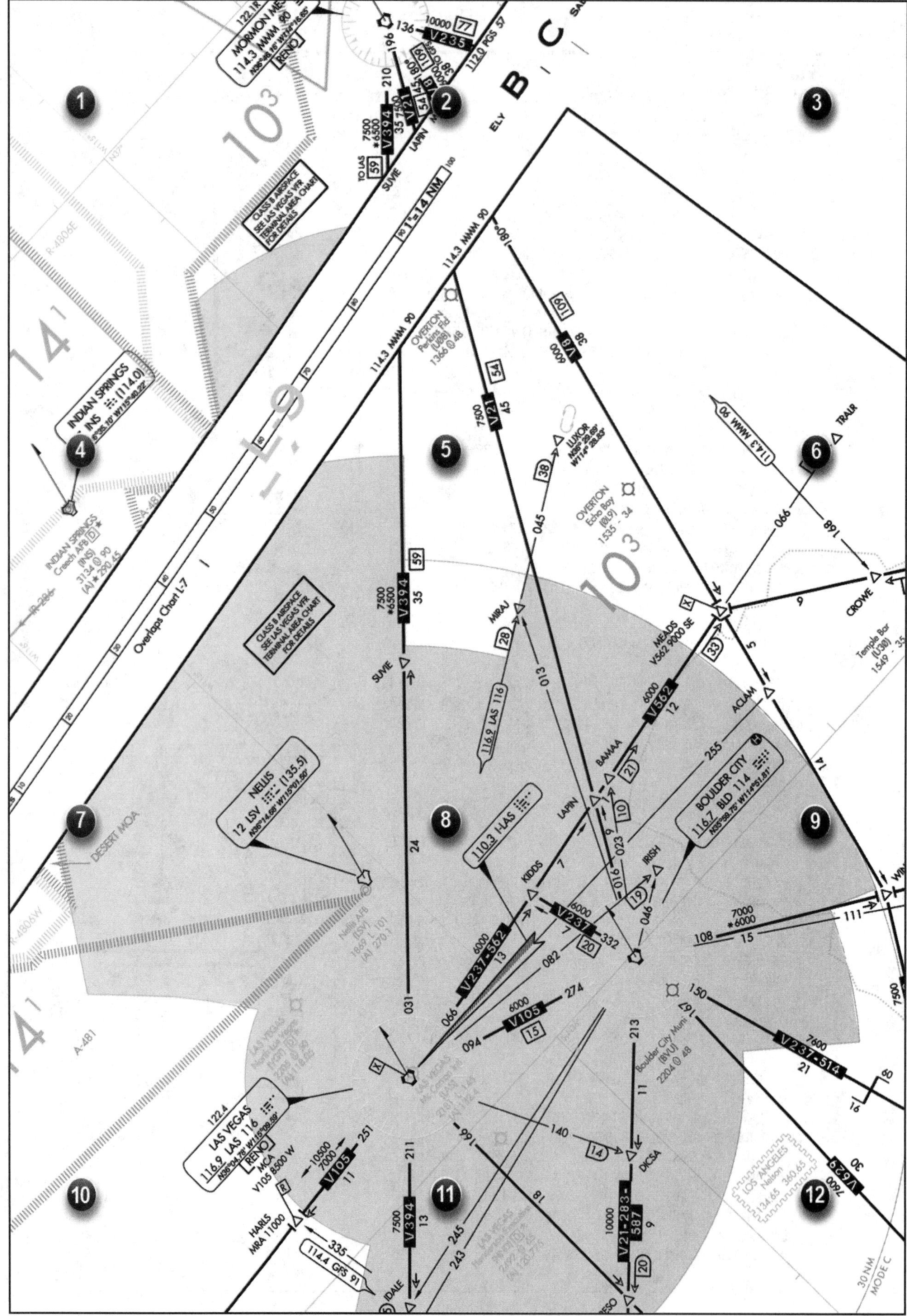

Figure 186. Low Altitude Airways.

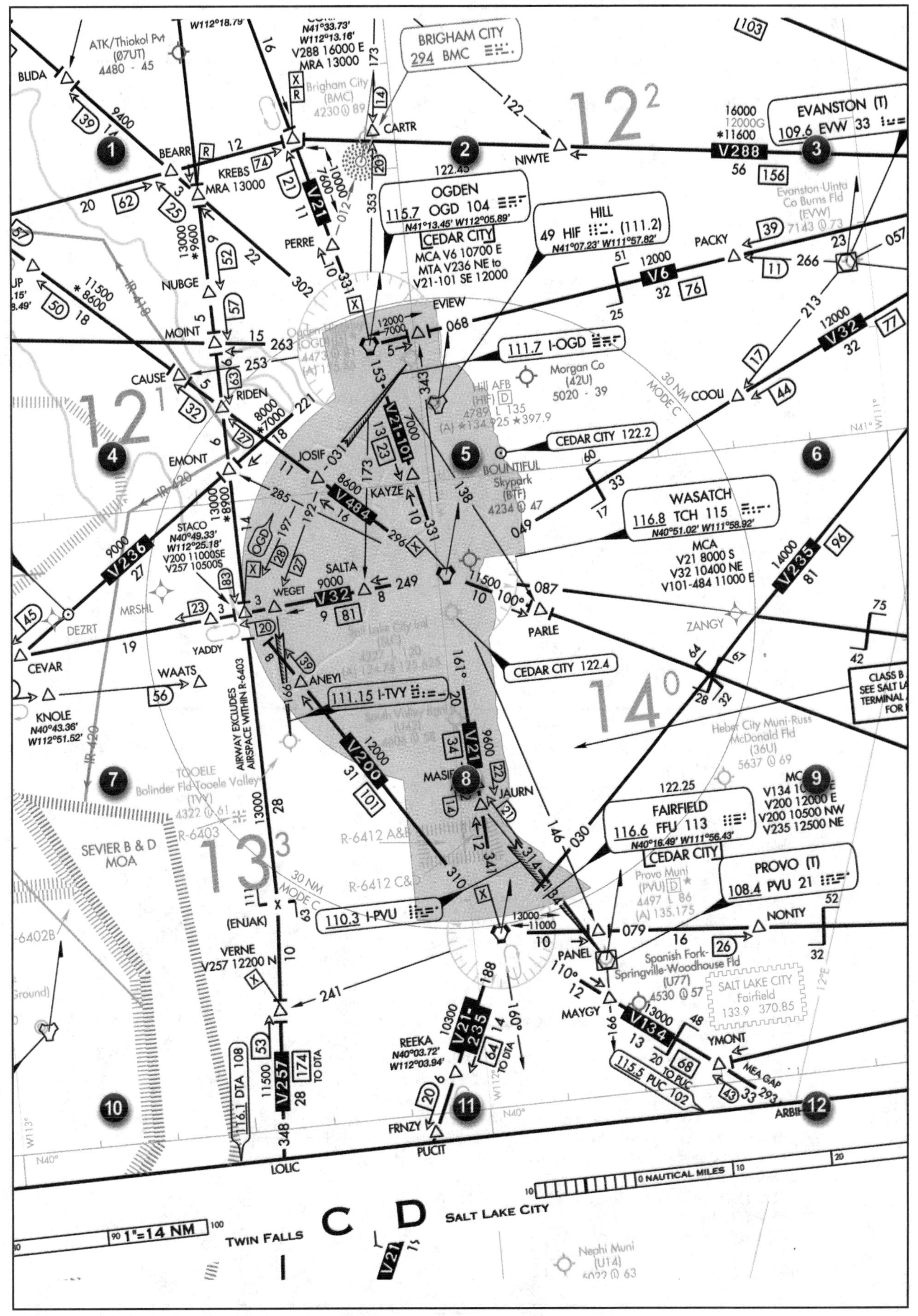

Figure 187. Low Altitude Airways.

PRICE

CARBON CO RGNL/BUCK DAVIS FLD (PUC)(KPUC) 3 E UTC–7(–6DT) N39°36.84´ W110°45.09´ **DENVER**
5957 B S2 **FUEL** 100LL, JET A OX 1, 2 NOTAM FILE PUC **H–3E, L–9D**
RWY 18–36: H8313X100 (ASPH–PFC) D–40 MIRL **IAP**
RWY 18: PAPI(P2L)—GA 4.0° TCH 45´. Fence. 1.9% down.
RWY 36: MALSF. PAPI(P4L)—GA 3.0° TCH 52´. 1.6% up.
RWY 14–32: H4514X75 (ASPH) S–13 MIRL 1.1% up NW
RWY 32: Road.
RWY 07–25: H3541X75 (ASPH) S–12.5 1.0% up E
RWY 25: Thld dsplcd 228´. Road.
AIRPORT REMARKS: Attended Mon–Fri 1400–0100Z‡, Sat–Sun 1500–0000Z‡. 24 hr self svc fuel avbl with credit card. Refuse dump 1/2 mile SW Rwy 36 thld—occasional smoke visibility hazard; bird hazard. Deer on and in the vicinity of arpt. Glider ops invof arpt SR–SS. Rwy 18 high voltage transmission line on extended centerline. Rwy 07 + 60´ drop off 520´ from rwy end. Rwy 14 + 40´ drop off 250´ from thld. Rwy 07–25 pavement cracking and separating. ACTIVATE MIRL Rwy 18–36 and Rwy 14–32 PAPI Rwy 36 and MALSF Rwy 36—CTAF. PAPI Rwy 18 opr continuously.
AIRPORT MANAGER: 435-637-9556
WEATHER DATA SOURCES: ASOS 135.425 (435) 637–2790.
COMMUNICATIONS: CTAF/UNICOM 122.8
RCO 122.2 (CEDAR CITY RADIO)
SALT LAKE CENTER APP/DEP CON 133.9
RADIO AIDS TO NAVIGATION: NOTAM FILE PUC.
(H) VORW/DME 115.5 PUC Chan 102 N39°36.19´ W110°45.21´ at fld. 5830/14E.
VOR portion unusable:
275°–300° byd 25 NM blo 12,000´
300°–330° byd 25 NM blo 13,500´
330°–010° byd 25 NM blo 17,300´
DME portion unusable:
275°–010° byd 27 NM blo 17,300´
275°–010° byd 35 NM
VOR/DME unusable:
010°–070° byd 25 NM blo 14,000´
200°–275° byd 27 NM blo 13,000´
ILS/DME 109.35 I–PUC Chan 30(Y) Rwy 36.

PROVO MUNI (PVU)(KPVU) 2 SW UTC–7(–6DT) N40°13.15´ W111°43.40´ **SALT LAKE CITY**
4497 B S4 **FUEL** 100, JET A OX 2, 4 TPA—See Remarks Class I, ARFF Index B **H–3D, L–9C, 11D**
NOTAM FILE PVU **IAP, AD**
RWY 13–31: H8599X150 (ASPH–PFC) S–65, D–85, 2S–108, 2D–140 HIRL
RWY 13: REIL. PAPI(P4L)—GA 3.0° TCH 42´. Rgt tfc.
RWY 31: PAPI(P2L)—GA 3.0° TCH 46´.
RWY 18–36: H6614X150 (ASPH) S–50, D–70, 2S–89, 2D–110 MIRL
RWY 18: PAPI(P2L)—GA 3.0° TCH 45´. Rgt tfc.
RWY 36: PAPI(P2L)—GA 3.0° TCH 46´.
RUNWAY DECLARED DISTANCE INFORMATION
RWY 13: TORA–8599 TODA–8599 ASDA–8599 LDA–8599
RWY 18: TORA–6614 TODA–6614 ASDA–6614 LDA–6614
RWY 31: TORA–8599 TODA–8599 ASDA–8599 LDA–8599
RWY 36: TORA–6614 TODA–6614 ASDA–6614 LDA–6614

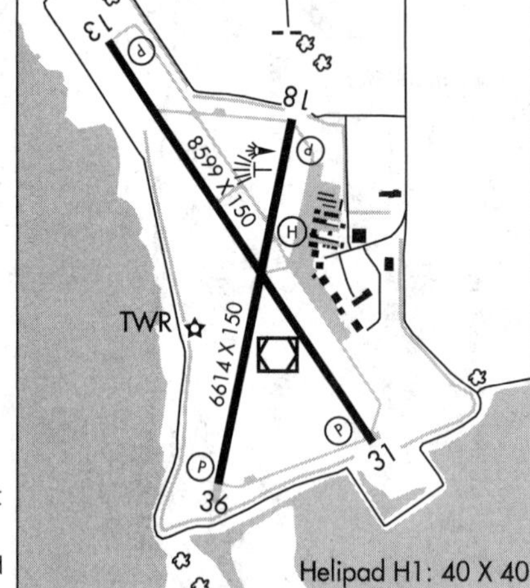

AIRPORT REMARKS: Attended Nov–May 1300–0400Z‡, Jun–Oct 1300–0500Z‡. For arpt svcs ctc 128.85. 24 hr PPR for unscheduled air carrier ops call airport manager 801–852–6715. Extensive flight training invof arpt. Use caution for extensive paragliding ops invof point of the mountain. Primary radar not avbl. Radar tfc advisories and svcs avbl for transponder equipped acft only. Be alert: helicopters arriving and departing from rwys and twys. TPA—5500(1003) single engine, 6000(1503) turbo/jet. NOTE: See Special Notice—Extensive Flight Training in vicinity of Provo Municipal Airport.
AIRPORT MANAGER: 801-852-6715
WEATHER DATA SOURCES: AWOS–3 135.175 (801) 373–9782. LAWRS.
COMMUNICATIONS: CTAF 125.3 **ATIS** 135.175
Ⓡ**SALT LAKE CITY APP/DEP CON** 118.85
TOWER 125.3 (1400–0400Z‡) **GND CON** 119.4
AIRSPACE: CLASS D svc airport 1400–0400Z‡ other times CLASS E.

Figure 188. Excerpt from Chart Supplement.

CONTINUED FROM PRECEDING PAGE

RADIO AIDS TO NAVIGATION: NOTAM FILE PVU.
(T) VORW/DME 108.4 PVU Chan 21 N40°12.90′ W111°43.28′ at fld. 4493/15E.
VOR/DME unusable:
350°–080° byd 10 NM
ILS/DME 110.3 I–PVU Chan 40 Rwy 13. Class IT. ILS/DME unmonitored when twr clsd.

• • • • • • • • • • • • • • • • • • •

HELIPAD H1: H40X40 (CONC)

RICHFIELD MUNI (RIF)(KRIF) 1 SW UTC–7(–6DT) N38°44.05′ W112°06.10′ **LAS VEGAS**
5318 B S4 **FUEL** 100LL, JET A NOTAM FILE CDC **H–3D, L–9C**
RWY 01–19: H7100X100 (ASPH) S–19 MIRL 0.5% up S **IAP**
RWY 01: PAPI(P2L)—GA 3.5°. Tree. Rgt tfc.
RWY 19: PAPI(P2L)—GA 3.5°. Pole.
AIRPORT REMARKS: Attended 1500–0000Z‡. For fuel after hours call 435–896–3053. ACTIVATE MIRL Rwy 01–19—CTAF.
AIRPORT MANAGER: 435-896-9413
WEATHER DATA SOURCES: AWOS–3 133.375 (435) 896–1775.
COMMUNICATIONS: CTAF/UNICOM 122.8
RCO 122.5 (CEDAR CITY RADIO)
SALT LAKE CENTER APP/DEP CON 133.6
RADIO AIDS TO NAVIGATION: NOTAM FILE CDC.
DELTA (H) VORTACW 116.1 DTA Chan 108 N39°18.13′ W112°30.33′ 135° 38.9 NM to fld. 4642/16E.
VOR portion unusable
045°–090° byd 25 NM blo 10,700′

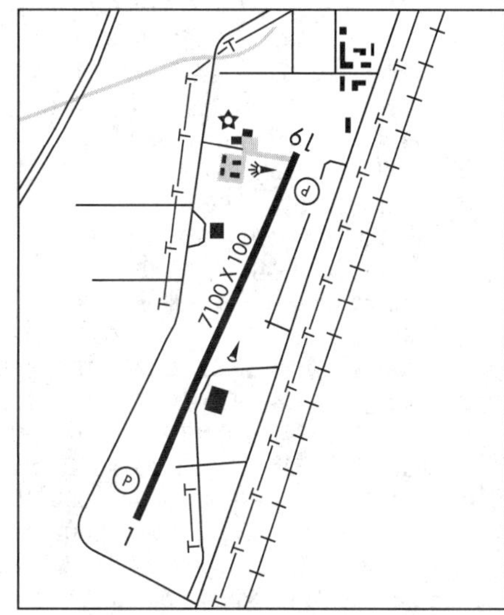

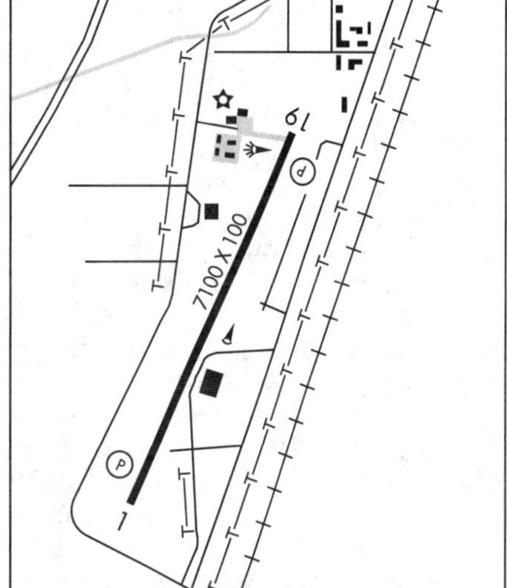

ROOSEVELT MUNI (74V) 3 SW UTC–7(–6DT) N40°16.71′ W110°03.08′ **SALT LAKE CITY**
5176 B S4 **FUEL** 100LL, JET A NOTAM FILE CDC **H–3E, L–9D, 11D**
RWY 07–25: H6501X75 (ASPH) S–12 MIRL 1.0% up W **IAP**
RWY 07: REIL. PAPI(P2L)—GA 3.0° TCH 40′. Brush.
RWY 25: REIL. PAPI(P2L)—GA 3.0° TCH 40′.
AIRPORT REMARKS: Attended Mon–Fri 1600–0100Z‡. For svc call 435–724–0539 or 435–722–5001. Fuel 24 hr credit card svc avbl. ACTIVATE MIRL Rwy 07–25, PAPI Rwy 07 and Rwy 25 and REIL Rwy 07 and Rwy 25—CTAF.
AIRPORT MANAGER: 435-722-5001
WEATHER DATA SOURCES: AWOS–3 118.975 (435) 722–4201.
COMMUNICATIONS: CTAF/UNICOM 122.8
MYTON RCO 112.7 T 122.1R (CEDAR CITY RADIO)
RADIO AIDS TO NAVIGATION: NOTAM FILE CDC.
MYTON (H) VOR/DME 112.7 MTU Chan 74 N40°08.95′ W110°07.62′ 010° 8.5 NM to fld. 5401/14E.

Figure 188A. Excerpt from Chart Supplement.

SALT LAKE CITY

SALT LAKE CITY INTL (SLC)(KSLC) P (ANG) 3 W UTC–7(–6DT) N40°47.30′ W111°58.67′ **SALT LAKE CITY**
4227 B S4 **FUEL** 100LL, JET A1+ OX 1, 2, 3, 4 LRA Class I, ARFF Index E **H–3D, L–9C, 11D**
NOTAM FILE SLC **IAP, AD**

RWY 16L–34R: H12002X150 (ASPH–GRVD) S–60, D–200, 2S–175, 2D–350, 2D/2D2–850 HIRL CL
RWY 16L: ALSF2. TDZL. PAPI(P4L)—GA 3.0° TCH 70′.
RWY 34R: ALSF2. TDZL. PAPI(P4L)—GA 3.0° TCH 73′.
RWY 16R–34L: H12000X150 (CONC–GRVD) S–60, D–200, 2S–175, 2D–350, 2D/2D2–850 HIRL CL
RWY 16R: ALSF2. TDZL. PAPI(P4L)—GA 3.0° TCH 73′.
RWY 34L: ALSF2. TDZL. PAPI(P4L)—GA 3.0° TCH 73′.
RWY 17–35: H9597X150 (ASPH–GRVD) S–60, D–200, 2S–175, 2D–350, 2D/2D2–850 HIRL CL
RWY 17: MALSR. TDZL. PAPI(P4R)—GA 3.0° TCH 76′.
RWY 35: MALSR. TDZL. PAPI(P4L)—GA 3.0° TCH 74′. Thld dsplcd 324′. Antenna.
RWY 14–32: H4892X150 (ASPH–GRVD) S–60, D–200, 2D–350, 2D/2D2–850 HIRL
RWY 14: PAPI(P4L)—GA 3.0° TCH 40′.
RWY 32: PAPI(P4L)—GA 3.0° TCH 41′.

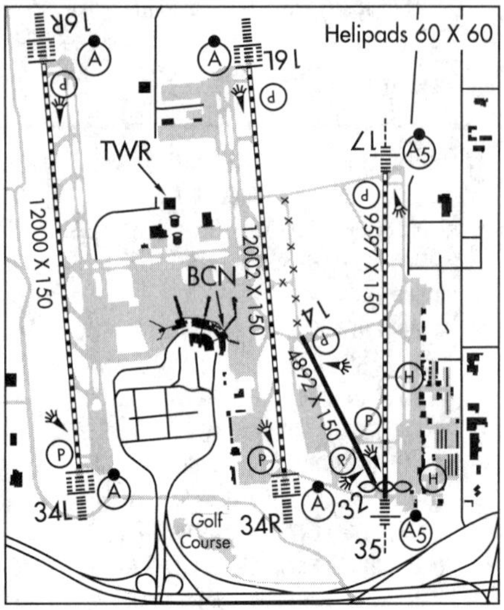

RUNWAY DECLARED DISTANCE INFORMATION

RWY 14:	TORA–4892	TODA–4892	ASDA–4892	LDA–4892
RWY 16L:	TORA–12002	TODA–12002	ASDA–12002	LDA–12002
RWY 16R:	TORA–12000	TODA–12000	ASDA–12000	LDA–12000
RWY 17:	TORA–9597	TODA–9597	ASDA–9597	LDA–9597
RWY 32:	TORA–4892	TODA–4892	ASDA–4892	LDA–4892
RWY 34L:	TORA–12000	TODA–12000	ASDA–12000	LDA–12000
RWY 34R:	TORA–12002	TODA–12002	ASDA–12002	LDA–12002
RWY 35:	TORA–9597	TODA–9597	ASDA–9597	LDA–9273

MILITARY SERVICE: JASU (MD–3M) (MA–1A) (M32A–60A) **FUEL** A++ avbl at ANG. (NC–100LL, A1+) **FLUID** LPOX **OIL** O–148(Mil)

AIRPORT REMARKS: Attended continuously. Flocks of birds on and invof arpt. Rwy 14–32 taxi ops only blo 1,200 ft RVR. Rwy 14–32 CLOSED blo 1200′ RVR. Due to tfc volume, local departure and arrival ops are discouraged and delays can be expected between 1700–1900Z‡ and 0300–0600Z‡. Rwy 34R deice pad construction Apr–2013–Sep–2014. See current NOTAMs for dates and additional information. South cargo apron access abeam Twy H2. Inner apron clsd between Twy H2 and apron spot 3. Twy Y rstd to wingspans less than 171′. Special VFR is not recommended at the arpt, if req, expect delays. Use caution for extensive paragliding ops invof point of the mountain. ASDE–X Surveillance System in use. Opr transponders with Mode C on all twys and rwys. Touchdown, midpoint and rollout rwy visual range Rwy 16L, Rwy 34R, Rwy 16R, Rwy 34L. Touchdown and rollout rwy visual range Rwy 17, Rwy 35. Flight Notification Service (ADCUS) avbl. NOTE: See Special Notices—Continuous Power Facilities.

AIRPORT MANAGER: 801-575-2401

WEATHER DATA SOURCES: ASOS (801) 328–3567 TDWR.

COMMUNICATIONS: D–ATIS 125.625 124.75 801–325–9749 **UNICOM** 122.95
RCO 122.4 (CEDAR CITY RADIO)
Ⓡ **SALT LAKE CITY APP/DEP CON** 120.9 (S of 41° latitude below 8000′) 121.1 (N of 41° latitude below 8000′) 124.3 (110°–160° above 8,000′) 124.9 (300°–340° above 8000′) 126.25 (250°–300° above 8000′) 128.1 (160°–250° above 8000′) 135.5 (340°–110° above 8000′).
TOWER 118.3 (Rwy 17–35 and Rwy 14–32) 119.05 (Rwy 16L–34R) 132.65 (Rwy 16R–34L)
GND CON 121.9 (Rwy 17–35 and Rwy 14–32) 123.775 (Rwy 16R–34L and Rwy 16L–34R) **CLNC DEL** 127.3
PRE–TAXI CLNC 127.3 **PRE–DEP CLNC** 127.3

AIRSPACE: CLASS B See VFR Terminal Area Chart

CONTINUED ON NEXT PAGE

Figure 189. Excerpt from Chart Supplement.

CONTINUED FROM PRECEDING PAGE

VOR TEST FACILITY (VOT) 111.0
RADIO AIDS TO NAVIGATION: NOTAM FILE SLC.
WASATCH (H) VORTACW 116.8 TCH Chan 115 N40°51.02′ W111°58.91′ 161° 3.7 NM to fld. 4220/16E.
VOR portion unusable:
015°–030° blo 26,000′
030°–050° byd 20 NM
050°–085° byd 20 NM blo 18,000′
085°–125° byd 30 NM blo 15,000′
360°–015° byd 20 NM blo 17,000′
DME unusable:
030°–080° byd 17 NM blo 17,000′
030°–080° byd 25 NM
080°–140° byd 17 NM blo 15,000′
080°–140° byd 25 NM
185°–220° byd 25 NM blo 16,000′
260°–290° byd 25 NM blo 11,000′
350°–360° byd 30 NM blo 16,000′
360°–030° byd 17 NM blo 16,000′
360°–030° byd 30 NM
TACAN AZIMUTH unusable:
030°–140°
ILS/DME 109.5 I–MOY Chan 32 Rwy 16L. DME also serves ILS Rwy 34R.
ILS/DME 111.9 I–UAT Chan 56 Rwy 16R. Class IIIE. DME also serves ILS Rwy 34L.
ILS/DME 111.5 I–BNT Chan 52 Rwy 17. Class – IE. DME also serves ILS Rwy 35.
ILS/DME 111.9 I–UUH Chan 56 Rwy 34L. Class IIIE. DME also serves ILS Rwy 16R.
ILS/DME 109.5 I–SLC Chan 32 Rwy 34R. Class IIIE. DME also serves ILS Rwy 16L.
ILS/DME 111.5 I–UTJ Chan 52 Rwy 35. DME service provided by ILS Rwy 17.

• • • • • • • • • • • • • • • • • •

HELIPAD HB: H60X60 (ASPH)
HELIPAD HF: H60X60 (ASPH)
HELIPORT REMARKS: Helipads B and F located on general aviation aprons. Lighted pole 51′ AGL 383′ ESE of Helipad B.

SOUTH VALLEY RGNL (U42) P (ARNG) 7 SW UTC–7(–6DT) N40°37.17′ W111°59.57′ **SALT LAKE CITY**
4606 B S4 **FUEL** 100LL, JET A OX 1 TPA—5406(800) NOTAM FILE CDC **H–3D, L–9C, 11D**
RWY 16–34: H5862X100 (ASPH) S–30, D–43 MIRL **IAP**
RWY 16: REIL. PAPI(P4L)—GA 3.0° TCH 40′. Rgt tfc.
RWY 34: REIL. PAPI(P4L)—GA 3.0° TCH 40′. Road.
AIRPORT REMARKS: Attended 1400–0400Z‡. Flocks of birds on and invof arpt. Use caution for extensive paragliding ops invof point of the mountain. ACTIVATE MIRL Rwy 16–34, REIL Rwy 16 and Rwy 34—CTAF. PAPI Rwy 16 and Rwy 34 opr continuously.
AIRPORT MANAGER: 801-575-2401
WEATHER DATA SOURCES: AWOS–3 134.425 (801) 562–0271. addl phone 801–566–2084.
COMMUNICATIONS: CTAF/UNICOM 122.7
Ⓡ **SALT LAKE CITY APP/DEP CON** 120.2 124.3
CLNC DEL 127.0
RADIO AIDS TO NAVIGATION: NOTAM FILE SLC.
WASATCH (H) VORTACW 116.8 TCH Chan 115 N40°51.02′ W111°58.91′ 166° 13.8 NM to fld. 4220/16E.

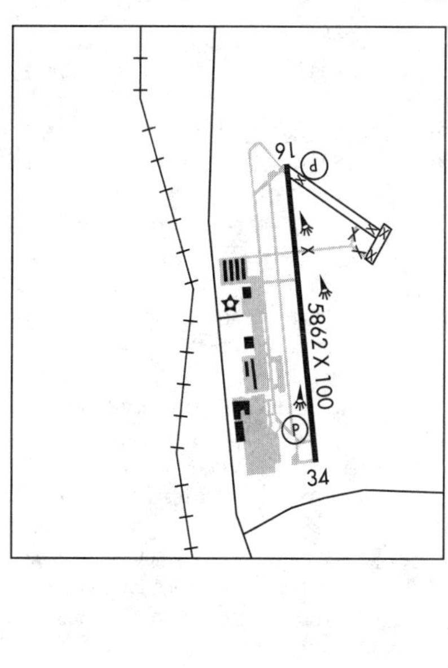

VOR portion unusable:
015°–030° blo 26,000′
030°–050° byd 20 NM
050°–085° byd 20 NM blo 18,000′
085°–125° byd 30 NM blo 15,000′
360°–015° byd 20 NM blo 17,000′
DME unusable:
030°–080° byd 17 NM blo 17,000′
030°–080° byd 25 NM
080°–140° byd 17 NM blo 15,000′
080°–140° byd 25 NM
185°–220° byd 25 NM blo 16,000′
260°–290° byd 25 NM blo 11,000′
350°–360° byd 30 NM blo 16,000′
360°–030° byd 17 NM blo 16,000′
360°–030° byd 30 NM
TACAN AZIMUTH unusable:
030°–140°

Figure 189A. Excerpt from Chart Supplement.

MINNEAPOLIS–ST PAUL INTL/WOLD–CHAMBERLAIN (MSP)(KMSP) P (AFRC ANG N) 6 SW **TWIN CITIES**
UTC–6(–5DT) N44°52.92′ W93°13.31′ **H–2J, L–12J, 14I, A**
842 B S4 **FUEL** 100LL, JET A OX 1, 3 LRA Class I, ARFF Index E NOTAM FILE MSP **IAP, AD**

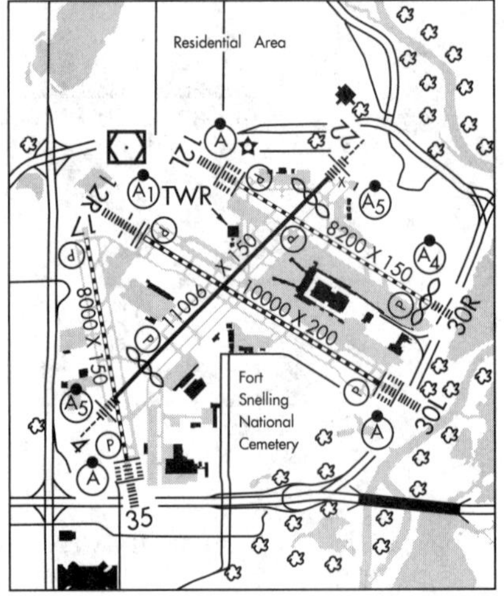

RWY 04–22: H11006X150 (CONC–GRVD) S–100, D–200, 2S–175, 2D–400, 2D/2D2–850 HIRL
RWY 04: MALSR. PAPI(P4L)—GA 3.0° TCH 76′. Thld dsplcd 1550′. Tree.
RWY 22: MALSR. PAPI(P4L)—GA 3.0° TCH 61′. Thld dsplcd 1000′. Tree.
RWY 12R–30L: H10000X200 (CONC–GRVD) S–100, D–200, 2S–175, 2D–400, 2D/2D2–850 HIRL CL
RWY 12R: ALSF1. TDZL. PAPI(P4L)—GA 3.0° TCH 66′. Tree. 0.3% down.
RWY 30L: ALSF2. TDZL. PAPI(P4L)—GA 3.0° TCH 78′. Tree.
RWY 12L–30R: H8200X150 (CONC–GRVD) S–100, D–200, 2S–175, 2D–400, 2D/2D2–850 HIRL CL
RWY 12L: ALSF2. TDZL. PAPI(P4L)—GA 3.0° TCH 79′. Tree. 0.3% down.
RWY 30R: MALSF. PAPI(P4L)—GA 3.0° TCH 71′. Thld dsplcd 200′. Tree.
RWY 17–35: H8000X150 (CONC–GRVD) S–100, D–200, 2S–175, 2D–400, 2D/2D2–850 HIRL CL
RWY 17: REIL. PAPI(P4R)—GA 3.0° TCH 60′. Tree.
RWY 35: ALSF2. TDZL. PAPI(P4L)—GA 3.0° TCH 71′.

LAND AND HOLD–SHORT OPERATIONS

LDG RWY	HOLD–SHORT POINT	AVBL LDG DIST
RWY 22	TWY K	8550
RWY 30L	TWY A9–W9	8150

RUNWAY DECLARED DISTANCE INFORMATION

RWY 04:	TORA–11006	TODA–11006	ASDA–11006	LDA–9456
RWY 12L:	TORA–8200	TODA–8200	ASDA–7620	LDA–7620
RWY 12R:	TORA–10000	TODA–10000	ASDA–10000	LDA–10000
RWY 17:	TORA–8000	TODA–8000	ASDA–8000	LDA–8000
RWY 22:	TORA–11006	TODA–11006	ASDA–11006	LDA–10006
RWY 30L:	TORA–10000	TODA–10000	ASDA–10000	LDA–10000
RWY 30R:	TORA–8200	TODA–8200	ASDA–8200	LDA–8000
RWY 35:	TORA–8000	TODA–8000	ASDA–8000	LDA–8000

ARRESTING GEAR/SYSTEM
RWY 12R: EMAS

MILITARY SERVICE: FUEL A++(Mil), A+ (C612–726–5700) (NC–100LL)

AIRPORT REMARKS: Attended continuously. Birds on and invof arpt. Training flights prohibited. General aviation flights must terminate at the FBO or US Customs unless approved by Airport Manager. All GA acft with less than 20 passengers that need to clear U.S. Customs should ctc 128.95 or 612–726–5700 prior to arr. All unscheduled acft at terminal 2–Humphrey are required to ctc terminal 2 gate ctl on 122.95 or call 612–726–5742 prior to arrival. All group V1 acft wingspan greater than 214′ need to contact airside ops at (612) 726–5111 prior to arrival to obtain (prior permission required) PPR. For noise abatement procedures call 612–726–9411. No stage 1 Category Civil acft, nighttime hrs are 0430–1200Z‡. Complex geometry at Rwy 04 approach end. Rwy 04 departures check compass to verify correct rwy heading. ASDE–X surveillance system in use. Opr transponders with mode C on all twys and rwys. Rwy 04 runway visual range avbl touchdown, rollout. Rwy 22 runway visual range avbl touchdown, rollout. Rwy 12R runway visual range avbl touchdown, midfield, rollout. Rwy 30L runway visual range avbl touchdown, midfield, rollout. Rwy 12L runway visual range avbl touchdown, midfield, rollout. Rwy 30R runway visual range avbl touchdown, midfield, rollout. Rwy 17 runway visual range avbl touchdown, midfield, rollout. Rwy 35 runway visual range avbl touchdown, midfield, rollout. Vehicles parked along south end of Twy S. Rwy status lgts are in operation. Ldg fee. Flight Notification Service (ADCUS) avbl. NOTE: See Special Notices—Intersection Departures During Period Of Darkness, Continuous Power Facilities.

AIRPORT MANAGER: 612–725–6464

WEATHER DATA SOURCES: ASOS (612) 725–0939 LLWAS. TDWR.

COMMUNICATIONS: D–ATIS ARR 135.35 (612) 726–9240 **D–ATIS DEP** 120.8 **UNICOM** 122.95
RCO 122.3 (PRINCETON RADIO)
Ⓡ **APP CON** 119.3 (N and E of arrival rwy and Rwy 17) 126.95 (S or W of arrival rwy and Rwys 04, 12R and 30L) 118.725 (Rwy 35)
TOWER 126.7 (Rwys 12R–30L and 04–22) 123.95 (Rwy 12L–30R) 123.675 (Rwy 17–35)
GND CON 121.9 (S) 121.8 (N) 127.925 (W) **CLNC DEL** 133.2 **GND METERING** 133.57
Ⓡ **DEP CON** 125.75 (N or W of arrival rwy) 124.7 (S or E of arrival rwy) 132.975

AIRSPACE: CLASS B See VFR Terminal Area Chart

Figure 191. Excerpt from Chart Supplement.

CONTINUED FROM PRECEDING PAGE

VOR TEST FACILITY (VOT) 111.0
RADIO AIDS TO NAVIGATION: NOTAM FILE MSP.
(H) VORW/DME 115.3 MSP Chan 100 N44°53.79′ W93°14.19′ 142° 1.1 NM to fld. 833/2E.
VOR portion unusable:
260°–270° blo 4,000′
ILS 109.3 I–APL Rwy 04. Glideslope unusable for coupled apchs blo 1,085′. LOC unusable byd 25° left and r of course.
ILS/DME 110.7 I–PJL Chan 44 Rwy 12L. Class III/E. DME also serves Rwy 30R. DME unusable byd 20° left of course.
ILS/DME 110.3 I–HKZ Chan 40 Rwy 12R. Class III/E. DME unusable byd 25° right of course.
LOC/DME 110.95 I–TJZ Chan 46(Y) Rwy 17.
LOC 110.5 I–SIJ Rwy 22.
ILS/DME 110.3 I–MSP Chan 40 Rwy 30L. Class IIE.
ILS/DME 110.7 I–INN Chan 44 Rwy 30R. Class IE.
ILS/DME 110.95 I–BMA Chan 46(Y) Rwy 35. Class IIIE.

MONTEVIDEO–CHIPPEWA CO (MVE)(KMVE) 2 N UTC–6(–5DT) N44°58.15′ W95°42.62′ **TWIN CITIES**
1035 B S4 **FUEL** 100LL NOTAM FILE MVE **L–12I, 14H**
RWY 14–32: H3995X75 (ASPH) S–14, D–18 MIRL 0.4% up NW **IAP**
RWY 14: REIL. PAPI(P4L)—GA 3.0° TCH 25′.
RWY 32: REIL. PAPI(P4L)—GA 3.0° TCH 25′.
RWY 03–21: 2385X165 (TURF) 0.5% up SW
AIRPORT REMARKS: Attended Mon–Sat 1400–2230Z‡, Sun 1900–2230Z‡. Fuel self serve, after hrs call 320–226–1483. Ultralights on and invof arpt. Rwy 03–21 not plowed winter months. Badger and gopher holes. Rwy 03–21 thlds and edges marked with yellow cones. Rwy 14–32 non frangible cages around REILS. ACTIVATE MIRL Rwy 14–32, REIL and PAPI Rwy 14 and REIL and PAPI Rwy 32—CTAF.
AIRPORT MANAGER: 320–269–4829
WEATHER DATA SOURCES: AWOS–3 111.6 MVE (320) 269–5830.
COMMUNICATIONS: CTAF/UNICOM 122.8
RCO 122.45 (PRINCETON RADIO)
MINNEAPOLIS CENTER APP/DEP CON 125.5
RADIO AIDS TO NAVIGATION: NOTAM FILE MVE.
(T) VORW/DME 111.6 MVE Chan 53 N44°58.36′ W95°42.73′ at fld. 1037/5E. **AWOS–3** VOR/DME unmonitored.

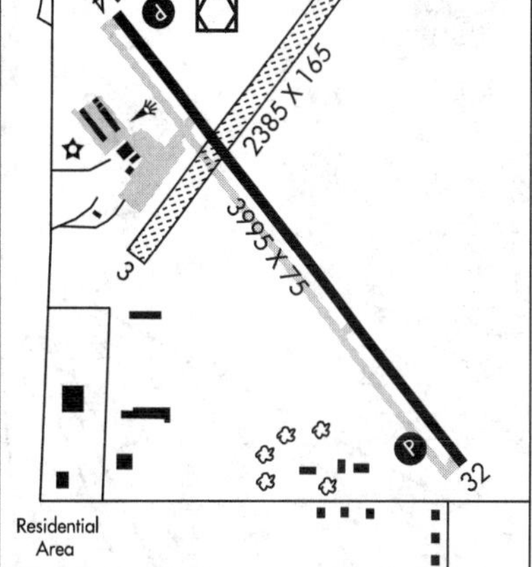

MONTZ N43°34.42′ W94°19.08′ NOTAM FILE FRM. **OMAHA**
NDB (LOM) 420 FQ 311° 6.0 NM to Fairmont Muni.

MOORHEAD MUNI (JKJ)(KJKJ) 4 SE UTC–6(–5DT) N46°50.36′ W96°39.84′ **TWIN CITIES**
918 B S4 **FUEL** 100LL, JET A TPA—1718(800) NOTAM FILE JKJ **L–14G**
RWY 12–30: H4300X75 (ASPH) MIRL **IAP**
RWY 12: REIL. PAPI(P4L)—GA 3.0° TCH 25′.
RWY 30: REIL. PAPI(P4L)—GA 3.0° TCH 25′. Tree.
AIRPORT REMARKS: Attended Mon–Fri 1400–2300Z‡. For svc after hrs call 218–287–1400. Self svc fuel avbl 24 hrs with credit card. Arpt underlies Fargo TRSA, Hector Intl Class D Airspace 3 miles NW of arpt. Noise abatement procedures in effect, ctc arpt manager 218–287–1400. ACTIVATE MIRL Rwy 12–30, REIL Rwy 12 and Rwy 30 and PAPI Rwy 12 and Rwy 30—CTAF.
AIRPORT MANAGER: 701–552–1865
WEATHER DATA SOURCES: AWOS–3 120.0 (218) 287–5049.
COMMUNICATIONS: CTAF/UNICOM 123.0
FARGO APP/DEP CON 120.4 (1200–0500Z‡)
MINNEAPOLIS CENTER APP/DEP CON 127.35
GCO 121.725 (FARGO APP AND PNM AFSS)
RADIO AIDS TO NAVIGATION: NOTAM FILE FAR.
FARGO (H) VORTACW 116.2 FAR Chan 109 N46°45.20′ W96°51.08′ 047° 9.3 NM to fld. 908/9E. **HIWAS.**
TACAN AZIMUTH unusable:
250°–275°

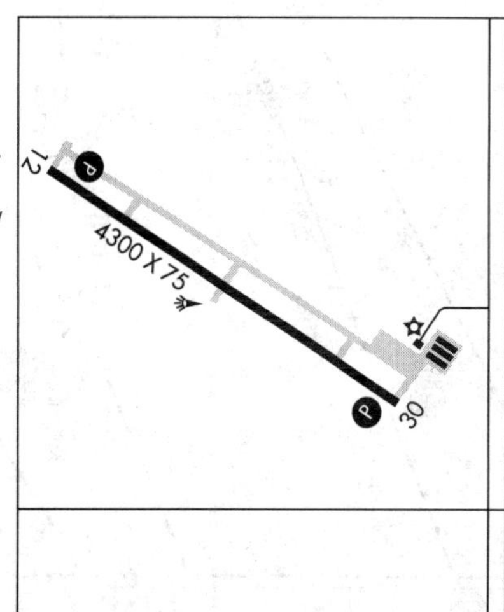

Figure 191A. Excerpt from Chart Supplement.

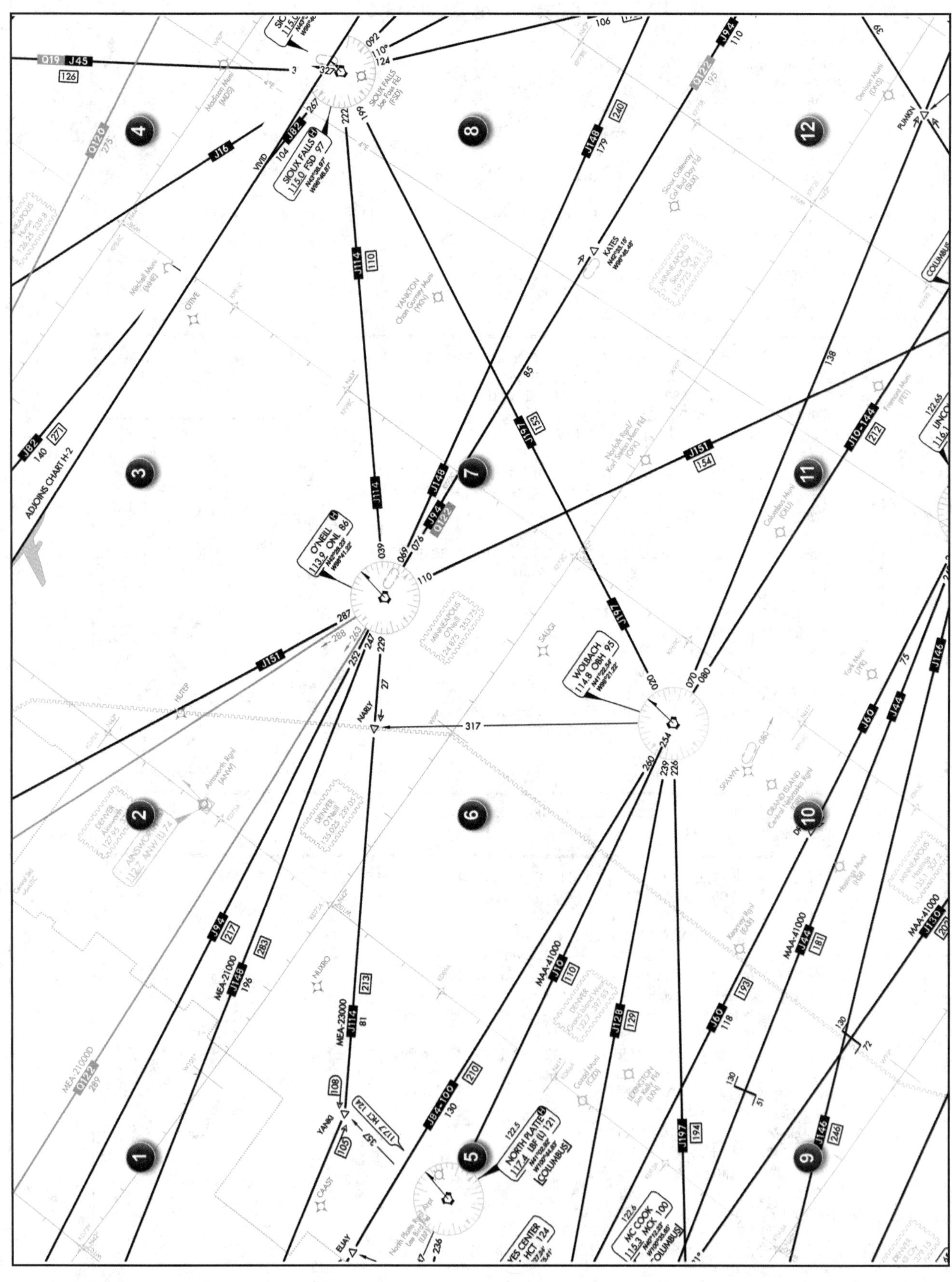

Figure 192. High Altitude Airways.

This page intentionally left blank.

EADS MUNI (9V7) 1 W UTC–7(–6DT) N38°28.51′ W102°48.65′ **WICHITA**
4245 NOTAM FILE DEN **L–10G**
RWY 17–35: H3860X60 (ASPH) MIRL
RWY 17: Road.
RWY 35: Road.
AIRPORT REMARKS: Unattended. Be alert, intensive USAF student training invof Colorado Springs and Pueblo Colorado. Rwy 17 +25′ bldgs 220′ right of centerline 108′ from rwy end. Rwy 17 has +17′ railroad 530′ from thld centerline, –4′ ditch 375′ from thld centerline. Apron area is milled asph. Twy and rwy have no markings. See Special Notices USAF 306 FTG Flight Training Areas, Vicinity of Colorado Springs and Pueblo Colorado.
AIRPORT MANAGER: 719-438-5590
COMMUNICATIONS: CTAF 122.9
RADIO AIDS TO NAVIGATION: NOTAM FILE LAA.
LAMAR (H) VORW/DME 116.9 LAA Chan 116 N38°11.83′ W102°41.25′ 329° 17.7 NM to fld. 3944/12E.

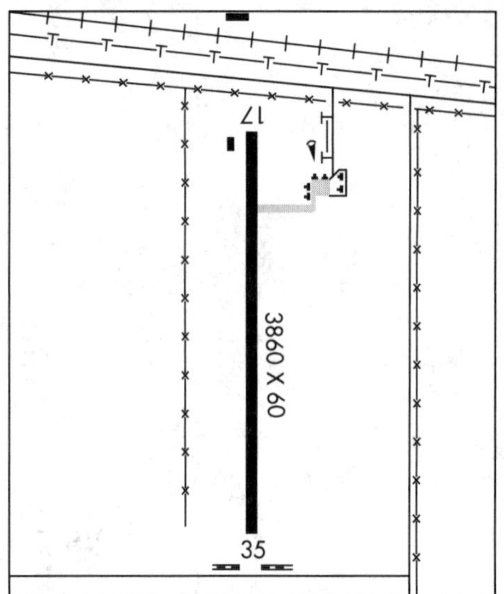

EAGLE CO RGNL (EGE)(KEGE) P (ARNG) 4 W UTC–7(–6DT) N39°38.57′ W106°54.96′ **DENVER**
6547 B S4 **FUEL** 100LL, JET A1, A1+ OX 1, 3 Class I, ARFF Index C NOTAM FILE EGE **H–3E, L–9E**
RWY 07–25: H9000X150 (ASPH–GRVD) S–75, D–140, 2S–175, 2D–255 HIRL **IAP, AD**
RWY 07: REIL. Tree. Rgt tfc. 0.9% up.
RWY 25: MALSR. PAPI(P4R)—GA 3.0° TCH 55′. Thld dsplcd 1000′. 1.0% down.
RUNWAY DECLARED DISTANCE INFORMATION
RWY 07: TORA–9000 TODA–9000 ASDA–9000 LDA–9000
RWY 25: TORA–9000 TODA–9000 ASDA–9000 LDA–8000
MILITARY SERVICE: FUEL A+ (1300–0400Z‡, C970–524–7700, OT $125 per hr.) (NC–100LL, A1, A1+) **FLUID** HPOX–RB
AIRPORT REMARKS: Attended May–Nov 1400–0400Z‡, Dec–Apr 1400–0600Z‡. Unscheduled air carrier operations with more than 30 passenger seats call arpt fire department 970–328–2688. High unmarked terrain all quadrants. Critical acft are Category D IV, B757–200 equivalent and lower. Ngt ops discouraged to pilots unfamiliar with arpt. Recommend all acft departing Rwy 25 initiate a left turn as soon as alt and safety permit to avoid high terrain. Rwy 25 PAPI only visible to 3° left of centerline due to terrain. Extensive military helicopter training ops sfc to 1000′ AGL within 25 NM radius Eagle Co Arpt 1330–0500Z‡. Rwy 07 touchdown runway visual range avbl. Rwy 25 touchdown runway visual range avbl. No snow removal or rwy monitoring between 0600Z‡ and 1300Z‡. Air carrier acft should not leave or enter Twy A east of Twy C–2. For twr hrs ctc ARFF at 970–328–2688. During hrs when twr clsd ACTIVATE HIRL Rwy 07–25, REIL Rwy 07, and MALSR Rwy 25—CTAF. PAPI Rwy 25 operates 24 hrs. U.S. Customs user fee arpt: regular office hrs Thu–Mon 1600–0000Z‡. After hrs svc avbl. Office 970–524–0490. After hrs 303–472–1125. Three hr advance notice required. Ldg fee.
AIRPORT MANAGER: 970-328-2680
WEATHER DATA SOURCES: AWOS–3 135.575 (970) 524–7386.
COMMUNICATIONS: CTAF 119.8 **ATIS** 135.575
RCO 122.2 (DENVER RADIO)
DENVER CENTER APP/DEP CON 128.65
TOWER 119.8 (1400–0200Z‡) **GND CON** 121.8 **CLNC DEL** 124.75
AIRSPACE: CLASS D svc 1400–0200Z‡ other times CLASS E.

Figure 198. Excerpt from Chart Supplement.

COLORADO

CONTINUED FROM PRECEDING PAGE

RADIO AIDS TO NAVIGATION: NOTAM FILE DEN.
SNOW (T) VORW/DME 109.2 SXW Chan 29 N39°37.77′ W106°59.47′ 065° 3.6 NM to fld. 8070/12E.
VOR/DME unmonitored 0600–1300Z‡.
VOR portion unusable:
310°–355°
VOR/DME unusable:
115°–135°
ILS/DME 109.75 I–ESJ Chan 34(Y) Rwy 25. Glideslope unmonitored.
LDA/DME 108.3 I–VAZ Chan 20 Rwy 25. LOC unusable byd 14 NM blo 10,940′. LOC unusable byd 15° left and right of course.

EASTON(VALLEY VIEW) (See GREELEY on page 248)

EMPIRE OCO N39°47.67′ W105°45.78′/12493 — DENVER L–9E
AWOS–3 134.325

ERIE MUNI (EIK)(KEIK) 3 S UTC–7(–6DT) N40°00.62′ W105°02.89′ — CHEYENNE L–10F, A IAP
5119 B S4 **FUEL** 100LL, JET A OX 3, 4 NOTAM FILE DEN
RWY 15–33: H4700X60 (CONC) S–12.5 MIRL 0.9% up S
RWY 15: REIL. PAPI(P2L)—GA 3.0° TCH 58′. Tree. Rgt tfc.
RWY 33: PAPI(P2L)—GA 3.0° TCH 52′. Hill.
AIRPORT REMARKS: Attended Mon–Sat 1500–0000Z‡, Sun 1500–2100Z‡. After hrs emerg ctc 303–870–5659. Self svc credit card fuel avbl 24 hrs. Rwy 15 has –2′ to –6′ ditches within 700′ of rwy end at various locations. Rwy 33 has –6′ to –12′ ditch 60′ left of centerline parallel to first 750′ of rwy. Rwy 33 has 30′ road 1350′ from thld outbound. Rwy 15–33 –2′ terrain 60′ to 70′ E of rwy centerline, full length. ACTIVATE MIRL Rwy 15–33 PAPI Rwy 15 and Rwy 33 and REIL Rwy 15 CTAF.
AIRPORT MANAGER: 303-664-0633
WEATHER DATA SOURCES: AWOS–3 133.825 (303) 604–4339.
COMMUNICATIONS: CTAF/UNICOM 123.0
® **DENVER APP/DEP CON** 126.1
RADIO AIDS TO NAVIGATION: NOTAM FILE BJC.
JEFFCO (H) VORW/DME 115.4 BJC Chan 101 N39°54.78′ W105°08.34′ 025° 7.2 NM to fld. 5737/11E.
VOR portion unusable:
226°–245° byd 36 NM blo 17,000′
246°–278° byd 30 NM blo 19,000′
279°–300° byd 34 NM blo 18,000′
DME unusable:
246°–278° byd 30 NM

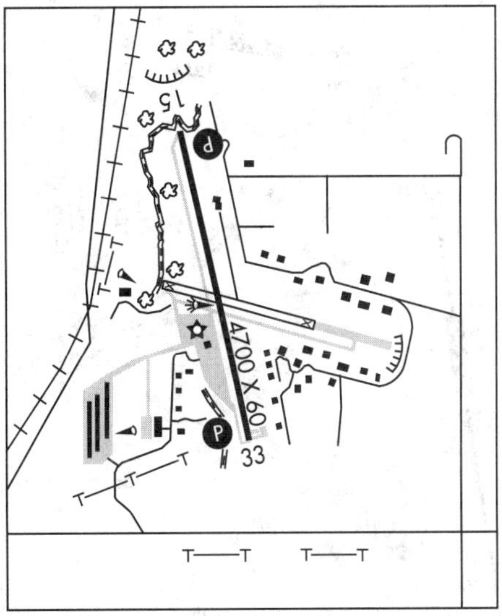

FALCON N39°41.41′ W104°37.26′ NOTAM FILE DEN. — DENVER H–3F, 5A, L–10G, A
(H) VORTACW 116.3 FQF Chan 110 225° 12.8 NM to Centennial. 5780/11E.
TACAN & DME unusable:
068°–088° byd 10 NM blo 11,500′

FORT COLLINS–LOVELAND MUNI (See FORT COLLINS/LOVELAND on page 246)

Figure 198A. Excerpt from Chart Supplement.

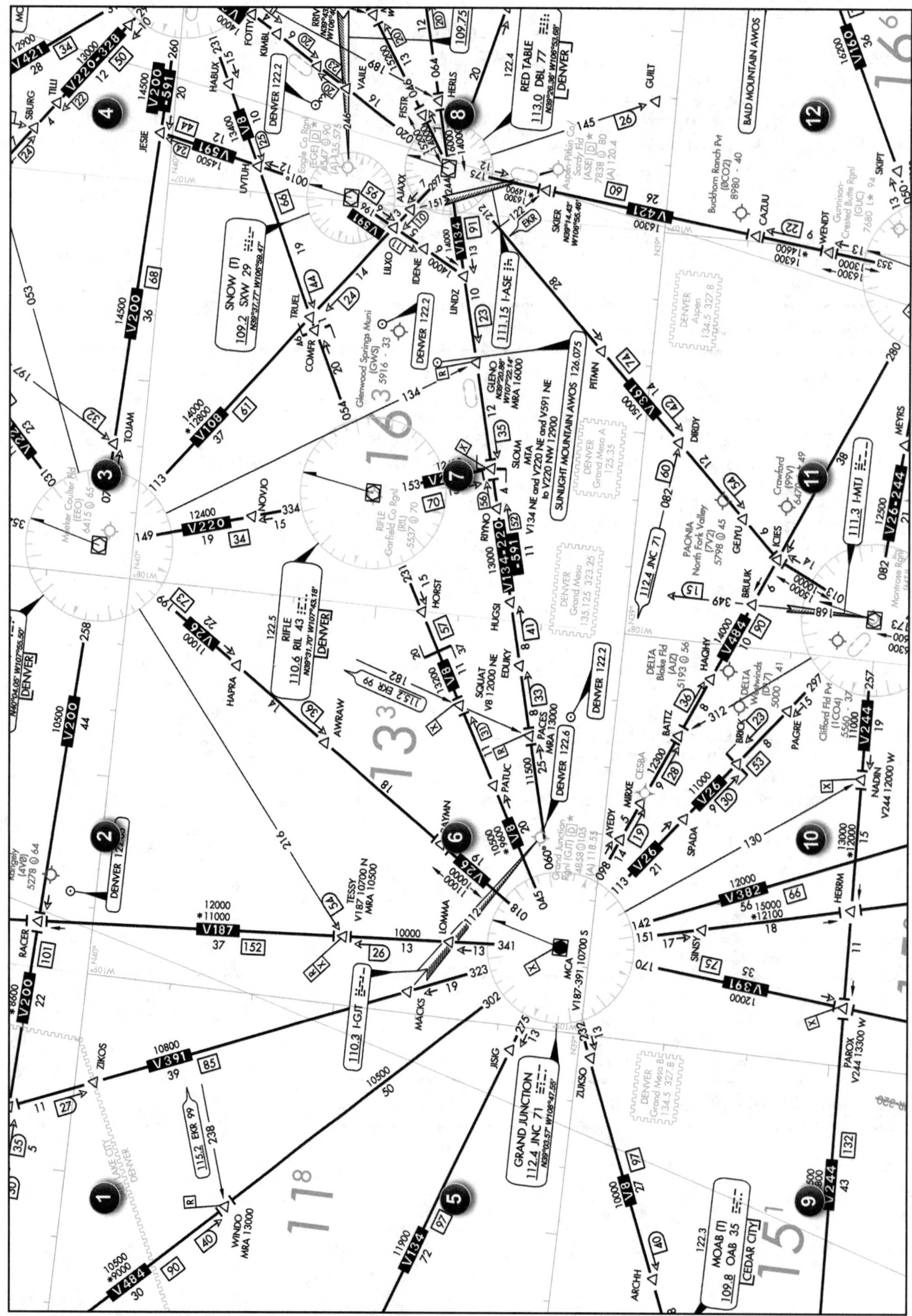

Figure 199. Low Altitude Airways.

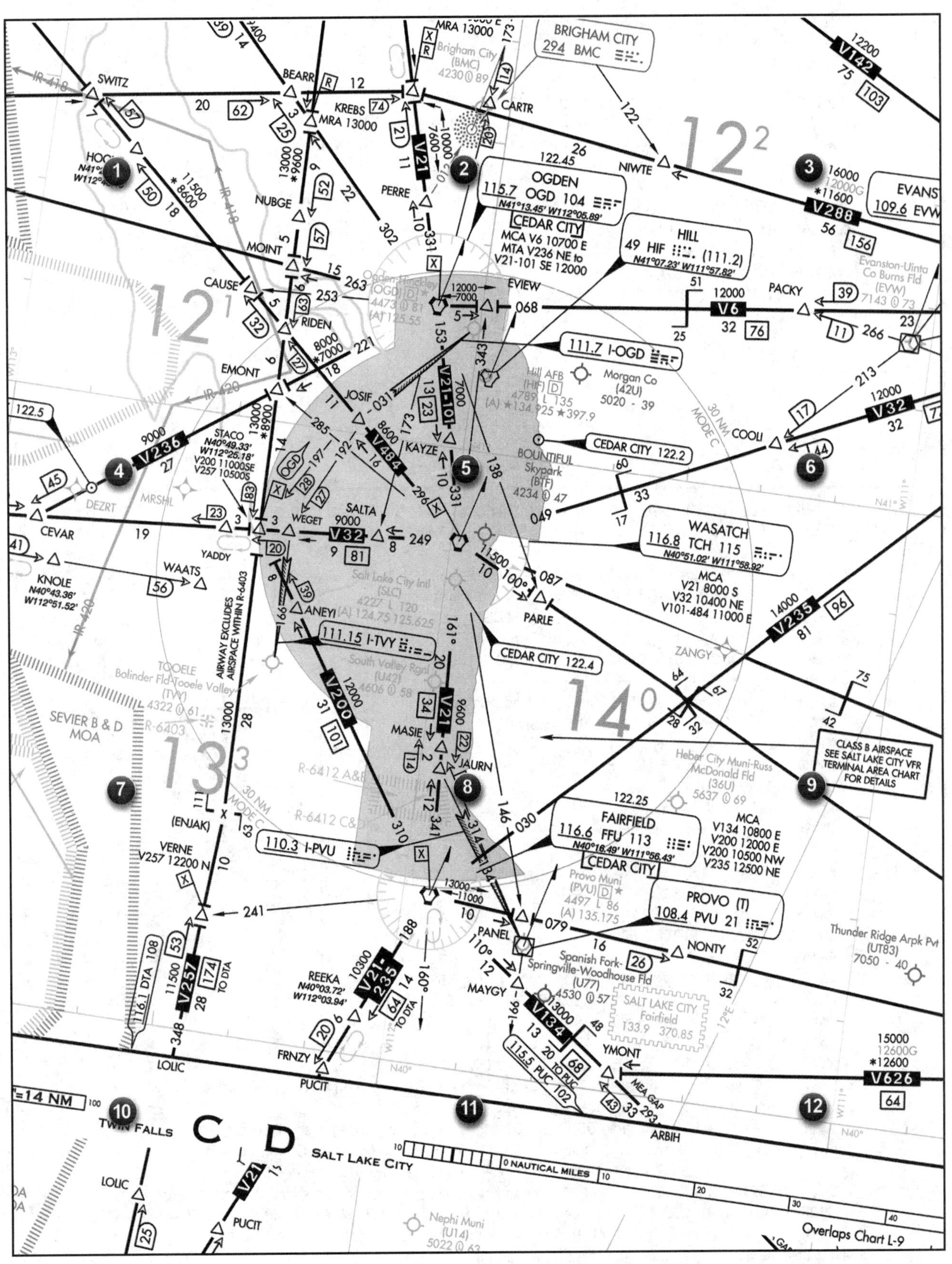

Figure 200. Low Altitude Airways.

NEPHI MUNI (U14) 3 NW UTC–7(–6DT) N39°44.20′ W111°52.20′ **LAS VEGAS**
5022 B **FUEL** 100LL, JET A NOTAM FILE CDC **H–3D, L–9C**
RWY 17–35: H6300X100 (ASPH) S–21, D–30 MIRL 0.6% up S **IAP**
RWY 17: REIL. PAPI(P2L)—GA 3.0° TCH 40′.
RWY 35: REIL. PAPI(P2L)—GA 3.0° TCH 40′.
AIRPORT REMARKS: Unattended. Fuel avbl 24 hrs, self svc credit card system. ACTIVATE MIRL Rwy 17–35, PAPI Rwy 17 and Rwy 35, and REIL Rwy 17 and Rwy 35—CTAF.
AIRPORT MANAGER: 435-623-0822
WEATHER DATA SOURCES: AWOS–3 118.275 (435) 623–1397.
COMMUNICATIONS: CTAF/UNICOM 122.8
Ⓡ **SALT LAKE CENTER APP/DEP CON** 127.825
RADIO AIDS TO NAVIGATION: NOTAM FILE PVU.
PROVO (T) VORW/DME 108.4 PVU Chan 21 N40°12.90′ W111°43.28′ 179° 29.5 NM to fld. 4493/15E.
VOR/DME unusable:
350°–080° byd 10 NM

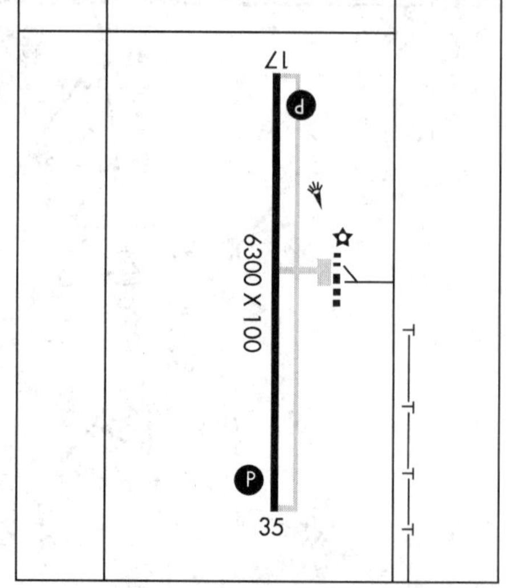

OGDEN–HINCKLEY (OGD)(KOGD) 3 SW UTC–7(–6DT) N41°11.74′ W112°00.78′ **SALT LAKE CITY**
4473 B S4 **FUEL** 100, JET A1+ OX 1, 2 TPA—See Remarks Class I, ARFF Index B **H–3D, L–9C, 11D**
NOTAM FILE OGD **IAP, AD**
RWY 03–21: H8103X150 (ASPH–GRVD) S–85, D–150, 2S–152 HIRL
RWY 03: MALS. PAPI(P4L)—GA 3.0° TCH 56′. Trees. 0.8% down.
RWY 21: PAPI(P4L)—GA 3.0° TCH 50′. Thld dsplcd 851′. Pole. Rgt tfc. 0.6% up.
RWY 16–34: H5195X100 (ASPH–GRVD) S–80, D–140 PCN 63 F/A/X/T MIRL 0.4% up S
RWY 16: REIL. PAPI(P4L)—GA 3.0° TCH 50′. Road. Rgt tfc.
RWY 34: REIL. PAPI(P4L)—GA 3.0° TCH 50′. Sign.
RWY 07–25: H3618X150 (ASPH) S–12.5 0.4% up W
RWY 07: VASI(V4L)—GA 3.5° TCH 50′.
RWY 25: Rgt tfc.

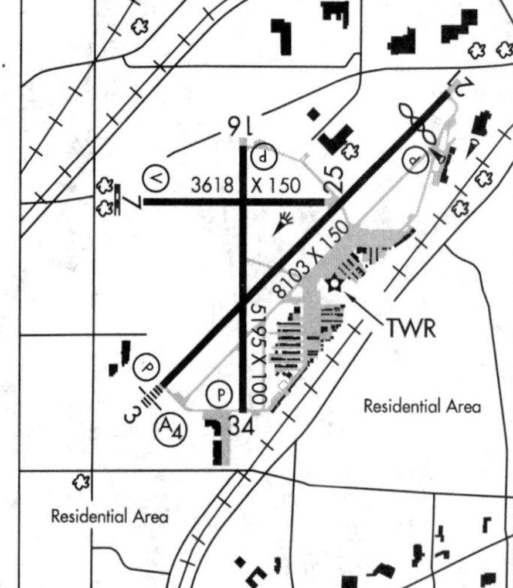

LAND AND HOLD–SHORT OPERATIONS

LDG RWY	HOLD–SHORT POINT	AVBL LDG DIST
RWY 03	07–25	4700
RWY 07	03–21	3500
RWY 21	16–34	4600
RWY 34	07–25	3880

RUNWAY DECLARED DISTANCE INFORMATION

RWY 03:	TORA–8103	TODA–8103	ASDA–7252	LDA–7252
RWY 07:	TORA–3618	TODA–3618	ASDA–3618	LDA–3618
RWY 16:	TORA–5195	TODA–5195	ASDA–5195	LDA–5195
RWY 21:	TORA–8103	TODA–8103	ASDA–8103	LDA–7252
RWY 25:	TORA–3618	TODA–3618	ASDA–3618	LDA–3618
RWY 34:	TORA–5195	TODA–5195	ASDA–5195	LDA–5195

AIRPORT REMARKS: Attended continuously. Parachute jumping on NE portion of arpt east of Twy A. No multiple approaches. Heavy volume of Military acft flying over Ogden Arpt at 5700′–6300′ MSL enroute to Hill AFB. No practice approaches—full stop ldgs only from 0500–1400Z‡. Rwy 07–25 numerous large and deep cracks, break–outs and ravelling. Rwy 07–25 massive crack–sealing has obliterated much of the marking. CLOSED to acft ops with more than 30 passenger seats except PPR, minimum 60 min notice required, call arpt manager 801–629–8223/336–7459/710–3706. No snow removal after twr closes. Arpt sfc condition unmonitored 0300–1400Z‡. TPA—5200(727) rqr due to interfacing tfc from Hill AFB. When twr clsd ACTIVATE HIRL Rwy 03–21, MIRL Rwy 16–34 and twy lgts—CTAF. Rwy 07–25 not avbl when twr clsd.
AIRPORT MANAGER: 801-629-8223
WEATHER DATA SOURCES: ASOS (801) 622–5600

Figure 201. Excerpt from Chart Supplement.

CONTINUED FROM PRECEDING PAGE

COMMUNICATIONS: CTAF 118.7 **ATIS** 125.55 **UNICOM** 122.95
RCO 122.45 (CEDAR CITY RADIO)
®**SALT LAKE CITY APP/DEP CON** 121.1
TOWER 118.7 (1400–0300Z‡) **GND CON** 121.7
AIRSPACE: CLASS D svc 1400–0300Z‡ other times CLASS E.
RADIO AIDS TO NAVIGATION: NOTAM FILE OGD.
(L) VORTACW 115.7 OGD Chan 104 N41°13.45′ W112°05.89′ 100° 4.2 NM to fld. 4223/14E.
VOR portion unusable:
030°–070° byd 25 NM blo 17,000′
070°–130° byd 15 NM
355°–030° byd 15 NM
TACAN and DME unusable:
255°–280° byd 30 NM blo 11,000′
355°–130° byd 15 NM
ILS/DME 111.7 I–OGD Chan 54 Rwy 03. Class IT. ILS/DME unmonitored when ATCT closed.
COMM/NAV/WEATHER REMARKS: Emerg frequency 121.5 not avbl at twr.

PANGUITCH MUNI (U55) 3 NE UTC–7(–6DT) N37°50.71′ W112°23.52′ — **LAS VEGAS H–3D, L–9C IAP**
6763 B S2 NOTAM FILE CDC
RWY 18–36: H5700X75 (ASPH) S–20 MIRL
RWY 18: PAPI(P2L)—GA 3.0° TCH 40′.
RWY 36: PAPI(P2L)—GA 3.0° TCH 40′.
AIRPORT REMARKS: Unattended. Antelope on and in vicinity of arpt during summer months. ACTIVATE MIRL Rwy 18–36 and PAPI Rwy 18 and Rwy 36—CTAF.
AIRPORT MANAGER: 435-676-8585
WEATHER DATA SOURCES: AWOS–3 133.125 (435) 676–8784.
COMMUNICATIONS: CTAF 122.9
®**SALT LAKE CENTER APP/DEP CON** 133.6
RADIO AIDS TO NAVIGATION: NOTAM FILE BCE.
BRYCE CANYON (H) VORTACW 112.8 BCE Chan 75 N37°41.35′ W112°18.23′ 321° 10.2 NM to fld. 9040/15E.

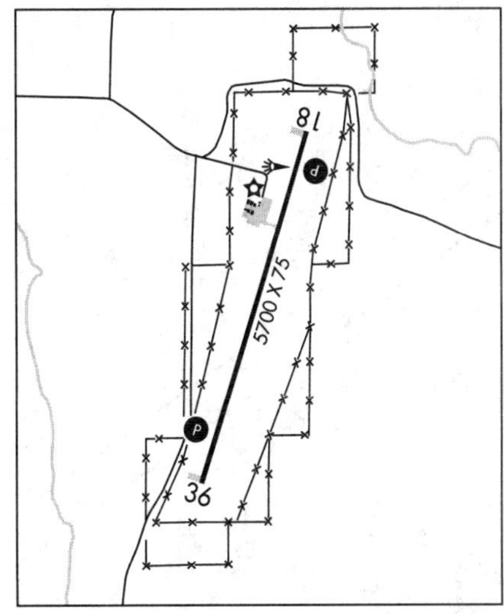

PAROWAN (1L9) 1 NE UTC–7(–6DT) N37°51.58′ W112°48.95′ — **LAS VEGAS H–3D, L–9C**
5930 B S3 **FUEL** 100LL, JET A OX 1, 2, 4 NOTAM FILE CDC
RWY 04–22: H5000X75 (ASPH) S–12.5 MIRL 1.3% up SW
RWY 04: REIL. PAPI(P2L)—GA 3.0° TCH 40′. Fence.
RWY 22: REIL. PAPI(P2L)—GA 3.0° TCH 40′. Road. Rgt tfc.
AIRPORT REMARKS: Attended 1500–0000Z‡. Prairie dog mounds and holes on rwy edges and twy. REIL Rwy 04 OTS indef. ACTIVATE MIRL Rwy 04–22, PAPI Rwy 04 and PAPI Rwy 22, REIL Rwy 04 and REIL Rwy 22—CTAF.
AIRPORT MANAGER: 435-477-8911
COMMUNICATIONS: CTAF/UNICOM 122.8
RADIO AIDS TO NAVIGATION: NOTAM FILE CDC.
CEDAR CITY (H) VORW/DME 117.3 CDC Chan 120 N37°47.24′ W113°04.09′ 054° 12.8 NM to fld. 5464/16E.
VOR/DME unusable:
060°–100° byd 20 NM
100°–135° byd 15 NM
135°–175° byd 20 NM
215°–255° byd 35 NM blo 10,500′

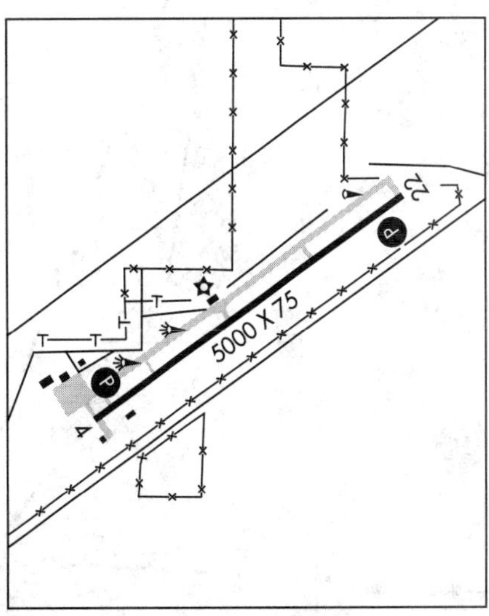

Figure 201A. Excerpt from Chart Supplement.

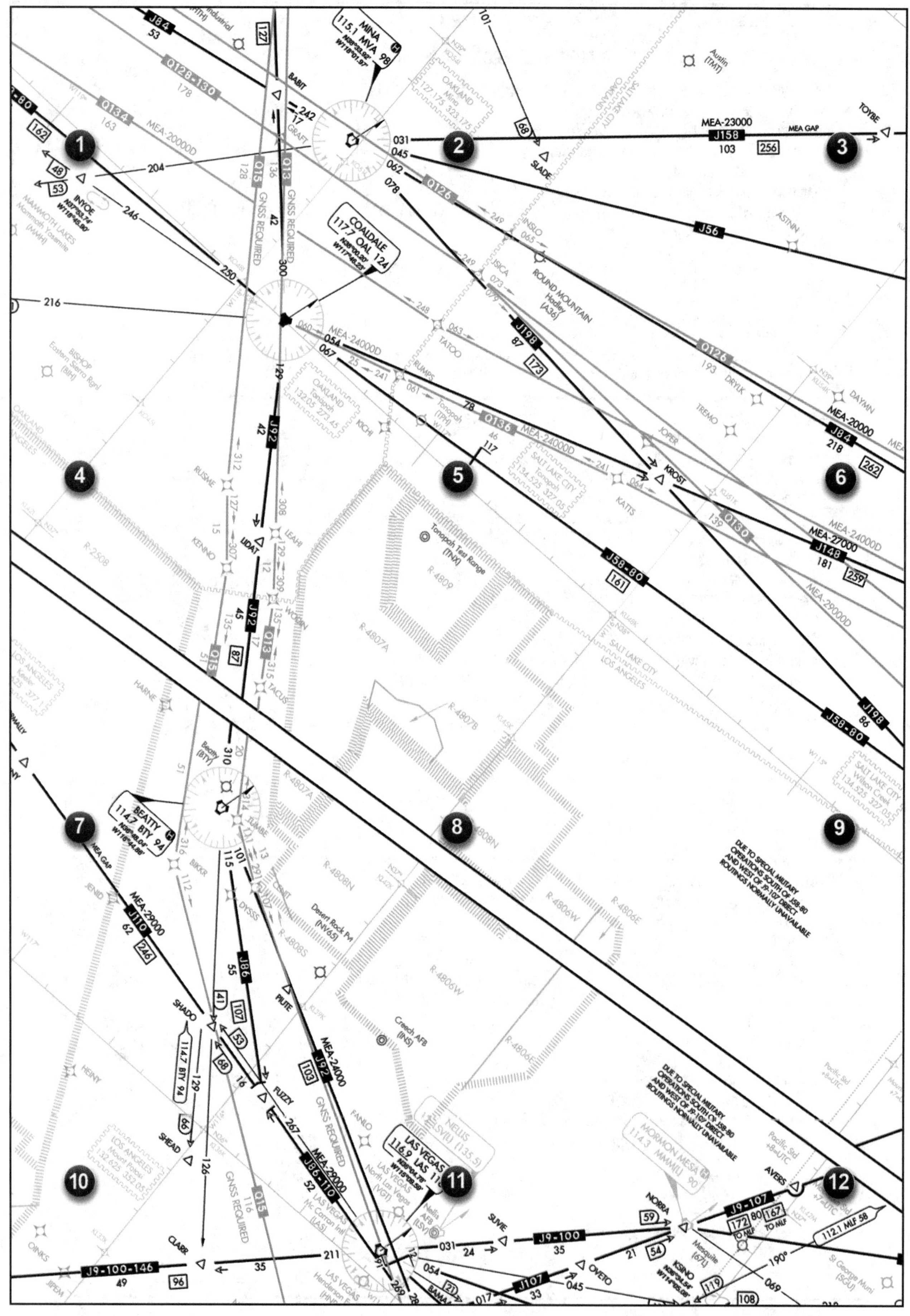

Figure 204. High Altitude Airways.

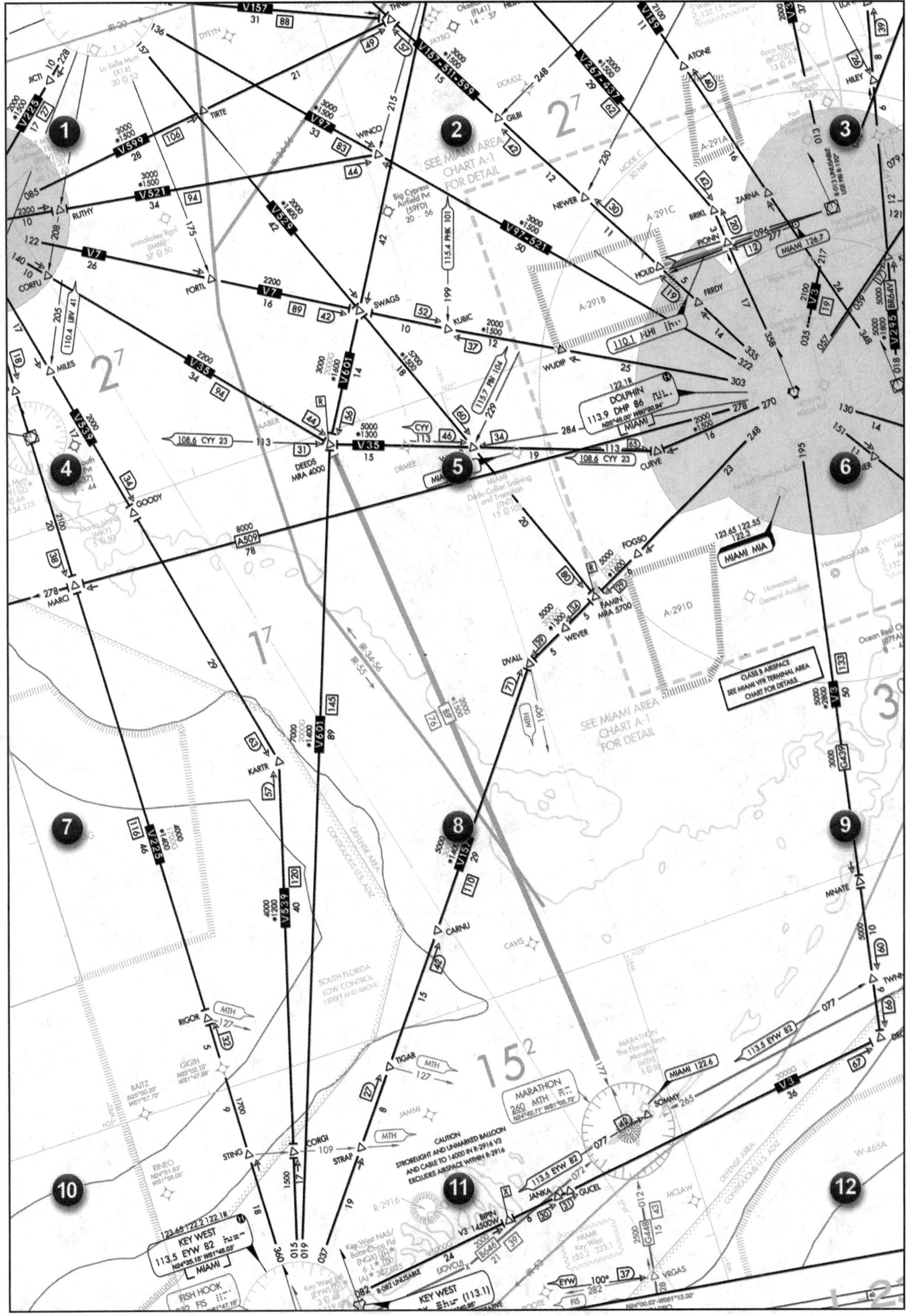

Figure 210. Low Altitude Airways.

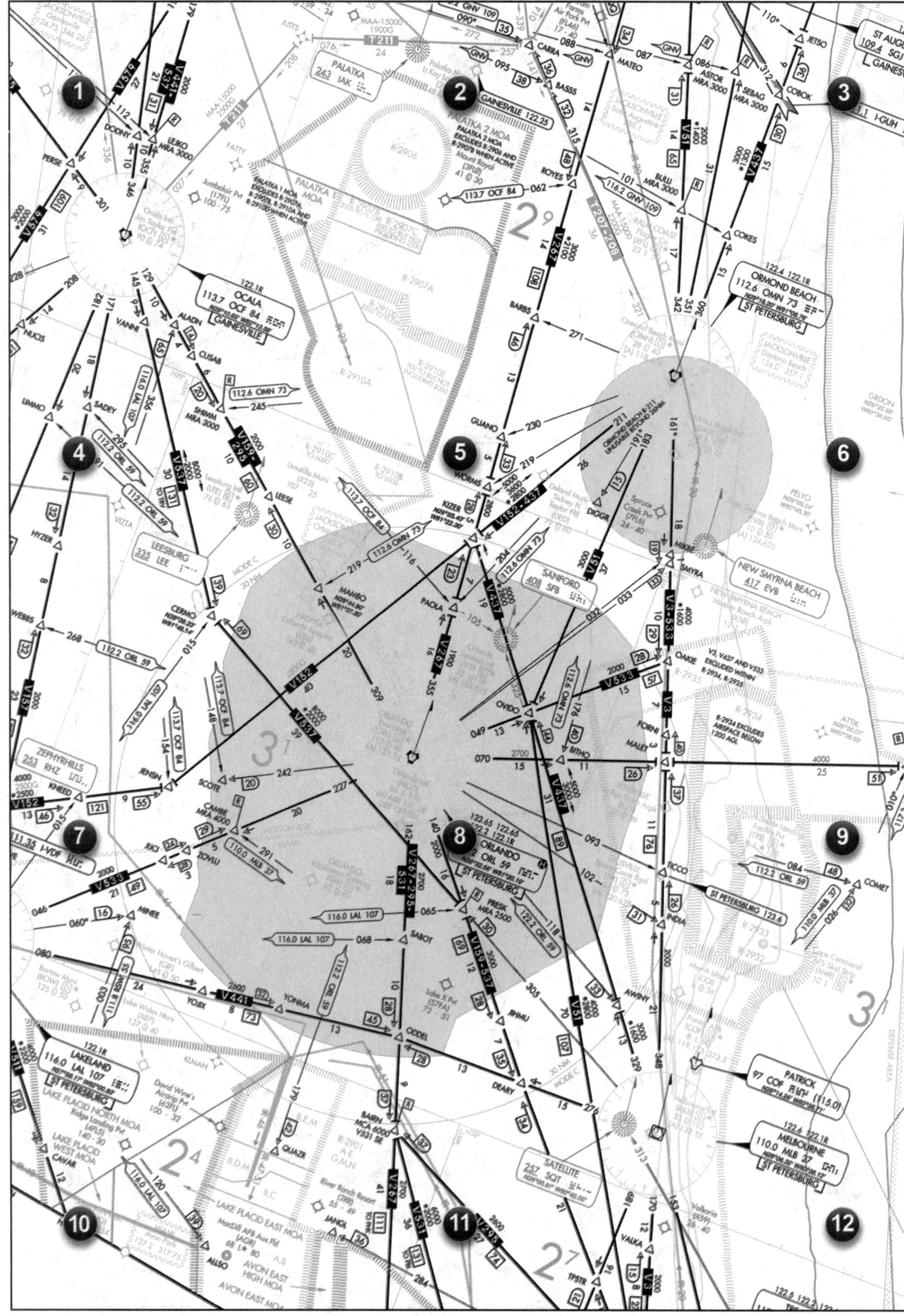

Figure 211. Low Altitude Airways.

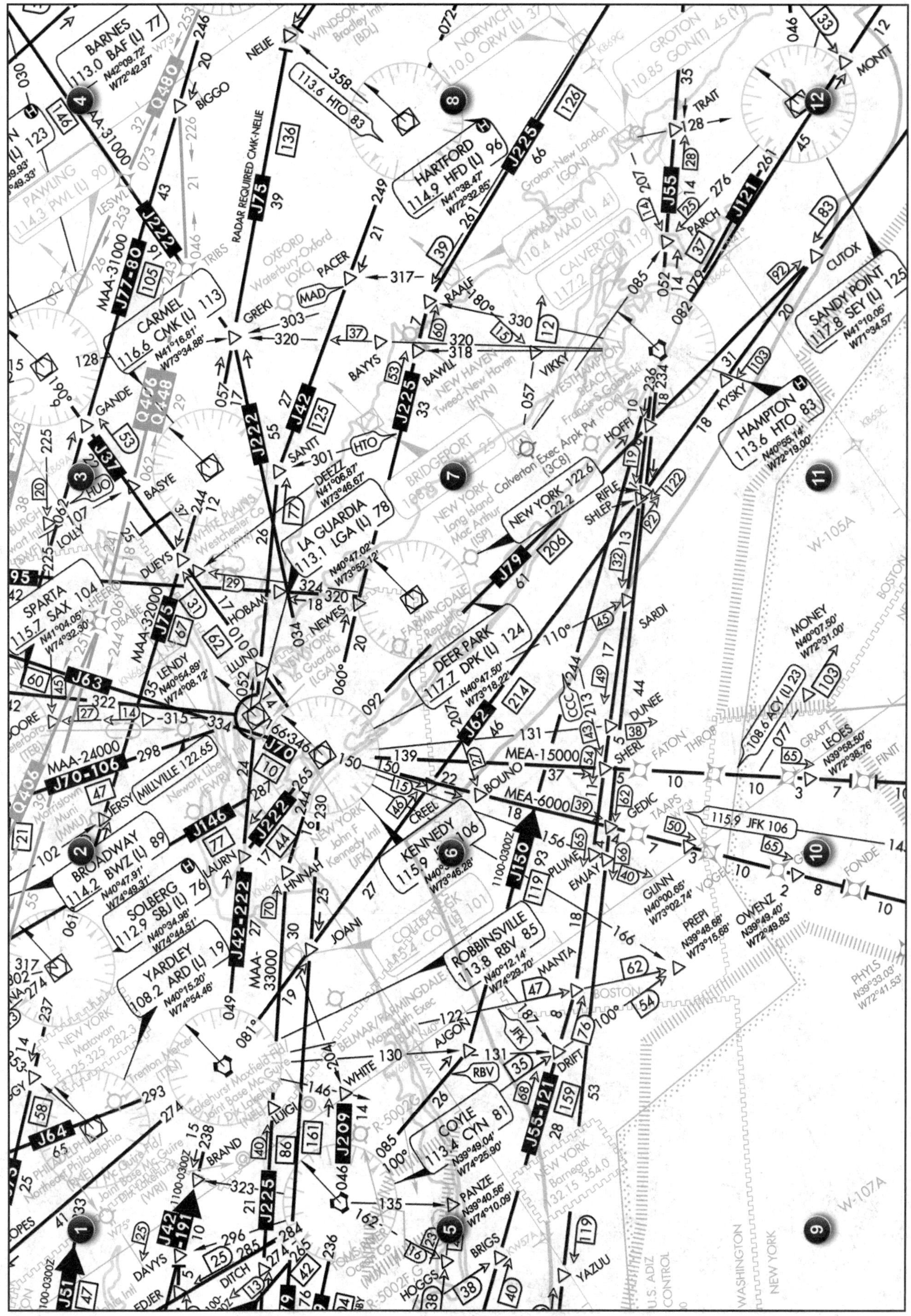

Figure 217. High Altitude Airways.

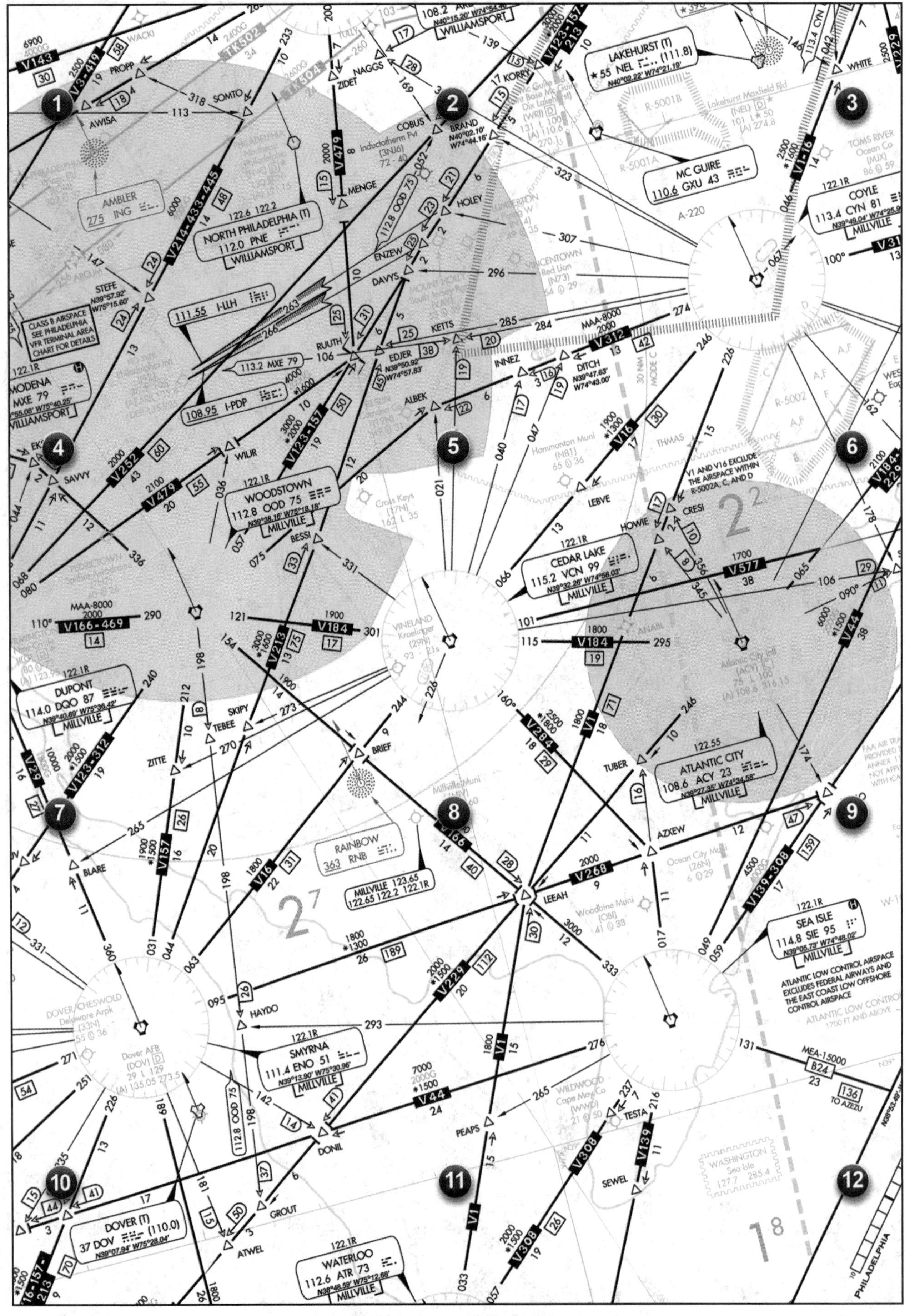

Figure 218. Low Altitude Airways.

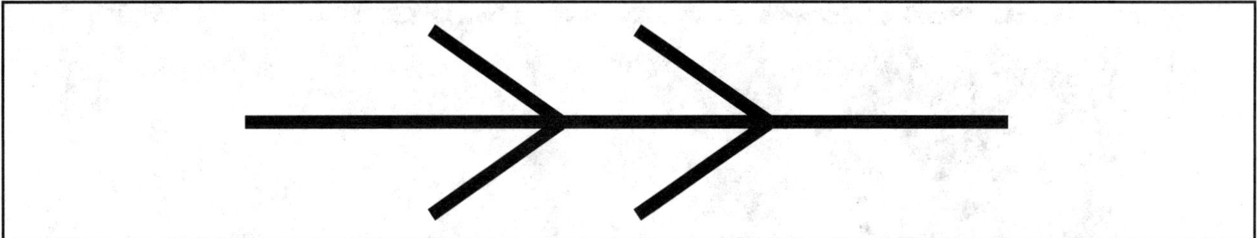

Figure 219. Chart and Navigation Symbol.

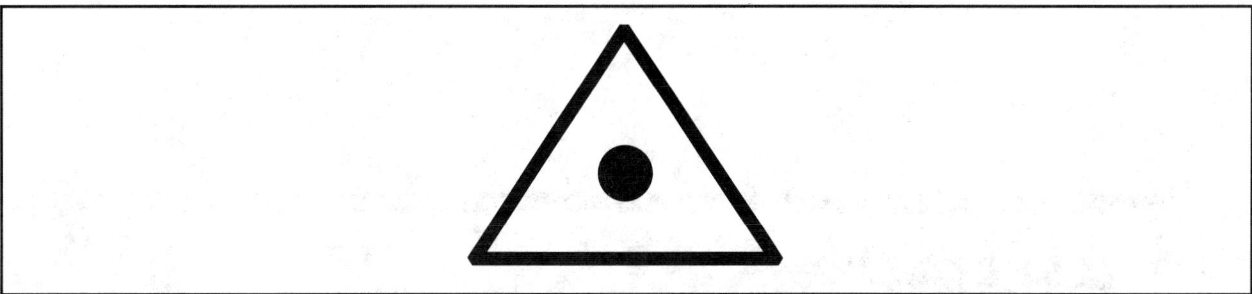

Figure 220. Chart and Navigation Symbol.

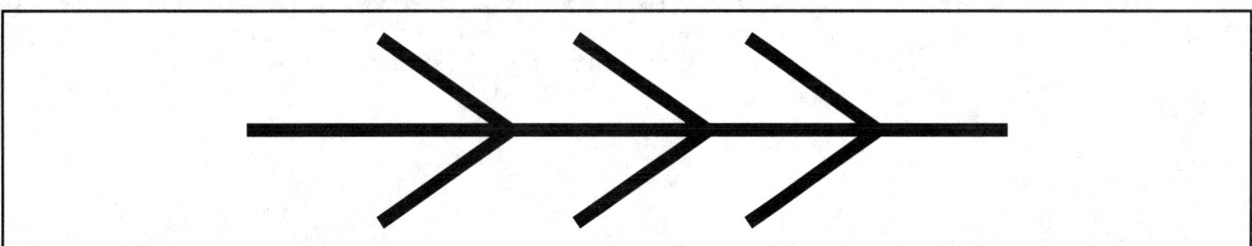

Figure 221. Chart and Navigation Symbol.

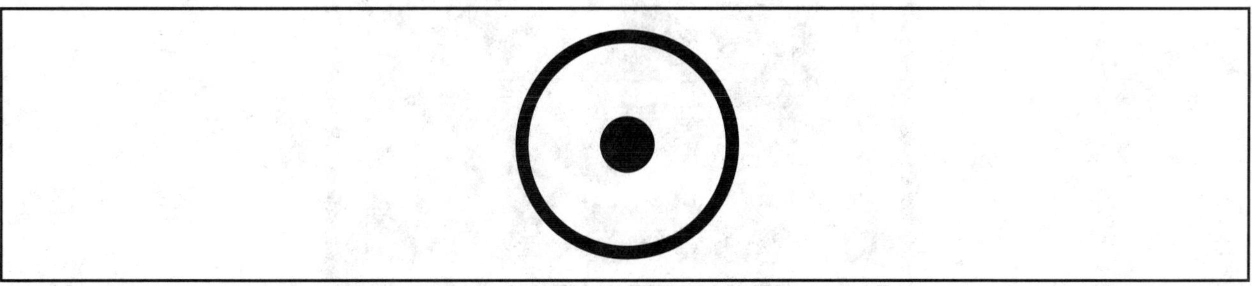

Figure 222. Chart and Navigation Symbol.

Figure 223. Airport Sign and Marking.

Figure 224. Airport Sign and Marking.

Figure 225. Airport Sign.

Figure 226. Airport Sign.

Figure 227. Airport Sign.

Figure 228. Airport Sign.

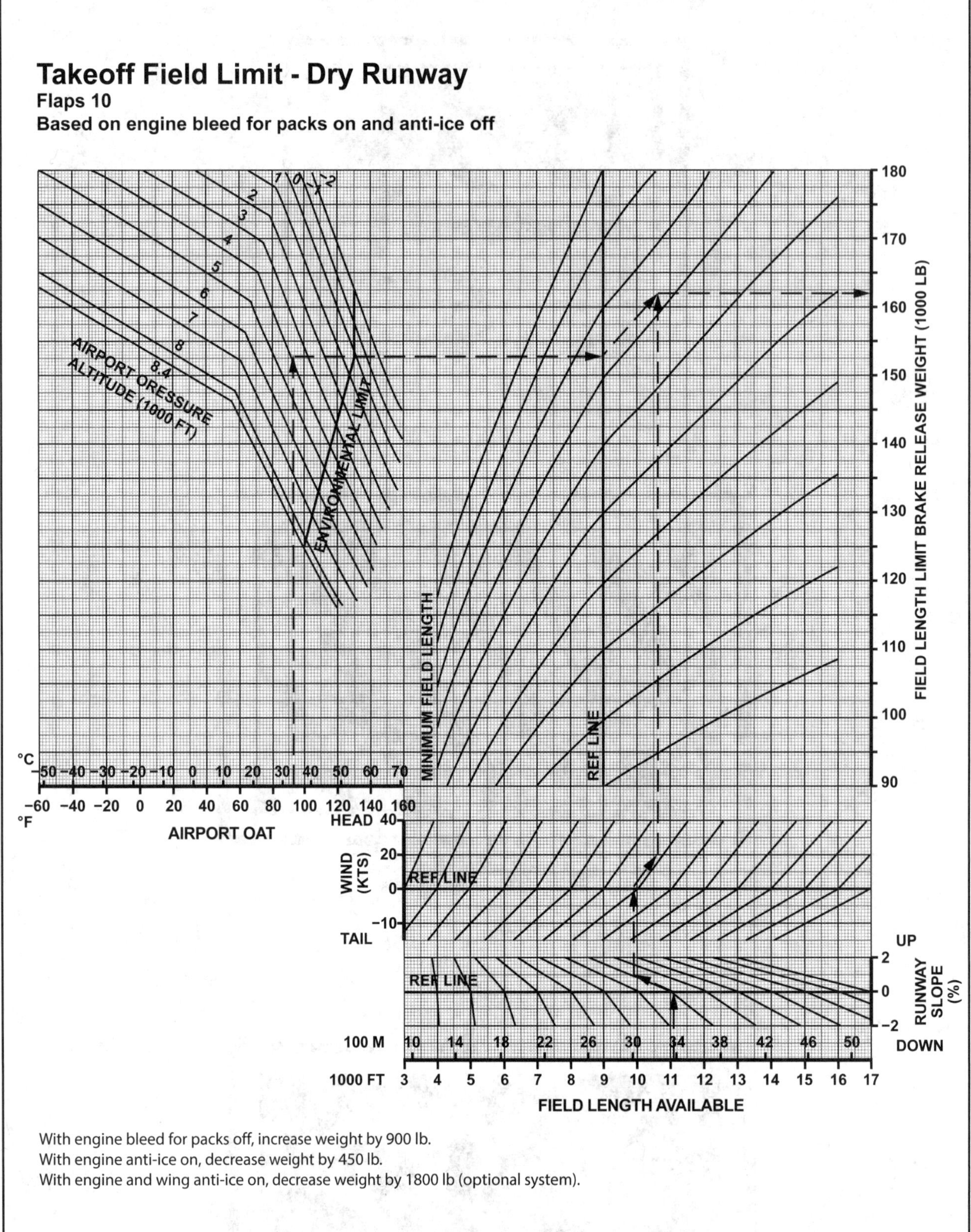

Takeoff Field Limit - Dry Runway
Flaps 10
Based on engine bleed for packs on and anti-ice off
AIRPORT ORESSURE ALTITUDE (1000 FT)
ENVIRONMENTAL LIMIT
MINIMUM FIELD LENGTH
REF LINE
FIELD LENGTH LIMIT BRAKE RELEASE WEIGHT (1000 LB)
°C
°F
AIRPORT OAT
HEAD
TAIL
WIND (KTS)
UP
DOWN
RUNWAY SLOPE (%)
100 M
1000 FT
FIELD LENGTH AVAILABLE
With engine bleed for packs off, increase weight by 900 lb.
With engine anti-ice on, decrease weight by 450 lb.
With engine and wing anti-ice on, decrease weight by 1800 lb (optional system).

Figure 229. Takeoff Field Limit—Dry Runway.

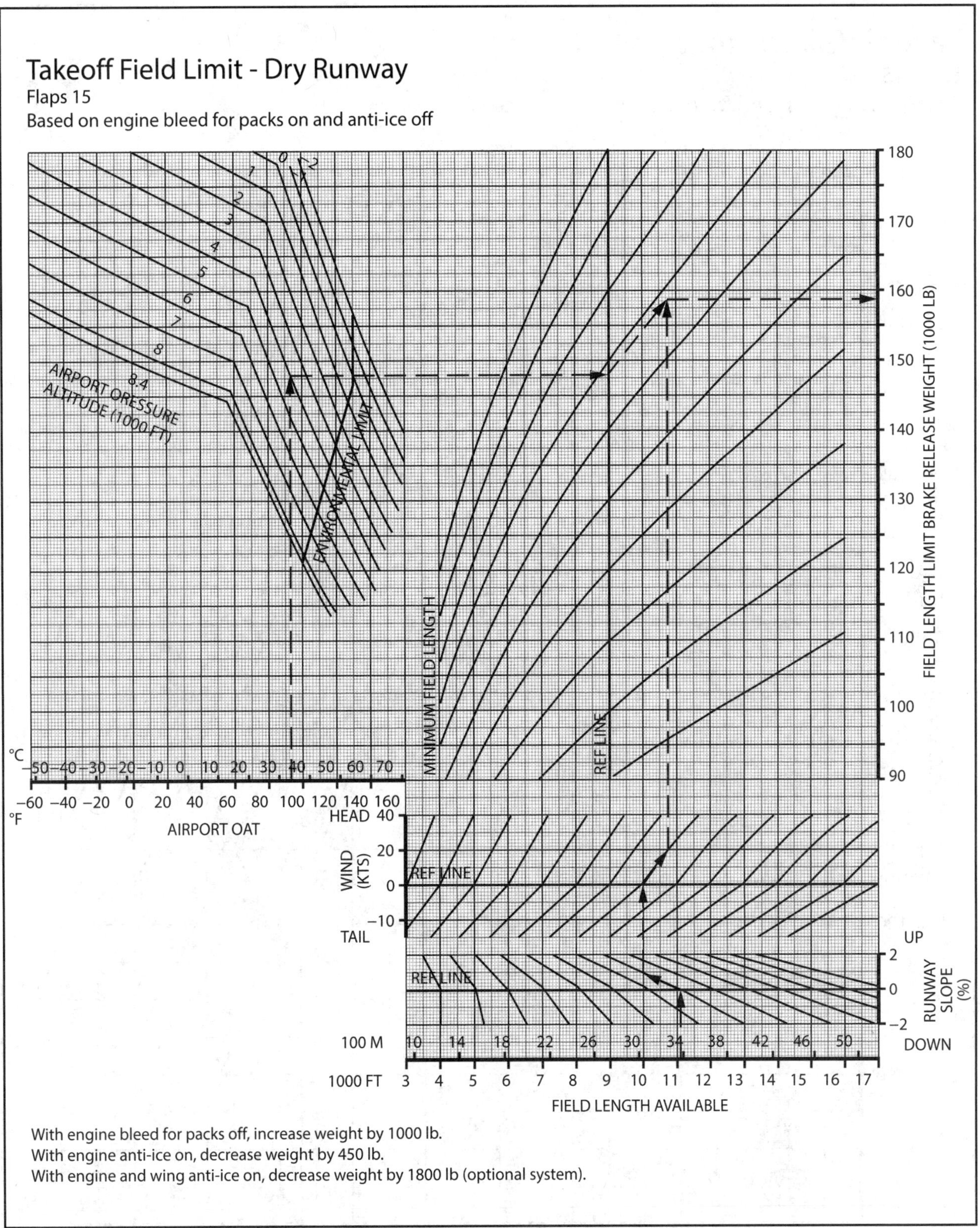

Figure 230. Takeoff Field Limit—Dry Runway.

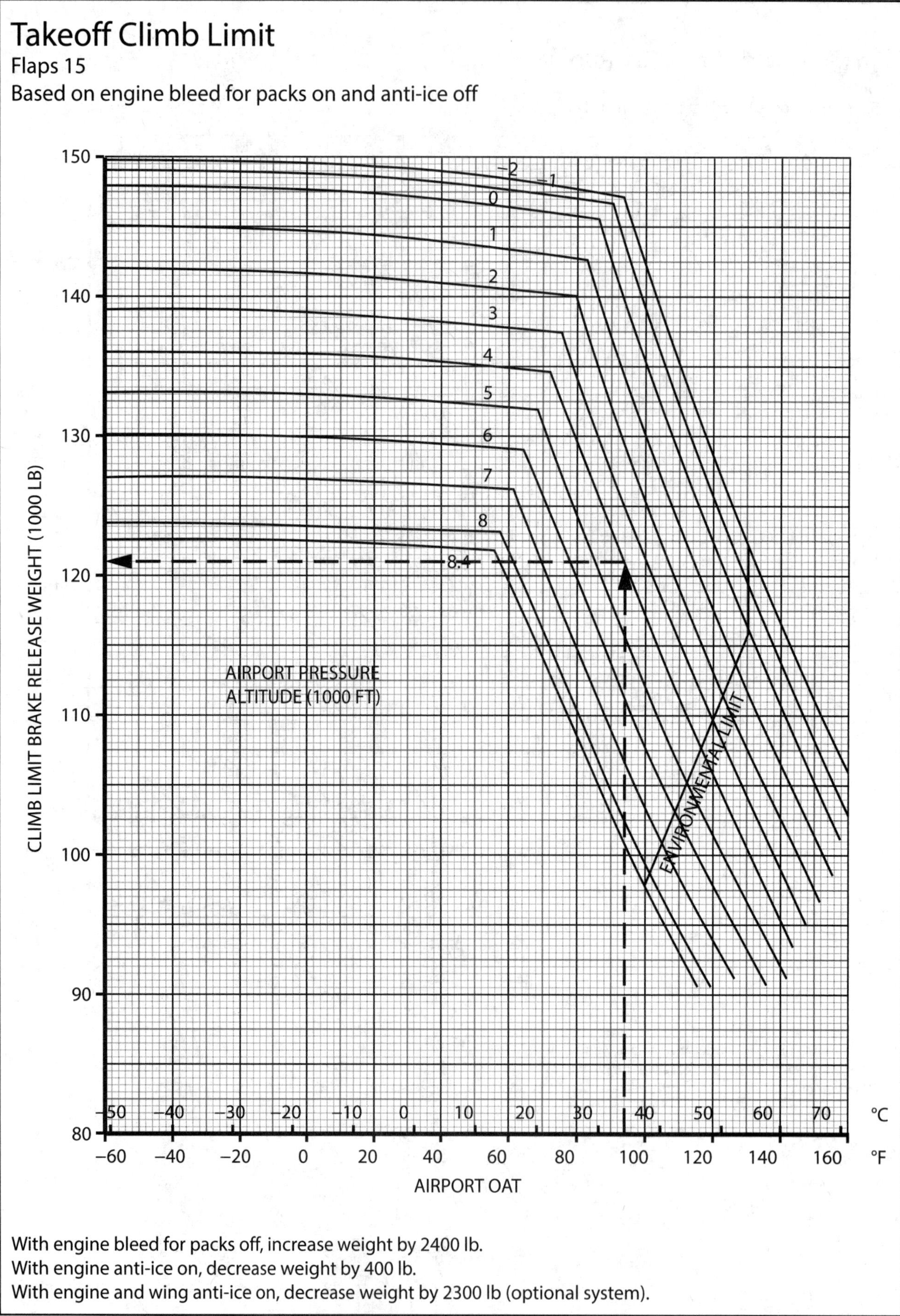

Figure 231. Takeoff Climb Limit.

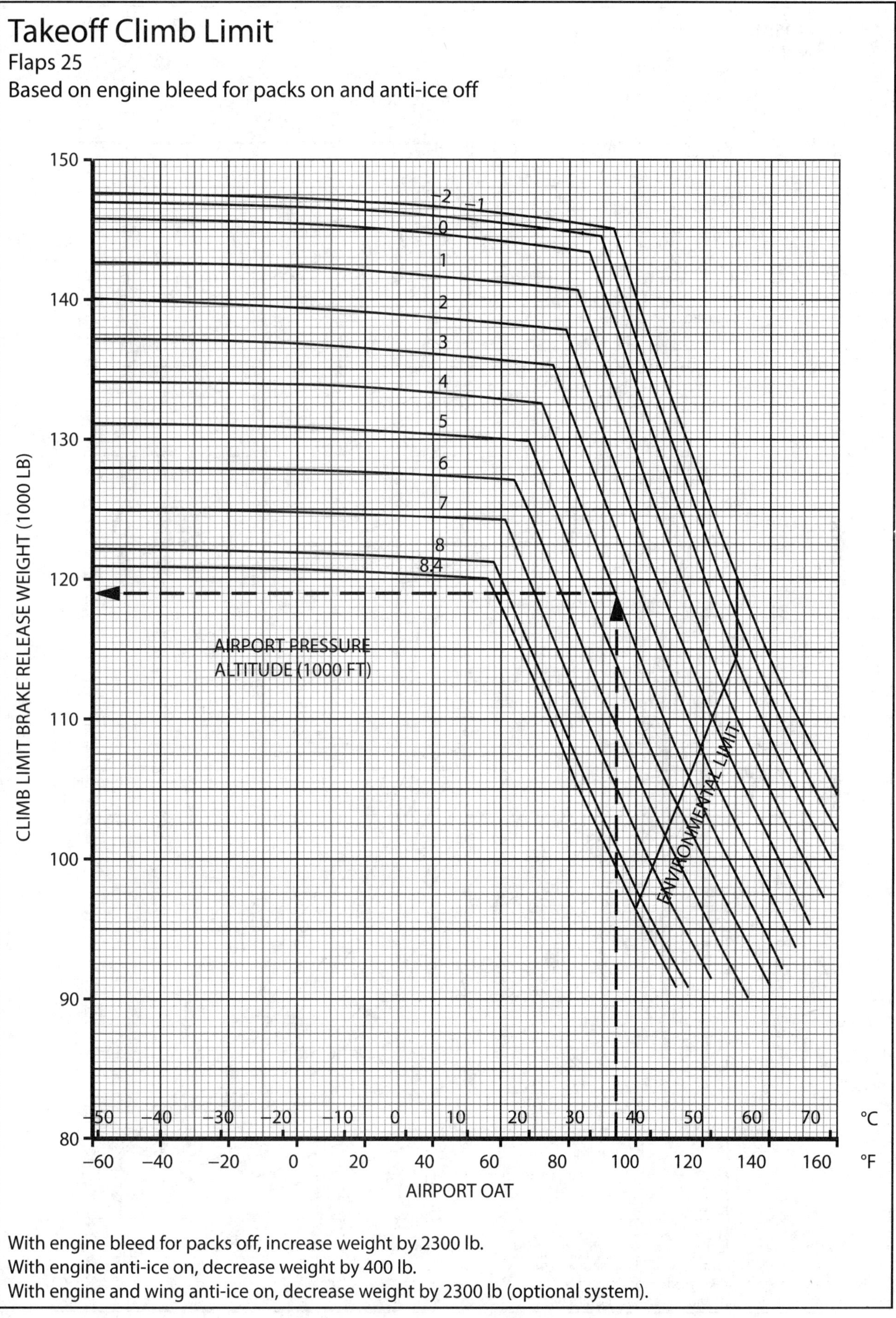

Figure 232. Takeoff Climb Limit.

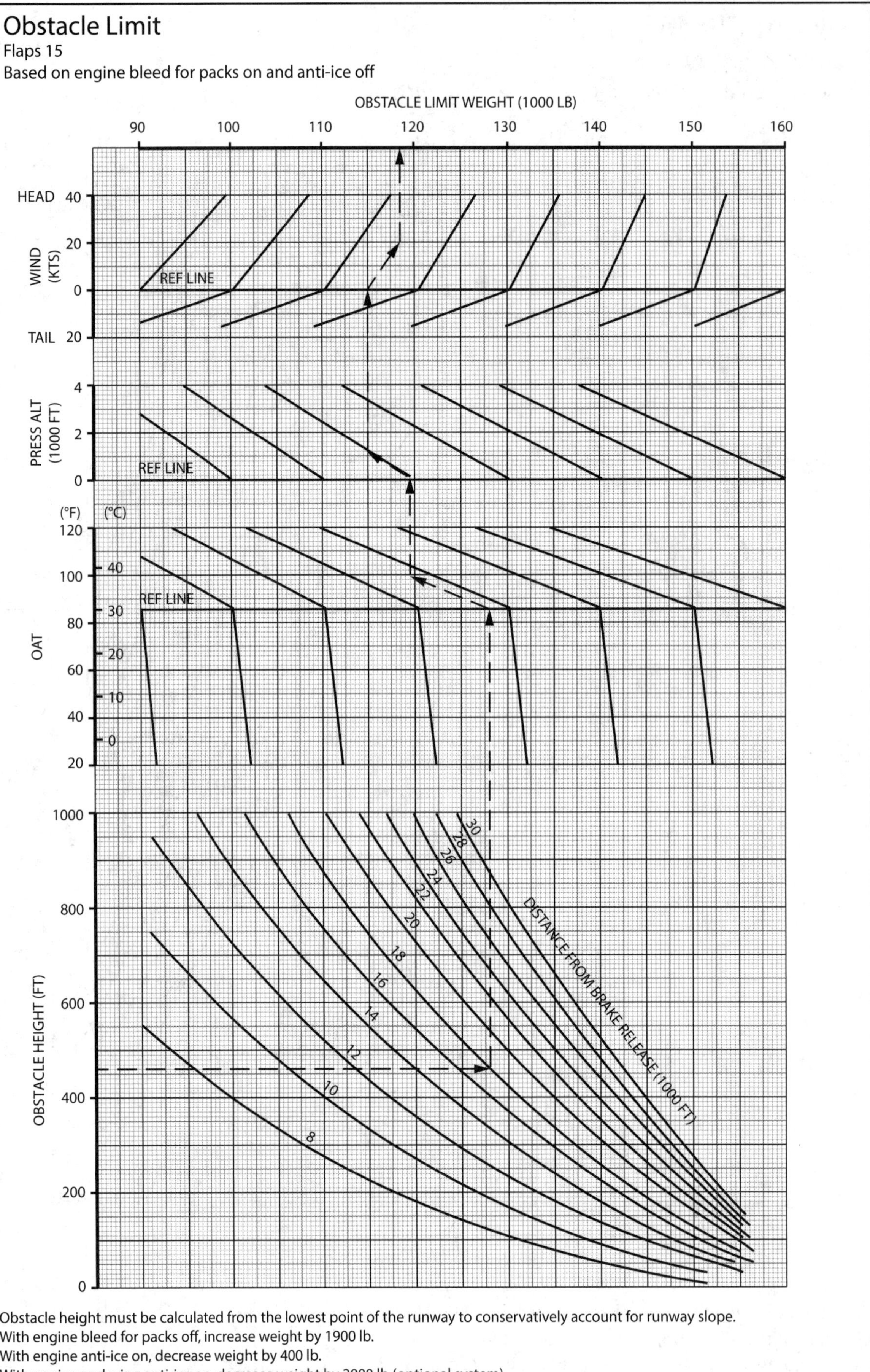
Obstacle Limit
Flaps 15
Based on engine bleed for packs on and anti-ice off
OBSTACLE LIMIT WEIGHT (1000 LB)
90
100
110
120
130
140
150
160
HEAD 40
20
WIND (KTS)
0
TAIL 20
REF LINE
PRESS ALT (1000 FT)
4
2
0
REF LINE
(°F) (°C)
120
100
80
60
40
20
40
30
20
10
0
OAT
REF LINE
OBSTACLE HEIGHT (FT)
1000
800
600
400
200
0
30
28
26
24
22
20
18
16
14
12
10
8
DISTANCE FROM BRAKE RELEASE (1000 FT)
Obstacle height must be calculated from the lowest point of the runway to conservatively account for runway slope.
With engine bleed for packs off, increase weight by 1900 lb.
With engine anti-ice on, decrease weight by 400 lb.
With engine and wing anti-ice on, decrease weight by 2000 lb (optional system).

Figure 233. Obstacle Limit.

Brake Energy Limits VMBE

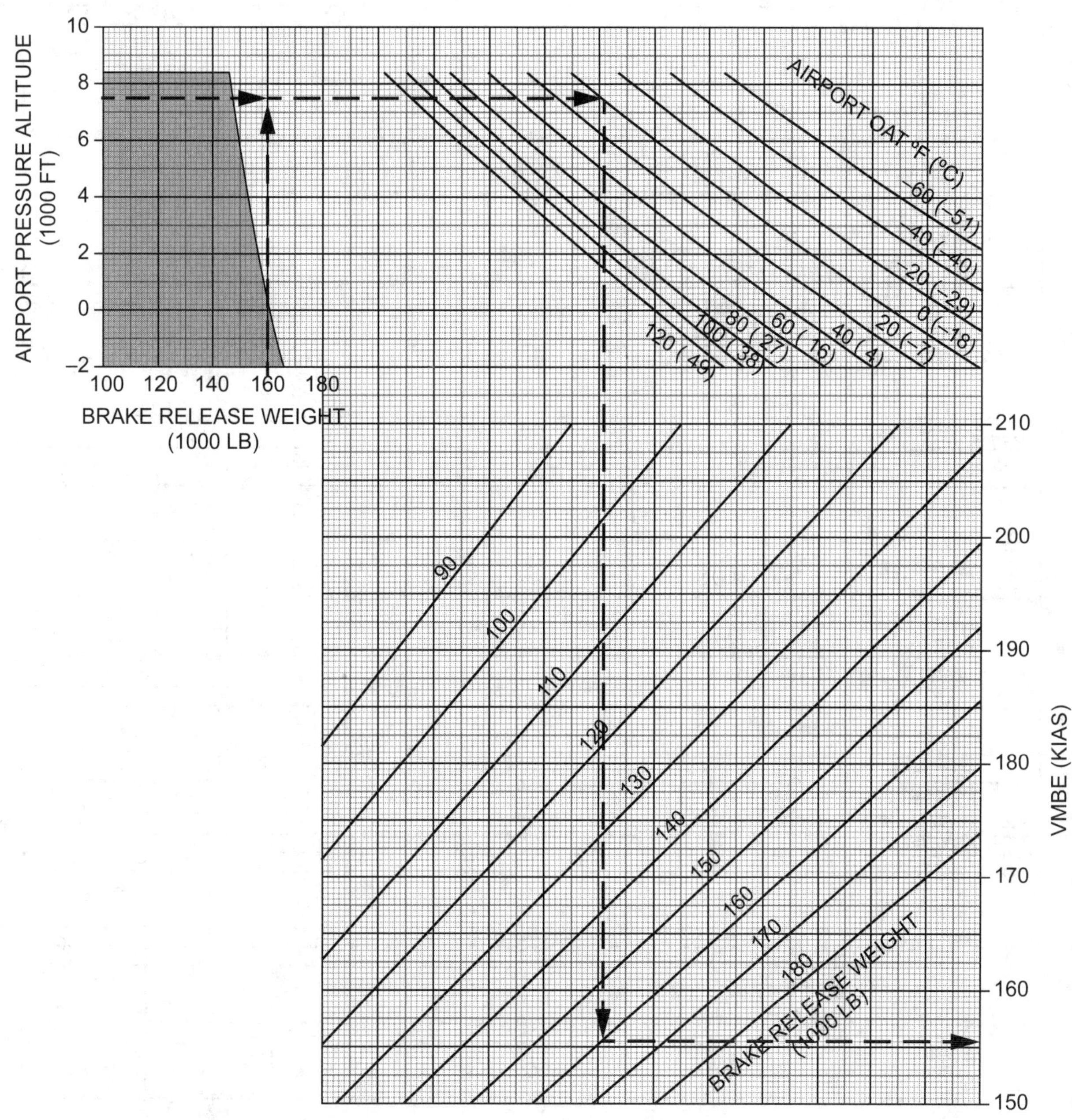

Check VMBE when outside shaded area or when operating with tailwind.
Increase VMBE by 2 knots per 1% uphill runway slope. Decrease VMBE by 3 knots per 1% downhi;; runway slope.
Increase VMBE by 4 knots per 10 knots headwind. Decrease VMBE by 18 knots per 10 knots tailwind.

Normal takeoff:
Decrease brake release weight by 1100 lb for each knot V1 exceeds VMBE.
Determine normal V1, VR, V2 speeds for lower brake release weight.

Improved climb takeoff:
Decrease climb weight improvement by 550 lb for each knot V1 exceeds VMBE.
Determine V1, VR, V2 speed increments for the lower climb weight improvement.

Figure 234. Brake Energy Limits VMBE.

Takeoff Speeds - Dry Runway

Flaps 10, 15 and 25

V1, VR, V2 for Max Takeoff Thrust

WEIGHT (1000 LB)	FLAPS 10			FLAPS 15			FLAPS 25		
	V1	VR	V2	V1	VR	V2	V1	VR	V2
170	138	140	145	136	136	141			
160	134	135	141	132	132	138	131	131	136
150	129	131	137	128	128	135	126	126	133
140	124	126	133	123	123	131	121	122	129
130	118	121	129	117	118	127	116	117	125
120	112	115	124	111	113	122	109	111	121
110	106	109	119	105	107	117	103	106	116
100	99	103	114	98	101	113	97	100	111
90	92	97	109	91	95	107	90	94	106

Check V1 (MCG).

V1, VR, V2 Adjustments*

TEMP		V1						VR						V2					
		PRESSURE ALTITUDE (1000 FT)						PRESSURE ALTITUDE (1000 FT)						PRESSURE ALTITUDE (1000 FT)					
°F	°C	-2	0	2	4	6	8	-2	0	2	4	6	8	-2	0	2	4	6	8
140	60	5	6	7	9			3	4	5	6			-2	-2	-2	-3		
120	49	3	4	5	7	8	10	2	3	4	5	6	6	-1	-1	-2	-2	-3	-3
100	38	1	2	3	5	6	8	1	1	2	3	4	5	0	-1	-1	-2	-2	-2
80	27	0	0	1	3	5	6	0	0	1	2	3	4	0	0	0	-1	-1	-2
60	16	0	0	1	2	3	4	0	0	1	1	2	3	0	0	0	0	-1	-1
-60	-51	0	0	1	2	3	3	0	0	1	1	2	3	0	0	0	0	-1	-1

Slope and Wind V1 Adjustments*

WEIGHT (1000 LB)	SLOPE (%)					WIND (KTS)							
	-2	-1	0	1	2	-15	-10	-5	0	10	20	30	40
170	-3	-1	0	1	1	-1	-1	-1	0	0	1	1	1
160	-3	-1	0	1	2	-1	-1	-1	0	0	1	1	1
150	-3	-1	0	1	2	-1	-1	-1	0	0	1	1	1
140	-2	-1	0	1	2	-2	-1	-1	0	0	1	1	1
130	-2	-1	0	1	2	-2	-1	-1	0	0	1	1	1
120	-2	-1	0	1	2	-2	-1	-1	0	0	1	1	1
110	-2	-1	0	1	2	-2	-1	-1	0	0	1	1	2
100	-2	-1	0	1	2	-2	-1	-1	0	0	1	2	2
90	-1	-1	0	1	1	-2	-1	-1	0	0	1	2	2

Clearway and Stopway V1 Adjustments *

NORMAL V1 (KIAS)	CLEARWAY MINUS STOPWAY (FT)								
	800	600	400	200	0	-200	-400	-600	-800
140	-3	-3	-3	-2	0	2	2	2	2
120	-3	-3	-3	-2	0	2	2	2	2
100	-3	-3	-2	-1	0	1	1	1	1

*V1 not to exceed VR.

Max Allowable Clearway for V1 Adjustment

FIELD LENGTH (FT)	4000	6000	8000	10000	12000	14000
MAX ALLOWABLE CLEARWAY (FT)	450	650	850	1000	1450	1550

V1 (MCG)

Max Takeoff Thrust

TEMP		PRESSURE ALTITUDE (FT)						
°F	°C	-2000	0	2000	4000	6000	8000	10000
160	71	102						
140	60	102	99	97	96			
120	49	104	102	98	96	94	92	90
100	38	110	107	103	100	96	92	90
80	27	112	111	109	105	101	97	93
60	16	112	112	109	107	104	101	97
-60	-51	113	113	110	108	105	102	100

Figure 237. Takeoff Speeds—Dry Runway.

Takeoff Speeds - Wet Runway

Flaps 10, 15 and 25

V1, VR, V2 for Max Takeoff Thrust

WEIGHT (1000 LB)	FLAPS 10			FLAPS 15			FLAPS 25		
	V1	VR	V2	V1	VR	V2	V1	VR	V2
170	133	139	145	133	136	141			
160	128	135	141	128	132	138	126	131	136
150	123	131	137	122	128	135	121	126	133
140	117	126	133	117	123	131	115	122	129
130	111	121	129	111	118	127	109	117	125
120	105	115	124	104	113	122	103	111	121
110	99	109	119	98	107	117	97	106	116
100	92	103	114	92	101	112	91	100	111
90	86	97	109	85	95	107	84	94	106

Check V1 (MCG).

V1, VR, V2 Adjustments*

TEMP		V1						VR						V2					
		PRESSURE ALTITUDE (1000 FT)						PRESSURE ALTITUDE (1000 FT)						PRESSURE ALTITUDE (1000 FT)					
°F	°C	-2	0	2	4	6	8	-2	0	2	4	6	8	-2	0	2	4	6	8
140	60	6	7	9	10			3	4	5	6			-2	-2	-2	-3		
120	49	4	4	6	8	9	11	2	3	4	4	5	6	-1	-1	-2	-2	-3	-3
100	38	1	2	3	5	7	9	1	1	2	3	4	5	0	-1	-1	-2	-2	-2
80	27	0	0	1	3	4	6	0	0	1	2	3	4	0	0	0	-1	-1	-2
60	16	0	0	1	2	3	4	0	0	1	1	2	3	0	0	0	0	-1	-1
-60	-51	0	0	1	2	3	4	0	0	1	1	2	3	0	0	0	0	-1	-1

Slope and Wind V1 Adjustments*

WEIGHT (1000 LB)	SLOPE (%)					WIND (KTS)							
	-2	-1	0	1	2	-15	-10	-5	0	10	20	30	40
170	-4	-2	0	2	4	-3	-2	-1	0	1	1	2	3
160	-4	-2	0	2	4	-3	-2	-1	0	1	1	2	3
150	-4	-2	0	2	4	-3	-2	-1	0	1	1	2	3
140	-4	-2	0	2	3	-4	-2	-1	0	1	1	2	3
130	-3	-1	0	1	3	-4	-3	-1	0	1	2	2	3
120	-3	-1	0	1	3	-4	-3	-1	0	1	2	2	3
110	-2	-1	0	1	2	-4	-3	-1	0	1	2	2	3
100	-2	-1	0	1	2	-4	-3	-1	0	1	2	2	3
90	-2	-1	0	1	2	-4	-3	-1	0	1	2	3	3

Stopway V1 Adjustments *

NORMAL V1 (KIAS)	STOPWAY (FT)				
	0	200	400	600	800
160	0	1	2	2	3
140	0	1	2	2	3
120	0	1	2	3	4
100	0	1	2	3	4

Use of clearway allowed on wet runways.
*V1 not to exceed VR.

V1 (MCG)

Max Takeoff Thrust

TEMP		PRESSURE ALTITUDE (FT)						
°F	°C	-2000	0	2000	4000	6000	8000	10000
160	71	102						
140	60	102	99	97	96			
120	49	104	102	98	96	94	92	90
100	38	110	107	103	100	96	92	90
80	27	112	111	109	105	101	97	93
60	16	112	112	109	107	104	101	97
-60	-51	113	113	110	108	105	102	100

Figure 238. Takeoff Speeds—Wet Runway.

Takeoff %N1

Based on engine bleeds for packs on, engine and wing anti-ice on or off

OAT (°F)	AIRPORT PRESSURE ALTITUDE (FT)												
	-2000	-1000	0	1000	2000	3000	4000	5000	6000	7000	8000	9000	10000
170	87.6	88.0	88.9	89.4	89.8	90.4	91.0	91.7	92.4	92.9	93.4	93.5	93.6
160	88.5	89.0	89.3	89.2	89.1	89.7	90.3	91.0	91.7	92.2	92.6	92.8	92.9
150	89.4	89.9	90.3	90.2	90.1	90.1	90.0	90.3	91.0	91.4	91.9	92.0	92.1
140	90.3	90.8	91.2	91.2	91.1	91.1	91.0	91.1	91.2	91.0	91.2	91.3	91.4
130	91.1	91.7	92.1	92.1	92.0	92.0	92.0	92.0	92.0	91.9	91.8	91.4	90.9
120	92.0	92.6	93.0	93.0	93.0	92.9	92.9	92.9	92.9	92.8	92.7	92.4	92.0
110	92.9	93.5	93.9	93.9	93.8	93.8	93.8	93.7	93.7	93.6	93.6	93.4	93.1
100	93.8	94.3	94.8	94.7	94.7	94.7	94.6	94.6	94.5	94.4	94.4	94.3	94.2
90	94.2	95.3	95.7	95.7	95.7	95.6	95.6	95.5	95.4	95.4	95.3	95.2	95.2
80	93.3	94.5	95.6	96.1	96.5	96.5	96.4	96.4	96.3	96.2	96.2	96.1	96.1
70	92.5	93.7	94.8	95.3	95.8	96.4	97.1	97.4	97.3	97.2	97.1	97.1	97.0
60	91.6	92.8	93.9	94.4	95.0	95.6	96.2	96.9	97.6	98.3	98.5	98.4	98.3
50	90.8	92.0	93.0	93.6	94.1	94.7	95.3	96.0	96.7	97.5	98.2	99.1	100.0
40	89.9	91.1	92.2	92.7	93.2	93.8	94.4	95.1	95.8	96.6	97.4	98.3	99.2
30	89.1	90.2	91.3	91.8	92.3	92.9	93.6	94.2	94.9	95.7	96.5	97.4	98.3
20	88.2	89.3	90.4	90.9	91.4	92.0	92.7	93.4	94.0	94.8	95.6	96.6	97.5
10	87.3	88.4	89.5	90.0	90.5	91.1	91.7	92.4	93.1	93.9	94.7	95.7	96.6
0	86.4	87.5	88.6	89.1	89.6	90.2	90.8	91.5	92.2	93.0	93.8	94.8	95.8
-10	85.5	86.6	87.6	88.1	88.6	89.3	89.9	90.6	91.3	92.1	92.9	94.0	94.9
-20	84.6	85.7	86.7	87.2	87.7	88.3	89.0	89.7	90.4	91.2	92.0	93.1	94.0
-30	83.6	84.7	85.7	86.2	86.7	87.4	88.0	88.7	89.4	90.2	91.1	92.2	93.1
-40	82.7	83.8	84.8	85.3	85.8	86.4	87.0	87.8	88.5	89.3	90.1	91.2	92.2
-50	81.7	82.8	83.8	84.3	84.8	85.4	86.1	86.8	87.5	88.3	89.2	90.3	91.3
-60	80.8	81.8	82.8	83.3	83.8	84.4	85.1	85.8	86.5	87.3	88.2	89.4	90.3

%N1 Adjustments for Engine Bleeds

BLEED CONFIGURATION	PRESSURE ALTITUDE (FT)												
	-2000	-1000	0	1000	2000	3000	4000	5000	6000	7000	8000	9000	10000
PACKS OFF	0.7	0.7	0.7	0.7	0.7	0.7	0.8	0.8	0.8	0.8	0.8	0.9	1.0

Figure 239. Takeoff % N1.

Stab Trim Setting

Max Takeoff Thrust

Flaps 1and 5

WEIGHT (1000 LB)	C.G. (%MAC)								
	9	11	13	16	20	24	28	30	33
160-180	8 1/2	8 1/2	8 1/2	7 3/4	6 3/4	6	5 1/4	4 3/4	4 1/4
140	8 1/2	8 1/2	8	7 1/4	6 1/2	5 1/2	4 3/4	4 1/2	3 3/4
120	8 1/2	8	7 1/2	6 1/2	5 3/4	5	4 1/4	4	3 1/4
80-100	6 3/4	6 1/2	6	5 1/2	5	4 1/4	3 1/2	3 1/4	2 3/4

Flaps 10, 15 and 25

WEIGHT (1000 LB)	C.G. (%MAC)								
	9	11	13	16	20	24	28	30	33
160-180	8 1/2	8 1/2	8 1/2	7 1/4	6 1/2	5 1/2	4 1/2	4 1/4	3 1/2
140	8 1/2	8 1/2	7 3/4	6 3/4	6	5	4 1/4	3 3/4	3
120	8 1/2	7 3/4	7	6	5 1/4	4 1/2	3 3/4	3 1/4	2 3/4
80-100	6 1/4	6	5 1/2	5	4 1/2	3 3/4	3	2 3/4	2 3/4

Figure 240. Stab Trim Setting.

This page intentionally left blank.

HOT SPOTS

An "airport surface hot spot" is a location on an aerodrome movement area with a history or potential risk of collision or runway incursion, and where heightened attention by pilots/drivers is necessary.

A "hot spot" is a runway safety related problem area on an airport that presents increased risk during surface operations. Typically it is a complex or confusing taxiway/taxiway or taxiway/runway intersection. The area of increased risk has either a history of or potential for runway incursions or surface incidents, due to a variety of causes, such as but not limited to: airport layout, traffic flow, airport marking, signage and lighting, situational awareness, and training. Hot spots are depicted on airport diagrams as open circles or polygons designated as "HS 1", "HS 2", etc. and tabulated in the list below with a brief description of each hot spot. Hot spots will remain charted on airport diagrams until such time the increased risk has been reduced or eliminated.

CITY/AIRPORT	HOT SPOT	DESCRIPTION*
CARLSBAD, CA		
MC CLELLAN-PALOMAR (CRQ)	HS 1	Large Jets may obscure twr visibility of small aircraft.
CHINO, CA		
CHINO (CNO)	HS 1	Twy D close proximity to Rwy 08L-26R.
	HS 2	Twy L close proximity to Rwy 03-21.
HAWTHORNE, CA		
JACK NORTHROP FIELD/ HAWTHORNE MUNI (HHR)	HS 1	Rwy 25 run-up area.
LONG BEACH, CA		
LONG BEACH (DAUGHERTY FLD) (LGB)	HS 1	Rwy 30 and Rwy 07L-25R, Twy A and Twy D.
	HS 2	Rwy 12-30 and Rwy 07L-25R, Twy B and Twy K.
	HS 3	Rwy 07R-25L, Twy B.
	HS 4	Rwy 07R-25L and Rwy 12-30, Twy J and Twy D.
	HS 5	Rwy 16R-34L, southwest ramp, Twy F and Twy B.
	HS 6	Rwy 34R and Rwy 07R-25L.
	HS 7	Rwy 12-30 cross every other rwy.
LOS ANGELES, CA		
LOS ANGELES INTL (LAX)	HS 1	Twy R not visible from the control twr.
PALM SPRINGS, CA		
PALM SPRINGS INTL (PSP)	HS 1	Twy C mistaken for Rwy 13R-31L or Rwy 13L-31R.
	HS 2	Int of Twy B and Twy C.
	HS 3	Twy B and Rwy 31R.
	HS 4	Twy C and Twy J.
RIVERSIDE, CA		
RIVERSIDE MUNI (RAL)	HS 1	Rwy 27, Twy C.
	HS 2	ATC non-visibility area.
SAN DIEGO, CA		
MONTGOMERY FLD (MYF)	HS 1	Rwy 10R-28L, Twy G and Twy H.
	HS 2	Rwy 28R and Rwy 28L, Twys G.
	HS 3	Rwy 28R and Rwy 28L, Twys F.
SANTA ANA, CA		
JOHN WAYNE ARPT-ORANGE COUNTY (SNA)	HS 1	Rwy 19L and Rwy 19R, Twy L and Twy K.
	HS 2	Rwy 19L and Rwy 19R, Twy H.
	HS 3	Twy A,Twy H, and Twy C.

(SEE CONTINUATION PAGE FOR MORE LISTINGS)

Figure 241. Hot Spots.

HOT SPOTS

(CONTINUED)

CITY/AIRPORT	HOT SPOT	DESCRIPTION*
SANTA BARBARA, CA		
SANTA BARBARA MUNI (SBA)	HS 1	Rwy 07-25, Twy C.
	HS 2	Rwy 15L and Rwy 15R, Twy C, wide pavement.
	HS 3	Rwy 15L-33R, Rwy 15R-33L, Rwy 07-25. Rwy 15L-33R and Rwy 15R-33L utilized for taxi.
	HS 4	Rwy 25, Twy H and Twy J.
SANTA MARIA, CA		
CAPTAIN G. ALLAN HANCOCK FLD (SMX)	HS 1	Twy A, Twy C, and Twy D.
	HS 2	Rwy 20 and Twy A.
	HS 3	Rwy 12 and Twy B.
VICTORVILLE, CA		
SOUTHERN CALIFORNIA LOGISTICS (VCV)	HS 1	Wrong rwy departure risk.

Figure 241A. Hot Spots.

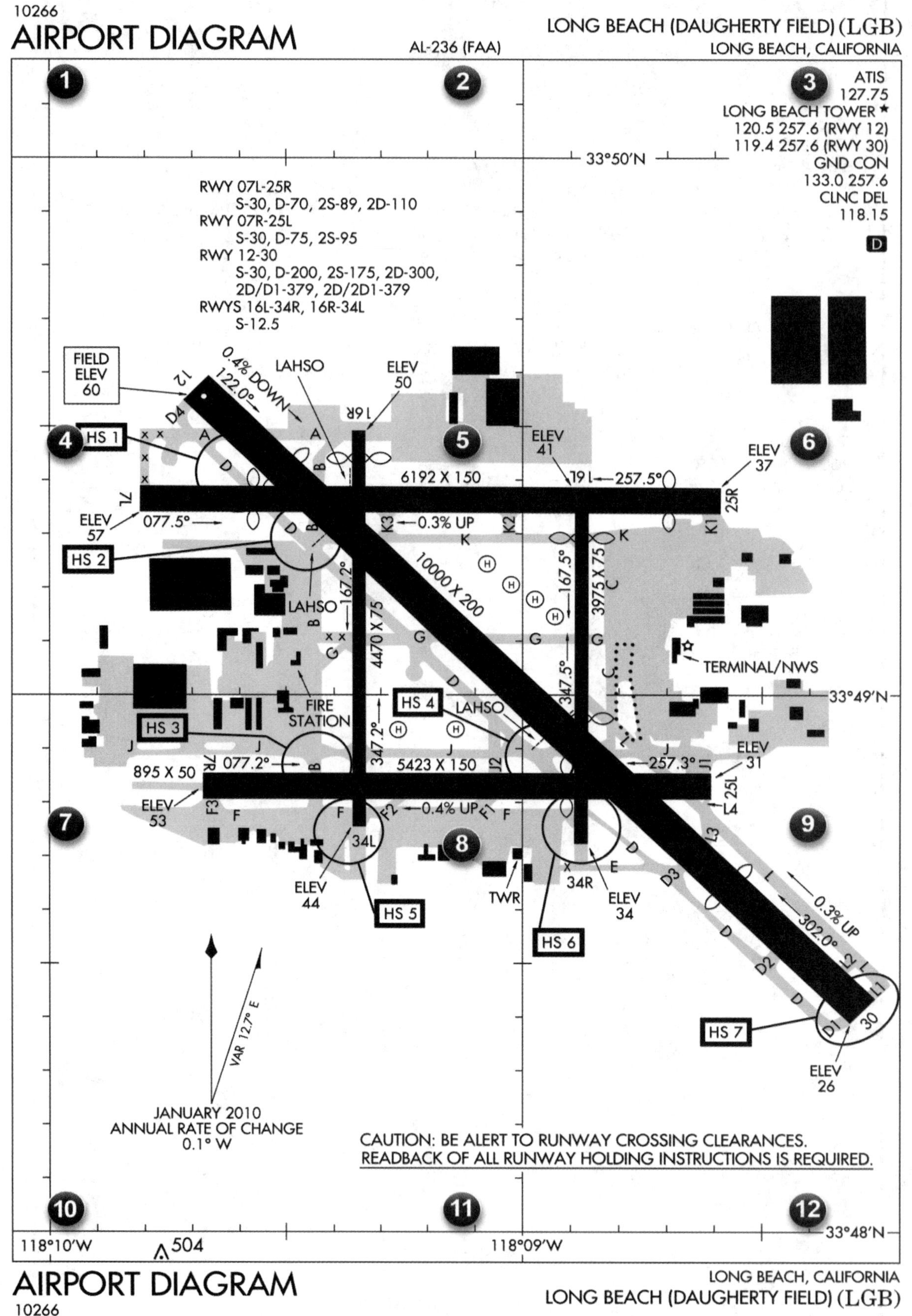

Figure 242. Airport Diagram (LGB).

11069

HOT SPOTS

An "airport surface hot spot" is a location on an aerodrome movement area with a history or potential risk of collision or runway incursion, and where heightened attention by pilots/drivers is necessary.

A "hot spot" is a runway safety related problem area on an airport that presents increased risk during surface operations. Typically it is a complex or confusing taxiway/taxiway or taxiway/runway intersection. The area of increased risk has either a history of or potential for runway incursions or surface incidents, due to a variety of causes, such as but not limited to: airport layout, traffic flow, airport marking, signage and lighting, situational awareness, and training. Hot spots are depicted on airport diagrams as open circles or polygons designated as "HS 1", "HS 2", etc. and tabulated in the list below with a brief description of each hot spot. Hot spots will remain charted on airport diagrams until such time the increased risk has been reduced or eliminated.

CITY/AIRPORT	HOT SPOT	DESCRIPTION*
DAYTONA BEACH, FL		
DAYTONA BEACH INTL (DAB)	HS 1	Int of Twy W and Twy S.
FORT LAUDERDALE, FL		
FORT LAUDERDALE-HOLLYWOOD INTL (FLL)	HS 1	Twy E at Rwy 09L-27R.
	HS 2	Twy D at Rwy 09L-27R.
	HS 3	Twy Q at Rwy 09L-27R.
	HS 4	Twy E int departure for Rwy 27L.
	HS 5	Twy departure risk. Twy B instead of Rwy 09L.
HOLLYWOOD, FL		
NORTH PERRY (HWO)	HS 1	Southbound on Twy D for Rwy 27R departures.
	HS 2	The hold line for Rwy 36L is also the hold line for Rwy 09R.
	HS 3	Aircraft taxiing on Twy L westbound to depart on Rwy 18R-36L.
MIAMI, FL		
MIAMI INTL (MIA)	HS 1	Short twy risk.
	HS 2	Short twy risk.
	HS 3	Rwy 27 and Rwy 30 wrong rwy departure risk.
	HS 4	Short twy between rwys.
MIAMI, FL		
OPA-LOCKA EXECUTIVE (OPF)	HS 1	Surface painted LOCATION and DIRECTION signs ONLY.
ORLANDO, FL		
ORLANDO SANFORD INTL (SFB)	HS 1	Twy C is beyond the Rwy 09C APCH hold sign and marking.
	HS 2	Hold line for Rwy 09R on Twy R northbound is adjacent to Twy S.
STUART, FL		
WITHAM FIELD (SUA)	HS 1	Intersecting rwys, wrong rwy departure risk.
	HS 2	Rwy 12 and Twy A1.

*See appropriate A/FD, Alaska or Pacific Supplement HOT SPOT table for additional information.

11069

Figure 243. Hot Spots.

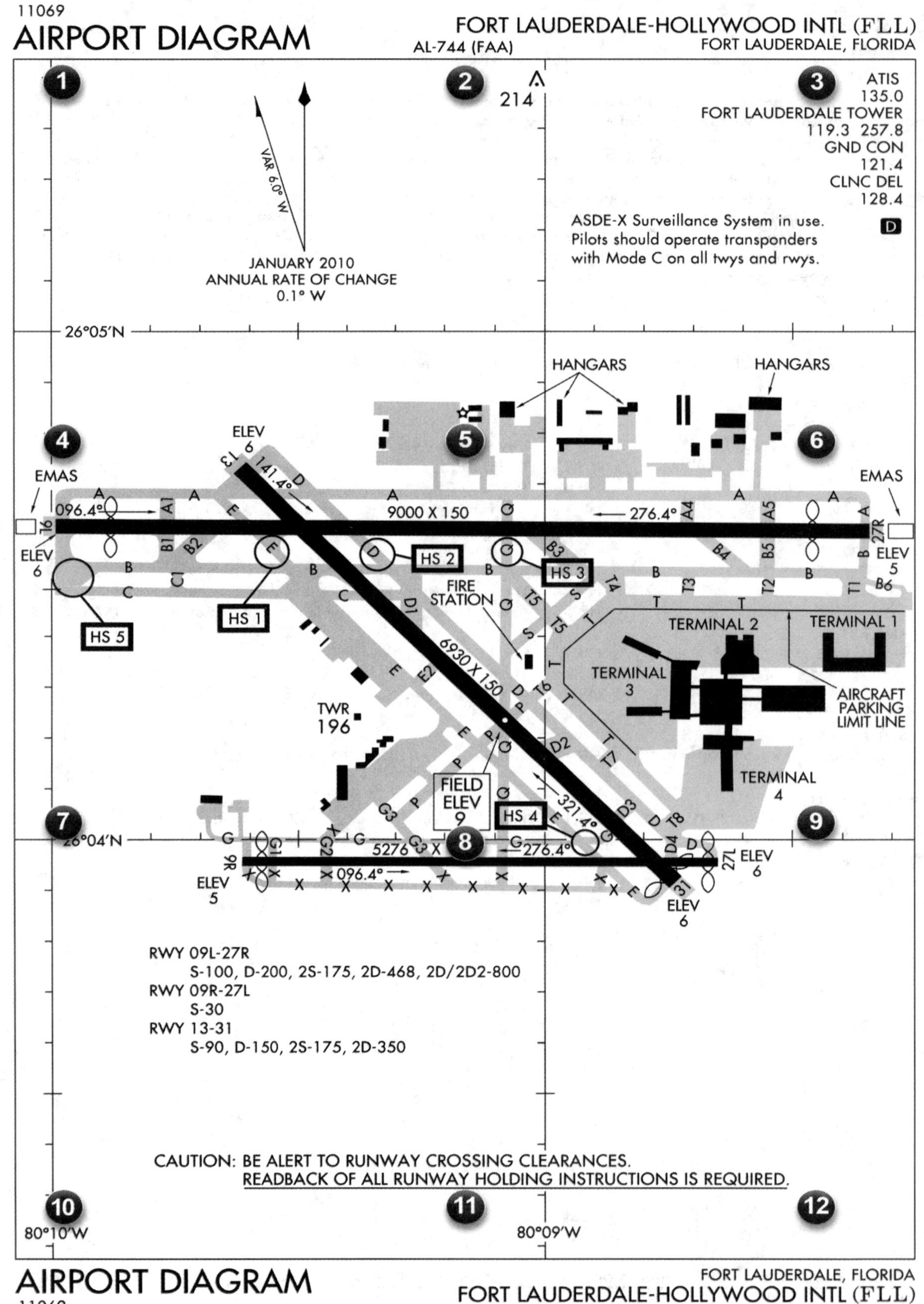

Figure 244. Airport Diagram (FLL).

This page intentionally left blank.

11069

HOT SPOTS

An "airport surface hot spot" is a location on an aerodrome movement area with a history or potential risk of collision or runway incursion, and where heightened attention by pilots/drivers is necessary.

A "hot spot" is a runway safety related problem area on an airport that presents increased risk during surface operations. Typically it is a complex or confusing taxiway/taxiway or taxiway/runway intersection. The area of increased risk has either a history of or potential for runway incursions or surface incidents, due to a variety of causes, such as but not limited to: airport layout, traffic flow, airport marking, signage and lighting, situational awareness, and training. Hot spots are depicted on airport diagrams as open circles or polygons designated as "HS 1", "HS 2", etc. and tabulated in the list below with a brief description of each hot spot. Hot spots will remain charted on airport diagrams until such time the increased risk has been reduced or eliminated.

CITY/AIRPORT	HOT SPOT	DESCRIPTION*
CHANDLER, AZ		
CHANDLER MUNI (CHD)	HS 1	Rwy 22R may be used as an alternate taxi route.
LAS VEGAS, NV		
HENDERSON	HS 1	Twy H, Twy G, and Rwy 17R.
EXECUTIVE (HND)	HS 2	Twy E and ramp area. High volume of traffic.
	HS 3	Twy A and run up area. Twy A being confused for Rwy 35L.
LAS VEGAS, NV		
McCARRAN INTL (LAS)	HS 1	Rwy 01R-19L, Twy S and the ramp.
	HS 2	Rwy 01R-19L and Rwy 01L-19R, Twy U.
	HS 3	Rwy 01R-19L and Rwy 01L-19R, Twy Y.
	HS 4	Rwy 07L and Rwy 01L, co-located rwy holding position markings.
	HS 5	Twy E.
LAS VEGAS, NV		
NORTH LAS VEGAS (VGT)	HS 1	Rwy 07, Twy G and Twy F.
	HS 2	Rwy 12R, Twy G.
	HS 3	Rwy 12R, Twy A and Twy B.
	HS 4	Rwy 12L, Twy A.
MESA, AZ		
FALCON FIELD (FFZ)	HS 1	Rwy 04R-22L, Twy B and Twy D.
MINDEN, NV		
MINDEN-TAHOE (MEV)	HS 1	Complex int.
	HS 2	Frequent crossings for sailplane operations.
OGDEN, UT		
OGDEN-HINCKLEY (OGD)	HS 1	Twy D intersects Rwy 25 at north edge of Rwy 03-21. Wrong rwy departure risk.
	HS 2	Confusing twy int in close proximity to rwy.
PHOENIX, AZ		
PHOENIX DEER VALLEY (DVT)	HS 1	Inadvertent Rwy 07R-25L crossings from Twy B5.
	HS 2	Inadvertent Rwy 07R-25L crossings from Twy B9.
PHOENIX, AZ		
PHOENIX-MESA GATEWAY (IWA)	HS 1	Twy V, Twy B, and Twy K complex int.
PHOENIX, AZ		
PHOENIX SKY HARBOR INTL (PHX)	HS 1	Pilots sometimes mistake Twy F for Rwy 07L or Rwy 07R.
	HS 2	Pilots sometimes cross Rwy 07L-25R at Twy F8, Twy F9, or Twy F10, without authorization.
	HS 3	Aircraft taxiing from southern ramps have turned onto Rwy 25L when given instructions to cross Rwy 25L at Twy H3.

(SEE CONTINUATION PAGE FOR MORE LISTINGS)

11069

Figure 245. Hot Spots.

11069

HOT SPOTS

(CONTINUED)

CITY/AIRPORT	HOT SPOT	DESCRIPTION*
PRESCOTT, AZ		
ERNEST A. LOVE FLD (PRC)	HS 1	Not visible from the twr.
	HS 2	Complex int.
	HS 3	Complex int.
	HS 4	Not visible from the twr.
	HS 5	Frequent rwy crossings.
PROVO, UT		
PROVO MUNI (PVU)	HS 1	Twy A and Twy A3 close proximity to ramp and rwys.
RENO, NV		
RENO/TAHOE INTL (RNO)	HS 1	Rwy 07-25, Twy A and Twy B.
	HS 2	Twy C and the ramp.
	HS 3	Rwy 16L, Twy C and Twy D.
SALT LAKE CITY, UT		
SALT LAKE CITY INTL (SLC)	HS 1	Hold line on apch end of Rwy 32 protects Rwy 35.
	HS 2	Confusing int. Twy K2 ramp in close proximity to Rwy 17-35.
	HS 3	Area not visible from control twr. Hold line at K1 in close proximity to ramp, protects Rwy 32 and Rwy 35.
	HS 4	Intermittent radio reception with ATC at apch end of Rwy 16L for some aircraft.
TUCSON, AZ		
RYAN FIELD (RYN)	HS 1	Rwy 33 and Rwy 06R, Twy B.
TUCSON, AZ		
TUCSON INTL (TUS)	HS 1	Twy A, Twy D and Twy A3, complex int.
	HS 2	Rwy 11L and Rwy 11R apch areas.
	HS 3	Rwy 29R and Rwy 29L.
	HS 4	Twy A5 and Twy A6 in close proximity of Rwy 11L-29R.

*See appropriate A/FD, Alaska or Pacific Supplement HOT SPOT table for additional information.

11069

Figure 245A. Hot Spots.

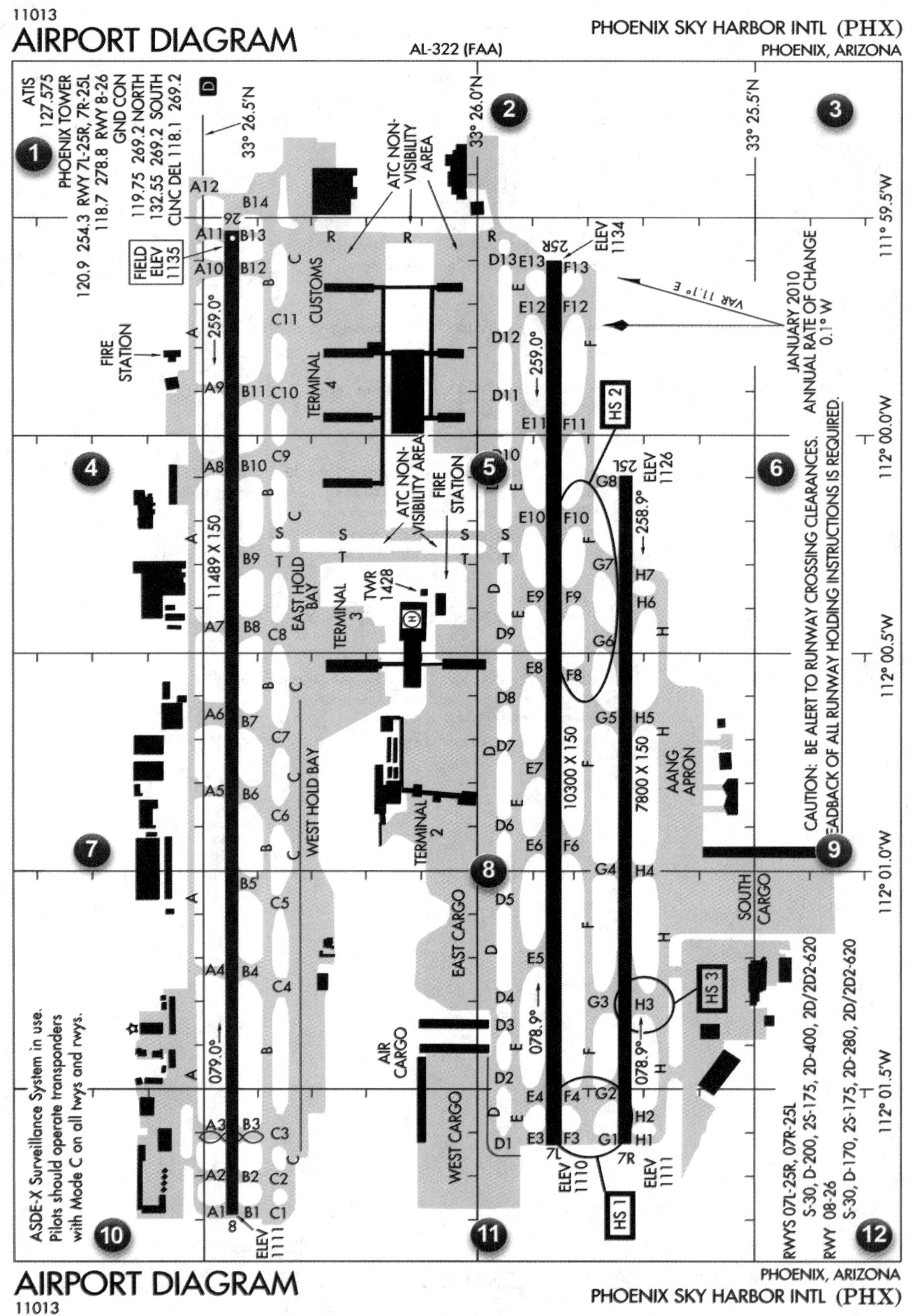

Figure 246. Airport Diagram (PHX).

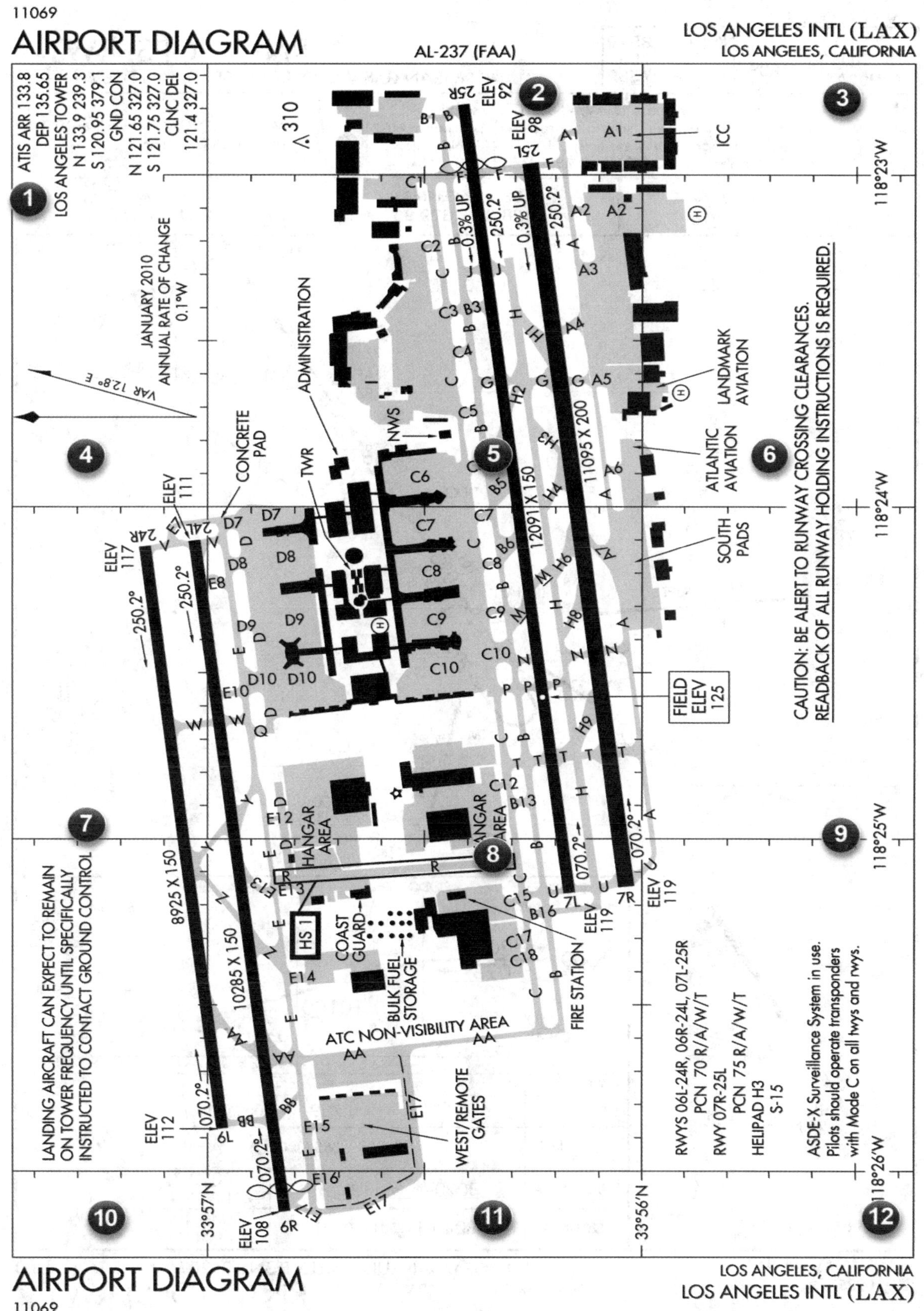

Figure 247. Airport Diagram (LAX).

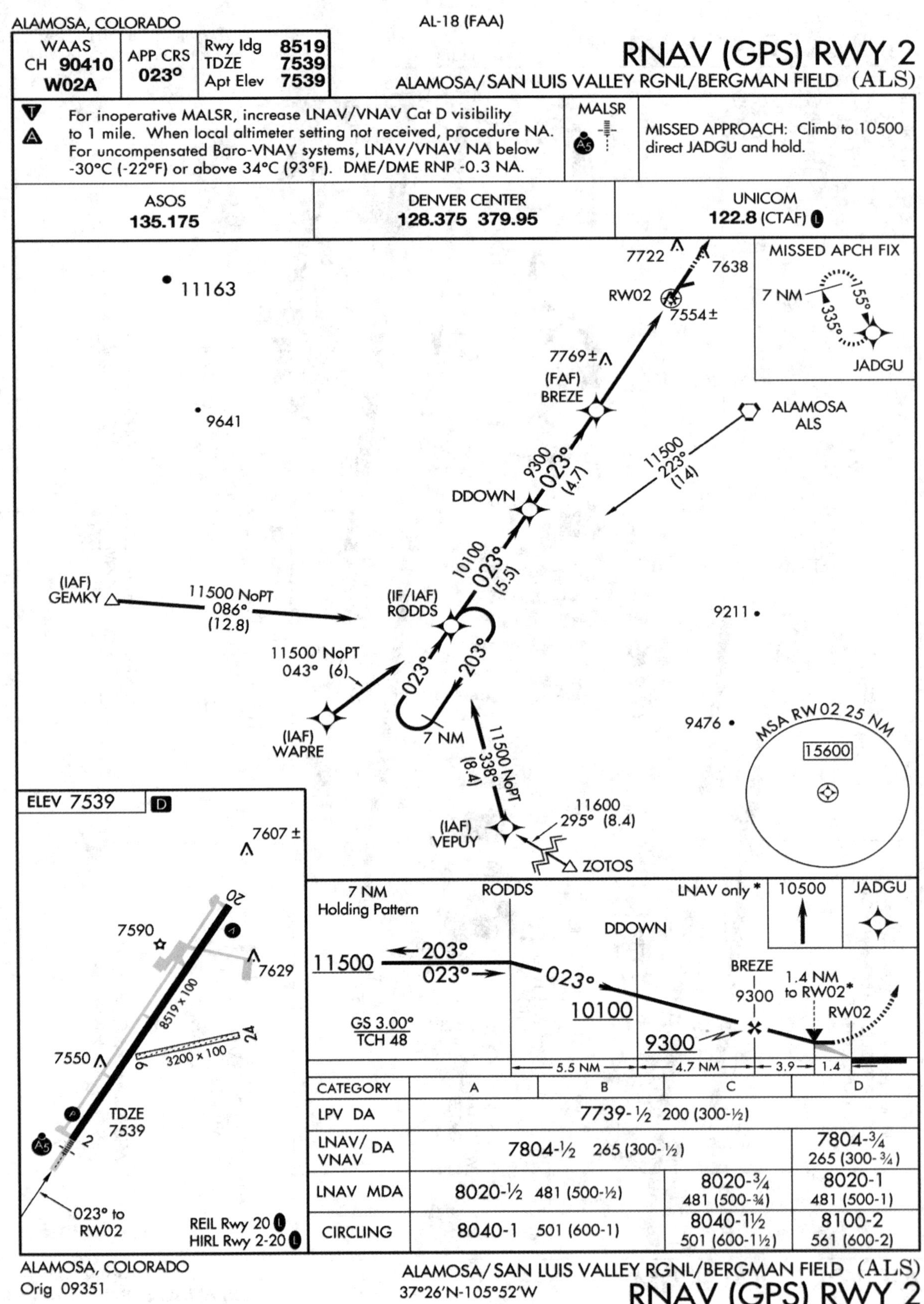

CATEGORY	A	B	C	D
LPV DA	7739-½ 200 (300-½)			
LNAV/VNAV DA	7804-½ 265 (300-½)			7804-¾ 265 (300-¾)
LNAV MDA	8020-½ 481 (500-½)		8020-¾ 481 (500-¾)	8020-1 481 (500-1)
CIRCLING	8040-1 501 (600-1)		8040-1½ 501 (600-1½)	8100-2 561 (600-2)

Figure 248. RNAV (GPS) RWY 2 (ALS).

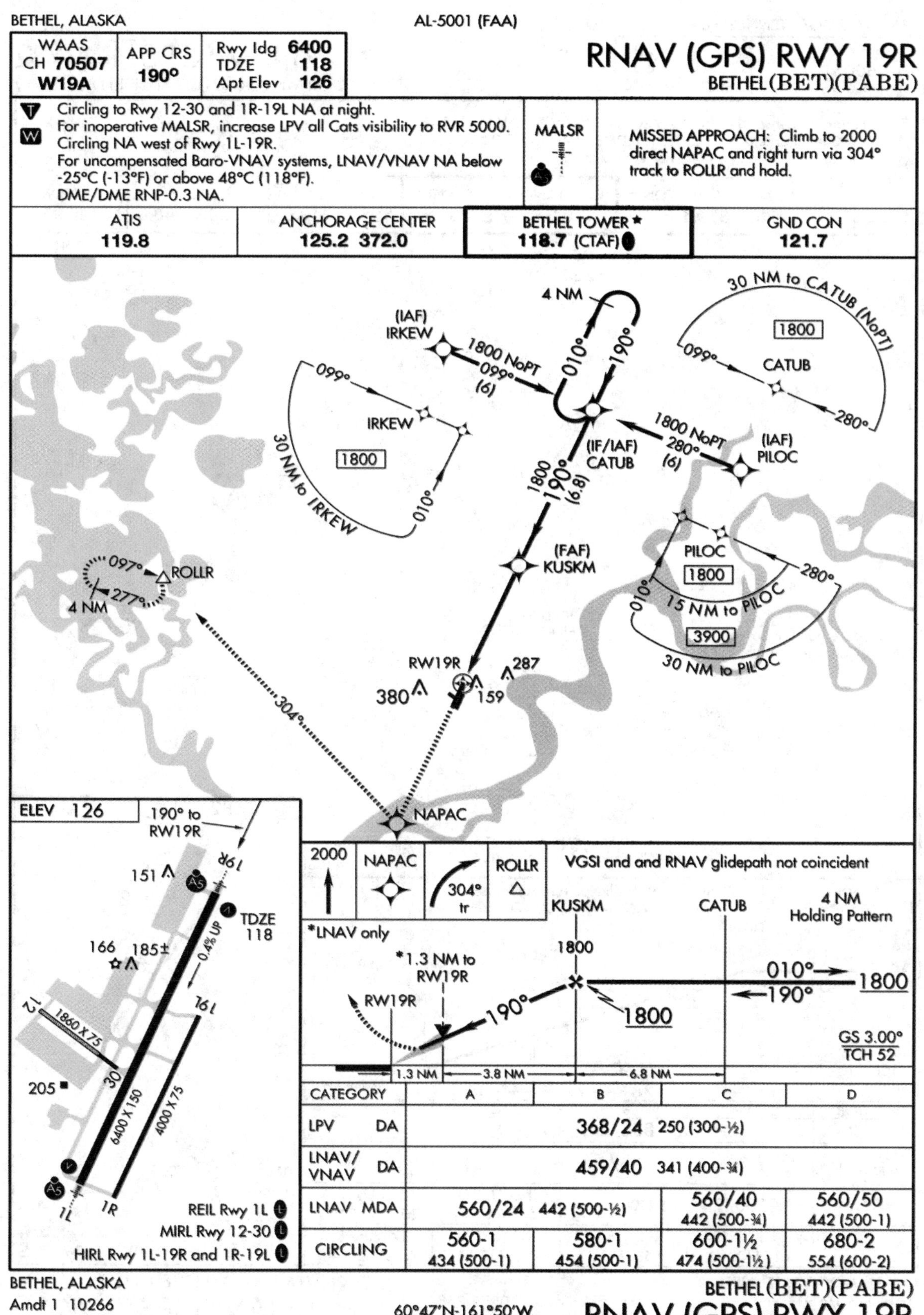

CATEGORY	A	B	C	D
LPV DA	368/24 250 (300-½)			
LNAV/VNAV DA	459/40 341 (400-¾)			
LNAV MDA	560/24 442 (500-½)		560/40 442 (500-¾)	560/50 442 (500-1)
CIRCLING	560-1 434 (500-1)	580-1 454 (500-1)	600-1½ 474 (500-1½)	680-2 554 (600-2)

Figure 249. RNAV (GPS) RWY 19R (BET) (PABE).

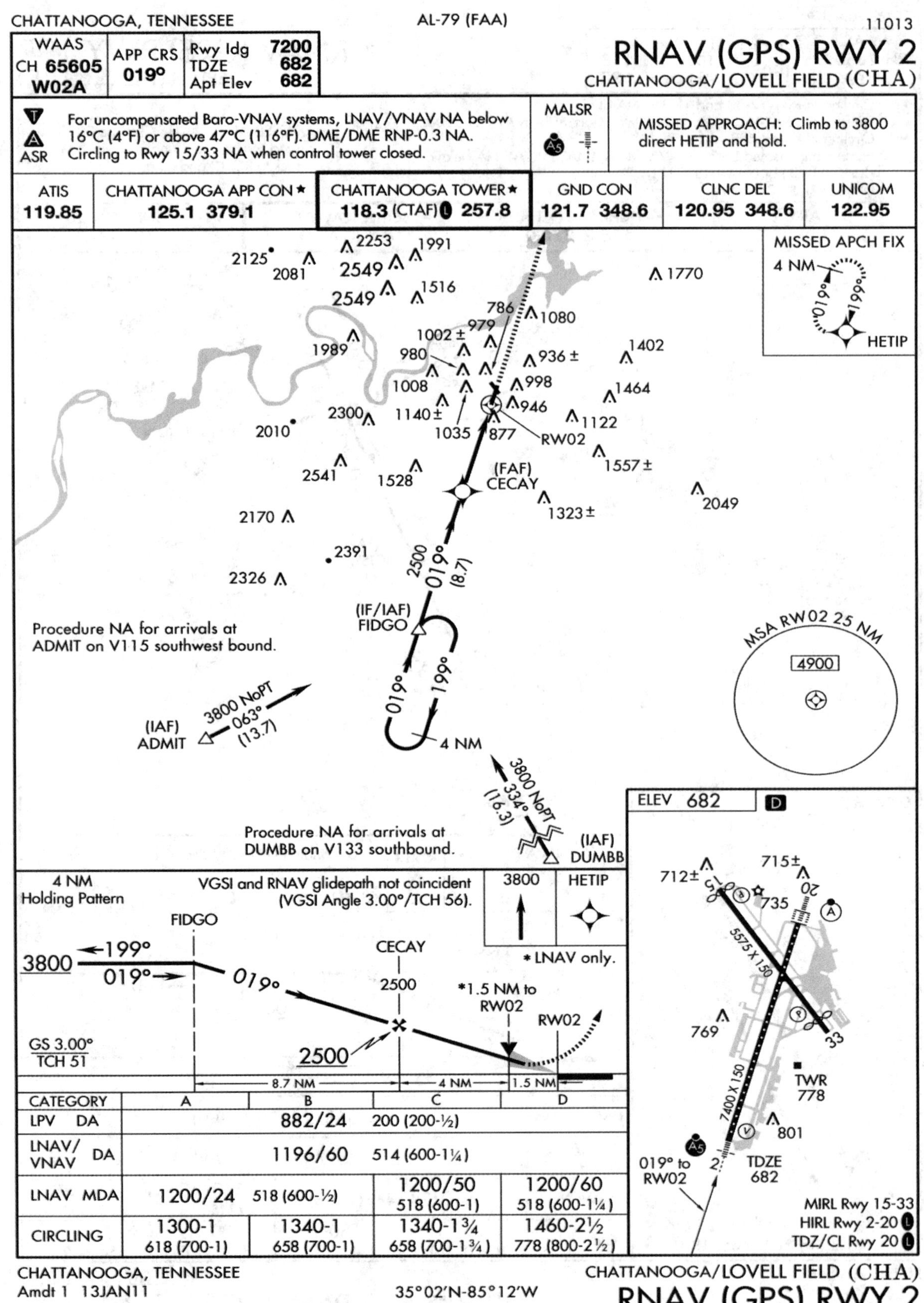

CATEGORY	A	B	C	D
LPV DA	882/24 200 (200-½)			
LNAV/VNAV DA	1196/60 514 (600-1¼)			
LNAV MDA	1200/24 518 (600-½)		1200/50 518 (600-1)	1200/60 518 (600-1¼)
CIRCLING	1300-1 618 (700-1)	1340-1 658 (700-1)	1340-1¾ 658 (700-1¾)	1460-2½ 778 (800-2½)

Figure 250. RNAV (GPS) RWY 2 (CHA).

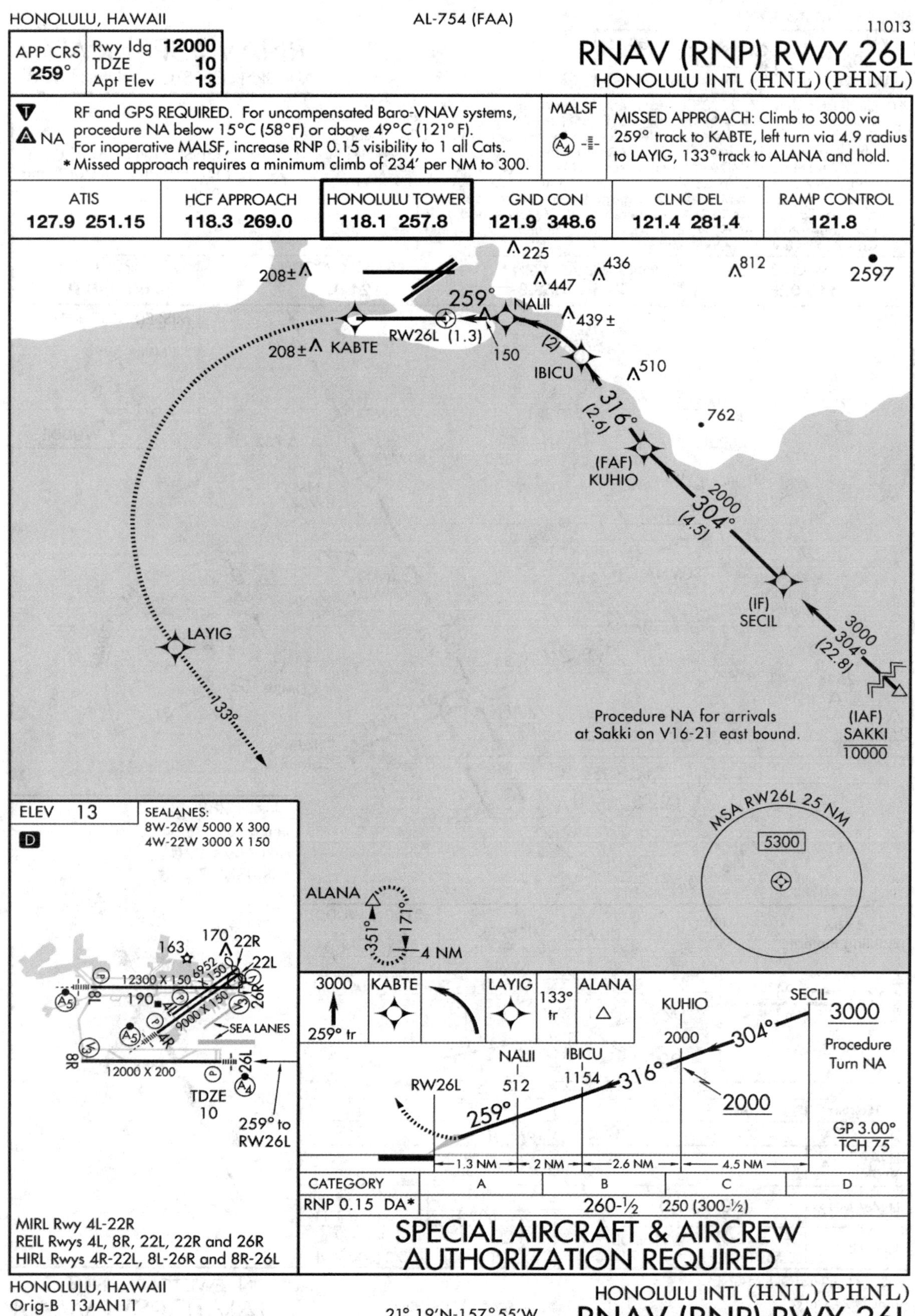

Figure 251. RNAV (RNP) RWY 26L (HNL) (PHNL).

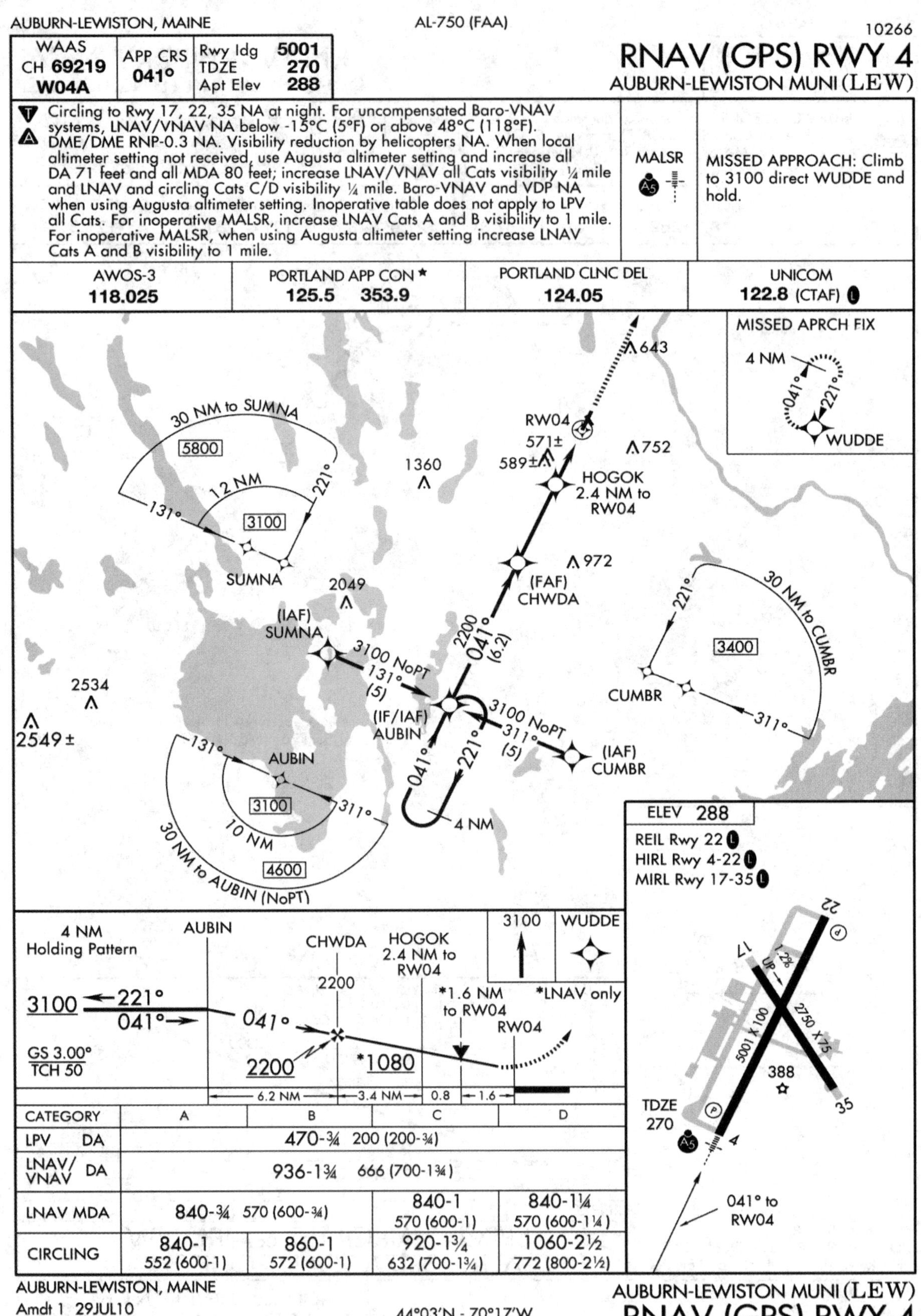

CATEGORY	A	B	C	D
LPV DA	470-¾ 200 (200-¾)			
LNAV/VNAV DA	936-1¾ 666 (700-1¾)			
LNAV MDA	840-¾ 570 (600-¾)		840-1 570 (600-1)	840-1¼ 570 (600-1¼)
CIRCLING	840-1 552 (600-1)	860-1 572 (600-1)	920-1¾ 632 (700-1¾)	1060-2½ 772 (800-2½)

Figure 252. RNAV (GPS) RWY 4 (LEW).

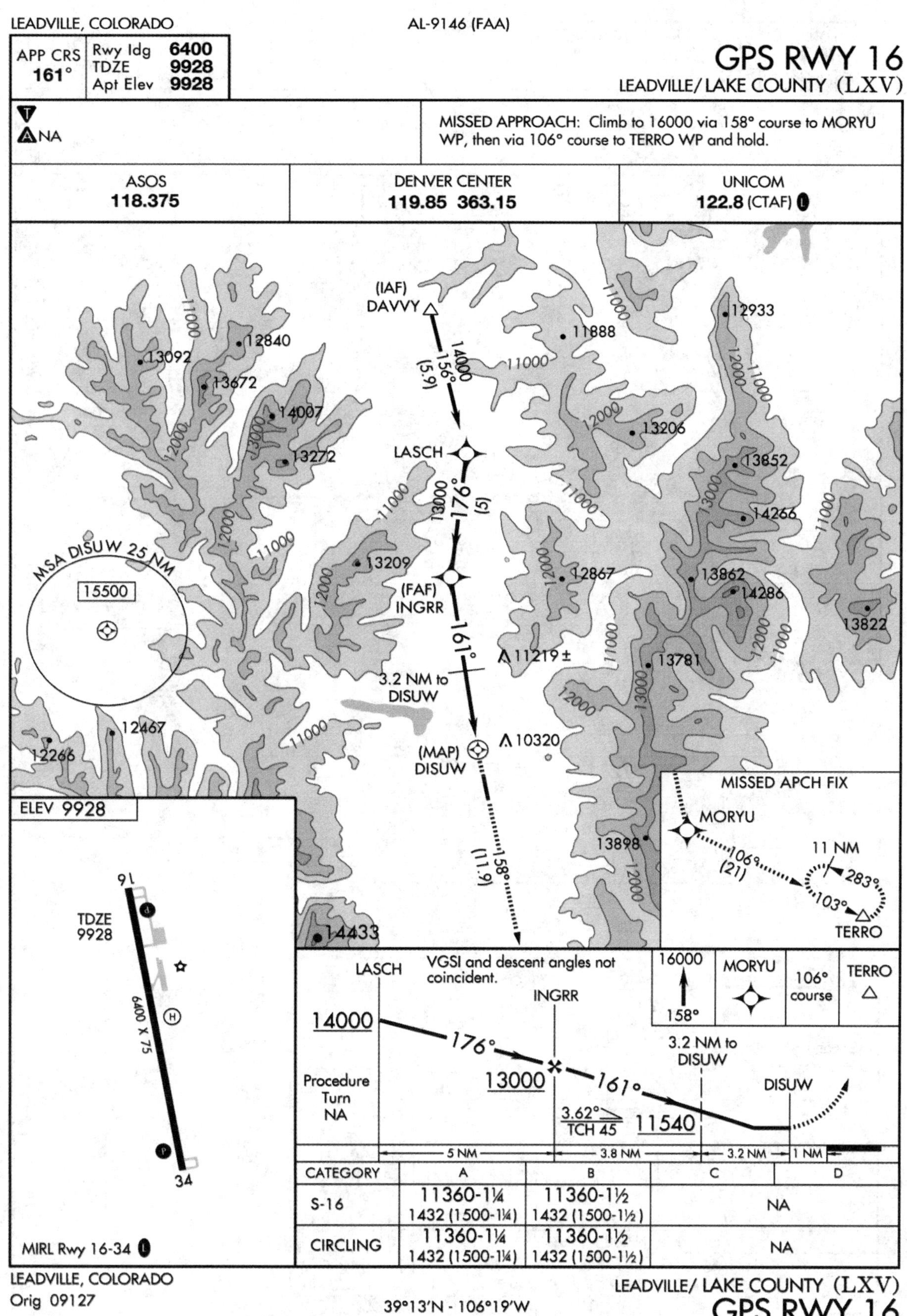

CATEGORY	A	B	C	D
S-16	11360-1¼ 1432 (1500-1¼)	11360-1½ 1432 (1500-1½)	NA	
CIRCLING	11360-1¼ 1432 (1500-1¼)	11360-1½ 1432 (1500-1½)	NA	

Figure 253. GPS RWY 16 (LXV).

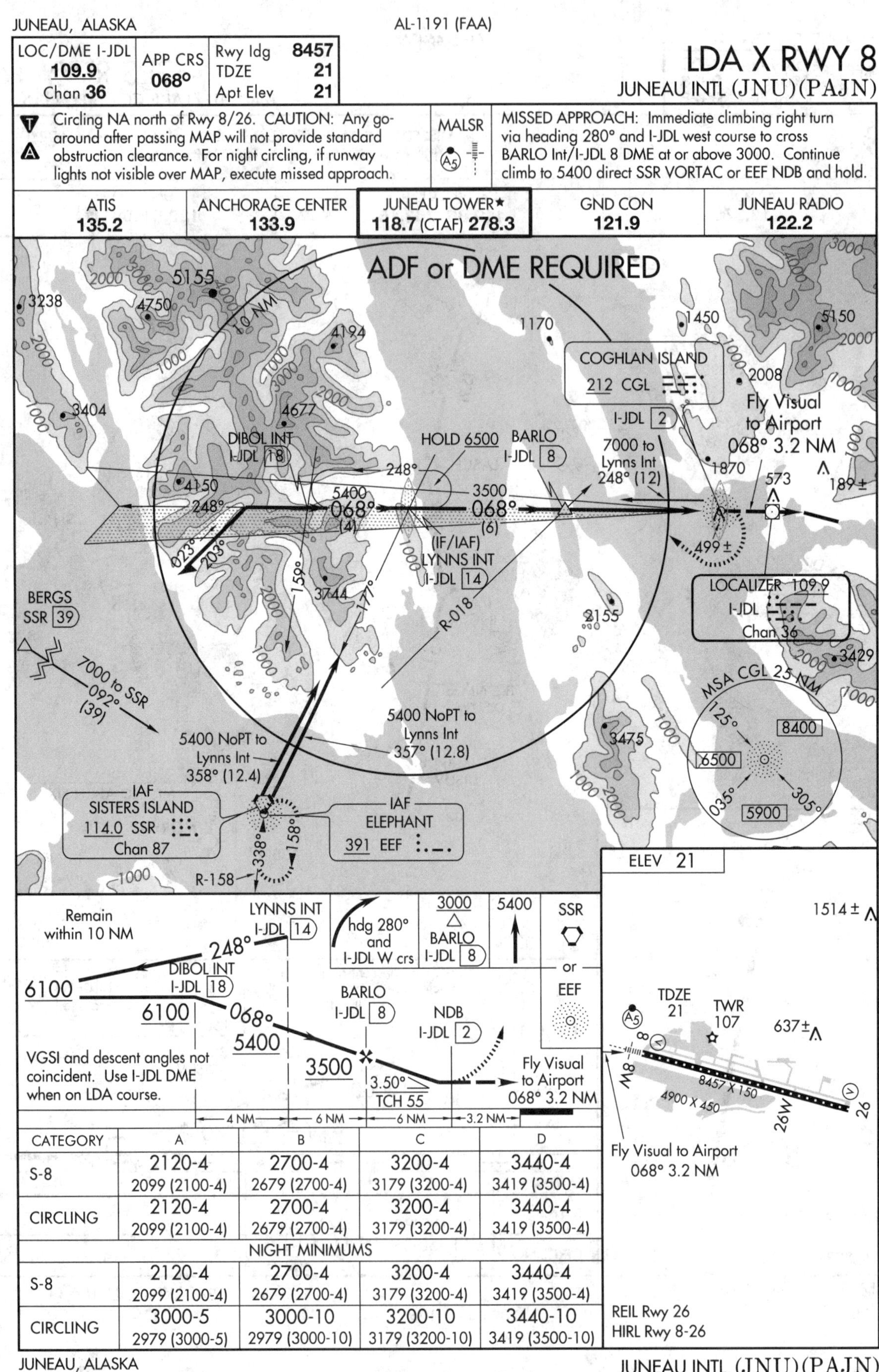

CATEGORY	A	B	C	D
S-8	2120-4 2099 (2100-4)	2700-4 2679 (2700-4)	3200-4 3179 (3200-4)	3440-4 3419 (3500-4)
CIRCLING	2120-4 2099 (2100-4)	2700-4 2679 (2700-4)	3200-4 3179 (3200-4)	3440-4 3419 (3500-4)
NIGHT MINIMUMS				
S-8	2120-4 2099 (2100-4)	2700-4 2679 (2700-4)	3200-4 3179 (3200-4)	3440-4 3419 (3500-4)
CIRCLING	3000-5 2979 (3000-5)	3000-10 2979 (3000-10)	3200-10 3179 (3200-10)	3440-10 3419 (3500-10)

Figure 254. LDA X RWY 8 (JNU) (PAJN).

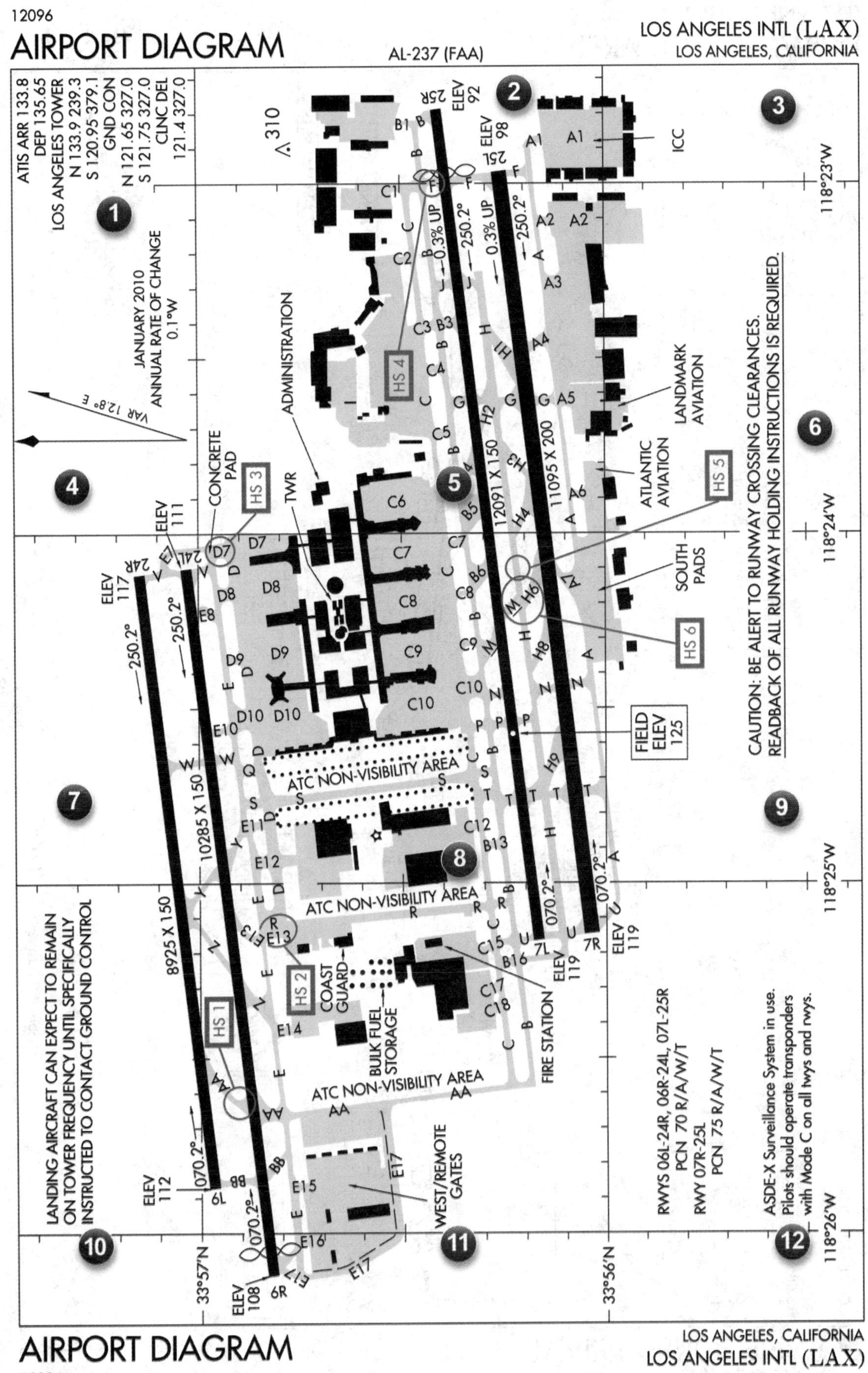

Figure 255. Airport Diagram (LAX).

(DOWNE.DOWNE4) 09351

DOWNE FOUR ARRIVAL

ST-237 (FAA)

LOS ANGELES INTL
LOS ANGELES, CALIFORNIA

PEACH SPRINGS
112.0 PGS
Chan 57
N35°37.48'-W113°32.67'
L-8, H-4

FL 250
229°
(120)

BUGGA
N34°43.13'
W115°43.11'

103
119

226°
(15)
102

DIKES
N34°36.17'
W115°59.22'

FL 230
(24)
87

EMMEY
N34°24.96'
W116°24.91'

63

14000
226°
(47)

TWENTYNINE PALMS
114.2 TNP
Chan 89
N34°06.73'-W115°46.19'
L-4, H-4

14000
254°
(48)

LAX
248°

PIONE
N34°05.67'
W116°44.33'

85

248°
(25)

HECTOR
112.7 HEC
Chan 74
N34°47.82'-W116°27.78'
L-7, H-4

10500
211°
(35)

PDZ 31
44

RESOR
N34°23.40'
W116°57.68'

40

210°
(30)

RUSTT
N34°02.89'
W117°14.55'

16

60

(8)

CIVET
N34°02.07'
W117°23.45'

10

R-030
R-046

PARADISE
112.2 PDZ
Chan 59

7000
248°
(12)
52

R-302

BINDY
N34°00.72' - W117°38.16'
TURBOJET VERTICAL NAVIGATION PLANNING INFORMATION
Expect clearance to cross at or above 12000'.

40
(17)

BASET
N33°58.72' - W117°58.71'
TURBOJET VERTICAL NAVIGATION PLANNING INFORMATION
Expect clearance to cross at 10000'.

R-003

(7)
23

R-327

SEAL BEACH
115.7 SLI
Chan 104

DOWNE
N33°57.86'
W118°07.42'

16

(17)
265°

R-068
R-085

SANTA MONICA
110.8 SMO
Chan 45
N34°00.61'
W118°27.40'

LOS ANGELES
113.6 LAX
Chan 83

259°
(19)

FILLMORE
112.5 FIM
Chan 72

R-158

WAKER
N34°01.90'
W118°50.00'

SOCAL APP CON
124.05 353.775
ATIS
133.8

N

NOTE: This arrival utilized for noise abatement between 0000 LCL and 0630 LCL.
NOTE: DME Required.

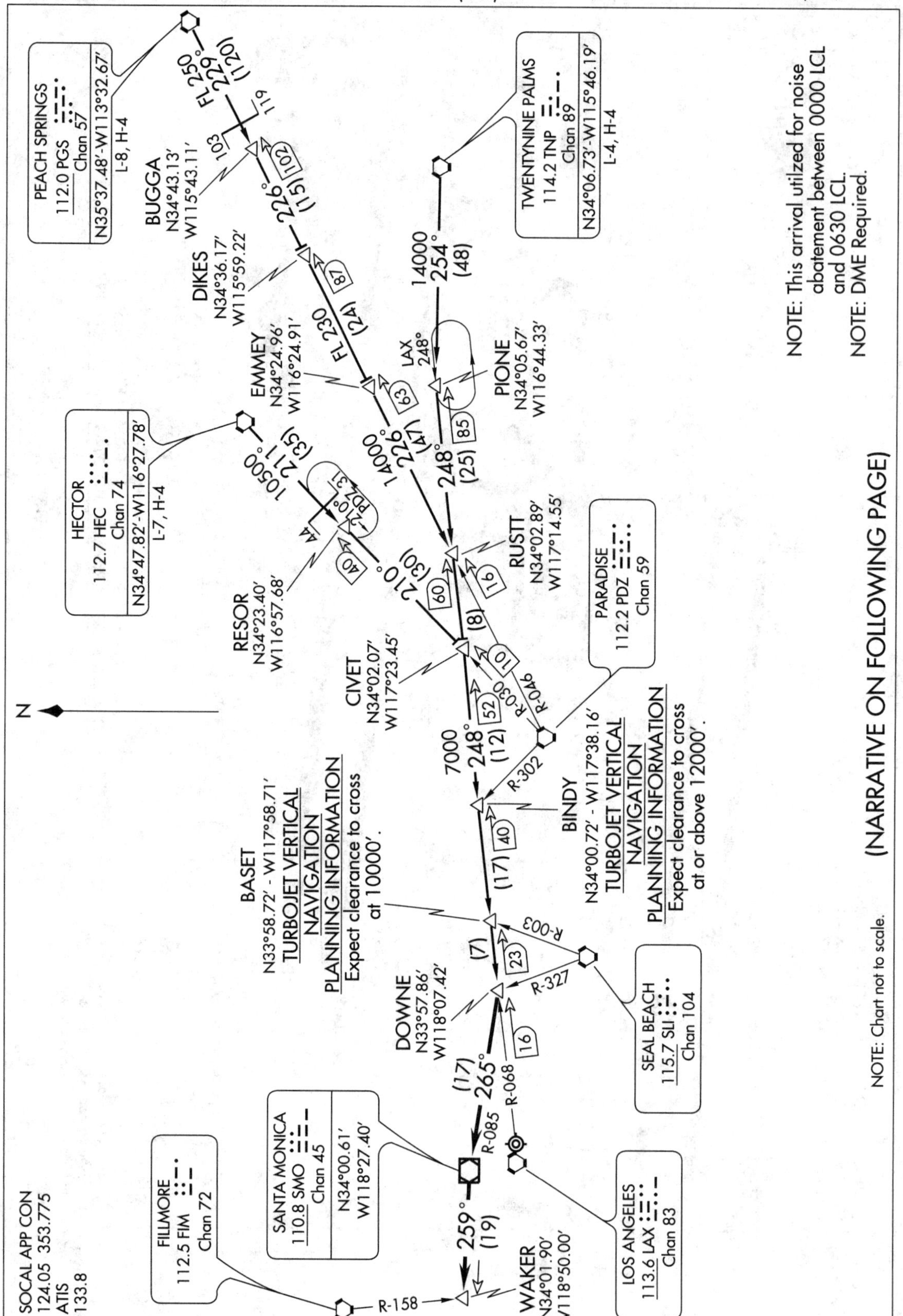

(NARRATIVE ON FOLLOWING PAGE)

NOTE: Chart not to scale.

DOWNE FOUR ARRIVAL
(DOWNE.DOWNE4) 09351

LOS ANGELES, CALIFORNIA
LOS ANGELES INTL

Figure 255A. DOWNE FOUR Arrival (DOWNE.DOWNE4).

(DOWNE.DOWNE4) 02276

DOWNE FOUR ARRIVAL

ST-237 (FAA)

LOS ANGELES INTL
LOS ANGELES, CALIFORNIA

ARRIVAL DESCRIPTION

HECTOR TRANSITION (HEC.DOWNE4): From over HEC VORTAC via HEC R-211 and PDZ R-030 to CIVET INT, then LAX R-068 to DOWNE INT. Thence....
PEACH SPRINGS TRANSITION (PGS.DOWNE4): From over PGS VORTAC via PGS R-229 and PDZ R-046 to RUSTT INT, then LAX R-068 to DOWNE INT. Thence....
TWENTYNINE PALMS TRANSITION (TNP.DOWNE4): From over TNP VORTAC via TNP R-254 to PIONE DME, then LAX R-068 to DOWNE INT.Thence....
....From DOWNE INT via SMO R-085 to SMO VOR/DME, then via SMO R-259 to WAKER INT, expect vector to final approach course for runways 6 and 7.

DOWNE FOUR ARRIVAL
(DOWNE.DOWNE4) 02276

LOS ANGELES, CALIFORNIA
LOS ANGELES INTL

Figure 255B. DOWNE FOUR Arrival (DOWNE.DOWNE4).

LOS ANGELES

LOS ANGELES INTL (LAX) 9 SW UTC–8(–7DT) N33°56.55′ W118°24.48′ **LOS ANGELES**

125 B S4 **FUEL** JET A OX 1, 3 LRA Class I, ARFF Index E NOTAM FILE LAX **COPTER**

RWY 07L–25R: H12091X150 (CONC–GRVD) PCN 70 R/A/W/T HIRL CL **H-4I, L-3E, 4G, 7B, A**

IAP, AD

RWY 07L: MALSR. TDZL. PAPI(P4L)—GA 3.0° TCH 59′. Rgt tfc.

RWY 25R: MALSR. Thld dsplcd 957′. Railroad. 0.3% up.

RWY 07R–25L: H11095X200 (CONC–GRVD) PCN 75 R/A/W/T HIRL CL

RWY 07R: MALSR. PAPI(P4L)—GA 3.0° TCH 57′. Pole. Rgt tfc.

RWY 25L: ALSF2. TDZL. Railroad. 0.3% up.

RWY 06R–24L: H10285X150 (CONC–GRVD) PCN 70 R/A/W/T HIRL CL

RWY 06R: MALSR. TDZL. PAPI(P4L)—GA 3.0° TCH 78′. Thld dsplcd 331′. Pole.

RWY 24L: MALSR. PAPI(P4R)—GA 3.0° TCH 79′. Rgt tfc.

RWY 06L–24R: H8925X150 (CONC–GRVD) PCN 70 R/A/W/T HIRL CL

RWY 06L: MALSR. PAPI(P4L)—GA 3.0° TCH 77′. Pole.

RWY 24R: ALSF2. TDZL. PAPI(P4L)—GA 3.0° TCH 73′. Sign. Rgt tfc.

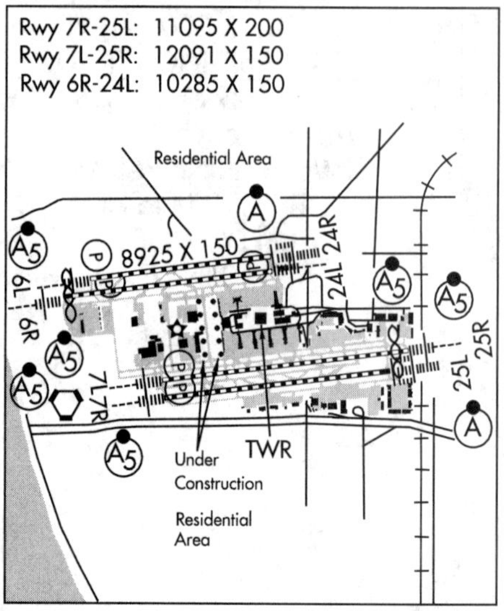

AIRPORT REMARKS: Attended continuously. Rwy 25L preferred emerg rwy. Numerous birds on and invof airport. Turbulence may be deflected upward from the blast fence 180′ E of Rwy 25R. ASDE–X Surveillance System in use: Pilots should operate transponders with Mode C on all twys and rwys. Tom Bradley International Gates: check LAWA (Los Angeles World Airport) rules and regulations for latest operating procedures. For B–777–300 and 300ER/A340–600 acft ops restrictions ctc LAX afld ops (310) 646–4265. Practice instrument approaches and touch and go landings are prohibited. Noise sensitive arpt. On westerly tkfs no turns before crossing shoreline. Over–ocean apchs utilized 0800–1430Z‡. Rwy 24R ALSF2 operates as SSALR till weather goes below VFR. Rwy 25L ALSF2 operates as SSALR until weather goes below VFR. Westbound B747–400 acft on Twy C prohibited from southbound turns onto Twy P. (Twy C–7, C–8, C–9 north of Twy C) and Twy D–7 south of Twy E will not accommodate B747 200 and larger acft. Twy D between Twy D–7 and D–8 (north of terminal one) restricted to B–767–300 and smaller acft. Taxilane D7 south of Twy E Rstd to 767–300 acft and smaller. Twy E–17, A340–600, B777–300/300ER acft northbound turn onto Twy E–17 from westbound Twy E prohibited. Twy E, A340–600, B777–300/300ER acft westbound turn onto Twy E from southbound Twy BB prohibited. Twy C–8, A340–600, B777–300/300ER acft prohibited on Twy C–8 between Twy B and Twy C. Twy C–9, A340–600, B777–300/300ER acft prohibited on Twy C–9 between Twy B and Twy C. A–380 ops ctc LAX afld opr (310) 646–4265 for acft movement procedures. West remote gates: acft use of open gates as taxi path is prohibited (gates 206, 207, 208, 209). A 700′X500′ clearway has been reestablished at west end of Rwy 24R. Touchdown, midpoint and rollout runway visual range avbl Rwy 06L, Rwy 24R, Rwy 06R, Rwy 24L, Rwy 07R, Rwy 25L, Rwy 07L, Rwy 25R. Simultaneous acft ops prohibited on Twy T and Twy H9 between Rwy 07L–25R and Rwy 07R–25L. Simultaneous acft ops prohibited on Twy H2 and Twy G between Rwy 07L–25R and Rwy 07R–25L. Overnight storage fee. Flight Notification Service (ADCUS) available. NOTE: See Special Notices—Noise Abatement Procedures, Continuous Power Facilities.

WEATHER DATA SOURCES: ASOS (310) 568-1486

COMMUNICATIONS: D-ATIS ARR 133.8 **D-ATIS DEP** 135.65 310-646-2297 **UNICOM** 122.95

Ⓡ**SOCAL APP CON** 128.5 (045°-089°), 124.9 (090°-224°), 124.5 (225°-044°) 124.3 (App from west)

TOWER 133.9 (N. complex), 120.95 (S. complex) 119.8

GND CON 121.75 (S. complex) 121.65 (N. complex) **CLNC DEL** 121.4 120.35

Ⓡ**SOCAL DEP CON** 125.2 (225°-044°) 124.3 (045°-224°) (Dep to west)

AIRSPACE: CLASS B See VFR Terminal Area Chart

RADIO AIDS TO NAVIGATION: NOTAM FILE LAX.

(H) VORTACW 113.6 LAX Chan 83 N33°55.99′ W118°25.92′ 050° 1.3 NM to fld. 182/15E.

VOR portion unusable:

270°-277° byd 25 NM blo 8,000′

277°-300° byd 10 NM blo 8,000′

277°-300° byd 28 NM blo 12,000′

VOR portion unusable:

175°-205° byd 10 NM blo 3,000′

Figure 256. Excerpt from Chart Supplement.

CONTINUED FROM PRECEDING PAGE

ILS/DME 108.5 I-UWU Chan 22 Rwy 06L. Class IE. DME also serves Rwy 24R.
ILS/DME 111.7 I-GPE Chan 54 Rwy 06R. Class IE. MM OTS indef. DME also serves Rwy 24L.
ILS/DME 111.1 I-IAS Chan 48 Rwy 07L. Class ID. MM OTS indef. Glideslope unusable byd 5° right of localizer course. DME also serves Rwy 25R.
ILS/DME 109.9 I-MKZ Chan 36 Rwy 07R. Class IT. GS unuseable 5° left and 4° right of course. Coupled approaches not applicable below 264 ' MSL. DME also serves Rwy 25L.
ILS/DME 111.7 I-HQB Chan 54 Rwy 24L. Class IE. DME also serves Rwy 06R.
ILS/DME 108.5 I-OSS Chan 22 Rwy 24R. Class IIIE. DME also serves Rwy 06L
ILS/DME 109.9 I-LAX Chan 36 Rwy 25L. Class IIIE.
ILS/DME 111.1 I-CFN Chan 48 Rwy 25R. Class IE. DME also serves Rwy 07L.

WHITEMAN (WHP) 1 E UTC–8(–7DT) N34°15.56´ W118°24.81´ **LOS ANGELES**
1003 B S4 **FUEL** 100LL, JET A OX 1, 3 TPA—2003(1000) NOTAM FILE WHP **COPTER**
RWY 12–30: H4120X75 (ASPH) S–12.5 MIRL 1.0% up NW **L–3E, 4G, 7B, A**
RWY 12: REIL. PAPI(P2R)—GA 3.8° TCH 40´. Thld dsplcd 729´. P-line. **IAP, AD**
RWY 30: REIL. PAPI(P2L)—GA 3.8° TCH 40´. Thld dsplcd 478´. P-line. Rgt tfc.

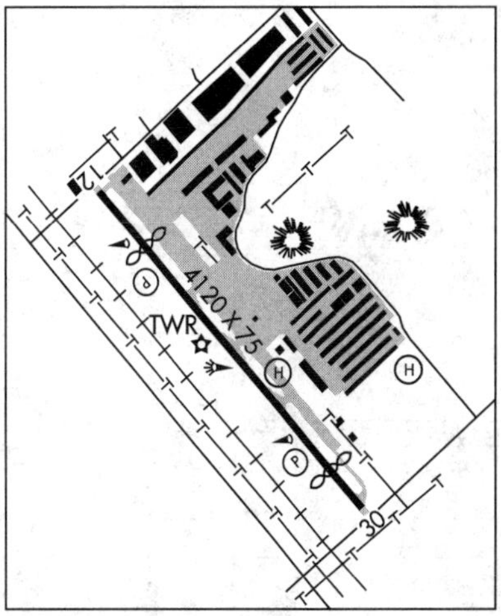

RUNWAY DECLARED DISTANCE INFORMATION
RWY 12: TORA–3442 TODA–4120 ASDA–3910 LDA–3181
RWY 30: TORA–3191 TODA–4120 ASDA–3940 LDA–3462
AIRPORT REMARKS: Attended continuously. Birds on and invof arpt. Helicopter ops 2500´ MSL (1500´ AGL) and below. Arpt CLOSED to helicopter training/pattern opr 0400–1600Z‡. Dirt infield areas. Helicopters advised to use care to prevent blasting dirt and debris onto movement areas.
WEATHER DATA SOURCES: AWOS-3PT 132.1 (818) 899-9820.
COMMUNICATIONS: CTAF 135.0 **ATIS** 132.1 818-899-9820
UNICOM 122.95
®**SOCAL APP/DEP CON** 120.4 134.2 (VNY 280°-BUR 050°) 134.2 (VNY 160°-VNY 280°)
TOWER 135.0 (1600-0400Z‡) **GND CON** 125.0
CLNC DEL For clnc del when ATCT clsd call Socal App 800-448-3724.
AIRSPACE: CLASS D svc 1600-0400Z‡ other times CLASS G
RADIO AIDS TO NAVIGATION: NOTAM FILE VNY.
VAN NUYS (L) VORW/DME 113.1 VNY Chan 78 N34°13.41´ W118°29.50´ 046° 4.4 NM to fld. 812/15E.
VOR/DME unusable:
010°-030° byd 20 NM blo 6,700´
030°-050° byd 25 NM blo 8,600´
330°-350° byd 25 NM blo 5,500´
350°-010° byd 15 NM blo 6,100´
DME unusable:
094°-096° byd 35 NM blo 5,000´
PACOIMA NDB (MHW) 370 PAI N34°15.58´ W118°24.80´ at fld. NOTAM FILE HHR. VFR only.
COMM/NAV/WEATHER REMARKS: Whiteman arpt altimeter setting not avbl.

LOS BANOS

LOS BANOS MUNI (LSN) 1 W UTC–8(–7DT) N37°03.83´ W120°52.19´ **SAN FRANCISCO**
121 B S2 **FUEL** 100LL, JET A TPA—921(800) NOTAM FILE RIU **L–3B**
RWY 14–32: H3801X75 (ASPH) S–23 MIRL **IAP**
RWY 14: REIL. PAPI(P2L)—GA 3.0° TCH 30´. Tree. Rgt tfc.
RWY 32: REIL. PAPI(P2L)—GA 3.0° TCH 38´. Tree.
AIRPORT REMARKS: Unattended. For cash fuel after hours call 209–827–7070. 24 hour automated fuel avbl with major credit card. Avoid overflight of houses south of arpt. No departures over housing areas to east of arpt. MIRL Rwy 14–32 preset low intensity until 0800Z‡. To increase intensity and ACTIVATE MIRL Rwy 14–32, REIL Rwy 14 and Rwy 32, and PAPI Rwy 14 and Rwy 32—CTAF.
WEATHER DATA SOURCES: AWOS-3 118.675 (209) 827-7084.
COMMUNICATIONS: CTAF/UNICOM 122.8
PANOCHE RCO 122.1R 112.6T (FRESNO RADIO)
®**NORCAL APP/DEP CON** 120.95
RADIO AIDS TO NAVIGATION: NOTAM FILE RIU.
PANOCHE (L) VORTAC 112.6 PXN Chan 73 N36°42.93´ W120°46.72´ 332° 21.3 NM to fld. 2060/16E.
VOR unusable:
230°-280° byd 7NM blo 9,000´

Figure 257. Excerpt from Chart Supplement.

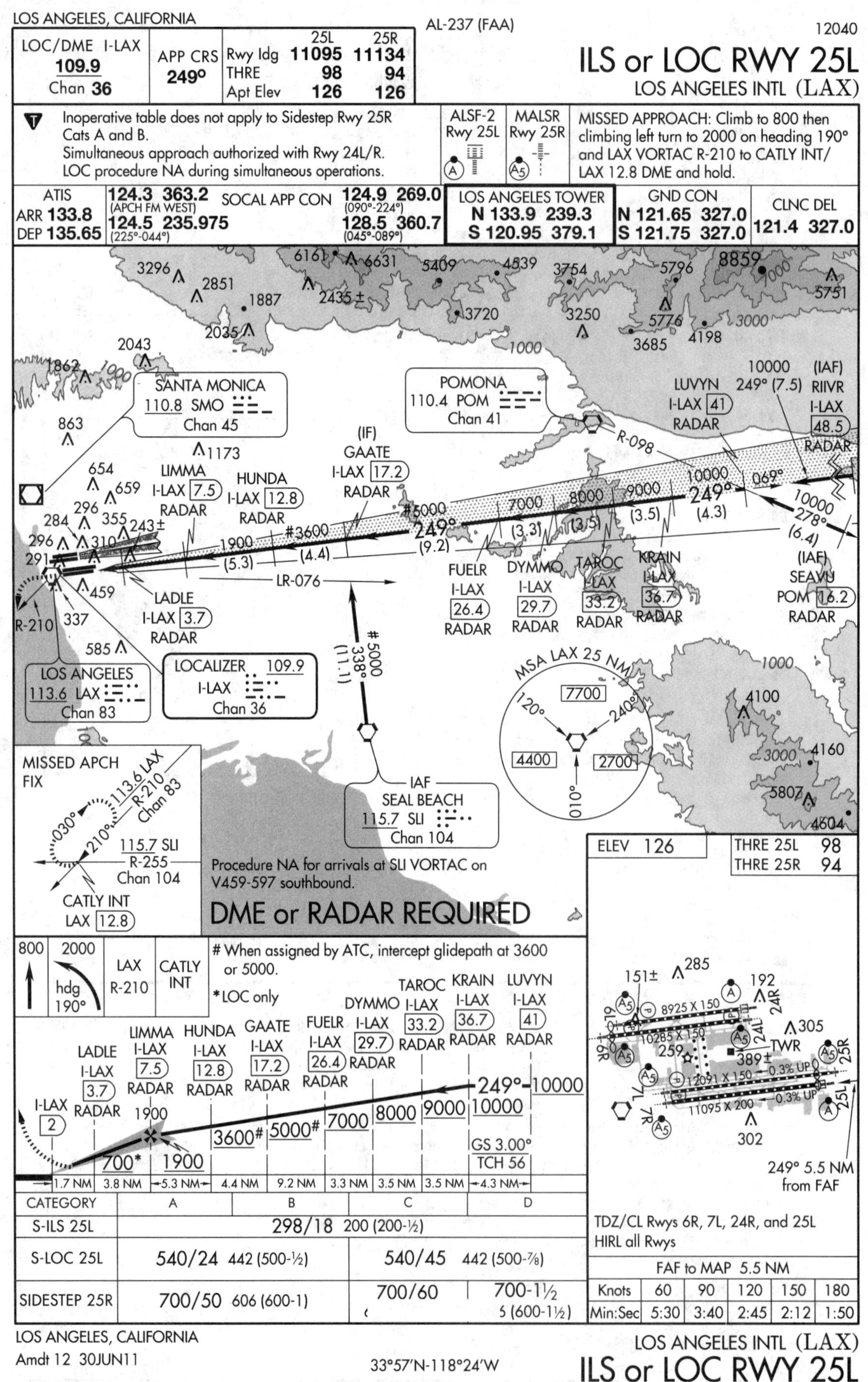

Figure 257A. ILS or ROC RWY 25L (LAX).

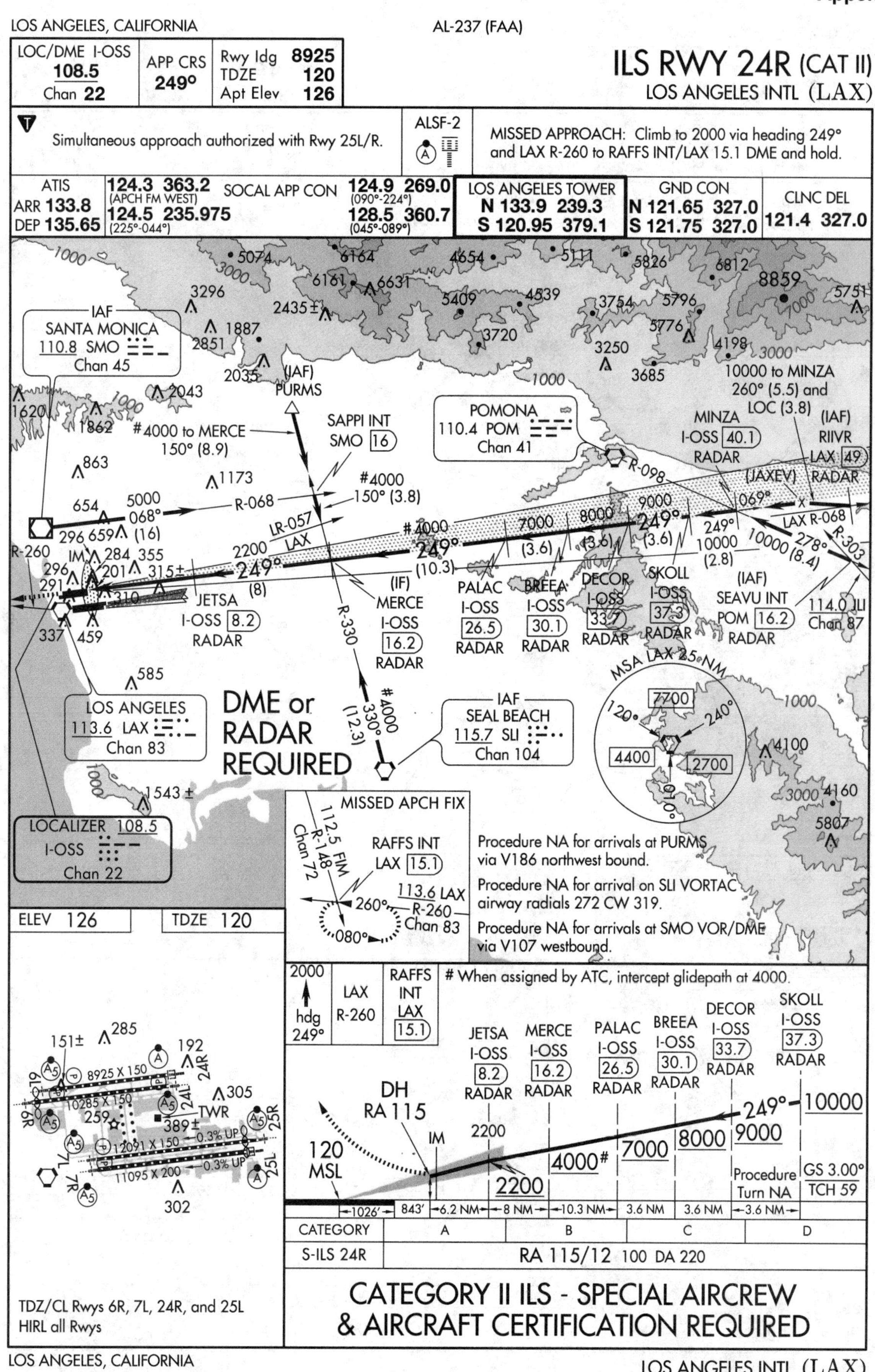

Figure 257B. ILS RWY 24R (CAT II) (LAX).

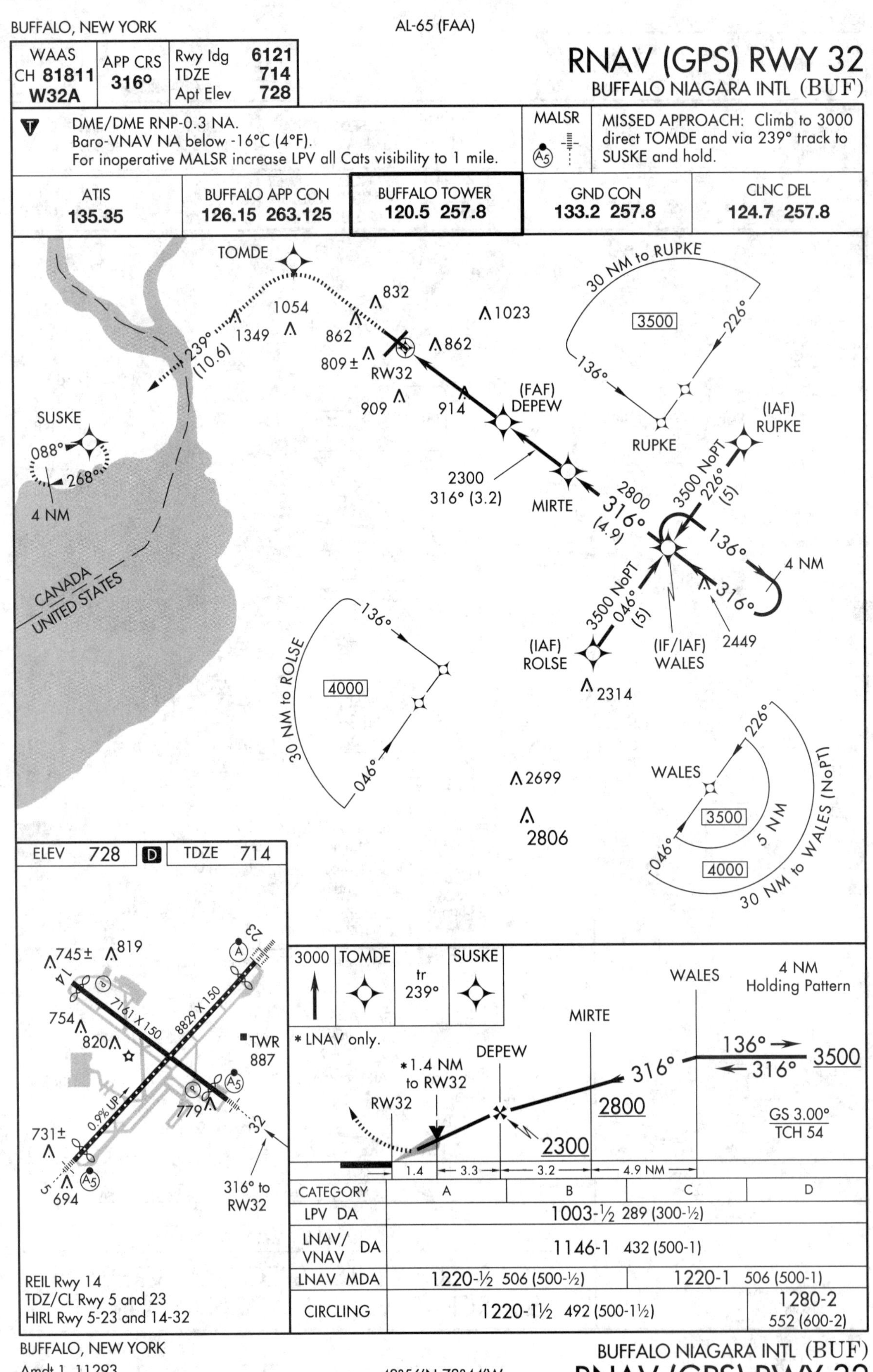

Figure 258. RNAV (GPS) RWY 32 (BUF).

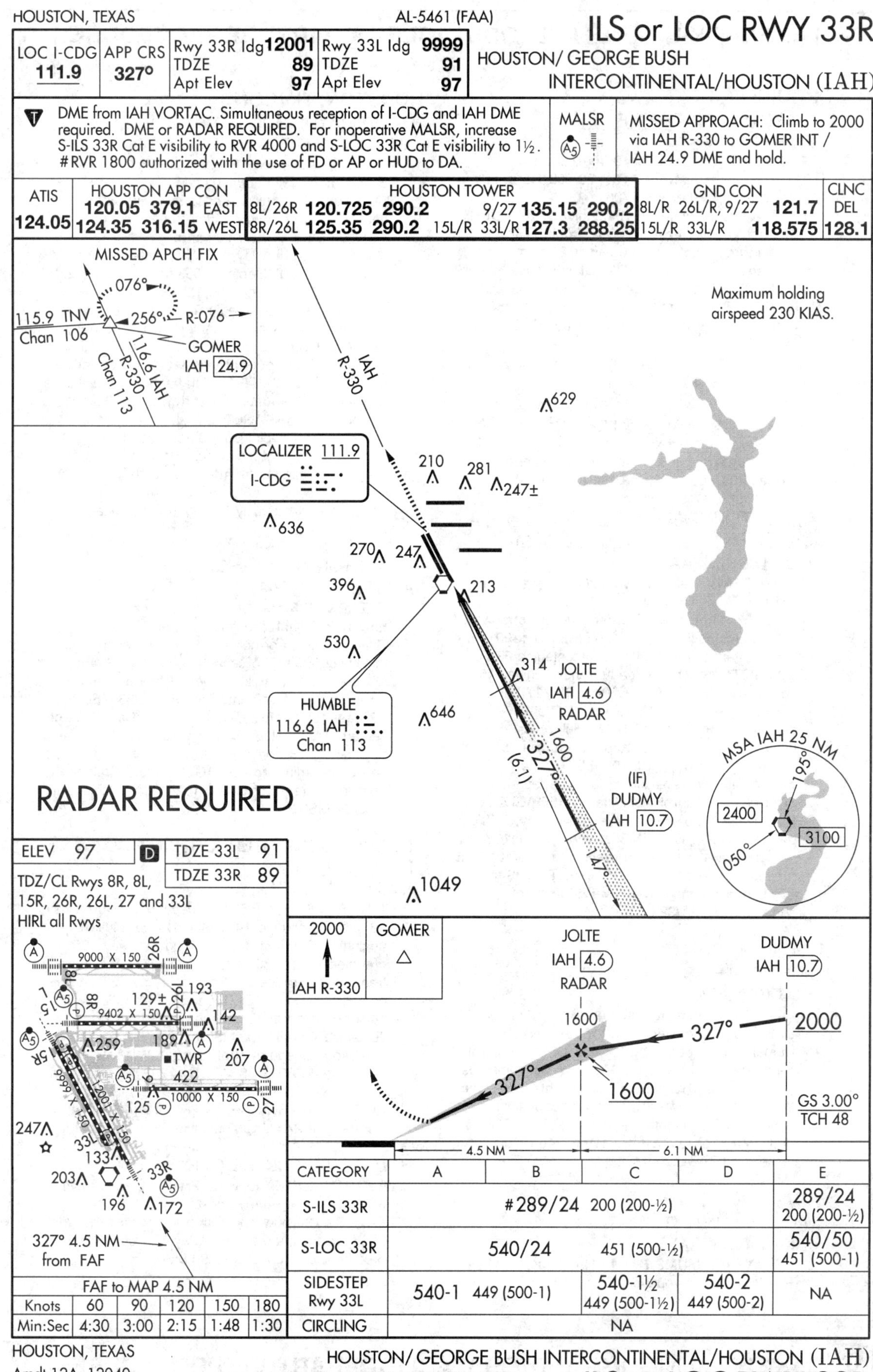

FAF to MAP 4.5 NM					
Knots	60	90	120	150	180
Min:Sec	4:30	3:00	2:15	1:48	1:30

CATEGORY	A	B	C	D	E
S-ILS 33R	#289/24 200 (200-½)				289/24 200 (200-½)
S-LOC 33R	540/24 451 (500-½)				540/50 451 (500-1)
SIDESTEP Rwy 33L	540-1 449 (500-1)		540-1½ 449 (500-1½)	540-2 449 (500-2)	NA
CIRCLING	NA				

Figure 259. ILS or LOC RWY 33R (IAH).

TAKEOFF MINIMUMS AND (OBSTACLE) DEPARTURE PROCEDURES

11349

CROCKETT, TX

HOUSTON COUNTY (DKR)
ORIG 11349 (FAA)

TAKE-OFF MINIMUMS: **Rwy 2,** 400-2 or std. w/min. climb of 280' per NM to 800. **Rwy 20,** 300-1½ or std. w/ min. climb of 459'per NM to 700.

NOTE: **Rwy 2,** multiple trees beginning 57' from DER, 61' right of centerline, up to 50' AGL/399' MSL. Multiple trees and terrain beginning 27' from DER, 109' left of centerline, up to 50' AGL/409' MSL. Tower 1.5 NM from DER, 2864' left of centerline 233' AGL/ 623' MSL. **Rwy 20,** multiple towers beginning 4567' from DER, 1025' right of centerline, up to 200' AGL/ 529' MSL.

EAGLE LAKE, TX

EAGLE LAKE

TAKE-OFF MINIMUMS: **Rwy 17,** 200-1, or std. with a min. climb of 420' per NM to 500.

NOTE: **Rwy 17,** tower 3068' from departure end of runway, 793' left of centerline, 192' AGL/317' MSL.

GALVESTON, TX

SCHOLES INTL AT GALVESTON (GLS)
AMDT 4 08157 (FAA)

TAKE-OFF MINIMUMS: **Rwy 17,** 300-1 or std. w/ min. climb of 502' per NM to 300.

NOTE: **Rwy 13,** bush 381' from departure end of runway, 533' left of centerline, 15' AGL/20' MSL. Fence 201' from departure end of runway, 490' left of centerline, 6' AGL/ 11' MSL. Tree 343' from departure end of runway, 468' right of centerline, 12' AGL/17' MSL. **Rwy 17,** building 3057' from departure end of runway, 339' left of centerline, 123' AGL/130' MSL. Multiple poles beginning 2034' from departure end of runway, 87' right of centerline, up to 60' AGL/70' MSL. Multiple transmission towers beginning 636' from departure end of runway, 551' right of centerline, up to 55' AGL/60' MSL. Tree 460' from departure end of runway, 316' right of centerline, 22' AGL/29' MSL. **Rwy 31,** multiple cranes beginning 4341' from departure end of runway, 1017' left of centerline, up to 131' AGL/ 131' MSL. **Rwy 35,** tree 730' from departure end of runway, 501' right of centerline, 27' AGL/32' MSL.

GIDDINGS, TX

GIDDINGS-LEE COUNTY (GYB)
ORIG 10210 (FAA)

NOTE: **Rwy 17,** numerous trees beginning 720' from DER, 58' right of centerline, up to 50' AGL/479' MSL. Numerous trees beginning 754' from DER, 340' left of centerline, up to 50' AGL/479' MSL. **Rwy 35,** numerous trees beginning 613' from DER, 272' right of centerline, up to 50' AGL/539' MSL. Numerous trees beginning 558' from DER, 265' left of centerline, up to 50' AGL/559' MSL. Vehicle on road 516' from DER, 246' left of centerline, 15' AGL/514' MSL.

HOUSTON, TX

DAN JONES INTL (T51)
ORIG 11321 (FAA)

TAKE-OFF MINIMUMS: **Rwy 17,** NA - numerous trees. **Rwy 35,** NA - numerous trees.

HOUSTON, TX (CON'T)

DAVID WAYNE HOOKS MEMORIAL (DWH)
AMDT 3 08157 (FAA)

TAKE-OFF MINIMUMS: **Rwys 17L, 35R,** NA-Environmental. **Waterways 17, 35,** NA - air traffic.

NOTE: **Rwy 17R,** multiple trees beginning 708' from departure end of runway, 68' left of centerline, up to 71' AGL/220' MSL. Multiple hangars beginning 433' from departure end of runway, 515' left of centerline, up to 37' AGL/182' MSL. DME antenna 653' from departure end of runway, 256' left of centerline, 13' AGL/162' MSL. Multiple trees and pole beginning 85' from departure end of runway, 294' right of centerline, up to 45' AGL/ 189' MSL. **Rwy 35L,** multiple trees and poles beginning 144' from departure end of runway, 32' left of centerline, up to 79' AGL/238' MSL. Multiple hangars and buildings beginning 85' from departure end of runway, 9' left of centerline, up to 53' AGL/202' MSL. Multiple trees, towers and pole beginning 100' from departure end of runway, 124' right of centerline, up to 93' AGL/247' MSL. Vehicle and road 315' from departure end of runway, on centerline 15' AGL/166' MSL. Building 894' from departure end of runway, 231' right of centerline, 23' AGL/173' MSL.

ELLINGTON FIELD (EFD)
AMDT 2 08157 (FAA)

NOTE: **Rwy 17R,** pole 1489' from departure end of runway, 817' right of centerline, 40' AGL/74' MSL. **Rwy 22,** antenna on building 1998' from departure end of runway, 598' right of centerline, 54' AGL/83' MSL. Obstruction light on glide slope 327' from departure end of runway, 543' left of centerline, 39' AGL/68' MSL. **Rwy 35R,** tree 1597' from departure end of runway, 32' left of centerline, 33' AGL/80' MSL. **Rwy 35L,** multiple trees beginning 1118' from departure end of runway, 679' right of centerline, up to 37' AGL/ 77' MSL. Crane 2352' from departure end of runway, 1024' left of centerline, 37' AGL/ 97' MSL.

GEORGE BUSH INTERCONTINENTAL/ HOUSTON (IAH)
AMDT 2 08157 (FAA)

NOTE: **Rwy 8L,** tree 2866' from departure end of runway, 921' left of centerline, 107' AGL/201' MSL. Multiple trees beginning 2750' from departure end of runway, 106' right of centerline, up to 80' AGL/174' MSL. **Rwy 15L,** multiple trees 2638' from departure end of runway, 758' right of centerline, up to 76' AGL/160' MSL. **Rwy 15R,** tower 1431' from departure end of runway, 591' left of centerline, 48' AGL/133' MSL. Antenna on glideslope 1469' from departure end of runway, 621' left of centerline, 49' AGL/133' MSL. **Rwy 26R,** pole 950' from departure end of runway, 660' right of centerline, 40' AGL/129' MSL. **Rwy 33R,** tree 2868' from departure end of runway, 1027' right of centerline, 73' AGL/172' MSL.

HOUSTON EXECUTIVE (TME)

DEPARTURE PROCEDURE: **Rwy 36,** Climb heading 355° to 700 before turning east.

NOTE: **Rwy 36,** power poles from left to right beginning 703' from departure end of runway, 623' left to 685' right of centerline, up to 32' AGL/196' MSL.

11349

TAKEOFF MINIMUMS AND (OBSTACLE) DEPARTURE PROCEDURES

SC-5

Figure 260. Takeoff Minimums and (Obstacle) Departure Procedures.

TAKEOFF MINIMUMS AND (OBSTACLE) DEPARTURE PROCEDURES

11349

HOUSTON, TX (CON'T)

HOUSTON-SOUTHWEST (AXH)
AMDT 5 08157 (FAA)

DEPARTURE PROCEDURE: **Rwy 9,** climb heading 089° to 2000 before turning left. **Rwy 27,** climb heading 269° to 2200 before turning right.

NOTE: **Rwy 9,** multiple hangars beginning 239' from departure end of runway, 360' right of centerline, up to 42' AGL/106' MSL. Multiple trees beginning 501' from departure end of runway, 355' right of centerline, up to 43' AGL/111' MSL. Multiple hangars beginning 119' from departure end of runway, 498' left of centerline, up to 41' AGL/105' MSL. Pole 332' from departure end of runway, 299' left of centerline, 43' AGL/97' MSL. Antenna 1172' from departure end of runway, 658' left of centerline, 51' AGL/115' MSL. Multiple trees beginning 558' from departure end of runway, 68' left of centerline, up to 58' AGL/122' MSL. **Rwy 27,** multiple trees beginning 1050' from departure end of runway, 40' left of centerline, up to 71' AGL/140' MSL. Vehicle and road 99' from departure end of runway, 291' right of centerline, 15' AGL/83' MSL. Multiple trees beginning 873' from departure end of runway, 514' right of centerline, up to 59' AGL/130' MSL. Multiple transmission poles beginning 1304' from departure end of runway, 131' right of centerline, up to 41' AGL/110' MSL.

LONE STAR EXECUTIVE (CXO)
AMDT 3 10266 (FAA)

NOTE: **Rwy 1,** trees beginning 194' from DER, 130' right of centerline, up to 100' AGL/374' MSL. Trees beginning 817' from DER, 15' left of centerline, up to 100' AGL/359' MSL. **Rwy 14,** trees and obstruction light on DME beginning 399' from DER, 80' right of centerline, up to 100' AGL/329' MSL. Trees beginning 640' from DER, 408' left of centerline, up to 100' AGL/329' MSL. **Rwy 19,** trees beginning 68' from DER, 64' right of centerline, up to 100' AGL/344' MSL. Trees beginning 1' from DER, 159' left of centerline, up to 100' AGL/339' MSL. **Rwy 32,** trees beginning 1785' from DER, 973' right of centerline, up to 100' AGL/339' MSL. Trees and vehicles on road beginning 603' from DER, 458' left of centerline, up to 100' AGL/354' MSL.

PEARLAND RGNL

DEPARTURE PROCEDURE: **Rwy 14,** climb heading 139° to 1600 before proceeding south through southwest. **Rwy 32,** climb heading 319° to 900 before proceeding on course.

NOTE: **Rwy 14,** multiple trees beginning 199' from departure end of runway, 226' right of centerline, up to 66' AGL/100' MSL. Vehicle on road 398' from departure end of runway, 405' left of centerline, 9' AGL/55' MSL. Trees 1287' from departure end of runway, 453' left of centerline, up to 56' AGL/90' MSL. **Rwy 32,** multiple trees beginning 690' from departure end of runway, 81' left of centerline, up to 79' AGL/128' MSL. Multiple poles beginning 745' from departure end of runway, 24' left of centerline, up to 40' AGL/80' MSL. Multiple trees and poles beginning 29' from departure end of runway, 11' right of centerline, up to 64' AGL/104' MSL. Building 237' from departure end of runway, 520' right of centerline, 32' AGL/72' MSL.

HOUSTON, TX (CON'T)

SUGAR LAND RGNL (SGR)
AMDT 7 08157 (FAA)

DEPARTURE PROCEDURE: **Rwy 17,** climb heading 170° to 1500 before turning eastbound. **Rwy 35,** climb heading 350° to 1100 before turning southbound.

NOTE: **Rwy 17,** multiple poles beginning 436' from departure end of runway, 172' right of centerline, up to 44' AGL/124' MSL. Railroad 110' from departure end of runway, 10' left of centerline, 23' AGL/104' MSL. Multiple poles beginning 135' from departure end of runway, 270' left of centerline, up to 44' AGL/ 111' MSL. **Rwy 35,** vehicle and road 65' from departure end of runway, 2' right of centerline, 15' AGL/ 96' MSL. Multiple trees beginning 37' from departure end of runway, 275' right of centerline, up to 81' AGL/164' MSL. DME antenna 380' from departure end of runway, 253' right of centerline, 24' AGL/100' MSL. Multiple trees beginning 83' from departure end of runway, 65' left of centerline, up to 81' AGL/155' MSL.

WEISER AIR PARK (EYQ)
AMDT 2 08157 (FAA)

TAKEOFF MINIMUMS: **Rwy 9,** 200-1 or std. w/ min. climb of 399' per NM to 400.

NOTE: **Rwy 9,** tank 4127' from departure end of runway, 1455' left of centerline, 147' AGL/282' MSL. **Rwy 27,** railroad 462' from departure end of runway, 555' left of centerline, 23' AGL/165' MSL. Vehicle and road 650' from departure end of runway, 7' left of centerline, 17' AGL/159' MSL.

WEST HOUSTON (IWS)
AMDT 3 09295 (FAA)

NOTE: **Rwy 15,** vehicles on roadway beginning abeam DER, left and right of centerline, up to 15' AGL/124' MSL. Building 177' from DER, 398' left of centerline, 18' AGL/ 126' MSL. Trees beginning 178' from DER, 289' right of centerline, up to 100' AGL/209' MSL. **Rwy 33,** building 265' from DER, 364' left of centerline, 33' AGL/143' MSL. Trees beginning 2706' from DER, 700' left of centerline, up to 100' AGL/214' MSL. Trees beginning 3159' from DER, 747' right of centerline, up to 100' AGL/216' MSL.

11349

SC-5

Figure 261. Takeoff Minimums and (Obstacle) Departure Procedures.

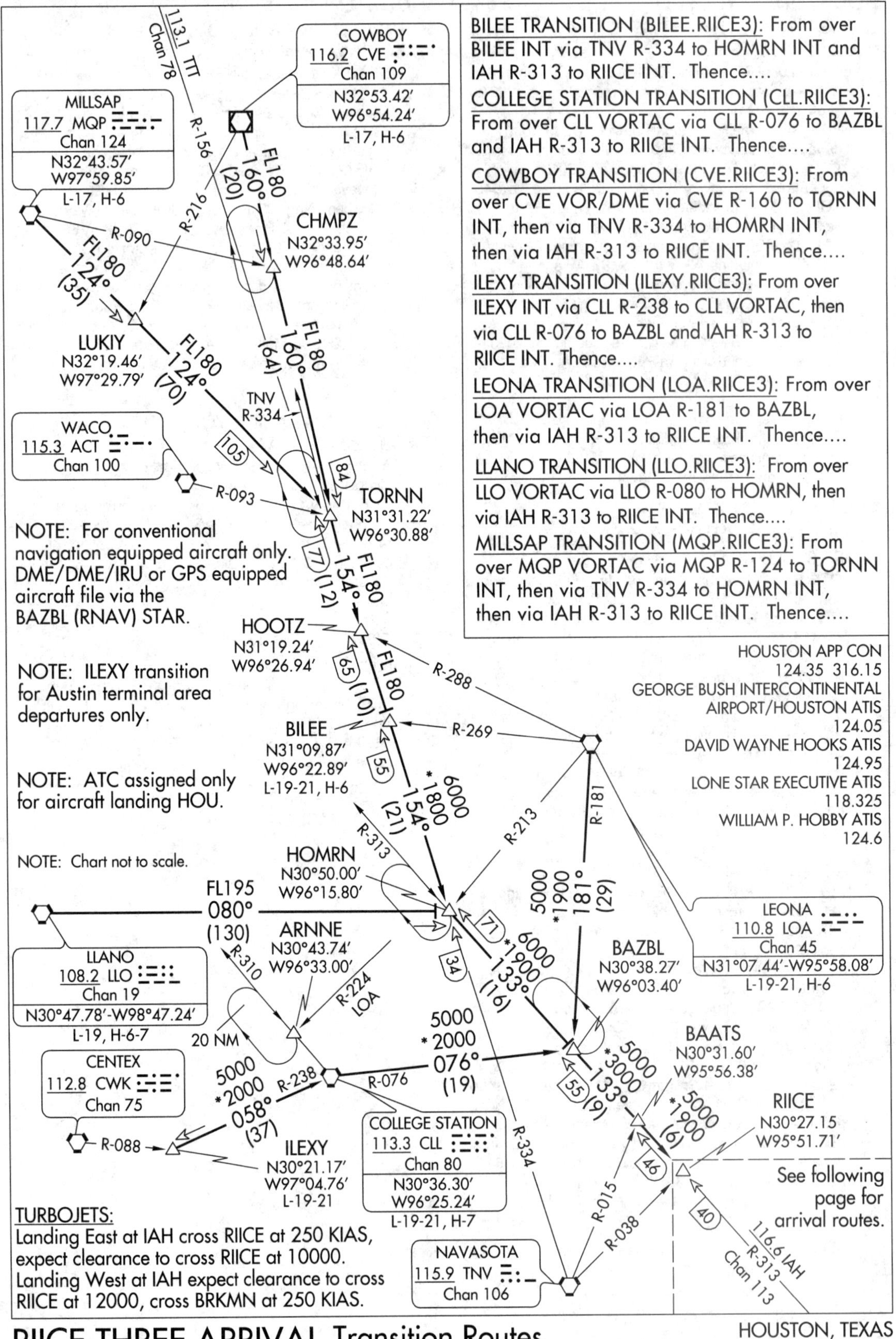
(RIICE.RIICE3) 12096
ST-5461 (FAA)
RIICE THREE ARRIVAL Transition Routes
HOUSTON, TEXAS
BILEE TRANSITION (BILEE.RIICE3): From over BILEE INT via TNV R-334 to HOMRN INT and IAH R-313 to RIICE INT. Thence....
COLLEGE STATION TRANSITION (CLL.RIICE3): From over CLL VORTAC via CLL R-076 to BAZBL and IAH R-313 to RIICE INT. Thence....
COWBOY TRANSITION (CVE.RIICE3): From over CVE VOR/DME via CVE R-160 to TORNN INT, then via TNV R-334 to HOMRN INT, then via IAH R-313 to RIICE INT. Thence....
ILEXY TRANSITION (ILEXY.RIICE3): From over ILEXY INT via CLL R-238 to CLL VORTAC, then via CLL R-076 to BAZBL and IAH R-313 to RIICE INT. Thence....
LEONA TRANSITION (LOA.RIICE3): From over LOA VORTAC via LOA R-181 to BAZBL, then via IAH R-313 to RIICE INT. Thence....
LLANO TRANSITION (LLO.RIICE3): From over LLO VORTAC via LLO R-080 to HOMRN, then via IAH R-313 to RIICE INT. Thence....
MILLSAP TRANSITION (MQP.RIICE3): From over MQP VORTAC via MQP R-124 to TORNN INT, then via TNV R-334 to HOMRN INT, then via IAH R-313 to RIICE INT. Thence....
COWBOY 116.2 CVE Chan 109 N32°53.42′ W96°54.24′ L-17, H-6
113.1 TTT Chan 78
MILLSAP 117.7 MQP Chan 124 N32°43.57′ W97°59.85′ L-17, H-6
R-156
R-216
R-090
FL180 160° (20)
CHMPZ N32°33.95′ W96°48.64′
FL180 124° (35)
LUKIY N32°19.46′ W97°29.79′
FL180 124° (70)
FL180 160° (64)
TNV R-334
WACO 115.3 ACT Chan 100
R-093
105
84
TORNN N31°31.22′ W96°30.88′
NOTE: For conventional navigation equipped aircraft only. DME/DME/IRU or GPS equipped aircraft file via the BAZBL (RNAV) STAR.
77
FL180 154° (12)
HOOTZ N31°19.24′ W96°26.94′
NOTE: ILEXY transition for Austin terminal area departures only.
65
FL180 (10)
R-288
BILEE N31°09.87′ W96°22.89′ L-19-21, H-6
R-269
NOTE: ATC assigned only for aircraft landing HOU.
55
6000 *1800 154° (21)
R-313
R-213
R-181
HOUSTON APP CON 124.35 316.15
GEORGE BUSH INTERCONTINENTAL AIRPORT/HOUSTON ATIS 124.05
DAVID WAYNE HOOKS ATIS 124.95
LONE STAR EXECUTIVE ATIS 118.325
WILLIAM P. HOBBY ATIS 124.6
NOTE: Chart not to scale.
HOMRN N30°50.00′ W96°15.80′
FL195 080° (130)
5000 *1900 181° (29)
LEONA 110.8 LOA Chan 45 N31°07.44′-W95°58.08′ L-19-21, H-6
ARNNE N30°43.74′ W96°33.00′
71
6000 *1900 133° (16)
BAZBL N30°38.27′ W96°03.40′
LLANO 108.2 LLO Chan 19 N30°47.78′-W98°47.24′ L-19, H-6-7
R-310
R-224 LOA
34
20 NM
5000 *2000 076° (19)
BAATS N30°31.60′ W95°56.38′
CENTEX 112.8 CWK Chan 75
5000 *2000 058° (37)
R-238
R-076
55
5000 *3000 133° (9)
RIICE N30°27.15′ W95°51.71′
5000 *1900 (6)
R-088
ILEXY N30°21.17′ W97°04.76′ L-19-21
COLLEGE STATION 113.3 CLL Chan 80 N30°36.30′ W96°25.24′ L-19-21, H-7
R-334
46
See following page for arrival routes.
R-015
R-038
40
116.6 IAH R-313 Chan 113
TURBOJETS:
Landing East at IAH cross RIICE at 250 KIAS, expect clearance to cross RIICE at 10000.
Landing West at IAH expect clearance to cross RIICE at 12000, cross BRKMN at 250 KIAS.
NAVASOTA 115.9 TNV Chan 106
RIICE THREE ARRIVAL Transition Routes
HOUSTON, TEXAS
(RIICE.RIICE3) 12096

Figure 262. RIICE THREE ARRIVAL Transition Routes (RIICE.RIICE3).

(RIICE.RIICE3) 10210 ST-5461 (FAA)

RIICE THREE ARRIVAL Arrival Routes

HOUSTON, TEXAS

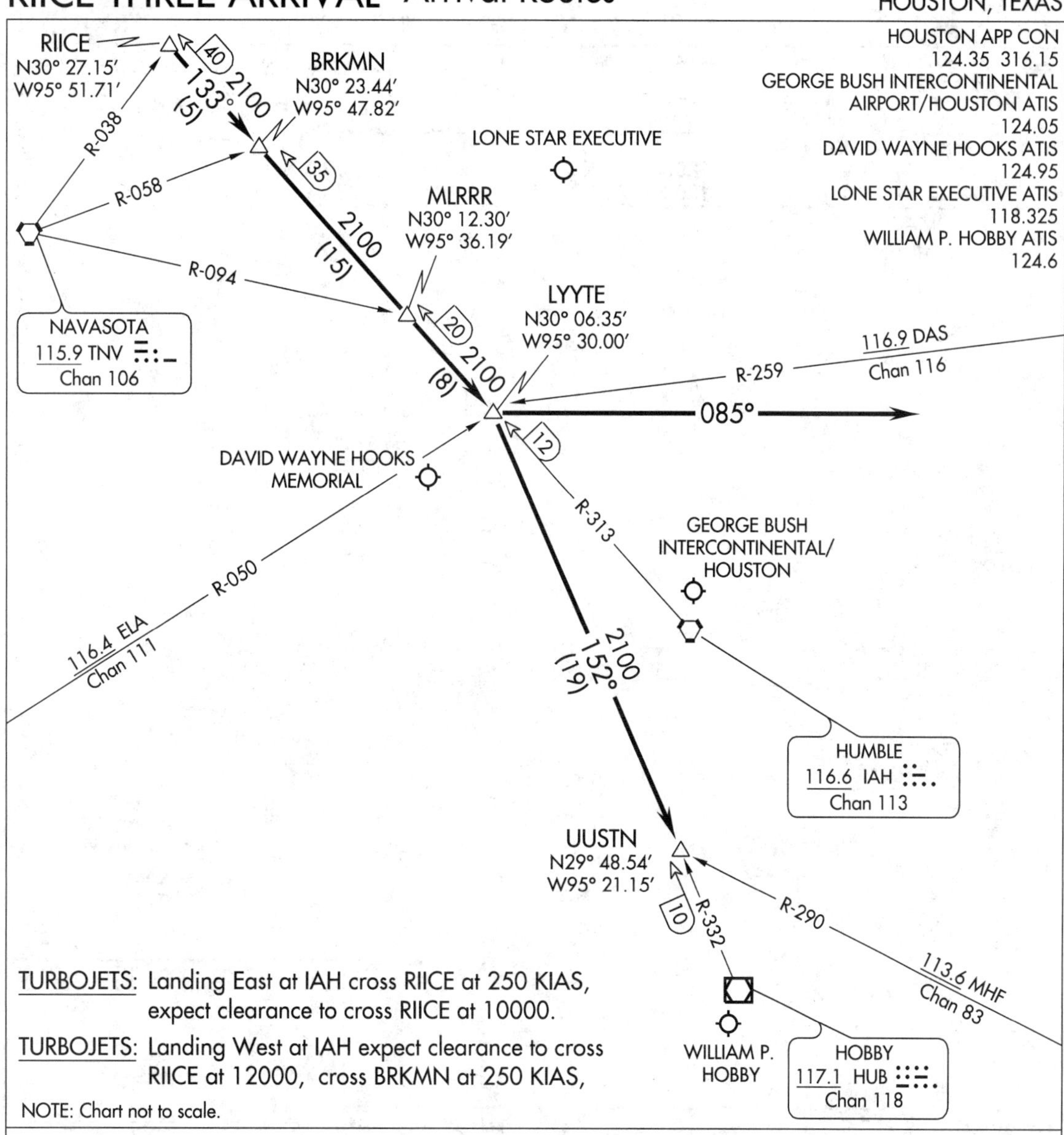

ARRIVAL ROUTE DESCRIPTION

GEORGE BUSH INTERCONTINENTAL/HOUSTON (IAH):

....From over RIICE INT via IAH R-313 to LYYTE INT.

LANDING RUNWAYS 26L/26R, 27: Fly heading 085° for vectors to final approach course.

LANDING ALL OTHER RUNWAYS: Expect vectors to final approach course at or prior to LYYTE INT.

WILLIAM P. HOBBY (HOU) (ATC ASSIGNED):

....From over RIICE INT via IAH R-313 to LYYTE INT, then via HUB R-332 to UUSTN INT, expect vectors to final approach course at or prior to UUSTN INT.

DAVID WAYNE HOOKS MEMORIAL (DWH) and LONE STAR EXCUTIVE (CXO):

....From over RIICE INT via IAH R-313 to LYYTE INT, expect vectors to final approach course at or prior to LYYTE INT.

RIICE THREE ARRIVAL Arrival Routes HOUSTON, TEXAS

(RIICE.RIICE3) 10210

Figure 263. RIICE THREE ARRIVAL Arrival Routes (RIICE.RIICE3).

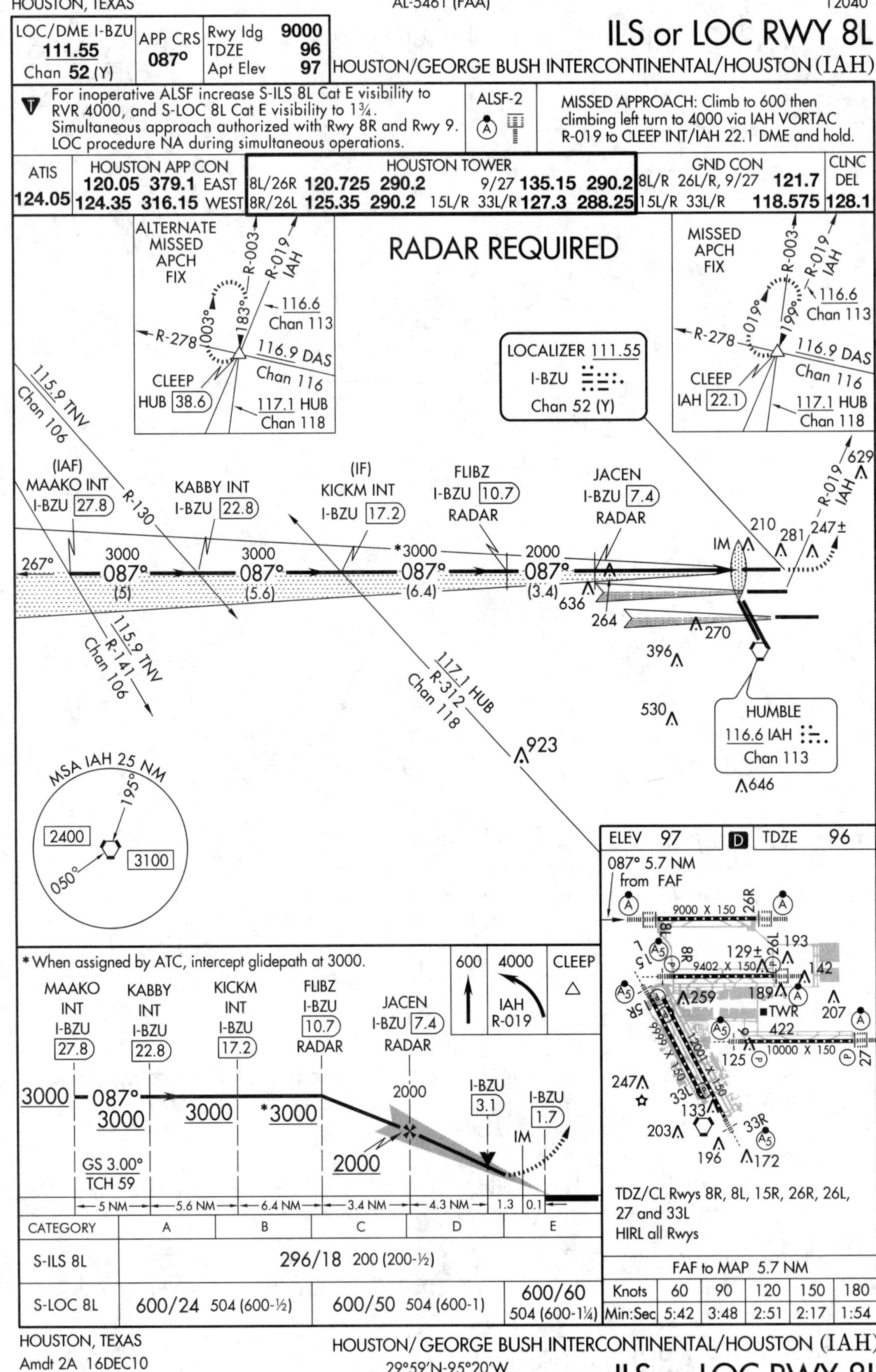

CATEGORY	A	B	C	D	E
S-ILS 8L	296/18 200 (200-½)				
S-LOC 8L	600/24 504 (600-½)		600/50 504 (600-1)		600/60 504 (600-1¼)

FAF to MAP 5.7 NM

Knots	60	90	120	150	180
Min:Sec	5:42	3:48	2:51	2:17	1:54

Figure 264. ILS or LOC RWY 8L (IAH).

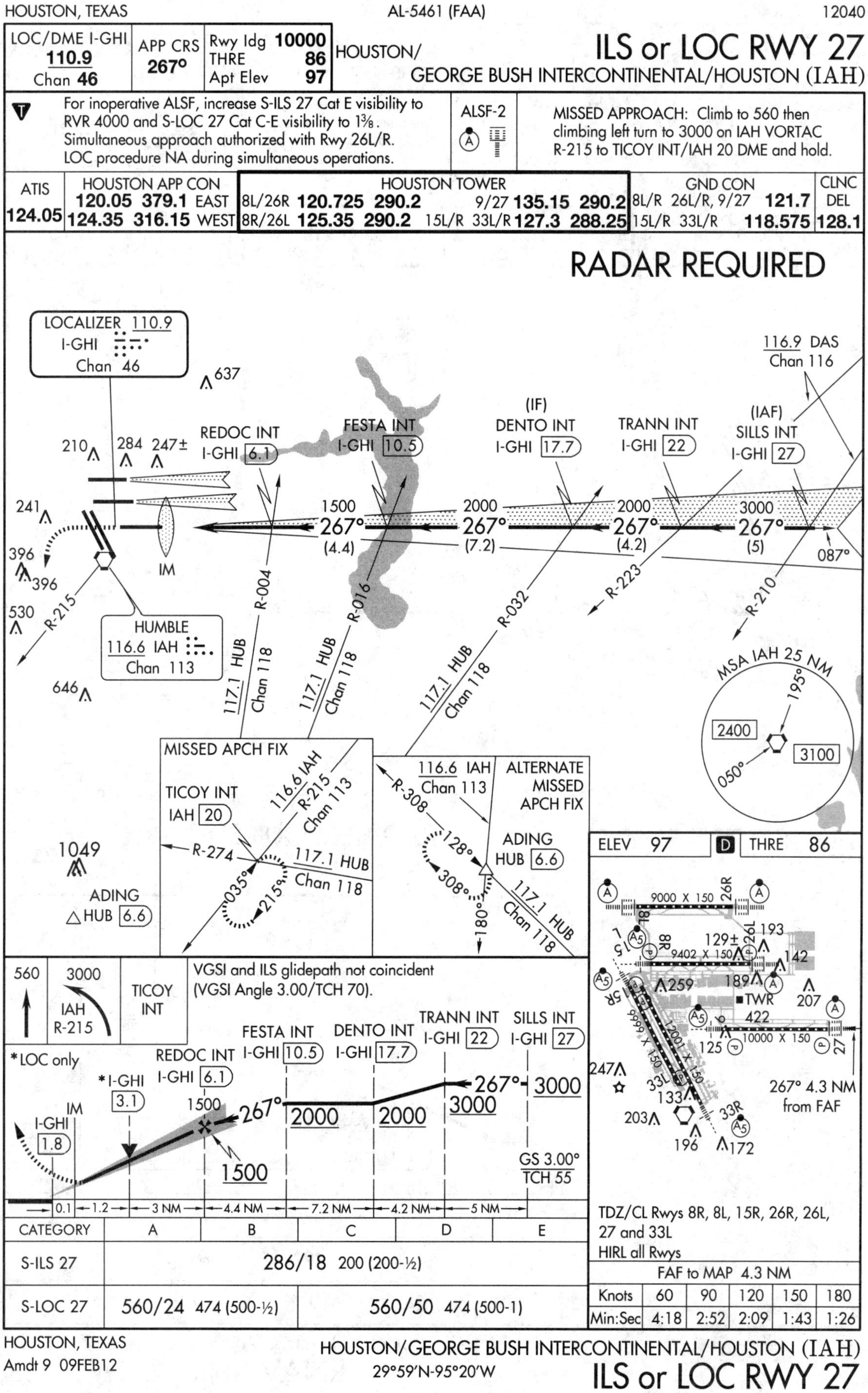

HOUSTON, TEXAS AL-5461 (FAA) 12040

LOC/DME I-GHI 110.9 Chan 46	APP CRS 267°	Rwy ldg 10000 THRE 86 Apt Elev 97

HOUSTON/ GEORGE BUSH INTERCONTINENTAL/HOUSTON (IAH)

ILS or LOC RWY 27

For inoperative ALSF, increase S-ILS 27 Cat E visibility to RVR 4000 and S-LOC 27 Cat C-E visibility to 1⅜. Simultaneous approach authorized with Rwy 26L/R. LOC procedure NA during simultaneous operations.

ALSF-2

MISSED APPROACH: Climb to 560 then climbing left turn to 3000 on IAH VORTAC R-215 to TICOY INT/IAH 20 DME and hold.

ATIS	HOUSTON APP CON	HOUSTON TOWER	GND CON	CLNC DEL
124.05	120.05 379.1 EAST 124.35 316.15 WEST	8L/26R 120.725 290.2 9/27 135.15 290.2 8R/26L 125.35 290.2 15L/R 33L/R 127.3 288.25	8L/R 26L/R, 9/27 121.7 15L/R 33L/R 118.575	128.1

RADAR REQUIRED

CATEGORY	A	B	C	D	E
S-ILS 27	286/18 200 (200-½)				
S-LOC 27	560/24 474 (500-½)		560/50 474 (500-1)		

FAF to MAP 4.3 NM

Knots	60	90	120	150	180
Min:Sec	4:18	2:52	2:09	1:43	1:26

HOUSTON, TEXAS
Amdt 9 09FEB12

HOUSTON/GEORGE BUSH INTERCONTINENTAL/HOUSTON (IAH)
29°59′N-95°20′W

ILS or LOC RWY 27

Figure 265. ILS or LOC RWY 27 (IAH).

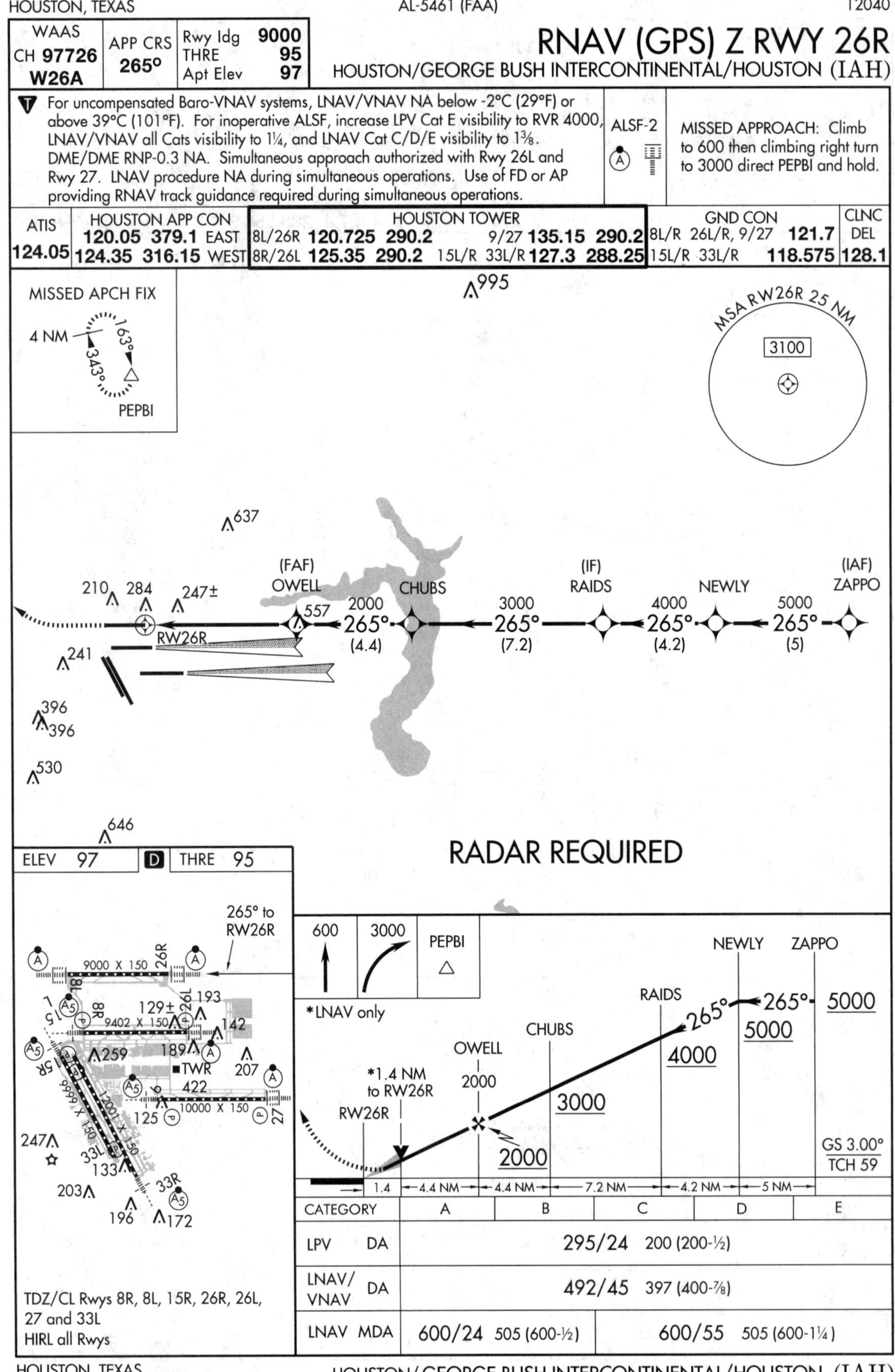
HOUSTON, TEXAS
AL-5461 (FAA)
12040
WAAS
CH 97726
W26A
APP CRS
265°
Rwy ldg 9000
THRE 95
Apt Elev 97
RNAV (GPS) Z RWY 26R
HOUSTON/GEORGE BUSH INTERCONTINENTAL/HOUSTON (IAH)
For uncompensated Baro-VNAV systems, LNAV/VNAV NA below -2°C (29°F) or above 39°C (101°F). For inoperative ALSF, increase LPV Cat E visibility to RVR 4000, LNAV/VNAV all Cats visibility to 1¼, and LNAV Cat C/D/E visibility to 1⅜. DME/DME RNP-0.3 NA. Simultaneous approach authorized with Rwy 26L and Rwy 27. LNAV procedure NA during simultaneous operations. Use of FD or AP providing RNAV track guidance required during simultaneous operations.
ALSF-2
MISSED APPROACH: Climb to 600 then climbing right turn to 3000 direct PEPBI and hold.
ATIS 124.05
HOUSTON APP CON 120.05 379.1 EAST 124.35 316.15 WEST
HOUSTON TOWER 8L/26R 120.725 290.2 9/27 135.15 290.2 8R/26L 125.35 290.2 15L/R 33L/R 127.3 288.25
GND CON 8L/R 26L/R, 9/27 121.7 15L/R 33L/R 118.575
CLNC DEL 128.1
MISSED APCH FIX
4 NM
163°
343°
PEPBI
MSA RW26R 25 NM
3100
(FAF) OWELL
CHUBS
(IF) RAIDS
NEWLY
(IAF) ZAPPO
2000 265° (4.4)
3000 265° (7.2)
4000 265° (4.2)
5000 265° (5)
RW26R
RADAR REQUIRED
ELEV 97
THRE 95
265° to RW26R
9000 X 150
9402 X 150
10000 X 150
TWR
TDZ/CL Rwys 8R, 8L, 15R, 26R, 26L, 27 and 33L
HIRL all Rwys
600
3000
PEPBI
*LNAV only
*1.4 NM to RW26R
GS 3.00°
TCH 59
1.4
4.4 NM
4.4 NM
7.2 NM
4.2 NM
5 NM
HOUSTON, TEXAS
Amdt 3 09FEB12
HOUSTON/ GEORGE BUSH INTERCONTINENTAL/HOUSTON (IAH)
29°59′N-95°20′W
RNAV (GPS) Z RWY 26R

CATEGORY		A	B	C	D	E
LPV	DA	295/24 200 (200-½)				
LNAV/VNAV	DA	492/45 397 (400-⅞)				
LNAV	MDA	600/24 505 (600-½)		600/55 505 (600-1¼)		

Figure 266. RNAV (GPS) Z RWY 26R (IAH).

(ANAHM3.SLI) 12040

ANAHEIM THREE DEPARTURE

SL-236 (FAA)

LONG BEACH (DAUGHERTY FIELD) (LGB)
LONG BEACH, CALIFORNIA

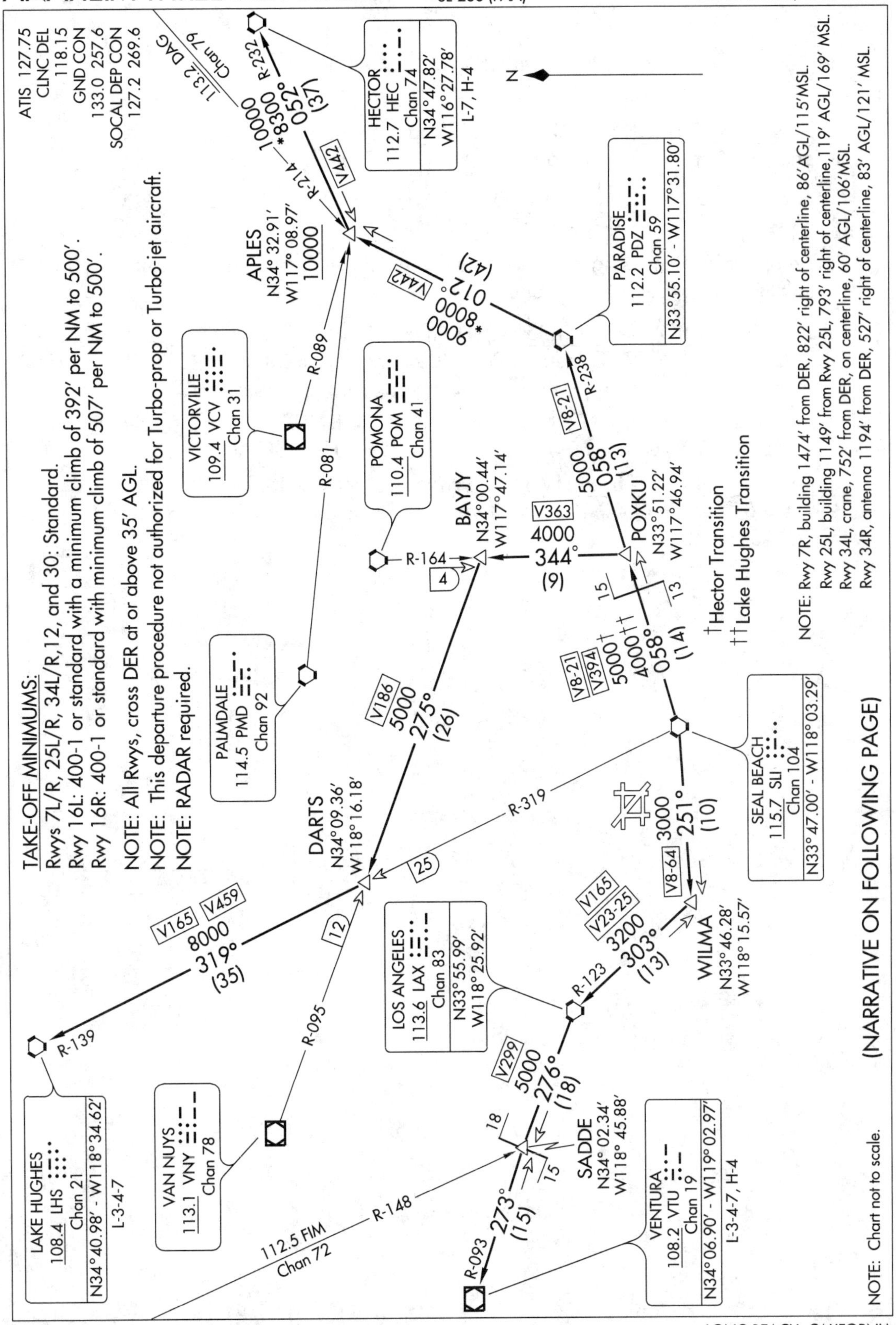

ATIS 127.75
CLNC DEL 118.15
GND CON 133.0 257.6
SOCAL DEP CON 127.2 269.6

TAKE-OFF MINIMUMS:
Rwys 7L/R, 25L/R, 34L/R,12, and 30: Standard.
Rwy 16L: 400-1 or standard with a minimum climb of 392′ per NM to 500′.
Rwy 16R: 400-1 or standard with minimum climb of 507′ per NM to 500′.

NOTE: All Rwys, cross DER at or above 35′ AGL.
NOTE: This departure procedure not authorized for Turbo-prop or Turbo-jet aircraft.
NOTE: RADAR required.

LAKE HUGHES
108.4 LHS
Chan 21
N34°40.98′ - W118°34.62′
L-3-4-7

VAN NUYS
113.1 VNY
Chan 78

PALMDALE
114.5 PMD
Chan 92

VICTORVILLE
109.4 VCV
Chan 31

113.2 DAG
Chan 79

APLES
N34° 32.91′
W117° 08.97′
10000

R-214
10000
*8300
052°
(37)
R-232

V442

HECTOR
112.7 HEC
Chan 74
N34°47.82′
W116°27.78′
L-7, H-4

R-139
V165 V459
8000
319°
(35)

R-095
R-081
R-089

DARTS
N34°09.36′
W118°16.18′

(12)
(25)

V186
5000
275°
(26)

POMONA
110.4 POM
Chan 41

R-164
(4)

BAYJY
N34°00.44′
W117°47.14′

V442
9000
*8000
012°
(42)

N

112.5 FIM
Chan 72
R-148

LOS ANGELES
113.6 LAX
Chan 83
N33°55.99′
W118°25.92′

R-093
273°
(15)
18
15

V299
5000
276°
(18)

SADDE
N34° 02.34′
W118° 45.88′

R-123
V165
V23-25
3200
303°
(13)

R-319

V363
4000
344°
(9)

V8-21
V394
5000†
4000††
058°
(14)
15
13

POXKU
N33°51.22′
W117°46.94′

5000
058°
(13)
V8-21
R-238

PARADISE
112.2 PDZ
Chan 59
N33°55.10′ - W117°31.80′

VENTURA
108.2 VTU
Chan 19
N34°06.90′ - W119°02.97′
L-3-4-7, H-4

V8-64
3000
251°
(10)

WILMA
N33°46.28′
W118°15.57′

SEAL BEACH
115.7 SLI
Chan 104
N33°47.00′ - W118°03.29′

†Hector Transition
††Lake Hughes Transition

NOTE: Rwy 7R, building 1474′ from DER, 822′ right of centerline, 86′AGL/115′MSL.
Rwy 25L, building 1149′ from Rwy 25L, 793′ right of centerline,119′ AGL/169′ MSL.
Rwy 34L, crane, 752′ from DER, on centerline, 60′ AGL/106′MSL.
Rwy 34R, antenna 1194′ from DER, 527′ right of centerline, 83′ AGL/121′ MSL.

NOTE: Chart not to scale.

(NARRATIVE ON FOLLOWING PAGE)

ANAHEIM THREE DEPARTURE
(ANAHM3.SLI) 12040
LONG BEACH, CALIFORNIA
LONG BEACH (DAUGHERTY FIELD) (LGB)

Figure 267. ANAHEIM THREE Departure (ANAHM3.SLI)(LGB).

(ANAHM3.SLI) 08045

ANAHEIM THREE DEPARTURE

SL-236 (FAA)

LONG BEACH (DAUGHERTY FIELD) (LGB)
LONG BEACH, CALIFORNIA

DEPARTURE ROUTE DESCRIPTION

HECTOR or LAKE HUGHES TRANSITION: Climb runway heading to 800′ then fly assigned heading for radar vectors to SLI VORTAC. Thence. . . .

VENTURA TRANSITION: Climb runway heading to 800′ then fly assigned heading for radar vectors to LAX VORTAC. Thence. . . .

. . . .via (transition) or (assigned route). Maintain assigned altitude. Expect clearance to filed altitude 10 minutes after departure.

HECTOR TRANSITION (ANAHM3.HEC): From over SLI VORTAC via SLI R-058 and PDZ R-238 to PDZ VORTAC, then via PDZ R-012 and HEC R-232 to HEC VORTAC.

LAKE HUGHES TRANSITION (ANAHM3.LHS): From over SLI VORTAC via SLI R-058 and PDZ R-238 to POXKU INT, then via POM R-164 to BAYJY INT, then via VNY R-095 to DARTS INT. Thence via SLI R-319 and LHS R-139 to LHS VORTAC.

VENTURA TRANSITION (ANAHM3.VTU): From over SLI VORTAC via SLI R-251 to WILMA INT, then via LAX R-123 to LAX VORTAC, then via LAX R-276 and VTU R-093 to VTU VOR/DME.

ANAHEIM THREE DEPARTURE
(ANAHM3.SLI) 08045

LONG BEACH, CALIFORNIA
LONG BEACH (DAUGHERTY FIELD) (LGB)

Figure 268. ANAHEIM THREE Departure (ANAHM3.SLI)(LGB).

(SENIC1.SENIC) 07354

SENIC ONE DEPARTURE (RNAV)

SL-236 (FAA)

LONG BEACH (DAUGHERTY FIELD) (LGB)
LONG BEACH, CALIFORNIA

ATIS 127.75
CLNC DEL 118.15
GND CON 133.0 257.6
LONG BEACH TOWER ★
120.5 257.6 (Rwy 12)
119.4 257.6 (Rwy 30)
SOCAL DEP CON 127.2 269.6

TAKE-OFF MINIMUMS
Rwys 7L/R, 12, 16L/R, 25L/R, 34L/R: NA- Air Traffic.
Rwy 30: ATC climb of 500′ per NM to 1500.
DAGGETT TRANSITION: Obstacle climb of 255′ per NM to 13000, ATC climb of 500′ per NM to 15000.

NOTE: DME/DME/IRU or GPS required.
NOTE: RNAV 1.
NOTE: Restricted to turbojet aircraft only.
NOTE: RADAR required.
NOTE: Some departures may be radar vectored to SENIC, LAHAB, PIGGN, or TRM VORTAC when needed for traffic.

TAKE-OFF OBSTACLE NOTES
Rwy 25R: FORD sign beginning 551′ from DER, 27′ right of centerline, up to 100′ AGL/159′ MSL.
Rwy 30: Railroad beginning 647′ from DER, on centerline, up to 27′ AGL/91′ MSL.
Mutiple antennas, rods, vents, and lights on building beginning 356′ from DER, 289′ left of centerline, up to 27′ AGL/87′ MSL.
Multiple poles beginning 2061′ from DER, 312′ left of centerline, up to 51′ AGL/124′ MSL.
Railroad beginning 207′ from DER, 485′ right of centerline, up to 25′ AGL/81′ MSL.
Multiple obstruction lights and poles beginning 632′ from DER 240′ right of centerline, up to 66′ AGL/142′ MSL.
Multiple trees beginning 1701′ from DER, 136′ right of centerline, up to 73′ AGL/146′ MSL.
Bldg 2617′ from DER, 802′ right of centerline, 63′ AGL/136′ MSL.

DAGGETT DAG
15000 034° (79)
SEBBY
15000 023° (12)
LAHAB 15000
005° (21)
N
1500
301°
MOXIE
093° (12)
SENIC
077° (29)
PIGGN
10000 103° (18)
RORBE
125° (54)
PILLO
077° (49)
IMPERIAL IPL
11000 074° (95)
THERMAL TRM

NOTE: Chart not to scale.

DEPARTURE ROUTE DESCRIPTION

TAKE-OFF RUNWAY 30: Climb heading 301° to 1500, then left turn direct MOXIE, Then via depicted route to SENIC. Thence....

....via assigned route/transition. Expect clearance to filed altitude 10 minutes after departure.

DAGGETT TRANSITION (SENIC1.DAG)
IMPERIAL TRANSITION (SENIC1.IPL)
THERMAL TRANSITION (SENIC1.TRM)

SENIC ONE DEPARTURE (RNAV)
(SENIC1.SENIC) 07354

LONG BEACH, CALIFORNIA
LONG BEACH (DAUGHERTY FIELD) (LGB)

Figure 269. SENIC ONE Departure (RNAV) (SENIC1.SENIC).

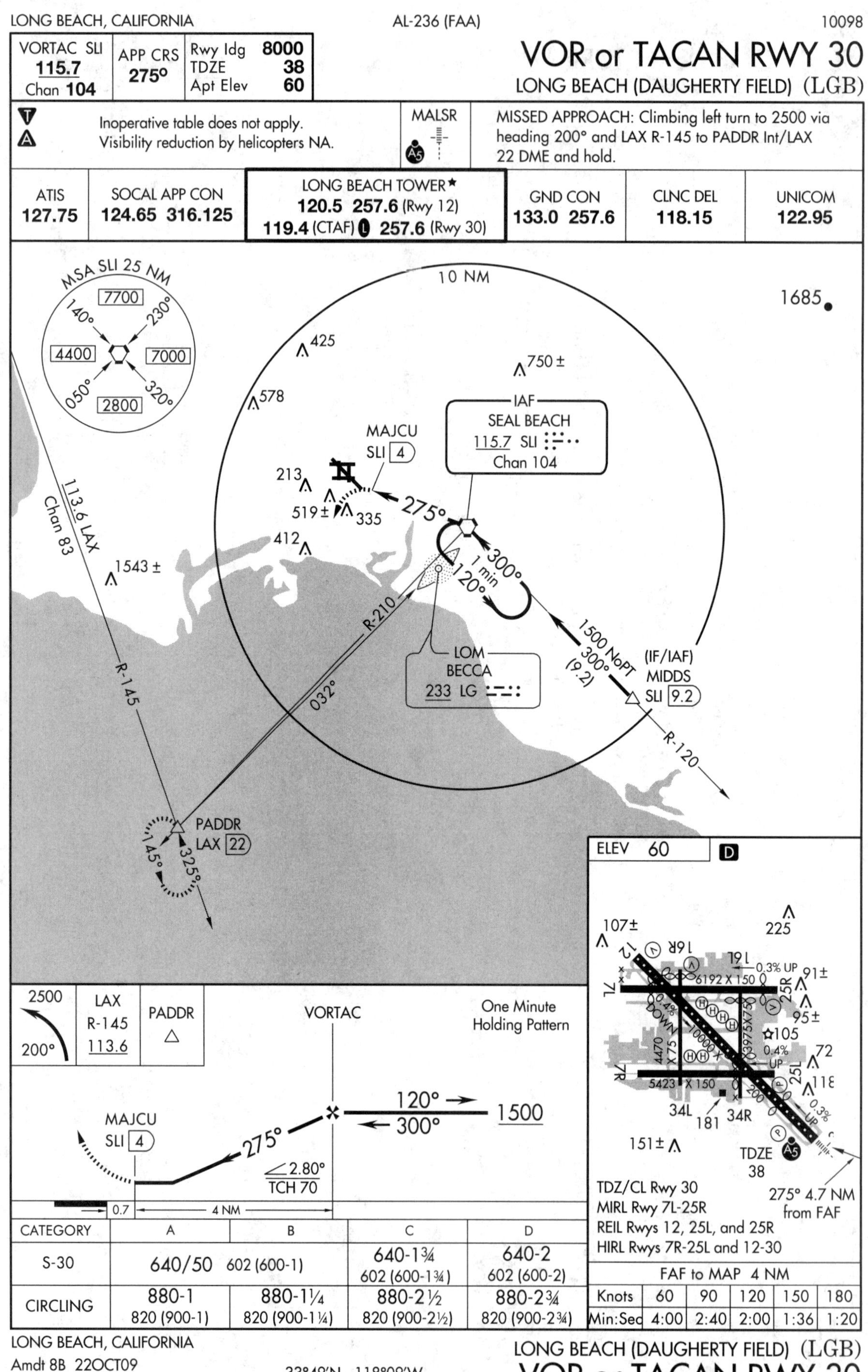

CATEGORY	A	B	C	D
S-30	640/50 602 (600-1)		640-1¾ 602 (600-1¾)	640-2 602 (600-2)
CIRCLING	880-1 820 (900-1)	880-1¼ 820 (900-1¼)	880-2½ 820 (900-2½)	880-2¾ 820 (900-2¾)

FAF to MAP 4 NM

Knots	60	90	120	150	180
Min:Sec	4:00	2:40	2:00	1:36	1:20

Figure 270. VOR or TACAN RWY 30 (LGB).

(IMPER1.IMPER) 11125

IMPER ONE DEPARTURE

SL-237 (FAA)

LOS ANGELES INTL (LAX)
LOS ANGELES, CALIFORNIA

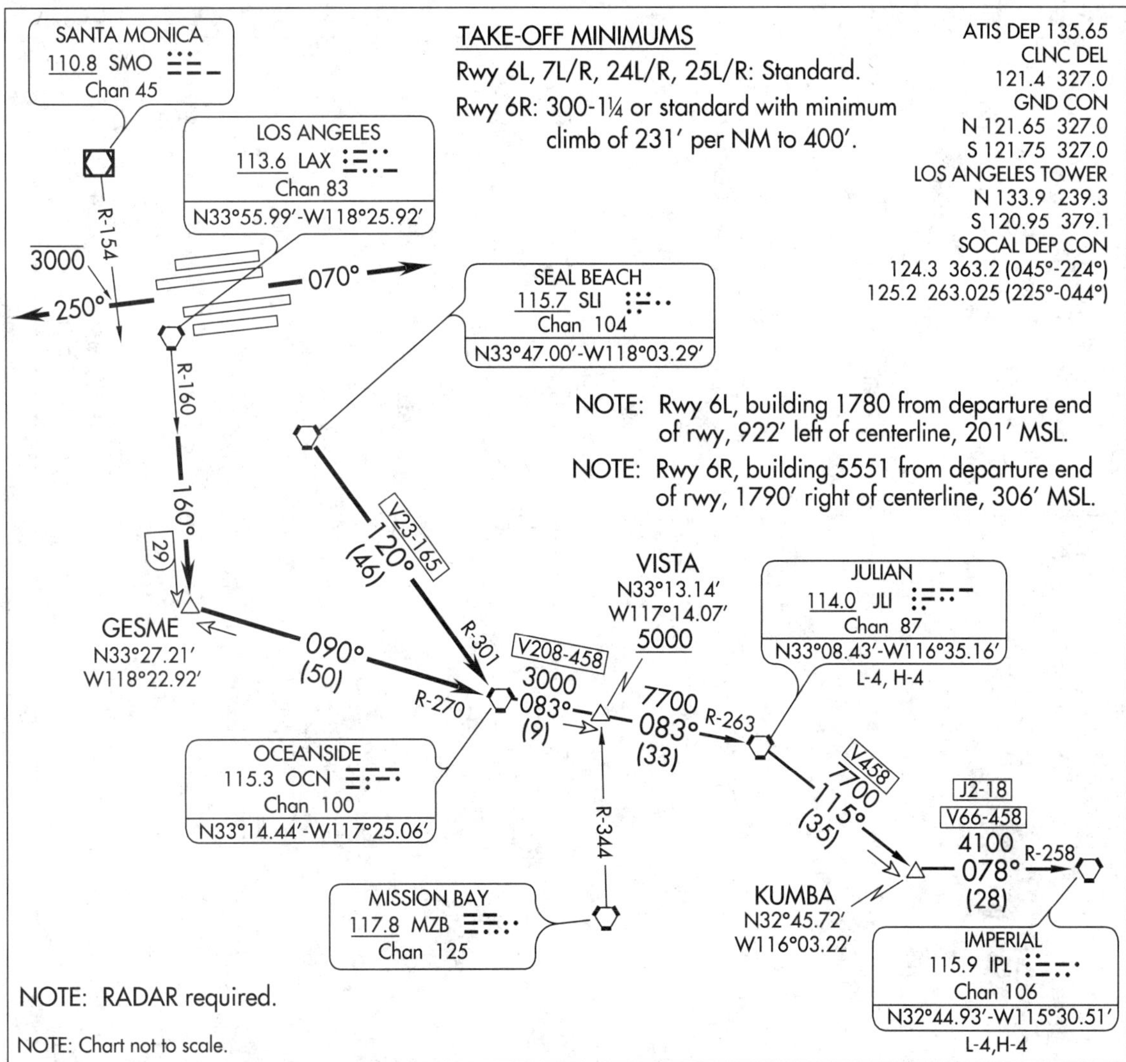

DEPARTURE ROUTE DESCRIPTION

TAKE-OFF RUNWAYS 6L/R, 7L/R: Climb via heading 070° for vector to SLI VORTAC, then via SLI R-120 and OCN R-301 to OCN VORTAC. Thence. . . .

TAKE-OFF RUNWAYS 24L/R, 25L/R: Climb via heading 250° to cross SMO R-154 at or below 3000. Then via radar vectors to join LAX R-160 to GESME INT. Then via OCN R-270 to OCN VORTAC. Thence. . . .

. . . .via (assigned transition) or (assigned route). All aircraft expect further clearance to filed flight level three minutes after departure.

LOST COMMUNICATIONS: If not in contact with Departure Control within five minutes after departure, climb to FL230 or filed altitude whichever is lower. Aircraft filing FL240 or above climb to filed altitude ten minutes after departure.

IMPERIAL TRANSITION (IMPER1.IPL): From over OCN VORTAC via OCN R-083 and JLI R-263 to JLI VORTAC. Then via JLI R-115 and IPL R-258 to IPL VORTAC.

JULIAN TRANSITION (IMPER1.JLI): From over OCN VORTAC via OCN R-083 and JLI R-263 to JLI VORTAC.

IMPER ONE DEPARTURE
(IMPER1.IMPER) 11125
LOS ANGELES, CALIFORNIA
LOS ANGELES INTL (LAX)

Figure 271. IMPER ONE Departure (IMPER1.IMPER)(LAX).

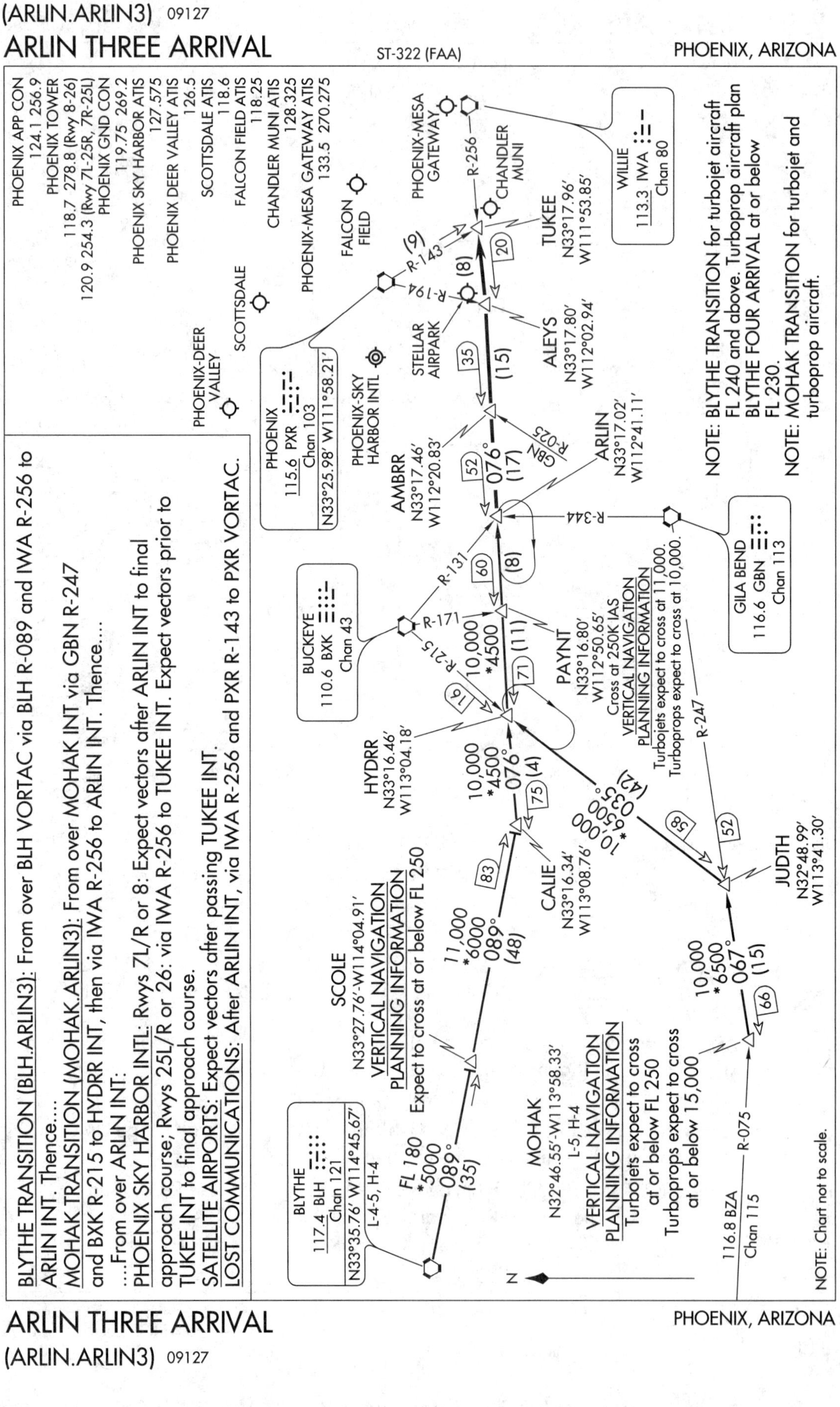

(ARLIN.ARLIN3) 09127

ARLIN THREE ARRIVAL

ST-322 (FAA)

PHOENIX, ARIZONA

PHOENIX APP CON
124.1 256.9
PHOENIX TOWER
118.7 278.8 (Rwy 8-26)
120.9 254.3 (Rwy 7L-25R, 7R-25L)
PHOENIX GND CON
119.75 269.2
PHOENIX SKY HARBOR ATIS
127.575
PHOENIX DEER VALLEY ATIS
126.5
SCOTTSDALE ATIS
118.6
FALCON FIELD ATIS
118.25
CHANDLER MUNI ATIS
128.325
PHOENIX-MESA GATEWAY ATIS
133.5 270.275

BLYTHE TRANSITION (BLH.ARLIN3): From over BLH VORTAC via BLH R-089 and IWA R-256 to ARLIN INT. Thence....
MOHAK TRANSITION (MOHAK.ARLIN3): From over MOHAK INT via GBN R-247 and BXK R-215 to HYDRR INT, then via IWA R-256 to ARLIN INT. Thence....
....From over ARLIN INT:
PHOENIX SKY HARBOR INTL: Rwys 7L/R or 8: Expect vectors after ARLIN INT to final approach course; Rwys 25L/R or 26: via IWA R-256 to TUKEE INT. Expect vectors prior to TUKEE INT to final approach course.
SATELLITE AIRPORTS: Expect vectors after passing TUKEE INT.
LOST COMMUNICATIONS: After ARLIN INT, via IWA R-256 and PXR R-143 to PXR VORTAC.

PHOENIX-DEER VALLEY
SCOTTSDALE
FALCON FIELD
PHOENIX-SKY HARBOR INTL
STELLAR AIRPARK
PHOENIX-MESA GATEWAY
CHANDLER MUNI

PHOENIX
115.6 PXR
Chan 103
N33°25.98′ W111°58.21′

BLYTHE
117.4 BLH
Chan 121
N33°35.76′ W114°45.67′
L-4-5, H-4

FL 180
*5000
089°
(35)

SCOLE
N33°27.76′-W114°04.91′
VERTICAL NAVIGATION PLANNING INFORMATION
Expect to cross at or below FL 250

11,000
*6000
089°
(48)

83

BUCKEYE
110.6 BXK
Chan 43

HYDRR
N33°16.46′
W113°04.18′

R-215
R-171
R-131
16
10,000
*4500
076°
(4)
75

CALIE
N33°16.34′
W113°08.76′

10,000
*4500
60
71
(11)

PAYNT
N33°16.80′
W112°50.65′
Cross at 250K IAS
VERTICAL NAVIGATION PLANNING INFORMATION
Turbojets expect to cross at 11,000.
Turboprops expect to cross at 10,000.

AMBRR
N33°17.46′
W112°20.83′

52
076°
(17)
(8)
GBN R-025
R-344

ARLIN
N33°17.02′
W112°41.11′

35
(15)
R-194
R-143
(9)
(8)
20
R-256

ALEYS
N33°17.80′
W112°02.94′

TUKEE
N33°17.96′
W111°53.85′

WILLIE
113.3 IWA
Chan 80

MOHAK
N32°46.55′-W113°58.33′
L-5, H-4
VERTICAL NAVIGATION PLANNING INFORMATION
Turbojets expect to cross at or below FL 250
Turboprops expect to cross at or below 15,000

116.8 BZA
Chan 115
R-075

10,000
*6500
067°
(15)
66

10,000
*6500
035°
(42)
58
52
R-247

JUDTH
N32°48.99′
W113°41.30′

GILA BEND
116.6 GBN
Chan 113

N

NOTE: BLYTHE TRANSITION for turbojet aircraft FL 240 and above. Turboprop aircraft plan BLYTHE FOUR ARRIVAL at or below FL 230.
NOTE: MOHAK TRANSITION for turbojet and turboprop aircraft.

NOTE: Chart not to scale.

ARLIN THREE ARRIVAL

PHOENIX, ARIZONA

(ARLIN.ARLIN3) 09127

Figure 272. ARLIN THREE Arrival (ARLIN.ARLIN3).

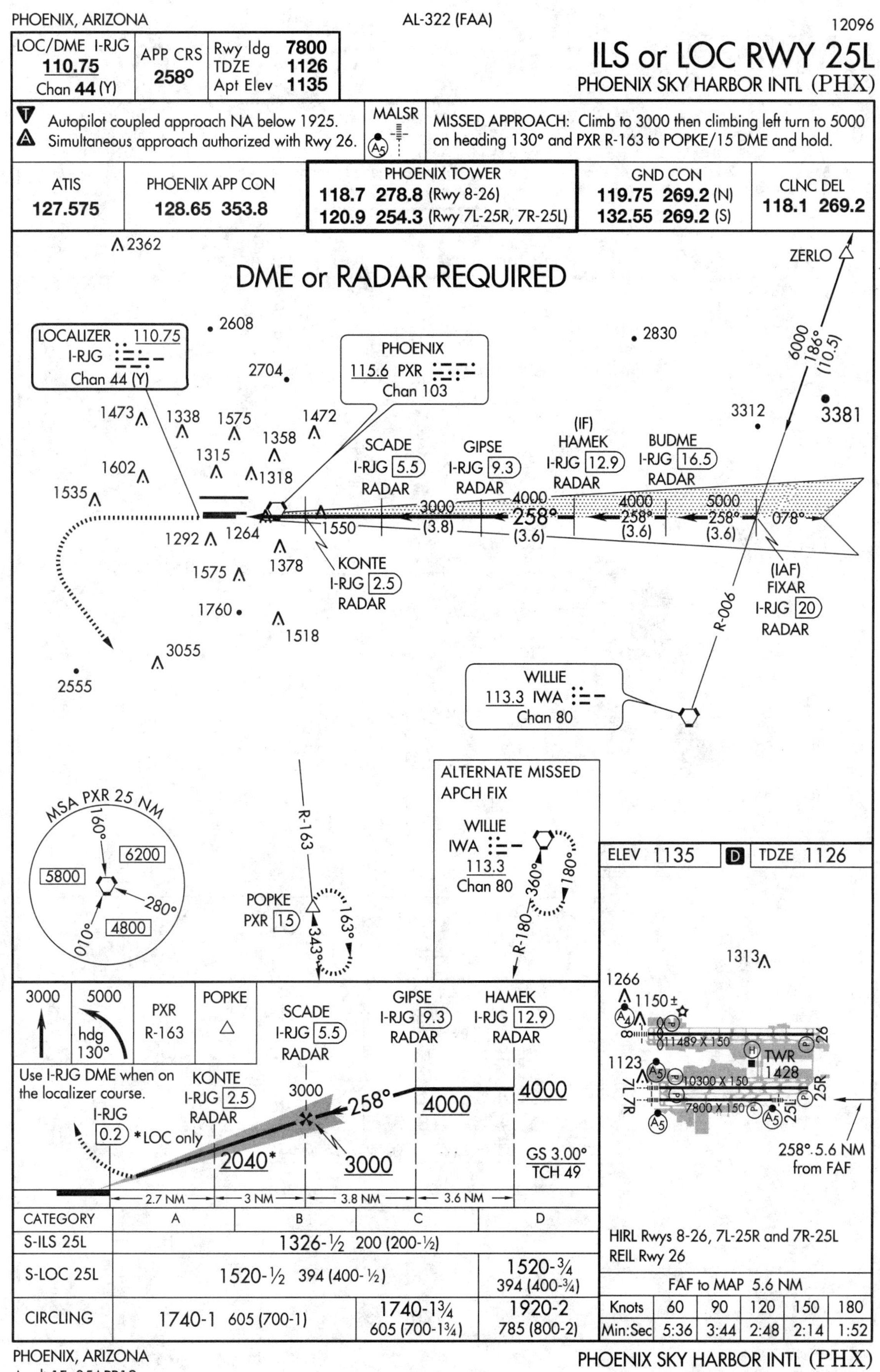

Figure 273. ILS or LOC RWY 25L (PHX).

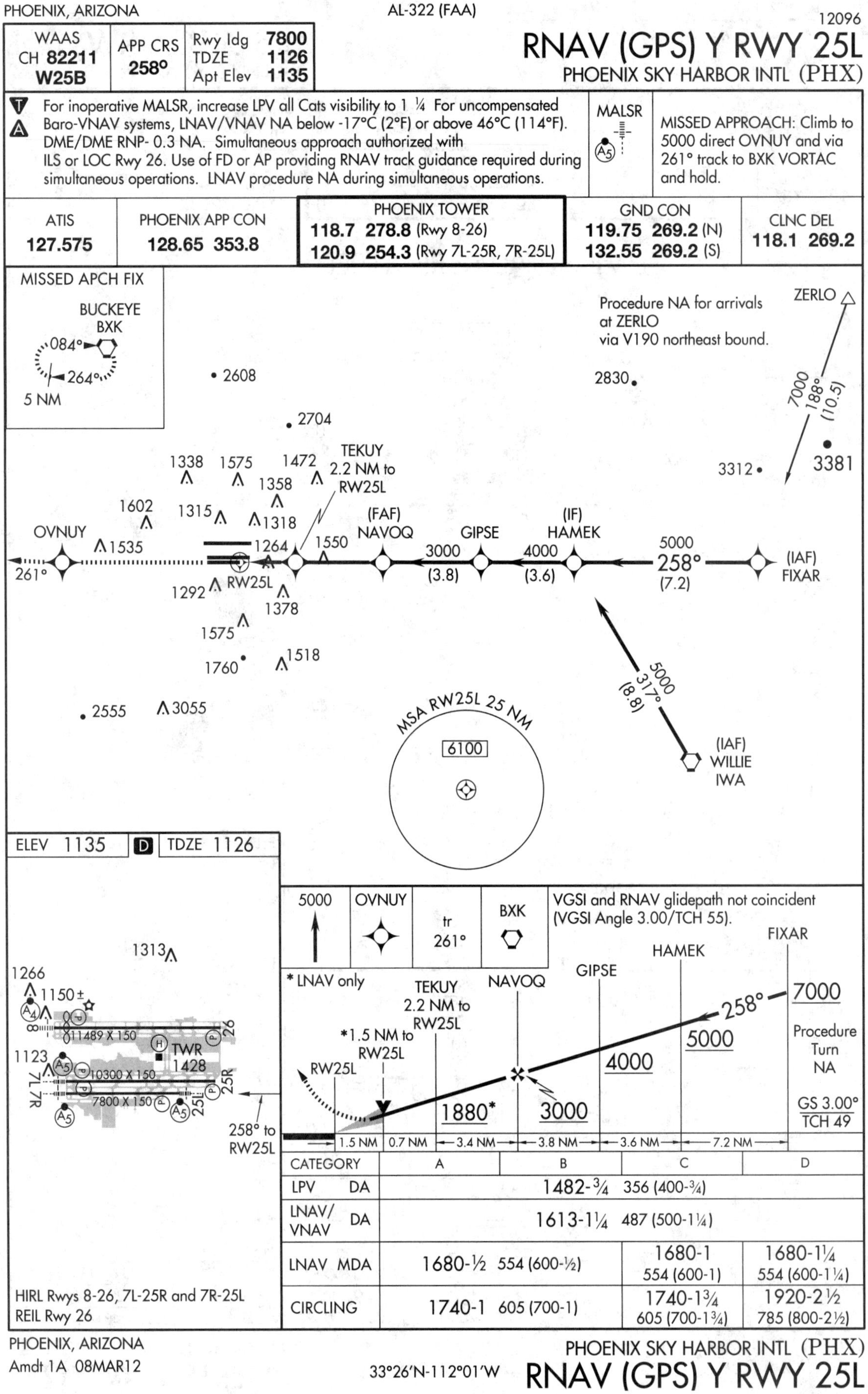
PHOENIX, ARIZONA
AL-322 (FAA)
12096
RNAV (GPS) Y RWY 25L
PHOENIX SKY HARBOR INTL (PHX)
WAAS CH 82211 W25B
APP CRS 258°
Rwy ldg 7800
TDZE 1126
Apt Elev 1135
For inoperative MALSR, increase LPV all Cats visibility to 1 ¼ For uncompensated Baro-VNAV systems, LNAV/VNAV NA below -17°C (2°F) or above 46°C (114°F). DME/DME RNP- 0.3 NA. Simultaneous approach authorized with ILS or LOC Rwy 26. Use of FD or AP providing RNAV track guidance required during simultaneous operations. LNAV procedure NA during simultaneous operations.
MALSR
MISSED APPROACH: Climb to 5000 direct OVNUY and via 261° track to BXK VORTAC and hold.
ATIS 127.575
PHOENIX APP CON 128.65 353.8
PHOENIX TOWER 118.7 278.8 (Rwy 8-26) 120.9 254.3 (Rwy 7L-25R, 7R-25L)
GND CON 119.75 269.2 (N) 132.55 269.2 (S)
CLNC DEL 118.1 269.2
MISSED APCH FIX
BUCKEYE BXK
084°
264°
5 NM
Procedure NA for arrivals at ZERLO via V190 northeast bound.
ZERLO
7000 188° (10.5)
OVNUY
261°
TEKUY 2.2 NM to RW25L
(FAF) NAVOQ
GIPSE
(IF) HAMEK
5000 258° (7.2)
(IAF) FIXAR
3000 (3.8)
4000 (3.6)
RW25L
5000 317° (8.8)
(IAF) WILLIE IWA
MSA RW25L 25 NM
6100
ELEV 1135
TDZE 1126
TWR 1428
11489 X 150
10300 X 150
7800 X 150
258° to RW25L
HIRL Rwys 8-26, 7L-25R and 7R-25L
REIL Rwy 26
5000
OVNUY
tr 261°
BXK
VGSI and RNAV glidepath not coincident (VGSI Angle 3.00/TCH 55).
* LNAV only
*1.5 NM to RW25L
1880*
3000
4000
5000
7000
Procedure Turn NA
GS 3.00°
TCH 49
1.5 NM
0.7 NM
3.4 NM
3.8 NM
3.6 NM
7.2 NM
CATEGORY A B C D
LPV DA 1482-¾ 356 (400-¾)
LNAV/VNAV DA 1613-1¼ 487 (500-1¼)
LNAV MDA 1680-½ 554 (600-½) 1680-1 554 (600-1) 1680-1¼ 554 (600-1¼)
CIRCLING 1740-1 605 (700-1) 1740-1¾ 605 (700-1¾) 1920-2½ 785 (800-2½)
PHOENIX, ARIZONA
Amdt 1A 08MAR12
33°26′N-112°01′W
PHOENIX SKY HARBOR INTL (PHX)
RNAV (GPS) Y RWY 25L

Figure 274. RNAV (GPS) Y RWY 25L (PHX).

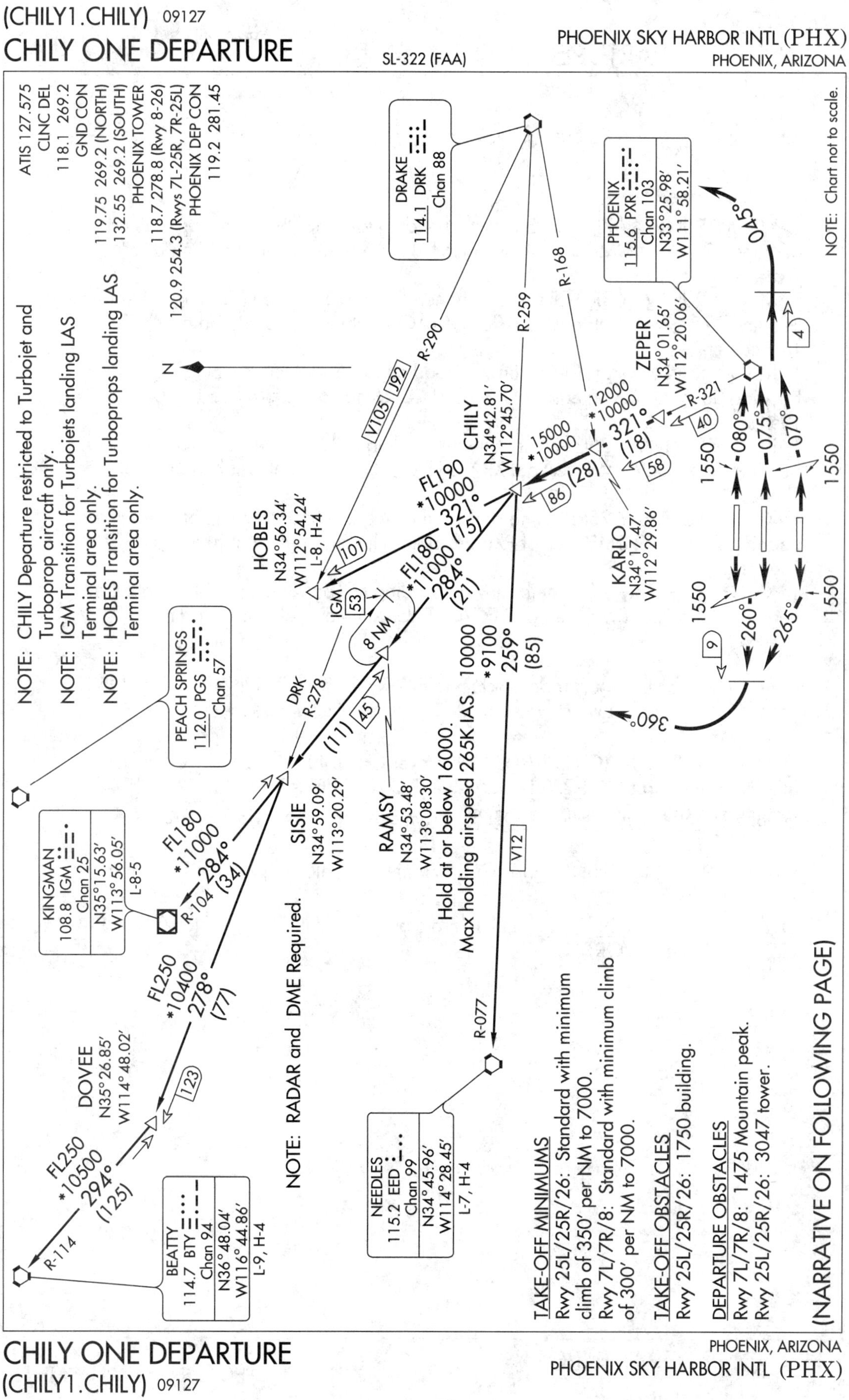

(CHILY1.CHILY) 09127

CHILY ONE DEPARTURE

SL-322 (FAA)

PHOENIX SKY HARBOR INTL (PHX)
PHOENIX, ARIZONA

ATIS 127.575
CLNC DEL
118.1 269.2
GND CON
119.75 269.2 (NORTH)
132.55 269.2 (SOUTH)
PHOENIX TOWER
118.7 278.8 (Rwy 8-26)
120.9 254.3 (Rwys 7L-25R, 7R-25L)
PHOENIX DEP CON
119.2 281.45

NOTE: CHILY Departure restricted to Turbojet and Turboprop aircraft only.
NOTE: IGM Transition for Turbojets landing LAS Terminal area only.
NOTE: HOBES Transition for Turboprops landing LAS Terminal area only.

NOTE: RADAR and DME Required.

NOTE: Chart not to scale.

N

KINGMAN
108.8 IGM
Chan 25
N35°15.63′
W113°56.05′
L-8-5

PEACH SPRINGS
112.0 PGS
Chan 57

BEATTY
114.7 BTY
Chan 94
N36°48.04′
W116°44.86′
L-9, H-4

DOVEE
N35°26.85′
W114°48.02′

R-114
FL250
*10500
294°
(125)

123
FL250
*10400
278°
(77)

R-104
FL180
*11000
284°
(34)

SISIE
N34°59.09′
W113°20.29′

DRK
R-278

HOBES
N34°56.34′
W112°54.24′
L-8, H-4

IGM
53
101
8 NM

RAMSY
N34°53.48′
W113°08.30′
Hold at or below 16000.
Max holding airspeed 265K IAS.

(11)
45
FL180
*11000
284°
(21)

FL190
*10000
321°
(15)

V105 J92
R-290

DRAKE
114.1 DRK
Chan 88

NEEDLES
115.2 EED
Chan 99
N34°45.96′
W114°28.45′
L-7, H-4

R-077
V12
10000
*9100
259°
(85)

CHILY
N34°42.81′
W112°45.70′

R-259
R-168

86
15000
*10000
(28)

KARLO
N34°17.47′
W112°29.86′

12000
*10000
321°
(18)
58

ZEPER
N34°01.65′
W112°20.06′

R-321
40

PHOENIX
115.6 PXR
Chan 103
N33°25.98′
W111°58.21′

360°
9
1550
260°
265°
1550
1550
080°
075°
070°
1550
4
045°

TAKE-OFF MINIMUMS
Rwy 25L/25R/26: Standard with minimum climb of 350′ per NM to 7000.
Rwy 7L/7R/8: Standard with minimum climb of 300′ per NM to 7000.

TAKE-OFF OBSTACLES
Rwy 25L/25R/26: 1750 building.

DEPARTURE OBSTACLES
Rwy 7L/7R/8: 1475 Mountain peak.
Rwy 25L/25R/26: 3047 tower.

(NARRATIVE ON FOLLOWING PAGE)

CHILY ONE DEPARTURE
(CHILY1.CHILY) 09127

PHOENIX, ARIZONA
PHOENIX SKY HARBOR INTL (PHX)

Figure 276. CHILY ONE Departure (CHILY1.CHILY)(PHX).

(CHILY1.CHILY) 02052

CHILY ONE DEPARTURE

SL-322 (FAA)

PHOENIX SKY HARBOR (PHX)
PHOENIX, ARIZONA

DEPARTURE ROUTE DESCRIPTION

TAKE-OFF RUNWAY 7L: Climb runway heading to 1550, then climbing left turn heading 075°, at 4 DME east of PXR VORTAC, climbing left turn heading 045°. Thence....
TAKE-OFF RUNWAY 7R: Climb runway heading to 1550, then climbing left turn heading 070°, at 4 DME east of PXR VORTAC, climbing left turn heading 045°. Thence....
TAKE-OFF RUNWAY 8: Climb runway heading to 1550, then climbing right turn heading 080°, at 4 DME east of PXR VORTAC, climbing left turn heading 045°. Thence....
TAKE-OFF RUNWAY 25L: Climb runway heading to 1550, then climbing right turn heading 265°, at 9 DME west of PXR VORTAC, climbing right turn heading 360°. Thence....
TAKE-OFF RUNWAY 25R: Climb runway heading to 1550, then climbing right turn heading 260°, at 9 DME west of PXR VORTAC, climbing right turn heading 360°. Thence....
TAKE-OFF RUNWAY 26: Climb runway heading to 1550, then climbing right turn heading 260°, at 9 DME west of PXR VORTAC, climbing right turn heading 360°. Thence....

....maintain 7000. Expect radar vectors to PXR R-321 to ZEPER INT then CHILY INT. Then via (transition). Expect filed altitude 3 minutes after departure.

BEATTY TRANSITION (CHILY1.BTY): From over CHILY INT via IGM R-104 to SISIE INT, then via DRK R-278 to DOVEE INT, then via BTY R-114 to BTY VORTAC.

HOBES TRANSITION (CHILY1.HOBES): From over CHILY INT via PXR R-321 to HOBES INT.

KINGMAN TRANSITION (CHILY1.IGM): From over CHILY INT via IGM R-104 to IGM VOR/DME.

NEEDLES TRANSITION (CHILY1.EED): From over CHILY INT via DRK R-259 and EED R-077 to EED VORTAC.

CHILY ONE DEPARTURE
(CHILY1.CHILY) 02052
PHOENIX, ARIZONA
PHOENIX SKY HARBOR (PHX)

Figure 277. CHILY ONE Departure (CHILY1.CHILY)(PHX).

(BUF3.BUF) 09127

BUFFALO THREE DEPARTURE SL-65 (FAA)

BUFFALO NIAGARA INTL (BUF)
BUFFALO, NEW YORK

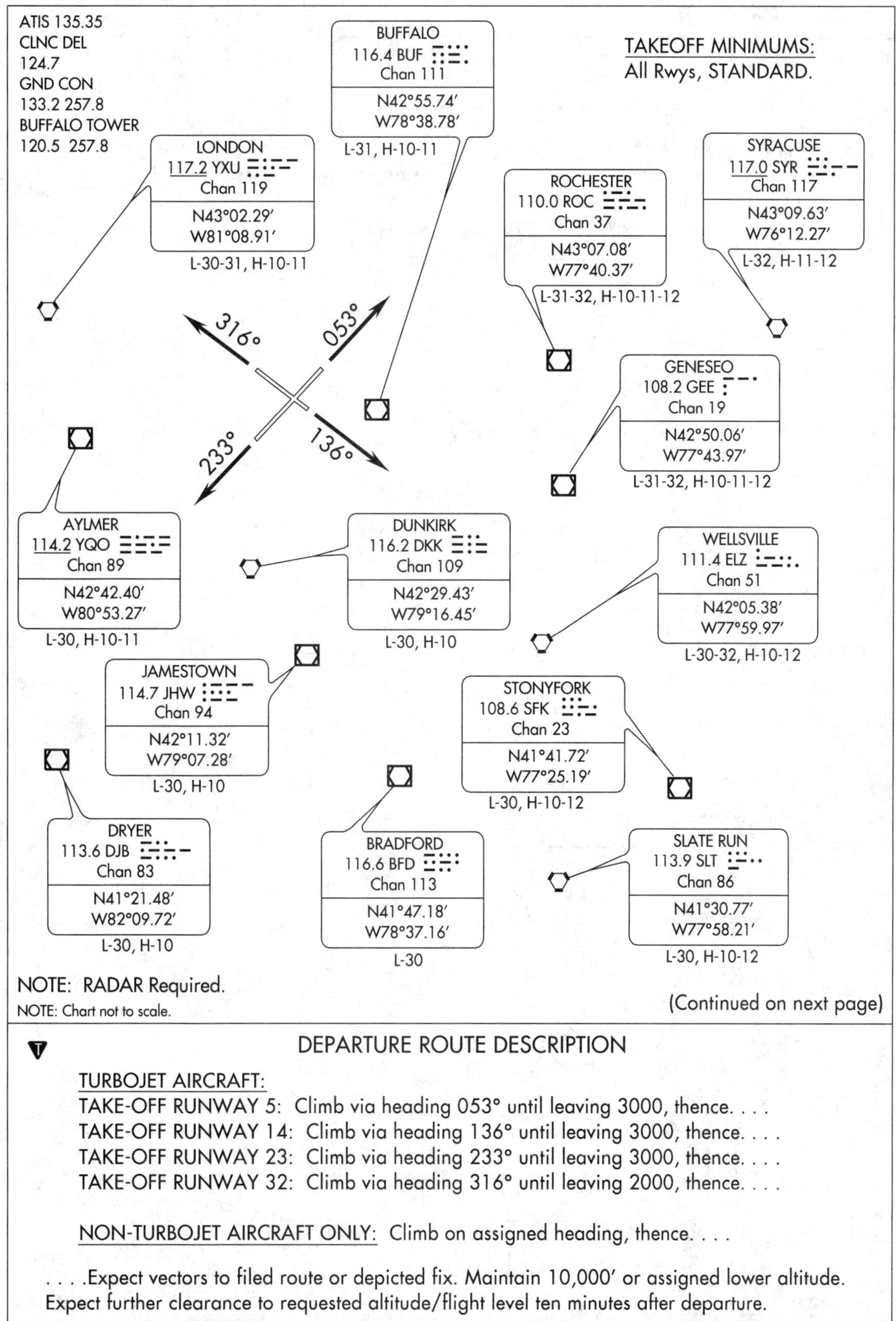

BUFFALO THREE DEPARTURE
(BUF3.BUF) 09127

BUFFALO, NEW YORK
BUFFALO NIAGARA INTL (BUF)

Figure 278. BUFFALO THREE Departure (BUF).

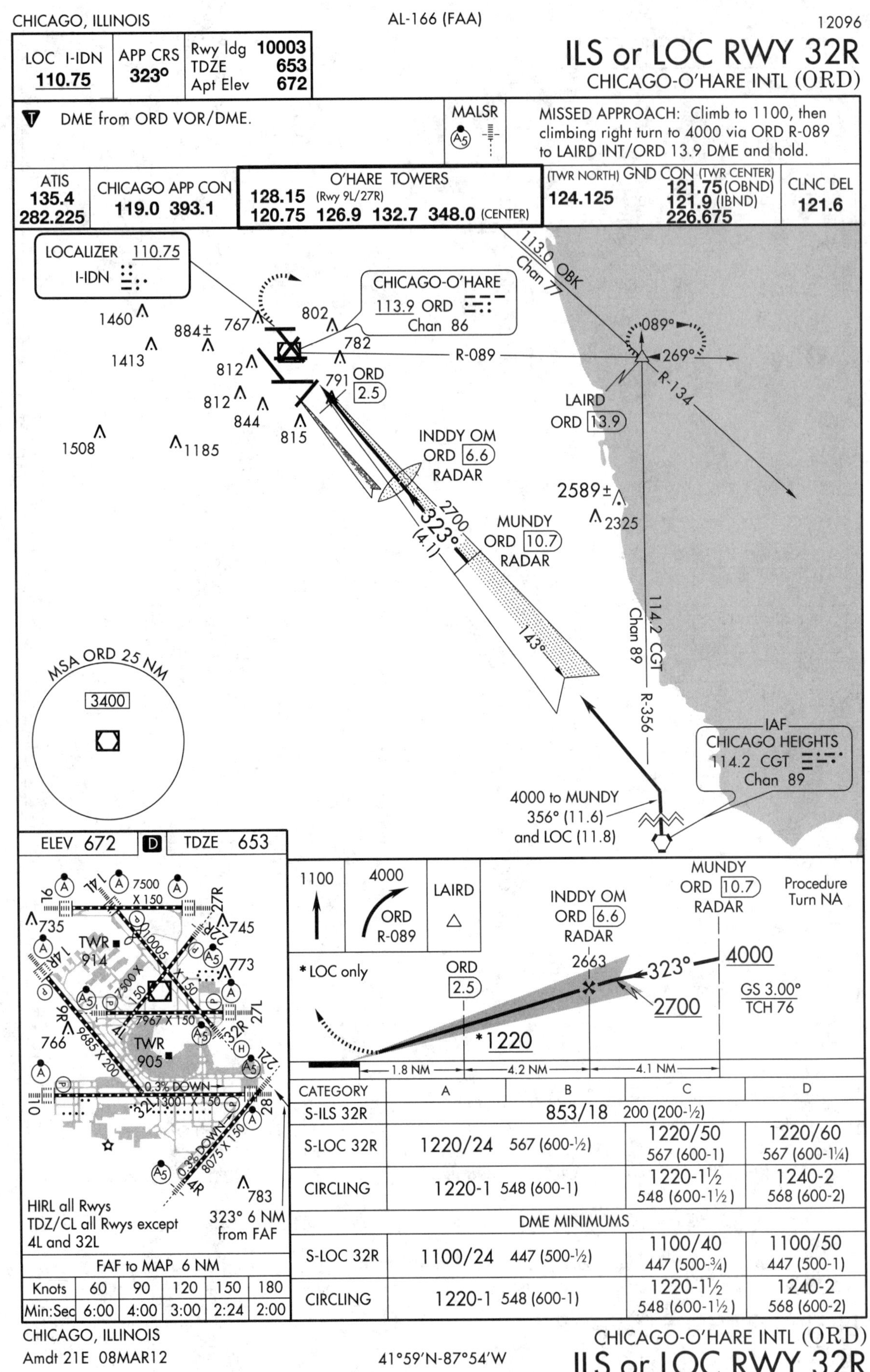

FAF to MAP 6 NM

Knots	60	90	120	150	180
Min:Sec	6:00	4:00	3:00	2:24	2:00

CATEGORY	A	B	C	D
S-ILS 32R	853/18 200 (200-½)			
S-LOC 32R	1220/24 567 (600-½)		1220/50 567 (600-1)	1220/60 567 (600-1¼)
CIRCLING	1220-1 548 (600-1)		1220-1½ 548 (600-1½)	1240-2 568 (600-2)
DME MINIMUMS				
S-LOC 32R	1100/24 447 (500-½)		1100/40 447 (500-¾)	1100/50 447 (500-1)
CIRCLING	1220-1 548 (600-1)		1220-1½ 548 (600-1½)	1240-2 568 (600-2)

Figure 279. ILS or LOC RWY 32R (ORD).

CHICAGO, ILLINOIS AL-166 (FAA) 12096

LOC/DME I-SAJ 111.75 Chan 54 (Y)	APP CRS 093°	Rwy ldg 7500 TDZE 668 Apt Elev 672

ILS or LOC RWY 9L
CHICAGO-O'HARE INTL (ORD)

Simultaneous approach authorized with Rwy 9R and 10.

ALSF-2

MISSED APPROACH: Climb to 1100 then climbing left turn to 4000 via OBK VOR/DME R-166 to OBK VOR/DME and hold.

ATIS	CHICAGO APP CON	O'HARE TOWERS	(TWR NORTH) GND CON (TWR CENTER)	CLNC DEL
135.4 282.225	119.0 393.1	128.15 (Rwy 9L/27R) 120.75 126.9 132.7 348.0 (CENTER)	124.125 121.75 (OBND) 121.9 (IBND) 226.675	121.6

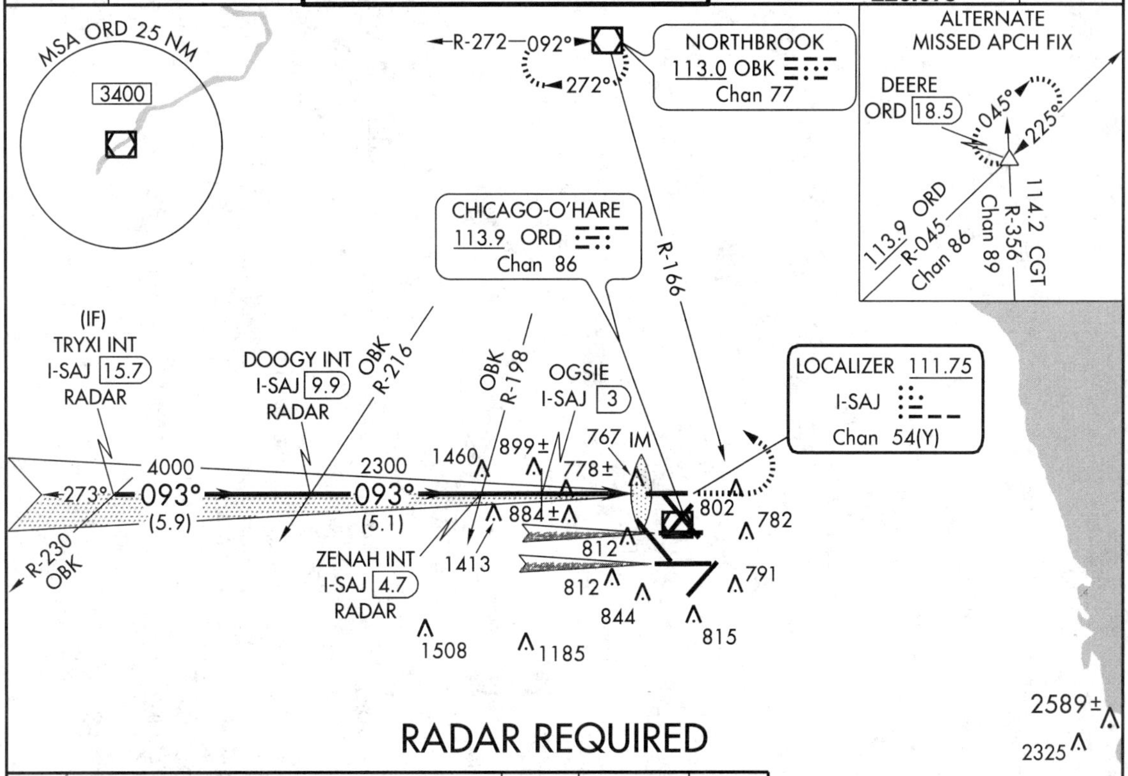

MSA ORD 25 NM 3400

R-272 092° 272°

NORTHBROOK 113.0 OBK Chan 77

ALTERNATE MISSED APCH FIX

DEERE ORD 18.5

045° 225°

113.9 ORD R-045 Chan 86

114.2 CGT R-356 Chan 89

CHICAGO-O'HARE 113.9 ORD Chan 86

R-166

(IF) TRYXI INT I-SAJ 15.7 RADAR

DOOGY INT I-SAJ 9.9 RADAR

OBK R-216

OBK R-198

OGSIE I-SAJ 3

767 IM

LOCALIZER 111.75 I-SAJ Chan 54(Y)

4000 273° 093° (5.9)

2300 093° (5.1)

1460 899± 778± 884± 1413 812 812 844 802 782 791 815 1508 1185

R-230 OBK

ZENAH INT I-SAJ 4.7 RADAR

2589± 2325

RADAR REQUIRED

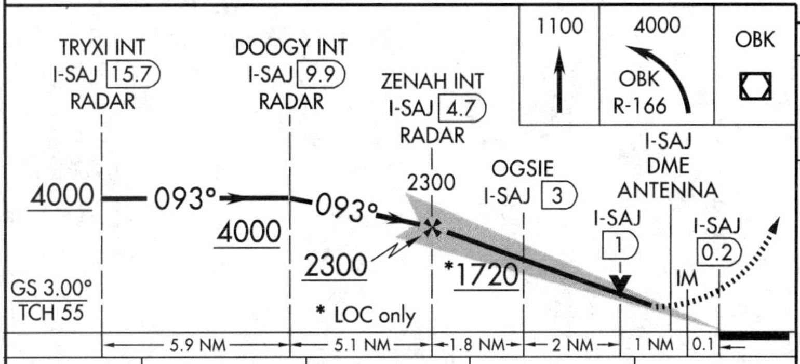

TRYXI INT I-SAJ 15.7 RADAR

DOOGY INT I-SAJ 9.9 RADAR

ZENAH INT I-SAJ 4.7 RADAR

1100	4000 OBK R-166	OBK

4000 093° 4000 093° 2300 2300

OGSIE I-SAJ 3

I-SAJ DME ANTENNA

I-SAJ 1

I-SAJ 0.2

IM

*1720

GS 3.00° TCH 55

* LOC only

5.9 NM 5.1 NM 1.8 NM 2 NM 1 NM 0.1

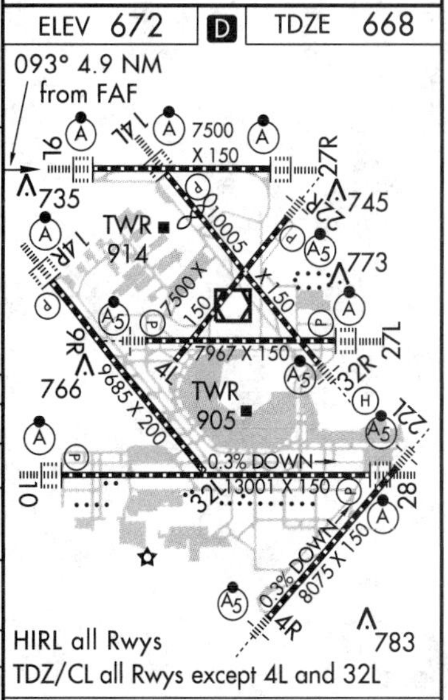

CATEGORY	A	B	C	D
S-ILS 9L	868/18 200 (200-½)			
S-LOC 9L	1720/40 1052 (1100-¾)	1720/50 1052 (1100-1)	1720-2½ 1052 (1100-2½)	
CIRCLING	1720-1¼ 1048 (1100-1¼)	1720-1½ 1048 (1100-1½)	1720-3 1048 (1100-3)	
OGSIE FIX MINIMUMS				
S-LOC 9L	1080/24 412 (500-½)		1080/40 412 (500-¾)	
CIRCLING	1220-1 548 (600-1)		1220-1½ 548 (600-1½)	1240-2 568 (600-2)

ELEV 672 TDZE 668

093° 4.9 NM from FAF

7500 X 150 10005 X 150 7500 X 150 7967 X 150 9685 X 200 13001 X 150 8075 X 150

TWR 914 TWR 905

735 745 773 766 783

0.3% DOWN 0.3% DOWN

9L 27R 14L 32R 14R 32L 9R 27L 4L 22R 4R 22L 10 28

HIRL all Rwys

TDZ/CL all Rwys except 4L and 32L

FAF to MAP 4.9 NM

Knots	60	90	120	150	180
Min:Sec	4:54	3:16	2:27	1:58	1:38

CHICAGO, ILLINOIS
Orig-D 08MAR12 41°59'N-87°54'W

CHICAGO-O'HARE INTL (ORD)
ILS or LOC RWY 9L

Figure 280. ILS or LOC RWY 9L (ORD).

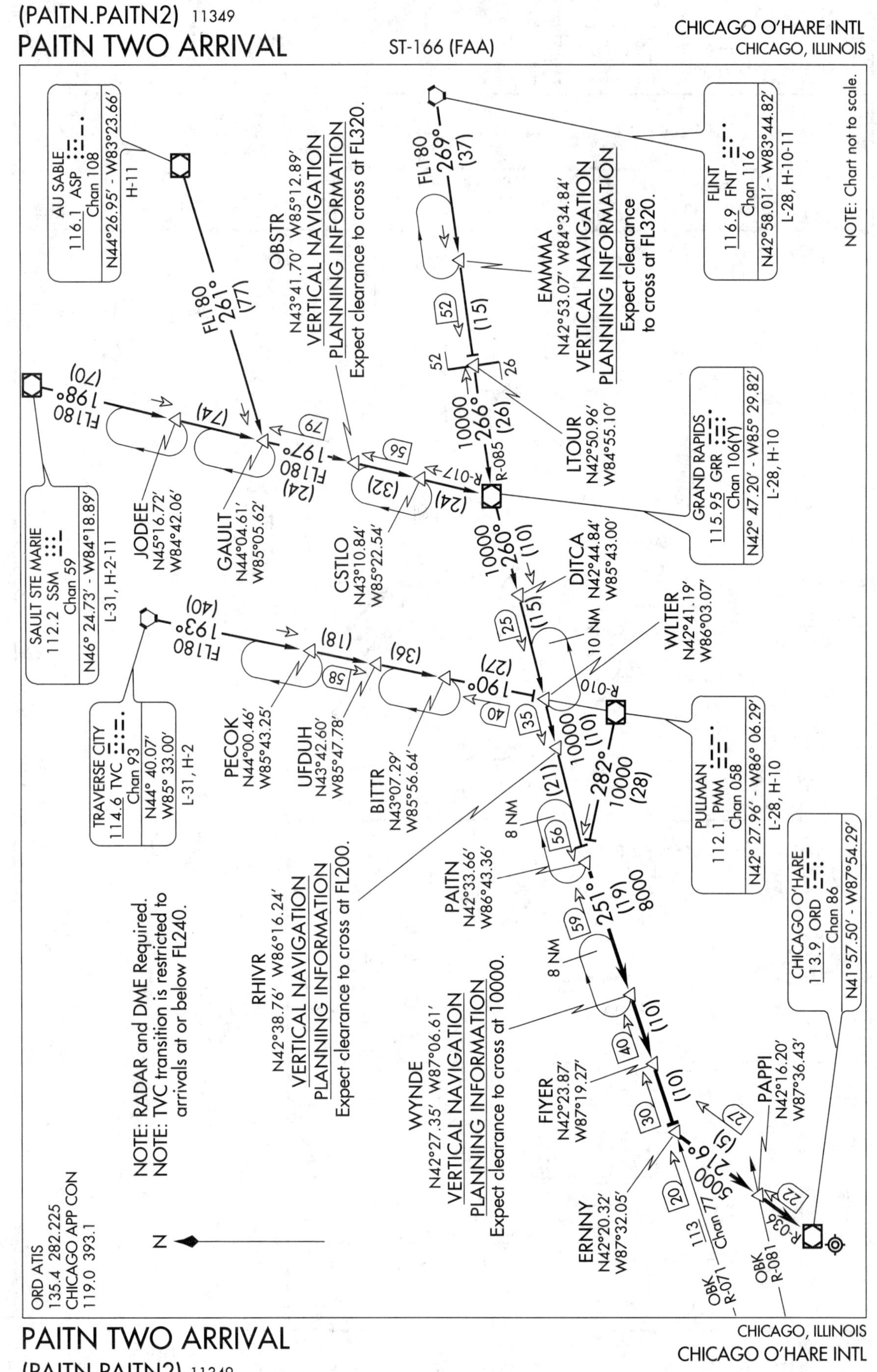

Figure 281. PAITN TWO Arrival (PAITN.PAITN2).

(PAITN.PAITN2) 11013

PAITN TWO ARRIVAL

ST-166 (FAA)

CHICAGO O'HARE INTL
CHICAGO, ILLINOIS

ARRIVAL ROUTE DESCRIPTION

AU SABLE TRANSITION (ASP.PAITN2): From over ASP VOR/DME via ASP R-261 to GAULT then via GRR R-017 to GRR VOR/DME then via GRR R-260 to PAITN. Thence....
FLINT TRANSITION (FNT.PAITN2): From over FNT VORTAC via FNT R-269 to LTOUR and GRR R-085 to GRR VOR/DME then via GRR R-260 to PAITN. Thence....
GRAND RAPIDS TRANSITION (GRR.PAITN2): From over GRR VOR/DME via GRR R-260 to PAITN. Thence....
PULLMAN TRANSITION (PMM.PAITN2): From over PMM VOR/DME via PMM R-282 to PAITN. Thence....
SAULT STE MARIE TRANSITION (SSM.PAITN2): From over SSM VOR/DME via SSM R-198 to GAULT then via GRR R-017 to GRR VOR/DME then via GRR R-260 to PAITN. Thence....
TRAVERSE CITY TRANSITION (TVC.PAITN2): From over TVC VORTAC via TVC R-193 to BITTR then via PMM R-010 to WLTER then via GRR R-260 to PAITN. Thence....

....From over PAITN via OBK VOR/DME R-071 to WYNDE/OBK 40 DME, then via OBK VOR/DME R-071 to FIYER/OBK 30 DME, then via OBK VOR/DME R-071 to ERNNY/OBK 20 DME, then via ORD VOR/DME R-036 to PAPPI/ORD 22 DME, then via ORD VOR/DME R-036 to ORD VOR/DME. Expect radar vectors to final approach course.

PAITN TWO ARRIVAL
(PAITN.PAITN2) 11013

CHICAGO, ILLINOIS
CHICAGO O'HARE INTL

Figure 282. PAITN TWO Arrival (PAITN.PAITN2).

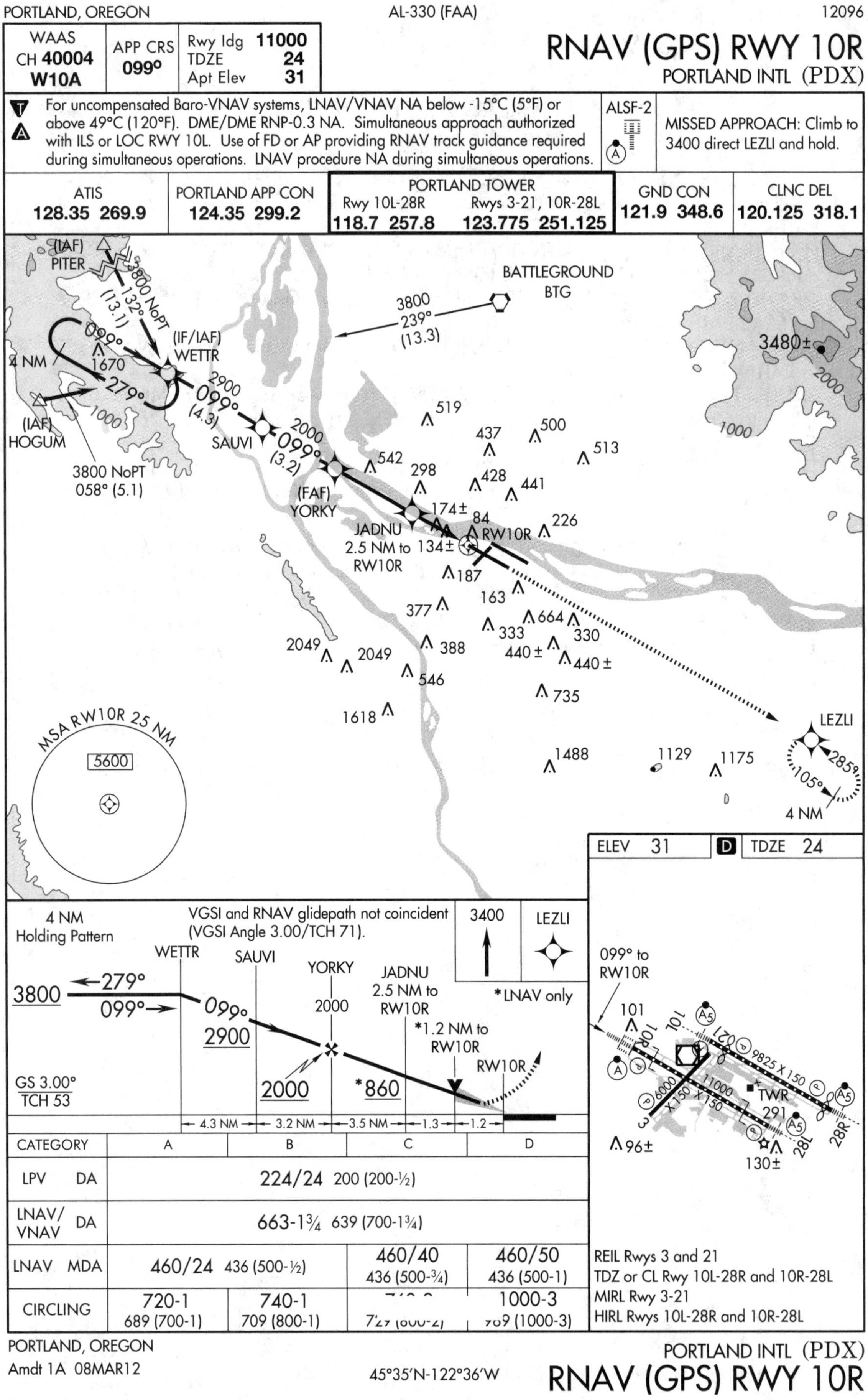

PORTLAND, OREGON | AL-330 (FAA) | 12096

WAAS CH 40004 W10A	APP CRS 099°	Rwy ldg 11000 TDZE 24 Apt Elev 31

RNAV (GPS) RWY 10R
PORTLAND INTL (PDX)

For uncompensated Baro-VNAV systems, LNAV/VNAV NA below -15°C (5°F) or above 49°C (120°F). DME/DME RNP-0.3 NA. Simultaneous approach authorized with ILS or LOC RWY 10L. Use of FD or AP providing RNAV track guidance required during simultaneous operations. LNAV procedure NA during simultaneous operations.

ALSF-2

MISSED APPROACH: Climb to 3400 direct LEZLI and hold.

ATIS	PORTLAND APP CON	PORTLAND TOWER Rwy 10L-28R	PORTLAND TOWER Rwys 3-21, 10R-28L	GND CON	CLNC DEL
128.35 269.9	124.35 299.2	118.7 257.8	123.775 251.125	121.9 348.6	120.125 318.1

(IAF) PITER — 3800 NoPT 132° (13.1)

BATTLEGROUND BTG — 3800 239° (13.3)

(IF/IAF) WETTR — 2900 099° (4.3)

(IAF) HOGUM — 3800 NoPT 058° (5.1)

4 NM — 099° — 279° — 1670

SAUVI — 2000 099° (3.2)

(FAF) YORKY

JADNU 2.5 NM to RW10R

RW10R

LEZLI — 285° — 105° — 4 NM

3480±

MSA RW10R 25 NM — 5600

ELEV 31 | TDZE 24

4 NM Holding Pattern

VGSI and RNAV glidepath not coincident (VGSI Angle 3.00/TCH 71).

3400 — LEZLI

3800 ← 279° / 099° →

WETTR — 099° — 2900

SAUVI — 2000

YORKY — 2000

JADNU 2.5 NM to RW10R

*1.2 NM to RW10R — *860

*LNAV only

RW10R

GS 3.00°
TCH 53

4.3 NM — 3.2 NM — 3.5 NM — 1.3 — 1.2

CATEGORY	A	B	C	D
LPV DA	224/24 200 (200-½)			
LNAV/VNAV DA	663-1¾ 639 (700-1¾)			
LNAV MDA	460/24 436 (500-½)		460/40 436 (500-¾)	460/50 436 (500-1)
CIRCLING	720-1 689 (700-1)	740-1 709 (800-1)	[illegible]	1000-3 [illegible]9 (1000-3)

099° to RW10R

101

9825 X 150

11000 X 150

6000 X 150

TWR

291

96±

130±

REIL Rwys 3 and 21
TDZ or CL Rwy 10L-28R and 10R-28L
MIRL Rwy 3-21
HIRL Rwys 10L-28R and 10R-28L

PORTLAND, OREGON
Amdt 1A 08MAR12

45°35′N-122°36′W

PORTLAND INTL (PDX)
RNAV (GPS) RWY 10R

Figure 283. RNAV (GPS) RWY 10R (PDX).

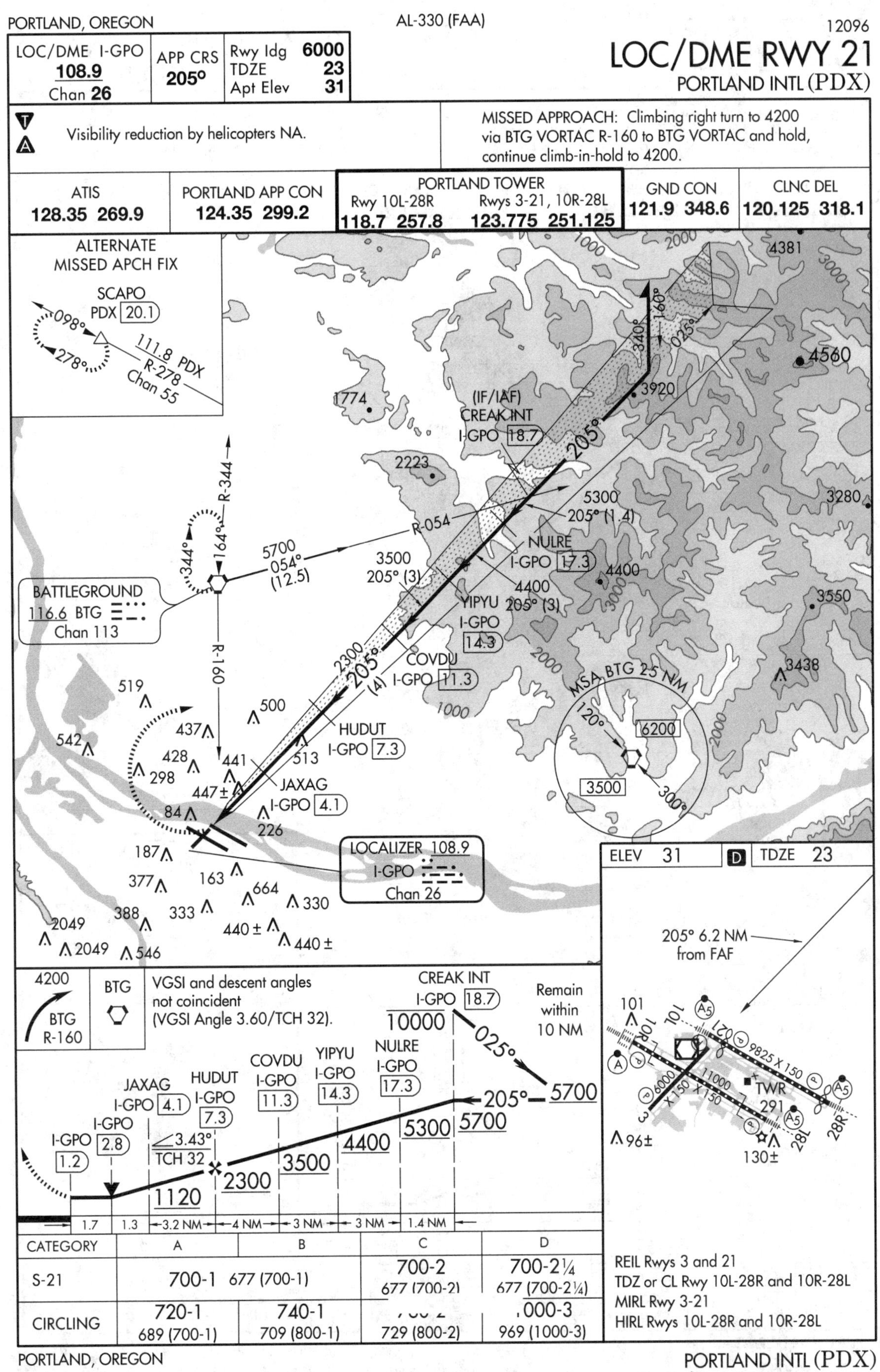

Figure 284. LOC/DME RWY 21 (PDX).

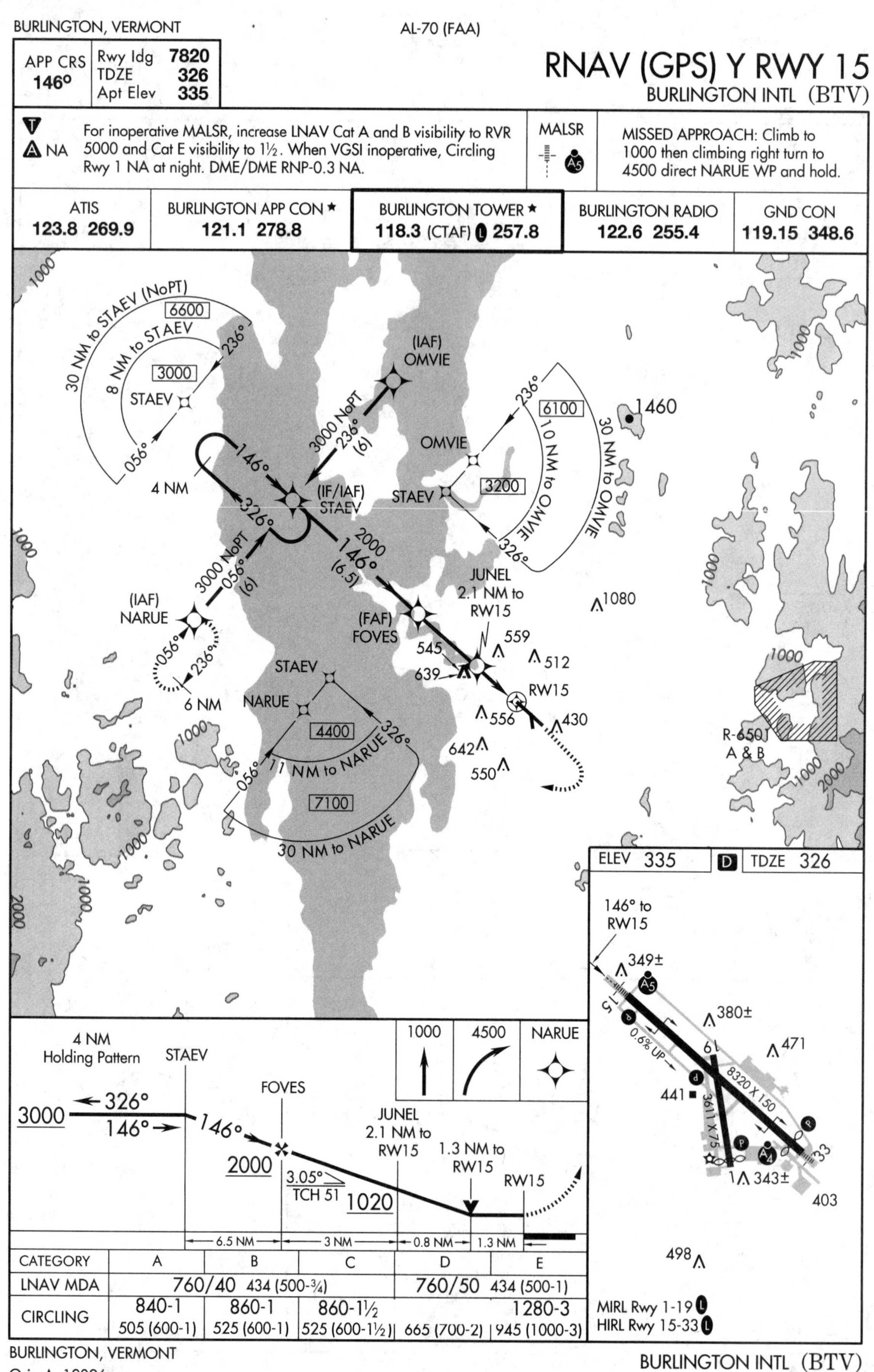

CATEGORY	A	B	C	D	E
LNAV MDA	760/40 434 (500-¾)			760/50 434 (500-1)	
CIRCLING	840-1 505 (600-1)	860-1 525 (600-1)	860-1½ 525 (600-1½)	665 (700-2)	1280-3 945 (1000-3)

Figure 285. RNAV (GPS) Y RWY 15 (BTV).

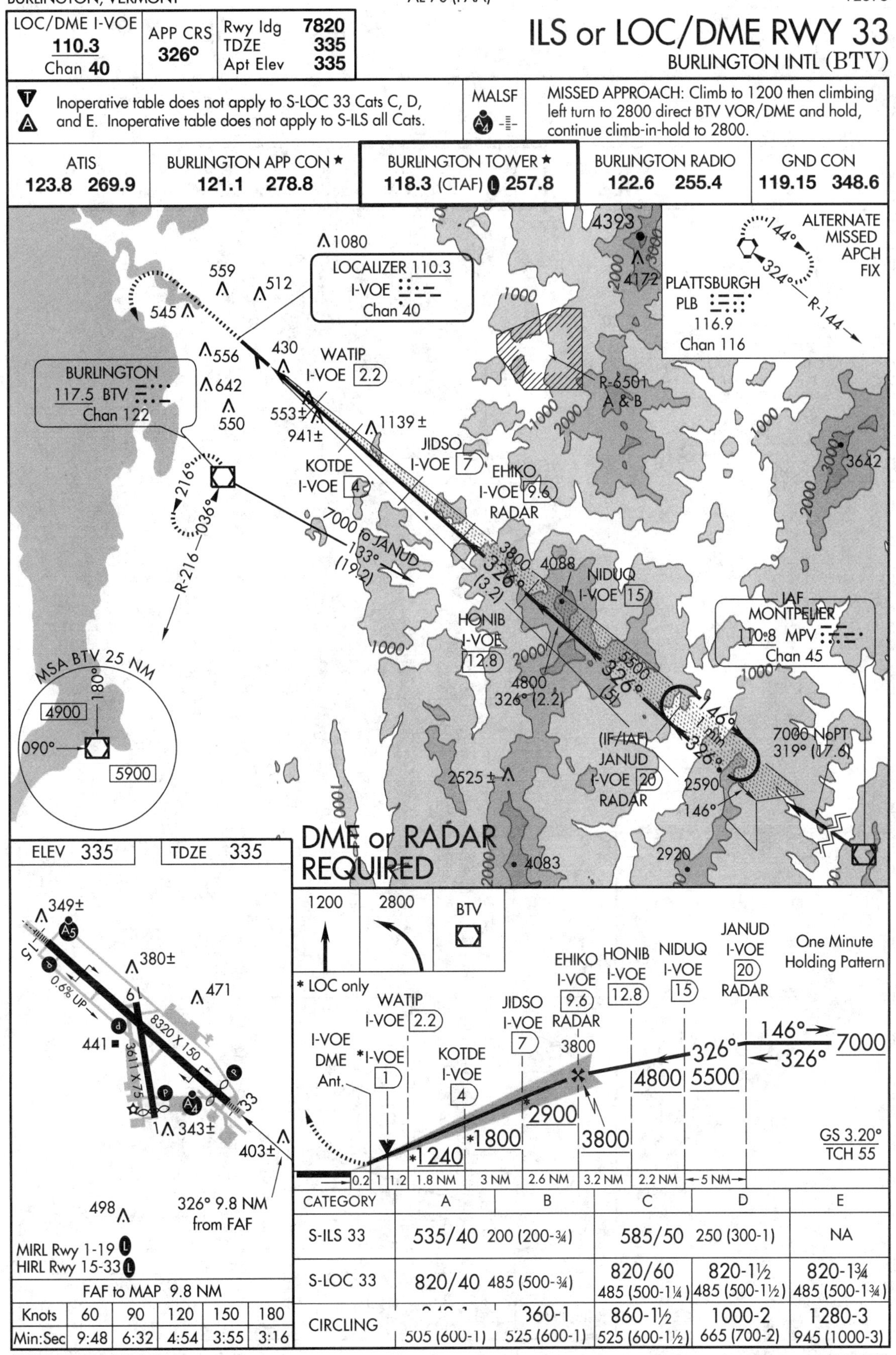
BURLINGTON, VERMONT
AL-70 (FAA)
12096
LOC/DME I-VOE
110.3
Chan 40
APP CRS
326°
Rwy ldg 7820
TDZE 335
Apt Elev 335
ILS or LOC/DME RWY 33
BURLINGTON INTL (BTV)
Inoperative table does not apply to S-LOC 33 Cats C, D, and E. Inoperative table does not apply to S-ILS all Cats.
MALSF
MISSED APPROACH: Climb to 1200 then climbing left turn to 2800 direct BTV VOR/DME and hold, continue climb-in-hold to 2800.
ATIS 123.8 269.9
BURLINGTON APP CON ★ 121.1 278.8
BURLINGTON TOWER ★ 118.3 (CTAF) 257.8
BURLINGTON RADIO 122.6 255.4
GND CON 119.15 348.6
ALTERNATE MISSED APCH FIX
PLATTSBURGH
PLB
116.9
Chan 116
R-144
LOCALIZER 110.3
I-VOE
Chan 40
BURLINGTON
117.5 BTV
Chan 122
WATIP I-VOE 2.2
JIDSO I-VOE 7
KOTDE I-VOE 4
EHIKO I-VOE 9.6 RADAR
NIDUQ I-VOE 15
HONIB I-VOE 12.8
R-6501 A & B
7000 to JANUD 133° (19.2)
3800 326° (3.2)
4800 326° (2.2)
5500 326° (5)
IAF MONTPELIER 110.8 MPV Chan 45
(IF/IAF) JANUD I-VOE 20 RADAR
7000 NoPT 319° (17.6)
146°
1 min
R-216
MSA BTV 25 NM
4900
5900
DME or RADAR REQUIRED
ELEV 335
TDZE 335
8320 X 150
3611 X 75
0.6% UP
326° 9.8 NM from FAF
MIRL Rwy 1-19
HIRL Rwy 15-33
FAF to MAP 9.8 NM
Knots 60 90 120 150 180
Min:Sec 9:48 6:32 4:54 3:55 3:16
1200
2800
BTV
* LOC only
One Minute Holding Pattern
I-VOE DME Ant.
*I-VOE 1
*1240
*1800
*2900
3800
4800
5500
326°
146°
7000
GS 3.20°
TCH 55
0.2 1 1.2 1.8 NM 3 NM 2.6 NM 3.2 NM 2.2 NM 5 NM
CATEGORY A B C D E
S-ILS 33 535/40 200 (200-¾) 585/50 250 (300-1) NA
S-LOC 33 820/40 485 (500-¾) 820/60 485 (500-1¼) 820-1½ 485 (500-1½) 820-1¾ 485 (500-1¾)
CIRCLING 505 (600-1) 360-1 525 (600-1) 860-1½ 525 (600-1½) 1000-2 665 (700-2) 1280-3 945 (1000-3)
BURLINGTON, VERMONT
Amdt 1 13JAN11
44°28'N - 73°09'W
BURLINGTON INTL (BTV)
ILS or LOC/DME RWY 33

Figure 286. ILS or LOC/DME RWY 33 (BTV).

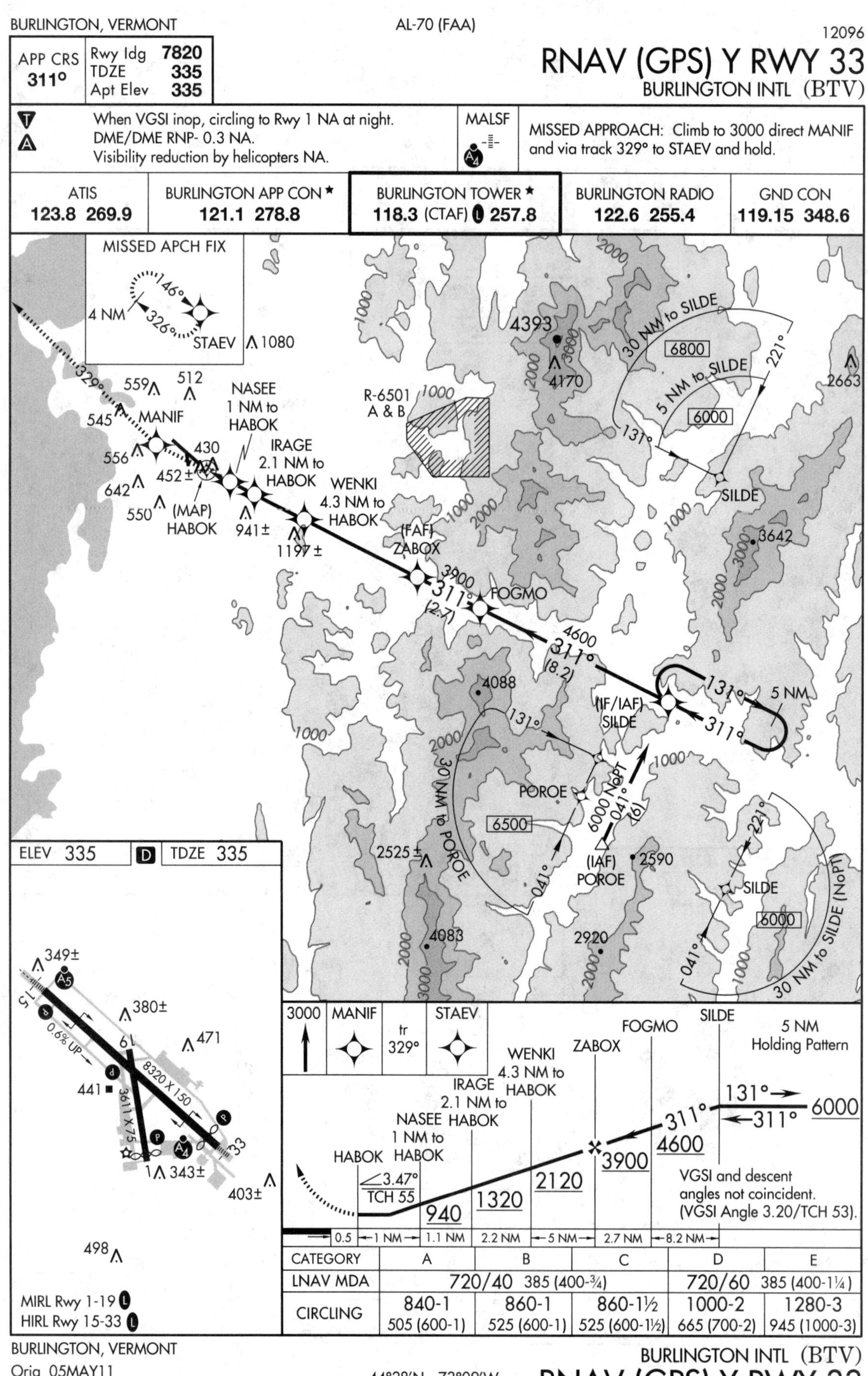

Figure 287. RNAV (GPS) Y RWY 33 (BTV).

(BTV6.BTV) 12096
SL-70 (FAA)
BURLINGTON SIX DEPARTURE
BURLINGTON INTL (BTV)
BURLINGTON, VERMONT
ATIS
123.8 269.9
BURLINGTON GND CON
119.15 348.6
BURLINGTON TOWER ★
118.3 257.8
BURLINGTON DEP CON
121.1 278.8
BURLINGTON RADIO
122.6 255.4
ST JEAN
115.8 YJN
Chan 105
N45°15.35′-W73°19.28′
L-32, H-11-12
SHERBROOKE
113.2 YSC
Chan 79
N45°18.99′-W71°47.29′
L-32, H-11
BANGOR
114.8 BGR
Chan 95
N44°50.51′
W68°52.44′
L-32, H-11
PLATTSBURGH
116.9 PLB
Chan 116
N44°41.10′-W73°31.36′
L-32, H-11-12
BERLIN
110.4 BML
Chan 41
N44°38.00′
W71°11.17′
L-32
MASSENA
114.1 MSS
Chan 88
N44°54.86′
W74°43.36′
L-32, H-11-12
MONTPELIER
110.8 MPV
Chan 45
N44°05.13′-W72°26.96′
L-32
SARANAC LAKE
109.2 SLK
Chan 29
N44°23.07′
W74°12.27′
L-32
BURLINGTON
117.5 BTV
Chan 122
N44°23.83′
W73°10.95′
L-32, H-11-12
LEBANON
113.7 LEB
Chan 84
N43°40.73′
W72°12.96′
L-32
WATERTOWN
109.8 ART
Chan 35
N43°57.13′
W76°03.88′
L-32, H-11-12
GLENS FALLS
110.2 GFL
Chan 39
N43°20.50′
W73°36.71′
L-32
KEENE
109.4 EEN
Chan 31
N42°47.66′
W72°17.51′
L-32-33,
H-11-12
SYRACUSE
117.0 SYR
Chan 117
N43°09.63′
W76°12.27′
L-32, H-11-12
CAMBRIDGE
115.0 CAM
Chan 97
N42°59.66′
W73°20.64′
L-32-34, H-11-12
ALBANY
115.3 ALB
Chan 100
N42°44.84′-W73°48.19′
L-32-33-34, H-10-11-12
TAKEOFF MINIMUMS:
Rwy 1: Standard with minimum climb of 360′ per NM to 6000.
Rwy 15: Standard with minimum climb of 375′ per NM to 5900.
Rwy 19: Standard with minimum climb of 345′ per NM to 5900.
Rwy 33: Standard with minimum climb of 340′ per NM to 5900.
NOTE: Radar required.
NOTE: Chart not to scale
(NARRATIVE ON FOLLOWING PAGE)
BURLINGTON SIX DEPARTURE
(BTV6.BTV) 12096
BURLINGTON, VERMONT
BURLINGTON INTL (BTV)

Figure 288. BURLINGTON SIX Departure (BTV).

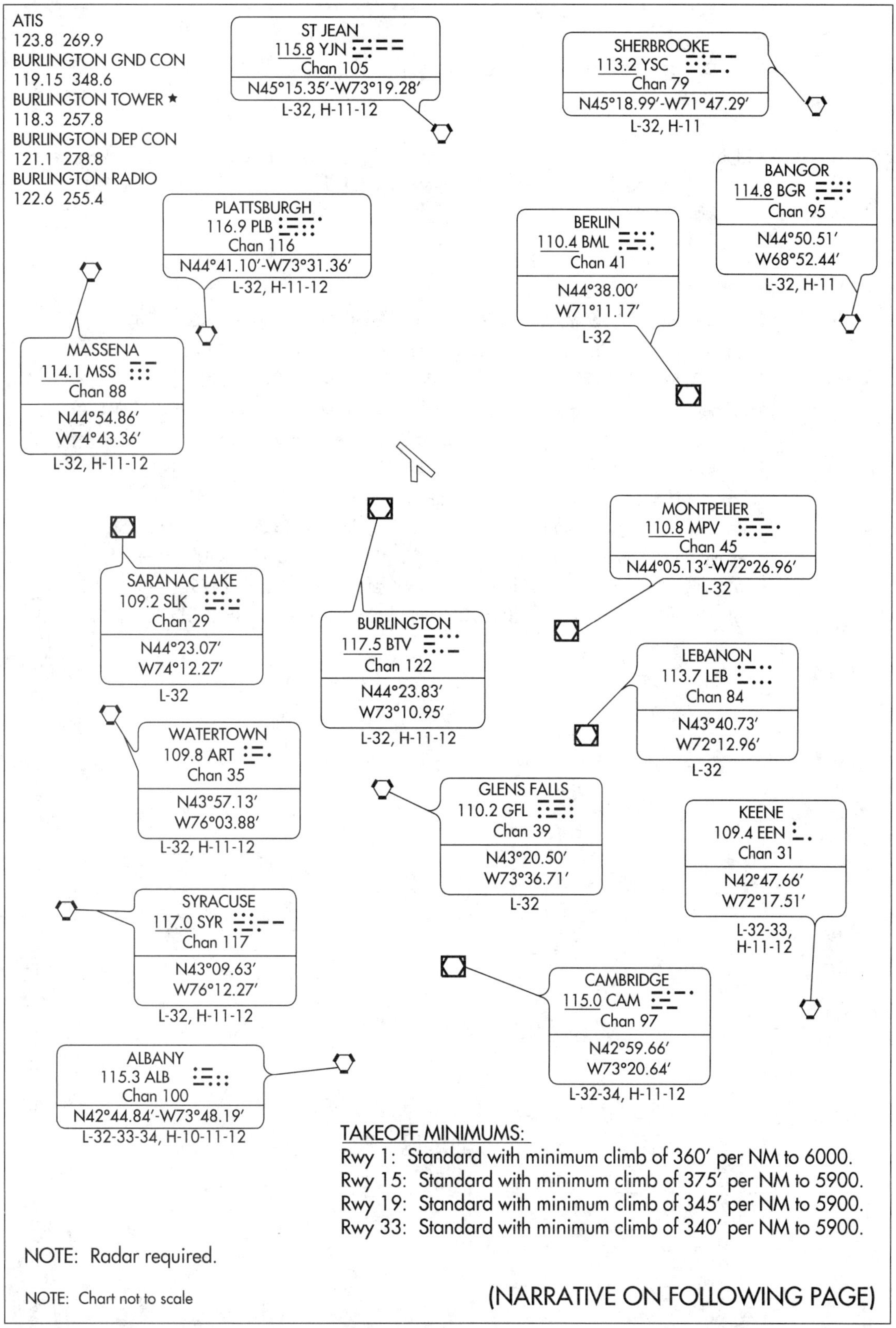

(BTV6.BTV) 10210 SL-70 (FAA)

BURLINGTON SIX DEPARTURE

BURLINGTON INTL (BTV)
BURLINGTON, VERMONT

DEPARTURE ROUTE DESCRIPTION

TAKEOFF RUNWAYS 1, 15, 19, 33: Climb on assigned heading for vectors to filed navaid, fix, or airway to 10000 or assigned lower altitude. Expect filed altitude ten minutes after departure.

TAKEOFF OBSTACLE NOTES:

Rwy 1: Trees beginning 1396′ from DER, 216′ right of centerline, up to 64′ AGL/384′ MSL.
Trees 1694′ from DER, 200′ left of centerline, up to 80′ AGL/380′ MSL.

Rwy 15: Bush 318′ from DER, 292′ left of centerline, up to 23′ AGL/343′ MSL.
Trees beginning 1418′ from DER, 358′ right of centerline, up to 27′ AGL/387′ MSL.
Hopper and trees beginning 1801′ from DER, 377′ left of centerline, up to 63′ AGL/403′ MSL.
Building 3453′ from DER, 1145′ left of centerline, 110′ AGL/430′ MSL.

Rwy 19: Trees beginning 168′ from DER, 24′ right of centerline, up to 56′ AGL/436′ MSL.
Trees beginning 172′ from DER, 184′ left of centerline, up to 93′ AGL/413′ MSL.

Rwy 33: Pole and trees beginning 971′ from DER, 755′ left of centerline, up to 97′ AGL/357′ MSL.
Trees beginning 1091′ from DER, 590′ right of centerline, up to 34′ AGL/334′ MSL.

BURLINGTON SIX DEPARTURE
(BTV6.BTV) 10210
BURLINGTON, VERMONT
BURLINGTON INTL (BTV)

Figure 289. BURLINGTON SIX Departure (BTV).

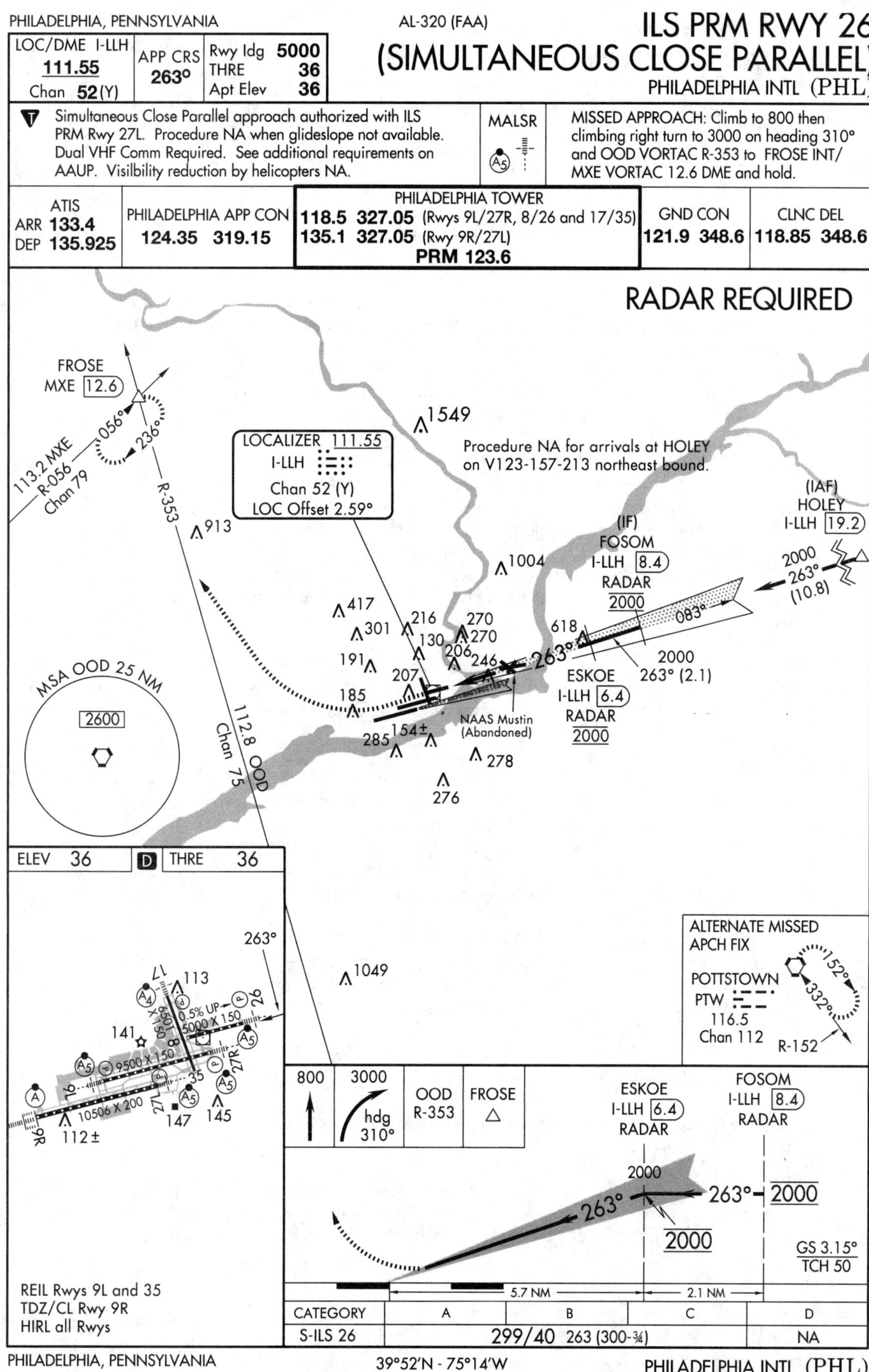

CATEGORY	A	B	C	D
S-ILS 26	299/40 263 (300-¾)			NA

Figure 290. ILS PRM RWY 26 (Simultaneous Close Parallel) (PHL).

ILS PRM RWY 26 Amdt 4 11237
(SIMULTANEOUS CLOSE PARALLEL) AL-320 (FAA)

PHILADELPHIA INTL (PHL)
PHILADELPHIA, PENNSYLVANIA

ATTENTION ALL USERS OF ILS PRECISION RUNWAY MONITOR (PRM)

Condensed Briefing Point:

*When instructed, immediately switch to the tower frequency and select the monitor frequency audio.

1. **ATIS.** When the ATIS broadcast advises that simultaneous ILS/PRM and LDA/PRM approaches are in progress, pilots should brief to fly the ILS/PRM 26 approach. If later advised to expect an ILS 26 approach, the ILS/PRM 26 chart may be used after completing the following briefing items:
   (a) Minimums and missed approach procedures are unchanged.
   (b) Monitor frequency no longer required.

2. **Dual VHF Communication required.** To avoid blocked transmissions, each runway will have two frequencies, a primary and a monitor frequency. The tower controller will transmit on both frequencies. The monitor controller's transmissions, if needed, will override both frequencies. Pilots will ONLY transmit on the tower controller's frequency, but will listen to both frequencies. Select the monitor frequency audio only when instructed by ATC to contact the tower. The volume levels should be set about the same on both radios so that the pilots will be able to hear transmissions on at least one frequency if the other is blocked.

3. **ALL "Breakouts"** are to be hand flown to assure that the manuever is accomplished in the shortest amount of time. Pilots, when directed by ATC to break off an approach, must assume that an aircraft is blundering toward their course and a breakout must be initiated immediately.

   (a) ATC Directed "Breakouts": ATC directed breakouts will consist of a turn and a climb or descent. Pilots must always initiate the breakout in response to an air traffic controller instruction. Controllers will give a descending breakout only when there are no other reasonable options available, but in no case will the descent be below minimum vectoring altitude (MVA) which provides at least 1000 feet required obstruction clearance. The MVA in the final approach segment is 1800 feet at Philadelphia Intl Airport.

   (b) Phraseology - "TRAFFIC ALERT": If an aircraft enters the "NO TRANSGRESSION ZONE" (NTZ), the controller will breakout the threatened aircraft on the adjacent approach. The phraseology for the breakout will be:

   "TRAFFIC ALERT, (aircraft call sign) TURN (left/right) IMMEDIATELY, HEADING (degrees), CLIMB/DESCEND AND MAINTAIN (altitude)".

4. **ILS Navigation** Decending on ILS glideslope ensures complying with any charted crossing restrictions.

Special pilot training required. Pilots who are unable to participate will be afforded appropriate arrival services as operational conditions permit and must notify the controlling ARTCC as soon as practical, but at least 100 miles from destination.

(SIMULTANEOUS CLOSE PARALLEL) 39° 52′N-75° 14′W PHILADELPHIA, PENNSYLVANIA
PHILADELPHIA INTL (PHL)
ILS PRM RWY 26 Amdt 4 11237

Figure 291. ILS PRM RWY 26 (Simultaneous Close Parallel) (PHL).

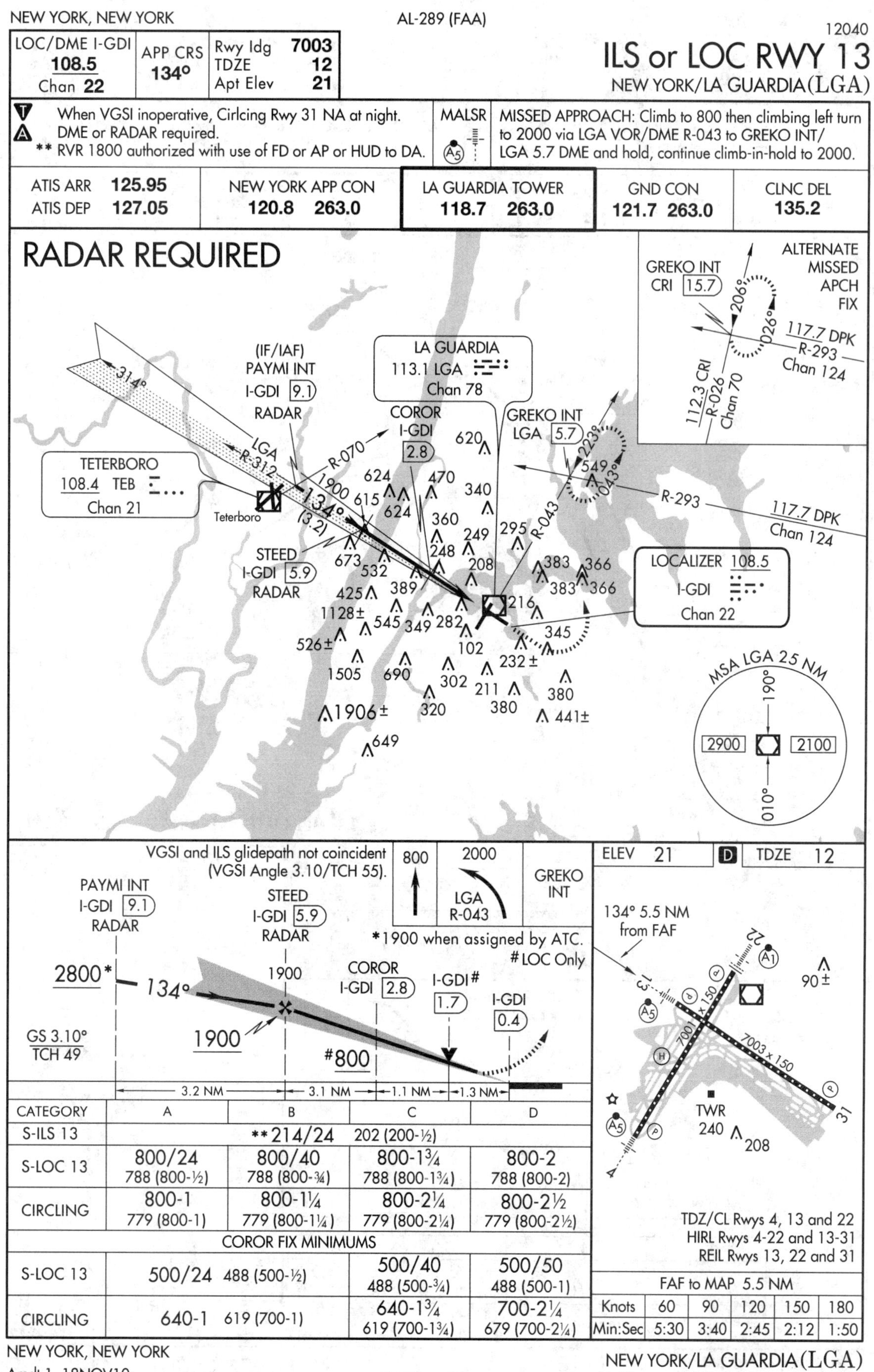

CATEGORY	A	B	C	D
S-ILS 13	**214/24		202 (200-½)	
S-LOC 13	800/24 788 (800-½)	800/40 788 (800-¾)	800-1¾ 788 (800-1¾)	800-2 788 (800-2)
CIRCLING	800-1 779 (800-1)	800-1¼ 779 (800-1¼)	800-2¼ 779 (800-2¼)	800-2½ 779 (800-2½)
COROR FIX MINIMUMS				
S-LOC 13	500/24 488 (500-½)		500/40 488 (500-¾)	500/50 488 (500-1)
CIRCLING	640-1 619 (700-1)		640-1¾ 619 (700-1¾)	700-2¼ 679 (700-2¼)

Knots	60	90	120	150	180
Min:Sec	5:30	3:40	2:45	2:12	1:50

Figure 292. ILS or LOC RWY 13 (LGA).

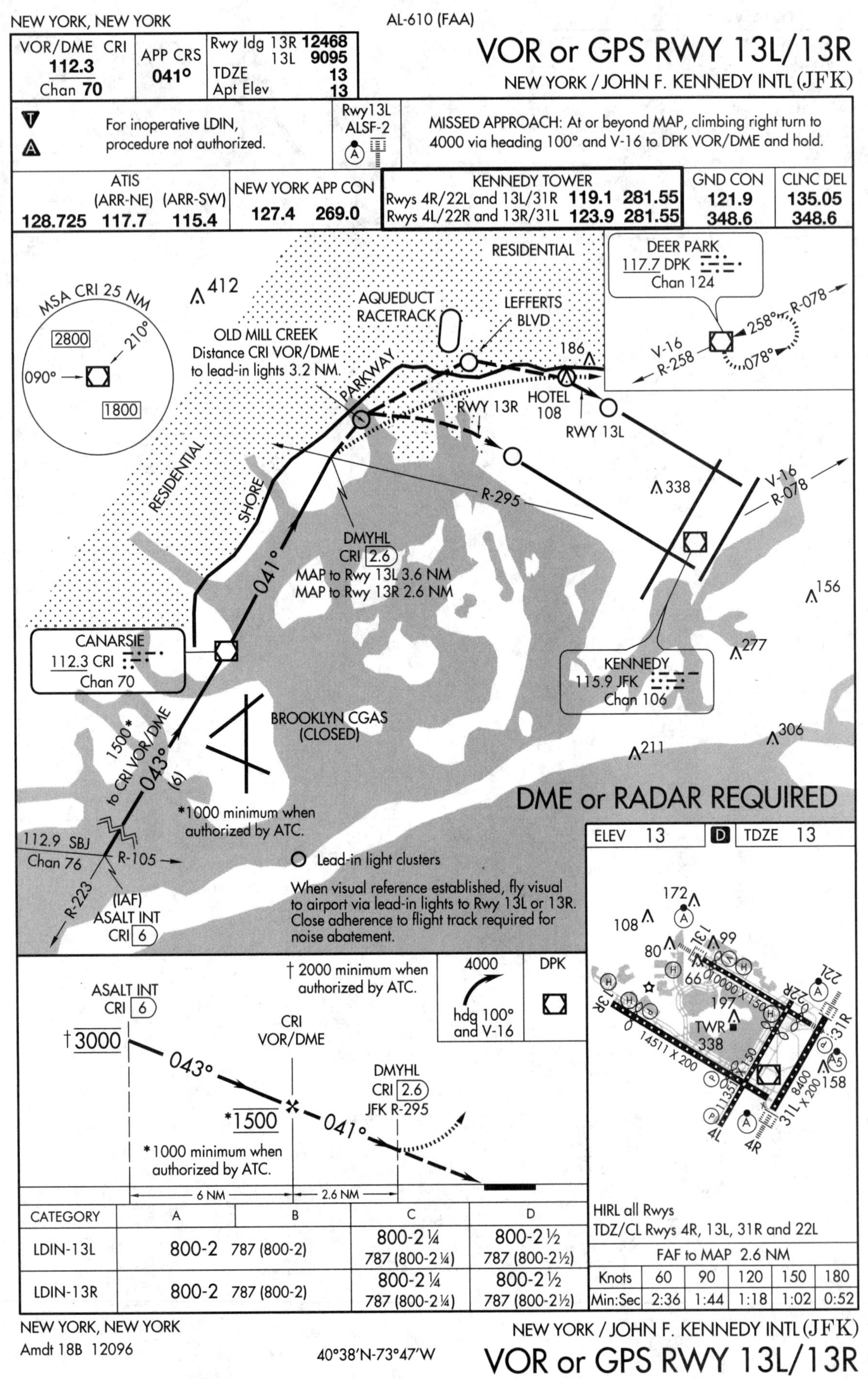

Figure 293. VOR or GPS RWY 13L/13R (JFK).

NEW YORK, NEW YORK AL-610 (FAA)

APP CRS 028°	Rwy ldg N/A TDZE N/A Apt Elev N/A

COPTER RNAV (GPS) 028°

NEW YORK/ JOHN F. KENNEDY INTL (JFK)

NA Proceed VFR from HELOG WP or conduct the specified missed approach. Limit final and missed approach airspeed to 70 KIAS. Use John F. Kennedy Intl altimeter setting.

MISSED APPROACH: Climbing left turn to 1800 direct COVIR WP and hold.

ATIS	ARR-NE	ARR-SW	NEW YORK APP CON
128.725	117.7	115.4	127.4 269.0

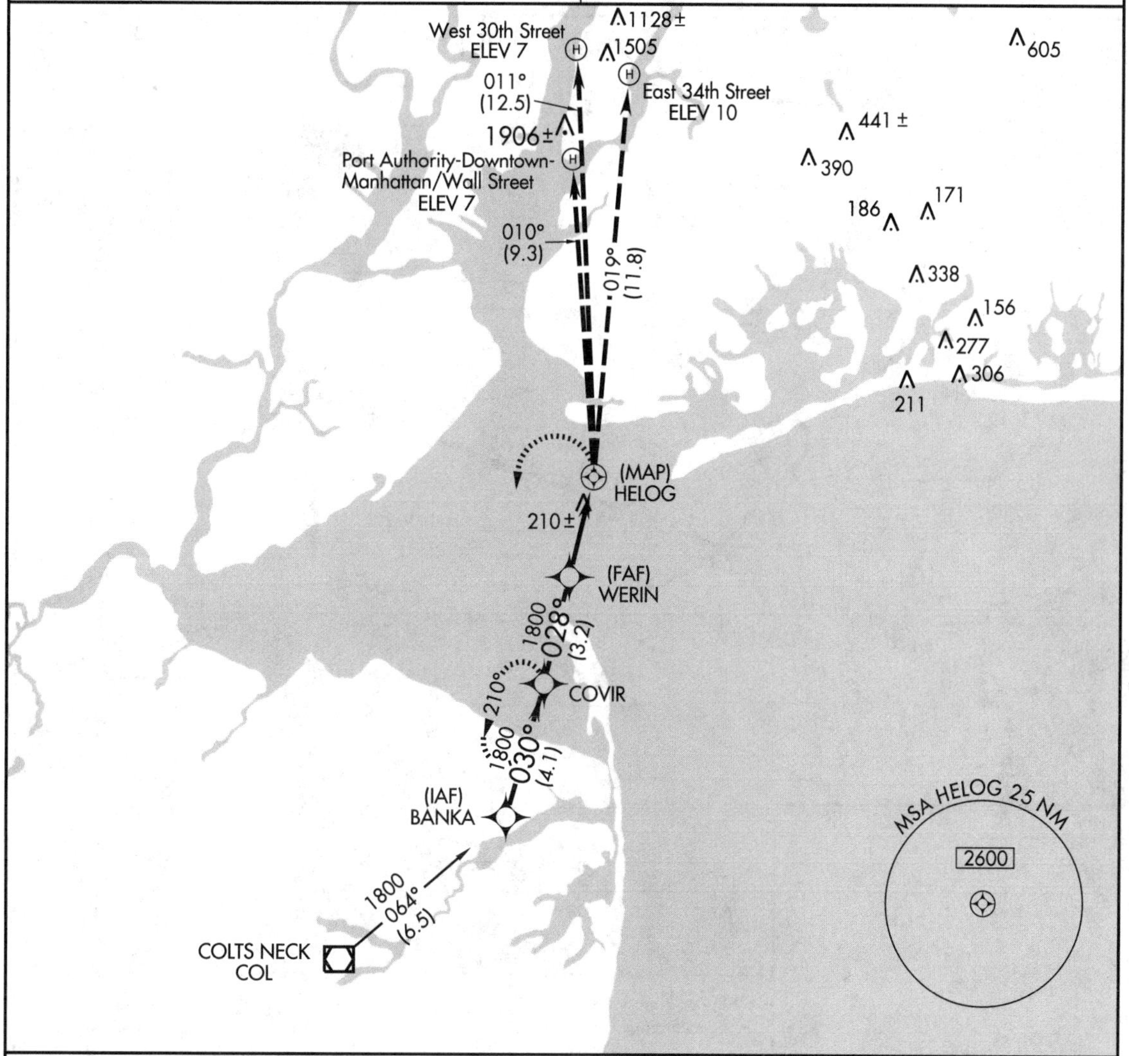

West 30th Street ELEV 7
1128±
1505
East 34th Street ELEV 10
605
011° (12.5)
1906±
441 ±
390
Port Authority-Downtown-Manhattan/Wall Street ELEV 7
186
171
010° (9.3)
019° (11.8)
338
156
277
306
211
(MAP) HELOG
210±
(FAF) WERIN
1800 028° (3.2)
210°
COVIR
1800 030° (4.1)
(IAF) BANKA
MSA HELOG 25 NM
2600
1800 064° (6.5)
COLTS NECK COL

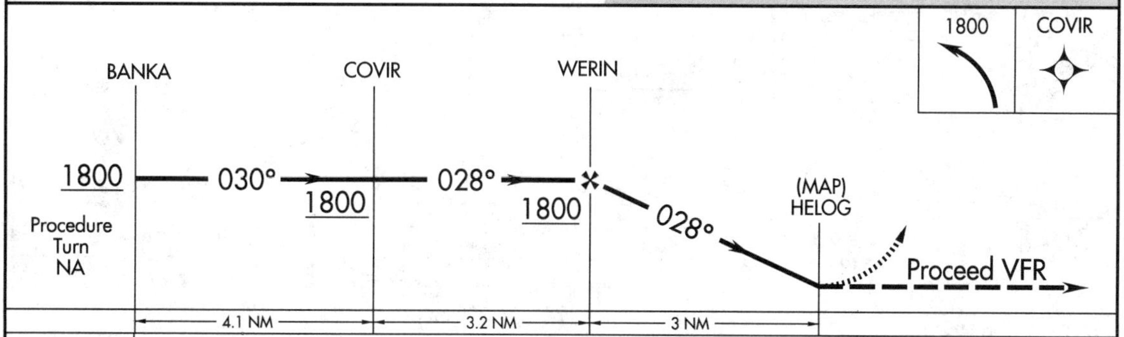

1800	COVIR

BANKA COVIR WERIN

1800 030° 1800 028° 1800 028° (MAP) HELOG

Procedure Turn NA

Proceed VFR

4.1 NM — 3.2 NM — 3 NM

CATEGORY	COPTER
H-028°	500-¾ 467 (500-¾)

NEW YORK, NEW YORK
Orig-A 11069

NEW YORK/ JOHN F. KENNEDY INTL (JFK)

40°38′N - 73°47′W COPTER RNAV (GPS) 028°

Figure 294. COPTER RNAV (GPS) 028° (JFK).

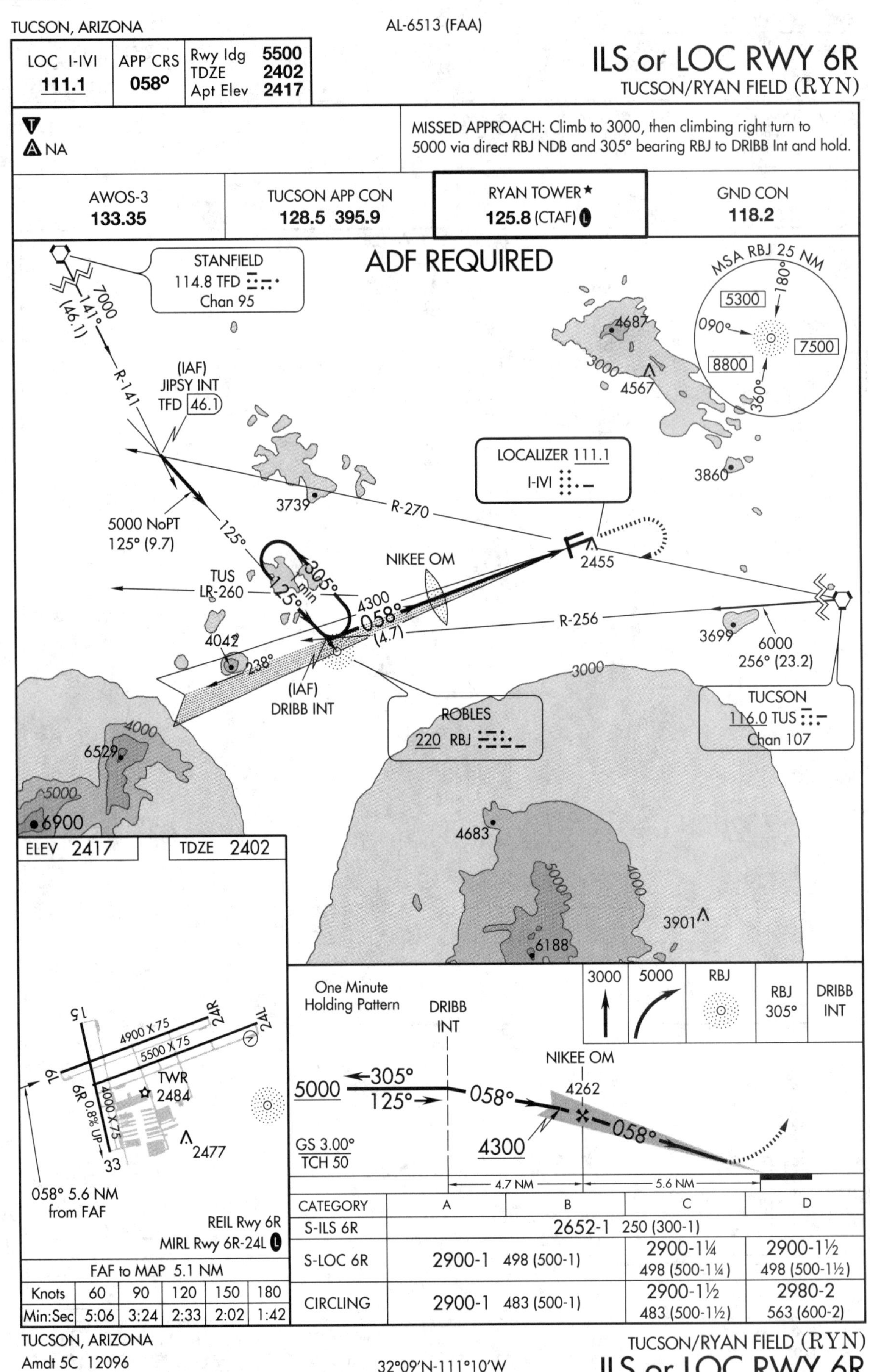

FAF to MAP 5.1 NM					
Knots	60	90	120	150	180
Min:Sec	5:06	3:24	2:33	2:02	1:42

CATEGORY	A	B	C	D
S-ILS 6R	2652-1 250 (300-1)			
S-LOC 6R	2900-1 498 (500-1)		2900-1¼ 498 (500-1¼)	2900-1½ 498 (500-1½)
CIRCLING	2900-1 483 (500-1)		2900-1½ 483 (500-1½)	2980-2 563 (600-2)

Figure 295. ILS or LOC RWY 6R (RYN).

TUCSON, ARIZONA

AL-6513 (FAA)

NDB RYN	APP CRS	Rwy ldg	5500
338	074°	TDZE	2400
		Apt Elev	2415

NDB/DME or GPS RWY 6R

TUCSON/ RYAN FIELD (RYN)

T A NA DME from TUS VORTAC. Simultaneous reception of RYN NDB and TUS DME required.

MISSED APPROACH: Climb to 5000 direct RYN NDB and hold.

AWOS-3	TUCSON APP CON	RYAN TOWER ★	GND CON
133.35	128.5 395.9	125.8 (CTAF) L	118.2

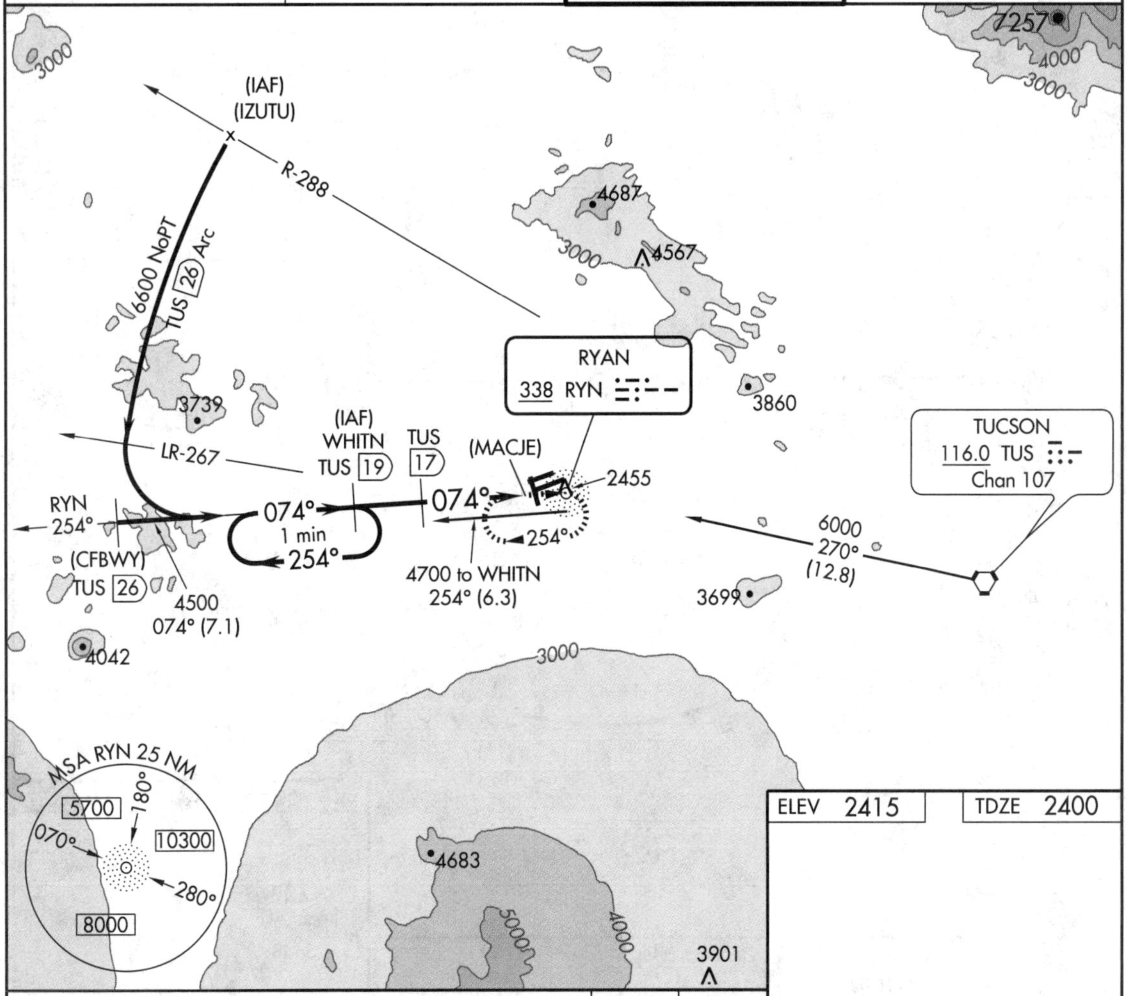

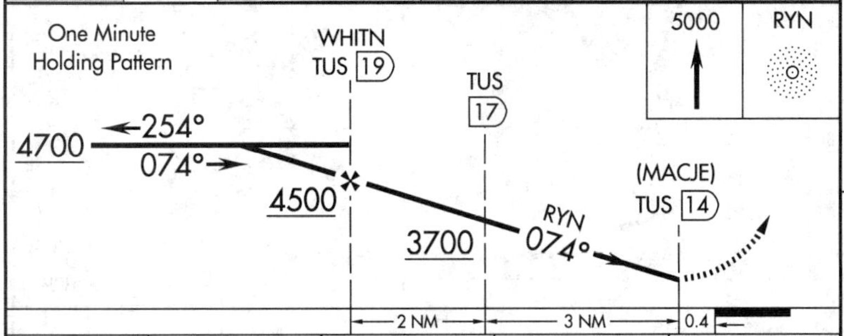

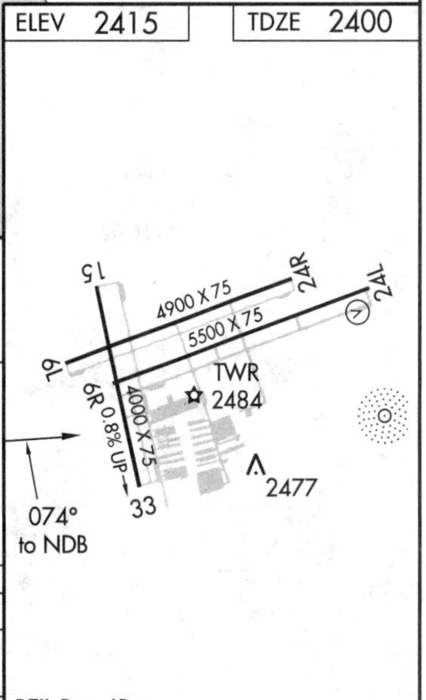

(IAF) (IZUTU)
R-288
6600 NoPT
TUS 26 Arc
7257
4000
3000
4687
4567
RYAN
338 RYN
3860
3739
(IAF) WHITN TUS 19
TUS 17
(MACJE)
2455
TUCSON
116.0 TUS
Chan 107
LR-267
RYN 254°
074°
1 min
254°
6000
270°
(12.8)
(CFBWY) TUS 26
4500
074° (7.1)
4700 to WHITN
254° (6.3)
3699
4042
MSA RYN 25 NM
180°
5700
070°
10300
280°
8000
4683
5000
3901

ELEV 2415 | TDZE 2400

One Minute Holding Pattern
WHITN TUS 19
TUS 17
4700
254°
074°
4500
3700
RYN 074°
(MACJE) TUS 14
5000
RYN
2 NM | 3 NM | 0.4

15
4900 X 75
24R
5500 X 75
24L
TWR 2484
6L
6R 0.8% UP
4000 X 75
2477
33
074° to NDB

CATEGORY	A	B	C	D
S-6R	3300-1¼	900 (900-1¼)	3300-2¾ 900 (900-2¾)	3300-3 900 (900-3)
CIRCLING	3300-1¼	885 (900-1¼)	3300-2¾ 885 (900-2¾)	3300-3 885 (900-3)

REIL Rwy 6R
MIRL Rwy 6R-24L L

TUCSON, ARIZONA
Amdt 1A 12096

32°09′N-111°10′W

TUCSON/ RYAN FIELD (RYN)

NDB/DME or GPS RWY 6R

Figure 296. NDB/DME or GPS RWY 16R (RYN).

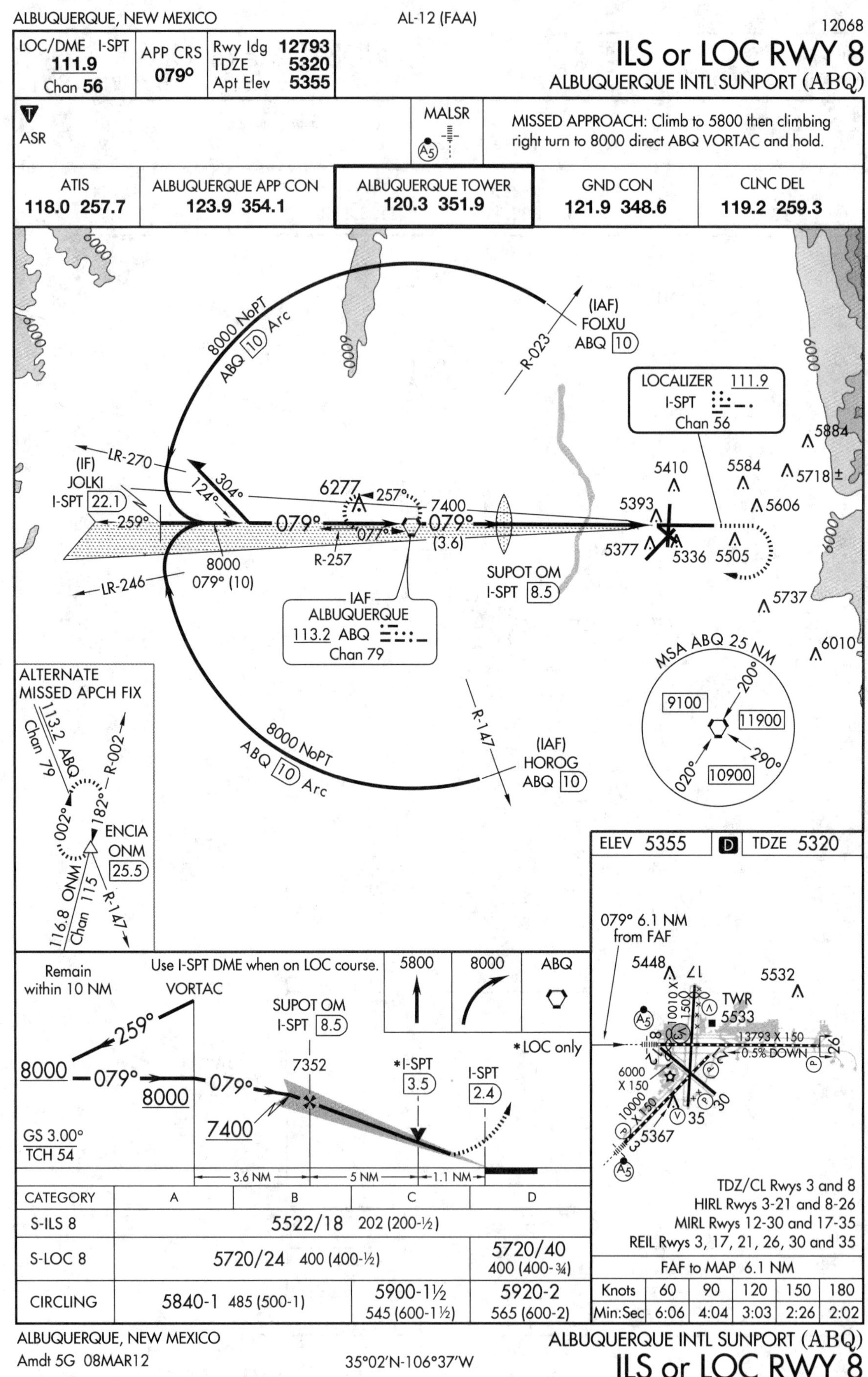

CATEGORY	A	B	C	D
S-ILS 8	5522/18 202 (200-½)			
S-LOC 8	5720/24 400 (400-½)			5720/40 400 (400-¾)
CIRCLING	5840-1 485 (500-1)		5900-1½ 545 (600-1½)	5920-2 565 (600-2)

Knots	60	90	120	150	180
Min:Sec	6:06	4:04	3:03	2:26	2:02

Figure 297. ILS or LOC RWY 8 (ABQ).

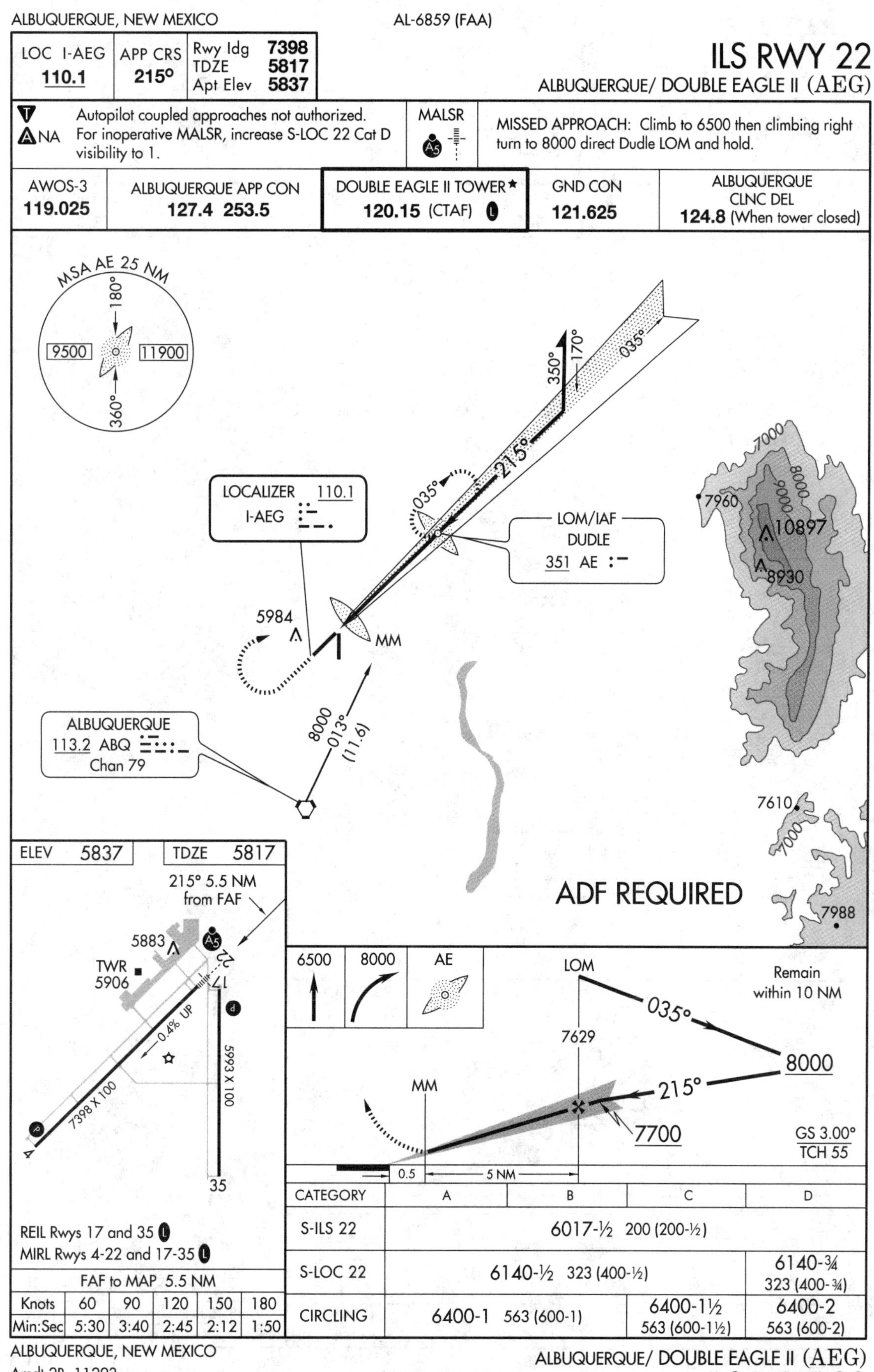

CATEGORY	A	B	C	D
S-ILS 22	6017-½ 200 (200-½)			
S-LOC 22	6140-½ 323 (400-½)			6140-¾ 323 (400-¾)
CIRCLING	6400-1 563 (600-1)		6400-1½ 563 (600-1½)	6400-2 563 (600-2)

FAF to MAP 5.5 NM					
Knots	60	90	120	150	180
Min:Sec	5:30	3:40	2:45	2:12	1:50

Figure 298. ILS RWY 22 (AEG).

CHICAGO/PROSPECT HEIGHTS/WHEELING, ILLINOIS AL-5028 (FAA)

LOC I-PWK 111.9	APP CRS 161°	Rwy ldg 5001 TDZE 643 Apt Elev 647

ILS or LOC RWY 16

CHICAGO EXECUTIVE (PWK)

If local altimeter setting not received, use Chicago-O'Hare Intl altimeter setting and increase all DAs 22 feet, and all visibilities ¼ mile; increase all MDAs 40 feet, and S-LOC Cat C and D visibilities ¼ mile. Visibility reduction by helicopters NA.

MISSED APPROACH: Climb to 1400 then climbing left turn to 2700 direct OBK VOR/DME and hold.

ATIS	CHICAGO APP CON	EXECUTIVE TOWER ★	GND CON	CLNC DEL	UNICOM
124.2	120.55 290.2	119.9 (CTAF)	121.7	124.7	122.95

RADAR REQUIRED

341° 206° 026° 161° R-343 163° 343°

IAF NORTHBROOK 113.0 OBK Chan 77

PAMME OM RADAR

840 830 818 1149 867± 967 759 834 822 834 881 1015 1460

LOCALIZER 111.9 I-PWK

MSA OBK 25 NM 2600 270° 3400 360°

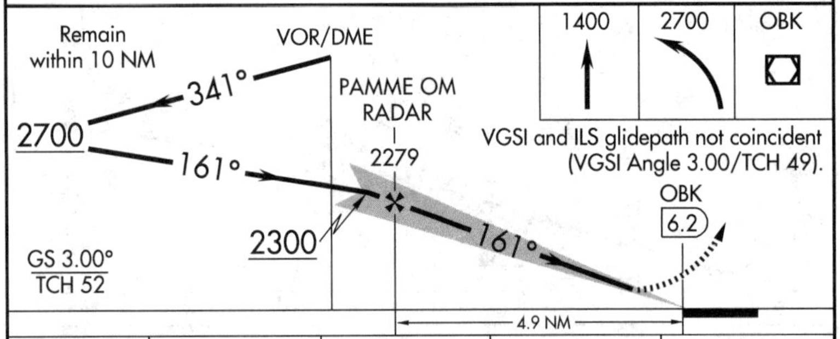

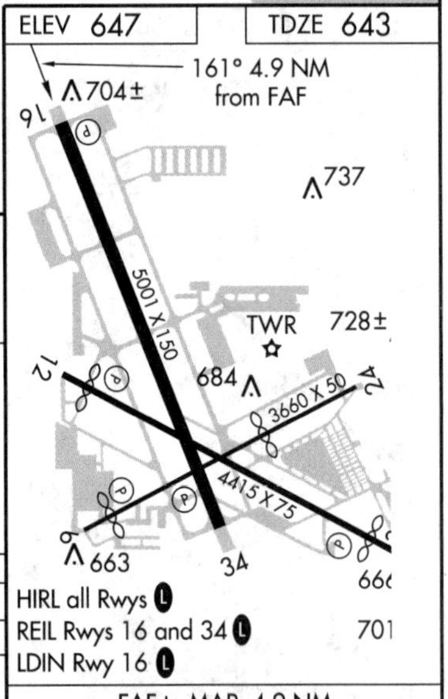

ELEV 647 TDZE 643

161° 4.9 NM from FAF

704± 737 728± TWR 684 663 666 701

5001 X 150 3660 X 50 4415 X 75

16 34 12 24

HIRL all Rwys

REIL Rwys 16 and 34

LDIN Rwy 16

Remain within 10 NM VOR/DME 341° 2700 161° PAMME OM RADAR 2279 2300 161° OBK 6.2

GS 3.00° TCH 52

4.9 NM

1400 2700 OBK

VGSI and ILS glidepath not coincident (VGSI Angle 3.00/TCH 49).

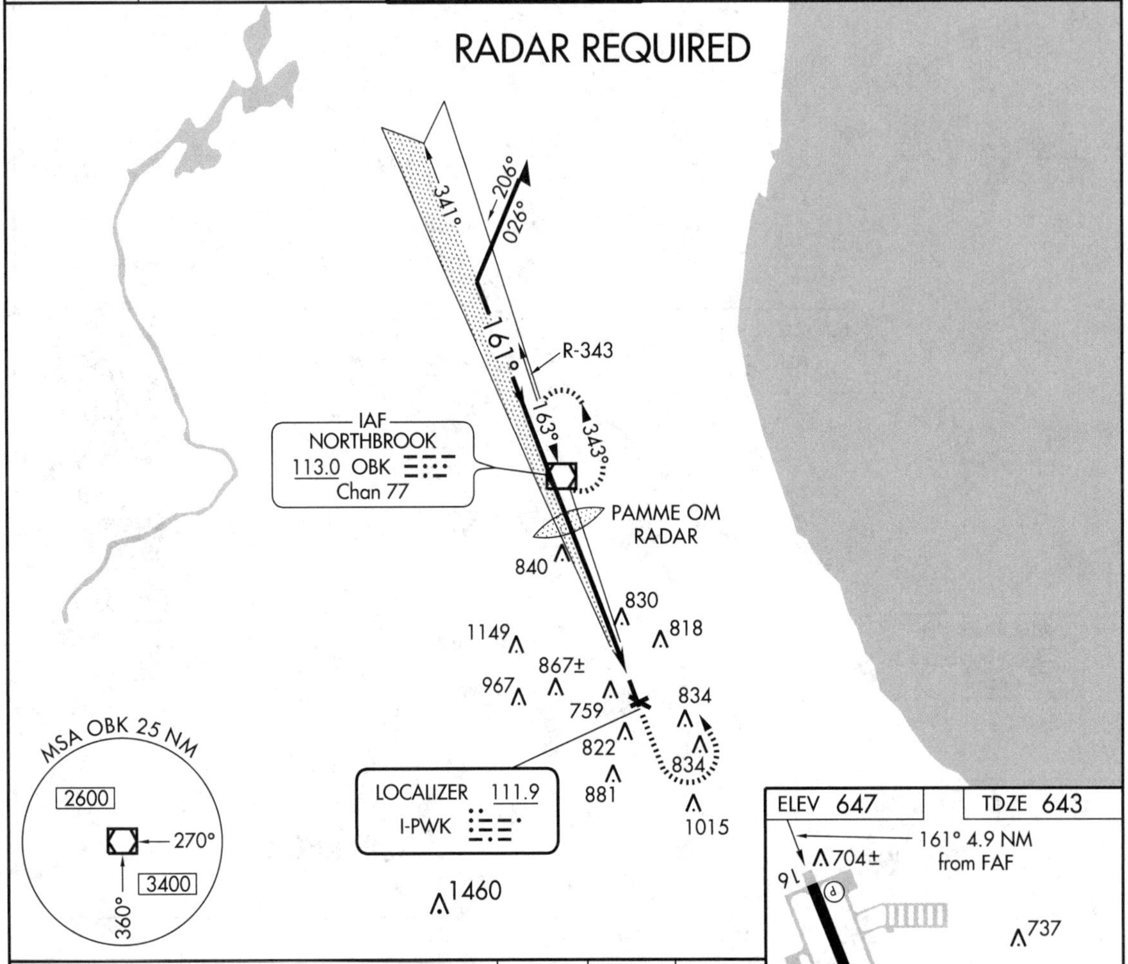

CATEGORY	A	B	C	D
S-ILS 16	893-¾ 250 (300-¾)			
S-LOC 16	1140-1 497 (500-1)		1140-1¼ 497 (500-1¼)	1140-1½ 497 (500-1½)
CIRCLING	1140-1 493 (500-1)		1140-1½ 493 (500-1½)	1200-2 553 (600-2)

FAF to MAP 4.9 NM

Knots	60	90	120	150	180
Min:Sec	4:54	3:16	2:27	1:58	1:38

CHICAGO/PROSPECT HEIGHTS/WHEELING, ILLINOIS

Amdt 2 12096

42°07'N-87°54'W

CHICAGO EXECUTIVE (PWK)

ILS or LOC RWY 16

Figure 299. ILS or LOC RWY 16 (PWK).

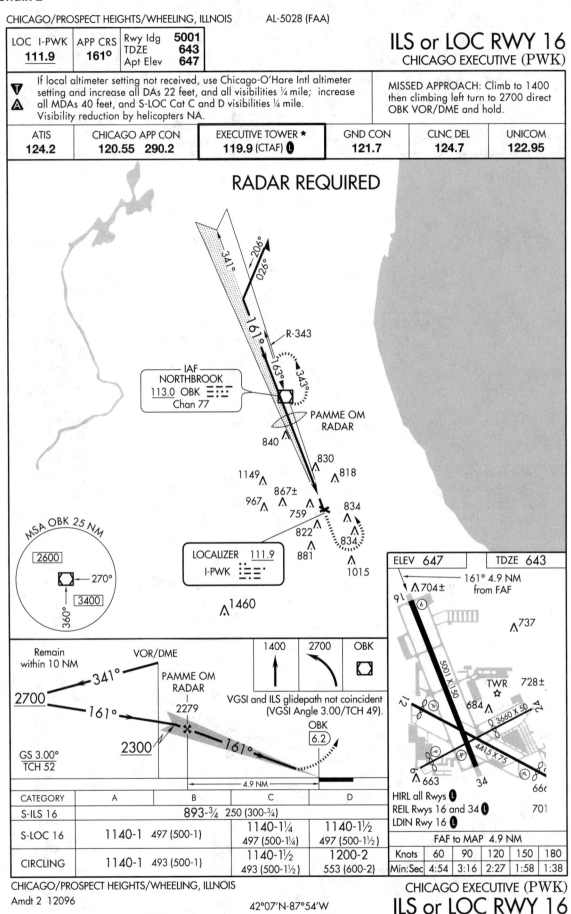

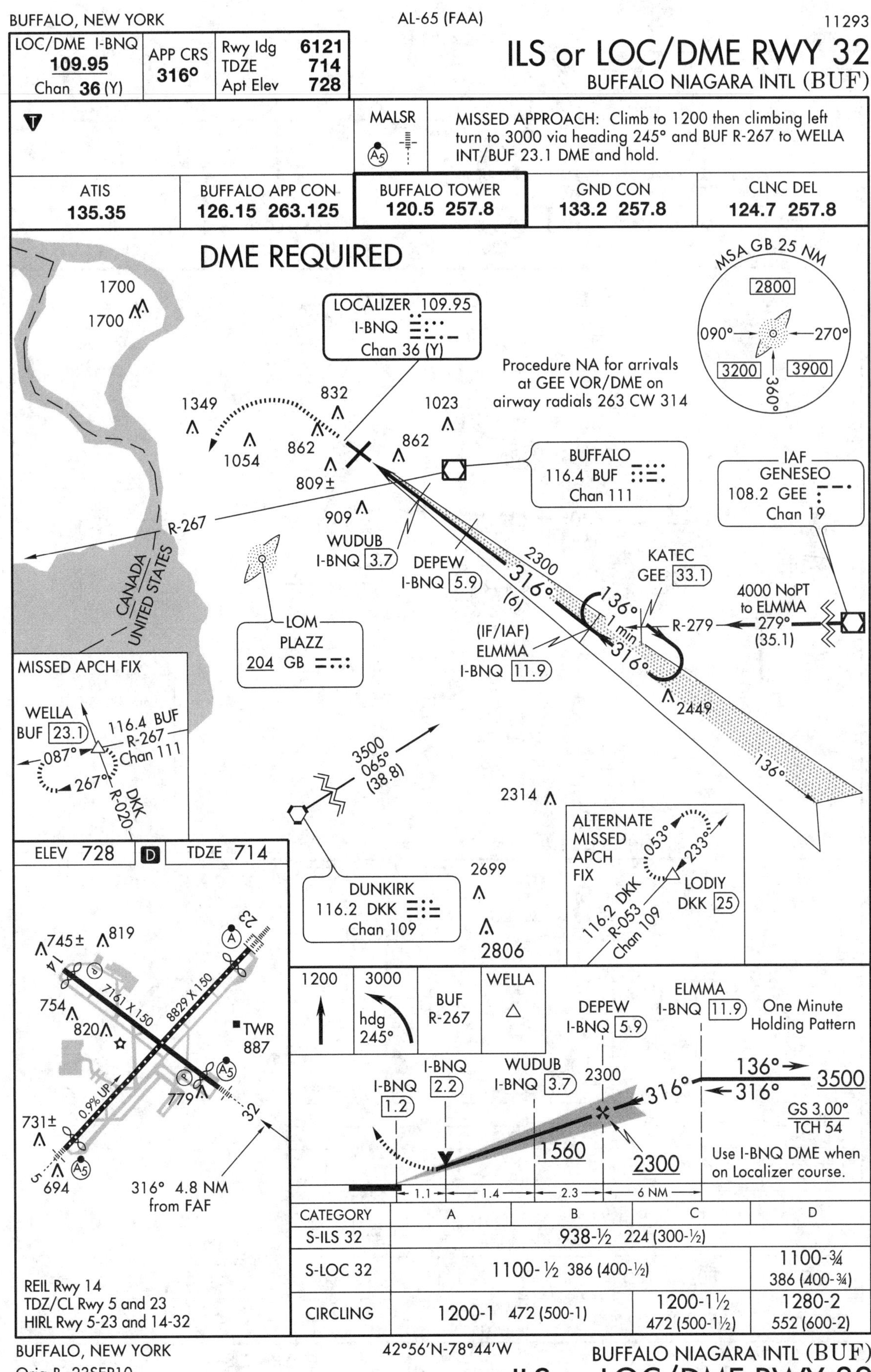

CATEGORY	A	B	C	D
S-ILS 32	938-½ 224 (300-½)			
S-LOC 32	1100-½ 386 (400-½)			1100-¾ 386 (400-¾)
CIRCLING	1200-1 472 (500-1)		1200-1½ 472 (500-1½)	1280-2 552 (600-2)

Figure 300. ILS or LOC/DME RWY 32 (BUF).

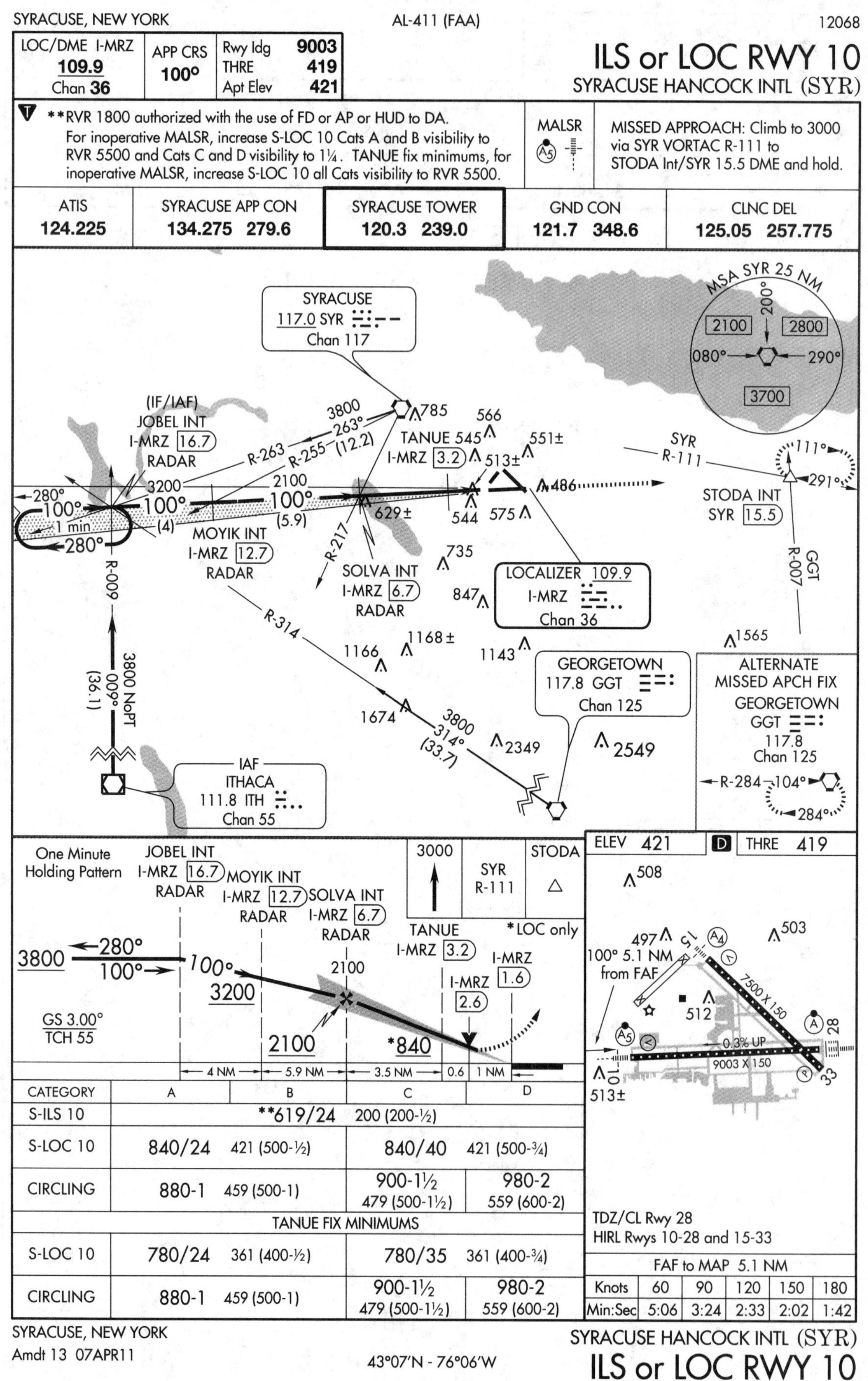

CATEGORY	A	B	C	D
S-ILS 10	**619/24 200 (200-½)			
S-LOC 10	840/24 421 (500-½)		840/40 421 (500-¾)	
CIRCLING	880-1 459 (500-1)		900-1½ 479 (500-1½)	980-2 559 (600-2)
TANUE FIX MINIMUMS				
S-LOC 10	780/24 361 (400-½)		780/35 361 (400-¾)	
CIRCLING	880-1 459 (500-1)		900-1½ 479 (500-1½)	980-2 559 (600-2)

TDZ/CL Rwy 28
HIRL Rwys 10-28 and 15-33

FAF to MAP 5.1 NM

Knots	60	90	120	150	180
Min:Sec	5:06	3:24	2:33	2:02	1:42

SYRACUSE, NEW YORK
Amdt 13 07APR11
43°07′N - 76°06′W
SYRACUSE HANCOCK INTL (SYR)
ILS or LOC RWY 10

Figure 301. ILS RWY 10 (SYR).

(POTOR2.POTOR) 10154

POTOR TWO DEPARTURE

SL-515 (FAA)

LEWISTON-NEZ PERCE COUNTY (LWS)
LEWISTON, IDAHO

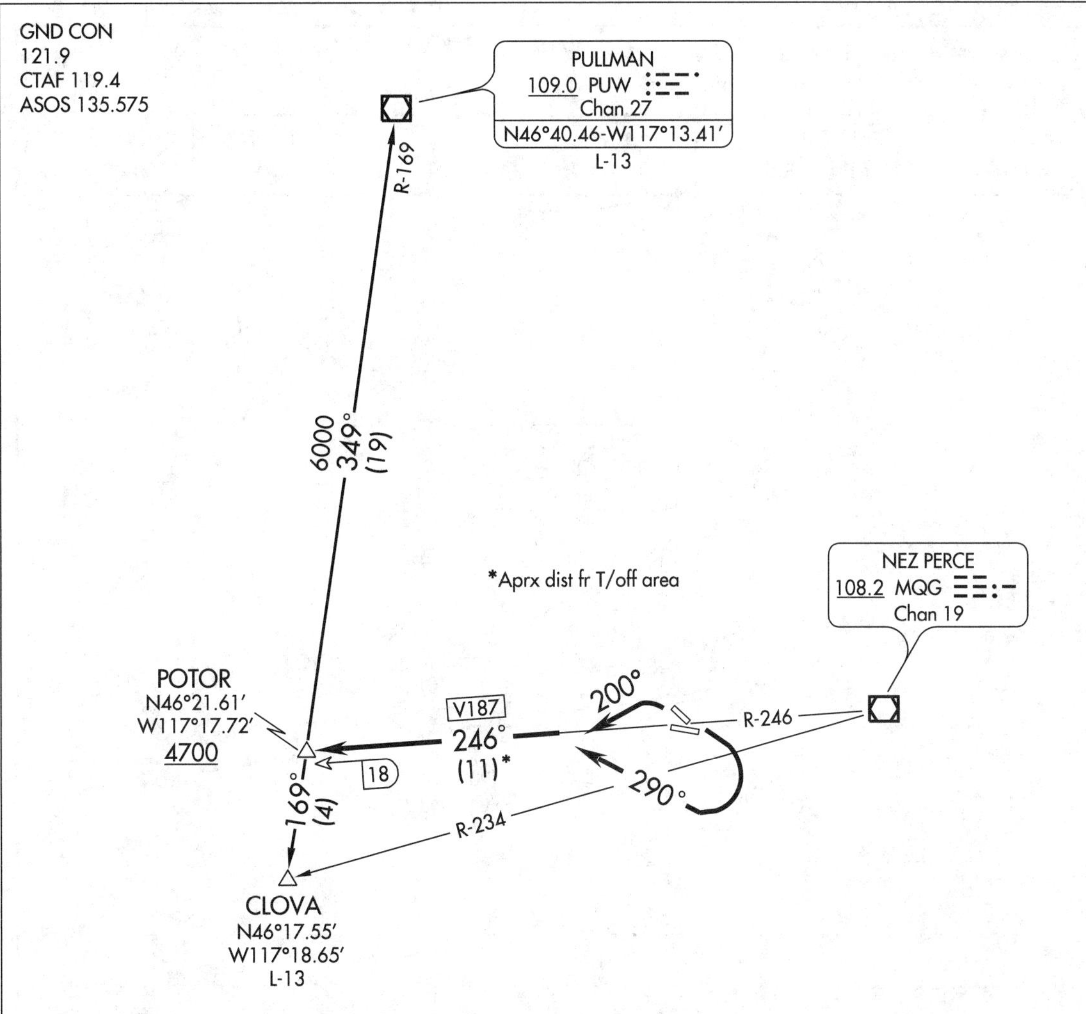

NOTE: Departures may be restricted to cross POTOR INT at 5000.

NOTE: Minimum climb required- Rwys 26 and 30-300′/NM to 4700′ (750 FPM/150K IAS, 1000 FPM/200K IAS).
Rwys 8 and 12-270′/NM to 4700′ (675 FPM/150K IAS, 900 FPM/200K IAS) or 4600′ ceiling and three miles visibility.

NOTE: Chart not to scale.

DEPARTURE ROUTE DESCRIPTION

TAKE-OFF RUNWAYS 8, 12: Turn right heading 290°. Thence....

TAKE-OFF RUNWAYS 26, 30: Turn left heading 200°. Thence....

....Intercept and proceed via MQG R-246 (V187) to POTOR INT. Thence via (assigned route) or (transition).

CLOVA TRANSITION (POTOR2.CLOVA): From over POTOR INT via PUW R-169 to CLOVA INT.

PULLMAN TRANSITION (POTOR2.PUW): From over POTOR INT via PUW R-169 to PUW VOR/DME.

POTOR TWO DEPARTURE
LEWISTON, IDAHO
LEWISTON-NEZ PERCE COUNTY (LWS)
(POTOR2.POTOR) 10154

Figure 302. POTOR TWO Departure (POTOR2.POTOR) (LWS).

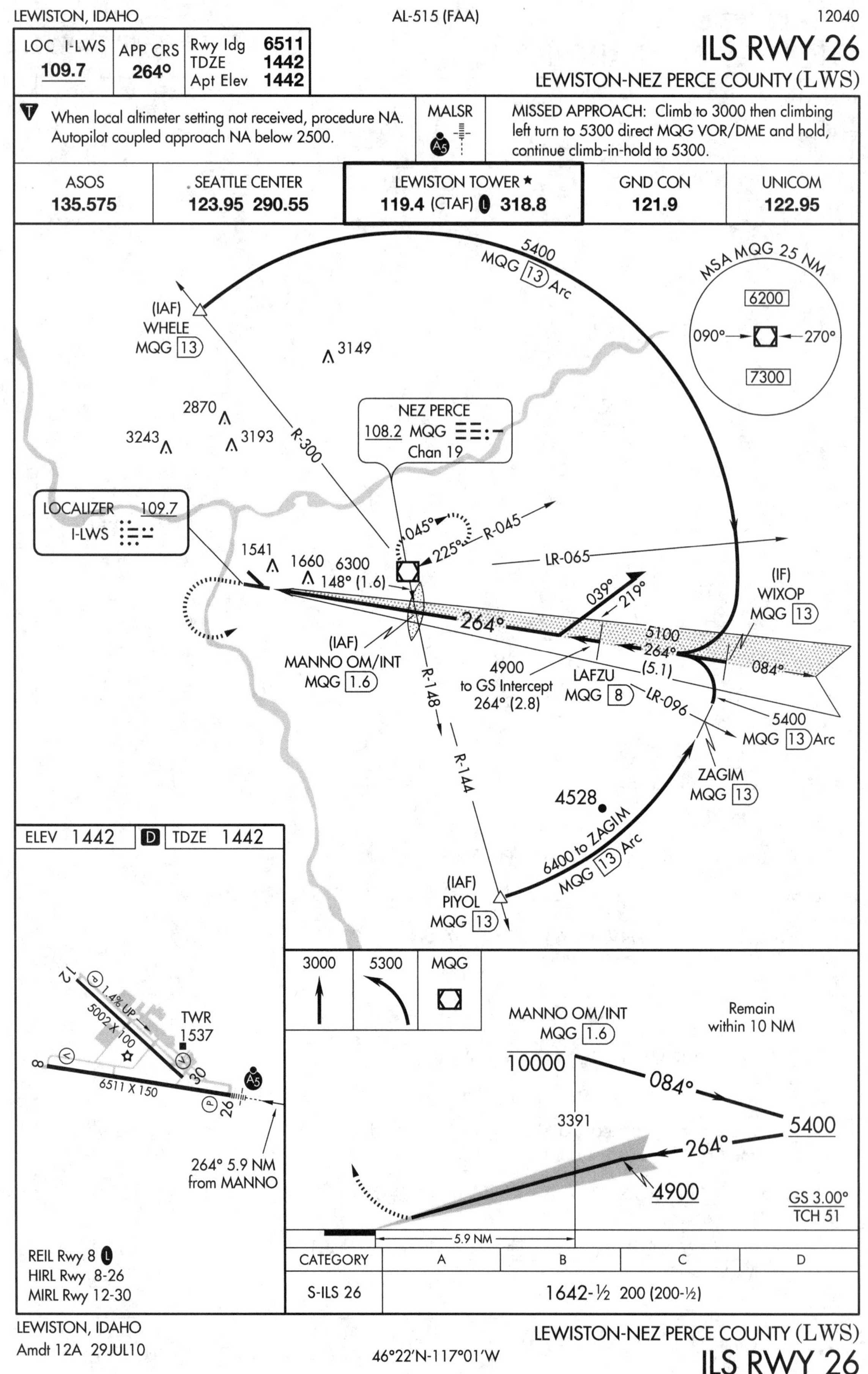

Figure 303. ILS RWY 26 (LWS).

HOQUIAM, WASHINGTON AL-889 (FAA) 12040

LOC/DME I-HQM 108.7 Chan 24	APP CRS 241°	Rwy ldg 5000 THRE 15 Apt Elev 18

ILS or LOC/DME RWY 24

HOQUIAM/ BOWERMAN (HQM)

When local altimeter setting not received, procedure NA. For inop MALSR, increase S-ILS Cat C visibility to 7/8 mile and S-LOC Cat C visibility to 1 5/8 mile. Circling NA northwest of Rwy 6-24.

MALSR

MISSED APPROACH: Climb to 2500 direct HQM VORTAC and hold.

ASOS	SEATTLE CENTER	UNICOM
135.775	128.3 269.0	122.7 (CTAF)

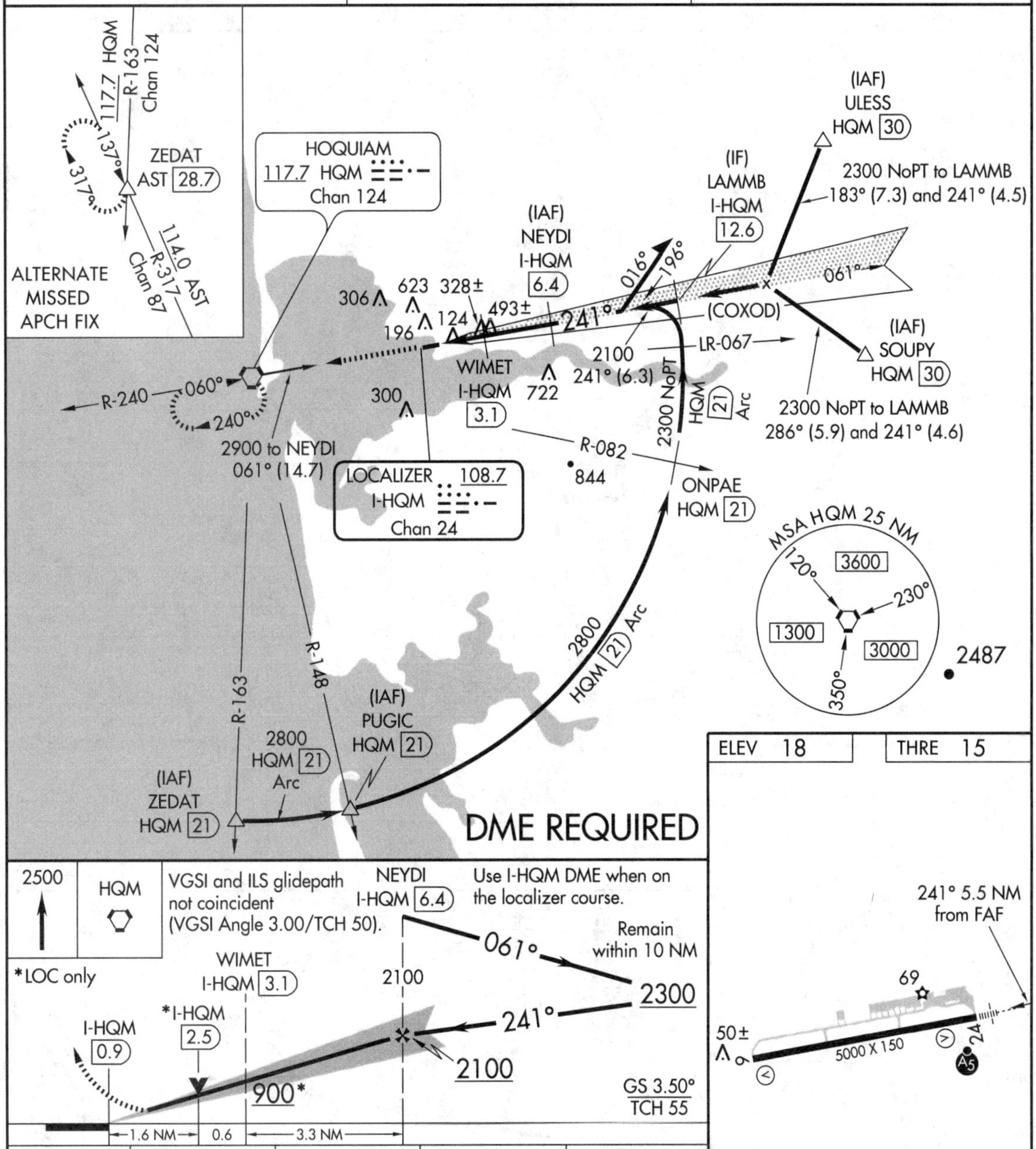

CATEGORY	A	B	C	D
S-ILS 24	215-½ 200 (200-½)		285-½ 270 (300-½)	NA
S-LOC 24	580-½ 565 (600-½)		580-1¼ 565 (600-1¼)	NA
CIRCLING	580-1 562 (600-1)		580-1⅝ 562 (600-1⅝)	NA

HOQUIAM, WASHINGTON
Amdt 4 09FEB12

HOQUIAM/ BOWERMAN (HQM)
46°58'N-123°56'W ILS or LOC/DME RWY 24

Figure 304. ILS or LOC/DME RWY 24 (HQM)

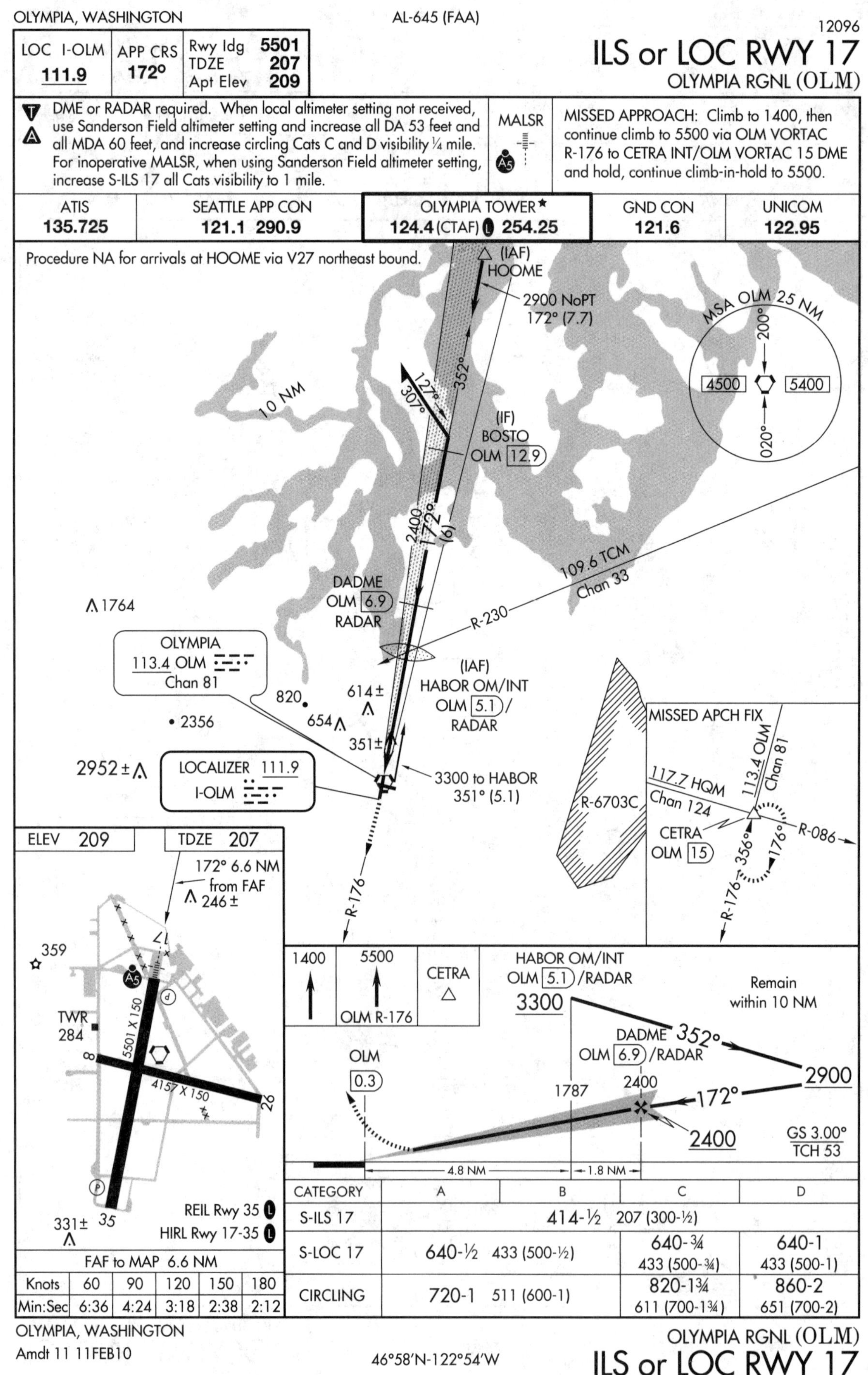

CATEGORY	A	B	C	D
S-ILS 17	414-½ 207 (300-½)			
S-LOC 17	640-½ 433 (500-½)		640-¾ 433 (500-¾)	640-1 433 (500-1)
CIRCLING	720-1 511 (600-1)		820-1¾ 611 (700-1¾)	860-2 651 (700-2)

Knots	60	90	120	150	180
Min:Sec	6:36	4:24	3:18	2:38	2:12

Figure 305. ILS or LOC RWY 17 (OLM).

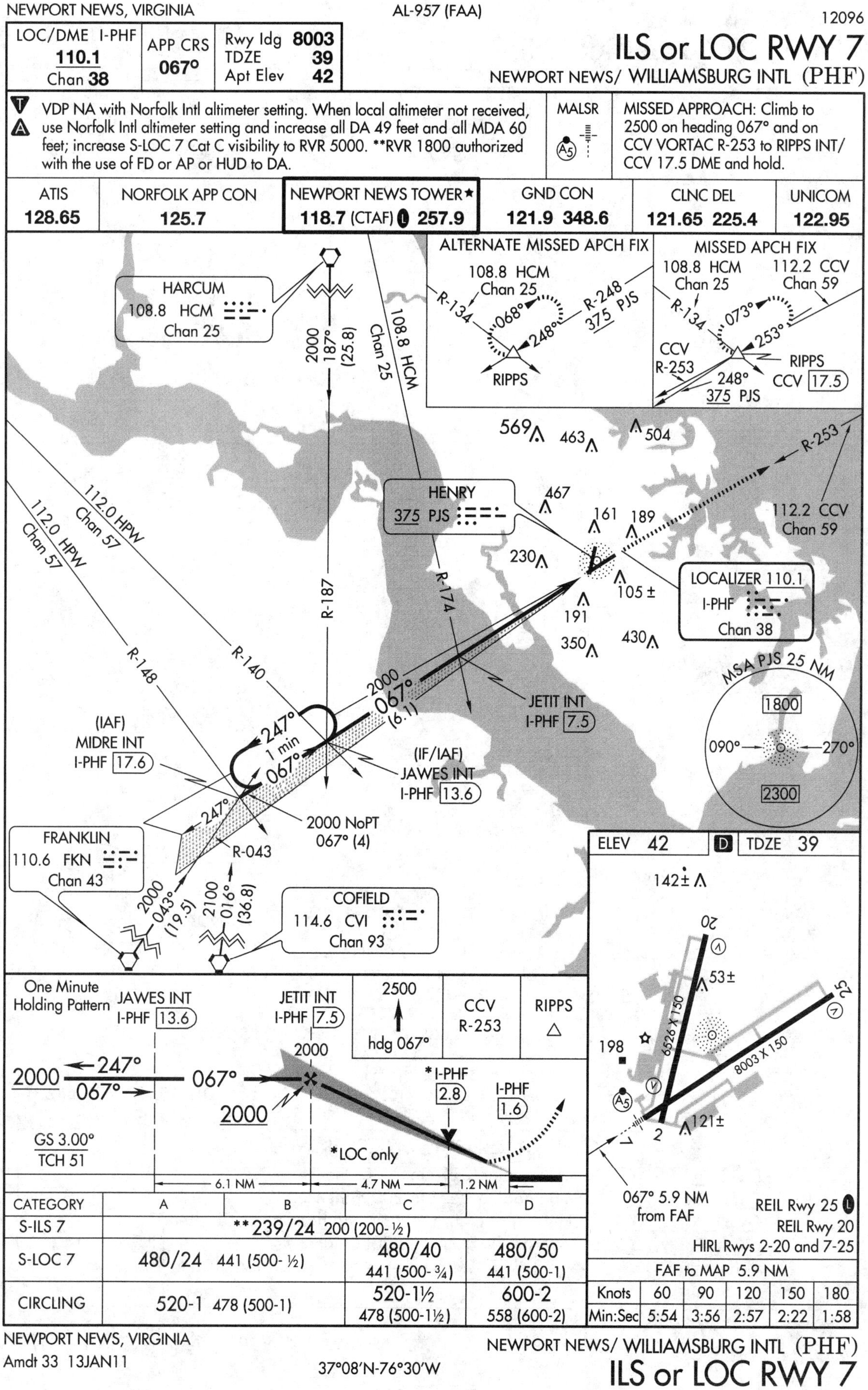

NEWPORT NEWS, VIRGINIA — AL-957 (FAA) — 12096

ILS or LOC RWY 7

NEWPORT NEWS/ WILLIAMSBURG INTL (PHF)

LOC/DME I-PHF	APP CRS	Rwy ldg 8003
110.1	**067°**	TDZE **39**
Chan **38**		Apt Elev **42**

VDP NA with Norfolk Intl altimeter setting. When local altimeter not received, use Norfolk Intl altimeter setting and increase all DA 49 feet and all MDA 60 feet; increase S-LOC 7 Cat C visibility to RVR 5000. **RVR 1800 authorized with the use of FD or AP or HUD to DA.

MALSR

MISSED APPROACH: Climb to 2500 on heading 067° and on CCV VORTAC R-253 to RIPPS INT/ CCV 17.5 DME and hold.

ATIS	NORFOLK APP CON	NEWPORT NEWS TOWER★	GND CON	CLNC DEL	UNICOM
128.65	**125.7**	**118.7** (CTAF) Ⓛ **257.9**	**121.9 348.6**	**121.65 225.4**	**122.95**

ALTERNATE MISSED APCH FIX: 108.8 HCM Chan 25; R-134; 068°; 248°; R-248; 375 PJS; RIPPS

MISSED APCH FIX: 108.8 HCM Chan 25; 112.2 CCV Chan 59; R-134; 073°; 253°; CCV R-253; 248°; 375 PJS; RIPPS; CCV 17.5

HARCUM 108.8 HCM Chan 25

2000 187° (25.8)

108.8 HCM Chan 25

569 463 504 467 161 189 230 105± 191 350 430

HENRY 375 PJS

R-253

112.2 CCV Chan 59

LOCALIZER 110.1 I-PHF Chan 38

112.0 HPW Chan 57

112.0 HPW Chan 57

R-187

R-174

R-140

R-148

MSA PJS 25 NM: 090°–270°; 1800; 2300

2000 067° (6.1)

JETIT INT I-PHF 7.5

247° 1 min 067°

(IAF) MIDRE INT I-PHF 17.6

(IF/IAF) JAWES INT I-PHF 13.6

247°

2000 NoPT 067° (4)

R-043

FRANKLIN 110.6 FKN Chan 43

2000 043° (19.5)

2100 016° (36.8)

COFIELD 114.6 CVI Chan 93

ELEV 42 — D — TDZE 39

142± 20 53± 198 6526 X 150 8003 X 150 25 121± 2 7

067° 5.9 NM from FAF

REIL Rwy 25 Ⓛ
REIL Rwy 20
HIRL Rwys 2-20 and 7-25

One Minute Holding Pattern

JAWES INT I-PHF 13.6

JETIT INT I-PHF 7.5

2500 hdg 067°

CCV R-253

RIPPS

2000 247° 067°

067° 2000

2000

*I-PHF 2.8

I-PHF 1.6

GS 3.00° TCH 51

*LOC only

6.1 NM — 4.7 NM — 1.2 NM

CATEGORY	A	B	C	D
S-ILS 7	**239/24 200 (200-½)			
S-LOC 7	480/24 441 (500-½)		480/40 441 (500-¾)	480/50 441 (500-1)
CIRCLING	520-1 478 (500-1)		520-1½ 478 (500-1½)	600-2 558 (600-2)

FAF to MAP 5.9 NM

Knots	60	90	120	150	180
Min:Sec	5:54	3:56	2:57	2:22	1:58

NEWPORT NEWS, VIRGINIA
Amdt 33 13JAN11

37°08′N-76°30′W

NEWPORT NEWS/ WILLIAMSBURG INTL (PHF)

ILS or LOC RWY 7

Figure 306. ILS or LOC RWY 7 (PHF).

(HENRY2.PHF) 08213

HENRY TWO DEPARTURE

SL-957 (FAA)

NEWPORT NEWS/WILLIAMSBURG INTL (PHF)
NEWPORT NEWS, VIRGINIA

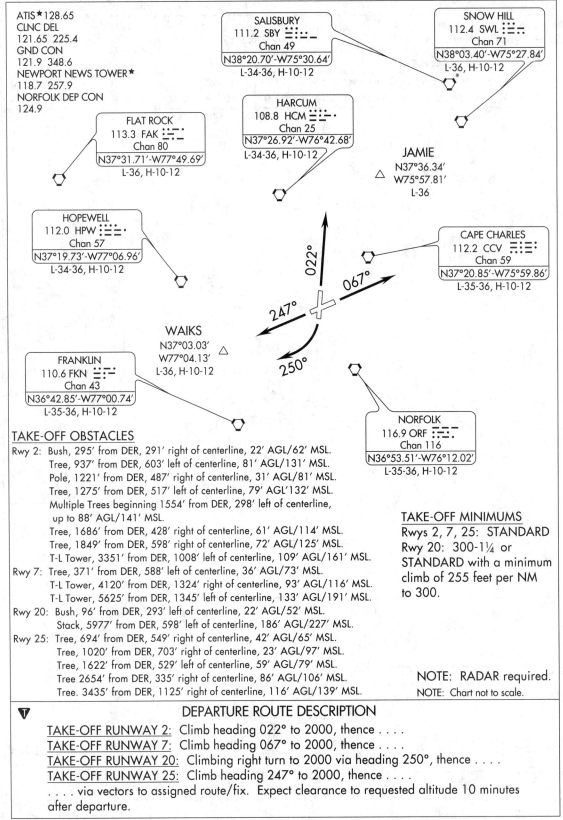

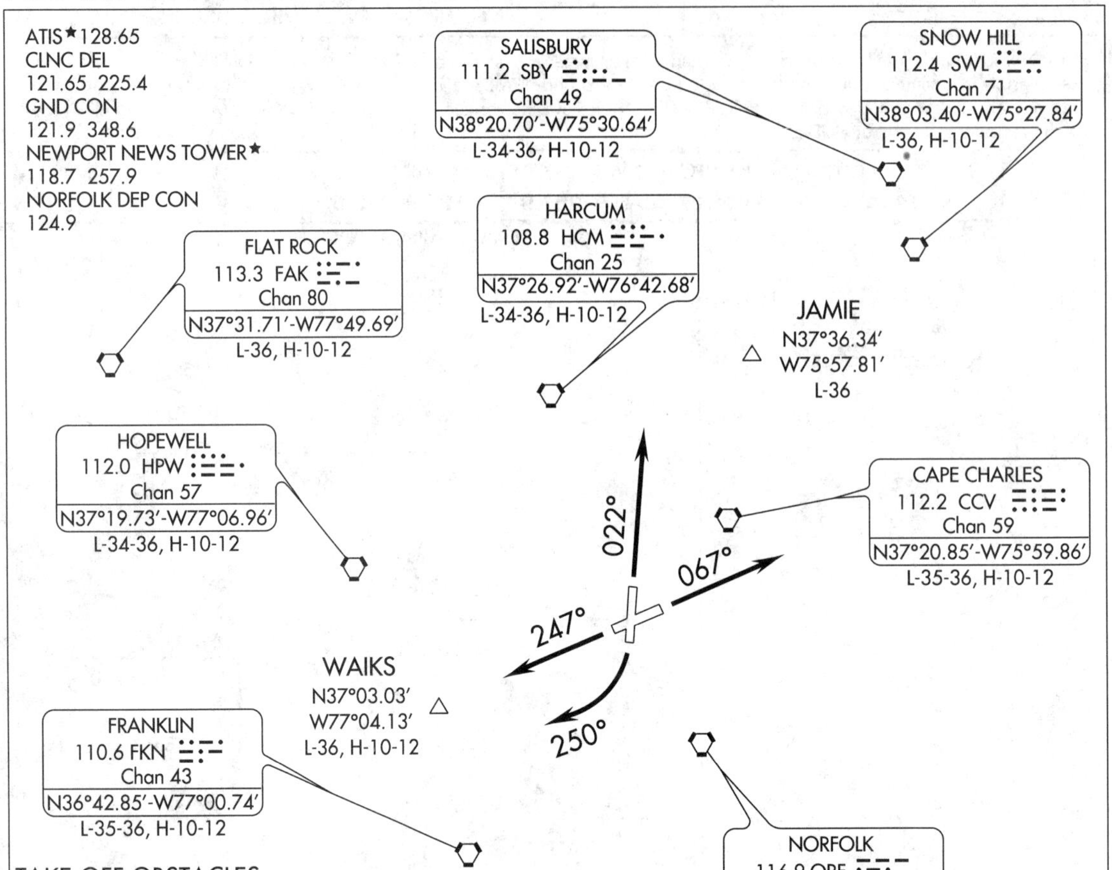

ATIS★128.65
CLNC DEL
121.65 225.4
GND CON
121.9 348.6
NEWPORT NEWS TOWER★
118.7 257.9
NORFOLK DEP CON
124.9

SALISBURY
111.2 SBY
Chan 49
N38°20.70′-W75°30.64′
L-34-36, H-10-12

SNOW HILL
112.4 SWL
Chan 71
N38°03.40′-W75°27.84′
L-36, H-10-12

FLAT ROCK
113.3 FAK
Chan 80
N37°31.71′-W77°49.69′
L-36, H-10-12

HARCUM
108.8 HCM
Chan 25
N37°26.92′-W76°42.68′
L-34-36, H-10-12

JAMIE
N37°36.34′
W75°57.81′
L-36

HOPEWELL
112.0 HPW
Chan 57
N37°19.73′-W77°06.96′
L-34-36, H-10-12

CAPE CHARLES
112.2 CCV
Chan 59
N37°20.85′-W75°59.86′
L-35-36, H-10-12

022°
067°
247°
250°

WAIKS
N37°03.03′
W77°04.13′
L-36, H-10-12

FRANKLIN
110.6 FKN
Chan 43
N36°42.85′-W77°00.74′
L-35-36, H-10-12

NORFOLK
116.9 ORF
Chan 116
N36°53.51′-W76°12.02′
L-35-36, H-10-12

TAKE-OFF OBSTACLES

Rwy 2: Bush, 295′ from DER, 291′ right of centerline, 22′ AGL/62′ MSL.
Tree, 937′ from DER, 603′ left of centerline, 81′ AGL/131′ MSL.
Pole, 1221′ from DER, 487′ right of centerline, 31′ AGL/81′ MSL.
Tree, 1275′ from DER, 517′ left of centerline, 79′ AGL′132′ MSL.
Multiple Trees beginning 1554′ from DER, 298′ left of centerline, up to 88′ AGL/141′ MSL.
Tree, 1686′ from DER, 428′ right of centerline, 61′ AGL/114′ MSL.
Tree, 1849′ from DER, 598′ right of centerline, 72′ AGL/125′ MSL.
T-L Tower, 3351′ from DER, 1008′ left of centerline, 109′ AGL/161′ MSL.

Rwy 7: Tree, 371′ from DER, 588′ left of centerline, 36′ AGL/73′ MSL.
T-L Tower, 4120′ from DER, 1324′ right of centerline, 93′ AGL/116′ MSL.
T-L Tower, 5625′ from DER, 1345′ left of centerline, 133′ AGL/191′ MSL.

Rwy 20: Bush, 96′ from DER, 293′ left of centerline, 22′ AGL/52′ MSL.
Stack, 5977′ from DER, 598′ left of centerline, 186′ AGL/227′ MSL.

Rwy 25: Tree, 694′ from DER, 549′ right of centerline, 42′ AGL/65′ MSL.
Tree, 1020′ from DER, 703′ right of centerline, 23′ AGL/97′ MSL.
Tree, 1622′ from DER, 529′ left of centerline, 59′ AGL/79′ MSL.
Tree 2654′ from DER, 335′ right of centerline, 86′ AGL/106′ MSL.
Tree. 3435′ from DER, 1125′ right of centerline, 116′ AGL/139′ MSL.

TAKE-OFF MINIMUMS

Rwys 2, 7, 25: STANDARD
Rwy 20: 300-1¼ or STANDARD with a minimum climb of 255 feet per NM to 300.

NOTE: RADAR required.
NOTE: Chart not to scale.

DEPARTURE ROUTE DESCRIPTION

TAKE-OFF RUNWAY 2: Climb heading 022° to 2000, thence . . . .
TAKE-OFF RUNWAY 7: Climb heading 067° to 2000, thence . . . .
TAKE-OFF RUNWAY 20: Climbing right turn to 2000 via heading 250°, thence . . . .
TAKE-OFF RUNWAY 25: Climb heading 247° to 2000, thence . . . .
. . . . via vectors to assigned route/fix. Expect clearance to requested altitude 10 minutes after departure.

HENRY TWO DEPARTURE
(HENRY2.PHF) 08213
NEWPORT NEWS, VIRGINIA
NEWPORT NEWS/WILLIAMSBURG INTL (PHF)

Figure 307. HENRY TWO Departure (HENRY2.PHF).

(VCN.VCN8) 12040 ST-320 (FAA)

CEDAR LAKE EIGHT ARRIVAL

PHILADELPHIA, PENNSYLVANIA

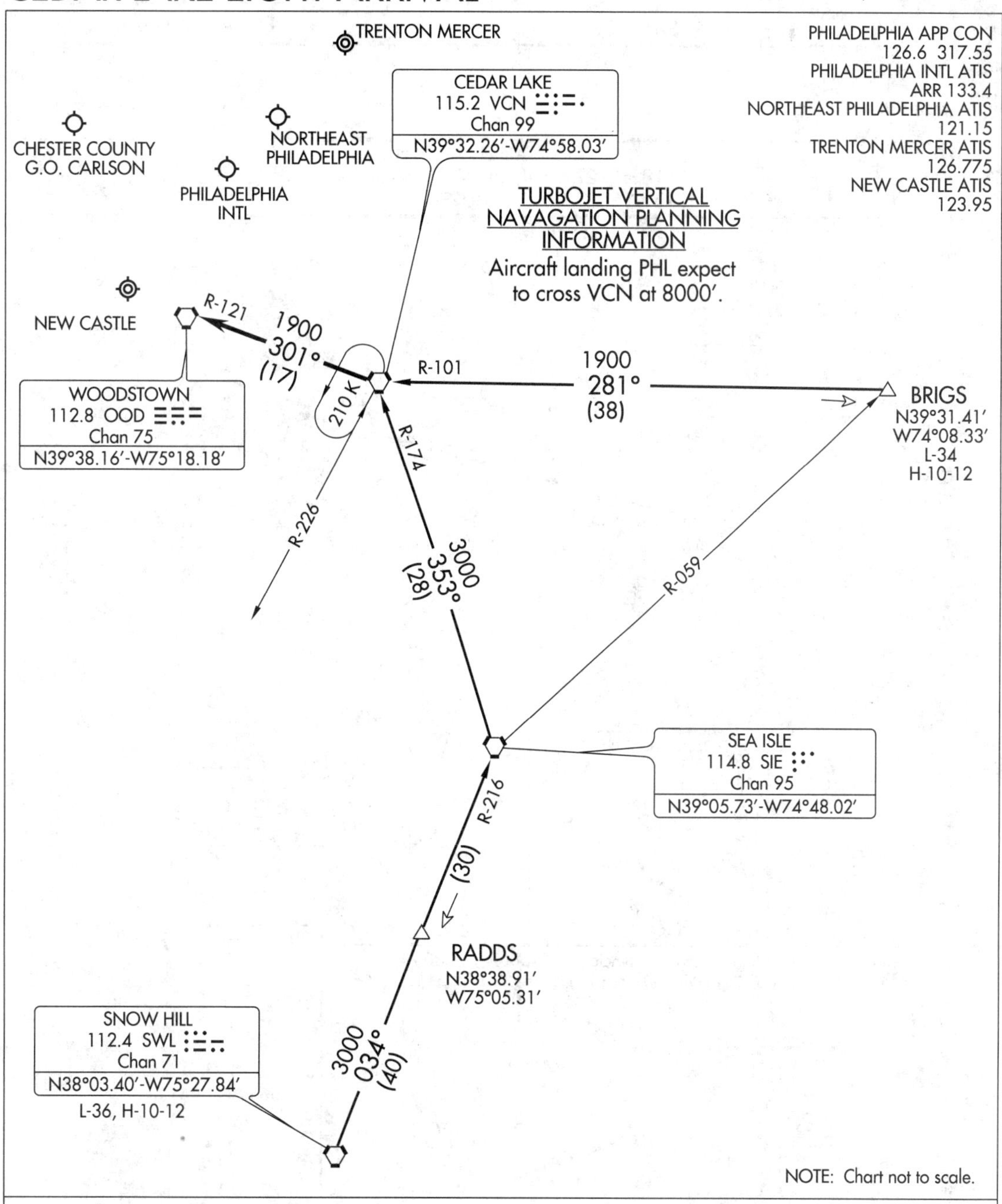

<u>BRIGS TRANSITION (BRIGS.VCN8)</u>: From over BRIGS INT via VCN R-101 to VCN VORTAC. Thence. . . .

<u>SNOW HILL TRANSITION (SWL.VCN8)</u>: From over SWL VORTAC via SWL R-034 and SIE R-216 to SIE VORTAC, then via the SIE R-353 and VCN R-174 to VCN VORTAC. Thence. . . .

. . . .From over VCN VORTAC: Turbojets expect radar vectors to final approach course. Non-Turbojets continue via the VCN R-301and the OOD R-121 to OOD VORTAC; expect radar vectors to final approach course.

CEDAR LAKE EIGHT ARRIVAL

PHILADELPHIA, PENNSYLVANIA

(VCN.VCN8) 12040

Figure 308. CEDAR LAKE EIGHT Arrival (VCN.VCN8).

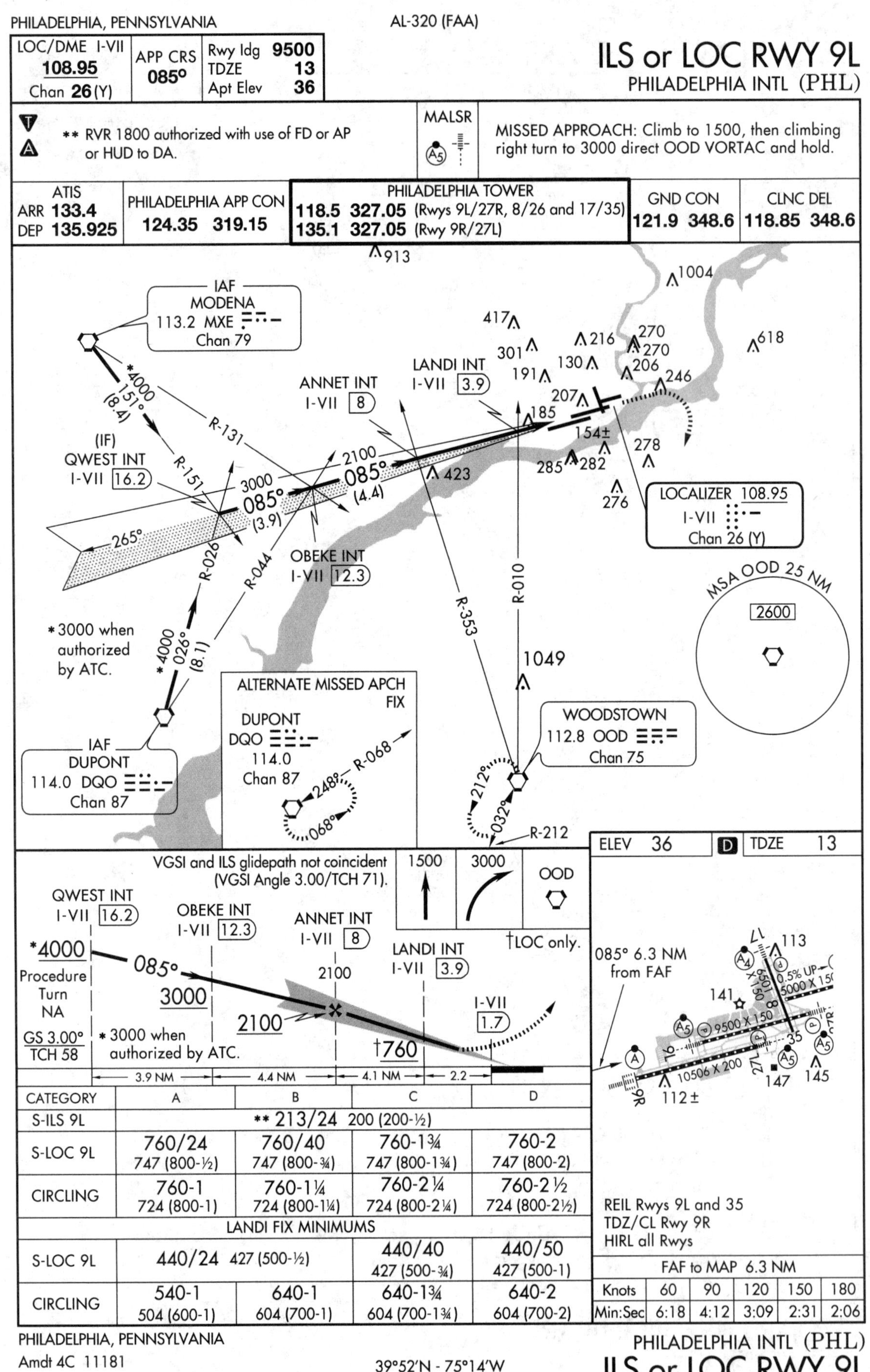

Figure 310. ILS or LOC RWY 9L (PHL).

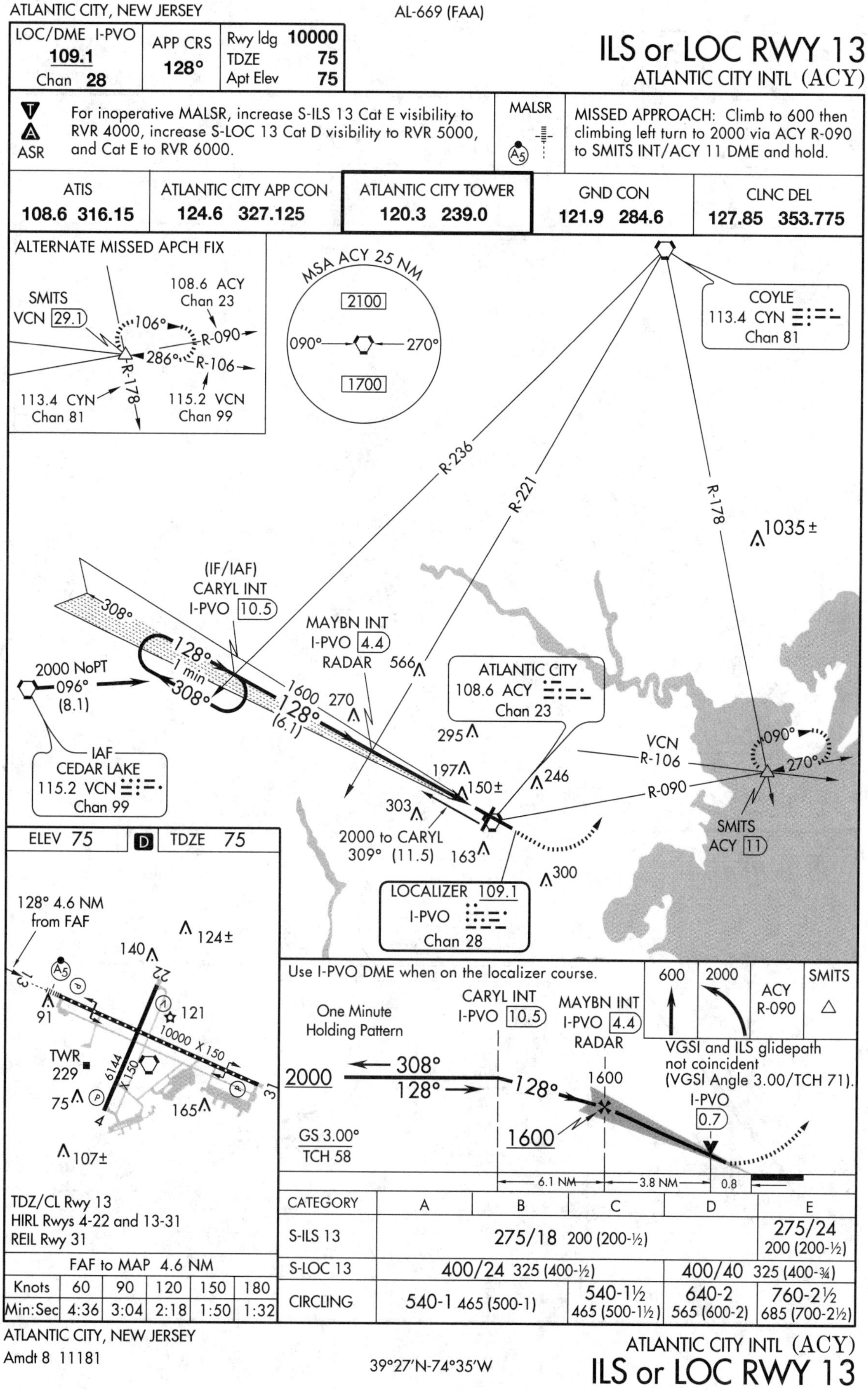

ATLANTIC CITY, NEW JERSEY AL-669 (FAA)

LOC/DME I-PVO 109.1 Chan 28	APP CRS 128°	Rwy ldg 10000 TDZE 75 Apt Elev 75

ILS or LOC RWY 13

ATLANTIC CITY INTL (ACY)

For inoperative MALSR, increase S-ILS 13 Cat E visibility to RVR 4000, increase S-LOC 13 Cat D visibility to RVR 5000, and Cat E to RVR 6000.

ASR

MALSR

MISSED APPROACH: Climb to 600 then climbing left turn to 2000 via ACY R-090 to SMITS INT/ACY 11 DME and hold.

ATIS	ATLANTIC CITY APP CON	ATLANTIC CITY TOWER	GND CON	CLNC DEL
108.6 316.15	124.6 327.125	120.3 239.0	121.9 284.6	127.85 353.775

ALTERNATE MISSED APCH FIX

SMITS VCN 29.1

108.6 ACY Chan 23

106° R-090 286° R-106 R-178

113.4 CYN Chan 81

115.2 VCN Chan 99

MSA ACY 25 NM

2100 090° 270° 1700

COYLE 113.4 CYN Chan 81

R-236 R-221 R-178

1035±

(IF/IAF) CARYL INT I-PVO 10.5

308° 128° 1 min 308°

2000 NoPT 096° (8.1)

MAYBN INT I-PVO 4.4 RADAR

566 1600 128° (6.1) 270

ATLANTIC CITY 108.6 ACY Chan 23

295 197 150± 246

IAF CEDAR LAKE 115.2 VCN Chan 99

VCN R-106 090° 270° R-090

303 2000 to CARYL 309° (11.5) 163

SMITS ACY 11

300

LOCALIZER 109.1 I-PVO Chan 28

ELEV 75 D TDZE 75

128° 4.6 NM from FAF

124± 140 A5 13 22 121 91 10000 X 150 TWR 229 6144 X 150 75 165 4 31 107±

TDZ/CL Rwy 13
HIRL Rwys 4-22 and 13-31
REIL Rwy 31

FAF to MAP 4.6 NM					
Knots	60	90	120	150	180
Min:Sec	4:36	3:04	2:18	1:50	1:32

Use I-PVO DME when on the localizer course.

600 2000 ACY R-090 SMITS

One Minute Holding Pattern

CARYL INT I-PVO 10.5

MAYBN INT I-PVO 4.4 RADAR

VGSI and ILS glidepath not coincident (VGSI Angle 3.00/TCH 71).

2000 308° 128° 128° 1600 1600

I-PVO 0.7

GS 3.00° TCH 58

6.1 NM 3.8 NM 0.8

CATEGORY	A	B	C	D	E
S-ILS 13	275/18 200 (200-½)				275/24 200 (200-½)
S-LOC 13	400/24 325 (400-½)			400/40 325 (400-¾)	
CIRCLING	540-1 465 (500-1)		540-1½ 465 (500-1½)	640-2 565 (600-2)	760-2½ 685 (700-2½)

ATLANTIC CITY, NEW JERSEY
Amdt 8 11181

39°27′N-74°35′W

ATLANTIC CITY INTL (ACY)

ILS or LOC RWY 13

Figure 311. ILS or LOC RWY 13 (ACY).

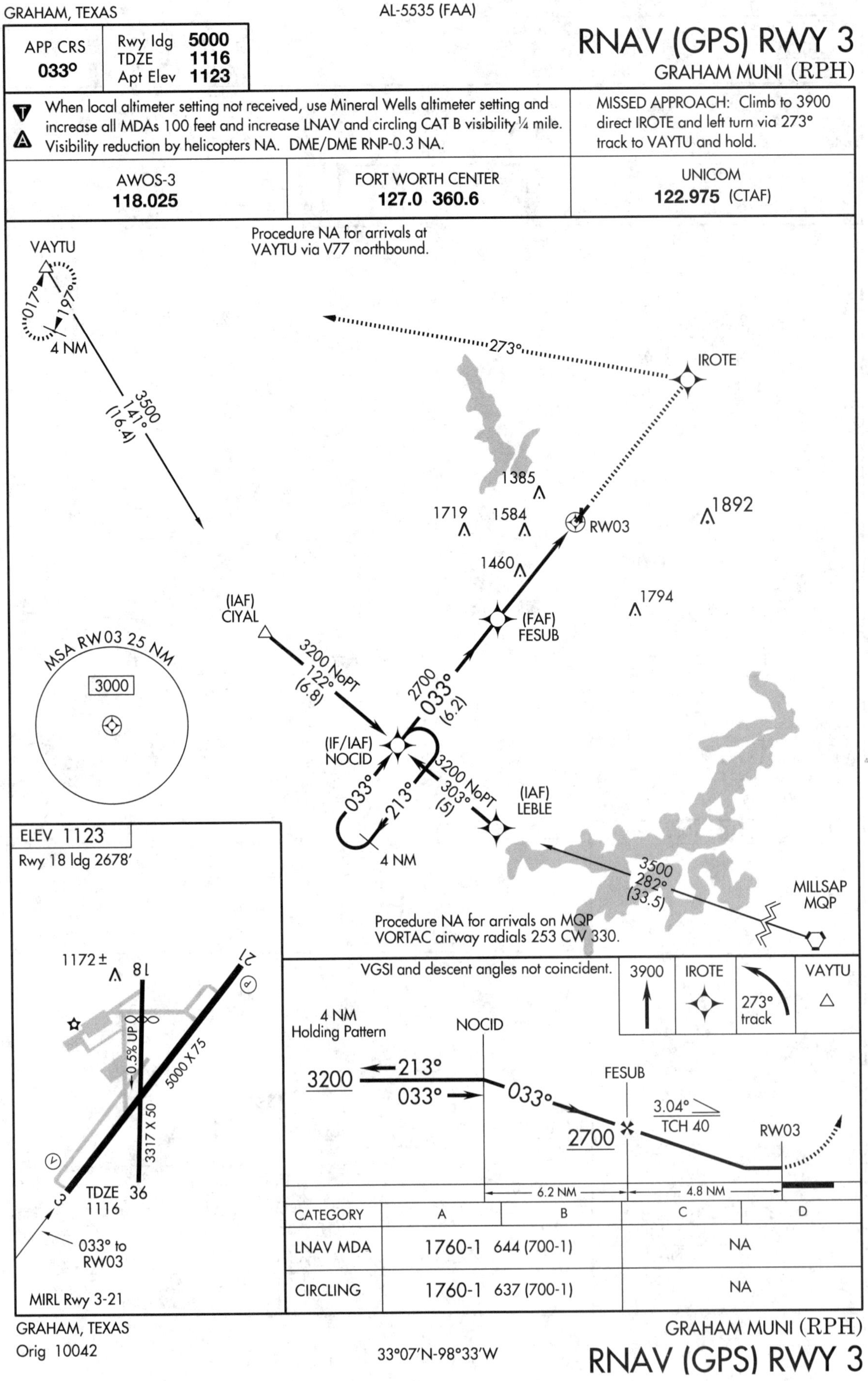

GRAHAM, TEXAS

AL-5535 (FAA)

RNAV (GPS) RWY 3

GRAHAM MUNI (RPH)

APP CRS	Rwy ldg 5000
033°	TDZE 1116
	Apt Elev 1123

T When local altimeter setting not received, use Mineral Wells altimeter setting and increase all MDAs 100 feet and increase LNAV and circling CAT B visibility ¼ mile.

A Visibility reduction by helicopters NA. DME/DME RNP-0.3 NA.

MISSED APPROACH: Climb to 3900 direct IROTE and left turn via 273° track to VAYTU and hold.

AWOS-3	FORT WORTH CENTER	UNICOM
118.025	**127.0 360.6**	**122.975** (CTAF)

Procedure NA for arrivals at VAYTU via V77 northbound.

VAYTU

017°

197°

4 NM

3500

141°

(16.4)

273°

IROTE

1385

1719

1584

1892

RW03

1460

1794

(IAF)
CIYAL

(FAF)
FESUB

MSA RW03 25 NM

3000

3200 NoPT

122°

(6.8)

2700

033°

(6.2)

(IF/IAF)
NOCID

033°

213°

3200 NoPT

303°

(5)

(IAF)
LEBLE

4 NM

3500

282°

(33.5)

MILLSAP
MQP

Procedure NA for arrivals on MQP VORTAC airway radials 253 CW 330.

ELEV 1123

Rwy 18 ldg 2678′

1172±

18

21

0.5% UP

5000 X 75

3317 X 50

3

TDZE 1116

36

033° to RW03

MIRL Rwy 3-21

VGSI and descent angles not coincident.

3900

IROTE

273° track

VAYTU

4 NM Holding Pattern

NOCID

3200

213°

033°

FESUB

033°

3.04°
TCH 40

2700

RW03

6.2 NM

4.8 NM

CATEGORY	A	B	C	D
LNAV MDA	1760-1 644 (700-1)		NA	
CIRCLING	1760-1 637 (700-1)		NA	

GRAHAM, TEXAS

Orig 10042

33°07′N-98°33′W

GRAHAM MUNI (RPH)

RNAV (GPS) RWY 3

Figure 312. RNAV (GPS) RWY 3 (RPH).

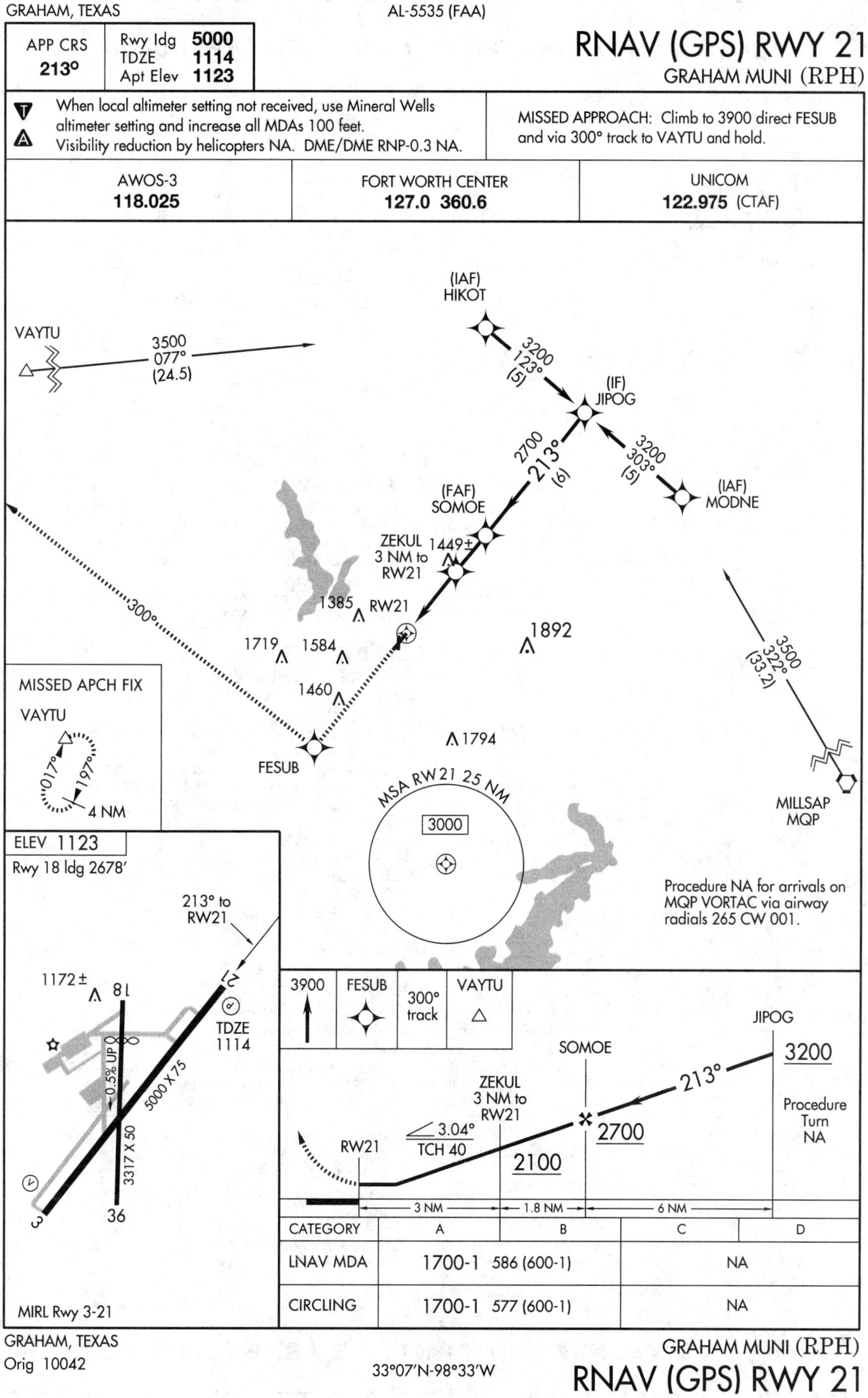

GRAHAM, TEXAS

AL-5535 (FAA)

APP CRS 213°	Rwy ldg 5000 TDZE 1114 Apt Elev 1123

RNAV (GPS) RWY 21

GRAHAM MUNI (RPH)

When local altimeter setting not received, use Mineral Wells altimeter setting and increase all MDAs 100 feet.
Visibility reduction by helicopters NA. DME/DME RNP-0.3 NA.

MISSED APPROACH: Climb to 3900 direct FESUB and via 300° track to VAYTU and hold.

AWOS-3	FORT WORTH CENTER	UNICOM
118.025	**127.0 360.6**	**122.975** (CTAF)

(IAF) HIKOT
VAYTU
3500 077° (24.5)
3200 123° (5)
(IF) JIPOG
2700 213° (6)
3200 303° (5)
(IAF) MODNE
(FAF) SOMOE
ZEKUL 3 NM to RW21
1449±
1385
RW21
300°
1719
1584
1892
1460
3500 322° (33.2)
MISSED APCH FIX
VAYTU
017°
197°
4 NM
FESUB
1794
MSA RW21 25 NM
3000
MILLSAP MQP
Procedure NA for arrivals on MQP VORTAC via airway radials 265 CW 001.

ELEV 1123
Rwy 18 ldg 2678′
213° to RW21
1172±
18
21
TDZE 1114
0.5% UP
5000 X 75
3317 X 50
36
3
MIRL Rwy 3-21

3900	FESUB	300° track	VAYTU

JIPOG
3200
Procedure Turn NA
SOMOE
213°
ZEKUL 3 NM to RW21
2700
3.04°
TCH 40
RW21
2100
3 NM
1.8 NM
6 NM

CATEGORY	A	B	C	D
LNAV MDA	1700-1 586 (600-1)		NA	
CIRCLING	1700-1 577 (600-1)		NA	

GRAHAM, TEXAS
Orig 10042

33°07′N-98°33′W

GRAHAM MUNI (RPH)

RNAV (GPS) RWY 21

Figure 313. RNAV (GPS) RWY 21 (RPH).

TAKE-OFF MINIMUMS AND (OBSTACLE) DEPARTURE PROCEDURES

12096

FORT WORTH, TX (CON'T)

FORT WORTH SPINKS

TAKE-OFF MINIMUMS: **Rwys 17L,35R**, NA. (Environmental)

DEPARTURE PROCEDURE: **Rwy 17R** climb heading 173° to 1200 before turning right.

NOTE: **Rwy 17R,** tree 4909' from departure end of runway, 1556' left of centerline, 60' AGL/830' MSL.

FORT WORTH NAS JRB (CARSWELL FLD)(KNFW)

FORT WORTH, TX 10014

Rwy 17, Cross DER at or above 6' AGL/656' MSL.

TAKE-OFF OBSTACLES: **Rwy 17,** rising terrain up to 670' MSL, 200'-600' from DER, 500'-560' right of centerline.

GAINESVILLE, TX

GAINESVILLE MUNI (GLE)

ORIG 09127 (FAA)

NOTE: **Rwy 17,** trees and poles beginning 1' from DER, 472' right and left of centerline, up to 25' AGL/819' MSL. **Rwy 30,** taxiways beginning 651' from DER, crossing centerline left to right 859' MSL. Trees and terrain beginning 2' from DER, 14' left and right of centerline, up to 64' AGL/890' MSL. **Rwy 35,** terrain, trees, poles, road, and vehicle beginning 149' from DER, 51' left of centerline, up to 95' AGL/940' MSL. Terrain and poles beginning 13' from DER, 85' right of centerline, up to 37' AGL/882' MSL.

GILMER, TX

FOX STEPHENS FIELD-GILMER MUNI (JXI)

ORIG 11293 (FAA)

DEPARTURE PROCEDURE: **Rwy 18,** climb heading 177° to 1000 before turning left.

NOTE: **Rwy 18,** trees beginning abeam the DER left and right of centerline, up to 100' AGL/500' MSL. **Rwy 36,** trees beginning abeam the DER left and right of centerline, up to 50' AGL/505' MSL.

GLADEWATER, TX

GLADEWATER MUNI (07F)

AMDT 1 11153 (FAA)

TAKE-OFF MINIMUMS: **Rwy 17,** 300-1¾ or std. w/min. climb of 285' per NM to 600. **Rwy 32,** 300-1. **Rwy 35,** Std. w/min. climb of 280' per NM to 1300 or 1100-2 ½ for climb in visual conditions.

DEPARTURE PROCEDURE: **Rwy 32,** climb heading 320° to 1100 before turning right. **Rwy 35,** for climb in visual conditions cross Gladewater Municipal Airport at or above 1200 before proceeding on course.

NOTE: **Rwy 14,** vehicles on roadway beginning 450' from DER, left and right of centerline, up to 17' AGL/311' MSL. Trees beginning 770' from DER, left and right of centerline, up to 100' AGL/394' MSL. Power lines 3524' from DER, left to right of centerline, 150' AGL/420' MSL. **Rwy 17,** vehicles on roadway beginning 212' from DER, left and right of centerline, up to 17' AGL/311' MSL. Trees beginning 624' from DER, left and right of centerline, up to 100' AGL/509' MSL. Power lines 1807' from DER, left to right of centerline, 150' AGL/439' MSL. **Rwy 32,** trees beginning 12' from DER, left and right of centerline, up to 100' AGL/429' MSL. **Rwy 35,** trees beginning 47' from DER, left and right of centerline, up to 100' AGL/429' MSL. Power lines 1.4 NM from DER, 844' right of centerline, 75' AGL/520' MSL.

GRAFORD, TX

POSSUM KINGDOM (F35)

ORIG-A 10154 (FAA)

TAKE-OFF MINIMUMS: **Rwy 20,** 400-2½ or std. w/ a min. climb of 212' per NM to 1500 or alternatively, with standard takeoff minimums and a normal 200' per NM climb gradient, takeoff must occur no later than 1600' prior to DER.

DEPARTURE PROCEDURE: **Rwy 20,** climb heading 204° to 1500 before turning left.

NOTE: **Rwy 2,** trees beginning 31' from DER, 22' left of centerline, up to 100' AGL/1099' MSL. Trees beginning 1023' from DER, 114' right of centerline, up to 100' AGL/1129' MSL. **Rwy 20,** vehicle on roadway 116' from DER, 498' right of centerline, 15' AGL/1024' MSL. Trees beginning 494' from DER, 126' right of centerline, up to 100' AGL/1109' MSL. Trees beginning 977' from DER, 115' left of centerline, up to 100' AGL/1109' MSL. Trees beginning 2.29 miles from DER, 1679' left of centerline, up to 100' AGL/1329' MSL.

GRAHAM, TX

GRAHAM MUNI

DEPARTURE PROCEDURE: **Rwys 17, 21,** climb runway heading to 2000 before proceeding on course.

NOTE: **Rwy 17,** light pole 21' from departure end of runway, 195' left of centerline, 30' AGL/1141' MSL. Light pole 86' from departure end of runway, 381' left of centerline, 50' AGL/1168' MSL.

GRANBURY, TX

GRANBURY RGNL (GDJ)

AMDT 2 11125 (FAA)

TAKE-OFF MINIMUMS: **Rwy 14,** 300-1.

DEPARTURE PROCEDURE: **Rwy 14,** climb heading 144° to 1700 before turning right.

NOTE: **Rwy 14,** vehicles on road beginning 1020' from DER, on centerline, 15' AGL/814' MSL. Trees and power poles beginning at DER, 75' right of centerline, up to 100' AGL/879' MSL. Trees, power poles, light poles and vehicles on road beginning at DER, 251' left of centerline, up to 100' AGL/899' MSL. **Rwy 32,** train on railroad tracks, transmission poles and tree beginning 339' from DER, 107' right of centerline, 76'AGL/845' MSL. Trees, vehicles on road and bush beginning 14' from DER, 198' left of centerline, up to 46' AGL/815' MSL.

GRAND PRAIRIE, TX

GRAND PRAIRIE MUNI (GPM)

AMDT 4 09295 (FAA)

DEPARTURE PROCEDURE: **Rwy 17,** climbing right turn to 2000 via heading 200° and TTT R-180 to NINAE/TTT 24 DME before proceeding on course. DME Required. **Rwy 35,** climb heading 356° to 1400 before turning south.

NOTE: **Rwy 17,** antenna 190' from DER, 456' right of centerline, 26' AGL/615' MSL. Road, multiple poles and signs beginning 570' from DER, 410' right of centerline, up to 31' AGL/620' MSL. Tree 1506' from DER, 517' right of centerline, 37' AGL/617' MSL. **Rwy 35,** tree 837' from DER, 204' left of centerline, up to 100' AGL/665' MSL. Pole 2687' from DER, 122' left of centerline, up to 75' AGL/653' MSL.

12096

TAKE-OFF MINIMUMS AND (OBSTACLE) DEPARTURE PROCEDURES

SC-2

Figure 314. Takeoff Minimums and (Obstacle) Departure Procedures.

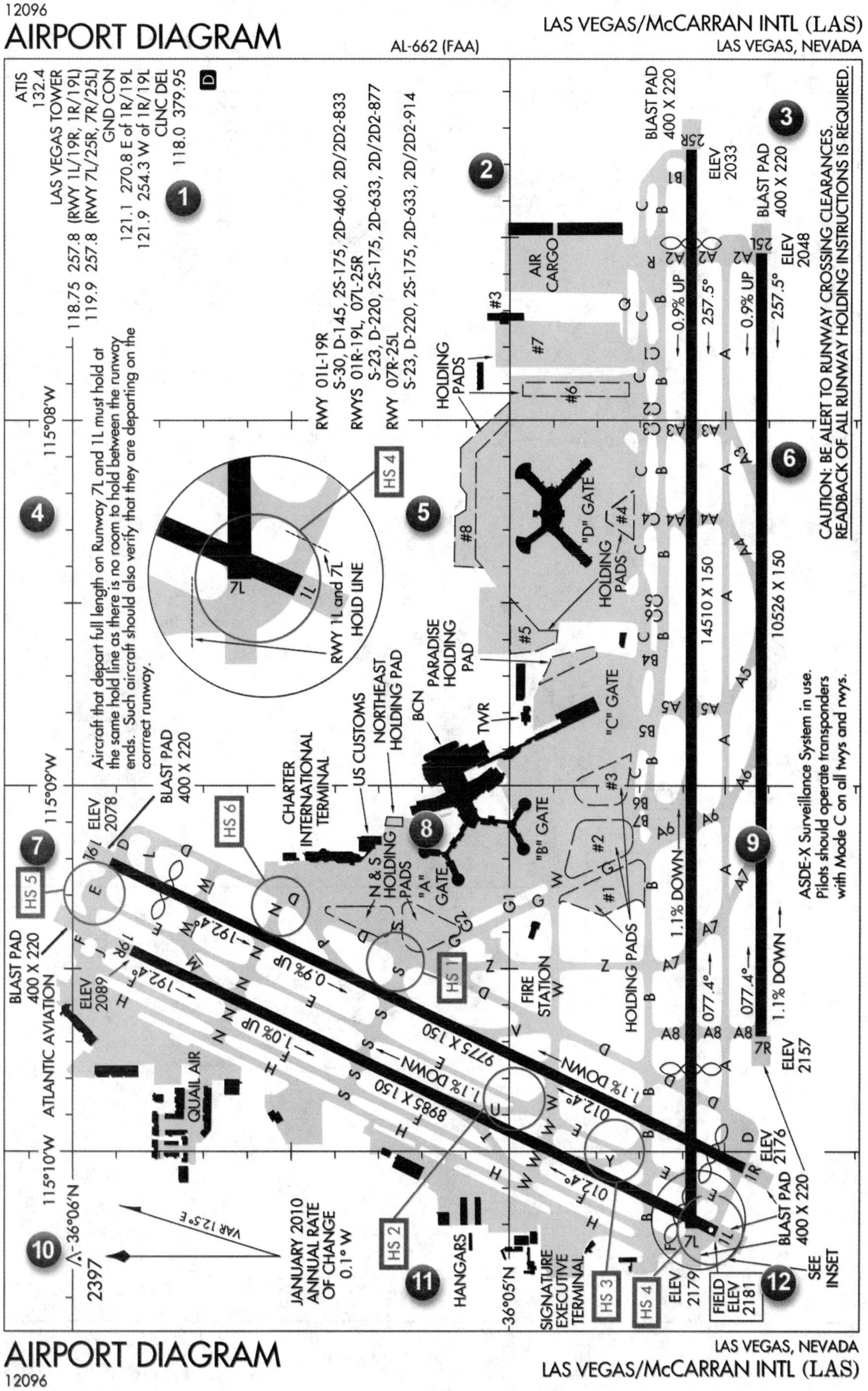

12096
AIRPORT DIAGRAM
AL-662 (FAA)
LAS VEGAS/McCARRAN INTL (LAS)
LAS VEGAS, NEVADA

ATIS 132.4
LAS VEGAS TOWER
118.75 257.8 (RWY 1L/19R, 1R/19L)
119.9 257.8 (RWY 7L/25R, 7R/25L)
GND CON
121.1 270.8 E of 1R/19L
121.9 254.3 W of 1R/19L
CLNC DEL
118.0 379.95

RWY 01L-19R
S-30, D-145, 2S-175, 2D-460, 2D/2D2-833
RWYS 01R-19L, 07L-25R
S-23, D-220, 2S-175, 2D-633, 2D/2D2-877
RWY 07R-25L
S-23, D-220, 2S-175, 2D-633, 2D/2D2-914

Aircraft that depart full length on Runway 7L and 1L must hold at the same hold line as there is no room to hold between the runway ends. Such aircraft should also verify that they are departing on the corrrect runway.

RWY 1L and 7L HOLD LINE

CAUTION: BE ALERT TO RUNWAY CROSSING CLEARANCES. READBACK OF ALL RUNWAY HOLDING INSTRUCTIONS IS REQUIRED.

ASDE-X Surveillance System in use. Pilots should operate transponders with Mode C on all twys and rwys.

JANUARY 2010 ANNUAL RATE OF CHANGE 0.1° W
VAR 12.5° E

BLAST PAD 400 X 220
ELEV 2033
ELEV 2048
ELEV 2078
ELEV 2089
ELEV 2157
ELEV 2176
ELEV 2179
FIELD ELEV 2181
14510 X 150
10526 X 150
9775 X 150
8985 X 150
257.5°
077.4°
192.4°
012.4°
0.9% UP
1.1% DOWN
1.0% UP
AIR CARGO
"D" GATE
"C" GATE
"B" GATE
"A" GATE
HOLDING PADS
PARADISE HOLDING PAD
NORTHEAST HOLDING PAD
N & S HOLDING PADS
US CUSTOMS
CHARTER INTERNATIONAL TERMINAL
BCN
TWR
FIRE STATION
ATLANTIC AVIATION
QUAIL AIR
HANGARS
SIGNATURE EXECUTIVE TERMINAL
SEE INSET
HS 1
HS 2
HS 3
HS 4
HS 5
HS 6
115°10'W
115°09'W
115°08'W
36°06'N
36°05'N
2397

AIRPORT DIAGRAM
12096
LAS VEGAS, NEVADA
LAS VEGAS/McCARRAN INTL (LAS)

Figure 315. Airport Diagram (LAS).

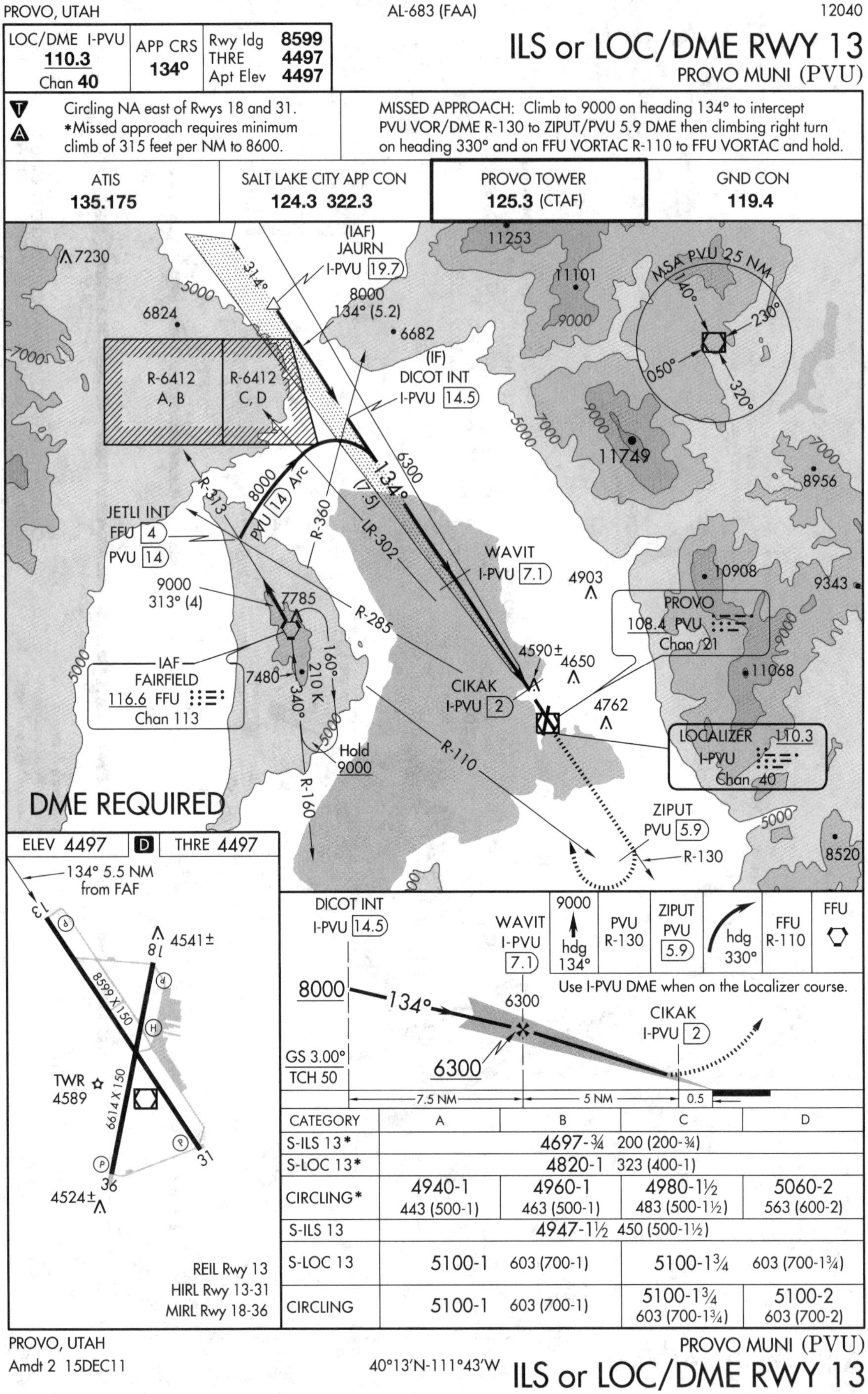

PROVO, UTAH | AL-683 (FAA) | 12040

LOC/DME I-PVU **110.3** Chan **40**	APP CRS **134°**	Rwy ldg **8599** THRE **4497** Apt Elev **4497**

ILS or LOC/DME RWY 13

PROVO MUNI (PVU)

Circling NA east of Rwys 18 and 31.
*Missed approach requires minimum climb of 315 feet per NM to 8600.

MISSED APPROACH: Climb to 9000 on heading 134° to intercept PVU VOR/DME R-130 to ZIPUT/PVU 5.9 DME then climbing right turn on heading 330° and on FFU VORTAC R-110 to FFU VORTAC and hold.

ATIS	SALT LAKE CITY APP CON	PROVO TOWER	GND CON
135.175	**124.3 322.3**	**125.3** (CTAF)	**119.4**

(IAF) JAURN I-PVU 19.7
8000 134° (5.2)
(IF) DICOT INT I-PVU 14.5
R-6412 A, B
R-6412 C, D
JETLI INT FFU 4 PVU 14
9000 313° (4)
PVU 14 Arc 8000
IAF FAIRFIELD 116.6 FFU Chan 113
210 K
Hold 9000
WAVIT I-PVU 7.1
CIKAK I-PVU 2
PROVO 108.4 PVU Chan 21
LOCALIZER 110.3 I-PVU Chan 40
ZIPUT PVU 5.9
R-130
R-110
R-285
R-160
R-313
R-360
LR-302
MSA PVU 25 NM
DME REQUIRED

ELEV 4497 | D | THRE 4497

134° 5.5 NM from FAF
8599 X 150
6614 X 150
TWR 4589
4541±
4524±
REIL Rwy 13
HIRL Rwy 13-31
MIRL Rwy 18-36

DICOT INT I-PVU 14.5
WAVIT I-PVU 7.1
9000 hdg 134°
PVU R-130
ZIPUT PVU 5.9
hdg 330°
FFU R-110
FFU
Use I-PVU DME when on the Localizer course.
8000
134°
6300
CIKAK I-PVU 2
GS 3.00°
TCH 50
7.5 NM | 5 NM | 0.5

CATEGORY	A	B	C	D
S-ILS 13*	4697-¾ 200 (200-¾)			
S-LOC 13*	4820-1 323 (400-1)			
CIRCLING*	4940-1 443 (500-1)	4960-1 463 (500-1)	4980-1½ 483 (500-1½)	5060-2 563 (600-2)
S-ILS 13	4947-1½ 450 (500-1½)			
S-LOC 13	5100-1 603 (700-1)		5100-1¾ 603 (700-1¾)	
CIRCLING	5100-1 603 (700-1)		5100-1¾ 603 (700-1¾)	5100-2 603 (700-2)

PROVO, UTAH
Amdt 2 15DEC11
40°13′N-111°43′W
PROVO MUNI (PVU)
ILS or LOC/DME RWY 13

Figure 316. ILS or LOC/DME RWY 13 (PVU).

(PROVO4.FFU) 09239

PROVO FOUR DEPARTURE (OBSTACLE) SL-683 (FAA) PROVO MUNI (PVU) PROVO, UTAH

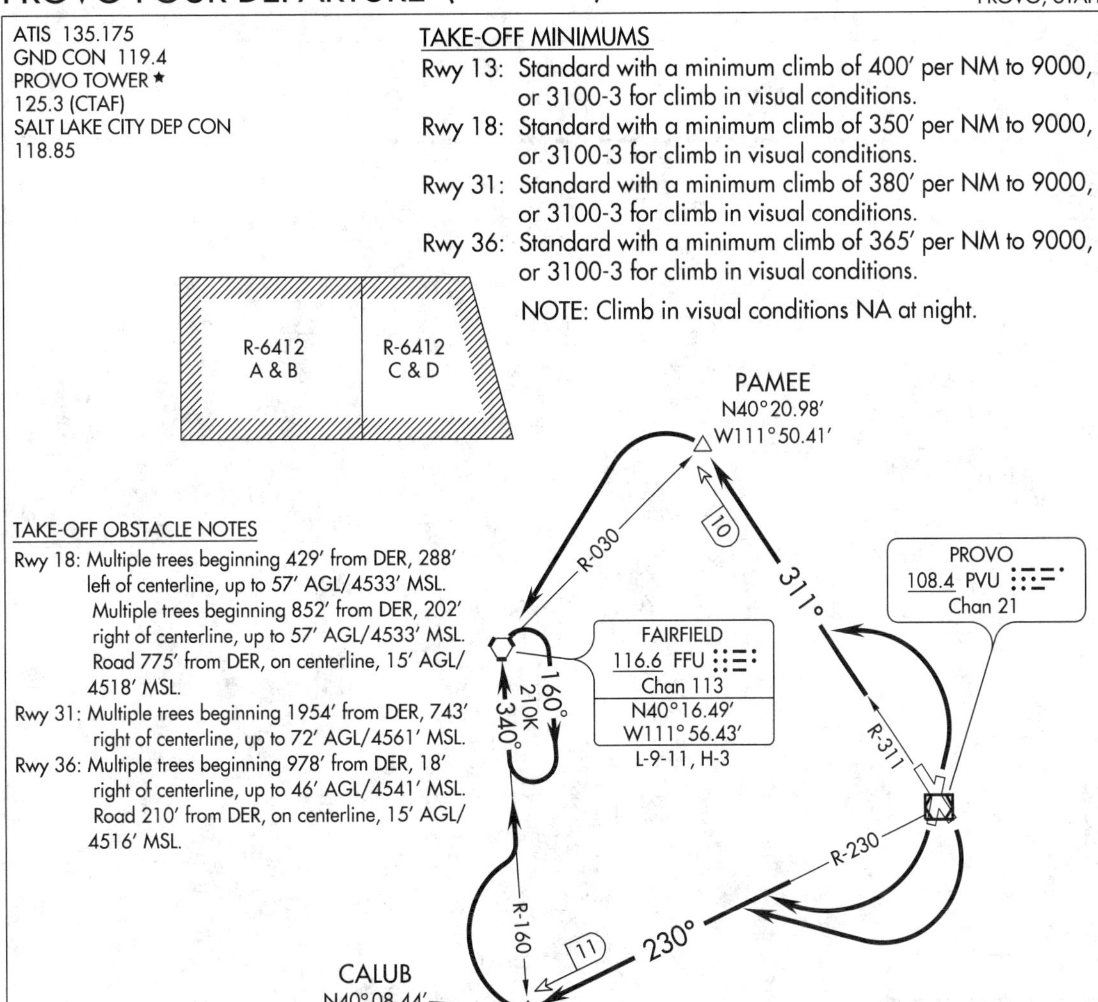
ATIS 135.175
GND CON 119.4
PROVO TOWER ★
125.3 (CTAF)
SALT LAKE CITY DEP CON
118.85
TAKE-OFF MINIMUMS
Rwy 13: Standard with a minimum climb of 400′ per NM to 9000, or 3100-3 for climb in visual conditions.
Rwy 18: Standard with a minimum climb of 350′ per NM to 9000, or 3100-3 for climb in visual conditions.
Rwy 31: Standard with a minimum climb of 380′ per NM to 9000, or 3100-3 for climb in visual conditions.
Rwy 36: Standard with a minimum climb of 365′ per NM to 9000, or 3100-3 for climb in visual conditions.
NOTE: Climb in visual conditions NA at night.
R-6412 A & B
R-6412 C & D
PAMEE
N40°20.98′
W111°50.41′
TAKE-OFF OBSTACLE NOTES
Rwy 18: Multiple trees beginning 429′ from DER, 288′ left of centerline, up to 57′ AGL/4533′ MSL. Multiple trees beginning 852′ from DER, 202′ right of centerline, up to 57′ AGL/4533′ MSL. Road 775′ from DER, on centerline, 15′ AGL/4518′ MSL.
Rwy 31: Multiple trees beginning 1954′ from DER, 743′ right of centerline, up to 72′ AGL/4561′ MSL.
Rwy 36: Multiple trees beginning 978′ from DER, 18′ right of centerline, up to 46′ AGL/4541′ MSL. Road 210′ from DER, on centerline, 15′ AGL/4516′ MSL.
R-030
10
311°
PROVO
108.4 PVU
Chan 21
FAIRFIELD
116.6 FFU
Chan 113
N40°16.49′
W111°56.43′
L-9-11, H-3
160°
210K
340°
R-311
R-230
R-160
11
230°
CALUB
N40°08.44′
W111°55.70′
NOTE: Chart not to scale.

DEPARTURE ROUTE DESCRIPTION

TAKE-OFF RUNWAYS 13, 18: Climbing right turn to 9000 via PVU VOR/DME R-230 to CALUB INT/PVU 11 DME and a right turn via FFU VORTAC R-160 to FFU VORTAC and hold. Thence.... or climb in visual conditions to cross Provo Muni Airport southwest bound at or above 7400, climb to 9000 via PVU R-230 to CALUB INT/PVU 11 DME and right turn via FFU R-160 to FFU VORTAC and hold. Thence...

TAKE-OFF RUNWAY 31: Climb to 9000 via PVU VOR/DME R-311 to PAMEE INT/PVU 10 DME and left turn direct FFU VORTAC and hold. Thence....
or climb in visual conditions to cross Provo Muni Airport northwest bound at or above 7400, climb to 9000 via PVU R-311 to PAMEE INT/PVU 10 DME and left turn direct FFU VORTAC and hold. Thence...

TAKE-OFF RUNWAY 36: Climbing left turn to 9000 via PVU VOR/DME R-311 to PAMEE INT/PVU 10 DME and left turn direct FFU VORTAC and hold. Thence....
or climb in visual conditions to cross Provo Muni Airport northwest bound at or above 7400, climb to 9000 via PVU R-311 to PAMEE INT/PVU 10 DME, and left turn direct FFU VORTAC and hold. Thence...

....Expect clearance for filed route and altitude within 10 minutes after departure.

PROVO FOUR DEPARTURE (OBSTACLE) PROVO, UTAH PROVO MUNI (PVU)

(PROVO4.FFU) 09239

Figure 317. PROVO FOUR Departure (Obstacle) (PROVO4.FFU) (PVU).

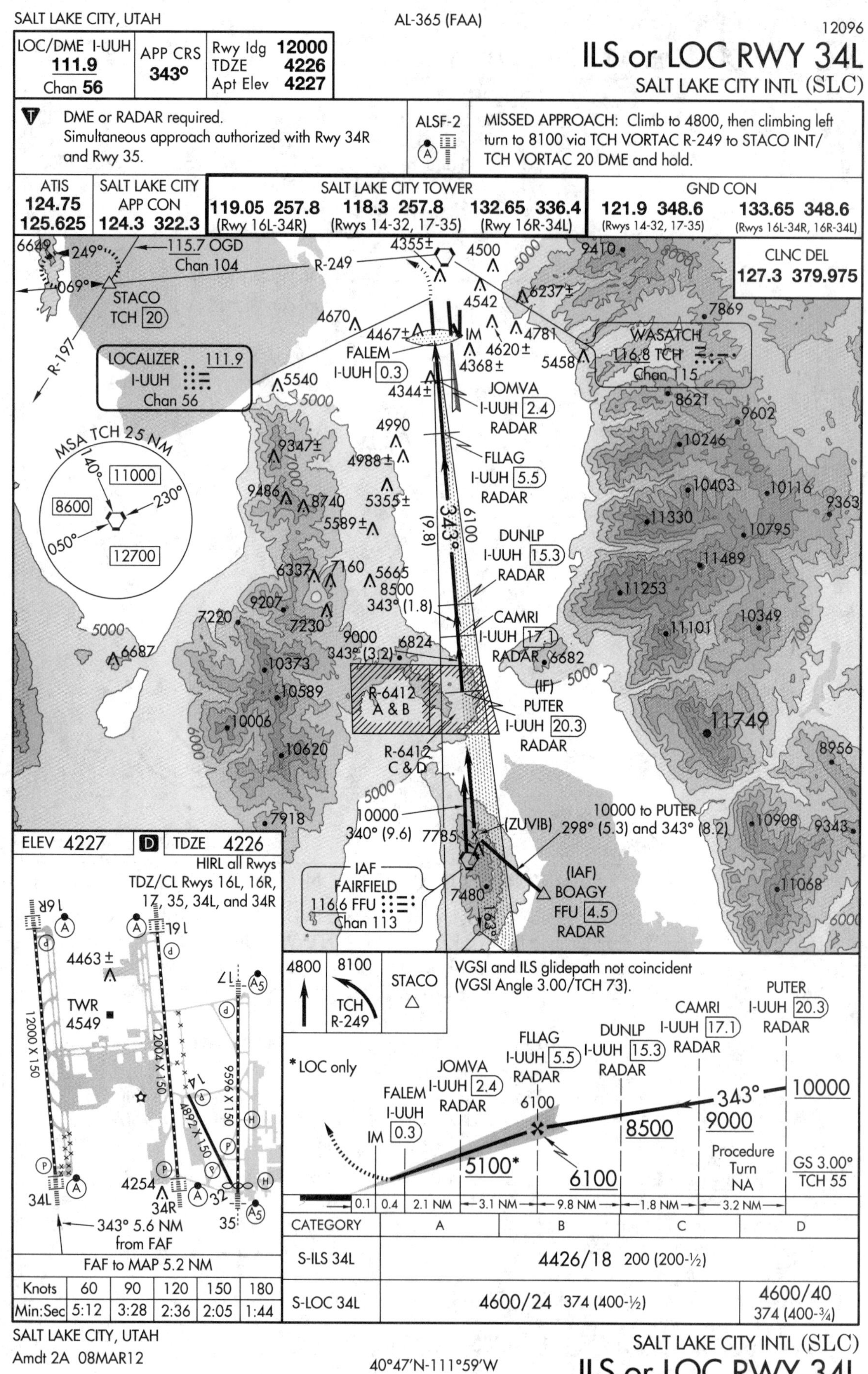

Figure 318. ILS or LOC RWY 34L (SLC).

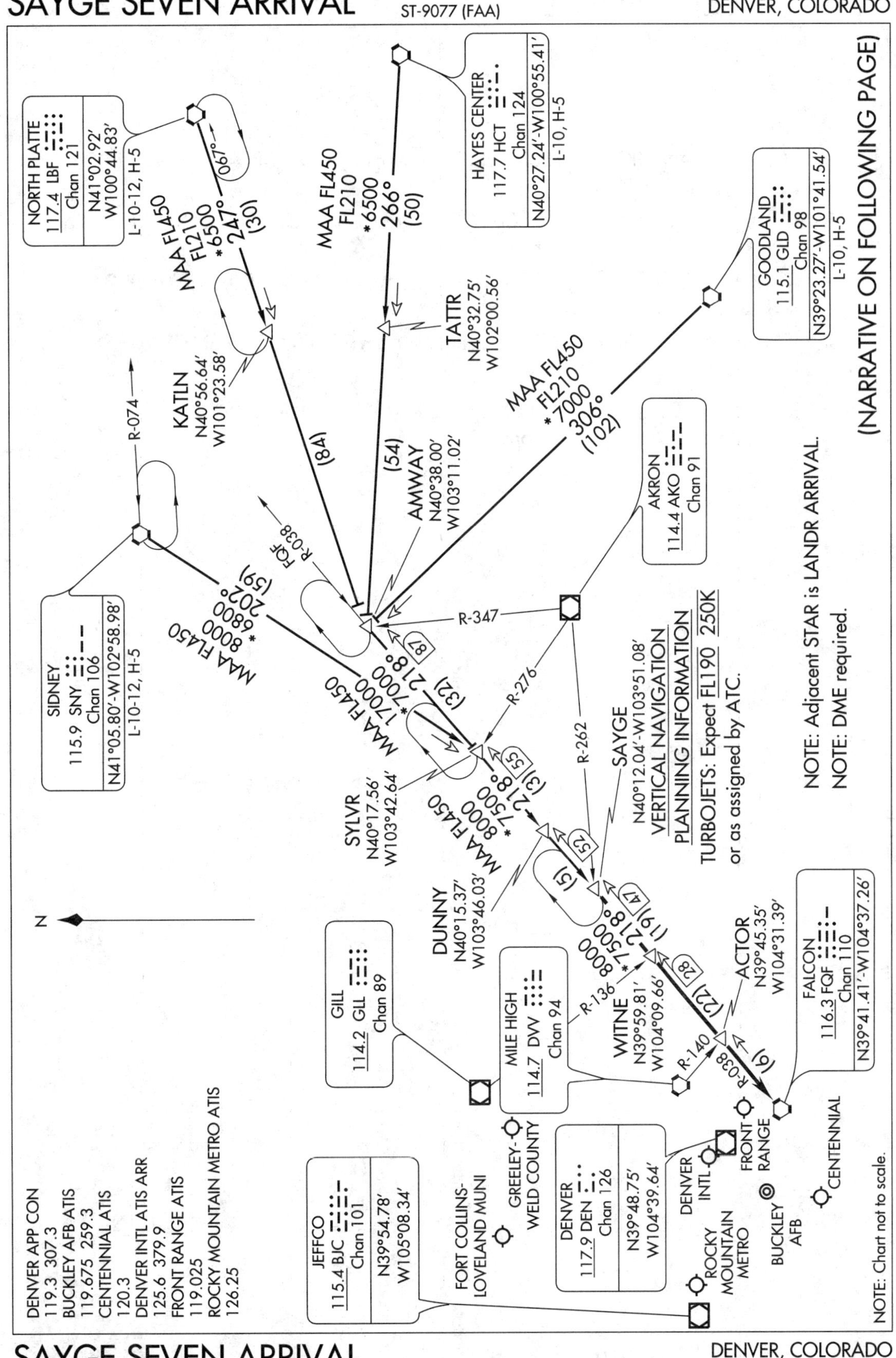

Figure 319. SAYGE SEVEN Arrival (SAYGE.SAYGE7).

(SAYGE.SAYGE7) 12096

SAYGE SEVEN ARRIVAL

ST-9077 (FAA) DENVER, COLORADO

ARRIVAL ROUTE DESCRIPTION

GOODLAND TRANSITION (GLD.SAYGE7): From over GLD VORTAC via GLD R-306 and FQF R-038 to SAYGE INT. Thence....

HAYES CENTER TRANSITION (HCT.SAYGE7): From over HCT VORTAC via HCT R-266 and FQF R-038 to SAYGE INT. Thence....

NORTH PLATTE TRANSITION (LBF.SAYGE7): From over LBF VORTAC via LBF R-247 and FQF R-038 to SAYGE INT. Thence....

SIDNEY TRANSITION (SNY.SAYGE7): From over SNY VORTAC via SNY R-202 and FQF R-038 to SAYGE INT. Thence....

....From over SAYGE INT via FQF R-038 to FQF VORTAC. Expect RADAR vectors to the final approach course at or before FQF VORTAC.

SAYGE SEVEN ARRIVAL DENVER, COLORADO

(SAYGE.SAYGE7) 12096

Figure 320. SAYGE SEVEN Arrival (SAYGE.SAYGE7).

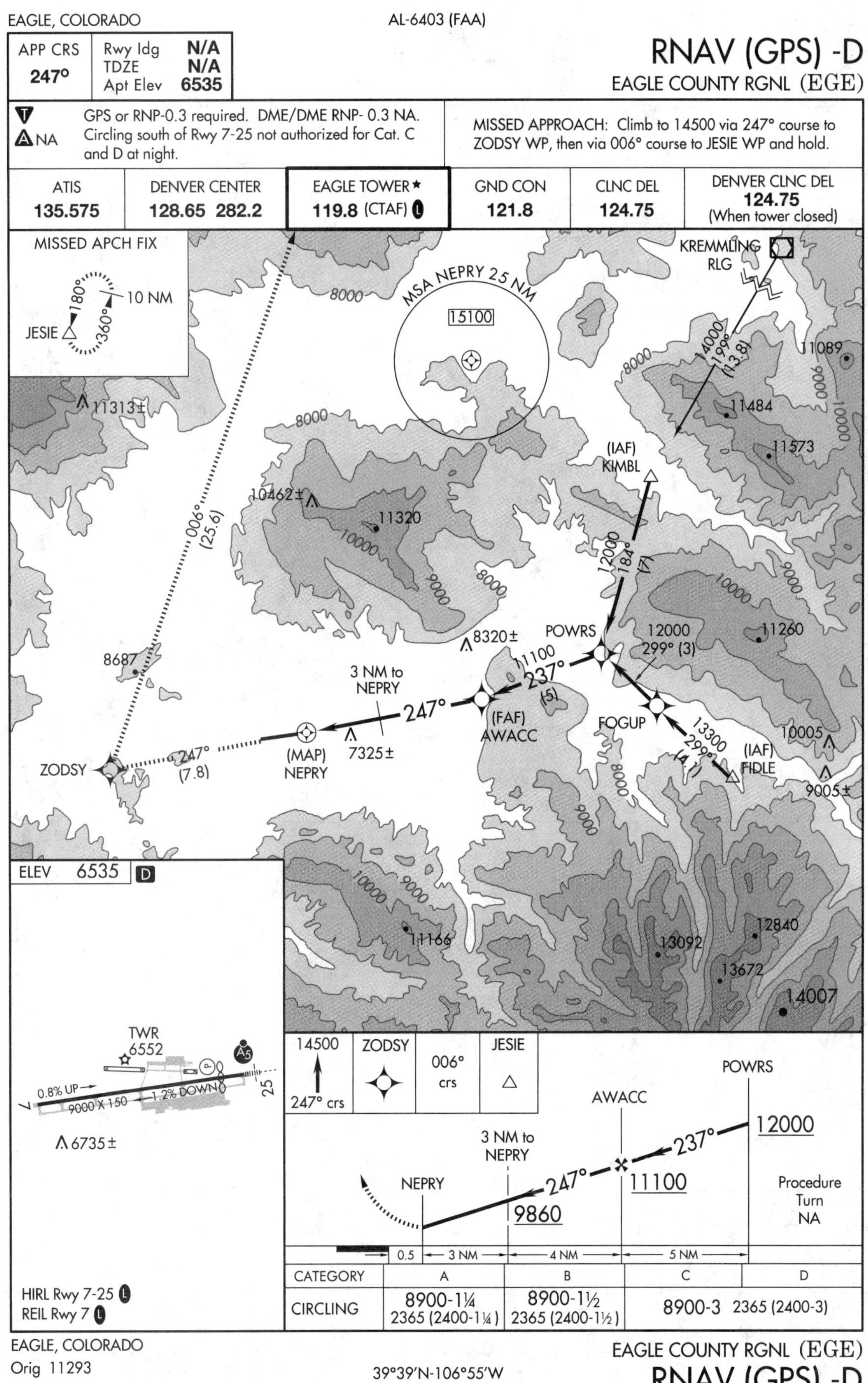

CATEGORY	A	B	C	D
CIRCLING	8900-1¼ 2365 (2400-1¼)	8900-1½ 2365 (2400-1½)	8900-3 2365 (2400-3)	

Figure 321. RNAV (GPS) –D (EGE).

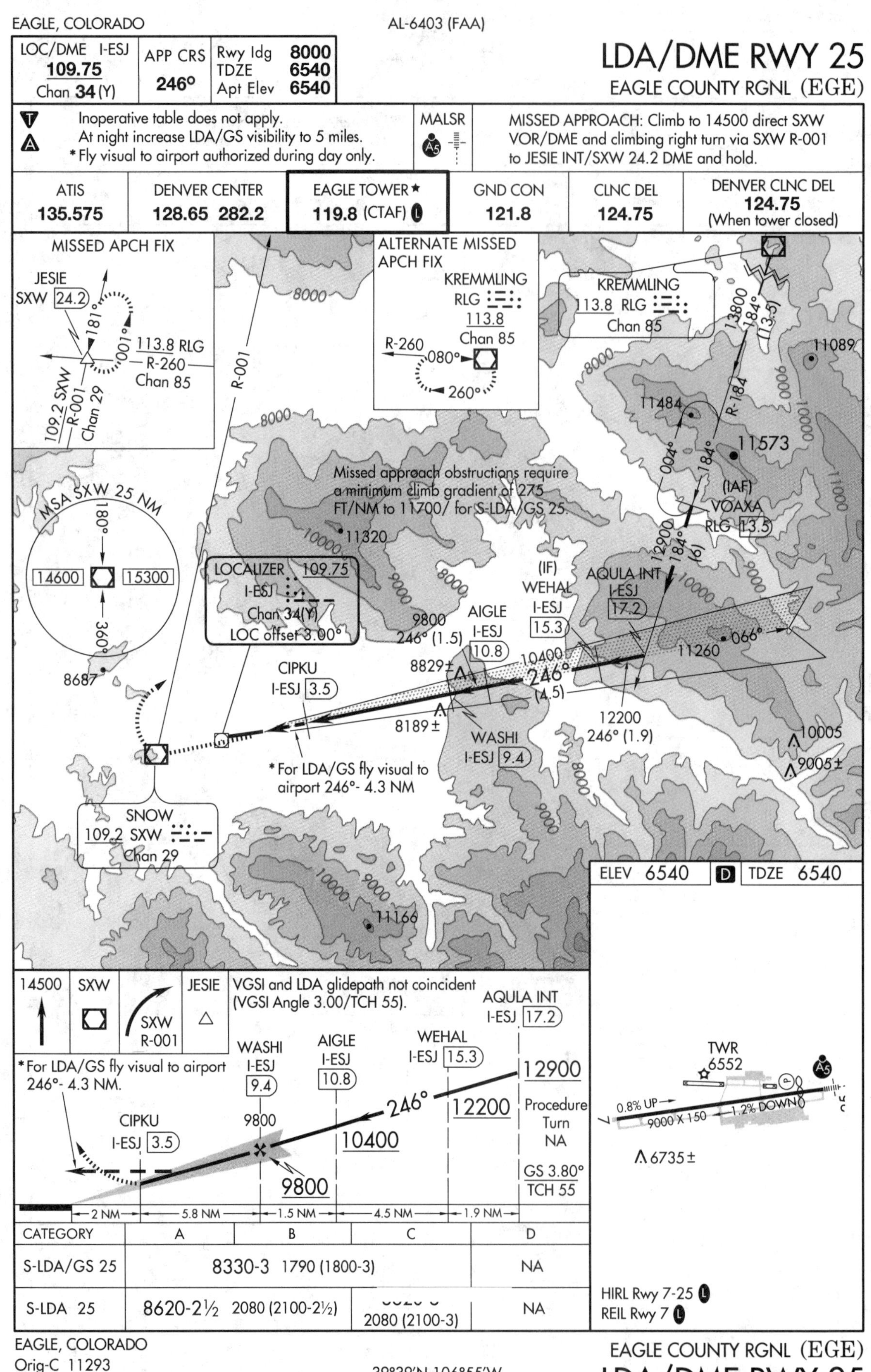

Figure 322. LDA/DME RWY 25 (EGE).

(GYPSM4.RLG) 12096 SL-6403 (FAA)

GYPSUM FOUR DEPARTURE (OBSTACLE)

EAGLE COUNTY RGNL (EGE)
EAGLE, COLORADO

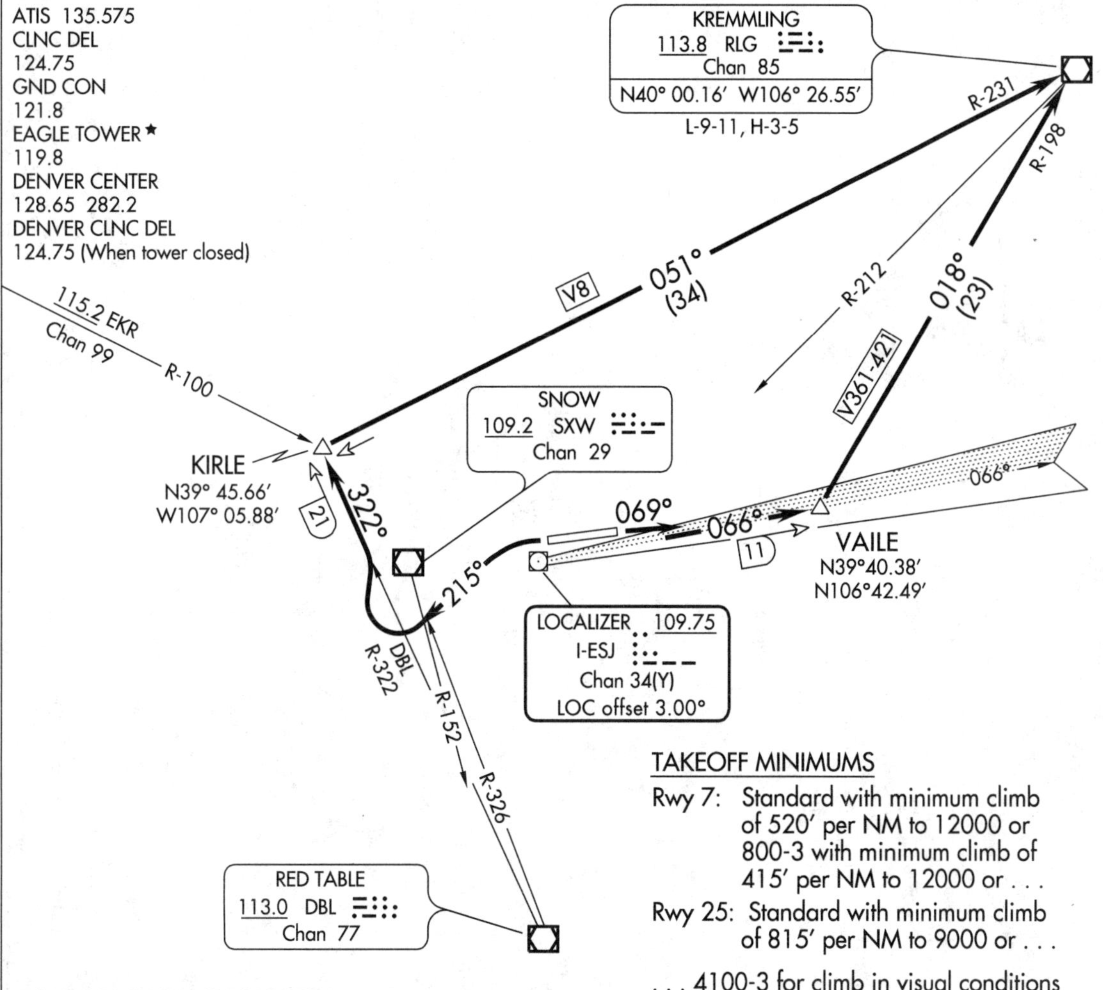

TAKEOFF OBSTACLE NOTES

Rwy 7: Windsock 99′ from DER, 352′ left of centerline, 12′ AGL/6552′ MSL.
OL on tower 2.2 NM from DER, 1688′ right of centerline, 57′ AGL/7057′ MSL.
Trees beginning 1.1 NM from DER, 1945′ right of centerline, up to 18′ AGL/7017′ MSL.
Tree 2.2 NM from DER, 3227′ right of centerline, 27′ AGL/7252′ MSL.

Rwy 25: Multiple trees beginning 1.6 NM from DER, 233′ left of centerline, up to 15′ AGL/7694′ MSL.
Pole 2 NM from DER, 111′ left of centerline, 14′ AGL/7333′ MSL.
Multiple trees beginning 1.4 NM from DER, 795′ right of centerline, up to 16′ AGL/7615′ MSL.
Multiple poles, tank, and OL on tower beginning 1.4 NM from DER, 77′ right of centerline, up to 37′ AGL/7716′ MSL.

NOTE: Chart not to scale.

DEPARTURE ROUTE DESCRIPTION

TAKEOFF RUNWAY 7: Climb heading 069° and I-ESJ northeast course to VAILE INT/I-ESJ 11 DME then turn left via RLG R-198 to RLG VOR/DME or . . .

TAKEOFF RUNWAY 25: Climbing left turn heading 215°, upon crossing SXW R-152 or DBL R-326 turn right via DBL R-322 to KIRLE INT/DBL 21 DME then turn right via RLG R-231 to RLG VOR/DME or . . .

. . . Climb in visual conditions to cross Eagle County Rgnl Airport northeast bound at or above 10500, then via RLG R-212 to RLG VOR/DME.

GYPSUM FOUR DEPARTURE (OBSTACLE)
(GYPSM4.RLG) 12096

EAGLE, COLORADO
EAGLE COUNTY RGNL (EGE)

Figure 323. GYPSUM FOUR Departure (Obstacle) (EGE).

(EKR1.EKR) 12096 SL-6403 (FAA)

MEEKER ONE DEPARTURE

EAGLE COUNTY RGNL (EGE)
EAGLE, COLORADO

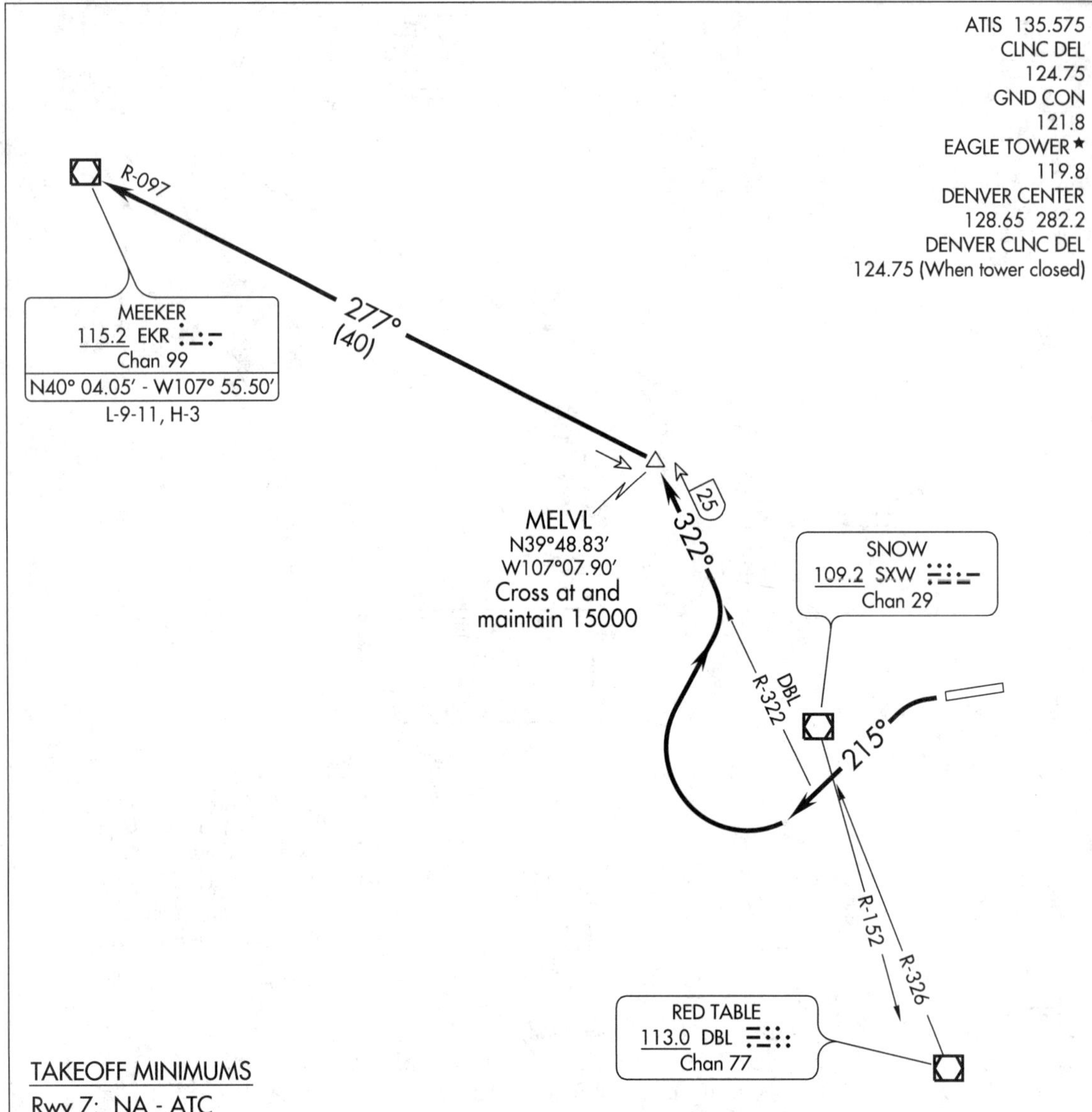

TAKEOFF MINIMUMS

Rwy 7: NA - ATC
Rwy 25: Standard with minimum climb of 815′ per NM to 15000.

TAKEOFF OBSTACLE NOTES

Rwy 25: Multiple trees beginning 1.6 NM from DER, 233′ left of centerline, up to 15′ AGL/7694′ MSL.
Pole 2 NM from DER, 111′ left of centerline, 14′ AGL/7333′ MSL.
Multiple trees beginning 1.4 NM from DER, 795′ right of centerline, up to 16′ AGL/7615′ MSL.
Multiple poles, tank and OL on tower beginning 1.4 NM from DER, 77′ right of centerline, up to 37′ AGL/7716′ MSL.

NOTE: Chart not to scale.

DEPARTURE ROUTE DESCRIPTION

TAKEOFF RUNWAY 25: Climbing left turn heading 215°, upon crossing SXW R-152 or DBL R-326 turn right via DBL R-322 to MELVL INT/DBL 25 DME then turn left via EKR R-097 to EKR VOR/DME. Cross MELVL at and maintain 15000, expect filed altitude 10 minutes after departure.

MEEKER ONE DEPARTURE
(EKR1.EKR) 12096

EAGLE, COLORADO
EAGLE COUNTY RGNL (EGE)

Figure 324. MEEKER ONE Departure (EGE).

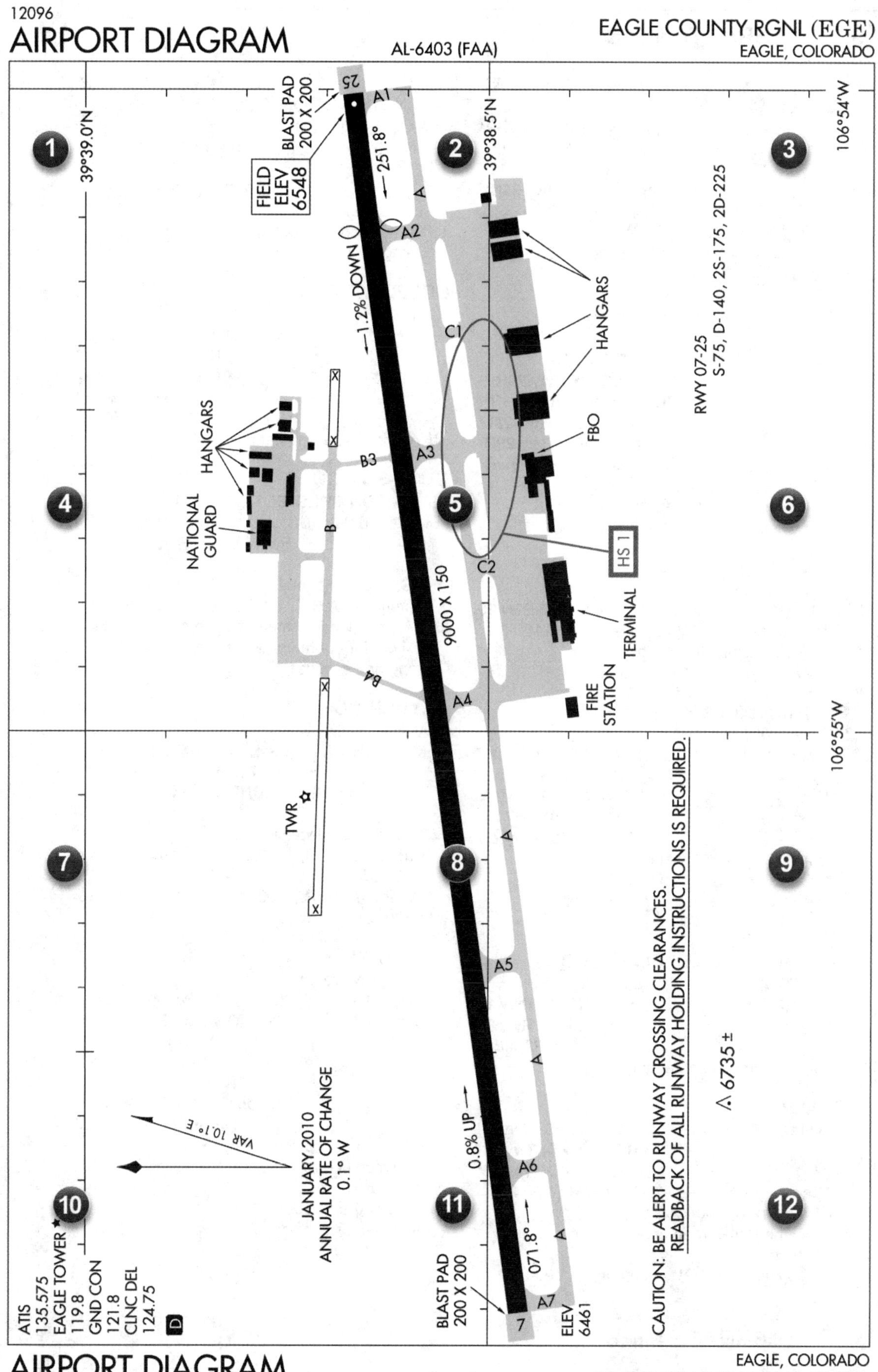

Figure 325. Airport Diagram (EGE).

ALTERNATE MINS

M2

12096

NAME — ALTERNATE MINIMUMS

DENVER, CO

CENTENNIAL (APA) ...... **ILS or LOC Rwy 35R**[1]
NDB Rwy 35R[2]
RNAV (GPS) Rwy 28[3,4]
RNAV (GPS) Rwy 35R[1,4]

[1]Categories A,B, 900-2; Category C, 900-2½, Category D, 900-2¾.
[2]Categories A,B, 1000-2; Categories C,D, 1000-3.
[3]Category D, 800-2¼.
[4]NA when local weather not available.

ROCKY MOUNTAIN METROPOLITAN
(BJC) .... **ILS or LOC Y Rwy 29R**[1,2,3]
ILS or LOC Z Rwy 29R[2,3]
RNAV (GPS) Rwy 29L[3]
RNAV (GPS) Rwy 29R[3]
VOR/DME Rwy 29L/R[2]

[1]ILS, Categories A, B, C, D, 700-2.
[2]NA when control tower closed.
[3]NA when local weather not available.

EAGLE, CO

EAGLE COUNTY
RGNL (EGE) .... **LDA/DME Rwy 25**

Categories A,B, 2100-2; Category C, 2100-3.
NA when control tower closed.
NA when local weather not available.

FARMINGTON, NM

FOUR CORNERS
RGNL (FMN) .... **ILS or LOC Rwy 25**[1,2]
RNAV (GPS) Rwy 5[3]
RNAV (GPS) Rwy 7[3]
RNAV (GPS) Rwy 23[4]
RNAV (GPS) Rwy 25[3]

[1]NA when control tower closed.
[2]ILS, Categories B,C,D, 700-2.
[3]NA when local weather not available.
[4]Category D, 800-2¼.

FORT COLLINS/LOVELAND, CO

FORT COLLINS-LOVELAND
MUNI (FNL) .... **RNAV (GPS) Rwy 15**
RNAV (GPS) Rwy 33
VOR/DME-A

NA when local weather not available.

GALLUP, NM

GALLUP MUNI (GUP) .... **RNAV (GPS) Rwy 6**[1,2]
RNAV (GPS) Rwy 24[3]
VOR Rwy 6[4]

[1]Categories A, B, 900-2; Category C, 900-2½; Category D, 900-3.
[2]NA when local weather not available.
[3]Category D, 900-3.
[4]Category C, 800-2¼; Category D, 900-3.

NAME — ALTERNATE MINIMUMS

GRAND JUNCTION, CO

GRAND JUNCTION
RGNL (GJT) .... **ILS or LOC Rwy 11**[1,2]
LDA/DME Rwy 29[3]
RNAV (GPS) Y Rwy 11[3]

[1]ILS, Category D, 700-2¼.
[2]NA when local weather not available.
[3]Category D, 800-2¼.

GREELEY, CO

GREELEY-WELD
COUNTY (GXY) .... **ILS or LOC Rwy 34**
RNAV (GPS) Rwy 16
RNAV (GPS) Rwy 27
RNAV (GPS) Rwy 34
VOR-A

NA when local weather not available.

GUNNISON, CO

GUNNISON-CRESTED
BUTTE RGNL (GUC) .... **ILS or LOC Rwy 6**[1]
RNAV (RNP) Rwy 6, 800-2¼
VOR or GPS-A[2,3]

[1]ILS,LOC, Categories A, B, C, 1600-3.
[2]Categories A,B,C, 1700-3;Cat D, 2300-3.
[3]NA when local altimeter setting not available except for operators with approved weather reporting service.

HAYDEN, CO

YAMPA
VALLEY (HDN) .... **ILS or LOC/DME Y Rwy 10**[1,2]
RNAV (GPS) Y Rwy 10[1,2]
RNAV (RNP) Z Rwy 10, 800-2¼[1]
VOR/DME-B[3]

[1]NA when local weather not availalbe.
[2]Categories A, B, 1200-2; Categories C, D, 1200-3.
[3]Categories A, B, 1300-2; Categories C, D, 1300-3.

HOBBS, NM

LEA COUNTY
RGNL (HOB) .... **ILS or LOC Rwy 3**[1]
LOC/DME BC Rwy 21[2]
RNAV (GPS) Rwy 3[3]
RNAV (GPS) Rwy 21[2]
RNAV (GPS) Rwy 30[2]
VOR/DME or TACAN Rwy 21[2]
VOR or TACAN Rwy 3[2]

[1]NA when control tower closed.
[2]NA when control tower closed, except standard for operators with approved weather reporting service.
[3]NA when local weather not available.

ALTERNATE MINS

12096

M2

SW-1

Figure 326. Alternate Minimums.

GUNNISON, COLORADO — AL-517 (FAA) — 10266

ILS or LOC RWY 6

GUNNISON-CRESTED BUTTE RGNL (GUC)

LOC/DME I-GUC 110.5 Chan 42	APP CRS 062°	Rwy ldg 9400 TDZE 7667 Apt Elev 7680

Circling NA at night. Inoperative table does not apply. When local altimeter setting not received, procedure NA. DME required. Visibility reduction by helicopters NA. Procedure NA when airport closed except by prior arrangement.

MALSF

MISSED APPROACH: Climb to 10000 then climbing right turn to 12000 via heading 180° and HBU VOR/DME R-050 to WIDIG/HBU 4 DME continue via HBU VOR/DME R-050 to HBU VOR/DME and hold.

AWOS-3	DENVER CENTER	UNICOM
135.075	125.35 354.05	122.7 (CTAF)

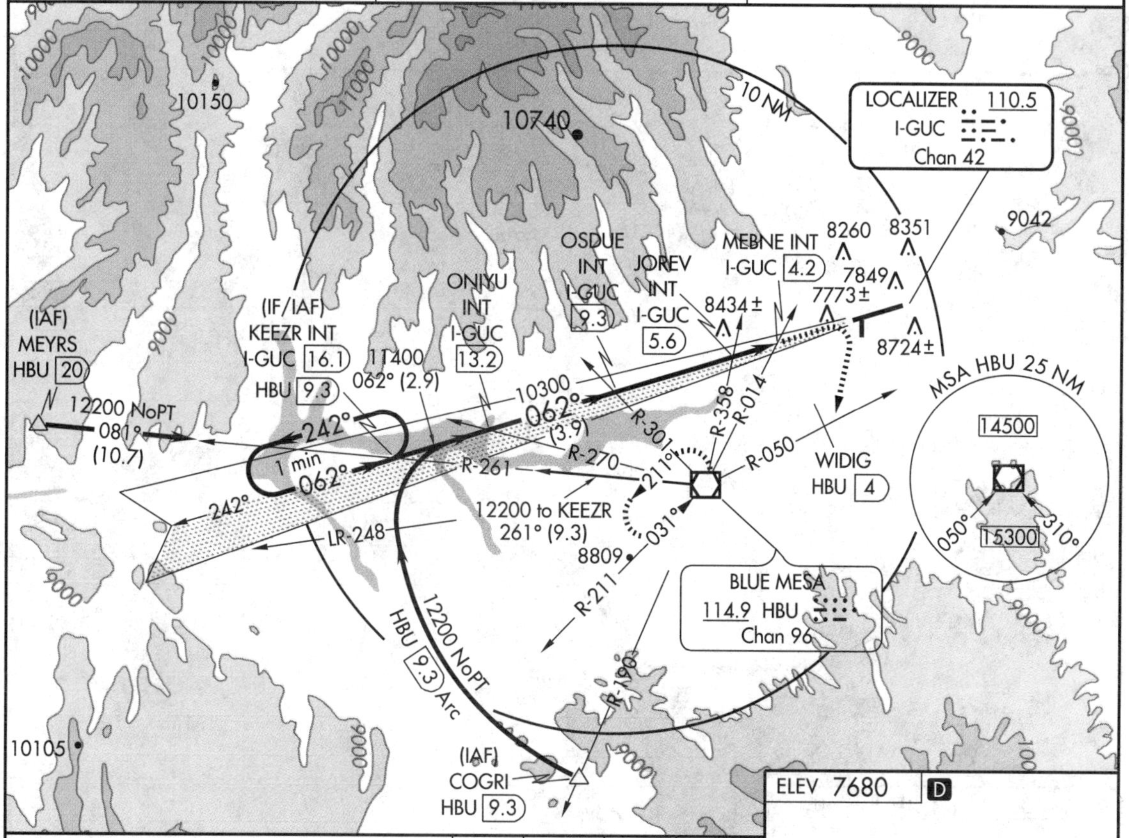

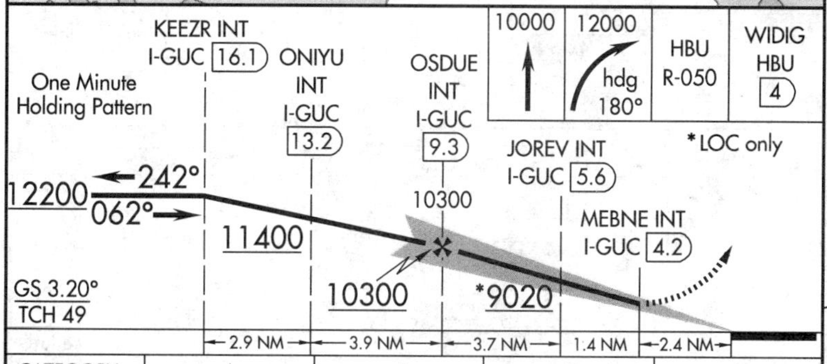

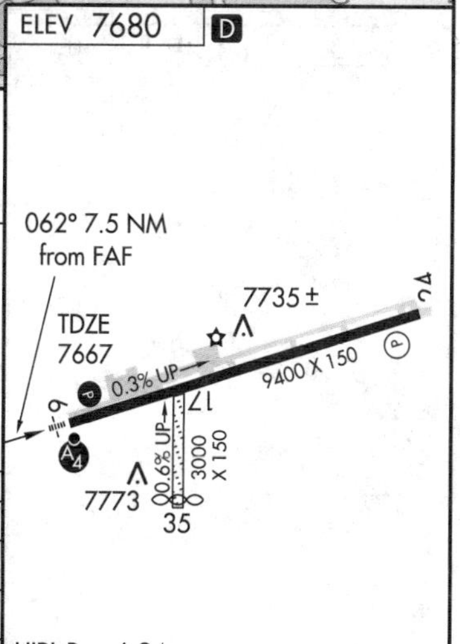

CATEGORY	A	B	C	D
S-ILS 6	8590-3 923 (1000-3)			NA
S-LOC 6	9020-3 1353 (1400-3)			
CIRCLING	9260-3 1580 (1600-3)			
JOREV FIX MINIMUMS				
S-LOC 6	8640-3 973 (1000-3)			
CIRCLING	9260-3 1580 (1600-3)			

FAF to MAP 5.1 NM

Knots	60	90	120	150	180
Min:Sec	5:06	3:24	2:33	2:02	1:42

GUNNISON, COLORADO
Amdt 5 22OCT09

38°32′N-106°56′W

GUNNISON-CRESTED BUTTE RGNL (GUC)

ILS or LOC RWY 6

Figure 327. ILS or LOC RWY 6 (GUC).

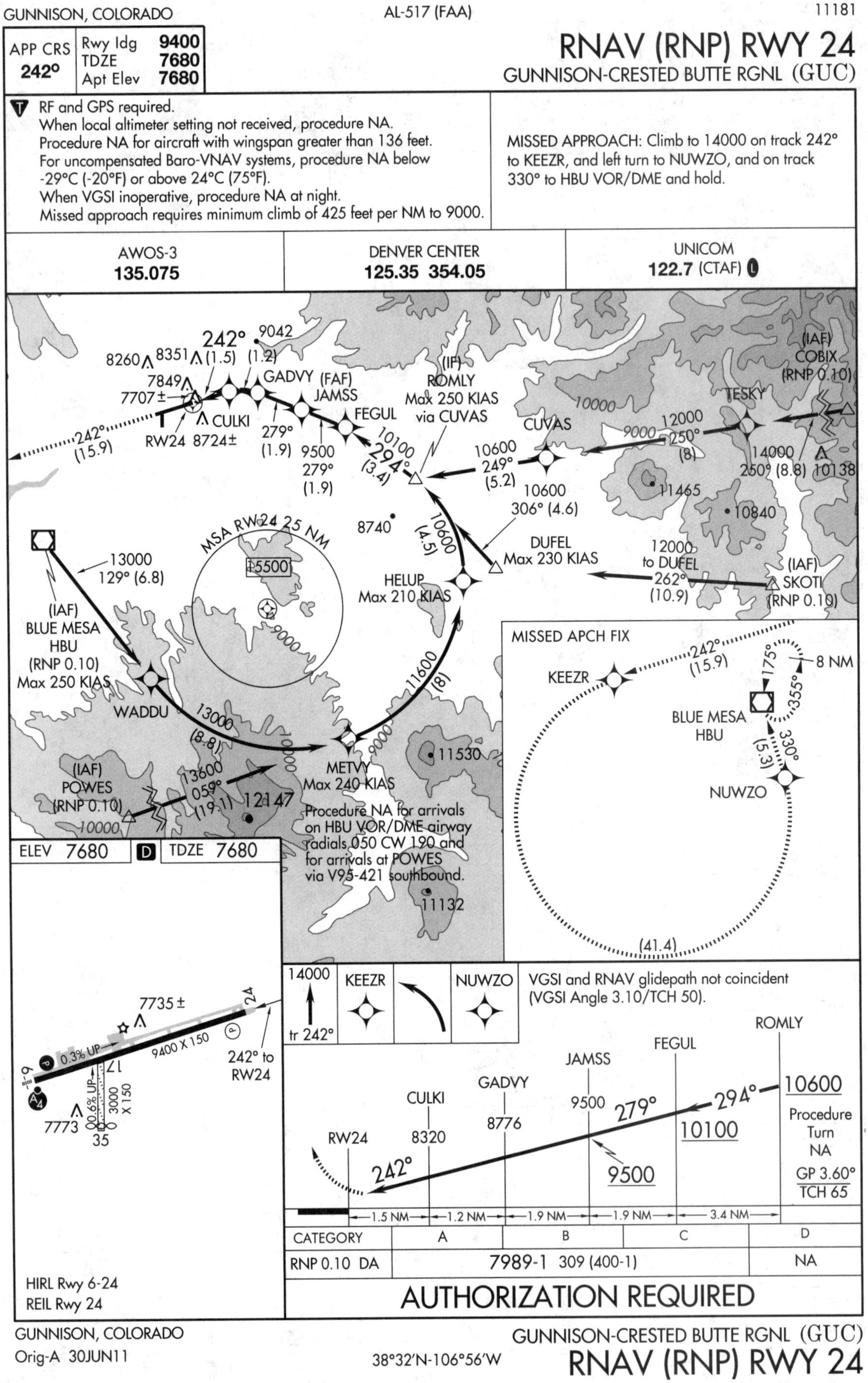
GUNNISON, COLORADO
AL-517 (FAA)
11181
APP CRS 242°
Rwy ldg 9400
TDZE 7680
Apt Elev 7680
RNAV (RNP) RWY 24
GUNNISON-CRESTED BUTTE RGNL (GUC)
RF and GPS required.
When local altimeter setting not received, procedure NA.
Procedure NA for aircraft with wingspan greater than 136 feet.
For uncompensated Baro-VNAV systems, procedure NA below -29°C (-20°F) or above 24°C (75°F).
When VGSI inoperative, procedure NA at night.
Missed approach requires minimum climb of 425 feet per NM to 9000.
MISSED APPROACH: Climb to 14000 on track 242° to KEEZR, and left turn to NUWZO, and on track 330° to HBU VOR/DME and hold.
AWOS-3 135.075
DENVER CENTER 125.35 354.05
UNICOM 122.7 (CTAF)
(IAF) COBIX (RNP 0.10)
TESKY
12000 250° (8)
14000 250° (8.8)
10138
CUVAS
10600 249° (5.2)
10600 306° (4.6)
(IF) ROMLY
Max 250 KIAS via CUVAS
10100 294° (3.4)
11465
10840
DUFEL
Max 230 KIAS
12000 to DUFEL 262° (10.9)
(IAF) SKOTI (RNP 0.10)
242° 9042
8260 8351 (1.5) (1.2)
7849
7707±
GADVY (FAF)
JAMSS
FEGUL
CULKI
RW24 8724±
279° (1.9)
9500 279° (1.9)
242° (15.9)
8740
10600 (4.5)
MSA RW24 25 NM
15500
HELUP
Max 210 KIAS
13000 129° (6.8)
(IAF) BLUE MESA HBU (RNP 0.10) Max 250 KIAS
WADDU
13000 (8.8)
11600 (8)
METVY
Max 240 KIAS
11530
(IAF) POWES (RNP 0.10)
13600 059° (19.1)
12147
Procedure NA for arrivals on HBU VOR/DME airway radials 050 CW 190 and for arrivals at POWES via V95-421 southbound.
11132
MISSED APCH FIX
KEEZR
242° (15.9)
175°
355°
8 NM
BLUE MESA HBU
330° (5.3)
NUWZO
(41.4)
ELEV 7680
TDZE 7680
7735±
0.3% UP
9400 X 150
242° to RW24
0.6% UP
3000 X 150
7773
HIRL Rwy 6-24
REIL Rwy 24
14000 tr 242°
KEEZR
NUWZO
VGSI and RNAV glidepath not coincident (VGSI Angle 3.10/TCH 50).
ROMLY
FEGUL
JAMSS
GADVY
CULKI
RW24
8320
8776
9500
279°
294°
10600
10100
9500
242°
Procedure Turn NA
GP 3.60°
TCH 65
1.5 NM
1.2 NM
1.9 NM
1.9 NM
3.4 NM
CATEGORY A B C D
RNP 0.10 DA 7989-1 309 (400-1) NA
AUTHORIZATION REQUIRED
GUNNISON, COLORADO
Orig-A 30JUN11
38°32'N-106°56'W
GUNNISON-CRESTED BUTTE RGNL (GUC)
RNAV (RNP) RWY 24

Figure 328. RNAV (RNP) RWY 24 (GUC).

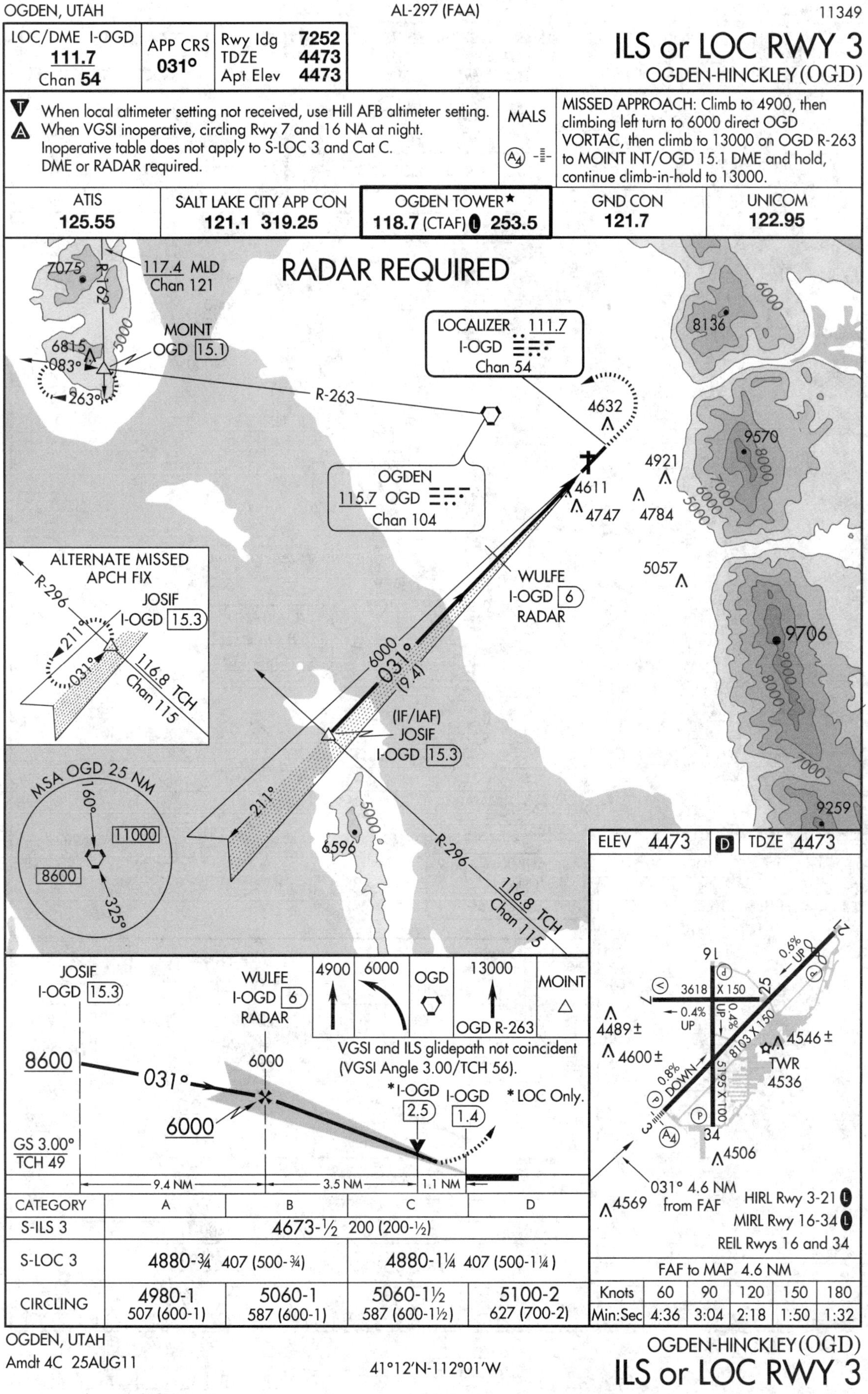
OGDEN, UTAH
AL-297 (FAA)
11349
ILS or LOC RWY 3
OGDEN-HINCKLEY (OGD)
LOC/DME I-OGD 111.7 Chan 54
APP CRS 031°
Rwy ldg 7252
TDZE 4473
Apt Elev 4473
When local altimeter setting not received, use Hill AFB altimeter setting.
When VGSI inoperative, circling Rwy 7 and 16 NA at night.
Inoperative table does not apply to S-LOC 3 and Cat C.
DME or RADAR required.
MALS
MISSED APPROACH: Climb to 4900, then climbing left turn to 6000 direct OGD VORTAC, then climb to 13000 on OGD R-263 to MOINT INT/OGD 15.1 DME and hold, continue climb-in-hold to 13000.
ATIS 125.55
SALT LAKE CITY APP CON 121.1 319.25
OGDEN TOWER★ 118.7 (CTAF) 253.5
GND CON 121.7
UNICOM 122.95
RADAR REQUIRED
117.4 MLD Chan 121
R-162
MOINT OGD 15.1
083°
263°
LOCALIZER 111.7 I-OGD Chan 54
R-263
OGDEN 115.7 OGD Chan 104
ALTERNATE MISSED APCH FIX
JOSIF I-OGD 15.3
R-296
211°
031°
116.8 TCH Chan 115
WULFE I-OGD 6 RADAR
6000 031° (9.4)
(IF/IAF) JOSIF I-OGD 15.3
MSA OGD 25 NM
160°
11000
8600
325°
ELEV 4473
TDZE 4473
HIRL Rwy 3-21
MIRL Rwy 16-34
REIL Rwys 16 and 34
031° 4.6 NM from FAF
TWR 4536
8103 X 150
5195 X 100
3618 X 150
VGSI and ILS glidepath not coincident (VGSI Angle 3.00/TCH 56).
*I-OGD 2.5
I-OGD 1.4
*LOC Only.
GS 3.00°
TCH 49
9.4 NM
3.5 NM
1.1 NM
CATEGORY A B C D
S-ILS 3 4673-½ 200 (200-½)
S-LOC 3 4880-¾ 407 (500-¾) 4880-1¼ 407 (500-1¼)
CIRCLING 4980-1 507 (600-1) 5060-1 587 (600-1) 5060-1½ 587 (600-1½) 5100-2 627 (700-2)
FAF to MAP 4.6 NM
Knots 60 90 120 150 180
Min:Sec 4:36 3:04 2:18 1:50 1:32
OGDEN, UTAH
Amdt 4C 25AUG11
41°12′N-112°01′W
OGDEN-HINCKLEY (OGD)
ILS or LOC RWY 3

Figure 329. ILS or LOC RWY 3 (OGD).

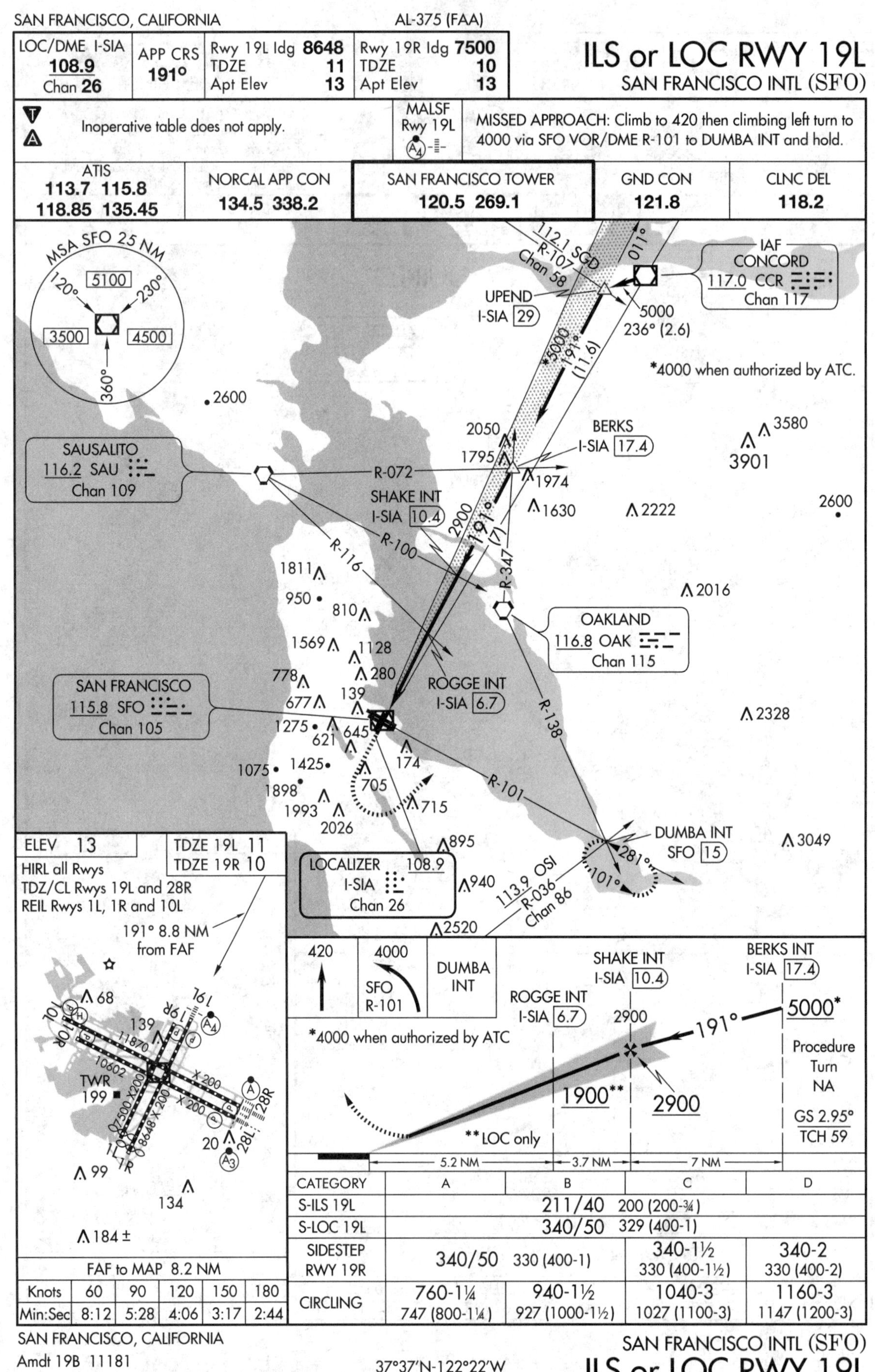

CATEGORY	A	B	C	D
S-ILS 19L	211/40 200 (200-¾)			
S-LOC 19L	340/50 329 (400-1)			
SIDESTEP RWY 19R	340/50 330 (400-1)		340-1½ 330 (400-1½)	340-2 330 (400-2)
CIRCLING	760-1¼ 747 (800-1¼)	940-1½ 927 (1000-1½)	1040-3 1027 (1100-3)	1160-3 1147 (1200-3)

Knots	60	90	120	150	180
Min:Sec	8:12	5:28	4:06	3:17	2:44

Figure 330. ILS or LOC RWY 19L (SFO).

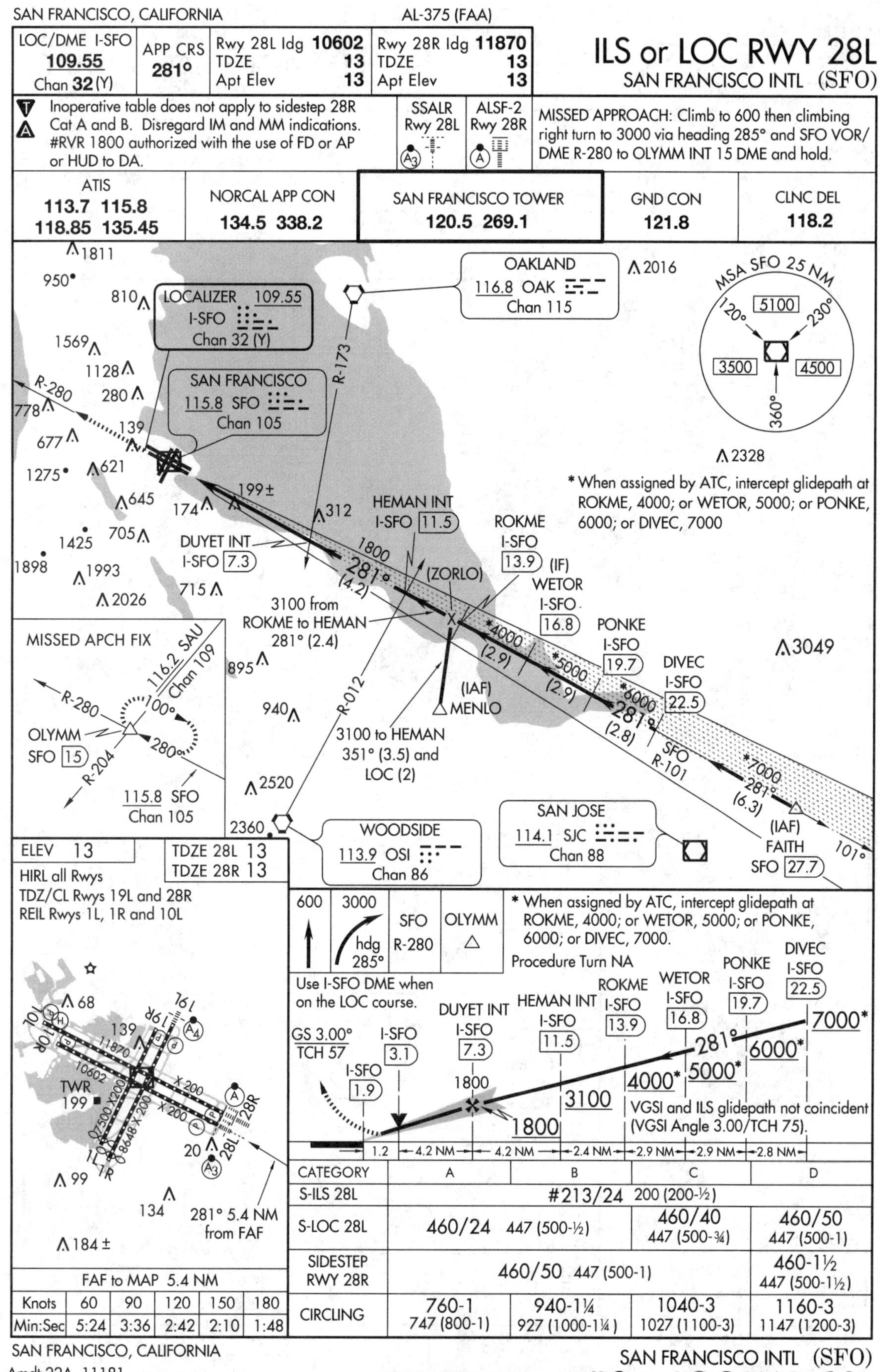

Knots	60	90	120	150	180
Min:Sec	5:24	3:36	2:42	2:10	1:48

CATEGORY	A	B	C	D
S-ILS 28L	#213/24 200 (200-½)			
S-LOC 28L	460/24 447 (500-½)		460/40 447 (500-¾)	460/50 447 (500-1)
SIDESTEP RWY 28R	460/50 447 (500-1)			460-1½ 447 (500-1½)
CIRCLING	760-1 747 (800-1)	940-1¼ 927 (1000-1¼)	1040-3 1027 (1100-3)	1160-3 1147 (1200-3)

Figure 331. ILS or LOC RWY 28L (SFO).

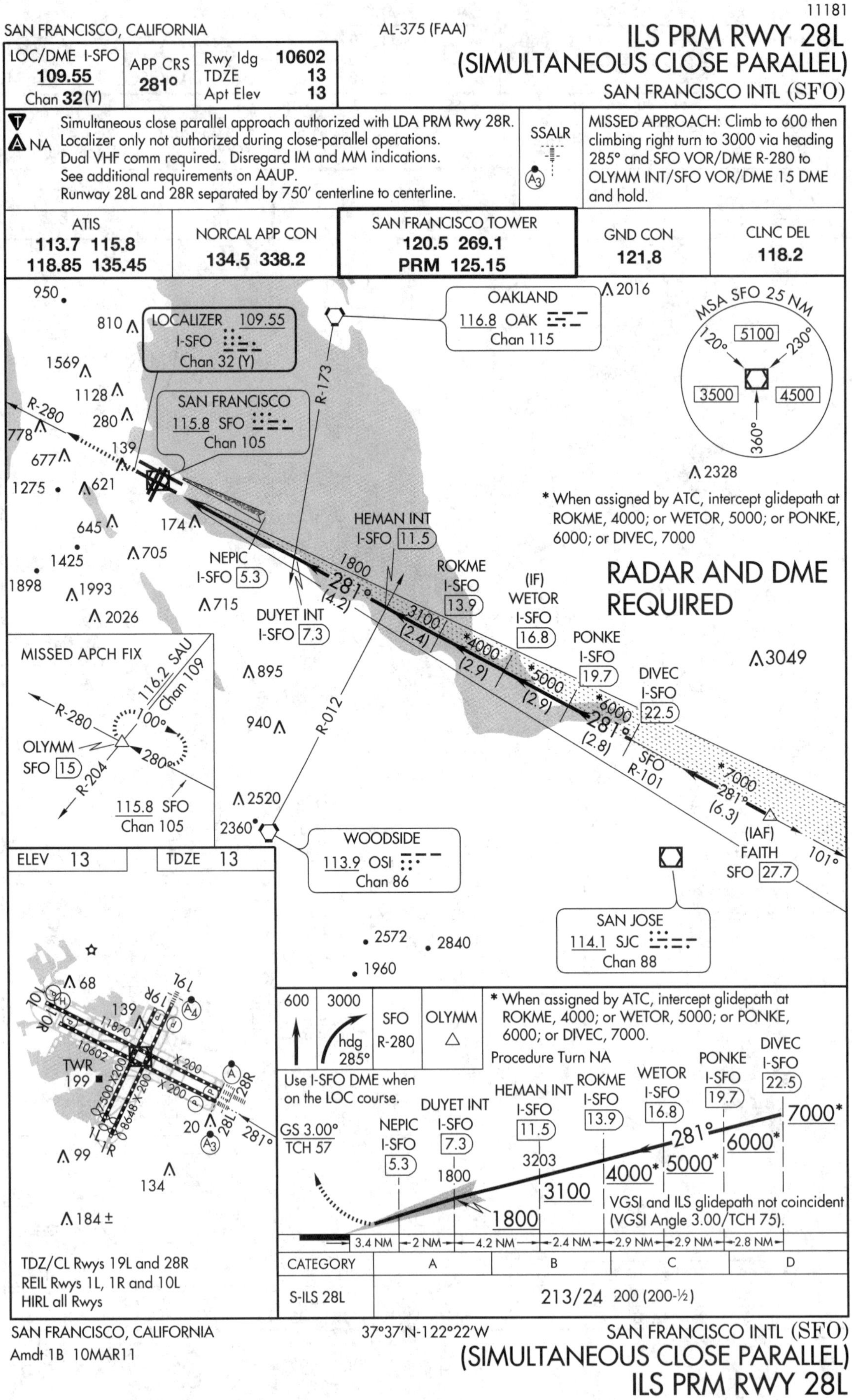
11181
SAN FRANCISCO, CALIFORNIA
AL-375 (FAA)
ILS PRM RWY 28L
(SIMULTANEOUS CLOSE PARALLEL)
SAN FRANCISCO INTL (SFO)
LOC/DME I-SFO 109.55 Chan 32 (Y)
APP CRS 281°
Rwy ldg 10602
TDZE 13
Apt Elev 13
Simultaneous close parallel approach authorized with LDA PRM Rwy 28R.
NA Localizer only not authorized during close-parallel operations.
Dual VHF comm required. Disregard IM and MM indications.
See additional requirements on AAUP.
Runway 28L and 28R separated by 750′ centerline to centerline.
SSALR
MISSED APPROACH: Climb to 600 then climbing right turn to 3000 via heading 285° and SFO VOR/DME R-280 to OLYMM INT/SFO VOR/DME 15 DME and hold.
ATIS 113.7 115.8 118.85 135.45
NORCAL APP CON 134.5 338.2
SAN FRANCISCO TOWER 120.5 269.1 PRM 125.15
GND CON 121.8
CLNC DEL 118.2
LOCALIZER 109.55 I-SFO Chan 32 (Y)
SAN FRANCISCO 115.8 SFO Chan 105
OAKLAND 116.8 OAK Chan 115
MSA SFO 25 NM
5100
3500
4500
120°
230°
360°
R-280
R-173
R-012
HEMAN INT I-SFO 11.5
NEPIC I-SFO 5.3
DUYET INT I-SFO 7.3
ROKME I-SFO 13.9
(IF) WETOR I-SFO 16.8
PONKE I-SFO 19.7
DIVEC I-SFO 22.5
* When assigned by ATC, intercept glidepath at ROKME, 4000; or WETOR, 5000; or PONKE, 6000; or DIVEC, 7000
RADAR AND DME REQUIRED
1800 281° (4.2)
3100 (2.4)
*4000 (2.9)
*5000 (2.9)
*6000 281° (2.8)
SFO R-101
*7000 281° (6.3)
(IAF) FAITH SFO 27.7
101°
MISSED APCH FIX
116.2 SAU Chan 109
R-280
100°
280°
OLYMM SFO 15
R-204
115.8 SFO Chan 105
WOODSIDE 113.9 OSI Chan 86
SAN JOSE 114.1 SJC Chan 88
ELEV 13
TDZE 13
TWR 199
10602
11870
8648 X 200
X 200
281°
TDZ/CL Rwys 19L and 28R
REIL Rwys 1L, 1R and 10L
HIRL all Rwys
600
3000
hdg 285°
SFO R-280
OLYMM
* When assigned by ATC, intercept glidepath at ROKME, 4000; or WETOR, 5000; or PONKE, 6000; or DIVEC, 7000.
Procedure Turn NA
Use I-SFO DME when on the LOC course.
GS 3.00° TCH 57
3203
1800
3100
4000*
5000*
6000*
7000*
VGSI and ILS glidepath not coincident (VGSI Angle 3.00/TCH 75).
3.4 NM
2 NM
4.2 NM
2.4 NM
2.9 NM
2.9 NM
2.8 NM
CATEGORY A B C D
S-ILS 28L 213/24 200 (200-½)
SAN FRANCISCO, CALIFORNIA
Amdt 1B 10MAR11
37°37′N-122°22′W
SAN FRANCISCO INTL (SFO)
(SIMULTANEOUS CLOSE PARALLEL)
ILS PRM RWY 28L

Figure 332. ILS PRM RWY 28L (Simultaneous Close Parallel) (SFO).

ILS PRM RWY 28L Amdt 1B 11069 AL-375 (FAA)
(SIMULTANEOUS CLOSE PARALLEL)

SAN FRANCISCO INTL (SFO)
SAN FRANCISCO, CALIFORNIA

ATTENTION ALL USERS PAGE (AAUP)

Condensed Briefing Points:

- Listen to the PRM monitor frequency when communicating with NORCAL approach control (135.65), no later than LOC intercept.
- Expect to be switched to SFO Tower (120.5) at NEPIC (I-SFO 5.3 DME).
- PRM monitor frequency may be de-selected after determining that the aircraft is on the tower frequency.

1. **ATIS.** When the ATIS broadcast advises that simultaneous ILS/PRM and LDA/PRM approaches are in progress, pilots should brief to fly the ILS/PRM 28L approach. If later advised to expect an ILS 28L approach, the ILS/PRM 28L chart may be used after completing the following briefing items:

(a) Minimums and missed approach procedures are unchanged.
(b) Monitor frequency no longer required.
(c) A different glideslope intercept altitude may be assigned when advised to expect the ILS 28L approach.

Simultaneous parallel approaches will only be offered/conducted when the weather is at least 2100 feet (ceiling) and 4 miles (visibility).

2. **Dual VHF Communication required.** To avoid blocked transmissions, each runway will have two frequencies, a primary and a PRM monitor frequency. The NORCAL approach controller will transmit on both frequencies. The PRM Monitor controller's transmissions, if needed, will override both frequencies. Pilots will ONLY transmit on the approach controller's frequency (135.65), but will listen to both frequencies. Select the PRM monitor frequency audio only when in contact with NORCAL approach control (135.65). The volume levels should be set about the same on both radios so that the pilots will be able to hear transmissions on at least one frequency if the other is blocked. The PRM monitor frequency may be de-selected passing NEPIC.

3. **ALL "Breakouts"** are to be hand flown to assure that the maneuver is accomplished in the shortest amount of time. Pilots, when directed by ATC to break off an approach, must assume that an aircraft is blundering toward their course and a breakout must be initiated immediately.

(a) ATC Directed "Breakouts:" ATC directed breakouts will consist of a turn and a climb or descent. Pilots must always initiate the breakout in response to an air traffic controller instruction. Controllers will give a descending breakout only when there are no other reasonable options available, but in no case will the descent be below minimum vectoring altitude (MVA) which provides at least 1000 feet required obstruction clearance. The MVA in the final approach segment is 1600 feet at San Francisco International Airport.

(b) Phraseology - "TRAFFIC ALERT:" If an aircraft enters the "NO TRANSGRESSION ZONE" (NTZ), the controller will breakout the threatened aircraft on the adjacent approach. The phraseology for the breakout will be:

"TRAFFIC ALERT, (aircraft call sign) TURN (left/right) IMMEDIATELY, HEADING (degrees), CLIMB/DESCEND AND MAINTAIN (altitude)".

4. Descending on (not above) the ILS glideslope ensures complying with any charted crossing restrictions and assists traffic on the LDA PRM 28R approach to mitigate possible wake turbulence encounters without destabilizing the LDA approach and creating a go-around.

5. **LDA Traffic:** While conducting this ILS/PRM approach to Runway 28L, other aircraft may be conducting the offset LDA/PRM approach to Runway 28R. These aircraft will approach from the right-rear and will re-align with 28R after making visual contact with the ILS traffic.

Special pilot training required. Pilots who are unable to participate will be afforded appropriate arrival services as operational conditions permit and must notify the controlling ARTCC as soon as practical, but at least 100 miles from destination.

(SIMULTANEOUS CLOSE PARALLEL)
ILS PRM RWY 28L Amdt 1B 11069 37°37'N-122°22'W

SAN FRANCISCO, CALIFORNIA
SAN FRANCISCO INTL (SFO)

Figure 333. ILS PRM RWY 28L (Simultaneous Close Parallel) (SFO).

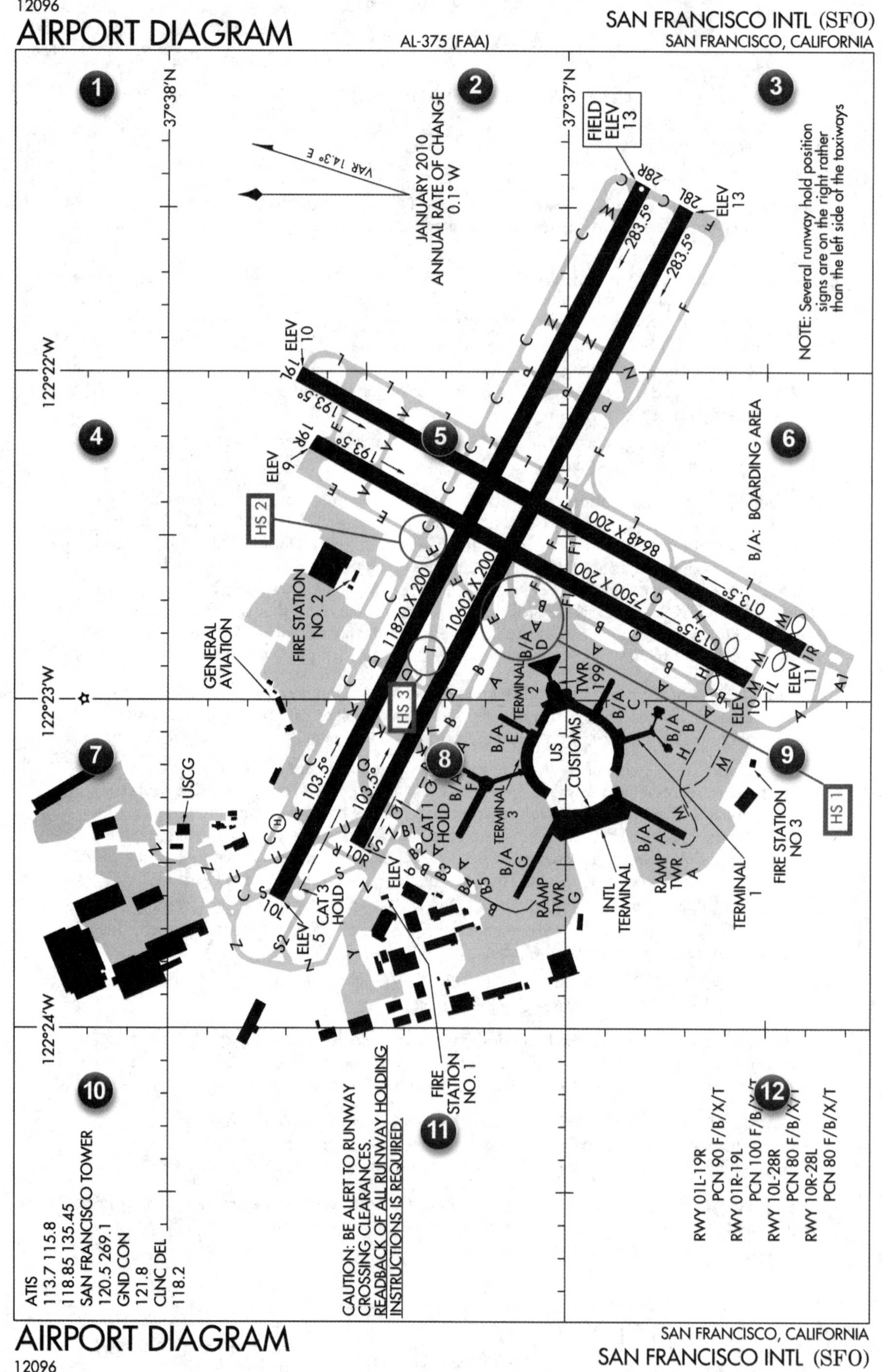

Figure 335. Airport Diagram (SFO).

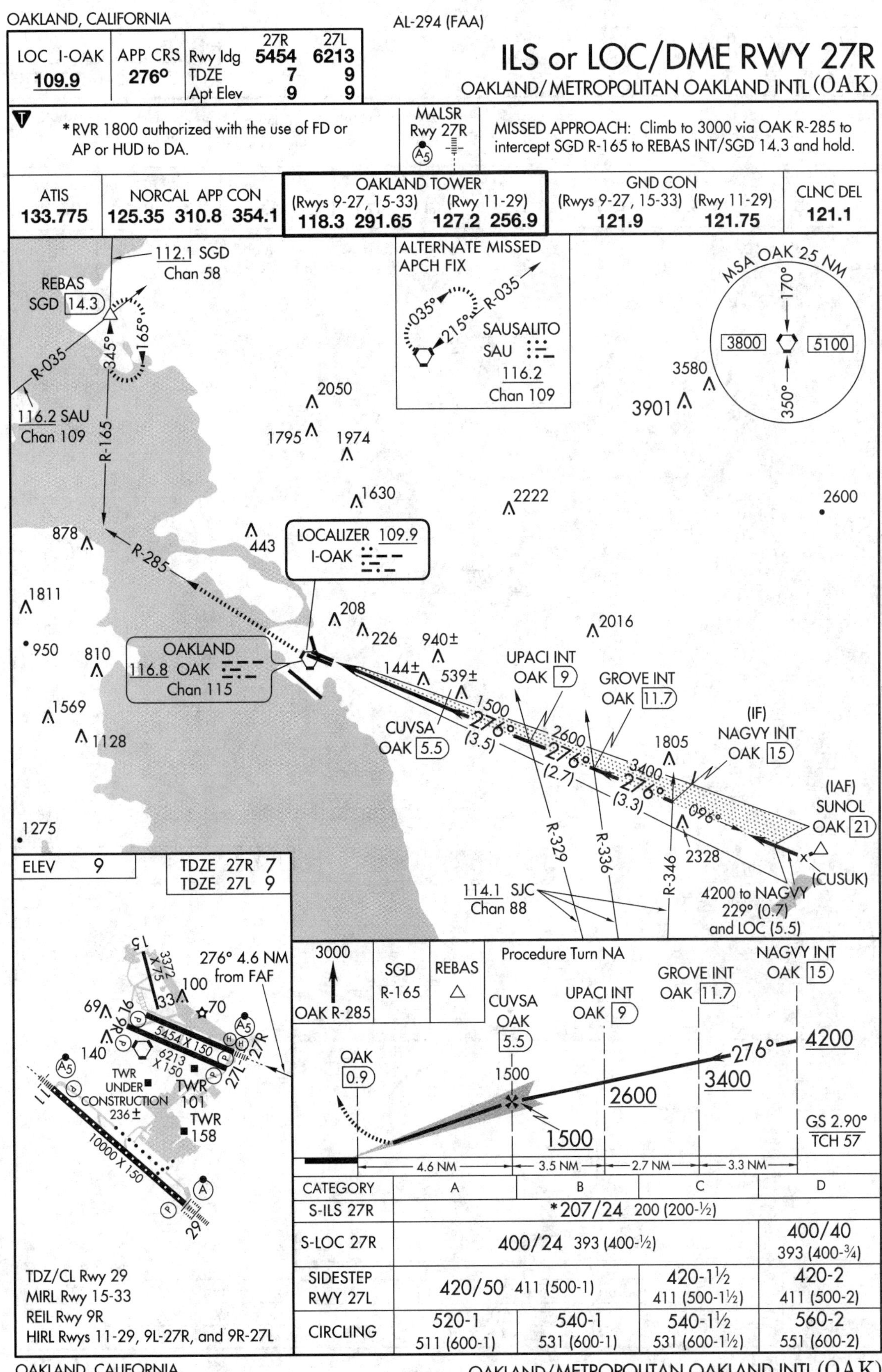

CATEGORY	A	B	C	D
S-ILS 27R	*207/24 200 (200-½)			
S-LOC 27R	400/24 393 (400-½)			400/40 393 (400-¾)
SIDESTEP RWY 27L	420/50 411 (500-1)		420-1½ 411 (500-1½)	420-2 411 (500-2)
CIRCLING	520-1 511 (600-1)	540-1 531 (600-1)	540-1½ 531 (600-1½)	560-2 551 (600-2)

Figure 336. ILS or LOC/DME RWY 27R (OAK).

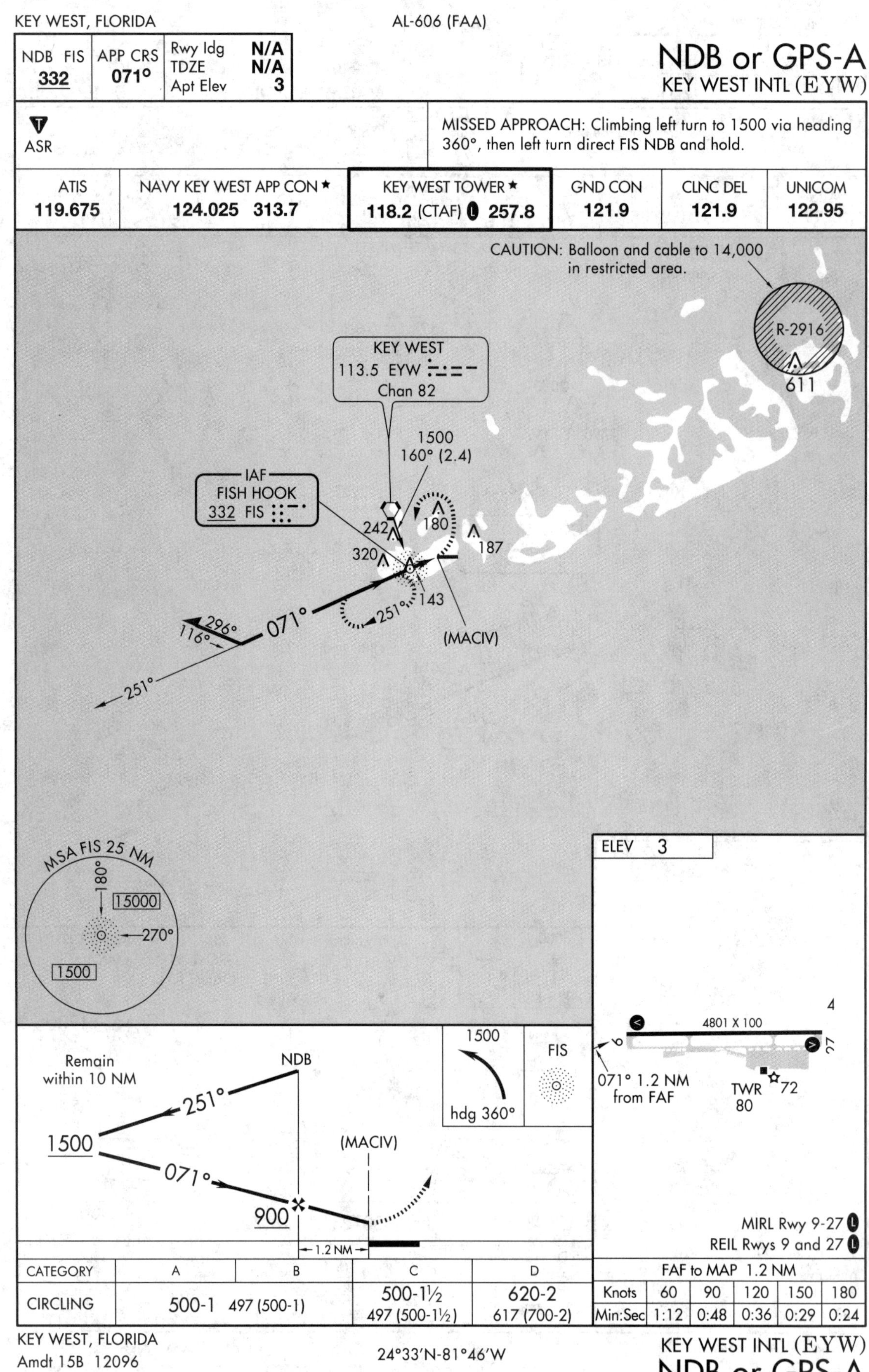

CATEGORY	A	B	C	D
CIRCLING	500-1	497 (500-1)	500-1½ 497 (500-1½)	620-2 617 (700-2)

FAF to MAP 1.2 NM

Knots	60	90	120	150	180
Min:Sec	1:12	0:48	0:36	0:29	0:24

Figure 337. NDB or GPS-A (EYW).

KEY WEST, FLORIDA — AL-606 (FAA)

WAAS CH 82100 W27A	APP CRS 273°	Rwy ldg 4801 TDZE 3 Apt Elev 3

RNAV (GPS) RWY 27

KEY WEST INTL (EYW)

DME/DME RNP-0.3 NA. If local altimeter setting not received, use Key West NAS/Boca Chica Fld altimeter setting.

ASR

MISSED APPROACH: Climb to 2400 direct ATNAW and via 003° track to CHETS and hold.

ATIS	NAVY KEY WEST APP CON ★	KEY WEST TOWER ★	GND CON	CLNC DEL	UNICOM
119.675	124.025 313.7	118.2 (CTAF) L 257.8	121.9	121.9	122.95

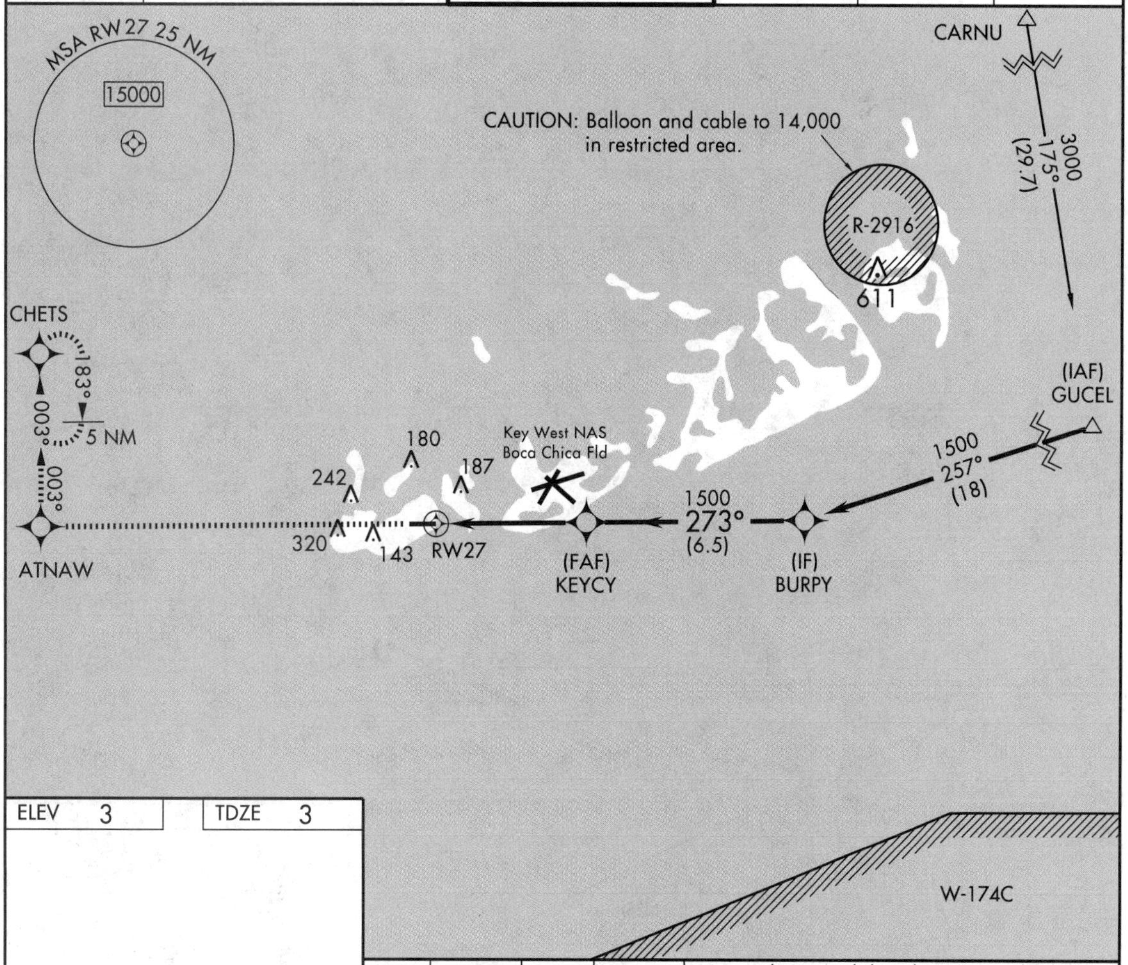

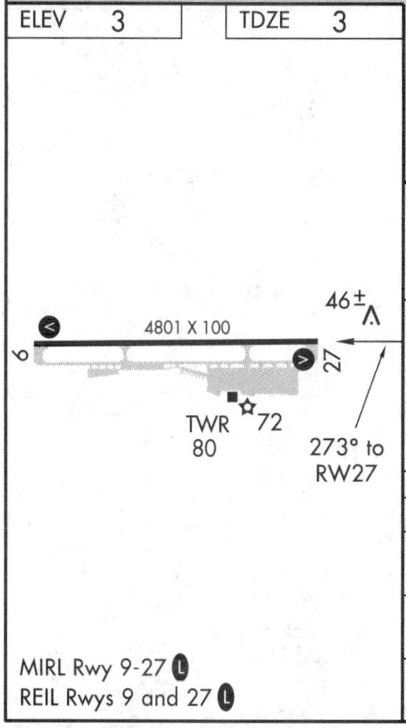

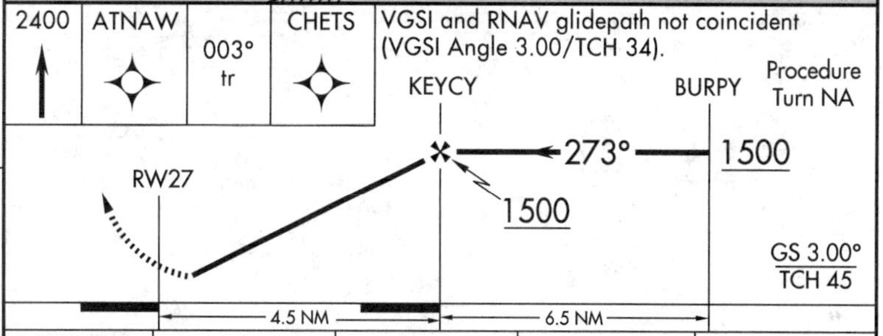

CATEGORY	A	B	C	D
LPV DA	253-1 250 (300-1)			
LNAV MDA	420-1 417 (500-1)		420-1¼ 417 (500-1¼)	
CIRCLING	500-1 497 (500-1)		500-1½ 497 (500-1½)	620-2 617 (700-2)

KEY WEST, FLORIDA
Orig 12096

24°33'N-81°46'W

KEY WEST INTL (EYW)
RNAV (GPS) RWY 27

Figure 338. RNAV (GPS) RWY 27 (EYW).

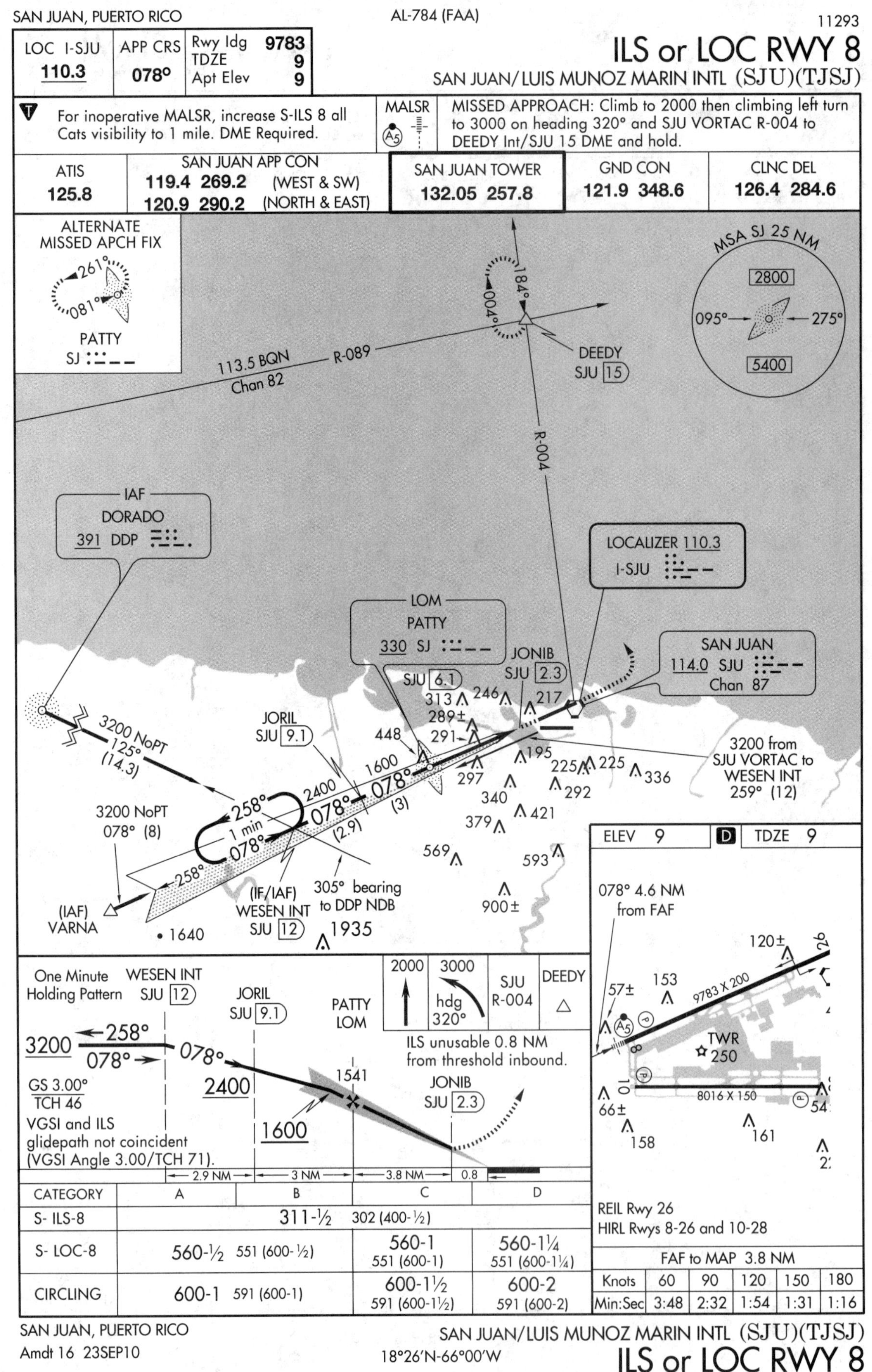

Figure 339. ILS or LOC RWY 8 (SJU) (TJSJ).

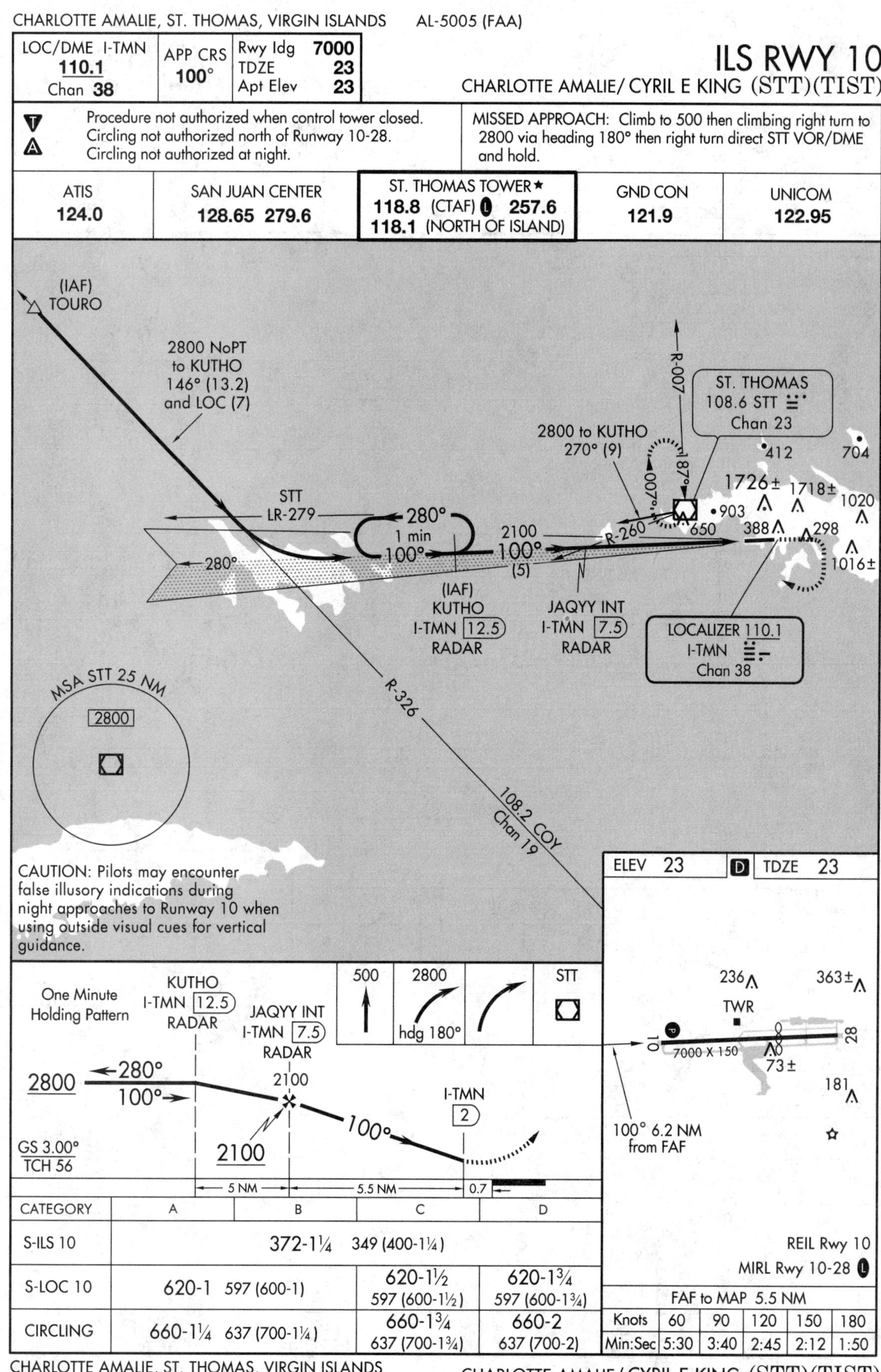

CATEGORY	A	B	C	D
S-ILS 10	372-1¼ 349 (400-1¼)			
S-LOC 10	620-1 597 (600-1)		620-1½ 597 (600-1½)	620-1¾ 597 (600-1¾)
CIRCLING	660-1¼ 637 (700-1¼)		660-1¾ 637 (700-1¾)	660-2 637 (700-2)

FAF to MAP 5.5 NM

Knots	60	90	120	150	180
Min:Sec	5:30	3:40	2:45	2:12	1:50

CHARLOTTE AMALIE, ST. THOMAS, VIRGIN ISLANDS
Amdt 1A 11181
18°20'N - 64°58'W
CHARLOTTE AMALIE/ CYRIL E KING (STT)(TIST)
ILS RWY 10

Figure 340. ILS RWY 10 (STT) (TIST).

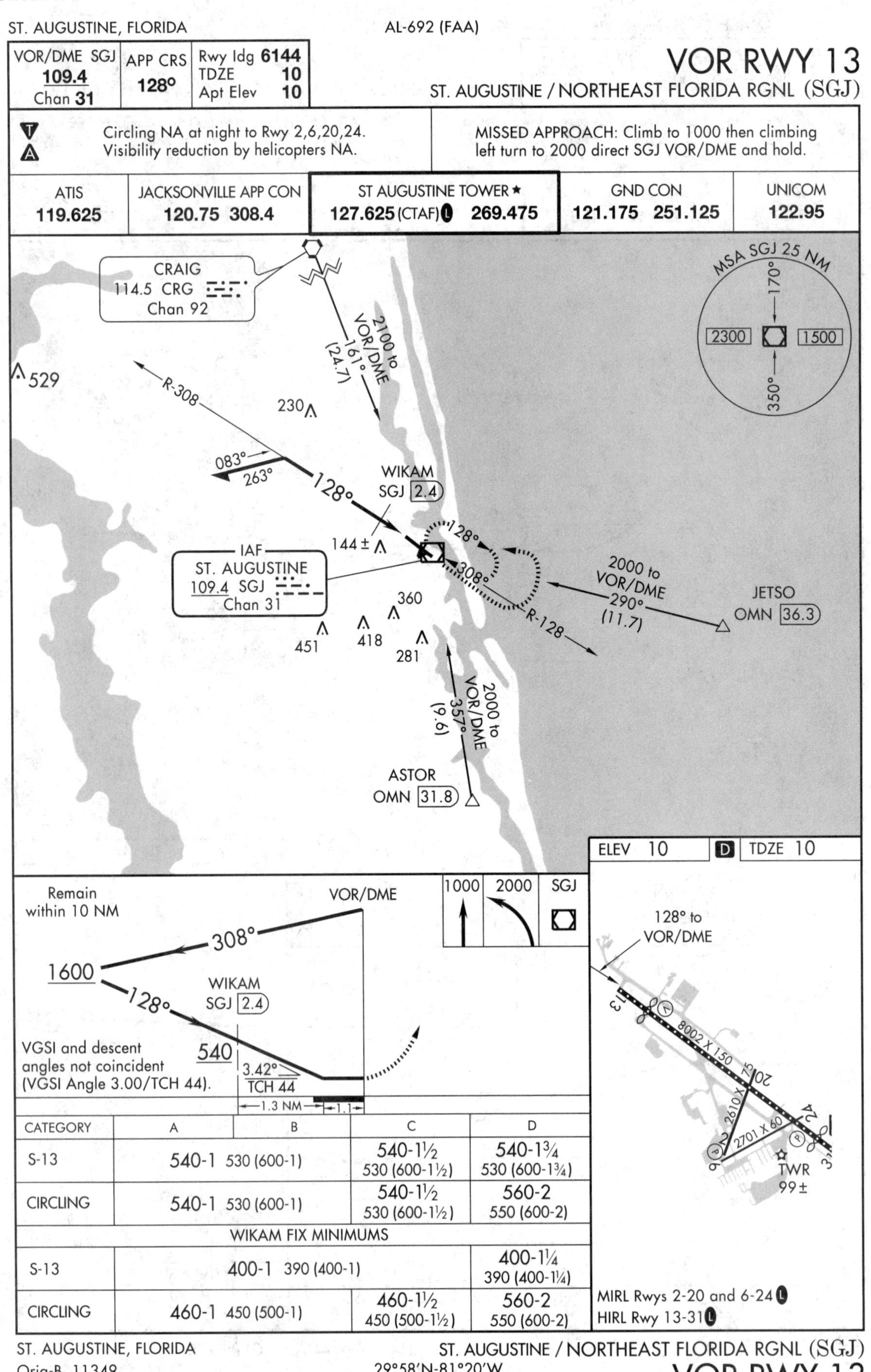

CATEGORY	A	B	C	D
S-13	540-1 530 (600-1)		540-1½ 530 (600-1½)	540-1¾ 530 (600-1¾)
CIRCLING	540-1 530 (600-1)		540-1½ 530 (600-1½)	560-2 550 (600-2)
WIKAM FIX MINIMUMS				
S-13	400-1 390 (400-1)			400-1¼ 390 (400-1¼)
CIRCLING	460-1 450 (500-1)		460-1½ 450 (500-1½)	560-2 550 (600-2)

Figure 341. VOR RWY 13 (SGJ).

ST. AUGUSTINE, FLORIDA

AL-692 (FAA)

WAAS CH 77711 W13A	APP CRS 130°	Rwy Idg 6144 TDZE 10 Apt Elev 10

RNAV (GPS) RWY 13

ST. AUGUSTINE / NORTHEAST FLORIDA RGNL (SGJ)

Baro-VNAV NA when using Jacksonville NAS/Towers Field altimeter setting. For uncompensated Baro-VNAV systems, LNAV/VNAV NA below -15°C (5°F) or above 48°C (118°F). DME/DME RNP-0.3 NA. Visibility reduction by helicopters NA. When local altimeter setting not received, use Jacksonville NAS/Towers Field altimeter setting and increase all DA 57 feet and all MDA 60 feet, increase LPV and LNAV/VNAV all Cats. visibility ¼ mile.

MISSED APPROACH: Climb to 2000 direct YUTKA and hold.

ATIS	JACKSONVILLE APP CON	ST AUGUSTINE TOWER ★	GND CON	UNICOM
119.625	120.75 308.4	127.625 (CTAF) 269.475	121.175 251.125	122.95

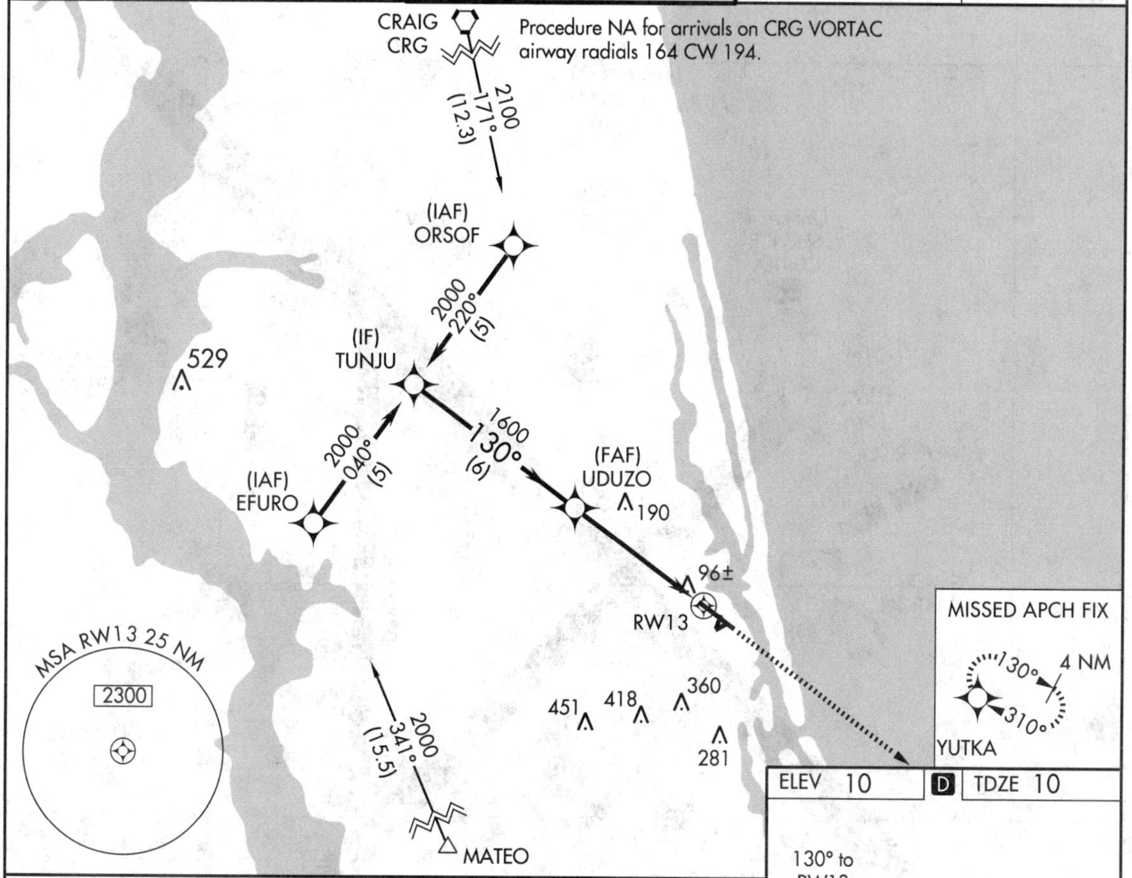

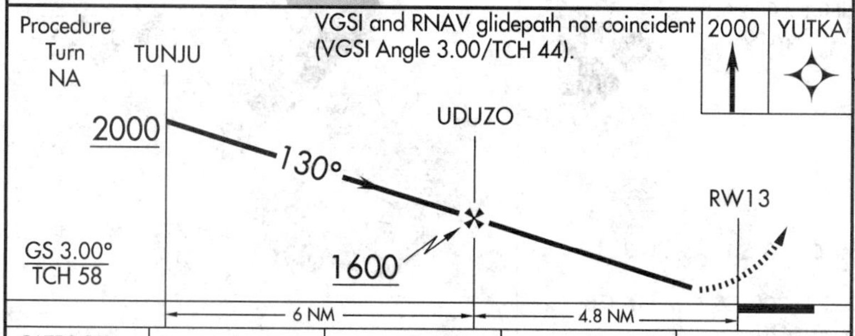

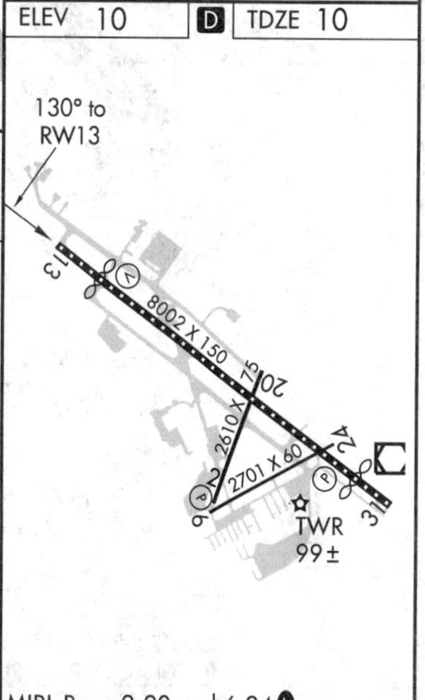

CATEGORY	A	B	C	D
LPV DA	357-1¼ 347 (400-1¼)			
LNAV/ VNAV DA	391-1¼ 381 (400-1¼)			
LNAV MDA	440-1 430 (500-1)		440-1¼ 430 (500-1¼)	440-1½ 430 (500-1½)
CIRCLING	460-1 450 (500-1)		460-1½ 450 (500-1½)	580-2 570 (600-2)

MIRL Rwys 2-20 and 6-24
HIRL Rwy 13-31

ST. AUGUSTINE, FLORIDA
Orig 11349

29°58′N-81°20′W

ST. AUGUSTINE / NORTHEAST FLORIDA RGNL (SGJ)

RNAV (GPS) RWY 13

Figure 342. RNAV (GPS) RWY 13 (SGJ).

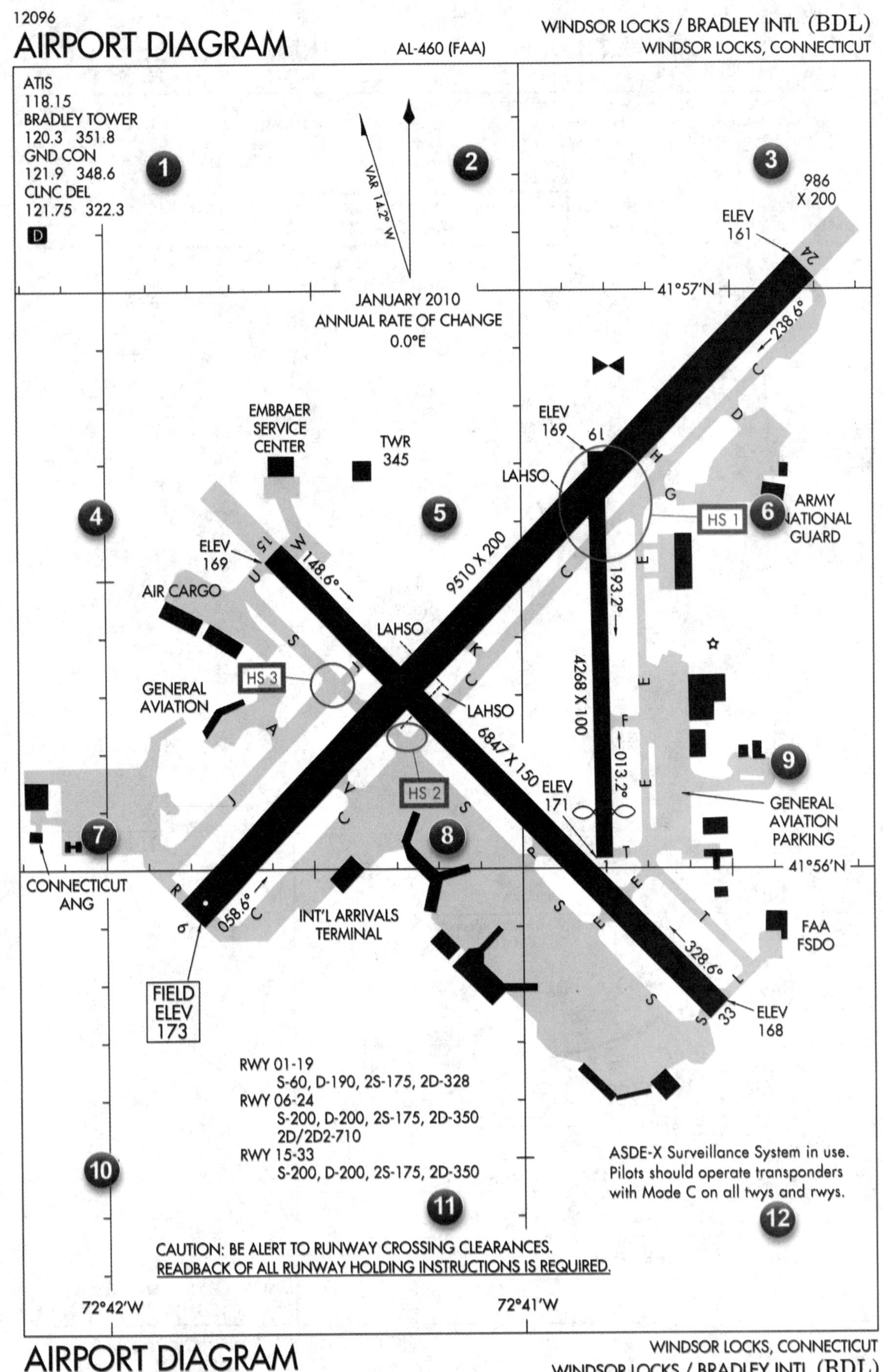

Figure 343. Airport Diagram (BDL).

WINDSOR LOCKS, CONNECTICUT AL-460 (FAA) 11321

LOC/DME I-BDL 111.1 Chan 48	APP CRS 058°	Rwy ldg 9509 THRE 173 Apt Elev 173

COPTER ILS or LOC RWY 6

WINDSOR LOCKS / BRADLEY INTL (BDL)

For inoperative ALSF-2, increase H-ILS 6 visibility to RVR 2400 and H-LOC 6 visibility to RVR 4000.

ALSF-2

MISSED APPROACH: Climb to 4000 then left turn direct BAF VORTAC and hold.

ATIS	BRADLEY APP CON	BRADLEY TOWER	GND CON	CLNC DEL
118.15	127.225 323.2	120.3 351.8	121.9 348.6	121.75 322.3

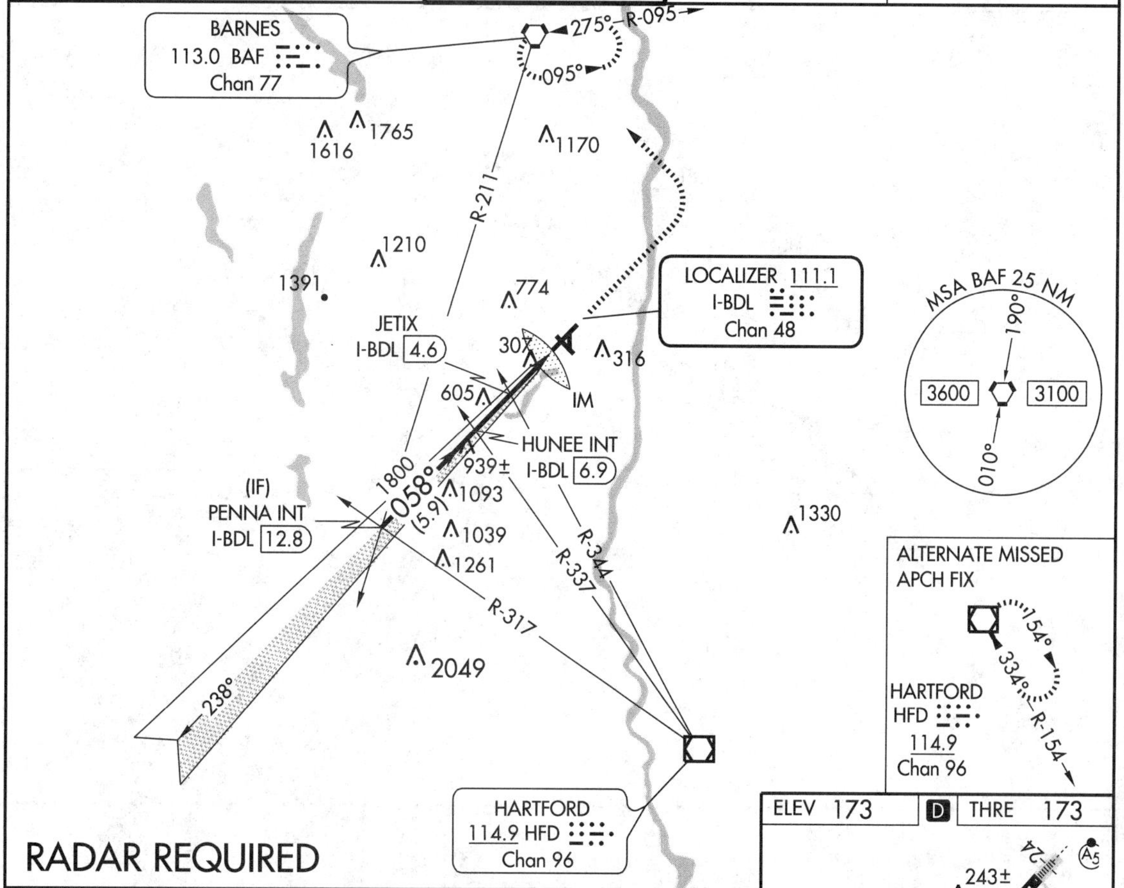

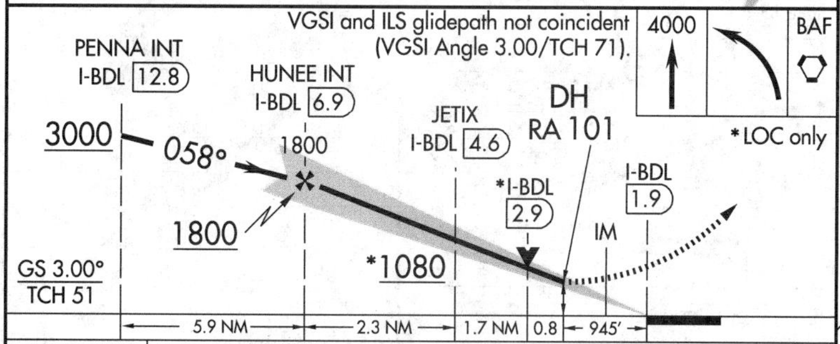

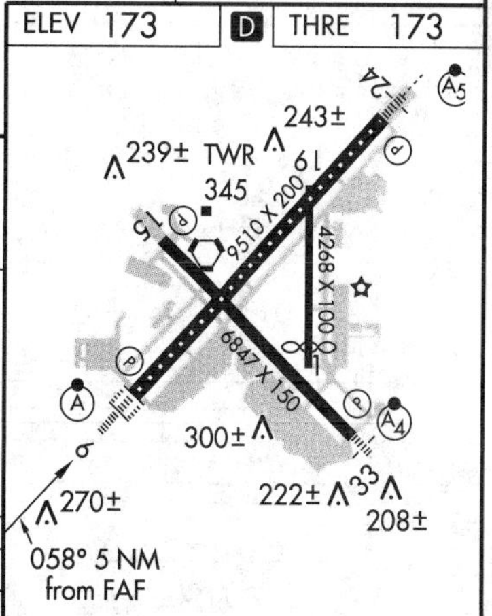

TDZ/CL Rwy 6 and 24
HIRL Rwys 6-24 and 15-33
MIRL Rwy 1-19
REIL Rwy 15

CATEGORY	COPTER
H-ILS 6	273/12 100 (100-¼)
H-LOC 6	1080/24 907 (1000-½)
JETIX FIX MINIMUMS	
H-LOC 6	560/24 387 (400-½)

COPTER ILS CATEGORY II - SPECIAL AIRCREW & AIRCRAFT CERTIFICATION REQUIRED

FAF to MAP 5 NM

Knots	60	90	120	150	180
Min:Sec	5:00	3:20	2:30	2:00	1:40

WINDSOR LOCKS, CONNECTICUT
Amdt 1 17NOV11 41°56'N-72°41'W

WINDSOR LOCKS / BRADLEY INTL (BDL)
COPTER ILS or LOC RWY 6

Figure 344. COPTER ILS or LOC RWY 6 (BDL).

WINDSOR LOCKS, CONNECTICUT | AL-460 (FAA) | 11293

ILS or LOC RWY 6

WINDSOR LOCKS / BRADLEY INTL (BDL)

LOC/DME I-BDL 111.1 Chan 48	APP CRS 058°	Rwy ldg 9509 THRE 173 Apt Elev 173

For inoperative ALSF-2, increase S-ILS 6 all Cats visibility to RVR 4000. JETIX Fix Minimums: For inoperative ALSF-2, increase S-LOC 6 Cat C, D visibility to RVR 6000.

ALSF-2

MISSED APPROACH: Climb to 4000 then left turn direct BAF VORTAC and hold.

ATIS	BRADLEY APP CON	BRADLEY TOWER	GND CON	CLNC DEL
118.15	127.225 323.2	120.3 351.8	121.9 348.6	121.75 322.3

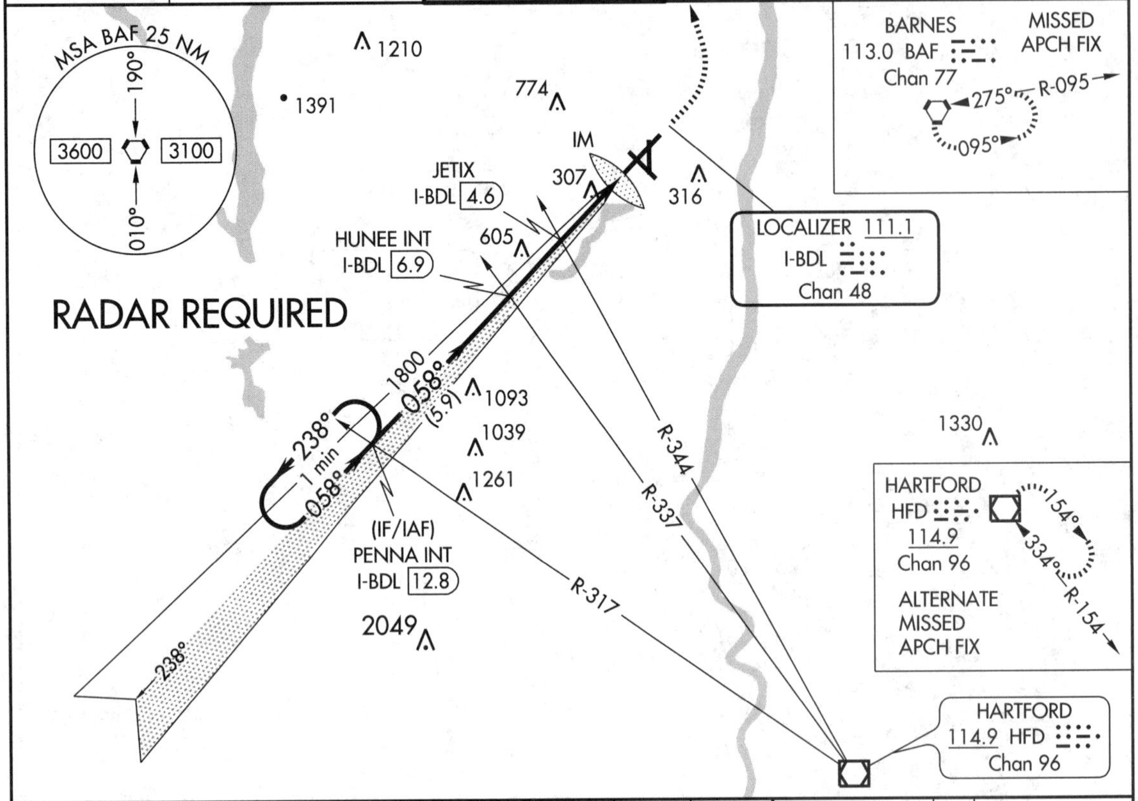

MSA BAF 25 NM
190°
3600
3100
010°

RADAR REQUIRED

1210
1391
774
IM
307
316
JETIX I-BDL 4.6
HUNEE INT I-BDL 6.9
605
LOCALIZER 111.1 I-BDL Chan 48
BARNES 113.0 BAF Chan 77
MISSED APCH FIX
275°
R-095
095°
1800
058°
(5.9)
1093
1039
1261
238°
1 min
058°
(IF/IAF) PENNA INT I-BDL 12.8
2049
238°
R-344
R-337
R-317
1330
HARTFORD HFD 114.9 Chan 96
154°
334°
R-154
ALTERNATE MISSED APCH FIX
HARTFORD 114.9 HFD Chan 96

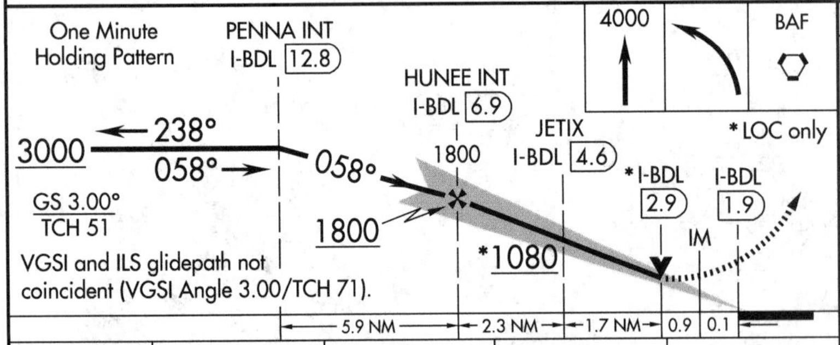

One Minute Holding Pattern
PENNA INT I-BDL 12.8
HUNEE INT I-BDL 6.9
JETIX I-BDL 4.6
4000
BAF
*LOC only
3000
238°
058°
058°
1800
1800
*1080
*I-BDL 2.9
I-BDL 1.9
IM
GS 3.00°
TCH 51
VGSI and ILS glidepath not coincident (VGSI Angle 3.00/TCH 71).
5.9 NM | 2.3 NM | 1.7 NM | 0.9 | 0.1

ELEV 173
THRE 173
243±
239± TWR 345
24
6
15
9510 X 200
4268 X 100
6847 X 150
1
19
300±
270±
222±
33
208±
058° 5 NM from FAF
TDZ/CL Rwy 6 and 24
HIRL Rwys 6-24 and 15-33
MIRL Rwy 1-19
REIL Rwy 15

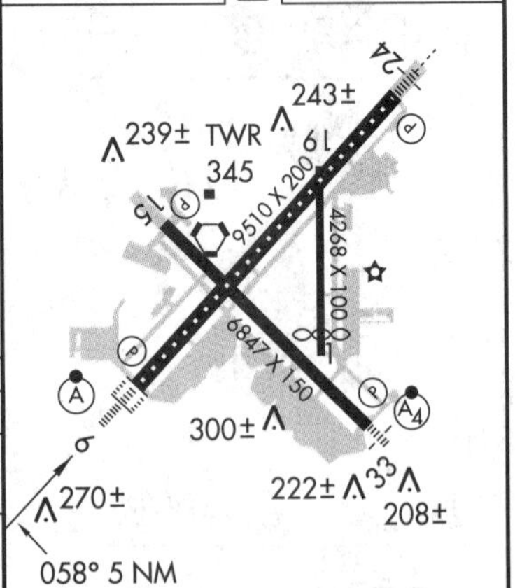

CATEGORY	A	B	C	D
S-ILS 6	373/18 200 (200-½)			
S-LOC 6	1080/40 907 (1000-¾)		1080-2 907 (1000-2)	
CIRCLING	1080-1¼ 907 (1000-1¼)		1080-2¾ 907 (1000-2¾)	1080-3 907 (1000-3)
JETIX FIX MINIMUMS				
S-LOC 6	560/24 387 (400-½)		560/35 387 (400-¾)	
CIRCLING	680-1 507 (600-1)		680-1½ 507 (600-1½)	940-2½ 767 (800-2½)

FAF to MAP 5 NM

Knots	60	90	120	150	180
Min:Sec	5:00	3:20	2:30	2:00	1:40

WINDSOR LOCKS, CONNECTICUT
Amdt 37 20OCT11
41°56′N-72°41′W
WINDSOR LOCKS / BRADLEY INTL (BDL)
ILS or LOC RWY 6

Figure 345. ILS or LOC RWY 6 (BDL).

(CSTL3.CCC) 11237 SL-460 (FAA)
COASTAL THREE DEPARTURE

WINDSOR LOCKS/ BRADLEY INTL (BDL)
WINDSOR LOCKS, CONNECTICUT

ATIS 118.15
CLNC DEL
121.75 322.3
GND CON
121.9 348.6
TOWER
120.3 351.8

1000
013°
328°
238°
148°

HARTFORD
114.9 HFD
Chan 96
N41°38.47'-W72°32.85'

2500
143°
(11)

THUMB
N41°31.40'
W72°21.53'

36
190°
(14)

YODER
N41°17.38'
W72°20.55'

22
R-010

R-057
237°
(30)

CALVERTON
117.2 CCC
Chan 119
N40°55.78'-W72°47.93'

KENNEDY
115.9 JFK
Chan 106

HAMPTON
113.6 HTO
Chan 83

7000
*3000
213°
(43)

18000
*3000
215°
(50)

R-139
R-150
R-236
R-234

SHERL
N40°15.34'
W73°07.30'
L-34, H-10-12

L456-461
J121
J174
L454-455-457-459

GEDIC
N40°08.77'
W73°12.12'
H-10-12

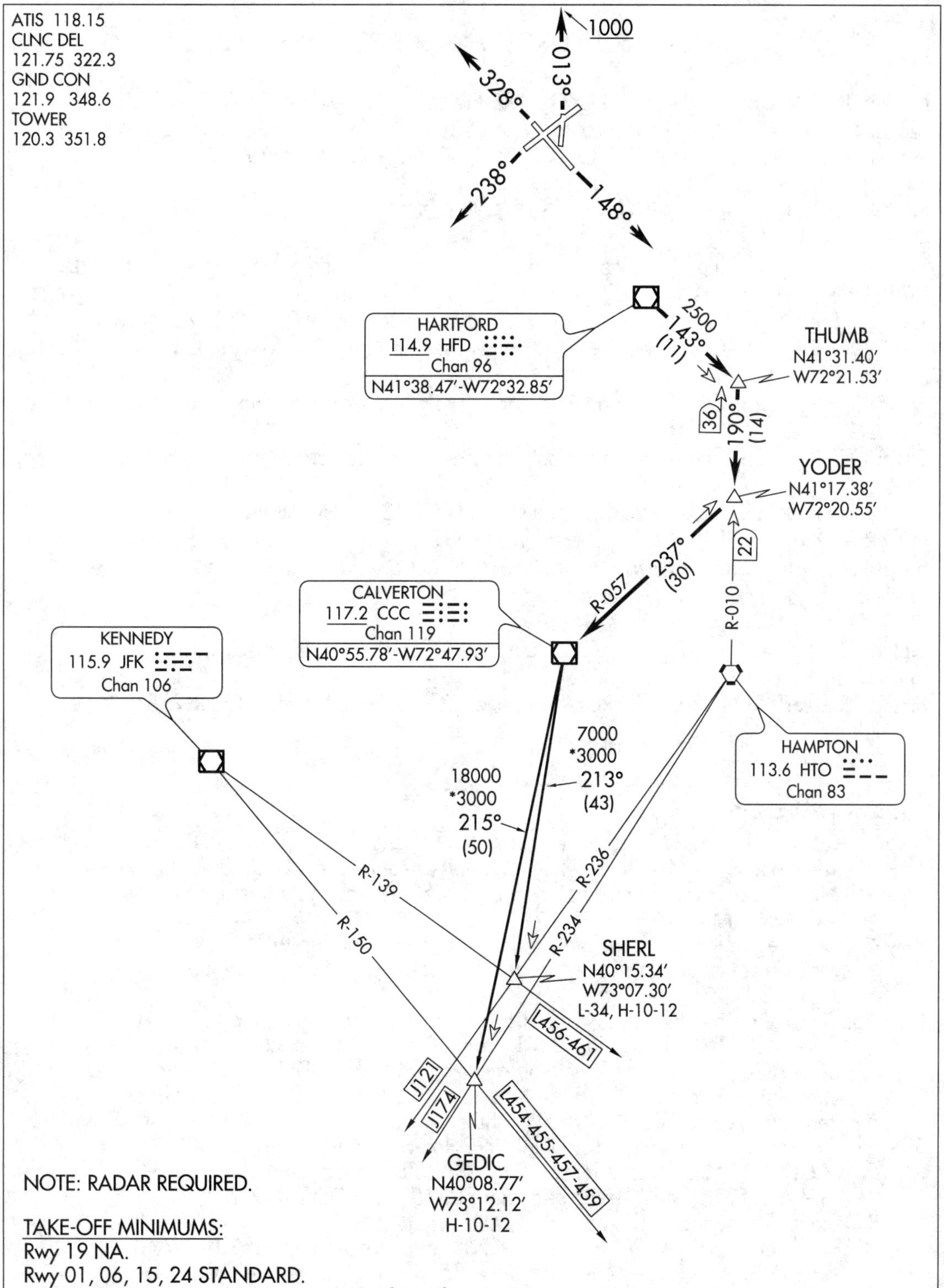

NOTE: RADAR REQUIRED.

TAKE-OFF MINIMUMS:
Rwy 19 NA.
Rwy 01, 06, 15, 24 STANDARD.
Rwy 33 STANDARD with minimum climb of 326 feet per NM to 1000.

NOTE: Chart not to scale.
(NARRATIVE ON FOLLOWING PAGE)

COASTAL THREE DEPARTURE
(CSTL3.CCC) 11237
WINDSOR LOCKS, CONNECTICUT
WINDSOR LOCKS/ BRADLEY INTL (BDL)

Figure 346. COASTAL THREE Departure (CSTL3.CCC).

(CSTL3.CCC) 10154 SL-460 (FAA)

COASTAL THREE DEPARTURE

WINDSOR LOCKS/ BRADLEY INTL (BDL)
WINDSOR LOCKS, CONNECTICUT

DEPARTURE ROUTE DESCRIPTION

NOTE: INITIAL DEPARTURE HEADINGS ARE PREDICATED ON AVOIDING NOISE SENSITIVE AREAS. FLIGHT CREW AWARENESS AND COMPLIANCE IS IMPORTANT IN MINIMIZING NOISE IMPACTS ON SURROUNDING COMMUNITIES.

NOTE: APPROPRIATE DEPARTURE CONTROL FREQUENCY TO BE ASSIGNED BY ATC.

TAKE-OFF RWY 1: Climb heading 013° to 1000 or as assigned for radar vectors to HFD VOR/DME, thence . . .
TAKE-OFF RWY 6: Fly assigned heading for radar vectors to HFD VOR/DME, thence . . .
TAKE-OFF RWY 15: Climb heading 148° or as assigned for radar vectors to HFD VOR/DME, thence . . .
TAKE-OFF RWY 24: Climb heading 238° or as assigned for radar vectors to HFD VOR/DME, thence . . .
TAKE-OFF RWY 33: Climb heading 328° or as assigned for radar vectors to HFD VOR/DME, thence . . .
. . . . From over HFD VOR/DME proceed via HFD R-143 to THUMB INT, then proceed via HTO R-010 to YODER INT, then proceed via CCC R-057 to CCC VOR/DME. Then via (transition) or (assigned route). Maintain 4000 or assigned altitude. Expect clearance to requested flight level ten minutes after departure.

GEDIC TRANSITION (CSTL3.GEDIC): From over CCC VOR/DME via CCC R-215 to GEDIC.
SHERL TRANSITION (CSTL3.SHERL): From over CCC VOR/DME via CCC R-213 to SHERL.

TAKE-OFF OBSTACLE NOTES:

Rwy 1: Vehicle on road 342′ from DER, 564′ left of centerline, 15′ AGL/184′ MSL. Trees beginning 441′ from DER, 493′ left of centerline, up to 100′ AGL/269′ MSL. Trees beginning 1884′ from DER, 45′ right of centerline, up to 100′ AGL/299′ MSL.

Rwy 6: Trees beginning 21′ from DER, 464′ left of centerline, up to 100′ AGL/249′ MSL. Trees beginning 1956′ from DER, 921′ right of centerline, up to 100′ AGL/239′ MSL.

Rwy 15: Vehicle on roadway 531′ from DER, 606′ left of centerline, up to 15′ AGL/186′ MSL. Trees beginning 2341′ from DER, 767′ left of centerline, up to 100′ AGL/244′ MSL. Vehicle on roadway 429′ from DER, 572′ right of centerline, up to 15′ AGL/186′ MSL. Tree 1520′ from DER, 786′ right of centerline, up to 100′ AGL/259′ MSL.

Rwy 24: Trees beginning 3066′ from DER, 599′ left of centerline, up to 100′ AGL/269′ MSL. OL on fence 1239′ DER, 784′ left of centerline, up to 45′ AGL/215′ MSL. Trees beginning 2345′ from DER, 489′ right of centerline, up to 100′ AGL/299′ MSL.

Rwy 33: Trees beginning 1590′ from DER, 275′ left of centerline, up to 100′ AGL/256′ MSL. Tower 2.4 NM from DER, 3534′ left of centerline, 104′ AGL/774′ MSL. Trees beginning 1618′ from DER, 264′ right of centerline, up to 100′ AGL/263′ MSL.

COASTAL THREE DEPARTURE
(CSTL3.CCC) 10154
WINDSOR LOCKS, CONNECTICUT
WINDSOR LOCKS/ BRADLEY INTL (BDL)

Figure 347. COASTAL THREE Departure (CSTL3.CCC).

TUCSON INTL (TUS) 6 S UTC–7 N32°06.97´ W110°56.46´ **PHOENIX**
2643 B S4 **FUEL** 100LL, JET A OX 1, 2, 3, 4 TPA—See Remarks AOE Class I, ARFF Index C **H–4J, L–5C**
NOTAM FILE TUS **IAP, AD**

RWY 11L–29R: H10996X150 (ASPH–GRVD) S–160, D–200, 2S–175, 2D–350, 2D/2D2–585 HIRL
RWY 11L: MALSR. PAPI(P4L)—GA 3.0° TCH 55´. 0.7% up..
RWY 29R: REIL. PAPI(P4L)—GA 3.0° TCH 76´. Ground. 0.5% down..
RWY 11R–29L: H8408X75 (ASPH) S–120, D–140, 2S–175, 2D–220 MIRL
RWY 11R: PAPI(P4L)—GA 3.0° Thld dsplcd 1410´. Rgt tfc. 0.7% up..
RWY 29L: REIL. Pole. 0.6% down..
RWY 03–21: H7000X150 (ASPH–GRVD) S–105, D–137, 2S–174, 2D–230, 2D/2D2–500 MIRL
RWY 03: Thld dsplcd 841´. Railroad.
RWY 21: REIL. PAPI(P4L)—GA 3.0° TCH 55´. Rgt tfc.

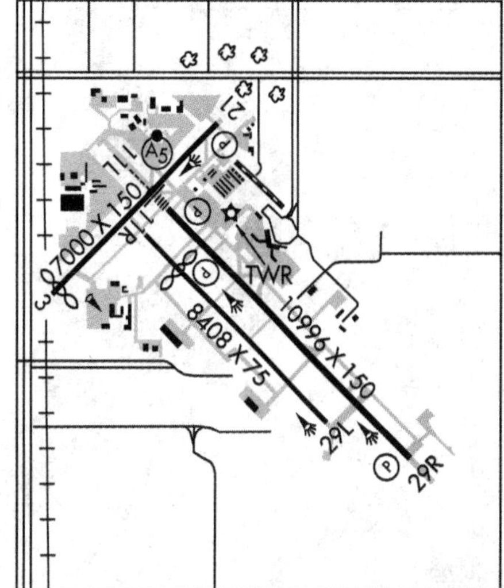

RUNWAY DECLARED DISTANCE INFORMATION
RWY 03: TORA–7000 TODA–7000 ASDA–7000 LDA–6160
RWY 21: TORA–6000 TODA–7000 ASDA–6000 LDA–6000

ARRESTING GEAR/SYSTEM
RWY 03 ← HOOK E5 (403´)
RWY 11L HOOK BAK-12B(B) (1220´ OVRN) BAK-14 BAK-12B(B) (1000´)
BAK-14 BAK-12B(B) (1215´) HOOK BAK-12B(B) (128´ OVRN) **RWY 29L**

AIRPORT REMARKS: Attended continuously. Air carriers use Rwy 11L–29R. Rwy 11R–29L rstd to acft with wing span less than 73´ and ldg speed less than 120 kt. Acft dep Rwy 11R required to attain at least 400´AGL prior to starting turn. No B–747 training except PPR; no flight training 0500–1300Z except PPR, call Flightline Office 520–573–8128. Rwy 11L–29R gross weight limit: DC–10–10 315,000 lbs, DC–10–30/40 400,000 lbs, L–1011–1 325,000 lbs, L–1011–100/200 340,000 lbs. Rwy 03–21 gross weight limit: DC–10–10 300,000 lbs DC–10–30/40 375,000 lbs, L–1011–01 310,000 lbs, L–1011–100/200 315,000 lbs. Helicopter ops located south of Rwy 11R–29L and west of Twy A13. TPA–3443 (800) small acft, 4043 (1400) large/heavy turbojet acft. B–747 acft taxi with inboard engines only. Rwy 11L touchdown runway visual range avbl. Twy T-general aviation twy 30,000 lbs. or less. Portions of Twy D not visible from twr due to hangars. Twy A5 limited to 70,000 lbs or less. REIL Rwy 29L and Rwy 29R dalgt hrs only. Ldg fee. Flight Notification Service (ADCUS) avbl. NOTE: See Special Notices—Glider Operations Northwest of Tucson, Arizona, U.S. Special Customs Requirement.

WEATHER DATA SOURCES: ASOS (520) 889-7236. **HIWAS** 116.0 TUS.LLWAS.

COMMUNICATIONS: ATIS 123.8 520-741-1177 **UNICOM** 122.95
TUCSON RCO 122.2 (PRESCOTT RADIO)
MOUNT LEMMON RCO 122.4 (PRESCOTT RADIO)
Ⓡ**APP/DEP CON** 125.1 (Rwy 11 090°-285°) (Rwy 29 275°-065°) 119.4 (Rwy 11 286°-089°) (Rwy 29 066°-274°)
TOWER 118.3 119.0 **GND CON** 124.4 **CLNC DEL** 126.65

AIRSPACE: CLASS C svc ctc **APP CON**

RADIO AIDS TO NAVIGATION: NOTAM FILE TUS.
(H) VORTACW 116.0 TUS Chan 107 N32°05.71´ W110°54.89´ 301° 1.8 NM to fld. 2672/12E. **HIWAS.**
VORTAC unusable:
050°-080° byd 30 NM blo 13,000´
350°-020° byd 30 NM blo 13,000´
DME unusable:
155°-165° byd 35 NM blo 13,000´
ILS/DME 111.7 I-TUS Chan 54 Rwy 11L. Localizer backcourse unusable byd 15 NM blo 7,200´. Backcourse unusable byd 10° right of course.

VALLE (See GRAND CANYON on page 39)

Figure 348. Excerpt from Chart Supplement.

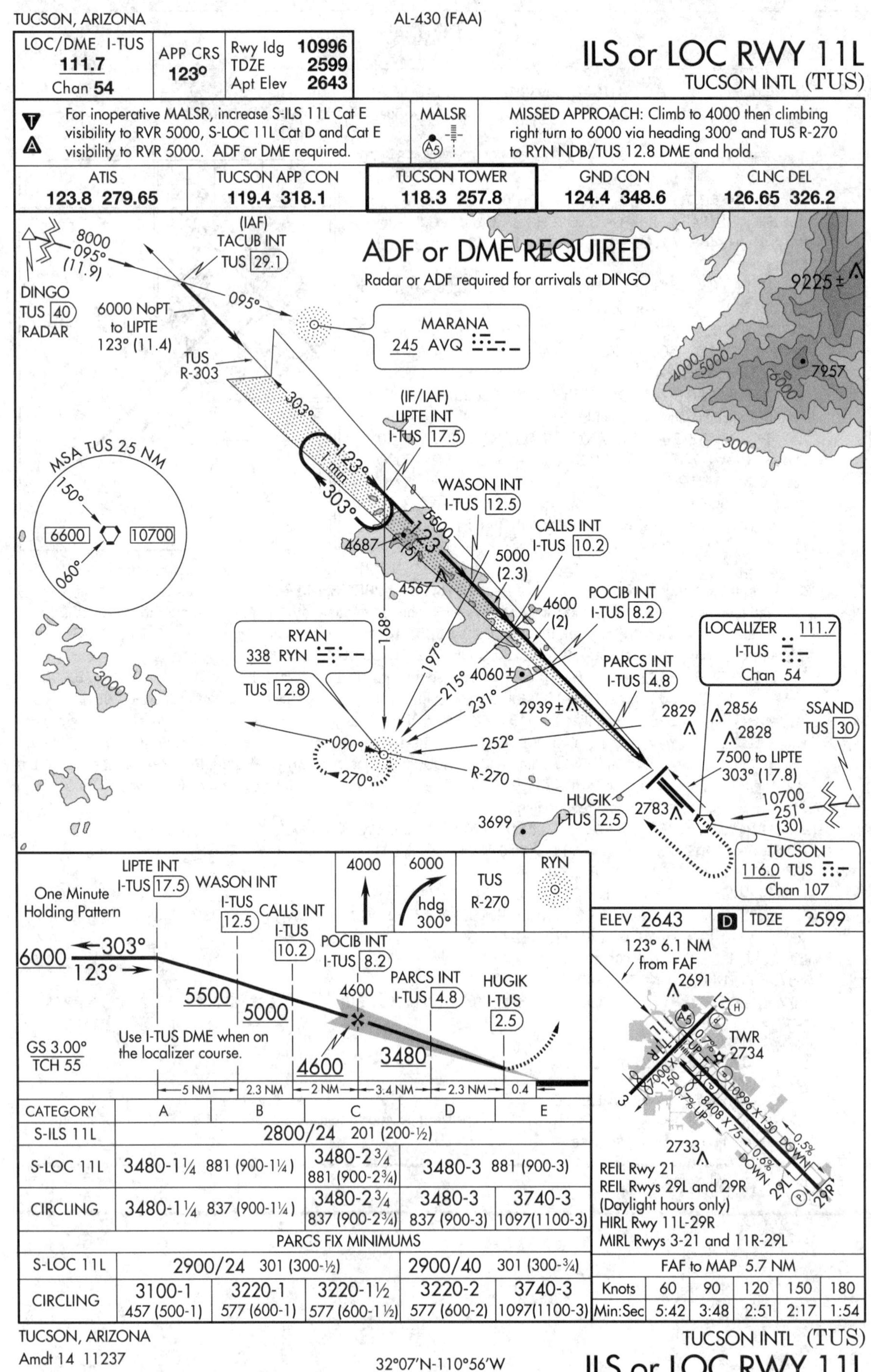

Figure 349. ILS or LOC RWY 11L (TUS).

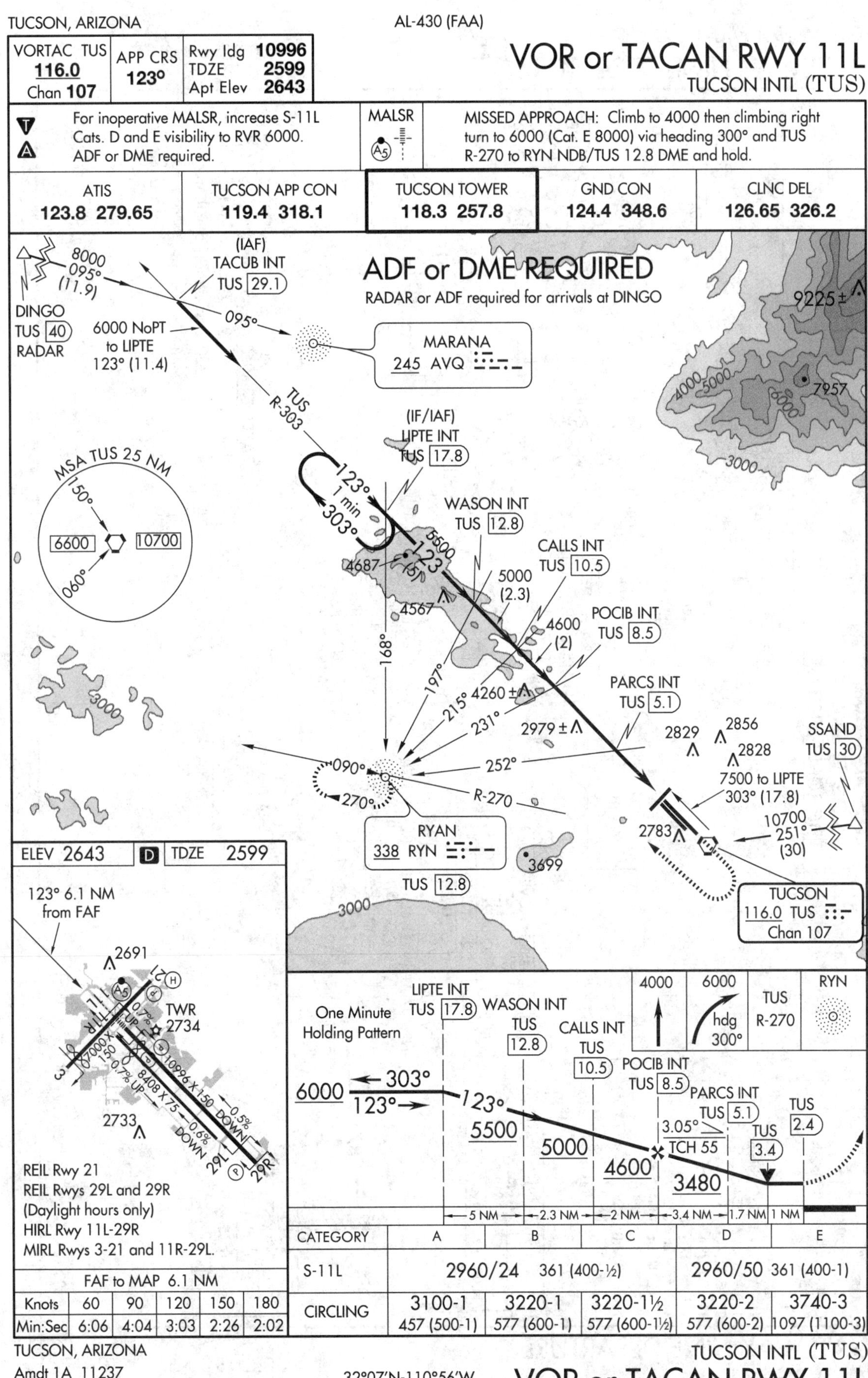

FAF to MAP 6.1 NM					
Knots	60	90	120	150	180
Min:Sec	6:06	4:04	3:03	2:26	2:02

CATEGORY	A	B	C	D	E
S-11L	2960/24 361 (400-½)			2960/50 361 (400-1)	
CIRCLING	3100-1 457 (500-1)	3220-1 577 (600-1)	3220-1½ 577 (600-1½)	3220-2 577 (600-2)	3740-3 1097 (1100-3)

Figure 350. VOR or TACAN RWY 11L (TUS).

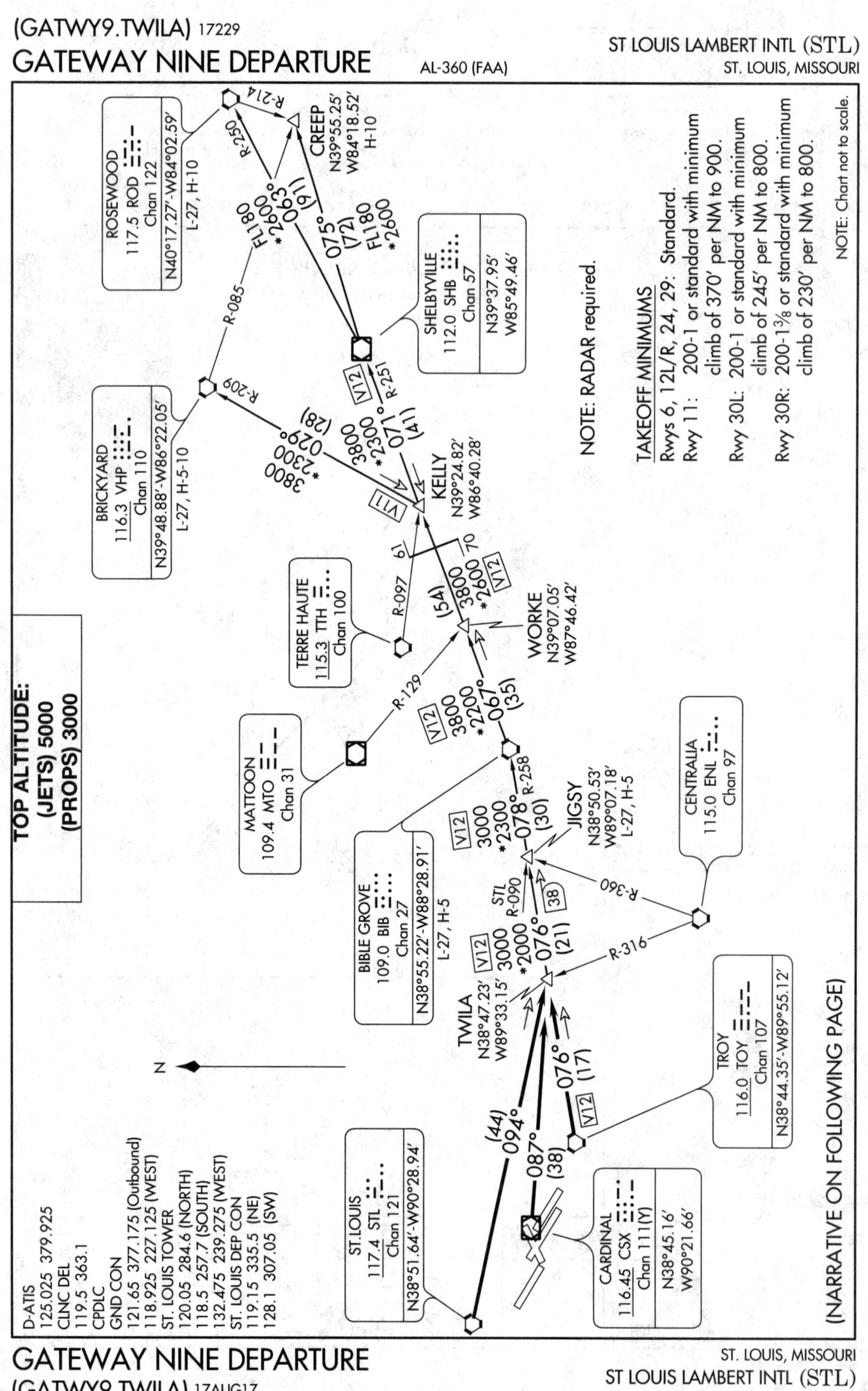

Figure 351. GATEWAY NINE Departure (GATWY9.TWILA).

(GATWY9.TWILA) 17229

GATEWAY NINE DEPARTURE AL-360 (FAA)

ST LOUIS LAMBERT INTL (STL)
ST. LOUIS, MISSOURI

DEPARTURE ROUTE DESCRIPTION

Climb on assigned heading for vector to appropriate route.

JETS: Maintain 5000 or assigned altitude, thence. . . .
PROPS: Maintain 3000 or assigned altitude, thence. . . .

. . . .from over CSX R-087 or over TOY VORTAC on TOY R-076 or over STL VORTAC on STL R-094 to TWILA INT. Then on (transition), expect clearance to filed altitude 10 minutes after departure.

BIBLE GROVE TRANSITION (GATWY9.BIB): From over TWILA on TOY R-076 to JIGSY, then on BIB R-258 to BIB VORTAC.

BRICKYARD TRANSITION (GATWY9.VHP): From over TWILA on TOY R-076 to JIGSY, then on BIB R-258 to BIB VORTAC, then on BIB R-067 to WORKE, then on BIB R-067 and SHB R-251 to KELLY, then on VHP R-209 to VHP VORTAC.

CREEP TRANSITION (GATWY9.CREEP): From over TWILA on TOY R-076 to JIGSY, then on BIB R-258 to BIB VORTAC, then on BIB R-067 to WORKE, then on BIB R-067 and SHB R-251 to KELLY, then on SHB R-251 to SHB VOR/DME, then on SHB R-075 to CREEP.

JIGSY TRANSITION (GATWY9.JIGSY): From over TWILA on TOY R-076 to JIGSY.

ROSEWOOD TRANSITION (GATWY9.ROD): From over TWILA on TOY R-076 to JIGSY, then on BIB R-258 to BIB VORTAC, then on BIB R-067 to WORKE, then on BIB R-067 and SHB R-251 to KELLY, then on SHB R-251 to SHB VOR/DME, then on SHB R-063 and ROD R-250 to ROD VORTAC.

GATEWAY NINE DEPARTURE
(GATWY9.TWILA) 17AUG17

ST. LOUIS, MISSOURI
ST LOUIS LAMBERT INTL (STL)

Figure 351A. GATEWAY NINE Departure (GATWY9.TWILA).

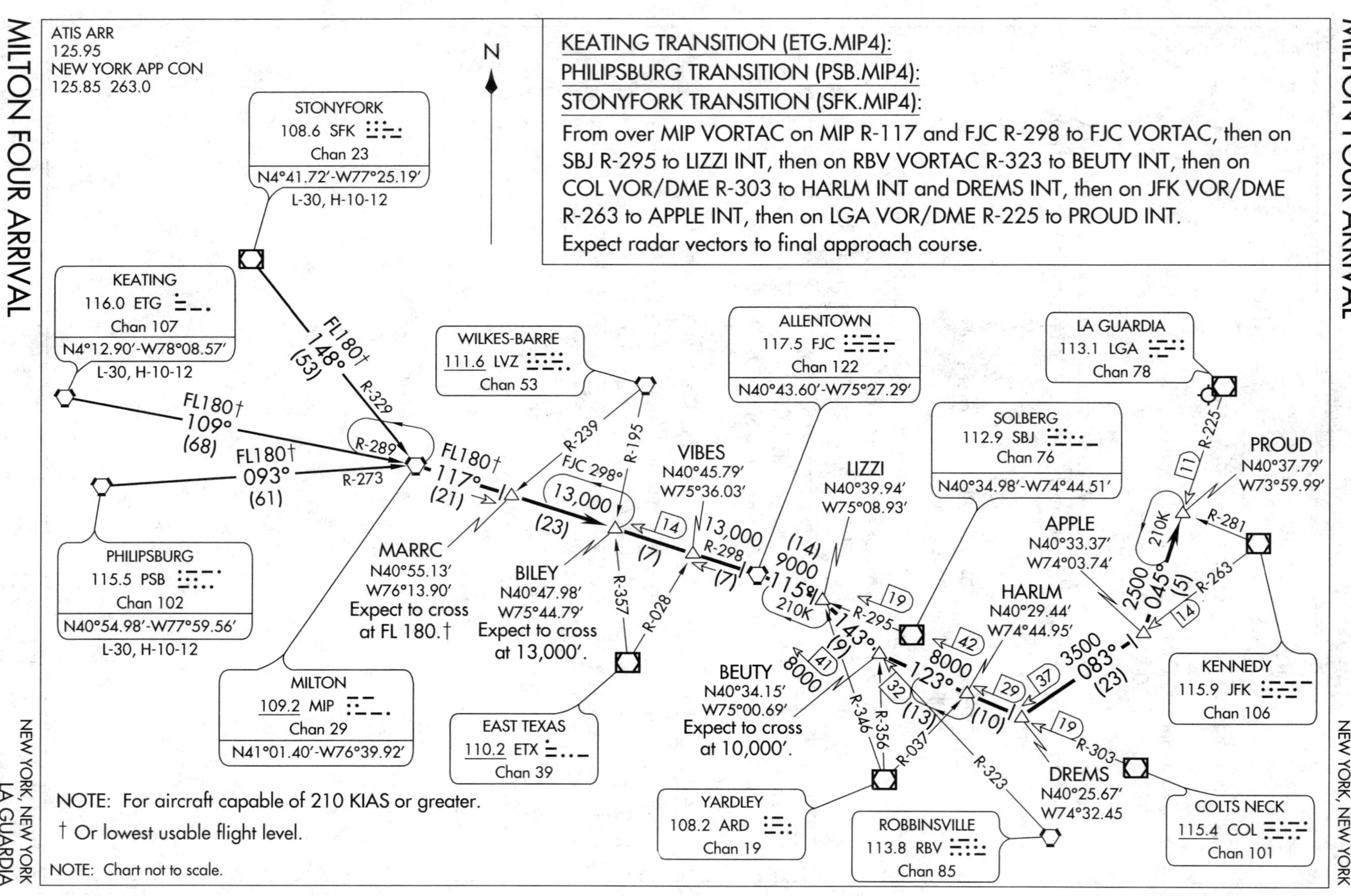

Figure 352. MILTON FOUR Arrival (MIP.MIP4).

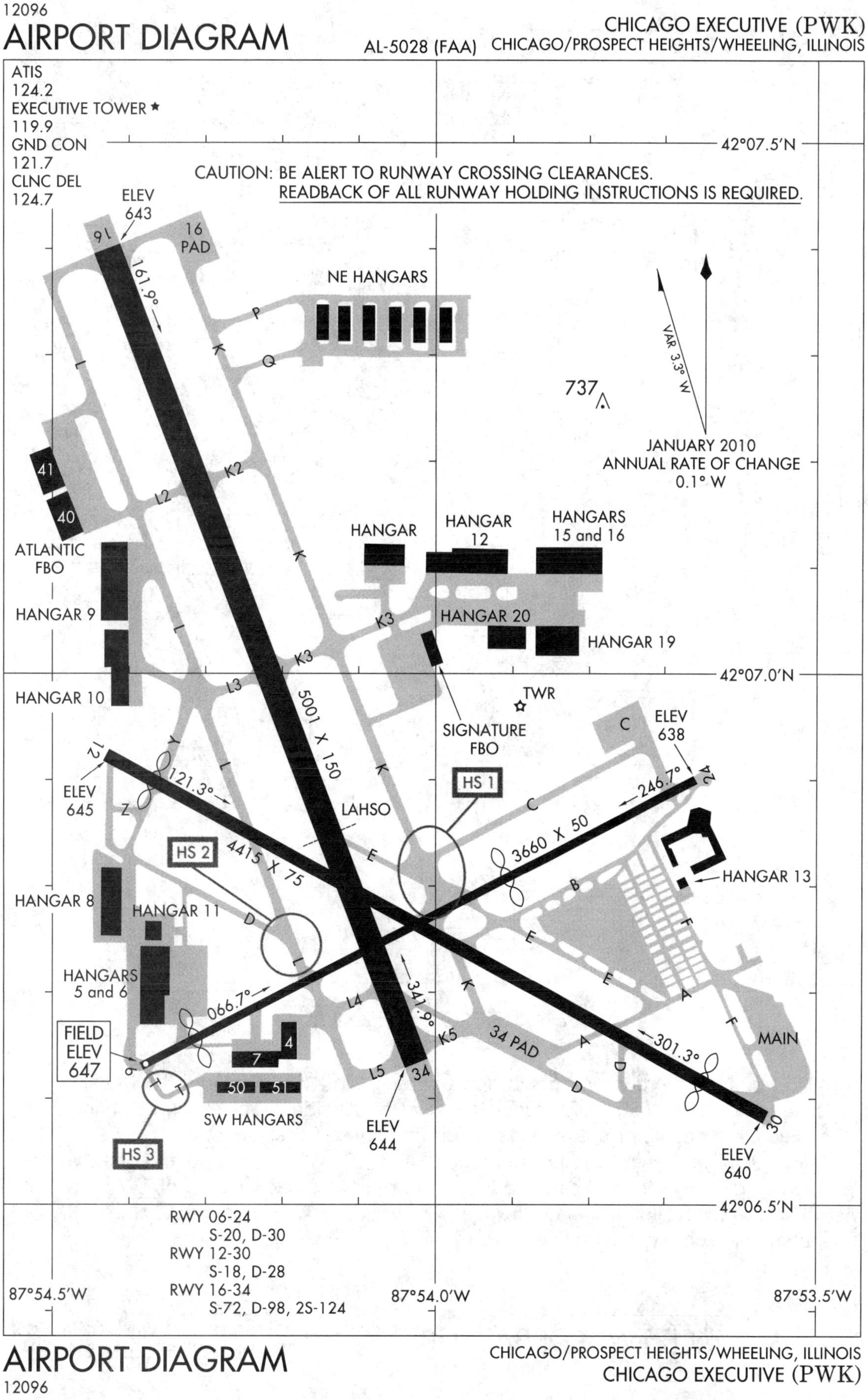

12096

AIRPORT DIAGRAM

AL-5028 (FAA)

CHICAGO EXECUTIVE (PWK)
CHICAGO/PROSPECT HEIGHTS/WHEELING, ILLINOIS

ATIS
124.2
EXECUTIVE TOWER ★
119.9
GND CON
121.7
CLNC DEL
124.7

42°07.5′N

CAUTION: BE ALERT TO RUNWAY CROSSING CLEARANCES.
READBACK OF ALL RUNWAY HOLDING INSTRUCTIONS IS REQUIRED.

ELEV
643
16
16
PAD
161.9°
NE HANGARS
P
K
Q
L
737
VAR 3.3° W
JANUARY 2010
ANNUAL RATE OF CHANGE
0.1° W
41
40
K2
L2
ATLANTIC
FBO
HANGAR 9
HANGAR
HANGAR
12
HANGARS
15 and 16
K
HANGAR 20
K3
HANGAR 19
L
K3
42°07.0′N
HANGAR 10
L3
5001 X 150
TWR
SIGNATURE
FBO
C
ELEV
638
12
Y
L
K
HS 1
246.7°
24
121.3°
ELEV
645
Z
LAHSO
C
3660 X 50
HS 2
4415 X 75
E
B
HANGAR 13
HANGAR 8
HANGAR 11
D
F
E
L
HANGARS
5 and 6
K
E
A
066.7°
L4
341.9°
F
FIELD
ELEV
647
4
7
K5
34 PAD
A
MAIN
301.3°
6
L5
34
D
T
T
50
51
D
SW HANGARS
ELEV
644
30
HS 3
ELEV
640
42°06.5′N

RWY 06-24
S-20, D-30
RWY 12-30
S-18, D-28
RWY 16-34
S-72, D-98, 2S-124

87°54.5′W
87°54.0′W
87°53.5′W

AIRPORT DIAGRAM
12096
CHICAGO/PROSPECT HEIGHTS/WHEELING, ILLINOIS
CHICAGO EXECUTIVE (PWK)

Figure 353. Airport Diagram (PWK).

12096 SL-5028 (FAA)

PAL-WAUKEE TWO DEPARTURE

CHICAGO EXECUTIVE (PWK)
CHICAGO/PROSPECT HEIGHTS/WHEELING, ILLINOIS

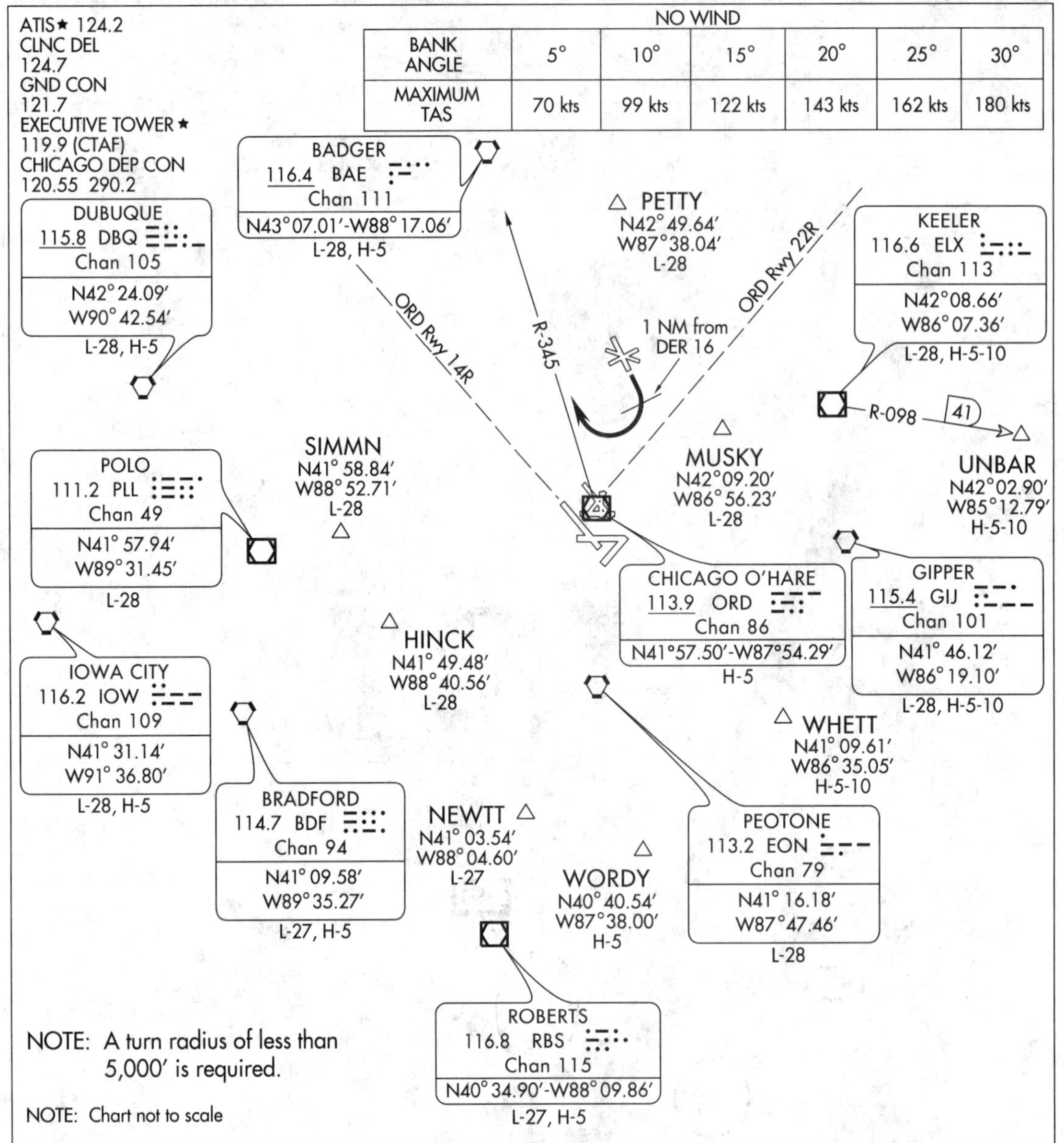

▼

DEPARTURE ROUTE DESCRIPTION

All aircraft expect radar vectors to appropriate navaid/fix; maintain 3000 feet or assigned altitude. Expect clearance to requested altitude/flight level (three minutes for jet/turbo engine or five minutes for piston engines) after departure.

TAKE-OFF RUNWAY 16: Start right turn within 1 NM of departure end of runway and complete turn to assigned heading east of R-345 of the ORD VOR/DME. This will insure separation from the runway 14R final approach course at O'Hare Intl. If unable to comply, advise Executive Tower prior to take-off.

PAL-WAUKEE TWO DEPARTURE
CHICAGO/PROSPECT HEIGHTS/WHEELING, ILLINOIS
CHICAGO EXECUTIVE (PWK)
12096

Figure 354. PAL-WAUKEE TWO Departure (PWK).

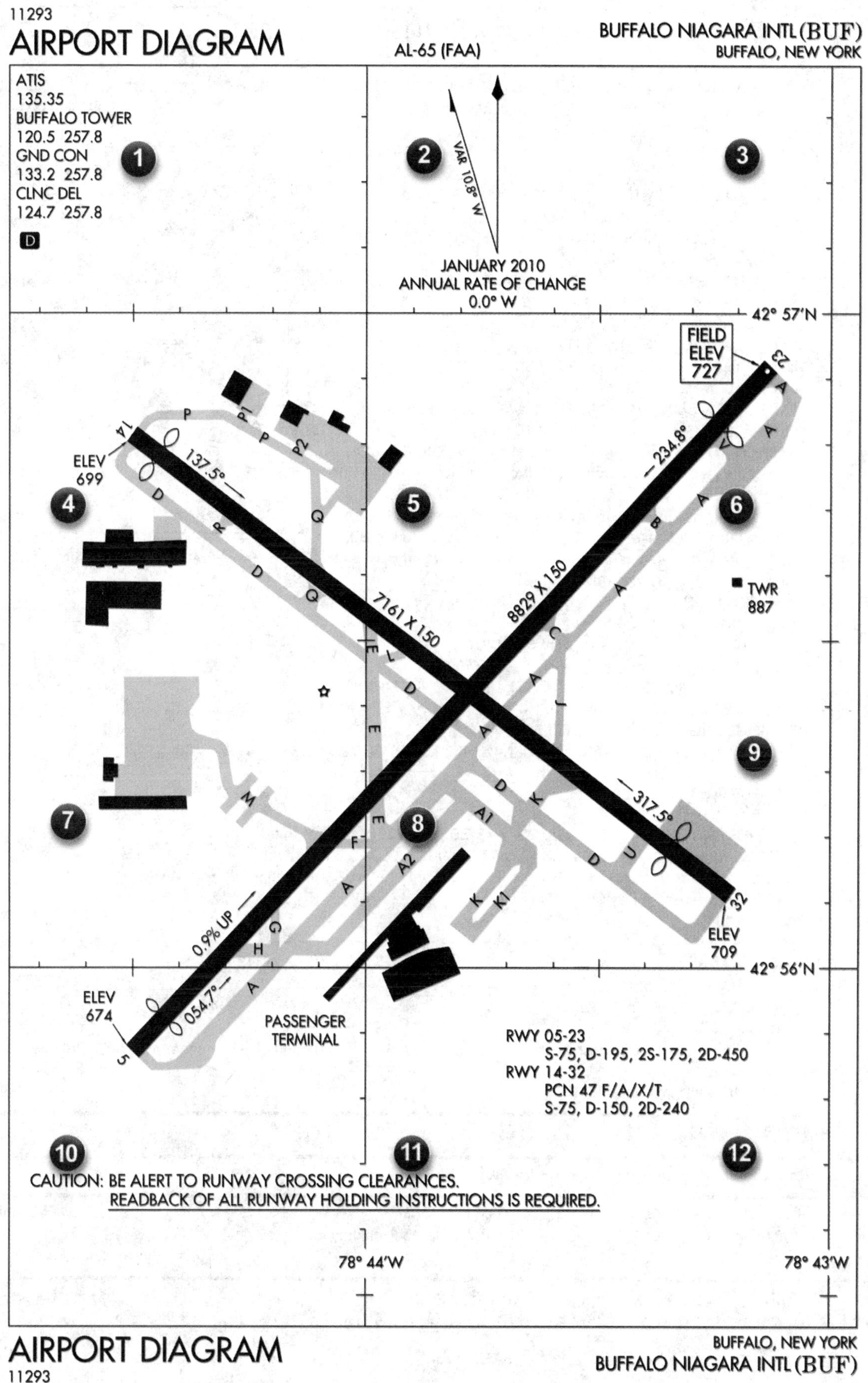

Figure 355. Airport Diagram (BUF).

BUFFALO NIAGARA INTL (BUF) 5 E UTC-5(-4DT) N42°56.43' W78°43.84' **DETROIT**
727 B S4 **FUEL** 100LL, JET A OX 1, 2, 3, 4 LRA Class I, ARFF Index D **H–10H, 11B, L–31E**
NOTAM FILE BUF **IAP, AD**

RWY 05–23: H8829X150 (ASPH–GRVD) S–75, D–195, 2S–175, 2D–450 HIRL CL
RWY 05: MALSR. TDZL. Thld dsplcd 535'. Bldg. 0.9% up.
RWY 23: ALSF2. TDZL. Thld dsplcd 725'. Tree.
RWY 14–32: H7161X150 (ASPH–GRVD) S–75, D–150, 2D–240 PCN 47 F/A/X/T HIRL
RWY 14: REIL. PAPI(P4L)—GA 3.0° TCH 45'. Thld dsplcd 320'. Tree.
RWY 32: MALSR. REIL. PAPI(P4L)—GA 3.0° TCH 54'. Thld dsplcd 720'. Sign.

RUNWAY DECLARED DISTANCE INFORMATION
RWY 05: TORA–8827 TODA–8827 ASDA–8292 LDA–7757
RWY 14: TORA–7161 TODA–7161 ASDA–6441 LDA–6121
RWY 23: TORA–8827 TODA–8827 ASDA–8292 LDA–7567
RWY 32: TORA–7161 TODA–7161 ASDA–6841 LDA–6121

AIRPORT REMARKS: Attended continuously. Heavy concentration of gulls, blackbirds, and starlings up to 5000 ft on and invof arpt. Deer on and invof arpt. Twy K1 clsd 0200–1300Z‡ daily. Twy A SW runup area/holding bay marked design group 3 acft (generally B727 or smaller), unavbl design group 4 (includes but not limited to B757, DC8). For fixed–base operator svcs ctc 131.75; for cargo svcs ctc 122.95. Rwy 23 ALSF2 unmonitored. Ldg fee. Flight Notification Service (ADCUS) available.
WEATHER DATA SOURCES: ASOS (716) 635–0532. WSP.
COMMUNICATIONS: D–ATIS 135.35
RCO 122.6 122.2 122.1R (BUFFALO RADIO)
®**APP DEP/CON** 126.15 (053°–233°) 126.5 (234°–052°)
TOWER 120.5 **GND CON** 133.2 **CLNC DEL** 124.7 **PRE–TAXI CLNC** 124.7
AIRSPACE: CLASS C svc continuous, ctc **APP CON**
RADIO AIDS TO NAVIGATION: NOTAM FILE BUF.
(H) VOR/DME 116.4 BUF Chan 111 N42°55.74' W78°38.78' 288° 3.8 NM to fld. 730/08W.
VOR/DME unusable:
036°–261° blo 11,000' 276°–305° blo 6000'
262°–275° blo 2300'
KLUMP NDB (LOM) 231 BU N43°00.02' W78°39.05' 233° 5.0 NM to fld.
PLAZZ NDB (LOM) 204 GB N42°52.43' W78°48.99' 053° 5.5 NM to fld.
ILS 111.3 I–BUF Rwy 23. Class IE. LOM KLUMP NDB. Glideslope unusable byd 5° rgt of course.
ILS 108.5 I–GBI Rwy 05. Class IA. LOM PLAZZ NDB.
ILS/DME 109.95 I–BNQ Chan 36(Y) Rwy 32.

CLARENCE AERODROME (D51) 5 NE UTC-5(-4DT) N43°04.00' W78°40.99' **DETROIT**
589 NOTAM FILE BUF
RWY 10–28: 2500X67 (TURF) LIRL
RWY 10: Fence. **RWY 28:** Trees.
AIRPORT REMARKS: Unattended. Ultralights on and invof arpt. Rwy 10–28 outlined with cones. ACTIVATE LIRL Rwy 10–28—122.7.
COMMUNICATIONS: CTAF/UNICOM 122.7

BUFFALO–LANCASTER RGNL (See LANCASTER)

BURRELLO–MECHANICVILLE (See MECHANICVILLE)

CALVERTON N40°55.78' W72°47.93' NOTAM FILE ISP. **NEW YORK**
(L) VORW/DME 117.2 CCC Chan 119 219° 7.2 NM to Brookhaven. 85/13W. **COPTER**
VOR portion unusable 280°–290° byd 25 NM. **H–10I, L–33B, 34I**

CAMBRIDGE N42°59.66' W73°20.64' NOTAM FILE BTV. **NEW YORK**
(L) VORW/DME 115.0 CAM Chan 97 159° 7.5 NM to Bennington State, Vt. 1490/14W. **H–11C, 12J, L–32G, 34J**
HIWAS.
DME unusable 050°–130° beyond 20 NM below 9000'.

Figure 356. BUFFALO THREE Departure (BUF).

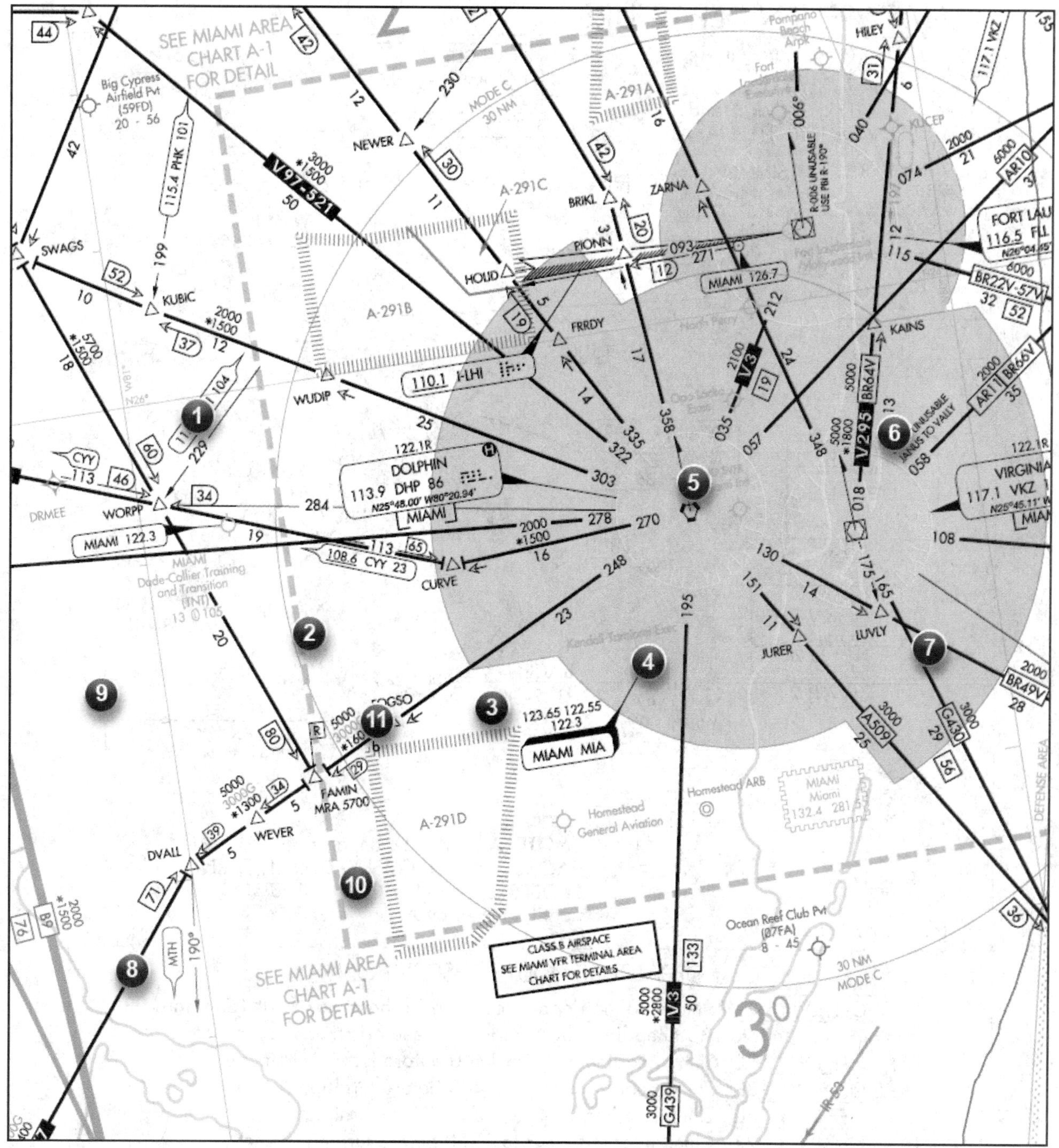

Figure 357. Low Altitude Airways.

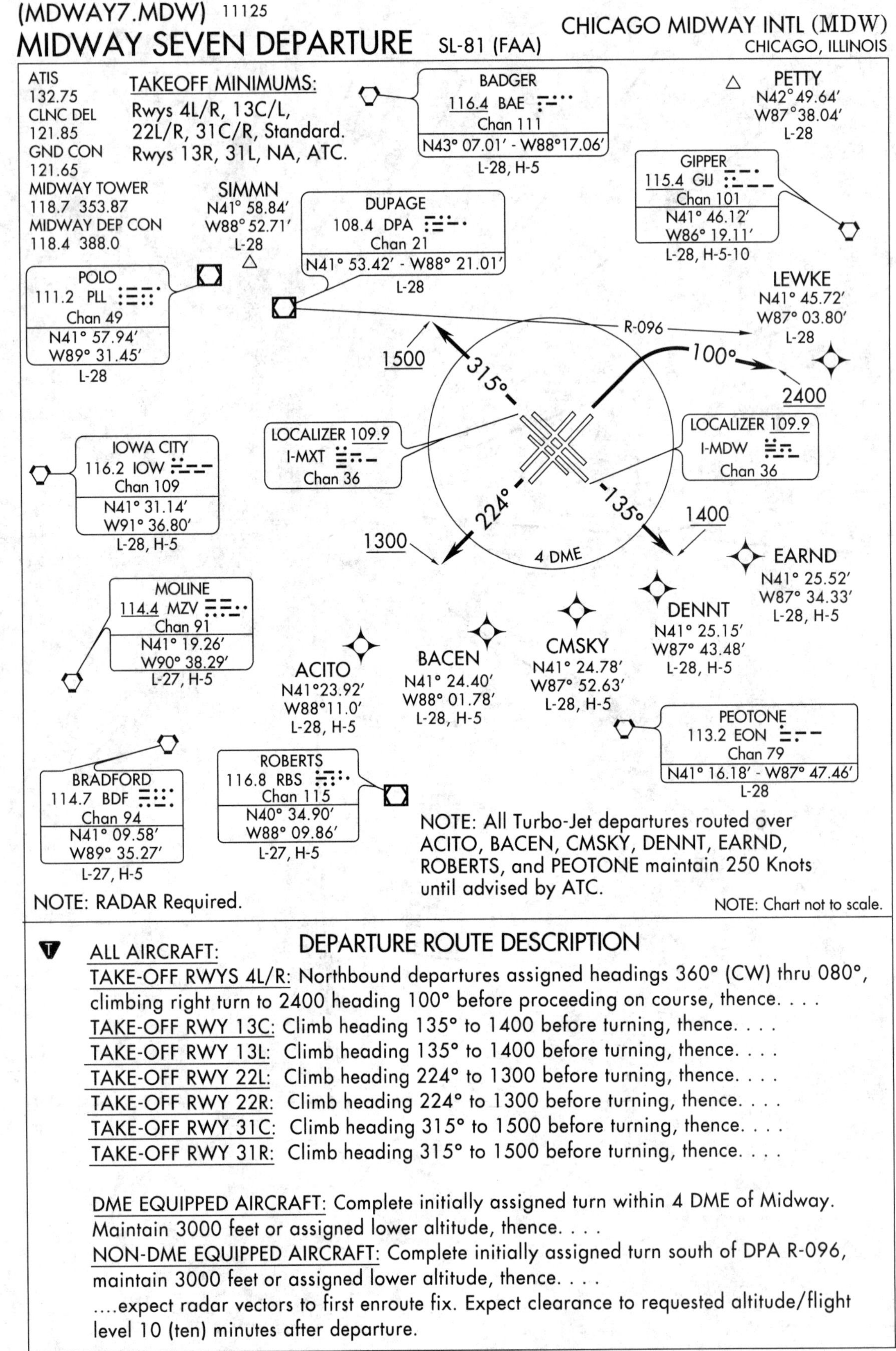

DEPARTURE ROUTE DESCRIPTION

ALL AIRCRAFT:

TAKE-OFF RWYS 4L/R: Northbound departures assigned headings 360° (CW) thru 080°, climbing right turn to 2400 heading 100° before proceeding on course, thence. . . .
TAKE-OFF RWY 13C: Climb heading 135° to 1400 before turning, thence. . . .
TAKE-OFF RWY 13L: Climb heading 135° to 1400 before turning, thence. . . .
TAKE-OFF RWY 22L: Climb heading 224° to 1300 before turning, thence. . . .
TAKE-OFF RWY 22R: Climb heading 224° to 1300 before turning, thence. . . .
TAKE-OFF RWY 31C: Climb heading 315° to 1500 before turning, thence. . . .
TAKE-OFF RWY 31R: Climb heading 315° to 1500 before turning, thence. . . .

DME EQUIPPED AIRCRAFT: Complete initially assigned turn within 4 DME of Midway. Maintain 3000 feet or assigned lower altitude, thence. . . .
NON-DME EQUIPPED AIRCRAFT: Complete initially assigned turn south of DPA R-096, maintain 3000 feet or assigned lower altitude, thence. . . .
....expect radar vectors to first enroute fix. Expect clearance to requested altitude/flight level 10 (ten) minutes after departure.

MIDWAY SEVEN DEPARTURE (MDWAY7.MDW) 11125

CHICAGO, ILLINOIS
CHICAGO MIDWAY INTL (MDW)

Figure 358. MIDWAY SEVEN Departure (MDW).

(MDWAY7.MDW) 08325
MIDWAY SEVEN DEPARTURE SL-81 (FAA)

CHICAGO MIDWAY INTL (MDW)
CHICAGO, ILLINOIS

TAKEOFF OBSTACLE NOTES:

NOTE: RWY 4L, Fence 18 feet from DER, 257 feet left of centerline, 12 feet AGL/616 feet MSL. Vehicle plus road 143 feet from DER, 163 feet left of centerline, 16 feet AGL/620 feet MSL. Bldg 251 feet from DER, 217 feet left of centerline, 26 feet AGL/630 feet MSL. Sign 1,912 feet from DER, 330 feet left of centerline, 88 feet AGL/692 feet MSL. Multiple Lt poles and trees beginning 375 feet from DER, 98 feet right of centerline, up to 75 feet AGL/679 feet MSL.
NOTE: RWY 4R, LOC 300 feet from DER, on centerline, 10 feet AGL/614 feet MSL. Lt pole and multiple trees beginning 40 feet from DER, 369 feet left of centerline, up to 75 feet AGL/679 feet MSL. Blast fence 277 feet from DER, 45 feet left of centerline, 9 feet AGL/613 feet MSL. Tower 3,983 feet from DER, 1,142 feet left of centerline, 109 feet AGL/708 feet MSL. Multiple lt poles and trees beginning 96 feet from DER, 21 feet right of centerline, up to 53 feet AGL/657 feet MSL. Train beginning 1,483 feet from DER, 570 feet right of centerline, 48 feet AGL/654 feet MSL.
NOTE: RWY 13C, LOC 248 feet from DER, on centerline, 8 feet AGL/619 feet MSL. Bldg 101 feet from DER, 254 feet left of centerline, 14 feet AGL/625 feet MSL. Trees beginning 288 feet from DER, 459 feet left of centerline, up to 76 feet AGL/680 feet MSL. Trees beginning 109 feet from DER, 402 feet right of centerline, up to 86 feet AGL/700 feet MSL.
NOTE: RWY 13L, Multiple poles and trees beginning 362 feet from DER, 215 feet left of centerline, up to 71 feet AGL/675 feet MSL. Trees beginning 1,136 feet from DER, 54 feet right of centerline, up to 76 feet AGL/680 feet MSL.
NOTE: RWY 22L, Multiple poles and trees beginning 74 feet from DER, 375 feet left of centerline, up to 70 feet AGL/689 feet MSL. Multiple poles and trees beginning 465 feet from DER, 49 feet right of centerline, up to 60 feet AGL/679 feet MSL. Tank 4,100 feet from DER, 161 feet right of centerline, 109 feet AGL/728 feet MSL.
NOTE: RWY 22R, Multiple poles and trees beginning 575 feet from DER, 168 feet left of centerline, up to 58 feet AGL/677 feet MSL. Tank 4,100 feet from DER, 161 feet left of centerline, 109 feet AGL/728 feet MSL. Fence 198 feet from DER, 3 feet right of centerline, 12 feet AGL/630 feet MSL. Trees beginning 183 feet from DER, 65 feet right of centerline, up to 72 feet AGL/686 feet MSL.
NOTE: RWY 31C, LOC 239 feet from DER, on centerline, 10 feet AGL/617 feet MSL. Trees beginning 452 feet from DER, 454 feet left of centerline, up to 63 feet AGL/667 feet MSL. Spire 2,207 feet from DER, 699 feet left of centerline, 78 feet AGL/684 feet MSL. Multiple poles and trees beginning 142 feet from DER, 28 feet right of centerline, up to 73 feet AGL/672 feet MSL. DME 183 feet from DER, 309 feet right of centerline, 17 feet AGL/624 feet MSL. Sign 1,528 feet from DER, 270 feet right of centerline, 52 feet AGL/652 feet MSL. Tank 5,576 feet from DER, 1,430 feet right of centerline, 162 feet AGL/756 feet MSL.
NOTE: RWY 31R, Multiple poles and trees beginning 379 feet from DER, 49 feet left of centerline, up to 65 feet AGL/664 feet MSL. Pole and trees beginning 70 feet from DER, 50 feet right of centerline, up to 68 feet AGL/667 feet MSL.

MIDWAY SEVEN DEPARTURE
(MDWAY7.MDW) 08325

CHICAGO, ILLINOIS
CHICAGO MIDWAY INTL(MDW)

Figure 359. MIDWAY SEVEN Departure (MDW).

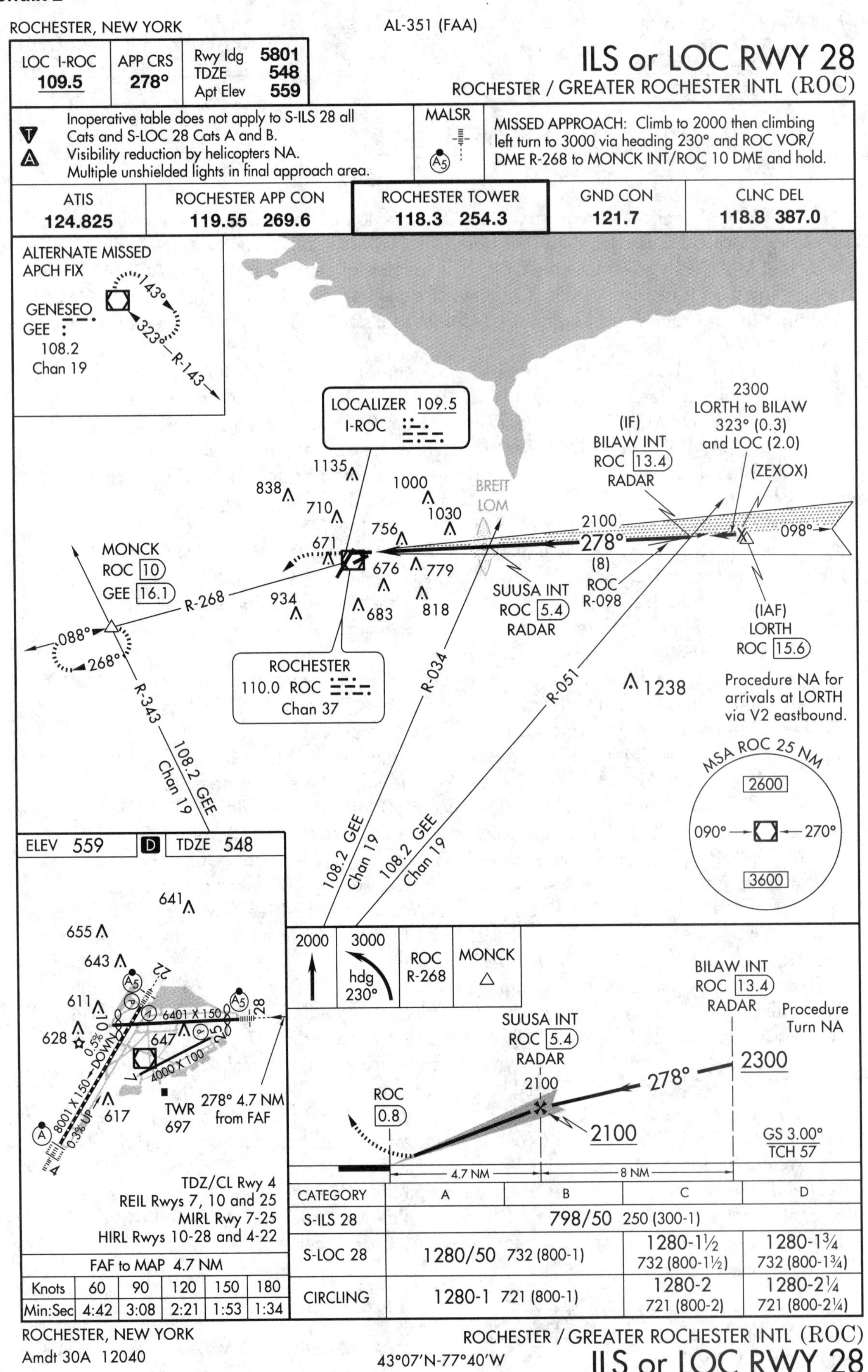

FAF to MAP 4.7 NM					
Knots	60	90	120	150	180
Min:Sec	4:42	3:08	2:21	1:53	1:34

CATEGORY	A	B	C	D
S-ILS 28	798/50 250 (300-1)			
S-LOC 28	1280/50 732 (800-1)		1280-1½ 732 (800-1½)	1280-1¾ 732 (800-1¾)
CIRCLING	1280-1 721 (800-1)		1280-2 721 (800-2)	1280-2¼ 721 (800-2¼)

ROCHESTER, NEW YORK
Amdt 30A 12040
43°07′N-77°40′W
ROCHESTER / GREATER ROCHESTER INTL (ROC)
ILS or LOC RWY 28

Figure 360. ILS or LOC RWY 28 (ROC).

(TUS7.TUS) 09183

TUCSON SEVEN DEPARTURE

SL-430 (FAA)

TUCSON INTL (TUS)
TUCSON, ARIZONA

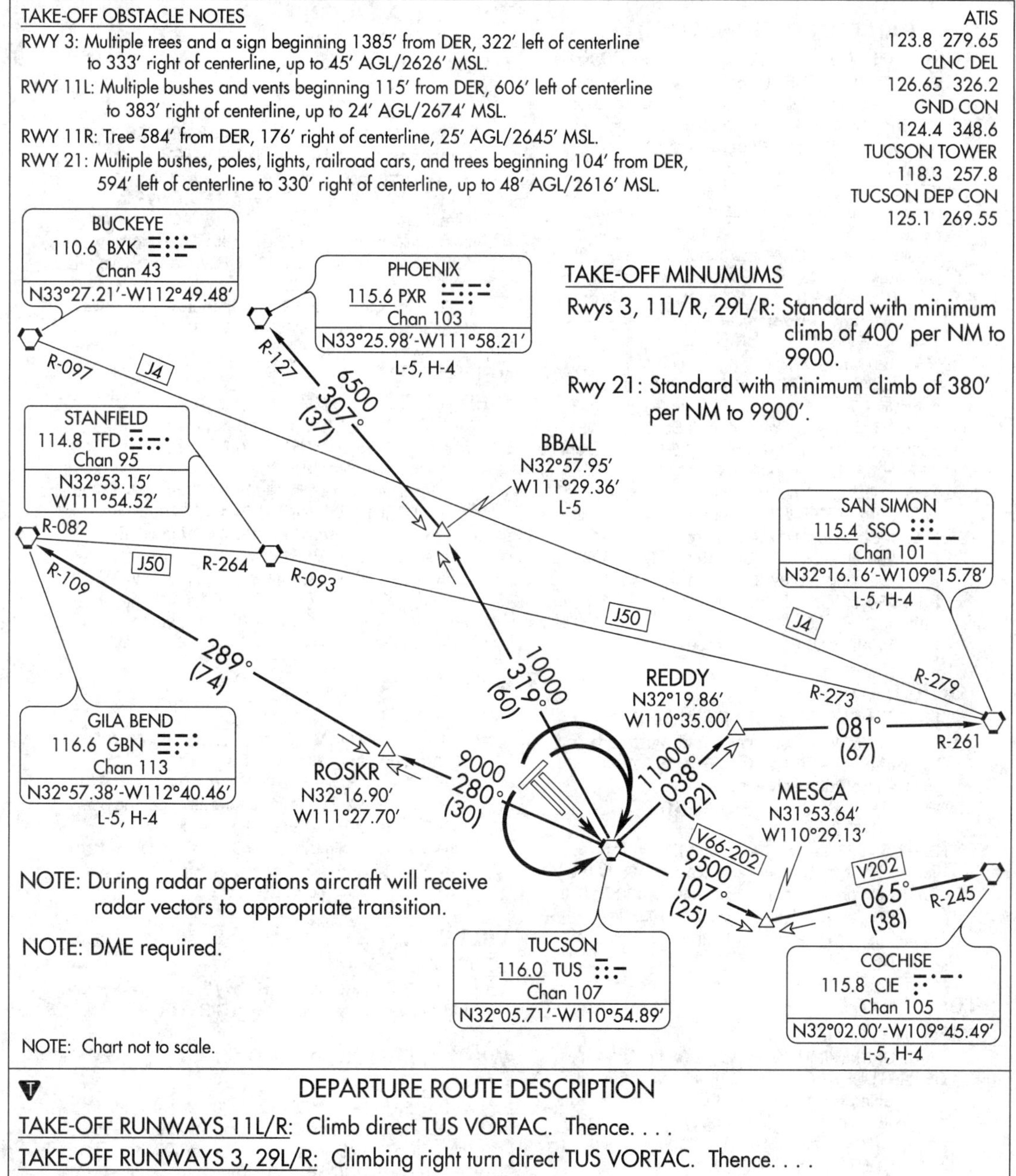
TAKE-OFF OBSTACLE NOTES
RWY 3: Multiple trees and a sign beginning 1385′ from DER, 322′ left of centerline to 333′ right of centerline, up to 45′ AGL/2626′ MSL.
RWY 11L: Multiple bushes and vents beginning 115′ from DER, 606′ left of centerline to 383′ right of centerline, up to 24′ AGL/2674′ MSL.
RWY 11R: Tree 584′ from DER, 176′ right of centerline, 25′ AGL/2645′ MSL.
RWY 21: Multiple bushes, poles, lights, railroad cars, and trees beginning 104′ from DER, 594′ left of centerline to 330′ right of centerline, up to 48′ AGL/2616′ MSL.
ATIS
123.8 279.65
CLNC DEL
126.65 326.2
GND CON
124.4 348.6
TUCSON TOWER
118.3 257.8
TUCSON DEP CON
125.1 269.55
TAKE-OFF MINUMUMS
Rwys 3, 11L/R, 29L/R: Standard with minimum climb of 400′ per NM to 9900.
Rwy 21: Standard with minimum climb of 380′ per NM to 9900′.
BUCKEYE
110.6 BXK
Chan 43
N33°27.21′-W112°49.48′
PHOENIX
115.6 PXR
Chan 103
N33°25.98′-W111°58.21′
L-5, H-4
STANFIELD
114.8 TFD
Chan 95
N32°53.15′
W111°54.52′
BBALL
N32°57.95′
W111°29.36′
L-5
SAN SIMON
115.4 SSO
Chan 101
N32°16.16′-W109°15.78′
L-5, H-4
GILA BEND
116.6 GBN
Chan 113
N32°57.38′-W112°40.46′
L-5, H-4
ROSKR
N32°16.90′
W111°27.70′
REDDY
N32°19.86′
W110°35.00′
MESCA
N31°53.64′
W110°29.13′
TUCSON
116.0 TUS
Chan 107
N32°05.71′-W110°54.89′
COCHISE
115.8 CIE
Chan 105
N32°02.00′-W109°45.49′
L-5, H-4
R-097
J4
R-127
6500
307°
(37)
R-082
J50
R-264
R-093
R-109
289°
(74)
10000
319°
(60)
J50
J4
R-279
R-273
081°
(67)
R-261
9000
280°
(30)
11000
038°
(22)
V66-202
9500
107°
(25)
V202
065°
(38)
R-245
NOTE: During radar operations aircraft will receive radar vectors to appropriate transition.
NOTE: DME required.
NOTE: Chart not to scale.

DEPARTURE ROUTE DESCRIPTION

TAKE-OFF RUNWAYS 11L/R: Climb direct TUS VORTAC. Thence. . . .

TAKE-OFF RUNWAYS 3, 29L/R: Climbing right turn direct TUS VORTAC. Thence. . . .

TAKE-OFF RUNWAY 21: Climbing left turn direct TUS VORTAC. Thence. . . .

. . . . via assigned transition. Maintain 17000, expect clearance to filed altitude 10 minutes after departure.

BBALL TRANSITION (TUS7.BBALL): From over TUS VORTAC via TUS R-319 to BBALL INT.

COCHISE TRANSITION (TUS7.CIE): From over TUS VORTAC via TUS R-107 and CIE R-245 to CIE VORTAC.

GILA BEND TRANSITION (TUS7.GBN): From over TUS VORTAC via TUS R-280 and GBN R-109 to GBN VORTAC.

PHOENIX TRANSITION (TUS7.PXR): From over TUS VORTAC via TUS R-319 and PXR R-127 to PXR VORTAC.

SAN SIMON TRANSITION (TUS7.SSO): From over TUS VORTAC via TUS R-038 and SSO R-261 to SSO VORTAC.

TUCSON SEVEN DEPARTURE
TUCSON, ARIZONA
TUCSON INTL (TUS)
(TUS7.TUS) 09183

Figure 361. TUCSON SEVEN Departure (TUS7.TUS).

L12

TAKE-OFF MINIMUMS AND (OBSTACLE) DEPARTURE PROCEDURES

12096

TONOPAH TEST RANGE (KTNX)

TONOPAH , NV. . . . . AMDT 1 12096

DEPARTURE PROCEDURE: **Rwy 14:** 1000-3 with minimum climb of 320 ft/NM to 10,700 or 2700-3 for Climb in Visual Conditions. Climb on a heading between 325º CW to 155º from departure end of runway or Climb in Visual Conditions to cross KZ-KTNX airport at or above 8100 MSL before proceeding on course. **Rwy 32:** 1000-3 with minimum climb of 260 ft/NM to 5900 or 2700-3 for Climb in Visual Conditions. Climb on a heading between 295º CW to 005º from departure end of runway or Climb in Visual Conditions to cross KZ-KTNX airport at or above 8100 MSL before proceeding on course.

TAKE-OFF OBSTACLES: **Rwy 14,** Terrain, 5582' MSL, 1204' from DER, 823' right of centerline. Terrain, 5565' MSL, 63' from DER, 517' right of centerline. Terrain, 5564' MSL, 46' from DER, 480' right of centerline. Terrain, 5561' MSL, 0' from DER, 353' right of centerline. Terrain, 5558' MSL, 62' from DER, 200' right of centerline. Terrain, 5561' MSL, 14' from DER, 292' right of centerline. Terrain, 5561' MSL, 0' from DER, 287' right of centerline. Terrain, 5559' MSL, 0' from DER, 222' right of centerline. Surveyed terrain, 5560' MSL, 215' from DER, 427' right of centerline. **Rwy 32,** Terrain, 5476' MSL, 0' from DER, 500' left of centerline. Terrain, 5476' MSL, 19' from DER, 465' left of centerline. Terrain, 5476' MSL, 110' from DER, 529' left of centerline.

TOOELE, UT

BOLINDER FIELD-TOOELE VALLEY

TAKE-OFF MINIMUMS: **Rwy 17,** std. with a min. climb of 490' per NM to 11000. **Rwy 35,** std. with a min. climb of 360' per NM to 9000.

DEPARTURE PROCEDURE: Use STACO DEPARTURE.

NOTE: **Rwy 17,** tree 794' from departure end of runway, 277' right of centerline, 35' AGL/4380' MSL. Tree 967' from departure end of runway, 432' right of centerline, 35' AGL/4394' MSL. Tree 1023' from departure end of runway, 313' right of centerline, 35' AGL/4395' MSL.

TUCSON, AZ

MARANA RGNL

TAKE-OFF MINIMUMS: **Rwys 3, 12,** N/A-Obstacles

DEPARTURE PROCEDURE: **Rwy 21,** climb to 6500 via heading 360° and TUS R-308 to TOTEC Int/TUS 57 DME, then as filed. **Rwy 30,** climb to 6500 via heading 303° intercept TUS R-308 above 3500, to TOTEC INT/TUS 57 DME, then as filed.

NOTE: **Rwy 21,** road 192' from departure end of runway, 527' left of centerline 15' AGL/2034' MSL.

RYAN FIELD (RYN)
AMDT 3 10210 (FAA)

TAKE-OFF MINIMUMS: **Rwys 6L, 15, 24R, 33,** NA, ATC.

DEPARTURE PROCEDURE: **Rwys 6R, 24L,** use ALMON DEPARTURE.

TUCSON, AZ (CON'T)

TUCSON INTL (TUS)
AMDT 4A 08241 (FAA)

TAKE-OFF MINIMUMS: **Rwy 3,** 300-1¾ or std. w/ min. climb of 228' per NM to 3000.

DEPARTURE PROCEDURE: **Rwys 3, 29L, 29R,** climbing right turn direct to TUS VORTAC. **Rwys 11L, 11R** climb via runway heading to 4000 then climbing left turn direct TUS VORTAC. **Rwy 21,** climbing left turn direct to TUS VORTAC. **All aircraft** continue climbing in holding pattern (NW, right turns, 128° inbound) to depart TUS VORTAC at or above 9000.

NOTE: **Rwy 3,** tower 9215' from departure end of runway, 1689' left of centerline, 246' AGL/2831' MSL.

VERNAL, UT

VERNAL RGNL

TAKE-OFF MINIMUMS: **Rwy 16**, 1500-2 or std with a min. climb of 250' per NM to 7000'. **Rwy 25**, 1500-2 or std. with a min. climb of 390' per NM to 7000. **Rwy 34**, 1600-2 pr std. with a min. climb of 330' per NM to 7000'.

DEPARTURE PROCEDURE: **Rwys 7, 34**, turn right. **Rwys 16, 25**, turn left. **All aircraft** climb direct VEL. Aircraft departing V391 S-bound climb on course. All others climb in holding pattern (SE, right turns, 322° inbound). Aircraft SW-bound V208 depart VEL at or above 8400', all others depart VEL at or above 9500'. Continue climb on course to MEA or assigned altitude.

WENDOVER, UT

WENDOVER

TAKE-OFF MINIMUMS: **Rwy 26,** standard wit h a min. climb of 300' per NM to 7000. **Rwy 30**, NA.

DEPARTURE PROCEDURE: **Rwys 8, 12, 26,** climbing left turn direct BVL VORTAC. Aircraft departing BVL VORTAC R-330 CW R-150 climb on course. All others continue climb in BVL VORTAC holding pattern (Hold NE right turns, 247° inbound) to cross at or above 7400, then climb on course.

WILLCOX, AZ

COCHISE COUNTY

DEPARTURE PROCEDURE: **Rwy 3,** turn right. **Rwy 21,** turn left. **All aircraft** climb direct CIE VORTAC.

WINDOW ROCK, AZ

WINDOW ROCK

TAKE-OFF MINIMUMS: **Rwy 2**, 700-2 or std. with a min. climb of 500' per NM to 8000. **Rwy 20,** 600-2 or std. with a min. climb of 260' per NM to 8200.

DEPARTURE PROCEDURE: **Rwy 2**, turn right. **Rwy 20,** turn left direct to GUP VORTAC before proceeding on course.

NOTE: **Rwy 2,** terrain 3832' from departure end of runway, 1025' right of centerline, 6926' MSL. Poles 5220' from departure end of runway, 245' right of centerline, 180' AGL/6922' MSL. Tower 7067' from departure end of runway, 3072' left of centerline, 71' AGL/7316' MSL. Terrain 7449' from departure end of runway, 1612' left of centerline, 6991' MSL. Terrain 8776' from departure end of runway, 1851' left of centerline, 7109' MSL. Tree 9665' from departure end of runway, 1326' right of centerline, 7340' MSL. Tree 11326' from departure end of runway, 355' left of centerline, 7351' MSL. **Rwy 20,** trees 1018' from departure end of runway, 620' left of centerline, 30' AGL/6768' MSL.

12096

TAKE-OFF MINIMUMS AND (OBSTACLE) DEPARTURE PROCEDURES

Figure 362. Takeoff Minimums and (Obstacle) Departure Procedures.

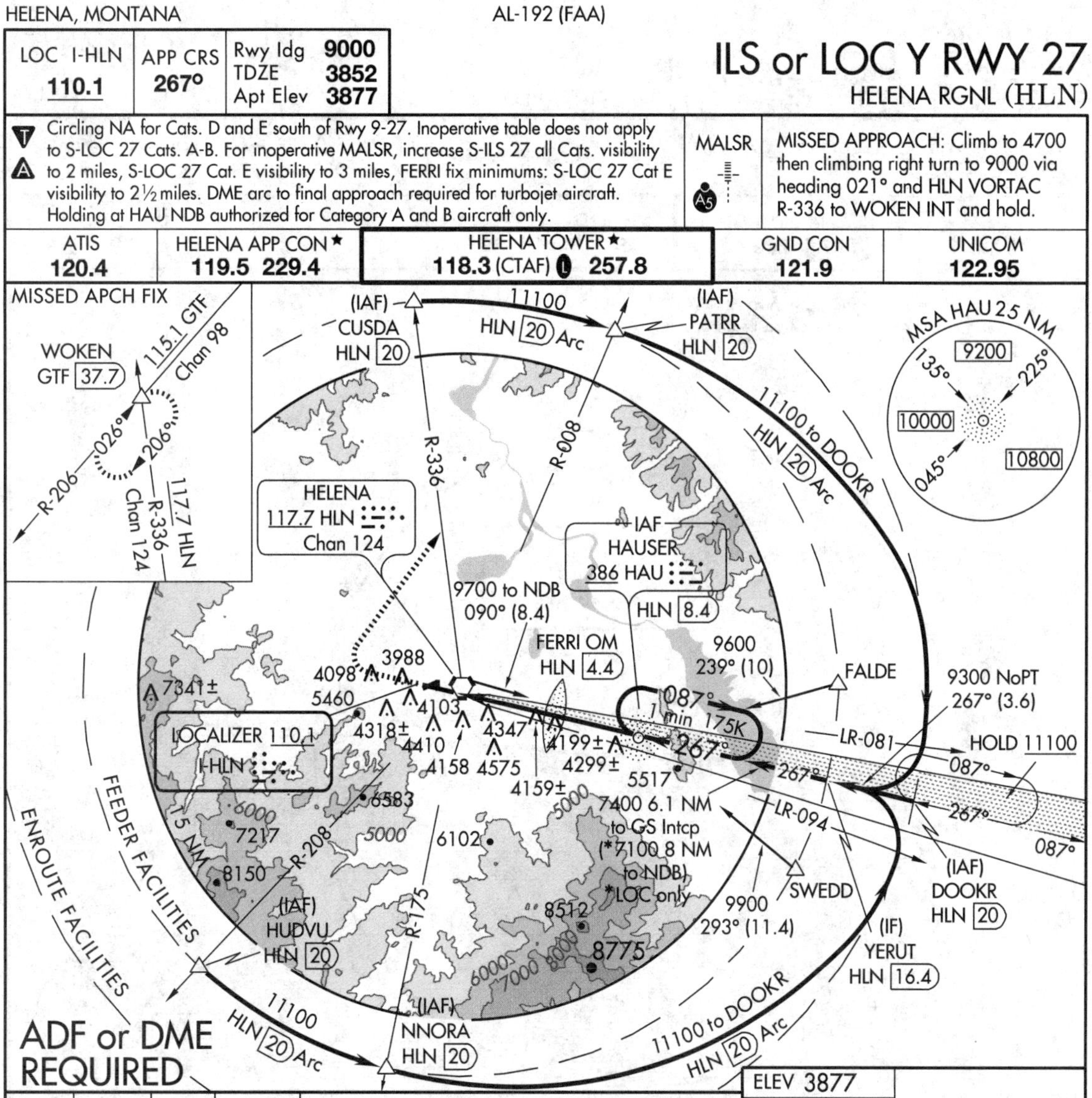

HELENA, MONTANA AL-192 (FAA)

LOC I-HLN 110.1	APP CRS 267°	Rwy ldg 9000 TDZE 3852 Apt Elev 3877

ILS or LOC Y RWY 27

HELENA RGNL (HLN)

Circling NA for Cats. D and E south of Rwy 9-27. Inoperative table does not apply to S-LOC 27 Cats. A-B. For inoperative MALSR, increase S-ILS 27 all Cats. visibility to 2 miles, S-LOC 27 Cat. E visibility to 3 miles, FERRI fix minimums: S-LOC 27 Cat E visibility to 2½ miles. DME arc to final approach required for turbojet aircraft. Holding at HAU NDB authorized for Category A and B aircraft only.

MALSR

MISSED APPROACH: Climb to 4700 then climbing right turn to 9000 via heading 021° and HLN VORTAC R-336 to WOKEN INT and hold.

ATIS	HELENA APP CON ★	HELENA TOWER ★	GND CON	UNICOM
120.4	119.5 229.4	118.3 (CTAF) Ⓛ 257.8	121.9	122.95

MISSED APCH FIX
WOKEN GTF 37.7
115.1 GTF Chan 98
026° 206° R-206
117.7 HLN R-336 Chan 124

(IAF) CUSDA HLN 20
11100 HLN 20 Arc
(IAF) PATRR HLN 20
MSA HAU 25 NM 9200 10000 10800 135° 225° 045°
11100 to DOOKR HLN 20 Arc
R-336 R-008
HELENA 117.7 HLN Chan 124
IAF HAUSER 386 HAU HLN 8.4
9700 to NDB 090° (8.4)
FERRI OM HLN 4.4
9600 239° (10)
FALDE
9300 NoPT 267° (3.6)
HOLD 11100 087° 267°
1 min 175K 087° 267°
LR-081 LR-094
(IAF) DOOKR HLN 20
7341± 4098 3988 5460 4103 4318± 4410 4347 4199± 4299± 4158 4575 4159± 5517 6583 7217 8150 6102 8512 8775
LOCALIZER 110.1 I-HLN
7400 6.1 NM to GS Intcp (*7100 8 NM to NDB) *LOC only
9900 293° (11.4)
SWEDD
(IF) YERUT HLN 16.4
R-208 R-175 15 NM
FEEDER FACILITIES
ENROUTE FACILITIES
(IAF) HUDVU HLN 20
11100 HLN 20 Arc
(IAF) NNORA HLN 20
11100 to DOOKR HLN 20 Arc

ADF or DME REQUIRED

4700 9000 021° HLN R-336 117.7 WOKEN
*LOC only

NDB HLN 8.4 6742
FERRI OM HLN 4.4 5426
One Minute Holding Pattern
087° 7400 267° 7100* 7400 5400*
GS 3.00° TCH 55
4.7 NM 4 NM

ELEV 3877
267° 8.7 NM from FAF
9 27 5 23 16 34 4644 X 75 6989 X 75 9000 X 150 1.2% UP 0.3% DOWN 1.7% UP
3951 3984 TDZE 3852 4174

CATEGORY	A	B	C	D	E
S-ILS 27	4402-1½ 550 (600-1½)				
S-LOC 27	5400-1¼ 1548 (1600-1¼)	5400-1½ 1548 (1600-1½)	5400-2½ 1548 (1600-2½)		
CIRCLING	5400-1¼ 1523 (1600-1¼)	5400-1½ 1523 (1600-1½)	5400-3 1523 (1600-3)		
FERRI FIX MINIMUMS *					
S-LOC 27	4560-½ 708 (700-½)		4560-1½ 708 (700-1½)	4560-1¾ 708 (700-1¾)	4560-2 708 (700-2)
CIRCLING	4640-1 763 (800-1)		4740-2½ 863 (900-2½)	4740-2¾ 863 (900-2¾)	4840-3 963 (1000-3)

REIL Rwy 9 Ⓛ
MIRL Rwys 5-23 and 16-34 Ⓛ
HIRL Rwy 9-27 Ⓛ

FAF to MAP 8.7 NM

Knots	60	90	120	150	180
Min:Sec	8:42	5:48	4:21	3:29	2:54

HELENA, MONTANA
Amdt 2 10098
46° 36'N - 111° 59'W
HELENA RGNL (HLN)
ILS or LOC Y RWY 27

Figure 363. ILS or LOC Y RWY 27 (HLN).

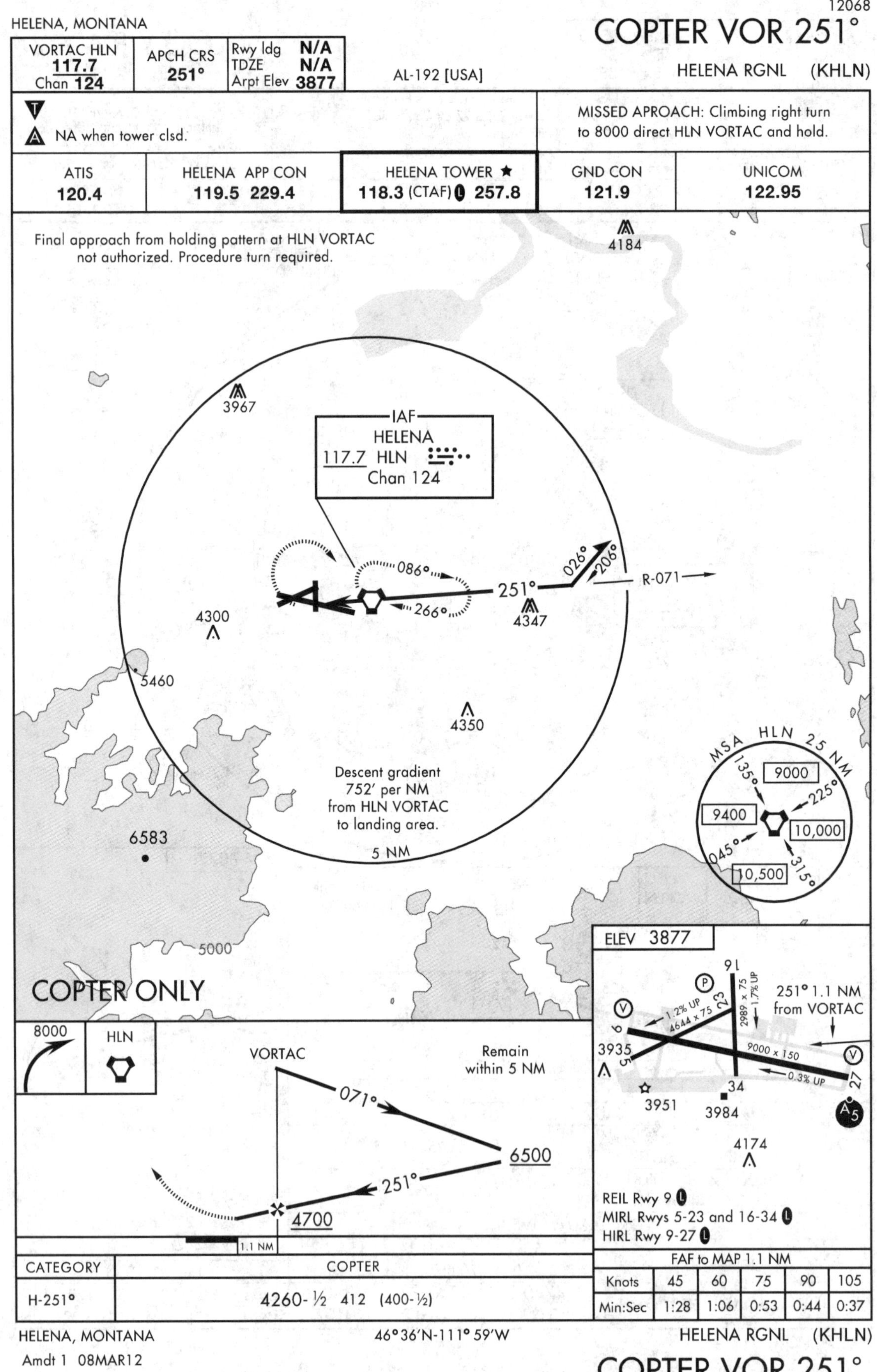

CATEGORY	COPTER
H-251°	4260-½ 412 (400-½)

FAF to MAP 1.1 NM					
Knots	45	60	75	90	105
Min:Sec	1:28	1:06	0:53	0:44	0:37

Figure 364. COPTER VOR 251° (KHLN).

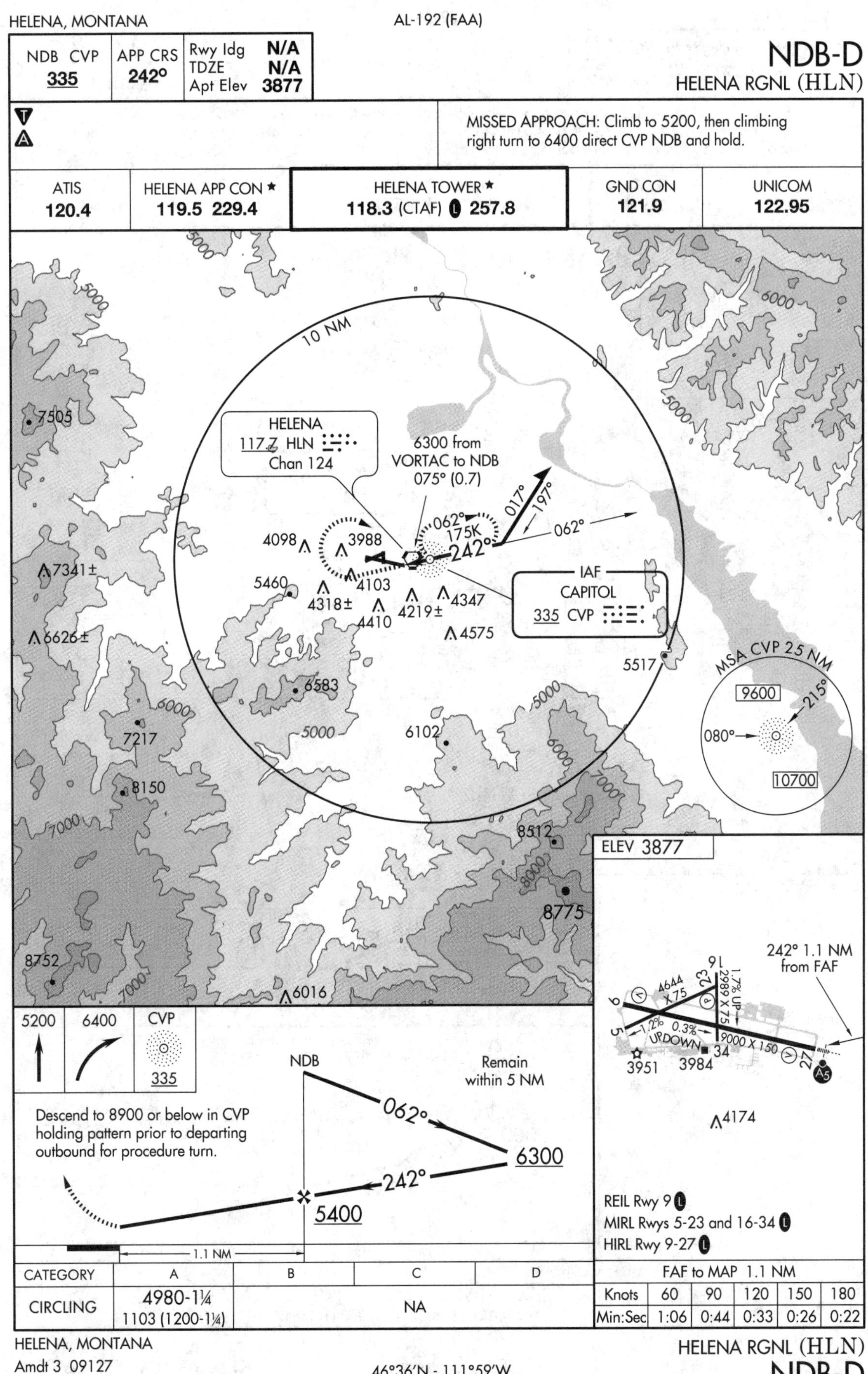
HELENA, MONTANA
AL-192 (FAA)
NDB CVP 335
APP CRS 242°
Rwy ldg N/A
TDZE N/A
Apt Elev 3877
NDB-D
HELENA RGNL (HLN)
MISSED APPROACH: Climb to 5200, then climbing right turn to 6400 direct CVP NDB and hold.
ATIS 120.4
HELENA APP CON ★ 119.5 229.4
HELENA TOWER ★ 118.3 (CTAF) 257.8
GND CON 121.9
UNICOM 122.95
10 NM
HELENA 117.7 HLN Chan 124
6300 from VORTAC to NDB 075° (0.7)
062° 175K
242°
017°
197°
062°
IAF CAPITOL 335 CVP
MSA CVP 25 NM
9600
215°
080°
10700
7505
7341±
6626±
4098
3988
5460
4103
4318±
4410
4219±
4347
4575
5517
6583
7217
5000
6102
8150
7000
6000
8512
8000
8775
8752
6016
ELEV 3877
242° 1.1 NM from FAF
4644 X 75
2989 X 75
1.7% UP
1.2% UP
0.3% DOWN
9000 X 150
3951
3984
4174
REIL Rwy 9
MIRL Rwys 5-23 and 16-34
HIRL Rwy 9-27
5200
6400
CVP 335
NDB
Remain within 5 NM
Descend to 8900 or below in CVP holding pattern prior to departing outbound for procedure turn.
062°
6300
242°
5400
1.1 NM
CATEGORY A B C D
CIRCLING 4980-1¼ 1103 (1200-1¼) NA
FAF to MAP 1.1 NM
Knots 60 90 120 150 180
Min:Sec 1:06 0:44 0:33 0:26 0:22
HELENA, MONTANA
Amdt 3 09127
46°36'N - 111°59'W
HELENA RGNL (HLN)
NDB-D

Figure 365. NDB-D (HLN).

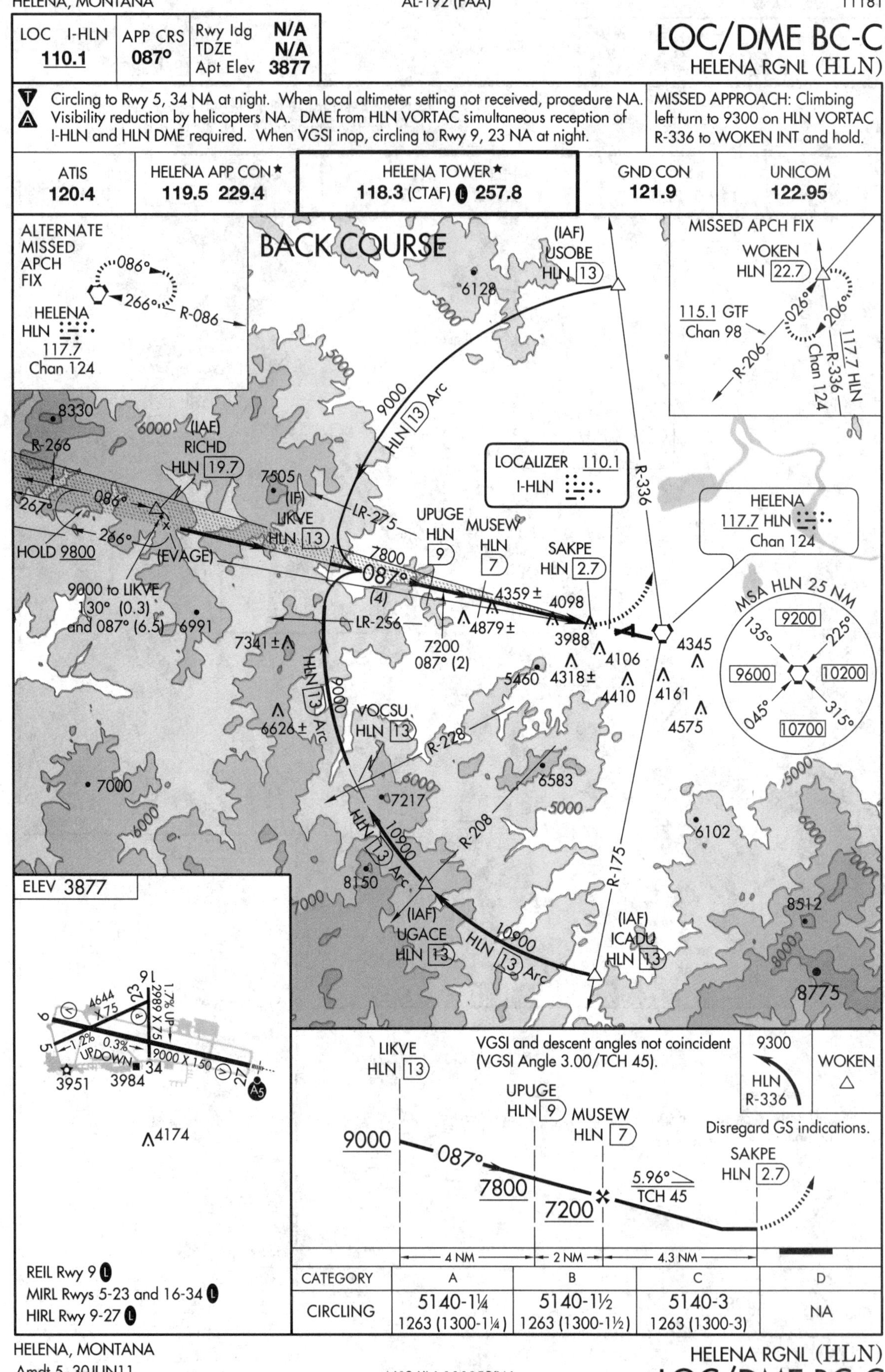

Figure 366. LOC/DME BC-C (HLN).

(MSP5.MSP) 12040 MINNEAPOLIS-ST PAUL INTL/WOLD-CHAMBERLAIN (MSP)

MINNEAPOLIS FIVE DEPARTURE

SL-264 (FAA) MINNEAPOLIS, MINNESOTA

ATIS DEP 120.8
CLNC DEL
133.2
MINNEAPOLIS DEP CON
SOUTH or EAST 124.7 357.4
NORTH or WEST 125.75 357.4
MINNEAPOLIS TOWER
123.95 273.55 (12L-30R)
126.7 273.55 (12R-30L, 4-22)
123.675 273.55 (17-35)

FARGO
116.2 FAR
Chan 109
N46°45.20'-W96°51.13'
L-14, H-2

DULUTH
112.6 DLH
Chan 73
N46°48.13'-W92°12.17'
L-14, H-2

BRAINERD
116.9 BRD
Chan 116
N46°20.89'-W94°01.55'
L-14, H-2

Rwy 17
(For assigned 230° CW 285°)
3500

FLYING CLOUD
117.7 FCM
Chan 124

MINNEAPOLIS
115.3 MSP
Chan 100

GREEN BAY
115.5 GRB
Chan 102
N44°33.31'-W88°11.69'
L-28-31, H-2

ABERDEEN
113.0 ABR
Chan 77
N45°25.04'-W98°22.12'
L-12-14, H-2

MSP 7

DME aircraft Rwy 12L/12R
(For assigned 060° CW 100°)
3500

RAPID CITY
112.3 RAP
Chan 70
N43°58.56'-W103°00.74'
L-12, H-2

NODINE
117.9 ODI
Chan 126
N43°54.74'-W91°28.05'
L-28, H-2

Rwy 30L/30R
(For assigned 220° CW 360°)
3500

R-010

Non DME Aircraft
Rwy 12L/12R
(For assigned 060° CW 100°)
3500

FARMINGTON
115.7 FGT
Chan 104

SIOUX FALLS
115.0 FSD
Chan 97
N43°38.97'-W96°46.87'
L-12, H-2-5

FORT DODGE
113.5 FOD
Chan 82
N42°36.67'-W94°17.69'
L-12, H-5

ROCHESTER
112.0 RST
Chan 57
N43°46.98'-W92°35.80'
L-12-28, H-2

DELLS
117.0 DLL
Chan 117
N43°33.05'-W89°45.82'
L-28, H-2-5

O'NEILL
113.9 ONL
Chan 86
N42°28.23'-W98°41.22'
L-12, H-5

OMAHA
116.3 OVR
Chan 110
N41°10.03'-W95°44.21'
L-10-12, H-5

DES MOINES
117.5 DSM
Chan 122
N41°26.26'-W93°38.91'
L-12-27, H-5

ST JOSEPH
115.5 STJ
Chan 102
N39°57.63'-W94°55.51'
L-10, H-5

KANSAS CITY
113.25 MCI
Chan 79 (Y)
N39°17.12'-W94°44.22'
L-10-27, H-5

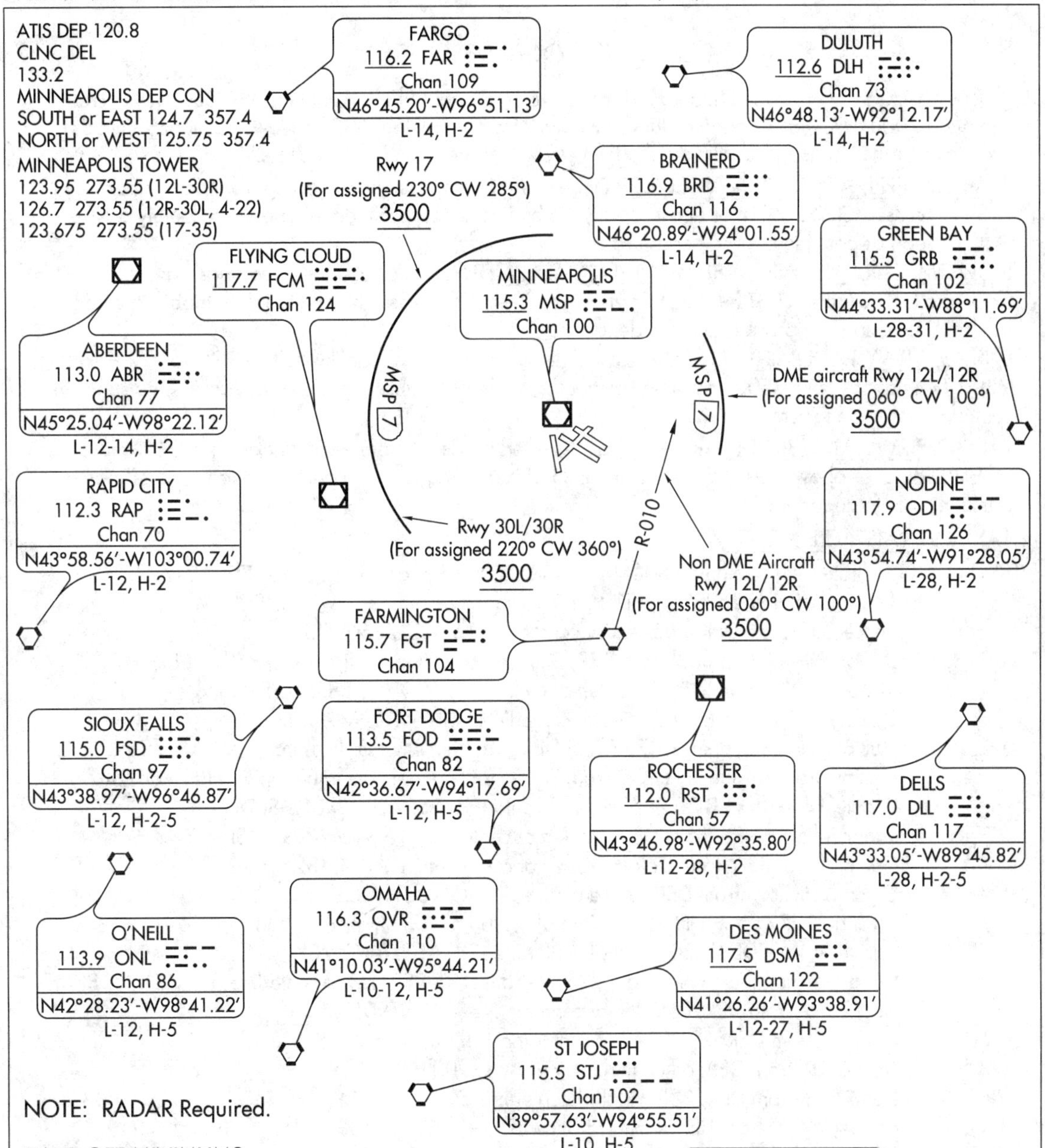

NOTE: RADAR Required.

TAKE-OFF MINIMUMS:
Rwy 4, 12L/R, 17, 22: Standard.
Rwy 30L: Standard with minimum climb of 210' per NM to 2100.
Rwy 30R: Standard with minimum climb of 220' per NM to 2100.
Rwy 35: Standard with minimum climb of 219' per NM to 2100.

DEPARTURE CROSSING RESTRICTIONS:
Runway 12L/R DME aircraft requires an ATC climb gradient of 546' per NM to 3500.
Runway 12L/R Non-DME aircraft requires an ATC climb gradient of 594' per NM to 3500.
Runway 17 requires an ATC climb gradient of 465' per NM to 3500.
Runway 30L/R requires an ATC climb gradient of 380' per NM to 3500.

(NARRATIVE ON FOLLOWING PAGE) NOTE: Chart not to scale.

MINNEAPOLIS FIVE DEPARTURE MINNEAPOLIS, MINNESOTA
(MSP5.MSP) 12040 MINNEAPOLIS-ST PAUL INTL/WOLD-CHAMBERLAIN (MSP)

Figure 367. MINNEAPOLIS FIVE Departure (MSP5.MSP).

(MSP5.MSP) 11349 MINNEAPOLIS-ST PAUL INTL/WOLD-CHAMBERLAIN (MSP)

MINNEAPOLIS FIVE DEPARTURE

SL-264 (FAA) MINNEAPOLIS, MINNESOTA

DEPARTURE ROUTE DESCRIPTION

ALL RUNWAYS: Fly assigned heading for radar vectors to join filed/assigned route. Turbojet aircraft maintain 7000 or lower assigned altitude, all other aircraft maintain 5000 or lower assigned altitude. Expect clearance to assigned altitude/flight level 10 (ten) minutes after departure.

DME EQUIPPED AIRCRAFT RWY 12L/12R DEPARTURES: For assigned heading from 060° clockwise to 100°, cross MSP 7 DME at or above 3500, maintain assigned altitude. If unable to comply advise ATC as soon as possible prior to departure.

NON-DME EQUIPPED AIRCRAFT RWY 12L/12R DEPARTURES: For assigned headings from 060° clockwise to 100°, cross FGT R-010 at or above 3500, maintain assigned altitude. If unable to comply, advise ATC as soon as possible prior to departure.

TAKE-OFF RWY 17 DEPARTURES: For assigned headings from 230° clockwise to 285° cross MSP 7 DME at or above 3500, maintain assigned altitude. If unable to comply, advise ATC as soon as possible prior to departure.

TAKE-OFF RWYS 30L/30R DEPARTURES: For assigned headings from 220° clockwise to 360° cross MSP 7 DME at or above 3500, maintain assigned altitude. If unable to comply, advise ATC as soon as possible prior to departure.

TAKE-OFF OBSTACLE NOTES:

RWY 04: Multiple trees beginning 800′ from DER, 264′ left of centerline, up to 75′ AGL/921′ MSL.
Rod on building 2528′ from DER, 1175′ left of centerline, 78′ AGL/922′ MSL.
Fence 803′ from DER, 585′ left of centerline, 15′ AGL/860′ MSL.
Ant on OL building 456′ from DER, 319′ left of centerline, 13′ AGL/850′ MSL.
LT poles 1932′ from DER, 718′ left of centerline, 45′ AGL/885′ MSL.
Stack 4535′ from DER, 481′ left of centerline, 139′ AGL/949′ MSL.

RWY 12R: Multiple trees beginning 1477′ from DER, 407′ left of centerline, up to 86′ AGL/851′ MSL.
Multiple trees beginning 1426′ from DER, 124′ right of centerline, up to 111′ AGL/847′ MSL.
LT pole 1408′ from DER, 746′ right of centerline, 85′ AGL/843′ MSL.
Radar reflector 983′ from DER, 32′ left of centerline, 15′ AGL/829′ MSL.
Pipe on bldg, 826′ from DER, 576′ left of centerline, 10′ AGL/825′ MSL.
OL on LOC 766′ from DER, on centerline, 7′ AGL/821′ MSL.

RWY 17: Antenna 1272′ from DER, 562′ right of centerline, 57′ AGL/891′ MSL.
Pole 409′ from DER, 530′ right of centerline, 29′ AGL/866′ MSL.
Wind direction indicator on bldg 2619′ from DER, 881′ left of centerline, 97′ AGL/918′ MSL.
Bldg 2619′ from DER, 859′ left of centerline, 84′ AGL/905′ MSL.
LT 1176′ from DER, 291′ right of centerline, 11′ AGL/875′ MSL.
Tree 2619′ from DER, on centerline, 79′ AGL/900′ MSL.

RWY 22: Tree 2906′ from DER, 833′ right of centerline, 94′ AGL/934′ MSL.
Hopper 1717′ from DER, 456′ left of centerline, 48′ AGL/888′ MSL.

RWY 30L: Multiple trees beginning 1113′ from DER, 701′ left of centerline, up to 80′ AGL/919′ MSL.
Tree 1230′ from DER, 633′ right of centerline, 30′ AGL/877′ MSL.
Ground 28′ from DER, 490′ right of centerline, 0′ AGL/844′ MSL.

RWY 30R: Bldg 1056′ from DER, 198′ left of centerline, 13′ AGL/853′ MSL.
Multiple trees beginning 3010′ from DER, 334′ left of centerline, up to 94′ AGL/940′ MSL.
LT pole 1849′ from DER, 698′ right of centerline, 17′ AGL/871′ MSL.
Fence 1327′ from DER, 667′ right of centerline, 8′ AGL/857′ MSL.
Tree 3703′ from DER, 350′ right of centerline, 67′ AGL/914′ MSL.
Rod on pole 3143′ from DER, 47′ right of centerline, 38′ AGL/898′ MSL.

RWY 35: Tree 175′ from DER, 398′ right of centerline, 73′ AGL/883′ MSL.
Multiple trees beginning 1989′ from DER, 351′ left of centerline, up to 65′ AGL/902′ MSL.
Multiple buildings beginning 5.5 NM from DER, 1787′ left of centerline, up to 811′ AGL/1743′ MSL.

MINNEAPOLIS FIVE DEPARTURE MINNEAPOLIS, MINNESOTA

(MSP5.MSP) 11349 MINNEAPOLIS-ST PAUL INTL/WOLD-CHAMBERLAIN (MSP)

Figure 368. MINNEAPOLIS FIVE Departure (MSP5.MSP).

MINNEAPOLIS, MINNESOTA AL-264 (FAA) 12068

LOC/DME I-PJL 110.7 Chan 44	APP CRS 120°	Rwy ldg 7620 TDZE 839 Apt Elev 841

ILS or LOC RWY 12L

MINNEAPOLIS-ST PAUL INTL/WOLD-CHAMBERLAIN (MSP)

For inop ALSF, increase S-ILS 12L Cat E visibility to RVR 4000 and S-LOC 12L Cat E visibility to 2½ mile. For inop ALSF when using AASUN fix minimums, increase S-LOC Cat E visibility to 1½ mile. Simultaneous approach authorized with Rwy 12R.

ALSF-2

MISSED APPROACH: Climb to 1500, then climbing left turn to 4000 via heading 350° and FCM VOR/DME R-046 to WHISK INT/GEP 17.5 DME and hold.

ATIS	MINNEAPOLIS APP CON	MINNEAPOLIS TOWER	GND CON	CLNC DEL
ARR 135.35 239.275 DEP 120.8	119.3 335.5	123.95 273.55 (12L-30R) 126.7 273.55 (12R-30L, 4-22) 123.675 273.55 (17-35)	N 121.8 348.6 S 121.9 348.6 W 127.925	133.2

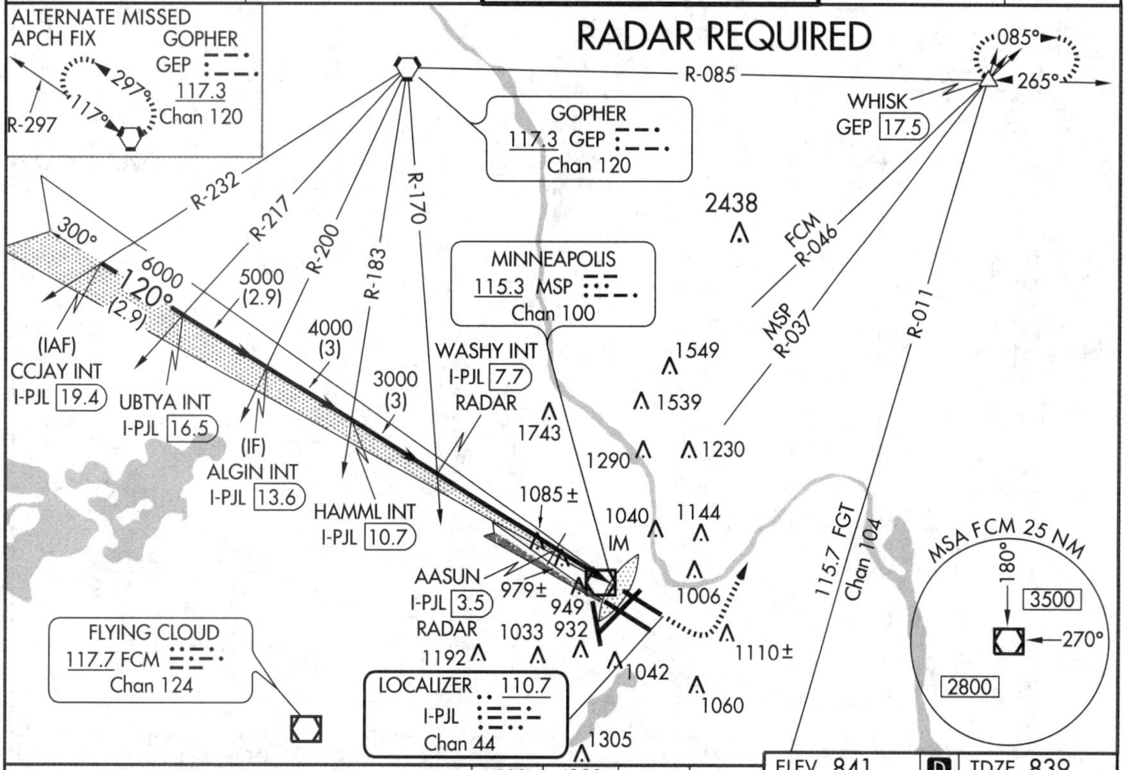

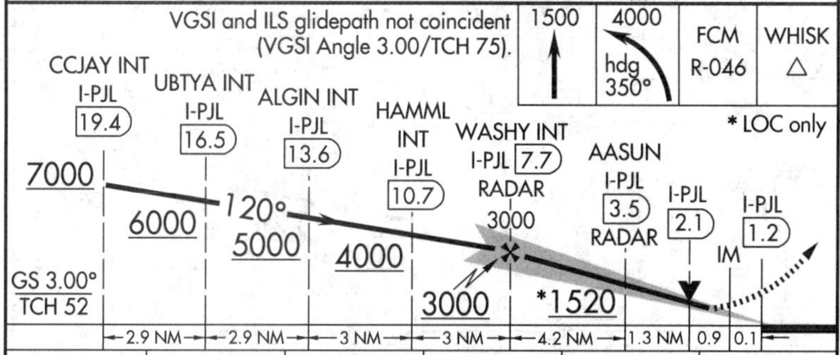

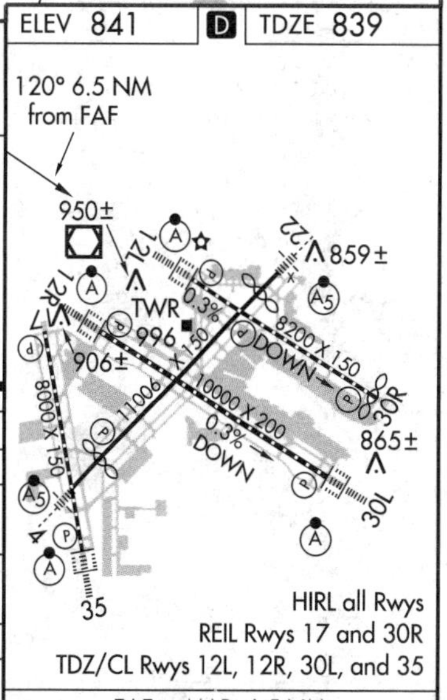

CATEGORY	A	B	C	D	E
S-ILS 12L	1039/18 200 (200-½)				
S-LOC 12L	1520/24 681 (700-½)		1520-1½ 681 (700-1½)	1520-1¾ 681 (700-1¾)	1520-2 681 (700-2)
CIRCLING	1520-1 679 (700-1)		1520-2 679 (700-2)	1520-2¼ 679 (700-2¼)	1660-3 819 (900-3)
AASUN FIX MINIMUMS					
S-LOC 12L	1240/24 401 (400-½)		1240/40 401 (400-¾)		1240/50 401 (400-1)
CIRCLING	1360-1 519 (600-1)		1360-1½ 519 (600-1½)	1460-2 619 (700-2)	1660-3 819 (900-3)

FAF to MAP 6.5 NM

Knots	60	90	120	150	180
Min:Sec	6:30	4:20	3:15	2:36	2:10

MINNEAPOLIS, MINNESOTA
Amdt 8A 08MAR12

MINNEAPOLIS-ST PAUL INTL/WOLD-CHAMBERLAIN (MSP)
44°53'N-93°13'W

ILS or LOC RWY 12L

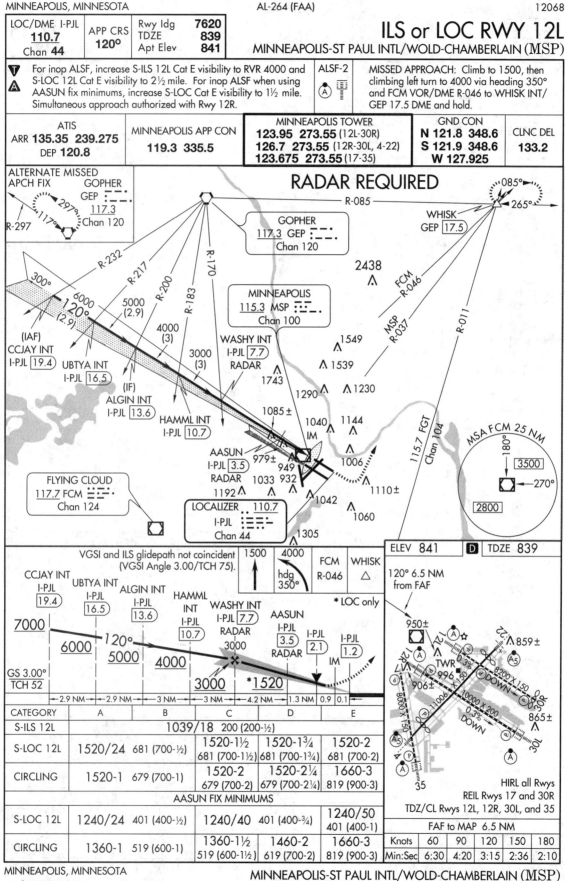

Figure 369. ILS or LOC RWY 12L (MSP).

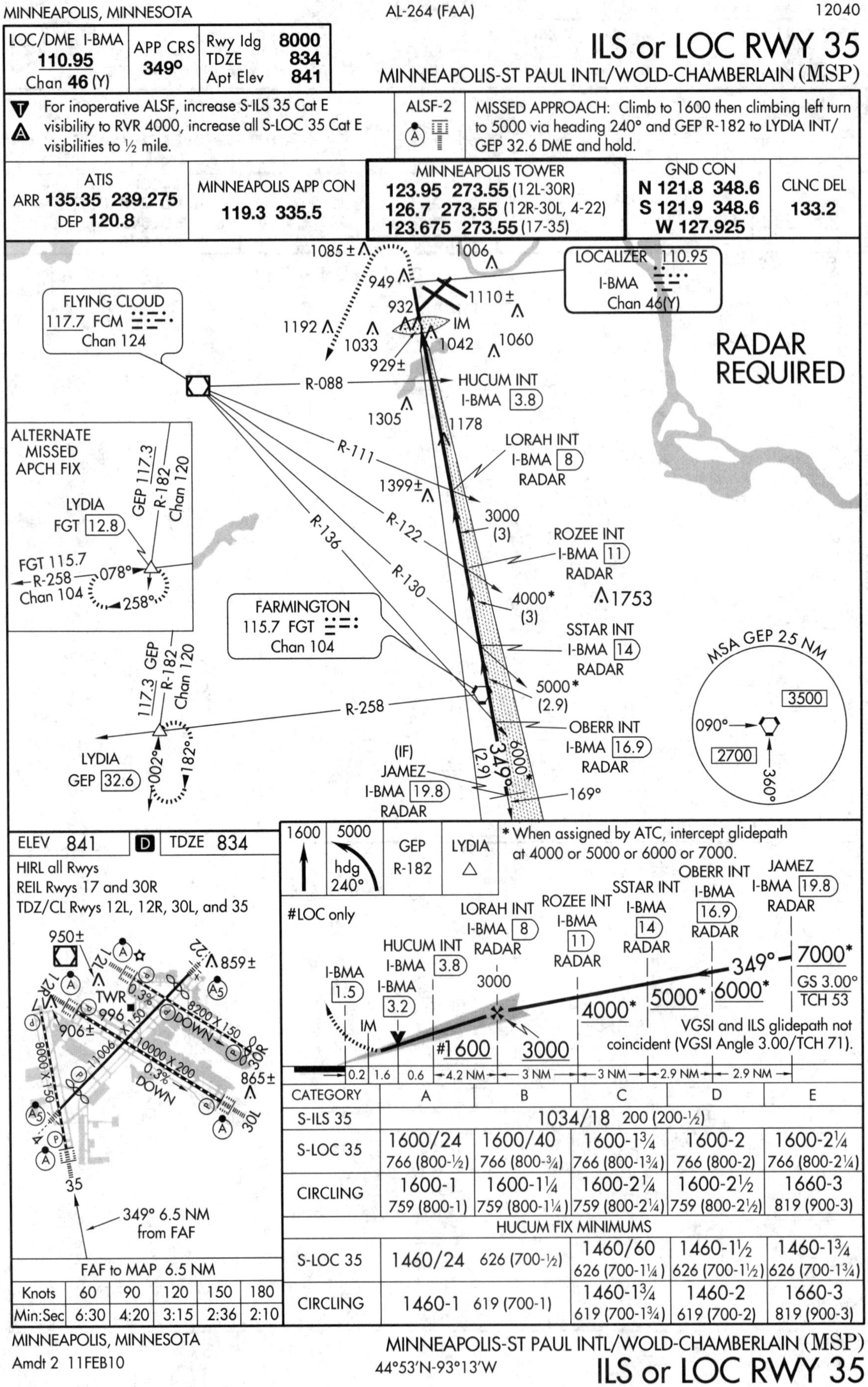
MINNEAPOLIS, MINNESOTA
AL-264 (FAA)
12040
LOC/DME I-BMA 110.95 Chan 46 (Y)
APP CRS 349°
Rwy ldg 8000
TDZE 834
Apt Elev 841
ILS or LOC RWY 35
MINNEAPOLIS-ST PAUL INTL/WOLD-CHAMBERLAIN (MSP)
For inoperative ALSF, increase S-ILS 35 Cat E visibility to RVR 4000, increase all S-LOC 35 Cat E visibilities to ½ mile.
ALSF-2
MISSED APPROACH: Climb to 1600 then climbing left turn to 5000 via heading 240° and GEP R-182 to LYDIA INT/GEP 32.6 DME and hold.
ATIS ARR 135.35 239.275 DEP 120.8
MINNEAPOLIS APP CON 119.3 335.5
MINNEAPOLIS TOWER 123.95 273.55 (12L-30R) 126.7 273.55 (12R-30L, 4-22) 123.675 273.55 (17-35)
GND CON N 121.8 348.6 S 121.9 348.6 W 127.925
CLNC DEL 133.2
LOCALIZER 110.95 I-BMA Chan 46(Y)
FLYING CLOUD 117.7 FCM Chan 124
RADAR REQUIRED
1085±
1006
949
1110±
932
IM
1192
1033
1042
1060
929±
R-088
HUCUM INT I-BMA 3.8
1305
1178
ALTERNATE MISSED APCH FIX
R-111
LORAH INT I-BMA 8 RADAR
GEP 117.3 R-182 Chan 120
LYDIA FGT 12.8
1399±
3000 (3)
R-122
ROZEE INT I-BMA 11 RADAR
R-136
FGT 115.7 R-258 Chan 104
078°
258°
R-130
4000* (3)
1753
FARMINGTON 115.7 FGT Chan 104
SSTAR INT I-BMA 14 RADAR
MSA GEP 25 NM
3500
090°
2700
360°
117.3 GEP R-182 Chan 120
5000* (2.9)
R-258
OBERR INT I-BMA 16.9 RADAR
LYDIA GEP 32.6
002°
182°
(IF) JAMEZ I-BMA 19.8 RADAR
349° (2.9)
6000*
169°
ELEV 841
TDZE 834
HIRL all Rwys
REIL Rwys 17 and 30R
TDZ/CL Rwys 12L, 12R, 30L, and 35
950±
859±
TWR 996
906±
12L
12R
22
4
8200 X 150
0.3% DOWN
11006 X 150
10000 X 200
0.3% DOWN
30R
30L
865±
8000 X 150
17
35
349° 6.5 NM from FAF
1600
5000 hdg 240°
GEP R-182
LYDIA
* When assigned by ATC, intercept glidepath at 4000 or 5000 or 6000 or 7000.
#LOC only
I-BMA 1.5
HUCUM INT I-BMA 3.8
I-BMA 3.2
LORAH INT I-BMA 8 RADAR
ROZEE INT I-BMA 11 RADAR
SSTAR INT I-BMA 14 RADAR
OBERR INT I-BMA 16.9 RADAR
JAMEZ I-BMA 19.8 RADAR
IM
3000
#1600
3000
4000*
5000*
6000*
349°
7000*
GS 3.00° TCH 53
VGSI and ILS glidepath not coincident (VGSI Angle 3.00/TCH 71).
0.2 1.6 0.6 4.2 NM 3 NM 3 NM 2.9 NM 2.9 NM
FAF to MAP 6.5 NM
MINNEAPOLIS, MINNESOTA
Amdt 2 11FEB10
MINNEAPOLIS-ST PAUL INTL/WOLD-CHAMBERLAIN (MSP)
44°53′N-93°13′W
ILS or LOC RWY 35

Knots	60	90	120	150	180
Min:Sec	6:30	4:20	3:15	2:36	2:10

CATEGORY	A	B	C	D	E
S-ILS 35	1034/18 200 (200-½)				
S-LOC 35	1600/24 766 (800-½)	1600/40 766 (800-¾)	1600-1¾ 766 (800-1¾)	1600-2 766 (800-2)	1600-2¼ 766 (800-2¼)
CIRCLING	1600-1 759 (800-1)	1600-1¼ 759 (800-1¼)	1600-2¼ 759 (800-2¼)	1600-2½ 759 (800-2½)	1660-3 819 (900-3)
HUCUM FIX MINIMUMS					
S-LOC 35	1460/24 626 (700-½)		1460/60 626 (700-1¼)	1460-1½ 626 (700-1½)	1460-1¾ 626 (700-1¾)
CIRCLING	1460-1 619 (700-1)		1460-1¾ 619 (700-1¾)	1460-2 619 (700-2)	1660-3 819 (900-3)

Figure 370. ILS or LOC RWY 35 (MSP).

(LANDR.LANDR6) 12096

LANDR SIX ARRIVAL

ST-9077 (FAA)

DENVER, COLORADO

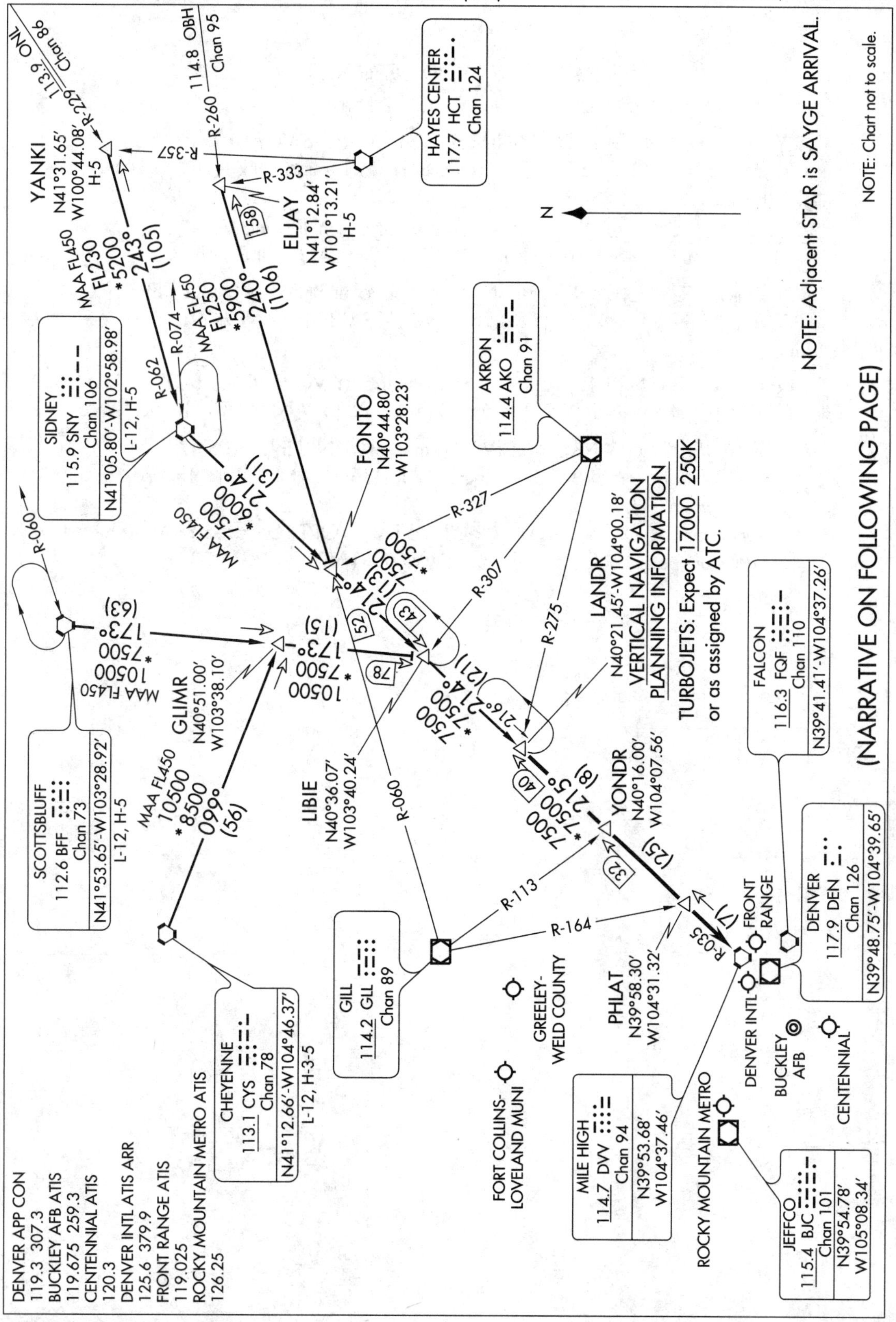

DENVER APP CON
119.3 307.3
BUCKLEY AFB ATIS
119.675 259.3
CENTENNIAL ATIS
120.3
DENVER INTL ATIS ARR
125.6 379.9
FRONT RANGE ATIS
119.025
ROCKY MOUNTAIN METRO ATIS
126.25

VERTICAL NAVIGATION PLANNING INFORMATION

TURBOJETS: Expect 17000 250K or as assigned by ATC.

NOTE: Adjacent STAR is SAYGE ARRIVAL.

NOTE: Chart not to scale.

(NARRATIVE ON FOLLOWING PAGE)

LANDR SIX ARRIVAL

DENVER, COLORADO

(LANDR.LANDR6) 12096

Figure 371. LANDR SIX Arrival (LANDR.LANDR6).

(LANDR.LANDR6) 12096

LANDR SIX ARRIVAL

ST-9077 (FAA)

DENVER, COLORADO

ARRIVAL ROUTE DESCRIPTION

CHEYENNE TRANSITION (CYS.LANDR6): From over CYS VORTAC via CYS R-099 and BFF R-173 to LIBIE INT; then via SNY R-214 and DVV R-035 to LANDR INT. Thence . . . .

ELJAY TRANSITION (ELJAY.LANDR6): From over ELJAY INT via GLL R-060 to FONTO INT, then via SNY R-214 and DVV R-035 to LANDR INT. Thence . . . .

SCOTTSBLUFF TRANSITION (BFF.LANDR6): From over BFF VORTAC via BFF R-173 to LIBIE INT; then via SNY R-214 and DVV R-035 to LANDR INT. Thence . . . .

SIDNEY TRANSITION (SNY.LANDR6): From over SNY VORTAC via SNY R-214 to FONTO INT, then via SNY R-214 and DVV R-035 to LANDR INT. Thence . . . .

YANKI TRANSITION (YANKI.LANDR6): From over YANKI INT via SNY R-062 to SNY VORTAC; then via SNY R-214 and DVV R-035 to LANDR INT. Thence . . . .

. . . . From over LANDR INT via DVV R-035 to DVV VORTAC. Expect RADAR vectors to the final approach course at or before DVV VORTAC.

LANDR SIX ARRIVAL

DENVER, COLORADO

(LANDR.LANDR6) 12096

Figure 372. LANDR SIX Arrival (LANDR.LANDR6).

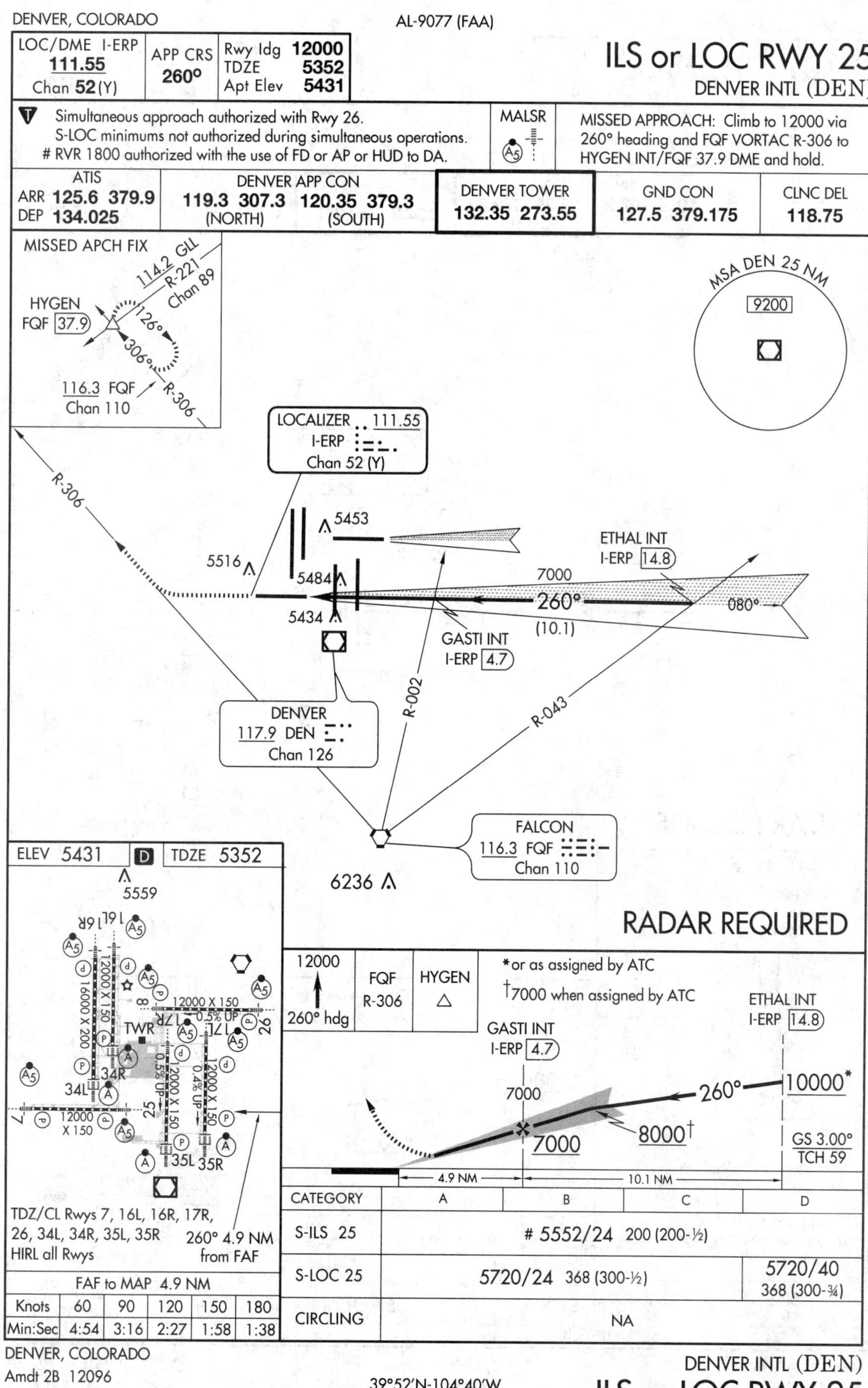

FAF to MAP 4.9 NM					
Knots	60	90	120	150	180
Min:Sec	4:54	3:16	2:27	1:58	1:38

CATEGORY	A	B	C	D
S-ILS 25	# 5552/24 200 (200-½)			
S-LOC 25	5720/24 368 (300-½)			5720/40 368 (300-¾)
CIRCLING	NA			

Figure 373. ILS or LOC RWY 25 (DEN).

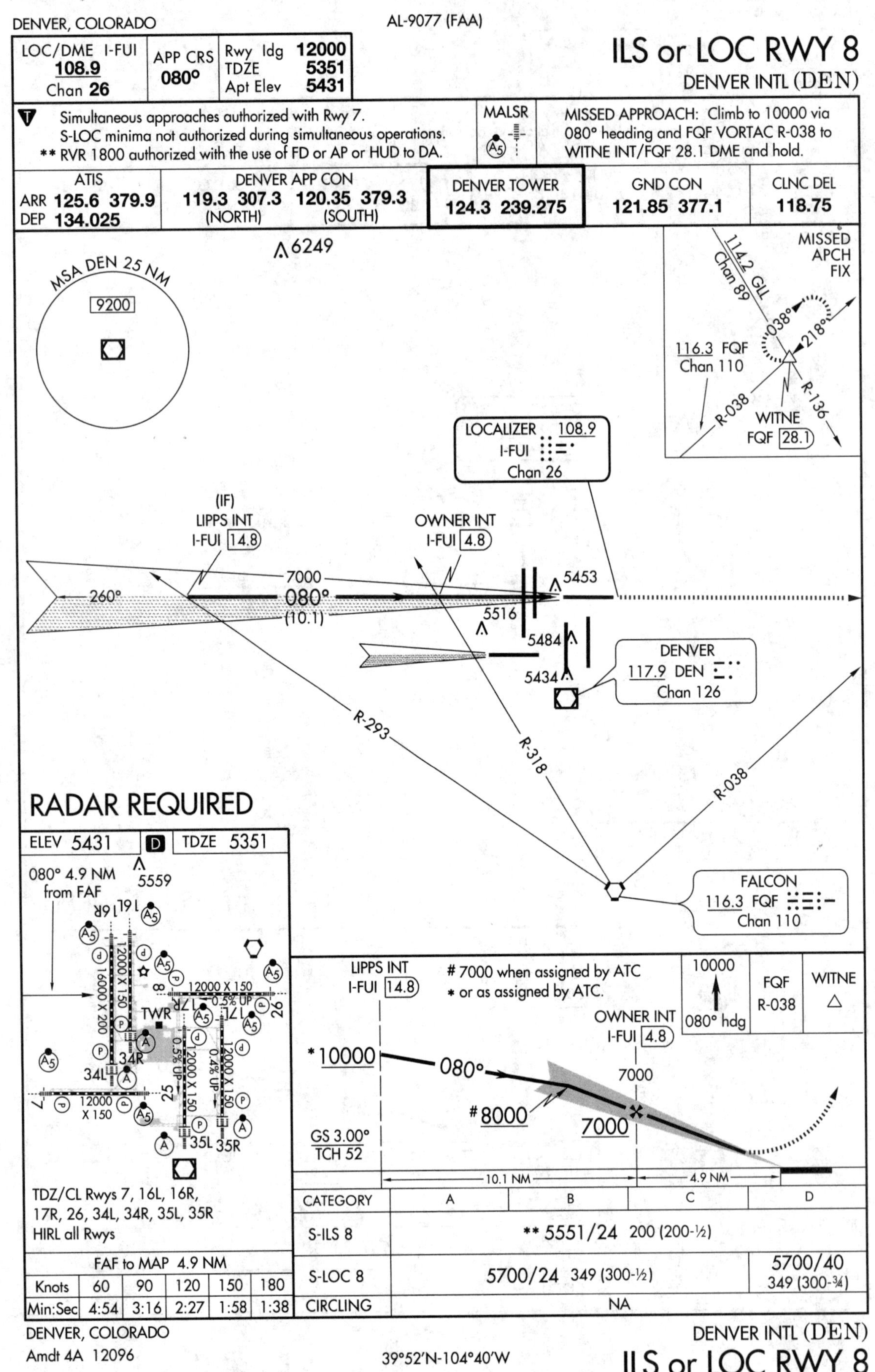

FAF to MAP 4.9 NM					
Knots	60	90	120	150	180
Min:Sec	4:54	3:16	2:27	1:58	1:38

CATEGORY	A	B	C	D
S-ILS 8	** 5551/24 200 (200-½)			
S-LOC 8	5700/24 349 (300-½)			5700/40 349 (300-¾)
CIRCLING	NA			

Figure 374. ILS or LOC RWY 8 (DEN).

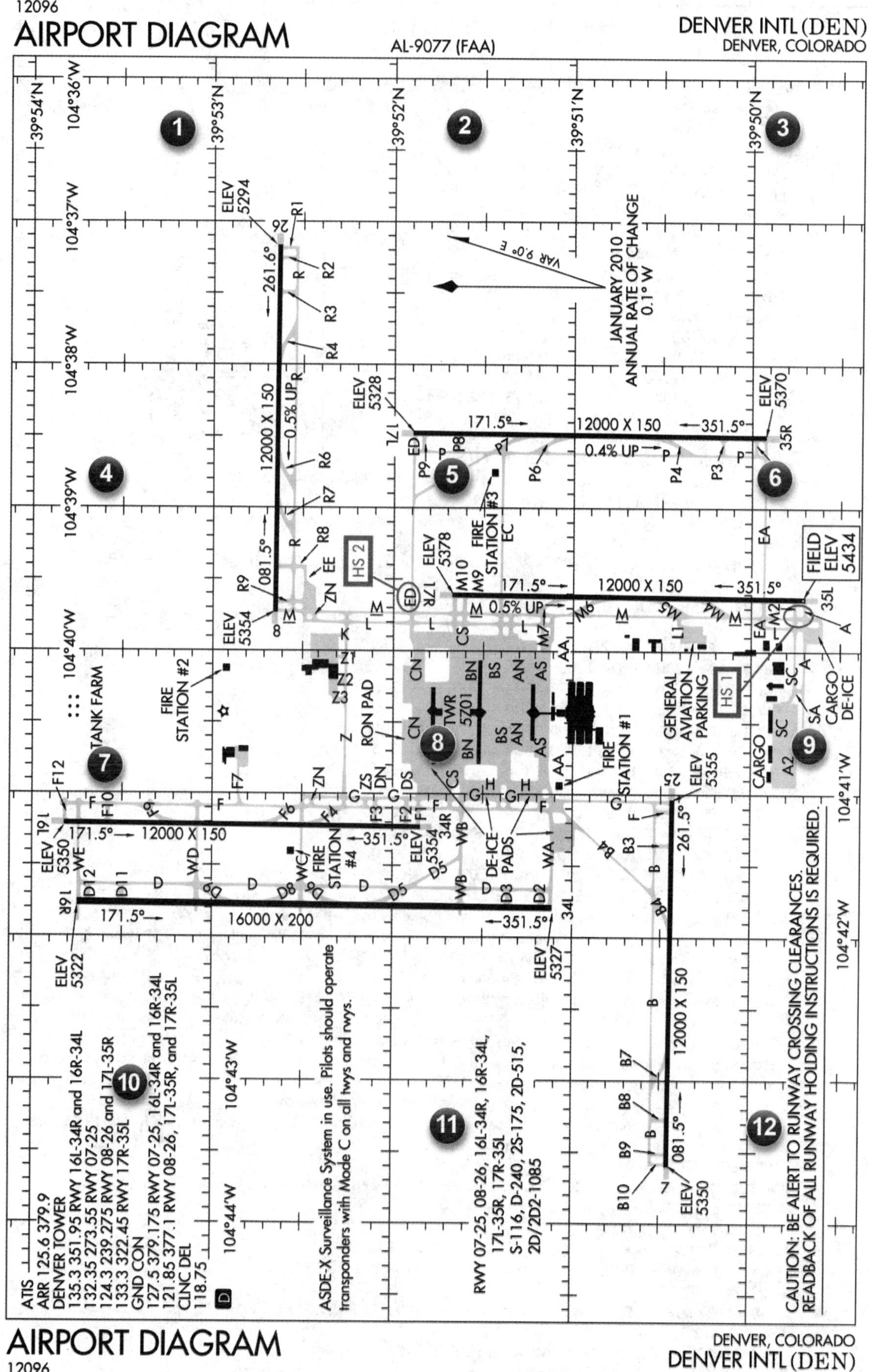

Figure 375. Airport Diagram (DEN).

COLORADO

DENVER INTL (DEN) 16 NE UTC–7(–6DT) N39º51.70′ W104º40.39′ **DENVER**
5434 B S4 **FUEL** 100, 100LL, JET A, MOGAS OX 1, 3 Class I, ARFF Index E **H–3F, 5A, L–10F, A**
NOTAM FILE DEN **IAP, AD**

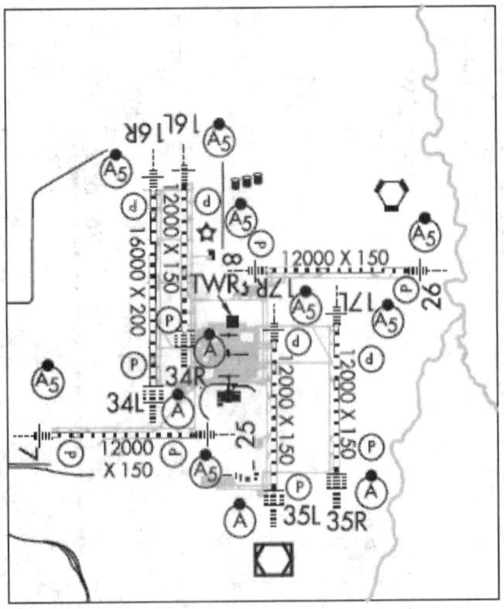

RWY 16R–34L: H16000X200 (CONC–GRVD) S–116, D–240, 2S–175, 2D–515, 2D/2D2–1085 PCN 92 R/B/W/T HIRL CL
RWY 16R: MALSR. TDZL. PAPI(P4R)—GA 3.0º TCH 55′.
RWY 34L: ALSF2. TDZL. PAPI(P4L)—GA 3.0º TCH 50′.
RWY 07–25: H12000X150 (CONC–GRVD) S–116, D–240, 2S–175, 2D–515, 2D/2D2–1085 PCN 92 R/B/W/T HIRL CL
RWY 07: MALSR. TDZL. PAPI(P4R)—GA 3.0º TCH 55′.
RWY 25: MALSR. PAPI(P4L)—GA 3.0º TCH 59′.
RWY 08–26: H12000X150 (CONC–GRVD) S–116, D–240, 2S–175, 2D–515, 2D/2D2–1085 PCN 92 R/B/W/T HIRL CL
RWY 08: MALSR. PAPI(P4L)—GA 3.0º TCH 52′.
RWY 26: MALSR. TDZL. PAPI(P4L)—GA 3.0º TCH 55′. 0.5% up.
RWY 16L–34R: H12000X150 (CONC–GRVD) S–116, D–240, 2S–175, 2D–515, 2D/2D2–1085 PCN 92 R/B/W/T HIRL CL
RWY 16L: MALSR. TDZL. PAPI(P4L)—GA 3.0º TCH 60′.
RWY 34R: ALSF2. TDZL. PAPI(P4L)—GA 3.0º TCH 59′.
RWY 17L–35R: H12000X150 (CONC–GRVD) S–116, D–240, 2S–175, 2D–515, 2D/2D2–1085 PCN 92 R/B/W/T HIRL CL
RWY 17L: MALSR. PAPI(P4L)—GA 3.0º TCH 55′. 0.4% up.
RWY 35R: ALSF2. TDZL. PAPI(P4R)—GA 3.0º TCH 59′.
RWY 17R–35L: H12000X150 (CONC–GRVD) S–116, D–240, 2S–175, 2D–515, 2D/2D2–1085 PCN 92 R/B/W/T HIRL CL
RWY 17R: MALSR. TDZL. PAPI(P4L)—GA 3.0º TCH 60′. 0.5% up.
RWY 35L: ALSF2. TDZL. PAPI(P4R)—GA 3.0º TCH 57′.

RUNWAY DECLARED DISTANCE INFORMATION
RWY 07: TORA–12000 TODA–12000 ASDA–12000 LDA–12000
RWY 08: TORA–12000 TODA–13000 ASDA–12000 LDA–12000
RWY 16L: TORA–12000 TODA–12000 ASDA–12000 LDA–12000
RWY 16R: TORA–16000 TODA–16000 ASDA–16000 LDA–16000
RWY 17L: TORA–12000 TODA–12000 ASDA–12000 LDA–12000
RWY 17R: TORA–12000 TODA–12000 ASDA–12000 LDA–12000
RWY 25: TORA–12000 TODA–13000 ASDA–12000 LDA–12000
RWY 26: TORA–12000 TODA–12000 ASDA–12000 LDA–12000
RWY 34L: TORA–16000 TODA–16000 ASDA–16000 LDA–16000
RWY 34R: TORA–12000 TODA–13000 ASDA–12000 LDA–12000
RWY 35L: TORA–12000 TODA–12000 ASDA–12000 LDA–12000
RWY 35R: TORA–12000 TODA–12000 ASDA–12000 LDA–12000

AIRPORT REMARKS: Attended continuously. Waterfowl and migratory bird activity invof arpt year round. ASDE–X Surveillance System in use: Pilots should opr transponders with Mode C on all twys and rwys. Arpt maintains clearways (500′ X 1000′). 1.25% slope) on departure Rwy 08, Rwy 26, and Rwy 34R. RVR Rwy 07 touchdown, rollout, RVR Rwy 25 touchdown, rollout, RVR Rwy 08 touchdown, rollout, RVR Rwy 26 touchdown, rollout, RVR Rwy 16L touchdown, midfield, rollout, RVR Rwy 34R touchdown, midfield, rollout, RVR Rwy 17L touchdown, midfield, rollout, RVR Rwy 35R touchdown, midfield, rollout, RVR Rwy 17R touchdown, midfield, rollout, RVR Rwy 35L touchdown, midfield, rollout. RVR Rwy 16R touchdown, midfield, rollout, RVR Rwy 34L touchdown, midfield, rollout. Overhead passenger bridge on South side of concourse `A′ provides 42 ft tail and 118 ft wingspan clearance when on twy centerline. Insufficient twy corner fillet pavement in the SE corner of the Twy M/M2 intersection for acft with wingspan over 107 ft. Informal rwy use program is in effect 24 hours a day. For additional noise abatement information contact airport management at 303–342–4200. Customs avbl with prior permission. Ldg fee. Flight Notification Service (ADCUS) avbl. NOTE: See Special Notices—Continuous Power Facilities.
WEATHER DATA SOURCES: ASOS (303) 342-0838 LLWAS-NE. TDWR.
COMMUNICATIONS: D-ATIS ARR 125.6 303-342-0819 **D-ATIS DEP** 134.025 303-342-0820 **UNICOM** 122.95
RCO 122.2 122.35 (DENVER RADIO)
RCO 123.65 (DENVER RADIO)
Ⓡ**APP CON** 119.3 124.95 (North) 120.35 126.55 (South) **FINAL CON** 120.8
TOWER 132.35 (Rwy 07-25) 135.3 (Rwy 16L-34R, Rwy 16R-34L) 133.3 (Rwy 17R-35L) 124.3 (Rwy 08-26 and 17L-35R)
GND CON 127.5 (Rwy 07-25, Rwy 16L-34R and Rwy 16R-34L) 121.85 (Rwys 08-26, 17L-35R and 17R-35L)
CLNC DEL 118.75
Ⓡ**DEP CON** 128.25 (East) 127.05 (North) 126.1 (West) 128.45 (South)
AIRSPACE: CLASS B See VFR Terminal Area Chart
RADIO AIDS TO NAVIGATION: NOTAM FILE DEN.

Figure 376. Excerpt from Chart Supplement.

COLORADO

CONTINUED FROM PRECEDING PAGE

(H) VORW/DME 117.9 DEN Chan 126 N39°48.75′ W104°39.64′ 338° 3.0 NM to fld. 5452/11E.
ILS/DME 111.55 I-DZG Chan 52(Y) Rwy 07. Class IE.
ILS/DME 108.9 I-FUI Chan 26 Rwy 08.
ILS/DME 111.1 I-LTT Chan 48 Rwy 16L. Class IE.
ILS/DME 111.9 I-DQQ Chan 56 Rwy 16R.
ILS/DME 110.15 I-BXP Chan 38(Y) Rwy 17L. Class IE.
ILS/DME 108.5 I-ACX Chan 22 Rwy 17R. Class IE.
ILS/DME 111.55 I-ERP Chan 52(Y) Rwy 25. Class IE.
ILS/DME 108.9 I-JOY Chan 26 Rwy 26. Class IE.
ILS/DME 111.9 I-DXU Chan 56 Rwy 34L. Class IIIE.
ILS/DME 111.1 I-OUF Chan 48 Rwy 34R. Class IIIE.
ILS/DME 108.5 I-AQD Chan 22 Rwy 35L.
ILS/DME 110.15 I-DPP Chan 38(Y) Rwy 35R. Class IIIE.
COMM/NAV/WEATHER REMARKS: Emerg frequency 121.5 not avbl at twr.

FRONT RANGE (FTG) 19 E UTC–7(–6DT) N39°47.12′ W104°32.59′ **DENVER**
5512 B S4 **FUEL** 100LL, JET A OX 1, 2 TPA—6500(988) NOTAM FILE FTG **H–5A, L–10F, A**
IAP, AD
RWY 08–26: H8000X100 (ASPH) S–28, D–40 HIRL
RWY 08: REIL. PAPI(P2L)—GA 3.0° TCH 50′. Rgt tfc. 0.5% up.
RWY 26: MALSR. PAPI(P2L)—GA 3.0° TCH 50′. 0.4% down.
RWY 17–35: H8000X100 (ASPH) S–34, D–75 MIRL
RWY 17: REIL. PAPI(P4L)—GA 3.0° TCH 50′. 0.5% up.
RWY 35: MALSR. PAPI(P4L)—GA 3.0° TCH 50′. Rgt tfc.
AIRPORT REMARKS: Attended 1400–0400Z‡. For svc after hrs call 303–208–8536. 24 hr credit card 100LL self fueling station. Be alert, intensive USAF student training invof Colorado Springs and Pueblo Colorado. Noise sensitive areas SE, S and SW of arpt. Avoid flights blo 1,000 ft over populated areas. Blue and yellow reflectors along Twy A, B, C, E edges. ACTIVATE MIRL Rwy 17–35, HIRL Rwy 08–26, PAPI Rwy 08, Rwy 26, Rwy 17 and Rwy 35 and REIL Rwy 08 and Rwy 17, MALSR Rwy 26 and Rwy 35—CTAF. See Special Notices—USAF 306 FTG Flight Training Areas, Vicinity of Colorado Springs and Pueblo Colorado.

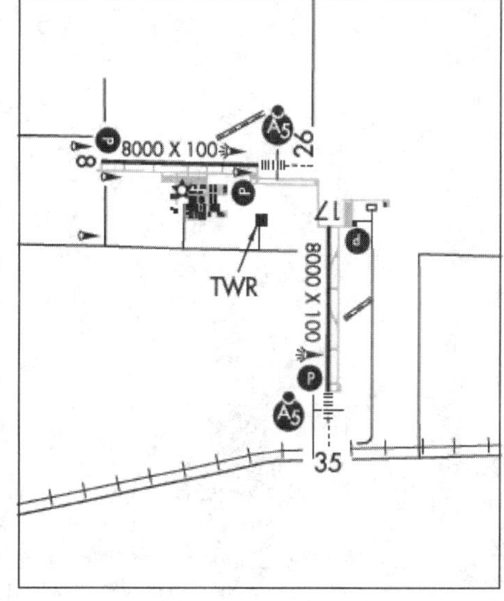

WEATHER DATA SOURCES: AWOS-3 119.025 (303) 261-9104.
COMMUNICATIONS: CTAF 120.2 **ATIS** 119.025 **UNICOM** 122.95
DENVER APP/DEP CON 128.2
TOWER 120.2 (1400-0400Z‡) **GND CON** 124.7 **CLNC DEL** 124.7
DENVER CLNC DEL 121.75 (0400-1400Z‡)
AIRSPACE: CLASS D svc 1400-0400Z‡ other times CLASS G
RADIO AIDS TO NAVIGATION: NOTAM FILE DEN.
DENVER (H) VORW/DME 117.9 DEN Chan 126 N39°48.75′ W104°39.64′ 096° 5.7 NM to fld. 5452/11E.
SKIPI NDB (LOM) 321 FT N39°47.51′ W104°26.05′ 255° 5.1 NM to fld. Unmonitored.
ILS/DME 110.9 I-FZR Chan 46 Rwy 17.
ILS/DME 109.3 I-FTG Chan 30 Rwy 26. LOM SKIPI NDB. Unmonitored.
ILS/DME 110.9 I-VWT Chan 46 Rwy 35.

Figure 377. Excerpt from Chart Supplement.

(MCCRN3.LAS) 09351 SL-662 (FAA)

MCCARRAN THREE DEPARTURE

LAS VEGAS/MC CARRAN INTL (LAS)
LAS VEGAS, NEVADA

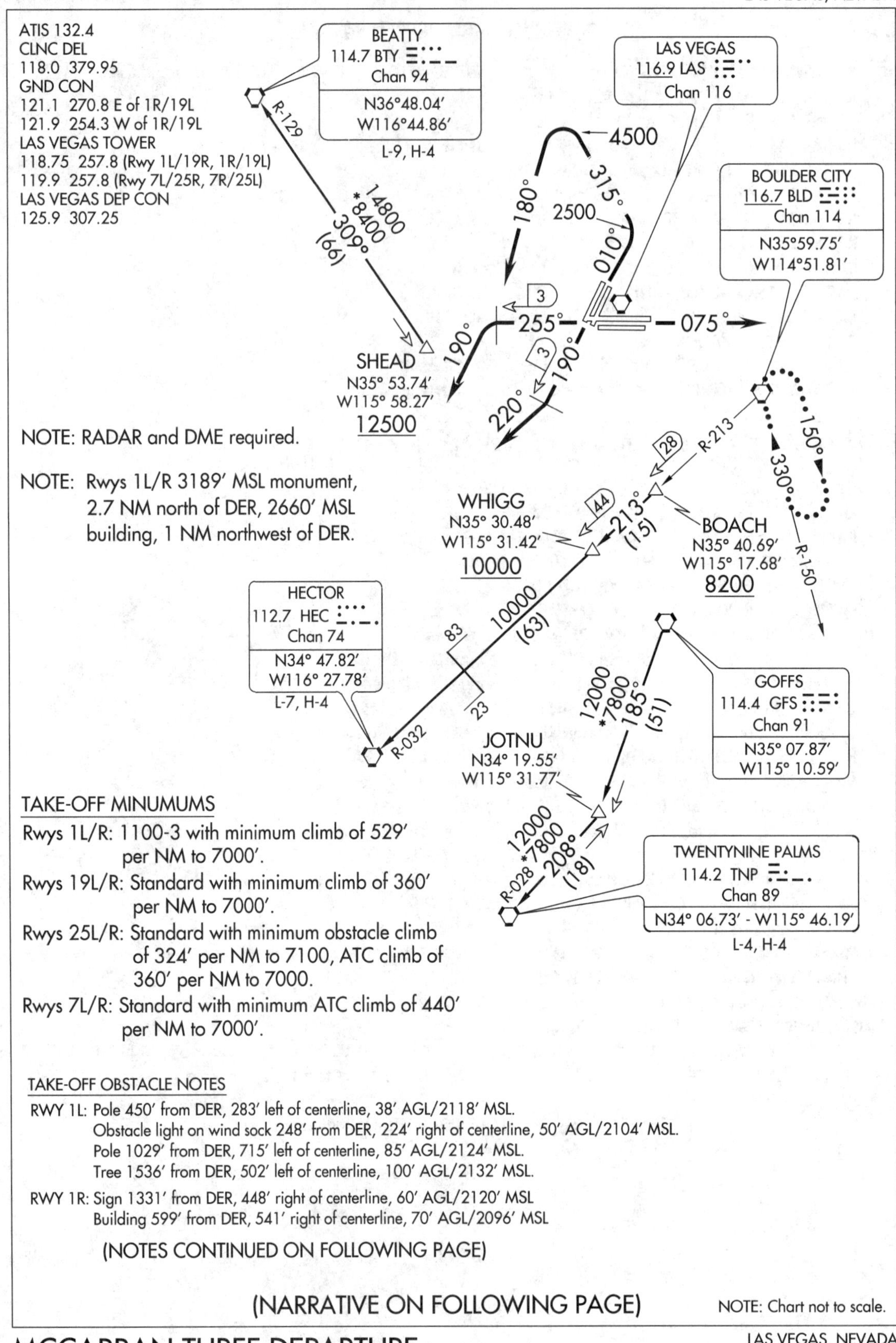

Figure 378. MCCARRAN THREE Departure (MCCRN3.LAS).

(MCCRN3.LAS) 09351 SL-662 (FAA)

MCCARRAN THREE DEPARTURE

LAS VEGAS/MC CARRAN INTL (LAS)
LAS VEGAS, NEVADA

DEPARTURE ROUTE DESCRIPTION

TAKE-OFF RUNWAYS 1L/R: Climb via heading 010° to 2500′, then climbing left turn via heading 315° to 4500′, then climbing left turn heading 180°, thence ....

TAKE-OFF RUNWAYS 7L/R: Climb via heading 075°, thence ....

TAKE-OFF RUNWAYS 19L/R: Climb via heading 190° until LAS VORTAC 3 DME, then right turn via heading 220°, thence ....

TAKE-OFF RUNWAYS 25L/R: Climb via heading 255° until LAS VORTAC 3 DME, then left turn via heading 190°, thence ....

....via radar vectors to transition or assigned route, maintain 7000′, expect clearance to filed altitude 2 minutes after departure.

LOST COMMUNICATIONS: If no contact with ATC upon reaching 7000′, proceed direct BLD VORTAC, then climb in BLD VORTAC holding pattern to the appropriate MEA for route of flight.

BEATTY TRANSITION (MCCRN3.BTY): From over SHEAD INT via BTY R-129 to BTY VORTAC.

HECTOR TRANSITION (MCCRN3.HEC): From over BOACH INT via BLD R-213 and HEC R-032 to HEC VORTAC.

TWENTY NINE PALMS TRANSITION (MCCRN3.TNP): From over GFS VORTAC via GFS R-185 to JOTNU INT, then via TNP R-028 to TNP VORTAC.

TAKE-OFF OBSTACLE NOTES (CONTINUED)

RWY 25R: Light pole 3115′ from DER, 1033′ right of centerline, 109′ AGL/2301′ MSL.
Light on pole 1.5 NM from DER, 2836′ left of centerline, 124′ AGL/2457′ MSL.
Light pole 1.7 NM from DER, 2965′ left of centerline, 139′ AGL/2469′ MSL.
Light on pole 1100′ from DER, 508′ left of centerline, 47′ AGL/2226′ MSL.
Building 1822′ from DER, 652′ left of centerline, 46′ AGL/2238′ MSL.
Building 2202′ from DER, 596′ left of centerline, 44′ AGL/2246′ MSL.
Rod on building 534′ from DER, 369′ left of centerline, 33′ AGL/2202′ MSL.
Road 678′ from DER, 16′ right of centerline, 35′ AGL/2201′ MSL.
Light on localizer antenna 533′ from DER, 32′ AGL/2195′ MSL.

RWY 25L: Pole 2860′ from DER, 813′ left of centerline, 57′ AGL/2236′ MSL.
Sign 3672′ from DER, 1302′ left of centerline, 57′ AGL/2256′ MSL.
Antenna on building 1002′ from DER, 251′ left of centerline, 34′ AGL/2183′ MSL.
Pole 3677′ from DER, 145′ left of centerline, 67′ AGL/2249′ MSL.

RWY 7L: Tree 1257′ from DER, 789′ left of centerline, 85′ AGL/2077′ MSL.
Light pole 747′ from DER, 441′ right of centerline, 62′ AGL/2057′ MSL.
Tree 1007′ from DER, 557′ right of centerline, 70′ AGL/2062′ MSL.

RWY 7R: Light on wind sock 102′ from DER, 300′ right of centerline, 30′ AGL/2051′ MSL.

RWY 19L: Pole 1394′ from DER, 533′ right of centerline, 36′ AGL/2236′ MSL.
Sign 2181′ from DER, 1062′ right of centerline, 50′ AGL/2256′ MSL.
Rod on building 2921′ from DER, 581′ right of centerline, 50′ AGL/2262′ MSL.
Pole 2633′ from DER, 319′ right of centerline, 40′ AGL/2246′ MSL.

RWY 19R: Pole 1135′ from DER, 619′ right of centerline, 65′ AGL/2249′ MSL.
Pole 756′ from DER, 618′ right of centerline, 50′ AGL/2231′ MSL.
Sign 2182′ from DER, 125′ right of centerline, 50′ AGL/2256′ MSL.
Pole 1396′ from DER, 403′ left of centerline, 55′ AGL/2236′ MSL.
Rod on building 197′ from DER, 441′ right of centerline, 30′ AGL/2202′ MSL.
Rod on building 2922′ from DER, 356′ left of centerline, 50′ AGL/2262′ MSL.

MCCARRAN THREE DEPARTURE
(MCCRN3.LAS) 09351
LAS VEGAS, NEVADA
LAS VEGAS/MC CARRAN INTL (LAS)

Figure 379. MCCARRAN THREE Departure (MCCRN3.LAS).

CALIFORNIA

SAN FRANCISCO INTL (SFO) 8 SE UTC–8(–7DT) N37°37.14´ W122°22.49´ **SAN FRANCISCO**
13 B S4 **FUEL** 100, 100LL, JET A OX 1, 2, 3, 4 LRA Class I, ARFF Index E **H–3B, L–2F, 3B, A**
NOTAM FILE SFO **IAP, AD**

RWY 10L–28R: H11870X200 (ASPH–GRVD) PCN 80 F/B/X/T HIRL CL
RWY 10L: REIL. PAPI(P4L)—GA 3.0° TCH 80´. Tower.
RWY 28R: ALSF2. TDZL. PAPI(P4L)—GA 3.0° TCH 70´. Rgt tfc.
RWY 10R–28L: H10602X200 (ASPH–GRVD) PCN 80 F/B/X/T HIRL CL
RWY 10R: PAPI(P4L)—GA 3.0° TCH 75´. Tower. Rgt tfc.
RWY 28L: SSALR. PAPI(P4L)—GA 3.0° TCH 75´.
RWY 01R–19L: H8648X200 (ASPH–GRVD) PCN 100F/B/X/T HIRL CL
RWY 01R: REIL. Thld dsplcd 238´. Tree.
RWY 19L: MALSF. TDZL. PAPI(P4L)—GA 3.0° TCH 75´.
RWY 01L–19R: H7500X200 (ASPH-CONC–GRVD) PCN 90 F/B/X/T HIRL CL
RWY 01L: REIL. Thld dsplcd 491´.
RWY 19R: PAPI(P4L)—GA 3.0° TCH 73´.

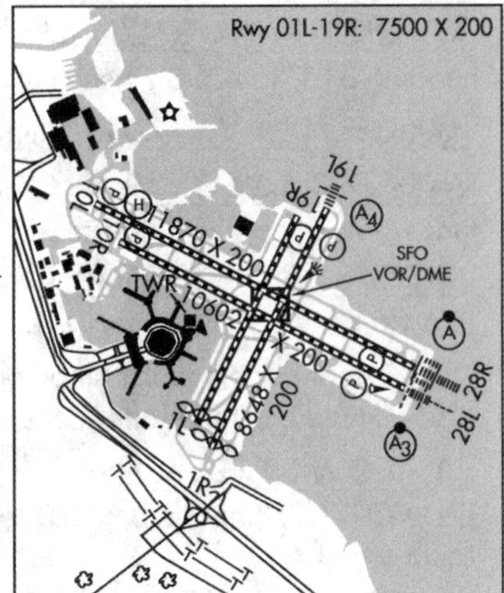

AIRPORT REMARKS: Attended continuously. PAEW AER 28L, Rwy 28R and Rwy 19L indef. Flocks of birds feeding along shoreline adjacent to arpt, on occasions fly across various parts of arpt. Due to obstructed vision, SFO twr is able to provide only limited arpt tfc control svc on Twy A between gates 88 and 89. Twr personnel are unable to determine whether this area is clear of traffic or obstructions. Rwy 10 preferred rwy between 0900–1400Z‡ weather and flight conditions permitting. Simultaneous ops in effect all rwys. Helicopter ldg area marked on Twy (C) west of Twy (R) opr for civil and military use. Noise sensitive arpt. For noise abatement procedures ctc arpt noise office Monday–Friday 1600–0100Z‡ by calling 650–821–5100. Airline pilots shall strictly follow the painted nose gear lines and no oversteering adjustment is permitted. No grooving exists at arpt rwy intersections. Rwy 01L–19R, 01R–19L, Rwy 10R–28L, Rwy 10L–28R grooved full length except at rwy intersections. B747, B777, A330, A340 or larger acft are restricted from using Twy A1 when B747–400, A340–600 or larger acft are holding short of Rwy 01R on Twy A. 747–400´s shall taxi at a speed of less than 10 miles per hour on all non–restricted taxiways on the terminal side of the intersecting rwys. All outbound Twy Y heavy aircraft with a wingspan of 171´ or greater under power prohibited from entering westbound Twy Z. Ramp clsd to acft with wingspan over 117´ at Terminal 1, gate C41 indef. Movement speed of not more than 5 miles per hour is required when two 747–400´s pass or overtake each other on parallel taxiways A and B. Rwy 19L MALSF has a NSTD length of 1115´ with 3 sequenced flashers. Ldg fee. Flight Notification Service (ADCUS) available. NOTE: See Special Notices—Intersection Departures During Period of Darkness, Expanded Charted Visual Flight Procedures. Continuous Power Facilities, Special Noise Abatement Procedures, Special Noise Abatement Procedures—Preferential Runways.

WEATHER DATA SOURCES: ASOS (650) 872-0246 LLWAS.

COMMUNICATIONS: D-ATIS 135.45 118.85 115.8 113.7 650-877-3585/8422 **UNICOM** 122.95
Ⓡ**NORCAL APP CON** 135.65 (S) 133.95
TOWER 120.5 **GND CON** 121.8 **CLNC DEL** 118.2 **PRE TAXI CLNC** 118.2
Ⓡ**NORCAL DEP CON** 135.1 (SE-W) 120.9 (NW-E)

AIRSPACE: CLASS B See VFR Terminal Area Chart

RADIO AIDS TO NAVIGATION: NOTAM FILE SFO.
(L) VORW/DME 115.8 SFO Chan 105 N37°37.17´ W122°22.43´ at fld. 13/17E.
VOR DME unusable:
025°-065° byd 30 NM blo 18,000´
035°-055° byd 12 NM blo 6,500´
150°-190° byd 25 NM blo 4,500´
190°-260° byd 10 NM blo 4,500´
260°-295° byd 35 NM blo 3,000´
295°-330° byd 20 NM blo 8,000´
BRIJJ NDB (LOM) 379 GW N37°34.33´ W122°15.59´ 282° 6.2 NM to fld. LOM unusable 160°-195° byd 6 NM.
ILS/DME 108.9 I-SIA Chan 26 Rwy 19L. Class IE. Ry 19L glideslope deviations are possible when critical areas are not required to be protected. Acft operating invof glideslope transmitter. Pilots should be alert for momentary localizer course excursions due to large aircraft operating in vicinity of localizer antenna.
ILS/DME 109.55 I-SFO Chan 32(Y) Rwy 28L. Class IE.
ILS/DME 111.7 I-GWQ Chan 54 Rwy 28R. Class IIIE. LOM BRIJJ NDB. LOM unusable 160°-195° byd 6 NM.
LDA/DME 110.75 I-FNP Chan 44(Y) Rwy 28R.

Figure 380. Excerpt from Chart Supplement.

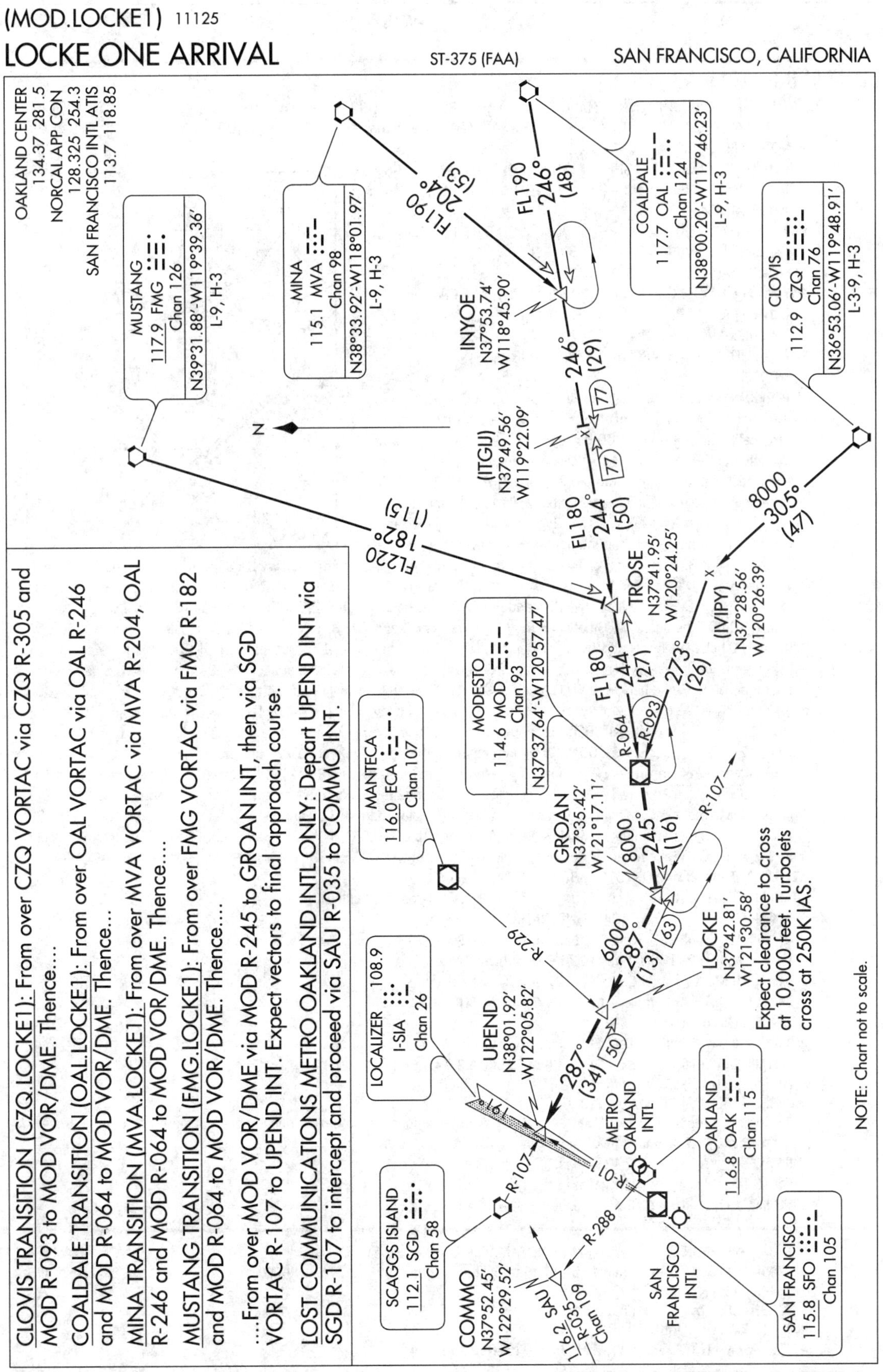
(MOD.LOCKE1) 11125
LOCKE ONE ARRIVAL
ST-375 (FAA)
SAN FRANCISCO, CALIFORNIA
OAKLAND CENTER
134.37 281.5
NORCAL APP CON
128.325 254.3
SAN FRANCISCO INTL ATIS
113.7 118.85
MUSTANG
117.9 FMG
Chan 126
N39°31.88′-W119°39.36′
L-9, H-3
MINA
115.1 MVA
Chan 98
N38°33.92′-W118°01.97′
L-9, H-3
COALDALE
117.7 OAL
Chan 124
N38°00.20′-W117°46.23′
L-9, H-3
CLOVIS
112.9 CZQ
Chan 76
N36°53.06′-W119°48.91′
L-3-9, H-3
FL190 204° (53)
FL190 246° (48)
INYOE
N37°53.74′
W118°45.90′
246° (29)
(ITGIJ)
N37°49.56′
W119°22.09′
FL180 244° (50)
FL220 182° (115)
8000 305° (47)
TROSE
N37°41.95′
W120°24.25′
(IVIPY)
N37°28.56′
W120°26.39′
FL180 244° (27)
273° (26)
R-064
R-093
MODESTO
114.6 MOD
Chan 93
N37°37.64′-W120°57.47′
MANTECA
116.0 ECA
Chan 107
GROAN
N37°35.42′
W121°17.11′
8000 245° (16)
R-107
R-229
6000 287° (13)
LOCKE
N37°42.81′
W121°30.58′
Expect clearance to cross at 10,000 feet. Turbojets cross at 250K IAS.
LOCALIZER 108.9
I-SIA
Chan 26
UPEND
N38°01.92′
W122°05.82′
287° (34)
METRO OAKLAND INTL
OAKLAND
116.8 OAK
Chan 115
R-011
R-107
R-288
SCAGGS ISLAND
112.1 SGD
Chan 58
COMMO
N37°52.45′
W122°29.52′
116.2 SAU
R-035
Chan 109
SAN FRANCISCO INTL
SAN FRANCISCO
115.8 SFO
Chan 105
NOTE: Chart not to scale.
CLOVIS TRANSITION (CZQ.LOCKE1): From over CZQ VORTAC via CZQ R-305 and MOD R-093 to MOD VOR/DME. Thence....
COALDALE TRANSITION (OAL.LOCKE1): From over OAL VORTAC via OAL R-246 and MOD R-064 to MOD VOR/DME. Thence....
MINA TRANSITION (MVA.LOCKE1): From over MVA VORTAC via MVA R-204, OAL R-246 and MOD R-064 to MOD VOR/DME. Thence....
MUSTANG TRANSITION (FMG.LOCKE1): From over FMG VORTAC via FMG R-182 and MOD R-064 to MOD VOR/DME. Thence....
....From over MOD VOR/DME via MOD R-245 to GROAN INT, then via SGD VORTAC R-107 to UPEND INT. Expect vectors to final approach course.
LOST COMMUNICATIONS METRO OAKLAND INTL ONLY: Depart UPEND INT via SGD R-107 to intercept and proceed via SAU R-035 to COMMO INT.
LOCKE ONE ARRIVAL
(MOD.LOCKE1) 11125
SAN FRANCISCO, CALIFORNIA

Figure 381. LOCKE ONE Arrival (MOD.LOCKE1).

CALIFORNIA

OAKLAND

METROPOLITAN OAKLAND INTL (OAK) 4 S UTC–8(–7DT) N37°43.28′ W122°13.24′ **SAN FRANCISCO**
9 B S4 **FUEL** 100LL, JET A OX 1, 2, 3, 4 TPA—See Remarks LRA Class I, ARFF Index D **H–3B, L–2F, 3B, A**
NOTAM FILE OAK **IAP, AD**

RWY 11–29: H10000X150 (ASPH–GRVD) PCN 71 F/A/W/T HIRL CL
RWY 11: MALSR. PAPI(P4L)—GA 2.75° TCH 65′. Rgt tfc.
RWY 29: ALSF2. TDZL. PAPI(P4L)—GA 3.0° TCH 71′.
RWY 09R–27L: H6213X150 (ASPH–GRVD) PCN 97 F/B/W/T HIRL
RWY 09R: REIL. PAPI(P4R)—GA 3.0° TCH 50′.
RWY 27L: PAPI(P4L)—GA 3.0° TCH 71′.
RWY 09L–27R: H5454X150 (ASPH–GRVD) PCN 69 F/C/W/T HIRL
RWY 09L: PAPI(P4R)—GA 3.0° TCH 49′.
RWY 27R: MALSR. PAPI(P4L)—GA 2.9° TCH 57′. Bldg. Rgt tfc.
RWY 15–33: H3372X75 (ASPH) S–12.5 MIRL
RWY 33: Rgt tfc.

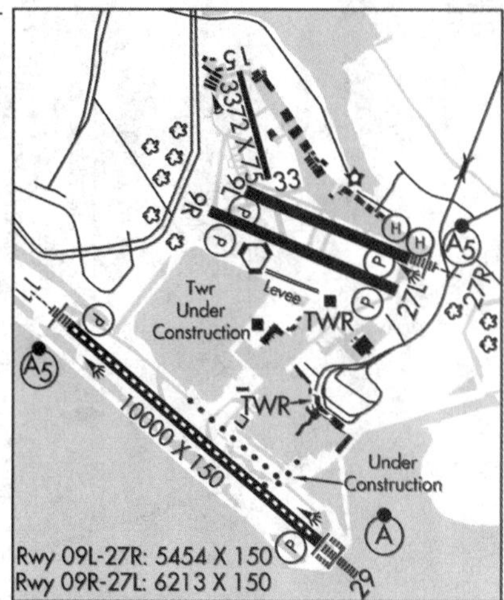

AIRPORT REMARKS: Attended continuously. Rwy 15–33 CLOSED to air carrier acft. Birds on and invof arpt. Acft with experimental or limited certification having over 1,000 horsepower or 4,000 pounds are restricted to Rwy 11–29. 24 hr Noise abatement procedure–turbojet and turbofan powered acft, turboprops over 17,000 lbs, four engine reciprocating powered acft, and surplus Military acft over 12,500 lbs should not depart Rwy 27L and Rwy 27R or land on Rwy 09L and Rwy 09R. For noise abatement information ctc noise abatement office at 510–563–6463. Intersection of Twy B, Twy W and Twy V not visible from twr. Twy K between Rwy 33 and Twy D and portions of Twy D not visible from twr. Twy A, Twy E, Twy G, Twy H between Rwy 27R and Twy C max acft weight 150,000 lbs. Twy G and Twy H between Rwy 27L and Rwy 27R, max acft weight 12,500 lbs. Twy P max acft weight 24,000 lbs single, 40,000 lbs dual. Twy C between Rwy 27R and Twy G and Twy B, Twy J, and Twy D max acft weight 9,000,000 lbs. Twy C between Twy G and Twy J max acft weight 25,000 lbs single, 175,000 lbs dual, 4,000,000 lbs tandem. Twy C between Twy J and Twy F max acft weight 25,000 lbs single, 150,000 lbs dual. 155,000 lbs tandem (dual tandem not authorized). Twy K between Twy D and intersection Twy F, Twy L, Twy K max acft weight 25,000 lbs single, 115,000 lbs dual, 140,000 lbs tandem. Twy K between Rwy 9R and intersection Twy F, Twy L, Twy K max acft weight 25,000 lbs single, 115,000 lbs dual, 140,000 lbs tandem. Twy K between Rwy 9R and intersection Twy F, Twy L, Twy K max acft weight 25,000 lbs single, 45,000 lbs dual, tandem not authorized. Preferential rwy use program in effect 0600–1400Z‡. North fld preferred arrival Rwy 27L, north fld preferred departure Rwys 09R or 27R. If these Rwys unacceptable for safety or twr instruction then Rwy 11–29 must be used. Noise prohibitions not applicable in emerg or whenever Rwy 11–29 is closed due to maintenance, safety, winds or weather. 400′ blast pad Rwy 29 and 500′ blast pad Rwy 11. Rwys 29, 27R and 27L distance remaining signs left side. TPA—Rwy 27L 606(597), TPA—Rwy 27R 1006(997). Ldg fee may apply for Rwy 11–29, rwy commercial ops and tiedown, ctc afld ops 510–563–3361. Flight Notification Service (ADCUS) avbl.

WEATHER DATA SOURCES: ASOS (510) 383-9514 **HIWAS** 116.8 OAK.

COMMUNICATIONS: D-ATIS 133.775 (510) 635-5850 (N and S Complex) **UNICOM** 122.95
OAKLAND RCO 122.2 122.5 (OAKLAND RADIO)
®**NORCAL APP CON** 125.35 (East) 135.65 (South) 135.1 (West) 134.5 120.9
®**NORCAL DEP CON** 135.1 (West) 120.9 (Northwest)
OAKLAND TOWER 118.3 (N Complex) 127.2 (S Complex) 124.9
GND CON 121.75 (S Complex) 121.9 (N Complex) **CLNC DEL** 121.1

AIRSPACE: CLASS C svc ctc **APP CON**

RADIO AIDS TO NAVIGATION: NOTAM FILE OAK.
OAKLAND (H) VORTACW 116.8 OAK Chan 115 N37°43.56′ W122°13.42′ at fld. 10/17E. **HIWAS.**
DME unusable:
335°-065° byd 30 NM blo 8,000′
ILS 111.9 I-AAZ Rwy 11. Class IE. Glideslope deviations are possible when critical areas are not required to be protected. Acft operating invof glideslope transmitter.
ILS 109.9 I-OAK Rwy 27R. Class IE.
ILS 108.7 I-INB Rwy 29. Class IIIE.

COMM/NAV/WEATHER REMARKS: Emerg frequency 121.5 not avbl at twr.

OAKLAND N37°43.56′ W122°13.42′ NOTAM FILE OAK. **SAN FRANCISCO**
(H) VORTACW 116.8 OAK Chan 115 at Metropolitan Oakland Intl. 10/17E. **HIWAS.** **H–3A, L–2F, 3B, A**
DME unusable:
335°-065° byd 30 NM blo 8,000′
RCO 122.2 122.5 (OAKLAND RADIO)
ASOS OAK N37°43.28′ W122°13.24′. (510) 383-9514.

Figure 382. Excerpt from Chart Supplement.

FLORIDA

KEY WEST INTL (EYW) 2 E UTC -5(-4DT) N24°33.37' W81°45.57' **MIAMI**
3 B S4 **FUEL** 100, JET A AOE Class I, ARFF Index IB NOTAM FILE EYW **L–21D, 23C**
RWY 09–27: H4801X100 (ASPH–GRVD) S–75, D–125, 2D–195 MIRL **IAP, AD**
RWY 09: REIL. VASI(V4L)—GA 3.0° TCH 34'. Rgt tfc.
RWY 27: REIL. VASI(V4L)—GA 3.0° TCH 34'.
ARRESTING GEAR/SYSTEM
RWY 09: EMAS

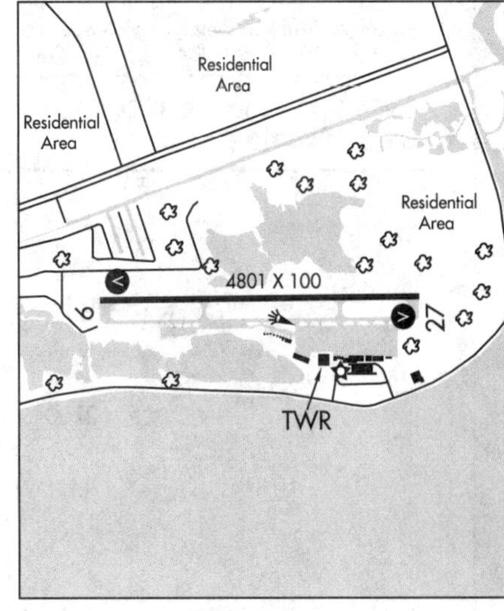

AIRPORT REMARKS: Attended 1200–0400Z‡. Parachute Jumping. Numerous flocks of birds on and in the vicinity of airport. Departing VFR acft requested to maintain rwy heading until reaching fld boundary, then execute turns for N or S dep. Restricted area R–2916 located 14 NM NE of arpt has strobe–lgtd and marked balloon and cable to 14,000 ft. Extremely noise sensitive area. Urge no ops 0400–1200Z‡. Use NBAA close in noise abatement procedures other times. Local ordinance rqr engine runups in designated area on N side commercial ramp from 0400–1200Z‡ and fines. PPR for unscheduled air carrier operations with more than 30 passenger seats 0430–1045Z‡; Call arpt manager 305–809–5200. PPR for acft exceeding rwy weight bearing capacity; call arpt manager 305–809–5200. Intensive military jet tfc S and E of arpt; acft entering arpt tfc area from SE through W. Enter arpt tfc area blo 2000'; refer to MIAMI VFR Terminal Area Chart for suggested VFR flyway routes. Twy A5 and Twy A6 not visible from twr. ACTIVATE MIRL Rwy 09–27, VASI/REIL Rwys 09–27—CTAF. Flight Notification Service (ADCUS) available. NOTE: See Special Notices—U.S. Special Customs Requirement.
WEATHER DATA SOURCES: ASOS 119.65 (305) 292–4046. **HIWAS** 113.5 EYW.
COMMUNICATIONS: CTAF 118.2 **ATIS** 119.675 **UNICOM** 122.95
RCO 122.1R 113.5T (MIAMI RADIO)
RCO 123.65 122.2 (MIAMI RADIO)
Ⓡ **NAVY KEY WEST APP/DEP CON** 124.025 126.575 (1200–0300Z‡) Ⓡ **MIAMI CENTER APP/DEP CON** 133.5 (0300–1200Z‡)
TOWER 118.2 (1200–0200Z‡) **GND CON** 121.9 **CLNC DEL** 121.9
AIRSPACE: CLASS D svc 1200–0200Z‡ other times CLASS G.
RADIO AIDS TO NAVIGATION: NOTAM FILE EYW.
(H) VORTAC 113.5 EYW Chan 82 N24°35.15' W81°48.03' 127° 2.9 NM to fld. 10/01E.
HIWAS. VOR unusable 040°–050°, 210°–240°.
FISH HOOK NDB (HW) 332 FIS N24°32.90' W81°47.18' 076° 1.5 NM to fld.
ASR (1100–0300Z‡)
COMM/NAV/WEATHER REMARKS: FSS freqs 123.65 and 122.2 unusable 330°–015° beyond 20 NM below 1500'. VORTAC unusable 121°–139°. Acft overflying SIMPL, ACRUZ, CANOA, and MAXIM shall ctc Miami Center 10 minutes prior to crossing the Miami flight information region 132.2.

Figure 383. Excerpt from Chart Supplement.

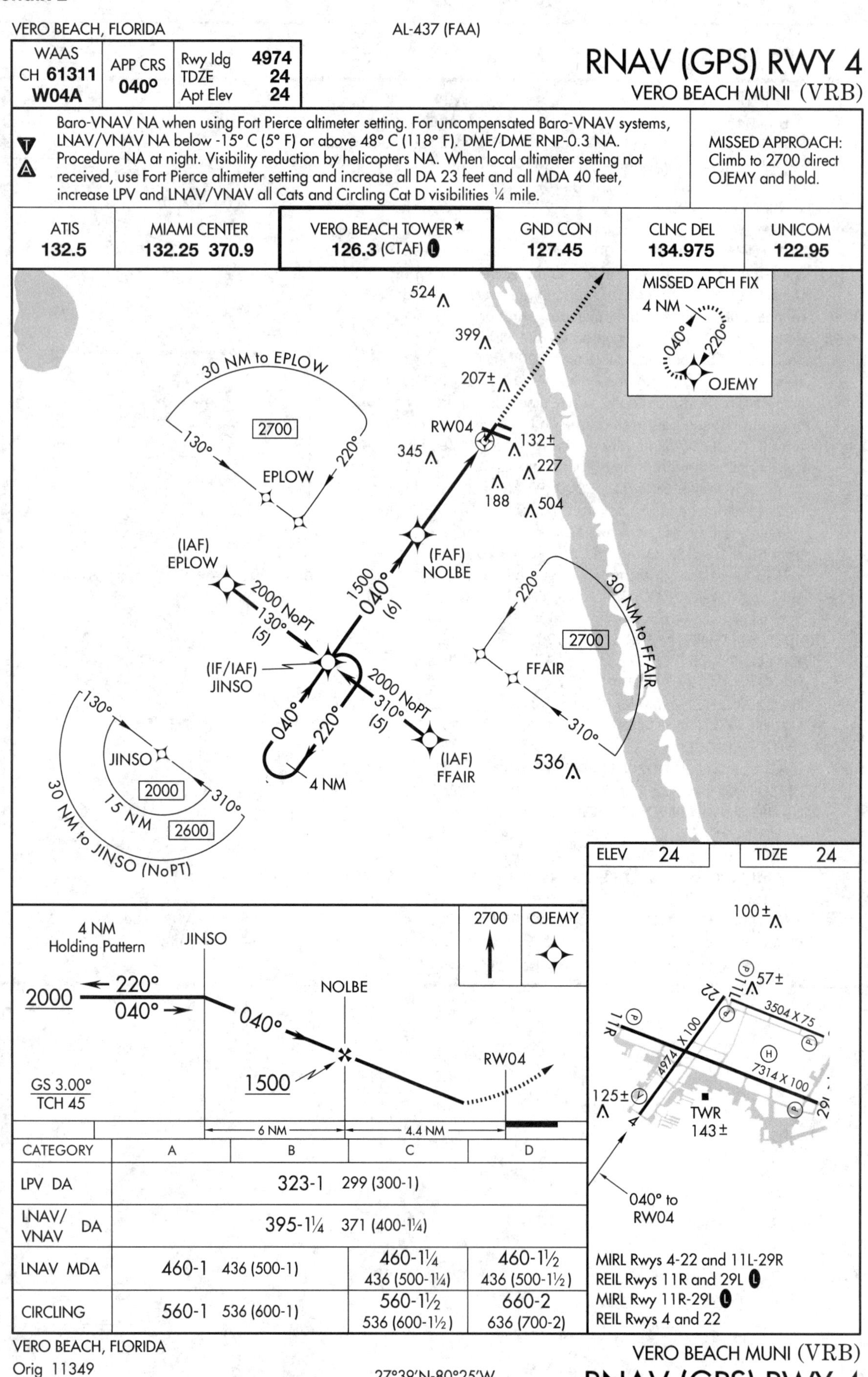

CATEGORY	A	B	C	D
LPV DA	323-1 299 (300-1)			
LNAV/VNAV DA	395-1¼ 371 (400-1¼)			
LNAV MDA	460-1 436 (500-1)		460-1¼ 436 (500-1¼)	460-1½ 436 (500-1½)
CIRCLING	560-1 536 (600-1)		560-1½ 536 (600-1½)	660-2 636 (700-2)

MIRL Rwys 4-22 and 11L-29R
REIL Rwys 11R and 29L
MIRL Rwy 11R-29L
REIL Rwys 4 and 22

VERO BEACH, FLORIDA
Orig 11349
27°39′N-80°25′W
VERO BEACH MUNI (VRB)
RNAV (GPS) RWY 4

Figure 384. RNAV (GPS) RWY 4 (VRB).

VERO BEACH MUNI (VRB) 1 NW UTC-5(-4DT) N27°39.33' W80°25.08' **MIAMI**
24 B S4 **FUEL** 100, JET A OX 1, 2 TPA—See Remarks Class IV, ARFF Index A **H–8I, L–24F**
NOTAM FILE VRB **IAP, AD**
RWY 11R–29L: H7314X100 (ASPH–GRVD)
S–85, D–115, 2S–146, 2D–220 MIRL
RWY 11R: REIL. PAPI (P4L)—GA 3.0° TCH 41'. Trees.
RWY 29L: REIL. PAPI(P4L) TCH 58'.
RWY 04–22: H4974X100 (ASPH–GRVD) S–30, D–115, 2S–146, 2D–220 MIRL
RWY 04: REIL. VASI(V4L)—GA 3.0° TCH 45'.Trees.
RWY 22: REIL. PAPI(P4L)—GA 3.0° TCH 42'. Trees.
RWY 11L–29R: H3504X75 (ASPH) S–12.5 MIRL
RWY 11L: PAPI(P2L)—GA 3.0° TCH 37'. Tree.
RWY 29R: PAPI(P2L)—GA 3.5° TCH 35'. Poles. 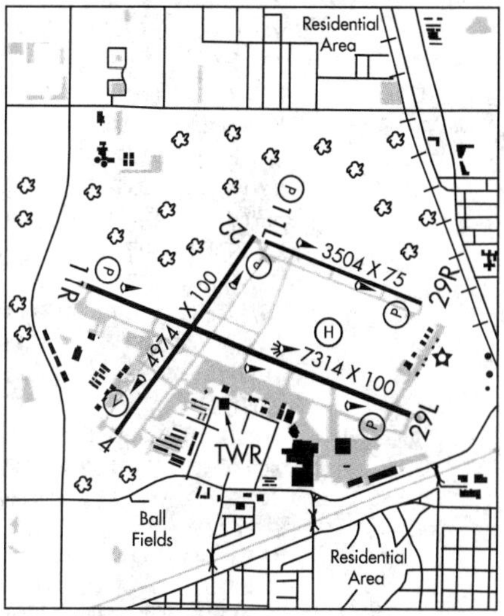
LAND AND HOLD SHORT OPERATIONS

LANDING	HOLD SHORT POINT	DIST AVBL
RWY 29L	04/22	4700

AIRPORT REMARKS: Attended 1200–0200Z‡. Rwy 04–22 CLOSED when twr clsd. TPA 1024(1000) large acft 1524(1500). Rwy 11L–29R CLOSED when twr clsd. CLOSED to air carrier ops with more than 30 passenger seats except 24 hrs PPR, call arpt manager 772–978–4930. No intersection departures except by ATC req. Noise sensitive arpt. Jet acft use NBAA noise abatement procedures. Voluntary local noise abatement procedures in effect call 772–978–4930. No touch and go ops 0300–1200Z‡ except PPR. Extensive flight training. ACTIVATE MIRL Rwy 11R–29L and REIL Rwy 11R and Rwy 29L—CTAF.
WEATHER DATA SOURCES: ASOS (772) 978–9535. **HIWAS** 117.3 VRB.
COMMUNICATIONS: CTAF 126.3 **ATIS** 132.5 **UNICOM** 122.95
RCO 122.1R 117.3T (ST PETERSBURG RADIO)
RCO 122.5 122.2 (ST PETERSBURG RADIO)
Ⓡ **MIAMI CENTER APP/DEP CON** 132.25
TOWER 126.3 133.15 (1200–0200Z‡) **GND CON** 127.45 **CLNC DEL** 134.975
AIRSPACE: CLASS D svc 1200–0200Z‡ other times CLASS E.
RADIO AIDS TO NAVIGATION: NOTAM FILE VRB.
(H) VORTAC 117.3 VRB Chan 120 N27°40.71' W80°29.38' 114° 4.1 NM to fld. 11/04W. **HIWAS.**

VIRGINIA KEY N25°45.11' W80°09.27' NOTAM FILE MIA. **MIAMI**
(H) VOR/DME 117.1 VKZ Chan 118 293° 7.8 NM to Miami Intl. 12/04W. **H–8I, L–23C, A**
VOR portion unusable 020°–064° byd 20 NM blo 4500', 091°–104° byd 30 NM blo 3000', 279°–284° byd 25 NM blo 7500', 285°–319° byd 15 NM blo 7500', 320°–335° byd 25 NM blo 3000'.
RCO 122.1R 117.1T (MIAMI RADIO)

WAKUL N30°19.57' W84°21.50' NOTAM FILE TLH. **JACKSONVILLE**
NDB (HW/LOM) 379 TL 007° 4.2 NM to Tallahassee Rgnl. **H–8G, L–21D, 22I**

WAKULLA CO (See PANACEA)

WARRINGTON N30°28.69' W86°31.25' NOTAM FILE CEW. **NEW ORLEANS**
(T) TACAN Chan 2 DWG (134.5) at Eglin AFB 118/00°E. **L–21C, 22H**

Figure 385. Excerpt from Chart Supplement.

WINDSOR LOCKS

BRADLEY INTL (BDL) 3 W UTC–5(–4DT) N41°56.35' W72°41.00' **NEW YORK**
173 B S4 **FUEL** 100LL, JET A OX 1, 2, 3, 4 TPA—See Remarks **H–10I, 11D, 12K, L–33C, 34I**
LRA Class I, ARFF Index D NOTAM FILE BDL **IAP, AD**

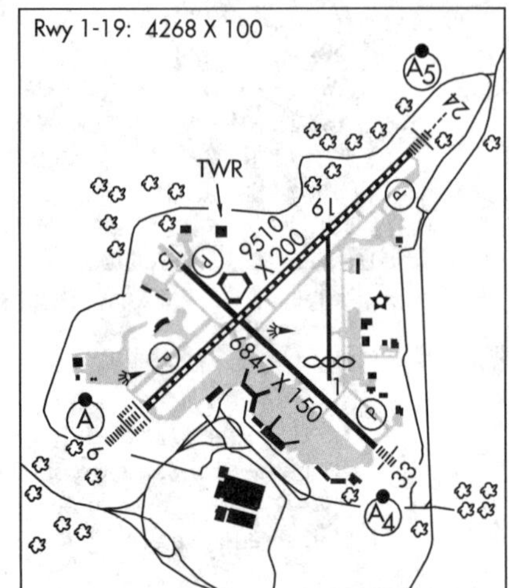

RWY 06–24: H9510X200 (ASPH–GRVD) S–200, D–200, 2S–175, 2D–350, 2D/2D2–710 HIRL CL
RWY 06: ALSF2. TDZL. PAPI(P4L)—GA 3.0° TCH 71'. Trees.
RWY 24: MALSR. TDZL. PAPI(P4L)—GA 3.0° TCH 71'. Trees.
RWY 15–33: H6847X150 (ASPH–GRVD) S–200, D–200, 2S–175, 2D–350 HIRL
RWY 15: REIL. PAPI(P4L)—GA 3.5°TCH 61'. Trees.
RWY 33: MALSF. PAPI(P4R)—GA 3.0°TCH 72'. Trees.
RWY 01–19: H4268X100 (ASPH) S–60, D–190, 2S–175, 2D–328 MIRL
RWY 01: Thld dsplcd 475'. Acft. **RWY 19:** Trees.

LAND AND HOLD SHORT OPERATIONS

LANDING	HOLD SHORT POINT	DIST AVBL
RWY 06	01–19	6000
RWY 24	15–33	5850
RWY 33	06–24	4550

RUNWAY DECLARED DISTANCE INFORMATION

RWY 01:	TORA–4268	TODA–4268	ASDA–4268	
RWY 06:	TORA–9509	TODA–9509	ASDA–9509	LDA–9509
RWY 15:	TORA–6847	TODA–6847	ASDA–6847	LDA–6847
RWY 19:				LDA–4268
RWY 24:	TORA–9509	TODA–9509	ASDA–9509	LDA–9509
RWY 33:	TORA–6847	TODA–6847	ASDA–6847	LDA–6847

AIRPORT REMARKS: Attended continuously. Numerous birds frequently on or invof arpt. No training flights; no practice apchs; no touch and go ldgs between: Mon–Sat 0400–1200Z‡ and Sun 0400–1700Z‡. Rwy 01–19 open for acft with wingspan less than 79'. Rwy 01 CLOSED for arrivals to all fixed wing acft. Rwy 19 CLOSED for departures to all fixed wing acft. Twy J clsd between S and R to acft with wing spans in excess of 171 ft. Air National Guard ramp PAEW barricaded adjacent northeast side. ASDE–X Surveilance System in Use. Pilots should operate transponders with Mode C on all twys and rwys. Rwy 33 touchdown RVR avbl. TPA—1873(1700) heavy acft. Rwy 06 visual glideslope indicator and glidepath not coincident. Rwy 24 visual glideslope indicator and glidepath not coincident. Rwy 33 visual glideslope indicator and glidepath not coincident. Ldg fee for business, corporate and revenue producing acft. Flight Notification Service (ADCUS) available. NOTE: See Special Notices–Land and Hold Short Lights.

WEATHER DATA SOURCES: ASOS (860) 627–9732. WSP.

COMMUNICATIONS: D-ATIS 118.15 (860–386–3570) **UNICOM** 122.95
WINDSOR LOCKS RCO 122.3 (BRIDGEPORT RADIO)
Ⓡ **BRADLEY APP CON** 123.95 (176°–240°) 125.35 (241°–060°) 127.8 (061°–175° and HFD area)
Ⓡ **BRADLEY DEP CON** 123.95 (176°–240°) 125.35 (241°–060°) 127.8 (061°–175° and HFD area)
TOWER 120.3 **GND CON** 121.9 **CLNC DEL** 121.75

AIRSPACE: CLASS C svc continuous ctc **APP CON**

RADIO AIDS TO NAVIGATION: NOTAM FILE BDL.
(T) VORTACW 109.0 BDL Chan 27 N41°56.46' W72°41.32' at fld. 160/14W.
ILS/DME 111.1 I–BDL Chan 48 Rwy 06. Class IIIE.
ILS/DME 108.55 I–IKX Chan 22(Y) Rwy 33. Class IE.
ILS/DME 111.1 I–MYQ Chan 48 Rwy 24. Class IT. DME unusable from .4 NM inbound to Rwy 24.

YALESVILLE HELIPORT (4C3) 2 N UTC–5(–4DT) N41°29.51' W72°48.67'
65 B **FUEL** 100LL, JET A NOTAM FILE BDR
HELIPAD H1: H65X65 (CONC)
HELIPORT REMARKS: Attended 1400–2300Z‡. Pilots unfamiliar with heliport ctc 203–294–8800 prior to arrival for a briefing on current procedures. ACTIVATE rotating bcn—123.5
COMMUNICATIONS: CTAF/UNICOM 123.05

Figure 386. Excerpt from Chart Supplement.

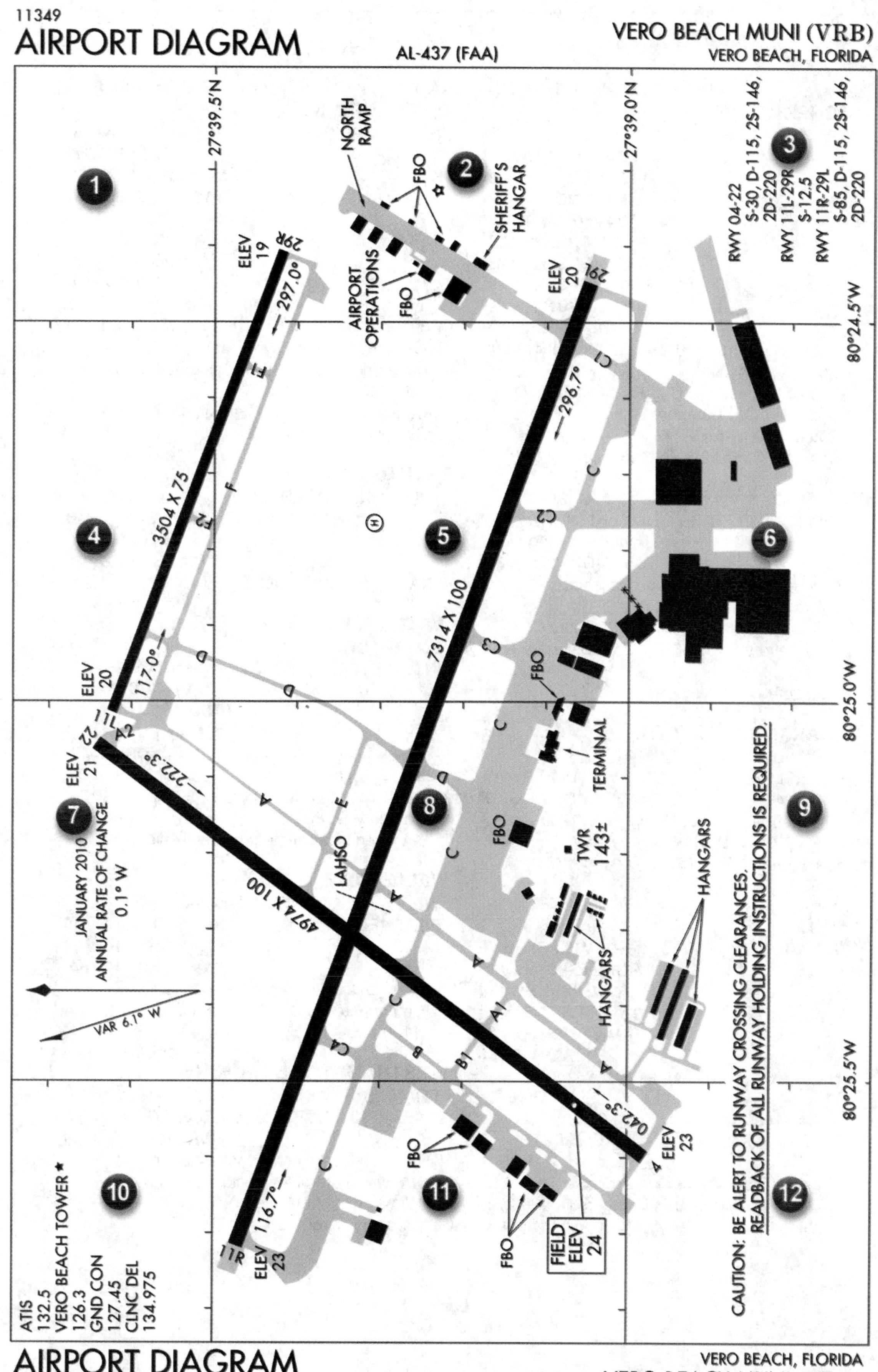

Figure 387. Airport Diagram (VRB).

ALTERNATE MINS

M4

12096

NAME ALTERNATE MINIMUMS

ROCHESTER, NY

GREATER ROCHESTER
INTL (ROC) .... **ILS or LOC Rwy 4**[1]
ILS or LOC Rwy 22[1]
ILS or LOC Rwy 28[2]
RNAV (GPS) Rwy 4[3]
RNAV (GPS) Rwy 22[3]
RNAV (GPS) Rwy 25[3]
RNAV (GPS) Rwy 28[4]
VOR Rwy 4[3]
VOR/DME Rwy 4[3]

[1]ILS, Category D, 700-2¼. LOC, Category D, 800-2¼.
[2]ILS, Categories A,B,C, 800-2; Category D, 800-2¼. LOC, Category D, 800-2¼.
[3]Category D, 800-2¼.
[4]Category C, 800-2¼; Category D, 800-2½.

ROME, NY

GRIFFISS INTL (RME) .... **ILS or LOC Rwy 33**[12]
RNAV (GPS) Rwy 15[3]
RNAV (GPS) Rwy 33[3]

NA when local weather not available.
[1]NA when control tower closed.
[2]ILS, Categories A, B, 700-2; Category C, 800-2; Category D, 800-2½. LOC, Category D, 800-2½.
[3]Category D, 800-2½.

SARANAC LAKE, NY

ADIRONDACK
RGNL (SLK) .... **VOR/DME Rwy 5**[1]
VOR or GPS Rwy 9[2]

[1]Category A, 1100-2; Category B, 1200-2; Categories C,D, 1200-3.
[2]Categories A,B, 1400-2; Categories C,D, 1400-3.

SHIRLEY, NY

BROOKHAVEN (HWV) .... **RNAV (GPS) Rwy 6**
RNAV (GPS) Rwy 15
RNAV (GPS) Y Rwy 24
RNAV (GPS) Z Rwy 24
RNAV (GPS) Rwy 33
VOR Rwy 6

NA when local weather not available.

SUSSEX, NJ

SUSSEX (FWN) .... **RNAV (GPS) Rwy 3**[1]
VOR-A[2]

NA when local weather not available.
[1]Categories A, B, 900-2; Category C, 900-2½.
[2]Categories A, B, 1400-2; Category C, 1400-3.

NAME ALTERNATE MINIMUMS

TETERBORO, NJ

TETERBORO (TEB) .... **ILS or LOC Rwy 6**[1]
ILS RWY 19[1]
RNAV (GPS) Y Rwy 6[3]
RNAV (RNP) Z Rwy 6, 800-2¼
VOR/DME-A[2]
VOR/DME-B[2]
VOR/DME Rwy 6[3]
VOR Rwy 24[4]

[1]ILS, Categories A,B, 800-2; Category C, 800-2¼; Category D, 900-2¾. LOC, Category C, 800-2¼; Category D, 900-2¾.
[2]Categories A,B, 1000-2; Categories C,D, 1000-3.
[3]Category C, 800-2¼; Category D, 900-2¾.
[4]Categories B,C,D, 1000-3.

TRENTON, NJ

TRENTON MERCER (TTN) .... **ILS Rwy 6**
NDB or GPS Rwy 6
VOR or GPS-A
VOR or GPS Rwy 24

NA when control tower closed.

WATERTOWN, NY

WATERTOWN
INTL (ART) .... **ILS or LOC Rwy 7**[1]
RNAV (GPS) Rwy 7[2]
RNAV (GPS) Rwy 10[3]
RNAV (GPS) Rwy 28[3]
VOR Rwy 7[2]

[1]ILS, Categories A, B, C, 700-2; Category D 700-2¼. LOC, Category D, 800-2¼.
[2]Category D, 800-2¼.
[3]NA when local weather not available.

WELLSVILLE, NY

WELLSVILLE MUNI ARPT,TARANTINE
FIELD (ELZ) .... **RNAV (GPS) Rwy 10**
RNAV (GPS) Rwy 28
VOR-A[1]

NA when local weather not available.
[1]Categories A,B, 1100-2; Categories C,D, 1100-3.

WESTHAMPTON BEACH, NY

FRANCIS S.
GABRESKI (FOK) .... **ILS or LOC Rwy 24**[1]
RNAV (GPS) Rwy 24

NA when local weather not available.
[1]NA when control tower closed.
[2]NA when control tower closed.
[3]Category D, 800-2¼.

ALTERNATE MINS

12096

NE-2

Figure 388. IFR Alternate Minimums.

Airspeed limitations and their operational significance are shown in Airspeed Limitations Chart.

	SPEED	KCAS	KIAS	REMARKS
V_{MO}	Maximum Operating Speed	175	175	Do not exceed this speed in any operation.
V_A	Maneuvering Speed: 8750 Pounds 7500 Pounds 6250 Pounds 5000 Pounds	 148 137 125 112	 148 137 125 112	Do not make full or abrupt control movements above this speed.
V_{FE}	Maximum Flap Extended Speed: UP – 10° Flaps 10° – 20° Flaps 20° – Full	 175 150 125	 175 150 125	Do not exceed these speeds with the given flap settings.
	Maximum Open Window Speed	175	175	Do not exceed this speed with window open.

Figure 389. CE-208—Airspeed Limitations.

Illustrations and materials were used with permission from Cessna Aircraft Company.

CONDITIONS:
8,750 Pounds
Power Lever **IDLE**
FUEL CONDITION Lever **HIGH IDLE**

MOST REARWARD CENTER OF GRAVITY

Flap Setting	Angle of Bank							
	0°		30°		45°		60°	
	KIAS	KCAS	KIAS	KCAS	KIAS	KCAS	KIAS	KCAS
UP	63	78	68	84	75	93	89	110
10°	58	69	62	74	69	82	82	98
20°	53	63	57	68	63	75	75	89
FULL	48	60	52	64	57	71	68	85

MOST FORWARD CENTER OF GRAVITY

Flap Setting	Angle of Bank							
	0°		30°		45°		60°	
	KIAS	KCAS	KIAS	KCAS	KIAS	KCAS	KIAS	KCAS
UP	63	78	68	84	75	93	89	110
10°	60	70	64	75	71	83	85	99
20°	54	64	58	69	64	76	76	91
FULL	50	61	54	66	59	73	71	86

NOTE

1. Altitude loss during a stall recovery may be as much as 300 feet from a wings-level stall, and even greater from a turning stall.
2. KIAS values are approximate.

Figure 390. CE-208—Stall Speeds.

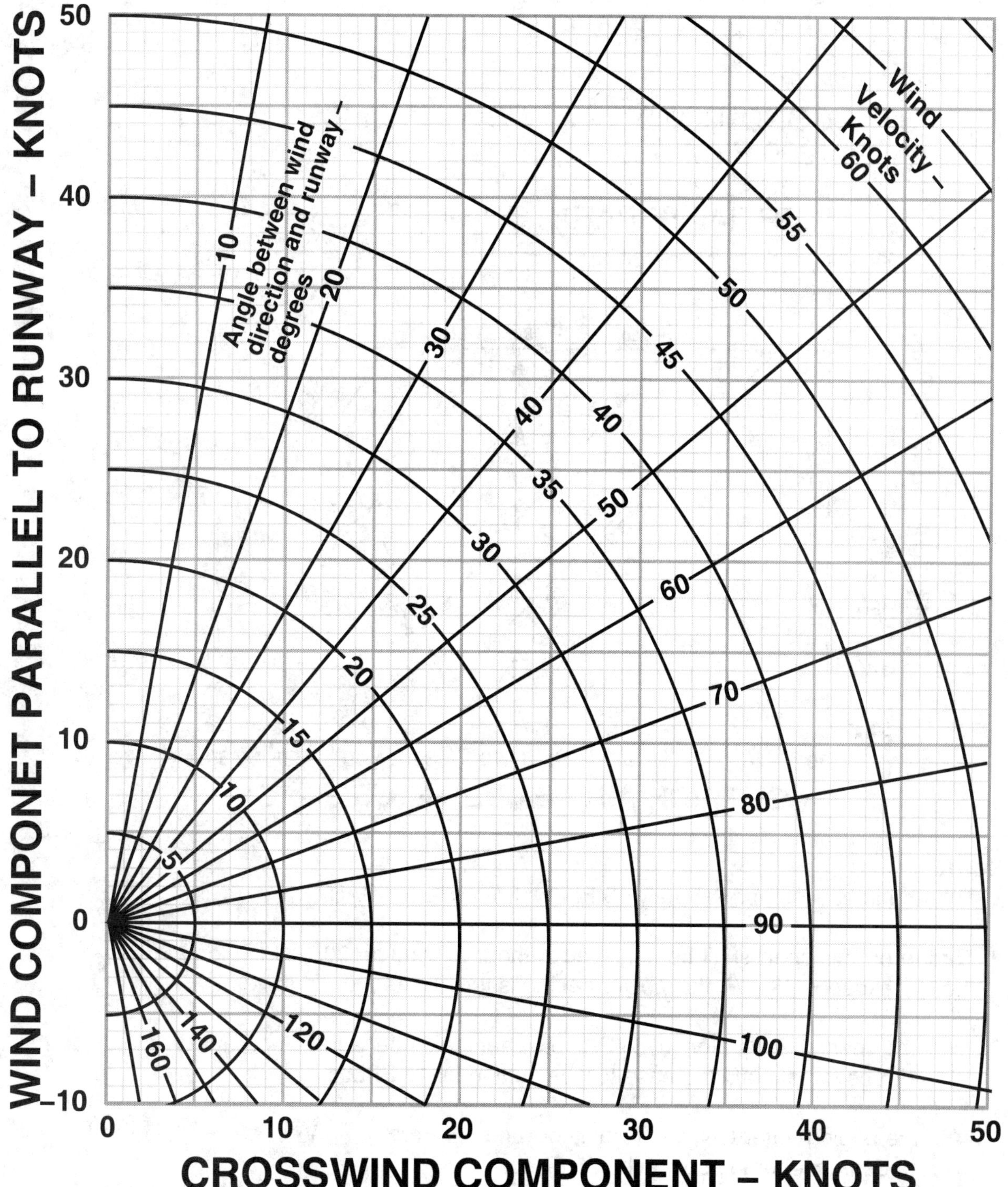

NOTE

Maximum demonstrated crosswind velocity is 20 knots (not a limitation).

Figure 391. CE-208—Wind Components.

Illustrations and materials were used with permission from Cessna Aircraft Company.

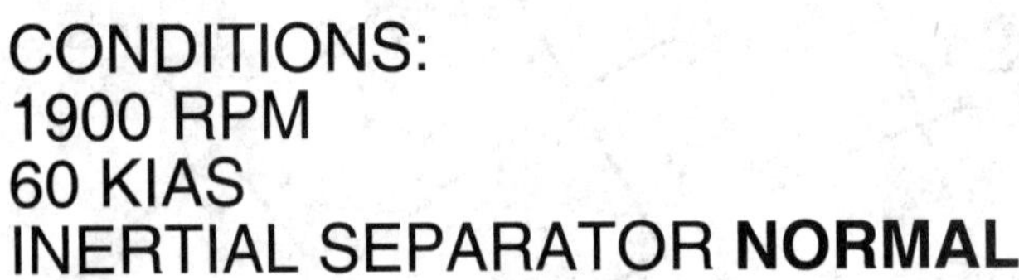

CONDITIONS:
1900 RPM
60 KIAS
INERTIAL SEPARATOR NORMAL

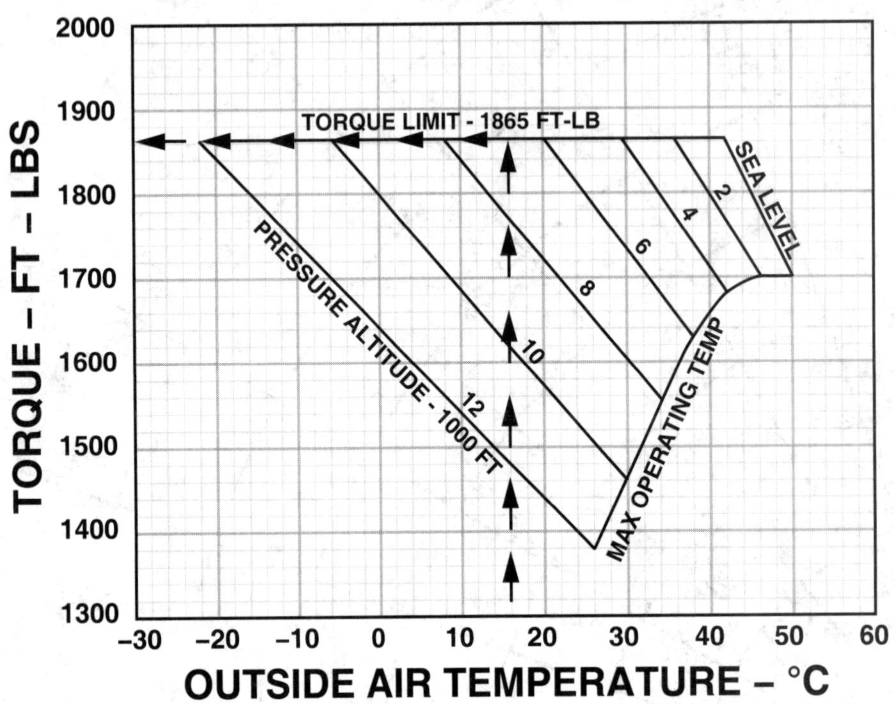

NOTE

1. Torque increases approximately 10 Ft-Lbs from 0 to 60 KIAS.

2. Torque on this chart shall be achieved without exceeding 805 °C ITT or 101.6 N_g. When the ITT exceeds 765 °C, this power setting is time limited to 5 minutes.

3. With the inertial separator in BYPASS, where altitude and temperature do not permit 1865 Ft-Lbs for takeoff, decrease torque setting by 15 Ft-Lbs.

4. With the cabin heater ON, where altitude and temperature do not permit 1865 Ft-Lbs for takeoff, decrease torque setting by 65 Ft-Lbs.

Figure 392. CE-208—Maximum Engine Torque for Takeoff.

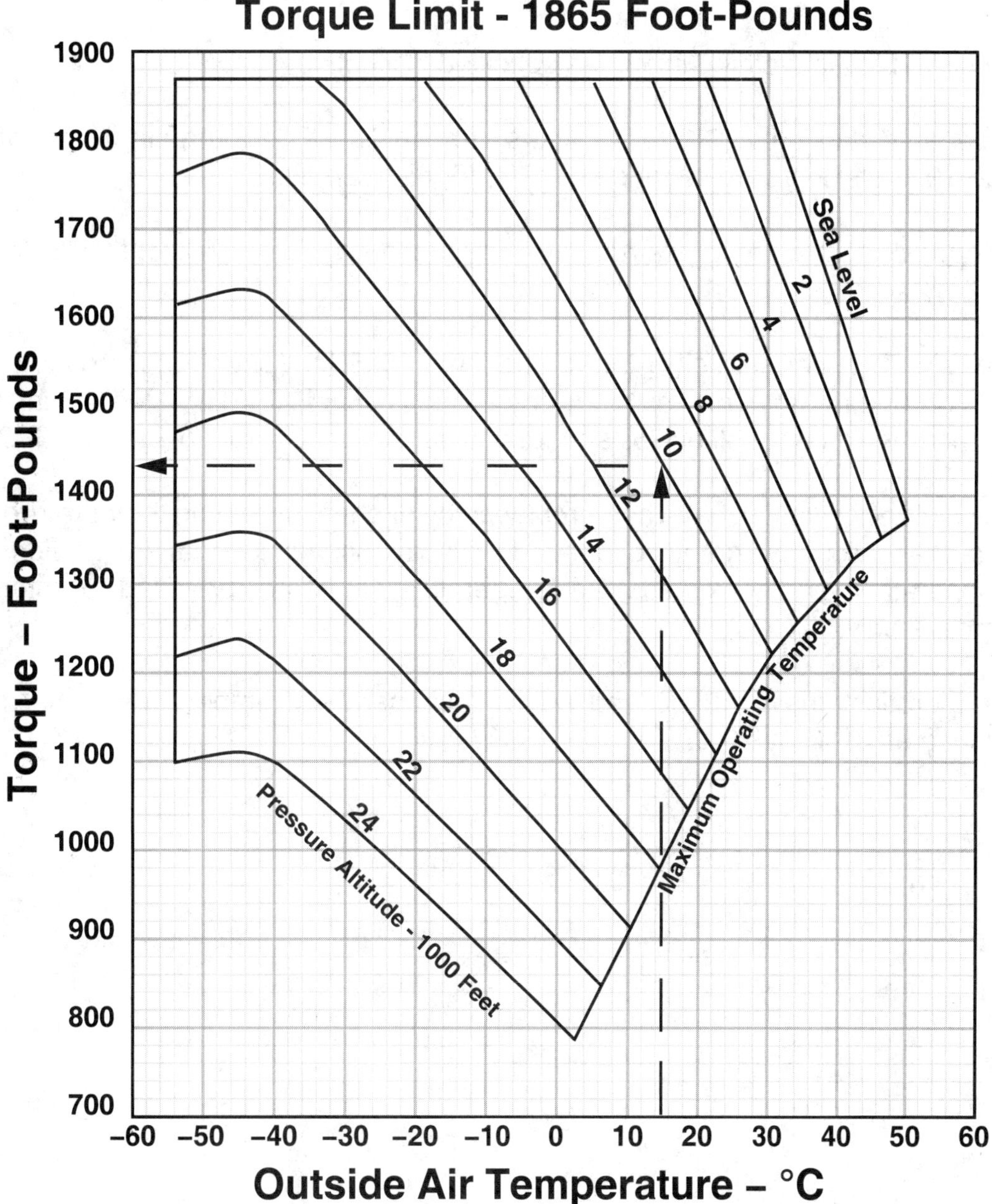

NOTE

1. Torque on this chart shall be achieved without exceeding 765 °C ITT or 101.6 N_g.

2. With the inertial separator in BYPASS, decrease torque setting by 100 Foot-Pounds.

3. With the cabin heater ON, decrease torque setting by 80 Foot-Pounds.

Figure 393. CE-208—Maximum Engine Torque for Climb.

Illustrations and materials were used with permission from Cessna Aircraft Company.

CARGO POD INSTALLED
SHORT FIELD TAKEOFF DISTANCE

NOTE

The following general information is applicable to all SHORT FIELD TAKEOFF DISTANCE Charts.

1. Use short field takeoff technique as specified in Section 4.

2. Decrease distance by 10% for 11 knots of headwind. For operation with a tailwind of up to 10 knots, increase distance by 10% for each 2 knots.

3. For operation on a dry, grass runway, increase distance by 15% of the "Ground Roll" figure.

4. With takeoff power set below the torque limit (1865 foot-pounds), increase distances (both ground roll and total distance) by 3% for INERTIAL SEPARATOR in BYPASS and increase ground roll by 5% and total distance by 10% for CABIN HEAT ON.

5. Where distance values have been replaced by dashes, operating temperature limits of the airplane would be greatly exceeded. The distance values that are provided, where the operation slightly exceeds the temperature limits, are provided for interpolation purposes only.

6. For operation above 40 °C and below the operating temperature limits, increase distance at 40 °C by 20%.

Figure 394. CE-208—Cargo Pod Installed—Short Field Takeoff Distance.

CARGO POD INSTALLED
SHORT FIELD TAKEOFF DISTANCE

CONDITIONS:
Flaps **20°**
1900 RPM
CABIN HEAT **OFF**
INERTIAL SEPARATOR **NORMAL**

Paved, Level, Dry Runway
Zero Wind
Lift Off: 70 KIAS
Speed at 50 Feet: 83 KIAS

8750 Pounds

Pressure Altitude (Feet)	–10 °C		0 °C		10 °C	
	Grnd Roll (Feet)	Total Dist To Clear 50 Foot Obst	Grnd Roll (Feet)	Total Dist To Clear 50 Foot Obst	Grnd Roll (Feet)	Total Dist To Clear 50 Foot Obst
Sea Level	1205	2160	1280	2295	1365	2430
2000	1360	2430	1455	2580	1545	2740
4000	1550	2745	1655	2920	1760	3105
6000	1765	3115	1890	3325	2015	3540
8000	2025	3560	2165	3805	2345	4125
10000	2335	4090	2585	4580	2930	5325
12000	2875	5155	3270	6030	3745	7175

Pressure Altitude (Feet)	20 °C		30 °C		40 °C	
	Grnd Roll (Feet)	Total Dist To Clear 50 Foot Obst	Grnd Roll (Feet)	Total Dist To Clear 50 Foot Obst	Grnd Roll (Feet)	Total Dist To Clear 50 Foot Obst
Sea Level	1445	2570	1535	2720	1625	2870
2000	1645	2905	1745	3075	1910	3400
4000	1875	3295	1995	3510	2290	4135
6000	2145	3765	2435	4370	2805	5195
8000	2670	4815	3065	5715	3565	7005
10000	3370	6350	3915	7790	---	---
12000	4350	8865	5130	11755	---	---

Figure 395. CE-208—Cargo Pod Installed—Short Field Takeoff Distance.
Illustrations and materials were used with permission from Cessna Aircraft Company.

CARGO POD INSTALLED
FLAPS UP TAKEOFF DISTANCE

NOTE

The following general information is applicable to all FLAPS UP TAKEOFF DISTANCE Charts.

1. Use Type II, Type III, or Type IV anti-ice fluid takeoff technique as specified in Section 4.
2. Decrease distance by 10% for each 11 knots of headwind. For operation with a tailwind of up to 10 knots, increase distance by 10% for each 2 knots.
3. For operation on a dry, grass runway, increase distance by 15% of the "Ground Roll" figure.
4. With takeoff power set below the torque limit (1865 foot-pounds), increase distances (both ground roll and total distance) by 3% for INERTIAL SEPARATOR in BYPASS and increase ground roll by 5% and total distance by 10% for CABIN HEAT ON.

Figure 396. CE-208—Cargo Pod Installed—Flaps Up Takeoff Distance.

CARGO POD INSTALLED
RATE OF CLIMB - TAKEOFF FLAP SETTING
FLAPS 20°

CONDITIONS:
Takeoff Power
1900 RPM

INERTIAL SEPARATOR **NORMAL**

Weight (Pounds)	Pressure Altitude (Feet)	Climb Speed (KIAS)	Rate of Climb - Feet Per Minute (FPM)				
			–40 °C	–20 °C	0 °C	20 °C	40 °C
8750	Sea Level	92	875	855	835	815	795
	2000	90	860	835	815	795	730
	4000	89	835	815	790	765	645
	6000	88	815	790	765	740	555
	8000	87	785	760	735	620	435
	10000	85	760	730	665	500	---
	12000	84	725	680	540	380	---
8300	Sea Level	91	955	940	920	900	880
	2000	89	940	920	895	875	810
	4000	88	915	895	870	850	725
	6000	86	895	870	845	820	630
	8000	85	865	840	815	700	505
	10000	84	835	810	745	575	---
	12000	82	805	760	615	450	---
7800	Sea Level	89	1055	1035	1020	1000	980
	2000	87	1035	1015	995	975	910
	4000	86	1015	995	970	950	820
	6000	85	990	965	945	920	720
	8000	83	965	940	915	795	595
	10000	82	935	905	840	665	---
	12000	80	905	855	710	540	---
7300	Sea Level	88	1160	1145	1130	1110	1090
	2000	86	1145	1125	1105	1085	1020
	4000	85	1125	1105	1080	1060	925
	6000	84	1100	1075	1055	1030	825
	8000	82	1075	1050	1025	900	690
	10000	81	1045	1015	950	765	---
	12000	79	1015	965	810	635	---

G208B675-00

NOTE

1. **Do not exceed torque limit for takeoff per MAXIMUM ENGINE TORQUE FOR TAKEOFF chart. When ITT exceeds 765 °C, this power setting is time limited to 5 minutes.**

2. With climb power set below the torque limit, decrease rate of climb by 20 FPM for INERTIAL SEPARATOR set in BYPASS and 45 FPM for CABIN HEAT ON.

3. Where rate of climb values have been replaced by dashes, operating temperature limits of the airplane would be greatly exceeded. The rates of climb that are provided included, where the operation slightly exceeds the temperature limit, are provided for interpolation purposes only.

Figure 397. CE-208—Cargo Pod Installed—Rate of Climb—Takeoff Flap Setting.

CARGO POD INSTALLED
CLIMB GRADIENT - TAKEOFF
FLAPS UP

CONDITIONS:
Takeoff Power
1900 RPM

Zero Wind
INERTIAL SEPARATOR **NORMAL**

Weight (Pounds)	Pressure Altitude (Feet)	Climb Speed (KIAS)	Climb Gradient - Feet/Nautical Mile (FT/NM)				
			–40 °C	–20 °C	0 °C	20 °C	40 °C
8750	Sea Level	68	735	695	655	620	475
	2000	69	695	655	615	580	390
	4000	69	660	615	580	500	305
	6000	70	620	580	545	410	230
	8000	70	580	540	475	330	165
	10000	71	545	505	390	250	---
	12000	72	505	420	305	180	---
8300	Sea Level	66	810	770	725	690	535
	2000	66	770	730	685	650	445
	4000	67	730	690	650	565	360
	6000	68	690	645	610	470	280
	8000	68	650	605	540	380	210
	10000	69	610	570	445	300	---
	12000	69	570	475	355	225	---
7800	Sea Level	61	910	860	815	775	615
	2000	62	865	820	775	735	515
	4000	62	820	775	730	640	425
	6000	62	780	730	690	540	340
	8000	63	735	690	615	445	265
	10000	63	690	645	515	360	---
	12000	63	645	550	420	280	---
7300	Sea Level	59	1020	970	920	875	700
	2000	59	975	920	875	830	595
	4000	59	925	875	830	730	500
	6000	59	880	830	780	620	405
	8000	59	830	780	700	520	330
	10000	59	785	735	595	430	---
	12000	59	735	630	490	340	---

G208B675-00

NOTE

1. **Do not exceed torque limit for takeoff per MAXIMUM ENGINE TORQUE FOR TAKEOFF chart. When ITT exceeds 765 °C, this power setting is time limited to 5 minutes.**
2. With climb power set below the torque limit, decrease climb by 10 FT/NM for INERTIAL SEPARATOR set in BYPASS and 40 FT/NM for CABIN HEAT ON.
3. Where climb gradient values have been replaced by dashes, operating temperature limits of the airplane would be greatly exceeded. The climb gradients that are included, where the operation slightly exceeds the temperature limit, are provided for interpolation purposes only.

Figure 398. CE-208—Cargo Pod Installed—Climb Gradient—Takeoff.

CARGO POD INSTALLED
TIME, FUEL, AND DISTANCE TO CLIMB
MAXIMUM RATE OF CLIMB

CONDITIONS:

FLAPS **UP** — Zero Wind

1900 RPM — INERTIAL SEPARATOR **NORMAL**

Weight (Pounds)	Pressure Altitude (Feet)	Climb Speed (KIAS)	Climb From Sea Level								
			20 °C Below Standard			Standard Temperature			20 °C Above Standard		
			Time (min)	Fuel (lbs)	Dist (NM)	Time (min)	Fuel (lbs)	Dist (NM)	Time (min)	Fuel (lbs)	Dist (NM)
8750	Sea Level	104	0	0	0	0	0	0	0	0	0
	4,000	104	4	32	8	5	33	8	6	38	10
	8,000	104	9	64	16	9	66	17	12	80	24
	12,000	102	14	98	25	15	105	29	22	132	43
	16,000	96	20	136	37	23	152	45	35	202	71
	20,000	88	28	186	54	36	219	72	69	349	142
	24,000	79	49	278	93	75	388	152	---	---	---
8300	Sea Level	103	0	0	0	0	0	0	0	0	0
	4,000	103	4	29	7	4	30	7	5	34	9
	8,000	103	8	58	14	8	60	15	11	72	21
	12,000	101	13	89	23	14	95	26	19	116	37
	16,000	95	18	123	33	21	135	40	30	172	60
	20,000	87	25	165	47	31	189	61	51	265	104
	24,000	77	40	233	76	54	287	106	---	---	---
7800	Sea Level	101	0	0	0	0	0	0	0	0	0
	4,000	101	4	26	6	4	27	6	4	30	8
	8,000	101	7	52	13	8	54	14	10	63	18
	12,000	99	11	80	20	12	84	22	16	100	31
	16,000	92	16	110	29	18	119	34	25	145	49
	20,000	84	22	146	41	27	163	51	40	210	79
	24,000	74	33	198	62	42	229	81	88	395	178
7300	Sea Level	99	0	0	0	0	0	0	0	0	0
	4,000	99	3	24	5	3	24	6	4	27	7
	8,000	99	7	47	11	7	49	12	9	55	16
	12,000	97	10	72	18	11	75	20	14	87	27
	16,000	89	14	99	25	16	105	30	21	124	41
	20,000	80	20	129	35	23	141	43	32	173	63
	24,000	70	29	171	52	34	191	65	55	260	108

NOTE:

1. **Torque set at 1865 foot-pounds or lesser value must not exceed maximum climb ITT of 765 °C or Ng of 101.6%.**
2. Add 35 pounds of fuel for engine start, taxi, and takeoff allowances.
3. With INERTIAL SEPARATOR set in BYPASS, increase time, fuel, and distance numbers by 1% for every 2000 feet of climb and for CABIN HEAT ON, increase time, fuel, and distance numbers by 1% for every 1000 feet of climb.
4. Where time, fuel, and distance values have been replaced by dashes, an appreciable rate of climb for the weight shown cannot be expected.

Figure 399. CE-208—Cargo Pod Installed—Time, Fuel and Distance To Climb.

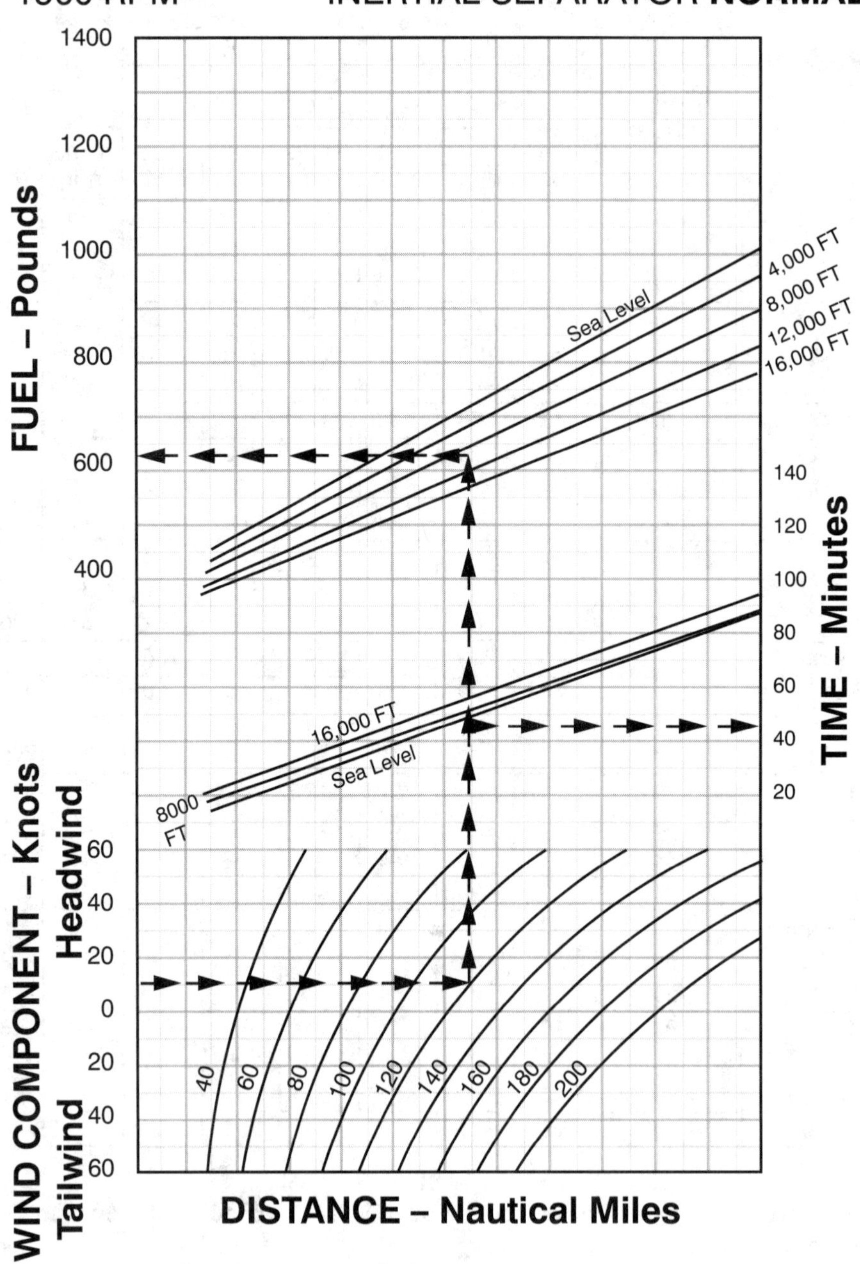

NOTE

1. Fuel required includes the fuel used for engine start, taxi, takeoff, maximum climb from sea level, descent to sea level and 45 minutes reserve. Time required includes the time during a maximum climb and descent.

2. With INERTIAL SEPARATOR in BYPAS, increase time by 4% and fuel by 2% or CABIN HEAT ON, increase time by 3% and fuel by 2%.

Figure 400. CE-208—Cargo Pod Installed—Fuel and Time Required.

Illustrations and materials were used with permission from Cessna Aircraft Company.

CARGO POD INSTALLED
SHORT FIELD LANDING DISTANCE

NOTE

The following general information is applicable to all SHORT FIELD LANDING DISTANCE Charts.

1. Use short field landing technique as specified in Section 4.
2. Decrease distance by 10% for every 11 knots of headwind. For operation with a tailwind of up to 10 knots, increase distance by 10% for every 2 knots.
3. For operation on a dry, grass runway, increase distance by 40% of the "Ground Roll" figure.
4. If a landing with flaps UP is necessary, increase the approach speed by 15 KIAS and allow for 40% longer distances.
5. Use of maximum reverse thrust after touchdown reduces ground roll distance by approximately 10%.
6. Where distance values have been replaced by dashes, operating temperature limits of the airplane would be greatly exceeded. The distance values that are included, where the operation slightly exceeds the temperature limit, are provided for interpolation purposes only.

Figure 401. CE-208—Cargo Pod Installed—Short Field Landing Distance.

Illustrations and materials were used with permission from Cessna Aircraft Company.

CARGO POD INSTALLED
SHORT FIELD LANDING DISTANCE

CONDITIONS:
Flaps **FULL**
Zero Wind
Maximum Braking
PROP RPM Lever **MAX**
Paved, Level, Dry Runway

POWER Lever **IDLE** after clearing obstacles. **BETA** range (lever against spring) after touchdown.

8500 Pounds

Speed at 50 Feet: 78 KIAS

Pressure Altitude (Feet)	-10 °C		0 °C		10 °C	
	Grnd Roll (Feet)	Total Dist To Clear 50 Foot Obst	Grnd Roll (Feet)	Total Dist To Clear 50 Foot Obst	Grnd Roll (Feet)	Total Dist To Clear 50 Foot Obst
Sea Level	835	1625	865	1670	900	1715
2000	900	1715	935	1765	965	1815
4000	965	1815	1005	1865	1040	1920
6000	1040	1920	1080	1975	1120	2030
8000	1125	2035	1165	2095	1210	2155
10000	1215	2160	1260	2220	1305	2285
12000	1310	2295	1360	2360	1410	2430

Pressure Altitude (Feet)	20 °C		30 °C		40 °C	
	Grnd Roll (Feet)	Total Dist To Clear 50 Foot Obst	Grnd Roll (Feet)	Total Dist To Clear 50 Foot Obst	Grnd Roll (Feet)	Total Dist To Clear 50 Foot Obst
Sea Level	930	1765	965	1810	995	1855
2000	1000	1860	1035	1910	1070	1960
4000	1075	1970	1115	2020	1150	2070
6000	1160	2085	1200	2140	1240	2195
8000	1250	2210	1295	2270	1340	2330
10000	1350	2345	1400	2410	---	---
12000	1460	2495	1510	2560	---	---

Figure 402. CE-208—Cargo Pod Installed—Short Field Landing Distance.

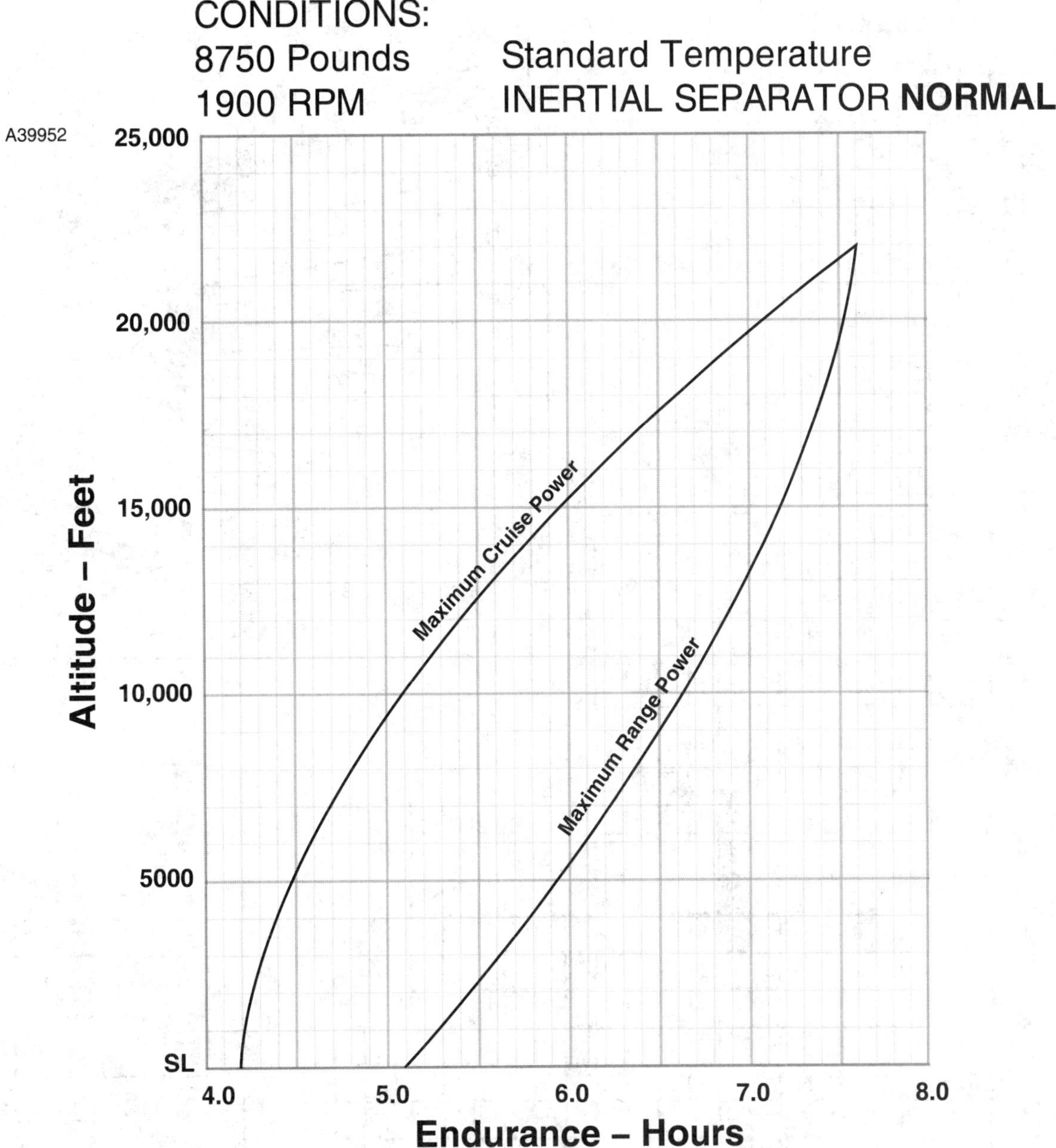

NOTE

1. This chart allows for the fuel used for engine start, taxi, takeoff, climb and descent. The time during a maximum climb and the time during descent are included.
2. With INERTIAL SEPARATOR in BYPASS, decrease endurance by 2%, or CABIN HEAT ON, decrease endurance by 3%.

Figure 403. CE-208—Without Cargo Pod—Endurance Profile—45 Minutes Reserve—2224 Pounds Useable Fuel.

Illustrations and materials were used with permission from Cessna Aircraft Company.

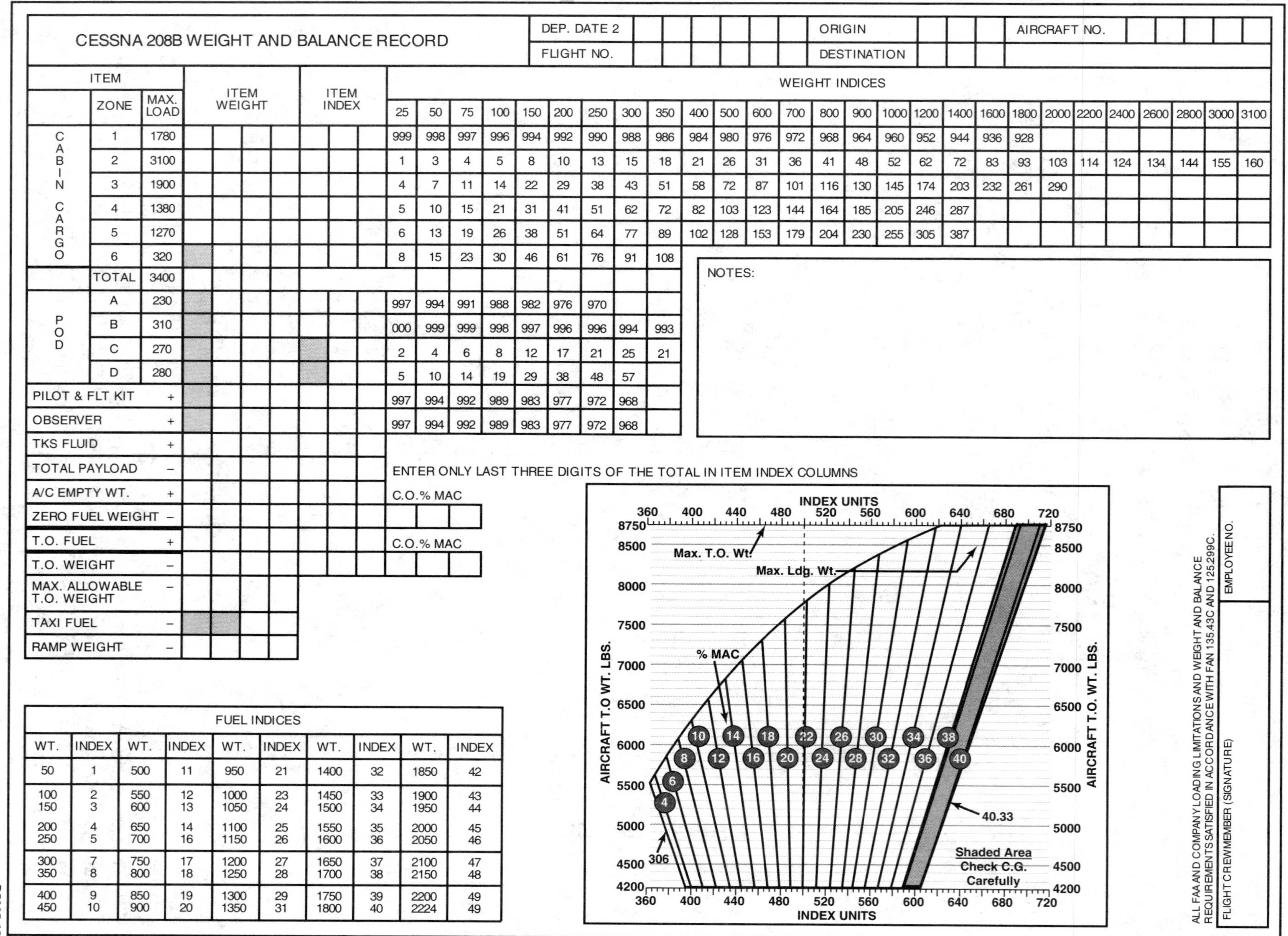

CESSNA 208B WEIGHT AND BALANCE RECORD

DEP. DATE 2		ORIGIN		AIRCRAFT NO.	
FLIGHT NO.		DESTINATION			

ITEM	ZONE	MAX. LOAD	ITEM WEIGHT	ITEM INDEX	25	50	75	100	150	200	250	300	350	400	500	600	700	800	900	1000	1200	1400	1600	1800	2000	2200	2400	2600	2800	3000	3100
CABIN	1	1780			999	998	997	996	994	992	990	988	986	984	980	976	972	968	964	960	952	944	936	928							
CABIN	2	3100			1	3	4	5	8	10	13	15	18	21	26	31	36	41	48	52	62	72	83	93	103	114	124	134	144	155	160
CABIN	3	1900			4	7	11	14	22	29	38	43	51	58	72	87	101	116	130	145	174	203	232	261	290						
CARGO	4	1380			5	10	15	21	31	41	51	62	72	82	103	123	144	164	185	205	246	287									
CARGO	5	1270			6	13	19	26	38	51	64	77	89	102	128	153	179	204	230	255	305	387									
CARGO	6	320			8	15	23	30	46	61	76	91	108																		
	TOTAL	3400																													
POD	A	230			997	994	991	988	982	976	970																				
POD	B	310			000	999	999	998	997	996	996	994	993																		
POD	C	270			2	4	6	8	12	17	21	25	21																		
POD	D	280			5	10	14	19	29	38	48	57																			
PILOT & FLT KIT +					997	994	992	989	983	977	972	968																			
OBSERVER +					997	994	992	989	983	977	972	968																			
TKS FLUID +																															
TOTAL PAYLOAD –																															
A/C EMPTY WT. +																															
ZERO FUEL WEIGHT –																															
T.O. FUEL +																															
T.O. WEIGHT –																															
MAX. ALLOWABLE T.O. WEIGHT –																															
TAXI FUEL –																															
RAMP WEIGHT –																															

NOTES:

ENTER ONLY LAST THREE DIGITS OF THE TOTAL IN ITEM INDEX COLUMNS

C.O.% MAC

C.O.% MAC

FUEL INDICES

WT.	INDEX	WT.	INDEX	WT.	INDEX	WT.	INDEX	WT.	INDEX
50	1	500	11	950	21	1400	32	1850	42
100	2	550	12	1000	23	1450	33	1900	43
150	3	600	13	1050	24	1500	34	1950	44
200	4	650	14	1100	25	1550	35	2000	45
250	5	700	16	1150	26	1600	36	2050	46
300	7	750	17	1200	27	1650	37	2100	47
350	8	800	18	1250	28	1700	38	2150	48
400	9	850	19	1300	29	1750	39	2200	49
450	10	900	20	1350	31	1800	40	2224	49

ALL FAA AND COMPANY LOADING LIMITATIONS AND WEIGHT AND BALANCE REQUIREMENTS SATISFIED IN ACCORDANCE WITH FAN 135.43C AND 125.299C.

FLIGHT CREWMEMBER (SIGNATURE)	EMPLOYEE NO.

D5115-13

Figure 404. CE-208—Weight and Balance Record (Load Manifest).

Illustrations and materials were used with permission from Cessna Aircraft Company.

WEIGHT AND BALANCE RECORD (LOAD MANIFEST)

MAXIMUM STRUCTURAL WEIGHTS	
MAX RAMP	8785 LBS
MAX TAKEOFF	8750 LBS
MAX LANDING	8500 LBS

INDEX FORMULA

BASIC AIRPLANE INDEX = $\frac{WT\ (ARM - 192)}{500} + 500$
LOAD ITEM INDEX = $\frac{WT\ (ARM - 192)}{500}$ = (IF NEG. SUBTRACT FROM 1,000)

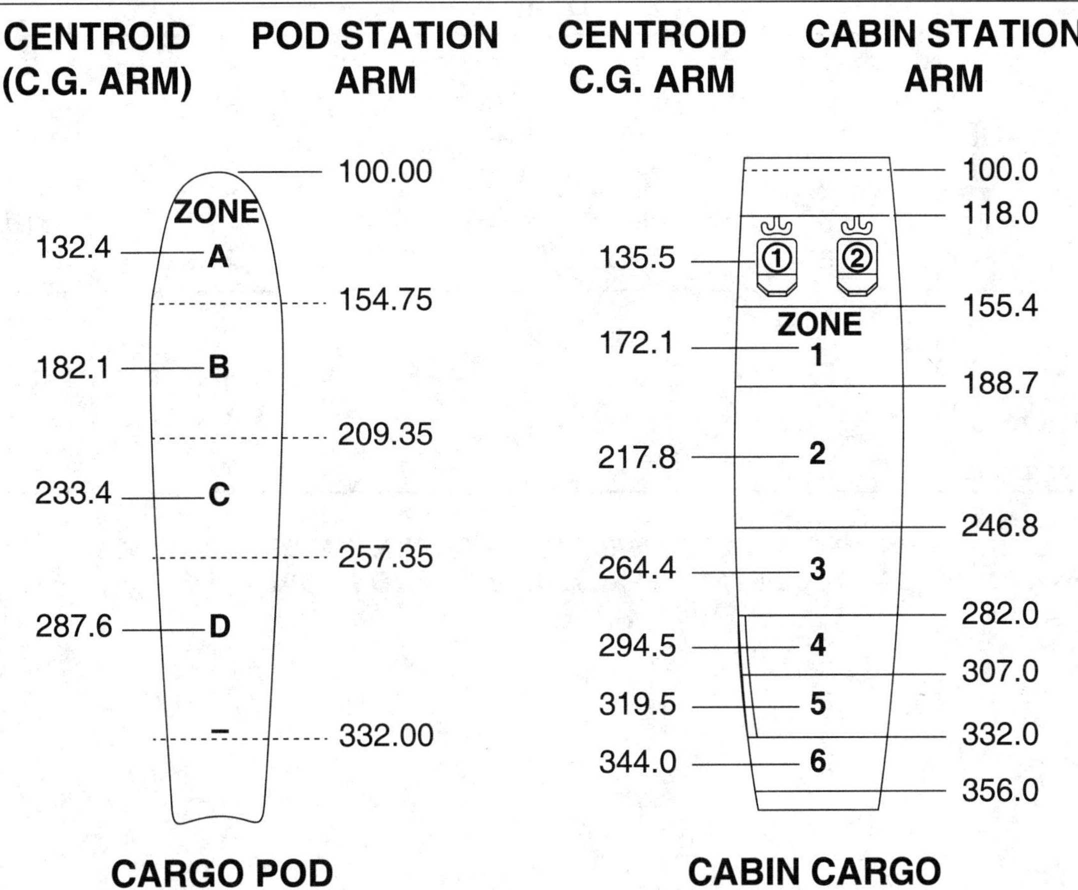

Figure 405. CE-208—Weight and Balance Record (Load Manifest).
Illustrations and materials were used with permission from Cessna Aircraft Company.

CARGO POD

The airplane may be equipped with a 111.5 cubic foot capacity cargo pod attached to the bottom of the fuselage. The pod is divided into four compartments (identified as Zones A, B, C, and D) by bulkheads and has a maximum floor loading of 30 pounds per square foot and maximum load weight limit of 1090 pounds. Each compartment has a loading door located on the left side of the pod. The doors are hinged at the bottom, and each has two latches. When the latch handles are rotated to the horizontal position with the doors closed, the doors are secured. Refer to the Pod Internal Dimension and Load Markings and Cargo Pod Loading Arrangements figures for additional details.

MAXIMUM ZONE/COMPARTMENT LOADINGS

Maximum zone loadings are as follows:

Weight Limits (Pounds)					
	Zone/ Compartment	Volume (Cubic Feet)	*Secured by Tie-downs	**Unsecured Using Partitions or in Cargo Pod	C.G. (Station Location)
FUSELAGE	1	52.9	1780	415	172.1
	2	109.0	3100	860	217.8
	3	63.0	1900	495	264.4
	4	43.5	1380	340	294.5
	5	40.1	1270	315	319.5
	6	31.5	320	245	344.0
CARGO POD	A	23.4	---	230	132.4
	B	31.5	---	310	182.1
	C	27.8	---	270	233.4
	D	28.8	---	280	287.6

*** THIS IS THE MAXIMUM CARGO ALLOWED IN THE BAY INDICATED.**
****DENSITY MUST BE 7.9 LBS/FT^3 OR LESS AND BAY 75% OR MORE FULL.**

Figure 406. CE-208—Cargo Pod and Maximum Zone/Compartment Loadings.

Illustrations and materials were used with permission from Cessna Aircraft Company.

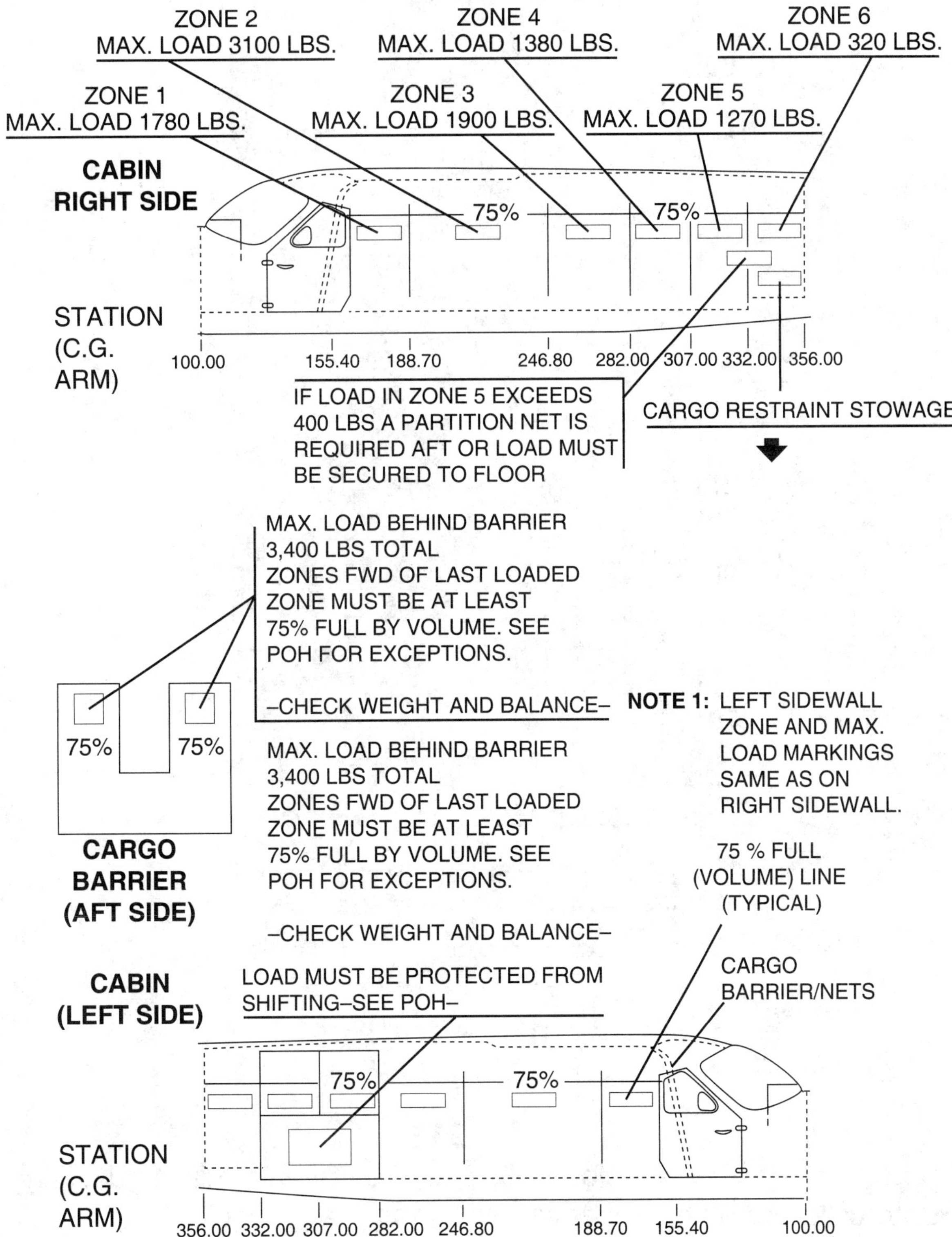

Figure 407. CE-208—Cabin Internal Load Markings (Cargo Version).

Illustrations and materials were used with permission from Cessna Aircraft Company.

MAXIMUM CARGO SIZES

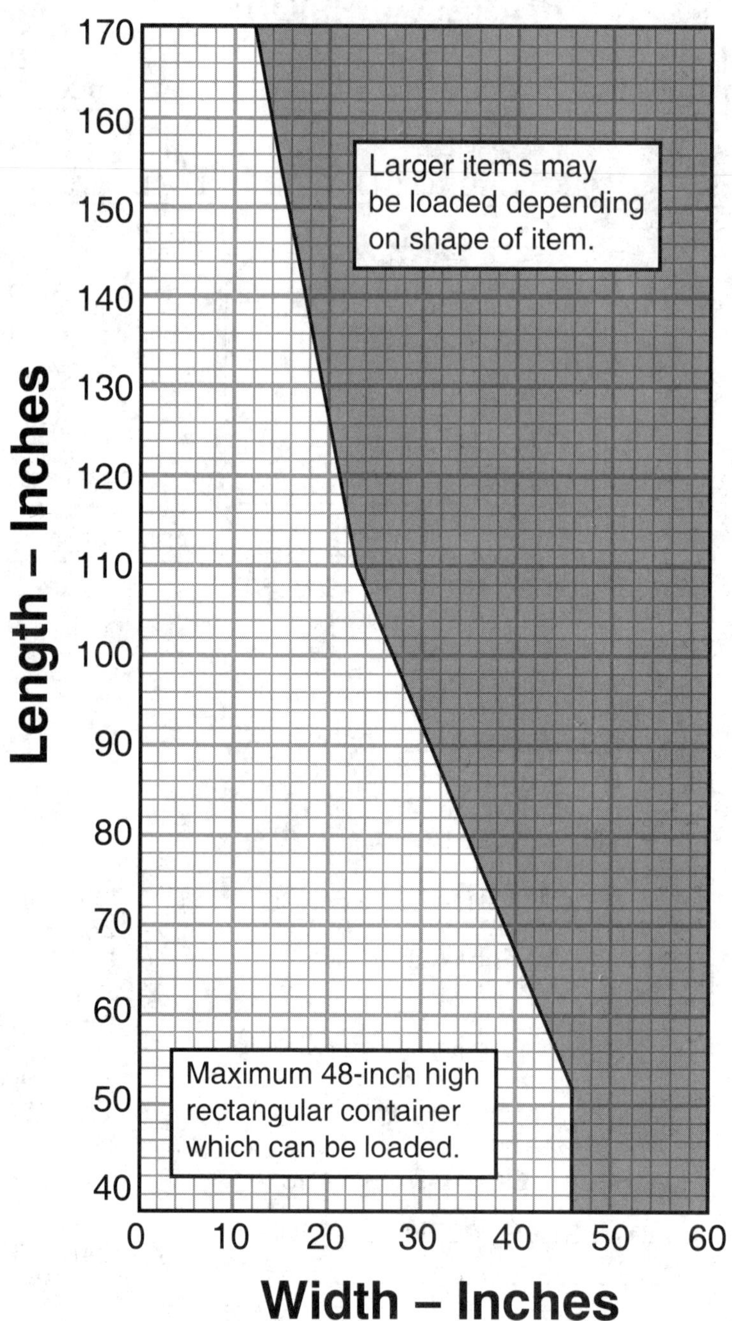

NOTE

1. Approximately one inch clearance allowed from sidewall and ceiling.
2. Subtract roller height and pallet thickness, if applicable.

Figure 408. CE-208—Maximum Cargo Sizes.

Illustrations and materials were used with permission from Cessna Aircraft Company.

CARGO POD INSTALLED
SHORT FIELD LANDING DISTANCE

CONDITIONS:
Flaps **FULL**
Zero Wind
Maximum Braking
PROP RPM Lever **MAX**
Paved, Level, Dry Runway

POWER Lever **IDLE** after clearing obstacles. **BETA** range (lever against spring) after touchdown.

8500 Pounds

Speed at 50 Feet: 78 KIAS

Pressure Altitude (Feet)	-10 °C		0 °C		10 °C	
	Grnd Roll (Feet)	Total Dist To Clear 50 Foot Obst	Grnd Roll (Feet)	Total Dist To Clear 50 Foot Obst	Grnd Roll (Feet)	Total Dist To Clear 50 Foot Obst
Sea Level	835	1625	865	1670	900	1715
2000	900	1715	935	1765	965	1815
4000	965	1815	1005	1865	1040	1920
6000	1040	1920	1080	1975	1120	2030
8000	1125	2035	1165	2095	1210	2155
10000	1215	2160	1260	2220	1305	2285
12000	1310	2295	1360	2360	1410	2430

Pressure Altitude (Feet)	20 °C		30 °C		40 °C	
	Grnd Roll (Feet)	Total Dist To Clear 50 Foot Obst	Grnd Roll (Feet)	Total Dist To Clear 50 Foot Obst	Grnd Roll (Feet)	Total Dist To Clear 50 Foot Obst
Sea Level	930	1765	965	1810	995	1855
2000	1000	1860	1035	1910	1070	1960
4000	1075	1970	1115	2020	1150	2070
6000	1160	2085	1200	2140	1240	2195
8000	1250	2210	1295	2270	1340	2330
10000	1350	2345	1400	2410	---	---
12000	1460	2495	1510	2560	---	---

Figure 409. CE-208—Weight and Moment Tables—Pilot and Front Passenger.

WEIGHT AND MOMENT TABLES
10 PLACE COMMUTER
Crew and Passengers (Single Commuter Seating)

Weight (Pounds)	Pilot/Front Passenger Seats 1 and 2 (Arm = 135.5 Inch)	Aft Passengers Seats			
		3 and 4 (Arm = 173.9 Inch)	5 and 6 (Arm = 209.9 Inch)	7 and 8 (Arm = 245.9 Inch)	9 and 10 (Arm = 281.9 Inch)
	Moment (Inch-Pound/1000)				
1	0.1	0.2	0.2	0.2	0.3
2	0.3	0.3	0.4	0.5	0.6
3	0.4	0.5	0.6	0.7	0.8
4	0.5	0.7	0.8	1.0	1.1
5	0.7	0.9	1.0	1.2	1.4
6	0.8	1.0	1.3	1.5	1.7
7	0.9	1.2	1.5	1.7	2.0
8	1.1	1.4	1.7	2.0	2.3
9	1.2	1.6	1.9	2.2	2.5
10	1.4	1.7	2.1	2.5	2.8
20	2.7	3.5	4.2	4.9	5.6
30	4.1	5.2	6.3	7.4	8.5
40	5.4	7.0	8.4	9.8	11.3
50	6.8	8.7	10.5	12.3	14.1
60	8.1	10.4	12.6	14.8	16.9
70	9.5	12.2	14.7	17.2	19.7
80	10.8	13.9	16.8	19.7	22.6
90	12.2	15.7	18.9	22.1	25.4
100	13.6	17.4	21.0	24.6	28.2
200	27.1	34.8	42.0	49.2	56.4
300	40.7	52.2	63.0	73.8	84.6

EXAMPLE:

To obtain moments for a 185 pound passenger in seat 5, add moments shown for 100 pounds (21.0), 80 pounds (16.8), and 5 pounds (1.0) for a total moment of 38.8 inch-pound/1000.

NOTE:

The airplane may be configured with left single commuter seats installed on the right side, and right single commuter seats installed on the left side. Actual seat location should be noted when computing airplane weight and balance.

Figure 410. CE-208—Weight and Moment Tables—10 Place Commuters.

Illustrations and materials were used with permission from Cessna Aircraft Company.

WEIGHT AND MOMENT TABLES

FUEL (JET FUEL WITH DENSITY OF 6.7 POUNDS/GALLON AT 60 °F)

Gallons	Weight Pounds	Moment Inch-Pound/1000 (Arm Varies)	Gallons	Weight Pounds	Moment Inch-Pound/1000 (Arm Varies)
5	34	6.8	175	1173	238.4
10	67	13.6	180	1206	245.2
15	101	20.4	185	1240	252.0
20	134	27.2	190	1273	258.8
25	168	34.0	195	1307	265.7
30	201	40.8	200	1340	272.5
35	235	47.6	205	1374	279.3
40	268	54.4	210	1407	286.1
45	302	61.2	215	1441	292.9
50	335	68.0	220	1474	299.7
55	369	74.8	225	1508	306.5
60	402	81.6	230	1541	313.3
65	436	88.4	235	1575	320.1
70	469	95.2	240	1608	326.9
75	503	102.0	245	1642	333.7
80	536	108.8	250	1675	340.5
85	570	115.7	255	1709	347.3
90	603	122.5	260	1742	354.1
95	637	129.3	265	1776	360.9
100	670	136.1	270	1809	367.7
105	704	142.9	275	1843	374.5
110	737	149.7	280	1876	381.2
115	771	156.6	285	1910	388.0
120	804	163.4	290	1943	394.8
125	838	170.2	295	1977	401.6
130	871	177.0	300	2010	408.4
135	905	183.8	305	2044	415.2
140	938	190.6	310	2077	422.0
145	972	197.5	315	2111	428.8
150	1005	204.3	320	2144	435.6
155	1039	211.1	325	2178	442.4
160	1072	217.9	327	2189	444.7
165	1106	224.7	330	2211	449.1
170	1139	231.5	332	2224	451.7

Figure 411. CE-208—Weight and Moment Tables—Fuel.

Illustrations and materials were used with permission from Cessna Aircraft Company.

WEIGHT AND MOMENT TABLES
CARGO (CABIN LOCATIONS)

Weight (Pounds)	Zone 1 (Arm = 172.1 Inch)	Zone 2 (Arm = 217.8 Inch)	Zone 3 (Arm = 264.4 Inch)	Zone 4 (Arm = 294.5 Inch)	Zone 5 (Arm = 319.5 Inch)	Zone 6 (Arm = 344.0 Inch)
	Moment (Inch-Pound/1000)					
1	0.2	0.2	0.3	0.3	0.3	0.3
2	0.3	0.4	0.5	0.6	0.6	0.7
3	0.5	0.7	0.8	0.9	1.0	1.0
4	0.7	0.9	1.1	1.2	1.3	1.4
5	0.9	1.1	1.3	1.5	1.6	1.7
6	1.0	1.3	1.6	1.8	1.9	2.1
7	1.2	1.5	1.9	2.1	2.2	2.4
8	1.4	1.7	2.1	2.4	2.6	2.8
9	1.5	2.0	2.4	2.7	2.9	3.1
10	1.7	2.2	2.6	2.9	3.2	3.4
20	3.4	4.4	5.3	5.9	6.4	6.9
30	5.2	6.5	7.9	8.8	9.6	10.3
40	6.9	8.7	10.6	11.8	12.8	13.8
50	8.6	10.9	13.2	14.7	16.0	17.2
60	10.3	13.1	15.9	17.7	19.2	20.6
70	12.0	15.2	18.5	20.6	22.4	24.1
80	13.8	17.4	21.2	23.6	25.6	27.5
90	15.5	19.6	23.8	26.5	28.8	31.0
100	17.2	21.8	26.4	29.5	32.0	34.4
200	34.4	43.6	52.9	58.9	63.9	68.8
300	51.6	65.3	79.3	88.4	95.9	103.2
400	68.8	87.1	105.8	117.8	127.8	
500	86.1	108.9	132.2	147.3	159.8	
600	103.3	130.7	158.6	176.7	191.7	
700	120.5	152.5	185.1	206.2	223.7	
800	137.7	174.2	211.5	235.6	255.6	
900	154.9	196.0	238.0	265.1	287.6	
1000	172.1	217.8	264.4	294.5	319.5	
2000		435.6				
3000		653.4				

EXAMPLE:

To obtain moments for 350 pounds of cargo in Zone 1, add moments shown in Zone 1 for 300 pounds (51.6) and 50 pounds (8.6) for a total moment of 60.2 inch-pound/1000.

Figure 412. CE-208—Weight and Moment Tables—Cargo (Cabin Locations).

Illustrations and materials were used with permission from Cessna Aircraft Company.

WEIGHT AND MOMENT TABLES
CARGO (CARGO POD LOCATIONS)

Weight Pounds	Zone A (Arm = 132.4 Inch)	Zone B (Arm = 182.1 Inch)	Zone C (Arm = 233.4 Inch)	Zone D (Arm = 287.6 Inch)
	Moment (Inch-Pound/1000)			
1	0.1	0.2	0.2	0.3
2	0.3	0.4	0.5	0.6
3	0.4	0.5	0.7	0.9
4	0.5	0.7	0.9	1.2
5	0.7	0.9	1.2	1.4
6	0.8	1.1	1.4	1.7
7	0.9	1.3	1.6	2.0
8	1.1	1.5	1.9	2.3
9	1.2	1.6	2.1	2.6
10	1.3	1.8	2.3	2.9
20	2.6	3.6	4.7	5.8
30	4.0	5.5	7.0	8.6
40	5.3	7.3	9.3	11.5
50	6.6	9.1	11.7	14.4
60	7.9	10.9	14.0	17.3
70	9.3	12.7	16.3	20.1
80	10.6	14.6	18.7	23.0
90	11.9	16.4	21.0	25.9
100	13.2	18.2	23.3	28.8
200	26.5	36.4	46.7	57.5
300		54.6		

EXAMPLE:
To obtain moments for 48 pounds of cargo in Zone A, add moments shown in Zone A for 40 pounds (5.3) and 8 pounds (1.1) for a total moment of 6.4 inch-pound/1000.

Figure 413. CE-208—Weight and Moment Tables—Cargo (Cargo POD Locations).
Illustrations and materials were used with permission from Cessna Aircraft Company.

SAMPLE LOADING PROBLEM

(CARGO LOADING SHOWN)	SAMPLE AIRPLANE		YOUR AIRPLANE	
	Weight Pounds	Moment Inch-Pound/1000	Weight Pounds	Moment Inch-Pound/1000
1. Basic Empty Weight (Use the data pertaining to your airplane as it is presently equipped (includes unusable fuel and full oil).	5005	929.4	5005	929.4
2. Usable Fuel (332 Gallons Max)	2224	451.7		
3. Pilot (Seat 1) (STA. 133.5 to 146.5)	170	23.1	200	
4. Front Passenger (Seat 2) (STA 133.5 to 146.5)				
5. Aft Passengers (Commuter Seating):				
STA. 173.9				
STA. 209.9				
STA. 245.9				
STA. 281.9				
6. Baggage/Cargo (Cabin Locations):				
Zone 1 (STA. 155.40 to 188.70)	120	20.6		
Zone 2 (STA. 188.70 to 246.80)	416	90.6		
Zone 3 (STA. 246.80 to 282.00)	200	52.9		
Zone 4 (STA. 282.00 to 307.00)	200	58.9		
Zone 5 (STA. 307.00 to 332.00)	200	63.9		
Zone 6 (STA. 332.00 to 356.00)	50	17.2		
7. Baggage/Cargo (Cargo Pod Locations):				
Zone A (STA. 100.00 to 154.75)	50	6.6		
Zone B (STA. 154.75 to 209.35)	50	9.1		
Zone C (STA. 209.35 to 257.35)	50	11.7		
Zone D (STA. 257.35 to 332.00)	50	14.4		
8. **RAMP WEIGHT AND MOMENT**	8785	1750.1		
9. Fuel Allowance (for engine start, taxi, and runup)	–35	–7.0		
10. **TO WEIGHT AND MOMENT** (Subtract Step 9 from Step 8)	8750	1743.1		

11. Locate this point (8750 at 1743.1) on the Center of Gravity Moment Envelope, and since this point falls within the envelope, the loading is acceptable.

NOTE:

Refer to the Weight and Moment Tables for weight and moment of crew, passengers, usable fuel, and cargo being carried. Refer to Cabin Internal Loading Arrangements for aft passengers seating arrangements.

Figure 414. CE-208—Sample Loading Problem.

CENTER OF GRAVITY LIMITS

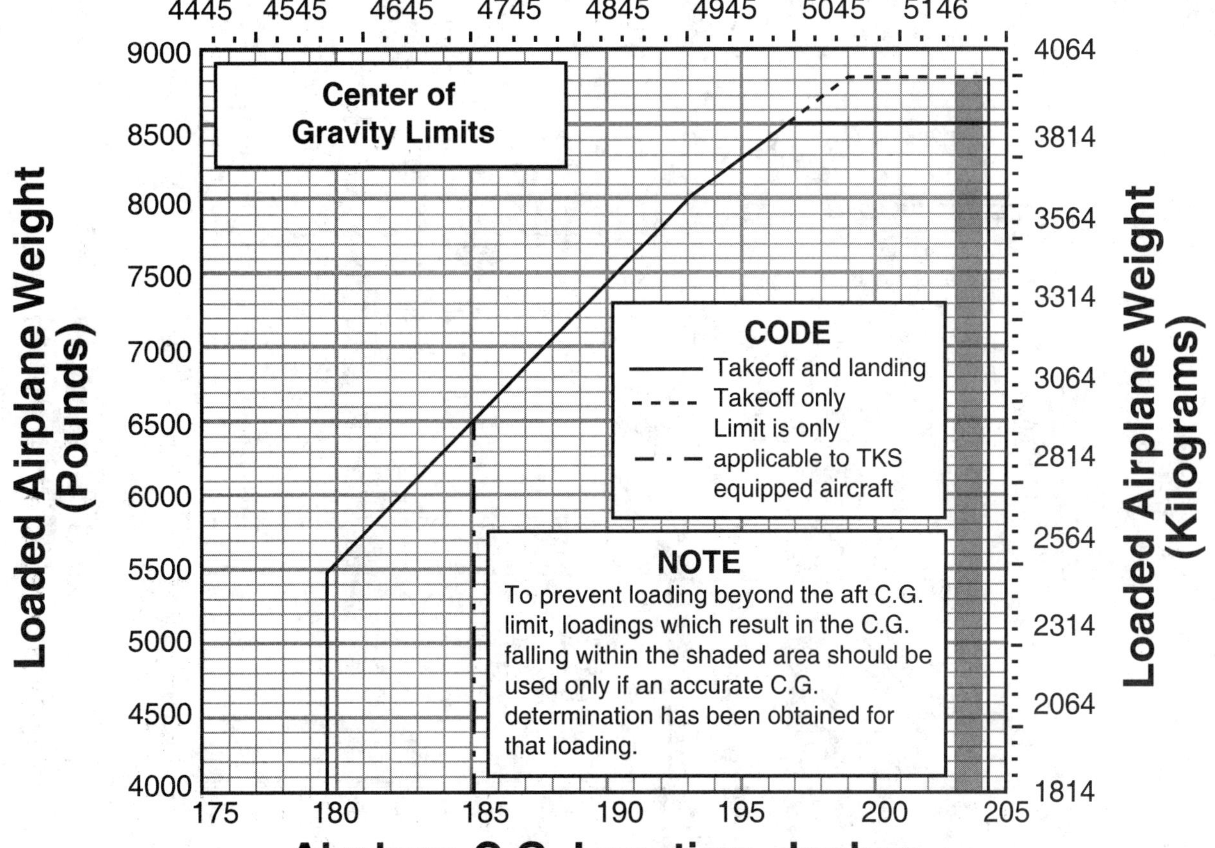

WARNING

It is the responsibility of the pilot to make sure that the airplane is loaded correctly. Operation outside of prescribed weight and balance limitations could result in an accident and serious or fatal injury.

Figure 415. CE-208—Center of Gravity Limits.

Illustrations and materials were used with permission from Cessna Aircraft Company.

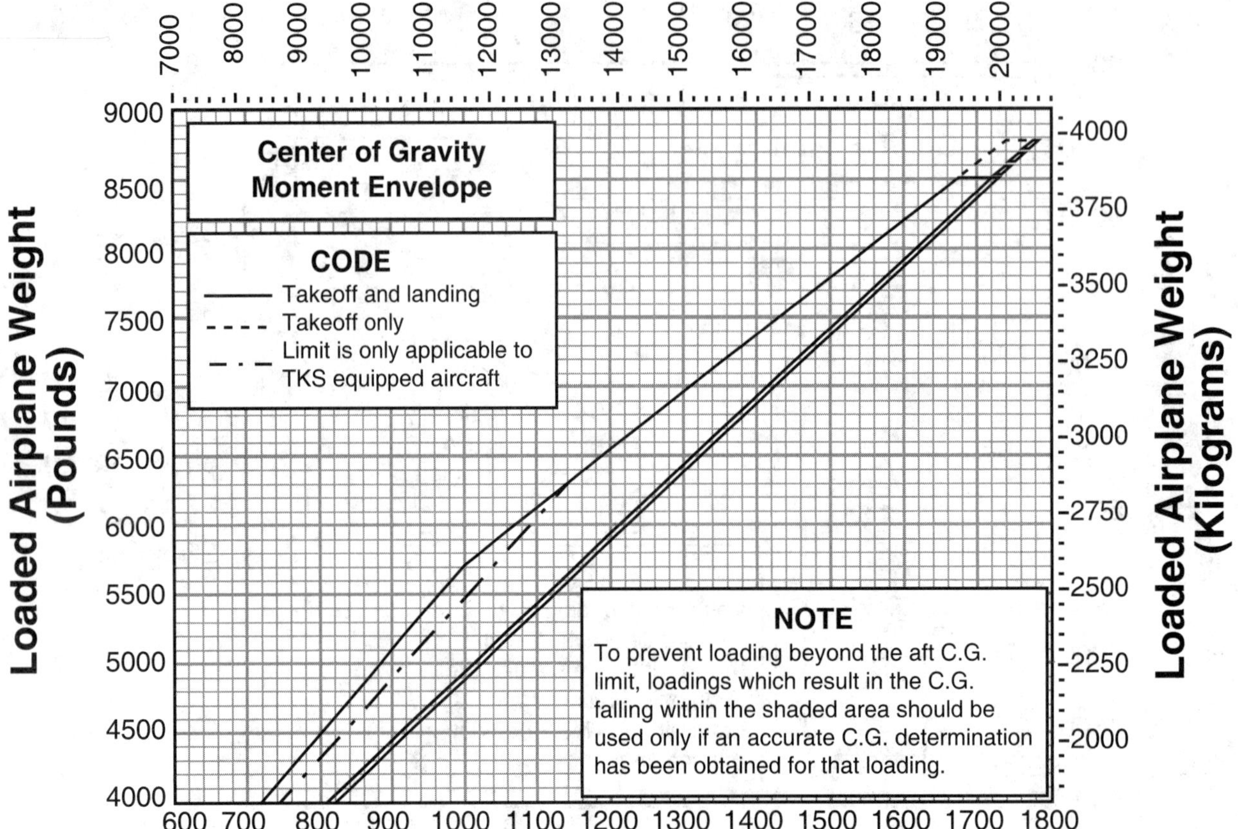

WARNING

Because loading personnel may not always be able to achieve an ideal loading, a means of protecting the C.G envelope is provided by supplying an aft C.G. location warning (shaded area) between 38.33% MAC and the maximum aft C.G. of 40.33% MAC on the center of gravity moment envelope. Points falling within this shaded area should be used only if accurate C.G. determination for cargo loadings can be obtained.

It is the responsibility of the pilot to make sure that the airplane is loaded correctly. Operation outside of prescribed weight and balance limitations could result in an accident and serious or fatal injury.

Figure 416. CE-208—Center of Gravity Moment Envelope.

Illustrations and materials were used with permission from Cessna Aircraft Company.

1. INTRODUCTION

Observance of the limitations included in this chapter is mandatory.

2. KINDS OF AIRPLANE OPERATION

The airplane is certified in the transport category for day and night operations, in the following conditions when the equipment and instruments required by the airworthiness and operating regulations are approved, installed, and in an operable condition:

- VFR and IFR
- Flight in icing conditions

The airplane is certified for ditching when the safety equipment specified by the applicable regulations is installed.

The airplane is certified capable of RVSM operations in accordance with the FAA "Interim guidance material on the approval of operations/aircraft for RVSM operations," 91-RVSM, dated June 30, 1999 and with the JAA Temporary Guidance Leaflet, TGL No. 6, Revision 1, RVSM. <1030>

NOTE

Compliance with these FAA and JAA standards does not constitute an operational approval. <1030>

RVSM operations must not be commenced or continued unless all of the required equipment specified in the RVSM Required Equipment List table is operational. <1030>

RVSM Required Equipment List <1030>	
Equipment	**Requirements for RVSM**
Autopilot	Must be operational.
Altitude Alerting System	Must be operational.
Altitude Reporting Transponder (2)	One (1) must be operational.
Air Data Computers (2)	Two (2) must be operational.

Effectivity:

- On airplanes registered in the Republic of Argentina:
  - The Necessary equipment for the different kinds of operations must comply with the applicable Argentinean regulation. <DNA>

Figure 417. CRJ 900—Limitations.

Illustrations and materials were used with permission from Bombardier.

1. STRUCTURAL WEIGHT LIMITATION

Weight	kg	lb	Airplane Option Code
Medium Ramp Weight (MRW)	36628	80750	
	36 613	80719	<2217>
	37108	81810	<2002>
	37535	82750	<2004>
	38222	84265	<2006>
	38555	85000	<2005>
Medium Takeoff Weight (MTOW)	36514	80500	
	36500	80469	<2217>
	36995	81560	<2002>
	37421	82500	<2004>
	37995	83765	<2006>
	38329	84500	<2005>
Maximum Landing Weight (MLW)	33339	73500	
	34065	75100	<2005> or <2006>
Maximum Zero Fuel Weight (MZFW)	31751	70000	
	32092	70750	<2005> or <2006>
Minimum Flight Weight	20412	45000	

NOTE

The Maximum Take-off Weight (MTOW) and/or Maximum Landing Weight (MLW) may be further limited due to performance considerations.

Figure 418. CRJ 900—Limitations—Structural Weight.
Illustrations and materials were used with permission from Bombardier.

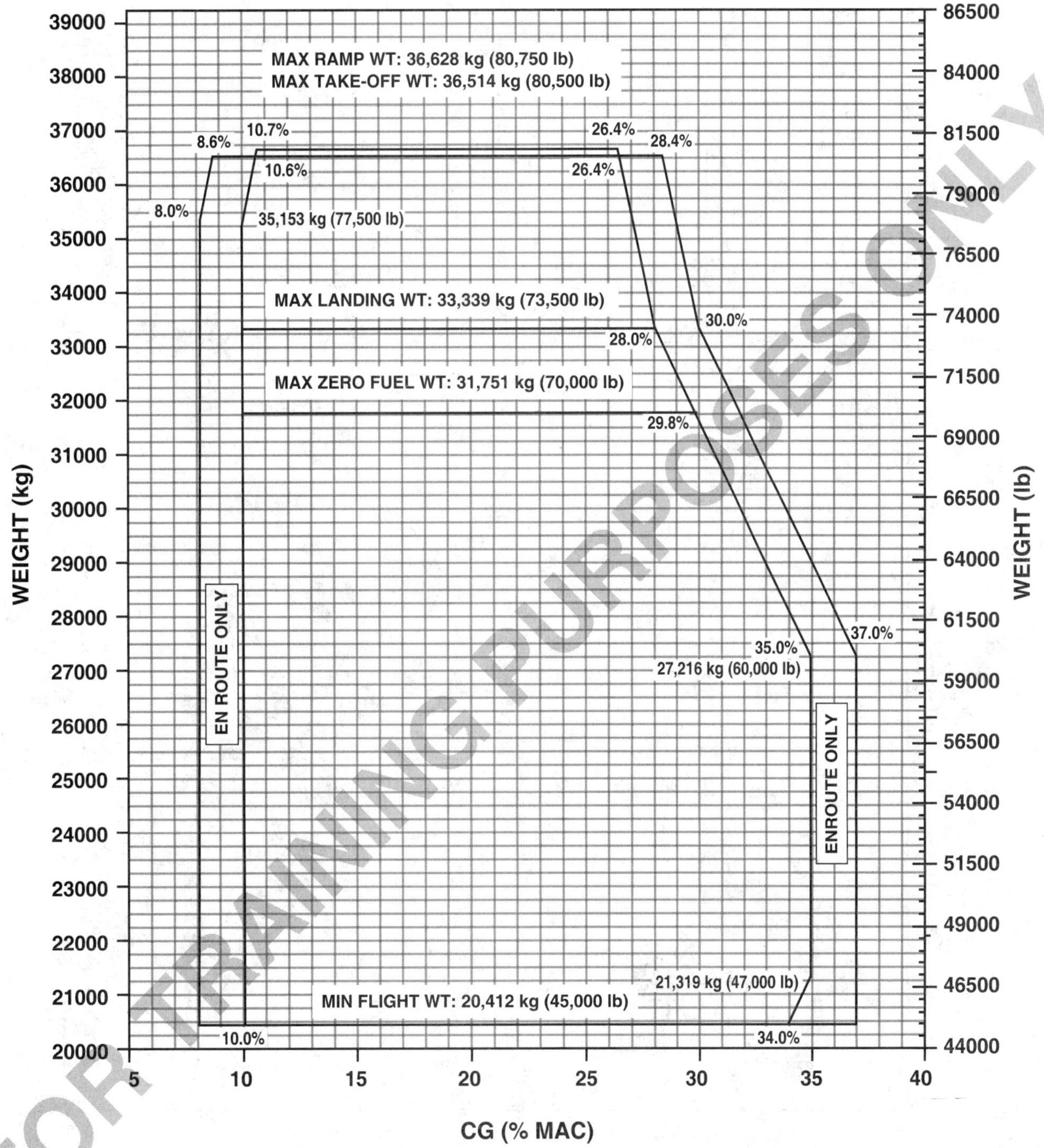

WEIGHT (kg)

39000
38000
37000
36000
35000
34000
33000
32000
31000
30000
29000
28000
27000
26000
25000
24000
23000
22000
21000
20000

WEIGHT (lb)

86500
84000
81500
79000
76500
74000
71500
69000
66500
64000
61500
59000
56500
54000
51500
49000
46500
44000

MAX RAMP WT: 36,628 kg (80,750 lb)
MAX TAKE-OFF WT: 36,514 kg (80,500 lb)

8.6%
10.7%
26.4%
28.4%
10.6%
26.4%
8.0%
35,153 kg (77,500 lb)

MAX LANDING WT: 33,339 kg (73,500 lb)

30.0%
28.0%

MAX ZERO FUEL WT: 31,751 kg (70,000 lb)

29.8%

EN ROUTE ONLY

37.0%
35.0%
27,216 kg (60,000 lb)

ENROUTE ONLY

21,319 kg (47,000 lb)
MIN FLIGHT WT: 20,412 kg (45,000 lb)
10.0%
34.0%

5 10 15 20 25 30 35 40

CG (% MAC)

Figure 419. CRJ 900—Center of Gravity Limits.
Illustrations and materials were used with permission from Bombardier.

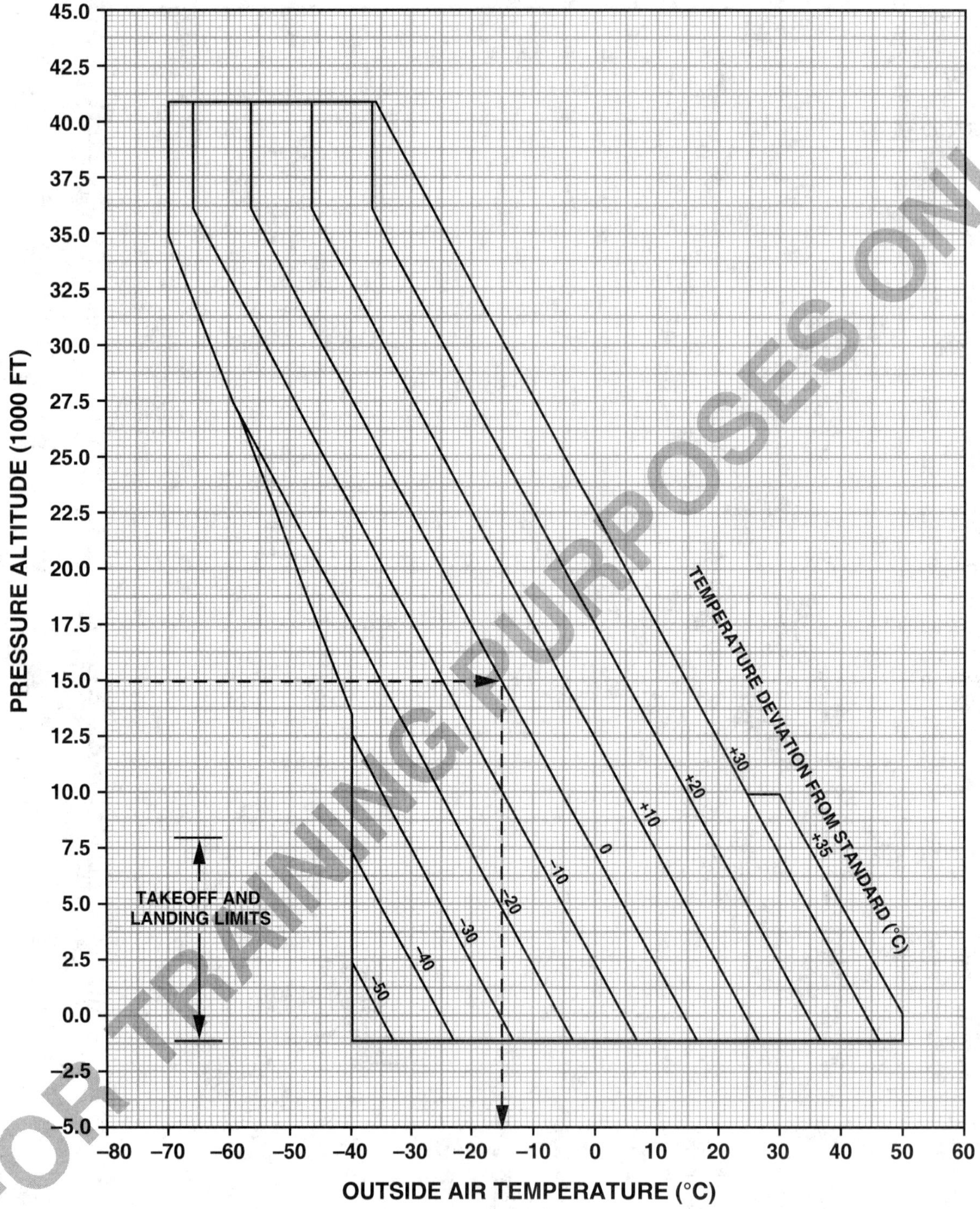

Figure 420. CRJ 900—Altitude and Temperature Operating Limits.
Illustrations and materials were used with permission from Bombardier.

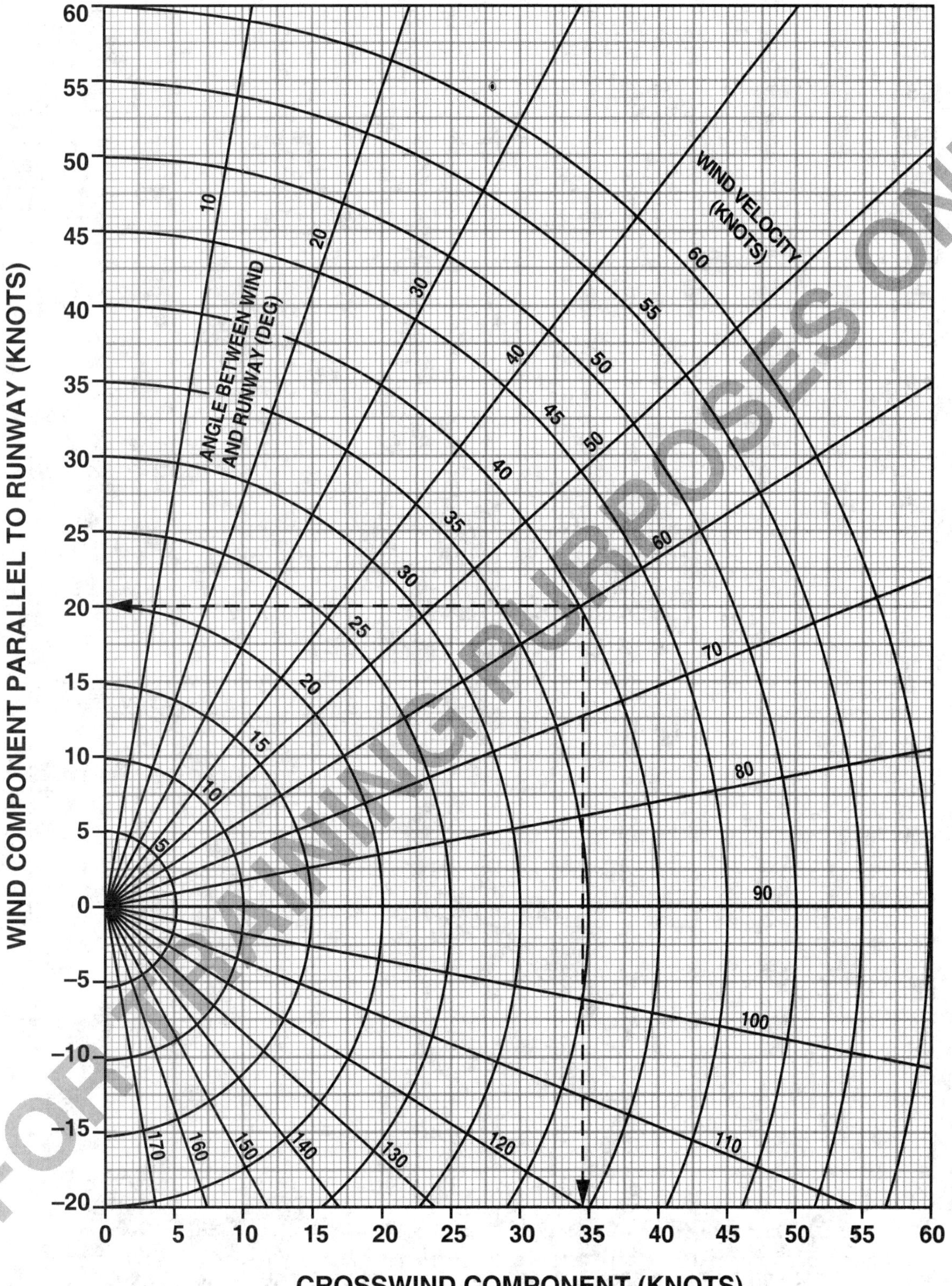

Figure 421. CRJ 900—Performance—Wind Component.
Illustrations and materials were used with permission from Bombardier.

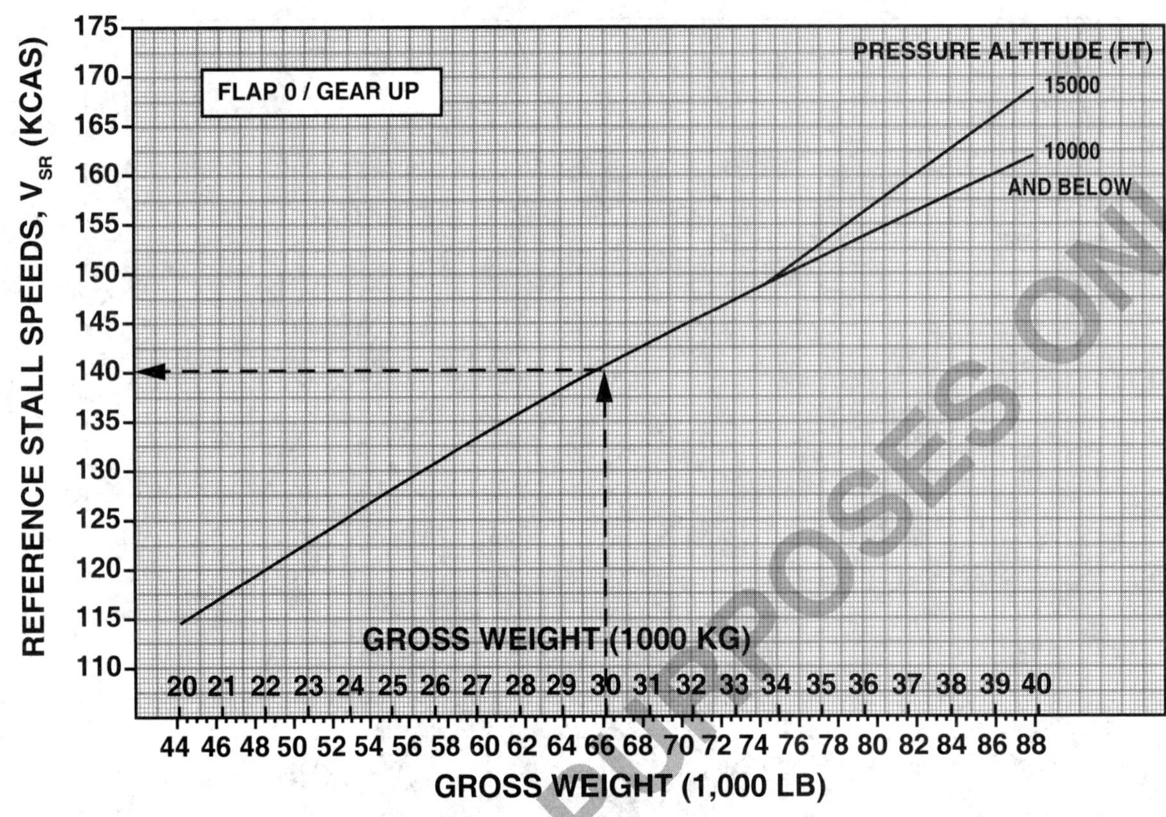

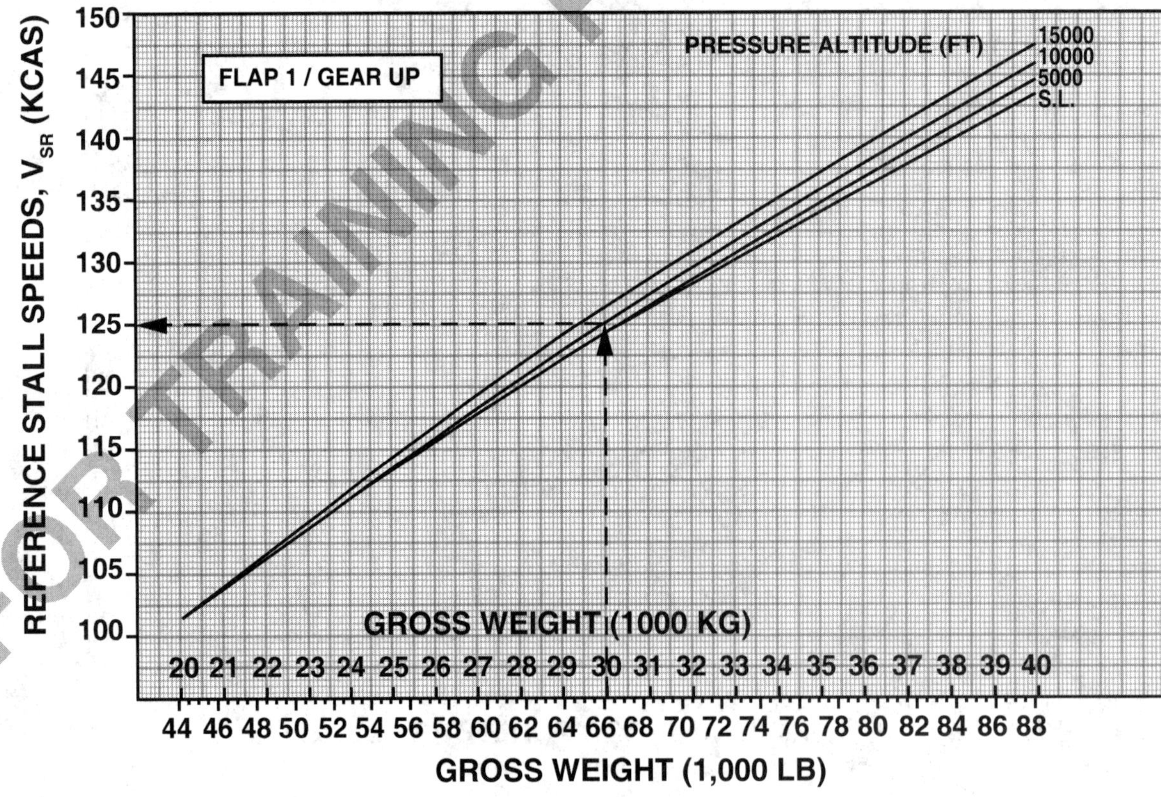

Figure 422. CRJ 900—Performance—Stall Speeds, V_{SR}.

Illustrations and materials were used with permission from Bombardier.

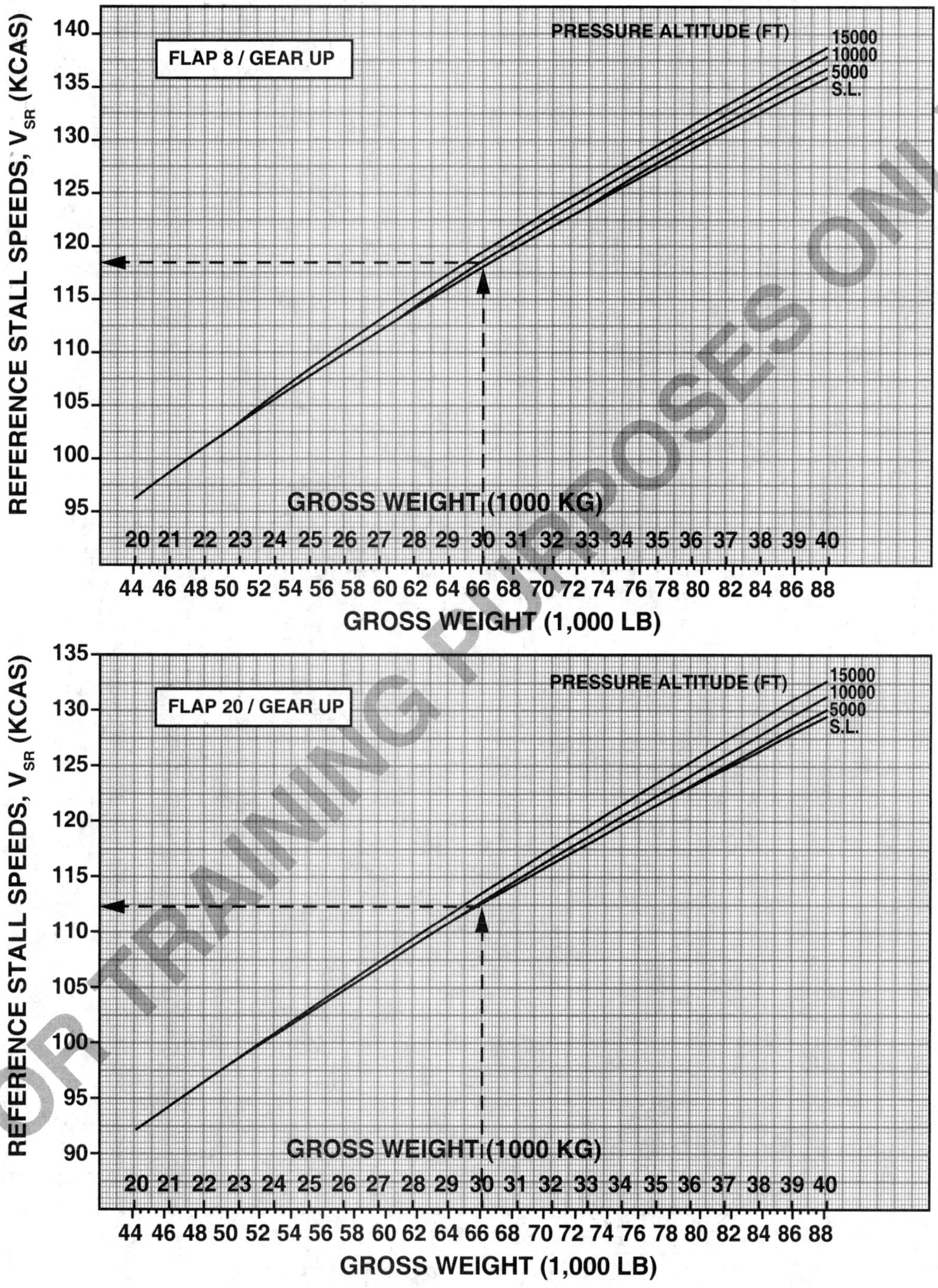

Figure 423. CRJ 900—Performance—Stall Speeds, V_{SR}.
Illustrations and materials were used with permission from Bombardier.

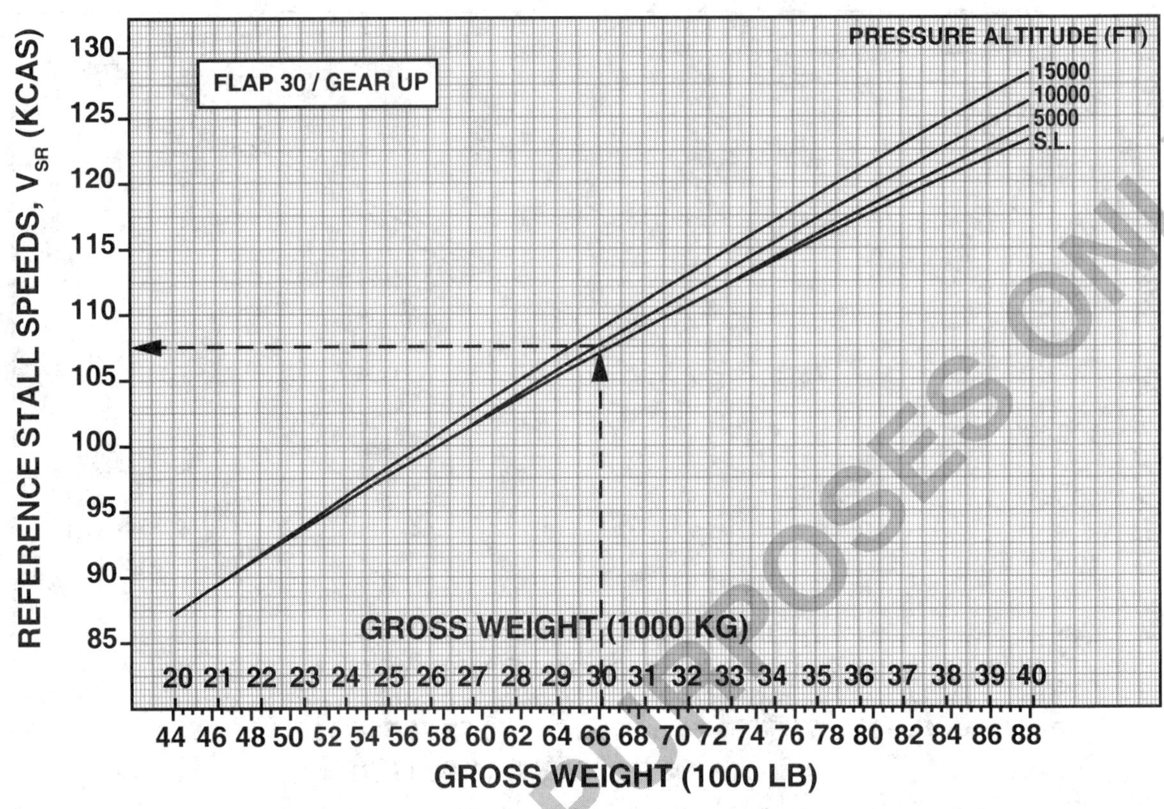

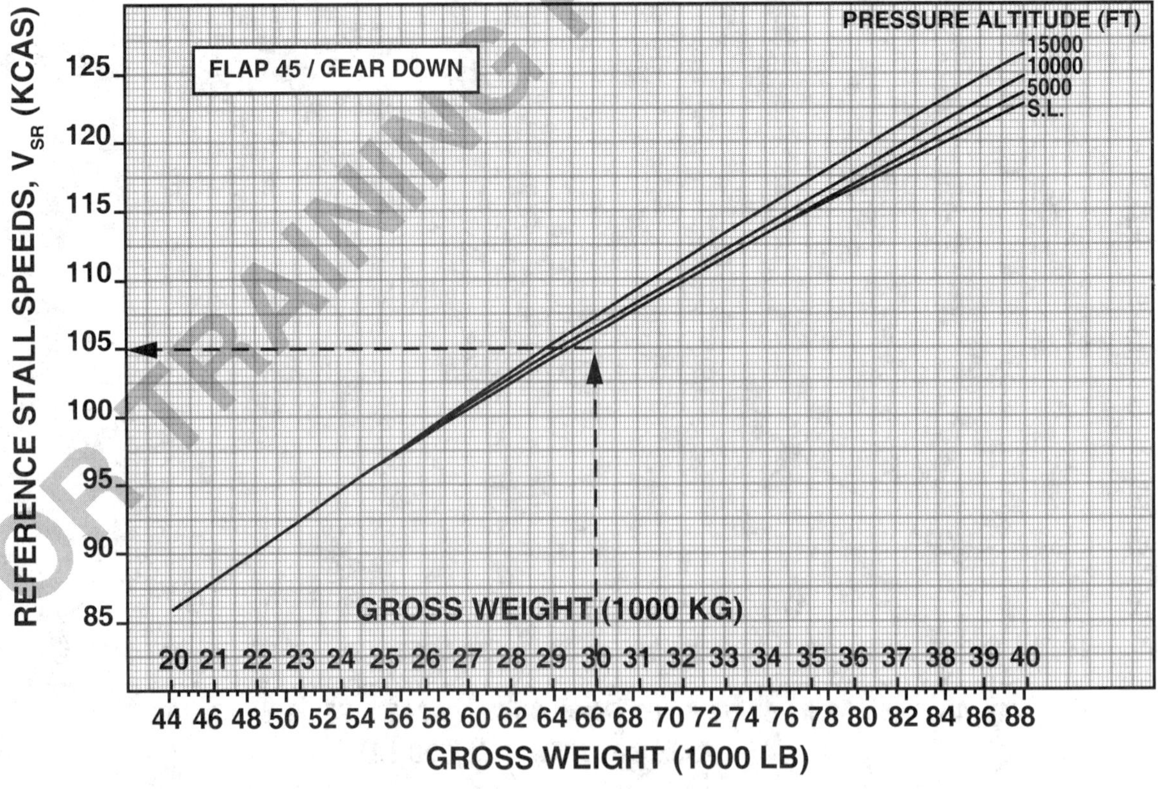

Figure 424. CRJ 900—Performance—Stall Speeds, V_{SR}.

Illustrations and materials were used with permission from Bombardier.

B. Maneuvering Capabilities

The maneuvering capabilities are shown in Figure 426. Figure 426 shows the maneuver margin (bank angle and/or g-load factor) for a given weight, CG, altitude and speed combination. Alternatively, for a given load factor, Figure 426 shows the altitude and speed margins for a given weight, CG and speed combination.

Maneuvering capability is defined relative to buffet onset or stick shaker activation, whichever occurs first.

Example A:

Associated conditions:

Airplane gross weight	= 33000 kg (72,750 lb)
Center of Gravity (CG)	= 20% MAC
Indicated Mach No.	= 0.770
Pressure altitude	= 35000 feet

Example A in Figure 426, for the given associated conditions (enter Figure 426 from the indicated Mach number scale), shows that the maneuvering capability is equal to 1.70 g or a bank angle of 54 degrees.

Example B:

Associated conditions:

Airplane gross weight	= 33000 kg (72,750 lb)
Centre of Gravity (CG)	= 20% MAC
Pressure altitude	= 37000 feet
Required maneuvering capability	= 1.30 g (or approximately 40-degree bank)

Example B in Figure 426, for the given associated conditions (enter Figure 426 from the load factor [or bank angle] scale towards the gross weight scale), shows the following speed margins:

- Low speed = 0.680 M
- High speed = 0.845 M

Operating at a speed greater than 0.680 M and lower than 0.845 M at 37000 feet will ensure that a minimum maneuvering capability of 1.30 g before stick shaker activation or buffet onset, will be maintained for the conditions in Example B.

Following the same example, the maximum altitude at a speed of 0.77 M, before stick shaker activation or buffet onset for the required maneuvering capability of 1.30 g is 40,600 feet, as marked by an X in Figure 426.

Figure 425. CRJ 900—Performance—Maneuvering Capabilities.
Illustrations and materials were used with permission from Bombardier.

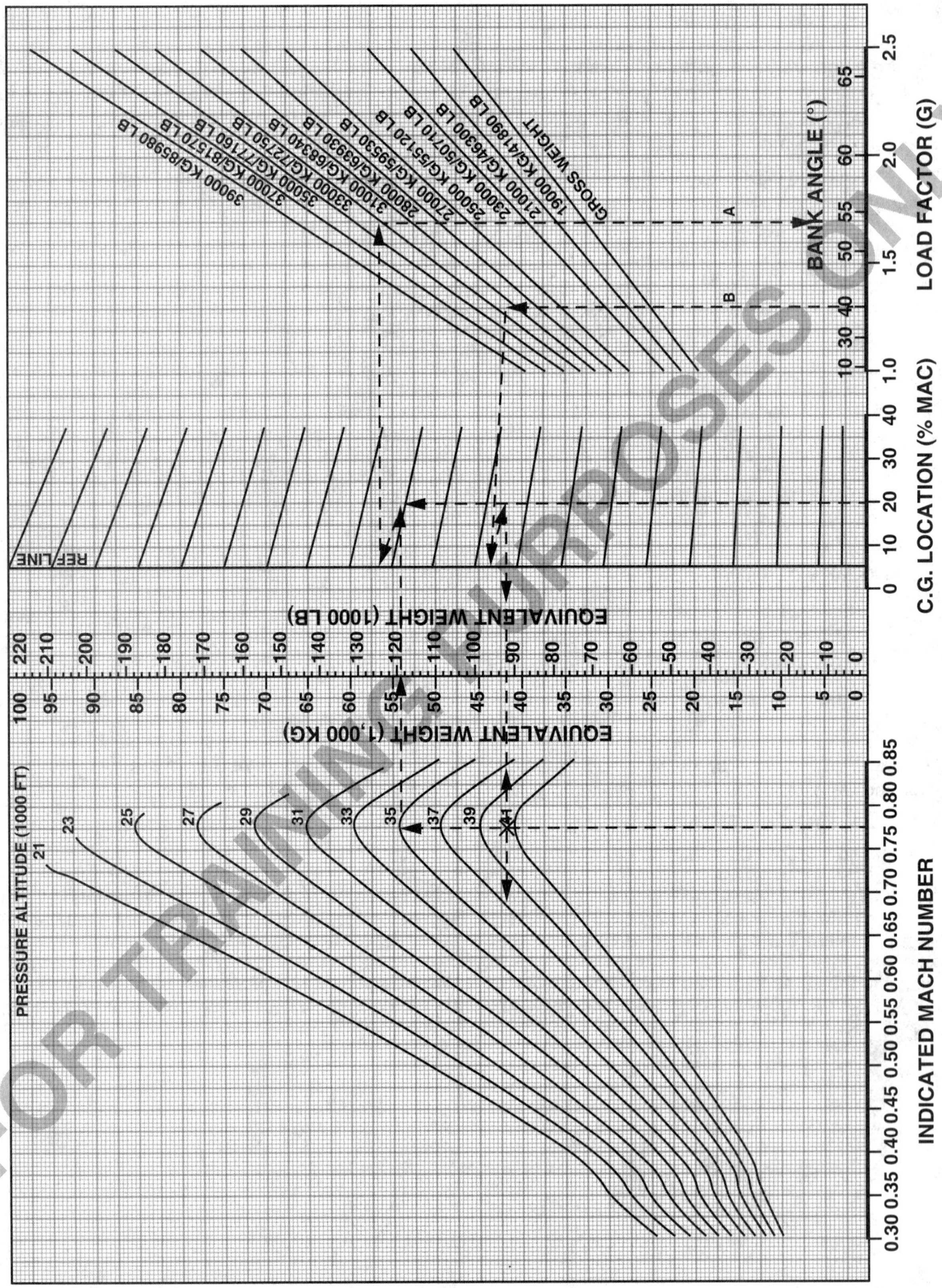

Figure 426. CRJ 900—Performance—Maneuvering Capabilities.

Illustrations and materials were used with permission from Bombardier.

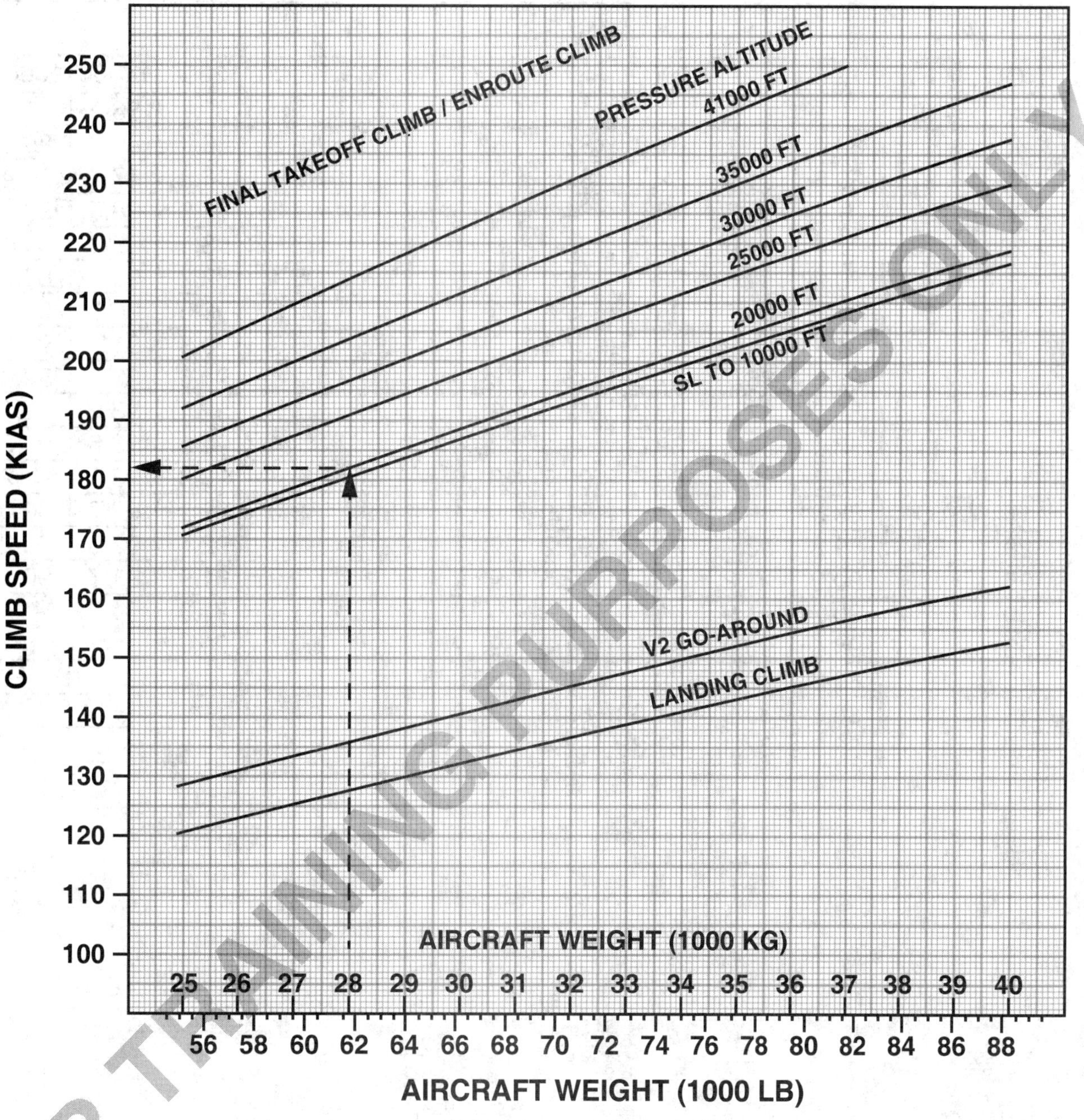

FINAL TAKEOFF CLIMB / ENROUTE CLIMB
PRESSURE ALTITUDE
41000 FT
35000 FT
30000 FT
25000 FT
20000 FT
SL TO 10000 FT
V2 GO-AROUND
LANDING CLIMB
CLIMB SPEED (KIAS)
250 240 230 220 210 200 190 180 170 160 150 140 130 120 110 100
AIRCRAFT WEIGHT (1000 KG)
25 26 27 28 29 30 31 32 33 34 35 36 37 38 39 40
56 58 60 62 64 66 68 70 72 74 76 78 80 82 84 86 88
AIRCRAFT WEIGHT (1000 LB)

Figure 427. CRJ 900—Performance—Climb Speeds.
Illustrations and materials were used with permission from Bombardier.

OAT		PRESSURE ALTITUDE (Feet)									
(°C)	(°F)	–1,000	0	2000	4000	6000	8000	10000	12000	14000	16000
–45	–49								85.1	86.0	85.8
–40	–40	80.0	81.1	81.8	82.8	83.6	84.3	85.2	86.0	86.8	86.6
–35	–31	80.8	81.9	82.7	83.6	84.5	85.2	86.0	86.8	87.7	87.4
–30	–22	81.6	82.7	83.5	84.4	85.3	86.0	86.8	87.6	88.5	88.3
–25	–13	82.4	83.5	84.3	85.2	86.1	86.8	87.6	88.4	89.3	89.1
–20	–4	83.2	84.3	85.1	86.0	86.9	87.6	88.4	89.2	90.1	89.9
–15	5	84.0	85.1	85.9	86.8	87.7	88.4	89.2	90.0	90.9	90.7
–10	14	84.7	85.9	86.7	87.6	88.5	89.2	90.0	90.8	91.7	91.5
–5	23	85.5	86.7	87.5	88.4	89.3	90.0	90.8	91.6	92.4	92.0
0	32	86.3	87.4	88.2	89.2	90.1	90.8	91.6	92.4	93.2	92.1
5	41	87.0	88.2	89.0	90.0	90.8	91.6	92.4	93.2	93.6	91.8
10	50	87.8	88.9	89.8	90.7	91.6	92.3	93.1	93.3	93.2	91.2
15	59	88.5	89.7	90.5	91.5	92.4	92.9	93.0	92.9	92.7	90.6
20	68	89.2	90.4	91.3	92.2	92.7	92.6	92.4	92.4	92.3	90.2
25	77	90.0	91.2	92.0	92.3	92.2	92.1	92.0	91.9	91.7	90.1
30	86	90.7	91.9	91.8	91.7	91.6	91.5	91.4	91.3	91.2	
35	95	90.4	90.9	90.9	91.0	90.9	90.8	90.7	90.6		
40	104	89.3	89.8	89.9	89.9	89.9	90.1				
45	113	88.1	88.6	88.6	88.7	88.9					
50	122	86.8	87.3	87.3	87.4						

Figure 428. CRJ 900—Thrust Settings—Normal Takeoff Thrust Setting (All Engines Operating), %N_1 Engine Bleeds Closed—Static to 65 KIAS.

Illustrations and materials were used with permission from Bombardier.

OAT		PRESSURE ALTITUDE (Feet)									
(°C)	(°F)	–1000	0	2000	4000	6000	8000	10000	12000	14000	16000
–45	–49								84.2	85.0	84.9
–40	–40	79.4	80.5	81.2	82.1	82.9	83.6	84.3	85.1	85.8	85.7
–35	–31	80.2	81.3	82.1	83.0	83.7	84.4	85.1	85.9	86.6	86.5
–30	–22	81.0	82.1	82.9	83.8	84.6	85.2	86.0	86.7	87.4	87.3
–25	–13	81.8	82.9	83.7	84.6	85.4	86.0	86.8	87.5	88.2	88.1
–20	–4	82.6	83.7	84.5	85.4	86.2	86.8	87.6	88.3	89.0	88.9
–15	5	83.4	84.5	85.3	86.2	87.0	87.6	88.3	89.1	89.8	89.7
–10	14	84.1	85.3	86.0	87.0	87.7	88.4	89.1	89.8	90.6	90.5
–5	23	84.9	86.0	86.8	87.7	88.5	89.1	89.9	90.6	91.3	91.1
0	32	85.6	86.8	87.6	88.5	89.3	89.9	90.6	91.3	92.0	90.9
5	41	86.4	87.5	88.3	89.2	90.0	90.7	91.4	91.9	92.0	90.3
10	50	87.1	88.3	89.1	90.0	90.8	91.4	91.8	91.8	91.4	89.7

Figure 429. CRJ 900—Thrust Settings—Normal Takeoff Thrust Setting (All Engines Operating), %N_1 Cowl Anti-ice On, PACK On—Static to 65 KIAS.

Illustrations and materials were used with permission from Bombardier.

OAT		PRESSURE ALTITUDE (Feet)									
(°C)	(°F)	–1000	0	2000	4000	6000	8000	10000	12000	14000	16000
–45	–49								86.4	86.5	87.4
–40	–40	82.3	83.4	84.1	84.9	85.8	86.6	87.2	87.2	87.3	88.2
–35	–31	83.1	84.3	84.9	85.7	86.6	87.4	88.0	88.0	88.2	89.1
–30	–22	83.9	85.1	85.8	86.6	87.4	88.2	88.8	88.8	89.0	89.9
–25	–13	84.7	85.9	86.6	87.4	88.2	89.0	89.6	89.6	89.8	90.7
–20	–4	85.5	86.7	87.4	88.2	89.0	89.8	90.4	90.4	90.6	91.3
–15	5	86.3	87.5	88.2	88.9	89.8	90.6	91.1	90.9	91.0	90.1
–10	14	87.1	88.3	89.0	89.7	90.6	91.4	91.2	91.3	91.3	89.5
–5	23	87.9	89.0	89.7	90.5	91.4	91.5	91.4	91.4	91.4	88.6
0	32	88.6	89.8	90.5	91.3	91.7	91.6	91.5	91.5	91.5	87.4
5	41	89.4	90.6	91.3	91.9	91.8	91.4	91.4	91.2	91.2	86.8
10	50	90.1	91.3	92.0	92.0	91.5	91.1	91.0	90.9	89.9	86.4

Figure 430. CRJ 900—Thrust Settings—Go Around or APR Thrust Setting (One Engine Inoperative), %N_1 Wing and Cowl Anti-ice On, PACK On—140 KIAS.

Illustrations and materials were used with permission from Bombardier.

SAT		PRESSURE ALTITUDE (Feet)							
(°C)	(°F)	0	5000	10000	15000	20000	25000	30000	35000
–70	–94							87.8	89.0
–65	–85						87.0	88.6	89.9
–60	–76					86.6	87.9	89.5	90.8
–55	–67					87.4	88.8	90.4	91.7
–50	–58				86.4	88.3	89.6	91.2	92.5
–45	–49			85.0	87.2	89.2	90.5	92.1	93.3
–40	–40	81.4	83.7	85.8	88.1	90.0	91.3	92.9	93.1
–35	–31	82.3	84.6	86.7	88.9	90.8	92.2	93.6	92.4
–30	–22	83.1	85.4	87.5	89.7	91.6	93.0	92.8	91.5
–25	–13	83.9	86.2	88.3	90.6	92.5	93.7	92.2	89.9
–20	–4	84.7	87.1	89.2	91.4	93.3	93.4	91.4	89.0
–15	5	85.5	87.9	90.0	92.2	93.8	92.6	90.7	88.8
–10	14	86.3	88.7	90.8	93.0	93.6	91.8	89.9	88.5
–5	23	87.1	89.5	91.5	93.5	92.8	91.1	89.7	
0	32	87.8	90.2	92.3	93.2	92.0	90.3	89.6	
5	41	88.6	91.0	92.7	92.4	91.3	90.0		
10	50	89.4	91.8	92.4	91.7	90.7	89.9		

Figure 431. CRJ 900—Thrust Settings—Maximum Continuous Thrust Setting (One Engine Inoperative), %N_1 Cowl Anti-ice On, PACK On—170 KIAS.

Illustrations and materials were used with permission from Bombardier.

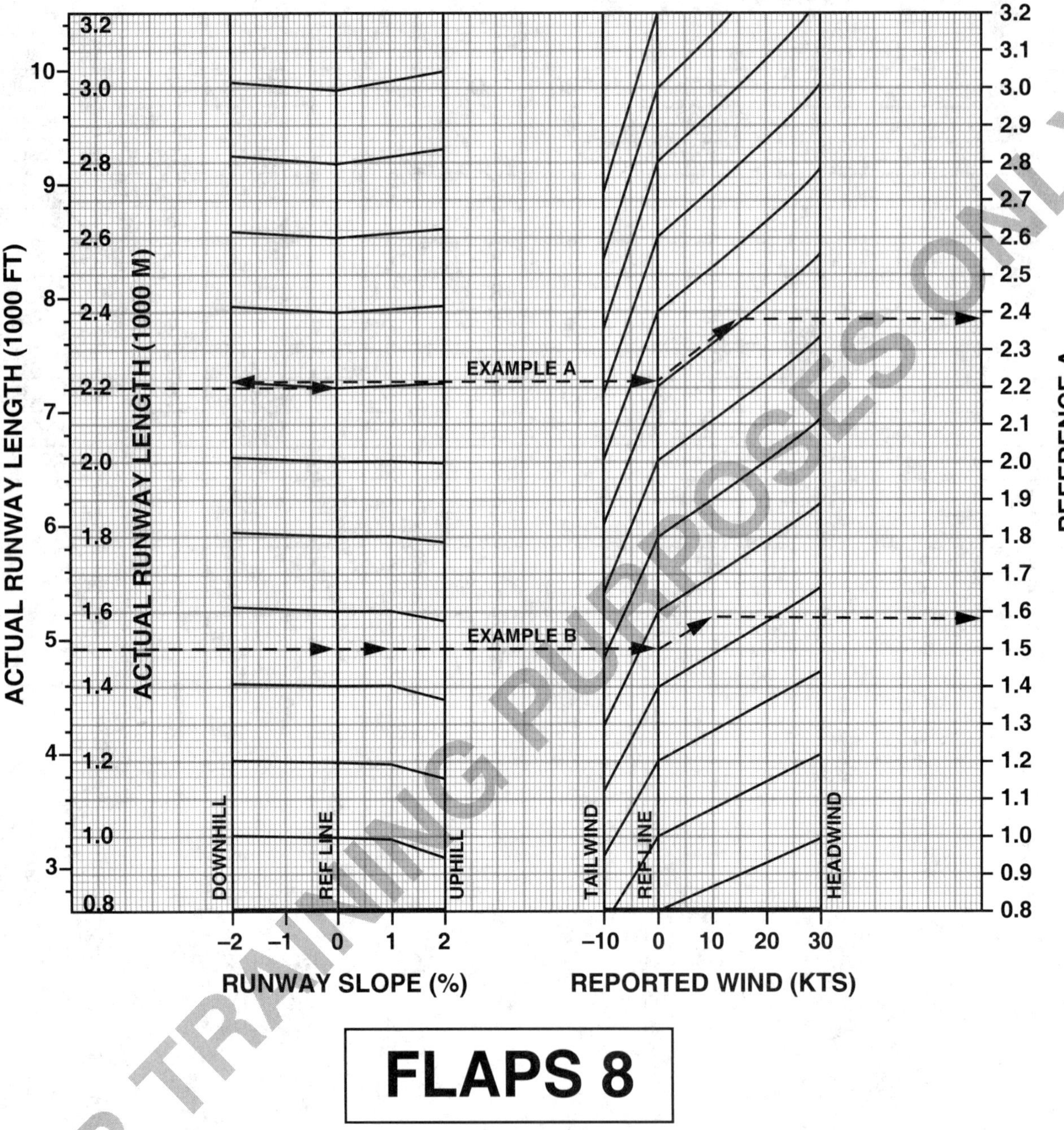

Figure 432. CRJ 900—Takeoff Performance—Takeoff Weight Limited by Field Length Requirements, Dry Runway—V_{MC} Limited, FLAPS 8

Illustrations and materials were used with permission from Bombardier.

D. Takeoff Weight Limited by Field Length Requirements, Dry Runway - One Engine Inoperative, FLAPS 8

The maximum takeoff weight limited by field length requirements on a dry runway, with one engine inoperative for a FLAPS 8 takeoff, is given by Figure 435, Figure 436, or Figure 437. The following charts take into account the accelerate-stop distance available, the actual length of the runway and the clearway, the airport pressure altitude, and the effects of runway slope, prevailing wind conditions and temperature for varying bleed configurations.

NOTE

1. If a rolling takeoff procedure will be performed, subtract 60 meters (200 feet) from the actual runway length and the available accelerate-stop distance, prior to determining the takeoff weight.

2. If the intersection of the actual runway length and available accelerate-stop distance falls to the right of the curve for a V_1/V_R of 1, project horizontally to the left from this intersection until the 1.0 V_1/V_R curve is reached. Use a V_1/V_R of 1.0 and the corresponding Reference A value at this point.

Figure 434. CRJ 900—Takeoff Performance—Takeoff Weight Limited by Field Length Requirements, Dry Runway—One Engine Inoperative, FLAPS 8

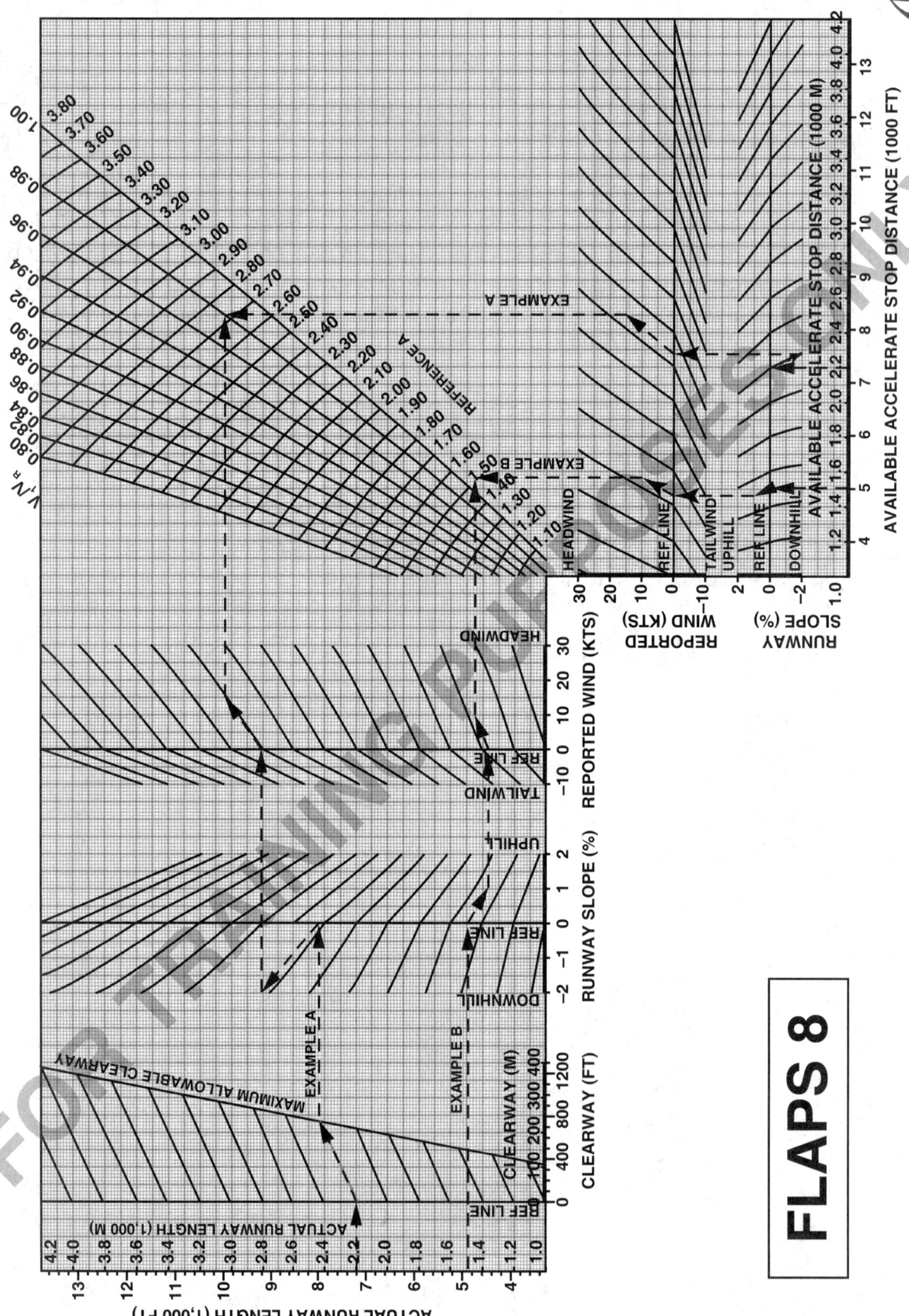

Figure 435. CRJ 900—Takeoff Performance—Takeoff Weight Limited by Field Length Requirements, Dry Runway—One Engine Inoperative, FLAPS 8

Illustrations and materials were used with permission from Bombardier.

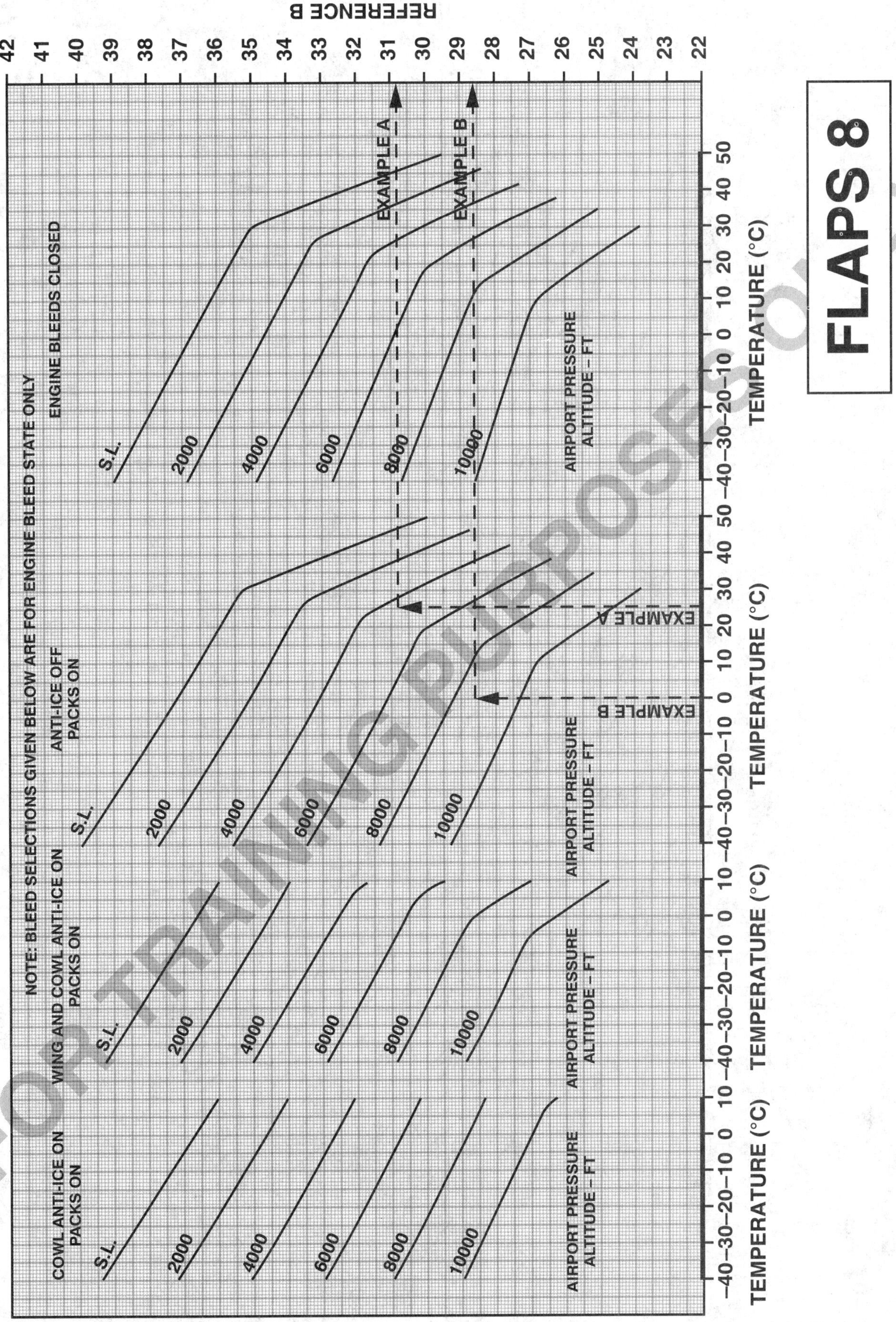

FLAPS 8

REFERENCE B

NOTE: BLEED SELECTIONS GIVEN BELOW ARE FOR ENGINE BLEED STATE ONLY

COWL ANTI-ICE ON
PACKS ON

WING AND COWL ANTI-ICE ON
PACKS ON

ANTI-ICE OFF
PACKS ON

ENGINE BLEEDS CLOSED

AIRPORT PRESSURE ALTITUDE – FT

TEMPERATURE (°C)

EXAMPLE A

EXAMPLE B

Figure 436. CRJ 900—Takeoff Performance—Takeoff Weight Limited by Field Length Requirements, Dry Runway—One Engine Inoperative, FLAPS 8

Illustrations and materials were used with permission from Bombardier.

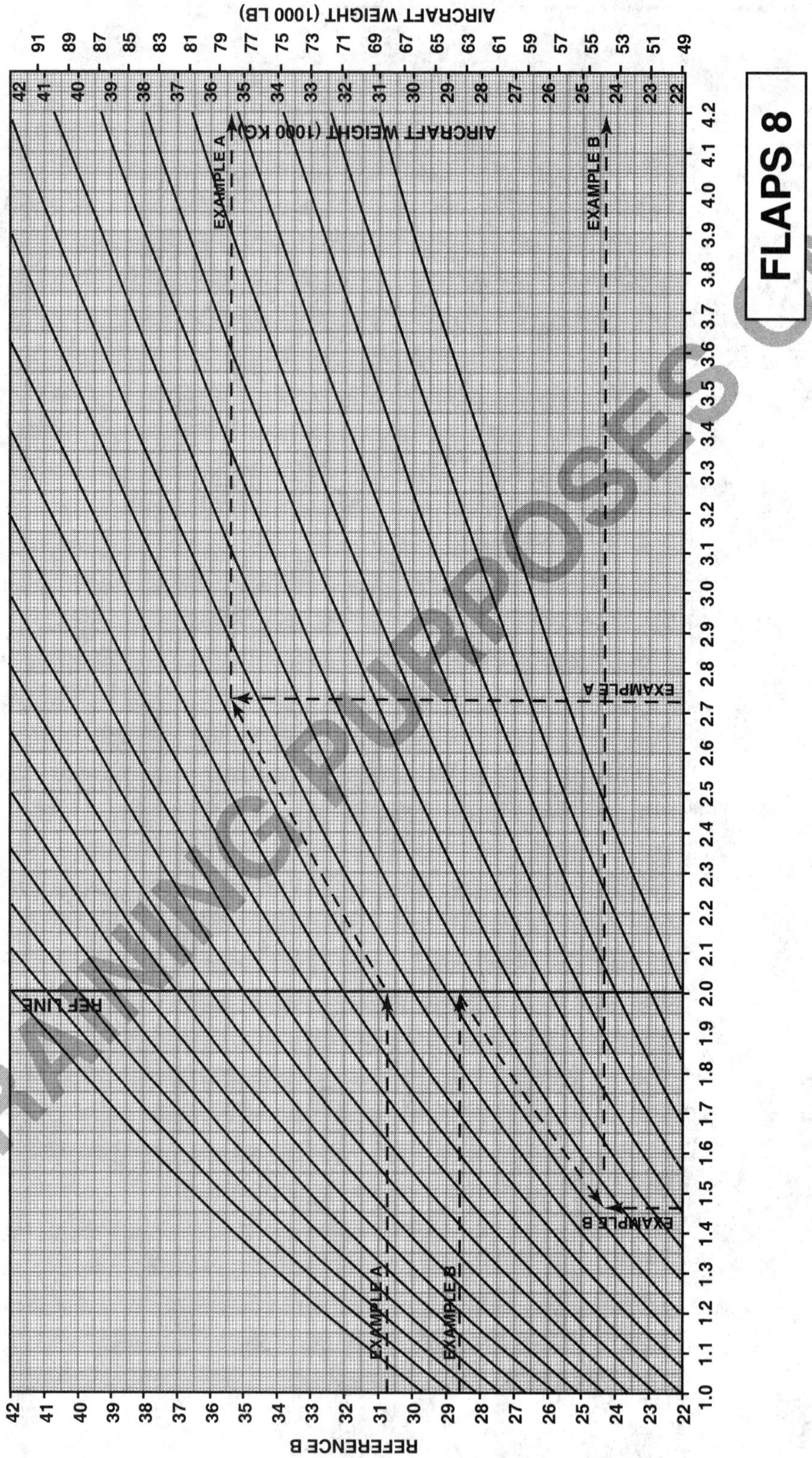

FLAPS 8

Figure 437. CRJ 900—Takeoff Performance—Takeoff Weight Limited by Field Length Requirements, Dry Runway—One Engine Inoperative, FLAPS 8

Illustrations and materials were used with permission from Bombardier.

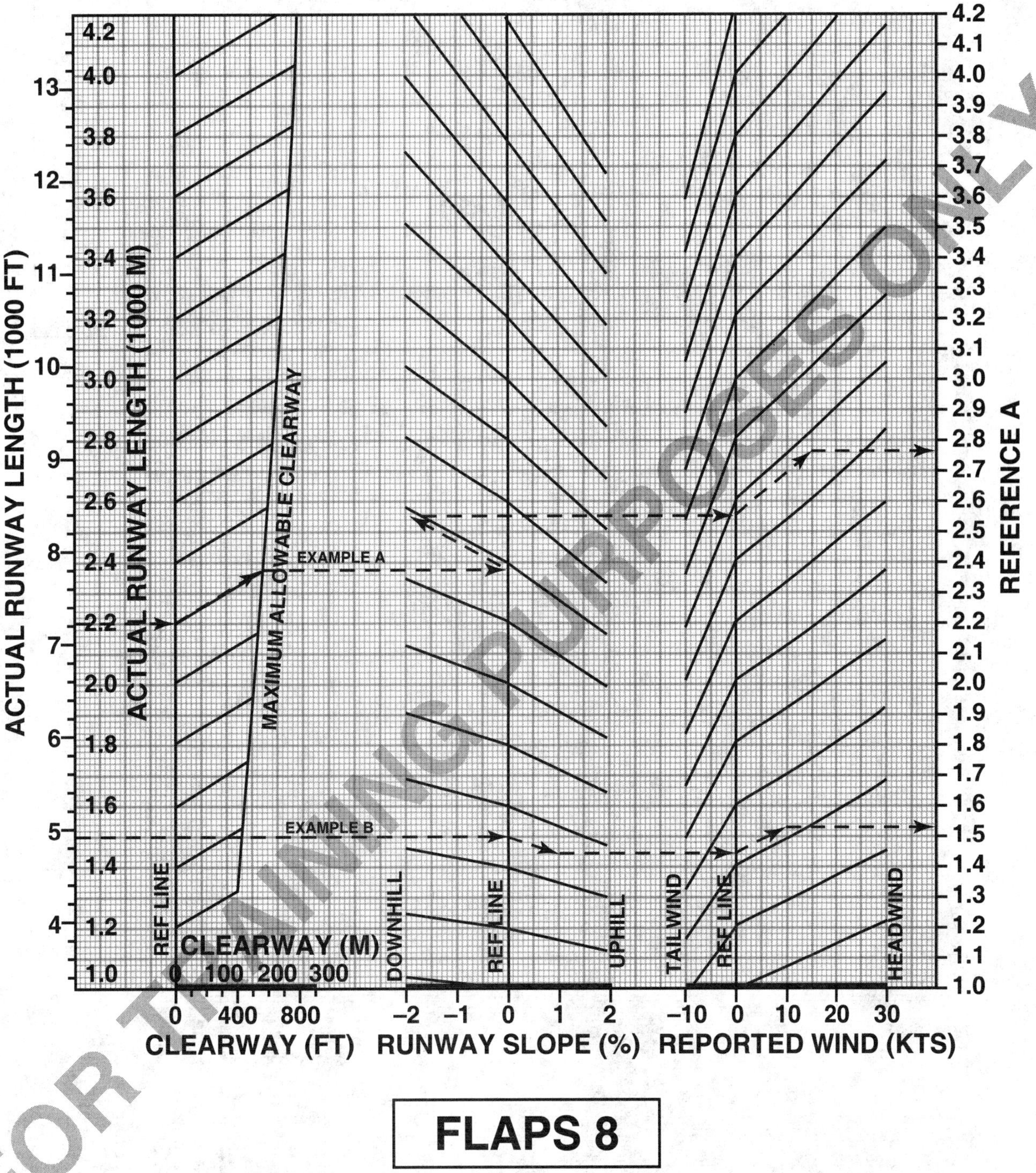

Figure 438. CRJ 900—Takeoff Performance—Takeoff Weight Limited by Field Length Requirements—All Engines Operating, FLAPS 8

Illustrations and materials were used with permission from Bombardier.

FLAPS 8

REFERENCE B

NOTE: BLEED SELECTIONS GIVEN BELOW ARE FOR ENGINE BLEED STATE ONLY

ENGINE BLEEDS CLOSED

ANTI-ICE OFF
PACKS ON

WING AND COWL ANTI-ICE ON
PACKS ON

COWL ANTI-ICE ON
PACKS ON

S.L. 2000 4000 6000 8000 10000

AIRPORT PRESSURE
ALTITUDE – FT

TEMPERATURE (°C)

EXAMPLE A

EXAMPLE B

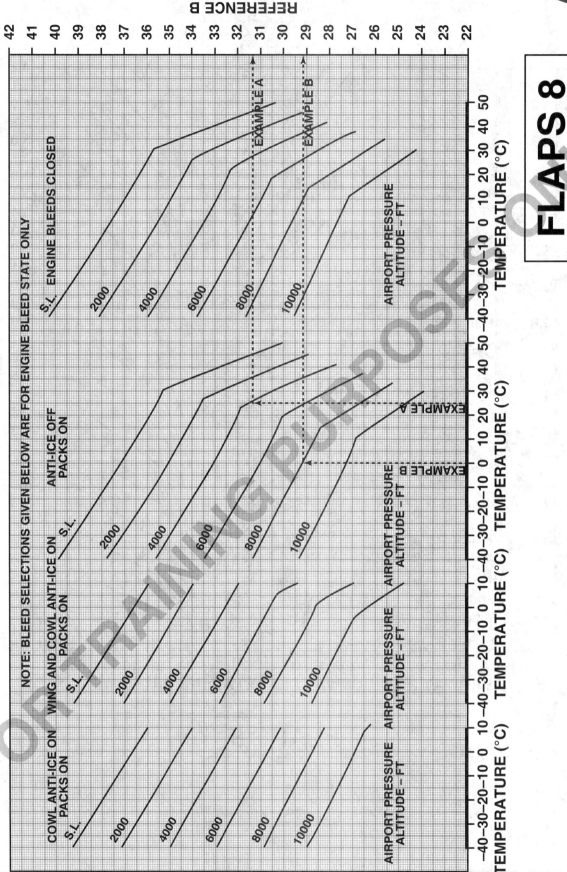

Figure 439. CRJ 900—Takeoff Performance—Takeoff Weight Limited by Field Length Requirements—All Engines Operating, FLAPS 8

Illustrations and materials were used with permission from Bombardier.

AIRCRAFT WEIGHT (1000 LB)

AIRCRAFT WEIGHT (1000 KG)

REFERENCE B

REF LINE

EXAMPLE A

EXAMPLE B

FLAPS 8

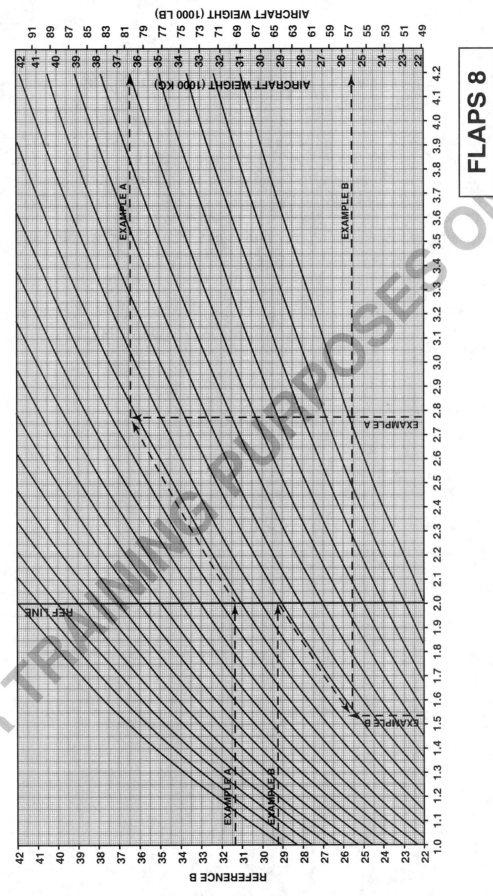

Figure 440. CRJ 900—Takeoff Performance—Takeoff Weight Limited by Field Length Requirements—All Engines Operating, FLAPS 8

Illustrations and materials were used with permission from Bombardier.

J. Takeoff Weight Limited by Field Length Requirements, Dry Runway — Minimum Control Speed (V_{MC}) Limited, FLAPS 20

The maximum takeoff weight limited by field length requirements on a dry runway for a FLAPS 20 takeoff, limited by V_{MC} is given by Figure 442, or Figure 443. The following charts are applicable to both the all engines operating and one engine inoperative cases. The first chart takes into account the actual length of the runway and the effects of runway slope and prevailing wind conditions. The subsequent charts cater to the effects of airport pressure altitude and temperature for varying bleed configurations to determine the takeoff weight.

NOTE

If a rolling takeoff procedure will be performed, subtract 60 meters (200 feet) from the actual runway length, prior to determining the takeoff weight.

Figure 441. CRJ 900—Takeoff Performance—Takeoff Weight Limited by Field Length Requirements, Dry Runway—Minimum Control Speed (V_{MC}) Limited, FLAPS 20.

FLAPS 20

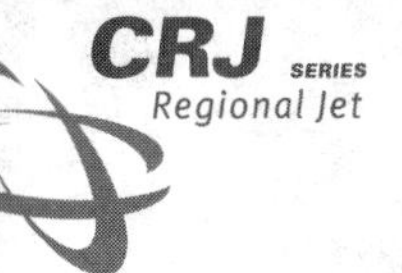

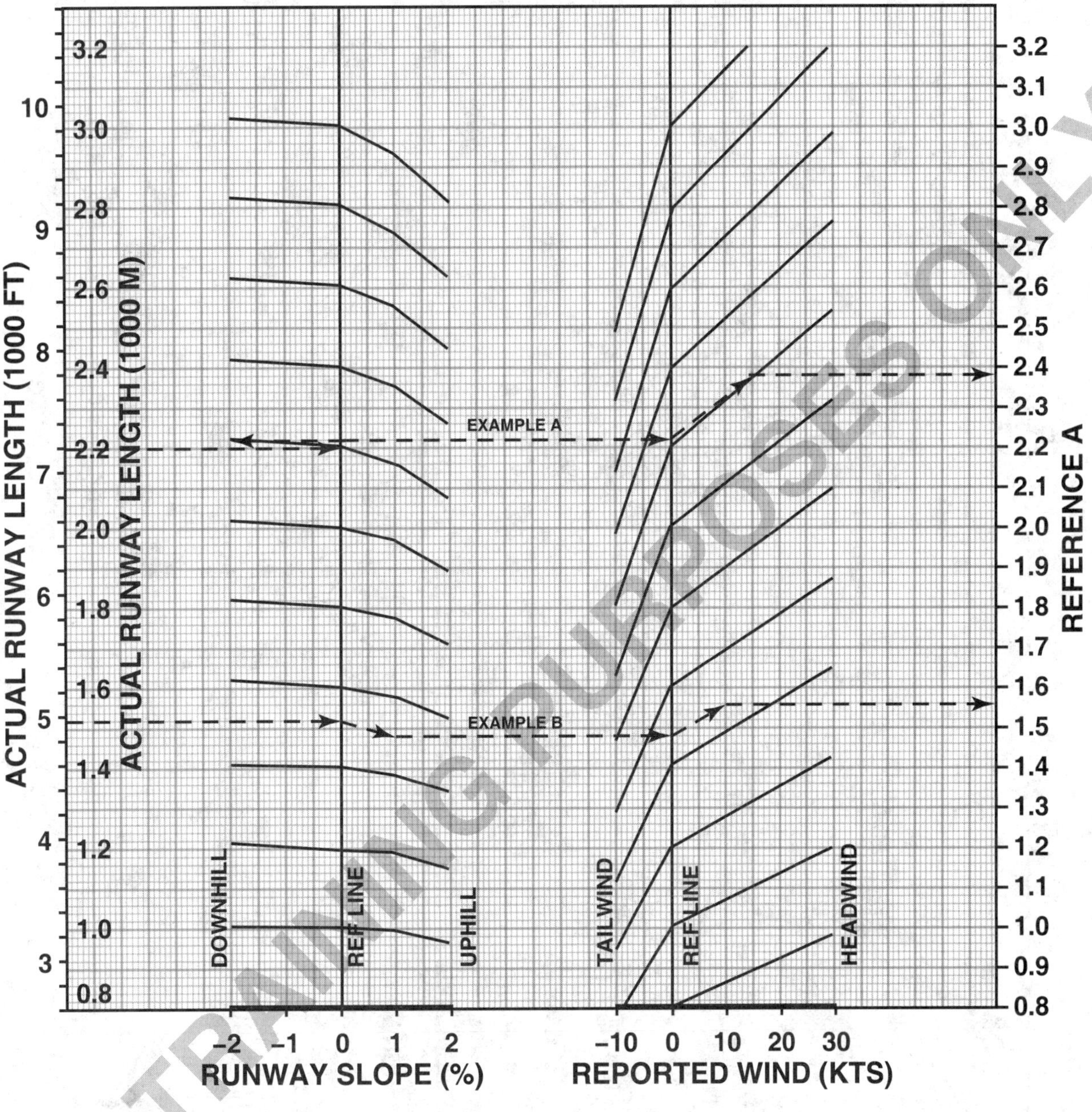

Figure 442. CRJ 900—Takeoff Performance—Takeoff Weight Limited by Field Length Requirements, Dry Runway—V_{MC} Limited, FLAPS 20.

Illustrations and materials were used with permission from Bombardier.

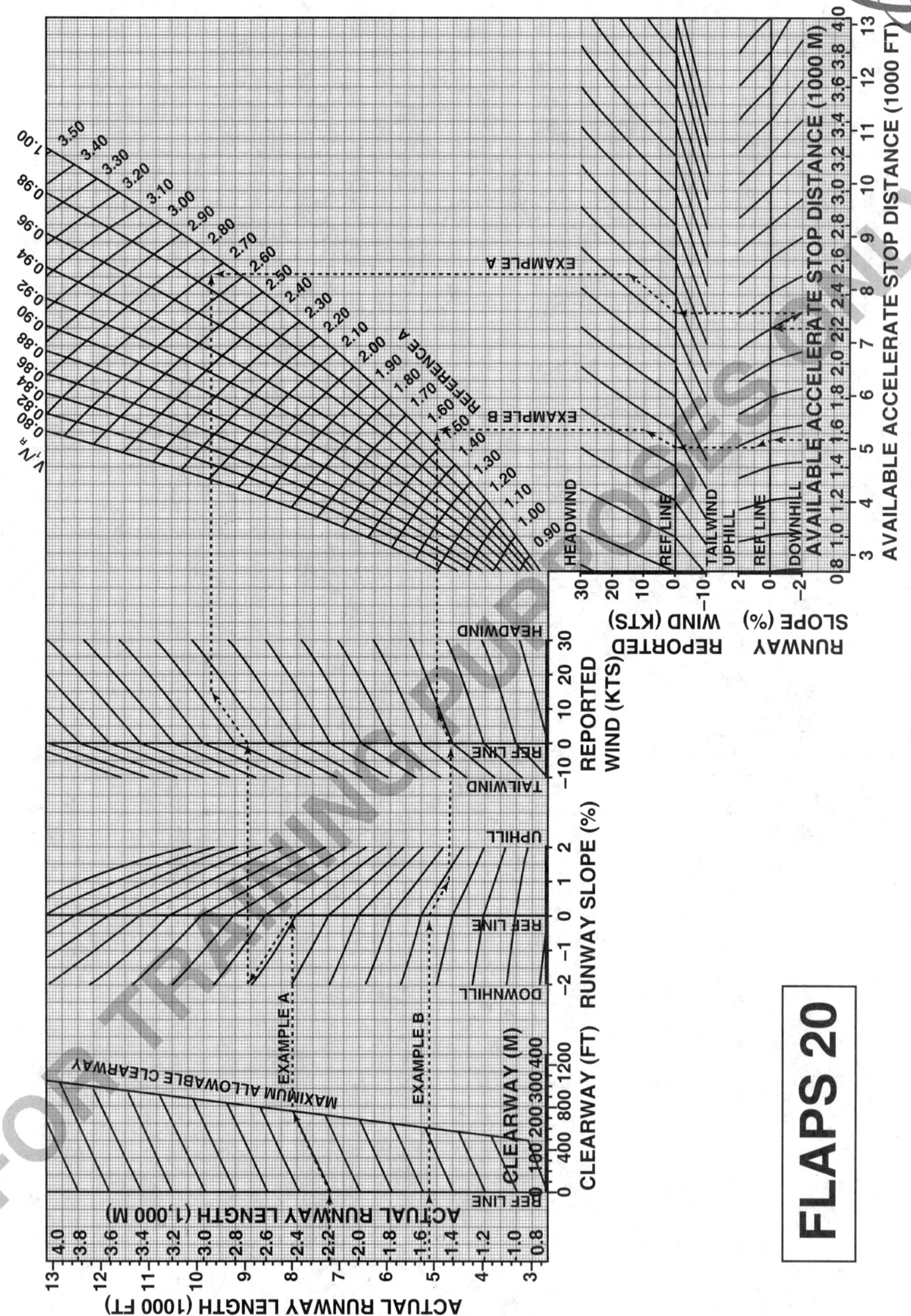

Figure 444. CRJ 900—Takeoff Performance—Takeoff Weight Limited by Field Length Requirements, Dry Runway—One Engine Inoperative, FLAPS 20.

Illustrations and materials were used with permission from Bombardier.

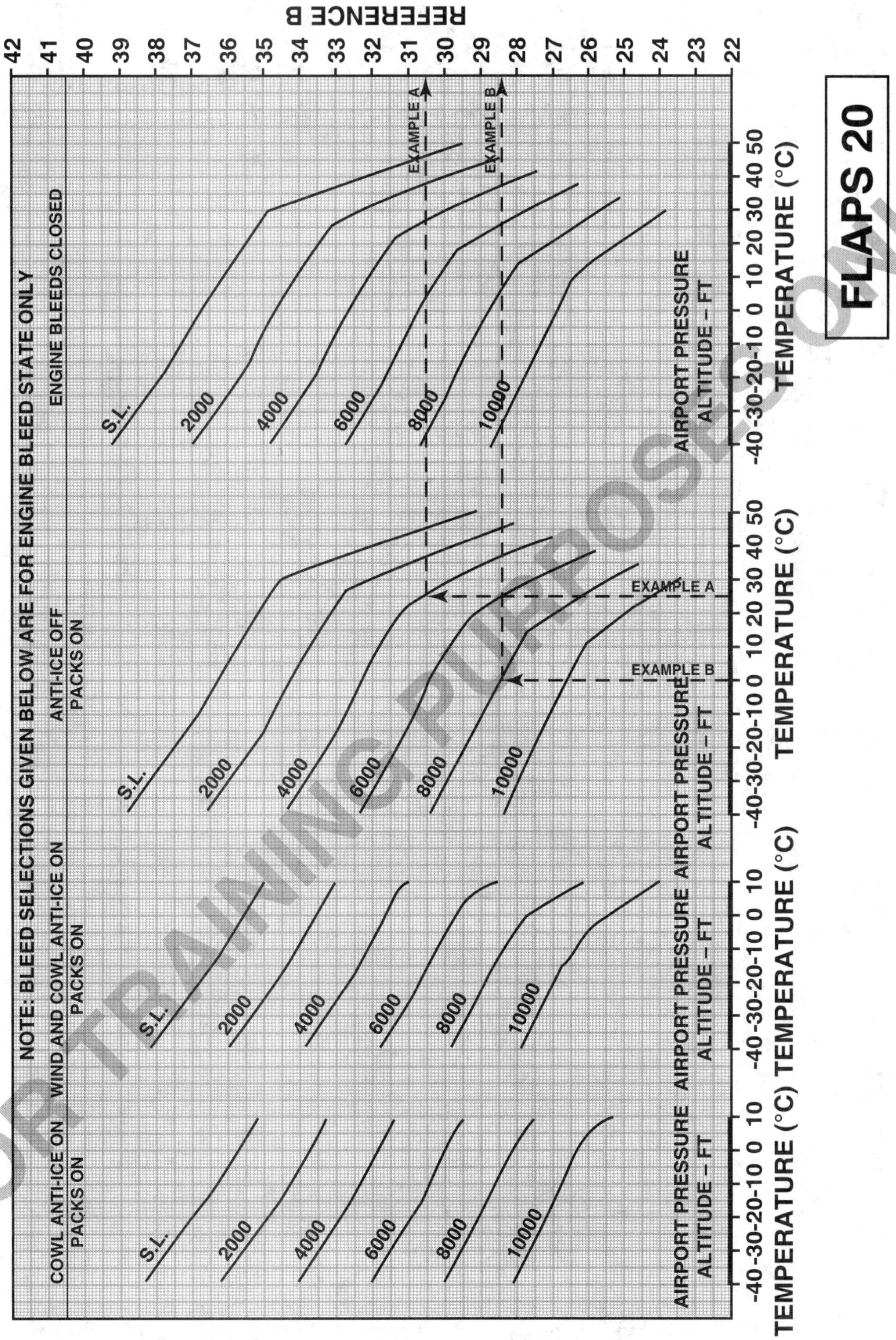

Figure 445. CRJ 900—Takeoff Performance—Takeoff Weight Limited by Field Length Requirements, Dry Runway—One Engine Inoperative, FLAPS 20.

Illustrations and materials were used with permission from Bombardier.

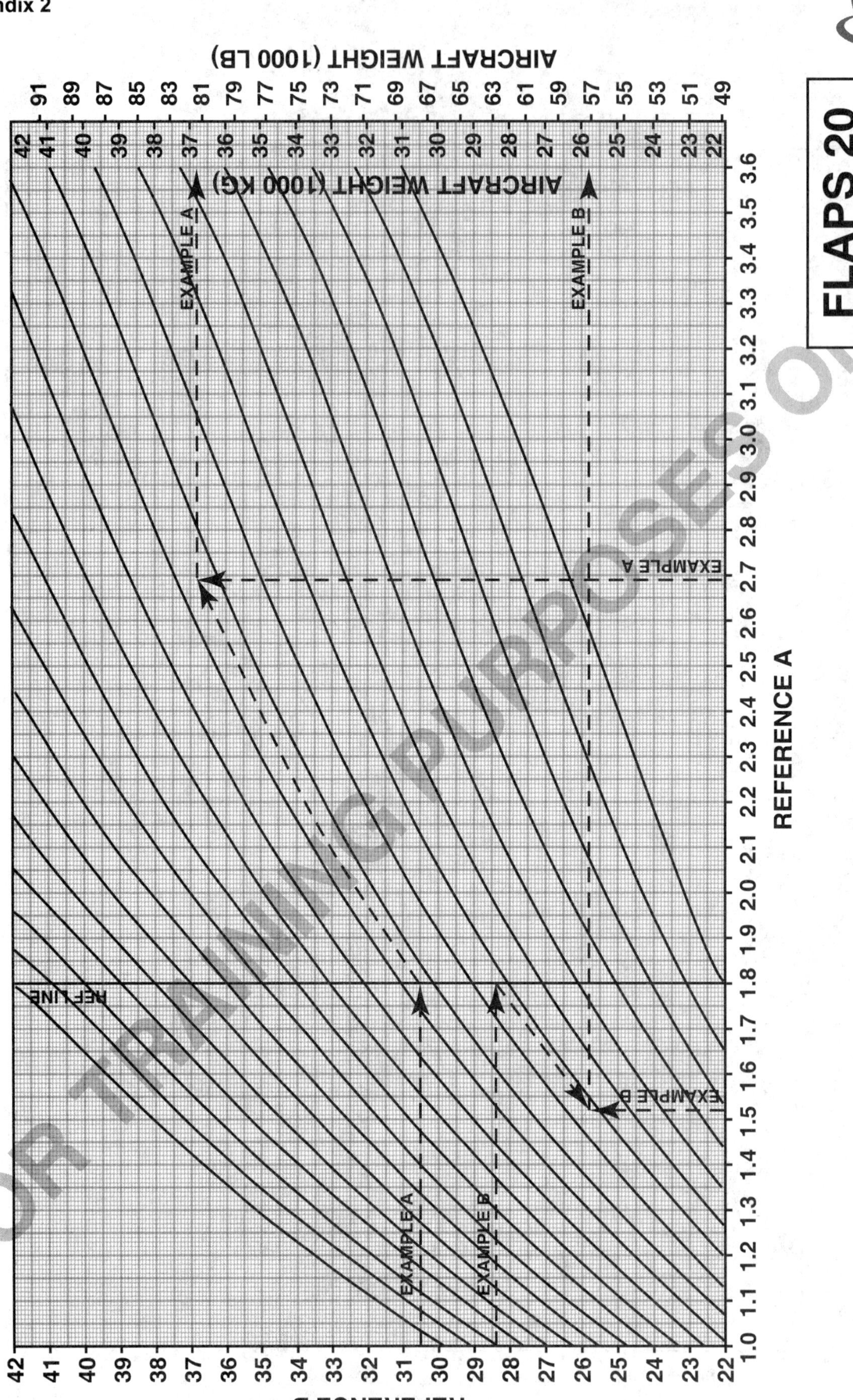

Figure 446. CRJ 900—Takeoff Performance—Takeoff Weight Limited by Field Length Requirements, Dry Runway—One Engine Inoperative, FLAPS 20.

Illustrations and materials were used with permission from Bombardier.

This page intentionally left blank.

S. Takeoff Weight Limited by Climb Requirements – FLAPS 8

The maximum takeoff weight limited by climb requirements for a FLAPS 8 takeoff is determined from Figure 448 for varying conditions of temperature and airport pressure altitude, taking into account the effects of different anti-icing and engine bleed configurations.

NOTE:

With the APU on, subtract 350 kg (772 lb) from the weight derived from Figure 448.

Example:

Associated conditions:

Temperature	= 10 °C
Airport pressure altitude	= 4,000 feet
Wing and cowl anti-ice	= Off
PACK	= On
APU	= Off

Enter Figure 448 from the temperature scale under the appropriate configuration of anti-ice and engine bleeds. As shown in the example, the maximum takeoff weight limited by climb requirements is found to be 41,050 kg (90,490 lb).

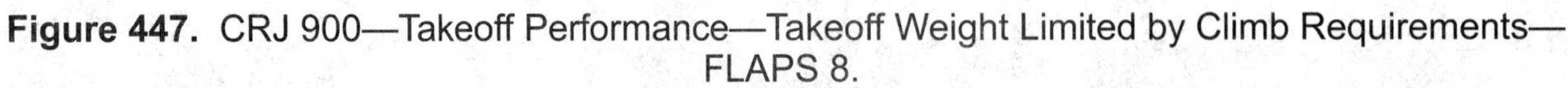

Figure 447. CRJ 900—Takeoff Performance—Takeoff Weight Limited by Climb Requirements—FLAPS 8.

Illustrations and materials were used with permission from Bombardier.

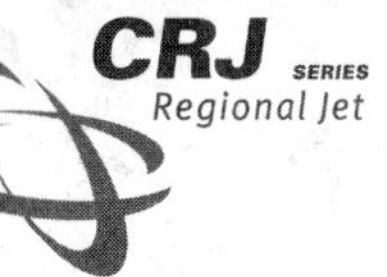

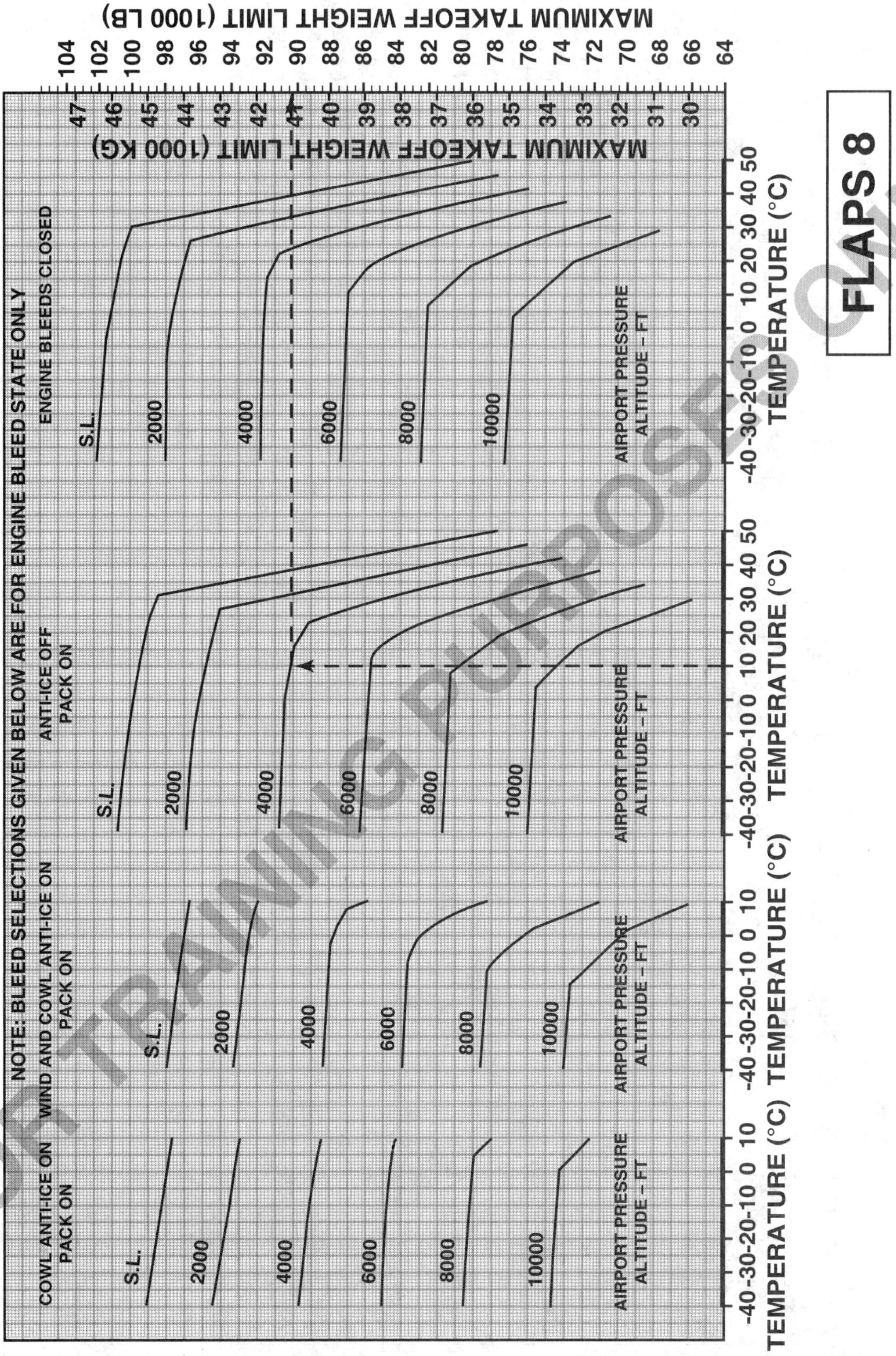

MAXIMUM TAKEOFF WEIGHT LIMIT (1000 LB)
MAXIMUM TAKEOFF WEIGHT LIMIT (1000 KG)
NOTE: BLEED SELECTIONS GIVEN BELOW ARE FOR ENGINE BLEED STATE ONLY
ENGINE BLEEDS CLOSED
ANTI-ICE OFF
PACK ON
WIND AND COWL ANTI-ICE ON
PACK ON
COWL ANTI-ICE ON
PACK ON
AIRPORT PRESSURE ALTITUDE – FT
S.L.
2000
4000
6000
8000
10000
TEMPERATURE (°C)
FLAPS 8

Figure 448. CRJ 900—Takeoff Performance—Takeoff Weight Limited by Climb Requirements—FLAPS 8.

Illustrations and materials were used with permission from Bombardier.

FLAPS 20

NOTE: BLEED SELECTIONS GIVEN BELOW ARE FOR ENGINE BLEED STATE ONLY

COWL ANTI-ICE ON PACK ON

WIND AND COWL ANTI-ICE ON PACK ON

ANTI-ICE OFF PACK ON

ENGINE BLEEDS CLOSED

MAXIMUM TAKEOFF WEIGHT LIMIT (1000 LB)

MAXIMUM TAKEOFF WEIGHT LIMIT (1000 KG)

AIRPORT PRESSURE ALTITUDE – FT

TEMPERATURE (°C)

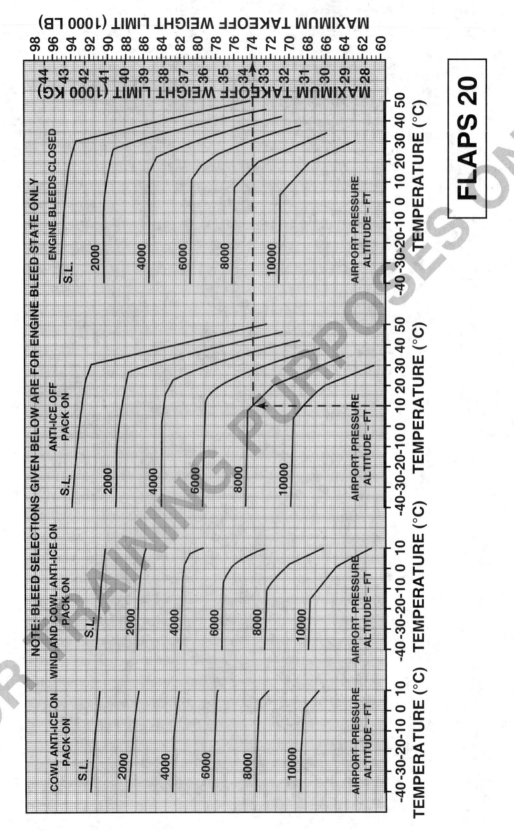

Figure 449. CRJ 900—Takeoff Performance—Takeoff Weight Limited by Climb Requirements—FLAPS 20.

Illustrations and materials were used with permission from Bombardier.

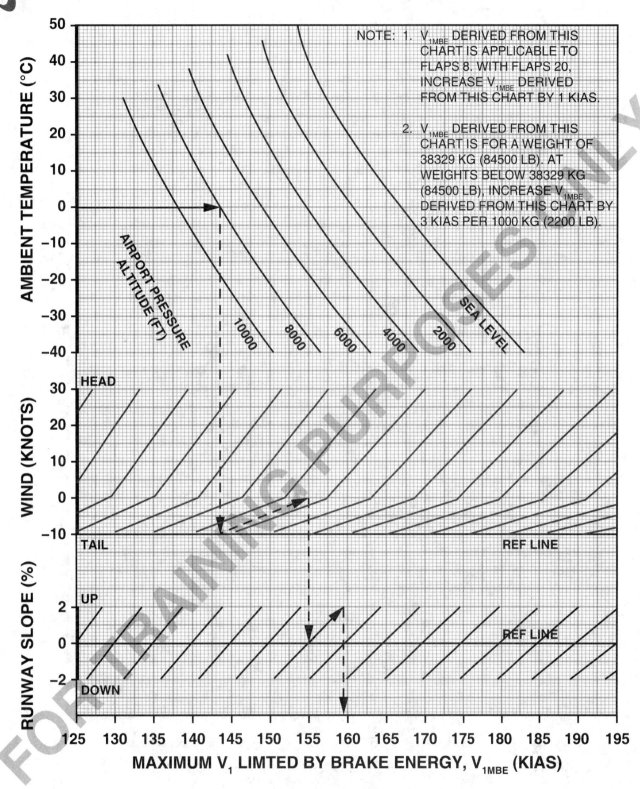

Figure 450. CRJ 900—Takeoff Performance—Maximum V_1 Limited by Brake Energy (V_{1MBE})—FLAPS 8.

Illustrations and materials were used with permission from Bombardier.

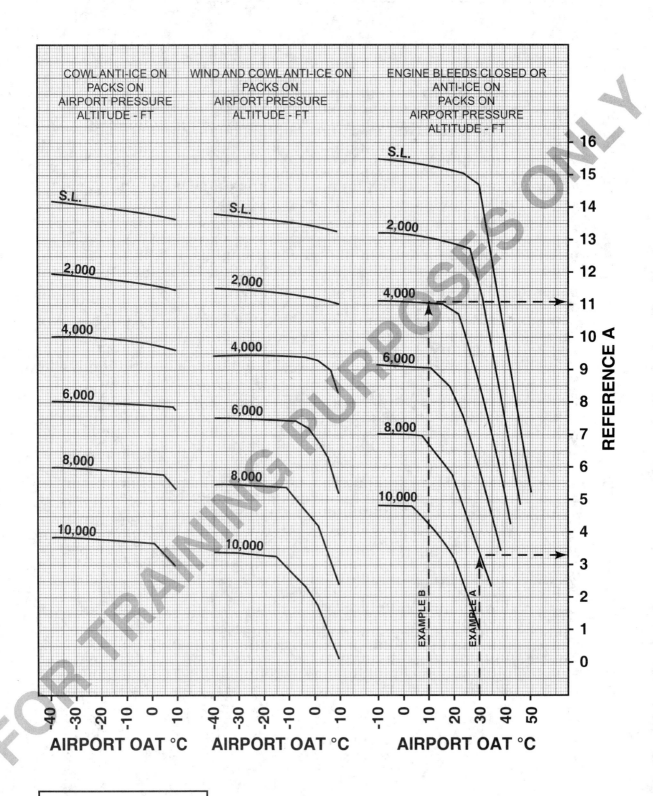

Figure 451. CRJ 900—Takeoff Performance—Takeoff Speeds—FLAPS 8.
Illustrations and materials were used with permission from Bombardier.

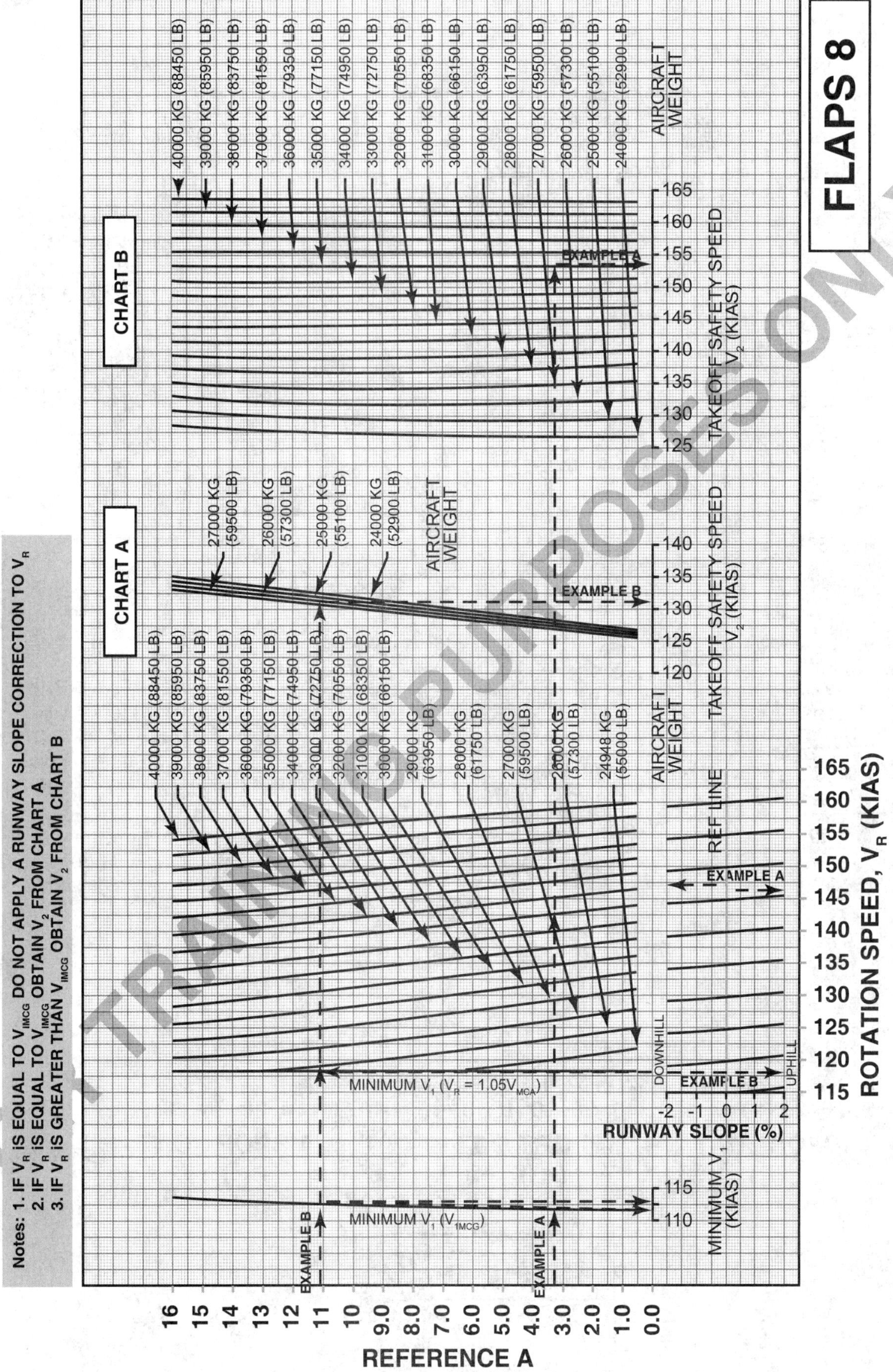

Figure 452. CRJ 900—Takeoff Performance—Takeoff Speeds—FLAPS 8.

Illustrations and materials were used with permission from Bombardier.

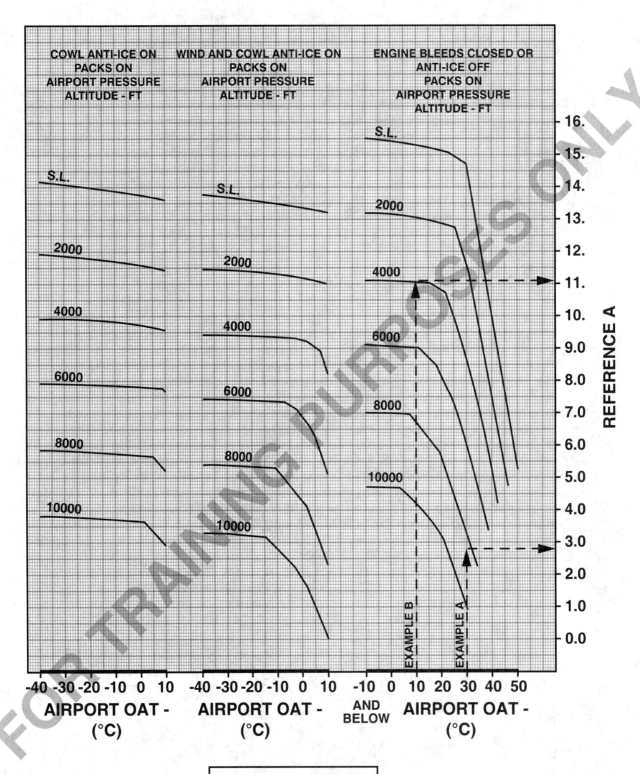

Figure 453. CRJ 900—Takeoff Performance—Takeoff Speeds—FLAPS 20.
Illustrations and materials were used with permission from Bombardier.

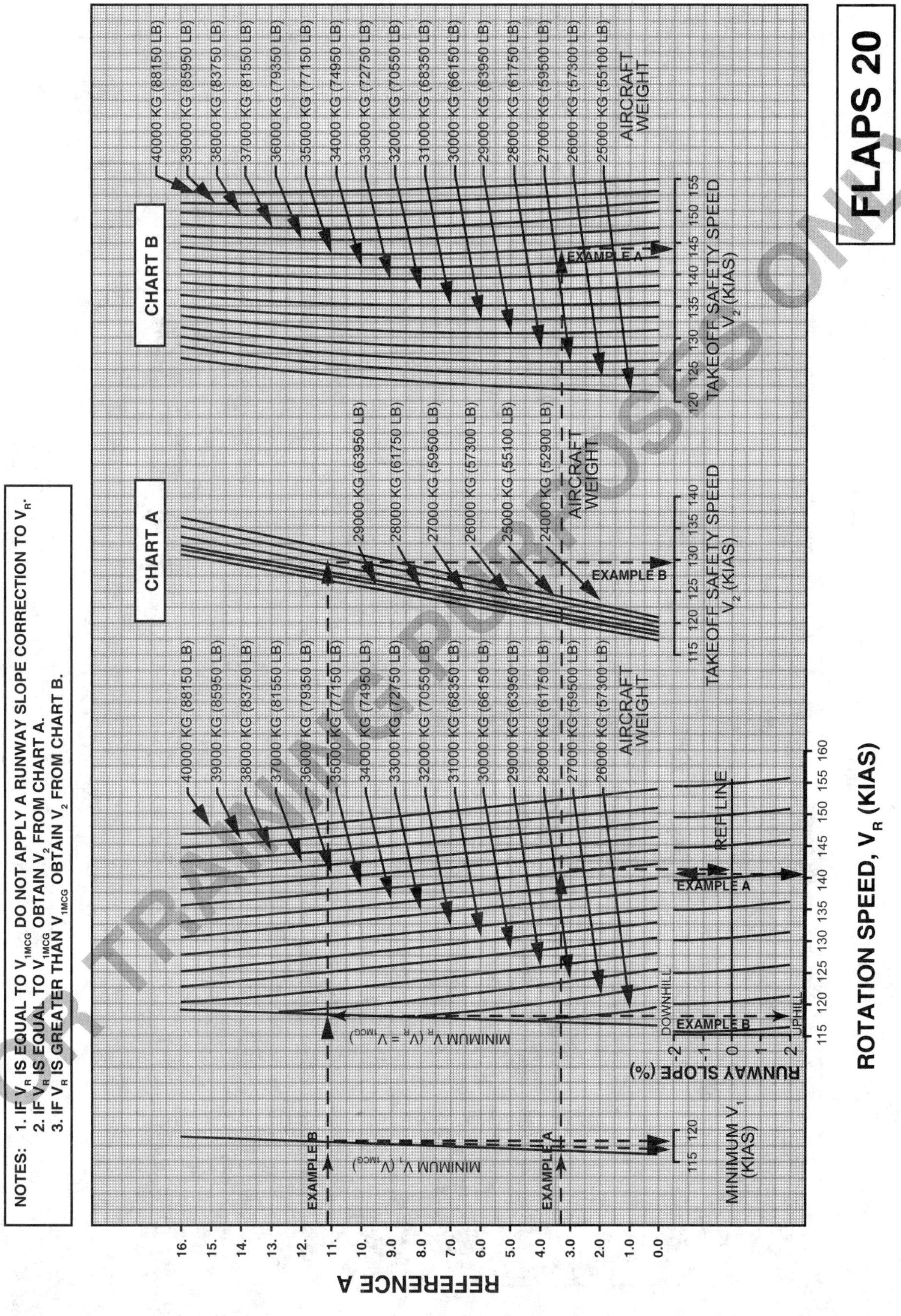

FLAPS 20

NOTES: 1. IF V_R IS EQUAL TO V_{1MCG} DO NOT APPLY A RUNWAY SLOPE CORRECTION TO V_R.
2. IF V_R IS EQUAL TO V_{1MCG} OBTAIN V_2 FROM CHART A.
3. IF V_R IS GREATER THAN V_{1MCG} OBTAIN V_2 FROM CHART B.

REFERENCE A: 16. 15. 14. 13. 12. 11. 10. 9.0 8.0 7.0 6.0 5.0 4.0 3.0 2.0 1.0 0.0

MINIMUM V_1 (V_{1MCG})
MINIMUM V_1 (KIAS): 115 120
EXAMPLE A
EXAMPLE B

MINIMUM V_R ($V_R = V_{1MCG}$)

AIRCRAFT WEIGHT: 40000 KG (88150 LB), 39000 KG (85950 LB), 38000 KG (83750 LB), 37000 KG (81550 LB), 36000 KG (79350 LB), 35000 KG (77150 LB), 34000 KG (74950 LB), 33000 KG (72750 LB), 32000 KG (70550 LB), 31000 KG (68350 LB), 30000 KG (66150 LB), 29000 KG (63950 LB), 28000 KG (61750 LB), 27000 KG (59500 LB), 26000 KG (57300 LB)

RUNWAY SLOPE (%): DOWNHILL 2 1 0 1 2 UPHILL
REF LINE
EXAMPLE A
EXAMPLE B
ROTATION SPEED, V_R (KIAS): 115 120 125 130 135 140 145 150 155 160

CHART A
AIRCRAFT WEIGHT: 29000 KG (63950 LB), 28000 KG (61750 LB), 27000 KG (59500 LB), 26000 KG (57300 LB), 25000 KG (55100 LB), 24000 KG (52900 LB)
EXAMPLE B
TAKEOFF SAFETY SPEED V_2 (KIAS): 115 120 125 130 135 140

CHART B
AIRCRAFT WEIGHT: 40000 KG (88150 LB), 39000 KG (85950 LB), 38000 KG (83750 LB), 37000 KG (81550 LB), 36000 KG (79350 LB), 35000 KG (77150 LB), 34000 KG (74950 LB), 33000 KG (72750 LB), 32000 KG (70550 LB), 31000 KG (68350 LB), 30000 KG (66150 LB), 29000 KG (63950 LB), 28000 KG (61750 LB), 27000 KG (59500 LB), 26000 KG (57300 LB), 25000 KG (55100 LB)
EXAMPLE A
TAKEOFF SAFETY SPEED V_2 (KIAS): 120 125 130 135 140 145 150 155

Figure 454. CRJ 900—Takeoff Performance—Takeoff Speeds—FLAPS 20.
Illustrations and materials were used with permission from Bombardier.

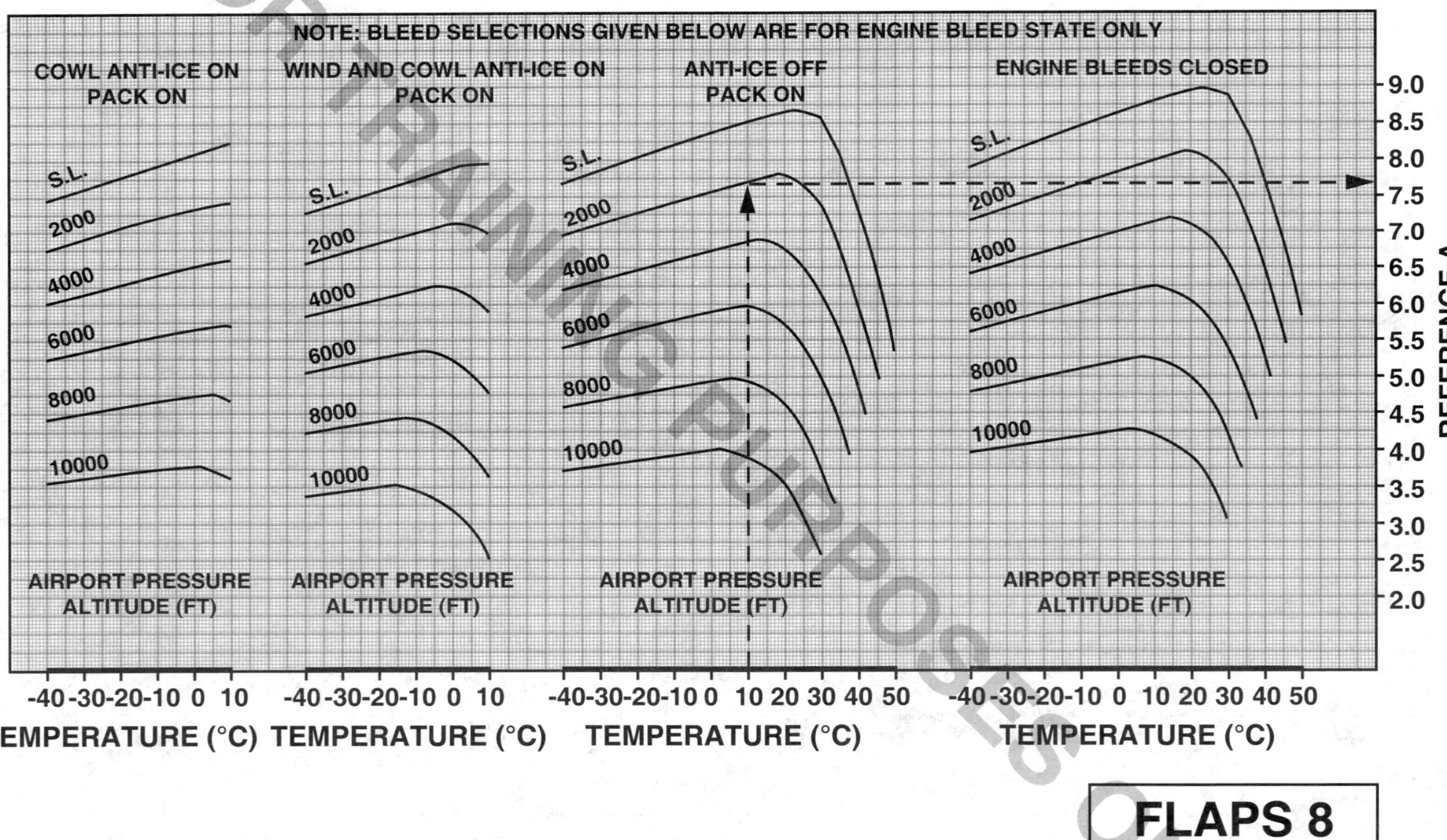

Figure 455. CRJ 900—Obstacle Clearance—Maximum Engine-out Level-off Height—FLAPS 8.

Illustrations and materials were used with permission from Bombardier.

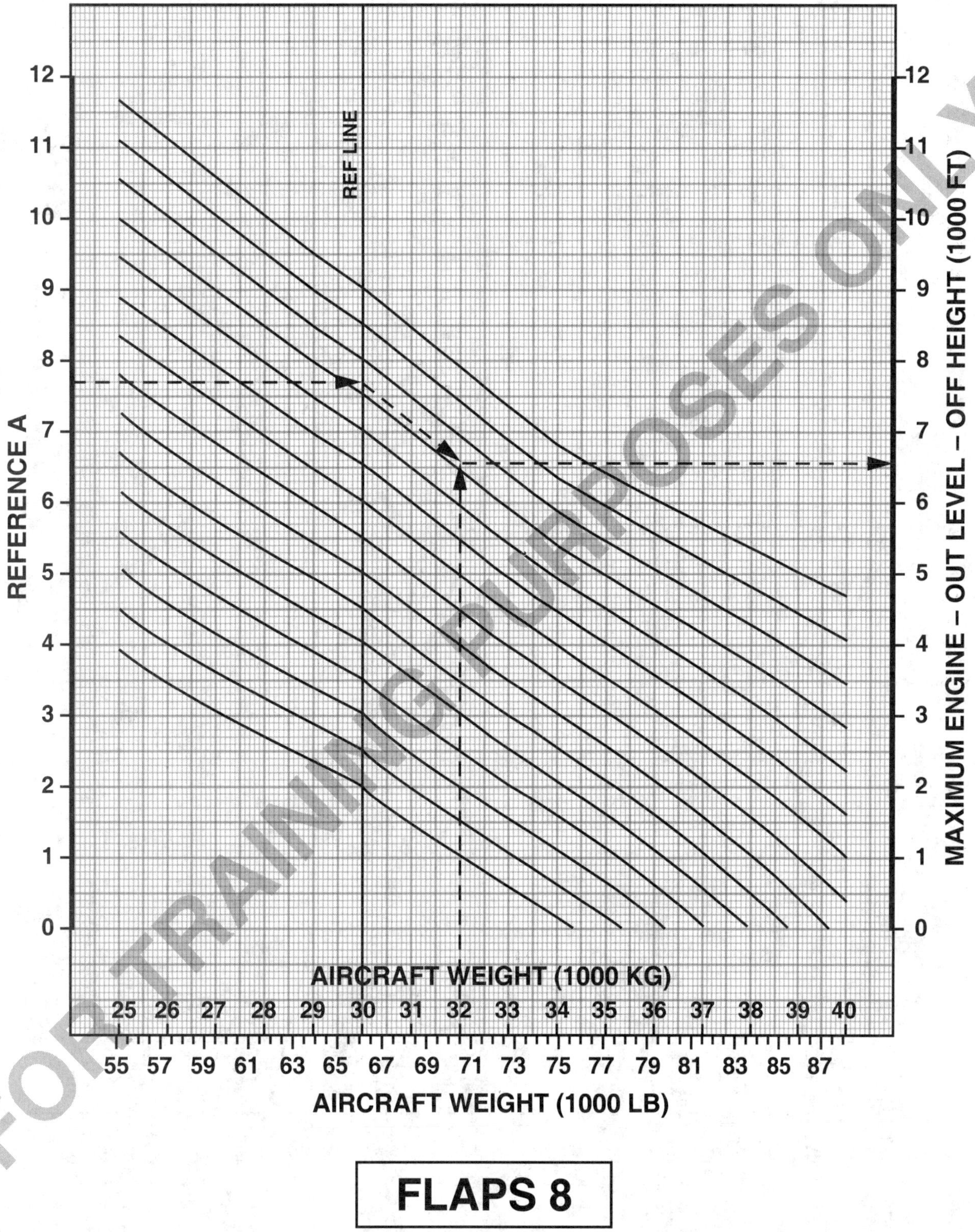

Figure 456. CRJ 900—Obstacle Clearance—Maximum Engine-out Level-off Height—FLAPS 8.

Illustrations and materials were used with permission from Bombardier.

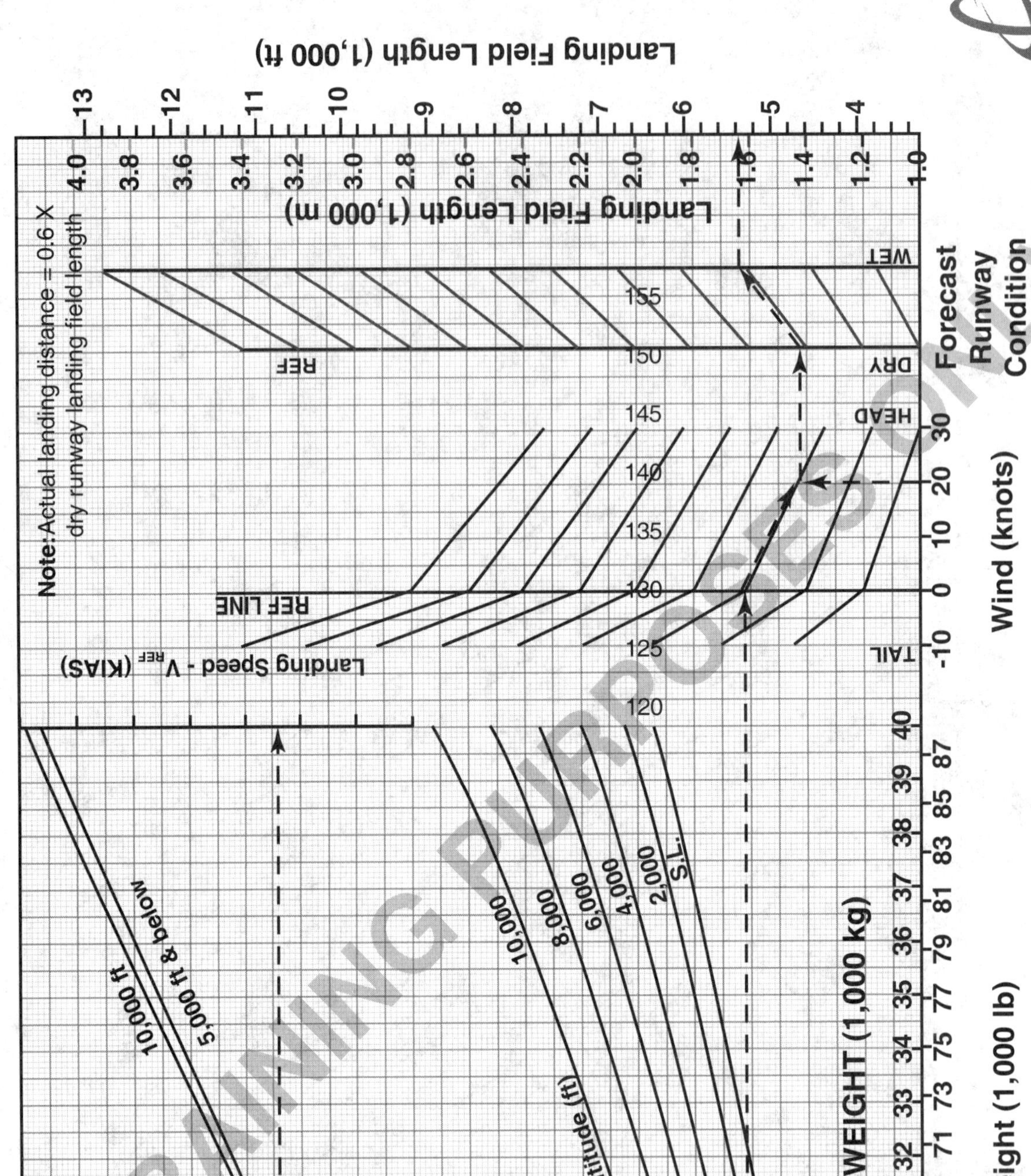

Figure 457. CRJ 900—Landing Performance—Landing Field and Landing Speed—FLAPS 45.

Illustrations and materials were used with permission from Bombardier.

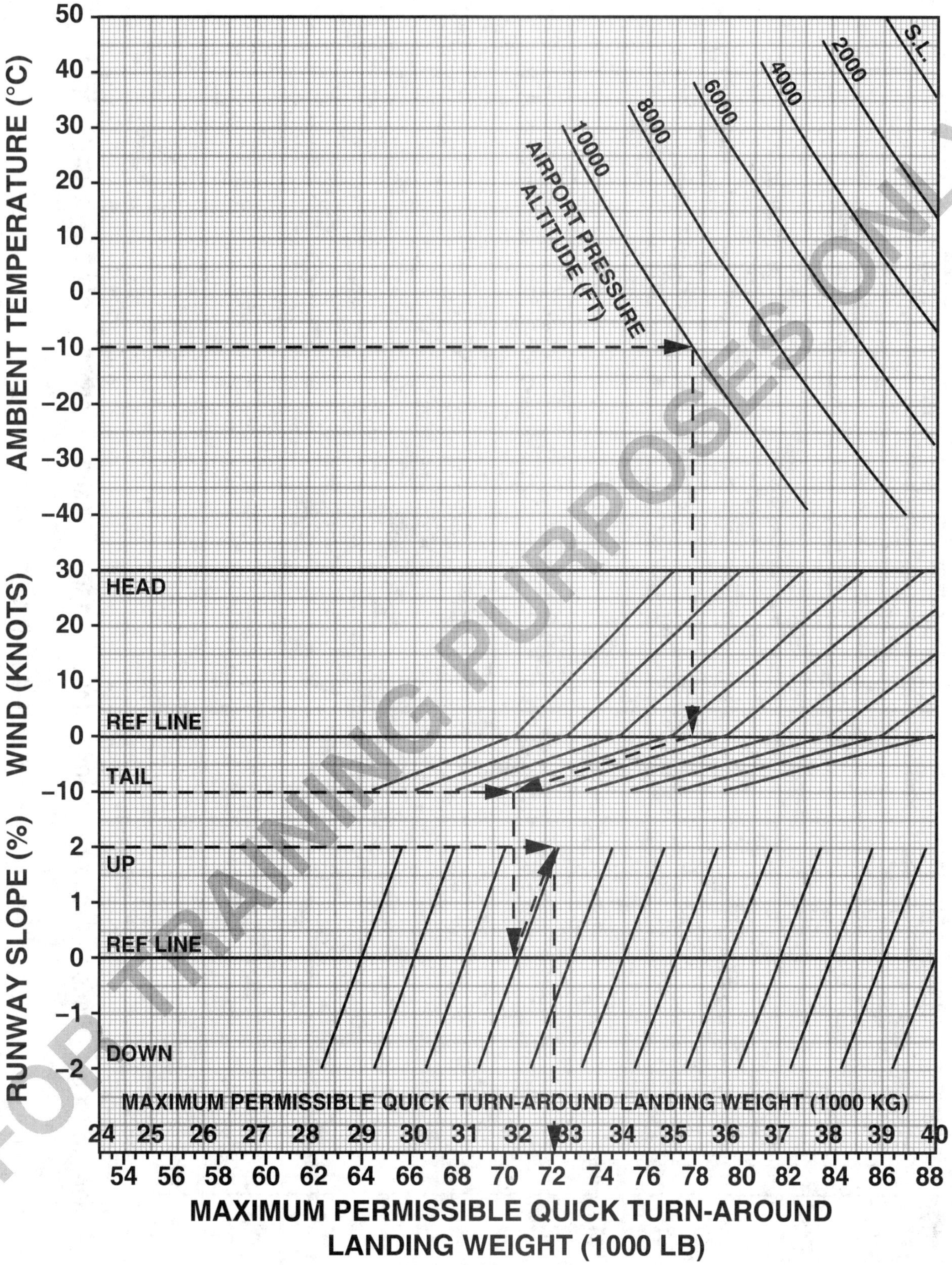

AMBIENT TEMPERATURE (°C)

50
40
30
20
10
0
−10
−20
−30
−40

S.L.
2000
4000
6000
8000
10000

AIRPORT PRESSURE ALTITUDE (FT)

WIND (KNOTS)

30
HEAD
20
10
REF LINE
0
TAIL
−10

RUNWAY SLOPE (%)

2
UP
1
REF LINE
0
−1
DOWN
−2

MAXIMUM PERMISSIBLE QUICK TURN-AROUND LANDING WEIGHT (1000 KG)

24 25 26 27 28 29 30 31 32 33 34 35 36 37 38 39 40

54 56 58 60 62 64 66 68 70 72 74 76 78 80 82 84 86 88

MAXIMUM PERMISSIBLE QUICK TURN-AROUND LANDING WEIGHT (1000 LB)

Figure 458. CRJ 900—Landing Performance—Maximum Permissible Quick Turn-around Landing Weight.

Illustrations and materials were used with permission from Bombardier.

ASSUMPTIONS:
- ISA
- 210 lb taxi and APU
- 160 lb take-off (1 min.)
- 100 lb approach (2 min.)
- Reserve fuel:
100 nm alternate 45 min.
holding at diversion altitude
- CF34-8C5 Engines
- OWE 47250 lb
- Climb & Descent speeds:
250 KCAS/0.70 M

MAX FUEL 19450 LB

MTOW 82500 LB

MZFW 70000 LB

86 PAX @ 200 LB

1722 NM RANGE

STILL AIR RANGE (NM)

400 600 800 1000 1200 1400 1600 1800 2000 2200 2400 2600

PAYLOAD (1000 LB)

24 22 20 18 16 14 12 10 8 6 4 2 0

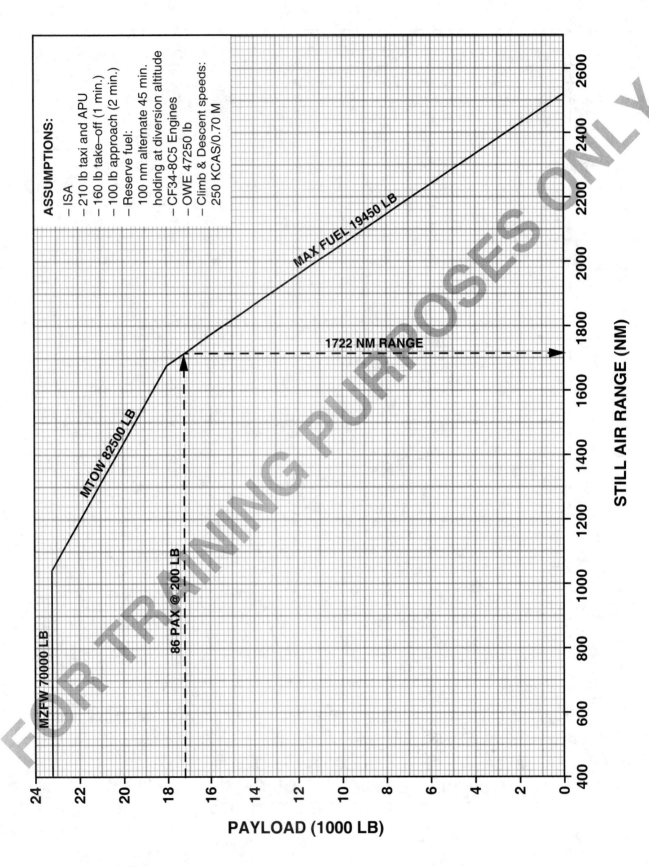

Figure 459. CRJ 900—Airport Planning Manual—Payload/Range.
Illustrations and materials were used with permission from Bombardier.

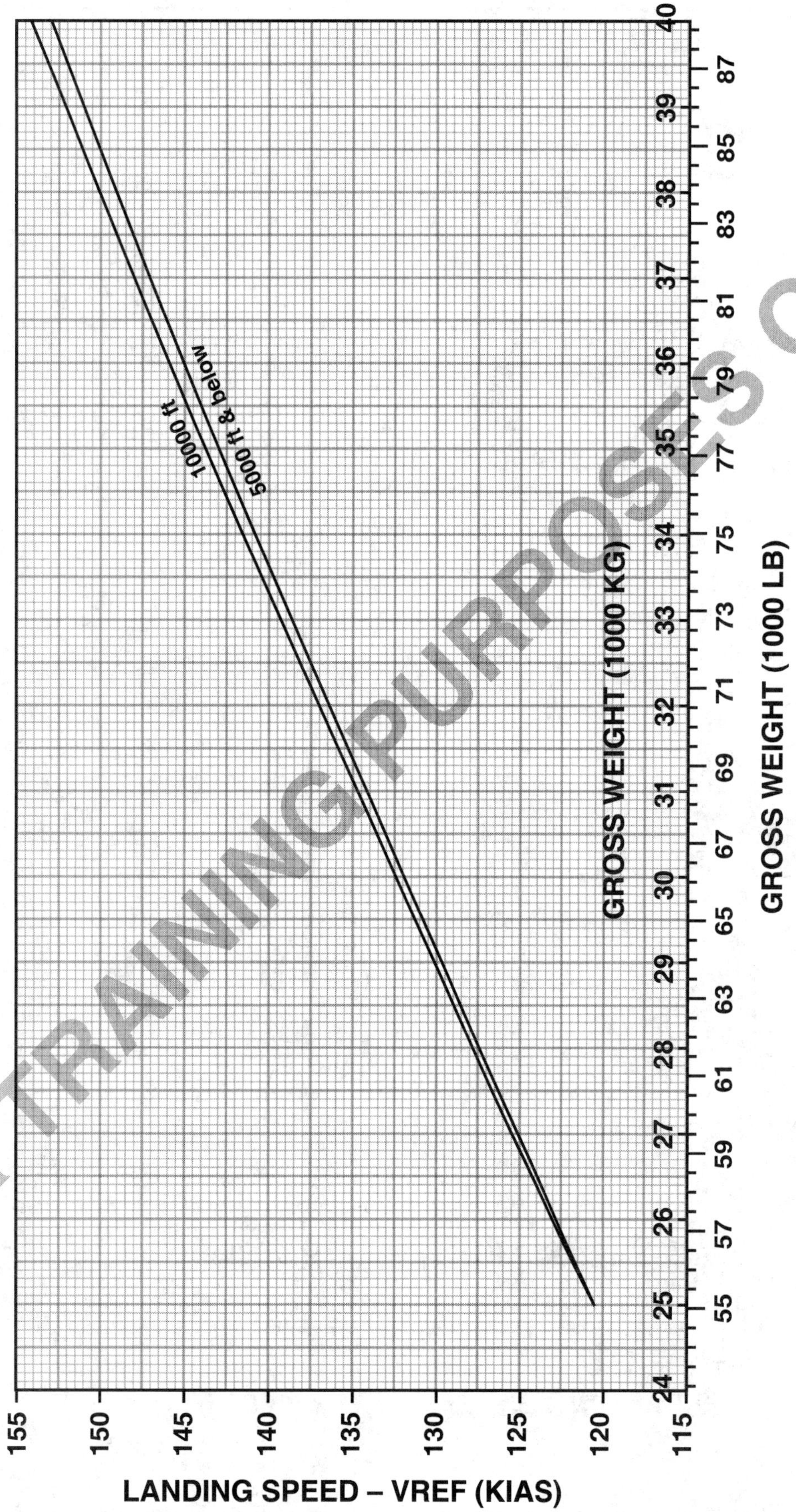

GROSS WEIGHT (1000 KG)

24 25 26 27 28 29 30 31 32 33 34 35 36 37 38 39 40

GROSS WEIGHT (1000 LB)

55 57 59 61 63 65 67 69 71 73 75 77 79 81 83 85 87

10000 ft

5000 ft & below

155 150 145 140 135 130 125 120 115

LANDING SPEED – VREF (KIAS)

Figure 460. CRJ 900—Airport Planning Manual—Flaps at 45 Degrees/Slats Extended.

Illustrations and materials were used with permission from Bombardier.

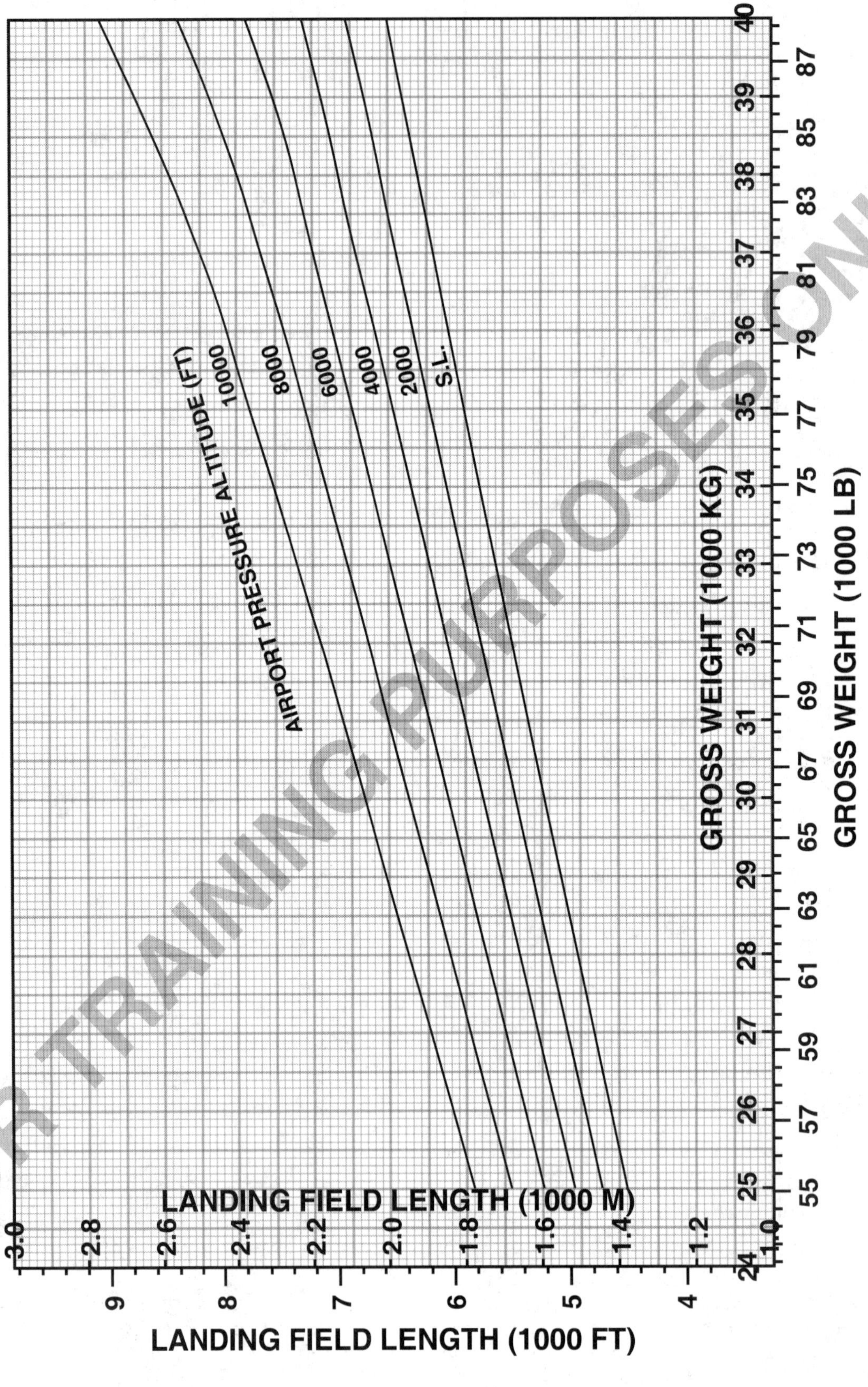

AIRPORT PRESSURE ALTITUDE (FT)
10000
8000
6000
4000
2000
S.L.

GROSS WEIGHT (1000 KG)
24 25 26 27 28 29 30 31 32 33 34 35 36 37 38 39 40

GROSS WEIGHT (1000 LB)
55 57 59 61 63 65 67 69 71 73 75 77 79 81 83 85 87

LANDING FIELD LENGTH (1000 M)
3.0 2.8 2.6 2.4 2.2 2.0 1.8 1.6 1.4 1.2 1.0

LANDING FIELD LENGTH (1000 FT)
9 8 7 6 5 4

Figure 461. CRJ 900—Airport Planning Manual—Landing Field Length—Flaps at 45 Degrees/ Slats Extended.

2.2 WEIGHT AND LOADING

2.2.1 MAXIMUM STRUCTURAL WEIGHT LIMITS

	Basic Gross Weight MS 4-201539	Intermediate Gross Weight MS 4-208807	High Gross Weight MS 4-308907	Enhanced High Gross Weight MS 4-309238
Ramp Weight	28,077 kg (61,900 lb)	29,089 kg (64,130 lb)	29,347 kg (64,700 lb)	29,665 kg (65,400 lb)
Maximum Takeoff Weight	27,987 kg (61,700 lb)	28,998 kg (63,930 lb)	29,257 kg (64,500 lb)	29,574 kg (65,200 lb)
Maximum Landing Weight	27,442 kg (60,500 lb)	28,009 kg (61,750 lb)	28,009 kg (61,750 lb)	28,123 kg (62,000 lb)
Maximum Zero Fuel Weight	25,174 kg (55,500 lb)	25,855 kg (57,000 lb)	25,855 kg (57,000 lb)	26,308 kg (58,000 lb)
Minimum Structural Design Weight	14,403 kg (31,753 lb)	14,403 kg (31,753 lb)	14,403 kg (31,753 lb)	14,403 kg (31,753 lb)

NOTE:
Maximum takeoff weight and maximum landing weight may be reduced by performance requirements of Section 5.

2.2.2 CENTER OF GRAVITY LIMITS (LANDING GEAR DOWN)

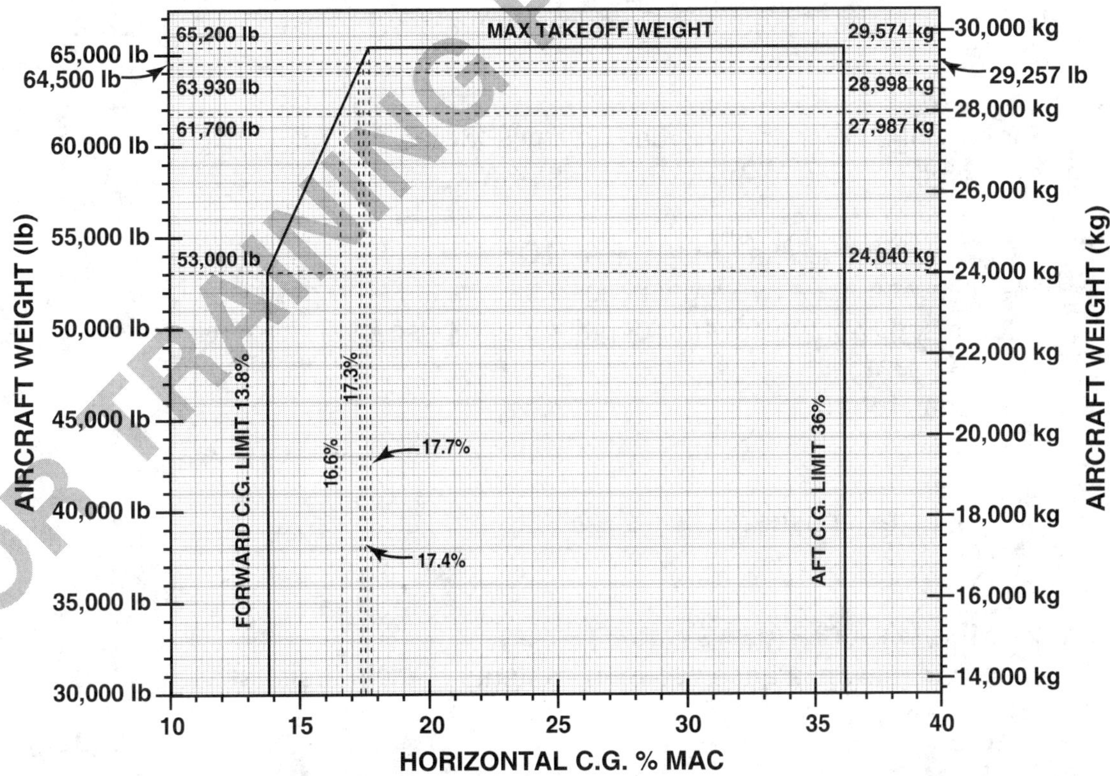

Figure 462. Q400—Weight and Loading—Maximum Structural Weight Limits.
Illustrations and materials were used with permission from Bombardier.

The Center of Gravity (C.G.) limits at all weights with landing gear extended are as follows:

1. Forward limit:
   387.16 inches aft of the reference datum (13.8% M.A.C.) for all weights up to 24,040 kg (53,000 lb).

   Slopes from 387.16 inches aft of the reference datum (13.8% M.A.C.) at 24,040 kg (53,000 lb) to 390.84 inches (17.7% M.A.C.) at 29,574 kg (65,200 lb).

2. Aft limit:
   408.14 inches aft of the reference datum (36.0% M.A.C.) at all weights.
   If these C.G. limits are met wtth the airplane landing gear extended, safe limits in flight are automatically achieved (see Figure 2-2-1, CG Limits).

2.2.3 LOADING INSTRUCTIONS

The airplane must always be loaded (i.e. crew, passengers, fuel, freight and baggage) to remain within the weight and centre of gravity limits in paragraphs 2.2.1 and 2.2.2.

Procedures for calculating weight and centre of gravity of a loaded airplane are contained in the Weight and Balance Manual (PSM 1-84-8 or 1-84-8M).

2.2.4 LOADING LIMITS

For baggage compartment loading limits for the various configurations, refer to the Cargo Loading Manual (PSM 1-84-8A).

2.2.5 MANEUVERING LIMIT LOAD FACTORS

The following maneuvering limit load factors limit the permissible angle of bank in turns and limit the severity of pull-up and push-over maneuvers.

Flap retracted	+2.5 g –1.0 g
Flap extended	+2.0 g 0.0 g

2.2.6 MAXIMUM LATERAL ASYMMETRY

Maximum fuel imbalance between contents of main fuel tanks is 272 kg (600 lb).

Figure 463. Q400—Weight and Loading—Center of Gravity Limits (Landing Gear Down).

d. The maximum permissible take-off and landing weights may be further limited by available runway lengths (sub-sections 5.5 and 5.11), obstacle clearance (sub-section 5.6) and brake energy (sub-section 5.12).

e. The maximum permissible take-off and landing weight is not limited by maximum tire speed at weight-altitude-temperatures, wind speeds and runway gradients shown on the performance charts included in this section.

5.1.5 MINIMUM CONTROL SPEEDS

The minimum control speeds, air, are as follows:

V_{MCA} (Flap 15°) 91 kt CAS
(Flap 10°) 95 kt CAS
(Flap 5°) 98 kt CAS
(Flap 0°) 113 kt CAS

V_{MCL} (Flap 35°) 92 kt CAS
(Flap 15°) 96 kt CAS
(Flap 10°) 99 kt CAS
(Flap 5°) 100 kt CAS

The minimum control speeds, ground, are as follows:

V_{MCG} (Flap 15°) 89 kt CAS
(Flap 10°) 89 kt CAS
(Flap 5°) 89 kt CAS

5.1.6 USE OF PERFORMANCE DATA AND CHARTS

a. Altitudes: All altitudes are pressure altitudes.

b. Outside Air Temperature (OAT) is the ambient air temperature. In flight, cockpit indicated Static Air Temperature (SAT) is equal to OAT. At rest, on the ground,the indicated SAT may be higher than the OAT.

c. Performance data given at a weight of 18,000 kg (39,680 lb) must be used for weights below 18,000 kg (39,680 lb).

d. Performance data shown at ISA –20 °C must be used for temperatures below ISA –20 °C.

e. Performance data shown for 20 kt headwind must be used for headwinds greater than 20 kt.

f. Performance data shown for altitudes at sea level must be used for altitudes below sea level.

Figure 464. Q400—Weight and Loading—Minimum Control Speeds.
Illustrations and materials were used with permission from Bombardier.

Q400 DASH 8
The Quiet One

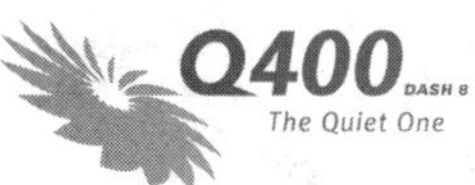

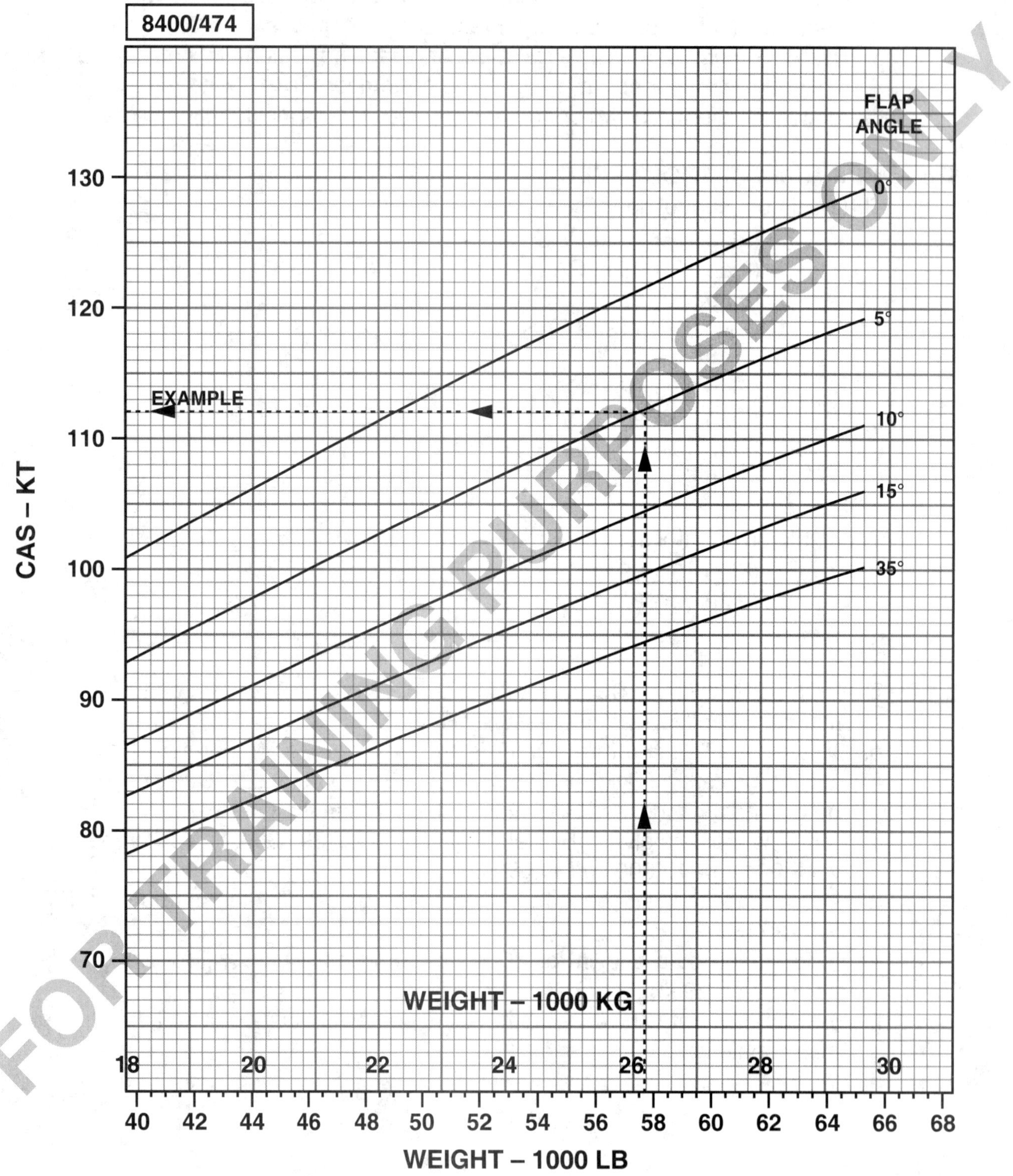

8400/474
FLAP ANGLE
0°
5°
10°
15°
35°
EXAMPLE
CAS – KT
130
120
110
100
90
80
70
WEIGHT – 1000 KG
18
20
22
24
26
28
30
40
42
44
46
48
50
52
54
56
58
60
62
64
66
68
WEIGHT – 1000 LB
FOR TRAINING PURPOSES ONLY

Figure 465. Q400—Weight and Loading—Reference Stall Speeds (V_{SR}).

Illustrations and materials were used with permission from Bombardier.

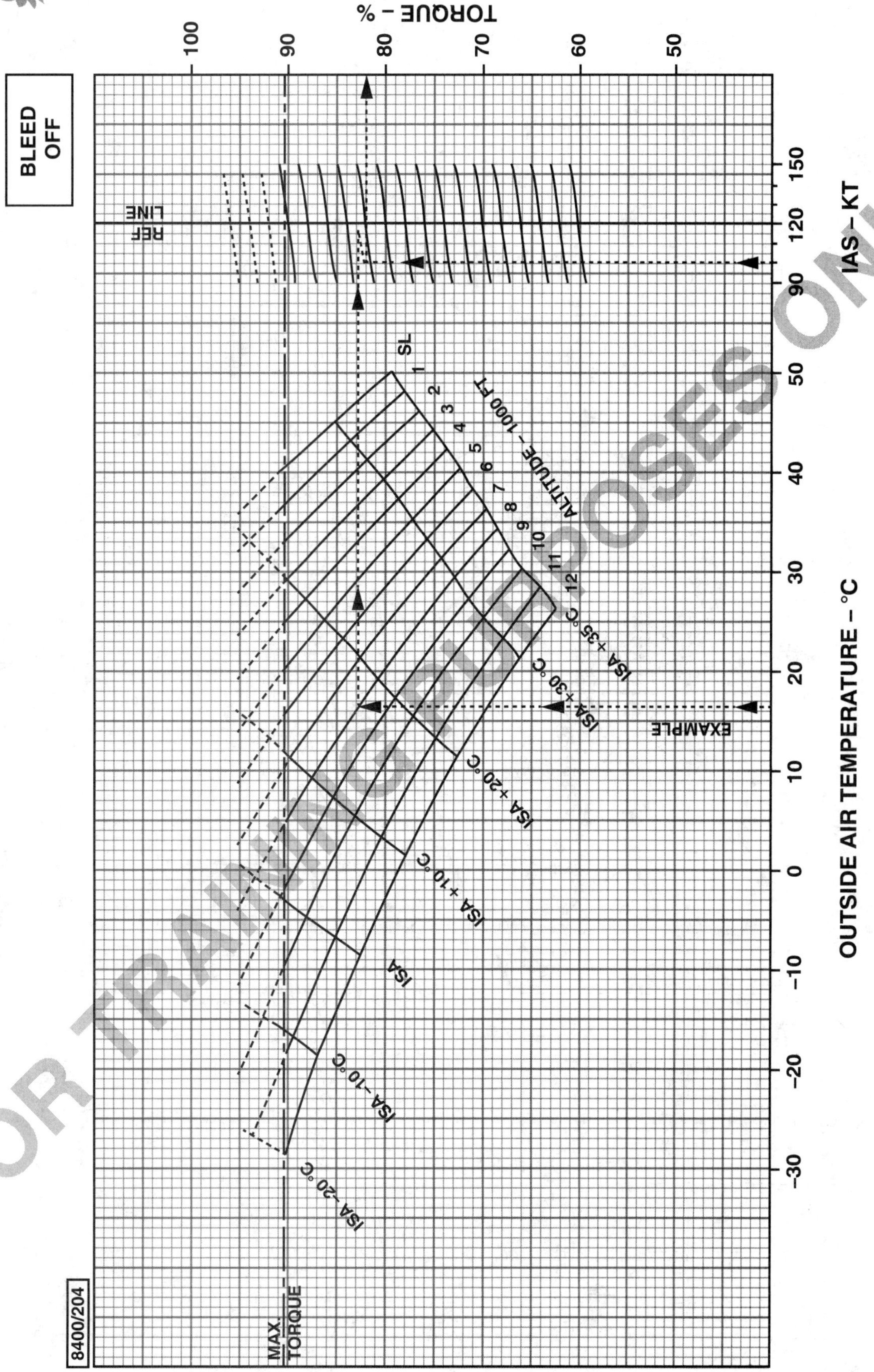

BLEED OFF

TORQUE – %

100 90 80 70 60 50

REF LINE

IAS – KT

90 120 150

SL 1 2 3 4 5 6 7 8 9 10 11 12

ALTITUDE – 1000 FT

ISA +35 °C

ISA +30 °C

ISA +20 °C

ISA +10 °C

ISA

ISA –10 °C

ISA –20 °C

EXAMPLE

MAX. TORQUE

OUTSIDE AIR TEMPERATURE – °C

50 40 30 20 10 0 –10 –20 –30

8400/204

Figure 468. Q400—Normal Takeoff Power Torque Setting (In-Flight) Propeller RPM–1020 Deicing Systems ON or OFF.

Illustrations and materials were used with permission from Bombardier.

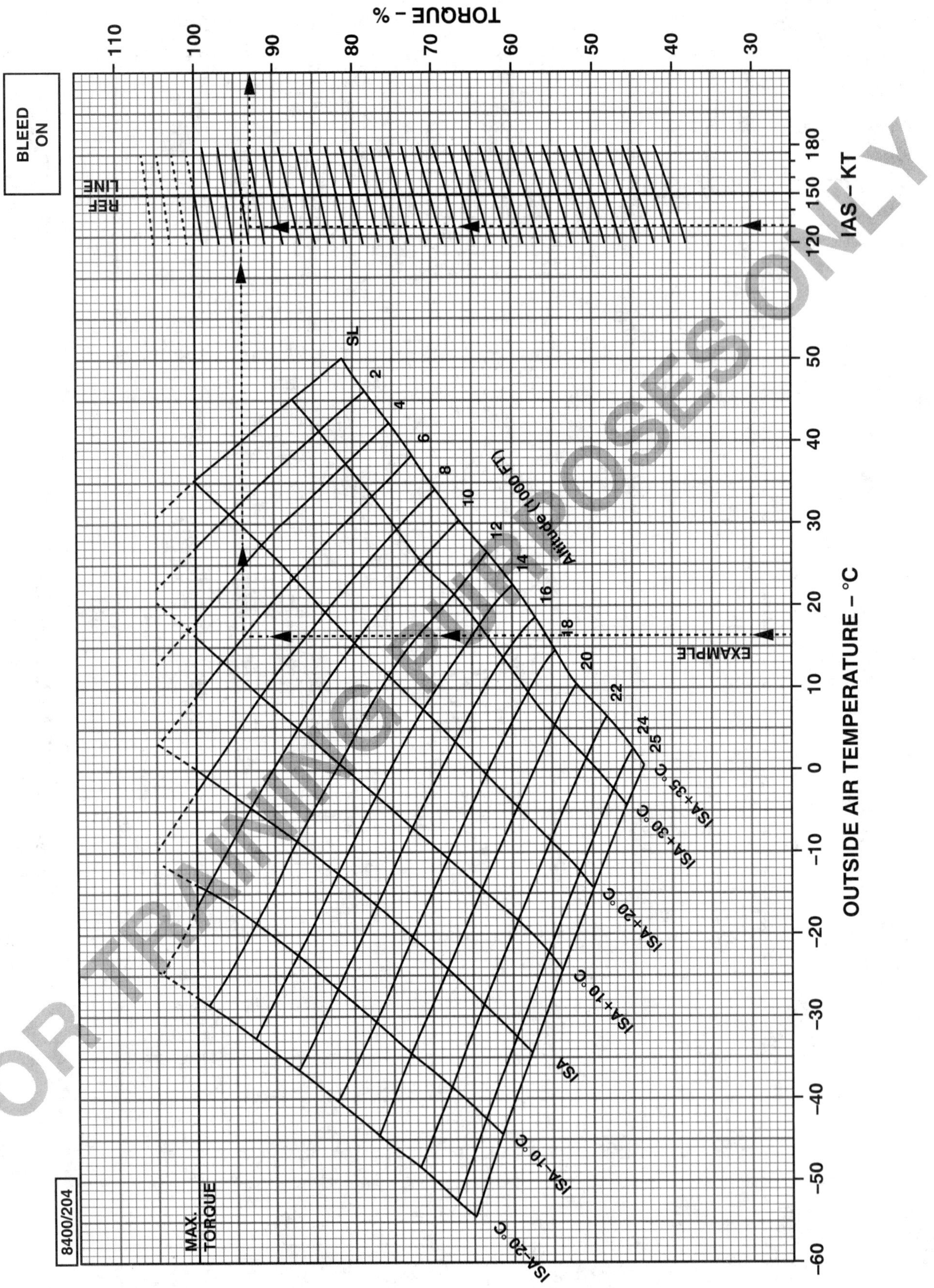

Figure 469. Q400—Maximum Continuous Power Torque Setting (In-Flight) Propeller RPM–1020 Deicing Systems ON or OFF.

Illustrations and materials were used with permission from Bombardier.

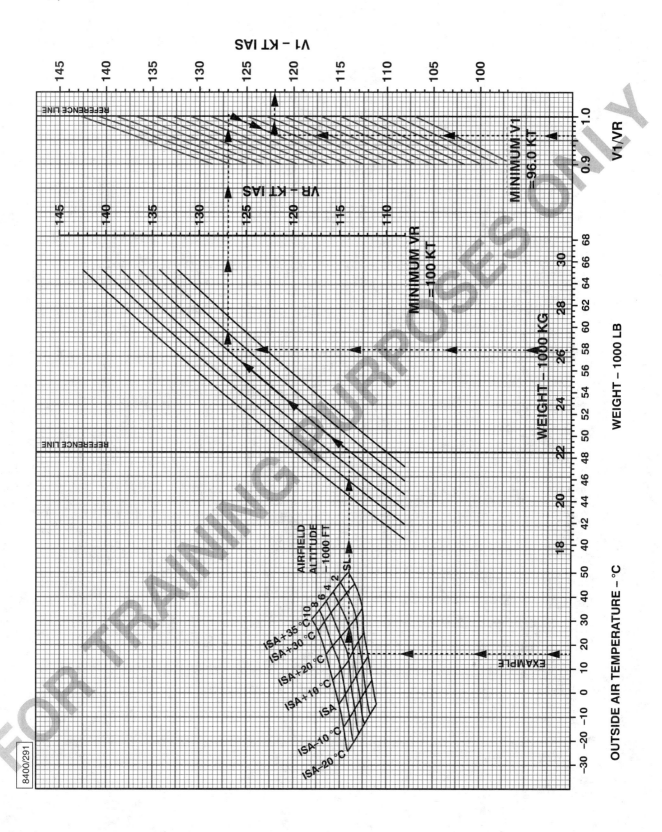

Figure 470. Q400—Rotation Speed V_R and Conversion of V_R and V_1/V_R Ratio to V_1—Flap 15°.

Illustrations and materials were used with permission from Bombardier.

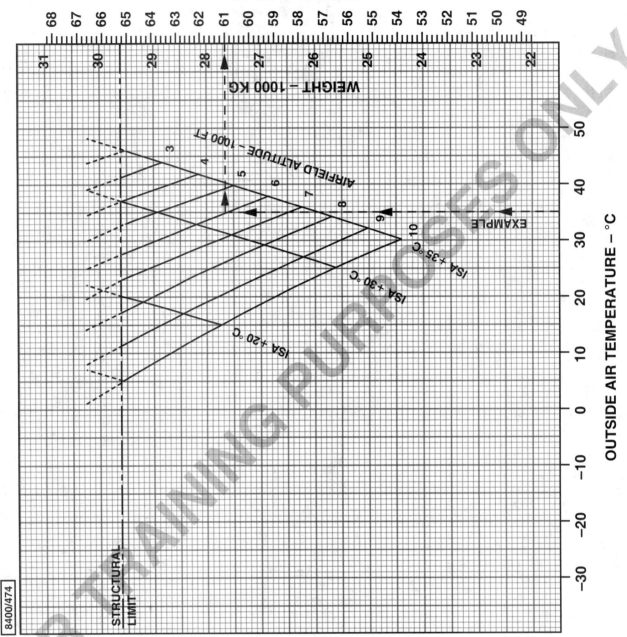

Figure 473. Q400—Maximum Permissible Takeoff Weight (WAT Limit)—Takeoff Flap 5°.

Illustrations and materials were used with permission from Bombardier.

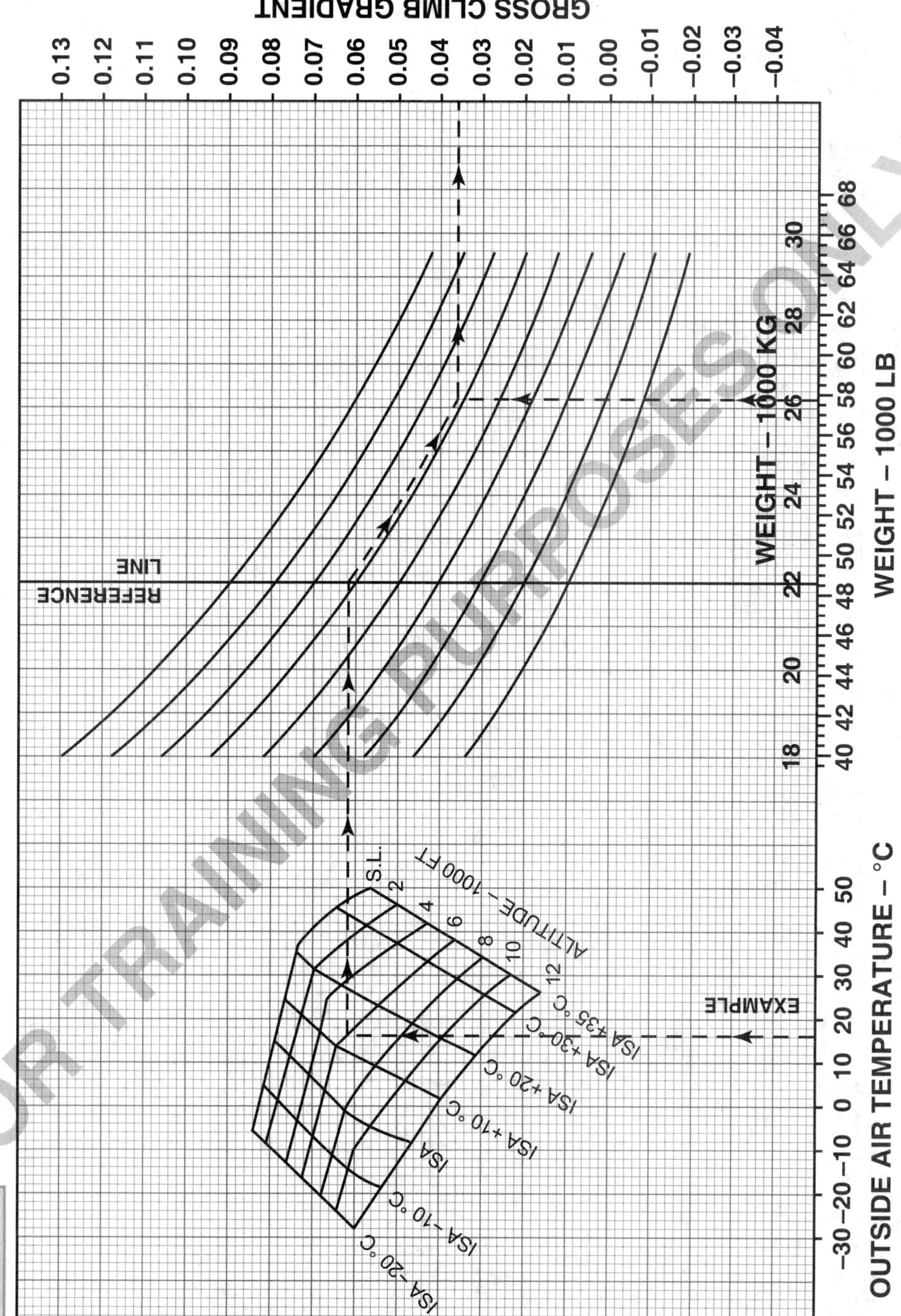

Figure 474. Q400—First Segment Takeoff Gross Climb Gradient One Engine Inoperative—Flap 5°.

Illustrations and materials were used with permission from Bombardier.

GROSS CLIMB GRADIENT

0.16 0.15 0.14 0.13 0.12 0.11 0.10 0.09 0.08 0.07 0.06 0.05 0.04 0.03 0.02 0.01 0.00 –0.01

REFERENCE LINE

WEIGHT – 1000 KG

18 20 22 24 26 28 30

WEIGHT – 1000 LB

40 42 44 46 48 50 52 54 56 58 60 62 64 66 68

OUTSIDE AIR TEMPERATURE – °C

–30 –20 –10 0 10 20 30 40 50

ALTITUDE – 1000 FT

SL 2 4 6 8 10 12

ISA –20 °C

ISA –10 °C

ISA

ISA +10 °C

ISA +20 °C

ISA +30 °C

ISA +35 °C

EXAMPLE

8400/291

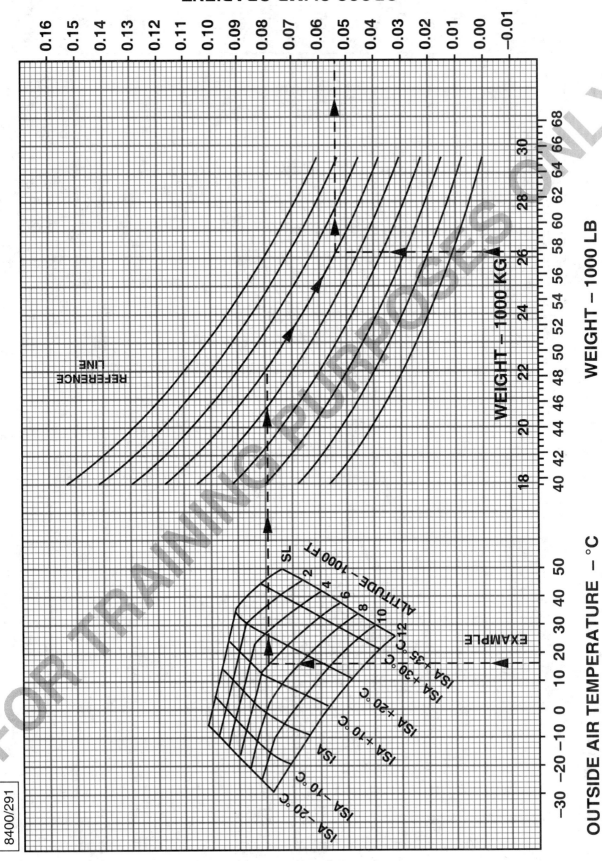

Figure 475. Q400—Second Segment Takeoff Gross Climb Gradient One Engine Inoperative—Flap 5°.

Illustrations and materials were used with permission from Bombardier.

TAKEOFF RUN REQUIRED –
ZERO WIND, ZERO RUNWAY SLOPE – 1000 FT

-100 METERS

REFERENCE LINE

V1/VR

WEIGHT – 1000 KG

WEIGHT – 1000 LB

AIRFIELD ALTITUDE – 1000 FT

EXAMPLE

OUTSIDE AIR TEMPERATURE – °C

8400/291

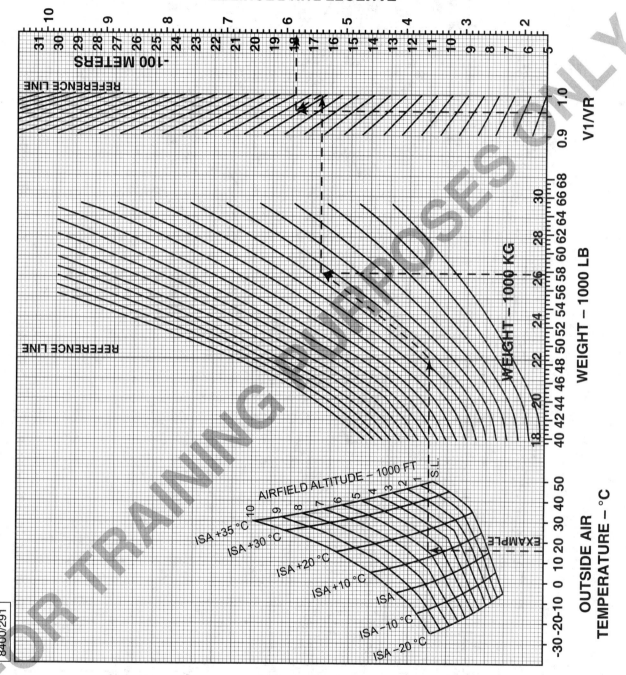

Figure 476. Q400—Takeoff Distance Required—Zero Wind, Zero Runway Slope—Flap 10°.

Illustrations and materials were used with permission from Bombardier.

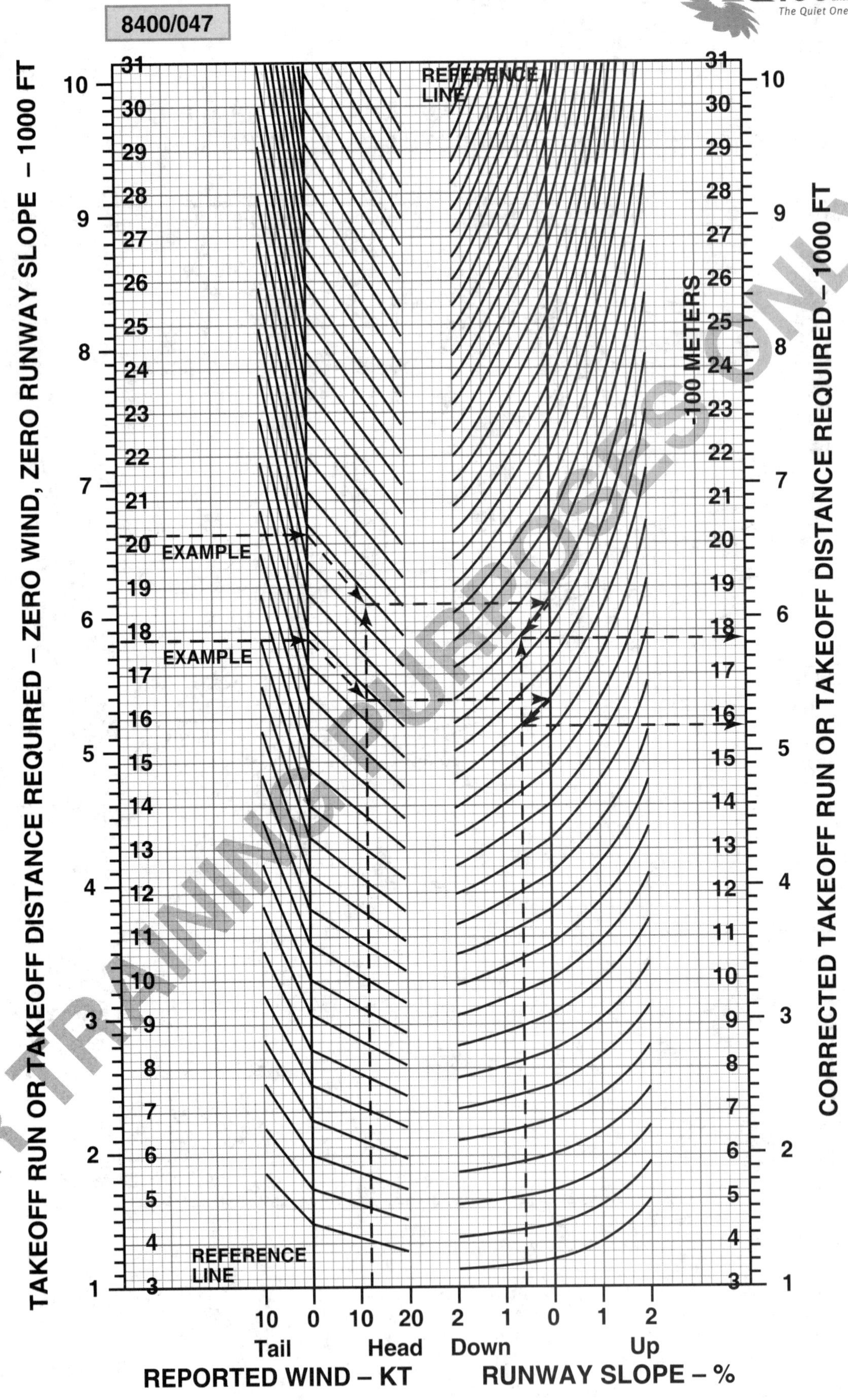

Figure 477. Q400—Takeoff Run and Takeoff Distance Required Wind and Runway Slope Correction—Flap 5°.

Illustrations and materials were used with permission from Bombardier.

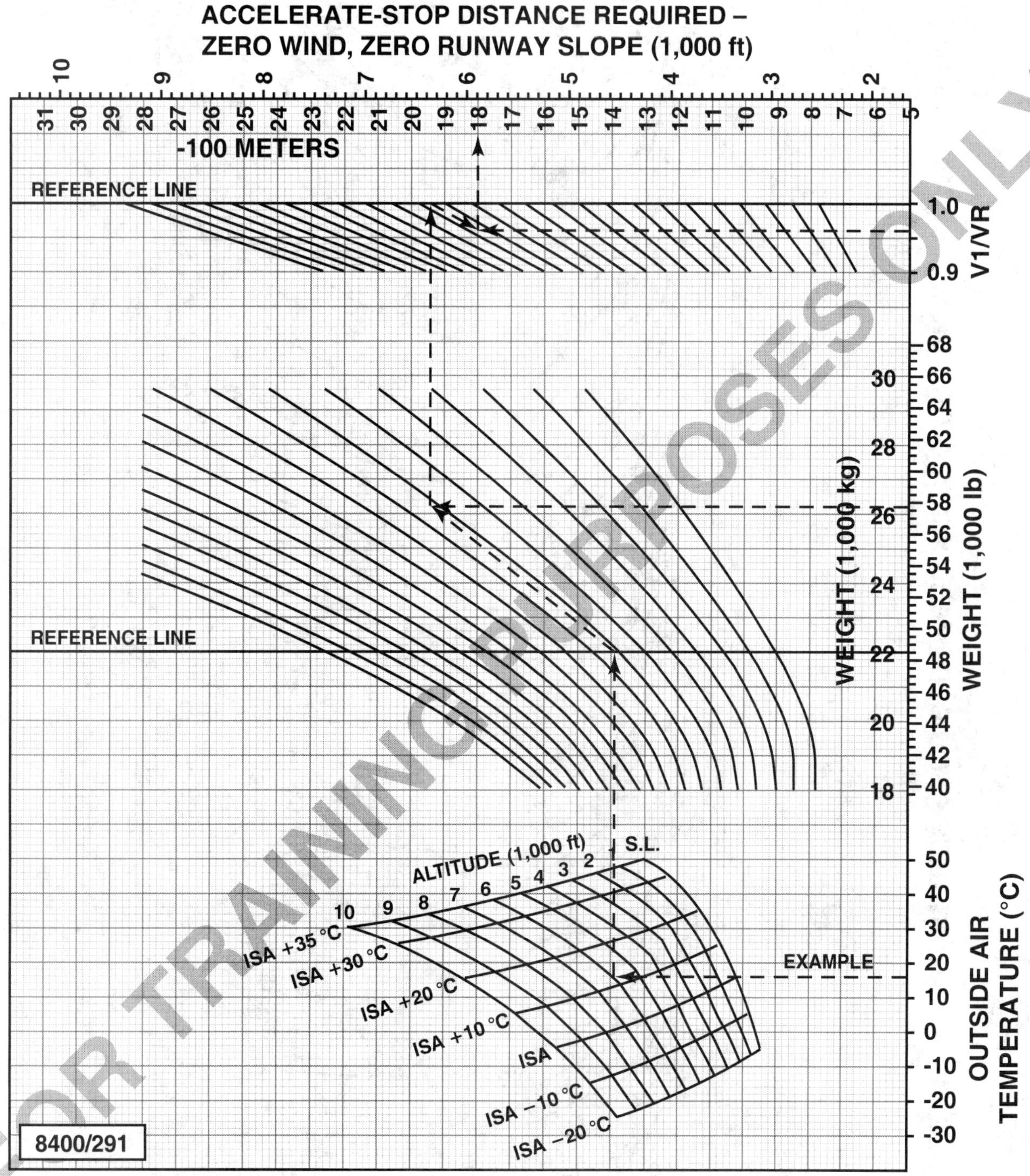

ACCELERATE-STOP DISTANCE REQUIRED – ZERO WIND, ZERO RUNWAY SLOPE (1,000 ft)

10 9 8 7 6 5 4 3 2

31 30 29 28 27 26 25 24 23 22 21 20 19 18 17 16 15 14 13 12 11 10 9 8 7 6 5

-100 METERS

REFERENCE LINE

1.0
0.9
V1/VR

68 66 64 62 60 58 56 54 52 50 48 46 44 42 40
WEIGHT (1,000 lb)

30 28 26 24 22 20 18
WEIGHT (1,000 kg)

REFERENCE LINE

ALTITUDE (1,000 ft)
S.L. 2 3 4 5 6 7 8 9 10

ISA +35 °C
ISA +30 °C
ISA +20 °C
ISA +10 °C
ISA
ISA −10 °C
ISA −20 °C

EXAMPLE

50 40 30 20 10 0 -10 -20 -30
OUTSIDE AIR TEMPERATURE (°C)

8400/291

Figure 478. Q400—Accelerate—Stop Distance Required—Zero Wind, Zero Runway Slope Flap 5°.

Illustrations and materials were used with permission from Bombardier.

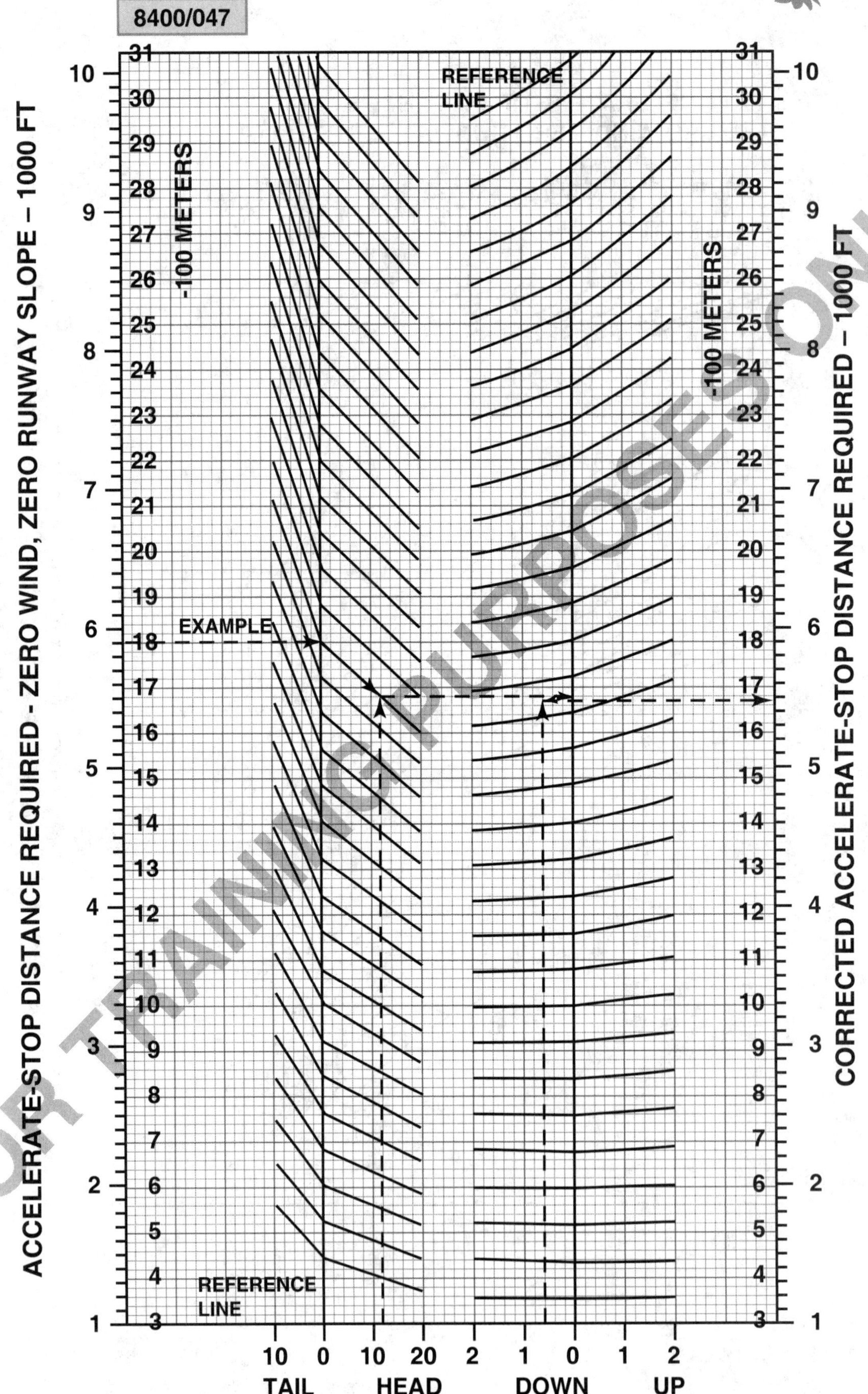

Figure 479. Q400—Accelerate-Stop Distance Required Wind and Runway Slope Correction—Flap 5°.

Illustrations and materials were used with permission from Bombardier.

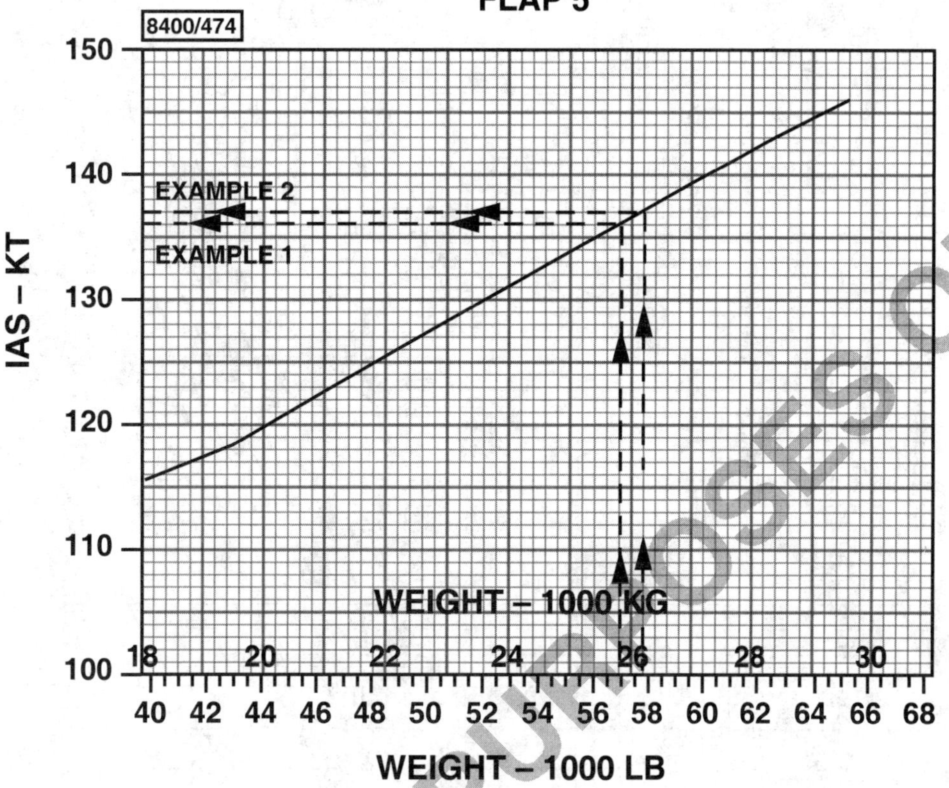

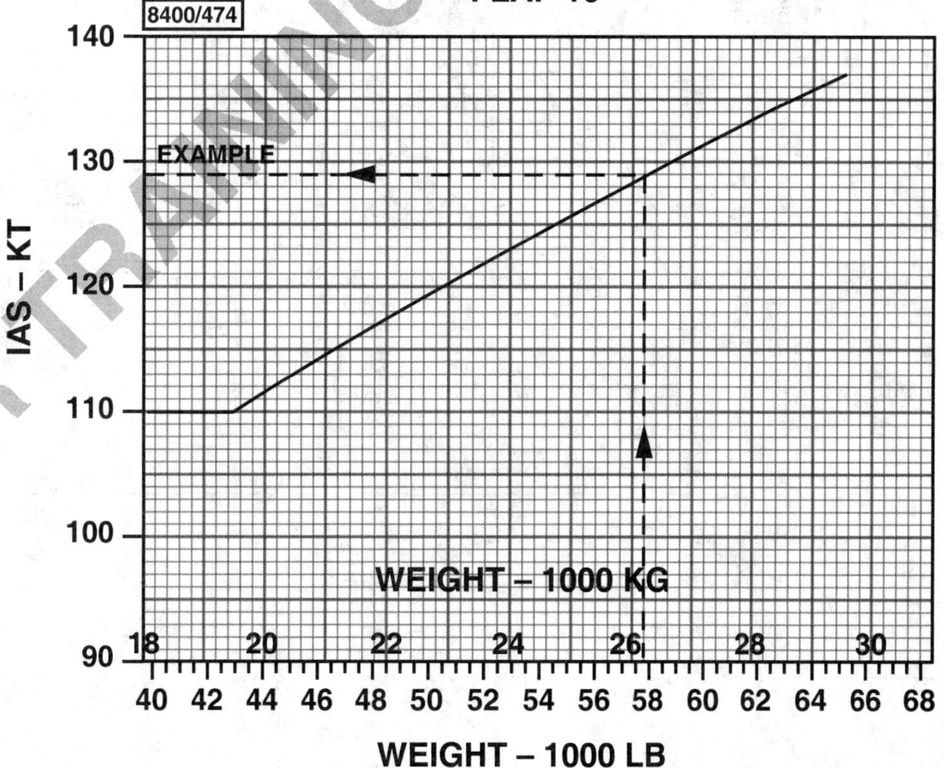

Figure 480. Q400—Flap Retraction Initiation Speed—Flap 5° and Flap 10°.
Illustrations and materials were used with permission from Bombardier.

8400/263

REF LINE

ISA −20 °C
ISA −10 °C
ISA
ISA +10 °C
ISA +20 °C
ISA +30 °C
ISA +35 °C

ALTITUDE – 1000 FT
12
10
8
6
4
2
S.L.

EXAMPLE

−30 −20 −10 0 10 20 30 40 50 100 110 120 130 140 150 160 170 180

OUTSIDE AIR TEMPERATURE – °C

IAS – KT

1000 METERS
9 10 11 12 13 14 15 16 17 18 19 20 21 22 23 24 25 26 27 28 29 30 31 32 33 34 35 36 37 38 39 40 41 42 43

RADIUS OF TURN – 1000 FT
3 4 5 6 7 8 9 10 11 12 13 14

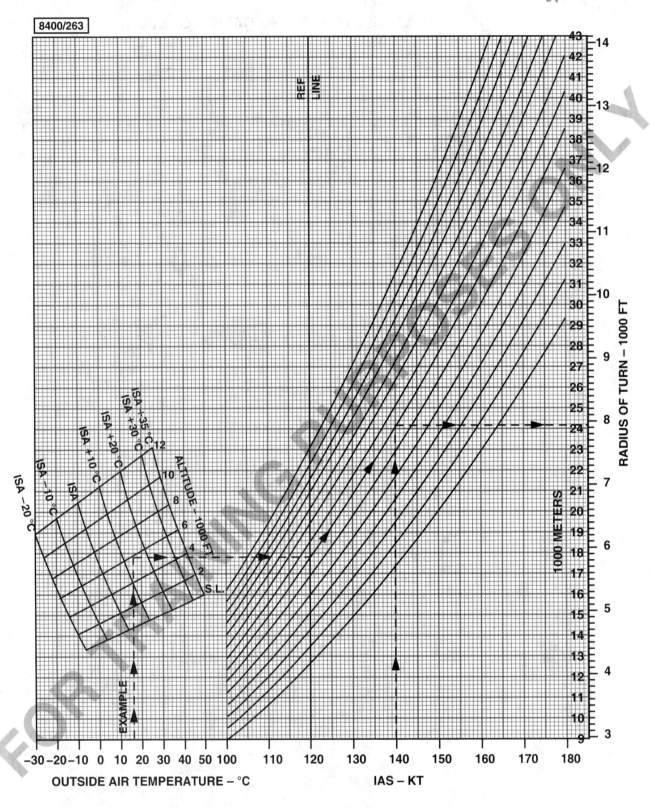

Figure 481. Q400—Net Takeoff Flight Path—Radius of Steady 15° Banked Turn.

Illustrations and materials were used with permission from Bombardier.

8400/291A

ISA −20 °C
ISA −10 °C
ISA
ISA +5 °C
ISA +10 °C
ISA +15 °C
ISA +20 °C
ISA +25 °C
ISA +30 °C
ISA +35 °C

EXAMPLE

WEIGHT – 1000 KG
18 19 20 21 22 23 24 25 26 27 28 29 30

WEIGHT – 1000 LB
40 42 44 46 48 50 52 54 56 58 60 62 64 66 68

ALTITUDE – 1000 FT
30 25 20 15 10 5

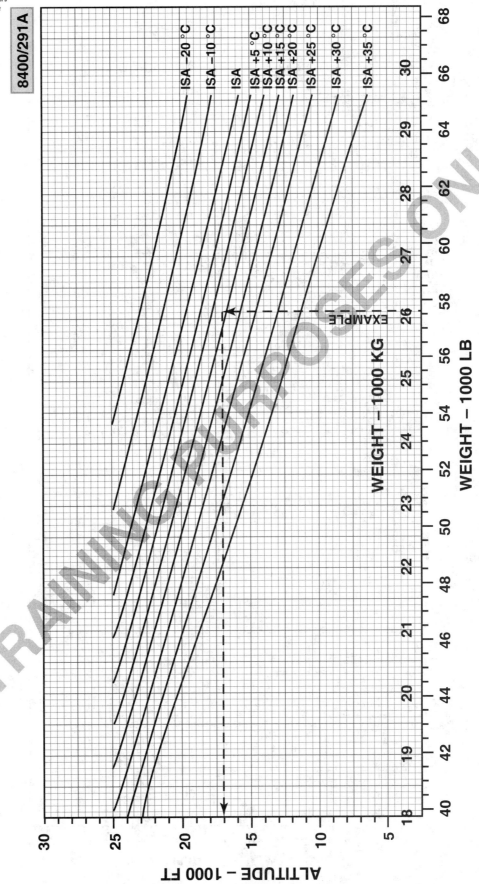

Figure 482. Q400—Enroute Climb Ceiling—One Engine Inoperative (Based on Zero Net Climb Gradient).

Illustrations and materials were used with permission from Bombardier.

Landing Speeds

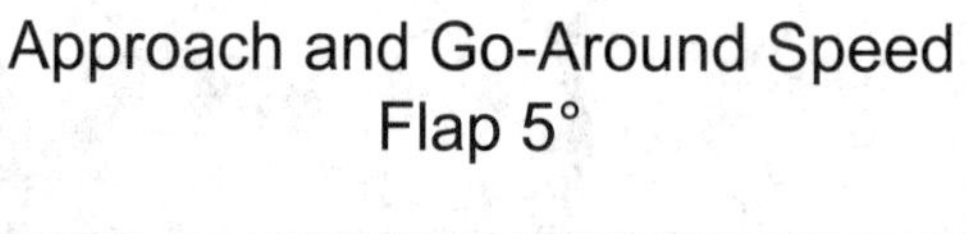

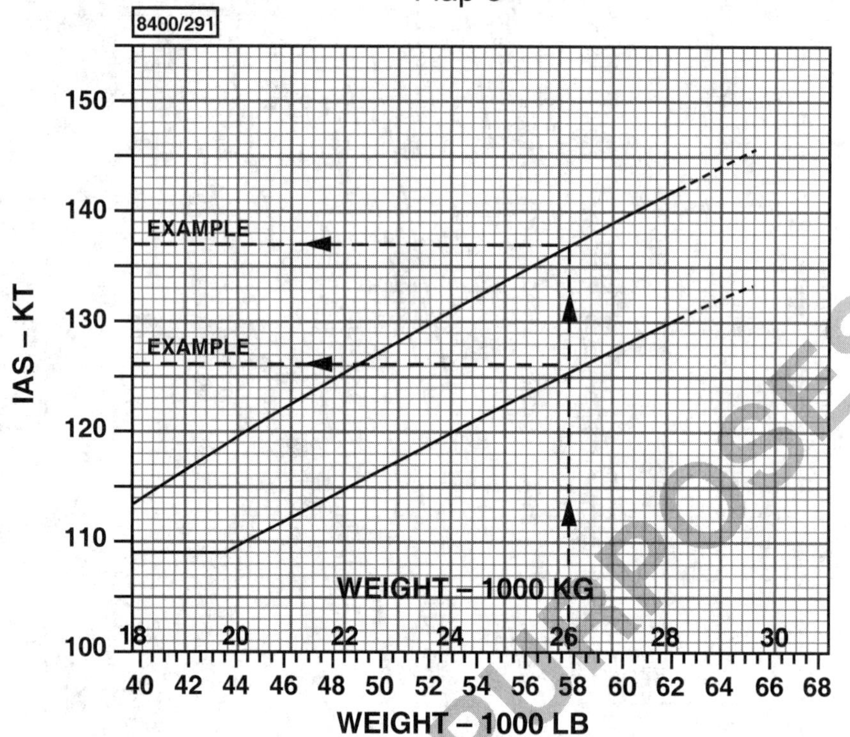

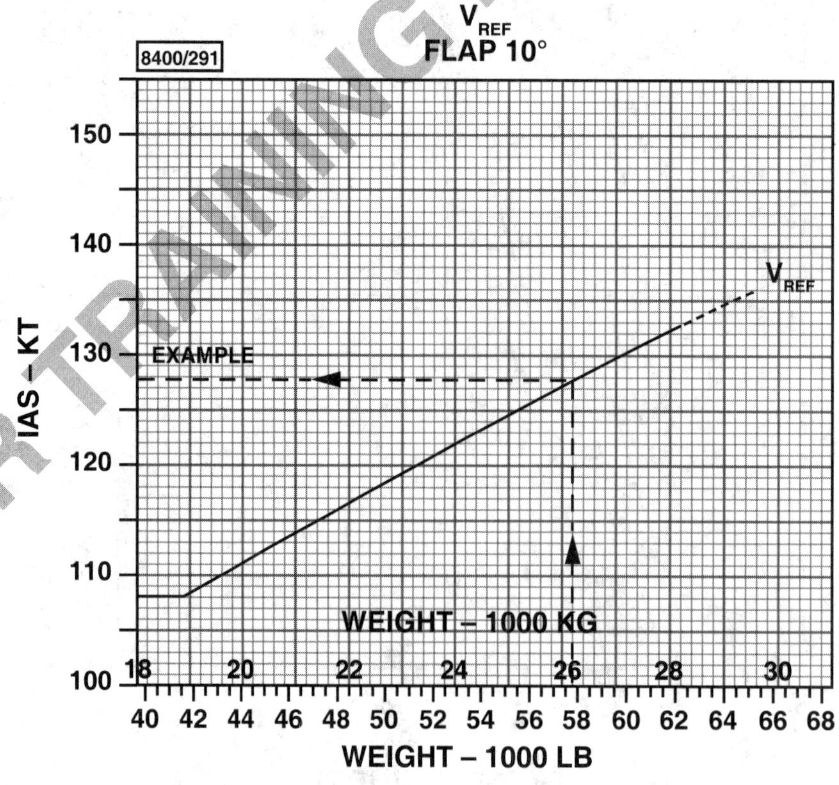

Figure 483. Q400—Approach, Go-Around, and V_{REF} Speeds.

Illustrations and materials were used with permission from Bombardier.

WEIGHT – 1000 LB

WEIGHT – 1000 KG

AIRFIELD ALTITUDE – 1000 FT

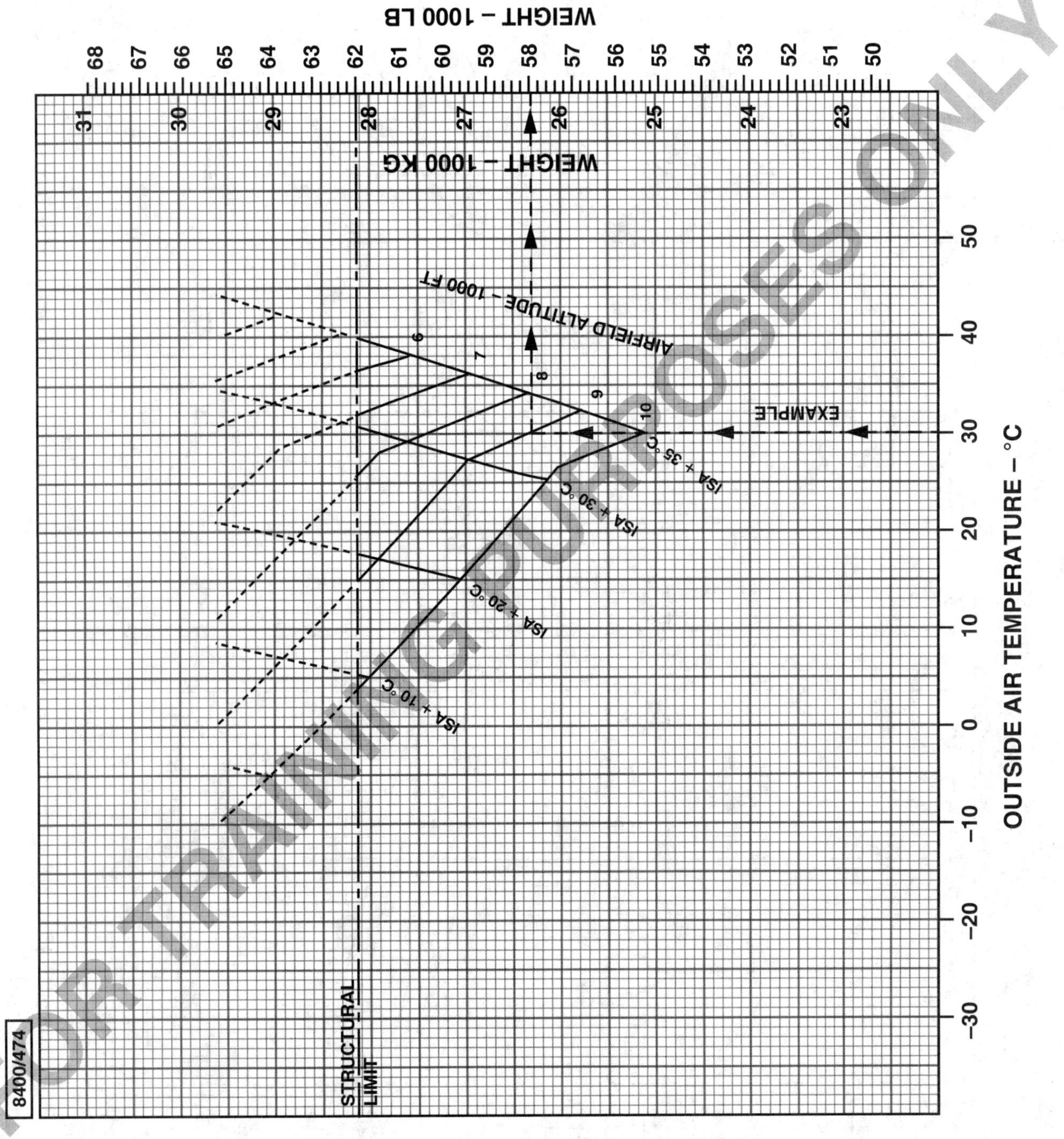

EXAMPLE

ISA + 35 °C

ISA + 30 °C

ISA + 20 °C

ISA + 10 °C

STRUCTURAL LIMIT

OUTSIDE AIR TEMPERATURE – °C

8400/474

Figure 484. Q400—Maximum Permissible Landing Weight (WAT LImit)
Landing Flap 10°, Approach Flap 5°.

Illustrations and materials were used with permission from Bombardier.

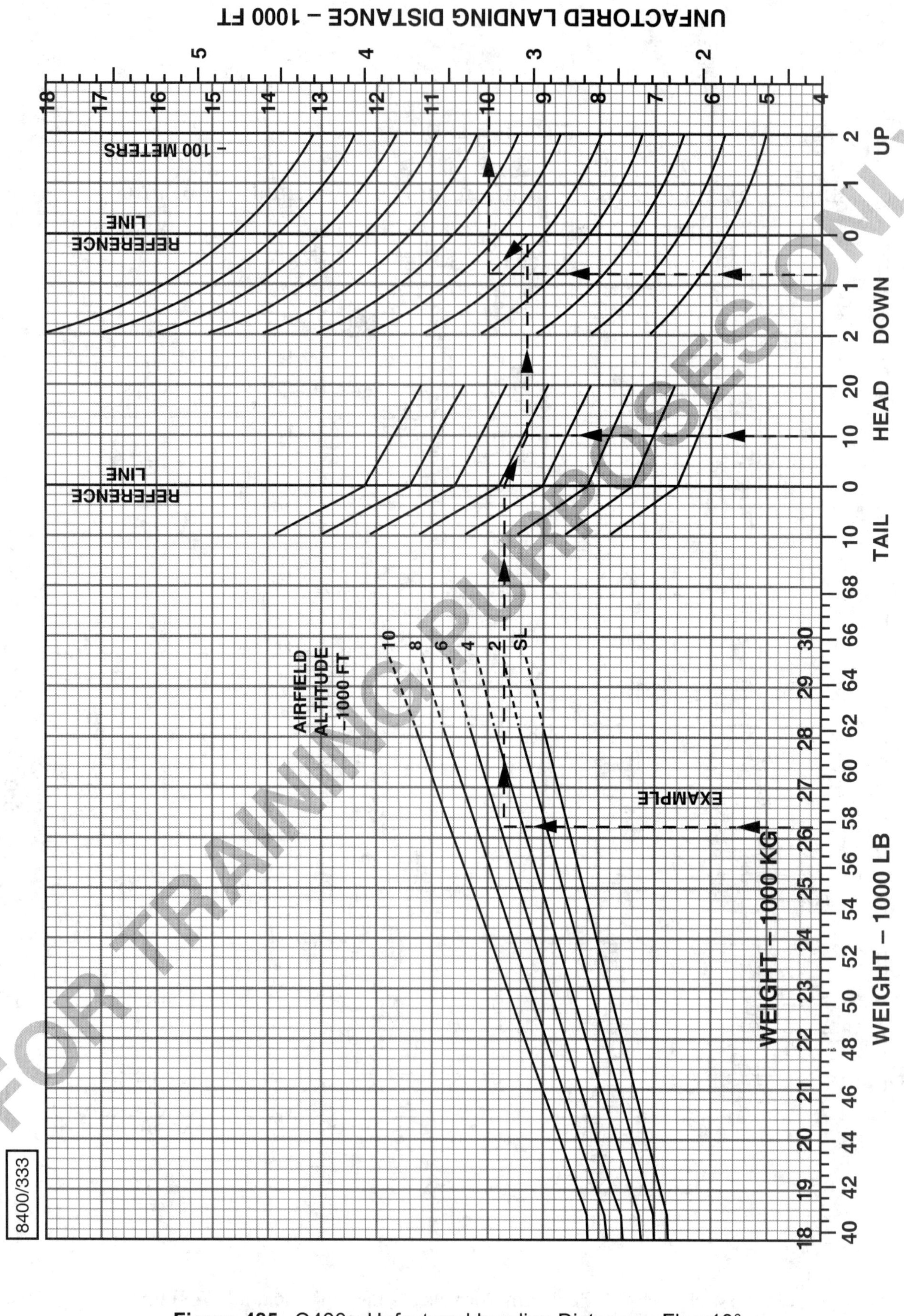

8400/333

Figure 485. Q400—Unfactored Landing Distance—Flap 10°.

Illustrations and materials were used with permission from Bombardier.

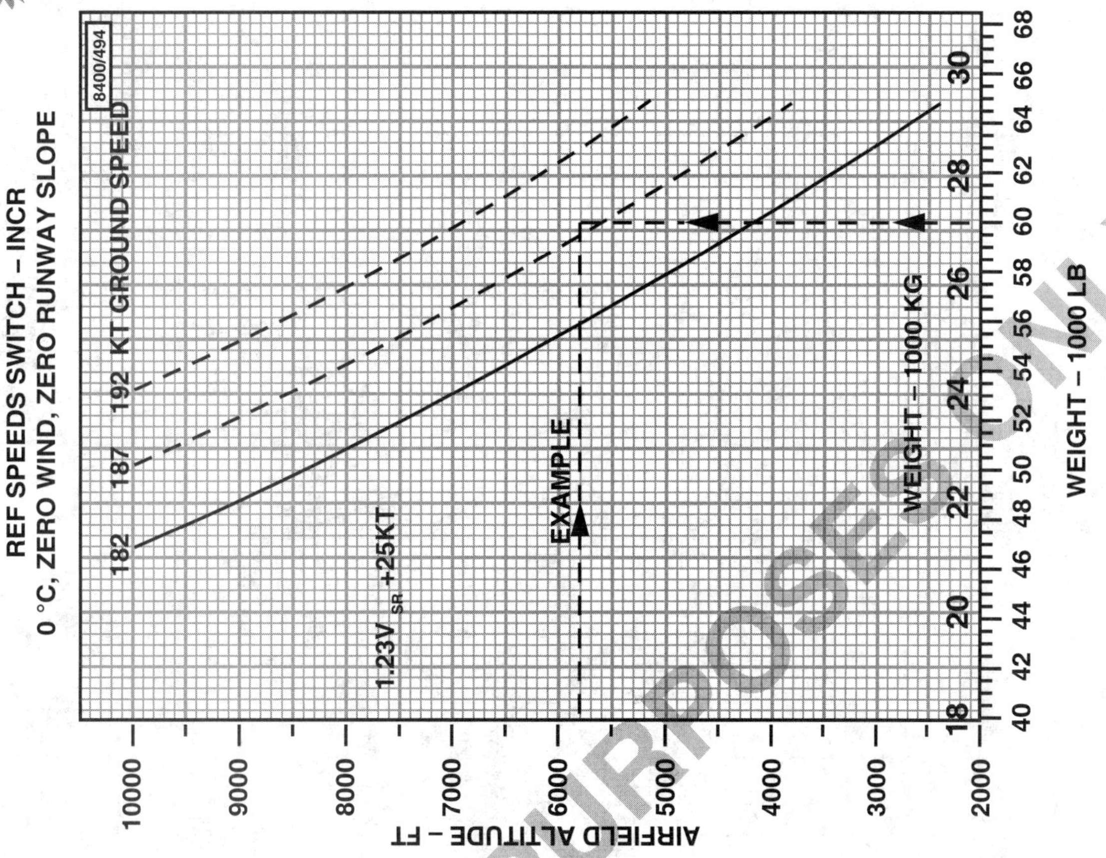

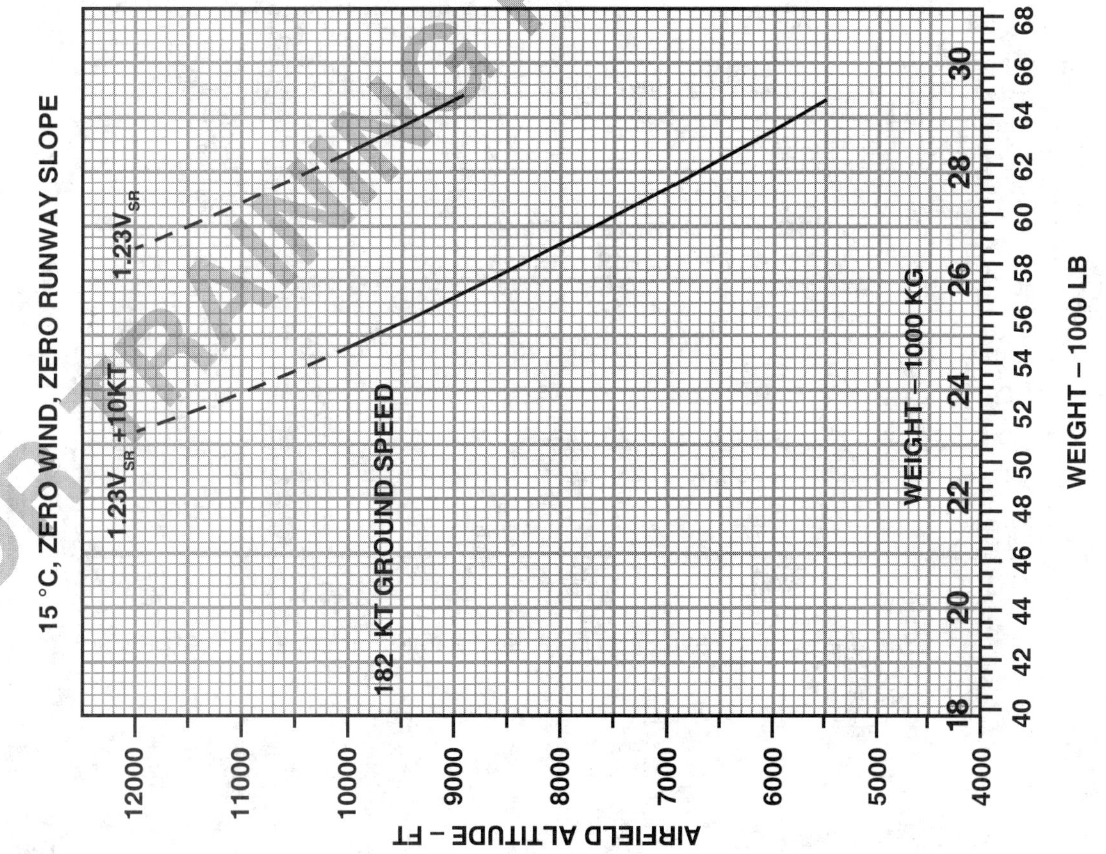

REF SPEEDS SWITCH – INCR
0 °C, ZERO WIND, ZERO RUNWAY SLOPE

8400/494

182 187 192 KT GROUND SPEED

$1.23V_{SR}$ +25KT

EXAMPLE

AIRFIELD ALTITUDE – FT

WEIGHT – 1000 KG

WEIGHT – 1000 LB

15 °C, ZERO WIND, ZERO RUNWAY SLOPE

$1.23V_{SR}$ +10KT

$1.23V_{SR}$

182 KT GROUND SPEED

AIRFIELD ALTITUDE – FT

WEIGHT – 1000 KG

WEIGHT – 1000 LB

Figure 486. Q400—Expected Touch Down Speeds—Abnormal Flap Landing (Flap 0°).

Illustrations and materials were used with permission from Bombardier.

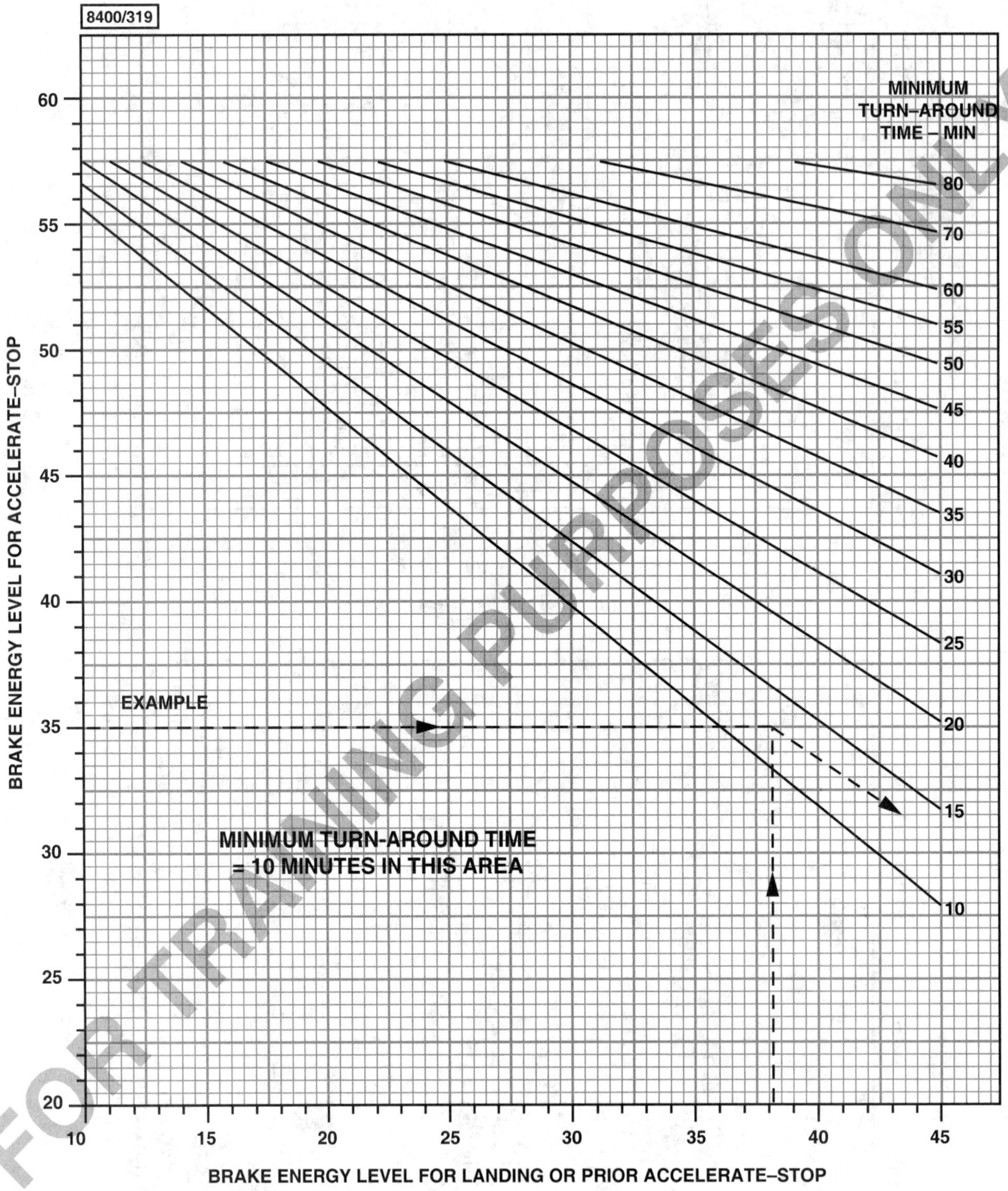

Figure 487. Q400—Minimum Turn-Around Time

Illustrations and materials were used with permission from Bombardier.

Table A to Part 117—Maximum Flight Time Limits for Unaugmented Operations Table

Time of report (acclimated)	Maximum flight time (hours)
0000–0459	8
0500–1959	9
2000–2359	8

Table B to Part 117—Flight Duty Period: Unaugmented Operations

Scheduled time of start (acclimated time)	Maximum flight duty period (hours) for lineholders based on number of flight segments.						
	1	2	3	4	5	6	7+
0000–0359	9	9	9	9	9	9	9
0400–0459	10	10	10	10	9	9	9
0500–0559	12	12	12	12	11.5	11	10.5
0600–0659	13	13	12	12	11.5	11	10.5
0700–1159	14	14	13	13	12.5	12	11.5
1200–1259	13	13	13	13	12.5	12	11.5
1300–1659	12	12	12	12	11.5	11	10.5
1700–2159	12	12	11	11	10	9	9
2200–2259	11	11	10	10	9	9	9
2300–2359	10	10	10	9	9	9	9

Table C to Part 117—Flight Duty Period: Augmented Operations

Scheduled time of start (acclimated time)	Maximum flight duty period (hours) for lineholders based on number of pilots.					
	Class 1 rest facility		Class 2 rest facility		Class 3 rest facility	
	3 pilots	4 pilots	3 pilots	4 pilots	3 pilots	4 pilots
0000–0559	15	17	14	15.5	13	13.5
0600–0659	16	18.5	15	16.5	14	14.5
0700–1259	17	19	16.5	18	15	15.5
1300–1659	16	18.5	15	16.5	14	14.5
1700–2359	15	17	14	15.5	13	13.5

Figure 488. 14 CFR part 117 Tables A, B, and C.

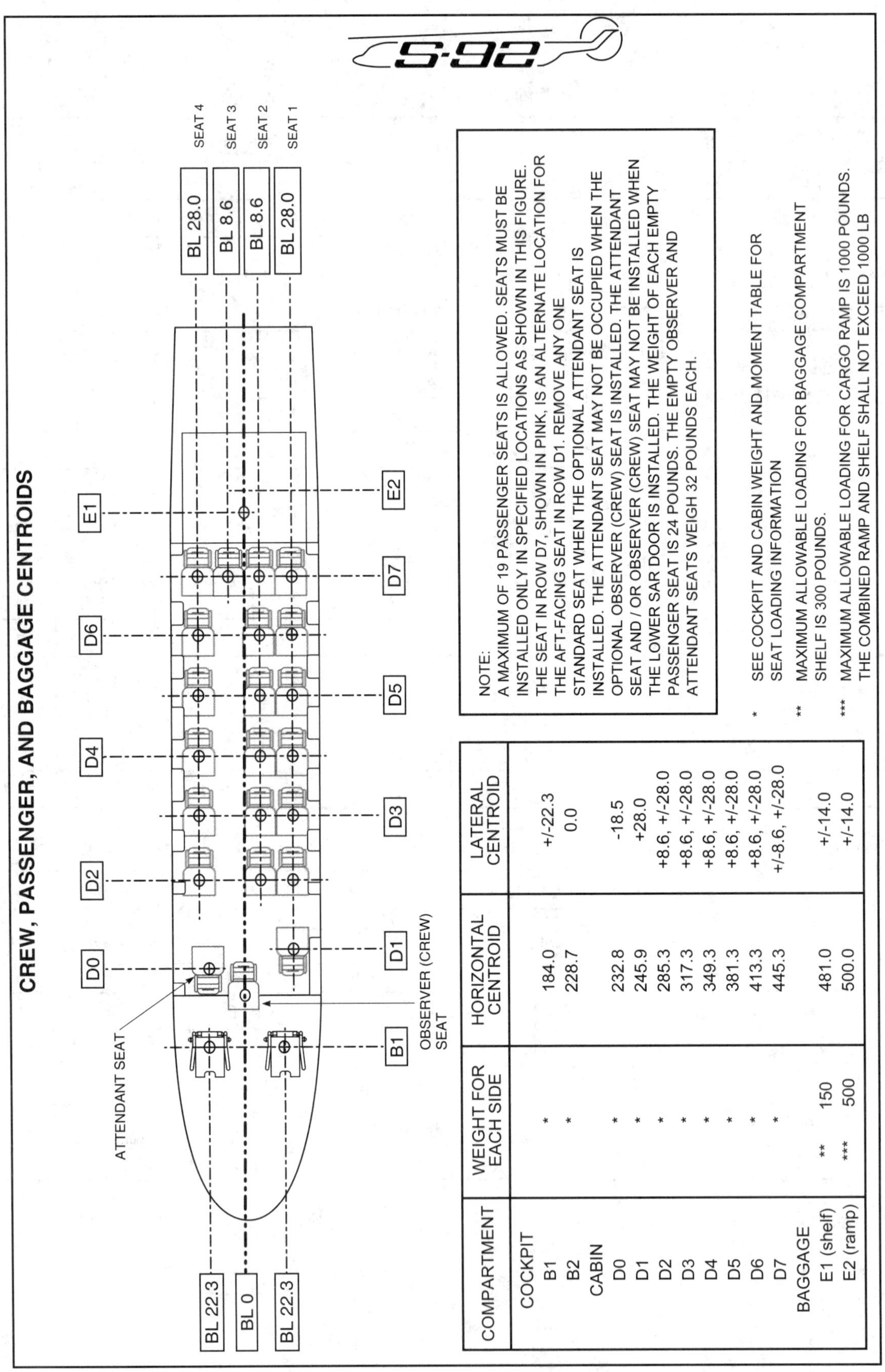

COMPARTMENT	WEIGHT FOR EACH SIDE	HORIZONTAL CENTROID	LATERAL CENTROID
COCKPIT			
B1	*	184.0	+/-22.3
B2	*	228.7	0.0
CABIN			
D0	*	232.8	-18.5
D1	*	245.9	+28.0
D2	*	285.3	+8.6, +/-28.0
D3	*	317.3	+8.6, +/-28.0
D4	*	349.3	+8.6, +/-28.0
D5	*	381.3	+8.6, +/-28.0
D6	*	413.3	+8.6, +/-28.0
D7	*	445.3	+/-8.6, +/-28.0
BAGGAGE			
E1 (shelf)	** 150	481.0	+/-14.0
E2 (ramp)	*** 500	500.0	+/-14.0

NOTE:
A MAXIMUM OF 19 PASSENGER SEATS IS ALLOWED. SEATS MUST BE INSTALLED ONLY IN SPECIFIED LOCATIONS AS SHOWN IN THIS FIGURE. THE SEAT IN ROW D7, SHOWN IN PINK, IS AN ALTERNATE LOCATION FOR THE AFT-FACING SEAT IN ROW D1. REMOVE ANY ONE STANDARD SEAT WHEN THE OPTIONAL ATTENDANT SEAT IS INSTALLED. THE ATTENDANT SEAT MAY NOT BE OCCUPIED WHEN THE OPTIONAL OBSERVER (CREW) SEAT IS INSTALLED. THE ATTENDANT SEAT AND / OR OBSERVER (CREW) SEAT MAY NOT BE INSTALLED WHEN THE LOWER SAR DOOR IS INSTALLED. THE WEIGHT OF EACH EMPTY PASSENGER SEAT IS 24 POUNDS. THE EMPTY OBSERVER AND ATTENDANT SEATS WEIGH 32 POUNDS EACH.

* SEE COCKPIT AND CABIN WEIGHT AND MOMENT TABLE FOR SEAT LOADING INFORMATION

** MAXIMUM ALLOWABLE LOADING FOR BAGGAGE COMPARTMENT SHELF IS 300 POUNDS.

*** MAXIMUM ALLOWABLE LOADING FOR CARGO RAMP IS 1000 POUNDS. THE COMBINED RAMP AND SHELF SHALL NOT EXCEED 1000 LB

Figure 489. S-92—Personnel and Baggage Centroids.

WEIGHT (LBS)	COCKPIT PILOT & COPILOT B1 HORIZONTAL ARM=184.0 MOM/1000	COCKPIT PILOT & COPILOT B1 LATERAL ARM=+/-22.3 MOM/1000	COCKPIT OBSERVER B2 HORIZONTAL ARM=226.7 MOM/1000	COCKPIT OBSERVER B2 LATERAL ARM=00.0 MOM/1000	CABIN PASSENGERS D0 HORIZONTAL ARM=232.8 MOM/1000	D1 HORIZONTAL ARM=245.9 MOM/1000	D2 HORIZONTAL ARM=285.3 MOM/1000	D3 HORIZONTAL ARM=317.3 MOM/1000	D4 HORIZONTAL ARM=349.3 MOM/1000	D5 HORIZONTAL ARM=381.3 MOM/1000	D6 HORIZONTAL ARM=413.3 MOM/1000	D7 HORIZONTAL ARM=445.3 MOM/1000	D0 LATERAL ARM=18.5 MOM/1000	D1 THROUGH D7 LATERAL ARM=+/-8.6 MOM/1000	D1 THROUGH D7 LATERAL ARM=+/-28.0 MOM/1000	TRANSITION BAGGAGE/CARGO E1 HORIZONTAL ARM=481.00 MOM/1000	E2 HORIZONTAL ARM=500.0 MOM/1000	E1 & E2 LATERAL ARM=+/-14.0 MOM/1000
50	9	+/-1	11	0	12	12	14	16	17	19	21	22	-1	+/-0	+/-1	24	25	+/-1
60	11	+/-1	14	0	14	15	17	19	21	23	25	27	-1	+/-1	+/-2	29	30	+/-1
70	13	+/-2	16	0	16	17	20	22	24	27	29	31	-1	+/-1	+/-2	34	35	+/-1
80	15	+/-2	18	0	19	20	23	25	28	31	33	36	-1	+/-1	+/-2	38	40	+/-1
90	17	+/-2	21	0	21	22	26	29	31	34	37	40	-2	+/-1	+/-3	43	45	+/-1
100	18	+/-2	23	0	23	25	29	32	35	38	41	45	-2	+/-1	+/-3	48	50	+/-1
110	20	+/-2	25	0	26	27	31	35	38	42	45	49	-2	+/-1	+/-3	53	55	+/-2
120	22	+/-3	27	0	28	30	34	38	42	46	50	53	-2	+/-1	+/-3	58	60	+/-2
130	24	+/-3	30	0	30	32	37	41	45	50	54	58	-2	+/-1	+/-4	63	65	+/-2
140	26	+/-3	32	0	33	34	40	44	49	53	58	62	-3	+/-1	+/-4	67	70	+/-2
150	28	+/-3	34	0	35	37	43	48	52	57	62	67	-3	+/-1	+/-4	72	75	+/-2
160	29	+/-4	37	0	37	39	46	51	56	61	66	71	-3	+/-1	+/-4	77	80	+/-2
170	31	+/-4	39	0	40	42	49	54	59	65	70	76	-3	+/-1	+/-5	82	85	+/-2
180	33	+/-4	41	0	42	44	51	57	63	69	74	80	-3	+/-2	+/-5	87	90	+/-3
190	35	+/-4	43	0	44	47	54	60	66	72	79	85	-4	+/-2	+/-5	91	95	+/-3
200	37	+/-4	46	0	47	49	57	63	70	76	83	89	-4	+/-2	+/-6	96	100	+/-3
210	39	+/-5	48	0	49	52	60	67	73	80	87	94	-4	+/-2	+/-6	101	105	+/-3
220	40	+/-5	50	0	51	54	63	70	77	84	91	98	-4	+/-2	+/-6	106	110	+/-3
230	42	+/-5					66	73	80	88	95	102		+/-2	+/-6	111	115	+/-3
240	44	+/-5					68	76	84	92	99	107		+/-2	+/-7	115	120	+/-3
250	46	+/-6					71	79	87	95	103	111		+/-2	+/-7	120	125	+/-4
260	48	+/-6					74	82	91	99	107	116		+/-2	+/-7	125	130	+/-4
270	50	+/-6					77	86	94	103	112	120		+/-2	+/-8	130	135	+/-4
280	52	+/-6					80	89	98	107	116	125		+/-2	+/-8	135	140	+/-4
290	53	+/-6					83	92	101	111	120	129		+/-2	+/-8	139	145	+/-4
300	55	+/-7					86	95	105	114	124	134		+/-3	+/-8	144	150	+/-4
310	57	+/-7					88	98	108	118	128	138		+/-3	+/-9		155	+/-4
320	59	+/-7					91	102	112	122	132	142		+/-3	+/-9		160	+/-4
330	61	+/-7					94	105	115	126	136	147		+/-3	+/-9		165	+/-5
340	63	+/-8					97	108	119	130	141	151		+/-3	+/-10		170	+/-5
350	64	+/-8					100	111	122	133	145	156		+/-3	+/-10		175	+/-5
360	66	+/-8					103	114	126	137	149	160		+/-3	+/-10		180	+/-5
370	68	+/-8					106	117	129	141	153	165		+/-3	+/-10		185	+/-5
380	70	+/-8					108	121	133	145	157	169		+/-3	+/-11		190	+/-5
390	72	+/-9					111	124	136	149	161	174		+/-3	+/-11		195	+/-5
400	74	+/-9					114	127	140	153	165	178		+/-3	+/-11		200	+/-6
410	75	+/-9					117	130	143	156	169	183		+/-4	+/-11		205	+/-6
420	77	+/-9					120	133	147	160	174	187		+/-4	+/-12		210	+/-6
430	79	+/-10					123	136	150	164	178	191		+/-4	+/-12		215	+/-6
440	81	+/-10					126	140	154	168	182	196		+/-4	+/-12		220	+/-6
450							128	143	157	172	186	200		+/-4	+/-13		225	+/-6
460							131	146	161	175	190	205		+/-4	+/-13		230	+/-6
470							134	149	164	179	194	209		+/-4	+/-13		235	+/-7
480							137	152	168	183	198	214		+/-4	+/-13		240	+/-7
490							140	155	171	187	203	218		+/-4	+/-14		245	+/-7
500							143	159	175	191	207	223		+/-4	+/-14		250	+/-7
510							146	162	178	194	211	227		+/-4	+/-14		255	+/-7
520							148	165	182	198	215	232		+/-4	+/-15		260	+/-7
530							151	168	185	202	219	236		+/-5	+/-15		265	+/-7
540							154	171	189	206	223	240		+/-5	+/-15		270	+/-8

Figure 490. S-92—Cockpit and Cabin Weight and Moment Table.

S-92

WEIGHT (LBS)	COCKPIT		COCKPIT		CABIN											TRANSITION		
	PILOT & COPILOT		OBSERVER		PASSENGERS											BAGGAGE/CARGO		
	B1	B1	B2	B2	D0	D1	D2	D3	D4	D5	D6	D7	D0	D1 THROUGH D7		E1	E2	E1 & E2
	HORIZONTAL ARM=184.0 MOM/1000	LATERAL ARM=+/-22.3 MOM/1000	HORIZONTAL ARM=228.7 MOM/1000	LATERAL ARM=00.0 MOM/1000	HORIZONTAL ARM=232.8 MOM/1000	HORIZONTAL ARM=245.9 MOM/1000	HORIZONTAL ARM=285.3 MOM/1000	HORIZONTAL ARM=317.3 MOM/1000	HORIZONTAL ARM=349.3 MOM/1000	HORIZONTAL ARM=381.3 MOM/1000	HORIZONTAL ARM=413.3 MOM/1000	HORIZONTAL ARM=445.3 MOM/1000	LATERAL ARM=18.5 MOM/1000	LATERAL ARM=+/-8.6 MOM/1000	LATERAL ARM=+/-28.0 MOM/1000	HORIZONTAL ARM=481.0 MOM/1000	HORIZONTAL ARM=500.0 MOM/1000	LATERAL ARM=+/-14.0 MOM/1000
550							157	175	192	210	227	245		+/-5	+/-15		275	+/-8
560							160	178	196	214	231	249		+/-5	+/-16		280	+/-8
570							163	181	199	217	236	254		+/-5	+/-16		285	+/-8
580							165	184	203	221	240	258		+/-5	+/-16		290	+/-8
590							168	187	206	225	244	263		+/-5	+/-17		295	+/-8
600							171	190	210	229	248	267		+/-5	+/-17		300	+/-8
610							174	194	213	233	252	272		+/-5	+/-17		305	+/-9
620							177	197	217	236	256	276		+/-5	+/-17		310	+/-9
630							180	200	220	240	260	281		+/-5	+/-18		315	+/-9
640							183	203	224	244	265	285		+/-6	+/-18		320	+/-9
650							185	206	227	248	269	289		+/-6	+/-18		325	+/-9
660							188	209	231	252	273	294		+/-6	+/-18		330	+/-9
670												298		6	+/-19		335	+/-9
680												303		6	+/-19		340	+/-10
690												307		6	+/-19		345	+/-10
700												312		6	+/-20		350	+/-10
710												316		6	+/-20		355	+/-10
720												321		6	+/-20		360	+/-10
730												325		6	+/-20		365	+/-10
740												330		6	+/-21		370	+/-10
750												334		6	+/-21		375	+/-11
760												338		7	+/-21		380	+/-11
770												343		7	+/-22		385	+/-11
780												347		7	+/-22		390	+/-11
790												352		7	+/-22		395	+/-11
800												356		7	+/-22		400	+/-11
810												361		7	+/-23		405	+/-11
820												365		7	+/-23		410	+/-11
830												370		7	+/-23		415	+/-12
840												374		7	+/-24		420	+/-12
850												379		7	+/-24		425	+/-12
860												383		7	+/-24		430	+/-12
870												387		7	+/-24		435	+/-12
880												392		8	+/-25		440	+/-12
890																	445	+/-12
900																	450	+/-13
910																	455	+/-13
920																	460	+/-13
930																	465	+/-13
940																	470	+/-13
950																	475	+/-13
960																	480	+/-13
970																	485	+/-14
980																	490	+/-14
990																	495	+/-14
1000																	500	+/-14

NOTE:
CAUTION MUST BE TAKEN TO ENSURE THAT PASSENGER OR BAGGAGE/CARGO COMPARTMENT LOADING DOES NOT CAUSE THE AIRCRAFT MAXIMUM WEIGHT OR CENTER OF GRAVITY OR CENTER OF GRAVITY LIMITS TO BE EXCEEDED.

Figure 491. S-92—Cockpit and Cabin Weight and Moment Table.

USABLE FUEL WEIGHT AND MOMENT TABLE

FUEL SYSTEM - 2 TANKS								
CAPACITY = 760 GALLONS								
TOTAL WT (LB)	HORIZONTAL MOM/1000	LAT=+/-60.3 MOM/1000	TOTAL WT (LB)	HORIZONTAL MOM/1000	LAT=+/-60.3 MOM/1000	TOTAL WT (LB)	HORIZONTAL MOM/1000	LAT=+/-60.3 MOM/1000
100	36	+/-6	1900	685	+/-115	3600	1303	
200	73	+/-12	2000	722	+/-121	3700	1339	
300	109	+/-18	2100	758	+/-127	3800	1375	
400	144	+/-24	2200	794	+/-133	3900	1412	
500	180	+/-30	2300	831	+/-139	4000	1448	
600	215	+/-36	2400	867	+/-145	4100	1484	
700	251	+/-42	2500	903	+/-151	4200	1521	
800	287	+/-48	**2565		+/-155	4300	1557	
900	323	+/-54	2600	940		4400	1593	
1000	359	+/-60	2700	976		4500	1630	
1100	395	+/-66	2800	1012		4600	1666	
1200	431	+/-72	2900	1049		4700	1702	
1300	468	+/-78	3000	1085		4800	1739	
1400	504	+/-84	3100	1121		4900	1775	
1500	540	+/-90	3200	1158		5000	1812	
1600	577	+/-96	3300	1194		5100	1848	
1700	613	+/-103	3400	1230		*5130	1859	
1800	649	+/-109	3500	1267				

* THIS REPRESENTS THE APPROXIMATE MAXIMUM WEIGHT AND MOMENT / 1000 FOR FULL FUEL WITH JET-A AT STANDARD CONDITIONS (60 °F / 15 °C).

** THIS REPRESENTS THE APPROXIMATE MAXIMUM WEIGHT AND MOMENT / 1000 FOR FULL FUEL IN ONE SPONSON, LEFT OR RIGHT HAND SIDE

NOTE:
- THE TOTAL USABLE CAPACITY OF 380 U.S. GALLONS PER TANK IS BASED ON CALCULATION.
- SEE FIGURE 2-15 FOR A PLOT OF FUEL C.G. AT VARIOUS FUEL WEIGHTS

Figure 492. S-92—Usable Fuel Weight and Moment Table.

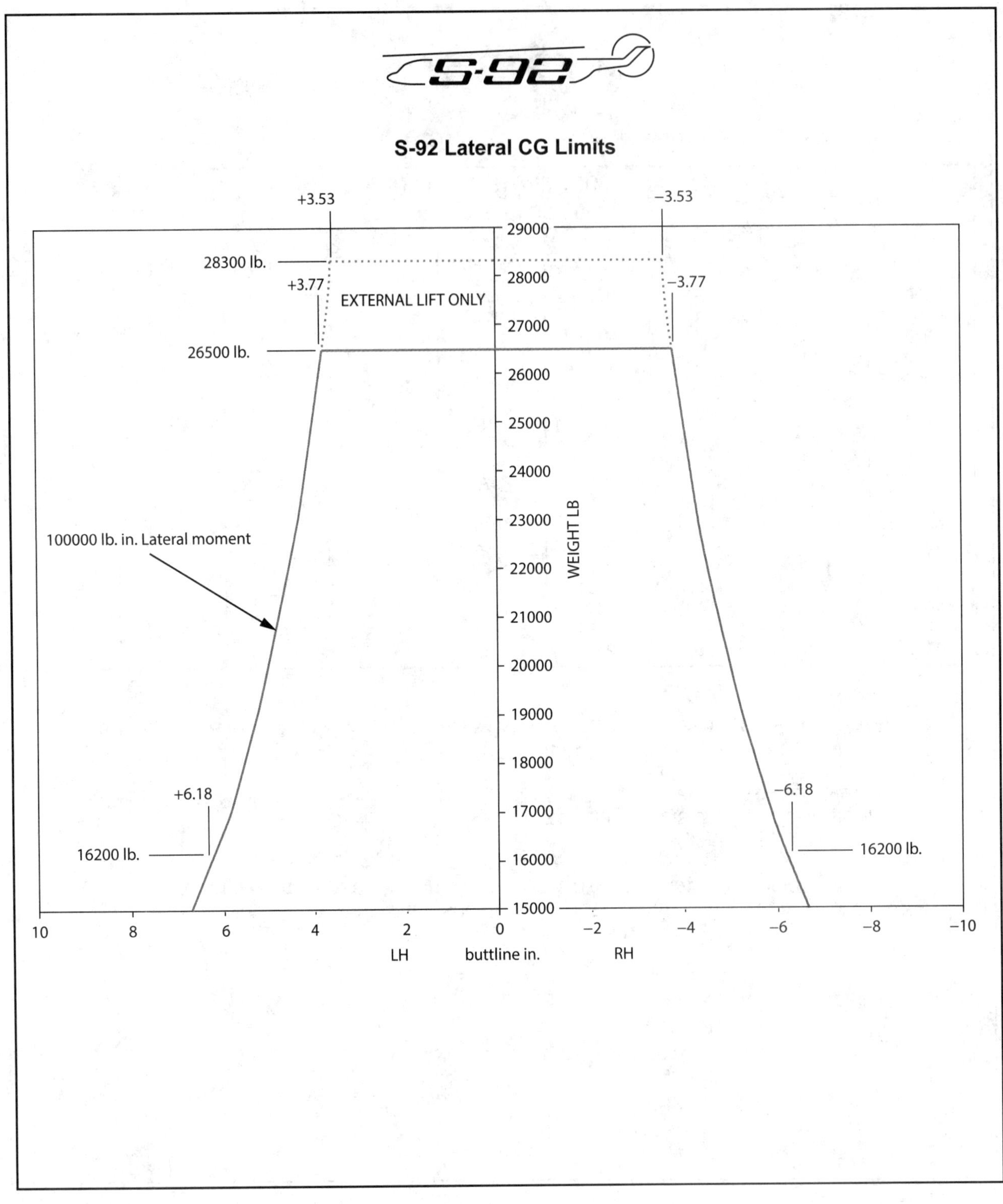

Figure 493. S-92—Lateral CG Limits.

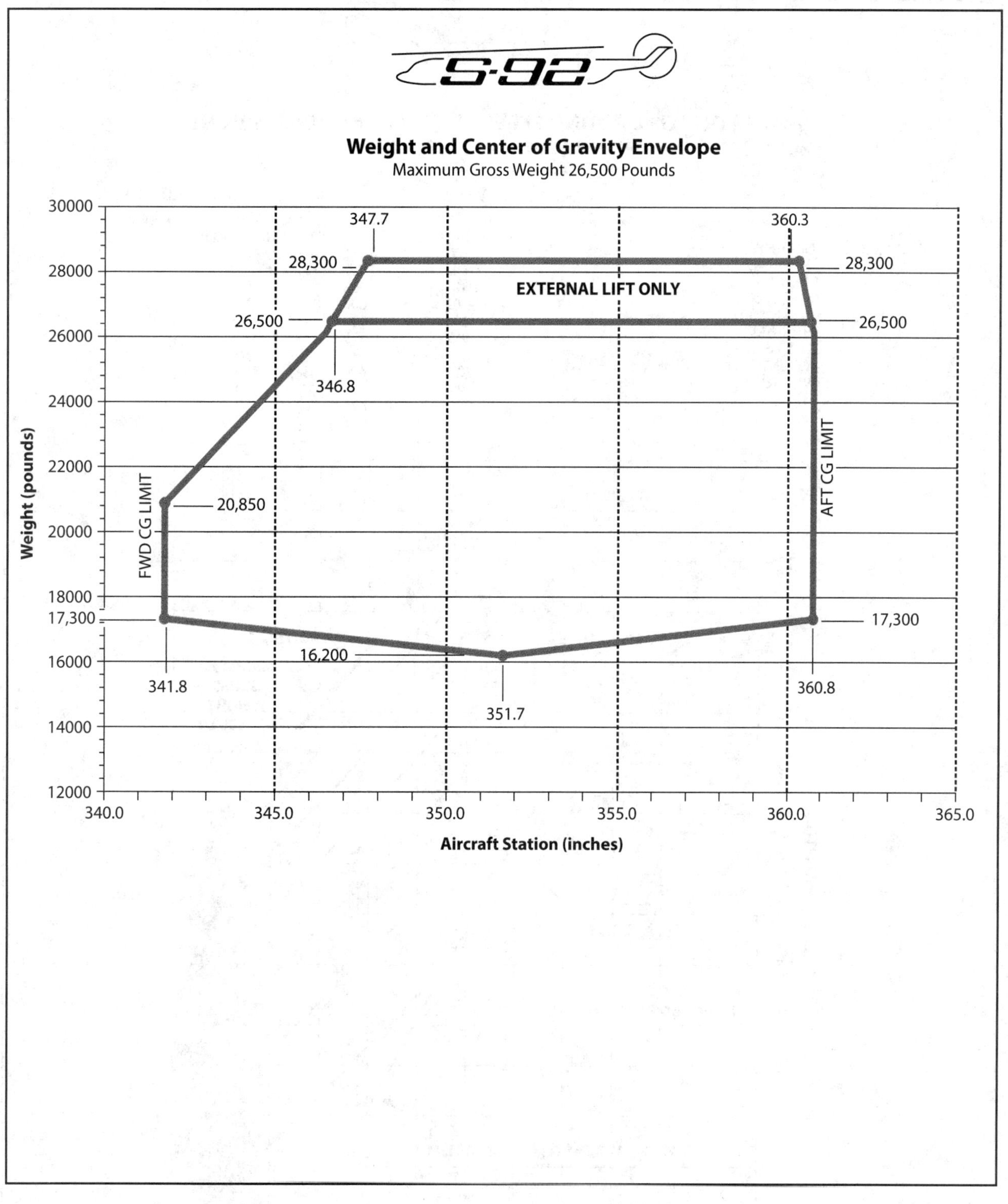

Figure 494. S-92—Weight and Center of Gravity Envelope.

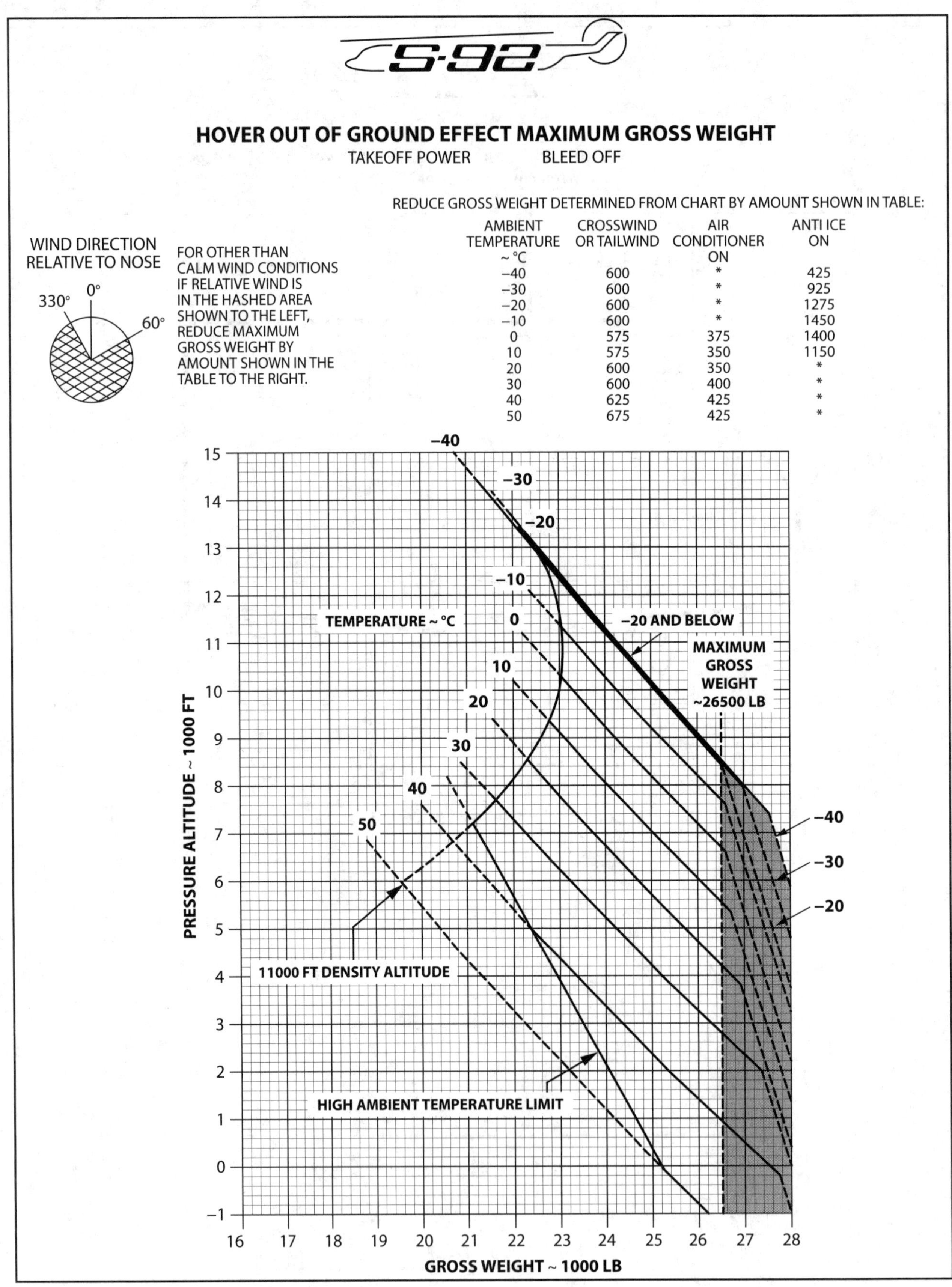

AMBIENT TEMPERATURE ~ °C	CROSSWIND OR TAILWIND	AIR CONDITIONER ON	ANTI ICE ON
−40	600	*	425
−30	600	*	925
−20	600	*	1275
−10	600	*	1450
0	575	375	1400
10	575	350	1150
20	600	350	*
30	600	400	*
40	625	425	*
50	675	425	*

Figure 495. S-92—Hover Out of Ground Effect Maximum Gross Weight.

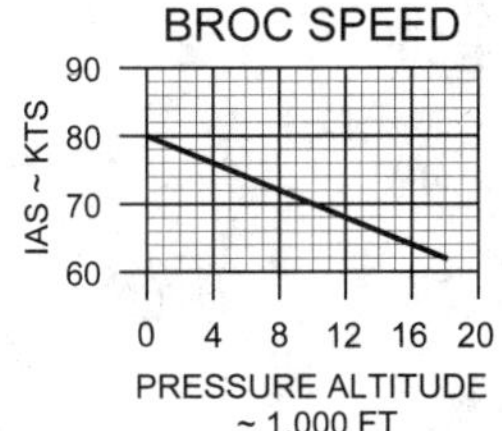

FORWARD CLIMB PERFORMANCE

DUAL ENGINE
BEST RATE OF CLIMB SPEED
GEAR UP

MAXIMUM CONTINUOUS POWER
105% Nr
< 14,000 FT HP

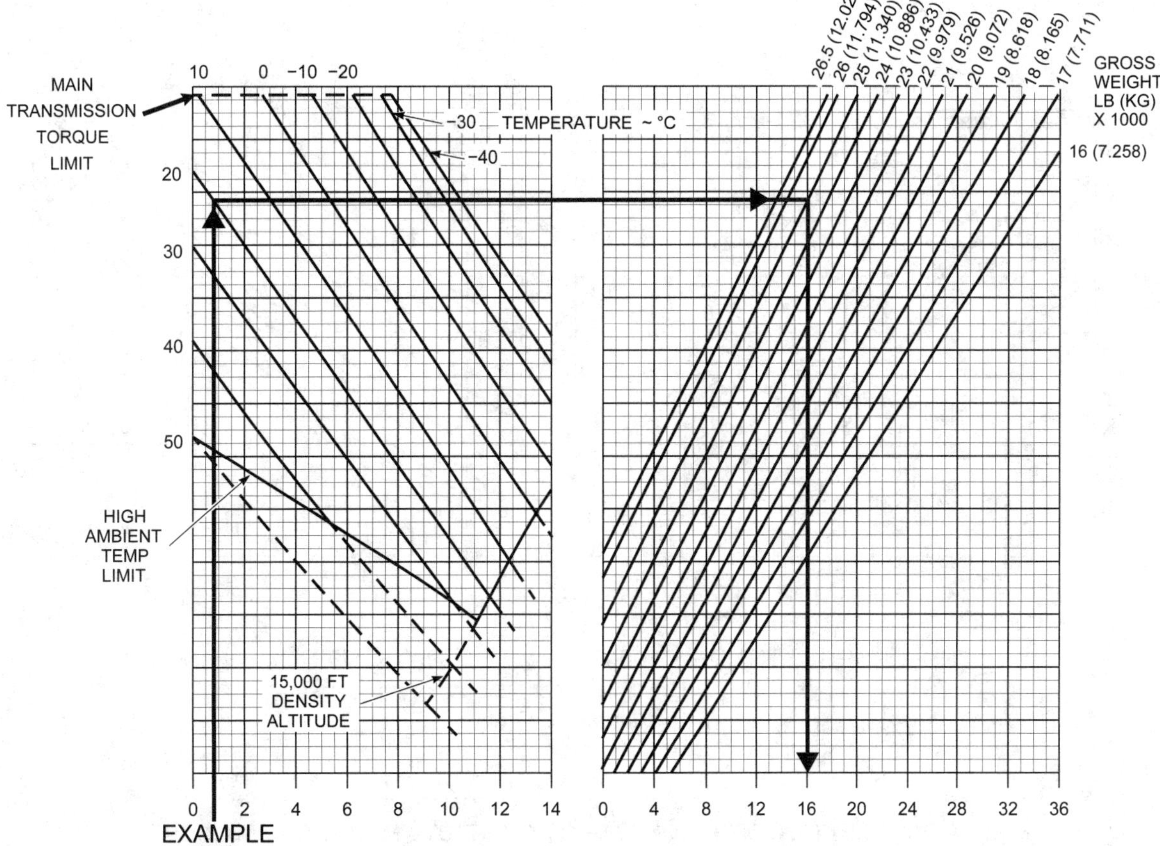

DASHED LINES ARE FOR INTERPOLATION ONLY

REDUCE RATE OF CLIMB DETERMINED FROM CHART BY AMOUNT SHOWN IN TABLE

GROSS WEIGHT-LB	REDUCTION ANTI-ICE ON	REDUCTION AIR CONDITIONER ON	REDUCTION BLEED AIR ON	REDUCTION BLEED AIR AND ANTI-ICE ON	REDUCTION LANDING GEAR DOWN	REDUCTION RESCUE HOIST	REDUCTION RIPS AND ANTI-ICE ON FOR ALTITUDES ≤4000FT	REDUCTION RIPS AND ANTI-ICE ON FOR ALTITUDES >4000FT
16,000	100	105	750	750	45	15	1225	1225
18,000	90	90	600	650	40	15	1100	1100
20,000	85	80	500	600	40	15	975	975
22,000	75	75	475	550	35	15	850	950
24,000	75	75	450	500	35	15	725	1125
26,000	70	70	450	450	35	15	600	1275
26,500	70	70	450	450	35	15	600	1300

Figure 497. S-92—AEO Forward Climb Performance, Best Rate of Climb Speed.

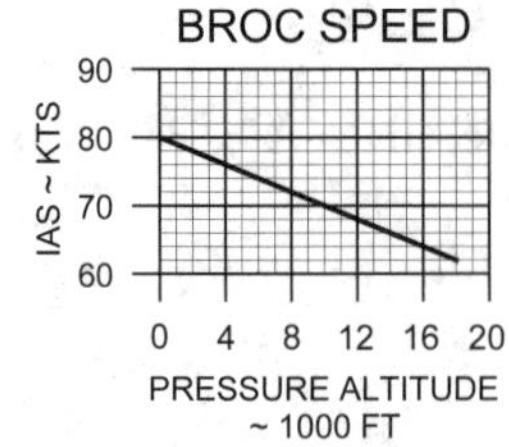

FORWARD CLIMB PERFORMANCE

SINGLE CT7−8A ENGINE
BEST RATE OF CLIMB SPEED
GEAR UP

MAXIMUM CONTINUOUS POWER
100% Nr

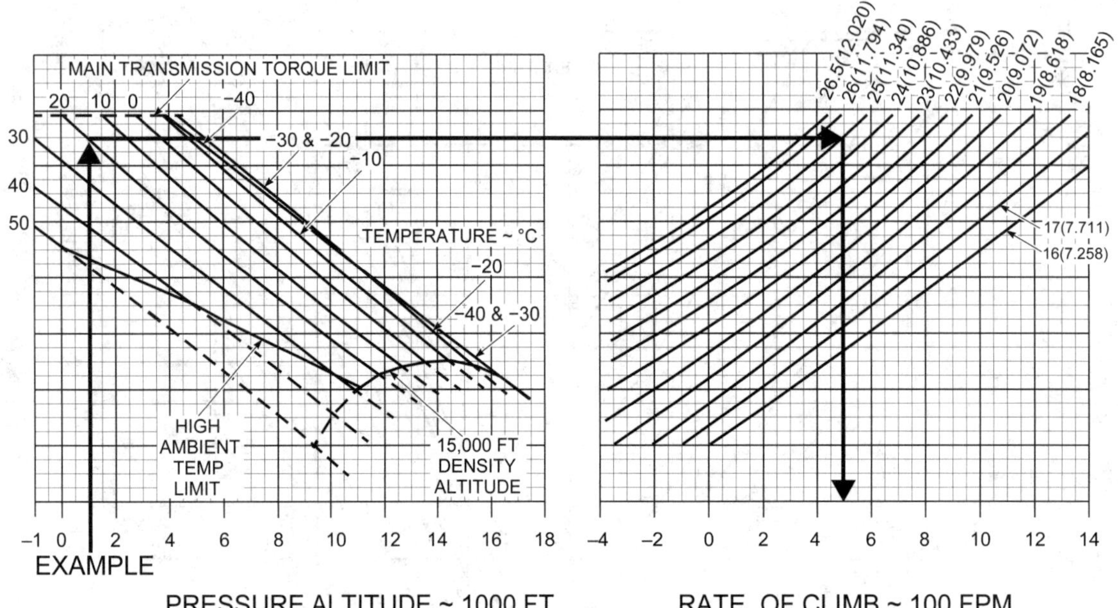

DASHED LINES ARE FOR INTERPOLATION ONLY

REDUCE RATE OF CLIMB DETERMINED FROM CHART BY AMOUNT SHOWN IN TABLE

GROSS WEIGHT-LB	REDUCTION ANTI-ICE ON	REDUCTION AIR CONDITIONER ON	REDUCTION LANDING GEAR DOWN	REDUCTION RESCUE HOIST INSTALLED	REDUCTION RIPS ON (MANUAL HEAVY MODE) ANTI-ICE ON
16,000	110	105	50	15	650
18,000	100	95	45	15	590
20,000	95	90	45	15	530
22,000	90	85	40	15	490
24,000	90	85	40	15	460
26,000	85	80	35	15	440
26,500	85	80	35	15	440

Figure 498. S-92—OEI Forward Climb Performance, Best Rate of Climb Speed.

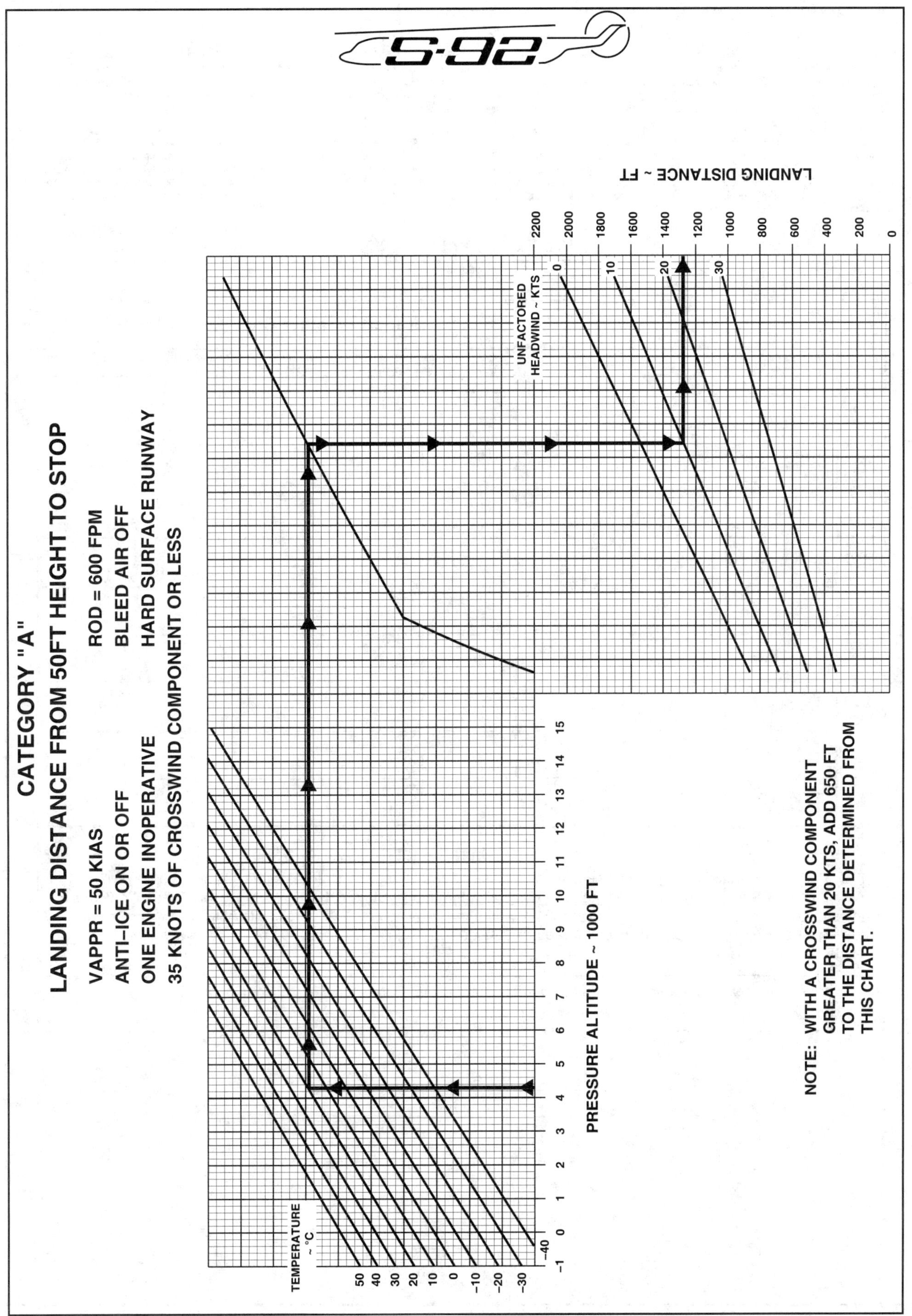

Figure 499. S-92—Category "A" Landing Distance From 50 ft. Height to Stop.

PRIVACY ACT STATEMENT: This statement is provided pursuant to the Privacy Act of 1974, 5 USC § 552a: The authority for collecting this information is contained in 49 U.S.C. §§ 40113, 44702, 44703, 44709, and 14 C.F.R. Part 6 - [Part 61, 63, 65, or 67. The principal purpose for which the information is intended to be used is to allow you to submit your flight plan. Submission of the data is voluntary. Failure to provide all required information may result in you not being able to submit your flight plan. The information collected on this form will be included in a Privacy Act System of Records known as DOT/FAA 847, titled "Aviation Records on Individuals" and will be subject to the routine uses published in the System of Records Notice (SORN) for DOT/FAA 847 (see www.dot.gov/privacy/privacyactnotices).

Paperwork Reduction Act Statement: A federal agency may not conduct or sponsor, and a person is not required to respond to, nor shall a person be subject to a penalty for failure to comply with a collection of information subject to the requirements of the Paperwork Reduction Act unless that collection of information displays a currently valid OMB Control Number. The OMB Control Number for this information collection is 2120-0026. Public reporting for this collection of information is estimated to be approximately 2.5 minutes per response, including the time for reviewing instructions, searching existing data sources, gathering and maintaining the data needed, completing and reviewing the collection of information. All responses to this collection of information are required to obtain or retain a benefit per 14 CFR Part 91. Send comments regarding this burden estimate or any other aspect of this collection of information, including suggestions for reducing this burden to the FAA at: 800 Independence Ave. SW, Washington, DC 20591, Attn: Information Collection Clearance Officer, ASP-110.

Approved OMB No. 2120-0026
Exp. 7/31/2020

Pre-Flight Pilot Checklist

Aircraft Identification			Time of Briefing			
Weather (Destination) (Alternate)	☐ Present	Remarks	**Report Weather Conditions Aloft**			
	☐ Forecast		*Report immediately weather conditions encountered---particularly cloud tops, upper cloud layers, thunderstorms, ice, turbulence, winds and temperature*			
			Position	Altitude	Time	Weather Conditions
Weather (En Route)	☐ Present					
	☐ Forecast					
	☐ Pireps					
Winds Aloft	Best Crzg. Alt.					
Nav. Aid & Comm. Status.	☐ Destination					
	☐ En Route					
Airport Conditions	☐ Destination					
	☐ Alternate					
ADIZ	☐ Airspace Restrictions					

Civil Aircraft Pilots

FAR Part 91 states that each person operating a civil aircraft of U S. registry over the high seas shall comply with Annex 2 to the Convention of International Civil Aviation, International Standards - Rules of the Air. Annex 2 requires the submission of a flight plan containing items 1-1 9 prior to operating any flight across international waters. Failure to file could result in a civil penalty not to exceed $1,000 for each violation (Section 901 of the Federal Aviation Act of 1958, as amended).

International briefing information may not be current or complete. Data should be secured, at the first opportunity, from the country in whose airspace the flight will be conducted.

Figure 500. FAA International Flight Plan Form - Pre-Flight Pilot Checklist.

Approved OMB No. 2120-0026
Exp. 7/31/2020

U S Department of Transportation
Federal Aviation Administration

International Flight Plan

PRIORITY <=FF

ADDRESSEE(S) <=

FILING TIME

ORIGINATOR <=

SPECIFIC IDENTIFICATION OF ADDRESSEE(S) AND / OR ORIGINATOR

3 MESSAGE TYPE <=(FPL

7 AIRCRAFT IDENTIFICATION —

8 FLIGHT RULES —

TYPE OF FLIGHT — <=

9 NUMBER —

TYPE OF AIRCRAFT

WAKE TURBULENCE CAT. /

10 EQUIPMENT — / <=

13 DEPARTURE AERODROME —

TIME <=

15 CRUISING SPEED —

LEVEL

ROUTE

<=

16 DESTINATION AERODROME

TOTAL EET HR MIN

ALTN AERODROME

2ND ALTN AERODROME <=

18 OTHER INFORMATION —

<=

SUPPLEMENTARY INFORMATION (NOT TO BE TRANSMITTED IN FPL MESSAGES)

19 ENDURANCE HR MIN —E/

PERSONS ON BOARD P/

EMERGENCY RADIO R/ UHF U VHF V ELT E

SURVIVAL EQUIPMENT / POLAR P DESERT D MARITIME M JUNGLE J

JACKETS / LIGHT L FLUORES F UHF U VHF V

DINGHIES
NUMBER CAPACITY COVER
D / C

COLOR <=

AIRCRAFT COLOR AND MARKINGS
A/

REMARKS
N / <=

PILOT-IN-COMMAND
C/)<=

FILED BY	ACCEPTED BY	ADDITIONAL INFORMATION

FAA Form 7233-4 (7/15)

Figure 500A. FAA International Flight Plan Form.

PRIVACY ACT STATEMENT: This statement is provided pursuant to the Privacy Act of 1974, 5 USC § 552a: The authority for collecting this information is contained in 49 U.S.C. §§ 40113, 44702, 44703, 44709, and 14 C.F.R. Part 6 - [Part 61, 63, 65, or 67. The principal purpose for which the information is intended to be used is to allow you to submit your flight plan. Submission of the data is voluntary. Failure to provide all required information may result in you not being able to submit your flight plan. The information collected on this form will be included in a Privacy Act System of Records known as DOT/FAA 847, titled "Aviation Records on Individuals" and will be subject to the routine uses published in the System of Records Notice (SORN) for DOT/FAA 847 (see www.dot.gov/privacy/privacyactnotices).

Paperwork Reduction Act Statement: A federal agency may not conduct or sponsor, and a person is not required to respond to, nor shall a person be subject to a penalty for failure to comply with a collection of information subject to the requirements of the Paperwork Reduction Act unless that collection of information displays a current valid OMB Control Number. The OMB Control Number for this information collection is 2120-0026. Public reporting for this collection of information is estimated to be approximately 2.5 minutes per response, including the time for reviewing instructions,completing and reviewing the collection of information. All responses to this collection of information are mandatory per14 CFR Part 91. Comments concerning the accuracy of this burden and suggestions for reducing the burden should be directed to the FAA at: 800 Independence Ave. SW, Washington, DC 20591, Attn: Information Collection Clearance Officer, ASP-110.

Form Approved: OMB No. 2120-0026 Exp. 7/31/2020

FLIGHT PLAN U.S. DEPARTMENT OF TRANSPORTATION FEDERAL AVIATION ADMINISTRATION	(FAA USE ONLY) ☐ PILOT BRIEFING ☐ VNR ☐ STOPOVER	TIME STARTED	SPECIALIST INITIALS

1. TYPE	2. AIRCRAFT IDENTIFICATION	3. AIRCRAFT TYPE / SPECIAL EQUIPMENT	4. TRUE AIRSPEED	5. DEPARTURE POINT	6. DEPARTURE TIME		7. CRUISING ALTITUDE
					PROPOSED (Z)	ACTUAL (Z)	
VFR IFR DVFR			KTS				

8. ROUTE OF FLIGHT

9. DESTINATION (Name of airport and city)	10. EST. TIME ENROUTE		11. REMARKS
	HOURS	MINUTES	

12. FUEL ON BOARD		13. ALTERNATE AIRPORT(S)	14. PILOT'S NAME, ADDRESS & TELEPHONE NUMBER & AIRCRAFT HOME BASE	15. NUMBER ABOARD
HOURS	MINUTES		17. DESTINATION CONTACT/TELEPHONE (OPTIONAL)	

16. COLOR OF AIRCRAFT	CIVIL AIRCRAFT PILOTS. FAR Part 91 requires you file an IFR flight plan to operate under instrument flight rules in controlled airspace. Failure to file could result in a civil penalty not to exceed $1,000 for each violation (Section 901 of the Federal Aviation Act of 1958, as amended). Filing of a VFR flight plan is recommended as a good operating practice. See also Part 99 for requirements concerning DVFR flight plans.

FAA Form 7233-1 (8-82)
Electronic Version (Adobe)

CLOSE VFR FLIGHT PLAN WITH ______________ FSS ON ARRIVAL

MILITARY STOPOVER (FAA USE ONLY)

TYPE ☐ IFR ☐ VFR	AIRCRAFT IDENTIFICATION	AIRCRAFT TYPE/SPECIAL EQUIPMENT	REMARKS
DEPARTURE POINT	DESTINATION	ETA	

TAS	DEP. PT	ETD	ALTITUDE	ROUTE OF FLIGHT	DESTINATION	ETE	REMARKS
KTS							
KTS							
KTS							
KTS							
REMARKS							INITIALS

FAA Form 7233-1 (8-82) Electronic Version (Adobe)

Figure 501. FAA Domestic Flight Plan Form.

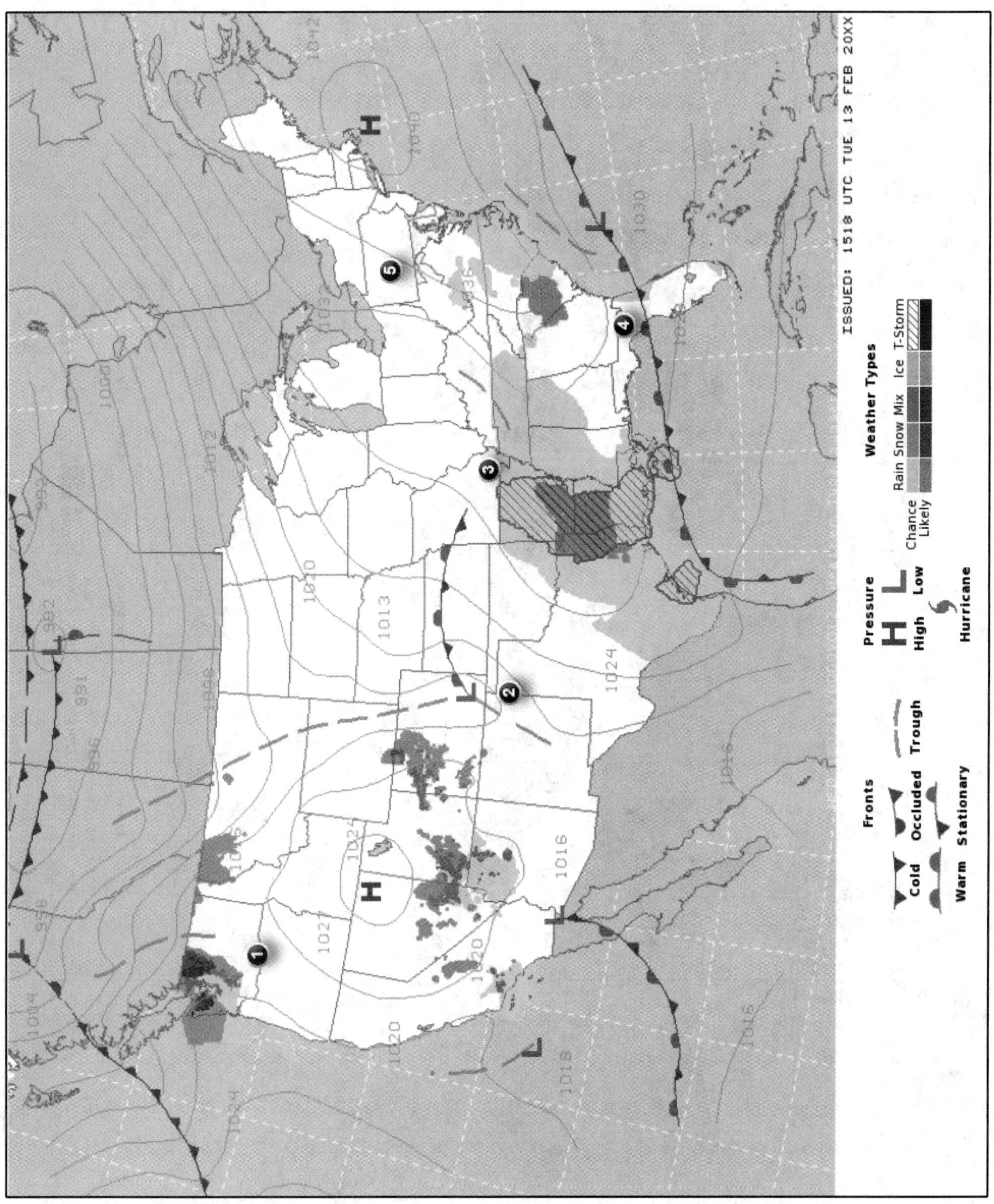

Figure 502. Weather Prediction Center (WPC) Surface Prog Chart.

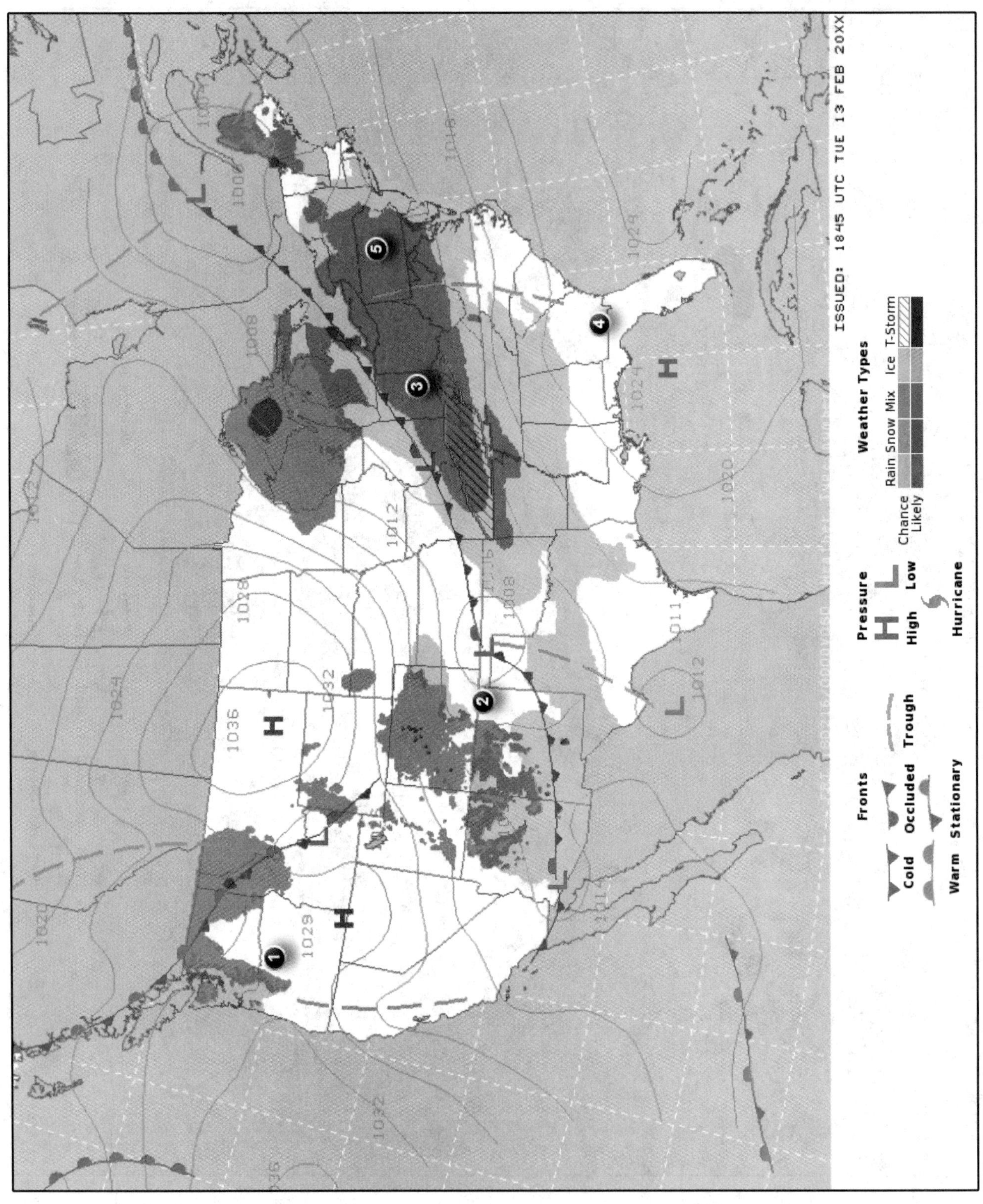

Figure 503. Weather Prediction Center (WPC) Surface Prog Chart.